ACRONYMS AND INITIALISMS
DICTIONARY

OTHER GALE PUBLICATIONS

REVERSE ACRONYMS AND INITIALISMS DICTIONARY—First Edition. Based on **ACRONYMS AND INITIALISMS DICTIONARY**, 3rd Edition, this "backwards dictionary" is the key to the commonly abbreviated forms for 80,000 terms. Entries arranged alphabetically by the term or phrase which has been acronymized.

ENCYCLOPEDIA OF BUSINESS INFORMATION SOURCES—Second Edition. Arranged according to subjects, entries in the first volume contain full references to sources of information important to executives and researchers. The second volume provides the same kinds of details on geographic subjects, on which the arrangement of the volume is based.

NATIONAL FACULTY DIRECTORY—Annual. An alphabetical list of names, with departmental affiliations and full institutional addresses, of over 413,000 faculty members at junior colleges, colleges, and universities in the United States.

CONTEMPORARY AUTHORS—Annual. A bio-bibliographical reference offering detailed information on more than 3,000 current authors each year. Distinctive features: unabridged bibliographies, sidelights, critical and biographical sources, work in progress. No duplication among volumes; cumulatively indexed.

AUTHOR BIOGRAPHY SERIES—Reference Book Reprints. Collective biographical works including Allibone, Duyckinck, and others.

ENCYCLOPEDIA OF ASSOCIATIONS—Seventh Edition. Volume 1: National Associations of the United States, detailed descriptions of nearly 17,000 national, nonprofit membership organizations. With 43,750-item keyword/alphabetical index. Volume 2: Geographic-Executive Index, a two-part index to material in Volume 1. Volume 3: **NEW ASSOCIATIONS AND PROJECTS,** quarterly supplements to Volume 1. Cumulatively indexed.

STATISTICS SOURCES—Third Edition. A subject guide to data on industrial, business, social, educational, financial, and other topics for the United States and selected foreign countries. With entries on 11,000 subjects from Abaca to Zoologists.

MANAGEMENT INFORMATION GUIDE SERIES—Authoritative, comprehensive, carefully indexed guides to the literature of such major business and governmental areas as Accounting, Commercial Law, Computers, Insurance, Communication, Transportation, Public Relations, and Economic and Business History.

BOOKMAN'S PRICE INDEX—The five volumes now available contain listings for over 250,000 antiquarian books and periodicals selected from the catalogs issued by leading rare book sellers, specialist dealers, and O.P. bookmen. Gives all essential details.

DIRECTORY OF SPECIAL LIBRARIES AND INFORMATION CENTERS—Second Edition. Volume 1 contains information about more than 13,000 special libraries, information centers, and documentation centers in the U.S. and Canada. Volume 2: Geographic-Personnel Index. Volume 3: **NEW SPECIAL LIBRARIES,** a periodic supplement to Volume 1.

RESEARCH CENTERS DIRECTORY—Fourth Edition. Covers 5,500 university-related and other nonprofit research units. Entries are indexed by name of research center and sponsoring institution. **NEW RESEARCH CENTERS,** a quarterly supplement to RCD; each issue averages about 200 listings.

ACRONYMS AND INITIALISMS DICTIONARY

Fourth Edition

*A Guide to Alphabetic Designations, Contractions, Acronyms,
Initialisms, and Similar Condensed Appellations*

Covering: Aerospace, Associations, Biochemistry, Business and Trade, Domestic
and International Affairs, Education, Electronics, Genetics, Government, Labor,
Medicine, Military, Pharmacy, Physiology, Politics, Religion, Science, Societies, Sports,
Technical Drawings and Specifications, Transportation, and Other Fields.

Edited By

Ellen T. Crowley
and
Robert C. Thomas

Contributing Editors

Harry Schecter
Former Chairman
Government Printing Office Style Board

Harvey Wolf
Staff Scientist, Data Systems Division
Hughes Aircraft Company

Miriam M. Steinert
Editorial Consultant

GALE RESEARCH COMPANY · BOOK TOWER · DETROIT, MICHIGAN

GALE EDITORIAL STAFF
for
ACRONYMS AND INITIALISMS DICTIONARY

Fourth Edition

Editors
Ellen T. Crowley
Robert C. Thomas

Editorial Assistant
Donna Wood

Editorial Staff

Dorothy Dockterman   Laura Morrison
Stephenie Koehn   Nell Sachs

This edition will be supplemented by

New Acronyms and Initialisms—1974
New Acronyms and Initialisms—1975

Copyright © 1960, 1965, 1968, 1969, 1970, 1971, 1972, 1973
Gale Research Company
Printed in the United States of America

**Library of Congress
Cataloging in Publication Data**

Gale Research Company.
  Acronyms and initialisms dictionary.

  First published in 1960 under title: Acronyms
dictionary.
  1. Acronyms. 2. Abbreviations. I. Crowley,
Ellen T., ed. II. Thomas, Robert C., ed. III. Title.
PE 1693.G3   423'.1   73-568

CONTENTS

ACKNOWLEDGMENTS

For suggestions, contributions of terms, permission to take material from personal or published sources, and for other courtesies during the preparation of previous editions and the present one, the editors are indebted to the following:

The contributing editors, named and identified on the title page, who assisted materially in expanding earlier editions to this volume's present size and scope.

O. T. Albertini, Personnel Directorate, Joint Chiefs of Staff, Department of Defense

A. Marjorie Taylor, editor, Language of World War II

Data Processing Division, International Business Machines Corp. (publishers of IBM Glossary for Information Processing)

B-G-R Division, Associated Spring Corp. (publishers of Civilian's Dictionary, a dictionary of wartime abbreviations)

Eric Partridge, author of A Dictionary of Slang and Unconventional English; A Dictionary of Abbreviations, with Special Attention to War-Time Abbreviations; and other books

Edwin B. Steen, Professor of Anatomy and Physiology, Western Michigan University

Mamie Meredith, late Professor of English, University of Nebraska

Robert E. Lacey, journalist

Roy Hubbard, journalist

Morgan Oates, librarian, Detroit Free Press

James Aguirre, staff writer and editor, Quality Evaluation Laboratory, United States Naval Weapons Station, Concord, California

Edith Thompson

Ethel M. Fair

David Glagovsky

William A. Taylor, Chief of the Terminology Section, Directorate of Administration, HQ US Air Force

National Library of Medicine

In addition, many suggestions concerning individual terms to be included or subjects to be covered have been received from individual users, and have been most helpful. The editors invite all such comments and suggestions, and will make every effort to incorporate them in future editions.

PREFACE TO

THE FOURTH EDITION

Because the preface to the second edition (1965) which explains the nature, purpose, and editorial practices of AID is thorough and is still relevant, that preface is reprinted on pages x-xiii, and the points made therein will not be covered here.

The preface to the third edition (1970) traced developments in the use of acronyms and initialisms during the late sixties -- the proliferation of these terms in particularly dynamic fields, such as aerospace and data processing; their growing popularity in political and social movements; and the widespread use of "prefabricated" acronyms, those chosen for their catchy suitability and then fleshed out with more-or-less appropriate words.

Because nearly three years have passed since publication of that third edition, however, some note should be taken of further changes and developments.

The number of terms comprising AID-3 (80,000) has now swelled to nearly 103,000 for AID-4 -- evidence enough that the popularity of acronyms and initialisms shows few signs of diminishing.

Growth continues to be strong in the same areas that AID-3 noted, but other trends are also noticeable in the additions, changes, and updating offered in AID-4.

Twentieth-Century Living as Reflected in AID

Among the new terms are many which have been prominent in headlines of recent years -- NICRA (Northern Ireland Civil Rights Association), NAG (National Action Group, an antibusing organization), COLC (Cost of Living Council), and NEP (New Economic Policy), the last two being products of the Nixon Administration. Recycling of acronyms is apparently not unheard-of -- NEP for New Economic Policy has appeared in earlier editions of AID in reference to a USSR program of 1921-28.

The "skyjacking" of aircraft was a rare occurrence only a few years ago; now a weapon-detecting device known as a GAMMA (Guns and Magnetic Material Alarm) seeks to prevent the increasing frequency of these incidents. MS has long been a familiar term for Manuscript or Multiple Sclerosis, but in the last few years the feminist movement has popularized its use as a nondiscriminating form of address for both married and nonmarried women.

As the renown of graffiti elevates it almost to an art form, comes the marketing of a graffiti-removing chemical for its ruder samples: the DWR, or Dirty Word Remover. And the growing interest in mysticism has greatly popularized the practice of TM, Transcendental Meditation. In some cases acronyms have already been proposed for so-far nonexistent situations. SANSAN has been suggested for San Francisco, San Diego - a possible "super-city" formed by the growth and merger of these California cities with all towns in between.

Occasionally one even has a choice of the term used. During 1972, the Committee to Re-Elect the President was alternately referred to as CRP or CREEP, depending, perhaps, on one's political affiliation.

Extensive Updating Increases Usefulness

New entries in AID-4 are not limited to recently coined terms. Added since the third edition are a great many academic degrees and such diverse references as RaM-BaM, for the 12th-century Jewish philosopher Rabbi Moses ben Maimon (Maimonides), and SATCHMO, for the late trumpeter Louis Armstrong's early nickname, "Satchel Mouth."

In addition, an effort has been made to update many terms from earlier editions. Obsolete entries were not deleted, but merely noted or cross-referenced.

Changes in the Selective Service System classifications are reflected in the addition of 2-S and the notice that 4-E is obsolete, among other modifications. Translations have been added to numerous foreign entries, and refinements since AID-3 will be noted among many chemical and biochemical terms.

Perhaps the most extensive updating is apparent in New York Stock Exchange symbols, which have been revised through mid-1972 -- the first such changes since the second edition. Over 600 NYSE symbols appear for the first time in AID-4.

Abbreviations Debut

For several editions, it has been AID policy not to emphasize abbreviations, defined for our purposes as a shortened form of a single word (TUE for Tuesday), while acronyms and initialisms are considered to be shortened forms of two or more words or of an entire phrase (RADAR for Radio Detection and Ranging).

With AID-4, over 1000 abbreviations are listed for the first time, laying the foundation for more nearly definitive coverage in future editions. It is the editors' intention that any listed abbreviation be considered to reflect usage only; it does not necessarily represent the only correct form of the term.

The Business Trend toward Acronyms and Initialisms

Among the trends noticed in editing this edition was the growing popularity of acronyms and initial-isms on both Wall Street and Madison Avenue.

Most consumers are familiar with SUNOCO (Sun Oil Company), NECCO (New England Confectionery Company), and NABISCO (National Biscuit Company). Within the past few years many other companies have jumped on the acronymic brandwagon.

The Electric Storage Battery Company became ESB, Inc.; the Radio Corporation of America officially took its more familiar initials and became RCA Corporation; the Shoe Corporation of America became SCOA Industries, Inc. There have been some indications, however, that the saturation point may have been reached; and at least one company has reversed the procedure. General Cable Corporation, which had changed its name to GCC, has now reverted to its original name.

Dr. Michael E. Rappeport of Opinion Research Corporation may have touched on the reasons for a possible reversal of this trend, when he spoke before the 1972 meeting of the United States Trademarks Association: "The decision to move to an acronym made up of the initials of a corporate name can play havoc with the recognition factor of companies. . . . A survey of men-on-the-street has indicated that a once familiar corporate name has drifted into anonymity for lack of ability to identify the meaning of ABC Corporation."

The Acronymic Population Explosion

The ever-enlarging ACRONYMS AND INITIALISMS DICTIONARY testifies to the growing predilection for abbreviating, truncating, and telescoping all manner of words and phrases on all levels of communication. The Germans have humorously, and perhaps rightfully, labeled the practice with an abbreviation of its own -- ABKUEFI (Abkuerzungsfimmel, or Abbreviation Craze).

Voice of Dissent

There have been rumblings of discontent with ABKUEFI through the years. In 1971, in a lecture presented before the International Congress of Pharmaceutical Sciences, Dr. Anatole Sliosberg, of the International Federation of Translators, expressed his dismay over the abuses of "abbreviomania":

> ...whenever you open a scientific, technical, or economic publication, or even a daily newspaper, you are immediately struck by the number of apparently meaningless letter or syllable combinations which the most knowledgeable reader cannot decipher without the aid of a dictionary or a keen sense of divination."

He examined the thriving growth of initialese from post-hieroglyphic symbols up to the modern passion for it, which has particularly mushroomed since World War II.

Dr. Sliosberg's was not a voice in the wilderness. He cited such impressive company as Seneca and Justinian I, who had spoken out against the abuse of abbreviations in manuscripts in their own day. He added that "the laws of France [since the 14th century] still forbid the use of abbreviations in legal documents, civil registers, and brokers' books."

From Aphaereses to Sigla

Several types of abbreviations were detailed by Dr. Sliosberg, among them sigla ("the single initial letter of each element. . . MP = Military Police"); aphaereses ("formed by dropping one or more syllables from the beginning. . . phone = telephone"); apocopes ("formed by dropping one or more syllables from the end. . . kilo = kilogramme"); and portmanteau words ("formed by combining the beginning of one word and the end of another. . . smog = smoke and fog").

He pointed out that, of sigla alone, "nearly 12 million five-letter combinations could be formed, each one having an unlimited number of meanings, depending on language and user!"

Need for a Guide Evident

In the face of this extensive evidence, one can hardly argue that the burgeoning acronym and initialism population is anything but overwhelming. However, the abbreviation of terms is also convenient, speedy, and well-suited to the highly technical world of today. It is not likely to be abandoned, and may not even be curtailed to any extent, despite Dr. Sliosberg's suggestion that "an international commission, including both linguistic specialists and representatives of widely ranging disciplines, should pay especial attention to establishing a universally accepted list of abbreviations and sigla, and then making periodic updates."

Since population control of acronyms and initialisms seems unlikely at present, the editors of ACRONYMS AND INITIALISMS DICTIONARY will continue to guide AID users through this expanding maze of linguistic shorthand. Suggestions and comments will be welcomed.

PREFACE TO
THE SECOND EDITION, 1965

It is four years since the first edition of the ACRONYMS DICTIONARY appeared, and high time for a new one because those years have been particularly eventful.

In that period, LASERS and MASERS began to spark creative imaginations. JFK played his shockingly brief role as President and was succeded by LBJ. COMSAT (Communications Satellite Corporation) was chartered to develop the potential of TELSTAR. New miracle drugs and chemicals with lengthy compound names became widely known, and were speedily tagged with short, memorable acronyms, such as DNA for genetics' Deoxyribonucleic Acid, and LSD (sometimes, LSD 25) for the hallucinatory drug, Lysergic Acid Diethylamine Tartrate.

Breakneck progress in electronics and space research brought new concepts, new projects, new instruments and weapons. It also brought new acronyms to save precious inches of newsprint and precious seconds of broadcast time, to serve as cloaks of military secrecy, and as spotlights on products, ideas, and programs which the public is expected to support, admire, or purchase.

Acronym Idea Not New

These and other developments, however, merely extend an age-old practice, for acronyms have been doing this kind of job for centuries. Roman soldiers carried standards engraved with the letters SPQR, from the Latin for Senate and People of Rome. They nailed a sign lettered INRI onto a cross in Judea.

The idea of using initials and telescope words (COMSAT is an example of the latter) to say things faster or more dramatically came early to America, also; but the word acronym (from the Greek akros, tip, and onyma, name) was not coined until 1943.

Seventeen years later the ACRONYMS DICTIONARY (believed to be the first book composed of this type of material) was published, and the subject attracted increased importance and interest. The book speedily won a place in Winchell's GUIDE TO REFERENCE BOOKS (Fourth Supplement), and LIBRARY JOURNAL included the title in its annual roster of Best Reference Books.

But no dictionary can be the final word in a field which grows as rapidly as acronyms, and it has always been the publisher's intention to bring out a revised and updated edition of the ACRONYMS DICTIONARY as soon as sufficient new material could be compiled. This edition has been delayed for a longer time than anticipated, but the delay has been advantageous in at least one respect: It allowed more time for numerous suggestions to be received from users of the first edition, and gave the editors four years in which to gather an unprecedented, unequaled store of acronyms and initialisms for the second edition.

Thanks to users' suggestions and to the lengthy research period, the new book is considerably thicker and infinitely more valuable than its predecessor. It has about 45,000 entries and nearly 775 pages, as opposed to 12,000 entries and 211 in the first edition.

Expansion Results from Two Causes

This nearly fourfold increase in size comes primarily from two causes:

1) Gaps have been filled and new words have been added to expand considerably the coverage provided in the previous edition for military, governmental, aerospace, labor, data processing, and voluntary association names and terminology.

2) Thousands of entries have been added, covering such fields as genetics, biochemistry, technical specifications, education, politics, railroading, domestic affairs, religion, sports, medicine, international commerce, and many other areas which did not receive major attention in the first edition.

Many medical terms, for example, have been added—both scientific and not-so-scientific. Among the former are LOP, an initialism for Left Occiput Posterior, a type of fetal position, and AC, the abbreviation of the Latin for "before meals," a term often encountered in doctors' prescriptions. Among the less scientific are such terms as TLC, a prescription much easier for the patient to take than many—it means Tender, Loving Care—and DOA, for Dead on Arrival.

Designations for stocks traded on the New York Stock Exchange have been added for the convenience of investment-minded readers. These include AAC (American Cement Corporation) and DCS (Distillers Corporation—Seagrams, Ltd.), but there are many others, such as ABT (Abbott Laboratories), which are more nearly symbols than initialisms or acronyms.

Some stocks have picked up nicknames, often based on verbalizations of their initials or trading symbols, and these are also mentioned; they include "Pizza" for Pacific International Express (NYSE symbol: PIE), and "Alice" for Allis-Chalmers.

Military terms, virtually a backbone of the first edition, have been augmented. The user will find many additional modern terms, plus more old standbys such as D & D (Drunk and Disorderly), DFR (Dropped From Rolls), and DI (Drill Instructor—and incidentally the title of a movie about the Marines). From such sources as a dictionary of wartime abbreviations, compiled by Eric Partridge, the editors have taken by permission numerous colorful terms, typified by CMAR (the reversed initials of Royal Army Medical Corps), meaning "Can't Manage a Rifle." And the user of this new edition can perhaps feel more secure by knowing that in addition to DEWLINE the country is now protected by AAEW (Atlantic Airborne Early Warning).

ADCOMSUBORDCOMPHIBSPAC

There's even a bravura specimen all but the most trusting readers will want to look up to convince themselves it is real. It is ADCOMSUBORDCOMPHIBSPAC (possibly the longest term in the book), which is the Navy's short-form name for Administrative Command, Amphibious Forces, Pacific Fleet, Subordinate Command.

Terms which are striking for reasons other than their length are those of the type represented by WAVES, ACTION, CARE, and JOBS, all of which are believed to have been constructed to convey a certain impression for a certain purpose, then fleshed out with more-or-less appropriate words which fit the catchy acronyms. Undoubtedly created the same way were ZIP and ABCD, Post Office Department designations for Zone Improvement Plan and Accelerated Business Collection and Delivery.

By far the largest proportion of terms in the ACRONYMS AND INITIALISMS DICTIONARY is made up of items which are specifically identified with the United States. Foreign terms are assuming an increasing importance, however, because of constantly closer association—politically, economically, and socially—between the United States and the rest of the world. The editors have therefore attempted to include as many as possible of the terms most likely to be encountered by the businessman, government official, student of political affairs, or the citizen who wishes to be informed.

As a result, this edition contains in the aggregate several thousand acronyms and initialisms based on Russian, French, German, Italian, Spanish, Japanese, and other major languages. Together, they represent—as do the terms based on English phrases and names—a source which is probably not duplicated anywhere else.

For example, the acronyms of international association names have been included because, since they are international, their activities are presumed to include Americans. Many terms, of course, have a military origin; and since World War II, which spawned so many acronyms, was the joint concern of several nations, many military terms from Great Britain and other countries appear for the first time in this edition. Foreign political parties, and their often-related labor unions, are also included, since the names and acronyms of such organizations are commonly encountered by the reader of magazines and daily newspapers in the United States.

Sweden is represented by, among others, AG (Company), while recent events in Algeria are recalled by OAS (Organisation de l'Armee Secrete). French terms are prevalent among international organizations because of the status French still enjoys as a major language of diplomacy. Examples are CGT (Confederation Generale de Travail), AATNU (Administration de l'Assistance Technique des Nations Unies), and AEP (Agence Europeene de Productivite).

Both DNB and ADN are listed. One is West Germany's news agency, Deutsche Nachrichtenburo; the other is Allgemeine Deutsche Nachrichtendienst, its counterpart in the DDR (Deutsche Demokratische Republik). Russia is represented by, for example, AD and ADD, initialisms for the Russian words meaning Air Division and Strategic Bombing Force, and by acronyms for the Soviet Republic's various secret police groups.

Foreign-car watchers are reminded that Germany's DKW is spelled out as Das Kleine Wunder (The Little Wonder), while American railroad car watchers can find that PAE and GHH are the AAR (Association of American Railroads) symbols for cars of the Peoria & Eastern Railroad and the Galveston, Houston & Henderson Railroad.

Finally, the new edition contains many more examples of slang terms than the previous volume. Among items included for the first time in this edition are such oddments as AD, a drug addict, and DVOT and SOS, both disparaging GI terms for unpopular items of Army cuisine.

Research Shows Comprehensive Guide Needed

Colorful, startling, interesting though the foregoing examples are, they are not included in the AID for those reasons alone. Besides being amusing, it is also true that identification or explanation of each of the terms in this volume may be of importance to the understanding of a modern reader, just as all the terms in an unabridged dictionary—any one of which might apparently be omitted without harm—are also each of potential importance.

Ready identification and comprehension of such terms as AE, SNCC, SORE, RNA, COIN, and thousands of others are necessary to understand newspapers and other common reading materials. A recent study at the University of Florida, however, indicated that even acronyms encountered every day by the average reader are often not widely understood, pointing up the need for a guide to common terms as well as the more exotic.

In the Florida survey, resulting from a journalism seminar which raised the question of how well newspaper readers understand the many initials they encounter, more than three hundred individuals were interviewed. They were confronted with sample initialisms, both alone and in the context of the headlines, and researchers concluded that the terms register with surprisingly small numbers of people. For example, only eight percent recognized GAO.

Accordingly, it seemed desirable for the editors to cast their nets as widely as possible in securing material for the new edition, and that they have done. They hope that this revised and enlarged version of the popular first edition will be equally valuable.

EDITORIAL POLICIES

Determining the subject areas to be covered in such a book as this is not nearly so difficult as deciding on the type of terms to be selected from each field. In other words, "Where should the line be drawn?"

Acronyms are, strictly speaking, words made from the tips of other words—but the question immediately arises, "How large a tip?" Some students of language hold out for syllables, and accept only such terms as ARBOR, from the virological term, Arthropod Borne, or BASEC, for Base Section, a military term. Some others might go one step further and accept terms such as BAFCOM, Basic Armed Forces Communication (Plan), or BART, Brooklyn Army Terminal.

One of the most common usages of acronym-like terms, however, is in the shortening of governmental, organizational, technical and other designations by the use of initial letter "tips" only of words in these designations. AID (Agency for International Development), SCLC (Southern Christian Leadership Conference), PC (Peace Corps), and thousands of similar terms are examples of this practice. Some refer to such terms, not as acronyms, but as initialisms or "abecedisms."

Which of these points of view is linguistically correct is not important here; and, quite possibly, there is no single correct way of forming what is known today as an acronym. The essential point which concerned the editors was that no user of the book should be disappointed because the term for which he sought an explanation was omitted on a technicality. It was decided, therefore, to include in this edition of AID all terms of the types described above, whether they met one or another of the definitions of acronym or not, so long as they might be thought to be an acronymic term when encountered in reading or conversation.

Should Shortened Terms Be Pronounced?

On this point, the editors suggest that you let your conscience—and whatever common usage you know of—be your guide. Pronunciation is almost entirely a matter of choice. Some people pronounce acronyms, whenever possible, as if they were complete words. Others prefer to rattle off the individual letters. Telescope words are almost invariably pronounced as words—and, indeed, very likely have come into being because they make conversationally manageable terms which are very cumbersome when used in full. NAWAS (the National Warning System of Civil Defense) and GESTAPO (from Geheime Staats Polizei) are examples of such terms.

Occasionally, an initialism will acquire an unofficial stray letter or sound which never appears in print, but which renders the term pronounceable. SNCC (Student National [formerly, Nonviolent] Coordinating Committee), for example, is widely pronounced "Snick." For such cases as this, discreet and careful listening is essential.

To Capitalize or Not to Capitalize?

It is comparatively rare, and is becoming even less common, for initialisms to be written any way other than in all capital letters, without periods. There are occasional exceptions, especially in scientific or technical notation (names of chemical elements, for example), but it appears that the overwhelming tendency is toward the use of all capitals and the omission of all periods. The capitalization of initialisms for common nouns, such as TV for Television, is typical.

The editors have speculated on the reasons for the tendency to use all capitals, without periods, and found no single answer. It seems significant, however, that the equipment which is more and more being used for records and/or for communication—such as Teletypes, computer printout units, punched cards, etc.—almost invariably has only uppercase letters, and, except for the Teletype, a relatively limited capacity for characters, punctuation, and spacing.

Therefore, the practice adopted in the first edition of writing acronyms uniformly in capitals and without periods or space between letters has been, in general, followed for the subsequent editions. The expansion of the scope of the volumes, however, has resulted in the use of certain types of material not covered in the first edition, to which the general rule could not logically be applied.

Unlike certain other types of acronyms which might be written in various ways, academic degrees, for example, often include both capital and lowercase letters; the degree of Bachelor of Science may be abbreviated as BS, but it is also often used as B Sc, and it would not have been appropriate to apply the "all capital" rule to material of this type. Also, although conjunctions, prepositions, and articles are usually ignored in the formation of an initialism, they are occasionally found in such instances as C of C and B of B for Chamber of Commerce and Bureau of the Budget, respectively; obviously, these could not be written COFC or BOFB.

Arrangement of Terms

Terms are arranged in alphabetical order, according to the acronym. If the same acronym has more than one meaning, the various meanings are arranged alphabetically. Spacing within the term does not affect alphabetizing, and lowercase letters occurring in an acronym do not affect its alphabetical position.

Acronyms and initialisms involving the same letters occur in a variety of forms, and this arbitrary order was established for the various possible arrangements:

Straight forms of the acronym . . . . BS
Hyphenated forms of the acronym. B-S
Forms of the acronym using the diagonal. . . . . B/S
Forms of the acronym with ampersand or other symbols . . . . . B & S
Forms of the acronym with conjunctions or prepositions . . . . . B of S
Forms of the acronym with numbers B2S

With respect to arrangement of terms and their meanings, it should be kept in mind that the point of view of the book, or the point of reference for the user, is an acronym rather than its meaning. Therefore, it is deliberate when there are two successive listings of, for example, the International Air Line Stewards and Stewardesses Association under slightly different initialisms, both of which were encountered in one or another of the various sources used to compile this dictionary.

A

A . . . . About
A . . . . Absent
A . . . . Absolute (Temperature in Fahrenheit degrees)
A . . . . Absolvo (I acquit) (Used by Romans in criminal trials)
A . . . . Abstracts
A . . . . Abundant (With respect to occurrence of species)
A . . . . Academician or Academy
A . . . . Acceleration
A . . . . Accepted
A . . . . Accommodation
A . . . . Ace
A . . . . Acre
A . . . . Act, Acting, Active, or Activity
A . . . . Adenine
A . . . . Adjective
A . . . . Adjutant
A . . . . Administration
A . . . . Admiral
A . . . . Adult
A . . . . Aerospace
A . . . . After
A . . . . Afternoon
A . . . . Air
A . . . . Aircraft, Airman, or Airplane
A . . . . Alaskan Standard Time (Aviation)
A . . . . Alphabetic
A . . . . Alternate (Approach and landing charts) (Aviation)
A . . . . Altimeter
A . . . . Altitude Difference (Navigation)
A . . . . Alto
A . . . . Amateur
A . . . . America or American
A . . . . Ampere
A . . . . Amphibian or Amphibious
A . . . . Amplification; Amplifier
A . . . . Amplitude (Physics)
A . . . . Anaconda Company (NYSE symbol)
A . . . . Androecium (Botany)
A . . . . Anglian
A . . . . Angstrom Unit (of light)
A . . . . Anno or Annus
A . . . . Annual
A . . . . Anode (Technical drawings)
A . . . . Anonymous
A . . . . Answer (In transcripts)
A . . . . Ante (Before)
A . . . . Anterior
A . . . . Antiquo (I oppose) (Used by Romans to signify a negative vote)
A . . . . Anus
A . . . . Apostle (Church calendars)
A . . . . Approved
A . . . . April
A . . . . Aqua
A . . . . Arctic (Air mass) (Meteorological symbol)
A . . . . Are (A unit of area in the metric system)
A . . . . Area
A . . . . Argon (Chemical element) (Also see Ar)
A . . . . Army
A . . . . Arousal
A . . . . Article
A . . . . Artillery
A . . . . Asked
A . . . . Assistant Captain (Worn on assistant captains' uniforms) (Hockey)

A . . . . Assists (in putting a man out) (Baseball)
A . . . . Associate (in an academic degree)
A . . . . Association
A . . . . Asymmetric
A . . . . At
A . . . . Atom, Atomic, or Atomic Weight
A . . . . Attack (Designation for all US military aircraft)
A . . . . Attack (Men's lacrosse position)
A . . . . Attendance (Sports)
a . . . . Atto (A prefix meaning divided by 10 to the 18th power)
A . . . . Auditory
A . . . . Augmentation (Music)
A . . . . Auricle
A . . . . Ausgabestelle (Distribution point) (German military – World War II)
A . . . . Australian
A . . . . Author
A . . . . Automobile
A . . . . Hail (Meteorological symbol)
A . . . . Mass Number (Symbol)
A (Bomb) . . . . Atom Bomb
A1 . . . . First Class or First Quality
A-1 . . . . Personnel Section of an Air Staff; also, officer in charge of this section (Air Force)
A-2 . . . . Intelligence Section of an Air Staff; also, officer in charge of this section (Air Force)
A-3 . . . . Operations and Training Section of an Air Staff; also, officer in charge of this section (Air Force)
A-4 . . . . Materiel and Supply Section of an Air Staff; also, officer in charge of this section (Air Force)
1-A . . . . Selective Service Class (for Registrant Available for Military Service)
2-A . . . . Selective Service Class (for Registrant Deferred Because of Civilian Occupation [Other than Agriculture] or Non-Degree Study
3-A . . . . Selective Service Class (for Registrant Deferred by Reason of Extreme Hardship to Dependents; or Registrant with a Child or Children)
4-A . . . . Selective Service Class (for Registrant with Sufficient Prior Active Service to Satisfy Requirements of Law [Veteran])
AA . . . . Absolute Altitude (Navigation)
AA . . . . Access Authorization
AA . . . . Achievement Age (Psychology)
AA . . . . Acting Appointment
AA . . . . Activation Analysis
AA . . . . Addicts Anonymous
AA . . . . Adenylic Acid
AA . . . . Administrative Assistant (to the Army Secretary)
AA . . . . Aerolineas Argentinas (Argentine airline)
AA . . . . Affected Areas
AA . . . . Air-to-Air
AA . . . . Airborne Alert
AA . . . . Airman Apprentice
AA . . . . Alcoholics Anonymous
AA . . . . All (text) After (specified point) (Message handling)
AA . . . . Aluminum Company of America (NYSE symbol) (Wall Street slang names: "Ack Ack" or "All American")
AA . . . . American Airlines, Inc.
AA . . . . American Association (Baseball league)
AA . . . . Amino Acid
AA . . . . Analytical Abstracts
AA . . . . Anglo-American
AA . . . . Ann Arbor R. R. (AAR code)
AA . . . . Anterior Aorta
AA . . . . Anthranilic Acid
AA . . . . Antiaircraft (Military)
AA . . . . Antibody Activity

AA . . . . Apollo Applications (NASA program)
AA . . . . Appropriate Authority (Office of Censorship) (World War II)
AA . . . . Approximate Absolute
AA . . . . Arithmetic Average
AA . . . . Arlington Annex (Navy Department)
AA . . . . Armature Accelerator
AA . . . . Arrival Angle
AA . . . . Associate in Accounting
AA . . . . Associate in Arts
AA . . . . Athletic Association
AA . . . . Atomic Absorption
AA . . . . Augustiniani Assumptionis (Assumptionists)
AA . . . . Author's Alteration (Printing)
AA . . . . Auto Acquisition (RADAR)
AA . . . . Automobile Association (British)
AA . . . . Auxi-Atome (French association)
AA . . . . Aviation Annex (Air Force)
AA . . . . Aviatsionnaya Armiya (Russian - Air Army)
AA . . . . Sisters Auxiliaries of the Apostolate (Roman Catholic religious order)
A-A . . . . Air-to-Air
A/A . . . . Advice of Allotment
A/A . . . . Air-to-Air
A/A . . . . Analysis of Accounts
A/A . . . . Angle of Attack (Military)
AAA . . . . Agricultural Adjustment Act
AAA . . . . Agricultural Adjustment Administration (or Agency)
AAA . . . . Agricultural Aircraft Association
AAA . . . . Alaska (Officially, name is spelled out); sometimes Alas.
AAA . . . . Allied Artists of America
AAA . . . . Amateur Astronomers Association
AAA . . . . Amateur Athletic Association
AAA . . . . American Abstract Artists
AAA . . . . American Academy of Advertising
AAA . . . . American Academy of Allergy
AAA . . . . American Academy of Art
AAA . . . . American Accordionists' Association
AAA . . . . American Accounting Association
AAA . . . . American Albino Association
AAA . . . . American Airship Association
AAA . . . . American Angus Association
AAA . . . . American Antarctic Association
AAA . . . . American Anthropological Association
AAA . . . . American Arbitration Association
AAA . . . . American Art Association (Predecessor of Parke-Bernet, New York)
AAA . . . . American Association of Anatomists
AAA . . . . American Astronomers Association
AAA . . . . American Australian Association
AAA . . . . American Automobile Association
AAA . . . . Anglo-American Associates (An organization)
AAA . . . . Antiaircraft Armament
AAA . . . . Antiaircraft Artillery
AAA . . . . Antique Airplane Association
AAA . . . . Appraisers Association of America
AAA . . . . Approved As Amended
AAA . . . . Archives of American Art
AAA . . . . Army Audit Agency
AAA . . . . Associate in Applied Arts
AAA . . . . Associated Agents of America
AAA . . . . Association of Attenders and Alumni of The Hague Academy of International Law
AAA . . . . Association of Average Adjusters of the United States
AAA . . . . Authorization Accounting Activity (DOD)
AAA . . . . Awaiting Aircraft Availability
AA & A . . . . . . Armor, Armament and Ammunition
AA of A . . . . . Ambulance Association of America
AAAA . . . . . . American Association for the Advancement of Atheism
AAAA . . . . . . American Association of Advertising Agencies
AAAA . . . . . . American Association of Audio Analgesia
AAAA . . . . . . Army Aviation Association of America
AAAA . . . . . . Associated Actors and Artistes of America
AAAB . . . . . . American Association of Architectural Bibliographers
AAAC . . . . . . American Association for the Advancement of Criminology
AAAC . . . . . . Antiaircraft Artillery Command
AAACE . . . . . American Association of Agricultural College Editors
AAAD . . . . . . American Athletic Association for the Deaf
AAAE . . . . . . American Association of Airport Executives
AAAEE . . . . . American Afro-Asian Educational Exchange
AA Ag . . . . . . Associate in Arts in Agriculture
AAAI . . . . . . Affiliated Advertising Agencies International
AAAIMH . . . . . American Association for the Abolition of Involuntary Mental Hospitalization

AAAIS . . . . . . Advanced Army Airborne Indicating System
AAAIS . . . . . . Antiaircraft Artillery Intelligence Service (Army)
AAAIWD . . . . . American Association of Aluminum Importers & Warehouse Distributors (Later, American Metal Importers Association)
AAAL . . . . . . Abolish All Abortion Laws
AAAL . . . . . . American Academy of Arts and Letters
AAALAC . . . . . American Association for Accreditation of Laboratory Animal Care
AAAN . . . . . . American Academy of Applied Nutrition
AAAOC . . . . . Antiaircraft Artillery Operation Center
AAAR . . . . . . Association for the Advancement of Aeronautical Research (France)
AAAR . . . . . . Association for the Advancement of Aging Research
AAARC . . . . . Antiaircraft Artillery Reception Center
AAAS . . . . . . American Academy of Arts and Sciences
AAAS . . . . . . American Academy of Asian Studies
AAAS . . . . . . American Association for the Advancement of Science
AAA & S . . . . . Associate in Arts in Arts and Science
AAASS . . . . . American Association for the Advancement of Slavic Studies
AAASUSS . . . . Association of Administrative Assistants and Secretaries to United States Senators
AAAUS . . . . . Association of Average Adjusters of the United States
AAB . . . . Aircraft Accident Board
AAB . . . . Aircraft Armament Bulletin (Navy)
AAB . . . . American Association of Bioanalysts
AAB . . . . Army Air Base
AAB . . . . Army Aviation Board
AAB . . . . Artichoke Advisory Board
AAB . . . . Aviation Armament Bulletin
AA/B . . . . . . Anti-Aircraft Balloon
AABB . . . . . . American Association of Blood Banks
AABC . . . . . . Accrediting Association of Bible Colleges
AABC . . . . . . All-American Bronze Club
AABC . . . . . . American Amateur Baseball Congress
AABC . . . . . . American Austin-Bantam Club
AABC . . . . . . Association for Advancement of Blind Children
AABD . . . . . . Aid to the Aged, Blind, or Disabled
AABEVM . . . . . Association of American Boards of Examiners in Veterinary Medicine
AABFS . . . . . . Amphibious Assault Bulk Fuel System (Navy)
AABGA . . . . . American Association of Botanical Gardens and Arboretums
AABM . . . . . . Airborne Anti-Ballistic Missiles
AABM . . . . . . Association of American Battery Manufacturers
AABM . . . . . . Australian Association of British Manufacturers
AABNCP . . . . . Advanced Airborne Command Post
AABS . . . . . . All Attitude-Indicator Bombing System
AABT . . . . . . Association for Advancement of the Behavioral Therapies
AABTM . . . . . American Association of Baggage Traffic Managers
AA Bus . . . . . . Associate in Arts in Business
AABW . . . . . . American Association of Book Wholesalers
AABY . . . . . . As Amended By (Army)
AAC . . . . Acoustical Absorption Coefficient
AAC . . . . Acoustical Attenuation Constant
AAC . . . . Aerial Ambulance Company (Army)
AAC . . . . Aeronautical Advisory Council
AAC . . . . Aeronautical Approach Chart (Military)
AAC . . . . Air Approach Control
AAC . . . . Aircraft Armament Change
AAC . . . . Alaskan Air Command (Air Force)
AAC . . . . Alumnae Advisory Center
AAC . . . . Amateur Athletic Club
AAC . . . . American Academy of Criminalistics
AAC . . . . American Alpine Club
AAC . . . . American Alumni Council
AAC . . . . American Archery Council
AAC . . . . American Association of Criminology
AAC . . . . American Cement Corp. (NYSE symbol)
AAC . . . . Amplitude Absorption Coefficient
AAC . . . . Anno Ante Christum (In the Year Before Christ)
AAC . . . . Antiaircraft Command
AAC . . . . Antiaircraft Common (Projectile)
AAC . . . . Armor and Arms Club
AAC . . . . Army Air Corps
AAC . . . . Association of American Choruses
AAC . . . . Association of American Colleges
AAC . . . . Atomic Absorption Coefficient
AAC . . . . Automatic Aperture Control
AAC . . . . Automatic Autocollimator
AAC . . . . Automotive Advertisers Council
AAC . . . . Aviation Armament Change
AACA . . . . . . Allied Control Commission for Austria
AACA . . . . . . Antique Automobile Club of America
AACA . . . . . . Automotive Air Conditioning Association
AACB . . . . . . Aeronautics and Astronautics Coordinating Board (NASA)

AACB . . . . Allied Control Commission for Bulgaria
AACB . . . . Aviation and Astronautics Coordinating Board (NASA/DOD)
AACBC . . . . . Association of College Baseball Coaches
AACBP . . . . . . American Academy of Crown and Bridge Prosthodontics
AACC . . . . . . American Association of Cereal Chemists
AACC . . . . . . American Association of Clinical Chemists
AACC . . . . . . American Association for Contamination Control
AACC . . . . . . American Association of Credit Counselors
AACC . . . . . . American Automatic Control Council
AACC . . . . . . Association for the Aid of Crippled Children
AACC . . . . Automatic Approach Control Coupler (Aerospace)
AACCC . . . . . All-American Conference to Combat Communism
AACCLA . . . . . Association of American Chambers of Commerce in Latin America
AACCN . . . . . American Association of Critical-Care Nurses
AACCP . . . . . American Association of Colleges of Chiropody-Podiatry
AACE . . . . . . American Association for Cancer Education
AACE . . . . . . American Association of Cost Engineers
AACFT . . . . . . Army Aircraft
AACG. . . . . . . Allied Control Council for Germany
AACG . . . . . . American Association for Crystal Growth
AACH. . . . . . . Allied Control Commission for Hungary
AACHS . . . . . . Afro-American Cultural and Historical Society
AACI . . . . Allied Control Commission for Italy
AACI . . . . American Association for Conservation Information
AACIGO . . . . Association of American and Canadian Importers of Green Olives
AACJ . . . . Allied Control Council for Japan
AACL . . . . Affect Adjective Check List (Psychology)
AACM . . . . . . African Anti-Colonial Movement of Kenya
AACM . . . . . . American Academy of Compensation Medicine
AACO . . . . . . American Association of Certified Orthoptists
AACO . . . . . . Assault Airlift Control Officer
AACOMS . . . . Army Area Communications System
AACP . . . . . . Air Carrier Contract Personnel
AACP . . . . . . American Academy for Cerebral Palsy
AACP . . . . . . American Academy of Child Psychiatry
AACP . . . . . . American Association of Colleges of Pharmacy
AACP . . . . . . American Association of Colleges of Podiatry
AACP . . . . . . American Association of Commerce Publications (Later, American Chamber of Commerce Executives Communications Council)
AACP . . . . . . American Association of Convention Planners
AACP . . . . . . American Association of Correctional Psychologists
AACPR . . . . . American Association for Cleft Palate Rehabilitation
AACPS . . . . . . American Association of Clinic Physicians and Surgeons
AACR . . . . . . Allied Control Commission for Rumania
AACR . . . . . . American Association for Cancer Research
AACR . . . . . . American Association of Conservators and Restorers
AACR . . . . . . Anglo-American Cataloging Rules
AACRAO . . . . American Association of Collegiate Registrars and Admissions Officers
AA-C & Ref Tech . . Associate in Air-Conditioning and Refrigeration Technology
AACS . . . . Airborne Astrographic Camera System (Air Force)
AACS . . . . . . Airways and Air Communications Service (Air Force)
AACS . . . . . . Army Airways Communications System
AACS . . . . . . Army Alaska Communication System (Air Force)
AACSB . . . . . American Association of Collegiate Schools of Business
AACSL . . . . . American Association for the Comparative Study of Law
AACSM. . . . . . Airways and Air Communications Service Manual
AACT . . . . . . American Association of Commodity Traders
AACTE . . . . . American Association of Colleges for Teacher Education
AACUBO . . . . American Association of College and University Business Officers
AAD . . . . Active Acoustic Device
AAD . . . . Admission and Disposition (Military)
AAD . . . . Air Assault Division (Army)
AAD . . . . Aircraft and Armament Development
AAD . . . . Aircraft Assignment Directive
AAD . . . . Alloxazine Adenine Dinucleotide
AAD . . . . American Academy of Dentists
AAD . . . . American Academy of Dermatology
AAD. . . . . Arlans Department Stores, Inc. (NYSE symbol)
AAD. . . . . Arms & Ammunition Division (Army)
AAD . . . . Army Air Defense
AAD . . . . Association of American Dentists
AADA . . . . . . Advanced Air Depot Area (Air Force)
AADA. . . . . . . Antiaircraft Defense Area
AADA . . . . . . Army Air Defense Area
AADC. . . . . . . Advanced Avionic Digital Computer (Naval Air Systems Command)
AADC. . . . . . . Antiaircraft Director Center
AADC . . . . . . Army Air Defense Command(er)
AADC. . . . . . . Arnold Air Development Center (Air Force)
AADC. . . . . . . Association of American Dance Companies
AADCM . . . . . Awaiting Action Deck Court-Martial
AADCP . . . . . Army Air Defense Command Post

AADE . . . . . . American Academy of Dental Electrosurgery
AADE . . . . . . American Association of Dental Editors
AADE . . . . . American Association of Dental Examiners
AADIS . . . . . . Army Air Defense Information Service
AADLA . . . . . Art and Antique Dealers League of America
AADM . . . . . . American Academy of Dental Medicine
A Adm. . . . . . Associate in Administration
AADN . . . . . . American Association of Doctors' Nurses
AADO. . . . . . . Accepted Alternative Designation Of
AADOO . . . . Army Air Defense Operations Office(r)
AADPA . . . . . American Academy of Dental Practice Administration
AA & DPD . . . . Appropriation Accounts and Data Processing Division (Ministry of Agriculture, Fisheries, and Food) (British)
AADS . . . . . . Advanced Air Defense System
AADS . . . . . . American Association of Dental Schools
AADS . . . . . . Army Air Defense System (Formerly, FABMDS)
AADS . . . . . . Automatic Aircraft Diagnostic System
AADV . . . . . . Acquisition Aid Vehicle (Army)
AADW . . . . . . Advanced Air Defense Weapon
AAE . . . . Aerospace Ancillary Equipment
AAE . . . . Amerace Esna Corporation (NYSE symbol)
AAE . . . . American Academic Environments, Inc.
AAE . . . . American Association on Emeriti
AAE . . . . American Association of Endodontists
AAE . . . . American Association of Engineers
AAE . . . . Apparent Activation Energy
AAE . . . . Army Aviation Element
AAE . . . . Army Aviation Engineers
AAEA . . . . . . American Agricultural Editors' Association
AAEC . . . . . . Association of American Editorial Cartoonists
AAEC . . . . . . Attitude Axis Emergency Control (Aerospace)
AAEC . . . . . . Australian Atomic Energy Commission
AAEE . . . . . . Airplane & Armament Experimental Establishment (British)
AAEE . . . . . . American Academy of Environmental Engineers
A Ae E . . . . . . Associate in Aeronautical Engineering
AAEH . . . . . . Association to Advance Ethical Hypnosis
AAEP . . . . . . American Association of Equine Practitioners
AAES . . . . . . American Association of Evangelical Students
AAESWB . . . . Army Airborne Electronics & Special Warfare Board (Army)
AAEW. . . . . . . Atlantic Airborne Early Warning (Military)
AAF . . . . Acetylaminofluorene
AAF . . . . Agglutination Activating Factor (Medicine)
AAF . . . . Agricultural Aids Foundation
AAF . . . . American Advertising Federation
AAF . . . . American Air Filter Company, Inc. (NYSE symbol)
AAF . . . . American Architectural Foundation
AAF . . . . American Astronautical Federation
AAF . . . . Amino Acid Formula (Biochemistry)
AAF . . . . Army Air Forces
AAF . . . . Army Airfield
AAF . . . . Atlantic Amphibious Force (Navy)
AAFAS . . . . . Army Air Forces Aid Society (World War II)
AAFB . . . . . . Andrews Air Force Base
AAFB . . . . . . Army and Air Force Base
AAFB . . . . . . Army Air Force Board
AAFB . . . . . . Auxiliary Air Force Base
AAFBD . . . . . Army and Air Force Exchange and Motion Picture Services Board of Directors (DOD)
AAFBS . . . . . Army Air Forces Bombardier School
AAFBTC . . . . . Army Air Forces Basic Training Center
AAFBU . . . . . Army Air Forces Base Unit
AAFC . . . . . . Air Accounting and Finance Center (Air Force)
AAFC . . . . . . Airborne Audio Frequency Coder
AAFC . . . . . . All-America Football Conference (Major league 1946-49, merged with NFL 1950)
AAFC . . . . . . Antiaircraft Fire Control
AAFC . . . . . . Army Air Forces Center
AAFC . . . . . . Association of Advertising Film Companies
AAFCC . . . . . Army Air Force Classification Center
AAFCE . . . . . Allied Air Force, Central Europe
AAFCFTC . . . . Army Air Force Central Flying Training Command
AAFCO . . . . . Association of American Feed Control Officials
AAFCO . . . . . Association of American Fertilizer Control Officials
A-AFCPB. . . . . Army-Air Force Clemency and Parole Board
AAFCTTC . . . . Army Air Force Central Technical Training Command
AAFCWF . . . . Army and Air Force Central Welfare Fund
AAFCWF . . . . Army and Air Force Civilian Welfare Fund
AAFE . . . . . . Advanced Applications Flight Experiment (NASA)
AAFE . . . . . . American Association of Feed Exporters
AAFE . . . . . . American Association of Forms Executives
AAFEC . . . . . Army Air Forces Engineer Command

AAFEFTC..... Army Air Force Eastern Flying Training Command
AAFEMPS .... Army and Air Force Exchange and Motion Picture Service
AAFES ...... Army and Air Force Exchange Service
AAFETTC..... Army Air Force Eastern Technical Training Command
AAFFTD ..... Army Air Force Flying Training Detachment
AAFG....... Amino Acid Formula with Glutamate (Biochemistry)
AAFGH...... Al-Anon Family Group Headquarters
AAFGS...... Army Air Forces Gunnery School
AAFH....... Academy of American Franciscan History
AAFIF....... Automated Air Facilities Intelligence File (Naval Oceanographic Office)
AAFIS....... Army Air Forces Intelligence School
AAFM ...... American Association of Feed Microscopists
AAFMTO .... Army Air Force Headquarters, Mediterranean Theater of Operations
AAFMC...... Army Air Forces Materiel Center
AAFMPS ..... Army and Air Force Motion Picture Service
AAFNE...... Allied Air Force Northern Europe
AAFNS...... Army Air Forces Navigation School
AAFOIC ..... Army Air Force Officer in Charge
AAFP .... American Academy of Family Physicians (Formerly, American Academy of General Practice)
AAFPFS(P).... Army Air Forces Pre-Flight School (Pilot)
AAFPOA ..... Army Air Forces, Pacific Ocean Areas
AAFPOA ADMIN .. Army Air Forces, Pacific Ocean Areas (Administrative)
AAFPS ...... Army and Air Force Postal Service
AAFPS ...... Army Air Forces Pilot School
AAFRC ...... American Association of Fund-Raising Counsel
AAFS .... American Academy of Forensic Sciences
AAFS .... American Association of Foot Specialists
AAFS .... Amphibious Assault Fuel System
AAFS .... Association for the Advancement of Family Stability
AAFS .... Atomic Absorption Flame Spectrometer
AAFSAT...... Army Air Forces School of Applied Tactics (World War II)
AAFSC ...... Additional Air Force Specialty Code
AAFSC ...... Army Air Forces Service Command
AAFSE ...... Allied Air Force Southern Europe
AAFSS ...... Advanced Aerial Fire Support System (Army)
AAFSSO ..... Advanced Aerial Fire Support System Office (Army)
AAFSW...... Association of American Foreign Service Women
AAFTAC ..... Army Air Forces Tactical Center (World War II)
AAFTAD ..... Army Air Forces Training Aids Division (World War II)
AAFTC ...... Army Air Forces Training Command (World War II)
AAFTS ...... Army Air Forces Technical School
AAFTTC ..... Army Air Forces Technical Training Command (World War II)
AAFWB...... Army and Air Force Wage Board
AAFWFTC .... Army Air Force Western Flying Training Command
AAFWTTC .... Army Air Forces Western Technical Training Command
AAG .... Air Adjutant-General
AAG .... Assistant Adjutant-General
AAG .... Association of American Geographers
AAGBA...... American Angora Goat Breeders' Association
AAGC ...... American Association for Gifted Children
AAGCM ..... Awaiting Action General Court-Martial
AAGFO ..... American Academy of Gold Foil Operators
AAGMS ..... Antiaircraft Guided Missile System
AAGO ...... Associate of American Guild of Organists
AAGp....... Aeromedical Airlift Group (Air Force)
AAGP....... American Academy of General Practice (Later, American Academy of Family Physicians)
AAGR ...... Air-to-Air Gunnery Range
A Agri ..... Associate in Agriculture
AAGS ...... All-America Gladiolus Selections
AAGUS ..... American Association of Genito-Urinary Surgeons
AAGS....... Army Air-Ground System
AAH....... Air Arc Heater
AAH....... American Academy of Homiletics
AAHA...... American All-Hobbies Association
AAHA ..... American Animal Hospital Association
AAHA...... American Association of Handwriting Analysts
AAHA...... American Association of Homes for the Aging
AAHA...... American Association of Hospital Accountants
AAHA ..... Awaiting Action (of) Higher Authority (Army)
AAHBE...... Anglo-American-Hellenic Bureau of Education
AAHC...... American Albino Horse Club
AAHC...... American Association of Hospital Consultants
AAHD...... American Academy of the History of Dentistry
AAHDC..... American Association of Hospital Dental Chiefs
AAHE...... American Association for Higher Education
AAHE...... American Association of Housing Educators
AAHE...... Associate in Arts in Home Economics
AAHH...... Air Arc Heater Housing
AAHM...... American Association for the History of Medicine

AAHM ...... Association of Architectural Hardware Manufacturers
AAHP ...... American Association for Hospital Planning
AAHP ...... American Association of Hospital Podiatrists
AAHP ...... American Association for Humanistic Psychology
AAHPA ...... American Association of Hospital Purchasing Agents
AAHPER ..... American Association for Health, Physical Education and Recreation
AAHPhA .... American Animal Health Pharmaceutical Association
AAHQ ..... Allied Air Headquarters
AAHS....... American Aviation Historical Society
AAI .... African-American Institute
AAI .... Agricultural Ammonia Institute
AAI .... Air-to-Air Identification
AAI .... Air-to-Air Intercept
AAI .... Airborne Alert Indoctrination
AAI .... Aircraft Armaments, Incorporated
AAI .... Alfred Adler Institute
AAI .... All Attitude Indicator
AAI .... Allied Armies in Italy
AAI .... American Association of Immunologists
AAI .... American Audio Institute
AAI .... Angle of Approach Indicator (Aviation)
AAI .... Angle of Attack Indicator
AAI .... Atlantic Art Institute
AAI .... Azimuth Angle Increment
AAIA ...... Association of American Indian Affairs
AAIAN ..... Association for the Advancement of Instruction about Alcohol and Narcotics
AAIB .... American Association of Instructors of the Blind
AAIC .... Allied Air Intelligence Center
AAIC .... American Amateur Inventors Club
AAICD ...... American Association of Imported Car Dealers
AAID .... American Academy of Implant Dentures
AAID .... American Association of Industrial Dentists
AAID .... Arithmetic Array Identification
AAIE .... American Association of Industrial Editors
AAIE .... American Association of Industrial Engineers
AAII........ Association for the Advancement of Invention and Innovation (Patent lobby)
AAIL .... Airborne Argon Ion LASER
AAIM ...... American Association of Industrial Management
AAIN ...... American Association of Industrial Nurses
AAIP .... Academic Administration Internship Program
AAIS .... Antiaircraft Artillery Intelligence Service
AAIT .... American Association of Inhalation Therapists
AAJ .... Arab Airways (Jerusalem) Ltd.
AAJ .... Augmented Air Jet
AAJC .... American Association of Junior Colleges
AAJCS ...... Anglo-American Joint Chiefs of Staff
AAJE .... American Association for Jewish Education
AAJR .... American Academy for Jewish Research
AAJS .... American Association of Jesuit Scientists
AAJSA ...... American Association of Journalism School Administrators
AAL........ Acoustical Absorption Loss
AAL .... Aid Association for Lutherans
AAL........ Aircraft Approach Limitation
AAL........ All American Life & Financial Corp. (NYSE symbol)
AAL........ Ames Aeronautical Laboratory (Air Force)
AAL........ Arctic Aerospace Laboratory (Air Force)
AAL........ Arctic Approach Limitation
AAL Agri ... Aviation Armament Laboratory (Navy) (Later, Naval Air Development Center)
AALA ...... American Auto Laundry Association
AALA ...... American Automotive Leasing Association
AALA....... Associate in Arts in Liberal Arts
AALC ...... African-American Labor Center (AFL-CIO)
AALC ...... Amplified Automatic Level Control (Air Force)
AALCI ...... Ateitis Association of Lithuanian Catholic Intellectuals
AALL ...... American Association of Law Libraries
AALMG .... Anti-Aircraft Light Machine Gun
AALPP ...... American Association for Legal and Political Philosophy
AALS ...... American Association of Language Specialists
AALS ...... Association of American Law Schools
AALS ...... Association of American Library Schools
AALT ...... American Association of Library Trustees
AALU ...... Association for Advanced Life Underwriting
AALUE ..... Asymptotically Admissible Linear Unbiased Estimator (Statistics)
AAM ...... Acoustic Analysis Memo (Navy)
AAM ...... Air-to-Air Missile
AAM ...... American Academy of Microbiology
AAM ...... American Association of Museums
AAM ...... American Medicorp, Inc. (NYSE symbol)

ACRONYMS AND INITIALISMS DICTIONARY

AAM . . . . Anti-Antimissile Missile
AAM . . . . Army Aircraft Maintenance
AAM . . . . Australian Air Mission
A/AM . . . . Air-to-Air Missile
AAMA . . . . . . American Academy of Medical Administrators
AAMA . . . . . . American Agricultural Marketing Association
AAMA . . . . . . American Apparel Manufacturers Association
AAMA . . . . . . American Association of Medical Assistants
AAMA . . . . Architectural Aluminum Manufacturers Association
AAMBP . . . . . Association of American Medical Book Publishers
AAMC . . . . . . American Association of Marriage Counselors
AAMC . . . . . . American Association of Medical Clinics
AAMC. . . . . . . Army Artillery and Missile Center
AAMC . . . . . . Army Aviation Materiel Command
AAMC . . . . . . Association of American Medical Colleges
AAMC . . . . . . Australian Army Medical Corps
AAMCH . . . . . American Association for Maternal and Child Health
AAMD . . . . . . American Association on Mental Deficiency
AAMD . . . . . . Association of Art Museum Directors
AAMES . . . . . . American Association for Middle East Studies
AAMF. . . . . . . American Association of Music Festivals
AAMFC . . . . . American Association of Marriage and Family Counselors
AAMG . . . . . . Anti-Aircraft Machine Gun
AAMGA . . . . American Association of Managing General Agents
AAMGE . . . . . Air-to-Air Missile Guidance Element
AAMI . . . . . . American Association of Machinery Importers
AAMI . . . . Association for the Advancement of Medical Instrumentation
AAMI . . . . . . Association of Allergists for Mycological Investigations
AAMID . . . . . . Accomplishment of Assigned Mission Impeded by Deadline (Army)
AAMIH . . . . . American Association for Maternal and Infant Health
AAML . . . . . . Arctic Aeromedical Laboratory (Air Force)
AAML . . . . . . Army Aviation Materiel Laboratory
AAMLS . . . . . . Association of Accredited Medical Laboratory Schools
AAMMC . . . . American Association of Medical Milk Commissions
AAMP . . . . . . American Academy of Maxillofacial Prosthetics
AAMR. . . . . . . American Academy on Mental Retardation
AAMREP . . . . Air-to-Air Missile Weapon System Flight Report
AAMRL . . . . . American Association of Medical Record Librarians
AAMS . . . . Airborne Auxiliary Memory System
AAMS . . . . American Air Mail Society
AAMS . . . . Army Aircraft Maintenance Shop
AAMS . . . . Army Artillery & Missile School
AAMU . . . . . . Army Advanced Marksmanship Unit
AAMVA . . . . . American Association of Motor Vehicle Administrators
AAMW . . . . . . Association of Advertising Men and Women (Later, Advertising and Marketing Association)
AAN . . . . American Academy of Neurology
AAN . . . . American Academy of Nutrition
AAN . . . . American Association of Neuropathologists
AAN . . . . American Association of Nurserymen
AAN . . . . Aminoacetonitrile (Organic chemistry)
AANA . . . . . . American Association of Nurse Anesthetists
AANM . . . . . . American Association of Nurse-Midwives
AANN . . . . . . American Association of Neurosurgical Nurses
AANO . . . . . . Albanian-American National Organization
AANP. . . . . . . Aircraft Accident Notification Procedures and Bureau Responsibilities (Manual)
AANR . . . . . . American Association of Newspaper Representatives
AANS . . . . . . American Academy of Neurological Surgery
AAO . . . . Academy of Applied Osteopathy
AAO . . . . American Academy of Optometry
AAO . . . . American Academy of Organ
AAO . . . . American Association of Ophthalmology
AAO . . . . American Association of Orthodontists
AAO . . . . Anti-Air Output
AAO . . . . Authorized Acquisition Objective (Army)
AAOA . . . . . . Ambulance Association of America
AAOA . . . . . . Auxiliary to the American Osteopathic Association
AAOC . . . . . . American Association of Osteopathic Colleges
AAOC . . . . . . Antiaircraft Operations Center (Air Force)
AAOD . . . . . . Army Aviation Operating Detachment
AAODC . . . . . American Association of Oilwell Drilling Contractors
AAOG . . . . . . American Association of Obstetricians and Gynecologists
AAOM . . . . . . American Academy of Occupational Medicine
AAOM . . . . . . American Academy of Oral Medicine
AAOME . . . . . American Association of Osteopathic Medical Examiners
AAONMS . . . . Imperial Council of the Ancient Arabic Order of the Nobles of the Mystic Shrine for North America
AAOO . . . . . . American Academy of Ophthalmology and Otolaryngology
AAOP. . . . . . . American Academy of Oral Pathology
AAOP. . . . . . . Antiaircraft Observation Post

AAOR. . . . . . . American Academy of Oral Roentgenology
AAOS . . . . . . American Academy of Orthopaedic Surgeons
AAOT . . . . . . American Association of Orthoptic Technicians
AAP. . . . . Academy of American Poets
AAP . . . . Advise If Able to Proceed (Aviation)
AAP . . . . Aerodynamics Advisory Panel (AEC)
AAP . . . . Aircraft Assembly Plant
AAP . . . . Allied Administrative Publication
AAP . . . . American Academy of Pediatrics
AAP . . . . American Academy of Pedodontics
AAP . . . . American Academy of Periodontology
AAP . . . . American Academy of Psychotherapists
AAP . . . . American Association of the Professions
AAP . . . . Analog Antenna Positioner
AAP . . . . Apollo Applications Program (NASA)
AAP . . . . Association for the Advancement of Psychoanalysis
AAP . . . . Association for the Advancement of Psychotherapy
AAP . . . . Association of American Physicians
AAP . . . . Association of American Publishers (Formerly, ABPC and AEPI)
AAP . . . . Association for Applied Psychoanalysis
AAPA . . . . . . American Amateur Press Association
AAPA . . . . . . American Association of Physical Anthropologists
AAPA . . . . . . American Association of Port Authorities
AAPB . . . . . . American Association of Pathologists and Bacteriologists
AAPC . . . . . . Advertising Agency Production Club of New York
AAPC . . . . . . All African Peoples' Conference
AAPC . . . . . . American Association of Pastoral Counselors
AAPC . . . . . . American Association of Political Consultants
AAPCC . . . . . . American Association of Poison Control Centers
AAPCC . . . . . . American Association of Psychiatric Clinics for Children
AAPCM . . . . . Association of American Playing Card Manufacturers
AAPCO . . . . . Association of American Pesticide Control Officials
AAPD . . . . . . American Academy of Physiologic Dentistry
AAPE . . . . . . American Academy of Physical Education
AAPG . . . . . . American Association of Petroleum Geologists
AAPH . . . . . . American Association on Professional Hypnologists
AAPHD . . . . . American Association of Public Health Dentists
AAPHP . . . . . American Association of Public Health Physicians
AAPIU . . . . . . Allied Aerial Photographic Interpretation Unit (Obsolete)
AAPL . . . . Afro-American Patrolmen's League
AAPL . . . . American Artists Professional League
AAPL . . . . American Association of Petroleum Landmen
AAPM . . . . . . American Association of Physicists in Medicine
AAPM . . . . . . Army Aviation Planning Manual
AAPMR . . . . . American Academy of Physical Medicine and Rehabilitation
AAPO . . . . Advanced Aircraft Programs Office
AAPO . . . . Apollo Applications Program Office (NASA)
AAPOR . . . . . American Association for Public Opinion Research
AAPPP . . . . . . American Association of Planned Parenthood Physicians
AAPRM . . . . . American Association of Passenger Rate Men
AAPS . . . . Airborne Angular Position Sensor
AAPS . . . . American Association of Plastic Surgeons
AAPS . . . . American Association for the Promotion of Science
AAPS . . . . Association for Ambulatory Pediatric Services
AAPS . . . . Association of American Physicians and Surgeons
AAPSC . . . . . . Afro-Asian Peoples Solidarity Council
AAPSE . . . . . . American Association of Professors in Sanitary Engineering
AAPSS. . . . . . . American Academy of Political and Social Science
AAPT. . . . . . . American Association of Physics Teachers
AAPT . . . . Association of Asphalt Paving Technologists
AAPTO . . . . . . American Association of Passenger Traffic Officers
AAQ . . . . Architectural Association Quarterly
AAQM . . . . . . Acting Assistant Quartermaster (Marine Corps)
AAR. . . . . After Action Report (Military)
AAR . . . . Against All Risks (Business and trade)
AAR . . . . Air Augmented Rocket
AAR . . . . Aircraft Accident Record (Military)
AAR . . . . Aircraft Accident Report
AAR . . . . Alternate Acquisition RADAR
AAR . . . . American Academy of Religion
AAR . . . . American Academy in Rome
AAR . . . . Army Area Representative
AAR . . . . Association of American Railroads
AAR . . . . Association of American Rhodes Scholars
AAR . . . . Automotive Affiliated Representatives
AARA . . . . . . American Arab Relief Agency
A Arch . . . . . . Associate in Architecture
AARD . . . . . . American Academy of Restorative Dentistry
AARDCO . . . . Association of American Railroad Dining Car Officers
AARDL . . . . . Artillery Ammunition and Rocket Development Laboratory (Army)
AARDS . . . . . . Australian Advertising Rate and Data Service

AARGCE . . . . . Association of American Rod and Gun Clubs in Europe
AARL . . . . Army Aeronautical Research Center (Ames Research Center) (Army)
AARM . . . . . . Advanced Anti-Radiation Missile
AARP . . . . American Association of Retired Persons
AARP . . . . Annual Advance Retainer Pay
AARPS . . . . . . Air Augmented Rocket Propulsion System
AARR . . . . Argonne Advanced Research Reactor (AEC)
AARRB . . . . . . Army Aircraft Requirements Review Committee
AARS . . . . Air Force Aerospace Rescue and Recovery Service
AARS . . . . All-America Rose Selections
AARS . . . . American Association of Railroad Superintendents
AARS . . . . American Association of Railway Surgeons
AARS . . . . Anonymous Arts Recovery Society
AARS . . . . Army Aircraft Repair Ship
AARS . . . . Army Amateur Radio System
AARS . . . . Automated Attendance Reporting System
AART . . . . American Association for Rehabilitation Therapy
AART . . . . American Association of Religious Therapists
AARTA . . . . . . American Association of Railroad Ticket Agents
AARTS . . . . . . Association of Advanced Rabbinical and Talmudic Schools (Formerly, Council of Roshay Hayeshivoth)
AARV . . . . Aerial Armored Reconnaissance Vehicle
AARWBA . . . . . American Auto Racing Writers and Broadcasters Association
AAS . . . . Aberdeen Art Society
AAS . . . . Abort Advisory System (NASA)
AAS . . . . Academiae Americanae Socius (Fellow of the American Academy)
AAS . . . . Academy of Applied Science
AAS . . . . Achievement Anxiety Scale (Psychology)
AAS . . . . Adjusted Air Speed (Navigation)
AAS . . . . Advanced Antenna System (Air Force)
AAS . . . . Airborne Antenna System
AAS . . . . Aircraft Airworthiness Section
AAS . . . . Airport Advisory Service
AAS . . . . Alert Area Supervisor (Military)
AAS . . . . All-America Selections
AAS . . . . American Amaryllis Society
AAS . . . . American Antiquarian Society
AAS . . . . American Association of Suicidology
AAS . . . . American Astronautical Society
AAS . . . . American Astronomical Society
AAS . . . . Analog Alarm Section
AAS . . . . Angular Acceleration Susceptibility (Orientation)
AAS . . . . Annual Average Score
AAS . . . . Arithmetic Assignment Statement
AAS . . . . Army Air Service
AAS . . . . Army Attaché System
AAS . . . . Arnold Air Society
AAS . . . . Associate in Applied Science
AAS . . . . Associate in Secretarial Science
AAS . . . . Associated Spring Corp. (NYSE symbol)
AAS . . . . Association for Asian Studies
AAS . . . . Atomic Absorption Spectrometer (or Spectroscopy)
AASA . . . . . . Administrative Assistant to the Secretary of the Army
AASA . . . . . . Afro-American Student Association
AASA . . . . . . American Association of School Administrators
AASACM . . . . American Association of Swiss Alpine Club Members
AASB . . . . American Association of Small Business
AASC . . . . Allied Air Support Command (Mediterranean)
AASC . . . . American Association of Specialized Colleges
AASC . . . . Army Area Signal Center
AASCM . . . . . . Awaiting Action Summary Court-Martial
AASCO . . . . . Association of American Seed Control Officials
AASD . . . . Antiaircraft Self-Destroying
AASDJ . . . . . . American Association of Schools and Departments of Journalism
AASE . . . . American Academy of Safety Education
AASE . . . . . . Association for Applied Solar Energy
AASEC . . . . . . American Association of Sex Educators and Counselors
AASFE . . . . . . American Association of Sunday and Feature Editors
AASG . . . . Association of American State Geologists
AAS & GP . . . . American Association of Soap and Glycerin Producers
AASHO . . . . . American Association of State Highway Officials
AASI . . . . Advertising Agency Service Interchange
AASL . . . . American Association of School Librarians
AASL . . . . Antiaircraft Searchlight
AASLH . . . . . . American Association for State and Local History
AASLT . . . . . Air Assault (Army)
AASM . . . . . . Association of American Steel Manufacturers
AASND . . . . . American Association for Study of Neoplastic Diseases
AASO . . . . . . Association of American Ship Owners
AASP . . . . American Association of Sheep Practitioners

AASP . . . . American Association for Social Psychiatry
AASP . . . . American Association of Stratigraphic Palynologists
AASPA . . . . . . American Association of School Personnel Administrators
AASPRC . . . . . American Association of Sheriff Posses and Riding Clubs
AASq . . . . Aeromedical Airlift Squadron (Air Force)
AASR . . . . Advanced Army System Requirements
AASR . . . . Airport and Airways Surveillance RADAR (Air Force)
AASR . . . . American Association of Securities Representatives
AASR . . . . Ancient Accepted Scottish Rite (Masonic)
AASRE . . . . . . American Association of Schools of Religious Education
AASRI . . . . . . Arctic and Antarctic Scientific Research Institute
AASR-NMJ . . . Supreme Council, Ancient Accepted Scottish Rite of Freemasonry, Northern Masonic Jurisdiction
AASR-SMJ . . . . Supreme Council 33°, Ancient and Accepted Scottish Rite of Freemasonry, Southern Masonic Jurisdiction
AASS . . . . Advanced Airborne Surveillance Sensor
AASS . . . . American Association for Social Security
AASS . . . . Americanae Antiquarianae Societatis Socius (Fellow of the American Antiquarian Society)
AASS . . . . Automatic Abort-Sensing System (NASA)
AAST . . . . American Association for the Surgery of Trauma
AASW . . . . . . Airborne Antisubmarine Warfare
AASWI . . . . . . American Aid Society for the West Indies
AAT . . . . Antiaircraft Technician
AAT . . . . Attitude Acquisition Technique
AAT . . . . Attitude Angle Transducer
AATA . . . . American Association of Teachers of Arabic
AATA . . . . American Automobile Touring Alliance
AATB . . . . Advanced Amphibious Training Base (Navy)
AATB . . . . Army Aviation Test Board
AATC . . . . Anti-Aircraft Training Center (Navy)
AATC . . . . Army Aviation Test Command (ATEC)
AATCAN . . . . . Army Air Traffic Control and Navigation System
AATCC . . . . . American Association of Textile Chemists and Colorists
AATCLC . . . . . American Association of Teachers of Chinese Language and Culture
AATCM . . . . . . Academy of Air Traffic Control Medicine
AATE . . . . Avionics Automatic Transmission Line
AATEA . . . . . . American Association of Teacher Educators in Agriculture
AA Tech . . . . . Associate in Automotive Technology
AA Ter Ed . . . . Associate in Arts in Terminal Education
AATESL . . . . . American Association of Teachers of English as a Second Language
AATF . . . . American Association of Teachers of French
AATG . . . . American Association of Teachers of German
AATI . . . . American Association of Teachers of Italian
AATNU . . . . . . Administration de l'Assistance Technique des Nations Unies
AATOC . . . . . Airhead Air Traffic Coordination Center (Army)
AATP . . . . American Academy of Tuberculosis Physicians
AATPA . . . . . . American Association of Traveling Passenger Agents
AATR . . . . Apollo Applications Test Requirements (NASA)
AATRACEN . . . Anti-Aircraft Training Center (Navy)
AATRI . . . . . . Army Air Traffic Regulation and Identification
AATRIS . . . . . . Army Air Traffic Regulation and Identification System
AATS . . . . American Academy of Teachers of Singing
AATS . . . . American Association of Theological Schools
AATS . . . . American Association for Thoracic Surgery
AATS . . . . Automatic Altitude Trim System (Helicopter) (Navy)
AATS . . . . Automatic Anti-Theft System (Electronic lock)
AATSEEL . . . . . American Association of Teachers of Slavic and East European Languages
AATSP . . . . . . American Association of Teachers of Spanish and Portuguese
AATT . . . . American Association for Textile Technology
AAT & TC . . . . Anti-Aircraft Training & Test Center (Navy)
AATU . . . . Association of Air Transport Unions
AATUF . . . . . . All-African Trade Union Federation
AAU . . . . Administrative Area Unit (Army)
AAU . . . . Amateur Athletic Union
AAU . . . . Angular Accelerometer Unit
AAU . . . . Association of American Universities
AAUN . . . . . . American Association for the United Nations (Later, United Nations Association of the United States)
AAUP . . . . American Association of University Professors
AAUP . . . . Association of American University Presses
AAUP-UAES . . . American Association of University Professors of Urban Affairs and Environmental Sciences
AAUTC . . . . . . Army Aviation Unit Training Command
AAUTI . . . . . . American Association of University Teachers of Insurance
AAUW . . . . . . American Association of University Women
AAV . . . . Airborne Assault Vehicle
AAV . . . . Antiaircraft Volunteer
AAVA . . . . American Association of Veterinary Anatomists
AAVB . . . . American Association of Veterinary Bacteriologists

AAVC . . . . . . Anomalous Atrioventricular Conduction (Cardiology)
AAVCS . . . . . Automatic Aircraft Vectoring Control System (Air Force)
AAVD. . . . . . Automatic Alternate Voice/Data (Data processing)
AAVMC . . . . . Association of American Veterinary Medical Colleges
AAVN . . . . . . American Association of Veterinary Nutritionists
AAVN . . . . . . Army Aviation
AAVP . . . . . . American Association of Veterinary Parasitologists
AAVRO . . . . . American Association of Variable Star Observers
AAVRPHS . . . . American Association for Vital Records and Public Health Statistics
AAVS . . . . . . Aerospace Audio Visual Service (Air Force)
AAVS . . . . . . American Anti-Vivisection Society
AAVSC . . . . . American Association of Volunteer Services Coordinators
AAVSO . . . . . American Association of Variable Star Observers
A Av Tech . . . . Associate in Aviation Technology
AAW . . . . Advertising Association of the West
AAW . . . . Aeromedical Airlift Wing (Air Force)
AAW . . . . Anti-Air Warfare
AAWB . . . . . . American Association of Workers for the Blind
AAWC. . . . . . All-African Women's Conference
AAWC . . . . . . Australian Advisory War Council
AAWD . . . . . . Association of American Women Dentists
AAWE . . . . . . Association of American Wives of Europeans
AAWEX. . . . . . Anti-Air Warfare Exercises (Navy)
AAWF. . . . . . . Auxiliary Aviation Weather Facility (FAA)
AAWg. . . . . . . Aeromedical Airlift Wing (Air Force)
AAWM . . . . . . American Association of Women Ministers
AAWPI . . . . . . Association of American Wood Pulp Importers
AAWS. . . . . . . Airborne Alert Weapon System
AAWS. . . . . . . Anti-Air Warfare Systems (Navy)
AAWS. . . . . . . Automatic Attack Warning System
AAWWW . . . . . Amalgamated Association of Wistful War Wives (World War II)
AAXICO . . . . . American Air Export & Import Company
AAYM . . . . . . American Association of Youth Museums
AAYPL . . . . . . Atlantic Association of Young Political Leaders
AAZPA . . . . . American Association of Zoological Parks and Aquariums
AB . . . . Able-Bodied Seaman
AB . . . . Abortion Patient (Medicine)
AB . . . . Accessories Bulletin
AB . . . . Adapter Booster
AB . . . . Adapter, Bulkhead
AB . . . . Aerial Burst Bombs
AB . . . . Aeronautical Board (Air Force)
AB . . . . After Body
AB . . . . Afterburner
AB . . . . Aid to the Blind
AB . . . . Air Bags
AB . . . . Air Base
AB . . . . Air Bomber
AB . . . . Airborne
AB . . . . Airman Basic
AB . . . . Aktiebolaget (Swedish word for company)
Ab . . . . Alabamine (Chemical element) (Superseded by astatine)
AB . . . . All (text) Before (specified point) (Message handling)
AB . . . . Alliance Balkanique
AB . . . . Ambac Industries, Inc. (NYSE symbol)
AB . . . . American Bosch Arma Corporation (NYSE symbol) (Delisted)
AB . . . . American Bureau of Shipping
AB . . . . Anchor Bolt (Technical drawings)
AB . . . . Anheuser-Busch, Inc.
AB . . . . Anterior Burster (Neuron)
Ab . . . . Antibody (Immunology)
AB . . . . Arctic Bibliography (A publication)
AB . . . . Armor Board
AB . . . . Artium Baccalaureus (Bachelor of Arts)
AB . . . . Assembly Bill (in state legislatures)
AB . . . . Associate in Business
AB . . . . At Bat (Baseball)
AB . . . . Audio Bandwidth
AB . . . . Aviation Battalion (Army)
AB . . . . Aviation Boatswain's Mate
AB . . . . Crane Ship (Navy symbol)
AB . . . . Graduate in Arts (An academic degree)
A-B . . . . Allen-Bradley Company
A/B . . . . Afterburner (on jet engines)
A/B . . . . Air Blast
A/B . . . . Airborne
A/B . . . . Aircraft Bulletin
A/B . . . . Airman Basic
A/B . . . . Architectural Barriers
A & B . . . . . . Assault and Battery
ABA . . . . Aaron Burr Association

ABA . . . . Abscisic Acid (Biochemistry)
ABA . . . . Air Brake Association
ABA . . . . Aktiebolaget Aero Transport (Swedish Airlines)
ABA . . . . Aktiebolaget Atomenergi (Swedish nuclear development company)
ABA . . . . American Badminton Association
ABA . . . . American Bakeries Co. (NYSE symbol)
ABA . . . . American Bakers Association
ABA . . . . American Bandmasters Association
ABA . . . . American Bankers Association
ABA . . . . American Bantam Association
ABA . . . . American Bar Association
ABA . . . . American Basketball Association (League of professional basketball players)
ABA . . . . American Battleship Association
ABA . . . . American Bell Association
ABA . . . . American Berkshire Association
ABA . . . . American Board Association
ABA . . . . American Booksellers Association
ABA . . . . American Bowhunters Association
ABA . . . . American Brazilian Association
ABA . . . . American Bridge Association
ABA . . . . American, British, Australian (Military)
ABA . . . . American Buddhist Association
ABA . . . . Aminobutyric Acid
ABA . . . . Annual Budget Authorization
ABA . . . . Antoniani Benedictini Armeni (Mechitarists)
ABA . . . . Armadillo Breeders Association
ABA . . . . Associate in Business Administration
ABA . . . . Ayrshire Breeders' Association
ABAA . . . . . . Antiquarian Booksellers Association of America
ABAC . . . . . . Abraham Baldwin Agricultural College (Georgia)
ABACUS . . . . . Air Battle Analysis Center, United States Air Force
ABACUS . . . . . Aktiebolaget Atomenergi Computer-Based User-Oriented Service
ABACUS . . . . Autonetics Business and Control United Systems, Inc. (Data processing)
ABAD . . . . . . Air Battle Analysis Division (Air Force)
ABAG . . . . . . Association of Bay Area Governments (Northern California)
ABAKO. . . . . . Alliance des Bakongo (Alliance of the Bakongo People)
ABAKWA. . . . . Alliance de Baboma-Bateke du Kwamouth (Alliance of Baboma-Bateke People of Kwamouth)
ABAMP . . . . . Absolute Ampere
ABAR . . . . . . Advanced (or Alternate) Battery Acquisition RADAR
ABAS . . . . . . American Board of Abdominal Surgery
ABA/TCP . . . . American Bar Association Traffic Court Program
ABATE . . . . . Alliance des Bateke (Alliance of Bateke)
ABATU . . . . . Advanced Base Air Task Unit
ABATU . . . . . Advanced Base Aviation Training Unit (Navy)
ABAZI . . . . . . Alliance des Bayanzi (Alliance of Bayanzis)
ABB . . . . Ablating Blunt Body
ABB . . . . Akron & Barberton Belt R. R. (AAR code)
ABB . . . . American Board of Bioanalysis
ABB . . . . Automatic Back Bias (RADAR)
ABB . . . . Axisymmetric Blunt Body
ABBA . . . . . . American Blind Bowling Association
ABBA . . . . . . American Brahman Breeders Association
ABB-A . . . . . . American Board of Bio-Analysis
ABBB . . . . . . Association of Better Business Bureaus
AB (Bible) . . . . Bachelor of Arts in Bible
ABBR . . . . . . Abbreviation
ABBRA . . . . . American Boat Builders & Repairers Association
ABBREV . . . . . Abbreviation
ABBT . . . . . . Animated Backlighted Burtek Trainer
ABC . . . . ABC Consolidated Corporation (NYSE symbol) (Delisted)
ABC . . . . A Better Chance (Scholarship program for the underprivileged)
ABC . . . . Abridged Building Classification for Architects, Builders, and Civil Engineers
ABC . . . . Academia Brasileira de Ciencias (Brazil)
ABC . . . . Aconite, Belladonna, and Chloroform (Liniment compound)
ABC . . . . Action for Brain-Injured Children (An organization)
ABC . . . . Advanced Biological Capsule
ABC . . . . Advanced Biomedical Capsule
ABC . . . . Advancing Blade Concept (Helicopter)
ABC . . . . Aerated Bread Company
ABC . . . . Afghan Border Crusade
ABC . . . . After Bottom Center (Valve position)
ABC . . . . Air Bath Chamber
ABC . . . . Air Bubble Craft
ABC . . . . Alcoholic Beverage Control (Board)
ABC . . . . Ale, Bread and Cheese
ABC . . . . Algemene Bedrijfsgroepen Centrale (General Union of Workers in Miscellaneous Industries) (Netherlands)
ABC . . . . Allocations for Budgetary Control

ABC . . . . Alum, Blood, and Charcoal (A method of deodorizing by addition of a compound of these) (Medicine)
ABC . . . . American Baptist Convention
ABC . . . . American Beagle Club
ABC . . . . American Beveren Club
ABC . . . . American Bibliographical Center
ABC . . . . American Bloodhound Club
ABC . . . . American-Born Chinese
ABC . . . . American Bowling Congress
ABC . . . . American Boxer Club
ABC . . . . American Brahma Club
ABC . . . . American, British, and Canadian
ABC . . . . American-British Conversation (as ABC-1, 1941 report that set forth allied worldwide strategy) (World War II)
ABC . . . . American Brittany Club
ABC . . . . American Broadcasting Companies, Inc. (NYSE symbol)
ABC . . . . Amities Belgo-Congolaises (Belgian-Congolese Friendship Association)
ABC . . . . Antigen-Binding Capacity (Immunology)
ABC . . . . Any Boy Can (Program)
ABC . . . . Apparel Business Control (System) (Data processing)
ABC . . . . Approach by Concept (Information retrieval)
ABC . . . . Architectural Barriers Committee
ABC . . . . Argentina, Brazil, Chile
ABC . . . . Atomic, Biological and Chemical (as, ABC Officer, ABC Warfare)
ABC . . . . Audit Bureau of Circulations
ABC . . . . Australian Broadcasting Commission
ABC . . . . Australian Broadcasting Corporation
ABC . . . . Automatic Bandwidth Control (Air Force)
ABC . . . . Automatic Bar Checker
ABC . . . . Automatic Bass Compensation (Radio)
ABC . . . . Automatic Bass Control
ABC . . . . Automatic Bias Compensation (Air Force)
ABC . . . . Automatic Bias Control
ABC . . . . Automatic Blip Counter
ABC . . . . Automatic Boiling-Column Reactor
ABC . . . . Automatic Brightness Control
ABC . . . . Automotive Booster Clubs International
ABC . . . . Refers to federal-aid program for improvement of (A) primary highway system, (B) secondary highway system, and (C) extensions of federal-aid primary and secondary highway systems in urban areas.
AB & C . . . . . Atlanta, Birmingham and Coast Railroad Company
ABCA . . . . . . American, British, Canadian, and Australian
ABCA . . . . . . American Building Contractors Association
ABCA . . . . . . American Business Communication Association
ABCA . . . . . . Antique Bottle Collectors Association
ABCA . . . . . . Army Bureau of Current Affairs (To encourage British soldiers to think and talk about what they were fighting for) (World War II)
ABCAIRSTD . . . American-British-Canadian Air Standardization Agreement
ABC-ASP . . . American-British-Canadian Army Standardization Program
ABCB . . . . . . Air-Blast Circuit Breaker
ABCB . . . . . . American Bottlers of Carbonated Beverages
ABCC . . . . . . Association of British Chambers of Commerce
ABCC . . . . . . Atomic Bomb Casualty Commission
ABCCC . . . . . Airborne Battlefield Command and Control Center
ABCCTC . . . . Advanced Base Combat Communication Training Center (Pearl Harbor)
ABCD . . . . . . Accelerated Business Collection and Delivery (US Post Office)
ABCD . . . . . . Action for Boston Community Development
ABCD . . . . . . Advanced Base Construction Depot
ABCD . . . . . . Agency for Business and Career Development
ABCD . . . . . . Airway opened, Breathing restored, Circulation restored, and Definitive therapy (Medicine)
ABCD . . . . . . America, Britain, China, and Dutch East Indies (The ABCD Powers) (World War II)
ABCD . . . . . . American Society of Bookplate Collectors and Designers
ABCD . . . . . . Associated Baby Carriage Dealers
ABCD . . . . . . Atomic, Biological, Chemical and Damage Control
ABCD . . . . . . Awaiting Bad Conduct Discharge (Military)
ABCDEF . . . . . American Boys Club in Defense of Errol Flynn (Facetious organization)
ABCDEFGHIJ . . Automobile Builders' Combination Designed Especially for Getting Hitler including Japan (Suggested name for Automotive Council for War Production) (World War II)
AB in CE . . . . Bachelor of Arts in Civil Engineering
ABCFM . . . . . . American Board of Commissioners for Foreign Missions
ABCH . . . . . . American Board of Clinical Hypnosis
AB in Ch E . . . . Bachelor of Arts in Chemical Engineering
ABCM . . . . . . Aviation Chief Boatswain's Mate
ABCMR . . . . . Army Board for Correction of Military Records
ABCO . . . . . . Advanced Base Components (Military)
ABCOP . . . . . American Board for Certification in Orthotics and Prosthetics
ABCP . . . . . . Association of Blind Chartered Physiotherapists

ABC POL SCI . . Advance Bibliography of Contents: Political Science (and Government) (A publication)
ABCR . . . . . . Association for Beautiful Colorado Roads
ABCRA . . . . . American-Byelorussian Cultural Relief Association
ABCRS . . . . . . American Board of Colon and Rectal Surgery
ABCS . . . . . . Advisory Board for Cooperative Systems (of ICIREPAT)
ABCS . . . . . . American Board on Counseling Services
ABCS . . . . . . Automatic Blip Counter System
ABCS . . . . . . Automatic Broadcasting Control System (Japan)
ABCSP . . . . . American-British-Canadian Standardization Program
ABCW . . . . . . American Bakery and Confectionery Workers' International Union
ABD . . . . Access Block Diagram
ABD . . . . Advanced Base Depot (Navy)
ABD . . . . Advanced Base Dock
ABD . . . . All But The Dissertation (PhD candidates)
ABD . . . . American Board of Dermatology
ABD . . . . Average Business Day (Bell System)
ABDA . . . . . . Australian-British-Dutch-American
ABDACOM . . . Advanced Base Depot Area Command
ABDACOM . . . American-British-Dutch-Australian Supreme Command (1942)
ABDAFLOAT . . . American-British-Dutch-Australian Naval Operational Command (1942)
ABDAIR . . . . . American-British-Dutch-Australian Air Operational Command (1942)
ABDARM . . . . American-British-Dutch-Australian Army Operational Command
ABDC . . . . . . After Bottom Dead Center
ABDE . . . . . . Airport Bird Detection Equipment
ABDFC . . . . . American Bouvier des Flandres Club
ABDI . . . . . . Administrative Board -- Dress Industry
ABDL . . . . . . Automatic Binary Data Link
ABDPH . . . . . American Board of Dental Public Health
ABE . . . . Air Burst Effect
ABE . . . . Airborne Bombing Evaluation
ABE . . . . Amphenol Corporation (NYSE symbol)
ABEA . . . . . . American Baptist Education Association
ABEA . . . . . . American Broncho-Esophagological Association
ABEC . . . . . . Amphenol-Borg Electronics Corporation
ABEC . . . . . . Annular Bearing Engineers Committee
AB Ed . . . . . . Bachelor of Arts in Education
AB in EE . . . . Bachelor of Arts in Electrical Engineering
ABEPH . . . . . American Board of Examiners in Psychological Hypnosis
ABEPP . . . . . American Board of Examiners in Professional Psychology
ABES . . . . . . Aerospace Business Environment Simulator (Computer-programmed management game)
ABES . . . . . . American Biblical Encyclopedia Society
ABETS . . . . . . Airborne Beacon Electronic Test Set
ABEX . . . . . . Ab Extra (From Without)
ABF . . . . Absolutely Bloody Final (Especially with reference to a drink)
ABF . . . . Aircraft Battle Force (Navy)
ABF . . . . American Bar Foundation
ABF . . . . American Beekeeping Federation
ABF . . . . Arbeiter-und-Bauern-Fakultaet
ABF . . . . Audio Bandpass Filter
ABFA . . . . . . Azobisformamide
ABFC . . . . . . Advanced Base Functional Component (DOD)
ABFLO . . . . . Association of Bedding and Furniture Law Officials
ABFM . . . . . . American Board of Foreign Missions
ABFM . . . . . . Association of Business Forms Manufacturers
ABFMS . . . . . American Baptist Foreign Mission Society (Congo--Leopoldville)
ABG . . . . Air Base Group (Navy)
ABG . . . . American Ship Building Co. (NYSE symbol)
ABG . . . . Anti-Backlash Gear
ABG . . . . Aural Bearing Generator
ABG . . . . Axiobuccogingival
ABGA . . . . . . American Brussels Griffon Association
ABGP . . . . . . Air Base Group (Air Force)
AB in H Ec . . . Bachelor of Arts in Home Economics
ABHH . . . . . . Association of Baptist Homes and Hospitals
ABHJ . . . . . . Angle Bulkhead Jack
ABHMS . . . . . American Baptist Home Mission Societies
ABHP . . . . . . American Board of Health Physics
ABHS . . . . . . American Baptist Historical Society
ABI . . . . Advance Book Information (Publishing)
ABI . . . . American Butter Institute
ABI . . . . Arbeiter-und-Bauern-Inspektion
ABI . . . . Associacao Brasileira de Imprensa (Brazilian press association)
ABIM . . . . . . American Board of Internal Medicine
ABIM . . . . . . American Board of International Missions
ABIOL . . . . . Advanced Base Initial Outfitting List (Military)
ABJ . . . . Abacus Fund (NYSE symbol)
ABJ . . . . Adhesively Bonded Joint (or Junction)
ABJ . . . . Angle Bulkhead Jack
AB in J . . . . . . Bachelor of Arts in Journalism

ABJS .... Association of Bone and Joint Surgeons
ABK .... American Brake Shoe Co. (NYSE symbol) (Delisted)
ABKUFI...... Abkuerzungsfimmel (Abbreviation Craze)
ABL .... Air Blast Loading
ABL .... Alameda Belt Line (AAR code)
ABL .... All Busy Low (AT & T)
ABL .... Allegheny Ballistics Laboratory
ABL .... American Bulgarian League
ABL .... Army Biological Laboratory
ABL .... Assembly Breakdown List
ABL .... Atlas Basic Language (Data processing)
ABL .... Automated Biological Laboratory (NASA)
ABL .... Axiobuccolingual
ABLA .... Amateur Bicycle League of America
ABLA .... American Business Law Association
ABLB........ Alternate Binaural Loudness Balancing (Audiometry)
ABLC .... American Brown Leghorn Club
ABLE .... Acquisition Based on Consideration of Logistic Effects (Air Force)
ABLE .... Activity Balance Line Evaluation (PERT)
ABLE .... Agricultural-Biological Literature Exploitation (Systems study of National Agricultural Library)
ABLE .... Autonetics Base-Line Equipment
ABLES....... Airborne Battlefield Light Equipment System (Army)
ABLG .... Anti-Backlash Gear
ABLI........ Abraham Lincoln Birthplace National Monument
ABLS .... Atlas Biomedical Literature System
ABLS .... Bachelor of Arts in Library Science
ABLSS ...... Advanced Ballistic-Type Logistic Spacecraft System
ABLUE ...... Asymptotically Best Linear Unbiased Estimator (Statistics)
ABM........ American Building Maintenance (NYSE symbol)
ABM .... Antiballistic Missile (Air Force)
ABM .... Associate in Business Management
ABM........ Atomic Beam Method
ABM .... Automated Batch Mixing (Data processing)
ABM........ Aviation Boatswain's Mate (Navy rating)
ABMA....... American Boiler Manufacturers' Association & Affiliated Industries
ABMA ...... American Brush Manufacturers Association
ABMA ...... Army Ballistic Missile Agency
ABMAC ..... American Bureau for Medical Aid to China
ABMAG ..... Aviation Boatswain's Mate, Arresting Gear and Barriers (Navy rating)
ABMC ...... American Battle Monuments Commission (Independent government agency)
ABMCP...... Aviation Boatswain's Mate, Catapult (Navy rating)
ABMD ...... Air Ballistics Missile Division (Air Force)
ABMDA...... Advanced Ballistic Missile Defense Agency
AB in ME .... Bachelor of Arts in Mechanical Engineering
ABMEWS .... Antiballistic Missile Early Warning System (Air Force)
ABMGA ..... Aviation Boatswain's Mate, Gasoline System (Navy rating)
ABMIS ...... Airborne Ballistic Missile Intercept System
ABMJ .... American Board of Missions to the Jews
ABMM ...... Antiballistic-Missile Missile
ABMPH ..... Aviation Boatswain's Mate, Plane Handler (Navy rating)
ABMR ...... Atlantic Ballistic Missile Range
ABMRF ..... American Business Men's Research Foundation
ABMS .... American Bureau of Metal Statistics
ABMU....... American Baptist Missionary Union
ABN........ Aerodrome Beacon
ABN........ Airborne
ABN........ American Bank Note Co. (NYSE symbol) (Delisted)
ABN........ Antibolshevic Bloc of Nations
ABNCP ...... Airborne Command Post
ABNE .... Association for the Benefit of Non-contract Employees
ABNI .... Available But Not Installed
ABNINF ..... Airborne Infantry (Military)
ABNM ...... American Board of National Missions
ABNS .... American Board of Neurological Surgery
ABO .... Accessory Boring Organ (of a gastropod)
ABO .... American Board of Ophthalmology
ABO .... American Board of Opticianry
ABO .... American Board of Orthodontics
ABO .... American Board of Otolaryngology
ABO .... Association of Buying Offices
ABO........ Astable Blocking Oscillator
ABOG ...... American Board of Obstetrics and Gynecology
AB ONE .... Air Bases Command, 1st Naval District
ABOPS ..... Association of Business Officers of Preparatory Schools
ABOS....... American Board of Oral Surgery
ABOS....... American Board of Orthopaedic Surgery
ABOSS ..... Advanced Bombardment System
ABP .... Absolute Boiling Point
ABP .... Adapter, Binding Post
ABP .... Airborne Beacon Processor

ABP .... American Board of Pathology
ABP .... American Board of Pediatrics
ABP .... American Board of Pedodontics
ABP .... American Board of Periodontology
ABP .... American Board of Prosthodontics
ABP .... American Broadcasting-Paramount Theatres (NYSE symbol; later, ABC)
ABP .... American Business Press
ABP .... Arterial Blood Pressure
ABP .... Associated Business Publications
ABPA ...... Advanced Base Personnel Administration
ABPC ...... American Book Publishers Council (Later, AAP)
ABPCA ..... Aluminum Building Products Credit Association
ABPD ...... American Board of Pediatric Dermatology
ABPE ...... Acute Bovine Pulmonary Emphysema (Cattle disease)
ABPF ...... Audio Bandpass Filter
ABPG ...... Advanced Base Proving Ground
ABPH ...... American Board of Psychological Hypnosis
ABPM ...... American Board of Preventive Medicine
ABPMR ..... American Board of Physical Medicine and Rehabilitation
ABPN ...... American Board of Psychiatry and Neurology
ABPO ...... Advanced Base Personnel Officer
ABPR ...... Association of Baptist Professors of Religion
ABPR ...... Association of British Picture Restorers
ABPRBC ..... American Barred Plymouth Rock Bantam Club
ABPRC ..... American Barred Plymouth Rock Club
ABPRC ..... American Buff Plymouth Rock Club
ABPS ...... Airborne Beacon Processing System
ABPS ...... American Board of Plastic Surgery
ABPU ...... Advanced Base Personnel Unit
ABPW ...... Agency Broadcast Producers Workshop
ABQ........ Admiralty Berthing Officer (British)
ABR .... Adhesive Bonding Repair
ABR .... American Board of Radiology
ABR .... American Commercial Lines, Inc. (NYSE symbol) (Delisted)
ABR .... Amphibian Boat Reconnaissance Aircraft
ABR .... Real-Aerovias Brasil, SA (Brazilian international airline)
ABRA ...... American Buckskin Registry Association
ABRACADABRA.. Abbreviations and Related Acronyms Associated with Defense, Astronautics, Business and Radio-electronics (Raytheon Company publication)
ABRB ...... Advanced Base Receiving Barracks
ABRD ...... Advanced Base Repair Depot
ABRD ...... Advanced Base Reshipment Depot
ABRDA ..... American Bill of Rights Day Association
ABRE ...... Army Board of Review for Eliminations
AB (Rel) .... Bachelor of Arts with Religious Major
ABRES...... Advanced Ballistic Re-Entry System (BSD)
ABS .... Absent
ABS .... Acrylonitrile-Butadiene-Styrene (Organic chemistry)
ABS .... Air Base Simulator (Air Force)
ABS .... Air Base Squadron (Air Force)
ABS .... Air-Break Switch
ABS .... Air Breathing System
ABS .... Albertsons, Inc. (NYSE symbol)
ABS .... Alkyl Benzenesulfonate (Organic chemistry)
ABS .... American Begonia Society
ABS .... American Behavioral Scientist (A periodical)
ABS .... American Bible Society
ABS .... American Board of Surgery
ABS .... American Boxwood Society
ABS .... American Bryological Society
ABS .... American Budgerigar Society
ABS .... American Bureau of Shipping
ABS .... Animal Behavior Society
ABS .... Antenna Base Spring
ABS .... Associate in Business Science
ABS .... Associated Biomedic Systems, Inc.
ABS .... Association on Broadcasting Standards
ABS .... Aux Bons Soins de (Care of, c/o)
ABSA ...... Association of British Secretaries in America
ABSAP ..... Air-Borne Search and Attack Plotter
ABSC ...... Automatic Blip-Scan Counter
ABSCM...... Association of Boys & Students Clothing Manufacturers
ABSCS ..... Automatic Blip-Scan Counter System
ABSD ...... Advance Base Section Dock (Floating drydock, first used in World War II)
ABSD ...... Advanced Base Supply Depot
AB in Sec Ed .. Bachelor of Arts in Secondary Education
ABSIE ...... American Broadcasting Station in Europe (OWI)
ABSM ...... Aktiebolaget Svenska Metallverken
ABSMA ...... American Bleached Shellac Manufacturers Association

ABSSOP .....Committee for the Application of the Behavioral Sciences to the Strategies of Peace
ABT ....Abbott Laboratories (NYSE symbol)
ABT ....All Body Type (Army)
ABT ....American Ballet Theater
ABT ....Animated Burtek Trainer
ABT ....Auxiliary Ballast Tank
ABTA ......American Board of Trial Advocates
ABTA ......American Bridge Teachers' Association
ABTD ......Automatic Bulk Tape Degausser
ABTF.......Airborne Task Force
ABTICS .....Abstract and Book Title Index Card Service (Iron and Steel Institute) (British)
ABTSS ......Airborne Transponder Subsystem
ABTTA ......American Bridge, Tunnel and Turnpike Association
ABTU ......Advanced Base Torpedo Unit
ABTU ......Advanced Base Training Unit
ABTU ......Air Bombers Training Unit (Navy)
ABU ....Alliance Biblique Universelle
ABV ....Afferent Branchial Vein
ABV ....Air Blast Valve
ABV ....Air Bubble Vehicle
ABW ....Air Base Wing (Air Force)
ABW ....American Baptist Women
ABW ....Associated Brewing Company (NYSE symbol)
ABW ....Autobond Welder
ABW ....Automated Batch Weighing
ABWA......American Bottled Water Association
ABWA......American Business Women's Association
ABWA......American Business Writing Association
ABWA .....Associated Business Writers of America
ABWC .....American Buff Wyandotte Club
ABWE ......Association of Baptists for World Evangelism
ABWG .....Air Base Wing (Air Force)
ABWIK ......Assault and Battery with Intent to Kill
ABWRC.....Army Biological Warfare Research Center
ABY ....A. M. Byers Company (NYSE symbol) (Delisted)
ABYC......American Boat and Yacht Council
ABYC.......Antique Boat and Yacht Club
AC........Account Control
AC ....Accountants and Controllers
Ac........Actinium (Chemical element)
AC........Adapter Cable
AC........Adjustment–Calibration
AC........Admiral Commanding
AC........Adrenal Cortex (Medicine)
AC........Adrenocorticoid (Medicine)
AC........Advertising Council
AC ....Advisory Circular
AC ....Aerodynamic Center
AC ....Aeronautical Approach Charts (Air Force)
AC ....Aeronautical Center (FAA)
AC........After Christ
AC ....Air Conduction
AC ....Air Controlman
AC ....Air Corps
AC ....Aircraft
AC ....Aircraft Commander
AC ....Aircraftman (RAF and RCAF)
AC........Airframe Change
AC ....Alaskan Command (Military)
AC........Algoma Central & Hudson Bay Railway Company (AAR code)
AC........Allis–Chalmers Corporation
AC........Alpine Club (British)
AC ....Alternating Current
AC........Altocumulus (Meteorology)
AC........American Can Company (NYSE symbol)
AC........Amphibious Corps (Marine Corps)
AC........Analytic(al) Chemist
AC........Anastomosing Cell
AC........Anglican Communion
AC........Anno Christi (In the Year of Christ)
AC ....Anodal Closure (Medicine)
AC........Anodal Contraction
AC........Answer Construct
AC........Ante Christum (Before Christ)
AC........Ante Cibum (Before Meals) (Medicine)
AC........Ante–Communion
AC........Anti–Corrosive
AC........Apostolic Church
AC ....Approach Chart

AC ....Architect of the Capitol
AC........Arctic Circle
AC ....Arithmetic Computation Test (Military)
AC ....Armored Cable
AC........Army Corps
AC ....Asbestos Cement (Technical drawings)
AC ....Asphaltic Concrete
AC ....Assistant Cashier (Banking)
AC ....Associate in Commerce
AC ....Athletic Club (Usually in combination with proper noun, as, DAC, Detroit Athletic Club)
AC ....Atlantic Charter
AC ....Atlantic Congress
AC........Atlas Centaur (Missile)
AC ....Auditor Camerae (Auditor of the Papal Treasury)
AC........Author's Correction (Printing)
AC ....Automatic Computer
AC........Automatic Control
AC........Automobile Club
AC........Auxiliary Command
AC........Availability Code
AC ....Aviation Cadet
AC ....Axiocervical
AC ....Azimuth Comparator
AC........Collier (Navy symbol)
A–C........Alternating Current
A/C ....Absolute Ceiling (Aerospace)
A/C ....Account Current (Business and Trade)
A/C ....Accounts
A/C ....Air Commodore (RAF and RCAF)
A/C ....Aircraft
A/C ....Aircraft Commander
A/C.......Alter Course (As used in a navigator's log)
A/C.......Approach Control (Aviation)
A/C ....Aviation Cadet (Air Force)
A/1C ......Airman First Class
A/2C ......Airman Second Class
A/3C ......Airman Third Class
ACA ....Accounts Control Area
ACA ....Adjacent Channel Attenuation
ACA ....Administrative Committee on Administration (UN)
ACA ....Aero Club of America
ACA ....Affenpinscher Club of America
ACA ....Airflow Club of America
ACA ....Airlift Clearance Authority
ACA ....Airplane Change Analysis
ACA ....Akita Club of America
ACA ....Alaska Coastal Airlines
ACA.......Allied Control Authority (Allied German Occupation Forces)
ACA ....American Cadet Alliance
ACA ....American Camping Association
ACA ....American Canoe Association
ACA ....American Carnivals Association
ACA ....American Casting Association
ACA ....American Cat Association
ACA ....American Cemetery Association
ACA.......American Cheerleader Association
ACA ....American Chiropractic Association
ACA ....American Civic Association
ACA ....American Collectors Association
ACA ....American College of Allergists
ACA ....American College of Anesthesiologists
ACA ....American College of Apothecaries
ACA.......American Communications Association
ACA.......American Commuters Association
ACA ....American Composers Alliance
ACA ....American Congregational Association
ACA.......American Consumer Industries, Inc. (NYSE symbol) (Delisted)
ACA ....American Correctional Association
ACA ....American Corriedale Association
ACA ....American Cryptogram Association
ACA ....American Crystallographic Association
ACA ....Americans for Constitutional Action
ACA.......Arcata National Corp. (NYSE symbol)
ACA ....Arts Councils of America
ACA ....Associate in Commercial Arts
ACA ....Associate of the Institute of Chartered Accountants (British)
ACA ....Associated Chiropodists of America
ACA ....Associated Councils of the Arts
ACA ....Association Canado–Americaine
ACA ....Association of Commuter Airlines

ACA....... Association of Correctional Administrators
ACA....... Australian Council for Aeronautics
ACA ...... Automatic Circuit Analyzer
ACA....... Azimuth Control Amplifier
ACA....... United States Advisory Committee on the Arts
ACAAR ..... Action Committee on American-Arab Relations
ACAB....... Army Contract Adjustment Board
ACABQ...... Advisory Committee on Administrative and Budgetary Questions (UN)
ACAC....... Allied Container Advisory Committee
ACAC...... American College Admissions Center
ACAC...... American Croatian Academic Club
ACAC...... Association of College Admissions Counselors (Later, NACAC)
ACACW ..... Athletic Conference of American College Women (Became ARFCW)
ACAD ...... Academician (or Academy)
ACAD ...... Acadia National Park
ACAD ...... American Conference of Academic Deans
ACAD....... Automotive Committee for Air Defense (World War II)
ACAE....... American Council for the Arts in Education
ACAF....... Amphibious Corps, Atlantic Fleet (Marine Corps)
ACAH....... Acylcholine Acyl-Hydrolase
ACAI....... American Christian Association for Israel (Later, American-Israel Cultural Foundation)
ACAL....... Aircraft Change Application List
ACAM ...... Apollo Computer Address Matrix (NASA)
ACAMR ..... Associate Committee on Aviation Medical Research (Canada)
ACAN ...... Army Command and Administrative Network (Domestic and oversea integrated system of fixed radio, wire, cable, and associated communications facilities)
ACAP....... American Council on Alcohol Problems
ACAP...... Army Contract Appeals Panel
ACAP....... Automatic Circuit Analysis Program
ACAPA..... American Concrete Agricultural Pipe Association
ACAR....... Associacao de Credito e Assistencia Rural (Association of Credit and Rural Assistance) (Brazil)
ACAS ...... Association of Casualty Accountants and Statisticians
ACAS ...... Automatic Collision Avoidance System (Aviation)
ACAS(I) .... Assistant Chief of Staff (Intelligence) (Army)
ACAST ...... Advisory Committee on Applications of Science and Technology (UNESCO)
ACB....... Advertising Checking Bureau
ACB....... Air Circuit Breaker
ACB ...... Air Crew System Bulletin
ACB ...... Airmen Classification Battery (Military tests)
ACB........ Amphibious Construction Battalion
ACB........ Annoyance Call Bureau (Pest telephone control)
ACB........ Army Classification Battery (of tests)
ACB........ Asbestos-Cement Board (Technical drawings)
ACB .... Association Canadienne des Bibliotheques (Canadian Library Association) (Also known as CLA)
ACB .... Association of Customers' Brokers
ACB ...... Association of the Customs Bar
ACBA ...... Academy of Comic Book Artists
ACBA ...... American Charbray Breeders Association
ACB of A ... Associated Credit Bureaus of America
ACBB ...... American Council for Better Broadcasts
ACBCT ..... Automatic Circuit Board Card Tester
ACBFC ..... Academy of Comic-Book Fans and Collectors
ACBFC ..... American Church Building Fund Commission
ACBL ...... American Commercial Barge Line Company (AAR code)
ACBL ...... American Contract Bridge League
ACBLF ..... Association Canadienne des Bibliothecaires de Langue Francaise
ACBM....... Advisory Committee for Biology and Medicine (AEC)
ACBM...... Associated Corset and Brassiere Manufacturers
ACBM ...... Atomic Cesium Beam MASER
ACBMAG.... Aviation Chief Boatswain's Mate, Arresting Gear and Barriers
ACBMCP.... Aviation Chief Boatswain's Mate, Catapult
ACBMGA ... Aviation Chief Boatswain's Mate, Gasoline System
ACBMPH.... Aviation Chief Boatswain's Mate, Plane Handler
ACBS .... Accrediting Commission for Business Schools
ACBS .... Alert Crew Billet Security
ACBT .... Automatic Circuit Board Tester
ACBWS...... Automatic Chemical Biological Warning System
ACC........ Abilene Christian College (Texas)
ACC........ Account
ACC........ Accounting Careers Council
ACC........ Accounting Classification Code
ACC........ Action Change Card
ACC........ Administrative Committee on Coordination (of the United Nations) (Aviation)
ACC........ Air Center Commander
ACC........ Air Component Command (Military)
ACC........ Air Control Center (Military)

ACC....... Air Coordinating Committee (Governmental policy body for civil aviation in US; terminated, 1962)
ACC .... Air Crew System Change
ACC........ Airborne Control Computer
ACC........ Alaskan Collectors Club
ACC .... Allied Chemical Corporation
ACC........ Allied Control Commission (World War II)
ACC........ Allied Control Council
ACC........ Alpena Community College (Michigan)
ACC........ Alternating Current Circuit
ACC........ Altocumulus Castellatus (Meteorology)
ACC ...... American Chesapeake Club
ACC ...... American College of Cardiology
ACC ...... American Concert Choir
ACC ...... American Conference of Cantors
ACC ...... American Crafts (formerly, Craftsmen's) Council
ACC .... Annual Contributions Contract (Public housing development)
ACC ...... Antenna Control Console
ACC........ Appleton-Century-Crofts (Publisher)
ACC........ Area Control Center (Aviation)
ACC........ Army Chemical Center
ACC........ Army Cooperation Command (British)
ACC........ Assiduously Capable Crossworder
ACC ...... Association of Choral Conductors
ACC ...... Astronomical Great Circle Course
ACC ...... Atlantic Christian College (North Carolina)
ACC........ Atlantic Coast Conference (College sports)
ACC........ Auburn Community College (New York)
ACC........ Audio Control Center
ACC........ Automatic Color Control
ACC........ Automatic Contrast Control
A-CC ...... Antiphlogistic-Corticoid Conditioning Effect (Medicine)
ACCA ..... Aeronautical Chamber of Commerce of America
ACCA ..... American Clinical and Climatological Association
ACCA ..... American College of Clinic Administrators
ACCA...... American Commercial Collectors Association
ACCA...... American Correctional Chaplains Association
ACCA...... American Cotton Cooperative Association
ACCA...... Antenna Counterbalance Cylinder Assembly
ACCA ..... Art Collectors Club of America
ACCA...... Associated Colleges of the Chicago Area (AEC)
ACCANT .... Allied Command Atlantic
ACCAP ..... Autocoder to COBOL Conversion Aid Program (Data processing)
ACCASP .... Air Coordinating Committee, Airspace Subcommittee
ACCB ...... Aircraft Change Control Board (DOD)
ACCB ...... Aircraft Configuration Control Board (DOD)
ACCC ......Advisory Council on College Chemistry
ACCC...... Alternate Command and Control Center (Air Force)
ACCC ..... American Council of Christian Churches
ACCCA ..... American Catholic Correctional Chaplains Association
ACC & CE .. Association of Consulting Chemists and Chemical Engineers
ACCCF...... American Concert Choir and Choral Foundation
ACCCI ..... American Coke and Coal Chemicals Institute
ACC/COM ... Air Coordinating Committee Communications Subcommittee
ACCE ..... American Chamber of Commerce Executives
AC-CEF ..... Allis-Chalmers Critical Experimental Facility
ACCEL ...... Automatic Circuit Card Etched Layout
ACCESS ..... Action Coordinating Committee to End Segregation in the Suburbs
ACCESS ..... Afloat Consumption Cost and Effectiveness Surveillance System (Navy)
ACCESS ..... Aircraft Communication Control and Electronic Signaling System (Air Force)
ACCESS ..... American College of Cardiology Extended Study Services
ACCESS ..... Automated Control and Checking of Electrical Systems Support
ACCESS ..... Automatic Computer-Controlled Electronic Scanning System (National Bureau of Standards)
ACCESS ..... Automatic Crane Control Storage System
ACCFA ..... Agricultural Credit Cooperative Farmers' Association (Philippines)
ACCHAN .... Allied Command Channel (NATO)
ACCI ...... Accident Injury
ACCI ...... American Cottage Cheese Institute
ACCL...... American Council of Christian Laymen (Later, Laymen's Commission of the American Council of Christian Churches)
ACCL....... Army Coating and Chemical Laboratory
ACCM ...... Acoustic Counter-Countermeasures (Navy)
ACCM ...... American College of Clinic Managers
ACC/MET .... Air Coordinating Committee Meteorological Subcommittee
ACCN ...... Associated Court and Commercial Newspapers
ACCNET ..... Army Command and Control Network
ACCO ...... American Cyanamid Company
ACCO ...... Associate of the Canadian College of Organists
Ac Co A .... Acetyl Coenzyme A

ACCOM . . . . . Accommodate
ACCOM . . . . . Accompany
ACCOMP. . . . . Accomplish
ACCOR . . . . . Army COMSEC (Communications Security) Central Office of Record
ACCORDS . . . . Acoustic Correlation and Detection System
ACCP . . . . . . Advisory Committee on Civilian Policy (World War II)
ACCP . . . . . . American College of Chest Physicians
ACCPA . . . . . . Army Chemical Center Procurement Agency
ACCR . . . . . . Accrue(d)
ACCR . . . . . . American Christian Committee for Refugees (Post-World War II, Europe)
ACCR . . . . . . American Council on Chiropractic Roentgenography (Later, Roentgenology)
ACCRA . . . . . . American Chamber of Commerce Researchers Association
ACCRED . . . . . Accredited
ACCRY . . . . . . Accuracy
ACCS . . . . . . Aircraft Communications System
ACCS . . . . . . American Christmas Crib Society
ACCS . . . . . . Automatic Checkout & Control System
ACCSIC . . . . . Atomic Collision Cross Sections Information Center (ORNL)
ACCSq . . . . . . Airborne Command Control Squadron (Air Force)
ACCT . . . . . . Account(ant)
ACCUS . . . . . . Automobile Competition Committee for the United States
ACCW . . . . . . Alternating Current Continuous Wave
ACCY . . . . . . Accessory
ACCY . . . . . . Accountancy
ACD . . . . . . Absolute Cardiac Dullness
ACD. . . . . . . Acid-Citrate-Dextrose (Medicine)
ACD . . . . . . Administrative Commitment Document
ACD. . . . . . . Allied Chemical Corporation (NYSE symbol)
ACD. . . . . . . Alternating Current Dump
ACD . . . . . . American College of Dentists
ACD . . . . . . Antenna Control Display
ACD . . . . . . Automatic Call Distributor (Telephone system)
ACD. . . . . . . Automatic Contour Digitizer
ACDA . . . . . . American Choral Directors Association
ACDA . . . . . . Arms Control and Disarmament Agency
ACDA. . . . . . Aviation Combat Development Agency (CDC)
ACDC. . . . . . Administrative Communications Distribution Center (Air Force)
ACDC . . . . . . Army Combat Developments Command
ACDC . . . . . . Auburn-Cord-Duesenberg Club
AC-DC . . . . . A Bisexual Person (Pun on electricity's 'AC or DC' -- alternating current or direct current)
A-C/D-C . . . . Alternating Current/Direct Current
ACDHA . . . . . American Cream Draft Horse Association
ACDNT. . . . . . Accident
ACDO . . . . . . Air Carrier District Office
ACDS . . . . . . Advanced Command Data System
ACDS . . . . . . Automatic Comprehensive Display System
ACDTR . . . . . Airborne Central Data Tape Recorder
ACDU. . . . . . Active Duty
ACDUBLI. . . . . Active Duty Obligation (DOD)
ACDUINS . . . . Active Duty Under Instruction (Navy)
ACDUTRA . . . . Active Duty Training (Military)
ACE . . . . . . Acceptance Checkout Equipment (NASA)
ACE . . . . . . Adrenal Cortical Extract
ACE . . . . Aerospace Control Environment (Air Force)
ACE . . . . Air Collection and Enrichment
ACE . . . . Alcohol, Chloroform, Ether (An early anesthetic mixture)
ACE . . . . Allied Command Europe (NATO)
ACE . . . . Ambush Communication Equipment (Military)
ACE . . . . . . American Cinema Editors
ACE . . . . . . American Council on Education
ACE . . . . Animated Computer Education
ACE . . . . Army Corps of Engineers
ACE . . . . Assessment of Combat Effectiveness (Army)
ACE . . . . . . Associated Corpuscular Emission
ACE . . . . . . Association for Comparative Economics
ACE . . . . . . Association of Conservation Engineers
ACE . . . . Attitude Control Electronics
ACE . . . . Automated Cost Estimates
ACE . . . . Automatic Checkout Equipment
ACE . . . . Automatic Circuit Exchange
ACE . . . . . . Automatic Computing Engine
ACE . . . . . . Automatic Continuity Equipment
ACE . . . . . . Automatic Continuous Evaporation
ACE . . . . . . Automatic Control Equipment
ACE . . . . Auxiliary Conversion Equipment
ACE . . . . Aviation Construction Engineers (Military)
ACEA . . . . . . Air Line Communication Employees Association
ACEARTS. . . . . Airborne Countermeasures Environment and RADAR Target Simulation
ACEC . . . . . . Army Communications & Electronic Command

ACEC . . . . . . Ateliers de Construction Electriques de Charleroi (Atomic power plant) (Belgium)
ACED . . . . . . Aerospace Crew Equipment Development
AC Ed . . . . . Associate in Commercial Education
ACEF . . . . . . Adult Christian Education Foundation
ACEF . . . . . . Asian Cultural Exchange Foundation
ACEF . . . . . . Association of Commodity Exchange Firms
ACEI . . . . . . Association for Childhood Education International
ACEJ . . . . . . American Council on Education for Journalism
ACEL . . . . . . Aerospace Crew Equipment Laboratory
ACEL . . . . . . Air Crew Equipment Laboratory (Navy)
ACEM . . . . . . American Crystallographic Association
ACEM . . . . . . Aviation Chief Electrician's Mate (Navy)
ACEMIS . . . . . Army Communications and Electronics Management Information System
ACEN . . . . . . Assembly of Captive European Nations
ACEORP . . . . . Automotive and Construction Equipment Overhaul and Repair Plant (Navy)
ACEP . . . . . . Advisory Committee on Export Policy
ACEP . . . . . . American College of Emergency Physicians
ACEP . . . . . . American Council for Emigres in the Professions
ACEPD . . . . . Automotive and Construction Equipment Parts Depot (Navy)
ACE REP. . . . . Allied Command Europe Report
ACERP . . . . . Advanced Communications-Electronics Requirements Plan (Air Force)
ACES . . . . . . Air Collection Engine System
ACES . . . . . . Air Collection & Enrichment System
ACES . . . . . . American Catholic Esperanto Society
ACES . . . . . . Americans for the Competitive Enterprise System
ACES . . . . . . Association Corporative des Etudiants en Sciences (France)
ACES . . . . . . Association for Counselor Education and Supervision
ACES . . . . . . Automatic Checkout and Evaluation System (Air Force)
ACES . . . . . Automatic Control Evaluation Simulator (Space flight training machine)
ACESIA . . . . . American Council for Elementary School Industrial Arts
ACEUR . . . . . Allied Command Europe
ACF . . . . ACF Industries, Inc. (NYSE symbol)
ACF . . . . Alternate Communications Facility (Military)
ACF . . . . American Car and Foundry
ACF . . . . American Checker Federation (Governing body for sport in US)
ACF . . . . American Chess Foundation
ACF . . . . American Choral Foundation
ACF . . . . American Culinary Federation
ACF . . . . . . Association of Consulting Foresters
ACF . . . . Axisymmetrical Conical Flow
ACFA . . . . . . American Cat Fanciers Association
ACFA . . . . . . Association of Commercial Finance Attorneys
ACFC . . . . . . Association of Commercial Finance Companies of New York
ACFC . . . . . . Aviation Chief Fire Controlman
ACFEA . . . . . . Air Carrier Flight Engineers Association
ACFEL . . . . . . Arctic Construction & Frost Effects Laboratory (Army)
ACFFTU . . . . . All Ceylon Federation of Free Trade Unions
ACFG. . . . . . Automatic Continuous Function Generation (Data processing)
ACFI . . . . . . Advisory Committee on Flight Information (FAA)
ACFL . . . . . . Atlantic Coast Football League
ACFN . . . . . . American Committee for Flags of Necessity
ACFO . . . . . . American College of Foot Orthopedists
ACFR . . . . . . Advisory Council on Federal Reports
ACFR . . . . . . American College of Foot Roentgenologists
ACFS . . . . . . American College of Foot Surgeons
ACFT . . . . . . Aircraft
ACFT . . . . . . Aircraft Flying Training
ACFTU . . . . . . All-China Federation of Trade Unions (Communist China)
AcG . . . . . . Accelerator Globulin (Medicine)
ACG . . . . Advanced Concepts Group
ACG . . . . Air Cargo Express, Inc.
ACG . . . . Air Cargo Glider
ACG . . . . Airborne Coordinating Group
ACG . . . . . . Airline Carriers of Goods
ACG . . . . . . Alpha Control Guidance
ACG . . . . . . Alternating Current Generator
ACG . . . . . . American College of Gastroenterology
ACG . . . . . . American Council on Germany
ACG . . . . . . Area Coordination Group (Army)
ACG. . . . . . . Assistant Commissary General
ACG . . . . . . Association for Corporate Growth
ACG . . . . . . Auto Car Guard
ACG . . . . . . Automatic Correlation Guidance
ACGA . . . . . . American Cranberry Growers' Association
ACGBI . . . . . . Automobile Club of Great Britain and Ireland (Later, Royal Automobile Club)
ACGC . . . . . . American Checkered Giant Club (Later, American Checkered Giant Rabbit Club)
ACGD . . . . . . Association for Corporate Growth and Diversification
ACGF. . . . . . American Child Guidance Foundation

ACGG . . . . . . Associate Committee of Geodesy and Geophysics (Canada)
ACGIH . . . . . . American Conference of Governmental Industrial Hygienists
ACGM . . . . . . Aircraft Carrier General Memorandum
ACGp . . . . . . Area Coordination Group (Air Force)
ACGP . . . . . . Army Career Group
ACGPOMS . . . American College of General Practitioners in Osteopathic Medicine and Surgery
ACGRC . . . . . American Checkered Giant Rabbit Club
ACGS . . . . . . American Council on German Studies
ACGSq . . . . . . Aerial Cartographic and Geodetic Squadron (Air Force)
A Ch . . . . Acetylcholine
ACH . . . . Adrenal Cortical Hormone
ACH . . . . Aircrafthand (British)
ACHA . . . . . . American Catholic Historical Association
ACHA . . . . . American College Health Association
ACHA . . . . . American College of Hospital Administrators
ACHA . . . . . American Coon Hunters Association
ACHDWU . . . . All-Ceylon Harbor and Dock Workers' Union
AChE . . . . . . Acetylcholinesterase
ACHE . . . . . . Alabama Commission on Higher Education
A Chem . . . . . Associate in Chemistry
ACHR . . . . . . American Council of Human Rights
ACHS . . . . . . American Catholic Historical Society
ACHS . . . . . . Association College Honor Societies
ACI . . . . Adjacent Channel Interference
ACI . . . . Adult-Child Interaction (Test)
ACI . . . . Agence Congolaise d'Information (Congolese Information Agency) (Congo--Brazzaville)
ACI . . . . Air Combat Information
ACI . . . . Air Combat Intelligence (Navy)
ACI . . . . Air Commuter, Incorporated
ACI . . . . Air-Controlled Interception
ACI . . . . Airborne Controlled Intercept (Air Force)
ACI . . . . Alliance Cooperative Internationale
ACI . . . . Alloy Casting Institute
ACI . . . . Altitude Command Indicator
ACI . . . . American Carpet Institute (Later, CRI)
ACI . . . . American Concrete Institute
ACI . . . . Atlas Chemical Industries, Inc. (NYSE symbol) (Delisted)
ACI . . . . Automatic Car Identification (Railroads)
ACI . . . . Automatic Control Instrumentation
ACI . . . . Azione Cattolica Italiana
ACIA . . . . . . Associated Cooperage Industries of America
ACIAS . . . . . . American Council of Industrial Arts Supervisors
ACIASAO . . . . . American Council of Industrial Arts State Association Officers
ACIATE . . . . . American Council of Industrial Arts Teacher Education
ACIBU . . . . . . Association des Commercants Indigenes du Burundi (Association of Indigenous Merchants of Burundi)
ACIC . . . . . . Aeronautical Chart and Information Center (Air Force)
ACIC . . . . . . Allied Captured Intelligence Center (US and British)
ACIC . . . . . . Auxiliary Combat Information Center
ACICAFE . . . . . Association du Commerce et de l'Industrie du Cafe dans la CEE (Association for the Coffee Trade and Industry in the EEC)
ACII . . . . Associate Chartered Insurance Institute (British)
ACIIB . . . . American Civilian Internee Information Bureau
ACIID . . . . A Critical Insight into Israel's Dilemmas (Jewish student newspaper)
ACIL . . . . American Council of Independent Laboratories
ACIM . . . . . . American Committee on Italian Migration
ACIM . . . . . . Axis Crossing Interval Meter (SONAR)
ACINT . . . . . . Acoustic Intelligence (Military)
ACIO . . . . Air Combat Intelligence Office(r) (Navy)
ACIOPJF . . . . Association Catholique Internationale des Œuvres de Protection de la Jeune Fille
ACIP . . . . Active Certificate Information Program (for stock certificates) (Data processing)
ACIP . . . . Attack Center Indicator Panel
ACIR . . . . Advisory Commission on Intergovernmental Relations
ACIR . . . . . . Automotive Crash Injury Research
AC/IREF . . . . . American Chapter, International Real Estate Federation
ACIS . . . . Advanced Credit Information System
ACIS . . . . Aircraft Crew Interphone System
ACIS . . . . American Committee for Irish Studies
ACIS . . . . Associate of the Chartered Institute of Secretaries (British)
ACIWLP . . . . . American Committee for International Wild Life Protection
ACJ . . . . American Committee on Japan
ACJ . . . . American Council for Judaism
ACJ . . . . Attitude Control Jet
ACJA . . . . . . American Congregation of Jews from Austria
ACK . . . . Acknowledge
ACK . . . . Acknowledgment Character (Data processing)
ACK . . . . Altitude Conversion Kit

ACK . . . . Armstrong Cork Company (NYSE symbol)
ACL . . . . Adjective Check List
ACL . . . . Aeronautical Computers Laboratory (Navy)
ACL . . . . Aircraft Circular Letter
ACL . . . . Allowable Cabin Load (in an aircraft)
ACL . . . . Allowable Cargo Load
ACL . . . . American Classical League
ACL . . . . American Commercial Lines, Inc.
ACL . . . . American Committee for Liberation
ACL . . . . Antigen-Carrier Lipid
ACL . . . . Association of Cinema Laboratories
ACL . . . . Association for Computational Linguistics
ACL . . . . Atlantic Coast Line R. R. (AAR code)
ACL . . . . Automatic Carrier Landing System (Navy)
ACL . . . . Aviation Circular Letter
ACLA . . . . . . American Comparative Literature Association
ACLA . . . . . . American Cotton Linter Association
ACLA . . . . . . American Country Life Association
ACLA . . . . . . Anti-Communist League of America
ACLAM . . . . . American College of Laboratory Animal Medicine
ACLAN . . . . . American Comparative Literature Association Newsletter
ACLANT . . . . . Allied Command Atlantic (NATO)
ACLD . . . . . . Association for Children with Learning Disabilities
ACLG . . . . . . Air-Cushion Landing Gear
ACLM . . . . . . American College of Legal Medicine
ACLO . . . . . . Agena Class Lunar Orbiter
ACLO . . . . . . Association of Cooperative Library Organizations
ACLPS . . . . . Academic Clinical Laboratory Physicians and Scientists
ACLRR . . . . . Atlantic Coast Line Railroad
ACLS . . . . . . All-Weather Carrier Landing System (Navy)
ACLS . . . . . . American Council of Learned Societies
ACLS . . . . . . Automated Control and Landing System (Navy)
ACLS . . . . . . Automatic Carrier Landing System (Air Force)
ACLU . . . . . . American Civil Liberties Union
ACLU . . . . . . American College of Life Underwriters
ACLV . . . . . . Accrued Leave (Military)
ACM . . . . Acoustic Countermeasures (Navy)
ACM . . . . Active Counter Measures
ACM . . . . Additional Crew Member (Military)
ACM . . . . Air Chief Marshal (British)
ACM . . . . Air Combat Maneuvering
ACM . . . . Air Commerce Manual
ACM . . . . Air Court Martial
ACM . . . . American Campaign Medal
ACM . . . . American College of Musicians
ACM . . . . American Conservatory of Music
ACM . . . . Asbestos-Covered Metal (Technical drawings)
ACM . . . . Associated Colleges of the Midwest
ACM . . . . Association for Computing Machinery
ACM . . . . Authorized Controlled Material Order
ACM . . . . Automatic Clutter Mapping
ACM . . . . Automatic Coating Machine
ACM . . . . Auxiliary Mine Layer (Navy symbol)
ACM . . . . Aviation Chief Metalsmith
ACM . . . . Axon Cylinder Membrane
ACMA . . . . . . Acidproof Cement Manufacturers Association
ACMA . . . . . . Air Carrier Mechanic Association
ACMA . . . . . . Alumina Ceramic Manufacturers Association
ACMA . . . . . . American Certified Morticians Association
ACMA . . . . . . American Circus Memorial Association
ACMA . . . . . . American Comedy Museum Association
ACMA . . . . . . American Cutlery Manufacturers Association
ACMA . . . . . . Army Class Manager Activity
ACMAF . . . . . Association des Classes Moyennes Africaines (African Middle Classes Association)
ACMC . . . . . . Area Combined Movements Center
ACMD . . . . . . Advanced Concepts and Missions Division (NASA)
ACME . . . . . . Adult Community Movement for Equality (Civil rights)
ACME . . . . . . Advanced Computer for Medical Research (Stanford University)
ACME . . . . . . Advisory Council on Medical Education
ACME . . . . . . Advisory Council for Minority Enterprise (White House)
ACME . . . . . . Aircraft Component Mating Evaluation
ACME . . . . . . Antenna Contour Measuring Equipment
ACME . . . . . . Association of Consulting Management Engineers
ACME . . . . . . Attitude Control and Maneuvering Electronics
ACMES . . . . . Attitude Control and Maneuver Electronic System
ACMF . . . . . . Air Corps Medical Forces
ACMF . . . . . . American Corn Millers' Federation
ACMF . . . . . . Australian Commonwealth Military Forces
ACMI . . . . . . American Cotton Manufacturers Institute
ACMM . . . . . . Aviation Chief Machinist's Mate

ACMMC . . . . . Aviation Chief Machinist's Mate, Carburetor Mechanic
ACMMF. . . . . . Aviation Chief Machinist's Mate, Flight Engineer
ACMMH . . . . . Aviation Chief Machinist's Mate, Hydraulic Mechanic
ACMMI. . . . . . Aviation Chief Machinist's Mate, Instrument Mechanic
ACMMP . . . . . Aviation Chief Machinist's Mate, Propeller Mechanic
ACMMT. . . . . . Aviation Chief Machinist's Mate, Gas Turbine Mechanic
ACMP. . . . . . . Amateur Chamber Music Players
ACMRR . . . . . . Advisory Committee on Marine Resources Research
ACMRU . . . . . . Audio Commercial Message Repeating Unit (Device delivering a
           recorded commercial from cigarette vending machines)
ACMS. . . . . . . Advanced Configuration Management System
ACMS . . . . . . Army Command Management System
ACMT. . . . . . . American College of Medical Technologists
ACMT. . . . . . . American Commission on Ministerial Training
ACN . . . . Activity Control Number
ACN . . . . All Concerned Notified
ACN . . . . American College of Neuropsychiatrists
ACN . . . . American Council on NATO
ACN . . . . Ante Christum Natum (Before the Birth of Christ)
ACN . . . . Artificial Cloud Nucleation (Rainmaking)
ACN . . . . Assignment Control Number (Army)
ACN . . . . Authorized Code Number
ACN . . . . Automatic Celestial Navigation (Air Force)
ACNA . . . . . . Advisory Council on Naval Affairs
ACNA . . . . . . Arctic Institute of North America
ACNB. . . . . . . Australian Commonwealth Naval Board (Navy)
ACNEE . . . . . . Action Committee for Narcotics Education and Enforcement
ACNHA . . . . . American College of Nursing Home Administrators
ACNM . . . . . . American College of Nurse-Midwifery
ACNO . . . . . . Assistant Chief of Naval Operations
ACNOT . . . . . Accident Notice (Aviation)
ACNOT . . . . . Assistant Chief of Naval Operations (Transportation)
ACNS . . . . . . American Council for Nationalities Service
ACNS . . . . . . Associated Correspondents News Service
ACNY . . . . . . Adventurers Club of New York
ACO . . . . Acme Steel Company (NYSE symbol) (Delisted)
ACO . . . . Action Cut-Out
ACO . . . . Administrative Contracting Officer (Navy)
ACO . . . . Agricultural Climatological Office (Department of Commerce)
ACO . . . . Alpha Cut-Off
ACO . . . . American Academy of Optometry
ACO . . . . Anodal Closing Odor
ACO . . . . Atico Mortgage Investors (NYSE symbol)
ACO . . . . Atomic Coordination Office (British)
ACO . . . . Attack Cut Out (Military)
ACOA . . . . . . American Committee on Africa
ACOC . . . . . . Area Communications Operations Center
AC/OC . . . . . Air Co-operation Command (British Royal Air Force)
ACOE . . . . . . Automatic Checkout Equipment
ACOF. . . . . . . Attendant Control of Facilities (Western Electric)
ACOG . . . . . . Aircraft on Ground
ACOG . . . . . . American College of Obstetricians and Gynecologists
ACOHA . . . . . American College of Osteopathic Hospital Administrators
ACOI . . . . . . American College of Osteopathic Internists
A Com . . . . . . Associate in Commerce
ACOM . . . . . . Aviation Chief Ordnanceman
ACOMARS. . . . Association of Centers of Medieval and Renaissance Studies
ACOMT. . . . . . Aviation Chief Ordnanceman, Turret Mechanic
ACONA . . . . . Advisory Council on Naval Affairs of the Navy League
ACONDA . . . . Activities Committee on New Directions for ALA (American Library
           Association)
ACOOG . . . . . American College of Osteopathic Obstetricians and Gynecologists
ACOP. . . . . . . Airborne Corps Operation Plan (Military)
ACOP. . . . . . . American College of Osteopathic Pediatricians
ACORDD . . . . Action Council of Regional Dissemination Directors
ACORN . . . . . Acronym-Oriented Nut
ACORN . . . . . Automated Conversion Routine
ACORN . . . . . Automatic Checkout and Recording Equipment
ACOS . . . . . . American College of Osteopathic Surgeons
ACOS. . . . . . . Arms Control Observation Satellite
ACOUSTINT . . Acoustical Intelligence (Military)
ACO(W) . . . . . Atomic Coordinating Office (Washington, DC) (British Defense Staff)
ACP. . . . . Accion Democratica Popular (Popular Democratic Action) (Political party
           in Costa Rica)
ACP. . . . . Acyl Carrier Protein
ACP. . . . . Adaptive Control Process
ACP. . . . . Additive Color Process
ACP . . . . Advanced Computational Processor (Data processing)
ACP . . . . Advanced Cooperative Project (NASA)
ACP . . . . Aerospace Computer Program (Air Force)
ACP. . . . . Agence Congolaise de Presse (Congolese Press Agency) (Leopoldville)

ACP. . . . . . . Agricultural Conservation Program (Department of Agriculture)
ACP. . . . . . . Air Control Point
ACP. . . . . . . Airborne Command Post (Air Force)
ACP. . . . . . . Aircraft Communication Procedures (Navy)
ACP. . . . . . . Airlift Command Post
ACP. . . . . . . Airline Carriers of Passengers
ACP. . . . . . . Alarm Control Panel
ACP. . . . . . . Allied Communications Publications (Military)
ACP. . . . . . . Altimeter Check Point (Aviation)
ACP . . . . American College of Pharmacists
ACP . . . . American College of Physicians
ACP. . . . . . . Ammunition Control Point
ACP. . . . . . . Analytical Computer Program
ACP . . . . Animal Care Panel
ACP. . . . . . . Anodal Closing Picture
ACP. . . . . . . Anti-Comintern Pact
ACP. . . . . . . Apparent Candle Power
ACP. . . . . . . Area Command Post
ACP. . . . . . . Armament Control Panel
ACP. . . . . . . Associate of the College of Preceptors (British)
ACP. . . . . . . Associate Collegiate Players
ACP . . . . Associated Church Press
ACP . . . . Associated Collegiate Press
ACP. . . . . . . Associated Construction Publications
ACP. . . . . . . Association of Clinical Pathologists
ACP. . . . . . . Association of Correctional Psychologists
ACP. . . . . . . Atmospheric Contamination Potential
ACP. . . . . . . Attack Center Panel
ACP. . . . . . . Auxiliary Check Point
ACP . . . . Azimuth Change Pulse
ACPA . . . . . . Affiliated Chiropodists-Podiatrists of America
ACPA . . . . . . American Capon Producers Association
ACPA . . . . . . American Catholic Philosophical Association
ACPA . . . . . . American Catholic Psychological Association
ACPA . . . . . . American Cleft Palate Association
ACPA . . . . . . American College Personnel Association
ACPA . . . . . . American Concrete Paving Association
ACPA . . . . . . American Concrete Pipe Association
ACPA . . . . . . Association of Computer Programmers and Analysts
A-CPA . . . . . . Asbestos-Cement Products Association
ACPAE . . . . . . Association of Certified Public Accountant Examiners
ACPATT . . . . . All Commands Process as Attached (Army)
ACPC . . . . . . American Christian Palestine Committee
ACPC . . . . . . American Council of Parent Cooperatives
ACPCC . . . . . American Council of Polish Cultural Clubs
ACPD . . . . . . Army Control Program Directive
ACPE . . . . . . American Council on Pharmaceutical Education
ACPF . . . . . . Amphibious Corps, Pacific Fleet
ACPI . . . . . . Assistant Chief Patrol Inspector (Immigration and Naturalization
           Service)
ACPIC . . . . . . American Council for Private International Communications, Inc.
           (Proposed corporation to replace Radio Free Europe)
ACPL . . . . . . Atlas Crew Procedures Laboratory
ACPM . . . . . . American College of Preventive Medicine
ACPM . . . . . . Attitude Control Propulsion Motors
ACPMR. . . . . . American Congress of Physical Medicine and Rehabilitation
ACPO. . . . . . . Accion Cultural Popular (Basic education organization) (Colombia)
ACPP . . . . . . Adrenocorticopolypeptide
ACPPD . . . . . Average Cost Per Patient Day (Medicine)
ACPRA . . . . . American College Public Relations Association
ACPS . . . . . . American Coalition of Patriotic Societies
ACPS . . . . . . Auxiliary Control Propulsion System (NASA)
ACPSAHMWA. . American Commission for Protection and Salvage of Artistic and
           Historical Monuments in War Areas (World War II)
ACPU. . . . . . . Auxiliary Computer Power Unit
ACQ . . . . Acquisition
ACQ . . . . Acquittal
ACQ . . . . All Courses and Quadrants (Aviation)
ACQT. . . . . . . Aviation Cadet Qualifying Test
ACR. . . . . Abandon Call and Retry
ACR. . . . . Abstracts of Classified Reports
ACR. . . . . Active Cavity Radiometer
ACR. . . . . Adjacent Channel Rejection
ACR. . . . . Advanced Capabilities Radar
ACR. . . . . Advanced Confidential Report
ACR. . . . . Aerial Combat Reconnaissance
ACR. . . . . Aircraft Control Room
ACR. . . . . Airfield Control RADAR (Air Force)
ACR. . . . . Alaskan Communications Region (Air Force)
ACR. . . . . Allied Commission on Reparations
ACR. . . . . American Academy in Rome

ACR	American College of Radiology
ACR	American Council for Romanians
ACR	Americans for Children's Relief
ACR	Ammunition Condition Report
ACR	Anti-Circular Run (Navy)
ACR	Approach Control RADAR
ACR	Armored Cavalry Regiment
ACR	Armored Cruiser (Navy symbol)
ACR	Assistant Chief for Research
ACR	Automatic Card Reader
ACR	Automatic Compression - Release
ACR	Auxiliary Computer Room (Apollo) (NASA)
AC & R	American Cable & Radio Corporation
ACRA	American Collegiate Retailing Association
ACRA	American Cotswold Record Association
ACRAF	Artists Civil Rights Assistance Fund (Defunct)
ACRB	Army Council of Review Boards
ACRC	Air Compressor Research Council
ACRD	Automatic Compression - Release Device
ACRE	Advanced Chemical Rocket Engine (Air Force)
ACRE	Associate Citizens for Responsible Education (Group opposing sex education in schools)
ACRE	Automatic Checkout and Readiness Equipment
ACRES	Airborne Communication Relay Station (Air Force)
ACRH	Argonne Cancer Research Hospital (Illinois)
ACRI	American Cocoa Research Institute
ACRL	Association of College and Research Libraries
ACRM	Aviation Chief Radioman
A/CRMD	Association for Children with Retarded Mental Development
ACRONYM	A Contrived Reduction of Nomenclature Yielding Mnemonics (Humorous interpretation of the term)
ACRP	Airborne Communications Reconnaissance Platform
ACRP	Airborne Communications Reconnaissance Program
ACRP	Army Cost Reduction Program
ACRPP	Association pour la Conservation et la Reproduction Photographique de las Presse
ACRR	American Council on Race Relations
ACRS	Advisory Committee on Reactor Safeguards (AEC)
ACRS	Automatic Chemical Reaction System
ACRT	Aviation Chief Radio Technician
ACRV	Armored Command and Reconnaissance Vehicle
ACRW	American Council of Railroad Women
ACS	Accumulator Switch
ACS	Activity Characteristics Sheet (Agency for International Development)
ACS	Adaptive Control System
ACS	Advance Count Switch
ACS	Affinely Connected Space
ACS	Agena Control System (NASA)
ACS	Aircraft Communications System
ACS	Aircraft Control and Surveillance (Air Force)
ACS	Airline Charter Service
ACS	Alaskan Communications System (Military)
ACS	Alternating Current Synchronous
ACS	American Camellia Society
ACS	American Canal Society
ACS	American Cancer Society
ACS	American Carnation Society
ACS	American Ceramic Society
ACS	American Cetacean Society
ACS	American Chemical Society
ACS	American College of Surgeons
ACS	American Colonization Society
ACS	American Crystal Sugar Company (NYSE symbol)
ACS	American Cultural Society
ACS	Analog Computer System
ACS	Annealed Copper-Covered Steel
ACS	Anodal Closing Sound
ACS	Anterior Convex Side
ACS	Antireticular Cytotoxic Serum
ACS	Apollo Communications System (NASA)
ACS	Armament Control System (Air Force)
ACS	Army Calibration System
ACS	Army Community Service
ACS	Art Center School
ACS	Assistant Chief of Staff
ACS	Associate in Commercial Science
ACS	Association of Clinical Scientists
ACS	Association of Council Secretaries
ACS	Attitude-Control System (Aerospace)
ACS	Audio Communications System
ACS	Autograph Card Signed

ACS	Automatic Control System
ACS	Automatic Counter System
ACS	Azimuth Control System
A/CS	Aircraft Security Vessel
AC of S	Assistant Chief of Staff (Army)
ACSA	Allied Communications Security Agency
ACSA	American Cotton Shippers Association
ACSA	Aqua-Cat Catamaran Sailing Association
ACSA	Association of Collegiate Schools of Architecture
AC/SAF	Assistant Chief of Staff, Air Force
ACSAP	Automated Cross-Section Analysis Program (Data processing)
ACSC	Air Carrier Service Corporation
ACSC	Air Command Staff College (Air Force)
ACSC	American Council on Schools and Colleges
ACSC	Applied Communications Systems Center (AT & T)
ACSC	Army Computer Systems Command (Also, CSC)
ACSC	Association of Casualty and Surety Companies
ACSC	Association of Colleges and Secondary Schools (Defunct)
AC & SC	Air Command and Staff College (of the Air University)
ACSC-E	Assistant Chief of Staff for Communications - Electronics
ACSD	Army Communications - Service Division
ACSDO	Air Carrier Safety District Office
ACSEA	Air Command, Southeast Asia
ACSEB	Aviation Clothing and Survival Equipment Bulletin
ACSF	Attack Carrier Striking Force
ACSFOR	Assistant Chief of Staff for Force Development (Army)
ACSGp	Area Coordination Subgroup (Air Force)
ACSI	Assistant Chief of Staff for Intelligence (Army)
ACSIF	Alaska Communication System Industrial Fund
ACSIL	Admiralty Centre for Scientific Information and Liaison (England)
ACSL	Standing Lenticular Altocumulus (Meteorology)
ACSM	American College of Sports Medicine
ACSM	American Congress on Surveying and Mapping
ACSMA	American Cloak and Suit Manufacturers Association
ACSN	Association of Collegiate Schools of Nursing
ACSOC	Acoustical Society of America
ACSP	Advanced Control Signal Processor (for spacecraft)
ACSP	Advisory Council on Scientific Policy
ACSPA	Australian Council of Salaried and Professional Associations
ACSR	Advanced Combat Surveillance RADAR
ACSR	Aluminum Cable Steel Reinforced
ACSR	Aluminum Conductor Steel Reinforced
ACSRC	Assistant Chief of Staff for Reserve Components (Army)
ACSS	Air Command and Staff School
ACSS	American Catholic Sociological Society
ACSS	American Cheviot Sheep Society
ACSS	Analog Computer Subsystem
ACSS	Army Chief of Support Services
AC & SS	Air Command and Staff School
ACS/S & A	Assistant Chief of Staff, Studies and Analysis (Air Force)
ACSSAVO	Association of Chief State School Audio-Visual Officers
ACSSN	Association of Colleges and Secondary Schools for Negroes
ACSSR	Ammunition Consolidated Stock Status Report
ACST	Army Clerical Speed Test
ACSU	Army Civil Services' Union (Singapore)
ACT	Acetate Cloth Tape
ACT	Act in Crisis Today (Fund sponsored by the Lutheran Church in America)
ACT	Action for Children in Trouble (An organization)
ACT	Action for Children's Television (An organization)
ACT	Active
ACT	Advanced Core Test
ACT	Air Combat Tactics
ACT	Air Control Team (Air Force)
ACT	Air Cushion Trailer (or Transporter)
ACT	Aircrew (or Airman) Classification Test
ACT	Algebraic Compiler and Translator
ACT	Allied Chemical Technology (Trademark)
ACT	Alpha Counter Tube
ACT	Alumina Ceramic Test
ACT	American College Testing (Program)
ACT	American Conservatory Theatre
ACT	Antenna Cross Talk
ACT	Area Correlation Tracker (Air Force)
ACT	Armored Cavalry Trainer (Army)
ACT	Army Chemical Typewriter (Data processing)
ACT	Arnold Constable Corporation (NYSE symbol) (Delisted)
ACT	Associated Container Transportation
ACT	Association of Catholic Teachers
ACT	Australian Capital Territory
ACT	Auto-lock Channel Tuning (TV)

ACT . . . . Automatic Cable Tester
ACT . . . . Automatic Capacitor Tester
ACT . . . . Automatic Checkout Technician (or Technique)
ACT . . . . Automatic Circuit Tester
ACT . . . . . . Automatic Code Translation (Data processing)
ACT . . . . Automatic Component Tester
ACT . . . . Aviation Classification Test
ACT . . . . Azimuth Control Torquer
ACTA . . . . . . Air Coach Transport Association
ACTA . . . . . . American Community Theatre Association
ACTA . . . . . . Automatic Centrifugal Tinning Apparatus
ACTB . . . . . . Aircrew Classification Test Battery
ACTC . . . . . . Association of Community Travel Clubs
ACTC . . . . . . Bureau of Air Commerce Type Certificate
ACTD . . . . . . Attitude Control Torquing Device
ACTER . . . . . . Anti-Counter-Measures Trainer
ACTFL . . . . . . American Council on the Teaching of Foreign Languages
ACTG . . . . Acting
ACTG . . . . . . Advance Carrier Training Group (Navy)
ACTH . . . . . . Adrenocorticotropic Hormone
ACTH . . . . . . Arbitrary Correction to Hit (Gunnery term) (Navy)
ACTIAC . . . . . Arms Control Technical Information and Analysis Center (Department of State)
ACT/IC . . . . . . Active--In Commission (Vessel status)
ACTION . . . . . Allegheny Council to Improve our Neighborhoods
ACTION . . . . . American Council to Improve Our Neighborhoods (Defunct)
ACTIONS . . . . Allocation and Control Through Identification of Ongoing Situations (New York City police system)
ACT/IS . . . . . . Active--In Service (Vessel status)
ACTIV . . . . . Army Concept Team in Vietnam
ACTL . . . . . . American College of Trial Lawyers
ACTM . . . . . . Association of Cotton Textile Merchants of New York
ACTMC . . . . . . Army Clothing, Textile & Materiel Center
ACTN . . . . Action
ACTO . . . . Action Officer (Army)
ACT/OC . . . . . Active--Out of Commission (Vessel status)
ACTOR . . . . . Askania Cine-Theodolite Optical-Tracking Range
ACT/OS . . . . . Active--Out of Service (Vessel status)
ACTP . . . . . . Adrenocorticotrophic Polypeptide
ACTPC . . . . . . Acting Pay Clerk
ACTPO . . . . . . Accountable Property Officer (Army)
ACTR . . . . . . Air Corps Technical Report
ACTREP . . . . . Activities Report (Shipping)
ACTRUS . . . . . Automatically Controlled Turbine Run-Up System (Navigation)
ACTS . . . . . . Acoustic Control and Telemetry System
ACTS . . . . . . Air Corps Tactical School
ACTS . . . . . . Air Crew Training System
ACTS . . . . . . Airlines Computer Tracing System (Luggage retrieving system)
ACTS . . . . . . Arc Current Time Simulator
ACTS . . . . . . Association for Christian Training and Service
ACTS . . . . . . Automatic Computer Telex Services
ACTSECNAV . . . Acting Secretary of the Navy
ACTU . . . . . . Association of Catholic Trade Unionists
ACTU . . . . . . Australian Council of Trade Unions
ACTV . . . . . . Activate
ACTY . . . . . . Activity
ACU . . . . Acceleration Compensation Unit
ACU . . . . Alarm Control Unit (Bell System)
ACU . . . . American Church Union
ACU . . . . American Congregational Union
ACU . . . . American Conservative Union
ACU . . . . . . American Cycling Union
ACU . . . . Antenna Control Unit
ACU . . . . Association of College Unions
ACU . . . . . . Autocycle Union (British)
ACU . . . . Automatic Calling Unit
ACU . . . . Auxiliary Conditioning Unit
ACUCM . . . . . . Association of College and University Concert Managers
ACUE . . . . . . American Committee of United Europe
ACUHO . . . . . Association of College and University Housing Officers
ACUIIS . . . . . Association of Colleges and Universities for International-Intercultural Studies
ACUNY . . . . . Associated Colleges of Upper New York
ACUP . . . . . . Association of College and University Printers
ACURA . . . . . Association for the Coordination of University Religious Affairs
ACURIL . . . . . Association of Caribbean University and Research Institute Libraries
ACUS . . . . . . Administrative Conference of the United States (A federal government body)
ACUS . . . . . . Atlantic Council of the United States
ACUTE . . . . . Accountants Computer-Users Technical Exchange
ACV . . . . Actual Cash Value

ACV . . . . . . Air-Cushion Vehicle
ACV . . . . Alberto-Culver Company (NYSE symbol)
ACV . . . . Armored Combat Vehicle
ACV . . . . . . Associate, College of Violinists
ACV . . . . . . Auxiliary Aircraft Carrier (Navy symbol)
ACVA . . . . . . Advisory Committee on Voluntary Foreign Aid
ACVAFS . . . . . American Council of Voluntary Agencies for Foreign Service
ACVC . . . . . . American Council of Venture Clubs
ACVC . . . . . . Army Commercial Vehicle Code
ACVE . . . . . . Accelerometer Calibration Vibration Exciter
ACVFA . . . . . . Advisory Committee on Voluntary Foreign Aid (Department of State)
ACVP . . . . . . American College of Veterinary Pathologists
ACVV . . . . . . Afrikaanse Christelike Vrouevereniging
ACW . . . . . . Airborne Collision Warning
ACW . . . . . . Air(craft) Control and Warning (Military)
ACW . . . . . . Aircraftwoman (British)
ACW . . . . . . Alternating Continuous Waves (Radio)
ACW . . . . . . American Chain of Warehouses
AC & W . . . . . Air Communications and Weather (Group) (Navy)
AC & W . . . . . Aircraft and Warning (Squadrons)
ACWA . . . . . . Amalgamated Clothing Workers of America
ACWA . . . . . . Automatic Car Wash Association International
ACWC . . . . . . Advisory Committee on Weather Control
ACWF . . . . . . Army Central Welfare Fund
ACWL . . . . . Army Chemical Warfare Laboratory
ACWO . . . . . . Aircraft Control and Warning Officer
ACWRON . . . . Aircraft Control and Warning Squadron (ADC)
ACWRRE . . . . American Cargo War Risk Reinsurance Exchange
ACWS . . . . . . Aircraft Control and Warning System (ADC)
AC & WS . . . . Aircraft Control and Warning Stations (Military)
ACWW . . . . . . Associated Country Women of the World
ACY . . . . Akron, Canton & Youngstown R. R. (AAR code)
ACY . . . . American Cyanamid Company (NYSE symbol)
ACYD . . . . . . Association of Cotton Yarn Distributors
ACYOA . . . . . Armenian Church Youth Organization of America
ACYPL . . . . . American Council of Young Political Leaders
AD . . . . A Drink
AD . . . . Abwehrdienst (Counterintelligence service) (German military – World War II)
AD . . . . Access Door
AD . . . . Accessions Document (Air Force)
AD . . . . Accion Democratica (Democratic Action) (Venezuelan political party)
AD . . . . Active Duty
AD . . . . Addict (Drug) (Slang)
AD . . . . Aden Airways
AD . . . . Adenoid Degenerative (Viruses) (Medicine)
AD . . . . After Date
AD . . . . Agnus Dei (Lamb of God)
AD . . . . Air Defense (Air Force)
AD . . . . Air Depot
AD . . . . Air Division
AD . . . . Air-Dried (Lumber)
AD . . . . Airdrome
AD . . . . Airframe Design (Division), Bureau of Aeronautics (Navy)
AD . . . . Airworthiness Directive
AD . . . . Alpha Delta (Society)
AD . . . . Alternate Days
AD . . . . Amplifier Detector
AD . . . . Amsted Industries, Inc. (NYSE symbol)
AD . . . . Analgesic Dose
AD . . . . Analog to Digital
AD . . . . Androstenedione (Hormone)
AD . . . . Anima Dulcis (Sweet Soul)
AD . . . . Anno Domini (In the Year of Our Lord)
AD . . . . Anodal Deviation
AD . . . . Ante Diem (Before the Day)
AD . . . . Appellate Division (Legal)
AD . . . . Archduke
AD . . . . Architectural Design (A publication)
AD . . . . Area Discriminator (SAGE)
AD . . . . Area Drain (Technical drawings)
AD . . . . Arithmetic Device
AD . . . . Army Depot
AD . . . . Army Digest (A publication)
AD . . . . Assembly-Disassembly
AD . . . . Assembly District
AD . . . . Assured Destruction (Capability) (of missiles)
AD . . . . ASTIA Document
AD . . . . Athletic Director
AD . . . . Atlantic & Danville Railway (AAR code)
AD . . . . Attention Display (Military communications device)
AD . . . . Australia Day

AD	Autograph Document
AD	Automatic Detection (Air Force)
AD	Automatic Display
AD	Average Deviation (Statistics)
AD	Aviation Daily
AD	Aviation Machinist's Mate (Navy rating)
AD	Aviatsionnaya Diviziya (Russian term for an air division)
AD	Avoidable Delay
AD	Destroyer Tender (Navy symbol)
AD	Doctor of Arts
A/D	Air Depot
A/D	Airdrome (or Aerodrome)
A/D	Analog-to-Digital (Data conversion)
A-to-D	Analog-to-Digital (Converter) (Data processing)
ADA	Advisory Area (Aviation)
ADA	Aerojet Differential Analyzer
ADA	Air Defense Area (Army)
ADA	Air Defense Artillery (Air Force)
ADA	Airborne Data Automation
ADA	American Dairy Association
ADA	American Dehydrators Association
ADA	American Dental Association
ADA	American Dermatological Association
ADA	American Diabetes Association
ADA	American Dietetic Association
ADA	Americans for Democratic Action
ADA	Amplifier Detector Assembly
ADA	Angular Differentiating-Integrating Accelerometer
ADA	Arming Device Assemblies (Army)
ADA	Assistant District Attorney
ADA	Atomic Development Authority (Proposed by Bernard Baruch to exercise control over those aspects of atomic energy inimical to global security, never organized)
ADA	Audio Distribution Amplifier
ADA	Authority Directing Arrest or Confinement (Military)
ADA	Automatic Data Acquisition
ADA	Automobile Dealers Association
ADA	Average Daily Attendance
AD-A	Air Density A (Explorer satellite)
ADAA	Air-Driven Air Amplifier
ADAA	American Dental Assistants Association
ADAA	Art Dealers Association of America
ADAC	Acoustic Data Analysis Center
ADAC	Air Defense Artillery Complex
ADAC	Allgemeiner Deutscher Automobil Club (Prewar; Germany)
ADAC	Auxiliary Data Annotation Set
ADAC	Aviation Development Advisory Committee
ADACC	Automatic Data Acquisition and Computer Complex (Air Force)
ADACIOM . . .	Associated Drug and Chemical Industries of Missouri
ADAD	Air Defense Artillery, Director (Air Force)
ADALINE	Adaptive Linear Neuron (Medicine)
ADAM	Adams National Historic Site
ADAM	Advanced Data Management
ADAM	Agriculture Department's Automated Manpower
ADAM	Air Base Damage Assessment Model
ADAM	Air Deflection and Modulation (Air Force)
ADAM	Automatic Distance and Angle Measurement
ADAML	Advise by Airmail (Army)
ADANDAC . . .	Administrative and Accounting Purposes
ADAOD	Air Defense Artillery Operations Detachment
ADAOO	Air Defense Artillery Operations Officer
ADAP	Airport Development Aid Program (FAA)
ADAPS	Automatic Display and Plotting System
ADAPSO	Association of Data Processing Service Organizations (Includes American and Canadian companies)
ADAPT	Adaption of Automated Program Tools
ADAPT	Analog Digital Automatic Program Tester
ADAPTS	Air-Deliverable Anti-Pollution Transfer System
ADAR	Advanced Design Array RADAR
ADAR	Air Defense Area
ADARCO	Advise Date of Reporting in Compliance with Orders (Navy)
ADAS	Agricultural Development and Advisory Service (British)
ADAS	Airborne Data Acquisition System
ADAS	Auxiliary Data Annotation Set (or System)
ADASP	Air Defense Annual Service Practice
ADAT	Automatic Data Accumulation and Transfer
ADAVAL	Advise Availability (Army)
ADB	Apollo Data Bank (NASA)
ADB	Arctic Drift Barge
ADB	Asian Development Bank
ADB	Australian Dictionary of Biography

ADB	Bachelor of Domestic Arts
ADBC	American Defenders of Bataan and Corregidor
ADBD	Active Duty Base Date (Navy)
ADBS	Association Francaise des Documentalistes et des Bibliothecaires Specialises
ADC	Active Duty Commitment
ADC	Advance Delivery of Correspondence (Military)
ADC	Aerophysics Development Corporation
ADC	Aerospace Defense Command (Air Force) (Formerly, Air Defense Command)
ADC	Agricultural Development Council
ADC	Aid to Dependent Children
ADC	Aide-de-Camp (Military)
ADC	Air Data Computers (or Computing)
ADC	Air Data Converter
ADC	Air Development Center (Air Force)
ADC	Air Diffusion Council
ADC	Airborne Digital Computer (Air Force)
ADC	Aircraft Directives Configuration (Navy)
ADC	Alaska Defense Command (Known to many of the soldiers who served in it as "All Damn Confusion") (World War II)
ADC	All Damn Confusion
ADC	Amateur Dramatic Club (British)
ADC	American Deserters Committee, France
ADC	American Distilling Company (NYSE symbol)
ADC	Analog-to-Digital Converter
ADC	Anodal Duration Contraction
ADC	Antenna Dish Control
ADC	Apollo Display Console
ADC	Area Data Center
ADC	Art Directors Club
ADC	Assistant Division Commander
ADC	Authorized Data Chain
ADC	Automatic Drift Control
ADC	Aviation Development Council
ADC	Axiodistocervical
AD & C	Ammunition Distribution and Control (Military)
ADCAD	Airways Data Collection and Distribution (Data processing)
ADCAT	Air Defense Control and Targets Office (Army)
ADCC	Air Defense Control Center (Air Force)
ADCC	American Devon Cattle Club
ADCC	Area Damage Control Center (Army)
ADCC	Associated Day Care Centers
ADCCC	Air Defense Command Commendation Certificate
ADCCCS	Air Defense Command, Control and Coordination System
ADCI	American Die Casting Institute
ADCII	American Die Casting Institute, Incorporated
ADCIR	Administrative Circular
ADCO	Air Defense Communications Office
ADCOC	Area Damage Control Center (Army)
ADCOM	Administrative Command
ADCOMINPAC . .	Administrative Command, Minecraft, Pacific Fleet
ADCOMPHIBSPAC . .	Administrative Command, Amphibious Forces, Pacific Fleet
ADCOMSUBORDCOMPHIBSPAC . .	Administrative Command, Amphibious Forces, Pacific Fleet, Subordinate Command
ADCON	Administrative Control
ADCON	Advance Concepts for Terrain Avoidance
ADCON	Advise or Issue Instructions to All Concerned
ADCON	Analog Digital Converter
ADCONSEN . .	(With the) Advice and Consent of the Senate
ADCOP	Area Damage Control Party (Army)
ADCOP	Associate Degree Completion Program (Navy)
ADCP	Advanced (Flight) Control Programmer
ADCP	Air Defense Command Post
ADCS	Advanced Defense Communications Satellite
ADCS	Air Data Computing System
ADCS	Automated Document Control System
ADCSP	Advanced Defense Communications Satellite Program
ADCUS	Advise Customs (Aviation)
ADD	Abstracts of Declassified Documents
ADD	Acoustic Discrimination of Decoys
ADD	Aerospace Defense Division (Air Force)
ADD	Aerospace Digital Development
ADD	American Dialect Dictionary
ADD	Analog Data Digitizer
ADD	Analog-Digital-Designer (Trademark)
ADD	Aviatsiia Dalnego Deistviia (Long-range Aviation) (Strategic bombing force of USSR)
ADDA	Air Defense Defended Area (Army)
ADDAR	Automatic Digital Data Acquisition and Recording
ADDC	Air Defense Direction Center (Air Force)
ADDC	Alignment and Diagnostic Display Console

ACRONYMS AND INITIALISMS DICTIONARY

ADDC ...... Association of Desk and Derrick Clubs of North America
ADDER ...... Automatic Digital-Data-Error Recorder
ADDL .... Aircraft Dummy Deck Landing (Navy)
ADDL .... Anti-Digit Dialing League
ADDNL...... Additional
ADDP....... Air Defense Defended Point (Army)
ADDPEP...... Aerodynamic Deployable Decelerator Performance Evaluation Program
ADDRESOR ... Analog-to-Digital Data Reduction System for Oceanographic Research
ADDS .... Apollo Document Descriptions Standards (NASA)
ADDS .... Astro Digital Doppler Speedometer (Electronics)
ADDS .... Automatic Data Digitizing System (Air Force)
ADDT .... Angular Distribution Data Tape
ADDU ...... Additional Duty
ADE .... After Delivery Economies
ADE .... Air Defense Element
ADE .... Air Density Explorer (Satellite)
ADE .... Alpha Disintegration Energy
ADE .... Alphanumeric Display Equipment
ADE .... Animal Disease Eradication Division (of ARS, Department of Agriculture)
ADE .... Approved (or Authorized) Data Element
ADE .... Armament Design Establishment (British)
ADE .... Assistant Division Engineer (Army)
ADE .... Association of Departments of English
ADE .... Automated Design Engineering
ADE .... Automatic Data Evaluation
ADEA .... American Driver Education Association
ADEA .... Association Belge pour le Developpement Pacifique de l'Energie Atomique
           (Belgian Association for the Peaceful Development of Atomic Energy)
ADEC .... Aiken Dahlgren Electronic Calculator
ADEDU ...... Assistant Director for Education (Vietnam)
ADEDY...... Anotati Diokisis Enosios Demosion Ypallilon (Supreme Council of Civil
           Servants) (Greece)
ADEH .... Aluminum Diethyl Hydride
ADELA ...... Atlantic Community Development Group for Latin America (Joint US -
           European private investment company)
ADEM .... Automatic Data Equalized Modem
ADEP .... Air Depot (Army)
ADEP .... Association pour le Developpement de l'Exportation des Vins de Bordeaux
ADEPO ..... Automatic Dynamic Evaluation by Programmed Organizations
ADEPT ...... A Distinctly Empirical Prover of Theorems
ADEPT ...... Agricultural and Dairy Educational Political Trust
ADEPT ...... Automatic Data Extractor and Plotting Table
ADEPT ...... Automatic Dynamic Evaluation by Programmed Test
ADES .... Automatic Digital Encoding System (Air Force)
ADETEM ..... Association pour le Developpement des Techniques de Marketing
ADF .... Acoustic Depth Finder
ADF .... After Deducting Freight
ADF .... Air Defense Force
ADF .... Air Development Force
ADF .... Air Direction Finder
ADF .... All Dielectric Filter
ADF .... Archdiocesan Development Fund (Catholic)
ADF .... Army Distaff Foundation
ADF .... Assured Destruction Force (Military)
ADF .... Automatic Direction Finder (Army)
ADF .... Auxiliary Detonation Fuze
ADFAP ..... Automatic Direction Finding Approach
ADFC ...... Adiabatic Film Cooling
ADFC ...... Air Defense Filter Center (Military)
ADFG ...... Alaska Department of Fish and Game
ADFI ...... American Dog Feed Institute
ADFL ...... Association of Departments of Foreign Languages
ADFOR ..... Adriatic Force (Military)
ADFS ...... American Dentists for Foreign Service
ADFS ...... Automatic Direction Finding System
ADFSC ..... Automatic Data Field Systems Command (Army)
ADG .... Advance Development Group (Army)
ADG .... Air Defense Group
ADG .... Antenna Directive Gain
ADG .... Average Daily Gain (of weight) (Cattle)
ADG .... Axiodistogingival
ADG .... Degaussing Vessel (Navy symbol)
ADGA ...... American Dairy Goat Association
ADGB ...... Air Defense of Great Britain
ADGE....... Air Defense Ground Environment (NATO)
ADGp....... Air Defense Group (Air Force)
ADGRU ..... Advisory Group (Military)
ADH .... Academy of Dentistry for the Handicapped
ADH .... Alcohol Dehydrogenase
ADH .... Antidiuretic Hormone (Vasopressin)
ADHA ...... American Dental Hygienists' Association

ADHCA ..... Advise this Headquarters of Complete Action (Army)
ADHI .... Area Defense Homing Interceptor
ADI .... Acceptable Daily Intake
ADI .... Acoustical Door Institute
ADI .... Air Defense Institute
ADI .... Air Defense Intercept (Air Force)
ADI .... Air Distribution Institute
ADI .... Alien Declared Intention
ADI .... Alternating Direction Implicit (Algorithm)
ADI .... Altitude Direction Indicator
ADI .... American Documentation Institute (Later, American Society for
           Information Science)
ADI .... Anti-Detonation Injection
ADI .... Attitude Director Indicator
ADI .... Automatic Direction Indicator
ADI .... Axiodistoincisal
AD/I .... Air Density/Injun (Explorer satellite)
ADIC ...... American Dental Interfraternity Council
ADIC ...... Analog-to-Digital Conversion System
A Dies Tech ... Associate in Diesel Technology
ADIL ...... Air Defense Identification Line (Air Force)
AD INTEL CEN.. Advanced Intelligence Center
ADIOS ...... Automatic Digital Input-Output System (Air Force)
ADIP ...... Air Defense, Interdiction and Photographic
ADIPU ...... Advise Whether Individual May Be Properly Utilized in Your
           Installation (Army)
ADIRS...... ADIS (Australasian Drug Information Services) Drug Information
           Retrieval System
ADIS ...... Air Defense Integrated System (Military)
ADIS ...... Airborne Digital Instrumentation System
ADIS ...... Australasian Drug Information Services
ADIS ...... Automatic Data Interchange System
ADIS ...... Automatic Diffemic Identification of Speakers (University of Bonn)
ADIT ...... Analog Digital Integrating Translator (Data processing)
A DIV...... Air Division (Air Force)
ADIZ ...... Air Defense Identification Zone (Air Force, FAA)
ADJ........ Adjective
ADJ........ Adjunct
ADJ........ Adjustment
ADJ........ Adjutant
ADJ........ Angle Deception Jamming
Adj A ...... Adjunct in Arts
ADJS ...... Angle Deception Jamming System
ADJUST ..... Center for the Administration of Justice (American University)
ADK....... Attach-Detach Kit
ADL........ Acceptable Defect Level
ADL........ Acoustic Delay Line
ADL........ Activities of Daily Living (Medicine)
ADL........ Admiral Corporation (NYSE symbol)
ADL........ Airborne Data Link
ADL........ Antenna Dummy Load
ADL .... Anti-Defamation League of B'nai B'rith
ADL .... Apollo Documentation List (NASA)
ADL .... Arthur D. Little, Inc.
ADL........ Authorized Data List (DOD)
ADL........ Automatic Data Link (Air Force)
ADLATAD .... Advise Latest Address (Military)
ADLM....... Aerial Delivered Land Mine
ADLO....... Air Defense Liaison Officer
ADLOG ..... Advance Logistical Command (Army)
ADLR ...... Automated Direct Labor Reporting
ADLS ...... Air Dispatch Letter Service (Navy)
ADLS ...... Airborne Data Link System
ADLTDE ..... Association of Dark Leaf Tobacco Dealers and Exporters
ADM .... Administration
ADM .... Admiral
ADM .... Advanced Development Model
ADM .... Affiliated Dress Manufacturers, Inc.
ADM .... Air Decoy Missile
ADM .... Air Defense Missile
ADM .... Archer-Daniels-Midland Company (NYSE symbol)
ADM .... Area Defense Missile
ADM .... Atomic Demolition Munition
ADM .... Automated Depot Maintenance
ADM .... Automatic Degreasing Machine
ADM .... Average Daily Membership
ADMA ...... American Drug Manufacturers' Association
ADMA ...... Automatic Drafting Machine
ADMA....... Aviation Distributors and Manufacturers Association
ADMAP...... Advise by Air Mail As Soon As Practicable
ADMCEN .... Administration Center

ADMG . . . . . . Assistant Deputy Military Governor (US Military Government, Germany)
ADMI . . . . . . American Dry Milk Institute
ADMIN . . . . . . Administration
ADMIN . . . . . . Administrative (Administrator, etc.)
ADMINI . . . . . . Administrative Instructions
ADMINO . . . . . Administrative Orders
ADMIRE . . . . . Automatic Diagnostic Maintenance Information Retrieval (Data processing)
ADML . . . . . . Average Daily Member Load
ADMO . . . . . . Air Defense Management Office
ADMRA . . . . . American and Delaine-Merino Record Association
ADMRL . . . . . Application Data Material Readiness List (DOD)
ADMS . . . . . . Assistant Director of Medical Services
ADMS . . . . . . Asynchronous Data Multiplexer Synchronizer
ADMS . . . . . . Atmospheric Diffusion Measuring System
ADMS . . . . . . Automated Depot Maintenance Study
ADMS . . . . . . Automatic Digital Message Switch
ADMSC . . . . . Automatic Digital Message Switching Center (AUTODIN)
ADMSG . . . . . Advise by (Electronically Transmitted) Message (Army)
ADMSLBN . . . . Air Defense Missile Battalion (Army)
ADN . . . . . . Accession Designation Number (Military)
ADN . . . . . . Adiponitrile (Chemical)
ADN . . . . . . Allgemeiner Deutscher Nachrichtendienst (General German Press Agency) (East Germany)
ADN . . . . . . Ashley, Drew & Northern Railway Company (AAR code)
ADNAC . . . . . Air Defense of North American Continent (Army)
ADNOK . . . . . Advise If Not Correct
ADO . . . . . . Advanced Development Objective (Air Force)
ADO . . . . . . Air Defence Officer (British Navy)
ADO . . . . . . Audio Decode Oscillator
ADO . . . . . . Axiodisto-Occlusal
ADOC . . . . . . Air Defense Operations Center (Air Force)
ADOGA . . . . . American Dehydrated Onion and Garlic Association
ADOIT . . . . . Automatically Directed Outgoing Intertoll Trunk (Bell System)
ADONIS . . . . . Automatic Digital On-Line Instruments System
ADOPE . . . . . Automatic Decisions Optimizing Predicted Estimates
ADOS . . . . . . Assistant Director of Ordnance Services (British)
ADOS . . . . . . Astronautical Defensive-Offensive System
ADOT . . . . . . Automatic Digital Optical Tracker (Army)
ADOT . . . . . . Automatically Directed Outgoing Trunk (Bell Laboratories)
ADP . . . . . . Academy of Denture Prosthetics
ADP . . . . . . Adenosine Diphosphate
ADP . . . . . . Advanced Development Plans (Air Force)
ADP . . . . . . Agence Dahomeene de Presse (Dahomean Press Agency)
ADP . . . . . . Air Defense Position (Military)
ADP . . . . . . Airborne Data Processor (Air Force)
ADP . . . . . . Airport Development Program
ADP . . . . . . Allied Products Corporation (NYSE symbol)
ADP . . . . . . Alpha Delta Phi (Fraternity)
ADP . . . . . . Alpha Delta Pi (Sorority)
ADP . . . . . . Ammonium Dihydrogen Phosphate
ADP . . . . . . Anatuberculina Diagnostica Petragnani (Petragnani Diagnostic Anatuberculin) (Medicine)
ADP . . . . . . Animal Disease and Parasite Research Division (of ARS, Department of Agriculture)
ADP . . . . . . Area Distribution Panel
ADP . . . . . . Automatic Data Plotter
ADP . . . . . . Automatic Data Processing
ADPB . . . . . . Air Defense Planning Board
ADPC . . . . . . Automatic Data Processing Center
ADPE . . . . . . Automatic Data Processing Equipment
ADPE . . . . . . Auxiliary Data Processing Equipment
ADPESO . . . . . Automatic Data Processing Equipment Selection Office (Navy)
ADPI . . . . . . Association Internationale d'Etudes pour la Protection des Investissements
ADPL . . . . . . Average Daily Patient Load
ADPLS . . . . . Automated Drawing Parts List System
ADPM . . . . . . Automatic Data Processing Machine
ADPP . . . . . . Automatic Data Processing Programs
ADPS . . . . . . Automatic Data Processing Systems
ADPSC . . . . . Automatic Data Processing Service Center
ADPSO . . . . . Association of Data Processing Service Organizations
ADPU . . . . . . Airborne Digital Processing Unit
ADR . . . . . . Accepted Dental Remedies (A publication)
ADR . . . . . . Advisory Route (Aviation)
ADR . . . . . . Airborne Digital Recorder
ADR . . . . . . Aircraft Direction Room
ADR . . . . . . Alianza Democratica Revolucionaria
ADR . . . . . . American Depositary Receipt
ADR . . . . . . Analog-Digital Recorder
ADR . . . . . . Angle Data Recorder
ADR . . . . . . Asset Depreciation Range (Treasury Department system)
ADR . . . . . . Aviation Design Research (Navy)

ADRAC . . . . . Automatic Digital Recording and Control
ADRB . . . . . . Army Disability Review Board
ADRB . . . . . . Army Discharge Review Board
ADRC . . . . . . Automatic Data Rate Changer
ADRDE . . . . . Advise Reason for Delay (Aviation)
ADRDE . . . . . Air Defense Research and Development Establishment
A Dr & Dgn . . . Associate in Drafting and Design
ADREP . . . . . Automatic Data Processing Resource Estimating Procedures
ADRES . . . . . Army Data Retrieval Engineering System
ADRIS . . . . . . Association for the Development of Religious Information Systems
ADRIS . . . . . . Automatic Dead Reckoning Instrument Systems (Canadian) (Navigation)
ADROBN . . . . Airdrome Battalion (Military)
ADRS . . . . . . Address
ADRS . . . . . . Airborne Digital Recording System
ADRT . . . . . . Analog Data Recorder Transcriber
ADS . . . . . . Academie des Sciences (Academy of Science)
ADS . . . . . . Accessory Drive System
ADS . . . . . . Accurately Defined Systems (Data processing)
ADS . . . . . . Advanced Data System (DOD)
ADS . . . . . . Advanced Display System
ADS . . . . . . Advanced Diving System
ADS . . . . . . Aerial Delivery System
ADS . . . . . . Air Defense Sector (Air Force)
ADS . . . . . . Air Defense System
ADS . . . . . . Air Development Station (Navy)
ADS . . . . . . Aircraft Development Service (Air Force)
ADS . . . . . . Airport Data System (FAA)
ADS . . . . . . Allied Mills, Inc. (NYSE symbol)
ADS . . . . . . American Daffodil Society
ADS . . . . . . American Dahlia Society
ADS . . . . . . American Denture Society
ADS . . . . . . American Dialect Society
ADS . . . . . . Anti-Coincidence Detection System
ADS . . . . . . Antidiuretic Substance
ADS . . . . . . Arctic Drift Station
ADS . . . . . . Arctic Drilling System
ADS . . . . . . Army Dental Service
ADS . . . . . . Association of Diesel Specialists
ADS . . . . . . Aston Dark Space
ADS . . . . . . Autograph Document Signed
ADS . . . . . . Automatic Digital Switch
ADS . . . . . . Automatic Door Seal (Technical drawings)
ADS . . . . . . Azione Dynamico-Specifico (Dynamic-Specific Action) (Medicine)
ADSA . . . . . . Air-Derived Separation Assurance (Aviation)
ADSA . . . . . . American Dairy Science Association
ADSA . . . . . . American Dental Society of Anesthesiology
ADSA . . . . . . Atomic Defense Support Agency
ADSAF . . . . . Automatic Data System within the Army in the Field
ADSAS . . . . . Air-Derived Separation Assurance System
ADSAT . . . . . Anomalous Dispersion Spherical Array Target (for increasing radio reflectivity)
ADSC . . . . . . Active Duty Service Commitment (Military)
ADSC . . . . . . Advanced Section Communication Zone (World War II)
ADSC . . . . . . Air Defense Systems Command
ADSC . . . . . . Automatic Data Service Center
ADSC . . . . . . Average Daily Service Charge (Hospitals)
ADSCOM . . . . Advanced Shipboard Communications
ADSCP . . . . . Advanced Defense Satellite Communications Project
AD SEC . . . . . Advanced Section (Military)
ADSEC . . . . . Air Defense System Engineering Committee
ADSG . . . . . . Atomic Defense and Space Group (Westinghouse Electric Corporation)
ADSHIPDA . . . . Advise Shipping Data
ADSHPDAT . . . Advise Shipping Date
ADSID . . . . . . Air Defense Systems Integration Division (Air Force)
ADS (ISA) . . . . Assistant Secretary of Defense (International Security Affairs)
ADSL . . . . . . Assembly Department Shortage List
ADSL . . . . . . Authorized Depot Stockage List (Army)
ADSM . . . . . . American Defense Service Medal
ADSMO . . . . . Air Defense System Management Office (Air Force)
ADSN . . . . . . Accounting and Disbursing Station Number (Air Force)
ADSO . . . . . . Aerospace Defense Systems Officer (Air Force)
ADSO . . . . . . Assistant Division Supply Officer (Army)
ADSO . . . . . . Automatic Display Switching Oscilloscope
ADSOC . . . . . Administrative Support Operations Center
ADSP . . . . . . Automatic Dispatching Stick Repeater
ADSPN . . . . . Advise Disposition (Aviation)
ADSS . . . . . . Aircraft Damage Sensing System
ADSS . . . . . . Analysis of Digitized Seismic Signals (Data processing)
ADSTADIS . . . . Advise Status and/or Disposition (Army)
ADSTKOH . . . Advise Stock on Hand (Army)
ADSUP . . . . . Automatic Data Systems Uniform Practices

ADT . . . . Adenosine Triphosphate (Chemical)
ADT . . . . Advanced Design Team
ADT . . . . Airborne Digital Timer
ADT . . . . American District Telegraph Co. (Alarm systems)
ADT . . . . Anything That You Desire (Notation in a placebo prescription) (Medicine)
ADT . . . . Assured Depot Task
ADT . . . . Atomic Damage Template (Military drafting)
ADT . . . . Automatic Data Translator
ADT . . . . Average Daily Traffic
ADTA . . . . . . American Dental Trade Association
ADTAC . . . . . . Automatic Digital Tracking Analyzer Computer (Data processing)
ADTC . . . . . . Armament Development Test Center (Air Force)
ADTD . . . . . . Apollo Docking Test Device (Aerospace)
ADTECH . . . . Advanced Decoy Technology
ADTIC . . . . . . Arctic-Desert-Tropic Information Center (Air Force)
ADTSC . . . . . . Auto Dealers Traffic Safety Council
ADTSEA . . . . . American Driver and Traffic Safety Education Association
ADTU . . . . . . Automatic Digital Test Unit
ADTU . . . . . . Auxiliary Data Translator Unit
ADU . . . . Acceleration-Deceleration Unit
ADU . . . . Accumulation Distribution Unit
ADU . . . . Adapter Unit
ADU . . . . Aircraft Delivery Unit (Air Force)
ADU . . . . Analog Delay Unit
ADU . . . . Analog Display Unit
ADU . . . . Arc Detector Unit
ADV . . . . Advance(ment)
ADV . . . . Advanced Development Vehicle
ADV . . . . Adverb
ADV . . . . Adversus (Against) (Latin)
ADV . . . . Advertisement
ADV . . . . Advisory
ADV . . . . Airborne Digital Voltmeter
ADV . . . . American Dual Vest Fund Inc. (NYSE symbol)
ADV . . . . Arc Drop Voltage
ADVALT . . . . . Advice of Allotment
Adv Cert in Ed . . Advanced Certificate in Education
Adv Cert in Mus Ed . . Advanced Certificate in Music Education
ADVDISC . . . . Advance Discontinuance of Allotment
ADVDLA-DEP . . Advance Payment of Dislocation Allowance to Dependents (Air Force)
ADV INTEL CEN . . Advanced Intelligence Center (Navy)
ADVISOR . . . . Advanced Integrated Safety and Optimizing Computer
ADVMOS . . . . Advanced Military Occupational Specialty (Army)
ADVON . . . . . Advanced Echelon (Marine Corps)
ADVON . . . . . Advanced Operations Unit (Navy)
ADVPMT . . . . . Advance Payment
ADVS . . . . . . Advise
ADVSR . . . . . . Advisor
ADVSY . . . . . . Advisory
ADVUL . . . . . Air Defense Vulnerability Simulation
ADW . . . . Air Defense Warning (Air Force)
ADW . . . . Air Defense Weapon
ADW . . . . Air Denial Weapon
ADW . . . . Arbeitsgemeinschaft der Waehlerinnen (Association of Women Voters) (Germany)
ADW . . . . Assault with Deadly Weapon
ADW . . . . Automated Data Wiring
ADWA . . . . . . Atlantic Deeper Waterways Association
ADWC . . . . . . Air Defense Weapons Center (Air Force)
ADWCP . . . . . Automated Digital Weather Communications Program (Air Force)
ADWKP . . . . . Air Defense Warning Key Point
ADWS . . . . . . Automatic Digital Weather Switch (Air Force)
ADX . . . . Adams Express Company (NYSE symbol)
ADX . . . . Air Defense Exercise
ADX . . . . Automatic Data Exchange
AE . . . . Abort Electronics (Apollo) (NASA)
AE . . . . Account Executive
AE . . . . Accrued Expenditure
AE . . . . Added Entry
AE . . . . Aeon
AE . . . . Aeromedical Evacuation
AE . . . . Aeronautical Engineer
AE . . . . Aerospace Education
AE . . . . Affect Elaboration (Scale) (Psychology)
AE . . . . Agricultural Engineer
AE . . . . Agricultural Engineering Research Division (of ARS, Department of Agriculture)
AE . . . . Air Escape (Technical drawings)
AE . . . . Airborne Electronics
AE . . . . Airborne Equipment Division, Bureau of Aeronautics (Navy)
AE . . . . Aircraft Equipment

AE . . . . Aktiebolaget Atomenergi (Stockholm)
AE . . . . All England
AE . . . . Aminoethyl
AE . . . . Ammunition Ship (Navy symbol)
AE . . . . Apostle and Evangelist (Church calendars)
AE . . . . Application Engineering
AE . . . . Arbeitseinheit
AE . . . . Architect-Engineer
AE . . . . Armor, Artillery, and Engineers Aptitude Area (Army)
AE . . . . Army in Europe
AE . . . . Assistant Engineer
AE . . . . Associate in Education
AE . . . . Associate in Engineering
AE . . . . Atmospheric Entry
AE . . . . Austral English or Australian English
AE . . . . Autoimmune Encephalomyelitis
AE . . . . Aviation Electrician's Mate (Navy rating)
A/E . . . . Absorptivity-Emissivity (Ratio)
A & E . . . . . . Appropriation and Expense
A & E . . . . . . Architectural and Engineering
A & E . . . . . . Armament & Electronics (Air Force)
A & E . . . . . . Azimuth and Elevation
A and E . . . . Airframe and Engine
AEA . . . . Abort Electronics Assembly (Apollo) (NASA)
AEA . . . . Active Element Array
AEA . . . . Actors' Equity Association
AEA . . . . Actual Expenses Allowable (Military)
AEA . . . . Adult Education Association of the USA
AEA . . . . Advanced Engine Aerospike
AEA . . . . Aft End Assembly
AEA . . . . Agence Europeenne d'Approvisionnement
AEA . . . . Air Entraining Agent (Freight)
AEA . . . . American Economic Association
AEA . . . . American Education Association
AEA . . . . American Engineering Association
AEA . . . . American Enterprise Association
AEA . . . . American Export Airlines
AEA . . . . Antenna Elevation Angle
AEA . . . . Artists Equity Association
AEA . . . . Associate in Engineering Administration
AEA . . . . Atomic Energy Act
AEA . . . . Atomic Energy Authority (British)
AEA . . . . Automatic Error Analysis
AEA . . . . Automotive Electric Association
AEAF . . . . . . Allied Expeditionary Air Force (World War I)
AEAO . . . . . . Airborne Emergency Actions Officer (SAC)
AEAONMS . . . Ancient Egyptian Arabic Order Nobles of the Mystic Shrine
AEAP . . . . . . Alliance Europeenne des Agences de Presse
AEAS . . . . . . Automatic Equalization/Analyzation System
AEB . . . . Advanced Engine Bell
AEB . . . . Airborne and Electronics Board (Army)
AEB . . . . Art Exhibitions Bureau
AE-B . . . . . . Atmosphere Explorer B (Satellite)
AEBR . . . . . . Airborne Electron Beam Recorder
AEBSTA . . . . . Atomic Energy Bureau of Science and Technics Agency (Japan)
AEC . . . . Agricultural Economics Division (of AMS, Department of Agriculture)
AEC . . . . Airship Experimental Center (Navy)
AEC . . . . Alaska Engineering Commission (Later, the Alaska Railroad)
AEC . . . . Aluminum Extruders Council
AEC . . . . American Engineering Council
AEC . . . . Analog Electronic Computer
AEC . . . . Architects' Emergency Committee
AEC . . . . Army Education Center
AEC . . . . Army Educational Corps (British)
AEC . . . . Army Electronics Command
AEC . . . . Assembled Electronic Component
AEC . . . . Association of Education Committees (British)
AEC . . . . Association of Episcopal Colleges
AEC . . . . Association Europeenne de Ceramique
AEC . . . . Atlantic & East Carolina Railway (AAR code)
AEC . . . . Atlas Educational Center
AEC . . . . Atomic Energy Commission
AEC . . . . Automatic Exciter Control
AEC . . . . Automatic Exposure Control
AEC . . . . Average Electrode Current
AECB . . . . . . Atomic Energy Control Board (Canada)
AECC . . . . . . Aeromedical Evacuation Control Center (Military)
AECL . . . . . . Atomic Energy of Canada, Limited
AECM . . . . . . Atomic Energy Commission Manual
AECO . . . . . . Aeromedical Evacuation Control Officer (Military)
AECP . . . . . . Airman Education and Commissioning Program

AECP . . . . Army Extension Course Program
AECS . . . . Advanced Engine Control System
AECT . . . . Association for Educational Communications and Technology
        (Formerly, DAVI)
AECT . . . . Automatic Exposure Control Technique
AECTR . . . . . . American Emergency Committee for Tibetan Refugees
AED . . . . Academy for Educational Development
AED . . . . Aeromedical Education Division (FAA)
AED . . . . Aeronautical Engineering Duty (Navy)
AED . . . . Airborne Equipment Division
AED . . . . ALGOL Extended for Design
AED . . . . Ammunition Engineering Directorate (Army)
AED . . . . Anaelectrodiabatic (Nuclear wave)
AED . . . . Artium Elegantium Doctor (Doctor of Fine Arts)
A Ed . . . . Associate in Education
AED . . . . Associated Equipment Distributors
AED . . . . Association of Electronic Distributors
AED . . . . Astro-Electronics Division (RCA)
AED . . . . Atomkernenergie-Dokumentation
AED . . . . Automated Engineering Design
AEDB . . . . . . Apollo Engineering Documentation Board
AEDC . . . . . . Arnold Engineering Development Center (Air Force)
AEDD . . . . . . Air Engineering Development Division (Air Force)
AEDE . . . . . . Airplane Economic Design Evaluator (Boeing Co.)
AEDE . . . . . . Association Europeenne des Enseignants (European Association of Teachers)
AEDO . . . . . . Aircraft Engineering District Office
AEDS . . . . . . Advanced Electric Distribution System
AEDS . . . . . . Airport Engineering Data Sheet (FAA)
AEDS . . . . . . Association of Educational Data Systems
AEDS . . . . . . Atomic Energy Detection System (AEC)
AEDT . . . . . . Association Europeenne des Organisations Nationales des Commercants
        Detaillants en Textiles (European Association of National Organizations
        of Textile Manufacturers)
AEDU . . . . . . Admiralty Experimental Diving Unit (British)
AEE . . . . Absolute Essential Equipment
AEE . . . . Aileen, Inc. (NYSE symbol)
AEE . . . . Associate in Engineering
AEE . . . . Atomic Energy Establishment
AEEA . . . . . . Aminoethylethanolamine
AEEC . . . . . . Airlines Electronic Engineering Committee
AEEF . . . . . . Association Europeenne des Exploitations Frigorifiques (European Associa-
        tion of Refrigeration Enterprises)
AEEL . . . . . . Aeronautical and Electronic Engineering Laboratory (Navy)
AEEL . . . . . . Arctic Environmental Engineering Laboratory (University of Alaska)
AEEM . . . . . . Airborne Electronic Equipment Modification (Aviation)
AEEN . . . . . . Agence Europeenne pour l'Energie Nucleaire
AEEW . . . . . . Atomic Energy Establishment, Winfrith (England)
AEF . . . . Advertising Educational Foundation
AEF . . . . Aerospace Education Foundation
AEF . . . . Afrique Equatoriale Francaise (French Equatorial Africa)
AEF . . . . After England Failed (Soldier slang for American Expeditionary Force
        in World War I)
AEF . . . . Airborne Equipment Failure (Air Force)
AEF . . . . Aircraft Engineering Foundation
AEF . . . . Allied Expeditionary Force
AEF . . . . American Economic Foundation
AEF . . . . American European Foundation
AEF . . . . American Expeditionary Forces
AEF . . . . Americans for Economic Freedom
AEF . . . . Armenian Educational Foundation
AEF . . . . Artists Equity Fund
AEF . . . . Aviation Engineer Force
AEF . . . . Centre d'Action Europeenne Federaliste
AEFC . . . . . . Alkaline Electrolyte Fuel Cell
AEFR . . . . . . Aurora, Elgin & Fox River Electric R. R. (AAR code)
AEFS . . . . . . Anti-Exposure Flight Suit
AEG . . . . Active Element Group (QCR)
AEG . . . . Air Encephalogram (Medicine)
AEG . . . . Allgemeine Elektrizitaets-Gesellschaft (Germany)
AEG . . . . Association of Engineering Geologists
AEGF . . . . . . Association des Etudiants Guineens de France (Association of Guinean
        Students in France)
AEGIS . . . . . . Active Electronic Gimballess Inertial System
AEGIS . . . . . . An Existing Generalized Information System (Data processing)
AEGp . . . . . . Aeromedical Evacuation Group (Air Force)
AEH . . . . Antenna Effective Height
AEHA . . . . . . Army Environmental Health Agency
AEHHC . . . . . Association of Educators of Homebound and Hospitalized Children
AEHL . . . . . . Army Environmental Health Laboratory
AEI . . . . Acrylic Eye Illustrator (Medical)
AEI . . . . Aerial Exposure Index

AEI . . . . Aerospace Education Instructor
AEI . . . . Air Express International
AEI . . . . American Enterprise Institute for Public Policy Research
AEI . . . . Annual Efficiency Index (Army)
AEI . . . . Arctic Enterprises, Incorporated (NYSE symbol)
AEI . . . . Associated Electrical Industry, Ltd. (British)
AEI . . . . Association des Ecoles Internationales
AEI . . . . Auto Enthusiasts International
AEI . . . . Average Efficiency Index
AEI . . . . Azimuth Error Indicator
AEIB . . . . . . Association for Education in International Business
AEIC . . . . . . Association of Edison Illuminating Companies
AEIL . . . . . . American Export Isbrandtsen Lines
AEIOU . . . . . . Albertus Electus Imperator Optimus Vivat (Inscription used by Albert
        II, 15th-century German king)
AEIOU . . . . . . Aller Ehren Ist Oesterreich Voll (Austria Is Crowned with All Honor)
        (Variation of 15th-century inscription)
AEIOU . . . . . . Aller Erst Ist Oesterreich Verdorben (Variation of 15th-century
        inscription)
AEIOU . . . . . . Alles Erdreich Ist Oesterreich Unterthan (Variation of 15th-century
        inscription)
AEIOU . . . . . . Archidux Electus Imperator Optime Vivat (Inscription used by Frederick
        III, 15th-century German king)
AEIOU . . . . . . Austria Erit In Orbe Ultima (Austria Will Be the Last in the World)
        (Variation of 15th-century inscription)
AEIOU . . . . . . Austriae Est Imperare Orbi Universo (Variation of 15th-century
        inscription)
AEIOU . . . . . . Austria's Empire Is Overall Universal (Variation of 15th century
        inscription)
AEIPPR . . . . . . American Enterprise Institute for Public Policy Research
AEIS . . . . Associate of the Educational Institute of Scotland
AEJ . . . . Aluminum Extension Jacket
AEJ . . . . Association for Education in Journalism
AEJI . . . . . . Association of European Jute Industries
AEK . . . . Aircraft Ejection Kit
AEL . . . . Acceptor Energy Level
AEL . . . . Admiralty Engineering Laboratory (Great Britain)
AEL . . . . Aeronautical Engine Laboratory (Navy)
AEL . . . . Aerospace Electronics Laboratories
AEL . . . . Aircraft Engine Laboratory
AEL . . . . Aircraft Equipment List
AEL . . . . Allowance Equipage List
AEL . . . . Aluminum Electrical Lead
AEL . . . . American Emigrants' League
AEL . . . . Animal Education League (Defunct)
AEL . . . . Appalachia Education Laboratory
AEL . . . . Association of Equipment Lessors
AEL . . . . Atomic Energy Level
AEL . . . . Audit Error List
AEL . . . . Automation Engineering Laboratory
AELE . . . . . . Americans for Effective Law Enforcement
AELE . . . . . . Association Europeenne de Libre-Echange (European Free Trade Association)
A El Ed . . . . . Associate in Elementary Education
AELMRP . . . . . . Atomic Energy Labor Management Relations Panel
AELO . . . . . . Aeromedical Evacuation Liaison Officer (Air Force)
AELTC . . . . . . All England Lawn Tennis Club
AEM . . . . Advance Engineering Memorandum
AEM . . . . Aeronautical Mobile
AEM . . . . Aircraft and Engine Mechanic
AEM . . . . American Meter Company (NYSE symbol) (Delisted)
AEM . . . . Association of Electronic Manufacturers
AEM . . . . Association des Etudiants Malgaches (Association of Malagasy Students)
AEM . . . . Aviation Electrician's Mate
AEMC . . . . . . Albert Einstein Medical Center
AEMC . . . . . . American Electro Metal Corporation
AEMCO . . . . . Aircraft Engineering Maintenance Company
AEM-ED . . . . . Association of Electronic Manufacturers, Eastern Division
AEMO . . . . . . Advance Engineering Material Order
AEMO . . . . . . African Elected Members Organization
AEMS . . . . . . American Engineering Model Society
AEMSA . . . . . Army Electronics Material Support Agency
AEMT . . . . . . Automatically Erectable Modular Torus
AEN . . . . Adaption Error Note
AEN . . . . Advance Evaluation Note
A En . . . . . . Associate in English
AENF . . . . . . Association des Etudiants Nigeriens en France (Association of Niger
        Students in France)
AENG . . . . . . Airways Engineer
A Eng . . . . . . Associate in Engineering
A Eng Elect . . . Associate in Engineering Electronics
A Engr . . . . . . Associate in Engineering

AEO........ Air Engineer Officer
AEO .... Appeals Examining Office (CSC)
AEO........ Arbeitsgemeinschaft Ehemaliger Offiziere
AEO .... Assistant Experimental Officer (Ministry of Agriculture, Fisheries, and Food) (Also, AExO and AXO) (British)
AEOB....... Advanced Engine Overhaul Base
AEOM ...... Association des Etudiants d'Origine Malgache (Association of Students of Malagasy Origins Studying in France)
AEOO ...... Aeromedical Evacuation Operations Office(r) (Air Force)
AEOP ...... Amend Existing Orders Pertaining To
AEOS....... Ancient Egyptian Order of Sciots, Supreme Pyramid
AEP .... Accrued Expenditure Paid
AEP .... Adult Education Program
AEP .... Agence Europeenne de Productivite
AEP .... American Electric Power System (Group of investor-owned public utility companies) (NYSE symbol)
AEP .... Apollo Experiment Pallet (Aerospace)
AEP .... Automatic Extracting Program
AEP .... Average(d) Evoked Potential
AE & P...... Ambassador Extraordinary and Plenipotentiary (Diplomacy)
AEPEM ..... Association of Electronic Parts and Equipment Manufacturers
AEPG .... Army Electronic Proving Ground
AEPI........ American Educational Publishers Institute (Later, AAP)
AEPS .... Advanced Extravehicular Protective System (NASA)
AEPS .... Aircraft Electrical Power System
AER .... Abbreviated Effectiveness Report (Air Force)
AER .... Aeronautical Engineering Report
AER .... After Engine Room
AER .... Airman Effectiveness Report (Air Force)
AER .... Antenna Effective Resistance
AER .... Army Emergency Relief
AER .... Association Europeenne pour l'Etude du Probleme des Refugies
AER .... Auditory Evoked Response
AER .... Average Evoked Response
AERA ...... American Educational Research Association
AERA ...... Automotive Engine Rebuilders Association
AERB ...... Army Education Requirements Board
AERC ...... Association of Executive Recruiting Consultants
AERCAB .... Advanced (or Aircrew) Escape/Rescue Capability (Navy – Air Force)
AERE .... Atomic Energy Research Establishment (of United Kingdom Atomic Energy Authority) (Harwell, England)
AERI........ Automotive Exhaust Research Institute
AERIS ...... Airborne Electronic Ranging Instrumentation System
AERL .... Aero-Elastic Research Laboratory (MIT)
AERL .... Avco-Everett Research Laboratory
AERM....... Aerographer's Mate
AERNO...... Aeronautical Equipment Reference Number (Military)
AERO ...... Aeronautics
AERO ...... Automatic Earnings Recomputation Operation (Social Security)
AEROBEE..... Aerojet/Bumblebee (Navy missile)
AEROCOM ... Aeronautical Communications Equipment Corporation
AER OF...... Aerological Officer
AEROFLOT ... Soviet Air Line
AEROHEAT ... Aerodynamic Heating
AEROSPACE... Aeronautics and Space
AEROSPACECOM .. Aerospace Communications
AERS .... Aircraft Equipment Requirement Schedule
AERS .... Atlantic Estuarine Research Society
AERT .... Acceptable Environmental Range Test
AERTEL...... Association Europeenne Rubans, Tresses, Tissus Elastiques (European Ribbon, Braid and Elastic Material Association)
AES .... Advanced Extravehicular Suit (NASA)
AES .... Aerospace Electrical Society
AES .... Aerospace and Electronic Systems
AES .... Agricultural Estimates Division (of AMS, Department of Agriculture)
AES .... Air and Earth Shock
AES .... Aircraft Ejection Seat
AES .... Aircraft Electrical Society
AES .... Airways Engineering Society
AES .... American Electrochemical Society
AES .... American Electroencephalographic Society
AES .... American Electromechanical Society
AES .... American Electronical Society
AES .... American Electroplaters' Society
AES .... American Entomological Society
AES .... American Epidemiological Society
AES .... American Epilepsy Society
AES .... American Equilibration Society
AES .... American Ethnological Society
AES .... American Eugenics Society
AES .... Apollo Earth-Orbiting Station (Aerospace)

AES .... Apollo Experiment Support
AES .... Apollo Extension System (NASA)
AES .... Area Electronic Supervisor
AES .... Army Excess Property
AES .... Army Exchange Service (Centralized the control of PX's in US) (World War II)
AES .... Array Element Study
AES .... Artificial Earth Satellite (NASA)
AES .... Astronomical Explorer Satellite
AES .... Atlantic Estuarine Society
AES .... Audio Engineering Society
AES .... Auger Electron Spectrometry (or Spectroscopy)
AES .... Automatic External Standard(ization) (Radioactivity measurement)
AES .... Auxiliary Encoder System
AE & S...... Air Equipment and Support
AESA ...... American Educational Studies Association
AESAP ..... Army Entertainment Scholarships and Awards Program
AESB ...... Architect-Engineers -- Spanish Bases
AESBOW..... Association of Engineers and Scientists of the Bureau of Naval Weapons (Later, ANWES)
AESC ...... American Engineering Standards Committee
AESC ...... Automatic Electronic Switching Center
AESE ...... Association of Earth Science Editors
AES(I)...... Association of Engineers and Scientists (Independent)
AESIR ...... Aerospace Instrumentation Range Station
AESOP ..... Artificial Earth Satellite Observation Program (Navy)
AESOP ..... Automated Engineering and Scientific Optimization Program (NASA)
AESP ...... Auxiliary Engineering Signal Processor
AESq ...... Aeromedical Evacuation Squadron (Air Force)
AESQ ...... Air Explorer Squadron
AESS ...... Aircraft Ejection Seat System
AET .... Aerlinte Eireann Teoranta (Irish Air Lines)
AET .... Aetna Life & Casualty Co. (NYSE symbol)
AET .... Aminoethylisothiuronium (Chemical)
AET .... Approximate Exposure Time
AET .... Associate in Electrical Technology
AETA ...... American Educational Theatre Association
AETA ...... Antique Engine and Thresher Association
AETAC ..... Aviation Electronic Technician's Mate, Combat Aircrewman
AETD ...... Aero-Electronic Technology Department (Navy)
AETE ...... Aerospace Engineering Test Establishment (Canada)
AETFAT..... Association pour l'Etude Taxonomique de la Flore d'Afrique Tropicale
AETM...... Aviation Electronic Technician's Mate
AETR ...... Advanced Engineering Test Reactor (AEC)
AETR ...... Advanced Epithermal Thorium Reactor
AETS ...... Association for the Education of Teachers in Science
AEU .... Accrued Expenditure Unpaid
AEU........ Amalgamated Engineering Union (Australia)
AEU........ Amalgamated Engineering Union (Rhodesia and Nyasaland)
AEU .... American Ethical Union
AEU .... Army Exhibit Unit
AEUS ...... Absolute Electrical Unit Scale
AEV .... Aerothermodynamic Elastic Vehicle
AEVAC...... Air Evacuation
AEW........ Airborne (or Aircraft) Early Warning (Station)
AEW........ Airborne Electronic Warfare
AEW .... American Education Week
AEW .... Appalachian Power (NYSE symbol)
AEWA....... Airborne Early Warning Aircraft
AEWC ..... Airborne Early Warning and Control (Army)
AEW & C.... Airborne Early Warning and Control (Army)
AEWES ..... Army Engineers Waterways Experiment Station
AEWF ...... Airborne Early Warning Fighter
AEWRON .... Airborne Early Warning Squadron
AEWS....... Advanced Earth Satellite Weapon System (Air Force)
AEWTU...... Airborne Early Warning Training Unit
AEX .... American Export Industries Company (NYSE symbol)
AExO....... Assistant Experimental Officer (Ministry of Agriculture, Fisheries, and Food) (Also, AEO and AXO) (British)
AF .... Acid-Fast
AF .... Acre-Foot
AF .... Ad Finem (At the End; To the End)
AF .... Admiral of the Fleet
AF .... Advance Freight (Shipping)
AF .... Aeronautically Fixed
AF .... Aggregation Factor (Biochemistry)
AF .... Air Filter
AF .... Air Force
AF .... Air Foundation
AF .... Air France
AF .... Alternating Field

AF . . . . Alternating Flow
AF . . . . Aluminium Federation
AF . . . . American Fabrics (A publication)
AF . . . . American & Foreign Power Company, Inc. (NYSE symbol) (Wall Street slang name: "Airforce") (Delisted)
AF . . . . America's Future
AF . . . . Amplification Factor
AF . . . . Anglo-French
AF . . . . Anterior (Part of) Foot
AF . . . . Army Force
AF . . . . Arthritis Foundation
AF . . . . Artilleriefuehrer (Division artillery commander) (German military - World War II)
AF . . . . Asiatic Fleet
AF . . . . Atrial Fibrillation (Medicine)
AF . . . . Audio Frequency (Electronics)
AF . . . . Automatic Following (RADAR)
AF . . . . Automation Foundation
AF . . . . Aviation Facilities
AF . . . . Store Ship (Navy symbol)
A/F . . . . Airfile
A & F . . . . . . Accounting and Finance
A & F . . . . . . Agriculture and Forestry Committee (US Senate)
A & F . . . . . . Aircraft and Facilities (Navy appropriation)
A & F . . . . . . Arming and Fuzing
AF2 . . . . Popular Name for an Identification Card issued to Air Force Military Personnel and Certain Civilian Personnel
2-A-F . . . . . . Selective Service Class (for Man Physically Disqualified for Military Service but Engaged in Work in the National Health, Safety, or Interest) (Obsolete)
AFA . . . . Actors' Fund of America
AFA . . . . Advertising Federation of America
AFA . . . . Aerophilatelic Federation of the Americas
AFA . . . . . . Air Force Academy
AFA . . . . Air Force Association
AFA . . . . Alien Firearms Act
AFA . . . . Allergy Foundation of America
AFA . . . . Amateur Fencing Association
AFA . . . . . . American Federation of Arts
AFA . . . . . . American Federation of Astrologers
AFA . . . . American Finance Association
AFA . . . . American Flag Association of the US
AFA . . . . American Forces in Action (Military)
AFA . . . . American Forensic Association
AFA . . . . American Forestry Association
AFA . . . . American Foundrymen's Association
AFA . . . . American Fracture Association
AFA . . . . American Freedom Association
AFA . . . . . . Armed Forces Act
AFA . . . . Army Finance Association
AFA . . . . Army Flight Activity
AFA . . . . Associate of the Faculty of Actuaries (British)
AFA . . . . Associate in Fine Arts
AFA . . . . Association of Federal Appraisers
AFA . . . . Association of Federal Architects
AFA . . . . Audio Frequency Amplifier
AFA . . . . Automatic Field Assistant
AFA . . . . Azimuth Followup Amplifier
AFAA . . . . . . Adult Film Association of America
AFAA . . . . . . American Fighter Aces Association
AFAA . . . . . . Automatic Fire Alarm Association
AFAADS . . . . . Advanced Forward Area Air Defense System
AFAADW . . . . . Advanced Forward Area Air Defense Weapon
AFAAEC . . . . . Air Force Academy and Aircrew Examining Center
AFA Art . . . . . Associate in Fine Arts in Art
AFAB . . . . . . Air Force Academy Board
AFAB . . . . . . Air Force Audit Branch
AFABBN . . . . . American Friends of the Anti-Bolshevik Bloc of Nations
AFAC . . . . . . Air Force Armament Center
AFAC . . . . . . Allied Finance Adjusters Conference
AFAC . . . . . . American Fisheries Advisory Committee
AFAC . . . . . . Association des Fonctionnaires et Agents de la Colonie (Association of Civil Servants and Agents of the Colony) (European civil servants) (East Congo)
AFAC . . . . . . Automatic Field Analog Computer
AFA Dance . . . Associate in Fine Arts in Dance
AFADO . . . . . Association of Food and Drug Officials
AFA Drama . . . Associate in Fine Arts in Drama
AFADVMC . . . . Air Force Advanced Management Class
AFAE . . . . . . American Foundation on Automation and Employment
AFAF . . . . . . Atlantic Fleet Amphibious Force (Navy)

AFAFC . . . . . . Air Force Accounting and Finance Center
AFAFFO . . . . Air Force Aerospace Fuels Field Office
AFAG . . . . . . Air Force Advisory Group
AFAI . . . . . . Air Force Agent Installation
AFAITC . . . . . Armed Forces Air Intelligence Training Center
AFAIU . . . . . . American Friends of the Alliance Israelite Universelle
AFAK . . . . . . Armed Forces Assistance to Korea (Military)
AFAL . . . . . . Air Force Avionics Laboratory
AF & AM . . . . Ancient Free and Accepted Masons
AFA Mus . . . . Associate in Fine Arts in Music
AFAO . . . . . . Approved Force Acquisition Objective (Army)
AFAP . . . . . . Association Francaise pour l'Augmentation de la Productivite (France)
AFAPL . . . . . Air Force Aero-Propulsion Laboratory
AFAR . . . . . . Airborne Fixed Array RADAR
AFAR . . . . . . Automatic False Alarm Rate
AFAR . . . . . . Azores Fixed Acoustic Range (NATO)
AFAS . . . . . . Air Flow Actuated Switch
AFAS . . . . . . Air Force Aid Society
AFAS . . . . . . American Fine Arts Society
AFASD . . . . . Air Force Aeronautical Systems Division
AFASE . . . . . Association for Applied Solar Energy
AFA-SEF . . . . Air Force Association - Space Education Foundation
AFATL . . . . . Air Force Armament Technology Laboratory
AFAUX . . . . . Air Force Auxiliary Field
AFB . . . . Acid-Fast Bacillus
AFB . . . . Air Force Base
AFB . . . . Air Force Bulletin
AFB . . . . American Farm Bureau
AFB . . . . American Foundation for the Blind
AFB . . . . Anti-Friction Bearing
AFBDA . . . . . Anti-Friction Bearing Distributors Association
AFBF . . . . . . American Farm Bureau Federation
AFBMA . . . . . Air Force Ballistic Missile Arsenal
AFBMA . . . . . Anti-Friction Bearing Manufacturers Association
AFBMC . . . . . Air Force Ballistic Missile Committee
AFBMD . . . . . Air Force Ballistic Missile Division
AFBMTC . . . . Air Force Ballistic Missile Training Center
AFBO . . . . . . Approved Force Budget Objective (Army)
AFBR . . . . . . Air Force Board of Review
AFBS . . . . . . American and Foreign Bible Society
AFBSD . . . . . Air Force Ballistic Systems Division
AFBU . . . . . . Air Force Base Unit
AFC . . . . Air Force Council (Advisory board to Air Force)
AFC . . . . Air Force Cross (British)
AFC . . . . Aluminum Field Coil
AFC . . . . American Finance Conference
AFC . . . . American Flag Committee
AFC . . . . American Football Conference (of NFL)
AFC . . . . American Foxhound Club
AFC . . . . American Freedom Center
AFC . . . . Analog to Frequency Converter
AFC . . . . Apollo Flight Control (NASA)
AFC . . . . Army Field Commands
AFC . . . . Army Finance Center
AFC . . . . Atomic Fuel Corporation (Japan)
AFC . . . . Audio Frequency Coder
AFC . . . . Automatic Flight Control (Aerospace)
AFC . . . . Automatic Frequency Control (Electronics)
AFC . . . . Average Fixed Cost
AFC . . . . Aviation Fire Controlman
AFC . . . . Axial Flow Compressor
AFCA . . . . . . American Football Coaches Association
AFCA . . . . . . Armed Forces Chemical Association
AFCA . . . . . . Armed Forces Communications Association
AFCAL . . . . . Association Francaise de Calcul
AFCAN . . . . . Analogue Factor Calibration Network
AFCC . . . . . . Air Force Combat Command
AFCC . . . . . . Air Force Communication Center
AFCC . . . . . . Air Force Component Commander
AFCC . . . . . . Assault Fire Command Console (Army)
AFCCDC . . . . Air Force Command and Control Development Center
AFCCE . . . . . Association of Federal Communications Consulting Engineers
AFCCP . . . . . Air Force Component Command Post
AFCCS . . . . . Air Force Command and Control System
AFCD . . . . . . Air Force Cryptologic Depot
AFCE . . . . . . Allied Forces Central Europe (Air Force)
AFCE . . . . . . American Foundation for Continuing Education
AFCE . . . . . . Armed Forces Chemical Association
AFCE . . . . . . Automatic Flight Control Equipment
AFCEA . . . . . Armed Forces Communications & Electronics Association
AFCEL . . . . . Air Force Contractor Experience List

AFCENT . . . . . Air Forces, Central Europe
AFCENT . . . . . Allied Forces Center
AFCENT . . . . . Allied Forces in Central Europe (NATO)
AFCET. . . . . . . Association Francaise pour la Cybernetique Economique et Technique
AFCG. . . . . . . American Fine China Guild
AFCI. . . . . American Foot Care Institute
AFCK . . . . Antenna Field Charge Kit
AFCM. . . . . . . Air Force Commendation Medal
AFCM . . . . . . Association of First Class Mailers
AFCMA . . . . . . Aluminum Foil Container Manufacturers Association
AFCMD. . . . . . Air Force Contract Management Division
AFCN. . . . . . . American Friends of the Captive Nations
AFCO . . . . . . Air Force Contracting Officer
AFCOA . . . . . . Air Force Contracting Office Approval
AFCCM . . . . . AFTN (Aeronautical Fixed Telecommunications Network) Communications Center (FAA)
AFCOM . . . . . Air Force Communications (Satellite)
AFCOMMSTA . . Air Force Communications Station
AFCOMSEC . . . Air Force Communications Security
AFCOMSECM . . Air Force Communications Security Manual
AFCON . . . . . Air Force Controlled (Units)
AFCOS . . . . . . Armed Forces Courier Service
AFCP . . . . Advanced Flight Control Programmer
AFCP . . . . Air Force Command Post
AFCR . . . . American Federation for Clinical Research
AFCR . . . . American Fund for Czechoslovak Refugees
AFCRC . . . . . . Air Force Cambridge Research Center (Obsolete)
AFCRL . . . . . . Air Force Cambridge Research Laboratories
AFCRP . . . . . . Air Force Cost Reduction Program
AFCS . . . . Active Federal Commissioned Service
AFCS . . . . Adaptive Flight Control System
AFCS . . . . Air Force Communications Service (or System)
AFCS . . . . Automatic Flight Control System (Air Force)
AFCSL . . . . . . Air Force Communications Security Letter
AFCSM . . . . . Air Force Communications Security Manual
AFCSS . . . . . . Air Force Communications Support System
AFCU . . . . American and Foreign Christian Union
AFCVC . . . . . . Vice Chief of Staff (Air Force)
AFCWB . . . . . American Federation of Catholic Workers for the Blind
AFCWF . . . . . . Air Force Civilian Welfare Fund
AFD . . . . Air Force Depot
AFD . . . . Amplitude-Frequency Distortion
AFD . . . . April Fools' Day
AFD . . . . Arithmetic Function Designator
AFD . . . . Association of Food Distributors
AFD . . . . Association of Footwear Distributors
AFD . . . . Automated Flaw Detector
AFD . . . . Automatic Fast Demagnetization
AFD . . . . Auxiliary, Floating Dock (Navy symbol)
AFDAP . . . . . . Air Force Data Automation Planning Concepts (Manual)
AFDAP . . . . . . Assistant for Development Planning (Air Force)
AFDASTA . . . . Air Force Data Station
AFDAT . . . . . . Air Force Directorate of Advanced Technology
AFDATACOM . Air Force Data Communications System
AFDB . . . . African Development Bank
AFDB . . . . Air Force Decorations Board
AFDB . . . . Large Auxiliary Floating Dry Dock (Navy symbol)
AFDC . . . . Agriculture and Fishery Development Corporation (South Korea)
AFDC . . . . Aid to Families with Dependent Children
AFDCB . . . . . . Armed Forces Disciplinary Control Board
AFDCCO . . . . Air Force Departmental Catalog Coordinating Office
AFDCS . . . . . . American First Day Cover Society
AFDCUF . . . . . Aid to Families with Dependent Children of Unemployed Fathers
AFDC-UP . . . . Aid to Families With Dependent Children - Unemployed Parents (HEW)
AFDDC . . . . . . Deputy Chief of Staff, Development (Air Force)
AFDE . . . . American Fund for Dental Education
AFDEA . . . . . . American Funeral Directors and Embalmers Association
AFDFO . . . . . . Development Field Office (Air Force)
AFDIERSS . . . . Air Force Departmental Industrial Equipment Reserve Storage Site
AFDL . . . . Small Auxiliary Floating Dry Dock (Navy symbol)
AFDM . . . . . . Medium Auxiliary Floating Dry Dock (Navy symbol)
AFDO . . . . Air Force Duty Officer
AFDO . . . . . . Assistant Fighter Director Office (Navy)
AFDOA . . . . . . Armed Forces Dental Officers Association
AFDOUS . . . . . Association of Food and Drug Officials of the United States
AFDP . . . . Army Force Development Plan
AFDRB . . . . . . Air Force Disability Review Board
AFDRB . . . . . . Air Force Discharge Review Board
AFDRD . . . . . . Director of Research and Development (Air Force)
AFDRQ . . . . . Director of Requirements (Air Force)
AFDS . . . . Associated Funeral Directors Service

AFDS . . . . Auxiliary Fighter Director Ship
AFDSDC . . . . . Air Force Data System Design Center
AFE . . . . Aerospace Facilities Engineer
AFE . . . . Air Force in Europe
AFE . . . . Allowed Failure Effect
AFEA . . . . American Farm Economic Association
AFEA . . . . American Film Export Association
AFEB . . . . Armed Forces Epidemiological Board
AFEES. . . . . . . Armed Forces Examining and Entrance Stations
AFEI . . . . Association of Finnish Electric Industries
AFEM . . . . Armed Forces Expeditionary Medal
AFEMS . . . . . . Air Force Equipment Management System
AFEPBA . . . . . Armed Forces Enlisted Personnel Benefit Association
AFERB . . . . . . Air Force Educational Requirements Board
AFERC . . . . . . Air Force Edwards Research Center
AFES . . . . Air Force Exchange Service
AFES . . . . American Far Eastern Society
AFES . . . . Armed Forces Examining Station
AFESD . . . . . . Air Force Electronic Systems Division
AFETR . . . . . . Air Force Eastern Test Range
AFETS. . . . . . . Air Force Engineering and Technical Service
AFEWES . . . . . Air Force Electronic Warfare Evaluation Simulator
AFEX . . . . Air Forces Europe Exchange
AFF . . . . Affairs
AFF . . . . Army Field Forces
AFF . . . . Axisymmetrical Flow Field
AFFA . . . . Air Freight Forwarders Association
AFFC . . . . Air Force Finance Center
AFFC . . . . Aluminum Foil Field Coil
AFFDL . . . . . . Air Force Flight Dynamics Laboratory
AFFE . . . . Air Force Far East
AFFE . . . . Army Forces Far East
AFFF . . . . American Fish Farmers Federation
AFFF . . . . Aqueous Film-Forming Foam (Firefighting chemical for ships)
AFFFA. . . . . . . American Forged Fitting and Flange Association
AFFI . . . . American Frozen Food Institute (Formerly, NAFFP)
AFFJ . . . . American Fund for Free Jurists
AFFLC . . . . . . Air Force Film Library Center
AF(F)MMIU . . . Amphibious Forces Ordnance Material Mobile Instruction Unit
AFFS . . . . American Federation of Film Societies
AFFTC . . . . . . Air Force Flight Test Center (AFSC)
AFFTC . . . . . . Air Force Flying Training Command
AFFUS . . . . . . Association of the Free French in the United States
AFG . . . . American Friends of Greece
AFG . . . . Analog Function Generator
AFG . . . . Antenna Field Gain
AFGC . . . . American Forage and Grassland Council
AFGCM . . . . . Air Force Good Conduct Medal
AFGE . . . . American Federation of Government Employees
AFGIS . . . . . . Aerial Free Gunnery Instructions School(s)
AFGM . . . . . . American Federation of Grain Millers
AFGR . . . . Approved Force Gross Requirement (Army)
AFGU . . . . Aerial Free Gunnery Unit
AFGW . . . . . . American Flint Glass Workers Union of North America
AFGWC . . . . . Air Force Global Weather Central
AFGWRP . . . . . Air Force Global Weather Reconnaissance Program
AFGWU . . . . . American Flint Glass Workers Union of North America
AFH . . . . Air Force Hospital
AFH . . . . American Foundation for Homoeopathy
AFH . . . . Antenna Feed Horn
AFHA . . . . Armed Forces Hostess Association
AFHC . . . . Air Force Headquarters Command
AFHC . . . . Association of Fair Housing Committees
AFHF . . . . Air Force Historical Foundation
AFHF . . . . American Foot Health Foundation
AFHQ . . . . . . Air African Force Headquarters
AFHQ . . . . . . Air Force Headquarters
AFHQ . . . . . . Allied Forces Headquarters (Might refer to any theater of war) (World War II)
AFHQ (CIC). . . Allied Force Headquarters (Counter Intelligence Corps)
AFHQPS . . . . . Allied Force Headquarters Petroleum Section
AFHRL . . . . . . Air Force Human Resources Laboratory
AFHU . . . . American Friends of Hebrew University
AFHW . . . . . . American Federation of Hosiery Workers
AFI . . . . African/Indian Ocean (Aviation)
AFI . . . . Air Filter Institute
AFI . . . . Air Flow Indicator
AFI . . . . American Fiber Institute
AFI . . . . American Film Institute
AFI . . . . American Forest Institute
AFI . . . . American Friends of Israel

AFI . . . . Armed Forces Institute
AFI . . . . Association of Federal Investigators
AFI . . . . Atlantic Refining Company (NYSE symbol)
AFI . . . . Automatic Fault Isolation
AFIA . . . . . . American Foreign Insurance Association
AFIC . . . . . . Air Force Intelligence Center
AFICCS . . . . . Air Force Integrated Command and Control System
AFICE . . . . . . Air Forces, Iceland
AFID . . . . . . Arithmetic Function Identifier
AFIE . . . . . . American Federation of Italian Evangelicals
AFIE . . . . Armed Forces Information and Education
AFIED . . . . . . Armed Forces Information and Education Division
AFIF . . . . Air Force Industrial Fund
AFIF . . . . Armed Forces Information Film
AFII . . . . American Federation of International Institutes
AFINS . . . . . . Airways Flight Inspector
AFIO . . . . Approved Force Inventory Objective (Army)
AFIO . . . . . . Authorization for Interceptor Operations
AFIP . . . . Armed Forces Information Program
AFIP . . . . . . Armed Forces Institute of Pathology
AFIPS . . . . . American Federation of Information Processing Societies
AFIR . . . . . . Air Force Installation Representative
AFIRE . . . . . . Association of Fundamental Institutions of Religious Education
AFIRO . . . . . . Air Force Installation Representative Officer
A-FIRST . . . . . Advanced - Far Infrared Search/Track
AFIS . . . . . . Armed Forces Information School
AFISM . . . . . . Aluminum-Free Inorganic Suspended Material
AFISR . . . . . . Air Force Industrial Security Regulations
AFIT . . . . Air Force Institute of Technology
AFIT . . . . Automatic Fault Isolation Test
AFITAE . . . . . Association Francaise des Ingenieurs et Techniciens de l'Aeronautique et de l'Espace
AFJ . . . . Air Force Jet
AFJA . . . . . . Association Francaise des Journalistes Agricoles
AFJCE . . . . . . American Federation of Jews from Central Europe
AFJKT . . . . . . Air Force Job Knowledge Test
AFJROTC . . . . Air Force Junior Reserve Officers Training Corps
AFKAG . . . . . . Air Force Cryptographic Aid, General
AFL . . . . Abstract Family of Languages
AFL . . . . . . Air Force Letter
AFL . . . . Air Force Liaison
AFL . . . . American Federation of Labor
AFL . . . . American Football League (Reorganized as part of AFC and NFC)
AFL . . . . Association for Family Living
AFL . . . . Automatic Fault Location
AFLA . . . . . . Amateur Fencers League of America
AFLA . . . . . . American Foreign Law Association
AFLA . . . . . . Asian Federation of Library Associations
AFLAT . . . . . . Air Force Language Aptitude Test
AFLC . . . . . . Air Force Logistics Command (Formerly, Air Materiel Command)
AFLCA . . . . . American Fur Liner Contractors Association
AFL-CIO . . . . . American Federation of Labor and Congress of Industrial Organizations
AFL-CIO DAP . . AFL-CIO Demonstration Arts Project
AFLCL . . . . . . Air Force Logistic Command Letter (Formerly, AMCL)
AFLCM . . . . . . Air Force Logistic Command Manual (Formerly, AMCM)
AFLCON . . . . . Air Force Logistics Communications Network
AFLD . . . . . . Airborne Fraunhofer Line Discriminator
AFLD . . . . . . Airfield
AFLI . . . . . . Air Force Legislative Item
AFLL . . . . . . Army Fuels and Lubricant Laboratory
AFLMC . . . . . . Air Force Logistics Management Center
AFLP . . . . . . Armed Forces Language Program
AFLSA . . . . . . Air Force Longevity Service Award
AFM . . . . Accredited Farm Manager (Designation given by American Society of Farm Managers and Rural Appraisers)
AFM . . . . Air Force Manuals
AFM . . . . Air Force Medal (British)
AFM . . . . Air Force Museum
AFM . . . . American Federation of Musicians of the US and Canada
AFM . . . . Annular Fire Missile
AFM . . . . . . Anti-Friction Metal
AFM . . . . Armed Forces Management
AFM . . . . Associated Fur Manufacturers
AFM . . . . Automatic Flight Management
AFMA . . . . . . American Feed Manufacturers Association
AFMA . . . . . . American Fur Merchants' Association
AFMA . . . . . . Armed Forces Management Association
AFMBT . . . . . Artificial Flower Manufacturers Board of Trade
AFMCC . . . . . Air Freight Motor Carriers Conference
AFMDC . . . . . Air Force Machinability Data Center
AFMDC . . . . . Air Force Missile Development Center (AFSC)

AFME . . . . . . American Friends of the Middle East
AFMED . . . . . Allied Forces Mediterranean (NATO)
AFMF . . . . . . Air Fleet Marine Force
AFMFIC . . . . . Associated Factory Mutual Fire Insurance Companies
AFMFP . . . . . Aircraft Fleet Marine Force Pacific
AFMH . . . . . . American Foundation for Mental Hygiene
AFMIDPAC . . . US Army Forces, Middle Pacific (Official name for the theater of war more commonly called MIDPAC) (World War II)
AF -- MIPR . . . Air Force -- Military Interdepartmental Purchase Requests
AFML . . . . . . Air Force Materials Laboratory
AFML . . . . . . Armed Forces Medical Library (Became National Library of Medicine, 1956)
AFMMFO . . . . Air Force Medical Materiel Field Office
AFMPA . . . . . Air Force Medical Publications Agency
AFMPA . . . . . Armed Forces Medical Procurement Agency
AFMPC . . . . . Assistant for Materiel Program Control (Air Force)
AFMR . . . . . . American Foundation for Management Research
AFMR . . . . . . Antiferromagnetic Resonance
AFMR . . . . . . Armed Forces Master Records (Solicited phonograph records, and money to buy records, for the armed forces) (World War II) (Cf. RFOFM)
AFMRB . . . . . Air Force Material Review Board
AFMS . . . . . . Air Force Medical Service
AFMS . . . . . . Airborne Frequency Multiplexing System
AFMS . . . . . . American Federation of Mineralogical Societies
AFMSC . . . . . Air Force Medical Specialist Corps
AFMTC . . . . . Air Force Missile Test Center
AFN . . . . Active Filter Network
AFN . . . . Air Force Finance Center
AFN . . . . Alaska Federation of Natives
AFN . . . . American Forces Network
AFN . . . . . . Armed Forces Network (Military)
AFN . . . . Average Failure Number
AFNA . . . . . . Air Force - Navy
AFNA . . . . . . American Federation of Negro Affairs
AFNB . . . . . . Armed Forces News Bureau
AFNC . . . . . . Air Force Nurse Corps
AFNCOAR . . . . Air Force Noncommissioned Officer Academy (Graduate) Ribbon
AFNE . . . . . . Allied Forces Northern Europe
AFNE . . . . . . American Forces Network, Europe
AFNEA . . . . . Air Force NOTAM Exchange Area
AFNEO . . . . . Air Force NOTAM Exchange Office
AF NETF . . . . . Air Force Nuclear Engineering Test Facility (Reactor)
AFNETSTA . . . Air Force Networks Station
AFNORTH . . . . Allied Forces Northern Europe (NATO)
AFNRD . . . . . Air Force National Range Division
AFNY . . . . . . Alliance Francaise de New York
AFO . . . . Accounting and Finance Office(r)
AFO . . . . Airports Field Office
AFO . . . . Atlantic Fleet Organization
AFOAR . . . . . Air Force Office of Aerospace Research (AFSC)
AFOAS . . . . . Air Force Office of Aerospace Sciences (AFOAR)
AFOAT . . . . . Air Force Office of Atomic Energy
AFOAT . . . . . Assistant for Atomic Energy (Air Force)
AFOB . . . . . . American Foundation for Overseas Blind
AFOC . . . . . . Air Force Operations Center
AFODC . . . . . Deputy Chief of Staff, Operations (Air Force)
AFOEP . . . . . Air Force Officer Education Program
AFOIC . . . . . . Air Force Officer in Charge
AFOQT . . . . . Air Force Officer Qualifying Test
AFORA . . . . . Air Force Office of Research Analysis
AFORD . . . . . Air Force Overseas Replacement Depot (World War II)
AFOREP . . . . . Air Force Operational Report
AFORG . . . . . Air Force Overseas Replacement Group
AFOS . . . . . . Air Force Objective Series (Papers)
AFOSCR . . . . . Air Force Organization Status Change Report
AFOSR . . . . . Air Force Office of Scientific Research
AFOTC . . . . . Air Force Operational Test Center
AFOUA . . . . . Air Force Outstanding Unit Award
AFOUAR . . . . Air Force Outstanding Unit Award Ribbon
AFP . . . . Agence France Presse (French Press Agency)
AFP . . . . Air Force Pamphlet
AFP . . . . Air Force Plant
AFP . . . . Alternate Flight Plan
AFP . . . . American Federation of Police
AFP . . . . American Federation of Priests
AFP . . . . Americans for Peace (An organization)
AFP . . . . Annual Funding Program (Army)
AFP . . . . Armed Forces of the Philippines
AFP . . . . Armed Forces Police
AFP . . . . Associated Fantasy Publishers
AFP . . . . Association of Federal Photographers

AFP . . . . Association of Flock Processors
AFP . . . . Authority for Purchase
A & FP . . . . . . American and Foreign Power Company
AFPA . . . . Association Nationale pour la Formation Professionnelle des Adultes
AFPAC . . . . . . US Army Forces in the Pacific (World War II)
AFPB . . . . Air Force Personnel Board
AFPC . . . . Air Force Personnel Council
AFPC . . . . Air Force Procurement Circulars
AFPC . . . . American Food for Peace Council
AFPC . . . . Armed Forces Policy Council
AFPCB . . . . . . Armed Forces Pest Control Board
AFPD . . . . Armed Forces Police Detachment
AFPDAB . . . . . Air Force Physical Disability Appeal Board
AFPDC . . . . . . Deputy Chief of Staff Personnel (Air Force)
AFPDP . . . . . . Director of Personnel Planning (Air Force)
AFPE . . . . American Foundation for Pharmaceutical Education
AFPE . . . . American Foundation for Political Education
AFPEA . . . . . . Air Force Packaging Evaluation Agency
AFPEB . . . . . . Air Force Professional Entertainment Branch
AFPFL . . . . . . Anti-Fascist People's Freedom League (Burma)
AFPG . . . . Air Force Personnel Processing Group
AFPH . . . . American Federation of the Physically Handicapped
AFPI . . . . Air Force Procurement Instructions
AFPI . . . . American Forest Products Industries
AFPJ . . . . American Federation for Polish Jews
AFPL . . . . Air Force Packaging Laboratory
AFPO . . . . Air Force Property Officer
AFPP . . . . Air Force Procurement Procedures
AFPPA . . . . . . American Federation of Poultry Producers Associations
AFPPG . . . . . . American Foundation for Psychoanalysis and Psychoanalysis in Groups
AFPR . . . . Air Force Plant (or Project) Representative
AFPR . . . . Armed Forces Procurement Regulations
AFPRDS . . . . . Air Force Petroleum Retail Distribution Station
AFPRO . . . . . . Air Force Plant Representative Office
AFPS . . . . Armed Forces Press Service
AFPT . . . . Air Force Personnel Test
AFPTRC . . . . . Air Force Personnel and Training Research Center
AFPU . . . . Air Force Postal Unit
AFQAR . . . . . . Air Force Quality Assurance Representative
AFQC . . . . Air Force Quality Control
AFQCR . . . . . . Air Force Quality Control Representative
AFQT . . . . Armed Forces Qualification Test
AFQTVA . . . . . Armed Forces Qualification Test, Verbal Arithmetic Subtest
AFR . . . . Acceptable Failure Rate
AFR . . . . Access Function Register
AFR . . . . Air Force Regulations
AFR . . . . Air Force Reserve
AFR . . . . American Friends of Refugees
AFR . . . . Artillery Flash Ranging (Army)
AFRA . . . . American Farm Research Association
AFRA . . . . Armed Forces Reserve Act of 1952, as Amended
AFRA . . . . Average Freight Rate Assessment (Shipping)
AFRAMS . . . . . Air Force Recoverable Assembly Management System
AFRAP . . . . . . American Foundation of Religion and Psychiatry
AFRASIA . . . . . Africa and Asia
AFRB . . . . Air Force Retiring Board
AFRBA . . . . . . Armed Forces Relief and Benefit Association
AFRC . . . . Air Force Records Center
AFRC . . . . Armed Forces Reserve Center
AFRCE . . . . . . Air Force Regional Civil Engineers
AFRCSTC . . . . . Air Force Reserve Combat Support Training Center
AFRCTC . . . . . Air Force Reserve Combat Training Center
AFRD . . . . Air Force Research Division
AFRD . . . . Air Force Reserve Division
AFRD . . . . Association of Fund-Raising Directors
AFRES . . . . . . Air Force Reserve
AFRESBSGP . . . Air Force Reserve Regions Base Support Group
AFRESM . . . . . Armed Forces Reserve Medal
AFRESNAVSQ . . Air Force Reserve Navigation Squadron
AFRESR . . . . . . Air Force Reserve Regions
AFRESRGP . . . . Air Force Reserve Regions Group
AFRESS . . . . . Air Force Reserve Sectors
AFRF . . . . American Freedom of Residence Fund
AFRF . . . . American Friends of Russian Freedom (Later, American Friends of Refugees)
AFRFI . . . . . . American Friends of Religious Freedom in Israel
AFRFTC . . . . . Air Force Reserve Flying Training Center
AFRI . . . . Applied Forest Research Institute (Syracuse University)
AFRICOBRA . . . African Commune of Bad Relevant Artists (Chicago)
AFRKB . . . . . . American Federation of Retail Kosher Butchers
AFRM . . . . . . Armed Forces Reserve Medal (US)

AFRO . . . . . . African Regional Organization
AFRO . . . . Air Force Reserve Orders
AFROASI . . . . . Authority for Removal of Accepted Spacecraft Installations
AFROIC . . . . . Air Force Resident Officer in Charge
AFROTC . . . . . Air Force Reserve Officers Training Corps
AFRP . . . . American Foundation of Religion and Psychiatry
AFRPC . . . . . . Air Force Reserve Policy Committee
AFRPL . . . . . . Air Force Rocket Propulsion Laboratories
AFRR . . . . Air Force Reserve Region
AFRRGp . . . . . Air Force Reserve Recovery Group
AFRRI . . . . . . Armed Forces Radiobiology Research Institute
AFRS . . . . Advanced Fighter RADAR System
AFRS . . . . Air Force Rescue Service
AFRS . . . . Air Force Reserve Sector
AFRS . . . . Armed Forces Radio Service (Military)
AFRSTC . . . . . Air Force Reserve Specialist Training Center
AFRTD . . . . . . Air Force Research and Technology Division
AFRTS . . . . . . Armed Forces Radio and Television Service (or System)
AFS . . . . Active Fuzing System
AFS . . . . Aerial Fire Support
AFS . . . . Aeronautical Fixed Service
AFS . . . . Air Force Specialty
AFS . . . . Air Force Station
AFS . . . . Air Force Supply
AFS . . . . Airline Feed System
AFS . . . . Airway Facilities Service (FAA)
AFS . . . . Airways Facility Shop
AFS . . . . American Feline Society
AFS . . . . American Fern Society
AFS . . . . American Fertility Society
AFS . . . . American Field Service
AFS . . . . American Finance System (NYSE symbol)
AFS . . . . American Fisheries Society
AFS . . . . American Folklore Society
AFS . . . . American Foundrymen's Society
AFS . . . . American Fuchsia Society
AFS . . . . Antenna Feed System
AFS . . . . Armed Forces Radiobiology Research Institute
AFS . . . . Atlantic Ferry Service (World War II)
AFS . . . . Atomic Fluorescence Spectroscopy
AFS . . . . Atomic Frequency Standard
AFS . . . . Automatic Frequency Stabilization
AFS . . . . Auxiliary Fire Service (British)
AFS . . . . Aviation Facilities Service (of FAA)
AFS . . . . Azimuth Followup System
AFS . . . . Combat Store Ship (Navy symbol)
AFSA . . . . Air Force Sergeants Association
AFSA . . . . American Flight Strips Association
AFSA . . . . American Foreign Service Association
AFSA . . . . Armed Forces Security Agency
AFSAB . . . . . . Air Force Scientific Advisory Board
AFSAG . . . . . . Armed Forces Security Agency
AFSAM . . . . . . Air Force School of Aviation Medicine
AFSAS . . . . . . Advanced Fire Support Avionics System
AFSAW . . . . . . Air Force Special Activities Wing
AFSBO . . . . . . American Federation of Small Business Organizations
AFSC . . . . Air Force Service Center (or Command)
AFSC . . . . Air Force Specialty Code
AFSC . . . . Air Force Staff College
AFSC . . . . Air Force Supply Catalog
AFSC . . . . Air Force Systems Command
AFSC . . . . American Federation of Soroptimist Clubs
AFSC . . . . American Friends Service Committee
AFSC . . . . Armed Forces Staff College
AFSCA . . . . . . Amalgamated Flying Saucers Clubs of America
AFSCC . . . . . . Air Force Special Communications Center
AFSCC . . . . . . Armed Forces Supply Control Center (DOD)
AFSCF . . . . . . Air Force Satellite Control Facility
AFSCME . . . . . American Federation of State, County and Municipal Employees
AFSCS . . . . . . Army Field Stock Control System
AFSD . . . . Air Force Supply Directive
AFSec . . . . . . Air Force Section
AFSF . . . . Air Force Stock Fund
AFSHEW . . . . . Association of Former Secretaries of (the Department of) Health, Education, and Welfare (Mythical group)
AFSI . . . . Aviation Financial Services, Incorporated
AFSIP . . . . . . Air Force Standard Intelligence Publication
AFSMAAG . . . . Air Force Section, Military Assistance Advisory Group
AFSN . . . . . . Air Force Serial Number
AFSN . . . . . . Air Force Service Number
AFSN . . . . . . Air Force Stock Number

AFSO . . . . Air Force Service Office
AFSOUTH . . . . Allied Forces Southern Europe (NATO)
AFSPA . . . . . . American Foreign Service Protective Association
AFSPBRSIO . . . Armed Forces Surplus Property Bidders Registration and Sales Information Office (Later, Defense Surplus Bidders Control Office)
AFSR . . . . Advanced Foreign System Requirements
AFSR . . . . Argonne Fast Source Reactor
AFSS . . . . Air Force Security Service
AFSS . . . . Air Force Service Statement
AFSSC . . . . . . Armed Forces Supply Support Center (Merged with Defense Logistics Services Center)
AFSSD . . . . . . Air Force Space Systems Division
AFSSO . . . . . . Air Force Special Security Office(r)
AFSSOP . . . . . Air Force Security Service Office of Production
AFST . . . . Assured Field Shop Task
AFSTC . . . . . . Air Force Space Test Center (Now, Western Test Range)
AFSTC . . . . . . Army Foreign Science and Technology Center
AFSTE . . . . . . Association for Field Services in Teacher Education
AFSTRIKE . . . . Air Force Strike Command
AFSU . . . . Auxiliary Ferry Service Unit
AFSUB . . . . . . Army Air Forces Anti-Submarine Command
AFSWA . . . . . . Armed Forces Special Weapons Agency
AFSWA . . . . . . Assistant Secretary of War for Air
AFSWC . . . . . . Air Force Special Weapons Center (AFSC)
AFSWP . . . . . . Armed Forces Special Weapons Project
AFT . . . . Acetate Film Tape
AFT . . . . Air Freight Terminal
AFT . . . . American Federation of Teachers
AFT . . . . Annual Field Training (Army)
AFT . . . . Anterior Fold from Typhlosole
AFT . . . . Automatic Fine Tuning
AFT . . . . Automatic Flight Termination
AFTA . . . . Atlantic Free Trade Area
AFTAC . . . . . . Air Force Technical Application Center
AFTB . . . . Air Force Test Base
AFTBC . . . . . . Air Flow Thermal Balance Calorimeter
AFTC . . . . Airborne Flight Training Command
AFTC . . . . American Fair Trade Council
AFTC . . . . American Fox Terrier Club
AFTCA . . . . . . Amateur Field Trial Clubs of America
AFTE . . . . American Federation of Technical Engineers
AFTF . . . . Air Force Task Force
AFTM . . . . American Foundation for Tropical Medicine
AFTMA . . . . . . American Fishing Tackle Manufacturers Association
AFTN . . . . Aeronautical Fixed Telecommunications Network
AFTO . . . . Air Force Technical Order
AFTOSB . . . . Air Force Technical Order Standardization Board
AFTRA . . . . . . American Federation of Television and Radio Artists
AFTRC . . . . . . Air Force Training Command
AFTRCC . . . . . Aerospace and Flight Test Radio Coordinating Council
AFTS . . . . Automatic Flexible Test Station
AFTTH . . . . . . Air Force Technical Training Headquarters
AFTU . . . . Air Force Test Unit
AFU . . . . Advanced Flying Unit (Air Force)
AFU . . . . American Fraternal Union
AFU . . . . Assault Fire Unit (Army)
AFU . . . . Auxiliary Functional Unit (Data link)
AFUPO . . . . . . Air Force Unit Post Office
AFUS . . . . Air Force of the United States
AFUS . . . . Armed Forces of the United States
AFV . . . . Aerospace Flight Vehicle
AFV . . . . American Friends of Vietnam
AFV . . . . Armored Fighting Vehicle (Marine Corps)
AFV . . . . Armored Force Vehicle
AFVA . . . . Air Force Visual Aid
AFVG . . . . Anglo-French Variable-Geometry (Combat aircraft)
AFVN . . . . Armed Forces Vietnam Network
AFW . . . . Air Force Weapon
AFW . . . . Army Field Workshop
AFW . . . . Axial Flow Wheel
AFWA . . . . . . Air Force with Army
AFWAB . . . . . Army Fixed Wing Aptitude Battery
AFWAR . . . . . Air Force Personnel on Duty with Army
AFWB . . . . . . Air Force Welfare Board
AFWC . . . . . . American Federation of World Citizens
AFWESPAC . . . US Army Forces, Western Pacific
AFWET . . . . . . Air Force Weapons Effectiveness Testing
AFWETS . . . . . Air Force Weapons Effectiveness Testing System
AFWL . . . . . . Air Force Weapons Laboratory
AFWL . . . . . . Armed Forces Writers League
AFWN . . . . . . Air Force Personnel on Duty with Navy

AFWOFS . . . . Air Force Weather Observing and Forecasting System
AFWR . . . . . . Approved Force War Reserves
AFWR . . . . . . Atlantic Fleet Weapons Range (Navy)
AFWS . . . . . . Advanced Filament Wound Structure
AFWST . . . . . Armed Forces Women's Selection Test
AFWTR . . . . . Air Force Western Test Range
AFWYU . . . . . American Foundation for World Youth Understanding
AFXF . . . . . . Advanced Flash X-Ray Facility
AFYMOSAP . . . Additional Fiscal Year Move Is Authorized by the Secretary of the Army Per
AG . . . . Accountant General
AG . . . . Action Group (Nigeria)
AG . . . . Adjutant General, Office of the
AG . . . . Advanced Guard
AG . . . . Aerographer's Mate (Navy rating)
AG . . . . Aerojet-General Corporation
AG . . . . Aeronautical Standards (Group), Bureau of Aeronautics (Navy)
AG . . . . Aerospace Group
AG . . . . Against Grain
AG . . . . Agency
AG. . . . . Agent General
AG . . . . Air Gage
AG . . . . Air-to-Ground (Communications, missiles, etc.)
AG . . . . Air Group
AG . . . . Aktiengesellschaft (Joint Stock Company) (Germany)
AG . . . . Alignment Group
AG . . . . Allegheny Ludlum Industries, Inc. (NYSE symbol)
AG . . . . And Gate (Data processing)
AG . . . . Anderson Galleries
AG . . . . Anti-Gas (Military)
Ag . . . . Antigen (Immunology)
Ag . . . . Argentum (Silver) (Chemical element)
AG . . . . Armed Guard
AG . . . . Armor Grating (Technical drawings)
AG . . . . Arresting Gear and Barriers (Navy)
AG . . . . Artists Guild
AG . . . . Attorney General
AG . . . . Auditor General (Military)
AG . . . . Aufklaerungsgruppe (Air forces reconnaissance unit) (German military - World War II)
AG . . . . Axiogingival
AG. . . . . Escort Research (Navy ship symbol)
AG. . . . . Miscellaneous (Navy ship symbol)
AG . . . . SONAR Research Ship (Navy symbol)
AG . . . . Technical Research Ship (Navy symbol)
A-G . . . . Arresting Gear (Aviation)
A/G . . . . Air-to-Ground (Photo, missile, etc.)
A/G . . . . Aircraft Arresting Gear
AGA . . . . Abrasive Grain Association
AGA . . . . Accelerated Growth Area (Embryology)
AGA . . . . Adjutants General Association of the United States
AGA . . . . Aerodromes, Air Routes and Ground Aids (Aviation)
AGA . . . . Air-to-Ground-to-Air (Air Force)
AGA . . . . Alabama Gas Corporation (NYSE symbol)
AGA . . . . American Gas Association
AGA . . . . American Gastroenterological Association
AGA . . . . American Gastroscopic Society
AGA . . . . American Genetic Association
AGA . . . . American Glassware Association
AGA . . . . American Go Association
AGA . . . . American Goiter Association
AGA . . . . American Gold Association
AGA . . . . American Guppy Association
AGA . . . . Animal Guild of America
AGA . . . . As Good As
AGA . . . . Associated Geographers of America
AGA . . . . Astrologers' Guild of America
AGA . . . . Average Global Automobile (Emissions to atmosphere)
A/G/A . . . . . . Air-to-Ground-to-Air
AGAA . . . . . . American Guild of Animal Artists
AGAA . . . . . . Automatic Gain Adjusting Amplifier
AGAC . . . . . . Aero Geo Astro Corporation (Fairchild division)
AGAC . . . . . . American Guild of Authors and Composers
AGACS . . . . . Air-Ground-Air Communications System
AGACS . . . . . Automatic Ground/Air/Communications System
AGAFBO . . . . Atlantic & Gulf American Flag Berth Operators
AGALA . . . . . Authors Guild of the Authors League of America
AGANI . . . . . Apollo Guidance and Navigation Information
AGARD . . . . . Advisory Group for Aerospace Research and Development (NATO) (Formerly, Advisory Group for Aeronautical Research and Development)
AGAS . . . . . . Aviation Gasoline (Navy)

AGATE . . . . . . Air-to-Ground Acquisition and Tracking Equipment
AGAUS . . . . . . Adjutants General Association of United States
AGAVE . . . . . Automatic Gimbaled-Antenna Vectoring Equipment (Air Force)
AGB . . . . Accessory Gear Box
AGB . . . . American General Bond Fund, Inc. (NYSE symbol)
AGB . . . . Any Good Brand
AGB . . . . Association of Governing Boards of Universities and Colleges
AGB . . . . Icebreaker (Navy ship symbol)
AGBA . . . . . . Alexander Graham Bell Association for the Deaf
AGBA . . . . . . American Galloway Breeders' Association
AGBC . . . . . . Avocado Growers Bargaining Council (Formerly, AGC)
AGBI . . . . . . Artists' General Benevolent Institution (British)
AGBUA . . . . . Armenian General Benevolent Union of America
AGC . . . . Adjutant General's Corps
AGC . . . . Aerojet-General Corporation
AGC . . . . Air Ground Chart
AGC . . . . Alaska Game Commission (Terminated, 1959)
AGC . . . . American General Insurance Company (NYSE symbol)
AGC . . . . American Grassland Council
AGC . . . . Amphibious Force Flagship (Navy symbol)
AGC . . . . Apollo Guidance Computer
AGC . . . . Armed Guard Center
AGC . . . . Army Advisory Group, China
AGC . . . . Associated General Contractors of America
AGC . . . . Automatic Gain Control (Electronics)
AGC . . . . Avocado Growers Council
AGCA . . . . . . Associated General Contractors of America
AGCA . . . . . Automatic Ground-Controlled Approach (RADAR)
AGCC . . . . . Air-Ground Communications Channel
AGCC . . . . . American Guernsey Cattle Club
AGCF . . . . . . Air Ground Correlation Factor
AGCG . . . . . Associated Granite Craftsmens Guild
AGCI . . . . . . Automatic Ground-Controlled Intercept
AGCL . . . . . . Automatic Ground-Controlled Landing
AGCMDL . . . . Army Good Conduct Medal
AGCO . . . . . Air-Ground Cooperation Officer
AGCRSP . . . . Army Gas-Cooled Reactor Systems Program
AGCT . . . . . . Army General Classification Test
AGCTS . . . . . Armed Guard Center Training School
AGCY . . . . . . Agency
AGD . . . . . . Academy of General Dentistry
AGD . . . . . . Adjutant General's Department (Army)
AGD . . . . . . Aircraft Gunfire Detector
AGD . . . . . . American Gage Design Committee
AGD . . . . . . Auditor General's Department (Air Force)
AGD . . . . . . Seagoing Dredge (Navy symbol)
AGDA . . . . . American Gasoline Dealers Association
AGDA . . . . . American Gun Dealers Association
AGDE . . . . . Escort Research Ship (Navy symbol)
AGDS . . . . . American Gage Design Standard
AGE . . . . Aerospace Ground Equipment
AGE . . . . Affiliated Government Employees' Distributing Co. (California)
AGE . . . . Amarillo Grain Exchange
AGE . . . . Associate in General Education
AGE . . . . Auditory Gross Error
AGE . . . . Automatic Ground Equipment
AGE . . . . Automatic Guidance Electronics
AGE . . . . Auxiliary Ground Equipment
AGEC . . . . . Army General Equipment Command
AGED . . . . . Advisory Group on Electron Devices (Army)
AGED . . . . . Aerospace Ground Equipment Department
AGED . . . . . Army Group Effects Department
A in G Ed . . . . Associate in General Education
AGEFAN . . . . . Association Generale des Etudiants de France en Afrique Noire (General Association of French Students in Black Africa)
AGEH . . . . . . Hydrofoil Research Ship (Navy symbol)
AGEHR . . . . . American Guild of English Handbell Ringers
AGEOCP . . . . Aerospace Ground Equipment Out of Commission for Parts (Air Force)
AGEP . . . . . . Advisory Group on Electronic Parts (Military)
AGER . . . . . . Environmental Research Ship (Navy symbol)
AGERS . . . . . Auxiliary General Electronics Research Ship (Navy)
AG & ES . . . . American Gas & Electric System
AGET . . . . . . Advisory Group on Electronic Tubes (DOD)
AGF . . . . Alternating Gradient Focusing
AGF . . . . Army Ground Forces
AGF . . . . Miscellaneous Command Ship (Navy symbol)
AGFA . . . . . . Aktien Gesellschaft fuer Anilin Farben
AGFL . . . . . . Airborne Ground Fire Locator
AGFLS . . . . . Airborne Ground Fire Locating System
AGFRTS . . . . . Air and Ground Forces Resources and Technical Staff (Army)
AGFSA . . . . . . American Ground Flat Stock Association

AGFSR . . . . . . Aircraft Ground Fire Suppression and Rescue (Air Force)
AGFSRS . . . . . Aircraft Ground Fire Suppression and Rescue Systems (DOD)
AGG . . . . Agent to the Governor-General (British)
AGG . . . . Aguirre Co. (NYSE symbol)
AGGD . . . . . . Apollo Guidance Ground Display (Aerospace)
AGGR . . . . . . Air-to-Ground Gunnery Range
AGGS . . . . . . American Good Government Society
AGHTM . . . . . Association Generale des Hygienistes et Techniciens Municipaux
AGI . . . . Adjusted Gross Income
AGI . . . . Alliance Graphique Internationale
AGI . . . . American Geographical Institute
AGI . . . . American Geological Institute
AGI . . . . Annee Geophysique Internationale (International Geophysical Year)
AGI . . . . Annual General Inspection (Army)
AGI . . . . Artistes Graphiques Internationales (International Graphical Alliance)
AGIC . . . . . . Air-Ground Information Center
AGIFORS . . . . Airline Group, International Federation of Operational Research Societies
AGIL . . . . . . Airborne General Illumination Light
AGILE . . . . . . Autonetics General Information Learning Equipment
AGIO . . . . . . Armed Guard Inspection Officer
AGIP . . . . Azienda Generale Italiana Petroli (Italian petroleum enterprise)
AGIS . . . . . . Air-Ground Integration System
AGIS . . . . . . Armed Guard Inspection Service
AGIT-PROP . . . Agitation and Propaganda (Military)
AGKO . . . . . . Arginine, Glutamate, alpha-Ketoglutarate Oxalacetate
AGL . . . . Above Ground Level
AGL . . . . Abteilungsgewerkschaftaleitung
AGL . . . . Airborne Gun Laying
AGL . . . . Argon Gas LASER
AGL . . . . Argon Glow Lamp
AGL . . . . Lighthouse Tender (Navy symbol)
AGLC . . . . . . Air-to-Ground Liaison Code (Air Force)
AGLO . . . . . . Air Ground Liaison Officer (Marine Corps)
AGLR . . . . . . Airborne Gun Laying RADAR
AGLS . . . . . . Association of General and Liberal Studies
AGLT . . . . . . Airborne Gun Laying for Turrets
AGM . . . . . . Air-to-Ground Missile
AGM . . . . . . Amalgamated Sugar Company (NYSE symbol)
AGM . . . . . . American Guild of Music
AGM . . . . . . Assistant General Manager (AEC)
AGM . . . . . . Missile Range Instrumentation Ship (Navy symbol)
A/G/M . . . . . Air-to-Ground Missile
AGMA . . . . . American Gear Manufacturers Association
AGMA . . . . . American Guild of Musical Artists
AGMA . . . . . Assistant General Manager for Administration (AEC)
AGMA . . . . . Athletic Goods Manufacturers Association
AGMC . . . . . Aerospace Guidance and Metrology Center (Air Force)
AGMEPS . . . . Advisory Group on Management of Electronic Parts Specifications
AGMIA . . . . . Assistant General Manager for International Activities (AEC)
AGMIS . . . . . Adjutant General Management Information System
AGMK . . . . . African Green Monkey Kidney (Cells)
AGMO . . . . . Assistant General Manager for Operations (AEC)
AGMPP . . . . . Assistant General Manager for Plans and Production (AEC)
AGMR . . . . . Major Communication Relay Ship (Navy symbol)
AGMRD . . . . . Assistant General Manager for Research and Development (AEC)
AGMSA . . . . . American Gem and Mineral Suppliers Association
AGMTI . . . . . Air-to-Ground Moving Target Indicator
AGN . . . . . . Aerojet-General Nucleonics (of Aerojet-General Corporation)
AGN . . . . . . Articles for the Government of the Navy
AGNIS . . . . . Apollo Guidance & Navigation Industrial Support (Army)
AGO . . . . . . Adjutant General's Office (Army)
AGO . . . . . . Administration Group Office
AGO . . . . . . Air Gunnery Officer
AGO . . . . . . American Guild of Organists
AGO . . . . . . Attorney General's Opinion
AGO . . . . . . Auditor General's Office
AGOR . . . . . . Auxiliary General Oceanographic Research (Ships) (NOO)
AGOR . . . . . . Oceanic Research Ship (Navy symbol)
AGOS . . . . . Air-Ground Operations Section, School, or System
AGOS . . . . . Aviation Gunnery Officers School
AGP . . . . . . Adjutant General Pool (for Army officers)
AGP . . . . . . Agence Guineene de Presse (Guinean Press Agency)
AGP . . . . . . Aircraft Grounded for Lack of Parts
AGP . . . . . . Aircraft Gun Pod
AGP . . . . . . Army Ground Pool (for officers)
AGP . . . . . . Motor Torpedo Boat Tender (Navy symbol)
AGPA . . . . . American Group Psychotherapy Association
AGPA . . . . . Ammunition Group - Picatinny Arsenal
AGPDC . . . . . Aeronutronic General Perturbations Differential Correction Program
AGPI . . . . . . Automatic Ground Position Indicator (Military)
AGPM . . . . . . Associated Glass and Pottery Manufacturers

AGPMR . . . . . . Agricultural Property Management Regulations
AGPR . . . . Agricultural Procurement Regulations
AGR . . . . Advanced Gas Cooled Reactor (Nuclear energy) (British)
AGR . . . . Anticipatory Goal Response (Medicine)
AGR . . . . Autonetics Generalized Reset
AGR . . . . RADAR Picket Ship (Navy symbol)
AGRCO . . . . . American Graves Registration Command
AGREE . . . . . . Advisory Group on Reliability of Electronics Equipment (Military)
AGRF . . . . American Geriatric Research Foundation
AGRS . . . . American Graves Registration Service
AGS . . . . Abort Guidance Section (Apollo) (NASA)
AGS . . . . Advanced Guidance System
AGS . . . . Agencies
AGS . . . . Airborne Gunsight
AGS . . . . Aircraft General Standards (British)
AGS . . . . Alabama Great Southern R. R. (AAR code)
AGS . . . . Allied Geographic Section (Southwest Pacific)
AGS . . . . Alternating Gradient Synchrotron (AEC)
AGS . . . . Alternating Guidance Section
AGS . . . . American Gem Society
AGS . . . . American Geographical Society
AGS . . . . American Geriatrics Society
AGS . . . . American Gesneria Society
AGS . . . . American Gloxinia Society
AGS . . . . American Goat Society
AGS . . . . American Graphological Society
AGS . . . . American Gynecological Society
AGS . . . . Armed Guard School(s)
AGS . . . . Army General Staff
AGS . . . . Artificial Gravity Structure
AGS . . . . Associate in General Studies
AGS . . . . Association of Graduate Schools (in Association of American Universities)
AGS . . . . Automatic Gain Stabilization
AGS . . . . Spalding (A. G.) & Bros., Inc. (NYSE symbol) (Delisted)
AGS . . . . Surveying Ship (Navy symbol)
AGSC . . . . . . Coastal Surveying Ship (Navy symbol)
AGSCC . . . . . Army General Supplies Commodity Center
AGSCPO . . . . Army General Staff Civilian Personnel Office, Office of the Chief of
        Staff, US Army
AGSL . . . . Satellite Launching Ship (Navy symbol)
AGSM . . . . . . American Gold Star Mothers
AGSPW . . . . . . Association of Girl Scout Professional Workers
AGSR . . . . All-Weather Ground Surveillance RADAR
AGSS . . . . American Geographical and Statistical Society
AG(SS) . . . . . . Auxiliary Submarine (Navy symbol)
AGSS . . . . High-Speed Target Submarine (Navy symbol)
AGT . . . . Adage Graphics Terminal
AGT . . . . Aircraft Gas & Turbine
AGT . . . . Alabama Great Southern R. R. Corporation (NYSE symbol)
AGTA . . . . Airline Ground Transportation Association
AGTE . . . . Association of Group Travel Executives
AGTOA . . . . . American Greyhound Track Operators Association
AGTR . . . . Technical Research Ship (Navy symbol)
AGU . . . . American Geophysical Union
AGV . . . . Aniline Gentian Violet
AGVA . . . . . . American Guild of Variety Artists
AGW . . . . Actual Gross Weight (Railroads)
AGW . . . . Air Gap Width
AGW . . . . Allowable Gross (takeoff) Weight (for an aircraft)
AGWAR . . . . . Adjutant General, War Department (Obsolete)
AGWI . . . . American Gulf West Indies Company
AGZ . . . . Actual Ground Zero (Nuclear explosions)
AH . . . . Adult Heart
AH . . . . Airfield Heliport
AH . . . . Allis-Chalmers Corp. (NYSE symbol) (Wall Street slang name: "Alice")
AH . . . . Alter Heading (Navigation)
AH . . . . Ampere Hour
AH . . . . Animal Husbandry Research Division (of ARS, Department of Agriculture)
AH . . . . Anno Hebraico (In the Hebrew Year) (Latin)
AH . . . . Anno Hegirae (In the Year of the Hegira) (The flight of Mohammed from
        Mecca)
AH . . . . Army Hospital
AH . . . . Hospital Ship (Navy symbol)
A-H . . . . Ampere-Hour
A & H . . . . . . Arm and Hammer (Brand of soda)
AHA . . . . Adirondack Historical Association
AHA . . . . Agricultural and Horticultural Engineering Abstracts
AHA . . . . American Habonim Association (Later, Labor Zionist Alliance)
AHA . . . . American Hardboard Association
AHA . . . . American Heart Association
AHA . . . . American Hereford Association

AHA . . . . American Historical Association
AHA . . . . American Homeowners Association (Commercial firm)
AHA . . . . American Hospital Association
AHA . . . . American Hotel Association
AHA . . . . American Humane Association
AHA . . . . American Humanist Association
AHA . . . . American Hypnotherapy Association
AHA . . . . American Hypnotists' Association
AHA . . . . Anterior Hypothalamic Area
AHA . . . . Association of Handicapped Artists
AHAM . . . . . . Association of Home Appliance Manufacturers
AHAUS . . . . . Amateur Hockey Association of the United States
AHB . . . . Air Heater Blower
AHC . . . . Academy of Hospital Counselors
AHC . . . . Allan Hancock College (California)
AHC . . . . Amerada Hess Corporation (NYSE symbol)
AHC . . . . American Hardware Corporation (NYSE symbol) (Delisted)
AHC . . . . American Helicopter Company
AHC . . . . American Hellenic Congress
AHC . . . . American Horticultural Council
AHC . . . . American Hospital Corps
AHC . . . . Appaloosa Horse Club
AHC . . . . Army Hospital Corps
AHC . . . . Assault Helicopter Company (Army)
AHC . . . . Austin Healey Club
AHC . . . . Automatic Headway Control
AHCA . . . . . Afghan Hound Club of America
AHCA . . . . . . American Hockey Coaches Association
AHCEI . . . . . . American Histadrut Cultural Exchange Institute
AHCRA . . . . . Arabian Horse Club Registry of America
AHCS . . . . . . American Hungarian Catholic Society
AHD . . . . American Agricultural Chemical Co. (NYSE symbol) (Delisted)
AHD . . . . American Heritage Dictionary
AHD . . . . Arc Heating Device
AHDGA . . . . . American Hot Dip Galvanizers Association
AHDME . . . . . Association of Hospital Directors of Medical Education
AHE . . . . Associate in Home Economics
AHE . . . . Association for Higher Education (of the NEA)
AHE . . . . Association for Human Emergence
AHEA . . . . . . American Home Economics Association
AH Ec . . . . . . Associate in Home Economics
AHEL . . . . . . Army Human Engineering Laboratory
AHEM . . . . . . Association of Hydraulic Equipment Manufacturers
AHES . . . . . . American Humane Education Society
AHF . . . . American Health Foundation
AHF . . . . American Heritage Foundation
AHF . . . . American Hobby Federation
AHF . . . . American Hospital Formulary (A publication)
AHF . . . . American Humanics Foundation
AHF . . . . American Hungarian Federation
AHF . . . . Antihemolytic (or Antihemophilic) Factor (Factor VIII – Hematology)
AHF . . . . Associated Health Foundation
AHF . . . . Azad Hind Fauj (Indian National Army)
AHFRAC . . . . . Army Human Factors Research Advisory Committee
AHFRDC . . . . . Army Human Factors Research and Development Committee
AHFS . . . . . . American Hospital Formulary Service
AHG . . . . American High-Density Gradient
AHG . . . . Antihemophilic Globulin
AHG . . . . Anti-Human Globulin (Consumption test) (Medicine)
AHGMR . . . . . Ad Hoc Group on Missile Reliability
AHH . . . . Arc Heater Housing
AHHS . . . . . . American Hackney Horse Society
AHI . . . . American Honey Institute
AHI . . . . Animal Health Institute
AHIL . . . . Association of Hospital and Institution Libraries (of ALA)
AHIS . . . . American Hull Insurance Syndicate
AHL . . . . Acetate Halftone Litho (Du Pont)
AHL . . . . American Hockey League
AHL . . . . Auroral Hydrogen Line
AHLE . . . . . . Auroral Hydrogen Line Emission
AHLHS . . . . . American Hungarian Library and Historical Society
AHLI . . . . American Home Lighting Institute
AHLMA . . . . . . American Home Laundry Manufacturers Association
AHM . . . . Ampere-Hour Meter
AHMA . . . . . . Advanced Hypersonic Manned Aircraft
AHMA . . . . . . Allied Hat Manufacturers Association
AHMA . . . . . . American Hardware Manufacturers Association
AH & MA . . . . American Hotel and Motel Association
AHMC . . . . . . Association of Hospital Management Committees
AHMD . . . . . . Airborne Helmet Mounted Display
AHMI . . . . Appalachian Hardwood Manufacturers, Incorporated

AHMJ . . . . . . Arc-Heated Materials Jet (Langley Research Center)
AHMS . . . . . . American Home Mission Society
AHNA . . . . . . Accredited Home Newspapers of America
AHO . . . . American Hoist & Derrick Co. (NYSE symbol)
AHP . . . . Air Horsepower (Air Force)
AHP . . . . Allied Hydrographic Publication
AHP . . . . Alpha Portland Cement Company (NYSE symbol; later, APC)
AHP . . . . American Home Products Corp. (NYSE symbol)
AHP . . . . Army Heliport
AHP . . . . Association for Humanistic Psychology
AHP . . . . Evacuation Hospital Ship (Navy symbol)
AHPA . . . . . . Accumulator High Pressure Air
AHPA . . . . . . American Horse Protection Association
AHPR . . . . . . Academy of Hospital Public Relations
AHPS . . . . . . Auxiliary Hydraulic Power Supply
AHPS-CWPS . . . American Historical Philatelic Society – Civil War Philatelic Society
AHQ . . . . Air Headquarters
AHQ . . . . Allied Headquarters
AHQ . . . . Army Headquarters
AHR . . . . Academy of Human Rights
AHR . . . . Aqueous Homogeneous Reactor (AEC)
AHR . . . . Association for Health Records
AHRA . . . . . . American Hot Rod Association
AHRCO . . . . . . Allegheny Housing Rehabilitation Corporation
AHRL . . . . . . Arctic Health Research Laboratory (HEW)
AHRS . . . . . . Attitude Heading Reference System
AHRU . . . . . . Armor Human Research Unit
AHRU . . . . . . Aviation Human Research Unit (Army)
AHS . . . . Ablative Heat Shield
AHS . . . . Agricultural History Society
AHS . . . . American Harp Society
AHS . . . . American Hearing Society
AHS . . . . American Helicopter Society
AHS . . . . American Hemerocallis Society
AHS . . . . American Hibiscus Society
AHS . . . . American Horticultural Society
AHS . . . . American Hospital Society
AHS . . . . American Hospital Supply Corporation (NYSE symbol)
AHS . . . . American Humane Society
AHS . . . . American Hypnodontic Society
AHS . . . . Anno Humanae Salutis (In the Year of Human Salvation)
AHS . . . . Antenna Homing System
AHS . . . . Arlington Hall Station (Army)
AHS . . . . Association of Hungarian Students in North America
AHS . . . . Augustana Historical Society
AHS . . . . Aviation Historical Society
AHSA . . . . . . American Hampshire Sheep Association
AHSA . . . . . . American Horse Shows Association
AHSA . . . . . . Association of Hospital Security Administrators
AHSM . . . . . . Alpha Hand and Shoe Monitor (Radiation detection)
AHSR . . . . . . Air Height Surveillance RADAR
AHSS . . . . . . Association of Home Study Schools
AHST . . . . . . Association of Highway Steel Transporters
AHT . . . . Acoustic Homing Torpedo
AHV . . . . Ad Hanc Vocem (At This Word)
AHWG . . . . . . Ad Hoc Working Group (Army)
AI . . . . Aaland Islands
AI . . . . Active Ingredient
AI . . . . Ad Interim (In the Meantime)
AI . . . . Admiralty Islands
AI . . . . Agricultural Index
AI . . . . Agudath Israel (Union of Israel) (World organization of Orthodox Jews)
AI . . . . Air Inspector
AI . . . . Air Installations
AI . . . . Air(borne) Intercept (RADAR) (Air Force)
AI . . . . Aircraft Interception (Air Force)
AI . . . . Airways Inspector
AI . . . . Alianza Interamericana
AI . . . . All Iron
AI . . . . American Institute
AI . . . . Amplifier Input
AI . . . . Angle Iron
AI . . . . Anglo-Indian
AI . . . . Anglo-Irish
AI . . . . Anglo-Israelism or Anglo-Israelite
AI . . . . Anno Inventionis (In the Year of the Discovery) (Latin)
AI . . . . Antenna Impedance
AI . . . . Anti-Icing (Technical drawings)
AI . . . . Anxiety Index (Psychology)
AI . . . . Aortic Insufficiency (Medicine)
AI . . . . Applications and Industry

AI . . . . Aptitude Index
AI . . . . Arctic Institute
AI . . . . Army Intelligence
AI . . . . Articulation Index
AI . . . . Artificial Insemination (Medicine)
AI . . . . Artificial Intelligence
AI . . . . Astrologers International
AI . . . . Atomics International (of North American Aviation, Inc.)
AI . . . . Auditory Induction
AI . . . . Axioincisal
AI . . . . Azimuth Indicator
A/I . . . . Air Inspector
A/I . . . . Aptitude Index
A & I . . . . . . Abstracting and Indexing
A & I . . . . . . Agricultural and Industrial (in a college name)
A & I . . . . . . Alteration and Improvement Program (Navy)
AIA . . . . Advise If Able (Aviation)
AIA . . . . Aerospace Industries Association of America
AIA . . . . Agudath Israel of America
AIA . . . . Aircraft Industries Association
AIA . . . . American Institute of Architects
AIA . . . . American Insurance Association
AIA . . . . American International Academy
AIA . . . . American International Association for Economic and Social Development
AIA . . . . American Inventors Association
AIA . . . . Anti-Intrusion Alarm
AIA . . . . Archaeological Institute of America
AIA . . . . Argentine Interplanetary Association
AIA . . . . Associate of the Institute of Actuaries (British)
AIA . . . . Association of Industrial Advertisers
AIA . . . . Association of Insurance Advertisers
AIA . . . . Association of Insurance Attorneys
AIA . . . . Association Internationale d'Allergologie (International Association of Allergology)
AIAA . . . . . . Aerospace (formerly, Aircraft) Industries Association of America
AIAA . . . . . . American Industrial Arts Association
AIAA . . . . . . American Institute of Aeronautics and Astronautics
AIAA . . . . . . Association of International Advertising Agencies
AIAA-TIS . . . . Technical Information Service (of American Institute of Aeronautics and Astronautics)
AIAC . . . . . . Association Internationale d'Archeologie Classique
AIAE . . . . . . Associate Institute of Automobile Engineers
AIAF . . . . . . American Institute of Architects Foundation
AIAG . . . . . . Association Internationale des Assureurs Contre la Grele (International Association of Hail Insurers)
AIAL . . . . . . Association of International Institute of Arts and Letters
AIAOS . . . . . . Academic Instructor and Allied Officer School (Military)
AIAR . . . . . . American Institute of Aerological Research
AIART . . . . . . Associazione Italiana Ascoltatori Radio Telespettatori
AIAS . . . . . . Anti-Intrusion Alarm Set
AIAS . . . . . . Army Institute of Advanced Studies
AIAW . . . . . . Association for Intercollegiate Athletics for Women
AIB . . . . Aircraft Instrument Bulletin
AIB . . . . American Institute of Baking
AIB . . . . American Institute of Banking
AIB . . . . Anthracite Information Bureau (Defunct)
AIB . . . . Associate of the Institute of Bankers (British)
AIB . . . . Association of Investment Brokers
AIB . . . . Associazione Italiana Biblioteche
AIBA . . . . . . American Industrial Bankers Association
AIBA . . . . . . Association of International Border Agencies
AIBA . . . . . . Association Internationale de Boxe Amateur (International Amateur Boxing Association)
AIBEA . . . . . . All-India Bank Employees' Association
AIBEF . . . . . . All-India Bank Employees' Federation
AIBM . . . . . . Association Internationale des Bibliotheques Musicales
AIBNRM . . . . . American Institute of Bolt, Nut and Rivet Manufacturers (Later, Industrial Fasteners Institute)
AIBS . . . . American Institute of Biological Sciences
AIC . . . . Academie Internationale de la Ceramique
AIC . . . . Accelerator Information Center (ORNL)
AIC . . . . Activity Identification Code (Navy)
AIC . . . . Advanced Intelligence Center
AIC . . . . Aerodynamic-Influence Coefficient
AIC . . . . Aircraft in Commission
AIC . . . . Aircraft Industry Conference (Navy)
AIC . . . . Air Interception and Control(ler) (RADAR)
AIC . . . . Allied Intelligence Committee (London)
AIC . . . . American Institute of Chefs
AIC . . . . American Institute of Chemists

AIC .... American Institute of Constructors
AIC .... American Institute of Cooperation
AIC .... American Institute of Criminology
AIC .... American International College (Massachusetts)
AIC .... American Investment Company (NYSE symbol)
AIC .... American Italian Congress
AIC .... Ammunition Identification Code
AIC .... Apollo Intermediate Chart (NASA)
AIC .... Army Industrial College
AIC .... Army Intelligence Center
AIC .... Art Information Center
AIC .... Associate of the Institute of Chemistry (British)
AIC .... Attack Information Center
AIC .... Automatic Intercept Center (Bell System)
AICA ...... American Institute of Commemorative Art
AICA ...... American-International Charolais Association
AICA ...... Aminoimidazolecarboxylic Acid (Organic chemistry)
AICA ...... Association Internationale pour le Calcul Analogique
AICA ...... Association Internationale des Critiques d'Art
AICB ...... Association des Interets Coloniaux Belges (Merged with AIIB into FEC)
AICB ...... Association Internationale Contre le Bruit
AICBM ..... Anti-Intercontinental Ballistic Missile
AICC ...... All-India Congress Committee
AICC ...... American Immigration and Citizenship Conference
AICC ...... Association Internationale de Chimie Cerealiere
AICCC ..... American Institute of Child Care Centers
AICCF ..... Association Internationale du Congres des Chemins de Fer
AICCP...... Association of Interstate Commerce Commission Practitioners
AICE ...... American Institute of Chemical Engineers
AICE ...... American Institute of Consulting Engineers
AICE ...... American Institute of Crop Ecology
AICE ...... Associate of the Institute of Civil Engineers (British)
AI-CE...... Atomic International – Combustion Engineering
AIChE...... American Institute of Chemical Engineers
AICI ...... Apparel Industry Committee on Imports
AICMA ..... Association Internationale des Constructeurs de Materiel Aeronautique
AICMR ..... Association Internationale des Constructeurs de Materiel Roulant (International Association of Rolling Stock Builders)
AICO ...... Action Information Control Officer (Navy)
AICO ...... American Insulator Corporation
AICP ...... Association of Independent Composers and Performers
AICP ...... Atomic Incident Control Plan
AICPA ..... American Institute of Certified Public Accountants
AICPOA .... Advanced Intelligence Center, Pacific Ocean Areas
AICRIP .... All India Coordinated Rice Improvement Program
AICS ...... Air Induction Control System (Air Force)
AICS ...... American Institute of Ceylonese Studies
AICS ...... Association Internationale du Cinema Scientifique
AICS ...... Automatic Inlet Control System
AICT ...... Atlantic Information Centre for Teachers
AICT ...... Automatic Integrated Circuit Tester
AID .... Abortion Information Data Bank (of Zero Population Growth, Inc.)
AID .... Accident, Incident, Deficiencies
AID .... Acronyms and Initialisms Dictionary (A reference publication)
AID .... Active Integral Defense
AID .... Aeronautical Inspection Directorate (British)
AID .... Agency for International Development (State Department)
AID .... Ailing-In Difficulty
AID .... Air Information Division (Library of Congress)
AID .... Airline Interline Development
AID .... Airport Information Desk
AID .... Alliance Internationale de la Diffusion par Fil (International Alliance for Diffusion by Wire)
AID .... American Institute of Decorators (Later, AIID)
AID .... American Instructors of the Deaf
AID .... Americans of Italian Descent (An organization)
AID .... Analytical Instrument Development, Inc.
AID .... Antijamming Display
AID .... Army Information Digest
AID .... Army Intelligence Department (British)
AID .... Articles Contributed for Intelligence and Dollars (Education program)
AID .... Artificial Insemination by Donor (Medicine)
AID .... Association of Institutional Distributors
AID .... Association for International Development
AID .... Association Internationale pour le Developpement
AID .... Attached Inflatable Decelerator (Aerodynamics)
AID .... Auditory Information Display
AID .... Automatic Interaction Detection (or Detector) (Data processing)
AID .... Avalanche Injection Diode
AIDA ...... Associated Independent Dairies of America
AIDA ...... Association Internationale de la Distribution des Produits Alimentaires

AIDA ...... Association Internationale du Droit de l'Assurance
AIDA ...... Attention-Interest-Desire-Action (Formula) (Marketing)
AIDA ...... Automated Inspection of Data
AIDA ...... Automatic Instrumented Diving Assembly
AIDA ...... Automobile Information Disclosure Act
AIDAC ..... Assistance Information and Data Acquisition Center (Navy)
AIDAP ..... Automatic Inspection, Diagnostic and Prognostic (System) (Army)
AIDAPS..... Automatic Inspection, Diagnostic and Prognostic Systems (Army)
AIDAS ..... Advanced Instrumentation and Data Analysis System
AIDAT ..... Automatic Integrated Dynamic Avionics Tester
AIDC ...... American Industrial Development Council
AIDD ...... American Institute for Design and Drafting
AIDE ...... Adapted Identification Decision Equipment
AIDE ...... Airborne Insertion Display Equipment
AIDE ...... Aircraft Installation Diagnostic Equipment
AIDE ...... Association Internationale des Distributions d'Eau
AIDES...... American Independent Designers and Engineers Society
AIDIS ..... Asociacion Interamericana de Ingenieria Sanitaria (Inter-American Association of Sanitary Engineering)
AIDJEX..... Arctic Ice Dynamics Joint Experiment (National Science Foundation)
AIDP ...... Association Internationale de Droit Penal
AID/PEP ... Agency for International Development/Private Enterprise Promotion
AIDR ...... Aerospace Internal Data Report (Air Force)
AIDS ...... Action Information Display System
AIDS ...... Administrative Information Data System
AIDS ...... Advanced Integrated Data System
AIDS ...... Airborne Inertial (or Integrated) Data System
AIDS ...... Aircraft Integrated Data System
AIDS ...... Air Force Intelligence Data Handling System (ESD)
AIDS ...... Army Information and Data Systems
AIDS ...... Association of Interior Decor Specialists
AIDS ...... Automated Information and Documentation System
AIDS ...... Automated Intelligence Data System (Air Force)
AIDS ...... Automation Instrument Data Service (Computer-based industrial information system) (British)
AIDSCOM ... Army Information and Data Systems Command
AIDT ...... Association Interparlementaire du Tourisme
AIE .... Acceptance Inspection Equipment (Army)
AIE .... Airborne Interceptor Equipment
AIEA ...... Agence Internationale de l'Energie Atomique
AIEA ...... Association Internationale des Etudiants en Agriculture
AIEC ...... All-Industry Electronics Conference
AIEC ...... American Indian Ethnohistorical Conference
AIECA..... Associated Independent Electrical Contractors of America
AIECF..... American Indian and Eskimo Cultural Foundation
AI Ed ..... Associate in Industrial Education
AIED ...... Association Internationale des Etudiants Dentaires
AIEE....... American Institute of Electrical Engineers (Later, IEEE)
AIEE....... Association des Instituts d'Etudes Europeennes
AIEJI ..... Association Internationale des Educateurs de Jeunes Inadaptes
AIEP....... Association Internationale des Usagers d'Embranchements Particuliers (International Association of Users of Private Sidings)
AIEPE ..... Association Internationale des Ecoles Privees Europeennes
AIER....... American Institute for Economic Research
AIERI ..... Association Internationale des Etudes et Recherches sur l'Information
AIESEC..... Association Internationale des Etudiants en Sciences Economiques et Commerciales
AIESEE ..... Association Internationale d'Etudes du Sud-Est Europeen (International Association of South-East European Studies)
AIESEP ..... Association Internationale des Ecoles ou Institut Superieurs d'Education Physique et Sportive (International Association of Schools or Higher Institutes of Physical and Sportive Education)
AIESS ..... Association Internationale des Ecoles de Service Social
AIEST ..... Association Internationale d'Experts Scientifiques du Tourisme
AIETA...... Airborne Infrared Equipment for Target Analysis
AIF .... Air Intelligence Force
AIF .... Air Interceptor Fuze
AIF .... Alliance Internationale des Femmes, Droits Egaux, Responsabilites Egales
AIF........ American Institute of France
AIF........ Amphibian Imperial Force
AIF........ Arbeitsgemeinschaft fuer Industrielle Forschung (Cooperative Group for Industrial Research) (Germany)
AIF .... Army Industrial Fund
AIF .... Atomic Industrial Forum
AIF .... Audience Interest Factor
AIF........ Australian Imperial Forces
AIFB ...... American Institute of Financial Brokers
AIFCS...... Airborne Interception Fire Control System (Air Force)
AIFD ...... Alaska Institute for Fisheries Development
AIFD ...... American Institute of Food Distributors
AIFE....... American Institute for Exploration

AIFEE	All-India Federation of Electricity Employees
AIFI	Automatic Inflight Insertion
AIFLD	American Institute for Free Labor Development
AIFM	Association Internationale des Femmes Medecins
AIFM	Automatic Integrating Fluctuation Meter
AIFR	American Institute of Family Relations
AIFRB	American Institute of Fishery Research Biologists
AIFS	Advanced Instruction Flying School
AIFS	American Institute for Foreign Study
AIFT	American Institute for Foreign Trade
AIFT	Audio Input Frequency Tolerance
AIFTA	Anglo-Irish Free Trade Area (British)
AIFURC	Assignment Instructions were Furnished your Command
AIG	Address Indicating Group (Data processing)
AIG	Adjutant Inspector General (Military)
AIG	Artificial Intelligence Group (MIT)
AIG	Assistant Inspector General (Military)
AIG	Association Internationale de Geodesie
AIGA	American Institute of Graphic Arts
AIGA	Association Internationale de Geomagnetisme et d'Aeronomie
AIGM	Association Internationale de Grands Magasins
AIGS	All-Inertial Guidance System
AIH	American Institute of Homeopathy
AIH	Artificial Insemination by Husband (Medicine)
AIH	Asociacion Internacional de Hispanistas
AIH	Association Internationale de l'Hotellerie
AIH	Association Internationale d'Hydrologie Scientifique
AIHA	American Indian Historical Association
AIHA	American Industrial Hygiene Association
AIHA	American Italian Historical Association
AIHA	Autoimmune Hemolytic Anemia (Medicine)
AIHED	American Institute for Human Engineering and Development
AIHP	American Institute of the History of Pharmacy
AIHR	American Indian Horse Registry
AIHS	American-Irish Historical Society
AIHS	Aspen Institute for Humanistic Studies
AIHS	Association Internationale d'Hydrologie Scientifique
AIHSC	Auto Industries Highway Safety Committee
AII	Aerial Inspection Instrument
AII	Air-India International (Airline)
AII	American Interprofessional Institute
AII	Army Intelligence Interpreter
AII	Automatic Imagery Interpretation
AII	Automation Industries, Incorporated (NYSE symbol)
AIIA	Association of International Insurance Agents
AIIB	Association des Interets Industriels au Congo (Merged with AICB into FEC)
AIIC	Army Imagery Intelligence Corps
AIIC	Association Internationale des Interpretes de Conference
AIID	American Institute of Interior Designers (Formerly, AID)
AIIE	American Institute of Industrial Engineers
AIIEA	All-India Insurance Employees' Association
AIIRM	Association Internationale des Interets Radio-Maritimes
AIIS	American Institute for Imported Steel
AIIS	American Institute of Indian Studies
AIIS	American Institute of Iranian Studies
AIISUP	Association Internationale d'Information Scolaire Universitaire et Professionnelle
AIJD	Association Internationale de Juristes Democrates (International Association of Democratic Lawyers)
AIJE	Association des Industries du Jute Europeennes
AIJE	Association Internationale des Juges des Enfants
AIJP	Association Internationale des Journalistes Philateliques (International Association of Philatelic Journalists)
AIJWF	All-India Jute Textile Workers' Federation
AIKD	American Institute of Kitchen Dealers
AIL	Advance Information Letter (Military)
AIL	Aeronautical Instruments Laboratory (Military)
AIL	Aerospace Instrumentation Laboratory (Air Force)
AIL	Air Intelligence Liaison (British)
AIL	Airborne Instruments Laboratory (Mineola, New York)
AIL	American Institute of Laundering (Later, IFI)
AIL	American Israeli Lighthouse
AIL	Argon Ion LASER
AIL	Art Institute of Light
AIL	Association of International Libraries
AIL	Association Internationale de Limnologie Theorique et Appliquee
AIL	Audio Input Level
AIL	Aviation Instrument Laboratory (Navy)
AILA	American Institute of Landscape Architects
AILAS	Airborne Integrated Light Avionics System
AILAS	Automatic Instrument Landing Approach System (RADAR)
AILAS	Automatic Instrument Low Approach System (RADAR)
AILC	Association Internationale de Litterature Comparee
AILO	Air Intelligence Liaison Officer (British)
AILS	Advanced Integrated Landing System
AILS	Airborne Infrared Live Scanner
AILS	Automatic Instrument Landing System (Aviation)
AILSA	American Indian Law Students Association
AIM	Abstracts of Instructional Materials in Vocational and Technical Education (A periodical of ERIC)
AIM	Academy of Interscience Methodology
AIM	Active Inert Missile
AIM	Add, Initial, Multiprecision
AIM	Adhesive Insulation Material
AIM	Aerothermodynamic Integration Model
AIM	Africa Inland Mission
AIM	Aid for International Medicine (An organization)
AIM	Air Intercept Missile
AIM	Air Isolated Monolithic (Circuit)
AIM	Airborne Infrared Mapper
AIM	Airman's Information Manual (FAA)
AIM	Alarm Indicating Monitor
AIM	American Institute of Maintenance
AIM	American Institute of Management
AIM	American Institute of Musicology
AIM	Army Installation Management
AIM	Associate in Industrial Management
AIM	Associated Industries of Massachusetts
AIM	Association of Innerspring Manufacturers
AIM	Association for the Integration of Management
AIM	Association Internationale de la Mutualite
AIM	Association of Interracial Marriages
AIM	Australian Inland Mission
AIM	Automotive Industrial Motor
AIMA	American Industrial Music Association
AIMACC	Air Materiel Command Compiling (System)
AIMACO	Air Material Computer (Air Force)
AIMBW	American Institute of Men's and Boys' Wear
AIMC	American Institute of Medical Climatology
AIME	American Institute of Mining, Metallurgical and Petroleum Engineers
AIME	Associate of the Institute of Mechanical Engineers
AIMEA	Association Internationale des Metiers et Enseignements d'Art
AIMF	American International Music Fund
AIMH	Academy of International Military History
AIMI	Airborne Infrared Measurement Instrument
AIMILO	Army/Industry Materiel Information Liaison Office
AIMME	See AIME, for which sometimes used erroneously
AIMMPE	American Institute of Mining, Metallurgical, and Petroleum Engineers
AIMO	Audibly Instructed Manufacturing Operations (Military)
AIMOSACGP	Assignment Instructions Will Include MOS (Military Occupational Specialty) within Army Career Group
AIMP	Air Intercept Missile Package
AIMP	Anchored Interplanetary Monitoring Platform
AIMPA	Association Internationale de Meteorologie et de Physique de l'Atmosphere
AIMS	Advanced Inertial Measurement System
AIMS	Advanced Intercontinental Missile System
AIMS	Air Traffic Control RADAR Beacon / Identification Friend or Foe / Mark XII / System
AIMS	Airborne Integrated Maintenance System
AIMS	Aircraft Identification Military System
AIMS	American Institute for Marxist Studies
AIMS	American Institute for Mental Studies
AIMS	American Institute of Merchant Shipping
AIMS	American International Managers Society
AIMS	Army Integrated Decision Equipment
AIMS	Army Integrated Meteorological Systems (AEC)
AIMS	Association for International Medical Study
AIMS	Automated Industrial Management System
AIMU	American Institute of Marine Underwriters
AIN	Addressograph-Multigraph Corporation (NYSE symbol)
AIN	American Institute of Nutrition
AIN	Assembly Identification Number
AIN	Association of Interpretive Naturalists
AINA	Arctic Institute of North America
AINL	Association of Immigration and Nationality Lawyers
AINM	Assistant Inspector Navy Materiel
AINO	Assistant Inspector of Naval Ordnance
AINP	Association Internationale des Numismates Professionnels
AINSE	Argonne Institute of Nuclear Science and Engineering (AEC)
AINSE	Australian Institute of Nuclear Science and Engineering
AINSMAT	Assistant Inspector Naval Material

AInstP . . . . . . Associate of the Institute of Physics (British)
AInstPI . . . . . Associate of the Institute of Patentees and Inventors (British)
AINTSEC . . . . Air Intelligence Section (Army)
AIO . . . . Action Information Organization
AIO . . . . Activity, Interest, and Opinion (Factor Scores) (Marketing)
AIO . . . . Air Installation Office
AIO . . . . Airborne Interceptor Officer
AIO . . . . Allied Interrogating Organization
AIO . . . . Americans for Indian Opportunity
AIO . . . . Arecibo Ionospheric Observatory (Puerto Rico)
AIO . . . . Army Inventory Objective
AIOA . . . . . . American Iron Ore Association
AIOCC . . . . . Associate Infantry Officer Career Course (Army)
AIOCC . . . . . Association Internationale d'Organisateurs de Courses Cyclistes
AIOD . . . . . . Automatic Identified Outward Dialing
AIOK of M . . . Ancient and Illustrious Order Knights of Malta
AIOP . . . . . . Analog Input/Output Package (Data processing)
AIOP . . . . . . Association Internationale d'Oceanographie Physique
AIOP . . . . . . Association Internationale d'Orientation Professionnelle
AIOW . . . . . . Association of Independent Optical Wholesalers
AIP . . . . Ablative Insulative Plastic
AIP . . . . Aeronautical Information Publication (FAA)
AIP . . . . Agence Ivoirienne de Presse (Ivorian Press Agency)
AIP . . . . Air Intake Panel
AIP . . . . Airborne Instrumentation Platform
AIP . . . . Alternate Inspection Policy
AIP . . . . American Institute of Parliamentarians
AIP . . . . American Institute of Physics
AIP . . . . American Institute of Planners
AIP . . . . Army Information Program
AIP . . . . Arylene Isopropylidene Polymers (Organic chemistry)
AIPA . . . . . . American Indian Press Association
AIPA . . . . . . American Ionospheric Propagation Association
AIPA . . . . . . Association Internationale de Psychologie Appliquee
AIPAC . . . . . . American Israel Public Affairs Committee
AIPC . . . . . . American Institute for Political Communication
AIPC . . . . . . Association Internationale de Prophylaxie de la Cecite
AIPC . . . . . . Association Internationale des Palais des Congres
AIPC . . . . . . Association Internationale des Ponts et Charpentes
AIPCE . . . . . . Association des Industries du Poisson de la CEE
AIPCN . . . . . . Association Internationale Permanente des Congres de Navigation
AIPCR . . . . . . Association Internationale Permanente des Congres de la Route
AIPD . . . . . . Associated Industrial Photographic Dealers (Defunct)
AIPDWF . . . . All-India Port and Dock Workers' Federation
AIPE . . . . . . American Institute of Park Executives
AIPE . . . . . . American Institute of Plant Engineers
AIPEPO . . . . . Association Internationale de Presse pour l'Etude des Problemes
          d'Outre-mer
AIPEU . . . . . . American Institute on Problems of European Unity
AIPG . . . . . . American Institute of Professional Geologists
AIPH . . . . . . Association Internationale des Producteurs de l'Horticulture
AIPLU . . . . . . American Institute for Property and Liability Underwriters
AIPPI . . . . . . Association Internationale pour la Protection de la Propriete
          Industrielle
AIPR . . . . . . American Institute of Pacific Relations (Defunct)
AIPS . . . . . . Association Internationale de la Presse Sportive
AIPS . . . . . . Association Internationale pour le Progres Social
AIPS . . . . . . Automatic Indexing and Proofreading System
AIQ . . . . Animal Inspection and Quarantine Division (of ARS, Department of
          Agriculture)
AIR . . . . Accelerated Item Reduction (Military)
AIR . . . . Acoustic Intercept Receiver
AIR . . . . Action for Industrial Recycling (An organization)
AIR . . . . Aeronautical (or Aerospace) Information Report
AIR . . . . Air Control Products, Inc. (NYSE symbol)
AIR . . . . Air Injection Reactor
AIR . . . . Air Intercept Rocket
AIR . . . . Airborne Interceptor Rocket
AIR . . . . Aircraft Incident Report (Navy)
AIR . . . . All-India Radio
AIR . . . . American Industrial Real Estate Association
AIR . . . . American Institute of Refrigeration (Defunct)
AIR . . . . American Institutes for Research in the Behavioral Sciences
AIR . . . . Antenna Input Resistance
AIR . . . . Army Intelligence Reserve
AIR . . . . Association for Institutional Research
AIR . . . . Associazione Italiana Razzi
AIRA . . . . . . Air Attache (Air Force)
AIRA . . . . . . Air Force Attache
AIRAC . . . . . . Atmospheric Infrared Attenuation Coefficient
AIRACS . . . . . . Aircraft Acquisition and Support

AIRAD . . . . . . Air Administrative Net (Army)
AIRAD . . . . . . Airmen's Advisory (A notice to airmen)
AIRAF . . . . . . Aircraft, Asiatic Fleet
AIRARMUNIT . . Aircraft, Armament Unit
AIRASDEVLANT . Aircraft Anti-Submarine Development Detachment, Atlantic Fleet
AIRBASECOM . . Air Base Commander
AIRBATFORPAC . . Aircraft Battle Force, Pacific Fleet
AIRBM . . . . . . Anti-Intermediate Range Ballistic Missile
AIRBO . . . . . . Association Internationale pour les Recherches au Bas Fourneau
          d'Ougree
AIRBR . . . . . . Association Internationale du Registre des Bateaux du Rhin
AIRC . . . . . . Association of International Relations Clubs
AIRCENT . . . . . Allied Air Forces, Central Europe (Formerly AAFCE)
AIRCEY . . . . . Air Ceylon Limited (Airline)
AIRCO . . . . . . Air Coordinator (Air Force)
AIRCOM . . . . . Aerospace Communications Complex (Air Force)
AIRCOM . . . . Air Force Communications Program
AIRCOM . . . . Airways Communications System
AIRCOMD . . . . Air Command Net (Army)
AIRCOMNET . . Air Communications Network
AIRCON . . . . . Automated Information and Reservation Computer Operated Network
AIRDEFCOM . . Air Defense Commander
AIRDEVRON . . Air Development Squadron
AIREA . . . . . . American Institute of Real Estate Appraisers
AIRELO . . . . . Air Electrical Officer
AIRENGPROPACCOVERHAUL . . Airplane Engine, Propeller and Accessory Overhaul (Navy)
AIREO . . . . . . Air Engineer Officer
AIREP . . . . . . Aircraft Report
AIREPDIV . . . . Aircraft Repair Division
AIREPDN . . . . Aircraft Repair Division
AIREVAC . . . . Air Evacuation
AIREVACWING . . Air Evacuation Wing
AIREW . . . . . . Airborne Infrared Early Warning
AIRF . . . . Aircraft Instrument Repair Facility
AIRF . . . . All-India Railwaymen's Federation
AIRF . . . . Assignment Instructions Remain Firm (Army)
AIRFERONS . . . Air Ferry Squadrons (Navy)
AIRFMFPAC . . . Aircraft, Fleet Marine Force, Pacific
AIRFORWARD . . Shore-Based Air Force, Forward Area, Central Pacific
AIRGI . . . . . . Airman's Guide (A publication)
AIRGLO . . . . . . Airborne Infrared Gunfire Locator
AIRGRP . . . . . . Air Group
AIRH . . . . Association Internationale de Recherches Hydrauliques
AIRHC . . . . . . Alaska International Rail and Highway Commission (Terminated, 1961)
AIRIS . . . . Air Store Issuing Ship
AIRL . . . . Aeronautical Icing Research Laboratory
AIRLANT . . . . . Air Forces, Atlantic Fleet (Navy)
AIRLO . . . . . . Air Liaison Officer
AIRLORDS . . . . Airlines Load Optimization Recording and Display System (Airport
          passenger-moving sidewalk)
AIRM . . . . Airborne Infrared Mapper
AIRMET . . . . . Airmen's Meteorological Information
AIRMG . . . . . . Aircraft, Machine Gunner
AIRNAVAID . . . Air Navigational Aid (Navy)
AIRNORSOLS . . Aircraft, Northern Solomons
AIRNORTH . . . Allied Air Forces Northern Europe
AIROPNET . . . Air Operational Network (Air Force)
AIROPS . . . . . Air Operations
AIRP . . . . Associazione Italiana Relazioni Pubbliche (Italian public relations
          organization)
AIRPAC . . . . . . Air Forces, Pacific Fleet
AIRPAC (ADV) . . Air Forces Pacific Advanced
AIRPAC (PEARL) . . Air Forces Pacific, Pearl Harbor
AIRPACSUBCOMFORD . . Air Forces Subordinate Command, Forward Area
AIRPAP . . . . . . Air Pressure Analysis Program (Bell System)
AIRS . . . . Airborne Infrared Radiometer System
AIRS . . . . Airborne Integrated Reconnaissance System
AIRS . . . . Automatic Information Retrieval System
AIRSCOFORPAC . . Aircraft Scouting Force, Pacific Fleet
AIRSHIPGR . . . Airship Group
AIRSHIPRON . . Airship Squadron
AIRSOLS . . . . . Air Solomons Command (US)
AIRSOPAC . . . Aircraft, South Pacific Force
AIRSOUTH . . . Allied Air Forces Southern Europe
AIRSOWESPAC . . Aircraft, Southwest Pacific Force (Navy)
AIRSTORDEP . . . Air Stores Depot (Navy)
AIRTRAINRON . . Air Training Squadron (Navy)
AIRTRANSRON . . Air Transport Squadron
AIRTRANSRONLANT . . Air Transport Squadron, Atlantic
AIRTRANSRONPAC . . Air Transport Squadron, Pacific
AIRTRANSRONWESTCOAST . . Air Transport Squadron, West Coast

AIRVAN . . . . . . Air-mobile Van (Trailer unit for use on ground or in air) (Military)
AIRXRS . . . . . . American Industrial Radium and X-Ray Society
AIS . . . . Ablating Inner Surface
AIS . . . . Academic Instructors School (Air Force)
AIS . . . . Advanced Information Systems Company
AIS . . . . Aeronautical Information Service
AIS . . . . Air Intelligence Service
AIS . . . . Airborne Infrared Spectrometer
AIS . . . . America-Italy Society
AIS . . . . American Iris Society
AIS . . . . Anti-Icing System (Aircraft)
AIS . . . . Apollo Instrumentation Ships (NASA)
AIS . . . . Army Intelligence School
AIS . . . . Army Intelligence & Security
AIS . . . . Association Internationale de la Savonnerie et de la Detergence
AIS . . . . Association Internationale de la Soie
AIS . . . . Association Internationale de Sociologie
AIS . . . . Attitude Indicating System
AIS . . . . Automated Instrumentation System
AIS . . . . Automatic Intercept System (Bell System)
AIS . . . . Automatic Interplanetary Station (USSR)
AIS . . . . International Association of Semiotics
AISA . . . . . . American Institute of Supply Associations (Formerly, AIWPHSA)
AISA . . . . . . Analytical Isoelectrofocusing Scanning Apparatus (Analytical chemistry)
AISC . . . . . . American Institute of Steel Construction
AISC . . . . . . Association of Independent Software Companies
AISC . . . . . . Association Internationale des Skal Clubs
AISE . . . . Association Internationale des Sciences Economiques
AISE . . . . Association of Iron and Steel Engineers
AISI . . . . American Iron and Steel Institute
AISI . . . . American-Italy Society, Incorporated
AISJ . . . . Association Internationale des Sciences Juridiques
AISM . . . . . . Association Internationale de Signalisation Maritime
AISM . . . . . . Association Internationale des Societes de Microbiologie
AIS-MEBA . . . . Association of Industrial Scientists (affiliated with) Marine Engineers
     Beneficial Association (A union)
AISP . . . . Association Internationale de Science Politique
AISPIT . . . . . . Association Internationale de Seismologie et de Physique de l'Interieur
     de la Terre
AISS . . . . Airborne Infrared Surveillance Set
AISS . . . . Association Internationale de la Securite Sociale
AIT . . . . Advanced Individual Training (Army)
AIT . . . . Alliance Internationale de Tourisme
AIT . . . . American Industrial Transport, Inc.
AIT . . . . Army Intelligence Translator
AIT . . . . Association Internationale des Travailleurs (International Association of
     Workers) (France)
AIT . . . . Automatic Information Test (Military)
AIT . . . . Automotive Information Test
AITA . . . . Act Inside the Army (European antiwar group)
AITA . . . . Advanced Individual Training Available (Military)
AITA . . . . . . Air Industries and Transports Association
AITA . . . . . . Association Internationale du Theatre d'Amateurs
AITC . . . . Action Information Training Center
AITC . . . . . . Air Intelligence Training Center
AITC . . . . . . American Institute of Timber Construction
AITF . . . . All in the Family (TV program)
AITI . . . . Aero Industries Technical Institute
AITIT . . . . . . Association Internationale de la Teinture et de l'Impression Textile
     (International Association of Textile Dyers and Printers)
AITU . . . . . . Alliance of Independent Telephone Unions
AITUC . . . . . All-India Trade Union Congress
AIU . . . . Abort Interface Unit (NASA)
AIU . . . . Action for Interracial Understanding
AIU . . . . Alliance Israelite Universelle
AIU . . . . Allied Independent Unions (Lebanon)
AIU . . . . Association Internationale des Universites
AIUFFAS . . . . . Association Internationale des Utilisateurs de Files de Fibres Artificielles
     et Synthetiques
AIUM . . . . . . American Institute of Ultrasonics in Medicine
AIUS . . . . . . Associazione Internazionale Uomo nello Spazis
AIV . . . . Accelerated Inverse Voltage
AIV . . . . Association Internationale de Volcanologie
AIVM . . . . . . Association Internationale pour les Voiles Minces (en Beton)
AIVP . . . . . . American Institute of Vocal Pedagogy
AIW . . . . Asbestos Insulated Wire
AIW . . . . International Union, Allied Industrial Workers of America
AIWI . . . . . . American Industrial Writing Institute
AIWO . . . . . . Agudas Israel World Organization
AIWPHSA . . . . American Institute of Wholesale Plumbing and Heating Supply
     Associations (Later, AISA)

AJ . . . . Air Jordan (Airline)
AJ . . . . A.J. Industries, Inc. (NYSE symbol)
AJ . . . . Alloy Junction
AJ . . . . Alma & Jonquieres R. R. (AAR code)
AJ . . . . Antijamming (RADAR)
AJ . . . . Arc Jet
AJ . . . . Architects Journal
AJ . . . . Associate in Journalism
AJ . . . . Associate Justice (US Supreme Court)
AJA . . . . Adjacent
AJA . . . . American Jewish Archives
AJAG/CIV . . . . Assistant Judge Advocate General for Civil Law (Army)
AJAG/MIL . . . . Assistant Judge Advocate General for Military Law (Army)
AJAI . . . . Anti-Jamming, Anti-Interference
AJAQ . . . . Army Job Activities Questionnaire
AJASS . . . . . . African Jazz Art Society Studios
AJAZ . . . . American Jewish Alternatives to Zionism
AJB . . . . Administration of Justice Branch (US Military Government, Germany)
AJBA . . . . Association de la Jeunesse Bakoko (Association of Bakoko Youth)
AJBC . . . . American Junior Bowling Congress
AJBP . . . . Association of Jewish Book Publishers
AJC . . . . Alvin Junior College (Texas)
AJC . . . . American Jewish Committee
AJC . . . . American Jewish Conference
AJC . . . . American Jewish Congress
AJC . . . . Association de la Jeunesse Camerounaise (Cameroonian Youth Association)
AJC . . . . Austin Junior College (Minnesota)
AJCAF . . . . . . Association of Jewish Chaplains of the Armed Forces
AJCC . . . . . . Alternate Joint Communications Center
AJCC . . . . . . American Jersey Cattle Club
AJCCA . . . . . . American Jewish Correctional Chaplains Association
AJCRW . . . . . Association of Jewish Community Relations Workers
AJCU . . . . . . Air Jet Control Unit
AJD . . . . Anti-Jam Display
AJDC . . . . . . American Joint Distribution Committee
AJE . . . . Adult Jewish Education
AJENAKO . . . . Association des Jeunesse Nationalistes du Kongo (Association of
     Nationalist Youth of the Congo) (Leopoldville)
AJEUNAL . . . . Alliance de Jeunesse Angolaise pour la Liberte (Alliance of Angolan
     Youth for Freedom)
AJF . . . . Anti-Jam Frequency
AJFH . . . . Anti-Jam Frequency Hopper
AJH . . . . Anti-Jam Hopper
AJHC . . . . . . American Jewish History Center
AJHS . . . . . . American Jewish Historical Society
AJI . . . . American Jewish Institute
AJL . . . . Association of Jewish Libraries
AJLA . . . . . . Association of the Junior Leagues of America
AJLAC . . . . . . American Jewish League Against Communism
AJLI . . . . American Jewish League for Israel
AJLO . . . . . . Avalanching Junction Light Output
AJM . . . . Association de la Jeunesse Mauritienne (Mauritanian Youth Association)
AJMA . . . . . . American Jesuit Missionary Association
AJPA . . . . . . American Jewish Press Association
AJPC . . . . . . American Jewish Periodical Center
AJPC . . . . . . American Jewish Physicians' Committee
AJPRS . . . . . . American Jewish Public Relations Society
AJQ . . . . Army Job Questionnaire
AJR . . . . Artemus-Jellico Railroad Company
AJRC . . . . . . American Junior Red Cross
AJS . . . . American Journal of Science
AJS . . . . American Journal of Sociology
AJS . . . . American Judicature Society
AJS . . . . Angle Jamming System
AJS . . . . Anti-Jam Synthesizer
AJSA . . . . . . American Junior Shorthorn Association
AJSC . . . . . . Association of Jewish Sponsored Camps
AJSS . . . . . . American Jewish Society for Service
AJSS . . . . . . Australian Joint Staff Service
AJT . . . . Advanced Jet Trainer
AJT . . . . Anti-Jam Technique
AJTI . . . . Association on Japanese Textile Imports
AJTR . . . . . . Allowance Prescribed in Joint Travel Regulations (Military)
AJVD . . . . . . Abrupt Junction Varactor Doubler
AK . . . . Above Knee (Medicine)
AK . . . . Adaption Kit (Army)
AK . . . . Alaska
AK . . . . Allied Kommandatura
AK . . . . Amplitude Keyed
AK . . . . Anterior (Wall of) Kidney
AK . . . . Arbeitskraft

AK	Aviation Storekeeper (Navy rating)
AK	Avtomat Kalashnikov (Submachine Gun) (USSR)
AK	Cargo Ship (of any type)
AKA	Also Known As
AKA	American Kitefliers Association
AKA	Attack Cargo Ship (Navy symbol)
AKBS	Advanced Kinematic Bombing System
AKC	American Kennel Club
AKC	Associate of King's College (London)
AKCL	Associate of King's College London
AKD	Allied Kid Company (NYSE symbol) (Delisted)
AKD	Cargo Ship, Dock (Navy symbol)
AKEL	Anorthotion Komma Ergazomanou Laou (Reform Party of the Working People) (Cyprus)
AKF	American-Korean Foundation
AKF	Anken Chemical & Film Corporation (NYSE symbol) (Delisted)
AKF	Refrigerated Cargo Ship (World War II)
AKFM	Antokon'ny Kongresin' ny Fahaleovantenan' i Madagasikara (Party for the Congress for the Independence of Madagascar)
AKFM	Association of Knitted Fabrics Manufacturers
AKGA	American Knit Glove Association
AKI	Alaska Interstate Co. (NYSE symbol)
AKK	Alpha Kappa Kappa (Fraternity)
AKL	Light Cargo Ship (Navy symbol)
AKMIL	Akademi Militer Nasional
AKN	Net Cargo Ship (Navy symbol)
AKNF	Adair-Koshland-Nemethy-Filmer (Enzyme model)
AKP	Alpha Kappa Psi (Fraternity)
AKR	Vehicle Cargo Ship (Navy symbol)
AKS	General Stores Issue Ship (Navy symbol)
AK(SS)	Cargo Submarine (Navy symbol)
AKU	Algemene Kunstzijde Unie (Commercial firm) (Netherlands) (Later, AKZO)
AKURON.	Autonetics Kalman Utilization of Reference for Optimal Navigation
AKV	Cargo Ship and Aircraft Ferry (Navy symbol)
AKWV	Algemene Katholieke Werkgeversvereniging
AKZO	Algemene Kunstzijde Unie (AKU) - Koninklijke Zout-Organon (KZO) (Two companies whose merger formed AKZO)
AL	Absolute Limen (Psychophysics)
AL	Accession List
AL	Accidental Loss (AEC)
AL	Acoustics Laboratory
AL	Acquisition Logistician
AL	Adaptation Level
AL	Aeronautical Laboratory
AL	Aerophysics Laboratory
AL	Air Letter
AL	Air Liaison
AL	Air Lock (Technical drawings)
AL	Aircraft Logistics (Division), Bureau of Aeronautics (Later, NASC) (Navy)
AL	Alabama
AL	Alcan Aluminium Limited (NYSE symbol)
AL	Allegheny Airlines, Inc.
AL	All Lengths (Lumber)
AL	Almanor R. R. (AAR code)
AI	Aluminum (Chemical element)
AL	American League (Baseball)
AL	American Legion
AL	Angle Lock
AL	Anglo-Latin (Language, speech, grammar)
AL	Anno Lucis (In the Year of Light)
AL	Annual Leave (US Civil Service)
AL	Antenna Laboratory
AL	Approach and Landing Charts (Aviation)
AL	Arm Length
AL	Assembly Language (Data processing)
AL	Assumed Latitude (Navigation)
AL	Astronomical League
AL	Astronuclear Laboratory (Westinghouse Electric Corporation)
AL	Astropower Laboratory (Douglas Aircraft Corporation)
AL	Autograph Letter
AL	Aviation Electronicsman (Military)
AL	Avionics Laboratory (Air Force)
AL	Axiolingual
AL	Laureate of Arts
AL	Lightship (Navy symbol)
ALA	Alabama
ALA	Alanine (Amino acid)
ALA	Alliance for Labor Action (An organization)
ALA	Amalgamated Lithographers of America (Later, Lithographers and Photoengravers International Union)
ALA	American Landrace Association

ALA	American Laryngological Association
ALA	American Latvian Association in the United States
ALA	American Legion Auxiliary
ALA	American Liberal Association
ALA	American Library Association
ALA	American Literary Anthology
ALA	Aminolevulinic Acid (Biochemistry)
ALA	Antenna Lightning Arrester
ALA	Arc Lamp Assembly
ALA	Army Launch Area
ALA	Assembly of Librarians of the Americas
ALA	Associate in Liberal Arts
ALA	Associate of the Library Association (British)
ALA	Authors League of America
ALA	Automobile Legal Association
ALAA	Associate of the London Association of Certified and Corporate Accountants (British)
ALAAR	Air Launched Air Recoverable Rocket
ALABM	Air Launched Anti-Ballistic Missile
ALABOL	Algorithmic and Business Oriented Language
ALACP	American League to Abolish Capital Punishment
ALAD	Arid Lands Agricultural Development (Program) (Middle East)
ALADLO	All Air Defense Liaison Officers (in region)
ALAI	Association Litteraire et Artistique Internationale
ALAIRS	Advanced Low Altitude Reconnaissance Sensor
ALALC	Asociacion Latino Americana de Libre Comercio (Latin American Free Trade Association) (Also uses initials LAFTA)
ALAMCABCO. .	All American Cable Company
ALANF	Army Land Forces
ALANO	All Accident Notice Offices (Aviation)
ALARM	Automatic Light Aircraft Readiness Monitor
ALARR	Air Launched, Air Recoverable Rocket
ALART	Army Low-Speed Air Research Tasks
ALARTC	All Air Route Traffic Control Centers (in region)
ALAS	Alaska
ALAS	Aminolevulinic-Acid Synthetase (Biochemistry)
ALAS	Association for Latin American Studies (Defunct)
ALASC	Aircraft Launching Accessory Service Change
ALAT	Army Language Aptitude Test
ALB	Aircraft Launching Bulletin
ALB	Alcon Laboratories (NYSE symbol)
ALB	Automobile Labor Board
ALBA	American Lawn Bowling Association
ALBA	American Leather Belting Association
ALBC	Anti-LASER Beam Coating
ALBI	Air-Launched Ballistic Intercept
ALBI	Air Launched Boost Intercept
ALBIS	Atmosphere Launched Boost Intercept System
ALBM	Air-Launched Ballistic Missile
ALBO	Automatic Line Buildout (Bell Laboratories)
ALBUS	All Bureaus (Navy)
ALC	Alabama Central R. R. (AAR code)
ALC	American Lancia Club
ALC	American Langshan Club
ALC	American Life Convention
ALC	Analytical Liquid Chromatograph
ALC	Antenna Loading Coil
ALC	Artificial Luminous Cloud
ALC	Assembly Language Coding
ALC	Associated Lutheran Charities (Later, Lutheran Social Welfare Conference of America)
ALC	Automatic Level Control
ALC	Automatic Load Control
ALC	Axiolinguocervical
ALCA	American Leather Chemists Association
ALCA	Associated Landscape Contractors of America
ALCAC	Airlines Communications Administrative Council
ALCAN	Alaska-Canada (Highway)
ALCANUS	Alaska, Canada, United States
ALCAPP	Automatic List Classification and Profile Production
ALCC	Airborne Launch Control Center
ALCC	Airlift Control Center
ALCE	Airlift Control Element
ALCEA	Air Line Communication Employees Association
ALCH	Approach Light Contact Height
ALCO	Airlift Coordinating Office(r)
ALCO	Airlift Launch Control Officer (Air Force)
ALCO	Airlift Liaison Coordination Officer
ALCO	American Locomotive Company
ALCOA	Aluminum Company of America
ALCOM	Alaska Command (Military)

ALCOM	Algebraic Compiler (or Computer)
ALCOM	All Commands (A dispatch to all commands in an area) (Navy)
ALCON	All Concerned (Army)
ALCOP	Alternate Command Post (Military)
ALCOR	ARPA (Advanced Research Projects Agency)/Lincoln C-Band Observable RADAR (Army)
ALCORCEN	Air Logistic Coordination Center
ALCS/C	All AT (Air Traffic Service) Combined Station/Centers (in region)
ALCS/T	All AT (Air Traffic Service) Combined Station/Towers (in region)
ALCU	Altocumulus (Meteorology)
ALCW	American Lutheran Church Women
ALD	Acceptable Limit for Dispersion
ALD	Airborne Line Discriminator
ALD	American Library Directory
ALD	At a Later Date
ALDA	Air Line Dispatchers Association
ALDA	Allied Linens and Domestics Association
ALDA	American Land Development Association
ALDC	Army Logistics Data Center
ALDEP	Automated Layout Design Program (IBM)
ALDP	Automatic Language Data Processing
ALDPS	Automated Logistics Data Processing System
ALDRI	Automatic Low Date Rate Input
ALDS	Apollo Launch Data System (NASA)
ALE	Automated Large Experiment (NASA)
ALEA	Air Line Employees Association, International
ALEAA	American Lithuanian Engineers' and Architects' Association
ALECS	Air Force – Los Alamos EMP (Electromagnetic Pulse) Calibration Simulator
ALEM	Apollo Lunar Exploration Mission (NASA)
ALEMS	Apollo Lunar Excursion Module Sensors (Aerospace)
ALERT	American Library for Education, Research and Training
ALERT	Automated Linguistic Extraction and Retrieval Technique
ALERT	Automatic Logging Electronic Reporting and Telemetering System (Maintains surveillance over petroleum wells and pipelines)
ALERT	Automatic Logical Equipment Readiness Tester
ALERT	Automatic Logician Evaluation Readiness Tester
ALERTS	Airborne LASER Equipment Real Time Surveillance
ALERTS	Associated Library and Educational Research Team for Survival (Group of Lorton Reformatory inmates publishing a newsletter)
ALES	American Labor Education Service
ALESCO	American Library and Educational Service Company
ALF	American Life Foundation (Press)
ALF	American Loan Fund
ALF	Automatic Lead Former
ALF	Automatic Letter Facer
ALF	Auxiliary Landing Field
ALFA	Air Lubricated Free Attitude
ALFA	Air Lubricated Free Axis Trainer (NASA)
ALFAA	All Federal Aviation Administration Field Offices and Personnel
ALFORD	Appalachian Laboratory for Occupational Respiratory Diseases
ALFRED	Associative Learning from Relative Environmental Data
ALFSE	Allied Land Forces Southern Europe
ALFSEA	Allied Land Forces South East Asia
ALFSS	All Flight Service Stations (in region)
ALFT	Airlift
ALG	Advanced Landing Ground (Air Force)
ALG	Aircraft Landing Gear
ALG	Antilymphocyte Globulin (Used in heart transplants)
ALG	Axiolinguogingival
ALGCU	Association of Land Grant Colleges and Universities
ALGEC	Algorithmic Language for Economic Problems
ALGLYN	Aluminum Glycinate
ALGM	Air-Launched Guided Missile (Military)
ALGOL	Algebraic Oriented Language
ALGOL	Algorithmic Language (Data processing)
AL of H	American Legion of Honor
ALHA	American Labor Health Association
ALI	Agricultural Limestone Institute
ALI	Airborne LASER Illuminator
ALI	American Ladder Institute
ALI	American Law Institute
ALI	Arc Lamp Igniter
ALI	Arm Length Index
ALI	Arthur Little, Incorporated
ALI	Automotive Lift Institute
ALIA	American Life Insurance Association
ALIADS	Alaskan Integrated Air Defense System
ALIANSA	Alimentos para Animales, SA (Feed plant) (Guatemala)
ALIAS	Algebraic Logic Investigation of Apollo Systems
ALIATCS	All International Air Traffic Communications Stations

ALIAZO	Alliance of Natives of Zombo (Angola)
ALIC	Association of Life Insurance Counsel
ALICE	Adiabatic Low-Energy Injection and Capture Experiment
ALICE	Alaskan Integrated Communications Exchange
ALICS	Advanced Logistics Information and Control System (Air Force)
ALIFSS	All International Flight Service Stations (in region)
ALIM	Air-Launched Intercept Missile
ALIMDA	Association of Life Insurance Medical Directors of America
ALIRATS	Airborne LASER Illuminator Ranging and Tracking System
ALIS	Advanced Life Information System (Data processing)
A Lit	Associate in Literature
ALIT	Automatic Line Insulation Tester
ALITALIA	Aerolinee Italiane Internazionali (Italian International Airline)
A Litt	Associate in Letters
ALJ	Administrative Law Judge (Federal trial examiner)
ALL	Accelerated Learning of Logic
ALL	Acute Lymphocytic Leukemia (Medicine)
ALL	Adams-Millis Corporation (NYSE symbol)
ALL	Address Locator Logic
ALL	Admiralty List of Lights (British)
ALL	Aircraft Landing Lamp
ALL	American Liberation League
ALL	Arc LASER Light
ALL	Argon LASER Lining
ALL	Augustana Luther League
ALLA	Allied Long Lines Agency
ALLNAVSTAS	All Naval Stations
ALLOC	Allocate (or Allocation)
ALLP	Arc LASER Light Pump
ALLP	Audiolingual Language Programing
ALLS	Apollo Lunar Logistic Support
ALM	Advanced List of Materials
ALM	Air Launched Missile
ALM	Allied Maintenance Corp. (NYSE symbol)
ALM	American Leprosy Missions
ALM	Apollo Lunar Module
ALM	Arkansas & Louisiana Missouri Railway Company (AAR code)
ALM	Audio Level Meter
ALM	Augmented Lunar Module
ALMA	Adoptees Liberty Movement Association
ALMA	Alphanumeric Language for Music Analysis
ALMA	American Lace Manufacturers Association
ALMA	Association of Labor Mediation Agencies
ALMA	Association of Literary Magazines of America
ALMAJCOM	All Major Commands
ALMC	Army Logistics Management Center (Obsolete)
ALMDA	Airlock Multiple Docking Adapter (Aerospace)
ALMIDO	Amplitude and Latency Measuring Instrument with Digital Output
ALMILACT	All Military Activities
ALMO	Army Logistics Manpower Office (Merged with Operations Personnel Office)
ALMS	Air-Launched Missile System
ALMS	Analytic Language Manipulation System
ALN	Albany & Northern Railway Company (AAR code)
ALN	Allen Group (NYSE symbol)
ALN	Ammunition Lot Number
ALN	Anterior Lateral Nerve
ALN	Armee de la Liberation Nationale (National Liberation Army) (Algeria)
ALNA	Armee de Liberation Nationale de l'Angola (Angolan Army of National Liberation)
ALNAV	All Navy and Marine Corps Activities (A dispatch to all activities in an area)
ALNAVSTA	All Naval Stations (A dispatch to all Naval stations in an area)
ALNICO	Aluminum, Nickel, Cobalt (Alloy)
ALNK	Armee de Liberation Nationale Kamerounaise (Cameroonese National Liberation Army)
ALNOT	Alert Notice
ALNTS	Automatic Liquid Nitrogen Transfer System
ALO	Advanced Lunar Operation
ALO	Air Liaison Officer (US Air Force, British Navy)
ALO	Allied Liaison Office
ALO	Aloha Airlines, Incorporated
ALO	Alternate Launch Officer (Air Force)
ALO	Amalgamated Lace Operatives of America
ALO	American Liaison Office
ALO	Apollo Lunar Orbit (Air Force)
ALO	Arm Length Order
ALO	Army Liaison Officer
ALOA	Amalgamated Lace Operatives of America
ALOA	Amalgamated Lithographers of America
ALOA	Assembly of Librarians of the Americas

ALOA . . . . Associated Locksmiths of America
ALOC . . . . . . Air Line of Communication (Air Force)
ALOC . . . . . Alternate Launch Officer Console (Air Force)
ALOO . . . . . . Albuquerque Operations Office
ALOREP . . . . . Airlift Operational Report
ALOT . . . . Airborne Lightweight Optical Tracker
ALOTM . . . . . . Allotment
ALOTS . . . . . . Airborne Lightweight Optical Tracking System (Air Force)
ALP . . . . Advanced Lunar Projects
ALP . . . . Air Liaison Party
ALP . . . . Airborne Line Printer
ALP . . . . Allied Liaison and Protocol
ALP . . . . Allied Logistic Publication (Military)
ALP . . . . Ambulance Loading Post (Military)
ALP . . . . American Labor Party
ALP . . . . Anterior Lobe of Pituitary (Gland)
ALP . . . . Assembly Language Program (Data processing)
ALP . . . . Australian Labor Party
ALP . . . . Automated Learning Process
ALPA . . . . Air Line Pilots Association
ALPA . . . . . . American Legion Press Association
ALPA . . . . . . International Air Line Pilots Association
ALPAC . . . . . Automatic Language Processing Advisory Committee (National Research Council)
ALPAI . . . . Air Line Pilots Association, International
ALPAK . . . . . . Algebra Package
ALPB . . . . . . Aircraft Logistics Planning Board
ALPB . . . . . . American Lutheran Publicity Bureau
ALPBC . . . . . . American League of Professional Baseball Clubs
ALPCA . . . . . . Auto License Plate Collectors Association
ALPEC . . . . . . Ammunition Loading Production Engineering Center (Army)
ALPERSCOM. . . All Personnel Communication (Military)
ALPETH . . . . . Aluminum and Polyethylene
ALPHA . . . . . . Alkali Plasma Hall Accelerator
ALPHA . . . . . . Automated Literature Processing, Handling, and Analysis
ALPL . . . . Advanced Lunar Projects Laboratory
ALPO . . . . Allegheny Portage Railroad National Historic Site
ALPO . . . . . . Association of Lunar and Planetary Observers
ALPPA . . . . . . Agriculture and Livestock Professional Photographers Association
ALPR . . . . Argonne Low Power Reactor (AEC)
ALPRA . . . . . . American Lithuanian Press and Radio Association
ALPS . . . . Advanced Linear Programing System
ALPS . . . . . . Advanced Liquid Propulsion System (NASA)
ALPS . . . . . . Applied LASER Projects Staff
ALPS . . . . . . Automatic License Plate Scanning
ALPURCOMS . . All-Purpose Communications System
ALQS . . . . Aliquippa & Southern R. R. (AAR code)
ALR . . . . Allright Auto Parks, Inc. (NYSE symbol)
ALR . . . . Amagat-Leduc Rule
ALR . . . . American Law Reports
ALR . . . . Automatic Level Recorder
ALRA . . . . . . Associated Legislative Rabbinate of America
ALRAFAC . . . . All RADAR Air Traffic Control Facilities in Region
ALRC . . . . . . Anti-Locust Research Center (British)
ALRCFA . . . . . American Lithuanian Roman Catholic Federation Ateitis
ALRCOL . . . . . American Lithuanian Roman Catholic Organist Alliance
ALRCP . . . . . . Army Long Range Capabilities Plan
ALRCWA . . . . . American Lithuanian Roman Catholic Women's Alliance
ALREMP . . . . . Aircraft Launch and Recovery Equipment Maintenance Program (Navy)
ALREP . . . . Air Launched Report (Navy)
ALRH . . . . Apollo Lunar Radioisotopic Heater (NASA)
ALRI . . . . Advanced Long-Range Interceptor
ALRI . . . . Airborne Long-Range Input
ALRI . . . . Airborne Long-Range Intercept
ALRI . . . . Airborne Long-Range RADAR Input
ALROS . . . . . . American Laryngological, Rhinological and Otological Society
ALRR . . . . Ames Laboratory Research Reactor (AEC)
ALRS . . . . Admiralty List of Radio Signals (British)
ALRTF . . . . Army Long-Range Technological Forecast
ALS . . . . Advanced Logistics Spacecraft
ALS . . . . Air Logistics Service (or System) (Military)
ALS . . . . Airborne Live Scanner
ALS . . . . Aircraft Landing System
ALS . . . . Allied Stores Corporation (NYSE symbol)
ALS . . . . Alton & Southern R. R. (AAR code)
ALS . . . . American Lessing Society
ALS . . . . American Liszt Society
ALS . . . . American Littoral Society (For underwater study of shore life)
ALS . . . . American Luxembourg Society
ALS . . . . Amyotrophic Lateral Sclerosis
ALS . . . . Anticipated Life Span

ALS . . . . Antilymphocyte Serum
ALS . . . . Approach and Landing Simulator
ALS . . . . Approach Light System
ALS . . . . Associate of the Linnaean Society (British)
ALS . . . . Associative List Selection
ALS . . . . Autograph Letter Signed
ALS . . . . Automatic Landing System
ALS . . . . Automatic Level Setting
ALS . . . . Azimuth Laying Set
A/LS . . . . Approach Light System (Aviation)
ALSA . . . . American Law Student Association
ALSAA . . . . . Americans (of Lebanese-Syrian Ancestry) for America
ALSAC . . . . . . Aiding Leukemia Stricken American Children (Fund-raising organization)
ALSAC . . . . . . American Lebanese Syrian Association Charities
ALSAFECOM . . All Safety Commands (Air Force)
ALSAM . . . . . Air-Launched Ship-Attack Missile
ALSAM . . . . . . Air-Launched Surface Attack Missile
ALSC . . . . American Lumber Standards Committee
ALSCC . . . . . . Apollo Lunar Surface Closeup Camera (Apollo 11) (NASA)
ALSCP . . . . . . Appalachian Land Stabilization and Conservation Program
ALSD . . . . Apollo Lunar Surface Drill (NASA)
ALSE . . . . Apollo Lunar Surface Experiment
AL SEA FRON . . Alaskan Sea Frontier
AL SEC . . . . . . Alaskan Sector
ALSEP . . . . . . Apollo Lunar Surface Experiments Package (NASA)
ALSI . . . . Aluminum Silicon (An alloy)
ALSK . . . . Alaska R. R. (AAR code)
ALSOR . . . . . . Air Launch Sounding Rocket
ALSRC . . . . . . Apollo Lunar Sample Return Container (NASA)
ALSS . . . . Airline System Simulator
ALSS . . . . Apollo Logistic Support System (Army)
ALSS . . . . Association of Lutheran Secondary Schools
ALSS . . . . International Air Line Stewards and Stewardesses Association
ALSSAI . . . . . . Air Line Stewards and Stewardesses Association, International
ALST . . . . Alaska Standard Time
ALST . . . . Altostratus (Meteorology)
ALT . . . . Accelerated Life Testing
ALT . . . . Administrative Lead Time
ALT . . . . Aer Lingus TTA
ALT . . . . Alternate
ALT . . . . Altimeter
ALT . . . . Altitude
ALTA . . . . . Airline Traffic Association
ALTA . . . . Alberta (Canadian province)
ALTA . . . . American Land Title Association
ALTA . . . . American Library Trustee Association
ALTA . . . . Association of Local Transport Airlines
ALTAC . . . . . . Algebraic Translator and Compiler
ALTAIR . . . . . . Advanced Research Projects Agency Long-Range Tracking and Instrument RADAR
ALTAN . . . . . Alternate Alerting Network (Air Force)
ALTAPE . . . . . . Automatic Line Tracer and Programming Equipment
ALTARE . . . . . . Automatic Logic Testing and Recording Equipment
ALTF . . . . Airlift Task Force
ALTID . . . . Alteration Identification
ALTLIB . . . . . . Alternate Library (Computer program) (NASA)
ALTN . . . . Alternate
ALTRAN . . . . . Algebraic Translator
ALTRV . . . . . . Altitude Reservation (Air Force)
ALTS . . . . Advanced Lunar Transportation Systems
ALTS . . . . National Lithuanian Society of America
ALT & S . . . . . Alton and Southern Railroad
ALTU . . . . Adder, Logical, and Transfer Unit (Computer)
ALU . . . . Arithmetic Logic Unit (Data processing)
ALUE . . . . Admissible Linear Unbiased Estimator (Statistics)
ALUSLO . . . . . US Naval Liaison Officer
ALUSNA . . . . . US Naval Attache
ALUSNOB . . . . US Naval Observer
ALV . . . . Air Launched Vehicle
ALW . . . . Air Launched Weapon
ALW . . . . Allowance
ALW . . . . Arch-Loop-Whorl (Basis of Galton's System of Fingerprint Classifications)
ALW . . . . Association of Lithuanian Workers
ALWL . . . . Army Limited War Laboratory
ALWLA . . . . . . American Lithuanian Workers Literary Association
ALX . . . . Alexander's Inc. (NYSE symbol)
ALZ . . . . Assault Landing Zone
AM . . . . Academy of Management
AM . . . . Acquisition Manager
AM . . . . Addressograph Multigraph Corporation
AM . . . . Administrative Manual

AM	Air Marshal (British)
AM	Air Medal (Air Force)
AM	Air Ministry (British)
AM	Aircooled Motor
AM	Airlock Module (NASA)
AM.	Airmail
AM	Albert Medal (British)
AM	Alpes Maritimes
AM	America(n)
AM	American Machinist (A publication)
Am.	Americium (Chemical element)
AM	Amperemeter
AM	Amplitude Modulation (Electronics)
AM	Angular Momentum
AM	Anno Mundi (In the Year of the World)
AM	Ante Meridian (or Meridiem) (Forenoon)
AM	Anti-Materiel (Munitions)
AM	Armour & Company (NYSE symbol)
AM	Arms Material
AM	Assignment Memorandum (Army)
AM.	Associate Member
AM	Atomic Migration
AM	Automedica Corporation
AM	Auxiliary Memory
AM	Ave Maria
AM	Aviation Medicine
AM	Aviation Metalsmith
AM	Aviation Structural Mechanic (Navy rating)
AM	Awaiting Maintenance
AM	Axiomesial
AM	Master of Arts
AM	Mine Vessel (Navy symbol)
AM	Mistress of Arts
A & M	Agricultural and Mechanical (in a college name)
A & M	Antitrust and Monopoly Subcommittee (US Senate)
AMA	Academy of Model Aeronautics
AMA	Acoustical Materials Association
AMA	Advanced Minuteman Accelerometer
AMA	Agricultural Marketing Administration (World War II)
AMA	Air Materiel Area (Air Force)
AMA	Aircraft Manufacturers Association
AMA	Ambulance Manufacturers Association
AMA	American Machinery Association
AMA	American Management Association
AMA	American Maritime Association
AMA	American Marketing Association
AMA	American McAll Association
AMA	American Medical Association
AMA	American Ministerial Association
AMA	American Missionary Association
AMA	American Monument Association
AMA	American Motel Association
AMA	American Motorcycle Association
AMA	American Municipal Association (Later, National League of Cities)
AMA	American Mutual Alliance (Insurance association)
AMA	Amfac, Inc. (NYSE symbol)
AMA	Archery Manufacturers Association
AMA	Arena Managers Association
AMA	Associate of the Museums Association
AMA	Australian Medical Association
AMA	Automatic Message Accounting
AMA	Automobile Manufacturers Association (Later, MVMA)
A & MA	Advertising and Marketing Association
AMAA	Adhesives Manufacturers Association of America
AMAA	Armenian Missionary Association of America
AMAA	Army Mutual Aid Association
AMAA	Association of Medical Advertising Agencies
AMAC	Aircraft Monitor and Control
AMAC	Arlington Memorial Amphitheater Commission
AMAC	Automated Multiparameter Analyzer for Cells
AMA-CIPP. . . .	American Medical Association Committee on Insurance and Prepayment Plans
AMACUS	Automated Microfilm Aperture Card Updating System (Army)
AMADA	Archery Manufacturers and Dealers Association
AMA-ERF	American Medical Association Education and Research Foundation
AMAFA.	Air Mass and Frontal Analysis (Meteorology)
AMAG	American Mission for Aid to Greece
AMAI	Arena Managers Association, Incorporated
AMAL	Aero-Medical Acceleration Laboratory
AMAL.	American Medical Acceleration Laboratory
AMAL.	Aviation Medical Acceleration Laboratory (Air Force)
AMALG	Amalgamated
AMAR.	Antimissile Array RADAR
AMARS	Air Mobile Aircraft Refueling System
AMARS	Automatic Message Address Routing System
AMARS	Autonetics Modular Airborne RADAR System
AMAS.	Advanced Midcourse Active System
AMAS	American Military Assistance Staff
AMASCP.	Air Material Area Stock Control Point
AMAT	American Mission for Aid to Turkey
AMATC	Air Material Armament Test Center
AMAX	American Metal Climax, Inc.
AMB.	Aerospace Medicine and Biology
AMB	Air-Launched Missile Bulletin
AMB.	Aircraft Maintenance Base
AMB.	Airways Modernization Board (Functions transferred to FAA)
AMB.	Ambient Noise Background
AMB.	Ambulance
AMB.	American Brands, Inc. (NYSE symbol)
AMB	Antimotorboat
AMB.	Armament Material Bulletin
AMB.	Army Maintenance Board
AMB	Asbestos Mill Board (Technical drawings)
AMB	Astronomy Missions Board (NASA)
AMB	Bachelor of Mechanic Arts
AMBAC.	American Bosch Arma Corporation
AMBBA	Associated Master Barbers and Beauticians of America
AMBEL	Ambiguity Eliminator (Electronics)
AMBIT	Augmented Built-In Test
AMBLADS	Advise Method, Bill of Lading, and Date Shipped
AMBOP.	American Board of Oral Pathology
AMBOT.	Art Material Board of Trade
AMBRL	Army Medical Biomechanical Research Laboratory
AMBUC.	National Association American Business Clubs
AMBV.	Auxiliary Mexican Border Veterans
AMC	Advanced Minuteman Computer
AMC	Aerospace Manufacturers Council
AMC	Aerospace Medical Command (Air Force)
AMC	Air-Launched Missile Change
AMC	Air Mail Center
AMC	Air Materiel Command (Later, Air Force Logistics Command)
AMC	Aircraft Manufacturers Council
AMC	Aircraft Manufacturing Company
AMC	Aircraft Motion Compensation
AMC	Alarm Monitor Computer
AMC	Albertus Magnus College (Connecticut)
AMC	Amador Central R. R. (AAR code)
AMC	American International Corporation (NYSE symbol) (Delisted)
AMC	American Maritime Cases
AMC	American Mining Congress
AMC	American Mission to the Chinese
AMC	American Mothers Committee
AMC	American Motors Corporation
AMC	American Movers Conference
AMC	American Music Center
AMC	American Music Conference
AMC	Angular Motion Compensator
AMC	Animal Medical Center
AMC	Anti-Malaria Campaign
AMC	Appalachian Mountain Club
AMC	Armament Material Change
AMC	Army Materiel Command
AMC	Army Medical Center
AMC	Army Medical Corps
AMC	Army Missile Command
AMC	Army Mobility Command
AMC	Army Munitions Command
AMC	Art Material Club
AMC	Association of Management Consultants
AMC	Association of Municipal Corporations (British)
AMC	Associative Memory Computer
AMC	Automatic Message Counting
AMC	Automatic Mission Control
AMC	Automatic Mixture Control
AMCA	Advanced Material Concepts Agency (Army)
AMCA	Air Moving and Conditioning Association
AMCA	Alaskan Malamute Club of America
AMCA	American Medical Curling Association
AMCA	American Mosquito Control Association
AMCA	Associated Male Choruses of America
AM & CA	Air Moving and Conditioning Association
AMCB.	Aluminum Manufacturers Credit Bureau

AMCB...... American Medical Center for Burma
AMCB...... Army Materiel Command Board
AMCBW ..... Amalgamated Meat Cutters and Butcher Workmen of North America
AMCC ..... American Mexican Claims Commission (Terminated, 1947)
AMCC ..... Association of Manufacturers of Confectionery and Chocolate
AMCCDO .... Army Materiel Command Catalog Data Office
AMCCOMNET . Air Material Command Communications Network
AMCD ...... Addressograph Multigraph Copier Duplicator
AMCEA...... Advertising Media Credit Executives Association
AMCEC...... Allied Military Communications Electronics Committee
AMCFASC .... Army Materiel Command Facilities and Services Center
AMCHQ ..... Air Materiel Command (later, Air Force Logistics Command) Headquarters
AMCL...... Air Materiel Command (later, Air Force Logistics Command) Letter
AMCLO ..... Air Materiel Command (later, Air Force Logistics Command) Logistics Office(r)
AMCM ...... Air Materiel Command (later, Air Force Logistics Command) Manual
AMCMFO .... Air Materiel Command (later, Air Force Logistics Command) Missile Field Office
AMCMS ..... Airborne Mine Countermeasure System
AMCOA ..... AiResearch Manufacturing Company of Arizona
AMCODE .... AMEX Computerized Order Display and Execution System (American Stock Exchange)
AMCOM ..... AMEX (American Stock Exchange) Communications (Network)
AMCON ..... American Consul
AMCONREPO.. American Consular Reporting Officer
AMCR...... Air Materiel Command Regulations
AMCROSS .... American Red Cross
AMCS...... Airborne Missile Control System
AMCS...... Aircraft Mounted Control System
AMCS ...... Army Mobilization Capabilities Study
AMCS...... Association of Military Colleges and Schools
AMCSA...... Army Materiel Command Support Activity
AMCSS...... Airborne Missile Control Subsystem
AMCTSO..... Air Materiel Command Test Site Office
AMD .... Administrative and Miscellaneous Duties (RAF)
AMD ...... Advance Manufacturing Directive
AMD ...... Aero-Mechanics Department (Navy)
AMD ...... Aerospace Medical Division (Air Force)
AMD ...... Air Movement Data (Air Force)
AMD ...... Air Movement Designator (Army)
AMD ...... Approved Marine Devices Co.
AMD ...... Army Medical Department
AMD ...... Automated Maintenance Depot
AMD ...... Automatic Map Display
AMD ...... Auxiliary Memory Drum
AMDA ...... Advances for Mutual Defense Assistance
AMDA ...... Airline Medical Directors Association
AMDAG ..... American Decartelization Agency (Post-World War II)
AMDC ...... Army Missile Development Center
AMDEL...... Australian Mineral Development Laboratory
AMDF....... Army Master Data File
AMDG ...... Ad Majorem Dei Gloriam (To the Greater Glory of God)
AMDI ...... Automatic Miss Distance Indicator
AMDLEVAC ... Aeromedical Evacuation (Later, AME)
AMDOC ..... American Doctors (An organization)
AMDP...... Aircraft Maintenance Delayed for Parts (Military)
AMDR ...... Advance Missile Deviation Report
AMDS ...... Association of Military Dental Surgeons
AMDSB...... Amplitude Modulation, Double Sideband
AMDT....... Active Maintenance Down Time
AME ...... Accord Monetaire Europeen
AME ...... Aerospace Materials Information
AME...... Admiralty Mining Establishment (British)
AME ...... Advanced Master of Education
AME...... Aeromedical Evacuation
AME........ African Methodist Episcopal (Church)
AME........ Ametek, Inc. (NYSE symbol)
AME........ Angle Measuring Equipment
AME........ Anti-Multipath Equipment
AME........ Associated Memory Equipment
AME........ Aviation Medical Examiner
AMEA...... Apparel Manufacturing Executives Association
AMEC....... Airframe Manufacturing Equipment Committee
AMECOS..... Automatic Measuring Computing and Sorting
AME/COTAR .. Angle Measuring Equipment, Correlation Tracking and Ranging
AMEDD ..... Army Medical Department
AMEDS...... Army Medical Service
AMEG ...... Association for Measurement and Evaluation in Guidance
AMEL...... Aero-Medical Equipment Laboratory
AMEMB...... American Embassy
AMEMIC..... Association of Mill and Elevator Mutual Insurance Companies
AMER....... America(n)

AMER ...... American Middle East Relief
AMERADC .... Army Mobility Equipment Research & Development Center
AMERICAL.... Americans in New Caledonia (Army's 23rd infantry; acronym used as name of division. Active in World War II, disbanded 1945; reactivated 1967-71)
AMERIND .... American Indian
AMEROSE .... American Committee of OSE
AMERWAX.... American Wax Importers and Refiners Association
AMES ...... Aeromedical Evacuation System
AMES....... Air Ministry Experimental Station
AMES....... Association of Marine Engineering Schools (British)
AMET ...... Africa – Middle East Theater (World War II)
AMETA ..... Army Management Engineering Training Agency
AMEX ...... American Express Company
AMEX ...... American Stock Exchange
AMEXCO .... American Express Company
AMEZ....... African Methodist Episcopal Zion (Church)
AMF .... Air Mail Facility (Post Office)
AMF........ Air Mail Field
AMF .... Air Materiel Force
AMF ...... Allied Mobile Force (NATO)
AMF........ American Messianic Fellowship
AMF........ AMF, Inc. (Formerly, American Machine & Foundry Company) (NYSE symbol)
AMF....... Annual Material Forecast (Military)
AMF ...... Army Management Fund
AMFA ...... Aircraft Mechanics Fraternal Association
AMFA....... Association Medicale Franco-Americaine
AMF(A) ..... Allied Mobile Force (Air) (NATO)
AMFEA...... Air Materiel Force, European Area
AMFFA...... American Medical Fly Fishing Association
AMFGC ..... Association of Midwest Fish and Game Commissioners
AMFIE ...... Association of Mutual Fire Insurance Engineers
AMFIS ...... Automatic Microfilm Information System
AMF(L) ..... Allied Mobile Force (Land) (NATO)
AMFPA...... Air Materiel Force, Pacific Area
AMFPS ...... Association of Mutual Fund Plan Sponsors
AMFUR...... Amplified Failure or Unsatisfactory Report
AMG .... Aircraft Machine Gunner
AMG ...... Albertus Magnus Guild
AMG ...... Allied Military Government (of occupied territory) (Post-World War II)
AMG ...... American Military Government
AMG ...... American Mission to Greeks
AMG ...... Amplitude Modulation Generator
AMG ...... Applied Mathematics Group
AMG ...... Automatic Magnetic Guidance
AMGOT ..... Allied Military Government of Occupied Territory
AMGP ...... Association of Medical Group Psychoanalysts
AMGRA ..... American Milk Goat Record Association
AMGS ...... Acceleration Monitoring Guidance System
AMH ...... Alaska Military Highway
AMH ...... Association of Marian Helpers
AMHA ...... American Motor Hotel Association
AMHC ...... Association of Mental Hospital Chaplains
AMHF ...... American Mental Health Foundation
AMHS....... American Material Handling Society
AMHS....... Association of Methodist Historical Societies
AMHT....... Automated Multiphasic Health Testing
AMI........ Advanced Manned Interceptor (US Air Force Artillery Spotting Division Interceptor)
AMI........ Aerospace Materials Information
AMI........ Air Mileage Indicator (Navigation)
AMI........ Aircraft Multiplex Intercommunications
AMI........ American Maritime Institute (Later, Society for Maritime History)
AMI........ American Meat Institute
AMI........ American Medical International (NYSE symbol)
AMI........ American Military Institute
AMI........ American Museum of Immigration
AMI........ American Mushroom Institute
AMI........ Apogee Motor Igniter
AMI........ Association of Medical Illustrators
AMIA ...... American Metal Importers Association
AMIA....... American Mutual Insurance Alliance
AMIA....... Angular Magnetic-Hydrodynamic Integrating Accelerometer
AMIADB ..... Army Member, Inter-American Defense Board
AMIC....... Aerospace Materials Information Center (Air Force)
AMICA...... Automobile Mutual Insurance Company of America
AMICE ...... Associate Member of the Institution of Civil Engineers (British)
AMICH...... American Marine Insurance Clearing House
AMICOM .... Army Missile Command
AMIE ...... Association of Mutual Insurance Engineers

AMIEE . . . . . . Associate Member of the Institution of Electrical Engineers (British)
AMIF . . . . American Marine Insurance Forum
AMIF . . . . American Meat Institute Foundation
AMIGOS . . . . . Americans Mutually Interested in Giving Others a Start (An organization)
AMIH . . . . Association for Middle-Income Housing
AMIMechE . . . . Associate Member of the Institution of Mechanical Engineers
AMIMinE . . . . Associate Member of the Institution of Mining Engineers (British)
AMIN . . . . Advertising and Marketing International Network
AMINCO . . . . . American Instrument Company
AMIND . . . . . American Indian
AMInstCE . . . . Associate Member of the Institution of Civil Engineers (Later, AMICE) (British)
AMInstT . . . . . Associate Member of the Institute of Transport (British)
AMINTAPHIL . . American Section of the International Association for Philosophy of Law and Social Philosophy
AMIS . . . . Advanced Management Information Service (or System) (Air Force)
AMIS . . . . Air Movements Information Section
AMIS . . . . Aircraft Movement Information Service (Air Force)
AMIS . . . . Aircraft Multiplex Intercommunications System
AMIS . . . . Amistad Recreation Area (National Park Service designation)
AMIS . . . . Army Information System
AMISIBR . . . . . American Marine Insurance Syndicate for Insurance of Builder's Risks
AMITA . . . . . . American-Italian Women of Achievement
AMJ . . . . Assemblee Mondiale de la Jeunesse
AMKO . . . . . . American Mothers of Korean Orphans
AML . . . . Aberdeen Marine Laboratory
AML . . . . Acute Myeloblastic Leukemia (Medicine)
AML . . . . Acute Myelocytic Leukemia (Medicine)
AML . . . . Admiralty Materials Laboratory (British)
AML . . . . Aero Medical Laboratory
AML . . . . Aeronautical Materials Laboratory
AML . . . . Allied Military Liaison (Balkans) (World War II)
AML . . . . American Mail Line
AML . . . . American Meteorite Laboratory
AML . . . . Application Module Library (IBM)
AML . . . . Applied Mathematics Laboratory
AML . . . . Approved Materials List (NASA)
AML . . . . Armee-Munitionslager (Army ammunition depot) (German military – World War II)
AML . . . . Army Medical Library (Became Armed Forces Medical Library, 1952; later, NLM)
AML . . . . Automatic Machine Loading
AML . . . . Automatic Magazine Loading
AML . . . . Auxiliary Mine Layer
AML . . . . Aviation Material Laboratories (Army)
AMLC . . . . . . Aerospace Medical Laboratory (Clinical) (Air Force)
AMLG . . . . . . Allied Military Headquarters, Greece
AMLI . . . . Americans for a Music Library in Israel
AMLLV . . . . . . Advanced Multipurpose Large Launch Vehicle
AMLO . . . . . . Aeromedical Liaison Office(r) (Air Force)
AMLP . . . . . . Amplitude Modulation Link Program
AMLS . . . . . . Master of Arts in Library Science
AMLSU . . . . . . Air Ministry Local Staff Union (Singapore)
AMM . . . . . . Adaptive Mathematical Model
AMM . . . . . . Air-Mining Mission (Military)
AMM . . . . . . American Metal Climax, Inc. (NYSE symbol; later AMX)
AMM . . . . . . Anomalous Magnetic Moment
AMM . . . . . . Antimissile Missile (Air Force)
AMM . . . . . . Associated Millinery Men
AMM . . . . . . Association Medicale Mondiale
AMM . . . . . . Aviation Machinist's Mate (Navy rating)
AMM . . . . . . Master of Mechanic Arts
AMMA . . . . . American Millinery Manufacturers Association
AMMA . . . . . American Museum of Marine Archaeology
AMMAC . . . . Aviation Machinist's Mate, Combat Aircrewman (Navy rating)
AMMC . . . . . Aviation Machinist's Mate, Carburetor Mechanic (Navy rating)
AMMF . . . . . Aviation Machinist's Mate, Flight Engineer (Navy rating)
AMMH . . . . . Aviation Machinist's Mate, Hydraulic Mechanic (Navy rating)
AMMI . . . . . . American Merchant Marine Institute
AMMI . . . . . . Aviation Machinist's Mate, Instrument Mechanic (Navy rating)
AMMIC . . . . . Armament Maintenance Management Information Center (Navy)
AMMIP . . . . . Aviation Materiel Management Improvement Program (Military)
AMMIS . . . . . Aircraft Maintenance Manpower Information System (Air Force)
AMMISCA . . . American Military Mission to China
AMMLA . . . . American Merchant Marine Library Association
AMMO . . . . . Ammunition
AMMO . . . . . . Army Mobile Missile Operation
AMMP . . . . . Advanced Manned Missions Program
AMMP . . . . . Approved Modernization Maintenance Program
AMMP . . . . . Aviation Machinist's Mate, Propeller Mechanic (Navy rating)

AMMR . . . . . Advanced Multimission RADAR
AMMR . . . . . Aircraft Maintenance Manpower Requirement
AMMRC . . . . . Army Materials and Mechanics Research Center
AMMRL . . . . . Aircraft Maintenance Material Readiness List (Navy)
AMMSDO . . . . Antimissile Missile and Space Defense Office
AMMT . . . . . . Aviation Machinist's Mate, Turret Mechanic (Navy rating)
AMMTR . . . . . Antimissile Missile Test Range (Military)
AMN . . . . Airman
AMN . . . . Ameron, Inc. (NYSE symbol)
AMN . . . . Atomic Mass Number
AMND . . . . . . Amend(ment)
AMNH . . . . . American Museum of Natural History
AMNIP . . . . . Adaptive Man-Machine Nonarithmetic Information Processing (Documentation)
AMNL . . . . . . Army Medical Nutrition Laboratory
AmnM . . . . . . Airman's Medal
AMO . . . . Accredited Management Organization (Designation given by Institute of Real Estate Management)
AMO . . . . Advance Material Order
AMO . . . . Air Ministry Order (British)
AMO . . . . Aircraft Material Officer
AMO . . . . Alternate Molecular Orbital
AMO . . . . American Motors Corporation (NYSE symbol) (Wall Street slang name: "Ammo")
AMO . . . . Assistant Medical Officer
AMOAP . . . . . Associated Marine Officers Association of the Philippines
AMOB . . . . . . Ancient Mystic Order of Bagmen of Bagdad Imperial Guild
AMOCC . . . . . American Mission for Opening Closed Churches
AMOCO . . . . American Oil Company
AMOCOM . . . Army Mobility Command
AMORC . . . . . Ancient Mystical Order Rosae Crucis (Rosicrucian Order)
AMOS . . . . . . Acoustic, Meteorological & Oceanographic Survey
AMOS . . . . . Additionally Awarded Military Occupational Specialty
AMOS . . . . . Aerospace Maintenance and Operational Status
AMOS . . . . . . Ancient Mystic Order of Samaritans
AMOS . . . . . . ARPA (Advanced Research Projects Agency) Mid-Course Optical Observatory
AMOS . . . . . Associative Memory Organizing System
AMOS . . . . . . Automatic Meteorological Observation (or Observing) Station (or System)
AMP . . . . Acid Mucopolysaccharides
AMP . . . . Acquisition Management Plan (Navy)
AMP . . . . Adaptation Mathematical Processor
AMP . . . . Add, Multi-Precision
AMP . . . . . . Additional Military Production
AMP . . . . Adenosinemonophosphate (Adenylic acid)
AMP . . . . Advanced Manned Penetrator
AMP . . . . Advanced Minuteman Platform
AMP . . . . Air Mail Pioneers
AMP . . . . Aircraft-Missile Project
AMP . . . . American Melting Point
AMP . . . . Ammonium Molybdophosphate
AMP . . . . AMP Incorporated (NYSE symbol)
AMP . . . . Ampere
AMP . . . . Another Mother for Peace (Antiwar organization) (Also, AM/P)
AMP . . . . Applied Mathematics Panel (of NDRC) (World War II)
AMP . . . . Area Mail Processing (US Postal Service)
AMP . . . . Army Materiel Plan
AMP . . . . Army Mine Planter
AMP . . . . Aseptic Maintenance by Pressurization (NASA)
AMP . . . . Australian Mutual Provident Society (Insurance)
AMP . . . . Avalanche Mode Photodiode
AMP . . . . . . Aviation Modernization Program
AM/P . . . . Another Mother for Peace (Antiwar organization) (Also, AMP)
AMPA . . . . . . American Manganese Producers Association
AMPA . . . . . . Associated Motion Picture Advertisers
AMPA . . . . . . Azimuth Mark Pulse Amplifier
AMPAC . . . . . American Medical Political Action Committee
AMPAS . . . . . Academy of Motion Picture Arts and Sciences
AMPC . . . . . . Automatic Message Processing Center
AMPC . . . . . . Auxiliary Military Pioneer Corps (British)
AMPCO . . . . Associated Missile Products Corporation
AMPD . . . . . . Army Mobilization Program Directive
AMPERE . . . . . APL Management Planning and Engineering Resources Evaluation (Navy)
AMPERE . . . . . Atomes et Molecules par Etudes Radio-Electriques (Switzerland)
AMPFTA . . . . American Military Precision Flying Teams Association
AMPFUR . . . . Amplifying Failure, Unsatisfactory or Removal Report
AMPH . . . . . . Amphibian
AMPH . . . . . . Amphibious
AMPH . . . . . . Association of Management in Public Health
Amphetamine . . Alpha-methyl-phen-ethyl-amine
AMPHFORLANT . . Amphibious Force, Atlantic

AMPHFORMED .. Amphibious Force, Mediterranean
AMPHFORPAC .. Amphibious Force, Pacific
AMPHIB ..... Amphibious
AMPHIBEX.... Amphibious Exercise (Navy; Marine Corps)
AMPHIBFOR .. Amphibious Forces
AMPHIBFORCENPAC .. Amphibious Forces, Central Pacific
AMPIC ...... Atomic and Molecular Processes Information Center (ORNL)
AMPLAS .... Apparatus Mounted in Plastic
AMPP .... Arctic Meteorology Photographic Probe
AMPP .... Association of Motion Picture Producers
AMPPD ...... Army Mobilization Planning and Programing Directive
AMPPGD..... Army Mobilization Planning and Programing Guidance Document
AMPR .... Aeronautical Manufacturers Planning Report
AMPR .... Aircraft Manufacturer's Progress Report
AMPR .... Automatic Manifold Pressure Regulator (Aircraft)
AMPS .... Accrued Military Pay System
AMPS .... Acid Mucopolysaccharide
AMPS .... Advanced Manned Penetrator System
AMPS .... Amazing Magic Pivot Swing (Training device for baseball batter's rear foot)
AMPS .... American Metered Postage Society
AMPS .... Army Mine Planter Service
AMPS .... Army Motion Picture Service
AMPS .... Associated Music Publishers (Musical slang)
AMPS .... Automatic Message Processing System (USAERDL)
AMPSS ..... Advanced Manned Penetrator Strike System
AMPSS ..... Advanced Manned Precision Strike System (Proposed Air Force plane)
AMQ ...... American Medical Qualification (British)
AMQ ...... Apparent Molar Quantity
AMR....... Abnormal Mission Routine
AMR....... Activity Metabolic Rate
AMR ...... Advance Material Request
AMR ...... Aerospace Medical Research
AMR....... Air Movement Recorder
AMR....... Airborne Magnetic Recorder
AMR....... Airman Military Record (Air Force)
AMR....... Altitude Marking RADAR
AMR....... American Airlines, Inc. (NYSE symbol)
AMR....... Annee Mondiale du Refugie
AMR....... Applied Mechanics Reviews
AMR....... Arcata & Mad River R. R. (AAR code)
AMR....... Atlantic Missile Range (Later, Eastern Test Range)
AMR....... Automatic Message Recording (or Registering)
AM(R)...... Master of Arts in Research
AMRA...... American Metal Repair Association (Defunct)
AMRA ..... Army Materials Research Agency
AMRAC ..... Anti-Missile Research Advisory Council
AMRAD...... Air Munitions Requirements and Developments Committee (Military)
AMRAD ..... ARPA (Advanced Research Projects Agency) Measurements RADAR (Raytheon)
AMRC ..... Advanced Metals Research Corporation
AMRC ..... Army Mathematics Research Center (Madison, Wisconsin)
AMRC...... Army Mobility Research Center
AMRC...... Association of Medical Record Consultants
AMRC...... Automotive Market Research Council
AMRCA..... American Miniature Racing Car Association
AMRD...... Army Missile and Rocket Directorate
AMRDC..... Association of Medical Rehabilitation Directors and Coordinators
AMR & DL.... Air Mobility Research & Development Laboratory (Army) (Also, USAMR & DL)
AMRD-NASC.. Army Missile and Rockets Directorate -- NATO Supply Center
AMREP ...... Aircraft/Missile Maintenance - Production Compression Report
AMRF....... Amended Route of Flight (Aviation)
AMRI .... Association of Missile and Rocket Industries
AMRL .... Aerospace Medical Research Laboratory (Air Force)
AMRL ...... Army Medical Research Laboratory
AMRNL ..... Army Medical Research & Nutrition Laboratory
AMROO ..... Atlantic Missile Range (Later, Eastern Test Range) Operations Office
AMRPD ...... Applied Manufacturing Research and Process Development
AMRV...... Astronaut Maneuvering Research Vehicle (NASA)
AMS....... Administrative Management Society
AMS .... Advanced Meteorological System
AMS....... Advanced Minuteman System
AMS....... Advanced Missile System
AMS....... Aeronautical Material Specification
AMS....... Aeronautical Mobile Service
AMS....... Aerospace Material Specification
AMS....... Agricultural Marketing Service (Formerly, CMS) (Department of Agriculture)
AMS....... Air Management Station
AMS....... Air Mass

AMS........ Air Missile System
AMS........ Airborne Maintenance System
AMS........ Alarm Monitoring System
AMS........ Altitude Measurement System
AMS........ American Magnolia Society
AMS........ American Mathematical Society
AMS........ American Meteor Society
AMS........ American Meteorological Society
AMS........ American Microchemical Society
AMS........ American Microscopical Society
AMS........ American Mohammedan Society (Later, Moslem Mosque, Inc.)
AMS........ American Montessori Society
AMS........ American Museum of Safety
AMS........ American Musicological Society
AMS........ Apollo Mission Simulator
AMS........ Arbetsmarknadsstyrelsen (Labor-Market Agency) (Sweden)
AMS .... Army Management Structure
AMS........ Army Map Service (Later, Army Topographic Command)
AMS........ Army Medical Service(s) (British)
AMS........ Artillery and Missile School (Army)
AMS........ Assets Management System
AMS........ Association of Messenger Services
AMS........ Association of Museum Stores
AMS........ Authority for Material Substitution
AMS........ Automatic Monitoring System (Aviation)
AMS........ Autopilot Mode Selector
AMS........ Aviation Structural Mechanic (Navy)
AMS........ Avionics Maintenance Shop
AMS........ Motor Minesweeper (Navy symbol)
AMSA ...... Advanced Manned Strategic Aircraft (Air Force)
AMSA ..... Advanced Mutual Security Act
AMSA ...... American Meat Science Association
AMSA...... American Metal Stamping Association
AMSA...... Anterior Middle Suprasylvian Association (Area of cat cortex)
AMSA...... Australian Marine Sciences Association
AMSAA...... Army Materiel Systems Analysis Agency
AMSAC..... American Society of African Culture
AMSAM..... Antimissile Surface-to-Air Missile
AMSAS ..... Advanced Manned Strategic Aircraft
AMSAT ...... Radio Amateur Satellite Corp.
AMSC...... Allied Military Staff Conference (Quebec, Yalta, etc.) (World War II)
AMSC....... American Miniature Schnauzer Club
AMSC....... Army Medical Specialist Corps
AMSC ..... Army Mobility Support Center
AMSCO .... American Mineral Spirits Company
AMSCO .... Army Medical Supply Control Officer
AMSE ...... Aircraft Maintenance Support Equipment
AmSECT .... American Society of Extra-Corporeal Technology
AMSEF ...... Anti-Mine-Sweeping Explosive Float
AMSGS ..... Army Medical Service Graduate School
AMSI .... Atlantic Merchant Shipping Instructions
AMSL .... Above Mean Sea Level (Navigation)
AMSL .... Applied Mathematics and Statistics Laboratory (Stanford University)
AMSMH ..... Association of Medical Superintendents of Mental Hospitals
AMSO ...... Ammunition Shipment Order (Army)
AMSOC ..... American Miscellaneous Society
AMSP ...... Allied Military Security Publication
AMSP .... Army Master Study Program
AMSq ...... Avionics Maintenance Squadron (Air Force)
AMSRDC .... Army Medical Service Research and Development Command
AMSS ...... Advanced Manned Space Simulator
AMSS ...... Advanced Meteorological Sounding System
AMSS ...... American Milking Shorthorn Society
AMSS ...... Army Medical Service School
AMSS ...... Automatic Master Sequence Selector
AMSSB ...... Amplitude Modulation, Single-Sideband
AMSTAN .... American Radiator and Standard Sanitary Corp.
AMSTS ...... Automatic Multiparameter Semiconductor Test Set
AMSUS ..... Association of Military Surgeons of the United States
AMSYA..... American Medical Sailing and Yachting Association
AMT........ Acme-Cleveland Corp. (NYSE symbol)
AMT........ Active Maintenance Time
AMT........ Advanced Manufacturing Technology
AMT........ Aerial Mail Terminal
AMT........ Alkali-Metal Turbine
AMT........ American Medical Technologists
AMT........ Amount
AMT........ Amplitude Modulated Transmitter
AMT........ Angular Mapping Transformation (Data processing)
AMT........ Apogee Motor Timer
AMT .... Associate in Mechanical Technology

AMT . . . . Associate in Medical Technology
AMT. . . . . . . Astrograph Mean Time (Navigation)
AMT. . . . . . . Automatic Moon Tracking
AMT. . . . . . . Automatic Motor Tester
AMT. . . . . . . Available Machine Time
AMT . . . . . . Master of Arts for Teachers
AMT . . . . . . Master of Arts in Teaching
AM(T). . . . . . Master of Arts in Teaching
AM in T . . . . . Master of Arts in Teaching
AMTA . . . . . . Airborne Moving Target Attack
AMTA. . . . . . . American Massage and Therapy Association
AMTA. . . . . . . American Medical Tennis Association
AMTANK . . . . Amphibious Tank (Military)
AMTB . . . . . Anti-Motor Torpedo Boat
AMTC. . . . . . Air Material Armament Test Center
AMTC. . . . . . American Manchester Terrier Club
AMTC . . . . . . Army Missile Test Center
AMTCL . . . . . Association for Machine Translation and Computational Linguistics (Later,
                 Association for Computational Linguistics)
AMTDA. . . . . American Machine Tool Distributors Association
AMTEA . . . . . American Machine Tool Export Associates
AMTF . . . . . . Air Mobile Task Force
AMTI . . . . . . Airborne Moving Target Indicator (Air Force)
AMTIDE . . . . . Aircraft Multipurpose Test Inspection & Diagnostic Equipment
AMTK . . . . . . Amphibious Tank
AMTPI. . . . . . . Associate Member of the Town Planning Institute (British)
AMTRAC . . . . Amphibious Tractor (Amphibian Tractor)
Amtrak . . . . . . American Track (National Railroad Passenger Corporation;
                 formerly, Railpax)
AMTRAN . . . . Automatic Mathematical Translator (NASA)
AMU . . . . . . Air Mileage Unit (Navigation)
AMU . . . . . . Air Mission Unit (Air Force)
AMU . . . . . . American Malacological Union
AMU . . . . . . Army Marksmanship Unit
AMU . . . . . . Army Medical Unit
AMU . . . . . . Associated Midwestern Universities, Inc.
AMU . . . . . . Astronaut Maneuvering Unit (Gemini) (NASA)
AMU . . . . . . Atomic Mass Unit
AMU . . . . . . Auxiliary Memory Unit
AMUCOM . . . . Army Munition Command
AMUNC . . . . . Army Munitions Command
AMURT . . . . . . Ananda Marga Universal Relief Team (India)
AMUUS . . . . . Association of Marine Underwriters of the United States
AMV. . . . . . . Alfalfa Mosaic Virus
AMV . . . . . . Association Mondiale Veterinaire
AMV . . . . . . Astable Multi-Vibrator
AMV . . . . . . Avian Myeloblastosis Virus
AMVER. . . . . Atlantic Merchant Vessel Report
AMVER. . . . . Automated Merchant Vessel Report (Coast Guard)
AMVERS . . . . Atlantic Merchant Vessel Report System
AMVETS . . . . American Veterans of World War II
AMVM . . . . . Administrative Motor Vehicle Management
AMW . . . . . . Actual Measurement Weight (Railroad)
AMW . . . . . . Antimateriel Warhead
AMW . . . . . . Association of Married Women
AMWA . . . . . American Medical Women's Association
AMWA . . . . . American Medical Writers' Association
AMWD . . . . . Advanced Millimeter Wave Device
AMWG . . . . . Academy of Master Wine Growers
AMWH . . . . . Antimateriel Warhead
AMX . . . . . . American Metal Climax, Inc. (NYSE symbol)
AMX . . . . . . Automatic Message Exchange
AMZ . . . . . . American Seating Company (NYSE symbol)
AN. . . . . Above-Named
AN . . . . Acid Number
AN . . . . Acide Nucléique (French) (Medicine)
AN . . . . Acrylonitrile (Chemical)
AN . . . . Advanced Navigator (Air Force)
AN . . . . Aerodynamics Note
AN . . . . Air Force-Navy
AN . . . . Air Navigation
AN . . . . Airco, Inc. (Formerly, Air Reduction Company, Inc.) (NYSE symbol)
AN . . . . Alphanumeric
AN . . . . Ammonium Nitrate
AN . . . . Anglo-Norman
AN . . . . Apalachicola Northern R. R. (AAR code)
AN . . . . Army and Navy
AN . . . . Army-Navy Joint Type Ordnance
AN . . . . Army/Navy Number
AN . . . . Arrival Notice (Shipping)
AN . . . . Associate in Nursing

AN . . . . Atomic Number
AN . . . . Net Laying Ship (Navy symbol)
A-N. . . . . . . Anglo-Norman
A/N. . . . . . . Acidic and Neutral (Chemical analysis)
A/N . . . . . . Allied/Neutral (Military)
A/N. . . . . . . Army/Navy Number
ANA . . . . . . Aerojet Network Analyzer
ANA . . . . . . Air Force-Navy Aeronautical
ANA . . . . . . American Naprapathic Association
ANA . . . . . . American Nature Association
ANA . . . . . . American Neurological Association
ANA . . . . . . American Newspaper Association
ANA . . . . . . American Numismatic Association
ANA . . . . . . American Nurses' Association
ANA . . . . . . Antibodies to Nuclear Antigen (Immunology)
ANA . . . . . . Army-Navy Aeronautical
ANA . . . . . . Association of National Advertisers
ANA . . . . . . Australian National Airways
ANA . . . . . . Automatic Network Analyzer
ANACDUTRA . . Annual Active Duty for Training (Army)
ANACOM . . . . Analog Computer
ANAD . . . . . Anniston Army Depot
ANADP . . . . . Association of North American Directory Publishers
ANAF. . . . . . Army-Navy-Air Force
ANAFJ . . . . . Army-Navy-Air Force Journal (A publication)
ANALIT . . . . . Analysis of Automatic Line Insulation Test (Bell System)
ANAPO . . . . . Alianza Nacional Popular (Colombian political party)
ANARC . . . . . Association of North American Radio Clubs
ANARE . . . . . Australian National Antarctic Research Expeditions
ANATRAN . . . Analog Translator (Data processing)
ANAV . . . . . . Area Navigation
ANB . . . . . . Army-Navy-British
ANBS . . . . . Armed Nuclear Bombardment Satellite
ANC . . . . . . Academy of the New Church
ANC . . . . . . African National Congress (South Africa; Northern Rhodesia)
ANC. . . . . . . Air Force-Navy-Civil
ANC . . . . . . Air Navigation Conference
ANC . . . . . . Airborne Navigation Computer
ANC . . . . . . All Numbers Calling (Telephone)
ANC . . . . . . American National Cowbelles
ANC . . . . . . American News Company (NYSE symbol) (Delisted)
ANC . . . . . . Ancorp National Services, Inc. (NYSE symbol)
ANC . . . . . . Arlington National Cemetery
ANC . . . . . . Armee Nationale Congolaise (Congolese National Army)
ANC . . . . . . Army-Navy-Commerce
ANC . . . . . . Army Nurse Corps
ANCA . . . . . Allied Naval Communications Agency
ANCA . . . . . American National Cattlemen's Association
ANCA. . . . . . Armenian National Council of America
ANCAM . . . . Association of Newspaper Classified Advertising Managers
ANCE. . . . . . Assemblee des Nations Captives d'Europe
ANCHA . . . . . American National Committee to Aid Homeless Armenians
ANCHEP . . . . American National Council for Health Education of the Public
ANCI . . . . . . Asociacion Nacional de Comerciantes y Industriales
ANCIF . . . . . Automated Nautical Chart Index File (System) (DOD)
ANCLAV . . . . Automatic Navigation Computer for Land and Amphibious Vehicles
ANCOA . . . . . Aerial Nurse Corps of America
ANCOVA . . . . Analysis of Covariance
ANCR. . . . . . Aircraft Not Combat Ready
ANCS. . . . . . Airborne Night Classification System
ANCWA . . . . American Naturalized Citizen Welfare Association
ANCXF . . . . . Allied Naval Commander Expeditionary Forces
ANCYL. . . . . . African National Congress Youth League
AND. . . . . . . Air Force-Navy Design
AND . . . . . . Air Navigation Device
AND . . . . . . Alphanumeric Display
AND . . . . . . Army-Navy Design
ANDB. . . . . . Air Navigation Development Board (Functions absorbed by the FAA)
ANDE. . . . . . Alphanumeric Display Equipment
ANDL . . . . . . Army Nuclear Defense Laboratory
ANDRO . . . . Arma Non-Destructive Readout
ANDS. . . . . . Advanced Navy Display System
ANDUS . . . . . Anglo-Dutch-United States
ANE. . . . . . . Acoustic Noise Environment
ANE. . . . . . . Aeronautical & Navigation Electronics Association
ANE . . . . . . Aerospace and Navigational Electronics
ANEEG. . . . . Army, Navy Electronics Evaluation Group
ANEF. . . . . . American-Nepal Education Foundation
ANERA . . . . . American Near East Refugee Aid (An organization)
ANERAC . . . . Annual Northeast Regional Antipollution Conference
ANEXGOVT . . At No Expense to the Government

ANF........	Air Navigation Facility
ANF........	Allied Nuclear Force
ANF........	American Nurses' Foundation
ANF	Anchored Filament
ANF........	Army News Features
ANF	Atlantic Nuclear Force (NATO)
ANFE......	Aircraft Not Fully Equipped
ANFO	Ammonium Nitrate and Fuel Oil (Explosive)
ANG	Acoustic Noise Generator
ANG	Air National Guard
ANG	Alarm Network Group
ANG	American Natural Gas Company (NYSE symbol)
ANG	American Newspaper Guild
ANG	Applied Naturalist Guild
ANG	Army National Guard (Military)
ANGAU	Australia-New Guinea Administrative Unit (World War II)
ANGELL.....	Acronymic Nonsense Game to Eliminate Lack of Loot
ANGELL.....	Associated Nursery Guides Emphatically Lacking in Leisure
ANGLICO....	Air and Naval Gunfire Liaison Company (Military)
ANGPC	Air National Guard Policy Council
ANGUS	Air National Guard of the United States
ANHA	American Nursing Home Association
ANHS	American Natural Hygiene Society
ANI	Agencia Nacionale de Informacoes (National Information Agency) (Portugal)
ANI	American National Insurance Company
ANI	Atmosphere Normale Internationale (International Normal Atmosphere)
ANI	Automatic Number Identification (Telephone)
ANICA	Associazione Nazionale Industrie Cinematografiche ed Affini
ANICO......	American National Insurance Company
ANIM	Association of Nuclear Instrument Manufacturers
ANIP	Army-Navy Instrumentation Program
ANIRC	Annual National Information Retrieval Colloquium
ANITA	A New Inspiration to Arithmetic
ANJSB	Army-Navy Joint Specifications Board
ANK	Alphanumeric Keyboard (Data processing)
ANK	American Enka Corporation (NYSE symbol) (Delisted)
ANKB.......	Alphanumeric Keyboard (Data processing)
ANL.......	Allen Industries, Inc. (NYSE symbol) (Delisted)
ANL	Annoyance Level (Aircraft noise)
ANL	Argonne National Laboratory (AEC)
ANL	Army Natick Laboratory
ANL	Automatic Noise Limiter (Electronics)
ANL	Net Laying Ship (Navy symbol)
ANL ID	Argonne National Laboratory, Idaho Division
ANLSC	Additive Noise Linear Sequential Circuit
ANMB	Army-Navy Munitions Board (Later, Munitions Board)
ANMC	Assistant Navy Mail Clerk
ANMCC	Alternate National Military Command Center
ANNA	Army, Navy, NASA, Air Force Geodetic Satellite
ANO	Above Named Officer (Army orders)
ANO	Air Navigation Office
ANO	Air Navigation Order
ANO	Alphanumeric Output (Data processing)
ANO	Austin, Nichols & Company, Inc. (NYSE symbol) (Delisted)
ANORS......	Anticipated Not Operationally Ready, Supply
ANOV	Analysis of Variance (Also, ANOVA)
ANOVA	Analysis of Variance (Also, ANOV)
ANP.......	Aircraft Nuclear Power
ANP	Aircraft Nuclear-Powered Program (Air Force)
ANP.......	Aircraft Nuclear Propulsion
ANPA	American Newspaper Publishers Association
ANPB	Army-Navy Petroleum Board
ANPC	Air-Nitrogen Pressurization Control
ANPC	American Nail Producers Council
ANPD	Aircraft Nuclear Propulsion Department (Navy)
ANPI	Associazione Nazionale Partigiani d'Italia
ANPM	African Nationalist Pioneer Movement
ANPO	Aircraft Nuclear Propulsion Office (of AEC) (Defunct)
ANPOD	Antenna Positioning Device
ANPP	Aircraft Nuclear Propulsion Program
ANPP	Army Nuclear Power Program
ANPP	Association of Negro Press Photographers
ANPPF	Aircraft Nuclear Power Plant Facility
ANPPPC	Army-Navy Petroleum Pool, Pacific Coast
ANPT	Aeronautical National Taper Pipe Threads
ANR.......	Angelina & Neches River R. R. (AAR code)
ANRA	Air Navigation Radio Aids
ANRAC......	Aids Navigation Radio Control (Military)
ANRC	American National Red Cross
ANRC.......	Animal Nutrition Research Council

ANRT	Association Nationale de la Recherche Technique (France)
ANS........	Active Network Synthesis
ANS........	Airborne Navigation Sensor
ANS........	American Name Society
ANS........	American Newcomen Society
ANS........	American Nuclear Society
ANS........	American Numismatic Society
ANS........	American Nutrition Society
ANS........	Answer
ANS........	Army News Service
ANS........	Army Newspaper Service (Military)
ANS........	Army Nursing Service (British)
ANS	Astronomical Netherlands Satellite
ANS	Astronomical Satellite
ANS........	Autograph Note Signal
ANS........	Autograph Note Signed
ANS........	Automatic Navigation System
ANS	Autonomic Nervous System (Medicine)
ANS........	Autonomous Navigation System
ANSA.......	Agenzia Nazionale Stampa Associata (Associated National Press Agency) (Italy)
ANSA.......	Aminonaphtholsulfonic Acid (Organic chemistry)
ANSA.......	Automatic New Structure Alert (Chemistry)
ANSAM	Anti-Missile Surface to Air Missile
ANSC......	American Nuclear Science Corporation
ANSC	Army and Navy Staff College (Redesignated National War College, 1946)
ANSC.......	Autonomous Navigation System Concept
ANSCOL	Army and Navy Staff College (See ANSC)
ANSCR	Alphanumeric System for Classification of Recordings
ANSER	Analytic Services, Inc.
ANSETT	Ansett Airways Pty., Ltd.
ANSI	American National Standards Institute (Formerly, ASA and USASI)
ANSIA	Army-Navy Shipping Information Agency
ANSIC	Aerospace Nuclear Safety Information Center
ANSO	Assistant Naval Stores Officer
ANSP	Academy of Natural Science, Philadelphia
ANSR	Advanced Naval System Requirements
ANSS......	American Nature Study Society
ANSS	Associate of the Normal School of Science
ANSW	Anti-Nuclear Submarine Warfare (Navy)
ANT........	Antenna
ANT	Antenna Noise Temperature
ANT	A. N. Tupolev (Initialism used as designation for Russian aircraft designed by Tupolev)
ANTA......	American National Theatre and Academy
ANTAC	Air Navigation and Tactical Control
ANTACCS	Advanced Navy Tactical Command and Control System
ANTC.......	Air Navigation Traffic Control
ANTCOMDUSARCARIB ..	Antilles Command, United States Army Caribbean
ANTI	Antietam National Battlefield Site
ANTILOG	Antilogarithm
ANTOR......	Assembly of National Tourist Office Representatives in New York
ANTS	Advanced Naval Training School
ANTS	Andover Newton Theological School
ANTS	Automatic Nitrogen Transfer System
ANTU	Air Navigation Training Unit
ANTU.......	Alpha-Naphthylthiourea (Organic chemistry)
ANTUF	All-Nigeria Trade Union Federation
ANU	Airframe Nose Up
ANU	Army and Navy Union, USA
ANUL.......	Australian National University (Canberra)
ANULAE	Amalgamated National Union of Local Authorities Employees' Federation of Malaya
ANV........	Army of Northern Virginia (Civil War)
ANVAR	Agence Nationale pour la Valorisation de la Recherche (France)
ANVO	Accept No Verbal Orders
ANWA	Abstracts of New World Archaeology
ANWC	American Newspaper Women's Club
ANWCG	Army Nuclear Weapon Coordination Group
ANWES......	Association of Naval Weapons, Engineers and Scientists
ANWG	Apollo Navigation Working Group (NASA)
ANZAAS.....	Australian and New Zealand Association for the Advancement of Science
ANZAC	Australia-New Zealand Army Corps
ANZUS.....	Australia, New Zealand, and the United States (The Anzus Pact Nations)
AO	Abwehroffizier (Counterintelligence officer) (German military – World War II)
AO	Access Opening (Technical drawings)
AO........	Account of
AO	Accounts Office (Army)
AO	Acridine Orange (Dye)
AO........	Action Officer

ACRONYMS AND INITIALISMS DICTIONARY

AO . . . . Administrative Operations
AO . . . . Administration Office
AO . . . . Adult Operculum
AO . . . . Aeronautical Order
AO . . . . Airdrome Officer
AO . . . . American Optical Company
AO . . . . Among Others
AO . . . . Amplifier Output
AO . . . . And Others
AO . . . . Anodal Opening
AO . . . . Arkansas & Ozarks Railway (AAR code)
AO . . . . Astronomical Observatory
AO . . . . Atomic Orbital (Chemistry)
AO . . . . Audio Oscillator
AO . . . . Authorized Order
AO . . . . Automatic Observer
AO . . . . Aviation Ordnanceman
AO . . . . Oiler (Navy ship symbol)
A/O . . . . Account of (Business and trade)
1-A-O . . . . . . Selective Service Class (for a Conscientious Objector Available for Noncombatant Military Service Only)
AOA . . . . Administration on Aging (HEW)
AOA . . . . American Conservation Association
AOA . . . . American Onotoanalytic Association
AOA . . . . American Optometric Association
AOA . . . . American Ordnance Association
AOA . . . . American Orthopaedic Association
AOA . . . . American Orthopsychiatric Association
AOA . . . . American Osteopathic Association
AOA . . . . American Overseas Airlines
AOA . . . . American Overseas Association
AOA . . . . Amphibious Objective Area (Navy)
AOA . . . . Angle of Attack (Military)
AOA . . . . At or Above (Aviation)
AOA . . . . Atlantic Ocean Area
AOAA . . . . . . Aminooxyacetic Acid
AOAC . . . . . . Army Ordnance Ammunition Command (Merged with Munitions Command)
AOAC . . . . . . Association of Official Analytical Chemists (Formerly, Agricultural)
AOACB . . . . . . Aviation Ordnanceman, Combat Aircrewman, Air Bomber
AOAD . . . . . . Army Operating Availability Data
AOAI . . . . . . Angle-of-Attack Indicator
AOAO . . . . . . Advanced Orbiting Astronautical Observatory
AOAO . . . . . . American Osteopathic Academy of Orthopedics
AOAT . . . . . . Allowed Off Aircraft Time
AOB . . . . Administrative Operations Branch (NTIS)
AOB . . . . Advanced Operational Base (Navy)
AOB . . . . Air Order of Battle
AOB . . . . Airborne Optical Beacon
AOB . . . . Alcohol on Breath (Police term)
AOB . . . . Angle of Bank
AOB . . . . Angle of Beam
AOB . . . . Association des Originaires de Bandounga (Association of Natives of Bandounga)
AOB . . . . At or Below (Aviation)
AOBMO . . . . . Army Ordnance Ballistic Missile Office
AOBSR . . . . . . Air Observer (Military)
AOC . . . . Air Officer Commanding (British)
AOC . . . . Air Officer Commanding (Marine Corps)
AOC . . . . Air Oil Cooler
AOC . . . . Air Operations Center (Air Force)
AOC . . . . Airport Operators Council
AOC . . . . American Ophthalmological Color (Chart)
AOC . . . . American Optical Company (NYSE symbol) (Delisted)
AOC . . . . American Orthoptic Council
AOC . . . . Anodal Opening Contraction (Medicine)
AOC . . . . Architect of the Capitol (US)
AOC . . . . Army Operations Center (in the Pentagon)
AOC . . . . Army Ordnance Corps
AOC . . . . Attached to Other Correspondence
AOC . . . . Attock Oil Company (Pakistan)
AOC . . . . Automatic Operation Control
AOC . . . . Automatic Output Control
AOC . . . . Automatic Overload Circuit
AOC . . . . Aviation Officer Candidate (Navy)
AOCA . . . . . . American Osteopathic College of Anesthesiologists
AOC in CBAFO . . Air Officer Commanding in Chief British Air Force Occupation
AOCD . . . . . . American Osteopathic College of Dermatology
AOCEO . . . . . Army Ordnance Combat Equipment Office
AOCM . . . . . . Aircraft Out of Commission for Maintenance (Air Force)
AOCO . . . . . . Atomic Ordnance Cataloging Office
AOCP . . . . . . Aircraft Out of Commission for (Lack of) Parts (Military)

AOCP . . . . . . American Osteopathic College of Pathologists
AOCP . . . . . . American Osteopathic College of Proctology
AOCPMR . . . . . American Osteopathic College of Physical Medicine and Rehabilitation
AOCR . . . . . . Advanced Optical Character Reader
AOCR . . . . . . Aircraft Operating Cost Report
AOCR . . . . . . American Osteopathic College of Radiology
AOCR . . . . . . American Osteopathic College of Rheumatology
AOCS . . . . . . American Oil Chemists' Society
AOD . . . . Academy of Oral Dynamics
AOD . . . . Air Officer of the Day (Air Force)
AOD . . . . Airfield Operations Designator
AOD . . . . Airlift Operations Directive
AOD . . . . Ancient Order of Druids
AOD . . . . Angle of Descent
AOD . . . . Army Ordnance Department
AOD . . . . As-Of Date
AOD . . . . Auriculo-Osteodysplasia
AODRA . . . . . American Oxford Down Record Association
AODS . . . . . . All Ordnance Destruct System
AODS . . . . . . Atlas (Missile) Operational Data Summary
AOE . . . . Aerodrome of Entry
AOE . . . . Airborne Operational Equipment
AOE . . . . Association of Overseas Educators
AOE . . . . Auditing Order Error
AOE . . . . Fast Combat Support Ship (Navy symbol)
AOEHI . . . . . American Organization for the Education of the Hearing Impaired
AOEM . . . . . Automotive Original Equipment Manufacturers
AOER . . . . . . Army Officers' Emergency Reserve (British)
AOES . . . . . . Arctic Ocean Environment Simulator
AOF . . . . Active Optical Fuze
AOF . . . . Afrique Occidentale Francaise (French West Africa)
AOF . . . . American Optometric Foundation
AOF . . . . Ancient Order of Foresters
AOFC . . . . . . Ancient Order of Foresters of California
AOFS . . . . . . Active Optical Fuzing System
AOG . . . . Aircraft on Ground (Navy)
AOG . . . . Aztec Oil & Gas Co. (NYSE symbol)
AOG . . . . Gasoline Tanker (Navy symbol)
AOGM . . . . . Army of Occupation of Germany Medal
AOGMS . . . . . Army Ordnance Guided Missile School
AOGO . . . . . Advanced Orbiting Geophysical Observatory
AOH . . . . Ancient Order of Hibernians in America
AOH . . . . Apollo Operations Handbook (NASA)
AOH . . . . Aviator's Oxygen Helmet
AOH . . . . Awaiting Office Hours
AOH . . . . Awaiting Overhaul
AOHA . . . . . . American Osteopathic Hospital Association
AOHS . . . . . . American Osteopathic Historical Society
AOI . . . . Advance Ordering Information
AOIC . . . . . . Assistant Officer in Charge (DOD)
A OIL . . . . . . Aviation Oil
AOIV . . . . . . Automatically Operated Inlet Valve
AOJ . . . . Acquire on Jam
AOJS . . . . . . Association of Orthodox Jewish Scientists
AOJT . . . . . . Association of Orthodox Jewish Teachers
AOK . . . . All Out of Kilter (Slang)
A-OK . . . . . . Expression meaning in perfect working order (Popularized during early development of NASA's space program)
AOL . . . . Absent Over Leave (Navy)
AOL . . . . Apco Oil Corporation (NYSE symbol)
AOL . . . . Atlantic Oceanographic Laboratories (of Environmental Science Services Administration)
AOLM . . . . . Apollo Orbiting Laboratory Module (NASA)
AOLO . . . . . Advanced Orbital Launch Operations
AOLR . . . . . . Amplifier Open Loop Response
AOLS . . . . . . Association of Our Lady of Salvation
AOM . . . . . . Army of Occupation Medal (Germany-Japan) (US)
AOM . . . . . . Association of Operative Millers
AOM . . . . . . Aviation Ordnanceman (Navy rating)
AOMA . . . . . Apartment Owners and Managers Association of America
AOMAC . . . . . Aviation Ordnanceman, Combat Aircrewman (Navy rating)
AOMB . . . . . Aviation Ordnanceman, Bombsight Mechanic (Navy rating)
AOMC . . . . . Army Ordnance Missile Center
AOMC . . . . . Army Ordnance Missile Command (Later, Missile Command)
AOML . . . . . Atlantic Oceanographic and Meteorological Laboratories (NOAA)
AOMP . . . . . Artisans Order of Mutual Protection
AOMSA . . . . . Army Ordnance Missile Support Agency
AOMT . . . . . Aviation Ordnanceman, Turret Mechanic
AO-N . . . . . . Administrative Office-Navy
AOND . . . . . Administrative Office, Navy Department
AOO . . . . . . American Oceanic Organization

AOO . . . . Anodal Opening Odor
AOO . . . . Aviation Ordnance Officer
AOOR . . . . . . American Academy of Oral Roentgenology
AOP. . . . . Advanced On-Board Processor (Computer)
AOP. . . . . Association of Osteopathic Publications (Defunct)
AOP. . . . . Atomic Ordnance Platoon
AOP. . . . . Automatic Operations Panel
AOPA. . . . . . . Aircraft Owners and Pilots Association
AOPA. . . . . . . American Orthotics and Prosthetics Association
AOPL. . . . . . . Association of Oil Pipe Lines
AOPU. . . . . . . Asian Oceanic Postal Union (China, Korea, Philippines, Thailand)
ACPV. . . . . . . Air-Operated Plastic Valve
AOQ . . . . Average Outgoing Quality (Quality control term)
AOQ . . . . Aviation Officers' Quarters
AOQL . . . . . . Average Outgoing Quality Level
AOQL . . . . . . Average Outgoing Quality Limit (QCR)
AOR . . . . Advance List of Oversea-Returnees for Reassignment (Army)
AOR . . . . Air Operations Room
AOR. . . . . Airborne Overland RADAR
AOR . . . . Angle of Reflection
AOR. . . . . Antenna Ohmic Resistance
AOR. . . . . Army Operational Research
AOR. . . . . Assembly Operations Record
AOR . . . . Replenishment Fleet Tanker (Navy symbol)
AORC. . . . . . . Association of Official Racing Chemists
AORL . . . . . . Apollo Orbital Research Laboratory
AORN . . . . . . Association of Operating Room Nurses
AORT . . . . Association of Operating Room Technicians
AOS . . . . Acquisition of Signal
AOS . . . . Activity Operating Schedule
AOS . . . . Add or Subtract
AOS. . . . . Air Oil Separator
AOS. . . . . American Ophthalmological Society
AOS. . . . . American Orchid Society
AOS. . . . . American Oriental Society
AOS. . . . . American Otological Society
AOS. . . . . Amplifier Output Stage
AOS. . . . . Ancient Order of Shepherds
AOS . . . . Angle of Site
AOS . . . . Anodal Opening Sound
AOS . . . . Azimuth Orientation System (Military)
AOSA. . . . . . . Association of Official Seed Analysts
AOSAP. . . . . . Airway Operations Specialist (Airport)
AOSC. . . . . . . Association of Oilwell Servicing Contractors
AOSE. . . . . . . American Order of Stationary Engineers
AOSEA . . . . . American Office Supply Exporters Association
AOSG . . . . . . Airways Operations Specialist (General)
AOSL . . . . . . Authorized Organizational Stockage List (Army)
AOSO . . . . . . Advanced Orbiting Solar Observatory (NASA)
AOSP. . . . . . . Automatic Operating and Scheduling Program (Data processing)
AOSPS . . . . . American Otorhinologic Society for Plastic Surgery (Later, American Academy of Facial Plastic and Reconstructive Surgery)
AOSPV . . . . . Airways Operations Supervisor
AOSS. . . . . . . Airways Operations Specialist
AOSS. . . . . . . Americanae Orientalis Societatis Socius (Fellow of the American Oriental Society)
AO(SS) . . . . . Submarine Oiler (Navy ship symbol)
AOT. . . . . Acquisition on Target
AOT. . . . . Active on Target
AOT. . . . . Alignment Optical Telescope
AOT. . . . . Angle on Target
AOT. . . . . Antarctic Observation Team
AOT. . . . . Askania Optical Tracker
AOT. . . . . Automotive Old Timers
AOT. . . . . Auxiliary Output Tester
AOT. . . . . Average Operation Time
AOTA. . . . . . . American Occupational Therapy Association
AOTC . . . . . . Aviation Officers Training Corps
AOTE . . . . . . Amphibious Operational Training Element
AOTE. . . . . . . Associated Organizations for Teacher Education
AOTOS . . . . . Admiral of the Ocean Sea (Annual award of US Merchant Marine; title originally bestowed on Christopher Columbus by the Spanish government)
AOU . . . . Air Operated Unit
AOU. . . . . American Ornithologists' Union
AOU . . . . Azimuth Orientation Unit (Military)
AOUSC. . . . . . Administrative Office of United States Courts
AOUW . . . . . Ancient Order United Workmen
AOW . . . . Articles of War
AOWC . . . . . Army Ordnance Weapons Command
AOWS . . . . . . Aircraft Overhaul Work Stoppage

AOX . . . . Associated Oil Company (American Stock Exchange symbol)
AP . . . . Above Proof
AP . . . . Academic Press, Inc. (Publishers)
AP . . . . Access Panel (Technical drawings)
AP . . . . Access Permit or Access Permittee (AEC)
AP . . . . Account Paid
AP . . . . Accounts Payable
AP . . . . Acidproof
AP . . . . Action Potential (of auditory nerve)
AP . . . . Adapter Panel
AP . . . . Additional Premium (Insurance)
AP . . . . Admiralty Pattern (The right procedure, the correct thing to do) (British)
AP . . . . Advanced Post (Military)
AP . . . . Advanced Procurement
AP . . . . Advice of Payment
AP . . . . Aerial Port
AP . . . . Aft Perpendicular (Naval engineering)
AP . . . . Agency Procedure
AP . . . . Aiming Point
AP . . . . Air Police; by extension, a person who is a member of the Air Police
AP . . . . Air Position
AP . . . . Air Publication (Navy)
AP . . . . Airplane
AP . . . . Airplane Pilot
AP . . . . Airport
AP . . . . Alco Products, Inc. (NYSE symbol; later, ASN)
AP . . . . Alignment Periscope
AP . . . . Alkaline Phosphatase (Enzyme)
AP . . . . All-Purpose
AP . . . . Alum Precipitated
AP . . . . American Paper Co.
AP . . . . American Psychologist (A publication)
AP . . . . Ammonium Perchlorate
AP . . . . Ammunition Point
AP . . . . Ampco-Pittsburgh Corp. (NYSE symbol)
AP . . . . Anal Pore
AP . . . . Andhra Pradesh
AP . . . . Angle Point
AP . . . . Anomalous Propagation (Electronics)
AP . . . . Anteprandial (Before Dinner) (Medicine)
AP . . . . Anterior Pituitary
AP . . . . Antipersonnel
AP . . . . Aortic Pressure
AP . . . . Arithmetic Progression
AP . . . . Armor-Piercing (Army)
AP . . . . As Prescribed
AP . . . . As Purchased
AP . . . . Ascent Phase
AP . . . . Assessment Paid
AP . . . . Assistant Paymaster
AP . . . . Associated Press
AP . . . . Assumed Position (Navigation)
AP . . . . Atmospheric Pressure
AP . . . . Atomic Powered
AP . . . . Author's Proof
AP . . . . Automatic Programming
AP . . . . Autopilot
AP . . . . Aviapolk (Russian term for an air regiment)
AP . . . . Aviation Pilot (Navy)
AP . . . . Awaiting Parts
AP . . . . Small Hail (Meteorology)
AP . . . . Transport (Navy ship symbol)
A/P . . . . Airplane
A/P . . . . Allied Papers
A/P . . . . Antennas & Propagation
A/P . . . . Authority to Pay or Purchase
A/P . . . . Automatic Pilot
A & P . . . . . . Airframe and Powerplant (Aviation)
A & P. . . . . . . Great Atlantic & Pacific Tea Company
APA . . . . Administrative Procedures Act (1946)
APA . . . . Advanced Programs Authorization
APA . . . . Aerovias Panama Airways
APA . . . . Agricultural Publishers Association
APA . . . . Airline Passengers Association
APA . . . . All Party Alliance (British)
APA . . . . Alliance of Poles of America
APA . . . . Allied Pilots Association
APA . . . . Amalgamated Printers' Association
APA . . . . American Patients Association
APA . . . . American Pax Association
APA . . . . American Philological Association

APA . . . . American Philosophical Association
APA . . . . American Photoengravers Association
APA . . . . . . American Physiotherapy Association
APA . . . . . . American Pilots' Association
APA . . . . American Plywood Association
APA . . . . . . American Podiatry Association
APA . . . . American Polygraph Association
APA . . . . American Poultry Association
APA . . . . American Protective Association (Late-19th-century organization opposed
           to so-called encroachments of the Catholic Church in the US;
           initialism was also used by Catholics as an epithet for Protestants)
APA . . . . American Protestant Association
APA . . . . American Psychiatric Association
APA . . . . American Psychoanalytic Association
APA . . . . American Psychological Association
APA . . . . American Psychotherapy Association
APA . . . . American Pulpwood Association
APA . . . . Animation Producers' Association
APA . . . . Antenna Pattern Analyzer
APA . . . . Apache Corp. (NYSE symbol)
APA . . . . Apache Railway Company (AAR code)
APA . . . . Appropriation Purchases Account
APA . . . . Archconfraternity of Perpetual Adoration
APA . . . . Architectural Photographers Association
APA . . . . Assistance Payments Administration (HEW)
APA . . . . Associate in Public Administration
APA . . . . Association of Paroling Authorities
APA . . . . Association of Port Authorities
APA . . . . Association for the Protection of the Adirondacks
APA . . . . . . Associative Principle for Addition (New math)
APA . . . . . . Attack Transport (Navy symbol)
APA . . . . Auxiliary Personnel, Attack (Navy designation for combat landing craft)
           (World War II)
APA . . . . . . Axial Pressure Angle (Gears)
APAA . . . . . . American Physicians Art Association
APAC . . . . . . Aerial Photographic Analysis Center
APAC . . . . . . Airborne Parabolic Arc Computer
APAC . . . . . . AiResearch Parabolic Analog Computer
APAC . . . . . . American Puppet Arts Council
APAC . . . . . . Area Planning-Action Councils
APACHE . . . . Accelerator for Physics and Chemistry of Heavy Metals
APACHE . . . . Analog Programming and Checking (Data processing)
APACHE . . . . Application Package for Chemical Engineers
APACL . . . . . Asian Peoples' Anti-Communist League
APACS . . . . . Adaptive Planning and Control Sequence (Marketing)
APAD . . . . . . Acetylpyridine-Adenine Dinucleotide
APADS . . . . . Automatic Programmer and Data System (Air Force)
APAF . . . . . . Antipernicious Anemia Factor (Hematology)
APAG . . . . . . Atlantic Political Advisory Group (NATO)
APAK . . . . . . Association Professionnelle Apolitique du Katanga (Non-Political
           Professional Association of Katanga)
APAL . . . . . . American Puerto-Rican Action League
APANY . . . . . Association of Personnel Agencies of New York
APAR . . . . . . Adaptive Phase Array RADAR
APAR . . . . . . Authorized Program Analysis Report (Data processing)
APAR . . . . . . Automatic Programming and Recording (Data processing)
APART . . . . . Alliance of Pan American Round Tables
APAS . . . . . . Automatic Performance Analysis System
APATS . . . . . Antenna Pattern Test System (Army)
APATS . . . . . Automatic Programmer and Test System
APAW . . . . . Association of Philippine-American Women
APB . . . . Accounting Principles Board (American Institute of Certified Public
           Accountants)
APB . . . . All Points Bulletin (Police call)
APB . . . . American Program Bureau (Lectures)
APB . . . . Antipersonnel Bomb (Military)
APB . . . . Army Packaging Board
APB . . . . Self-Propelled Barracks Ship (Navy symbol)
APB . . . . Sisters Adorers of the Precious Blood (Roman Catholic religious order)
APBA . . . . . . American Power Boat Association
APBA . . . . . . Associated Press Broadcasters Association
APBE . . . . . . Association for Professional Broadcasting Education
APBHR . . . . . American Part-Blooded Horse Registry
APBI . . . . . . Advanced Planning Briefing for Industry
APBPA . . . . . Association of Professional Ball Players of America
APC . . . . Accelerated Pacification Campaign (South Vietnam)
APC . . . . Acoustical Phase Constant
APC . . . . Acoustical Plaster Ceiling (Technical drawings)
APC . . . . Acoustical Propagation Constant
APC . . . . Address Plate Cabinet
APC . . . . Adenoidal-Pharyngeal-Conjunctival (Viruses) (Medicine)

APC . . . . Adjustable Pressure Conveyor
APC . . . . Advanced Programming Course (Data processing)
APC . . . . Advanced Propulsion Cooling
APC . . . . Aeronautical Planning Chart (Military)
APC . . . . Aerospace Primus Club
APC . . . . All Peoples Congress (Sierra Leone)
APC . . . . Alpha Portland Industries (NYSE symbol)
APC . . . . American Parents Committee
APC . . . . American Philatelic Congress
APC . . . . American Pointer Club
APC . . . . American Pomeranian Club
APC . . . . American Power Conference
APC . . . . Analog to Pressure Converter
APC . . . . Annular Primary Combustor
APC . . . . Appalachian Power Company
APC . . . . Approach Control (Aviation)
APC . . . . Approach Power Compensator
APC . . . . Area Positive Control (FAA)
APC . . . . Arkansas Polytechnic College
APC . . . . Armor-Piercing Capped (Ammunition)
APC . . . . Armored Personnel Carrier
APC . . . . Army Pay Corps
APC . . . . Army Petroleum Center
APC . . . . Army Pictorial Center
APC . . . . Army Policy Council
APC . . . . Army Postal Clerk
APC . . . . Aspirin, Phenacetin, and Caffeine Compound (Slang translation is,
           "All Purpose Capsules")
APC . . . . Associated Pimiento Canners
APC . . . . Association of Private Camps
APC . . . . Association of Pulp Consumers
APC . . . . Atomic Power Construction, Ltd.
APC . . . . Auto-Plot Controller
APC . . . . Autographed Presentation Copy
APC . . . . Automatic Phase Control
APC . . . . Automatic Pressure Conveyor
APC . . . . Azote et Produits Chimiques (France)
APC . . . . Small Coastal Transport (Navy symbol)
A/PC . . . . . . Autopilot Capsule
APCA . . . . . . Air Pollution Control Association
APCA . . . . . . American Petroleum Credit Association
APCA . . . . . . American Planning and Civic Association (Later, Urban America, Inc.)
APCA . . . . . . Audio Peak Clipping Amplifier
APCCA . . . . . American Protestant Correctional Chaplains Association
APCCLA . . . . Aviation Petroleum Coordinating Committee, Latin American
APCD . . . . . . Air Pollution Control District
APCD . . . . . . Association of Philippine Coconut Desiccators
APCEC . . . . . Army Precommission Extension Course
APCEF . . . . . Advanced Power Conversion Experimental Facility
APCG . . . . . . Aperture Plate Character Generator
APCHE . . . . . Automatic Programmed Checkout Equipment
APCI . . . . . . Armor-Piercing-Capped Incendiary (Ammunition)
APCI . . . . . . Association of Pulp Consumers, Incorporated
APCIT . . . . . Armor-Piercing-Capped Incendiary with Tracer (Ammunition)
APCK . . . . . . Association for Promoting Christian Knowledge (Church of Ireland)
APCL . . . . . . Atomic Power Construction, Limited
APCM . . . . . . American Presbyterian Congo Mission
APCM . . . . . . Asiatic-Pacific Campaign Medal
APCN . . . . . . Active Pulse Compression Network
APCN . . . . . . Anno Post Christum Natum (In the Year after Christ Was Born)
APCNY . . . . . Analytical Psychology Club of New York
APCO . . . . . . Air Pollution Control Office (Environmental Protection Agency) (Formerly,
           NAPCA)
APCO . . . . . . Appomattox Court House National Historic Park
APCO . . . . . . Associated Public-Safety (formerly, Police) Communications Officers
APCOL . . . . . All-Pakistan Confederation of Labor
APCON . . . . . Approach Control (FAA)
APCOPPLSRF . . Analysis & Program for Calculation of Optimum Propellant Performance
           for Liquid & Solid Rocket Fuels
APCP . . . . . . Activation Project Control Plan
APC/QC . . . . . Armored Personnel Carrier/Qualification Course (Army)
APCS . . . . . . Air Photographic and Charting Service
APCS . . . . . . American Pencil Collectors Society
APCS . . . . . . American Portuguese Cultural Society
APCS . . . . . . Approach Power Compensator System (Navy)
APCS . . . . . . Approach Power Control Set
APCT . . . . . . Armor-Piercing-Capped with Tracer (Ammunition)
APCV . . . . . . Air Piloted Control Valve
APD . . . . Adjustable Pitch Device
APD . . . . Advanced Planning Document
APD . . . . Advanced Program Development

APD . . . . Aerospace Power Division (Air Force)
APD . . . . Aiming Point Determination
APD . . . . Air to Pneumatic Distribution (Aerospace)
APD . . . . Air Procurement Directive (Air Force)
APD . . . . Air Procurement District (Air Force)
APD . . . . Air Products & Chemicals, Inc. (NYSE symbol)
APD . . . . Albany Port District R. R. (AAR code)
APD . . . . Analog-to-Pulse Duration
APD . . . . Angular Position Digitizer
APD . . . . Area Postal Directory
APD . . . . Army Pay Department
APD . . . . Automated Powder Diffractometer
APD . . . . Average Particle Diameter
APD . . . . High-Speed Transport (Navy symbol)
APDA . . . . . . American Parkinson Disease Association
APDA . . . . . . American Power Drinkers Association
APDA . . . . . . Appliance Parts Distributors Association
APDA . . . . . . Army Physical Disability Activity
APDA . . . . . . Atomic Power Development Associates, Inc.
APDA . . . . . . Auxiliary Pump-Drive Assembly
APDAB . . . . . . Army Physical Disability Appeal Board
APDC . . . . . . Air Procurement District Commander
APDC . . . . . . Ammonium Pyrrolidine Dithiocarbamate
APDO . . . . . . Airport District Office
APDS . . . . . . Advanced Planning Data Sheet
APDSMS . . . . . Advanced Point Defense Surface Missile System (Navy)
APE . . . . Advanced Production Engineering
APE . . . . Aerial Port of Embarkation
APE . . . . Alfven Propulsion Engine (Aerospace)
APE . . . . Ammunition Peculiar Equipment
APE . . . . Anchor Placement Equipment
APE . . . . Anterior Pituitary Extract
APE . . . . Assemblee Parlementaire Europeenne
APE . . . . Assistant Project Engineer
APE . . . . Atomic Photoelectric Effect
APE . . . . Automatic Positioning Equipment
APE . . . . Available Power Efficiency
APEA . . . . . . Antenna Pattern Error Analysis
APEA . . . . . . Association Parlementaire Europe-Afrique (Eur-African Parliamentary Association)
APECO . . . . . American Photograph Equipment Company
AP Ed . . . . . . Associate in Physical Education
APEI . . . . Associated Poultry and Egg Industries
APEL . . . . . . Aeronautical Photographic Experimental Laboratory
APELSCOR . . Architects, Professional Engineers, Land Surveyors Council on Registration
APEQS . . . . . Airborne Photography of the Eclipse of the Quiet Sun
APER . . . . . . Antipersonnel (Projectile)
APEX . . . . . . Advance-Purchase Excursion (Airline fare)
APEX . . . . . . Air Pollution Exercise
APF . . . . Acidproof Floor (Technical drawings)
APF . . . . Adjustable Pawl Fastener
APF . . . . Administrative Flagship (Navy symbol)
APF . . . . American Physicians Fellowship for the Israel Medical Association
APF . . . . American Progress Foundation
APF . . . . American Psychological Foundation
APF . . . . Animal Protein Factor
APF . . . . Association of Pacific Fisheries
APF . . . . Automatic Press Feed
APFA . . . . . . Accelerator Pulsed Fast Assembly
APFA . . . . . . American Pipe Fittings Association
APFA . . . . . . Appalachian Finance Association
APFC . . . . . . American Printed Fabrics Council
APFRI . . . . . . American Physical Fitness Research Institute, Inc.
APG . . . . Aberdeen Proving Ground (Army)
APG . . . . Accessory Pedal Ganglia
APG . . . . Air Proving Ground
APG . . . . American Pewter Guild
APG . . . . Antenna Power Gain
APG . . . . Application Program Generator (Data processing)
APG . . . . Army Planning Group
APG . . . . Army Proving Grounds
APG . . . . Association for Precision Graphics
APG . . . . Astronomiae Professor Greshamii (Professor of Astronomy at Gresham College, London)
APG . . . . Supporting Gunnery Ship (Navy symbol)
APGA . . . . . . American Personnel and Guidance Association
APGA . . . . . . American Public Gas Association
APGBRL . . . . Aberdeen Proving Ground – Ballistics Research Laboratory
APGC . . . . . . Air Proving Ground Center
APGC . . . . . . Air Proving Ground Command

APGCE . . . . . . Air Proving Ground Center – Eglin Air Force Base
APGCU . . . . . . Autopilot Ground Control Unit
APG/HEL . . . . Aberdeen Proving Ground – Human Engineering Laboratory
APG/OBDC . . . Aberdeen Proving Ground – Ordnance Bomb Disposal Center
APH . . . . Access Permit Holder
APH . . . . American Printing House for the Blind
APH . . . . Anterior Pituitary Hormone (Medicine)
A Ph . . . . Associate in Philosophy
APH . . . . Association of Private Hospitals
APH . . . . Automatic Parts Handler
APH . . . . Aviator's Protective Helmet
APH . . . . Sir Allan Patrick Herbert (British humorist)
APH . . . . Transport (Fitted to evacuate wounded) (Navy)
APhA . . . . . . American Pharmaceutical Association
APHA . . . . . . American Pinto Horse Association
APHA . . . . . . American Polled Hereford Association
APHA . . . . . . American Protestant Hospital Association
APHA . . . . . . American Public Health Association
APHB . . . . . . American Printing House for the Blind
APHE . . . . . . Armor Piercing High Explosive
APHF . . . . . . American Poultry and Hatchery Federation
APHIS . . . . . . Animal and Plant Health Inspection Service (Department of Agriculture)
APHS . . . . . . American Poultry Historical Society
API . . . . Academic Press, Incorporated
API . . . . Acceptable Periodic Inspection
API . . . . Advanced Performance Interceptor
API . . . . Air Position Indicator (Air Force)
API . . . . Alabama Polytechnic Institute
API . . . . Amalgamated Publishers, Incorporated
API . . . . American Paper Institute
API . . . . American Paramedical Institute (Honolulu)
API . . . . American Petroleum Institute
API . . . . American Potash Institute
API . . . . American Press Institute (Columbia University)
API . . . . Americans for Progressive Israel
API . . . . Angle Position Indicator
API . . . . Antecedent Precipitation Index
API . . . . Antenna Position Indicator
API . . . . Appreciation of Capital, Protection, Income (Finance)
API . . . . Archconfraternity of Prayer for Israel
API . . . . Armor-Piercing Incendiary (Ammunition)
API . . . . Association Phonetique Internationale
API . . . . Automated Pronunciation Instructor
APIC . . . . . . Alliance des Patriotes Independents du Congo (Alliance of Independent Patriots of the Congo)
APIC . . . . . . Alliance des Proletaires Independents du Congo (Alliance of Independent Proletarians of the Congo)
APIC . . . . . . American Political Item Collectors (An organization)
APIC . . . . . . Apollo Parts Information Center (NASA)
APIC . . . . . . Army Photo Interpretation Center
APIC . . . . . . Automatic Power Input Controller
APICON . . . . Aircraft Position Information Converter (Air Force)
APICP . . . . . . Association for the Promotion of the International Circulation of the Press (Distipress)
APICS . . . . . . Air Pollution Information and Computation System
APICS . . . . . . American Production and Inventory Control Society
APID . . . . . . Army Photo Interpretation Detachment
APID . . . . . . Association of Photographic Importers and Distributors
APIE . . . . . . Antioch Program for Interracial Education (Antioch College)
API-HH . . . . . Americans for Progressive Israel – Hashomer Hatzair
APIM . . . . . . Association Professionnelle International des Medicins
APIPOCC . . . . Appropriating Property in Possession of Common Carrier (FBI standardized term)
APIR . . . . . . American Petroleum Institute Research
APIT . . . . . . Armor Piercing Incendiary Tracer (Ammunition)
APJ . . . . American Power Jet Company
APJ . . . . Angle Panel Jack
APJA . . . . . . Appliance Parts Jobbers Association
APKCA . . . . . Associated Pot and Kettle Clubs of America
APL . . . . A Programming Language (Data processing)
APL . . . . Advance Procurement List
APL . . . . Aero-Propulsion Laboratory (Air Force)
APL . . . . Allowance Parts List
APL . . . . American Poetry League
APL . . . . Anterior Pituitary-Like (Hormone) (Biochemistry)
APL . . . . Aperture Lip
APL . . . . APL Corp. (NYSE symbol)
APL . . . . Applied Physics Laboratory (Johns Hopkins University)
APL . . . . Approved Parts List
APL . . . . Army Personnel Letter
APL . . . . Army Promotion List

APL . . . . Assembly Part List
APL . . . . Automatic Phase Lock
APL . . . . Automatic Production Line
APL . . . . Automotive Pigeon Loft
APL . . . . Average Picture Level
APL . . . . Barracks Ship (Nonself-propelled) (Navy symbol)
APLA . . . . . . American Patent Law Association
APLA . . . . . . Armenian Progressive League of America
APLA . . . . . . Aviation Pilot, Airship (Navy)
APLC . . . . . . Automated Parking Lot Control
APL/JHU . . . . . Applied Physics Laboratory, Johns Hopkins University
APLO . . . . . . Aerial Port Liaison Office(r) (Air Force)
APLS . . . . . . American Plant Life Society
APLS . . . . . . Apparel Performance Level Standards (Pronounced "Apples")
APLU . . . . . . Automatic Program Loading Unit
APM. . . . . . . Academy of Psychosomatic Medicine
APM . . . . Acid Precipitable Material (Chemistry)
APM. . . . . . . Aim-Point-Miss
APM. . . . . . . Air Permeability Meter
APM . . . . Air Provost Marshal
APM. . . . . . . Alarm Panel Monitor
APM. . . . . . . Aluminum Powder Metallurgy
APM . . . . American People's Mobilization (First called American Peace Mobilization) (World War II)
APM . . . . Anti-Personnel Missile
APM. . . . . . . Applied Magnetics (NYSE symbol)
APM. . . . . . . Assistant Paymaster (Marine Corps)
APM. . . . . . . Assistant Provost Marshal
APM. . . . . . . Association of Professors of Medicine
APM. . . . . . . Association of Professors of Missions
APM. . . . . . . Association for Psychoanalytic Medicine
APM . . . . Associative Principle for Multiplication (New math)
APM. . . . . . . Mechanized Artillery Transport (Navy symbol)
APMA . . . . . . Absorbent Paper Manufacturers Association
APMA . . . . . . Advance Payment of Mileage Authorized (Army)
APMA . . . . . . Automatic Phonograph Manufacturers Association
APMALTA . . . . Advance Payment of Monetary Allowance in Lieu of Transportation is Authorized (Army)
APMC. . . . . . Academy of Psychologists in Marital Counseling
A/P MCU . . . . Autopilot Monitor and Control Unit
APME . . . . . . Area Precipitation Measurement Equipment
APME . . . . . . Associated Press Managing Editors Association
APMI . . . . . . American Powder Metallurgy Institute
APMMRI . . . . . Automatic Point Marking, Measuring and Recording Instrument
APMR . . . . . . Association for Physical and Mental Rehabilitation
APMT . . . . . . Antenna Pattern Measurement Test (Army)
APN. . . . . . . All Pass Network
APN. . . . . . . Nonmechanized Artillery Transport (Navy symbol)
APNA. . . . . . American Power Net Association
APNL . . . . . . Army Personnel Newsletter
APNRP . . . . . American-Polish National Relief for Poland
APO. . . . . . . Abteilungsparteiorganisation
APO. . . . . . . Accountable Property Officer
APO. . . . . . . Advanced Post Office (Military)
APO . . . . Air Force Post Office
APO . . . . Air Post Office
APO. . . . . . . Air Procurement Office
APO. . . . . . . Air Programs Office (Environmental Protection Agency)
APO. . . . . . . American Potash & Chemical Corporation (NYSE symbol) (Delisted)
APO. . . . . . . Andean Pact Organization (Chile, Peru, Bolivia, Ecuador, Colombia)
APO . . . . Animal Procurement Office (Military)
APO . . . . Annual Program Objectives (Navy)
APO . . . . Area Petroleum Office(r)
APO. . . . . . . Army Post Office
APO . . . . Asian Productivity Organization
APOAF . . . . . All Present or Accounted For
APOC. . . . . . Army Point of Contact
APOD . . . . . . Aerial Port of Debarkation (Air Force)
APOE . . . . . . Aerial Port of Embarkation (Air Force)
APOG . . . . . . Aerial Port Group
APOPA . . . . . Association of Private Office Personnel Agencies
APOR . . . . . . Advisory Panel for Operations Research
APOS . . . . . . Advanced Polar Orbiting Satellite
APOTA . . . . . Automatic Positioning Telemetering Antenna
APP . . . . Advance Procurement Plan (Navy)
APP . . . . Advanced Planetary Probe
APP . . . . Advanced Project Planning
APP . . . . Air Parcel Post
APP . . . . Air Pollution Potential
APP . . . . Antenna Position Programmer
APP . . . . Antipodal Propagation Phenomena

APP . . . . Appendix
APP . . . . Applied Psychology Panel (of NDRC) (World War II)
APP . . . . Army Procurement Procedure
APP . . . . Association of Professional Photogrammetrists
APP . . . . Associative Parallel Processor (Data processing)
APP . . . . Automatic Plate Processor
APP . . . . Automatic Position Planning
APP . . . . Auxiliary Pneumatics Panel
APP . . . . Auxiliary Power Plant
APP . . . . Troop Barge, Class A (Navy symbol)
APPA . . . . . . Advise Present Position and Altitude (Aviation)
APPA . . . . . . American Paper and Pulp Association
APPA . . . . . . American Professional Practice Association
APPA . . . . . . American Psychopathological Association
APPA . . . . . . American Public Power Association
APPA . . . . . . Association for the Preservation and Presentation of the Arts
APPAC . . . . . Aviation Petroleum Products Allocation Committee
APPAC-L . . . . Aviation Petroleum Products Allocation Committee, London
APPAR . . . . . . Apparatus
APPB . . . . . . Airborne Provisioning Parts
APPC . . . . . . Automatic Power Plant Checker
APPCON. . . . . Approach Control (Air Force)
APPD . . . . . . Aviation Personnel Planning Data (Navy)
APPECS . . . . . Adaptive Pattern Perceiving Electronic Computer System
APPI. . . . . . . Advance Planning Procurement Information (Army)
APPI . . . . International Association for the Promotion and Protection of Private Foreign Investments
APPL . . . . . . Applicable
APPLE . . . . . . Advanced Propulsion Packaged Liquid Engine
APPLE . . . . . . Apollo Payload Exploration
APPM . . . . . . Association of Publication Production Managers
APPMA . . . . . American Pet Products Manufacturers Association
APPME . . . . . American Professors for Peace in the Middle East
App ME . . . . . Applied Mechanics Engineer (An academic degree)
APPN . . . . . . Appropriation
A/P POI . . . . Autopilot Positioning Indicator
APPR . . . . . . Apprehend (or Apprehension)
APPR . . . . . . Approval (or Approve)
APPR . . . . . . Army Package Power Reactor
APPRC . . . . . American Partridge Plymouth Rock Club
APPROX . . . . Approximately
APPT. . . . . . . Appointment
APPTU . . . . . All-Pakistan Post and Telegraph Union
APR . . . . Aerial Photographic Reconnaissance
APR . . . . Agency Progress Report
APR . . . . Air Pictorial Service
APR . . . . Air Priority Rating
APR . . . . Airman Performance Report
APR . . . . All Purpose Room
APR . . . . Annual Progress Report
APR . . . . Antenna Position Recorder
APR . . . . Anti-Plugging Relay
APR . . . . Apprentice
APR . . . . April
APR . . . . Association of Petroleum Re-Refiners
APR . . . . Association of Publishers Representatives
APR . . . . Automatic Pattern Recognition
APR . . . . Automatic Production Recording
APR . . . . Automatic Programming and Recording
APR . . . . Available Power Response
APR . . . . Rescue Transport (Navy symbol)
APRA . . . . . . Aircraft Production Resources Agency
APRA . . . . . . Alianza Popular Revolucionaria Americana (Peruvian political party)
APRA . . . . . . American Petroleum Refiners Association
APRA . . . . . . American Public Relations Association
APRA . . . . . . Army Pulsed Experimental Research Assembly
APRA . . . . . . Automotive Parts Rebuilders Association
APRAC . . . . . Air Pollution Research Advisory Committee
APRC . . . . . . Army Personnel Research Committee
APRC . . . . . . Army Physical Review Council
APRC . . . . . . Association for Promoting the Reform of Convocation (British)
APRCAS . . . . . All Purpose Rocket for Collecting Atmospheric Soundings (Navy)
APRE . . . . . . Aerospace Photographic Reconnaissance Equipment
APRE . . . . . . Air Procurement Region, Europe
APREQS . . . . . Approval Requests (Military)
APRF . . . . . . All-Pakistan Railwaymen's Federation
APRF . . . . . . Army Pulse Radiation Facility
APRFE . . . . . . Air Procurement Region, Far East
APRI . . . . . . Air Priority
APRIL . . . . . . Aquaplaning Risk Indicator for Landings
APRIL . . . . . . Automatically Programed Remote Indication Logged

APRL . . . . Army Prosthetics Research Laboratory
APRO . . . . Aerial Phenomena Research Organization
APRO . . . . Army Personnel Research Office
APROCOLIN . . Association Professionelle de Colons Individuels (Professional Association of Colonials)
APROSOMA. . . Association pour la Promotion Sociale de la Masse (Association for the Social Betterment of the People) (Rwanda and Burundi)
APRRB. . . . . . . Airman Performance Report Review Board
APRRN . . . . . . Advance Personnel Requirements Research Note
APRS . . . . American Performing-Rights Society
APRS . . . . Applied Physics Research Section
APRS . . . . Army Personnel Research Service
APRS . . . . Automatic Position Reference System
APRT. . . . . . . Airport
APRTA . . . . . . Associated Press Radio and Television Association
APRX . . . . Approximate
APS . . . . Aborigines Protection Society
APS . . . . Academy of Political Science
APS . . . . Accelerated Photosynthetic System (Sewage purification)
APS & . . . . Accelerometer Parameter Shift
APS . . . . Accessory Power Supply
APS . . . . Adenosine Phosphosulfate
APS . . . . Advanced Personnel System
APS . . . . Advanced Photosynthetic System
APS . . . . Agence de Presse Senegalese (Senegalese Press Agency)
APS . . . . Air Pictorial Service
APS . . . . Air Pressure Switch
APS . . . . Airborne Pulse Search RADAR
APS . . . . Allegheny Power System
APS . . . . American Metal Products Company (NYSE symbol) (Delisted)
APS . . . . American Peace Society
APS . . . . American Pediatric Society
APS . . . . American Penstemon Society
APS . . . . American Peony Society
APS . . . . American Pheasant Society
APS . . . . American Philatelic Society
APS . . . . American Philosophical Society
APS . . . . American Physical Society
APS . . . . American Physiological Society
APS . . . . American Phytopathological Society
APS . . . . American Plant Selections
APS . . . . American Poinsettia Society
APS . . . . American Polar Society
APS . . . . American Pomological Society
APS . . . . American Primrose Society
APS . . . . American Proctologic Society
APS . . . . American Prosthodontic Society
APS . . . . American Protestant Society
APS . . . . American Psychosomatic Society
APS . . . . Ammonium Persulfate
APS . . . . Amplifier Power Supply
APS . . . . Angstrom Pyrheliometric Scale
APS . . . . Angular Position Sensor
APS . . . . Army Pilot School
APS . . . . Army Postal Service
APS . . . . Ascent Propulsion System (NASA)
APS . . . . Assimilations Per Second
APS . . . . Association of Photo Sensitizers
APS . . . . Atmospheric Pollution Sensor
APS . . . . Attitude Propulsion Subsystem
APS . . . . Autograph Postcard Signed
APS . . . . Automated Production System
APS . . . . Automatic Pilot System
APS . . . . Auxiliary Power Supply
APS . . . . Auxiliary Propulsion System (or Subsystem) (Apollo) (NASA)
APS . . . . Mine Laying Submarine (Navy symbol)
APSA . . . . American Political Science Association
APSA . . . . American Psychologists for Social Action
APSA . . . . Ammunition Procurement & Supply Agency (Army)
APSaA . . . . . . American Psychoanalytic Association
APSC . . . . Arizona Public Service Company
APSC . . . . Austin Peay State College (Tennessee)
AP & SC . . . . . Army Port and Service Command
APSCO . . . . . . Associated Public-Safety Communications Officers
APSE . . . . Abstracts of Photographic Science and Engineering Literature
APSET. . . . . . . Aviation Personnel and Survival Equipment Team (Navy)
APSGD . . . . . . Army Procurement-Sharpe General Depot
APSI. . . . . Advanced Propulsion Subsystem Integration (Air Force)
APSO . . . . Allied Petroleum Service Organization
APSO . . . . Association of Poultry Slaughterhouse Operators
APSQ . . . . Advance Payment of Subsistence and Quarters

APSq . . . . Aerial Port Squadron (Air Force)
APSS . . . . Advanced Planetary Spacecraft System
APSS . . . . American Polled Shorthorn Society
APSS . . . . Army Printing and Stationery Services (British)
APSS . . . . Associated Public School Systems
APSS . . . . Association for the Psychophysiological Study of Sleep
AP(SS) . . . . . . Transport Submarine (Navy symbol)
APT . . . . Advanced Passenger Train (British)
APT . . . . Airmen Proficiency Test
APT . . . . Alum Precipitated Toxoid (Medicine)
APT . . . . American Playwrights Theatre
APT . . . . Aminopropylisothiourea
APT . . . . Analog Program Tape
APT. . . . . Apartment
APT . . . . Arizona Photopolarimeter Telescope
APT . . . . Armed Propaganda Team (Military)
APT . . . . Armor Piercing with Tracer (Ammunition)
APT . . . . Army Parachute Team
APT . . . . Association for Poetry Therapy
APT . . . . Automatic Picture Taking (or Transmission) (NASA)
APT . . . . Automatic Position Telemetering
APT . . . . Automatic Programming for Tools
APT . . . . Automatically Programed Tools
APT . . . . Automation Planning and Technology
APT . . . . Troop Barge, Class B (Navy symbol)
APTA . . . . American Physical Therapy Association
APTA . . . . American Pioneer Trails Association
APTA . . . . American Platform Tennis Association
APTA . . . . . . Aptitude Area
APTD . . . . Aid to the Permanently and Totally Disabled (HEW)
APTI. . . . . Actions Per Time Interval
APTIC. . . . . . . Air Pollution Technical Information Center (of National Air Pollution Control Administration)
APTO . . . . Association for Psychiatric Treatment of Offenders
APTPDA . . . . . Advance Payment of Travel Per Diem Authorized (Army)
APTR . . . . Advanced Pressure Tube Reactor
APTS . . . . Automatic Picture Transmission Subsystem (NASA)
APTS . . . . Automatic Programmer and Test System (Army)
APTU . . . . African Postal and Telecommunications Union
APTW. . . . . . . Asiatic-Pacific Theater of War
APU . . . . Acoustica Propellant Utilization
APU . . . . Airborne Processing Unit
APU . . . . Arab Postal Union
APU . . . . Army Postal Unit
APU . . . . Audio Playback Unit
APU . . . . Auxiliary Power Unit (Air Force)
APU . . . . Auxiliary Propulsion Unit
APUC . . . . Area Production Urgency Committee
APUC . . . . Association for Promoting Unity of Christendom
APUHS . . . . . . Automatic Program Unit High Speed (Component of ADIS)
APULS . . . . . . Automatic Program Unit Low Speed (Component of ADIS)
APUPA . . . . . . Alien, Penumbral, Umbral, Penumbral, Alien
A-Put . . . . Associate Pulmonary Technologist (Academic degree)
APV . . . . Air Piloted Valve
APV . . . . Transport and Aircraft Ferry (Navy symbol)
APVA . . . . Association for the Preservation of Virginia Antiquities
APW . . . . Accelerated Public Works (Program) (Interior Department)
APW . . . . American Prisoner of War
APW . . . . Architectural Projected Window (Technical drawings)
APW . . . . Association of Petroleum Writers
APW . . . . Augmented Plane Wave
APWA. . . . . . . American Public Welfare Association
APWA. . . . . . . American Public Works Association
APWD. . . . . . . Aircraft Proximity Warning Device
APWI . . . . Air Prisoner of War Interrogation
APWIB . . . . . . American Prisoner of War Information Bureau
APWO . . . . . . Assistant Public Works Officer
APWP. . . . . . . Accelerated Public Works Program (Interior Department)
APWR. . . . . . . American Polish War Relief (Post-World War II)
APWS . . . . Aircraft Proximity Warning System
APWU. . . . . . . American Postal Workers Union
APWUS . . . . . . Association of Polish Women of the United States
APX . . . . Ampex Corporation (NYSE symbol)
APY . . . . Apeco Corp. (Formerly, American Photocopy Equipment Company) (NYSE symbol)
AQ . . . . Accomplishment Quotient
AQ . . . . Achievement Quotient
AQ . . . . Any Quantity
AQ . . . . Assimulatory Quotient
AQ . . . . Attainment Quotient
AQ . . . . Australian Quarterly (A publication)

AQ	Aviation Fire Control Technician (Navy rating)
AQA	Air Quality Act
AQAB	Air Quality Advisory Board
AQB	Army Qualification Battery (of tests)
AQC	Associate of Queen's College (London)
AQC	Automatic Quench Calibration (or Correction)
AQCR	Air Quality Control Region (Environmental Protection Agency)
AQDM	Air Quality Display Model
AQE	Airman Qualifying Examination
AQGV	Azimuth Quantized Gated Video (Air Force)
AQHA	American Quarter Horse Association
AQIC	Anima Quiescat in Christo (May His [or Her] Soul Repose in Christ)
AQL	Acceptable Quality Level (Quality control)
AQL	Average Quality Level (or Limit)
AQM	Assistant Quartermaster
AQMC	Army Quartermaster Corps (Merged with Supply & Maintenance Command)
AQMG	Assistant Quartermaster General
AQN	Azimuthal Quantum Number
AQP	Aeroquip Corporation (NYSE symbol) (Delisted)
AQREC	Army Quartermaster Research and Engineering Command
AQT	Applicant Qualification Test (Navy)
AQU	Aquila Airways, Ltd.
AR	Aberdeen & Rockfish R. R. (AAR code)
AR	Account Receivable
AR	Achievement Ratio
AR	Acid Resisting (Technical drawings)
AR	Acknowledgment of Receipt
AR	Acoustic Reflex
AR	Acoustic Research, Inc. (Electronics firm)
AR	Acquisition RADAR
AR	Action Register
AR	Active Resistance (Occupational therapy)
AR	Administrative Ruling (US)
AR	Aerodynamic Report
AR	Age Replacement
AR	Air Receive
AR	Air Refueling
AR	Air Regulator
AR	Air Requirement (DOD)
AR	Air Resistance
AR	Airman Records (Air Force)
AR	Airman Recruit
AR	Airship Rigger
AR	Alarm Reaction (Physiology)
AR	All Rail (Railroad)
AR	All Risks
AR	Allocated Reserve
AR	Amendment Request (Navy)
AR	American Smelting & Refining Company (NYSE symbol)
AR	Amphibian Reconnaissance (Military)
AR	Analytical Reagent (Chemistry)
AR	Anno Regni (In the Year of the Reign of)
AR	Annual Report
AR	Annual Return
AR	Anode Reaction
AR	Anti-Racketeering
AR	Apical Region
AR	Approved for Release
AR	Area of Resolution
Ar	Argon (Chemical element; preferred form, but also see A)
AR	Arizona Review (A publication)
AR	Arkansas
AR	Armored Reconnaissance
AR	Army Regulations
AR	Army Reserve
AR	Arrival and Return (Shipping)
AR	Artificial Respiration
AR	As Required
AR	Aspect Ratio
AR	Associate in Retailing
AR	Attenuation Reaction
AR	Audio Response
AR	Automatic Radio (Electronics firm)
AR	Automatic Rifleman (DOD)
AR	Autonomous Republic
AR	Average Rating
AR	Average Revenue
AR	Avionics Requirements
AR	Avis de Reception (Return receipt)
AR	Bomber (AR-2, etc.) (Russian aircraft symbol)
AR	Repair Ship (Navy symbol)

A/R	All Risks (Business and trade)
A & R	Approved and Removed
A & R	Assembly and Repair
AR II	American Revolution II Committee
ARA	Academy of Rehabilitative Audiology
ARA	Accelerated Readiness Analysis
ARA	Accredited Rural Appraiser (Designation given by American Society of Farm Managers and Rural Appraisers)
ARA	Adapter, Right Angle
ARA	Aerial Rocket Artillery
ARA	Aerospace Research Association
ARA	Agricultural Research Administration (Department of Agriculture) (Superseded by ARS, 1953)
ARA	Airborne RADAR Approach (Aviation)
ARA	Aircraft Replaceable Assemblies
ARA	Allied Research Association, Inc.
ARA	Amateur Rocketeers of America
ARA	American Radio Association
ARA	American Railway Association
ARA	American Recreational Activities
ARA	American Relief Administration Association
ARA	American Reloaders Association
ARA	American Remount Association
ARA	American Rental Association
ARA	American Repossessors Association
ARA	American Republics Area (State Department)
ARA	American Retreaders Association
ARA	American Revenue Association
ARA	American Rheumatism Association
ARA	American Royal Association
ARA	Analog RADAR Absorber
ARA	ARA Services, Inc. (Formerly, Automatic Retailers of America Inc.) (NYSE symbol)
ARA	Arab Relief Agency
ARA	Arcade & Attica Corporation (AAR code)
ARA	Area Redevelopment Act (Labor Department)
ARA	Area Redevelopment Administration (Department of Commerce)
ARA	Artists' Representatives Association
ARA	Assigned Responsible Agency (DOD)
ARA	Associate of the Royal Academy (British)
ARA	Associates for Radio Astronomy
ARA	Average Response Amplitude
ARA	Society of American Registered Architects
ARAA	Aerodrome RADAR/Radio Approach Aid
ARAA	American Registry of Architectural Antiquities
ARAA	American Russian Aid Association
ARAAV	Armored Reconnaissance Airborne Assault Vehicle
ARAB	American Riding Association of Berlin (Post-World War II)
ARAC	Aerospace Research Applications Center (Indiana University) (NASA)
ARAC	Area Airports Checked
ARAC	Army RADAR Approach Control Facility
ARAD	Airborne RADAR and Doppler
ARAD	Average Response Amplitude Data
ARADCOM ...	Army Air Defense Command
ARADMAC....	Army Aeronautical Depot Maintenance Center (AMC--ASMC)
ARADSCH ...	Army Air Defense School
ARAE	American Retail Association Executives
ARAL	Association to Repeal Abortion Laws
ARAL	Automatic Record Analysis Language
ARAM	Associate of the Royal Academy of Music (British)
ARAM	Association of Railroad Advertising Managers
ARAMCO	Arabian-American Oil Company
ARAP	Aeronautical Research Association of Princeton
ARAS	Ascending Reticular Activating System
ARAS	Association of Regular Army Sergeants
ARAT	Advise (names of) Representatives, Accommodations, and Transportation (desired) (Army)
ARAT	Automatic Random Access Transport
ARAV	Army Aviator
AR Av Bad	Army Aviator Badge
AR Av MO Bad ..	Army Aviation Medical Officer's Badge
ARB	Air Registration Board (British)
ARB	Air Research Bureau
ARB	Air Resources Board (California)
ARB	Aircraft Reactors Brand
ARB	Aircraft Recovery Bulletin
ARB	American Research Bureau
ARB	APCHE (Automatic Program Checkout Equipment) Relay Box
ARB	Armored Rifle Battalion
ARB	Army Rearming Base
ARB	Army Retiring Board

ARB . . . . ASTIA (Armed Services Technical Information Agency) Report Bibliography
ARB . . . . Automatic RADAR Beacon
ARB . . . . Battle Damage Repair Ship (Navy symbol)
ARBA . . . . . . American Rabbit Breeders Association
ARBA . . . . . . American Road Builders' Association
ARBA . . . . . . American Romney Breeders' Association
ARBA . . . . . . Associated Retail Bakers of America
ARBBA . . . . . . American Railway Bridge and Building Association
ARBC . . . . . . American Revolution Bicentennial Commission
ARBHC . . . . . Association of Registered Bank Holding Companies
ARBOR . . . . . Argonne Boiling Reactor (Nuclear power project) (Proposed)
ARBOR . . . . . Arthropod-Borne (Virology)
ARBS . . . . . . Automatic RADAR Beacon Sequencer
ARC . . . . Aboriginal Research Club
ARC . . . . Addiction Research Center (National Institute of Mental Health)
ARC . . . . Advanced Reentry Concepts
ARC . . . . Aeronautical Research Council (British)
ARC . . . . Aerospace Remote Calculator
ARC . . . . Aerospace Research Chamber
ARC . . . . Agricultural Relations Council
ARC . . . . Agricultural Research Center (Agriculture Department)
ARC . . . . Agricultural Research Council (British)
ARC . . . . Aiken Relay Calculator
ARC . . . . Air Reserve Center
ARC . . . . Airborne Radio Communicating
ARC . . . . Airborne Research Capsule
ARC . . . . Airworthiness Requirements Committee
ARC . . . . Alexander R. R. (AAR code)
ARC . . . . Altitude Rate Command
ARC . . . . Amerada Petroleum Corporation (NYSE symbol) (Later, AHC)
ARC . . . . American National Red Cross
ARC . . . . American Railway Cases (Legal)
ARC . . . . American Red Cross
ARC . . . . American Rehabilitation Committee
ARC . . . . Ames Research Center (NASA)
ARC . . . . Amphibious Research Craft
ARC . . . . Analyzer-Recorder-Controller
ARC . . . . Annual Report Council
ARC . . . . Antigen-Reactive Cell
ARC . . . . Appalachian Regional Commission
ARC . . . . Area of Responsibility Centre (Aviation)
ARC . . . . Associated Retail Confectioners of North America
ARC . . . . Association of Rehabilitation Centers
ARC . . . . Atlantic Research Corporation
ARC . . . . Atlantic Richfield Company (NYSE symbol)
ARC . . . . Atomedic Research Center
ARC . . . . Augmentation Research Center (Stanford Research Institute)
ARC . . . . Automatic Range Control
ARC . . . . Automatic Rate Changer
ARC . . . . Automatic Ratio Control
ARC . . . . Automatic Reset Counter
ARC . . . . Autopilot Rate Control
ARC . . . . Auxiliary Roll Control
ARC . . . . Average Response Computer
ARC . . . . Cable Repairing or Laying Ship (Navy symbol)
ARC . . . . Foundation for the Arts, Religion and Culture
ARCA . . . . . . American Rehabilitation Counseling Association
ARCA . . . . . . American Retail Coal Association
ARCA . . . . . . Associate of the Royal College of Art (British)
ARCA . . . . . . Association of Romanian Catholics of America
ARCA . . . . . . Automobile Racing Club of America
ARCADE . . . . . Automatic RADAR Control and Data Equipment
ARCAS . . . . . . All Purpose Rocket for Collecting (or Carrier for) Atmospheric Soundings (Navy)
ARCAS . . . . . Automatic RADAR Chain Acquisition System (Air Force)
ARCB . . . . . . Association of Reserve City Bankers
ARCC . . . . . . American Restaurant China Council
ARCCF . . . . . American Red Cross Children's Fund
ARCE . . . . . . Amphibious River Crossing Equipment (Military)
ARCEA . . . . . American Railway Car Export Association
ARCH . . . . . . Arches National Monument
ARCH . . . . . . Architects Renewal Committee of Harlem
ARCH . . . . . . Articulated Computing Hierarchy (British)
ARCH . . . . . . Automated Reports Control Handling
Arch E . . . . . . Architectural Engineer (Academic degree)
ARCI . . . . . . Aid Refugee Chinese Intellectuals
ARCI . . . . . . American Railway Car Institute
ARCM . . . . . . Associate of the Royal College of Music (British)
ARCO . . . . . . Agricultural Research Center Operations (of ARS, Department of Agriculture)
ARCO . . . . . . Aircraft Resources Control Office

ARCO . . . . . . Airspace Reservation Coordination Office (Canadian)
ARCO . . . . . . Associate of the Royal College of Organists (British)
ARCO . . . . . . Atlantic Richfield Company
ARCOM . . . . . Army Commendation Medal (US)
ARCOM . . . . . Army Reserve Command
ARCON . . . . . Advanced Research Consultants
ARCOV . . . . . Army Combat Operations Vietnam
ARCP . . . . . . Air Refueling Control Point
ARCRA . . . . . Arabian Horse Club Registry of America
ARCS . . . . . . Achievement Rewards for College Scientists (Foundation)
ARCS . . . . . . Air Resupply and Communication Service
ARCS . . . . . . Associate of the Royal College of Science (British)
ARCS . . . . . . Association of Retail Candy Shops
ARCSA . . . . . Aviation Requirements for the Combat Structure of the Army
ARCT . . . . . . Air Refueling Control Time
ARCT . . . . . . Army Radio Code Aptitude Test
ARCUS . . . . . Associated Retail Confectioners of the US
ARD . . . . Accelerated Rural Development
ARD . . . . Acute Respiratory Disease (Medicine)
ARD . . . . Advanced Research Division
ARD . . . . Air Reserve District
ARD . . . . American Research & Development Corp. (NYSE symbol)
ARD . . . . Armament Research Development (British)
ARD . . . . Army Renegotiation Division (of ASRB)
ARD . . . . Association of Research Directors
ARD . . . . Automatic Release Date (Military)
ARD . . . . Auxiliary Repair Dry Dock (Non-self-propelled) (Navy ship symbol)
ARD . . . . Average Response Data
AR & D . . . . . Air Research and Development
ARDA . . . . . . Advanced Reactor Development Associates
ARDA . . . . . . American Railway Development Association
ARDA . . . . . . Analog Recording Dynamic Analyzers (Data processing)
ARDBC . . . . . American Rubberband Duckpin Bowling Congress
ARDC . . . . . . Aberdeen Research & Development Center
ARDC . . . . . . Air Research and Development Center (Later, Air Force System Command)
ARDC . . . . . . Air Research and Development Command
ARDC . . . . . . American Racing Driver's Club
ARDC . . . . . . Auxiliary Floating Dry Dock, Concrete (Navy symbol)
ARDCA . . . . . Air Research and Development Command – Andrews Air Force Base
ARDCM . . . . . Air Research and Development Command Manual
ARDE . . . . . . Aircraft and Rocket Design Engineers
ARDE . . . . . . Armaments Research and Development Establishment (British)
ARDF . . . . . . Airborne Radio Direction Finding
ARDG . . . . . . Army Research and Development Group
ARDG(E) . . . . . Army Research and Development Group (Europe)
ARDG(FE) . . . . Army Research and Development Group (Far East)
ARDIS . . . . . . Army Research and Development Management Information System
ARDM . . . . . . Medium Auxiliary Repair Dry Dock (Navy symbol)
ARDME . . . . . Automatic RADAR Data Measuring Equipment
ARDME . . . . . Automatic Range Detector and Measuring Equipment
ARDP . . . . . . Army Requirements Development Plan
ARDS . . . . . . Aviation Research and Development Service (of FAA)
ARE . . . . Acoustic Radiation Element
ARE . . . . Air Reactor Experiment
ARE . . . . Aircraft Recovery Equipment
ARE . . . . Anion-Responsive Electrode
Ar E . . . . Architectural Engineer
ARE . . . . Arlen Realty & Development Corp. (NYSE symbol)
ARE . . . . Associate in Religious Education
ARE . . . . Association for Research and Enlightenment
ARE . . . . Asymptotic Relative Efficiency (Statistics)
ARE . . . . Automatic Record Evaluation
ARE . . . . Auxiliary Rocket Engine
AREA . . . . . . Aerovias Ecuatoriana, SA
AREA . . . . . . American Railway Engineering Association
AREA . . . . . . American Recreational Equipment Association
AREA . . . . . . Army Reactor Experimental Area (Army)
AREA . . . . . . Association of Records Executives and Administrators
AREBA . . . . . Accelerated Reeducation of Emotions, Behavior and Attitudes (Rehabilitation program)
AREC . . . . . . Agricultural Research and Educational Center (American University of Beirut)
AREC . . . . . . Amateur Radio Emergency Corps (of ARPSC)
AREFS . . . . . Air Refueling Squadron
A Rel . . . . . . Associate in Religion
ARELEM . . . . Arithmetic Element Program
ARENA . . . . . Adoption Resource Exchange of North America
ARENTS . . . . ARPA (Advanced Research Projects Agency) Environmental Test Satellites
AREP . . . . . . Air Refueling Egress Point
ARES . . . . . . Advanced Research EMP (Electromagnetic Pulse) Simulator
ARES . . . . . . Advanced Rocket Engine Storable

ARES . . . . Association of Real Estate Syndicators
ARES . . . . Automatic Record Evaluation System
ARESTEM . . . . . A Recording Stray Energy Monitor
ARETS . . . . Arizona Regional Ecological Test Site (Department of the Interior)
AREUEA . . . . . American Real Estate and Urban Economics Association
ARF . . . . Advertising Research Foundation
ARF . . . . Aeronautical Research Foundation
ARF . . . . African Research Foundation
ARF . . . . Air Reserve Forces
ARF . . . . American Rationalist Federation
ARF . . . . American Rehabilitation Foundation
ARF . . . . American Retail Federation
ARF . . . . American Rose Foundation
ARF . . . . Animal Research Facilities
ARF . . . . Apparel Research Foundation
ARF . . . . Armour Research Foundation
ARF . . . . Arthritis and Rheumatism Foundation
ARF . . . . Automatic Return Fire (ARPA)
ARFA . . . . . . Allied Radio Frequency Agency
ARFA . . . . . . Armenian Revolutionary Federation of America
ARFC . . . . . . Air Reserve Flying Center (Air Force)
ARFCOS . . . . . Armed Forces Courier Service
ARFCOSTA . . . Armed Forces Courier Station
ARFCW . . . . . . Athletic and Recreation Federation of College Women
ARFMSR . . . . . Air Reserve Forces Meritorious Service Ribbon
ARFOR . . . . . . Area Forecast (Aviation)
ARFORA . . . . . Asociatiunea Reuniunilor Femeilor Ortodoxe Romane-Americane
ARFPC . . . . . . Air Reserve Forces Policy Committee
ARFPDS . . . . . Air Reserve Forces Personnel Data System
ARG . . . . Aerolineas Argentinas (Airline)
ARG . . . . Aethylen-Rohrleitungs-Gesellschaft (West Germany)
ARG . . . . Amphibious Ready Group
ARG . . . . Arginine (Amino acid)
ARG . . . . Atlas Reliability Group
ARG . . . . Internal Combustion Engine Repair Ship (Navy symbol)
ARGA . . . . . . Antique Radio Guild of America
ARGA . . . . . . Appliance, Range, Adjust (Data processing)
ARGCA . . . . . American Rice Growers Cooperative Association
ARGMA . . . . . Army Rocket and Guided Missile Agency
ARGONAUT . . Argonne Nuclear Assembly for University Training
ARGR . . . . . . Association for Research in Growth Relationships
ARGS . . . . . . American Rock Garden Society
ARGUS . . . . . . Analytical Reports Gathering and Updating System (Navy)
ARGUS . . . . . . Associative Registers for Generalized User Switching (Computer typesetting system)
ARGUS . . . . . Automatic Routine Generating and Updating System (Data processing)
ARH . . . . Ammunition Railhead
ARH . . . . Anchor Hocking Corporation (NYSE symbol)
ARH . . . . Antenna RADOME Heater
ARH . . . . Anti-Radiation Homer
ARH . . . . Heavy-Hull Repair Ship (Navy symbol)
ARHA . . . . . . Associate of the Royal Hibernian Academy
ARHCO . . . . . Atlantic Richfield Hanford Company
ARI . . . . Aerial Radiac Instrument
ARI . . . . Agricultural Research Institute
ARI . . . . Air-Conditioning and Refrigeration Institute
ARI . . . . Allied Research Institute
ARI . . . . Aluminum Research Institute
ARI . . . . American Rayon Institute
ARI . . . . Authority Is Requested to Inter (the remains of) (Army)
ARIA . . . . . . Administration, Ryukyu Islands, Army
ARIA . . . . . . Adult Reading Improvement Association
ARIA . . . . . . American Radio Importers Association
ARIA . . . . . . American Risk and Insurance Association
ARIA . . . . . . Apollo Range Instrumentation Aircraft (NASA)
ARIB . . . . . . Asphalt Roofing Industry Bureau
ARIBA . . . . . . Associate of the Royal Institute of British Architects
ARIC . . . . . . Associate of the Royal Institute of Chemistry (British)
ARIEM . . . . . Army Research Institute of Environment Medicine
ARIES . . . . . . Advanced RADAR Information Evaluation System
ARIES . . . . . . Atmospheric Research Information Exchange Study
ARIES . . . . . . Authentic Reproduction of an Independent Earth Satellite
ARIF . . . . Association pour le Retablissment des Institutions et Oeuvres Israelites en France
ARIMS . . . . . Airborne RADAR Inflight Monitoring System
ARINCO . . . . Aeronautical Radio, Incorporated
ARINOA . . . . Association of Russian Imperial Naval Officers in America
ARIP . . . . . . Air Refueling Ingress Point (FAA)
ARIP . . . . . . Air Refueling Initial Point (Air Force)
ARIP . . . . . . Automatic Rocket Impact Predictor
ARIS . . . . . . Advanced Range Instrumentation Ship

ARIS . . . . . . Advanced Range Instrumentation Systems
ARIS . . . . . . Advanced Research Instrument System, Inc.
ARIS . . . . . . Aerial Radiac Instrument System
ARIS . . . . . . Aeronautical Research Institute of Sweden
ARIS . . . . . . Airborne Range Instrumentation Station
ARIS . . . . . . Aircraft Research Instrumentation System
ARIS . . . . . . Atlantic Range Instrumentation Ship
ARIS . . . . . . Attitude and Rate Indicating System
ARIS . . . . . . Automatic Recording Infrared Spectrometer
ARIST . . . . . . Annual Review of Information Science and Technology (Journal)
ARISTOTLE . . . Annual Review and Information Symposium on the Technology of Training, Learning, and Education (DOD)
ARIT . . . . . . American Registered Inhalation Therapist (Academic degree)
ARIT . . . . . . American Registry of Inhalation Therapists
ARIT . . . . . . American Research Institute in Turkey
ARIZ . . . . . . Arizona
ARK . . . . . . Arkansas
ARK . . . . . . Reconnaissance Seaplane (Russian symbol)
ARKLA . . . . . Arkansas-Louisiana Gas Company
ARL . . . . . . Acceptable Reliability Level (Quality control)
ARL . . . . . . Admiralty Research Laboratory (British)
ARL . . . . . . Aerial Reconnaissance Laboratory
ARL . . . . . . Aeronautical Research Laboratory (OAR)
ARL . . . . . . Aerospace Research Laboratory (Air Force)
ARL . . . . . . Age Run Length
ARL . . . . . . American Roque League
ARL . . . . . . Applied Research Laboratory (of John Hopkins University)
ARL . . . . . . Arctic Research Laboratory
ARL . . . . . . Army Radiation Laboratory
ARL . . . . . . Association of Research Libraries
ARL . . . . . . Landing Craft Repair Ship (Navy symbol)
ARLD . . . . . . Army Logistics Research & Development
ARLIS . . . . . Arctic Research Laboratory Island (A floating ice island in the Arctic Ocean) (Navy)
ARLO . . . . . . Air Reconnaissance Liaison Officer
ARLO . . . . . . Army Liaison Officer
ARLO . . . . . . Art Reference Libraries of Ohio
ARLS . . . . . . Automatic Resupply Logistics System
ARLSEA . . . . . Active-Retired Lighthouse Service Employees' Association
ARM . . . . . . Abstracts of Research and Related Materials in Vocational and Technical Education (A periodical of ERIC)
ARM . . . . . . All Risk Management (Insurance)
ARM . . . . . . Alliance Reformee Mondiale
ARM . . . . . . Amateur Radio Monitor
ARM . . . . . . Anhysteretic Remanence
ARM . . . . . . Anti-RADAR Missile
ARM . . . . . . Anti-Radiation Missile
ARM . . . . . . Applied Research Management
ARM . . . . . . Armstrong Rubber Company (NYSE symbol)
ARM . . . . . . Army Ready Materiel
ARM . . . . . . Association of Railway Museums
ARM . . . . . . Aviation Radioman
ARM . . . . . . Heavy Machinery Repair Ship (Navy symbol)
ARMA . . . . . . Accumulator Reservoir Manifold Assembly
ARMA . . . . . American Records Management Association
ARMA . . . . . American Registry of Medical Assistants
ARMA . . . . . Army Attache (Military)
ARMAC . . . . . Aviation Radioman, Combat Aircrewman (Navy)
ARMACS . . . . Aviation Resources Management and Control System
ARMADA . . . . American Record Merchandisers and Distributors Association
ARMAN . . . . Artificial Methods Analyst
ARMATSC . . . Army Materiel Status Committees
ARMD . . . . . . American Red Mogen Dovid for Israel
ARMD . . . . . . Armored
ARMEA . . . . . American Railway Magazine Editors Association
ARMF . . . . . . Advanced Reactivity Measurement Facility (AEC)
ARMH . . . . . Academy of Religion and Mental Health
ARMI . . . . . . American Rack Merchandisers Institute
ARMI . . . . . . American Research Merchandising Institute
ARMIP . . . . . Accounting and Reporting Management Improvement Program (Army)
ARMISH . . . . United States Military Mission with the Iranian Army
ARMM . . . . . Analysis and Research of Methods for Management
ARMM . . . . . Association of Reproduction Materials Manufacturers
ARMMA . . . . American Railway Master Mechanics' Association
ARMMS . . . . . Automated Reliability and Maintenance Management System (Navy)
ARMS . . . . . . ADPE (Automatic Data Processing Equipment) Resources Management System
ARMS . . . . . . Advanced Receiver Model System
ARMS . . . . . . Aerial Radiological Measurements and Survey (Program)
ARMS . . . . . . Aerial Radiological Measuring (or Monitoring) System
ARMS . . . . . . Application of Remote Manipulators in Space (Robot) (NASA)

ARMS . . . . Automatic Radiation Monitoring System
ARMT . . . . Armament
ARMTE . . . . . . Army Missile Test and Evaluation
ARMU . . . . Associated Rocky Mountain Universities (AEC)
ARN . . . . Airborne Radio Navigation
ARN . . . . Atmospheric Radio Noise
ARNA . . . . Army with Navy (personnel)
ARNA . . . . Association of Radio-Television News Analysts
ARNE . . . . Accion Revolucionaria Nacional Ecuatoriana (National Revolutionary Action) (Political party in Ecuador)
ARNG . . . . . . Army National Guard
ARNGUS . . . . . Army National Guard of the United States
ARNMD . . . . . Association for Research in Nervous and Mental Disease
ARNO . . . . . . Air Indicator Not Operating (Aviation)
ARO . . . . After Receipt of Order
ARO . . . . Air Radio Officer
ARO . . . . Airborne Range Only (RADAR ranging set for use with various gun computers)
ARO . . . . Applied Research Objective
ARO . . . . Army Research Office
ARO . . . . Army Routine Order (Military)
ARO . . . . Aro Corporation (NYSE symbol)
ARO . . . . Asian Regional Organization
ARO . . . . Assistant Research Officer (Ministry of Agriculture, Fisheries, and Food) (British)
ARO . . . . Association for Research in Ophthalmology
AROC . . . . . . Air Rescue Operations Center (Air Force)
AROD . . . . Airborne Ranging and Orbit Determination System
ARO-D . . . . . . Army Research Office-Durham
ARODS . . . . . . Airborne RADAR Orbital Determination System
ARO-E . . . . . . Army Research Office-Europe
ARO-FE . . . . . Army Research Office - Far East
ARO-ICFTU . . . Asian Regional Organization - International Federation of Free Trade Unions
ARO-J . . . . . . Army Research Office-Japan
AROTC . . . . . . Air Reserve Officers' Training Corps (Air Force)
AROU . . . . . . Aviation Repair and Overhaul Unit
AROY . . . . American Romanian Orthodox Youth
ARP . . . . Advanced Reentry Program (Aerospace)
ARP . . . . Advanced Research Projects
ARP . . . . Aerodrome Reference Point
ARP . . . . Aeronautical (or Aerospace) Recommended Practice
ARP . . . . Aerospace Recommended Practice (NASA)
ARP . . . . Aerospace Reference Project (Formerly, Aerospace Technology Division) (Library of Congress)
ARP . . . . Air Raid Precautions (British) (World War II)
ARP . . . . Airborne RADAR Platform (Air Force)
ARP . . . . Aircrew Respiratory Protection
ARP . . . . Airport Reference Point
ARP . . . . Alternator Research Package
ARP . . . . American Registry of Pathologists
ARP . . . . American Relief for Poland
ARP . . . . Ammunition Refilling Point
ARP . . . . Analytical Rework Program (Navy)
ARP . . . . Antenna Radiation Pattern
ARP . . . . Area Redevelopment Program
ARP . . . . Army Research Plan
ARP . . . . Associated Reformed Presbyterian
ARP . . . . Association for Realistic Philosophy
ARP . . . . Association of Retired Persons International
ARPA . . . . . . Advanced Research Projects Agency (Military)
ARPA . . . . . . Association pour les Recherches sur les Parodontopathies
ARPAC . . . . . . Agricultural Research Policy Committee (Department of Agriculture)
ARPAS . . . . . . Air Reserve Pay and Allowance System
ARPAT . . . . . . Advanced Research Projects Agency Terminal
ARPC . . . . . . Air Raid Precautions Controller (British)
ARPC . . . . Air Reserve Personnel Center (Air Force)
ARPC . . . . . . Annual Report Producers Council
ARPM . . . . . . Average Revenue Per Message
ARPN . . . . Aircraft and Related Procurement, Navy
ARPO . . . . . . Air Raid Precautions Officer (British)
ARPO . . . . . . Applied Research Program
ARPO . . . . . . Arkansas Post National Memorial
ARPS . . . . . . Aerospace Research Pilot School (Air Force)
ARPS . . . . . . Air Reserve Pay System
ARPSC . . . . . . Amateur Radio Public Service Corps
ARPSE . . . . . . Aerospace Research Pilot School - Edwards Air Force Base
ARPT . . . . . . American Registry of Physical Therapists
ARPT . . . . . . Army Registry of Physical Therapists
ARPU . . . . . . American Racing Pigeon Union
ARQ . . . . Annual Review Questionnaire (Military)

ARQ . . . . Automatic Request
ARR . . . . Advanced Restricted Report
ARR . . . . Aeronautical Radionavigation RADAR
ARR . . . . Air Regional Representative
ARR . . . . Airborne Radio Receiver
ARR . . . . Altitude Referenced Radiometer
ARR . . . . Anno Regni Regis (or Reginae) (In the Year of the King's [or Queen's] Reign)
ARR . . . . Antenna Radiation Resistance
ARR . . . . Anti-Repeat Relay
ARR . . . . Armour Research Foundation Reactor
ARR . . . . Army Retail Requirements
ARR . . . . Arrival (or Arrive)
ARRC . . . . . . Aerospace Rescue and Recovery Center
ARRC . . . . . . Air Reserve Records Center
ARRC . . . . . . American Road Race of Champions
ARREP . . . . . . Arrival Report (Navy)
ARREPISIC . . . Arrival Report Immediate Superior in Command (Navy)
ARRF . . . . . . Automatic Recording and Reduction Facility
ARRGp . . . . . . Aerospace Rescue and Recovery Group (Air Force)
ARRHA . . . . . . American RSROA Roller Hockey Association
ARRL . . . . . . Aeronautical Radio and RADAR Laboratory (Navy)
ARRL . . . . . . American Radio Relay League
ARROTCA . . . . Army Reserve and ROTC Affairs
ARRS . . . . . . Aerospace Rescue and Recovery Service (Air Force)
ARRS . . . . . . American Roentgen Ray Society
ARRS . . . . . . Attitude-Referenced Radiometer Study (NASA)
ARRSq . . . . . . Aerospace Rescue and Recovery Squadron (Air Force)
ARRT . . . . . . American Registry of Radiologic Technologists
ARRT . . . . . . American Revolution Round Table
ARRTC . . . . . . Aerospace Rescue and Recovery Training Center (Air Force)
ARRUS . . . . . . Arrived Within Continental Limits of US (Navy)
ARRWg . . . . . . Aerospace Rescue and Recovery Wing (Air Force)
ARS . . . . Active Repeater Satellite (Air Force)
ARS . . . . Advanced Reconnaissance Satellite
ARS . . . . Advanced Record System (Air Force)
ARS . . . . Advanced Reentry System (Aerospace)
ARS . . . . Advanced Rescue System (Proposed VTOL aircraft)
ARS . . . . Aerial Reconnaissance and Security
ARS . . . . Aeronautical Research Scientist
ARS . . . . Aerospace Research Satellite
ARS . . . . Agricultural Research Service (Department of Agriculture)
ARS . . . . Air Regulating Squadron
ARS . . . . Air Rescue Service (Air Force)
ARS . . . . Airborne Ranging System
ARS . . . . Airborne Refrigeration System
ARS . . . . Alpha Ray Spectrometer
ARS . . . . American Radium Society
ARS . . . . American Recorder Society
ARS . . . . American Recreation Society
ARS . . . . American Repair Service
ARS . . . . American Rhinologic Society
ARS . . . . American Rhododendron Society
ARS . . . . American Rocket Society (Later, AIAA)
ARS . . . . American Rose Society
ARS . . . . Angular Rate Sensor
ARS . . . . Anno Reparatæ Salutis (In the Year of Our Redemption)
ARS . . . . Apollo Reentry Ship (Aerospace)
ARS . . . . Area Re-Supply
ARS . . . . Armenian Relief Society
ARS . . . . Army Relief Society
ARS . . . . Asbestos Roof Shingles (Technical drawings)
ARS . . . . Atmosphere Revitalization Section (Apollo) (NASA)
ARS . . . . Augustan Reprint Society
ARS . . . . Automatic Recording Spectrometer
ARS . . . . Salvage Ship (Navy symbol)
Ar S . . . . Sister of Arts
ARSA . . . . . . Allied Railway Supply Association
ARSA . . . . . . Associate of the Royal Scottish Academy
ARSA . . . . . . Associate of the Royal Society of Art (British)
ARSA . . . . . . Austrian RADAR Site Analysis
ARSAP . . . . . . Army Small Arms Program
ARSB . . . . Air Reconnaissance Support Battalion
ARSBA . . . . . . American Rambouillet Sheep Breeders Association
ARSC . . . . . . Aircraft Repair and Supply Center
ARSC . . . . . . Analog Rotation Speed Control
ARSC . . . . . . Association for Recorded Sound Collections
ARSC . . . . . . Association Royale Sportive Congolaise (Congolese Royal Sporting Association)
ARSD . . . . . . Aviation Repair Supply Depot
ARSD . . . . . . Salvage Lifting Vessel (Navy symbol)

ARSE . . . . Alpha Ray Spectrometric Equipment
ARSEM . . . . . . Army Registry of Special Educational Materials
ARSIP . . . . Arrears in Pay (Military)
ARSL . . . . Associate of the Royal Society of Literature
ARSM . . . . Associate of the Royal School of Mines (British)
ARSM . . . . Associate of the Royal Society of Musicians (British)
ARSP . . . . Aerospace Research Support Program (Air Force)
ARSP . . . . Archiv fuer Rechts- und Sozialpolitik (A publication)
ARSR . . . . Air Route Surveillance RADAR
ARSS . . . . American Radiator and Standard Sanitary Corporation
ARST . . . . Aerial Reconnaissance and Security Troop
ARST . . . . Salvage Craft Tender (Navy ship symbol)
ARSTRIKE . . . . (US) Army Strike (STRICOM)
ARSTS . . . . . . Air Reserve Specialist Training Squadron
ARSV . . . . Armored Reconnaissance Scout Vehicle (Army)
ART . . . . Accredited Record Technician
ART . . . . Admissible Rank Test (Statistics)
ART . . . . Advanced Research and Technology
ART . . . . Air Reserve Technician
ART . . . . Airborne Radiation Thermometer
ART . . . . Alarm Reporting Telephone
ART . . . . Alert Reaction Time
ART . . . . American Radiography Technologists (An organization)
ART . . . . Animated Reconstruction of Telemetry
ART . . . . Arc Resistance Tester
ART . . . . Arithmetic Reading Test (Military)
ART . . . . Arithmetic Reasoning Test
ART . . . . Article
ART . . . . Automatic Radiating Tester
ART . . . . Automatic Range Tracker
ART . . . . Automatic Reporting Telephone
ART . . . . Aviation Radio Technician
ARTA . . . . . . Association of Retail Travel Agents
ARTAC . . . . . . Advanced Reconnaissance and Target Acquisition Capabilities
ARTC . . . . . . Air Route Traffic Control
ARTC . . . . . . Aircraft Research and Testing Committee
ARTC . . . . . . Auxiliary Rescue Team Chief (Air Force)
ARTCC . . . . . . Air Route Traffic Control Center
ARTCS . . . . . . Advanced RADAR Traffic Control System
Art D . . . . . . Doctor of Arts
ARTL . . . . . . Awaiting Results of Trial (Military)
ARTLF . . . . . . Association of Railway Trainmen and Locomotive Firemen
ARTNA . . . . . . Association of Radio-Television News Analysts
ARTOC . . . . . Army Tactical Operations Central
ARTP . . . . . . Air Reserve Technician Program (Air Force)
ARTP . . . . . . Army Rocket Transportation System
ARTRAC . . . . . Advanced Range Testing, Reporting, and Control
ARTRON . . . . . Artificial Neuron
ARTS . . . . . . Advanced RADAR Traffic Control System (Air Force)
ARTS . . . . . . Annual Research Task Summary
ARTS . . . . . . Arkansas Research Test Station
ARTS . . . . . . Army Research Task Summary
ARTS . . . . . . Automated RADAR Terminal System
ARTS . . . . . . Automatic Resistance Test Set
ARTU . . . . . . Automatic Range Tracking Unit (Military)
ARTY . . . . . . Artillery
ARU . . . . Acoustic Resistance Unit
ARU . . . . Aeromedical Research Unit (Army)
ARU . . . . Air Reserve Unit
ARU . . . . American Railway Union
ARU . . . . Analog Remote Unit
ARU . . . . Attitude Reference Unit
ARU . . . . Audio Response Unit (Credit card verification)
ARUG . . . . . . Air Reserve Unit (General Training)
ARUNK . . . . . Arrival Unknown (Aviation)
ARUSNP . . . . Air Reserve Unit (General Training, Nonpay)
ARUSP . . . . . . Air Reserve Unit (General Training, Pay)
ARV . . . . Aeroballistic Reentry Vehicle
ARV . . . . Aerospace Research Vehicle
ARV . . . . Afferent Renal Vein
ARV . . . . Aircraft Repair Ship (Navy symbol)
ARV . . . . Alternate Record-Voice
ARV . . . . American Revised Version (of the Bible)
ARV . . . . Armored Recovery Vehicle
ARV . . . . Army Vietnam
ARV . . . . Arvin Industries, Inc. (NYSE symbol)
ARVA . . . . . . Aircraft Repair Ship (Aircraft)
ARVE . . . . . . Aircraft Repair Ship (Engine)
ARVH . . . . . . Aircraft Repair Ship (Helicopter) (Navy symbol)
ARVIDA . . . . . Arthur Vining Davis Corporation
ARVN . . . . Army of the Republic of Vietnam (South Vietnam)

ARVSG . . . . . . Air Reserve Volunteer Support Group
ARW . . . . Air-Conditioning and Refrigeration Wholesalers
ARW . . . . Air Raid Warden
ARW . . . . Air Raid Warning (Air Force)
ARW . . . . Arkansas Western Railway Company (AAR code)
ARW . . . . Atmospheric Radio Wave
ARW . . . . Attitude Reaction Wheel
ARWA . . . . . . American Right of Way Association
ARWAB . . . . . Army Rotary Wing Aptitude Battery
ARWC . . . . . . Army War College
ARWI . . . . . . Association of Russian War Invalids of First World War
ARX . . . . Air Regenerative Exhaust
AS . . . . Abilene & Southern Railway Company (AAR code)
AS . . . . Academy of Sciences
AS . . . . Account Sales
AS . . . . Acquisitions Section (Resources and Technical Services Division of ALA)
AS . . . . Action Socialiste (Socialist Action) (Congo)
AS . . . . Adapter, Straight
AS . . . . Add-Subtract
AS . . . . Aeronautical Standards
AS . . . . Aerospace Standards
AS . . . . Aerospace Studies (AFROTC)
AS . . . . After Sight
AS . . . . Air Screw
AS . . . . Air Section
AS . . . . Air Service
AS . . . . Air Specification
AS . . . . Air Speed
AS . . . . Air Staff (Air Force)
AS . . . . Air Station
AS . . . . Air Surveillance (Air Force)
AS . . . . Airless Spraying
AS . . . . Airports Service (of FAA)
AS . . . . Airscoop
AS . . . . Alongside
AS . . . . Altostratus (Meteorology)
AS . . . . Aluminum and Steel (Freight)
AS . . . . Aluminium Suisse (SA)
AS . . . . American Speech (A periodical)
AS . . . . Amertool Services
AS . . . . Anglo-Saxon
AS . . . . Anno Salvatoris (or Salutis) (In the Year of Salvation)
AS . . . . Anthranilate Synthetase
AS . . . . Antiserum
AS . . . . Antisubmarine
AS . . . . Aortic Stenosis (Medicine)
AS . . . . Apollo Saturn (NASA)
AS . . . . Applied Science
AS . . . . Apprentice Seaman
AS . . . . Aqueous Solution
AS . . . . Area Surveillance
AS . . . . Armco Steel Corporation (NYSE symbol)
AS . . . . Armed Services Committee (US Senate)
AS . . . . Armor School (Army)
AS . . . . Army Security
AS . . . . Army Staff
As . . . . Arsenic (Chemical element)
AS . . . . Arteriosclerosis (Medicine)
AS . . . . Artificial Satellite
AS . . . . As Stated
AS . . . . Ascendance-Submission (Psychology)
AS . . . . Ascent Stage (Aerospace)
AS . . . . Associate in Science
as . . . . Asymmetric (Chemistry)
AS . . . . At Sight
AS . . . . Atmosphere and Space
AS . . . . Audio Sensitivity
AS . . . . Augmentation System
AS . . . . Augmented Surveyor
AS . . . . Automatic Sprinkler (Technical drawings)
AS . . . . Aviaeskadra (Russian term for an air squadron)
AS . . . . Sister of Arts
AS . . . . Submarine Tender (Navy symbol)
A-S . . . . Anglo-Saxon
A/S . . . . Airspeed
A/S . . . . Aktieselskapet- (Joint stock company) (Norwegian)
A/S . . . . Antisubmarine
A/S . . . . As Stated
A/S . . . . Aux Soins de (Care of, c/o)
ASA . . . . Abort Sensor Assembly (Apollo) (NASA)
ASA . . . . Acetylsalicylic Acid (Aspirin)

ASA . . . . Acoustical Society of America
ASA . . . . Actuarial Society of America
ASA . . . . Adjustable Shock Absorber
ASA . . . . African Studies Association
ASA . . . . Alaska Airlines, Inc.
ASA . . . . Aluminum Siding Association
ASA . . . . Amateur Softball Association of America
ASA . . . . American Saluki Association
ASA . . . . American Scientific Affiliation
ASA . . . . American Sentic Association
ASA . . . . American Shellfisheries Association
ASA . . . . American Shorthorn Association
ASA . . . . American Sightseeing Association
ASA . . . . American Snowmobile Association
ASA . . . . American Society for Abrasives
ASA . . . . American Society for Aesthetics
ASA . . . . American Society of Agronomy
ASA . . . . American Society of Anesthesiologists
ASA . . . . American Society of Appraisers
ASA . . . . American Society of Auctioneers
ASA . . . . American Sociological Association
ASA . . . . American Sociometric Association
ASA . . . . American-South African Investment Company Ltd. (NYSE symbol)
ASA . . . . American Soybean Association
ASA . . . . American Standards Association (Later, USASI; then, ANSI)
ASA . . . . American Statistical Association
ASA . . . . American Stockyards Association
ASA . . . . American Student Association
ASA . . . . American Studies Association
ASA . . . . American Subcontractors Association
ASA . . . . American Sunbathing Association
ASA . . . . American Surgical Association
ASA . . . . Anterior Sorting Area
ASA . . . . Anthroposophical Society in America
ASA . . . . Anti-Static Additive
ASA . . . . Area Scanning Alarm
ASA . . . . Armenian Students Association of America
ASA . . . . Army Seal of Approval
ASA . . . . Army Security Agency (Later, Defense Security Agency)
ASA . . . . Assistant Secretary of the Army
ASA . . . . Associated Stenotypists of America
ASA . . . . Association of Southeast Asia
ASA . . . . Association for the Study of Abortion
ASA . . . . Atomic Security Agency (Army)
ASA . . . . Auditory Sensation Area
ASA . . . . Aviation Supply Annex
ASA . . . . Azimuth Servo Assembly
AS of A . . . . . Assistant Secretary of the Army
ASAA . . . . Armenian Students Association of America
ASAB . . . . Atlanta & Saint Andrews Bay Railway (AAR code)
ASAC . . . . Active Satellite Attitude Control
ASAC . . . . . . Air Service Area Command
ASAC . . . . . . Altostratus and Altocumulus (Meteorology)
ASAC . . . . American Society of Agricultural Consultants
ASAC . . . . American-Southern Africa Council
ASAC . . . . Antisubmarine Air Control (Navy)
ASAC . . . . Army Study Advisory Committee
AS of AC . . . . American Society of Arms Collectors
ASACS . . . . . . Airborne Surveillance And Control System (ASD)
ASAE . . . . . . American Society of Agricultural Engineers
ASAE . . . . . . American Society of Association Executives
AS of AF . . . . Assistant Secretary of the Air Force
ASA (FM) . . . . Assistant Secretary of the Army (Financial Management)
ASAFMA . . . . . Assistant Secretary of the Air Force (Materiel)
ASAGAD . . . . . American Society for Advancement of General Anesthesia in Dentistry
ASAH . . . . American Society of Association Historians
ASAH . . . . . . American Squadron of Animal Historians
ASAHC . . . . . American Society of Architectural Hardware Consultants
ASAHP . . . . . . Association of Schools of Allied Health Professions
ASAI . . . . American Society of Ancient Instruments
ASA (I & L) . . . Assistant Secretary of the Army (Installations & Logistics)
ASAIO . . . . . . American Society for Artificial Internal Organs
ASAMN . . . . . American Society of Anthropometric Medicine and Nutrition
ASAMPE . . . . . Allied States Association of Motion Picture Exhibitors
ASA(M & RA). . Assistant Secretary of the Army (Manpower and Reserve Affairs)
ASAMS . . . . . . Austere Surface-to-Air Missile System
ASAO . . . . . . Association for Social Anthropology in Oceania
ASAP . . . . . . American Society of Adlerian Psychology
ASAP . . . . . . American Society of Animal Production
ASAP . . . . . . Analog System Assembly Pack
ASAP . . . . . . Antisubmarine Attack Plotter (Navy)

ASAP . . . . . . Army Scientific Advisory Panel
ASAP . . . . . . As Soon As Possible
ASAP . . . . . . Automated Statistical Analysis Program
ASAPR . . . . . . Accelerated Strike Aircraft Program Requirement (DOD)
ASARB . . . . . . Association of Statisticians of American Religious Bodies
ASARCO . . . . . American Smelting and Refining Company
ASA (R & D). . . Assistant Secretary of the Army (Research & Development)
ASAS . . . . . . Alternate Stability Augmentation System (Aerospace)
ASAS . . . . . . American Society of Abdominal Surgery
ASAS . . . . . . American Society of Animal Science
ASAS . . . . . . Army Security Agency School (Merged with Defense Security Agency School)
ASAS . . . . . . Association of South-East Asian States
ASAT . . . . . . Air Search Attack Team (Military)
ASAT . . . . . . Arbeitsgemeinschaft Satellitentragersystem (Germany)
ASATOM . . . . . Association pour les Stages et l'Accueil des Techniciens d'Outre-Mer (Association for the Reception and Instruction of Overseas Technicians)
ASATTU . . . . . Antisubmarine Attack Teacher Training Unit
ASAU . . . . . Air Search Attack Unit (Military)
ASB . . . . Air Safety Board
ASB . . . . Air Staff Board
ASB . . . . Aircraft Safety Beacon
ASB . . . . Aircraft Services Base
ASB . . . . Allied Staff, Berlin
ASB . . . . American Society of Bariatrics
ASB . . . . Anti-Shock Body
ASB . . . . Asymmetrical Sideband
ASB . . . . Automated Status Board
AS & B . . . . . Aloin, Strychnine, and Belladonna (Pills)
ASBA . . . . . . American Shorthorn Breeders Association
ASBA . . . . . . American Skibob Association
ASBA . . . . . . American Southdown Breeders' Association
ASBA . . . . . . Association of Ship Brokers and Agents
ASBC . . . . . . American Safety (formerly, Seat) Belt Council
ASBC . . . . . . American Society of Biological Chemists
ASBC . . . . . . American Society of Brewing Chemists
ASBCA . . . . . . Armed Services Board of Contract Appeals
ASBD . . . . . . Advanced Sea Based Deterrent (Navy)
ASBDA . . . . . American School Band Directors' Association
ASBE . . . . . . American Society of Bakery Engineers
ASBE . . . . . . American Society of Body Engineers
ASB & I . . . . . Aloin, Strychnine, Belladonna, and Ipecac (Pills)
ASBIPC . . . . . . American Sugar Beet Industry Policy Committee
ASBLY . . . . . . Assembly
ASBM . . . . . . Associate in Business Management
ASBO . . . . . . Association of School Business Officials of the United States and Canada
ASBPA . . . . . . American Shore and Beach Preservation Association
ASBPE . . . . . American Society of Business Press Editors
ASC . . . . Abbe Sine Condition
ASC . . . . Acme Markets, Inc. (NYSE symbol)
ASC . . . . Action Socialiste Congolaise (Congolese Socialist Action)
ASC . . . . Adams State College (Colorado)
ASC . . . . Adhesive and Sealant Council
ASC . . . . Administrative Service Centers
ASC . . . . Aeronautical Systems Center (Air Force)
ASC . . . . Aerospace Static Converter
ASC . . . . Agnes Scott College (Georgia)
ASC . . . . Agricultural Stabilization and Conservation
ASC . . . . Air Service Command
ASC . . . . Air Support Command
ASC . . . . Air Support Control
ASC . . . . Air Systems Command (Navy)
ASC . . . . Aircraft Service Change
ASC . . . . Alabama State College
ASC . . . . Albany State College (Georgia)
ASC . . . . Allowance Source Code (Military)
ASC . . . . Altered State of Consciousness
ASC . . . . Alternate Squadron Commander (Air Force)
ASC . . . . American Safety Council
ASC . . . . American Sailing Council
ASC . . . . American Security Council
ASC . . . . American Silk Council
ASC . . . . American Society of Cartographers
ASC . . . . American Society of Cinematographers
ASC . . . . American Society of Criminology
ASC . . . . American Society for Cybernetics
ASC . . . . American Society of Cytology
ASC . . . . American Spaniel Club
ASC . . . . Analog Signal Correlator
ASC . . . . Analog Strip Chart

ASC . . . . Annapolis Science Center
ASC . . . . Anti-Static Compound
ASC . . . . Applied Science Corporation
ASC . . . . Arizona State College
ASC . . . . Arkansas State College
ASC . . . . Arlington State College (Texas)
ASC . . . . Army Service Corps
ASC . . . . Army Signal Corps
ASC . . . . Army Specialist Corps
ASC . . . . Army Subsistence Center
ASC . . . . Asian Socialist Conference
ASC . . . . Assigned Service Contractor
ASC . . . . Associate in Science in Commerce
ASC . . . . Associated Sandblasting Contractors
ASC . . . . Associated Schools of Construction
ASC . . . . Astronautical Society of Canada
ASC . . . . Astronautics Support Center
ASC . . . . Atlantic Seaboard Circuit (Horse racing)
ASC . . . . Aughey Spark Chamber
ASC . . . . Automatic Scan Counter
ASC . . . . Automatic Sensitivity Control
ASC . . . . Automatic Switching Center
ASC . . . . Automatic System Control
ASC . . . . Auxiliary Switch (Breaker) Normally Closed
AS & C . . . . . Aerospace Surveillance and Control
ASCA . . . . . . American School Counselor Association
ASCA . . . . . . American-Serbian Cultural Association
ASCA . . . . . . American Shrimp Canners Association
ASCA . . . . . . American Society for Church Architecture
ASCA . . . . . . American Society of Consulting Arborists
ASCA . . . . . . American Society of Contemporary Artists
ASCA . . . . . American Standard Chinchilla Association
ASCA . . . . . . Association for Sickle Cell Anemia
ASCA . . . . . . Automatic Subject Citation Alert (Institute for Scientific Information)
ASCAA . . . . . Automobile Seat Cover Association of America
ASCAC . . . . . Anti-Submarine Classification Analysis Center (Navy)
ASCAIA . . . . Association of Student Chapters, American Institute of Architects
ASCAM . . . . . Aerospace Catalog Automated Microfilm, Inc.
ASCAP . . . . . American Society of Composers, Authors and Publishers
ASCAS . . . . . All-Service Close Air Support (Military)
ASCAT . . . . . Analog Self-Checking Automatic Tester
ASCATS . . . . . Apollo Simulation Checkout and Training System
ASCC . . . . . . Air Standardization Coordinating Committee
ASCC . . . . . . American Society of Concrete Constructors
ASCC . . . . . . Army Strategic Communications Command
ASCC . . . . . . Automatic Sequence Controlled Calculator (First all-automatic calculating machine)
ASCCA . . . . . Automobile Seat Cover Association of America
ASCD . . . . . . Association for Supervision and Curriculum Development
ASCE . . . . . . Abrupt Space Charge Edge (Algorithm)
ASCE . . . . . . American Society of Christian Ethics
ASCE . . . . . . American Society of Civil Engineers
ASCE . . . . . . Association of Safety Council Executives
ASCENT . . . . . Assembly System for Central Processor (UNIVAC)
ASCET . . . . . . American Society of Certified Engineering Technicians
ASCGW . . . . . Action-Study Center for a Governed World
ASCH . . . . . . American Society of Church History
ASCH . . . . . . American Society of Clinical Hypnosis
ASCHE . . . . . American Society of Chemical Engineers
ASCH-ERF . . . . American Society of Clinical Hypnosis - Education and Research Foundation
ASCI . . . . . . American Society for Clinical Investigation
ASCI . . . . American Society of Construction Inspectors
ASCID . . . . . . Altered States of Consciousness Induction Device
ASCII . . . . . . American Standard Code for Information Interchange (Department of Commerce)
ASCL . . . . . . Advanced System Concepts Laboratory (Army)
ASCL . . . . . . American Sugar Cane League of the USA
ASCLU . . . . . American Society of Chartered Life Underwriters
ASCM . . . . . . American Society of Chinese Medicine
ASCM . . . . . . Association of Sprocket Chain Manufacturers (Defunct)
ASCMA . . . . . American Sprocket Chain Manufacturers Association
ASCN . . . . . . American Society for Clinical Nutrition
ASCO . . . . . . Associated Spring Corporation
ASCO . . . . . . Association of Schools and Colleges of Optometry
ASCO . . . . . . Auxiliary Sustainer Cut-Off
ASCOFAM . . . Association Mondiale de Lutte Contre la Faim
ASCOM . . . . . Area Service Command (Army)
ASCOM . . . . . Army Service Command
ASCOMACE . . . Association des Constructeurs de Machines a Coudre de la CEE (Association of Sewing Machine Manufacturers of the EEC)

ASCOP . . . . . . Applied Science Corporation of Princeton
ASCORE . . . . . Automatic Shipboard Checkout and Readiness Equipment
ASCP . . . . . . Air Standardization Coordination Program (NATO)
ASCP . . . . . . American Society of Clinical Pathologists
ASCP . . . . . . American Society of Consultant Pharmacists
ASCP . . . . . . American Society of Consulting Planners
ASCP . . . . . . Army Strategic Capabilities Plan
ASCR . . . . . . Advanced Sodium Cooled Reactor
ASCR . . . . . . American Society of Chiropodical Roentgenology
ASCR . . . . . . Analog Strip Chart Recorder
ASCRA . . . . . American Standard Chinchilla Rabbit Association
ASCRO . . . . . Active Service Career for Reserve Officers
ASCS . . . . . . Aerospace Surveillance and Control Squadron (Air Force)
ASCS . . . . . . Agricultural Stabilization and Conservation Service (Department of Agriculture)
ASCS . . . . . . American Society of Corporate Secretaries
ASCS . . . . . . Attitude and Spin Control Subsystem (NASA)
ASCS . . . . . . Automatic Scan Counter System
ASCS . . . . . . Automatic Stabilization & Control System
ASCU . . . . . . Air Support Control Units
ASCU . . . . . . Alarm System Control Unit
ASCU . . . . . . Armament Station Control Unit
ASCU . . . . . . Association of State Colleges and Universities
ASCU . . . . . . Automatic Scanning Control Unit
ASCUFRO . . . . Association of State Colleges and Universities Forestry Research Organizations
ASCUS . . . . . Association for School, College, and University Staffing
ASCVD . . . . . Arteriosclerotic Cardiovascular Disease
ASD . . . . Adjustable Speed Drive
ASD . . . . Adult Services Division (of American Library Association)
ASD . . . . Advanced Ship Development
ASD . . . . Advanced Systems Division (IBM)
ASD . . . . Aeronautical System Development
ASD . . . . Aeronautical Systems Division (AFSC)
ASD . . . . Aerospace Systems Division
ASD . . . . Airspace Docket
ASD . . . . All Saints' Day
ASD . . . . Alside, Inc. (NYSE symbol) (Delisted)
ASD . . . . Alternate Source Development
ASD . . . . American Society of Dowsers
ASD . . . . Army Shipping Document
ASD . . . . Artillery Spotting Division
ASD . . . . Assignment Selection Date (Military)
ASD . . . . Assistant Secretary of Defense
ASD . . . . Associated Surplus Dealers (An organization)
ASD . . . . Association for Social Design
ASD . . . . Association of Steel Distributors
ASD . . . . Atomic Solution Diffusion
ASD . . . . Automated Structural Design (NASA)
ASD . . . . Aviation Supply Depot
ASDA . . . . . . American Safe Deposit Association
ASDA . . . . . . American Seafood Distributors Association
ASDA . . . . . . American Stamp Dealers Association
ASDA . . . . . . Association of Structural Draftsmen of America
ASDA . . . . . . Atomic and Space Development Authority
ASD(A) . . . . . Assistant Secretary of Defense (Administration)
ASDAE . . . . . Association of Seventh-Day Adventist Educators
AsDB . . . . . . Asian Development Bank
ASDC . . . . . . Aeronomy and Space Data Center (National Oceanic and Atmospheric Administration)
ASDC . . . . . . American Society of Dentistry for Children
ASD (C) . . . . . Assistant Secretary of Defense (Comptroller)
ASDE . . . . . . Airport Surface Detection Equipment
ASDE . . . . . . American Society of Danish Engineers
ASDEC . . . . . Applied Systems Development Evaluation Center
ASDEC . . . . . Automatic Selection of Digital Electronic Computers
ASDEFORLANT . . Antisubmarine Defense Forces, Atlantic (Navy)
ASDEFORPAC . . Antisubmarine Destroyer Forces, Pacific (Navy)
ASDEVLANT . . Antisubmarine Development Detachment, Atlantic Fleet
ASDG . . . . . . Aircraft Storage & Disposition Group (Air Force)
ASDG . . . . . . Antisubmarine Defense Group
ASD/H & M . . Assistant Secretary of Defense (Health and Medical)
ASDI . . . . . . Automatic Selective Dissemination of Information
ASDIC . . . . . Antisubmarine Detection Investigation Committee (Actually, a device rather than a group of persons) (World War I)
ASDIC . . . . . Armed Services Documents Intelligence Center
ASD (I & L) . . . Assistant Secretary of Defense (Installations & Logistics)
ASDIRS . . . . . Army Study Documentation and Information Retrieval System
ASD/ISA . . . . Assistant Secretary of Defense (International Security Affairs)
ASDJ . . . . . . American Society of Disk Jockeys
ASDM . . . . . . America's Society of Divorced Men (Elgin, Illinois)

ASD (M)	Assistant Secretary of Defense (Manpower)
ASD/MP & R	Assistant Secretary of Defense (Manpower, Personnel, and Reserves)
ASD(M & RA)	Assistant Secretary of Defense (Manpower and Reserve Affairs)
ASDO	Aviation Safety District Office
ASDP	Automatic Shot Dispensing Pump
ASD (PA)	Assistant Secretary of Defense (Public Affairs)
ASD/P & I	Assistant Secretary of Defense (Properties and Installations)
ASDR	Airport Surface Detection (RADAR)
ASDR	American Society of Dental Radiographers
ASD/R & D	Assistant Secretary of Defense (Research and Development)
ASD/R & E	Assistant Secretary of Defense (Research and Engineering)
ASD(SA)	Assistant Secretary of Defense (Systems Analysis)
ASD/S & L	Assistant Secretary of Defense (Supply and Logistics)
ASDSVN	Army Switched Data and Secure Voice Network
ASDVS	American Society of Directors of Volunteer Services
ASE	Active Seismic Experiment (NASA)
ASE	Aerospace Support Equipment
ASE	Airborne Search Equipment
ASE	Aircraft Search Equipment
ASE	Aircraft Stores Establishment (Navy)
ASE	All-Steel Equipment, Inc.
ASE	Allowable Steering Error
ASE	American Society of Engineers
ASE	American Society of Enologists
ASE	American Stock Exchange
ASE	Associate in Engineering
ASE	Association of Senior Engineers of the Naval Ship System Command (Formerly, ASEBS)
ASE	Association for Stamp Exhibitions
ASE	Audio Support Equipment
ASE	Australasian Society of Engineers
ASE	Automatic Stabilization Equipment
ASE	Automatic Support Equipment
ASEA	Allmanna Svenska Electriska Aktiebolaget (Sweden)
ASEA	American Society for Eastern Arts
ASEA	American Society of Engineers and Architects
ASEAN	Association of Southeast Asian Nations (Formerly, Association of Southeast Asia)
ASEB	Aeronautics and Space Engineering Board
ASEBS	Association of Senior Engineers of the Bureau of Ships (Later, ASE)
ASEC	Airworthiness Standards Evaluation Committee (FAA)
ASEC	Allied Secretariat (Allied German Occupation Forces)
ASEC	American Standard Elevator Codes
ASECA	Association for Education and Cultural Advancement (South Africa)
ASECH	Acetylselenocholine
ASECNA	Agency for the Security of Air Navigation
ASECS	American Society for Eighteenth-Century Studies
ASED	Ammoniaque Synthetique et Derives (Belgium)
ASEE	American Society for Engineering Education
A/SEE	Antisubmarine Experimental Establishment
ASEF	Association of Stock Exchange Firms (Later, Securities Industry Association)
ASEIB	American Sanitary Engineering Intersociety Board
ASEP	Advanced Science Education Program (National Science Foundation)
ASEP	American Society of Electroplated Plastics
ASEP	American Society for Experimental Pathology
ASEPELT	Association Scientifique Europeenne pour la Prevision Economique a Moyen et Long Terme (European Scientific Association for Medium and Long-Term Economic Forecasts)
ASER	Amplification by Stimulated Emission of Radiation
A Se S	Associate in Secretarial Science
ASESA	Armed Services Electro-Standards Agency
ASESB	Armed Services Explosives Safety Board
ASESBD	Armed Services Explosives Safety Board (Army)
A Se Sc	Associate in Secretarial Science
ASESS	Aero-Space Environment Simulation System
ASETC	Armed Services Electron Tube Committee
AS & EWD	Air, Surface and Electronic Warfare Division (Navy)
ASF	Additional Selection Factor
ASF	Advisory Support Force (Military)
ASF	Aerospace Security Force
ASF	Aircraft Services Facility
ASF	Alaskan Sea Frontier (Navy)
ASF	American-Scandinavian Foundation
ASF	Ammunition Storage Facility (Military)
ASF	Amperes per Square Foot
ASF	Arithmetic Statement Function
ASF	Army Service Forces
ASF	Army Stock Fund
ASF	Assignable Square Feet
ASF	Association of State Foresters
ASF	Atomic Scattering Factor
ASF	Automatic Store and Forward
ASF	Automotive Safety Foundation
ASFA	American Science Film Association
ASFA	American Steel Foundrymen's Association
ASFALEC	Association des Fabricants de Laits de Conserve des Pays de la CEE (Association of Powdered Milk Manufacturers of the EEC)
A/SFDO	Antisubmarine Fixed Defenses Officer
ASFEC	Arab States Fundamental Education Centre
ASFG	Atmospheric Sound-Focusing Gain
ASFIR	Active Swept-Frequency Interferometer RADAR (RADC)
ASFISS	Advance Simulation Facility Interconnection and Setup System (Air Force)
ASFLH	American Society of the French Legion of Honor
ASFMRA	American Society of Farm Managers and Rural Appraisers
ASFS	American Seamen's Friend Society
ASFS	American Society for Friendship with Switzerland
ASFSA	American School Food Service Association
ASFSE	American Swiss Foundation for Scientific Exchange
ASFTCU	Army Service Forces Training Center Unit
ASFTRNTRARONPAC	Auxiliary Service Force, Transition Training Squadron, Pacific
ASG	Administrative Support Group (Army)
ASG	Advanced Studies Group (Air Force)
ASG	Aeronautical Standards Group (Military)
ASG	Air Service Group (Air Force)
ASG	Aircraft Supply Group
ASG	Airless Spray Gun
ASG	American Society of Genealogists
ASG	Antenna Steering Group
ASG	Army Surgeon General
ASG	Association of Student Governments
ASG	Automatic Spray Gun
ASGA	Advertising Specialty Guild of America
ASGAN	Assistant Secretary General for Air Navigation (ICAO)
ASGCA	American Society of Golf Course Architects
ASGD	American Society of Geriatric Dentistry
ASGE	American Society for Gastrointestinal Endoscopy
ASGE	Association for the Study of the Grants Economy
ASGLS	Advanced Space Ground Link Subsystem
ASGM	American Scripture Gift Mission
ASGN	Assign(ment)
ASGp	Aeronautical Standards Group (Air Force)
ASGPP	American Society of Group Psychotherapy & Psychodrama
ASGRO	Armed Services Graves Registration Office
ASGS	American Scientific Glassblowers Society
ASGS	Assistant Secretary General Staff
ASH	Action on Smoking and Health (Antismoking organization)
ASH	American Society of Hematology
ASH	Armature Shunt
ASH	Ashland Oil, Inc. (NYSE symbol)
ASH	Assault Support Helicopter (Military)
ASHA	American School Health Association
ASHA	American Shire Horse Association
ASHA	American Social Health Association
ASHA	American Social Hygiene Association
ASHA	American Speech and Hearing Association
ASHA	American Suffolk Horse Association
ASHACE	American Society of Heating and Air Conditioning Engineers
ASHAE	American Society of Heating and Air-Conditioning Engineers (Later, ASHRAE)
ASHBA	American Saddle Horse Breeders Association
ASHBA	American Scotch Highland Breeders' Association
ASHC	All States Hobby Club
ASHD	Arteriosclerotic Heart Disease
ASHE	American Society for Hospital Engineers (of American Hospital Association)
ASHET	American Society for Hospital Education and Training
ASHF	American Swedish Historical Foundation and Museum
ASHFSA	American Society for Hospital Food Service Administrators (of the American Hospital Association)
ASHG	American Society of Human Genetics
ASHP	American Society of Hospital Pharmacists
ASHPA	American Society for Hospital Personnel Administration
ASHPS	American Scenic and Historic Preservation Society
ASHRAE	American Society of Heating, Refrigerating and Air-Conditioning Engineers (Formerly, ASHAE)
ASHS	American Society for Horticultural Science
ASHVE	American Society of Heating and Ventilating Engineers
ASI	Advanced Scientific Instruments
ASI	Aerospace Static Inverter

ASI . . . . Aerospace Studies Institute (Air Force)
ASI . . . . Africa Service Institute of New York
ASI . . . . Air Society, International
ASI . . . . Airspeed Indicator (Aviation)
ASI . . . . Alphabetic Subject Index (A publication)
ASI . . . . Alphabetical Subject Index
ASI . . . . Althydusamband Islands (Icelandic Federation of Labor)
ASI . . . . Altimeter Setting Indicator (Aviation)
ASI . . . . Amended Shipping Instruction
ASI . . . . American Society of Indexers
ASI . . . . American Soybean Institute
ASI . . . . American Specification Institute
ASI . . . . American Swedish Institute
ASI . . . . Anti-Saturation Inverter
ASI . . . . Augmented Spark Igniter
ASI . . . . Augustana Swedish Institute
ASI . . . . Aviation Services, Incorporated
ASI . . . . Azimuth Speed Indicator
ASIA . . . . Airlines Staff International Association
ASIA . . . . American Society of Industrial Auctioneers
ASIA . . . . American Stone Importers Association
ASIA . . . . Army Signal Intelligence Agency
ASIA . . . . Asian Studies in America
ASIA . . . . Automotive Service Industry Association
ASIC . . . . Air Service Information Circular
ASIC . . . . Area Security Information Center
ASICA . . . . . . Association Internationale pour le Calcul Analogique
ASID . . . . American Society of Industrial Designers
ASID . . . . Association of Sports Information Directors
ASID . . . . Automatic Station Identification Device
ASIDIC . . . . . . Association of Scientific Information Dissemination Centers
ASIF . . . . Airlift Service Industrial Fund (Military)
ASIGCEN . . . . Area Signal Center (Army)
ASIH . . . . American Society of Ichthyologists and Herpetologists
ASII . . . . American Science Information Institute
ASIL . . . . American Society of International Law
ASILS . . . . Association of Student International Law Societies
ASIM . . . . American Society of Insurance Management
ASIM . . . . American Society of Internal Medicine
ASIM . . . . Associate in Industrial Management
ASIP . . . . Aircraft Structural Integrity Program
ASIPRE . . . . . Army Snow, Ice and Permafrost Research Establishment
ASIRC . . . . . . Aquatic Sciences Information Retrieval Center (University of Rhode Island)
ASIRC . . . . . . Armed Services Industrial Readiness Council
ASIS . . . . Abort Sensing & Implementation System
ASIS . . . . American Society for Industrial Security
ASIS . . . . American Society for Information Science (Formerly, American Documentation Institute)
ASIS . . . . Ammunition Stores Issue Ship
ASIS . . . . Assateague Island National Seashore (National Park Service designation)
ASIWPCA . . . . . Association of State and Interstate Water Pollution Control Administrators
ASJA . . . . Assistant Staff Judge Advocate (Air Force)
ASJSA . . . . . . American Society of Journalism School Administrators
ASK . . . . Adjustable Stroke Kit
ASK . . . . Aircraft Station Keeper
ASK . . . . Amplitude Shift Keying
ASK . . . . Astronaut Survival Kit
ASKS . . . . Automatic Station Keeping System
ASKT . . . . American Society of Knitting Technologists
ASL . . . . Abbe's Sine Law
ASL . . . . Above Sea Level
ASL . . . . Advanced Systems Laboratory
ASL . . . . Aeronautical Structures Laboratory (Navy)
ASL . . . . American Association of State Libraries
ASL . . . . American Shuffleboard Leagues
ASL . . . . American Sign Language (for the deaf)
ASL . . . . Antistreptolysin
ASL . . . . Applied Science Laboratory
ASL . . . . Army Standards Laboratory
ASL . . . . Association of Standards Laboratories
ASL . . . . Association for Symbolic Logic
ASL . . . . Astigmatic Spectral Line
ASL . . . . Astrosurveillance Science Laboratory
ASL . . . . Atmospheric Sciences Laboratory
ASL . . . . Authorized Stockage List (Army)
ASL . . . . Automated Soft Lander (Aerospace)
ASL . . . . Average Service Life
ASL . . . . Aviation Systems Laboratory
ASLA . . . . American Society of Landscape Architects

ASLA . . . . Association of State Library Agencies (Formerly, Association of State Libraries)
ASLB . . . . Atomic Safety and Licensing Board (AEC)
ASLBM . . . . . . Antisubmarine Launched Ballistic Missile
ASLE . . . . American Society of Lubrication Engineers
ASLH . . . . American Society for Legal History
ASLI . . . . American Savings and Loan Institute
Aslib . . . . No longer used as an acronym; this style adopted as formal name when ASLIB (Association of Special Libraries and Information Bureaux) merged in 1949 with British Society for International Bibliography
AS & LL . . . . . American Savings and Loan League
ASLNY . . . . . . Art Students' League of New York
ASLO . . . . American Society of Limnology and Oceanography
ASLP . . . . Association of Special Libraries of the Philippines
ASLRA . . . . . . Association of State Labor Relations Agencies
ASLRRA . . . . . American Short Line Railroad Association
ASLS . . . . Associazione Sindacati Lavoratore della Somalia (Workers' Trade Union Association of Somalia)
ASLT . . . . Advanced Solid Logic Technology
ASLT . . . . Assault
ASM . . . . Advanced Surface Missile
ASM . . . . Aerospace Structural Material
ASM . . . . Air-to-Surface Missile (Air Force)
ASM . . . . American Society of Mammalogists
ASM . . . . American Society for Metals
ASM . . . . American Society for Microbiology
ASM . . . . Antarctica Service Medal (US)
ASM . . . . Antenna Switching Matrix
ASM . . . . Aviation School of Medicine
ASM . . . . Avionics Shop Maintenance
ASMA . . . . . . Aerospace Medical Association
ASMA . . . . . . American Ski Manufacturers' Association
ASMA . . . . . . American Society of Music Arrangers
ASMC . . . . . . Army Supply & Maintenance Command
ASMC . . . . . . Aviation Surface Material Command (Army)
ASMD . . . . . . Association of Science Museum Directors
ASME . . . . . . American Society of Magazine Editors
ASME . . . . . . American Society of Mechanical Engineers
ASME . . . . . . Association for the Study of Medical Education
ASMFC . . . . . . Atlantic States Marine Fisheries Commission
ASMHBA . . . . . American Society of Mental Hospital Business Administrators
ASMI . . . . Airfield Surface Movement Indicator
ASMIC . . . . . . American Society of Military Insignia Collectors
ASMM . . . . . . American Society for Metals Monographs
ASMMA . . . . . American Supply and Machinery Manufacturers Association
ASMOLV . . . . . Afford Service Member Opportunity to Apply for Ordinary Leave (Army)
ASMP . . . . . . American Society of Magazine Photographers
ASMP . . . . . . Army Survival Measures Plan
ASMPA . . . . . . Armed Services Medical Procurement Agency
ASMPE . . . . . . American Society of Motion Picture Engineers (Later, ASMPTE)
ASMPTE . . . . . American Society of Motion Picture and Television Engineers (Formerly ASMPE)
ASMRO . . . . . . Armed Services Medical Regulating Office
ASMS . . . . Advanced Surface Missile System
ASMS . . . . Advanced Synchronous Meteorological Satellite
ASMS . . . . American Society of Maxillofacial Surgeons
ASMS . . . . Associate in Science in Medical Secretarial
ASMSA . . . . . . Army Signal Material (or Missile) Support Agency
ASMT . . . . American Society of Medical Technologists
ASN . . . . Alco Standard Corp. (NYSE symbol)
ASN . . . . Allotment Serial Number
ASN . . . . American Society of Naturalists
ASN . . . . Army Serial Number
ASN . . . . Army Service Number
ASN . . . . Asparagine (Amino acid)
ASN . . . . Assistant Secretary of the Navy
ASN . . . . Associate in Nursing
ASN . . . . Associate in Nursing Science
ASN . . . . Atomic Strike Net
ASN . . . . Average Sample Number (Quality control)
ASN . . . . Axially Symmetric Nozzle
ASNA . . . . . . Advertising Specialty National Association
ASNA . . . . . . Arctic Slope Native Association
ASNE . . . . American Society of Naval Engineers
ASNE . . . . American Society of Newspaper Editors
ASNEMGE . . . . Association des Societes Nationales Europeennes et Mediterraneennes de Gastroenterologie
ASN (FM) . . . . . Assistant Secretary of the Navy (Financial Management)
ASNLH . . . . . . Association for the Study of Negro Life and History
ASNP . . . . Army Student Nurse Program
ASN(R & D) . . Assistant Secretary of the Navy (Research and Development)

ASNT	American Society for Nondestructive Testing (Atomic energy)
AS of NY	Australian Society of New York
ASO	Accommodation Sales Order
ASO	Administrative Service Office
ASO	Air Signal Officer
ASO	Air Staff Officer
ASO	Air Staff Orientation
ASO	Air Surveillance Officer (Air Force)
ASO	Alarm System Operation
ASO	American Society for Oceanography
ASO	American Society of Orthodontists
ASO	American Sokol Educational and Physical Culture Organization
ASO	Ammunition Supply Officer
ASO	Area Supply Officer (Army)
ASO	Assistant Secretary's Office (Navy)
ASO	Auxiliary Switch (Breaker) Normally Open (Electricity)
ASO	Aviation Supply Office (Air Force)
ASOA	Avicultural Society of America
ASOAP	Army Spectrometric Oil Analysis Program
ASOC	Air Support Operations Center (Air Force)
ASOL	American Symphony Orchestra League
ASOOA	American Society of Ophthalmologic & Otolaryngologic Allergy
ASOP	Army Strategic Objectives Plan
ASOP	Automatic Operating and Scheduling Program
ASOP	Aviation Supply Office Philadelphia (Navy)
ASOR	American Schools of Oriental Research
ASOS	American Society of Oral Surgeons
ASOS	Assistant Supervisor of Shipbuilding (Navy)
ASOS	Automatic Storm Observation Service (AFCRL)
ASOTS	Africa South of the Sahara (Military)
ASP	Active SONAR Processor
ASP	Advanced Study Program
ASP	Advanced System Planning (Air Force)
ASP	Aerospace Plane
ASP	Afro-Shirazi Party (Zanzibar)
ASP	Air Superiority Mission
ASP	Airborne Support Platform (Army)
ASP	Airspace Subcommittee (ACC)
ASP	All-Altitude Spin Projected (Munition)
ASP	Aluminum Silicate Pigment
ASP	American Selling Price
ASP	American Society of Papyrologists
ASP	American Society of Parasitologists
ASP	American Society of Perfumers
ASP	American Society of Periodontists
ASP	American Society of Pharmacognosy
ASP	American Society of Photogrammetry
ASP	Ammunition Supply Point
ASP	Amphibious Supply Platform (Army)
ASP	Annual Service Practice (Firings) (Military)
ASP	Anti-Ship Phoenix
ASP	Antisubmarine Patrol
ASP	Apollo Simple Penetrometer (NASA)
ASP	Area Specialist Program (Air Force training program)
ASP	Army Strategic Plan (A document)
ASP	Aspartic Acid (Amino acid)
ASP	Association-Storing Processor (Data processing)
ASP	Astronomical Society of the Pacific
ASP	Atmosphere Sounding Projectile
ASP	Atomic Strike Plan
ASP	Attached Support Processor (Data processing)
ASP	Augmented Support Period (or Plan)
ASP	Automated Spooling Priority (Data processing)
ASP	Automatic Schedule Procedures
ASP	Automatic Services and Products
ASP	Automatic Servo Plotter
ASP	Automatic Specimen Positioning
ASP	Automatic Switching Panel
ASP	Automatic Synthesis Program
ASP	Auxiliary Spacecraft Power
ASP	Average Speech Power
ASPA	American Society for Personnel Administration
ASPA	American Society of Practicing Architects
ASPA	American Society for Public Administration
ASPA	Armed Services Petroleum Agency
ASPA	Armed Services Procurement Act
ASPAB	Armed Services Patent Advisory Board (DOD)
ASPAC	Asian and Pacific Council
ASPAU	African Scholarship Program of American Universities (Joint undertaking, headquartered in Cambridge, Mass., to provide aid to African applicants for admission to American universities)

ASPB	American Society of Professional Biologists
ASPB	Armed Services Petroleum Board
ASPB	Assault Support Patrol Boat (Navy symbol)
ASPC	American Sheep Producers Council
ASPC	American Shetland Pony Club
ASPC	American Society for the Prevention of Crime
ASPC	Analysis Spare Parts Change
ASPCA	American Society for the Prevention of Cruelty to Animals
ASPCGA	Atomic Strike Plan Control Group Alternate
ASPD	American Society for Preventive Dentistry
ASPDA	American Society of Professional Draftsmen and Artists
ASPDA	Association of State Planning and Development Agencies
ASPDE	Automatic Shaft-Position Data Encoder
ASPDM	American Society of Psychosomatic Dentistry and Medicine
ASPE	American Society of Psychopathology of Expression
ASPEP	Association of Scientists and Professional Engineering Personnel
ASPER	Assembly System for the Peripheral Processors
ASPERS	Armed Services Procurement Regulations
ASPET	American Society for Pharmacology and Experimental Therapeutics
ASPH	Association of Schools of Public Health
ASPHRS	Asphalt Roof Shingles (Technical drawings)
ASPHV	Association of State Public Health Veterinarians
ASPIC	Armed Services Personnel Interrogation Center
ASPIRE	Achieve Successful Performance, Intensify Reliability Effort
ASPIRE	Advanced Special Projects in Radiation Effects
ASPIRE	Associated Students Promoting Individual Rights for Everyone
ASPMA	American Smoking Pipe Manufacturers Association
ASPN	American Society of Precision Nailmakers
ASPO	American Society of Planning Officials
ASPO	American Society for Psychoprophylaxis in Obstetrics
ASPO	Antisubmarine Systems Project Office (Navy)
ASPO	Apollo Spacecraft Program Office
ASPP	Alloy-Steel Protective Plating
ASPP	American Society of Picture Professionals
ASPP	American Society of Plant Physiologists
ASPP	American Society of Polar Philatelists
ASPP	Association for Sane Psychiatric Practices
ASPPA	Armed Services Petroleum Purchasing Agency
ASPPF	Association of Seminary Professors in the Practical Fields
ASPPO	Armed Services Procurement Planning Officer
ASPPR	Association of Sugar Producers of Puerto Rico
ASPR	American Society for Psychical Research
ASPR	Armed Services Procurement Regulation
ASPR	Armed Services Procurement Regulations (Committee)
ASPRL	Armament Systems Personnel Research Laboratory (Air Force)
ASPRS	American Society of Plastic and Reconstructive Surgeons
ASPS	Acoustic Ship Positioning System
ASPS	Automatic Specimen Positioning System
ASPSC	Association of State and Provincial Safety Coordinators
ASPSPOM	American Society for the Preservation of Sacred, Patriotic and Operatic Music
ASPT	American Society of Plant Taxonomists
ASQ	Administrative Science Quarterly
ASQC	American Society for Quality Control
ASQDE	American Society of Questioned Document Examiners
ASR	Acceptance Summary Report
ASR	Advanced Surveillance RADAR
ASR	Advanced Systems Requirements
ASR	Air-Sea-Rescue
ASR	Air Search RADAR
ASR	Air (or Area) Surveillance RADAR
ASR	Airborne Scanning Radiometer
ASR	Airport Surveillance RADAR
ASR	American Society of Rocketry
ASR	Amstar Corp. (Formerly, American Sugar Company) (NYSE symbol)
ASR	Annual Summary Report
ASR	Approved System Requirement
ASR	Area Surveillance RADAR
ASR	Association of Southeastern Railroads
ASR	Atmospheric Sound Refraction
ASR	Atomic Strike Recording
ASR	Automatic Send and Receive
ASR	Automatic Sprinkler Riser (Technical drawings)
ASR	Automatic Step Regulator
ASR	Auxiliary Submarine Rescue (Ship) (Navy)
ASR	Available Supply Rate
ASR	Aviation Safety Regulation
ASR	Submarine Rescue Vessel (Navy symbol)
AS/R	Automatic Send/Receive (Communications equipment)
ASRA	American Shropshire Registry Association
ASRA	Automatic Stereo Recording Amplifier

ASRB . . . . Armed Services Renegotiation Board
ASRB . . . . Army Security Review Board
ASRBA . . . . . . American Satin Rabbit Breeders' Association
ASRC . . . . Air-Sea Rescue Craft
ASRC . . . . . . American Synthetic Rubber Corporation
ASRD . . . . Advanced Systems Research Department
ASRD . . . . Aircraft Shipment Readiness Date (Army)
ASRDI . . . . Aerospace Safety Research and Data Institute (Lewis Research Center)
            (NASA)
ASRDL . . . . . . Army Signal Research and Development Laboratory
ASRE . . . . . . Admiralty Signal and RADAR Establishment (British)
ASRE . . . . . . American Society of Refrigerating Engineers
ASREC . . . . . . American Society of Real Estate Counselors
ASRF . . . . . . American Seed Research Foundation
ASRI . . . . Aluminum Smelters Research Institute
ASRL . . . . . . Aeroelastic and Structures Research Laboratory (MIT)
ASRM . . . . . . American Society of Range Management
ASRNH . . . . . American Society for Russian Naval History
ASROC . . . . . Antisubmarine Rocket (Navy)
ASRPA . . . . . Army Signal Radio Propagation Agency
ASRR . . . . . . American Society for Reformation Research
ASRS . . . . . . Advanced Strategic Reconnaissance System (Air Force)
ASRS . . . . . . Airborne Satellite Receiving Station
ASRS . . . . . . Amalgamated Society of Railway Servants (New Zealand)
ASRS . . . . . . Anglo-Soviet Recognition Signals
ASRS . . . . . . Auxiliary Support Reaction System
ASRSC . . . . . Armed Services Research Specialists Committee
ASRT . . . . . . Air Support RADAR Team (Marine Corps)
ASRT . . . . . . American Society of Radiologic Technologists
ASS . . . . Accessory Supply System
ASS . . . . Advanced Space Station
ASS . . . . Aerosol Sampling System
ASS . . . . Aerospace Surveillance System
ASS . . . . Air Sampling System
ASS . . . . Air Surveillance System
ASS . . . . Airborne Surveillance Set
ASS . . . . Altitude Sensing System
ASS . . . . Analog Simulation System
ASS . . . . Anterior Superior Spine
ASS . . . . Army Special Staff
ASS . . . . Associate in Secretarial Science
ASS . . . . Associate in Secretarial Studies
ASS . . . . Automatic Stabilization System
ASS . . . . Automatic Start-up System (Reactor)
ASS . . . . Autopilot Surface Servo
ASSA . . . . . . American Shetland Sheepdog Association
ASSA . . . . . . American Society for the Study of Arteriosclerosis
ASSA . . . . Area Supply Support Activity
ASSA . . . . Army Signal Supply Agency
ASSA . . . . Cargo Submarine (Navy symbol)
ASSANEF . . . . . Association des Anciens Eleves des Ecoles des Freres Chretiennes
            (Association of Former Students of Catholic Schools)
ASSAW . . . . . . Aerospace Surveillance and Warning
ASSB . . . . Avionics Subsystem for Strategic Bombers
AS & SB . . . . . Automated Systems and Services Branch (NTIS)
ASSBT . . . . . . American Society of Sugar Beet Technologists
ASSC . . . . Army Subsistence Supply Center (Merged with Defense Subsistence Supply
            Center)
ASSCI . . . . . . American Section of the Societe de Chimie Industrielle
ASSCN . . . . . . Association
ASSDD . . . . . . Association of Summer Session Deans and Directors
ASSE . . . . . . American Society of Safety Engineers
ASSE . . . . . . American Society of Sanitary Engineering
ASSE . . . . . . American Society of Swedish Engineers
ASSE . . . . . . Association Suisse des Syndicats Evangeliques (Swiss Federation of
            Protestant Trade Unions)
ASSE . . . . . . Automation System for Scientific Experiments
ASSERON . . . . Army Service Squadron (Corresponds to Navy's CASU)
ASSESS . . . . . . Analytical Studies of Surface Effects of Submerged Submarines (Navy)
ASSET . . . . . . Advanced System Synthesis and Evaluation Technique (Lockheed Aircraft)
ASSET . . . . . . Aerothermodynamic/Elastic Structural Systems Environmental Test
            (Military)
ASSET . . . . . . American Society of Scientific and Engineering Translators
ASSET . . . . . . American-South African Study and Educational Trust
ASSET . . . . . . Automated Spares Simulation Estimating Technique (Boeing)
ASSH . . . . . . American Society for Surgery of the Hand
ASSILEC . . . . . Association de l'Industrie Laitiere de la CEE (Milk Industry Association
            of the EEC)
ASSINSEL . . . . Association Internationale des Selectionneurs Professionnels pour la
            protection des Obtentions Vegetales (International Plant Breeders
            Association for the Protection of New Varieties)

ASSIPORT . . . . Association des Interets Portuaires
AS & SL . . . . . All Ships and Stations Letters
ASSM . . . . . . Authorization for Sale of Salvage Material
ASSMPE . . . . . Allied States Association of Motion Picture Exhibitors
ASSN . . . . . . Association
ASSOBELA . . . Association des Batetela de Lodja (Association of Batetelas of Lodja)
ASSOC . . . . . Associate (or Association)
ASSOCD . . . . . Associated
ASSOFECAM . . Association pour l'Emancipation de la Femme Camerounaise (Association
            for the Emancipation of Cameroonian Women)
ASSORECO . . . Association des Ressortissants du Haut et du Moyen Congo (Association of
            Natives of the Upper and Middle Congo)
ASSOSIRACI . . Association des Sinistres et Repatries de Cote d'Ivoire (Association of the
            Wounded and Repatriates of the Ivory Coast)
ASSP . . . . Aerospace Systems Security Program
ASSP . . . . Transport Submarine (Navy symbol)
ASSR . . . . . . American Society for the Study of Religion
ASSR . . . . . . Autonomous Soviet Socialist Republic
ASSRA . . . . . American Single Shot Rifle Association
ASSRON . . . . . Air Service Support Squadron (Army)
ASSS . . . . . . Aerospace Systems Safety Society
ASSS . . . . . . American Society for the Study of Sterility
ASSS . . . . . . American Suffolk Sheep Society
ASSS . . . . . . Associate in Science in Secretarial Studies
ASST . . . . . . Advanced Supersonic Transport
ASST . . . . . . American Society for Steel Treating
ASST . . . . . . Assistant
ASST . . . . . . Association of Social Science Teachers
ASST . . . . . . Association of Supervisory Staff and Technicians (British)
ASST . . . . . . Azienda de Stato per i Servizi Telefonici (Italy)
ASSU . . . . . . American Sunday School Union
ASSUC . . . . . . Association des Organisations Professionnelles du Commerce des Sucres
            pour les Pays de la CEE (Association of Sugar Trade Organizations for
            the EEC Countries)
AST . . . . Abort-Scan Table (NASA)
AST . . . . Absolute Space-Time
AST . . . . Action Sociale Tchadienne (Chadian Social Action)
AST . . . . Action Speed Tactical
AST . . . . Add-Subtract Time
AST . . . . Administrative-Supply Technician (Army)
AST . . . . Aerial Survey Team
AST . . . . Aerospace Technology (NASA)
AST . . . . Air Surveillance Technician (Air Force)
AST . . . . American Standard, Inc. (NYSE symbol)
AST . . . . Area Specialist Team (Army)
AST . . . . Army Satellite Tracking Center
AST . . . . Army Specialized Training
AST . . . . Association for Student Teaching
AST . . . . At Same Time
AST . . . . Atlantic Standard Time
AST . . . . Atomized Suspension Technique
ASTA . . . . . . Aerial Surveillance and Target Acquisition (Military)
ASTA . . . . . . American Seed Trade Association
ASTA . . . . . . American Society of Travel Agents
ASTA . . . . . . American Spice Trade Association
ASTA . . . . . . American String Teachers Association
ASTA . . . . . . American Surgical Trade Association
ASTAS . . . . . Antiradar Surveillance and Target Acquisition System
ASTC . . . . . . Advanced Satellite Tracking Center
ASTC . . . . . . American Sealyham Terrier Club
ASTC . . . . . . American Shih Tzu Club
ASTC . . . . . . Appalachian State Teachers College (North Carolina)
ASTC . . . . . . Arkansas State Teachers College
ASTC . . . . . . Aroostook State Teachers College (Maine)
ASTCDPD . . . . Association of State and Territorial Chronic Disease Program Directors
ASTD . . . . . . Air-Supported Threat Defense (Army)
ASTD . . . . . . American Society of Teachers of Dancing
ASTD . . . . . . American Society for Training and Development
ASTD . . . . . . American Society of Training Directors
ASTD . . . . . . Area Scale Temperature Display
ASTDD . . . . . Association of State and Territorial Dental Directors
ASTDLHS . . . . Association of State and Territorial Directors of Local Health Services
ASTDPHN . . . . Association of State and Territorial Directors of Public Health Nursing
ASTE . . . . . . American Society of Tool Engineers
ASTE . . . . . . Association for the Study of Soviet-Type Economies
ASTEC . . . . . Advanced Solar Turbo-Electric Conversion
ASTEC . . . . . American Steamship Traffic Executives Committee
ASTEC . . . . . Antisubmarine Technical Evaluation Center (Military)
ASTER . . . . . . Antisubmarine Terrier
ASTHE . . . . . . Average Straight Time Hourly Earnings
ASTHMA . . . . A Society to Help the Morale of Asthmatics

ASTHO . . . . . . Association of State and Territorial Health Officers
ASTI . . . . Applied Science and Technology Index
ASTIA . . . . . . Armed Services Technical Information Agency (Later, Defense Documentation Center)
ASTL . . . . Approved Supplier Tab List
ASTM . . . . . . American Society for Testing and Materials
ASTMC . . . . . ARS Structures and Materials Committee
ASTME . . . . . American Society of Tool and Manufacturing Engineers (Later, SME)
ASTMH . . . . . American Society of Tropical Medicine and Hygiene
ASTMS . . . . . Association of Scientific, Technical, and Management Staffs (British)
ASTND . . . . . Association of State and Territorial Nutrition Directors
ASTOR . . . . . Antisubmarine Torpedo Ordnance Rocket (Navy)
ASTP . . . . . . Army Specialized Training Program (World War II)
ASTPHLD . . . Association of State and Territorial Public Health Laboratory Directors
ASTPHND . . . . Association of State and Territorial Public Health Nutrition Directors
ASTR . . . . . . Aerospace Systems Test Reactor (Formerly, Aircraft Shield Test Reactor)
ASTR . . . . . . American Society for Theatre Research
ASTRA . . . . . Adapted Swimming-Pool Tank Reactor, Austria
ASTRA . . . . . Advanced Static Test Recording Apparatus
ASTRA . . . . . Air Space Transportation
ASTRA . . . . . Air Staff Training (Air Force)
ASTRA . . . . . Application of Space Techniques Relating to Aviation (International Civil Aviation Organization)
ASTRA . . . . . Astronomical and Space Techniques for Research on the Atmosphere (National Science Foundation project)
ASTRA . . . . . Automatic Sorting, Testing, Recording Analysis
ASTRAC . . . . Arizona Statistical Repetitive Analog Computer
ASTREC . . . . . Atomic Strike Evaluation Center
ASTREC . . . . Atomic Strike Recording System (Air Force)
ASTRID . . . . . Association Scientifique et Technique pour la Recherche en Informatique Documentaire
ASTRO . . . . . Advanced Spacecraft Truck/Trainer/Transport Reusable Orbiter
ASTRO . . . . . Aerodynamic Spacecraft Two-Stage Reusable Orbiter
ASTRO . . . . . Air Space Travel Research Organization
ASTRO . . . . . America's Sound Transportation Review Organization (AAR)
ASTRO . . . . . Artificial Satellite Time and Radio Orbit
ASTROS . . . . Automated Shell Theory for Rotating Structures (NASA)
ASTS . . . . . . American Sabbath Tract Society
ASTSECAF . . . . Assistant Secretary of Air Force
ASTSECNAV . . Assistant Secretary of Navy
ASTSECNAVAIR . . Assistant Secretary of the Navy for Air
ASTT . . . . . . American Society of Traffic and Transportation
ASTT . . . . . . Associate in Science in Teacher Training
ASTU . . . . . . Air Support Test Unit
ASTU . . . . . . Air Support Training Units
ASTU . . . . . . Army Specialized Training Unit
ASTU . . . . . . Automatic Systems Test Unit
ASTWg . . . . Aerospace Test Wing (Air Force)
ASU . . . . Administrative Service Unit
ASU . . . . Aircraft Scheduling Unit
ASU . . . . Aircraft Starting Unit
ASU . . . . Allied Supermarkets, Inc. (NYSE symbol)
ASU . . . . American Snowshoe Union
ASU . . . . American Student Union
ASU . . . . Area Service Unit
ASUBJSCD . . . . Army Subject Schedule
ASUC . . . . . . American Society of University Composers
ASUC . . . . . . Associated Students of the University of California
ASUD . . . . . . Aerovia Sud Americana
ASULGC . . . . Association of State Universities and Land-Grant Colleges
ASUPP . . . . . Air Supply
ASUS . . . . . . Associazione Studentesca Universitaria della Somalia (University Students' Association of Somalia)
ASUSSR . . . . . Academy of Science (Union of Soviet Socialist Republics)
ASUT . . . . . . Adapter Sub-Unit Tester
ASUUS . . . . . Amateur Skating Union of the United States
ASV . . . . Acceleration Switching Valve
ASV . . . . Aerothermodynamic Structural Vehicle (Air Force)
ASV . . . . Air Solenoid Valve
ASV . . . . . . Air-to-Surface Vessel
ASV . . . . Airborne Surface Vessel Detection (RADAR device)
ASV . . . . American Standard Version (of the Bible, 1901)
ASV . . . . Angle Stop Valve (Technical drawings)
ASV . . . . Anode Supply Voltage
ASV . . . . Anodic Stripping Voltammetry (Chemical analysis)
ASV . . . . Arithmetic Simple Variable
ASV . . . . . . Automatic Self-Verification
ASV . . . . Automatic Shuttle Valve
ASVAB . . . . . Armed Services Vocational Aptitude Battery (Tests)
ASVO . . . . . . American Society of Veterinary Ophthalmology
ASVPP . . . . . . American Society of Veterinary Physiologists and Pharmacologists

ASVS . . . . . . Airborne Stabilized Viewing System
ASW . . . . Air to Surface Weapon
ASW . . . . Antisubmarine Warfare
ASW . . . . Artificial Seawater
ASW . . . . Assistant Secretary of War
ASW . . . . Astronaut Work Station (NASA)
ASWA . . . . . Americon Society of Women Accountants
ASWA . . . . . American Steel Warehouse Association
A/SWA . . . . . Aviation/Space Writers Association
ASWAAF . . . . Arms and Services with the Army Air Forces
ASW/AAW . . . . Anti-Submarine Warfare and Anti-Air Warfare
ASWAC . . . . . Antisubmarine Warfare Advisory Committee
ASWAF . . . . . Arms and Services on duty with Air Force
ASWB . . . . . . Antisubmarine Warfare Barriers (Military)
ASWBPL . . . . Armed Services Whole Blood Processing Laboratory
ASWC . . . . . . Army Special Warfare Center
ASWCR . . . . . Airborne Surveillance Warning and Control RADAR (ASD/ADC)
ASWD . . . . . . Army Special Weapons Depot
ASWE . . . . . Admiralty Surface Weapon Establishment (British)
ASWEPS . . . . Antisubmarine Warfare Environmental Prediction System (Navy)
ASWEPS . . . . Antisubmarine Warfare Weapon Electronic Prediction System
ASWG . . . . . . American Steel and Wire Gage
ASWH . . . . . . Advise Soldier Write Home
ASWL . . . . . . Antisubmarine Warfare Laboratory (Military)
ASWLC . . . . . American Shortwave Listeners Club
ASWO . . . . . . (Naval) Air Stations Weekly Orders
ASWORG . . . . Antisubmarine Warfare Operational Research Group (World War II)
ASWS . . . . . . Antisubmarine Warfare Systems (Navy)
ASWSAG . . . . Antisubmarine Warfare Systems Analysis Group (Navy)
ASWSPO . . . . Antisubmarine Warfare, Special Projects Office
ASWTC . . . . . Antisubmarine Warfare Training Center (Navy)
ASWTNS . . . . Antisubmarine Warfare Tactical Navigation System (Navy)
ASWTRACEN . . Antisubmarine Warfare Training Center
ASWTU . . . . . Antisubmarine Warfare Training Unit
ASWU . . . . . . Antisubmarine Warfare Unit (Navy)
ASW/UW . . . . Antisubmarine Warfare / Underwater Warfare
ASXT . . . . . . American Society of X-Ray Technicians
ASYA . . . . . . American Stock Yards Association
ASYMCA . . . . Association of Secretaries Young Men's Christian Associations
ASZ . . . . American Society of Zoologists
ASZ . . . . American Sterilizer Co. (NYSE symbol)
ASZD . . . . . . American Society for Zero Defects
AT . . . . Acceptance Tester
AT . . . . Acceptance Trials (Shipbuilding)
AT . . . . Access Time
AT . . . . Achievement Test
AT . . . . Across Tape (Curve)
AT . . . . Action Taken
AT . . . . Adapter, Tee
AT . . . . Advanced Trainer (Air Force)
AT . . . . Aerial Torpedo
AT . . . . Air Technician (Air National Guard)
AT . . . . Air Temperature
AT . . . . Air Traffic Service (of FFA) (Also known as ATS)
AT . . . . Air Transmit
AT . . . . Air Transport (Military)
AT . . . . Airtight (Technical drawings)
AT . . . . Ambient Temperature
AT . . . . American Terms (Grain trade)
AT . . . . American Tobacco Company (NYSE symbol) (Later, AMB)
AT . . . . Aminotransferase (Enzyme)
AT . . . . Ampere-Turn (Technical drawings)
AT . . . . Analysis Time
AT . . . . Angle Template
AT . . . . Antitank
AT . . . . Antitorpedo
AT . . . . Armament Test
AT . . . . Assay Ton
At . . . . Astatine (Chemical element)
AT . . . . Astronomical Time
AT . . . . Atlantic Standard Time
AT . . . . Atomic Time
AT . . . . Automatic Test
AT . . . . Automatic Ticketing
AT . . . . Auxiliary Timer
AT . . . . Aviation Electronic Technician (Navy rating)
AT . . . . Awaiting Transportation
AT . . . . Tug, Ocean-Going (Navy symbol)
A/T . . . . Action Taken
A/T . . . . Action Time (Air Force)
A/T . . . . American Terms (Business and trade)

A/T . . . . Anti-Tank
A/T . . . . Anti-Torpedo (Nets)
A/T . . . . Attack Teacher
A & T . . . . . . Acceptance and Transfer
A & T . . . . Agricultural and Technical (in a college name)
A & T . . . . Assemble and Test
AT-7 . . . . Hexachlorophene
AT-10. . . . . . Antitetany Preparation #10
ATA . . . . Actual Time of Arrival
ATA . . . . Advertising Typographers Association of America
ATA . . . . Air to Air
ATA . . . . Air Transport Association of America
ATA . . . . Air Turbine Alternator
ATA . . . . Alimentary Toxic Aleukia
ATA . . . . . . Amateur Trapshooting Association
ATA . . . . . . American Taxicab Association
ATA . . . . American Taxpayers Association
ATA . . . . . . American Teachers Association
ATA . . . . . . American Thyroid Association
ATA . . . . American Title Association
ATA . . . . . . American Topical Association
ATA . . . . . . American Trainers Association
ATA . . . . . . American Transit Association
ATA . . . . . . American Translators Association
ATA . . . . . . American Travel Association
ATA . . . . . . American Tree Association
ATA . . . . . . American Trucking Associations
ATA . . . . . . American Tunaboat Association
ATA . . . . . . Appropriation Transfer Account
ATA . . . . . . Army Transportation Association
ATA . . . . . . Associate Technical Aide
ATA . . . . . . Associate in Technical Arts
ATA . . . . . . Association for Academic Travel Abroad
ATA . . . . . . Association of Technical Artists
ATA . . . . . . Atlantic Treaty Association
ATA . . . . . . Automatic Tracking Antenna
ATA . . . . . . Auxiliary Ocean Tug (Navy symbol)
ATA . . . . . . Azimuth Torquer Amplifier
ATAA . . . . . . Advertising Typographers Association of America
ATAA . . . . . . Air Transport Association of America
ATAAD . . . . . Antitank Assault Air Defense
ATABCS . . . . . Airborne Tactical Air Battle Control System
ATABE . . . . . Automatic Target and Battery Evaluation (Military)
ATABW . . . . . American Trade Association for British Woolens
ATAC . . . . . . Army Tank-Automotive Center (or Command)
ATACC . . . . . Airborne Tactical Air Control Capability (Air Force)
ATACCS . . . . Advanced Tactical Air Command and Control System
ATAD . . . . . . Absent on Temporary Additional Duty (Navy)
ATAD . . . . . . Air Technical Analysis Division
ATAD . . . . . . Atlanta Army Depot
ATAD . . . . . . Automatic Target Designation
ATAE . . . . . . American Trade Association Executives (now ASAE)
ATAE . . . . . . Associated Telephone Answering Exchanges
ATAF . . . . . . Agricultural Technical Assistance Foundation
ATAF . . . . . . Allied Tactical Air Force
ATAG . . . . . . Air Training Advisory Group
ATALA . . . . . Association pour l'Etude et le Developpement de la Traduction
          Automatique et de la Linguistique Appliquee
ATAM . . . . . . Automotive Trade Association Managers
ATAP . . . . . . Apollo Telemetry Aircraft Project
ATAR . . . . . . Above Transmitted As Received
ATAR . . . . . . Acquisition Tracking and Recognition (Aviation)
ATAR . . . . . . Advanced Tactical Avionics RADAR
ATAR . . . . . . Air-to-Air Recovery (Air Force)
ATAR . . . . . . Air-to-Air Visual Recognition (Aviation)
ATAR . . . . . . Antitank Aircraft Rocket
ATAR . . . . . . Automated Travel Agents Reservation
ATARS . . . . . Anti-Terrain Avoidance RADAR
ATAS . . . . . . Academy of Television Arts and Sciences
ATAS . . . . . . Air Traffic (Area) Supervisor
ATAS . . . . . . Air Transport Auxiliary Service (British)
ATAS . . . . . . Association of Telephone Answering Services
ATAS . . . . . . Automatic Test Analysis System
ATAS . . . . . . Automatic Three-Axis Stabilization
ATAS . . . . . . Automatic Tracking Antenna System
ATAW . . . . . . Advanced Tactical Assault Weapon
ATB . . . . . . Aeration Test Burner (Heating)
ATB . . . . Air Transport Bureau (ICAO)
ATB . . . . Aircraft Technical Bulletin
ATB . . . . All Trunks Busy (Communications)
ATB . . . . Amphibious Training Base (Navy)

ATB . . . . Anti-Tactical Ballistic Missile
ATB . . . . Antitank Battery (Military)
ATB . . . . Arctic Test Branch (Army)
ATB . . . . Army Transportation Board
ATB . . . . Artillery Test Board (Army)
ATB . . . . Asphalt-Tile Base (Technical drawings)
ATB . . . . Association for Tropical Biology
ATBA . . . . . . Association of Theatre Benefit Agents
ATBI . . . . . . Allied Trades of the Baking Industry
ATBM . . . . . . Advanced Tactical Ballistic Missile (AMC--Missile)
ATBM . . . . . . Anti-Tactical Ballistic Missile
ATBM . . . . . . Average Time Between Maintenance
ATBT . . . . . . Acoustic Telemetry Bathythermometer
ATC . . . . Ablative Thrust Chamber
ATC . . . . Acoustical Test Chamber
ATC . . . . Acoustical Tile Ceiling (Technical drawings)
ATC . . . . Active Thermal Control
ATC . . . . Active Transfer Command
ATC . . . . Advertising Training Center (New York City)
ATC . . . . Aerial Tuning Condenser
ATC . . . . After Top Center (Valve position)
ATC . . . . Air Traffic Conference
ATC . . . . Air Traffic Control (Air Force)
ATC . . . . Air Training Command (Air Force)
ATC . . . . Air Training Corps (Royal Air Force) (British)
ATC . . . . Air Transport Command (Military)
ATC . . . . Air Transport Committee (ICAO)
ATC . . . . Aircraft Technical Committee
ATC . . . . Airport (or Airway) Traffic Control
ATC . . . . Allergic to Combat (A play on the initialism for the Air Transport
          Command)
ATC . . . . Alpine Tourist Commission
ATC . . . . Annotated Tax Cases
ATC . . . . Annular Turbojet Combustor
ATC . . . . Apollo Time Conditioner (NASA)
ATC . . . . Appalachian Trail Conference
ATC . . . . Approved Type Certificate (Governmental airworthiness certification
          for planes)
ATC . . . . Arctic Test Center (Army)
ATC . . . . Armament Test Center (Military)
ATC . . . . Armored Troop Carrier (Navy)
ATC . . . . Army Topographic Command (Formerly, Army Map Service)
ATC . . . . Army Training Center
ATC . . . . Army Transportation Corps
ATC . . . . Arnold Transit Company (AAR code)
ATC . . . . Assistant Test Conductor
ATC . . . . Associated Traffic Clubs of America
ATC . . . . Automatic Tap Changing
ATC . . . . Automatic Target Counting
ATC . . . . Automatic Temperature Compensation
ATC . . . . Automatic Temperature Control
ATC . . . . Automatic Train Control
ATC . . . . Automatic Tuning Control
ATC . . . . Average Total Cost
ATCA . . . . . . Air Traffic Conference of America
ATCA . . . . . . Air Traffic Control Association
ATCA . . . . . . Airedale Terrier Club of America
ATCA . . . . . . American Teilhard de Chardin Association
ATCA . . . . . . Attitude and Translation Control Assembly
ATCAC . . . . . Air Traffic Control Advisory Committee (Department of Transportation)
ATCAR . . . . . Association des Tshokwe de Congo Belge, de l'Angola, et de la Rhodesie
          (Association of Belgian Congolese, Angolan and Rhodesian Tshokwe)
ATCAS . . . . . Air Traffic Control Automation System
ATCBGS . . . . Air Traffic Control Beacon Ground Station
ATCBI . . . . . . Air Traffic Control Beacon Interrogator
ATCC . . . . . . Aerial Target Control Central
ATCC . . . . . . Aerospace Traffic Control Center
ATCC . . . . . . Air Traffic Control Center (Air Force)
ATCC . . . . . . Air Traffic Control Communication
ATCC . . . . . . American Type Culture Collection
ATCC . . . . . . Atlantic Division Transport Control Center (Hq)
ATCCC . . . . . Advanced Tactical Command and Control Capabilities
ATCC (L) . . . . Allied Tanker Coordinating Committee in London
ATCC (W) . . . . Allied Tanker Coordinating Committee in Washington
ATCE . . . . . . Ablative Thrust Chamber Engine (NASA)
ATCE . . . . . . Automatic Test and Checkout Equipment
ATCEU . . . . . Air Traffic Control Experimental Unit
ATCF . . . . . . Air Traffic Control Facility
ATCH . . . . . . Attach(ment)
ATCL . . . . . . Air Traffic Control Line
ATCLO . . . . . Amphibious Training Command Liaison Officer

ATCMU ..... Associated Third Class Mail Users
ATCO ...... Air Taxi-Commercial Operator
ATCO ...... Air Traffic Control Officer (Air Force)
ATCO ...... Air Traffic Coordinating Officer
ATCOM ..... Atlantic Computer Microfilming Corp.
ATCOM ..... Atoll Commander (In Pacific operations) (World War II)
ATCOR ..... Air Traffic Control Operations Representative
ATCOR ..... Air Traffic Coordinator
ATCOREU ... Air Traffic Coordinator Europe
ATCORUS ... Air Transport Coordinator for the United States
ATCOS ..... Atmospheric Composition Satellite (NASA)
ATCRB ..... Air Traffic Control RADAR Beacon (Air Force)
ATCRBS .... Air Traffic Control RADAR Beacon System
ATCRS ..... Air Traffic Control RADAR System
ATCRU ..... Air Traffic Control RADAR Unit
ATCS ...... Air Traffic Communications Station
ATCS ...... Air Traffic Control Specialist
ATCSS ..... Air Traffic Control Signaling System
ATCT ...... Air(port) Traffic Control Tower
ATCT ...... Air Traffic Control Transponder
ATCU ...... Attitude and Translation Control Unit
ATD .... Absent (on) Temporary Duty
ATD .... Actual Time of Departure
ATD .... Aerospace Technology Division (Formerly, Aerospace Information Division; now, ARP) (Library of Congress)
ATD .... Air Transportable Dispensary
ATD .... Air Turbine Drive
ATD .... Airlift and Training Division (Air Force)
ATD .... Anthropomorphic Test Dummy
ATD .... Armament Test Division
ATD .... Assistant Test Director
ATD .... Audio Tone Decoder
ATD .... Automatic Tape Degausser
ATD .... Automatic Teaching Device
ATDA ...... Alternate Target Docking Adapter (NASA)
ATDA ...... American Train Dispatchers Association
ATDA ...... Augmented Target Docking Adapter (Gemini) (NASA)
ATDC ...... After Top Dead Center (Valve position)
ATDC ...... Association of Thalidomide-Damaged Children
ATD/LC .... Aerospace Technology Division/Library of Congress
ATDLP ..... Apollo Trajectory Decision Logic Prototype
ATDO ...... Airways Technical District Office
ATDP ...... Air Traffic Data Processor
ATDPS ..... Airborne Tactical Data Processing System
ATDS ...... Air Tactical Data System (Marine Corps)
ATDS ...... Airborne Tactical Data System
ATDS ...... Airborne Technical Data System
ATDS ...... Airways Technical District Supervisor
ATDS ...... Automatic Telemetry Decommutation System (Air Force)
ATDS ...... Aviation Tactical Data System
ATE .... Aerospace Test Equipment
ATE .... Air-Turbo Exchanger
ATE .... Airborne Teletypewriter Equipment
ATE .... Airplane Test Equipment
ATE .... Altitude Transmitting Equipment (FAA)
ATE .... Associated Telephone Exchanges
ATE .... Atlantic City Electric Company (NYSE symbol)
ATE .... Automatic Test Equipment
AT (E) ..... Administration of Territories (Europe)
ATEA ...... American Technical Education Association
ATEA ...... American Toy Export Association
ATEC ...... Agence Transequatoriale des Communications (Trans-Equatorial Communications Agency) (of CCEAE)
ATEC ...... Army Test and Evaluation Command (AMC)
ATEGG ..... Advanced Turbine Engine Gas Generator (Air Force)
ATEKAD .... Akademi Tehnik Angkatan Darat
ATEL ...... Audio Techniques and Evaluation Laboratory (NASA)
ATEM ...... Aircraft Test Equipment Modification
ATEN ...... Association Technique pour l'Energie Nucleaire
ATEP ...... Advanced Technical Education Program
ATEP ...... Augmented Thermally Electric Propulsion
ATER ...... Automatic Testing, Evaluation and Reporting
ATERM ..... Air Terminal
ATESL ..... Association of Teachers of English as a Second Language
ATEWA ..... Automatic Target Evaluator and Weapon Assignor
ATEWS ..... Advanced Tactical Electronic Warfare System
ATF .... Acceptance Test Facility
ATF .... Actual Time of Fall
ATF .... Air Task Force
ATF .... Antarctic Task Force
ATF .... Army Training Film

ATF .... Asphalt-Tile Floor (Technical drawings)
ATF .... Australian Task Force
ATF .... Automatic Target Follower
ATF .... Automatic Terrain Following (Army)
ATF .... Aviation Turbine Fuel
ATF .... Fleet Ocean Tug (Navy symbol)
ATFA ...... Acetyltrifluoroacetate
ATFAC ..... American Turpentine Farmers Association Cooperative
ATFO ...... Airways Technical Field Office
ATFOS ..... Alignment and Test Facility for Optical Systems (Navy)
ATFP ...... Alliance of Television Film Producers
ATFR ...... Automatic Terrain-Following RADAR
ATFRAM .... Airborne Time/Frequency Range/Altitude Monitor
ATG .... Accordion Teachers' Guild
ATG .... Advanced Technology Group (Navy)
ATG .... Air-to-Ground (Military)
ATG .... Air Turbine Generator
ATG .... Antenna Test Group (Army)
ATG .... Antitank Gun (Military)
ATG .... Automatic Test Grading
ATGAR ..... Antitank Guided Air Rocket
ATGM ...... Antitank Guided Missile
ATGSB ..... Admission Test for Graduate Study in Business
ATH .... Above the Horizon
ATH .... Air Transportable Hospital
A Th ...... Associate in Theology
ATH .... Athlone Industries, Inc. (NYSE symbol)
ATH .... August Thyssen Huette (German steel producer)
ATHESA .... Automatic Three-Dimensional Electronic Scanned Array
ATHODYD ... Aero-Thermo-Dynamic-Duct
ATI .... Actual Time of Interception
ATI .... Aerial Tuning Inductance
ATI .... Air Technical Index
ATI .... Air Technical Information (Used by Armed Services Technical Information Agency to accession and identify documents)
ATI .... Air Technical Intelligence (Air Force)
ATI .... Amtel Inc. (NYSE symbol)
ATI .... Asbestos Textile Institute
ATI .... Associate of the Textile Institute (British)
ATI .... Association of Technical Institutions
ATI .... Automation Techniques, Incorporated
ATI .... Average Total Inspection (QCR)
ATIBT ..... Association Technique Internationale des Bois Tropicaux
ATIC ...... Aerospace Technical Intelligence Center
ATIC ...... Association Technique de l'Importation Charbonniere
ATID ...... American Trade and Industrial Development
ATIL ...... Air Target Intelligence Liaison Program (Air Force)
ATIP ...... Association Technique de l'Industrie Papetiere
ATIS ...... Adirondack Trail Improvement Society
ATIS ...... Air Technical Intelligence Study (Air Force)
ATIS ...... Allied Translation and Intelligence Section
ATIS ...... Automatic Terminal Information Service (Aviation)
ATISC ..... Air Technical Intelligence Services Command (Air Force)
ATJ .... Association of Teachers of Japanese
ATJC ...... Annular Turbojet Combustor
ATJS ...... Advanced Tactical Jamming System (Aircraft)
ATKSC ..... Attack Surveillance Committee (or Coverage) (Army)
ATL .... Acoustic Test Laboratory
ATL (E) .... Active Time List (Data processing)
ATL .... Advanced Technology Laboratory (Navy)
ATL .... Aeronautical Turbine Laboratory (Navy)
ATL .... American Tariff League
ATL .... Anti-Trust Law
ATL .... Armament Technology Division (Air Force)
ATL .... Artificial Transmission Line
ATL .... Atlanta, Ga. (Airport symbol)
ATL .... Atlantic
ATL .... Automatic Test Line
ATL .... Automatic Turret Lathe
ATL .... Tank Landing Craft (Navy symbol)
ATLA ...... American Theological Library Association
ATLA ...... American Trial Lawyers Association (Formerly, NACCA)
ATLAS ..... Abbreviated Test Language for Avionic Systems
ATLAS ..... Automated Tape Label Assignment System
ATLAS ..... Automatic Tape Load Audit System
ATLB ...... Air Transport Licensing Board (British)
ATLIS ..... Army Technical Library Improvement Studies
ATM .... Air Atlas/Air Maroc
ATM .... Air Traffic Management
ATM .... Air Turbine Motor
ATM .... Amici Thomae Mori

ATM	Antitank Missile (Air Force)
ATM	Apollo Telescope Mount (NASA)
ATM	Arc Tangent Mechanism
ATM	Associated Tobacco Manufacturers
ATM	Atmosphere
ATM	Authentication Maneuver (Aviation)
ATM	Auxiliary Tape Memory (Spacecraft guidance)
ATM	Axial Turbo Machine
ATMA	American Textile Machinery Association
ATMA	Association Technique Maritime et Aeronautique (France)
ATMC	Air Transport Movement Control Center
ATMDC	Apollo Telescope Mount Digital Computer (NASA)
ATMI	American Textile Manufacturers Institute
ATMN	Amalgamated Tin Mines of Nigeria
ATMP	Air Target Materials Program
ATMS	Automatic Transmission Measuring System
ATMS	Automatic Trunk Measuring System (Bell System)
ATMU	Aircraft Torpedo Maintenance Unit
ATN	Actual Test Number (NASA)
ATN	Alabama, Tennessee & Northern R. R. (AAR code)
ATNO	Atomic Number
ATNP	Assistencia aos Tuberculosos de Norte de Portugal
ATO	Academy of Teachers of Occupations
ATO	Action Technical Order
ATO	Aeronautical Telecommunications Operator
ATO	Air Tactics Officer (Air Force)
ATO	Air Terminal Officer (Air Force)
ATO	Aircraft Technical Order
ATO	Aircraft Transfer Order
ATO	Alpha Tau Omega
ATO	Ammunition Technical Officer (Ireland)
ATO	Area Traffic Officer
ATO	Assisted Take-Off (British aviation and rocket term)
ATO	A-T-O, Inc. (NYSE symbol)
ATO	Ocean Tug, Old (Navy symbol)
ATOA	American Tung Oil Association
ATOCI	Association de Traducteurs et Reviseurs des Organisations et Conferences Intergouvernementales
ATOE	American Theatre Organ Enthusiasts
ATOG	Allowable Takeoff Gross (Weight)
ATOLL	Automatic Test of Launch Language
ATOM	Analog Tree-Organized Multiplexer
ATOM	Astronomical Telescope Orientation Mount (NASA)
ATOMDEF	Atomic Defense
ATOMDEV	Atomic Device (Military)
ATOMS	Automated Technical Order Maintenance Sequences (or Systems) (Boeing)
ATON	Aids to Navigation
ATONU	Assistance Technique de l'Organisation des Nations Unies
ATORP	Anti-Torpedo
ATORP	Atomic Torpedo (Military)
ATOS	Assisted Take-Off System
ATOS	Association of Temporary Office Services
ATOT	Actual Time Over Target
ATOT	Angle Track on Target (Military)
ATP	Acceptance Test Procedure
ATP	Actual Time of Penetration (Aviation)
ATP	Adenosine Triphosphate
ATP	Advanced Test in Psychology
ATP	Air Traffic Procedures
ATP	Allied Tactical Publication
ATP	Allied Technical Publication (Navy)
ATP	Alternate Target Point
ATP	American Theater Productions, Inc.
ATP	Anti-Torque Pedal
ATP	Army Training Program
ATP	Associated Transport, Inc. (NYSE symbol)
ATP	Association of Technical Professionals
ATP	At (Time or Place) (Aviation)
ATP	Authority to Proceed
ATPA	Auxiliary Turbopump Assembly
ATPAM	Association of Theatrical Press Agents and Managers
ATP-ASCP	Army Transportation Plan in Support of the Army Strategic Capabilities Plan
ATPC	Association of Temporary Personnel Contractors
ATPF	Armament Test Preparation Facility
ATPI	American Textbook Publishers Institute
ATPM	Association of Teachers of Preventive Medicine
ATPOS	Atomic Post-Strike Analysis Report
ATPR	Advanced Triga Prototype Reactor
ATPR	Annual Technical Progress Report
ATPS	Automatic Type Placement System

ATPU	Air Transport Pressurizing Unit
ATR	Advanced Tactical RADAR
ATR	Advanced Test Reactor (AEC)
ATR	Air-Launched Trainer Rocket
ATR	Air Traffic Regulations
ATR	Air Transport Rating
ATR	Air Turbo Rocket
ATR	Aircraft Trouble Report
ATR	Ambient Temperature Range
ATR	Analog Tape Recorder
ATR	Antitank Regiment (Military)
ATR	Anti-Transmit-Receive
ATR	Attenuated Total Reflectance (Used in field of analytical instruments)
ATR	Automatic Target Recognition
ATR	Aviation Training Record
ATR	Rescue Ocean Tug (Navy symbol)
ATRA	American Toy Retailers Association
ATRA	Automatic Transmission Rebuilders Association
ATRAN	Automatic Terrain Recognition and Navigation Guidance System
ATRAX	Air Transportable Communications Complex
ATRC	Air Traffic Regulation Center
ATRC	Air Training Command
ATRC	Anti-Tracking Control
ATRC	Army Transportation Research Command
ATRCE	Advanced Test Reactor Critical Experiment (AEC)
ATRD	Automatic Target Recognition Device
ATREP	Air Traffic Representative
ATRHTRBAA . . .	Association to Remind Husbands to Remember Birthdays and Anniversaries (Probably mythical)
ATRI	Artists Technical Research Institute
ATRID	Automatic Target Recognition Identification & Detection
ATRIS	Air Traffic Regulation Identification System (Army)
ATRLS	Actual Time of Release (Aviation)
ATRO	Acting Transportation Officer
ATRO	Actual Time of Return to Operation
ATRON	Atlantic Squadron
ATRR	Antitrust & Trade Regulation Report (of Bureau of National Affairs)
ATRS	Assembly Test Recording System
ATRT	Anti-Transmit-Receive Tube
ATS	Absolute Temperature Scale
ATS	Acoustic Transmission System
ATS	Acquisition Target and Search
ATS	Acquisition and Tracking System
ATS	Administrative Terminal System (IBM)
ATS	Advanced Technological Satellite
ATS	Aeronautical Training Society
ATS	Air Tactical School (Air Force)
ATS	Air Traffic Section
ATS	Air Traffic Service (of FAA) (Also known as AT)
ATS	Air Transportable SONAR
ATS	Air Turbine Starter
ATS	American Technical Society
ATS	American Temperance Society
ATS	American Therapeutic Society
ATS	American Thesaurus of Slang
ATS	American Thoracic Society
ATS	American Tract Society
ATS	American Trudeau Society
ATS	American-Turkish Society
ATS	Antitetanus Serum
ATS	Anxiety Tension State
ATS	Applications Technology Satellite (NASA)
ATS	Army Transport Service
ATS	Arturo Toscanini Society
ATS	Associated Technical Services, Inc.
ATS	Associates Investment Company (NYSE symbol)
ATS	Astronomical Time Switch
ATS	Attitude Thrustor System
ATS	Automated Trading System (NYSE computer)
ATS	Automatic Telemetry System
ATS	Automatic Test Scoring
ATS	Automatic Test System
ATS	Auxiliary Territorial Service (British women's service) (World War II)
ATS	Auxiliary Tug Salvage (Navy)
ATS	Salvage Tug (Navy symbol)
ATSA	Aero Transportes, SA (Mexican airline)
ATSA	American Tramp Shipowners Association
ATSAC	Association of Theatre Screen Advertising Companies (Defunct)
ATSC	Air Technical Service Command
ATSC	Army Technical Service Corps
ATSD(AE)	Assistant to the Secretary of Defense (Atomic Energy)

ATSF .... Atchison, Topeka & Santa Fe Railway Company (AAR code)
AT & SF ..... Atchison, Topeka and Santa Fe Railway Company
ATSFSD ...... Air Traffic Service Flight Services Division (FAA)
ATSIT .... Automatic Techniques for Selection and Identification of Targets
ATSOCC ..... Applications Technology Satellite Operations Control Center (NASA)
ATSQMC ..... Army Transport Service Quartermaster Corps
ATSR .... Argonne Thermal Source Reactor (AEC)
ATSS .... Acquisition and Tracking Seeker Subsystem
ATSS .... Association of Track and Structure Suppliers
ATSSS .... Air Transportable SONAR Surveillance System
ATST .... Atlantic Standard Time
ATSU .... Air Travel Security Unit
ATT .... Accelerated Test Technology
ATT .... Air Traffic Transponder
ATT .... American Telephone and Telegraph Company
ATT .... Army Training Test
ATT .... Average Task Time
AT & T ..... American Telephone and Telegraph Company
ATTA .... American Tin Trade Association
ATTC .... Amarillo Technical Training Center
ATTC .... Atlantic Transportation Terminal Command (Army)
ATTC .... Aviation Technical Training Center
ATTD .... Alcohol and Tobacco Tax Division (Internal Revenue Service)
ATTD .... Avalanche Transit Time Diode
ATTE .... Automatic Transistor Test Equipment
ATTF .... Advanced Technical Training Facility (Military)
ATTM .... At This Time
ATTM .... Authorization to Transfer Material
ATTN .... Attention
ATTS .... American Tax Token Society
ATTS .... American Time Travel Society
ATTS .... Automatic Telemetry Tracking System
ATTY .... Attorney
ATU .... Advanced Training Unit
ATU .... Alcohol Tax Unit (US Treasury Department)
ATU .... Alliance of Independent Telephone Unions
ATU .... Amalgamated Transit Union
ATU .... Automatic Tracking Unit
ATUC .... Aden Trade Union Congress
ATUC .... African Trade Union Confederation (Confederation Syndical Africaine)
ATUC .... Average Total Unit Cost
ATUCH ...... American Trade Union Council for Histadrut
ATUC(SR) .... African Trades Union Congress of Southern Rhodesia
ATUF .... Austrian Trade Union Federation
ATV .... Active Tattic Vibration
ATV .... Advanced Test Vehicle
ATV .... Air Test Vehicle
ATV .... Akademiet for de Tekniska Videnskaber (Academy of Technical
             Sciences) (Denmark)
ATV .... All-Terrain Vehicle
ATV .... Associated Television Ltd. (British independent, commercial television
             company)
ATV .... Automatic Threshold Variation
ATVC .... Automatic Thrust Vector Control (NASA)
ATVM .... Attenuator-Thermoelement Voltmeter
ATW .... Aerospace Test Wing
ATW .... Air Transport Wing
ATW .... American Theatre Wing
ATW .... Atlantic & Western R. R. (AAR code)
AT/W .... Atomic Hydrogen Weld
ATWg .... Air Transport Wing (Air Force)
ATWS .... Adjustable Thermal Wire Stripper
ATWS .... Automatic Track-While-Scan (RADAR)
ATWT .... Atomic Weight
ATXPL ...... Atomic Explosion
ATYPI ...... Association Typographique Internationale
ATZ .... Airdrome Traffic Zone
AU .... Ad Usum (According to Custom)
AU .... Air University
AU .... Alma Urbis (Beloved City, Rome)
AU .... American University
AU .... Angstrom Unit (of light)
AU .... Arbitrary Unit
AU .... Arithmetic Unit
AU .... Associated Universities
AU .... Astronomical Unit
Au .... Aurum (Gold) (Chemical element)
AUA .... Allied Underwear Association
AUA .... American Unitarian Association
AUA .... American Urological Association
AUA .... Argonne Universities Association

AUA .... Associated Unions of America
AUA .... Association of University Anesthetists
AUA .... Association of University Architects
AUAS ...... Academy of Underwater Arts and Sciences
AUB .... American University of Beirut (Lebanon)
AUBBER .... Associated University Bureaus of Business and Economic Research
AUBC ...... Association of Universities of the British Commonwealth
AUBV ...... Air University Board of Visitors
AUC .... Ab Urbe Condita (From the founding of the city, refers especially
            to Rome)
AUC .... Association of Uptown Converters
AUC .... Atlantic Union College (Massachusetts)
AUCA ...... American Unitarian Christian Association
AUCC ...... Association of Universities and Colleges of Canada
AUCCTU .... All Union Central Council of Trade Unions (USSR)
AUCOA ..... Association of United Contractors of America
AUD .... Aldens, Inc. (NYSE symbol) (Delisted)
AUD .... Audit(or)
AUD .... Automatic Data Processing (NYSE symbol)
AUDACIOUS .. Automatic Direct Access to Information with the On-line
            UDC (Universal Decimal Classification) System
AUDAR ..... Autodyne Detection and Ranging
AUDGENAV... Auditor General of the Navy
AUDI ...... Societe Internationale d'Audiologie
AUDIT ..... Aircraft Unitized Diagnostic Inspection and Test (Boeing)
AUDIT ..... Auditory Input Task (Data processing)
AUDIT ..... Automatic Unattended Detection Inspection Transmitter (Raytheon)
AUDRE ..... Audio Response (International Harvester Co. computer)
AUDREY .... Automatic Digit Recognition
AUE .... Association des Universitaires d'Europe
AUEC ...... Association of University Evening Colleges
AUET ...... Armored, Universal Engineer Tractor
AUFS ...... American Universities Field Staff
AUG .... August
AUG. ...... Augusta R. R. (AAR code)
AUGU ...... Augmenting Unit (Navy)
AuH2O ..... Goldwater, Barry (Chemical symbols for gold and water; used to
            refer to the 1964 Republican presidential candidate)
AUI .... Associated Universities, Incorporated
AUJ .... Air-to-Umbilical Junction Box
AUJS ...... Advanced Universal Jamming System
AUL .... Air University Library
AUL .... Average Useful Life
AULR ...... Attrition, Utilization and Loss Rate
AUM .... Air-to-Underwater Missile (Air Force)
AUM .... Animal-Unit Month
AUM .... Association of Umbrella Manufacturers and Supplies
AUM .... Automatic Canteen Company of America (NYSE symbol) (Delisted)
AUN .... Absque Ulla Nota (Unmarked; literally, without any marking or note)
AUNT ...... Alliance for Undesirable but Necessary Tasks (From book title, "The
            Woman from AUNT")
AUNT ...... Automatic Universal Translator
AUOD ...... Alliance Universelle des Ouvriers Diamantaires
AUP .... Air University Press
AUPA ...... Association of Unclaimed Property Administrators
AUPE ...... Amalgamated Union of Public Employees (Singapore)
AUPELF ..... Association d'Universites Partiellement ou Entierement de Langue
            Francaise
AUPG ...... American University Publishers Group, Ltd.
AUPHA ..... Association of University Programs in Hospital Administration
AUR .... Aircraft Utilization Report
AUR .... Association of University Radiologists
AURA ...... Association of Universities for Research in Astronomy (National Science
            Foundation)
AURBO ..... Aurora Borealis
AUS .... Army of the United States
AUS .... Augusta & Summerville R. R. (AAR code)
AUSA ...... Association of the United States Army
AUSBCM .... Apollo Unified S-Band Circuit Margin (Program) (NASA)
AUSCOR .... Automatic Scanning Correlator
AUSS ...... American Union of Swedish Singers
AUSS ...... Association of University Summer Sessions
AUT .... Advanced Unit Training (Army)
AUTEC ..... Atlantic Undersea Test and Evaluation Center (Navy) (Acronym also used
            to refer to device for detection, amplification, and transmission of
            undersea noise)
AUTH ...... Authority (or Authorization; Authorize)
AUTH ...... Authorized
AUTHAB .... Authorized Abbreviation
AUTHGR .... Authority Granted
AUTHN ..... Authentication

AUTO....... Automatic
AUTODIN .... Automatic Digital Information Network (DOD)
AUTOLABS ... Automatic Low Altitude Bombing System
AUTOMAP.... Automatic Machining Program
AUTOMAST ... Automatic Mathematic Analysis and Symbolic Translation (Data processing)
AUTOMET .... Automatic Meteorological Correction (A missile guidance technique)
AUTON ..... Automation
AUTONET ... Automatic Network Display
AUTOP..... Automatic Pistol
AUTOPIC .... Automatic Personal Identification Code
AUTOPOS .... Automatic Trains, Protection, Operation and Supervision (Washington, DC, subway monitor)
AUTOPROMT.. Automatic Programming of Machine Tools
AUTOPSY ... Automatic Operating System (IBM)
AUTOSATE ... Automated Data System Analysis Technique
AUTOSCRIPT .. Automated System for Composing, Revising, Illustrating, and Phototypesetting
AUTOSERVCEN .. Automated Service Center
AUTOSEVCOM.. Automatic Secure Voice Communications
AUTOSPOT ... Automatic System for Positioning Tools
AUTO-STATIS.. Automatic Statewide Theft Inquiry System (California Highway Patrol)
AUTOSTRAD... Automated System for Transportation Data (Military)
AUTOSYN.... Automatically Synchronous (Trade name) (Motor)
AUTOTRAN ... Automatic Translation
AUTOVON ... Automatic Voice Network (DOD)
AUTRA ..... Automobile Utility Trailer Rental Association
AUTRAN ..... Automatic Target Recognition Analysis
AUU .... Association of Urban Universities
AUV........ Administrative Use Vehicle (Military)
AUV .... Armored Utility Vehicle
AUW .... Advanced Undersea Weapons
AUW .... Airframe Unit Weight
AUW ..... All Up Weight (Aviation)
AUWE....... Admiralty Underwater Weapons Establishment (British)
AUWS....... Automatic Unmanned Weather Station
AUX........ Auxiliary
AUXOPS.... Auxiliary Operational Members (Coast Guard)
AUXRC ..... Auxiliary Recording Control (Circuit) (Bell System)
AV .... Acid Value
AV .... Actual Value
AV........ Ad Valorem (According to Value)
AV........ Advanced Voyager
AV........ Aerospace Vehicle
AV .... Afferent Vessel
AV .... Air Vent
AV........ American Viewpoint
AV........ Anglo-Vernacular
AV........ Anno Vixit (He Lived [a given number of] Years)
AV........ Anti-Vehicle (Munitions)
AV........ Appalachian Volunteers (Antipoverty agency)
AV........ Arbeitsverwendungsfaehig (Fit for labor duty only) (German military - World War II)
AV........ Artillery Volunteers
AV........ Association Value (Psychology)
AV .... Atrioventricular
AV........ Audio-Visual
AV........ Auriculo Ventricular
AV .... Authorized Version (or King James Version of the Bible, 1611)
AV........ Avco Corporation (NYSE symbol)
AV........ Avenue
AV........ Average Variability
AV........ Seaplane Tender (Navy symbol)
A-V....... Atrioventricular
AVA .... American Vecturist Association
AVA .... American Vocational Association
AVA....... Audio/Visual Annunciator
AVA .... Azimuth vs. Amplitude
AVAL...... Available (or Availability)
AVATI ...... Asphalt and Vinyl Asbestos Tile Institute
AVB .... Advanced Aviation Base Ship (Navy symbol)
AVB....... Analog Video Bandwidth
AVBA...... Association of Volunteer Bureaus of America
AVBAD..... Army Aviator Badge
AVBAT..... Aviation Battalion (Army)
AVC....... Acceleration Vector Control
AVC....... Altitude Velocity Chart
AVC ...... American Veterans Committee
AVC ...... American Viewcard Club
AVC....... Arc Vacuum Cast

AVC........ Army Volunteers Corps (British)
AVC........ Association of Vitamin Chemists
AVC....... Automatic Vibration Control
AVC....... Automatic Voltage Clamp
AVC ...... Automatic Volume Control (Radio)
AVC....... AVC Corporation (Formerly, American Viscose Corporation)
AVC........ Average Variable Costs
AVC........ Large Catapult Lighter (Navy symbol)
AVCAD .... Aviation Cadet
AVCAL..... Aviation Coordinated Allowance List (Navy)
AVCIR ..... Aviation Crash Inquiry Research
AVCN ..... Antero-Ventral Cochlear Nucleus
AVCOM .... Aviation Command (Army)
AVCS....... Advanced Vidicon Camera System
AVCS...... Assistant Vice Chief of Staff
AVCS...... Atrioventricular Conduction System (Cardiology)
AVC of SA ... Assistant Vice Chief of Staff, Army
AVD....... Air Velocity Detector
AVD........ Anode Voltage Drop
AVD....... Army Veterinary Department
AVD....... Army Victualling Department (British)
AVD....... Automatic Voice Data
AVD....... Automatic Voltage Digitizer
AVD....... Seaplane Tender, Destroyer (Navy symbol)
AVDA ..... American Venereal Disease Association
AVDA...... Avenida (Avenue)
AVDD...... Advanced Vehicle Design Department
AVDO...... Aerospace Vehicle Distribution Office(r) (Air Force)
AVDP...... Aided Visual Development Program
AVDU...... Audio-Visual Display Unit
AVE....... Aerospace (or Airborne) Vehicle Equipment
AVE....... Automatic Volume Expansion
AVE....... Avenue
AVEA...... American Veterinary Exhibitors' Association
AVEC...... Automatic Vibration Exciter Control
AVEM ..... Association of Vacuum Equipment Manufacturers
AVENS..... Audiovisual Education in Neurosurgery
AVENSA.... Aerovias Venezolanas, SA (Venezuelan airline)
AVERA..... American Vocational Education Research Association
AVERT..... Automatic Verification, Evaluation and Readiness Tester
AVF....... Availability Factor
AVFR ...... Available for Reassignment
AVG ...... Aircraft Escort Vessel (Navy symbol)
AVG ...... American Volunteer Group (Flying Tigers) (World War II)
AVG ...... Average
AVGAS..... Aviation Gasoline
AVH........ Aircraft Rescue Boat (Navy symbol)
AVH....... Average Heading
AVI ...... Airborne Vehicle Identification
AVI ...... Association Universelle d'Aviculture Scientifique
AVI .... Association of Veterinary Inspectors
AVIA ...... Aviation Pay (Navy)
AVIATECA ... Empresa Guatemalteca de Aviacion
AVID ...... Advanced Visual Information Display
AVID...... Airborne Vehicle Identification
AVIEN ..... Aviation Engineering Corporation
AVIONICS ... Aviation Electronics
AVIS ...... Active Vibration Isolation System
AVIS ...... Audio-Visual Information System
AVISPA..... Aerovias Interamericanas de Panama, SA
AVJ........ Anti-Vibration Joint
AVJC...... Antelope Valley Junior College (California)
AVL........ Allport-Vernon-Lindzey (Study of values)
AVL....... Angle Versus Length (Data processing)
AVL....... Approved Vendors List
AVL....... Aroostook Valley R. R. (AAR code)
AVL ...... Associated Veterinary Laboratories
AVLABS .... Aviation Laboratories (Army)
AVLB ...... Armored Vehicle Launched Bridge (Military)
AVLF ...... Airborne Very Low Frequency
AVLM...... Anti-Vehicle Land Mine
AVLUB ..... Aviation Lubricant
AVM ...... Air Velocity Meter
AVM ...... Air Vice-Marshal (British)
AVM ...... Airborne Vibration Monitor
AVM ...... Automatic Vehicle Monitoring (Antihijack device)
AVM ...... Automatic Voting Machine
AVM ...... Aviation Medical
AVM ...... Guided Missile Ship (Navy symbol)
AVMA ..... American Veterinary Medical Association
AVMF....... Aviatsiya Voenno Morskikh Flota (Soviet naval aviation) (USSR)

AVMH. . . . . . . Available Manhours
AVN . . . . AVIANCA (Aerovias Nacionales de Colombia, SA; Colombian airline)
AVN . . . . Aviation
AVNENGRBN. . Aviation Engineer Battalion (Marine Corps)
AVNG . . . . . . Afferent Vein to Nephridial Gland
AVNL . . . . . . Automatic Video Noise Leveling (Air Force)
AVNL . . . . . . Automatic Video Noise Limited
AVNMED . . . . Aviation Medicine (Military)
AVNOJ . . . . . Antifasisticko Vece Narodnog Oslobodenja Jugoslavije
AVNU . . . . . . Aviation Unit (Marine Corps)
AVO . . . . Avoid Verbal Orders
AVOIL . . . . . . Aviation Oil (Military)
AVOLO . . . . . Automatic Voice Link Observation
AVP . . . . Arginine Vasopressin
AVP. . . . . . . Army Validation Program
AVP . . . . Automatic Variable Perforating
AVP . . . . Avon Products, Inc. (NYSE symbol)
AVP . . . . Small Seaplane Tender (Navy symbol)
AVPA . . . . . . American Veneer Package Association
AVR . . . . Aircraft Rescue Vessel (Navy symbol)
AVR. . . . . . . Automatic Voice Relay
AVRE . . . . . . Assault Vehicle, Royal Engineers (British)
AVRS . . . . . . American Veterinary Radiology Society
AVS . . . . Adjustable Voltage Screwdown
AVS . . . . Aided Visual System
AVS . . . . Air Valve Silencer
AVS . . . . Airborne Viewing System
AVS . . . . Altitude Vertical Scale
AVS . . . . . . American Vacuum Society
AVS . . . . American Vegan Society
AVS . . . . Anti-Vivisection Society
AVS. . . . . . . Association for Voluntary Sterilization
AVS . . . . Aviation Supply Ship (Navy symbol)
AVSA . . . . . . African Violet Society of America
AVSC . . . . . . Audio-Visual Support Center (Army)
AVSCOM . . . . Army Aviation Systems Command
AVSCOM . . . Aviation and Surface Material Command (Air Force)
AVSEP . . . . . . Audio Visual Superimposed Electrocardiogram Presentation
AVST . . . . . . Automated Visual Sensitivity Tester
AVSYCOM . . . Aviation Systems Command (Army)
AVT . . . . Adult Vocational Training (HEW)
AVT . . . . Air Velocity Transducer
AVT . . . . Air Vibrating Table
AVT . . . . Applications Vertical Test Program (Communication Satellite program)
AVT . . . . Arginine Vasotocin
AVT . . . . Audiovisual Tutorial
AVT . . . . . . Auxiliary Aircraft Transport (Navy symbol)
AVT . . . . Available Time
AVT . . . . Aviation Medicine Technician (Navy)
AVT . . . . Avnet, Incorporated (NYSE symbol)
AVTP . . . . . . Adult Vocational Training Program (HEW)
AVU . . . . American Vegetarian Union
AVUS . . . . . . Automobil Versuchs- und Untersuchungs Strecke (Automobile Test Track)
AVV. . . . . . . Algemeen Vrijzinning Vakverbond in Nederland (General Liberal Labor Federation) (Netherlands)
AVV . . . . Avvocato
AVVI . . . . . . Altitude-Vertical Velocity Indicator
AVW . . . . Average Width
AVY . . . . Avery Products Corp. (NYSE symbol)
AW . . . . A. A. Weinman (Designer's mark, when appearing on US coins)
AW . . . . Above Water
AW . . . . Acid Waste
AW . . . . Actual Weight
AW . . . . Ahnapee & Western Railway Company (AAR code)
AW . . . . Air Warning
AW . . . . Air-to-Water
AW . . . . Airwork, Ltd.
AW . . . . Air-World Company
AW . . . . Alignment Window
AW . . . . All Water
AW . . . . All-Weather (As applied to fighter aircraft, etc.)
AW . . . . All Widths (Lumber)
AW . . . . Alternate Weapon
AW . . . . Anti-Wear
AW . . . . Arm Width
AW . . . . Arming Wire (Bombs)
AW . . . . Army-Wide
AW . . . . Articles of War (Army)
AW . . . . Atomic Warfare
AW . . . . Atomic Weight
AW . . . . Automatic Weapons

AW . . . . Aviation Week
AW . . . . Distilling Ship (Navy symbol)
A/W. . . . . . . Actual Weight (Business and trade)
AWA . . . . . . Acoustic Wave Analysis
AWA . . . . . . Advise When Able
AWA . . . . . . Air Warfare Analysis Section (British)
AWA . . . . . . All Wave Antenna
AWA . . . . . . All-Weather Attack
AWA . . . . . . Allied Workers' Association (Philippines)
AWA . . . . . . Aluminum Wares Association
AWA . . . . . . American Warehousemen's Association
AWA . . . . . . American Watch Association
AWA . . . . . . American Waterfowl Association
AWA . . . . . . American Wine Association
AWA . . . . . . American Woman's Association
AWA . . . . . . Anstalt zur Wahrung der Auffuehrungsrechte
AWA . . . . . . Antique Wireless Association
AWA . . . . . . Assist Work Authorization
AWA . . . . . . Association of Women in Architecture
AWA . . . . . . Atmospheric Winds Aloft
AWA . . . . . . Audio Wave Analyzer
AWA . . . . . . Aviation/Space Writers Association
AWAC . . . . . Airborne Weapon and Control
AWACS . . . . Airborne Warning and Control System (Air Force)
AWADS . . . . Adverse Weather Aerial Delivery System (Ordnance delivery method)
AWADS. . . . . All Weather Aerial Delivery System
AWAG . . . . . American Wit and Gags (Book title)
AWAPA . . . . Academy of Wind and Percussion Arts
AWAR . . . . . Area Weighted Average Resolution (Photography)
AWARE . . . . . Addiction Workers Alerted to Rehabilitation and Education (New York City)
AWARE . . . . Adirondack World Affairs Resources for Education
AWARE . . . . Association for Women's Active Return to Education
AWARS . . . . . Airborne Weather and Reconnaissance System
AWAS. . . . . . Acoustic Wave Analysis System
AWAS. . . . . . Air Warfare Analysis Section (British)
AWAS . . . . . American Waldensian Aid Society
AWASP . . . . Advance Weapon Ammunition Support Point
AWB. . . . . . . Agricultural Wages Board (British)
AWB . . . . . . Association of Women Broadcasters
AWBC . . . . . American Women Buyers Club
AWBE . . . . . Automatic Weather Broadcast Equipment
AWC . . . . . . Air War College
AWC . . . . . . Airborne Weapons Control
AWC . . . . . . Alma White College (New Jersey)
AWC . . . . . . American Watershed Council
AWC . . . . . . American Whippet Club
AWC . . . . . . American Wood Council
AWC . . . . . . American Wool Council
AWC . . . . . . Anaconda Wire & Cable Company (NYSE symbol) (Delisted)
AWC . . . . . . Angelic Warfare Confraternity
AWC . . . . . . Army War College
AWC . . . . . . Army Weapons Command (AMC)
AWC . . . . . . Art Workers Coalition
AWC . . . . . . Assisting Work Center
AWC . . . . . . Australian Wool Commission
AWCAP. . . . . Air War College Associate Program
AWCI. . . . . . Aircraft and Weapons Control Interceptor
AWCIS . . . . . Aircraft and Weapons Control Interceptor System
AWCO . . . . . Area Wage and Classification Office
AWCOA . . . . American Wrestling Coaches and Officials Association (Later National Collegiate Athletic Association of Wrestling Coaches and Officials)
AWCS. . . . . . Agency-Wide Coding Structure
AWCS . . . . . Air Weapons Control System (Air Force)
AWCS. . . . . . Automatic Warning and Control System
AWCS. . . . . . Automatic Weapons Control System
AWD . . . . . . Air Warfare Division (Navy)
AWD . . . . . . American War Dads
AWD . . . . . . Astrogeodetic World Datum
AWD . . . . . . Average Working Depth
AWDA . . . . . American War Dads Auxiliary
AWDA . . . . . Automotive Warehouse Distributors Association
AWDISCOM . . Awaiting Disciplinary Action this Command (Army)
AWDMA . . . . Aluminum Window and Door Manufacturers Association
AWDR. . . . . . Advanced Weapon Delivery RADAR
AWDS. . . . . . Automated Wire Data System
AWE . . . . . . Accepted Weight/Estimate (Ships)
AWE . . . . . . Advise When Established (Aviation)
AWE . . . . . . Average Weekly Earnings
AWECOM . . . . Army Weapons Command
AWF. . . . . . . Acceptable Workload Factor (Management)

AWF	Adjoint Wave Function
AWF	Adrenal Weight Factor
AWF	All Weather Flare
AWF	Art for World Friendship
AWF	Aviation Weather Facility
AWFI	American Wood Fabric Institute
AWG	American Wire Gage (Standard)
AWH	American Women's Hospitals
AWH	Association of Western Hospitals
AWHA	American Walking Horse Association
AWHA	Australian Women's Home Army
AWHDA	American Wholesale Horticultural Dealers Association
AWHS	American Women's Hospitals Service
AWI	All-Weather Interceptor
AWI	American Watchmakers Institute
AWI	Animal Welfare Institute
AWI	Architectural Woodwork Institute
AWI	Arm Width Index
A & WI	Atlantic and West Indies
AWIU	Aluminum Workers International Union
AWIU(I)	Allied Workers International Union (Independent)
AWK	American Water Works Company, Inc. (NYSE symbol)
AWK	Americans Want to Know (An organization)
AWL	Absent with Leave
AWL	Administrative Weight Limitation (Military)
AWL	All-Weather Landing (Aviation)
AWL	Association for a World Language
AWL	Average Work Load
AWLF	African Wildlife Leadership Foundation
AWLS	All-Weather Landing System
AWM	American War Mothers
AWM	Arc Welding Machine
AWM	Association of Woman Mathematicians
AWM	Automatic Writing Machine
AWM	Awaiting Maintenance
AWMA	Aluminum Window Manufacturers Association
AWMA	American Walnut Manufacturers Association
AWMA	Automatic Welding Machinery Association
AWMC	Advanced Weapon Monitoring System
AWMC	Army Weapons & Mobility Command
AWMPA	Association of Women of the Motion Picture Industry
AWN	Activation Work Notice
AWN	Aston Whole Number
AWN	Automated Weather Network (Air Force)
AWNCS	Automated Weather Network Coordinating Station (Air Force)
AWNY	Advertising Women of New York
AWO	Accounting Work Order
AWO	Agricultural Workers' Organization
AWO	American Waterways Operators
AWOC	Agricultural Workers Organizing Committee (AFL-CIO)
AWOC	All-Weather Operations Committee (ATA)
AWOL	A Wolf on the Loose (Slang)
AWOL	Absent Without Official Leave (Military)
AWOL	After Women or Liquor (Slang)
AWP	Antisubmarine Warfare Programs (Navy)
AWP	Atlanta & West Point R. R. (AAR code)
AWP	Awaiting Parts
A & WP	Atlanta and West Point Rail Road Company
AWPA	American Wood-Preservers' Association
AWPI	American Wood Preservers Institute
AWR	Adaptive Waveform Recognition
AWR	Army War Room
AWR	Association of Western Railways
AWRA	American Water Resources Association
AWRD	Air Warfare Research Department (Navy)
AWRE	Atomic Weapons Research Establishment (British)
AWRIS	Army War Room Information System
AWRNCO	Aircraft Warning Company (Marine Corps)
AWRS	Airborne Weather RADAR System
AWRS	Aircraft Weapons Release Set
AWRS	Aviation Weather Reporting Station
AWRT	American Women in Radio and Television
AWS	Adjustable Wire Stripper
AWS	Air Warning Service (or System)
AWS	Air Warning Squadron (Marine Corps)
AWS	Air Weapon Systems (Air Force)
AWS	Air Weather Service (Air Force)
AWS	Air Wing Staffs
AWS	Aircraft Warning Service (Military)
AWS	American War Standards
AWS	American Watercolor Society
AWS	American Welding Society
AWS	American Wine Society
AWS	Attack Warning System (Civil Defense)
AWS	Automatic Weather Station
AWS	Automatic Welding System
AWS	Aviation Weather Service (of National Weather Service)
AWSA	Air Warfare Systems Analysis
AWSA	Airborne Wave-Guide Slotted Array
AWSA	American Water Ski Association
AWSAA	Airborne Wave-Guide Slot Array Antenna
AWSCOM	Advance Weapons Support Command
AWSCPA	American Woman's Society of Certified Public Accountants
AWSM	Air Weather Service Manual
AWSO	Assembly Work Schedule Order
AWSTG	Air Weather Service Training Guide
AWT	Advanced Waste Treatment (of water)
AWT	Aeroelastic Wind Tunnel
AWT	Anechoic Water Tank
AWT	Arc-Jet Wind Tunnel
AWTAO	Association of Water Transportation Accounting Officers
AWTAS	Automated Weapons Test Analysis System
AWTE	Association for World Travel Exchange
AWTG	Atomic Weapons Training Group (DASA)
AWTMS	All-Weather Topographic Mapping System (Army)
AWTTP	Apollo Wind-Tunnel Testing Program (NASA)
AWU	Aluminum Workers International Union
AWU	Associated Western Universities
AWU	Associated Workers' Union (Philippines)
AWU	Atomic Weight Unit
AWU	Australian Workers' Union
AWVS	American Women's Voluntary Services (World War II)
AWW	Algers, Winslow & Western Railway Company (AAR code)
AWWA	American Water Works Association
AWWA	American White-Water Affiliation
AWWA	Armenian Women's Welfare Association
AWWI	American Wash and Wear Institute
AWWM	Automatic Wire Wrap Machine
AWWPA	American Wire Weavers Protective Association
AWWS	Automated Want and Warrant System (Data processing system used in police work)
AWWU	American Watch Workers Union
AWYDC	All-Weather Yaw Damper Computer
AX	Atlantic Coast Line R.R. Company (NYSE symbol) (Delisted)
AX	Attack Experimental
AX	Aviation ASW (Antisubmarine Warfare) Technician (Navy rating)
AXBT	Aircraft Expendable Bathythermograph
AXD	Alpha Xi Delta (Sorority)
AXF	Advanced X-Ray Facility
AXFL	Axial Flow
AXL	Arc Xenon Lamp
AXO	Aaxico Air Lines
AXO	Akzona Inc. (NYSE symbol)
AXO	Assistant Experimental Officer (Ministry of Agriculture, Fisheries, and Food) (Also AEO and AExO) (British)
AXP	Allied Exercise Publication
AXPS	Air Express
AXR	AMREP Corporation (NYSE symbol)
AXSIGCOMM .	Axis or Axes of Signal Communication
AXT	Address to Index, True
AY	Allegheny & Western Railway Company (NYSE symbol) (Delisted)
AY	Allied Youth
AYA	American Yachtsmen's Association
AYC	Aerodynamic Yaw Coupling
AYC	American Yorkshire Club
AYC	American Youth Congress
AYCC	American Yugoslav Claims Committee
AYCP	Aerodynamic Yaw Coupling Parameters
AYD	American Youth for Democracy
AYD	Association of Yarn Distributors
AYF	American Youth Foundation
AYF	Antiyeast Factor
AYF	Armenian Youth Federation of America
AYH	American Youth Hostels
AYI	Academic Year Institute (National Science Foundation)
AYI	Angle of Yaw Indicator
AYJUSA	Association of Yugoslav Jews in the U.S.A.
AYL	Anderson, Clayton and Company (NYSE symbol)
AYM	Ancient York Mason
AYP	Alaska Yukon Pioneers
AYP	Allegheny Power System, Inc. (NYSE symbol)
AYRS	Amateur Yacht Research Society

ACRONYMS AND INITIALISMS DICTIONARY

AYS . . . . Agni Yoga Society
AYSS . . . . Allegheny & South Side R. R. (AAR code)
AZ . . . . Active Zone
AZ . . . . Airship Tender (Navy symbol)
AZ . . . . ALITALIA (Aerolinee Italiane Internazionali, Italian airline)
AZ . . . . Aluminium-Zentrale eV
AZ . . . . Arizona
AZ . . . . Atlas Corporation (NYSE symbol)
AZ . . . . Aviation Maintenance Administrationman (Navy rating)
AZ . . . . Azimuth
AZA . . . . Aleph Zadik Aleph (Society)
AZAR . . . . Adjustable Zero Adjustable Range
AZC . . . . American Zionist Council
AZEL . . . . Azimuth-Elevation (Air Force)
AZF . . . . American Zionist Federation
AZGS . . . . . . Azusa Ground Station
AZI . . . . American Zellter, Incorporated
AZI . . . . American Zinc Institute

AZII . . . . American Zinc Institute, Incorporated
AZKW . . . . . . Amt fuer Zoll und Kontrolle des Warenverkehrs
AZO . . . . Alpha Zeta Omega
AZON . . . . . Azimuth Only
AZOV . . . . . Aufschlagzuender ohne Verzoegerung (Nondelay fuze) (German military – World War II)
AZP . . . . Arizona Public Service Company (NYSE symbol)
AZRAN . . . . . Azimuth and Range
AZRU . . . . . . Aztec Ruins National Monument
AZS . . . . Alloyed Zinc Sheet
AZS . . . . Automatic Zero Set
AZT . . . . Ascheim-Zondek Test (Medicine)
AZT . . . . Azusa Transponder
AZTB1 . . . . . . Azusa Transponder B-1
AZTB2 . . . . . . Azusa Transponder B-2
AZTC . . . . Azusa Transponder Coherent
AZUSA . . . . . Azimuth, Speed, Altitude
AZYC . . . . . . American Zionist Youth Commission

B

B . . . . Bachelor
B . . . . Bacillus (Bacteriology)
B . . . . Back
B . . . . Bag
B . . . . Baht (Monetary unit in Siam)
B . . . . Balboa (Monetary unit in Panama)
B . . . . Baldwin-Lima-Hamilton Corporation (NYSE symbol) (Delisted)
B . . . . Bale
B . . . . Ball
B . . . . Ballistic
B . . . . Balloon Ceiling (Meteorology)
B . . . . Bancus (Bench)
B . . . . Band
B . . . . Bandwidth (Also, BW)
B . . . . Baptist
B . . . . Bar
B . . . . Barber (Charles E.) (Designer's mark, when appearing on US coins)
B . . . . Barge
B . . . . Barn (Unit of area for measuring cross-section) (Nuclear physics)
B . . . . Barometric pressure correction
B . . . . Baron
B . . . . Base
B . . . . Bass or Basso (Music)
B . . . . Bat
B . . . . Bath
B . . . . Battery
B . . . . Battle
B . . . . Baume
B . . . . Bay (Maps and charts)
B . . . . Bayou (Maps and charts)
B . . . . Beacon (Aviation)
B . . . . Beak
B . . . . Bearing (Angle)
B . . . . Before
B . . . . Beginning of Precipitation (Meteorology)
B . . . . Bel (Ten decibels)
B . . . . Belga (Monetary unit in Belgium)
B . . . . Bering Standard Time (Aviation)
B . . . . Beva (A prefix meaning multiplied by one billion; same as "giga")
B . . . . Bible
B . . . . Bicuspid (Dentistry)
B . . . . Bid or Buyer (NYSE symbol)
B . . . . Biplane
B . . . . Bishop (Chess)
B . . . . Bishop (Ecclesiastical)
B . . . . Bitch
B . . . . Black (Buoy)
B . . . . Blend
B . . . . Blessed
B . . . . Blue (Aviation)
B . . . . Boat
B . . . . Boatswain
B . . . . Boilermaker (Navy)
B . . . . Boils At
B . . . . Bolivar (Monetary unit in Venezuela)
B . . . . Boliviano (Monetary unit in Bolivia)
B . . . . Bomb
B . . . . Bomber (Designation for US military aircraft)
B . . . . Bomber Field
B . . . . Bond
B . . . . Bonded
B . . . . Book
B . . . . Booster

B . . . . Born
B . . . . Boron (Chemical element)
B . . . . Breadth or Beam (of a ship)
B . . . . Brightness
B . . . . British
B . . . . Broken
B . . . . Brother, Brotherhood
B . . . . Built for British (As suffix to plane designation)
B . . . . Bulb
B . . . . Bulletin
B . . . . Buoyancy
B . . . . Butcher (Navy)
B . . . . Mean barometric pressure
B . . . . Polar radius of earth
°B . . . . Degree Baume
B4 . . . . Before
1B . . . . First Base(man) (Baseball)
2B . . . . Second Base(man) (Baseball)
2B . . . . Two-base hits (Baseball)
3B . . . . Third Base(man) (Baseball)
3B . . . . Three-base hits (Baseball)
5B . . . . Bald man with Bridgework, Bifocals, Baywindow, and Bunions (A humorous unofficial Selective Service Class)
2-B . . . . Selective Service Class (for Man Deferred or Deferrable from Military Service Because of His Necessity to War Production) (Obsolete)
4-B . . . . Selective Service Class (for Public Officials Deferred by Law)
BA . . . . Bachelor of Agriculture
BA . . . . Bachelor of Arts
BA . . . . Bank Angle
Ba . . . . Barium (Chemical element)
BA . . . . Base Activation
BA . . . . Base Assembly
BA . . . . Basic Agreement
BA . . . . Basic Authorization
BA . . . . Battery Adjust
BA . . . . Beach Abort
BA . . . . Binary Add
BA . . . . Biological Abstracts (A publication)
BA . . . . Blind Approach (Flying)
BA . . . . Blood Agar
BA . . . . Boeing Company (NYSE symbol)
BA . . . . Books Abroad (A publication)
BA . . . . Boolean Algebra
BA . . . . Boston & Albany R. R. (AAR code)
BA . . . . Braking Action (Aviation)
BA . . . . Braniff Airlines
BA . . . . Breaks Above
BA . . . . Breathing Apparatus
BA . . . . Bridge Amplifier
BA . . . . British Academy
BA . . . . British Admiralty
BA . . . . British Aluminium Co., Ltd.
BA . . . . British America
BA . . . . British Army
BA . . . . British Association
BA . . . . Bromoaceton (Chemical gas)
BA . . . . Bromoacetyl
BA . . . . Buccoaxial
BA . . . . Budget Activity (Navy)
BA . . . . Budget Authorization
BA . . . . Buenos Aires
BA . . . . Buffer Amplifier
BA . . . . Bureau of Accounts (Treasury Department)

BA . . . . Bureau of Apprenticeship (Labor Department)
BA . . . . Busted Aristocrat (A cadet officer reduced to the ranks) (Military slang)
BA . . . . Graduate in Arts
B/A . . . . Bureau of Aeronautics (Later, Naval Air Systems Command) (Navy)
B & A . . . . Boston and Albany Railroad
BAA . . . . Bachelor of Applied Arts
BAA . . . . Billeting & Accommodations Advisory (Military communications)
BAA . . . . . . Brewers Association of America
BAA . . . . British Astronomical Association
BAA . . . . Broadband Active Analyzer
BAA . . . . Budget Activity Account (Army)
BAA . . . . Bureau of African Affairs (Department of State)
B of AA . . . . . Bachelor of Aeronautical Administration
BAAF . . . . . . Brigade Airborne Alert Force (Military)
BAAL . . . . . . Black Academy of Arts and Letters
BAAN . . . . . . Budget Authorization Account Number
BAAR . . . . . . Board for Aviation Accident Research (Army)
BAARINC . . . . Booz-Allen Applied Research, Incorporated
BAAS . . . . British Association for American Studies
BA in A & Sci . . Bachelor of Arts in Arts and Sciences
BAATC . . . . . . Bay Area Army Terminal Center
BAB . . . . Babbitt (B. T.), Inc. (NYSE symbol) (Delisted)
BAB . . . . Blood Agar Base (Growth medium)
BAB . . . . Budget Advisory Board
BABA . . . . . . Boys' Apparel Buyers Association
BA in BA . . . . . Bachelor of Arts in Business Administration
BABC . . . . . . Black American Baptist Churchmen (An organization)
BA in B & E . . . Bachelor of Arts in Business and Economics
BABS . . . . The Babbage Society
BABS . . . . . . Beam Approach Beacon System (Aviation)
BABS . . . . . . Blind Approach Beacon System (for aircraft) (British)
BABS . . . . . . Blind Approach Beam System (Flying)
BABT . . . . . . Brotherhood of Associated Book Travelers
BAC . . . . Bache and Company (NYSE symbol)
B Ac . . . . Bachelor of Accounts
BAC . . . . Bacterial Adherent Colonies
BAC . . . . Barometric Altitude Control
BAC . . . . Bell Aircraft Corporation
BAC . . . . Belmont Abbey College (North Carolina)
BAC . . . . Below All Clouds
BAC . . . . Bendix Aviation Corporation
BAC . . . . Benzalkonium Chloride
BAC . . . . Binary Asymmetric Channel
BAC . . . . Bipolar Active-Plastic Cell
BAC . . . . Black Affairs Council (Unitarian-Universalist)
BAC . . . . Blood Alcohol Concentration (Sobriety test)
BAC . . . . Blower Access Cover
BAC . . . . Boating Anti-Pollution Council
BAC . . . . Boeing Aircraft Corporation
BAC . . . . Bristol Aeroplane Company
BAC . . . . British Air Commission (Washington)
BAC . . . . British Aircraft Corporation
BAC . . . . Buccoaxiocervical
BAC . . . . Budget Advisory Committee (Army)
BAC . . . . Bureau of Air Commerce
BAC . . . . Business Advisory Council
BACA . . . . . . British Advisory Committee for Aeronautics
BACAIC . . . . . Boeing Airplane Company Algebraic Interpretive Computing System
B Acc . . . . . . Bachelor of Accountancy
BACC . . . . . . British-American Coordinating Committee (Turkey)
B Acc's . . . . . Bachelor of Accounts
BACCC . . . . . Base Activation Central Control Committee
BACE . . . . . . Bachelor of Air Conditioning Engineering
BACE . . . . . . Basic Automatic Checkout Equipment
BACE . . . . . . British Association of Consulting Engineers
BAC Eng . . . . Bachelor of Air Conditioning Engineering
BA in Cer A . . Bachelor of Arts in Ceramic Art
BA Chem . . . . Bachelor of Applied Chemistry
BACI . . . . . . Brazilian American Cultural Institute
BA Class . . . . Bachelor of Arts - Classical
BACLIN . . . . . Baroclinic
BACO . . . . . . Base Activation Change Order
BACP . . . . . . Business Advisory Committee on Procurement (DOD)
BACS . . . . . . Backup Acquisition System
BACU . . . . . . Battle Area Control Unit (Military)
BAD . . . . Berlin Airlift Device (Military award)
BAD . . . . British Admiralty Delegation (to Washington)
BAD . . . . Department of Bantu Administration and Development (An agency of South African government)
BADA . . . . . . Base Air Depot Area (Air Force)
BADA . . . . . . British Antique Dealers' Association

BADAS . . . . . . Binary Automatic Data Annotation System
BADC . . . . . . Binary Asymmetric Dependent Channel
BADGE . . . . . . Base Air Defense Ground Environment (Air Force)
BADIC . . . . . . Biological Analysis Detection Instrumentation & Control
BADL . . . . . . Badlands National Monument
B Adm . . . . . Bachelor of Administration
B Adm Eng . . Bachelor of Administrative Engineering
B of Adv Art & Des . . Bachelor of Advertising Arts and Design
BAE . . . . Bachelor of Aeronautical Engineering
B Ae . . . . Bachelor of Aeronautics
BAE . . . . Bachelor of Agricultural Engineering
BAE . . . . Bachelor of Architectural Engineering
BAE . . . . Bachelor of Art Education
BAE . . . . Bachelor of Arts in Education
BAE . . . . Beacon Antenna Equipment
BAE . . . . British Admiralty Establishment
BAE . . . . Bureau for Africa and Europe (AID)
BAE . . . . Bureau of Agricultural Economics (Department of Agriculture) (Functions dispersed, 1953)
BAE . . . . Bureau of American Ethnology (of the Smithsonian Institution)
B of AE . . . . . Bachelor of Aeronautical Engineering
BA in E & B . . . Bachelor of Arts in Economics and Business
BA Ed . . . . . . Bachelor of Art Education
BA Ed . . . . . . Bachelor of Arts in Education
B Ae E . . . . . . Bachelor of Aeronautical Engineering
BA in E Ed . . . . Bachelor of Arts in Elementary Education
B Ae Eng . . . . Bachelor of Aeronautical Engineering
BAEF . . . . . . Belgian American Educational Foundation
B/AERE . . . . . British Atomic Energy Research Establishment
B Aero E . . . . Bachelor of Aeronautical Engineering
B Ae S . . . . . Bachelor of Aeronautical Science
B Ae Sc . . . . Bachelor of Aeronautical Science
BAF . . . . Belgian Air Force
BAF . . . . Brith Abraham Foundation
BAF . . . . British Air Force
BA & F . . . . . . Budget, Accounting and Finance
BAFA . . . . . . Bul Bul Academy of Fine Arts (Dacca, Pakistan)
BAFCOM . . . . Basic Armed Forces Communication Plan
BAFGOPI . . . . Boston Area Faculty Group on Public Issues
BAFO . . . . . . Base Accounting and Finance Office (Air Force)
BAFT . . . . . . Bankers Association for Foreign Trade
BAFVC . . . . . Bids Accepted for the Following Vacancies
B Ag . . . . Bachelor of Agriculture
BAG . . . . Bag All Garbage
BAG . . . . Baggage
BAG . . . . Ballistic Attack Game
BAG . . . . Beta Absorption Gauge
BAG . . . . Bloc Africain de Guinee (African Bloc of Guinea)
BAG . . . . Buccoaxiogingival
B Ag E . . . . . Bachelor of Agricultural Engineering
B Agr . . . . . . Bachelor of Agriculture
BAGR . . . . . . Bureau of Aeronautics General Representative (Navy) (Obsolete)
B Agr E . . . . . Bachelor of Agricultural Engineering
BAGRED . . . . . Bureau of Aeronautics General Representative, Eastern District (Navy) (Obsolete)
B Agr S . . . . . Bachelor of Agricultural Science
B Agr Sc . . . . Bachelor of Agricultural Science
BAGRWD . . . . . Bureau of Aeronautics General Representative, Western District (Navy) (Obsolete)
BAGS . . . . . . Bullpup All-Weather Guidance System (Naval Ordnance Systems Command)
BAH . . . . Basic Adaptive Hardware
BAH Re . . . . . Bachelor of Arts in Human Relations
BAI . . . . Baccalaurius in Arte Ingeniaria (Bachelor of Engineering)
BAI . . . . Baird-Associates, Incorporated
BAI . . . . Bank Administration Institute (Formerly, National Association for Bank Audit, Control and Operation)
BAI . . . . Base Activation Instruction
BAI . . . . Basic Incorporated (NYSE symbol)
BAI . . . . Bureau of Animal Industry (Department of Agriculture)
BAIC . . . . . . Binary Asymmetric Independent Channel
BAIC . . . . . . Bureau of Agricultural and Industrial Chemistry (Department of Agriculture)
BAID . . . . . . Boolean Array Identifier
BAINS . . . . . . Basic Advanced Integrated Navigation System
BAIR . . . . . . Bureau for the Advancement of Independent Retailing
BAIR . . . . . . Bureau of Aeronautics Industrial Reserve
BAIS . . . . Bulletin Articles Information Subsystem (Data processing)
BAIT . . . . Bacterial Automated Identification Technique
BAJ . . . . Bachelor of Arts in Journalism
BA in J . . . . . Bachelor of Arts in Journalism

BAK . . . . Baker Industries, Inc. (American Stock Exchange symbol)
BAK . . . . Broadband Antenna Kit
BAKOPDASU . . Badan Koordinasi Pembangunan Daerah Sumatera Utara
BAL . . . . Balance
BAL . . . . Base Authorization List
BAL . . . . Basic Assembly Language (Data processing)
BAL . . . . Biological Assessment Laboratory
BAL . . . . Bonanza Airlines, Inc.
BAL . . . . British Anti-Lewisite (A drug)
BALANCE . . . . Basic and Logically Applied Norms – Civil Engineering
BALAST . . . . . Balloon Astronomy
BALC . . . . Brotherhood of the American Lutheran Church
BALDNY . . . . . Ballistic Density
BALIC . . . . . . Board of Action on Letter of Intent Conversion (Navy)
BALL . . . . Ballistic
BALL . . . . Bay Area Leg Lovers (San Francisco group opposing below-the-knee
  fashions introduced in 1970)
BALLAD . . . . Ballistic LORAN Assist Device
BALLUTE . . . . Balloon Parachute
BALLWIN . . . . Ballistic Winds
BALOG . . . . . Base Logistical Command
BALPA . . . . . . Balance of Payments
BALPA . . . . . . British Airline Pilots Association
BALSPACON . . Balance of Space to Space Control Agencies
BALTAP . . . . . . Allied Command Baltic Approaches (NATO)
BALUBAKAT . . Association des Baluba du Katanga (Association of the Baluba of Katanga)
BALUN . . . . . . Balance-to-Unbalance Network
BALUN . . . . . Balancing Unit (Radio)
BALUTE . . . . . Balloon Parachute
BALWND . . . . Ballistic Wind
BAM . . . . Bachelor of Applied Mathematics
BAM . . . . Bachelor of Arts in Music
BAM . . . . Ballistic Advanced Missile
BAM . . . . Black Action Movement
BAM . . . . Bowling Apparel Manufacturers of America
BAM . . . . Bradley Aberration Method
BAM . . . . British Air Ministry
BAM . . . . Broadcasting AM
BAMA . . . . . Boys Apparel and Accessories Manufacturers Association
BAMA . . . . . . British Automobile Manufacturers Association
BAMBI . . . . . Ballistic Missile Bombardment (or Boost) Interceptor (Military)
BAMBI . . . . . Bayesian, Analysis Modified By Inspection (Computer)
BAMC . . . . . . Brooke Army Medical Center
BAMCO . . . . . British Air Ministry Control Office
BA in M Ed . . . Bachelor of Arts in Music Education
BAMG . . . . . . Browning Aircraft Machine Gun
BAMIRAC . . . . Ballistic Missile Radiation Analysis Center
BAMN . . . . . . By Any Means Necessary
BAMO . . . . . Bureau of Aeronautics Material Officer (Navy) (Obsolete)
BAMR . . . . . . Bureau of Aeronautics Maintenance Representative (Navy) (Obsolete)
BAMRO . . . . . Bureau of Aeronautics Maintenance Repair Officer (Navy) (Obsolete)
BAMRRO . . . . Bureau of Aeronautics Maintenance Resident Representative Office
  (Navy) (Obsolete)
BAMS . . . . . . Broadcast to Allied Merchant Ships
BAMSR . . . . . British Admiralty Maintenance and Supply Representative
BAN . . . . Base Activation Notice
BAN . . . . Best Asymptotically Normal (Estimates) (Econometrics)
BAN . . . . Bionics Adaptive Network
BA of NA . . . . Bnei Akiva of North America
BANANAS . . . Benevolent Association for Naming All Nonentities After Schools
BAND . . . . . . Bandelier National Monument
BANDES . . . . . National Bank for Social and Economical Development (Cuba)
BANIR . . . . . . Bombing & Navigation Inertial Reference
BankPAC . . . . Bankers Political Action Committee (Fund-raising for national elections)
BA Non-Class . . Bachelor of Arts – Non-Classical
BAO . . . . Bachelor of Art of Oratory
BAO . . . . Bachelor of Obstetrics
BAO . . . . Budget and Accounting Officer (Military)
BAO . . . . Bundes-abgabenordnung (Austria)
BAOR . . . . . . British Army of the Rhine (NATO/NORTHAG)
BAP . . . . Band Amplitude Product
BAP . . . . Basic Assembler Program
BAP . . . . Benzyl-Aminophenol (Organic chemistry)
BAP . . . . Best Adaptive Path (NASA)
BAP . . . . Boeing Associated Products
BAP . . . . Butte, Anaconda & Pacific Railway (AAR code)
BAPCO . . . . . Bahrein Petroleum Company
BAPCT . . . . . . Bachelor of Arts in Practical Christian Training
BAPE . . . . . . Base Plate
BAPEKAN . . . . Badan Pengawas Kegiatan Aparatur Negara (Indonesia)
BAPL . . . . Bettis Atomic Power Laboratory (AEC)

BAPREPT . . . . . Beds and Patients Report
BAPS . . . . Bureau of Air Pollution Sciences
BAQ . . . . Bachelor Airmen's Quarters (Air Force)
BAQ . . . . Basic Allowance for Quarters
BAR . . . . Babinet Absorption Rule
B Ar . . . . Bachelor of Architecture
BAR . . . . Bacille Acido-Resistant (Acid-Fast Bacillus) (Medicine)
BAR . . . . Bangor & Aroostook R. R. (AAR code)
BAR . . . . Battery Acquisition RADAR
BAR . . . . Board of Appeals and Review
BAR . . . . Browning Automatic Rifle
BAR . . . . Budget Adjustment Request
BAR . . . . Buffer Address Register
BAR . . . . Bureau of Aeronautics Representative (Navy) (Obsolete)
B & AR . . . . . Bangor and Aroostook Railroad Company
BARA . . . . . . Bureau d'Analyse et de Recherche Appliquees (Bureau of Analysis and
  Applied Research)
BARB . . . . . . British Angular Rate Bombsight
BARC . . . . . . Barge, Amphibious, Resupply, Cargo
BARC . . . . . . Bhabha Atomic Research Centre (India)
BARC . . . . . . British Aeronautical Research Committee
BARCAP . . . . Barrier Combat Air Patrol (Navy)
B Arc E . . . . . Bachelor of Architectural Engineering
B Arch . . . . . . Bachelor of (or in) Architecture
B Arch (Arch) . . Bachelor of Architecture in Architecture
B Arch (ArchE) . . Bachelor of Architecture in Architectural Engineering
B Arch in City Pl . Bachelor of Architecture in City Planning
B Arch Des . . . Bachelor of Architectural Design
B Arch Eng . . . Bachelor of Architectural Engineering
B Ar E . . . . . . Bachelor of Architectural Engineering
BA in Rel Ed . . Bachelor of Arts in Religious Education
BARLANT . . . . Atlantic Barrier Patrol (Eastern seaward extension of the DEW Line)
BARM . . . . . . British Admiralty Repair Mission
BARN . . . . . . Bombing & Reconnaissance Navigation
BARPAC . . . . . Pacific Barrier Patrol (Military)
BARR . . . . . . Bureau of Aeronautics Resident Representative
B & ARR . . . . Boston & Albany Railroad
BARS . . . . . . Backup Attitude Reference System
BARS . . . . . . Ballistic Analysis Research System
BARS . . . . . . Baryon-Isobar Rest System
BARS . . . . . . Budget Analysis Reporting System
B Ar Sc . . . . . Bachelor of Arts and Sciences
BARSTUR . . . . Barking Sands Tactical Underwater Range (Naval Oceanographic Office)
BART . . . . . . Bay Area Rapid Transit (San Francisco area, California)
BART . . . . . . Brooklyn Army Terminal
BARTD . . . . . Bay Area Rapid Transit District (San Francisco, California)
BARV . . . . . . Beach Armored Recovery Vehicle
BARZREX . . . . Bartok Archives Z-Symbol Rhythm Extraction (Data processing)
BAS . . . . Bachelor of Agricultural Science
BAS . . . . Bachelor of Applied Science
BAS . . . . Bachelor of Arts in Speech
BAS . . . . Basic Airspeed (Flying)
BAS . . . . Basic Allowance for Subsistence
BAS . . . . Basic Angle System
BAS . . . . Behavioral Approach Scale (Psychology)
BAS . . . . Block Automation System (NYSE trading computer)
BAS . . . . Bomb Alarm System (Air Force)
BAS . . . . Bomb Assembly Spares
BAS . . . . Books-Across-the-Sea (Project)
BAS . . . . Boolean Assignment Statement (Mathematics)
BAS . . . . Brazilian-American Society
BAS . . . . Brazilian American Survey (A publication)
Bas Adv Tra . . . Basic Advance Training
BA Sc . . . . . . Bachelor of Agricultural Science
BA Sc . . . . . . Bachelor of Applied Science
BASC . . . . . . Base Activation Statistical Control
BASC . . . . . . Berlin Air Safety Center
BASD . . . . . . Basic Active Service Date
BASE . . . . . . Basic Army Strategic Estimate (A document)
BASE . . . . . . Brokerage Accounting System(s) Elements (IBM computer program)
BASEC . . . . . . Base Section
BASEFOR . . . . . Base Force
BASESERVUNIT . . Base Service Unit
BASF . . . . . . Badische Anilin-und Soda-Fabrik (Chemical company) (West Germany)
BASH . . . . . . Baroque All Style High (Acronym is title of silk screen by Sculptor
  Eduardo Paolozzi)
BASIC . . . . . . Banking and Securities Industry Committee
BASIC . . . . . . Basic Appraisal System for Incoming Components
BASIC . . . . . . Battle Area Surveillance and Integrated Communications System
  (Marine Corps)
BASIC . . . . . . Bedell Advertising Selling Improvement Corporation

BASIC . . . . . . Beginner's Algebraic Symbolic Interpretive Compiler (Data processing)
BASIC . . . . . . Beginner's All Purpose Symbolic Instruction Code (Data processing)
BASIC . . . . . . Biological Abstracts' Subjects in Context (Documentation)
BASIC (English) . . British-American Scientific International Commercial English
BASICPAC . . . . Basic Package Computer (Army)
BASICPAC . . . . BASIC Processor and Computer
BASIS . . . . Budgetary and Scheduling Information System
BASO . . . . Base Accountable Supply Officer (Air Force)
BASO . . . . . . Bureau of Aeronautics Shipment Order (Navy) (Obsolete)
BASOPS . . . . . Base Operations Office
BA in Sp . . . . . Bachelor of Arts in Speech
B/ASRE . . . . . . British Admiralty Signal RADAR Establishment
B As S . . . . Bachelor of Association Science
BASS . . . . Bass Anglers Sportsman Society
BASS . . . . Behavioral and Social Sciences
B As Sc . . . . . . Bachelor of Association Science
BAT . . . . Bates Manufacturing Co., Inc. (NYSE symbol)
BAT . . . . Battalion Antitank Rifle (Military)
BAT . . . . Biomedical Application Teams (NASA)
BAT . . . . Blind Approach Training (Air Force)
BAT . . . . Boeing Air Transport
BAT . . . . British-American Tobacco
BAT . . . . Bureau of Apprenticeship and Training (Department of Labor)
BAT . . . . Bureau de l'Assistance Technique
BAT . . . . Butler Air Transport, Ltd.
BATA . . . . . . Black American Travel Association
BATCRULANT . . Battleships and Cruisers, Atlantic Fleet
BATCRUPAC . . . Battleships and Cruisers, Pacific Fleet
BATCS . . . . . . Breakdown Air Traffic Control Services
BATDIV . . . . . . Battleship Division
BATE . . . . Base Activation Test Equipment
BATES . . . . . . Ballistic Test Evaluation and Sealing
BATFOR . . . . . Battle Force
BATH . . . . Best Alignment (or Available) True Heading
BATH . . . . . . Boron Carbide, Aluminum, Titanium Hydride
BATLANT . . . . Battleships, Atlantic Fleet
BATM . . . . British Admiralty Technical Mission (World War II)
BATM . . . . . . Bureau of Air Traffic Management
BATO . . . . . . Balloon-Assisted Takeoff (Air Force)
BATPAC . . . . . Battleships, Pacific Fleet
BATRON . . . . . Battleship Squadron
BATROP . . . . . Baratropic
BATRS . . . . . . British Amateur Tape Recording Society
BATS . . . . Business Air Transport Service
BATSHIP . . . . . Battleship
BATSHIPSBATFORPAC . . Battleships, Battle Force, Pacific Fleet
BATSHIPSLANT . . Battleships, Atlantic Fleet
BATSHIPSPAC . . Battleships, Pacific Fleet
BATV . . . . Bureau for Adult Thalidomide Victims (West Germany)
BAU . . . . Baseband Assembly Unit
BAU . . . . British Absolute Unit
B Au E . . . . . . Bachelor of Automobile Engineering
B Au Eng . . . . Bachelor of Automobile Engineering
BAVA . . . . . . Byelorussian-American Veteran Association
BAVE . . . . . . Bureau of Adult and Vocational Education (Office of Education)
BAVTE . . . . . . Bureau of Adult, Vocational, and Technical Education (HEW)
BAW . . . . Babcock & Wilcox Company (NYSE symbol)
BAW . . . . Bare Aluminum Wire
BAWA . . . . . . Burley Auction Warehouse Association
BAWHA . . . . . Bide-A-Wee Home Association
BAWI . . . . . . Balance Agriculture with Industry Program
BAX . . . . Baxter Laboratories, Inc. (NYSE symbol)
BAYCANDDC . . Bayonet Candelabra Double Contact
BAZA . . . . . . Byelorussian-American Association in the U.S.A.
BB . . . . B and Better (Lumber)
BB . . . . Bachelor of Bacteriology
BB . . . . Backbord (Portside) (German military)
BB . . . . Bail Bond
BB . . . . Ball Bearing (Technical drawings)
BB . . . . Balloon Barrage
BB . . . . Bank Book
BB . . . . Bank Burglary
BB . . . . Bare Base (Air Force)
BB . . . . Barrels or Boxes (Freight)
BB . . . . Bases on Balls (Baseball)
BB . . . . Battleship (Navy symbol)
BB . . . . Below Bridges (Navigation)
BB . . . . Beobachtung (Observation) (German military)
BB . . . . Berlin Brigade
BB . . . . Bernard Berenson (American art critic, 1865-1959)
BB . . . . Bill Book (Shipping)

BB . . . . Birmingham Belt R. R. (AAR code)
BB . . . . A Bitter and Burton (Drink served in British public houses)
BB . . . . Blood Bank
BB . . . . Bloody Bastard
BB . . . . Blowback
BB . . . . Blue Book (Directory of proprietaries)
BB . . . . B'nai B'rith
BB . . . . Bomb Bay (of an aircraft)
BB . . . . Bomber (BB-1, etc.) (Russian aircraft symbol)
BB . . . . Bottom Bounce (SONAR propagation mode) (Navy)
BB . . . . Branch Bill
BB . . . . Breaker Block
BB . . . . Breaks Below
BB . . . . Brigitte Bardot (French motion picture star)
BB . . . . British Blue (A British sailor)
BB . . . . Broadcast Bureau (of FCC)
BB . . . . Brush Border (of intestinal epithelial cell) (Cell physiology)
BB . . . . Bulletin Board
BB . . . . Bureau of Biologics (FDA)
BB . . . . Bureau of the Budget (Later, OMB)
BB . . . . Burroughs Bibliophiles
BB . . . . A Bust Bodice
B-B . . . . Butane-Butene Fraction
B/B . . . . Baby Incendiary Bomb
B/B . . . . Both-to-Blame (Shipping)
B/B . . . . Bottled in Bond (Wines and spirits)
B & B . . . . Bell and Bell (Technical drawings)
B & B . . . . Benedictine and Brandy
B & B . . . . Brown and Bigelow (Division of Standard Packaging Corporation)
B & B . . . . National Block and Bridle Club
B or B . . . . . . Brass or Bronze (Top) (Freight)
B to B . . . . . . Back to Back (Technical drawings)
BBA . . . . Bachelor of Business Administration
BBA . . . . Banque Belge d'Afrique (Belgian African Bank)
BBA . . . . Bermuda Benevolent Association
BBA . . . . Big Brothers of America
BBA . . . . Bishop Baraga Association
BBA . . . . Born Before Arrival (of mother at hospital) (Medicine)
BBA . . . . Box Association of America
BBA . . . . Broad Band Antenna
BBA . . . . Bureau of Budget Approval (Obsolete)
BBAA . . . . . . Bridal and Bridesmaids Apparel Association
B Bac . . . . . . Bachelor of Bacteriology
BB Ad . . . . . . Bachelor of Business Administration
BB Adm . . . . . Bachelor of Business Administration
BBB . . . . Bags, Barrels or Boxes (Freight)
BBB . . . . Basic Boxed Base
BBB . . . . Best Berlin Broadcast (Radio program broadcast from Berlin by Robert H. Best, former South Carolina journalist) (World War II)
BBB . . . . Better Business Bureau
BBB . . . . Blood Brain Barrier (Neurology)
BBC . . . . Bachelor of Beauty Culture
BBC . . . . Bachelor of Building Construction
BBC . . . . Barrels, Boxes or Crates (Freight)
BBC . . . . Battery Booster Cable
BBC . . . . Before Bottom Center (Valve position)
BBC . . . . Blockhouse Battery Charger
BBC . . . . British Broadcasting Corporation (State-operated radio and television)
BBC . . . . Bromobenzyl Cyanide (Tear gas)
BBC . . . . Brown, Boveri and Company (Germany)
BBC . . . . Brush Beryllium Company
BBC . . . . Building Block Concept (Army--ROAD concept)
B of BC . . . . . Bachelor of Building Construction
BBCW . . . . . . Bare Beryllium Copper Wire
BBDC . . . . . . Before Bottom Dead Center
BBDE . . . . . . Berlin Brigade
BBD & O . . . . Batten, Barton, Durstine and Osborn (Advertising agency)
BB Ed . . . . . . Bachelor of Business Education
BB & EM . . . . . Bed, Breakfast, and Evening Meal (Travel industry)
BBF . . . . Better Boys Foundation
BBF . . . . Boron Based Fuel
BBF . . . . International Brotherhood of Boilermakers, Iron Shipbuilders, Blacksmiths, Forgers and Helpers
BBFI . . . . Baptist Bible Fellowship International
BBG . . . . Benziger Bruce & Glencoe, Inc.
BBG . . . . Berlin Border Guard (East German)
BBG . . . . Board of Broadcasting Governors
BBG . . . . Bodenbearbeitungsgerate
BBG . . . . Guided Missile Capital Ship (Navy symbol)
BBGA . . . . . . Belgian Begonia Growers Association
BBGKY . . . . . Bogoliubov-Born-Green-Kirkwood-Yvon (Plasma kinetic theory hierarchy)

BBH . . . . Battalion Beachhead (Army)
BBHF . . . . B'nai B'rith Hillel Foundation
BBI . . . . Barbecue Briquet Institute
BBI . . . . Biscuit Bakers Institute
BBI . . . . Buxom Belle, International
BBIA . . . . Billiard and Bowling Institute of America
B Bib Art . . . . . Bachelor of Biblical Arts
B Bi Ch . . . . . Bachelor of Biological Chemistry
B Bi Chem . . . . Bachelor of Biological Chemistry
B Bi E . . . . . . Bachelor of Biological Engineering
B Bi Eng . . . . Bachelor of Biological Engineering
BBII . . . . Brass and Bronze Ingot Institute
BBIM . . . . Buoyant Ballistic Inertial Missile
BBIP . . . . British Books in Print
B Bi Phy . . . . Bachelor of Biological Physics
B Bi Sc . . . . . Bachelor of Biological Sciences
BBJ . . . . Ball Bearing Joint
BBK . . . . Bobbie Brooks, Inc. (NYSE symbol)
BBK . . . . Bread Board Kit
BB/KR . . . . Brown, Boveri/Krupp Reaktorbau (Germany)
BBL . . . . Barrel
BBL . . . . Big Brothers League
BBL . . . . Blue Bell Inc. (NYSE symbol)
BBL . . . . Buys Ballot Law
BBM . . . . Bachelor of Business Management
BBM . . . . Break-Before-Make
BBM . . . . Building Block Monochromator
BBN . . . . Balloon-Borne Nephelometer
BBN . . . . Bolt, Beranek and Newman, Inc. (American Stock Exchange symbol)
BBO . . . . Barber Oil Corporation (NYSE symbol)
BBP . . . . Bavarian Border Police (Germany)
BBP . . . . Boxes, Barrels or Packages (Freight)
BBP . . . . Building Block Principle
BBPN . . . . Balloon-Borne Polar Nephelometer
BBPS . . . . Behavior-Based Personnel Systems
BBPS . . . . Bureau of Biological and Physical Sciences (of FDA)
BBQ . . . . Brooklyn, Bronx and Queens (New York City slang for nightclub or restaurant which has fallen out of favor with the pacesetters)
BBR . . . . Balloon-Borne Radio
BBR . . . . Black Body Radiator
BBRC . . . . Ball Brothers Research Corporation
BBRR . . . . Brookhaven Beam Research Reactor (AEC)
BBRS . . . . Balloon-Borne Radio System
BBS . . . . Bachelor of Business Science
BBS . . . . Barber Suggestibility Scale (Psychology)
BBS . . . . Bare Base Set (Air Force)
BBS . . . . British Bryological Society
BBSA . . . . Bridge and Building Supply Association
BB Sc . . . . Bachelor of Business Science
BBSI . . . . Beauty and Barber Supply Institute
BBSJ . . . . Ball Bearing Swivel Joint
BBT . . . . Backlight Burtek Trainer
BBT . . . . Ball Bearing Torque
BBT . . . . Basal Body Temperature (Physiology)
BBT . . . . Black Ball Transport, Inc. (AAR code)
BBT . . . . Buck-Boost Transformer
BBTA . . . . British Bureau of Television Advertising
BBU . . . . Beefmaster Breeders Universal
BBVS . . . . B'nai B'rith Vocational Service
BBW . . . . Bare Brass Wire
BBW . . . . B'nai B'rith Women
BBWAA . . . . . . Baseball Writers' Association of America
BBWC . . . . Broad Band Waveguide Circulator
BBWR . . . . Bezpartyjny Blok Wspolpracy z Rzadem (Nonpartisan Bloc of Cooperation with the Government) (Poland)
BBYO . . . . B'nai B'rith Youth Organization
BC . . . . Baccalaureus Chirurgiae (Bachelor of Surgery)
BC . . . . Bachelor of Chemistry
BC . . . . Bachelor of Classics
BC . . . . Bachelor of Commerce
BC . . . . Back-Connected (Technical drawings)
BC . . . . Back Course (Aviation)
BC . . . . Bad Character
BC . . . . Bad Check
BC . . . . Ballistic Camera
BC . . . . Bank for Cooperatives
BC . . . . Bare Copper
BC . . . . Barium Crown
BC . . . . Barrel Coating
BC . . . . Base Collector
BC . . . . Bass Clarinet

BC . . . . Bathy-Conductograph
BC . . . . Battery Chargers (Military)
BC . . . . Battery Commander (Army)
BC . . . . Battle Cruiser
BC . . . . Beam Collimator
BC . . . . Before Christ
BC . . . . Before Computer
BC . . . . Before the Crash (i.e., before the 1929 stock market collapse) (Slang)
BC . . . . Before Croonery (Musical slang)
BC . . . . Beginning Climb (Aviation)
BC . . . . Bell Cord (Technical drawings)
BC . . . . Berlin Command (Allied German Occupation Forces)
BC . . . . Between Centers (Technical drawings)
BC . . . . Bibliographic Classification (System of library classification devised by Henry Evelyn Bliss)
BC . . . . Binary Code
BC . . . . Binary Counter
BC . . . . Black Code (Law passed after the Civil War limiting the rights of Negroes in the South)
BC . . . . Bogus Check
BC . . . . Bolt Circle (Technical drawings)
BC . . . . Bomber Command
BC . . . . Bone Conduction
BC . . . . Boro-Carbon
BC . . . . Boston College
BC . . . . Bottom Center (Valve position)
BC . . . . Bottom Chord
BC . . . . Boxes or Crates (Freight)
BC . . . . Breguet Cruise (SST)
BC . . . . Brightness Contrast
BC . . . . British Columbia (A Canadian province)
BC . . . . British Council
BC . . . . Broadcast Control
BC . . . . Broadcasting
BC . . . . Brunswick Corporation (NYSE symbol)
BC . . . . Bubble Chamber
BC . . . . Buccal Cartilage
BC . . . . Buccal Commissure
BC . . . . Bulkhead Connector
BC . . . . Burden Center
BC . . . . Bureau of the Census
BC . . . . Bureau of Consultation (Federal Trade Commission)
BC . . . . Bureau of Customs (Department of the Treasury)
BC . . . . Burroughs Corporation
BC . . . . Bursting Charge (Military)
B/C . . . . Bales of Cotton (Shipping)
B & C . . . . Ball and Chain (Slang for a wife)
B & C . . . . Banking and Currency Committee (US Senate)
BCA . . . . Bachelor of Commercial Arts
BCA . . . . Basenji Club of America
BCA . . . . Battery Control Area
BCA . . . . Best Cruise Altitude
BCA . . . . Bilderberg Continuum Atmosphere
BCA . . . . Billiard Congress of America
BCA . . . . Bliss Classification Association
BCA . . . . Blood Color Analyzer
BCA . . . . Blue Cross Association
BCA . . . . Board of Contract Appeals (AEC)
BCA . . . . Bovine Carbonic Anhydrase
BCA . . . . Boys' Clubs of America
BCA . . . . Briard Club of America
BCA . . . . British Colonial Airlines, Inc.
BCA . . . . Bulldog Club of America
B/C of A . . . . . British College of Aeronautics
BCAC . . . . British Conference on Automation and Computation
B Can L . . . . . Bachelor of Canon Law
BCAP . . . . Bipartite Civil Aviation Panel
BCB . . . . Battery Control Building
BCB . . . . Binary Code Box
BCB . . . . Broadcast Band
BCB . . . . Button Cell Battery
BCC . . . . Baltimore College of Commerce (Maryland)
BCC . . . . Battery Control Central (Army)
BCC . . . . Beam Coupling Coefficient
BCC . . . . Behavior Classification Checklist (Psychology)
BCC . . . . Benard Convection Cell
BCC . . . . Berkshire Community College (Massachusetts)
BCC . . . . Bethune-Cookman College (Florida)
BCC . . . . Body-Centered Cubic (Crystallography)
BCC . . . . Boise Cascade Corporation (NYSE symbol)
BCC . . . . Briar Cliff College (Iowa)

BCC	British Crown Colony
BCC	Broadcast Control Center
BCC	Bureau Central de Compensation
BCCA	Beer Can Collectors of America
BCCA	Buick Collector's Club of America
BCCFSUA	Barn Cleaner, Cattle Feeder and Silo Unloader Association
BCCO	Base Consolidation Control Office
BCCUS	Belgian Chamber of Commerce in the United States
BCCW	Bare Copper Clad Wire
BCD	Bad Conduct Discharge (Army)
BCD	Battle Correlator Display
BCD	Behind Completion Date
BCD	Binary Coded Decimal (Data processing)
BCD	Business Cycle Developments (A publication of Bureau of the Census)
BCDA	Biscuit and Cracker Distributors Association
BCDC	Bay Conservation and Development Commission (San Francisco)
BCDC	Binary Coded Decimal Counter
BCDD	Base Construction Depot Detachment (Navy)
BCDP	Battery Control Data Processor
BCE	Bachelor of Chemical Engineering
BCE	Bachelor of Christian Education
BCE	Bachelor of Civil Engineering
BCE	Base Civil Engineer (Military)
BCE	Before the Common Era (Jewish equivalent of BC)
BCE	Bench Checkout Equipment
BCE	British Columbia Electric Company, Ltd. (AAR code)
BCE	Bubble Chamber Experiment
BC Ed	Bachelor of Commercial Education
B Ce Eng	Bachelor of Cement Engineering
BCEM	Bureau of Community Environmental Management (HEW)
B Cer E	Bachelor of Ceramic Engineering
B Cer Eng	Bachelor of Ceramic Engineering
BCEX	Bundle Controlled Expansion
BCF	Bachelor of City Forestry
BCF	Bandpass Crystal Filter
BCF	Basic Control Frequency
BCF	Bulked Continuous Fiber (Carpeting)
BCF	Bureau of Commercial Fisheries (Later, National Marine Fisheries Service)
BCFSK	Binary Code Frequency Shift Keying (SAGE)
BCG	Bacillus Calmette-Guerin (TB vaccine)
BCG	Ballistocardiogram (Medicine)
BCG	Bicolor Guaiac (Test)
BCG	Bidirectional Categorical Grammar
BCG	Bucking Current Generator
BCG	Buffalo Creek & Gauley R. R. (AAR code)
B Ch	Baccalaureus Chirurgiae (Bachelor of Surgery)
B Ch	Bachelor of Chemistry
BCH	Basal Cell Hyperplasia (Medicine)
BCH	Beech Creek R. R. Co. (NYSE symbol)
BCH	Binary Coded Hollerith
B Ch D	Baccalaureus Chirurgiae Dentium (Bachelor of Dental Surgery)
B Ch E	Bachelor of Chemical Engineering
B Chem	Bachelor of Chemistry
B Chem E	Bachelor of Chemical Engineering
B Ch Eng	Bachelor of Chemical Engineering
B Chir	Baccalaureus Chirurgiae (Bachelor of Surgery)
B Chr Ed	Bachelor of Christian Education
BCI	Barro Colorado Island (Canal Zone) (Site of Smithsonian Tropical Research Institute)
BCI	Battery Condition Indicator
BCI	Binary-Coded Information
BCI	Biomedical Communications Inventory (National Library of Medicine)
BCI	Bituminous Coal Institute
BCI	Bluff Creek Industries R. R. (AAR code)
BCI	Brazilian Coffee Institute
BCI	Broadcast Interference (Communications)
BCI	Bureau of Contract Information
BCIRA	British Cast Iron Research Association
BCIS	Binary Constitution Information Service
BCIU	Business Council for International Understanding
BCJC	Bay City Junior College (Michigan)
BCJS	Bureau for Careers in Jewish Service
BCK	Buffalo Creek R. R. (AAR code)
BCL	Bachelor of Civil Law
BCL	Bachelor of Commercial Law
BCL	Behavioral Checklist (Psychology)
BCL	Books for College Libraries (A publication of ALA)
BCL	Broadcast Listener (Amateur radio)
BCM	Bachelor of Church Music
BCM	Balance Calibration Machine
BCM	Battery Control and Monitor
BCM	Blunt Conical Model
BCM	Body Cell Mass
BCM	Boston Conservatory of Music
BCMA	Biscuit and Cracker Manufacturers' Association
BCMR	Board for Correction of Military Records
BCN	Beacon
BCN	Biomedical Communications Network (Proposed) (National Library of Medicine)
BCN	British Commonwealth of Nations
BCNU	Bischloroethylnitrosourea (Organic chemistry)
BCNY	Brazilian Center of New York
BCO	Battery Control Officer (Army)
BCO	Binary-Coded Octal (SAGE)
BCO	Booster Cut-Off
BCOA	Bituminous Coal Operators Association
BCOA	Borzoi Club of America
BCOB	Booster Cut-Off Backup
BCOE	Bench Checkout Equipment
BCOI	British Central Office of Information
B Com	Bachelor of Commerce
B Com Adm . . .	Bachelor of Commercial Administration
B Comm	Bachelor of Commerce
BCP	Bachelor of City Planning
BCP	Basutoland Congress Party
BCP	Battery Command Post
BCP	Beam Candle Power
BCP	Blue Cross Plan (Health insurance)
BCP	Bootstrap Commissioning Program (Air Force)
BCP	Budget Change Proposal
BCPO	British Commonwealth Producers' Organization
BCPS	Beam Candle Power Seconds
BCPSG	British Caribbean Philatelic Study Group
B Cr	Bachelor of Criminology
BCR	Bard (C.R.) Inc. (NYSE symbol)
BCR	Battery Control RADAR
BCR	Bituminous Coal Research, Inc.
BCRA	Bureau Centrale de Reseignements et d'Action (Free French)
BCRV	Blunt Conical Reentry Vehicle
BCS	Bachelor of Chemical Science
BCS	Bachelor of Commercial Science
BCS	Bardeen-Cooper-Schrieffer (Theory)
BCS	Basic Contract Specification
BCS	Battle Cruiser Squadron
BCS	Beam Communications Set
BCS	Bengal Civil Service
BCS	Bidirectional Category System
BCS	Blip Counter System
BCS	Bombing Computer Set
BCS	British Computer Society
BCS	Broadcast Communications System
BCS	Brothers of Charity of Spokane (Roman Catholic religious order)
BC Sc	Bachelor of Commercial Science
BC Se	Bachelor of Commercial Service
BCSE	Board of US Civil Service Examiners
BCSH	Barat College of the Sacred Heart (Illinois)
BCSS	Bishops' Committee for the Spanish Speaking
BCST	Broadcast
BCT	Bachelor of Christian Training
BCT	Bandwidth Compression Technique
BCT	Basic Combat Training
BCT	Battalion Combat Team
BCT	Body-Centered Tetragonal (Crystallography)
BCTD	Building and Construction Trades Department (AFL-CIO)
BCTN	Baja California - Territorio Norte
BCTS	Baja California - Territorio Sur
BCTU	Basutoland Congress of Trade Unions
BCU	Bay Cabinet Unit
BCURA	British Coal Utilization Research Association
BCUSA	Buddhist Center of the United States of America
BCV	Ball Check Valve
BCV	Brightness Contrast Value
BCW	Bakery and Confectionery Workers' International Union of America
BCW	Bare Copper Wire
BCW	Bobbin Coil Winder
BCW	Buffer Control Word (Data processing)
BCWD	Biological and Chemical Warfare Division (DOD)
BCWIU of A . . .	Bakery and Confectionery Workers' International Union of America
BCWVA	British Commonwealth War Veterans
BCX	Beech Aircraft Corporation (NYSE symbol)
BCZ	Berlin Control Zone (Allied German Occupation Forces)
BD	Bachelor of Divinity

BD . . . . Back Dividends
BD . . . . Base Detonating
BD . . . . Base Diameter
BD . . . . Basic Democrats (Pakistan)
BD . . . . Battle Dress (Military)
BD . . . . Beam Degrader
BD . . . . Beginning Descent (Aviation)
BD . . . . Behavioral Differential
BD . . . . Belladonna ("Deadly-nightshade" plant, or medicinal extract from it)
BD . . . . Bend Down
BD . . . . Benzoylated
BD . . . . Benzoylated DEAE (Diethylaminoethyl) (Cellulose)
BD . . . . Berlin District (Allied German Occupation Forces)
BD . . . . Bernoulli Disk
BD . . . . Binary Decoder (Data processing)
BD . . . . Binary Divide
BD . . . . Bit Density
BD . . . . Blowing Dust (Meteorology)
BD . . . . Board
BD . . . . Bomb Disposal
BD . . . . Bonner Durchmusterung (Star chart)
BD . . . . Booster Development
BD . . . . Boulevard
BD . . . . Bursal Dependent (Cells) (Immunology)
B/D . . . . Bank Draft
B/D . . . . Barrels Per Day
B/D . . . . Bills Discounted
B/D . . . . Binary to Decimal (Data processing)
B/D . . . . Brought Down (Business and trade)
B & D . . . . . . Black and Decker (Commercial firm)
B7D . . . . Buyer has 7 Days to Take Up (Securities brokerage)
BDA . . . . Bachelor of Domestic Arts
BDA . . . . Bachelor of Dramatic Art
BDA . . . . Battle Damage Assessment
BDA . . . . Bomb Damage Assessment
BDA . . . . Booster-Distribution Amplifier
BDA . . . . British Dental Association
BDAC . . . . . . Bureau of Drug Abuse Control (Absorbed by Bureau of Narcotics and Dangerous Drugs of Department of Justice)
BDAM . . . . . . Basic Direct Access Method (Data processing)
BDART . . . . . . Battle Damage Assessment and Reporting Team
BDB . . . . Big Dumb Booster
BDB . . . . Bjerrum Double Band
BDC . . . . Back-up Digital Computer
BDC . . . . Bentley Drivers Club
BDC . . . . Berlin Document Center (Allied German Occupation Forces)
BDC . . . . Binary Decimal Counter (Data processing)
BDC . . . . Bomb Data Center (International Association of Chiefs of Police)
BDC . . . . . . Book Development Council (British)
BDC . . . . . . Bottom Dead Center (Engineering)
BDC . . . . Bureau of Domestic Commerce (Formerly, Business and Defense Services Administration and Office of Field Services) (Department of Commerce)
BDC . . . . Bureau International de Documentation des Chemins de Fer (International Office of Railway Documentation)
BDC . . . . Burndy Corporation (NYSE symbol)
BDCT . . . . . . Bradford Durfee College of Technology (Later, Southeastern Massachusetts Technical Institute)
BDD . . . . Balzac Deflection Door
BDD . . . . Binary to Decimal Decoder (Data processing)
BDD . . . . Binary Digital Data (Data processing)
BDD . . . . Binary-to-Digital Decoder (Data processing)
BDDI . . . . . . Beading Die
BD D & M . . . . Board of Decorations and Medals (Navy)
BDE . . . . Beta Disintegration Energy
BDE . . . . Bright Display Equipment
BDE . . . . British Destroyer Escort
BDE . . . . Escort Vessel (Lend-lease to Great Britain)
BD in E . . . . . Bachelor of Divinity in Education
BDELT . . . . . . Brigade Landing Team (Army)
B Des . . . . . . Bachelor of Design
B Des A Ed . . . Bachelor of Design in Art Education
BDF . . . . Base Detonating Fuze
BDFGA . . . . . Bio-Dynamic Farming and Gardening Association
BDG . . . . Bloc Democratique Gabonais (Gabonese Democratic Bloc)
BDGC . . . . . . Bad Conduct Discharge, General Court-Martial, After Confinement in Prison (Navy)
BDGI . . . . . . Bad Conduct Discharge, General Court-Martial, Immediate (Navy)
BDGP . . . . . . Bad Conduct Discharge, General Court-Martial, After Violation of Probation (Navy)
BDH . . . . Bearing, Distance, and Heading
BDH . . . . British Drug Houses, Ltd.

BDHCA . . . . . . Belgian Draft Horse Corporation of America
BDHI . . . . Bearing, Distance, Heading Indicator
BDHSA . . . . . Bomb Director High Speed Aircraft
BDI . . . . Bearing Deviation Indicator (Aerospace)
BDI . . . . Biological Damage Indicator
BDI . . . . Bundesverband der Deutschen Industrie (Federation of German Industry)
BDI . . . . Bureau of Dairy Industry (Department of Agriculture) (Functions transferred to ARS, 1953)
BDIAC . . . . . . Battelle-Defender Information Analysis Center (Battelle Memorial Institute)
BDIAS . . . . . . Battelle - Defender Information Analysis Center
BDIC . . . . . . Battelle - Defense Information Center
B Did . . . . . . Bachelor of Didactics
B Di E . . . . . . Bachelor of Diesel Engineering
B Di Eng . . . . Bachelor of Diesel Engineering
B Dipl . . . . . . Bachelor of Diplomacy
BDJ . . . . Brans-Dicke-Jordan (Scalar-tensor theory)
BDK . . . . Black & Decker Mfg. Co. (NYSE symbol)
BDL . . . . Bachelor of Divine Literature
BDL . . . . Base of Dorsal Lip
BDL . . . . Battery Data Link (Air Force)
BDL . . . . Beach Discharge Lighter
BDL . . . . Best Dressed List
BDLS . . . . . . Battery Data Link System (Air Force)
BDLTEA . . . . Burley and Dark Leaf Tobacco Export Association
BDM . . . . Binary Delta Modulation
BDM . . . . Bomber Defense Missile (Air Force)
BDO . . . . Boom Defense Officer
BDP . . . . Bechuanaland Democratic Party
BDP . . . . Brookes Deflection Potentiometer
BDPA . . . . . . Bureau of Data Processing and Accounts (Social Security Administration)
BDPEC . . . . . . Bureau of Disease Prevention and Environmental Control
BDPI . . . . Base Data Processing Installation
BDPI . . . . Bureau de Developpement et de Promotion Industriels (Bureau of Industrial Promotion and Development) (Malagasy Republic)
BDPO . . . . . . Business Data Processing Operation
BDPS . . . . . . Brigade Data Processing System
BDR . . . . Bomb Damage Repair
B Dr Art . . . . Bachelor of Dramatic Art
BDRC . . . . . . Becton, Dickinson Research Center
BDRI . . . . . . Bright Display RADAR Indicator
BDS . . . . Bachelor of Dental Surgery
BDS . . . . Base Data System
BDS . . . . Beitrage zur Danziger Statistik (Danzig)
BDS . . . . Binary Decode Scaler
BDS . . . . Biological Defense System
BDS . . . . Biological Detection System
BDS . . . . Bomb Damage Survey
BDS . . . . Bomb Director Set (or System)
BDS . . . . Bomb-Disposal Squad
BDS . . . . Bonded Double Silk
BDS . . . . Brass Divider Strip (Technical drawings)
BDS . . . . British Defence Staff
BDSA . . . . . . Business and Defense Services Administration (Later, BDC) (Department of Commerce)
BD Sc . . . . . . Bachelor of Dental Science
BDSD . . . . . . Base Detonating, Self-Destroying
BDSI . . . . Bad Conduct Discharge, Sentence of Summary Court-Martial, Immediate
BDSP . . . . . . Bad Conduct Discharge, Summary Court-Martial, After Violation of Probation
BDT . . . . Back Door Trot (i.e., a call of nature) (Obsolete slang)
BDT . . . . Beam Deflection Tube
BDT . . . . Binary Deck to Tape (Data processing)
BDT . . . . Burst Delay Timer
BDU . . . . Barograph Display Unit
BDU . . . . Basic Display Unit (Data processing)
BDU . . . . Battery Display Unit (Army)
BDU . . . . Bomb, Dummy Unit
BDV . . . . Bend-Down Virginia (A picked-up stub of a cigarette)
BDVP . . . . . . Bezirksbehoerde der Deutschen Volkspolizei
BDW . . . . . . Buffered Distilled Water (Chemistry)
BDX . . . . Becton, Dickinson & Co. (NYSE symbol)
BE . . . . Bachelor of Education
BE . . . . Bachelor of Elocution
BE . . . . Bachelor of Engineering
BE . . . . Bachelor of English
BE . . . . Bachelor of Expression
BE . . . . Baltimore & Eastern R. R. (AAR code)
BE . . . . Band Elimination
BE . . . . Bank of England

BE . . . . Bank Error
BE . . . . Base Ejection
BE . . . . Basic Encyclopedia (Army)
BE . . . . Belgium (NATO)
BE . . . . Bell End
BE . . . . Benguet Consolidated, Inc. (NYSE symbol)
Be . . . . Beryllium (Chemical element)
BE . . . . Biennial
BE . . . . Bill of Exchange
BE . . . . Binding Energy
BE . . . . Bird Electronic Co.
BE . . . . Board of Education
BE . . . . Booster Engine
BE . . . . British Element
BE . . . . British Empire
BE . . . . Bucyrus-Erie Company
BE . . . . Buddhist Era
BE . . . . Bureau of Economics (Federal Trade Commission)
B/E . . . . Bill of Entry (Business and trade)
B/E . . . . Bill of Exchange (Business and trade)
B & E . . . . . . Breaking & Entering
B of E . . . . . . Bank of England
B of E . . . . . . Board of Education
BEA . . . . Barn Equipment Association
BEA . . . . British East Africa
BEA . . . . British Electrical Authority
BEA . . . . British European Airways Corporation
BEA . . . . Bureau of Economic Affairs (Department of State)
BEA . . . . Bureau of European Affairs (Department of State)
BE-A . . . . Beacon Explorer A (Satellite)
BEAA . . . . Business Education Administrators Association
BEAB . . . . British Electrical Approvals Board
BEAC . . . . Boeing Electronic Analog Computer
BEACON. . . . . British European Airways Computerized Office Network
BEAM. . . . . . . Building Equipment Accessories and Materials (Program) (Canada)
BEAMA . . . . . British Electrical and Allied Manufacturers
BEAMS . . . . . Base Engineer Automated Management System
BEAPA . . . . . Bureau of East Asian and Pacific Affairs (Department of State) (Formerly, Bureau of Far Eastern Affairs)
BEAR . . . . Biological Effects of Atomic Radiation
BEARA . . . . . British Electronic and Applied Research Association
BEART. . . . . . Beaver Army Terminal
BEAVER. . . . . Be Ever Alert, Vigilant / Error Removal (United States Air Force Security System's acronym for the Zero Defects Program)
BEB . . . . Beach Erosion Board (Army)
BEB . . . . Best Ever Bottled (Wines and spirits)
BE-B. . . . . . . Beacon Explorer B (Satellite)
B Ec . . . . Bachelor of Economics
BEC . . . . Bachelor of Engineering Construction
BEC . . . . Base Equipment Container
BEC . . . . Base Examination Course
BEC . . . . Base Extension Course
BEC . . . . Beckman Instruments, Inc. (NYSE symbol) (Wall Street slang name: "Becky")
BEC . . . . Bioelectrochemistry
BEC . . . . Bowles Engineering Corporation
BEC . . . . British Engineers Club
BEC . . . . Bureau of Employees' Compensation (Department of Labor)
BEC . . . . Bureau Europeen du Cafe
BEC . . . . Business Electronics Computer (Used in training)
BECA . . . . . . Bureau of Educational and Cultural Affairs (Department of State)
BECE . . . . . . Bachelor of Electro-Chemical Engineering
BECEG . . . . . Bureau Europeen de Controle et d'Etudes Generales
BECG . . . . . . Bipartite Economics Control Group (Post-World War II, Germany)
BECKTRAN . . . Beckman Translation (Computer language) (Beckman Instrument, Inc.)
BECO. . . . . . . Booster Engine Cutoff (Rocketry)
BE & CWLC . . British Empire and Commonwealth Weight-Lifting Council
B Ed . . . . Bachelor of Education
BED . . . . Bachelor of English Divinity
BED . . . . Board of Educational Development (University of California, Berkeley)
BEDAC . . . . . Burst Error Detection and Correlation
BEDOC . . . . . Beds Occupied
BEDT . . . . . . Brooklyn Eastern District Terminal R. R. (AAR code)
BEE . . . . Bachelor of Electrical Engineering
BEE . . . . Bond Edge Energy
BEE . . . . Books for Equal Education
B of EE (Com Opt) . . Bachelor of Electrical Engineering, Communication Option
BEEF. . . . . . . Base Engineer Emergency Force (Air Force)
BEEF. . . . . . . Business and Engineering Enriched FORTRAN (UNIVAC)
BEEM . . . . . . Beech Mountain R. R. (AAR code)
BEEN . . . . . . Bureau d'Etude de l'Energie Nucleaire

BEEP. . . . . . . Battalion Equipment Evaluation Program (DOD)
BEEP. . . . . . . Bureau Europeen de l'Education Populaire (European Bureau of Adult Education)
B of EE (Power Opt) . . Bachelor of Electrical Engineering, Power Option
BEER. . . . . . . Bombardment Etch Rate
BEF . . . . Band Elimination Filter
BEF . . . . Bonus Expeditionary Force
BEF . . . . Brazilian Expeditionary Force
BEF . . . . British Expeditionary Forces
BEF . . . . Buffered Emitter Follower
BEFT. . . . . . . Bureau of Education for Fair Trade
BEH . . . . Bureau of Education for the Handicapped (Office of Education)
BEHVL . . . . . Behavioral
BEI . . . . Banque Europeenne d'Investissement
BEI . . . . Bridgeport Engineering Institute (Connecticut)
BEI . . . . Budget Executives Institute
BEI . . . . Butanol-Extractable Iodine (Chemistry)
BEIA. . . . . . . Bureau d'Education Ibero-Americain
BEID. . . . . . . Behavioral Effects of Infectious Diseases (Army)
BEJE. . . . . . . Bureau Europeen de la Jeunesse et de l'Enfance
BEK . . . . A. S. Beck Shoe Corporation (American Stock Exchange symbol)
B EI . . . . Bachelor of Elocution
BEL . . . . Bachelor of English Literature
BEL . . . . Basic Equipment List
BEL . . . . Belden Corp. (NYSE symbol)
BELC . . . . . . Bureau pour l'Enseignement de la Language et de la Civilisation Francaises a l'Etranger (France)
BELCRK . . . . Bell Crank
B Ele . . . . . . Bachelor of Elements
BELLREL . . . . Bell Laboratories Library Real-Time Loan System
BEM . . . . Bachelor of Engineering of Mines
BEM . . . . Bachelor of Mining Engineering
BEM . . . . Beaufort & Morehead R. R. (AAR code)
BEM . . . . Beaunit Corporation (NYSE symbol) (Delisted)
BEM . . . . . . British Empire Medal
BEM . . . . Bureau of Executive Manpower (Civil Service Commission)
BEM . . . . Business Executives Move for Vietnam Peace
BEMA . . . . . . Bakery Equipment Manufacturers Association
BEMA . . . . . . Business Equipment Manufacturers Association
BEMAC . . . . . British Exports Marketing Advisory Committee
BEMAR . . . . . Backlog of Essential Maintenance and Repair
BEMB . . . . . . Bituminous Equipment Manufacturers Bureau
BEMO . . . . . . Base Equipment Management Office (Air Force)
B En . . . . Bachelor of English
BEN . . . . Benrus Corp. (American Stock Exchange symbol)
BEN . . . . Bureau d'Etudes Nucleaire (Belgium)
BENA . . . . . . Belgian Engineers in North America
BENA . . . . . . British Empire Naturalist Association
BENCOM. . . . . Beneficial Communications (Computer system) (Beneficial Management Corp.)
BENDEX . . . . Beneficiary Data Exchange System (between state welfare agencies and the Social Security Administration)
BENEF . . . . . . Beneficiary
BENELUX . . . . Belgium, Netherlands, Luxembourg (Economic union)
B Eng A . . . . . Bachelor of Agricultural Engineering
BENREP. . . . . BIG BEN Report (WW II)
B Ent . . . . . . Bachelor of Entomology
BENT . . . . . . Beginning Evening Nautical Twilight
B & ENT & PL. . Breaking and Entering in Nighttime and Petty Larceny
BEOC . . . . . . Battery Echelon Operating Control
BEOL . . . . . . Bent's Old Fort National Historic Site
BEP . . . . Bachelor of Engineering Physics
BEP . . . . Budget Execution Plan
BEP . . . . Bureau of Engraving and Printing (Treasury Department)
B of EP . . . . . Bachelor of Engineering Physics
BEPD . . . . . . Bureau of Educational Personnel Development (HEW)
BE Phy . . . . . Bachelor of Engineering Physics
BEPI . . . . Budget Estimates Presentation Instructions
BEPI . . . . Bureau d'Etudes et des Participations Industries
BEPO . . . . . . British Experimental Pile Operation (Atomic energy)
BEPOC . . . . . Burrough's Electrographic Printer-Plotter for Ordnance Computing
BEPQ . . . . . . Bureau of Entomology and Plant Quarantine (Department of Agriculture) (Functions transferred to ARS, 1953)
BEQ . . . . Bachelor Enlisted Quarters
BER . . . . Bearings, Inc. (NYSE symbol)
BER . . . . BIT Error Rate (Data processing)
BER . . . . Budget Execution Review (Military)
BER . . . . Bureau of Economic Regulation (of CAB)
BER . . . . Bureau of Equipment and Recruiting (Navy)
BERA . . . . . . Business Education Research Associates
BERC . . . . . . Biomedical Engineering Research Corporation (Illinois)

BERC . . . . Black Economic Research Center
BERCOMB . . . . Berlin Commission British (Post-World War II)
BERF . . . . Business Education Research Foundation
BERH . . . . Board of Engineers for Rivers and Harbors (Army)
B & ERS . . . . . Boat and Engine Repair Shop (Coast Guard)
BERSEAPAT . . . Bering Sea Patrol (Navy)
BES . . . . Bachelor of Engineering Sciences
BES . . . . Bachelor of Science in Engineering
BES . . . . Balanced Electrolyte Solution (Physiology)
BES . . . . Booster Exhaust Stream
BES . . . . Bose-Einstein Statistics
BES . . . . Buildings and Equipment Section (Library Administration Division of ALA)
BES . . . . Bureau of Employment Security (Labor)
BESA . . . . British Engineering Standards Association
BESE . . . . Bureau of Elementary and Secondary Education (Office of Education)
BESEP . . . . . . Base Electronics System Engineering Plan
BESI . . . . Black Educational Services, Incorporated
BESRL . . . . . . Behavioral Science Research Laboratory (Army)
BESS . . . . Binary Electromagnetic Signal Signature
BEST . . . . Ballastable Earthmoving Sectionalized Tractor (Formerly, UET) (Army)
BEST . . . . Better Electronic Service Technicians
BEST . . . . Black Efforts for Soul in Television (An organization)
BEST . . . . Business EDP Systems Technique
BEST . . . . Business Equipment Software Techniques (Data processing)
BESTS . . . . . . Belgian Educational Student Travel Service
BET . . . . Best-Estimate Trajectory (Apollo) (NASA)
BET . . . . Brunauer-Emmett-Teller (Physics equation)
BET . . . . Business Experience Training (Program) (Chase Manhattan Bank)
BETA . . . . Business Equipment Trade Association
BETFOR . . . . . Headquarters British Element Trieste Forces
BEU . . . . British Empire Union
BEUC . . . . Bureau Europeen des Unions Consommateurs
BeV . . . . Billion Electron Volts
BEW . . . . Board of Economic Warfare (World War II)
B Ex . . . . Bachelor of Expression
BEXEC . . . . . Budget Execution (Army)
BF . . . . Bachelor of Finance
BF . . . . Bachelor of Forestry
BF . . . . Back-Feed
BF . . . . Back Folded (Freight)
BF . . . . Banque de France (Bank of France)
BF . . . . Basal Fold
BF . . . . Base Funded
BF . . . . Base Fuze
BF . . . . Batch Fabrication
BF . . . . Beam Forming
BF . . . . Beat-Frequency
BF . . . . Belgian Fourragere
BF . . . . Bloody Fool
BF . . . . Boiler Feed (Technical drawings)
BF . . . . Bold Face (Printing term)
BF . . . . Bona Fide (In good faith)
BF . . . . Bonœ Feminœ (To the good woman)
BF . . . . Both Faces (Technical drawings)
BF . . . . Bottom Face (Technical drawings)
BF . . . . Boy Friend (Slang)
BF . . . . Brandon Films, Inc.
BF . . . . Brought Forward
BF . . . . Budd Company (NYSE symbol)
B/F . . . . Brought Forward (Business and trade)
B & F . . . . Bell and Flange (Technical drawings)
BF1 . . . . Virus Isolated from Bovine Feces (Medicine)
2-B-F . . . . Selective Service Class (for Man Physically Disqualified for Military Service but Necessary to War Production) (Obsolete)
BFA . . . . Bachelor of Fine Arts
BFA . . . . Balloon Federation of America
BFA . . . . Broadcasting Foundation of America
BFA . . . . Bureau of Finance and Administration (US Postal Service)
BFA in DA . . . . Bachelor of Fine Arts in Dramatic Art
BFA in Ed . . . . Bachelor of Fine Arts in Education
BFA in Mus . . . Bachelor of Fine Arts in Music
BFA in PS . . . . Bachelor of Fine Arts in Painting and Sculpture
BFA in Sp . . . . . Bachelor of Fine Arts in Speech
BFB . . . . Broad-Flanged Beam
BFB . . . . Bundesverband der Freien Berufe
BFBS . . . . British Forces Broadcasting Service
BFBS . . . . British and Foreign Bible Society
BFC . . . . Bellefonte Central R. R. (AAR code)
BFC . . . . Bending Feedback Control
BFC . . . . Bohr Frequency Condition
BFC . . . . . . Broadcasting and Film Commission

BFC . . . . Budget and Forecast Calendarization
BFC . . . . Buffalo Forge Company (NYSE symbol)
BFC . . . . Bureau of Foreign Commerce (Commerce Department, abolished 1961)
BFCA . . . . Bichon Frise Club of America
BFCF . . . . Bremerton Freight Car Ferry, Inc. (AAR code)
BFCSD . . . . . . International Union of United Brewery, Flour, Cereal, Soft Drink and Distillery Workers of America
BFCT . . . . Boiler Feed Compound Tank (Technical drawings)
BFCU . . . . . . Bureau of Federal Credit Unions (Social Security Administration)
BFD . . . . Big Fine Deal
BFD . . . . Boolean Function Designator
BFDC . . . . Battalion Fire Distribution Center
BFDC . . . . Bureau of Foreign and Domestic Commerce (In Department of Commerce; functions later dispersed)
BFE . . . . Bachelor of Forest Engineering
BFE . . . . Beam-Forming Electrode
BFE . . . . Board for Fundamental Education
BFE . . . . Bureau for Far East (AID)
BFEA . . . . Bureau of Far Eastern Affairs (Department of State)
BF Eng . . . . . . Bachelor of Forest Engineering
BFF . . . . Buffered Flip-Flop
BFG . . . . B. F. Goodrich Company
BfG . . . . Bank fuer Gemeinwirtschaft (Frankfurt, Germany)
BFG . . . . Brute Force Gyro
BFH . . . . Bundesfinanzhof
BFI . . . . British Film Institute
BFI . . . . Browning-Ferris Industries (NYSE symbol)
BFI . . . . Business Forms Institute
BFID . . . . Boolean Function Identifier
BFJ . . . . Booster Fuel Jacket
BFL . . . . Bachelor of Family Life
BFL . . . . Back Focal Length
BFL . . . . Books for Libraries (Program)
BFM . . . . Barium Ferrite Magnet
BFM . . . . Basic Field Manual (Military)
BFMA . . . . Business Forms Management Association
BFMDS . . . . . . Base Flight Management Data System
BFN . . . . British Forces Network
BFO . . . . Beat Frequency Oscillator
BFOQ . . . . . . Bona Fide Occupational Qualification
BFORM . . . . . . Budget Formulation (Army)
BFP . . . . Batters Faced by Pitcher (Baseball)
BFP . . . . Biological False Positive
BFP . . . . Boiler Feed Pump (Technical drawings)
BFP . . . . Bottom Finding Pinger
BFPPS . . . . . . Bureau of Foods, Pesticides, and Product Safety (FDA)
BFPV . . . . Bona Fide Purchaser for Value (of a security, or other negotiable instrument) (Law)
BFR . . . . Barrier Film Rectifier
BFR . . . . Blast Furnace Research, Inc.
BFR . . . . Block Format Recording
BFRL . . . . Basic Facility Requirements List (Navy)
BFRS . . . . Bio-Feedback Research Society
BFS . . . . Bachelor of Foreign Service
BFS . . . . Band Filter Set
BFS . . . . Board of Foreign Scholarships (Department of State)
BFS . . . . Bureau of Family Services (of SSA)
BFSO . . . . Base Fuel Supply Officer
BFT . . . . Bachelor of Foreign Trade
BFT . . . . Batch Fabrication Technique
BFTSS . . . . . . Bohemian Free Thinking School Society
BFU . . . . Benjamin Franklin University (Washington, DC)
BFUP . . . . Board of Fire Underwriters of the Pacific
BFUSA . . . . . . Basketball Federation of the United States of America
BFW . . . . Boiler Feed Water (Technical drawings)
BFX . . . . Best Foods, Inc. (American Stock Exchange symbol)
BFZ . . . . Branch of Fall Zero
BG . . . . Back Gear (Technical drawings)
BG . . . . Background
BG . . . . Basal Groove
BG . . . . Battle Group
BG . . . . Beach Group
BG . . . . Before Girls (i.e., before women became part of armed forces) (Military)
BG . . . . Benny Goodman (Clarinetist)
BG . . . . Bezirksgericht
BG . . . . Bluish Green
BG . . . . Brigadier General
BG . . . . Briggs Manufacturing Company (NYSE symbol) (Delisted)
BG . . . . British Guiana
B/G . . . . Bonded Goods (Business and trade)
B & G . . . . Barton & Guestier (Wine)

BGA	American Belted Galloway Cattle Breeders' Association
BGA	Barre Granite Association
BGA	Bernard Geis Associates (Publisher) (Obsolete)
BGA	Blue-Green Algae (Water purification)
BGA	Blue-Green Algae Virus (Medicine)
BGAL	British Guiana Airways, Ltd. (A national airline)
BGB	Booksellers of Great Britain
BGB	Buergerliches Gesetzbuch
BGC	Bailiff Grand Cross
BGC	Blood Group Class
BGCC	Bowling Green College of Commerce (Later, a division of Western Kentucky State College)
BGCG	Battery Guidance Command Group
BGD	Billion Gallons per Day
BGDA	Blue Grass Depot Activity (Army)
BGE	Bachelor of Geological Engineering
BGE	Baltimore Gas & Electric Company (NYSE symbol)
BGE	Bull General Electric
BGE	Butyl Glycidyl Ether
B Ge E	Bachelor of Geological Engineering
B Ge Eng	Bachelor of Geological Engineering
B Gen Ed	Bachelor of General Education
BGFE	Boston Grain and Flour Exchange
BGFRS	Board of Governors, Federal Reserve System
BGG	Black Granite Gage
BGG	Booster Gas Generator
BGG	Bovine Gamma Globulin
BGG	Briggs and Stratton Corporation (NYSE symbol)
BGH	Burroughs Corporation (NYSE symbol)
BGK	Bhatnagar-Gross-Krook (Equation)
BGLA	Business Group for Latin America
BGLT	Battle Group Landing Team
BGM	Basegram (Navy)
BGM	Buglemaster (Navy)
BGMA	British Gear Manufacturing Association
BGN	Board on Geographic Names (Department of the Interior)
BGPDC	Brouwer General Perturbations Differential Correction Program
BGPP	Beneficiary Government Production Program
BGPW	Bare Gold Plated Wire
BGR	Basal Granule
BGR	Bombing and Gunnery Range
B-G-R	Barnes-Gibson-Raymond Division, Associated Spring Corporation
BGRR	Brookhaven Graphite Research Reactor (AEC)
BGRV	Boost Glide Reentry Vehicle (Air Force)
BGS	Bachelor of General Studies
BGS	Backup Gimbal Servo
BGS	Beta Gamma Sigma
BGS	Bigelow-Sanford, Inc. (NYSE symbol) (Delisted)
BGS	Brigadier, General Staff (British Army)
BGS	Brothers of Good Shepherd (Roman Catholic religious order)
BGSS	Battalion Ground Surveillance Section (Army)
BGSU	Bowling Green State University (Ohio)
BGT	Bender-Gestalt Test
BGT	Budget Industries, Inc. (NYSE symbol)
BGTB	Brazilian Government Trade Bureau
BGU	British Guiana
BH	Bachelor of Hebrew
BH	Bachelor of Humanics
BH	Base Hospital (Military)
BH	Baskets or Hampers (Freight)
BH	Bath & Hammondsport R. R. (AAR code)
BH	Blasthole
BH	Bloody Hell (British)
BH	Boiler House (Technical drawings)
BH	Borehole
BH	Brigade Headquarters (Army)
BH	Brinell Hardness
BH	British Hovercraft
BH	Bung-Hole (i.e., cheese) (British slang)
B of H	Board of Health
BHA	Bachelor of Hospital Administration
BHA	Base Helix Angle (NASA)
BHA	Bleed Hose Assembly
BHA	Bus History Association
BHA	Butylated Hydroxyanisole (Chemical)
BHAD	Broach Adapter
BH Adm	Bachelor of Hospital Administration
BHB	Bush Terminal Buildings (NYSE symbol) (Later, BSH)
BHC	Benedictine Heights College (Oklahoma)
BHC	Benzene Hexachloride (An insecticide)
BHC	Better Heating-Cooling Council

BHC	Bore Hole Capsule
BHC	Born-Haber Cycle
BHC	British High Commissioner
BHC	Journeymen Barbers, Hairdressers, Cosmetologists and Proprietors' International Union of America
BHCA	Bassett Hound Club of America
BHD	Beachhead
BHD	Binary Homing Device
BHE	Bureau of Higher Education (Office of Education)
BH Ec	Bachelor of Home Economics
BHF	Background Heat Flux
BHF	Business History Foundation
BHFX	Broach Fixture
BHG	Baeuerliche Handelsgesellschaft
BHG	Booth-Henry-Gorin (Equations for calculation of net charge and valence of molecule)
BHHMC	Board of Hospitals and Homes of the Methodist Church
BHI	Bureau of Health Insurance (Social Security Administration)
BHI	Bureau Hydrographique International (International Hydrographic Bureau)
BHIF	Better Highways Information Foundation (Defunct)
BHJ	Bulkhead Jack
BHK	Baby Hamster Kidney
BHK	Bohack Corp. (American Stock Exchange symbol)
BHL	Bachelor of Hebrew Letters
BHL	Bachelor of Hebrew Literature
BHL	Bachelor of Humane Letters
BHL	Bohn Aluminum and Brass Corporation (NYSE symbol) (Delisted)
BHLA	Ben Hur Life Association
BHM	Buckingham Corporation (NYSE symbol) (Delisted)
BHM	Bureau of Health Manpower
BHMA	Builders' Hardware Manufacturers Association
BHMO	Blue Hill Meteorological Observatory (Harvard University)
BHN	Brinell Hardness Number
BHN	Brotherhood of the Holy Name
BHNHE	Bureau of Human Nutrition and Home Economics (Department of Agriculture) (Functions transferred to ARS, 1953)
BHO	Branch Hydrographic Office
B Ho Ec	Bachelor of Household Economy
B Hor	Bachelor of Horticulture
B Ho Sc	Bachelor of Household Science
BHP	Boiler Horsepower
BHP	Brake Horsepower
BHP	Brashear-Hastings Prism
BHQ	Brigade Headquarters (Army)
BHR	Basal Heart Rate
BHR	Biotechnology & Human Research
BHR	Bulkhead Receptacle
BHRA	British Hydromechanics Research Association
BHRI	Brewers Hop Research Institute
BHS	Bachelor of Home Science
BHS	Basic Hole System
BHS	Bonhomie & Hattiesburg Southern R. R. (AAR code)
BHS	Bore Hole Seismometer
BHS	Broadway-Hale Stores, Inc. (NYSE symbol)
BHS	Bureau of Health Services (PHS)
BHS	Burlesque Historical Society
BHT	Brotherhood of the Holy Trinity
BHT	Butylated Hydroxytoluene
BHTC	Black Hills Teachers College (Later, Black Hills State College) (South Dakota)
B Hu	Bachelor of Humanities
BHW	Bell and Howell Company (NYSE symbol)
BHWR	Boiling Heavy Water Reactor (AEC)
BHXU	Brayton Heat Exchanger Unit
B Hy	Bachelor of Hygiene
BHY	Belding Heminway Company, Inc. (NYSE symbol)
BHZ	Berliner Handelszentrale
BI	Background Investigation
BI	Balch Institute (Philadelphia, Pa.)
BI	Base Ignition
BI	Basic Infantry
BI	Battlefield Illumination (Army)
BI	Bermuda Islands
Bi	Bismuth (Chemical element)
BI	Bobov in Israel
BI	Bodily Injury (Insurance)
BI	Branch Immaterial
BI	British India
BI	Buffer Index
BI	Bureau of Investigation (Federal Trade Commission)
BI	National Biscuit Company (NYSE symbol) (Later, NAB)

B/I . . . . Battery Inverter
B & I . . . . Base and Increment (Technical drawings)
B & I . . . . Billeting and Inventory (Military)
B or I . . . . Brass or Iron (Freight)
BIA . . . . Bachelor of Industrial Arts
BIA . . . . Bee Industries Association
BIA . . . . Bicycle Institute of America
BIA . . . . Board of Immigration Appeals (Department of Justice)
BIA . . . . Boating Industry Association
BIA . . . . Boost, Insertion & Abort
BIA . . . . Booster Interstage Assembly
BIA . . . . Braille Institute of America
BIA . . . . British Insurance Association
BIA . . . . Bureau of Indian Affairs (Department of the Interior)
BIA . . . . Bureau of Insular Affairs (Originally, part of War Department; functions transferred to Department of the Interior, 1939)
BIA . . . . Bureau Issues Association (Philately)
BIA . . . . Real-Aerovias Brasil (Airline)
BIAA . . . . . Bureau of Inter-American Affairs (Department of State)
BIAC . . . . . . Bioinstrumentation Advisory Council
BIAD . . . . . Bureau International d'Anthropologie Differentielle
BIAPS . . . . . . Battery Inverter Accessory Power Supply
BIAR . . . . Base Installation Action Requirements
BI Arch . . . . . Bachelor of Interior Architecture
BI Arch E . . . . Bachelor of Interior Architectural Engineering
BI Arch Eng . . . Bachelor of Interior Architectural Engineering
BIAS . . . . Battlefield Illumination Airborne System
BIAS . . . . Brooklyn Institute of Arts and Sciences
BIAT . . . . Burn-In/Aging Tester
BIATA . . . . . . British Independent Air Transport Association
BIB . . . . Baby Incendiary Bomb
BIB . . . . Biennale of Illustrations Bratislava
BIB . . . . Biographical Information Blank
BIB . . . . Bipartite Board (Post-World War II, Germany)
BIB . . . . Bottled in Bond (Wines and spirits)
BIBA . . . . Babson Institute of Business Administration (Massachusetts)
BIBD . . . . Balanced Incomplete Block Design (Mathematics)
BIBE . . . . Big Bend National Park
BIBO . . . . . . Bureau of International Business Operations (Department of Commerce)
BIBS . . . . Built-In Breathing System
BIC . . . . Baha'i International Community
BIC . . . . Battlefield Information Center (Army)
BIC . . . . Bibas In Christo (May You Live in Christ)
BIC . . . . Biodeterioration Information Centre (British)
BIC . . . . Biographical Inventory Creativity
BIC . . . . Biomedical Instrumentation Consultant
BIC . . . . Bombardment-Induced Conductivity
BIC . . . . Bureau International de la Chaussure et du Cuir
BIC . . . . Bureau International du Cinema
BIC . . . . Bureau of International Commerce (Department of Commerce)
BIC . . . . Bureau International des Containers
BICA . . . . . . Bighorn Canyon National Recreation Area
BICC . . . . . . Battlefield Information Control Center (Army)
BICC . . . . . . British Insulated Collender's Cable
BICC . . . . . . Business and Industrial Coordinating Council
BICE . . . . . . Bureau International Catholique de l'Enfance
BICEMA . . . . British Internal Combustion Engine Manufacturers' Association
BICEP . . . . . . British Industrial Collaborative Exponential Program
BICIV . . . . . . Bipartite Civil Service Advisors (Post-World War II, Germany)
BICO . . . . . . Bipartite Control Office (Post-World War II, Germany)
BICOM . . . . . Bipartite Communications Panel (Post-World War II, Germany)
BID . . . . Bachelor of Industrial Design
BID . . . . Bis in Die (Twice a Day) (Medicine)
BID . . . . Blow in Door
BID . . . . Brought In Dead (Medical notation)
B of ID . . . . . Bachelor of Interior Design
BIDAP . . . . . . Bibliographic Data Processing Program (for Keyword Indexing)
BIDEC . . . . . Binary to Decimal Converter (Data processing)
BIDEC . . . . . . Bipartite Decartelization Commission (Berlin) (Post-World War II, Germany)
BIDESC . . . . . Bipartite Decartelization Sub-Commission (Minden) (Post-World War II, Germany)
BIDO . . . . . . British Industrial Development Office (Through foreign branches, encourages investments in Britain from abroad)
BIDS . . . . Bendix Integrated Data System
BIE . . . . Bachelor of Industrial Engineering
BIE . . . . Binaural Intensity Effect
BIE . . . . Bureau International d'Education
BIE . . . . Bureau International des Expositions
BIE . . . . Business-Industry-Education (Days) (Usually sponsored by chambers of commerce)
BIECO . . . . . . Bipartite Economic Panel (Post-World War II, Germany)

BIECO/RAIL . . . Bipartite Economic Panel Railway Supplies Committee (Post-World War II, Germany)
BIEE . . . . British Institute of Electrical Engineers
BIEM . . . . . . Bureau International de l'Edition Mecanique
BI Eng . . . . . Bachelor of Industrial Engineering
BIF . . . . Bombardier's Information File
BIF . . . . British Industries Fair
BIF . . . . British Industries Federation
BIF & A . . . . . Bipartite Food and Agriculture Panel (Post-World War II, Germany)
BIFIN . . . . . . Bipartite Finance Panel (Post-World War II, Germany)
BIFR . . . . Before Encountering Instrument Flight Rules Conditions
BIG . . . . Best in Group
BIG . . . . Big Three Industries Inc. (NYSE symbol)
BIG . . . . Biological Isolation Garment (NASA)
BIGECO . . . . Bipartite Economic Control Group (Post-World War II, Germany)
BIGENA . . . . Bibliography and Index of Geology Exclusive of North America (American Geological Institute)
BIGFET . . . . . Bipolar Insulated Gate Field Effect Transistor (Bell Laboratories)
BIH . . . . Bureau International de l'Heure (International Bureau of Time)
BIHO . . . . . . Big Hole National Battlefield
BII . . . . Background Illumination Intensity
BII . . . . Biosophical Institute, Incorporated
BIIA . . . . British Institute of Industrial Art
BIICC . . . . . . Bureau International d'Information des Chambres de Commerce
BIIL . . . . Basic Issue Item List (Army)
BIK . . . . Bickford's, Inc. (American Stock Exchange symbol)
BIL . . . . Basic Insulation Level
BIL . . . . Blue Indicator Light
BIL . . . . Bulk Items List
BILA . . . . . . Bible Institute of Los Angeles
BILA . . . . . . Bureau of International Labor Affairs (Department of Labor)
BILB . . . . . . Built-In Light Beacon
BILE . . . . . . Balanced Inductor Logical Element
BILI . . . . Basic Issue List Items (Army)
BIM . . . . Bachelor of Industrial Management
BIM . . . . Basic Industrial Materials (Program) (Navy)
BIM . . . . Best in Match
BIM . . . . Biographical Inventory for Medicine
BIM . . . . Blade Inspection Method
BI-M . . . . . . Bimonthly
B of IM . . . . . Bachelor of Industrial Management
BIMA . . . . . . Business and Industry Management Abstracts
BIMAC . . . . . Bistable Magnetic Core (Data processing)
BIMCAM . . . . British Industrial Measuring and Control Apparatus Manufacturers' Association
BIMRAB . . . . BUWEPS (Bureau of Naval Weapons) [Obsolete] - Industry Material Reliability Advisory Board
BIMS . . . . . . Battlefield Integration Management System (Army)
BIN . . . . Bell Information Network
BIN . . . . Binary
BINAC . . . . . Binary Automatic Computer
BINCOS . . . . Binder Control Subsystem
B Ind . . . . . . Bachelor of Industry
B Ind E . . . . . Bachelor of Industrial Engineering
B Ind Ed . . . . . Bachelor of Industrial Education
B Ind Mgt . . . . . Bachelor of Industrial Management
BINOVC . . . . Break in Overcast (Meteorology)
B Int L . . . . . Bachelor of International Law
BIO . . . . Base Installation Officer
BIO . . . . Biological Information-Processing Organization
BIO . . . . Branch Intelligence Officer
BIOA . . . . . . Bureau of International Organization Affairs (Department of State)
BIODEF . . . . . Biological Defense
BIOL . . . . . . Biology (or Biological)
BIOLDEF . . . . . Biological Defense (Military)
BIOLOP . . . . Biological Operations (Military)
BIOLWPN . . . . Biological Weapons (Military)
BIOLWPNSYS . . Biological Weapon System (Army)
BIOMOD . . . . Biochemical Modeling (Data processing system)
BIOPACK . . . . Biological Packs
BIOR . . . . . . Business Input/Output Rerun
BIORED . . . . . Biological Resources Development Teams
BIOREP/CHEMREP . . . Biological/Chemical Attack Report
BIOS . . . . . . Biological Investigation of Outer Space (NASA)
BIOS . . . . . . Biological Satellite (NASA)
BIOSC . . . . . British Intelligence Objectives Subcommittee
BIOSIS . . . . . Biological Sciences Information Service (of Biological Abstracts)
BIOT . . . . . . British Indian Ocean Territory
BIOWAR . . . . Biological Warfare
BIP . . . . Balloon Interrogation Package
BIP . . . . Banco Industrial del Peru (Industrial Bank of Peru)

BIP . . . . Bismuth Iodoform Paraffin
BIP . . . . Books in Print (A reference publication)
BIP . . . . Bureau of International Programs (Department of Commerce)
BIPAC . . . . . Business-Industry Political Action Committee
BIPAD . . . . . . Binary Pattern Detector
BIPAD . . . . . . Bureau of Independent Publishers and Distributors
BIPCA . . . . . . Bureau International Permanent de Chimie Analytique pour les Matieres
    Destinees a l'Alimentation del'Homme et des Animaux (Permanent
    International Bureau of Analytical Chemistry of Human and Animal Food)
BIPCO . . . . . . Built-in-Place Component (Electronics)
BIPD . . . . Biparting Door
BIPE . . . . Bureau d'Informations et de Previsions Economiques (France)
BIPM . . . . . . Bureau International des Poids et Mesures (International Bureau of
    Weights and Measures)
BIR . . . . Break-In Relay
BIR . . . . Bureau of Intelligence and Research (Department of State)
BIR . . . . Bureau of Internal Revenue (Treasury Department) (Later, Internal
    Revenue Service)
BIR . . . . Bureau International de la Recuperation (International Reclamation Bureau)
BIRD . . . . Banque Internationale pour la Reconstruction et le Developpement
    (International Bank for Reconstruction and Development; also known as
    the World Bank)
BIRDIE . . . . . Battery Integration and RADAR Display Equipment (Air defense system)
B Ir E . . . . . . Bachelor of Irrigation Engineering
BIRE . . . . British Institute of Radio Engineers
B Ir Eng . . . . Bachelor of Irrigation Engineering
BIRI . . . . . . Brewing Industries Research Institute
BIRISPT . . . . . Bureau International de Recherche sur les Implications Sociales du
    Progres Technique
BIRPI . . . . Bureaux Internationaux Reunis pour la Protection de la Propriete
    Intellectuelle (United International Bureau for the Protection of
    Intellectual Property) (Later, WIPO)
BIRS . . . . British Institute of Recorded Sound
BIRT . . . . Bolt Installation and Removal Tool
Bi S . . . . . . Bachelor of Biological Sciences
BIS . . . . Bank for International Settlements
BIS . . . . Best in Show
BIS . . . . Board of Inspection and Survey (Navy)
BIS . . . . Brain Information Service (UCLA)
BIS . . . . British Information Services
BIS . . . . British Interplanetary Society
BIS . . . . Bureau of Inspection and Survey
BIS . . . . Bureau Interafricain des Sols et de l'Economie Rurale
BIS . . . . Bureau International du Scoutisme
BIS . . . . Burn-In Screening
BIS . . . . Business Information System (Bell Laboratories)
BIS . . . . Business Intelligence Services, Ltd. (British)
BISAM . . . . . Basic Indexed Sequential Access Method (Data processing)
BISCUS . . . . . Business Information System/Customer Service (Bell System)
BISEC . . . . . . Bipartite Secretariat (Post-World War II, Germany)
BISF . . . . . . British Iron and Steel Federation
BISFA . . . . . . Bureau International pour la Standardisation de la Rayonne et des
    Fibres Synthetiques (International Bureau for the Standardization of
    Man-Made Fibres)
BISITS . . . . . . British Iron and Steel Industry Translation Service
BISMAPS . . . . Business Information System Modeling and Planning System (Bell Labora-
    tories)
BISMRA . . . . . Bureau of Inter-Industrial Statistics & Multiple Regression Analysis
BISNC . . . . . British India Steam Navigation Company
BISP . . . . Business Information System Programs (Bell System)
BISRA . . . . . . British Iron and Steel Research Association
BISS . . . . Bio-Isolator Suit System
BISSC . . . . . . Baking Industry Sanitation Standards Committee
BIST . . . . Built-In Self-Test
BIT . . . . Bachelor of Industrial Technology
BIT . . . . Band Ignitor Tube
BIT . . . . Binary Digit (Data processing)
BIT . . . . Born-Infeld Theory
BIT . . . . Built-In Test(ing) (RADAR)
BIT . . . . Bureau International du Travail (International Labour Office)
BITA . . . . . . British Industrial Truck Association
BITE . . . . Built-In Test Equipment
BITN . . . . . . Bilateral Iterative Network
BITO . . . . . . Burnishing Tool
BITS . . . . Binary Digits (Data processing)
BITS . . . . . . Binary Intersystem Transmission Standard
BIU . . . . Bureau International des Universites
BIW . . . . Bath Industries, Inc. (Formerly, Bath Iron Works Corp.) (NYSE symbol)
BIW . . . . . . Battle Injury or Wound
BI-W . . . . . . Biweekly
BIX . . . . Binary Information Exchange

BIZMAC . . . . . Business Machine Computer
BJ . . . . Bachelor of Journalism
BJ . . . . Back Judge (Football)
BJ . . . . Barrage Jammers (RADAR)
BJ . . . . Blair (John) & Co. (NYSE symbol)
BJ . . . . Bulkhead Jack
BJA . . . . Ball Joint Actuator
BJA . . . . Basic Journal Abstracts (A publication of American Chemical Society)
BJA . . . . Burlap and Jute Association
BJC . . . . Babinet Jamin Compensator
BJC . . . . Baltimore Junior College (Maryland)
BJC . . . . Bennett Junior College (New York)
BJC . . . . Bismarck Junior College (North Dakota)
BJC . . . . Boise Junior College (Idaho)
BJC . . . . Boone Junior College (Iowa)
BJC . . . . Bradford Junior College (Massachusetts)
BJC . . . . Brainerd Junior College (Minnesota)
BJC . . . . British Jewish Cockney
BJC . . . . Brotherhood of the Jungle Cock
BJCEB . . . . . . British Joint Communications-Electronics Board (Military)
BJCPA . . . . . Baptist Joint Committee on Public Affairs
BJD . . . . Beam (James B.) Distilling Company (NYSE symbol) (Delisted)
BJ Ed . . . . . . Bachelor of Jewish Education
BJEP . . . . . . Bureau on Jewish Employment Problems
BJF . . . . Ball Joint Fitting
BJM . . . . Bluejacket's Manual (Navy)
BJP . . . . Bachelor of Jewish Pedagogy
BJS . . . . British Joint Services
BJSM . . . . . . British Joint Services Mission
BJSM . . . . . . British Joint Staff Mission
BJU . . . . Beach Jumper Unit
BJU . . . . Bob Jones University (South Carolina)
BK . . . . Bank of New York Co., Inc. (NYSE symbol)
BK . . . . Bauernkorrespondent
BK S . . . . . . Below Knee (Medicine)
Bk . . . . Berkelium (Chemical element)
BK . . . . Berlin Kommandatura
BK . . . . Blaw-Knox Company (NYSE symbol) (Delisted)
BK . . . . Blendkoerper (Frangible-glass smoke grenade) (German military –
    World War II)
BKA . . . . Bee Keepers Association
BKA . . . . Broadband Klystron Amplifier
BKDI . . . . . . Brake Die
BKI . . . . Better Kitchens Institute
BKKI . . . . . . Badan Kongress Kebathinan Indonesia
BKLT . . . . . . Booklet
BKO . . . . Baker Oil Tools, Inc. (NYSE symbol)
BKO . . . . Barkhausen-Kurz Oscillator
BKP . . . . Buckeye Pipe Line Company (NYSE symbol) (Delisted)
BKP . . . . Bulgarska Komunisticheska Partiia (Bulgarian Communist Party)
BKS . . . . Blutkorpersenkung (Blood Sedimentation Rate) (Medicine)
BKV . . . . Betriebskollektivvertrag
BKY . . . . Berkey Photo, Inc. (NYSE symbol)
BL . . . . Bachelor of Laws
BL . . . . Bachelor of Letters
BL . . . . Bachelor of Literature
BL . . . . Background Listening (Music)
BL . . . . Bank Larceny
BL . . . . Base Line (Technical drawings)
BL . . . . Beak Line
BL . . . . Bill of Lading
BL . . . . Biological Laboratory
BL . . . . Black Letter (Type)
BL . . . . Bombline
BL . . . . Bonanza Air Lines, Incorporated
BL . . . . Bottom Layer (Technical drawings)
BL . . . . Boundary Layer
BL . . . . Breadth-Length
BL . . . . Breech Loading (Weapon)
BL . . . . British Legion
BL . . . . Buccolingual
BL . . . . Building Line (Technical drawings)
BL . . . . Bureau of Litigation (Federal Trade Commission)
BL . . . . Burkitt's Lymphoma
BL . . . . Butt Line (Technical drawings)
BL . . . . Buttock Line (Technical drawings)
BL . . . . Graduate in Letters
B/L . . . . Bill of Lading
B & L . . . . . . Building and Loan (Association)
BLA . . . . Bachelor of Landscape Architecture
BLA . . . . Bachelor of Liberal Arts

BLA . . . . Baltimore & Annapolis R. R. (AAR code)
BLA . . . . Baptist Life Association
BLA . . . . Base Loaded Antenna
BLA . . . . Belgian Linen Association
BLA . . . . Bills of Lading Act
BLA . . . . Black Liberation Army
BLA . . . . Bracket and Linkage Assembly
BLA . . . . Bureau for Latin America (AID)
BLA . . . . Graduate in Liberal Arts
BLAC . . . . . . British Light Aviation Center
BLADE . . . . . . Base Level Automation of Data through Electronics
BLADE . . . . . . Bell Laboratories Automatic Device
BLADES. . . . . . Bell Laboratories Automatic Design System
BLADING . . . . Bill of lading (Military)
BLADS . . . . . . Bell Laboratories Automatic Design System
B La L . . . . . . Bachelor of Latin Letters
BLAM . . . . . . Ballistically Launched Aerodynamic Missile
BL Arch . . . . . Bachelor of Landscape Architecture
BLAST. . . . . . . Black Legal Action for Soul in Television (Student legal action organization)
BLB . . . . Boy's Life Brigade
BLBG . . . . . . Biological Laboratory, Brunswick, Georgia (US Bureau of Commercial Fisheries)
BLBSB. . . . . . Better Light Better Sight Bureau
BLC . . . . Barrier Layer Cell
Bl C . . . . Blood Culture (Bacteriology)
BLC . . . . Blue Line Copy
BLC . . . . Boundary-Layer Control
BLC . . . . British Lighting Control
BLC . . . . Broadband Latching Circulator
BLCA . . . . . . Black Canyon of the Gunnison National Monument
BLCE . . . . . . Base Line Calibration Equipment
BLD . . . . Below Limit of Detection
BLD . . . . Boulevard
BLD . . . . Bullard Company (NYSE symbol) (Delisted)
BLDCS . . . . . . Bureau of Laundry and Dry Cleaning Standards
BL Des . . . . . . Bachelor of Landscape Design
BLDG . . . . . . Building
Bldg E . . . . . . Building Engineer
BLDI. . . . . . . Blank Die
BLE . . . . Bachelor of Library Economics
BLE . . . . Bessemer and Lake Erie R. R. (AAR code)
BLE . . . . Blunt Leading Edge
BLE . . . . Brotherhood of Locomotive Engineers
B & LE . . . . . Bessemer and Lake Erie Railroad Company
BL Ec . . . . . . Bachelor of Library Economics
BLEDCO . . . . . Brooklyn Local Economic Development Corporation
BL Eng . . . . . . Bachelor of Landscape Engineering
BLESMA . . . . . British Limbless Ex-Service Men's Association
BLESSED . . . . . Bell Little Electrodata Symbolic System for the Electrodata
BLESTO-VIII. . . Bears, Lions, Eagles, Steelers, Vikings, Colts, Dolphins, and Bills (Computerized scouting combine for professional football teams; name comprises membership teams)
BLET. . . . . . . Bureau of Libraries and Educational Technology (Office of Education)
BLEU . . . . . . Belgium-Luxembourg Economic Union
BLEU . . . . . . Blind Landing Experimental Unit (Aviation)
BLF . . . . Byelorussian Liberation Front
BLFE. . . . . . . Brotherhood of Locomotive Firemen and Enginemen
BLG . . . . Bell and Gossett Company (NYSE symbol) (Delisted)
BLH . . . . Baldwin-Lima-Hamilton Company, Inc.
BLH . . . . British Legion Headquarters
BLI . . . . Bachelor of Literary Interpretation
BLI . . . . Basic Learning Institute
BLI. . . . . Bliss and Laughlin Industries, Inc. (NYSE symbol)
BLIC. . . . . . . Bureau de Liaison des Industries du Caoutchouc de la CEE
BLIMPRON . . . Blimp Squadron
BLIP . . . . Background-Limited Infrared Photoconductor
BLIP . . . . Big Look Improvement Program
BLIP . . . . Boundary Layer Instrument Package (Meteorology)
BLIS . . . . Bell Laboratories Interpretive System (Data processing)
B Lit . . . . Bachelor of Letters
B Lit . . . . Bachelor of Literature
B Litt . . . . . . Bachelor of Letters
B Litt . . . . . . Bachelor of Literature
BLJ . . . . Bachelor of Letters in Journalism
BLJ . . . . Bumper Lift Jack
BLL . . . . Bachelor of Latin Letters
BLL . . . . Bachelor of Laws
BLL . . . . Base of Lateral Lip
BLL . . . . Bell Intercontinental Corporation (NYSE symbol) (Delisted)
BLLE. . . . . . . Balanced Line Logical Element

BLM . . . . Bachelor of Landscape Management
BLM . . . . Bimolecular Lipid Membrane
BLM . . . . Book-Library-Management (System)
BLM . . . . Bureau of Land Management (Department of the Interior)
BLMPS. . . . . . Base Level Military Personnel System
BLMR . . . . . . Bureau of Labor-Management Reports (Department of Labor)
BLMRA . . . . . British Leather Manufacturers Research Association
BLN . . . . Balloon
BLO . . . . Bombardment Liaison Officer (Navy)
BLO . . . . British Liaison Officer
BLO . . . . Butt Line Zero
BLOC . . . . . . Block Oriented Compiler
BLODI . . . . . . Block Diagram Compiler
BLOWS . . . . . British Library of Wildlife Sound
BLP . . . . Ball Lock Pin
BLP . . . . Bela Lyons Pratt (Designer's mark, when appearing on US coins)
BLP. . . . . Blaettchenpulver (Flake powder) (German military – World War II)
BLP . . . . Blue Line Print
BLP . . . . Bombing Landplane
BL & P . . . . . . Blind Loaded and Plugged (Projectile)
BLPC . . . . . . Backward Limit Photocell
BLPZZ . . . . . . Bent Logarithmically Periodic Zig-Zags
BLR . . . . Ballistic Research Laboratories (Army)
BLR . . . . Barrier Layer Rectifier
BLR . . . . Breech-Loading Rifle
BLRG . . . . . . Breech-Loading Rifled Guns
BLRI . . . . Blue Ridge Parkway (National Park Service designation)
BLS . . . . Bachelor of Library Science
BLS . . . . Balanced Line System
BLS . . . . Balloon Launching Station
BLS . . . . Band Limited Signal
BLS . . . . Beech-Nut Life Savers, Inc. (NYSE symbol) (Delisted)
BLS . . . . Bell Log System
BLS . . . . Blood and Lymphatic System
Bl S . . . . Blood Sugar (Medicine)
BLS . . . . Boundary Layer Separation
BLS . . . . Broadband Latching Switch
BLS . . . . Brooklyn Law School
BLS . . . . Bureau of Labor Standards (Department of Labor)
BLS . . . . Bureau of Labor Statistics (Department of Labor)
BLSB. . . . . . . Ball-Lock Separation Bolt
BL Sc . . . . . . Bachelor of Library Science
BLSJICP . . . . . Beam Lead Sealed Junction Integrated Circuit Package
BLSS . . . . Base Level Self-Sufficiency (Air Force)
B Lt . . . . Bachelor of Literature
BLT . . . . Bacon, Lettuce and Tomato (Sandwich) (Waitress's call to a short order cook)
BLT . . . . Battalion Landing Team
Bl T . . . . Blood Type (Medicine)
BLT . . . . Boat Landing Team
BLT . . . . But Less Than
BL & T . . . . . . Blind Loaded and Traced (Projectile)
BLTDA . . . . . . Burley Leaf Tobacco Dealers Association
BLTI . . . . Better Lawn and Turf Institute
BLU . . . . Bomb, Live Unit
BLUE . . . . . . Best Linear Unbiased Estimator (Statistics)
BLV . . . . British Legion Village
BLVD . . . . . . Boulevard
BLZ . . . . Boundary Layer Zone
BM . . . . Bachelor of Mathematics
BM . . . . Bachelor of Medicine
BM . . . . Bachelor of Music
BM . . . . Bachelor of Physic
BM. . . . . Back Marker (Aviation)
BM. . . . . Ballistic Missile
BM . . . . Basal Metabolism
BM. . . . . Base Maintenance (Air Force)
BM. . . . . Basilar Membrane (Cell physiology)
BM. . . . . Beam Monitor
BM. . . . . Beata Maria (The Blessed Virgin)
BM. . . . . Beatae Memoriae (Of Blessed Memory)
BM . . . . Before Marriage
BM. . . . . Bench Mark (In surveying)
BM . . . . Bending Moment
BM. . . . . Bimonthly
BM. . . . . Binary Multiply
BM. . . . . Bishop and Martyr (Church calendars)
BM. . . . . Board Measure (Lumber)
BM. . . . . Boatswain's Mate
BM. . . . . Bonae Memoriae (Of Happy Memory)
BM. . . . . Bone Marrow

BM .... Bordmechaniker (Flight engineer) (German military - World War II)
BM......... Boston & Maine R. R. (AAR code)
BM .... Bowel Movement (Medicine)
BM......... Branch Material (Military)
BM......... Branch Memorandum
BM .... Breech Mechanism (of a weapon)
BM......... Brigade Major
BM......... Brightness Merit
BM......... British Museum (London)
BM......... Bronze Medal
BM......... Buccal Mass
BM......... Buffer Module
BM .... Bureau of Medicine (of FDA)
BM......... Bureau of Mines (Department of the Interior)
BM......... Bureau of the Mint (Department of the Treasury)
BM......... Burgomaster
BM......... Monitor (Navy symbol)
B/M........ Bill of Material
B & M ...... Boston and Maine Railroad
BM1 .... Boatswain's Mate 1st class
BM2 .... Boatswain's Mate 2nd class
BMA ...... Bachelor of Municipal Administration
BMA....... Balanced Magnetic Amplifier
BMA....... Berman Leasing Company (NYSE symbol) (Delisted)
BMA....... Bible Memory Association, International
BMA ...... Bicycle Manufacturers Association
BMA....... Body Mounted Accelerometer
BMA....... British Medical Association
BMA....... British Midland Airways
BMA....... British Military Authority
B Ma E ..... Bachelor of Marine Engineering
B Ma Eng .... Bachelor of Marine Engineering
BMAR ..... Ballistic Missile Acquisition RADAR
B Mar E .... Bachelor of Marine Engineering
BMAT/S .... Ballistic Missile Analyst Technician-Specialist
BMB....... Ballistic Missile Branch
BMB....... British Metrication Board
BMB....... Broadcast Measurement Bureau
BMBDR ..... Bombardier (Military)
BMBR ...... Bomber (Air Force)
BMC....... Ballistic Missile Center (Air Material Command)
BMC....... Ballistic Missile Checker
BMC....... Bearing Mounted Clutch
BMC....... Binary Magnetic Core
BMC....... Blue Mountain College (Mississippi)
BMC....... Boehringer Mannheim Corporation (Chemical industry supplier)
BMC....... British Motor Corporation Ltd.
BMC....... Bryn Mawr College (Pennsylvania)
BMC....... Bulk Molding Compound
BMC ...... Bureau of Motor Carriers (ICC)
BMC ...... Joint Brazil-United States Military Commission
BMC/AMC.... Ballistic Missile Center, Air Materiel Command (Obsolete)
BMCBB ..... Boatswain's Mate, Construction Battalion, Boatswain
BMCBS ..... Boatswain's Mate, Construction Battalion, Stevedore
BMCET/S .... Ballistic Missile Checkout Equipment Technician-Specialist
BMCO ..... Ballistic Missile Construction Office
BMCS ...... Ballistic Missile Cost Study
BMCS ...... Bureau of Motor Carrier Safety (Department of Transportation)
BMCT ...... Beginning Morning Civil Twilight
BMD....... Ballistic Missile Defense
BMD....... Ballistic Missile Division (Air Research and Development Center)
BMD....... Base Maintenance Division
BMDC ..... Ballistic Missile Defense Committee
BMDCP ..... Battalion Mortar and Davy Crockett Platoon (Army)
BMDF...... Black Mesa Defense Fund
BMDMB..... Ballistic Missile Defense Missile Battalion (Army)
BMD-NEAT ... Ballistic Missile Defense - Nuclear Effects and Threat
            Committee (Army)
BMDNS ..... Basic Mission Design Number and Series
BMDS...... Ballistic Missile Defense System (Air Force)
BMDS ...... Base Mail Distribution Scheme (Air Force)
BMDSB ..... Ballistic Missile Defense Surveillance Battalion (Army)
BME....... Bachelor of Mechanical Engineering
BME....... Bachelor of Mining Engineering
BME....... Bachelor of Music Education
BME....... Bachelor of Music in Education
BME....... Beaver, Meade & Englewood R. R. (AAR code)
BME....... Bio-Medical Electronics
BME....... Born-Mayer Equation
BME ...... Brotherhood of Marine Engineers (Later merged with MEBA)
BMEA ...... Building Maintenance Employers Association

BMEA ...... Building Material Exhibitors Association
BME (Aero Option) .. Bachelor of Mechanical Engineering (Aeronautical Option)
BMEC ...... Ball Manufacturers Engineers Committee
B Med ..... Bachelor of Medicine
BM Ed ..... Bachelor of Music Education
B Med Sc .... Bachelor of Medical Science
BM Eng .... Bachelor of Mechanical Engineering
BMEP ...... Brake Mean Effective Pressure
B Met...... Bachelor of Metallurgy
B Metal E .... Bachelor of Metallurgical Engineering
B Met E .... Bachelor of Metalurgical Engineering
B Met Eng ... Bachelor of Metallurgical Engineering
BMETO ..... Ballistic Missiles European Task Organization (Military)
BMEWS..... Ballistic Missile Early Warning System (Air Force)
BMF....... Bene Merenti Fecit (He Erected This to the Well-Deserving)
BMF....... Betriebsmittelfonds
BMF....... Boron Metal Fiber
BMF ...... Business Mail Foundation
BMFA...... Boston Museum of Fine Arts
BMG....... Browning Machine Gun
B Mgt E ..... Bachelor of Management Engineering
BMH....... British Motor Holdings
BMI ...... Ballistic Missile Interceptor (Air Force)
BMI ...... Barley and Malt Institute
BMI ...... Battelle Memorial Institute
BMI ...... Book Manufacturers Institute
BMI .... Bravais-Miller Indices
BMI .... Broadcast Music, Incorporated
B Mic ..... Bachelor of Microbiology
BMIC ...... Bureau of Mines Information Circular
B Mi E ..... Bachelor of Mining Engineering
B Mi Eng... Bachelor of Mining Engineering
BMIGT/M ... Ballistic Missile Inertial Guidance Technician-Mechanic
BMILS ..... Bottom-Mounted Impact Locations System (Missile technology)
BMJ....... British Medical Journal
BML ...... Bachelor of Modern Languages
BML ...... Belfast & Moosehead Lake R. R. (AAR code)
BML ...... Bible Meditation League
BML-BS ..... British Matchbox Label and Booklet Society
BMLET/R .... Ballistic Missile Launch Equipment Technician-Repairman
BMLO ..... Ballistic Missile Logistics Office
BMLUS ..... Business Men's League of the United States
BMM ...... Bachelor of Mining and Metallurgy
BMM ...... Ballistic Missile Manager
BMM ...... Baptist Mid-Missions
BMM ...... Benthic Metabolism Measurement
BMMA ..... Beverage Machinery Manufacturers Association
BMMG ..... Ballistic Missiles Management Group (Air Force)
BMN ...... Base Manager's Notice
BMN ...... British Merchant Navy
BMNH ..... British Museum of Natural History (London)
BMNT..... Beginning Morning Nautical Twilight (Navigation)
BMO ...... Ballistic Missile Office(r) (Air Force)
BMO ...... Beach Modulator Oscillator
BMO ...... Bond Molecular Orbitals
BMOC ..... Ballistic Missile Orientation Course
BMOC ..... Big Machine on Campus (Computer)
BMOC ..... Big Man on Campus (Slang)
BMOM ..... Base Maintenance and Operations Model
BMORT..... Ballistic Missile Operational Training Readiness
BMP....... Bricklayers, Masons and Plasterers' International Union of America
BMPA...... Broadband Microwave Power Amplifier
BMPR ..... Bimonthly Progress Report
BMR....... Basal Metabolic Rate
BMR....... Basal Metabolism Reading (Medicine)
BMR....... Basic Military Requirement
BMR....... Boston and Maine R. R. (NYSE symbol) (Delisted)
BMR....... Brookhaven Medical Reactor (AEC)
BMRC...... Brookhaven Medical Research Center
BMRMO .... Balance Mobilization Reserve Materiel Objective (Army)
B & MRR .... Boston & Maine Railroad
BMRS ...... Ballistic Missile Reentry Systems
BMS ...... Bachelor of Marine Science
BMS ...... Bachelor of Mechanical Science
BMS ...... Ballistic Missile Ship (Navy)
BMS ...... Basic Meteorological Services
BMS ...... Behavior Monitor System
BMS ...... Bemis Co., Inc. (NYSE symbol)
BMS ...... Berlin Mills R. R. (AAR code)
BMS ...... Biomedical Monitoring System
BMS ...... Bloc des Masses Senegalaises (Bloc of the Senegalese Masses)

BMS . . . . Blow Molding System
BMS . . . . Bomb Maintenance Spares
BMS . . . . Breathing Metabolic Simulator (IBM)
BMS . . . . British Ministry of Supply
BMS . . . . Bureau of Medical Services (Public Health Service)
BMS . . . . Bureau of Medicine and Surgery (Navy)
BMS . . . . Bypass Monochrome Signal
BM Sc . . . . . . Bachelor of Mechanical Science
BMSF . . . . . . Ballistic Missile Surface Force
BMSM . . . . . . British Merchant Shipping Mission
BMSO . . . . . . Base Medical Supply Office(r) (Air Force)
BMSO . . . . . . Blue Mountain Seismological Observatory
BMSRC . . . . . . Boatswain's Mate, Ship Repair, Crane Operator
BMSRDE . . . . . British Ministry of Supply Research and Development Establishment
BMSRR . . . . . Boatswain's Mate, Ship Repair, Rigger
BMSRS . . . . . Boatswain's Mate, Ship Repair, Canvasman
B Ms Sc . . . . . Bachelor of Mechanical Sciences
BMT . . . . Bachelor of Medical Technology
BMT . . . . Basic Military Training
BMT . . . . Basic Motion-Time Study
BMT . . . . Bene Merenti (To the Well-Deserving)
BMT . . . . Boston & Maine Transportation R. R. (AAR code)
BMT . . . . Brooklyn-Manhattan Transit Corporation (A New York City subway line)
BMTD . . . . . . Ballistic Missile Terminal Defense
BMTP . . . . . . Bureau of Mines Technical Paper
BMTS . . . . . . Ballistic Missile Target System
BMTS . . . . . . Basic Military Training School
B Mu . . . . . . Bachelor of Music
BMU . . . . Beach Master Unit (Navy)
BMU . . . . Bureau of Manpower Utilization (World War II)
B Mus . . . . . . Bachelor of Music
B Mus E . . . . . Bachelor of Music Education
B Mus Ed . . . . Bachelor of Music in Education
B Mus (PSM) . . . Bachelor of Music in Public School Music
BMV . . . . Base Mount Valve
BMV . . . . Beata Maria Virgo (Blessed Mary the Virgin)
BMV . . . . Bistable Multi-Vibrator
BMV . . . . Bromegrass Mosaic Virus
BMW . . . . . . Bare Molybdenum Wire
BMW . . . . . . Bayrische Motoren Werke (Bavarian Motor Works) (German automobile manufacturer; initialism used as name of its cars)
BMWCCA . . . . BMW (Bavarian Motor Works) Car Club of America
BMWE . . . . . . Brotherhood of Maintenance of Way Employees
BMWS . . . . . Ballistic Missiles Weapon System (Air Force)
BMY . . . . Bristol-Myers Company (NYSE symbol)
BN . . . . Bachelor of Nursing
BN . . . . Banknote
BN . . . . Battalion (Military)
BN . . . . Bauxite & Northern Railway Company (AAR code)
BN . . . . Binary Number
BN . . . . Bloody Nuisance (British)
BN . . . . Blowing Sand (Meteorology)
BN . . . . Bolt and Nut
BN . . . . Borden, Inc. (NYSE symbol) (Wall Street slang name: "Moo Moo")
BN . . . . Boron Nitride (Fiber)
BN . . . . Brazilian Navy
BN . . . . Bull Nose
BN . . . . Bureau of Narcotics (Treasury Department) (Absorbed by BNDD of Department of Justice)
BN . . . . Burlington Northern (Railroad)
BN . . . . But Not
B/N . . . . Bombing/Navigation
B Na . . . . Bachelor of Navigation
BNA . . . . Basle (Basel) Nomina Anatomica (Basel Anatomical Nomenclature) (Medicine)
BNA . . . . Brazil Nut Association
BNA . . . . British North America
BNA . . . . Bureau of National Affairs
BNAF . . . . . . Brazil Nut Advertising Fund
BN Arch . . . . . Bachelor of Naval Architecture
BNAS . . . . . . British Naval Air Service
BNAS . . . . . . British Naval Air Staff
BNB . . . . Banque Nationale de Belgique (National Bank of Belgium)
BNB . . . . British National Bibliography
BNB . . . . British North Borneo
BNC . . . . BanCal Tri-State Corporation (NYSE symbol)
BNC . . . . Bethany Nazarene College (Oklahoma)
BNC . . . . Board of Navy Commissioners
BNC . . . . Brasenose College (Oxford)
BNCA . . . . . . Bureau of National Capital Airports (of FAA)
BNCF . . . . . . Biblioteca Nazionale Centrale Florence (Italy)

BNCI . . . . . . Banque Nationale pour le Commerce et l'Industrie (National Bank for Commerce and Industry)
BNCOQ . . . . . Bachelor Noncommissioned Officers' Quarters
BNCSR . . . . . . British National Committee on Space Research
BNCW . . . . . Bare Nickel Chrome Wire
BND . . . . Benzoylated-Naphthoylated DEAE (Diethylaminoethyl)
BND . . . . Bond Industries, Inc. (NYSE symbol)
BND Sc . . . . . Bundes Nachrichtendienst (Intelligence-gathering agency of the Federal Republic of Germany)
BNDD . . . . . . Bureau of Narcotics and Dangerous Drugs (Formerly, Bureau of Narcotics and Bureau of Drug Abuse Control) (Department of Justice)
BNDE . . . . . . Banco Nacional do Desanvolvimento Economico (National Economic Development Bank) (Brazil)
BNDRY . . . . . Boundary
BNE . . . . Bachelor of Naval Engineering
BNE . . . . Bathymetric Navigation Equipment
BNE . . . . But Not Exceeding
BNEC . . . . . . British Nuclear Energy Conference
BN Ed . . . . . . Bachelor of Nursing Education
BN Eng . . . . . Bachelor of Naval Engineering
BNEP . . . . . . Basic Naval Establishment Plan
BNES . . . . . . British Nuclear Energy Society
BNESA . . . . . Bureau for Near East and South Asia (AID)
BNESAA . . . . Bureau of Near Eastern and South Asian Affairs (Department of State)
BNF . . . . Bomb Nose Fuze
BNF . . . . Boron Nitride Fiber
BNF . . . . Brand Names Foundation
BNF . . . . Braniff Airways, Inc. (NYSE symbol)
BNF . . . . British National Formulary (A publication in pharmacy)
BNF . . . . British Nuclear Forum
BNFMRA . . . . British Non-Ferrous Metals Research Association
BNG . . . . Bureau of Natural Gas (of FPC)
BNGS . . . . . . Bomb Navigation Guidance System
BNHL . . . . . . Boston Neighborhood Hockey League
BNHQ . . . . . . Battalion Headquarters (Marine Corps)
BNHSC . . . . . Boston National Historic Sites Commission (Government agency, discontinued 1960)
BNI . . . . Bengal Native Infantry
BNI . . . . Burlington Northern, Incorporated (NYSE symbol)
BNK . . . . Bangor Punta Corporation (NYSE symbol)
BNKCPA . . . . Bureau National Kamerunais pour la Conference des Peuples Africains (Cameroonian National Bureau for African Peoples Conference)
BNL . . . . Battelle Northwest Laboratories
BNL . . . . Beneficial Corp. (NYSE symbol) (Wall Street slang name: "Big Nose Louie")
BNL . . . . Brookhaven National Laboratory (AEC)
BNLO . . . . . . British Naval Liaison Officer
BNLUS . . . . . British Naval Liaison (Office) US Navy (London)
BNM . . . . Bureau de Normalisation de la Mecanique (France)
BNML . . . . . . Bitter National Magnet Laboratory
BNMRA . . . . . British Non-Ferrous Metals Research Association
BNO . . . . Bipartite News Office (Post-World War II, Germany)
BNOC . . . . . . British National Opera Company
BNOV . . . . . . But Not Over
BNP . . . . Background Noise Power
BNP . . . . Bureau of Naval Personnel
BNP . . . . Bureau of Naval Personnel Publications
BNPCL . . . . . . Bureau of Naval Personnel Circular Letters
BNS . . . . Bachelor of Naval Science
BNS . . . . Bachelor of Nursing Science
BNS . . . . Binary Number System (Data processing)
BNS . . . . Bombing-Navigation System
BNS . . . . Broadcasters Nonprofit Satellite Service (Ford Foundation)
BNS . . . . Brown & Sharpe Manufacturing Co. (NYSE symbol)
BNS . . . . Bureau of Naval Ships (Obsolete)
BN Sc . . . . . . Bachelor of Nursing Science
BNSFCP . . . . . Battalion Shore Fire Control Party
BNU . . . . Basic Notch Unit
BNU . . . . Benson Needham Univas (International advertising network)
BNW . . . . . . Bureau of Naval Weapons (Obsolete)
BNX . . . . British Nuclear Export Executives (Group to promote export of nuclear power stations of British design)
BNYD . . . . . . Boston Navy Yard
BNYD . . . . . . Bureau of Navy Yards and Docks (Later, NFEC)
BO . . . . Bachelor of Oratory
BO . . . . Bachelor of Osteopathy
BO . . . . Back Order
BO . . . . Bad Order (i.e., requiring repair)
BO . . . . Bail Out
BO . . . . Baltimore & Ohio R. R. Company (NYSE symbol) (Delisted)
BO . . . . Base Order

BO . . . . Beat Oscillator
BO . . . . Blackout
BO . . . . Blanking Oscillator
BO . . . . Blockhouse Operation
BO . . . . Blocking Oscillator
BO . . . . Blowoff
BO . . . . Board of Ordnance
BO . . . . Body Odor (Slang)
BO . . . . Boiled (Linseed) Oil
Bo . . . . Boltzmann number
BO . . . . Botanical (or Biological) Origin
BO . . . . Box Office (Theatrical slang)
BO . . . . Branch Office
BO . . . . Broker's Order (Finance)
BO . . . . Bureau of Ordnance (Navy) (Functions transferred to Bureau of Naval Weapons, 1960; and later to Naval Ordnance Systems Command)
bo . . . . Burnout (Subscript)
BO . . . . Buyer's Option (Business and trade)
B-O . . . . Boil-Off
B/O . . . . Brought Over (Business and trade)
B & O . . . . . . Baltimore and Ohio Railroad Company (Later, Chessie System)
B & O . . . . . . Band and Orchestra (Musical slang)
BOA . . . . Basic Ordering Agreement
BOA . . . . Bipolar Operational Amplifier
BOA . . . . . . Born on Arrival (Medicine)
BOA . . . . Break-Off Altitude
BOA . . . . Broad Ocean Area
BOAC . . . . . . British Overseas Airways Corporation
BOADICEA . . . British Overseas Airways Digital Information Computer for Electronic Automation
BOA-MILS . . . . Broad Ocean Area - Missile Impact Locating System (Navy)
BOAR . . . . . . Board of Action on Redetermination (Navy)
BOASI . . . . . . Bureau of Old-Age and Survivors Insurance (of the Social Security Administration)
BOAT . . . . . . Better Occupational Awareness Training
BOAT/US . . . . Boat Owners Association of the United States
BOB . . . . Beginning of Business
BOB . . . . Bureau of the Budget (Later, OMB)
BOB . . . . Business Opportunity Bank (Institute for New Enterprise Development)
BOBR . . . . . . Boring Bar
BOBS . . . . . . Beacon Only Bombing System
BOC . . . . Battery Operations Center (Air Force)
BOC . . . . Bayes Operating Characteristic
BOC . . . . Bevitron Orbit Code
BOC . . . . Bingham Oceanographic Collection
BOC . . . . Block-Oriented Computer
BOC . . . . Blowout Coil
BOC . . . . Body-on-Chassis (Technical drawings)
BOC . . . . Brittany Oceanological Center
BOC . . . . Butyloxycarbonyl (Organic chemistry)
BOCA . . . . . . Boat Owners Council of America
BOCA . . . . . . Building Officials Conference of America
BOCES . . . . . . Boards of Cooperative Educational Services
BOCF . . . . . . Bureau of Commercial Fisheries (Department of the Interior)
BOCOL . . . . . Basic Operating Consumer-Oriented Language (Data processing)
BOCT . . . . . . Baltimore & Ohio Chicago Terminal R. R. (AAR code)
B & OCT . . . . . Baltimore and Ohio Chicago Terminal Railroad Company
BOD . . . . Beneficial Occupancy Date
BOD . . . . Biochemical Oxygen Demand (Water pollution)
BOD . . . . Blackout Door (Military)
BOD . . . . . . Boeing on Dock
BOD . . . . . . Buy-Off Date
BODEPE . . . . . Boiler Design and Performance
BODN . . . . . . Bowdon Railway Company (AAR code)
BODU . . . . . . Bureau of Ordnance Design Unit (Navy)
BOE . . . . Bachelor of Oral English
BOE . . . . Bottom of Edge
BOE . . . . Bureau of Enforcement
BOF . . . . Barium Oxide Ferrite
BOF . . . . Base Oxygen Furnace (Steelmaking)
BOF . . . . Beurre, Oeufs, Fromages (Butter, Eggs, Cheese)
BOF . . . . Binary Oxide Film (Memory)
BOF . . . . Building Owners Federation of Mutual Fire Insurance Companies
BOFADS . . . . . Business Office Force Administration Data System (Bell System)
BOG . . . . Bank Officers Guild
BOG . . . . Brigade of Guards
BOH . . . . Beautiful Old House
BOH . . . . Break-Off Height (Aviation)
BOH . . . . Bureau of Ordnance and Hydrography (Navy)
BOI . . . . Basis of Issue (Army)
BOI . . . . Board of Investments (Philippines)

BOI . . . . Break of Inspection
BOIA . . . . . . Bureau of Indian Affairs (Department of the Interior)
BOJ . . . . Booster Jettison
BOJ . . . . Bourjois, Inc. (American Stock Exchange symbol)
BOK . . . . Book-of-the-Month Club, Inc. (NYSE symbol)
BOL . . . . Bachelor of Oriental Language
BOL . . . . Bausch & Lomb, Inc. (NYSE symbol)
BOLD . . . . . . Bibliographic On-Line Library Display (Data processing)
BOLM . . . . . . Bureau of Land Management (Department of the Interior)
BOLO . . . . . . Be On the Lookout For
BOLOVAC . . . . Bolometric Voltage and Current (Voltage measurement) (National Bureau of Standards)
BOLSA . . . . . . Bank of London & South America, Ltd.
BOLT . . . . . . Basic Occupational Language Training
BOLT . . . . . . Beam of Light Transistor
BOLTOP . . . . Better on Lips Than on Paper (Put at the end of a letter with kisses) (British)
BOM . . . . Base Operation Manager
BOM . . . . Bills of Materials
BOM . . . . Binary Order of Magnitude (Data processing)
BOM . . . . Board on Medicine (of the National Academy of Sciences)
BOM . . . . Born-Oppenheimer Method
BOM . . . . . . Bureau of Mines
BOMAP . . . . . Barbados Oceanographic and Meteorological Analysis Project
BOMARC . . . . Boeing-Michigan Aeronautical Research Center
BOMC . . . . . Book-of-the-Month Club
BOMCOM . . . . Bomber Command (Army)
BOMEX . . . . . Barbados Oceanographic and Meteorological Experiment
BOMFOG . . . . The Brotherhood of Man under the Fatherhood of God (Journalistic slang for political platitudes; taken from a speech by Hubert H. Humphrey)
BOMID . . . . . Branch Office, Military Intelligence Division (Army)
BOMP . . . . . . Bill of Material Processor
BOMREP . . . . Bombing Report
BOMRON . . . . Bombing Squadron
BONA . . . . . Bachad Organization of North America
BONIS . . . . . Bibliography of Old Norse-Icelandic Studies
BONUS . . . . . Benevolent Order of Nurses Under Sedation
BONUS . . . . . Boiling Nuclear Superheat Reactor (AEC)
BOOK . . . . . Built-in Orderly Organized Knowledge (Learning device)
BOOR . . . . . . Bureau of Outdoor Recreation (Department of the Interior)
BCOST . . . . . Bettering Oregon's Opportunity for Saving Talent (Educational project)
BOP . . . . Association for Balance of Political Power
BOP . . . . Balance of Payments
BOP . . . . Base of Preference Program (for reenlisting airmen)
BOP . . . . Basic Operation Plan (Army)
BOP . . . . Basic Oxygen Process (Steel furnace)
BOP . . . . Bathyscaphe Oceanographic Program
BOP . . . . Binary Output Program
BOP . . . . Blowout Preventer
BOP . . . . The Boy's Own Paper (Late nineteenth- and early twentieth-century periodical) (British)
BOP . . . . Building Optimization Program (Data processing)
BOP . . . . Burn-Out Proof
BOPAT . . . . . Border Patrol
B Opt . . . . . . Bachelor of Optometry
BOQ . . . . . . Bachelor Officers' Quarters (Army)
B Or . . . . . . Bachelor of Oratory
BOR . . . . Belady Optimum Replacement (Algorithm) (Data processing)
BOR . . . . Board of Review (Army)
BOR . . . . Borg-Warner Corporation (NYSE symbol)
BOR . . . . Bureau of Operating Rights
BOR . . . . Bureau of Outdoor Recreation (Department of the Interior)
BOR . . . . Bureau of Reclamation (Department of the Interior)
BORAM . . . . . Block Oriented Random Access Memory (Data processing)
BORAX . . . . . Boiling Reactor Experiments (AEC)
BORE . . . . . . Beryllium Oxide Reactor Experiment (Formerly, EBOR) (AEC)
B Orient . . . . . Bachelor of Oriental Studies
BORM . . . . . . Bureau of Raw Materials for American Vegetable Oils and Fats Industries
B & O RR . . . . Baltimore & Ohio Railroad
B Or Sc . . . . . Bachelor of the Science of Oratory
BORU . . . . . . Boat Operating and Repair Unit (Navy)
BOS . . . . Base Operating Support
BOS . . . . Basic Oblate Spheroid
BOS . . . . Basic Operating System
BOS . . . . Boston, Massachusetts (Airport symbol)
BOSEY . . . . . . Board of Supply, Executive Yuan (Responsible for removing surplus US war material to China from Guam)
BOSFW . . . . . Bureau of Sport Fisheries and Wildlife (Department of the Interior)
BOSH . . . . . . Bottom Oriented Shrimp Harvester

BOSNYWASH..	Boston, New York, Washington (Proposed name for possible "super-city" formed by growth and mergers of other cities)
BOSO......	Bureau of Ordnance Shipment Order
BOSOR......	Buckling of Shells of Revolution
BOSOX......	Boston Red Sox (Baseball team)
BOSP......	Bioastronautics Orbital Space Program (Air Force)
BOSS......	Bett's Open Shop System
BOSS......	Bioastronautic Orbiting Space Station
BOSS......	Biological Orbiting Space Station (Air Force)
BOSS......	Boeing Operational Supervisory System
BOSS......	Bomb Orbital Strategic System
BOSS......	Broad Ocean Scoring System (Missiles)
BOSS......	Bureau for State Security (South Africa)
BOSS-WEDGE..	Bomb Orbital Strategic System - Weapon Development Glide Entry
BOSU......	Bioastronautics Operational Support Unit
BOT.......	Balance of Trade
BOT.......	Beginning of Tape (Data processing)
BOT.......	Board of Trade (British)
BOTH......	Bombing Over The Horizon
BOTOSS.....	Bottom Topography Survey System (Naval Oceanographic Office)
BOTU(FW)....	Basic Operational Training Unit (Fixed Wing)
BOTU(RW)....	Basic Operational Training Unit (Rotary Wing)
BOU.......	Boat Operating Unit (Navy)
BOU.......	Bourns, Inc. (NYSE symbol)
BOU.......	British Ornithologists' Union
BOUMAC....	Boulder Laboratory Macrosystem (National Bureau of Standards)
BOV.......	Brown Oil of Vitriol
BOV.......	Burn-Out Velocity
BOVC......	Base of Overcast (Meteorology)
BOW......	Beryllium Oxide Washer
BOW......	Blackout Window (Military)
BOWA.....	Booker T. Washington National Monument
BOWP......	Black Ordinary Working People
BOYC......	Boyne City R. R. (AAR code)
BP........	Bachelor of Painting
BP........	Bachelor of Pedagogy
BP........	Bachelor of Pharmacy
BP........	Bachelor of Philosophy
BP........	Back Pressure
BP........	Bandpass
BP........	Base Percussion
BP........	Base Plate (Technical drawings)
BP........	Base Point
BP........	Base Procured
BP........	Basic Pay
BP........	Battery Package
BP........	Beach Party
BP........	Beatissime Pater (Most Holy Father)
BP........	Beautiful People (Slang for the wealthy, world-traveling, party-going set)
BP........	Before Present
BP........	Below Proof
BP........	Benzyprene (Chemistry)
BP........	Between Perpendiculars (Technical drawings)
BP........	Bill of Parcels
BP........	Bill(s) Payable
BP........	Biotic Potential
BP........	Birthplace
BP........	Black Powder
BP........	Blackout Preparedness
BP........	Blood Pressure
BP........	Blueprint
BP........	Board of Parole (Department of Justice)
BP........	Boiler Plate
BP........	Boiler Pressure
BP........	Boiling Point
BP........	Bolted Plate (Technical drawings)
BP........	Bonum Publicum (The Public Good)
BP........	Border Patrol
BP........	Boron Plastic
BP........	British Petroleum Company (NYSE symbol)
BP........	British Pharmacopoeia (A publication in pharmacy)
BP........	British Public (Slang)
BP........	Budget Program
BP........	Bureau of Power (of FPC)
BP........	Bureau of Prisons (Department of Justice)
BP........	By-Pass
BP........	Union Bag-Camp Paper Corporation (NYSE symbol) (Delisted)
B/P.......	Blueprint
B/P.......	Board President
B & P......	Bid and Proposal
B of P......	Breach of Promise

B Pa.......	Bachelor of Painting
BPA.......	Bachelor of Professional Arts
BPA.......	Bachelor of Public Administration
BPA.......	Balloon Platoon of America
BPA.......	Beam Plasma Amplification
BPA.......	Billiard Players Association of America
BPA.......	Biological Photographic Association
BPA.......	Bonneville Power Administration (Department of the Interior)
BPA.......	Border Patrol Academy
BPA.......	Bovine Plasma Albumin
BPA.......	Broadcasters' Promotion Association
BPA.......	Budget Project Account (Military)
BPA.......	Bureau of Public Assistance (Social Security Administration)
BPA.......	Business Publications Audit of Circulation
BPAA......	Bowling Proprietors' Association of America
BPAA-DAD...	Bowling Proprietors Association of America - Duckpin Activities Department
BPAC......	Better Packaging Advisory Council
BPAC......	Budget Program Activity Code
BP Adm.....	Bachelor of Public Administration
BPB.......	Bachelor of Physical Biology
BPB.......	Badan Perdjoangan Buruh (Board for the Defense of Labor Interest) (Indonesia)
BPB.......	Base Planning Board
BPBD......	International Alliance of Bill Posters, Billers and Distributors of US and Canada
BPBW......	Bare Phosphor Bronze Wire
BPC.......	Back-Pressure Control
BPC.......	Band Pass Crystal
BPC.......	Battery Park City (New York City)
BPC.......	Belco Petroleum Corporation (NYSE symbol)
BPC.......	Boost Protective Cover (Apollo) (NASA)
BPC.......	British Pharmaceutical Codex (A publication in pharmacy)
BPC.......	British Productivity Council
BPC.......	British Purchasing Commission
BPC.......	Bureau of Provisions and Clothing (Navy)
BPCC......	Better Postcard Collectors' Club
BPCD......	Barrels Per Calendar Day (Petroleum)
BPCDI......	Brookhaven Portable Cesium Developmental Irradiator Unit (AEC)
BPCF......	Band Pass Crystal Filter
BPCI......	Bulk Packaging and Containerization Institute
BP/CP......	Base Procured/Central Procured
BPCS......	Business Periodicals Circulation Services (Harcourt Brace Jovanovich)
B Pd......	Bachelor of Pedagogy (or Pedagogies)
BPD.......	Barrels Per Day
BPD.......	Basic Planning Document (Military)
BPD.......	Basic Products Corporation (NYSE symbol) (Delisted)
BPD.......	Bikini Photo Drone
BPD.......	British Society of Posters Designers
BPD.......	Bureau of the Public Debt
BPD.......	Doctor of Bio-Psychology
BPDC......	Berkeley Particle Data Center
BPDP......	Brotherhood of Painters, Decorators and Paperhangers of America (Also known as B of PDPH of A)
B of PDPH of A..	Brotherhood of Painters, Decorators and Paperhangers of America (Also known as BPDP)
B Pe.......	Bachelor of Pedagogy
BPE.......	Bachelor of Physical Education
BPE.......	Back Porch Effect
BPE.......	Best Preliminary Estimate
BPE.......	Binaural Phase Effect
BPE.......	Bit-Plane Encoding
BPE.......	Boiling Point Elevation
BPE.......	Bremen Port of Embarkation (Germany)
BPEC......	Building Products Executives Conference
B Ped......	Bachelor of Pedagogics (or Pedagogy)
BP Ed.....	Bachelor of Physical Education
BPED......	Basic Pay Entry Date
B Pe E.....	Bachelor of Petroleum Engineering
B Pe Eng....	Bachelor of Petroleum Engineering
BPE-LCA....	Board of Parish Education, Lutheran Church in America
B Pet E.....	Bachelor of Petroleum Engineering
BPF.......	Bandpass Filter
BPF.......	Baptist Peace Fellowship
BPF.......	British Plastic Federation
BPF.......	Bromine Pentafluoride
BPFILO.....	British Pacific Fleet Intelligence Liaison Officer
BPFLO.....	British Pacific Fleet Liaison Officer
BPFP......	Bechuanaland Protectorate Federal Party
BPG.......	Blood Pressure Gauge
BPG.......	Boron Pyrolytic Graphite

BPGC . . . . Bearing Per Gyro Compass (Navigation)
B Ph . . . . Bachelor of Philosophy
BPH . . . . Bachelor of Public Health
BPH . . . . Barrels Per Hour
B-P-H . . . . . . Botanico-Periodicum-Huntianum (Book title)
B Pharm . . . . . Bachelor of Pharmacy
B Ph C . . . . . . Bachelor of Pharmaceutical Chemistry
BPHE . . . . Bachelor of Public Health Engineering
BPH Ed . . . . . Bachelor of Public Health Education
BPH Eng . . . . . Bachelor of Public Health Engineering
B Phil . . . . . . Bachelor of Philosophy
BPHN . . . . . . Bachelor of Public Health Nursing
B Pho . . . . . . Bachelor of Photography
B Ph S . . . . . . Bachelor of Physical Science
B Phy . . . . . . Bachelor of Physics
BPI . . . . Bio-Degradable Plastics, Incorporated
BPI . . . . BITS Per Inch (Data processing)
BPI . . . . Bituminous Pipe Institute
BPI . . . . Board of Patent Interferences (of Patent Office)
BPI . . . . Book Production Industry (A journal)
BPI . . . . Bookman's Price Index (A reference publication listing rare books and
          their list prices)
BPI . . . . Boost Phase Intercept (DCD)
BPI . . . . Break-Point Instruction
BPI . . . . Bureau of Plant Industry (Department of Agriculture)
BPI . . . . Bureau of Public Inquiries
BPI . . . . Businessmen for the Public Interest (Chicago-based group)
BPI . . . . Buying Power Index
BPI . . . . Bytes Per Inch (Data processing)
BPICA . . . . . . Bureau Permanent International des Constructeurs d'Automobiles
B-PID . . . . . . Book - Physical Inventory Difference (AEC)
BPISAE . . . . . Bureau of Plant Industry, Soils, and Agricultural Engineering
          (Department of Agriculture) (Functions transferred to ARS, 1953)
BPITT . . . . . . Bureau Permanent Interafricain de la Tse-Tse et de la Trypanosomiase
BPJ . . . . Balanced Pressure Joint
BPJC . . . . Bay Path Junior College (Massachusetts)
BPKK . . . . . . Bezirksparteikontrollkommission
BPL . . . . Bachelor of Patent Law
BPL . . . . Band Pressure Level
BPL . . . . Beta-Propiolactone (Chemical)
BPL . . . . Brass Pounders League (Unit of American Radio Relay League)
BPL . . . . Burst Position Locator
B/PL . . . . Book-Plate (Bibliography)
BPM . . . . Beam Positioning Magnet
BPM . . . . Beats Per Minute (Cardiology)
BPM . . . . Bible Protestant Missions
BPMA . . . . . . Barrier Paper Manufacturers Association
BPMEL . . . . . . Base Precision Measurement Equipment Laboratory
BPMS . . . . . . Blood Pressure Measuring System
BPN . . . . Balloon-borne Polar Nephelometer
BPN . . . . Band Pass Network
BPN . . . . Bloody Public Nuisance (British slang)
BPN . . . . Budget Project Number (Navy)
BPN . . . . Bureau Politique National (National Political Bureau) (Of the Guinean
          PDG)
BPO . . . . Base Post Office
BPO . . . . Base Procurement Office (Air Force)
BPO . . . . Benzoyl Peroxide
BPO . . . . Betriebsparteiorganisation
BPO . . . . British Post Office
BPOC . . . . . . Before Proceeding on Course (Aviation)
BPOE . . . . . . Benevolent and Protective Order of Elks
B Pol Sc . . . . . Bachelor of Political Science
BPO-WOW . . . Benevolent Protective Order--Wolves of the World (Limited, not-too-
          serious order)
BPP . . . . Bechuanaland People's Party
BPP . . . . Border Patrol Police (Thailand)
BPP . . . . Bubble Pulse Period
BPPG . . . . . . Bureau Planned Procurement Guide (Navy)
BPPSJ . . . . . . Balanced Pressure Plane Swivel Joint
BPR . . . . American Book Publishing Record
BPR . . . . Banana Plug Resistor
BPR . . . . Battery Powered Recorder
BPR . . . . Bimonthly Progress Report
BPR . . . . Biweekly Progress Report
BPR . . . . Blood Pressure Recorder
BPR . . . . Bridge Plotting Room (Navy)
BPR . . . . Bureau of Public Roads (Department of Transportation)
BPR . . . . Bypass Ratio
BPRA . . . . . . Baptist Public Relations Association
BPRF . . . . . . Bullet Proof (Army)

BPRMA . . . . . . Bank Public Relations and Marketing Association
BPRO . . . . . . Blind Persons Resettlement Officer (Department of Employment) (British)
BPRO . . . . . . Branch Public Relations Office
BPRS . . . . . . Brief Psychiatric Rating Scale
B Ps . . . . Bachelor of Psychology
BPS . . . . Base Postal Section (Air Force)
BPS . . . . Beacon Processing System
BPS . . . . Behavioral Pharmacology Society
BPS . . . . Biophysical Society
bps . . . . BITS (Binary Digits) Per Second (Data processing)
BPS . . . . Blanked Picture Signal
BPS . . . . Bloc Populaire Senegalais (Senegalese People's Bloc)
BPS . . . . Blowout Pipe System
BPS . . . . British Plain Spirits
BPS . . . . Buoy Power Supply
BPS . . . . Bureau of Product Safety (Department of Commerce)
BPSA . . . . . . Bachelor of Public School Art
BPSC . . . . . . Bearing Per Standard Compass (Navigation)
BPSD . . . . . . Barrels Per Stream Day (Petroleum)
BPSH . . . . . . Bashkimet Profesionale te Shqiperise (Union of Albanian Trade Unions)
BPSH . . . . . . Border Patrol Sector Headquarters
BPSJ . . . . Balanced Pressure Swivel Joint
BPSM . . . . . . Bachelor of Public School Music
BPSN . . . . . . Budget Project Symbol Number
BPSS . . . . . . Base Perimeter Security System
BPSS . . . . . . Base Procurement Service Stores (Air Force)
B Ps Sc . . . . . Bachelor of Psychic Sciences
BPSTGC . . . . . Bearing Per Steering Gyro Compass
B Ps Th . . . . . Bachelor of Psychotherapy
BPT . . . . Band Pass Transformer
BPT . . . . Base Point
BPT . . . . Beginning Procedure Turn (Aviation)
BPTEU . . . . . . Bombay Port Trust Employees' Union (India)
BPTO . . . . . . BMEWS (Ballistic Missile Early Warning System) Performance Test
          Outline
BPU . . . . Base Production Unit (Army)
BPU . . . . Basic Pole Unit
BPV . . . . Bordetella Pertussis Vaccine
BPW . . . . Bare Platinum Wire
BPW . . . . Board of Public Works
BPW . . . . Business and Professional Women's Foundation
BPWC . . . . . . International Federation of Business and Professional Women Clubs
BPWMA . . . . . Buff and Polishing Wheel Manufacturers Association
B Py . . . . Bachelor of Pedagogy
BQ . . . . Before Queues (Referring to pre-World War II period) (British slang)
BQ . . . . Bene Quiescat (May He or She Rest Well)
B & Q . . . . . . Barracks and Quarters (Army)
BQB . . . . British-American Tobacco Company (American Stock Exchange symbol)
BQEP . . . . . . Brief Qualification Evaluation Program
BQLI . . . . Brooklyn, Queens, Long Island (Section of New York Times)
BQM . . . . Base Quartermaster (Marine Corps)
BR . . . . Bank Rate
BR . . . . Bank Robbery
BR . . . . Bank Roll (Slang)
BR . . . . Basic Research
BR . . . . Bedroom
BR . . . . Bedroom Steward (In the first class aboard an ocean liner)
BR . . . . Bend Radius
BR . . . . Bill of Rights
BR . . . . Bills Receivable
BR . . . . Birmingham Revision (of BNA) (British medical)
BR . . . . Block Replacement
BR . . . . Boilermaker (Navy rating)
BR . . . . Bomber Reconnaissance Aircraft
BR . . . . Braced and Racked (Freight)
BR . . . . Brake Relay
BR . . . . Branch
BR . . . . Branch Report
BR . . . . Breeder Reactor (AEC)
BR . . . . Briefing Room (Navy)
BR . . . . British
BR . . . . British Railways
BR . . . . British Revision (of BNA) (Medicine)
Br . . . . Bromine (Chemical element)
BR . . . . Bronze
BR . . . . Brown (Buoy) (Maps and charts)
BR . . . . Buffer Register (Data processing)
BR . . . . Builder's Risk (Insurance)
BR . . . . Bulkhead Receptacle
BR . . . . Bunker-Ramo Corp. (NYSE symbol)
BR . . . . Bureau of Reclamation (Department of the Interior)

BR . . . . Butadiene Rubber
B or R . . . . . . Bales or Rolls (Freight)
BRA . . . . Beam Ride Actuator
BRA . . . . Bench Replaceable Assembly
BRA . . . . Boston Redevelopment Authority
BRA . . . . **Building Renovating Association**
BRAB . . . . . . **Building Research Advisory Board**
BRAC . . . . . . Britannica Reading Achievement Center
BRAC . . . . . . Brotherhood of Railway and Airline Clerks
B Ra E . . . . . . **Bachelor of Radio Engineering**
B Ra Eng . . . . **Bachelor of Radio Engineering**
BRAF . . . . Braking Action Fair (Aviation)
BRAG . . . . . . Braking Action Good (Aviation)
BRAINS . . . . . . Behavior Replication by Analog Instruction of the Nervous System
(Electrical stimulation of the brain)
BRAL . . . . Bureau de Renseignements et d'Action, Londres (Free French)
BRALUP . . . . . . Bureau of Resource Assessment and Land Use Planning
BRAMATEC . . . Brain Mapping Technique
BRAN . . . . Braking Action Nil (Aviation)
BRANE . . . . . . Bombing RADAR Navigation Equipment
BRAP . . . . Braking Action Poor (Aviation)
BRAS . . . . . . **Ballistic Rocket Air Suppression**
BRASO . . . . . **Branch Aviation Supply Office (Navy)**
BRASS . . . . . . BEEF (Base Engineer Emergency Forces) Reporting, Analysis, and Status
System (Air Force)
BRASS . . . . . . Bottom Reflection Active SONAR System
BRAXP . . . . . Braking Action Extremely Poor (Aviation)
BRB . . . . Ballistic Reentry Body
BRB . . . . Bundesratsbeschluss
BRBC . . . . . . Burro Red Blood Cells
BRBZC . . . . . Brass, Bronze or Copper (Freight)
BRC . . . . **Base Residence Course**
BRC . . . . Behavioral Research Council (for Scientific Inquiry into the Problems of
Men in Society)
BRC . . . . Belt Railway Company of Chicago (AAR code)
BRC . . . . . . **Beveren Rabbit Club**
BRC . . . . Biological Radio Communications
BRC . . . . Biological Research Center (Philippines)
BRC . . . . Broadcast Rating Council
BRC . . . . Brotherhood of Railway Carmen of America (AFL-CIO)
BRC . . . . Burlingame Research Center
BR of C . . . . . **Belt Railway Company of Chicago**
BRCA . . . . . . Bryce Canyon National Park
BRC of A . . . . **Brotherhood Railway Carmen of America**
BRCR . . . . . . Brices Crossroads National Battlefield Site
BRCS . . . . . . BMEWS (Ballistic Missile Early Warning System) Rearward Communications
System
BRCS . . . . . . **British Red Cross Society**
BRD . . . . Ball Reduction Drive
BRD . . . . Base (or Basic) Retirement Date (Air Force)
BRD . . . . Bellofram Rolling Diaphragm
BRD . . . . Blank Recording Disc
BRD . . . . Bomb Release Distance (Army)
BRD . . . . Bundesrepublik Deutschland (Federal Republic of Germany)
BRDA . . . . . . Boxboard Research and Development Association
BRDC . . . . . . Bare Refractory, Double Containment (Boiler) (NASA)
BRDT . . . . . . Bayesian Reliability Demonstration Test
B Re . . . . . . **Bachelor of Religion**
BRE . . . . **Bachelor of Religious Education**
BRE . . . . Bureau of Research and Engineering (US Postal Service)
BRECOM . . . . Broadcast Radio Emergency Communication (Air Force)
BR Ed . . . . . . **Bachelor of Religious Education**
B Re E . . . . . **Bachelor of Refrigeration Engineering**
B Re Eng . . . . **Bachelor of Refrigeration Engineering**
BREMA . . . . . British Radio Equipment Manufacturers Association
BREN . . . . . . Bare Reactor Experiment at Nevada
BRER . . . . Basic Radiation Effects Reactor (AEC)
BRF . . . . **Blood Research Foundation**
BRF . . . . Borman's Inc. (Formerly, Borman Food Stores) (NYSE symbol)
BRF . . . . **Brain Research Foundation**
BRF . . . . Branchial Filament
BRG . . . . **Bearing**
BRGBLN . . . . . Barrage Balloon
BRGM . . . . . . Bureau de Recherches Geologiques et Minieres (France)
BRH . . . . Brush Holder
BRH . . . . Bureau of Radiological Health (FDA)
BRI . . . . Banque des Reglements Internationaux (Bank for International Settlements)
BRI . . . . Bearing Range Indicator
BRI . . . . **Biological Research Institute**
BRI . . . . Book Review Index (A publication)
BRI . . . . Brand Rating Index Corporation

BRI . . . . . . **Building Research Institute**
B-RI . . . . Burlington-Rock Island Railroad Company
BRIG . . . . Brigadier
BRIGEN . . . . . **Brigadier General**
BRIG GEN . . . . **Brigadier General**
BRIGHED . . . . **Brigade Headquarters (Army)**
BRIMM . . . . . . Blessed Religious Institute of Mercenary Missionaries
BRIT . . . . Britain (or British)
BRITE . . . . . . Bright RADAR Indicator-Tower Equipment
BRJ . . . . Barco Rotary Joint
BRJ . . . . Blind Riveted Joint
BRK . . . . Brach (E. J.) & Sons (NYSE symbol) (Delisted)
BRK . . . . Brockway Glass Co., Inc. (NYSE symbol)
BRKHIC . . . . . Breaks in Higher Overcast (Meteorology)
BRL . . . . **Babe Ruth League**
BRL . . . . Ballistic Research Laboratories (Military)
BRL . . . . Behavioral Research Laboratories
BRL . . . . Bionetics Research Laboratory
BRL . . . . **Bomb Release Line**
BRLESC . . . . . Ballistic Research Laboratories Electronic Scientific Computer
BRLG . . . . . . Bomb, Radio, Longitudinal, Generator-Powered
BRLO . . . . . . British Routing Liaison Officer (World War II)
BRM . . . . Baseline Reference Mission
BRM . . . . Brimstone R. R. (AAR code)
BRM . . . . British Racing Motors
BRMA . . . . . . **Braided Rug Manufacturers Association**
BRN . . . . Brown & Root-Northrop
BRO . . . . **British Routing Office**
BRO . . . . **Brush-Off (Slang)**
BROFICON . . . **Broadcast Fighter Control (Military)**
BROI . . . . Branch Operating Instructions (Military)
BROOM . . . . . Ballistic Recovery of Orbiting Man
BROS . . . . . . Brothers
BRP . . . . Beacon Ranging Pulse
BRPM . . . . . . Bureau de Recherches et de Participations Minieres
BRPRA . . . . . British Rubber Products Research Association
BR & PRY . . . . Buffalo, Rochester & Pittsburg Railway
BRQM . . . . . . **Brigade Quartermaster (Marine Corps)**
BRR . . . . Battelle Research Reactor (AEC)
BRR . . . . **Bridge Receiving Room (Navy)**
BRR . . . . Brookhaven Research Reactor (AEC)
BRRL . . . . . . British Road Research Laboratory
BR/RL . . . . . . Bomb Rack/Rocket Launcher
BRS . . . . Ballistic Recording System
BRS . . . . Balloon Radio System
BRS . . . . Boron Reinforced Structure
BRS . . . . Break Request Signal (Data processing)
BRS . . . . Brotherhood of Railroad Signalmen
BRS . . . . Building Research Station (British)
BRS . . . . Bureau of Railroad Safety (Department of Transportation)
BRS . . . . Business Radio Service
B of RS . . . . . **Brotherhood of Railroad Signalmen**
BRSC . . . . . . **Brotherhood of Railway and Steamship Clerks, Freight Handlers,**
Express and Station Employees
BRSF . . . . Biafra Relief Services Foundation
BRT . . . . Base Resistance Transistor
BRT . . . . Belgische Radio en Televisie
BRT . . . . BMEWS (Ballistic Missile Early Warning System) Test Report
BRT . . . . Bolt Removal Tool
BRT . . . . Brooklyn Rapid Transit Company (A New York City subway line) (Became
BMT)
BRT . . . . **Brotherhood of Railroad Trainmen**
BRT . . . . Bruttoregistertonne (Gross Registered Ton) (Germany)
BRTE . . . . Bachelor of Radio and Television Engineering
BRT Eng . . . . . Bachelor of Radio and Television Engineering
BRU . . . . **Boat Repair Unit (Navy)**
BRU . . . . Brayton Rotating Unit
B Ru E . . . . . **Bachelor of Rural Engineering**
B Ru Eng . . . . **Bachelor of Rural Engineering**
BRUSA . . . . . **British-United States Agreement (Circuits)**
BRV . . . . Ballistic Reentry Vehicle
BRVMA . . . . . British Radio Valve Manufacturers' Association
BRY . . . . **Beatrice Foods Company (NYSE symbol)**
BRZ . . . . Breeze Corporation (American Stock Exchange symbol)
BS . . . . **Bachelor of Science**
BS . . . . **Bachelor of Science in Pure Science**
BS . . . . **Bachelor of Surgery**
BS . . . . Backspace
BS . . . . **Balance Sheet**
BS . . . . Baroswitch
BS . . . . Base Shell

BS	Base Skirt
BS	Basic Sediment (Petroleum)
BS	Basilian Salvatorian Fathers (Roman Catholic religious order)
BS	Battery Simulator
BS	Battle Squadron (Navy)
BS	Battle Star (Military)
BS	Battleship Squadron
BS	Beam Steering
BS	Beam Stop
BS	Berlin Sector (Allied German Occupation Forces)
BS	Beta Spectrometer
BS	Bethlehem Steel Corporation (NYSE symbol) (Wall Street slang name: "Bessie")
BS	Bill of Sale
BS	Bill of Sight
BS	Bill of Store
BS	Binary Subtract
BS	Biometric Society
BS	Biophysical Society
BS	Birmingham Southern R. R. (AAR code)
BS	Bishop Suffragan
BS	Blood Sugar
BS	Blowing Snow (Meteorology)
BS	Blue Steel (Guns)
BS	Body Shell
BS	Bomb Service
BS	Both Sides (Technical drawings)
BS	Bottom Sediment (Maps and charts)
BS	Bottom Settlings (of crude oil in storage)
BS	Brada-Svejda (Tumor) (Medicine)
BS	British Standard
BS	Broadcasting Station
BS	Bull Session (Slang for a random conversation)
BS	Bullsling(er) (Bowdlerized version)
BS	Bureau of Ships (Later, Naval Ship Systems Command)
BS	Bureau of Standards
BS	Graduate in Science
B/S	Behind Schedule
B/S	Bill of Sale
B & S	Beams and Stringers (Technical drawings)
B & S	Bell and Spigot (Technical drawings)
B & S	Booster and Sustainer
B & S	Brown and Sharpe (Gage)
B and S	Brandy and Soda
B of S	Bureau of Standards
B1S	Beaded One Side (Lumber)
B2S	Beaded Two Sides (Lumber)
BSA	Bachelor of Science in Agriculture
BSA	Bachelor of Scientific Agriculture
BSA	Bank Stationers Association
BSA	Basic Standardization Agreement (Military)
BSA	Basic Stock Allowance (DOD)
BSA	Bearing Specialists Association
BSA	Benzene Sulfonic Acid
BSA	Bible Sabbath Association
BSA	Bibliographical Society of America
BSA	Birmingham Small Arms, Inc.
BSA	Bistrimethylsilylacetamide
BSA	Blind Service Association
BSA	Blue Streak Request (Military)
BSA	Board of Scientific Affairs
BSA	Body Surface Area
BSA	Bohr-Sommerfeld Atom
BSA	Botanical Society of America
BSA	Bovine Serum Albumin
BSA	Boy Scouts of America
BSA	British South Africa
BSA	Bureau of Supplies and Accounts (Later, NSUPSC) (Navy)
BSAA	British South American Airways
BSA Adm	Bachelor of Science in Agricultural Administration
BSAC	Brotherhood of Shoe and Allied Craftsmen
BS (Acc)	Bachelor of Science in Accounting
BS in Acc	Bachelor of Science in Accounting
BS in AD	Bachelor of Science in Agricultural Education
BS Adv	Bachelor of Science in Advertising
BSAE	Bachelor of Science in Aeronautical Engineering
BSAE	Bachelor of Science in Architectural Engineering
BS in AE	Bachelor of Science in Administrative Engineering
BS in AE	Bachelor of Science in Aeronautical Engineering
BS in AE	Bachelor of Science in Architectural Engineering
BS Ae E	Bachelor of Science in Aeronautical Engineering

BSAE-E	Bachelor of Science in Aeronautical Engineering - Electronics Major
BS in Ae E	Bachelor of Science in Aeronautical Engineering
BS (AE Elec)	Bachelor of Science with Aeronautical Engineering Electives
BS in Aero Adm	Bachelor of Science in Aeronautical Administration
BS (Aero E)	Bachelor of Science in Aeronautical Engineering
BS in Aero E	Bachelor of Science in Aeronautical Engineering
BSAF	Bids Solicited As Follows
BS Ag	Bachelor of Science in Agriculture
BS in Ag	Bachelor of Science in Agriculture
BS in Ag (DM)	Bachelor of Science in Agriculture in Dairy Manufacturing
BS in Ag E	Bachelor of Science in Agricultural Engineering
BS in Ag & Ed	Bachelor of Science in Agriculture and Education
BS Agr	Bachelor of Science in Agriculture
BS in Agr & Chem	Bachelor of Science in Agriculture and Chemistry
BS in Agr E	Bachelor of Science in Agricultural Engineering
BS in Agr Ed	Bachelor of Science in Agricultural Education
BS in Agr Eng	Bachelor of Science in Agricultural Engineering
BSAL	Base Spares Allowance List
BS in AM	Bachelor of Science in Agricultural Administration
BS (A Math)	Bachelor of Science in Applied Mathematics
BSAME	Bachelor of Science in Aircraft Maintenance Engineering
BS in AN	Bachelor of Science in Agricultural Engineering
BS Arch	Bachelor of Science in Architecture
BS in Arch	Bachelor of Science in Architecture
BS Arch (Arch)	Bachelor of Science in Architecture in Architecture
BS Arch (Arch E)	Bachelor of Science in Architecture in Architectural Engineering
BS Arch E	Bachelor of Science in Architectural Engineering
BSAS	British Ship Adoption Society
B Sa Sc	Bachelor of Sacred Sciences
BSAT	Bachelor of Science in Air Transportation
BSB	Bachelor of Science in Business
BSBA	Bachelor of Science in Business Administration
BS in BA	Bachelor of Science in Business Administration
BSB Ad	Bachelor of Science in Business Administration
BS in B Ad	Bachelor of Science in Business Administration
BSB Ed	Bachelor of Science in Business Education
BS in B Ed	Bachelor of Science in Business Education
BS in Biol	Bachelor of Science in Biology
BS in BMS	Bachelor of Science in Basic Medical Sciences
BS BSF	Boot or Shoes, or Boot or Shoe Findings (Freight)
BS Bus	Bachelor of Science in Business
BS in Bus	Bachelor of Science in Business
BS Bus Ad	Bachelor of Science in Business Administration
BS in Bus Ad	Bachelor of Science in Business Administration
BS in Bus Ed	Bachelor of Science in Business Education
BS (Bus-MR)	Bachelor of Science in Business - Medical Records
BSC	Bachelor of Christian Science
B Sc	Bachelor of Science
BSC	Bachelor of Science in Commerce
BSC	Backspace Contact
BSC	Balkan Supply Center (Navy)
BSC	Barber-Scotia College (North Carolina)
BSC	Base Security Council (Air Force)
BSC	Basic-Message Switching Center (Data processing)
BSC	Beltsville Space Center (NASA)
BSC	Bemidji State College (Minnesota)
BSC	Bengal Staff Corps
BSC	Billet Sequence Code
BSC	Binary Symmetric Channel
BSC	Binary Synchronous Communication (Data processing)
BSC	Biological Stain Commission
BSC	Biomedical Sciences Corps (Air Force)
BSC	Biomedical Signal Conditioner
BSC	Birmingham Southern College (Alabama)
BSC	Blip-Scan Counter
BSC	Bluefield State College (West Virginia)
BSC	Body Support Cradle
BSC	Bolted Separable Connector
BSC	Brethren Service Commission
BSC	British Steel Corporation
BSC	British Sugar Corporation
BSC	British Supply Council
BSC	Burley Stabilization Corporation
BSC	Business Service Center
B Sc	Graduate in Science
B Sc	Mistress of Science
BS in C	Bachelor of Science in Commerce
BSCA	Belgian Sheepdog Club of America
BSCA	Binary Synchronous Communications Adapter (Data processing)
B Sc Agr	Bachelor of Science in Agriculture

B Sc in Agr Engr .. Bachelor of Science in Agricultural Engineering
BS in Cart .... Bachelor of Science in Cartography
BSCBA ...... Brown Swiss Cattle Breeders Association of the USA
BS in C & BA .. Bachelor of Science in Commercial and Business Administration
B Sc in Bact .. Bachelor of Science in Bacteriology
B Sc in CE .... Bachelor of Science in Civil Engineering
B Sc (Dn) .... Bachelor of Science in Dianoetics
BSCE .... Bachelor of Science in Civil Engineering
BS in CE..... Bachelor of Science in Chemical Engineering
BS in CE..... Bachelor of Science in Civil Engineering
BS in C & Ec .. Bachelor of Science in Commerce and Economics
B Sc Econ .... Bachelor of Science in Economics
B Sc in EE .... Bachelor of Science in Electrical Engineering
BS in CE – Music..Bachelor of Science in Christian Education – Music
BSc(Eng) ..... Bachelor of Science (Engineering)
BS in Cer .... Bachelor of Science in Ceramics
BS (Cer E).... Bachelor of Science in Ceramic Engineering
BS in Cer E .. Bachelor of Science in Ceramic Engineering
BS in Cer Tech .. Bachelor of Science in Ceramic Technology
B Sc F....... Bachelor of Science in Forestry
B Sc For ..... Bachelor of Science in Forestry
B-SCH ...... Bomber (Russian aircraft symbol)
BS in Ch..... Bachelor of Science in Chemistry
BS Ch E ..... Bachelor of Science in Chemical Engineering
BS in Ch E.... Bachelor of Science in Chemical Engineering
B Sc in HE.... Bachelor of Science in Home Economics
BS (Ch E Elect) . Bachelor of Science with Chemical Engineering Electives
BS Chem E ... Bachelor of Science in Chemical Engineering
BS in Chem E .. Bachelor of Science in Chemical Engineering
BS in Chem Tech.. Bachelor of Science in Chemical Technology
BS Ch Eng.... Bachelor of Science in Chemical Engineering
BS in Ch Eng.. Bachelor of Science in Chemical Engineering
BS in Chm .... Bachelor of Science in Chemistry
BS in Chm E .. Bachelor of Science in Chemical Engineering
B Sch Mus ... Bachelor of School Music
B Sc L ...... Bachelor of the Science of Law
B Sc in ME ... Bachelor of Science in Mechanical Engineering
B Sc in Med .. Bachelor of Science in Medicine
B Sc in Med Tech .. Bachelor of Science in Medical Technology
B Scn .... Bachelor of Scientology
BS in CN .... Bachelor of Science in Chemical Engineering
B Sc in Nurs .. Bachelor of Science in Nursing
B Sc O ...... Bachelor of the Science of Oratory
BSCO ...... Bethlehem Steel Co. (Form preferred by the company)
B Sc in Occ Ther.. Bachelor of Science in Occupational Therapy
BS Com...... Bachelor of Science in Communications
BS in Com .... Bachelor of Science in Commerce
BS in Com & Bus .. Bachelor of Science in Commerce and Business
BS in Com Ed.. Bachelor of Science in Commercial Education
BS in Comm ... Bachelor of Science in Commerce
BS in Comm Rec .. Bachelor of Science in Community Recreation
B Sc in Opt... Bachelor of Science in Optometry
BSCP .... Biological Sciences Communication Project (American Institute of Biological Sciences)
BSCP .... British Standard Code of Practice
B Sc in Phar .. Bachelor of Science in Pharmacy
B Sc in Phys ... Bachelor of Science in Physics
B Sc in Phys Ther .. Bachelor of Science in Physical Therapy
BSCRA ...... British Steel Castings Research Association
BS Cr E ...... Bachelor of Science in Ceramic Engineering
B Sc in Rest Mgt..Bachelor of Science in Restaurant Management
BSCS .... Biological Sciences Curriculum Study
BSCS........ Blip-Scan Counter System
B Sc in Soc Adm .. Bachelor of Science in Social Administration
BSCTE....... Bell System Center for Technical Education
B Sc Tech .... Bachelor of Technical Science
BSD .... Bachelor of Didactic Science
BSD .... Bachelor of Science in Design
BSD .... Ballistic System Division (AFSC)
BSD .... Beam Steering Device
BSD .... BIT (Binary Digit) Storage Density (Data processing)
BSD .... Blast Suppression Device
BSD .... Blue Stellar Object (Astronomy)
BSD .... Burst Slug Detection
BSDC .... Binary Symmetric Dependent Channel
BSDC .... British Space Development Company
BS in Dent.... Bachelor of Science in Dentistry
BS Des ..... Bachelor of Science in Design
BS Des (Dec Des) .. Bachelor of Science in Design in Decorative Design
BSDF .... Beet Sugar Development Foundation
BS in DH..... Bachelor of Science in Dental Hygiene

BSD Hyg ..... Bachelor of Science in Dental Hygiene
BS Di .... Bachelor of Scientific Didactics
BSDL .... Boresight Datum Line (Military)
BSE .... Bachelor of Sanitary Engineering
BSE .... Bachelor of Science in Education
BSE .... Bachelor of Science in Engineering
BSE .... Backscatter Electron
BSE .... Base Support Equipment (Military)
BSE .... Bethe-Saltpeter Equation
BSE .... Birmingham & Southeastern R. R. (AAR code)
BSE .... Boston Edison Company (NYSE symbol)
BSE .... Breast Self-Examination (for Cancer) (Medicine)
BSE .... Building Service Employees' International Union
BSE .... Bureau of Steam Engineering (Navy)
BS in E ..... Bachelor of Science in Education
BS in E ..... Bachelor of Science in Engineering
B Se A ..... Bachelor of Secretarial Arts
BSE (Ae E) ... Bachelor of Science in Engineering in Aeronautical Engineering
BS Ec ...... Bachelor of Science in Economics
BS in Ec ..... Bachelor of Science in Economics
BSE (CE)..... Bachelor of Science in Engineering and Civil Engineering
BSE (Ch E) ... Bachelor of Science in Engineering in Chemical Engineering
B Sec Sc .... Bachelor of Secretarial Science
BS Ed ...... Bachelor of Science in Education
BSED .... Ballistic Systems Education Division (Air University) (Air Force)
BS in Ed ..... Bachelor of Science in Education
BSEE .... Bachelor of Science in Electrical Engineering
BSEE .... Bachelor of Science in Elementary Education
BS in EE ..... Bachelor of Science in Electrical Engineering
BSE (EE) ..... Bachelor of Science in Engineering in Electrical Engineering
BSE (EM) ..... Bachelor of Science in Engineering in Engineering Mechanics
BSE (Geod & Surv) .. Bachelor of Science in Engineering in Geodesy and Surveying
BSE (Ind E).... Bachelor of Science in Engineering in Industrial Engineering
BSEL .... Bachelor of Science and English Literature
BS El E ...... Bachelor of Science in Electronic Engineering
BS in Elect Eng . Bachelor of Science in Electronic Engineering
BS El Ed ..... Bachelor of Science in Elementary Education
BS Elem ..... Bachelor of Science in Elementary Education
BSEM .... Bachelor of Science in Engineering of Mines
BS in EM ..... Bachelor of Science in Engineering of Mines
BSE (Mat E) ... Bachelor of Science in Engineering in Materials Engineering
BS in E Math .. Bachelor of Science in Engineering Mathematics
BSE (ME)..... Bachelor of Science in Engineering in Mechanical Engineering
BSE (Met E) ... Bachelor of Science in Engineering in Metallurgical Engineering
BSE (M & Ind E) .. Bachelor of Science in Engineering in Mechanical and Industrial Engineering
BSE (Nav Arch & Mar E).. Bachelor of Science in Engineering in Naval Architecture and Marine Engineering
BS Eng ..... Bachelor of Sanitary Engineering
BS in Eng..... Bachelor of Science in Engineering
BS Engr Ad ... Bachelor of Science in Engineering Administration
BS Engr Phys.. Bachelor of Science in Engineering Physics
BS Engr Sci ... Bachelor of Science in Engineering Science
BS Eng Sci ... Bachelor of Science in Engineering Sciences
BSEP .... Bachelor of Science in Engineering Physics
BS in EP ..... Bachelor of Science in Engineering Physics
BSE Phys ..... Bachelor of Science in Engineering Physics
BS in E Phys .. Bachelor of Science in Engineering Physics
BSERBN...... Base Service Battalion (Marine Corps)
BSES .... Bachelor of Science in Engineering Sciences
BS in ES ..... Bachelor of Science in Engineering Sciences
BSE Sc ...... Bachelor of Science in Engineering Sciences
B Se St ...... Bachelor of Secretarial Studies
BSF .... Bachelor of Science in Forestry
BSF .... Ball Spinning Friction
BSF .... Baltic Student Federation
BSF .... Bandwidth Shape Factor
BSF .... Blade Slap Factor (Helicopter)
BSF .... British Salonica Force
BSF .... British Standard Fine Thread
BSF .... Bulk Shielding Facility (ORNL)
BSFC .... Brake Specific Fuel Consumption
BS (Fin) ..... Bachelor of Science in Finance
BS in Fin .... Bachelor of Science in Finance
BSFM .... Bachelor of Science in Forest Management
BSF Mgt ..... Bachelor of Science in Fisheries Management
BS For...... Bachelor of Science in Forestry
BS in For..... Bachelor of Science in Forestry
BSFS .... Bachelor of Science in Foreign Service
BS in FS ..... Bachelor of Science in Foreign Service
BS Fsty ..... Bachelor of Science in Forestry

BSFT . . . . Bachelor of Science in Fuel Technology
BSFW . . . . . . Bureau of Sport Fisheries and Wildlife (of USFWS)
BS in Fy . . . . . Bachelor of Science in Forestry
BSG . . . . Base Spares Group
BSG . . . . Beam Steering Group
BSG . . . . Betriebssportgemeinschaft
BSGE . . . . Bachelor of Science in General Engineering
BS in GE . . . . . Bachelor of Science in General Engineering
BS in Ge E . . . Bachelor of Science in Geological Engineering
BS in Gen Bus . . Bachelor of Science in General Business
BS Gen Ed . . . Bachelor of Science in General Education
BS in Gen Eng . . Bachelor of Science in General Engineering
BS in Gen Nurs . . Bachelor of Science in General Nursing
BS in Gen Sci . . Bachelor of Science in General Science
BS in Gen Std . . Bachelor of Science in General Studies
BS in Geod & Surv Bachelor of Science in Geodesy and Surveying
BS (Geog) . . . . Bachelor of Science in Geography
BS (Geol) . . . . Bachelor of Science in Geology
BS Geol E . . . . Bachelor of Science in Geological Engineering
BS in Geol E . . Bachelor of Science in Geological Engineering
BS Ggr . . . . . . Bachelor of Science in Geography
BS Gl . . . . Bachelor of Science in Geology
BS Gl E . . . . . Bachelor of Science in Geological Engineering
BSG Mgt . . . . . Bachelor of Science in Game Management
BSGP . . . . . . Base Support Group (Air Force)
BS Gph . . . . . . Bachelor of Science in Geophysics
BS in Gph E . . . Bachelor of Science in Geophysical Engineering
BSGS . . . . Base Support Group System (Air Force)
BS in GS . . . . . Bachelor of Science in General Studies
BS in GSM . . Bachelor of Science in General Science and Mathematics
BS in GWE . . Bachelor of Science in Group Work Education
BSH . . . . Bush Universal, Inc. (NYSE symbol)
BSHA . . . . . . Bachelor of Science in Hospital Administration
BS in HD . . . . Bachelor of Science in Home Economics Education
BSHE . . . . . . Bachelor of Science in Health Education
BSHE . . . . . . Bachelor of Science in Home Economics
BS (HE) . . . . . Bachelor of Science in Home Economics
BS in HE . . . . Bachelor of Science in Home Economics
BS H Ec . . . . Bachelor of Science in Home Economics
BS in H Ec . . . Bachelor of Science in Home Economics
BS in H Econ . . Bachelor of Science in Home Economics
BS in H Ed . . . Bachelor of Science in Health Education
BSHP . . . . . . Beginning Standard Holding Procedure (Aviation)
BS in HPE . . . Bachelor of Science in Health and Physical Education
BS in H & PE . . Bachelor of Science in Health and Physical Education
BS in H & RA . . Bachelor of Science in Hotel and Restaurant Administration
BSI . . . . Baker Street Irregulars
BSI . . . . British Solomon Islands
BSI . . . . British Standards Institution (Promulgates manufacturing standards and specifications)
BSI . . . . Building Stone Institute
BSIA . . . . . . Bead and Stone Importers Association
BS in IA . . . . . Bachelor of Science in Industrial Arts
BSIAP . . . . . . Beginning Straight-In Approach (Aviation)
BSIB . . . . . . Boy Scouts International Bureau
BSIC . . . . . . Binary Symmetric Independent Channel (Data processing)
BSIE . . . . . . Bachelor of Science in Industrial Education
BSIE . . . . . . Bio-Sciences Information Exchange (Smithsonian Institution)
BS in IE . . . . Bachelor of Science in Industrial Engineering
BS in IE & M . . Bachelor of Science in Industrial Engineering and Management
BSIM . . . . . . Bachelor of Science in Industrial Management
BS in IM . . . . Bachelor of Science in Industrial Management
BS in Ind Art . . Bachelor of Science in Industrial Art
BS in Ind Ch . . Bachelor of Science in Industrial Chemistry
BS in Ind E . . Bachelor of Science in Industrial Engineering
BS in Ind Ed . . Bachelor of Science in Industrial Education
BS Ind Eng . . . Bachelor of Science in Industrial Engineering
BS Ind Mgt . . . Bachelor of Science in Industrial Management
BSIR . . . . . . Bachelor of Science in Industrial Relations
BSIRA . . . . . . British Scientific Instrument Research Association
BSIT . . . . . . Bachelor of Science in Industrial Technology
BSJ . . . . Bachelor of Science in Journalism
BSJ . . . . Balanced Swivel Joint
BSJ . . . . Ball and Socket Joint
BS in J . . . . . Bachelor of Science in Journalism
BS Jr . . . . . . Bachelor of Science in Journalism
BSK . . . . Back Shunt Keying
BSL . . . . Bachelor of Sacred Literature
BSL . . . . Bachelor of Science in Languages
BSL . . . . Bachelor of Science in Law
BSL . . . . Bachelor of Science in Linguistics

BSL . . . . Back Stage Left (A stage direction)
BSL . . . . Billet Split Lens
BSL . . . . Biot-Savart Law
BSL . . . . Botanical Society, London
BSL . . . . Building Service League
BSLA . . . . . . Bachelor of Science in Landscape Architecture
BS Lab Rel . . . Bachelor of Science in Labor Relations
BSL Arch . . . . Bachelor of Science in Landscape Architecture
BS in Lat . . . . Bachelor of Science in Latin
BSLF . . . . Bulgarian Socialist Labor Federation (Defunct)
BSLM . . . . . . Bachelor of Science in Landscape Management
BS in LP . . . . Bachelor of Science in Land Planning
BSLS . . . . . . Bachelor of Science in Library Science
BS in LS . . . . Bachelor of Science in Library Service
BS in L & S . . . Bachelor of Science in Letters and Science
BS in LT . . . . Bachelor of Science in Laboratory Technology
BSL & W . . . . Beaumont, Sour Lake & Western Railway Company
BSM . . . . Bachelor of Sacred Music
BSM . . . . Bachelor of School Music
BSM . . . . Bachelor of Science in Medicine
BSM . . . . Bachelor of Science in Music
BSM . . . . Battalion Sergeant-Major (Army)
BSM . . . . Battery Sergeant-Major
BSM . . . . Bi-Stable Multivibrator
BSM . . . . Bottom SONAR Marker
BSM . . . . Braked Servomotor
BSM . . . . Bronze Star Medal
BS in MA . . . . Bachelor of Science in Mechanical Arts
BS in Math . . . Bachelor of Science in Applied Mathematics
BS in Math Stat . . Bachelor of Science in Mathematical Statistics
BSMCP . . . . . . Blue Shield Medical Care Plans
BS in Md . . . . Bachelor of Science in Medical Technology
BSME . . . . . . Bachelor of Science in Mechanical Engineering
BSME . . . . . . Bachelor of Science in Mining Engineering
BSME . . . . . . Bachelor of Science in Music Education
BS (ME) . . . . . Bachelor of Science in Mechanical Engineering
BS in ME . . . . Bachelor of Science in Mechanical Engineering
BS in Mech . . . Bachelor of Science in Engineering Mechanics; or Bachelor of Science in Mechanics
BS in Mech Eng . . Bachelor of Science in Mechanical Engineering
BS in Mech Ind . Bachelor of Science in Mechanical Industries
BSM Ed . . . . . Bachelor of Science in Music Education
BS in Med . . . . Bachelor of Science in Medicine
BS in Med Rec . . Bachelor of Science in Medical Records
BS in Med Rec Lib . . Bachelor of Science in Medical Records Librarianship
BS in Med S . . . Bachelor of Science in Basic Medical Science
BS in Med Sc . . Bachelor of Science in Medical Secretarial Science
BS Med T . . . . Bachelor of Science in Medical Technology
BS Med Tech . . Bachelor of Science in Medical Technology
BS in Med Tech . . Bachelor of Science in Medical Technology
BS in M Educ . . Bachelor of Science in Music Education
BS (ME Elect) . Bachelor of Science with Mechanical Engineering Electives
BS in M Engr . . Bachelor of Science in Mechanical Engineering
BS Met . . . . . . Bachelor of Science in Meteorology
BS in Met . . . . Bachelor of Science in Metallurgy
BS in Met . . . . Bachelor of Science in Meteorology
BS Met E . . . . Bachelor of Science in Metallurgical Engineering
BS in Met E . . Bachelor of Science in Metallurgical Engineering
BS Met Eng . . Bachelor of Science in Metallurgical Engineering
BS in Met Engin . . Bachelor of Science in Metallurgical Engineering
BS Mg E . . . . Bachelor of Science in Mining Engineering
BS in Mgt Engr . . Bachelor of Science in Management Engineering
BS in Mgt Sc . . Bachelor of Science in Management Science
BS Min . . . . . . Bachelor of Science in Mineralogy
BS in Min . . . . Bachelor of Science in Mining
BS Min E . . . . Bachelor of Science in Mining Engineering
BS in Min E . . Bachelor of Science in Mining Engineering
BS in Min Eng . . Bachelor of Science in Mining Engineering
BS Mng E . . . . Bachelor of Science in Mining Engineering
BSMO . . . . . . Base Supply Management Office (Air Force)
BSMP . . . . . . Brussels Sprouts Marketing Program
BS in MRL . . . . Bachelor of Science in Medical Record Library Science
BS in MS . . . . Bachelor of Science in Military Science
BSMT . . . . . . Bachelor of Science in Medical Technology
BSMT . . . . . . Board of Schools of Medical Technology
BS (MT) . . . . . Bachelor of Science in Medical Technology
BS in MT . . . . Bachelor of Science in Medical Technology
BS Mt E . . . . Bachelor of Science in Metallurgical Engineering
BS Mu . . . . . . Bachelor of Sacred Music
BS in Mu Ed . . Bachelor of Science in Music Education
BS Mus . . . . . Bachelor of Sacred Music

BS Mus . . . . . . Bachelor of School Music
BS Mus . . . . . . Bachelor of Science in Music
BS Mus Ed . . Bachelor of Science in Music Education
BS in Mus Ed . . Bachelor of Science in Musical Education
BSMV . . . . . . Barley Stripe Mosaic Virus
BSN . . . . Bachelor of Science in Nursing
BS in N . . . . . Bachelor of Science in Nursing
BSNA . . . . . . Bachelor of Science in Nursing Administration
BSNA . . . . . . Bureau of Salesmen's National Associations
BS in Nat G Engin . . Bachelor of Science in Natural-Gas Engineering
BS in Nat Hist . . Bachelor of Science in Natural History
BSNE . . . . . . Bachelor of Science in Nursing Education
BS in NE . . . . Bachelor of Science in Nursing Education
BSN Ed . . . . . Bachelor of Science in Nursing Education
BS in N Ed . . . . Bachelor of Science in Nursing Education
BS in Nr . . . . . Bachelor of Science in Nursing
BS in NS . . . . . Bachelor of Science in Natural Science
BS in N Sc . . . Bachelor of Science in Natural Science
BS Nurs . . . . . Bachelor of Science in Nursing
BS in Nurs . . . . Bachelor of Science in Nursing
BS in Nurs Ed . . Bachelor of Science in Nursing Education
BS in Nurs Ed . . Bachelor of Science in Nursing Education
BSNY . . . . . . Bible Seminary in New York
BSO . . . . Bachelor of the Science of Oratory
B So . . . . Bachelor of Sociology
BSO . . . . Base Supply Officer (Navy)
BSO . . . . Bomb Safety Officer (Navy)
BSO . . . . Boston Symphony Orchestra
BSO . . . . British Supply Office
BSOAL . . . . . . Bank-Share Owners Advisory League
BS in Occ Ther . . Bachelor of Science in Occupational Therapy
BS in Ocean . . . Bachelor of Science in Oceanography
BS in OH . . . . Bachelor of Science in Ornamental Horticulture
BSOIW . . . . . . International Association of Bridge, Structural and Ornamental Iron Workers
BS (Opt) . . . . . Bachelor of Science in Optometry
BS in Opt . . . . Bachelor of Science in Optics
BS in Opt . . . . Bachelor of Science in Optometry
BS Orn Hort . . . Bachelor of Science in Ornamental Horticulture
BS in Ortho . . . Bachelor of Science in Orthoptics
B So Sc . . . . . . Bachelor of Social Science
B So Se . . . . . . Bachelor of Social Service
BSOT . . . . . . Bachelor of Science in Occupational Therapy
BS in OT . . . . . Bachelor of Science in Occupational Therapy
B So W . . . . . . Bachelor of Social Work
BSP . . . . Bachelor of Science in Pharmacy
B Sp . . . . Bachelor of Speech
BSP . . . . Baltimore Steam Packet Company (AAR code)
BSP . . . . Bell System Practices
BSP . . . . BMEWS (Ballistic Missile Early Warning System) Specification
BSP . . . . British Socialist Party
BSP . . . . British Standard Pipe
BSP . . . . Bromsulphalein (Trademark) (Medicine)
BSPA . . . . . . Bachelor of Science in Public Administration
BSPA . . . . . . Black Students Psychological Association
BS in PA . . . . Bachelor of Science in Practical Arts
BS in PA . . . . Bachelor of Science in Public Administration
BS in PAL . . . . Bachelor of Science in Practical Arts and Letters
BSPE . . . . . . Bachelor of Science in Physical Education
BS (PE) . . . . . Bachelor of Science in Physical Education
BS in PE . . . . Bachelor of Science in Petroleum Engineering
BS in PE . . . . Bachelor of Science in Physical Education
BS in P Ed . . . Bachelor of Science in Physical Education
BS (Per & Ind Rel) . . Bachelor of Science in Personnel and Industrial Relations
BS in Pet . . . . Bachelor of Science in Petroleum
BS in Pet Engin . . Bachelor of Science in Petroleum Engineering
BS in Petr E . . . Bachelor of Science in Petroleum Engineering
BS Ph . . . . . . Bachelor of Science in Pharmacy
BSPH . . . . . . Bachelor of Science in Public Health
BS in Ph . . . . Bachelor of Science in Pharmacy
BS Phar . . . . . Bachelor of Science in Pharmacy
BS in Phar . . . . Bachelor of Science in Pharmacy
BSPHN . . . . . Bachelor of Science in Public Health Nursing
BS in PHN . . . . Bachelor of Science in Public Health Nursing
BS in PHPM . . Bachelor of Science in Public Health and Preventative Medicine
BS Ph Th . . . . Bachelor of Science in Physical Therapy
BS in Phy Ed . . Bachelor of Science in Physical Education
BS Phys . . . . . Bachelor of Science in Physics
BS in Phys Ed . . Bachelor of Science in Physical Education
BS in Phys Th . . Bachelor of Science in Physical Therapy
BS in Phys Ther . . Bachelor of Science in Physical Therapy

BSPL . . . . . . Behavioral Science Programming Language
BSPM . . . . . . Battlefield Systems Project Management
BSPO . . . . . BMEWS (Ballistic Missile Early Warning System) System Program Office
BS in Prac Arts . Bachelor of Science in Practical Arts
BS in Pr Ge . . Bachelor of Science in Professional Geology
BS in Pr Met . . Bachelor of Science in Professional Meteorology
BS in PSM . . . . Bachelor of Science in Public School Music
BSPT . . . . . . Bachelor of Science in Physical Therapy
BS (PT) . . . . . Bachelor of Science in Physical Therapy
BS in PT . . . . Bachelor of Science in Physical Therapy
BSPW . . . . . . Bare Silver Plated Wire
BSQ . . . . Bachelor Sergeant Quarters (Air Force)
BSR . . . . Bachelor of Science in Recreation
BSR . . . . Back Stage Right (A stage direction)
BSR . . . . Backspace Recorder
BSR . . . . Balloon Supported Rocket
BSR . . . . Basal Skin Resistance
BSR . . . . Battle Short Relay
BSR . . . . Blip-Scan Ratio
BSR . . . . Board of Standards Review (American National Standards Institute)
BSR . . . . Boilermaker, Ship Repair (Navy)
BSR . . . . Brain Stimulation Reinforcement
BSR . . . . Bulk Shielding Reactor
BSR . . . . Butane Secondary Refrigerant
BSRA . . . . . . British Ship Research Association
BS in RAH . . . . Bachelor of Science in Range Animal Husbandry
BSRAP . . . . . . Beginning Standard Range Approach (Aviation)
BS in RE . . . . Bachelor of Science in Religious Education
BS Rec . . . . . Bachelor of Science in Recreation
BS in Rec . . . . Bachelor of Science in Recreation
BS in Rec Lead . Bachelor of Science in Recreation Leadership
BS Ret . . . . . Bachelor of Science in Retailing
BSRL . . . . . . Boeing Scientific Research Laboratories
BSRO . . . . . . Beitrage zur Statistik der Republik Osterreich (Austria)
BSRRO . . . . . . Begin Standard RADAR Refuel Orbit (Aviation)
BSRT . . . . . . Bachelor of Science in Radiological Technology
BS in RT . . . . Bachelor of Science in Radiological Technology
BSS . . . . Bachelor of Sanitary Science
BSS . . . . Bachelor of Science in Science
BSS . . . . Bachelor of Secretarial Science
BSS . . . . Bachelor of Social Science(s)
BSS . . . . Balanced Salt Solution
BSS . . . . Basic Shaft System
BSS . . . . Beam Steering System
BSS . . . . Bibliographical Services Section (of a library)
BSS . . . . Bibliography of Soil Science (An abstracts journal)
BSS . . . . BOMARC Squadron Simulator
BSS . . . . British Standard Specifications
BSS . . . . Bronze Service Star (Military award)
BSS . . . . Bulletin de Statistique Suisse (Switzerland)
BSS . . . . Bureau of State Services (of Public Health Service)
BSSA . . . . . . Bachelor of Science in Secretarial Administration
BS in San E . . . Bachelor of Science in Sanitary Engineering
BS in San Sci . . Bachelor of Science in Sanitary Science
BS Sc . . . . . . Bachelor of Sanitary Science
BS Sc E . . . . . Bachelor of Science in Science Engineering
BSSE . . . . . . Bachelor of Science in Secondary Education
BS Sec . . . . . Bachelor of Science in Secondary Education
BS (Sec Adm) . . Bachelor of Science in Secretarial Administration
BS Sec Ed . . . . Bachelor of Science in Secondary Education
BS (Sec Ed) . . . Bachelor of Science in Secondary Education
BS in Sec Ed . . Bachelor of Science in Secondary Education
BS in Sec Sc . . . Bachelor of Science in Secretarial Science
BS in Sec Sc . . . Bachelor of Science in Secretarial Science
BS in Soc Serv . . Bachelor of Science in Social Service
BS in Soc St . . . Bachelor of Science in Social Studies
BS (Soc Wk) . . . Bachelor of Science in Social Work
BS Sp . . . . . . Bachelor of Science in Speech
BSSP . . . . . . Broadband Solid State Preamplifier
BS in Spec Flds . Bachelor of Science in Special Fields
BSSR . . . . . . Bureau of Social Sciences Research, Inc.
BSSRS . . . . . . British Society for Social Responsibility in Science
BSSRS . . . . . . Bureau of Safety and Supply Radio Services
BSSS . . . . . . Bachelor of Science in Secretarial Studies
BSSS . . . . . . Bachelor of Science in Social Science
BS (SS) . . . . . Bachelor of Science in Social Science
BS in SS . . . . Bachelor of Science in Social Science
BS in S Sc . . . . Bachelor of Science in Social Science
BSS Sci . . . . . Bachelor of Science in Secretarial Science
BS in Stat . . . . Bachelor of Science in Statistics
BS in Struc E . . Bachelor of Science in Structural Engineering

BSSW . . . . Bare Stainless Steel Wire
BST . . . . Bachelor of Sacred Theology
BST . . . . Bachelor of Science in Teaching
B St . . . . Bachelor of Statistics
BST . . . . Beam Steering Transducer
BST . . . . Beam-Switching Tube
BST . . . . Beobachtungsstelle (Observation post) (German military – World War II)
BST . . . . Bereitschaftsstellung (Line of support) (German military – World War II)
BST . . . . Best & Company, Inc. (NYSE symbol) (Delisted)
BST . . . . Blood Serological Test (Medicine)
BST . . . . Bore Sight Tunnel
BST . . . . Brief Stimulus Therapy (Psychology)
BST . . . . British Summer Time
BS & T . . . . . . Blood, Sweat and Tears (Rock music group)
BSTC . . . . Ball State Teachers College (Indiana)
B St E . . . . . . Bachelor of Structural Engineering
BS in TE . . . . Bachelor of Science in Textile Engineering
B St Eng . . . . Bachelor of Structural Engineering
BS in Text . . . . Bachelor of Science in Textiles
BSTFA . . . . . . Bis(trimethylsilyl)trifluoroacetamide (Organic chemistry)
BS in Th . . . . Bachelor of Science in Physical and Occupational Therapy
BST & IE . . . . Bachelor of Science in Trade and Industrial Engineering
BSTR . . . . Booster (Military)
BS Trans . . . . Bachelor of Science in Transportation
BSU . . . . Base Service Unit (Navy)
BSU . . . . Black Students Union
BSUB . . . . . . Ball and Socket Upper Bearing
B Sur . . . . . . Bachelor of Surgery
BSUS . . . . . . Bolivarian Society of the United States
BSUT . . . . . . Beam Steering Ultrasonic Transducer
BSV . . . . Boolean Simple Variable (Mathematics)
BS in Voc Ag . . Bachelor of Science in Vocational Agriculture
BS in Voc Ed . . Bachelor of Science in Vocational Education
BSW . . . . Bare Steel Wire
BSW . . . . Boot and Shoe Workers' Union
BS & W . . . . . Basic Sediment and Water (In crude oil)
BSWM . . . . . . Bureau of Solid Waste Management (Environmental Protection Agency)
BSYM . . . . . . Boy Savior Youth Movement
B Sy Th . . . . . Bachelor of Systematic Theology
BSZ . . . . Ballistic Systems Zeus (Aerospace)
BS in ZS . . . . Bachelor of Science in Zoological Sciences
BT . . . . Bachelor of Teaching
BT . . . . Bachelor of Theology
BT . . . . Bacillus Thuringiensis
BT . . . . Bankers Trust New York Corp. (NYSE symbol)
BT . . . . Baronet
BT . . . . Basic Trainer (Air Force)
BT . . . . Bathythermal Traces
BT . . . . Bathythermograph
BT . . . . Beam Rider – Terrier
BT . . . . Berth Terms
BT . . . . Blind Toss
BT . . . . Block Template
BT . . . . Blue Tetrazolium (A dye)
BT . . . . Board of Trade
BT . . . . Boilerman (Navy rating)
BT . . . . Bomber Transport (Air Force)
BT . . . . Broader Term (Cross-reference) (Indexing)
BT . . . . Builder's Trials (Shipbuilding)
BT . . . . Bus (Electrical Conductor) Tie (Technical drawings)
B of T . . . . . . Board of Trade
BTA . . . . Better Than Average
BTA . . . . Big Thicket Association
BTA . . . . . . Blood Transfusion Association
BTA . . . . Board of Tax Appeals
BTA . . . . Brith Trumpeldor of America
BTA . . . . British Tourist Authority (Formerly, British Travel Association)
BTAM . . . . . . Basic Telecommunications Access Method (Data processing)
BTAO . . . . . . Bureau of Technical Assistance Operations (UN)
BTAP . . . . . . Bond Trade Analysis Program (IBM)
BTB . . . . Basic Test Battery (Navy)
BTB . . . . Braided Tube Bundle
BTB . . . . Bromthymol (or Bromothymol) Blue (A dye)
BTB . . . . Bus Tie Breaker
BTBC . . . . . . Boehm Test of Basic Concepts (Psychology)
BTC . . . . . . Bachelor of Textile Chemistry
BTC . . . . . . Basic Training Center (Military)
BTC . . . . Before Top Center (Valve position)
BTC . . . . Below Threshold Change (Air Force)

BTC . . . . Bench Test Console
BTC . . . . Beryllium Thrust Chamber
BTC . . . . Bicycle Touring Club (British)
BTC . . . . BIT (Binary Digit) Time Counter (Data processing)
BTC . . . . Business Training College
B of TC . . . . . Bachelor of Textile Chemistry
BTCA . . . . . . Basic Tables of Commissioning Allowances (Navy)
BTCA . . . . . . Border Terrier Club of America
BTCA . . . . . . Boston Terrier Club of America
BTCA . . . . . . Bull Terrier Club of America
BTCC . . . . . . Broome Technical Community College (New York)
B of TCC . . . . Board of Trade of the City of Chicago
BTCG . . . . . . Bipartite Transport Control Group (Post-World War II, Germany)
BT Ch . . . . . . Bachelor of Textile Chemistry
BTD . . . . Bachelor of Textile Dyeing
BTD . . . . Balanced Tape Drive
BTD . . . . Bias Telegraph Distortion
BTD E . . . . . . Bomb Testing Device
BTD . . . . Bulk Tape Degausser
BTDA . . . . . . Benzophenone Tetracarboxylic Dianhydride
BTDC . . . . . . Before Top Dead Center
BT Des . . . . . . Bachelor of Textile Design
BTDL . . . . . . Back Transient Diode Logic (Data processing)
BTE . . . . Bachelor of Textile Engineering
BTE . . . . Battery Terminal Equipment
BTE . . . . Blunt Trailing Edge
BTE . . . . Boltzmann Transport Equation
BTE . . . . Bourdon Tube Element
BTE . . . . Brayton Turboelectric Engine
BTE . . . . British Troops in Egypt
BTE . . . . Bulk Tape Eraser
B of TE . . . . . Bachelor of Textile Engineering
B of TE . . . . . Bureau of Ordnance Fleet Test Equipment (Obsolete)
B Tech . . . . . . Bachelor of Technology
BTEE . . . . . . Brayton Turboelectric Engine
BT Eng . . . . . . Bachelor of Textile Engineering
BTF . . . . Bomb Tail Fuse
BTG . . . . Ball Tooth Gear
BTG . . . . Battery Timing Group
BTG . . . . Beacon Trigger Generator
BTG . . . . Burst Transmission Group
BTGCA . . . . . Burley Tobacco Growers Cooperative Association
BTGJ . . . . . . Ball Tooth Gear Joint
B Th . . . . Bachelor of Theology
BTH . . . . British Thomson-Houston Company
BTH . . . . Bulk Transfer Hose
BTHA . . . . . . British Travel and Holidays Association
BTHU . . . . . . British Thermal Unit (Also, BTU)
BTI . . . . Bank and Turn Indicator
BTI . . . . Boston Theological Institute
BTI . . . . Boy's Towns of Italy
BTI . . . . British Technology Index
BTIS . . . . Bureau of Transportation and International Services (US Postal Service)
BTJ . . . . Ball Tooth Joint
BTJ . . . . Board of Trade Journals
B of TKC . . . . Board of Trade of Kansas City
BTL . . . . Behind the Line (Air Force)
BTL . . . . Bell Telephone Laboratories
BTL . . . . Between Layers (Aviation)
BTL . . . . BTL Corporation (Formerly, Butler Brothers)
BTM . . . . Ballast Tank Meter
BTM . . . . Bellows Tankage Module
BTM . . . . Blast Test Missile
BTM . . . . British Trade Mission
BTM . . . . Brushless Torque Motor
B of TM . . . . . Bachelor of Textile Management
BTMA . . . . . . Boat Trailer Manufacturers Association
BTMA . . . . . . Bow Tie Manufacturers Association
BTMA . . . . . . Braided Trimming Manufacturers Association
BTN . . . . Brussels Tariff Nomenclature (EEC)
BTO . . . . Big-Time Operator (Slang)
BTO . . . . Bombing Through Overcast (By means of RADAR equipment)
BTO . . . . Branch Transportation Office(r) (Army)
BTO . . . . Brussels Treaty Organization (Became Western European Union)
BTP . . . . BMEWS (Ballistic Missile Early Warning System) Test Procedure
BTP . . . . Braille Technical Press
BTP II . . . . . . Boston Tea Party II (An organization)
BTPS . . . . Body Temperature and Pressure, Saturated
BTR . . . . Ballast Tube Resistor
BTR . . . . Barrel-Tile Roof (Technical drawings)
BTR . . . . Block Tape Recorder

BTR . . . . Broadcast and Television Receivers
BTRY. . . . . . . Battery
BTS . . . . Barrier Terminal Strip
BTS . . . . Base of Terminal Service (for airmen)
BTS . . . . Basic Training School
BTS . . . . Battery Test Set
BTS . . . . Beacon Tracking System
BTS . . . . Beam Transport System
BTS . . . . Bio-Telemetry System
BTS . . . . Blessed Trinity Society
BTS . . . . Board of Thoracic Surgery
BTS . . . . Boolean Time Sequence
BTS . . . . Brazilian Thorium Sludge
BTS . . . . Broadcast Transmission Systems
BTSB. . . . . . . Bound to Stay Bound Books, Inc.
BTST. . . . . . . Busy-Tone Start Lead
BTT . . . . Bachelor of Textile Technology
BTT . . . . Beginning to Tape Test
BTU . . . . Basutoland Congress of Trade Unions
BTU . . . . Board of Trade Unit (British)
BTU . . . . British Thermal Unit(s) (Also, BTHU)
BTUC . . . . . . Burma Trade Union Congress
BTV . . . . Blast Test Vehicle
BTVOR . . . . . . (Weather) Broadcast Terminal Very-High Frequency Omni-Range
BTW . . . . Bare Tungsten Wire
BTW . . . . Bimetal Turbine Wheel
BTW . . . . Boat Wave
BTX . . . . Benzene, Toluene, and Xylene
BU . . . . Base Unit (Air Force)
BU . . . . Bend Up
BU . . . . Boston University
BU . . . . Brilliant Uncirculated (Condition of coins) (Numismatics)
BU . . . . Brooklyn Union Gas Company (NYSE symbol) (Wall Street slang name: "Bug")
BU . . . . Builder (Navy rating)
BU . . . . Buoy Boat
BUA . . . . Booster Umbilical Assembly
BUA . . . . Booster Union Assembly
BUA . . . . British United Airways
BUAER . . . . . Bureau of Aeronautics (Later, Naval Air Systems Command)
BUAIR. . . . . . Bureau of Aeronautics (Later, Naval Air Systems Command)
BuB . . . . Bureau of the Budget (Later, OMB)
BUBUD . . . . . Bureau of the Budget (Later, OMB)
BUCO. . . . . . Build-Up Control Organization
BUCON . . . . . Bureau of Construction and Repair (Navy)
BUCOP . . . . . British Union Catalogue of Periodicals
BUC & R . . . . Bureau of Construction and Repair (Navy)
BUCU . . . . . . Burring Cutter
BUD . . . . Budget
BUD . . . . Budget Office (Army)
BUDC . . . . . . Back-Up Digital Computer
BUDOCKS . . . . Bureau of Yards and Docks (Later, NFEC) (Navy)
BUDR . . . . . . Bromodeoxyuridine (Cancer drug)
BUDR . . . . . . Bromouracial Deoxyriboside
BUDS . . . . . . Back-Up Digital System
BUENG. . . . . . Bureau of Engineering (Navy) (Obsolete)
BUF . . . . Black United Front
BUF . . . . British Union of Fascists
BUG. . . . . . . Brooklyn Union Gas Co.
BUG. . . . . . . Buccal Ganglion
BUG. . . . . . . Budget Finance Plan (NYSE symbol)
BUG. . . . . . . Bugler (Navy)
BUIA . . . . . . British United Island Airways
BUIC . . . . . . Backup Interceptor Control (Air Force emergency system)
BUIC . . . . . . Bureau (of Naval Personnel) Unit Identification Code
BUICS. . . . . . Back-Up Interceptor Control System
BUILD. . . . . . Bi-University Institutional Liaison for Development
BUIS . . . . . . Buck Island Reef National Monument
BUISYS. . . . . . Barrier Up Indicator System
BUJ . . . . Baccalaureus Utriusque Juris (Bachelor of Both Laws; i.e., Canon and Civil Laws)
BUL . . . . Bulletin
BUL . . . . Bullock's, Inc. (NYSE symbol) (Delisted)
BUM. . . . . . . Break-Up Missile
BuM . . . . Bureau of Mines
BUMED . . . . . Bureau of Medicine and Surgery (Navy)
BUMIFOM . . . . Bureau Minier de la France d'Outre-Mer (Mining Bureau of Overseas France)
BUMP . . . . . . Boston University Marine Program
BUM & S . . . . . Bureau of Medicine and Surgery (Navy)

BUN. . . . . . . Blood Urea Nitrogen (Physiology)
BUNAV. . . . . . Bureau of Navigation (Navy) (Obsolete)
BUNO . . . . . . Bureau Number (Aircraft identification) (Navy)
BUNY. . . . . . . Board of Underwriters of New York
BUORD . . . . . Bureau of Ordnance (Later, Naval Ordnance Systems Command)
BUP . . . . Back-Up Plate
BUP . . . . Bend Up (Technical drawings)
BUP . . . . British United Press
BUPERS . . . . . Bureau of Naval Personnel
BUPERSCONINSTRBIL . . Bureau of Personnel Controlled Instructor Billets (Navy)
BUPP. . . . . . . Back-Up Plate, Perforated
BUPS . . . . . . Beacon, Ultra Portable "S" Band (Navy)
BUR . . . . Burbank, Calif. (Airport symbol)
BUR . . . . Bureau
BUR . . . . Burlington Industries, Inc. (NYSE symbol)
B Urb Pl . . . . . Bachelor of Urban Planning
BUREC . . . . . . Bureau of Reclamation (Department of the Interior)
BUS . . . . Bank of the United States
BUS . . . . Business
BUSAC . . . . . . Bureau of Ships [Obsolete] Analog Computer
BUSANDA . . . . Bureau of Supply and Accounts (Later, Naval Supply Systems Command)
BUSARB . . . . . British - United States Amateur Rocket Bureau
BUSCI . . . . . . British-United States Convoy Instructions
BUSH . . . . . . Bush Terminal R. R. (AAR code)
BUSH . . . . . . Buy United States Here (Program to procure US-made supplies from overseas subsidiaries of US firms)
BUSHIPS . . . . . Bureau of Ships (Later, Naval Ship Systems Command)
BUSIVISIT . . . . Business Visit (Program) (United States Travel Service)
BUSL . . . . . . Buoy Boat, Stern Loading
BUSRA . . . . . . British-United States Routing Agreement (Shipping)
BUSS . . . . Buoy Underwater Sound Signal
BUSTDS . . . . . Bureau of Standards
BUT . . . . Basic Unit Training
BUT . . . . Bureau of University Travel
BUV . . . . Backscatter Ultraviolet
BUVS . . . . . . Backscatter Ultraviolet Spectrometer
BUWEPS . . . . . Bureau of Naval Weapons (Obsolete)
BUWEPSFLEREADREP . . Bureau of Naval Weapons [Obsolete] Fleet Readiness Representative
BUWEPSFLEREADREPCEN . . Bureau of Naval Weapons [Obsolete] Fleet Readiness Representative, Central
BUWEPSFLEREADREPLANT . . Bureau of Naval Weapons [Obsolete] Fleet Readiness Representative, Atlantic
BUWEPSFLEREADREPPAC . . Bureau of Naval Weapons [Obsolete] Fleet Readiness Representative, Pacific
BUWEPS FR . . . Bureau of Naval Weapons [Obsolete], Fleet Readiness
BUWEPSINST . . . Bureau of Naval Weapons [Obsolete] Instruction
BUWEPSREP . . . Bureau of Naval Weapons [Obsolete] Representative
BUYAC . . . . . . Buying Activity (Air Force)
BUY & D . . . . . Bureau of Yards and Docks (Later, NFEC) (Navy)
BV . . . . Balanced Voltage
BV . . . . Beata Virgo (Blessed Virgin)
BV . . . . Beatitudo Vestra (Your Holiness)
BV . . . . Bellows Valve
BV . . . . Bene Vixit (He Lived a Good Life)
BV . . . . Bible Version (As opposed to the Prayer Book version of the Psalms)
BV . . . . Blessed Virgin
BV . . . . Blood Volume
BV . . . . Blow Valve
BV . . . . Bonnet Valve
BV . . . . Book Value (Business and trade)
BV . . . . Breakdown Voltage
BV . . . . Bundesvorstand
BV . . . . Bureau Voucher (Army)
B/V . . . . Book Value
BVA . . . . Bachelor of Vocational Agriculture
BVA . . . . Blinded Veterans Association
BVA . . . . Board of Veterans Appeals (VA)
BVA . . . . Bulova Watch Company, Inc. (NYSE symbol)
BVAL . . . . . . Blackman's Volunteer Army of Liberation (An organization)
BVBRF . . . . . . Blood Vessel of Branchial Filament
BVC . . . . Buena Vista College (Iowa)
BVD . . . . Beacon Video Digitizer
BVD . . . . Boeing, Vega, Douglas
BVD . . . . BVD Company (Initials stand for Bradley, Voorhies, and Day, organizers of the company, and have come to be used as a generic term for underwear)
BVDT . . . . . . Brief Vestibular Disorientation Test
BVE . . . . Bachelor of Vocational Education
BVE . . . . Bivariate Exponential (Distribution) (Statistics)

BVG . . . . Berliner Verkehrs-Gesellschaft
BVI . . . . Better Vision Institute
BVL . . . . Bowlers' Victory Legion
BVLS . . . . . . Battery-Voltage Limit System
BVM . . . . Bachelor of Veterinary Medicine
BVM. . . . . Beata Virgo Maria (Blessed Virgin Mary)
BVO. . . . . Brominated Vegetable Oil (Soft drink additive)
BVOR . . . . . . (Weather) Broadcast Very-High Frequency Omni-Range
BVP . . . . Beacon Video Processor
BVP . . . . Blood Vessel of Pinnule
BVP . . . . Blood Vessel Prostheses
BVP . . . . Booster Vacuum Pump
BVP . . . . Boundary Value Problem
BVPP . . . . . . Blood Vessel of Palp
BVPS . . . . . . Beacon Video Processing System
BVPS . . . . . . Booster Vacuum Pump System
BVR . . . . Balanced Valve Regulator
BVR . . . . Black Void Reactor
BVRO . . . . . . Base Vehicle Reporting Officer
BVRR . . . . . . Bureau of Veterans Reemployment Rights (Department of Labor)
BVRS . . . . . . Breadboard Visual Reference System
BVS . . . . Bachelor of Veterinary Science
BVS . . . . Bachelor of Veterinary Surgery
BVS . . . . Bevier & Southern R. R. (AAR code)
BVS . . . . Buddhist Vihara Society
BVS . . . . Buoyant Venus Station (NASA)
BVS . . . . Bureau of Vital Statistics
BVW . . . . Binary Voltage Weigher
BW. . . . . Bacteriological Warfare
BW . . . . Bacteriological Warhead
BW. . . . . Bandwidth
BW. . . . . Basal Web
BW. . . . . Below Water
BW. . . . . Bendix-Westinghouse Automotive Air Brake Company
BW . . . . Biological Warfare
BW . . . . Birth Weight
BW. . . . . Biweekly
BW . . . . Black Watch (British military unit)
BW . . . . Blood Wassermann (Medicine)
BW . . . . Blunted Wedge
BW . . . . Board of Works (British)
BW . . . . Body Whorl
BW. . . . . Bonded Warehouse
BW. . . . . Bonded Winery
BW. . . . . Borg-Warner Corporation
BW . . . . Both Ways (Technical drawings)
BW . . . . Business Week (A magazine)
B & W . . . . . . Babcock and Wilcox Company
B & W . . . . . . Black and White (Photography)
B & W . . . . . . Bread and Water
B & W. . . . . . . Brown & Williamson Tobacco Corp.
BWA . . . . Backward Wave Amplifier
BWA . . . . Baptist World Alliance
BWA. . . . . Bent Wire Antenna
BWA. . . . . Boxing Writers Association
BWA . . . . Building Waterproofers Association
BWAA . . . . . . Bowling Writers Association of America
BWAR . . . . . . Budget Workload Analysis Report (Navy)
BWB . . . . Brown & Bigelow (NYSE symbol)
BWBR . . . . . . Bureau of Naval Weapons [Obsolete] Branch Representative
BWC . . . . Backward-Wave Converter
BWC . . . . . . Baldwin Wallace College (Ohio)
BWC . . . . . . Baltic Women's Council
BWC. . . . . Basic Weight Controller
BWC. . . . . Board of War Communications (World War II)
BWC. . . . . Bonded Wine Cellar
BWC. . . . . British War Cabinet
BWC . . . . . . Broadband Waveguide Circulator
BWC. . . . . Bureau Weather Control
B/WCC . . . . . . Bomb to Warhead Conversion Components
BWCP . . . . . . Base Wire Communications Program (Air Force)
BWCP . . . . . . Bench Welder Control Panel
BW/CW. . . . . . Biological Warfare/Chemical Warfare
BWD . . . . Bacillary White Diarrhea (Veterinary medicine)
BWDA . . . . . . Bicycle Wholesale Distributors Association
BWE . . . . Bachelor of Welding Engineering
BWF . . . . Bailett Weighting Function
BWF . . . . Breit-Wigner Formula
BWF . . . . British Wool Federation
BWF . . . . Burst Wave Form

BWF . . . . Butt Welded Filter
BWFRR . . . . . Bureau of Naval Weapons [Obsolete] Fleet Readiness Representative
BWG . . . . Bestwall Gypsum Company (NYSE symbol) (Delisted)
BWG . . . . Birmingham Wire Gage
BWGMSB. . . . . Bright Wire Goods Manufacturers Service Bureau
BWH . . . . Blower Wheel Housing
BWI . . . . British West Indies
BWIA . . . . . . British West Indian Airways, Ltd.
BWIU . . . . Building Workers' Industrial Union (Australia)
BWK. . . . . Batch Weighing Kit
BWK . . . . Brillouin-Wentzel-Kramers (Physics)
BWL . . . . Belt Work Line
BWL . . . . Biological Warfare Laboratory
BWLT . . . . . . Bow Light
BWM . . . . International Broom and Whisk Makers' Union of America
BWMB. . . . . . . British Wool Marketing Board
BWN . . . . Brown Co. (NYSE symbol)
BWO . . . . Backward Wave Oscillator
BWOC . . . . . . Big Woman on Campus (Slang)
BWOS. . . . . . . Backward Wave Oscillator Synchronizer
BWOT . . . . . . Backward Wave Oscillator Tube
BWP . . . . Ballistic Wind Plotter
BWP. . . . . Basic War Plan (Navy)
BWP . . . . Bureau of Work Programs (Department of Labor)
BWPA . . . . . . Backward Wave Parametric Amplifier
BWPA . . . . . . Backward Wave Power Amplifier
BWR . . . . Bandwidth Ratio
BWR . . . . Biweekly Report
BWR . . . . Boiling Water Reactor (AEC)
BWR . . . . Bureau of Naval Weapons [Obsolete] Representative
BWRA . . . . . . British Welding Research Association
BWRL . . . . . . Bollweevil Research Laboratory (Department of Agriculture)
BWRL . . . . . . Bureau of War Risk Litigation
BWRS . . . . . . British War Relief Society (in US)
BWRWS . . . . . Biological Warfare Rapid Warning System (Army)
BWS . . . . Batch Weighing System
BWS . . . . Battlefield Weapons System
BWS . . . . Beaufort Wind Scale
BWS . . . . Beveled Wood Siding (Technical drawings)
BWS . . . . Biological Weapons System
BWS . . . . British Water Color Society
BWS . . . . Brown Group, Inc. (Formerly, Brown Shoe Company, Inc.) (NYSE symbol)
BWSC. . . . . . . Boys of Woodcraft Sportsmen's Clubs
BWSL . . . . . . Battlefield Weapons Systems Laboratory
BWSO . . . . . . Backward Wave Sweep Oscillator
BWT . . . . Boeing Wind Tunnel
BWT . . . . Bohr-Wheeler Theory
BWT . . . . Both Way Trunk
BWTA . . . . . . Boston Wool Trade Association
BWTF . . . . . . Bank Wire Transfer of Funds
BWTP . . . . . . Bureau of Work-Training Programs (Department of Labor)
BWTR . . . . . . Babcock and Wilcox Test Reactor
BWTSDS . . . . . Base Wire and Telephone System Development Schedule (Air Force)
BWV . . . . Back-Water Valve
BWVA . . . . . . British War Veterans of America
BX . . . . Base Exchange
BX . . . . Bendix Corporation (NYSE symbol)
BXK . . . . Broadband X-Band Klystron
BY . . . . Billion Years
BY . . . . Blowing Spray (Meteorology)
BY . . . . Bucyrus-Erie Company (NYSE symbol)
BY . . . . Budget Year
BYAA . . . . . . Byelorussian Youth Association of America
BYC . . . . Brewers Yeast Council
BYD . . . . Bureau of Yards and Docks (Later, NFEC)
BYDV . . . . . . Barley Yellow Dwarf Virus
BYK . . . . Bayuk Cigars, Inc. (NYSE symbol)
BYM-AG. . . . . Bornu Youth Movement-Action Group Alliance (Nigeria)
BYMS. . . . . . . British Yard Motor Minesweepers
BYO. . . . . Bring Your Own (Liquor) (Party invitation notation)
BYOB . . . . . . Bring your Own Booze (or Bottle) (Party invitation notation)
BYPU . . . . . . Baptist Young People's Union
BYT . . . . Bright Young Things (The younger set) (British)
BYU . . . . Brigham Young University (Utah)
BZ . . . . Bild Zeitung (Picture newspaper) (Germany)
BZ . . . . Blank when Zero
BZ . . . . Bnai Zion
BZA . . . . Board of Zoning Adjustment
BZA . . . . Bombenzielapparat (Bomb sight) (German military - World War II)

BZFX . . . . Brazing Fixture
BZG . . . . Bombenzielgeraet (Bomb sight) (German military – World War II)
BZH . . . . Benzaldehyde
BZOH . . . . Benzoic Acid

BZPCA . . . . . . British Zone Petroleum Coordinating Authority (Post-World War II, Germany)
BZ Sc . . . . . . Bachelor of Zoological Science
BZW . . . . Bare Zirconium Wire
BZW . . . . Be Zichungs Weise (Respectively) (German)

C

C . . . . Acceleration Correction
C . . . . Cable
C . . . . Caecum
C . . . . Caesar
C . . . . Calm (i.e., no wind)
C . . . . Calorie
C . . . . Can (Buoy) (Maps and charts)
C . . . . Canadian
C . . . . Canceled
C . . . . Candle (Illumination)
C . . . . Canine Tooth (Dentistry)
C . . . . Canon
C . . . . Capacitance
C . . . . Cape (Maps and charts)
C . . . . Captain
C . . . . Captain (Worn on captain's uniform) (Hockey)
C . . . . Caput (Head)
C . . . . Carat (Unit of measure for precious stones equal to 200 milligrams; see also meaning re gold)
C . . . . Carat (Signifies a twenty-fourth part; i.e., 24-carat gold is pure gold, 12-carat gold is half gold, half other substances)
C . . . . Carbon (Chemical element)
C . . . . Cargo/Transport (Designation for all US military aircraft)
C . . . . Case
C . . . . Cash (NYSE symbol)
C . . . . Cast
C . . . . Castle
C . . . . Catalog
C . . . . Catcher (Baseball)
C . . . . Cathode
C . . . . Catholic
C . . . . Caught (by) (In cricket)
C . . . . Cause
C . . . . Celsius (Centigrade) Temperature Scale
C . . . . Cent
C . . . . Centavo (Monetary unit in many Spanish-American countries)
C . . . . Center (A position in football, lacrosse, basketball)
c . . . . Centi (A prefix meaning divided by 100)
C . . . . Centigrade (Celsius)
C . . . . Centime (Monetary unit in France)
C . . . . Centimeter
C . . . . Cento (Composition compiled from other works)
C . . . . Central
C . . . . Central Standard Time (Aviation)
C . . . . Centum (Hundred)
C . . . . Century
C . . . . Certified
C . . . . Chairman
C . . . . Chancellor
C . . . . Chancery
C . . . . Change (Army) (Used in combinations only)
C . . . . Chapter
C . . . . Charlotte (North Carolina) (Mint mark, when appearing on US coins)
C . . . . Chief
C . . . . Child
C . . . . Choppy, Short, or Cross Sea
C . . . . Chronometer Time
C . . . . Chrysler Corporation (NYSE symbol)
C . . . . Church
C . . . . Circa (About)
C . . . . Circling (Approach and landing charts) (Aviation)
C . . . . Circuit
C . . . . Circular

C . . . . Circum
C . . . . Circumference
C . . . . Cirrus
C . . . . Class (Used with number for Navy rating as: 1c; i.e., first class)
C . . . . Clearance
C . . . . Clockwise
C . . . . Cloudy
C . . . . Coast Guard (Military flight identification prefix)
C . . . . Cobalt
C . . . . Cocaine (Slang)
C . . . . Codex
C . . . . Coefficient
C . . . . Cognate
C . . . . Cold
C . . . . College
C . . . . Color
C . . . . Color Index (Astronomy)
C . . . . Colt
C . . . . Combat (In unit designations and symbols only)
C . . . . Command Paper
C . . . . Commandant (Coast Guard)
C . . . . Commander; as: CNAB (Commander Naval Air Bases)
C . . . . Commissary (Marine Corps)
C . . . . Common Meter
C . . . . Common Time
C . . . . Companion
C . . . . Compass
C . . . . Complex
C . . . . Compliance
C . . . . Compression of Earth
C . . . . Comptroller
C . . . . Concentration
c . . . . Concentration by volume (Chemistry)
C . . . . Condemned
C . . . . Condemno (I Condemn) (Used by Romans in criminal trials)
C . . . . Conductivity
C . . . . Conductor
C . . . . Confessor
C . . . . Confidential
C . . . . Congius (Apothecaries' gallon)
C . . . . Congregation
C . . . . Congress
C . . . . Conservative (Politics)
C . . . . Constable
C . . . . Constant
C . . . . Consul
C . . . . Contact
C . . . . Continental
C . . . . Contra
C . . . . Contraction
C . . . . Contralto
C . . . . Control
C . . . . Copper
C . . . . Copy
C . . . . Copyright
C . . . . Cord
C . . . . Cordoba (Monetary unit) (Nicaragua)
C . . . . Corolla
C . . . . Corps
C . . . . Correction
C . . . . Cost
C . . . . Cotton
C . . . . Coulomb (Quantity of electricity)

C	Count
C	Coupon
C	Course (Navigation)
C	Course Angle (Navigation)
C	Court
C	Cousin
C	Cove
C	Created
C	Crowned
C	Cruiser
C	Cubic
C	Cum
C	Cup(s)
C	Curate, Curacy
C	Curie(s) (Unit of measurement of radiation)
C	Currency
C	Current
C	Cushion Lift
C	Cycle (Electricity)
C	Cylinder
C	Cytosine
C	Minor league baseball league classification (Sixth highest rank, for a league composed of teams from cities with aggregate population of 150,000 to 250,000)
C	One Hundred (Roman numeral)
C	One Hundred Dollar Bill (C Note) (Slang)
C	Protected Cruiser
c	Speed of light in vacuum (Symbol)
C (Bomb)	Cobalt Bomb
°C	Degree Celcius
C^{14}	Radioactive Carbon (Key substance for determination of age of objects by measurement of radioactivity)
C3	Command, Control, and Communications
4C	Community Coordinated Child Care Program (Also, CCCC)
1-C	Selective Service Class (for a Member of Armed Forces of the US, the National Oceanic and Atmospheric Administration, or the Public Health Service)
2-C	Selective Service Class (for Registrant Deferred from Military Service Because of Agricultural Occupation)
4-C	Selective Service Class (for Aliens Not Currently Liable for Military Service)
1/C	Single Conductor
2/C	Two-Conductor (Wire or cable)
3/C	Three-Conductor (Wire or cable)
4/C	Four-Conductor (Wire or cable)
CA	Assistant Commandant (Coast Guard)
Ca	Calcium (Chemical element)
CA	Calibrated Altitude (Navigation)
CA	California
CA	Canada (NATO)
CA	Cancer
CA	Candy Apple (Bowdlerized version)
CA	Capital Account
CA	Capital Airlines, Inc.
CA	Capital Asset
CA	Carbonic Anhydrase (Biochemistry)
CA	Cariolis Absorber
CA	Cartographic Assistant (Ministry of Agriculture, Fisheries, and Food) (British)
CA	Catecholamine (Biochemistry)
CA	Centare (Unit of area in metric system)
CA	Central Airways
CA	Central America
CA	Cephalic Artery
CA	Certificate of Airworthiness
CA	Charge d'Affaires (State Department Foreign Service)
CA	Chartered Accountant
CA	Checks Anonymous
CA	Chemical Abstracts (A publication)
CA	Chief Accountant
CA	Choline-Adrenalin (Test) (Medicine)
CA	Chronological Age (Psychology)
CA	Church Association (British)
Ca	Circa (About)
CA	Civil Affairs
CA	Civil Authorities
CA	Claim Agent (Insurance)
CA	Clear and Add
CA	Clerical Aptitude (Test)
CA	Clerical Assistant (British)
CA	Clipping Amplifier

CA	Coast Artillery
CA	Co-Axial
CA	Cold Air
CA	Coll'arco (With the bow) (Music)
CA	Combat Aircrew(man)
CA	Commandant Assistant (Coast Guard)
CA	Commercial Agent
CA	Commercial Air
CA	Commitment Authorization
CA	Compensation Act (Forms)
CA	Compressed Air
CA	Comptroller of the Army
CA	Computer Assembly
CA	Confederate Army
CA	Consular Agent
CA	Contemporary Authors (A biographical reference book)
CA	Continental Airways
CA	Contingencies of the Army
CA	Contract Administrator
CA	Contract Authorization
CA	Control Assembly
CA	Controlled Atmosphere
CA	Controller of Accounts
CA	Convening Authority
CA	Convention Africaine (African Covenant)
CA	Cor Anglais (English Horn)
CA	Corpus Allatum
CA	Cosmopolitan Associates
CA	Cost Account(ant)
CA	Council Accepted (Medicine)
CA	County Attorney
CA	Court of Appeal
CA	Cover Aft
CA	Cranial Academy
CA	Credit Account
CA	Croup-Associated (Virology)
CA	Crown Agent
CA	Ctenidial Analog
CA	Cuenta Abierta (Open Account) (Business and trade) (Spain)
CA	Curates' Alliance (British)
CA	Curing Agent
CA	Current Account
CA	Current Assets
CA	Heavy Cruiser (Navy symbol)
CA	United States Court of Appeals (Formerly, United States Circuit Court of Appeals)
C/A	Capital Account (Business and trade)
C/A	Coat of Arms
C/A	Cost of Arms (Army)
C/A	Credit Account (Business and trade)
C & A	Chicago and Alton Railroad Company
C & A	Classification and Audit
C & A	Compartment and Access (Technical drawings)
C & A	Contract and Administration
C of A	Certificate of Airworthiness
CAA	Caging Amplifier Assembly
CAA	Cantors Assembly of America
CAA	Catholic Anthropological Association
CAA	Catholic Art Association
CAA	Central African Airways Corporation
CAA	Central American Airways (Kentucky)
CAA	Chaplains' Aid Association
CAA	Chief of Army Aviation
CAA	Chile-American Association
CAA	Circular Aperture Antenna
CAA	Citizens Assessment Administration
CAA	Civil Aeronautics Administration (Later, part of FAA)
CAA	Civil Aeronautics Authority
CAA	Clean Air Act
CAA	Collectors of American Art
CAA	College Art Association of America
CAA	Commission on Art and Antiquities
CAA	Community Action Agencies (Department of Labor)
CAA	Computer Amplifier Alarm
CAA	Conference of Asian Affairs
CAA	Correctional Administrators Association of America
CAA	Cremation Association of America
CAA	Crime Aboard Aircraft
CAA	Croatian Academy of America
CAA	Cyanoacrylate Adhesive
CAAA	California Agricultural Aircraft Association

CAAA.......	Chief of Army Audit Agency
CAAA.......	Coast Artillery (Antiaircraft)
CAAA.......	College Art Association of America
CAAA	Composers, Authors and Artists of America
CA(AA)......	Coast Artillery (Antiaircraft)
CAAAL	Classified Abstract Archive of the Alcohol Literature
CAAB.......	California Asparagus Advisory Board
CAAB.......	California Avocado Advisory Board
CAAC.......	Civilian Aviation Advisory Committee (Air Defense Planning Board)
CAAC.......	College Admissions Assistance Center
CAAC.......	Combat Alert Aircrew (Air Force)
CAADRP	Civil Aircraft Airworthiness Data Recording Program (British)
CAAF.......	Chief, Army Air Forces
CAAF.......	Combined Allied Air Forces
CAAG	Civil Aviation Advisory (or Assistance) Group
CAAHA	Council on Arteriosclerosis of the American Heart Association
CAAN	Continental Advertising Agency Network (Later, Advertising and Marketing International Network)
CAAR.......	Compressed Air Accumulator Rocket
CAAS.......	Canadian Association for American Studies
CAAS.......	Chinese Association for the Advancement of Science
CAAS.......	Combined Arms and Support (Army)
CAAS.......	Computer-Aided Approach Spacing (Aviation)
CAA-WTS	Civil Aviation Authority -- War Training Service
CAB.......	Captive Air Bubble (Surface effect ship)
CAB	Cellulose Acetate-Butyrate (Chemical)
CAB.......	Chicago Alliance of Businessmen
CAB.......	Civil Aeronautics Board (Independent government agency)
CAB.......	Civil Aeronautics Bulletin
CAB.......	Civil Air Branch (Air Force)
CAB.......	Collating and Binding
CAB.......	Commonwealth Agricultural Bureaux
CAB.......	Consumers' Advisory Board
CAB.......	Contract Appeals Board (VA)
CAB.......	Cooperative Analysis of Broadcasting
CABA.......	Charge Account Bankers Association
CABAL	Clifford, Arlington, Buckingham, Ashley, Lauderdale (Ministers of Charles II of England)
CABB	Captured Air Bubble Boat (Navy)
CABEI.......	Central American Bank for Economic Integration
C-ABM......	Chinese-Oriented Antiballistic Missile System (Army)
CABMA......	Canadian Association of British Manufacturers and Agencies
CABMA......	College Athletic Business Managers Association
CABPP	Commission for Acceleration of Black Participation in Psychology
CABR.......	Cabrillo National Monument
CABRA	Copper and Brass Research Association
CAC.......	Cable Access Cover
CAC.......	California Aeronautics Commission
CAC.......	Canadian Armoured Corps
CAC	Cardiac Accelerator Center (Physiology)
CAC	Caribbean Air Command (Air Force)
CAC.......	Catholic Anthropological Conference
CAC	Central American Club of New York
CAC	Changing to Approach Control (Aviation)
CAC.......	Chief of Air Corps
CAC	Cigarette Advertising Code, Inc.
CAC.......	Citizens Advocate Center (Antipoverty organization)
CAC.......	Civil Administration Committee (US Military Government, Germany)
CAC.......	Clear All Channels
CAC	Coast Artillery Corps (Army)
CAC.......	College Admissions Center
CAC	Combat Air Crew
CAC	Comite Administratif de Coordination (des Nations Unies) (Aviation)
CAC	Commander Air Center
CAC	Commonwealth Aircraft Corporation, Ltd. (Australia)
CAC.......	Complete Address Constant
CAC.......	Computer-Assisted Counseling (Proposed for Air Force)
CAC.......	Consolidated Aircraft Corporation (Later, General Dynamics Corporation)
CAC	Consolidated Athletic Commission
CAC.......	Constant Alert Cycle
CAC	Consumer's Advisory Council
CAC	Contact Approach Control (Aviation)
CAC.......	Contact Area Commander
CAC.......	Continental Air Command (Air Force)
CAC.......	Continental Army Command
CAC.......	Control and Coordination (Army)
CAC.......	CONVAIR (Consolidated-Vultee Aircraft Corp.) Astronautics Corporation (Later, General Dynamics Corporation)
CAC.......	Cooperation and Coordination
CAC	Correction Action Committee
CAC	Current Actions Center

CACA	Carlsbad Caverns National Park
CACA	Chinese American Citizens Alliance
CACA	Citizens Association for the Care of Animals
CACA.......	Council Against Communist Aggression
CACC.......	Civil Avaition Communication Center (Canada)
CACCE	Council of American Chambers of Commerce in Europe
CACEED	Conference of Americans of Central and Eastern European Descent
CACH.......	Canyon de Chelly National Monument
CACHE	Computer Aids for Chemical Engineering Education (National Academy of Engineering)
CACHE	Computer-Controlled Automated Cargo Handling Envelope
CACI	Community Arts Councils, Incorporated
CACI	Consolidated Analysis Centers, Incorporated
CACL	Canadian Association of Children's Librarians
CACL	Castle Clinton National Monument
CACM	Central American Common Market
CACO	Cape Cod National Seashore (National Park Service designation)
CACR.......	Clean Air Car Race
CACR	Council for Agricultural and Chemurgic Research
CACS	California Aqueduct Control System
CACS	Continental Airways and Communications Service (Air Force)
CACSW......	Citizens' Advisory Council on the Status of Women
CACT.......	Civil Air Carrier Turbojet
CACT	Command Automatic Card Tester
CACUCS	Conference of Administrators of College and University Counseling Services
CACUL	Canadian Association of College and University Libraries
CACW	Chinese-American Composite Wing (Air Force)
CAC & W....	Continental Air Control and Warning
CACWV......	Committee to Aid Cold War Veterans
CAD........	Cadiz R. R. (AAR code)
CAD........	Canadian Air Division
CAD........	Cartridge-Activated Devices (Military)
CAD	Cash Against Documents (Banking)
CAD	Center Area Discrete (Channel)
CAD........	Central Aircraft Dispatch
CAD........	Chief of Air Defense
CAD........	Civil Affairs Division (Military)
CAD........	Comite d'Aide au Developpement (OCDE)
CAD........	Commutated Aerial Direction
CAD	Compensated Avalanche Diode
CAD........	Computation and Analysis Division (NASA)
CAD........	Computer Access Device
CAD........	Computer-Aided Design
CAD........	Computer-Assisted Diagnosis
CAD........	Continuous Acceleration Device
CAD........	Contract Award Date
CAD........	Corrective Action Directive
CADA	Campus Americans for Democratic Action
CADA	Centre d'Analyse Documentaire pour l'Archeologie
CADA.......	Clear Air Dot Angle
CADC.......	Central Air Data Computer
CADC	Combined Administrative Committee
CADC.......	Continental Air Defense Command (Air Force)
CADCO	Core and Drum Corrector
CADD.......	Combat Air Delivery Division (Air Force)
CADDAD.....	Central Analog Data Distributing and Computing
CADDE	Central Automatic Digital Data Encoder (NASA)
CADEL	Comite pour la Defense de la Legalite (Committee for Legal Defense) (Dahomey)
CADET	Computer-Aided Design and Electrical Test
CADET	Computer-Aided Design Experiment Translator
CADETRON ...	Cadet Practice Squadron
CADF.......	Central Air Defense Force
CADF.......	Commutated Antenna Direction Finder
CADF	Contract Administrative Data File
CADFISS	Computation and Data Flow Integrated Subsystem
CADI	Central Apollo Data Index (NASA)
CADIC	Chemical Analysis Detection Instrumentation Control
CADIC	Compagnie Africaine des Ingenieurs-Conseils
CADIC	Computer-Aided Design of Integrated Circuits
CADIN	Continental Air Defense Integration, North (Air Force)
CADIZ	Canadian Air Defence Identification Zone
CADM	Central German Administrative Department (Economic) Committee (US Military Government, Germany)
CADM	CONUS (Continental United States) Air Defense Modernization
CADO	Central Air Documents Office
CADO	Chief, Airport District Office (FAA)
CADO.......	Current Actions Duty Officer (Air Force)
CADOCS.....	Carrier Aircraft Data Operations Control System (Navy)

CADPIN . . . . . Customs Automatic Data Processing Intelligence Network (Treasury Department)
CADPO. . . . . . Communications and Data Processing Operation
CADRC . . . . . . Combined Air Documents Research Center
CADS . . . . . . Cellular Absorbed Dose Spectrometer
CADS . . . . . . Central Air Data System (Air Force)
CADS . . . . . . Continental Air Defense System (Air Force)
CADSS . . . . . Combined Analog-Digital Systems Simulator (Data processing)
CADW . . . . . . Civil Air Defense Warning
CAE . . . . Canadian Aviation Electronics
CAE . . . . Carrier Aircraft Equipment
CAE . . . . Centro Anglo-Espanol
CAE . . . . Chartered Association Executive (Designation given by American Society of Association Executives)
CAE . . . . Chicago Aurora & Elgin Railroad Corporation (AAR code)
CAE . . . . Chief Activation (or Administrative) Engineer
CAE . . . . Compagnie Europeenne d'Automatisme (Became part of Compagnie Internationale d'Informatique)
CAE . . . . Continental Aviation and Engineering Corporation
CAEA . . . . . . California Aviation Education Association
CAEA . . . . . . Central American Economics Association
CAEC . . . . . . Committee of the Acta Endocrinologica Countries
CAEL . . . . . . Consolidated Aerospace Equipment List
CAEM . . . . . . Certified Assistant Export Manager (Designation given by American Society of International Executives)
CAER . . . . . . Chief Aerographer
CAERM . . . . . Chief Aerographer's Mate
CAES . . . . . . Connecticut Agricultural Experiment Station
CAF . . . . Canadian Force
CAF . . . . Central African Federation (Disbanded Dec. 31, 1963)
CAF . . . . Chinese Air Force (Nationalist)
CAF . . . . Clean Assembly Facility
CAF . . . . Cleared As Filed
CAF . . . . Clerical, Administrative & Fiscal (Used with number, as, CAF-6, to indicate grade of position) (Civil Service)
CAF . . . . Cloth Assistance Factor (Textiles)
CAF . . . . CNA Financial Corp. (NYSE symbol)
CAF . . . . Complete Assembly for Ferry (Air Force)
CAF . . . . Congressional Action Fund
CAF . . . . Conjunctive Alteration File
CAF . . . . Continental Air Forces
CAF . . . . Cost and Freight
CAF . . . . Cout, Assurance, Fret (Cost, Insurance, Freight)
CAF . . . . Critical Area Flag
CAF . . . . Curates' Augmentation Fund (British)
CAFA . . . . . . Chicago Academy of Fine Arts
CAFAC . . . . . . Commander All Forces, Aruba-Curacao
CAFAF . . . . . . Commander, Amphibious Force, Atlantic Fleet
CAFB . . . . . . Charleston Air Force Base
CAFB . . . . . . Cooke Air Force Base (Later, VAFB)
C of AFCH. . . . Chief of Air Force Chaplains
CAFD . . . . . . Contact Analog Flight Display
CAFEA-ICC . . . Commission on Asian and Far Eastern Affairs of the International Chamber of Commerce
CAFEE . . . . . Critical Assembly Fuel Element Exchange (AEC)
CAFIT . . . . . . Computer-Assisted Fault Isolation Test
CAFM . . . . . . Commercial Air Freight Movement
CAFMS . . . . . Continental Association of Funeral and Memorial Societies
CAFO. . . . . . Command Accounting and Finance Office
CAFRAD . . . . . Centre Africain de Formation et de Recherche Administratives pour la Developpement (African Training and Research Center in Administration for Development)
CAFSC . . . . . Control Air Force Specialty Code
CAFT . . . . . . Combined Agencies Field Team (US Military Government, Germany)
CAFT . . . . . . Consolidated Advance Field Teams
CAFTA . . . . . Central American Free Trade Area
CAG . . . . Carrier Air Group (Navy)
CAG . . . . Catholic Accountants Guild
CAG. . . . . . . Civil Air Guard (British)
CAG. . . . . . . Combat Applications Group
CAG . . . . Combat Arms Group (Army)
CAG . . . . Combined Arms Group (Army)
CAG . . . . Commander of the Air Group (Navy)
CAG. . . . . . . Commercial Artists' Guild
CAG . . . . Committee on Autonomous Groups
CAG . . . . Composers-Authors Guild
CAG . . . . Computer Applications Group (Air Force)
CAG . . . . Concert Artist Guild
CAG . . . . Constant Altitude Glide
CAG . . . . Guided Missile Heavy Cruiser (Navy symbol)
CAGA . . . . . . Catholic Actors Guild of America

CAGA . . . . . . Church Architectural Guild of America
CAGC . . . . . . Clutter Automatic Gain Control
CAGC . . . . . . Coded Automatic Gain Control
CAGE. . . . . . . California Almond Growers Exchange
CAGE . . . . . . Canadian Air-Ground Environment
CAGE. . . . . . . Compiler and Assembler by General Electric
CAGE. . . . . . . Convicts' Association for a Good Environment
CAGEL . . . . . Consolidated Aerospace Ground Equipment List
CAGI . . . . . . Compressed Air and Gas Institute
CAG(N) . . . . . Guided Missile Heavy Cruiser (Nuclear propelled) (Navy symbol)
CAGNY . . . . . Chemical Advertisers Group of New York
CAGR . . . . . . Casa Grand Ruins National Monument
CAGS . . . . . . Certificate of Advanced Graduate Study
CAH. . . . . . . Calumet & Hecla, Inc. (NYSE symbol) (Delisted)
CAH. . . . . . . Congenital Adrenal Hyperplasia (Medicine)
CAHA . . . . . . Cape Hatteras National Seashore (National Park Service designation)
CAHPER . . . . . Canadian Association for Health, Physical Education, and Recreation
CAHR. . . . . . . Council for the Advancement of Hospital Recreation
CAHS. . . . . . . Comprehensive Automation of the Hydrometeorological Service
CAI . . . . Canadian Aeronautical Institute
CAI . . . . Canvas Awning Institute
CAI . . . . Chinese Army in India
CAI . . . . Club Alpino Italiano
CAI . . . . Club Atletico Independiente
CAI . . . . Coded Acoustic Interrogator
CAI . . . . Computer Analog Input
CAI . . . . Computer Applications, Incorporated
CAI . . . . Computer-Assisted Instruction
CAI . . . . Conference Aeronautique Internationale
CAI . . . . Configuration Acceptance Inspection
CAI . . . . Configuration Audit Inspection (Army)
CAI . . . . Conjunctive Alteration Indicator
CAI . . . . Constructive Action, Incorporated
CAI . . . . Counselor Activity Inventory (Guidance)
CAIA . . . . . . Clock Assemblers and Importers Association
CAID . . . . . . Convention of American Instructors of the Deaf
CAIDO . . . . . . Chief Advisor, International District Office (FAA)
CAIFO . . . . . . Chief Advisor, International Field Office (FAA)
CAIMS . . . . . Conventional Ammunition Integrated Management System
CAINS . . . . . Carrier Aircraft Inertial Navigation System
CAIOP . . . . . . Computer Analog Input-Output
CAIP . . . . . . Catholic Association for International Peace
CAIR . . . . . . Cost Analysis Information Report (Air Force)
CAIRA . . . . . Central Automated Inventory and Referral Activity (Organization for operation of CAIRS) (Air Force)
CAIRC . . . . . Caribbean Air Command (Air Force)
CAIRS. . . . . . . Central Automated Inventory and Referral System (Air Force)
CAIRS. . . . . . . Computer-Assisted Interactive Resources Scheduling System
CAIS . . . . . . Canadian Association for Information Science
CAISIM . . . . . Computer-Assisted Industrial Simulation (Army)
CAITS . . . . . Chemical Agent Identification Training Set
CAJ . . . . Caulked Joint
CAJ . . . . Consumers' Association of Jamaica
CAK . . . . Conical Alignment Kit
CAK . . . . Cube Alignment Kit
CAL . . . . Calculated Average Life
CAL . . . . Calendar
CAL . . . . Caliber
CAL . . . . California
CAL . . . . Calorie
CAL . . . . Center for Applied Linguistics
CAL . . . . Command Authorization List
CAL . . . . Compressed Air Loudspeaker
CAL . . . . Computer-Assisted Learning
CAL . . . . Conservation Analytical Laboratory (Smithsonian Institution)
CAL . . . . Continental Air Lines, Inc. (NYSE symbol)
CAL . . . . Continuity Accept Limit
CAL . . . . Conversational Algebraic Language (Adaptation of JOSS language) (Data processing)
CAL . . . . Cornell Aeronautical Laboratory
CAL . . . . Course Author Language (Data processing)
CALA . . . . . . Combined Administrative Liquidating Agency (Microfilmed SHAEF documents for each participating country after SHAEF was disbanded) (Post-World War II)
CALC . . . . . . Calculated
CALCAV . . . . . Clergy and Laymen Concerned about Vietnam
CALCOFI . . . . California Cooperative Oceanic Fishery Investigations
CALF . . . . . . Combined Allied Land Forces
CALIB . . . . . . Calibrate
CALIBN . . . . . Calibration
CALIF. . . . . . . California

CALIT . . . . . . California Institute of Technology (Also, CALTECH or CIT)
CALL . . . . Composite Aeronautical Load List
CALL . . . . Counseling at the Local Level (Small Business Administration)
CALM . . . . . . Catapult Arresting Gear and Landing Aids Maintenance (Aviation)
CALM . . . . . . Child Abuse Listening Mediation (An organization)
CALM . . . . . . Citizens Against Legalized Murder (Opposes death penalty for criminals)
CALM . . . . . . Collected Algorithm for Learning Machines (Data processing)
CALM . . . . . . Computer-Assisted Library Mechanization
CALMS . . . . . Continuous Automatic Line Monitoring System
CALO . . . . . . Cape Lookout National Seashore (National Park Service designation)
CALOGSIM . . Computer-Assisted Logistics Simulation (Army)
CALOLL . . . . . Catholic Aviation League of Our Lady of Loreto
CALROSA . . . . Committee on American Library Resources on South Asia (Later, CALROSEA)
CALROSEA . . . Committee on American Library Resources on Southeast Asia (Formerly, CALROSA)
CALSU . . . . . . Combat Airlift Support Unit (Air Force)
CALTECH . . . . California Institute of Technology (Also, CALIT or CIT)
CALUTRON . . . California University Cyclotron
CAM . . . . Administrative Management Division (Coast Guard)
CAM . . . . Camouflage
CAM . . . . Catapult Aircraft Merchantship (Used by British RAF to catapult Hurricane fighter planes from ships to defend convoys from enemy bombers) (World War II)
CAM . . . . Central Address Memory (Data processing)
CAM . . . . Central American Mission
CAM . . . . Checkout & Maintenance
CAM . . . . Chief, Aircraft Maintenance
CAM . . . . Christian Amendment Movement
CAM . . . . Circular Area Method
CAM . . . . Civil Aeronautics Manual
CAM . . . . Civil Air Mission
CAM . . . . Commercial Air Movement Number
CAM . . . . Composite Army-Marine
CAM. . . . . . . Computer Address Matrix
CAM . . . . Computer-Aided Manufacturing
CAM . . . . Computer Assisted Maintenance
CAM . . . . Consolidated Aircraft Maintenance
CAM . . . . Content-Addressable Memory (Data processing)
CAM. . . . . . . Contract Air Mail
CAM . . . . Contract Audit Manual
CAM . . . . Contractor-Acquired Materiel
CAM . . . . Crassulacean Acid Metabolism (Biochemistry)
CAM . . . . Cruise and Maintain (Aviation)
CAMA . . . . . . Civil Aerospace Medical Association
CAMAE . . . . . Central Air Materiel Area, Europe
CAMAL . . . . . Continuously Airborne Missile Launching and Low-Level (Penetration) (Air Force)
CAMAR . . . . . Common Aperture Multifunction Array RADAR
CAMCOS . . . . Computer-Assisted Maintenance Planning and Control System
CAMEA . . . . . Comite des Applications Militaires de l'Energie Atomique (France)
CAMECA . . . . Compagnie d'Applications Mecaniques a l'Electronique au Cinema et a l'Atomistique (French company which invented Scopitone, a coin-operated machine which projects musical movies in places of entertainment)
CAMEL . . . . . Collapsible Airborne Military Equipment Lifter
CAMEL . . . . . Critical Aeronautical Material and Equipment List
CAMELOT . . . . Cultural Auction of Many Extraordinary Lots of Treasure (St. Louis, Missouri)
CAMEN . . . . . Centro Autonomo Militaire Energia Nucleare (Italy)
CAMEO . . . . . Capitol Area Motion Pictures Education Organization (Washington, DC)
CAMESA . . . . Canadian Military Electronics Standards Agency
CA/MG . . . . . Civil Affairs/Military Government
CAMI . . . . . . Civil Aeromedical Institute
CAMI . . . . . . Coated Abrasives Manufacturers Institute
CAMI . . . . . . Continuing Action Maintenance Instruction
CAMM . . . . . Chlor-Alkali-Market Model
CAMMIS . . . . Command Aircraft Maintenance Manpower Information System
CAMO . . . . . Capulin Mountain National Monument
CAMO . . . . . Consolidated Administrative Management Organization (AID)
CAMP . . . . . . Cabin Air Manifold Pressure
CAMP . . . . . . Command and Management Presentation (Marine Corps)
CAMP . . . . . . Computer Applications of Military Problems (Computer users' group)
CAMP . . . . . . Computer-Assisted Management of Portfolios
CAMP . . . . . . Computer-Assisted Menu Planning
CAMP . . . . . . Computerized Aircraft Maintenance Program
CAMP . . . . . . Continuous Air Monitoring Program (Public Health Service)
CAMP . . . . . . Cooperative African Microfilm Project
CAMP . . . . . . Council on Abandoned Military Posts - USA
CAMP . . . . . . Cyclic Adenosine Monophosphate (Also, cAMP) (Biochemistry)
CAMPS . . . . . Centralized Automated Military Pay System

CAMPS . . . . . Cooperative Area Manpower Planning System
CAMPUS . . . . Comprehensive Analytical Method of Planning in the University Sphere (Cost simulation technique)
CAMRB . . . . . Central Aircrew Medical Review Board
CAMROC . . . . Cambridge Radio Observatory Committee
CAMS . . . . . . Chartiers Aero-Maritime de la Seine (France)
CAMS . . . . . . Coastal Antimissile System
CAMS . . . . . . Containerized Avionics Maintenance System
CAMS . . . . . . Cybernetic Anthropomorphous Machine Systems (Robot) (Army)
CAMSI . . . . . Canadian, American Merchant Shipping Instructions
CAMSI . . . . . Canadian Association of Medical Students and Interns
CAMSI . . . . . Confidential Admiralty Merchant Shipping Instructions
CAMSIM . . . . Computer-Assisted Maintenance Simulation (Army)
CAMSTA . . . . Cameron Station (Army)
CAMTMTS . . . . Central Area, Military Traffic Management and Terminal Service
CAN . . . . Cajun Nike (US Navy missile)
CAN . . . . Canister
CAN . . . . Citizens Against Noise
CAN. . . . . . . Configuration Accounting Number
CAN. . . . . . . Consumer Action Now (An organization)
CAN. . . . . . . Correlation Air Navigation
CAN . . . . Cost Account Number
CANA . . . . . . Christian Anti-Narcotic Association
CANA . . . . . . Czech American National Alliance
CANAIRDEF . . . Air Defense Command Headquarters, St. Hubert, Province of Quebec, Canada
CANAIRDIV . . . Canadian Air Division Headquarters (Allied Air Forces in Europe)
CANAIRFAX . . Maritime Group Headquarters, Halifax, Nova Scotia, Canada
CANAIRHED . . . Air Force Headquarters, Ottawa, Ontario, Canada
CANAIRLIFT . . . Air Transport Command Headquarters, Rockcliffe, Ontario, Canada
CANAIRLON . . Air Member, Canadian Joint Staff, London, England
CANAIRMAT . . Air Material Command Headquarters, Ottawa, Ontario, Canada
CANAIRNEW . . Senior Royal Canadian Air Force Liaison Officer, St. Johns Newfoundland, Canada
CANAIRNORWEST . . North-West Air Command Headquarters, Edmonton, Alberta, Canada
CANAIRPEG . . . Canadian 14th Air Training Group Headquarters, Winnipeg
CANAIRTAC . . Canadian Tactical Air Command Headquarters
CANAIRTRAIN . . Canadian Air Training Command Headquarters
CANAIRVAN . . 12th Air Defense Group Headquarters, Vancouver, British Columbia, Canada
CANAIRWASH . Air Member, Canadian Joint Staff, Washington, DC
CANAS . . . . . Naval Air Station (Canadian Navy)
CANAVAT . . . Naval Attaché (Canadian Navy)
CANAVBRIT . . Naval Member, Canadian Joint Staff, London, England
CANAVCHARGE . Senior Officer (or Officer in Charge) at (Canadian Navy)
CANAVHED . . . Naval Headquarters, Ottawa, Ontario, Canada
CANAVSTORES . . Naval Stores Officer (Canadian Navy)
CANAVUS . . . Canadian Member, Canadian Joint Staff, Washington, DC
CANCARAIRGRP . . Carrier Air Group (Canadian military)
CANCOMDESFE . . Commander, Canadian Destroyers, Far East
CANCOMDESFLOT 1 . . Commander, First Canadian Destroyer Flotilla
CANCOMDESLANT . . Commander, Canadian Destroyers, Atlantic
CANCOMDESPAC . . Commander, Canadian Destroyers, Pacific
CANCOMFLT . . Senior Officer Afloat (Canadian Navy)
CANCOMFLTLANT . . Senior Officer Afloat Atlantic (Canadian Navy)
CANCOMFLTPAC . . Senior Officer Afloat Pacific (Canadian Navy)
CANCOMNEW . . Canadian Naval Commander Newfoundland
CANCON . . . . Canadian Control System (For convoys in Canadian Coastal Zone)
CAND . . . . . . Candidate
CANDEP . . . . . Royal Canadian Navy Depot
CANDESFE . . . Canadian Destroyers Far East
CANDESFLOT 1 . . 1st Canadian Destroyer Flotilla
CANDESLANT . . Canadian Destroyers Atlantic
CANDESPAC . . Canadian Destroyers Pacific
CAN DO . . . . . Consolidated Accelerated Navy Documentation Organization
CANDR . . . . . Construction and Repair
CANDR . . . . . Convoy and Routing (Section)
CANDU . . . . . Canadian Deuterium Uranium
CANDY . . . . . Cigarette Advertising Normally Directed to Youth (Student legal action organization)
CANEL . . . . . Connecticut Advanced Nuclear Engineering Laboratory
CANF . . . . . . Combined Allied Naval Forces
CANFLAGLANT . . Flag Officer, Atlantic Coast (Canadian Navy)
CANFLAGPAC . . Flag Officer, Pacific Coast (Canadian Navy)
CANFSWPA . . . Combined Allied Naval Forces, Southwest Pacific Area
CANFSWPAOPPLAN . . Combined Allied Naval Forces Southwest Pacific Ocean Area Operating Plan
CANLANT . . . . Canadian Atlantic Subarea (Canadian Navy)
CANLF . . . . . . United States Committee to Aid the National Liberation Front of South Vietnam

CANO . . . . . . Catalog Number
CANRESLANT . . Senior Officer Reserve Fleet East Coast (Canadian Navy)
CANRESPAC . . Senior Officer Reserve Fleet West Coast (Canadian Navy)
CANSAF . . . . . Canadian Sales Finance Long Form Report
CAN/SDI . . . . Canadian Selective Dissemination of Information
CANSERVCOL . . Canadian Services College
CANTAT . . . . . Canadian Transatlantic Telephone Cable
CANU . . . . . . Convention African National Union (Nyasaland)
CAN-UK . . . . . Canada-United Kingdom
CANUKUS . . . . Canada-United Kingdom-United States (Agreement)
CANUKUS JCECS . . Canadian-United Kingdom-United States Joint Communications-
                Electronics Committees
CAN-US . . . . . Canada - United States
CANUSE . . . . . Canadian-United States Eastern Power Complex
CANY . . . . . . Canyonlands National Park
CAO . . . . Carolina Freight Carriers (NYSE symbol)
CAO . . . . Central Accounting Office (Air Force)
CAO . . . . Chief Administrative Officer
CAO . . . . . . City Administrative Office
CAO . . . . Civil Affairs Officer (Navy)
CAO . . . . Collateral Action Officer (Army)
CAO . . . . . . Contract Administration Office
CAO . . . . . . Cost Analysis Organization (Navy)
CAO . . . . Cretans' Association Omonia
CAOCS . . . . . Carrier Aircraft Operational Compatibility System (Navy)
CAOE . . . . . . Contractor-Acquired Operational Equipment
CAOF . . . . . . Catholic Association of Foresters
CAOPT . . . . . Council of American Official Poultry Tests
CAORE . . . . . Canadian Army Operational Research Establishment
CAOS . . . . . . Completely Automatic Operational System
CAO SOP . . . . Coordination of Atomic Operations - Standing Operating Procedures
CAP . . . . Campaign Against Pollution
CAP . . . . Canadian Association of Pathologists
CAP . . . . Capacity
CAP . . . . Capital
CAP . . . . Capital Airlines, Inc.
CAP . . . . Card Assembly Program
CAP . . . . Catapult and Arresting-Gear Pool (Navy)
CAP . . . . Central Africa Party (Southern Rhodesia)
CAP . . . . Central Arizona Project (Federal water-and-power project, similar to
                TVA)
CAP . . . . Chief Aviation Pilot (Navy, Coast Guard)
CAP . . . . Chloracetophenone (Organic chemistry)
CAP . . . . Chloro-Aluminum Phthalocyanine
CAP . . . . Christian Action Party (Puerto Rico)
CAP . . . . Civil Air Patrol
CAP . . . . Classroom Assembly Program
CAP . . . . Clean Air Projector
CAP . . . . Cleaner Air Package
CAP . . . . Collection Agency Practices
CAP . . . . Collection Agency Project (Student legal action organization)
CAP . . . . College of American Pathologists
CAP . . . . Combat Air Patrol
CAP . . . . Commencing at a Point
CAP . . . . Common Agricultural Policy (Common Market)
CAP . . . . Community Action Program (Office of Economic Opportunity)
CAP . . . . Community Alert Patrol
CAP . . . . Composers' Autograph Publications (An organization)
CAP . . . . Computer-Aided Production
CAP . . . . Computer-Assisted Printing
CAPA . . . . . . Computerized Assignment of Personnel (Military)
CAP . . . . Condenser Absolute Pressure
CAP . . . . Console Action Processor
CAP . . . . Contract Administration Panel (Military)
CAP . . . . Contractor-Acquired Property
CAP . . . . Council on Advanced Programming
CAP . . . . Cropland Adjustment Program
CAP . . . . Current Assessment Plan
CAPA . . . . . . Central Arizona Project Association
CAPA . . . . . . Comite Argentino Permanente de Aeronautica
CAPAC . . . . . Composers, Authors and Publishers Association of Canada
CAPAL . . . . . Computer and Photographic Assisted Learning
CAPAV . . . . . Committee on Atmospheric Problems of Aerospace Vehicles
                (American Meteorological Society)
CAPC . . . . . . Civil Aviation Planning Committee
CAPCHE . . . . . Component Auto-Programmed Checkout Equipment (Aerospace)
CAPCOM . . . . Capsule Communications (or Communicator)
CAPCP . . . . . Civil Air Patrol Coastal Patrol (Wartime)
CAPCRA . . . . Cooperative Agricole des Producteurs de Cereales de la Region d'Arras
CAPE . . . . . . Committee on Assessing the Progress of Education
CAPE . . . . . . Communication Automatic Processing Equipment

CAPE . . . . . . Council on American Private Education
CAPERTSIM . . . Computer-Assisted Program Evaluation Review-Technique Simulation (Army)
CAPG . . . . . . Civil Air Patrol Guard
CAPI . . . . . . Center for the Analysis of Public Issues (Princeton, NJ)
CAPISM . . . . Comite d'Action Politique et Sociale pour l'Independance de Madagascar
              (Political and Social Committee for Malagasy Independence)
CAPL . . . . . . Control Assembly Parts List (Aerospace)
CAPM . . . . . . Computer-Aided Patient Management
CAPP . . . . . . Conference of Actuaries in Public Practice
CAPPA . . . . . Crusher and Portable Plant Association
CAPPI . . . . . . Constant Altitude Plan Position Indicator (Aviation)
CAPPS . . . . . Council for the Advancement of the Psychological Professions and Sciences
CAPRA . . . . . Composers' Autograph Publications Records Association
CAPRI . . . . . . Coded Address Private Radio Intercommunications
CAPRI . . . . . . Computerized Advance Personnel Requirements Information (or
              Inventory) (Navy)
CAPS . . . . . . Christian Association for Psychological Studies
CAPS . . . . . . Clearinghouse on Counseling and Personnel Services (ERIC)
CAPS . . . . . . Computer-Aided Pipe Sketching (System) (Du Pont)
CAPS . . . . . . Control & Auxiliary Power Supply System
CAPS . . . . . . Creative Artists Public Service
CAPSEP . . . . . Capsule Separation (Aerospace)
CAPSHIPFOR . . Capacity Ships Force
CAPT . . . . . . Captain
CAPU . . . . . . Coast African People's Union (Kenya)
CAPUC . . . . . Coordinating Area Production Urgency Committee
CAPWSK . . . . Collision Avoidance, Proximity Warning, Station Keeping Equipment
              (Military)
CAR . . . . Carter Wallace, Inc. (NYSE symbol)
CAR . . . . Center for Aging Research
CAR . . . . Channel Address Register (Data processing)
CAR . . . . Chief Airship Rigger
CAR . . . . Chief, Army Reserve
CAR . . . . Civil Aeronautical Regulation (of FAA)
CAR . . . . Civil Air Reserve
CAR . . . . Cloud-Top Altitude Radiometer
CAR . . . . Community Antenna Relay (Service) (FCC)
CAR . . . . Conditioned Avoidance Response
CAR . . . . Configuration Audit Review
CAR . . . . Contract Authorization Request
CAR . . . . Corrective Action Reply
CAR . . . . Corrective Action Report
CAR . . . . Corrective Action Request
CAR . . . . United States Army Caribbean
CARA . . . . . . Cargo and Rescue Aircraft
CARA . . . . . . Center for Applied Research in the Apostolate
CARA . . . . . . Check Area Airports
CARA . . . . . . Chinese American Restaurant Association
CARA . . . . . . Combat Aircrew Recovery Aircraft
CARA . . . . . . Compagnie d'Applications et de Recherches Atomiques (France)
CARAIRGROUP . . Carrier Air Group
CARATOM . . . . Compagnie d'Applications et de Recherches Atomiques (France)
CARB . . . . . . California Air Resources Board
CARBASORD . . Carry Out Unexecuted Portion Basic Orders
CARBOPOL . . . Carboxypolymethylene
CARC . . . . . . Coast Artillery Reserve Corps
CARD . . . . . . Card Automated Reproduction and Distribution System (Library of Congress)
CARD . . . . . . Civil Aviation Research and Development (NASA)
CARD . . . . . . Coded Automatic Reading Device
CARD . . . . . . Compact Automatic Retrieval Device (or Display) (Data processing)
CARDA . . . . . Continental Airborne Reconnaissance for Damage Assessment (Air Force)
CARDAN . . . . Centre d'Analyse et de Recherche Documentaires pour l'Afrique Noire
CARDE . . . . . Canadian Armament Research and Development Establishment
CARDIAC . . . . Cardboard Illustrative Aid to Computation (Data processing)
CARDIV . . . . . Carrier Division (Navy)
CARDS . . . . . Combat Aircraft Recording and Data System
CARE . . . . . . Capitol Reef National Monument
CARE . . . . . . Clinical and Administrative Research (System)
CARE . . . . . . Clothing Articles Require Explanation (Student legal action organization)
CARE . . . . . . Cooperative for American Relief Everywhere (Formerly: Cooperative
              for American Remittances to Europe; Cooperative for American
              Remittances to Everywhere)
CAREL . . . . . Central Atlantic Regional Educational Laboratory
CARETS . . . . . Central Atlantic Regional Ecological Test Site (Department of the
              Interior)
CARF . . . . . . Center Airman Record File (Air Force)
CARF . . . . . . Central Airspace Reservation Facility
CARF . . . . . . Central Altitude Reservation Facility
CARF . . . . . . Commission on Accreditation of Rehabilitation Facilities
CARG . . . . . . Corporate Accountability Research Group (Formed by consumer-advocate
              Ralph Nader)

CARI . . . . Civil Aeromedical Research Institute (FAA)
CARIB . . . . . . Caribbean
CARIBCOM . . . Caribbean Command (Military)
CARIBSEAFRON . . Caribbean Sea Frontier (Navy)
CARIC . . . . . . Contractor All-Risk Incentive Contract (Air Force)
CARIFTA . . . . . Caribbean Free Trade Association
CARIH . . . . . . Children's Asthma Research Institute and Hospital (Denver, Colorado)
CARISMA . . . . Corrections to Applied Research Laboratories Ion-Sputtering Mass
    Analyzers (Data processing)
CARL . . . . Calibration Requirements List
CARLA . . . . . . Code Actuated Random Load Apparatus
CARMOCS . . . . Continental Army and Major Overseas Commands Systems
CARN . . . . Committee for Amnesty and National Recognition (Cameroon)
CARO . . . . Combined Arms Research Office
CAROT . . . . . . Centralized Automatic Recording on Trunks (Bell Laboratories)
CARP . . . . Citizens Concerned About Radiation Pollution (Organization in
    Denver, Colorado)
CARP . . . . Computed Air Release Point
CARP . . . . Construction of Aircraft and Related Procurement
CARPAC . . . . . Carriers, Pacific Fleet (Navy)
CARPAS . . . . . Comision Asesora Regional de Pesca el Atlantico Sud-Occidental
    (Southwest Atlantic Fishery Commission)
CARPLE . . . . . . Cartilla Electoral Para el Plebiscito (Colombia)
CARQUAL . . . . Carrier Qualification (Navy)
CARQUALS . . . Carrier Qualification Landings
CARR . . . . Carrier
CARR . . . . Carrollton R. R. (AAR code)
CARR . . . . Customer Acceptance Readiness Review (Apollo) (NASA)
CARROTC . . . . Chief, (US) Army Reserve and Reserve Officers Training Corps Affairs
CARRS . . . . . . Close-in Automatic Route Restoral System (NORAD)
CARS . . . . Collision Avoidance RADAR Simulator (Maritime)
CARS . . . . Combat Arms Regimental System (Army)
CARS . . . . Community Antenna Relay Service
CARS . . . . Computer-Aided Routing System
CART . . . . Centralized Automatic Recorder and Tester
CARTASKFOR . . Carrier Task Force (Navy)
CARW . . . . Carolina Western R. R. (AAR code)
CAS . . . . Calibrated Air Speed
CAS . . . . California Academy of Science
CAS . . . . Cambrian Airways, Ltd.
CAS . . . . Canadian Astronautical Society
CAS . . . . Casual(ty)
CAS . . . . Chemical Abstracts Service
CAS . . . . Chicago Academy of Science
CAS . . . . Chief of Air Staff
CAS . . . . Child Attitudes Survey (Education)
CAS . . . . Civil Affairs Section
CAS . . . . Civil Air Surgeon (of FAA)
CAS . . . . Close Air Support (Military)
CAST . . . . Coded Armaments System
CAS . . . . Collision-Avoidance System (Aviation)
CAS . . . . Combined Activities System (Vietnam) (Air Force)
CAS . . . . Communication Analysis Section
CAS . . . . Communications Antenna Sleeve
CAS . . . . Compensating Air Supply
CAS . . . . Complete Assembly for Strike
CAS . . . . Compressed Air Spraying
CAS . . . . Continental Air Services
CAS . . . . Contract Administration Service (DOD)
CAS . . . . Control Augmentation System
CAS . . . . Controls Assembly Set
CAS . . . . Cooperative Applications Satellite (France) (NASA)
CAS . . . . Courier Air Service
CAS . . . . Current Awareness Service (Cryogenic literature bibliography) (Cryogenic
    Data Center)
CASA . . . . Castillo de San Marcos National Monument
CASA . . . . Chinese Art Society of America
CASA . . . . Construcciones Aeronauticas, SA (Spain)
CASB . . . . Cost Accounting Standards Board (US)
CASBO . . . . . . Conference of American Small Business Organizations
CASBS . . . . . . Center for Advanced Study in the Behavioral Sciences
CASC . . . . Council for the Advancement of Small Colleges
CASCAN . . . . . Casualty Canceled (Navy)
CASCO . . . . . . Canadian Australian Line
CASCOR . . . . . Casualty Corrected (Navy)
CASCP . . . . . . Caribbean Area Small Craft Project
CASCU . . . . . . Commander Aircraft Support Control Unit (Navy)
CASD . . . . Carrier Aircraft Service Detachment (Marine Corps)
CASD . . . . Carrier Aircraft Service Division (Navy)
CASDAC . . . . . Computer-Aided Ship Design and Construction
CASDIV . . . . . . Carrier Aircraft Service Division (Navy)

CASDO . . . . . . Computer Applications Support and Development Office (Navy)
CASDOS . . . . . Computer-Assisted Detailing of Ships
CASDS . . . . . . Center for Advanced Study in the Developmental Sciences
CASE . . . . Commission on Accreditation of Service Experiences
CASE . . . . Committee on Academic Science and Engineering (Federal Council for
    Science and Technology)
CASE . . . . Committee on the Atlantic Salmon Emergency
CASE . . . . Common Access Switching Equipment
CASE . . . . Computer Automated Support Equipment
CASE . . . . Coordinated Aerospace Supplier Evaluation
CASE . . . . Council of Administrators of Special Education
CASE . . . . Council for Advancement of Secondary Education
CASEA . . . . . . Center for the Advanced Study of Educational Administration
CASF . . . . Composite Air Strike Force (Air Force)
CASH . . . . Citizens Alliance for Self-Help
CASH . . . . Committee on Administrative Services of Hospitals
CASI . . . . Canadian Aeronautics and Space Institute
CASL . . . . Committee of American Steamship Lines
CASL-CI . . . . . Confederation Africaine des Syndicats Libre de Cote d'Ivoire (African
    Confederation of Free Trade Unions of the Ivory Coast)
CASL-FO . . . . Confederation Africaine des Syndicats Libres-Force Ouvriere (African
    Confederation of Free Trade Unions - Workers' Force) (Cameroon,
    Chad, Gabon)
CASL-FO-RC . . Confederation Africaine des Syndicats Libres - Force Ouvriere -
    Republique Centafricaine (African Confederation of Free Trade Unions -
    Workers' Force - Central African Republic)
CASL-HV . . . . . Confederation Africane des Syndicats Libres de la Haute Volta (African
    Confederation of Free Trade Unions of the Upper Volta)
CASM . . . . Cyclic Air Sampling Monitor
CASMT . . . . . . Central Association of Science and Mathematics Teachers
CASO . . . . Canada Southern R. R. (AAR code)
CASOFF . . . . . Control and Surveillance of Friendly Forces
CASP . . . . Capability Support Plan
CASP . . . . Country Analysis and Strategy Paper (Bureau of Inter-American Affairs)
    (State Department)
CASR . . . . Center Surveillance RADAR
CASREP . . . . . Casualty Report(s) (Navy)
CASS . . . . Carrier Aircraft Support Study (Navy)
CASS . . . . Command Active Sonobuoy System (Navy)
CASS . . . . Computer Automatic Scheduling System
CASS . . . . Computerized Algorithmic Satellite Scheduler (NASA)
CASSA . . . . . . CONARC (Continental Army Command) Automated System Support
    Agency (Army)
CASSANDRA . . Chromatogram Automatic Soaking Scanning and Digital
    Recording Apparatus
CASSI . . . . Chemical Abstracts Service Source Index
CASSIS . . . . . . Communication and Social Science Information Service (Canadian
    research collection network)
CASSP . . . . . . Central Ammunition Supply Status Point
CAST . . . . Cartoon Archetypical Slogan Theater (London)
CAST . . . . Center for Application of Sciences and Technology
CAST . . . . Clearinghouse Announcements in Science and Technology (CFSTI)
    (Obsolete; see SAST)
CAST . . . . Committee Against Student Terrorism (Student group opposed to
    disruptive campus demonstrations) (Wayne State University, Detroit)
CASTE . . . . . . Collision Avoidance System Technical Evaluation
CASTS . . . . . . Canal Safe Transit System
CASU . . . . Carrier Aircraft Service Unit (Navy)
CASU (F) . . . . . Combat Aircraft Service Unit (Navy)
CASUM . . . . . . Civil Affairs Summary (Navy)
CASW . . . . Church Association for Seamen's Work
CASW . . . . Council for the Advancement of Science Writing
CASWO . . . . . . Confidential and Secret Weekly Orders (Naval Air Stations)
CAT . . . . Cabin Air Temperature (Aviation)
CAT . . . . California Achievement Test
CAT . . . . Camper Alert Team (for missile sites) (Air Force)
CAT . . . . Carburetor Air Temperature (Aviation)
CAT . . . . Cartridge Assembly Test
CAT . . . . Catapult
CAT . . . . Category
CAT . . . . Caterpillar Tractor Co. (NYSE symbol) (Wall Street slang name: "Cat")
CAT . . . . Celestial Atomic Trajectile
CAT . . . . Centralized Automatic Testing
CAT . . . . Child's Apperception Test (Psychology)
CAT . . . . Civil Action Team
CAT . . . . Civil Air Transport (Free China's International Airline)
CAT . . . . Civilian Actress Technician (Term for professional actresses who worked
    under Army Special Services Division in soldier shows) (World War II)
CAT . . . . Classical Analytic Technique
CAT . . . . Clear Air Turbulence (Aviation)
CAT . . . . Clerical Aptitude Test

CAT . . . . College Ability Test
CAT . . . . Combined Acceptance Trials
CAT . . . . Comite de l'Assistance Technique de l'ONU
CAT . . . . Command and Triangulation
CAT . . . . Computer-Aided Teaching
CAT . . . . Computer of Average Transients
CAT . . . . Confederation Autonome de Travail (Autonomous Confederation of Labor)
CAT . . . . Control and Assessment Team
CAT . . . . Converted Aerial Targets
CAT . . . . Copper Alloy Tubing
CAT . . . . Current Adjusting Type
CATA . . . . . . Compania Amazonia Textil de Aniagem (Commercial firm) (Brazil)
CATA . . . . . . Cushion Air Tread Articulate (Vehicle) (Army)
CATB . . . . . . Coast Artillery Training Battalion
CATC . . . . . . Confederation Africaine des Travailleurs Croyants (African Confederation of Believing Workers)
CATC . . . . . . Continental Oil, Atlantic Refining, Tidewater Oil, and Cities Service (Group of companies joined together for mutual drilling ventures)
CATCC . . . . . Carrier Air Traffic Control Center (Navy)
CATCH . . . . . Computer Analysis of Thermo-Chemical (Data tables)
CATCO . . . . . Catalytic Construction Company
CATCUSAF . . . Commander, Amphibious Training Command United States Atlantic Fleet
CATDO . . . . . Chief Airways Technical District Office
CATE . . . . . . Current ARDC (Air Research and Development Command) Technical Efforts (DOD program)
CATF . . . . . . Chinese Air Task Force
CATFO . . . . . Chief Airways Technical Field Office
CATMN. . . . . Consolidated Air Target Material Notices (NOO)
CATNIP. . . . . Computer-Assisted Technique for Numerical Indexing Purposes
CATO. . . . . . Catoctin Mountain Park (National Park Service designation)
CATOR . . . . . Combined Air Transport Operations Room (Allied office, World War II)
CATP . . . . . . Classified Area Term Pass
CATR . . . . . . Central Air Transport
CATRALA . . . . Car and Truck Renting and Leasing Association
CATS . . . . . . Chicago Area Transportation Study
CATS . . . . . . Civil Affairs Training School (Navy)
CATS . . . . . . Communications and Tracking System
CATS . . . . . . Comprehensive Analytical Test System
CATS . . . . . . Compute Air-Trans Systems, Inc.
CATS . . . . . . Computer-Assisted Test Shop
CATS . . . . . . Computer Automated Test System (AT & T)
CATT . . . . . . Consumers' Association of Trinidad and Tobago
CATT . . . . . . Conveyorized Automatic Tube Tester (Data processing)
CATU . . . . . . Combat Aircrew Training Unit (Navy)
CATU . . . . . . Confederation of Arab Trade Unions
CATV . . . . . . Cabin Air Temperature Valve
CATV . . . . . . Cable Television
CATV . . . . . . Community Antenna Television (FCC)
CAU . . . . Caucasian
CAU . . . . Congress of American Unions
CAUEOI . . . . . Caucasian Except as Otherwise Indicated (Army)
CAUFN. . . . . . Caution Advised Until Further Notice (Aviation)
CAUNC . . . . . Comite d'Action de L'Union Nationale des Cabindais (Action Committee for the National Association of the People of Cabinda)
CAUS . . . . . . Color Association of the United States
CAUSA . . . . . Compania Aeronautics Uruguaya, SA
CAUSE . . . . . College and University System Exchange
CAUSE . . . . . Counselor Advisor University Summer Education (Department of Labor program)
CAUT . . . . . . Caution
CAUTION . . . . Citizens Against Unneccessary Tax Increases and Other Nonsense (St. Louis organization)
CAUTRA . . . . Coordinateur Automatique de Traffic
CAV. . . . . . . Constant Angular Velocity
CAV. . . . . . . Continuous Airworthiness Visit
CAVD. . . . . . Completion, Arithmetic, Vocabulary, Directions (Psychology)
CAVE . . . . . . Catholic Audio-Visual Educators Association
CAVORT . . . . Coherent Acceleration & Velocity Observations in Real Time
CAVT . . . . . . Constant Absolute Vorticity Trajectory
CAVU. . . . . . Ceiling and Visibility Unlimited (Meteorology)
CAW. . . . . . . Caesars World, Inc. (NYSE symbol)
CAW . . . . . . Cam Action Wheel
CAW . . . . . . Channel Address Word (Data processing)
CAWC . . . . . Committee on Air and Water Conservation (American Petroleum Institute)
CAWG . . . . . Coaxial Adapter Wave-Guide
CAWS. . . . . . Common Aviation Weather Subsystem
CAWU. . . . . . Clerical and Administrative Workers Union (British)
CAWU. . . . . . Commercial and Allied Workers' Union (Somali Republic)
CAX. . . . . . . Community Automatic Exchange (Telephone)
CAX . . . . Conrac Corp. (NYSE symbol)
CAY. . . . . . . Carey (The Philip) Mfg. Co. (NYSE symbol) (Delisted)

CB . . . . Cadmium Bronze
CB . . . . Capacitor Bank
CB . . . . Cape Breton Island
CB . . . . Cast Brass
CB . . . . Catapult Bulletin
CB . . . . Catch Basin (Technical drawings)
CB . . . . Cavalry Brigade
CB . . . . Cement Base (Technical drawings)
CB . . . . Census Bureau (Commerce Department)
CB . . . . Center of Buoyancy
CB . . . . Chemical and Biological (Warfare) (Formerly, CBR)
CB . . . . Chief Boilermaker (Navy)
CB . . . . Children's Bureau (of SSA)
CB . . . . Chirurgiae Baccalaureus (Bachelor of Surgery)
CB . . . . Circuit Breaker
CB . . . . Citizens Band (A radio frequency band for limited-range, two-way voice communications by persons without technical training or standard operator licenses)
CB . . . . Coated on the Back Side (Carbonless paper)
CB . . . . Cobalt Bomb (Nuclear)
CB . . . . Code Book
CB . . . . Col Basso (With the bass)
Cb . . . . Columbium (A chemical element; modern name is niobium)
CB . . . . Commercial Bank
CB . . . . Common Battery (Electronics; or in technical drawings)
CB . . . . Companion of the (Order of the) Bath (British)
CB . . . . Compass Bearing (Navigation)
CB . . . . Condition Bit (Data processing)
CB . . . . Conference Board (Formerly, National Industrial Conference Board)
CB . . . . Confidential Book (British Navy)
CB . . . . Confidential Bulletin
CB . . . . Confinement to Barracks (A military punishment)
CB . . . . Construction Battalion (Navy)
CB . . . . Continuous Blowdown
CB . . . . Contrabass
CB . . . . Contract Brief
CB . . . . Control Branch (Military)
CB . . . . Corned Beef (Restaurant slang)
CB . . . . Corps Brandenburgia
CB . . . . Counter Battery
CB . . . . County Borough
CB . . . . Crash Boat
CB . . . . Crew Boat
CB . . . . Cumulative Bulletin (US Internal Revenue Service)
CB . . . . Cumulonimbus (Meteorology)
CB . . . . Currency Bond
CB . . . . Large Cruiser (Navy symbol)
C/B . . . . Cash Book
C of B . . . . . . Confirmation of Balance (Banking)
CBA. . . . . Candy Brokers Association of America
CBA . . . . Caribbean Atlantic Airlines, Inc. (of Puerto Rico)
CBA . . . . Catholic Biblical Association of America
CBA . . . . Catholic Broadcasters Association
CBA . . . . Chemical Bond Approach
CBA . . . . Chesapeake Bay Annex (Navy)
CBA . . . . Christian Booksellers Association
CBA . . . . Clydesdale Breeders Association of the United States
CBA . . . . Cocoa Beach Apollo
CBA . . . . Community Broadcasters Association
CBA . . . . Consumer Bankers Association
CBA . . . . Cruising Boats of America, Inc.
CBAA . . . . . . Cleveland Bay Association of America
CBAA . . . . . . Conservative Baptist Association of America
CBAA . . . . . . Corset and Brassiere Association of America
CBAC . . . . . . Chemical-Biological Activities (A publication of Chemical Abstracts Service)
CBAF . . . . . . Cobalt Base Alloy Foil
CBAICP . . . . . Chemical and Biological Accident and Incident Control Plan (Army)
CBALS. . . . . . Carrier Borne Air Liaison Section
CBANY . . . . . Covered Button Association of New York
CBAR . . . . . . Counterbore Arbor
CBARC . . . . . Conference Board of Associated Research Councils
CBAS . . . . . . Chemical Bond Approach Study
CBAT . . . . . . Central Bureau of Astronautical Telegrams
CBB . . . . Catholic Big Brothers
CBBA . . . . . . Christian Brothers Boys Association
CBBI . . . . . . Cast Bronze Bearing Institute
CBBII . . . . . . Council of the Brass and Bronze Ingot Industry
CBBU . . . . . . Construction Battalion Base Unit (Obsolete)
CBC. . . . . Cadmium Bronze Connector
CBC. . . . . Cambridge Bicycle Club (British)

CBC . . . . Canadian Broadcasting Corporation (State-operated radio and television)
CBC . . . . Carbon County Railway Company (AAR code)
CBC . . . . Cauchy Boundary Condition
CBC . . . . Cerebro-Buccal Commissure
CBC . . . . Children's Book Council
CBC . . . . Christian Brothers College (Tennessee)
CBC . . . . Circuit Board Card
CBC . . . . Coffee Brewing Center
CBC . . . . Coldwell, Banker & Company (NYSE symbol)
CBC . . . . Columbia Bible College (South Carolina)
CBC . . . . Complete Blood Count (Medicine)
CBC . . . . Conservative Book Club
CBC . . . . Construction Battalion Center (Navy)
CBC . . . . Contraband Control (Navy)
CBC . . . . Corset and Brassiere Council
CBC . . . . Tactical Command Ship, Large (Navy symbol)
CBCC . . . . . . Common Bias, Common Control
CBCC . . . . . . Conviction by Civil Court
CBCMA . . . . . Carbonated Beverage Container Manufacturers Association
CBCMC . . . . . Carbonated Beverage Can Makers Committee
CBCT . . . . . . Circuit Board Card Tester
CBCU . . . . . . Counterbore Cutter (Tool)
CBD . . . . Board of Review, Discharges and Dismissals (Coast Guard)
CBD . . . . Cash Before Delivery
CBD . . . . Central Business District
CBD . . . . Closed Bladder Drainage (Medicine)
CBD . . . . Commerce Business Daily
CBD . . . . Common Bile Duct (Medicine)
CBD . . . . Constant Bit Density (Control feature of magnetic tape recorders) (Data processing)
CBD . . . . Construction Battalion Detachment (Navy)
CBDNA . . . . . College Band Directors National Association
CBE . . . . Carbon Black Export
CBE . . . . Cesium Bombardment Engine
CBE . . . . Chemical Binding Effect
CBE . . . . Circuit Board Extractor
CBE . . . . Command Budget Estimates (Military)
CBE . . . . Commander of the (Order of the) British Empire
CBE . . . . Compression Bonding Encapulation
CBE . . . . Conference of Business Economists
CBE . . . . Consumer Buying Expectations Survey (Bureau of the Census) (Formerly, Quarterly Survey of Intentions)
CBE . . . . Cooper Industries, Inc. (Formerly, Cooper-Bessemer Corporation) (NYSE symbol)
CBE . . . . Council for Basic Education
CBE . . . . Council of Biology Editors
CBEA . . . . . . Catholic Business Education Association
CBEA . . . . . . Christian Brothers Education Association
CBEL . . . . . . The Cambridge Bibliography of English Literature
CBF . . . . Cerebral Blood Flow (Medicine)
CBF . . . . Colonial Bishoprics' Fund (British)
CBFC . . . . . . Copper & Brass Fabricators Council
CBFFTA . . . . . Copper and Brass Fabricators Foreign Trade Association (Later, Copper and Brass Fabricators Council)
CBFMS . . . . . Conservative Baptist Foreign Mission Society
CBG . . . . Corticosteroid-Binding Globulin (Endocrinology)
CBH . . . . Circuit Board Holder
CBHA . . . . . . Council for Biology in Human Affairs
CBI . . . . Carbonated Beverage Institute
CBI . . . . Central Bible Institute (Missouri)
CBI . . . . Chesapeake Bay Institute (Johns Hopkins University)
CBI . . . . China-Burma-India Theater (World War II)
CBI . . . . Coffee Brewing Institute
CBI . . . . Collective Bargaining Institute (New York City)
CBI . . . . Complete Background Investigation
CBI . . . . Compound Batch Identification (Data processing)
CBI . . . . Computer-Based Instruction (Education)
CBI . . . . Conditional Breakpoint Instruction
CBI . . . . Confederation of British Industry
CBI . . . . Controlled Batch Identification
CBI . . . . Cumulative Book Index
CB & I . . . . . . Chicago Bridge & Iron Company
CBIO . . . . . . Counterbattery Intelligence Officer (Army)
CBIS . . . . Campus-Based Information System (National Science Foundation)
CBIVA . . . . . China-Burma-India Veterans Association
CBJ . . . . Common Bulkhead Joint
CBJA . . . . . . Central Bureau for the Jewish Aged
CBJO . . . . . . Co-ordinating Board of Jewish Organizations for Consultation with ECOSOC
CBL . . . . Cable
CBL . . . . Carlyle Barton Laboratory

CBL . . . . Caustic Boundary Layer (Acoustics)
CBL . . . . Chesapeake Biological Laboratories (University of Maryland)
CBL . . . . Commercial Bill of Lading
CBL . . . . Conemaugh & Black Lick R. R. (AAR code)
CBL . . . . Configuration Breakdown List
CBL . . . . Supreme Council Catholic Benevolent Legion
CB/L . . . . . . Commercial Bill of Lading
CBLANT . . . . . Construction Battalions, Atlantic
CBLFA . . . . . . Corn Belt Livestock Feeders Association
CBLO . . . . . . Chief Bombardment Liaison Officer (Navy)
CBLS . . . . . . Carrier Borne Air Liaison Section (Navy)
CBM . . . . Ceramic-Based Microcircuit
CBM . . . . Certified Ballast Manufacturers Association
CBM . . . . Chemical-Biological Munitions
CBM . . . . Chesebrough-Pond's Inc. (NYSE symbol)
CBM . . . . Chief Boatswain's Mate
CBM . . . . Cigar Box Manufacturers
CBM . . . . Communications Buffer Memory (Data processing)
CBM . . . . Constant Boiling Mixture
CBM . . . . Continental Ballistic Missile
CBMA . . . . . . Chief Boatswain's Mate Acting
CBMC . . . . . . Communaute de Travail des Brasseurs du Marche Commun (Working Committee of Common Market Brewers)
CBMC . . . . . . Corregidor-Bataan Memorial Commission (Government agency)
CBMCBB . . . . Chief Boatswain's Mate, Construction Battalion, Boatswain
CBMCBS . . . . Chief Boatswain's Mate, Construction Battalion, Stevedore
CBMCI . . . . . Christian Business Men's Committee International
CBMKR . . . . . Chief Boilermaker (Coast Guard)
CBMM . . . . . Chief Boatswain's Mate A (Master-at-Arms)
CBMS . . . . . . Conference Board of the Mathematical Sciences
CBMSRC . . . . Chief Boatswain's Mate, Ship Repair, Crane Operator
CBMSRR . . . . Chief Boatswain's Mate, Ship Repair, Rigger
CBMSRS . . . . Chief Boatswain's Mate, Ship Repair, Canvasman
CBMU . . . . . . Construction Battalion Maintenance Unit (Navy)
CBMU . . . . . . Current Bit Monitor Unit
CBN . . . . Columbian Carbon Company (NYSE symbol)
CBN . . . . Commission on Biochemical Nomenclature (IUPAC)
CBO . . . . Conference of Baltic Oceanographers
CBO . . . . Carborundum Company (NYSE symbol)
CBO . . . . Clarksville Branch Office (AEC)
CBO . . . . Coding Board Officer
CBO . . . . Counter-Battery Officer
CBOB . . . . . . Collegiate Basketball Officials Bureau (Later, Eastern College Basketball Association)
CBOC . . . . . . Completion of Bed Occupancy Care (VA)
CBOI . . . . . . Complete Basis of Issue (Army)
CBP . . . . Ceramic Beam Pentode
CBP . . . . Constant Boiling Point
CBPAC . . . . . Construction Battalions, Pacific
CBPC . . . . . . Canadian Book Publishers' Council
CBPF . . . . . . Centro Brasileiro de Pesquisas Fisicas (Brazilian Center for Physics Research)
CBPI . . . . Conditional Break-Point Instruction
CBPO . . . . . . Consolidated Base Personnel Office
CBQ . . . . Chicago, Burlington & Quincy R. R. (AAR code)
CBQ . . . . Civilian Bachelor Quarters (Air Force)
CB & Q . . . . . Chicago, Burlington & Quincy Railroad Company
CBR . . . . Budget and Requirements Division (Coast Guard)
CBR . . . . California Bearing Ratio (Aviation)
CBR . . . . Chemical-Bacteriological-Radiological
CBR . . . . Chemical, Biological, and Radiological Warfare (Later, CB)
CBR . . . . Circuit Board Rack
CBRA . . . . . . Chemical, Biological, Radiological Agency (Military)
CBRA . . . . . . Copper and Brass Research Association
CBRC . . . . . . Chemical, Biological, and Radiological Center
CBRD . . . . . . Construction Battalion Replacement Depot
CBRE . . . . . . Chemical, Biological, and Radiological Element (Military)
CBREG . . . . . Chemical-Biological-Radiological Engineering Group (Army)
CBRM . . . . . . Charger-Battery-Regulator Module (NASA)
CBRN . . . . . . Chemical, Biological, Radiological and Nuclear (Army)
CBRS . . . . . . Chemical, Biological, and Radiological Section (Military)
CBRS . . . . . . Child Behavior Rating Scale
CBRS . . . . . . Chiropody Bibliographical Research Society
CBS . . . . Center Back Stage (A stage direction)
CBS . . . . Central Bibliographic System (Library of Congress)
CBS . . . . Central Bureau of Statistics (Netherlands)
CBS . . . . Chronic Brain Syndrome (Medicine)
CBS . . . . Church Building Society (British)
CBS . . . . Close Boundary Sentry (Military)
CBS . . . . Coarse Bearing Servo
CBS . . . . Coastal Base Section (Name changed to Continental Advance Section) (World War II)

CBS	Columbia Broadcasting System, Inc. (NYSE symbol)
CBS	Compact Buoy System
CBS	Complex Behavior Simulator
CBS	Conference on British Studies
CBS	Confraternity of the Blessed Sacrament
CBS	Connector Backing Shell
CBS	Consolidated Balance Sheet
CBS	Controlled Barrier System
CBSA	Catholic Bible Society of America
CBSC	Common Bias, Single Control
CBSR	Chief Boilermaker, Ship Repair
CBSR	Coupled Breeding Superheating Reactor
CBT	Cabot Corp. (NYSE symbol)
CBT	Cesium Beam Tube
CBT	Chicago Board of Trade
CBT	Cincinnati Board of Trade
CBT	Cooperative Bureau for Teachers
CBTI	Combat Intelligence
CBTS	California Baptist Theological Seminary
CBTS	Cesium Beam Time Standard
CBU	City & Suburban Homes Company (American Stock Exchange symbol)
CBU	Cluster Bomb Unit (Military)
CBU	Collective Bargaining Unit
CBU	Construction Battalion Unit
CBW	Catholic Book Week
CBW	Chemical and Biological Warfare
CBW	Chemical and Biological Weapons
CBW	Constant Bandwidth
CBWA	Copper and Brass Warehouse Association
CBWC	Corset and Brassiere Women's Club
CBWR	Coos Bay Wagon Road (Lands) (Department of Interior)
CBX	C-Band Transponder (Radio)
CBZ	Carbobenzoxy (Organic chemistry)
CC	Calcium Cyclamate (Chemistry)
CC	Call Contract
CC	Canadian Club (A whiskey)
CC	Cans or Cartons (Freight)
CC	Cape Colony (British Empire)
CC	Capsule Communicator
CC	Carbon Copy
CC	Card Code
CC	Career Control
CC	Caribbean Commission (Later, Caribbean Organization)
CC	Carriage Control
CC	Carson City (Nevada) (Mint mark, when appearing on US coins)
CC	Cash Credit
CC	Cashier's Check
CC	Cast Copper
CC	Catholic Clergyman
CC	Catholic Curate
CC	Central Computer
CC	Central Console
CC	Centrifugal Coating
CC	Cerebral Commissure
CC	Chamber of Commerce
CC	Change Course
CC	Channel Command (Military) (Refers to English Channel)
CC	Chess Club
CC	Chief of Chaplains (Army)
CC	Chief Clerk
CC	Chief Complaint (Medicine)
CC	Chronometer Correction
CC	Chrysler Corporation
CC	Circuit Closing
CC	Circuit Court
CC	Circulating Copy
CC	Circumnavigators Club
CC	Cirrocumulus (Meteorology)
CC	City Council(lor)
CC	Civil Commotion
CC	Classification of Characteristics (Navy)
CC	Clerk of the (Privy) Council (British)
CC	Clerk of the Crown (British)
CC	Closing Coil
CC	Coastal Command (British Royal Air Force)
CC	Code Control
CC	Code Converter
CC	Coefficient of Correlation (Mathematics)
CC	Collectors Club
CC	Colon Classification (Library science)
CC	Color Code (as, for types of wire) (Technical drawings)

CC	Color Compensation (Photography)
CC	Color Contrast
CC	Color Correction (Color printing)
CC	Combat Center (Military)
CC	Combat Command (Initialism may be followed by a number as, CC2, to indicate a specific, numbered command) (Army)
CC	Combat Control (Army)
CC	Combat Correspondent
CC	Command Center
CC	Command Computer
CC	Command Control (Military)
CC	Command Ship (Navy symbol)
CC	Commercial Credit Company (NYSE symbol) (Delisted)
CC	Commission Certified (Bacteriology)
CC	Common Carrier
CC	Common Council(man)
CC	Communication Center
CC	Communications Central (Military)
CC	Companion of the Order of Canada
CC	Company Commander
CC	Compass Course
CC	Compound Cathartic (Pills)
CC	Computation Center
CC	Computer Calculator
CC	Conditioning Container
CC	Configuration Control
CC	Confined to Camp (Military)
CC	Connecting Carrier
CC	Connector Circuit
CC	Constructing Contractor
CC	Construction Corps
CC	Consules (Consuls)
CC	Contemporary Civilization (University course)
CC	Continuation Clause
CC	Continuous Casting (Metalworking)
CC	Contra Credit (Banking)
CC	Control Center
CC	Control Circuit
CC	Cooling Coil
CC	Coordinate Converter
CC	Corpora Cardiaca (Endocrinology)
CC	Corrugated or Cupped (Freight)
CC	Cost Center
CC	Council of Churches
CC	Council of Conservationists
CC	Counterclockwise
CC	Country Club
CC	Country Code
CC	County Circuit (As in "CC Rider," i.e., a traveling preacher)
CC	County Commissioner
CC	County Council
CC	County Court
CC	Cricket Club
CC	Critical Condition (Medicine)
CC	Cross Channel
CC	Cross Correlation
CC	Cross Couple
CC	Crown Colony
CC	Crystal Control
CC	Crystal Current
CC	Cubic Centimeter(s)
CC	Cubic Contents
CC	Curling Club
CC	Current Complaints (Medicine)
CC	Current Cost
CC	Cycling Club
CC	Tactical Command Ship (Navy symbol)
C/C	Change of Course (Aviation)
C & C	Command and Control
C of C	Chamber of Commerce
C-in-C	Commander-in-Chief
C to C	Center to Center (Technical drawings)
CCA	Cable Commuter Airlines
CCA	California Central Airlines
CCA	Cancel Corridor Assignment (Aviation)
CCA	Caribbean Conservation Association
CCA	Carrier Controlled Approach (Aircraft carrier RADAR landing system)
CCA	Cash Clothing Allowance
CCA	Cecchetti Council of America
CCA	Cellular Cellulose Acetate
CCA	Cellular Concrete Association

CCA. . . . . . . Central Computer Accounting
CCA. . . . . . . Chick Cell Agglutination (Vaccine potency test)
CCA. . . . . . . Chief of Civil Affairs (Army)
CCA. . . . . . . Chief Clerk of the Admiralty
CCA. . . . . . . Chihuahua Club of America
CCA. . . . . . . Chimpanzee Coryza Agent
CCA. . . . . . . Circuit Court of Appeals
CCA. . . . . . . Citizens for Clean Air
CCA. . . . . . . Citizens' Councils of America
CCA. . . . . . . City Center Arts (A publication)
CCA. . . . . . . Cloud Chamber Analysis
CCA. . . . . . . Clown Club of America
CCA. . . . . . . College Characteristics Analysis
CCA. . . . . . . Collie Club of America
CCA. . . . . Combat Command A
CCA. . . . . . . Comics Code Authority (Regulatory body for comic book and comic
         magazine publishing industry)
CCA. . . . . . . Committee for Conventional Armaments
CCA. . . . . . . Compass Control Alarm
CCA. . . . . . . Component Checkout Area
CCA. . . . . . . Computer Corporation of America
CCA. . . . . . . Conservative Clubs of America
CCA. . . . . . . Consumers Cooperative Association
CCA. . . . . . . Container Corporation of America
CCA. . . . . . . Continental Control Area (FAA)
CCA. . . . . . . Controlled Circulation Audit (Name changed to Business Publications
         Audit of Circulation)
CCA. . . . . . . Corduroy Council of America
CCA. . . . . . . Council of Consumer Advisers
CCA. . . . . . . Cruising Club of America
CCA. . . . . . . United States Circuit Court of Appeals (See CA)
CCAAFB . . . . . Cape Canaveral Auxiliary Air Force Base (Obsolete)
CCAC . . . . . California College of Arts and Crafts
CCAC. . . . . . Central Computer Accounting Corporation
CCAC. . . . . . Combined Civil Affairs Committee
CCAC/L . . . . . Combined Civil Affairs Committee, London Subcommittee
CCAC/S . . . . . Combined Civil Affairs Committee, Supply Subcommittee
CCAE . . . . . . Council of Canning Association Executives
CCAF . . . . . . Chinese Communist Air Force
CCAI . . . . . . Chamber of Commerce of the Apparel Industry
CCAIC . . . . . Catholic College Admissions and Information Center
CCAO. . . . . . Chief Civil Affairs Officer (Navy)
CCAP . . . . . . Citizens Crusade Against Poverty
CCAP . . . . . . Communications Control Applications Program
CCAR . . . . . . Central Conference of American Rabbis
CCAS . . . . . . Comprehensive Close Air Support
CCAT . . . . . . Comite de Coordination de l'Assistance Technique (ONU)
CCATNA. . . . . Combined Committee on Air Training in North America
CCATS . . . . . . Communications, Command and Telemetry Systems
CCB . . . . Campbell Colpitts Bridge (Electronics)
CCB . . . . Capital Cities Broadcasting Corp. (NYSE symbol)
CCB . . . . Change Control Board
CCB . . . . Close Control Bombing (Air Force)
CCB . . . . Combat Command B
CCB . . . . Combined Communications Board
CCB . . . . Command and Control Boat (Navy symbol)
CCB . . . . Common Carrier Bureau (of FCC)
CCB . . . . Configuration Control Board (DOD)
CCB . . . . Contraband Control Base (Navy)
CCB . . . . Control Complications Bronchiques (Vaccine for "bronchial complaints")
         (Medicine)
CCB . . . . Convertible Circuit Breaker
CCBA . . . . . . Central Canada Broadcasting Association
CCBA . . . . . . Chinese Consolidated Benevolent Association
CCBD . . . . . . Configuration Control Board Directive
CCBP . . . . . . Combined Communications Board Publications
CCBS . . . . . . Clear Channel Broadcasting Service
CCBV . . . . . . Central Circulating Blood Volume (Physiology)
CCC. . . . . . . California College of Chiropody
CCC. . . . . . . Cambridge Communication Corporation
CCC. . . . . . . Campus Crusade for Christ
CCC. . . . . . . Caribbean Conservation Corporation
CCC. . . . . . . Catalytic Construction Company
CCC. . . . . . . Cathode Closure Contraction
CCC. . . . . . . Cedar Crest College (Pennsylvania)
CCC. . . . . . . Centerville Community College (Iowa)
CCC. . . . . . . Central Classification Committee (International Federation for
         Documentation)
CCC. . . . . . . Central Computer Complex
CCC. . . . . . . Central Criminal Court (British)
CCC. . . . . . . Chief Cable Censor (Navy)

CCC. . . . . . . Chow Chow Club
CCC. . . . . . . Civilian Conservation Corps (Created, 1937; liquidated, 1943)
CCC. . . . . . . Classified Control Clerk (Army)
CCC. . . . . . . Closed Cycle Cooler
CCC. . . . . . . Combat Command C
CCC. . . . . . . Combined Coordinating Committee
CCC. . . . . . . Command and Control Center (Air Force)
CCC. . . . . . . Commercial Contract Change
CCC. . . . . . . Commodity Credit Corporation (Department of Agriculture)
CCC. . . . . . . Communications Control Console
CCC. . . . . . . Component Change Control (Navy)
CCC. . . . . . . Computer Communications Console
CCC. . . . . . . Computer Control Company
CCC. . . . . . . Conseil de la Cooperation Culturelle (Council for Cultural Cooperation)
         (of the Council of Europe)
CCC. . . . . . . Consumer Credit Counselors
CCC. . . . . . . Continental Can Company (NYSE symbol)
CCC. . . . . . . Corpus Christi College (Cambridge and Oxford)
CCC. . . . . . . Council of Community Churches
CCC. . . . . . . Customs Co-operation Council
CC & C . . . . . Command Control and Communications (Air Force)
CCCA . . . . . . Catholic Civics Clubs of America (Defunct)
CCCA . . . . . . Classic Car Club of America
CCCB . . . . . . Component Change Control Board (DOD)
CCCC . . . . . . Cape Cod Community College (Massachusetts)
CCCC . . . . . . Chrome Card Collectors Club
CCCC . . . . . . Community Coordinated Child Care Program (Also, 4C)
CCCC . . . . . . Conference on College Composition and Communication
CCCC . . . . . . Consolidated Computer and Control Center
CCCD . . . . . . California Center for Community Development
CCCE . . . . . . Caisse Centrale de Co-operation Economique
CCCE . . . . . . Certified Consumer Credit Executive (Designation awarded by
         International Consumer Credit Association)
CCCE . . . . . . Closed Cycle Cryogenic Equipment
CCCF . . . . . . Central Committee on Communications Facilities
CCCI . . . . . . Candy, Chocolate and Confectionery Institute
CCCI . . . . . . Compagnie du Congo pour le Commerce et l'Industrie (Congo Commerce
         and Industry Company)
CCCL . . . . . . Catholic Council on Civil Liberties
CCCL . . . . . . Citizens Committee for Constitutional Liberties
CCCL . . . . . . Cleveland, Cincinnati, Chicago & St. Louis Railway (AAR code)
CCCMMM . . . . Closed Chest Cardiac Massage and Mouth-to-Mouth (Resuscitation)
CCCO. . . . . . Central Committee for Conscientious Objectors
CCCP . . . . . . Council on Cooperative College Projects
CC & CP. . . . . Command Control and Communications Program (Air Force)
CCCR . . . . . . Communication and Command Control Requirements
CCCS . . . . . . Central Control Computer System
CCCS . . . . . . Colonial and Continental Church Society (British)
CCCS . . . . . . Current Contents Chemical Sciences (A publication)
CCCTU . . . . . Central Council of Ceylon Trade Unions
CCCUNY. . . . . City College of City University of New York
CCD. . . . . . . Cell Current Density
CCD. . . . . . . Center for Curriculum Development
CCD. . . . . . . Central Command Decoder
CCD. . . . . . . Central Commissioning Detail (Navy)
CCD. . . . . . . Charge Coupled Device (Bell Laboratories)
CCD. . . . . . . City (or County) Civil Defense Director
CCD. . . . . . . Civil Censorship Division (US Military Government, Germany)
CCD. . . . . . . Cold Cathode Discharge
CCD. . . . . . . Combat Center Director
CCD. . . . . . . Combat Command D
CCD. . . . . . . Command and Control Director (Air Force)
CCD. . . . . . . Commander of Coast Defenses
CCD. . . . . . . Computer-Controlled Display
CCD. . . . . . . Condensed Chemical Dictionary
CCD. . . . . . . Conference of the Committee on Disarmament (Formerly, ENDC)
CCD. . . . . . . Confraternity of Christian Doctrine
CCD. . . . . . . Construction Completion Date
CCD. . . . . . . Core Current Driver
CCD. . . . . . . Cost Center Determination
CCD. . . . . . . Countercurrent Distribution (Analytical chemistry)
CCDA . . . . . . Commercial Chemical Development Association
CCDC . . . . . . Canadian Communicable Disease Center
CCDC . . . . . . Cape Cod Direction Center (Air Force)
CCDC . . . . . . Central Control and Display Console
CCDD . . . . . . Command and Control Development Division (Air Force)
CCDL . . . . . . Camera Confederale del Lavoro (Confederal Chamber of Labor) (Italy/
         Trieste)
CCDP . . . . . . Churchmen's Commission for Decent Publications
CCDP . . . . . . Cooperative College Development Program
CCDS . . . . . . Consultative Committee for the Definition of the Second

CCDS . . . . . . Control Circuits Design Section
CCDSO . . . . . Command and Control Defense Systems Office
CCDVT . . . . . Caisse Centrale de Depots et Vriements de Titres
CCDW . . . . . Carrying Concealed Deadly Weapon
CCE . . . . Certified Chamber Executive (Designation awarded by American Chamber of Commerce Executives)
CCE . . . . Cesium Contact Engine
CCE . . . . Chief, Corps of Engineers (Army)
CCE . . . . Clapeyron-Clausius Equation
CCE . . . . Combat Communications Equipment (Military)
CCE . . . . Combat Control Elements (Army)
CCE . . . . Conseil des Communes d'Europe
CCE . . . . Contract Change Estimate
CCE . . . . Contractor Change Evaluation
CCE . . . . Crusade for a Cleaner Environment
CCEBS . . . . . Committee for the Collegiate Education of Black Students
CCEI . . . . . . Colorado Committee for Environmental Information
CCEP . . . . . . Cabinet Committee for Economic Policy
CCEP . . . . . . Commission Consultative des Etudes Postales (de l'Union Postale Universelle)
CCESO . . . . . Committee on Contributions for Elective State Officials
CCESUSA . . . . Catholic Church Extension Society of the United States of America
CCETI . . . . . . Commission Consultative des Employes et des Travailleurs Intellectuels (de l'OIT)
CCEX . . . . . . Clad Controlled Expansion
CCF . . . . Cancer Cytology Foundation of America
CCF . . . . Captain, Coastal Forces
CCF . . . . Central Computing Facility (NASA)
CCF . . . . Chinese Communist Forces
CCF . . . . Christian Children's Fund
CCF . . . . Circular Crystal Facet
CCF . . . . Citizens' Council Forum
CCF . . . . Combined Cadet Force (British equivalent of US ROTC)
CCF . . . . Common Cold Foundation
CCF . . . . Communication Central Facility (Air Force)
CCF . . . . Compressed Citation File
CCF . . . . Cook United, Inc. (NYSE symbol)
CCF . . . . Cooperative Commonwealth Federation
CCF . . . . Corps Contingency Force (Army)
CCF . . . . Cross Correlation Function
CCF . . . . Socialistic Co-operative Commonwealth Federation (Former Canadian political party; later, NDP)
CCFA . . . . . . Cancer Cytology Foundation of America
CCFA . . . . . . Children's Cancer Fund of America
CCFC . . . . . . Citizens Committee for a Free Cuba
CCFE . . . . . . Commercial Customer-Furnished Equipment
CCFET . . . . . . Captain, Coastal Forces, Eastern Theater
CCFF . . . . . . Crew-Compartment Fit and Function (Apollo) (NASA)
CCFLSA . . . . . Citizens Committee on the Fair Labor Standards Act
CCFMC . . . . . Center for the Coordination of Foreign Manuscript Copying (Library of Congress)
CCFR . . . . . . Constant Current Flux Reset
CCFRA . . . . . Cancelled Concurrent with Next Federal Register Amendment
CCFSA . . . . . Certified Cold Fur Storage Association
CCFT . . . . . . Controlled Current Feedback Transformer
CCG . . . . Change Control Group
CCG . . . . Choral Conductors Guild
CCG . . . . Commandant of the Coast Guard
CCG . . . . Committee for Constitutional Government
CCG . . . . Commodity Coordination Groups
CCG . . . . Constant Current Generator
CCG . . . . Control Commission for Germany
CCGA . . . . . . California Cactus Growers Association
CCGD . . . . . . Commander, Coast Guard District
CCGE . . . . . . Cold Cathode Gage Experiment (Apollo) (NASA)
CCGEU . . . . . Confederation of Central Government Employees' Unions (India)
CCH . . . . Citizenship Clearing House
CCH . . . . Commerce Clearing House (A publishing company)
CCH . . . . Committee on Cosmic Humanism
CCH . . . . Cube Corner Holder
C of CH . . . . . Chief of Chaplains (Army)
CCHE . . . . . . California Coordinating Council for Higher Education
CCHEP . . . . . Cement-Coated Heavy Epoxy
CCHS . . . . . . Conference of California Historical Societies
CCHS . . . . . . Congregational Christian Historical Society
CCI . . . . Calcium Chloride Institute
CCI . . . . Canadian Credit Institute
CCI . . . . Cancer Care, Incorporated (of the National Cancer Foundation)
CCI . . . . CCI Corp. (NYSE symbol)
CCI . . . . Chambre de Commerce Internationale (International Chamber of Commerce)

CCI . . . . Christians Concerned for Israel
CCI . . . . Chronic Coronary Insufficiency (Medicine)
CCI . . . . Circuit Condition Indicator
CCI . . . . College Characteristics Index (A questionnaire)
CCI . . . . Command Control Interface (Army)
CCI . . . . Compactor Company, Incorporated
CCI . . . . Component Cost Index
CCI . . . . Concordia Collegiate Institute (New York)
CCI . . . . Control Current Impedance
CCI . . . . Corrugated Container Institute
CCI . . . . Corrugated, Cupped or Indented (Freight)
CCI . . . . Cotton Council International
CCI . . . . Council on Consumer Information
CCIA . . . . . . Commission of the Churches on International Affairs
CCIA . . . . . . Console Computer Interface Adapter
CCIA . . . . . . Consumer Credit Insurance Association
CCIAH . . . . . Clearinghouse Committee for Information on the Arts and Humanities
CCIC . . . . . . Comite Catholique International de Coordination Aupres de l'Unesco
CCIC . . . . . . Comite Consultatif International du Coton (International Cotton Advisory Committee)
CCIC . . . . . . Concerned Citizens Information Council (Group opposing sex education in schools)
CCICA . . . . . Catholic Commission on Intellectual and Cultural Affairs
CCID . . . . . . Control Channel Information Demodulator
CCIG . . . . . . Cold Cathode Ion Gage
CCIL . . . . . . Commander's Critical Item List (Army)
CCIP . . . . . . Commission du Commerce International des Produits de Base (Nations Unies)
CCIP . . . . . . Continuously Computed Impart Point (Type of bombing sighting system) (Air Force)
CCIR . . . . . . Comite Consultatif International des Radiocommunications (International Radio Consultative Committee)
CCIR . . . . . . Consultative Committee, International Radio (Department of State)
CCIS . . . . . . Cold-Cathode Ion Source
CCIS . . . . . . Command Control Information System
CCIT . . . . . . Comite Consultatif Internationale Telegraphique (International Telephone Consultative Committee) (Later, CCITT)
CCITT . . . . . Comite Consultatif Internationale Telegraphique et Telephoniques (International Telegraph and Telephone Consultative Committee) (ITU)
CCIVS . . . . . . Coordinating Committee for International Voluntary Service
CCIW . . . . . . Canada Centre for Inland Waters
CCIZT . . . . . . Committee of Control of the International Zone of Tangier
CCJ . . . . Conference of Chief Justices
CCJC . . . . . . Chicago City Junior College (Illinois)
CCJC . . . . . . Custer County Junior College (Montana)
CCJO . . . . . . Consultative Council of Jewish Organizations
CCK . . . . Campbell's Creek R. R. (AAR code)
CCK . . . . Central College of Kentucky
CCK . . . . Chief Cook
CCK . . . . Crown Cork & Seal Company, Inc. (NYSE symbol)
CCK(B) . . . . . Chief Cook (Baker)
CCK(C) . . . . . Chief Cook (Commissary)
CCL . . . . Caribbean Congress of Labor
CCL . . . . Carolina, Clinchfield & Ohio Railway (NYSE symbol)
CCL . . . . Centenary College of Louisiana
CCL . . . . Coating and Chemical Laboratory (Army)
CCL . . . . Combat Command L
CCL . . . . Communications Circular Letter (Navy)
CCL . . . . Computer Control Loading
CCL . . . . Conference on Christianity and Literature
CCL . . . . Convective Condensation Level
CCLA . . . . . . Committee on Cooperation in Latin America (of The National Council of Churches of Christ in the USA)
CCLA . . . . . . Correspondence Chess League of America
CCLJ . . . . . . Central Committee of Lithuanian Jurists
CCLM . . . . . . Coordinating Council of Literary Magazines
CCLS . . . . . . Court of Claims
CCLSR . . . . . Court of Claims Reports
CCLU . . . . . . Confederation of Citizens Labor Union (Philippines)
CCM . . . . Chief Carpenter's Mate
CCM . . . . Cloud Camera Multiplexer
CCM . . . . Combat Cargo Mission (Air Force)
CCM . . . . Combined Cipher Machine
CCM . . . . Combined Coding Machine
CCM . . . . Commodity Class Manager
CCM . . . . Constant Current Modulation
CCM . . . . Controlled Carrier Modulation
CCM . . . . Counter-Countermeasures (Military)
CCM . . . . Cross-Country Movement (Maps)
CCM . . . . Crowell-Collier and Macmillan (Publishers)
CCMA . . . . . . Card Clothing Manufacturers Association

CCMA . . . . . . Civilian Clothing Maintenance Allowance (Army)
CCMC . . . . . . Coincident-Current Magnetic Core
CCMCBB . . . . . Chief Carpenter's Mate, Construction Battalion, Builder
CCMCBD . . . . . Chief Carpenter's Mate, Construction Battalion, Draftsman
CCMCBE . . . . . Chief Carpenter's Mate, Construction Battalion, Excavation Foreman
CCMCBS . . . . . Chief Carpenter's Mate, Construction Battalion, Surveyor
CCMCC . . . . . . Continuing Committee on Muslim-Christian Cooperation
CCMD. . . . . . . Chrysler Corporation Missile Division
CCMD. . . . . . . Continuous Current-Monitoring Device
CCMLO. . . . . . Chief Chemical Officer (Army)
CCMR. . . . . . Central Contract Management Region (Air Force)
CCMRD. . . . . . Coordinating Committee on Materials Research and Development
          (Executive Office of the President)
CCMS. . . . . . Central Cardiac Monitoring System
CCMS. . . . . . Committee on the Challenges of Modern Society (NATO)
CCMSRB . . . . . Chief Carpenter's Mate, Ship Repair, Boatbuilder--Wood
CCMSRJ . . . . . Chief Carpenter's Mate, Ship Repair, Joiner
CCMTA. . . . . . Cape Canaveral Missile Test Annex (Later, KSC)
CCMTC. . . . . . Cape Canaveral Missile Test Center (Later, KSC)
CCN . . . . . . Chris-Craft Industries, Inc. (NYSE symbol)
CCN. . . . . . . Cloud Condensation Nuclei (Fog)
CCN . . . . . . Command Control Number (Air Force)
CCN . . . . . . Communication Control Number
CCN . . . . . . Configuration Control Number
CCN . . . . . . Contract Change Notification
CCNR. . . . . . Citizens Committee on Natural Resources
CCNRA. . . . . . Central Council of National Retail Associations
CCNSC. . . . . . Cancer Chemotherapy National Service Center
CCNT. . . . . . Chief Controller (Air Force)
CCNY. . . . . . Canadian Club of New York
CCNY. . . . . . Carnegie Corporation of New York
CCNY. . . . . . Chemists' Club (of New York)
CCNY . . . . . City College of New York (Later, City University of New York)
CCO . . . . . . Calf Certifying Officer (Ministry of Agriculture, Fisheries, and Food)
          (British)
CCO . . . . . . Chicago College of Osteopathy
CCO. . . . . . . Chief Chemical Officer (Army)
CCO. . . . . . . Classified Control Officer
CCO. . . . . . . Contract Change Order
CCO. . . . . . . Convoy Control Officer (Navy)
CCO . . . . . . Coordinating Committee on Oceanography
CCO. . . . . . . Corporate Contract Officer
CCO. . . . . . . Crystal-Controlled Oscillator
CCO. . . . . . . Current-Controlled Oscillator
CC-O. . . . . . Composite Cut-Off (Aerospace)
CC/O. . . . . . Composite Checkout (Aerospace)
CCOC . . . . . . Command Control Operations Center (Army)
CCP . . . . . . Cable Connector Panel
CCP . . . . . . Ceco Corporation (NYSE symbol)
CCP . . . . . . Center for Community Planning (HEW)
CCP . . . . . . Chinese Communist Party
CCP . . . . . . Cibachrome-Print (Color photography)
CCP . . . . . . Command Control Panel
CCP . . . . . . Command Control Post
CCP . . . . . . Commission on College Physics
CCP . . . . . . Communications Control Panel
CCP . . . . . . Conciliation Commission for Palestine (of the UN)
CCP . . . . . . Consolidated Cryptologic Program (Army)
CCP . . . . . . Continuous Correlation Processing
CCP . . . . . . Contract Change Proposal
CCP . . . . . . Court of Common Pleas
CCP . . . . . . Credit Card Purchase
CCP . . . . . . Critical Compression Pressure
CCP . . . . . . Cropland Conversion Program
CCP . . . . . . Cross-Check Procedure
CCPA . . . . . . Cemented Carbide Producers Association
CCPA . . . . . . Cloud Chamber Photographic Analysis
CCPA . . . . . . Committee for Congested Production Areas
CCPA . . . . . . Consumer Credit Protection Act (1969)
CCPA . . . . . . Court of Customs and Patent Appeals
CCPE . . . . . . Canadian Council of Professional Engineers
CCPF . . . . . . Comite Central de la Propriete Forestiere de la CEE (Central
          Committee on Forest Property for the EEC)
CCPF . . . . . . Commander-in-Chief, Pacific Fleet
CCPG. . . . . . Chemical Corps Proving Ground
CCPI . . . . . . Consultative Committee for Public Information (UN)
CCPM. . . . . . Constant-Choice Perceptual Maze Test
CCP/ML . . . . . Communist Party of the Phillipines/Marxist-Leninist
CCPO. . . . . . Central Civilian Personnel Office (Military)
CCPO. . . . . . Comite Central Permanent de l'Opium
CCPR . . . . . . Coherent Cloud Physics RADAR

CCPR . . . . . . Comite Consultatif de Photometrie et de Radiometrie (Formerly, Advisory
          Committee on Photometry)
CCPS . . . . . . Consultative Committee for Postal Studies (UPU)
CCR . . . . . . Catholic Committee for Refugees
CCR . . . . . . Central Communication Region (Air Force)
CCR . . . . . . Circulation Control Rotor (Navy)
CCR . . . . . . Closed-Cycle Refrigerator
CCR . . . . . . Combat Center Remoted (Military)
CCR . . . . . . Combat Command R
CCr . . . . . . Combat Crew (Air Force)
CCR . . . . . . Command Control Receiver
CCR . . . . . . Commission Centrale pour la Navigation du Rhin (Central Commission
          for the Navigation of the Rhine)
CCR . . . . . . Commission on Civil Rights
CCR . . . . . . Complex Chemical Reaction
CCR . . . . . . Computer Character Recognition
CCR . . . . . . Consumable Case Rocket
CCR . . . . . . Contract Change Release (or Request)
CCR . . . . . . Control Circuit Resistance
CCR . . . . . . Cooperative College Registry
CCR . . . . . . Credit Card Reader
CCR . . . . . . Creedence Clearwater Revival (Rock music group)
CCR . . . . . . Critical Compression Ratio
CCR . . . . . . Cross-Channel Rejection
CCR . . . . . . Crystal Can Relay
CCR . . . . . . Cube Corner Reflector
CCRC . . . . . . Chemical Corps Research and Development Command (Army)
CCRC . . . . . . Combat Crew Replacement Center (World War II)
CCRDC . . . . . Chemical Corps Research and Development Command (Military)
CCRR . . . . . . Conference Committee for Refugee Rabbis
CCRT . . . . . . Check Collectors Round Table
CCRU . . . . . . Complete Crew
CCRZ . . . . . . Climb to and Cruise (Aviation)
CCS . . . . . . Call Seconds (Bell Laboratories)
CCS . . . . . . Cape Cod System (Air Force)
CCS . . . . . . Carrier Color Signal
CCS . . . . . . Cast Carbon Steel
CCS . . . . . . Casualty Clearing Station (Military)
CCS . . . . . . Cataloging and Classification Section (of RTSD) (Library science)
CCS . . . . . . Catholic Committee on Scouting
CCS . . . . . . Center for Comparative Sociology
CCS . . . . . . Central Certificate Service (NYSE)
CCS . . . . . . Central Certificate System (Stock exchange automation program)
CCS . . . . . . Central Cooperative Society (United Arab Republic)
CCS . . . . . . Centurion Colidar System
CCS . . . . . . Change Control System
CCS . . . . . . Chief Commissary Steward
CCS . . . . . . Church of Christ, Scientist
CCS . . . . . . Circular Cylindrical Shell
CCS . . . . . . Collective Call Sign (Radio)
CCS . . . . . . Combined Chiefs of Staff (DOD)
CCS . . . . . . Command and Communications System (NASA)
CCS . . . . . . Command, Control, Support (Army)
CCS . . . . . . Command and Control System
CCS . . . . . . Committee for Collective Security
CCS . . . . . . Compass Control System
CCS . . . . . . Component Control Section
CCS . . . . . . Composers Cooperative Society
CCS . . . . . . Computer Campaign Services (Data processing firm in field of politics)
CCS . . . . . . Confidential Cover Sheet
CCS . . . . . . Consiliul Central al Sindicatelor (Central Council of Trade Unions)
          (Romania)
CCS . . . . . . Contaminant Control System
CCS . . . . . . Continuous Commercial Service (Equipment specifications)
CCS . . . . . . Contrast Contour Seeker
CCS . . . . . . Controlled Combustion System (Antipollution device for automobiles)
CCS . . . . . . Conveyor Control System
CCS . . . . . . Council of Communication Societies
CCS . . . . . . Custom Contract Service (IBM)
CCS . . . . . . Hundred-Call-Second (Tables for telephone trunk loading)
CC & S . . . . . Central Computer and Sequencer (NASA)
CCSA . . . . . . Common Control Switching Arrangement (AT & T)
CCSA . . . . . . Council for Christian Social Action (United Church of Christ)
CCSATU . . . . . Coordinating Council of South African Trade Unions
CCSAU . . . . . Committee for Corporate Support of American Universities
CCSB . . . . . . Control Commission Shipping Bureau (Allied German Occupation Forces)
CCSB . . . . . . Credit Card Service Bureau (of America)
CCSC . . . . . . Central Connecticut State College
CCSC . . . . . . Civil Affairs Staff Center (Wimbledon, England)
CCSC . . . . . . Confederation Camerounaise des Syndicats Chretiens (Confederation of
          Believing Workers of the Cameroon)

CCSC . . . . . . Congregational Christian Service Committee
CCS-C . . . . . Central Coordinating Staff, Canada
CCSEP . . . . . Cement Coated Single Epoxy
CCSF . . . . . . City College of San Francisco
CCSF . . . . . . Commander, Caribbean Sea Frontier (Navy)
CCSFI . . . . . Canned Chop Suey Foods Industry
CCSG . . . . . . Computer Components & System Group
CCSL . . . . . . Camp Coles Signal Laboratory (Army)
CCSL . . . . . . Citizens Conference on State Legislatures
CCSL . . . . . . Communications and Control Systems Laboratory
CCSL . . . . . . Confederation Congolaise des Syndicats Libres (Congolese Confederation of Free Unions) (Brazzaville)
CCSM . . . . . . Confederation Chretienne des Syndicats Malgaches (Christian Confederation of Malagasy Unions)
CCSN . . . . . . Conference of Catholic Schools of Nursing
CCSPP . . . . . Clergy Counseling Service for Problem Pregnancies
CCSS . . . . . . Cooperative College-School Science (Program) (National Science Foundation)
CCSSO . . . . . Council of Chief State School Officers
CCST . . . . . . Centennial Centre of Science and Technology
CCST . . . . . . Center for Computer Sciences and Technology (National Bureau of Standards)
CCSTD . . . . . Chief Commissary Steward
CCSTP . . . . . Cubic Centimeters at Standard Temperature and Pressure (Also CSTP)
CCSU . . . . . . Computer Cross Select Unit
CCT . . . . C-Band Communications Transponder
CCT . . . . Cathode Closure Tetanus
CCT . . . . Cauchy Convergence Test
CCT . . . . Central California Traction Company (AAR code)
CCT . . . . Cesium Contact Thruster
CCT . . . . Chocolate-Colored Tablet (Pharmacy)
CCT . . . . Clarkson College of Technology (New York)
CCT . . . . Combat Control Team
CCT . . . . Combat Crew Training
CCT . . . . Communications Control Team (Military)
CCT . . . . Complex Coordination Test
CCT . . . . Confrerie des Chevaliers du Tastevin
CCT . . . . Constant Current Transformer
CCT . . . . Controlled Cord Traction (Medicine)
CCT . . . . Council for Clinical Training
CCT . . . . Crystal-Controlled Transmitter
CC/T . . . . . . Combined Center/Tower (Aviation)
CCTA . . . . . . Cape Canaveral Test Annex (Obsolete) (Aerospace)
CCTA . . . . . . Commission de Cooperation Technique en Afrique (Commission for Technical Cooperation in Africa)
CCTA . . . . . . Coordinating Committee of Technical Assistance
CCTC . . . . . . Chemical Corps Technical Command (Army)
CCTE . . . . . . Council on Cooperation in Teacher Education (Defunct)
CCTEP . . . . . Cement Coated Triple Epoxy
CCTP . . . . . . Center City Transportation Program
CCTS . . . . . . Canaveral Council of Technical Societies
CCTS . . . . . . Combat Crew Training School (Air Force)
CCTS . . . . . . Combat Crew Training Squadron (TAC)
CCTUO . . . . . Coordinating Committee of Trade Union Organizations (Ceylon)
CCTV . . . . . . Closed Circuit Television
CCTWg . . . . . Combat Crew Training Wing (Air Force)
CCU . . . . Camera Control Unit
CCU . . . . Catholic Central Union
CCU . . . . Central Control Unit
CCU . . . . Chart Comparison Unit
CCU . . . . Comite Consultatif des Unites (Advisory Committee on Units)
CCU . . . . Common Control Unit (Army)
CCU . . . . Communication Control Unit
CCU . . . . Computer Control Unit
CCU . . . . Coronary Care Unit (of a hospital)
CCU . . . . Council on Christian Unity
CCU . . . . Coupling Control Unit
CCU . . . . Crewman Communications Umbilical (Apollo) (NASA)
CCU . . . . Croatian Catholic Union of the USA
CCU . . . . Czech Catholic Union
CCUA . . . . . . Catholic Central Union of America
CCUAP . . . . . Computer Cable Upkeep Administrative Program (Bell System)
CCUN . . . . . . Collegiate Council for the United Nations
CCUP . . . . . . Commission Consultative Universitaire de Pedagogie (Belgium)
CCURR . . . . . Canadian Council on Urban and Regional Research
CCUS . . . . . . Chamber of Commerce of the United States
CCUS . . . . . . Cleared Customs (Aviation)
CCV . . . . Color Contrast Value
CCV . . . . Combat Command V
CCV . . . . Congregatio a Sacro Corde Jesu (Congregation of the Priests of the Sacred Heart)

CCV . . . . Control Configured Vehicle (Air Force)
CCV . . . . Coolant Control Valve
CCW . . . . Caldwell College for Women (New Jersey)
CCW . . . . Carrying Concealed Weapon
CCW . . . . Channel Command Word (Data processing)
CCW . . . . Charles City Western Railway Company (AAR code)
CCW . . . . Cosmetic Career Women
CCW . . . . Counterclockwise
CCWAD . . . . . Conference of Church Workers Among the Deaf
CCWHP . . . . . Coordinating Committee on Women in the Historical Profession
CCWL . . . . . . Catholic Council on Working Life
CCWO . . . . . . Commercial Communications Work Order (Air Force)
CCWO . . . . . . Cryptocenter Watch Officer
CC WR HDR . . Canvas-Covered Wire Rope Handrail (Aerospace)
CCX . . . . Continental Copper & Steel Industries, Inc. (NYSE symbol)
CCXD . . . . . . Computer-Controlled X-Ray Diffractometer
CCYUA . . . . . Catholic Central Youth Union of America
CCZA . . . . . . Canadian Coastal Zone Atlantic
CCZP . . . . . . Canadian Coastal Zone Pacific
Cd . . . . Cadmium (Chemical element)
CD . . . . Calendar Day
CD . . . . Camouflage Detection (Often, in regard to a special photographic film, as, "CD film") (Military)
CD . . . . Canada Dry Corporation (NYSE symbol) (Delisted)
cd . . . . Candela (Formerly, Candlepower)
CD . . . . Canine Distemper (Veterinary medicine)
CD . . . . Canine Dose (Pharmacology)
CD . . . . Capacitor Diode
CD . . . . Carried Down
CD . . . . Cash Discount
CD . . . . Central District
CD . . . . Certificate of Deposit (Banking)
CD . . . . Certificate of Destruction
CD . . . . Cesarean Delivered (Medicine)
CD . . . . Chancery Division
CD . . . . Change Directive
CD . . . . Chief of Division
CD . . . . Circular Dispersion
CD . . . . Civil Defense
CD . . . . Classification of Defects
CD . . . . Clock Driver
CD . . . . Coast Defense(s)
CD . . . . Coin Dimple
CD . . . . Cold-Drawn (Metal)
CD . . . . Colla Destra (With the Right Hand)
CD . . . . College Discovery (Educational project for disadvantaged youngsters)
CD . . . . Combat Development
CD . . . . Commerce Department
CD . . . . Commercial Dock
CD . . . . Commission du Danube (Danube Commission)
CD . . . . Common Denominator
CD . . . . Common Digitizer (FAA)
CD . . . . Communicable Disease (or a patient with such a disease) (Medicine)
CD . . . . Companion Dog (Degree of obedience training)
CD . . . . Completely Denatured
CD . . . . Confidential Document (Navy)
CD . . . . Congressional District
CD . . . . Conning Director (Navy)
CD . . . . Consular Declaration
CD . . . . Contagious Diseases
CD . . . . Contract Definition (Navy)
CD . . . . Converging-Diverging
CD . . . . Convulsive Dose
CD . . . . Cordoba Durchmusterung (Star chart)
CD . . . . Corps Diplomatique (Diplomatic Corps)
CD . . . . Countdown (Aerospace)
CD . . . . Crystal Diode
CD . . . . Crystal Driver
CD . . . . Current Density
CD . . . . Current Driver
C-D . . . . CONVAIR (Consolidated-Vultee Aircraft Corp.) Daingerfield (Later, General Dynamics/Daingerfield) (Aerospace)
C/D . . . . Certificate of Deposit
C/D . . . . Command Destruct (Aerospace)
C/D . . . . Contract Definition
C/D . . . . Count Down
C & D . . . . . . Chemist and Druggist
C & D . . . . . . Collection and Delivery (Business and trade)
C & D . . . . . . Collection and Distribution (Transportation)
C & D . . . . . . Communications and Data
C & D . . . . . . Construction and Development

C & D . . . . . . Controls and Displays
CD/50 . . . . . . Median Curative Dose
CDA . . . . Canadian Dental Association
CDA . . . . Catholic Daughters of America
CDA . . . . . . Civil Defense Agency
CDA . . . . . . Combined Development Agency (Anglo-American uranium procurement)
CDA . . . . Command Data Acquisition
CDA . . . . Community Development Agency
CDA . . . . Compania Dominicana de Aviacion, SA (Dominican Republic airline)
CDA . . . . Control Data Corporation (NYSE symbol)
CDA . . . . Copper Development Association
C d'A . . . . Corps d'Afrique
CDA . . . . National Society of Colonial Dames of America
CDAAA . . . . . . Committee to Defend America by Aiding the Allies (Active prior to US entry into World War II)
CDAC . . . . . . Civil Defense Advisory Council
CDAE . . . . . . Civil Defense Adult Education
CDANC . . . . . Committee for the Development of Art in Negro Colleges
CDAP . . . . . . Civil Damage Assessment Program (Army)
CDAS . . . . . . Central Data Acquisition System
CDAS . . . . . . Command and Data Acquisition Station (Aerospace)
CDB . . . . Caliper Disk Brake
CDB . . . . Capacitance Decode Box
CDB . . . . Caribbean Development Bank (UN)
CDB . . . . Cast Double Base
CDB . . . . Central Data Bank
CDB . . . . Combat Development Branch
CDB . . . . Current Data Bit (Data processing)
CDBN . . . . . . Column-Digit Binary Network
CDC . . . . Calculated Date of Confinement (Medicine)
CDC . . . . California Debris Commission (Army)
CDC . . . . . . Call Directing Code
CDC . . . . Canada Development Corporation
CDC . . . . . . Capsule Drive Core
CDC . . . . Career Development Center
CDC . . . . Career Development Course
CDC . . . . Caribbean Defense Command(er)
CDC . . . . Center for Disease Control (Formerly, Communicable Disease Center) (Atlanta) (Public Health Service)
CDC . . . . Central Digital Computer
CDC . . . . Ceramic Disc Capacitor
CDC . . . . Chemical Development Corporation (Geneva, Switzerland)
CDC . . . . Chenodeoxycholic Acid (Bile constitutent)
CDC . . . . Child Development Consultant
CDC . . . . Citizens' Defense Corps
CDC . . . . Civil Defense Coordinator
CDC . . . . Clamped Dielectric Constant
CDC . . . . Classified Document Control
CDC . . . . Coaxial Directional Coupler
CDC . . . . Code Directing Character (Data processing)
CDC . . . . Colonial Development Corporation
CDC . . . . Combat Development Command (Army)
CDC . . . . Command and Data-Handling Console (DSIF)
CDC . . . . Command Destruct Control (Aerospace)
CDC . . . . Commissioners of District of Columbia
CDC . . . . Community Development Corporation
CDC . . . . Company Data Coordinator
CDC . . . . Computer Display Channel
CDC . . . . Configuration Data Control
CDC . . . . Continental Dorset Club
CDC . . . . Contract Data Coordinator
CDC . . . . Control Data Corporation
CDC . . . . Control Distribution Center
CDC . . . . Copper Data Center (Battelle Memorial Institute)
CDC . . . . Countdown Clock
CDC . . . . Cryogenic Data Center (National Bureau of Standards)
CDC . . . . Cumberland Railway & Coal Company (AAR code)
CDCA . . . . . . Chefs de Cuisine Association of America
CD & CC . . . . Central Data and Cataloging Center
CDCD . . . . . . Certificate of Disposition of Classified Documents
CDCD . . . . . . Counter-Double-Current Distribution (Analytical chemistry)
CDCDSCA . . . . Children's Dress, Cotton Dress, and Sportwear Contractors Association
CDCE . . . . . . Central Data-Conversion Equipment
CDCEC . . . . . Combat Development Committee Experimentation Center (Army)
CDCIA . . . . . . Combat Development Command Infantry Agency (Army)
CDC-INTA . . . Combat Development Command - Intelligence Agency (Army)
CDCM . . . . . . Carbon Dioxide Concentrating (or Concentrator) Module
CDCR . . . . . . Center for Documentation and Communication Research (Case-Western Reserve University)
CDCR . . . . . . Control Drawing Change Request
CDCS . . . . . . Central Data Collection System

CDCS . . . . . . Civil Defense Countermeasures System
CDCS . . . . . . Construction Dollar Control System (AT & T)
CDCU . . . . . . Communications Digital Control Unit
CDD . . . . Castilejo-Dalitz-Dyson
CDD . . . . Central Data Display
CDD . . . . Certificate of Disability Discharge (Military)
CDD . . . . Chart Distribution Data
CDD . . . . Coded Decimal Digit
CDD . . . . Color Data Display
CDD . . . . Command Destruct Decoder
CDD . . . . Computer-Directed Drawing
CDD . . . . Conference on Dual Distribution
CDD . . . . Cosmic Dust Detector
CDD . . . . Cratering Demolition Device
CDD . . . . Cunningham Drug Stores, Inc. (NYSE symbol)
CDDA . . . . . . Canadian Diamond Drilling Association
CDDGP . . . . . Commander, Destroyer Development Group, Pacific (Navy)
CDDI . . . . . . Computer-Directed Drawing Instrument
CDDP . . . . . . Canadian Department of Defence Production
CDDT . . . . . . Countdown Demonstration Test (NASA)
CDE . . . . Cadence Industries Corp. (NYSE symbol)
CDE . . . . Carbon Dioxide Economizer
CDE . . . . Civil Director of Economics
CDE . . . . Contamination-Decontamination Experiment (AEC)
CDEC . . . . . . Combat Development Experimentation Center (Army)
CDEE . . . . . . Chemical Defense Experimental Establishment (British)
CDEF . . . . . . Committee on the Development of Engineering Faculties
CDEI . . . . . . Control Data Education Institutes
CDEK . . . . . . Computer Data Entry Keyboard
CDEOS . . . . . Civil Defense Emergency Operations System
CDF . . . . Class Determination and Finding
CDF . . . . Combat Defense Force
CDF . . . . Combined Distribution Frame (RADAR)
CDF . . . . Command Decoder Filter
CDF . . . . Community Development Foundation
CDF . . . . Confined Detonating Fuze
CDF . . . . Constant Current Fringes
CDF . . . . Cumulative Distribution Function (Statistics)
CDFAB . . . . . California Dried Fig Advisory Board
CDFC . . . . . . Commonwealth Development Finance Company Limited (Joint government and private agency in London established to aid businesses elsewhere in British Commonwealth)
CDFEA . . . . . California Dried Fruit Export Association
cd/ft . . . . . . Candela Per Square Foot
CDG . . . . Capacitor Diode Gate
CDG . . . . . . Circular Diffraction Grating
CDG . . . . Coder-Decoder Group (Army)
CDG . . . . Costume Designers Guild
CDGA . . . . . . California Date Growers Association
CDGM . . . . . Child Development Group of Mississippi
CDH . . . . Constant Delta Height (Aerospace)
CDH . . . . Constant Differential Height
CDHW . . . . . International Association of Cleaning and Dye House Workers
CDI . . . . Cargo Disposition Instructions
CDI . . . . Church Defence Institution (British)
CDI . . . . Classified Defense Information (Military)
CDI . . . . Collector Diffusion Isolation (Electronics)
CDI . . . . Commission du Droit International (ONU)
CDI . . . . Computer-Directed Instrument
CDI . . . . Contractor's Demonstration Inspection
CDI . . . . Course Deviation Indicator (Aviation)
CDI . . . . Cutting Die Institute
CDIF . . . . . . Controller/Director Information File
CDL . . . . Cable Delay Line
CDL . . . . Carbon Dioxide LASER
CDL . . . . Central Dental Laboratories (Army)
CDL . . . . Central Dockyard Laboratory (British)
CDL . . . . Ceramic Delay Line
CDL . . . . Citizens for Decent Literature
CDL . . . . Coaxial Diode Limiter
CDL . . . . Common Display Logic (Data processing)
CDL . . . . Condor Data Link
CDL . . . . Constant Delay Line
CDL . . . . Contract Deficiency Listing
CDL . . . . Cronar Dot Litho (Du Pont)
CDLS . . . . . . Condor Data Link System
CDLS(W) . . . . Canadian Defence Liaison Staff (Washington)
CDM . . . . Certified Decal Manufacturers
CDM . . . . Chief Decision Makers
CDM . . . . Coded Division Multiplex
CDM . . . . Contractor Developed Material

cd/m² . . . . . . Candela Per Square Meter
CDMA . . . . . . Code Division Multiple Access
CDMS . . . . . . Coherent Doppler Measurement System
CDN . . . . . . Chicago Daily News (A newspaper)
CDN . . . . . . Coded Decimal Notation
CDN . . . . . . Convergent-Divergent Nozzle
CDO . . . . . . California Disaster Office
CDO . . . . . . Change Design Order (Navy)
CDO . . . . . . Combat Development Office
CDO . . . . . . Command Duty Officer (Navy)
CDO . . . . . . Communications Duty Officer
CDO . . . . . . Community Dial Office
CDOA . . . . . . Car Department Officers Association
CDOG . . . . . . Combat Development Objective Guide (CDC)
CDOS . . . . . . Controlled Date of Separation (Military)
CDP . . . . . . Central (or Command) Data Processor
CDP . . . . . . Cerro Corporation (NYSE symbol)
CDP . . . . . . Certificate in Data Processing
CDP . . . . . . Certified Data Processor
CDP . . . . . . Checkout Data Processor (RADAR)
CDP . . . . . . Combat Development Project (Army)
CDP . . . . . . Common Depth Point
CDP . . . . . . Communications Data Processor (Electronics)
CDP . . . . . . Company Distributing Point (Army)
CDP . . . . . . Compound Diffraction Projector
CDP . . . . . . Compressor Discharge Pressure
CDP . . . . . . Concept Definition Proposal
CDP . . . . . . Confidence Development Plan
CDP . . . . . . Constant Deviation Prism
CDP . . . . . . Contract Definition Phase (DOD)
CDP . . . . . . Cornu Double Prism
CDP . . . . . . Coronary Drug Project
CDP . . . . . . Correlated Data Processor
CDP . . . . . . Cost Data Plan
CDP . . . . . . Critical Decision Point
CDP . . . . . . Crosslinked Dextran Polymer
CDP . . . . . . Cytidine Diphosphate
C-DP . . . . . . Comptroller-Directors of Programs (Army)
CDPC . . . . . . Central Data Processing Computer
CDPIE . . . . . . Command Data Processor Interface Equipment
CDR . . . . . . Cargo Delivery Receipt
CDR . . . . . . Civil Defense Receiver
CDR . . . . . . Command Destruct Receiver (Military)
CDR . . . . . . Command Distribution Rack
CDR . . . . . . Commission des Reparations (Reparation Commission)
CDR . . . . . . Complete Design Release (Navy)
CDR . . . . . . Consolidated Cigar Corporation (NYSE symbol) (Delisted)
CDR . . . . . . Constant Dose Range (Radiation in atmosphere)
CDR . . . . . . Controlled Dynamic Range
CDR . . . . . . Council on Documentation Research (Defunct)
CDR . . . . . . Countdown Deviation Request (Aerospace)
CDR . . . . . . Critical Design Review
CDR . . . . . . Current Directional Relay
CDRA . . . . . . Civil Defense Research Associates
CDRB . . . . . . Canadian Defense Research Board
CDRE . . . . . . Chemical Defence Research Establishment (British)
CDRL . . . . . . Contract Data Requirements List
CDRT . . . . . . Committee on Diagnostic Reading Tests
CDRU . . . . . . Child Development Research Unit (Nigeria)
CDRX . . . . . . Critical Damping Resistance External
CDS . . . . . . Cargo Delivery System
CDS . . . . . . Cash on Delivery Service
CDS . . . . . . Cathode Dark Space
CDS . . . . . . Central Distribution System (Publications) (Navy)
CDS . . . . . . Certificate of Deposit
CDS . . . . . . Certified Documentary Specialist (Designation given by American Society of International Executives to persons in international trade)
CDS . . . . . . Chamber of Destination of Ships
CDS . . . . . . Chemical Discriminator System
CDS . . . . . . Climatological Data Sheet (Air Force)
CDS . . . . . . Cold-Drawn Steel
CDS . . . . . . Color Data System
CDS . . . . . . Color Difference Signal
CDS . . . . . . Command Destruct System
CDS . . . . . . Commander, Destroyer Squadron (Navy)
CDS . . . . . . Communications and Data Subsystems
CDS . . . . . . Compact Depth Sounder
CDS . . . . . . Companion of the Distinguished Service Order
CDS . . . . . . Compatible Duplex System
CDS . . . . . . Comprehensive Display System
CDS . . . . . . Compressed Data Storage

CDS . . . . . . Computer Data Switchboard
CDS . . . . . . Conceptual Design Study
CDS . . . . . . Congregation of the Divine Spirit (Roman Catholic women's religious order)
CDS . . . . . . Construction-Differential Subsidy (Authorized by Merchant Marine Act of 1936)
CDS . . . . . . Construction Dollar Spreading (System) (AT & T)
CDS . . . . . . Container Delivery System (Military)
CDS . . . . . . Controlled Delivery System
CDS . . . . . . Count Dracula Society
CDSA . . . . . . Country Dance Society of America
CDSE . . . . . . Computer-Driven Simulation Environment (FAA)
CDSHA . . . . . . Country Day School Headmasters Association of the US
CDSM . . . . . . Consolidated Defense Supply Material
CDSO . . . . . . Commonwealth Defense Service Organization
CDSR . . . . . . Contractual Data Status Reporting System
CDSR . . . . . . Controlled Deployment Specular Reflector (Army)
CDSRS . . . . . . Consolidated Delivery Status Report System
CDSS . . . . . . Compressed Data Storage System
C & DSS . . . . . Communication and Data Subsystem
CDST . . . . . . Central Daylight Saving Time
CDT . . . . . . Central Daylight Time
CDT . . . . . . Command Destruct Transmitter (Military)
CDT . . . . . . Compressed-Data Tape
CDT . . . . . . Consecutive Duty Tour (Air Force)
CDT . . . . . . Continuous Duty Target
CDT . . . . . . Control Data Terminal
CDT . . . . . . Coordinate Data Transmission
CDT . . . . . . Countdown Demonstration Test
CDT . . . . . . Countdown Time
CDTC-V . . . . . Combat Development and Test Center - Vietnam
CDTE . . . . . . Council for Distributive Teacher Education
CDTEC . . . . . . Combat Development Technical Evaluation Center
CDTS . . . . . . Constant-Depth Temperature Sensor (Oceanography)
CDTS . . . . . . Continuous Duty Target Source
CDU . . . . . . Cable Distribution Unit (Aerospace)
CDU . . . . . . Central Display Unit
CDU . . . . . . Christlich-Demokratische Union (Christian Democratic Union) (West German political party)
CDU . . . . . . Classification Decimale Universelle (Universal Decimal Classification)
CDU . . . . . . Coastal Defense RADAR for Detecting U-boats
CDU . . . . . . Command Destruct Unit (Army)
CDU . . . . . . Control Data Unit
CDU . . . . . . Control and Diagnostic Unit (Data processing)
CDU . . . . . . Coupling Data Unit
CDU . . . . . . Coupling Display Unit
CDUCE . . . . . . Christian Democratic Union of Central Europe
CDUEP . . . . . . Civil Defense University Extension Program
CDV . . . . . . Carte-de-Visite (Visiting Card)
CDVO . . . . . . Civilian Defense Volunteer Office
CDW . . . . . . Carrying a Dangerous Weapon (Police term)
CDW . . . . . . Chilled Drinking Water (Aerospace)
CDW . . . . . . Civil Defense Warning
CDWR . . . . . . Chilled Drinking Water Return (Aerospace)
CDX . . . . . . Companion Dog, Excellent (Degree of obedience training)
CDX . . . . . . Control Differential Transmitter
CDZ . . . . . . Chef der Zivilverwaltung (Chief of Civil Affairs Section) (German military - World War II)
CE . . . . . . Canada East
CE . . . . . . Caveat Emptor (Let the Buyer Beware)
CE . . . . . . Celestial Equator
Ce . . . . . . Cerium (Chemical element)
CE . . . . . . Chancellor of the Exchequer (British)
CE . . . . . . Chemical Engineer
CE . . . . . . Chief Engineer (Navy)
CE . . . . . . Chief of Engineers (Army)
CE . . . . . . Christian Era
CE . . . . . . Chronometer Error (Navigation)
CE . . . . . . Church of England
CE . . . . . . Circular Error (Military)
CE . . . . . . Civil Engineer (Navy)
CE . . . . . . College English (A periodical)
CE . . . . . . Combustion Engineering (Navy)
CE . . . . . . Common Emitter
CE . . . . . . Common Era
CE . . . . . . Communications-Electronics
CE . . . . . . Communications Equipment
CE . . . . . . Compass Error (Navigation)
CE . . . . . . Compression Engine
CE . . . . . . Computer Engineer
CE . . . . . . Concept Exploration
CE . . . . . . Conspicuity Enhancement (Aviation)

ACRONYMS AND INITIALISMS DICTIONARY

CE . . . . Construction Electrician (Navy rating)
CE . . . . Corps of Engineers (Army) (Merged with General Equipment Command)
CE . . . . Cost Effectiveness
CE . . . . Council of Europe
CE . . . . Counter-Espionage
CE . . . . Customer Engineer
CE . . . . Customs and Excise
CE . . . . Cuvee Extra
C-E . . . . Campbell-Ewald Company (Advertising agency)
C-E . . . . Communications-Electronics
C & E . . . . . . Chicago and Erie Railroad Company
C & E . . . . . . Clothing and Equipage
C & E . . . . . . Communications and Electronics
C & E . . . . . . Construction and Equipment
C of E . . . . . . Church of England
C of E . . . . . . The Comedy of Errors (by Shakespeare)
C of E . . . . . . Corps of Engineers
CEA . . . . Cambridge Electron Accelerator (AEC)
CEA . . . . Canadian Electrical Association
CEA . . . . Carcinoembryonic Antigen (Biochemistry)
CEA . . . . Catholic Economic Association
CEA . . . . Cessna Aircraft Company (NYSE symbol)
CEA . . . . Chinese Exclusion Act
CEA . . . . Church Evangelism Association
CEA . . . . Church Extension Association (British)
CEA . . . . Circular Error Average (Military)
CEA . . . . Clearinghouse on Educational Administration (ERIC)
CEA . . . . Coal Exporters Association of the United States
CEA . . . . College English Association
CEA . . . . Comite Europeen des Assurances (European Insurance Committee)
CEA . . . . Commissariat a l'Energie Atomique (France)
CEA . . . . Commission Economique pour l'Afrique
CEA . . . . Commodity Exchange Authority (Department of Agriculture)
CEA . . . . Confederation des Educateurs Americains
CEA . . . . Confederation Europeenne de l'Agriculture (European Confederation of Agriculture)
CEA . . . . Conservation Education Association
CEA . . . . Construction Equipment Advertisers
CEA . . . . Cooperative Education Association
CEA . . . . Correctional Education Association
CEA . . . . Council of Economic Advisers (to the President)
CEAA . . . . . . Center for Editions of American Authors
CEAA . . . . . . Centre Europeen d'Aviation Agricole
CEAA . . . . . . Council of European-American Associations
CEAC . . . . . . Citizens Educational Advisory Committee
CEAC . . . . . . Commission Europeenne de l'Aviation Civile (European Civil Aviation Commission)
CEAC . . . . . . Committee on European Airspace Coordination (NATO)
CEAC . . . . . . Consulting Engineers Association of California
CEAEO . . . . . . Commission Economique pour l'Asie et l'Extreme-Orient
CEAL . . . . . . Committee on East Asian Libraries
CEAN . . . . . . Centre d'Etudes pour les Applications de l'Energie Nucleaire (Belgium)
CEANAR . . . . . Commission on Education in Agriculture and Natural Resources (National Research Council)
CEAP . . . . . . Comite d'Entente et d'Action Politique (Committee for Understanding and Political Action)
CEAPD . . . . . . Central Air Procurement District
CEASA . . . . . . Centro Estadual de Abastecimento SA (State Central Supply Company) (Brazil)
CEASD . . . . . . Conference of Executives of American Schools for the Deaf
CEASD . . . . . . Corporate Engineering and Sales Directive
CEASRS . . . . . Civil Engineer Automated Specification Retrieval System (Air Force)
CEB . . . . Comite Electrotechnique Belge
CEB . . . . Comite Europeen du Beton (European Committee for Concrete)
CEB . . . . Council of Employee Benefits
CEB . . . . Cryogenic Expulsive Bladder
CEBAR . . . . . . Chemical, Biological, Radiological Warfare
CEBELCOR . . . . Centre Belge d'Etude de la Corrosion
CEBJ . . . . . . Commission of Editors of Biochemical Journals
CEBM . . . . . . Corona, Eddy Current, Beta Ray, Microwave
CEBMCA . . . . . Corps of Engineers Ballistic Missile Construction Agency (Army)
CEBMCO . . . . . Corps of Engineers Ballistic Missile Construction Office (COE/BSD)
CEBR . . . . . . Cedar Breaks National Monument
CEBUS . . . . . . Confirmed Exposure but Unconscious (Advertising)
CEC . . . . Canadian Electrical Code
CEC . . . . Capsule End Cover
CEC . . . . Center for Educational Change (University of California, Berkeley)
CEC . . . . Central Economic Committee
CEC . . . . Centralized Electronic Control (Navy)
CEC . . . . Centre Europeen de la Culture (European Cultural Center)
CEC . . . . Ceramic Educational Council

CEC . . . . Citizen Exchange Corps
CEC . . . . Civil Engineer Corps (Army)
CEC . . . . Coal Experts Committee (Allied German Occupation Forces)
CEC . . . . Combined Environment Centrifuge
CEC . . . . Combined Environmental Chamber
CEC . . . . Commodity Exchange Commission
CEC . . . . Commonwealth Economic Committee
CEC . . . . Commonwealth Edison Company (Chicago)
CEC . . . . Communications & Electronics Command
CEC . . . . Communications-Electronics Committee
CEC . . . . Consolidated Electrodynamics Corporation
CEC . . . . Consolidated Electronics Corporation
CEC . . . . Consulting Engineers Council
CEC . . . . Continental Entry Charts (Air Force)
CEC . . . . Council for Exceptional Children
CEC . . . . Criminological Executives Club
CEC . . . . Cryogenics Engineering Conference
CECA . . . . . . Communaute Europeenne du Charbon et de l'Acier (European Coal and Steel Community)
CECA . . . . . . Council on Economic and Cultural Affairs (Rockefeller Brothers Fund, Ford Foundation activity)
CECAL . . . . . Commission Episcopale de Cooperation Apostolique Canada-Amerique Latine
CECB . . . . . . Conseil Europeen du Cuir Brut (European Untanned Leather Council)
CECC . . . . . . Communaute Europeenne de Credit Communal (European Municipal Credit Community)
CECH . . . . . . Comite Europeen de la Culture du Houblon (European Hop Growers Committee)
CECIL . . . . . Compact Electronic Components Inspection Laboratory
CECIOS . . . . . From the French for European Council of International Committee of Scientific Management
CECL . . . . . . Civil Engineering Computer Laboratory (MIT)
CECL . . . . . . Conference of Eastern College Librarians
CECLB . . . . . Comite Europeen de Controle Laitierbeurrier
CECMRL . . . . . Communications-Electronics Consolidated Mobilization Reserve List
CECO . . . . . . Chandler Evans Corporation
CECOGp . . . . . Civil Engineer Construction Operations Group (Air Force)
CECOS . . . . . Civil Engineers Corps Officers School (Navy)
CECR . . . . . . Central European Communication Region (Air Force)
CECS . . . . . . Charge Exchange Cross Section
CECS . . . . . . Communications-Electronics Coordinating Section (NATO)
CECT . . . . . . Comite Europeen de la Chaudronnerie et de la Tolerie (European Committee for Boilermaking and Kindred Steel Structures)
CED . . . . Captured Enemy Documents
CED . . . . Committee for Economic Development
CED . . . . Communaute Europeenne de Defense (European Defense Community)
CED . . . . Communications-Electronics Doctrine (Series of Air Force manuals)
CED . . . . Constant Energy Differences
CED . . . . Council on Education of the Deaf
C/ED . . . . . . Clothing and Equipment Development Branch (Army)
CEDAC . . . . . Central Differential Analyzer Control
CEDAC . . . . . Cooling Effect Detection and Control
CEDAL . . . . . Centro de Estudios Democraticos de America Latina
CEDAM . . . . . Casa Editrice Dott. A. Milani (Italian publisher)
CEDAM . . . . . Club de Exploraciones y Deportes Actuaticos de Mexico AC
CEDAM . . . . . Conservation, Exploration, Diving, Archeology, Museums (Acronym is used as name of an international organization interested in these five subjects)
CEDAMEL . . . . Centre d'Etudes et de Distribution des Appareils et du Materiel de l'Enseignement Linguistique
CEDB . . . . . . Church Executive Development Board
CEDESE . . . . . Communaute Europeenne des Etudiants en Sciences Economiques
CEDICOL . . . . Centre d'Information des Combustibles Liquides
CEDIT . . . . . Centro Didattico Telefonico (Telephone Teaching Center) (Italy)
CEDOPI . . . . . Centre d'Etudes Documentaires de Propriete Industrielle
CEDPO . . . . . Communications-Electronics Doctrinal Projects Office (Air Force)
CEE . . . . Captured Enemy Equipment (Military)
CEE . . . . Carbon Electrode Equipment
CEE . . . . Combat Emplacement Excavator
CEE . . . . Commission Economique pour l'Europe (Nations Unies)
CEE . . . . Communaute Economique Europeenne (European Economic Community)
CEE . . . . Communication Electronics Element (Army)
CEE . . . . International Commission on Rules for the Approval of Electrical Equipment
CEEA . . . . . . Catholic Educational Exhibitors Association
CEEA . . . . . . Communaute Europeenne de l'Energie Atomique
CEEB . . . . . . College Entrance Examination Board
CEEC . . . . . . Committee for European Economic Cooperation (Marshall Plan) (Post-World War II)
CEEF . . . . . . Clergy Economic Education Foundation
CEEMA . . . . . Conference Europeenne des Experts Meteorologistes de l'Aeronautique

CEEN . . . . Centre d'Etude de l'Energie Nucleaire (Belgium) (Also known as NERC)
CEEP. . . . . . . Centre Europeen d'Etudes de Population (European Center for Population Studies)
CEER . . . . Chemical Economy & Engineering Review (A publication)
CEERA . . . . . . Conference Europeenne des Experts Radiotelegraphistes de l'Aeronautique
CEF . . . . Canadian Expeditionary Forces
CEF . . . . Captain (Commanding) Escort Forces (Navy)
CEF . . . . Carrier Elimination Filter
CEF . . . . Catalogue de l'Edition Francaise
CEF . . . . Centro de Estudios Familiares y de Poblacion
CEF . . . . Channeling Effect Factor
CEF . . . . Chick Embryo Fibroblasts
CEF . . . . Chief Executives Forum
CEF . . . . Chinese Expeditionary Force
CEF . . . . Citizens for Educational Freedom
CEF . . . . Clearinghouse on Educational Facilities (ERIC)
CEF . . . . Cloth Elongation Factor (Textiles)
CEF . . . . Commission Europeenne des Forets
CEF . . . . Complementary Emitter Follower
CEF . . . . Contemporary Evaluation Form (Army)
CEF . . . . Corps Expeditionaire Francais
CEF . . . . Costruzioni Esercizio Ferrovie, SA
CEF . . . . Creative Education Foundation
CEFACD . . . . . Comite Europeen des Fabricants d'Appareils de Chauffage et de Cuisine Domestiques (European Committee of Manufacturers of Domestic Heating and Cooking Appliances)
CEFCTU . . . . . Central European Federation of Christian Trade Unions
CEFF . . . . Controlled Energy Flow Forming
CEFI. . . . . . . Child Evangelism Fellowship International
CEFIC . . . . . . Centre Europeen des Federations de l'Industrie Chimique (European Center of Chemical Manufacturers' Federations)
CEFOAM . . . . Checkout Equipment for Onboard Automatic Maintenance
CEFS . . . . . . Comite Europeen des Fabricants de Sucre (European Committee of Sugar Manufacturers)
CEFSR . . . . . . Committee for Evaluating the Feasibility of Space Rocketry (Navy Bureau of Aeronautics) (Obsolete)
CEFYM . . . . . Central European Federal Youth Movement
CEG. . . . . . . Central Aguirre Sugar Company (NYSE symbol) (Delisted)
CEG. . . . . . . Centro de Estudios Gaudinistas
CEGB . . . . . . Central Electricity Generating Board (British)
CEGB . . . . . . Central Electricity Governing Board
CEGROB . . . . . Communaute Europeenne des Associations du Commerce de Gros de Biere des Pays Membres de la CEE (European Community of Associations of the Wholesale Beer Trade of the EEC)
CEGS . . . . . . Council for Economic Growth and Security (Defunct)
CEGS . . . . . . Council on Education in the Geological Sciences
CEH . . . . Conference Europeenne des Horaires des Trains de Voyageurs (European Passenger Timetable Conference)
CEH . . . . Cutler-Hammer, Inc. (NYSE symbol; later, CH)
CEHC . . . . . . Canever English History Club
CEHS . . . . . . Civilian Employee Health Service
CEHSA . . . . . Consumer and Environmental Health Services Administration (HEW)
CEI . . . . Chicago & Eastern Illinois R. R. (AAR code)
CEI . . . . Chicago Evangelistic Institute
CEI . . . . Comitato Elettrotechnico Italiano
CEI . . . . Commission Electrotechnique Internationale (International Electrotechnical Commission)
CEI . . . . Committee for Environmental Information
CEI . . . . Communication Electronic Instructions
CEI . . . . Communications Engineering and Installation Department (Army)
CEI . . . . Compagnia Edizioni Internazionali SPA
CEI . . . . Consolidated Electronics Industries Corporation (NYSE symbol) (Delisted)
CEI . . . . Contract End Item
CEI . . . . Cost Effectiveness Index
CEI . . . . Council for Engineering Institution
CEI . . . . Cycle Engineers' Institute
C & EI . . . . . Chicago and Eastern Illinois Railroad Company
CEIA . . . . . . Communications Engineering and Installation Agency
CEIBOIS . . . . . Confederation Europeenne des Industries du Bois
CEIF. . . . . . . Council of European Industrial Federations
CEIN . . . . . . Contract End Item Number
CEIP. . . . . . . Carnegie Endowment for International Peace
CEIP. . . . . . . Communications-Electronics Implementation Plan (For major air command requirements within the Communications-Electronics area) (Air Force)
CEIPA . . . . . . Communications-Electronics Implementation Plan Amendment
CEIR . . . . . . Corporation for Economics and Industrial Research (Subsidiary of Control Data Corporation)
CEIS . . . . . . Cost and Economic Information System (DOD)
CEJ . . . . Compagnie Europeenne de la Jeunesse
CEL . . . . Celestial
CEL . . . . Central European Line (Oil pipeline)

CEL . . . . Central Louisiana Electric Co. (NYSE symbol)
CEL . . . . Civil Engineering Laboratory (Navy)
CEL . . . . Combat Elevation Launch
CEL . . . . Constitutional Educational League
CEL . . . . Cosine Emission Law
CEL . . . . Council on Engineering Laws
CEL . . . . Critical Experiment Laboratory
CEL . . . . Cryogenic Engineering Laboratory (National Bureau of Standards)
CELACS . . . . . Confidential Employment Listing (American Chemical Society)
CELADE . . . . . Centro Latinoamericana de Demografia (Latin American Demographic Center)
CELAM . . . . . Conseil Episcopal Latino-Americain (Latin American Episcopal Council)
CELC . . . . . . Commonwealth Education Liaison Committee
CELEG . . . . . Centre d'Etude des Litteratures d'Expression Graphique
CELESCOPE . . . Celestial Telescope (OAO)
CELG . . . . . . Certificat d'Etudes Litteraires Generales (France)
CELIMAC . . . . Comite Europeen de Liaison des Industries de la Machine a Coudre (European Liaison Committee for the Sewing Machine Industries)
CELL . . . . . . Continuing Education Learning Laboratory (of Youth Pride, Inc.)
CELNUCO . . . . Comite Europeen de Liaison des Negociants et Utilisateurs de Combustibles (European Liaison Committee of Fuel Merchants and Users)
CELT . . . . . . Classified Entries in Lateral Transposition (Indexing)
CEM . . . . Captured Enemy Material
CEM . . . . Chief Electrician's Mate
CEM . . . . Circular Electric Mode
CEM . . . . Combination Export Management (Small Business Administration)
CEM . . . . Communications-Electronics-Meteorological
CEM . . . . Compagnie Electromecanique (Swiss-German electrical equipment company)
CEM . . . . Cost Element Monitor (Air Force)
CEM . . . . Council of European Municipalities
CEM . . . . Counter Electromotive Cell
CEMA . . . . . . Canadian Electrical Manufacturers' Association
CEMA . . . . . . Chicago Envelope Manufacturers Association
CEMA . . . . . . Comite Europeen des Groupements de Constructeurs de Machines Agricoles (European Committee of Associations of Manufacturers of Machinery)
CEMA . . . . . . Conveyor Equipment Manufacturers Association
CEMA . . . . . . Council for the Encouragement of Music and the Arts (Later, Arts Council)
CEMAP . . . . . Cotton Export Market Acreage Program
CEMB . . . . . . Communication-Electronic-Meteorological Board (Air Force)
CEMCBC . . . . . Chief Electrician's Mate, Construction Battalion, Communications
CEMCBD . . . . . Chief Electrician's Mate, Construction Battalion, Draftsman
CEMCBG . . . . . Chief Electrician's Mate, Construction Battalion, General
CEMCBL . . . . . Chief Electrician's Mate, Construction Battalion, Line and Station
CEMCO . . . . . Continental Electronics Manufacturing Company
CEMF . . . . . . Counter Electromotive Force
CEMI . . . . . . Committee on Emergency Medical Identification
CEMIRT . . . . . Civil Engineering Maintenance, Inspection, Repair, and Training Team (Air Force)
CEMLA . . . . . Centro de Estudios Monetarios Latino-Americanos (Center for Latin-American Monetary Studies)
CEMO . . . . . . Canada Emergency Measures Organization (Civil Defense)
CEMO . . . . . . Command Equipment Management Office (Military)
CEMON . . . . . Customer Engineering Monitor (IBM)
CEMPAC . . . . . Communications-Electronics-Meteorology Program Aggregate Code
CEMREL . . . . . Central Midwest Regional Educational Laboratory
CEMS . . . . . . Central Electronic Management System
CEMS . . . . . . Chemical Education Material Study
CEMS . . . . . . Civil Engineer Management System
CEMSq . . . . . Communications and Electronics Maintenance Squadron
CEMSRG . . . . . Chief Electrician's Mate, Ship Repair, General Electrician
CEMSRS . . . . . Chief Electrician's Mate, Ship Repair, Shop Electrician
CEMSRT . . . . . Chief Electrician's Mate, Ship Repair, IC Repairman
CEMT . . . . . . Conference Europeenne des Ministres des Transports (European Conference of Ministers of Transport)
CEN . . . . Center (or Central)
CEN . . . . Central Airlines, Inc.
CEN . . . . Centre d'Etudes de l'Energie Nucleaire (Belgium)
CEN . . . . Comite Europeen de Coordination des Normes (European Committee for Coordination of Standards)
CEN . . . . Commission pour l'Etude des Nuages (OMI)
C & EN . . . . . Chemical and Engineering News (A publication of American Chemical Society)
CE/NAVFAC . . Army Corps of Engineers/Naval Facilities Engineering Command
CENC . . . . . . Centre d'Etudes Nucleaires de Cadarache (France)
CENCATS . . . . Central Pacific Combat Air Transport Service
CENCOMMRGN . . Central Communications Region (Military)
CEND . . . . . . Combustion Engineering Nuclear Division (AEC)
CENDRAFT . . . Central Drafting Officer (Navy)
CENECA . . . . . Centre National des Expositions et Concours Agricoles
CENEUR . . . . . Central European

CENFAM..... Centro Nazionale per la Fisica della Atmosfera e la Meteorologia (Italy)
C of ENGRS .. Chief of Engineers (Army)
CENIC...... Centro Nacional de Investigaciones Cientificas
CENID...... Centro Nacional de Informacion y Documentacion
CENO...... Central Naval Ordnance Management Information System
CENPAC..... Central Pacific Area (Navy)
CENPACFOR ... Central Pacific Forces
CENS....... Censor(ship)
CENS....... Centre d'Etudes Nucleaires de Saclay (France)
CENSER ..... Census Servomechanism and Tape Handler
CENTAG..... Central (European) Army Group (NATO)
CENTAUM.... Committee on Education Needs for Teen-Age Unwed Mothers
CENTCOM ... Central Pacific Communications Instructions
CENTCON ... Centralized Control Facility
CENTI...... Centre pour le Traitement de l'Information
CENTO...... Central Treaty Organization (Formerly Baghdad Pact)
CENTPACBACOM.. Central Pacific Base Command (Navy)
CENTREX .... Central Terminal Exchange
CEO....... Casualty Evacuation Officer
CEO....... Chemical Engineering Operations (MIT)
CEO....... Chief Executive Officer
CEO....... Command Education Officer (British military)
CEO....... Command Entertainments Officer (British military)
CEO....... Communications-Electronics Officer (Air Force)
CEO....... Customs Enforcement Officer (Treasury)
CEOA...... Central European Operating Agency (NATO)
CEOAS..... Corps of Engineers Office of Appalachian Studies (Army)
CEOP...... Communaute Europeenne des Organisations de Publicitaires (European Community of Advertising Organizations)
CEP .... Capital Expenditure Proposal
CEP .... Circle of Equal Probability
CEP .... Circular Error Probable (Nuclear bombing)
CEP .... Color Evaluation Program
CEP .... Computer Entry Punch
CEP .... Concentrated Employment Program (Department of Labor) (Also known as CIEP)
CEP .... Confederatione Europeenne d'Etudes Phytosanitaires (European Committee for Plant Protection Research)
CEP .... Conference on Economic Progress
CEP .... Cotton Equalization Program
CEP .... Council on Economic Priorities
CEPA...... Civil Engineering Program Applications
CEPA...... Consumers Education and Protective Association
CEPACC ..... Chemical Education Planning and Coordinating Committee (American Chemical Society)
CEPAL ...... Commission Economique pour l'Amerique Latine (UN)
CEPC...... Comite Europeen pour les Problemes Criminels (Conseil de l'Europe)
CEPCEO ..... Comite d'Etude des Producteurs de Charbon d'Europe Occidentale
CEPE ...... Central Experimental and Proving Establishment (Canada)
CEPE ...... Centre d'Etudes Phylosociologiques et Ecologiques (France)
CEPE ...... Cylindrical Electrostatic Probe Experiment
CEPES..... Centro de Estudos e Planejamento Economico e Social (Brazil)
CEPES..... Comite Europeen pour le Progres Economique et Social
CEPETI ..... Comissao Especial para Execucao do Plano de Melhoramento e Expansao do Ensino Tecnico e Industrial (Brazil)
CEPI...... Circulo de Escritores y Poetas Iberoamericanos
CEPL....... Conference Europeenne des Pouvoirs Locaux
CEPM...... Civil Engineer Preventive Maintenance (Air Force)
CEPO...... Central Eastern Personnel Organization (Computerized scouting combine for professional football teams)
CEPO...... Central European Pipeline Office (NATO)
CEPPC ..... Central Europe Pipeline Policy Committee (NATO)
CEPR...... Council on Education in Professional Responsibility
CEPS ...... Civil Engineering Problems
CEPS ...... Command Module Electrical Power System (Air Force)
CEPS ...... Commonwealth Edison - Public Service
CEPS ...... Council for the Education of the Partially Seeing
CEPT ...... Conference Europeenne des Administrations des Postes et des Telecommunications (European Conference of Postal Telecommunications Administrations)
CEQ ...... Council on Environmental Quality (of Federal Council on Science and Technology)
CER .... Capital Expenditure Request
CER .... Central Illinois Light Company (NYSE symbol)
CER .... Civil Engineering Report
CER .... Climb Enroute (Aviation)
CER .... Commanders Evaluation Report (Army)
CER .... Community Educational Resources
CER .... Complete Engine Repair
CER .... Complete Engineering Release
CER .... Conditioned Emotional Response (Psychology)

CER .... Cost Estimating Relationship
C & ER..... Combustion and Explosives Research
CERA...... Central Electric Railfans' Association
CERAMAL .... Ceramic and Alloy (NASA)
CERB ...... Coastal Engineering Research Board (Army)
CERC ...... Central Engine Room Control
CERC ...... Coastal Engineering Research Center (Army)
CERCA..... Centre de Recherches pour Combustibles Atomiques (France)
CERCHAR .... Centre d'Etudes et Recherches des Charbonnages de France
CERD ...... Central Evidence of Research and Development Reports
CERDOC..... Centre d'Etudes et Recherches Documentaires (France)
Cer E...... Ceramic Engineer
CERE ...... Comite Europeen pour les Relations Economiques
CEREA ..... Centre de Regroupement Africain (Center for African Regroupment) (Congo-Leopoldville)
CEREL ...... Civil Engineering and Evaluation Laboratory (Navy)
CERES..... Comite d'Etudes Regionales Economiques et Sociales
CERGH ..... Centre d'Etudes et de Recherches Geologiques et Hydrogeologiques
CERI....... Centre for Educational Research and Innovation (OECD)
CERL...... Cambridge Electronic Research Laboratory
CERL...... Central Electricity Research Laboratories (British)
CERL...... Commercial Equipment Requirement List
CERL...... Construction Engineering Research Laboratory (Army)
CERLI...... Cooperative Educational Research Laboratory, Incorporated
CERMA..... Centre d'Etudes et de Recherches de Medecine Aeronautique (France)
CERMET..... Ceramic and Metal (NASA)
CERN...... Conseil Europeen pour la Recherche Nucleaire (Now Organisation Europeene pour la Recherche Nucleaire)
CERP....... Civil Engineering Report of Performance
CERP....... Current Economic Reporting Program (Department of State)
CERRC ..... Complete Engine Repair Requirements Card (DOD)
CERT ...... Certificate (or Certification)
CES .... Caribbean Educational Service
CES .... Central (Nervous System) Excitatory State
CES .... Closed Ecological System
CES .... College d'Enseignement Secondaire (France)
CES .... Comite Economique et Social (of CEE)
CES .... Commercial Earth Station
CES .... Committee on Economic Security (Terminated as formal agency, 1936, but continued informally for some time thereafter)
CES .... Committee to Eradicate Syphilis
CES .... Comparative Education Society
CES .... Comprehensive Export Schedule (US)
CES .... Compressor End Seal
CES .... Conference on European Security (Proposed by US)
CES .... Constant Elasticity of Substitution (Industrial production)
CES .... Control Electronics Section (Apollo) (NASA)
CES .... Controlled Environmental System (NASA)
CES .... Cooperative Extension Service (Department of Agriculture)
CES .... Cost Effectiveness Study
CES .... Crew Escape System
CESA ...... Canadian Engineering Standards Association (Became Canadian Standards Association)
CESA ...... Cooperative Educational Service Agency (National Science Foundation)
CESAC..... Communications-Electronics Scheme Accounting and Control (Air Force)
CESAR ..... Capsule Escape and Survival Applied Research (Aerospace)
CESB ...... Center for Experimental Studies in Business (University of Minnesota)
CESD ...... Centre Europeen de Formation des Statisticiens-Economistes des Pays en Voie de Developpement (France)
CESE ...... Captured Enemy Signal Equipment (Military)
CESE....... Civil Engineer Support Equipment (Army)
CESEMI...... Computer Evaluation of Scanning Electron Microscope Image
CESF....... Commander, Eastern Sea Frontier (Navy)
CESG ...... Cryogenic Electrically Suspended Gyroscope
CESI....... Closed Entry Socket Insulator
CESI....... Council for Elementary Science International
CESK ...... Cable End Sealing Kit
CESL ...... Camp Evans Signal Laboratory (Army)
CESL ...... Civil Engineering Systems Laboratory (University of Illinois)
CESMA ..... Centro Experienze e Studi di Marketing
CESO ...... Council of Engineers and Scientists Organizations
CESP...... Centrais Electricas de Sao Paulo SA (Brazil)
CESP...... Centre d'Etudes des Supports de Publicite (France)
CESP...... Correlation Echo Sound Processor (Oceanography)
CESPE..... Centro Studi Politica Economica (of the Italian Communist Party)
CESR ...... Canadian Electronic Sales Representatives
CESS ...... Council of Engineering Society Secretaries
CESSI ..... Church of England Sunday School Institute
CESSLGO .... Continuing Education Service for State and Local Government Officials
CET .... Capsule Elapsed Time (Aerospace)
CET .... Center for Educational Technology

CET . . . . Centre Europeen de Traduction (European Translations Center)
CET . . . . Commission Europeenne du Tourisme
CET . . . . Common External Tariff (for EEC countries)
CET . . . . Controlled Environment Testing
CET . . . . Cooperative English Test
CET . . . . Critical Experiment Tank
CET . . . . Cumulative Elapsed Time
CETA . . . . Centre de' Etudes pour la Traduction Automatique (Center for the Study of Automatic Translation) (France)
CETA . . . . Corrosion Evaluation and Test Area (NASA)
CETC . . . . Corps of Engineers Technical Committee (Army)
CETEC . . . . . . Consolidated Engineering Technology Corporation
CETEX . . . . . Committee on Contamination of Extra-Terrestrial Exploration (NASA)
CETG . . . . . . Civil Effects Test Group (DASA and AEC)
CETHEDEC. . . . Centre d'Etudes Theoriques de la Detection et des Communications
CETI . . . . . . Communication with Extraterrestrial Intelligence (Radioastronomy)
CETIE . . . . . . Centre Technique International de l'Embouteillage (International Technical Center of Bottling)
CETIS . . . . . . Centre de Traitement de l'Information Scientifique (EURATOM)
CETO . . . . . . Centre for Educational Television Overseas (British)
CETO . . . . . . Civil Effects Test Operations (DASA and AEC)
CETR . . . . . . Consolidated Edison Thorium Reactor (AEC)
CETS . . . . . . Church of England Temperance Society
CETS . . . . . . Conference Europeene des Telecommunications par Satellite
CETS . . . . . . Contractor Engineering and Technical Services
CEU . . . . Christian Endeavor Union
CEU . . . . Coupler Electronics Unit
CEV . . . . Centre d'Essais en Vol (France)
CEV . . . . Combat Engineer Vehicle
CEV . . . . Convoy Escort Vessel
CEV . . . . Cryogenic Explosive Valve
CEVAT . . . . . Combined Environmental, Vibration, Acceleration, Temperature (Aerospace)
CEVM. . . . . . Consumable Electrode Vacuum Melting
CEW. . . . . . . Caravan of East and West
CEW. . . . . . . Circular Electric Wire
CEW. . . . . . . Copi-Elgot-Wright (Electronics)
CEWA . . . . . . Combined Economic Warfare Agencies
CEWMS. . . . . Church of England Working Men's Society
CEX . . . . Charge Exchange
CEX . . . . Civil Effects Experiments (DASA and AEC)
CEX . . . . Corn Exchange Bank (NYSE symbol)
CEY . . . . Century Electric Company (NYSE symbol)
CEYMS . . . . . Church of England Young Men's Society
CEZA . . . . . . Comite Europeen d'Etudes de Zoologie Agricole
CF . . . . Cable, Functional
CF . . . . Cable, Fuzing or Firing
Cf . . . . Californium (Chemical element)
CF . . . . Cannot Find
CF . . . . Cantus Firmus (Plain Chant)
CF . . . . Cape Fear Railways, Inc. (AAR code)
CF . . . . Carbolfuchsin (A dye)
CF . . . . Carbon Film
CF . . . . Carried Forward (Accounting)
CF . . . . Carrier-Free (Radioisotope)
CF . . . . Carrier Frequency (Radio)
CF . . . . Cathode Follower
CF . . . . Cement Floor (Technical drawings)
CFS . . . . Center Field(er) (Baseball)
CF . . . . Center Fire
CF . . . . Center of Flotation
CF . . . . Center Forward (Soccer position)
CF . . . . Center Frequency
CF . . . . Central Files
CF . . . . Centrally Funded
CF . . . . Centrifugal Force
CF . . . . CF & I Steel Corp. (Formerly, Colorado Fuel & Iron Corporation) (NYSE symbol)
CF . . . . Change in Formula
CF . . . . Change (or Changing) to Frequency (followed by number) (Communications)
CF . . . . Chaplain to the Forces (British)
CF . . . . Chief of Finance (Army)
CF . . . . Christmas Factor (Physiology)
CF . . . . Chromosomal Fraction
CF . . . . Circuit Finder
CF . . . . Citrovorum Factor (Physiology)
CF . . . . Clarissima Femina (Most Illustrious Woman)
CF . . . . Coastal Frontier (Military)
CF . . . . Coated on the Front Side (Carbonless paper)
CF . . . . Commutation Factor

CF . . . . Company First (A mealtime whimsicality for use when guests are present)
CF . . . . Complement Fixation (Immunology)
CF . . . . Concept Formulation (DOD)
CF . . . . Conservation Foundation
CF . . . . Constant Frequency (Pulse component)
CF . . . . Contract Formulation
CF . . . . Controlled Facility (Aerospace)
CF . . . . Conversion Factor
CF . . . . Copy Furnished (Army)
CF . . . . Correlation Factor
CF . . . . Corresponding Fellow
CF . . . . Count Forward (Data processing)
CF . . . . Counterfire (Military)
CF . . . . Counting Fingers (Psychology)
CF . . . . Cover Forward
CF . . . . Crude Fiber
CF . . . . Cubic Feet
CF . . . . Cystic Fibrosis (Medicine)
CF . . . . Flying-Deck Cruiser (Navy symbol)
C/F . . . . Contract Formulation
C & F . . . . . . Commerce and Finance
C & F . . . . . . Cost and Freight (Business and trade)
C of F . . . . . Chief of Finance (Army)
C of F . . . . . Custodian of Fund
CFA . . . . California Freezers Association
CFA . . . . Call for Action (An organization)
CFA . . . . Cat Fanciers' Association
CFA . . . . Chartered Financial Analyst (Designation given by Institute of Chartered Financial Analysts)
CFA . . . . Chief of Field Artillery
CFA . . . . Circus Fans Association of America
CFA . . . . Cleared for Approach
CFA . . . . Cognizant Field Activity
CFA . . . . Commission of Fine Arts (Independent government agency)
CFA . . . . Communaute Financiere Africaine
CFA . . . . Community Facilities Administration (of HHFA) (Terminated)
CFA . . . . Companions of the Forest of America
CFA . . . . Compass Failure Annunciator
CFA . . . . Complete Freund's Adjuvant
CFA . . . . Concept Feasibility Analysis
CFA . . . . Congregatio Fratrum Cellitarum seu Alexianorum (Alexian Brothers) (Roman Catholic religious order)
CFA . . . . Consumer Federation of America
CFA . . . . Council on Fertilizer Application
CFA . . . . Cowl-Flap Angle (Air Force)
CFA . . . . Crossed-Field Amplifier (Air Force)
CFA . . . . Current Files Area
CF & A . . . . . Chief of Finance and Accounting (Army)
CFAA . . . . . . Cooperative Finance Association of America
CFAC . . . . . . Citizens Foreign Aid Committee (Defunct)
CFAD . . . . . . Commander, Fleet Air Detachment
CFAE . . . . . . Centre de Formation en Aerodynamique Experimentale
CFAE . . . . . . Contractor-Furnished Aerospace Equipment
CFAE . . . . . . Council for Financial Aid to Education
CFAO . . . . . . Compagnie Francaise de l'Afrique Occidentale
CFAP . . . . . . Cleared for Approach (Aviation)
CFAR . . . . . . Constant False Alarm Rate (Air Force)
CFAS . . . . . . Catholic Fine Arts Society
CFAT . . . . . . Carnegie Foundation for the Advancement of Teaching
CFAW. . . . . . Commander, Fleet Air Wing
CFAW. . . . . . Committee of French American Wives
CFB . . . . Carey Foster Bridge (Electronics)
CFB . . . . Coated Front and Back (Carbonless Paper)
CFB . . . . Combined Food Board (United States, United Kingdom, and Canada) (World War II)
CFC . . . . C-Band Frequency Converter
CFC . . . . California Fashion Creators
CFC . . . . Campus-Free College
CFC . . . . Carbon Fiber-Reinforced Composite
CFC . . . . Central Fire Control (Military)
CFC . . . . Central Forms Committee
CFC . . . . Chief Fire Controlman
CFC . . . . Colony-Forming Cells
CFC . . . . Combined Federal Campaign (Army)
CFC . . . . Complex Facility Console (Aerospace)
CFC . . . . Consolidated Freight Classification
CFC . . . . Contract Finance Committee (Military)
CFC . . . . Controlled Force Circulation (Boilers)
CFC . . . . Crossed-Film Cryotron

ACRONYMS AND INITIALISMS DICTIONARY

CFC . . . . From the Latin for Congregation of Christian Brothers (Formerly, Christian Brothers of Ireland) (Roman Catholic religious order)
CFCA . . . . . . California Fish Canners Association
CFCA . . . . . . Camp Fire Club of America
CFCA . . . . . . Confederation Francaise de la Cooperation Agricole
CFCA . . . . . . Crested Fowl Club of America
CFCB . . . . . . Computer Format Control Buffer
CFCE . . . . . . Conseil des Federations Commerciales d'Europe (Council of European Commercial Federations)
CFCF . . . . . . Central Flow Control Facility
CFCO . . . . . . Chief Fire Controlman, Operator
CFCRFC . . . . Chewings Fescue and Creeping Red Fescue Commission
CFCS . . . . . . Chief Fire Controlman, Submarines
CFD . . . . Consolidated Foods Corporation (NYSE symbol)
CFDA . . . . . . Cooperative Food Distributors of America
CFDA . . . . . . Council of Fashion Designers of America
CFDTS . . . . . Cold Flow Development Test System (AEC)
CFE . . . . California Fruit Exchange
CFE . . . . Cathode Flicker Effect
CFE . . . . Central Fighter Establishment (British)
CFE . . . . Committee for a Free Estonia
CFE . . . . Contractor-Furnished Equipment
CFE . . . . Controlled Flash Evaporation
CFEA . . . . . . College Fraternity Editors Association
CFEP . . . . . . Committee on Fair Employment Practices (World War II)
CFEP . . . . Council on Foreign Economic Policy (Functions transferred to Secretary of State, 1961)
CFES . . . . . . Canadian Federation of Engineers and Scientists
CFF . . . . California Packing Corporation (NYSE symbol) (Delisted)
CFF . . . . Capuchin Franciscan Friary
CFF . . . . Cat Fanciers' Federation
CFF . . . . Christian Freedom Foundation
CFF . . . . Cold Flow Facility
CFF . . . . Conical Flow Field
CFF . . . . Critical Flicker Frequency (Psychophysical test)
CFF . . . . Critical Fusion Frequency
CFFA . . . . . . Crested Fowl Fanciers' Association
CFFC . . . . . . Counterflow Film Cooling
CFFP . . . . Cooperative Forest Fire Prevention (Forest Service, Department of Agriculture)
CFG . . . . Camp Fire Girls
CFG . . . . CPC International, Inc. (Formerly, Corn Products Company) (NYSE symbol)
CFGM . . . . . . Committee for a Free Gold Market
CFH . . . . Cubic Feet per Hour
CFI . . . . California Fig Institute
CFI . . . . California Financial Corporation (NYSE symbol)
CFI . . . . Certified Flight Instructor (Aviation)
CFI . . . . Chief Flying Instructor (British Royal Air Force)
CFI . . . . Cost, Freight, and Insurance (Business and trade)
CFIA . . . . . . Center for Independent Action
CFIA . . . . . . Chinese Federation of Industrial Associations
CFIE . . . . Conseil des Federations Industrielles d'Europe (Council of European Industrial Federations)
CFJO . . . . . . Council of Federated Jewish Organizations
CFK . . . . Confidence Firing Kit
CFL . . . . Canadian Football League
CFL . . . . Ceylon Federation of Labor
CFL . . . . Chinese Federation of Labor (Nationalist China)
CFL . . . . Close Focus Lens
CFL . . . . Club Francais du Livre (French Book Club)
CFL . . . . Committee for a Free Latvia
CFL . . . . Committee for a Free Lithuania
CFL . . . . Constant Feed Lubricator
CFL . . . . Context Free Language
CFL . . . . Continental Football League
CFLA . . . . . . Catholics for Latin America
CFLI . . . . Catholic Family Life Insurance
CFLI . . . . Clay Flue Lining Institute
CFLN . . . . . . Comite Francais Liberation Nationale
CFLT . . . . . . Courtesy Flight (Aviation)
CFM . . . . Cathode Follower Mixer
CFM . . . . Center Frequency Modulation
CFM . . . . . . Chill-Down Flow Meter
CFM . . . . . . Christian Family Movement
CFM . . . . Confirm
CFM . . . . Contingency for Movement
CFM . . . . Council of Foreign Ministers
CFM . . . . Crystal Frequency Multiplier
CFM . . . . Cubic Feet per Minute
CFMA . . . . . . Church Furniture Manufacturers Association

CFMS . . . . . . Chained File Management System (IBM)
CFMS . . . . . . Combined Field Maintenance Shop (Army)
CFMU . . . . . . Chinese Foreign Missionary Union
CFMU . . . . . . Compagnie Francaise des Minerais d'Uranium
CFO . . . . Canceling Former Order
CFO . . . . Ceramic Fiber Optics
CFO . . . . Channel for Orders (Business and trade)
CFO . . . . Chief Financial Officer
CFO . . . . Complex Facility Operator (Aerospace)
CFO . . . . Connection Fitting Out (Navy)
CFO . . . . Consolidated Function Ordinary (IBM)
CFOC . . . . . . Contractor Fin Opener Crank
CFOR . . . . . . COMSEC (Communications Security) Field Office of Record (Army)
CFOT . . . . . . Crossed Field Output Tube
CFP . . . . Carrier Frequency Pulse
CFP . . . . Change Flight Plan
CFP . . . . Cold Front(al) Passage (Meteorology)
CFP . . . . Compagnie Francaise des Petroles (France)
CFP . . . . Concentracion de Fuerzas Populares (Concentration of Popular Forces) (Political party in Ecuador)
CFP . . . . Concept Formulation Package (Air Force)
CFP . . . . Congregatio Fratrum Pauperum (Brothers of the Poor of St. Francis) (Roman Catholic religious order)
CFP . . . . Contractor-Furnished Property (Air Force)
CFP . . . . Cystic Fibrosis of the Pancreas
CFPP . . . . . . Concept Formulation Program Plan
CFPS . . . . . . Crossed Field Plasma Sheath
CFP/TDP . . . . . Concept Formulation Package - Technical Development Plan (Air Force)
CFQ . . . . California Folklore Quarterly (A publication)
CFR . . . . Carbon-Film Resistor
CFR . . . . Catastrophic Failure Rate
CFR . . . . Code of Federal Regulations
CFR . . . . Committee on Friendly Relations Among Foreign Students
CFR . . . . Compagnie Francaise de Raffinage
CFR . . . . Contact Flight Rules (Same as VFR) (Meteorology)
CFR . . . . Cooperative Fuels Research (Committee)
CFR . . . . Council on Foreign Relations
CFR . . . . Cumulative Failure Rate
CFRD . . . . . . Confidential, Formerly Restricted Data
CFRE . . . . . . Circulating Fuel Reactor Experiment (AEC)
CFRM . . . . . . Continuous Fiber Reinforcing Mat (Fiberglass)
CFRM . . . . . . Contract Financial Reporting Manual
CFRP . . . . . . Carbon-Fiber Reinforced Plastic
CFS . . . . Carrier Frequency Shift
CFS . . . . Cassegrain Feed System
CFS . . . . Center Frequency Stabilization (Radio)
CFS . . . . Central Flying School (Royal Air Force) (British)
CFS . . . . Cesium Feed System
CFS . . . . Combined File Search (Data processing)
CFS . . . . Composite Feed System
CFS . . . . Contract Field Service
CFS . . . . Contract Financial Status
CFS . . . . Counter Filling System
CFS . . . . Critical Field Strength
CFS . . . . Cryogenic Fluid Storage
CFS . . . . Cubic Feet per Second
CFS . . . . Cystic Fibrosis Society
CFSA . . . . . . California Flyers School of Aeronautics
CFSA . . . . . . College Fraternity Secretaries Association
CFSC . . . . . . Cryogenic Fluid Storage Container
CFSEB . . . . . . Conference of Funeral Service Examining Boards of the United States
CFSI . . . . Confederation Francaise des Syndicats Independents (French Confederation of Independent Unions)
CFSLP . . . . . . Center for Short-Lived Phenomena (Smithsonian Institution)
CFSOA . . . . . . College Fraternity Scholarship Officers Association
CFSR . . . . . . Commission on Financial Structure and Regulation (White House)
CFSR . . . . . . Contract Fund Status Report (Army)
CFSS . . . . Combined File Search Strategy
CFSS . . . . . . Committee of French Speaking Societies
CFSSB . . . . . . Central Flight Status Selection Board (Air Force)
CFSTI . . . . Clearinghouse for Federal Scientific and Technical Information (Later, NTIS) (National Bureau of Standards)
CFSTR . . . . . . Continuous Flow Stirred Tank Reactor
CFT . . . . Coated Foam Tape
CFT . . . . Cold Flow Test
CFT . . . . Complement-Fixation Test
CFT . . . . Continuous Fourier Transport
CFT . . . . Contract Field Technician
CFT . . . . Crossed Field Tube
CFTB . . . . . . Control Flight Test Bed
CFTC . . . . . . Central Flying Training Command (AAFCFTC)

CFTC . . . . . . Confederation Francaise des Travailleurs Chretiens (French Confederation of Christian Workers)
CFTH . . . . . . Compagnie Francaise Thomson Houston
CFTMA . . . . . Caster and Floor Truck Manufacturers Association
CFTS . . . . . . Captive Firing Test Set (Aerospace)
CFTU . . . . . . Confederation of Free Trade Unions (India)
CFU . . . . Colony Forming Units
CFU . . . . Control Functional Unit (Data link)
CFU . . . . Corn-Equivalent Feed Unit
CFU . . . . Croatian Fraternal Union of America
CFVD . . . . . . Constant Frequency Variable Dot
CFW . . . . CONVAIR (Consolidated-Vultee Aircraft Corp.) Fort Worth (Later, General Dynamics/Fort Worth) (Aerospace)
CFWS . . . . . . Conversion to the Federal Wage System
CFX . . . . Congregatio Fratrum Sancti Francisci Xaverii (Brothers of St. Francis Xavier) (Roman Catholic religious order)
CFY . . . . Current Fiscal Year
CG . . . . Camera Gun
CG . . . . Captain-General
CG . . . . Captain of the Guard
CG . . . . Cargo Glider (Military)
CG . . . . Categorical Grammar
CG . . . . Center of Gravity
cg . . . . Centigram
CG . . . . Central of Georgia Railway Company (AAR code)
CG . . . . Cerebral Ganglion
CG . . . . Chorionic Gonadotropin (Endocrinology)
CG . . . . Civil Guard (Air Force)
CG . . . . Clutter Gate
CG . . . . Coast Guard
CG . . . . Coincidence Gate
CG . . . . Coldstream Guards (British)
CG . . . . Columbia Gas System, Inc. (NYSE symbol)
CG . . . . Combat Group
CG . . . . Command Guidance (Aerospace)
CG . . . . Commanding General (Military)
CG . . . . Commissary General
CG . . . . Complete Games (Baseball)
CG . . . . Comptroller General
CG . . . . Consul General
CG . . . . Consultative Group (NATO)
CG . . . . Control Group
CG . . . . Crushed or Ground
CG . . . . Current Gain
CG . . . . Guided Missile Cruiser (Navy symbol)
C & G . . . . . . Ceramic and Graphite Information Center (Air Force)
C & G . . . . . . Columbus and Greenville Railway Company
C & G . . . . . . Control and Guidance
C de G . . . . . Croix de Guerre (French decoration for gallantry in the field)
C of G . . . . . . Convenience of the Government
CGA . . . . Canadian Gas Association
CGA . . . . Cargo's Proportion of (General) Average (Business and trade)
CGA . . . . Caribbean Gamefishing Association
CGA . . . . Carrier Group Alarm (Telephone communications)
CGA . . . . Certified General Accountant
CGA . . . . Certified Graphoanalyst
CGA . . . . Coast Guard Academy
CGA . . . . Coast Guard Auxiliary
CGA . . . . Compressed Gas Association
CGA . . . . Confederation Generale de l'Agriculture (France)
CGA . . . . Contrast Gate Amplifier
C of GA . . . . . Central of Georgia Railway Company
CGAAF . . . . . . Commanding General, Army Air Forces
CGAB . . . . . . Coast Guard Air Base
CGACTEUR . . Coast Guard Activities Europe
CGAES . . . . . Coffee Growers' Association of El Salvador
CGAIRDET . . . . Coast Guard Air Detachment
CGARY . . . . . . Central of Georgia Railway
CGAS . . . . . . Coast Guard Air Station
CGAT . . . . . . Confederation Generale Africaine du Travail (African General Confederation of Labor)
CGB . . . . Ceramics & Graphite Branch (Air Force)
CGB . . . . Christlicher Gewerkschaftsbund Deutschlands (Confederation of German Christian Trade Unions) (West Germany)
CGB . . . . Convert Gray to Binary
CGBASE . . . . . Coast Guard Base
CGC . . . . Calavo Growers of California
CGC . . . . Ceramic Gold Coating
CGC . . . . Clebsch-Gordan Coefficients
CGC . . . . Coast Guard Cutter
CGC . . . . Colorado Interstate Corp. (NYSE symbol)

CGC . . . . Computer Guidance Corporation
CGC . . . . Confederation Generale des Cadres (General Confederation of Supervisory Employees) (France)
CGC . . . . Critical Grid Current
CGC . . . . Cruise Guidance Control
CGCE . . . . . . Comptoir Guineen du Commerce Exterieur (Guinean Foreign Trade Agency)
CGCRUITSTA . . Coast Guard Recruiting Station
CGCT . . . . . . Confederation Generale Camerounaise du Travail (Cameroonian General Confederation of Workers)
CGD . . . . Christliche Gewerkschaftsbewegung Deutschlands (Christian Trade Union Movement of Germany) (West Germany)
CGD . . . . Coast Guard Depot
CGD . . . . Coast Guard District
CGD . . . . Comptroller General's Decision
CGDIST . . . . . Coast Guard District
CGDO . . . . . . Coast Guard District Office
CGE . . . . Chadwick-Goldhaber Effect
CGE . . . . Chicago & Eastern Illinois R. R. Company (NYSE symbol)
CGE . . . . Compagnie Generale d'Electricite (General Electric Company)
CGEN . . . . . . Consul General
CGF . . . . Carrier Gas Fusion (Chemistry)
CGF . . . . Chemotaxis-Generating Factor
CGF . . . . Coarse Glass Frit
CGF . . . . College of Great Falls (Montana)
CGFAB . . . . . . Catholic Guild for All the Blind
CGFP . . . . . . Calcined Gross Fission Product
CGG . . . . Chicago Pneumatic Tool Company (NYSE symbol)
CGG . . . . Continuous Grinding Gage
CGGBT . . . . . . China, Glass, Giftware Board of Trade
CGGCM . . . . . Coast Guard Good Conduct Medal
CGGP . . . . . . Conference Group on German Politics
CGH . . . . Cape of Good Hope
CGH . . . . Chorionic Gonadotropin, Human (Endocrinology)
CGH . . . . Clevite Corporation (NYSE symbol)
CGI . . . . Chadbourn, Incorporated (NYSE symbol)
CGI . . . . Cruise Guide Indicator (Aircraft)
CGIBT . . . . . . Commanding General, India-Burma Theater (World War II)
CGIC . . . . . . Ceramic & Graphite Information Center (Air Force)
CGIF . . . . . . Cherry Growers and Industries Foundation
CGIL . . . . . . Confederazione Generale Italiana del Lavoro (Italian General Confederation of Labor)
CGK . . . . Cathode Grid Capacitance
CGKT . . . . . . Confederation Generale Kamerounaise du Travail (Cameroonese General Labor Confederation)
CGL . . . . Center-of-Gravity Locator
CGL . . . . Coast Guard League
CGL . . . . Continuous Gas LASER
CGL . . . . Controlled Ground Landing
CGL . . . . Corrected Geomagnetic Latitude
CGLASTA . . . . Coast Guard Light Attendant Station
CGLBSTA . . . . Coast Guard Lifeboat Station
CGLIHA . . . . . Coastwise-Great Lakes and Inland Hull Association
CGLORSTA . . . Coast Guard LORAN Transmitting Station
CGLS . . . . . . Coast Guard LORAN Station
CGLTSTA . . . . Coast Guard Light Station
CGM . . . . Centigram(s)
CGM . . . . Central Gray Matter (Physiology)
CGM . . . . Chief Gunner's Mate
CGM . . . . Ciliated Groove to Mouth
CGM . . . . Connecticut General Mortgaging & Realty Investments (NYSE symbol)
CGM . . . . Conspicuous Gallantry Medal (British)
CGMB . . . . . . Commanding General, Marine Base
CGMCBG . . . . Chief Gunner's Mate, Construction Battalion, Armorer
CGMCBP . . . . . Chief Gunner's Mate, Construction Battalion, Powderman
CGMO . . . . . . Coast and Geodetic Magnetic Observatory
CGMTO . . . . . Commanding General, Mediterranean Theater of Operations (World War II)
CG(N) . . . . . . Guided Missile Cruiser (Nuclear-propelled) (Naval ship designation)
CGO . . . . Can Go Over (Newspapers)
CGO . . . . Committee on Government Operations
CGO . . . . Comptroller General Opinion
CGO . . . . Contracts Group Office
CGOB . . . . . . Coast Guard Operating Base
CGOFE . . . . . . CONVAIR (Consolidated-Vultee Aircraft Corp.; later, General Dynamics) Government-Owned Facilities and Equipment (Aerospace)
CGOPHEOSE . . Consultative Group on Potentially Harmful Effects of Space Experiments
CGOS . . . . . . Combat Gunnery Officers School (Army Air Forces)
CGOU . . . . . . Coast Guard Oceanographic Unit
CGP . . . . Coastal States Gas Producing Company (NYSE symbol)
CGP . . . . Current Geographical Publications (Periodical)
CGPAA . . . . . . China, Glass and Pottery Association of America
CGPF . . . . . . Church of God Peace Fellowship

CGPM ...... Conference Generale des Poids et Mesures (General Conference on Weights and Measures)
CGPM ...... Conseil General des Peches pour la Mediterranee (General Fisheries Council for the Mediterranean)
CGPSq ...... Cartographic and Geodetic Processing Squadron (Air Force)
CGR ...... Captured Gamma Ray
CGR .... Carriers & General Corporation (NYSE symbol)
CGR .... Coast Guard Reserve
CGR .... Crime on Government Reservation
CGRA .... Canadian Good Roads Association
CGRADSTA .. Coast Guard Radio Station
CGRS ...... Central Gyro Reference System
CGS ...... Catholic Guardian Society
cgs .... Centimeter-Gram-Second
CGS ...... Chef des Generalstabs des Heeres (Chief of General Staff of the Army) (German military - World War II)
CGS ...... Chief of the General Staff (in the field) (British military)
CGS .... Chromatographic Separation
CGS .... Coast and Geodetic Survey (Later, National Ocean Survey)
CGS .... Commission on Government Security
CGS .... Community Guidance Service
CGS ...... Confederation Generale des Syndicats (General Confederation of Trade Unions) (Congo--Leopoldville)
CGS .... Council of Graduate Schools in the United States
C & GS ..... Coast and Geodetic Survey (Later, National Ocean Survey)
C & GS ..... Command and General Staff (Army)
CGSBN ...... Consortium for Graduate Study in Business for Negroes
CGSC .... Command and General Staff College
C & GSC .... Command and General Staff College (Military)
CGSFU ..... Ceramic Glazed Structural Facing Units (Technical drawings)
CGSI ...... Confederation Generale des Syndicats Independents (General Confederation of Independent Unions) (Algeria)
CGSL ...... Confederazione Generale Somala dei Lavoratori (Somali General Confederation of Workers)
CGSE ...... Centimeter-Gram-Second-Electrostatic
CGSLB ...... Centrale Generale des Syndicats Liberaux de Belgique (General Federation of Liberal Unions of Belgium)
CGSM ...... Centimeter-Gram-Second-Electromagnetic
CGSS ...... Cryogenic Gas Storage System
C & GSS .... Command & General Staff School (Army)
CGSSC ..... Columbia Gas System Service Corporation
CGSTA ..... Coast Guard Station
CGSUB ..... Ceramic Glazed Structural Unit Base (Technical drawings)
CGSUPCEN ... Coast Guard Supply Center
CGSUS ..... Council of Graduate Schools in the United States
CGT .... Canada & Gulf Terminal Railway (AAR code)
CGT .... Confederation Generale du Travail (General Confederation of Labor)
CGT .... Confederation Generale des Travailleurs (South Vietnam)
CGT .... Corrected Geomagnetic Time
CGT .... Current Gate Tube
CGTA ...... Confederation Generale des Travailleurs Africains (General Confederation of African Workers) (Former French Equatorial Africa)
CGTFL ..... California Grape and Tree Fruit League
CGT-FO ..... Confederation Generale du Travail-Force Ouvriere (General Confederation of Labor - Workers' Force)
CGTM ...... Command Guided Tactical Missile
CGTRASTA ... Coast Guard Training Station
CGTS ...... Coast and Geodetic Tide Station
CGTS ...... Coast Guard Training Station
CGU .... Ceramic Glazed Units (Technical drawings)
CGU .... Church Guilds Union (British)
CGUSCONARC.. Commanding General United States Continental Army Command
CGUSFET .... Commanding General, United States Forces, European Theater (World War II)
CGV .... Critical Grid Voltage
CGVS .... Ciliated Grove to Ventral Sac
CGW .... Chicago Great Western Railway (NYSE symbol) (Delisted)
CGW .... Corning Glass Works
C & GWRY ... Chicago & Great Western Railway
CGWU ...... Commercial and General Workers' Union (Rhodesia and Nyasaland)
CGYD .... Coast Guard Yard
CH .... Candle Hours (Illumination)
CH .... Case Harden (Metal) (Technical drawings)
CH .... Central Heating
CH .... Chain
CH .... Chain Home (Aviation)
CH .... Champion
CH .... Chaplain
CH .... Chapter
CH .... Chicago Helicopter Airways, Inc. (Also, CHA)
CH .... Chief

CH .... Child(ren)
CH .... Church
CH .... Clearing House (Banking)
CH .... Clothing and Housing Research Division (of ARS, Department of Agriculture)
CH .... Coach House
CH .... Companion of Honour (British)
CH .... Compass Heading
CH .... Conquering Hero (British, for returning soldiers)
CH .... Continental Can Company, Inc. (NYSE symbol)
CH .... Court House
CH .... Custom House
CH .... Cutler-Hammer, Inc. (NYSE symbol)
C-H .... Cutler-Hammer, Inc.
CHA .... Cable-Harness Analyzer
CHA .... Catholic Hospital Association of the United States and Canada
CHA .... Chicago Helicopter Airways, Inc. (Also, CH)
CHA .... Chronic Hemolytic Anemia
CHA .... Community Health Association
CHA .... Crop Husbandry Adviser (Ministry of Agriculture, Fisheries, and Food) (British)
CHA .... Cyclohexylamine
CHABA ..... Committee on Hearing, Bio-Acoustics, and Biomechanics (Military)
ChAc ...... Choline Acetylase (Biochemistry)
CHACOM .... Chain of Command
CHAD ...... Charleston Army Depot
CHAER ..... Chief Aerographer
CHAFB ..... Chanute Air Force Base
CHAIR ..... Chairman
CHAL ...... Chalmette National Historical Park
CHALICE..... Compressional Heating and Linear Injection Cusp Experiment
CHAM ...... Chamizal National Memorial
CHAMCHIKIAN .. Charter of American Chapters of the International Kinetics Institute - Atomic and Nuclear
CHAMPION... Compatible Hardware and Milestone Program for Integrating Organizational Needs (AFSC)
CHAMPUS .... Civilian Health and Medical Program of the Uniformed Services (Army)
CHANCE..... Complete Help and Assistance Necessary for College Education (Project)
CHAOS...... Cannon Hunters Association of Seattle
CHAOTIC .... Computer and Human-Assisted Organization of a Technical Information Center (National Bureau of Standards)
CHAP ...... Chapter
CHAP ...... Charring Ablation Program (NASA)
CHAP ...... Child Health Associate Program
CHAP ...... Children Have a Potential (Program for handicapped or disturbed children of Air Force personnel)
CHAP ...... Contractor Held Air Force Property
CHAP ...... Convective Heating and Ablation Program
CHARGUID ... Character Guidance (Army)
CHARM...... CAA (Civil Aeronautics Authority) High-Altitude Remote Monitoring
CHART ..... Clearing House for Augmenting Resources for Training (DOD)
CHART ..... Computerized Hierarchy and Relationship Table
CHASE...... Cut Holes and Sink 'em (Navy ammunition disposal project)
Ch B ...... Bachelor of Chemistry
ChB .... Bachelor of Surgery
CHB .... Cargo Handling Battalion (Army) (Obsolete)
CHB .... Chain Belt Company (NYSE symbol)
CHB .... Chain Home Beamed (Aviation)
Ch B ...... Chirurgiae Baccalaureus (Bachelor of Surgery)
CHBOSN..... Chief Boatswain
CHBUAER .... Chief of the Bureau of Aeronautics (Navy) (Obsolete)
CHBUDOCKS .. Chief of the Bureau of Yards and Docks (Navy) (Obsolete)
CHBUMED .... Chief of the Bureau of Medicine and Surgery (Navy)
CHBUORD .... Chief of the Bureau of Ordnance (Navy) (Obsolete)
CHBUPERS ... Chief of the Bureau of Naval Personnel
CHBUSANDA . Chief of the Bureau of Supplies and Accounts (Navy) (Obsolete)
CHBUSHIPS ... Chief of the Bureau of Ships (Navy) (Obsolete)
CHC .... Chaplain Corps
CHC .... Checker Motors Corporation (NYSE symbol)
CHC .... Chestnut Hills College (Pennsylvania)
CHC .... Choke Coil
CHC .... College of the Holy Cross (Massachusetts)
CHC .... Confederate High Command
CHC .... Crouse-Hinds Company
CHC .... Cyclohexylamine Carbonate (Used in paper preservation)
CHCA ...... Chaco Canyon National Monument
CHCARP ..... Chief Carpenter (Navy)
CHCH .... Chickamauga and Chattanooga National Military Park
CHCIVENGS .. Chief of Civil Engineers (Army)
CHCK .... Chief Cook (Navy)
CHCW .... Conference for Health Council Work

CHD . . . . Chelsea Industries, Inc. (NYSE symbol)
CHD . . . . Coronary Heart Disease (Medicine)
Ch D . . . . Doctor of Chemistry
C(H & D) . . . . Center (Hospital and Domiciliary) (Veterans Administration)
CH and D . . . . Cold, Hungry and Dry (Slang)
CHE . . . . Cargo Handling Equipment
Ch E . . . . Chemical Engineer
ChE . . . . Cholinesterase
CHEAM . . . . . . Centre de Hautes Etudes Administratives sur l'Afrique et l'Asie Modernes
     (Center for Advanced Administrative Study on Modern Africa and Asia)
CHEAR . . . . . Council on Higher Education in the American Republics (Later, ICHE)
CHEBYTOP . . . . Chebychev Trajectory Optimization Program
CHECO . . . . . . Contemporary Historical Examination Current Operations (Air Force)
CHEF . . . . . . Citizens Honest Elections Foundation
CHEKA . . . . . Chrezvychainaya Komissiya (Extraordinary commission; Soviet secret police
     organization, 1917-21)
CHEL . . . . . . Chain Home Extra Low (Aviation)
CHELEC . . . . . Chief Electrician
CHEM . . . . . . Chemical (or Chemist)
CHEM . . . . . . Chemical Education Materials (Study)
CHEM . . . . . . Chemistry
ChemTeC . . . . . Chemical Technicians Curriculum (Project)
CHEMTREC . . . Chemical Transportation Emergency Center (Washington, DC)
CHEOPS . . . . . Chemical Operations System
CHESS . . . . . Community Health Environmental Surveillance Studies
CHF . . . . Chock Full O'Nuts Corporation (NYSE symbol) (Wall Street slang name:
     "Nuts")
CHF . . . . Congestive Heart Failure (Medicine)
CHF . . . . Critical Heat Flux (Nuclear)
CH of F . . . . . Chaplain of the Fleet (British)
CHFS . . . . . . Central (Atom) Hyperfine Structure
CHG . . . . Change
CHG . . . . Chicago Milwaukee Corp. (NYSE symbol)
CHGFA . . . . . Costs Chargeable to Fund Authorization (Army)
CHGPAA . . . . Costs Chargeable to Purchase Authorization Advice
CHG . . . . Cross Hatch Generator
CHGUN . . . . Chief Gunner
CHH . . . . Cheswick & Harmar R. R. (AAR code)
CHI . . . . Champlin Oil & Refining Company (NYSE symbol) (Delisted)
CHI . . . . Concordia Historical Institute
CHI . . . . Crouse-Hinds Co. (NYSE symbol)
CHIAA . . . . . Crop-Hail Insurance Actuarial Association
CHIC . . . . . . Cermet Hybrid Integrated Circuit
CHICAGORILLA . . Chicago Gorilla (Slang for a desperado gunman)
CHICODER . . . Chinese Language Encoder
CHICOM . . . . . Chinese Communist
CHID . . . . . . Community Human and Industrial Development, Inc. (OEO)
CHIDE . . . . . . Committee to Halt Indoctrination and Demoralization in Education
     (Group opposing sex education in schools)
CHIEF . . . . . . Controlled Handling of Internal Executive Functions (UNIVAC)
CHILD . . . . . . Cognitive Hybrid Intelligent Learning Device
CHILD . . . . . . Community Helps in Life Development
CHINA . . . . . Chronic Infectious Neuropathic Agents
CHINAT . . . . . Chinese Nationalist
CHINFO . . . . Chief of Information (Navy)
CHIPITTS . . . . . Chicago-Pittsburgh (Proposed name for possible "super-city" formed by
     growth and mergers of other cities)
CHIPS . . . . . . Chemical Engineering Information Processing System
CHIR . . . . . . Chiricahua National Monument and Fort Bowie National Historic Site
Chir Doct . . . . Chirurgiae Doctor (Doctor of Surgery)
CHIS . . . . . . Channel Islands National Monument
CHISOX . . . . . Chicago White Sox (Baseball team)
CHJ . . . . Colel Hibath Jerusalem
CHJ . . . . Society of the Devotees of Jerusalem
CH-JM . . . . . Carnegie Hall - Jeunesses Musicales
CHL . . . . Central Hockey League
CHL . . . . Chain Home Low (Aviation)
CHL . . . . Chemical New York Corp. (NYSE symbol)
CHL . . . . Confinement at Hard Labor (Army)
CHL . . . . Cronar Halftone Litho (Du Pont)
CHM . . . . Chamber
CHM . . . . Champion Spark Plug Company (NYSE symbol)
Ch M . . . . Chirurgiae Magister (Master of Surgery)
CHM . . . . Compound Handling Machine
CHM . . . . Congregation of Humility of Mary (Roman Catholic women's religious order)
CHMACH . . . . Chief Machinist (Navy)
CHMK . . . . . . Chung-Hau Min Kuo (Republic of China)
CHMN . . . . . . Chairman
CHN . . . . Carbon, Hydrogen, Nitrogen
CHN . . . . College of the Holy Names (New York)
CHNAVAIRSHIPTRA . . Chief of Naval Airship Training

CHNAVMIS . . . Chief, Naval Mission
CHNL . . . . Channel
CHNOPS . . . . . Carbon, Hydrogen, Nitrogen, Oxygen, Phosphorus, and Sulfur
     (Compounds)
CHO . . . . Chinese Hamster Ovarian (Tumor)
CHO . . . . Chinese Hamster Ovary (Cells)
CHOB . . . . . . Cannon House Office Building
CHOH . . . . . . Chesapeake and Ohio Canal National Monument
CHOKE . . . . . . Care How Others Keep the Environment (An organization)
ChON . . . . . . Chasti Osobogo Naznacheniia (Elements of Special Designation)
     (Political police units attached to the armed forces) (USSR)
CHOP . . . . . . Change of Operational Control
CHOP . . . . . . Changeover Point (Aviation)
CHORD . . . . . Change my Operation Order (Military)
CHORI . . . . . . Chief of Office of Research and Inventions
CHOVR . . . . . . Changeover
CHP . . . . Cherry Point (Navy)
CHP . . . . Chihuahua Pacific R. R. (AAR code)
CHP . . . . Comhuriyet Halk Partisi (Turkey)
CHP . . . . Comprehensive Health Planning (A requirement for HEW grants to
     local agencies)
CHP . . . . Council of Housing Producers
CHP . . . . Ferrocarril de Chihuahua al Pacifico, SA (AAR code)
CH-P . . . . . . Challenge Position (Dancing)
CHPCLK . . . . Chief Pay Clerk (Navy)
CHPHAR . . . . Chief Pharmacist (Navy)
CHPHOT . . . . Chief Photographer (Navy)
CHQ . . . . Corps Headquarters (Army)
CHQMCLK . . . Chief Quartermaster Clerk (Coast Guard)
CHR . . . . Chestnut Ridge Railway Company (AAR code)
CHR . . . . Constant Hazard Ratio
CHR . . . . Coordinated Hungarian Relief
C-HR . . . . . . Candle Hour
ChrDem . . . . . Christian Democrats
CHRELE . . . . Chief Radio Electrician (Navy)
CHRG . . . . . . Charge
CHRI . . . . . . Christiansted National Historic Site
CHRIE . . . . . . Council on Hotel, Restaurant, and Institutional Education
CHRIS . . . . . . Cancer Hazards Ranking and Information System
CHRIST . . . . . Christians Heeding Righteousness Instead of Satanic Tyranny
     (Conservative organization)
ChrSoc . . . . . Christian Socialist
CHS . . . . Capitol Historical Society (Washington, DC)
CHS . . . . Catholic Homiletic Society
CHS . . . . Chloracetophenone Solution (Tear gas)
CHS . . . . Church Historical Society
CHS . . . . Circus Historical Society
CHS . . . . Community Health Service (HEW)
CHS . . . . Constant Heat Summation
CHS . . . . Crime on High Seas
CHSAA . . . . . Catholic High Schools Athletic Association
CHSCLK . . . . Chief Ship's Clerk
CHSM . . . . . . China Service Medal
CHT . . . . Cathode Heating Time
CHT . . . . Ceramic-Heated Tunnel (Langley Research Center)
CHT . . . . Charactron Tube
CHT . . . . Convective Heat Transfer
CHT . . . . Cylinder-Head Temperature
CHTG . . . . . . Charting
CHTORP . . . . Chief Torpedoman
CHTT . . . . . . Chicago Heights Terminal Transfer R. R. (AAR code)
CHU . . . . Centigrade Heat Unit
CHUM . . . . . . Chart Updating Manual (Air Force)
CHUM . . . . . . Computers and the Humanities (A periodical)
CHV . . . . Carl Hanser Verlag (Publisher)
CHV . . . . Chattahoochee Valley Railway Company (AAR code)
CHW . . . . . . Chesapeake Western Railway (AAR code)
CHW . . . . Chilled Water (Aerospace)
CHW . . . . Cold Heading Wire
CHW . . . . Cold and Hot Water
CHW . . . . Constant Hot Water (British)
CHX . . . . Chiro-Xylographic (Type of block book)
CHY . . . . Cherry-Burrel Corporation (American Stock Exchange symbol)
CI . . . . Call Indicator (Data processing)
CI . . . . Cambria & Indiana Railway (AAR code)
CI . . . . Capability Inspection (Air Force)
CI . . . . Carcinogenic Index
CI . . . . Cast Iron
CI . . . . Center of Impact
CI . . . . Central Interval
CI . . . . Centromeric Indices (Chromosomes)

CI . . . . Cephalic Index (Anthropology)
CI . . . . Channel Islands
CI . . . . Characteristic Independence
CI . . . . Chemical Ionization
CI . . . . Chief of Information (Army)
CI . . . . Chief Inspector
CI . . . . Chief Instructor
CI . . . . Chlorine Institute
CI . . . . CI Mortgage Group (NYSE symbol)
CI . . . . Circuit Interrupter
CI . . . . Cirrus (Meteorology)
CI . . . . Civitan International
CI . . . . Classification Inventory (Military)
CI . . . . Clean Identification Decal (Aerospace)
CI . . . . Close-In
CI . . . . Coefficient of Intelligence
CI . . . . Color Index (Medicine)
CI . . . . Colour Index (Numerical listing of dyes) (British)
CI . . . . Combat Interviews
CI . . . . Combustion Institute
CI . . . . Comfort Index
CI . . . . Communication Information
CI . . . . Compression Ignition (Engine)
CI . . . . Computer Indicator
CI . . . . Concept Identification (Psychology)
CI . . . . Configuration Interaction (Quantum mechanics)
CI . . . . Configuration Item
CI . . . . Congressional Interference
CI . . . . Consular Invoice
CI . . . . Continental Baking Company (NYSE symbol) (Wall Street slang name: "Coney Island") (Delisted)
CI . . . . Coordinate Index
CI . . . . Cordage Institute
CI . . . . Cost Inspector
CI . . . . Cost and Insurance (Business and trade)
CI . . . . Counter-Intelligence
CI . . . . Craft Inclination (Aerospace)
CI . . . . Criminal Investigation (Military)
CI . . . . Critical Influence
CI . . . . Crown of India (Imperial Order of the)
Ci . . . . Curie(s) (Unit of measurement of radiation)
CI . . . . Cut In
CI . . . . Lady of the Order of the Crown of India
C/I . . . . Carrier-to-Interference Ratio (Data processing)
C/I . . . . Certificate of Insurance
C & I . . . . Classification and Index (Air Force)
C & I . . . . Cost and Insurance
CIA . . . . California Institute of the Arts
CIA . . . . Casein Importers Association
CIA . . . . Center for Interreligious Affairs
CIA . . . . Central Intelligence Agency (of the US)
CIA . . . . Centre International des Antiparasitaires
CIA . . . . Chief Inspector of Armaments
CIA . . . . China Institute in America
CIA . . . . Cigar Institute of America
CIA . . . . Collegium Internationale Allergologicum
CIA . . . . Commission Internationale d'Analyses
CIA . . . . Compagnie Industriale Aerospaziale
CIA . . . . Computer Interface Adaptor
CIA . . . . Confederation Internationale des Accordeonistes (International Confederation of Accordionists)
CIA . . . . Conseil International des Archives (International Council on Archives)
CIA . . . . Controllers Institute of America
CIA . . . . Cork Institute of America
CIA . . . . Correctional Industries Association
CIA . . . . Cotton Importers Association
CIA . . . . Cotton Insurance Association
CIA . . . . Council on Islamic Affairs
CIAA . . . . . . Central Intercollegiate Athletic Association
CIAA . . . . . . Cheese Importers Association of America
CIAA . . . . . . Coordinator of Inter-American Affairs
CIAC . . . . . . Career Information and Counseling (Air Force)
CIAC . . . . . . Council for Inter-American Cooperation
CIAD . . . . . . Counter-Intelligence Analysis Division (DOD)
CIAFMA . . . . Centre International de l'Actualite Fantastique et Magique
CIAGO . . . . . . Chemische Industrie AKU(Algemene Kunstzidie Unie)-Goodrich (Belgium)
CIAI . . . . Comite International d'Aide aux Intellectuels
CIAL . . . . . . Communaute Internationale des Associations de Librairis (International Community of Booksellers Associations)
CIAME . . . . . . Commission Interministerielle des Appareils de Mesure Electriques et Electroniques (France)

CIANDE . . . . . Civil Information and Education Section of Allied Headquarters (World War II)
CIAO . . . . . . Conference Internationale des Africanistes de l'Ouest
CIAO . . . . . . Congress of Italian-American Organizations
CIAP . . . . . . Climatic Impact Assessment Program (of high altitude aircraft)
CIAP. . . . . . . Comite Interamericano de la Alianza para el Progreso (Inter-American Committee of the Alliance for Progress)
CIAPG . . . . . . Confederation Internationale des Anciens Prisonniers de Guerre (International Confederation of Former Prisoners of War)
CIAPS. . . . . . . Customer-Integrated Automated Procurement System
CIARA . . . . . . Conference Internationale Administrative des Radiocommunications Aeronautiques
CIAS . . . . . . California Institute of Asian Studies (An evening graduate school)
CIAT . . . . . . Crew Initiated Automatic Test
CIB . . . . Central Intelligence Board
CIB . . . . Centralized Intercept Bureau (Bell System)
CIB. . . . . COBOL (Common Business-Oriented Language) Information Bulletin (Air Force)
CIB . . . . Combat Infantryman's Badge
CIB . . . . Communaute Internationale Baha'ie (Baha'i International Community)
CIB . . . . Conseil International du Batiment pour la Recherche, l'Etude et la Documentation (International Council for Building Research, Studies and Documentation)
CIB . . . . Conseil International du Ble
CIB . . . . Criminal Intelligence Bureau
CIBA . . . . . . Chemical Industry in Basle
CIBE . . . . . . Confederation Internationale des Betteraviers Europeens (International Confederation of European Sugar Beet Growers)
CIBS. . . . . . . Cosmetic Industry Buyers' and Suppliers' Association
CIC . . . . Card Inventory Control
CIC . . . . Cardiac Inhibition Center (Physiology)
CIC . . . . Catholic Interracial Council
CIC . . . . Cedar Rapids & Iowa City Railway Company (AAR code)
CIC . . . . Chemical Industry Council
CIC . . . . Chemical Institute of Canada
CIC . . . . Cloud in Cell
CIC . . . . Codex Iuris Canonici (Code of Canon Law)
CIC . . . . Combat Information Center (Navy)
CIC . . . . Combat Intercept Control
CIC . . . . Combined Intelligence Committee
CIC . . . . Comite International de la Conserve
CIC . . . . Command Information Center
CIC . . . . Commander-in-Chief (Air Force)
CIC . . . . Commission Internationale du Chataignier
CIC . . . . Committee on Institutional Cooperation (Big Ten universities and University of Chicago)
CIC . . . . Common-Impression Cylinder
CIC . . . . Compensated Ion Chamber
CIC . . . . Complex Integrated Circuit
CIC . . . . Computer Instruments Corporation
CIC . . . . Concrete Industries Council
CIC . . . . Confederation Internationale de la Coiffure (International Conference of the Hairdressing Trade)
CIC . . . . Conseil International de la Chasse (International Hunting Council)
CIC . . . . Conseil International des Compositeurs
CIC . . . . Content Indication Codes
CIC . . . . Continental Corp. (NYSE symbol)
CIC . . . . Coordinator for Industrial Cooperation (Functions ceased, 1937)
CIC . . . . Corporate Information Center
CIC . . . . Counter-Intelligence Corps (Military)
CIC . . . . Critical Issues Council
CIC . . . . Customer Identification Code
CICA . . . . . . Canadian Institute of Chartered Accountants
CICA . . . . . . Confederation Internationale du Credit Agricole (International Confederation for Agricultural Credit)
CICA . . . . . . Council of International Civil Aviation
CICAE . . . . . . Confederation Internationale des Cinemas d'Art et d'Essai (International Experimental and Art Film Theatres Confederation)
CICAF. . . . . . . Compagnie Industrielle de Combustibles Atomiques Frittes (France)
CICAR . . . . . . Cooperative Investigations for the Caribbean and Adjacent Regions (UNESCO)
CICC . . . . . . Catholic Interracial Council of Chicago
CICC . . . . . . Conference Internationale des Charites Catholiques (International Conference of Catholic Charities)
CICCA . . . . . . Centre International de Coordination pour la Celebration des Anniversaires
CICE . . . . . . Centre d'Information des Chemins de Fer Europeens (Information Center of the European Railways)
CICEP. . . . . . . Conseil Interamericain du Commerce et de la Production
CICF. . . . . . . Chambre des Ingenieurs - Conseils de France

CICF . . . . . . Confederation Internationale des Corps de Fonctionnaires (International Confederation of Public Service Officers)
CICG . . . . . . Centre International du Commerce de Gros
CICIAMS. . . . . Comite International Catholique des Infirmieres et Assistantes Medico-Sociales (International Committee of Catholic Nurses)
CICIN . . . . . . Conference on Interlibrary Communications and Information Networks
CICIREPATO. . . Committee for International Co-operation in Information Retrieval Among Examining Patent Offices
CICM . . . . . . Commission Internationale Catholique pour les Migrations (International Catholic Migration Commission)
CICM . . . . . . Congregatio Immaculati Cordis Mariae (Congregation of the Immaculate Heart of Mary) (Roman Catholic men's religious order)
CICNY . . . . . Catholic Interracial Council of New York
CICOP . . . . . Catholic Inter-American Cooperation Program
CICP. . . . . . . Committee to Investigate Copyright Problems
CICP. . . . . . . Confederation Internationale du Credit Populaire (International Confederation for Popular Credit)
CICPE. . . . . . Comite d'Initiative pour le Congres du Peuple Europeen
CICR . . . . . . Comite International de la Croix-Rouge (International Committee of the Red Cross)
CICRA . . . . . Centre International pour la Coordination des Recherches en Agriculture
CICRC . . . . . Commission Internationale Contre le Regime Concentrationnaire
CICS . . . . . . Commercial or Industrial and Control Service Data System
CICS . . . . . . Customer Information Central System (Library of Congress)
CICT . . . . . . Commission on International Commodity Trade
CICT . . . . . . Conseil International du Cinema et de la Television (International Film and Television Council)
CICU . . . . . . Cirrocumulus (Meteorology)
CICU . . . . . . Commission for Independent Colleges and Universities (Pennsylvania)
CICWO. . . . . Combat Information Center Watch Officer
CID . . . . Central Institute for the Deaf
CID . . . . Change in Design
CID . . . . Cleanliness Identification (Label) (Aerospace)
CID . . . . Comite International de Dachau
CID . . . . Comite International des Derives Tensio-Actifs (International Committee of Tensio-Active Derivatives)
CID . . . . Commercial Import Division (Vietnam)
CID . . . . Commission for International Development
CID . . . . Committee for Industrial Development (UN)
CID . . . . Committee on Interest and Dividends (Federal Reserve Board)
CID . . . . Communication Implementation Directive (Air Force)
CID . . . . Component Identification
CID . . . . Council for Independent Distribution
CID . . . . Criminal Investigation Department (Often loosely referred to as Scotland Yard) (British)
CID . . . . Criminal Investigation Detachment
CID . . . . Criminal Investigation Division (Army)
CID . . . . Cubic Inch Displacement
CIDA . . . . . . Canadian International Development Agency (Formerly, External Aid Office)
CIDA . . . . . . Centre d'Information et de Documentation Atlantique (Brussels, Belgium)
CIDA . . . . . . Centre International de Developpement de l'Aluminium
CIDA . . . . . . Comite Intergouvernemental du Droit d'Auteur
CIDADEC. . . . . Confederation Internationale des Associations d'Experts et de Conseils (International Confederation of Associations of Experts and Consultants)
CIDALC. . . . . . Comite International pour la Diffusion des Arts et des Lettres par le Cinema (International Committee for the Diffusion of Arts and Literature through Cinema)
CIDC . . . . . . Construction Industry Development Council (Canada)
CIDCOMED . . . Council for Interdisciplinary Communication in Medicine
CIDE . . . . . . Comision de Inversiones y Desarrollo Economico (Uruguay)
CIDEM . . . . . . Centro Interamericano de Musica (Inter-American Music Center)
CIDEM . . . . . . Consejo Interamericano de Musica (Inter-American Music Council)
CIDEP. . . . . . Centre International de Documentation Concernant les Expressions Plastiques
CIDERE. . . . . Civil Defense Report
CIDESA. . . . . Centre International de Documentation Economique et Sociale Africaine (International Center for African Social and Economic Documentation)
CIDESCO . . . . Comite Internationale d'Esthetique et de Cosmetologie (International Committee for Aesthetics and Cosmetology)
CIDG . . . . . . Civilian Irregular Defense Groups (Military)
CIDITVA . . . . Centre International de Documentation de l'Inspection Technique des Vehicules Automobiles
CIDNP . . . . . Chemically Induced Dynamic Nuclear Polarization
CIDOC. . . . . . Centro Intercultural de Documentacion (Center for Intercultural Documentation) (Cuernavaca, Mexico)
CIDS . . . . . . Chemical Information Data System (Army)
CIDSS. . . . . . Comite International pour le Documentation des Sciences Sociales (International Committee for Social Sciences Documentation)
CIDSTAT . . . . Civil Disturbance Status Reporting (Army)

CID-UNATI . . . Comite d'Information et de Defense - Union Nationale des Artisans et Travailleurs Independents
CIE . . . . Catering Industry Employee (A publication)
CIE . . . . Centre International de l'Enfance (International Children's Center)
CIE . . . . Cesium Ion Emission
CIE . . . . Cleveland Institute of Electronics
CIE . . . . Coherent Infrared Energy
CIE . . . . Comite International des Echanges Pres la Chambre de Commerce Internationale
CIE . . . . Commission Internationale de l'Eclairage (International Commission on Illumination)
CIE . . . . Common Ion Effect
CIE . . . . Commonwealth Institute of Entomology (British)
CIE . . . . Companion of the (Order of the) Indian Empire (British)
CIE . . . . Customs Information Exchange (An arm of US Customs Bureau)
CIE-AF . . . . . Certified International Executive - Air Forwarding (Designation given by American Society of International Executives)
CIEB. . . . . . . Chilean Iodine Educational Bureau
CIEC . . . . . . Centre International des Engrais Chimiques
CIEC . . . . . . Commission Internationale de l'Etat Civil (International Commission on Civil Status)
CIEC . . . . . . Confederation Interamericaine d'Education Catholique (Inter-American Confederation of Catholic Education)
CIEC . . . . . . Conseil International des Employeurs du Commerce (International Council of Commerce Employers)
CIEE. . . . . . . Council on International Educational Exchange
CIE-EM . . . . . Certified International Executive - Export Management (Designation given by American Society of International Executives)
CIEF. . . . . . . Comite International d'Enregistrement des Frequences (International Frequency Registration Board)
CIE-F . . . . . . Certified International Executive - Forwarding (Designation given by American Society of International Executives)
CIEG . . . . . . Center for International Economic Growth (Defunct)
CIEM . . . . . . Conseil International pour l'Exploration de la Mer (International Council for the Exploration of the Sea)
CIEN . . . . . . Commission Interamericaine d'Energie Nucleaire (Inter-American Nuclear Energy Commission)
CIENES. . . . . Centro Interamericano de Ensenanza de Estadistica
CIEO . . . . . . Catholic International Education Office
CIEP. . . . . . . Committee on International Exchange of Persons
CIEP. . . . . . . Concentrated Impact Employment Program (Also known as CEP)
CIEP. . . . . . . Council on International Economic Policy
CIEPS . . . . . Conseil International de l'Education Physique et Sportive
CIER. . . . . . . Centre Interamericain d'Education Rurale
CIER. . . . . . . Commission for International Educational Reconstruction
CIES . . . . . . Comite International des Entreprises a Succursales (International Association of Chain Stores)
CIETA. . . . . . Centre International d'Etudes des Textiles Anciens (International Research Centre on Ancient Textiles)
CIETB . . . . . Centre Intercontinental d'Etudes de Techniques Biologiques
CIE-TM . . . . . Certified International Executive - Traffic Management (Designation given by American Society of International Executives)
CIF. . . . . Capacitor Input Filter
CIF. . . . . Carriage, Insurance, and Freight
CIF. . . . . Central Index File
CIF. . . . . Central Information File
CIF. . . . . Central Instrumentation Facility (NASA)
CIF. . . . . Central Integration Facility
CIF. . . . . China International Foundation
CIF. . . . . Cohesive Intermolecular Force
CIF. . . . . Cold-Insoluble Fibrinogen
CIF. . . . . Conseil International des Femmes (International Council of Women)
CIF. . . . . Construction Industry Foundation
CIF. . . . . Consumer Interests Foundation
CIF. . . . . Cost, Insurance, and Freight (Business and trade)
CIF. . . . . Cultural Integration Fellowship
CIFAX . . . . . Enciphered Facsimile Communications
CIFC . . . . . . Cost, Insurance, Freight, and Charges
CIFC . . . . . . Cost, Insurance, Freight, and Commission
CIFCO . . . . . Civilians in Foreign Communications Operations (Military)
CIFE. . . . . . . Centre International de Formation Europeenne
CIFE. . . . . . . Comite International du Film Ethnographique
CIFE. . . . . . . Conseil International du Film d'Enseignement (International Council for Educational Films)
CIFE. . . . . . . Cost, Insurance, Freight, and Exchange
CIFES . . . . . Comite International du Film Ethnographique et Sociologique (International Committee on Ethnographical and Sociological Films)
CIFI. . . . . . . Catholic Institute of the Food Industry
CIFI. . . . . . . Cost, Insurance, Freight, and Interest
CIFJ. . . . . . . Centre International du Film pour la Jeunesse
CIFLT . . . . . . Cost, Insurance, Freight, London Terms

CIFP. . . . . . . Cancel IFR (Instrument Flight Rules) Flight Plan
CIFTA. . . . . . Comite International des Federations Theatrales d'Amateurs de Langue Francaise
CIG . . . . Chemical Ion Generator
CIG . . . . Comite International de Geophysique (International Geophysical Committee)
CIG . . . . Counter Intelligence Group (Military)
CIGA . . . . . . Compagnia Italiana del Grande Alberghi (Italian hotel chain)
CIGB . . . . . . Commission Internationale des Grands Barrages de la Conference Mondiale de l'Energie
CIGR . . . . . . Commission Internationale du Genie Rural (International Commission of Agricultural Engineering)
CIGRE. . . . . . Conference Internationale des Grands Reseaux Electriques (International Conference on Large High Tension Electric Systems)
CIGS . . . . . . Chief of the Imperial General Staff (British)
CIGTF. . . . . . Central Inertial Guidance Test Facility (Air Force)
CIH . . . . Committee for Italic Handwriting (Defunct)
CIHA . . . . . . Comite International d'Histoire de l'Art (International Committee on the History of Art)
CII. . . . . Chartered Insurance Institute
CII. . . . . Compagnie Internationale d'Informatique (Formed by merger of SEA and CAE)
CII. . . . . Conseil International des Infirmieres (International Council of Nurses)
CII. . . . . Council of International Investigators
CII. . . . . Criminal Identification and Investigation
CII. . . . . Current Indicator and Integrator
CIIA . . . . Canadian Institute of International Affairs
CIIA . . . . Commission Internationale des Industries Agricoles (International Commission for Agricultural Industries)
CIIC . . . . Counterintelligence Interrogation Center (Military)
CIIM . . . . Centre International d'Information de la Mutualite
CIIR . . . . Central Institute for Industrial Research
CIITC . . . . . . Confederation Internationale des Industries Techniques du Cinema
CIIUAP . . . . . Commission on Increased Industrial Use of Agricultural Products
CIJ . . . . Commission Internationale de Juristes (International Commission of Jurists)
CIJ . . . . Cour Internationale de Justice
CIJC . . . . Construction Industry Joint Conference
CIJE . . . . Current Index to Journals in Education
CIK . . . . Chickasha Cotton Oil Company (NYSE symbol) (Delisted)
CIL . . . . Canadian Industries, Limited
CIL . . . . Certificate in Lieu (of)
CIL . . . . Chicago, Indianapolis & Louisville R. R. (AAR code)
CIL . . . . Commercial Instrument Landing
CIL . . . . Critical Item List
C/I/L. . . . . . . Computer/Information/Library Sciences (Abstracts)
CILA . . . . Centro Interamericano de Libros Academicos (Inter-American Scholarly Book Center)
CILA . . . . Council of International Lay Associations
CILB. . . . . . . Commission Internationale de Lutte Biologique Contre les Ennemis des Cultures
CILC . . . . Confederation Internationale du Lin et du Chanvre (International Linen and Hemp Confederation)
CILET . . . . . . Circular Letter
CILFA. . . . . . Centro Industrial de Laboratorios Farmaceuticos Argentinos
CILOPGO . . . . Comite International de Liaison des Gynecologues et Obstetriciens
CILPE . . . . . . Confederation Internationale de Liaison Entre Producteurs d'Energie Electrique
CILS. . . . . . . Cossor Instrument Landing System (Aviation)
CIM . . . . Capital Investment Model (Navy)
CIM . . . . Cavitation Intensity Meter
CIM . . . . Chicago & Illinois Midland Railway Company (AAR code)
CIM . . . . China Inland Mission
CIM . . . . Cleveland Institute of Music (Ohio)
CIM . . . . Communications Improvement Memorandum (Military)
CIM . . . . Communications Interface Modules (Data processing)
CIM . . . . Compound Inserting Machine
CIM . . . . Computer Input Media
CIM . . . . Computer Input Microfilming
CIM . . . . Conductance Increase Mechanism
CIM . . . . Congres International des Fabrications Mecaniques
CIM . . . . Congres Islamique Mondial
CIM . . . . Conseil International de la Musique
CIM . . . . Convention Internationale Concernant le Transport des Marchandises par Chemins de Fer
CIM . . . . Cork Insulation Material
CIM . . . . Council for Independent Managers
CIM . . . . Crystal Impedance Meter
CIM . . . . Curtis Institute of Music (Pennsylvania)
C & IM . . . . . Chicago & Illinois Midland Railway Company
CIMA . . . . . . Channel Industries Mutual Aid (Houston, Texas, firefighting group)
CIMA . . . . . . Construction Industry Manufacturers Association

CIMA . . . . . . Creek Indian Memorial Association
CIMAC . . . . . Conseil International des Machines a Combustion (International Council on Combustion Engines)
CIMAe . . . . . Commission Internationale de Meteorologie Aeronautique (OMI)
CIMAS . . . . . Conference Internationale de la Mutualite et des Assurances Sociales
CIMBA . . . . . Contractor Installation Make or Buy Authorization
CIMC . . . . . . Commanders' Internal Management Conference (Air Force)
CIMC . . . . . . Committee for International Municipal Cooperation
CIMCEE . . . . Comite des Industries de la Moutarde de la CEE (EEC Committee for the Mustard Industries)
CIMCO. . . . . Card Image Correction (Data processing)
CIME . . . . . . Chartered Institute of Marine Engineers
CIME . . . . . . Comite Intergouvernemental pour les Migrations Europeennes (Intergovernmental Committee for European Migration)
CIMM . . . . . Canadian Institute of Mining & Metallurgy
CIMM. . . . . . Constant Impedance Mechanical Modulation
CIMMS . . . . . Civilian Information Manpower Management System (Navy)
CIMMYT . . . . Centro Internacional de Mejoramiento de Maiz y Trigo (Mexico) (International Maize and Wheat Improvement Center)
CIMO. . . . . . Commission des Instruments et des Methodes d'Observation (OMI)
CIM-OMF . . . China Inland Mission Overseas Missionary Fellowship (Later, Overseas Missionary Fellowship)
CIMP . . . . . . Conseil International de la Musique Populaire (International Folk Music Council)
CIMPM . . . . . Comite International de Medecine et de Pharmacie Militaires (International Committee of Military Medicine and Pharmacy)
CIMR . . . . . . Commander's Internal Management Review (Also known as Black Saturday) (Military)
CIMS . . . . . . Civilian Information Management (or Manpower) System (Navy)
CIMS . . . . . . Communications Instructions for Merchant Ships (Navy)
CIMTP. . . . . . Congres Internationaux de Medecine Tropicale et de Paludisme (International Congresses on Tropical Medicine and Malaria)
CIMU . . . . . . Compatibility-Integration Mock-Up
CIN . . . . Chemical Industry Notes (A publication)
CIN . . . . Cincinnati Gas & Electric Company (NYSE symbol)
CIN . . . . Commission Internationale de Numismatique (International Numismatic Commission)
CIN . . . . Communication Identification Navigation
CIN . . . . Criminal, Immoral, and Narcotic
CINA . . . . . . Commission Internationale de Navigation Aerienne
CINC . . . . . . Commander-in-Chief
CINCAC . . . . Commander-in-Chief, Continental Air Command
CINCAF . . . . Commander-in-Chief, Allied Forces
CINCAF . . . . Commander-in-Chief, (US) Asiatic Fleet
CINCAFLANT. . Commander-in-Chief, Air Force Atlantic Command
CINCAFMED . . Commander-in-Chief, Allied Forces Mediterranean (NATO)
CINCAFPAC . . Commander-in-Chief, (US) Army Forces in the Pacific
CINCAFSTRIKE. . Commander-in-Chief, Air Force Strike Command
CINCAIREASTLANT. . Air Commander-in-Chief Eastern Atlantic Area
CINCAL . . . . . Commander-in-Chief, Alaskan Command
CINCALAIRCENEUR. . Commander-in-Chief, Allied Air Forces, Central Europe
CINCARIB . . . Commander-in-Chief, Caribbean
CINCARLANT. . Commander-in-Chief, (US) Army Forces, Atlantic
CINCARPAC . . Commander-in-Chief, (US) Army Forces, Pacific
CINCARSTRIKE. . Commander-in-Chief, Army Strike Command
CINCAWI . . . Commander-in-Chief, America West Indies Station (British)
CINCA & WI. . Commander-in-Chief, Atlantic and West Indies
CINCBPF . . . . Commander-in-Chief, British Pacific Fleet
CINCCONAD. . Commander-in-Chief, Continental Air Defense Command
CINCEASTLANT. . Commander-in-Chief, Eastern Atlantic Area (NATO)
CINCEI. . . . . . Commander-in-Chief, East Indies Station (British)
CINCENT . . . . Commander-in-Chief, Allied Forces Central Europe
CINCEUR . . . . Commander-in-Chief, Europe
CINCFE . . . . . Commander-in-Chief, Far East
CINCFESTA . . . Commander-in-Chief, Far East Station (British)
CINCHAN. . . . Commander-in-Chief Channel and S. North Sea (NATO)
CINCLANT . . . Commander-in-Chief, Atlantic (US Navy and Allies)
CINCLANTFLT. . Commander-in-Chief, Atlantic Fleet
CINCMAIRCHAN. . Allied Maritime Air Commander-in-Chief, Channel
CINCMEAFSA. . Commander-in-Chief, Middle East/Southern Asia and Africa South of the Sahara (Military)
CINCMED . . . Commander-in-Chief, Mediterranean
CINCNAVEASTLANTMED. . Commander-in-Chief, (US) Naval Forces, Eastern Atlantic and Mediterranean
CINCNE . . . . . Commander-in-Chief, (US) Northeast Command
CINCNEDE . . . Commander-in-Chief, Netherlands Forces in the East
CINCNELM . . . Commander-in-Chief, Naval Forces, Eastern Atlantic and Mediterranean (Military)
CINCNORAD. . Commander-in-Chief, North American Air Defense
CINCNOREUR. . Commander-in-Chief, Northern Europe
CINCNORTH . . Commander-in-Chief, Allied Forces Northern Europe (NATO)

CINCONAD... Commander-in-Chief, Continental Air Defense Command
CINCPAC.... Commander-in-Chief of the Pacific Fleet (World War II)
CINCPACAF... Commander-in-Chief, Pacific Air Forces
CINCPAC-CINCPOA.. Commander-in-Chief, (US) Pacific Fleet and Pacific Ocean Areas
CINCPACFLT.. Commander-in-Chief, Pacific Fleet
CINCPACHEDPEARL.. Commander-in-Chief, (US) Pacific Fleet Headquarters, Pearl Harbor
CINCPACREP.. Commander-in-Chief, Pacific Representative
CINCPOA.... Commander-in-Chief, Pacific Ocean Areas (Military)
CINCPOAHEDPEARL.. Commander-in-Chief, Pacific Ocean Areas Headquarters, Pearl Harbor
CINCSA..... Commander-in-Chief, South Atlantic Station (British)
CINCSAC.... Commander-in-Chief, Strategic Air Command
CINCSO..... Commander-in-Chief, (US) Southern Command
CINCSOUTH.. Commander-in-Chief, Allied Forces Southern Europe (NATO)
CINCSPECOMME.. Commander-in-Chief, Specified Command, Middle East
CINCSTRIKE.. Commander-in-Chief, Strike Forces (Military)
CINCTAC.... Commander-in-Chief, Tactical Air Command
CINCUNC.... Commander-in-Chief, United Nations Command
CINCUS..... Commander-in-Chief, United States Fleet (Obsolete)
CINCUSAFE... Commander-in-Chief, United States Air Forces in Europe
CINCUSAFLANT.. Commander in Chief, United States Air Force Atlantic
CINCUSAFSTRIKE.. Commander in Chief, United States Air Force Strike
CINCUSAREUR.. Commander-in-Chief, United States Army, Europe
CINCUSARPAC.. Commander-in-Chief, United States Army, Pacific
CINCUSNAVEUR.. Commander-in-Chief, United States Naval Forces, Europe
CINCWESTLANT.. Commander-in-Chief Western Atlantic Area (NATO)
CIND....... Central Indiana Railway Company (AAR code)
CIND....... Chief Intercept Director
CIND....... Computer Index of Neutron Data
CINDA...... Computer Index of Neutron Data
CINDA-3G... Chrysler Improved Numerical Differencing Analyzer for Third-Generation Computers
CINE....... Council on International Nontheatrical Events
CINFAC..... Counterinsurgency Information Analysis Center
CINFAC..... Cultural Information Analysis Center (American University)
CINFO...... Chief of Information
CINFR...... Central Institute for Nutrition and Food Research (Netherlands)
CINL....... Cumulative Index to the Nursing Literature
CINOA..... Confederation Internationale des Negociants en Oeuvres d'Art (International Confederation of Art Dealers)
CINS...... CENTO (Central Treaty Organization) Institute of Nuclear Science
CINS...... Cryogenic Inertial Navigating System
CINTA..... Compania Nacional de Turismo Aereo (Chilean airline)
C Int C..... Canadian Intelligence Corps
CINTC..... Chief, Intelligence Corps
CINU...... Centre d'Information des Nations Unies
CINVA..... From the Spanish for Inter-American Housing and Planning Center
CINWMD.... Committee on Interpretation of the Nation-Wide Marine Definition
CIO....... Central Input-Output Multiplexer (Data processing)
CIO....... Combat Intelligence Officer (Navy)
CIO....... Comite International Olympique
CIO....... Command Issuing Office(r)
CIO....... Commission Internationale d'Optique (International Commission for Optics)
CIO....... Committee of Industrial Organization
CIO....... Common Item Order
CIO....... Congress of Industrial Organizations
CIO....... Conventional International Origin
CIOA...... Center for Information on America
CIOMR..... Comite Interallie des Officiers Medecins de Reserve (Interallied Committee of Medical Reserve Officers)
CIOMS..... Council for International Organizations of Medical Sciences
CIOPAC..... Congress of Industrial Organizations, Political Action Committee
CIOS...... Combined Intelligence Objectives Subcommittee
CIOS...... Combined Intelligence Operations Section (Navy)
CIOS...... Comite International de l'Organisation Scientifique (International Committee for Scientific Management)
CIOSTA..... Commission International e pour l'Organisation Scientifique du Travail en Agriculture (International Committee of Scientific Management in Agriculture)
CIP........ Capital Investment Program
CIP........ Capsule Internal Programmer
CIP........ Cascade Improvement Program
CIP........ Cast-Iron Pipe (Technical drawings)
CIP........ Cataloging in Publication (Formerly, CIS) (Library science)
CIP........ Catholic Institute of the Press
CIP........ Catholic Intercontinental Press
CIP........ Central Illinois Public Service Company (NYSE symbol)
CIP........ Chief Industrial Property
CIP........ Civilian Institution Program
CIP........ Class Improvement Plan (Navy)
CIP........ Clean in Place

CIP....... College International de Podologie (International College of Podology)
CIP....... Comite International de Photobiologie (International Committee of Photobiology)
CIP....... Command Information Program (Military)
CIP....... Commercial Import Program
CIP....... Commission Internationale du Peuplier (International Poplar Commission)
CIP....... Common Input Processor
CIP....... Community Improvement Program
CIP....... Component Improvement Program
CIP....... Compool Interpreter Program
CIP....... Consolidated Instrument Package (Atmospheric research)
CIP....... Consolidated Intelligence Program
CIP....... Control Inlet Panel (Aerospace)
CIP....... Conversion in Place (Aerospace)
CIP....... Cost Improvement Program
CIP....... Council of International Programs for Youth Leaders and Social Workers
CIP....... Current Injection Probe
CIP....... Custom Interest Profile
CIPA...... Committee for Independent Political Action
CIPAC..... Collaborative International Pesticides Analytical Council (England)
CIPAP..... Changes in Itinerary to Proceed to Additional Places (Military)
CIPASH..... Committee for International Program in Atmospheric Sciences and Hydrology (UN)
CIPC...... Centre International Provisoire de Calcul
CIPC...... Combined Intelligence Priorities Committee (US and British) (London, World War II)
CIPC...... Comite International Permanent de la Conserve (International Permanent Committee on Canned Foods)
CIPEMAT..... Centre International pour l'Etude de la Marionnette Traditionnelle (International Center for Research on Traditional Marionettes)
CIPER..... Central Inventory of Production Equipment Records (Army)
CIPHER..... Calculations of Patient and Hospital Education Resources (Data processing)
CIPHONY.... Cipher and Telephony Equipment (Military)
CIPL...... Comite International Permanent de Linguistes (Permanent International Committee of Linguists)
CIPM...... Comite International des Poids et Mesures (International Committee on Weights and Measures)
CIPM...... Council for International Progress in Management
CIPO...... Conseil International pour la Preservation des Oiseaux (International Council for Bird Preservation)
CIPP...... Conseil Indo-Pacifique des Peches (Indo-Pacific Fisheries Council)
CIPPP...... Cooperative International Pupil-to-Pupil Program
CIPR...... Commission Internationale de Protection Contre les Radiations
CIPR...... Corporate Industrial Preparedness Representative (Military)
CIPRA..... Cast Iron Pipe Research Association
CIPRA..... Commission Internationale pour la Protection des Regions Alpines
CIPROFOLC... Centro de Investigaciones y Promociones Folcloricas
CIPS...... Canadian Information Processing Society
CIPS...... Cesium Ion Propulsion System
CIPSH...... Conseil International de la Philosophie et des Sciences Humaines (International Council for Philosophy and Humanistic Studies)
CIQ...... Confoederatio Internationalis ad Qualitates Plantarum Edulium Perquirendas (International Association for Quality Research on Food Plants)
CIR....... Canada-India Reactor
CIR....... Center for Inter-American Relations
CIR....... Circuit
CIR....... Color Infrared (Image)
CIR....... Commission on Industrial Relations (Department of Employment) (British)
CIR....... Commission on Intergovernmental Relations
CIR....... Commissioners of Inland Revenue (British)
CIR....... Committee of Interns and Residents
CIR....... Common IFR (Instrument Flight Rules) Room (Aviation)
CIR....... Continental Illinois Realty (NYSE symbol)
CIR....... Cost Information Reports (DOD)
CIR....... Courant-Isaacson-Rees (Method)
CIR....... Court of Industrial Relations (Philippines)
CIR....... Crime on Indian Reservation
CIR....... Current Industrial Reports (Census Bureau)
CIR....... Current Instruction Register
CIRA...... Comite International Radioaeronautique
CIRA...... Committee on International Reference Atmosphere
CIRA...... COSPAR (Committee on Space Programs for Earth Observation) International Reference Atmosphere
CIRADS..... Counter-Insurgency Research and Development System
CIRAS...... Center for Industrial Research and Science
CIRC...... Centralized Information Reference and Control
CIRC...... Circular
CIRC...... Circulation
CIRCAL..... Circuit Analysis (Data processing)

CIRCCE . . . . . Confederation Internationale de la Representation Commerciale de la Communaute Europeenne (International Confederation of Commercial Representation in the European Community)

CIRCLTR . . . . . Circular Letter (Military)

CIRCUS. . . . . . Calculation of Indirect Resources and Conversion to Unit Staff (Data processing)

CIRE. . . . . City of Refuge National Historic Park

CI Rel . . . . . . Certificate in Industrial Relations

CIRES . . . . . . Communication Instructions for Reporting Enemy Sightings (Navy)

CIRF. . . . . . . Centre International d'Information et de Recherche sur la Formation Professionnelle

CIRF. . . . . . . Corn Industries Research Foundation

CIRFS . . . . . . Comite International de la Rayonne et des Fibres Synthetiques (International Rayon and Synthetic Fibres Committee)

CIRGA . . . . . . Critical Isotope Reactor, General Atomics

CIRIA . . . . . . Construction Industry Research and Information Association (British)

CIRIEC . . . . . . Centre International de Recherches et d'Information sur l'Economie Collective (International Center of Research and Information on Public and Cooperative Economy)

CIRIS . . . . . . Completely Integrated Range Instrumentation System (NASA)

CIRM . . . . . . Centro Internazionale Radio-Medico (International Radio Medical Center; gives emergency medical advice to ships at sea)

CIRM . . . . . . Comite International Radio-Maritime (International Maritime Radio Committee)

CIRP. . . . . . . College Internationale de Recherches pour la Production (International Institution for Production Engineering Research)

CIRVIS . . . . . . Communications Instructions for Reporting Visual (or Vital) Intelligence Sightings (Military)

CIS . . . . Cataloging in Source (Later, CIP)

CIS . . . . Catholic Information Society

CIS . . . . Center of International Studies (MIT)

CIS . . . . Central (Nervous System) Inhibitory State

CIS . . . . Central Installation Supply (Air Force)

CIS . . . . Central Instructor School

CIS . . . . Centro de Investigaciones Sociales (Social Research Center) (Colombia)

CIS . . . . Cesium Ion Source

CIS . . . . Close-in Support (Military)

CIS . . . . Communication and Instrumentation System

CIS . . . . Composition Information Services (Commercial firm)

CIS . . . . Conference of Internationally-Minded Schools

CIS . . . . Configuration Information System

CIS . . . . Congressional Information Service (Commercial firm)

CIS . . . . Continental Insurance Company (NYSE symbol) (Wall Street slang name: "Coney Island Sand") (Delisted)

CIS . . . . Corrosion Interception Sleeve

CIS . . . . Cost Information System

CIS . . . . Cost Inspection Service (Navy)

CIS . . . . Council for Intersocietal Studies

CIS . . . . Coupled Impedance Synthesis

CIS . . . . Credito Industriale Sardo (Sardinia)

CIS . . . . Cryogenic Instrumentation System

CIS . . . . Current Information Selection (IBM)

CISA . . . . . . Canadian Intercollegiate Sailing Association

CISA . . . . . . Council for Independent School Aid

CISAC . . . . . . Confederation Internationale des Societes d'Auteurs et Compositeurs (International Confederation of Societies of Authors and Composers)

CISAI . . . . . . Comite International de Soutien aux Antifascistes Iberiques

CISBH. . . . . . Comite International de Standardisation en Biologie Humaine (International Committee for Standardization in Human Biology)

CISC . . . . Confederation Internationale des Syndicats Chretiens (International Federation of Christian Trade Unions)

CIS & DB . . . . Comprehensive Information System and Data Base

CISE. . . . . . . Centro Informazioni Studi Esperienze

CISF. . . . . . . Confederation Internationale des Sages Femmes

CISH . . . . . . Comite International des Sciences Historiques (International Committee for Historical Sciences)

CISJA. . . . . . Comite International de Solidarite Avec la Jeunesse Algerienne

CISL. . . . . . . Confederation Internationale des Syndicats Libres (International Confederation of Free Trade Unions)

CISL. . . . . . . Confederazione Italiana Sindacati Lavoratori (Italian Confederation of Labor Unions)

CISL. . . . . . . Confederazione Italiana di Sindacati Liberi (Italian Confederation of Free Workers)

CISM . . . . . . Conseil International du Sport Militaire (International Military Sports Council)

CISNAL . . . . . Confederazione Italiana Sindacati Nazionali Lavoratori (Italian Confederation of National Workers' Unions)

CISO . . . . . . Comite International des Sciences Onomastiques (International Committee of Onomastic Sciences)

CISPF . . . . . . Cast Iron Soil Pipe Foundation

CISPI . . . . . . Cast Iron Soil Pipe Institute

CISPM . . . . . . Confederation Internationale des Societes Populaires de Musique

CISPR. . . . . . . Comite International Special des Perturbations Radioelectriques (International Committee on Radio Interference)

CISS. . . . . . . Comite International des Sports Silencieux (International Committee of the Silent Sports)

CISS. . . . . . . Conference Interamericaine de Securite Sociale (Inter-American Conference on Social Security)

CISS. . . . . . . Conference Internationale de Service Social (International Conference of Social Service)

CISS. . . . . . . Conseil International des Sciences Sociales (International Social Science Council)

CIST. . . . . . . Co-orbital Interceptor Scoring Technique

CISW . . . . . . California Institute of Social Welfare

CIT . . . . California Institute of Technology (Also, CALTECH or CALIT)

CIT. . . . . Call-in Time (Military communications)

CIT . . . . Carnegie Institute of Technology (Later, Carnegie-Mellon University) (Pennsylvania)

CIT. . . . . Case Institute of Technology (Later, Case Western Reserve University)

CIT . . . . CIT Financial Corp. (NYSE symbol)

CIT . . . . Citation

CIT . . . . Citizen

CIT. . . . . Comite International de Television (International Television Committee)

CIT . . . . Comite International des Transports par Chemins de Fer (International Rail Transport Committee)

CIT. . . . . Compressor Inlet Temperature

CIT . . . . Conseil International des Tanneurs (International Council of Tanners)

CIT. . . . . Contact Ion Thruster

CIT . . . . Controlled Interceptor Trainer (Aerospace)

CIT. . . . . Counselor-in-Training (for summer camps)

CITA . . . . . . Commission Internationale de Tourisme Aerien

CITA . . . . . . Committee for the Implementation of Textile Agreements

CITA . . . . . . Confederation Internationale des Ingenieurs Agronomes (International Confederation of Technical Agricultural Engineers)

CITAB. . . . . . Computer Instruction and Training Assistance for the Blind

CITAM . . . . . Centre International de la Tapisserie Ancienne et Moderne

CITCE . . . . . . Comite International de Thermodynamique et de Cinetique Electro-Chimiques (International Committee of Electro-Chemical Thermodynamics and Kinetics)

CITE. . . . . . . Capsule Integrated Test Equipment

CITE. . . . . . . Compression Ignition Turbine Engine

CITE . . . . . . Consolidated Index of Translations into English

CITE. . . . . . . Contractor Independent Technical Effort (DOD)

CITE. . . . . . . Controller Input Test Equipment

CITE. . . . . . . Council of Institute of Telecommunication Engineers

CITE . . . . . . Current Information Tapes for Engineers

CITEJA . . . . . . Comite Internationale d'Experts Juridiques Aeriens (International Technical Committee of Aerial Legal Experts)

CITEL . . . . . . Committee for the Inter-American Telecommunications

CITEN . . . . . . Comite International de la Teinture et du Nettoyage (International Committee for Dyeing and Dry Cleaning)

CITI . . . . Confederation Internationale des Travailleurs Intellectuels (International Confederation of Professional and Intellectual Workers)

CITI . . . . Congress of the International Theater Institute

CITIGO . . . . . Citizens for Good Government (Political fund of Ling-Temco-Vought, Inc.)

CITL. . . . . . . Canadian Industrial Traffic League

CITM . . . . . . Certified International Traffic Manager (Designation given by American Society of International Executives)

CITTA. . . . . . Comite International des Fabricants de Tapis et de Tissus d'Ameublement (International Committee of Manufacturers of Carpets and Furnishing Fabrics)

CIU . . . . Central Interpretation Unit (Military)

CIU . . . . Computer Interface Unit

CIU . . . . Congress of Independent Unions

CIU . . . . Congress of Irish Unions

CIU . . . . Coopers' International Union of North America

CIUS . . . . . . Conseil International des Unions Scientifiques (International Council of Scientific Unions)

CIUS . . . . . . County and Intermediate Unit Superintendents (of NEA)

CIUSS. . . . . . Catholic International Union for Social Service

CIV . . . . Civil(ian)

CIV . . . . Code Inserter Verifier (Air Force)

CIV . . . . Commission Internationale du Verre (International Commission on Glass)

CIV . . . . Convention Internationale Concernant le Transport des Voyageurs et des Bagges par Chemins de fer (International Convention Concerning the Carriage of Passengers and Luggage by Rail)

CIVCLO . . . . . Civilian Clothing

CIVIC. . . . . . Civic Issues Voluntary Information Council (Michigan)

CIV-M-MARP. . Civilian Mobilization Manpower Allocation/Requirements Plan

CIVPERSINS. . . Civilian Personnel Information System (Army)

CIW . . . . California Institution for Women

CIW. . . . . . . Carnegie Institution of Washington

CIW . . . . Ceramic Insulated Wire
CIW . . . . Chicago & Illinois Western R. R. (AAR code)
CIWG . . . . . . Camera Industries of West Germany
CIWP . . . . . . Counter Intelligence Working Party (US Military Government, Germany)
CJ . . . . Chief Judge
CJ . . . . Chief Justice (Various supreme courts)
CJ . . . . Congregatio Iosephitarum (Josephite Fathers) (Roman Catholic religious order)
CJ . . . . Conseil de la Jeunesse (Youth Council) (Senegal, Mali, Upper Volta, Niger and Dahomey)
CJ . . . . Construction Joint (Technical drawings)
CJ . . . . Corpus Juris (Body of Law)
CJ . . . . Creuzfelat-Jabok (Neurological disorder)
CJ . . . . US Pipe & Foundry Company (NYSE symbol) (Delisted)
CJA . . . . Classic Jaguar Association
CJA . . . . Conseil de la Jeunesse d'Afrique (African Youth Council) (Senegal)
CJA . . . . United Brotherhood of Carpenters and Joiners of America
CJBT . . . . . . Costume Jewelry Board of Trade of New York
CJC . . . . Cambridge Junior College (Massachusetts)
CJC . . . . Casper Junior College (Wyoming)
CJC . . . . Cazenovia Junior College (New York)
CJC . . . . Centenary Junior College (New Jersey)
CJC . . . . Centralia Junior College (Washington)
CJC . . . . Chipola Junior College (Florida)
CJC . . . . Cisco Junior College (Texas)
CJC . . . . Citrus Junior College (California)
CJC . . . . Clarendon Junior College (Texas)
CJC . . . . Coahoma Junior College (Mississippi)
CJC . . . . Compton Junior College (California)
CJC . . . . Congress for Jewish Culture
CJCI . . . . . . Conseil de la Jeunesse de Cote d'Ivoire (Ivory Coast Youth Council)
CJCS . . . . . . Chairman, Joint Chiefs of Staff
CJCW . . . . . . Colby Junior College for Women (New Hampshire)
CJD . . . . Doctor of Criminal Jurisprudence
CJFWF . . . . . Council of Jewish Federations and Welfare Funds
CJI . . . . Central Juvenile Index
CJI . . . . Concrete Joint Institute
CJIA . . . . . . Comite Juridique International de l'Aviation
CJIS . . . . . . Criminal Justice Information System
CJM . . . . Congregatio Jesu et Mariae (Eudist Fathers)
CJM . . . . . . Congres Juif Mondial (World Jewish Congress)
CJMCAG . . . . Conference on Jewish Material Claims Against Germany
CJO . . . . Communications Jamming Operator
CJO . . . . Council of Jewish Organizations in Civil Service
CJP . . . . Cornu-Jellet Prism
CJR . . . . Columbia Journalism Review
CJRL . . . . . . Criminal Justice Reference Library (University of Texas)
CJS . . . . Canadian Joint Staff
CJS . . . . Copper Jacketed Steel
CJS . . . . Cotton, Jute or Sisal (Freight)
CJSA . . . . . . Costume Jewelry Salesmen's Association
CJSPA . . . . . Conference of Jesuit Student Personnel Administrators
CJSS . . . . . . Conference on Jewish Social Studies
CJTA . . . . . . Costume Jewelry Trade Association
CJTF . . . . . . Commander, Joint Task Force
CJTF . . . . . . Crossroads Joint Task Force (Atomic weapons testing)
CJZ . . . . Cable Jacket Zipper
CK . . . . Check(ed)
CK . . . . Collins & Aikman Corporation (NYSE symbol)
CK . . . . Crystal Kit
C to K . . . . . Curious to Know (An inquisitive customer) (Merchandising slang)
CKA . . . . Catholic Knights of America
CKAFS . . . . . Cape Kennedy Air Force Station
CKB . . . . Caequot Kite Balloon
CKB . . . . Cork Base
CKBD . . . . . . Cork Board
CKCL . . . . . . Chicago-Kent College of Law
CKD . . . . Completely Knocked Down (i.e., disassembled, as a toy or piece of furniture which must be assembled before use)
CKE . . . . Castle & Cooke, Inc. (NYSE symbol)
CKF . . . . Christ the King Foundation
CKF . . . . Cork Floor
CKFM . . . . . . Check Form (Tool)
CKGA . . . . . . Check Gage (Tool)
CKIC . . . . . . Chemical Kinetics Information Center (National Bureau of Standards)
CKL . . . . Clark Equipment Company (NYSE symbol)
CKN . . . . Crocker National Corp. (NYSE symbol)
CKO . . . . Clark Oil & Refining Corp. (NYSE symbol)
CKP . . . . Cayley-Klein Parameter
CKS . . . . Chiang Kai-shek
CKS . . . . Chicago, Kalamazoo & Saginaw Railway (AAR code)

CKS . . . . Christian Knowledge Society (Also known as Society for Promoting Christian Knowledge)
CKSA . . . . . . Catholic Kolping Society of America
CKSG . . . . . . Catholic Knights of St. George
CKSNI . . . . . Cape Kennedy Space Network, Incorporated
CKSO . . . . . . Condon, Kinzua & Southern R. R. (AAR code)
CKT . . . . Circuit
CL . . . . Calamus Length
CL . . . . Carload
CL . . . . Carload Lot (Commerce)
CL . . . . Celtic League
CL . . . . Center Line
CL . . . . Centiliter
CL . . . . Central Line
Cl . . . . Chlorine (Chemical element)
CL . . . . Circuit Layout (AT & T)
CL . . . . Circular Letter
CL . . . . Civil Law
CL . . . . Clarendon Laboratory (Oxford University)
CL . . . . Class
CL . . . . Climatic Laboratory (Military)
CL . . . . Close
CL . . . . Colgate-Palmolive Company (NYSE symbol)
CL . . . . Common Law
CL . . . . Comparative Literature (A publication)
CL . . . . Concentration Length
CL . . . . Confidence Limits
CL . . . . Connecting Line
CL . . . . Consolidated Listing
CL . . . . Contact Lost (RADAR)
CL . . . . Control Logic
CL . . . . Conversion Loss
CL . . . . Corpus Luteum (Endocrinology)
CL . . . . Cost of Living
CL . . . . Course Line (Aviation)
CL . . . . Crane Load
CL . . . . Critical List (Medicine)
CL . . . . Crystallographic Laboratory (MIT)
CL . . . . Cyclotron Laboratory
CL . . . . Light Cruiser (Navy symbol)
C-L . . . . Canadair, Limited (Division of General Dynamics Corporation) (Montreal)
C/L . . . . Cash Letter (Banking)
C/L . . . . Circular Letter
C of L . . . . . Cost of Living
CLA . . . . California Library Association
CLA . . . . Canadian Library Association (Also known as ACB)
CLA . . . . Canadian Lumbermen's Association
CLA . . . . Catholic Library Association
CLA . . . . Center Line Average
CLA . . . . Chinese Laundry Association
CLA . . . . Christian Labor Association of the United States of America
CLA . . . . Church League of America
CLA . . . . Clear and Add
CLA . . . . Coaxial Line Attenuator
CLA . . . . College Language Association
CLA . . . . Colonial Corporation of America (NYSE symbol) (Delisted)
CLA . . . . Commonwealth Library Association (British)
CLA . . . . Communication Line Adapters
CLA . . . . Comparative Literature Association
CLA . . . . Conservative Library Association
CLA . . . . Council for Latin America
C & LA . . . . . Cargo and Loading Analysis
CLAA . . . . . . Anti-Aircraft Light Cruiser (Navy symbol)
CLAA . . . . . . Centre Lyonnais d'Applications Atomiques (France)
CLAC . . . . . . Closed-Loop Approach Control
CLAC . . . . . . Combined Liberated Areas Committee
CLAD . . . . . . Collect Adapter
CLAH . . . . . . Conference on Latin American History
CLAM . . . . . . Chemically-fueled Low Altitude Missile (Air Force program)
CLAM . . . . . . Clear Air Mass
CLAM . . . . . . Comite Permanent de Liaison de l'Agrumiculture Mediterraneenne (Liaison Committee for Mediterranean Citrus Fruit Culture)
CLAMP . . . . . Chemical Low Altitude Missile Puny
CLAMTI . . . . . Clutter-Locked Airborne Moving Target Indicator (Air Force)
CLANS . . . . . Computerized Link Analysis System
CLAO . . . . . . Contact Lens Association for Optometry
CLAR . . . . . . Clarification (or Clarify)
CLARA . . . . . Cornell Learning and Recognizing Automaton
CLARK . . . . . Combat Launch and Recovery Kit
CLAS . . . . . . Catholic Ladies Aid Society
CLAS . . . . . . Classify

CLAS . . . . Communications Link Analyzer System
CLAS . . . . Crowd, Lift, Actuate, Swing (Backhoe controls for tractors)
CLASB . . . . . . Citizens League Against the Sonic Boom
CLASC . . . . . . Confederacion Latinoamericana de Sindicalistas Cristianos (Latin American Federation of Christian Trade Unionists)
CLASP. . . . . . . Clients Lifetime Advisory Service Program (Insurance)
CLASP. . . . . . . Composite Launch & Spacecraft Program
CLASP. . . . . . . Computer Language for Aeronautics and Space Programing (NASA)
CLASP. . . . . . . Computer Launch and Separation Problem
CLASS . . . . . . Carrier Landing-Aid Stabilization System (Navy)
CLASS . . . . . . Class Action Study and Survey (Student legal action organization)
CLASS . . . . . . Classification
CLASS . . . . . . Close Air Support System
CLASS . . . . . . Computer-Based Laboratory for Automated School System
CLASS . . . . . . Current Literature Alerting Search Service (of BIOSIS)
CLASSICS . . . . Classification or Identification of Covert Satellites
CLASSMATE. . . Computer Language to Aid and Stimulate Scientific, Mathematical, and Technical Education
CLAT . . . . Communication Line Adapters for Teletype
CLAT . . . . Confederation of Latin-American Teachers
CLATT. . . . . . . Comite Latinoamericano de Textos Teologicos
CLAW . . . . . . Clustered Atomic Warhead
CLB . . . . Bachelor of Civil Law
CLB . . . . Civil Liberties Bureau (Forerunner of the American Civil Liberties Union)
CLB . . . . Constant Level Balloon
CLB . . . . Crash Locator Beacon (Air Force)
CLBW . . . . . . Closed Loop Bandwidth
CLC . . . . Cadillac-LaSalle Club
CLC . . . . Canadian Labour Congress
CLC . . . . Catholic Ladies of Columbia
CLC . . . . Columbia & Cowlitz Railway Company (AAR code)
CLC . . . . Compressive Load Cell
CLC . . . . Computerized Lubrication Control (Sun Oil Co.)
CLC . . . . Consolidated Leasing Corporation of America (NYSE symbol)
CLC . . . . Cost of Living Council (Acronym pronounced "click")
CLC . . . . Course Line Computer
CLC . . . . Tactical Command Ship (Navy symbol)
CLC . . . . Task Fleet Command Ship (Navy symbol)
C & LC . . . . . . Capitals and Lower Case (Printing)
CLCC . . . . Closed Loop Continuity Check (Aerospace)
CLCD . . . . Clearinghouse and Laboratory for Census Data (of Center for Research Data)
CLCM . . . . . . Council of Lutheran Church Men
CLCO . . . . Claremont & Concord Railway Company (AAR code)
CLD . . . . Children with Learning Disabilities
CLD . . . . Civil Liaison Division (Army)
CLD . . . . Cost Laid Down
CLD . . . . Doctor of Civil Law
CLDAS . . . . . . Clinical Laboratory Data Acquisition System (Data processing)
CLDO . . . . Central Load Dispatching Office (US Military Government, Germany)
CLDWN . . . . . Cool Down
CLE . . . . Chicago Livestock Exchange
CLE . . . . Cleveland (Ohio) (Airport symbol)
CLE . . . . Continuing Legal Education
CLEAN . . . . . . California League Enlisting Action Now (Antiobscenity group)
CLEAN . . . . . . Committee for Leaving the Environment of America Natural
CLEAR . . . . . . Center for Labor Education and Research (University of Colorado)
CLEAR . . . . . . Center for Lake Erie Area Research (Ohio State University)
CLEAR . . . . . . Civic Leaders for Ecological Action and Responsibility (Connecticut)
CLEAR . . . . . . Closed-Loop Evaluation and Reporting System
CLEAR . . . . . . Compiler, Executive Program, Assembler Routines
CLEAR . . . . . . Components Life Evaluation and Reliability
CLEAR . . . . . . County Law Enforcement Applied Regionally
CLEC . . . . Closed Loop Ecological Cycle (Aerospace)
CLEF . . . . Civil Liberties Educational Foundation
CLEM . . . . Cargo Lunar Excursion Module
CLEO . . . . Council for Legal Education Opportunity
CLEP . . . . College-Level Examination Program (of College Entrance Examination Board)
CLER . . . . Comite de Liaison des Etudiants Revolutionnaires (French student group)
CLERES . . . . . . Centre de Liaison des Etudes et Recherches Economiques et Sociales (France)
CLETS . . . . . . California Law Enforcement Telecommunications System
CLF . . . . Cleveland-Cliffs Iron Company (NYSE symbol)
CLF . . . . Critical Link Factor
CLFMI . . . . . . Chain Link Fence Manufacturers Institute
CLFT . . . . Crippled Leap-Frog Test
CLG . . . . Change to Lower Grade (Army)
CLG . . . . Closed Loop Gain
CLG . . . . Columbus & Greenville Railway Company (AAR code)
CLG . . . . Guided Missile Light Cruiser (Navy symbol)

CLGA . . . . Composers and Lyricists Guild of America
CLGC . . . . Civilian Labor Group Center (Army)
CLGSFU . . . . . Clear Glazed Structural Facing Units (Technical drawings)
CLGN . . . . Guided Missile Light Cruiser (Nuclear powered) (Navy symbol)
CLGSO . . . . . . Civilian Labor Group Special Orders (Army)
CLGSUB . . . . . Clear Glazed Structural Unit Base (Technical drawings)
CLGW . . . . . . United Cement, Lime and Gypsum Workers International Union
CLH . . . . Cedars of Lebanon Hospital
CLHU . . . . Computer Laboratory of Harvard University
CLI . . . . Calamus Length Index
CLI . . . . Capacitor Leakage Indicator
CLI . . . . Coach Lace Institute
CLI . . . . Coherent LASER Illumination
CLI . . . . Coin Level Indicator (Telephone communications)
CLI . . . . Control Level Item
CLI . . . . Core Logic Intervalometer
CLI . . . . Cost-of-Living Index
CLIA . . . . Clinical Laboratory Improvement Act
CLIC . . . . Commercial Loan Insurance Corporation
CLIC . . . . Cooperating Libraries in Consortium
CLICK . . . . . . Commerce, Labor, Industry Corporation of Kings County (Brooklyn, NY)
CLIF . . . . Cliffside R. R. (AAR code)
CLIFS . . . . Cost, Life, Interchangeability, Function, and Safety (Navy)
CLIM . . . . Climactic
CLIMMAR . . . . Centre de Liaison International des Marchands de Machines Agricoles et Reparateurs (International Liaison Center for Agricultural Machinery Distributors and Maintenance)
CLIN . . . . Contract Line Item Number (Army)
CLIP . . . . Cancel Launch in Progress (Air Force)
CLIP . . . . Compiler Language for Information Processing
CLIP . . . . Country Logistics Improvement Program (Air Force)
CLIPS . . . . Coincident Light Information Photographic Strips
CLIS . . . . Clearinghouse for Library and Information Sciences
CLITRAVI . . . . Centre de Liaison des Industries Transformatrices de Viandes de la CEE
CLIU . . . . Catholic Life Insurance Union
CLIV . . . . Core Logic Intervalometer
CLJ . . . . Control Joint
CLJC . . . . Copiah-Lincoln Junior College (Mississippi)
CLK & . . . . . . Clerk
CLK . . . . Clock
CLK . . . . Hunter-Killer Ship (Navy symbol)
CLKWZ . . . . . Clockwise
CLL . . . . Catholic Listener Library (Later, Maynard Listener Library)
CLL . . . . Chief of Legislative Liaison (Army)
CLL . . . . Cholesterol Lowering Lipid (Biochemistry)
CLL . . . . Confederation of Lebanese Labor
CLL . . . . Continental Oil Company (NYSE symbol)
CLLA . . . . Commercial Law League of America
CLLW . . . . . . Council for Lay Life and Work
CLM . . . . Cislunar Landing Mission
CLMA . . . . . . Certified Livestock Markets Association
CLMA . . . . . . Cigarette Lighter Manufacturers Association
CLMA . . . . . . Clothing Monetary Allowance
CLMA . . . . . . Contact Lens Manufacturers Association
CLMC . . . . . . Catholic Lay Mission Corps
CLML . . . . . . Chicago Linear Music Language
CLML . . . . . . Current List of Medical Literature
CLMO . . . . . . Coordinator and Liaison Maintenance Officer
CLMS . . . . . . Clinical Laboratory Management System (Data processing)
CLN . . . . Clipper Negative
CLNAI . . . . . . Comitato de Liberazione Nazionale per l'Alta Italia
CLNC . . . . . . Clearance
CLNT . . . . . . Coolant
CLO . . . . Celotex Corporation (NYSE symbol) (Delisted)
CLO . . . . Civil Liaison Officer (Army)
CLO . . . . Clean Lube Oil
CLO . . . . Coleco Industries (NYSE symbol)
CLO . . . . Computer Lock-On
CLO . . . . Concentric Line Oscillator
CLO . . . . Congressional Liaison Office
CLOAX . . . . . Corrugated-Laminated Coaxial (Cable)
CLODA . . . . . Closing Date
CLOPP . . . . . . Continuous Level of Production Plan
CLOTO . . . . . Close This Office
CLP . . . . Campbell-Larsen Potentiometer
CLP . . . . Clarendon & Pittsford R. R. (AAR code)
CLP . . . . Clipper Positive
CLP . . . . Confederation of Labor in the Philippines
CLP . . . . Congress Liberation Party (Nyasaland)
CLP . . . . Continuous Line Plotter
CLP . . . . Criminal Law and Procedure

CLP . . . . Cross Linked Polyethylene (Organic chemistry)
CL & P. . . . . . Connecticut Light and Power Company
CLR . . . . Central London Underground Railway
CLR . . . . Centurion LASER Range-Finder
CLR . . . . City of London Rifles (British)
CLR . . . . Computer Language Recorder
CLR . . . . Coordinating Lubricant and Equipment Research Committee
            (Coordinating Research Council)
CLR . . . . Council on Library Resources
CLRAP . . . . . . Catholic League for Religious Assistance to Poland
CLRAP. . . . . . . Cleared As Planned
CLRC . . . . Central Labor Relations Commission (Japan)
CLRI. . . . . Central Leather Research Institute (British)
CLRU . . . . Cambridge Language Research Unit
CLS . . . . Cable Laying Ship
CLS . . . . Cam Limit Switch
CLS . . . . Canon Law Society of America
CLS . . . . Cislunar Space
CLS . . . . Close Lunar Satellite
CLS . . . . Closed-Loop Support (Army)
CLS . . . . Compatible LASER System
CLS . . . . Constant Level Speech
CLS . . . . Consular Law Society
CLSA . . . . Conservation Law Society of America
CLSA . . . . Cooperative Logistic Support Arrangement (Military)
CLSC . . . . Chautauqua Literary and Scientific Circle
CLSC . . . . COMSEC (Communications Security) Logistic Support Center (Army)
CLSC . . . . Confederation Luxembourgeoise des Syndicats Chretiens (Confederation
            of Christian Trade Unions of Luxembourg)
CLSD . . . . Closed
CLSF. . . . . Committee for Latvian Song Festival in USA
CLSG . . . . Closing
CLSR . . . . Closure
CLSS . . . . Communication Link Subsystem
CLSU . . . . COMSEC (Communications Security) Logistic Support Unit (Army)
CLT . . . . Central Limit Theorem (Statistics)
CLT . . . . Clerical Technician, Medical (Navy)
CLT . . . . Clinical Laboratory Technician
CLT . . . . Closed Loop Telemetry
CLT . . . . Communication Line Terminal (Data processing)
CLT . . . . Computer Language Translator
CLT . . . . Council of the Living Theatre
CLT . . . . Crippled Leap-Frog Test
CLTA . . . . Chinese Language Teachers Association
CLTE . . . . Commissioned Loss to Enlisted Status (Revocation of an officer's
            appointment)
CLTS . . . . Chicago Lutheran Theological Seminary
CLU . . . . Central Logic Unit
CLU . . . . Certified Life Underwriter (Insurance)
CLU . . . . Ceylon Labor Union
CLU . . . . Chartered Life Underwriter
CLU . . . . Circuit Line Up
CLU . . . . Cluett, Peabody & Company, Inc. (NYSE symbol)
CLUE . . . . Clinical Literature Untoward Effects (Service published by International
            Information Institute)
CLUG. . . . . . . Community Land Use Game (Urban-planning game)
CLUMP . . . . . . Compool Look-Up Memory Print
CLUP . . . . Consolidated Labor Union of the Philippines
CLURT . . . . . . Come, Let Us Reason Together (Labor mediators' slogan)
CLUS . . . . Continental Limits, United States
CLUSA . . . . . . Continental Limits, United States of America (Navy)
CLUSA . . . . . . Cooperative League of the United States of America
CLV . . . . Clarissimus Vir (Most Illustrious Man)
CLVP . . . . Craft, Landing, Vehicle - Personnel
CLW. . . . . Catholic Library World (Official journal of Catholic Library Association)
CLW. . . . . Council for a Livable World
CLWG . . . . . . Clear Wire Glass (Technical drawings)
CLWP . . . . Committee for Liquidation of German War Potential (Allied German
            Occupation Forces)
CLX . . . . Clorox Co. (NYSE symbol)
CLX . . . . Continuous Lightweight Exterior
CLY . . . . County of London Yeomanry (British)
CLZ . . . . Copper, Lead or Zinc (Freight)
CM . . . . Carat (Metric)
CM . . . . Carboxymethyl
CM . . . . Career Motivation
CM . . . . Carpenter's Mate
CM . . . . Causa Mortis (On Occasion of Death)
CM . . . . Cell Membrane
CM . . . . Center of Mass
CM . . . . Center Matched (Technical drawings)

CM . . . . Centimeter
CM . . . . Certificated Master (or Mistress)
CM . . . . Chairman's Memorandum
CM . . . . Chief Metalsmith
CM . . . . Chirurgiae Magister (Master of Surgery)
CM . . . . Christian Mission
CM . . . . Chrom-Moly
CM . . . . Circular Measure
CM . . . . Circular Mil (Wire measure)
CM. . . . . Cochlear Microphonics (Response) (Auditory testing)
CM . . . . Columellar Muscle
CM . . . . Command Module
CM . . . . Common Meter (Music)
CM . . . . Communications Multiplexer
CM . . . : . . . Computer Module
CM . . . . Confidential Memorandum
CM . . . . Configuration Management
CM . . . . Congregatio Mariae (Fathers of the Company of Mary)
CM . . . . Congregatio Missionis (Lazarists)
CM . . . . Congregatio Missionis Sancti Vicentii a Paulo (Congregation of the
            Mission, or Vincentians) (Roman Catholic men's religious order)
CM . . . . Construction and Machinery
CM . . . . Construction Mechanic (Navy rating)
CM . . . . Continental Marines
CM . . . . Continuous Monitor
CM . . . . Controlled Minefield (Navy)
CM . . . . Core Memory
CM . . . . Corrective Maintenance
CM . . . . Corresponding Member
CM . . . . Countermarked
CM . . . . Countermeasure
CM . . . . Countermortar
CM . . . . Court-Martial
CM . . . . Credit Memo
CM . . . . Cruiser Minelayer
CM . . . . Cub Master (Scouting)
CM . . . . Cumulative Mortality (Radiology)
CM . . . . Cumulonimbus Mammatus (Meteorology)
Cm. . . . . Curium (Chemical element)
CM . . . . Medal of Courage of the Order of Canada
CM . . . . Mine Layer (Navy symbol)
C/M. . . . . Communications Multiplexer (Data processing)
C/M. . . . . Control and Monitoring (Aerospace)
C/M. . . . . Counts Per Minute
C & M . . . . . . Coal and Mining
C & M . . . . . . Construction and Machinery
C of M. . . . . . Certificate of Merit
cm³ . . . . Cubic Centimeter
CMA . . . . California Maritime Academy
CMA . . . . Canadian Medical Association
CMA . . . . Candle Manufacturers Association
CMa. . . . . Canis Major (IAU)
CMA . . . . Casket Manufacturers Association of America
CMA . . . . Center for Marine Affairs (Scripps Institution of Oceanography)
CMA . . . . Chinese Merchants Association
CMA . . . . Chocolate Manufacturers Association of the USA
CMA . . . . Christian and Missionary Alliance
CMA . . . . Cigar Manufacturers Association of America
CMA . . . . Circular Mil Area
CMA . . . . Civil-Military Affairs
CMA . . . . Classified Mail Address
CMA . . . . Clothespin Manufacturers of America
CMA . . . . Clothing Maintenance Allowance
CMA . . . . Clothing Manufacturers Association of the USA
CMA . . . . Colleges of Mid-America (An organization)
CMA . . . . Colorado Mining Association
CMA . . . . Communication Managers Association
CMA . . . . Complex Modulus Apparatus
CMA . . . . Computer-Marked Assignment (Education) (British)
CMA . . . . Confederate Memorial Association
CMA . . . . Conical Monopole Antenna
CMA . . . . Contract Maintenance Activity
CMA . . . . Convert Makers of America
CMA . . . . Corps Maintenance Area
CMA . . . . Country Music Association
CMA . . . . Court of Military Appeals
CMA . . . . Crucible Manufacturers Association
CMAA . . . . . . Chief Master at Arms
CMAA . . . . . . Church Music Association of America
CMAA . . . . . . Cigar Manufacturers Association of America
CMAA . . . . . . Club Managers Association of America

CMAA ...... Cocoa Merchants' Association of America
CMAA ...... Comics Magazine Association of America
CMAB ...... Clothing Maintenance (or Monetary) Allowance, Basic (Army)
CMAC ...... Capital Military Assistance Command
CMACL ...... Composite Mood Adjective Check List (FAA)
CMACP ...... Conseil Mondial pour l'Assemblee Constituante des Peuples
CMAIISS ...... Clothing Monetary Allowance, Initial Issue (Army)
CMAIWAC ... Clothing Monetary Allowance Initial (Women's Army Corps)
CMAK ...... Conical Monopole Antenna Kit
CMAL ...... Clothing Monetary Allowance List (Military)
CMAL ...... Controlled Multiple Address Letter
CMAM ...... Chief Mailman
CMAO ...... Court-Martial Appointing Order
CMAP ...... Charge Material Allocation Processor
CMAR ...... Can't Manage a Rifle (Formed by reversing the initials of Royal
    Army Medical Corps) (British) (World War I)
CMAS ...... Clergy Mutual Assurance Society (British)
CMAS ...... Clothing Maintenance Allowance, Standard (Air Force)
CMAS ...... Clothing Monetary Allowance, Standard (Army)
CMAS ...... Complete Mixing Activated Sludge
CMAS ...... Confederation Mondiale des Activities Subaquatiques (World Underwater
    Federation)
CMAS ...... Council for Military Aircraft Standards
CMAT ...... Cigar Manufacturers Association of Tampa
CMB ...... Carbolic Methylene Blue
CMB ...... Chase Manhattan Corp. (NYSE symbol)
CMB ...... Coastal Motor-Boat
CMB ...... Combat Maneuver Battalion(s) (Army)
CMB ...... Compagnie Maritime Belge
CMB ...... Corrective Maintenance Burden
CMBNY ...... China Medical Board of New York
CMBT ...... Combat
CMC ...... Carboxymethylcellulose
CMC ...... Catholic Microfilm Center
CMC ...... Center for Mass Communication (Columbia University)
CMC ...... Chemical Materials Catalog
CMC ...... Christian Medical Council
CMC ...... Claremont Men's College (California)
CMC ...... Clark Memorial College (Mississippi)
CMC ...... Clutter Mapper Card
CMC ...... Color Mixture Curve
CMC ...... Combined Meteorological Committee
CMC ...... Command Module Computer (NASA)
CMC ...... Commandant of the Marine Corps
CMC ...... Committee for Modern Courts
CMC ...... Communications Mode Control
CMC ...... Contact-Making Clock
CMC ...... Control Magnetization Curve
CMC ...... Coordinated Manual Control
CMC ...... Corporate Mountaineers Cult
CMC ...... Council of Mennonite Colleges
CMC ...... Critical Micelle Concentration
CMC ...... Curved Motion Cutter
CMCB ...... Carpenter's Mate, Construction Battalion
CMCBB ...... Carpenter's Mate, Construction Battalion, Builder
CMCBD ...... Carpenter's Mate, Construction Battalion, Draftsman
CMCBE ...... Carpenter's Mate, Construction Battalion, Excavation Foreman
CMCC ...... Central Marine Chamber of Commerce
CMCC ...... Classified Matter Control Center
CMCC ...... Conference of Mutual Casualty Companies
CMCH ...... Company of Military Collectors & Historians
CMCM ...... Commandant of the Marine Corps Memorandum
CMCSA ...... Canadian Manufacturers of Chemical Specialties Association
CMD ...... Capital Military District (Vietnam)
CMD ...... Carboxymuconolactone Decarboxylase
CMD ...... Central Meridian Distance (NASA)
CMD ...... Colonial Medical Department (British)
CMD ...... Command
CMD ...... Common Meter Double (Music)
CMD ...... Configuration Management Division
CMD ...... Core Memory Driver
CM & D ...... Counter Measures and Deception (RADAR)
CMDAC ...... Current Mode Digital-to-Analog Converter
CMDC ...... Central Milk Distributive Committee (British)
CMDJA ...... Country Music Disk Jockeys Association
CMDN ...... Catalog Management Data Notification (Army)
CMDO ...... Calcutta Metropolitan Development Organization
CMDO ...... Consolidated Material Distribution Objectives (Air Force)
CMDR ...... Commander
CMDS ...... Centralized Message Data System (AT&T)
CME ...... Centrifuge Moisture Equivalent

CME ...... Christian Methodist Episcopal (Church)
CME ...... College of Medical Evangelists (Los Angeles, California)
CME ...... Colloid Microthruster Experiment
CME ...... Commission on Missionary Education (Later, Department of Education
    for Missions)
CME ...... Common Mode Error
CME ...... Conference Mondiale de l'Energie (World Energy Conference)
CM & E ...... Chemical Marketing and Economics
C & ME ...... Civil and Mining Engineer
CMEA ...... Central Medical Establishment, Aviation (Air Force)
CMEA ...... Council for Middle Eastern Affairs
CMEA ...... Council for Mutual Economic Assistance (Communist-bloc nations)
    (Also known as COMECON)
CMEC ...... Chemical Marketing and Economics
CMEMA ...... Chicago and Midwest Envelope Manufacturers Association
CMERA ...... Conference Mondiale des Experts Radiotelegraphistes de l'Aeronautique
CMET ...... Coated Metal
CMEU ...... Colombo Municipal Employees' Union (Ceylon)
CMF ...... C-Band Monopulse Feed
CMF ...... Calcium- and Magnesium-Free
CMF ...... Cardinal Mindszenty Foundation
CMF ...... Cartesian Mapping Function
CMF ...... Chocolate Milk Foundation
CMF ...... Christian Missionary Fellowship
CMF ...... Circular Mil Foot
CMF ...... Citizen Military Forces (New Guinea)
CMF ...... Coherent Memory Filter
CMF ...... Color Mixture Function
CMF ...... Combat Mission Folder
CMF ...... Composite Medical Facility
CMF ...... Congregatio Missionariorum Filiorum Immaculati Cordis Beatae Maria
    Virginia (Congregation of Missionary Sons of the Immaculate Heart of
    the Blessed Virgin Mary, or Claretian Fathers) (Roman Catholic
    religious order)
CMF ...... Court-Martial Forfeiture
CMFC ...... China Man-Made Fiber Corporation (Taiwan)
CMFL ...... Commission on Marriage and Family Life (of NCC)
CMFSW ...... Calcium- and Magnesium-Free Synthetic Seawater
CMG ...... Central Machine Gun
CMG ...... Chief Marine Gunner
CMG ...... Color Marketing Group (An organization)
CMG ...... Companion of the Order of St. Michael and St. George (British)
CMG ...... Control Movement Gyro(scope) (NASA)
CMH ...... Cambridge Medieval History (A publication)
CMH ...... Chief of Military History (Department of the Army)
CMH ...... Company of Military Historians
CMH ...... Congressional Medal of Honor
CMHA ...... California Mental Health Analysis (Testing)
C-MHA ...... Confidential - Modified Handling Authorized (Military)
CMHCA ...... Community Mental Health Centers Act
CMHS ...... Congressional Medal of Honor Society
CMI ...... Can Manufacturers Institute
CMi ...... Canis Minor (IAU)
CMI ...... Caribbean Meteorological Institute
CMI ...... Comite Maritime International (International Maritime Committee)
CMI ...... Comite Meteorologique International
CMI ...... Command Maintenance Inspection (Army)
CMI ...... Commission Mixte Internationale pour les Experiences Relatives a la
    Protection des Lignes de Telecommunication et des Canalisations
    Souterraines
CMI & E ...... Computer Managed Instruction
CMI ...... Continental Mortgage Investors (NYSE symbol)
CMI ...... Cornell Medical Index
CMI ...... Cumulative Monthly Issue (Material)
CMIA ...... Coal Mining Institute of America
CMIA ...... Command Management Inventory Accounting (Army)
CMIA ...... Cultivated Mushroom Institute of America
CMIP ...... Cost Management Improvement Program
CMIR ...... Common Mode Input Resistance
CMIU of A ... Cigar Makers' International Union of America
CMJ ...... Church Mission of Jews
CMK ...... Carnation Company (American Stock Exchange symbol)
CMK ...... Chassis Marking Kit
CML ...... Chicago Midway Laboratory (Army)
CML ...... Chief Moulder (Navy)
CML ...... Chronic Myelocytic (or Myeloid or Myelogenous) Leukemia (Medicine)
CML ...... Collimated Monochromatic Light
CML ...... Common Machine Language (Data processing)
CML ...... Components & Materials Laboratory
CML ...... Computer Managed Laboratory
CML ...... Critical Mass Laboratory

CML........ Current Mode Logic
CMLA....... Concordia Mutual Life Association
CMLC...... Chemical Corps (Army)
CMLC...... Civilian/Military Liaison Committee
CMLCBL..... Chemical Corps Biological Laboratories (Army)
CMLCENCOM.. Chemical Corps Engineering Command
CMLCMATCOM.. Chemical Corps Material Command
CMLCRDCOM.. Chemical Corps Research and Development Command
CMLCRECOM.. Chemical Corps Research and Engineering Command
CMLCTNGCOM.. Chemical Corps Training Command
CMLE....... Carboxymuconate Lactonizing Enzyme
CMLOPS..... Chemical Operations (Army)
CMLS...... Confederate Memorial Literary Society
CMM .... Chemical Milling Machine
CMM ...... Chief Machinist's Mate
CMM ...... Coherent Microwave Memory
CMM ...... Commission for Maritime Meteorology (World Meteorological
            Organization)
CMM ...... Congregatio Missionariorum de Mariannhill (Congregation of Mariannhill
            Missionaries, or Mariannhill Fathers) (Roman Catholic religious order)
CMM ...... Coordinate Measuring Machine
CMM ...... Cutting or Molding Machine
CMMB ...... Catholic Medical Mission Board
CMMCBE..... Chief Machinist's Mate, Construction Battalion, Equipment Operator
CMMG ..... Chief Machinist's Mate, Industrial Gas Generating Mechanic
CMMG ..... Civilian Manpower Management Guides (Navy)
CMMI....... Civilian Manpower Management Instruction (Navy)
CMMI....... Command Maintenance Management Inspection (Military)
CMML ..... Christian Missions in Many Lands
CMML ..... Civilian Manpower Management Letters (Navy)
CMMR ..... Chief Machinist's Mate, Refrigeration
CMMR ..... Confirmed and Made a Matter of Record (Army)
CMMS ..... Carbon Monoxide Measuring System
CMMS ..... Chief Machinist's Mate, Shop
CMMS ..... Columbia Mental Maturity Scale (Psychology)
CMMSRO.... Chief Machinist's Mate, Ship Repair, Outside Machinist C
CMN .... Callahan Mining Corporation (NYSE symbol)
CMN .... Cerium Magnesium Nitrate
CMNS ...... Committee on Mediterranean Neogene Stratigraphy
CMO .... Cardiac Minute Output (Physiology)
CMO .... Chicago, St. Paul, Minneapolis & Omaha R. R. (AAR code)
CMO ...... Chief Maintenance Officer
CMO ...... Chief Medical Officer (Military)
CMO ...... Configuration Management Office
CMO ...... Controlled Materials Officer
CMO ...... Court-Martial Orders (Navy)
CMO ...... Crystal Marker Oscillator
CMOMM..... Chief Motor Machinist's Mate
CMOMSRD.... Chief Motor Machinist's Mate, Ship Repair, Diesel Engineering Mechanic
CMOMSRG .. Chief Motor Machinist's Mate, Ship Repair, Gasoline Engineering
            Mechanic
CMOPE...... Confederation Mondiale des Organisations de la Profession Enseignante
            (World Confederation of Organizations of the Teaching Profession)
            (Also known as WCOTP)
CMOS....... Capper Military Occupational Specialty (Army)
CMOS ...... Complementary Metal Oxide Semiconductor
CMOSM ..... Configuration Management Operating Systems Manual
CMP....... Cast Metal Part
CMP....... Command Module Pilot (Apollo) (NASA)
CMP....... Congruent Melting Point
CMP....... Console Message Processor (Data processing)
CMP....... Contemporary Music Project
CMP....... Contract Monitoring Point
CMP....... Controlled Materials Plan (of War Production Board) (World War II)
CMP....... Controlled Materials Production
CMP....... Corps of Military Police (British)
CMP....... Corrugated Metal Pipe (Technical drawings)
CMP....... Cytosine Monophosphate
CMPA...... Church Music Publishers Association
CMPAA ..... Certified Milk Producers Association of America
CMPF ...... Central Meat Processing Facility (Army)
CMPF ...... Cumulative Preferred (A class of stock)
CMPHE ..... Conference of Municipal Public Health Engineers
CMPL ...... Critical Materials Parts List
CMPNT...... Component
CMPS ...... Centimeters Per Second
CMPS ...... Colosseum of Motion Picture Salesmen
CMPT ...... Component
CMQ ...... Coal Mining and Quarrying
CMR....... Canadian Mounted Rifles
CMR....... Cape Mounted Rifles (British)

CMR........ Cerebral Metabolic Rate (Physiology)
CMR........ Chase Manhattan Mortgage & Realty Trust (NYSE symbol)
CMR........ College Militaire Royal (Canada)
CMR........ Committee on Medical Research (Subdivision of OSRD) (World War II)
CMR........ Common Mode Rejection
CMR........ Communications Monitoring Report
CMR........ Communications Moon Relay (System) (NASA)
CMR........ Consolidated Mail Room (Air Force)
CMR........ Continental Motors Corporation (NYSE symbol) (Delisted)
CMR........ Contract Management Region
CMR........ Countdown Modification Request (Aerospace)
CMR........ Counter Mortar RADAR
CMR........ Court-Martial Report(s)
CMR........ Court of Military Review
CMR........ Customer Material Return
CMRA....... Chemical Market Research Association
CMRED...... Council on Marine Resources and Engineering Development
CMRI....... Children's Medical Relief International
CMRI....... Command Maintenance Readiness Inspection (Military)
CMRLW..... Cape Mounted Rifles, Left Wing (British)
CMRR....... Common Mode Rejection Ratio
CMRRW..... Cape Mounted Rifles, Right Wing (British)
CMRS...... Countermeasures Receiving System
CMS....... Cable Marking System
CMS....... Cambridge Monitor System
CMS....... Canadian Micrographic Society
CMS....... Center for Maritime Studies
CMS....... Chicago Medical School
CMS....... Christian Medical Society
CMS....... Church Missionary Society
CMS....... Clay Minerals Society
CMS....... Cleaning Management Station
CMS....... College Music Society
CMS....... Common Manpower Standards
CMS....... Common Mode Signal
CMS....... Comprehensive Medical Society
CMS....... Condor Missile System
CMS....... Conservation Materials and Services
CMS....... Construction Maintenance Supervisor
CMS....... Consumer Marketing Service (Later, Agricultural Marketing Service)
            (Department of Agriculture)
CMS....... Consumers Power Company (NYSE symbol)
CMS....... Contemporary Music Society
CMS........ Cross-Section Measurement System
C & MS..... Consumer and Marketing Service (Department of Agriculture)
CMSA....... Canning Machinery and Supplies Association
CMSAF...... Chief Master Sergeant of the Air Force
CMSC...... Catalina Marine Science Center
CMSC...... Central Missouri State College
CMSCI...... Council of Mechanical Specialty Contracting Industries
CMSE...... Center for Materials Science and Engineering (MIT)
CMSER..... Commission on Marine Science, Engineering, and Resources
CMSGT...... Chief Master Sergeant
CMS/LC ..... Chamber Music Society of Lincoln Center
CMSM ...... Conference of Major Superiors of Men of the USA
CM-SM ..... Command Module - Service Module (Combined) (NASA)
CMSR...... Carpenter's Mate, Ship Repair
CMSRB ..... Carpenter's Mate, Ship Repair, Boatbuilder--Wood
CMSRB ..... Chief Metalsmith, Ship Repair, Blacksmith
CMSRC..... Carpenter's Mate, Ship Repair, Carpenter
CMSRC..... Chief Metalsmith, Ship Repair, Coppersmith
CMSRJ ..... Carpenter's Mate, Ship Repair, Joiner
CMSRK ..... Carpenter's Mate, Ship Repair, Caulker--Boat
CMSRN..... Carpenter's Mate, Ship Repair, Cement Worker--Concrete
CMSRS..... Carpenter's Mate, Ship Repair, Shipwright
CMSRS ..... Chief Metalsmith, Ship Repair, Sheet Metal Worker
CMSS...... Commission on Molecular Structure and Spectroscopy
CM & STP... Chicago, Milwaukee & St. Paul Railway
CM ST P & P... Chicago, Milwaukee, St. Paul and Pacific Railroad Company
CMSW ..... Conference of Major Religious Superiors of Women's Institutes of the
            United States of America
CMT........ California Mastitis Test
CMT........ Card Module Tester
CMT........ Code Matching Technique
CMT........ Commissary Technician, Medical
CMT........ Computer Memory Tester
CMT........ Concora Medium Test
CMT........ Council on Medical Television
CMT........ Craig Mountain Railway (AAR code)
CMTA....... Chinese Musical and Theatrical Association
CMTC....... Citizens' (or Civilian) Military Training Camp

CMTC....... Combined Military Transportation Committee
CMTCU...... Communications Message Traffic Control Unit (Air Force)
CMTI....... Celestial Moving Target Indicator
CMTM...... Capsule Mechanical Training Model
CMTM...... Communications and Telemetry
CMTT....... Joint Committee on Television Transmission
CMU........ Carnegie-Mellon University
CMU........ Ceylon Mercantile Union
CMU........ Church Missionary Union (British)
CMU........ Colliery Mazdoor Union (India)
CMUS....... Chief Musician (Navy rating)
CMU/WA .... Committee on Man's Underwater Activities
CMV........ Common Mode Voltage
CMV........ Controlled Multivibrator
CMV .... Cytomegalovirus
CMVM ...... Contact-Making Voltmeter
CMVR ...... Common Mode Voltage Range
CMW .... Circular Magnetic Wave
CMW .... Cold Molecular Weld
CMY .... Chemway Corporation (NYSE symbol) (Delisted)
CMZ .... Cincinnati Milacron, Inc. (NYSE symbol)
CMZ .... Compagnie Maritime du Zaire
CN .... Canadian National Railways (AAR code)
CN .... Canet Nordenfelt Gun
CN........ Careless and Negligent Driving (Traffic offense charge)
CN .... Case of Need
CN........ Central Airlines, Inc.
CN........ Cetane Number
CN........ Change Notice
CN........ Charter New York Corp. (NYSE symbol)
CN........ Chloracetophenone
CN .... Circular Note
CN........ Code Napoleon
CN........ Collective Negotiations
CN........ Commonwealth Nation
CN........ Compass North
CN........ Consignment Note
CN........ Coordination Number
CN........ Cover Note (Insurance)
CN........ Cuban Navy
CN........ Cumulonimbus (Meteorology)
CN........ Cupro Nickel
CN........ New York Central R. R. Company (Delisted; now Penn Central) (NYSE symbol)
C/N........ Consignment Note (Business and trade)
C/N........ Credit Note (Shipping)
CNA ...... Canadian Northwest Atlantic Area
CNA ...... Canadian Nuclear Association
CNA ...... Center for Naval Analysis
CNA ...... Centrale Nucleaire des Ardennes
CNA ...... Chief of Naval Air
CNA ...... Code Not Allocated
CNA ...... Continental National America (Insurance group)
CNA ...... Cosmic Noise Absorption
CNAA ..... Council for National Academic Awards (British)
CNAADTRA ... Chief of Naval Air Advanced Training (Formerly, CNAOPTRA)
CNAB..... Commander, Naval Air Bases
CNABATRA ... Chief of Naval Air Basic Training
CNAC ...... China National Aviation Corps
CNAD....... Conference of National Armaments Directors (Air Force)
CNAE ...... Comissao Nacional de Atividades Espaciais (Brazil)
CNAINTERMTRA.. Chief of Naval Air Intermediate Training (Later, CNABTRA)
CNAIT ...... Chief of Naval Air Intermediate Training
CNAOPTRA ... Chief of Naval Air Operational Training (Later, CNAADTRA)
CNAOT...... Chief of Naval Air Operational Training
CNAPRIMTRA.. Chief of Naval Air Primary Training (Later, CNARFSTRA)
CNAPT...... Chief of Naval Air Primary Training
CNARESTRA... Chief of Naval Air Reserve Training
CNARFSTRA... Chief of Naval Air Primary Training
CNAS...... Chief of Naval Air Services (British)
CNAS ..... Civil Navigation Aids System
CNAT...... Chief of Naval Air Training
CNAT...... Commission Nationale de l'Amenagement du Territoire
CNATE...... Chief of Naval Airships Training and Experimentation
CNATECHTRA .. Chief of Naval Air Technical Training
CNATEC (LTA) .. Commander, Naval Air Technical Training (Lighter Than Air)
CNATRA..... Chief of Naval Air Training
CNATT..... Chief of Naval Air Technical Training
CNAVANTRA .. Chief of Naval Air Advanced Training
CNB........ Canadian Breweries, Ltd. (NYSE symbol)
CNB........ Canadian Naval Board

CNB....... Commander, Naval Base
CNC ...... Carson-Newman College (Tennessee)
CNC ...... Cenco Instruments Corporation (NYSE symbol)
CNC....... Chief Naval Censor
CNC ...... Chief of Naval Communications (Formerly, DNC)
CNC ...... Czechoslovak National Council
CNCA ..... Council for National Cooperation in Aquatics
CNCP...... Center for New Corporate Priorities
CNCR...... Concurrent
CND ...... Campaign for Nuclear Disarmament
CND ...... Canadian Dredge & Dock Company, Ltd. (American Stock Exchange symbol)
CND ...... Chief of Naval Development
CND ...... Code Names Dictionary (A reference publication)
CND ...... Sisters of the Congregation of Notre Dame (Roman Catholic religious order)
CNDI ..... Combination Die
CNDO ..... Chief Navy Disbursing Officer
CNDO ..... Complete Neglect of Differential Overlap (Theory) (Method used for calculation of chemical structure)
CNDP...... Continuing Numerical Data Projects
CNDR...... Consiglio Nazionale delle Ricerche (National Research Council) (Italy)
CNE ...... Canadian National Exhibition (Held annually in Toronto)
CNEA...... Comision Nacional de Energia Atomica (National Commission for Atomic Energy) (Mexico)
CNEEMA..... Centre National d'Etudes et d'Experimentation du Machinisme Agricole
CNEL...... Community Noise Equivalent Level
CNEN ..... Comision Nacional de Energia Nuclear (National Commission for Nuclear Energy) (Mexico)
CNEN ..... Comitato Nazionale per l'Energia Nucleare (National Nuclear Energy Committee) (Italy)
CNEP...... Cable Network Engineering Program (Bell System)
CNES...... Centre National d'Etudes Spatiales (National Center for Space Studies) (France)
CNET...... Centre National d'Etudes des Telecommunications (France)
CNEUPEN .... Commission Nationale pour l'Etude de l'Utilisation Pacifique de l'Energie Nucleaire (Belgium)
CNEWA ..... Catholic Near East Welfare Association
CNEXO ..... Centre National pour l'Exploitation des Oceans (France)
CNF....... Commander, Naval Forces
CNF....... Conjunctive Normal Formula
CNF....... Consolidated Freightways, Inc. (NYSE symbol)
CNFS...... California National Fuchsia Society
CNG ...... Commander, Northern Group
CNG ...... Connecticut Natural Gas Corporation
CNG ...... Consolidated Natural Gas Company (NYSE symbol)
CNGA ..... California Natural Gas Association
CNGB ..... Chief, National Guard Bureau (Department of the Army)
CNGS ..... Christlich-Nationaler Gewerkschaftsbund der Schweiz (Swiss Federation of National-Christian Trade Unions)
CNH ...... Central Hudson Gas & Electric Corporation (NYSE symbol)
CNHI ..... Committee for National Health Insurance
CNHM ..... Chicago Natural History Museum
CNHS..... Center for Neo-Hellenic Studies
CNHS..... Cherokee National Historical Society
CNI ...... Centrale Nucleaire Interescaut (A nuclear power station) (Belgium)
CNI ...... Chief of Naval Intelligence
CNI ...... Committee for Nuclear Information (Later, Committee for Environmental Information)
CNI ...... Communication, Navigation, and Identification
CNIB ..... Canadian National Institute for the Blind
CNIE ..... Comision Nacional de Investigaciones Espaciales (Argentina)
CNIM ..... Confederation Nationale des Instituteurs Malagaches (National Confederation of Malagascan Teachers)
CNIPA ..... Committee of National Institutes of Patent Agents
CNIPTG ..... Communications, Networks and Information Processing Theory Group (MIT)
CNIT ...... Confederation Nationale Independante des Travailleurs (National Independent Confederation for Workers) (Belgium)
CNJ....... Central Railroad Company of New Jersey (ARR code)
CNJC...... Cable Network Joint Committee
CNK ...... Crompton & Knowles Corporation (NYSE symbol)
CNL ...... Cancel(lation)
CNL...... Carrier Noise Level
CNL...... Circuit Net Loss
CNL....... Columbia, Newberry & Laurens R. R. (AAR code)
CNLA ..... Council of National Library Associations
CNLCI ..... Comite National pour la Liberation de la Cote d'Ivoire (National Committee for the Liberation of the Ivory Coast)
CNLDP..... Committee for National Land Development Policy
CNM ...... Chief of Naval Material
CNMO ..... Canadian Naval Mission Overseas

CNO . . . . Chief of Naval Operations
CNO-AE . . . . . Council of National Organizations for Adult Education
CNOB . . . . . . Commander, Naval Operating Base
CNOBO . . . . . Chief of Naval Operations Budget Office
CNOCOM/MIS. . Chief of Naval Operations Command / Management Information System
CNOCY . . . . . Council of National Organizations for Children and Youth
CNOM . . . . . . Chief of Naval Operations Memorandum
CNOM/CMCM. . Chief of Naval Operations Memorandum and Commandant of the
    Marine Corps Memorandum (Joint)
CNOR . . . . . . Cincinnati Northern R. R. (AAR code)
CNO & TP . . . Cincinnati, New Orleans and Texas Pacific Railway Company
CNOUS . . . . . Centre National des Oeuvres Universitaires et Scolaires (France)
CNP. . . . . Chief of Naval Personnel (The Second Sea Lord) (British)
CNP. . . . . Consecutive Number Printer
CN/PNL . . . . . Contractors Panel (Aerospace)
CNPq . . . . Conselho Nacional de Pesquisas (Brazil)
C & NPRR . . . Chicago & Northern Pacific Railroad
CNPS . . . . Caucus for a New Political Science
CNR. . . . . Canadian National Railways
CNR. . . . . Carboxy-Nitroso Rubber
CNR. . . . . Carrier-to-Noise Ratio
CNR. . . . . Cellular Neoprene Rubber
CNR. . . . . Change(s) to Navy Regulations
CNR. . . . . Change Notice Request
CNR. . . . . Chief of Naval Research
CNR. . . . . College of New Rochelle (New York)
CNR. . . . . Composite Noise Rating
CNR. . . . . Conseil National de la Resistance (France)
CNR. . . . . Consiglio Nazionale delle Ricerche (National Research Council) (Italy)
CNR . . . . Container Corporation of America (NYSE symbol) (Delisted)
CNR. . . . . Contractual Nontechnical Report
CNRA. . . . . . . Conseil National de la Revolution Algerienne (National Council of the
    Algerian Revolution)
CNRG. . . . . . . Conseil National de la Revolution de la Guinee Dite Portugaise (National
    Revolutionary Council of So-called Portuguese Guinea)
CNRM . . . . . . Centre National de Recherches Metallurgiques (Belgium)
CNRN . . . . . . Comitato Nazionale per le Ricerche Nucleari (Italy) (Now, CNEN)
CNRS . . . . Centre National de la Recherche Scientifique (National Center of
    Scientific Research) (France)
CNRT . . . . . . Chief, Naval Reserve Training
CNS . . . . Camp Newspaper Service
CNS. . . . . Canada Southern Railway Company (NYSE symbol)
CNS. . . . . Canadian Naval Service
CNS. . . . . Canadian News Service
CNS . . . . Central Nervous System (Physiology)
CNS. . . . . Chloracetophenone Solution
CNS. . . . . Common Number System
CNS. . . . . Congress of Neurological Surgeons
CNS. . . . . Control Net System (Chiefly British)
CNS. . . . . Copley News Service
CNSG. . . . . . . Consolidated Nuclear Steam Generator
CNSL . . . . Counsel(ing) (or Counselor)
CNSM . . . . . . Chicago North Shore & Milwaukee R. R. (AAR code)
CNSM . . . . . . Confederation Nationale des Syndicats du Mali (National Confederation
    of Malian Unions)
CNSS . . . . Canadian National Steamships (AAR code)
CNSY. . . . . . . Charleston Naval Shipyard
CNSYD. . . . . . Charleston Naval Shipyard
CNT. . . . . Celestial Navigation Trainer
CNT. . . . . Confederacion Nacional de Trabajo (National Confederation of Labor)
    (In Exile) (Spain)
CNT. . . . . Confederation Nationale du Travail (National Confederation of Labor)
    (France)
CNT. . . . . Conselho Nacional do Trabalho (Brazil)
CNTC. . . . . . . Centrale National des Travailleurs Croyants de Senegal (National
    Believing Workers of Senegal)
CNTC . . . . . . Confederation Nationale des Travailleurs Croyants de Senegal (National
    Confederation of Believing Workers of Senegal)
CNTCCI . . . . . Centrale National des Travailleurs Croyants de Cote d'Ivoire (National
    Union of Believing Workers of the Ivory Coast)
CNTCLKWZ . . . Counterclockwise
CNTG . . . . . . Confederation National des Travailleurs de Guinee (National Confed-
    eration of Guinean Workers)
CNTP . . . . Cincinnati, New Orleans & Texas Pacific Railway (AAR code)
CNTP . . . . Committee for a National Trade Policy
CNTS . . . . Chief, Naval Transportation Service
CNTU. . . . . . . Confederation of National Trade Unions
CNUIP . . . . . . Commission des Nations Unies pour l'Inde et le Pakistan
CNUURC . . . . Commission des Nations Unies pour l'Unification et le Relevement
    de la Coree

CNV . . . . Christlijk Nationaal Vakverbond in Nederland (National Federation
    of Christian Workers) (Protestant) (Netherlands)
CNV . . . . City Investing Company (NYSE symbol)
CNV . . . . Contingent Negative Variation
CNVA . . . . . . Committee for Nonviolent Action
CNW . . . . Chicago & North Western Railway Company (AAR code)
C & NW . . . . . Chicago and North Western Railway Company
CNWA . . . . . . Charleston Naval Weapons Annex
CNWDI. . . . . . Critical Nuclear Weapons Design Information
CO . . . . Cardiac Output (Physiology)
CO . . . . Caribbean Organization (An international governmental body, of which
    the US is a member)
CO . . . . Carried Over (Bookkeeping)
CO . . . . Castor Oil
CO. . . . . Cathode Ray Oscillator
CO. . . . . Central Office
CO. . . . . Chain Operator
CO . . . . Change Order
CO. . . . . Chesapeake & Ohio--Chesapeake Dist. R. R. (AAR code)
CO . . . . Chesapeake & Ohio Railway Company (NYSE symbol)
CO . . . . Chief of Ordnance (Army)
CO. . . . . Cleanout
CO . . . . Clerical Officer (British)
CO . . . . Close-Open
Co . . . . Cobalt (Chemical element)
CO . . . . Colonial Office (British)
CO . . . . Colorado
CO . . . . Combined Operations
CO . . . . Command Operations (Army)
CO . . . . Command Orders
CO . . . . Commanding Officer
CO . . . . Commissioner for Oaths
CO . . . . Communications Officer (Navy)
CO. . . . . Company
CO . . . . Components Only
CO . . . . Congregation of the Oratory (Oratorians) (Roman Catholic men's
    religious order)
CO . . . . Conjugi Optimo (To My Excellent Husband)
CO . . . . Conscientious Objector
CO . . . . Continental Air Lines, Inc.
CO . . . . Contracting Officer (Also, KO)
CO . . . . Copyright Office (US)
CO. . . . . Corporate Office
CO . . . . County
CO . . . . Cross-Over (Genetics)
CO . . . . Crown Office (British)
CO . . . . Crystal Oscillator
CO . . . . Cut Out
C/O. . . . . Care Of
C/O. . . . . Case Of
C/O. . . . . Cash Order
C/O . . . . Certificate of Origin
C/O. . . . . Change Order
C/O. . . . . Checkout
C/O. . . . . Complains Of (Medicine)
C & O . . . . . . Chesapeake & Ohio Railway (Later, Chessie System)
C & O . . . . . . Controllability and Observability
CO⁶⁰ . . . . . . Radioactive Cobalt
COA . . . . California Olive Association
COA . . . . Carwash Operators Association
COA . . . . Change of Assignment
COA . . . . Change Order Account
COA . . . . Chief of Operations Analysis
COA. . . . . . . Coenzyme A
COA . . . . Coherent Optical Array
COA . . . . College of Aeronautics (British)
COA . . . . Committee on Accreditation (American Library Association)
COA . . . . Compass Operation Alarm
COA . . . . Comptroller of the Army
COA . . . . Cordova Airlines, Inc.
COA . . . . Cruiser Olympia Association
COA . . . . Current Operating Allowances
CO(A) . . . . . . Change Order (Aircraft)
COAC . . . . . . Commanding Officer, Atlantic Coast
COAC . . . . . . Council on Adoptable Children
COACT. . . . . . Combat Activity Report (Navy)
COAD . . . . . . Columbus Army Depot
COAHR . . . . . Committee on Appeal for Human Rights
COAIREVACRON . . Commanding Officer, Air Evacuation Squadron
COAL . . . . . . Consolidated Ordnance Allowance List (Navy)
COAM . . . . . . Company-Owned and Maintained

COAP . . . . . . Combat Optimization and Analysis Program (Air Force)
COAS . . . . . . Council of the Organization of American States (OAS)
COAS. . . . . . . Crew Optical Alignment Sight (Apollo) (NASA)
COASP . . . . . . Coordinated Aircraft/Stores Program (Navy)
COASTA . . . . . Conference of Officers of Affiliated States and Territorial Associations
COAT. . . . . . . Coherent Optical Array Techniques
COAX . . . . . . Coaxial
COB. . . . . Central Obrera Boliviana
COB. . . . . Ceramic Oceanographic Buoy
COB. . . . . Change Order Board
COB. . . . . Close of Business (With date)
COB. . . . . . . Committee of Combined Boards
COB. . . . . . . Congregation of Oblates of Bethany (Roman Catholic women's religious order)
COBATAME . . . Committee of Black Americans for Truth about the Middle-East
COBCCEE . . . . Comite des Organisations de la Boucherie-Charcuterie de la CEE (Committee of Butchery Organizations of the EEC)
COBECC . . . . . Central Ohio Biomedical Engineering Community Council
COBEO. . . . . . National Conference of Black Elected Officials
COBESTCO . . . Computer-Based Estimating Technique for Contractors
COBI . . . . Coded Biphase
COBOL . . . . . . Common Business-Oriented Language (Data processing)
COBQ . . . . . . Cum Omnibus Bonis Quiescat (May He or She Repose with All Good Souls)
COBRA . . . . . . Compatible on Board Ranging
COBRA . . . . . . Computerized Boolean Reliability Analysis (Boeing)
COBS . . . . Caesarean-Originated, Barrier-Sustained (Mice)
COBSI . . . . . . Committee on Biological Sciences Information (NAS/NRC)
COBT . . . . . . Chicago Open Board of Trade
COC . . . . Cathode Opening Contraction
COC . . . . Certificate of Competency (Small Business Administration)
COC . . . . Change of Contract
COC . . . . Change Order Conference
COC . . . . Chief of Chaplains (Navy)
COC . . . . Chlorate Oxygen Candle
COC . . . . Clergy Orphan Corporation (British)
COC . . . . Climb on Course (Aviation)
COC . . . . Code of Conduct (Military)
COC . . . . Columbus & Southern Ohio Electric Company (NYSE symbol)
COC . . . . Combat Operations Center (Air Force)
COC . . . . Commissioned Officer Corps (National Oceanic and Atmospheric Administration)
COC . . . . Committee of Concern
COC . . . . Contempt of Court
COC . . . . Cultuur-en Ontspanningscentrum (Center for Culture and Recreation, an association of homosexuals) (Holland)
COC . . . . Customer-Originated Change
COCB. . . . . . . Crossed Olivocochlear Bundles (Hearing)
COCCEE . . . . . Comite des Organisations Commerciales des Pays de la CEE (Committee of Commercial Organizations in the EEC Countries)
COCEEE . . . . . Committee on Captured Enemy Electronics Equipment
COCITEF . . . . . Comissao de Coordenacao e Implementacao de Tecnicas Financeiras (Brazil)
COCO . . . . . . Contractor Owned, Contractor Operated (Military)
CO/CO . . . . . Contractor Owned / Contractor Operated (Facilities) (Military)
COCOA . . . . . Critical Terrain; Obstacles; Cover and Concealment; Observation and Fields of Fire; Avenues of Approach (Military)
COCOAS . . . . CONARC (Continental Army Command) Class One Automated System (Army)
COCOCAM . . . Comite de Coordination Camerounaise (Committee for Cameroonese Coordination)
COCODE . . . . Compressed Coherency Detection (RADAR technique)
COCOM . . . . . Coordinating Committee
COCOSEERS . . Coordinating Committee for Slavic and East European Library Resources
COCP. . . . . . . Crossed Olivocochlear Potential (Hearing)
COCU . . . . . . Consultation on Church Union
COCWA . . . . . Coin-Op Car Wash Association
COD . . . . Carrier-On-Deck (Navy carrier-based aircraft)
COD . . . . Carrier Onboard Delivery (Naval aviation)
COD . . . . Cash on Delivery
COD . . . . Certificates of Deposit (Banking)
COD . . . . Chemical Oxygen Demand
COD . . . . Coherent Optical Device
COD . . . . Collect on Delivery
COD. . . . . Condensed or Dried
COD. . . . . Crack Opening Displacement
CODA . . . . . . Committee on Drugs and Alcohol
CODA . . . . . . Coulee Dam National Recreation Area
CODAC . . . . . Coordination of Operating Data by Automatic Computer
CODAG . . . . . Combined Diesel and Gas (Turbine)
CODAM . . . . . Contractor-Oriented Data Abstract Modules (Air Force)
CODAN . . . . . Carrier-Operated Device, Antinoise (Radio)

CODAN . . . . . Coded Weather Analysis (Navy)
CODAP. . . . . . Control Data Assembly Program
CODAR. . . . . . Coherent Display Analyzing and Recording
CODAR. . . . . . Correlation Display Analyzing and Recording
CODASYL. . . . Conference on Data Systems Languages (Data processing)
CODATA . . . . Committee on Data for Science and Technology (National Bureau of Standards)
CODCAVE. . . . Committee on Decentralization of Controls after V-E Day (War Production Board)
CODE . . . . . . Committee on Donor Enlistment
CODE. . . . . . . Controller Decision Evaluation
CODED. . . . . . Computer Design of Electronic Devices
CODEIN . . . . . Computerized Drawing Electrical Information
CODEMAC . . . Comite des Demenageurs du Marche Commun
CODEP . . . . . Council for a Department of Peace
CODES . . . . . . Commutating Detection System
CODESA . . . . Centro Operacional del Desarrollo (Operational Center for Development) (Colombia)
CODEXAL . . . . Conseil Europeen du "Codex Alimentarius"
CODIA . . . . . Comite pour le Developpement des Activities Intellectuelles en Afrique (Committee for the Development of Intellectual Activities in Africa)
CODIC . . . . . Computer-Directed Communications
CODIP . . . . . Hague Conference on Private International Law
CODIPHASE . . Coherent Digital Phased Array System (ARPA)
CODIS . . . . . . Completed Discharge
CODIT . . . . . . Computer Direct to Telegraph
CODORAC . . . Coded Doppler RADAR Command
CODOT . . . . . Classification of Occupations and Directory of Occupational Titles (Formerly, MOLOC) (British)
CODSIA . . . . . Council of Defense and Space Industry Associations
COE. . . . . Cab Over Engine (Type of truck)
COE. . . . . Central Office Equipment
COE . . . . Certificate of Eligibility (Navy)
COE. . . . . Complete Operating Equipment
COE. . . . . Cone Mills Corporation (NYSE symbol)
COE . . . . Conseil Oecumenique des Eglises (World Council of Churches)
COE. . . . . Corps of Engineers
CO(E) . . . . . . Change Order (Electronic)
COEBG. . . . . . Commission on Organization of the Executive Branch of the Government
COED. . . . . . . Char Oil Energy Development (Project of Office of Coal Research)
COED. . . . . . . Computer-Operated (or -Oriented) Electronic Display
COED. . . . . . . Concentration on Engineering Design
COED. . . . . . . Concise Oxford English Dictionary
COEES . . . . . . Central Office Equipment Engineering System (Bell System)
COEFF . . . . . . Coefficient
COEL . . . . Chain Overseas Extremely Low (Aviation)
COEPR . . . . . . Council on Education in Professional Responsibility (Law)
COEPS . . . . . . Cortically Originating Extra-Pyramidal System (Physiology)
COESA . . . . . . Committee on Extension to the Standard Atmosphere
COEV. . . . . . . Canadian Ocean Escort Vessel
COF. . . . . Canadian Order of Foresters
COF. . . . . Catholic Order of Foresters
COF. . . . . Computer Operations Facility
COF. . . . . Cut-Off Frequency
COFAFCH . . . . Chief of Air Force Chaplains
COFALEC . . . . Comite des Fabricants de Levure de Panification de la CEE (Committee of Bread Yeast Manufacturers of the EEC)
COFCH . . . . . Chief of Chaplains
COFENGRS . . Chief of Engineers
COFF . . . . Chief of Finance
COFF . . . . Cut Off (Military)
COFI . . . . Committee on Fisheries (Food and Agriculture Organization)
COFIMPAC . . . Compagnie Francaise Industrielle et Miniere du Pacifique (French commercial firm)
COFINATOME . . Compagnie de Financement de l'Industrie Atomique (France)
COFO . . . . . . Council of Federated Organizations (in field of civil rights in Mississippi)
COFORD. . . . . Chief of Ordnance
COFRC . . . . . . Chevron Oil Field Research Company
COFRON. . . . . Coastal Frontier (Coast Guard)
COFRS . . . . . . Computerized Freight Remittance System (Pronounced "coffers")
COFS . . . . Chief of Staff
COFSA . . . . . . Chief of Staff, United States Army
COFT . . . . Chief of Transportation
COFT . . . . Commander, Fleet Train
COFT . . . . Conduct of Fire Trainer
COG . . . . Cognizant
COG . . . . Commander of the Guard (Military)
COG . . . . Compact Orbital Gears, Ltd.
COG . . . . Computer Operations Group
COG . . . . Control Orbitron Gauge
COG . . . . Convenience of the Government

COG . . . . Council of Governments (Voluntary organizations of municipalities and counties)
COGARD . . . . Coast Guard
COGAS . . . . . Coal (into) Gas (Process)
COGB . . . . . . Certified Official Government Business
COGO . . . . . . Coordinate Geometry (Computer language)
COGS . . . . . . Continuous Orbital Guidance System
COGSA . . . . . Carriage of Goods by Sea Act
COH . . . . Commodore Hotel, Inc. (NYSE symbol) (Delisted)
COHO . . . . . . Coherent Oscillator (RADAR)
COHO . . . . . . Council of Health Organizations
COHQ . . . . . . Combined Operations Headquarters
COHVENT. . . . Coherent Event (Trademark)
COI . . . . Central Office of Information (British)
COI . . . . Commission Oceanographique Intergouvernementale (Intergovernmental Oceanographic Commission)
COI . . . . Communications Operations Instructions (Air Force)
COI . . . . Conjugi (To My Husband or Wife)
COI . . . . Continental Investment Corp. (NYSE symbol)
COI . . . . Course of Instruction (Navy)
Co-I . . . . Co-Investigator
COIC . . . . . . Combined Operational Intelligence Center (Navy)
COID . . . . . . Council of Industrial Design (England)
COIN . . . . . . California Olive Industry News
COIN . . . . . . Committee on Information Needs
COIN . . . . . . Complete Operating Information (Data processing)
COIN . . . . . . Continuation Incentive Pay (Proposed) (Army)
COIN . . . . . . Counter-Insurgency (Guerrilla warfare term)
COINS . . . . . Committee on Improvement of National Statistics (Inter-American)
COINS . . . . . Computer and Information Sciences
COINS . . . . . Computerized Information System
COINS . . . . . Control in Information Systems
COINS . . . . . Cooperative Intelligence Network System (Proposed) (Navy)
COIT . . . . . . Central Office of the Industrial Tribunal (Department of Employment) (British)
COIU . . . . . . Congress of Independent Unions
COK. . . . . . . Cook Paint & Varnish Company (American Stock Exchange symbol)
COL. . . . . . . Chain Overseas Low (Aviation)
COL. . . . . . . Coherent Optical LASER
COL. . . . . . . Colonel (Military)
COL. . . . . . . Column
COL . . . . . . Computer-Oriented Language (Data processing)
COL . . . . . . Cost of Living
COL . . . . . . Crisis on Location (Psychological test)
CO-L . . . . . . Colatitude (Navigation)
COLA. . . . . . Committee on Library Automation (American Library Association)
COLA. . . . . . Constant Output Level Adapter
COLA. . . . . . Cost of Living Allowance
COLANFORASCU . . Commanding Officer, Landing Force Air Support Control Unit
COLASL . . . . . Compiler, Los Alamos Scientific Laboratories
COLC. . . . . . Cost of Living Council (US)
COLD. . . . . . Chronic Obstructive Lung Disease (Medicine)
COLD. . . . . . Coherent Light Detector
COLE . . . . . . College of Our Lady of the Elms (Massachusetts)
COLED . . . . . Combat Loss and Expenditure Data
COLED-V . . . . Combat Loss and Expenditure Data - Vietnam
COLEQUAP . . . Consumer Level Quality Audit Program
COLEX . . . . . CIRC (Central Information Reference and Control) On-Line Experiment
COLIDAR . . . . Coherent Light Detecting and Ranging (RADAR) (Hughes Aircraft)
COLIME . . . . . Comite de Liaison des Industries Metalliques Europeennes
COLINGO . . . Compile On-Line and Go (Data processing)
COLL . . . . . . Collect
COLM . . . . . . Colorado National Monument
COLM . . . . . . Column
COLMGP. . . . . Column Gap (Army)
COLO . . . . . . Colonial National Historic Park
COLO . . . . . . Colorado
COLOD . . . . . Completed Loading (Navy)
COLOG . . . . . Cologarithm
COLPA . . . . . National Jewish Commission on Law and Public Affairs
COLQUAP. . . . Consumer Level Quality Audit Program
COLT . . . . . . Communication Line Terminator
COLT . . . . . . Computerized On-Line Testing
COLT . . . . . . Council on Library Technology
COLTS . . . . . Contrast Optical LASER Tracking Subsystem (Missile guidance)
COLYAHAR . . . Columbia, Yale, Harvard (Used to refer to a project involving the medical libraries of these universities)
COM . . . . Checkout Operations Manual
COM . . . . Command
COM . . . . Commander (Navy)
COM . . . . Commissioned Officers Mess (Navy)

COM . . . . Computer Output Microfilm(ing)
COM . . . . Copper Oxide Modulator
COM . . . . County Office Manager
C/OM . . . . . . Clothing and Organic Materials Laboratory
C & OM. . . . . Clothing and Organic Materials (Army)
COMAC . . . . . Commander, Military Airlift Command
COMAC . . . . . Continuous Multiple Access Collator (Data processing)
COMAF . . . . . Comite des Constructeurs de Materiel Frigorifique de la CEE (Committee of Manufacturers of Refrigeration Equipment of the EEC)
COMAIR . . . . . Commander Air Forces (Navy)
COMAIR . . . . . Commander Aircraft (Navy)
COMAIR . . . . Commercial Air Service (Pty.) Ltd.
COMAIRBALTAP . . Commander, Allied Air Forces Baltic Approaches
COMAIRCANLANT . . Air Commander Canadian Atlantic Subarea
COMAIRCENT . . Commander, Allied Air Forces Central Europe
COMAIRCENTLANT . . Air Commander Central Atlantic Subarea
COMAIRLANT . . Commander Air Force, Atlantic Fleet
COMAIRNORECHAN. . Air-Commander, Nore Subarea Channel
COMAIRNORLANT . . Air-Commander Northern Atlantic Subarea
COMAIRNORTH . . Commander, Allied Air Forces Northern Europe
COMAIRPAC . . Commander Air Force, Pacific Fleet
COMAIRPLYMCHAN . . Air-Commander, Plymouth Subarea Channel
COMAIRSHIPGR . . Commander, Airship Group
COMAIRSOLS . Commander Air Forces, Solomons
COMAIRSOPAC . . Commander Aircraft, South Pacific Force
COMAIRSOUTH . . Commander, Allied Air Forces Southern Europe
COMAIRTRANS . . Commander Air Transport
COMAIRTRANSRON . . Commander Air Transport Squadron
COMALAIRNOREUR. . Commander, Allied Air Forces, Northern Europe
COMALAMGRU . . Commander Alameda Group
COMALNAVNOREUR . . Commander, Allied Naval Forces, Northern Europe
COMALSEC . . . Commander Alaskan Sector
COMANBAT. . . Combat Maneuver Battalion(s) (Army)
COMANTDEFCOM . . Commander, Antilles Defense Command
COMAP . . . . . Committee for the Alliance for Progress (Commerce Department)
COMAR . . . . . Computer, Aerial Reconnaissance
COMARCARAREA . . Commander, Marshalls-Carolines Area
COMAREGRU . . Commander, Mare Island Group
COMART. . . . . Commander, Marine Air Reserve Training
COMASE . . . . . Companhia Agricola de Sergipe (State of Sergipe, Brazil)
COMAT . . . . . Commodore Air Train (Navy)
COMATS . . . . Commander, Military Air Transport Service
COMB . . . . . . Combination (or Combine)
COMB . . . . . . Combustion
COMB . . . . . . Console Oriented Model Building (Data processing)
COMBALTAP . . Allied Command Baltic Approaches (NATO)
COMBASFRANCE. . Commander, (US) Ports and Bases, France
COMBAT. . . . . Cost-Oriented Models Built to Analyze Tradeoffs
COMBATDIV . . Commander, Battleship Division
COMBATLANT. . Commander, Battleships, Atlantic Fleet
COMBATPAC . . Commander, Battleships, Pacific Fleet
COMBENECHAN. . Commander, BENELUX Subarea Channel
COMBISLANT. . Commander, Bay of Biscay Atlantic Subarea (NATO)
COMBOMRON. . Commander, Bombing Squadron
COMBQUARFOR . . Combined Quarantine Force (US/Venezuela/Dominican Republic/ Argentina)
COMBRAX . . . . Commodore, Royal Canadian Navy Barracks at (place)
COMBREMGRU. . Commander, Bremerton Group
COMBRESTCHAN . . Commander, Brest Subarea Channel
COMBSNGRU. . Commander, Boston Group
COMCABCO . . Commercial Cable Company
COMCAM . . . . Compressible Cell and Maker
COMCANLANT . . Commander, Canadian Atlantic Subarea (NATO)
COMCARSTRIKFOR . . Commander, Carrier Striking Force
COMCARSTRIKGRUONE . . Commander, Carrier Striking Group One
COMCARSTRIKGRUTWO . . Commander, Carrier Striking Group Two
COMCAS. . . . . Computer-Oriented Modal Control and Appraisal System
COMCASU . . . Commander, Carrier Aircraft Service Unit
COMCBLANT. . Commander, Naval Construction Battalions, Atlantic Fleet
COMCBPAC. . . Commander, Naval Construction Battalions, Pacific Fleet
COMCENPAC . Commander, Central Pacific
COMCENTAG. . Commander, Central Army Group, Central Europe
COMCENTLANT. . Commander, Central Atlantic Subarea (NATO)
COMCHASNGRU . . Commander, Charleston Group
COMCHERCHAN . . Commander, Cherbourg Subarea Channel
COMCM . . . . Communication Countermeasures
COMCOLUMGRU . Commander, Columbia River Group
COMCOMRON . . Commander, Composite Squadron
COMCON. . . . Combat Control (Army)
COMCONSUP . . Combat, Control, Support (Army)

COMCRUDESFLOT. . Commander, Cruiser, Destroyer, Flotilla (Initialism always followed by a number) (Navy)
COMCRUDESLANT . . Commander, Cruiser-Destroyer Force Atlantic (Navy)
COMCRUDESPAC . . Commander, Cruiser-Destroyer Forces, Pacific
COMCRUDIV . . Commander, Cruiser Division
COMCRULANT . . Commander, Cruiser Forces, Atlantic Fleet
COMCRUPAC . . Commander, Cruisers, Pacific Fleet
COMCRUSCORON . . Commander, Cruiser Scouting Squadron
COMD . . . . . . Command
COMDAC . . . . Comite d'Action en France
COMDEC . . . . Command Decision & Movement Control Charts
COMDES . . . . Commander, Destroyers
COMDESDIV . . Commander, Destroyer Division
COMDESLANT . . Commander, Destroyers, Atlantic Fleet
COMDESPAC . . Commander, Destroyers, Pacific Fleet
COMDESRON . . Commander, Destroyer Squadron
COMDG . . . . . Commanding
COMDGEN . . . Commanding General
COMDG OF . . . Commanding Officer
COMDIEGOGRU . . Commander, San Diego Group
COMDO . . . . . Commando
COMDOC . . . . Combat Documentation
COMDR . . . . . Commander
COMDT . . . . . Commandant
COMDTMARCORPS . . Commandant, US Marine Corps
COMDTNOB . . Commandant, Naval Operating Base
COMDTNY. . . . Commandant, Navy Yard
COMDTUSCG . . Commandant, United States Coast Guard
COMDTUSMC . . Commandant, United States Marine Corps
COM(D) WA . . Commodore, (Destroyers) Western Approaches (British)
COMECON . . . Council for Mutual Economic Assistance (Poland, Russia, East Germany, Czechoslovakia, Romania, Bulgaria, Hungary) (Also known as CMEA)
COMEDCENT . . Commander, Central Mediterranean
COMEDEAST . . Commander, Eastern Mediterranean
COMEDNOREAST . . Commander, Northeast Mediterranean Area
COMEDOC . . . Commander, Western Mediterranean
COMEDSOUEAST . . Commander, Southeast Mediterranean
COMEINDORS . . Composite Mechanized Information and Document Retrieval System
COMET. . . . . . Coherent Electromagnetic Energy Transmission
COMET. . . . . . Computer-Operated Management Evaluation Technique (AEC-Army)
COMET. . . . . . Continental (United States) Meteorological Teletype System (Navy)
COMET. . . . . . Cost Measurement Technique
COMETEC-GAZ . . Comite d'Etudes Economiques de l'Industrie du Gaz (Economic Research Committee of the Gas Industry)
COMEX . . . . . Compagnie Maritime d' Expertise
COMEXDIV . . . Commander, Experimental Division (Navy)
COMFAIR . . . . Commander, Fleet Air
COMFAIRWESTPAC . . Commander, Fleet Air, Western Pacific
COMFAIRWING . . Commander, Fleet Air Wing
COMFAIRWINGNORLANT . . Commander, Fleet Air Wing Northern Atlantic
COMFIGHTRON . . Commander, Fighting Squadron
COMFIVEATAF . . Commander, Fifth Allied Tactical Air Force
COMFLAGRU . . Commander, Florida Group
COMFLDCOMDASA . . Commander, Field Command, Defense Atomic Support Agency
COMFLOGWING . Commander, Fleet Logistic Air Wing
COMFLTBASTILLES . . Commander, (US) Atlantic Fleet Bases, Antilles
COMFOURATAF . . Commander, Fourth Allied Tactical Air Force, Central Europe
COMGEN . . . . Commanding General
COMGENMED . . Commanding General, (US) Army Forces, Mediterranean Theater of Operations
COMGENPOA . . Commanding General, (US) Army Forces, Pacific Ocean Areas
COMGENTEN . . Commanding General, Tenth Army
COMGIB . . . . . Commander, Gibraltar (Navy)
COMGIBMED . . Commander, Gibraltar-Mediterranean Command
COMGREPAT . . Commander, Greenland Patrol
COMHAWSEAFRON . . Commander, Hawaiian Sea Frontier (Navy)
COMHEDRON . . Commander, Headquarters Squadron
COMIBOL . . . . Corporacion Minera de Bolivia
COMIC . . . . . Colorant Mixture Computer (Du Pont trademark)
COMICEDEFOR . Commander, Iceland Defense Force
COMILOG. . . . Compagnie Miniere de l'Ogooue (Ogooue Mining Company) (Gabon)
COMIN . . . . . Commander, Minecraft (Navy)
COMINCH . . . Commander-in-Chief (US fleet)
COMINDIV . . . Commander, Minecraft Division (Navy)
COMINFORM . Communist Information
COMINGRP. . . Commander, Mine Group
COMINGRPOK . . Commander, Mine Group Okinawa
COMINLANT. . Commander, Mine Force, Atlantic Fleet
COMINPAC. . . Commander, Minecraft, Pacific Fleet
COMINRON . . Commander, Mine Squadron

COMINST . . . . Communications Instructions (Navy)
COMINT. . . . . Communications Intelligence (Air Force)
COMINTERN . . Communist International
COMIT . . . . . . Computing System, Massachusetts Institute of Technology
COMJAM . . . . Communications Jamming (Military)
COMJEF . . . . . Commander, Joint Expeditionary Force (Military)
COMKD . . . . . Completely Knocked Down (Freight)
COML . . . . . Columbia & Millstadt R. R. (AAR code)
COML . . . . . . Commercial
COMLANDCENT . . Commander, Allied Land Forces Central Europe
COMLANDJUT. . Commander, Allied Land Forces Schleswig-Holstein and Jutland
COMLANDMARK. . Commander, Allied Land Forces Denmark
COMLANDNORWAY . . Commander, Allied Land Forces Norway
COMLANDSCHLESWIG . . Commander, Allied Land Forces Schleswig-Holstein
COMLANDSOUTH . . Commander, Allied Land Forces Southern Europe
COMLANDSOUTHEAST . . Commander, Allied Land Forces Southeastern Europe
COMLANDZEALAND . . Commander, Allied Land Forces Zealand
COMLBEACHGRU . . Commander, Long Beach Group
COMLO . . . . . Combined Operations Material Liaison Officer
COMLO . . . . . Compass Locator
COMLOGNET . . Combat Logistics Network (DOD)
COMM . . . . . . Communication(s)
COMMAIRCENTLANT . . Commander, Maritime Air Central Subarea (NATO)
COMMAIRCHAN . . Commander, Allied Maritime Air Force Channel (NATO)
COMMAIREASTLANT . . Commander, Maritime Air Eastern Atlantic Area (NATO)
COMMAIRNORECHAN . . Commander, Maritime Air Nore Subarea Channel
COMMAIRNORLANT . . Commander, Maritime Air Northern Subarea (NATO)
COMMAIRPLYMCHAN . . Commander, Maritime Air Plymouth Subarea Channel
COMMAND. . . . Command Model for Analysis and Design
COMMARIANAS . . Commander, Marianas
COMMCEN . . . Communications Center
COMMDET . . . Commissioning Detail
COMMEL . . . . Communications Electronics
COMMFACMEDME . . Communication Facilities Mediterranean and Middle East
COMMFU . . . . Complete Utter Monumental Military Foul Up (Bowdlerized version)
COMMO. . . . . Communications Officer
COMMR . . . . . Commissioner
COMMSECACT . Communication Security Activity
COMMSUPACT . Communication Supplementary Activity
COMMSUPDET . Communication Supplementary Detachment
COMNAB . . . . Commander, Naval Air Bases
COMNAS (EA) . . Commodore, Naval Air Stations, East Africa (British)
COMNAV . . . . Navy Command (Part of North American Air Defense Command)
COMNAVAIR . . Commander, Naval Air Force
COMNAVAIRLANT . . Commander, Naval Air Forces, Atlantic Fleet
COMNAVAIRPAC . . Commander, Naval Air Forces, Pacific Fleet
COMNAVBALTAP . . Commander, Allied Naval Forces Baltic Approaches
COMNAVCENT . . Commander, Allied Naval Forces Central Europe
COMNAVEASTLANTMED . . Commander, (US) Naval Forces, Eastern Atlantic and Mediterranean
COMNAVEU . . Commander, (US) Naval Forces in Europe
COMNAVFE . . Commander, (US) Naval Forces, Far East
COMNAVFORGER . . Commander, Naval Forces, Germany
COMNAVFORJAPAN . . Commander, Naval Forces, Japan
COMNAVGER . . Commander, (US) Naval Forces, Germany
COMNAVICE . . Commander, Naval Forces, Iceland
COMNAVJAP . . Commander, Naval Activities, Japan
COMNAVMARIANA . . Commander, Naval Forces Mariana
COMNAVNAW . . Commander, (US) Naval Forces, Northwest African Waters
COMNAVNON . . Commander, Allied Naval Forces, North Norway
COMNAVNORTH . . Commander, Allied Naval Forces, Northern Europe
COMNAVSCAP . . Commander, Allied Naval Forces, Scandinavian Approaches
COMNAVSUPPACT . . Commander, Naval Support Activity
COMNAVZOR . . Commander, (US) Naval Forces, Azores
COMNEED . . . Communications Need
COMNET . . . . Communications Network (Military)
COMNEWLONGRU . . Commander, New London Group
COMNORASDEFLANT . . Commander, North American Anti-Submarine Defense Force, Atlantic (NATO)
COMNORECHAN . . Commander, Nore Subarea Channel
COMNORLANT . . Commander, Northern Atlantic Subarea (NATO)
COMNORPAC . . Commander, North Pacific Force
COMNORTHAG . . Commander, Northern Army Group, Central Europe
COMNORVAGRU . . Commander, Norfolk Group
COMNYKGRU . . Commander, New York Group
COMO . . . . . . Coherent Master Oscillator
COMO . . . . . . Communications Officer
COMO . . . . . . Comprehensive Model
COMOCEANLANT . . Commander, Ocean Atlantic Subarea (NATO)
COMOI . . . . . Committee on Manpower Opportunities in Israel
COMOPDEVFOR . . Commander, Operational Development Force (Navy)

COMOPTEVFOR .. Commander, Operational Test and Evaluation Force (Navy)
COMOROCLANT .. Commander, Maritime Forces, Morocco
COMORSEAFRON .. Commander, Moroccan Sea Frontier Forces
COMORTEXGRU .. Commander, Orange, Texas, Group; Inactive Fleet, Atlantic Fleet
COMP........ Complement
COMP........ Component
COMP........ Composite
COMP........ Computation
COMP........ Computer
COMPAC .... Computer Program for Automatic Control
COMPACT.... Combined Passive Active Detection (RADAR)
COMPACT.... Committee to Promote Action (Poverty program)
COMPACT.... Compatible Algebraic Compiler and Translator
COMPACT.... Computer Programmed Automatic Checkout & Test System
COMPACT.... Computerization of World Facts
COMPAD .... Combined Office Material Procurement and Distribution
COMPARE .... Console for Optical Measurement and Precise Analysis of Radiation
     from Electronics
COMPAS .... Combined Metropolitan Phoenix Arts (Phoenix, Arizona)
COMPAS..... Committee on Physics & Society (of American Institute of Physics)
COMPASEAFRON .. Commander, Panama Sea Frontier
COMPASS .... Compiler-Assembler
COMPASS .... Comprehensive Assembly System (Data processing)
COMPASU.... Commander, Patrol Aircraft Service Unit
COMPATENFC.. Compassionate Reassignment Not Favorably Considered (Army)
COMPATPLANEREPRONSPAC .. Command Patrol Plane Replacement Squadrons Pacific
COMPATRON .. Commander, Patrol Squadron
COMPDES .... Compensator Design (Data processing)
COMPENDEX. Computerized Engineering Index (of Engineering Index, Inc.)
COMPGEN ... Comptroller General (Navy)
COMPGENDEC .. Comptroller General Decisions (Navy)
COMPHIB .... Commander, Amphibious Force
COMPHIBEU .. Commander, Amphibious Force, Europe
COMPHIBFOR .. Commander, Amphibious Force (Navy)
COMPHIBLANT .. Commander, Amphibious Force, Atlantic Fleet
COMPHIBNAW.. Commander, (US) Amphibious Force, Northwest African Waters
COMPHIBPAC .. Commander, Amphibious Force, Pacific Fleet
COMPHIBRON .. Commander, Amphibious Squadron
COMPHILAGRU .. Commander, Philadelphia Group
ComplEE ..... Companion of the Institution of Electrical Engineers
COMPL...... Complete
COMPLAN ... Communications Plan
COMPLYMCHAN .. Commander, Plymouth Subarea Channel
COMPMR ..... Commander, Pacific Missile Range
COMPO ..... Council of Motion Picture Organizations
COMPOOL ... Common Pool
COMPOOL ... Communications Pool
COMPORON .. Composite Squadron
COMPS...... Consolidation of Military Pay Services (Strategic Air Command proposal)
COMPT...... Comptroller
COMR ...... Court of Military Review
COMRAC .... Combat Radius Capability (Military)
COMRAT..... Commuted Ration (Military)
COMREC..... Care-Oriented Medical Record (University of Alabama)
COMROUTE... Commander-in-Chief, (US Fleet), Convoy and Routing Section
COMSANFRANGRU .. Commander, San Francisco Group
COMSAT .... Communications Satellite Corporation (Assignee of operational and de-
     velopmental responsibilities for Telstar and other international com-
     munications space devices)
COMSCORON .. Commander, Scouting Squadron
COMSEAFRON .. Commander, Sea Frontier (Navy)
COMSEC..... Communications Security (Military)
COMSERFORSOPACSUBCOM .. Commander, Service Force, South Pacific Subordinate
     Command
COMSERV.... Commander, Service Force
COMSERVLANT .. Commander, Service Force, Atlantic Fleet
COMSERVPAC .. Commander, Service Force, Pacific Fleet
COMSERVRON .. Commander, Service Squadron
COMSERVSOWESPAC .. Commander, Service Force, Southwest Pacific
COMSIXATAF.. Commander, Sixth Allied Tactical Air Force
COMSN ..... Commission
COMSOAL ... Computer Method of Sequencing Operations for Assembly Lines
COMSOC .... Communications Spacecraft Operation Center
COMSOEASTPAC .. Commander, Southeast Pacific Force
COMSOLANT.. Commander, South Atlantic Force
COMSOPAC .. Commander, South Pacific
COMSOTFE ... Commander, Support Operations Task Force Europe
COMSOWESPAC .. Commander, Southwest Pacific Force
COMSQN .... Communications Squadron (Marine Corps)
COMSTAC.... Commission on Standards and Accreditation of Services for the Blind
COM-STAT ... Computer Stock Timing and Analysis Technique

COM-STEP ... Computerized Spot Television Evaluation and Processing (Advertising)
COMSTOCKGRU .. Commander, Stockton Group
COMSTRIKEFLTLANT.. Commander, Striking Fleet, Atlantic (NATO)
COMSTRIKFLTLANT.. Commander, Striking Fleet Atlantic
COMSTRIKFORSOUTH .. Commander, Naval Striking and Support Forces, Southern Europe
COMSTS ..... Commander, Military Sea Transportation Service (Navy)
COMSTSELMAREA.. Commander, Military Sea Transportation Service, Eastern Atlantic
     and Mediterranean Area
COMSTSGULFSUBAREA .. Commander, Military Sea Transportation Service, Gulf Subarea
COMSTSLANTAREA.. Commander, Military Sea Transportation Service, Atlantic Area
COMSTSMIDPACSUBAREA .. Commander, Military Sea Transportation Service,
     Mid-Pacific Subarea
COMSTS/MIS.. Commander, Military Sea Transportation Service / Management
     Information System (Navy)
COMSTSNORPACSUBAREA .. Commander, Military Sea Transportation Service, Northern
     Pacific Subarea
COMSTSPACAREA .. Commander, Military Sea Transportation Service, Pacific Area
COMSTSWESTPACAREA .. Commander, Military Sea Transportation Service, West Pacific
     Area
COMSUBACLANT .. Commander, Submarine Allied Command, Atlantic
COMSUBASE .. Commander, Submarine Base
COMSUBDIV .. Commander, Submarine Division
COMSUBEASTLANT.. Commander, Submarine Force, Eastern Atlantic (NATO)
COMSUBLANT .. Commander, Submarine Force, Atlantic (Navy)
COMSUBMED.. Commander, Submarines, Mediterranean
COMSUBMEDNOREAST .. Commander, Submarines, Northeast Mediterranean
COMSUBPAC .. Commander, Submarine Force, Pacific (Navy)
COMSUBRON .. Commander, Submarine Squadron
COMSUBS .... Commander, Submarines
COMSUBSLANT .. Commander, Submarines, Atlantic Fleet
COMSUBSPAC .. Commander, Submarine Force, Pacific Fleet
COMSUBSSOWESPAC .. Commander, Submarines, Southwest Pacific Force
COMSUBTRAFAC .. Commander, Submarine Training Facilities
COMSUBWESTLANT .. Commander, Submarine Force, Western Atlantic Area
COMSUP..... Combat Support Units (Army)
COMSY...... Commissary
COMSYMP ... Communist Sympathizer
COMSYSTR ... Commissary Store (Army)
COMT ...... Catecholamine-O-Methyl-Transferase
COMT ...... Commit
COMTAC.... Commander, Tactical Air Command
COMTACGRU . Commander, Tacoma Group
COMTAFNORNOR .. Commander, Allied Tactical Air Force North Norway
COMTAFSONOR .. Commander, Allied Tactical Air Force, South Norway
COMTASKFORNON .. Commander, Allied Task Forces North Norway
COMTBFLOT .. Commander, Motor Torpedo Boat Flotilla
COMTBRON .. Commander, Motor Torpedo Boat Squadron
COMTBRONTRACENT .. Commander, Motor Torpedo Boat Squadron Training Center
COMTEC .... Computer Micrographic Technology Users Group
COMTECHREP. Complementary Technical Report (Military)
COMTEXGRU.. Commander, Texas Group
COMTONGRU .. Commander, Tongue Point Group, Inactive Fleet, Pacific Fleet
COMTORPRON .. Commander, Torpedo Squadron
COMTRAINCARRONPAC .. Commander, Carrier Training Squadron, Pacific Fleet
COMTRAN ... Commercial Translator
COMTRANSDIV .. Commander, Transport Division
COMTRANSGR .. Commander, Transport Group
COMTRANSGRSOPAC .. Commander, Transport Group, South Pacific Force
COMTRANSPHIB .. Commander, Transports, Amphibious Force
COMTRANSPHIBLANT .. Commander, Transports, Amphibious Force, Atlantic Fleet
COMTRANSPHIBPAC .. Commander, Transports, Amphibious Force, Pacific Fleet
COMTWOATAF .. Commander, Second Allied Tactical Air Force
COMUKADR .. Commander, United Kingdom Air Defense Region
COMUL ..... Complement-Fixation for Murine Leukemia (Test) (Immunology)
COMUSAFSO.. Commander, United States Air Forces Southern Command
COMUSARSO.. Commander, United States Army Forces Southern Command
COMUSBASFRANCE .. Commander, US Ports and Bases, France
COMUSFAIRWINGMED .. Commander, United States Fleet Air Wing Mediterranean
COMUSFORAZ.. Commander, United States Forces Azores
COMUSJAPAN.. Commander, United States Forces in Japan
COMUSKOREA.. Commander, United States Forces in Korea
COMUSLANT.. Commander, US Atlantic Subarea
COMUSMACTHAI .. Commander, United States Military Assistance Command, Thailand
COMUSMACV .. Commander, United States Military Assistance Command, Vietnam
COMUSMILGP .. Commander, United States Military Group
COMUSTDC... Commander, United States Taiwan Defense Command
COMUTRON .. Commander, Utility Squadron
COMUTWING .. Commander, Utility Wing
COMUTWINGSERVLANT .. Commander, Utility Wing, Service Force, Atlantic
COMUTWINGSERVPAC .. Commander, Utility Wing, Service Force, Pacific
COMYARD ... Commander of the Dockyard at (place)

COMZ . . . . . . Communications Zone
CON . . . . Cast-Out-Nines
CON . . . . . . Commission on the Nomenclature of Organic Chemistry (IUPAC)
CON . . . . Continental
CON . . . . Control(ler)
CONAB. . . . . . Commanding Officer, Naval Advanced Base
CONAB . . . . . Commanding Officer, Naval Air Base
CONAC . . . . . Continental Air Command
CONACYT. . . . Consejo Nacional de Ciencia y Tecnica (Argentina)
CONAD . . . . . Continental Advance Section (Originally called Coastal Base Section) (World War II)
CONAD . . . . . Continental Air Defense Command (Navy, Army, and Air Force)
CONAIR . . . . . Commanding Officer, Naval Air Wing
CONAKAT . . . Confederation des Associations du Katanga (Confederation of Katangan Associations)
CONALT. . . . . CONARC (Continental Army Command) Alternate Headquarters Plan
CONALT. . . . . Construction and Repair, Alteration (Coast Guard)
CONAR . . . . . Commanding Officer's Narrative Report
CONAR . . . . . Continental Army
CONARC . . . . Continental Army Command (now responsible for induction, processing, training of active duty personnel)
CONARESTRAPROG . . Connection Naval Air Reserve Training Program
CONAS . . . . . Commanding Officer, Naval Air Station
CONC . . . . . . Concentration
CONCA . . . . . Continue Calling Until
CONCOMO . . Convoy Commodore
CONCP. . . . . . Conference des Organisations Nationales des Colonies Portugaises (Conference of National Organizations of Portuguese Colonies)
COND . . . . . . Commanding Officer, Naval Divisions (Canada)
COND . . . . . . Condition
CONDEF. . . . . Contract Definition
CONDEL. . . . . Conselho Deliberativo
CONDESE . . . . Conselho de Desenvolvimento Economico de Sergipe (State of Sergipe, Brazil)
CONDR . . . . . Conductor
CONE . . . . . . Collectors of Numismatic Errors
CONE . . . . . . Controller Error
CONEA . . . . . Confederation of National Educational Associations
CONELRAD . . . Control of Electromagnetic Radiations (Purpose is to deny the enemy aircraft the use of electromagnetic radiations for navigation, while still providing essential services)
CONEX . . . . . Container Express (Army)
CONF. . . . . . . Conference
CONF. . . . . . . Confidential
CONF. . . . . . . Confine(ment)
CONFBUL. . . . Confidential Bulletin (Navy)
CONFED. . . . . Confederation
CONFIDAL . . . Conjugate Filter Data Link
CONFLEX . . . . Conditional Reflex
CONFMOD . . . Confidential - Modified Handling Authorized
CONFORM . . . Contract Formulation
CONG . . . . . . Congress
CONGA . . . . . Concept Game (A war game)
CONGEN . . . . Consul General
CONGINT . . . Interest by Member of Congress
CONGRESS . . . Contiguous Node Group Restoral Supervision and Switching
CONHYDROLANT . . Confidential Hydrographic Office (Later, Naval Oceanographic Office) Reports - Atlantic (Navy)
CONICYT . . . . Comision Nacional de Investigacion Cientifica y Tecnologica (Chile)
CONIE . . . . . . Comision Nacional de Investigacion del Espacio (Spanish space commission)
CONLIS . . . . . Committee on National Library Information Systems
CONN . . . . . . Connecticut
CONN . . . . . . Connellan Airways, Ltd.
CONNORPAC. . . Commander, (US) Naval Forces, Northern Pacific
CONOBJTR . . Conscientious Objector
CONOCO . . . . Continental Oil Company
CONOPS . . . . Continental United States Operations (Army)
CONPASP . . . . Construction Project Alternative Selection Program (Bell System)
CONPASS . . . . Consortium of Professional Associations to Supervise Studies of Special Programs for the Improvement of Instruction in American Education
CONPRESDU . . Continue Present Duty (Military)
CONPY . . . . . Contact Party (Army)
CONRAD . . . . Computerized National Range Documentation
CONREC . . . . Conference for Reconciliation, Restitution Fund
CONREP . . . . . CONARC (Continental Army Command) Emergency Relocation Plan
CONROUTE. . . Convoy and Routing Section (US Fleet)
CONS . . . . . . Carrier-Operated Noise Suppression
CONSA . . . . . Consular Shipping Advisor
CONSALD. . . . Committee on South Asian Libraries and Documentation
CONSCAN . . . Conical Scan

CONSCIENCE . . Committee on National Student Citizenship in Every National Case of Emergency
CONSD . . . . . Commanding Officer, Naval Supply Depot
CONS-GEN. . . Consul-General
CONSO . . . . . Consolan Facility (Aviation)
CONSOL . . . . Consolidate
CONSSTOCS . . Contingency Support Stocks (Army)
CONST. . . . . . Constant
CONST. . . . . . Construct(ion)
CONSTRANS . . Conceptual Thought Random Net Simulation
CONT . . . . . . Continent
CONT. . . . . . . Continue
CONTAC . . . . Conference on the Atlantic Community
CONTACT. . . . Conformal Tactical Array
CONTAX . . . . Consumers and Taxpayers
CONTD . . . . . Continued
CONTH . . . . . Continue to Hold (Aviation)
CONTR. . . . . . Contract(or)
CONTRAIL . . . Condensation Trail (in the air)
CONTRAN . . . Control Translator
CONTREAT . . . Continue Treatment (Navy)
CONUS . . . . . Continental United States
CONUSAMDW. . Continental United States and the Military District of Washington (Refers to the numbered armies in that area)
CONUS INTEL. . Continental United States Intelligence (Domestic intelligence project) (Army)
CONUS OTH. . Continental United States Over-the-Horizon (RADAR system)
CONUS OTH-B. . Continental United States Over-the-Horizon-Backscatter (RADAR system)
CONV . . . . . . Convalescent
CONVAIR . . . . Consolidated-Vultee Aircraft Corporation (Later, General Dynamics)
CONVDD . . . . Converted Destroyer
CONVL . . . . . Conventional
COO . . . . Chicago Operations Office (of AEC)
COO . . . . Chief Ordnance Officer
COO . . . . College of Optometry of Ontario
COO . . . . Committee on Organization (American Library Association)
COO . . . . Cooper Laboratories, Inc. (NYSE symbol)
COO . . . . Council of Oriental Organizations
COOBSRON . . Commanding Officer, Observation Squadron
COOK . . . . . . Cook Transit R. R. (AAR code)
COOP . . . . . . Continuity of Operations Plan (Army)
COOP-JCS . . . Continuity of Operations of the Organization of the Joint Chiefs of Staff
COOPLAN . . . Continuity of Operations Plan (Navy)
COORD . . . . . Coordinate (or Coordination)
COORS. . . . . . Communications Outage Restoral Section (ADC)
COOS . . . . . . Chemical Orbit-to-Orbit Shuttle (NASA)
COP. . . . . Cam Operated Plunger
COP. . . . . Capillary Osmotic Pressure (Physiology)
COP. . . . . Capsule Observation Panel
COP. . . . . Career Opportunities Program (US Office of Education)
COP. . . . . City of Prineville Railway (AAR code)
COP. . . . . Coefficient of Performance
COP. . . . . Coherent Optical Processor
COP. . . . . Combat Outpost
COP. . . . . Command Objective Plan (Air Force)
COP. . . . . Commissary Operating Program (Air Force)
COP. . . . . Computer Optimization Package (or Program)
COP. . . . . Constable on Patrol
COP. . . . . Continuity of Operations Plan
COP. . . . . Control of Operation Programs
COP. . . . . Custom of the Port (Shipping)
COP . . . . Customer Owned Property
COPA. . . . . . . Center for Overseas Program Analysis (Department of State)
COPA . . . . . . Comite des Organisations Professionnelles Agricoles de la CEE (Committee of Professional Agricultural Organizations in the EEC)
COPA. . . . . . . Compania Panamena de Aviacion, SA
COPAC. . . . . . Continuous Operation Production Allocation and Control (Data processing)
COPAG . . . . . Collision Prevention Advisory Group (US)
COPAN . . . . . Command Post Alerting Network
COPANT. . . . . Comite Panamericano de Normes Tecnicas (Buenos Aires) (Also known as PASC)
COPAR. . . . . . Computerized Operational Audit Routine
COPARS . . . . . Contractor-Operated Parts Stores (Military)
COPB. . . . . . . Children's Organization for Peace and Brotherhood
COP/B . . . . . . Command Operating Program/Budget (DOD)
COPCOM . . . . Controllers' Procedures Committee (Aviation)
COPD. . . . . . . Chronic Obstructive Pulmonary Disease
COPDAF . . . . . Continuity of Operations Plan, Department of the Air Force
COPE. . . . . . . Campership Outdoor Program of Education (Federal antipoverty program)
COPE. . . . . . . Carbon Monoxide Pollution Experiment (NASA/General Electric)
COPE. . . . . . . Career Oriented Preparation for Employment (Federal antipoverty program)

COPE . . . . . . Chronic Obstructive Pulmonary Emphysema (Medicine)
COPE . . . . . . Committee for Original People's Entitlement (Eskimo claim to Canadian land)
COPE . . . . . . Committee on Parenthood Education
COPE . . . . . . Committee on Political Education (AFL-CIO)
COPE . . . . . . Communications Oriented Processing Equipment
COPE . . . . . . Concepts of Postal Economics (A series of newsletters of Mail Advertising Corporation)
COPE . . . . . . Congress on Optimum Population and Environment
COPE . . . . . . Console Operator Proficiency Examination
COPE . . . . . . Consortium of Publishers for Employment
COPE . . . . . . Council on Population and Environment
COPE . . . . . . Custodian of Postal Effects (Military)
COPECIAL. . . . Comite Permanent des Congres Internationaux pour l'Apostolat des Laics
COPED . . . . . Cooperative Project for Educational Development (Office of Education)
COPEP . . . . . Committee on Public Engineering Policy (National Academy of Engineering)
COPERS . . . . . Commission Preparatoire Europeenne de Recherches Spatiales
COPES . . . . . . Committee on Program Evaluation and Support (American Library Association)
COPES . . . . . . Community-Oriented Programs Environment Scale (Psychosocial assessment test)
COPES . . . . . . Conceptually Oriented Program in Elementary Science
COPH . . . . . . National Congress of Organizations of the Physically Handicapped
COPL . . . . . . Combat Outpost Line
COPL . . . . . . Committee for Oil Pipe Lines
COPO. . . . . . Chief, Office of Personnel Operations (Army)
COPQE. . . . . . Commanding Officer, Port of Embarkation
COPP . . . . . . Cobaltiprotoporphyrin (Medicine)
COPP . . . . . . Combined Operations Pilotage Party
COPPS . . . . . Committee on Power Plant Siting (National Academy of Engineering)
COPR . . . . . . Copper Range R. R. (AAR code)
COPR . . . . . . Critical Officer Personnel Requirement (Air Force)
COPREX . . . . . Coprecipitation X-Ray Fluorescence Spectroscopy
COPRL . . . . . Command Operations Priority Requirements List (Air Force)
COPROD. . . . . Coal Production Committee
COPS . . . . . . Catalytic Optimum Profit-Sharing
COPS . . . . . . Chrysler Optical Processing Scanner
COPS . . . . . . Circuit Order Preparation (or Processing) System (AT & T)
COPS . . . . . . Coherent Optical Processing System
COPS . . . . . . College of Osteopathic Physicians and Surgeons
COPSI . . . . . Council of Profit Sharing Industries
COPSS . . . . . . Committee of Presidents of Statistical Societies
COPT . . . . . . Completed Procedure Turn (Aviation)
COPTRAN . . . . Communication Optimization Program Translator (NASA)
COR. . . . . . . Cardiac Output Recorder
COR. . . . . . . Carrier-Operated Relay
COR. . . . . . . Cash on Receipt
COR. . . . . . . Center for Operations Research (MIT)
COR. . . . . . . Circular of Requirements
COR. . . . . . . Coherent Optical Receiver
COR. . . . . . . Combat Operations Report
COR. . . . . . . Committee of Responsibility
COR . . . . Communications Operations Report (Air Force)
COR. . . . . . . Concentric-Orbit Rendezvous (NASA)
COR. . . . . . . Conditioned Orientation Reflex
COR. . . . . . . Contactor, Running
COR. . . . . . . Contracting Officer Representatives (Army)
COR. . . . . . . Copper Oxide Rectifier
CORA. . . . . . Coherent RADAR Array
CORA . . . . . . Commission on Religion in Appalachia
CORA. . . . . . Conditioned Reflex Analogue
CORAD. . . . . Correlation RADAR
CORAL . . . . . Class-Oriented Ring-Associated Language (Data processing)
CORAL . . . . . Command Radio Link
CORAL . . . . . Comparison of Recognition Algorithms (US Postal Service)
CORAL . . . . . Correlated Radio Link
CORAL . . . . . Council of Research and Academic Libraries
CORAM . . . . . Colles et Resines Adhesives du Midi (France)
CORAS . . . . . Corridor Assignment (Aviation)
CORBFUS . . . . Copy of Reply Be Furnished this Office (Army)
CORC . . . . . . Chief, Office of Reserve Components (Army)
CORC. . . . . . Conventional Ordnance Release Computer
CORC . . . . . . Cornell Computing Language
CORCO . . . . . Commonwealth Oil Refining Company (Puerto Rico)
CORD. . . . . . Chief of Ordnance (Army)
CORD. . . . . . Cohort Research Development Program
CORD. . . . . . Commissioned Officer Residency Deferment (Program of Public Health Service)
CORD. . . . . . Committee on Research in Dance
CORD. . . . . . Computer with On-Line Remote Devices (National Bureau of Standards)

CORD. . . . . . Consortium Research Development (Office of Education)
CORD. . . . . . Coordinating of Research and Development (Navy)
C of ORD . . . . Chief of Ordnance (Army)
CORDE . . . . . Corporacion Dominicana de Empresas Estatales (Dominican Republic)
CORDIC . . . . . Coordinate Rotation Digital Computer
CORDPO . . . . Correlated Data Printout (Electronics)
CORDPO-SORD . . Correlated Data Printout - Separation of RADAR Data
CORDS . . . . . . Civil Operations Revolutionary (or Rural) Development Support (South Vietnam pacification program)
CORDS . . . . . . Coherent On Receive Doppler System (RADAR)
CORE . . . . . . Coherent-On-Receive
CORE . . . . . . Committee on Research Evaluation (US)
CORE . . . . . . Competitive Operational Readiness Evaluation (Air Force)
CORE . . . . . . Computer-Oriented Reporting Efficiency
CORE . . . . . . Congress of Racial Equality
CORECA . . . . Comite pour la Reunification du Camaroon (Committee for the Reunification of the Cameroons)
CORELAP . . . . Computerized Relationship Layout Planning
COREN. . . . . . Combustibili per Reattori Nucleari (A nuclear power company) (Italy)
COREP . . . . . Combined Overload Repair Control
CORESTA . . . . Centre de Cooperation pour les Recherches Scientifiques Relatives au Tabac
CORFO. . . . . . Corporacion de Fomento de la Produccion (Industrial promotion agency) (Chile)
CORG. . . . . . Combat Operational Reserve Group
CORM . . . . . Council on Optical Radiation Measurement
CORMOSEA . . Committee on Research Materials on Southeast Asia
CORNET . . . . Corporation Network (Telephone communications)
CORO . . . . . . Coronado National Memorial
COROIPAS . . . Conferences on Research on International Peace and Security (Founded International Peace Research Association)
CORONA . . . . Control Rod Analysis
COROS . . . . . Collectors of Religion on Stamps
CORP . . . . . . Corporal
CORP . . . . . . Corporation
CORPAL . . . . Control Room Patching and Labeling
CORPPIN. . . . . Corporeal Pin (Method of tuberculin and histoplasmin testing) (Medicine)
CORPS . . . . . Comprehensive Radiance Profile Synthesizer
CORR . . . . . . Correct(ed) (or Correction)
CORR . . . . . . Correspondence
CORRAL . . . . Computer-Oriented Retrieval of Auto Larcenists
CORRESP . . . . Corresponding
CORS . . . . . . Canadian Operational Research Society
CORSAIR . . . . Computer-Oriented Reference System for Automatic Information Retrieval
CORST . . . . . . Council of Resident Stock Theatres
CORTDIV. . . . . Escort Division
CORTS . . . . . . Conversion of Range Telemetry Systems
COS. . . . . . . Cash-on-Shipment
COS. . . . . . . Central Opera Service
COS. . . . . . . Ceskoslovenska Obec Sokolska (Czechoslovakia)
COS. . . . . . . Charity Organization Society (British)
COS. . . . . . . Chief of Section
COS. . . . . . . Chief of Staff
COS. . . . . . . Civilian Occupational Specialty
COS. . . . . . . Clinical Orthopaedic Society
COS. . . . . . . Compatibility Operating System (Data processing)
COS. . . . . . . Conceptual Operational System
COS. . . . . . . Condemned or Suppressed
COS. . . . . . . Contactor, Starting
COS. . . . . . . Cooper Ornithological Society
COS. . . . . . . Copperweld Steel Company (NYSE symbol)
COS. . . . . . . Cosine
COSA. . . . . . Corps Service Area (Army)
COSAL . . . . . Coordinated Shipboard (or Shorebased) Allowance List (Navy)
COSAM . . . . . Co-Site Analysis Model (Data processing)
COSAR . . . . . Compression Scanning Array RADAR (Raytheon)
COSATI . . . . . Committee of Scientific and Technical Information (Federal Council for Science and Technology)
COSC. . . . . . Canadian Chiefs of Staff Committee
COSC. . . . . . Combat Operations Specialist Course (Air Force)
COSC. . . . . . Combined Operational Service Command
COSCOM . . . . Corps Support Command (Army)
COSCTRACEN . . Commanding Officer, Submarine Chaser Training Center
COSD. . . . . . Combined Operations Supply Depot
COSD. . . . . . Council of Organizations Serving the Deaf
COSEC . . . . . . Coordinating Secretariat of National Unions of Students (in Africa)
COSECTBASE . . Commanding Officer, Section Base (Navy)
COSEP . . . . . Committee on Special Educational Projects (Cornell University)
COSERV . . . . National Council for Community Services to International Visitors
COSH. . . . . . Cosine, Hyperbolic
COSHD. . . . . . Committee for Oil Shale Development

COSI . . . . . . Committee on Scientific Information (Federal Council for Science and Technology)
COSIDA . . . . . College Sports Information Directors of America
COSIP . . . . . . College Science Improvement Program (National Science Foundation)
COSMD . . . . . Combined Operations Signal Maintenance Depot
COSMEP . . . . . Cooperative of Small Magazine Editors and Publishers
COSMIC . . . . . Computer Software Management & Information Center (NASA facility at University of Georgia)
COSMO . . . . . Combined Operations Signal Maintenance Officer
COSMON . . . . Component Open/Short Monitor
COSMOS . . . . Centralization of Supply Management Operations Projects (Army)
COSMOS . . . . Console Oriented Statistical Matrix Operator System (Data processing)
COSO . . . . . . Combined Operations Signal Officer
COSOF . . . . . . Conseil des Organizations Syndicales d'Union Francaise (Council of Labor Unions of the French Union)
COSOMA . . . . Comite de Solidarite de Madagascar (Madagascar Solidarity Committee)
COSOS . . . . . Conference on Self-Operating Systems (Data processing)
COSPA . . . . . . Council of Student Personnel Associations
COSPAR . . . . . Committee on Space Research (of the International Council of Scientific Unions)
COSPAR . . . . . Consultative Group on Potentially Harmful Effects on Space Research
COSPEAR . . . . Committee on Space Programs for Earth Observation (National Academy of Sciences)
COSPUP . . . . . Committee on Science and Public Policy (National Academy of Sciences)
COSR . . . . . . Committee on Space Research
COSR . . . . . . Cut-Off Shear (Tool)
COSRIMS . . . . Committee on Support of Research in the Mathematical Sciences (National Academy of Sciences)
COSRO . . . . . Conical Scan-on-Receive Only
COSSAC . . . . . Chief of Staff to Supreme Allied Commander (Europe) (World War II)
COSSLOA . . . . Coin Operated Self-Service Laundry Owners' Association
COST . . . . . . Congressional Office of Science and Technology
COST . . . . . . Contaminated Oil Settling Tank
COST . . . . . . Cost-Oriented Systems Technique
COST . . . . . . Council of Stock Theatres
CO-STAR . . . . Combat Service to the Army
COSTEP . . . . Commissioned Officer Student Training and Extern Program (Public Health Service)
COSTS . . . . . . Committee on Sane Telephone Service
COSU . . . . . . Combined Operations Scout Unit
COSVN . . . . . Central Office of South Vietnam (North Vietnamese high command in the South)
COSY . . . . . . Checkout Operating System
COT . . . . Cathode Opening Tetanus
COT . . . . Checkout Time
COT . . . . Colt Industries, Inc. (NYSE symbol)
COT . . . . Commander of Troops (for a parade or review) (Military)
COT . . . . Consecutive Oversea Tour (Military)
COT . . . . Consolidated Operability Trial
COT . . . . Contralateral Optic Tectum
COT . . . . Cotangent
COT . . . . Coty, Inc. (NYSE symbol) (Delisted)
COTA . . . . . . Cinetheodolite Orientation Target Array
COTA . . . . . . Confirming Telephone (or message) Authority Of
COTAL . . . . . Confederacion de Organizaciones Turisticas de la America Latina (Confederation of Tourist Organizations of Latin America)
COTAR . . . . . Correlated Orientation Tracking and Range system (Satellite and missile tracking term) (RADAR)
COTAR-AME . . Correlation Tracking and Ranging Angle Measuring Equipment
COTAR-DAS . . Correlation Tracking and Ranging Data Acquisition System
COTAR-DME . . Correlation Tracking and Ranging Data Measuring Equipment
COTAT . . . . . Correlation Tracking and Triangulation
COTC . . . . . . Canadian Overseas Telecommunications Corporation
COTC . . . . . . Commander, Fleet Operational Training Command
COTCLANT . . . Commander, Fleet Operational Training Command, Atlantic Fleet
COTCPAC . . . . Commander, Fleet Operational Training Command, Pacific Fleet
COTCPACSUBCOM . . Commander, Fleet Operational Training Command, Pacific Subordinate Command
COTH . . . . . . Cotangent, Hyperbolic
CO-TIE . . . . . Cooperation via Televised Instruction in Education (Colorado State University)
COTP . . . . . . Captain of the Port (Coast Guard)
COTP . . . . . . Commanding Officer's Tactical Plan (Navy)
COTR . . . . . . Cockpit Orientation Trainer (Aviation)
COTR . . . . . . Contracting Officers' Technical Representative (Army)
COTS . . . . . . Checkout Test Set
COU . . . . Courtaulds, Ltd. (American Stock Exchange symbol)
COUGH . . . . . Congregation Organized by United Genial Hackers
COUNT . . . . . Computer-Operated Universal Test
COUP . . . . . . Congress of Unrepresented People
COUSNAB . . . Commander of United States Naval Advanced Base (Weser River, Germany)

COUSS . . . . . Commanding Officer, United States Ship
COV . . . . Calculus of Variation (NASA)
COV . . . . Check-Out Valve
COV . . . . Coefficient of Variation
COV . . . . Concentrated Oil of Vitriol
COV . . . . Counter-Operating Voltage
COV . . . . Cross-Over Value (Genetics)
COV . . . . Cut-Off Voltage
COV . . . . Cutout Valve
COVAM . . . . . Capture Orbit Vehicle Assembly Mode
COVER . . . . . Cut-Off Velocity & Range
COVFF . . . . . Coverings, Facing or Floor (Freight)
COWA . . . . . Council for Old World Archaeology
COWAR . . . . . Committee on Water Research (International Council of Scientific Unions)
COWLR . . . . . Conference on Oriental-Western Literary Relations
COWP . . . . . . Cowpens National Battlefield Site
COWRR . . . . . Committee on Water Resources Research (US)
COX . . . . Cox Broadcasting Corp. (NYSE symbol)
COXCBS . . . . Coxswain, Construction Battalion, Stevedore
COXSRR . . . . Coxswain, Ship Repair, Rigger
COXSRS . . . . Coxswain, Ship Repair, Canvasman
COY . . . . Career Opportunities for Youth
COZI . . . . . . Communications Zone Indicator (Air Force)
CP . . . . Canadian Pacific, Ltd. (Formerly, Canadian Pacific Railway Company) (NYSE symbol)
CP . . . . Canadian Press
CP . . . . Candle Power (Physics)
CP . . . . Cape Province (of South Africa)
CP . . . . Capillary Pressure (Physiology)
CP . . . . Carbamyl Phosphate
CP . . . . Carriage Paid
CP . . . . Cat Pack ("Women's Wear Daily" slang for jetsetters)
CP . . . . Catch Phrase
CP . . . . Center of Pressure
CP . . . . Centipoise
CP . . . . Central Press
CP . . . . Central Processor (Data processing)
CP . . . . Central Provinces (Later, Madhya Pradesh, India)
CP . . . . Centrally Procured
CP . . . . Cerebral Palsy (Medicine)
CP . . . . Cesspool
CP . . . . Chamber Pressure
CP . . . . Change Package
CP . . . . Character Printer (Data processing)
CP . . . . Charge Parity
CP . . . . Check Point
CP . . . . Chemically Pure (Chemistry)
CP . . . . Chief Patriarch
CP . . . . Circular Pitch (Technical drawings)
CP . . . . Circular Polarization
CP . . . . Civil Power
CP . . . . Civil Procedure (Legal)
CP . . . . Clarissima Puella (Most Illustrious Maiden)
CP . . . . Claw Plate (Technical drawings)
CP . . . . Clay Pipe (Technical drawings)
CP . . . . Clerk of the Peace
CP . . . . Clinical Pathology
CP . . . . Clock Phase
CP . . . . Clock Pulse
CP . . . . Closed Position (Dancing)
CP . . . . Code of Practice
CP . . . . Code of Procedure (Legal)
CP . . . . Code Proficiency (Amateur radio)
CP . . . . Cold-Punched (Metal)
CP . . . . Colla Parte (With the solo part) (Music)
CP . . . . Command Pilot
CP . . . . Command Post (Military)
CP . . . . Common Pleas (Legal)
CP . . . . Common Prayer
CP . . . . Communication Personnel (Marine Corps)
CP . . . . Communications Processor
CP . . . . Communist Party
CP . . . . Component Parts
CP . . . . Computed Point (Navigation)
CP . . . . Concrete Piercing
CP . . . . Concurrent Planometric (A discrimination task)
CP . . . . Conductive Plastic
CP . . . . Conference Paper
CP . . . . Congregatio Passionis (Passionists) (Roman Catholic men's religious order)
CP . . . . Connector Panel
CP . . . . Constant Property

CP . . . . Constrained Procedure
CP . . . . Construction Permit (FCC)
CP . . . . Contact Party
CP . . . . Control Panel
CP . . . . Control Point
CP . . . . Control Post (RADAR)
CP . . . . Control Procedures
CP . . . . Control Program
CP . . . . Co-Pilot
CP . . . . Cost & Performance
CP . . . . Cost Proposal
CP . . . . Court of Probate (Legal)
CP . . . . Cover Point (Lacrosse position)
CP . . . . Crack Propagation
CP . . . . Creatine Phosphate (Phosphocreatine; see PC) (Biochemistry)
CP . . . . Crystal Palace, Sydenham (British)
CP . . . . Crystalline or Powdered
CP . . . . Current Paper
CP . . . . Cushioning Pads
CP . . . . Cuticular Plate (Biology)
CP . . . . Cutie Pie (Survey meter for radiation)
CP . . . . Cylindrical Perforated
C/P . . . . Change Package
C/P . . . . Charter Party (Transportation)
C/P . . . . Control Panel
C & P . . . . . . Care and Preservation (Army)
C to P . . . . . . Confined to Post
CP-5 . . . . Chicago Pile-5 (Nuclear heavy-water-research reactor)
CPA . . . . Canadian Pacific Airlines, Ltd.
CPA . . . . Canvas Products Association International
CPA . . . . Cash Purchasing Agent
CPA . . . . Catholic Press Association
CPA . . . . Central Pacific Area (Hawaiian area) (World War II)
CPA . . . . Certified Public Accountant
CPA . . . . Church Penitentiary Association (British)
CPA . . . . Civilian Production Administration (Became part of Office of Temporary Controls, 1946)
CPA . . . . . . Civilian Property Agent
CPA . . . . Clay Products Association
CPA . . . . Closest Position of Approach (Navigation)
CPA . . . . Color Phase Alternation
CPA . . . . . . Commonwealth Preference Area
CPA . . . . . . Commutative Principle for Addition (New math)
CPA . . . . . . Concrete Pipe Association
CPA . . . . Constant Potential Accelerator
CPA . . . . Consumer Protection Agency (Proposed) (HEW)
CPA . . . . Controlled Products Area
CPA . . . . Cooperative Publication Association
CPA . . . . Cost Planning and Appraisal
CPA . . . . Coudersport & Port Allegany R. R. (AAR code)
CPA . . . . Creative Printers of America
CPA . . . . Critical Path Analysis
CPA . . . . Cycle Parts and Accessories Association
CPAA . . . . . . Cultured Pearl Association of America
CPAA . . . . . . Current Physics Advance Abstracts
CPAB . . . . . . California Prune Advisory Board
CPAB . . . . . . Cling Peach Advisory Board
CPAD . . . . . . Central Pay Accounts Division (Navy)
CP Adm . . . . . Certificate in Public Administration
CPAF . . . . . . Cost Plus Award Fee
CPAGA . . . . . . California Prune and Apricot Growers Association
CPAL . . . . . . Canadian Pacific Air Line
CPAO . . . . . . Canoga Park Area Office (AEC)
CPAP . . . . . . Continuous Positive Airway Pressure (Medicine)
CPAP . . . . . . Control Parameter Assembly Program
CPAS . . . . . . Church Pastoral Aid Society (British)
CPAWS . . . . . Computer-Planning and Aircraft-Weighing Scales
CPB . . . . Campbell Soup Company (NYSE symbol)
CPB . . . . Censorship Policy Board
CPB . . . . Contractors Pump Bureau
CPB . . . . Corporation for Public Broadcasting
CP (b) . . . . . . Communist Party (Bolsheviks)
CPBA . . . . . . Competitive Protein-Binding Analysis
CPBC . . . . . . Central Pacific Base Command (Hawaiian Islands) (World War II)
CPBL . . . . . . Capable (or Capability)
CPC . . . . Canadian Postal Corps (Later, RCPC)
CPC . . . . Card Programmed Calculator (Data processing)
CPC . . . . Cement-Plaster Ceiling (Technical drawings)
CPC . . . . Ceramic-Wafer Printed Circuit
CPC . . . . Cerebro-Pedal Commissure
CPC . . . . Characters Per Column

CPC . . . . Chief Pay Clerk (Navy)
CPC . . . . Chief Planning and Control Staff (Coast Guard)
CPC . . . . Chronic Passive Congestion (Medicine)
CPC . . . . Church Pensions Conference
CPC . . . . Church Periodical Club
CPC . . . . Citizens for Parental Control (Group opposing sex education in schools)
CPC . . . . Civilian Personnel Circular (Army)
CPC . . . . Clerk of the Privy Council (British)
CPC . . . . Clinical Pathology Conference
CPC . . . . Clock Pulsed Control
CPC . . . . College Placement Council
CPC . . . . Color Pack Camera
CPC . . . . Column Position Counter
CPC . . . . Computer Process Control
CPC . . . . Corn Products Company (Commercial firm)
CPC . . . . Curtis Publishing Company (NYSE symbol) (Delisted)
CPC . . . . Custodial, Protective and Crafts (US government workers)
CPC . . . . Cyclic Permutation Code
CPC . . . . Cyclic Program Control
CPCC . . . . . . Chicago Playing Card Collectors
CPCI . . . . . . Cross-Pointer Course Indicator
CPCIZ . . . . . . Comite Permanent des Congres Internationaux de Zoologie
CPC & N . . . . Certificate of Public Convenience and Necessity
CPCS . . . . . . Coast Phase Control System (Army)
CPCS . . . . . . Conversion Process Controller System
CPCS . . . . . . Cyclic Pitch Control Stick
CPCT . . . . . . Committee to Protect our Children's Teeth
CPCU . . . . . . Chartered Property and Casualty Underwriter
CPCU . . . . . . Council of Protestant Colleges and Universities
CPCU . . . . . . Custody Pending Completion of Use
CPD . . . . Central Postal Directory (Army)
CPD . . . . Central Procurement Division (Marine Corps)
CPD . . . . Charterers Pay Dues
CPD . . . . Circuit Protection Device
CPD . . . . Citrate-Phosphate-Dextrose (Anticoagulant)
CPD . . . . Civilian Personnel Division
CPD . . . . Coaxial Power Divider
CPD . . . . . . Combat Potential Display (SAGE) (Air Force)
CPD . . . . Commercial Product Development
CPD . . . . Commercial Program Development
CPD . . . . Common Pleas Division
CPD . . . . Consolidated Programming Document
CPD . . . . Contact Potential Difference
CPD . . . . Counter-Propaganda Directorate (British)
CPD . . . . Cycles Per Day
Cp D . . . . Doctor of Chiropody
CPDA . . . . . . Copper Products Development Association
CPDA . . . . . . Council for Periodical Distributors Associations
CPDCET . . . . . Centre de Perfectionnement pour le Developpement et la Cooperation Economique et Technique (France)
CPDD . . . . . . Command Post Digital Display (SAGE) (Air Force)
CPE . . . . Cable Pressurization Equipment
CPE . . . . Cathodic Protection Equipment
CPE . . . . Cellulose Polyethylene
CPE . . . . Central Processing Element
CPE . . . . Central Programmer and Evaluator
CPE . . . . Chlorinated Polyethylene (Dow Chemical)
CPE . . . . Circular Probable Error
CPE . . . . Collective Protection Equipment
CPE . . . . Comite de Politique Economique (OCDE)
CPE . . . . Congres du Peuple Europeen
CPE . . . . Continuous Particle Electrophoresis
CPE . . . . Contractor Performance Evaluation
CPE . . . . Cytopathogenic Effect
CPEA . . . . . . College Physical Education Association
CPEA . . . . . . Concentrated Phosphate Export Association
CPEA . . . . . . Cooperative Program in Educational Administration
CPEB . . . . . . Council for Professional Education for Business
CPEB . . . . . . Cryogenic Positive Expulsion Bladder
CPEG . . . . . . Contractor Performance Evaluation Group
CPEHS . . . . . . Consumer Protection and Environmental Health Service (US government)
CPEM . . . . . . Conference on Precision Electromagnetic Measurements
CPEP . . . . . . Committee on Public Engineering Policy
CPEP . . . . . . Contractor Performance Evaluation Plan (Army)
CPEQ . . . . . . Corporation of Professional Engineers of Quebec
CPER . . . . . . Contractor Personnel Employment Report
CPES . . . . . . Contractor Performance Evaluation System
CPET . . . . . . Charged Particle Electrostatic Thruster
CPEx . . . . . . Command Post Exercise
CPF . . . . Central Post Fund (Army)
CPF . . . . Chlorine Pentafluoride

CPF . . . . Church Pension Fund
CPF . . . . Compagnie du Polyisoprene Francais
CPF . . . . Complete Power Failure (Aviation)
CPF . . . . Conditional Peak Flow (Biology)
CPF . . . . Cotton Plant - Fargo Railway Company (AAR code)
CPF . . . . Creative Playthings Foundation (Defunct)
CPFF . . . . Cost Plus Fixed Fee (Business and trade)
CPFR . . . . Continuous Page Facsimile Recorder
CPG . . . . Candidate Pass Generator (NASA)
CPG . . . . Clock Pulse Generator
CPG . . . . College Publishers Group
CPG . . . . Controlled-Pore Glass (Corning)
CPG . . . . Cotton Piece Goods
CPGA . . . . California Persimmon Growers Association
CPGA . . . . China Pottery and Glassware Association
CPGAF . . . . . . Commission on Population Growth and the American Future (Presidential commission)
CPGC . . . . Course Per Gyro Compass (Navigation)
CPH . . . . Capitas Holding Corp. (NYSE symbol)
CPH . . . . Central Powerhouse
CPH . . . . Certificate in Public Health
CPH . . . . Close-Packed Hexagonal (Metallography)
CPH . . . . Counts Per Hour
CPHA . . . . Commission on Professional and Hospital Activities
CPHM . . . . Chief Pharmacist's Mate
CPHMDP . . . . . Chief Pharmacist's Mate, Dental Prosthetic Technician
CPHM(RPA) . . . Chief Pharmacist's Mate (Radium Plaque Adaptometer Operator)
CPHO . . . . Chief Photographer (Navy rating)
CPHOM . . . . . . Chief Photographer's Mate
CPHV . . . . Conference of Public Health Veterinarians
CPI . . . . California Personality (or Psychological) Inventory
CPI . . . . Caltex Pacific Indonesia
CPI . . . . Characters Per Inch (Typesetting)
CPI . . . . Chief Patrol Inspector (Immigration and Naturalization Service)
CPI . . . . Chief of Public Information (Army)
CPI . . . . Clay Pipe Institute
CPI . . . . Commission Permanente Internationale de l'Acetylene, de la Soudure Autogene et des Industries Qui S'y Rattachent
CPI . . . . Commission on Personnel Interchange (Presidential)
CPI . . . . Commission Phytosanitaire Interafricaine
CPI . . . . Communist Party of India
CPI . . . . Community Products, Incorporated
CPI . . . . Constitutional Psychopathic Inferior
CPI . . . . Consumer Price Index (Economics)
CPI . . . . Crash Position Indicator (Air Force)
CPI . . . . Crop Protection Institute
CPI . . . . Customs Port Investigator (Treasury)
CPI . . . . Public Information Division (Coast Guard symbol)
CPIA . . . . Chemical Propulsion Information Agency
CPIA . . . . Close-Pair Interstitial Atom
CPIAF . . . . Cost-Plus-Incentive-Award Fee
CPIB . . . . Chlorophenoxyisobutyrate (Chemical)
CPIC . . . . Charged Particles Information Center (ORNL)
CPIC . . . . Combined Photographic Interpretation Center
CPIC . . . . Cost Price of the Items Canceled
CPIF . . . . Cost-Plus-Incentive-Fee
CPIF . . . . Cost Plus Intended (or Interim) Fee
CP-ILS . . . . . . Correlation-Protected Instrument Landing System
CPIP . . . . Computer Pneumatic Input Panel
CPIP . . . . Computer Program Implementation Process
CPIRA . . . . Carbon Paper and Inked Ribbon Association
CPIT . . . . Contract Price of Items Terminated
CPIT . . . . Cost Price of the Items Terminated
CPIUS . . . . Comite Permanent International d'Urbanisme Souterrain
CPIV . . . . Comite Permanent International du Vinaigre (Marche Commun)
CPJ . . . . Conoseal Pipe Joint
CPJI . . . . Cour Permanente de Justice Internationale
CPK . . . . Central Pastry Kitchen (Army)
CPK . . . . Corey-Pauling-Koltun
CPL . . . . Carolina Power & Light Company (NYSE symbol)
CPL . . . . Cement Plaster
CPL . . . . Civilian Personnel Letter
CPL . . . . Collective Pitch Lever
CPL . . . . Columns Per Line
CPL . . . . Combined Programming Language (Data processing)
CPL . . . . Common Program Language (Data processing)
CPL . . . . Common Pulse Line
CPL . . . . Communist Party of Lesotho (Basutoland)
CPL . . . . Corporal (Military)
CPL . . . . Council of Planning Librarians
CPL . . . . Critical Path Length

CPLA . . . . Conference for Progressive Labor Action
CPL&D . . . . . . Civilian Personnel Letters and Dispatches
CPLEE . . . . Charged Particle Lunar Environment Experiment (NASA)
CPLIA . . . . Contracting Plasterers' and Lathers' International Association
CPLR . . . . Coupler
CPLT . . . . Camino, Placerville & Lake Tahoe R. R. (AAR code)
CPM . . . . Capsule Positioning Mechanism
CPM . . . . Cards Per Minute (Data processing)
CPM . . . . Cathode Pulse Modulation
CPM . . . . Central Path Method (Data processing)
CPM . . . . Certified Property Manager (Designation given by Institute of Real Estate Management)
CPM . . . . Characters Per Minute
CPM . . . . Chief Patternmaker (Navy rating)
CPM . . . . Coloured Progressive Matrices
CPM . . . . Combat Air Patrol Mission (Air Force)
CPM . . . . Command Processor Module
CPM . . . . Common Particular Metre (Music)
CPM . . . . Commutative Principle for Multiplication (New math)
CPM . . . . Congregation of Priests of Mercy (Fathers of Mercy) (Roman Catholic religious order)
CPM . . . . Cost Per Thousand (Advertising)
CPM . . . . Counts Per Minute
CPM . . . . Critical Path Method (Management) (Electronics) (PERT)
CPM . . . . Current Physics Microform
CPM . . . . Cycles Per Minute
CPMA . . . . Computer Peripheral Manufacturers Association
CPME . . . . Conseil Parlementaire du Mouvement Europeen
CPNC . . . . Cameroons People's National Congress
CPNU . . . . Conference des Plenipotentiaires
CPO . . . . Central Project Office (of ARS, Department of Agriculture)
CPO . . . . Changing Path of Operation
CPO . . . . Chief Petty Officer (Navy)
CPO . . . . Circular Parking Orbit (Aerospace)
CPO . . . . Civilian Personnel Office(r)
CPO . . . . Cloud Physics Observatory (University of Hawaii)
CPO . . . . Code Practice Oscillator
CPO . . . . Command-Post Officer
CPO . . . . Command Pulse Output
CPO . . . . Component Pilot Overhaul (Navy)
CPO . . . . Controlled Precision Oscillator
CPO . . . . Cost Proposal Outline
CPOC . . . . Clay Pigmented Organic Coating
CPOR . . . . Centro de Preparacao de Oficiais de Reserva (Brazil)
CPOS . . . . Civilian Personnel Occupational Standards (Military)
CPOSMA . . . . . Conference of Presidents and Officers of State Medical Associations
CPP . . . . Champion Papers, Inc. (NYSE symbol) (Delisted; later, US Plywood-Champion Papers, Inc.)
CPP . . . . Children's Plea for Peace
CPP . . . . Civilian Personnel Pamphlet (Military)
CPP . . . . Committee on Political Parties
CPP . . . . Communist Party of the Philippines
CPP . . . . Conductive Plastic Potentiometer
CPP . . . . Control and Protection Panel
CPP . . . . Convention People's Party (Ghana)
CPP . . . . Council of Psychoanalytic Psychotherapists
CPP . . . . Current Papers in Physics
CPP . . . . Cyclopentenophenanthrene
CPPA . . . . Canadian Pulp and Paper Association
CPPA . . . . Classroom Periodical Publishers Association
CPPA . . . . Coated and Processed Paper Association
CPPA . . . . Conference for Progressive Political Action
CPPC . . . . Cost Plus a Percentage of Cost
CPPCA . . . . . . California Probation, Parole, and Correctional Association
CPPCC . . . . . . Chinese People's Political Consultative Conference
CPPD . . . . Consumers Public Power District
CPPL . . . . Civilian Personnel and Payroll Letter (Military)
CPPM . . . . Civilian Personnel Procedures Manual (Military)
CPP/ML . . . . . . Communist Party of the Philippines/Marxist-Leninist
CPPO . . . . Controlled Production Planning Officer
CPPS . . . . Combined Procurement Processing Series
CPPS . . . . Composite Professional Performance Score
CPPS . . . . Congregatio Pretiosissimi Sanguinis (Society of the Most Precious Blood) (Roman Catholic men's religious order)
CPPS . . . . Critical Path Planning and Scheduling
CPQ . . . . Children's Personality Questionnaire
CPQ . . . . Civil Procedures, Quebec
CPR . . . . Cam Plate Readout
CPR . . . . Canadian Pacific Railway
CPR . . . . Cardiopulmonary Resuscitation (Medicine)
CPR . . . . Center for Political Research

CPR . . . . Center for Population Research
CPR . . . . Chemicals, Plastic Research
CPR . . . . Chinese People's Republic
CPR . . . . Citizens for Parents' Rights (Group opposing sex education in schools)
CPR . . . . Civilian Personnel Regulation (Military)
CPR . . . . Cloud Physics Radiometer
CPR . . . . Committee on Polar Research (US)
CPR . . . . Component Pilot Rework (Navy)
CPR . . . . Consolidated Progress Report
CPR . . . . Crew Provisioning Report
CPR . . . . Cut Paraboloidal Reflector
CPRA . . . . Chemical Public Relations Association
CPRA . . . . Congo Protestant Relief Agency
CPRB . . . . Combined Production and Resources Board (World War II)
CPRC . . . . Chrysler Products Restorers Club
CPRC . . . . Civilian Payroll Circular
CPRE . . . . Council for the Preservation of Rural England
CPRG . . . . Computer Personnel Research Group
CPRH . . . . Conference on Peace Research in History
CPRI . . . . Canadian Peace Research Institute
CPRR-NEA . . . . Commission on Professional Rights and Responsibilities of the NEA
CPRS . . . . Canadian Public Relations Society
C PRTR . . . . . . Chief Printer (Navy rating)
CPRTRL . . . . . . Chief Printer, Lithographer (Navy rating)
CPRTRM . . . . . Chief Printer, Offset Process (Navy rating)
CPS . . . . Cabinet Pressurization System
CPS . . . . Cathode Potential Stabilized
CPS . . . . Catholic Pamphlet Society of the United States
CPS . . . . Central Processing System
CPS . . . . Cephalo Pedal Sinus
CPS . . . . Certified Professional Secretary (Designation given by National
　　　　　　　　　Secretaries Association)
CPS . . . . Change Processing Station
CPS . . . . Characters Per Second (Data processing)
CPS . . . . Circuit Provision System (AT & T)
CPS . . . . Civilian Public Service
CPS . . . . Close Packed Structure
CPS . . . . College of Physicians & Surgeons
CPS . . . . College Placement Council
CPS . . . . Color Picture Signal
CPS . . . . Columbia Pictures Industries (NYSE symbol)
CPS . . . . Command Personnel Summary
CPS . . . . Commission on the Patent System
CPS . . . . Comparative Political Studies (A publication)
CPS . . . . Computer Power Supply
CPS . . . . Computer Program Specification
CPS . . . . Computer Programming Service
CPS . . . . Comrey Personality Scales
CPS . . . . Condensation Pressure Spread
CPS . . . . Conference on the Public Service
CPS . . . . Congregational Publishing Society
CPS . . . . Constitutional Psychopathic State
CPS . . . . Consumer Purchasing Service
CPS . . . . Contract Pilot School
CPS . . . . Contract(or) Plant Services
CPS . . . . Control Panel Subassembly
CPS . . . . Control Power Supply
CPS . . . . Control Pressure System
CPS . . . . Conversational Programming System (Data processing)
CPS . . . . Crew Procedures Simulator
CPS . . . . Critical Path Scheduling (or System)
CPS . . . . Crossfield Plasma Sheath
CPS . . . . Current Population Survey (Census Bureau)
CPS . . . . Custos Privati Sigilli (Keeper of the Privy Seal) (British)
cps . . . . Cycles Per Second (Later, Hz)
CPSA . . . . Canadian Political Science Association
CPSA . . . . Catholic Poetry Society of America
CPSA . . . . Civil and Public Services Association (British)
CPSA . . . . Communist Party of South Africa
CPSAC . . . . . . Cycles Per Second Alternating Current
CPSAH . . . . . . Committee to Promote the Study of Austrian History
CPSD . . . . Cross Power Spectral Density
CPSE . . . . Carr-Purcell Spin-Echo
CPSG . . . . Common Power Supply Group
CPSK . . . . Cathodic Protection Survey Kit
CPSO . . . . Cumberland Plateau Seismological Observatory
CPSR . . . . Contractor Procurement System Review (DOD)
CPSR . . . . Cost and Performance Summary Report (Army)
CPSS . . . . Central Processing Subsystem
CPSS . . . . Common Program Support System
CPSS . . . . Component Percentage Shipment Schedule

CPSU . . . . Calcutta Port Shramik Union (India)
CPSU . . . . Central Processor Sub-Unit
CPSU . . . . Communist Party of the Soviet Union
CPT . . . . Caribou Performance Test
CPT . . . . Casement Projected Transom (Technical drawings)
CPT . . . . Ceramic Planar Tube
CPT . . . . Chicago Produce Terminal Company (AAR code)
CPT . . . . Civilian Pilot Training (Became War Training Service) (World War II)
CPT . . . . Cockpit Procedure Trainer (Air Force)
CPT . . . . Color Pyramid Technic (Projective test)
CPT . . . . Colored People's Time (Slang)
CPT . . . . Consolidated Pilot Training Program (Air Force)
CPT . . . . Continuous Performance Test (Psychology)
CPT . . . . Crew Procedures Trainer
CPT . . . . Critical Path Technique (PERT)
CPT . . . . Cryogenic Pressure Transducer
CPT . . . . Crystal Pressure Transducer
CPT . . . . Current Physics Titles (A publication)
CPTC . . . . Central Processor Test Console
CPTF . . . . Central Plains Turfgrass Foundation
CPTP . . . . Civil Pilot Training Program
CPTR . . . . Chief Painter (Navy rating)
CPTRV . . . . . . Chief Painter, Aircraft (Navy rating)
CPU . . . . Caudate-Putamen Complex (Anatomy)
CPU . . . . Central Processing Unit (Data processing)
CPU . . . . Children's Peace Union
CPU . . . . Church Peace Union
CPU . . . . Commonwealth Press Union
CPURMC . . . . . Committee to Promote Uniformity in the Regulation of Motor Carriers
CPUSA . . . . . . Communist Party, United States of America
CPV . . . . Compania Peruana de Vapores (Peruvian Line)
CPVC . . . . Chlorinated Polyvinyl Chloride
CPVR . . . . Committee on Procedure and Valuation of Reparations (Allied German
　　　　　　　　　Occupation Forces)
CPW . . . . Club of Printing Women of New York
CPW . . . . Commercial Projected Window (Technical drawings)
CPWU . . . . . . Ceylon Plantation Workers' Union
CPX . . . . Command Post Exercise
CPX . . . . Copper Range Company (NYSE symbol)
CPY . . . . Clopay Corporation (American Stock Exchange symbol)
CPZ . . . . Chlorpromazine
CQ . . . . Call to Quarters (General call preceding transmission of radio signals)
CQ . . . . Caribbean Quarterly (A publication)
CQ . . . . Charge of Quarters (Army)
CQ . . . . Chloroquine (Antimalarial drug)
CQ . . . . Commercial Quality
CQ . . . . Communications Satellite Corp. (NYSE symbol)
CQ . . . . Conceptual Quotient (Psychology)
CQ . . . . Conditionally Qualified
CQ . . . . Congressional Quarterly, Inc.
CQ . . . . Creativity Quotient (Testing term)
C/Q . . . . Certificate of Assignment of Quarters (Navy)
CQA . . . . Component Quality Assurance
CQAP . . . . Component Quality Assurance Program
CQC . . . . Citizens for a Quieter City (New York City)
CQC . . . . Crop Quality Council
CQD . . . . Come Quick -- Danger
CQD . . . . Customary Quick Dispatch
CQI & R . . . . . Cent. Qualifications Inventory & Referral System (Army Ordnance)
CQM . . . . Chief Quartermaster (Navy)
CQM . . . . Circuit Quality Monitor
CQM . . . . Crystal Quartz Modern
CQMC . . . . . . Chief Quartermaster Clerk (Navy)
CQMS . . . . . . Company Quartermaster-Sergeant
CQP . . . . Capacitor Qualification Program
CQT . . . . Capacitor Qualification Test
CQTP . . . . Capacitor Qualification Test Program
CQTU . . . . . . Carrier Qualification Training Unit
CQU . . . . College Qualification Tests
CR . . . . Caledonian Railway
CR . . . . Calendrier Republicain (Republican Calendar)
CR . . . . Call Request
CR . . . . Camera Repairman (Navy rating)
CR . . . . Carolus Rex (King Charles)
CR . . . . Carriage Return
CR . . . . Carrier's Risk (Shipping)
CR . . . . Cathode Ray
CR . . . . Cathode Reaction
CR . . . . Centennial Review (A publication)
CR . . . . Center of Resistance
CR . . . . Cerebral Ridge

CR . . . . Change Recommendation
CR . . . . Change Release (Military)
CR . . . . Change Request
CR . . . . Channels Ratio
CR . . . . Characteristic Relief
CR . . . . Chemical Report
CR . . . . Chief Ranger
Cr . . . . Chromium (Chemical element)
CR . . . . Civil Rights
CR . . . . Class Rate
CR . . . . Classification Research
CR . . . . Classified Register
CR . . . . Clinical Record (Medicine)
CR . . . . Clot Retraction (Medicine)
CR . . . . Cold-Rolled (Metal)
CR . . . . Combat Ready
CR . . . . Combat Reserve (Military)
CR . . . . Command Register
CR . . . . Commendation Ribbon
CR . . . . Commodity Rate
CR . . . . Community of the Resurrection
CR . . . . Company's Risk (Insurance)
CR . . . . Competing Risks
CR . . . . Complete Round (Technical drawings)
CR . . . . Compression Ratio
CR . . . . Computing Reviews
CR . . . . Conditioned Reflex (or Response)
CR . . . . Conference Report
CR . . . . Congregatio Resurrectionis (Congregation of the Resurrection, or Resurrectionist Fathers) (Roman Catholic religious order)
CR . . . . Congregation of Clerics Regular (Theatine Fathers) (Roman Catholic religious order)
CR . . . . Congressional Record
CR . . . . Connaught Rangers (British military)
CR . . . . Consolidated Report
CR . . . . Consumers' Research (Service reporting results of tests on consumers' goods)
CR . . . . Continuous Rod
CR . . . . Contract(or) Report
CR . . . . Control Relay
CR . . . . Controlled Rectifier
CR . . . . Cost Reimbursement
CR . . . . Count Reverse
CR . . . . Crane Company (NYSE symbol)
CR . . . . Credit
CR . . . . Credit Requisition
CR . . . . Creditable Record
CR . . . . Creek (Maps and charts)
CR . . . . Crew Rest (Military)
CR . . . . Critical Ratio
CR . . . . Crops Research Division (of ARS, Department of Agriculture)
CR . . . . Crossroads (Maps and charts)
CR . . . . Cryptographer (Navy rating)
CR . . . . Crystal Rectifier
CR . . . . Currency Regulation
CR . . . . Current Rate
CR . . . . Custos Rotulorum (Keeper of the Rolls) (British)
C/R . . . . Change of Rating
C/R . . . . Change Request
C/R . . . . Contract Requirement
C/R . . . . Cuenta y Riesgo (For Account and Risk of) (Business and trade) (Spain)
C & R . . . . . Bureau of Construction and Repair (of Navy) (Until 1940)
C & R . . . . . . Convoy and Routing Section (Navy)
C and R . . . . . . Construction and Repair (Coast Guard)
CRA . . . . California Redwood Association
CRA . . . . Cassegrain Reflector Antenna
CRA . . . . Cave Research Associates
CRA . . . . Central Research Agency (Cuc Nghien-Chu Trung-Uong) (North Vietnamese intelligence agency)
CRA . . . . Central Retinal Artery
CRA . . . . Centralized Referral Activity (Military)
CRA . . . . Centro Ricerche Aerospaziali (Italy)
CRA . . . . Civil Rights Act
CRA . . . . Command Relationship Agreements (Army)
CRA . . . . Commander, Royal Artillery (Division level) (British)
CRA . . . . Community Research Associates
CRA . . . . . . Composite Research Aircraft
CRA . . . . Continuing Resolution Authority (Military)
CRA . . . . Control Relay Automatic
CRA . . . . Control Repeater Amplifier
CRA . . . . Corn Refiners Association

CrA . . . . Corona Australis (Astronomy)
CRA . . . . Cosmic Ray Altimeter
CRA . . . . Crew Reception Area (Apollo) (NASA)
CRAB . . . . Caging Retainer and Boresight (Air Force)
CRAB . . . . California Raisin Advisory Board
CRAC . . . . . . Community Relations Advisory Council (Military)
CRACC . . . . . Communication and RADAR Assignment Coordinating Committee
CRACCUS . . . . Comite Regional d'Afrique Centrale pour la Conservation et l'Utilisation du Sol
CRAE . . . . Combat Readiness Assessment Exercise (Navy)
CRAF . . . . . . Civil Reserve Air Fleet (Department of Commerce)
CRAFREP . . . . Civil Reserve Air Fleet Summary Report
CRAFT . . . . . . Changing Radio Automatic Frequency Transmission
CRAFT . . . . . . Comparing Reading Approaches in First Grade Teaching
CRAFT . . . . . . Computerized Relative Allocation of Facilities Technique (IBM)
CRAFT. . . . . . Continuous Random Analog to Frequency Transmission
CRAG . . . . Carrier Replacement Air Group
CRAGS . . . . . Chemistry Records and Grading System (Data processing)
CRALOG . . . . Council of Relief Agencies Licensed for Operation in Germany (Post-World War II)
CRAM . . . . . . Card Random Access Memory (Data processing)
CRAM . . . . Collapsible Rollup Antenna Mast
CRAM . . . . Computer Reliability Analysis Method
CRAM . . . . Conditional Relaxation Analysis Method
CRAM . . . . Contractual Requirements, Recording, Analysis & Management (Air Force)
CRAMSHIP . . . Complete Round Ammunition Shipment
CRAN . . . . . . Cross Scan Terrain-Avoidance Displays
CRAP . . . . . . Centres Regionaux d'Action Pedagogique (France)
CRAP . . . . . . Committee on Rhetoric, Administration, and Perspicacity (Satirical bureaucracy term)
CRAR . . . . . . Committee for the Recovery of Archaeological Remains
CRAR . . . . . . Critical Reliability Action Report
CRAS . . . . . . Coder and Random Access Switch
CRASC . . . . . Commander, Royal Army Service Corps (British)
CRASH . . . . . Citizens to Reduce Airline Smoking Hazards (Student legal action organization)
CRASH . . . . . Citizens Responsible Action for Safety on the Highways
CRASH . . . . . Community Resource and Self-Help, Inc. (Pennsylvania organization)
CRASH . . . . . Countermeasures Related to Alcohol Safety on the Highways (Vermont)
CRASH . . . . . Creep in Axisymmetric Shells
CRAW . . . . . . Carrier Replacement Air Wing (Navy)
CRAW . . . . . . Combat Readiness Air Wing
CRAZI . . . . . . Count Routine Applied to Zero Input (Computer program)
CRB . . . . Cab Research Bureau
CRB . . . . Clutch Release Bearing
CRB . . . . Container Repair Building
CrB . . . . Corona Borealis (Astronomy)
CRB . . . . Council of Review Board (Army)
CRB . . . . Crop Reporting Board
CRB . . . . Customer Records and Billing (Bell System)
CRBA . . . . . . Christian Record Benevolent Association
CRBE . . . . Conversational Remote Batch Entry (Data processing)
CRBF . . . . . . Christian Record Braille Foundation
CRBL . . . . Charles River Breeding Laboratories
CRBP . . . . Colorado River Basin Project
CRBR . . . . Controlled Recirculation Boiling Water Reactor (AEC)
CRC . . . . Cambridge Research Center (Air Force)
CRC . . . . Cardiovascular Reflex Conditioning
CRC . . . . Carriage Return Contact
CRC . . . . Central Requirements Committee
CRC . . . . Central Rhine Commission (Post-World War II)
CRC . . . . Ceramic Refraction Coating
CRC . . . . Chemical Research Consultants, Inc.
CRC . . . . Chemical Resistant Coating
CRC . . . . Chemical Rubber Company
CRC . . . . Chief of Reserve Components (Army)
CRC . . . . Civil Rights Commission
CRC . . . . Colorado Research Corporation
CRC . . . . Column Research Council of Engineering Foundation
CRC . . . . Combat Reporting Center
CRC . . . . Combined Rubber Committee
CRC . . . . Command Reporting Center
CRC . . . . Communications Relay Center (Air Force)
CRC . . . . Complete Round Chart
CRC . . . . Computer Response Corporation
CRC . . . . COMSEC (Communications Security) Repair Center
CRC . . . . Condition Reservation Code (Army)
CRC . . . . Consistency Recording Controller
CRC . . . . Contract Requirement Card
CRC . . . . Control and Reporting Center (Air Force)
CRC . . . . Cooperative Research Council

CRC .... Coordinating Research Council
CRC .... Copper Recovery Corporation
CRC .... Copy Research Council
CRC .... Corinth & Counce R. R. (AAR code)
CRC .... Cost Reimbursement Contract
CRC .... Crescent Petroleum Corporation (NYSE symbol) (Delisted)
CRC .... Crew Chief (Military, especially Air Force)
CRC .... Cyclic Redundancy Check (Data processing)
CRC .... Czechoslovak Red Cross
CRCAT ..... Combat Readiness Categories (Navy)
CRCC ...... Consolidated Record Communications Center (Army)
CRCH ...... Crew Chief
CRCL ...... Clearinghouse for Research in Child Life (Federal Security Administration)
CRCP ...... Committee of Religious Concern for Peace
CRCPI ..... Coordinating Research Council of the Petroleum Industry
CRCR ...... Center for Rate Controlled Recordings
CRCS ...... Cardiovascular Reflex Conditioning System
CRCS ...... Clerici Regulares Congregationis Somaschæ (Somaschi Fathers)
CRCSU ..... Clinical Record Cover Sheet (Army medical)
CRCSU ..... Ceylon Railway Clerical Service Union
CRD .... Capacitor-Resistor Diode
CRD .... Central Recruiting Division
CRD .... Chief of Research and Development (Army)
CRD .... Chronic Respiratory Disease (Medicine)
CRD .... Civil Rights Division (Department of Justice)
CRD .... Committee on Reciprocal Deliveries (Allied German Occupation Forces)
CRD .... Complete Reaction of Degeneration (Physiology)
CRD .... Confidential Restricted Data
CRD .... Creditthrift Financial Corp. (NYSE symbol)
CR & D ..... Chief, Research & Development (Army)
CRDC ...... Columbia Research and Development Corporation
CRDF ...... Canadian Radio-Direction Finding or Finder
CRDF ...... Cathode-Ray Direction Finding (RADAR)
CRDL ...... Chemical Research & Development Laboratories (Army)
CRDM ...... Chief RADARman (Navy rating)
CRDM ..... Control Rod Drive Mechanism Study
CRDP ...... Civil Rights Documentation Project
CR & DP ... Cooperative Research & Development Program
CRDS ...... Colgate Rochester Divinity School (New York)
CRDS ...... Component Repair Data Sheets
CRDSD ..... Current Research and Development in Scientific Documentation (A publication)
CRE .... Cation-Responsive Electrode
CRE .... Cauchy-Riemann Equation
CRE .... Chief Radio Electrician (Navy rating)
CRE .... Combat Readiness Evaluation (Army)
CRE .... Commander, Royal Engineers (British)
CRE .... Compton Recoil Electron
CRE .... Corrosion Resistant
CREATE ..... Carpet Research, Engineering, Aesthetics, Technological Evaluation (Dow Chemical Company)
CREATE ..... Center for Research and Evaluation in Applications of Technology in Education (Palo Alto, California)
CREATE ..... Computational Requirements for Engineering and Simulation, Training and Education (Time-sharing computer complex) (Air Force)
CREATION ... Cultural and Recreational Education Achieved Through Investigations Ordinarily Neglected (University course)
CREC ...... Combat Readiness Evaluation Criteria (Navy)
CRECON ..... Counterreconnaissance (Army)
CREDIF ..... Centre de Recherches et d'Etudes pour la Diffusion du Francais (France)
CREDO ...... Chaplains' Relevance to the Emerging Drug Order (Navy)
CREDOC ..... Centre de Recherches et de Documentation sur la Consommation (France)
CREEP ...... Committee to Re-Elect the President (Also, CRP) (1972)
CREF ...... College Retirement Equities Fund
CREF ...... Cross Reference
CREFAL ..... Centro Regional de Education Fundamental para la America Latina (Mexico)
CREI ...... Capitol Radio Engineering Institute (Now known only by initialism)
CREL ...... Cold Regions Engineering Laboratory
CRES ...... Corrosion-Resistant Steel
CRESME ..... Centro Richerche Economiche, Sociologiche e di Mercato nell 'Edilizia
CRESS ...... Center for Research in Social Systems (American University)
CRESS ...... Clearinghouse on Rural Education and Small Schools (ERIC)
CRESS ...... Combined Reentry Effort in Small Systems
CREST ...... Committee on Rural Economic and Social Trends
CREST ...... Consolidated Reporting and Evaluating System, Tactical (Computer program) (Air Force)
CREST ...... Crew Escape and Rescue Techniques (Air Force)
CRET ...... Cathode Ray Electron Tube
CRET ...... Commission Regionale Europeenne du Tourisme

CREWTAF .... Crew Training Air Force
CRF .... Calendar Reform Foundation
CRF .... Capacitor Resonance Frequency
CRF .... Capital Recovery Factor
CRF .... Cathode Ray Furnace
CRF .... Christian Rural Fellowship
CRF .... Citizens' Research Foundation
CRF .... Conservation and Research Foundation
CRF .... Constitutional Rights Foundation
CRF .... Continuous Reinforcement
CRF .... Control Relay Forward
CRF .... Copeland Corporation (NYSE symbol)
CRF .... Corticotropin Release Factor (Endocrinology)
CRF .... Cosmic Ray Flux
CRF .... Credit Research Foundation
CRF .... Cross-Reference File
CRF .... Cryptographic Repair Facilities
CRFA ...... Czechoslovak Rationalist Federation of America
CRFUSAIC ... Central Records Facility, United States Army Intelligence Center
CRG .... Catalytic Rich Gas
CRG .... Classification Research Group (British)
CRG .... Cosmic Ray Gas
CRH .... Canal-Randolph Corp. (NYSE symbol)
CRH .... Control Relay, Hand
CRH .... Council on Religion and the Homosexual
CRHH ...... Cold Rolled Half Hard
CRHS ...... Competent Reliability History Survey (Navy)
CRI .... Caribbean Research Institute (College of the Virgin Islands)
CRI .... Carpet and Rug Institute (Formerly, ACI)
CRI .... Cellulose Research Institute (Syracuse University)
CRI .... Centre de Recherches et d'Irradiations (France)
CRI .... Christian Research Institute
CRI .... Circuit Reliability Improvement
CRI .... Collins Radio Company (NYSE symbol)
CRI .... Committee for Reciprocity Information (A federal government body)
CRI .... Communications Research Institute
CRI .... Complex Refraction Index
CRI .... Composer Recordings, Incorporated (Recording label)
CRI .... Conflict Resolution Inventory (Psychology)
CR & I ..... Chicago River and Indiana Railroad Company
CRIA ...... Committee to Rescue Italian Art
CRIA ...... Council on Religion and International Affairs
CRIC ...... Canonici Regulares Immaculate Conceptionis (Canons Regular of the Immaculate Conception)
CRICISAM ... Center for Research in College Instruction of Science and Mathematics
CRICKET ..... Cold Rocket Instrument Carrying Kit
CRICO ...... Committee for the Revision of the Criminal Code (Allied German Occupation Forces)
CRIFO ...... Civilian Research, Interplanetary Flying Objects
CRIG ...... Capacitor Rate-Integrating Gyroscope
CRIL ...... Consolidated Repairable Item List
CRIM ...... Criminal
CRIME ...... Censorship Records and Information (Middle East, Military)
CRIO ...... COMSEC (Communications Security) Regional Issuing Office (Military)
CRI & P ..... Chicago, Rock Island and Pacific Railway Company
CRIS .... Command Retrieval Information System
CRIS .... Council for Religion in Independent Schools
CRIS .... Counterintelligence Records Information System (Army)
CRIS .... Current Research Information System (Department of Agriculture)
CRISCO ..... Cream Received in Separating Cottonseed Oil
CRITHOUS.... Critical Housing Shortage at (named place) (Army)
CRITICOMM ... Critical Intelligence Communications System (Air Force)
CRJE ...... Conversational Remote Job Entry (Data processing)
CRJWA ...... Council of Religious Jewish Workers of America
CRK .... Campbell Red Lake Mines, Ltd. (NYSE symbol)
CRK .... Clean Room Kit
CRL .... Cadmium Red Line
CRL .... Cambridge Research Laboratory
CRL .... Canonici Regulares Lateranenses (Canons Regular of the Lateran)
CRL .... Cathode Ray Lamp
CRL .... Center for Research Libraries
CRL .... Certified Record Librarian
CRL .... College & Research Libraries (Official journal of ACRL)
CRL .... Control Relay Latch
CRLA ...... California Rural Legal Assistance (Antipoverty program)
CRLA ...... Crater Lake National Park
CRLLB ...... Center for Research on Language and Language Behavior (University of Michigan)
CRLR ...... Chemical & Radiological Laboratories (Army)
CRLT ...... Central Research Laboratory of Tashiba

CRM . . . . Centre de Reflexion sur le Monde Non Occidental (Center for the Study of the Non-Occidental World)
CRM . . . . Change Request Material
CRM . . . . Chief Radioman (Navy rating)
CRM . . . . Clerici Regulares Minores (Clerks Regular Minor, Mariani)
CRM . . . . Clinch River Mile (AEC)
CRM . . . . Cloud-Croft Radiation Measurement
CRM . . . . Combat Readiness Medal
CRM . . . . Command Receiver Monitor
CRM . . . . Communications/Research/Machines, Inc. (Publisher)
CRM . . . . Conceptual Reference Mission (NASA)
CRM . . . . Confusion Reflector Material
CRM . . . . Control Relay Master
CRM . . . . Counter-RADAR Measures (or Missile)
CRM . . . . Counter Rate Meter (Radioactivity)
CRM . . . . Cross-Reacting Material (Immunology)
CR/M . . . . Crew Member
CRMA . . . . . . Commercial Refrigerator Manufacturers Association
CRMB . . . . . . Combined Raw Materials Board (US and Britain) (Washington)
CRMD . . . . . . Class for Retarded in Mental Development
CRMD . . . . . . Clerici Regulares Matris Dei (Clerks Regular of the Mother of God)
CRMI . . . . . . Clerici Regulares Ministrantes Infirmis (Clerks Regular Attendant on the Sick, Camillini, Camilliani)
CRMO . . . . . Craters of the Moon National Monument
CRMPT . . . . . Commendation Ribbon with Metal Pendant
CRMR . . . . . . Continuous-Reading Meter Relay
CRMS . . . . . . Center for Research in Management Science (University of California)
CRMSS . . . . . Central Registry of Magazine Subscription Solicitors
CRMWD . . . . . Colorado River Municipal Water District
CRN . . . . Carolina & Northwestern Railway Company (AAR code)
CRN . . . . Cermet Resistor Network
CRN . . . . Complement Requiring Neutralizing
cRNA . . . . . . Chromosomal Ribonucleic Acid (Genetics)
CRNC . . . . . . College Republican National Committee
CRO . . . . Carded for Record Only
CRO . . . . . . Cathode-Ray Oscilloscope or Oscillograph
CRO . . . . Central Records Office
CRO . . . . Chromally American Corp. (NYSE symbol)
CRO . . . . Civil Readjustment Officer
CRO . . . . Civilian Repair Organization (Aircraft)
CRO . . . . Contractor Resident Office
CROACUS . . . . Comite Regional Ouest-Africain pour la Conservation et l'Utilisation du Sol
CROC . . . . . . Committee for Rejection of Obnoxious Commercials
CROC . . . . . . Computer Review and Orientation Course
CROCP . . . . . Committee for Review of Our China Policy
C(RO & H) . . . Center (Regional Office and Hospital) (Veterans Administration)
C(RO & INS) . . Center (Regional Office and Insurance) (Veterans Administration)
CROP . . . . . . Christian Rural Overseas Program
CROS . . . . . . Computerized Reliability Organization System
CROS . . . . . . Contralateral Routing of Offside Signals (Hearing aid)
CROSS . . . . . Committee to Retain Our Segregated Schools (Group in Arkansas, organized to oppose STOP)
CROSS . . . . . Computerized Rearrangements of Special Subjects (or Subject Specialties)
CROSS . . . . . Counter Revolutionary Organization on Salvation and Service
CROSSBOW . . . Computer Retrieval of Organic Structures Based on Wiswesser
CROSSPATE . . . Coordinative Retrieval of Selectively Sorted Permuted Analogue-Title Entries (Data Processing)
CROW . . . . . . Counter-Rotating Optical Wedge
CROWCASS . . . Central Registry of War Criminals and Security Suspects (Organization which used crime detection methods to ferret out German war criminals) (World War II)
CRP . . . . Central R. R. of Pennsylvania (AAR code)
CRP . . . . Clauson Rolling Platform
CRP . . . . Committee to Re-Elect the President (Also, CREEP) (1972)
CRP . . . . Community Renewal Program
CRP . . . . Component Reliability Prediction
CRP . . . . Compton Recoil Particle
CRP . . . . Congregatio Reformatorium Praemonstratensium (Premonstratensians)
CRP . . . . Conservation Reserve Program
CRP . . . . Control and Reporting Post (RADAR) (Air Force)
CRP . . . . Controlled Referral Plan
CRP . . . . Cooperative Research Program (Military and US Office of Education)
CRP . . . . Cosmic Ray Particle
CRP . . . . Cost Reduction Program
CRP . . . . Creative Protein
CRP . . . . Cryogenic Refrigerator Program
CRPAG . . . . . Calendar Reform Political Action Group
CRPB . . . . . . Comite de Relevement du Peuple Bassa (Committee for the Aid of the Bassa People)
CRPL . . . . . . Central Radio Propagation Laboratory

CRPM . . . . . . Combined Registered Publication Memoranda
CRPM . . . . . . Communication Registered Publication Memoranda
CRPO . . . . . . Consolidated Reserve Personnel Office (Air Force)
CRQ . . . . Commutation of Rations and Quarters (Military)
CRQ . . . . Current Requirements
CRR . . . . Carrier Corporation (NYSE symbol)
CRR . . . . Center for Radiation Research (National Bureau of Standards)
CRR . . . . Chinese Refugee Relief
CRR . . . . Churchill Research Range (Air Force)
CRR . . . . Clinchfield R. R. (AAR code)
CRR . . . . Clutter Rejection RADAR
CRR . . . . Consumer's Reliability Risk
CRR . . . . Cost Reduction Report
CRRC . . . . . . Cold Regions Research Company
CRREL . . . . . Cold Regions Research and Engineering Laboratory (Army)
CRRI . . . . . . Central Rice Research Institute (India)
CRRL . . . . . . Contour Rolls
CRR of NJ . . . Central Railroad Company of New Jersey
CRRS . . . . . . Combat Readiness Rating System (Air Force)
CRS . . . . Calibration Requirements Summary
CRS . . . . Camp Reception Station (A kind of field hospital) (British)
CRS . . . . Career Reserve Status (Air Force)
CRS . . . . Carolina Southern Railway Company (AAR code)
CRS . . . . Carpenter Technology Corp. (Formerly, Carpenter Steel Company) (NYSE symbol)
CRS . . . . Catholic Relief Services
CRS . . . . Catholic Renascence Society
CRS . . . . Center for Radiation Research (National Bureau of Standards)
CRS . . . . Centralized Referral System
CRS . . . . Chain RADAR System
CRS . . . . Child Rearing Study
CRS . . . . Chinese Restaurant Syndrome (Malady affecting some people while eating in Chinese restaurants)
CRS . . . . Clericorum Regularium Somaschensium (Somascan Fathers) (Roman Catholic religious order)
CRS . . . . Coarse
CRS . . . . Cold Rolled Steel
CRS . . . . Community Relations Service (Department of Justice)
CRS . . . . Compagnies Republicaines de Securite (France)
CRS . . . . Congressional Research Service (Formerly, Legislative Reference Service) (Library of Congress)
CRS . . . . Cooperative Recreation Service
CRS . . . . Cosmic Ray Shower
CRS . . . . Countermeasures Receiving Set
CRS . . . . Creation Research Society
CRS . . . . Crew Reserve Status (Military)
CRSD . . . . . . Contractor Required Shipment Date
CRSG . . . . . . Classification Research Study Group
CRSI . . . . . . Concrete Reinforcing Steel Institute
CRS-NCWC . . . Catholic Relief Services - National Catholic Welfare Conference (Later, Catholic Relief Services - US Catholic Conference)
CRSP . . . . . . Clerici Regulares Pauperum Matris Dei Scholarum Piarum (Clerks Regular of the Poor Men of the Mother of God for Pious Schools; Piarists)
CRSP . . . . . . Clerici Regulares Sancti Pauli (Barnabites)
CRSP . . . . Colorado River Storage Project (Department of the Interior)
CRSP . . . . Criminally Receiving Stolen Property
CRSR . . . . . . Center for Radiophysics and Space Research (Cornell University)
CRSS . . . . . . Chemically Rigidized Space Structure
CRSS . . . . . . Collectors of Religion on Stamps Society
CRSTPA . . . . . Columbia River Salmon and Tuna Packers Association
CRT . . . . C-Band RADAR Transponder
CRT . . . . Cathode-Ray Tube
CRT . . . . Cathode-Ray Typesetting
CRT . . . . Certain-teed Products Corporation (NYSE symbol)
CRT . . . . Charactron Tube
CRT . . . . Chief Radio Technician (Navy rating)
CRT . . . . Clerici Regulares Theatini (Theatines)
CRT . . . . Cold-Rolled and Tempered (Metals)
CRT . . . . Combat Rated Thrust (Navy)
CRT . . . . Combat Reaction Time
CRT . . . . Combat Readiness Training or Trainer
CRT . . . . Combined Radiation Test
CRT . . . . Counter Recovery Time
CRTC . . . . . . Cavalry Replacement Training Center
CRTO . . . . . . Cathode Ray Tube Oscillograph
CRTOG . . . . . Cartographer (or Cartography)
CRTS . . . . . . Cathode Ray Tube Shield
CRTS . . . . . . Constant Returns to Scale (Econometrics)
CRTS . . . . . . Controllable RADAR Target Simulator
CRTT . . . . Cathode Ray Tube Tester
CRTU . . . . . . Combined Receiving and Transmitting Unit

CRTV . . . . Composite Reentry Test Vehicle
CRU . . . . Collective Reserve Unit (International finance)
CRU . . . . Combined Rotating Unit (AEC)
CRU . . . . Computer Resource Unit
CRU . . . . Control Relay Unlatch
CRUBATFOR . . . Cruisers, Battle Force (Navy)
CRUD . . . . Chalk River Unidentified Deposit
CRUDESPAC . . Cruiser-Destroyer Force, Pacific Fleet (Navy symbol)
CRUDIV . . . . . Cruiser Division (Navy)
CRUEI . . . . Centre Italien pour les Relations Universitaires avec l'Etranger (Italy)
CRUEL . . . . . . Commission on Reform of Undergraduate Education and Living (University of Illinois)
CRUITNOP . . . . Recruiting Station and Office of Naval Officer Procurement
CRUITSTA . . . . Recruiting Station
CRULANT . . . . Cruiser Force, Atlantic Fleet (Navy symbol)
CRULANTFLT . . Cruisers, Atlantic Fleet
CRUPAC . . . . . Cruisers, Pacific Fleet
CRUPACFLT . . . Cruisers, Pacific Fleet
CRU SCO FOR . . Cruiser Scouting Force
CRUSCORON . . Cruiser Scouting Squadron
CRUSK . . . . . . Center for Research on Utilization of Scientific Knowledge (University of Michigan)
CRUZEIRO . . . Servicos Aereos Cruzeiro do Sul
CRV . . . . Certificate of Reasonable Value (Veterans Administration)
CRV . . . . Chrome Vanadium
CRV . . . . Comment Recevez-Vous?
CRV . . . . Committee of Returned Volunteers
CRV . . . . Conditional Release Violator (FBI standardized term)
CRW . . . . Community Radio Watch
CRW . . . . Crowell-Collier & Macmillan Inc. (NYSE symbol)
CRWA . . . . . . Community Resources Workshop Association
CRWAD . . . . . . Conference of Research Workers in Animal Diseases
CRWM . . . . . . Committee on Radioactive Waste Management
CRWMP . . . . . Commendation Ribbon with Metal Pendant (US)
CRWO . . . . . . Coding Room Watch Officer (Navy)
CRWP . . . . . . Census Registration Working Party (US Military Government, Germany)
CRWRC . . . . . . Christian Reformed World Relief Committee
CRYPTA . . . . . Cryptanalysis (Air Force)
CRYPTO . . . . . Cryptographic (or Cryptography)
CRZ . . . . Close Reconnaissance Zone (Army)
CRZWTR . . . . . Cruise Well to Right (Aviation)
CRZZ . . . . . . Centralna Rada Zwiazkow Zawodowych (Central Council of Trade Unions) (Poland)
CS . . . . Cable Ship (Followed by name of cable-laying ship)
CS . . . . Call Sign
CS . . . . Capital Stock
CS . . . . Carbon Steel
CS . . . . Carrier Stability
CS . . . . Cast Steel
CS . . . . Cast Stone
CS . . . . Caught Stealing (Baseball)
CS . . . . Cechoslovakische Statistik (Czechoslovakia)
CS . . . . Center Section
CS . . . . Center Stage (A stage direction)
CS . . . . Centistere (Metric)
cs . . . . Centistoke
CS . . . . Centrifugal Spraying
CS . . . . Cephalic Sinus
CS . . . . Cesarean Section (Medicine)
Cs . . . . Cesium (Chemical element)
CS . . . Change Sheet (Marine Corps)
CS . . . . Channel Status
CS . . . . Characteristic Slope
CS . . . . Check Sorter
CS . . . . Chief of Section
CS . . . . Chief of Staff (Army, Air Force)
CS . . . . Christian Science
CS . . . . Cirrostratus (Meteorology)
CS . . . . Cities Service Company (NYSE symbol)
CS . . . . Civil Service
CS . . . . Clear and Subtract
CS . . . . Clerk to the Signet (British)
CS . . . . Close Support (Army)
CS . . . . Closed Shell
CS . . . . Clymer System
CS . . . . Coaling Station (As part of a symbol)
CS . . . . Coco Solo, Canal Zone
CS . . . . Cognitive Stimulation (Experimental psychology)
CS . . . . Cognizance Symbol
CS . . . . Colla Sinistra (With the Left Hand)
CS . . . . Color Specification

CS . . . . Colorado & Southern Railway Company (AAR code)
CS . . . . Command Selector
CS . . . . Commissary Store (Navy)
CS . . . . Commissaryman (Navy rating)
CS . . . . Commit Stop
CS . . . . Common Slavic (Language)
CS . . . . Common and Standard (Items)
CS . . . . Common Steel (Projectile)
CS . . . . Communication Station
CS . . . . Communications System
CS . . . . Community Service
CS . . . . Company of the Savior (Roman Catholic women's religious order)
CS . . . . Complex Spikes
CS . . . . Component Specification
CS . . . . Composite Service (Army)
CS . . . . Concurrent Stereometric (A discrimination task)
CS . . . . Conditioned Stimulus (Psychology)
CS . . . . Conestoga Society
CS . . . . Congregatio Missionariorum a Sancto Carlo (Congregation of the Missionary Fathers of St. Charles) (Formerly, PSSC) (Roman Catholic religious order)
CS . . . . Contract Surgeon (Military)
CS . . . . Contracts Station
CS . . . . Control Scanner
CS . . . . Control Set
CS . . . . Control Signal
CS . . . . Convergent Stereoscopic (Photography)
CS . . . . Cooperative Society
CS . . . . Copper or Steel (Freight)
CS . . . . Core Shift
CS . . . . Corticosteroid (Endocrinology)
CS . . . . Cost Sharing
CS . . . . Counselor Structured
CS . . . . Counter-Sabotage
CS . . . . Counting Switch
CS . . . . Court of Session
CS . . . . Cross-Section
CS . . . . Cruiser Squadron
CS . . . . Ctenidial Sinus
CS . . . . Cumulative Sun
CS . . . . Current Series (Army)
CS . . . . Current Source
CS . . . . Current Strength
CS . . . . Custos Sigilli (Keeper of the Seal) (British)
CS . . . . Cutting Specification
CS . . . . Cycle Shift
CS . . . . Scout Cruiser (Navy symbol)
C/S . . . . Call Sign (or Signal) (Radio)
C/S . . . . Certificate of Service (Military)
C/S . . . . Change of Status
C/S . . . . Chief of Staff
C/S . . . . Cycles Per Second (Also see Hz) (Aviation)
C & S . . . . Colorado and Southern Railway Company
C and S . . . . . Clean and Sober (Slang)
C of S . . . . . . Chief of Section
C of S . . . . . . Chief of Staff (Army)
C to S . . . . . . Carting to Shipside
CS3 . . . . Combat Service Support System
C3S . . . . College Chemistry Consultants Service
C3S . . . . Curriculum Committee on Computer Science (of the Association for Computing Machinery)
CSA . . . . Canadian Standards Association
CSA . . . . Caricaturists Society of America
CSA . . . . Catalog Services Association
CSA . . . . Catch Society of America
CSA . . . . Cebu Stevedores Association (Philippines)
CSA . . . . Central Supply Association
CSA . . . . Ceskoslovenske Aerolinie (Czechoslovak Airline)
CSA . . . . Chief Special Artificer (Navy rating)
CSA . . . . Chief of Staff, United States Army
CSA . . . . China Society of America
CSA . . . . Chopper Stabilized Amplifier
CSA . . . . Cigar Smokers of America
CSA . . . . College Stores Association
CSA . . . . Combat Surveillance Agency (Signal Corps)
CSA . . . . Commercial Service Area (Military)
CSA . . . . Commercial-Service Authorization (Military)
CSA . . . . Communications Service Authorization
CSA . . . . Community Service Activities (AFL-CIO)
CSA . . . . Community Services Administration (HEW)
CSA . . . . Confederate Stamp Alliance

CSA . . . . Confederate States of America
CSA . . . . Confederate States Army
CSA . . . . Confederation Syndicale Africaine (African Trade Union Confederation)
CSA . . . . Configuration Status Accounting
CSA . . . . Conical Scan Antenna
CSA . . . . Conseil Scientifique pour l'Afrique au Sud de Sahara (Scientific Council for Africa South of the Sahara)
CSA . . . . Consular Shipping Adviser
CSA . . . . Correctional Service Associates
CSA . . . . Cross Service Agreement
CSA . . . . Current Source Amplifier
CSA . . . . Cymbidium Society of America
CSA . . . . Czechoslovak Society of America
CSA . . . . Sisters of the Congregation of St. Agnes (Roman Catholic religious order)
C of SA . . . . . Chief of Staff, Army
CSAA . . . . Child Study Association of America
CSAB . . . . . . California Strawberry Advisory Board
CSAB . . . . . . Combined Shipping Adjustment Board (World War II)
CSAC . . . . . . Cameron State Agricultural College (Oklahoma)
CSAC . . . . . . Central Ships Alignment Console (Navy)
CSAC . . . . . . Citizens Stamp Advisory Committee (US Postal Service)
CSAC . . . . . . Civil Service Association of Canada
CSAC . . . . . . Connors State Agricultural College (Oklahoma)
CSAD . . . . . . Capsule Systems Advanced Development
CSAD . . . . . . Chief Special Artificer, Synthetic Training Devices (Navy rating)
CSAF . . . . . . Chief of Staff, United States Air Force
CSAFM . . . . . Chief of Staff Air Force Memorandum
CSAGI . . . . . . Comite Special de l'Annee Geophysique Internationale (Special Committee for the International Geophysical Year) (Superseded by CIG)
CSAI . . . . Chief Special Artificer, Instruments (Navy rating)
CSAITR . . . . . Chief Special Artificer, Instruments, Typewriter and Office Equipment Repairman (Navy rating)
CSAIWR . . . . . Chief Special Artificer, Instruments, Watch Repairman (Navy rating)
CSAM . . . . . . Chief of Staff, Army Memorandum (Air Force)
CSAO . . . . . . Chief Special Artificer, Optical (Navy rating)
CSAR . . . . . . Communications Satellite Advanced Research (AFSC)
CSARS . . . . . . Close Support Artillery Rocket System
CSASA . . . . . Czechoslovak Society of Arts and Sciences in America
CSATC . . . . . Climb so as to Cross (Aviation)
CSATR . . . . . Climb so as to Reach (Aviation)
CSAV . . . . . . Compania Sud America de Vapores (Chilean Line)
CSB . . . . Bachelor of Christian Science
CSB . . . . Catholic Slovak Brotherhood
CSB . . . . Center Stage Back (A stage direction)
CSB . . . . Central Statistical Board (Functions taken over by Bureau of the Budget, 1940)
CSB . . . . Christian Science Teacher
CSB . . . . Civil Service Board
CSB . . . . College of Saint Benedict (Minnesota)
CSB . . . . Combined S-Band
CSB . . . . Combustible Storage Building
CSB . . . . Committee for Safe Bicycling
CSB . . . . Concrete Splash Block (Technical drawings)
CSB . . . . Congregatio Sancti Basilii (Basilians)
CSB . . . . Congregation of St. Brigid (Roman Catholic women's religious order)
CSB . . . . Consolidated Spot (TV) Buying (General Foods advertising)
CSB . . . . Copper Shielding Braid
CSBA . . . . . . Columbia Sheep Breeders Association of America
CSBN . . . . . . Captured Steam Bubble Nuclear
CSC . . . . Cadmium-Sulfide Cell
CSC . . . . Cardinal Stritch College (Wisconsin)
CSC . . . . Cartel des Syndicats Caledoniens (Federation of New Caledonian Trade Unions)
CSC . . . . Cartridge Storage Case
CSC . . . . Central Security Control (Military)
CSC . . . . Central State College (Ohio, Oklahoma)
CSC . . . . Change Schedule Chart
CSC . . . . Child Safety Council
CSC . . . . Children's Self-Conceptions Test
CSC . . . . Christian Service Corps
CSC . . . . Citizens' Service Corps
CSC . . . . Civil Service Club (British)
CSC . . . . Civil Service Commission
CSC . . . . Civilian Screening Center
CSC . . . . Classic Stage Company
CSC . . . . Clock Start Command
CSC . . . . Clothing and Survival Equipment Change (Navy)
CSC . . . . Coastal Surveillance Center
CSC . . . . Coil Stock Cradle
CSC . . . . College of Saint Catherine (Minnesota)
CSC . . . . Colorado State College (Later, University of Northern Colorado)

CSC . . . . Combat Support Company (Army)
CSC . . . . Combined Shipbuilding Committee (World War II)
CSC . . . . Command Selector Control
CSC . . . . Command and Staff College (Air Force)
CSC . . . . Commercial Solvents Corporation
CSC . . . . Commercial Steamship Company
CSC . . . . Commonwealth Scientific Committee
CSC . . . . Commonwealth Service Corps
CSC . . . . Communications Satellite Corporation
CSC . . . . Communications Sub Committee (Allied German Occupation Forces)
CSC . . . . Communications Switchboard Console
CSC . . . . Communications Systems Center
CSC . . . . Comprehensive Self-Check (Computer)
CSC . . . . Computer Sciences Corporation (NYSE symbol)
CSC . . . . Computer Systems Command (Army) (Also, ACSC)
CSC . . . . COMSAT Corporation
CSC . . . . Concordia Seminary College (Missouri)
CSC . . . . Confederation des Syndicats Chretiens de Belgique (Confederation of Christian Trade Unions) (Belgium)
CSC . . . . Congregatio a Sancta Cruce (Fathers and Brothers of Holy Cross)
CSC . . . . Congressional Secretaries Club
CSC . . . . Consolidation Coal Company (NYSE symbol) (Delisted)
CSC . . . . Conspicuous Service Cross (British)
CSC . . . . Construction Scheduling and Coordination (AT & T)
CSC . . . . Continental Shelf Crawler
CSC . . . . Continuous Service Certificate (Navy)
CSC . . . . Cosecant
CSC . . . . Cryogenic Storage Container
CSC . . . . Culver Stockton College (Missouri)
CSC . . . . Cylinder Stroke Control
CS/C . . . . Combined Station/Center (Aviation)
C & SC . . . . . Capitals and Small Capitals (Printing)
CSCA . . . . . . Central States College Association
CSCAA . . . . . College Swimming Coaches Association of America
C-SCAN . . . . . Carrier System for Control Approach of Naval Aircraft
CSCC . . . . . . Confederation des Syndicats Chretiens du Congo (Confederation of Christian Syndicates of the Congo) (Leopoldville)
CSCC . . . . . . Council of State Chambers of Commerce
CSCE . . . . . . Conference on Security and Cooperation in Europe
CSCF . . . . . . California State College at Fresno
CSCFE . . . . . Civil Service Council for Further Education (British)
CSCH . . . . . . Cosecant, Hyperbolic
CSChE . . . . . Canadian Society for Chemical Engineering
CSCJ . . . . . . Center for Studies in Criminal Justice
CSCLK . . . . . Chief Ship's Clerk
CSCNC . . . . . Committee on Scholarly Communications with Mainland China
CScO . . . . . . Chief Scientific Officer (Ministry of Agriculture, Fisheries, and Food) (Also, CSO) (British)
C-SCOPE . . . . Cathode-Ray Screen (Air Force)
CSCS . . . . . . Civil Service Cooperative Society (British)
CSCS . . . . . . Cost Schedule and Control System
CSCSL . . . . . Coe's Scrapbook Clipping Service of Laingsburg
CS & CSS . . . . Christmas Seal and Charity Stamp Society
CSCU . . . . . . Countersink Cutter
CSCW . . . . . . Church Society for College Work
CSD . . . . Calibrated Sweep Delay
CSD . . . . Children's Services Division (of ALA)
CSD . . . . Christian Science Teacher (Used only by those teachers who had received instruction directly from Mary Baker Eddy)
CSD . . . . Civil Service Department (British)
CSD . . . . Command Signal Decoder
CSD . . . . Constant-Speed Drives
CSD . . . . Contract Support Detachment
CSD . . . . Cortical Spreading Depression
CSD . . . . Crew Systems Division (NASA)
CSD . . . . Doctor of Christian Science
CSDH . . . . . . Council of Societies in Dental Hypnosis
CSDI . . . . . . Center for the Study of Democratic Institutions
CSDIC . . . . . Combined Services Detailed Interrogation Center
CSDICNOI . . . Combined Services Detailed Interrogation Center-- Non-Operational Intelligence
CSDP . . . . . . Command Supply Discipline Program (Army)
CSDP . . . . . . Coordinated Ship Development Plan (Navy)
CSDP . . . . . . Customer Service Department Procedure
CSDR . . . . . . Cross Section Data Reduction
CSDS . . . . . . Communication Signal Distribution System
CSDS . . . . . . Constant Speed Drive/Starter
CSE . . . . Certificate of Secondary Education (British)
CSE . . . . Civil and Sanitary Engineering
CSE . . . . Cold Start Entry (Data processing)
CSE . . . . College of Saint Elizabeth (New Jersey)

CSE . . . . Commission on Science Education
CSE . . . . Communications Support Element (Military)
CSE . . . . Competitive Study Engineer
CSE . . . . Containment Systems Experiment (AEC)
CSE . . . . Control and Switching Equipment (RADAR)
CSE . . . . Control Systems Engineering
CSE . . . . Core Storage Element
CSEA . . . . California State Electronics Association
CSEA . . . . Civil Service Employees Association
CSEC . . . . Clothing and Survival Equipment Change
CSED . . . . Consolidated Ship Electronic Design (Navy)
CSED . . . . Coordinated Ship Electronic Design
CSEERI . . . . . . Comite Scientifique pour l'Etude des Effets des Radiations Ionisantes
CSEIP . . . . Center for the Study of the Evaluation of Instructional Programs
CS En . . . . Certificate in Sales Engineering
CSEP. . . . . Communications Security Education Program
CSEU . . . . Confederation of Shipbuilding and Engineering Unions (British)
CSF . . . . Caribbean Sea Frontier
CSF . . . . Casualty Staging Facility (Military)
CSF . . . . Center Stage Front (A stage direction)
CSF . . . . Central Switching Facility
CSF . . . . Cerebrospinal Fluid
CSF . . . . Chi-Squared Function
CSF . . . . Chief Shipfitter (Navy rating)
CSF . . . . Civil Service Forum
CSF . . . . College of Saint Francis (Illinois)
CSF . . . . Combat Support Force
CSF . . . . Community Systems Foundation
CSF . . . . Compagnie de Telegraphie Sans Fil (Electronics concern) (France)
CSF . . . . Correctional Service Federation - USA
CSF . . . . Cylindrically Symmetrical Field
CSFA . . . . California School of Fine Arts
CSFA . . . . Citizens' Scholarship Foundation of America
CSFCBM . . . . . Chief Shipfitter, Construction Battalion, Mechanical Draftsman (Navy rating)
CSFCBP. . . . . . Chief Shipfitter, Construction Battalion, Pipe Fitter and Plumber (Navy rating)
CSFCBR. . . . . . Chief Shipfitter, Construction Battalion, Rigger (Navy rating)
CSFCBS . . . . . Chief Shipfitter, Construction Battalion, Steel Worker (Navy rating)
CSFCBW . . . . . Chief Shipfitter, Construction Battalion, Welder (Navy rating)
CSFI. . . . . Company Standard Form Instruction
CSFPSC. . . . . . Commander, Subordinate Command, Service Force Pacific Fleet (Navy rating)
CSFSR . . . . . . Chief Shipfitter, Ship Repair (Navy rating)
CSFSRP . . . . . Chief Shipfitter, Ship Repair, Pipe Fitter and Plumber (Navy rating)
CSFSRW . . . . . Chief Shipfitter, Ship Repair, Welder (Navy rating)
CSG. . . . . Combat Service Group (Army)
CSG. . . . . Combined Studies Group (Central Intelligence Agency operation in Southeast Asia)
CSG. . . . . Console Set Group
CSG. . . . . Control Synthetic Gas (Process)
CSG. . . . . Council of State Governments
CSGB. . . . . . . Cartophilic Society of Great Britain
CSGp . . . . Combat Support Group (Air Force)
CSGUS . . . . . Clinical Society of Genito-Urinary Surgeons
CSH . . . . College of the Sacred Heart (Puerto Rico)
CSHS . . . . Chief Superintendent of Hydrographic Supplies
CSI . . . . Canned Salmon Institute
CSI . . . . Cellulose Sponge Institute
CSI . . . . Center for the Study of Instruction (of NEA)
CsI. . . . . Cesium Iodide
CSI . . . . Chemical Substructure Index (Trademark)
CSI . . . . Coelliptic Sequence Initiation (Aerospace)
CSI . . . . Colonial Stores, Incorporated (NYSE symbol)
CSI . . . . Commission Sericicole Internationale (International Sericultural Commission)
CSI . . . . Companion of the Star of India
CSI . . . . Company Source Inspection
CSI . . . . Concentric Sequence Initiation (Aerospace)
CSI . . . . Construction Specifications Institute
CSI . . . . Construction Surveyors Institute
CSI . . . . Contractor Standard Item
CSI. . . . . CONUS (Continental United States) Sustaining Increment (Army)
CSI . . . . Correct Seating Institute
CSI . . . . Counseling Satisfaction Inventory (Education)
CSIGC . . . . . . Chief, Signal Corps (Army)
CSIGO . . . . . . Chief Signal Officer
CSIP. . . . . Comprehensive School Improvement Project
CSIR . . . . Corpo di Spedizione Italiano in Russia
CSIR . . . . Council for Scientific and Industrial Research (South Africa)
CSIRO . . . . . . Commonwealth Scientific and Industrial Research Organisation (British Commonwealth)

CSIRT . . . . . . Comite Scientifique International de Recherches sur les Trypanosomiases
CSISRS . . . . . Cross-Section Information Storage and Retrieval System (AEC)
CSIT. . . . . Comite Sportif International du Travail (International Workers Sport Committee)
CSJ . . . . Congregatio Sancti Joseph (Congregation of St. Joseph) (Roman Catholic men's religious order)
CSJCA . . . . . . Central Sephardic Jewish Community of America
CSK . . . . Cable Splicing Kit
CSK . . . . Cathodic Survey Kit
CSK . . . . Chesapeake Corporation of Virginia (NYSE symbol)
CSK . . . . Chief Storekeeper
CSK . . . . Comite Special du Katanga
CSK . . . . Cooperative Study of the Kuroshio (UNESCO)
CSKCB . . . . . Chief Storekeeper, Construction Battalion, Stevedore (Navy rating)
CSKD . . . . . . Chief Storekeeper, Disbursing (Navy rating)
CSKH . . . . . . Countersunk Head
CSKO. . . . . . . Countersink Other Side
CSKT . . . . . . Chief Storekeeper, Technical (Navy rating)
CSKV . . . . . . Chief Storekeeper, Aviation (Navy rating)
CSL . . . . Carlisle Corporation (NYSE symbol)
CSL . . . . Chicago Short Line Railway Company (AAR code)
CSL . . . . Coaxial Slotted Line
CSL . . . . Coles Signal Laboratory (Army)
CSL . . . . Combat Surveillance Laboratory
CSL . . . . Command Signal Limiter
CSL . . . . Comparative Systems Laboratory (Case-Western Reserve University)
CSL . . . . Computer Sensitive (or System) Language (Data processing)
CSL . . . . Confederazione Somala dei Lavoratori (Somali Workers Confederation)
CSL . . . . Conseil Superieur de Livre (Canada)
CSL . . . . Console
CSL . . . . Control and Simulation Language
CSL . . . . Control Systems Laboratory (University of Illinois)
CSL . . . . Co-ordinated Science Laboratory (University of Illinois)
CSLA . . . . . . Church and Synagogue Library Association
CSLC . . . . . . Confederation des Syndicats Libres du Congo (Leopoldville) (Merger of FGTK, APIC, SNTC) (Congolese Free Trade Union Federation)
CSLEA . . . . . . Center for the Study of Liberal Education for Adults
CSLP . . . . . . Center for Short-Lived Phenomena (Miami) (Smithsonian Institution)
CSLS . . . . . . Civil Service Legal Society (British)
CSM. . . . . Cast Metals Federation (Formerly, Gray and Ductile Iron Founders' Society, Malleable Founders' Society, and Steel Founders' Society of America)
CSM . . . . Cerebrospinal Meningitis (Medicine)
CSM . . . . Ceskoslovensky Svaz Mladeze (Czechoslovakia)
CSM . . . . Chief Signalman (Navy rating)
CSM . . . . Chief of Staff Memorandum (Military)
CSM . . . . Christian Science Monitor (A newspaper)
CSM. . . . . Close-Support Mission (Air Force)
CSM. . . . . Coaxial Switching Matrix
CSM. . . . . Coffin Strategic Missile
CSM. . . . . College of Saint Mary (Nebraska)
CSM. . . . . College of San Mateo (California)
CSM. . . . . Colorado School of Mines
CSM. . . . . Combustion Stability Monitor
CSM. . . . . Command and Service Module (NASA)
CSM. . . . . Commission for Synoptic Meteorology
CSM. . . . . Company Sergeant-Major
CSM. . . . . Composite Signal Mixer
CSM. . . . . Continental Shelf Mining
CSM . . . . Continuous Sampler Monitor (Radioactivity)
CSM . . . . Corn, Soybean, and Milk (Products) (Main ingredients of a formulated food)
CSM . . . . Corn Soybean Mixture
CSM . . . . Cottonseed Meal
CSM. . . . . Council of the Southern Mountains
CSM . . . . Council for the Study of Mankind
CSM . . . . Master of Christian Science
CSMA. . . . . . . Chemical Specialties Manufacturers Association
CSMC . . . . . . Catholic Students' Mission Crusade
CSMI . . . . . . Company Sergeant-Major Instructor (British Army)
CSMOL. . . . . . Control Station Manual Operating Level
CSMP. . . . . . . Continuous System Modeling Program (Computer)
CSMP. . . . . . . Current Ship's Maintenance Project
CSMPS . . . . . Computerized Scientific Management Planning System
CSMS . . . . . . College of Saint Mary of the Springs (Ohio)
CSMT. . . . . . . Circuit Switching Magnetic Tape
CSN . . . . Catholic Scholarships for Negroes
CSN. . . . . Cincinnati Bell Inc. (NYSE symbol)
CSN. . . . . Circuit Switching Network
CSN. . . . . Companhia Siderurgica Nacional (Steel producer) (Brazil)
CSN. . . . . Confederate States Navy

CSN . . . . Contract Serial Number
CSN . . . . Contract Surgeon (Military)
CSN . . . . Control Symbol Number
CSNF . . . . Common Source Noise Figure
CSNY . . . . Canadian Society of New York
CSN & Y . . . . Crosby, Stills, Nash, and Young (Rock music group)
CSNYS . . . . . Canal Society of New York State
CSO . . . . Central Selling Organization (London diamond exchange)
CSO . . . . Central Sign Off
CSO . . . . Central Statistical Office (British)
CSO . . . . Chained Sequential Operation
CSO . . . . Chemically Stable Oxide
CSO . . . . Chief Scientific Officer (Ministry of Agriculture, Fisheries, and Food) (Also, CScO) (British)
CSO . . . . Chief Signal Officer (Army)
CSO . . . . Chief Staff Officer
CSO . . . . Coastal States Organization
CSO . . . . Communication Standing Order
CSO . . . . Complex Safety Officer (Air Force)
CSO . . . . Cross Service Order (Military)
CSOM . . . . . . Chief SONARman (Navy rating)
CSOMH . . . . Chief SONARman, Harbor Defense
CSOP . . . . Commission to Study the Organization of Peace
CSP . . . . Camas Prairie R. R. (AAR code)
CSP . . . . Central Signal Processor
CSP . . . . Chaplain Service Personnel (Air Force)
CSP . . . . Chief Specialist (Navy rating)
CSP . . . . Coder Sequential Pulse
CSP . . . . Coherent Signal Processor
CSP . . . . Combined Staff Planners
CSP . . . . Combustion Engineering, Inc. (NYSE symbol)
CSP . . . . Communications Security Publication
CSP . . . . Community Shelter Plan (Civil Defense)
CSP . . . . Company Standard Practice
CSP . . . . Computer Simulation Program
CSP . . . . Concurrent Spare Parts
CSP . . . . Congregatio Sancti Pauli (Paulists) (Roman Catholic men's religious order)
CSP . . . . Contents of Selected Periodicals (A publication)
CSP . . . . Continuous Stratification Profiler
CSP . . . . Control Signal Processor (for spacecraft)
CSP . . . . Controlled Surface Porosity
CSP . . . . Controlled Surface Process
CSP . . . . Coproduction for Security Program (United States and Italy)
CSP . . . . Corporation Standard Practice
CSPA . . . . . . California State Psychological Association
CSPA . . . . . . Catholic School Press Association
CSPA . . . . . . Chesapeake Seafood Packers Association
CSPA . . . . . . Chief Specialist, Physical Training Instructor (Navy rating)
CSPA . . . . . . Clay Sewer Pipe Association
CSPA . . . . . . Columbia Scholastic Press Association
CSPAA . . . . . Columbia Scholastic Press Advisers Association
CSPAA . . . . . . Conference de Solidarite des Pays Afro-Asiatiques
CSPC . . . . . . California State Polytechnical College
CSPC . . . . . . Cost and Schedule Planning and Control
C/SPCS . . . . . Cost/Schedule Planning Control Specification
CSPG . . . . . . Common Source Power Gain
CSPHA . . . . . . Conference of State and Provincial Health Authorities of North America
CSPI . . . . Center for Science in the Public Interest (Formed by consumer-advocate Ralph Nader)
CSPI . . . . College Student Personnel Institute
CSPM . . . . . . Communication Security Publication Memorandum (Army)
CSPMP . . . . . Chief Specialist, Motion Picture Production (Navy rating)
CSPO . . . . . . Chief Specialist, Petroleum Inspector (Navy rating)
CSPO . . . . . . Communications Satellite Project Office
CSPOS . . . . . Community Shelter Planning Officer, State (Civil Defense)
CSPPHLD . . . . Conference of State and Provincial Public Health Laboratory Directors
CSPPLB . . . . . Chief Specialist, Laboratory (Navy rating)
CSPPPG . . . . . Chief Specialist, Photogrammetry (Navy rating)
CSPPVM . . . . Chief Specialist, V-Mail (Navy rating)
CSPR . . . . . . Chief Specialist, Identification (Navy rating)
CSPR . . . . . . Chief Specialist, Recruiter (Navy rating)
CSPS . . . . . . Chief Specialist, Personnel Supervisor (Navy rating)
CSPS . . . . . . Chief Specialist, Shore Patrol and Security (Navy rating)
CSPS . . . . . . Coherent Signal Processing System (Army)
CSPS . . . . . . Committee to Save the Peace Symbol (Student legal action organization)
CSPT . . . . . . Chief Specialist, Teacher (Navy rating)
CSP-T . . . . . . Contents of Selected Periodicals - Technical (A publication)
CSPTLT . . . . . Chief Specialist, Link Trainer Instructor (Navy rating)
C of SptS . . . . Chief of Support Services (Army)
CSPV . . . . . . Chief Specialist, Transport Airman (Navy rating)

CSPW . . . . . Chief Specialist, Chaplain's Assistant (Navy rating)
CSPX . . . . . Brothers of St. Pius X (Roman Catholic religious order)
CSPX . . . . . Chief Specialist, All Designators (Navy)
CSPY . . . . . . Chief Specialist, Control Tower Operator (Navy rating)
CSQ . . . . Coastal Sentry Quebec
CSQ . . . . Cryptofacility Security Questionnaire (Army)
CSR . . . . Center for Space Research (MIT)
CSR . . . . Central & South West Corporation (NYSE symbol)
CSR . . . . Certified Shorthand Reporter
CSR . . . . Chartered Stenographic Reporter
CSR . . . . Chief of Staff Regulations
CSR . . . . Civil Service Retirement
CSR . . . . Civil Service Rule
CSR . . . . Clamped Speed Regulator
CSR . . . . Coaxial Single-Pole Relay
CSR . . . . College of Saint Rose (New York)
CSR . . . . Combat Surveillance RADAR
CSR . . . . Communications Satellite Relay
CSR . . . . Conference on Science and Religion
CSR . . . . Configuration Selection Register
CSR . . . . Contract Status Report
CSR . . . . Copper Sulfide Rectifier
CSR . . . . Corps Specifications Revision
CSR . . . . Corrected Sedimentation Rate (Medicine)
CSR . . . . Critical Shortage Report
CSR . . . . Custom Spherical Resins
CSRC . . . . . . Communication Science Research Center (Battelle Memorial Institute)
CSRDF . . . . . Civil Service Retirement and Disability Fund
CSRO . . . . . . Consolidated Standing Route Order (Army)
CSRO . . . . . . Contract Service Rework Orders
CSRS . . . . . . Cooperative State Research Service (Department of Agriculture)
CSRV . . . . . . Civil Service Rifle Volunteers (British)
CSS . . . . CBPO (Consolidated Base Personnel Office) Strength Summary Card
CSS . . . . Certificate of Sanitary Science (Cambridge)
CSS . . . . Chicago South Shore & South Bend R. R. (AAR code)
CSS . . . . Chief of Support Services (Army)
CSS . . . . City Stores Company (NYSE symbol)
CSS . . . . Coded Switch System (to permit or deny the ability to arm nuclear weapons in strategic aircraft)
CSS . . . . College of Saint Scholastica (Minnesota)
CSS . . . . Color Sync Signal
CSS . . . . Combat Service Support (Army)
CSS . . . . Commit Sequence Summary
CSS . . . . Committee on State Sovereignty
CSS . . . . Commodity Stabilization Service (Name changed to Agricultural Stabilization and Conservation Service, 1961)
CSS . . . . Communications Subsystem
CSS . . . . Computer System Stimulator
CSS . . . . Confederate States Ship
CSS . . . . Confederated Spanish Societies
CSS . . . . Conference of State Societies
CSS . . . . Congregation of the Sacred Stigmata (Stigmatine Fathers and Brothers) (Roman Catholic religious order)
CSS . . . . Contractor Storage Site
CSS . . . . Control Stick Steering (Aviation)
CSS . . . . Coordinated Situation System
CSS . . . . Critical Shear Stress
CSSA . . . . . . Cactus and Succulent Society of America
CSSA . . . . . . Civil Science Systems Administration (Proposed for National Science Foundation)
CSSA . . . . . . Civil Service Supply Association (British)
CSSA . . . . . . Civilian Science Systems Administration (Proposed)
CSSA . . . . . . Clothing and Small Stores Account
CSSA . . . . . . Combat Service Support Area (Military)
CSSA . . . . . . Crop Science Society of America
CSSB . . . . . . Civilian Supervisory Selection Battery
CSSB . . . . . . Compatible Single Sideband
CSSCA . . . . . Circus Saints and Sinners Club of America
CSSCC . . . . . . Congregatio Sacratissimorum Cordium (Missionaries of the Sacred Hearts of Jesus and Mary)
CSSCO . . . . . Staff Communications Office, Office of the Chief of Staff (Army)
CSSDA . . . . . Council of Social Science Data Archives
CSSE . . . . . . Conference of State Sanitary Engineers
CSSEC . . . . . . Computer Systems Support and Evaluation Command
CSSF . . . . . . Clothing and Small Stores Fund
CSSF . . . . . . Congregation of the Sisters of St. Felix (Felician Sisters) (Roman Catholic religious order)
CSSG . . . . . . Combat Services Support Group (Army)
CSSI . . . . . . Coriolis Sickness Susceptibility Index (Orientation)
CSSJ . . . . . . Central States Speech Journal
CSSL . . . . . . Canada Steamship Lines R. R., Ltd. (AAR code)

CSSL . . . . Continuous System Simulation Language (Data processing)
CSSM . . . . . . Chief Ship's Service Man (Navy rating)
CSSMB . . . . . . Chief Ship's Service Man, Barber (Navy rating)
CSSMC . . . . . . Chief Ship's Service Man, Cobbler (Navy rating)
CSSML . . . . . . Chief Ship's Service Man, Laundryman (Navy rating)
CSSMT . . . . . . Chief Ship's Service Man, Tailor (Navy rating)
CSSN . . . . Common Source Spot Noise
CSSNF . . . . . . Common Source Spot Noise Figure
CSSO . . . . Consolidated Surplus Sales Office (Military - Merged with Defense Supply Agency)
CSSP . . . . Center for Studies of Suicide Prevention (National Institute of Mental Health)
CSSP. . . . . . . Combined Services Support Program (Navy)
CSSP . . . . . . Congregatio Sancti Spiritus (Fathers of the Holy Ghost)
CSSR . . . . Congregatio Sanctissimi Redemptoris (Redemptorists)
CSSR . . . . . . Consolidated Stock Status Report
CSSS . . . . Combat Service Support System (ADSAF)
CSSS . . . . . . Cross Spin Stabilization Systems
CSST. . . . . . . Compatible Sidelobe Suppression Technique
CSST . . . . . . Computer System Science Training (IBM)
CSSU . . . . . . Church Sunday School Union (British)
CST . . . . Capsule Systems Test (NASA)
CST . . . . . . Central Standard Time
CST . . . . . . Chief Steward (Navy rating)
CST . . . . College of Saint Teresa (Minnesota)
CST . . . . College of Saint Thomas (Minnesota)
CST . . . . Colloidal System Test
CST . . . . Combat Support Training (Military)
CST . . . . . . Combined Systems Test
CST . . . . . . Commit Start
CST . . . . . . Communications Surveillance Transistor
CST . . . . . . Complex Safety Technician (Air Force)
CST . . . . . . Conceptual Systems Test
CST . . . . . . Conical Shock Tube
CST . . . . . . Continuously Stirred Tank
CST . . . . . . Control System Test
CST . . . . . . Convulsive Shock Therapy
CST . . . . . . Council on Student Travel
CST . . . . . . Crystalline Style
CST . . . . . . Cycling Strength Test
CS/T . . . . . . Combined Station/Tower (Aviation)
CSTA . . . . . . Cloak and Suit Trucking Association
CSTA . . . . . . Combat Surveillance and Target Acquisition
CSTA . . . . . . Consolidating Station
CS & TAE . . . . Combat Surveillance and Target Acquisition Equipment (Military)
CSTAR . . . . . . Classified Scientific and Technical Aerospace Reports (NASA)
CSTATC . . . . . Combat Surveillance and Target Acquisition Training Command
CSTB . . . . . . Centre Scientifique et Technique du Batiment (Building research) (France)
CSTC . . . . . . Coppin State Teachers College (Maryland)
CSTDPHE. . . . . Conference of State and Territorial Directors of Public Health Education
CSTE . . . . . . Conference of State and Territorial Epidemiologists
CSTHOPHS . . . Conference of State and Territorial Health Officers with Public Health Service
CSTI. . . . . . . Chattanooga State Technical Institute (Tennessee)
CSTI. . . . . . . Clearinghouse for Scientific and Technical Information (Later, NTIS) (National Bureau of Standards)
CSTI. . . . . . . Control Surface Tie In
CStJ. . . . . . . Commander, Order of St. John of Jerusalem (British)
C-STOL . . . . . Controlled Short Takeoff and Landing (Acronym used for a type of aircraft) (Also, CTOL)
CSTP . . . . . . Cubic Centimeters at Standard Temperature and Pressure (Also CCSTP)
CSTPM & O . . . Chicago, St. Paul, Minneapolis and Omaha Railway Company
CSTR . . . . . . Continuously Stirred Tank Reactor
CSTU . . . . . . Combined Systems Test Unit
CSTV . . . . . . Confederation des Syndicats des Travailleurs du Viet-Nam (Confederation of Workers' Trade Unions of Viet-Nam) (South Vietnam)
CSU . . . . Casualty Staging Unit (Military)
CSU . . . . Central Statistical Unit (of VLRL)
CSU . . . . Central Switching Unit
CSU . . . . Christlich-Soziale Union (Political party in Bavaria connected with the CDU) (West Germany)
CSU . . . . Civil Service Union (British)
CSU . . . . Civilian Service Unit
CSU . . . . Colorado State University
CSU . . . . Combat Support Units (Army)
CSU . . . . Combined Shaft Unit
CSUCE . . . . . Conference of State Utility Commission Engineers
CSUSA . . . . . Copyright Society of the United States of America
CSV . . . . Cammed-Gear Speed Variator
CSV . . . . Cellular Size Volume
CSV . . . . Characteristic Statistical Value

CSV . . . . Clerici Sancti Viatoris (Clerics of St. Viateur) (Roman Catholic men's religious order)
CSV . . . . Conical Shell Vibration
CSV . . . . Corona Starting Voltage
CSVP . . . . . . Sisters of Charity of St. Vincent de Paul (Roman Catholic religious order)
CSW . . . . Command Surveillance and Weather
CSW . . . . Computing & Software, Inc. (NYSE symbol)
CSWE . . . . . . Council on Social Work Education
CSWI . . . . . . Commission for Synoptic Weather Information (IMO)
CSWP . . . . . . Civil Service Working Party (US Military Government, Germany)
CSWV . . . . . . Centraal Sociaal Werkgevers Verbond (Employers' organization) (Netherlands)
CSY . . . . Central Soya Company, Inc. (NYSE symbol)
CSZ . . . . Copper, Steel or Zinc (Freight)
CT . . . . Cable, Test
CT . . . . California Terms (Grain shipping)
CT . . . . Carbon Tetrachloride
CT . . . . Carrier Telephone Channel
CT . . . . Cartographer (Navy rating)
CT . . . . Casters and Towbar
CT . . . . Center Tap (Technical drawings)
CT . . . . Center Tap (of a winding) (Radio)
CT . . . . Central Time
CT . . . . Ceramic Tile (Technical drawings)
CT . . . . Certificated Teacher
CT . . . . Charge-Transfer (or intermolecular electron transfer)
CT . . . . Chief Telegrapher (Navy rating)
CT . . . . Chief of Transportation (Army)
CT . . . . China Theater (World War II)
CT . . . . Ciguatoxin
CT . . . . Circuit Theory
CT . . . . Clock Time
CT . . . . Close Tolerance
CT . . . . Coated Tablet (Pharmacy)
CT . . . . Code Telegram
CT . . . . Combat Team
CT . . . . Combined Trials (Shipbuilding)
CT . . . . Commercial Traveler
CT . . . . Communication Trench (Military)
CT . . . . Communications Technician
CT . . . . Communications Terminal
CT . . . . Compressed Tablet (Pharmacy)
CT . . . . Confirmatory Test (Army)
CT . . . . Connecticut
CT . . . . Connective Tissue
CT . . . . Contact Tension
CT . . . . Continuous Tone (Color printing)
CT . . . . Contour Template
CT . . . . Control Transformer
CT . . . . Corrective Therapist
CT . . . . Counter Timer
CT . . . . Crawler-Transporter
CT . . . . Critical Temperature
CT . . . . Crosstrail (Military)
CT . . . . Cubic Tonnage (Shipping)
CT . . . . Current Transformer
C/T . . . . Cable Transfer (of funds)
C & T . . . . . . Classification and Testing (Air Force)
C & T . . . . . . Contingency and Training (Army)
C of T . . . . . . Chief of Transportation (Army)
CTA . . . . Call Time Adjustor (Military communications)
CTA . . . . Caribbean Travel (formerly, Tourist) Association
CTA . . . . Chemical Toilet Association
CTA . . . . Chicago Transit Authority
CTA . . . . Children's Theatre Association (Formerly, CTC)
CTA . . . . Combined Target Area
CTA . . . . Committee on Thrombolytic Agents
CTA . . . . Common Table(s) of Allowances (Army)
CTA . . . . Communiquer a Toutes Adresses (To be circulated to all addresses)
CTA . . . . Contractor Technical Assistance
CTA . . . . Control Area (Aviation)
CTA . . . . Council for Technological Advancement
CTA . . . . Covered Threads Association
CTA . . . . Cum Testamento Annexo (With the Will Annexed)
CTAA . . . . . . Corporate Transfer Agents Association
CTAB . . . . . . Cetyltrimethylammonium Bromide
CTAF . . . . . . Crew Training Air Force
CTAL . . . . . . Confederacion de Trabajadores de America Latina (Confederation of Latin-American Workers)
CTAM . . . . . . Climb to and Maintain (Aviation)

CTAS . . . . Constant Temperature Anemometer System
CTAUA . . . . . . Catholic Total Abstinence Union of America
CTAX . . . . Climb to and Cross (Aviation)
CTB . . . . Calibration Test Box
CTB . . . . California Test Bureau (Psychology)
CTB . . . . Central Tracing Bureau (Post-World War II)
CTB . . . . Ceramic-Tile Base (Technical drawings)
CTB . . . . Coast Torpedo Boat (Navy symbol)
CTB . . . . Collateral Trust Bond
CTB . . . . Combined Travel Board (Allied German Occupation Forces)
CTB . . . . Command Telemetry Buoy
CTB . . . . Commercial Traffic Bulletin
CTB . . . . Companhia Telefonica Brasileira (A telecommunications company) (Brazil)
CTB . . . . Comprehensive Test Ban (of nuclear testing)
CTB . . . . Control Test Bed
CTB . . . . Controlled Temperature Bath
CTB . . . . Cooper Tire & Rubber Company (NYSE symbol)
CTBS . . . . Comprehensive Tests of Basic Skills
CTC . . . . Cam Timing Contact
CTC . . . . Carbon Tetrachloride
CTC . . . . Catholic Teachers College (Rhode Island)
CTC . . . . Central Training Council (Department of Employment) (British)
CTC . . . . Centralized Traffic Control (Railroad system)
CTC . . . . Certified Travel Counselor (Designation given by Institute of Certified Travel Agents)
CTC . . . . Chicago Teachers College
CTC . . . . Chicago Technical College
CTC . . . . Chief Turret Captain (Navy)
CTC . . . . Children's Theatre Conference (Later, CTA)
CTC . . . . Chlortetracycline (Antibiotic)
CTC . . . . Citizens' Training Corps
CTC . . . . Cleveland Trust Company
CTC . . . . Climate Test Chamber
CTC . . . . Cold Type Composition (Section of Printing Industries of America)
CTC . . . . Combined Training Center
CTC . . . . Compatibility Test Capsule
CTC . . . . Concordia Teachers College (Illinois, Nebraska)
CTC . . . . Constant Torque Compensation
CTC . . . . Continental Telephone Corporation (NYSE symbol)
CTC . . . . Continuity Test Current
CTC . . . . Controls Company of America (NYSE symbol) (Delisted)
CTC . . . . Counter Timer Control
CTC . . . . Cyclists' Touring Club
CT & C . . . . . . Quadripartite Trade & Commerce Committee (Allied German Occupation Forces)
CT & C . . . . . . Trade and Commerce Committee (US Military Government)
CTCA . . . . Cairn Terrier Club of America
CTCA . . . . Channel and Traffic Control Agency (of AACS)
CTCA . . . . Commission for Technical Cooperation for Africa
CTCC . . . . Change (or Changing) to Center Control (Aviation)
CTCC . . . . Contact Center Control (Aviation)
CTCC . . . . Continental Division, Transport Control Center (Hq)
CTCF . . . . Channel and Technical Control Facility (In a tape-relay station in the AIRCOMNET)
CTCI . . . . Classic Thunderbird Club International
CTCI . . . . Contract Technical Compliance Inspection
CTCLS . . . . . . Court of Claims
CTCP . . . . Contract Task Change Proposal
CTCS . . . . Consolidated Telemetry Checkout System (Air Force)
CTCU . . . . Channel and Traffic Control Unit (Subordinate unit of the Channel and Traffic Control Agency)
CTD . . . . Certified Test Data
CTD . . . . College Training Detachment
CTD . . . . Commander, Transportation Division
CTD . . . . Controlled Thermolytic Dissociation
CTD . . . . Council for Television Development
CTD . . . . Crew Task Demand
CTD . . . . Crew Task Detail
CTDA . . . . Custom Tailors and Designers Association of America
CTDC . . . . Chemical Thermodynamics Data Center (National Bureau of Standards)
CTDC . . . . Company Technical Document Center
CTDC . . . . Control Track Direction Computer
CTD (I) . . . . . . Truck Drivers, Chauffeurs and Helpers Union of Chicago and Vicinity
CTDS . . . . Code Translation Data System (Air Force)
CTDU . . . . Chicago Truck Drivers Union
CTE . . . . Car-Tours in Europe, Inc.
CTE . . . . Central Timing Equipment
CTE . . . . Central Translation Evidence
CTE . . . . Coefficient of Thermal Expansion
CTE . . . . Commander, Task Element
CTE . . . . Cross Track Error

CTEA . . . . Channel Transmission and Engineering Activation
CTF . . . . Canadian Teachers Federation
CTF . . . . Cavity Turnable Filter
CTF . . . . Central Task Force
CTF . . . . Ceramic-Tile Floor (Technical drawings)
CTF . . . . Ceramic Tube Fabrication
CTF . . . . Change (or Changing) to Tower Frequency (Aviation)
CTF . . . . Chlorine Trifluoride
CTF . . . . Commander, Task Force
CTF . . . . Common Test Facility
CTF . . . . Core Test Facility
CTF . . . . Correction to Follow
CTF . . . . Correctional Training Facility (Army)
CTFA . . . . Cosmetics, Toiletry and Fragrance Association (Formerly, TGA)
CTFE . . . . Chlorotrifluoroethylene
CTFM . . . . Continuous-Transmission Frequency Modulated (SONAR)
CTFO . . . . Controlled Tuning Fork Oscillator
CTG . . . . Combined Test Group
CTG . . . . Commander, Task Group
CTGH . . . . Cotangent, Hyperbolic
C Th . . . . Candidate of Theology
CTI . . . . Cambridge Technology, Incorporated
CTI . . . . Camera Timing Indicator
CTI . . . . Command Technical Inspection (Army)
CTI . . . . Complaint Type Investigation (Army)
CTI . . . . Contract Technical Instructor (Army)
CTI . . . . Cooling Tower Institute
CTI . . . . Crossroads Technical Instrumentation (Atomic weapons testing)
CTIC . . . . Cable Television Information Center
CTIF . . . . Comite Technique International de Prevention et d'Extincting du Feu (International Technical Committee for the Prevention and Extinction of Fire)
CTIF . . . . Commercial Travelers Insurance Federation
CTIO . . . . Cerro Tololo Inter-American Observatory (National Science Foundation)
CTIP . . . . Compagnia Tecnica Industrie Petroli (Italy)
CTJC . . . . Centralia Township Junior College (Illinois)
CTK . . . . Crimping Tool Kit
CTL . . . . California Testing Laboratory
CTL . . . . Carrier Tracking Loop
CTL . . . . Certified Tool List
CTL . . . . Combat Training Launch
CTL . . . . Complementary Transistor Logic (Data processing)
CTL . . . . Confidence Training Launch
CTL . . . . Constructive Total Loss
CTL . . . . Continental Steel Corporation (NYSE symbol)
CTL . . . . Control
CTL . . . . Core Transistor Logic
CTLI . . . . Combat Training Launch Instrumentation (Minuteman)
CTLI . . . . Command Training Launch Instrumentation
CTLI . . . . Confidence Training Launching Instrumentation
CTM . . . . Cable Testing Meter
CTM . . . . Catholic Traditionalist Movement
CTM . . . . Chief Torpedoman's Mate
CTM . . . . Close Talking Microphone
CTM . . . . Communications Terminal Modules (Data processing)
CTM . . . . Concordia Tract Mission
CTM . . . . Confederacion de Trabajadores de Mexico (Workers' Confederation of Mexico)
CTM . . . . Contract Termination Manual
CTM . . . . Contractor Technical Meeting
C & TM . . . . . . Clothing and Textile Materiel (Army)
CTMA . . . . Camping Trailer Manufacturers Association
CTMA . . . . Cutting Tool Manufacturers Association
CTMC . . . . . . Collapsible Tube Manufacturers Council
CTMC . . . . Communications Terminal Module Controller (Data processing)
CTMC . . . . . . Confederation des Travailleurs des Madagascar et Comores (Confederation of Workers of Madagascar and the Comores)
CTME . . . . . . Chief Torpedoman's Mate, Electrical
CTMM . . . . . . California Test of Mental Maturity
CTMP . . . . Contractor Technical Manual Plan (DOD)
CTMS . . . . Ceramic to Metal Seal
CTMV . . . . Chief Torpedoman's Mate, Aviation
CTN . . . . Cable Termination Network
CTN . . . . Canton R. R. (AAR code)
CTN . . . . Centre d'Etudes des Consequences Generales des Grands Techniques Nouvelles (Center for the Study of the General Results of New Technologies)
CTN . . . . Chemetron Corporation (NYSE symbol)
CTN . . . . Ctenidial Nerve
CTNDS . . . . . . Commercial Transport Navigation Display System
CTNE . . . . Compania Telefonica Nacionale de Espana

CTNF . . . . Controlled Thermonuclear Fusion
CTO . . . . Cavity Tuned Oscillator
CTO . . . . Central Torpedo Office
CTO . . . . Central Treaty Organization
CTO . . . . Circular Terminal Orbit (Aerospace)
CTO . . . . Cognizant Transportation Office(r) (Air Force)
CTO . . . . Commercial Transportation Officer
CTO . . . . Control Tower Operator (Army)
CTO . . . . Courier Transfer Office(r)
CTOA . . . . . . Creative Tour Operators Association
CTOC . . . . . . Communications Technical Operations Center (Air Force)
CTOC . . . . . . Corps Tactical Operations Center
CTOCU . . . . . Central Technical Order Control (or Coordination) Unit
CTOL . . . . . . Conventional Takeoff or Landing (Aircraft) (Also, C-STOL)
CTORP . . . . . Chief Torpedoman
CTP . . . . California Test of Personality (Education)
CTP . . . . Capacitor Test Program
CTP . . . . Central Maine Power Co. (NYSE symbol)
CTP . . . . Central Transfer Point
CTP . . . . Charge Transfer Photography
CTP . . . . Christmas Tree Pattern
CTP . . . . Command Translator and Programmer
CTP . . . . Conservez Taxe Payee (Retain Charge Paid)
CTP . . . . Coordinated Test Plan
CTP . . . . Cytosine Triphosphate
CTPB . . . . . . Carboxyl-Terminated Polybutadiene Binder
CTPB . . . . . . Central Tracing Policy Board (Post-World War II)
CTPEC . . . . . Coal Tar Pitch Emulsion Council
CTR . . . . C-Band Tracking RADAR
CTR . . . . Canaveral Test Report
CTR . . . . Carrier Telegraph Receiver
CTR . . . . Caterpillar Tractor Company (NYSE symbol; later, CAT) (Wall Street
           slang name: "Cat")
CTR . . . . Cavitation Tendency Ratio
CTR . . . . Center
CTR . . . . Central Tool Room
CTR . . . . Certification Test Requirement (NASA)
CTR . . . . Contractual Technical Report
CTR . . . . Controlled Thermonuclear Reaction (or Reactor) (AEC)
CTR . . . . Core Transistor Register
CTR . . . . Standing Committee for Controlled Thermonuclear Research
CTRI . . . . . . Catholic Tape Recorders, International
CTS . . . . Cartographic Test Standard (Air Force)
CTS . . . . Central Training Section (Air Force)
CTS . . . . Cesium Time Standard
CTS . . . . Charge Transfer Spectrum
CTS . . . . Chicago Theological Seminary
CTS . . . . Chief(s), Technical Services
CTS . . . . Circuit Test Set
CTS . . . . Command and Telemetry System (Aerospace)
CTS . . . . Communications and Tracking Subsystems
CTS . . . . Compass Tilt Signal
CTS . . . . Component Test Set
CTS . . . . Concordia Theological Seminary (Missouri)
CTS . . . . Contract Technical School
CTS . . . . Contract Termination Settlement
CTS . . . . Contractor Technical Services (Air Force)
CTS . . . . Courier Transfer Station
CTS . . . . Course Training Standard (Air Force)
CTS . . . . Cream of Tartar Substitute
CTS . . . . Critical Tool Service
CTS . . . . Crosier Theological Seminary (Minnesota)
CTS . . . . Cryogenic Temperature Sensor (or Source)
CTS . . . . CTS Corporation (NYSE symbol)
CTSA . . . . . . Catholic Theological Society of America
CTSB . . . . . . Combined Travel Security Board (Allied German Occupation Forces)
CTSE . . . . . . Chicago, Terre Haute & Southeastern R. R. (AAR code)
CTSP . . . . . . Contract Technical Services Personnel
CTSS . . . . . . Compatible Time-Sharing System (Data processing)
CTST . . . . . . Coaxial Triple-Stud Tuner
CTT . . . . Card-to-Tape Tape (Data processing)
CTT . . . . Carrousel Transfer Tube
CTT . . . . Central Trunk Terminals
CTT . . . . Compressed Tablet Triturate (Pharmacy)
CTT . . . . Corrugated TEFLON Tubing
CTT . . . . Crew Transfer Tunnel (NASA)
CTTC . . . . . Chanute Technical Training Center (Air Force)
CTTE . . . . . . Cintered Tungsten-Tantalum Emitter
CTTEE . . . . . . Committee
CTU . . . . Centigrade Thermal Unit
CTU . . . . Central Telephone & Utilities Corp. (NYSE symbol)

CTU . . . . Central Terminal Unit
CTU . . . . Combat Training Unit
CTU . . . . Commander, Task Unit
CTU . . . . Commercial Telegraphers' Union
CTU . . . . Committee for Time Uniformity
CTU . . . . Compatibility Test Unit
CTU . . . . Components Test Unit
CTU . . . . Conference on Transportation Unity
CTU . . . . Construction Training Unit
CTUC . . . . . . Central Trade Union Council (Czechoslovakia)
CTUF . . . . . . Ceylon Trade Union Federation
CTV . . . . Coaxial Thermal Voltmeter
CTV . . . . Commercial Television
CTV . . . . Confederacion de Trabajadores de Venezuela (Venezuelan Workers'
           Confederation)
CTV . . . . Constant Tangential Velocity
CTV . . . . Control Test Vehicles
CTVD . . . . . . Cinema Television Digest
CTW . . . . Can't Tell What (Accounting slang)
CTW . . . . Children's Television Workshop
CTW . . . . Counterweight
CTX . . . . Centex Corp. (NYSE symbol)
CTX . . . . Centrex (Bell System)
CTX . . . . Consolidated Textile Company (NYSE symbol) (Delisted)
CTY . . . . Century Industries Company, Inc. (American Stock Exchange symbol)
CTZ . . . . Control Zone
CTZ . . . . Corps Tactical Zone (Military)
CU . . . . Call-Us, Inc.
CU . . . . Catholic University
CU . . . . Chymotrypsin Unit
CU . . . . Clinical Unit
CU . . . . Close Up (A photograph or motion picture sequence taken from a
           short distance)
CU . . . . Closeup Crystal Unit (Piezoelectric)
CU . . . . Coefficient of Utilization
CU . . . . Columbia University (New York)
CU . . . . Construction Unit (Data processing)
CU . . . . Consumers Union of United States
CU . . . . Control Unit
Cu . . . . Copper (Chemical element)
CU . . . . Credit Union
CU . . . . Crosstalk Unit
CU . . . . Crystal Unit (Piezoelectric)
CU . . . . Cubic
CU . . . . Cumulus (Meteorology)
CUA . . . . Catholic University of America (Washington, DC)
CUA . . . . Confederated Unions of America
CUA . . . . Council for Urban Affairs
CUAC . . . . . Cambridge University Athletic Club
CUBC . . . . . . Cambridge University Boat Club
CUBE . . . . . . Cooperating Users of Burroughs Equipment (Data processing)
CUBI . . . . . . Centro Nazionale per il Catalogo Unico delle Biblioteche Italiane (Italy)
CUBS . . . . . . Congress for the Unity of Black Students
CUC . . . . Canadian Union College
CUC . . . . Crystal Unit Cell
CUCB . . . . . . Cumulus and Cumulonimbus (Meteorology)
CUCM . . . . . Cubic Centimeter
CUCOSS . . . . . California Universities Council on Space Sciences
CUD . . . . Craft Union Department (AFL-CIO)
CUD . . . . Cudahy Company (NYSE symbol) (Delisted)
CUDAT . . . . . Common User Data Terminal (Military)
CUDWR . . . . . Columbia University Division of War Research
CUE . . . . Center for Urban Education (New York)
CUE . . . . Communications Unit Executor
CUE . . . . Computer Update Equipment
CUE . . . . Cooperating Users' Exchange
CUE . . . . Culture, Understanding, and Enrichment (New York State Education
           Department project)
CUEBS . . . . . Commission on Undergraduate Education in the Biological Sciences
CUEPACS . . . . Congress of Unions of Employees in the Public and Civil Services
           (Malaya)
CUES . . . . . . College and University Environment Scales
CUF . . . . Catholics United for the Faith (An organization)
CUF . . . . Cumuliform (Meteorology)
CUF . . . . Federation of Catholic Universities
CUFR . . . . . . Cumulus Fractus (Meteorology)
CUG . . . . . . Common-User Group (SAGE)
CUGA . . . . . Cumberland Gap National Historical Park
CUGCO . . . . Confederation of Unions in Government Corporations and Offices
           (Philippines)
CUH . . . . Control Users Handbook

CUHL . . . . . . Columbia University Hudson Laboratory
CUI . . . . Chymotripsin Units Inhibited
CUIN . . . . . . Cubic Inch
CUL . . . . Canonical Unit of Length
CUL . . . . Culligan International Co. (NYSE symbol)
CUL . . . . See You Later (Telegrapher's slang)
CULL . . . . . . Corning Uniformity Limit Level
CUM . . . . . . Cambridge University Mission
CUM . . . . . . Central Unit-Memory
CUM. . . . . . . Cummins Engine Co., Inc. (NYSE symbol)
CUMM . . . . . Cubic Millimeter
CUMMFU . . . . Complete Utter Monumental Military Foul Up
CUMS. . . . . . Cambridge University Musical Society
CUMU . . . . . . Cubic Micron
CUN . . . . Cuneo Press, Inc. (NYSE symbol) (Delisted)
CUNA . . . . . . Credit Union National Association
CUNC . . . . . . Comite d'Union Nationale des Cabindais (Cabindan Committee of National Union)
CUNY . . . . . . City University of New York
CUP . . . . Cambridge University Press
CUP . . . . Columbia University Press
CUPA . . . . . . College and University Personnel Association
CU & PFC . . . Criminally Uttering and Publishing False (or Forged) Check
CUPID . . . . . . Combat Using Price Incentives Doctrine
CUPLE . . . . . . Cambridge University Press Limited Editions
CUPM. . . . . . Committee on the Undergraduate Program in Mathematics (Mathematical Association of America)
CUPR . . . . . . Catholic University of Puerto Rico
CUPS . . . . . . Consolidated Unit Personnel Section
CUPU . . . . . . Cambridge University Prayer Union
CU-PU-FU. . . National Clean Up - Paint Up - Fix Up Bureau
CUR . . . . Complex Utility Routine
CUR . . . . Current
CURAGI . . . . . Comite pour l'Utilisation des Resultats de l'Annee Geophysique Internationale (IGY Completion Committee)
CURB . . . . . . Curtis Bay R. R. (AAR code)
CURE . . . . . . Catholics United for Racial Equality
CURE . . . . . . Christians United for Responsible Entertainment
CURE . . . . . . Clean Urban River Environments (Project)
CURE . . . . . . Conference for Universal Reason and Ethics (Founded by motion picture actor Lew Ayres)
CURE . . . . . . Conference Upon Research and Education in World Government
CURE . . . . . . Council of Urban Rebuilding Enterprises
CURE . . . . . . Curecanti Recreation Area (National Park Service designation)
CURMCO . . . . City Urban Renewal Management Corporation (New York City)
CURR . . . . . . Currency
CURR . . . . . . Current
CURS . . . . . . Center for Urban and Regional Studies
CURTS . . . . . Common User Radio Transmission Sounding System
CURTS . . . . . Communications User Radio Transmission Sounding (Navy)
CURV . . . . . . Cable-Controlled Underwater Research Vehicle
CURV . . . . . . Controlled Unmanned Recovery Vehicle (Torpedo retrieving device)
CUS . . . . Continental United States
CUSA . . . . . . Catholic Union of the Sick in America
CUSARROTC . . Chief, United States Army Reserve and Reserve Officers Training Corps Affairs
CUSIP. . . . . . Committee on Uniform Security Identification Procedures (Banking)
CUSNO . . . . . Customs Has Been Notified (Aviation)
CUSO. . . . . . Canadian University Service Overseas
CUSR . . . . . . Central United States Registry (Army)
CUSRPG . . . . Canada-United States Regional Planning Group (NATO)
CUSS I . . . . . Continental, Union, Shell, and Superior (Ocean drilling barge; named after oil companies which financed its development)
CUST . . . . . . Custer Battlefield National Monument
CUST . . . . . . Custodian (or Custody)
CUT . . . . Canonical Unit of Time
CUT . . . . Comite d l'Unite Togolaise (Committee for Togolese Unity)
CUTAS . . . . . Committee on Uniform Traffic Accident Statistics
CUTC . . . . . . Combat Unit Training Center (Army)
CUTH . . . . . . Council of University Teaching Hospitals
CUTS . . . . . . Computer Utilized Turning System (Warner & Swasey)
CUVA. . . . . . Cuyahoga Valley Railway Company (AAR code)
CUW . . . . . . Committee on Undersea Warfare
CUYD. . . . . . Cubic Yard
CUZ. . . . . . . Cousins Mortgage and Equity Investors (NYSE symbol)
CV. . . . . Aircraft Carrier
CV. . . . . Cape de Verde Island
CV . . . . Cardiovascular (Medicine)
CV. . . . . Central Vermont Railway, Inc. (AAR code)
CV. . . . . Check Valve
CV. . . . . Chief Value

CV. . . . . Chikungunya Virus
CV . . . . Coefficient of Variation (Mathematics)
CV . . . . Colla Voce (With the Voice) (Music)
CV. . . . . Collection Voucher
CV. . . . . Combat Vehicle
CV. . . . . Command Vehicle
CV. . . . . Command Verification (NASA)
CV. . . . . Commercial Solvents Corporation (NYSE symbol)
CV. . . . . Common Version (Bible)
CV. . . . . Constant-Viscosity (Rubber)
CV. . . . . Continuous Vulcanization
CV. . . . . Continuously Variable
CV. . . . . Contrast Value
CV. . . . . Contributing Value (Shipping)
CV. . . . . Control Van
CV. . . . . Convertible (NYSE symbol)
CV. . . . . Counter Voltage
CV. . . . . Cruise Vehicle (Military)
CV. . . . . Single Cotton Varnish (Insulation)
C de V . . . . Carte de Visite (Visiting Card)
CVA . . . . . . Attack Aircraft Carrier (Navy symbol)
CVA. . . . . . . California Vehicle Act
CVA . . . . . . Cerebrovascular Accident (Medical term for stroke)
CVA . . . . . . Chance Vought Aircraft, Inc. (Obsolete)
CVA . . . . . . Columbia Valley Authority
CVA . . . . . . CONVAIR (Consolidated-Vultee Aircraft Corp.; later, General Dynamics) Astronautics
CVA . . . . . . Current Variable Attenuator
CVA. . . . . . . Heavy Aircraft Carrier (65,000 tons) (Navy ship designation)
CVAC. . . . . . Consolidated Vultee Aircraft Corporation
CVA(N) . . . . Attack Aircraft Carrier (Nuclear propelled)
CVB . . . . . . Combined VHF (Very High Frequency)-Band
CVB . . . . . . Large Aircraft Carrier (Navy symbol)
CVC . . . . . . Cesium Vapor Cathode
CVC . . . . . . Consonant-Vowel-Consonant (Form used in verbal learning and conditioning studies involving meaningfulness of nonsense syllables)
CVC . . . . . . Contactless Vacuum Controller
CVC . . . . . . Convalescent Camp (Military)
CVC . . . . . . Cryogenic Vacuum Calorimeter
CVCS . . . . . Cardiovascular Conditioning Suit
CVD . . . . . . Chemical Vapor Deposition
CVD. . . . . . . Column Valve Diaphragm
CVD. . . . . . . Communication Valve Development (British)
CVD. . . . . . . Current-Voltage Diagram
CVE . . . . . . Calibration Vibration Exciter
CVE . . . . . . Continuously Variable, for Emergency
CVE . . . . . . Customer-Vended Equipment
CVE . . . . . . Escort Aircraft Carrier (Navy symbol)
CVEH . . . . . Combat Vehicle (Army)
CVF . . . . . . Continuously Variable Filter
CVF . . . . . . Controlled Visual Flight
CVF . . . . . . Corporacion Venezolana de Fomento (Venezuelan Development Corporation)
CVFR . . . . . Controlled Visual Flight Rules
CVFS . . . . . Cesium Vapor Feed System
CVFS . . . . . Circular Variable Filter Spectrometer
CVG. . . . . . . Cincinnati (Ohio) - Covington (Ky.) (Airport symbol)
CVHA . . . . . Assault Helicopter Aircraft Carrier (Navy symbol)
CVHE . . . . . Escort Helicopter Aircraft Carrier (Navy symbol)
CVI . . . . . . Cape Verde Islands
CVI . . . . . . Cerebrovascular Insufficiency (Medicine)
CVI . . . . . . College of the Virgin Islands
CVI . . . . . . Colorado Video, Incorporated
CVI . . . . . . Current Variable Inductor
CVIS . . . . . Computerized Vocational Information System (Guidance program)
CVJM. . . . . . Christliche Vereine Junger Manner (Young Men's Christian Associations) (Germany)
CVK. . . . . . . Centerline Vertical Keel
CVL. . . . . . . Corpo Voluntari della Liberta
CVL . . . . . . Small Aircraft Carrier (Navy symbol)
CVLS . . . . . Central Vacuum Loading System
CVM . . . . . . Consumable Vacuum Melt (Steel)
CVM . . . . . . Council for a Volunteer Military
CVM . . . . . . Cylindrical Vibration Mount
CVMAS. . . . . Continuously Variable Mechanical Advantage Shifter
CVMP . . . . . Committee on Veterans Medical Problems (US)
CVN . . . . . . Casualty Vulnerability Number
CVNPA . . . . Carolinas-Virginia Nuclear Power Associates, Inc.
CVO . . . . . . Chief Veterinary Officer (Ministry of Agriculture, Fisheries, and Food) (British)
CVO . . . . . . Commander of the Royal Victorian Order
CVP . . . . . . Chemical Vapor Plating

CVR . . . . Carrier Vessel Reactor
CVR . . . . Ceramic Vacuum Relay
CVR . . . . Cockpit Voice Recorder
CVR . . . . Command Voltage Regulator
CVR . . . . Constant Velocity Recording
CVR . . . . Constant Voltage Reference
CVR . . . . Controlled Visual Rules (FAA)
CVRD . . . . . . Companhia Vale do Rio Doce (Brazil)
CVS . . . . ASW (Antisubmarine Warfare) Support Aircraft Carrier (Navy symbol)
CVS . . . . Cardiovascular System
CVS . . . . Committee on Valuation of Securities
CVS . . . . Common Video System
CVS . . . . Constant Volume Sampling (ACF Industries)
CVS . . . . Consumer Value Stores
CVS . . . . Covert Viewing System
CVSD . . . . . . Continuous Variable Slope Delta
CVSG . . . . . . Channel Verification Signal Generator
CVSSUS . . . . . Central Verband der Siebenburger Sachsen of the U.S.
CVT . . . . Central Vermont Railway, Inc.
CVT . . . . Training Aircraft Carrier (Navy ship symbol)
CVTC . . . . . . Confederation Vietnamienne du Travail Chretien (Vietnamese Confederation of Christian Labor) (South Vietnam)
CVTR . . . . . . Carolinas-Virginia Tube Reactor
CVU . . . . Constant Voltage Unit
CVU . . . . Utility Aircraft Carrier (Navy symbol)
CVV . . . . Control Variable Valve
CVW . . . . Attack Carrier Air Wing (Navy symbol)
CVWS . . . . . . Combat Vehicle Weapons System (AWC)
CVX . . . . Cleveland Electric Illum. Company (NYSE symbol)
CW . . . . Calls Waiting (Telephone communication)
CW . . . . Canada West
CW . . . . Canadian Welfare (A publication)
CW . . . . Carrier Wave (A form of radio transmission in code) (Navy)
CW . . . . Cell Wall
CW . . . . Chemical Warfare
CW . . . . Chemical Warhead
CW . . . . Child Welfare
CW . . . . Churchwarden
CW . . . . Clockwise
CW . . . . Cold Water (Technical drawings)
CW . . . . Colorado & Wyoming Railway Company (AAR code)
CW . . . . Commercial Weight
CW . . . . Computerworld (A publication)
CW . . . . Concealed Weapons
CW . . . . Continuous Wave (A form of radio transmission)
CW . . . . Control Word
CW . . . . Copper Weld
CW . . . . Cotton or Wool (Freight)
CW . . . . Cubic Weight
CW . . . . Curtiss-Wright Corporation (NYSE symbol)
C-W . . . . Chronometer Time Minus Watch Time (Navigation)
C-W . . . . Curtiss-Wright Corporation
C/W . . . . Chemical Warfare
C/W . . . . Counterweight
C & W . . . . . . Country and Western (Music)
CW2 . . . . Chief Warrant Officer 2 (Army)
CW3 . . . . Chief Warrant Officer 3 (Army)
CW4 . . . . Chief Warrant Officer 4 (Army)
CWA . . . . Canadian Western Approaches
CWAA . . . . . . Children's Wear Association
CWAA . . . . . . Chinese Women's Association
CWA . . . . Civil Works Administration (1933-1934)
CWA . . . . Cockcroft-Walton Accelerator
CWA . . . . Communication Workers Alliance (Philippines)
CWA . . . . Communications Workers of America
CWA . . . . Construction Writers Association
CWA . . . . Customer Work Authorization
CWAC . . . . . . Canadian Women's Army Corps
CWAR . . . . . . Continuous Wave Acquisition RADAR (Military)
CWAS . . . . . . Contractor's Weighted Average Share (in Cost Risk) (Accounting)
CWB . . . . Canadian Weekly Bulletin (A publication)
CWB . . . . Central Welsh Board
CWBCNA . . . . Credit Women's Breakfast Clubs of North America (Later, Credit Women - International)
CWBL . . . . . . Catholic Women's Benevolent Legion
CWBW . . . . . . Chemical Warfare - Bacteriological Warfare
CWC . . . . Cam Wedge Clamp
CWC . . . . Carpet Wool Council
CWC . . . . Ceylon Workers' Congress
CWC . . . . Charleston & Western Carolina Railway Company (AAR code)
CWC . . . . Clear Write Condition

CWC . . . . Cold War Council
CWC . . . . Colorado Woman's College
CWC . . . . Commonwealth of World Citizens
CWC . . . . Conventional (Non-Nuclear) War Capability
CWC . . . . Council of Women Citizens
CWC . . . . Country Women's Council, USA
CWC . . . . Curtiss-Wright Corporation
CWC . . . . National Committee for a Confrontation with Congress
C & WC . . . . . Charleston & Western Carolina Railway Company
CWCA . . . . . . Civil War Centennial Association
CWCC . . . . . . Civil War Centennial Commission
CWCCA . . . . . Cardigan Welsh Corgi Club of America
CWCCI . . . . . . Crayon, Water Color and Craft Institute
CWCS . . . . . . Combined Wheat Control Section (Allied German Occupation Forces)
CWD . . . . Civilian War Dead
CWD . . . . Conwood Corp. (NYSE symbol)
CWD . . . . Cyclotron Wave Device
CWDIC . . . . . . Cooperative Weapons Data Indexing Committee (AEC and DOD)
CWDWD . . . . . Committee for World Development and World Disarmament
CWE . . . . Cockcroft-Walton Experiment
CWE . . . . Coil Winding Equipment
CWE . . . . Commonwealth Edison Company (NYSE symbol)
CWE . . . . Contractor's Work Estimate (Military)
CWE . . . . Current Working Estimate (Military)
CWEA . . . . . . Caution and Warning Electronics Assembly (Apollo) (NASA)
CWF . . . . Christian Women's Fellowship
CWF . . . . Civilian Welfare Fund
CWF . . . . Composite Wave Filter
CWF . . . . Cornwell-Weisskoph Formula
CWF . . . . Cross Wind Force
CW/FM . . . . . . Continuous Wave Frequency Modulated
CWFS . . . . . . Crashworthy Fuel Systems (Aviation)
CWG . . . . Campaign for World Government
CWG . . . . Closed Wave-Guide
CWG . . . . Conformal Wire Grating
CWG . . . . Constant-Wear Garment (Apollo) (NASA)
CWG . . . . Continuous Wave Gas
CWG . . . . Corrugated Wire Glass (Technical drawings)
CWGA . . . . . . Catholic Writers Guild of America
CWI . . . . Chicago & Western Indiana R. R. (AAR code)
CWI . . . . Continuous Wave Illuminator
CWIC . . . . . . Competition with Industrial Cooperation
CWIF . . . . Continuous Wave Intermediate Frequency
CWIK . . . . . . Chemical World Index Key
CWIK . . . . . . Cutting with Intent to Kill
CWINJ . . . . . . Cold Weather Injury
CWIR . . . . Continuous Wave Illuminator RADAR (Military)
CWIS . . . . Cotton Warehouse Inspection Service
CWIT . . . . Concordance Words in Titles (Indexing)
CWL . . . . Chemical Warfare Laboratory
CWL . . . . Continuous Wave LASER
CWL . . . . Cornwall R. R. (AAR code)
CWL . . . . Cowles Communications, Inc. (NYSE symbol)
CWLA . . . . . . Child Welfare League of America
CWLR . . . . . . Chemical Warfare Laboratories (Army)
CWM . . . . Catholic Worker (Movement)
CWM . . . . Change Weight Manifest (Aviation)
CWM . . . . Coil Winding Machine
CWM . . . . Commercial Water Movement Number
CWMAA . . . . . Clock and Watch Manufacturers Association of America
CWMEWCC . . . Commission on World Mission and Evangelism of the World Council of Churches
CWMTU . . . . Cold Weather Materiel Test Unit
CWN . . . . Certificate of War Necessity (World War II)
CWO . . . . Cash with Order
CWO . . . . Chief Warrant Officer
CWO . . . . Commissioned Warrant Officer
CWO . . . . Commonwealth Oil Refining Co., Inc. (NYSE symbol)
CWO . . . . Communication Watch Officer
CWO . . . . Continuous Wave Oscillator
CWOHC . . . . . Commissioned Warrant Officer Hospital Corps
CWOIH . . . . . . Council of World Organizations Interested in the Handicapped
CWOP . . . . . . Cold Weather Operations (Military)
CWP . . . . Chicago, West Pullman & Southern R. R. (AAR code)
CWP . . . . Circulating Water Pump
CWP . . . . Civil Works Program
CWP . . . . Coal Workers' Pneumoconiosis (Medicine)
CWPC . . . . . . Cam Wedge Power Clamp
CWPC . . . . . . Canadian Women's Press Club (Later, Media Club of Canada)
CWPC . . . . . . Civil War Press Corps
CWPEA . . . . . . Childbirth Without Pain Education Association

CWPI . . . . . . Configuration Work Package Item (Army)
CWPM . . . . . . Correct Words Per Minute (Typewriting, etc.)
CWPS . . . . . . Civil War Philatelic Society
CWR . . . . . . California Western R. R. (AAR code)
CWRC . . . . . . Climb Well to Right of Course (Aviation)
CWRM . . . . . . Cell Water Removal Mechanism
CWRR . . . . . . Curtiss-Wright Research Reactor
CWRTNY . . . . . Civil War Round Table of New York
CWRU . . . . . . Case-Western Reserve University
CWS . . . . Canadian Wildlife Service
CWS . . . . Chemical Warfare Service (Army)
CWS . . . . . . Child Welfare Service
CWS . . . . Chilled Water Supply (Aerospace)
CWS . . . . . . Church World Service (of the National Council of Churches of Christ in the USA)
CWS . . . . . . Church World Services (Protestant and Eastern Orthodox Church Aid Project)
CWS . . . . Clockwise
CWS . . . . . . Cold-Water Soluble
CWS . . . . Community War Services (of FSA) (World War II)
CWS . . . . Complex Wiring System
CWS . . . . Consolidated Western Steel
CWS . . . . Continental Wage Schedule (Military)
CWS . . . . Control Wheel Steering
CWS . . . . . . Crew Weapons Sight
CWSD . . . . . . Continuous Wave Space Duplexed
CWSF . . . . . . Commander, Western Sea Frontier
CWSP . . . . . . College Work-Study Program
CWSRA . . . . . Chester White Swine Record Association
CWT . . . . . . Chemical Warfare Specialist, Medical (Navy rating)
CWT . . . . . . Chief Water Tender (Navy rating)
CWT . . . . Color Word Test
CWT . . . . Cooperative Wind Tunnel
CWT . . . . . . Council on World Tensions (Later, Institute on Man and Science)
CWTR . . . . . . Climb Well to Right (Aviation)
CWT . . . . . . Hundred Weight
CWU . . . . . . Chemical Workers' Union
CWU . . . . . . Composite Weighted Work Unit
CWV . . . . . . Catholic War Veterans of the USA
CWV . . . . . . Continuous-Wave Video
CWVA . . . . . Catholic War Veterans of the USA Ladies Auxiliary
CWVS . . . . . . College Women's Volunteer Service (World War II)
CWW . . . . . . Canadian Woodmen of the World
CX . . . . Central Exchange
CX . . . . Colorado & Southern Railway Co. (NYSE symbol)
CXC . . . . Clorox Chemical Company (NYSE symbol; later, CLX)

CX-HLS . . . . . Cargo Experimental, Heavy Logistic Support (Aircraft) (Air Force)
CXI . . . . Crosstell Input
CXO . . . . Crosstell Output
CXT . . . . Common External Tariff (Common Market)
CY . . . . Calendar Year
CY . . . . Chief Yeoman (Navy rating)
CY . . . . City Products Corporation (NYSE symbol) (Delisted)
CY . . . . Current Year
CY . . . . Cycle
CYA . . . . Carded Yarn Association
CYA . . . . Catholic Youth Adoration Society
CYA . . . . Covenant Youth of America
CYA . . . . Cover Your Anatomy (Army slang) (Bowdlerized version)
CYBORG . . . . . Cybernetic Organism (Concept of machine to alter man's bodily functions for space environment)
CYC . . . . Chicago Yellow Cab Company, Inc. (NYSE symbol) (Delisted)
CYC . . . . Chinese Youth Council
CYCO . . . . . . Central Yiddish Culture Organization
CYEE . . . . . . Central Youth Employment Executive (Department of Employment) (British)
CYI . . . . Coty International Corporation (NYSE symbol) (Delisted)
CYK . . . . Consider Yourself Kissed (Correspondence)
CYL . . . . Cyclops Corporation (Formerly, UCS) (NYSE symbol)
CYL . . . . Cylinder
CYM . . . . . . Cyprus Mines Corp. (NYSE symbol)
CYMA . . . . . Catholic Young Men's Association
CYNAP . . . . . Cytotoxicity Negative-Absorption Positive (Immunology)
CYO . . . . . . Catholic Youth Organization
CYO . . . . Council on Youth Opportunity (Disbanded 1971; functions taken over by Domestic Council and OMB)
CYP . . . . Cyprus Airways, Ltd.
CYS . . . . Cysteine (Amino acid)
CYSA . . . . . . Combed Yarn Spinners Association
CZ . . . . Canal Zone
CZ . . . . Celanese Corporation (NYSE symbol)
CZ . . . . Coahuila & Zacatecas AG Railway (AAR code)
CZ . . . . Combat Zone
CZ . . . . Communications Zone
CZB . . . . Carbon Zinc Battery
CZBA . . . . . . Canal Zone Biological Area (A preserve administered by the Smithsonian Institution)
CZC . . . . Chromated Zinc Chloride
CZG . . . . Canal Zone Government
CZJC . . . . . . Canal Zone Junior College
CZKR . . . . . . Czechoslovakian Kronen
CZPS . . . . . . Czechoslovak Philatelic Society
CZS . . . . Citizens and Southern Realty Investors (NYSE symbol)

D

d . . . . British penny (Derived from Latin "denarius")
D . . . . Dahlonega (Georgia) (Mint mark, when appearing on US coins)
D . . . . Dam
D . . . . Dame
D . . . . Damn
D . . . . Danger Area (Aviation)
D . . . . Dart Industries, Inc. (NYSE symbol)
D . . . . Date
D . . . . Datum
D . . . . Daughter
D . . . . Day (Approach and landing charts) (Aviation)
D . . . . Deacon
D . . . . Dead or Deceased
D . . . . Dean
D . . . . Debye
D . . . . Decessit (Died)
d . . . . Deci (A prefix meaning divided by 10)
D . . . . Deciduous
D . . . . Declination
D . . . . Defeated
D . . . . Defense (Men's lacrosse position)
D . . . . Degree
D . . . . Deleted
D . . . . Democrat
D . . . . Denarius, Denarii (Silver coin in Ancient Rome; gold coin in Roman Empire)
D . . . . Density
D . . . . Denver (Colorado) (Mint mark, when appearing on US coins)
D . . . . Depart
D . . . . Department
D . . . . Depositus (Laid to Rest)
D . . . . Depth
D . . . . Depth of Ship
D . . . . Deputy
D . . . . Descend(ing) (Aviation)
D . . . . Deserter
D . . . . Destroyed
D . . . . Deus (God)
D . . . . Deuterium (Radioisotope of Hydrogen, H^2)
d . . . . Deutero (Chemistry)
D . . . . Development
D . . . . Deviation
D . . . . Dexter (Right)
D . . . . Dextro (Configuration in chemical structure)
d . . . . Dextro(rotatory) (Chemistry)
D . . . . Diameter
D . . . . Died
D . . . . Dies (Day)
D . . . . Difference
d . . . . Differential of
D . . . . Differential Coefficient
D . . . . Differentiation (Calculus)
D . . . . Dime
D . . . . Dimensional
D . . . . Diopter
D . . . . Dip
D . . . . Director aircraft capable of controlling drones or missiles (Designation for all US military aircraft)
D . . . . Discharged
D . . . . Distance
D . . . . Dividend
D . . . . Division
D . . . . Doctor

D . . . . Document
D . . . . Dog
D . . . . Dollar
D . . . . Dominant (Applied to a species)
D . . . . Dominus (The Lord)
D . . . . Dorsal
D . . . . Dose (in prescriptions)
D . . . . Double
D . . . . Doublet
D . . . . Douglas Aircraft Company, Inc. (NYSE symbol) (Later, MD)
D . . . . Dowager
D . . . . Drachma (Monetary unit in Greece)
D . . . . Dragoons (Military) (British)
D . . . . Driving
D . . . . Drizzling
D . . . . Drone Plane (Navy symbol)
D . . . . Droppable Fuel Tank (Suffix to plane designation)
D . . . . Druids (Freemasonry)
D . . . . Duchess
D . . . . Duke
D . . . . Dulcis (Dear One)
D . . . . Duodecimo
D . . . . Dust (Meteorology)
D . . . . Dutch
D . . . . Duty (Navy)
D . . . . Dyne (Unit of force)
D . . . . Five Hundred (Roman numeral)
D . . . . Penny (Nail size)
D (Day) . . . . . General military term designating the day on which a specific action is planned to commence; by extension, the beginning of any activity of importance
1-D . . . . Selective Service Class (for Qualified Member of Reserve Component, or Student Taking Military Training, Including ROTC and Accepted Aviation Cadet Applicant)
2-D . . . . Selective Service Class (for Registrant Deferred Because of Study for the Ministry)
3-D . . . . Selective Service Class (for Man Deferred from Military Service Because Induction Would Cause Extreme Hardship and Privation to a Wife, Child or Parent) (Obsolete)
3-D . . . . Three-Dimensional (Pictures or films)
4-D . . . . Dead, Dying, Diseased, Disabled (Food processors' classification of animals unfit for use)
4-D . . . . Selective Service Class (for a Minister of Religion)
DA . . . . Data Analysis
DA . . . . Data Automation
DA . . . . Data Available
DA . . . . Decimal Add
DA . . . . Defense Aid (Lend-Lease) (World War II)
DA . . . . Define Area
da . . . . Deka (A prefix meaning multiplied by ten)
DA . . . . Delayed Action (Bomb or shell fuze)
DA . . . . Delayed Action (Pharmacy)
DA . . . . Delayed Arming (of explosive device)
DA . . . . Denmark (NATO)
DA . . . . Density Altitude (Navigation)
DA . . . . Dental Apprentice
DA . . . . Department of Agriculture
DA . . . . Department of the Army
DA . . . . Deployment Assembly (Skylab) (NASA)
DA . . . . Deposit Account (Banking)
DA . . . . Deputy Administrator
DA . . . . Design Authorization
DA . . . . Detergent Aid

DA . . . . Detroit Arsenal (Army)
DA . . . . Dictionary of Americanisms
DA . . . . Difference Amplifier
DA . . . . Differential Amplifier
DA . . . . Digestive Anlage
DA . . . . Digital Alternator
DA . . . . Diploma in Anesthetics
DA . . . . Direct Action (Bomb or shell fuze)
DA . . . . Disassemble
DA . . . . Discharge Afloat
DA . . . . Discrete Address
DA . . . . Dislocation Allowance (Military)
DA . . . . Dissolved Acetylene
DA . . . . Distribution Amplifier
DA . . . . District Attorney
DA . . . . Division Artillery (Army)
DA . . . . Doctor of Arts
DA . . . . Documentary Bill for Acceptance
DA . . . . Documentation Abstracts (A journal)
DA . . . . Documents against Acceptance, or Documents for Acceptance
DA . . . . Documents Attached
DA . . . . Dominion Atlantic Railway (AAR code)
DA . . . . Donor-Acceptor
DA . . . . Don't Answer
DA . . . . Dopamine (Biochemistry)
DA . . . . Double Acting
DA . . . . Double Aged (Metals)
DA . . . . Dragon Airways, Ltd.
DA . . . . Drift Angle (Navigation)
DA . . . . Dummy Antenna
DA . . . . Dunlap and Associates, Inc.
DA . . . . National Council, Daughters of America
D/A . . . . Days after Acceptance (Business and trade)
D/A . . . . Deposit Account (Banking)
D/A . . . . Documents upon Acceptance of Draft
D of A . . . . . . Daughters of America
D of A . . . . . . Department of Agriculture
D-to-A . . . . . . Digital-to-Analog (Converter) (Data processing)
DAA . . . . Data Automation Activity
DAA . . . . Department of Aeronautics and Astronautics (MIT)
DAA . . . . Dependents Assistance Act
DAA . . . . Diacetone Acrylamide (Chemistry)
DAA . . . . Diaminoacetanilide (Chemistry)
DAA . . . . Doctor of Applied Arts
DAA . . . . Durene Association of America
DAAA . . . . . . Department of the Army Administrative Area
DAA & AM . . . Defense Aid (Lend-Lease) Aircraft and Aeronautical Material (World War II)
DAACA . . . . . Department of the Army Allocation Committee, Ammunition
DAAD . . . . . . Deutscher Akademischer Austauschdienst (German Academic Exchange Service)
DAAE . . . . . . Defense Aid (Lend-Lease) Administration Expenses (World War II)
DAAG . . . . . . Deputy Assistant Adjutant-General
DA-AHEW . . . . Department of the Army Plan for Assistance in Department of Health, Education, and Welfare
DAAI & OC . . . Defense Aid (Lend-Lease) Agricultural, Industrial and Other Commodities (World War II)
DAALPS . . . . . Detachment d'Armee des Alpes
DAAP . . . . . . Diamylamyephosphonate
DAAS . . . . . . DOD (Department of Defense) Automatic Addressing System
DAATCO . . . . . Department of the Army Air Traffic Coordinating Officer
DAATL . . . . . . Detachment d'Armee de l'Atlantique
DAB . . . . Destroyer Advisory Board
DAB . . . . Deutsches Arzneibuch (Medicine)
DAB . . . . Devereux Adolescent Behavior (Rating scale) (Psychology)
DAB . . . . Diaminobenzidine
DAB . . . . Dictionary of American Biography
DAB . . . . Display Attention Bits (Data processing)
DABLC . . . . . . Director, Advanced Base Logistics Control (Navy)
DABOA . . . . . Director, Advanced Base Office, Atlantic (Navy)
DABOP . . . . . Director, Advanced Base Office, Pacific (Navy)
DABS . . . . . . Discrete Address Beacon System
DAC . . . . Data Acquisition Center (NASA)
DAC . . . . Data Acquisition Computer
DAC . . . . Data Acquisition Controller
DAC . . . . Data Analysis Console
DAC . . . . Deductible Average Clause (Insurance)
DAC . . . . Defenders of the American Constitution
DAC . . . . Department of the Army Civilian
DAC . . . . Design Augmented by Computer
DAC . . . . Development Assistance Committee (OECD)

DAC . . . . Diallyl Chlorendate
DAC . . . . Digital-to-Analog Converter
DAC . . . . Digital Arithmetic Center
DAC . . . . Direct Air Cycle
DAC . . . . Disablement Advisory Committee (Department of Employment) (British)
DAC . . . . Display Analysis Console
D Ac . . . . Doctor of Accounts
DAC . . . . Domestic Affairs Council (Replaced Urban Affairs Council, Rural Affairs Council and Cabinet Committee on Environment) (White House)
DAC . . . . Double Action Cylinder
DAC . . . . Douglas Aircraft Company
DAC . . . . Drug Abuse Council
DAC . . . . Durex Abrasives Corporation
DAC . . . . National Society, Daughters of the American Colonists
DACA . . . . . . Department of Army Certificate of Achievement
DACAN . . . . . Douglas Aircraft Co. of Canada
DACAN . . . . . Standing Group Distribution and Accounting Agency, NATO
DACAS . . . . . Damage Assessment and Casualty Report (Military)
DACC . . . . . . DeHavilland Aircraft Company, Canada
DACC . . . . . . Department of the Army Communications Center
DACC . . . . . . Direct Access Communications Channels
D Acc . . . . . . Doctor of Accountancy (or Accounting)
DACCC . . . . . Defense Area Communications Control Center
DACCS . . . . . Department of the Army Command and Control System
DACE . . . . . . Department of the Army Alternate Command and Control Element
DACE . . . . . . Doctor of Air Conditioning Engineering
DAC Eng . . . . Doctor of Air Conditioning Engineering
DA Chem . . . . Doctor of Applied Chemistry
DACI . . . . . . Direct Adjacent Channel Interference
DACL . . . . . . Dynamic Analysis and Control Laboratory (MIT)
DACO . . . . . Douglas Aircraft Corporation Overseas (Obsolete)
DACOM . . . . Datascope Computer Output Microfilmer
DACON . . . . Data Controller
DACON . . . . Digital-to-Analog Converter
DACOR . . . . . Data Correction (IBM)
DACOR . . . . . Data Correlator
DACOR . . . . . Diplomatic and Consular Officers, Retired
DACOWITS . . . Defense Advisory Committee on Women in the Services
DACPO . . . . . Data Count Printout (Data processing)
DACRP . . . . . Department of the Army Communication Resources Plan
DACRYLON . . . Dacron and Nylon
DACS . . . . . . Data Acquisition and Correction System (Data processing)
DACS . . . . . . Discrete Address Communications System
DAD . . . . Data Automation Digest (A publication) (Air Force)
DAD . . . . Deputy Assistant Director
DAD . . . . Digital Angle Data
DAD . . . . Directional Aerial Disposal (Insecticide spray)
DAD . . . . Directorate of Armament Development
DAD . . . . Documents Against Discretion (Banking)
DAD . . . . . . Double-Acting Door (Technical drawings)
DADAC . . . . . Department of the Army Distribution/Allocation Committee
DADAC . . . . . Digital-to-Analog Deck Angle Converter (Navy)
DADC . . . . . . Digital Air Data Computer
DADCAP . . . . Dawn and Dusk Combat Air Patrol
DADCMI . . . . . Department of the Army Policy for Disclosure of Classified Military Information (to foreign government)
DADE . . . . . . Data Acquisition and Decommutation Equipment
DADEE . . . . . Dynamic Analog Differential Equation Equalizer
DADIC . . . . . Data Dictionary
DADIT . . . . . Daystrom Analog-to-Digital Integrating Translator
D Adm . . . . . Doctor of Administration
DADMCS . . . . Department of Army Decoration for Meritorious Civilian Service
D Adm Eng . . . Doctor of Administrative Engineering
DAD/MSD . . . . Deputy Assistant Director for Management Support Division (Vietnam)
DADO . . . . . . Data Automation Design Office (Air Force)
DADOS . . . . . Deputy Assistant Director of Ordnance Stores (Military)
DAD/PE . . . . . Deputy Assistant Director for Plans and Evaluation (Vietnam)
DAD/POD . . . . Deputy Assistant Director for the Psychological Operations Division (Vietnam)
DADR . . . . . . Digital Angle Data Recorder
DAE . . . . Dictionary of American English
DAE . . . . Director of Army Education (British)
DAE . . . . District Airport Engineer
D Ae . . . . Doctor of Aeronautics
DAE . . . . Doctor of Art Education
DAEA . . . . . . Dimethyl Aminoethyl Acetate (Organic chemistry)
DAEC . . . . . . Danish Atomic Energy Commission
D Ae E . . . . . Doctor of Aeronautical Engineering
D Ae Eng . . . . Doctor of Aeronautical Engineering
DAEMON . . . . Data Adaptive Evaluator and Monitor
D Aero E . . . . Doctor of Aeronautical Engineering

DAES . . . . . . Division of Adult Education Service (of NEA)
D Ae S . . . . . . Doctor of Aeronautical Science
D Ae Sc . . . . . Doctor of Aeronautical Science
DAF . . . . Dansk Astronautisk Forening (Danish Astronautical Society)
DAF . . . . Data Acquisition Facility (of STADAN)
DAF . . . . Demonstration Air Force
DAF . . . . Department of Agriculture and Fisheries (Scotland)
DAF . . . . Department of the Air Force
DAF . . . . Departure Airfield
DAF . . . . Deutsche Arbeitsfront (German Workers Front) (Post-World War II)
DAF . . . . Van Doorn's Automobile Fabrieken (Dutch automobile manufacturer; acronym used as name of its cars)
DAFC . . . . . . Departure Airfield Control
DAFC . . . . . . Digital Automatic Frequency Control
DAFCCS . . . . Department of the Air Force Command and Control System (Air Force)
DAFCG . . . . . Departure Airfield Control Group
DAFD . . . . . . Dayton Air Force Depot
DAFD . . . . . . Department of the Army Forward Depot
DAF & E . . . . . Defense Aid (Lend-Lease) Facilities and Equipment (World War II)
DAFFO . . . . . . Dansk Forening til Fremme of Opfindelser (Danish Society for Furthering Inventions)
DAFICCS . . . . . Department of the Air Force Integrated Command and Control Systems
DAFIE . . . . . . Directorate for Armed Forces Information and Education (Military)
DAFS . . . . Department of Agriculture and Fisheries for Scotland (British)
DAFS . . . . Duty Air Force Specialty
DAFSC . . . . . . Duty Air Force Specialty Code
DAFSO . . . . . . Department of the Air Force Special Order
DAFT . . . . Digital/Analog Function Table (Data processing)
DAG . . . . Deputy Adjutant-General
DAG . . . . Deutsche Angestellten Gewerkschaft (German Salaried Employees' Union) (West Germany)
DAG . . . . Development Assistance Group
D Ag . . . . Doctor of Agriculture
DAGC . . . . . . Delayed Automatic Gain Control
DAGMAR . . . . Drift and Ground-Speed Measuring Airborne RADAR
DAGO . . . . . . District Aviation Gas Office (Navy)
D Agr . . . . Doctor of Agriculture
D Agr E . . . . . . Doctor of Agricultural Engineering
D Agr Eng . . . . Doctor of Agricultural Engineering
D Agr S . . . . . Doctor of Agricultural Science
D Agr Sc . . . . . Doctor of Agricultural Science
DAH . . . . Dictionary of American History
DAH . . . . Disordered Action of the Heart (Medicine)
DAI . . . . Death from Accidental Injuries (Military)
DAI . . . . Drift Angle Indicator
DAIP . . . . Department of the Army Intelligence Plan
DAIR . . . . Direct Altitude and Identity Readout (FAA)
DAIR . . . . Driver Aid, Information and Routing (Data processing)
DAIRE . . . . . . Direct Altitude and Identification Readout Equipment (Aviation)
DAIRS . . . . . . Dial Access Information Retrieval System
DAIS . . . . Defense Automatic Integrated Switch (Army communications system)
DAISY . . . . . . Data Acquisition and Interpretation System
DAISY . . . . . . Double Precision Automatic Interpretive System
DAIU . . . . Digital to Analog Interface Unit
DAJS . . . . Distributed Area Jamming System (Air Force)
DAL . . . . Dallas (Texas) (Airport symbol)
DAL . . . . Delta Air Lines, Inc. (NYSE symbol)
DAL . . . . Deutsche Akademie der Landwirtschaftswissenschaften
DAL . . . . Directional Arm Lock
DAL . . . . Distribution Authority List
DAL . . . . Dog at Large (Humorous notation put on letters that cannot be delivered) (British postmen's slang)
DAL . . . . Drawing Assembly List
DALA . . . . delta-Aminolevulinic Acid (Biochemistry)
DALC . . . . Deployment Area Location Code (Army)
DALC . . . . Divided Access Line Circuit
DALC . . . . Dynamic Asynchronous Logic Circuit
DALE . . . . Drug Abuse Law Enforcement (Justice Department)
DALO . . . . Defense Attaché Liaison Officer
DALS . . . . Double-Acting Limit Switch
DALT . . . . Drop Altitude
DALTO . . . . . . Doman Approach Landing Take-Off
DALTS . . . . . . Data Link Test Set
DALVP . . . . . . Delay Enroute Authorized as Ordinary Leave Provided It Does not Interfere with Reporting Date
DAM . . . . Data Addressed Memory (Data processing)
DAM . . . . Data Association Message
DAM . . . . Defended Area Model (Army)
DAM . . . . Definition, Analysis, and Mechanization
DAM . . . . Descriptor Attribute Matrix
DAM . . . . Diallyl Maleate

DAM . . . . Digitized Analog Magnetogram
DAM . . . . Downrange Antimissile Program (Army)
DAMA . . . . . . Department of the Army Materiel Annex
DAME . . . . . . Defense Against Methods of Entry (Military intelligence)
DAME . . . . . . Data Acquisition and Monitoring Equipment (Electronics)
DAM II-EE . . . Defended Area Model II Engagement Evaluation (Army)
DAM II-EP . . . Defended Area Model II Engagement Planning (Army)
DAMIS . . . . . . Department of the Army Management Information System
DAMIT . . . . . . Data Analysis (Program) of Massachusetts Institute of Technology
DAMMO . . . . . Directorate of Ammunition (Military) (Canada)
DAMN . . . . . . Diaminomaleonitrile (Organic chemistry)
DAMP . . . . . . Department of the Army Materiel Program
DAMP . . . . . . Downrange Antimissile Measurement Program (RADAR)
DAMPR . . . . . Digital Automatic Multiple Pressure Recorder (Lewis Research Center)
DAMPS . . . . . Data Acquisition Multiprogramming System (Data processing)
DAMP/TVPB . . Department of the Army Motion Picture/Television Production Board
DAMP/TVPP . . Department of the Army Motion Picture/Television Production Program
DAMR(W) . . . . Director of Aircraft Maintenance and Repair (Washington) (Navy)
DAMS . . . . . . Defense Against Missiles Systems
DAMV . . . . . . Destruction of Aircraft or Motor Vehicles
DAMV . . . . . . Double-Air Movement Valve
DAMW . . . . . . Deutsches Amt fuer Material und Warenpruefung
DAMWO . . . . Department of the Army Modification Work Order
DAN . . . . Deacon and Nike (Research rocket)
daN . . . . Dekanewton
DAN . . . . Deposit Account Number
DANA . . . . . . Deutsche Allgemeine Nachrichten Agentur (German general news agency, sponsored by US newspapermen as a successor to the NAZI-controlled DNB) (Post-World War II)
DANBIF . . . . . . Danske Boghandleres Importrfrening (Danish Booksellers Import Association)
DANK . . . . . . German-American National Congress
DAO . . . . Defense Attaché Office
DAO . . . . District Accounting Office(r) (Navy)
DAO . . . . District Aviation Office(r) (Navy)
DAO . . . . Division Air Officer
DAO . . . . Division Ammunition Office (Army)
DAO . . . . Divisional Agricultural Officer (Ministry of Agriculture, Fisheries, and Food) (British)
DAO . . . . Doctor of Art of Oratory
DAO . . . . Duly Authorized Officer
DAO & OS . . . Defense Aid Ordnance and Ordnance Stores (Lend-Lease)
DA-OPRR . . . . Department of the Army Plan for (Possession, Control and) Operation of Railroads
DAP . . . . Data Automation Panel (Air Force)
DAP . . . . Data Automation Proposal
DAP . . . . Delayed Alpha Particle
DAP . . . . Democratic Action Party (Malaysia)
DAP . . . . Depot Acceptance Procedures
DAP . . . . Diallyl Phthalate (Organic chemistry)
DAP . . . . Diammonium Phosphate (Fertilizer)
DAP . . . . Diazepam (Chemistry)
DAP . . . . Diffused Alloy Power
DAP . . . . Digital Autopilot
DAP . . . . Dihydroxyacetone Phosphate
DAP . . . . Dipeptidyl Aminopeptidase (An enzyme)
DAP . . . . Directed Audit Program
DAP . . . . Director of Army Programs
DAP . . . . Division of Air Pollution (Public Health Service)
DAP . . . . Do All Possible
D-A-P . . . . . . Draw a Person (Psychological test)
DAP & E . . . . . Diploma in Applied Parasitology and Entomology (British)
DAPEP . . . . . . Department of Army Panel on Environmental Physiology
DAPG . . . . . . Deutsch-Amerikanische Petroleum Gesellschaft (German-American Petroleum Society)
DAPG . . . . . . Drug & Allied Products Guild
DAPHNE . . . . Dido and Pluto Handmaiden for Nuclear Experiments (Nuclear reactor at Harwell, England)
DAPN . . . . . . Directional Antenna Phasing Network
DAPS . . . . . . Direct Access Programming System (Data processing)
DAQMG . . . . . Deputy Assistant Quartermaster General
DAR . . . . Daily Activity Report (Military)
DAR . . . . Damned Average Raiser (A diligent student) (Slang)
DAR . . . . Data Acquisition Recorder
DAR . . . . Data Automation Requirement
DAR . . . . Daughters of the American Revolution
DAR . . . . Defense Acquisition RADAR
DAR . . . . Differentiation with Asymmetrical Reinforcement
DAR . . . . Digital Angle Recorder
DAR . . . . Director of Army Research
DAR . . . . Driver Augmented Readout (Data processing)

DARA . . . . Deutsche Arbeitgemeinschaft fuer Rechen-Anlagen (A data processing association)
DARAS . . . . . . Direction and Range Acquisition System
DARC . . . . Data Acquisition and Reports Control (Army)
DARCEE. . . . . . Demonstration and Research Center for Early Education (George Peabody College, Nashville)
D Arch . . . . . . Doctor of Architecture
D Arch Des . . . Doctor of Architectural Design
D Arch E . . . . Doctor of Architectural Engineering
D Arch Eng . . . Doctor of Architectural Engineering
DARE . . . . Differential Analyzer Replacement
DARE . . . . Documentation Automated Retrieval Equipment
DARE . . . . Doppler and Range Evaluation
DARE . . . . Drug Addiction Rehabilitation Enterprise
DARES . . . . . . Data Analysis and Reduction System
DARF . . . . Defense Atomic Research Facility
DARK . . . . Discrimination Analysis Technique Adapted and Refined at Kwajalein (Army)
D Ark . . . . . . Doctor of Archaeology
DARME . . . . . . Director, Armament Engineering (Military) (Canada)
DARMS . . . . . . Drifting Automatic Radiometeorological Station
DARR . . . . Department of Army Regional Representative
DARRIS . . . . . Department of Army Requisitioning, Receipt, and Issue System
DARS . . . . Data Acquisition Recording System
DARS . . . . Data Acquisition and Reduction System
DARS . . . . Decommutation and Readout System (Data processing)
DARS . . . . Department of the Army Relocation Sites
DARS . . . . Digital Adaptive Recording System (Data processing)
DARS . . . . Digital Attitude Reference System
D Ar Sc . . . . . Doctor of Arts and Sciences
DART . . . . Daily Automatic Rescheduling Technique (Data processing)
DART . . . . Data Analysis Recording Tape
DART . . . . Data Reduction Translator
DART . . . . Decomposed Ammonia Radioisotope Thruster (Aerospace)
DART . . . . Deployable Automatic Relay Terminal (Air Force)
DART . . . . Depot Automatic Rescheduling Technique
DART . . . . Development of Advanced Rate Techniques
DART . . . . Directional Automatic Realignment of Trajectory
DART . . . . Dual Axis Rate Transducer (A gyroscope)
DARTS . . . . . . Digital Azimuth Range Tracking System
DAS . . . . Data Acquisition System
DAS . . . . Data Administration Section
DAS . . . . Data Automation System (or Subsystem) (NASA)
DAS . . . . Data Collection System
DAS . . . . Datatron Assembly System
DAS . . . . Date Arrived Station (Military)
DAS . . . . Defense Attaché System (Department of State)
DAS . . . . Deficiency Analysis Summary
DAS . . . . Delivered Alongside Ship
DAS . . . . Dialdehyde Starch
DAS . . . . Digital Altimeter Scanner
DAS . . . . Digital Analog Simulator
DAS . . . . Digital Attenuator System
DAS . . . . Dipole Antenna System
DAS . . . . Direct Air Support (Military)
DAS . . . . Direct Automotive Support
DAS . . . . Director of Administrative Services (US Military Government, Germany)
DAS . . . . Division of Atmospheric Surveillance (Environmental Protection Agency)
DAS . . . . Doctor of Applied Science
D As . . . . Doctor of Astronomy
DAS . . . . Dramatic Authors' Society (British)
DASA . . . . . . Defense Atomic Support Agency
DASA-DC . . . . Defense Atomic Support Agency Data Center
DASC . . . . . . Defense Automotive Supply Center
DASC . . . . . . Direct Air Support Center
DA Sc . . . . . . Doctor of Applied Science
DASCOTAR . . . Data Acquisition System, Correlation Tracking and Ranging (Air Force)
DASD . . . . . . Department of the Army Shipping Document
DASD . . . . . . Deputy Assistant Secretary of Defense
DASD . . . . . . Direct Access Storage Device (Data processing)
DASE . . . . . . Defense Against Sound Equipment (Military intelligence)
DAS & E . . . . Defense Aid (Lend-Lease) Services and Expenses (World War II)
DASEB . . . . . Department of the Army Suitability Evaluation Board
DASF . . . . . . Defense Aid (Lend-Lease) Special Fund (World War II)
DASF . . . . . . Direct Air Support Flight (Military)
DASH . . . . . . Delta Airlines Special Handling (for small packages)
DASH . . . . . . Destroyer Antisubmarine Helicopter
DASH . . . . . . Drone Antisubmarine Helicopter (Air Force, Navy)
DASL . . . . . . Department of the Army Strategic Logistics (Study)
DASM. . . . . . Director of Advanced Systems Management
DASO . . . . . . Demonstration and Shakedown Operations (Military)

DASO . . . . . . Department of the Army Special Order
DASOP . . . . . Demonstration and Shakedown Operation Piggyback (Kit)
DASP . . . . . . Departamento Administrativo do Servico Publico (Administrative Department of Public Service) (Brazil)
DASP . . . . . . Director of Advanced Systems Planning
DASPO . . . . . Department of the Army Special Photographic Office
DASq . . . . . . Direct Air Support Squadron (Air Force)
DASR . . . . . . Data Acquisition Statistical Recorder
D As S . . . . . Doctor of Association Science
D As Sc . . . . . Doctor of Association Science
DASSO . . . . . Data Systems Support Office
DASSO . . . . . Department of the Army Systems Staff Officer
DAST . . . . . . Directorate of Advanced Systems Technology
DAST . . . . . . Division for Advanced Systems Technology
DASTARD . . . Destroyer Antisubmarine Transportable Array Detector
DASY . . . . . . Data Analysis System
DAT . . . . Delayed Action Tablet (Pharmacy)
DAT . . . . Design Approval Test
DAT . . . . Desktop Analysis Tool (A publication)
DAT . . . . Detail Assembly Template
DAT . . . . Development Assist Test
DAT . . . . Differential Aptitude Test (Psychology)
DAT . . . . Director(ate) of Advanced Technology (Air Force)
DAT . . . . Docking Alignment Target (NASA)
DAT . . . . Drone Assisted Torpedo
DAT . . . . Duration Adjusting Type
DATA . . . . . . Defense Air Transportation Administration
DATA . . . . . . Development and Technical Assistance International
DATAC . . . . . Data Analog Computer
DATAC . . . . . Defense & Tactical Armament Control
DATAC . . . . . Digital Automatic Tester and Classifier
DATACOL . . . Data Collection
DATACOM . . . Data Communications
DATAR . . . . . Delegation General a l'Amenagement du Territoire et a l'Action Regionale (France)
DATAR . . . . . Digital Automatic Tracking and Ranging (or Remoting) (Air Force)
DATCOM . . . . Data Support Command (Army)
DATDC . . . . . Data Analysis and Technique Development Center
DATE . . . . . . Dash Automatic Test Equipment
DATE . . . . . . Data for Allotments Transmitted Electronically
DATE . . . . . . Digital Angular Torquing Equipment
DATEC . . . . . Digital Adaptive Technique for Efficient Communications
DATI . . . . . . Director of Army Technical Information
DATICO . . . . Digital Automatic Tape Intelligence Check-Out
DATO . . . . . . Disbursing and Transportation Office
DATO . . . . . . Discover America Travel Organizations, Inc. (Formerly, National Association of Travel Organizations, and Discover America, Inc.)
DATOR . . . . . Digital Data, Auxiliary Storage, Track Display, Outputs, and RADAR Display
DAT & OV . . . Defense Aid (Lend-Lease) Tanks and Other Vehicles (World War II)
DATR . . . . . . Design Approval Test Report
DATRAN . . . . Data Transmission Co.
DATRDA . . . . Defense Aid (Lend-Lease) Testing, Reconditioning, etc., of Defense Articles (World War II)
DATRIX . . . . . Direct Access to Reference Information (Xerox)
DATS . . . . . . Data Transmission System
DATS . . . . . . Despun Antenna Test Satellite (Air Force)
DATS . . . . . . Dynamic Accuracy Test Set (or System)
DATSC . . . . . Department of the Army Training and Support Committee
DATT . . . . . . Defense Attaché
DATUM. . . . . . Dokumentations- und Ausbildungszentrum fuer Theorie und Methode der Regionalforschung (Documentation and Training Center for Theory and Methods of Regional Research) (Germany)
DAU . . . . Data Acquisition Unit
DAU . . . . Declaration of Atlantic Unity
D Au E . . . . . Doctor of Automobile Engineering
D Au Eng . . . . Doctor of Automobile Engineering
DAV . . . . Disabled American Veterans
DAVA . . . . . . Disabled American Veterans Auxiliary
DAVC. . . . . . Delayed Automatic Volume Control
DAVI . . . . . . Department of Audiovisual Instruction (of NEA) (Later, AECT)
DAVI . . . . . . Dynamic Antiresonant Vibration Isolator
DAVID . . . . . Defense of Airborne Vehicles in Depth
DAV & OW . . . Defense Aid (Lend-Lease) Vessels and Other Watercraft (World War II)
DAVR . . . . . . Division of Adult and Vocational Research (US Office of Education)
DAW . . . . . . Dienstanweisung (Service regulations) (German military - World War II)
DAW . . . . . . Directorate of Atomic Warfare
DAWA . . . . . Danish American Women's Association
DAWG . . . . . Dynamic Air War Game (Military)

DAWID . . . . . . Device for Automatic Word Identification and Discrimination (Data processing)
DAWN . . . . . . Digital Automatic Weather Network
DAXBT . . . . . . Deep Airborne Expendable Bathythermograph (NOO)
DAY . . . . Dayco Corporation (NYSE symbol)
DAZ . . . . Deutsche Allgemeine Zeitung (German newspaper)
DAZD . . . . . . Double Anode Zener Diode
DB . . . . Bachelor of Divinity
DB . . . . Bomber (Russian aircraft symbol)
DB . . . . Daily Bulletin (Military)
DB . . . . Daimler-Benz (Name of German engine factory) (World War II)
DB . . . . Damned Bad
DB . . . . Day Book
DB . . . . Dead Band
dB . . . . Decibel (Unit of sound)
DB . . . . Decibel Meter (Radio equipment)
DB . . . . Depth Bomb (Military)
DB . . . . Deutsche Bundesbahn (West German railroad)
DB . . . . Diffused Base
DB . . . . Digital Block (Data processing)
DB . . . . Director Bomber (Air Force)
DB . . . . Dirty Book
DB . . . . Disciplinary Barracks
DB . . . . Dispersal Base (Military)
DB . . . . Display Buffer (Data processing)
DB . . . . Distribution Box (Technical drawings)
DB . . . . Dive Bomb
DB . . . . Dive Bomber Aircraft
DB . . . . Division Base (Army)
DB . . . . Double Biased (Relay)
DB . . . . Double Break
DB . . . . Dry Bulb (Thermometer, of a psychrometer) (Meteorology)
DB . . . . Durchfuehrungsbestimmung
DB . . . . Dynamic Braking
D/B . . . . Deposit Book
DB's . . . . Double Bottoms (Naval)
D & B . . . . . . Dun & Bradstreet, Inc.
DBA . . . . Danish Brotherhood in America
DBA . . . . . . Daytime Broadcasters Association
DBA . . . . Decibels, Adjusted (Communications)
DBA . . . . Dibenzanthracene (Chemical)
DBA . . . . . . Doctor of Business Administration
DBA . . . . Doing Business As (Followed by company name)
DBA . . . . Doing Business At
DBA . . . . Dolichos biflorus Agglutinin (Immunology)
DBA . . . . Duct Burner Augmentation
dB(A) . . . . Decibel A-Weighted
DB Ad . . . . . . Doctor of Business Administration
DB Adm . . . . . Doctor of Business Administration
DBB . . . . Detector Back Bias
DBB . . . . Detector Balanced Bias
DBB . . . . Deutsche Bauernbank
DBB . . . . Deutscher Beamtenbund (Federation of German Civil Service Officials) (West Germany)
DBC . . . . Decatur Baptist College (Iowa)
DBC . . . . Deputy Brigade Commander (Army)
DBC . . . . Desert Bighorn Council
DBC . . . . Diameter Bolt Circle (Technical drawings)
DBC . . . . Dictionnaire Biographique du Canada (More correctly, DCB/DBC)
DBC . . . . Digital-to-Binary Converter
DBC . . . . Doctor of Beauty Culture
DBC . . . . Don Bosco College (New Jersey)
DBC . . . . Dye-Binding Capacity
DBCAA . . . . . Dutch Belted Cattle Association of America
DBCATA . . . . Disposable Barrel Cartridge Area Target Ammunition (Weapon launcher)
DBCD . . . . . . Differential Base Current Drift
DBCO . . . . . . Digital Block Clock Oscillator (Data processing)
DBCO . . . . . . Dunbar Brothers Company, Division of Associated Spring Corporation
DBCP . . . . . . Dibromochloropropane (Chemical)
DBCP . . . . . . Double Bounce, Circularly Polarized
DBD . . . . Demokratische Bauernpartei Deutschlands (Democratic Peasants' Party) (East Germany)
DBD . . . . Detailed Budget Decision
DBD . . . . Diebold, Inc. (NYSE symbol)
DBD . . . . Digital Bargraph Display
DBD . . . . Double-Base Diode
DBD . . . . Double Beta Decay
DBDU . . . . . . Digital Bargraph Display Unit
DBE . . . . Dame Commander of the (Order of the) British Empire
DBE . . . . Dynamic Balancing Equipment
DBED . . . . . . Dibenzyl-Ethylene-Diamine (Penicillin)

DB Ed . . . . . . Doctor of Business Education
DBF . . . . Data Base File (Military)
DBF . . . . Drexel Bond Fund (NYSE symbol)
DBF . . . . Dual Bowl Feeder
DBFF . . . . . . Digital Block Flip-Flop (Data processing)
DBG . . . . Deutsche Buchgemeinschaft
DBG . . . . Deutsches Beamtengesetz (Germany)
DBH . . . . Diameter at Breast Height
DBH . . . . . . Division Beachhead (Army)
DBHP . . . . . . Drawbar Horsepower
DBI . . . . Differential Bearing Indicator
DBIA . . . . Digital Block Inverter Amplifier (Data processing)
D Bi Ch . . . . . Doctor of Biochemistry
D Bi Chem . . . . Doctor of Biochemistry
D Bi E . . . . . . Doctor of Biological Engineering
D Bi Eng . . . . . Doctor of Biological Engineering
DBIL . . . . Data Base Input Languages (Data processing)
D Bi Phy . . . . Doctor of Biological Physics
D Bi S . . . . . . Doctor of Biological Sciences
D Bi Sc . . . . . Doctor of Biological Sciences
DBK . . . . Data Bank
DBL . . . . Data Base Load (Data processing)
DBL . . . . Displaced Business Loan (Small Business Administration)
DBM . . . . Data Buffer Memory (Data processing)
DBM . . . . Data Bus Monitor
DBM . . . . . . Decibels (Referred to 1 Milliwatt in 600 Ohms)
DBM . . . . . . Doctor of Business Management
DBM . . . . Double Balanced Mixer
DBM . . . . Dry Bulk Material
DBMA . . . . . Distillate Burner Manufacturers Association
DBMS . . . . . . Director of Base Medical Services
DBMV . . . . . . Digital Block Multivibrator (Data processing)
DBN . . . . . . De Bonis Non (Of the goods not yet administered)
DBNA . . . . . . Digital Block Noninverting Amplifier (Data processing)
DBO . . . . Directorate of Biological Operations
DBO . . . . Dopaminebeta-Oxidase (Biochemistry)
DBO . . . . Dual Beam Oscilloscope
DBOI . . . . . . Developmental Basis of Issue (Military)
DBOMP . . . . . Data Base Organization and Maintenance Processor
DBP . . . . Deutsche Bundespost
DBP . . . . Drawbar Pull
DBPC . . . . . . Ditertiary-Butyl-para-Cresol (Organic chemistry)
DBPH . . . . . . Division for the Blind and Physically Handicapped (Library of Congress)
DBPO . . . . . . Data Buoy Project Office (National Oceanic and Atmospheric Administration)
DBR . . . . Disk, Balls, and Roller
DBR . . . . . . National Society, Daughters of the Barons of Runnemede
DBRI . . . . Danish Building Research Institute
DBRN . . . . . . Decibels Above Reference Noise (Communications)
DBS . . . . Despeciated Bovine Serum
DBS . . . . Dibutyl Sebacate
DBS . . . . Direct Broadcast Satellite
DBS . . . . Division of Biologics Standards (FDA)
DBS . . . . Doctor of Business Science
DBS . . . . Dodecyl Benzenesulfonate (Organic chemistry)
DBS . . . . Dominion Bureau of Statistics (Canada)
DBS . . . . Drama Book Specialists
DBS . . . . Drinking Behavior Scale (Test)
DBSC . . . . . . Digital Block Slave Clock
DB Sc . . . . . . Doctor of Business Science
DBSO . . . . . . District Base Service Office
DBST . . . . . . Digital Block Schmitt Trigger
DBT . . . . Double Base Transistor
DBT . . . . Dry Bulb Temperature
DBTT . . . . . . Ductile to Brittle Transition Temperature
DBUT . . . . . . Data Base Update Time
DBV . . . . De Badande Vannerna (Sweden)
DBV . . . . Decibel Referred to 1 Volt
DBVF . . . . . . Dual Bowl Vibratory Feeder
DBW . . . . . . Decibel Referred to 1 Watt
DBW . . . . Design Bandwidth
DBW . . . . Deutsche Babcock Wilcox Werke
DBW . . . . . . Differential Ballistic Wind
DBWC . . . . . . Differential Ballistic Wind Computer
DBWO . . . . . Differential Ballistic Wind Offset
DC . . . . Da Capo (Return to beginning) (Music)
DC . . . . "Daisy Cutter" (A type of World War II bomb)
DC . . . . Damage Control (Military)
DC . . . . Damage Controlman
DC . . . . Data Collection
DC . . . . Data Control

DC . . . . Daughters of Charity of St. Vincent de Paul (Roman Catholic religious order)
DC . . . . Daughters of the Cincinnati
DC . . . . Daughters of the Cross (Roman Catholic religious order)
DC . . . . Davy Crockett (A tactical atomic weapon) (Army)
DC . . . . Decade Counter
DC . . . . Decimal Classification
DC . . . . Deck Cargo
DC . . . . Deck Court
DC . . . . Defense Counsel
DC . . . . Definitive Contract
DC . . . . Delray Connecting R. R. (AAR code)
DC . . . . Dental Corps (Navy)
DC . . . . Department of Commerce
DC . . . . Deposited Carbon
DC . . . . Depth Charge (Aerial)
DC . . . . Deputy Chief
DC . . . . Deputy Consul
DC . . . . Destruct Charge
DC . . . . Deterioration Control
DC . . . . Development Characteristic
DC . . . . Deviation Clause
DC . . . . Device Control
DC . . . . Dewey Decimal Classification
DC . . . . Diagnostic Center
DC . . . . Dictaphone Corporation (NYSE symbol)
DC . . . . Digital Clock
DC . . . . Digital Comparator
DC . . . . Digital Computer
DC . . . . Dinero Contante (Cash) (Spain)
DC . . . . Dip Coating
DC . . . . Diphenylarsine Cyanide
DC . . . . Direct Command
DC . . . . Direct Current
DC . . . . Direct Cycle
DC . . . . Direction Center (SAGE) (RADAR)
DC . . . . Directional Coupler
DC . . . . Disarmament Commission (Also known as UNDC)
DC . . . . Disciples of Christ
DC . . . . Disorderly Conduct
DC . . . . Display Compartments (Freight)
DC . . . . Display Computer
DC . . . . Dissimilarity Coefficient (Numerical taxonomy)
DC . . . . District of Columbia
DC . . . . District Court
DC . . . . Division of Contracts
DC . . . . Doctor of Chiropractic
DC . . . . Doctor of Chiropraxis
DC . . . . Donor's Cells
DC . . . . Double Column
DC . . . . Double Contact (Switch)
DC . . . . Double Crochet
DC . . . . Partito Democrazia Cristiana (Christian Democrats) (Italy)
D & C . . . . . . Drug and Cosmetic Colors
D and C . . . . Dilation and Curettage (Of the uterus) (Obstetrics)
D of C . . . . . . Daughters of the Confederacy
D of C . . . . . . Department of Commerce
DCA . . . . Dachshund Club of America
DCA . . . . Dalmatian Club of America
DCA . . . . Data Correction Amplifier
DCA . . . . Defense Communications Agency (Military)
DCA . . . . Defense Contre Avion (French)
DCA . . . . Deflection Coil Amplifier
DCA . . . . Democratic Congress Alliance - Gambia
DCA . . . . Department of Civil Aviation (Australia)
DCA . . . . Deputy Chief of Staff for Administration
DCA . . . . Desoxycorticosterone Acetate
DCA . . . . Diamond Council of America
DCA . . . . Dichloroaniline
DCA . . . . Digital Computers Association
DCA . . . . Direct Current Amplifier
DCA . . . . Direct Current Arc
DCA . . . . Direction Center Active (SAGE) (RADAR)
DCA . . . . Distribution Contractors Association
DCA . . . . Doctor of Commercial Arts
DCA . . . . Double Conversion Adapter
DCA . . . . Drift Correction Angle
DCA . . . . Dynamics Corporation of America (NYSE symbol)
DCA . . . . Washington, DC (Airport symbol)
DCAA . . . . . . Defense Contract Audit Agency (DOD)
DCAC . . . . Defense Communications Agency Circular

DCAI . . . . Defense Communications Agency Instruction
DCAN . . . . . . Defense Communications Agency Notice
D Can L . . . . . Doctor of Canon Law
DCAO . . . . . . Digital Card And-Or Gate (Data processing)
DCAOC . . . . . Defense Communications Agency Operations Center
DCAP . . . . . . Deficiency Corrective Action Program (Surface Missile Systems)
DCAR . . . . Discrepancy and Corrective Action Report
DCAS . . . . Data Collection and Analysis System (NASA)
DCAS . . . . . . Defense Contract Administration Service (DOD)
DCAS . . . . . . Deputy Chief of the Air Staff (British)
DCAS . . . . . . Deputy Commander Aerospace System (Air Force)
DCASD . . . . . Defense Contract Administration Services District
DCASO . . . . . Defense Contract Administration Service Office
DCASPRO . . . Defense Contract Administration Service Plant Representative Office
DCASR . . . . . Defense Contract Administrative Service Region
DCAT . . . . . . Drug, Chemical and Allied Trades Association
DCB . . . . Defense Communications Board
DCB . . . . Design Certificate Board
DCB . . . . Devereux Child Behavior (Rating scale) (Psychology)
DCB . . . . Dictionary of Canadian Biography (More correctly, DCB/DBC)
DCB . . . . Distant-Control Boat
DCB . . . . Division Crime Buffer
DCB . . . . Double Cantilever Beam (Stress corrosion of aluminum alloy)
DCB/DBC . . . Dictionary of Canadian Biography/Dictionnaire Biographique du Canada
DCC . . . . Data Communications Channel
DCC . . . . Data Condition Code
DCC . . . . Defense Concessions Committee
DCC . . . . . . Defense Control Center
DCC . . . . Delayed Contact Closure
DCC . . . . . . Design Change Control
DCC . . . . Development Control Center
DCC . . . . Digital Control Computer
DCC . . . . . . District Communications Center (Navy)
DCC . . . . Division of Cataloging and Classification (Became CCS)
DCC . . . . Division of Consumer Credit (FTC)
DCC . . . . Dodge City College (Kansas)
DCC . . . . Double Cotton Covered (Insulation for certain types of magnet wire)
DCC . . . . Dow Chemical Company
DCC . . . . Dual Cam Clutch
DCCAO . . . . . Deputy Chief Civil Affairs Officer (US and Britain)
DCCB . . . . . . Defense Center Control Building (Army)
DCCC . . . . . . Defense Communications Control Center
DCCO . . . . . . Digital Card Clock Oscillator
DCCP . . . . . . Digital Computer Control Panel
DCCS . . . . . . Defense Communication Control System (Air Force)
DCCS . . . . . . Digital Camera Control System
DCCS . . . . . . Digital Command Communications System
DCCSA . . . . . Dictionary of Computer and Control Systems Abbreviations, Signs and Symbols
DCCU . . . . . . Data Communications Control Unit
DCD . . . . Defecation-Collection Device (Apollo) (NASA)
DCD . . . . Deflection Coil Drive
DCD . . . . Department of Community Development (Proposed Government department)
DCD . . . . . . Differential Current Density
DCD . . . . Digital Countdown Display (Data processing)
DCD . . . . Diode-Capacitor-Diode
DCD . . . . Direct Current Dump
DCD . . . . Don't-Care-a-Damn (British naval slang term for torpedo-boat destroyer) (World War I)
DCD . . . . Double Channel Duplex
DCDG . . . . . . Diode-Capacitor-Diode Gate (Data processing)
DCDMA . . . . . Diamond Core Drill Manufacturers Association
DCDP . . . . . . Defense Center Data Processing (Army)
DCDPO . . . . . Directorate for Civil Disturbance Planning and Operations (Army)
DCDR . . . . . . Direct Cycle Diphenyl Reactor
DCDS . . . . . . Digital Countdown Display System (Data processing)
DCDS . . . . . . Double Cotton Double Silk (Insulation)
DCDS . . . . . . Dual Channel Dual Speed
DCDT . . . . . . Direct-Current Differential Transformer
DCDU . . . . . . Data Collection and Distribution Units (Military)
DCE . . . . Dallas Cotton Exchange
DCE . . . . Department of Conservation and Environment (Proposed name for US Department of the Interior)
DCE . . . . Director(ate) of Civil Engineering (Air Force)
DCE . . . . Directorate of Communications - Electronics (ADC)
DCE . . . . . . Doctor of Civil Engineering
DCE . . . . Drive Control Equipment
DC Ed . . . . . . Doctor of Commercial Education
D Ce Eng . . . . Doctor of Cement Engineering
DCEO . . . . . . Defense Communications Engineering Office
D Cer E . . . . . Doctor of Ceramic Engineering

D Cer Eng . . . . Doctor of Ceramic Engineering
DCERR . . . . . . Depot Component/Equipment Rework Report (Navy)
DCF . . . . Data Collection Form (Civil Defense)
DCF . . . . Data Correlation Facility
DCF . . . . Deputy for Contract Financing (Air Force)
DCF . . . . Direct Centrifugal Flotation (Parasitology)
DCF . . . . Discounted Cash Flow
DCF . . . . Distribution Chart File
DCF . . . . Doctor of City Forestry
DCF . . . . Dynamic Coercive Force
DCFEM . . . . . . Dynamic Crossed-Field Electron Multiplication
DCFEM . . . . . . Dynamic Crossed Fields, Electric and Magnetic
DCFF . . . . Digital Card Flip-Flop (Data processing)
DCFG . . . . Direct Current Free Gyro
DCFT . . . . Double Coated Foam Tape
DCG . . . . Decisions of the Comptroller General
DCG . . . . Deputy Commanding General
DCG . . . . Deputy Commissary-General
DCG . . . . Diode Capacitor Gate
DCG . . . . Direct Current Generator
DCG . . . . Double Current Generator
DCG/CONARC . . Deputy Commanding General, Continental Army Command (Later, Deputy Commanding General, Training)
DCGO . . . . District Coast Guard Officer
DCGS . . . . . . Deputy Chief of the General Staff in the Field (British military)
DCG/T . . . . . . Deputy Commanding General, Training (CONARC) (Army)
D Ch . . . . Chirurgiae Doctor (Doctor of Surgery)
DCH . . . . Deep Case Hardened
DCH . . . . Denote Chassis
DCH . . . . Dicyclohexyl
DCH . . . . Diploma in Child Health
DCH . . . . District Chaplain (Navy)
DCHC . . . . . . Dunbarton College of Holy Cross (Washington, DC)
D Ch E . . . . . Doctor of Chemical Engineering
D Che E . . . . . Doctor of Chemical Engineering
D Chem E . . . . Doctor of Chemical Engineering
D Ch Eng . . . . Doctor of Chemical Engineering
D Chr Ed . . . . Doctor of Christian Education
DCHS . . . . . . Disciples of Christ Historical Society
DCI . . . . Defense Computer Institute
DCI . . . . Des Moines & Central Iowa R. R. (AAR code)
DCI . . . . Dielectric Constant Indicator
DCI . . . . Digital Clock Indicator
DCI . . . . Director of Central Intelligence
DCI . . . . Driving Car Intoxicated
DCIA . . . . Digital Card Inverting Amplifier (Data processing)
DCIB . . . . Data Communication Input Buffer
DCIC . . . . Defense Ceramic Information Center (Battelle Memorial Institute)
DCIGS . . . . . . Deputy Chief of the Imperial General Staff (British military)
DCII . . . . Defense Central Index of Investigations
DCIST . . . . . . Directory of Computerized Information in Science and Technology
DCJ . . . . Doctor of Criminal Jurisprudence
DCJC . . . . . . Dawson County Junior College (Montana)
DCL . . . . Design Capability Line (Army)
DCL . . . . Designer Choice Logic
DCL . . . . Detailed Check List
DCL . . . . Detroit College of Law
DCL . . . . Digital Computer Laboratory (MIT)
DCL . . . . Diners' Club, Inc. (NYSE symbol) (Delisted)
DCL . . . . Distillers Company Limited
DCL . . . . Division of Chemical Literature (ACS)
DCL . . . . Doctor of Canon Law
DCL . . . . Doctor of Civil Law(s)
DCL . . . . Doctor of Classical Literature
DCL . . . . Doctor of Commercial Law
DCL . . . . Dynamic Characteristic Load
DCLI . . . . Duke of Cornwall's Light Infantry (British)
DCLIR . . . . . . Dead Cat Lying in the Road (Traffic report)
DCM . . . . Deputy Chief of Mission (Diplomatic corps)
DCM . . . . Digital Circuit Module (Data processing)
DCM . . . . Director of Civilian Marksmanship (Army)
DCM . . . . Directorate for Classification Management (DOD)
DCM . . . . Distinguished Conduct Medal (British)
DCM . . . . District Court-Martial
DCM . . . . Doctor of Comparative Medicine
DCM . . . . Dominican Campaign Medal
DCM . . . . Double Common Meter (Music)
DCMA . . . . . . Defense Contract Management Agency
DCMA . . . . . . District of Columbia Manpower Administration
DCMA . . . . . . Dry Color Manufacturers Association
DCMA . . . . . . Duty Cycle Modulation Alternator

DCMD . . . . . . District of Columbia Military District
DCMH . . . . . . Data Collection Module, High Speed
DCMI . . . . Disclosure of Classified Military Information (to foreign governments)
DCML . . . . . . Data Collection Module, Low Speed
DCMS . . . . Data Control Multiplex System
DCMS . . . . . . Depot Command Management System
DCMT . . . . . . Diploma in Clinical Medicine of the Tropics (British)
DCMV . . . . . . Digital Card Multivibrator
DCN . . . . Dana Corporation (NYSE symbol)
DCN . . . . Depot Control Number
DCN . . . . Design Change Notice
DCN . . . . Development Change Notice
DCN . . . . Document Control Number
DCN . . . . Drawing Change Notice
DCNA . . . . . . Digital Card Noninverting Amplifier
DCNG . . . . . . District of Columbia National Guard
D Cn L . . . . . Doctor of Canon Law
DCNM . . . . . . Deputy Chief of Naval Material
DCNM(D) . . . . Deputy Chief of Naval Material, Development
DCNM(M & F) . . Deputy Chief of Naval Material, Material and Facilities
DCNM(M & O) . . Deputy Chief of Naval Material (Management and Organization)
DCNM(P & FM) . . Deputy Chief of Naval Material, Programs and Financial Management
DCNO . . . . . . Deputy Chief of Naval Operations
DCNOA . . . . . Deputy Chief of Naval Operations, Administration
DCNO(AIR) . . . Deputy Chief of Naval Operations (Air)
DCNO(D) . . . . Deputy Chief of Naval Operations (Development)
DCNOFOR . . . Deputy Chief of Naval Operations, Fleet Operations and Readiness
DCNO(L) . . . . Deputy Chief of Naval Operations (Logistics)
DCNO(M & NR) . Deputy Chief of Naval Operations for Manpower and Naval Reserve
DCNO(P & P) . . Deputy Chief of Naval Operations (Plans and Policies)
DCNO(P & R) . . Deputy Chief of Naval Operations, Personnel and Naval Reserve
DCNS . . . . . . Deputy Chief of Naval Staff (Marine Corps)
DCO . . . . Depth Cut Out (Navy)
DCO . . . . Deputy Commanding Officer
DCO . . . . Diploma of the College of Optics
DCO . . . . District Camouflage Office(r)
DCO . . . . District Clothing Office(r)
DCO . . . . District Communication Officer
DCO . . . . Divco-Wayne Corporation (NYSE symbol) (Delisted)
DCO . . . . Division Classification Officer
D Co . . . . Doctor of Cosmology
DCO . . . . Duke of Cambridge's Own (Military unit) (British)
DCO . . . . Duke of Connaught's Own (Military unit) (British)
DCOC . . . . . . Drain Cut-Off Current
DCOFS . . . . . . Deputy Chief of Staff
DCO(I) . . . . . . Director of Combined Operations (India)
D Com . . . . . . Doctor of Commerce
D Com Adm . . . Doctor of Commercial Administration
DCO(ME) . . . . Director of Combined Operations (Middle East)
D Compl L . . . . Doctor of Comparative Law
D Com Sc . . . . Doctor of Commercial Science
DCOR . . . . . . Defense Committee on Research (Air Force)
DCOT . . . . . . Distant Central Office Transceivers
DCP . . . . Data Collection Platform (National Weather Service)
DCP . . . . Depth Charge Projector
DCP . . . . Design Change Proposal
DCP . . . . Development Concept Paper
DCP . . . . Dicetyl Phosphate
DCP . . . . Digital Clock Pulse
DCP . . . . Diploma in Clinical Pathology
DCP . . . . Director of Civilian Personnel (Navy)
DCP . . . . Disaster Control Plan
DCP . . . . Display Control Panel
DCP . . . . Doctor of City Planning
DCPA . . . . . . Defense Civil Preparedness Agency (DOD)
DCPA . . . . . . Dichloropropionanilide
DCPB . . . . . . Departmental Civilian Personnel Branch
DCPG . . . . . . Digital Clock Pulse Generator
DCPI . . . . Deputy Chief Patrol Inspector (Immigration and Naturalization Service)
DCPO . . . . . . District Civilian Personnel Office(r)
DCPR . . . . . . Defense Contractor Planning Report
DCPR . . . . . . Deputy Chief of Staff for Plans and Research
DCPS . . . . . . Data Compression Processing System
DCPS . . . . . . Data Control Panel Submodule
DCPS . . . . . . Dynamic Crew Procedures Simulator
DCPT . . . . . . Direct Current Plasma Torch
DCPT . . . . . . Doctor of Chiropractic and Physiological Therapeutics
DCQM . . . . . . Digital Circuit Quality Monitor
DCR . . . . Data Conversion Receiver
DCR . . . . Data Coordinator and Retriever (Data processing)
DCR . . . . Decision Circuit Reception

DCR	Dental Corps, General Service (USNR officer designation)
DCR	Design Change Request
DCR	Detail Condition Register
DCR	Digital Concentration Readout (Data processing)
DCR	Digital Conversion Receiver
DCR	Direct Conversion Reactor
DCR	Direct Cortical Response
DCR	Direct-Current Restorer
DCR	District Chief Ranger (Ancient Order of Foresters)
DCR	Doctor of Comparative Religion
D Cr	Doctor of Criminology
DCR	Drawing Change Request
DCR	Drawing Copy Request
DCRB	Drawn Cup Roller Bearing
DCRE	Deputy Commandant Royal Engineers (British)
DCREO	Design Change Request Engineering Order
DCRF	Die Casting Research Foundation
DCRO	District Civil Readjustment Office(r)
DCRP	Department of City and Regional Planning (MIT)
DCRP	Developmental Cycle Research Plan
DCRP	Disaster Control Recovery Plan
DCRS	Data Collection and Reduction System
DCRSEO	Design Change Request Serial Engineering Order
DCS	Damage Control School (Navy)
DCS	Data Communications Subsystem
DCS	Data Conditioning System (NASA)
DCS	Data Conversion System
DCS	Data Correction System
DCS	Davis Computer Systems, Inc.
DCS	Defense Communications System
DCS	Delayed Coincidence Spectroscopy
DCS	Deputy Chief of Staff
DCS	Design Change Schedule
DCS	Digital Command System
DCS	Digital Communication System (Data processing)
DCS	Digital Control System
DCS	Digital Countdown System (Data processing)
DCS	Direct Current Sensor
DCS	Direction Center Standby (SAGE)
DCS	Distillers Corporation-Seagrams Ltd. (NYSE symbol)
DCS	Diversity Combiner System
DCS	Doctor of Christian Science
DCS	Doctor of Christian Service
DCS	Doctor of Commercial Science
DCS	Dorsal Column Stimulator (Pain killer)
DCS	Double Channel Simplex
DCS	Double Compton Scattering
DCS	Drone Control System
DCSA	Direct Current Servo Amplifier
DC of SA	Deputy Chief of Staff, Army
DC/SAF	Deputy Chief of Staff, Air Force
DCSAIROPNET . .	Defense Communications Systems Air Operational Network
DCSAR	Defense Contract Services Administration Region
DCSC	Defense Construction Supply Center
DCSC	Digital Card Slave Clock
DC Sc	Doctor of Commercial Science
DCS/C	Deputy Chief of Staff, Comptroller
DCS/D	Deputy Chief of Staff, Development
DCSDATANET . .	Defense Communications Systems Data Network
DC Se	Doctor of Commercial Service
DCS/I	Deputy Chief of Staff, Intelligence (Army)
DCS/INT	Deputy Chief of Staff, Intelligence (Air Force)
DC/SL	Deputy Chief of Staff, Logistics (Army)
DCSLOG	Deputy Chief of Staff, Logistics (Army)
DCSM	Deputy Chief of Staff, Materiel
DC/SMO	Deputy Chief of Staff, Military Operations (Army)
DCSO	Deputy Chief of Staff, Operations
DCSOA	Deputy Chief of Staff, Operations and Administration
DCSOPS	Deputy Chief of Staff for Military Operations (Army)
DCSP	Defense Communications Satellite Project
DCS/P	Deputy Chief of Staff, Personnel
DCS/PEAB	Defense Communications System – Personnel Emergency Actions Book
DCSPER	Deputy Chief of Staff for Personnel (Army)
DCS/P & O . . .	Deputy Chief of Staff for Plans and Operations
DCS/P & P . . .	Deputy Chief of Staff, Plans and Programs
DCSPR	Deputy Chief of Staff for Plans and Research (Army)
DCS/P & R . . .	Deputy Chief of Staff for Programs and Resources
DCSR	Dominican College of San Rafael (California)
DCS/RC	Deputy Chief of Staff, Reserve Components (Army)
DCS/R & D . . .	Deputy Chief of Staff, Research & Development (Army)
DCS/R & T . . .	Deputy Chief of Staff, Research and Technology
DCSS	Damage Control Suit System (Navy oxygen sensor)
DCS/S & L . . .	Deputy Chief of Staff, Systems and Logistics
DCST	Digital Card Schmitt Trigger
DCSTTYNET . . .	Defense Communications System Teletype Network
DCT	Data Conversion Transmitter
DCT	Decimal Code Translator
DCT	Department of Classroom Teachers (of NEA)
DCT	Depth-Charge Thrower
DCT	Depth Charges Track
DCT	Diode Curve Tracer
DCT	Direct Carbon Transfer
DCT	Disaster Control Team
DCT	Dissector Camera Tube
DCT	Doctor of Christian Theology
DCT	Doctor of Christian Training
DCT	Doklady Chemical Technology
DCTC	District of Columbia Teachers College
DCTL	Direct-Coupled Transistor Logic
DCTM	Direct Current Torque Motor
DCTSC	Defense Clothing and Textile Supply Center (Later, Defense Personnel Support Center) (DOD)
DC & TSC	Defense Clothing and Textile Supply Center (Later, Defense Personnel Support Center) (DOD)
DCTV	Digital Color Television
DCU	Data Collection Unit
DCU	Data Command Unit
DCU	Data Control Unit
DCU	Decade Counting Unit
DCU	Decimal Counting Unit
DCU	Digital Counting Unit
DCUA	Division of College and University Assistance (HEW)
DC (UN)	Disarmament Commission of the United Nations
DCUTL	Direct Coupled Unipolar Transistor Logic
DCV	Direct Current, Volts
DCV	Directional Control Valve
DCV	Double Check Valve
DCVG	Digital Control and Vector Generator
DCVR	Direct Current Voltage Reference (or Regulator)
DCW	Define Constant with Wordmark
DCW	National Society, Daughters of Colonial Wars
DCWO	Design Change Work Order
DCWV	Direct Current Working Volts
DCX	Direct Current Experiments (ORNL)
D Cx	Double Convex
DD	Daily Double (Horse racing)
DD	Dangerous Drugs (British)
DD	Day's Date
DD	Days after Date
DD	Days after Delivery
DD	Deadline Date
DD	Decimal Divide
DD	Dedit, Dedicavit (Gave, Dedicated)
DD	Deep-Drawn (Metals)
DD	Deferred Delivery (Especially, of securities)
DD	Delayed Delivery
DD	Delivered at Docks
DD	Deo Dedit (He Gave to God)
DD	Department of Defense
DD	Dependent Drainage (Medicine)
DD	Deputy Director
DD	Destroyer (Navy symbol)
DD	Development Directive
DD	Dichloropropene-Dichloropropane (Chemical)
DD	Differential Diagnosis (Medicine)
DD	Digital Display (SAGE)
DD	Discharged Dead (On a serviceman's papers)
DD	Dishonorable Discharge
DD	District Director
DD	Doctor of Divinity
DD	Doctor of Divinity in Metaphysics
DD	Dono Dedit (He or She Gave as a Gift)
DD	Donum Dedit; Dedicavit (Gave, Dedicated)
DD	Double Drift (As used in a navigator's log)
DD	Drawing Deviation
DD	Drum Demand
DD	Drydock
DD	du Pont (E.I.) de Nemours & Company (NYSE symbol)
DD	Due Date
DD	Duplex-Drive (Tank)
DD	Dutch Door (Technical drawings)

D/D	Days after Date (Business and trade)
D/D	Demand Draft
D/D	Donation on Discharge
D & D	Death and Dying (Medical course)
D & D	Desk and Derrick (Oil industry)
D & D	Direct and Distribution (Postal Service)
D & D	Drunk and Dirty (Military)
D & D	Drunk and Disorderly
D-to-D	Digital-to-Digital
DDA	Dental Dealers of America
DDA	Depth-Duration-Area
DDA	Digital Differential Analyzer
DDA	Directed Duty Assignment (Military)
DDA	Doctor of Dramatic Art
DDALV	Day's Delay Enroute Authorized Chargeable as Leave (Military)
DDAM	Dynamic Design Analysis Method (Navy)
DDAS	Digital Data Acquisition System
DDAS	Digital Data Archives System
DDAS (ET)	Deputy Director of Armament Supply (Eastern Theater)
DDB	Data Display Board (or Buffer) (Data processing)
DDB	Design Data Book
DDB	Dial Drive Belt
DDB	Digital Data Buffer (Data processing)
DDB	Double Declining Balance (Statistics)
DDB	Doyle Dane Bernbach, Inc. (Advertising agency)
DDC	Corvette (Navy symbol)
DDC	Dangerous Drug Cabinet (Lockable auxiliary to bathroom medicine chest)
DDC	Data Display Central
DDC	Data Distribution Center
DDC	Decision, Design, and the Computer (Symposium)
DDC	Deck Decompression Chamber (Undersea technology)
DDC	Defense Documentation Center for Scientific and Technical Information (DOD)
DDC	Dewey Decimal Classification
DDC	Diamond Dealers Club
DDC	Digital Data Converter
DDC	Direct Digital Control
DDC	Double Doped Crystal
DDC	Dual Diversity Comparator
D & DC	Drunk and Disorderly Conduct
DDCE	Digital Data Conversion Equipment
DDCO (I)	Deputy Director of Combined Operations (India)
DDCONUS . . .	Date Departed Continental United States (Military)
DDCP	Department of Defense Claimant Program
DDCS	Direct Digital Control System
DDD	Dat, Dicat, Dedicat (He Gives, Devotes, and Dedicates)
DDD	Deadline Delivery Date
DDD	Desired Delivery Date
DDD	Detailed Data Display
DDD	Diesel Direct Drive (Navy)
DDD	Direct Distance Dialing (Of telephone numbers for toll calls)
DDD	Dono Dedit Dedicavit (He Gave and Dedicated as a Gift)
DDD	Duplexed Display Distributor
DD in D	De Die in Diem (From Day to Day)
DDDA	Decimal Digital Differential Analyzer
DDDS	Digital Data Display System
DDE	Direct Digital Encoder
DDE	Escort Destroyer (Navy symbol)
DDEL	Defense Development and Engineering Laboratories (Military)
DDEP	Defense Development Exchange Program
D Des	Doctor of Design
DDF	Dental Documentary Foundation
DDF	Design Discharge Format
DDF	Design Disclosure Formats (Naval Applied Science Laboratory)
DDF	Dielectric Dissipation Factor
DDF	Military Order, Devil Dog Fleas
DDG	Data Display Generator
DDG	Dial Depth Gage
DDG	Digital Data Group
DDG	Digital Delay Generator
DDG	Digital Display Generator (SAGE)
DDG	Guided Missile Destroyer (Navy symbol)
DDGC	Dishonorable Discharge, General Court-Martial, after Confinement in Prison (Navy)
DDGE	Digital Display Generator Element
DDGI	Dishonorable Discharge, General Court-Martial, Immediate (Navy)
DDGP	Dishonorable Discharge, General Court-Martial, after Violation of Probation (Navy)
DDH	Digital Data Handling
DDHP	Deringer Duell Head Process
DDI	Data Display Indicator
DDI	Density Dependent Inhibition (of cell growth)
DDI	Depression Deviation Indicator
DDI	Depth Deviation Indicator
DDI	Directed Drawing Instrument
D Did	Doctor of Didactics
D Di E	Doctor of Diesel Engineering
D Di Eng	Doctor of Diesel Engineering
D Dipl	Doctor of Diplomacy
DDIR	District Directors of Internal Revenue (IRS)
DDIS	Document Data Indexing Set
DDK	Hunter Killer Destroyer (Navy ship symbol)
DDL	Data Definition Language
DDL	Data Distribution List
DDL	Det Danske Luftfartselskab A/S (Danish Airlines)
DDL	Digital Data Link
DDL	Digital Data Logger
DDL	Dispersive Delay Line
DDL	Doctor of Divine Literature
DDLDS	Date Departed Last Duty Station (Military)
DDM	Department of Data Management (VA)
DDM	Derived Delta Modulation
DDM	Difference in Depth Modulation
DDM	Digital Display Machine
DDM	Digital Display Makeup
DDM	Diploma in Dermatological Medicine (British)
DDM	Doctor of Dental Medicine
DDM	Double Diffused Mesa
DDM	Master of Dental Medicine
DDMI	Deputy Director of Military Intelligence
DDMOI	Deputy Director of Military Operations and Intelligence (British)
DDMP	Deep-Drawn Metal Part
DDMS	Department of Defense Manned Space Flight
DDMS	Deputy Director of Medical Services (British)
DDMS	Digital Data Measuring System
DDMT	Deputy Director of Military Training (British)
D Dn	Doctor of Design
DDNN	Dominis Nostris (To Our Lords)
DDNP	Diazonitrophenol
DDO	Deputy Director of Operations (Air Force)
DDO	Destroyers, Disbursing Office (Navy)
DDO	Diploma in Dental Orthopaedics (British)
DDO	District Dental Office(r) (Navy)
DDOCE	Digital Data Output Conversion Element
DDP	Department of Defense Production
DDP	Design Data Package
DDP	Digital Data Processor
DDP	Director(ate) of Development Planning (Air Force)
DDP	Dry Discharge Pump
DDPA	Delta Dental Plans Association
DDPC	DCSLOG (Deputy Chief of Staff for Logistics) Data Processing Center (Military)
DDPE	Digital Data Processing Equipment
DDPS	Digital Data Processing System
DDPS	Discrete Depth Plankton Sampler
DDPS	Discrimination Data Processing System
DDQ	Dimensions Description Questionnaire
DDR	Daily Demand Rate
DDR	Daughters of the Defenders of the Republic, USA
DDR	Daughters of the Divine Redeemer (Roman Catholic religious order)
DDR	Decoy Discrimination RADAR
DDR	Deutsche Demokratische Republik (German Democratic Republic) (East Germany)
DDR	Digital Data Receiver
DDR	Digital Data Recorder
DDR	Digital Demand Recorder
DDR	Diploma in Diagnostic Radiology (British)
DDr	Doctor of Divinity
DDR	Downrange Data Report
DDR	RADAR Picket Destroyer (Navy symbol)
DDRB	Danish Defense Research Board
DDRB	Data Requirements Review Board
DD & RB	Document Distribution and Reproduction Branch (NTIS)
DDRE	Director of Defense Research and Engineering (Army)
DDR & E	Defense Development Research and Engineering
DDR & E	Director of Defense Research and Engineering
DDRF	Degenerative Diseases Research Foundation
DDRH	Digital Data Recording Head
DDRI	Design Drafting Reference Information
DDRR	Directional Discontinuity Ring Radiator
DDRS	Digital Data Recording System
DDS	Damien-Dutton Society

DDS . . . . Data Display System
DDS . . . . Data Distribution System
DDS . . . . Deep-Diving System
DDS . . . . Design Disclosure Standard
DDS . . . . Diaminodiphenylsulfone (Antimalaria drug)
DDS . . . . Digital Data Servo
DDS . . . . Digital Data System
DDS . . . . Digital Display Scope
DDS . . . . Digital Drafting System
DDS . . . . Directory Development Study
DDS . . . . Distillation Desalination System
DDS . . . . Doctor of Dental Surgery
DDS . . . . Doppler Detection Station (Detection station on the Mid-Canada Line)
DDS . . . . Doppler Detection System
DDS . . . . Dose Detector System
DDS . . . . Dummy Director Set
DD Sc . . . . . . Doctor of Dental Science
DD Sc . . . . . . Doctor of Dental Surgery
DDSE . . . . Design Disclosure for Systems and Equipment
DDSM . . . . Decontrolled Defense Supply Material
DDST . . . . Deputy Director of Supply and Transport (British)
DDSU . . . . Digital Data Storage Unit (Data processing)
DD Sur . . . . . . Doctor of Dental Surgery
DDT . . . . Debye Dipole Theory
DDT . . . . Design and Drafting Techniques
DDT . . . . Dichlorodiphenyltrichloroethane (Chemistry)
DDT . . . . Digital Data Transceiver (Data processing)
DDT . . . . Digital Data Transmitter
DDT . . . . Digital Debugging Tape
DDT . . . . Doctor of Drugless Therapy
DDT . . . . Doppler Data Translator
DDT . . . . Dynamic Display Tester
DDTCA . . . . . . Dandie Dinmont Terrier Club of America
DDTE . . . . Digital Data Terminal Equipment
DDT & E . . . . . Design, Development, Test & Evaluation
DDTESM . . . . . Digital Data Terminal Equipment Service Module
DDTO . . . . District Domestic Transportation Office(r)
DDTS . . . . Direct Dial Telephone System
DDTV . . . . Dry Diver Transport Vehicle (Navy)
DDU . . . . Digital Display Unit
DDU . . . . Digital Distributing Unit
DDU . . . . Disc Data Unit
DDU . . . . Dual Diversity Unit
DDUS . . . . Date Departed United States (Army)
DDV . . . . Deck Drain Valve
DDV . . . . Deep-Diving Vehicle
DDY . . . . Dynayoke Deflection Yoke
DE . . . . Date of Entry (Military)
DE . . . . Date of Extension (Military)
DE . . . . Decision Element
DE . . . . Decision Error
DE . . . . Deck and Engineering Duties, General Service (USNR officer designation)
DE . . . . Deckle Edged (Paper)
DE . . . . Deep Etch (Lithography term)
DE . . . . Deere & Company (NYSE symbol)
DE . . . . Deflection Error (Military)
DE . . . . Delaware
DE . . . . Department of Education
DE . . . . Destroyer Escort (Navy symbol)
DE . . . . Development Engineering
DE . . . . Diesel-Electric
DE . . . . Digital Encoder
DE . . . . Director Error (Military)
DE . . . . Disk Electrophoresis
DE . . . . Distributive Education
DE . . . . District Engineer (Army)
DE . . . . Doctor of Entomology
DE . . . . Double End (Technical drawings)
DE . . . . Double-ended, Cylindrical Boiler
DE . . . . Double Entry (Bookkeeping)
DE . . . . Dynamic Engineer
DE's . . . . Destroyer Escorts (Navy)
DEA . . . . Dance Educators of America
DEA . . . . Data Exchange Agreement
DEA . . . . Department of Economic Affairs (Department of Agriculture)
DEA . . . . Dictionary of Electronics Abbreviations, Signs and Symbols
DEA . . . . Diethanolamine
DEA . . . . Diethylamine
DEA . . . . Dynamo Electric Amplifier
DEACON . . . . . Direct English Access and Control (Data processing)

DEADS . . . . . . Detroit Air Defense Sector (ADS)
DEAE . . . . Diethylaminoethyl
DEAE-D . . . . . Diethylaminoethyl Dextran
DEAL . . . . Decision Evaluation and Logic
DEAL . . . . Detachment Equipment Authorization List (Military)
DEAN . . . . Deputy Educators Against Narcotics
DEAP . . . . Division of Engineering and Applied Physics (Harvard University)
DEAPA . . . . . . Diethylaminopropylamine
DEAR . . . . Diamonds, Emeralds, Amethysts, and Rubies
DEB . . . . Decaying Extrastellar Body (Astronomy)
DEB . . . . Dental Examining Board
DEC . . . . Control Escort Vessel (Navy symbol)
DEC . . . . Data Equipment Company
DEC . . . . Davis and Elkins College (West Virginia)
DEC . . . . December
DEC . . . . Decimal Equivalent Chart
DEC . . . . Digital Equipment Corporation (NYSE symbol)
DEC . . . . Direct Energy Conversion
D Ec . . . . Doctor of Economics
DEC . . . . Drug Evaluation Center
DEC . . . . Dry Electrolytic Capacitor
DEC . . . . Dynamic Energy Conversion
DECA . . . . . . Descent Engine Control Assembly (Apollo) (NASA)
DECA . . . . . . Distributive Education Clubs of America
DECAL . . . . . . Decalcomania
DECAL . . . . . . Digital Equipment Corporation's Adaptation of Algorithmic Language (Data processing)
DECAN . . . . . . Distance-Measuring Equipment Command and Navigation
DECCO . . . . . . Defense Commercial Communications Office (Military)
DECD . . . . . . Deceased
DECEA . . . . . . Defense Communication Engineering Agency
DECELERON . . Decelerator and Aileron (NASA)
DECEO . . . . . . Defense Communications Engineering Office (Army)
DECH . . . . . . Diethylcyclohexane
DE Ch E . . . . . Doctor of Electro-Chemical Engineering
DECHEMA . . . . Deutsche Gesellschaft fuer Chemisches Apparatewesen
DE Ch Eng . . . . Doctor of Electro-Chemical Engineering
DECM . . . . . . Defense Electronic Countermeasures
DECN . . . . . . Decision
DECO . . . . . . Direct Energy Conversion Operation
DECOM . . . . . Decommissioned
DECOMP . . . . Decomposition Mathematical Programming System
D Econ . . . . . . Doctor of Economics
DECOR . . . . . Digital Electronic Continuous Ranging
DECS . . . . Decoration for Exceptional Civilian Service (Army civilian employee award)
DECUS . . . . . . Digital Equipment Computer Users Society
DED . . . . Director of the Education Department (British Navy)
D Ed . . . . Doctor of Education
DED . . . . Doctor of English Divinity
DEDA . . . . . . Data Entry and Display Assembly (Apollo) (NASA)
D Ed AS . . . . . Diploma in Education Administration and Supervision
DEDD . . . . . . Diesel Electric Direct Drive (Navy)
DEDE . . . . . . Density-Depth
DEDS . . . . . . Digital Error Detection Subsystem (Data processing)
DEDS . . . . . . Directory of Engineering Document Services (A publication)
DEE . . . . Digital Evaluation Equipment
DEE . . . . Digital Event Evaluator
DEE . . . . Doctor of Electrical Engineering
DE Eng . . . . . . Doctor of Electrical Engineering
DEEP . . . . . . Developmental Economic Education Program
DEER . . . . . . Deer Environment Ecology and Resources (An organization)
DEER . . . . . . Directional Explosive Echo Ranging
DEF . . . . Defense
DEFCON . . . . . Defense Readiness Condition
DEFLOWH . . . . Defense Liaison Officer to the White House
DEFREP . . . . . Defense Readiness Posture (Army)
DEFREPNAMA . . Defense Representative, North Atlantic Mediterranean Area
DEFSATCOM . . Defense Satellite Communication System
DEFSCAP . . . . Defense Standard Contract Administration Procedure
DEFSEC . . . . . Defense Sector (Navy)
DEFSIP . . . . . . Defense Scientists Immigration Program
DEFT . . . . . . Driven Equilibrium Fourier Transform
DEFT . . . . . . Dynamic Error-Free Transmission
DEG . . . . Degenerate Electron Gas
DEG . . . . Degree
DEG . . . . Guided Missile Destroyer Escort (Navy symbol)
DEGA . . . . . . Depth Gage
DEG and DEP . . Degaussing and Deperming (Navy)
DEGS . . . . . . Diethylene Glycol Succinate
DEH . . . . Departement Etranger Hachette

DEH . . . . Digital Encoder Handbook
DEHB . . . . . . Digital Encoder Handbook
DEHP . . . . . . Diethyl Hydrogen Phosphite
DEI . . . . Defense Electronics, Incorporated
DEI . . . . Design Engine Inspection
DEI . . . . Development Engineering Inspection
DEI . . . . Display Evaluation Index
DEI . . . . **Dutch East Indies**
DEIMOS . . . . . Development Investigation in Military Orbiting Systems
DEL . . . . Del Monte Corp. (NYSE symbol)
DEL . . . . Delaware
D El . . . . Doctor of Elements
DEL . . . . Doctor of English Literature
DEL . . . . Donor Energy Level
DEIA . . . . . . Dictionary of Electrical Abbreviations, Signs and Symbols
DELACCT . . . . Delinquent Account
DELE . . . . . . Delete
D El Ed . . . . . Diploma in Elementary Education
DELMARVA . . . Delaware, Maryland, Virginia
D Elo . . . . . . Doctor of Elocution
DELPHO . . . . Deliver by Telephone (Message handling)
DELRIBACO . . . Delaware River Basin Commission (Successor to INCODEL)
DELTA . . . . . Detailed Labor and Time Analysis (PERT)
DELTA . . . . . Differential Electronically Locking Test Accessory
DELTIC . . . . . **Delay Line Time Compression**
DEM . . . . Decoy Ejection Mechanism
DEM . . . . Democrat(ic)
DEM . . . . Dynamic Effect Model
DEMA . . . . . . **Diesel Engine Manufacturers Association**
DEMATRON . . . Distributed Emission Magnetron Amplifier
DEMIZ . . . . . DEW (Distant Early Warning) East Military Identification Zone
DEML . . . . . . Detached Enlisted Men's List (Army)
DEML(CIC) . . . Enlisted Men on Duty with the Counter Intelligence Corps (Army)
DEML(NG) . . . . Enlisted Men on Duty with the National Guard (Army)
DEML(OR) . . . . Enlisted Men on Duty with the Organized Reserves (Army)
DEML(ROTC) . . Enlisted Men on Duty with the Reserve Officers' Training Corps (Army)
DEMOD . . . . . Deployment Model (Army)
DEMON . . . . . Decision Mapping via Optimum Go-No Networks
DEMON . . . . . Digital Electric Monitor
DEMP . . . . . . Democratic Party (Slang)
DEMS . . . . . . **Defensively Equipped Merchant Ships**
DEMS . . . . . . Development Engineering Management System (Air Force)
DEMS . . . . . . Dynamic Effectiveness Model Study
DEN . . . . Denny's Restaurants, Inc. (NYSE symbol)
DEN . . . . Denver (Colo.) (Airport symbol)
DEN . . . . Diethylnitrosamine (Organic chemistry)
D En . . . . Doctor of English
DEN . . . . Dow Epoxy Novolac
DENALT . . . . . Density-Altitude (Computer)
DENDRAL . . . . Dendritic Algorithm (Organic molecules)
D Eng . . . . . . Doctor of Engineering
D Eng P . . . . . Doctor of Engineering Physics
D Eng Sc . . . . . Doctor of Engineering Science
DENPAY . . . . Dental Pay
DENS . . . . . . Density
DENT . . . . . . Directions for Education in Nursing via Teaching
D Ent . . . . . . Doctor of Entomology
DENTCORPS . . Dental Corps (Air Force)
DEO . . . . Deck Edge Outlet (Navy)
DEO . . . . District Engineer Officer (Army)
DEO . . . . Divisional Education Officer (British)
DEO . . . . Divisional Entertainments Officer (British)
DEO . . . . Doped Erbium Oxide
DEO . . . . Duke of Edinburgh's Own (Military unit) (British)
DEP . . . . Data Exchange Program
DEP . . . . Defense Electronic Products
DEP . . . . Deflection Error Probable (Military)
DEP . . . . Dense Electronic Population
DEP . . . . Depart(ure)
DEP . . . . Deposit(s)
DEP . . . . Depot
DEP . . . . Deputy
DEP . . . . Diethyl Pyrocarbonate (Chemical preservative)
DEP . . . . Double Ended Pivot
DEPA . . . . . . Defense Electric Power Administration (Department of the Interior)
DEPACTV . . . . . Depot Activity
DEPC . . . . . . Diethylpyrocarbonate (Antiseptic for wines)
DEPCDR(R & D) . . . Deputy Commander for Research and Development (Navy)
DEPCDR(SA) . . . Deputy Commander for Ship Acquisitions (Navy)
DEPDIRPACDOCKS . . Deputy Director Pacific Division, Bureau of Yards and Docks
(Later, NFEC) (Navy)

DEPERMSTA . . . Deperming and Flashing Station (Navy)
DE Phy . . . . . . Doctor of Engineering Physics
DEPI . . . . Differential Equations Pseudocode Interpreter
DEPN . . . . . . Dependent
DEPO . . . . . . Devils Postpile National Monument
DEPOS . . . . . Depositary
DEPREP . . . . . Deployment Reporting System
DEPSECDEF . . . Deputy Secretary of Defense
DEPSO . . . . . Department Standardization Office (Navy)
DEPSUM . . . . Daily Estimated Position Summary (Navy)
DEPSUM . . . . Deployment Summary Report (Air Force)
DEPT . . . . . . Department
DEPTEKRA . . . Departemen Tekstil dan Keradjinan Rakjat (Indonesia)
DEPU . . . . . . De Paul University (Illinois)
DEQUISA . . . . Desarrollo Quimico Industrial, SA (Spain)
DER . . . . Declining Error Rate
DER . . . . Dereco, Inc. (NYSE symbol)
DER . . . . Designated Engineer Representative (FAA title)
DER . . . . Destroyer Escort, RADAR (Navy symbol)
DER . . . . Document Error Report
De R . . . . Reaction of Degeneration (Neurology)
DERAX . . . . . Detection and Range (Early name for RADAR)
DERD . . . . . . **Diesel Electric Reduction Drive**
DERE . . . . . . Dounreay Experimental Reactor Establishment (British)
DERI . . . . Deep Electric Research Investigation (Navy)
DERM . . . . . . Delayed Echo RADAR Marker
DEROS . . . . . **Date Eligible for Return from Overseas**
DEROS . . . . . Date of Estimated Return from Overseas
DES . . . . Department of Education and Science (British)
DES . . . . Design Expansion System
DES . . . . Detroit Steel Corporation (NYSE symbol) (Delisted)
DES . . . . Diethylstilbestrol (Synthetic estrogen)
DES . . . . Differential Equation Solver
DES . . . . Digital Expansion System
DES . . . . Director of Engineer Stores Service (British)
DES . . . . Doctor of Engineering Science
DES . . . . Doctors Emergency Service (New York City)
DES . . . . Dow Education Systems (Dow Chemical Corp.)
DES . . . . Dual Exciter System
DES . . . . Ducosyn Excitation Switch
DES . . . . Dynamic Electro-Speaker
DESAF . . . . . Destroyers, Asiatic Fleet (Navy)
DESB . . . . . . Devereux Elementary School Behavior (Rating scale) (Psychology)
DESBATFOR . . . Destroyer Battle Force (Navy)
DESC . . . . . . Defense Electronic Supply Center (DSA)
DE Sc . . . . . . Doctor of Engineering Science
DESCOFOR . . . Destroyer Scouting Force (Navy)
DESCRUPAC . . . Destroyers/Cruisers, Pacific Fleet (Navy)
DESDIV . . . . . Destroyer Division (Navy)
DESEFF . . . . . Deserter's Effects (Military)
DESFLOT . . . . Destroyer Flotilla (Navy)
DESG . . . . . . Designate (or Designation)
DESIGNAP . . . Designated as Naval Aviation Pilot (Marine Corps)
DESILU . . . . . Desi-Lucille Arnaz Company
DESLANT . . . . Destroyer Force, Atlantic Fleet (Navy symbol)
DESO . . . . . . DeSoto National Memorial
DESO . . . . . . District Educational Services Officer (Navy)
DESOIL . . . . . Diesel Oil
DESOMS . . . . Deaf Sons of Master Masons
DESP . . . . . . Department of Elementary School Principals (of NEA)
DESPAC . . . . . Destroyers, Pacific Fleet
DESPORT . . . . Daily Equipment Status Report (Army)
DESREP . . . . . Destroyer Repair (Navy)
DESREP . . . . . Destroyer Representative (Navy)
DESRON . . . . Destroyer Squadron
DESS . . . . . . Department of Economics and Social Science (MIT)
DESSIM . . . . . Design Simulator
DESSOWESPAC . . Destroyers, Southwest Pacific Fleet
DESTN . . . . . . Destination
DESY . . . . . . Deutsches Elektron-Synchrotron (West Germany)
DET . . . . Design Evaluation Test
DET . . . . Detachment
DET . . . . Detection
DET . . . . Diethyltryptamine (Hallucinogenic drug)
DET . . . . Direct Energy Transfer
DETA . . . . . . Diethylenetriamine
DETA . . . . . . Divisao de Exploracao dos Transportes Aereos
DETAB . . . . . **Decision Tables**
DETAB-X . . . . Design Table, Experimental (Computer language)
DETALL . . . . . **Detached from Duty Indicated and from all Other Duty Assigned**
DETAP . . . . . . Decision Table Processor (Data processing)

DETC	Diethylthiacarbocyanine (Chemical)
DETO	Devils Tower National Monument
DETOC	Decision Table to COBOL Processor (Data processing)
DETRAN	Decision Table Translator (Data processing)
DETS	Digital Element Test Set
DETW	Detroit & Western R. R. (AAR code)
DEU	Data Exchange Unit
DEU	Duplicates Exchange Union (Library)
DEUCE	Digital Electronic Universal Calculating Engine
DEV	De Vilbiss Company (NYSE symbol) (Delisted)
DEV	Develop(ment)
DEVA	Death Valley National Monument
DEVAT	Depot Vehicle Automatic Tester
DEVR	Distortion-Eliminating Voltage Regulator
DEW	DELMARVA Power & Light Company (NYSE symbol)
DEW	Deutsche Edelstahlwerke Aktiengesellschaft (West Germany)
DEW	Direct Energy Weapon
DEW	Distant Early Warning (RADAR picket line) (Obsolete)
DEWA	Delaware Water Gap National Recreation Area
DEWAG	Deutsche Werbe-Anzeigen-Gesellschaft
DEWIZ	Distant Early Warning Identification Zone (Obsolete)
DEW LINE	Distant Early Warning Line (North American RADAR system) (Obsolete)
DEX	Decision Expediting (Graphic Sciences, Inc., copying machine)
DEX	Dexter Corp. (NYSE symbol)
D Ex	Doctor of Expression
DEXAN	Digital Experimental Airborne Navigator
DEXTER	Dental X-Ray Teaching and Training Replica
DF	Damage Free
DF	Data Folder
DF	Dead Freight (Shipping)
DF	Dean of the Faculty
DF	Decapacitation Factor
DF	Decontamination Factor
DF	Defender of the Faith
DF	Defensive Fire
DF	Degrees of Freedom
DF	Delay Fuse
DF	Dermatology Foundation
DF	Describing Function
DF	Destroyer Flotilla
DF	Direct Flight
DF	Direction-Finder (or Finding) (Radio aid to navigation)
DF	Disaccommodation Factor
DF	Disposition Form (Army)
DF	Dissipation Factor
DF	Distrito Federal (Mexico City)
DF	Doctor of Forestry
DF	Dorsal Fold
DF	Double Feeder (Line) (Technical drawings)
DF	Drag Friction
DF	Drive Fit (Technical drawings)
DF	Drop Forge
DF	Federal District (Mexico)
D & F	Determination and Finding
DFA	Defense Fisheries Administration (Abolished, 1953)
DFA	Design Fabrication Assembly
DFA	Designated Field Activity (DOD)
DFA	Deterministic Finite Automaton
DFA	Die Forged Aluminum
DFA	Digital Frequency Analyzer
DFA	Direction Finding Antenna
DFA	Doctor of Fine Arts
DFA	Dominant Feature Analysis
DFA	Dried Fruit Association of California
DFA	Drop Forging Association
DFAA	Dissolved Free Amino Acids
DFAC	Dried Fruit Association of California
DFAW	Direct Fire Anti-Tank Weapon
DFBPT	Digital Force Balance Pressure Transducer
DFC	Dial Financial Corporation (NYSE symbol)
DFC	Diffusion Formed Coating
DFC	Distinguished Flying Cross (US and British)
DFC	Drop Forged Clamp
DFC	Dry-Filled Capsules (Pharmacy)
DFC	Dust-Free Chamber
DFCA	Dual Fault Correction Actuator
DFCK	Development Finance Company of Kenya
DFCLS	Digital Flight Control and Landing System
DFCO	Duty Flying Control Officer (Navy)
DFCP	Division Funding Control Point
DFD	Demokratischer Frauenbund Deutschlands

DFD	Demolition Firing Device
DFD	Digital Flight Display
DFD	Digital Frequency Display
DFD	Dogs for Defense (Organization which trained dogs for armed services) (World War II)
DFDT	Difluorodiphenyltrichloroethane (Insecticide)
DFE	Debye-Falkenhagen Effect
DFE	Direction Finding Equipment
DFE	Division Force Equivalents (Army)
DFE	Doctor of Forest Engineering
DFEC	Douglas Fir Export Company
DF Eng	Doctor of Forest Engineering
DFF	Deutscher Fernsehfunk
DFF	Division Final Fade
DFG	Deutsche Forschungsgemeinschaft (German Research Association)
DFG	Deutsche Friedensgesellschaft
DFG	Digital Function Generator
DFG	Diode Function Generator
DFG	Discrete Frequency Generator
DFH	Defense Family Housing (Army)
DFH	Dual Filter Hybrid
DFI	Dark Field Illumination
DFI	Decorative Fabrics Institute
DFI	Diabetes Foundation, Incorporated
DFIC	Dehydrated Foods Industry Council
DFING	Radio Direction-Finding (Military)
DFIS	Digital Facsimile Interface System
DFISA	Dairy and Food Industries Supply Association
DFL	Democrat-Farmer-Labor (Party) (Minnesota)
DFL	Department of Family Life (Later, Commission on Marriage and Family Life) (of NCC)
DFL	Deutsche Forschungsanstalt fuer Luftfahrt
DFL	Deviation for Failure Location
DFL	Doctor of Family Life
DFL	Dry Film Lubricant
DFLC	Division of Foreign Labor Conditions (Department of Labor)
DFM	Decorative Furniture Manufacturers Association
DFM	Digital Frequency Meter (or Monitor)
DFM	Direct Flight Mode
DFM	Distinguished Flying Medal (British)
DFML	Dictionary of Folklore, Mythology, and Legend
DFMO	Doppler Filter Mixer-Oscillator (Electronics)
DFMS	Domestic and Foreign Missionary Society (British)
DFMSR	Directorate of Flight & Missile Safety Research (Air Force)
DFO	Dorsal Fold (Oesophagus)
DFOLS	Depth of Flash Optical Landing System (Navy)
DFP	Deviant Flight Plan
DFP	Difluorophosphate
DFP	Diisopropyl Fluorophosphate (A drug)
DFP	Diode Flat Pack
DFP	Dipole Flat Plate
DFP	Dry Film Processor
DFP	Dry Filter Processing
DFPA	Douglas Fir Plywood Association
DFPA	National Society, Daughters of Founders and Patriots of America
DFPS	Digital Ferrite Phase Shifter
DFR	Decreasing Failure Rate
DFR	Delayed Free Recall
DFR	Direction Finding Receiver
DFR	Dounreay Fast Reactor (British)
DFR	Dropped from Rolls
DFR	Dual-Frequency Receiver
DFR	Dust Free Room
DFRC	Distillers Feed Research Council
DFRIF	Defense Freight Railway Interchange Fleet (Army)
DFRP	Deficiency and Replacement
DFS	A Dictionary of Forces' Slang
DFS	Digital Field System
DFS	Digital Frequency Synthesizer
DFS	Direct Fire Simulator
DFS	Direct Fire System
DFS	Direct Forces Support (Military)
DFS	Direction Finding Set (or System)
DFS	Director of Flight Safety (Air Force)
DFS	Distance Finding Station
DFS	Doctor of Foreign Science
DFS	Doctor of Foreign Service
DFS	Doctor of Forest Science
DFS	Down Feeding Spindle
DFS	Dynamic Flight Simulator
DFSB	Defense Force Section Base (Navy)

DFSC . . . . Defense Fuel Supply Center (DOD)
DFSK . . . . Double Frequency Shift Keying (Radio)
DFSR . . . . Director(ate) of Flight Safety Research (Air Force)
DFSTN . . . . . . Direction Finding Station (Aviation)
DFT . . . . Deaerating Feed Tank
DFT . . . . Digital Filtering Technique
DFT . . . . Director, Fleet Training
DFT . . . . Discrete Fourier Transform
DFTMN . . . . . . Draftsman
DFU . . . . Difluorourea
DFVLR . . . . . . Deutsche Forschungs- und Versuchsanstalt fuer Luft- und Raumfahrt
              (West Germany)
DFW . . . . Director of Fortifications and Works (British)
DG . . . . Associated Dry Goods Corporation (NYSE symbol)
DG . . . . Dangerous Goods (Shipping)
DG . . . . Decigram
DG . . . . Degaussing
DG . . . . Dei Gratia (By the Grace of God)
DG . . . . Density Gradient
DG . . . . Deo Gratias (Thanks Be to God; or God Be Thanked)
DG . . . . Differential Generator
DG . . . . Digestive Gland
DG . . . . Diode Gate (Data processing)
DG . . . . Directional Gyro
DG . . . . Director General
DG . . . . Disc Grind (Technical drawings)
DG . . . . Displacement Gyro
DG . . . . Distinguished Graduate (Military)
DG . . . . Distinguished Guest (Hotel term)
DG . . . . Double Groove (Insulators)
DG . . . . Dragoon Guards (British)
D-G . . . . Director-General (UN)
DGA . . . . Directors Guild of America
DGA . . . . Durum Growers Association of the United States
DGALA . . . . . Dramatists Guild of the Authors League of America
DGAMS . . . . . Director-General of Army Medical Services (British)
DGAV . . . . . . Director-General of Armoured Vehicles (British)
DGB . . . . Deutscher Gewerkschaftsbund fuer das Gebiet der Bundesrepublik
              Deutschland und Berlin (German Trade Union Federation for the Area
              of the Federal Republic and Berlin) (West Germany)
DGB . . . . Disk Gap Band (Parachute)
DGBC . . . . . . Digital Geoballistic Computer
DGC . . . . Digital Geoballistic Computer
DGCA . . . . . . Director-General of Civil Aviation (British)
DGCC . . . . . . Director-General of Civilian Clothing (British)
DGD . . . . Diesel Geared Drive (Navy)
DGD . . . . Dynamic Gravity Detector
DGDG . . . . . . Distributor-to-Group Display Generator
DGDP . . . . . . Double Groove, Double Petticoat (Insulators)
DGE . . . . Davisson-Gernier Experiment
DGE . . . . Density Gradient Electrophoresis
DGE . . . . Dual Gage Expander
D Ge E . . . . . . Doctor of Geological Engineering
D Ge Eng . . . . Doctor of Geological Engineering
DGES . . . . Division of Graduate Education in Science (National Science Foundation)
DGFG . . . . . . Director General of the Foreign Service (Department of State)
DGFI . . . . Deutsches Geodaetisches Forschungsinstitut (Munich, Germany)
DGG . . . . Department of Geology and Geophysics (MIT)
DGG . . . . Deutsche Grammophon Gesellschaft (Phonograph recording company)
DGG . . . . Dynamic Gravity Generator
DGHP . . . . . . Drive-Gearhead Package
DGI . . . . Date Growers' Institute
DGKC . . . . . . Deutsche Gesellschaft fuer Klinischen Chemie
DGL . . . . Doped Glass LASER
DGLR . . . . . . Deutsche Gesellschaft fuer Luft- und Raumfahrt (West Germany)
DGM . . . . Data Gathering Monitoring (System)
DGM . . . . Defense Guidance Memorandum
DGM . . . . Deputy General Manager (AEC)
DGM . . . . Deputy Grand Master (Masonry)
DGM . . . . Directional Gyro Mode
DGM . . . . Dummy Guided Missile
DG-MG . . . . Diesel Geared-Motor Geared (Navy)
DGMS . . . . . . Director-General of Medical Services (British)
DGMS . . . . . . Division of General Medical Sciences (of National Institutes of Health)
DGO . . . . Degaussing Officer
DGO . . . . Diploma in Gynecology and Obstetrics
DGO . . . . Directional Gyro Operation
DGON . . . . . . Deutsche Gesellschaft fuer Ortung und Navigation (West Germany)
DGP . . . . Data Generating Program
DGP . . . . Destruction of Government Property
DGP . . . . Director-General of Production (British Air Ministry)

DGP . . . . Drive-Gearhead Package
DGP . . . . Dry Gas Pump
DGPH . . . . . . Deutsche Gesellschaft fuer Photographie (West Germany)
DGR . . . . Denver & Rio Grande Western R.R. Company (NYSE symbol) (Delisted)
DGR . . . . Director of Graves Registration (British)
DGRD . . . . . . Director-General of the Research Department (British)
DGRO . . . . . . Degaussing Range Officer
DGRR . . . . . . Deutsche Gesellschaft fuer Raketentechnik und Raumfahrt (German
              Society for Rocket Research and Space Flight)
DGRST . . . . . . Delegation Generale a la Recherche Scientifique et Technique (France)
DGS . . . . Digital Ground System
DGS . . . . Director of Ground Safety (Air Force)
DGS . . . . Display Generation System
DGS . . . . Don't Give a Spit (Slang) (Bowdlerized version)
DGSC . . . . . . Defense General Supply Center
DGSJ . . . . Druggist's Guild of St. James
DG Tn . . . . . . Director-General of Transportation Services (British)
DGTO . . . . . . Degaussing Technical Officer
DGW . . . . Double Gypsy Winch
DGWO . . . . . . Degaussing Wiping Officer
DGWS . . . . . . Division for Girls' and Women's Sports (of American Association for
              Health, Physical Education, and Recreation; also used in a book title)
DGZ . . . . Desired Ground Zero (Bombing)
DH . . . . Dayton-Hudson Corporation (NYSE symbol)
DH . . . . Deadhead (Freight)
DH . . . . Decision Height (Aviation)
DH . . . . DeHavilland (Aircraft Company, Ltd.)
DH . . . . Dehydrogenase (Biochemistry)
DH . . . . Delaware & Hudson Company (NYSE symbol) (Delisted)
DH . . . . Design Handbook
DH . . . . Disorderly House
DH . . . . Display Hold
DH . . . . Doctor of Humanics
DH . . . . Doctor of Humanities
D & H . . . . . . Delaware and Hudson Railroad
D & H . . . . . . Dressed and Headed (Lumber)
DHA . . . . Dairy Husbandry Adviser (Ministry of Agriculture, Fisheries, and Food)
              (British)
DHA . . . . Dehydroabietic Acid
DHA . . . . . . Dehydroepiandrosterone (Chemical)
DHA . . . . Dependent Housing Area (Army)
DHA . . . . Dihydroanthracene (Chemical)
DHA . . . . . . Doctor of Hospital Administration
DHA . . . . . . Double Heave Amplitude
DH Adm . . . . . Doctor of Hospital Administration
DHC . . . . Defense Homes Corporation (World War II)
D & HCO . . . . Delaware & Hudson Company
DHCY . . . . . . Division of Handicapped Children and Youth (HEW)
DHD . . . . Double Heat-Sink Diode
DHDI . . . . Drophammer Die
DHDS . . . . . . Data Handling and Display Subsystem
DHE . . . . Data Handling Equipment
DHE . . . . Debye-Hueckel Equation
DHE . . . . . . Department of Home Economics (of NEA)
DHE . . . . Dielectric Heating Equipment
DH Ec . . . . . . Doctor of Home Economics
DH Ec . . . . . . Doctor of Household Economy
DHEP . . . . . . Detailed Human Engineering Plan
DHEW . . . . . . Department of Health, Education, and Welfare
DHF . . . . Dengue Hemorrhagic Fever
DHFA . . . . . . Double-Conductor, Heat and Flame-Resistant, Armor (Cable)
DHFK . . . . . . Deutsche Hochschule fuer Koerperkultur
DHG . . . . Dihydroxyethylglycinate (Chemical)
DHH . . . . Doctor of Honorary Humanities
DHI . . . . Directional Horizon Indicator
DHI . . . . Dunhill International, Incorporated (NYSE symbol) (Delisted)
DHIA . . . . . . Dairy Herd Improvement Association
DHIR . . . . . . Dairy Herd Improvement Registry
DHIRS . . . . . Director Headquarters Induction and Recruiting Station (Marine Corps)
DHL . . . . Doctor of Hebrew Letters
DHL . . . . Doctor of Hebrew Literature
DHL . . . . Doctor of Humane Letters
DH Lit . . . . . . Doctor of Hebrew Literature
DH Lit . . . . . . Doctor of Hebrew Letters
DH Litt . . . . . Doctor of Hebrew Literature
DHM . . . . Dillingham Corp. (NYSE symbol)
DHM . . . . Diocesan Home Missionary
DHM . . . . Dry Honing Machine
DHMA . . . . . . Drapery Hardware Manufacturers Association
DHO . . . . District Historical Office(r) (Navy)
D Hor . . . . . . Doctor of Horticulture

D Ho Sc . . . . . Doctor of Household Science
DHP . . . . Developed Horsepower
DHPA . . . . . . Degree of Honor Protective Association
DHQ . . . . Division Headquarters (Army)
DHQ . . . . Mean Diurnal High Water Inequality
DHS . . . . Data Handling System
DHS . . . . Despun Heat Shield
DHS . . . . Doctor of Humanitarian Service
DHS . . . . Dry Heat Sterilization
DHSS . . . . . . Department of Health and Social Security (British)
DHT . . . . Dihydrotestosterone (Endocrinology)
D Hu . . . . Doctor of Humanities
DHUD . . . . . . Department of Housing and Urban Development
D Hu L . . . . . Doctor of Humane Letters
D Hum . . . . . Doctor of Humanities
DHV . . . . Deutscher Handels- und Industrieangestellten-Verband (Association of Clerical Employees of Germany) (West Germany)
DHV . . . . Duck Hepatitis Virus
DHVA . . . . . . De Haas-van Alphen (Effect)
DHW . . . . . . Double-Hung Windows (Technical drawings)
DHY . . . . Deuterated Hydrogen Y (Type of zeolite)
DHY . . . . Develet Hava Yollari (Airline)
D Hyg . . . . . . Doctor of Hygiene
DHZ . . . . Deutsche Handelszentrale
DHZ . . . . Deutsche Hydrographische Zeitschrift
DI . . . . Dark Ignition
DI . . . . Dead Indian (Careless man) (Army slang)
DI . . . . Defence Intelligence (British)
DI . . . . Defense Information
DI . . . . De-Icing
DI . . . . Delay Indefinite (Aviation)
DI . . . . Deviation Indicator
DI . . . . Diabetes Insipidus
DI . . . . Difference Index (Protein calculation) (Biochemistry)
DI . . . . Digital Input (Data processing)
DI . . . . Direct Investor
DI . . . . Directivity Index
DI . . . . Director(ate) of Installations (Air Force)
DI . . . . Discomfiture Index (Weather)
DI . . . . Distinctive Insignia (Military)
DI . . . . District Inspector (Ministry of Agriculture, Fisheries, and Food) (British)
DI . . . . District Inspector (Navy)
DI . . . . Document Identifier (Military)
DI . . . . Doppler Inertial
DI . . . . Double Injection
DI . . . . Dresser Industries, Inc. (NYSE symbol)
DI . . . . Drill Instructor (Marine Corps)
DI . . . . Drug Information
DI . . . . Due In
DI . . . . Fighter (Russian aircraft symbol)
DI . . . . Flight Path Deviation Indicator (Navigation)
D of I . . . . . . Department of Interior
DIA . . . . Date of Initial Appointment
DIA . . . . Defense Intelligence Agency (Formerly JJ-2)
DIA . . . . Deutscher Innen- und Aussenhandel
DIA . . . . Diamond Shamrock Corp. (Formerly, Diamond Alkali Co.) (NYSE symbol)
DIA . . . . Dig-In Angle
DIA . . . . Doctor of Industrial Arts
DIA . . . . Documentation et Information Africaines (African Documentation and Information (Catholic News Agency)
DIA . . . . Drug Information Association
DIA . . . . Dulles International Airport (FAA)
DIAC . . . . . . Defense Industry Advisory Council (Later, IAC)
DIAC . . . . . . Dilodothyroacetic Acid (Biochemistry)
DIAC . . . . . . Directorate of Internal Affairs & Communications (Allied German Occupation Forces)
DIAD . . . . . . Drum Information Assembler and Dispatcher
DIAGE . . . . . . Defense Industry Advisory Group Europe
DIAI . . . . Defense Intelligence Agency Instruction
DIALGOL . . . . Dialect of Algorithmic Language
DIAM . . . . . . Diameter
DIAMAT . . . . . Dialektischer Materialismus
DIAN . . . . Decca Integrated Airborne Navigator
DIANE . . . . . . Digital Integrated Attack and Navigation Equipment
DIANE . . . . . . Distance Indicating Automatic Navigation Equipment
DIANE . . . . . . Duct Integrity and Nozzle Efficiency
DIAPAS . . . . . Diabetes Personalized Alerting Service
DI Arch . . . . . Doctor of Interior Architecture
DI Arch E . . . . Doctor of Interior Architectural Engineering
DI Arch Eng. . . Doctor of Interior Architectural Engineering
DIAS . . . . Dynamic Inventory Analysis System (Data processing)

DIB . . . . Department of Information and Broadcasting (India)
DIB . . . . Department Information Bulletin
DIB . . . . Design Information Bulletin
DIB . . . . Deutsche Investitionsbank
DIB . . . . Dictionary of International Biography (A publication)
DIB . . . . Dielectric Infrared Beamsplitter
DIB . . . . Domestic and International Business (Department of Commerce)
DIBA . . . . . . Digital Integral Ballistic Analyzer
DIC . . . . Dairy Industry Committee
DIC . . . . Data Input Clerk
DIC . . . . Data Insertion Converter
DIC . . . . Dependency and Indemnity Compensation (Military)
DIC . . . . Detailed Interrogation Center (Navy)
DIC . . . . Division of Industrial Cooperation (MIT)
DIC . . . . Document Identifier Code
DICAB . . . . . . Directive Coordinated and Approved by Budget Director (Air Force)
DICASS . . . . . Directional Command Active Sonobuoy System (Navy)
DICBM . . . . . . Defense Intercontinental Ballistic Missile
DICBM . . . . . . Depressed-Trajectory Intercontinental Ballistic Missile
DICE . . . . Digital Integrated Circuit Element
DICE . . . . Digitally Interlaced Countermeasures Equipment
DICEF . . . . . . Digital Communications Experimental Facility (Air Force)
DICNAVAB . . . . Dictionary of Naval Abbreviations
DICO . . . . Discovery (or Dissemination) of Information through Co-operative Organization
DICODE . . . . . Digital Correlation Demonstrator
DICON . . . . . . Digital Communication through Orbiting Needles
DICOSE . . . . . Digital Communications System Evaluator
DICR . . . . Daily Inspection Call Record
DICT . . . . Dictionary
DID . . . . Daily Intelligence Digest
DID . . . . Data Input Display (Data processing)
DID . . . . Data Item Description (DOD)
DID . . . . Digital Information Display (SAGE)
DID . . . . Direct Inward Dialing (Method of bypassing central switchboards in telephoning extensions from outside)
DID . . . . Division of Isotopes Development (of AEC)
DID. . . . . Double Isotope Derivative
DID . . . . Drum Information Display
DIDA . . . . Dynamic Instrumentation Digital Analyzer
DIDAC . . . . . . Digital Data Computer
DIDAD . . . . . . Digital Data Display (Data processing)
DIDAP . . . . . . Digital Data Processor
DIDAS . . . . . . Dynamic Instrumentation Data Automobile System (Telemetering system for auto test tracks)
DIDC . . . . Data Input Display Console (Data processing)
DIDD . . . . Dynamic Integrated Data Display
DIDDS . . . . . . Dynamic Integrated Data Display System
DI/DES . . . . . . Vessels Disposed of by Sinking, Burning, Abandoning or Other Means of Destruction
DIDF . . . . Dual Input Describing Function (Data processing)
DI/DO . . . . . . Data Input/Data Output (Data processing)
DIDOC . . . . . . Desired Image Distribution Using Orthogonal Constraints (Illinois Institute of Technology)
DIDP . . . . Diisodecyl Phthalate (Organic chemistry)
DIDS . . . . Decision Information Distribution System
DIDS . . . . Defense Integrated Data System
DIDS . . . . Digital Information Display System (Data processing)
DIE . . . . Distance in Error
DIE . . . . Doctor of Industrial Engineering
DIE . . . . Double Injection Effect
DIEAGE . . . . . Defense Industry Export Advisory Group
DIECO . . . . . . Defense Item Entry Control Office (Military)
DIECP . . . . . . Defense Item Entry Control Program (Army)
DIED . . . . Department of Industrial and Economic Development (of Ohio) (Now defunct)
DIEL . . . . Diesel Electric
DI Eng . . . . . . Doctor of Industrial Engineering
DIER . . . . Departmental Industrial Equipment Reserve (Navy)
DIF . . . . Difference (or Differential)
DIF . . . . Direction Finder (Radio)
DIF . . . . Division of International Finance (of FRS)
DIF . . . . Duty Involving Flying (Navy)
DIFAD . . . . . . Digitally Integrated Fleet Air Defense
DIFAR . . . . . . Directional Frequency Analysis and Recording System
DI/FLC . . . . . . Vessels in Forward Areas Transferred to State Dept. Foreign Liquidation Corp.
DIFM . . . . Due in from Maintenance (Air Force)
DIFOT . . . . . . Duty in a Flying Status Involving Operational or Training Flights
DIFOTECH . . . . Duty Involving Operational or Training Flights as a Technical Observer (Air Force)

DIFOTINS .... Duty Involving Operational or Training Flights under Instruction (Air Force)
DIFR........ Diesel Fruit Vessel
DIG .... Deputy Inspector-General
DIG .... Detonator Inspection Gage
DIG .... Di Giorgio Corporation (NYSE symbol)
DIG .... Digital
DIGACC .... Digital Guidance and Control Computer
DIGICCM .... Digital Communications
DIG-IT ...... Dramatic Interpretation of the Ghetto through Improvisational Theater (Washington, DC)
DIGITAC .... Digital Tactical Airborne Computer
DIGS .... Delta Inertial Guidance System (NASA)
DIGS .... Deputy Inspector General for Safety (Air Force)
DIH .... Departement International Hachette
DIH .... Diploma in Industrial Health (British)
DIHEST ...... Direct Induced High Explosive Simulation
DII......... Diode Ion Injector
DIIO........ District Industrial Incentive Office(r) (Navy)
DIIP........ Defense Inactive Item Program
DIL .... Doctor of International Law
DIL .... Doppler-Inertial-LORAN
DIL .... Double Injection Luminescence
DILS........ Doppler Inertial LORAN System
DIM .... Dardo de Investigacion Meteorologica (Argentina)
DIM .... Deutsches Institut fuer Marktforschung
DIM .... District Industrial Manager (Navy)
DIM .... Dynamic Impedance Measurement
DIMA .... Detroit Institute of Musical Arts
DIMA .... Direct Imaging Mass Analyzer
DIMAPA ..... Dimethylaminopropylamine
DIMATE ..... Depot-Installed Maintenance Automatic Equipment
DIME .... Division of International Medical Education (Association of American Medical Colleges)
DIMES ...... Defense-Integrated (or Improved) Management Engineering System (Navy)
DIMES ...... Development of Improved Management Engineering Systems
DIMPLE..... Deuterium Moderated Pile Low Energy (Reactor)
DIMSA ...... Depot Integrated Maintenance Support Agreement (Air Force)
DIMSA ...... Distribuidora de Impresos SA (Mexico)
DIMUS ...... Digital (or Directional) Multibeam Steering (SONAR)
DIN .... Data Identification Number
DIN .... Deutsche Industrie-Normen (German Industrial Standards)
DIN .... Diana Stores Corporation (NYSE symbol) (Delisted)
DIN .... Do It Now (Category of service call for maintenance or repair work) (Air Force)
DIN .... Document Identification Number
DINA .... Digital Network Analyzer
DINA .... Direct Internal Noise Amplification
DINA .... Direct Noise Amplifier (Airborne RADAR Transmitter)
D Ind ...... Doctor of Industry
DINFOS .... Defense Information School
DINN .... Dual Input Null Network
DINO....... Deputy Inspector of Naval Ordnance
DINO....... Dinosaur National Monument
DIO .... District Intelligence Officer
DIO .... Duty Intelligence Officer (Air Force)
DIOB .... Digital Input/Output Buffer (Data processing)
DIOP .... Digital Input/Output Package (Data processing)
DIOP .... Diisooctyl Phthalate (Organic chemistry)
DIP .... Departamento de Imprensa e Propaganda (Brazil)
DIP .... Design Improvement Program
DIP .... Destruction of Interstate Property
DIP .... Digital Incremental Plotter
DIP .... Display Information Processor (Air Force)
DIP .... Disposition of Inactive Parts List
DIP .... Division of Industrial Participation (AEC)
DIP .... Document Improvement Program (DOD)
DIP .... Dormit In Pace (Sleeps in Peace)
DIP .... Dual In-Line Package (or Pulse)
DIPEC...... Defense Industrial Plant Equipment Center
DipEd ...... Diploma of Education
DIPL........ Diploma
DIPR........ Departmental Industrial Plant Reserve (Department of the Army)
DipRADA..... Diploma of Royal Academy of Dramatic Art
DIPROG .... Request Diagnosis, Prognosis, Present Condition (Army)
DIPS........ Development Information Processing System
DIR .... Department of Industrial Research
DIR .... Depot Inspection and Repair
DIR .... Director(ate)
DIR .... Disassembly and Inspection Report
DIR .... Doctrine of Incremental Reduction

DIRC .... Dithered Infrared Configuration
DIRCOL ..... Direction Cosine Linkage
D Ir E ...... Doctor of Irrigation Engineering
DIR/ECT ..... Director Project (Data processing) (Bell Laboratories)
D Ir Eng ..... Doctor of Irrigation Engineering
DIRFM ...... Director Field Maintenance (Army)
DIRINCO .... Direccion de Industria y Comercio
DIRLANTDOCKS .. Director Atlantic Division, Bureau of Yards and Docks (Obsolete)
DIRM .... Defense Intelligence Requirement Manual
DIRNAVHIST .. Director of Naval History
DIRNSA ..... Director, National Security Agency
DIRO .... District Industrial Relations Officer (Navy)
DIROCD ..... Director, Office of Civil Defense
DIRPACALDOCKS .. Director, Pacific and Alaskan Divisions, Bureau of Yards and Docks (Obsolete)
DIRPACDOCKS .. Director, Pacific Division, Bureau of Yards and Docks (Obsolete)
DIRPRO...... When Directed Proceed
DIRS .... Departmental Industrial Reserve System
DIRW .... Director of Women Marines
DIS .... Defense Intelligence School
DIS .... Defense Investigative Service
DIS .... Design Improvement Study
DIS .... Disney (Walt) Productions (NYSE symbol) (Wall Street slang name: "Mickey Mouse")
DIS .... Dissertation Inquiry Service (Xerox)
DIS .... Ductile Iron Society
DIS .... Dwarf Iris Society
DISA .... Dairy Industries Supply Association
DI/SAL...... Vessels Disposed of by Sale through Navy Material Redistribution Agency
DISBMT...... Disbursement
DISC .... Data Information System for Management Control (Military)
DISC .... Defense Industrial Supply Center
DISC .... Discontinue
DISC .... Domestic International Sales Corporation (Canada)
DISCH ...... Discharge
DISCO ...... Defense Industrial Security Clearance Office
DISCOM .... Digital Selective Communications
DISCOM .... Division Support Command (Army)
DI/SCP...... Vessels Disposed of by Scrapping (Navy)
DISCREP ..... Discrepancy Report
DISD .... Data and Information Systems Division
DISI........ Diode Ion Source Injector
DISN .... Diiminosuccinonitrile (Organic chemistry)
DISP........ Defense Industry Studies Program
DISP........ Dispensary
DISP........ DOD (Department of Defense) Industrial Security Program
DISREP ...... Discrepancy in Shipment Report (Army)
DIST........ Distance
DIST........ District
DISTAR...... Direct Instructional System for Teaching Arithmetic and Reading
DISTENGR ... District Engineer (Army)
DISTO ...... Defense Industrial Security Education and Training Office
DISTR....... Distribution
DISTRA ...... Distribution Authority (Army)
DISTRAM .... Digital Space Trajectory Measurement System (Raytheon)
DISTRIPRESS... Federation Internationale des Distributeurs de Presse
DISUM ...... Daily Intelligence Summary (Air Force)
DISYNDA .... Display of Synoptic Data
DISZ .... Dolgozo Ifjusay Szovetsege
DIT .... Detroit Institute of Technology
DIT .... Diiodotyrosine (Biochemistry)
DIT......... Domestic Independent Tour (Travel)
DIT .... Drexel Institute of Technology (Pennsylvania)
DIT......... Dual Input Transponder
DITA .... Diesel Tank Vessel
DITC .... Disability Insurance Training Council
DITDJENKRA .. Direktorat Djenderal Keradjinan Rakjat (Indonesia)
DITDJENTEKS.. Direktorat Djenderal Perindustrian Tekstil (Indonesia)
DI/TES ...... Vessels Disposed of by Using as Targets and Tests (Navy)
DI/TRN...... Vessels Transferred to Other Government Agencies and Miscellaneous Activities (Navy)
DITS........ Digital Television Spectrometer
DIU .... Data Interface Unit
DIU .... Destratification Impeller Unit
DIU .... Digital Insertion Unit
DIU .... Display Interface Unit
DIV .... Division(al)
DIV .... Dynamic Imagery Viewer
DIVA .... Digital Inquiry – Voice Answer
DIVAR ...... Diving Instrumentation Vehicle for Environmental and Acoustic Research
DIVART...... Division Artillery (Army)

DIVBASE . . . . . Division Base (Army)
DIVCOM . . . . Division Commander (Navy)
DIVEAR . . . . . . Driving Instrumentation Vehicle for Environmental and Acoustic Research
DIVENGR . . . . . Division Engineer (Army)
DIVHED . . . . . Division Headquarters (Army)
DIVIC . . . . . . Digital Variable Increment Computer
DIVOO . . . . . Division Ordnance Officer
DIVOT . . . . . . Digital-to-Voice Translator
DIVTAG . . . . . Division Through Army Group
DIW . . . . Design Information Worksheet
DI/WSA . . . . . Vessels Transferred to War Shipping Administration - Maritime Commission for Disposition (Navy)
DIWT . . . . . . Director of Inland Water Transport Service (British)
DIY . . . . Do-It-Yourself
DIZ . . . . Defense Identification Zone
DJ . . . . Diffused Junction
DJ . . . . Disc Jockey
DJ . . . . District Judge
DJ . . . . Doctor Juris (Doctor of Law)
DJ . . . . Dust Jacket (Paper cover for a hard-bound book)
D-J . . . . Dow Jones & Co. (Also, the stock market averages compiled by this company)
D of J . . . . . . Department of Justice
DJAG . . . . Deputy Judge Advocate General
DJB . . . . Drill Jig Bushing
DJC . . . . Danville Junior College (Illinois)
DJC . . . . Dixie Junior College (Utah)
DJCB . . . . . . Dominican Junior College of Blauvelt (New York)
DJD . . . . Degenerative Joint Disease
DJDS . . . . . Division of Juvenile Delinquency Service (of SSA)
DJE . . . . Deflected Jet Exhaust
DJF . . . . Descriptor Justification Form (ERIC)
DJI . . . . Dow-Jones Index
DJIA . . . . Dow-Jones Industrial Average
DJOT . . . . . . Delayed Jam on Target
DJP . . . . Doctor of Jewish Pedagogy
DJR . . . . Deutscher Jugendring
DJS . . . . Deception Jamming System
DJS . . . . Director Joint Staff (Military)
DJS . . . . Doctor of Judicial Science
DJS . . . . Doctor of Juridical Science
DJ Sc . . . . . . Doctor of Juridical Science
DJSM . . . . Director, Joint Staff Memorandum (Military)
DJT . . . . Doctor of Jewish Theology
DJ Th . . . . . . Doctor of Jewish Theology
D Jur . . . . . . Doctor of Jurisprudence
D Jur Sc . . . . . Doctor of Juridical Science
DK . . . . Dezimal-Klassifikation
DK . . . . Disbursing Clerk (Navy rating)
DK . . . . Don't Know
DK . . . . Dorsal (Kidney)
DKA . . . . Decca Records, Inc. (NYSE symbol) (Delisted)
DKB . . . . Decimal Keyboard (Data processing)
DKE . . . . Delta Kappa Epsilon (Society)
DKG . . . . . . Dekagram
DKL . . . . . . Dekaliter
DKM . . . . . . Dekameter
DKMS . . . . . . Dimitrovski Komunisticheski Mladezhki Suiuz (Bulgaria)
DKO . . . . . . Delay Key On
DKS . . . . Doniphan, Kensett & Searcy Railway (AAR code)
DKT . . . . Dahl-Kirkam Telescope
DKTC . . . . . . Dog Kidney Tissue Culture
DKW . . . . . . Das Kleine Wunder (Initialism used as name of German automobile, manufactured by Auto Union)
DKWT . . . . . . De Kalb & Western Transportation R. R. (AAR code)
DL . . . . Damage Limitation (Strategy) (in a war)
DL . . . . Danger List (Medicine)
DL . . . . Dark on Light
DL . . . . Data Link
DL . . . . Data Lists (DOD)
DL . . . . Day Letter (Telegraphy)
DL . . . . Days Lost (Military)
DL . . . . Dead Load
DL . . . . Deciliter
DL . . . . Delay Line
DL . . . . Delta Air Lines, Inc.
DL . . . . Department of Labor
DL . . . . Deputy Lieutenant
DL . . . . Destroyer Leader
DL . . . . Difference Limen (Physiology, psychology)
DL . . . . Diode Logic

DL . . . . Direct Labor
DL . . . . Disjunctively Linear
DL . . . . Doctor of Law
DL . . . . Doctor of Letters
DL . . . . Doctor of Literature
DL . . . . Dominical Letter
DL . . . . Doppellafette (Two-barreled mount) (German military – World War II)
DL . . . . Dorsal Lip
DL . . . . Down Left (The front left portion of a stage) (A stage direction)
DL . . . . Down Link (Data processing)
DL . . . . Drawing List (Engineering)
DL . . . . Frigate (Navy symbol)
D/L . . . . Data Link
D/L . . . . Demand Loan
D & L . . . . . . Distillate plus Loss
D of L . . . . . . Department of Labor
DLA . . . . Data Link Address
DLA . . . . Delay Line Assembly
DLA . . . . Democratic Labor Association (Philippines)
DLA . . . . Dislocation Allowance
DLA . . . . Divisional Land Agent (Ministry of Agriculture, Fisheries, and Food) (British)
DLA . . . . Doctor of Liberal Arts
D La L . . . . . . Doctor of Latin Letters
D Lang . . . . . . Doctor of Languages
DL Arch . . . . . Doctor of Landscape Architecture
DLAT . . . . . . Defense Language Aptitude Test (Army)
DLB . . . . Deposit Liquidation Board
DLC . . . . David Lipscomb College (Tennessee)
DLC . . . . Delay Line Case
DLC . . . . Delayed Clearance (Aviation)
DLC . . . . Development Loan Committee (Department of State)
DLC . . . . Digital Logic Circuit
DLC . . . . Direct Lift Control
DLC . . . . Disaster Loan Corporation
DLC . . . . Doctor of Celtic Literature
DLC . . . . Drummond Lighterage R. R. (AAR code)
DLC . . . . Dynamic Load Characteristics
DLCA . . . . . . Dairymen's League Cooperative Association
DLCA . . . . . . Dynamic Logic Chassis Analyzer
DLCC . . . . . . Division Logistics Control Center
DLCS . . . . . . Data-Line Concentration System (Bell System)
DLD . . . . Deadline Date (Air Force)
DL Des . . . . . . Doctor of Landscape Design
DLE . . . . Data Link Escape (Data processing)
DLE . . . . Disseminated Lupus Erythematosus (Medicine)
DLEA . . . . . . Double Leg Elbow Amplifier
DL Ec . . . . . . Doctor of Library Economics
DL Eng . . . . . Doctor of Landscape Engineering
D Let . . . . . . Doctor of Letters
DLF . . . . Data List File
DLF . . . . Development Loan Fund
DLF . . . . Diffraction Limited Focusing
DLF . . . . Drydock Launch Facility
DLFDU . . . . . . Data Line Flight Direction Unit
DLG . . . . Deutsche Landwirtschafts-Gesellschaft
DLG . . . . Deutsch-Lateinamerikanische Gesellschaft
DLG . . . . Guided Missile Frigate (Navy symbol)
DLG(N) . . . . . Guided Missile Frigate (Nuclear propelled) (Navy symbol)
DLI . . . . Defense Language Institute
DLI . . . . Doctor of Literary Interpretation
DLIC . . . . Detachments Left in Contact (Military)
DLIEC . . . . . . Defense Language Institute, East Coast Branch (Military)
DLIR . . . . Downward Looking Infrared (Air Force)
DLISC-EP . . . . Defense Language Institute Support Command – El Paso
D Lit . . . . Doctor of Letters (or Literature)
DLIWC . . . . . . Defense Language Institute, West Coast Branch (Military)
DLK . . . . Diamond Locking Knurl
DLL . . . . Dames of the Loyal Legion of the United States
DLL . . . . Dial Long Line (Bell System)
DLL . . . . Dillon Companies, Inc. (NYSE symbol)
DLL . . . . Doctor of Late Laws
DLL . . . . Double Length Line
DLLF . . . . . . Design Limit Load Factor
DLM . . . . Delay Line Memory
DLM . . . . Depot Level Maintenance (Air Force)
DLM . . . . Digital Logic Module
DLM . . . . Doctor of Landscape Management
DLM . . . . Double Long Meter (Music)
DLMTB . . . . . . Defense Logistics Management Training Board
DLN . . . . Daylin, Inc. (NYSE symbol)

DLN . . . . Double Length Number
DLNC . . . . . . Deputy Local Naval Commander
DLO . . . . Dead Letter Office (US Postal Service)
DLO . . . . Delayed Output (Data processing)
DLO . . . . Difference of Longitude (Navigation)
DLO . . . . Diploma in Laryngology and Otolaryngology (British)
DLO . . . . Dispatch Loading Only
DLO . . . . District Legal Office(r) (Navy)
DLO . . . . Double Local Oscillator
DLOC . . . . . . Division Logistical Operation Center
DLOGS . . . . . . Division Logistics System
DLP . . . . Damage Limiting Program
DLP . . . . Defense Language Program
DLP . . . . Democratic Labor Party (Australia)
DLP . . . . Director of Laboratory Programs (Navy)
DLPT . . . . . . Defense Language Proficiency Tests
DLQ . . . . Mean Diurnal Low Water Inequality
DLR . . . . Delay Line Register
DLR . . . . Developing Learning Readiness
DLR . . . . Doppler LASER RADAR
DLR . . . . Driving After License Revoked
DLR . . . . Dynamic Line (or Load) Regulation
DLRL . . . . . . Diffraction Limited Raman LASER
DLRO . . . . . . District Labor Relations Office(r) (Navy)
DLRV . . . . . . Dual Mode Lunar Roving Vehicle
DLS . . . . Data Link Set
DLS . . . . Data Link Simulator
DLS . . . . Data Logging System
DLS . . . . Debt Liquidation Schedule
DLS . . . . Digital Logic System
DLS . . . . Direct Least Squares (Econometrics)
DLS . . . . Doctor of Library Science
DLS . . . . Driving After License Suspended
DLSC . . . . . . Defense Logistics Services Center (Military)
DLSC . . . . . . Differential Logistics Services Center (AEC)
DL Sc . . . . . . Doctor of Library Science
DLSEF . . . . . . Division of Library Services and Educational Facilities (US Office of Education)
DLSIE . . . . . . Defense Logistics Studies Information Exchange (DOD)
DLST . . . . Division Logistics System Test (Army)
DLST/SEACAPS . . Division Logistics System Test/Seventh Army Card Processor System
DLT . . . . Data Link Terminal
DLT . . . . Data Link Translator
DLT . . . . Decision Logic Table (DOD)
DLT . . . . Deck Landing Training
DLT . . . . Deltona Corp. (NYSE symbol)
DLT . . . . Deutsche Landmaschinen und Traktorenindustrie
DLTDP . . . . . . Dilaurylthiodipropionate
DLTM . . . . . . Data Link Test Message
DLTS . . . . . . Deck Landing Training School
DLU . . . . Digitizer Logic Unit
DLU . . . . Display Logic Unit
DLW . . . . Delaware, Lackawanna & Western R. R. (AAR code)
DL & W . . . . . Delaware, Lackawanna and Western Railroad Company
DL & WRR . . . Delaware, Lackawanna & Western Railroad
DLZ . . . . Drop Landing Zone (Air Force)
DM . . . . Deacon and Martyr (Church calendars)
DM . . . . Debugging Mode
DM . . . . Decameter
DM . . . . Decamired
DM . . . . Decimal Multiply
DM . . . . Decimeter (Metric)
DM . . . . Decision Maker
DM . . . . Delta Modulation
DM . . . . Demand Meter
DM . . . . Design Manual
DM . . . . Design Memorandum
DM . . . . Destra Mano (Right Hand)
DM . . . . Destroyer Minelayer (Light minelayer)
DM . . . . Detector Mosaic
DM . . . . Detroit & Mackinac Railway Company (AAR code)
DM . . . . Deutsche Mark (German money)
DM . . . . Diastolic Murmur (Medicine)
DM . . . . Diesel-Mechanical
DM . . . . Diffused Mesa
DM . . . . Diis Manibus (To the Manes [Departed Souls])
DM . . . . Dioxane-Methanol (Scintillation solvent) (Bray solution)
DM . . . . Disease-a-Month (A publication)
DM . . . . Doctor of Mathematics
DM . . . . Doctor of Medicine
DM . . . . Doctor of Music

DM . . . . Documentation Manager (Air Force)
DM . . . . Dome Mines, Limited (NYSE symbol)
DM . . . . Draftsman (Navy rating)
DM . . . . Driver, Master
DM . . . . Master Diver (Navy)
DM . . . . Master of Divinity
D/M . . . . Demodulate/Modulate
D/M . . . . Disintegrations Per Minute
D & M . . . . . . Detroit and Mackinac Railway Company
D & M . . . . . . Dressed and Matched (Technical drawings)
D of M . . . . . . Dames of Malta
D of M . . . . . . Supreme Caldron, Daughters of Mokanna
DMA . . . . Dance Masters of America
DMA . . . . Data Management Analysis
DMA . . . . Defense Manpower Administration (Department of Labor) (Superseded by Office of Manpower Administration, 1953)
DMA . . . . Degraded Mission Assessment
DMA . . . . Delegation Ministerielle a l'Armement (France)
DMA . . . . Dental Manufacturers of America
DMA . . . . Direct Memory Address
DMA . . . . Director of Military Assistance
DMA . . . . Division of Military Application (AEC)
DMA . . . . Doctor of Municipal Administration
DMA . . . . Doctor of Musical Arts
DMA . . . . Drum Memory Assembly (Data processing)
DMAA . . . . . . Direct Mail Advertising Association
DMAC . . . . . . Dimethylacetamide
DM Adm . . . . . Doctor of Municipal Administration
D Ma E . . . . . . Doctor of Marine Engineering
D Ma Eng . . . . Doctor of Marine Engineering
DMAM . . . . . . Dimethyl Aminoethyl Methacrylate (Organic chemistry)
DMAP . . . . . . Direct Matrix Abstraction Process
DMAT . . . . . . Digital Module Automatic Tester
DMB . . . . Defense Mobilization Board (Terminated, 1958)
DMB . . . . Distinguished Marksmanship Badge
DMBA . . . . . . Dimethylbenzanthracene (Chemistry)
DMC . . . . Data Management Channel
DMC . . . . Degraded Mission Capability
DMC . . . . Digital Micro-Circuit
DMC . . . . Diversified Industries, Inc. (NYSE symbol)
DMCA . . . . . . Dependents' Medical Care Act (HEW)
DMCC . . . . . . Depot Maintenance Control Center (Army)
DMCCC . . . . . Deputy Missile Combat Crew Commander
DMCEUF . . . . . Delhi Municipal Corporation Employees' Unions' Federation (India)
DMCR . . . . . . Director, Marine Corps Reserve
DMCS . . . . . . Dimethyldichlorosilane (Organic chemistry)
DMD . . . . Doctor of Dental Medicine
DMD . . . . Doctor of Mathematics and Didactics
DMD . . . . Doctor of Medical Dentistry
DMD . . . . Dual Mode Display
DMD . . . . Dynamic Map Display
DMDHEU . . . . . Dimethylol Dihydroxyethyleneurea (Used to provide durable press finish in fabrics)
DME . . . . Design Margin Evaluation
DME . . . . Direct Measurements Explorer (Satellite)
DME . . . . Director of Medical Education
DME . . . . Distance Measuring Equipment (Navigation)
DME . . . . Distance Monitoring Equipment (Military)
DME . . . . Doctor of Mechanical Engineering
D Me . . . . Doctor of Metaphysics
DMEA . . . . . . Defense Minerals Exploration Administration (Interior Department)
DME-A . . . . . . Direct Measurements Explorer A (Satellite)
D Mech . . . . . Doctor of Mechanics
DME/COTAR . . Distance Measuring Equipment/Correlation Tracking and Ranging
DMED . . . . . . Digital Message Entry Device (Police and military communications)
DM Ed . . . . . . Doctor of Musical Education
DM Eng . . . . . Doctor of Mechanical Engineering
DMES . . . . . . Digital Message Entry System
DMET . . . . . . Defense Management Educating and Training
DMET . . . . . . Distance Measuring Equipment TACAN (or Touchdown)
D Met . . . . . . Doctor of Metallurgy
D Met E . . . . . Doctor of Metallurgical Engineering
D Met Eng . . . Doctor of Metallurgical Engineering
DMF . . . . Decayed, Missing, Filled (Dentistry)
DMF . . . . Dimethylformamide (Chemical)
DMG . . . . Damage
DMG . . . . Defense Marketing Group (AMA)
DMG . . . . Deputy Military Governor (US Military Government, Germany)
DMG . . . . Distinguished Military Graduate
DMG . . . . Diversified Mortgage Investors (NYSE symbol)
DMH . . . . Dimythal Hydrazine

DMH	Direct Man-Hours
DMH	Drop Manhole (Technical drawings)
DMH	Dual Mode Hydrazine
DMHR	Daughters of the Most Holy Redeemer (Roman Catholic religious order)
DMHS	Director of Medical and Health Services
DMI	Defense Mechanisms Inventory (Psychology)
DMI	Desmethylimipramine (Chemical)
DMI	Destratification Motor Impeller
DMI	Director of Military Intelligence (US, British)
DMI	Directorate of Missile Intelligence (Army)
DMI	Distance Measuring Instrument
DMIAA	Diamond Manufacturers and Importers Association of America
DMIC	Defense Metals Information Center
D Mic	Doctor of Microbiology
D Mi E	Doctor of Mining Engineering
D Mi Eng	Doctor of Mining Engineering
D Mil S	Doctor of Military Science
DMIP	Defense Materiel Interservicing Program (DOD)
DMIR	Duluth, Missabe & Iron Range Railway (AAR code)
DM & IR	Duluth, Missabe and Iron Range Railway
DMISA	Depot Maintenance Interservice Support Agreement (Military)
DMIU	Destratification Motor Impeller Unit
DMJ	Daughters of Mary and Joseph (Roman Catholic religious order)
DMJ	Doctor of Medical Jurisprudence
DMJP	Door Mounted Junction Panel
DMK	Dial Marking Kit
DMK	Dominick Fund, Inc. (NYSE symbol)
DMK	Dravida Munnetra Kazhagam (Political party in India seeking independent socialist state of Dravidanad)
DML	Dan River, Inc. (Formerly, Dan River Mills) (NYSE symbol)
DML	Demolition
DML	Digitized Message Link
DML	Doctor of Modern Languages
DML	Dual Mode LASER
DMLF	Descending Medial Longitudinal Fasciculus
DMM	Dansville & Mount Morris R. R. (AAR code)
DMM	Digital Multimeter
DMM	Directorate of Materiel Management
DMMB	Defense Medical Material Board
DMMC	Digital Multi-Meter Control
DMMCS	Dimethylmonochlorosilane (Organic chemistry)
DMMG	Displacement Method Matrix Generator
DMMH/FH	Direct Maintenance Manhours per Flight Hour (Navy)
DMN	Damon Corp. (NYSE symbol)
DMN	Dimethylnitrosoamine (Chemical carcinogen in cigarette smoke)
DMN	Dorsal Motor Nucleus (of the vagus)
DMNI	Device Multiplexing Nonsynchronized Inputs (Data processing)
DMO	Data Management Office(r) (Air Force)
DMO	Defense Mobilization Order
DMO	Dependent Meteorological Office
DMO	Diode Microwave Oscillator
DMO	Director of Manpower and Organization (Air Force)
DMO	Director(ate) of Military Operations
DMO	District Management Office
DMO	District Marine Officer (Navy)
DMO	District Material Officer (Navy)
DMO	District Medical Officer (Navy)
DMO	Documentation Management Officer (Air Force)
DMO	Dymo Industries, Inc. (NYSE symbol)
DMOI	Director of Military Operations and Intelligence
DMOS	Duty Military Occupational Specialty
DMOS	Dynamic Model Operations Section
DMP	Defense Manpower Policy
DMP	Director of Military Personnel (Air Force)
DMP	Disarmed Military Personnel
DMP	Display Maintenance Program
DMP	Documented Material Processed
DMPA	Defense Materials Procurement Agency
DMPEA	Dimethoxyphenylethylamine
DMPI	Desired Mean Point of Impact (Military)
DMPS	Deepwater Motion Picture System
DMQ	Director of Movements and Quartering (British)
DMR	Daily Mechanical Report
DMR	Date Material Required
DMR	Defective Materiel Report (Air Force)
DMR	Diploma in Medical Radiology
DMR	Director of Materiel Readiness (Army)
DMR	Directorate of Medical Research (Army)
DMR	Distributor-Manufacturer-Representative
DMRE	Diploma in Medical Radiology and Electrolysis (British)
DMRI	Data Material Required, Increasing Urgency (Navy)

D & MRR	Detroit and Mackinac Railroad
DMRT	Diploma in Medical Radio-Therapy (British)
DMS	Data Management System (Data processing)
DMS	Data Measuring System
DMS	Data Monitoring System
DMS	Data Multiplexing System
DMS	Decision Making System
DMS	Defense Marketing Survey
DMS	Defense Materials Service (of GSA)
DMS	Defense Materials System
DMS	Delta Milliohm Sensor
DMS	Delta Modulation System
DMS	Department of Medicine and Surgery (VA)
DMS	Destroyer Minesweeper (Navy symbol)
DMS	Differential Maneuvering Simulator (Aviation)
DMS	Digital Multiplexing Synchronizer (Data processing)
DMS	Diis Manibus Sacrum (Sacred to the Manes [Departed Souls])
DMS	Director of Medical Services
DMS	Director for Mutual Security
DMS	Disk Monitor System (Data processing)
DMS	Display Management System (IBM)
DMS	Distance Measuring System
DMS	Distinguished Military Students
DMS	Doctor of Mechanical Science
DMS	Doctor of Medical Science(s)
DMS	Doctor of Military Science
DMS	Documentation of Molecular Spectroscopy
DMS	Doppler Measurement System
DMS	Drum Memory System (Data processing)
DMSA	Diploma in Medical Services Administration (British)
DMSC	Defense Medical Supply Center (Later, Defense Personnel Support Center)
DM Sc	Doctor of Medical Science
DMSDS	Direct Mail Shelter Development System (Civil Defense)
DMSO	Dimethyl Sulfoxide (Chemical)
DMSP	Depot Maintenance Support Plan (Air Force)
DMSR	Director of Missile Safety Research (Air Force)
DMSS	Data Multiplex Subsystem (Data processing)
DMSS	Digital Multibeam Steering System
DMSS	Director of Medical and Sanitary Services (British)
DMST	Demonstrate
DMSTN	Demonstration
DMT	Dictaphone Machine Transcriber
DMT	Dimethyl Terephthalate
DMT	Dimethyltryptamine (A drug)
DMT	Direct Modulation Technique
DMT	Director of Military Training
DMT	Doctor of Medical Technology
DMTPS	Digital Magnetic Tape Plotting System
DMTR	Dounreay Materials Testing Reactor (British)
DMTS	Department of Mines and Technical Survey (Canada)
DMTS	Digital Module Test Set
DMU	Des Moines Union Railway Company (AAR code)
DMU	Destratification Motor Unit
DMU	Dual Maneuvering Unit (A spacecraft)
DMUP	Defense Materiel Utilization Program (DOD)
D Mus	Doctor of Music
D Mus A	Doctor Musical Arts
D Mus Ed	Doctor of Musical Education
DMV	Department of Motor Vehicles
DMVE	Dulbecco-Vogt Modified Eagle's (Medium for cell growth)
DMW	De-Mineralized Water
DMWR	Depot Maintenance Work Request (or Requirement) (Army)
DMX	Data Multiplex (Computer)
DMZ	Demilitarized Zone
DN	Date Number
DN	Day and Night (Approach and landing charts) (Aviation)
DN	Debit Note
DN	Decimal Number
DN	Delayed Neutron
DN	Dentalman (Nonrated enlisted man) (Navy)
DN	Department of the Navy
DN	Deutscher Normenausschuss
DN	Dialect Notes (A periodical)
DN	Diamond International Corporation (NYSE symbol)
DN	Dinitro-Ortho-Cresol (Insecticide and herbicide) (Also, DNOC)
DN	Doctor of Nursing
DN	Domino Nostro (To Our Lord)
DN	Dominus (Lord)
DN	Dominus Noster (Our Lord)
D : N	Dextrose : Nitrogen Ratio
DNA	Deoxyribonucleic Acid (Biochemistry, genetics)

DNA . . . . Deutscher Normenausschuss (German standards association)
DNA . . . . Director of Naval Accounts
D Na . . . . . . Doctor of Navigation
DNA . . . . Does Not Answer (Telephone operator's designation)
DNAD . . . . Director of Naval Air Division
DNAME . . . . . Department of Naval Architecture and Marine Engineering (MIT)
DN Arch . . . . . Doctor of Naval Architecture
D Na S . . . . . Doctor of Naval Science
D Na Sc . . . . Doctor of Naval Science
D Nat . . . . . . Doctor of Naturopathy
DNB . . . . Departure from Nuclear Boiling
DNB . . . . Deutsches Nachrichtenburo (German news agency)
DNB . . . . Dictionary of National Biography
DNB . . . . Dinitrobenzidine
DNB . . . . Dun & Bradstreet, Inc. (NYSE symbol)
DNC . . . . Democratic National Committee
DNC . . . . Departamento Nacional do Cafe (Brazil)
DNC . . . . Dinitrocellulose
DNC . . . . Director, Naval Communications
DNCB . . . . . . Dinitrochlorobenzene (Chemical)
DNCCC . . . . . Defense National Communications Control Center
DNCG . . . . . . Digital Null Command Generator
DNCINST . . . . Director, Naval Communication Instruction
DNCNOTE . . . Director, Naval Communications Notice
DND . . . . Demodulator Neon Driver
DND . . . . Department of National Defence (Canadian)
DNE . . . . Department of Nuclear Engineering (MIT)
DNE . . . . Director of Naval Equipment
DNE . . . . . . Director of Nursing Education
DNE . . . . . . Doctor of Naval Engineering
DNE . . . . Duluth & Northeastern R. R. (AAR code)
DN Ed . . . . . . Doctor of Nursing Education
DN Eng . . . . . Doctor of Naval Engineering
DNET . . . . . . Division of Nuclear Education and Training (of AEC)
DNF . . . . Disjunctive Normal Formula
DNFB . . . . . . Dinitrofluorobenzene
DNFST . . . . . Department of Nutrition, Food Science and Technology (MIT)
DNFYP . . . . . Department of the Navy Five-Year Program
DNG . . . . . . Distinguished Naval Graduate
DNG . . . . . . District of Columbia National Guard
DNG . . . . . . Dorsal (Nephridial Gland)
DNI . . . . Director of Naval Intelligence (US, British)
DNI . . . . Division of Naval Intelligence
DNJC . . . . . . Dominus Noster Jesus Christus (Our Lord Jesus Christ)
DNJC . . . . . . Nativitas Domini Nostri Jesu Christi (Nativity of Our Lord Jesus Christ)
DNL . . . . . . Det Norske Luftfartselkap (Norwegian Airlines)
DNL . . . . Director of Naval Laboratories
DNL . . . . Do Not Load (Instruction re a freight car)
DNMM . . . . . . Division of Nuclear Materials Management (of AEC)
DNMO . . . . . . District Naval Material Office
DNMR . . . . . Dynamic Nuclear Magnetic Resonance
DNMS . . . . . . Director of Naval Medical Services (Royal Australian Navy)
DNMS . . . . . . Division of Nuclear Materials Safeguards (AEC)
DNN . . . . Dansk Normal Nul (Oceanography)
DNO . . . . . . Director of Naval Operations
DNOC . . . . . Dinitro-Ortho-Cresol (Insecticide and herbicide) (Also, DN)
DNOP . . . . . . Director of Naval Officer Procurement
DNP . . . . Declared National Program (to share oceanographic data with other nations)
DNP . . . . Dinitrophenyl
DNP . . . . . . Drill Non-Pay Status (Naval Reserve)
DNPP . . . . . . Director, Navy Program Planning
DNPT . . . . . . Dinitrosopentamethylenetetramine
DNR . . . . Department of Natural Resources (Department of Agriculture)
DNR . . . . Director of Naval Recruiting (British)
DNR . . . . Does Not Run
DNRC . . . . . Democritus Nuclear Research Center (Greece)
DNRH . . . . . Director of Naval Records and History
DNRQ . . . . . . Did Not Receive Questionnaire
DNS . . . . Diaphragm Nerve Stimulation
DNS . . . . Director of Nuclear Safety (Air Force)
DNS . . . . Discrete Network Simulation
DNS . . . . . . Doctor of Nursing Science
DNS . . . . Doppler Navigation System
DN Sc . . . . . Doctor of Nursing Science
DNSP . . . . . . Departamento Nacional de Saude Publica (Brazil)
DNSR . . . . . . Director of Nuclear Safety Research (Air Force)
DNSS . . . . . . Defense Navigation Satellite System (Formerly, SSPN)
DNST . . . . . . Daughters of the Nile, Supreme Temple
DNT . . . . Developing Nations Tractor (Ford Motor Company)

DNT . . . . Dinitrotoluene (An explosive)
DNT . . . . Downtime
DNTA . . . . . . Dinitrosoterephthalamide
DNTS . . . . . . Director, Naval Transportation Service (Later, CNTS)
DNVP . . . . . . Deutschnationale Volkspartei (German National People's Party)
DNWS . . . . . . Discrete Network Simulation
DNY . . . . . . Donnelley (R. R.) & Sons Company (NYSE symbol)
DO . . . . Defense Order
DO . . . . Delivery Order
DO . . . . Dental Officer
DO . . . . Deviating Oscillator
DO . . . . Diesel Oil
DO . . . . Digital Output (Data processing)
DO . . . . Diploma in Ophthalmology
DO . . . . Direct Obligation
DO . . . . Direct Order
DO . . . . Director of Operations
DO . . . . Director's Office
DO . . . . Disbursing Officer
DO . . . . Dispersing Officer
DO . . . . Dissolved Oxygen
DO . . . . District Office (or Officer)
DO . . . . Ditto
DO . . . . Divisional Officer (Agricultural Development and Advisory Service) (British)
DO . . . . Divisional Orders
DO . . . . Doctor of Optometry
DO . . . . Doctor of Oratory
DO . . . . Doctor of Osteopathic Medicine and Surgery
DO . . . . Doctor of Osteopathy
DO . . . . Dominions Office (British)
DO . . . . Doric Corp. (NYSE symbol)
DO . . . . Due Out (Army)
DO . . . . Duty Officer (Military)
D/O . . . . Disbursing Officer
D & O . . . . . . Directors' and Officers' (Liability insurance)
DOA . . . . Date of Availability (Military)
DOA . . . . Dead on Arrival (Medicine)
DOA . . . . Defeat Opiate Addiction (An organization)
DOA . . . . Department of Agriculture
DOA . . . . Department of the Army
DOA . . . . Disabled Officers Association
DOAL . . . . . . Directorate of Airlift (Air Force)
DOB . . . . Date of Birth
DOB . . . . Daughters of Bilitis (An organization)
DOB . . . . Depth of Burial (of explosives)
DOB . . . . Detained on Board (Referring to seamen)
DOB . . . . Dispersed Operating Base (Air Force)
DOC . . . . Data, Operations, and Control
DOC . . . . Data Optimizing Computer
DOC . . . . Date of Change
DOC . . . . Decimal to Octal Conversion
DOC . . . . Delayed Opening Chaff
DOC . . . . Deoxycholate (Biochemistry)
DOC . . . . Deoxycorticosterone (Endocrinology)
DOC . . . . Department of Commerce
DOC . . . . Direct Operating Cost
DOC . . . . Doctor
DOC . . . . Dr. Pepper Company (NYSE symbol)
DOC . . . . Document
DOC . . . . Due-Out Cancellation (Military)
DOC . . . . Dynamic Overload Controls
DOCA . . . . . . Date of Change of Accountability (Military)
DOCA . . . . . . Date of Current Appointment (Military)
DOCA . . . . . . Defense Orientation Conference Association
DOCA . . . . . . Deoxycorticosterone Acetate (Endocrinology)
DOCC . . . . . . Defense Communications Agency Operations Center Complex
DOCE . . . . . . Date of Current Enlistment
DOCG . . . . . . Date of Rank in Current Grade (Military)
DOCGEN . . . . Document Generator
D Oc S . . . . . Doctor of Ocular Science
D Oc Sc . . . . Doctor of Ocular Science
DOCUS . . . . . . Display Oriented Compiler Usage System
DOD . . . . Department of Defense
DOD . . . . Detroit Ordnance District
DOD . . . . Died of Disease
DOD . . . . Direct Outward Dialing
DOD . . . . Director of Operations Division (British Navy)
DODAAD . . . . Department of Defense Activity Address Directory
DODAC . . . . . Department of Defense Ammunition Code
DODCAPS . . . . Department of Defense Central Automated Personnel System

ACRONYMS AND INITIALISMS DICTIONARY

DODCI . . . . . . Department of Defense Computer Institute
DODCLPMI . . . Department of Defense Consolidated List of Principal Military Items
DODD . . . . . . Department of Defense Directive
DODDAC . . . . Department of Defense Damage Assessment Center
DODEP . . . . . . Department of Defense Emergency Plans
DODEP . . . . . . Department of Defense Exercise Planning
DODFDCO . . . Department of Defense Foreign Disclosure Coordinating Office
DODGE . . . . . Department of Defense Gravity Experiment (Satellite)
DODGE-M . . . Department of Defense Gravity Experiment, Multipurpose
DODH . . . . . . Diimide Oxalic Acid Dihydrazide
DODHGCSO . . Department of Defense Household Goods Commercial Storage Office
DODHGFO . . . Department of Defense Household Goods Field Office
DODHSNS. . . . Department of Defense High School Newspaper Service
DODI . . . . Department of Defense Instruction
DODIC . . . . . Department of Defense Identification (or Item) Code
DODIER . . . . . Department of Defense Industrial Equipment Reserve
DODIS . . . . . Distribution of Oceanographic Data at Isentropic Levels
DODISS . . . . . Department of Defense Index of Specifications and Standards
DOD/MIS . . . . Department of Defense Management Information System
DODMPAC . . . Department of Defense Military Pay and Allowance Committee
DODMPRC . . . Department of Defense Military Personnel Records Center
DODMUL . . . . Department of Defense Master Urgency List
DODNACC . . . Department of Defense National Agency Check Center
DODPM . . . . . Department of Defense Military Pay and Allowances Entitlements Manual
DODPRT . . . . . Date of Departure (Army)
DODRE . . . . . . Department of Defense Research and Engineering
DODS . . . . Definitive Orbit Determination System (NASA)
DOE . . . . Date of Enlistment
DOE . . . . Deep Ocean Environment
DOE . . . . Doctor of Oral English
DOE . . . . Dyspnea on Exertion (Medicine)
D Oec . . . . . . Doctor Oeconomiae (Doctor of Economics)
DOES . . . . . . Defense Organization Entity Standards
DOES . . . . Defense Organization Entity System (DOD)
DOES . . . . Disk-Oriented Engineering System (Data processing)
DOETS . . . . . Dual-Object Electronic Tracking System
DOF . . . . Deep Ocean Floor
DOF . . . . Defenders of Furbearers
DOF . . . . Degree of Freedom
DOF . . . . Delivery on Field
DOF . . . . Demonstration of Operational Feasibility
DOFAB . . . . . Damned Old Fool About Books (Acronym created by Eugene Field)
DOFL . . . . . . Diamond Ordnance Fuze Laboratory (AMC) (Later, Harry Diamond Laboratories)
DOG . . . . Disgruntled Old Graduate (West Point)
DOG . . . . Double Chain Branch-Oblong Master Link-Grab Hook
DOG . . . . Drop Out Generator
DOH . . . . Deutscher Orden der Harugari (German Order of Harugari)
DOHC . . . . . . Double Overhead Camshaft (Automotive term)
DOI . . . . Deep Ocean Installation
DOI . . . . Department of the Interior
DOI . . . . Department Operating Instruction
DOI . . . . Descent Orbit Insertion (Aerospace)
DOI . . . . Died of Injuries (Army)
DOI . . . . Differential Orbit Improvement
DOI . . . . Directorate Office Instruction
DO/IT . . . . . . Digital Output/Input Translator
DOJ . . . . Department of Justice
DOK . . . . De Odeon Kring (The Odeon Club, for homosexuals) (Holland)
DOKK . . . . . . Dramatic Order Knights of Khorassan
DOL . . . . Department Of Labor
DOL . . . . Detached Officer's List (Army)
DOL . . . . Doctor of Oriental Languages
DOL . . . . Dollar
DOL . . . . Dynamic Octal Load
DOLA . . . . . . Dog Owners League of America
DOLARS . . . . Digital Off-Line Automatic Recording System
DOLARS . . . . Doppler Location and Ranging System
DOLITAC . . . . Department of Labor International Technical Assistance Corps
DOLLS . . . . . Delayed Opening Leaflet System (Military propaganda)
DOLO . . . . . . Disbursing Officers Liaison Office
DOLOA . . . . . Dog Owners League of America
DOM . . . . Datur Omnibus Mori (It is Allotted unto All to Die)
DOM . . . . Deo Optimo Maximo (To God, the Best and Greatest)
DOM . . . . Depth of Modulation
DOM . . . . Designing Out Maintenance
DOM . . . . Digital Ohmmeter
DOM . . . . Dirty Old Man (Slang)
DOM . . . . Division of Overseas Ministries (National Council of Churches)
DOM . . . . Domestic

DOM . . . . Dominus Omnium Magister (God the Master, or Lord, of All) (Motto of the Benedictine Order)
DOM . . . . A hallucinogenic drug, more commonly known as STP
DOMAR . . . . . Doppler Martin RADAR (Air Force)
DOMD . . . . . . Digital Oxygen Metering Device (Aerospace)
DOMREP . . . . Dominican Republic
DOMS . . . . . . Diploma in Ophthalmic Medicine and Surgery
DON . . . . Demand Order Number (Army)
DON . . . . Department of the Navy
DON . . . . Doppler Optical Navigation
DONMICS. . . . Department of the Navy Management Information Control System
DOO . . . . Director, Office of Oceanography (UNESCO)
DOO . . . . District Operations Office(r) (Navy)
DOO . . . . District Ordnance Office(r) (Navy)
DOO . . . . Division Ordnance Officer
DOOLAR . . . . . Deep Ocean Object Location and Recovery
DOOM . . . . . . Deep Ocean Optical Measurement
DOP. . . . . Designated Overhaul Point
DOP. . . . . Detachment of Patients
DOP. . . . . Developing-Out Paper
DOP. . . . . Dioctyl Phthalate (Also, Di-2-ethylhexyl Phthalate) (Organic chemistry)
DOPA . . . . . . Dihydroxyphenylalanine (Biochemistry)
DOPDF . . . . . . Doppler Direction-Finding Equipment
DOPE . . . . Double Odd Pass Even (System in game of bridge)
DOPF . . . . Duty Directed in Order is Being Performed For
DOPI . . . . Delay-On-Pull-In
DOPI . . . . Double O (Zero) Pass One (System in game of bridge)
DOPLOC . . . . . Doppler Phase Lock
D Opth . . . . . Doctor of Ophthalmology
DOR . . . . Date of Rank
DOR. . . . . Date of Request
DOR. . . . . Design Objective Reliability
D Or . . . . Doctor of Oratory
DOR. . . . . Dorr-Oliver, Inc. (NYSE symbol)
DOR. . . . . Drop on Request (Navy)
DORA. . . . . . . Defence of the Realm Act (British) (World War I)
DORA. . . . . . . Dynamic Operator Response Apparatus
DORAN . . . . . Doppler Range and Navigation (Electronics)
DORCG . . . . . Date of Rank, Current Grade (Air Force)
DORCMA . . . . Door Operator and Remote Controls Manufacturers Association
DORCSA . . . . . District Officer for Reserve Communication Supplementary Activities
DORE . . . . DOD (Department of Defense) Officer Record Examination
DORF . . . . Diamond Ordnance Radiation Facility (AEC)
DORIS . . . . . . Direct Order Recording and Invoicing System (A computer-based system of British petroleum companies)
DORPG. . . . . . Date of Rank, Permanent Grade (Air Force)
DORS . . . . . . Dynamic Operator Response System
D Or Sc . . . . . Doctor of the Science of Oratory
DOS. . . . . Date of Separation (Military)
DOS. . . . . Days of Supply (Rations)
DOS. . . . . Degenerate Oscillating System
DOS. . . . . Department of State
DOS. . . . . Dioctyl Sebacate (Organic chemistry)
DOS. . . . . Director of Ordnance Services (British military)
DOS. . . . . Discrete Orthonormal Sequence
DOS. . . . . Disk Operating System (Data processing)
DOS. . . . . Division of Operational Safety (AEC)
DOS . . . . Doctor of Ocular Science
DOS . . . . Doctor of Optical Science
DOS. . . . . Doctor of Optometric Science
DOSAAF . . . . . Dobrovol'noe Obshchestvo Sodeistviia Armii, Aviatsii, i Flotu (Voluntary Society for Cooperation with the Army, Aviation, and the Fleet) (USSR)
DOSAR . . . . . Dosimetry Applications Research Facility (AEC)
DO Sc . . . . . . Doctor of Optometric Science
DOSC. . . . . . . Dubois Oleic Serum Complex (Bacteriology)
DOSN . . . . . . Disbursing Office Serial Number
DOSV. . . . . . . Deep Oceanographic Survey Vehicle (Naval Oceanographic Office)
DOT. . . . . Deep-Ocean Technology
DOT. . . . . Deep Ocean Transponder
DOT. . . . . Deep Oceanic Turbulence
DOT. . . . . Delayed on Target
DOT. . . . . Department of Overseas Trade (British)
DOT . . . . Department of Transport (Canada)
DOT. . . . . Department of Transportation (US)
DOT. . . . . Department of the Treasury
DOT. . . . . Dependent Overseas Territory
DOT. . . . . Dictionary of Occupational Titles
DOT. . . . . Digital Output Timer (Data processing)
DOT. . . . . Duplex One-Tape System
DOTC. . . . . . . Data Observing Testing Console

DOTC . . . . Department of Transport (Canada)
DOTI . . . . Director of Operations, Training and Intelligence (Army)
DOTM . . . . . . Director of Naval Ordnance, Torpedoes, and Mines (Royal Australian Navy)
DOUCHE . . . . . Description of Underwater Contacts Hastily and Exactly (Navy slang)
DOUSER . . . . . Doppler Unbeamed Search RADAR
DOV . . . . Diaphragm Operated Valve
DOV . . . . Disbursing Officer's Voucher
DOV . . . . Distilled Oil of Vitriol
DOV . . . . Double Oil of Vitriol
DOV . . . . Dover Corporation (NYSE symbol)
DOVAP . . . . . Doppler, Velocity and Position (NASA)
DOW . . . . Density of Water
DOW . . . . Died of Wounds
DOW . . . . Dow Chemical Company (NYSE symbol)
DOW . . . . Duration of War
DOWB . . . . . . Deep Ocean Work Boat
DOWB . . . . . . Deep Operating Work Boat
DOWB . . . . . Director of Works and Buildings (British)
DOZ . . . . Dozen
DP . . . . By Direction of the President
DP . . . . Dash Pot (Relay)
DP . . . . Data Printer
DP . . . . Data Processing
DP . . . . De Profundis
DP . . . . Deck Piercing
DP . . . . Deep Penetration (Air Force)
DP . . . . Deep Pulse (Medicine)
DP . . . . Deflection Plate (Technical drawings)
DP . . . . Degree of Polymerization
DP . . . . Delivery Point
DP . . . . Dementia Praecox (or a patient with this condition) (Medical slang)
DP . . . . Democratic Party (Uganda)
DP . . . . Dental Prosthetic Technician
DP . . . . Department of the Pacific (Marine Corps)
DP . . . . Departure Point
DP . . . . Description Pattern
DP . . . . Design Proposal
DP . . . . Detrucking Point
DP . . . . Developing Proboscis
DP . . . . Dew Point
DP . . . . Dial Pulsing
DP . . . . Diametrical Pitch
DP . . . . Diastatic Power
DP . . . . Difference in Pressure
DP . . . . Differential Pressure
DP . . . . Diffused Planar
DP . . . . Digit Present
DP . . . . Dining Permit (Slang)
DP . . . . Diphenyl
DP . . . . Diphosgene
DP . . . . Direct Port (Transportation)
DP . . . . Directing Point
DP . . . . Director of Programs (Air Force, Army)
DP . . . . Discussion Paper
DP . . . . Disorderly Person
DP . . . . Dispensing Precaution
DP . . . . Displaced Person (Post-World War II)
DP . . . . Display Panel
DP . . . . Distribution Point
DP . . . . Doctor of Philosophy
DP . . . . Domestic Prelate
DP . . . . Donor's Plasma (Medicine)
DP . . . . Doppelposten (Double sentry) (German military - World War II)
DP . . . . Dorsal Pit
DP . . . . Double Petticoat
DP . . . . Double Play (Baseball)
DP . . . . Double Pole (Switch)
DP . . . . Double Purpose Gun
DP . . . . Drill Pay
DP . . . . Driving Power
DP . . . . Drop Point (Air Force)
DP . . . . Dry Point
DP . . . . Dual Purpose
DP . . . . Duty Paid
DP . . . . Duty Pay
DP . . . . Dynamic Programming
D/P . . . . Detained Pay
D/P . . . . Documents against Payment (Banking)
D/P . . . . Documents upon Payment of Draft
D & P . . . . . . Developing and Printing

D & P . . . . . . Drunk and Proud
D of P . . . . . . Degree of Pocahontas
DPA . . . . Data Processing Activities
DPA . . . . Defense Production Act
DPA . . . . Defense Production Administration
DPA . . . . Demonstration Programs Administration (HUD)
DPA . . . . Deutsche Presse-Agentur (West German news agency)
DPA . . . . Deutscher Personalausweis
DPA . . . . Diploma in Public Administration (British)
D Pa . . . . Doctor of Painting
DPA . . . . Doctor of Public Administration
DPA . . . . Driving Point Admittance
DP Adm . . . . . Doctor of Public Administration
DPAIAI . . . . . . Disregard Previous Assignment Instructions and Assign as Indicated (Army)
DPAS . . . . Discharged Prisoners' Aid Society (British)
D-PAT . . . . . . Drum Programmed Automatic Tester
DPB . . . . Data Plotting Board
DPB . . . . Deposit Passbook (Banking)
DPB . . . . Disability Policy Board (VA)
DPB . . . . Distinguished Pistol Badge
DPB . . . . . . Doctor of Physical Biology
DPB . . . . . . Document Processing Branch (NTIS)
DPBC . . . . . . Double Pole, Both Connected (Switch)
DPC . . . . Data Processing Centrals
DPC . . . . Data Processing Control
DPC . . . . Defence Production Chief (British)
DPC . . . . Defense Plant Corporation (Subsidiary of Reconstruction Finance Corporation) (Obsolete)
DPC . . . . Defense Procurement Circular
DPC . . . . Democratic Policy Committee
DPC . . . . Desert Protective Council
DPC . . . . Differential Pressure Control
DPC . . . . Digital Phase Comparator
DPC . . . . Digital Pressure Converter
DPC . . . . Digital Process Controller
DPC . . . . Displaced Persons Commission (Terminated, 1952)
DPC . . . . Display Power Control
DPC . . . . Documentation Processing Center (British)
DPC . . . . Doklady Physical Chemistry
DPCA . . . . . . Displaced Phase Center Antenna
DPCA . . . . . . Doberman Pinscher Club of America
DPCF . . . . . . Dorsal Peristomial Collar Fold
DPCS . . . . . . Difference Pressure Control Switch
DPCTE . . . . . . Data Processor and Computer Test Equipment
DPCU . . . . . . Digital Processing and Control Unit
DPD . . . . Data Processing Department
DPD . . . . Data Project Directive
DPD . . . . Diffusion Pressure Deficit
DPD . . . . Digital Phase Difference
DPD . . . . Diploma in Public Dentistry (British)
DPD . . . . . . Director, Personnel Department
DPD . . . . Director of Plans Division (British Navy)
DPD . . . . District Port Director (Navy)
D Pd . . . . Doctor of Pedagogy
DPDC . . . . . . Double Paper, Double Cotton (Insulation)
DPDI . . . . . . Dimple Die
DPDT . . . . . . Double Pole, Double Throw (Switch)
DPE . . . . Data Processing Equipment
DPE . . . . Distributor-to-Printer Electronics
DPE . . . . Doctor of Physical Education
DPE . . . . Duration of the Present Emergency (British) (World War II)
D Ped . . . . . . Doctor of Pedagogy
D Pe E . . . . . . Doctor of Petroleum Engineering
D Pe Eng . . . . . Doctor of Petroleum Engineering
DPF . . . . Data Processing Facility
DPF . . . . Dense Plasma Focus
DPF . . . . Depression Position-Finder
DPF . . . . Disciples Peace Fellowship
DPF . . . . DPF, Inc. (Formerly, Data Processing Financial & General Corp.) (NYSE symbol)
DPF . . . . Drill Press Feed
DPF . . . . Dynamic Pressure Feedback
DPFC . . . . . . Double Pole, Front Connected (Switch)
DPFT . . . . . . Desk, Double-Pedestal Flat-Top
DPG . . . . Data Processing Group
DPG . . . . Date of Permanent Grade
DPG . . . . Digital Pattern Generator
DPG . . . . Diphenylguanidine
DPG . . . . Diphosphoglycerate (Organic chemistry)
DPG . . . . Dugway Proving Ground (Army)
DPGp . . . . . . Data Processing Group (Air Force)

DPGR . . . . Dugway Proving Ground (Army)
DPH . . . . Department of Public Health
DPH . . . . Diphenylhydantoin
DPH . . . . Diploma in Public Health
DPH . . . . Disintegrations Per Hour
D Ph . . . . Doctor of Philosophy
DPH . . . . Doctor of Public Health
DPH . . . . Doctor of Public Hygiene
D Phar . . . . . . Doctor of Pharmacy
D Phar C . . . . . Doctor of Pharmaceutical Chemistry
D Ph C . . . . . . Doctor of Pharmaceutical Chemistry
D Phc . . . . Doctor of Pharmacology
DPHE . . . . Doctor of Public Health Engineering
DPH Ed . . . . . . Doctor of Public Health Education
DPH Eng . . . . . Doctor of Public Health Engineering
D Phil . . . . Doctor of Philanthropy
D Phil . . . . Doctor of Philosophy
D Ph M . . . . . . Doctor of Philosophy in Metaphysics
DPHN . . . . . . Doctor of Public Health Nursing
D Pho . . . . Doctor of Photography
D Ph S . . . . . . Doctor of Physical Science
D Ph Sc . . . . . Doctor of Physical Science
D Phy . . . . Doctor of Physics
DPI . . . . Data Processing Installation
DPI . . . . Deal Proneness Index (Marketing)
DPI . . . . Department of Public Information (of United Nations)
DPI . . . . Desired Point of Impact
DPI . . . . Director of Public Instruction
DPI . . . . Disposable Personal Income
DPI . . . . Duo-Plasmation Ion
DPII . . . . Dairy Products Improvement Institute
DPIO . . . . District Public Information Office(r) (Navy)
DPIP . . . . Dichlorophenolindophenol
DPIS . . . . Duo-Plasmation Ion Source
DPK . . . . Delta Psi Kappa (Society)
DPL . . . . Dayton Power & Light Company (NYSE symbol)
DPL . . . . Diagonal Proof Line (Technical drawings)
DPL . . . . Distribution Plot List
DPL . . . . Doctor of Patent Law
DPL . . . . Double Propellant Loading
DP & L . . . . . . Dallas Power & Light Company
DPLM . . . . Dual Pulse LASER Microwelder
DPLO . . . . District Postal Liaison Officer (Navy)
DPM . . . . Deflectable Photomultiplier
DPM . . . . Department Personnel Manual
DPM . . . . Designated Project Manager
DPM . . . . Designated for Prompt Mobilization
DPM . . . . Development Planning Memo
DPM . . . . Diploma in Psychological Medicine
DPM . . . . Disintegrations Per Minute
DPM . . . . Doctor of Physical Medicine
DPM . . . . Draft Presidential Memorandum (DOD)
DPM . . . . Drafting Practice Manual
DPMA . . . . Data Processing Management Association
DPMA . . . . . Dictionary of Physics and Mathematics Abbreviations, Signs and Symbols
DPMA . . . . . . Distributive Principle of Multiplication over Addition (New math)
DPMC . . . . . . Director of Personnel, Marine Corps
DPMOAP . . . . Society of Data Processing Machine Operators and Programmers
DPN . . . . Diphosphopyridine Nucleotide (Biochemistry) (See NAD)
DPNC . . . . . . Democratic Party of Nigeria and the Cameroons
DPNE . . . . . . Division of Peaceful Nuclear Explosives (of AEC)
DPO . . . . Data Processing Operation
DPO . . . . Depot Property Officer
DPO . . . . Development Planning Objective
DPO . . . . Diphenyl Oxide
DPO . . . . Distributing Post Office
DPO . . . . District Personnel Office(r) (Navy)
DPO . . . . District Postal Office(r) (Navy)
DPO . . . . . . Divisional Pests Officer (Ministry of Agriculture, Fisheries, and Food) (British)
DPO . . . . Double Pulse Operation
DPOB . . . . . . Date and Place of Birth
DPODP . . . . . Double-Precision Orbit Determination Program (NASA)
DPOL . . . . . . Political Directorate (Allied German Occupation Forces)
DPOP . . . . . . Data Printout Program
DPOW . . . . . Prisoners of War and Displaced Persons Directorate (Allied German Occupation Forces)
DPOWA . . . . Distributive, Processing and Office Workers Union of America
DPP . . . . Decentralized Printing Program (Army)
DPP . . . . Defense Procurement Program (DOD)

DPP . . . . Detailed Project Plan
DPP . . . . Development Program Plan
DPP . . . . Director of Personnel Planning (Air Force)
DPP . . . . Director of Procurement and Production (Army)
DPP . . . . Director of Public Prosecutions (British)
D Ph . . . . Dry Photo Process
DPPA . . . . . . Double Pumped Parametric Amplifier
DPPB . . . . . . Disaster Preparedness Planning Board
DPPC . . . . . . Data Processing Products Contract
DPPH . . . . . . Diphenylpicrylhydrazyl
DPPO . . . . . . Direct Procurement Petty Officer
DPPO . . . . . . District Publications and Printing Office
DPPT . . . . . . Director of Personnel Procurement and Training (Air Force)
DPQ . . . . Double Precision Quantity
DPR . . . . Data Processing Request
DPR . . . . Department Performance Rating
DPR . . . . Department of Physical Research (British)
DPR . . . . Depolymerized Rubber
DPR . . . . Development Planning Reports
DPR . . . . Director of Public Relations
DPR . . . . District Probate Registry
DPR . . . . Double Pulse Ranging
DPR . . . . Dual Pen Recorder
DPRK . . . . . . Democratic People's Republic of Korea
DPRO . . . . . . District Public Relations Office(r) (Navy)
DPRS . . . . . . Dynamic Preferential Runway System (Aviation)
DPS . . . . Data Present Signal
DPS . . . . Data-Processing System (SAGE)
DPS . . . . Defense Printing Service
DPS . . . . Delayed Printer Simulator
DPS . . . . Denison & Pacific Suburban Railway Company (AAR code)
DPS . . . . Descent Propulsion System (NASA)
DPS . . . . Development and Proof Services
DPS . . . . Dewan Pengurus Sementara (Provisional Management Board Section) (Indonesia)
DPS . . . . Dialectic Problem Solver
DPS . . . . Digital Phase Shifter
DPS . . . . Digital Plotter System
DPS . . . . Diode Phase Shifter
DPS . . . . Director of Personal Services (British Navy)
DPS . . . . Display Power Supply
DPS . . . . Doctor of Political Science
D Ps . . . . Doctor of Psychology
DPS . . . . Doctor of Public Service
DPS . . . . Document Processing System (Data processing)
DPS . . . . Dual Porosity Sinter
DPSA . . . . . . Data Processing Supplies Association
DPSA . . . . . . Doctor of Public School Art
DPSC . . . . . . Defense Personnel Support Center
DPSC . . . . . . Defense Petroleum Supply Center
DP Sc . . . . . . Doctor of Political Science
DPSD . . . . . . Dew Point Sensing Device
DPSD . . . . . . Dimensionless Power Spectral Density
DPSK . . . . . . Differentially Phase Shift Keying
DPSM . . . . . . Diode Phase Shifter Module
DPSM . . . . . . Doctor of Public School Music
DPSO . . . . . . Defense Projects Support Office (NASA)
DPSS . . . . . . Data Processing Subsystem
DPSS . . . . . . Department of Public Social Services
DPSS . . . . . . Director of Printing and Stationery Services (British military)
DPST . . . . . . Double Pole, Single Throw (Switch)
D Ps Th . . . . . Doctor of Psycho-Therapy
DPSW . . . . . . Differential Pressure Sea Water
DPT . . . . Design Proof Tests
DPT . . . . Development Prototype
DPT . . . . Dew Point Tester
DPT . . . . Director of Personnel and Training (Army)
DPTO . . . . . . District Property Transportation Office(r) (Navy)
DPTS . . . . . . Director of Physical Training and Sports (British Navy)
DPTT . . . . . . Double Pole, Triple Throw
DPTW . . . . . . Desk, Double-Pedestal Typewriter
DPU . . . . Data Processing Unit
DPU . . . . Digital Processing Unit
DPU . . . . Driver Propulsion Unit
D Pub Adm . . . . Doctor of Public Administration
DPUO . . . . . . Duty Directed is Being Performed for Unit Issuing Order
DPV . . . . Design Point Vehicle
DPV . . . . Dry Pipe Valve
DPW . . . . Department of Public Welfare
DPW . . . . Director of Prisoners of War (British) (World War II)
DPWO . . . . . . District Public Works Office

DQ	Deep Quest
DQ	Definite Quantity
DQ	Development Quotient
DQ	Direct Question (Legal testimony)
DQC	Data Quality Control
DQC	Dynamic Quality Control
DQCM	Data Quality Control Monitor
DQE	De Queen & Eastern R. R. (AAR code)
DQM	Data Quality Monitors
DQM	Depot Quartermaster (Marine Corps)
DQM	Digital Quality Monitor
DQMG	Deputy Quartermaster General
DQN	Depot Quartermaster, Norfolk, Virginia (Marine Corps)
DQP	Depot Quartermaster, Philadelphia, Pennsylvania (Marine Corps)
DQP	Diode Qualification Program
DQPH	Depot Quartermaster, Pearl Harbor, Hawaii (Marine Corps)
DQQ	Depot Quartermaster, Quantico, Virginia (Marine Corps)
DQR	Depot Quartermaster, Richmond, Virginia (Marine Corps)
DQSF	Depot Quartermaster, San Francisco, California (Marine Corps)
DQT	Diode Qualification Test
DQTP	Diode Qualification Test Program
DQU	Deganawidah-Quetzalcoatl University (Davis, California)
DQU	Duquesne Light Company (NYSE symbol)
DR	Dardanelle & Russellville R. R. (AAR code)
DR	Data Recorder
DR	Data Report
DR	Date of Rank
DR	Dead Reckoning
DR	Debit Request
DR	Decanus Ruralis (Rural Dean)
DR	Defensive Response (Psychology)
DR	Deficiency Report (Air Force)
DR	Degeneration Reaction
DR	Dental Recruit
DR	Dependents Rate (Air Force)
DR	Deposit Receipt
DR	Design Requirement
DR	Despatch Rider (British military)
DR	Detailed Report
DR	Detection RADAR
DR	Development Report
DR	Deviation Range
DR	Diesel Radial (Aircraft engine)
DR	Differential Rate
DR	Digital Resolver
DR	Dining Room
DR	Diploma in Radiology
DR	Direct Route
DR	Directive Antenna
DR	Discrimination RADAR
DR	Display Racks (Freight)
DR	District Railway (London)
DR	District Registry
DR	Division of Research (Navy)
DR	Dock Receipt
DR	Doctor
DR	Document Report
DR	Down Right (The front right portion of a stage) (A stage direction)
DR	Drachma
DR	Drill Regulations
DR	Drill Rod
DR	Drive
DR	Duplicating Requisition
DR	Dynamic Range
DR	National Distillers & Chemical Corporation (NYSE symbol)
DR	Reaction of Degeneration (Physiology)
D/R	Dead Reckoning
D/R	Direct/Reverse
D/R	Directional Radio
D/R	Dispatch Rider (Marine Corps)
D/R	Down Range
D & R	Distiller and Rectifier
DRA	Dead Reckoning Analyzer
DRA	Defense Reorganization Act
DRA	Dielectric Rod Antenna
DRA	Digital Recorder Analyzer
DRA	Doppler RADAR
DRA	Dude Ranchers' Association
DR & A	Data Reduction and Analysis
DR & A	Data Reporting and Accounting
DRAAG	Design Review and Acceptance Group (Reviews nuclear weapon designs for DOD)
DRAB	Downriver Residents Against Bowling
DRAC	Distributed Read Address Counter
DRAD	Drill Adapter
DRADS	Defense RADAR Degradation System
DRADS	Degradation of RADAR Defense Systems
Dr Ae	Doctor of Aviation
D Ra E	Doctor of Radio Engineering
D Ra Eng	Doctor of Radio Engineering
Dr Ae S	Doctor of Aeronautical Science
Dr Ae Sc	Doctor of Aeronautical Science
DRAI	Dead Reckoning Analog (or Analyzer) Indicator
DRA/INED	Development Research Associates Inc., Institute for New Enterprise Development
DRAM	Dynamic Random Access Mechanization
DRAMS	Digital Recording and Measuring System
DRANS	Data Reduction and Analysis System
DRAP	Dram, Apothecary
DRAPE	Data Recording and Processing Equipment
DRAPE	Digital Recording and Playback Equipment
DRAT	Data Reduction and Analysis Tape
DRAT	Demonstration Reliability Acceptance Test
DRAV	Dram, Aviordupois
DRB	Decade Resolver Bridge
DRB	Decimal Register Binary
DRB	Defence Research Board (Canada)
DRB	Design Review Board
DRBG	Drill Bushing
Dr Bi Ch	Doctor of Biological Chemistry
Dr Bi Phy	Doctor of Biophysics
DRC	Damage-Risk Criteria (Tolerable limits for noise exposure)
DRC	Data Rate Changer
DRC	Data Recording Camera
DRC	Data Reduction Center (or Complex)
DRC	Data Reduction Compiler
DRC	Data Return Capsule
DRC	Defense Research Corporation
DRC	Democratic Republic of the Congo
DRC	Direct-Reaction Calculation
DRC	Discoverer Recovery Capsule (NASA)
DRC	Division of Rehabilitation Counseling (of the APGA)
DRC	Dynamics Research Corporation
Dr Can L	Doctor of Canon Laws
DRCCC	Defense Regional Communications Control Center
DRCL	Defence Research Chemical Laboratories (Canada)
Dr Com	Doctor of Commerce
DRCPR	Differential Reactive Current Project Relay
Dr Cr Jus	Doctor of Criminal Jurisprudence
Dr CS	Doctor of Commercial Science
DRCT	Direct
DRCTY	Directory
Dr Cul S	Doctor of Cultural Science
Dr Cul Sc	Doctor of Cultural Science
DRD	Data Requirement Description (NASA)
DRD	Diesel Reduction Drive
DRD	Director(ate) of Research and Development (Air Force)
DRD	Diver Restraint Device
DRD	Division of Reactor Development (AEC)
Dr D	Doctor of Divinity
DRD	Documentary Research Division (Air Force)
DRD	Drum Read Driver (Data processing)
DRDS	Degradation RADAR Defense System
DRDT	Division of Reactor Development and Technology (AEC)
DRDTO	Detection RADAR Data Takeoff (Air Force)
DRE	Data Reduction Equipment
DRE	Defense Research Establishment (Israel)
DRE	Department of Rural Education (of NEA)
DRE	Direct Reading Encoder
DRE	Director of Religious Education
DRE	Director(ate) of Research and Engineering (Military)
DRE	District Reserve Equipment (Army)
D Re	Doctor of Religion
DRE	Doctor of Religious Education
DRE	Drachmae
DRE	Drewrys Limited USA, Inc. (NYSE symbol) (Delisted)
DREC	Detection RADAR Electronic Component
Dr Ec	Doctor of Economics
DRED	Data Routing and Error Detecting
DRED	Detection RADAR Environmental Display (Air Force)
DR Ed	Doctor of Religious Education

DREE . . . . Department of Regional Economic Expansion (Canada)
D Re E . . . . . . Doctor of Refrigeration Engineering
D Re Eng . . . . . Doctor of Refrigeration Engineering
DREGE . . . . . . Diabetes Retrieval Element Generator & Executor
Dr En . . . . Doctor of English
Dr Eng . . . . . . Doctor of Engineering
Dr of Eng . . . . Doctor of Engineering
Dr Ent . . . . . . Doctor of Entomology
DREPO . . . . . . District Reserve Electronics Program Officer
DRET . . . . Defence Research Establishment, Toronto (Canada)
DRET . . . . Direct Reentry Telemetry (Air Force)
DRETS . . . . . . Direct Reentry Telemetry System (Air Force)
DREWS . . . . . . Direct Readout Equatorial Satellite
DRF . . . . Dairy Remembrance Fund
DRF . . . . Data Reporting Form
DRF . . . . Deafness Research Foundation
DRF . . . . Diamond Radiation Facility
DRF . . . . Differential Reinforcement
DRF . . . . Direct Relief Foundation
DRF . . . . Discharge Ringing Frequency
DRF . . . . Division Ready Force (Army)
Dr F . . . . Doctor of Forestry
Dr Fi . . . . Doctor of Finance
DRFO . . . . . . Danube River Field Organization (Allied German Occupation Forces)
DRFR . . . . . . Division of Research Facilities and Resources (of National Institutes of Health)
DRFX . . . . . . Drill Fixture
DRG . . . . Defense Research Group (NATO)
DRG . . . . Digital Ranging Generator (Apollo) (NASA)
DRG . . . . Division of Research Grants (of National Institutes of Health)
Dr Ge . . . . . . Doctor of Geology
Dr Geo . . . . . . Doctor of Geography
Dr GP . . . . . . Doctor of Geopolitics
DRGW . . . . . . Denver & Rio Grande Western R. R. (AAR code)
D & RGW . . . . Denver & Rio Grande Western Railroad Company
DRH . . . . Digital Readout Head (Data processing)
DRHD . . . . . . Drill Head
Dr HL . . . . . . Doctor of Humanities of Learning
Dr Hor . . . . . . Doctor of Horticulture
Dr HS . . . . . . Doctor of Humanitarian Service
Dr Hy . . . . . . Doctor of Hygiene
DRI . . . . Data Reduction Interpreter
DRI . . . . Davenport, Rock Island & North Western Railway (AAR code)
DRI . . . . Defense Research Institute
DRI . . . . Denver Research Institute
DRI . . . . Desert Research Institute (University of Nevada)
DRI . . . . Dose Rate Instrumentation
DRI . . . . Dual Roll Idler
DRIFT . . . . . . Diversity Receiving Instrumentation for Telemetry
DRIFT . . . . . . Diversity Reliability Instantaneous Forecasting Technique
DRIFT . . . . . . Dynamic Reliability Instantaneous Forecasting Technique
DRIL . . . . Directorio Revolucionario Iberico de Liberta (Revolutionary Directorate for Iberian Liberation)
DRILL . . . . . . Delaware Rapid Interlibrary Loan and Reference Service
DRILS . . . . . . Defense Retail Interservice Logistic Support (Military)
DRINC . . . . . . Dairy Research, Incorporated
Dr Ind . . . . . . Doctor of Industry
DRIP . . . . Data Reduction Input Program (Data processing)
DRIP . . . . Digital Ray and Intensity Projector
DRIR . . . . Direct Readout Infrared
DRISS . . . . . . Digital Read-In Subsystem (Data processing)
DRJ . . . . Data Requirements Justification (Military)
DRJG . . . . . . Drill Jig
Dr JS . . . . . . Doctor of Judicial Science
Dr J Sc . . . . . Doctor of Judicial Science
Dr Jur . . . . . . Doctor of Laws
DRK . . . . Deutsches Rotes Kreuz
DRKL . . . . . . Defence Research Kingston Laboratory (Canada)
DRL . . . . Data Reduction Laboratory
DRL . . . . Data Retrieval Language (National Bureau of Standards)
DRL . . . . Defense Research Laboratory
DRL . . . . Digital Readout Light (Data processing)
DRL . . . . Directional Reference Locator
DRL . . . . Division of Reactor Licensing (AEC)
Dr Lit . . . . . . Doctor of Literature
Dr Litt . . . . . . Doctor of Letters
Dr LL . . . . . . Doctor of Laws
DRLS . . . . . . Despatch-Rider Letter-Service (British military)
Dr LS . . . . . . Doctor of Library Science
DRM . . . . Decay Rate Meter
DRM . . . . Dental Repair Technician (Navy)

DRM . . . . Design Reference Mission (NASA)
DRM . . . . Development Reactor Mockup
DRM . . . . Digital Radiometer
DRM . . . . Digital Range Machine
DRM . . . . Direction of Relative Movement (Navigation)
DRM . . . . Drafting Room Manual
DRMAJ . . . . . . Drum Major (Marine Corps)
DRME . . . . . . Direction des Recherches et Moyens d'Essais (France)
Dr Med . . . . . . Doctor of Medicine
DRMF . . . . . . Damon Runyon Memorial Fund for Cancer Research
DRMI . . . . . . Dual Radio Magnetic Indicator
DRML . . . . . . Defence Research Medical Laboratory (Canada)
DRMO . . . . . . District Records Management Office
DRMS . . . . . . Department of Defense Resource Management System
Dr MT . . . . . . Doctor of Mechanotherapy
Dr Mus . . . . . . Doctor of Music
DRN . . . . Daily Reports Notice (Air Force)
DRN . . . . Data Reference Number
DRN . . . . Documentation Revision Notice
DRN . . . . Double-Round Nose
DRNL . . . . . . Defence Research Northern Laboratory (Canada)
Dr N Ph . . . . . Doctor of Natural Philosophy
Dr N Sc . . . . . Doctor of the Natural Sciences
DRO . . . . Daily Receipt of Obligation (Military)
DRO . . . . Daily Report of Obligation (Navy)
DRO . . . . Day Room Orderly (Army)
DRO . . . . Destructive Readout
DRO . . . . Digital Readout Oscilloscope (Data processing)
DRO . . . . Direct Recording Oscillograph
DRO . . . . Director of Recruiting and Organization (British military)
DRO . . . . Disablement Resettlement Officer (Department of Education) (British)
DRO . . . . Divisional Routine Order(s)
DROD . . . . . . Delayed Readout Detector (Satellite instrument)
DRO-LA . . . . . . Defense Research Office, Latin America (US Army)
DROMDI . . . . . Direct Readout Miss Distance Indicator (Data processing)
DRON . . . . . . Data Reduction
DROO . . . . . . Digital Readout Oscilloscope (Data processing)
DROS . . . . . . Date Returned from Overseas
DROS . . . . . . Direct Readout Satellite
Dr O Sc . . . . . Doctor of the Science of Oratory
DROT . . . . . . Delayed Range on Target (Air Force)
DROWS . . . . . Direct Readout Weather Satellite
DRP . . . . Data Reduction Procedure (or Program)
DRP . . . . Dead Reckoning Plotter
DRP . . . . Deutsches Reichs-Patent (German patent)
DRP . . . . Digital Recording Process
DRP . . . . Doctor of Regional Planning
DRP . . . . Documentation Research Project (American Institute of Physics)
DRP . . . . Dorsal Root Potential
DRPA . . . . . . Delaware River Port Authority
Dr Pa . . . . . . Doctor of Painting
Dr PA . . . . . . Doctor of Public Administration
Dr of PE . . . . . Doctor of Physical Education
Dr PH . . . . . . Doctor of Public Health
Dr PH . . . . . . Doctor of Public Hygiene
Dr PH Hy . . . . Doctor of Public Health and Hygiene
Dr Phi . . . . . . Doctor of Philanthropy
Dr Phil . . . . . . Doctor of Philosophy
Dr Phil Nat . . . Doctor of Natural Philosophy
Dr Pho . . . . . . Doctor of Photography
Dr Phy . . . . . . Doctor of Physics
DRPL . . . . . . Drill Plate
Dr Pol Sci . . . . Doctor of Political Science
DRPR . . . . . . Drawing Practice
Dr Pr M . . . . . Doctor of Preventative Medicine
DRPS . . . . . . Dry Reed Pushbutton Switch
Dr P Sc . . . . . Doctor of Physical Science
DRR . . . . Descent Rate RADAR
DRR . . . . Digital RADAR Relay
DRR . . . . Direct Reading Receiver
DRR . . . . Diversity Reception Receiver
DRRB . . . . . . Data Requirements Review Board (DOD)
Dr of Rec . . . . Doctor of Recreation
DRRF . . . . . . Division Rapid Reaction Force (Army)
DRRI . . . . . . Defense Race Relations Institute (Air Force)
DRRL . . . . . . Digital RADAR Relay Link
DRS . . . . Data Recording Set
DRS . . . . Data Reduction System (Data processing)
DRS . . . . Data Relay Satellite
DRS . . . . Defense Research Sciences
DRS . . . . Digital RADAR Simulator

DRS . . . . Digital Readout System (Data processing)
DRS . . . . Digital Receiver Station (Data processing)
DRS . . . . Division of Research Services (of National Institutes of Health)
DRS . . . . Document Retrieval System
DRS . . . . Dry Reed Switch
DRS . . . . Dynamic Reflectance Spectroscopy
DRSC . . . . . . Direct RADAR Scope Camera
Dr Sc . . . . . . Doctor of Science
Dr Sci . . . . . . Doctor of Science
Dr Sci Nat . . . Doctor of Natural Sciences
Dr Sc Jur . . . Doctor of the Science of Jurisprudence
Dr Sc Pol . . . Doctor of Political Sciences
DRSCS . . . . . . Digital Range Safety Command System
DRSG . . . . . . Digital Recorder Signal Generator (Data processing)
DRSH . . . . . . Drill Shell
Dr So . . . . . . Doctor of Sociology
Dr So Sc . . . . . Doctor of Social Science
DRSR . . . . . . Direct RADAR Scope Recorder
DRSS . . . . . . Data Relay Satellite System (NASA)
DRT . . . . Daughters of the Republic of Texas
DRT . . . . Dead Reckoning Tracer (RADAR)
DRT . . . . Decade Ratio Transformer
DRT . . . . Deviation for Replacement Time
DRT . . . . Diagnostic Rhyme Test
DRT . . . . Digital Readout Timer (Data processing)
DRT . . . . Digital Rotary Transducer
DRT . . . . Diode Recovery Tester
DRT . . . . Direct Reading Totalizer
DRT . . . . Dome Removal Tool
DRTC . . . . . . Documentation Research and Training Centre (India)
DRTE . . . . . . Defence Research Telecommunication Establishment (Canada)
DRTE . . . . . . Doctor of Radio and Television Engineering
Dr Tech . . . . . Doctor of Technology
DRT Eng . . . . Doctor of Radio and Television Engineering
Dr Theol . . . . Doctor of Theology
DRTI . . . . Dual Roll Trough Idler
Dr T Med . . . . Doctor of Tropical Medicine
DRTP . . . . . . Drill Template
DRTR . . . . . . Dead Reckoning Trainer
DRU . . . . Demolition Research Unit
DRU . . . . Digital Range Unit
DRU . . . . Digital Remote Unit (Data processing)
DRU . . . . Disaccharide Repeating Unit
DRUB . . . . . . Digital Remote Unit Buffer (Data processing)
D Ru E . . . . . Doctor of Rural Engineering
D Ru Eng . . . . Doctor of Rural Engineering
DRUL . . . . . . Down-Range Up Link (Apollo) (NASA)
DRV . . . . Data Recovery Vehicle
DRV . . . . Deep Research Vehicle (or Vessel) (NOO)
DRV . . . . Democratic Republic of Vietnam (North Vietnam)
DRV . . . . Dravo Corp. (NYSE symbol)
DRVN . . . . . . Democratic Republic of Vietnam (Communist North Vietnam)
DRVS . . . . . . Drill Vise
DRWAW . . . . . Distillery, Rectifying, Wine & Allied Workers International Union of America
DRY . . . . Dreyfus Corp. (NYSE symbol)
DRZ . . . . Deep Reconnaissance Zone (Army)
DS . . . . Dal Segno (Repeat from the mark) (Music)
DS . . . . Danmarks Statistik (Denmark)
DS . . . . Data Systems Technician (Navy rating)
DS . . . . Date of Service (Military)
DS . . . . Day's Sight
DS . . . . Dead Space
DS . . . . Decanning Scuttle
DS . . . . Decimal Subtract
DS . . . . Decision and Switching
DS . . . . Define Symbol
DS . . . . Degree of Substitution
DS . . . . Delphian Society
DS . . . . Department of State
DS . . . . Depth Sounder
DS . . . . Design Specification
DS . . . . Design Standards
DS . . . . Detached Service (Army)
DS . . . . Detail Specification
DS . . . . Device Selector
DS . . . . Dial System
DS . . . . Difference Sensation (Psychology)
DS . . . . Dilute Strength (Chemistry)
DS . . . . Diode Switch
DS . . . . Dioptric Strength

DS . . . . Direct Support (Army)
DS . . . . Directing Staff
DS . . . . Director of Services (Air Force)
DS . . . . Discarding Sabot
DS . . . . Diver, Salvage (Navy)
DS . . . . Diving Saucer
DS . . . . Doctor of Science
DS . . . . Document Signed
DS . . . . Domestic Service (Equipment specification)
DS . . . . Donor's Serum (Physiology)
DS . . . . Double Stitch (Bookbinding)
DS . . . . Down Stage (Toward audience) (A stage direction)
DS . . . . Draft Stop (Technical drawings)
DS . . . . Drill Sergeant (Army)
DS . . . . Drive System
DS . . . . Drop Siding
DS . . . . Drug Store (US maps)
DS . . . . Drum Switch
DS . . . . Durham & Southern Railway Company (AAR code)
DS . . . . Duty Section (Air Force)
DS . . . . Duty Status (Air Force)
D-S . . . . Dada-Surrealism
D/S . . . . Days after Sight (Business and trade)
D/S . . . . Direct Support (Military)
D & S . . . . . . Dangerous and Suspicious
D of S . . . . . Daughters of Scotia
D of S . . . . . . Day of Supply (Military)
D of S . . . . . . Department of State
D of S . . . . . . Depot of Supplies (Marine Corps)
DSA . . . . Danish Sisterhood of America
DSA . . . . Dante Society of America
DSA . . . . Defense Shipping Authority
DSA . . . . Defense Supply Agency (DOD)
DSA . . . . Defense Supply Association
DSA . . . . Defense Systems Analysis (DOD)
DSA . . . . Design Schedule Analysis
DSA . . . . Dimensionally Stabilized Anode
DSA . . . . Direct Selling Association
DSA . . . . Discrete Sample Analyzer
DSA . . . . Division Service Area (Army)
DSA . . . . Doppler Spectrum Analyzer
DSA . . . . Drum Seiners Association
DSA . . . . Duluth, South Shore & Atlantic R. R. (AAR code)
DSA . . . . Duodecimal Society of America
DSA . . . . Dynamic Signal Analyzer
DSA . . . . Supreme Lodge of the Danish Sisterhood of America
DSAB . . . . . . Dictionary of South African Biography
DSABLSEVP . . . Disability Severance Pay
DSAC . . . . . . Deputy Supreme Allied Commander (Military)
DSAD . . . . . . Destruct Safe Arm Device
DSAFSM . . . . . Deputy System Manager (Army)
DSAG . . . . . . Defence Systems Analysis Group (Canada)
DSAH . . . . . . Defense Supply Agency Handbook
DSAM . . . . . . Defense Supply Agency Manual
DSAP . . . . . . Data Systems Automation Program
DSAR . . . . . . Data Sampling Automatic Receiver
DSAR . . . . . . Defense Supply Agency Regulation
DSARC . . . . . Defense Systems Acquisition Review Council
DSAS . . . . . . Direct Support Aviation Section
D Sa Sc . . . . . Doctor of Sacred Sciences
DSATC . . . . . Descend so as to Cross (Aviation)
DSATR . . . . . Descend so as to Reach (Aviation)
DSB . . . . Decade Synchro Bridge
DSB . . . . Defense Science Board (DOD)
DSB . . . . Divine Science Bachelor
DSB . . . . Double Sideband
DSB . . . . Drug Supervisory Body
DS in BA . . . . . Doctor of Science in Business Administration
DSBCO . . . . . Defense Surplus Bidders Control Office
DSBG . . . . . . Disbursing
DSBS . . . . . . Defense Science Board Subcommittee
DSBSC . . . . . Double-Sideband Suppressed Carrier
DSBTC . . . . . Double-Sideband Transmitted Carrier
DSB (UN) . . . . Drug Supervisory Body of the United Nations
DSBV . . . . . . Double-Seated Ball Valve
DSC . . . . Data Synchronizer Channel
DSC . . . . Debye-Sears Cell
DSC . . . . Decent Suit of Civvies (British slang military decoration) (World War I)
DSC . . . . Defense Supply Center
DSC . . . . Defense Supply Corporation (World War II)
DSC . . . . Defensiveness Scale for Children (Psychology)

DSC . . . . Delaware State College
DSC . . . . Depot Supply Center
DSC . . . . Die Sinkers Conference
DSC . . . . Differential Scanning Calorimeter (or Calorimetry)
DSC . . . . Differential Signal Control
DSC . . . . Discone Antenna
DSC . . . . Discrete System Concept
DSC . . . . Distinguished Service Cross (US and British)
DSC . . . . Doctor of Christian Science
DSC . . . . Doctor of Commercial Science
D Sc . . . . Doctor of Science
DSC . . . . Doctor of Surgical Chiropody
DSC . . . . Document Service Center
DSC . . . . Double Silk Covered (Wire)
DSC . . . . Down Stage Center (Toward audience) (A stage direction)
DSC . . . . Drain Saturation Current
DSC . . . . Duns Scotus College (Michigan)
DSC . . . . International Die Sinkers' Conference
DSCA . . . . . . Department of State Correspondents Association
DSCC . . . . . . Deep Space Communications Complex
DSCC . . . . . . Democratic Senatorial Campaign Committee
DSCC . . . . . . Division Support Control Center (Army)
D Sc Com . . Doctor of Science in Commerce
D Sc Econ . . . . Doctor of Science in Economics
D Sc (Eng) . . . . Doctor of Science (Engineering)
D Sch Mus . . . . Doctor of School Music
D Sc Hyg . . . . . Doctor of Science in Hygiene
D Sci . . . . . . Doctor of Science
D Sci H . . . . . Doctor of Science and Hygiene
D Sc L . . . . . . Doctor of the Science of Law
D Scn . . . . . . Doctor of Scientology
D Sc O . . . . . . Doctor of the Science of Oratory
D Sc Os . . . . Doctor of the Science of Osteopathy
DSCP . . . . . . Division Supply Control Point
DSCR . . . . . . District Sub-Chief Ranger (Ancient Order of Foresters)
DSCS . . . . . . Defense Satellite Communications System (DOD)
DSCS . . . . . . Desk Side Computer System (GE)
DSCS . . . . . . Digital Simulator Computer System
D Sc in VM . . Doctor of Science in Veterinary Medicine
DSD . . . . Data (or Disc) Storage Device
DSD . . . . Data Systems Designator
DSD . . . . Departmental Science Development (National Science Foundation)
DSD . . . . Diode Semiconductor Device
DSD . . . . Divine Science Doctor
DSD . . . . Dry Sterile Dressing (Medicine)
DSD . . . . Dual Speed Drive
DSDAR . . . . . . Deputy and Scientific Director of Army Research
DS & DH . . . . Data Switching and Data Handling
DS Di . . . . . . Doctor of Scientific Didactics
DSDP . . . . . . Deep Sea Drilling Project (National Science Foundation)
DSDT . . . . . . Discrete Space and Discrete Time
DSE . . . . Data Storage Equipment
DSE . . . . Data Systems Engineering
DSE . . . . Debye-Sears Effect
DSE . . . . Doctor of Sanitary Engineering
DSE . . . . Dynamic System Electronics
DSEA . . . . . . Data Storage Electronics Assembly (Apollo) (NASA)
D Se A . . . . . . Doctor of Secretarial Arts
DSEL . . . . . . Doctor of Science and English Literature
DS Eng . . . . . Doctor of Sanitary Engineering
D Se Sc . . . . . Doctor of Secretarial Science
D Se St . . . . . Doctor of Secretarial Studies
DSF . . . . Dairy Suppliers Foundation
DSF . . . . Data Scanning and Formatting
DSF . . . . Daughters of St. Francis of Assisi (Roman Catholic religious order)
DSF . . . . Day-Second-Foot (or Feet) (Measurement)
DSF . . . . Design Safety Factor
DSF . . . . . . Doctor of the Science of Forestry
DSFA . . . . . . Defense Solid Fuels Administration (Abolished, 1954)
DSFR . . . . . . Detailed System Functional Requirements
DSFU . . . . . . Danish Sailors' and Firemen's Union
DSG . . . . Deep Submergence Group
DSG . . . . Delta Smelta Guefelta
DSG . . . . Democratic Study Group
DSG . . . . Designer Shoe Guild
DSG . . . . Digital Signal Generator
DSG . . . . Direct Support Group (Army)
DS in Ge Engr . Doctor of Science in Geological Engineering
DSGN . . . . . . Design
DSGN . . . . . . Designate
DSGp . . . . . . Directed Studies Group (Air Force)

DS in Gp Engr . Doctor of Science in Geophysical Engineering
DSGS(CAR) . . . Deputy Secretary of the General Staff (Coordination and Reports) (Army)
DSI . . . . Dairy Society International
DSI . . . . Design Science Institute
DSI . . . . Distilled Spirits Institute
DSI . . . . Divisional Safety Inspector (Ministry of Agriculture, Fisheries, and Food) (British)
DSI . . . . Drinking Straw Institute
DSIA . . . . . . Diaper Service Industry Association
DSIATP . . . . . Defense Sensor Interpretation and Application Training Program
DSIF . . . . . . Deep Space Instrumentation Facility
DSIM . . . . . . Doctor of Science in Industrial Medicine
DSIR . . . . . . Department of Scientific and Industrial Research (of the Privy Council for Scientific and Industrial Research) (Great Britain)
DSIS . . . . . . Directorate of Scientific Information Service (Canada)
DSJ . . . . Doctor of the Science of Jurisprudence
DSKY . . . . . . Display and Keyboard (Data processing)
DSL . . . . Decalogue Society of Lawyers
DSL . . . . Deep Scattering Layer (Undersea plankton)
DSL . . . . Denver & Salt Lake R. R. (AAR code)
DSL . . . . Detroit Signal Laboratory (Army)
DSL . . . . Dickinson School of Law (Carlisle, Pennsylvania)
DSL . . . . Digital Simulation Language (Data processing)
DSL . . . . Directory of Special Libraries and Information Centers
DSL . . . . Doctor of Sacred Literature
DSL . . . . Down Stage Left (Toward audience) (A stage direction)
D & SL . . . . . Denver and Salt Lake Railway Company
DSM . . . . . . Danziger Statistische Mitteilungen (Danzig)
DSM . . . . . . Defense Suppression Missile
DSM . . . . . . Development of Substitute Materials
DSM . . . . . . Diagnostic and Statistics Manual (of mental disorders)
DSM . . . . . . Direction de Service de Securite Militaire (France)
DSM . . . . . . Direction of Systems Management
DSM . . . . . . Director of Supply and Maintenance (Army)
DSM . . . . . . Distinguished Service Medal (US and British)
DSM . . . . . . Doctor of Sacred Music
DSM . . . . . . Double Short Meter (Music)
DSMA . . . . . . Defense Supply Management Agency
DSMA . . . . . . Doll Supply Manufacturers Association
DS in Met Engr . . Doctor of Science in Metallurgical Engineering
DSMG . . . . . . Designated Systems Management Group (Air Force)
DSMP . . . . . . Daughters of St. Mary of Providence (Roman Catholic religious order)
DSMT . . . . . . Dual-Speed Magnetic Transducer
DSN . . . . . . Deep Space Network (NASA)
DSN . . . . . . Dennison Manufacturing Co. (NYSE symbol)
DSNM . . . . . Dimitrovski Suiuz na Narodnata Mladesh (Bulgaria)
DSO . . . . . . Data Systems Office
DSO . . . . . . De Soto, Inc. (NYSE symbol)
DSO . . . . . . Defense System Operator (ECM operator)
DSO . . . . . . Display Switching Oscilloscope
DSO . . . . . . Distinguished Service Order (British)
DSO . . . . . . District Sales Office
DSO . . . . . . District Security Office(r) (Navy)
DSO . . . . . . District Service Office(r) (Navy)
DSO . . . . . . District Supply Officer
DSO . . . . . . Division Signal Officer
DSO A . . . . . Doctor of the Science of Oratory
D So . . . . . . Doctor of Sociology
DSO . . . . . . Donora Southern R. R. (AAR code)
D Soc Sc . . . . Doctor of Social Science
D So Sc . . . . . Doctor of Social Science
D So Se . . . . . Doctor of Social Service
DSOT . . . . . . Daily Systems Operability Test (for surface-to-air missiles)
DSOTS . . . . . Demonstration Site Operational Test Series
DSP . . . . Decessit Sine Prole (Died without Issue)
DSP . . . . Deep Space Probe
DSP . . . . Deep Submergence Program
DSP . . . . Defense Standardization Program (DOD)
DSP . . . . Dentsply International, Inc. (Formerly, Dentists' Supply Company of N.Y.) (NYSE symbol)
DSP . . . . Deployable Solar Panel
DSP . . . . Designated Stock Point
DSP . . . . Deutsche Sex Partei (Political party) (Germany)
DSP . . . . Digital Strip Printer
DSP . . . . Display Simulation Program
DSP . . . . Distilled Spirits Plant
DSP . . . . Distributed System Program (Data processing)
DSP . . . . Distribution Point
D Sp . . . . . . Doctor of Speech
DSP . . . . Doppler Spectrum Processor

DSP . . . . Double Silver Plate
DSPE . . . . . . Division of Scientific Personnel and Education (National Science Foundation)
DS in PE . . . . . Doctor of Science in Petroleum Engineering
DSPLN . . . . . . Discipline
DSPN . . . . Disposition
DSPR . . . . . . Defense Supply Procurement Regulation (Military)
DS in PRE . . . Doctor of Science in Petroleum Refining Engineering
DSPS . . . . Digital Signal Processing System
DSQ . . . . Discharged to Sick Quarters
DSR . . . . Danmarks Radio
DSR . . . . Data Scanning and Routing
DSR . . . . Data Specification Request
DSR . . . . Daughters of St. Rita of the Immaculate Heart (Roman Catholic religious order)
DSR . . . . Defense Suppression Rocket
DSR . . . . Delayed Sound Reinforcement
DSR . . . . Differentiation with Symmetrical Reinforcement
DSR . . . . Digit Storage Relay
DSR . . . . Digital Shift Register
DSR . . . . Digital Stepping Recorder
DSR . . . . Direct Stage Recorder
DSR . . . . Director of Surveillance and Reconnaissance (Army)
DSR . . . . Distributed State Response
DSR . . . . Division of Sponsored Research (MIT)
DSR . . . . Document Status Report (Military)
DSR . . . . Down Stage Right (Toward audience) (A stage direction)
DSR . . . . Dummy Stowage Receptacle
DSR . . . . Dynamic Sideband Regulator
DSRC . . . . . . David Sarnoff Research Center (RCA)
DSRS . . . . . . Direct Scope Recording System
DSRV . . . . . . Deep Submergence Rescue Vehicle (Navy)
DSS . . . . Data Storage System
DSS . . . . Data Systems Specification
DSS . . . . Deep-Space Station
DSS . . . . Deep Submergence System (Navy)
DSS . . . . Deputy of Space Systems (Air Force)
DSS . . . . Digital Signal Synchronizer
DSS . . . . Digital Simulator System
DSS . . . . Digital Storage System
DSS . . . . Digital Subset
DSS . . . . Digital Subsystem
DSS . . . . Direct Station Selection
DSS . . . . Director(ate) of Statistical Services (Air Force)
DSS . . . . Doctor Sacrae Scripturae (Doctor of Holy Scripture)
DSS . . . . Doctor of Sanitary Science
DSS . . . . Doctor of Science in Surgery
DSS . . . . Doctor of Secretarial Science
DSS . . . . Doctor of Social Service
DSS . . . . Double Spot System
DSS . . . . Drum Storage System
DSS . . . . Dynamic Steady State
DS & S . . . . . . Data Systems and Statistics
DSS & A . . . . Duluth, South Shore and Atlantic Railway Company
DSSC . . . . . . Defense Subsistence Supply Center (Later, Defense Personnel Support Center)
DS Sc . . . . . . Doctor of Sanitary Science
DS Sc . . . . . . Doctor of Social Science
DSSCS . . . . . Defense Special Security Communications System (Pronounced "discus")
DSSD . . . . . . Direct Supply Support Depot (Military)
DSSM . . . . . . Drawing Stimulus Strategy Measure
DSSN . . . . . . Disbursing Station Symbol Number (Military)
DSSO . . . . . . Defense Surplus Sales Office
DSSO . . . . . . District Ships Service Office(r) (Navy)
DSSO . . . . . . Duty Space Surveillance Officer (Air Force)
DSSP . . . . . . Deep Submergence Systems Project (Navy)
DSSP . . . . . . Depot Support Supply Plan
DSSP . . . . . . Direct Supply Support Point (DOD)
DSSPO . . . . . Deep Submergence Systems Project Office
DSSPTO . . . . . Deep Submergence Systems Project Technical Office (Navy)
DSS & R . . . . . Document Storage Search and Retrieval (Air Force)
DSSRG . . . . . . Deep Submergence Systems Review Group (Navy)
DSST . . . . . . Driver Stage Silicon Transistor
DSSV . . . . . . Deep Submergence Search Vehicle (Research submarine) (Navy)
DSS-W . . . . . Defense Supply Service – Washington
DST . . . . Daylight Saving Time
DST . . . . Dermatology and Syphilology Technician (Navy)
DST . . . . . . Desensitization Test (Allergy)
DST . . . . Detailed System Test
DST . . . . Dielectric Strength Test
DST . . . . Digital Subscriber Terminal

DST . . . . Dihydrostreptomycin
DST . . . . Director of Supplies and Transport (British)
DST . . . . Disston, Inc. (NYSE symbol)
DST . . . . Doctor of Sacred Theology
D St . . . . Doctor of Statistics
DST . . . . Double Spot Tuning
DST . . . . Double Summer Time (Daylight Saving Time two hours ahead of Standard Time) (British)
DST . . . . Drop Survival Time
DSTDP . . . . . . Distearylthiodipropionate
DSTE . . . . . . Digital Subscriber Terminal Equipment
D St E . . . . . . Doctor of Structural Engineering
D St Eng . . . . Doctor of Structural Engineering
DStJ . . . . Dame Order of St. John of Jerusalem (British)
DSTP . . . . . . Director of Strategic Target Planning (Military)
DSTS . . . . . . Desk Side Time Shared (Data processing) (GE)
DSU . . . . Data Synchronization (or Synchronizer) Unit
DSU . . . . Decoder Switching Unit
DSU . . . . Device-Switching Unit
DSU . . . . Direct Support Unit
DSU . . . . Drum Storage Unit
DSUE . . . . . . A Dictionary of Slang and Unconventional English
DSUH . . . . . . Direct Suggestion Under Hypnosis
D Sur . . . . . . Doctor of Surgery
DSW . . . . Data Status Word
DSW . . . . Deep Sea Winch
DSW . . . . . . Director of Special Weapons (Army)
DSW . . . . . . Doctor of Social Welfare
DSW . . . . . . Doctor of Social Work
DSW . . . . Door Switch
DSW . . . . Drum Switch
D of S (W) . . . . Director of Stores (Washington) (Navy)
DSXBT . . . . . . Digitized Shipboard Expandable Bathythermograph (Naval Oceanographic Office)
DSY . . . . Dorsey Corp. (NYSE symbol)
D Sy Th . . . . . Doctor of Systematic Theology
DT . . . . Data Transmission
DT . . . . Date
DT . . . . Daylight Time
DT . . . . Dead Time
DT . . . . Dental Technician
DT . . . . Detroit Terminal R. R. (AAR code)
DT . . . . Digital Technique
DT . . . . Diphtheria, Tetanus (Medicine)
DT . . . . Distance Test
DT . . . . Diver, Second Class (Navy rating)
DT . . . . Doctor of Theology
DT . . . . Double Throw (Switch)
DT . . . . Double Time
DT . . . . Double Tube
DT . . . . Drain Tile (Technical drawings)
DT . . . . Dressed or Tanned (Freight)
DT . . . . Drop Test Report
DT . . . . Dual Tires
D–T . . . . Deuterium–Tritium Reaction (Fusion program)
DT's . . . . Delirium Tremens (Hallucinatory condition of advanced alcoholism)
D of T . . . . . . Department of the Treasury (Commonly TD, Treasury Department)
DTA . . . . Defense Transport Administration
DTA . . . . Detroit Tooling Association
DTA . . . . Development Test Article
DTA . . . . Diethylenetriamine
DTA . . . . Differential Thermal Analyzer (or Analysis)
DTA . . . . Disk Turbine Assembly
DTA . . . . Distributing Terminal Assembly (Electronics)
DTA . . . . Divisao de Exploracao dos Transportes Aereos (Angola Airline)
DTA . . . . Division Tactical Area (Army)
DTA . . . . Double Tape Armored (Heavy–duty telephone buried cable)
DTA . . . . Dual Trace Amplifier
DTAA . . . . . . Diamond Trade Association of America
DTAL . . . . . . David Taylor Aerodynamics Laboratory
DTAM . . . . . . Daily Traffic Assignment Model (Aviation)
DTAM . . . . . . Descend to and Maintain (Aviation)
DTAO . . . . . . During the Temporary Absence of (Military)
DTAS . . . . . . Data (or Digital) Transmission and Switching
DTAX . . . . . . Descend to and Cross (Aviation)
DTB . . . . Destroyer Tactical Bulletin
DTB . . . . Deviation Test Bridge
DTBP . . . . . . Di-Tert-Butyl Peroxide
DTC . . . . Dead Time Correction
DTC . . . . Decision Threshold Computer
DTC . . . . Defense Technical Center

DTC . . . . Depot Training Center
DTC . . . . Desert Test Center (Army)
DTC . . . . Desk Top Computer
DTC . . . . Differential Throttle Control
DTC . . . . Digital Tape Conversion
DTC . . . . Digital Television Camera
DTC . . . . Digital to Tone Converter
DTC . . . . Direct-to-Consumer (Sales)
DTC . . . . Disciplinary Training Center
DTC . . . . Display Test Chamber
DTC . . . . Doctor of Textile Chemistry
DTC . . . . Doppler Translation Channel
DT Ch . . . . . . Doctor of Textile Chemistry
DTCS . . . . . . Digital Tank Control (or Command) System
DTCS . . . . . . Digital Test Command System
DTD . . . . Dated
DTD . . . . Department of Tank Design (British)
DTD . . . . Detailed Test Description
DTD . . . . Doctor of Textile Dyeing
DT Des . . . . . Doctor of Textile Design
DTDS . . . . . . Digital Television Display System
DTE . . . . Data Terminal Equipment
DTE . . . . Data Transmitting Equipment
DTE . . . . Detroit Edison Company (NYSE symbol)
DTE . . . . Diamond Tool Engineering Company
DTE . . . . Digital Television Encoder
DTE . . . . Doctor of Textile Engineering
DTE . . . . Dual Track Etcher
DT & E . . . . . . Development, Test and Evaluation
DTEAS . . . . . Detection Track Evaluation and Assignment Systems (Navy)
D Tech Chem . . Doctor of Technical Chemistry
DT Eng . . . . . Doctor of Textile Engineering
DTF . . . . Daily Transaction File
DTF . . . . Data Transmission Feature (or Factor or Function)
DTF . . . . Drone Target (or Test) Facility
DTG . . . . Date-Time Group (Group of figures at head of radio or Teletype message indicating filing time)
DTG . . . . Display Transmission Generator
DTG . . . . Dual Track Geneva
D Th . . . . . . Doctor of Theology
DTI . . . . Department of Trade and Industry (British)
DTI . . . . Detroit, Toledo & Ironton R. R. (AAR code) (Nickname: Damned Tough and Independent)
DTI . . . . Distortion Transmission Impairment
DTI . . . . Division of Technical Information (AEC)
DTI . . . . Drug and Therapeutic Information
DT & I . . . . . Detroit, Toledo and Ironton Railroad Company
DTIE . . . . Division of Technical Information Extension (Later, Technical Information Center) (AEC)
DTL . . . . Dead Time Log
DTL . . . . Deltec International Limited (NYSE symbol)
DTL . . . . Diode-Transistor Logic
DTM . . . . Digital Television Monitor
DTM . . . . Diploma in Tropical Medicine
DTM . . . . Director of Telecommunications Management (Air Force)
DTM . . . . Doctor of Tropical Medicine
DTMB . . . . . . David Taylor Model Basin (Military)
DTMD . . . . . . Differential Temperature Measuring Device
DTM & H . . . . Diploma in Tropical Medicine and Hygiene (British)
DTMI . . . . . . Dairy Training and Merchandising Institute
DTMS . . . . . . Defense Traffic Management Service
DTMS . . . . . . Digital Test Measurement (or Monitor) System
DTN . . . . Diphtheria Toxin Normal (Medicine)
DTN . . . . Drug Trade News (A publication)
DTO . . . . Data Takeoff (Air Force)
DTO . . . . Detailed Test Objective
DTO . . . . Direct Turn-Over
DTO . . . . District Training Office(r) (Navy)
DTO . . . . District Transportation Officer
DTO . . . . Dollar Tradeoff
DTOC . . . . . . Division Tactical Operations Center
DTP . . . . Depth Telemetering Pinger
DTP . . . . Diode Test Program
DTP . . . . Diphtheria, Tetanus, Pertussis (Medicine)
DTP . . . . Directory Tape Processor
DTP . . . . Distal Tingling on Percussion (Medicine)
DTP . . . . Dolph-Tchebyscheff Pattern
DTP . . . . Doppler Techniques Proposal
DTP . . . . Double Test Position
DTP . . . . Drum Timing Pulse
DTPA . . . . . . Diethylenetriaminepentaacetic Acid (Chemical)

DTPH . . . . . . Diploma in Tropical Public Health (British)
DTPL . . . . . . Domain Tip Propagation Logic
DTR . . . . Daily Transaction Reporting
DTR . . . . Data Telemetering Register
DTR . . . . Data Transfer Rate
DTR . . . . Deep Tendon Reflex (Physiology)
DTR . . . . Digital Telemetering Register
DTR . . . . Division of Tax Research
DTRA . . . . . . Defense Technical Review Agency (Army)
DTRE . . . . . . Defence Telecommunications Research Establishment
DTREM . . . . . Dust, Thermal, and Radiation Engineering Measurements Package (NASA)
DTRM . . . . . . Dual Thrust Rocket Motor
DT/RSS . . . . . . Data Transmission/Recording Subsystem
DTS . . . . Data Test Station
DTS . . . . Data Transfer System (Army)
DTS . . . . Data Transmission System (Air Force)
DTS . . . . Department of Defense Transportation System
DTS . . . . Detector Tracker Switch
DTS . . . . Detroit & Toledo Shore Line R. R. (AAR code)
DTS . . . . Digital Telemetry System
DTS . . . . Diplomatic Telecommunications Service
DTS . . . . Doctor of Textile Science
DTS . . . . Doppler Tracking Station
DTS . . . . Double Throw Switch
DTS . . . . Dynamic Test System
DTSB . . . . . . Deutscher Turn und Sportbund
DTSD . . . . . . Director of Training and Staff Duties Division (British Navy)
DTSG . . . . . . Data Transmission Study Group
D & TSL . . . . . Detroit and Toledo Shore Line Railroad Company
DTSS . . . . . . Dartmouth Time-Sharing System (Data processing)
DTS-W . . . . . . Defense Telephone Service - Washington
DTT . . . . Diphtheria-Tetanus Toxoid
DTT . . . . Dithiothreitol
DTT . . . . Doctor of Textile Technology
DTT . . . . Duplicate Title Transferred (Library science)
DTTC . . . . . . Diethylthiatricarbocyanine
DTU . . . . Data Transformation Unit
DTU . . . . Digital Telemetry Unit
DTU . . . . Digital Test Unit
DTUTF . . . . . Digital Tape Unit Test Facility (NASA)
DTV . . . . Deutsche Taschenbuch Verlag (Publisher)
DTV . . . . Digital Television
DTV . . . . Dynamic Test Vehicle
DTVM . . . . . . Differential Thermocouple Voltmeter
DTVM . . . . . . Diploma in Tropical Veterinary Medicine
DTW . . . . Dry Tank Weight
DTWX . . . . . . Dial Teletypewriter Exchange
DTX . . . . Dominion Textile (Montreal and Toronto Stock Exchanges symbol)
DTZ . . . . Division Tactical Zone (Army)
DU . . . . Diagnosis Unknown (Medicine)
DU . . . . A Dictionary of the Underworld
DU . . . . Digital Unit
DU . . . . Dog Unit (Veterinary medicine)
DU . . . . Double Uptake (Boilers)
DU . . . . Du Bois Chemicals, Inc. (NYSE symbol) (Delisted)
DU . . . . Ducks Unlimited
DUA . . . . Digitronics Users Association
DUAL . . . . . . Data Use and Access Laboratories (Bureau of the Census)
DUBC . . . . . . Dublin University Boat Club
DUC . . . . Data Utilization Console
DUC . . . . Dense Upper Cloud
DUC . . . . Distinguished Unit Citation (Military)
DUCE . . . . . . Distinguished Unit Citation Emblem
DUCON . . . . . Duty Connection
DUCS . . . . . . Deep Underground Communications System
DUCS . . . . . . Defense Unit Classification System
DUDAT . . . . . Due Date
DUE . . . . Distinguished Unit Emblem
DUET . . . . . . Dual Emitter Transistor
DUFLY . . . . . Duty Involving Flying (Military)
DUFLYTECH . . . Duty Involving Flying as a Technical Observer (Military)
DUI . . . . Date Use Identifier
DUINS . . . . . . Duty Under Instruction
DUJ . . . . Juris Utriusque Doctor (Doctor of Both Laws; i.e., Canon and Civil Law)
DUK . . . . Duke Power Company (NYSE symbol)
DUKW . . . . . . Amphibious Truck, 2 1/2-ton Cargo
DUM . . . . Dublin University Mission
DUN . . . . Data Users' Note (NASA)
DUNC . . . . . . Deep Underwater Nuclear Counting
DUNS . . . . . . Data Universal Numbering System

DUO . . . . Datatron Users' Organization
DUP . . . . Duplan Corporation (NYSE symbol)
DUP . . . . Duplicate
DUP . . . . National Society, Daughters of Utah Pioneers
DUPC . . . . Displayed Under Program Control
DUPPA . . . . . . Dual Path Protection Arrangement (AT & T)
DUR . . . . Duro-Test Corporation (American Stock Exchange symbol)
DURC . . . . Dublin University Rowing Club
DUS . . . . Driver Units Speaker
DUSA . . . . . . Deputy Under Secretary of the Army
DUSAA . . . . . . Davison United States Army Airfield
DUSC . . . . . Deep Underground Support Center (Air Force)
DUSS . . . . . . Deep Underground Support System
DUSTA . . . . . . Duty Station (Navy)
DUT . . . . Device Under Test
DUT . . . . Diode Under Test
DUT . . . . Duplication Technician, Photolithography (Navy rating)
DUTOUT . . . . (For) Duty Outside the Continental Limits of the United States
DUVCW . . . . . Daughters of Union Veterans of the Civil War
DUW . . . . Director of Underwater Weapons (British)
DUWCAL . . . . Duluth Weapons Calibration System
DV . . . . Deo Volente (God Willing)
DV . . . . Dependent Variable
DV . . . . Differential Voltmeter
DV . . . . Dilute Volume (Chemistry)
DV . . . . Disbursement Voucher
DV . . . . Distemper Virus
DV . . . . Distinguished Visitor
DV . . . . Divisionsverfuegung; Divisionsverordnung (Divisional Order) (German military – World War II)
DV . . . . Douay Version (Bible)
DV . . . . Double Vibration (Cycles)
DV . . . . Durchgangsvermittlung (Long distance telephone exchange) (German military – World War II)
DVA . . . . Differential Voltage Amplifier
DVA . . . . Duration of Voluntary Apnea (Physiology)
DVB . . . . Department of Veterans Benefits (VA)
DVB . . . . Digital Video Bandwidth
DVD . . . . Delta Velocity Display
DVD . . . . Design Verification Demonstration
DVD . . . . Deutscher Veranstaltungsdienst
DVD . . . . Direct-View Device (Night vision)
DVDY . . . . . . Diving Duty (Military)
DVE . . . . Differential Vector Equation
DVE . . . . Duck Virus Enteritis (Duck plague)
DV Ed . . . . . . Doctor of Vocational Education
D Vet Med . . . . Doctor of Veterinary Medicine
DVF . . . . Dualbowl Vibratory Feeder
DVFE . . . . . . Director, Vehicle and Field Engineering (Military) (Canada)
DVFR . . . . . . Defense Visual Flight Rules
DVH . . . . Diploma in Veterinary Hygiene
DVL . . . . Delta Velocity Launch
DVL . . . . Deutsche Versuchsanstalt fuer Luftfahrt
DVL . . . . Distance Velocity Laboratory
DVL . . . . Dorsal Velar Lobe
DVM . . . . . . Digital Voltmeter
DVM . . . . . . Directional Variable Microphone
DVM . . . . . . Discontinuous Variational Method
DVM . . . . . . Displayed Virtual Machine
DVM . . . . . . Doctor of Veterinary Medicine
DVMS . . . . . Doctor of Veterinary Medicine and Surgery
DVO . . . . Decimal Voltage Output
DVO . . . . Divisional Veterinary Officer (Ministry of Agriculture, Fisheries, and Food) (British)
DVOM . . . . . . Digital Volt-Ohmmeter
DVOR . . . . . . Doppler VHF Omnirange
DVOT . . . . . . Delayed Voltage (or Velocity) on Target
DVOT . . . . . . Dog Vomit On Toast (Creamed beef or tuna on toast) (Military slang)
DVP . . . . Decessit Vita Patris (He, or She, Died during His, or Her, Father's Lifetime)
DVP . . . . Delta Velocity Planet
DVP . . . . Deutsche Volkspolizei
DVPDF . . . . . Dry Vacuum Pump Discharge Filter
DVPF . . . . . . Dry Vacuum Pump Filter
DVR . . . . Division of Vocational Rehabilitation (D.C.)
DVS . . . . Delta Valley & Southern Railway Company (AAR code)
DVS . . . . Director of Veterinary Services (British military)
DVS . . . . Doctor of Veterinary Science
DVS . . . . Doctor of Veterinary Surgery
DVS . . . . Doppler Velocity Sensor
DVS . . . . Dynamic Vacuum Seal

DV Sc . . . . . . Doctor of Veterinary Science
DVSC . . . . . . Doctor of Veterinary Surgery
DVSM . . . . . . Diploma in Veterinary State Medicine
DVST . . . . . . Direct-Viewing Storage Tube
DVT . . . . Design Verification Test
DW . . . . Dangerous Weapon
DW . . . . Daughters of Wisdom (Montfort Sisters) (Roman Catholic religious order)
DW . . . . Dead Weight
DW . . . . Dean Witter & Co., Inc. (NYSE symbol)
DW . . . . Deck Watch (A small chronometer) (Navy)
DW . . . . Delayed Weather
DW . . . . Distilled Water
DW . . . . Dock Warrant
DW . . . . Double Weight
DW . . . . Drop Wire
DW . . . . Drum Write
DW . . . . Dust Wrapper
DWA . . . . Deadly Weapon Act
DWA . . . . Died of Wounds Resulting from Action with Enemy
DWA . . . . Dirty Writers of America (Satirical)
DWA . . . . Double-Wire Armor
DWAC . . . . . . Director, Women's Army Corps (United States)
DWAC . . . . . . Distributed Write Address Counter
DWBA . . . . . . Distorted-Wave Born Approximation
DWBO . . . . . . District War Bond Office(r) (Navy)
DWC . . . . Dead Weight Capacity
DWC . . . . Democratic Workers' Congress (Ceylon)
DWD . . . . Deepest Working Depth
DWD . . . . Director of Wreck Disposal
DWD . . . . Driving While Drunk
DWD . . . . Drum Write Drive
DWDL . . . . . . Donald W. Douglas Laboratory (McDonnell Douglas Corp.)
DWET . . . . . . Directorate of Weapons Effect Tests
DWF . . . . Directional Warhead Fuze
DWG . . . . Dead Weight Gage
DWG . . . . Diamond Walnut Growers
DWG . . . . Drawing
DWG . . . . DWG Cigar Corporation (NYSE symbol) (Delisted)
DWI . . . . Descriptor Word Index
DWI . . . . Driving While Intoxicated (Police term)
DWI . . . . Durable Woods Institute
DWI . . . . Durum Wheat Institute
DWICA . . . . . . Deep Water Isotopic Current Analyzer (TVA)
DWL . . . . Designed Water Line (Technical drawings)
DWM . . . . . . Deutsche Waffen- und Munitionsfabriken (Name of German armament company) (World War II)
DWMI . . . . . . Diamond Wheel Manufacturers Institute
DWML . . . . . . Due West Motor Line R. R. (AAR code)
DWO . . . . Development Work Order
DWO . . . . Direct Writing Oscillograph
DWP . . . . Duluth, Winnipeg & Pacific Railway Company (AAR code)
DW & P . . . . . Duluth, Winnipeg and Pacific Railway Company
DWPO . . . . . . District War Plans Officer
DWR . . . . Digital Wired Recorder
DWR . . . . Dirty Word Remover (Graffiti-removing chemical)
DWR . . . . Duke of Wellington's Regiment (British Army)
DWRC . . . . . . Descend Well to Right of Course (Aviation)
DWS . . . . Deck Working Space
DWS . . . . Defense Weapons System
DWS . . . . Design Work Study
DWS . . . . Dorcas Welfare Society
DWS . . . . Drop Wood Siding (Technical drawings)
DWSA . . . . . . Director of Weapon Systems Analysis (Army)
DWSMC . . . . . Defense Weapons System Management Center
DWSO . . . . . . Drainage and Water Supply Officer (Ministry of Agriculture, Fisheries, and Food) (British)
DWSS . . . . . . Double Wipe Slide Switch
DWStK . . . . . . Deutsche Waffen Stillstandkommission (German Armistice Commission, in France) (World War II)
DWT . . . . Deadweight
DWT . . . . Deadweight Tester
DWT . . . . Deadweight Tons
DWT . . . . Deck Watch Time (Navigation)
DWT . . . . Dog Wags Tail (Airspace effects)
DWT . . . . Pennyweight
DWTF . . . . . . Daily and Weekly Till Forbidden (Advertising)
DWTR . . . . . . Descend Well to Right (Aviation)
DWTT . . . . . . Drop-Weight Tear Test
DWU . . . . Dakota Wesleyan University (South Dakota)
DWV . . . . Drain, Waste, and Vent (System)
DX . . . . Direct Exchange (Army)

DX . . . . Distance (Radio term)
DX . . . . Duplex Repeater (Teletypewriter designation for quality of reception)
DXC . . . . Data Exchange Control
DXC . . . . Penn-Dixie Cement Corporation (NYSE symbol)
DXI . . . . Direct Exchange Item (Army)
DXR . . . . Deep X-Ray
DXRT . . . . Deep X-Ray Therapy
DY . . . . Deflection Yoke
DY . . . . Dockyard
DY . . . . Duty
Dy . . . . Dysprosium (Chemical element)
DYA . . . . Deflection Yoke Amplifier
DYANA . . . . . Dynamic Analyzer
DYB . . . . Dynamic Braking
DYCON . . . . . Dynamic Control
DYCOP . . . . . . Dynamic Console for Operations Planners

DYF . . . . Damned Young Fools (Officers under the age of thirty) (British naval slang)
DYN . . . . Detectability of Yes-No
DYNAMO . . . . Dynamic Action Management Operations (BSD)
DYNAMO . . . . Dynamic Model
DYNA-SOAR . . Dynamic Soaring (Space flight)
DYSAC . . . . . . Digital Simulated Analog Computer
DYSTAC . . . . . Dynamic Storage Analog Computer
DYSTAL . . . . . Dynamic Storage Allocation Language (in FORTRAN) (Data processing)
DZ . . . . Dizygotic
DZ . . . . Doctor of Zoology
DZ . . . . Drop(ping) Zone (For parachute troops and gliders)
DZ . . . . Druckzuender (Pressure igniter) (German military – World War II)
DZA . . . . Drop Zone Area (Military)
DZCO . . . . . . Drop Zone Control Officer (Air Force)
DZR . . . . Double Zigzag Rectifier
DZSO . . . . Drop Zone Safety Officer (Army)

E

E . . . . Air Evacuation (Military aircraft identification prefix)
E . . . . Amphibian (Russian aircraft symbol)
E . . . . Awarded by US Government to firms which have increased exports
        substantially (Beginning early 1960's)
E . . . . Color Excess (Astronomy)
E . . . . Earl
E . . . . Earth (Wind triangle problems and relative movement problems)
E . . . . Easily
E . . . . East
E . . . . Easter
E . . . . Eastern
E . . . . Eastern Standard Time
E . . . . Eccentricity
E . . . . Edge (Lumber)
E . . . . Educated
E . . . . Efficiency or Efficient
E . . . . Egyptian
E . . . . Einsteinium (Chemical element) (Also see Es)
E . . . . Elasticity
E . . . . Eldest
E . . . . Electrode Potential
E . . . . Electromotive Force (Also, EMF)
E . . . . Electron
E . . . . Electronic Night Bombing Capability (When a plane designation)
E . . . . Ell
E . . . . Emergency (Symbol placed in neighborhood windows to indicate that
        resident will aid passing schoolchildren in the event of an emergency)
E . . . . Empty
E . . . . End (Football position)
E . . . . Ending of Precipitation (Meteorology)
E . . . . Energy
E . . . . Engine, Engineer, or Engineering
E . . . . English
E . . . . Entrance
E . . . . Epidermis
E . . . . Epinephrine
E . . . . Epistle
E . . . . Equatorial (Air mass)
E . . . . Erg
E . . . . Erie-Lackawanna R.R. Company (NYSE symbol) (Delisted)
E . . . . Errors (Baseball)
E . . . . Escudo (Monetary unit of Portugal and its territories)
E . . . . Esophagus
E . . . . Estimate or Estimated
E . . . . Evangelist (Church calendars)
E . . . . Evensong
E . . . . Evidence (Law)
E . . . . Excellence; Excellency; Excellent
E . . . . "Excellence in Production" (Army-Navy "E" awarded manufacturers)
        (World War II)
E . . . . Experimental, when precedes vessel classification (Navy)
E . . . . Export
E . . . . Exposure
E . . . . Eye
E . . . . Modulus of Elasticity
e . . . . Naperian (or natural) logarithm base (2.7182818)
E . . . . Sleet (Weather reports)
E . . . . Special electronics installation (Aviation designation used by all US
        military services)
E . . . . Torpedo Boat (German symbol)
E . . . . Water Vapor Pressure
E³ . . . . Education and Experience in Engineering (Illinois Institute of Technology
        program)

4-E . . . . Selective Service Class (for a Conscientious Objector Available for,
        Assigned to, or Released from Work of National Importance) (Obsolete)
EA . . . . East Africa
EA . . . . Eastern Air Lines, Inc.
EA . . . . Economic Adviser
EA . . . . Edgewood Arsenal (Army)
EA . . . . Educational Age
EA . . . . Egyptian Army
EA . . . . Electrocardiographic Amplifier
EA . . . . Electronic Associates, Inc. (NYSE symbol)
EA . . . . Emergency Area
EA . . . . Encyclopedia of Associations (Formerly, Encyclopedia of American
        Associations)
EA . . . . Enemy Aircraft
EA . . . . Engineer Rear Admiral (British)
EA . . . . Engineering Aide (Navy rating)
EA . . . . Enlistment Allowance
EA . . . . Enumeration Area (Statistics)
E/A . . . . Enemy Aircraft
EAA . . . . . . East African Airways
EAA . . . . . . Ecuadorean American Association
EAA . . . . . . Encyclopedia of American Associations (Later, Encyclopedia of
        Associations)
EAA . . . . . . Engineer in Aeronautics and Astronautics
EAA . . . . . . Engineering and Architects Association
EAA . . . . . . Epilepsy Association of America
EAA . . . . . . Equipment Approval Authority
EAA . . . . . . Ethyleneacrylic Acid (Organic chemistry)
EAA . . . . . . Experimental Aircraft Association
EAAA . . . . . . European Association of Advertising Agencies
EAAC . . . . . . European Agricultural Aviation Centre
EAAS . . . . . . European Association for American Studies
EABN . . . . . . Engineer Aviation Battalion (Military)
EAC . . . . . . East African Community
EAC . . . . . . Eastern Air Command (CBI Theater) (World War II)
EAC . . . . . . Educational Advisory Committee (AIAA)
EAC . . . . . . Effective Acoustic Center
EAC . . . . . . Effective Atomic Charge
EAC . . . . . . Ehrlich Ascites Carcinoma (Cells)
EAC . . . . . . Eire Army Corps
EAC . . . . . . Electro-Optical Area Correlator (Missile guidance system)
EAC . . . . . . End-Around Carry
EAC . . . . . . Engineer Amphibian Command (Had logistical rather than engineering
        mission, namely, to load, carry, and unload a complete infantry
        division) (World War II)
EAC . . . . . . Environmental Action Coalition
EAC . . . . . . Epiphany Apostolic College (New York)
EAC . . . . . . European Advisory Commission
EAC . . . . . . European Advisory Committee (Allied German Occupation Forces)
EAC . . . . . . Exhibitors Advisory Council
EAC . . . . . . Expected Approach Clearance (Aviation)
EACC . . . . . . East Asia Christian Conference
EACC . . . . . . Electronic Asset Control Center
EACNL . . . . . . Expect Approach Clearance Not Later Than (Aviation)
EACP . . . . . . European Area Communications Plan (Military)
EACRP . . . . . . European-American Committee on Reactor Physics
EACSO . . . . . . East African Common Services Organization
EAD . . . . . . Endo-Atmospheric Decoy
EAD . . . . . . Entry on Active Duty
EAD . . . . . . Equipment Allowance Document (Military)
EAD . . . . . . Estimated Availability Date (Military)
EAD . . . . . . Extended Active Duty
EADF . . . . . . Eastern Air Defense Force

EADI . . . . Electronic Attitude Direction Indicator
EADIZ . . . . . . Entering Air Defense Identification Zone
EAE . . . . Experimental Allergic Encephalomyelitis (Medicine)
EAEC . . . . East African Economic Community
EAEI . . . . Ecology Action Educational Institute
EAES . . . . European Atomic Energy Society
EAF . . . . Egyptian Air Force
EAF . . . . Emergency Action File (Air Force)
EAF . . . . Emery Air Freight Corporation (NYSE symbol)
EAFB . . . . . . Edwards Air Force Base
EAFB . . . . . . Eglin Air Force Base
EAG . . . . Electroantennogram
EAG. . . . . . . Equipment Advisory Group
EAG. . . . . . . Evaluation and Analysis Group (Navy)
EAG. . . . . . . Experimental Firing Ship (Navy symbol)
EAGA. . . . . . Episcopal Actors' Guild of America
EAGER . . . . . Electronic Audit Gager
EAGGF. . . . . European Agricultural Guidance and Guarantee Fund
EAGLE . . . . . Elevation Angle Guidance Landing Equipment
EAGS . . . . . . English and Germanic Studies
EAHF . . . . . . Eczema, Asthma, Hay Fever
EAI . . . . Education Audit Institute (Washington, DC)
EAI . . . . Electronic Associates, Incorporated
EAIA . . . . . . Early American Industries Association
EAID . . . . . . Equipment Authorization Inventory Data (Air Force)
EAID . . . . . . ESRO (European Space Research Organization) Advanced Imaging
          Detector (Satellite)
EAIDL . . . . . . Equipment Authorization Inventory Data Listing (Air Force)
EAJC . . . . . . Eastern Arizona Junior College
EAL . . . . Early American Life Insurance Association
EAL . . . . Eastern Air Lines, Inc. (NYSE symbol)
EAL . . . . Ehrenfest Adiabatic Law
EAL . . . . Electromagnetic Amplifying Lens
EAL . . . . Estimated (or Expected) Average Life
EAM. . . . . . . Electric (or Electronic) Accounting Machines
EAM. . . . . . . Ethnikon Apeleutherotikon Metopon (National Liberation Front) (Greece)
EAMC . . . . . . Eastern Atlantic & Mediterranean Command (DOD)
EAME . . . . . . Europe-Africa-Middle East
EAMECM. . . . . European-African-Middle Eastern Campaign Medal
EAMG . . . . . . Electric Arc Metallizing Gun
EAMHD. . . . . . Engineering Aspects of Magnetohydrodynamics
EAMTC . . . . . European Association of Management Training Centres
EAMTMTS . . . . Eastern Area, Military Traffic Management and Terminal Service
EAMU. . . . . . Electric Accounting Machine Unit
EAN. . . . . . . Effective Atomic Number
EAN. . . . . . . Emergency Action Notification (Civil Defense)
EAN. . . . . . . Equivalent Atomic Number
EAN. . . . . . . Expenditure Account Number
EANA . . . . . . Esperanto Association of North America
EANA . . . . . . European Alliance of News Agencies
EANDC . . . . . Edgewood Arsenal Nuclear Defense Center (Army)
EANDC . . . . . European-American Nuclear Data Committee (OECD)
EANS . . . . . . Emergency Action Notification System (White House Teletype network)
          (Civil Defense)
EAON . . . . . . Except as Otherwise Noted
EAOS . . . . . . Expiration of Active Obligated Service
EAP . . . . Educational Awareness Project
EAP . . . . Equivalent Air Pressure
EAP . . . . Eye Artifact Potential
EAPAUS . . . . . Employment Agencies Protective Association of the United States
EAPD . . . . . . Eastern Air Procurement District
EAPL . . . . . . Engineering Assembly Parts List
EAPR . . . . . . European Association for Potato Research
EAPS . . . . . . Engine Air Particle Separator
EAR . . . . Electronic Audio Recognition
EAR . . . . Escape and Rescue
EARB . . . . . . European Airlines Research Bureau
EARC . . . . . . Eastern Association of Rowing Colleges
EARC . . . . . . Extraordinary Administrative Radio Conference (ITU)
EARCCUS . . . . East African Regional Committee for Conservation and Utilisation of
          Soil
EARFLAP. . . . . Emergency Action Reporting for Logistics Action Programming
EARLPRADATE . .(At) Earliest Practicable Date
EAROPH . . . . . East Asia Regional Organization for Planning and Housing
EAROS . . . . . Electrically Alterable Read Only Store (Data processing)
EARP . . . . . . Equipment Allowance Revision Program
EARS . . . . . . Emergency Airborne Reaction System
EARS . . . . . . Environmental Analog Recording System
EAS . . . . Early American Society
EAS . . . . Earth Aspect Sensor
EAS . . . . Eastern Apicultural Society of North America

EAS . . . . Educational Analog Simulator
EAS . . . . End-Around Shift
EAS . . . . Enlisted Assignment System
EAS . . . . Equivalent Airspeed
EAS . . . . Error Analysis Study
EAS . . . . Estimated Air Speed
EAS . . . . Evaluation and Analysis Staff (Navy)
EAS . . . . Extended Area Service (Telephone communications)
EAS . . . . Extensive Air Shower
EASA . . . . . . Electrical Apparatus Service Association
EASA . . . . . . Emergency Air Force Staff Actions
EASB . . . . . . Electronic Area Support Base (Air Force)
EASCOMINT . . Extended Air Surveillance Communications Intercept (Air Force)
EASCON. . . . . Electronics and Aerospace Systems Convention
EASE . . . . . . Econolite Automatic Sensing Equipment
EASE . . . . . . Electrical Automatic Support Equipment
EASE . . . . . . Emigrant's Assured Savings Estate (Banking program)
EASE . . . . . . Engineering Automatic System for Solving Equations
EASEP . . . . . Early Apollo Scientific Experiments Payload (or Package) (NASA)
EASL . . . . . . Electroacoustic Systems Laboratory
EASL . . . . . . Engineering Analysis and Simulation Language (Data processing)
EASL . . . . . . Experimental Assembly and Sterilization Laboratory (NASA)
EASP . . . . . . Edgewood Arsenal Special Publication
EAST . . . . . . Electric-Arc Shock Tunnel (NASA)
EAST . . . . . . Experimental Army Satellite, Tactical
EASTAF. . . . . Eastern Transport Air Force
EASTCO . . . . . East Coast
EASTCOBASE. . East Coast Base
EASTCOMMRGN .. Eastern Communications Region (Military)
EASTCON. . . . Eastern Sea Frontier Control Local of Shipping in Gulf of Maine
EASTLANT. . . . Eastern Atlantic Area
EASTLANTMEDCOM .. Eastern Atlantic and Mediterranean Command (Military)
EASTOMP . . . . East-Ocean Meeting Point
EASTSEAFRON .. Eastern Sea Frontier
EASTT . . . . . . Experimental Army Satellite Tactical Terminals
EASY . . . . . . Early Acquisition System (Army)
EASY . . . . . . Efficient Assembly System
EASY . . . . . . Engine Analyzer Systems (Air Force)
EAT . . . . Earliest Arrival Time
EAT . . . . Electro-Aerosol Therapy (Medicine)
EAT . . . . Encoder Address Translator
EAT . . . . Estimated (or Estimating) Approach Time (Aviation)
EAT . . . . Expected Approach Time
EAT . . . . Experiments in Art and Technology, Inc.
EATI. . . . . . . Equipment and Tool Institute
EATM . . . . . . Edgewood Arsenal Technical Memorandum
EATR . . . . . . Edgewood Arsenal Technical Report
EATR . . . . . . Equilibrium Air Total Radiation
EATS . . . . . . Equipment Accuracy Test Station
EATS . . . . . . European Air Transport Service
EAUTC . . . . . Engineer Aviation Unit Training Center (Military)
EAV . . . . Effective Angular Velocity
EAV . . . . Engine Assembly Vehicle
EAV . . . . Explosive Actuated Valve
EAW . . . . . . Electric Arc Weld
EAX . . . . Electronic Automatic Exchange
EAZ . . . . Empfindlicher Aufschlagzuender (Superquick impact fuze) (German
          military - World War II)
EAZ . . . . Ethnographisch-Archaeologische Zeitschrift (A publication)
EB . . . . Early Burst (Premature explosion of a warhead)
EB . . . . Eastbound
EB . . . . Electric Boat
EB . . . . Electron Beam
EB . . . . Elementary Body
EB . . . . Encyclopaedia Britannica
EB . . . . Engine Bulletin
EB . . . . Engineer Battalion (Army)
EB . . . . Environment and Behavior (A publication)
EB . . . . Ethylene Dibromide
EB . . . . Executive Board
EB . . . . Eyepiece Box
E-B . . . . Estate-Bottling (Wine)
EBA . . . . Early Birds of Aviation
EBA . . . . Emergency Breathing Apparatus
EBA . . . . Ethoxybenzoic Acid (Dental cement)
EBA . . . . Experimental Behavioral Analyzer
EBB . . . . Extra Best Best (Steel wire)
EBBA . . . . . . Eastern Bird Banding Association
EBC . . . . Eastern Baptist College (Pennsylvania)
EBC . . . . Electron Beam Cutting (Engraving)
EBC . . . . Electronic Batch Control

EBC . . . . End Breguet Cruise (SST)
EBC . . . . European Bibliographical Center
EBC . . . . European Billiards Confederation
EBC . . . . European Brewery Convention
EBCDIC . . . . . Extended Binary-Coded Decimal Interchange Code (Data processing)
EBCG . . . . . . Experimental Buried Collector Gauge
EBD . . . . Equivalent Binary Digit
EBDC . . . . . . Enamel Bonded Double Cotton (Insulation)
EBDP . . . . . . Enamel Bonded Double Paper (Insulation)
EBDS . . . . . . Enamel Bonded Double Silk (Insulation)
EBE . . . . Electron Beam Evaporator
EBE . . . . Electron Binding Energy
EBEE . . . . . . Electron Beam Evaporation Equipment
EBF . . . . Economic and Business Foundation
EBF . . . . Electric Bomb Fuze
EBF . . . . Ennis Business Forms, Inc. (NYSE symbol)
EBG . . . . Electron Beam Generator
EBG . . . . Electron Beam Gun
EBI . . . . Equivalent Background Input
EBI . . . . Expanded Background Investigation
EBI . . . . Eye Ball In
EBIC . . . . . . Electron-Bombardment-Induced Conductivity (NASA)
EBICON . . . . Electron-Bombardment-Induced Conductivity
EBIS . . . . Encyclopedia of Business Information Sources (A publication) (Formerly, EGIS)
EBIS . . . . Exothermic Bimetallic Ignition System
EBK . . . . Embryonic Bovine Kidney
EBL . . . . Eastern Basketball League
EBL . . . . European Bridge League
EBM . . . . Early-Break-Make (Data Processing)
EBM . . . . Electron Beam Melted
EBM . . . . Electron Beam Method
EBMA . . . . . . Elastic Braid Manufacturers Association
EBMA . . . . . . Engine, Booster Maintenance Area
EBMD . . . . . . Electron Beam Mode Discharge
EBME . . . . . . Eagle's Basal Medium with Earle's Salts (Biochemistry)
EBNY . . . . . . Edition Bookbinders of New York
EBO . . . . Eye Ball Out
EBOR . . . . . . Experimental Beryllium Oxide Reactor (Later, BORE) (AEC)
EBP . . . . Electric Bilge Pump
EBP. . . . . Estradiol-Binding Protein (Biochemistry)
EBPA . . . . . . Electron Beam Parametric Amplifier
EBR . . . . Electron Beam Readout
EBR . . . . Electron Beam Recorder
EBR . . . . Electron Beam Regulator
EBR . . . . Emulsion Butadiene Rubber
EBR . . . . Epoxy Bridge Rectifier
EBR . . . . . . Experimental Breeder Reactor (AEC)
EBRD . . . . . . Export Business Relations Division (Department of Commerce)
EBS . . . . Electric Bond & Share Company (NYSE symbol) (Delisted)
EBS . . . . Electron Beam System
EBS . . . . Electronic Band Spectra
EBS . . . . Emergency Broadcast System (Formerly CONELRAD)
EBS . . . . Engine Breather Separator
EBS . . . . Ernest Bloch Society
EBS . . . . Extruded Bar Solder
EBSR . . . . . . Eye-Bank for Sight Restoration
EBT . . . . Earth-Based Tug (NASA)
EBT . . . . Electron Beam (Fluorescence) Technique
EBT . . . . Executive Business Transport (Aircraft)
EBU . . . . European Broadcasting Union
EBV . . . . Efferent Branchial Vein
EBV . . . . Electron Bombardment Vehicle
EBV . . . . Epstein-Barr Virus
EBW . . . . Effective Band Width
EBW . . . . Electronic Beam Welding
EBW . . . . Exploding Bridge Wire
EBWR . . . . . Experimental Boiling Water Reactor (Nuclear reactor)
EBYC . . . . . . European Bureau for Youth and Childhood
EC . . . . East Carolina Railway (AAR code)
EC . . . . East Central (Refers especially to London postal district)
EC . . . . Eastern Command (British)
EC . . . . Edge Connector
EC . . . . Educational Coordinates (Business firm)
EC . . . . Effective Conductivity
EC . . . . Electric Coding (Cipher) Machine Repairman (Navy rating)
EC . . . . Electrical Conductivity
EC . . . . Electrification Council
EC . . . . Electrocoating
EC . . . . Electron Capture
EC . . . . Electronic Computers

EC . . . . Electronic Conductivity
EC . . . . Electronic & Control
EC . . . . Electronic Counter
EC . . . . Electronics Chassis
EC . . . . Emergency Capability
EC . . . . En Cuenta (On Account) (Business and trade) (Spain)
EC . . . . Enamel Covered
EC . . . . Encyclopedia Canadiana
EC . . . . Engineer Captain (British Navy)
EC . . . . Engineering Changes
EC . . . . Engineering Construction
EC . . . . Engineering Corps
EC . . . . Enteric Coated (Pharmacy)
EC . . . . Entering Complaint (Medicine)
EC . . . . Enzyme Commission (of the International Union of Biochemistry)
EC . . . . Epidermal Cell
EC . . . . Episcopal Church
EC . . . . Error Correcting (Data processing)
EC . . . . Established Church
EC . . . . Excretory Cell
EC . . . . Exempli Causa (For the Sake of Example)
EC . . . . Exhaust Closes (Valve position)
EC . . . . Expansive Classification
EC . . . . Experimentation Command (Army)
EC . . . . Expiratory Center (Physiology)
EC . . . . Explorers Club
EC . . . . Extended Coverage (Insurance)
EC . . . . Extension and Conversion (Public buildings)
EC . . . . Extension Course
EC . . . . External Combustion
E in C . . . . . . Engineer-in-Chief
ECA . . . . Department of Economic Affairs of the United Nations
ECA . . . . Early Closing Association (British)
ECA . . . . East Coast Aeronautics, Inc.
ECA . . . . Economic Commission for Africa (of UN)
ECA . . . . Economic Control Agency (Allied German Occupation Forces)
ECA . . . . Economic Cooperation Act (of 1948)
ECA . . . . Economic Cooperation Administration (Administered aid under Marshall Plan; abolished, 1951)
ECA . . . . Eigenvalue Change Analysis
ECA . . . . Electronic Confusion Area
ECA . . . . Electronics Control Assembly
ECA . . . . Electronics Corporation of America
ECA . . . . Engineering Change Analysis
ECA . . . . Enter Control Area (Aviation)
ECA . . . . Environmental Control Administration (Later, EPA)
ECA . . . . Epoxy Curing Agent
ECA . . . . European Civil Affairs
ECA . . . . European Confederation of Agriculture
ECA . . . . Executive Chef Association
ECA . . . . Explosives Corporation of America
ECAB . . . . . . Employees' Compensation Appeals Board (Department of Labor)
ECAC . . . . . . Eastern College Athletic Conference
ECAC . . . . . . Electromagnetic Compatibility Analysis Center (FAA)
ECAC . . . . . . Engineering College Administrative Council
ECAC . . . . . . European Civil Aviation Conference
ECAD . . . . . . Engineer Control and Advisory Detachment (Air Force)
ECAD . . . . . . European Civil Affairs Division (US Military Government, Germany)
ECAFE . . . . . Economic Commission for Asia and the Far East (of UN)
ECAP . . . . . . Electric Companies' Advertising Program
ECAP . . . . . . Electronic Circuit Analysis Program
ECAP . . . . . . Environmental Compatability Assurance Program (Navy)
ECAPE . . . . . Exploratory Committee on Assessing the Progress of Education
ECAR . . . . . . European Civil Affairs Regiment
ECARS . . . . . Electronic Coordinatograph Readout System
ECAT . . . . . . Emergency Committee for American Trade
ECAT . . . . . . Equipment Category
ECB . . . . Eddy Current Brake
ECB . . . . Etched Circuit Board
ECBA . . . . . . Eastern College Basketball Association
ECBC . . . . . . Empress Chinchilla Breeders Cooperative
ECBMD . . . . . Emergency Committee to Boycott Mother's Day
ECB-P . . . . . Excellence-in-Competition Badge (Pistol) (Army)
ECB-R . . . . . Excellence-in-Competition Badge (Rifle) (Army)
E & CB1S . . . . Edge and Center Bead on One Side (Technical drawings)
E & CB2S . . . . Edge and Center Bead on Two Sides (Technical drawings)
ECC . . . . East Carolina College (North Carolina)
ECC . . . . Eddy Current Clutch
ECC . . . . Effective Creep Compliance
ECC . . . . El Camino College (California)
ECC . . . . Electrocardiocorder

ECC . . . . Electronic Calibration Center (National Bureau of Standards)
ECC . . . . Elgin Community College (Illinois)
ECC . . . . Emergency Combat Capability
ECC . . . . Emergency Conservation Committee
ECC . . . . Emergency Core Cooling (Nuclear)
ECC . . . . Employees' Compensation Commission
ECC . . . . English Ceramic Circle
ECC . . . . European Coordinating Committee
ECC . . . . European Cultural Centre
ECC . . . . Excitement, Choreiform Movements, and Circling (Characterizations of a medical syndrome)
ECC . . . . Experimental Computer Complex
ECCAA . . . . . . Executive Chefs de Cuisine Association of America
ECCANE . . . . . East Coast Conference on Aerospace and Navigational Electronics
ECCC . . . . . . Ecology Center Communications Council
ECCC . . . . . . European Command Coordination Committee (Military)
ECCDA . . . . . Eastern Connecticut Clam Diggers Association
ECCM . . . . . . Electronic Counter-Countermeasures
ECCP . . . . . . Engineering Concepts Curriculum Project
ECCP . . . . . . European Committee on Crime Problems
ECCP . . . . . . Executive Committee on Commercial Policy (Abolished, 1944)
ECCS . . . . . . Emergency Core Cooling Systems (AEC)
ECD . . . . Educational and Cultural Development Program
ECD . . . . Electric Control Drive
ECD . . . . Electrochemical Debarring
ECD . . . . Electronic Communications Division (Air Force)
ECD . . . . Endocardial Cushion Defect
ECD . . . . Energy Conversion Devices
ECD . . . . Equal Charge Displacement (Fission)
ECD . . . . Estimated Completion Date
ECDC . . . . . . Electrochemical Diffused-Collector Transistor
ECDC . . . . . . External Count-Down Clock
ECE . . . . Economic Commission for Europe (of UN)
ECE . . . . Economic Coverage Endorsement
ECE . . . . Eddy Current Energy
ECE . . . . Element Characteristics Equation
ECE . . . . Environmental Control Equipment
ECE . . . . Extended Coverage Endorsement (Insurance)
ECF . . . . Effective Cutoff Frequency
ECF . . . . Employees Compensation Fund
ECF . . . . Engineering Central Files
ECF . . . . "Evangelize China" Fellowship
ECF . . . . Experimental Cartographic Facility (Air Force)
ECF . . . . Externally Caused Failure
ECF . . . . Extracellular Fluid (Physiology)
ECFA . . . . . . European Committee on Future Accelerators (Nuclear energy)
ECFMG . . . . Educational Council For Foreign Medical Graduates
ECFMS . . . . . Educational Council for Foreign Medical Students
ECFSOV . . . . Episcopal Council for Foreign Students and Other Visitors, Inc.
ECG . . . . Electrocardiogram (Medicine) (Also, EKG)
ECG . . . . Electronic Component Group
ECGAI . . . . . Education Council of the Graphic Arts Industry
ECGD . . . . . . Exports Credit Guarantee Department
ECGS . . . . . . Evaporative Cooled Garment System (NASA)
ECH . . . . Echlin Manufacturing Company (NYSE symbol)
ECHO . . . . . . Electronic Computing Hospital-Oriented Group
ECHO . . . . . . Entero-Cytopathogenic Human Orphan (Virus)
ECHO . . . . . . Evidence for Community Health Organization (Part of Michigan Health Survey)
ECHO . . . . . . Evolution of Competing Hierarchical Organizations
ECHO . . . . . . Experimental Contract Highlight Operation (NASA)
ECI . . . . Electronic Communications, Incorporated
ECI . . . . Electronic Control Instrumentation
ECI . . . . Engineering Change Information
ECI . . . . Environmental Clearinghouse, Incorporated
ECI . . . . Error Cause Identification (Military)
ECI . . . . Extension Course Institute (Air Force)
ECI . . . . Extracorporeal Irradiation
ECIC . . . . . . Electric Consumers Information Committee
ECIC . . . . . . Export Credits Insurance Corporation (Canada)
ECIIB . . . . . . Enemy Civilian Internee Information Bureau (Military)
ECIIB(Br) . . . . Enemy Civilian Internee Information Bureau (Branch) (Military)
ECIMOT . . . . European Central Inland Movements of Transport
ECIS . . . . . . European Community Information Service
ECITO . . . . . European Central Inland Transport Organization
ECJC . . . . . . East Central Junior College (Mississippi)
ECJS . . . . . . East Coast Joint-Stock (British railroad)
ECK . . . . Eckerd (Jack) Corp. (NYSE symbol)
ECK . . . . Embryonic Chicken Kidney
ECK . . . . Emergency Communications Key
ECL . . . . East Coast Laboratory (Environmental Science Services Administration)

ECL . . . . Eddy Current Loss
ECL . . . . Egyptian Confederation of Labor (United Arab Republic)
ECL . . . . Electronic Components Laboratory
ECL . . . . Emitter-Coupled Logic
ECL . . . . Energy Conversion Laboratory (MIT)
ECL . . . . English Comprehension Level (Army)
ECL . . . . Equipment Component List (Army)
ECL . . . . European Calibration Line
ECLA . . . . . . Economic Commission for Latin America (of UN)
ECLC . . . . . . Emergency Civil Liberties Committee
ECLO . . . . . . Emitter-Coupled Logic Operator
ECLOF . . . . . Ecumenical Church Loan Fund
EC/LS . . . . . . Environmental Control/Life Support (NASA)
ECM . . . . Effective Complex Modulus
ECM . . . . Electric Coding (or Cipher) Machine
ECM . . . . Electrochemical Machining
ECM . . . . Electronic Counter Measure
ECM . . . . Embryonic Chicken Muscle
ECM . . . . Emergency Conservation Measures
ECM . . . . Emission Characteristics Monitor
ECM . . . . Ends Matched, Center (Lumber)
ECM . . . . Engine Condition Monitoring
ECM . . . . European Common Market
ECMA . . . . . . Eastern Cosmetic Manufacturers Association
ECMA . . . . . . Embalming Chemical Manufacturers Association (Defunct)
ECMA . . . . . . Engineering College Magazines Associated
ECMA . . . . . . European Computer Manufacturers' Association
ECMALGOL . . European Computer Manufacturers Association Algorithmic Language
ECMB . . . . . . European Conference on Molecular Biology
ECMBR . . . . . European Committee on Milk-Butter-fat Recording
ECM-D . . . . . Engineering Change Management-Development
ECME . . . . . . Electronic Circuit-Making Equipment (Data processing)
ECME . . . . . . Electronics Countermeasures Environment
ECMEA . . . . . European Conference of Meteorological Experts for Aeronautics
ECME (UN) . . . Economic Commission for the Middle East (Proposed) of the United Nations
ECMob . . . . . Electronic Countermeasures Observer
ECMP . . . . . . Electronic Countermeasures Program
ECMR . . . . . . Eastern Contract Management Region (Air Force)
ECMR . . . . . . Equipment Calibration Maintenance Record
ECMRA . . . . . European Chemical Market Research Association
ECMSN . . . . . Electronic Countermeasures Mission
ECMT . . . . . . European Conference of Ministers of Transport
ECN . . . . Engineering Change Notice
ECNG . . . . . . East Central Nuclear Group
ECNRT . . . . . Emitter-Controlled Negative Resistance Triode
ECO . . . . Economic Cooperation Organization
ECO . . . . Effective Citizens Organization
ECO . . . . Electron Coupled Oscillator
ECO . . . . Electronic Central Office
ECO . . . . Electronic Check-Out
ECO . . . . Electronic Contact Operate
ECO . . . . Engine Cut-Off (Aerospace)
ECO . . . . Engineering Change Order
ECO . . . . Environmental Control Organization (Proposed in 1970 by Walter J. Hickel, Secretary of the Interior)
ECO . . . . Environmental Crisis Operation (University of British Columbia)
ECO . . . . Equipment Control Officer (Air Force)
ECO . . . . European Coal Organization
ECO . . . . Exempted by Commanding Officer
ECOG . . . . . . Electrocorticogram (or -graphic)
ECOM . . . . . . Electronic Command (Army)
ECOMS . . . . . Early Capability Orbital Manned Station
ECON . . . . . . Economics (or Economist)
ECON . . . . . . Economy
ECONOMAN . . Effective Control of Manpower
ECOP . . . . . . Extension Committee on Organization and Policy
ECOSOC . . . . Economic and Social Council of the United Nations
ECOX . . . . . . Educational Communications on Exhibit (Commercial firm)
ECP . . . . Electrical Contact Plate
ECP . . . . Electrical Control Package
ECP . . . . Electrically Compensated Pyrometer
ECP . . . . Electromagnetic Compatibility Program (Air Force)
ECP . . . . Electronic Calculating Punch
ECP . . . . Electronic Circuit Protector
ECP . . . . Elliptical Cavity Pump
ECP . . . . Engineering Change Package
ECP . . . . Engineering Change Proposals
ECP . . . . Estradiol Cyclopentyl Propionate (Medicine)
ECP . . . . European Committee of Crop Protection
ECP . . . . Evaporative Cooling Processor

ECP . . . . Executive Control Program
ECPD . . . . . . Engineers Council for Professional Development
ECPI. . . . . . . Electronic Computer Programming Institute
ECPIP . . . . . . Electric Companies' Public Information Program
ECR . . . . Electrochemical Reaction
ECR . . . . Emitted Coherent Radiation
ECR . . . . Engineering Change Request (or Requirement) (NASA)
ECR . . . . Error Cause Removal (Management)
ECR . . . . Executive Control Routines
ECR . . . . External Channels Ratio
ECRA . . . . . . Electric Car Racing Association
ECRA . . . . . . Excess and Casualty Reinsurance Association
ECR/A . . . . . . Engineering Change Request/Authorization
ECRB . . . . . . Export Control Review Board
ECRC . . . . . . Electricity Council Research Center (British)
ECRC . . . . . . Electronic Component Reliability Center (Battelle Memorial Institute)
ECRC . . . . . . Engineering College Research Council
ECRC . . . . . . Engineering Contracts Requirement Committee
ECRDG . . . . . Electronic Component Research and Development Grant (Canada)
ECREA . . . . . European Conference of Radiotelegraphy Experts for Aeronautics
ECRS . . . . . . Economic and Contingency Reserve Stock (Military)
ECS . . . . Education Commission of the States
ECS . . . . Educational Career Services (An organization)
ECS . . . . Electrical Connector Subassembly
ECS . . . . Electrocardioscanner
ECS . . . . Electrochemical Society
ECS . . . . Electroconvulsive Shock
ECS . . . . Electronic Countermeasures System
ECS . . . . Electroshock Therapy
ECS . . . . Emperor's Clothes Syndrome
ECS . . . . Enable Control System
ECS . . . . Engine Control System
ECS . . . . Engineering Change Summary
ECS . . . . Environmental Chamber Shroud
ECS . . . . Environmental Control System (NASA)
ECS . . . . Etched Circuit Society
ECS . . . . Executive Control System
ECS . . . . Extended Core Storage (Data processing)
ECSA . . . . . . Episcopal Churchmen for South Africa
ECSA . . . . . . European Communication Security Agency
ECSA . . . . . . Expanded Clay and Shale Association
ECSC . . . . . . East Central State College (Oklahoma)
ECSC . . . . . . European Coal and Steel Community (France, West Germany, Italy, Benelux)
ECSCA . . . . . English Cocker Spaniel Club of America
ECSG . . . . . . Electronic Connector Study Group
ECSH . . . . . . Edgewood College of the Sacred Heart (Wisconsin)
ECSIL . . . . . . Experimental Cross Section Information Library (University of California, Livermore)
ECSO . . . . . . Enteritis Cytopathic Swine Orphan (Virus) (Medicine)
ECSOB . . . . . Eastern College Soccer Officials Bureau
ECSP . . . . . . Electronic Specialist
ECSS . . . . . . Extendable Computer System Simulator
ECSTASY. . . . Economical Storage and Access System (Data processing)
ECT . . . . Electroconvulsive Therapy (Medicine)
ECT . . . . Encyclopedia of Chemical Technology
ECT . . . . Enteric Coated Tablet (Pharmacy)
ECT . . . . Error Control Translator (or Transmitter)
ECT . . . . Estimated Completion Time
ECT . . . . Evaporative Cooling Techniques
ECT . . . . Exposure Control Technique
ECTAR . . . . . Electronic Tactical Action Report
ECTI. . . . . . . Eddy Current Testing Instrument
ECTI. . . . . . . Erie County Technical Institute (New York)
ECTL . . . . . . Emitter-Coupled Transistor Logic (Data processing)
ECTS . . . . . . Electric Circuit Test Set
ECTS . . . . . . Electrical Cable Test Set
ECTS . . . . . . European Conference on Telecommunications by Satellite
ECU . . . . Electrical Conversion Unit
ECU . . . . Electronic Cabling Unit
ECU . . . . Electronic Control Unit
ECU . . . . English Church Union
ECU . . . . Environmental Control Unit
ECV . . . . Electric Clock Valve
E & CV1S . . . . Edge and Center V on One Side
E & CV2S . . . . Edge and Center V on Two Sides
ECW . . . . Emergency Conservation Work (Succeeded by CCC, 1937, now obsolete)
ECW . . . . Episcopal Church Women
ED . . . . Consolidated Edison Company of New York, Inc. (NYSE symbol)
ED . . . . Doctor of Engineering
ED . . . . Eastern District (ATSC)

ED . . . . Economics Division (US Military Government, Germany)
ED . . . . Edge Distance
ED . . . . Edition
ED . . . . Editor
ED . . . . Education
ED . . . . Effective Dose
ED . . . . Efficiency Decoration (British)
ED . . . . Election District
ED . . . . Electric Dynamic (Motors)
ED . . . . Electrical Differential
ED . . . . Electron Devices
ED . . . . Emergency Department (of a hospital)
ED . . . . Enemy Dead
ED . . . . Engineering Data
ED . . . . Engineering Depot
ED . . . . Engineering Design
ED . . . . Engineering Division
ED . . . . Engineering Draftsman
ED . . . . Engineering Duty (Navy)
ED . . . . Enumeration District (Census)
ED . . . . Environmental Disruption
ED . . . . Equilibrium Dialysis (Analytical chemistry)
ED . . . . Error Detecting (Data processing)
ED . . . . Erythema Dose
ED . . . . Excused from Duty
ED . . . . Ex-Dividend
ED . . . . Executive Director
ED . . . . Existence Doubtful (Navigation charts)
ED . . . . Expanded Display
ED . . . . Explosive Device
ED . . . . External Device
ED . . . . Extra Duty (Marine Corps)
EDA . . . . Early Departure Authorized
EDA . . . . Economic Development Administration (Formerly, Office of Appalachian Assistance) (Department of Commerce)
EDA . . . . Electronic Differential Analyzer
EDA . . . . Electronic Digital Analyzer
EDA . . . . Error Detector Assembly
EDA . . . . Estimated Date of Arrival
EDA . . . . Ethylene Diamine
EDA2 . . . . . . Exhaust Deflection Angle
Ed A2 . . . . . . Advanced Degree in Education
EDAC . . . . . . Electronic Dive Angle Control
EDAC . . . . . . Equipment Distribution and Condition (Statistical reporting system) (Military)
EDAC . . . . . . Error Detection and Correction
EDALHAB . . . Engineering Design and Analysis Laboratory Habitat
EDAM . . . . . . Experiments, Drill and Maintenance
Ed B. . . . . . . Bachelor of Education
EDB . . . . Economic Defense Board (Later, Board of Economic Warfare) (World War II)
EDB . . . . Elongated Die Bushing
EDB . . . . Ethylene Dibromide (Chemical)
EDC . . . . Eastern Defense Command (Army)
EDC . . . . Economic Development Committee (Nickname: "Little Neddie") (British)
EDC . . . . Education Development Center (Formerly, ESI and IEI)
EDC . . . . Electro Development Corporation
EDC . . . . Electrode Dark Current
EDC . . . . Electronic Digital Computer
EDC . . . . Emergency Digital Computer
EDC . . . . Energy Distribution Curve (Electron)
EDC . . . . Error Detecting Code
EDC . . . . Estimated Date of Completion
EDC . . . . Ethylene Dichloride (Chemical)
EDC . . . . European Defence Community (NATO)
EDC . . . . Expect Departure Clearance (Aviation)
EDC . . . . Expected Date of Confinement (Obstetrics)
EDCG . . . . . . Error Detection Code Generator
EDCLMDA . . . Eastern Dry Cleaning and Laundry Machinery Distributors Association
EDCMR . . . . . Effective Date of Change of Morning Report
EDCOM . . . . . Editor and Compiler
EDCP . . . . . . Engineering Design Change Proposal
EDCPF . . . . . Environmental Data Collection and Processing Facility (Army)
EDCS . . . . . . Engineering Design Change Schedule
EDCSA . . . . . Effective Date of Change of Strength Accountability
EDCV . . . . . . Enamel Double Cotton Varnish (Insulation)
EDCW . . . . . . External-Device Control Word
Ed D . . . . . . Doctor of Education
EDD . . . . Eastern Development Division (Air Force)
EDD . . . . Economic Development District (EDA)
EDD . . . . Electric Displacement Density
EDD . . . . Electronic Data Display

EDD . . . . Electronic Dehydration Dryer
EDD . . . . English Dialect Dictionary
EDD . . . . Envelope Delay Distortion
EDD . . . . Estimated Delivery Date
EDD . . . . Expected Date of Delivery (Obstetrics)
EDDD . . . . . . Expanded Direct Distance Dialing (Telephone)
EDDF . . . . . . Error Detection and Decision Feedback
EDDFEC . . . . . Estimated Date of Departure Far East Command (Military)
EDDS . . . . . . Electron Devices Data Service (National Bureau of Standards)
EDDS . . . . . . Emergency Detection and Decision System
EDDS . . . . . . Ethylene-Diaminedisuccinic (Acid)
EDE . . . . Electronic Defense Evaluator
EDE . . . . Elliptic (or Exact) Differential Equation
EDE . . . . Empire District Electric Company (NYSE symbol)
EDES . . . . . . Ethnikos Demokratikos Ellenikos Stratos (Hellenic National Democratic Army) (Greek)
EDEVAL . . . . . Escuela de Derecho de Valparaiso
EDF . . . . Economics of Distribution Foundation
EDF . . . . Electric Depth Finder
EDF . . . . Electricite de France (National electric company)
EDF . . . . Engineering Data File
EDF . . . . Environmental Defense Fund
EDF . . . . European Development Fund
EDFO . . . . . . Economic Development Financing Organization (Greece)
EDFR . . . . . . Effective Date of Federal Recognition
EDFTGA . . . . . Eastern Dark-Fired Tobacco Growers Association
EDG . . . . Exploratory Development Goal (DOD)
EDGE . . . . . . Electronic Data Gathering Equipment
EDGE . . . . . . Experimental Display Generator
EDHE . . . . . . Experimental Data Handling Equipment
EDI . . . . Eckerd Drugs, Incorporated (NYSE symbol)
EDI . . . . Economic Development Institute (of the International Bank for Reconstruction and Development)
EDI . . . . Electron Diffraction Instrument
ED & I . . . . . Engineering, Design, and Inspection
EDIAC . . . . . . Engineering Decision Integrator and Communicator
EDICT . . . . . . Engineering Departmental Interface Control Technique
EDICT . . . . . . Engineering Document (or Drawing) Information Collection Task (or Technique)
EDIN . . . . . . Edinburgh
EDIS . . . . Edison National Historic Site
EDIS . . . . Engineering Data & Information System (Army)
EDIT . . . . Engineering Development Integration Test
EDIT . . . . Error Deletion by Iterative Transmission
EDITAR . . . . . Electronic Digital Tracking and Ranging
EDITS . . . . . . Experimental Digital Television System
EDL . . . . Edition Deluxe
EDL . . . . Educational Developmental Libraries, Inc.
EDL . . . . Electric Delay Line
EDL . . . . Electric Double Layer
EDL . . . . Electronic Defense Laboratory (Sylvania, Inc.)
EDL . . . . Engineering Development Laboratory
EDL . . . . Engineering Drawing List
EDLCC . . . . . . Electronic Data Local Communications Central
EDM . . . . Edgmoor & Manetta Railway (AAR code)
EDM . . . . Electrical Discharge Machining
EDM . . . . Electrodischarge Machine (or Machining)
EDM . . . . Electronic Drafting Machine
EDM . . . . Enforced Dipole Moment
EDM . . . . Engineering Data Management
EDM . . . . Engineering Design Machine
EDM . . . . Engineering Design Memorandum
EDM . . . . Engineering Development Model
EDM . . . . Engineering Drafting Machine
EDM . . . . Equipment Deadlined for Maintenance (Army)
EDM . . . . Exploratory Development Model
Ed M . . . . . . Master of Education
EDMA . . . . . . Ethylene Glycol Dimethacrylate
Ed M in BT Ed . . Master of Education in Business Teacher Education
EDMF . . . . . . Extended Data Management Facility
EDMICS . . . . . Engineering Data Management Information Control System (DOD)
Ed M in Phy Ed . . Master of Education in Physical Education
EDMS . . . . . . Engineering Data Management System
EDMS . . . . . . Engineering Data Micro-Reproduction System (DOD)
EDN . . . . Engine Deflector Nozzle
EDO . . . . Effective Diameter of Objective (Optics)
EDO . . . . Employee Development Officer
EDO . . . . Engineering Duty Officer (Military)
EDO . . . . Engineering Duty Only (Aeronautical)
EDO . . . . Experimental Development Operations
EDOC . . . . . . Effective Date of Change

EDOMP . . . . . . Educational Development of Military Personnel
EDP . . . . Economic Development Program
EDP . . . . Electronic Data Processing
EDP . . . . Electronic Display Panel
EDP . . . . Engineering Design Plan
EDP . . . . Epatite "Degenerative-Proliferativa" (A strain of mouse hepatitis virus) (Medicine)
EDP . . . . Equipment Deadlined for Parts
EDPA . . . . . . Exhibit Designers and Producers Association
EDPC . . . . . . Electronic Data Processing Center
EDPE . . . . . . Electronic Data Processing Equipment
EDPM . . . . . . Electronic Data Processing Machine (Also translated by some users of such equipment as "Every Damn Problem Multiplied")
EDPRESS . . . . . Educational Press Association of America
EDPS . . . . . . Electronic Data Processing System
EDPS . . . . . . Electronic Dew Point Sensor
EDPS . . . . . . Equipment Distribution Planning Studies (Army)
EDPT . . . . . . Electronic Data Processing Test
EDQA . . . . . . Electronic Devices Quality Assurance
EDR . . . . Electrodermal Response
EDR . . . . Electronic Decoy Rocket
EDR . . . . Engineering Department (or Division) Report)
EDR . . . . Equivalent Direct Radiation
EDR . . . . Expect Departure Release (Aviation)
EDR . . . . Exploratory Development Request (DOD)
EDR . . . . Exploratory Development Requirement (Navy)
EDRA . . . . . . Engineering Drawing Release Authorization
EDRCC . . . . . . Electronic Data Remote Communications Complex
Ed RD . . . . . . Doctor of Religious Education
EDRI . . . . Electronic Distributors' Research Institute
EDRS . . . . . . Education Document Reproduction Service
EDRS . . . . . . Engineering Data Retrieval System (Military)
EDRS . . . . . . ERIC (Educational Resources Information Center) Document Reproduction Service
EDRT . . . . . . Effective Date of Release from Training
EDS . . . . Echo Depth Sounder
Ed S . . . . Educational Specialist, or Specialist in Education
EDS . . . . Electronic Data Systems Corp. (NYSE symbol)
EDS . . . . Emergency Detection System
EDS . . . . Energy Depot Systems
EDS . . . . Engineering Data Systems (DOD)
EDS . . . . English Dialect Society
EDS . . . . Environmental Data Service (National Oceanic and Atmospheric Administration)
EDS . . . . Estimated Date of Separation
EDSA . . . . . . Effective Date of Change in Station Assignment (Military)
EDSAC . . . . . . Electronic Data Storage Automatic Computer
EDSAT . . . . . . (Center for) Educational Diffusion and Social Application of Satellite Telecommunications (University of Wisconsin)
EDSC . . . . . . Engineering Data Service Center (Air Force)
EDSD . . . . . . Electronic Defense Systems Division
Ed Sp . . . . . . Education Specialist
Ed Spec . . . . . Education Specialist
EDS & R . . . . . Engineering Data Storage and Retrieval (Army)
EDST . . . . . . Eastern Daylight Saving Time
EDST . . . . . . Electric Diaphragm Switch Technique (IBM)
EDSV . . . . . . Enamel Double Silk Varnish
EDT . . . . Eastern Daylight Time
EDT . . . . Effective Date of Training
EDT . . . . Engineering Design Test
EDT . . . . Equipment Downtime
EDT . . . . Estimated Delivery Times
EDT . . . . Ethylenediamine Tartrate (Organic chemistry)
EDTA . . . . . . Ethylenediaminetetraacetate (Organic chemistry)
EDTCC . . . . . . Electronic Data Traffic Control Center
EDTCC . . . . . . Electronic Data Transmission Communications Central
EDTR . . . . . . Experimental, Developmental, Test and Research
EDTS . . . . . . Electro-Depositer Technology Society
EDU . . . . Electronic Display Unit
EDU . . . . Experimental Diving Unit
EDUC . . . . . . Education
EDUCOM . . . . Educational Communications (Inter-University Communications Council)
EDV . . . . End-Diastolic Volume (Biology)
EDVAC . . . . . . Electronic Digital-Vernier Analog Computer
EDVAC . . . . . . Electronic Discrete Variable Automatic Computer
EDW . . . . Earth Departure Window
EDW . . . . El Dorado & Wesson Railway (AAR code)
EE . . . . Early English (Language, etc.)
EE . . . . Eastern Establishment (Politics)
EE . . . . Electrical Engineer(ing)
EE . . . . Electronic Engineering

EE .... Electronics to Electronics
EE .... Electronics Engineering Division (Coast Guard)
EE .... Elements of Expense (Army)
EE .... Embryo Extract
EE .... Engagement Effectiveness (Army)
EE .... Envoy-Extraordinary
EE .... Equine Encephalitis
EE .... Errors Excepted (Business and commerce)
EE .... Exoerythrocyte
EE .... Expiration of Enlistment
EE .... External Environment
EE .... Eye and Ear
E & E .... Evacuation and Evasion
E & E .... Evasion and Escape (Military)
E of E .... Expiration of Enlistment
E to E .... End to End (Technical drawings)
EEA .... Electrical Engineering Abstracts
EEA .... Electromagnetic Environment Analysis
EEA .... Electronic Engineering Association (British)
EEA .... Essential Elements of Analysis
EEA .... Ethylene-Ethyl Acrylate (Bakelite)
EEB .... Eastern Electricity Board (British)
EEC .... East Erie Commercial R. R. (AAR code)
EEC .... Electrical Export Corporation (Defunct)
EEC .... Emerson Electric Company
EEC .... Encased Elastic Cylinder
EEC .... English Electric Company, Ltd.
EEC .... Enlisted Evaluation Center (Army)
EEC .... European Economic Community (Common Market)
EEC .... Evaporative Emission Control (Antipollution device for automobiles)
EEC .... EXAMETNET Executive Committee (NASA)
EECA .... Engineering Economic Cost Analysis
EECE .... Emergency Economic Committee for Europe (A "Western Nation" organization) (Post-World War II)
EECOM...... Electrical, Environmental, and Communications
EECT .... End, Evening Civil Twilight (Navigation)
EED .... Electro-Explosive Device
EED .... Emergency Escape Device
EED .... European Enterprises Development Company (Luxembourg)
EEE .... Eastern Equine Encephalitis (Virus)
EEE .... Electrical, Electronic, and Electromechanical
EEE .... Electrical Engineering Exposition
EEE .... Electronic Equipment Engineering (A publication)
EEE .... Electronics Engineering Division (Coast Guard)
E in EE ...... Engineer in Electrical Engineering
EEEC .... Electromagnetic Energy Environment Criteria (Army)
EEES .... Electronic Equipment Environment Survey
EEF........ Egyptian Expeditionary Force (British military)
EEF .... Eisenhower Exchange Fellowships
EEF .... Erickson Educational Foundation
EEFI .... Essential Elements of Friendly Information (Army)
EEFT .... Electronic Environmental Test Facility
EEG .... Electroencephalogram or Electroencephalography (Medicine)
EEH .... Explorations in Economic History (Formerly, Explorations in Entrepreneurial History) (A publication)
EEI .... Edison Electric Institute
EEI........ Educational Expeditions International
EEI .... Environmental Equipment Institute
EEI........ Essential Elements of Information (Military)
EEIB .... Environmental Engineering Intersociety Board
EEIC....... Element of Expense/Investment Code
EEK .... Epoxy Experimental Kit
EEL .... Emergency Exposure Limits
EEL .... Engineering Electronics Laboratory
EEL .... Evans Electroselenium, Limited (as in EEL analyzer, used in biochemical analysis) (British)
EEM .... Eastern European Mission
EEM .... Effective Elastic Modulus
EEM .... Effective Engineering Management
EEM....... Electronic Equipment Modification
EEM .... Electrostatic Electron Microscope
EEM........ Engineering Experimental Memo
EEM .... Experienced Export Manager (Designation given by American Society of International Executives)
EEMK ...... Electronic Equipment Maintenance Kit
EE & MP .... Envoy Extraordinary and Minister Plenipotentiary (State Department)
EENT .... End, Evening Nautical Twilight (Navigation)
EENT .... Eyes, Ears, Nose, and Throat (Medicine)
EEO .... Equal Employment Opportunity
EEOC....... Equal Employment Opportunity Commission
EEP .... Earth Equatorial Plane

EEP .... Electrode Electrostatic Precipitator
EEP .... Emergency Essential Personnel
EEP .... Epsilon Eta Phi (Society)
EEP .... Experimental Education Program
EEPC .... India Engineering Export Promotion Council
EEPM .... Electrical and Electronic Properties of Materials
EEPNL ...... Estimated Effective Perceived Noise Level
EER .... Energy Efficiency Ratio (Home appliance electric output)
EER .... Envelope Elimination and Restoration
EER .... Equipment Evaluation Report
EER .... Expendable-Expendable-Reusable
EER .... Explosive Echo Ranging
EERA .... Electrical Equipment Representatives Association
EERC .... Explosive Echo Ranging Charge (Military)
EERI .... Earthquake Engineering Research Institute
EE & RM ..... Elementary Electrical and Radio Material (Training School) (Navy)
EES .... Educational Employment Service
EES .... Effectiveness Evaluation System
EES .... Electrical Equipment Shelter
EES .... Electronic Environment Simulator
EES .... Engineering Experiment Station
EES .... Enlisted Evaluation System
EES .... Environmental Engineering Section
EES .... Estonian Educational Society
EES .... European Exchange System
EES .... Evangelical Education Society of the Protestant Episcopal Church
EET .... Education Equivalency Test
EET .... Electrical Equipment Trailer
EET .... Engineering Evaluation Test
EET .... Epoxy-Encapsulated Transistor
EET .... Equator Earth Terminal
EET .... Estimated Elapsed Time (Aviation)
EET .... Explosive-to-Electric Transducer
EETF........ Electromagnetic Environmental Test Facility (Military)
EETP........ Engineering Evaluation Test Program
EETS........ Early English Text Society
EEUA .... Engineering Equipment Users Association
EEW .... Extraordinary Electromagnetic Wave
EEWG....... Emergency Egress Working Group
EEX .... Electronic Egg Exchange (Computer program)
EF .... Each Face (Technical drawings)
EF .... Elevation Finder (Military)
EF .... Elongation Factor (Protein biosynthesis)
EF .... Emitter Follower
EF .... English Finish (Paper)
EF .... Equivalent Focal Length (Optics)
EF .... Expeditionary Force
EF .... Experimental Flight
EF .... Extra Fine (Threads)
EF .... Extremely Fine (Condition) (Antiquarian book trade and numismatics)
EFA .... Entire Field Available (Aviation)
EFA .... Environmental Financing Authority (of Environmental Protection Agency)
EFA .... Essential Fatty Acids (Biochemistry)
EFAG .... Emergency Field Arresting Gear
EFAI........ Educational Foundation for the Apparel Industry
EFAS .... Electronic Flash Approach System
EFB .... Electric Feedback
EFC .... Earth Fixed Coordinate
EFC .... Electrical Field Current
EFC .... Electrochemical Fuel Cell
EFC .... Electronic Frequency Control
EFC .... Emergency Fleet Corporation (Defunct, 1936)
EFC .... Empire Financial Corporation (NYSE symbol)
EFC .... Equivalent Full Discharge
EFC .... European Forestry Commission
EFC .... Expect Further Clearance (Aviation)
EFCR .... Experimental Fast Ceramic Reactor
EFCS .... Engineer Functional Components System
EFCUA ..... Extreme Fuel - Critical, Unspecified Area
EFD .... Earliest Finish Date
EFD .... Early Failure Detection
EFD .... Electric Flux Density
EFD .... Electrofluid Dynamic (Process)
EFD .... Enemy Forward Disposition (Military)
EFD .... Energy Flux Density
EFD .... Engineered Fasteners Division (Townsend Company)
EFD .... Engineering Field Divisions (Military)
EFD .... Eurofund International, Inc. (NYSE symbol) (Delisted)
EFD .... Excused from Duty
EFE .... External Field Emission
EFEA .... Empresa Ferrocarriles del Estado Argentino

EFEC . . . . Efforts from Ex-Convicts (Organization in Washington, DC)
EFET . . . . Epoxy Field Effect Transistor
EFF . . . . Effect(ive)
EFF . . . . Electric Flow Field
EFF . . . . English for Foreigners
EFF . . . . European Furniture Federation
EFFBR . . . . Enrico Fermi Fast Breeder Power Reactor (AEC)
EFFF . . . . Electrical Field-Flow Fractionation (Electrochemical separation method)
EFFI . . . . Electronic Fiber Fineness Indicator
EFFI . . . . Electronic Forum for Industry (British)
EFFORPA . . . . . Elliptic Function First Order Ripple Phase Approximation
EFH . . . . E. F. Hutton & Co. (NYSE symbol)
EFI . . . . Elektrisitetsforsyningens Forskninginstitutt (Research Institute of Electricity Supply) (Norway)
EF & I . . . . . . Engineer, Furnish, and Install
EFICO . . . . Electrical Fitting Inventory Control Branch
EFICON . . . . . . Electronic Financial Control
EFINS . . . . Enrico Fermi Institute for Nuclear Studies (University of Chicago)
EFJG . . . . Educational Foundation for Jewish Girls
EFL . . . . Education Facilities Laboratories
EFL . . . . Effective Focal Length (Optics)
EFL . . . . English as a Foreign Language
EFLA . . . . Educational Film Library Association
EF & LTC . . . . Enemy Fuels and Lubricants Technical Committee
EFL-UAR . . . . . Egyptian Federation of Labor (United Arab Republic)
EFM . . . . Electric Field Meter
EFM . . . . Expeditionary Force Message (Low-rate cable or radio message selected from a list of standard wordings)
EFM . . . . Extensive Field Maintenance (Military)
EFMA . . . . Evangelical Foreign Missions Association
EFMC . . . . Educators Fund Management Corporation (of NEA)
EFMG . . . . Electric Fuse Manufacturers Guild
EFMI . . . . Elastic Fabric Manufacturers Institute
EFMO . . . . Effigy Mounds National Monument
EFNS . . . . Educational Foundation for Nuclear Science
EFP . . . . Effective Filtration Pressure (Physiology)
EFP . . . . End Forming Press
EFP . . . . Error-Free Performance
EFP . . . . Escaped Federal Prisoner
EFPH . . . . Equivalent Full-Power-Hour (FCC)
EFPH . . . . Evaluating Fallout Protection in Homes (Later, HFPS) (Civil Defense)
EFPW . . . . European Federation for the Protection of Waters
EFR . . . . Echo Free Room
EFR . . . . Effective Filtration Rate (Physiology)
EFR . . . . Electronic Failure Report
EFR . . . . Equipment Failure Rate
EFRAP . . . . Exchange Feeder Route Analysis Program (Bell System)
EFRC . . . . Edwards Flight Research Center (NASA)
EFRIS . . . . External Finished Reports Information Subsystem (Data processing)
EFS . . . . Electric Field-Induced Spectra
EFS . . . . Electric Field Strength
EFS . . . . Electronic Firing Switches (Military)
EFS . . . . Emergency Feeding Service (Civil Defense)
EFSORPA . . . . . Elliptic Function Second-Order Ripple Phase Approximation
EFSP . . . . Electrolytic Fused-Salt Process
EFSP . . . . Electronic Family Security Program (of Sun Life of Canada insurance company)
EFT . . . . Early Finish Time
EFT . . . . Electrostatically Focused Tube
EFT . . . . Embedded Figures Test (Psychology)
EFT . . . . Emergency Flight Termination
EFT . . . . Engineering Flight Test
EFT . . . . Experimental Flight Test
EFTA . . . . European Free Trade Association (Known as the "Outer Seven" as opposed to the "Inner Six" Common Market nations)
EFTC . . . . Edwards Flight Test Center
EFTC . . . . Elementary Flying Training School (British)
EFTI . . . . Engineering Flight Test Inspector
EFTO . . . . Encrypt for Transmission Only (Military)
EFTR . . . . Engineering Flight Test Report
EFTS . . . . Elementary Flying Training School (Navy)
EFU . . . . Eastern Gas & Fuel Associates (NYSE symbol)
EFV . . . . Electric Field Vector
EFY . . . . End of Fiscal Year
EG . . . . Edge Grain
EG . . . . Else Good (In good condition except for defects mentioned) (Antiquarian book trade)
EG . . . . Engineering Geologist
EG . . . . Environment Generator
EG . . . . Escort Group
EG . . . . Ethylene Glycol

EG . . . . Executive Generator
EG . . . . Exempli Gratia (For Example)
EG . . . . Experimental Group
EG . . . . Expert Gunner (Army)
E/G . . . . Engine-Generator
EGA . . . . Edge Gradient Analysis
EGA . . . . Export Guarantees Act
EGAA . . . . Emergency General Account of Advances
EGAD . . . . Electronegative Gas Detector
EGAD . . . . Electronic Ground Automatic Destruct
EGADS . . . . . . Electronic Ground Automatic Destruct Sequencer (Air Force)
EGAL . . . . Elevation Guidance for Approach and Landing
EGB . . . . Episcopal Guild for the Blind
EGC . . . . Electronic Gyro Compass
EGC . . . . Empire Gas Corporation (NYSE symbol)
EGC . . . . Exposure Growth Curve
EGCR . . . . Experimental Gas-Cooled Reactor (AEC)
EGD . . . . Electrogasdynamic (Generator)
EGDN . . . . Ethylene Glycol Dinitrate
EGE . . . . Elevated Glandular Epidermis
EGECON . . . . . Electronic Geographic Coordinate Navigation System
EGG . . . . EG & G, Inc. (NYSE symbol)
EGG . . . . Electric Glue Gun
EGI . . . . Explosive Gas Indicator
EGIS . . . . Executive Guide to Information Sources (A publication) (Later, EBIS)
EGJC . . . . Eagle Grove Junior College (Iowa)
EGLMT . . . . . . Ejector-Launcher, Guided Missile, Transporter
EGM . . . . European Glass Container Manufacturers' Committee
EGME . . . . Ethylene Glycol Monomethyl Ether
EGMTR . . . . . . Eglin Gulf Missile Test Range
EGNA . . . . Eucharistic Guard for Nocturnal Adoration
EGO . . . . Eccentric Geophysical Observatory (NASA)
EGO . . . . Electronic Grading Operator
EGP . . . . Eagle-Picher Company (NYSE symbol) (Later, EPI)
EGP . . . . Elliptical Gear Planetary
EGP . . . . Embezzlement of Government Property
EGP . . . . Exhaust Gas Pressure
EGR . . . . Embossed Groove Recording
EGR . . . . Exhaust Gas Recirculation (Engines)
EGRESS . . . . . . Emergency Global Rescue, Escape and Survival System (NASA)
EGRESS . . . . . . Evaluation of Glide Reentry Structural Systems
EGS . . . . Edge Guide System
EGS . . . . Electronic-Glide Slope
EGS . . . . Extension of the Gastric Shield
EGSE . . . . Electrical Ground Support Equipment
EGSIPS . . . . . . Electronic Guides for Standardizing Items of Procurement and Supply
EGSMA . . . . . . Engine Generator Set Manufacturers' Association
EGT . . . . Equivalent Gear Train
EGT . . . . Exhaust-Gas Temperature
EGTR . . . . Eglin Gulf Test Range
EGV . . . . Exit Guide Vane
EH . . . . Engine Hoods
EH . . . . Exercise Head
EHA . . . . Economic History Association
EHA . . . . Electric Heating Association
EHA . . . . Electro-Hydraulic Actuator
EHA . . . . Environmental Hygiene Agency (Army)
EHA . . . . Expect Higher Altitude (Aviation)
EHBF . . . . Extrahepatic Blood Flow (Medicine)
EHC . . . . Elastic Hysteresis Constant
EHC . . . . Emergency Housing Corporation
EHC . . . . Emory & Henry College (Virginia)
EHD . . . . Elastohydrodynamic
EHD . . . . Electrohydrodynamics
EHD . . . . Epizootic Hemorrhagic Disease (Veterinary medicine)
EHF . . . . Electrohydraulic Forming
EHF . . . . Experimental Husbandry Farm (British)
EHF . . . . Exponential Hazard Function
EHF . . . . Extremely High Frequency (Electronics, radio wave)
EHFA . . . . Electric Home and Farm Authority (Terminated, 1947)
EHI . . . . Emergency Homes, Incorporated
EHK . . . . Electrode Heater Kit
EHL . . . . Eastern Hockey League
EHL . . . . Effective Halflife (Nuclear science)
EHL . . . . Elasto-Hydrodynamic Lubrication
EHM . . . . Electrohydraulic Motor
EHME . . . . Employee Health Maintenance Examination
EHMO . . . . Extended Hueckel Molecular Orbit
EHP . . . . Effective Horsepower
EHP . . . . Electric Horsepower
EHP . . . . Electrical Hull Penetration

EHPA	Ethylhexyl Phosphoric Acid (Chemical)
EHPAC	Emergency Health Preparedness Advisory Committee
EHPM	Electrohydraulic Pulse Motor
EHR	Extra High Reliability
EHS	Earth Horizon Scanner
EHS	Earth-Lunar Horizon Sensor
EHS	Emergency Health Service (Civil Defense)
EHS	Environmental Health Services (US Government)
EHS	Experimental Horticulture Station (British)
EHT	Extra High Tension
EHTRC	Emergency Highway Traffic Regulation Center (Army)
EHU	Electric Heating Unit
EHV	Extra-High Voltage (FPC)
EHW	Extreme High Water
EHY	Engage High Yield
EI	East Indies
EI	Ecumenical Institute
EI	Electrical Insulation
EI	Electromagnetic Interference
EI.	Electron Impact (Mass spectrometry)
EI	Electronic Installation
EI	Electronic Interface
EI	Electronic Interference
EI	Emery Industries, Inc. (NYSE symbol)
EI	End Item
EI	Engineering Index
EI	Engineering Instruction
EI	Exposure Index (Photography)
EI	Extra-Illustrated
E-I	Engineering-Installation
E-I	Extraversion-Introversion (Jungian psychology)
E/I	Endorsement Irregular (Banking)
EIA	Electronic Industries Association
EIA	English in Action
EIA	Envelope Institute of America
EIA	Equipment Interchange Association
EIAC	Electronic Industries Association of Canada
EIA-J	Electronic Industries Association - Japan
EIASA.	Energia e Industrias Aragonesas Sociedad Anonima (Spain)
EIB.	Economic Impact Budget
EIB.	Electronic Information Bulletin (Navy)
EIB.	Electronics Information Branch (Navy)
EIB.	European Investments Bank
EIB.	Expert Infantryman Badge
E-IB.	Export-Import Bank
EIBAD.	Expert Infantryman Badge
EIB(W).	Export-Import Bank (of Washington)
EIC	Earth Inductor Compass
EIC	Earth-Ionosphere Cavity
EIC	East India Company
EIC	Electrically Insulated Coating
EIC	Emplaced Instrument Complex
EIC	Enamel Insulating Compound
EIC	Engineer-in-Charge
EIC	Engineering Information Center
EIC	Engineering Institute of Canada
EIC	Environment Information Center
EIC	Environmental Improvement Commission (Maine)
EIC	Equipment Identification Code
EIC	Equipment Interstage Container
EICM	Employer's Inventory of Critical Manpower
EICS.	East India Company's Service
EICS.	Electromagnetic Intelligence Collection System
EID	East India Dock
EID	Electronic Intrusion Detection
EID	End Item Designators
EIDAP.	Emitter Isolated Difference Amplifier Paralleling (Bell System)
EIDL.	Economic Injury Disaster Loan (Small Business Administration)
EIDS	Equipment Integration Design Section
EIDSO	Engineer Information and Data Systems Office (Army)
EIFAC.	European Inland Fisheries Advisory Committee
EIFF	Enemy Identification Friend or Foe
EIG	Emitter Identification Guide
EIGL	Eastern Intercollegiate Gymnastic League
EIL.	Electron Injection LASER
EIL.	Electronic Instruments, Limited (as in EIL electrode, used in biochemistry) (British)
EIL.	Experiment in International Living
EIL	Explosives Investigation Laboratory
EIM	Elastomeric Insulation Material
EIM	Excitability-Inducing Material (Biochemistry)

EIM	Explosives Investigation Memorandum (Navy)
EIM	Eyelet Installing Machine
EIMB	Electronics Installation and Maintenance Bulletin
EIMC	English Institute Materials Center
EIMO	Electronic Interface Management Office
EIMO	Engineering Interface Management Office
EIMS.	End Item Maintenance Sheets
EIN	Educational Information Network
EIN	Engineer Intelligence Note
EIN	Eulerian Iterative Nonsteady (Method)
EIO	Electric Induction Oven
EIO	Emergency Information Officer (Civil Defense)
EIOC	Equivalent Input Offset Current
EIOD	Equivalent Instruction or Duty
EIOV	Equivalent Input Offset Voltage
EIP	Economic Inventory Procedures (Army)
EIP	Electronic Installation Plan
EIP.	Environmental Improvement Program
EIP.	Experiment Implementation Plan (NASA)
EIR	East Indian Railway
EIR.	Eidgenoessisches Institut fuer Reaktoforschung (Switzerland)
EIR	Emergency Information Readiness (Civil Defense)
EIR.	Engineering Investigation Request
EIR.	Equipment Improvement Recommendations (Military)
EIR.	Equipment Improvement Report (DOD)
EIRD.	Experiment Integration Requirements Document (NASA)
EIRMA	European Industrial Research Management Association
EIRP	Effective Isotropically Radiated Power
EIS	Economic Information System
EIS.	Educational Institute of Scotland
EIS.	Electromagnetic Intelligence System (Air Force)
EIS.	End Interruption Sequence
EIS.	Epidemic Intelligence Service (of the Center for Diseases Control)
EIS.	Expendable Instrument System
EIS.	Experiment Information System
EIS.	Eyes in the Sky
EISC	Eastern Illinois State College
EIT.	Electrical Information Test
EIT.	Electrical Insulation Tape
EIT.	Electromagnetic Interference Testing
EIT.	Electron-Bombardment Ion Thrustor
EIT.	Electronic Installation Technician
EIT.	Engineer-in-Training
EIT.	Engineering Index Thesaurus
EITS	Educational and Industrial Testing Service
EIV	Effective Initial Value
EIV	Eigenverstaendigung (Intravehicular communication) (German military - World War II)
EIV	Engine Installation Vehicle
EIVR.	Exchange of Information, Visits and Reports
EIW	Enamel Insulated Wire
EJ	Elbow Jerk (Medicine)
EJ	Electronic Jamming
EJ	English Journal (A periodical)
EJA	Executive Jet Aviation, Inc.
EJC	Eccles-Jordan Circuit (Electronics)
EJC	Ellsworth Junior College (Iowa)
EJC	Ely Junior College (Minnesota)
EJC	Endicott Junior College (Massachusetts)
EJC	Engineers Joint Council
EJC	Espoir de la Jeunesse Camerounaise (Hope of the Cameroonese Youth)
EJC	Estherville Junior College (Iowa)
EJC	Eveleth Junior College (Minnesota)
EJC	Everett Junior College (Washington)
EJCC	Eastern Joint Computer Conference
EJE	Chicago Outer Belt R. R. (AAR code)
EJE	Electric Junction Equation
EJE	Elgin, Joliet & Eastern Railway Company (AAR code)
EJI	Expansion Joint Institute
EJMA	Educational Jewelry Manufacturers Association
EJMA	Expansion Joint Manufacturers Association
EJN	Endicott Johnson Corporation (NYSE symbol) (Delisted)
EJP.	Excitatory Junctional Potential (Electrophysiology)
EJR	East Jersey R. R. & Terminal Company (AAR code)
EJRMG	Edmond James Rothschild Memorial Group (Foundation)
EJS	East Jordan & Southern R. R. (AAR code)
EJS	Engineering Job Sheet
EJT.	Eccles-Jordan Trigger (Electronics)
EJT.	Engineering Job Ticket
EK	Eastman Kodak Company (NYSE symbol)
EK	Einschluss-Korper (Inclusion Body) (Medicine)

EKB . . . . Electronic Key Board
EKB . . . . Electronic Knowledge Bank
EKBS . . . . . . Electronic Keyboard System
EKC . . . . Eastman Kodak Company
EKD . . . . Evangelische Kirche Deutschlands
EKG . . . . Electrocardiogram (Medicine)
EKI . . . . Eregli Komurleri Isletmesi
EKM . . . . Edwald-Kornfeld Method
EKN . . . . Eta Kappa Nu (Fraternity)
EKNE . . . . . . Department of Elementary, Kindergarten, and Nursery Education (NEA)
            (Later, American Association of Elementary, Kindergarten, Nursery
            Educators)
EKO . . . . Eisenhuettenkombinat Ost
EKO . . . . Evreiskoe Kolonizatsionnoe Obshchestvo (Jewish Colonization Association)
EKP . . . . Eestimaa Kommunistlik Partei
EKP . . . . Epikeraprosthesis (Ophthalmology)
EKR . . . . East Kent Regiment
EKS . . . . Electrocardiogram Simulator
EKS . . . . Electronic Keyboard System
EKSC . . . . . . Eastern Kentucky State College
EKU . . . . Eureka Pipe Line Company (American Stock Exchange symbol)
eKv . . . . Electron Kilovolt
EKW . . . . Eisenbahnkesselwagen (Railway tank car) (German military -
            World War II)
EKW . . . . Electrical Kilowatts
EKY . . . . Electrokymogram
EL . . . . Each Layer (Technical drawings)
EL . . . . Eastern League (Baseball)
EL . . . . Economics Laboratory, Inc.
EL . . . . Education Level
EL . . . . Egg Length
EL . . . . Einfache Lafette (Single-barreled mount) (German military -
            World War II)
EL . . . . Elastic Limit
EL . . . . Election Laws
EL . . . . Electroluminescence
EL . . . . Electronics Laboratory
El . . . . Eline
EL . . . . Engineer Lieutenant (British Navy)
EL . . . . Epidemiological Laboratory (Air Force)
EL . . . . Erie-Lackawanna R. R. (AAR code)
EL2 . . . . Elongation in 2 Inches
ELA . . . . Eighth Lively Art (Advertising award)
ELA . . . . Electron Linear Accelerator
ELAL . . . . . . El Al Israel Airlines, Ltd.
ELAS . . . . . . Ellenikos Laikos Apeleutherotikos Stratos (Hellenic Peoples Army of
            Liberation) (Military arm of EAM) (Greece)
ELATE . . . . . Engineers' Language for Automatic Test Equipment
ELB . . . . Bachelor of English Literature
ELBA . . . . . . English Language Books Abroad (A publication)
ELC . . . . Extra Low Carbon
ELCD . . . . . . Evaporative Loss Control Device (Motor exhaust control)
ELCO . . . . . . Eliminate and Count (Coding) (Data processing)
ELD . . . . East Longitude Date
ELD . . . . Edge-Lighted Display
ELD . . . . Ehrlich-Lettre Hyperdiploid (Mouse ascites tumor)
ELD . . . . Electroluminescent Diode
ELD . . . . Electronic Lie Detector
ELD . . . . Energy Level Diagram
ELD . . . . Engineering Logic Diagram
ELD . . . . Error Logging Device
ELD . . . . Extra-Long Distance
ELDATRAWP . . . Electronic Data Transmission Working Party (Army)
ELDO . . . . . . European Launch Development Organization (Later, ESO)
ELDS . . . . Editorial Layout Display System
ELE . . . . Electronic Launching Equipment
ELE . . . . Emergency Lighting Equipment
ELE . . . . Engine Life Expectancy
ELEC . . . . . . Electric
ELEC . . . . . . European League for Economic Cooperation
ELECN . . . . . Electrician
ELECOM . . . . Electronic Computing
ELEM . . . . . . Elementary
ELETROBRAS . . Centrais Eletricas Brasileiras SA (Brazil)
ELEV . . . . Elevation
ELF . . . . Early Lunar Flare
ELF . . . . Ejected Lunar Flare
ELF . . . . Electroluminescent Ferroelectric
ELF . . . . Electronic Location Finder
ELF . . . . Ellipsometry, Low Field (Microscopy)
ELF . . . . Engine Lube Filter

ELF . . . . Eritrean Liberation Front (Ethiopia)
ELF . . . . European Landworkers Federation
ELF . . . . Explosive-Actuated Light Filter
ELF . . . . Explosive Lens Flashbinder
ELF . . . . Extremely Low Frequency
ELFC . . . . . . Electroluminescent Ferroelectric Cell
ELG . . . . El Paso Natural Gas Company (NYSE symbol)
ELG . . . . Emergency Landing Ground
ELG . . . . European Liaison Group (Army)
EL/G . . . . . . Emergency Landing Ground
ELGMT . . . . . Erector-Launcher, Guided Missile, Transportable
ELH . . . . Enol-Lactone Hydrolase
ELI . . . . Equitable Life Interpreter (Computer)
ELI . . . . Environmental Law Institute
ELI . . . . Extra Low Impurity (Metals)
ELI . . . . Extra-Low-Interstitial (Alloy)
ELIG . . . . . . Eligible
ELIM . . . . . . Eliminate
ELINT . . . . . . Electronic Intelligence
ELIT . . . . Electronics Information Test
ELJ . . . . Executive-Legislative-Judicial
ELL . . . . Equivalent Loudness Level
ELLA . . . . . . European Long Lines Agency (NATO)
ELM . . . . Eastern Atlantic and Mediterranean (Military)
ELM . . . . Element Load Model
ELM . . . . Endings (of nerves) to Lip Muscle
ELM . . . . Extended Lunar Module
ELM . . . . External Limiting Membrane
ELME . . . . . . Emitter Location Method
ELMEX . . . . . Elementos Electronics Mexicanos, SA (Mexico)
ELMINT . . . . Electromagnetic Intelligence
ELMO . . . . . . El Morro National Monument
ELMS . . . . . . Engineering Lunar Model Surface
ELMS . . . . . . Experimental Library Management System
ELMT . . . . . . Electronic Mechanic Technician
ELNA . . . . . . Esperanto League for North America
ELO . . . . Evangelical Literature Overseas
ELOI . . . . . . Emergency Letter of Instructions
ELOISE . . . . . European Large Orbiting Instrumentation for Solar Experiments
ELP . . . . Emulsified Liquid Propellant
ELP . . . . Engine Lube and Purge (System)
ELPE . . . . . . Electroluminescent-Photoelectric
ELPG . . . . . . Electric Light and Power Group
ELPHR . . . . . Experimental Low Temperature Process Heat Reactor
ELQC . . . . . . Electroluminescent Quantum Counter
ELR . . . . Engineering Laboratory Report
ELR . . . . English Literary Renaissance (A publication)
ELRA . . . . . . Electronic RADAR
ELRAC . . . . . Electronic Reconnaissance Accessory Set
ELRDL . . . . . Electronics Research and Development Laboratory
ELRIC . . . . . . Employers Labor Relations Information Committee
ELS . . . . Earth Landing System
ELS . . . . Electric Limit Switch
ELS . . . . Electrical System
ELS . . . . Electronic Specialty Company (NYSE symbol) (Delisted)
ELS . . . . Escanaba & Lake Superior R. R. (AAR code)
ELS . . . . Extra-Long Staple (Cotton)
ELSB . . . . . . Edge Lighted Status Board (Navy)
ELSEC . . . . . Electronic Security (Air Force)
ELSIE . . . . . . Electronic Letter Sorting and Indicator Equipment
ELSIE . . . . . . Emergency Life-Saving Instant Exit (Aircraft) (Air Force)
ELSS . . . . Emergency Life Support System
ELSS . . . . Emplaced Lunar Scientific Station
ELSS . . . . EVA (Extravehicular Activity) Life-Support System (NASA)
ELSSE . . . . . . Electronic Sky Screen Equipment (Air Force)
ELT . . . . Each Less Than
ELT . . . . Electrocardiography and Basal Metabolism Technician (Navy)
ELT . . . . Emergency Locator Transmitter
ELT . . . . English Language Teaching (A publication)
ELTC . . . . . . Enlisted Loss to Commissioned Status (Military)
ELTV . . . . . . Ejection Launch Test Vehicle
ELTW . . . . . . Enlisted Loss to Warrant Status (Military)
ELV . . . . Earth Launch Vehicle
ELV . . . . Extension Lay Volunteers
ELVIS . . . . . . Electroluminescent Vertical Indication System
ELW . . . . Extreme Low Water
ELWAR . . . . . Electronic Warfare
ELZC . . . . . . Emergency Lead-Zinc Committee
EM . . . . E. Merck (Laboratories)
EM . . . . Earl Marshal (British)
EM . . . . Earth Mass

EM . . . . Eastern Megalopolis (Proposed name for possible "super-city" formed by growth and mergers of other cities)
EM . . . . Economical Methods (A line of Varian spectrometers)
EM . . . . Education Manual (Military)
EM . . . . Efficiency Modulation
EM . . . . Electrician's Mate
EM . . . . Electrodeposition Memo
EM . . . . Electromagnetic
EM . . . . Electromechanical
EM . . . . Electromicroscopic
EM . . . . Electro-Motive Corporation
EM . . . . Electron Microprobe
EM . . . . End Matched
EM . . . . End of Medium (Data processing)
EM . . . . Engine Maintenance
EM . . . . Engineer Manager
EM . . . . Engineer of Mines (or Mining)
EM . . . . Engineering Management
EM . . . . Engineering Manual
EM . . . . Engineering Memorandum
EM . . . . English Market
EM . . . . Enlisted Man (or Men)
EM . . . . Episcopus et Martyr (Bishop and Martyr)
EM . . . . Epitaxial Mesa
EM . . . . Equitum Magister (Master of the Horse) (British)
EM . . . . Error Multiplier
EM . . . . Etna & Montrose R. R. (AAR code)
EM . . . . European Movement
EM . . . . Evangelist and Martyr (Church calendars)
EM . . . . Excerpta Medica (A publication)
EM . . . . Expanded Metal
EM . . . . Experimental Memo
EM . . . . External Memorandum
E-M . . . . Etat-Major (Headquarters) (French military)
E/M . . . . Electro-Mechanical (Rotary or linear actuators)
E & M . . . . . . Erection and Maintenance
EMA . . . . Electronic Maintenance Assembly
EMA . . . . Electronic Missile Acquisition
EMA . . . . Electronics Manufacturers Association
EMA . . . . Electronics Materiel Agency (Army)
EMA . . . . Emergency Movements Atomic (Military)
EMA . . . . Employment Management Association
EMA . . . . Engine Manufacturers Association
EMA . . . . Envelope Manufacturers Association
EMA . . . . Ethyl Methacrylate
EMA . . . . European Monetary Agreement
EMA . . . . Evaporated Milk Association
EMA . . . . Exposition Management Association
EMA . . . . Extended Mission Apollo (Aerospace)
EMAC . . . . Electromechanical Averaging Circuit
E-MAD . . . . . . Engine Maintenance and Disassembly (Building)
E-MAD . . . . . . Engineer-Maintenance Assembly-Disassembly (NERVA program)
EMAR . . . . Experimental Memory - Address Register
EMAS . . . . Emergency Message Authentication System (USEUCOM)
EMAS . . . . Employment Medical Advisory Service (Department of Employment) (British)
EMATS . . . . . . Emergency Message Automatic Transmission System (Air Force)
EMATS-AF . . . . Emergency Message Automatic Transmission System - Air Force
EMATS-JCS . . . Emergency Message Automatic Transmission System-Joint Chiefs of Staff
EMB . . . . Early-Make-Break (Data processing)
EMB . . . . Electronic Material Bulletin (Army)
EMB . . . . Embassy
EMB . . . . Engineering in Medicine and Biology
EMB . . . . Eosin-Methylene Blue (Dye combination)
EMB . . . . Experimental Model Basin (Navy)
EMBA . . . . Emba Mink Breeders Association
EMBERS . . . . . . Emergency Bed Request System (Data processing)
EMBO . . . . European Molecular Biology Organization
EMC . . . . Eastern Mennonite College (Virginia)
EMC . . . . Education Media Council
EMC . . . . Electromagnetic Compatibility
EMC . . . . Electromagnetic Cyclotron
EMC . . . . Electronic Material Change
EMC . . . . Electronic Modules Corporation
EMC . . . . Employee-Management Cooperation
EMC . . . . Encephalomyocarditis
EMC . . . . Engineer Maintenance Center
EMC . . . . Engineer Maintenance Control (Army)
EMC . . . . Engineered Military Circuit (Leased long lines established in continental US) (Military)
EMC . . . . Engineering Manpower Commission

EMC . . . . Entreprise Miniere et Chimique (France)
EMC . . . . Etched Metal Circuit
EMC . . . . Eye-Motion Camera
EMCB . . . . Electrician's Mate, Construction Battalion (Navy rating)
EMCBC . . . . . . Electrician's Mate, Construction Battalion, Communications (Navy rating)
EMCBD . . . . . . Electrician's Mate, Construction Battalion, Draftsman (Navy rating)
EMCBG . . . . . . Electrician's Mate, Construction Battalion, General (Navy rating)
EMCBL . . . . . . Electrician's Mate, Construction Battalion, Line and Station (Navy rating)
EMCC . . . . European Municipal Credit Community
EMCCC . . . . . . European Military Communications Co-ordinating Committee (NATO)
EMCCS . . . . . . Emergency Medical Command and Communications System
EMCE . . . . Eastern Montana College of Education
EMCEE . . . . . . Master of Ceremonies (Slang)
EMCON . . . . . Electron Microscopy Congress
EMCON . . . . . Emission Control
EMCP . . . . Electromagnetic Compatibility Program
EMCV . . . . Encephalomyocarditis Virus
EMD . . . . Electric-Motor-Driven
EMD . . . . Electro-Motive Division (General Motors Corporation)
EMD . . . . European Market Development
EMD . . . . Eye Movement Device
EMDI . . . . Energy Management Display Indicator
EMDI . . . . Engineering Manufacturing Division Instruction
EMDP . . . . Electromotive Difference of Potential
EMDS . . . . Electromechanical Development Section
EME . . . . Earth-Mars-Earth
EME . . . . Electromagnetic Environment
EME . . . . Environmental Measurements Experiment
E in ME . . . . . Engineer in Mechanical Engineering
EMEA . . . . Electronic Maintenance Engineering Association
EMEB . . . . East Midlands Electricity Board (British)
EMEC . . . . Electronics Maintenance Engineering Center (Navy)
EMEG . . . . Electromagnetic Environment Generator
EMEM . . . . Eagle's Minimum Essential Medium (Culture medium)
EMERGCONS . . Emergency Conditions (Military)
E Met . . . . Engineer of Metallurgy
EMETF . . . . . . Electromagnetic Environment Test Facility (Army)
EMF . . . . Electromotive Force
EMF . . . . Erythrocyte Maturation Factor (Physiology)
EMF . . . . European Motel Federation
EMF . . . . Every Morning Fixum (An old car) (Slang)
EMF . . . . Excerpta Medica Foundation
EMF . . . . Explosive Metal Forming
EMFF . . . . Electromagnetic Form Factor
EMFM . . . . Electromagnetic Flowmeter
EMG . . . . Electromagnetic Gyro
EMG . . . . Electromyogram
EMG . . . . Electromyographic
EMG . . . . Equipment Management Group
EMG . . . . Executive Mansion and Grounds (i.e., the White House and its grounds) (Executive Office of the President)
EMG . . . . Eye Movement Gauge
EM in Geol . . . Mining Engineer in Geology
EMH . . . . Educable Mentally Handicapped
EMH . . . . Emhart Corporation (NYSE symbol)
EMI . . . . Electromagnetic Interference
EMI . . . . Electronic Maintenance Inspector
EMI . . . . Electronic Memories, Incorporated
EMI . . . . EMI, Ltd. (Formerly, Electric & Musical Industries, Inc.) (NYSE symbol)
EMIC . . . . Emergency Maternity and Infant Care
EMIDEC . . . . . EMI (Electric and Musical Industries, Ltd.) Data Electronic Computer (Made by EMI Industries - Great Britain)
EMIE . . . . Educational Media Institutes Evaluation (Project)
EMIS . . . . Ecosystem of Machines Information System
EMIS . . . . Educational Management Information System
EMIS . . . . Electromagnetic Intelligence Systems
EMIS . . . . Extension Management Information System (Department of Agriculture)
EMISEC . . . . . . Emission Security
EMISS . . . . Electromolecular Instrument Space Simulator
EMIT . . . . Electromagnetic Interference Testing
EMIT . . . . Engineering Management Information Technique
EMJ . . . . Engineering & Mining Journal
EMJC . . . . East Mississippi Junior College
EMK . . . . Edward Moore Kennedy
EMK . . . . Electrical Meter Kit
EMK . . . . Electro-Motorische Kraft (Electromotive Force) (German)
EML . . . . Empire Lines, Inc.
EML . . . . Engineering Materials List (AEC)
EML . . . . Equipment Maintainance Log (Army)
EML . . . . Equipment Modification List

EML . . . . Experimental Meteorology Laboratory
EMLA . . . . Electromechanical Linear Actuator
EMM . . . . Electronic Memories & Magnetics Corp. (NYSE symbol)
EMM . . . . Emhart Manufacturing Company (NYSE symbol) (Later, EMH)
EMM . . . . Engineering Management Manual
EMMA . . . . Expeditious Monitor and Maintenance Analyst (Computer) (NASA)
EMMA . . . . Eye-Movement Measuring Apparatus
EMMCC . . . . . . Erection Mechanism Motor Control Center
EMO . . . . Embarkation Medical Official (British)
EMO . . . . Emergency Measures Organization (Canada)
EMO . . . . Environmental Medicine Officer (Military)
EMOS . . . . Earth Mean Orbital Speed (Aerospace)
EMOS . . . . Entry Military Occupational Specialty
EMP . . . . Electromagnetic Pulse
EMP . . . . Electromechanical Power
EMP . . . . Electromolecular Propulsion (Electrochemistry)
EMP . . . . Electron Microprobe
EMP . . . . Embden-Meyerhof-Parnas (Pathway) (Biochemistry)
EMP . . . . End of Month Payment
EMP . . . . Engineering Modification Proposal
EMPC . . . . Educational Materials Producers Council (National Audio-Visual Association)
EMPIRE . . . . . . Early Manned Planetary-Interplanetary Round Trip Experiment
EMPIRE . . . . . . Early Manned Planetary Interruptionless Reconnaissance Expedition
EMPT . . . . Electronic Maintenance Proficiency Test
EMQ . . . . Electromagnetic Quiet
EMR . . . . Eastern and Midlands Railway (British)
EMR . . . . Educable Mentally Retardate (or Retarded)
EMR . . . . Electromagnetic Radiation
EMR . . . . Electro-Mechanical Research, Inc.
EMR . . . . Electronic Moisture Recorder
EMR . . . . Emerson Electric Company (NYSE symbol)
EMR . . . . Engineering Malfunction Report
EMR . . . . Enlisted Manning Report (Air Force)
EMR . . . . Equipment Maintenance Record (Army)
EMR . . . . Executive Management Responsibility (Military)
EMR . . . . Executive Management Review
EMRG . . . . Electromagnetic Radiation Generator
EMRIC . . . . Educational Media Research Information Center
EMS . . . . Electromagnetic Submarine (Navy)
EMS . . . . Electromagnetic Surveillance (Air Force)
EMS . . . . Electromyosignal (Data processing)
EMS . . . . Electron Multiplex Switch
EMS . . . . Electronic Management System
EMS . . . . Electronic Medical System
EMS . . . . Emergency Medical Service
EMS . . . . Emergency Mission Support (Air Force)
EMS . . . . Emission Spectrograph
EMS . . . . Engine Management System (Army)
EMS . . . . Engineering Master Schedule
EMS . . . . Ente Minerario Siciliano
EMS . . . . Entry Monitor System (NASA)
EMS . . . . Environmental Mutagen Society
EMS . . . . Ethyl Methanesulfonate (Chemical mutagen)
EMS . . . . Experimental Monitoring Satellite
EMS . . . . Export Marketing Service (Department of Agriculture)
EMSA . . . . Electron Microscopy (formerly, Microscope) Society of America
EMSA . . . . Electronics Materiel Support Agency (Army)
EMSC . . . . Educational Media Selection Center (National Book Committee)
EMSC . . . . Electromechanical Stop Clock
EMSD . . . . Equipment Major Subdivision
EMSI . . . . Equipes Medico-Sociales Itinerantes
EMSKED . . . . . . Employment Schedule
EMSL . . . . Electronic Material Sciences Laboratory
EMSN . . . . External-Mix Spray Nut
EMSO . . . . Education Society
EMSO . . . . Electronic Memory Systems Organization (Burroughs Corporation)
EMSO . . . . European Mobility Service Office (Army)
EMSR . . . . Electrician's Mate, Ship Repair (Navy rating)
EMSR . . . . Electronic Material Shipment Request (Navy)
EMSRG . . . . . . Electrician's Mate, Ship Repair, General Electrician (Navy rating)
EMSRS . . . . . . Electrician's Mate, Ship Repair, Shop Electrician (Navy rating)
EMSRT . . . . . . Electrician's Mate, Ship Repair, I.C. Repairman (Navy rating)
EMSS . . . . Emergency Mission Support System
EMSS . . . . Experimental Manned Space Station (Air Force)
EMSTRP . . . . . . Equipment Management System Training Requirements Program (Navy)
EMSU . . . . Environmental Meteorological Support Unit (National Weather Service)
EMT . . . . Each More Than
EMT . . . . Early Missile Test
EMT . . . . Elapsed Maintenance Time
EMT . . . . Electrical Mechanical Tubing

EMT . . . . Electrical Metallic Tubing
EMT . . . . Electrician's Mate, Telephone (Coast Guard rating)
EMT . . . . Electronic Maintenance Technician (FAA)
EMT . . . . Electronic Mind Tester
EMT . . . . Elemental Method of Training
EMT . . . . Embalmer (Navy rating)
EMT . . . . Emergency Medical Tag
EMT . . . . Emergency Medical Technician - Ambulance
EMT . . . . Emergency Medical Treatment (Military)
EMT . . . . Engineering Model Transport
EMTECH . . . . . Electromagnetic Technology
EMTF . . . . Estimated Mean Time to Failure
EMTI . . . . Edge Mounted Threaded Inserts
EMTR . . . . Enlisted Master Tape Record (Army)
EMTTF . . . . . . Equivalent Mean Time to Failure
EMU . . . . Eastern Michigan University
EMU . . . . Electromagnetic Unit(s)
EMU . . . . European Mineworkers' Union (Zambia)
EMU . . . . Extravehicular Mobility Unit (Spacesuit)
EMV . . . . Egress Maintenance Vehicle
eMv . . . . Electron Megavolt
EMW . . . . Electrical Megawatt
EMW . . . . Electromagnetic Wave
EMW . . . . Electromagnetic Window
EMWF . . . . . . Electromagnetic Wave Form
EMX . . . . Electron Microprobe X-Ray Analyzer (ARL)
EMXA . . . . Electron Microprobe X-Ray Analyzer
EN . . . . Electronics News
EN . . . . Engineering Note
EN . . . . Engineman (Navy rating)
EN . . . . Esquimalt & Nanaimo Railway (AAR code)
EN . . . . Exception Noted
ENA . . . . Ecole Nationale d'Administration (France)
ENA . . . . English Newspaper Association
ENABLE . . . . . Education and Neighborhood Action for Better Living Environment
ENACT . . . . . . Environmental Action for Survival (An organization)
ENAL . . . . Ente Nazionale Assistenza Lavoratori (Italy)
ENC . . . . Eastern Nazarene College (Massachusetts)
ENC . . . . Electroencephalography Technician (Navy)
ENC . . . . Enlistment Cancelled
ENCA . . . . European Naval Communications Agency (NATO)
ENCAR . . . . . . Enclosed Cryocondenser for Air Recovery
ENCAT . . . . . . Ente Nazionale Consulenza Assistenza Tecnica
ENCMP . . . . . . Economists' National Committee on Monetary Policy
ENCO . . . . Energy Company (Slogan and brand name used by Humble Oil & Refining Company) (Later, Exxon)
ENCOM . . . . . United States Army Chemical Corps Engineering Command
END . . . . Earth Net Dial
END . . . . Electronic Null Detector
END . . . . Exaltation Newcastle Disease
ENDC . . . . Eighteen-Nation Disarmament Committee (or Conference) (Convened March 14, 1962; actually attended by 17 nations, with France absent) (Later, CCD)
ENDE . . . . Empresas Nacionales de Energia (Argentina)
ENDF . . . . Evaluated Nuclear Data File (AEC)
ENDOR . . . . . . Electron-Nuclear Double Resonance
ENDS . . . . European Nuclear Documentation System
ENE . . . . East-Northeast
ENEA . . . . European Nuclear Energy Agency
ENEL . . . . Ente Nazionale per l'Energia Elettrica (Italian National Electric Energy Agency)
ENEP . . . . Expanded Nutrition Education Program (New York State Cooperative Extension Service)
ENG . . . . Electronystagmography
ENG . . . . Engelhard Minerals and Chemical Corp. (NYSE symbol)
ENG . . . . Engine
ENG . . . . Engineer(ing)
ENG . . . . England (or English)
ENGBAT . . . . . Engineer Battalion (Army)
ENGCOMDC . . Engineer Commissioner, District of Columbia (Military)
Eng D . . . . Doctor of Engineering
ENGID . . . . . . Engine Identification Report (Air Force)
ENGR . . . . Engineer
Engr D . . . . . . Doctor of Engineering
ENGRG . . . . . Engineering
Eng Sc D . . . . . Doctor of Engineering Science
ENGSTAT . . . . Engine Status Report (Air Force)
ENI . . . . Ente Nazionale Idrocarburi (National Hydrocarbons Authority) (State-owned oil agency) (Italy)
ENIAC . . . . . . Electronic Numerical Integrator and Calculator
ENIG . . . . Electronic Nuclear Instrumentation Group

ENIT . . . . Ente Nazionale Italiano per il Turismo (Italy)
ENJC . . . . Ecole Normale Jacques Cartier
ENL . . . . Enlistment
ENL . . . . Equivalent Noise Level
ENMISA . . . . . Empresa Nacional Mineral del Sahara (Corporation owned by the Spanish government)
ENML . . . . End Mill
ENMU . . . . . . Eastern New Mexico University
ENORS . . . . . . Engine Not Operationally Ready – Supply (Air Force)
ENP . . . . Electroless Nickel Plating
ENR . . . . Equivalent Noise Ratio
ENR . . . . Excess Noise Ratio
ENRFOSCOMD . . En Route This Station from Oversea Command
ENRT . . . . En Route
ENS . . . . Ecole Normale Superieure (French teacher-training institution)
ENS . . . . Extended Nylon Shaft
ENSA . . . . . . Entertainments National Service Association (For British military forces)
ENSI . . . . Energia Nucleare Sud Italia (Italian nuclear power plant project)
ENSI . . . . Equivalent-Noise-Sideband Input
ENSP . . . . Engineering Specification (Air Force)
ENSURE . . . . . Expedited Non-Standard Urgent Requirements for Equipment (Army)
ENT . . . . Ears, Nose, and Throat
ENT . . . . Emergency Negative Thrust
ENT . . . . Equivalent Noise Temperature
ENTAC . . . . . . Engin Teleguide Anti-char (Antitank missile) (French)
ENTAC . . . . . . Entrance National Agency Check
ENV . . . . Equivalent Noise Voltage
ENV . . . . Erdbeernekrosevirus
ENVANAL . . . . Environmental Analysis (Program)
ENVMT . . . . . Environment(al)
ENW . . . . Effects of Nuclear Weapons (AEC-DOD book)
ENW . . . . Elgin National Industries, Inc. (Formerly, Elgin National Watch Co.) (NYSE symbol)
ENX . . . . Eaton Manufacturing Company (NYSE symbol) (Later, ETN)
EO . . . . Easter Offerings (to a church)
EO . . . . Education Officer (Military)
EO . . . . Electro-Optical
EO . . . . Engine Oil
EO . . . . Engineering Order
EO . . . . Entertainments Officer (British military)
EO . . . . Equal Opportunity (HUD)
EO . . . . Equipment Operator (Navy rating)
EO . . . . Errors and Omissions
EO . . . . Ethylene Oxide
EO . . . . Ex Officio
EO . . . . Executive Officer
EO . . . . Executive Order (Rule or regulation having the force of law, issued by the President with congressional authorization)
EO . . . . Exhaust Opens (Valve position)
EO . . . . Experimental Officer (Ministry of Agriculture, Fisheries, and Food) (Also, ExO and XO) (British)
EO . . . . Explosive Ordnance
E/O . . . . Engineering Opportunities (A journal)
EOA . . . . Economic Opportunity Act
EOA . . . . Effective On or About
EOA . . . . End of Address
EOA . . . . Epithelioma Mammaire (Epithelioma of the Breast) (Medicine)
EOA . . . . Essential Oil Association
EOA . . . . . . Examination, Opinion, and Advice (Medicine)
EOAR . . . . . . European Office of Aerospace Research (Air Force)
EOARDC . . . . . European Office Air Research and Development Command
EOB . . . . Educational Opportunity Bank
EOB . . . . Electronic Order of Battle
EOB . . . . End of Block
EOB . . . . End of Bombardment
EOB . . . . Enemy Order of Battle
EOB . . . . Executive Office Building (Washington, DC)
EOB . . . . Expense Operating Budget
EOC . . . . Eastern Oregon College
EOC . . . . Electronic Operations Center (Military)
EOC . . . . Emergency Operating Center (Civil Defense)
EOC . . . . End of Construction
EOC . . . . End of Course
EOC . . . . Enemy Oil Committee (US)
EOC . . . . Equipment Operational Control
EOC . . . . Erbium Oxide Crystal
EOC . . . . Error of Closure
EOC . . . . Ethylene Oxide Cycle
EOC . . . . Executive Officers Council
EOC . . . . Experimental Operations Center
EOCI . . . . Electric Overhead Crane Institute

EOCP . . . . . . Engine Out of Commission for Parts
EOCR . . . . Experimental Organic Cooled Reactor (AEC)
EOD . . . . Date of Entering Office
EOD . . . . Electro-Optic Display
EOD . . . . End of Date
EOD . . . . End of Day
EOD . . . . Entrance on Duty (Military)
EOD . . . . Ethylene Oxide Decontamination
EOD . . . . Every Other Day (Advertising)
EOD . . . . Explosive, Ordnance, and Demolition
EOD . . . . Explosive Ordnance Device
EOD . . . . Explosive Ordnance Disposal
EODB . . . . Explosive Ordnance Disposal Bulletin
EODC . . . . . . Explosive Ordnance Disposal Control (Army)
EODP . . . . Engineering Order Delayed for Parts
EODTC . . . . . . Electro-Optic Display Test Chamber
EOE . . . . Earth Orbit Ejection
EOE . . . . Earth Orbit Equipment
EOE . . . . Enemy Occupied Europe (World War II)
EOE . . . . Errors and Omissions Excepted
E and OE . . . . Errors and Omissions Excepted
EOED . . . . Earth Orbit Escape Device
EOEM . . . . Electronic Original Equipment Market
EOF . . . . Electro-Optic Force
EOF . . . . End of File (Data processing)
EOF . . . . Expected Operations Forecast (Aviation)
EOG . . . . Educational Opportunity Grant
EOG . . . . Effect on Guarantees
EOG . . . . Electrooculogram
EOG . . . . Electroolfactogram
EOGO . . . . . . Elliptical Orbiting Geological Observatory
EOGS . . . . . . Electrooptical Guidance Section
EOH . . . . Emergency Operation Headquarters (Army)
EOHP . . . . . . Except as Otherwise Herein Provided
EOJ . . . . End of Job
EOKA . . . . . . Ethnike Organosis Kypriakou Agonos (Greece)
EOL . . . . Economic Opportunity Act Loan
EOL . . . . End of Life
EOL . . . . End of Line (Communications)
EOLM . . . . . . Electro-Optical Light Modulator
EOLT . . . . End of Logic Tape
EOLV . . . . . . Electro-Optic Light Valve
EOM . . . . Earth Orbit Mission
EOM . . . . Electro-Optical Modulator
EOM . . . . End of Message
EOM . . . . End of Month
EOM . . . . Extra-Ocular Movements
EOP . . . . Electronic Overload Protection
EOP . . . . Electro-Optic Projector
EOP . . . . Emergency Operations Plan (Civil Defense)
EOP . . . . End of Part
EOP . . . . End of Program (Data processing)
EOP . . . . Engineering Operating Procedure
EOP . . . . Executive Office of the President
EOPF . . . . . . Extraoptic Photoreceptors
EOPF . . . . . . End of Powered Flight
EOQ . . . . Economic Order Quantity
EOQ . . . . End of Quarter
EOQC . . . . . . European Organization for Quality Control
EOR . . . . Earth Orbit Rendezvous (NASA)
EOR . . . . Electro-Optical Research
EOR . . . . End of Reel
EOR . . . . Explosive Ordnance Reconnaissance
EORA . . . . . . Explosive Ordnance Reconnaissance Agent (Army)
EORBS . . . . . . Earth Orbiting Recoverable Biological Satellite
EORC . . . . . . Emergency Operations Research Center
EORL . . . . . . Emergency Officers' Retired List (Army)
EORSA . . . . . . Episcopalians and Others for Responsible Social Action
EOS . . . . Earth Orbiting Shuttle (NASA)
EOS . . . . Edison Brothers Stores, Inc. (NYSE symbol)
EOS . . . . Electro-Optical Systems, Inc. (Subsidiary of Xerox Corporation)
EOS . . . . Eligible for Overseas Service
EOS . . . . Emergency Operations System
EOS . . . . Equation of State
EOSD . . . . . . Equipment on Station Date (Army)
EOSO . . . . . . Escort Oilers Supervising Officer
EOSP . . . . . . Economic Order and Stockage Procedure
EOSS . . . . . . Earth Orbital Space Station
EOST . . . . . . Emergency Operations Simulation Techniques (Civil Defense)
EOT . . . . End of Tape
EOT . . . . End-of-Transmission

EOTC	Electro-Optic Test Chamber
EOTD	Electro-Optical Tracking Device
EOTS	Electro-Optical Tracking System
EOU	Enemy Objective Unit (of US) (in London)
EOV	Electrically Operated Valve
EOW	Engineering Order Worksheet
EOWS	Electro-Optical Weapons System
EP	Eastward Position
EP	Electric Primer
EP	Electrical Panel
EP	Electrically Polarized (Relay)
EP	Electron Photon
EP	Electronic Package
EP	Electroplate
EP	Electro-Pneumatic
EP	Electrostatic Powder
EP	Elongated Punch
EP	En Passant (In passing) (Chess)
EP	En Route Penetration (Aviation)
EP	End Point (Distilling)
EP	End of Program
EP	Engineer Personnel (Marine Corps)
EP	Engineering Paper
EP	Engineering Practice
EP	Engineering Project
EP	Entrucking Point (Military)
EP	Enzyme Presoak (for laundry)
EP	Estimated Position (Navigation)
EP	Etched Plate
EP	Evening Prayer
EP	Evoked Potential
EP	Excess Profits
EP	An Experienced Playgoer (Theatrical)
EP	Explosion-Proof
EP	Extended Play
EP	External Pressure
EP	External Publication
E-P	Extreme Pressure
E/P	End-Paper (Bibliography)
E & P	Editor & Publisher (A publication)
E & P	Extraordinary and Plenipotentiary
EPA	Eastern Provincial Airways (Labrador)
EPA	Eastern Psychological Association
EPA	Eire Philatelic Association
EPA	Electron Probe Analyzer
EPA	Emergency Powers Act (British) (World War II)
EPA	Employee Plan Administrators
EPA	Environmental Protection Agency (Government agency formed in 1970)
EPA	European Productivity Agency
EPA	Evangelical Press Association
EPA	Exoatmospheric Penetration Aid
EPA	Export Pound Account (Special type of currency) (United Arab Republic)
EPAA	Educational Press Association of America (Later, EDPRESS)
EPAA	Employing Printers Association of America
EPAM	Elementary Perceiver and Memorizer
EPANY	Export Packers Association of New York
EPB	Engineering Process Bulletin
EPB	Erie & Pittsburgh R.R. Company (NYSE symbol) (Delisted)
EPB	External Proton Beam
EPBX	Electronic Private Branch Exchange
EPC	Eastern Pilgrim College (Pennsylvania)
EPC	Easy Processing Channel
EPC	Economic Policy Committee (OECD)
EPC	Editor's Presentation Copy
EPC	Educational Policies Commission
EPC	Electronic Program Control
EPC	Elementary Processing Centers
EPC	End Products Committee (of WPB) (World War II)
EPC	Engineering Part Card
EPC	Equipotential Cathode
EPCCS	Emergency Positive Control Communications System
EPCO	Engine Parts Coordinating Office (Navy)
EPCO	Engineer Procurement Office (Army)
EPCOT	Experimental Prototype Community of Tomorrow
EPD	Earliest Possible (or Practicable) Date
EPD	Eastern Procurement Division (Navy)
EPD	Eastern Production District (Navy)
EPD	Electric Power Distribution
EPD	Electronic Products Department
EPD	Enlisted Personnel Directorate (Army)
EPD	Enlisted Personnel Division (Navy)

EPD	Excess Profits Duty
EPD	Extra Police Duty (Extra cleaning chores) (Military)
EPDA	Educational Professional Development Assistance (Office of Education)
EPDA	Emergency Powers Defence Act (British) (World War II)
EPDA	Exhibit Producers and Designers Association
EPDC	Economic Power Dispatch Computer
EPDCC	Elementary Potential Digital Computing Component
EPDM	Ethylene-Propylene Diene Monomer
EPDO	Enlisted Personnel Distribution Office (Navy)
EPDOCONUS . .	Enlisted Personnel Distribution Office, Continental United States
EPDS	Electronic Parts Distributors' Show
EPE	Editorial Projects for Education
EPE	Electrostatic Probe Experiment
EPE	Emergency Passenger Exit
EPE	Energetic Particles Explorer (Satellite) (NASA)
EPE	Experimental and Proving Establishment (Canada)
EPE	Explosion-Proof Enclosure
EPEA	Experiment Pointing Electronic Assembly (NASA)
EPEAA	Employing Photo-Engravers Association of America
EPEC	Electric Programmer Evaluator Controller
EPEC	Emerson Programmer – Evaluator – Controller
EPEM	Electronic Parts and Equipment Manufacturers Association
EPF	Emergency Plant Facilities
EPF	Episcopal Pacifist Fellowship
EPF	Exophthalmos-Producing Factor (Endocrinology)
EPFL	East Pakistan Federation of Labor
EPG	Eggs Per Gram (Parasitology)
EPG	Electrolytic Plunge Grinder
EPG	Electronic Proving Ground (Army)
EPG	Electrostatic Power Generator
EPG	Emergency Power Generator
EPG	Eniwetok Proving Ground (AEC)
EPG	European Press Group
EPGA	Emergency Petroleum and Gas Administration (Department of the Interior)
EPGCR	Experimental Prototype Gas-Cooled Reactor
EPH	Electronic Package Housing
EPH	Explosion-Proof Housing
EPI	Eagle-Picher Industries, Inc. (NYSE symbol)
EPI	Earth Path Indicator
EPI	Ehrenreich Photo-Optical Industries, Inc.
EPI	Electronic Position Indicator
EPI	Elevation Position Indicator (Aviation)
EPI	Emergency Public Information (Civil Defense)
EPI	Engine Performance Indicator
EPI	Expanded Position Indicator
EPIC	Earth-Pointing Instrument Carrier (A satellite)
EPIC	Electric Properties Information Center
EPIC	Electronic Photochromic Integrating Cathode-Ray (Tube)
EPIC	End Poverty in California (Slogan used by Upton Sinclair during campaign as Democratic candidate for governor of California, 1934)
EPIC	Engineers Public Information Council
EPIC	Epitaxial Passivated Integrated Circuits
EPIC	Evaluator Programmer Integrated Circuit (NASA)
EPIC	Extended Performance & Increased Capability
EPIE	Educational Products Information Exchange
EPIREPT	Epidemiological Report
EPK	Equipotential Kathode
EPL	Early Programming Language (Data processing)
EPL	Elliptically Polarized Light
EPL	Excess Profits Levy (British)
EPLA	Electronics Precedence List Agency
EPM	Earth-Probe-Mars (NASA)
EPM	Educator's Purchasing Master (A publication)
EPM	Elastic Plastic Membrane
EPM	Electron Probe Microanalysis
EPM	Electronic Parts Manual
EPM	Engineering Procedures Manual
EPMA	Electronic Parts Manufacturers Association
EPMS	Engine Performance Monitoring System
EPMS	Engineering Project Management System
EPN	Effective Perceived Noise
EPNdB	Effective-Perceived-Noise Decibel Level (Aviation)
EPNG	El Paso Natural Gas Co.
EPNL	Effective Perceived Noise Level
EPNS	Electroplated Nickel Silver
EPO	Earth Parking Orbit (Apollo) (NASA)
EPO	Ekco Products Company (NYSE symbol) (Delisted)
EPO	Electrostatic Plasma Oscillator
EPO	European Patents Organization (Munich, West Germany)
EPO	Examination Procedure Outline (Weighing equipment)

EPO . . . . Experiment Performance Option
EPOC . . . . . . Eastern Pacific Oceanic Conference
EPOC . . . . . . Engineers Procurement Office, Chicago
EPOE . . . . End Piece of Equipment
EPOI . . . . Ehrenreich Photo-Optical Industries, Inc.
EPOMA . . . . . . Explosive and Pyrotechnic Ordnance Manufacturing Association
EPP . . . . Earth Physics Program
EPP . . . . Effective Program Projections
EPP . . . . Emergency Powder Package
EPP . . . . End Plate Potential
EPP . . . . Equipment Procurement Program
EPP . . . . Estimating Price Policy
EPPA . . . . . . Established Pattern of Psychodynamic Adaptation
EPPI . . . . Eastern Pennsylvania Psychiatric Institute
EPPI . . . . Electronic Programmed Procurement Information
EPPO . . . . . . European and Mediterranean Plant Protection Organization
EPPP . . . . Emergency Production Planning Program (Navy)
EPPS . . . . Edwards Personal Preference Scale (or Schedule) (Marketing)
EPPVS . . . . . . Emergency Propulsive Propellant Venting System
EPR . . . . Electron Paramagnetic Resonance
EPR . . . . Electronic Parts Reliability
EPR . . . . Electrophrenic Respiration (Medicine)
EPR . . . . Engine-Pressure Ratio
EPR . . . . Engineer Photographic and Reproduction (Marine Corps)
EPR . . . . Equipotential Region
EPR . . . . Ethylene Propylene Rubber
EPR . . . . Exhaust Pressure Ratio
EPR . . . . Explosion-Proof Relay
EPR . . . . Eye Point of Regard (NASA)
EPRA . . . . . . Eastern Psychiatric Research Association
EPRA . . . . . . Electronic Production Resources Agency (Military)
EPRD . . . . . . Electrical Power Requirements Data
EPRD . . . . . . Emergency Plans and Readiness Division (of OEP)
EPR/G . . . . . . End-Paper Rubbed, Else Good (Condition) (Antiquarian book trade)
EPS . . . . Earnings Per Share (Finance)
EPS . . . . El Paso Southern Railway Company (AAR code)
EPS . . . . Elastosis Perforans Serpiginosa (Medicine)
EPS . . . . Electric Propulsion System
EPS . . . . Electrical Power Subsystem
EPS . . . . Electrical Power Supply
EPS . . . . Embossing Press Station
EPS . . . . Emergency Power Supply
EPS . . . . Emergency Pressurization System
EPS . . . . Emergency Procurement Service
EPS . . . . Encoder Power Supply
EPS . . . . Engineering (or Engineered) Performance Standards
EPS . . . . Engineering Print System (Xerox)
EPS . . . . Engineering Procedures Services
EPS . . . . Engineering Purchase Specification
EPS . . . . Environmental Purification Systems, Inc.
EPS . . . . Equipment Policy Statement (Army)
EPS . . . . Equipotential Surface
EPS . . . . Equivalent Prior Sample (Information) (Statistics)
EPS . . . . European Physical Society
EPS . . . . Excitation Power Supply
EPS . . . . Executive Protection Service (Formerly, White House Police)
EPS . . . . Exophthalmos-Producing Substance (Endocrinology)
EPS . . . . Experiment Pointing System
EPS . . . . Experimental Procurement Service
EPS . . . . Eye Protection Shutter
EPSA . . . . . . Electrostatic Particle Size Analyzer
EPSC . . . . . . Emergency Petroleum Supply Committee
EPSI . . . . Earnings Per Share Issued (Finance)
EPSL . . . . Eastern Primary Standards Laboratory
EPSOC . . . . . . Earth-Physics Satellite Observation Campaign (Smithsonian Astrophysical Observatory)
EPSP . . . . . . Excitatory Postsynaptic Potential (Physiology)
EPST . . . . Encyclopedia of Polymer Science & Technology
EPT . . . . Economic Power Transmission
EPT . . . . Electrostatic Printing Tube
EPT . . . . Ethylene Propylene Terpolymer
EPT . . . . Excess Profits Tax
EPT . . . . External Pipe Thread (Technical drawings)
EPTA . . . . . . Expanded Program of Technical Assistance (UN)
EPTE . . . . . . Existed Prior to Enlistment (Especially, dependency)
EPTE . . . . . . Existed Prior to Entry
EPTI . . . . Existed Prior to Induction (Especially, dependency or physical defect)
EPTO . . . . . . Engineer Packaging Technical Office (Merged with General Equipment Command)
EPTS . . . . . . Existed Prior to Entry Service
EPU . . . . Electrical Power Unit

EPU . . . . Emergency Power Unit
EPU . . . . European Payments Union
EPUT . . . . . . Events Per Unit Time
EPV . . . . Electric Polarization Vector
EPV . . . . Electro-Pneumatic Valve
EPV . . . . External Pressure Vessel
EPVS . . . . . . Emergency Propellant Venting System
EPW . . . . Electric Pressure Wave
EPW . . . . Elliptically Polarized Wave
EPW . . . . Enemy Prisoner of War (Army)
EPWIB . . . . . . Enemy Prisoner of War Information Bureau
EPWIB(Br) . . . . Enemy Prisoner of War Information Bureau (Branch)
EPWS . . . . . . Emergency Production Weapons Schedule (Navy)
EQ . . . . Educational Quotient (Psychology)
EQ . . . . Encephalization Quotient
EQ . . . . Environmental Quality
EQ . . . . Equitable Life Mortgage & Realty Investors (NYSE symbol)
EQ . . . . Ethnic Quotient
EQA . . . . Equipment Quality Analysis
EQC . . . . Environmental Quality Control
EQC . . . . Externally-Quenched Counter
EQCC . . . . . . Entry Query Control Console
EQF . . . . Elswick Quick-Firing Gun
EQF . . . . Equity Funding Corp. of America (NYSE symbol)
EQK . . . . Equimark Corp. (NYSE symbol)
EQL . . . . Expected Quality Level
EQM . . . . Environmental Quality Magazine
EQMM . . . . . . Ellery Queen's Mystery Magazine
EQQ . . . . Electric Quadrupole-Quadrupole
EQS . . . . Equatorial Scatter
EQT . . . . Environmental Qualification Test
EQT . . . . Equation of Time (Navigation)
EQT . . . . Equitable Gas Company (NYSE symbol)
EQUIV . . . . . . Equivalent
ER . . . . The Earlham Review (A publication)
ER . . . . Earned Run (Baseball)
ER . . . . Earth Radii
ER . . . . Echo Ranging
ER . . . . Educational Ratio
ER . . . . Edwardus Rex (King Edward)
ER . . . . Effectiveness Report (Military)
ER . . . . Electronic Reconnaissance
ER . . . . Elizabetha Regina (Queen Elizabeth)
ER . . . . Emergency Request
ER . . . . Emergency Rescue
ER . . . . Emergency Room (Medicine)
ER . . . . Endoplasmic Reticulum (Cytology)
ER . . . . Engine Room (Force)
ER . . . . Engineering Release
ER . . . . Engineering Report
ER . . . . Environmental Resistance (Ecology)
ER . . . . Equipment Requirement
Er . . . . Erbium (Chemical element)
ER . . . . Error Relay
ER . . . . Equivalent Roentgen
ER . . . . Evaluation Report
ER . . . . Executive Reserve
ER . . . . Expert Rifleman
ER . . . . Explosives Report
ER . . . . Extended Range
ER . . . . Extended Release (Pharmacy)
ER . . . . External Report
ER . . . . External Resistance (Physics)
E/R . . . . En Route
E & R . . . . . . Engineering and Repair (Department) (Navy)
ERA . . . . Earned Run Average (of a baseball pitcher)
ERA . . . . Education & Religious Affairs (US Military Government, Germany)
ERA . . . . Electric Railroaders Association
ERA . . . . Electrical Research Association (British)
ERA . . . . Electron Ring Accelerator
ERA . . . . Electronic Reading Automation (Information retrieval)
ERA . . . . Electronic Replaceable Assembly
ERA . . . . Electronic Representatives Association
ERA . . . . Electronic Research Association (British)
ERA . . . . Emergency Relief Administration
ERA . . . . Engineering Release Authorization
ERA . . . . Engineering Research Associates
ERA . . . . Enzyme Rate Analyzer
ERA . . . . Equitable Reserve Association
ERA . . . . European Research Associates
ERAA . . . . . . Equipment Review and Authorization Activity (Military)

ERAC . . . . Electromagnetic Radiation Advisory Council
ERAC . . . . Electronic Random Action Control
ERAD . . . . En Route Radial (Aviation)
ERAN . . . . . . Examine and Repair As Necessary
ERAP . . . . Entreprise de Recherches et d'Activites Petrolieres (State-owned petroleum agency) (France)
ERAS . . . . Electronic Reconnaissance Access Set
ERASER . . . . . Elevated Radiation Seeking Rocket
ERB . . . . Earth Radiation Budget (NASA)
ERB . . . . Edgar Rice Burroughs (1875-1950) (Author of Tarzan books)
ERB . . . . Educational Records Bureau
ERB . . . . Equipment Review Board
ERB-dom . . . . . Edgar Rice Burroughs Domain (as in organization, Friends of ERB-dom)
ERBM . . . . Extended-Range Ballistic Missile
ERBOL . . . . . Escuelas Radiofonicas de Bolivia
ERC . . . . Earth Rate Compensation
ERC . . . . Economic Resources Corporation (OEO-Department of Labor project)
ERC . . . . Edge Reading Controller
ERC . . . . Eject Rocket Container
ERC . . . . El Reno College (Oklahoma)
ERC . . . . Electric Regulation Company
ERC . . . . Electron Reflection Coefficient
ERC . . . . Electronics Research Center (NASA)
ERC . . . . En-Route Chart (Aviation)
ERC . . . . Enlisted Reserve Corps
ERC . . . . Estonian Relief Committee
ERCA . . . . Educational Research Council of America
ER CAM . . . . . Eremitarum Camaldulensium (Monk Hermits of Camaldoli) (Roman Catholic religious order)
ERCN . . . . . . Employee Record Change Notice
ERCS . . . . Emergency Rocket Communications System
ERD . . . . Eastern Recruiting Division
ERD . . . . Electronic Research Directorate (Air Force)
ERD . . . . Emergency Reserve Decoration (British)
ERD . . . . Emergency Return Device (Aerospace)
ERD . . . . Equipment Readiness Date (Army)
ERD . . . . Equivalent Residual Dose
ERD . . . . Error Recording Device
ERD . . . . Evoked Response Detector
ERD . . . . Exponentially Retrograded Diode
ERDA . . . . Electronic Resources Development Agency
ERDA . . . . Electronics Research and Development Activity (Army)
ERDAA . . . . . . Electronics Research and Development Activity Analysis (Army)
ERDC . . . . East Region Development Corporation
ERDE . . . . Explosive Research and Development Establishment (British)
ERDL . . . . Electronic Research and Development Laboratory (Army)
ERDL . . . . Engineering Research and Development Laboratory (AMC)
ERDR . . . . Earth Rate Directional Reference
ERE . . . . Echo Range Equipment
ERE . . . . Edison Responsive Environment (Automated learning system)
ERE . . . . Encyclopedia of Religion and Ethics
EREF . . . . Energy Research and Education Foundation
EREP . . . . Earth Resources Experiment Package (NASA)
ERF . . . . Error Function
ERF . . . . Exponential Reliability Function
ERFA . . . . European Radio Frequency Agency (NATO)
ERFC . . . . Error Function Complementary
ERFPI . . . . Extended Range Floating Point Interpretive System
ERG . . . . Electromagnetic Radiation Generator
ERG . . . . Electroretinogram (Medicine)
ERG . . . . Engineer Reactors Group (Army)
ERGS . . . . Electronic (or Experimental) Route Guidance System (Road sign aid) (Bureau of Public Roads)
ERHS . . . . Evangelical & Reformed Historical Society
ERI . . . . Educational Research Information
ERI . . . . Elm Research Institute
ERI . . . . Employee Relations Index
ERI . . . . Environmental Research Institute
ERI . . . . Eyes Right
ERIC . . . . Educational Resources (formerly, Research) Information Center (Office of Education)
ERIC . . . . Electronic Remote and Independent Control
ERIC/CLIS . . . . Educational Resources Information Center/Clearinghouse for Library Information Sciences
ERICR . . . . . . Eleanor Roosevelt Institute for Cancer Research
ERIE . . . . Eastern Regional Institute for Education
ERIE . . . . Environmental Resistance Inherent in Equipment
ERIE . . . . Erie R. R. (AAR code)
ERILCO . . . . . Exchange of Ready for Issue in Lieu of Concurrent Overhaul
ERJ . . . . Extended-Range Juno (Survey meter for radiation)
ERJ . . . . External Ramjet

ERK . . . . Experimental Research Kit
ERL . . . . Electronics Research Laboratory (MIT)
ERL . . . . Environmental Research Laboratories (National Oceanic and Atmospheric Administration)
ERL . . . . ESSA (Environmental Science Services Administration) Research Laboratories
ERL . . . . European Requirements List (Military)
ERL . . . . Event Record Log
ERM . . . . Earth Reentry Module
ERM . . . . Earth Return Module
ERM . . . . Edge Reading Meter
ERM . . . . Effective Relaxation Modulus
ERM . . . . Electrical Research Memorandum
ERM . . . . Emergency Radiation Monitor
ERM . . . . Explosives Research Memorandum
ERMA . . . . Electrical Reproduction Method of Accounting
ERMA . . . . Electronic Recording Machine Accounting
ERMA . . . . Expansion Rate Measuring Apparatus
ERMU . . . . Experimental Remote Maneuvering Unit
ERN . . . . Educational Radio Network
ERN . . . . Explosives Research Note
ERNIE . . . . . . Electronic Random Number Indicating Equipment (Used for selecting winning premium savings bond numbers) (British)
ERNO . . . . Entwicklungsring Nord (Germany)
ERO . . . . Emergency Repair Overseer (Navy)
ERO . . . . European Regional Organization of the ICFTU
ERO . . . . European Research Office
EROP . . . . Executive Review of Overseas Programs (Army)
EROPA . . . . . . Eastern Regional Organization for Public Administration
EROS . . . . Earth Resources Observation Satellite (Environmental Science Services Administration)
EROS . . . . Eliminate Range Zero System (Aviation)
EROS . . . . Experimental Reflector Orbital Shot (NASA project)
EROWS . . . . . Expendable Remote Operating Weather Station (Air Force)
EROZ . . . . Elimination Range Zero (Air collision avoidance system)
ERP . . . . Early Receptor Potential (of the eye)
ERP . . . . Effective Radiated Power
ERP . . . . Electronic Requirement Plan (Navy)
ERP . . . . Emerson Radio & Phonograph Corporation (NYSE symbol) (Delisted)
ERP . . . . Engineering Release Package
ERP . . . . Engineering Requirements Plan (for Military Assistance Programs)
ERP . . . . Equipment Repair Parts
ERP . . . . Equipments Requirement Program
ERP . . . . Euler-Rodrigues Parameter
ERP . . . . European Recovery Program
ERP . . . . Event-Related Potential
ERP . . . . External Ramjet Program
ERPAL . . . . . . Electronic Repair Parts Allowance List (Navy)
ERPC . . . . Eastern Railroad Presidents Conference
ERPC . . . . Emerson Radio and Phonograph Corporation
ERPD . . . . Electronic Reconnaissance Procurement Division
ERPF . . . . Effective Renal Plasma Flow (Physiology)
ERPL . . . . Equipment Repair Parts List
ERPPO . . . . . . Engineer Repair Parts Packaging Office (Merged with General Equipment Command)
ER-PR . . . . . . Effectiveness Report – Performance Report (Air Force)
ERR . . . . Elk River Reactor (AEC)
ERR . . . . Engineering Research Report
ERRC . . . . Expendability, Recoverability, Reparability Cost
ERRDEP . . . . . Error Variance Dependent on Level (Statistical test)
ERRDF . . . . . . Earth Resources Research Data Facility
ERREAC . . . . . Employee Relocation Real Estate Advisory Council
ERRT . . . . Economic Research Round Table
ERS . . . . Earth Resources Satellite
ERS . . . . Economic Research Service (Department of Agriculture)
ERS . . . . Electronic Reconnaissance Set
ERS . . . . Elevated Radio System
ERS . . . . Emergency Relocation Site (Military)
ERS . . . . Engineering Release System
ERS . . . . Environmental Research Satellite (NASA)
ERS . . . . Equilibrium Radiation Spectra
ERS . . . . Expanded RADAR Service
ERS . . . . Experimental Research Society
ERSA . . . . Electronic Research Supply Agency
ERSA . . . . Embry-Riddle School of Aviation
ERSA . . . . Extended Range Strike Aircraft (for low-level missions) (Air Force)
ERSC . . . . Extended Range and Space Communication
ERSER . . . . . . Expanded Reactance Series Resonator
ERSP . . . . Earth Resources Survey Program
ERSR . . . . Equipment Reliability Status Report
ERT . . . . Educational Requirements Test

ERT . . . . Elementary Renewal Theorem
ERT . . . . Engine Rotor Tester
ERT . . . . Equipment Repair Time
ERT . . . . Exhibits Round Table (American Library Association)
ERTC . . . . . . Emergency Rescue Team Chief (Air Force)
ERTC . . . . . . Engineer Replacement Training Center
ERTS. . . . . . . Earth Resources Technology Satellite (NASA)
ERU . . . . Eastern Rugby Union of America
ERU . . . . English Rugby Union
ERV . . . . Efferent Renal Vein
ERV . . . . Expiratory Reserve Volume (Physiology)
ERW . . . . Electrical Resistance Weld
ERX . . . . Electronic Remote Switching
ERZ . . . . Extended Reconnaissance Zone (Army)
ES . . . . Earth Sciences Division (Army Natick Laboratories)
ES . . . . EASCO Corp. (Formerly, Eastern Stainless Steel Corporation) (NYSE symbol)
ES . . . . Echo Sounding
ES . . . . Econometric Society
ES . . . . Educational Specialist
ES . . . . Einheitliche Systematik (Library science)
Es . . . . Einsteinium (Chemical element) (Preferred form, but also see E)
ES . . . . Eldest Son
ES . . . . Electrochemical Society
ES . . . . Electromagnetic Storage
ES . . . . Electron Synchrotron (AEC)
ES . . . . Electronic Section (National Weather Service)
ES . . . . Electronic Shop Major (Coast Guard)
ES . . . . Electronic Standard
ES . . . . Electronic Switching
ES . . . . Electroshock (Medicine)
ES . . . . Electrostatic
ES . . . . Electrostatic Spraying
ES . . . . Electrostatic Storage
ES . . . . Eligible for Separation
ES . . . . Ellis Air Lines
ES . . . . Emergency Service
ES . . . . Endocrine Society
ES . . . . Engine-Sized
ES . . . . Engineering Standardization (Military)
ES . . . . Engineering Study
ES . . . . Enzyme Substrate (Biochemistry)
ES . . . . Equal Section (Technical drawings)
ES . . . . Equipment Section
ES . . . . Equipment Specification
ES . . . . Erkennungssignal (Recognition signal) (German military – World War II)
ES . . . . Executive Secretary
ES . . . . Experimental Station
ES . . . . Extension Service (Department of Agriculture)
ES . . . . Exterior Surface
ES . . . . Extra Series
ES . . . . Eye Stalk
E of S . . . . Expiration of Service
ESA . . . . Earth Station – Arabia
ESA . . . . Ecole Superieure d'Agriculture
ESA . . . . Ecological Society of America
ESA . . . . Economic Stabilization Agency (Terminated, 1953)
ESA . . . . Electrical Stress Analysis
ESA . . . . Electrically Supported (or Suspended) Accelerometer
ESA . . . . Electrolysis Society of America
ESA . . . . Electronic Surge Arrester
ESA . . . . Employment Standards Administration (Department of Labor)
ESA . . . . Engine Service Association
ESA . . . . Engineers and Scientists of America
ESA . . . . Entomological Society of America
ESA . . . . Epiphyllum Society of America
ESA . . . . Equalized Sidelobe Antenna
ESA . . . . Euthanasia Society of America
ESA . . . . Explosive Safe Area (NASA)
ESAA . . . . . . English Setter Association of America
ESAC . . . . . . Environmental Systems Applications Center (NASA)
ESADA . . . . . . Empire State Atomic Development Associates, Inc.
ESADE . . . . . . Escuela Superior de Administracion y Direccion de Empresas
ESAFT . . . . . . Electrically Steerable Antenna Feed Techniques
ESAIRA . . . . . Electronically Scanning Airborne Intercept RADAR Antenna
ESAN . . . . . . Escuela de Administracion de Negocios para Graduados (A graduate school of business administration) (Lima, Peru)
ESAOA . . . . . . Eastern Ski Area Operators Association
ESAPAC . . . . . Escuela Superior de Administracion Publica America Central (Costa Rica)
ESAR . . . . . . Electronically Steerable Array RADAR

ESARS . . . . . . Employment Service Automated (or Automatic) Reporting System (Department of Labor)
ESASC . . . . . Elementary School Administrative Supervisory Certificate
ESA (UN) . . . . Department of Economic and Social Affairs (of United Nations) (Later, Department of Social Affairs)
ESAUS . . . . . . Essential Oil Association of the United States
ESAUSA . . . . . Estonian Student Association in the United States of America
ESAWC . . . . . . Evaluation Staff, War College (Air Force)
ESAWR . . . . . . Early Settlers Association of the Western Reserve
ESB . . . . Earth Station – Brazil
ESB . . . . Economic Stabilization Board (World War II)
ESB . . . . Electrical Stimulation of the Brain
ESB . . . . Environmental Studies Board (National Academy of Sciences)
ESB . . . . ESB, Inc. (Formerly, Electric Storage Battery Co.) (NYSE symbol)
ESBC . . . . . . Electronics Small Business Council
ESBFCOA . . . . Eastern States Blast Furnace and Coke Oven Association
ESBR . . . . . . Electronic Stacked Beam RADAR
ESC . . . . Earth Station – Congo
ESC . . . . Eastern Simulation Council
ESC . . . . Economic and Social Council (of UN)
ESC . . . . Educational Systems Corporation
ESC . . . . Electric Surface Current
ESC . . . . Electromechanical Stop Clock
ESC . . . . Electronic Scan Converter
ESC . . . . Electronic Shop Computer
ESC . . . . Electronic Systems Center (Air Force)
ESC . . . . Electronic Systems Command (Formerly, Bureau of Ships) (Navy)
ESC . . . . Environmental Stress Crack(ing) (Plastics)
ESC . . . . Epoxy Spray Coater
ESC . . . . Equipment Section Container
ESC . . . . Equipment Serviceability Criteria (Military)
ESC . . . . Erythropoietin-Sensitive Stem Cells (Hematology)
ESC . . . . European Security Conference (Soviet-sponsored)
ESC . . . . European Space Conference
ESC . . . . Executive Seminar Center (Civil Service Commission)
ESCA . . . . . . Electron Spectroscopic Chemical Analysis
ESCA . . . . . . Executive Stewards' and Caterers' Association
ESCAPE . . . . . Expansion Symbolic Compiling Assembly Program for Engineers
ESCARFOR . . . . Escort Carrier Force
ESCAT . . . . . . Emergency Security Control of Air Traffic
ESCF . . . . . . Electronic Systems Compatibility Facility (NASA)
ESCH . . . . . . Earth Station – Chile
ESCL . . . . . . Electronic Systems Compatibility Laboratory (NASA)
ESCO . . . . . . Earth Station – Colombia
ESCO . . . . . . Engineers Supply Control Office (Army)
ESCORON . . . . Escort Scouting Squadron
ESCORTDIV . . . Escort Division
ESCORTFIGHTRON . . Escort Fighter Squadron
ESCP . . . . . . Earth Science Curriculum Project (Education)
ESCRG . . . . . . Escort Guard
ESCRU . . . . . . Episcopal Society for Cultural and Racial Unity
ESCS . . . . . . Eccentrically Stiffened Cylindrical Shell
ESCS . . . . . . Expanded Shale Clay and Slate Institute
ESCSI . . . . . . Expanded Shale Clay and Slate Institute
ESD . . . . Earliest Start Date
ESD . . . . Echo Sounding Device (Navigation)
ESD . . . . Electronic Systems Division (AFSC)
ESD . . . . Electroocular Symbol Display
ESD . . . . Electrostatic Storage Deflection
ESD . . . . Elongated Single Domain
ESD . . . . Estimated Shipping Date
ESDAC . . . . . . European Space Data Center
ESDC . . . . . . Equipment Sliding Drawer Cabinet
ESDR . . . . . . Electrical System Design Report
ESDS . . . . . . Elemental Standard Data System
ESDU . . . . . . Event Storage and Distribution Unit
ESE . . . . East-Southeast
ESE . . . . Electrical Support Equipment
ESE . . . . Electronic Stock Evaluator Corporation
ESE . . . . Electronic Support Equipment
ESE . . . . Electronic System Evaluator
ESE . . . . Environmental Simulation Equipment
ESEA . . . . . . Elementary and Secondary Education Act (of 1965)
ESEC . . . . . . Earth Station – Ecuador
ESEG . . . . . . Earth Station – Egypt
ESES . . . . . . Earth-Moon Space Exploration Study
ESF . . . . Eastern Sea Frontier
ESF . . . . Electrostatic Focusing (Electronics)
ESF . . . . Engineering Specification Files
ESF . . . . Erythropoietic Stimulating Factor (Physiology)
ESF . . . . Even Side Flat

ESFC . . . . Equivalent Specific Fuel Consumption
ESG . . . . Earth Station - Greece
ESG . . . . Electrically Suspended Gyro
ESG . . . . Electronic Sweep Generator
ESG . . . . Electrostatic Gyroscope
ESG . . . . Electrostatically Suspended Gyro
ESG . . . . Engineers' and Scientists' Guild
ESGA . . . . Electrically Supported (or Suspended) Gyro Accelerometer
ESH . . . . Equivalent Solar Hour (NASA)
ESHH . . . . Enthronement of the Sacred Heart in the Home
ESHK . . . . Earth Station - Hong Kong
ESHP . . . . Empire State Historical Publications (Series)
ESHP . . . . Equivalent Shaft Horsepower (Air Force)
ESHU . . . . Emergency Ship Handling Unit
ESI . . . . Earth Station - Iran
ESI . . . . Educational Services Incorporated (Became Education Development Center)
ESI . . . . Educreative Systems, Incorporated
ESI . . . . Electrical Specialties, Incorporated
ESI . . . . Executives' Secretaries, Incorporated
ESI . . . . Externally Specified Indexing
ESI . . . . Extremely Sensitive Information (Army)
ESIC . . . . Earth Station - Ivory Coast
ESIS . . . . Earth Station - Israel
ESIS . . . . Executive Selection Inventory System
ESJ . . . . Earth Station - Jordan
ESK . . . . Earth Station - Kenya
ESK . . . . Electrostatic Klystron
ESL . . . . Earth Station - Libya
ESL . . . . Egg Stalk Length
ESL . . . . Electromagnetic Systems Laboratories, Inc.
ESL . . . . Electronic Support Laboratory
ESL . . . . Electronic Systems Laboratory
ESL . . . . Engineering Societies Library
ESL . . . . English as a Second Language
ESL . . . . Esterline Corp. (NYSE symbol)
ESL . . . . Evans Signal Laboratory (Army)
ESL . . . . Exceeding Speed Limit
ESLAB . . . . European Space Laboratory
ESLJ . . . . East St. Louis Junction R. R. (AAR code)
ESLO . . . . European Space Launcher Organization
ESLT . . . . Equipment Section Leakage Test
ESM . . . . Earth Station - Mexico
ESM . . . . Edible Structure Material
ESM . . . . Edmund S. Muskie (Candidate for US vice president, 1968)
ESM . . . . Effectiveness Simulation Model
ESM . . . . Electronic Shop Minor (Coast Guard)
ESM . . . . Electronic Switch Module
ESM . . . . Energy Storage Modulator
ESM . . . . Engineering Schedule Memo
ESM . . . . Engineering Service Memo
ESM . . . . Escort Mission (Military)
ESMA . . . . Electronic Sales-Marketing Association
ESMA . . . . Engraved Stationery Manufacturers Association
ESMO . . . . Earth Station - Morocco
ESMR . . . . Electrically Scanned Microwave Radiometer (NASA)
ESMRI . . . . Engraved Stationery Manufacturers Research Institute
ESMT . . . . Electronic Shop Minor Telephone and Teletype (Coast Guard)
ESMWT . . . . Engineering, Science and Management War Training
ESN . . . . Educationally Sub-Normal
ESN . . . . Elastic Stop Nut Corporation of America (NYSE symbol) (Delisted)
ESN . . . . English-Speaking Nations (of NATO)
ESNA . . . . Elastic Stop Nut Corporation of America
ESO . . . . Educational Services Office(r) (Navy)
ESO . . . . Electronic Standards Office (Navy)
ESO . . . . Electronics Supply Office(r)
ESO . . . . Embarkation Staff Officer (British)
ESO . . . . Emergency Security Operations
ESO . . . . European Southern Observatory (La Silla Mountain, Chile)
ESO . . . . European Space Organization (Formerly, ELDO and ESRO)
ESOA . . . . Epiphyllum Society of America
ESOB . . . . Eastern Soccer Officials Bureau (Later, Eastern College Soccer Officials Bureau)
ESOC . . . . European Space Operations Center
ESOL . . . . English to Speakers of Other Languages (Program)
ESOMAR . . . . European Society for Opinion Surveys and Market Research
ESOPS . . . . Employment Service On-Line Placement System (Data processing)
ESP . . . . Economic Stabilization Policy (of Nixon Administration)
ESP . . . . Electronic Security Profile (of Equitable Life Assurance Society)
ESP . . . . Electronic Seismic Photography
ESP . . . . Electronic Standard Procedure
ESP . . . . Electrosensitive Programming

ESP . . . . Electrosonic Profiler
ESP . . . . Elevated Stabilized Platform (Aircraft)
ESP . . . . Energetic Storm Particle
ESP . . . . Engine Start Panel
ESP . . . . Engineering Schedule Plan
ESP . . . . Engineering Signal Processor
ESP . . . . Expandable Stored Program
ESP . . . . Extrasensory Perception
ESP . . . . Extravehicular Support Pack (NASA)
E & SP . . . . Equipment and Spare Parts
ESP-1 . . . . Elizabeth S. Priori-1 (Virus named after one of the scientists who isolated it)
ESPA . . . . Evening Student Personnel Association
ESPAR . . . . Electronically Steerable Phased Array RADAR (SPADATS)
ESPPI . . . . Expanding and Specialty Paper Products Institute
ESPWO . . . . Exigencies of the Service Having Been Such as to Preclude the Issuance of Competent Written Orders in Advance
ESQ . . . . Esquire
ESQ . . . . Esquire, Inc. (NYSE symbol)
ESQT . . . . Extended Sterilization Qualification Test
ESR . . . . East Surrey Regiment (British Army)
ESR . . . . Effective Signal Radiated
ESR . . . . Electron Spin Resonance
ESR . . . . Electronic Scanning RADAR
ESR . . . . Electroslag Refining
ESR . . . . Electroslag Remelting (Steel alloy)
ESR . . . . Engineering Summary Report
ESR . . . . Equipment Status Report (Air Force)
ESR . . . . Equivalent Series Resistance
ESR . . . . Equivalent Service Rounds (A standard for indicating gun erosion)
ESR . . . . Erythrocyte Sedimentation Rate (Physiology)
ESR . . . . Experimental Superheat Reactor (AEC)
ESR . . . . External Standard Ratio
ESRANGE . . . . . European Space Range (Sweden)
ESRD . . . . Equipment Shipment Ready Date (Army)
ESRF . . . . Electrical Systems Repair Facilities
ESRIN . . . . European Space Research Institute
ESRO . . . . European Space Research Organization (Later, ESO)
ESRP . . . . Emergency Substitute in a Regular Position (Education)
ESRS . . . . Electronic Scanning RADAR System
ESRS . . . . European Society for Rural Sociology
ESS . . . . Earth-Sighting Simulator (NASA)
ESS . . . . Earth Station - Sudan
ESS . . . . Educational Services Section (Navy)
ESS . . . . Educational Subscription Service, Inc.
ESS . . . . Electronic Scanning Spectrometer
ESS . . . . Electronic Security System
ESS . . . . Electronic Sequence Switching
ESS . . . . Electronic Surveillance System
ESS . . . . Electronic Switching System
ESS . . . . Elementary Science Study (National Science Foundation)
ESS . . . . Emergency Social Services (Civil Defense)
ESS . . . . Emplaced Scientific Station (NASA)
ESS . . . . Employment Security System (Department of Labor)
ESS . . . . Encyclopedia of the Social Sciences
ESS . . . . Energy Storage System
ESS . . . . Engine Start Signal
ESS . . . . Engineer Specialized Services
ESS . . . . Equipment Section Shell
ESS . . . . Erythrocyte-Sensitizing Substance (Medicine)
ESS . . . . Executive's Shopping Service
ESS . . . . Expendable Second Stage (Space shuttle) (NASA)
ESS . . . . Experiment Support System
ESS . . . . Experimental SAGE (Semi-Automatic Ground Environment) Sector
ESSA . . . . Earth Station - South Africa
ESSA . . . . Electronic Scanning and Stabilizing Antenna
ESSA . . . . Embassy Social Secretaries Association
ESSA . . . . Environmental Science Services Administration
ESSA . . . . Environmental Survey Satellite
ESSB . . . . Electronic Supply Support Base (Air Force)
ESSBR . . . . Electronically Scanned Stacked Beam RADAR (Program)
ESSC . . . . Earth Station - Scandinavia
ESSE . . . . Earth Station - Senegal
ESSEX . . . . Experimental Solid-State Exchange (Communication system)
ESSFL . . . . Electron Steady-State Fermi Level
ESSFLO . . . . Electronic Switching System Flow Chart
ESSFTA . . . . English Springer Spaniel Field Trial Association
ESSG . . . . Engineer Strategic Studies Group (Army)
ESSL . . . . Eastern Secondary Standards Laboratory
ESSM . . . . Emergency Ship Salvage Material (Navy)
ESSNSS . . . . Electronic Supply Segment of the Navy Supply System

ESSO . . . . Standard Oil (Trademark in foreign use only; superseded in US, 1973, by Exxon)
ESSOBA . . . . . Essor Social des Bashi (Social Development of the Bashi)
ESSP . . . . Elementary School Science Project
ESSPO . . . . . . Electronic Support Systems Project Office (Air Force)
ESSU . . . . Electronic Selective Switching Unit
ESSY . . . . Earth Station - Syria
EST . . . . Early Start Time
EST . . . . Earth Station - Turkey
EST . . . . Eastern Standard Time
EST . . . . Electronic Sequencer Timer
EST . . . . Electronic Shop Major Telephone and Teletype (Coast Guard)
EST. . . . . . . Electronic Social Transformation
EST . . . . Electroshock Therapy
EST . . . . Electrostatic Storage Tube
EST . . . . Embedded Sensor Technique
EST . . . . En-Route Support Team (Military)
EST . . . . Enlistment Screening Test
EST . . . . Epidemiology and Sanitation Technician (Navy)
EST . . . . Equilibrium Surface Thermochemistry
EST. . . . . . . Established
EST. . . . . . . Estimate(d)
ESTA . . . . . . Electroshock Therapy Apparatus
ESTAR. . . . . . Estimated Arrival Date
ESTB. . . . . . . Establish(ment)
ESTEC. . . . . . European Space Technology Center
E/S TIEP . . . . Engineering/Service Test and Independent Evaluation Program (Army)
ESTL. . . . . . . Electronic Systems Test Laboratory (NASA)
ESTO . . . . . . Engineer/Service Test Office
ESTP . . . . . . Electronic Systems Test Program (NASA)
ESTRACK. . . . . European Space Tracking and Telemetry Network
ESTU . . . . . . Electronic System Test Unit
ESU . . . . Electrostatic Unit(s)
ESU . . . . English-Speaking Union of the United States
ESU . . . . Europa Study Unit (An organization)
ESV . . . . Earth Satellite Vehicle (Air Force)
ESV . . . . Earth Station - Venezuela
ESV . . . . Elastic Space Vehicle
ESV . . . . Esophageal Valve
ESV . . . . Expanded Service Volume
ESV . . . . Experimental Safety Vehicle (Volkswagen)
ESV . . . . Extension Society Volunteers
ESWP . . . . . . Engineers' Society of Western Pennsylvania
ESWS . . . . . . Earth Satellite Weapon Systems
ESY . . . . Earth Station - Yugoslavia
ESY . . . . Episcopal Service for Youth
ET . . . . Easter Term
ET . . . . Eastern Time
ET . . . . Edge Thickness (Technical drawings)
ET . . . . Educational Therapy
ET . . . . Educational Training
ET . . . . Effective Temperature
ET . . . . Elapsed Time (Automobile racing)
ET . . . . Electric Telegraph
ET . . . . Electrical Time
ET . . . . Electrical Transcription (A phonograph recording) (Musical slang)
ET . . . . Electron Tube
ET . . . . Electronic Test(s)
ET . . . . Electronic Tube
ET . . . . Electronics Technician
ET . . . . Eltra Corporation (NYSE symbol)
ET . . . . Engineer Training
ET . . . . Engineering Test
ET . . . . English Translation
ET . . . . Environmental Test
ET . . . . Ephemeris Time
ET . . . . Equipment Time
ET . . . . European Theater
ET . . . . Expander Tube
ET . . . . Explosive Technology
ETA . . . . Engineering Task Assignment
ETA . . . . Estimated Target Assurance
ETA . . . . Estimated (or Expected) Time of Arrival
ETA . . . . European Tropospheric - Army
ETA . . . . Euzkadi Ta Azkatasuna (Long Live Basque Freedom) (An organization in Spain)
ETA . . . . Exception Time Accounting
ETA . . . . Expect to Arrive
ETAB . . . . . . Environmental Testing Advisory Board (Dow Chemical Co.)
ETAB . . . . . . Expanded Technical Assistance Board (UN)
ETAC . . . . . . Electrically Tuned Antenna Coupler

ETAC . . . . . . Environment Technical Applications Center (Ashville, NC) (Air Force)
ET AL. . . . . . Et Alibi (And Elsewhere)
ET AL. . . . . . Et Alii (And Others)
ETAP . . . . . . Expanded Technical Assistance Program (of UN)
ETAS . . . . . . Effective True Airspeed
ETB . . . . End of Transmission Block (Data processing)
ETB . . . . Equipment Transfer Bag (NASA)
ETB . . . . Estimated Time of Berthing (Navigation)
ETB's . . . . . . Elastic Top and Bottom (British naval slang for WREN's knickers)
ETBC . . . . . . East Texas Baptist College
ETC . . . . Electronic Temperature Control
ETC . . . . Electronic Toll Center (AT & T)
ETC . . . . Emergency Training Centre (British)
ETC . . . . Enclosed Track Conveyor
ETC . . . . Environmental Test Chamber
ETC . . . . Equal-Time Commutation
ETC . . . . Equipment Trust Certificate
ETC . . . . Estimated Time of Completion
ETC . . . . Et Cetera (And So Forth)
ETC . . . . European Translation Centre
ETC . . . . European Travel Commission
ETC . . . . Excess Three Code
ETCG . . . . . . Elapsed-Time Code Generator
ETCO . . . . . . Emergency Traffic Coordinating Officer (Army)
ETD . . . . Effective Transfer Date (Military)
ETD . . . . Engineering Test Directive
ETD . . . . Environments and Threats Directorate (Army)
ETD . . . . Estimated Time of Departure
ETD . . . . Event Time Digitizer
ETDAIP . . . . . Experimental Technology Development and Applications Incentives Program (National Bureau of Standards proposed program)
ETDE . . . . . . Experimental Target Designation Equipment
ETDP . . . . . . Emergency Traffic Disposition Plan (Military)
ETDP . . . . . . Estimated Time and Point of DEWIZ (Distant Early Warning Identification Zone) Penetration
ETE . . . . Emergency Transceiver Equipment
ETE . . . . Estimated Time En Route
ETEC . . . . . . Effective Thermal Expansion Coefficient
ETECG . . . . . . Electronics Test Equipment Coordination Group (Military)
ETEDS. . . . . . Electromagnetic Test Environment Data System
ETEL. . . . . . . Empreendimentos Tecnicos de Estradas Limitada
ETF. . . . . Eastern Task Force
ETF . . . . Electron-Transferring Flavoprotein (Biochemistry)
ETF . . . . Electronic Tuning Fork
ETF . . . . Electronically Tunable Filter
ETF . . . . Engine Test Facility
ETFAS. . . . . . Ente per la Trasformazione Fondiaria e Agraria in Sardegna (Italy)
ETFL. . . . . . . Each Thousand-Foot Level (Aviation)
ETFO . . . . . . Electronics Technical Field Office
ETG . . . . Electronic Turbine Governor
ETG . . . . External Thermal Garment
ETGT . . . . . . Equal To or Greater Than
ETH . . . . Eidgenoessische Technische Hochschule
ETH . . . . Extraterrestrial Hypothesis
ETI. . . . . Educational Travel, Incorporated
ETI. . . . . Elapsed Time Indicator
ETI. . . . . Electric Test Installation
ETI. . . . . Electric Tool Institute (Later, Power Tool Institute)
ETI. . . . . Encapsulated Toroidal Inductor
ETI. . . . . Engine Test Information
ETI . . . . Equipment and Tool Institute
ETI. . . . . Estimated Information (Aviation)
ETI. . . . . Estimated Time of Interception
ETI. . . . . European Transuranium Institute (West Germany)
ETI. . . . . Extraction Tool Insert
ETI. . . . . Extraterrestrial Intelligence
ETIC. . . . . . . Electron Tube Information Council
ETIC. . . . . . . Estimated Time in Commission (Army)
ETIL . . . . Economisch Technologisch Instituut in Limburg (Germany)
ETIYRA . . . . . El Toro International Yacht Racing Association
ETK . . . . Electron Tube Klystron
ETK . . . . Embryonic Turkey Kidney
ETL . . . . Electrical Testing Laboratories, Inc.
ETL . . . . Electronic Technology Laboratory (Air Force)
ETL . . . . Emergency Time Limit
ETL . . . . Engineer Topographic Laboratory (Army)
ETL . . . . Essex Terminal Railway (AAR code)
ETL . . . . Etching by Transmitted Light
ETLT . . . . Equal To or Less Than
ETM . . . . Elapsed Time Meter
ETM . . . . Electrical Tactical Map

ETM . . . . Electrical Time Measurement
ETM . . . . Electronic Technician's Mate (Navy rating)
ETM . . . . Extension Training Memorandum (Civil Defense)
ETM . . . . External Technical Memorandum
ETMA . . . . . . Educational Television for the Metropolitan Area
ETMB . . . . . . Electrical Techniques in Medicine and Biology
ETMG . . . . . . Electron Tube Management Group
ETMSR . . . . . Electronic Technician's Mate, Ship Repair (Navy rating)
ETMWG . . . . . Electronic Trajectory Measurements Working Group (IRIG)
ETN . . . . Eastern Technical Net (Air Force)
ETN . . . . Eaton Corporation (Formerly, Eaton Yale & Towne) (NYSE symbol)
ETN . . . . Electrical Terminal Nut
ETN . . . . Equipment Table Nomenclature
ETO . . . . Electronic Temperature Offset
ETO . . . . . . Emergency Test Operation
ETO . . . . ESSO (Standard Oil) Turbo Oil
ETO . . . . Estimated Time Off
ETO . . . . Estimated Time Over (Aviation)
ETO . . . . Ethylene Oxide
ETO . . . . European Theater of Operations (World War II)
ETO . . . . European Transport Organization (ECE)
ETO . . . . Express Transportation Order (Army)
ETOC . . . . . . Estimated Time Out of Commission
ETOG . . . . . . European Technical Operations Group
ETOUSA . . . . . European Theater of Operations, United States Army (World War II)
ETP . . . . Electrical Tough Pitch
ETP . . . . Electrolytic Tough Pitch (Copper)
ETP . . . . Electron Transfer (or Transporting) Particle
ETP . . . . Equivalent Top Product
ETP . . . . Estimated Time of Penetration (Aviation)
ETP . . . . Estimated Turnaround Point
ETPA . . . . . . Electronically Tunable Parametric Amplifier
ETR . . . . Eastern Test Range (Formerly, Atlantic Missile Range)
ETR . . . . Electron Tube Rectifier
ETR . . . . Electronic Trouble Report
ETR . . . . Electronically Tuned Receiver
ETR . . . . Engineering Test Reactor (AEC)
ETR . . . . Estimated Time of Repair
ETR . . . . Estimated Time of Return
ETR . . . . Export Traffic Release
ETR . . . . External Technical Report
ETR . . . . External Timing Register
ETRA . . . . . . Estimated Time to Reach Altitude
ETRC . . . . . . Engineering Test Reactor Critical Facility (AEC)
ETRO . . . . . . Estimated Time of Return to Operation (Military)
ETRT . . . . Electronically Tuned Receiver Tuner
ETRTO . . . . . . European Tyre and Rim Technical Organisation
ETS . . . . Educational Talent Search
ETS . . . . Educational Testing Service
ETS . . . . Edwards Test Station
ETS . . . . Electronic Telegraph System
ETS . . . . Electronic Test Set
ETS . . . . Electronic Test Stand
ETS . . . . Electronic Test Station
ETS . . . . Electronic Timing Set
ETS . . . . Electronic Translator System (Bell System)
ETS . . . . Engine Test Stands (NERVA program)
ETS . . . . Engineered Time Standards
ETS . . . . Engineering and Technical Service
ETS . . . . Episcopal Theological School
ETS . . . . Equal Time Spacing
ETS . . . . Estimated Time of Sailing (Navigation)
ETS . . . . Evaluation Trainers
ETS . . . . Evangelical Theological Society
ETS . . . . Expiration Term of Service
ETSAL . . . . . . Electronic Terms for Space Age Language
ETSC . . . . . . East Tennessee State College
ETSC . . . . . . East Texas State College
ETSG . . . . . . Elevated Temperature Strain Gage
ETSP . . . . . . Entitled to Severance Pay
ETSPL . . . . . . Equivalent Threshold Sound Pressure Level
ETSQ . . . . . . Electrical Time, Superquick
ETT . . . . Electron Tube, Triode
ETT . . . . Electronic Tensile Tester
ETT . . . . Electronically Tuned Tuner
ETT . . . . End of Tape Test
ETT . . . . Equipment Task Time
ETT . . . . Extended Time Tests
ETTA . . . . . . Evangelical Teacher Training Association
ETTO . . . . . . Extractor Tool
ETU . . . . Engineering Test Unit

ETU . . . . Ethylene Thiourea
ETV . . . . Educational Television
ETV . . . . Ejection Test Vehicle
ETV . . . . Engine Test Vehicle
ETV . . . . Epitaxial Tuning Varactor
ETVM . . . . . . Electrostatic Transistorized Voltmeter
ETWN . . . . . . East Tennessee & Western North Carolina R. R. (AAR code)
EU . . . . Electronics Unit
EU . . . . Elms Unlimited (Later, Elm Research Institute)
EU . . . . Engineering Unit
EU . . . . Entropy Unit
Eu . . . . Europium (Chemical element)
EU . . . . Evacuation Unit (Army)
EU . . . . Evangelical Union (British)
EU . . . . Experience Unit
E-U . . . . Etats-Unis (United States)
EUA . . . . Eastern Underwriters Association
EUA . . . . Eastern Utilities Associates (NYSE symbol)
EUB . . . . Estados Unidos do Brasil
EUB . . . . Evangelical United Brethren (Church)
EUC . . . . Euclid R. R. (AAR code)
EUCLID . . . . . . Experimental Use Computer, London Integrated Display
EUCOM . . . . . European Command (Military)
EUDAC . . . . . . European Distribution and Accounting Agency of the Military Committee, London (US Army)
EUDS . . . . . . Electronic Unit Design Section
EUF . . . . European Union of Federalists
EUM. . . . . . . European–Mediterranean (Military)
EUO . . . . Emergency Use Only
EUP . . . . Electric Utility Pump
EUR . . . . Emergency Unsatisfactory Report (Military)
EUR . . . . Equipment Unsatisfactory Report
EUR . . . . Europe
EURAFRICA . . . Europe and Africa
EURAILPASS. . . European Railway Passenger (Ticket)
EURAL . . . . . . European Air Lines
EURASAFRICA. . Europe, Asia, and Africa
EURATOM . . . European Atomic Energy Community
EURDA . . . . . . Etudes d'Urbanisme de Developpement et d'Amenagement (du Territoire)
EUREMAIL . . . . Conference Permanente de l'Industrie Europeenne de Produits Emailles
EUROCAE . . . . European Organization for Civil Aviation Electronics
EUROCOM . . . . Union Europeenne des Negociants en Combustibles (European Fuel Merchants Union)
EUROCONTROL . . European Organization for the Safety of Air Navigation
EUROMART . . . European Common Market
EUROPHOT. . . . Association Europeenne des Photographes Professionnels (European Association of Professional Photographers)
EUROSAC . . . . Federation Europeenne des Fabricants de Sacs en Papier a Grande Contenance (European Federation of Manufacturers of Multiwall Paper Sacks)
EUROSAT . . . . European Application Satellite Systems
EUROSPACE. . . European Industrial Space Study Group
EUROTOX . . . . Comite Europeen Permanent de Recherches sur la Protection des Populations contre les Risques de Toxicite a long Terme (Permanent European Research Committee for the Protection of the Population against the Hazards of Chronic Toxicity)
EUROVISION. . European Television
EUR/SV/LDO . . European Space Vehicle Launcher Development Organization
EUS . . . . Eastern United States
EUSA . . . . . . Eighth United States Army
EUSAR . . . . . . Eighth United States Army Rear
EUSEC . . . . . . Conference des Societes d'Ingenieurs de l'Europe Occidental et des Etats-Unis d'Amerique (Conference of Engineering Societies of Western Europe and the United States of America)
EUSEC . . . . . . European Communications Security and Evaluation Agency of the Military Committee, London (US Army)
EUSIDIC . . . . . European Association of Scientific Information Dissemination Centers
EUT . . . . Equipment Under Test
EUV . . . . Energetic Ultraviolet
EUV . . . . Extreme Ultraviolet (NASA)
EUVSH . . . . . . Equivalent Ultraviolet Solar Hour (NASA)
EUVT . . . . . . Extended Ultraviolet Transmission
EUVT . . . . . . Extreme Ultraviolet Telescope
EUW . . . . European Union of Women
EV . . . . Efferent Vessel
EV . . . . Eingang Vorbehalten (Rights reserved, i.e., copyrighted) (Germany)
eV . . . . Electron Volt(s)
EV . . . . English Version
EV . . . . Escort Vessels (Enemy)
EV . . . . Everett R. R. (AAR code)
EV . . . . Ex Voto (In Fulfillment of a Vow)

EVA . . . . Education Voucher Agency (Proposed for OEO experiment in education funding)
EVA . . . . Electronic Velocity Analyzer
EVA . . . . Electronic Vote Analysis (Election poll)
EVA . . . . Engineer Vice-Admiral (British)
EVA . . . . Escort Vessel Administration (World War II)
EVA . . . . Ethylene Vinyl Acetate (Copolymer)
EVA . . . . Extravehicular Activity (Aerospace)
EVA . . . . Extravehicular Astronaut
EVAC . . . . . . Evacuation
EVAL . . . . . . Evaluate (or Evaluation)
EVATA . . . . . Electronic-Visual-Auditory Training Aid
EVATRON . . . . Eccentric Variable-Angle Thermionic Rheostat
EVB . . . . Extruded Vinyl Bumper
EVC . . . . Educational Video Corporation
EVC . . . . Eenheidsvakcentrale (United Dutch Trade Union Central)
EVC . . . . Engineer Volunteer Corps (British)
EVC . . . . Error Vector Computer
EVC . . . . Executive Volunteer Corps
EVCS . . . . . . Extravehicular Communications System (NASA)
EVCS . . . . . . Extruded Vinyl Chamfer Strip
EVD . . . . Electro-Vacuum Drive
EVDE . . . . . . External Visual Display Equipment (Used in Apollo mission)
EVDF . . . . . . Eugene V. Debs Foundation
EVDP . . . . . . Engine Vibration Diagnostic Program
EVE . . . . Einstein Viscosity Equation
EVEA . . . . . . Extravehicular Engineering Activity
EVER . . . . . . Everglades National Park
EVESR . . . . . . ESADA (Empire State Atomic Development Associates, Inc.) Vallecitos Experimental Superheat Reactor
EVF . . . . Electromagnetic Vibrating Feeder
EVG . . . . Electric Vacuum Gyro
EVG . . . . Europaeische Verteidigungsgemeinschaft
EVI . . . . Encapsulated Variable Inductor
EVIF . . . . Emergency Virus Isolation Facility (National Cancer Institute)
EVIL . . . . . . Elevation Versus Integrated Log
EVM . . . . Electrostatic Voltmeter
EVM . . . . Elektronno-Vychislitel'naya Mashina (Electronic Calculating Machine) (Russia)
EVM . . . . Evacuation Mission (Air Force)
EVNG . . . . . . Efferent Vein from Nephridial Gland
EVNG . . . . . . Evangeline Railway Company (AAR code)
EVO . . . . Eisenbahn-Verkehrsordnung (Germany)
EVO . . . . Extravehicular Operation (Aerospace)
EVOP . . . . . . Evolutionary Operation
EVR . . . . Electronic Video Recording (CBS Laboratories' brand name for tape cartridges of TV programs)
EVR . . . . Eversharp, Inc. (NYSE symbol) (Delisted)
EVS . . . . Ecumenical Voluntary Service
EVS . . . . Electronic Valve Specification
EVS . . . . Electronic Voice Switching
EVS . . . . Electro-Optical Viewing System (Air Force)
EVS . . . . Electro-Optical Visual Sensors (Hughes Aircraft Co.)
EVS . . . . Emergency Venting System
EVS . . . . Engine Vertical Scale
EVS . . . . Extravehicular System (Aerospace)
EVS . . . . Extreme Value Statistics
EVS . . . . Eye-Voice Span
EVSS . . . . . . Extravehicular Space Suit (Aerospace)
EVSTC . . . . . . Extravehicular Suit Telemetry and Communication
EVT . . . . Elasticity, Viscosity and Thixotropy
EVT . . . . Emergency Veterinary Tag
EVT . . . . End Viewing Tube
EVT . . . . Envirotech (NYSE symbol)
EVT . . . . Expect Vector To (Aviation)
E/VTS . . . . . . Engine/Vehicle Test Stand
EVV . . . . English Versions
EVVA . . . . . . Extravehicular Visor Assembly (NASA)
EVW . . . . European Voluntary Worker
EVY . . . . Evans Products Company (NYSE symbol)
EW . . . . Early Warning (Air Force)
EW . . . . East Washington Railway Company (AAR code)
EW . . . . East-West
EW . . . . Egg Width
EW . . . . Eingetragenes Warenzeichen (Registered trademark) (Germany)
EW . . . . Electronic Warfare (Military)
EW . . . . Enlisted Woman or Women
EW . . . . Extensive Wound
EW . . . . Sleet Showers (Meteorology)
EWA . . . . East-West Acceleration
EWA . . . . East-West Airlines, Ltd.

EWA . . . . Education and World Affairs (An organization)
EWA . . . . Education Writers Association
EWA . . . . Engineering Work Assignment (or Authorization)
EWAS . . . . . . Economic Warfare Analysis Section
EWASER . . . . . Electromagnetic Wave Amplification by Simulated Emission of Radiation
EWB . . . . Bliss (E.W.) Company (NYSE symbol) (Delisted)
EWC . . . . Edward Walters College (Florida)
EWC . . . . Electric Water Cooler
EWCL . . . . . . Electromagnetic Warfare and Communications Laboratory
EW/CRP . . . . . Early Warning/Control and Reporting Post
EWCS . . . . . . European Wideband Communications System (Army)
EWD . . . . Economic Warfare Division (US) (London)
EWD . . . . Electronic Warfare Department
EWDI . . . . . . Electronic Wind Direction Indicator
EWEC . . . . . . Electromagnetic Wave Energy Converter (Solar energy conversion)
EWES . . . . . . Electronic Warfare Evaluation Simulator
EWES . . . . . . Engineering Waterways Experiment Station (Army)
EWF . . . . Early Warning Fighter
EWF . . . . Electronic Warfare
EWF . . . . Equivalent-Weight Factor
EWFH . . . . . . East-West Fine, Hundreds
EWFT . . . . . . East-West Fine, Tens
EWFU . . . . . . East-West Fine, Units
EWG . . . . Equipment Working Group
EWG . . . . Europaeische Wirtschaftsgemeinschaft (European Economic Community)
EWGETS . . . . . Electronic Warfare Ground Environment Threat Simulator
EWHA . . . . . . Eastern Women's Headwear Association
EWI . . . . Education with Industry
EWI . . . . Electronic Wiring Intercommunication
EWI . . . . Entered without Inspection (Usually applies to aliens who enter at other than a port of entry)
EWI . . . . Experiential World Inventory (Psycho-diagnostic test)
EWL . . . . Effective Wave Length
EWL . . . . Electronic Warfare Laboratory
EWM . . . . . . Edge-Wise Meter
EWM . . . . . . Electrical Welding Machine
EWMC . . . . . . Eli Whitney Metrology Center
EWO . . . . Electronic Warfare Office(r)
EWO . . . . Emergency War Operations
EWO . . . . Emergency War Order (Air Force)
EWO . . . . Engineering Work Order
EWOS . . . . . . Electronic Warfare Operational System (Air Force)
EWOT . . . . . . Electronic Warfare Officer Training
EWP . . . . Emergency War Plan
EWP . . . . Exploding Wire Phenomena
EWQ . . . . Exceptionally Well Qualified
EWR . . . . Early Warning RADAR (Air Force)
EWR . . . . Newark (New Jersey) (Municipal airport symbol)
EWRC . . . . . . European Weed Research Council
EWRT . . . . . . Electrical Women's Round Table
EWS . . . . Early Warning System
EWS . . . . East-West Speed
EWS . . . . Eduworld Society
EWS . . . . Emergency Water Supply
EWS . . . . Emergency Welfare Service (Civil Defense)
EWS . . . . Engineering Work Schedule
EWS . . . . Engineering Writing and Speech
EWSC . . . . . . Electric Water Systems Council
EWSF . . . . . . Electric Wave Section Filter
EWSI . . . . . . Electronic Wind Speed Indicator
EWT . . . . Eastern War Time (World War II)
EWT . . . . Electronic Warfare Trainer
EWT . . . . Expandable Wing Tank
EWTAD . . . . . Early Warning Threat Analysis Display
EWTES . . . . . Electronic Warfare Tactical Environment Simulation
EWTS . . . . . . Expandable Wing Tank Structure
EWTT . . . . . . Electronic Warfare Tactics Trainer
EWW . . . . . . Extended Work Week
EWWS . . . . . Electronic Warfare Warning System
EWWS . . . . . . ESSA (Environmental Science Services Administration) Weather Wire Service
EXACCT . . . . . Expenditure Account
EXAGT . . . . . . Executive Agent
EXAM . . . . . . Examination
EXAMETNET . . Experimental Inter-American Meteorological Rocket Network (NASA)
EXBEDCAP . . . . Expanded Bed Capacity
EXC . . . . Essex International, Inc. (NYSE symbol)
EXCELS . . . . . Expanded Communications - Electronics System (DOD)
EXCH . . . . . . Exchange
EXCL . . . . Excluding
EXCL . . . . Exclusive

EXCOA......	Explosives Corporation of America
EXDAMS.....	Extendable Debugging and Monitoring System (Data processing)
EXDIS......	Exclusive Distribution (Military security classification)
EXDIV......	Experimental Division
EXEC......	Executive
EXGA......	External Gage
EXIM.......	Export-Import Bank
EXMOVREP ...	Expedited Movement Report (Army)
EXO	Executive Officer
ExO........	Experimental Officer (Ministry of Agriculture, Fisheries, and Food) (Also, EO and XO) (British)
EXOS......	Executive Office of the Secretary (Navy)
EXP........	Exponential
EXPDIVUNIT ..	Experimental Diving Unit
EXPER......	Experiment(al)
EXPERT.....	Expanded Program Evaluation and Review Technique
EXPHO.....	Expedite Delivery by Telephone
EXPND.....	Expenditure
EXPO......	Extended-Range Poseidon (Navy)
EXREP......	Expedite Mail Reply

EXREQ	Extract of Requisition
EXSTA	Experimental Station
EXT	Extend (or Extension)
EXTAL	Extra Time Allowance
EXTLV	Extension of Leave (Army)
EXTM	Ex Testamento (In Accordance with the Testament of)
EXTRADOP ...	Extended Range Doppler
EY	Eger's Yellow
EY	Electron Yield
EY	Ethyl Corp. (NYSE symbol)
EYC	European Youth Campaign
EYD	Engineering Youth Day
EYM	Electron Yield Measurement
EYMS	Electron Yield Measurement System
EYOA......	Economic and Youth Opportunity Agency
EZ	Eastern Zone
EZ	Easy (Slang)
EZ	Electrical Zero
EZ	Extraction Zone (Military)
EZCO......	Extraction Zone Control Officer (Military)

F

F . . . . Cleared to the Fix (Aviation)
F . . . . Fahrenheit
F . . . . Failure
F . . . . Fair
F . . . . False
F . . . . Family
F . . . . Farad
F . . . . Faraday Constant
F . . . . Farthing (British monetary unit)
F . . . . Fast
F . . . . Father
F . . . . Fathom
F . . . . Feast
F . . . . Fecit (Did)
F . . . . Feedback
F . . . . Feet or Foot
F . . . . Feliciter (Happily)
F . . . . Fellow
F . . . . Female
F . . . . Feminine
f . . . . Femto (A prefix meaning divided by 10 to the 15th power)
F . . . . Fermi
F . . . . Fiat (Let There Be Made)
F . . . . Fiction
F . . . . Field
F . . . . Fighter (Aircraft)
F . . . . Filius (Son)
F . . . . Filly
F . . . . Filter
F . . . . Fine (Condition) (Antiquarian book trade and numismatics)
F . . . . Final Approach (Aviation)
F . . . . Final Target
F . . . . Finance or Financial
F . . . . Finish
F . . . . Fire
F . . . . Fireman (Navy rating)
F . . . . Firm
F . . . . Fitted as Flagship (Suffix to plane designation)
F . . . . Fixed (A continuous steady light) (Navigation)
F . . . . Flat
F . . . . Fleet
F . . . . Floods
F . . . . Florin (Same as gulden, monetary unit in Netherlands)
F . . . . Flower
F . . . . Flugzeug (Airplane) (German military)
F . . . . Fluid
F . . . . Fluid Ounce
F . . . . Fluorine (Chemical element)
F . . . . Focal length
F . . . . Fog (Weather)
F . . . . Folio (Book 30 centimeters and over in height)
F . . . . Following
F . . . . For
F . . . . Force
F . . . . Ford Motor Company (NYSE symbol) (Wall Street slang names: "Tin Lizzy" or "Flivver")
F . . . . Forma
F . . . . Formality
F . . . . Formed
F . . . . Formula
F . . . . Forte (Loud) (Music)
F . . . . Forward
F . . . . Foul

F . . . . Founded
F . . . . Fracture
F . . . . Fragile
F . . . . Fragmentation
F . . . . Franc(s) (French monetary unit)
F . . . . Fraser (James E.) (Designer's mark, when appearing on US coins)
F . . . . Frater (Brother)
F . . . . French
F . . . . Frequency
F . . . . Frequent (In mention of occurrence of species)
F . . . . Fresh Water (Load line mark)
F . . . . Friar
F . . . . From
F . . . . Fuel
F . . . . Fueler (Aircraft designation)
F . . . . Fugacity
F . . . . Full
F . . . . Function
F . . . . Furlong
F . . . . National Yeomen
F . . . . Photo-Reconnaissance (Aircraft designation)
F . . . . Ship being built by US for a foreign nation, when precedes vessel classification (Navy)
2F . . . . Two-seater Fighter Aircraft (Navy)
4F . . . . Fair, Fat, Fertile, and Forty (Medical slang describing women most susceptible to gall bladder attacks)
4-F . . . . Selective Service Class (for Man Not Qualified for Military Service)
FA . . . . Fairchild Aircraft
FA . . . . Family Allowance
FA . . . . Fatty Acid (Biochemistry)
FA . . . . Felonious Assault
FA . . . . Field Ambulance (Military)
FA . . . . Field Army
FA . . . . Field Artillery
FA . . . . Filterable Agent (Virology)
FA . . . . Financial Adviser
FA . . . . Finite Automaton
FA . . . . Fireman Apprentice
FA . . . . First Aid (Medicine)
FA . . . . First Attack (Men's lacrosse position)
FA . . . . Fluorescent Antibody
FA . . . . Folic Acid (Biochemistry)
FA . . . . Folklore Americas
FA . . . . Football Association (Controlling body of British soccer)
FA . . . . Forage Acre
FA . . . . Fortified Aqueous (Pharmacy)
FA . . . . Frankford Arsenal (Army)
FA . . . . Free of All Average (Insurance)
FA . . . . Free Alongside
FA . . . . Free Aperture (Technical drawings)
FA . . . . Free Astray
FA . . . . Freight Agent
FA . . . . Frequency Agility
FA . . . . Freund's Adjuvant
FA . . . . Friendly Aircraft
FA . . . . Full Action
FA . . . . Full Adder (Data processing)
FA . . . . Full Automatic
FA . . . . Functional Analysis
FA . . . . Fuzed Alloy
F/A . . . . Field Activities
F/A . . . . Fuel-Air (Ratio)
F & A . . . . . . Fore and Aft

FAA . . . . Family Allowance Class A
FAA . . . . Federal Aviation Administration (Formerly, Agency) (Independent government agency)
FAA . . . . Field Artillery Airborne
FAA . . . . Fireplace Association of America
FAA . . . . Fleet Air Arm (British)
FAA . . . . For an Approach To (Aviation)
FAA . . . . Foreman's Association of America
FAA . . . . Formalin, Acetic Acid, Alcohol (Solution)
FAA . . . . Foundation for American Agriculture
FAA . . . . Fraternal Actuarial Association
FAA . . . . Free of All Average (Insurance)
FAA . . . . Friends of Africa in America
FAAA . . . . . . First Allied Airborne Army (World War II)
FAA-AM . . . . Federal Aviation Administration - Office of Aviation Medicine
FAAAS . . . . . . Fellow of the American Association for the Advancement of Science
FAAB . . . . . . Family Allowance, Class A and B
FAAC . . . . . . Fellow of the American Association of Criminology
FAA/CAS . . . . Federal Aviation Administration - Canadian Air Services Committee
FAAD . . . . . . Forward Area Air Defense
FAADS . . . . . . Forward Area Air Defense System
FAADW . . . . . Forward Area Air Defense Weapon
FAAG . . . . . . First Advertising Agency Group
FAAN . . . . . . First Advertising Agency Network
FAAO . . . . . . Finance and Accounts Office (Army)
FAAO . . . . . . Fleet Aviation Accounting Office
FAAP . . . . . . Federal Aid to Airports Program (FAA)
FAAR . . . . . . Forward Area Alerting RADAR
FAA-RD . . . . . Federal Aviation Administration - Systems Research and Development Service
FAAS . . . . . . Fellow of the Academy of Arts and Sciences
FAAWTC . . . . . Fleet Anti-Air Warfare Training Center
FAB . . . . Family Allowance, Class B
FAB . . . . Fleet Air Base
FAB . . . . Forca Aerea Brasileira (Brazilian Air Force)
FAB . . . . Functional Adhesive Bonding
FABB . . . . . . Filene's (Boston) Automatic Bargain Basement
FABI . . . . Federation Royale des Association Belges d'Ingenieurs (Belgium)
FABIS . . . . . . Filmless Automatic Bond Inspection System
FABL . . . . Fire Alarm Bell
FABMDS . . . . Field Army Ballistic Missile Defense System
FABMIDS . . . . Field Army Ballistic Missile Defense System (Antimissile missile)
FABP . . . . . . Fatty Acid Binding Protein (Biochemistry)
F & ABR . . . . Food and Agriculture Branch (US Military Government, Germany)
FABRIC . . . . . . Frequency Assignment by Reference to Interference Charts
FABU . . . . . . Fleet Air Base Unit
FABU . . . . . . Fuel Additive Blender Unit
FABX . . . . . . Fire Alarm Box
FAC . . . . Facilities Associate Contractor
FAC . . . . Factor (Max) & Company (NYSE symbol)
FAC . . . . Failure Analysis Coordinator
FAC . . . . Federal Advisory Council
FAC . . . . Federal Aviation Commission
FAC . . . . Femoral Ash per Centimeter
FAC . . . . Field Accelerator
FAC . . . . Filter Address Correction
FAC . . . . Financial Administrative Control
FAC . . . . Fisheries Advisory Committee
FAC . . . . Fixed Air Capacitor
FAC . . . . Fleet Activities Command (Navy)
FAC . . . . Flettner Aircraft Corporation
FAC . . . . Fonds d'Aide et de Cooperation (Aid and Cooperation Fund) (France)
FAC . . . . Forward Air Control(ler) (Air Force)
FAC . . . . Frequency Allocation Committee (CCB)
FAC . . . . Frequency Analysis and Control
FACA . . . . . . Federal Alcohol Control Administration (Established, 1933; abolished, 1935)
FACA . . . . . . Fellow of the American College of Anesthesiologists
FACA . . . . . . Fellow of the American College of Apothecaries
FACC . . . . . . Fellow of the American College of Cardiologists
FACC . . . . . . Force Associated Control Communications (Military)
FACCA . . . . . Fellow of the Association of Certified and Corporate Accountants (British)
FACCONCEN . . Facilities Control Center (Army)
FACD . . . . . . Fellow of the American College of Dentists
FACD . . . . . . Foreign Area Consumer Dialing
FACE . . . . . . Facilities and Communication Evaluation (Army)
FACE . . . . . . Factory Automatic Checkout Equipment
FACE . . . . . . Federally Assisted Code Enforcement (Proposed HUD program)
FACE . . . . . . Field Artillery Computer Equipment
FACE . . . . . . Foundation for Accredited Chiropractic Education

FACET . . . . . . Fluid Amplifier Control Engine Test
FACETS . . . . . Franco-American Committee for Educational Travel and Studies
FACGD . . . . . Federation of American Citizens of German Descent
FACI . . . . First Article Configuration Inspection (Gemini) (NASA)
FACIL . . . . . . Facility
FACILE . . . . . . Fire and Casualty Insurance Library Edition
FACMTA . . . . Federal Advisory Council on Medical Training Aids
FACO . . . . . . Factory Assembly and Check-Out
FACOG . . . . . Fellow of the American College of Obstetricians and Gynecologists
FACP . . . . . . Fellow of the American College of Physicians
FACP . . . . . . Forward Air Control Post
FACR . . . . . . Fellow of the American College of Radiologists
FACR . . . . . . First Article Configuration Review (Army)
FACS . . . . . . Fast Attack Class Submarine
FACS . . . . . . Fellow of the American College of Surgeons
FACS . . . . . . Field Army Communication System
FACS . . . . . . Fine Attitude Control System (Aerospace)
FACS . . . . . . Flight Augmentation Control System (Aviation)
FACS . . . . . . Floating Decimal Abstract Coding System
FACS . . . . . . Fluid Amplifier Control System
FACS . . . . . . Fully Automatic Compiling System
FACSC . . . . . Frequency Allocation Coordinating Subcommittee (Canada)
FACSEA . . . . . Society for French American Cultural Services & Educational Aids
FACSI . . . . . . Federal Advisory Council on Scientific Information
FACSS . . . . . . Federation of Analytical Chemistry and Spectroscopy
FACT . . . . . . Fairchild Assured Component Test
FACT . . . . . . Field Audit and Completion Test (Market research)
FACT . . . . . . Fingerprint Automatic Classification Technique (Data processing)
FACT . . . . . . Flanagan Aptitude Classification Test (Psychology)
FACT . . . . . . Flexible Automatic Circuit Tester
FACT . . . . . . Flight Acceptance Composite Test (NASA)
FACT . . . . . . Fully Automatic Compiler-Translator
FACT . . . . . . Fully Automatic Compiling Technique
FACTER . . . . . Forward Air Controller Terminal
FACTS . . . . . . Facilities Action Control Target System (US Postal Service)
FACTS . . . . . . Facilities Administration Control and Time Schedule
FACTS . . . . . . Facsimile Transmission System
FACTS . . . . . . Field Army Calibration Team Support
FACTS . . . . . . National Food and Conservation Through Swine (An organization)
FAD . . . . Ferrite Array Demonstration (RADAR)
FAD . . . . First Article Demonstration
FAD . . . . Flavin-Adenine Dinucleotide (Biochemistry)
FAD . . . . Fleet Air Defense
FAD . . . . Fleet Air Detachment
FAD . . . . Flexible Automatic Depot
FAD . . . . Force/Activity Designator (Military)
FAD . . . . Free Air Delivered
F/AD . . . . . . Force/Activity Designator
FADAC . . . . . Field Artillery Data Computer (Military)
FADAP . . . . . Fleet Antisubmarine Data Analysis Program
FADD . . . . . . Fight Against Dictating Designers (Group opposing below-the-knee fashions introduced in 1970)
FADM . . . . . . Fleet Admiral
FADN . . . . . . Frente Anti-Communista de Defensa Nacional (Anti-Communist Front for National Defense) (Ecuador)
FADS . . . . . . Force Administration Data System (Bell System)
FADS . . . . . . Forward Area Deployment, Spain
FAE . . . . Final Approach Equipment
FAE . . . . Fuel Air Explosive
FAE . . . . Fund for the Advancement of Education
FAETU . . . . . Fleet Airborne Electronic Training Unit
FAETUA . . . . . Fleet Airborne Electronics Unit, Atlantic
FAETUPAC . . . Fleet Air Electronics Training Unit, Pacific (Later, FASOTRAGRUPAC; then, FASTTRAGRUPACFLT)
FAF . . . . Faellesrepraesentationen for Danske Arbejdsleder- og Tekniske Funktinaerforeninger (Council of Danish Supervisors' and Technical Employees' Associations)
FAF . . . . Fafnir Bearing Company (NYSE symbol) (Delisted)
FAF . . . . Fast Acting Fuse
FAF . . . . Final Approach Fix (Aviation)
FAF . . . . Financial Analysts Federation
FAF . . . . Fine Arts Foundation
FAF . . . . Flyaway Factory
FAF . . . . French Air Force
FAFP . . . . . . Foreign Area Fellowship Program
FAG . . . . Fraud Against the Government
FAGAIRTRANS . First Available Government Air Transportation (Navy)
FAGC . . . . . . Fast Automatic Gain Control
FAGLANT . . . . Fleet Assistance Group, Atlantic
FAGMS . . . . . Field Artillery Guided Missile (Air Force)
FAGp . . . . . . Finance and Accounting Group (Air Force)

FAGPAC . . . . . Fleet Assistance Group, Pacific
FAGS . . . . Federation of Astronomical and Geophysical Services
FAGS . . . . Fellow of the American Geographical Society
FAGT . . . . . . First Available Government Transportation
FAGTRANS . . . First Available Government Surface Transportation
FAGU . . . . Fleet Air Gunnery Unit
FAH . . . . Federation of American Hospitals
FAHA . . . . . . Finnish-American Historical Archives
FAHQT . . . . . . Fully Automatic, High Quality Translation
FAHSM . . . . . . Finnish American Historical Society of Michigan
FAI . . . . Federation Abolitionniste Internationale (International Abolitionist
        Federation)
FAI . . . . Federation Aeronautique Internationale (International Aeronautical
        Federation)
FAI . . . . Federazione Autonoma Indossatrici (Autonomous Federation of Models)
        (Italy)
FAI . . . . Frequency-Azimuth Intensity (RADAR)
FAIA . . . . Fellow of the American Institute of Architects
FAIB . . . . Federation des Associations Internationales Etablies en Belgique
        (Federation of International Associations Established in Belgium)
FAIC . . . . . . Fellow of the American Institute of Criminology
FAIF . . . . Field Automated Intelligence File
FAIME . . . . . . Foreign Affairs Information Management Effort (Computer) (Department
        of State)
FAIO . . . . Field Army Issuing Office
FAIR . . . . Fair Access to Insurance Requirements
FAIR . . . . Fair and Impartial Random Selection (System) (Military draft)
FAIR . . . . Fast Access Information Retrieval
FAIR . . . . Firearms and Individual Rights (A California organization)
FAIR . . . . . . Fleet Air (Wing)
FAIR . . . . Focus on Arms Information & Reassurance
FAIRDEX . . . . . Fleet Air Defense Exercise (Navy)
FAIRSHIPS . . . . Fleet Airships
FAIRSHIPWING. Fleet Airship Wing
FAIRTRANS . . . First Available Air Transportation
FAIRWESTPAC. . Fleet Air Wing, Western Pacific Area
FAIRWING . . . Fleet Air Wing
FAIS . . . . Force Air Intelligence Study (Air Force)
FAK . . . . Fly-Away Kit
FAK . . . . Freight, All Kinds (Railroad)
FAL . . . . Facilities Laboratory (National Center for Atmospheric Research)
FAL . . . . Falstaff Brewing Corporation (NYSE symbol)
FAL . . . . Finite Automaton Language
FAL . . . . Forces Armee Lao
FAL . . . . Frequency Allocation List
FAL . . . . Frontier Airlines, Inc.
FALD . . . . . . Finnish American League for Democracy
FALS . . . . Foreign Area and Language Study
FALT . . . . FADAC (Field Artillery Data Computer) Automatic Logic Tester
        (Military)
FALT . . . . . . Field Artillery Logic Tester (Army)
FAM . . . . Facilities Analysis Model (Data processing)
FAM . . . . Family
FAM . . . . Family Finance Corporation (NYSE symbol)
FAM . . . . Field Artillery Missile
FAM . . . . Foreign Air Mail
FAM . . . . Free at Mill (Business and trade)
F & AM . . . . Free and Accepted Masons
FAMA . . . . . . Federal Association of Management Analysts
FAMA . . . . . . Fellow of the American Medical Association
FAMA . . . . . . Fire Apparatus Manufacturers Association
FAMA . . . . . . Fondation pour l'Assistance Mutuelle en Afrique au Sud du Sahara
        (Foundation for Mutual Assistance in Africa South of the Sahara)
FAMAE . . . . . . Following Amendment Authorized Effective (followed by date)
FAMBSA . . . . Farmers and Manufacturers Beet Sugar Association
FAME . . . . . . Farmers' Allied Meat Enterprises Co-operative
FAME . . . . Fatty Acid Methyl Ester(s) (Biochemistry)
FAME . . . . . . Financial Analysis of Management Effectiveness (Department of
        Agriculture)
FAME . . . . . . Florida Association of Marine Explorers
FAME . . . . . . Forecasts, Appraisals, and Management Evaluations
FAME . . . . . . Future American Magical Entertainers (An organization)
FAMECE . . . . . Family of Military Engineer Construction Equipment
FAMF . . . . . . Floating Aircraft Maintenance Facility (Army)
FAMIS . . . . . . Financial and Management Information System (Naval Oceanographic
        Office)
FAMOS . . . . . . Fleet Air Meteorological Observation Satellite
FAMOS . . . . . . Fleet Applications of Meteorological Observations from Satellites
FAMOUS . . . . . Franco-American Midocean Undersea Treaty (Joint undersea program)
FAMS . . . . Field Army Messenger Service
FAMU . . . . Fleet Aircraft Maintenance Unit

FAMU . . . . . . Fuel Additive Mixture Unit
FANDT . . . . . . Fuel and Transportation (Navy)
FANG . . . . . . Flechette Area Neutralizing Gun
FANK . . . . Force Armee Nationale Khmer (Cambodian army)
FANTAC . . . . . Fighter Analysis Tactical Air Combat
FANUS . . . . . . Federazione fra le Associazioni Nazionali Ufficiali e Sottufficiali in
        Congedo Provenienti dal Servizio Effettivo (Federation of National
        Associations for Discharged Career Officers and Petty Officers) (Italy)
FANY . . . . . . First Aid Nursing Yeomanry (British women's organization formed to do
        medical transport work for the army; later did general transport work)
FANZCP . . . . . Fellow of the Australian and New Zealand College of Psychiatrists
FAO . . . . Field Audit Office
FAO . . . . Finance and Accounts Office(r) (Military)
FAO . . . . Finish All Over (Technical drawings)
FAO . . . . Fleet Accountant Officer (British)
FAO . . . . Fleet Administration Office
FAO . . . . Food and Agriculture Organization (of the United Nations)
FAO . . . . Free Albania Organization
FAOLU . . . . . . Federation of All Okinawan Labor Unions
FAOMELU . . . . Federation of All Okinawan Military Employees' Labor Unions
FAOUSA . . . . . Finance and Accounts Office(r), United States Army
FAP . . . . Facilities Assistance Program
FAP . . . . Family Assistance Plan (or Program)
FAP . . . . Fast Atmospheric Pulsation
FAP . . . . Federal Art Project
FAP . . . . Final Approach (Aviation)
FAP . . . . Finance and Accounting Policy (Army)
FAP . . . . Financial Analysis Program (IBM)
FAP . . . . Financial Assistance Program
FAP . . . . Fine Arts Philatelists
FAP . . . . First-Aid Post
FAP . . . . Fixed Action Pattern
FAP . . . . Floating-Point Arithmetic Package
FAP . . . . Food Additive Petition
FAP . . . . Foreign Air Program
FAP . . . . FORTRAN (Formula Translation) Assembly Program
FAP . . . . Frequency Allocation Panel
FAPA . . . . . . Fantasy Amateur Press Association
FAPA . . . . . . Filipino American Political Association
FAPA . . . . . . Flight Accrual Payment Action (Air Force)
FAPAP . . . . . . Federation des Personnels Africains de Police (Federation of African
        Police)
FAPC . . . . Fatty Acid Producers' Council
FAPCC . . . . . . Film, Air and Package Carriers Conference
FAPG . . . . . . Fleet Air Photographic Group
FAPHA . . . . . . Fellow of the American Public Health Association
FAPI . . . . Federazione Artisti e Professionisti Italiani (Italian Federation of the
        Arts and Professions)
FAPIG . . . . . . First Atomic Power Industry Group (Japan)
FAPO . . . . . . Field Army Petroleum Office
FAPR . . . . . . Federal Aviation Procurement Regulations
FAPRON . . . . . Fleet Air Photo Squadron
FAPS . . . . . . Fate of Atmospheric Pollutants Study
FAPS . . . . . . Fellow of the American Physical Society
FAPUSMCEB . . . Frequency Allocation Panel, United States Military Communications
        Electronics Board
FAQ . . . . Fair Average Quality
FAQ . . . . Free at Quay
FAR . . . . Failure Analysis Report
FAR . . . . False Alarm Rate
FAR . . . . Federal Aviation Regulations (FAA)
FAR . . . . Federation of Arab Republics (Formerly, UAR)
FAR . . . . First Alarm Register
FAR . . . . Fixed Array RADAR
FAR . . . . Flight Aptitude Rating
FAR . . . . Floor Area Ratio (in office buildings)
FAR . . . . Foreign Agricultural Relations Office
FAR . . . . Foreign Area Research Coordination Group (Department of State)
FAR . . . . Forward Acquisition RADAR
FAR . . . . Foundation for Administrative Research
FAR . . . . Frequency Adjusting Rheostat
FARADA . . . . Failure Rate Data (Program) (Navy)
FARC . . . . Field Artillery Replacement Center
FARE . . . . Foreign Assignment Resources Employees (FAA)
FARET . . . . . . Fast Reactor Engineering (or Experiment) Test (AEC)
FARGO . . . . . . Fourteen-o-one Automatic Report Generating Operation
FARK . . . . Forces Armee Kmer
FARMERS . . . . Frequency Agility RADAR Modifications to Existing RADAR
        Systems (DOD)
FARR . . . . . . Failure and Rejection Report
FARS . . . . Field Army Replacement System

FARSUL...... Federacao da Agricultura do Estado do Rio Grande do Sul
FAS .... Failure Analysis Section
FAS .... Fairbanks Air Service (Alaska)
FAS .... Fast Announcement Service (NTIS publication)
FAS .... **Federation of American Scientists**
FAS .... **Feel Augmentation System (Helicopters)**
FAS .... Fellow of the Antiquarian Society (British)
FAS .... Fellows in American Studies
FAS .... Field Alert Status (Army)
FAS .... Finnish-American Society
FAS .... Fire Support Aerial System
FAS .... Firsts and Seconds
FAS .... **Flight Advisory Service (FAA)**
FAS .... Flight Analysis Section
FAS .... **Flight Assistance Service**
FAS .... Focusing Array Study
FAS .... Followup Alarm System
FAS .... Force Accounting System (Army)
FAS .... **Foreign Agricultural Service (Department of Agriculture)**
FAS .... Foreign Aid Society (British)
FAS .... Foreign Area Specialist (Military)
FAS .... **Free Alongside Ship (Business and trade)**
FAS .... Frequency Assignment Subcommittee
FASA .... Field Army Service Area
FASA .... Fixed Area Scanning Alarm
FASA .... **Fleet Airships, Atlantic**
FASC .... Foreign Affairs Specialist Corps (State Department)
FASC .... **Foreign Agricultural Service Club**
FASCOM..... Field Army Support Command
FASE .... Fellow of the Antiquarian Society of Edinburgh
FASE .... Fundamentally Analyzable Simplified English (Data processing)
FASEB ...... **Federation of American Societies for Experimental Biology**
FASH .... Fraternal Association of Steelhaulers
FASO .... Forward Airfield Supply Organization
FASOR ...... Forward Area SONAR Research
FASOTRAGRUPAC... Fleet Aviation Specialized Operational Training Group, Pacific (Formerly, FAETUPAC; later FASOTRAGRUPACFLT) (Navy)
FASOTRAGRUPACFLT ... Fleet Aviation Specialized Operational Training Group, Pacific Fleet (Formerly, FASOTRAGRUPAC and FAETUPAC)
FASP .... **Fleet Airships, Pacific**
FASRON ..... Fleet Air(craft) Service Squadron
FASST....... Fly America's Supersonic Transport (Student group)
FAST .... Facility for Automatic Sorting and Testing
FAST .... Fast Automatic Shuttle Transfer (System) (Navy)
FAST .... Federal Assistance for Staff Training (Education)
FAST .... Federal Assistance Streamlining Taskforce (HEW)
FAST .... Fence Against Satellite Threats
FAST .... Field Data Applications, Systems, and Techniques
FAST .... First Atomic Ship Transport, Inc.
FAST .... Flexible Algebraic Scientific Translator
FAST .... Flight Advisory Service Test
FAST .... Fluorescent Antibody Staining Technique
FAST .... Foolproof Auditing and Sale of Tickets (in motion picture theaters)
FAST .... Foreign Area Specialist Training (Military)
FAST .... Formula and Statement Translator
FAST .... Friction Assessment Screening Test (for brake linings)
FAST .... Functional Analysis System Technique
FASTAR...... Frequency Angle Scanning, Tracking and Ranging
FASTI .... Fast Access to Systems Technical Information
FASTP....... **Foreign Area Specialist Training Program**
FAST RIPSAW . Financial Automation Systems Team for Writing Programs for Standardized Army-Wide Applications
FASTULANT... **Fleet Ammunition Ship Training Unit, Atlantic**
FASTUPAC.... **Fleet Ammunition Ship Training Unit, Pacific**
FAST-VAL .... Forward Air Strike Evaluation
FAT .... Factory Acceptance Test
FAT .... Fast Automatic Transfer
FAT .... Final Acceptance Trial
FAT .... **Final Assembly Test**
FAT .... **Fixed Asset Transfer**
FAT .... Flight Acceptance Test
FAT .... Free Air Temperature
FAT .... Fresno Air Terminal (California)
FATAB ...... Field Artillery Target Acquisition Battalion (Army)
FATAG ...... Field Artillery Target Acquisition Group (Army)
FATAL ...... Fully Automatic Test Algebraic Language
FATCAT ..... Film and Television Correlation Assessment Technique
FATDL ...... Frequency and Time-Division Data Link
FATE .... Fuze Arming Test Experiment
FATE .... Fuzing and Arming Test and Evaluation (Space vehicle)
FATEMETA.... Fakultas Teknologi dan Mekanisasi Pertanian

FATF .... Free Air Test Facility
FATIPEC ..... Federation d'Associations de Techniciens des Industries des Peintures, Vernis, Emaux et Encres d'Imprimerie de l'Europe Continentale (Federation of Associations of Technicians in the Paint, Varnishes, Enamels, and Printing-Ink Industries of Continental Europe)
FATOC...... **Field Army Tactical Operation Center**
FATRACS.... Field Army Tactical Random Access Communications System
FATRANS .... (Via) First Available Transportation
FATS .... Fight to Advertise the Truth about Saturates (Student legal action organization)
FATT .... Fracture Appearance Transition Temperature
FATU .... Fleet Air Tactical Unit
FAU .... **Flag Administrative Unit**
FAU .... Florida Atlantic University
FAU .... Frequency Allocation and Uses
FAUSST...... French-Anglo-United States Supersonic Transport
FAV .... **Favorable**
FAV .... Fixed-Angle Variable
FAVO....... **Fleet Aviation Officer (British)**
FAW....... Fawick Corporation (NYSE symbol) (Delisted)
FAW .... Fleet Air Wing
FAW .... **Forward Area Weapons (Military)**
FAW........ Friends of American Writers
FAWA....... **Federation of Asian Women's Associations**
FAWAF ..... Fleet Air Wings Atlantic Fleet (Navy)
FAWC ...... Franciscan Apostolate of the Way of the Cross
FAWCO ..... Federation of American Women's Clubs Overseas
FAWESP ..... Field Activity War and Emergency Support Plan
FAWOD ..... Furnish Assignment Instructions Without Delay
FAWS .... Flight Advisory Weather Service
FAWSHMOTRON .. Fast Wave Simple Harmonic Motion (A microwave tube device)
FAWTU ...... Fleet All-Weather Training Unit
FAWTULANT . **Fleet All Weather Training Unit, Atlantic**
FAWTUPAC . **Fleet All Weather Training Unit, Pacific**
FAX .... Facsimile
FAX .... Fuel Air Explosive
FB .... Fenian Brotherhood (Irish)
FB .... Fighter Bomber Aircraft
FB .... Film Bulletin
FB .... Fine Business (i.e., excellent) (Amateur radio)
FB .... **Fire Brigade**
FB .... First National Boston Corp. (NYSE symbol)
FB .... **Fishery Board**
FB .... **Flat Bar (Technical drawings)**
FB .... **Fluidized Bed**
FB .... **Flying Boat**
FB .... **Fog Bell (Navigation charts)**
FB .... **Foreign Body (Medicine)**
FB .... Forward Body
FB .... **Free Baptist**
FB .... Freight Bill
FB .... **Fullback (Football position)**
FB .... **Fumigation and Bath (Military)**
FB .... Function Button (Data processing)
F/B .... Fighter Bomber
F & B .... Fire and Bilge
FBA .... Fanned Beam Antenna
FBA .... **Federal Bar Association**
FBA .... Fellow of the British Academy
FBA .... **Fibre Box Association**
FBA .... **Figural Bottle Association**
FBAA ...... Fellow of the British Association of Accountants and Auditors
FBAA ...... Flying Boat Alighting Area
FBAA ...... Fur Brokers Association of America
FBACSI ..... **Fur Buyers Association, Coat and Suit Industry**
FBAO .... Farm Buildings Advisory Officer (Ministry of Agriculture, Fisheries, and Food) (British)
FBB .... Functional Breadboard System (Skylab) (NASA)
FBC .... Fallen Building Clause
FBC .... Fixed Bathtub Capacitor
FBC .... Friends Bible College (Kansas)
FBC .... Fully Buffered Channel
FBD .... Fibreboard Corp. (NYSE symbol)
FBD .... Free Board
FBD .... Free Body Diagram
FBDCA ..... French Bulldog Club of America
FBFM ...... Feedback Frequency Modulation
FBG .... Faberge, Inc. (NYSE symbol)
FBH .... **Federal Board of Hospitalization (Coordinated hospitalization activities of Army, Navy, and various government agencies; terminated, 1948)**
FBH .... Fire Brigade Hydrant

ACRONYMS AND INITIALISMS DICTIONARY

FBHDL ...... Force Beachhead Line
FBI .... Federal Bureau of Investigation
FBI .... Federation of British Industries
FBI's .... Forgotten Boys of Iceland (Nickname for US soldiers in Iceland) (World War II)
FBIS .... Foreign Broadcast Intelligence Service (of FCC) (World War II)
FBK .... Flat Back
FBL .... Federal Barge Lines R. R., Inc. (AAR code)
FBL .... Form Block Line
FBL .... Foundation for Better Living
FBLA .... Future Business Leaders of America
FBM .... Feet Board Measure
FBM .... Fleet Ballistic Missile
FBMP ...... Fleet Ballistic Missile Program (Navy)
FBMS ...... Fleet Ballistic Missile System
FBMWS ..... Fleet Ballistic Missile Weapon System
FBN .... Feed Back Network
FBNML ...... Francis Bitter National Magnet Laboratory (MIT)
FBO .... Federal Paper Board Company, Inc. (NYSE symbol)
FBO .... Fixed Base Operator (Provider of aviation [non-airline] services to users of airports)
FBO .... Foreign Building Office (of Department of State)
FBOA .... Fellow of the British Optical Association
FBOOM ..... Fort Benning Officers' Open Mess (Pronounced "fuhboom")
FBP .... Fighter Bomber Program
FBP .... Final Boiling Point
FBP .... Fleet Boat Pool
FBP .... Fluidized Bed Process
FBP .... Fuel Booster Pump
FBPC .... Foreign Bondholders Protective Council
FBPsS ...... Fellow of the British Psychological Society
FBR .... Fast Breeder Reactor (AEC)
FBR .... Fast Burn Rate
FBR .... Fast Burst Reactor
FBR .... Fireball Radius (Military)
FBR .... Fluidized Bed Reactor
FBRF .... Fast Burst Reactor Facility
FBRL .... Final Bomb Release Line
FBS .... Fasting Blood Sugar (Physiology)
FBS .... Fellow of the Botanical Society (British)
FBS .... Fetal Bovine Serum
FBS .... Fine Bearing Servo
FBS .... Forward Based Systems (US aircraft based outside the US and capable of carrying nuclear weapons to the USSR)
FBSA .... Filter Band Suppressor Assembly
FBSI .... Furniture and Bedding Spring Institute
FBU .... Fire Brigade Union
FBW .... Fly by Wire
FBY .... Future Budget Year
FC .... Compound Fracture (Medicine)
FC .... Congregatio Fratrum Caritate (Brothers of Charity) (Roman Catholic religious order)
FC .... Facilities Contract
FC .... Failure Count
FC .... Feature Count (Data processing)
FC .... Federal Cabinet (Australia)
FC .... Ferrite Core
FC .... Ferry Command (British Royal Air Force)
FC .... Fideicommissum (Bequeathed in Trust)
FC .... Field Camera
FC .... Field Command (Military)
FC .... Fieri Curavit (Caused to Be Made)
FC .... Fighter Command (Air Force)
FC .... File Copy
FC .... Filter Center
FC .... Finance Charge
FC .... Finance Corps
FC .... Fine Champagne
FC .... Fine Cognac
FC .... Fire Clay
FC .... Fire Control (of guns)
FC .... Fire Controlman
FC .... Fishery Council
FC .... Flight Charts
FC .... Flight Control
FC .... Flood Control
FC .... Flow Coating
FC .... Follow Copy (Printing)
FC .... Food Controller (British) (World War II)
FC .... Foot-Candle
FC .... Football Club

FC .... Foreign Currency
FC .... Fractocumulus (Meteorology)
FC .... Free Choice (Psychology)
FC .... Free Church (of Scotland)
FC .... Frequency Converter
FC .... Front-Connected
FC .... Functional Code
FC .... Fuze Committee (Military)
F/C .... Flight Certificate
FC's .... False Calves (Padding worn under tights by actors, to improve shape of their legs)
FCA .... Farm Credit Administration (Independent government agency)
FCA .... Fecal-Collection System (Apollo) (NASA) (See also DCD)
FCA .... Federal Committee on Apprenticeship
FCA .... Federal Communications Act
FCA .... Federal Council on Aging (Succeeded by President's Council on Aging, 1962)
FCA .... Federation of Canadian Artists
FCA .... Fellow of the Institute of Chartered Accountants (British)
FCA .... Fellowship of Christian Athletes
FCA .... Ferrite Control Amplifier
FCA .... Field Change Authorization
FCA .... Fighter Control Area (Military)
FCA .... Fire Control Area (Army)
FCA .... Fixed Coaxial Attenuator
FCA .... Flight Control Assemblies
FCA .... Free China Assistance
FCA .... French Computing Association
FCA .... Frequency Control and Analysis
FCAA ...... Florence Crittenton Association of America
FCAD ...... Field Contract Administration Division (of ONM)
FCAF ...... Frequency Control Analysis Facility
FCAP ...... Fellow of the College of American Pathologists
FCAS ...... Frequency Coded Armaments System
FCAT ...... Flight Composite Acceptance Test
FCB .... Facility Clearance Board (WPB)
FCB .... Fast Capacitor Bank
FCB .... Foote, Cone & Belding Communications, Inc. (NYSE symbol)
FCB .... Foreign Clearing Base
FCB .... Format Control Buffer
FCB .... Foundation for Commercial Banks
FCB .... Free Cutting Brass
FCB .... Fuel Cell Battery
FCBA ...... Federal Communications Bar Association
FCC .... Face-Centered Cubic (Crystallography)
FCC .... Falsely Claiming (US) Citizenship
FCC .... Family Communion Crusade
FCC .... Federal City College (Washington, DC)
FCC .... Federal Communications Commission (Independent government agency)
FCC .... Federal Construction Council
FCC .... Federal Consultative Council of South African Railways and Harbors Staff Association
FCC .... Federal Council of Churches
FCC .... Field Camera Control
FCC .... Field Control Center
FCC .... Fire Control Code
FCC .... First-Class Certificate
FCC .... Fixed Ceramic Capacitor
FCC .... Flat Conductor Cables
FCC .... Flight Communications Center
FCC .... Flight Control Container
FCC .... Flight Coordination Center
FCC .... Florida Christian College
FCC .... Florida Citrus Commission
FCC .... Fluid Catalytic Cracking
FCC .... Forbidden Combination Check
FCC .... Foreign Commerce Club of New York
FCC .... Fuel Cell Catalyst
FCCA ...... Farmers Chinchilla Cooperative of America
FCCA ...... Forestry, Conservation Communications Association
FCCA ...... Four Cylinder Club of America
FCCB ...... Field Configuration Control Board (Army)
FCCC ...... Flight Coordination Control Central
FCCI ...... Federal Clean Car Incentive Program
FCCN ...... Federal Communications Commission Network
FCCO ...... Fellow of the Canadian College of Organists
FCCO ...... Flight Change Control Order
FCCP ...... Fellow of the American College of Chest Physicians
FCCS ...... Fellow of the Corporation of Certified Secretaries (British)
FCCUS ..... French Chamber of Commerce of the United States
FCD .... Femoral Cortical Density

FCD	Fixed Center Drive
FCD	Flood Control District (Florida)
FCD	Food Control Diet
FCD	Four-Bar Cutter Device
FCD	Frequency Compression Demodulator
FCDA	Federal Civil Defense Administration (Transferred to Office of Defense and Civilian Mobilization, 1958; to Department of Defense and Office of Emergency Preparedness, 1961)
FCDA	Fuel Control Diaphragm Assembly
FC/DASA	Field Command, Defense Atomic Support Agency
FCDC	Fixed Ceramic Disc Capacitor
FCDG	Federal Civil Defense Guide
FCDN	Ferrocarril de Nacozari (AAR code)
FCDR	Failure Cause Data Report
FCDT	Four Coil Differential Transformer
FCE	Field Checkout Equipment
FCE	Fire Control Equipment
FCE	Fleet Civil Engineer
FCE	Flexible Critical Experiment
FCE	Foundation for Character Education
FCE	Frequency Converter Excitation
FCE	Friends Council on Education
FCECA	Fishery Committee for the Eastern Central Atlantic
FCEI	Facility Contract End Item
FCF	Family Camping Federation
FCF	First Charter Financial Corporation (NYSE symbol)
FCF	Free China Fund for Medical and Refugee Aid
FCF	Frequency Compressive Feedback
FCF	Fuel Cycle Facility (AEC)
FCF	Functional Check Flight (Air Force)
FCFA	Florida Commercial Fisheries Association
FCFC	Full-Coverage Film Cooling
FCF SE	Facility Checking Flight – Service Evaluation (Air Force)
FCG	Federation for Constitutional Government
FCG	Fernwood, Columbia & Gulf R. R. (AAR code)
FCG	Fire Control Group
FCG	Foreign Clearance Guide
FCGC	Flight Control Gyro Container
FCGCMA	Federation of Cash Grain Commission Merchants Associations
FCGP	Fellow of the College of General Practitioners
FCH	Flight Controllers Handbook
FCH	Foundation for Cooperative Housing
FCI	Fairchild Camera & Instrument Corporation (NYSE symbol)
FCI	Fashion Coordination Institute
FCI	Federal Crop Insurance
FCI	Flight Critical Items
FCI	Fluid Conductivity Indicator
FCI	Fluid Controls Institute
FCI	Franklin College of Indiana
F & CI	Food and Container Institute
FCIA	Foreign Credit Insurance Association (Export-Import Bank)
FCIB	Foreign Credit Interchange Bureau
FCIC	Fairchild Camera and Instrument Corporation
FCIC	Federal Crop Insurance Corporation (Department of Agriculture)
FCIF	Flight Crew Information File
FCII	Federated Council of Israel Institutions
FCII	Fellow of the Chartered Insurance Institute
FCIN	Frankfort & Cincinnati R. R. (AAR code)
FCIP	Field Cable Installation Platoon (Army)
FCIR	Facility Change Initiation Request
FCIS	Fellow of the Chartered Institute of Secretaries (British)
FCIU	Family Crisis Intervention Unit (New York Police Department)
FCJ	Society of the Sisters, Faithful Companions of Jesus (Roman Catholic religious order)
FCK	Field Change Kit
FCK	Filter Change Kit
FCK	Fuel Charge Kit
FCL	Fifth Avenue Coach Lines, Inc. (NYSE symbol) (Delisted)
FCL	Final Coordination Line (Military)
FCL	Fire Coordination Line (Military)
FCL	Flight Control Laboratory
FCL	Flux Current Loop
FCL	Fuze Cavity Lines (Projectile)
FCLP	Field Carrier Landing Passes (or Practice)
FCLTY	Facility
FCM	Fat Corrected Milk
FCM	Ferrocarril Mexicano (AAR code)
FCM	Fiber Composite Material
FCM	Filament Composite Material
FCM	Florida Citrus Mutual
FCM	Forged Chrom-Moly
FCM	Framing Camera Mopper
FCM	Fuel Cell Module
FCMSBR	Federal Coal Mine Safety Board of Review (Independent government agency)
FCMT	Flight Configuration Mode Test (Gemini) (NASA)
FCMU	Foot-Controlled Maneuvering Unit (Skylab) (NASA)
FCMV	Fuel Consuming Motor Vehicle
FCNA	Florida Citrus Nurserymen's Association
FCNL	French Committee of National Liberation (World War II)
FCNL	Friends Committee on National Legislation
FCO	Fellow of the College of Organists (British)
FCO	Files Control Office
FCO	Fire Control Operator (Army)
FCO	Fixed Cycle Operation
FCO	Flag Communications Officer (Navy)
FCO	Flying Control Officer (Navy)
FCO	Functional Check Out
FCOAC	Furnish Copies of Orders to Appropriate Commanders
FCOB	Flight Control Operations Branch (NASA)
FCOI	Fire Control Optical Instrument
FCP	Federal Catalog Program
FCP	Federazione dei Chimici e Petrolieri (Federation of Chemical and Petroleum Workers) (Italy)
FCP	Fellow of the College of Preceptors (British)
FCP	Ferrocarril del Pacifico (AAR code)
FCP	Field Command Post
FCP	Final Common Pathway (Neurology)
FCP	Fire Control Personnel (Marine Corps)
FCP	Fire Control Platoon (Army)
FCP	Function Control Package (Data processing)
FCP	Pacific F.C. del P. R. R. (AAR code)
FCPC	Fair Campaign Practices Committee
FCPC	Federal Committee on Pest Control
FCPC	Flat Computer Programming Center
FCPCP	Fleet Computer Programming Center, Pacific
FCPG	Federation of Catholic Physicians' Guilds
FCPO	First Class Post Office
FCPS	Fellow of the College of Physicians and Surgeons
FCR	Facility Capability Report (Military)
FCR	Facility Capability Review
FCR	Facility Change Request
FCR	Fast Ceramic Reactor (Program)
FCR	Fire Control RADAR
FCR	Fire Controlman, Range-Finder Operator (Navy rating)
FCR	Floating Control Regulator
FCR	Fuse Current Rating
FCRAA	Folding Chair Rental Association of America
FCRC	Federal Contract Research Center
FCRE	Foundation for Cotton Research and Education
FCRL	Flight Control Ready Light (System)
FCRU	Facilities Control Relay Unit (Army)
FCS	Facsimile Communications System
FCS	Fairchild Semiconductor
FCS	Farm Credit System (of FCA)
FCS	Farmer Cooperative Service (Department of Agriculture)
FCS	Federal Catalog System (of GSA)
FCS	Feedback Control System
FCS	Fellow of the Chemical Society (British)
FCS	Fetal Cow (or Calf) Serum
FCS	Fighter Command School (Air Force)
FCS	Fire Control Simulator
FCS	Fire Control System
FCS	Fire Controlman, Submarine (Navy)
FCS	Flame Control System
FCS	Flight Control Subsystem
FCS	Flowmeter Calibration Stand
FCS	Forged Carbon Steel
FCS	Free of Capture and Seizure (Insurance)
FC & S	Free of Capture and Seizure (Insurance)
FCSA	Forest Conservation Society of America
FCSC	Foreign Claims Settlement Commission
FCSG	Fire Control Sensor Group
FCSL	Fire Control System Laboratory
FCSLU	First Catholic Slovak Ladies Union
FCSPASTU . . .	Federation of Civil Service and Primary Aided School Teachers' Unions (Mauritius)
FCSS	Flight Control Systems Section
FCST	Federal Council for Science and Technology (Executive Office of President)
FCST	Flat Cable Stripping Tool
FCST	Forecast
FCSU	Fire Control Switching Unit

FCSU	First Catholic Slovak Union of the USA
FCSUM	**Federation of Civil Service Unions of Mauritius**
FCT	**Face-Centered Tetragonal (Crystallography)**
FCT	Fatigue Cracking Test
FCT	**Filament Center Tap**
FCT	Final Contract Trials (Navy)
FCT	**Fire Control Technician (Navy)**
FCT	Fire Control Trainer
FCT	Flux-Corrected Transport (Algorithm)
FCT	**Fraction Thereof**
FCTCSC	Flue-Cured Tobacco Cooperative Stabilization Corporation
FCTGA	**Flue-Cured Tobacco Growers Association**
FCTP	Fire Control Test Package
FCU	Fire Control Unit
FCU	Flight Control Unit
FCU	Force Control Unit
FCU	Frequency Converter Unit
FCUA	**Federated Clerks' Union of Australia**
FCUA	Fuel-Critical, Unspecified Area
FCUSA	Finance Center, United States Army
FCV	Flow Control Valve
FCW	Flyer Coil Winder
FCWA	Fellow of the Chartered Institute of Cost and Work Accountants (British)
FCWG	Frequency Control Working Group
FD	Central Foundry Company (NYSE symbol) (Later, GBI)
FD	**Fatal Dose**
FD	Federal Document
FD	Fidei Defensor (Defender of the Faith)
FD	Fighter Direction
FD	Finance Department
FD	Fire Department
FD	Fire Direction
FD	First Day (Philately)
FD	First Defense (Men's lacrosse position)
FD	First Down (Football)
FD	Floor Drain (Technical drawings)
FD	Focal Distance
FD	Fog Diaphone (Navigation charts)
FD	Food Distribution Division (of AMS, Department of Agriculture)
FD	Forced Draft
FD	Fourth Day (NYSE symbol)
FD	Frame Difference
FD	Free Delivery
FD	Free Discharge
FD	Free Dispatch
FD	Free Dock
FD	Free Drop
FD	Frequency Diversity (Radio)
FD	Frequency Divider
FD	Frequency Doublers
FD	Frequency Drift
FD	Front of Dash (Technical drawings)
FD	Full Dress (Colloquial reference to formal dress)
FD	**Full Dress (Military)**
FD	Full Duplex
FD	**Fuze Delay**
F & D	Findings and Determination
F & D	Freight and Demurrage (Shipping)
FDA	Ferrite Driver Amplifier
FDA	First Division Association (British)
FDA	Flying Dentists Association
FDA	Folded Dipole Antenna
FDA	Food Distribution Administration (Terminated, 1945)
FDA	Food and Drug Administration (of HEW)
FDA	Frequency Distortion Analyzer
FDA	Fronto-Dextra Anterior
FDAI	Feather and Down Association, Incorporated
FDAI	Flight Director Attitude Indicator
FDAS	**Field Depot Aviation Squadron (Air Force)**
FDAS	Frequency Distribution Analysis Sheet
FDATC	Flying Division Air Training Command
FDB	Faelliesforeningen for Danmarks Brugsforeninger (Denmark)
FDB	**Field Dynamic Braking**
FDB	**Fighter Dive-Bomber**
FDB	**Forced-Draft Blower**
FDC	Field Data Computer
FDC	Final Design Criteria
FDC	**Fire-Department Connection (Technical drawings)**
FDC	Fire Detection Center
FDC	**Fire Direction Center (Military)**
FDC	First-Day Cover (Philately)

FDC	Fixed Decade Capacitor
FDC	Flight Director Computer
FDC	Fluid Digital Computer
FDC	**Food, Drug and Cosmetic (Act)**
FDC	**Formation Drone Control (Navy)**
FDC	**Forward Direction Center (Air Force)**
FDC	Frequency Domain Coding
FDCPA	Food, Drug and Consumer Product Agency (Proposed successor to FDA) (HEW)
FDCS	**Fighter Director Control Schools (Navy)**
FDCT	Frequency Domain Coding Technique
FDD	**Floating Digital Drive**
FDD	**Floating Drydock (Navy)**
FDD	**Fondation Documentaire Dentaire**
FDD	Foreign Document Division (of CIA)
FDD	Franc de Droits (Free of charge)
FDDL	**Frequency Division Data Link (Radio)**
FDDM	Fort Dodge, Des Moines & Southern Railway Company (AAR code)
FDE	**Field Decelerator**
FDE	Flaw Detection Equipment
FDE	**Functional Differential Equation**
FDF	Failure Density Function
FDF	Flame Deflector Firex
FDF	Flush Door Fastener
FDG	Fermi-Dirac Gas
FDG	Fractional Doppler Gate
FDG	**Fur Dressers Guild**
FDGB	Freier Deutscher Gewerkschaftsbund (Trade union confederation, Russian Zone of Germany)
FDH	Floating Divide or Halt
FDI	**Federation Dentaire Internationale**
FDI	**Feeder Distribution Interface (Bell System)**
FDI	Field Discharge
FDI	Field Displacement Isolator
FDI	Flight Direction Indicator
FDI	Formal Documents Issued (Federal Power Commission)
FDI	Fuel Desulphurization, Incorporated
FDIC	**Federal Deposit Insurance Corporation (Independent government agency)**
FDIC	Fire Department Instructors Conference
FDIF	**Federation Democratique Internationale des Femmes (Women's International Democratic Federation)**
FDIS	Freeway Driver Information System
FDJ	Freie Deutsche Jugend (Free German Youth)
FDL	Fast Deployment Logistics (Ships) (Navy)
FDL	Federals, Inc. (NYSE symbol)
FDL	Fick Diffusion Law
FDL	Fixed Delay Line
FDL	Flight Dynamic Laboratory (Air Force)
FDL	Foremost (or Forward) Defended Localities (or Locations) (British)
FDL	Frequency Double LASER
FDL	Fuehrer der Luft (Air liaison officer with Navy) (German military – World War II)
FDLD	Frequency Doubling LASER Device
FDLH	Flight Determination Laboratory, Holloman Air Force Base
FDLI	Food and Drug Law Institute
FDLS	Fast Deployment Logistic Ship (Navy)
FDM	Faraday Disc Machine
FDM	Federated Development Co. (NYSE symbol)
FDM	Frequency Deviation Meter
FDM	Frequency Division Multiplex(ing) (Radio)
FDMA	Ferrocarril de Minatitlan al Carmen (AAR code)
FDMA	Fibre Drum Manufacturers Association (Defunct)
FDMA	Frequency-Division Multiple Access
FDMHA	**Frederick Douglass Memorial and Historical Association**
FDMIS	Force Development Management Information System (Army)
FDMS	Frequency-Division Multiplexing System
FDMVC	Frequency Division Multiplex Voice Communication
FDN	Field Designator Number (Air Force)
FDNET	**Fighter Direction Net (Navy)**
FDO	**Fighter Director Officer (Navy)**
FDO	Fire Direction Officer (Army)
FDO	**Fleet Dental Officer**
FDO	Flight Duty Officer (Air Force)
FDO	Food Distribution Order
FDP	Feasibility Demonstration Program
FDP	Field Developed Program (Data processing)
FDP	Fighter Development Program
FDP	Filii Divinae Providentiae (Sons of Divine Providence) (Roman Catholic religious order)
FDP	Flare Dispenser Pod
FDP	Florida Power Corporation (NYSE symbol)

FDP . . . . Foreign Duty Pay
FDP . . . . Forward Distribution Point (Military)
FDP . . . . Freedom Democratic Party (in Mississippi)
FDP . . . . **Freie Demokratische Partei (Free Democratic Party) (West Germany)**
FDP . . . . Fronto-Dextra Posterior
FDPC . . . . Fluorimetric Determination of Plasma Cortisol
FDPM . . . . Final Draft, Presidential Memorandum (DOD)
FDR . . . . Facility Data Report (AEC)
FDR . . . . Final Data Report
FDR . . . . Flight Data Recorder
FDR . . . . Formal Design Review
FDR . . . . Franklin Delano Roosevelt
FDR . . . . Frequency Diversity RADAR
FDRF . . . . **Financial Data Records Folder**
FDRG . . . . . . Fluid Dynamics Research Group (MIT)
FDRL . . . . . . Fluid Dynamics Research Laboratory (MIT)
FDRMA . . . . . . **Flooring Division, Rubber Manufacturers Association**
FDRPS . . . . . . Franklin D. Roosevelt Philatelic Society
FDS . . . . Faraday Dark Space
FDS . . . . Fast Diode Switch
FDS . . . . Fathometer Depth Sounder
FDS . . . . Federated Department Stores, Inc. (NYSE symbol)
FDS . . . . Fellow of Dental Surgery
FDS . . . . Feminine Deodorant Spray (Initialism used as brand name)
FDS . . . . Fermi-Dirac Statistics
FDS . . . . Fighter Director Ship (Navy)
FDS . . . . Finance Disbursing Section (Army)
FDS . . . . Fire Detection System
FDS . . . . Fire Distribution System
FDS . . . . Flexible Display System
FDS . . . . Flexible Drive Shaft
FDS . . . . Frame Difference Signal
FDSIS . . . . . . Flight Deck System Integration Simulator
FDSSR . . . . . . Flight Dynamics Staff Support Room (Apollo) (NASA)
FDT . . . . Fault Detection Tester
FDT . . . . **Fighter Director Tender (Navy)**
FDT . . . . Figure Drawing Test (Psychology)
FDT . . . . First Destination Transportation (Military)
FDT . . . . Flowing Gas Detonation Tube
FDT . . . . Fronto-Dextra Transversa
FDT . . . . Full Duplex Teletype
FDTK . . . . . . Floating Drift Tube Klystron
FDTU . . . . . . **Federation of Danish Trade Unions**
FDU . . . . Fairleigh Dickinson University (New Jersey)
FDU . . . . Fidelity Union Bancorp (NYSE symbol)
FDU . . . . Frequency Determining Unit
FDV . . . . Friend Disease Virus
FDV . . . . Full Duplex Vocoder
FDW . . . . Fine (Condition) in Dust Wrapper (Antiquarian book trade)
FDX . . . . Full Duplex
FE . . . . Failure Equation
FE . . . . Far East
FE . . . . Farm Economics Research Division (of ARS, Department of Agriculture)
FE . . . . Feliciana Eastern R. R. (AAR code)
FE . . . . Ferroelectric
Fe . . . . **Ferrum (Iron) (Chemical element)**
FE . . . . Field Engineer(ing)
FE . . . . Fighter Escort
FE . . . . Flame Emission
FE . . . . Flight Engineer(ing)
FE . . . . Fluid Extract (Pharmacy)
FE . . . . Fonetic English (for spelling words the way they sound)
FE . . . . Forest Engineer
FE . . . . Format Effector
F/E . . . . Fraudulent Enlistment
F & E . . . . Facilities and Equipment
FE⁵⁹ . . . . Radioactive Iron
FEA . . . . Failure Effect Analysis
FEA . . . . Federal Editors Association
FEA . . . . Federation Internationale pour l'Education Artistique
FEA . . . . Fiber-Embedding Approximation
FEA . . . . Field Effect Amplifier
FEA . . . . Field Evaluation Agency (Army)
FEA . . . . Followup Error Alarm
FEA . . . . **Foreign Economic Administration**
FEA . . . . Functional Economic Area
FEA . . . . Future Engineers of America
FEAA . . . . . . **Free Enterprise Awards Association**
FEAC . . . . . . Fairchild Engine and Airplane Corporation
FEAC . . . . . . Far Eastern Advisory Council

FEACCI . . . . Far-East-America Council of Commerce and Industry
FEACO . . . . . Federation Europeenne des Associations de Conseils en Organisation
(European Federation of Management Consultants Associations)
FEAF . . . . . . Far East Air Force
FEA(I) . . . . . . Federal Employees Association (Independent)
FEAICS . . . . . Federation Europeenne des Associations d'Ingenieurs de Securite et de
Chefs de Service de Securite
FEALOGFOR . . Far East Air Logistical Force
FEAMCOM . . . Far East Air Materiel Command
FEAN . . . . . . Federation des Enseignants d'Afrique Noire (Federation of Teachers of
Black Africa)
FEANF . . . . . Federation des Etudiants d'Afrique Noire en France (Federation of Students
of Black Africa in France)
FEANI . . . . . . Federation Europeenne d'Associations Nationales d'Ingenieurs (European
Federation of National Associations of Engineers)
FEAO . . . . . . Federation of European American Organizations
FEAPW . . . . . Federal Emergency Administration of Public Works (Consolidated into
Federal Works Agency and administered as PWA, 1939)
FEAR . . . . . . Free Expression of Appreciation or Revenge (Customer opinion campaign
operated by Bekins Van and Storage Company)
FEAST . . . . . . Food Education and Service Training
FEAT . . . . . . Final Engineering Acceptance Test (Apollo) (NASA)
FEAT . . . . . . Formal Evaluation Acceptance Test (Apollo) (NASA)
FEAT . . . . . . Frequency of Every Allowable Term
FEB . . . . **Fair Employment Board (of Civil Service Commission) (Abolished, 1955)**
FEB . . . . February
FEB . . . . Federal Executive Board (Civil Service Commission)
FEB . . . . Flight Evaluation Board
FEB . . . . Forca Expedicionaria Brasileira (Brazilian Expeditionary Force,
1944-1955)
FEB . . . . Functional Electronic Block
FEBA . . . . . . Forward Edge of the Battle Area (Army)
FEBNYC . . . . **Foreign Exchange Brokers of New York City**
FEBOSCO . . . . Federation des Scouts du Congo
FEBS . . . . Federation of European Biochemical Societies
FEBS . . . . Functional Electronic Blocks
FEC . . . . Facilities Engineering Command (Also, NFEC) (Formerly, Bureau of Yards
and Docks) (Navy)
FEC . . . . Far East Conference
FEC . . . . Far East Command
FEC . . . . Far Eastern Commission
FEC . . . . Farm Electrification Council
FEC . . . . Federation des Entreprises au Congo (Merger of AIIB and AICB)
FEC . . . . Ferroelectric Ceramic
FEC . . . . Fixed Electrolytic Capacitor
FEC . . . . **Florida East Coast R. R. (AAR code)**
FEC . . . . Fondation Europeenne de la Culture
FEC . . . . Foreign Economic Coordination (Office of)
FEC . . . . Foreign Exchange Cost
FEC . . . . Forward End Cap
FEC . . . . Franciscan Educational Conference
FEC . . . . Free Energy Change
FEC . . . . Free Europe Committee
FEC . . . . French Expeditionary Force
FECA . . . . . . Facilities Engineering and Construction Agency (HEW)
FECA . . . . . . Federal Employees Compensation Act
FECB . . . . . . Far East Combined Bureau (Singapore, 1940) (Military)
FECB . . . . . . Federation des Employes Congolais des Banques (Federation of Congolese
Bank Clerks)
FECEP . . . . . . Federation Europeenne des Constructeurs d'Equipement Petrolier
FECG . . . . . . Fetal Electrocardiography (Medicine)
FECL . . . . . . Federal Constitutional Law
FECOM . . . . . Far East Command (Military)
FECR . . . . . . Far East Communications Region (Air Force)
FECS . . . . . . Federation Europeenne des Fabricants de Ceramiques Sanitaires (European
Federation of Ceramic Sanitary-ware Manufacturers)
FECUA . . . . . Farmers' Educational & Cooperative Union of America
FED . . . . Federal
FED . . . . Federation
FED . . . . Field Effect Device
FEDA . . . . . . Foodservice Equipment Distributors Association (Formerly, FSEI)
FEDAC . . . . . Forward Error Detection and Correction
FEDAL . . . . . Failed Element Detection and Location
FEDECAME . . . Federacion Cafetalera de America (Central American Coffee Growers'
Federation)
FEDEKA . . . . Federation des Associations Tribales des Originaires du Kasai (Federation
of Associations of Kasai Tribes)
FEDOM . . . . . Fonds Europeen de Developpement pour les Pays et Territoires d'Outre-Mer
(European Development Fund for Overseas Countries and Territories)
FEDS . . . . . . Foreign Economic Development Service (Department of Agriculture)
FEDSTRIP . . . . . Federal Standard Requisitioning & Issue Procedure

FEE .... Field Engineering and Equipment (Military)
FEE .... Fill Exit Entry (Data processing)
FEE .... Foundation for Economic Education
F & EE ...... Film and Equipment Exchange (Army)
FE-EL ...... Ferroelectric-Electroluminescent
FEF .... Fast Extrusion Furnace
FEF........ Feline Embryonic Fibroblast
FEF .... Foundry Educational Foundation
FEF .... Free Energy Function
FEFAC ...... Federation Europeenne des Fabricants d'Aliments Composes pour Animaux
           (European Federation of Compound Animal Feeding Stuffs Manufacturers)
FEFCO ...... Federation Europeenne des Fabricants de Carton Ondule (European Feder-
           ation of Manufacturers of Corrugated Board)
FEGEMARE ... Federazione della Gente del Mare (Federation of Seamen) (Italy)
FEGLI....... Federal Employees' Group Life Insurance
FEGS .... Federation Employment and Guidance Service
FEHA .... Federal Hall National Memorial
FEHB .... Federal Employees Health Benefits
FEHBA ...... Federal Employees Health Benefits Act
FEHBP ...... Federal Employees Health Benefits Program
FEI .... Farm Equipment Institute
FEI......... Federal Executive Institute
FEI......... Federation Equestre Internationale (International Equestrian Federation)
FEI .... Financial Executives Institute
FEI......... Firing Error Indicator
FEI......... Free Europe, Incorporated
FEIA ...... Flight Engineers' International Association
FEIEA ...... Federation of European Industrial Editors' Associations
FEIS....... Fellow of the Educational Institute of Scotland
FEITC....... Federation Europeenne des Industries Techniques du Cinema
FEL .... Full Employment League
FELV ...... Feline Leukemia Virus (Also, FeLV)
FEM .... Federation Europeenne de la Manutention (European Mechanical Handling
           Federation)
FEM .... Federation Europeenne des Motels (European Motel Federation)
FEM ...... Field-Electron Microscopy
FEM ...... Field Emission Microscope
FEM ...... Field Evaluation Model
FEM ...... Finite Element Method
FEMA ...... Farm Equipment Manufacturers Association
FEMA ...... Fire Equipment Manufacturers Association
FEMA ...... Flavoring Extract Manufacturers Association of the US
FEMA ...... Foundry Equipment Manufacturers Association
FEMAS ..... Far East Merchants Association
FEMK .... Federation Europeenne des Masseurskinesitherapeutes Praticiens en
           Physiotherapie
FEMS ...... Field Electronic Maintenance Section (National Weather Service)
FEN .... Fairchild Industries, Inc. (NYSE symbol)
FEN .... Far East Network
FEN .... Federation de l'Education Nationale (Federation of National Education)
           (Malagasy)
FENALCO .... Federacion Nacional de Comerciantes (Colombia)
FENALPORTI .. Federazione Nazionale dei Lavoratori Portuali (National Federation of
           Port Workers) (Italy)
FENASYCOA .. Federation Nationale des Syndicats du Commerce Ouest Africain (National
           Federation of Commerce Unions - West Africa)
FENDRE ..... Forces to Eliminate No-Deposit/No-Return
FENEAL ..... Federazione Nazionale Edili, Affini e del Legno (National Federation
           of Building and Construction Workers) (Italy)
F Eng ...... Forest Engineer
FEO .... Flag Engineering Officer (British)
FEO .... Fleet Engineer Officer (British)
FEOF .... Foreign Exchange Operations Fund
FEP .... Fair Employment Practice
FEP .... Financial Evaluation Program (IBM)
FEP .... Flash Evaporator Plant
FEP ..... Fluorinated Ethylene-Propylene (Copolymer)
FEP .... Fore Edges Painted (Paper)
FEP .... Free Enterprise Personnel
FEPA .... Fair Educational Practice Act (New York, New Jersey, Massachusetts)
FEPA .... Fair Employment Practices Act
FEPA .... Far-Eastern Prehistory Association
FEPC .... Fair Employment Practice Committee (or Commission)
FEPC .... Farm Employment Practices Committee
FEPE........ Federation Europeenne de la Publicite Exterieure (European Federation
           of Outdoor Advertising)
FEPEM ...... Federation of European Petroleum Equipment Manufacturers
FEPP........ Foreign Excess Personal Property
FEQ .... Failure Equation
FER .... Final Engineering Report
FER .... Forward Engine Room

FERA ...... Federal Emergency Relief Administration (Liquidated, 1937)
FERES ...... Federation Internationale des Instituts de Recherches Socio-Religieuses
           (International Federation of Institutes for Socio-Religious Research)
FERF .... Financial Executives Research Foundation
FERIC ...... False Entries in Records of Interstate Carriers (FBI standardized term)
FERO .... Far East Research Office
FES .... Family Expenditure Survey (Department of Employment) (British)
FES .... Fast Erect System
FES .... Federal Executive Service
FES .... Federal Extension Service (Department of Agriculture)
FES .... Fellow of the Ethnological Society (British)
FES .... Field Emitting Surface
FES .... Field Engineering Service
FES .... Fluid to Electric Switch
FESA .... Fonetic English Spelling Association
FESE....... Field-Enhanced Secondary Emission
FESFP ...... Federation Europeenne des Syndicats de Fabricants de Parquets
FESO .... Federal Employment Stabilization Office (Functions transferred to
           National Resources Planning Board, 1939)
FESS........ Flight Experiment Shielding Satellite
FET .... Federal Excise Tax
FET .... Field Effect Transistor
FET .... Fleet Evaluation Trial (Navy)
FET........ Freeze-Etch Technique
FETAP...... Federation Europeenne des Transports Aeriens Prives
FETC .... Federal Excise Tax Council
FETF....... Flight Engine Test Facility
FETO ...... Factory Equipment Transfer Order
FETRIKAT .... Federation Generale des Tribes du Haut Katanga (General Federation of
           Tribes of North Katanga)
FETS ...... Field Effect Transistors
FEU .... Federated Engineering Union
FEUE ...... Federacion de Estudiantes Universitaries de Ecuador
FEUS ...... French Engineers in the United States
FEV .... Federacion de Estudiantes de Venezuela
FEV .... Forced Expiratory Volume (Physiology)
FEVA ...... Federal Employees Veterans Association
FEVAC ...... Ferroelectric Variable Capacitor
FEW .... Federally Employed Women (An organization)
FEWA ...... Farm Equipment Wholesalers Association
FEWG ...... Flight Evaluation Working Group
FEWO...... Fund for Education in World Order
FEX .... Fleet Exercise (Navy, Marine Corps)
FEY .... Forever Yours
FEZ .... Federation Europeenne de Zootechnie (European Federation for Animal
           Production)
FF .... Failure Factor
FF .... Farm Foundation
FF .... Fast Fatigue (Type of muscle contraction)
FF .... Fat Free (Biochemistry)
FF .... Festungsflak (Fortress antiaircraft artillery) (German military -
           World War II)
FF .... Fieri Fecit (Caused to Be Made)
FF .... Filmfacts (A publication)
FF .... Filtration Fraction (Physiology)
FF .... First Families (i.e., the aristocracy) (Slang)
FF .... Fixed Focus (Photography)
FF .... Fixing Fluid (Histology)
FF .... Flat Face (Diamonds)
FF .... Fleet Fighter (Air Force)
FF .... Fleet Flagship
FF .... Flexi-Filament
FF .... Folded Flat (Freight)
FF .... Folios (Leaves)
FF .... Following (Pages)
FF .... Force Field
FF .... Force Flagship
FF .... Ford Foundation
FF .... Foremanship Foundation
FF .... Form Feed
FF .... Fortissimo (Very loud) (Music)
FF .... Foster Father
FF .... Fragrance Foundation
FF .... Free Flight
FF .... Free French
FF .... Freight Forwarder
FF .... French Fourragere (Military)
FF .... French Fried
FF .... Front Focal Length (Optics)
FF .... Full-Fashioned
FF .... Full Field

F/F . . . . Flip-Flop (Electronics)
F & F . . . . Fire and Flushing
FF's . . . . First Families (Supposedly elite society) (Slang)
F & F . . . . . . Furniture and Fixtures
F of F . . . . . . Field of Fire (Military)
F to F . . . . Face to Face (Technical drawings)
FFA . . . . Federal Firearms Act
FFA . . . . Fellow of the Faculty of Actuaries (British)
FFA . . . . Flammability Fabrics Act
FFA . . . . Flygtekniska Forsoksanstalten (Sweden)
FFA . . . . For Further Assignment
FFA . . . . Forces Francaises en Allemagne (French Forces in Germany)
FFA . . . . Foundation for Foreign Affairs
FFA . . . . Free from Alongside
FFA . . . . Free from Average (Insurance)
FFA . . . . Free Fatty Acid (Biochemistry)
FFA . . . . Free Foreign Agency (or Agent) (Business and trade)
FFA . . . . Future Farmers of America
FFAC . . . . Forest Farmers Association Cooperative
FFAG . . . . Fixed-Field Alternating Gradient (Accelerator) (Nuclear energy)
FFAR . . . . Folding-Fin Aircraft Rocket
FFAR . . . . Forward-Fighting Aerial Rocket
FFAS . . . . Free Flight Analysis Section
FFAUS . . . . . . Federation of French Alliances in the United States
FFB . . . . Fat-Free Body
FFB . . . . Federal Farm Board (Name changed to Farm Credit Administration, 1933)
FFB . . . . Fluid Film Bearing
FFB . . . . Functional Flow Block
FFBD . . . . Functional Flow Block Diagram
FFC . . . . Family Fitness Council
FFC . . . . Farmers Federation Cooperative
FFC . . . . Federal Facilities Corporation (Dissolved, 1961)
FFC . . . . Federal Fire Council
FFC . . . . Fixed Film Capacitor
FFC's . . . . Folklore Fellows Communications (Journal)
FFC . . . . For Further Clearance (Aviation)
FFC . . . . Foreign Funds Control
FFC . . . . Free from Chlorine
FFCAA . . . . . Federation Francaise des Cooperatives Agricoles d'Approvisionnement
FFCAC . . . . . Federation Francaise des Cooperatives Agricoles de Cereales
FFCB . . . . . Federal Farm Credit Board (of FCA)
FFCSA . . . . . Florida Fresh Citrus Shippers Association
FFD . . . . Field Forcing (Decreasing)
FFD . . . . Formation Flight Display
FFD . . . . Forward Floating Depot (Army)
FFD . . . . Free Flight Data
FFD . . . . Friendly Forward Disposition
FFD . . . . Fuel Failure Detection
FFD . . . . Functional Flow Diagram
FFDA . . . . Flying Funeral Directors of America
FFD of A . . . . Federated Funeral Directors of America
FFDO . . . . . . Force Fighter Director Officer
FFE . . . . Forced Fault Entry (Data processing)
FF & E . . . . . . Furniture, Fixtures, and Equipment (Insurance)
FFEC . . . . . . Field-Free Emission Current
FFES . . . . . . Food Facilities Engineering Society
FFF . . . . Farm Film Foundation
FFF . . . . Fast Fission Factor
FFF . . . . Federal Co. (NYSE symbol)
FFF . . . . Federation of Free Farmers (Philippines)
FFF . . . . Field-Flow Fractionation (Chemical separation method)
FFF . . . . Flat or Folded Flat (Freight)
FFF. . . . . Fortissimo (Music)
FFFH . . . . . . American Freedom from Hunger Foundation
FFH . . . . Formerly Fat Housewife (Weight Watchers, International; advertising)
FFHC . . . . . . Freedom from Hunger Campaign
FFI . . . . Field Forcing (Increasing)
FFI . . . . Financial Federation, Inc. (NYSE symbol)
FFI . . . . Fit for Issue (Navy)
FFI . . . . Fluid Flow Indicator
FFI . . . . Forces Francaises de l'Interieur (France) (World War II)
FFI . . . . Free from Infection
FFI . . . . Freight Forwarders Institute
FFI . . . . Frozen Food Institute
FFI. . . . . Fuel Flow Indicator
FFL . . . . Federation of Free Labor (Philippines)
FFL . . . . Fiji Federation of Labor
FFL . . . . Fixed and Flashing (Signal Light) (Navigation charts)
FFL . . . . Forces Francaises Libres (Free French Forces)
FFL . . . . Front Focal Length
FFLT . . . . Familiarization Flight (Aviation)

FFM . . . . Fertilizantes Fosfatados Mexicanos (SA)
FFM . . . . Foundation for Microbiology
FFMA . . . . . . Fraternal Field Managers' Association
FFMC . . . . . . Federal Farm Mortgage Corporation (Established, 1934; assets transferred to Secretary of the Treasury, 1961)
FFMG . . . . . . Foundry Facings Manufacturers Group
FFMN . . . . . . Fixed Federal Monitoring Network (Aviation)
FFN . . . . Folded Flat or Nested (Freight)
FFNC . . . . . . First Fix Not Converted
FFO . . . . Forces Francaises de l'Ouest
FFO . . . . Formation Flight Operation
FFOB . . . . . . Flexible Fiber Optic Borescope
FFOB . . . . . . Forward Fighting Operating Base (Military)
FFOT . . . . . . Fast Frequency on Target
FFP . . . . Far Field Pressure
FFP . . . . Firm-Fixed Price (Government contracting)
FFP . . . . Fleet Frequency Plans
F & FP . . . . . . Force and Financial Program
FFPC . . . . . . Firm-Fixed Price Contract
FFPS . . . . Fellow of the Faculty of Physicians and Surgeons
FFR . . . . Fellow of the Faculty of Radiologists (British)
FFR . . . . Fixed Frequency Receiver
FFR . . . . Fleet Fighter Reconnaissance
FFR . . . . Folded Flow Reactor (AEC)
FFR . . . . Forsvarets Forskningsrad (Defense Board) (Denmark)
FFR . . . . Free Field Room
FFRC . . . . . . Fossil Fuel Resources Committee
FFRD . . . . . . Flip-Flop Relay Driver (Data processing)
FFRDC . . . . . Federally Funded Research and Development Center (National Science Foundation)
FFRR . . . . . . Full Frequency Range Recording
FFS . . . . Fat-Free Solids
FFS . . . . Flight Following Service (FAA)
FFS . . . . Food Fair Stores, Inc. (NYSE symbol)
FFS. . . . . Formatted File System (Defense Intelligence Agency)
FFSC . . . . . . From the Latin for Franciscan Brothers of the Holy Cross (Roman Catholic religious order)
FFSD . . . . . . Free Foil Switching Device
FFT . . . . Fast Fourier Transform
FFT . . . . Flicker Fusion Threshold
FFT . . . . For Further Transfer (to) (Military)
FFTA . . . . . . Frozen Fish Trades Association
FFTC . . . . . . Fixed Feed Through Capacitor
FFTF . . . . Fast Flux (or Fuels) Text Facility (AEC)
FFTR. . . . . . . Firefighter
FFTV . . . . . . Free Flight Test Vehicle
FFU . . . . Focus-Forming Unit(s) (Medical/biochemical research)
FFU . . . . Forskningens Faellesudvalg (Science Advisory Council) (Denmark)
FFV . . . . Fast Flying Vestibule (Old railroad term for a deluxe coach)
FFV's . . . . . . First Families of Virginia (Supposedly elite society) (Slang)
FFVA . . . . . . Florida Fruit and Vegetable Association
FFVF . . . . . . Freedoms Foundation at Valley Forge
FFW . . . . Federation of Free Workers (Philippines)
FFW . . . . Filoil Free Workers (Philippines)
FFWV . . . . . . Federation of French War Veterans
FFY . . . . Fanny Farmer Candy Shops (American Stock Exchange symbol)
FFZ . . . . Free Fire Zone (Army)
FG . . . . Fallschirmjaeger-Gewehr (Parachutist's rifle) (German military – World War II)
FG . . . . Fashion Group
FG. . . . . Female Groove
FG . . . . Field Goal (Football)
FG. . . . . Fine Grain
FG. . . . . Fire Guardsman (British) (World War II)
FG . . . . Flat Grain (Lumber)
FG. . . . . Flow Gauge
FG . . . . Fog Gong (Navigation charts)
FG. . . . . Fog Gun (Navigation charts)
FG. . . . . Foot Groove
FG. . . . . Foot Guards (British)
FG . . . . Forgotten Generation
FG. . . . . Forward Gate
FG. . . . . Frank Gasperro (Designer's mark, when appearing on US coins)
FG. . . . . Friction Glaze
FG. . . . . Fuel Gas
FG. . . . . Fully Good
FG. . . . . U.S. Fidelity & Guaranty Co. (NYSE symbol)
F & G . . . . . . Folded and Gathered (Printing)
FGA. . . . . . . Foreign General Agent
FGA. . . . . . . Foreign General Average (Insurance)
FGA. . . . . . . Free of General Average

FGAA . . . . Federal Government Accountants Association
FGAN . . . . . . Fertilizer Grade Ammonium Nitrate
FGB . . . . Familiengesetzbuch
FGB . . . . Fiber Glass Brush
FGBMFI . . . . . Full Gospel Business Men's Fellowship International
FGC . . . . Facility Group Control (Military)
FGC . . . . Federation Generale du Congo (Congolese General Federation)
FGC . . . . Fiber Glass Curtain
FGC . . . . Finished Goods Control
FGC . . . . Fixed Gain Control
FGC . . . . Fixed Glass Capacitor
FGC . . . . Friends General Conference
FGCB . . . . . . Fiber Glass Cone Brush
FGCM . . . . . . Field General Court-Martial
FGD . . . . Ferri-Gas Duplexer
FGD . . . . Fine Grain Data (Equipment) (RADAR)
FGE . . . . Fracto-Graphic Examination
FGF . . . . Filament-Wound Glass Fiber
FGFC . . . . . . Fixed Gas-Filled Capacitor
FGFSA . . . . . Florida Gift Fruit Shippers Association
FGGM . . . . . . Fort George G. Meade (Maryland)
FGH . . . . Fiber Glass Hull
FGH . . . . Flameless Gas Heater
FGH . . . . Flexible Gyro Header
FGHA . . . . . . Flexible Gyro Header Assembly
FGI . . . . Federation Graphique Internationale (International Graphical Federation)
FGJ . . . . Freezing Gas Jet
FGJA . . . . . . Flat Glass Jobbers Association
FGN . . . . Foreign
FGO . . . . Finance Group Office
FGO . . . . Flag Gunnery Officer
FGO . . . . Fleet Gunnery Officer
FGP . . . . Frontal Groove of Pinnule
FGPFL . . . . . Fixed and Group Flashing (Signal Light) (Navigation charts)
FGRF . . . . . . Forest Genetics Research Foundation
FGS . . . . Federazione Giovanile Socialista (Italy)
FGS . . . . Fellow of the Geological Society (British)
FGS . . . . Fischerei-Geraete-Station
FGS . . . . Flowing Gas Stream
FGS . . . . Friends of the Golden State
FGSA . . . . . . Fellow of the Geological Society of America
FGSM . . . . . . Fellow of Guildhall School of Music (British)
FGT . . . . Food Giant Markets, Inc. (NYSE symbol) (Delisted)
FGTB . . . . . . Federation Generale du Travail de Belgique (Belgian General Federation of Labor)
FGTK . . . . . . Federation Generale du Travail du Kongo (General Federation of Labor of the Congo) (Leopoldville)
FGTSA . . . . . Fur Garment Traveling Salesmen's Association
FGVT . . . . . . Forschungs-Gesellschaft Verfahrens-Technik (West Germany)
FH . . . . Flag Hoist
FH . . . . Flat Head (Screw)
FH . . . . Flight Hour
FH . . . . Fog Horn (Navigation charts)
FH . . . . Frequency Hopping (Modulation)
FH . . . . Friendship House
FHA . . . . Farmers Home Administration (Department of Agriculture)
FHA . . . . Federal Housing Administration (HUD)
FHA . . . . Fine Hardwoods Association
FHA . . . . Flexible Header Assembly
FHA . . . . Free-Heave Amplitude
FHA . . . . Friends Historical Association
FHA . . . . Future Homemakers of America
FHA . . . . Future Horsemen of America
FHAA . . . . . . Field Hockey Association of America
FHAS . . . . . . Federation of Hellenic American Societies of Greater New York
FHB . . . . Family Hold Back (i.e., take small portions) (A mealtime whimsicality for use when guests are present)
FHC . . . . Federal Housing Corporation
FHC . . . . Four-Horse Club (British)
FHC . . . . Freed-Hardeman College (Tennessee)
FHD . . . . Family Housing Division (Army)
FHDA . . . . . . Fir and Hemlock Door Association
FHDO . . . . . . Field Handling Design Objective
F & HE . . . . . Fridays and Holidays Excepted (Mohammedan)
FHFA . . . . . . Four-Conductor, Heat- and Flame-Resistant, Armor (Cable)
FHI . . . . Fair Housing, Incorporated
FHI . . . . Freedom House, Incorporated
FHIC . . . . . . Franciscan Hospitaller Sisters of the Immaculate Conception (Roman Catholic religious order)
FHIF . . . . . . Frequenting House of Ill Fame
FHIP . . . . . . Family Health Insurance Plan

FHK . . . . Shattuck (Frank G.) Company (NYSE symbol) (Delisted)
FHKKW . . . . . Flugbetriebstoff-Kesselkraftwagen (Aviation-gasoline tank truck) (German military – World War II)
FHL . . . . Forward Half-Line (Feed)
FHLB . . . . . . Federal Home Loan Bank
FHLBB . . . . . Federal Home Loan Bank Board (Independent government agency)
FHLS . . . . . . First Hungarian Literary Society
FHM . . . . Feedwater Heater Management
FHMA . . . . . . Family Housing Management (Army)
FHO . . . . Family Hands Off, or Family Hold Off (Indicates that a certain dish is not to be eaten by members of the family at a meal where guests are present)
FHP . . . . Fort Howard Paper Co. (NYSE symbol)
FHP . . . . Friction Horsepower
FHP . . . . Friends of Historical Pharmacy
FHR . . . . Federal Housing Representative (Australia)
FHR . . . . Fire Hose Rack
FHR . . . . Fisher Foods, Inc. (NYSE symbol)
FHR . . . . Fund for Human Rights
FHS . . . . Feminine Hygiene Spray
FHS . . . . Fetal Heart Sounds
FHS . . . . Forest History Society
FHSA . . . . . . Federal Hazardous Substances Act
FHSG . . . . . . Family Housing (Army)
FHT . . . . Free-Heave Test
FHTC . . . . . . Fixed High Temperature Capacitor
FHVC . . . . . . Fixed High Volt Capacitor
FHWA . . . . . . Federal Highway Administration (Department of Transportation)
FHY . . . . Fire Hydrant
FI . . . . Fabrication Instructions
FI . . . . Field Intensity
FI . . . . Fighter Interceptor
FI . . . . Films, Incorporated
FI . . . . Fixed Interval
FI . . . . Flood Insurance (HUD)
FI . . . . Flow Indicator
FI . . . . Forum Italicum (A publication)
FI . . . . Frontiers International
FIA . . . . Factory Insurance Association
FIA . . . . Federal Insurance Administration (HUD)
FIA . . . . Federated Ironworkers' Association of Australia
FIA . . . . Federation Internationale des Acteurs (International Federation of Actors)
FIA . . . . Federation Internationale de l'Automobile (International Automobile Federation)
FIA . . . . Fellow of the Institute of Actuaries (British)
FIA . . . . Financial Inventory Accounting
FIA . . . . Flatware Importers Association
FIA . . . . Flight Information Area
FIA . . . . Forging Industry Association
FIA . . . . Free Interstitial Atom
FIA . . . . Freedom of Information Act
FIA . . . . Full Interest Admitted
FIAA . . . . . . Federation Internationale d'Athletisme Amateur (International Federation of Amateur Athletics)
FIAB . . . . . . Federation Internationale des Associations de Bibliothecaires
FIABCI . . . . . . Federation Internationale des Administrateurs de Biens Conseils Immobiliers
FIAC . . . . . . Federation Interamericaine des Automobile Clubs
FIAC . . . . . . Flight Information Advisory Committee (FAA)
FIAD . . . . . . Federation Internationale des Associations des Distributeurs de Films
FIAD . . . . . . Flame Ionization Analyzer and Detector
FIAE . . . . . . Food Industry Association Executives
FIAEM . . . . . . Federation Internationale des Associations d'Etudiants en Medecine (International Federation of Medical Students Associations)
FIAeS . . . . . . Fellow of the Institute of Aeronautical Sciences (British)
FIAF . . . . Federation Internationale des Archives du Film (International Federation of Film Archives)
FIAI . . . . Federation Internationale des Associations d'Instituteurs (International Federation of Teachers' Associations)
FIAI . . . . Federazione Italiana Autoferrotramvieri e Internavigators (National Federation of Busdrivers, Streetcar Conductors) (Italy)
FIAIZA . . . . . . Federazione Italiana Addetti Industrie Zucchero e Alcole (Italian Federation of Workers in the Sugar and Alcohol Industry)
FIAJ . . . . Federation Internationale des Auberges de la Jeunesse (International Youth Hostel Federation)
FIAJF . . . . . . Federation Internationale des Amies de la Jeune Fille
FIALS . . . . . . Federazione Italiana Autonoma Lavoratori dello Spettacolo (Italian Autonomous Federation of Entertainment Workers)
FIAMC . . . . . . Federation Internationale des Associations des Medecins Catholiques (International Federation of Catholic Doctors)

FIANEI ...... Federation Internationale d'Associations Nationales d'Eleves Ingenieurs (International Federation of National Associations of Engineering Students)

FIAP .... Federation Internationale de l'Art Photographique (International Federation of Photographic Art)

FIAPF .... Federation Internationale des Associations de Producteurs de Films (International Federation of Film Producers' Associations)

FIAPL .... Federation Internationale des Associations de Pilotes de Ligne

FIARVEP ..... Federazione Italiana Agenti Rappresentanti Viaggiatorie e Paizzisti (Italian Federation of Commercial Agents and Travelers)

FIASA .... Financiera Industrial y Agropecuaria, SA (Guatemala)

FIAT .... Fabbrica Italiana Automobile, Torino (Italian automobile manufacturer; acronym used as name of its cars)

FIAT .... Field Information Agency, Technical (Under G-2, SHAEF)

FIATA .... Federation Internationale des Associations de Transitaires et Assimiles (International Federation of Forwarding Agents Associations)

FIATC .... Federation Internationale des Associations Touristiques de Cheminots (International Federation of Railwaymen's Travel Associations)

FIATE .... Federation Internationale des Associations de Travailleurs Evangeliques

FIAV .... Federation Internationale des Agences de Voyages

FIB .... Federation Internationale de Boules (International Bowling Federation)

FIB .... Federazione Italiana Bancari (Italian Federation of Bank Employees)

FIB .... Fellow of the Institute of Bankers (British)

FIB .... Fleet Installation Budget (Navy)

FIB .... Free into Barge

FIB .... Free into Bunker

FIBA .... Federation Internationale de Basketball Amateur (International Amateur Basketball Federation)

FIBAT .... Federation Independente des Batetelas (Independent Federation of Batetelas)

FIBC .... Federal Interagency Broadcast Committee

FIBEP .... Federation Internationale des Bureaux d'Extraits de Presse (International Federation of Press-Cutting Agencies)

FIBI .... Filed but Impracticable (to transmit)

FIBT .... Federation Internationale de Bobsleigh et de Tobogganing (International Bobsledding and Tobogganing Federation)

FIBTP .... Federation Internationale du Batiment et des Travaux Publics

FIC .... Fault Isolation Code

FIC .... Federal Information Center

FIC .... Federation of Insurance Counsel

FIC .... Fellow of the Institute of Chemistry (Later, FRIC) (British)

FIC .... Field Installed Connector

FIC .... Financial Inventory Control

FIC .... Flight Information Center

FIC .... Forest Industries Council

FIC .... Foundation for International Cooperation

FIC .... Fraternal Insurance Field Counselor (Designation given by Fraternal Field Managers' Association)

FIC .... Fratrum Instructionis Christianae (Brothers of Christian Instruction, or La Mennais Brothers) (Roman Catholic religious order)

FIC .... Frequency Interference Control

FICA .... Federal Insurance Contributions Act (Under which collections are made from employers and employees for OASDI benefits)

FICA .... Federation Internationale des Cheminots Antialcooliques (International Railway Temperance Union)

FICA .... Fraternal Insurance Counsellors Association

FICB .... Federal Intermediate Credit Bank

FICC .... Federation Internationale de Camping et de Caravanning (International Federation of Camping and Caravanning)

FICC .... Federation Internationale des Cine-Clubs (International Federation of Film Societies)

FICC .... Frequency Interference Control Center (Air Force)

FICCIA ...... Federation International des Cadres de la Chimie et des Industries Annexes

FICD .... Fellow of the International College of Dentists

FICE .... Federal Interagency Committee on Education

FICE .... Federation Internationale des Communautes d'Enfants (International Federation of Children's Communities)

FICEP .... Federation Internationale Catholique d'Education Physique et Sportive (International Catholic Federation for Physical and Sports Education)

FICIC .... Federation Internationale du Commerce et des Industries du Camping

FICJA .... Fellow of the International Criminal Justice Association

FICJF .... Federation Internationale des Conseils Juridiques et Fiscaux (International Federation of Legal Fiscal Consultants)

FICM .... Federation Internationale des Cadres des Mines

FICM .... From the Latin for Brothers of the Immaculate Heart of Mary (Roman Catholic religious order)

FICO .... Ford Instrument Company

FICP .... Federation Internationale des Clubs de Publicite

FICR .... Financial Inventory Control Report

FICS .... Fault Isolation Checkout System

FICS .... Federation Internationale des Chasseurs de Son (International Federation of Sound Hunters)

FICS .... Fellow of the International College of Surgeons

FICS .... Forecasting for Inventory Control System

FICSA .... Federation of International Civil Servants' Associations

FICT .... Federation Internationale de Centres Touristiques (International Federation of Tourist Centers)

FID .... Far Infrared Detector

FID .... Federation Internationale du Diabete (International Diabetes Federation)

FID .... Federation Internationale de Documentation (International Federation for Documentation)

FID .... Fidelity Mortgage Investors (NYSE symbol)

FID .... Field Intelligence Department

FID .... Flame-Ionization Detector

FID .... Foolproof Identification (System)

FIDAC .... Federazione Italiana Dipendenti da Aziende di Credito (Italian Federation of Credit Institution Employees)

FIDAC .... Film Input to Digital Automatic Computer

FIDACSYS ... Film Input to Digital Automatic Computer System

FIDAE .... Federazione Italiana Dipendenti Aziende Elettriche (Italian Federation of Electrical Workers)

FIDAG .... Federazione Italiana Dipendenti Aziende Gas (Italian Federation of Gas Workers)

FIDAQ .... Federation Internationale des Associations de Quincailliers et Marchands de Fer (International Federation of Ironmongers and Iron Merchants Associations)

FIDAT .... Federazione Italiana Dipendenti Aziende Telecomunicazioni (Italian Federation of Communications Workers)

FIDE .... Federation de l'Industrie Dentaire en Europe (Federation of the European Dental Industry)

FIDE .... Federation Internationale pour le Droit Europeen (International Federation for European Law)

FIDE .... Federation Internationale des Echecs (International Chess Federation)

FIDEGEP ..... Federation Interalliee des Evades de Guerre et des Passeurs

FIDEL .... Federazione Italiana Dipendenti Enti Local (Italian Federation of Local Government Employees)

FIDEM .... Federation Internationale des Editeurs de Medailles (International Federation of Medal Producers)

FIDEP .... Federazione Italiana Dipendenti da Enti Parastatali e di Diritto Pubblico (Italian Federation of Employees of Quasi-Governmental and State-Controlled Agencies)

FIDES .... Fonds d'Investissement pour le Developpement Economique et Social (UN)

FIDGA .... Federazione Italiana della Gente dell'Aria (Italian Federation of Airline Workers)

FIDI .... Federation Internationale des Demenageurs Internationaux (Federation of International Furniture Removers)

FIDIA .... Federation Internationale des Intellectuels Aveugles

FIDIC .... Federation Internationale des Ingenieurs-Conseils (International Federation of Consulting Engineers)

FIDJC .... Federation Internationale des Directeurs de Journaux Catholiques

FIDO .... Fallout Intensity Detector Oscillator

FIDO .... Flight Dynamics Officer (NASA)

FIDO .... Flight Inspection District Office

FIDO .... Fog, Intense, Dispersal of (NASA)

FIDO .... Fog Investigation and Dispersal Operation (System used on airfield landing strips) (World War II)

FIE .... Federation Internationale d'Escrime (International Fencing Federation)

FIE .... Florida Industries Exposition

FIE .... Foundation for Integrative Education

FIEC .... Federation Internationale des Associations d'Etudes Classiques (Internationa Federation of Associations of Classical Studies)

FIEJ .... Federation Internationale des Editeurs de Journaux et Publications (International Federation of Newspaper Publishers)

FIELDATA .... Field Data Computers (Army)

FIEM .... Federation Internationale de l'Enseignement Menager

FIEN .... Forum Italiano dell'Energia Nucleare

FIEP .... Federation Internationale d'Education Physique (International Federation for Physical Education)

FIEP .... Federation Internationale des Etudiants en Pharmacie

FIER .... Foundation for Instrumentation Education and Research

FIERF .... Forging Industry Educational and Research Foundation

FIESP .... Federation Internationale des Etudiants en Sciences Politiques

FIET .... Federation Internationale des Employes et des Techniciens

FIF .... Failure Indicating Fuse

FIF .... Fellow of the Institute of Fuels

FIF .... Ferric Ion Free

FIFA .... Federation Internationale du Film sur d'Art (International Federation of Films on Art)

FIFA .... Federation Internationale de Football Association (International Federation of Club Football)

FIFC .... Fur Information and Fashion Council

FIFCLC ...... Federation Internationale des Femmes de Carrieres Liberales et Commerciales (International Federation of Business and Professional Women)

FIFDU....... Federation Internationale des Femmes Diplomees des Universites (International Federation of University Women)

FIFO ...... First In, First Out (Inventory)

FIFO ...... Flight Inspection Field Office (FAA)

FIFO .... Floating Input - Floating Output

FIFO-H...... Flight Inspection Field Office, High Altitude

FIFOR....... Flight Forecast

FIFRA .... Federal Insecticide, Fungicide, and Rodenticide Act (Department of Agriculture)

FIFSP .... Federation Internationale des Fonctionnaires Superieurs de Police (International Federation of Senior Police Officers)

FIG .... Federation Internationale des Geometres (International Federation of Surveyors)

FIG .... Federation Internationale de Gymnastique (International Gymnastic Federation)

FIG .... Figure

FIG .... Flight Inspection Group (FAA)

FIGA .... Fretted Instrument Guild of America

FIGED ...... Federation Internationale des Grandes Entreprises de Distribution (International Federation of Distributors)

FIGHT ...... Freedom, Independence (formerly, Integration), God, Honor, Today (Organization in Rochester, New York)

FIGHTRON .... Fighting Squadron

FIGLU ...... Formimino-L-glutamic Acid (Organic chemistry)

FIGO .... Federation Internationale de Gynecologie et d'Obstetrique (International Federation of Gynecology and Obstetrics)

FIH .... Federation Internationale de Handball (International Handball Federation)

FIH .... Federation Internationale de Hockey (International Hockey Federation)

FIH .... Federation Internationale des Hopitaux (International Hospital Federation)

FIH .... Free in Harbor (Navigation)

FIHC .... Federation Internationale Halterophile et Culturiste

FIHU .... Federation Internationale de l'Habitation et de l'Urbanisme

FII .... Federal Item Identification

FIIC........ Flight Inspector In Charge

FIICPI ...... Federation Internationale des Ingenieurs-Conseils en Propriete Industrielle

FIIG........ Federal Item Identification Guides

FIIG........ Federal Item Inventory Group

FIIG........ Federation des Institutions Internationales Semi-Officielles et Privees Etablies a Geneve (Federation of Semi-Official and Private International Institutions Established in Geneva)

FIIGMO ..... Forget It, I've Got My Orders (Bowdlerized version) (Military slang)

FIIGSC...... Federal Item Identification Guides for Supply Cataloging

FIIN .... Federal Item Identification Number

FIIP .... Federation Internationale de l'Industrie Phonographique

FIJ......... Federation Internationale des Journalistes (International Federation of Journalists)

FIJ......... Federation Internationale de Judo (International Judo Federation)

FIJC........ Federation Internationale de la Jeunesse Catholique

FIJET ...... Federation Internationale des Journalistes et Ecrivains du Tourisme (International Federation of Tourism Journalists and Writers)

FIJL .... Federation Internationale des Journalistes Libres de l'Europe Centrale et Orientale et des Pays Baltes et Balkaniques

FIJM .... Federation Internationale des Jeunesses Musicales (International Federation of Young Musicians)

FIJPA....... Federation Internationale des Journalistes Professionnels de l'Aeronautique

FIJU........ Federation Internationale des Producteurs de Jus de Fruits (International Federation of Fruit Juice Producers)

FIL......... Federation Internationale de Laiterie (International Dairy Federation)

FIL......... Federation Internationale de Luge (International Luge Federation)

FIL .... Federazione Italiana del Lavoro (Italian Federation of Labor)

FIL......... Fellow of the Institute of Linguists (British)

FILA .... Federazione Italiana Lavoratori Abbigliamento (Italian Federation of Garment Workers)

FILAI ...... Federazione Italiana Lavoratori Ausiliari dell'Impiego (Italian Federation of Auxiliary Services)

FILAM ...... Federazione Italiana Lavoratori Albergo Mensa e Termali (National Union of Hotel and Restaurant Workers) (Italy)

FILC .... Federazione Italiana Lavoratori Chimici (Italian Federation of Chemical Workers)

FILCA ...... Federazione Italiana Lavoratori Costruzioni e Affini (Italian Federation of Construction and Related Workers)

FILCEA ..... Federazione Italiana Lavoratori Commercio e Aggregati (Italian Federation of Commercial and Associated Workers)

FILCEN...... Filter Center

FILDA ...... Federazione Italiana Lavoratori degli Acquedotti (Italian Federation of Aqueduct Workers)

FILDIR ...... Federation Internationale Libre des Deportes et Internes de la Resistance (International Free Federation of Deportees and Resistance Internees)

FILER .... File Information Language Executive Routine (Data processing)

FILIA ...... Federazione Italiana Lavoratori Industrie Alimentari (Italian Federation of Food Processing Workers)

FILIE .... Federazione Italiana Lavoratori Industrie Estrattive (Italian Federation of Workers in Mining Industries)

FILL........ Fleet Issue Load List (Navy)

FILLBAV ..... Federazione Italiana Lavoratori Legno-Boschivi -- Artistiche e Varie (National Federation of Carpenters, Lumbermen, Cabinetmakers) (Italy)

FILLEA ...... Federazione Italiana Lavoratori del Legno, dell'Edilizia e Industrie Affini (Italian Federation of Construction and Allied Workers)

FILM .... Federazione Italiana Lavoratori del Mare (Italian Federation of Merchant Seamen)

FILM ...... For Illustrating Legal Methods (Student legal action organization)

FILMSORT .... Microfilm Sorter (Electronics)

FILP .... Federazione Italiana Lavoratori dei Porti (Italian Federation of Longshoremen)

FILPC ...... Federazione Italiana Lavoratori Poligrafici e Cartai (Italian Federation of Printers and Paperworkers)

FILS .... Federazione Italiana Lavoratori dello Spettacolo (Italian Federation of Entertainment Workers)

FILS .... Federazione Italiana Lavoratori Statali (Italian Federation of Government Employees)

FILS .... Flarescan Instrument Landing System

FILSA ...... Federazione Italiana Lavoratori Sanatoriali (Italian Federation of Public Health Workers - Hospital and Sanatorium Employees)

FILSTA ..... Federazione Italiana Lavoratori Servizi Tributari e Assicuratori (Italian Federation of Tax Workers)

FILTAT ..... Federazione Italiana Lavoratori Trasporti ed Ausiliari del Traffico (Italian Federation of Transportation and Auxiliary Services)

FIM .... Fabric Insulation Material

FIM .... Failure Indication Modules

FIM .... Far Infrared MASER

FIM .... Fault Isolation Meter

FIM .... Federation Internationale Motocycliste (International Motorcycle Federation)

FIM .... Federation Internationale des Musiciens (International Federation of Musicians)

FIM .... Federazione Italiana Metal-Meccanici (Italian Metal Mechanic Workers' Federation)

FIM .... Fellow of the Institute of Metallurgists (British)

FIM .... Field Intensity Meter

FIM .... Field Ion Microscope (or Microscopy)

FIM .... First Mortgage Investors (NYSE symbol)

FIM .... Flight Information Manual

FIMATE...... Factory-Installed Maintenance Automatic Test Equipment

FIMEM ..... Federation Internationale des Mouvements d'Ecole Moderne

FIMIS ...... Financial Management Information System (Army)

FIMITIC ..... Federation Internationale des Mutiles et Invalides du Travail et des Invalides Civils (International Federation of Disabled Workmen and Civilian Invalids)

FIML ...... Full-Information Maximum Likelihood (Econometrics)

FIMMEMA .... Fikambanan' Ny Mpanoratra Sy Mpamoron-Kira Ary Editora Malagasy (Malagasy Republic)

FIMOC...... Federation Internationale des Mouvements Ouvriers Chretiens

FIMP .... Federation Internationale de Medecine Physique (International Federation of Physical Medicine)

FIMS .... Federation Internationale Medecine Sportive (International Federation of Sportive Medicine)

FIMS .... Field Intensity Measuring System

FIN .... Finance (or Financial)

FIN .... Futures Information Network

FINA ...... Federation Internationale de Natation Amateur (International Amateur Swimming Federation)

FINA ...... Following Items Not Available

FinAF ...... Finnish Air Force

FINAL ...... Financial Analysis Language

FINAST...... First National Stores

FINAT ...... Federation Internationale des Fabricants et Transformateurs d'Adhesifs et Thermo-Collants sur Papiers et Autres Supports (International Federation of Manufacturers and Converters of Pressure-Sensitive and Heatseals on Paper and Other Base Materials)

FIND .... Friendless, Isolated, Needy, Disabled (Project of National Council on the Aging - acronym used as name of New York City coffeehouse)

FINE .... Fighter Inertial Navigation System

FINEBEL .... France, Italy, Netherland, Belgium & Luxembourg (economic agreement)

FINNAIR..... Aero O/Y (Finnish Air Lines)

FINO .... Finance Officer (Army)

FInstP ...... Fellow of the Institute of Physics (British)

FInstPI...... Fellow of the Institute of Patentees and Inventors (British)

FINSUPSCOL .. Finance and Supply School (Coast Guard)

FIO . . . . Far Infrared Observation
FIO . . . . Federation Internationale d'Oleiculture (International Olive Growers
            Federation)
FIO . . . . Fleet Intelligence Officer
FIO . . . . Florida Institute of Oceanography
FIO . . . . Free In and Out
FIOCC . . . . . . Federation Internationale des Ouvriers de la Chaussure et du Cuir (Inter-
            national Shoe and Leather Worker's Federation)
FIOCES . . . . . . Federation Internationale des Organisations de Correspondances et
            d'Echanges Scolaires (International Federation of Organizations for
            School Correspondence and Exchange)
FIOM . . . . . . Federation Internationale des Ouvriers sur Metaux (International Metal-
            worker's Federation)
FIOM . . . . . . Federazione Impiegati e Operai Metallurgici (Federation of Metal
            Workers and Employees) (Italy)
FIORH . . . . . . Federation Internationale pour l'Organisation de Rencontres de Handicapes
            (International Federation for the Organization of Meetings for the
            Handicapped)
FIOT . . . . Federazione Impiegati Operai Tessili (Federation of Textile Workers)
            (Italy)
FIP . . . . Fabrica de Implementos, SA (Mexico)
FIP . . . . Fairly Important Person
FIP . . . . Falcon Improvement Program
FIP . . . . Far Infrared Pointer
FIP . . . . Federation Internationale Pharmaceutique (International Pharmaceutical
            Federation)
FIP . . . . Federation Internationale de Philatelie (International Philatelic Federation)
FIP . . . . Federation Internationale de la Precontrainte
FIP . . . . Federazione Italiana Pensionati (Italian Federation of Pensioners)
FIP . . . . Federazione Italiana Postelegrafonici (Italian Federation of Postal,
            Telegraph, and Telephone Workers)
FIP . . . . Fleet Improvement Program (Navy)
FIP . . . . Fleet Introduction Program
FIP . . . . Flight Instruction Program (Air Force)
FIP . . . . Free Instrument Package
FI/P . . . . Flight Inspection (Permanent)
FIPA . . . . Federation Internationale des Producteurs Agricoles (International Federa-
            tion of Agricultural Producers)
FIPACE . . . . . . Federation Internationale des Producteurs Auto-Consommateurs Industriels
            d'Electricite (International Federation of Industrial Producers of
            Electricity for Own Consumption)
FIPAGO . . . . . Federation Internationale des Fabricants de Papiers Gommes (International
            Federation of Gummed Paper Manufacturers)
FIPESO . . . . . . Federation Internationale des Professeurs de l'Enseignement Secondaire
            Officiel
FIPJF . . . . Federation Internationale des Producteurs de Jus de Fruits
FIPM . . . . Federation Internationale de Psychotherapie Medicale (International
            Federation for Medical Psychotherapy)
FIPP . . . . Far Infrared Pointer Package
FIPP . . . . Federation Internationale de la Presse Periodique (International Federation
            of the Periodical Press)
FIPP . . . . Federation Internationale pour la Protection des Populations
FIPP . . . . Fondation Internationale Penale et Penitentiaire (International Penal and
            Penitentiary Foundation)
FIPR . . . . Foundation for International Potash Research
FIPRA . . . . . . Federation Internationale de la Presse Agricole
FIPRESCI . . . . . Federation Internationale de la Presse Cinematographique (International
            Federation of the Cinematographic Press)
FIPS . . . . Federal Information Processing Standards
FIPS . . . . First Independent Political Success (Political campaigning)
FIPS . . . . Flight Inspection Positioning System
FIPSR . . . . . . Federal Information Processing Standards Register (National Bureau of
            Standards)
FIR . . . . Far Infrared
FIR . . . . Far Infrared Radiometer
FIR . . . . Fault Isolation Routine
FIR . . . . Federation Internationale des Resistants (International Federation of
            Resistance Movements)
FIR . . . . Field Intensity Receiver
FIR . . . . Films in Review (A publication)
FIR . . . . Firestone Tire & Rubber Company (NYSE symbol)
FIR . . . . Flight Information Region (FAA)
FIR . . . . Flight Inspection Report
FIR . . . . Food Irradiation Reactor (AEC)
FIR . . . . Fuel Indicator Reading
FIR . . . . Full Indicator Reading
FIR . . . . Functional Item Replacement (Program) (Navy)
FIRA . . . . Federation Internationale de Rugby Amateur (International Amateur Rugby
            Federation)
FIRAA . . . . . . Fire Insurance Research and Actuarial Association
FIRAV . . . . . . First Available (Military)

FIRB . . . . Flight Information Region Boundary
FIRC . . . . Forest Industries Radio Communications (Later, FIT)
FIRD . . . . Far Infrared Detector
FIRE . . . . Finance, Insurance, and Real Estate (Insurance)
FIRE . . . . Fingerprint Reader
FIRE . . . . Flight Investigation Reentry Environment
FIRE . . . . Flight in a Radiation Environment
FIRE . . . . Foundation for Insurance Reform and Education
FIREC . . . . . . Federation Internationale des Redacteurs en Chef
FIRE PLAN . . . . Fleet Improved Readiness by Expediting Procurement, Logistics and
            Negotiations (Navy)
FIRETRAC . . . . Firing Error Trajectory Recorder and Computer
FIRFLT . . . . . . First Fleet (Pacific) (Navy)
FIRL . . . . Fleet Issue Requirements List (Navy)
FIRL . . . . Franklin Institute Research Laboratories
FIRM . . . . Financial Information for Resources Management
FIRM . . . . Fleet Introduction of Replacement Models (Military)
FIRMA . . . . . . Firepower and Maneuver (Army)
FIRO . . . . Far Infrared Observation
FIRO . . . . Fundamental Interpersonal Relations Orientation
FIRP . . . . Far Infrared Pointer
FIRPP . . . . Far Infrared Pointer Package
FIRR . . . . Federal Institute for Reactor Research (Switzerland)
FIRS . . . . Federation Internationale de Roller-Skating (International Roller Skating
            Federation)
FIRST . . . . Fabrication of Inflatable Reentry Structures for Test (Air Force)
FIRST . . . . Far Infrared Search and Track
FIRST . . . . . . Financial Information Reporting System
FIRSTASKFLT . . First Task Fleet
FIRT . . . . Fertilizer Industry Round Table
FIRTS . . . . Following Individual Reported This Station (Army)
FIS . . . . Facilities Inventory Study
FIS . . . . Family Income Supplement (British)
FIS . . . . Far Infrared Search
FIS . . . . Far Infrared Spectrometer
FIS . . . . Federation Internationale des Centres Sociaux et Communautaires (Inter-
            national Federation of Settlements and Neighborhood Centers)
FIS . . . . Federation Internationale du Commerce des Semences (International
            Federation of the Seed Trade)
FIS . . . . Federation Internationale de Sauvetage
FIS . . . . Federation Internationale de Ski (International Ski Association)
FIS . . . . Field Information System
FIS . . . . Field Infrared Spectrometer
FIS . . . . Field Installation Simulator
FIS . . . . Field Instruction System
FIS . . . . Fighter Identification System
FIS . . . . Fighter-Intercepter Squadron (Air Force)
FIS . . . . Fischbach & Moore, Inc. (NYSE symbol)
FIS . . . . Fleet Introduction Site (Navy)
FIS . . . . Flight Information Service
FIS . . . . Foam in System
FIS . . . . Freedom Information Service
FISA . . . . Federation Internationale des Semaines d'Art
FISA . . . . Federation Internationale des Societes Aerophilateliques (International
            Federation of Aero-Philatelic Societies)
FISA . . . . Federation Internationale des Societes d'Avion
FISAIC . . . . . . Federation Internationale des Societes Artistiques et Intellectuelles de
            Cheminots (International Federation of Railwaymen's Art and Intellectual
            Societies)
FISAR . . . . Federal Institute for Snow and Avalanche Research
FISASCA . . . . Federazione Italiana Sindacati Addetti Servizi Commerciali ed Affini
            (Italian Federation of Commercial and Related Workers' Unions)
FISB . . . . Federal Internal Security Board (Formerly, Subversive Activities Control
            Board)
FISBA . . . . . . Federazione Italiana Salariati Braccianti Agricoli e Maestranze
            Specializzate Agricole e Forestali (Italian Federation of Permanent
            Unskilled and Skilled Agricultural Workers)
FISBTA . . . . . . Federazione Italiana Salariati, Braccianti e Tecnici Agricoli (Italian
            Federation of Permanent, Daily and Technical Agricultural Workers)
FISCA . . . . . . Flexible Integrated Solar Cell Assembly
FISCETCV. . . . . Federation Internationale des Syndicats Chretiens d'Employes, Techniciens,
            Cadres et Voyageurs de Commerce (International Federation of Christian
            Trade Unions of Salaried Employees, Technicians, Managers, and
            Commercial Travellers)
FISCM . . . . . . Federation Internationale des Syndicats Chretiens de la Metalurgie
            (International Federation of Christian Metalworkers Unions)
FISCOA. . . . . . Federation Internationale des Syndicats Chretiens d'Ouvriers Agricoles
            (International Federation of Christian Agricultural Workers Unions)
FISCOBB . . . . . Federation Internationale des Syndicats Chretiens d'Ouvriers du Batiment
            et du Bois (International Federation of Christian Trade Unions of
            Building and Wood Workers)

FISCTTH ..... Federation Internationale des Syndicats Chretiens des Travailleurs du Textile et de l'Habillement (International Federation of Christian Trade Unions of Textile and Clothing Workers)
FISD........ Federation Internationale de Stenographie et de Dactylographie
FISE........ Federation Internationale Syndicale de l'Enseignement (International Federation of Teachers' Unions)
FISEC....... Federation Internationale Sportive de l'Enseignement Catholique
FISEM ...... Federation Internationale des Societes d'Ecrivains-Medecins
FISEMA...... Federation Internationale et Syndicale des Employes de Madagascar (International Federation and Union of Malagasy Employees) (WFTU affiliate)
FISEMA ..... Firaisan'ny Sendika eran'i Madagaskara (Confederation of All Unions in Madagascar)
FISH........ Friends in Service Here (An organization)
FISH........ Fully Instrumented Submersible Housing (An oceanographic instrument)
FISITA ...... Federation Internationale des Societes d'Ingenieurs des Techniques de l'Automobile (International Federation of Automobile Engineers' and Technicians' Associations)
FISO .... Federazione Italiana Sindacato Ospedalieri (Italian Federation of Hospital Workers' Union)
FISP........ Federation Internationale des Societes de Philosophie (International Federation of Societies of Philosophy)
FISP........ Federazione Italiana Servizi Pubblici (Italian Federation of Public Services)
FISq .... Fighter Interceptor Squadron (Air Force)
FIST........ Fault Isolation by Semiautomatic Techniques (National Bureau of Standards)
FISU........ Federation Internationale du Sport Universitaire (International University Sports Federation)
FIT......... Fabrication, Integration, and Test
FIT......... Far Infrared Track
FIT......... Fashion Institute of Technology (New York)
FIT......... Fault Isolation Test
FIT......... Federal Income Tax
FIT .... Federation Internationale des Traducteurs (International Federation of Translators)
FIT........ First Indication of Trouble
FIT........ Fixed Interval Timer
FIT........ Flight Instrument Trainer
FIT........ Florida Institute of Technology
FIT........ Forest Industries Telecommunications (Formerly, FIRC)
FIT .... Forward Inspection Team (Military)
FIT........ Franchise Industry Training (High school dropout program) (Department of Labor)
FIT........ Free of Income Tax
FIT........ Free in Truck
FIT .... Fusion at the Inferred Threshold (Test) (Medicine)
FI/T .... Flight Inspection (Temporary)
FITA....... Federation Internationale de Tir a l'Arc (International Archery Federation)
FITAP...... Federation Internationale des Transports Aeriens Prives (International Federation of Private Air Transport)
FITBB ...... Federation Internationale des Travailleurs du Batiment et du Bois
FITC....... Fluorescein Isothiocyanate
FITCAL..... Feel, Inspect, Tighten, Clean, Adjust, Lubricate (A keyword representing operations in preventive maintenance of communications equipment) (Military)
FITCE...... Federation des Ingenieurs des Telecommunications de la Communaute Europeenne (Federation of Telecommunications Engineers in the European Community)
FITD....... Far Infrared Target Detector
FITE....... Fair International Trade Employment Committee
FITEC...... Federation Internationale du Thermalisme et du Climatisme (International Federation of Thermalism and Climatism)
FITGO ..... Floating Input to Ground Output
FITH....... Federation Internationale des Travailleurs de l'Habillement
FITH....... Fire-in-the-Hole (Burn) (NASA)
FITI....... Far Infrared Target Indicator
FITP....... Federation Internationale des Travailleurs du Petrole
FITP....... Federation Internationale des Travailleurs des Plantations
FITPASC.... Federation Internationale des Travailleurs des Plantations, de l'Agriculture et des Secteurs Connexes (International Federation of Plantation, Agricultural, and Allied Workers)
FITR....... Foundation for International Trade Research
FITT....... Federation Internationale de Tennis de Table (International Table Tennis Federation)
FITT....... Federation Internationale des Travailleurs de la Terre
FITU....... Federation of Independent Trade Unions (Lebanon)
FITW...... Federal Income Tax Withholding
FIU........ Forward Interpretation Unit (Military)
FIUS ...... Flax Institute of the United States
FIUS ...... French Institute in the United States

FIVAG ..... Federazione Italiana Venditori Ambulanti e Giornalai (Italian Federation of Street Vendors and Newspaper Sellers)
FIVB....... Federation Internationale de Volleyball (International Volleyball Federation)
FIVF....... Federazione Italiana Vigili del Fuoco (Italian Federation of Firemen)
FIVZ ...... Federation Internationale Veterinaire de Zootechnie
FIW .... Fiberglass Insulated Wire
FIW .... Fighter Interceptor Wing
FIW .... Free in Wagon
FIWC ...... Fiji Industrial Workers' Congress
FJ .... Field Judge (Football)
FJ .... Flush Joint (Diamond drilling)
FJ .... Fused Junction
FJA .... Future Journalists of America
FJC .... Fairbury Junior College (Nebraska)
FJC .... Federal Judicial Center
FJC .... Ferrum Junior College (Virginia)
FJC .... Fisher Junior College (Massachusetts)
FJC .... Flint Junior College (Michigan)
FJC .... Freeman Junior College (South Dakota)
FJC .... Friendship Junior College (South Carolina)
FJC .... Fullerton Junior College (California)
FJCC ...... Fall Joint Computer Conference
FJCEE..... Federation des Jeunes Chefs d'Entreprises d'Europe (European Federation of Young Managers)
FJCNY ..... Furriers Joint Council of New York
FJE .... Free Jet Expansion
FJG .... Fonda, Johnstown & Gloversville R. R. (AAR code)
FJI........ Frequency Jumper Identification
FJN .... Front Jednosci Narodowej (Polish Front of National Unity)
FJNA ...... Front des Jeunes Nationalistes Africains (National African Youth Front)
FJNF ...... Foundation for the Jewish National Fund
FJP .... Federation of Jewish Philanthropies of New York
F of JR ..... Fourth of July Road
FJQ....... Fedders Corporation (NYSE symbol)
FJSRL ..... Frank J. Seiler Research Laboratory (Air Force)
FJSTO..... Federation of Jewish Student Organizations
FJWO ..... Federation of Jewish Women's Organizations
FK .... Flat Keel (Shipbuilding)
FKBI ...... Fourdrinier Kraft Board Institute
FKC ...... Fellow of King's College (London)
FKCL ..... Fellow of King's College, London
FKH....... Forschungs Kommission fuer Hochspannungsfragen (Swiss)
FKM....... Fairbanks Morse & Company (NYSE symbol) (Later, COT)
FKQCP..... Fellow of the King's and Queen's College of Physicians, Ireland
FKS....... Franklin Simon & Company (NYSE symbol) (Delisted)
FKTU..... Federation of Korean Trade Unions (South Korea)
FL .... Falso Lectio (False reading, in a text)
FL .... Fatigue Limit
FL .... Federal League (Major league in baseball, 1914-15)
FL .... Flag Lieutenant (Naval)
FL .... Flashing (Signal Light) (Navigation)
FL .... Flight Level
FL .... Flight Lieutenant
FL .... Florida
FL .... Flow Line (Technical drawings)
FL .... Focal Length
FL .... Foot-Lambert
FL .... Foreign Language
FL .... Frontier Airlines, Inc.
FL .... Funnel Length
F@L........ Fathers-At-Large
FLA .... Fabric Laminators Association
FLA .... Federal Loan Administration
FLA .... Federal Loan Agency
FLA .... Fellow of the Library Association (British)
FLA .... Flight Article (Army)
FLA .... Florida
FLA .... Florida East Coast Railway Company (NYSE symbol)
FLA .... Foam Laminators Association
FLA .... Freie Letzeburger Arbechterverband (Free Luxembourg Workers' Federation)
FLAC ...... Florida Automatic Computer (Air Force)
FLACSO ..... Facultad Latinoamericana de Ciencias Sociales (Santiago, Chile)
FLAEI ...... Federazione Laboratori Aziende Elettriche Italiane (Federation of Workers for Italian Electrical Firms)
FLAG ...... Female Liberal Arts Graduate
FLAG ...... Flagstaff National Park Service Group
FLAGCENT ... Flag Officer Central Europe
FLAGRP ..... Florida Group (Navy)
FLAK ...... Fliegerabwehrkanone, Flugzeugabwehrkanone, or Fugabwehrkanone (German word for antiaircraft gun; acronym used for antiaircraft fire)
FLAK ...... Fondest Love and Kisses (Correspondence)

FLAM . . . . . . Forward Launched Aerodynamic Missiles
FLAME . . . . . . Friendship Loans to Latin American Endeavors, Inc.
FLAMR . . . . . . Forward Looking Advanced Multi-Mode RADAR
FLAMTI . . . . . . Forward-Looking Airborne Moving Target Indication
FLAP . . . . . . Federacion Latinoamericana de Parasitologos
FLAP . . . . . . First Level Adaptive Program
FLAP . . . . . . Flores Assembly Program (Data processing)
FLAR . . . . . . Forward-Looking Airborne RADAR
FLARE . . . . . . Florida Aquanaut Research Expedition (National Oceanic and Atmospheric Administration)
FLASH . . . . . . Flash Lights and Send Help (Florida highway driving aid)
FLASH FIRE . . . Flash Financial Report (for prospective overruns) (Navy)
FLAW . . . . . . Fleet Logistic Air Wing
FLB . . . . Family Life Bureau
FLB . . . . Federal Land Bank
FLB . . . . Foreign Language Bulletin
FLBA . . . . . . Federal Land Bank Association
FLBIN . . . . . . Floating-Point Binary
FLC . . . . Fault Locator Cable
FLC . . . . Federal Library Committee (Library of Congress)
FLC . . . . Federation of Lutheran Clubs
FLC . . . . Flat Load Cell
FLC . . . . Foreign Liquidation Commission
FLC . . . . Frequency and Load Controller
FLCR . . . . . . Fixed Length Cavity Resonance
FLD . . . . Ferret LASER Detector
FLD . . . . Field
FLD . . . . Fieldcrest Mills, Inc. (NYSE symbol)
FLD . . . . Fraunhofer Line Discriminator
FLDA . . . . . . Federal Land Development Authority (Malaysia)
FLDCK . . . . . . Field Cook (Marine Corps)
FLDCK(B) . . . . Field Cook (Baker) (Marine Corps)
FLDCK(C) . . . . Field Cook (Commissary) (Marine Corps)
FLDCOMDASA Field Command, Defense Atomic Support Agency
FLDEC . . . . . . Floating-Point Decimal
FLDI . . . . Flare Die
FLDMS . . . . . . Field Maintenance Shop (Army)
FLDO . . . . . . Field Officer
FLDO . . . . . . Final Limit, Down
FLDR . . . . . . Fluid Dram
FLE . . . . Fleetwood Enterprises, Inc. (NYSE symbol)
FLEA . . . . . . Flux Logic Element Array
FLEACT . . . . . Fleet Activities
FLEEP . . . . . . Flying Lunar Excursion Experimental Platform (NASA)
FLES . . . . Foreign Languages in Elementary Schools
FLETC . . . . . . Federal Law Enforcement Training Center
FLETRABASE . . . Fleet Training Base
FLETRAGRUWATE . . Fleet Training Group and Underway Training Element
FLEXEM . . . . . Flexible Energy Management
FLF . . . . Fault Location Facility (Aircraft)
FLF . . . . Final Limit, Forward
FLFT . . . . . . Full Load Frame Time (Term used in SAGE operations)
FLG . . . . Florida Gas Co. (NYSE symbol)
FLG . . . . Front de Libertacao de Guine (Guinean Liberation Front) (Portuguese Guinea)
FLGA . . . . . . Florida Lychee Growers Association
FLH . . . . Final Limit, Hoist
FLI . . . . Fault Location Indicator
FLI . . . . Federation Lainiere Internationale (International Wool Textile Organization)
FLI . . . . Flight Leader Identity (RADAR)
FLI . . . . Food Law Institute
FLI . . . . Forward Looking Infrared
FLI . . . . Funnel Length Index
FLIA . . . . . . Federation Life Insurance of America
FLIC . . . . Film Library Information Council
FLICON . . . . . Flight Control(ler)
FLICR . . . . . . Fluid Logic Industrial Control Relay
FLID . . . . . . Front de la Lutte pour l'Independence du Dahomey (Battle Front for the Independence of Dahomey)
FLIDAP . . . . . Flight Data Position
FLIDEN . . . . . Flight Data Entry (Device) (SAGE)
FLIDIT . . . . . Flight Line Detection and Isolation Techniques
FLIFO . . . . . . Flight Information
FLIMBAL . . . . Floated Inertial Measurement Ball
FLING . . . . . . Front de Lutte pour l'Independence de la Guinee (Battle Front for the National Independence of Portuguese Guinea)
FLINT . . . . . . Floating Interpretive Language (Princeton University)
FLIOP . . . . . . Flight Operations Planner
FLIP . . . . Film Library Instantaneous Presentation (Data processing)
FLIP . . . . Flight Information Plan
FLIP . . . . Flight Information Publication (Air Force)

FLIP . . . . Flight Launched Infrared Probe
FLIP . . . . Floated Lightweight Inertial Platform
FLIP . . . . Floating Indexed Point Arithmetic (Data processing)
FLIP . . . . Floating Instrument Platform (Navy)
FLIP . . . . Floating Laboratory Instrument Platform (Movable oceanographic research station)
FLIP . . . . Floating Point Interpretive Program (Data processing)
FLIPs . . . . . . Flight Information Publications (Air Force, Navy)
FLIR . . . . Forward Looking Infrared RADAR
FLIRAS . . . . . Forward Looking Infrared Attack Set
FLIRT . . . . . . Federal Librarians Round Table (American Library Association)
FLIRT . . . . . . First Ladies' International Racing Team (Group of women racing at Le Mans, France)
FLITE . . . . . . Future Lawyers Investigating Transportation Employment (Student legal action organization)
FLJTC . . . . . . Freeland League for Jewish Territorial Colonization
FLL . . . . Final Limit, Lower
FLLU . . . . . . Federation of Libyan Labor Unions
FLM . . . . Federation Lutherienne Mondiale (Lutheran World Federation)
FLM . . . . Fleming Co., Inc. (NYSE symbol)
FLM . . . . Flight Line Maintenance
FLM . . . . Fluidic Logic Module
FLM . . . . Frightened Little Man
FLM . . . . Fur, Leather and Machine (Workers Joint Board)
FLMI . . . . . . Fellow, Life Management Institute (Designation conferred by Life Office Management Association)
FLN . . . . Front de Liberation Nationale (National Liberation Front) (Algeria)
FLNK . . . . . . Force de Liberation Nationale Kamerunaise (National Cameroonian Liberation Force)
FLO . . . . Functional Line Organization
FLOA . . . . . . Federal Licensed Officers Association
FLOC . . . . . . For Love of Children (Organization)
FLODAC . . . . . Fluid-Operated Digital Automatic Computer
FLOG . . . . . . Fleet Logistics
FLOGWING . . Fleet Logistics Air Wing (Military)
FLOLS . . . . . Fresnel Lens Optical Landing System
FLOOD . . . . . Fleet Observation of Oceanographic Data (Navy)
FLOP . . . . . . Floating Octal Point (IBM)
FLORA . . . . . Fire Location RADAR
FLORL . . . . . Fluorescent Runway Lighting
FLOSY . . . . . Front for the Liberation of Occupied South Yemen
FLOX . . . . . . Fluorine-Liquid Oxygen
FLOZ . . . . . . Fluid Ounce
FLP . . . . Festlegepunkt (Reference point, a gunnery term) (German military – World War II)
FLP . . . . Fighting Landplane
FLP . . . . Flight Line Printer
FLP . . . . Foreign Language Program
FLP . . . . Front de Liberation Populaire (Quebec separatist group)
FLPA . . . . . . Foreign Language Press of America
FLQ . . . . Front de Liberation du Quebec (Separatist group)
FLR . . . . Field Loss Relay
FLR . . . . Final Limit, Reverse
FLR . . . . Fluor Corporation, Ltd. (NYSE symbol)
FLR . . . . Fluoroleucine Resistant (Mutant)
FLR . . . . Forward Looking RADAR
FLRNG . . . . . Flash Ranging
FLS . . . . Family Location Service
FLS . . . . Farm Labor Service (of USES)
FLS . . . . Federazione Lavoratori Somali (Somali Labor Federation)
FLS . . . . Fellow of the Linnaean Society (British)
FLS . . . . Florida Steel Corp. (NYSE symbol)
FLSA . . . . . . Flow Switch
FLSA . . . . . . Fair Labor Standards Act
FLSC . . . . . . Fixed Laboratory Standard Capacitor
FLSC . . . . . . Flexible Linear Shaped Charge
FLSIP . . . . . . Fleet Logistic Support Improvement Program
FLSP . . . . . . Fluorescein Labeled Serum Protein (Chemical)
FLSS . . . . . . Falcon Launching Saber System
FLSW . . . . . . Fleet Logistic Support Wing (Navy)
FLT . . . . Fault Locating Test
FLT . . . . Field Level Training
FLT . . . . Filing Time
FLT . . . . Filtrol Corporation (NYSE symbol) (Wall Street slang name: "Flit")
FLT . . . . Flight
FLT . . . . Flight Line Taxi
FLT . . . . Flight Line Tester
FLT . . . . Fork Lift Truck
FLT . . . . Foss Launch & Tug (AAR code)
FLTACT . . . . . Fleet Activities
FLTCERT . . . . . Flight Certificate

FLTGUNSCH . . Fleet Gunnery School
FLTL . . . . Flight Line
FLTLOSCAP . . . Fleet Liaison Officer, Supreme Commander Allied Powers (World War II)
FLTO . . . . Flight Officer (Air Force)
FLTP. . . . . Foreign Language Training Program (Air Force)
FLTREADREP. . . Fleet Readiness Representative
FLTSERVSCOL . . Fleet Service School
FLTSOUNDSCOL . . Fleet Sound School
FLTST . . . . Flight Steward
FLTTRACEN . . . Fleet Training Center
FLU . . . . Federation of Labor Unions (Lebanon)
FLU . . . . Final Limit, Up
FLUG . . . . Flugfelag Islands H. F. (Iceland Airways, Ltd.)
FLUL . . . . Federation of Labor Unions in Lebanon
FLV . . . . Friend Leukemia Virus
FLW . . . . International Fur and Leather Workers Union of United States and Canada
FLWIS . . . . Flood Warnings Issued
FLY . . . . Flying Tiger Corp. (NYSE symbol)
FLYTAF . . . . . . Flying Training Air Force
FLZO . . . . Farband Labor Zionist Order
FM . . . . Face Measurement
FM . . . . Facilities Maintenance
FM . . . . Factory Mutual System (Group of four insurance companies and an engineering organization)
FM . . . . Fan Marker (Aviation)
FM . . . . Feedback Mechanism
Fm . . . . Fermium (Chemical element)
FM . . . . Ferrite Metal
FM . . . . Fibrous Material
FM . . . . Field Maintenance
FM . . . . Field Manual
FM . . . . Field Marshal
FM . . . . Field Music (Marine Corps)
FM . . . . Figure of Merit
FM . . . . Filament Midtop
FM . . . . Fine Measurement
FM . . . . Flight Manual
FM . . . . Flight Mechanic
FM . . . . Foreign Mission
FM . . . . Formerly Married
FM . . . . Foundation Member
FM . . . . Fraternite Mondiale (World Brotherhood)
FM . . . . Frequency Meter
FM . . . . Frequency Modulation (Radio)
FM . . . . Frequency Multiplex
FM . . . . Frisker-Monitor (Radiation detection)
FM . . . . Full Moon (Moon phase)
FMA . . . . Fabricating Machinery Association
FMA . . . . Factory Materials Association
FMA . . . . Failure Mode Analysis
FMA . . . . Fellow of the Museums Association (British)
FMA . . . . Ferrite Manufacturers Association
FMA . . . . File Manufacturers Association
FMA . . . . Financial Management Association
FMA . . . . Flexicore Manufacturers Association
FMA . . . . . . Food Management Area
FMA . . . . Food Merchandisers of America
FMA . . . . Forging Manufacturers Association
FMA . . . . Fulfillment Managers Association (Formerly, SFMA)
FMACC . . . . . . Federation Mondiale des Anciens Combattants (World Veterans Federation)
FMACC. . . . . . Foreign Military Assistance Coordinating Committee
FMAL . . . . Funds Management Audit List (Military)
FMANA . . . . . Fire Marshals Association of North America
FMANU . . . . . Federation Mondiale des Associations pour les Nations Unies (World Federation of United Nations Associations)
FMAP . . . . . . Fan Marker Approach (Aviation)
FMAS . . . . Florida Marine Aquarium Society
FMASC . . . . . . Foreign Military Assistance Steering Committee
FMAW. . . . . . . First Marine Aircraft Wing
FMB . . . . Federal Maritime Board (1950-1961; functions transferred to FMC)
FMB . . . . Foreign Materiel Branch (Military)
FMB . . . . Frequency Modulation Broadcasters
FMBSA . . . . . . Farmers and Manufacturers Beet Sugar Association
FMC . . . . Facilities Management Contract
FMC . . . . Fatstock Marketing Corporation (British)
FMC . . . . Federal Maritime Commission (Independent government agency)
FMC . . . . Felt Manufacturers Council
FMC . . . . Ferrite Memory Core
FMC . . . . Film-Makers' Cooperative
FMC . . . . Fixed Mica Capacitor

FMC . . . . Fixed Mylar Capacitor
FMC . . . . Flexible Monte Carlo
FMC . . . . Flexible Motor Coupling
FMC . . . . FMC Corporation (NYSE symbol)
FMC . . . . Food Machinery Corporation (Later, FMC Corporation)
FMC . . . . Former Members of Congress (US)
FMC . . . . Forward Motion Compensation
FMC . . . . Franklin and Marshall College (Pennsylvania)
FMC . . . . Frequency-Modulated Cyclotron (AEC)
FMC . . . . Fuel Management Computer
FMCMA . . . . . Fraternal and Military Club Managers Association
FMCORP . . . . . Field Music Corporal (Marine Corps)
FMCPL . . . . . . Field Music Corporal (Marine Corps)
FMCR . . . . Fleet Marine Corps Reserve
FMCS . . . . . . Federal Mediation and Conciliation Service (Independent government agency)
FMCU . . . . Form Cutter
FM/CW . . . . . . Frequency-Modulated/Continuous-Wave (RADAR)
FMD . . . . Ferrous Metal Detector
FMD . . . . Ferry Movement Directives
FMD . . . . Fixtures Manufacturers and Dealers
FMD . . . . Foot-and-Mouth Disease (Veterinary medicine)
FMD . . . . Frequency of Minimum Delay
FMDA . . . . . . Frequency Modulation Development Association
FMDC . . . . . . Franciscan Missionary Sisters of the Divine Child (Roman Catholic religious order)
FMDI . . . . Form Die
FMDJ . . . . Federation Mondiale des Villes Jumelees (United Towns Organization)
FMDM . . . . . . Franciscan Missionaries of the Divine Motherhood (Roman Catholic women's religious order)
FMDM . . . . . . Frequency Modulation Deviation Meter
FMDV . . . . . . Foot-and-Mouth Disease Virus
FME . . . . Frequency-Measuring Equipment
FMEA . . . . . . Failure Mode and Effect Analysis
FMEA . . . . . . Flour Millers Export Association
FMEC . . . . . . Fur Merchants Employers Council
FMECA . . . . . Failure Mode, Effects and Criticality Analyses
FMEVA . . . . . Floating Point Means and Variance
FMF . . . . Fairmont Foods Company (NYSE symbol)
FMF . . . . Familial Mediterranean Fever
FMF . . . . Fleet Marine Force (Military)
FMF . . . . Florida Mango Forum
FMFB . . . . . . Frequency Modulation with Feedback
FMFIC . . . . . . Federation of Mutual Fire Insurance Companies
FMFLANT . . . . Fleet Marine Force, Atlantic
FMFM . . . . . . Fleet Marine Force Manual (Marine Corps)
FM-FM . . . . . . Frequency Modulation-Frequency Modulation
FMFPAC . . . . . Fleet Marine Force, Pacific Fleet (Navy, Marine Corps)
FMG . . . . Fabricated Metal Goods
FMG . . . . Flakmessgerat (Antiaircraft, gun-laying RADAR) (German)
FMG . . . . Foreign Medical Graduate (doing residency in US hospital)
FMG . . . . Frequency Modulation Generator
FMH . . . . Falling Mass Hazard
FmHA . . . . . . Farmers Home Administration
FMHC . . . . . . Federation of Mental Health Centers
FMHS . . . . . . Freely Moving Human Subject
FMI . . . . Fonds Monetaire International (International Monetary Fund)
FMI . . . . Free Motion Impedance
FMI . . . . Frequency Modulation Intercity Relay Broadcasting
FMIC . . . . . . Frequency Monitoring and Interference Control (Radio)
FMIC . . . . . . Fund Management Identification Code (Military)
FMIR . . . . . . Frustrated Multiple Internal Reflectance
FMJD . . . . . . Federation Mondiale de la Jeunesse Democratique (World Federation of Democratic Youth)
FMJFC . . . . . . Federation Mondiale des Jeunesses Feminines Catholiques
FML . . . . Feedback, Multiple Loop
FML . . . . Front Mounting Light
FMLP . . . . . . Field Mirror Landing Practice
FMM . . . . Ferromagnetic Material
FMM . . . . Fivondronamben'ny Mpiasa Malagasy (Confederation of Malagasy Workers)
FMM . . . . Franciscan Missionaries of Mary (Roman Catholic women's religious order)
FMM . . . . From the Latin for Brothers of Mercy (Roman Catholic religious order)
FMMA . . . . . . Floor Machine Manufacturers Association
FMMC . . . . . . Fixed Mylar Metallized Capacitor
FMMF . . . . . . Flexure Monitor Mounting Fixture
FMN . . . . Flavin Mononucleotide
F/M/N . . . . . . Faith-Man-Nature (from F/M/N Papers, National Council of Churches)
FMO . . . . Fast Moving Object
FMO . . . . Federal-Mogul Corporation (NYSE symbol)
FMO. . . . . . . Fleet Maintenance Office(r)
FMO. . . . . . . Fleet Medical Officer

FMO .... Flight Medical Officer (Air Force)
FMO .... Forms Management Officer (Army)
FMOP....... Frequency Modulation on the Pulse
FMP........ Ferrous Metal Powder
FMP........ **Field Maintenance Party (Aviation)**
FMP........ **Financial Management Plan**
FMP........ Fleet Modernization Plan (Navy)
FMP........ Fluid Motion Panel (of the British Aeronautical Research Council)
FMP........ Force Modernization Program
FMPA....... Federation Mondiale pour la Protection des Animaux (World Federation for the Protection of Animals) (Also known as WFPA and WTB)
FMPC....... **Federation of Motion Picture Councils**
FMPC....... Feed Materials Production Center (AEC)
FMPD....... Fort Monmouth Procurement Division
FMPEC..... **Financial Management Plan for Emergency Conditions**
FMPM....... Family Manned Planetary Mission
FM-PM...... Frequency Modulation - Phase Modulation (RADAR)
FMPO....... Fort Monmouth Procurement Office
FMPP....... Federal Merit Promotion Program
FMPP....... **Foundation of the Motion Picture Pioneers**
FMPS....... Functional Mathematical Programming System (Data processing)
FMQ........ Frequency-Modulated Quartz
FMR........ Final Meteorological Radiation
FMR........ Food Mart, Inc. (NYSE symbol) (Delisted)
FMR........ Frequency-Modulated RADAR
FMR........ Frequency-Modulated Receiver
FMR........ Funds Management Record (Military)
FMRA ...... **Foreign Media Representatives Association**
FMRC....... Fixed Motor Run Capacitor
FMRL....... Form Roll
FMRLY..... Formerly
FMRS....... **Federal Mediation and Reconciliation Service**
FMRT....... Final Meteorological Radiation Tape
FMS........ Fallout Monitoring Station (Civil Defense)
FMS........ Fat Mobilizing Substance
FMS........ **Federated Malay States**
FMS........ Federation Mondiale des Sourds (World Federation of the Deaf)
FMS........ Fellow of the Meteorological Society (British)
FMS........ Field Maintenance Squadron
FMS........ **Field Music School (Marine Corps)**
FMS........ Fighter Missile System
FMS........ Financial Management System
FMS........ Flexible Measuring System
FMS........ Flight Motion Simulator
FMS........ **Floating Machine Shop**
FMS........ Flow Measuring System
FMS........ Food Management System
FMS........ Foreign Military Sales
FMS........ Foreign Military Service
FMS........ Fort Myers Southern R. R. (AAR code)
FMS........ Fratres Maristae a Scholis (Marist Brothers) (Roman Catholic religious order)
FMS........ **Free-Machining Steel**
FMS........ Frequency Mixer Stage
FMS........ Frequency Multiplier Storer
FMS........ Fuze Maintenance Spares
FMSAEG.... Fleet Missile Systems Analysis and Evaluation Group (Navy)
FMSC...... Federal Manual for Supply Cataloging
FMSC...... Fixed Motor Starting Capacitor
FMSGT..... **Field Music Sergeant (Marine Corps)**
FMSI ...... Filii Mariae Salutis Infirmorum (Sons of Mary, Health of the Sick) (Roman Catholic religious order)
FMSI ...... **Friction Materials Standards Institute**
FMSJ....... Franciscan Missionaries of St. Joseph (Patricroft Sisters) (Roman Catholic religious order)
FMSL...... Fort Monmouth Signal Laboratory (Army)
FMSM...... Federation Mondiale pour la Sante Mentale (World Federation for Mental Health)
FMSO ..... **Fleet Material Support Office (Navy)**
FMSO...... Foreign Military Sales Order (Army)
FMSP ..... Foreign Military Sales Program (Army)
FMSq ..... Field Maintenance Squadron (Air Force)
FMST...... Frequency Mass Spectrometer Tube
FMSWR.... Flexible Mild Steel Wire Rope
FMT ...... **Flush Metal Threshold (Technical drawings)**
FMT ...... Frequency-Modulated Transmitter
FMT ...... Friction Measurement Test
FMTM...... Friction Materials Test Machine
FMTO...... Form Tool
FMTS ..... Federation Mondiale des Travailleurs Scientifiques (World Federation of Scientific Workers)

FMTS ...... Field Maintenance Test Station (Army)
FMU....... Force Measurement Unit
FMV....... Fair Market Value
FMVSS ..... Federal Motor Vehicle Safety Standard
FMW ...... First Main Watch
FMX ...... Full Mouth Radiograph (Dentistry)
FN........ Fabrique Nationale (d'Armes de Guerre, Societe Anonyme)
FN........ Fireman (Nonrated enlisted man) (Navy)
FN .... Flat or Nested (Freight)
FN........ Flat Nose (Projectile)
FN........ Flight Nurse
FN........ Fog Nautophone (Navigation charts)
FN........ Footnote
FN........ St. Louis-San Francisco Railway Company (NYSE symbol)
FNA ...... Flora North America Program
FNA....... **Following Named Airmen**
FNA....... Frequency Network Analyzer
FNB....... First Chicago Corp. (NYSE symbol)
FNB....... **Food and Nutrition Board**
FNC....... First National City Corp. (NYSE symbol)
FNC....... Fixed Niobium Capacitor
FNC....... Flexible Nylon Coupling
FNCB...... First National City Bank (New York City)
FNCC..... Federation Nationale des Cooperatives de Cereales
FNCE..... Fabricacion Nacional de Colorantes, SA
FNCETA .... Federation Nationale des Centres d'Etudes Techniques Agricoles
FNCUMA .... Federation Nationale des Cooperatives d'Utilisation de Materiel Agricole
FND....... Fast Neutron Dose
FND....... Frontal National Democratic (Rumania)
FNDEL ..... **Federazione Nazionale Dipendenti Enti Locali** (National Federation of Local Government) (Italy)
FNDS ..... **Federazione Nazionale delgi Statali** (Italian Federation of Government Employees)
FNE....... **Following Named Enlisted Personnel**
FNEORID .... **Following Named Enlisted Men Organization Indicated**
FNERAS .... **Following Named Enlisted Men Are Relieved Assignment**
FNGAA .... Federation Nationale des Groupements Agricoles d'Approvisionnement
FNH....... **Flashless Nonhygroscopic (Gunpowder)**
FNI ...... Federation Naturiste Internationale (International Naturist Federation)
FNI ...... **Following Named Individuals**
FNIE ..... Federation Nationale des Industries Electroniques Francaises (National Federation of French Electronics Manufacturers)
FNL....... Fansteel, Inc. (NYSE symbol)
FNLA...... **Fronte Nacional de Libertacao da Angola** (Angolan National Liberation Front)
FNM ...... Federal National Mortgage Association (NYSE symbol) (Wall Street slang name: "Fannie Mae")
FNM ...... Ferrocarriles Nacionales des Mexico (National Railroad of Mexico)
FNMA ..... Federal National Mortgage Association (Nickname: Fannie Mae)
FNO ...... **Following Named Officers**
FNOA ..... **Following Named Officers and Airmen**
FNOIO..... **Fleet Naval Ordnance Inspecting Officer**
FNOSS..... Federation Nationale des Organismes de Securite Sociale (France)
FNP....... **Fusion Point**
FNPA..... Foreign Numbering Plan Area (AT & T)
FNPOR..... **Federation of National Professional Organizations for Recreation**
FNR....... Ford Nuclear Reactor
FNRJ ..... Federationa Narodna Republika Jugoslavija (Yugoslavia)
FNRS ..... Federation Nationale Researche Scientifique (Belgium)
FNS ...... First National State Bancorp (NYSE symbol)
FNS ...... Food and Nutrition Service (Department of Agriculture)
FNS ...... Frontier Nursing Service (An organization)
FNS ...... Functional Neuromuscular Stimulation (Physiotherapy)
FNS ...... Functional Nomenclature Signal
FNT ...... Fenestra Incorporated (NYSE symbol) (Delisted)
FNTAPSCM ... **Federation Nationale des Travailleurs de l'Agriculture, des Plantations, et Secteurs Connexes de Madagascar** (National Federation of Workers of Agriculture, Plantations and Related Sectors of Madagascar)
FNU....... Forces des Nations Unies (United Nations Forces)
FNUR...... Fonds des Nations Unies pour les Refugies (United Nations Funds for Refugees)
FNV....... Federacion Nacional Velasquista (Political party in Ecuador)
FNVCA..... **Federazione Nazionale Vetro e Ceramica** (National Federation of Glass and Pottery Workers) (Italy)
FNWC ..... Fleet Numerical Weather Central (Navy)
FNWF..... Fleet Numerical Weather Facility
FNY....... French Navy
FO....... Factory Order
FO....... Fan Out
FO........ **Fast Operating (Relay)**
FO........ Fatty Oil

FO........ Field Office(r)
FO........ Field Order
FO........ Finance Officer
FO........ Fine Old
FO........ Firm Offer (Business and trade)
FO........ Fishery Officer (Ministry of Agriculture, Fisheries, and Food) (British)
FO........ Fitting Out (Navy)
FO........ Fixed Oil
FO........ Flag Officer (Navy)
FO........ Flat Oval (Technical drawings)
FO........ Flight Officer (Air Force)
FO........ Flight Order
FO........ Flintkote Company (NYSE symbol)
FO........ Flying Officer (British)
FO........ For Orders
FO........ Force Ouviere
FO........ Foreign Office
FO........ Forward Observer
FO........ Free Overside
FO........ Fuel Oil
FO........ Full Organ (Music)
FO........ Full Out (Flush left) (Typesetting)
FOA....... Fitting Out Availability (Navy)
FOA....... Football Officials Association
FOA....... Foreign Operations Administration
FOA....... Foresters of America
FOA....... Friends of Animals
FOA....... Fugitive Other Authorities (FBI standardized term)
FOB....... Federal Office Building
FOB....... Fiber Optics Bundle
FOB....... Fine Old Blend (Wines and spirits)
FCB....... First Overtone Band
FOB....... Forward Observer Bombardment
FOB....... Forward Operating Base (Air Force)
FOB....... Fractional Orbital Bombardment
FOB....... Free on Board
FOB....... Fresh Off the Boat
FOB....... Fuel on Board (Aviation)
FOBAA.... Flag Officer British Assault Area
FOBO...... Fort Bowie National Historic Site
FOBS...... Fiber Optics Borescope
FOBS...... Fractional Orbital Bombardment System
FOBTSU.... Forward Observer Target Survey Unit
FOC....... Final Operational Capability (Military)
FOC....... Fixed Oil Capacitor
FOC....... Flight Operations Center
FOC....... Follow-On Contract
FOC....... Forward Observer Colidar
FOC....... Free on Car
FOC....... Free of Charge (Business and trade)
FOC....... Fuel Oil Cooler
FOCA...... Fort Caroline National Memorial
FOCA...... Free and Open Church Association (British)
FOCAP.... Federacion Odontologica Centro America y Panama (Odontological Federation of Central America and Panama)
FOCCPAC ... Fleet Operations Control Center, Pacific Fleet
FOCI...... Farrand Optical Company, Incorporated
FOCL...... Fort Clatsop National Memorial
FCCOHANA .. Fourier Coefficient Harmonic Analyzer
FOCSL..... Fleet Oriented Consolidated Stock List (Navy)
FOCUS..... For Our Christian Understanding (Program)
FOCUS..... Form of Control Users System
FOCUS..... Formal Officer Career Utilization Structure (Military)
FOCWA.... Flag Officer Commanding West Africa (British)
FOD....... Field Officer of the Day (Army)
FOD....... Field Operations Department
FOD....... Flashblindness Orientation Device
FOD....... Flight Operations Directorate (Apollo) (NASA)
FOD....... Foreign Object Damage
FOD....... Free of Damage (Business and trade)
FODA..... Fort Davis National Historic Site
FODAAS.... Field On-Line Data Acquisition and Analysis System
FODO..... Fort Donelson National Military Park
FOE....... Ferro Corporation (NYSE symbol)
FOE....... Fraternal Order of Eagles
FOEP...... Frog Otolith Experiment Package (NASA)
FOES...... Fine Old Extra Special
FOEU...... Foreign Organizations' Employees Union
FOF....... Facts on File (Inc.)
FOF....... Field Observing Facility (of National Center for Atmospheric Research)
FOF....... Flight Operations Facility

FOF....... Fukuoka Occupation Force
FOF....... Full Octave Filter
FOF....... Fund of Funds
FOFA...... Friends of Free Asia
FOFATUSA ... Federation of Free African Trade Unions of South Africa
FO/FO/FS.... Fail Operational, Fail Operational, Fail Safe
FOFR...... Fort Frederica National Monument
FOG....... Field Operations Group
FOG....... Flow of Gold
FOG....... Frequency Offset Generator
FOGA..... Fashion Originators Guild of America
FOGSIG.... Fog Signal (Station)
FOI....... Field Operations Intelligence
FOI....... Fighter Officer for Interceptors (Member of the SAGE Command Post staff)
FOI....... Fleet Operational Investigation (NOO)
FOI....... Forced Oil Injection
FOI....... Freedom of Information (Army)
FOIC...... Flag Officer-in-Charge (British-controlled port)
FOIF...... Free Oceanographic Instrument Float
FOIR...... Field-of-Interest Register (DOD)
FOITAF..... Federacion Obrera de la Industria Tabaquera de Filipinas (Workers' Federation of the Tobacco Industry of the Philippines)
FOIU...... Flowmeter Ordering and Indicating Unit
FOJE...... Fort Jefferson National Monument
FOK....... Free of Knots
FOKEU..... Foreign Organizations Korean Employees' Union (South Korea)
FOL....... Fiber Optics LASER
FOL....... Fiber Optics Light
FOL....... Follow
FOL....... Friends of the Land
FOLA...... Fort Laramie National Historic Site
FOLIS...... Following Information Is Submitted (Army)
FOLNOAVAL.. Following Items Not Available
FOLR...... Forward Observer LASER Range-Finder
FOLS...... Fort Larned National Historic Site
FOM....... Fighter Officer for Missiles (Member of the SAGE Command Post staff)
FOM....... Figure of Merit
FOM....... Fishers of Men
FOMA..... Fort Matanzas National Monument
FOMC..... Federal Open Market Committee (of FRS)
FOMC..... Fort McHenry National Monument
FOMCAT.... Foreign Material Catalog
FOMOCO .... Ford Motor Company
FON....... Federation of Ontario Naturalists
FONAP..... Flag Officer, Naval Air, Pacific (British)
FONE...... Fort Necessity National Battlefield
FONECON ... Telephone Conversation
FONF...... Flag Officer Newfoundland (British)
FONJEP .... Fonds de Cooperation de la Jeunesse et de l'Education Populaire
FONOFF .... Foreign Office
FOO....... Forward Observation Officer (Military)
FOO....... Fraternal Order of Orioles
FOOT...... Follow-On Operational Test
FOP....... Fiber Optics Probe
FOP....... Financial Operating Plan
FOP....... Flight Operations Plan
FOP....... Forward Observation Post (Military)
FOP....... Fraternal Order of Police, Grand Lodge
FOP....... Grand Lodge, Ladies Auxiliary, Fraternal Order of Police
FOPEN..... Foliage Penetration (RADAR)
FOPI...... First-Order Polynomial Interpolator
FOPP...... Fiber Optics Photo Pickup
FOPP...... First-Order Polynomial Predictor
FOPR...... Full Out-Patient Rate
FOPR...... Society of Friends of Puerto Rico
FOPREP..... Force Packaging Report (Military)
FOPT...... Fiber Optics Photo Transfer
FOPU...... Fort Pulaski National Monument
FOQ....... Free on Quay (Business and trade)
FOR....... Federacion Obrera Revolucionaria (Mexican political party)
FOR....... Fellowship of Reconciliation
FOR....... Fore River Corporation (AAR code)
FOR....... Foremost-McKesson, Inc. (NYSE symbol)
FOR....... Free on Rail (Business and trade)
FOR....... Free on Road (Business and trade)
FORA..... Fort Raleigh National Historic Site
FORAC..... For Action
FORACS.... Fleet Operational Readiness Accuracy Check Sites (Navy)
FORAST.... Formula Assembler Translator
FORATOM.... Forum Atomique Europeen (European Atomic Forum)

FORC . . . . . . Formula Coder
FORD . . . . Foreign Office Research Department (British)
FORDACS . . . . Fuel-Oil Route Delivery and Control System (Computer-based system)
FORDS . . . . . . Floating Ocean Research & Development Station
FORE . . . . . . Foundation for Oceanographic Research and Education
FOREAMI . . . . Fonds Reine Elisabeth d'Assistance Medicale aux Indigenes (Queen Elisabeth Funds for Medical Assistance to the Natives)
FOREMAN. . . . . Form Retrieval and Manipulation Language
FORESDAT. . . . Formerly Restricted Data (Military)
FOREST. . . . . . Fast Order Radiation Effects Sampling Technique
FORF . . . . Forfeiture
FORJ . . . . Fellowship of Religious Journalists
FORM. . . . . . . Ferromagnetic Object Recognition Matrix
FORMA. . . . . . Fonds d'Orientation et de Regularisation des Marches Agricoles (French government food agency)
FORMA. . . . . . FORTRAN (Formula Translation) Matrix Analysis (Data processing)
FORMAC. . . . . Formula Manipulation Compiler (Data processing)
FORMPATPAC . . Formosa Patrol Force, US Pacific Fleet
FORPAC . . . . . Forecasting Passenger and Cargo
FORSTAT. . . . . Force Status Report (Military)
FORTRAN . . . . Formula Translation (Data processing)
FORTRUNCIBLE. . FORTRAN (Formula Translation) Style Runcible (Data processing)
FORTSK . . . . . For Task Force (Military)
FOS . . . . Follow-On Spares
FOS . . . . Free on Station
FOS . . . . Free on Steamer (Business and trade)
FOS . . . . Full Operational Status
FOSAT . . . . . . Fitting Out Supply Assistance Team (Navy)
FOSATS . . . . . Fleet Outfitting Supply Assistance Teams (Navy)
FOSD . . . . Functional Operational Sequence Diagram
FOSDIC . . . . Film Optical Sensing Device for Input to Computers (of the National Bureau of Standards)
FOSM. . . . . . . Fort Smith National Historic Site
FOSO. . . . . . . Flight Operations Scheduling Office (NASA)
FOSU . . . . . . Fort Sumter National Monument
FOSWAC. . . . . Family of Special Weapons Atomic Contractors
FOT . . . . Fifth-Order Theory
FOT . . . . Follow-on Operational Test
FOT . . . . Free on Truck (Business and trade)
FOT . . . . Frequency Optimum Traffic
FOT . . . . Frequency on Target
FOT . . . . Fuel-Oil Transfer
FOTALI . . . . . . Flag Officer Taranto and Adriatic and for Liaison
FOTF . . . . . . Folded Other Than Flat (Freight)
FOTM . . . . . . Friends of Old-Time Music (An organization)
FOUN . . . . . . Fort Union National Monument
FOUO. . . . . . . For Official Use Only
FOURATAF . . . Fourth Allied Tactical Air Force, Central Europe
FOUS . . . . . . Fort Union Trading Post National Historic Site
FOUSA . . . . . Finance Officer, United States Army
FOV. . . . . Field of View (or Vision)
FOVA. . . . . . Fort Vancouver National Historic Site
FOW . . . . . . First Open Water (Shipping)
FOW . . . . . . Free on Wagons (Business and trade)
FOW . . . . . . Friends of the Wilderness (An organization)
FOWABPF . . . . Flag Officer Western Area, British Pacific Fleet
FOWHM . . . . . Fuel Oil and Water Heater Manufacturers Association
FOWSAB . . . . . Federation of Women Shareholders in American Business
FOX . . . . Foxboro Company (NYSE symbol)
FP . . . . False Pretenses
FP . . . . Fecal Pellet
FP . . . . Feedback Positive
FP . . . . Feedback Potentiometer
FP . . . . Festpunkt (Reference point, a surveying term) (German military – World War II)
FP . . . . Field Punishment (Military)
FP . . . . Financial Plan
FP . . . . Fine Paper
FP . . . . Fire Plug
FP . . . . Fireplace
FP . . . . Fission Product
FP . . . . Fixed Price
FP . . . . Flagpole
FP . . . . Flash Point
FP . . . . Flat Point (Technical drawings)
FP . . . . Flavin Phosphate
FP . . . . Flavoprotein (Biochemistry)
FP . . . . Flight Pay
FP . . . . Flight Plan (Aviation)
FP . . . . Floating Policy (Insurance)
FP . . . . Fluorescent Particle

FP . . . . Foot Patrol
FP . . . . Foot-Pound
FP . . . . Fordyce & Princeton R. R. (AAR code)
FP . . . . Forest Patrol (Activity of Civil Air Patrol)
FP . . . . Former Priest
FP . . . . Forte Piano (Loud, then soft) (Music)
FP . . . . Forward Perpendicular
FP . . . . Freezing Point
FP . . . . Freight and Passenger Vessels (Army)
FP . . . . Full Period
FP . . . . Fully Paid
FP . . . . Pipefitter (Navy)
F/P . . . . Flat Pattern
FPA . . . . Failure Probability Analysis
FPA . . . . Fattori Proteici Animali (Medicine)
FPA . . . . Federal Professional Association
FPA . . . . Field Profit Analysis
FPA . . . . Fill Producers' Association
FPA . . . . Final Power Amplifier
FPA . . . . First Pennsylvania Corp. (NYSE symbol)
FPA . . . . Flat Plate Antenna
FPA . . . . Flexible Packaging Association
FPA . . . . Flight Path Analysis
FPA . . . . Flight Path Angle
FPA . . . . Flight Plan Approval
FPA . . . . Floating Point Arithmetic
FPA . . . . Flying Physicians Association
FPA . . . . Food Production Administration (World War II)
FPA . . . . Force Planning Analysis (Army)
FPA . . . . Foreign Policy Association
FPA . . . . Foreign Press Association
FPA . . . . Franklin Pierce Adams (1881-1960) (American newspaper columnist)
FPA . . . . Free of Particular Average (Insurance)
FPA . . . . Funding Program Advice (Military)
FPAA . . . . . . Federacion Panamericana de Asociaciones de Arquitectos (Panamerican Federation of Architects' Associations)
FPAA . . . . . . Flat Plate Array Antenna
FPAAC . . . . . . Free of Particular Average, American Conditions (Insurance)
FPAC . . . . . . Flight Path Analysis and Command (Team) (NASA)
FPAD . . . . . . Fund for Peaceful Atomic Development
FPAEC . . . . . . Free of Particular Average, English Conditions (Insurance)
FPAF . . . . . . Fixed Price Award Fee
FPANY . . . . . . Film Producers Association of New York
FPB . . . . Federal Petroleum Board (Department of the Interior)
FPB . . . . Fixed-Price Basis
FPB . . . . Flight Progress Board (Aviation)
FPBAA . . . . . . Folding Paper Box Association of America
FPBG . . . . . . Final Program and Budget Guidance
FPC . . . . Federal Pacific Electric Company (NYSE symbol) (Delisted)
FPC . . . . Federal Personnel Council (Civil Service Commission) (Abolished, 1954)
FPC . . . . Federal Power Commission (Independent government agency)
FPC . . . . Final Processing Center
FPC . . . . Firestone Plastics Company
FPC . . . . Firestone Polyvinyl Chloride
FPC . . . . Fish Protein Concentrate (For use in antistarvation programs)
FPC . . . . Fixed Paper Capacitor
FPC . . . . Fixed Photoflash Capacitor
FPC . . . . Fixed Point Calculation
FPC . . . . Fixed Polycarbonate Capacitor
FPC . . . . Fixed Precision Capacitor
FPC . . . . Fixed Price Call
FPC . . . . Fixed Price Contracts
FPC . . . . Fixed Program Computer
FPC . . . . Flexible Printed Circuit
FPC . . . . Flight Programmer Computer
FPC . . . . Floating Point Calculation
FPC . . . . Florida Presbyterian College (Later, Eckerd College)
FPC . . . . Food Packaging Council
FPC . . . . For Private Circulation
FPC . . . . Frank Phillip College (Texas)
FPC . . . . French Pressure Cell
FPC . . . . Friends Peace Committee
FPC . . . . Front Panel Control
FPC . . . . Frozen Pea Council
FPCA . . . . . . Fiber Producers Credit Association
FPCC . . . . . . Fixed Polycarbonate Capacitor
FPCC . . . . . . Fixed Printed Circuit Capacitor
FPCE . . . . . . Fission Products Conversion and Encapsulation (Plant) (AEC)
FPCH . . . . . . Foreign Policy Clearing House
FPCP . . . . . . Ferrocene Polymer Cure Process
FPCS . . . . . . Free Polar Corticosteroids (Endocrinology)

FPCS . . . . Freezing Point Calibration Standard
FPD . . . . Ferrite Phase Driver
FPD . . . . Flat Pack Diode
FPD . . . . Full Paid (NYSE symbol)
FPDI . . . . Flight Path Deviation Indicator
FPDI . . . . Food Processing Development Irradiator
FPDL . . . . . . Fission Products Development Laboratory (ORNL)
FPDS . . . . Fleet Probe Data System (Navy)
FPE . . . . Fairport, Painesville & Eastern R. R. (AAR code)
FPE . . . . Fixed Price with Escalation
FPEC . . . . . . Fixed Porcelain Enamel Capacitor
FPF . . . . Final Protective Fire (Artillery term)
FPF . . . . Fixed Price Firm
FPF . . . . Flexible Polyurethane Foam
FPF . . . . Full Power Frequency
FPFC . . . . . . Fixed Photoflash Capacitor
FPG . . . . . . Federal Pecan Growers
FPG . . . . . . Force Planning Guide (Army)
FPGAUS . . . . . Federated Pecan Growers' Associations of the United States
FPGL . . . . . . Flight Plan Gas Load (Air Force)
FPHA . . . . . . Federal Public Housing Authority (Functions transferred to Public Housing Administration, 1947)
FPHS . . . . . . Fallout Protection in Houses
FPI . . . . Fabry-Perot Interferometer
FPI . . . . Faded Prior to Interception (RADAR)
FPI . . . . Family Pitch In (i.e., eat freely of a given food) (A mealtime whimsicality for use when guests are present)
FPI . . . . Federal Personnel Intern (Program) (Civil Service Commission)
FPI . . . . Federal Prison Industries
FPI . . . . Federation Prohibitionniste Internationale (International Prohibition Federation)
FPI . . . . Fixed Price Incentive
FPI . . . . Fuel Pressure Indicator
FPIC . . . . . . Fixed Price Incentive Contract
FPIF . . . . . . Fixed Price Incentive Fee
FPIF . . . . . . Fixed Price Incentive Firm (Award) (Government contracting)
FPIF . . . . . . Fixed Price Incentive Force(s)
FPIS . . . . . . Family Planning Information Service
FPIS . . . . . . Fixed Price Incentive Successive
FPIS . . . . . . Forward Propagation by Ionospheric Scatter (Radio communication technique)
FPK . . . . Fixed Position Keyboard
FPL . . . . Family Protection League of USA
FPL . . . . Ferry-Potter Law
FPL . . . . Final Protective Line (Military)
FPL . . . . Flight Propulsion Laboratory
FPL . . . . Florida Power & Light Company (NYSE symbol)
FPL . . . . Forest Products Laboratory (Department of Agriculture)
FPL . . . . Frequency Phase Lock
FPLA . . . . . . Fair Packaging and Labeling Act
FPM . . . . Federal Personnel Manual
FPM . . . . Feet Per Minute
FPM . . . . First Pennsylvania Mortgage Trust (NYSE symbol)
FPMC . . . . . . Fixed Paper Metallized Capacitor
FPMR . . . . . . Federal Property Management Regulations
FPML . . . . . . Forest Products Marketing Laboratory (Forest Service)
FPN . . . . Fixed Pulse RADAR Navigation Aid
FPNO . . . . . . Flight Plan Not Received
FPO . . . . Federation of Prosthodontic Organizations
FPO . . . . Field Post Office (British military)
FPO . . . . Field Project Officer
FPO . . . . Fixed Path of Operation
FPO . . . . Fixed Point Operation
FPO . . . . Fixed Price Open
FPO . . . . Fleet Post Office
FPO . . . . Fuel Pressure Out
FPO . . . . Future Projects Office
FPP . . . . Fibreboard Paper Products Corporation (NYSE symbol) (Delisted)
FPP . . . . Foster Parents' Plan (An organization)
FPP . . . . From Present Position (Aviation)
FPPI . . . . Frozen Potato Products Institute
FPPS . . . . . . Flight Plan Processing System (British)
FPQINA . . . . . Federal Plant Quarantine Inspectors National Association
FPR . . . . Fair Pressure Ratio
FPR . . . . Farm Publications Reports
FPR . . . . Federal Procurement Regulations
FPR . . . . Field Personnel Record
FPR . . . . Final Progress Report
FPR . . . . Fixed Point Representation
FPR . . . . Fixed Price Redeterminations
FPR . . . . Flat-Plate Radiometer

FPR . . . . Flight Planned Route
FPR . . . . Floating Point Routine
FPR . . . . Foliage Penetration RADAR
FPR . . . . Full Power Response
FPRA . . . . . . Financial Public Relations Association
FPRA . . . . . . Fixed Price Redetermination Article
FPRC . . . . . . Flying Personnel Research Committee (British)
FPRC . . . . . . For Possible Reclearance (Aviation)
FPRF . . . . . . Fats and Proteins Research Foundation
FPRS . . . . . . Forest Products Radio Service
FPRS . . . . . . Forest Products Research Society
FPS . . . . Federal Prison System
FPS . . . . Federal Protective Service (Washington, DC)
FPS . . . . Feet Per Second
FPS . . . . Fellow of the Pharmaceutical Society
FPS . . . . Fellow of the Philological Society (British)
FPS . . . . Fellow of the Physical Society (British)
FPS . . . . Ferrite Phase Shifter
FPS . . . . Field Power Supply
FPS . . . . Fixed Plasma Sheath
FPS . . . . Fixed Point System
FPS . . . . Fixed Price Supply
FPS . . . . Fixed Pulse RADAR Search Equipment
FPS . . . . Flash Photolysis System
FPS . . . . Flight Preparation Sheet
FPS . . . . Floating Point System
FPS . . . . Fluid Power Society
FPS . . . . Fluid Power Supply (or System)
FPS . . . . Fluid Purification System
FPS . . . . Focus Projection and Scanning
FPS . . . . Foot-Pound-Second (System)
FPS . . . . Frames Per Second
FPS . . . . Franciscan Preparatory Seminary
FPS . . . . Front Populaire Soudanais (Sudanese Popular Front)
FPS . . . . Full Pressure Suit (Aerospace)
FPSC . . . . . . Foreign Petroleum Supply Committee
FPSC . . . . . . Forest Products Safety Conference
FPT . . . . Full Power Trial
FPT . . . . Functional Performance Time
FPTS . . . . . . Forward Propagation by Tropospheric Scatter (Radio communications technique)
FPTU . . . . . . Federation of Progressive Trade Unions (Zanzibar)
FPU . . . . First Production Unit
FPUR . . . . . . For the Purpose Of
FPV . . . . Fishery Protection Vessel
FPV . . . . Fowl Plague Virus
FPV . . . . Functional Proofing Vehicle
FPVPC . . . . . Federation of Paint and Varnish Production Clubs
FPW . . . . Flat Pack Welder
FPW . . . . Free Progressive Wave
FPWA . . . . . . Federation of Protestant Welfare Agencies
FPWA . . . . . . Further Particulars When Available
FPWS . . . . . . Flat Pack Welder System
FQ . . . . Fare Quotation (Airline)
FQ . . . . Film Quarterly (A publication)
FQ . . . . First Quarter (Moon phase)
FQ . . . . Fiscal Quarter
FQ . . . . Flight Qualification
FQA . . . . Fuqua Industries, Inc. (NYSE symbol)
FQF . . . . Front du Quebec Francais
FQH . . . . Filled Quartz Helix
FQI . . . . Fuel Quantity Indicator
FQIL . . . . . . Fuzed Quartz Incandescent Lamp
FQM . . . . Four Quadrant Multiplier
FQPA . . . . . . Flight Quality Photomultiplier Assembly
FQT . . . . Fused Quartz Tubing
FR . . . . Faculty Rating
FR . . . . Failure Rate
FR . . . . Failure Report
FR . . . . Fast Release (Relay)
FR . . . . Father
FR . . . . Fatigue Resistant
FR . . . . Feather River R. R. (AAR code)
FR . . . . Federal Register
FR . . . . Federal Republic
FR . . . . Federal Reserve
FR . . . . Field Report
FR . . . . Fighter Reconnaissance
FR . . . . Film Report
FR . . . . Final Report
FR . . . . Fineness Ratio

FR . . . . Fire (or Flame) Retardant (or Resistant)
FR . . . . Fireman Recruit
FR . . . . Fixed Ratio
FR . . . . Flash Ranging
FR . . . . Fleet Reserve (Navy)
FR . . . . Flocculation Reaction (Medicine)
FR . . . . Flood Relief Punt (Coast Guard)
FR . . . . Flow Recorder
FR . . . . Forced Removal
FR . . . . Foreign Relations Committee (US Senate)
FR . . . . Franc
FR . . . . France (NATO)
Fr . . . . Francium (Chemical element)
FR . . . . Freight Release
FR . . . . French
FR . . . . Frequency Range
FR . . . . Frequency Response
FR . . . . Friar
FR . . . . Friden, Inc. (NYSE symbol) (Delisted)
FR . . . . From
FR . . . . Fuel Remaining (Aviation)
FR . . . . Full Range
FR . . . . Full-Rate (Telegrams and cables)
FR . . . . Furlough Rations (Army)
FR . . . . Furness Railway (British)
F/R . . . . Fighter Reconnaissance (Air Force)
F & R . . . . . . Force and Rhythm (of Pulse) (Medicine)
F & R . . . . . . Functions and Responsibilities
FRA . . . . Farah Manufacturing Co., Inc. (NYSE symbol)
FRA . . . . Federal Railroad Administration
FRA . . . . Federal Regular Army (Federation of South Arabia)
FRA . . . . Federal Reserve Act
FRA . . . . Fleet Reserve Association
FRA . . . . Fluorescent Rabies Antibody (Immunology)
FRA . . . . Friction Reducing Agent (Chemicals)
FRAA . . . . . . Fleet Reserve Association Auxiliary
FRAC . . . . . . Fractionator Reflux Analog Computer
FRACHE . . . . . Federation of Regional Accrediting Commissions of Higher Education
FRACP . . . . . . Fellow of the Royal Australasian College of Physicians
FRACS . . . . . . Fellow of the Royal Australasian College of Surgeons
FRAeS . . . . . . Fellow of the Royal Aeronautical Society (British)
FRAG . . . . . . Fragment
FRAGBOMB . . . Fragmentation Bomb
FRAI . . . . Fellow of the Royal Anthropological Institute (British)
FRAIN . . . . . . Front Revolutionnaire Africain pour l'Independance Nationale des Colonies Portugaises (African Revolutionary Front for the National Independence of Portuguese Colonies)
FRAK . . . . . . Flak RADAR Automatic Kanon
FRAM . . . . . . Fleet Rehabilitation and Modernization (Navy)
FRAME . . . . . . Fund for the Replacement of Animals in Medical Experiments
FRAN . . . . . . Fleet Readiness Analysis (NORRS)
FRANY . . . . . . Fashion Reporters Award - New York
FRAP . . . . . . Fleet Readiness Assistance Program
FRAP . . . . . . Frente de Accion Popular (Popular Action Front) (Chile)
FRAP . . . . . . Front d'Action Politique
FRAS . . . . . . Fellow of the Royal Asiatic Society (British)
FRAS . . . . . . Fellow of the Royal Astronomical Society (British)
FRASCO . . . . . Foundation for Religious Action in the Social and Civil Order
FR and ASS . . . Fellow of the Royal and Antiquarian Societies (British)
FRAT . . . . . . Free Radical Assay Technique (Army drug test)
FRB . . . . Fast Rise Balloon
FRB . . . . Federal Reserve Banks (of FRS)
FRB . . . . Federal Reserve Board
FRB . . . . Flight Rated Bioinstrumentation
FRB . . . . Forschungs-Reaktor Berlin
FRBS . . . . . . Fellow of the Royal Botanic Society (British)
FRC . . . . Facility Review Committee
FRC . . . . Fasteners Research Council
FRC . . . . Federal Radiation Council
FRC . . . . Federal Radio Commission (Functions transferred to FCC, 1934)
FRC . . . . Federal Records Center (General Services Administration)
FRC . . . . Federal Records Council
FRC . . . . Federal Regional Center (Office of Civil Defense)
FRC . . . . Fiber Reinforced Composite
FRC . . . . Filipino Rehabilitation Commission (Post-World War II)
FRC . . . . Fishery Research Craft
FRC . . . . Fixed Radio Communication
FRC . . . . Flight Research Center (of NASA)
FRC . . . . Flow Recorder Controller
FRC . . . . Flowers' Roguish Cultivator
FRC . . . . Fram Corporation (NYSE symbol) (Delisted)

FRC . . . . Fresnel Reflection Coefficient
FRC . . . . Fuels Research Council
FRC . . . . Functional Residual Capacity (of the Lungs) (Medicine)
FR & CC . . . . . Free of Riot and Civil Commotion
FRCF . . . . . . Federation of Reconstructionist Congregations and Fellowships
FRCI . . . . Fellow of the Royal Colonial Institute (British)
FRCJ . . . . Fiber-Reinforced Composite Junction
FRCM . . . . . . Fellow of the Royal College of Music (British)
FRCO . . . . . . Fellow of the Royal College of Organists (British)
FRCOG . . . . . . Fellow of the Royal College of Obstetricians and Gynaecologists (British)
FRCOUSA . . . . Federation of Russian Charitable Organizations of the United States of America
FRCP . . . . . . Fellow of the Royal College of Physicians (British)
FRCS . . . . . . Fellow of the Royal College of Surgeons (British)
FRCSL . . . . . . Fellow of the Royal College of Surgeons of London
FRCTF . . . . . . Fast Reactor Core Test Facility (AEC)
FRCU . . . . . . Fractocumulus (Meteorology)
FRCVS . . . . . . Fellow of the Royal College of Veterinary Surgeons (British)
FRD . . . . Federal Reserve District
FRD . . . . Flight Readiness Demonstration
FRD . . . . Fluid Rate Damper
FRD . . . . Formerly Restricted Data (Military)
FRD . . . . Fraction Reliability Deviation
FRDN . . . . . . Ferdinand R. R. (AAR code)
FRE . . . . Field Representative Europe
FREB . . . . . . Federal Real Estate Board (Abolished, 1951)
FREC . . . . . . Federal Radio Education Committee
FRED . . . . . . Fast Reactivity Exclusion Device (Nuclear)
FRED . . . . . . Fiendishly Rapid Electronic Device
FRED . . . . . . Figure Reading Electronic Device (Information retrieval)
FREDI . . . . . . Flight Range and Endurance Data Indicator
FREJID . . . . . Frequency Jumper Identification
FREL . . . . . . Feltman Research & Engineering Laboratory (Army)
FREQ . . . . . . Frequency (or Frequent)
FRES . . . . . . Fellow of the Royal Empire Society (British)
FRES . . . . . . Fellow of the Royal Entomological Society (British)
FRES . . . . . . Fire Resistant
FRESCAN . . . . Frequency Scanning
FRESCANNAR . . Frequency Scan RADAR
FRESH . . . . . . Foil Research Supercavitating Hydrofoil
FRF . . . . Flight Readiness Firing
FRF . . . . Free French (World War II)
FRF . . . . Free Running Frequency
FRFE . . . . . . Field Representative Far East
FRFPS . . . . . . Fellow of the Royal Faculty of Physicians and Surgeons (British)
FRG . . . . Federal Republic of Germany
FRGp . . . . . . Field Record Group (Air Force)
FRGS . . . . . . Fellow of the Royal Geographical Society (British)
FRH . . . . Fellowship of Religious Humanists
FRH . . . . Frequency Response Histogram (Biometrics)
FRHB . . . . . . Foundation for Research on Human Behavior
FRHistS . . . . . Fellow of the Royal Historical Society
FRHS . . . . . . Fellow of the Royal Historical Society (British)
FRHS . . . . . . Fellow of the Royal Horticultural Society (British)
FRI . . . . Feeling Rough Inside (Slang)
FRI . . . . Fisheries Research Institute
FRI . . . . Flight Refueling, Incorporated
FRI . . . . Friday
FRIA . . . . . . Finnish Radio Industries Association
FRIBA . . . . . . Fellow of the Royal Institute of British Architects
FRIC . . . . . . Fellow of the Royal Institute of Chemistry (Formerly, FIC) (British)
FRINGE . . . . . File and Report Information Processing Generators (Data processing)
FRIP . . . . Fleet Readiness Improvement Plan
FRIPHH . . . . . Fellow of the Royal Institute of Public Health and Hygiene (British)
FRISCO . . . . . Fast Reaction Integrated Submarine Control
FRITALUX . . . . Union Economique France, Italie, Benelux
FRJM . . . . . . Full Range Joint Movement (Occupational therapy)
FRL . . . . Feltman Research Laboratory (Army)
FRL . . . . Field Requirements List
FRL . . . . Fuels Research Laboratory (MIT)
FRL . . . . Fuselage Reference Line
FRLA . . . . . . Federal Regulation of Lobbying Act
FRM . . . . Fiber-Reinforced Material
FRM . . . . Film Reading Machine
FRM . . . . Force Reaction Motor
FRM . . . . Foucault Rotating Mirror
FRM . . . . Frequency Meter
FRMetSoc . . . . Fellow of the Royal Meteorological Society (British)
FRMS . . . . . . Fellow of the Royal Microscopical Society (British)
FRN . . . . Floating Round
FRN . . . . Force Requirement Number (Army)

FRN . . . . Full-Round Nose (Diamond drilling)
FRNM . . . . Foundation for Research on the Nature of Man
FRNS . . . . Fellow of the Royal Numismatic Society (British)
FRO . . . . Fleet Records (or Resources) Office
FRO . . . . Flight Radio Officer (Aviation)
FROC . . . . Federated Russian Orthodox Clubs
FROF . . . . Fire Risk on Freight (Insurance)
FROF . . . . Freight Office
FROG . . . . Free Rocket Over Ground (USSR missile)
FROGS . . . . . . Fund Raising Organization Graphics Service
FROKA . . . . . . First Republic of Korea Army
FROLINAT . . . . Front de Liberation Nationale (Chad)
FROM . . . . Full Range of Movement (Occupational therapy)
FROST . . . . . . Floating Repair and Oil Storage Terminal
FROST . . . . . . Food Reserves on Space Trips
FRP . . . . Feather River Project
FRP . . . . Fiber-Reinforced Plastic(s)
FRP . . . . Filament-Reinforced Plastic
FRP . . . . Flag Register Processing
FRP . . . . Force Rendezvous Point (Military)
FRP . . . . Free Radical Photography
FRP . . . . Frequency Response Plotter
FRP . . . . Parachute Fragmentation Bomb
FR-PET . . . . . . Fiber-Reinforced Polyethylene Terephthalate (Glass)
FRR . . . . Failure and Replacement Report
FRR . . . . Full Reimbursement Rate
FRRB . . . . Fast Rise Reflective Balloon
FRRRB . . . . . . Fast Rise RADAR Reflective Balloon
FRRS . . . . Full Remaining Radiation Service (Unit) (Military)
FRRU . . . . Freight Receiving and Redistribution Unit
FRS . . . . Facilities Requirements Study
FRS . . . . Fast Retrieval Storage (Data processing)
FRS . . . . Federal Reserve System (Independent government agency)
FRS . . . . Fellow of the Royal Society (British)
FRS . . . . Flying Relay Station
FRS . . . . Franz Rosenzweig Society
FRSA . . . . Fellow of the Royal Society of Arts (British)
FRSAS . . . . . . Fast-Response Solar Array Simulator
FRSC . . . . Fellow of the Royal Society of Canada (British)
FRSE . . . . Fellow of the Royal Society of Edinburgh
FRSH . . . . Fellow of the Royal Society of Health (British)
FRSL . . . . Fellow of the Royal Society of Literature (British)
FRSL . . . . Forestry Remote Sensing Laboratory
FRSP . . . . Fredericksburg and Spotsylvania County Battlefield Memorial National Military Park
FRSS . . . . Fellow of the Royal Statistical Society
FRT . . . . Flight Rating Test
FRT . . . . Flight Readiness Test
FRT . . . . Flow Recording Transmitter
FRT . . . . Freight
FRT . . . . Frequency Response Tracer
FRTF . . . . Fixed Radio Transmission Facility
FRTO . . . . French Togoland
FRTP . . . . Fiberglass-Reinforced Thermoplastic
FRU . . . . Fleet Radio Unit
FRU . . . . Fleet Requirements Units (Aircraft)
FRUCOM . . . . . Federation Europeenne des Importateurs de Fruits Secs, Conserves, Epices et Miels (European Federation of Importers of Dried Fruits, Preserves, Spices, and Honey)
FRUGAL . . . . . FORTRAN (Formula Translation) Rules Used as a General Applications Language
FRUPAC . . . . . Fleet Radio Unit, Pacific
FRUSA . . . . . . Flexible Rolled-Up Solar Array (Air Force)
FRV . . . . Fishing Research Vessel
FS . . . . Factor of Safety
FS . . . . Faire Suivre (Please Forward)
FS . . . . Fallschirm (Parachute) (German military)
FS . . . . Far Side
FS . . . . Feasibility Study
FS . . . . Federal Specification
FS . . . . Federal Standard
FS . . . . Feedback, Stabilized
FS . . . . Feet Per Second (Ordnance)
FS . . . . Felix Schlag (Designer's mark, when appearing on US coins)
FS . . . . Fernschreiben (Teletype message) or Fernschreiber (Teletype) (German military)
FS . . . . Field Security (British Army detective police - a branch of Intelligence)
FS . . . . Field Service
FS . . . . File Separator (Data processing)
FS . . . . Filmstrip
FS . . . . Fin Stabilized (Rocketry)

FS . . . . Final Settlement
FS . . . . Financial Secretary
FS . . . . Finish Specification
FS . . . . Fire Station (Maps and charts)
FS . . . . Fire Support
FS . . . . Firing Set
FS . . . . First Stage
FS . . . . Fisher Scientific Co. (NYSE symbol)
FS . . . . Flame Shielding
FS . . . . Flameless, Smokeless (Gunpowder)
FS . . . . Fleet Surgeon
FS . . . . Flight Safety
FS . . . . Flight Sergeant (British Royal Air Force)
FS . . . . Flight Service
FS . . . . Flight Simulator
FS . . . . Flight Standards Service (FAA)
FS . . . . Floating Sign
FS . . . . Flow Switch
FS . . . . Fluid Switch
FS . . . . Flying Status
FS . . . . Fog Signal Station (Maps and charts)
FS . . . . Fog Siren (Maps and charts)
FS . . . . Foot Shock (Biometrics)
FS . . . . Foreign Service (State Department)
FS . . . . Forest Service (Later, Department of Natural Resources) (Department of Agriculture)
FS . . . . Forged Steel
FS . . . . Forward Scatter
FS . . . . Forward Support
FS . . . . Fractostratus (Meteorology)
FS . . . . Fracture, Simple (Medicine)
FS . . . . Freight Supply Vessel
FS . . . . Frequency Stability
FS . . . . Full Scale
FS . . . . Full and Soft (Dietetics)
FS . . . . Fullrack System
FS . . . . Function Set
FS . . . . Functional Selector
FS . . . . Fuselage Station
F/S . . . . Final Statement (Army)
F 1S . . . . Finish One Side (Technical drawings)
F 2S . . . . Finish Two Sides (Technical drawings)
FSA . . . . Fallout Shelter Analyst (or Analysis) (Civil Defense)
FSA . . . . Family Separation Allowance (Military)
FSA . . . . Farm Security Administration (Succeeded by Farmers Home Administration, 1946)
FSA . . . . Federal Security Administration (HEW)
FSA . . . . Federal Security Agency (Functions and units transferred to HEW, 1953)
FSA . . . . Fellow of the Society of Actuaries
FSA . . . . Fellow of the Society of Antiquaries (British)
FSA . . . . Fiat Secundum Artem (Let It Be Done According to Art) (Old medical term)
FSA . . . . Finance Service, Army
FSA . . . . Fire Support Area (Military)
FSA . . . . Flared Slot Antenna
FSA . . . . Flux Switch Alternator
FSA . . . . Foreign Service Availability (Military)
FSA . . . . Forward Support Area (Military)
FSA . . . . Fraternity Scholarship Association (Later, College Fraternity Scholarship Officers Association)
FSA . . . . Frequency Stability Analyzer
FSA . . . . Front Suspension Arm
FSA . . . . Future Scientists of America
FSAA . . . . Family Service Association of America
FSAA . . . . Fellow of the Society of Incorporated Accountants and Auditors (British)
FSAA . . . . Flight Simulator for Advanced Aircraft (NASA)
FSAC . . . . Fourth Stowage Adapter Container
FSAF . . . . Future Scientists of America Foundation
FSAICU . . . . . Federation of State Associations of Independent Colleges and Universities
FSAS . . . . Fellow of the Society of Antiquaries of Scotland
FSB . . . . Falange Socialista Boliviana (Bolivian Socialist Falange)
FSB . . . . Fallout Studies Branch (AEC)
FSB . . . . Federal Specifications Board
FSB . . . . Field Selection Board (Military)
FSB . . . . Fire Support Base (Army)
FSBC . . . . Florida State Board of Conservation
FSC . . . . Fairmont State College (West Virginia)
FSC . . . . Family Services Center (Military)
FSC . . . . Federal Safety Council
FSC . . . . Federal Stock Class

FSC .... Federal Supply Catalog
FSC .... Federal Supply Classification
FSC .... Federal Supply Code
FSC .... Fellowship of Southern Churchmen
FSC .... First-Stage Conduit
FSC .... Fixed Silicon Capacitor
FSC .... Fleet Satellite Communications
FSC .... Flexible Shielded Cable
FSCL .... Flight Service Center
FSC .... Florida Southern College
FSC .... Fluid Storage Container
FSC .... Flying Status Code
FSC .... Food Storage Cell
FSC .... Force Structure Committee
FSC .... Foreign Service Credits (Military)
FSC .... Foundation for the Study of Cycles
FSC .... Franklin Stores Corporation (NYSE symbol)
FSC .... Fratres Scholarum Christianarum (Brothers of the Christian Schools, or Christian Brothers) (Roman Catholic religious order)
FSC .... Frequency Shift Converter
FSC .... Fresno State College (California)
FSCC ...... Federal Surplus Commodities Corporation
FSCC ...... Fire Support Coordination Center (Military)
FSCC ...... First-Stage Conduit Container
FSCC ...... Food Surplus Commodities Corporation
FSCG ...... Federal Supply Classification Group
FSCI .... Frequency Space Characteristic Impedance
FSCJ ...... Congregatio Filiorum Sacratissimi Cordis Jesu (Sons of the Sacred Heart, or Verona Fathers) (Roman Catholic religious order)
FSCL ...... Fire Support Coordination Line (Military)
FSCM ...... Federal Supply Code for Manufacturers
FSCNHA ..... Federal Service Campaign for National Health Agencies
FSCOORD .... Fire Support Coordinator (Military)
FSCP .... Firing Site Command Post (Army)
FSCR ...... First Ship Configuration Review (Navy)
FSCS ...... Fire Support Coordination Section
FSCS ...... Flight Service Communications System
FSCS ...... Frequency Shift Communications System
FSCT ...... Floyd Satellite Communications Terminal
FSD .... Flight Support Division
FSD .... Flying Spot Digitizer
FSD .... Force Spectral Density
FSD .... Forecast Support Date
FSD .... Foreign Sea Duty
FSD .... Foster-Seeley Discriminator
FSD .... Fuel Supply Depot (Military)
FSD .... Full-Scale Deflection (Instrumentation)
FSDH ...... Forsyth School for Dental Hygienists
FSDO ...... Flight Standards District Office (FAA)
FSE .... Facilities System Engineer
FSE .... Family Stop Eating (A table signal) (Slang)
FSE .... Field Support Engineer
FSE .... Field Support Equipment (Military)
FSE .... Fill Start Entry (Data processing)
FSE .... Fire Support Element (Military)
FSE .... Fluid Shaft Encoder
FSE .... From the Latin for Brothers of the Holy Eucharist (Roman Catholic religious order)
FSEA ...... Food Service Executives' Association
FSEC ...... Federal Specifications Executive Committee
FSEC .... Federation des Syndicats de l'Enseignement du Cameroon (Federation of Teachers' Unions of the Cameroons)
FSEE .... Federal Service Entrance Examination (Civil Service)
FSEI .... Food Service Equipment Industry (Later, FEDA)
FSES ...... Federation of Swiss Employees' Societies
FSES ...... Friendly Society of Engravers and Sketchmakers
FSF .... Fibrin-Stabilizing Factor
FSF .... Fixed Sequence Format
FSF .... Flight Safety Foundation
FSFLP ...... Farm Storage Facility Loan Program
FSFMJC ..... Federation Senegalaise des Foyers et Maisons des Jeunes et de la Culture (Senegalese Federation of Hearth and Homes of Youth and Culture)
FSG .... Federal Supply Group
FSG .... Finite State Grammar
FSG .... Flexible Space Garment
FSGA ...... Four-Wire, Shipboard, General Use, Armored (Cable)
FSGB ...... Foreign Service Grievance Board (State Department)
FSGp ...... Federal Supply Group (Air Force)
FSH .... Federacion de Sociedades Hispanas
FSH .... First-Stage Hydraulics
FSH .... Follicle-Stimulating Hormone (Endocrinology)

FSHPC ...... Fort Sam Houston Purchasing and Contracting Office
FSI .... Federal Stock Item
FSI .... Federation Spirite Internationale (International Spiritualist Federation)
FSI .... Fellow of the Surveyors' Institute (British)
FSI .... Fire Service Instructors
FSI .... Force Structure Increase (Military)
FSI .... Foreign Service Institute (Department of State)
FSI .... Frame Sync Indication
FSI .... Free Sons of Israel
FSI .... International Society of Fire Service Instructors
FSIA .... Fellow of the Society of Industrial Artists (British)
FSIC .... Foreign Service Inspection Corps (Department of State)
FSIC .... Franciscan Sisters of the Third Order of the Immaculate Conception (Roman Catholic religious order)
FSIP .... Federal Shelter Incentive Program
FSIWA ..... Federation of Sewage and Industrial Wastes Association
FSJ .... Fratres Sancti Joseph (Brothers of St. Joseph) (Roman Catholic religious order)
FSJC ...... Fort Scott Junior College (Kansas)
FSJC ...... Fort Smith Junior College (Arkansas)
FSK .... Frequency Shift Keying (Radio)
FSL .... Family Strike Light (i.e., take small portions) (A mealtime whimsicality for use when guests are present)
FSL .... Federal Stock Listings
FSL .... Federation des Syndicats Libres des Travailleurs Luxembourgeois (Free Luxembourg Workers' Federation)
FSL .... Finite State Language
FSL .... Formal Semantic Language
FSL .... Full Stop Landing (Aviation)
FS/L .... Food Service/Lodging
FSLIC ...... Federal Savings and Loan Insurance Corporation (of FHLBB)
FSLUS ..... Federazione dei Sindacati Lavoratori Uniti della Somalia (Somali Federation of United Trade Unions)
FSM .... Fast Settle Mode
FSM .... Federation Syndicale Mondiale (World Federation of Trade Unions)
FSM .... Field Strength Meter
FSM .... First-Stage Motor
FSM .... First Surface Mirror
FSM .... Flight System Mockup
FSM .... Folded Sideband Modulation
FSM .... Free Speech Movement (University of California, Berkeley)
FSM .... Frequency Shift Modulation
FSMBUS .... Federation of State Medical Boards of the United States
FSMC ...... Federal Supply Manufacturers' Code (DOD)
FSMC ...... First-Stage Motor Container
FSMC ...... Fixed Silver Mica Capacitor
FSME ...... Fruehsommer-Meningoencephalitis
FSMS ...... Firing Set Maintenance Spares
FSMT ...... Fleet Service Mine Test (Navy)
FSMWI ..... Free Space Microwave Interferometer
FSMWO ..... Field Service Modification Work Order
FSN .... Federal Stock Number
FSN .... Filler Sensor Nozzle
FSN .... Fiscal Station Number (Military)
FSN .... French-Speaking Nations (NATO)
FSN .... Funksjonaersambandet i Norge (Employees Federation of Norway)
FSO .... Fabryka Samochodow Osbowych (Poland)
FSO .... Fast Settle Operation
FSO .... Field Security Officer (Military)
FSO .... Fleet Signals Officer (Naval)
FSO .... Fleet Supply Officer
FSO .... Flying Safety Officer (Air Force)
FSO .... Foreign Service Officer (Department of State)
FSO .... Frequency Sweep Oscillator
FSO .... Fuel Supply Office (Military)
FSO .... Full-Scale Output
FSO .... Funksjonaerenes Sentralorganisasjoh (Central Organization of Salaried Employees) (Norway)
FSOC ...... Fixed Stand-Off Capacitor
FSOTS ...... Foreign Service Officers' Training School
FSP .... Facility Security Program (World War II)
FSP .... Family Services Program (Military)
FSP .... Finger Sweat Print (Psychometrics)
FSP .... Fixed Sample-Size Procedure
FSP .... Food Stamp Program
FSP .... Force Sensing Probe
FSP .... Ford Satellite Plan (Communications)
FSP .... Foreign Service Pay
FSP .... Forward Supply Point (Military)
FSP .... Foundation for the Peoples of the South Pacific
FSP .... Frequency Shift Pulsing

FSP . . . . Frequency Standard, Primary
FSP . . . . From the Latin for Brothers of St. Patrick (Patrician Brothers) (Roman Catholic religious order)
FSPC . . . . Foundation for the Study of Primitive Culture
FSPPR . . . . . . Fast Supercritical Pressure Power Reactor
FSPT . . . . Federation of Societies for Paint Technology
FSR . . . . Fast Slew Rate
FSR . . . . Feedback Shift Register
FSR . . . . Fermi Selection Rules
FSR . . . . Field Service Regulations (Army)
FSR . . . . Field Service Representative
FSR . . . . Field Strength Radio
FSR . . . . Film Society Review (A publication)
FSR . . . . Fin Stabilized Rockets
FSR . . . . First Soviet Reactor
FSR . . . . Flight Safety Research
FSR . . . . Flight Simulation Report
FSR . . . . Flight Solar Reflectometer
FSR . . . . Flux Sensitive Resistor
FSR . . . . Foundation for Scientific Relaxation
FSR . . . . Frequency Scan RADAR
FSR . . . . Frequency Selective Relay
FSR . . . . Frequency Shift Receiver
FSR . . . . Frequency Shift Reflector
FSR . . . . From the Latin for Brothers of the Holy Rosary (Roman Catholic religious order)
FSR . . . . Full Scale Record (Instrumentation)
FSRA . . . . Federal Sewage Research Association
FSRB . . . . Flight Safety Review Board
FSRM . . . . . . First-Stage Rocket Motor
FSS . . . . Fabrique Suisse d'Explosifs
FSS . . . . Fear Survey Schedule (Psychology)
FSS . . . . Federal Sign & Signal Corp. (NYSE symbol)
FSS . . . . Federal Supply Schedule
FSS . . . . Federal Supply Service (of GSA)
FSS . . . . Fellow of the Statistical Society (British)
FSS . . . . Field Service Section (Military)
FSS . . . . Field Support System
FSS . . . . Fine Sun Sensor (NASA)
FSS . . . . Fire Support Ship
FSS . . . . Fleet Service School
FSS . . . . Flight Service Station (FAA)
FSS . . . . Flight Standards Service
FSS . . . . Flutter Suppression System (Aviation)
FSS . . . . Flying Spot Scanner
FSS . . . . Fog Signal Station (Coast Guard)
FSS . . . . Foreign Shore Service
FSSA . . . . Fellow of the Society of Science and Art (British)
FSSC . . . . Federazione Svizzera dei Sindicati Cristiani (Swiss Federation of National-Christian Trade Unions)
FSSC . . . . Foreign Student Service Council
FSSCN . . . . . . Federation Suisse des Syndicats Chretiens-Nationaux (Swiss Federation of National-Christian Trade Unions)
FSSD . . . . First-Stage Separation Device (Aerospace)
FSSD . . . . Foreign Service Selection Date
FSSE . . . . Federation des Societes Suisses d'Employes (Federation of Swiss Employees' Societies)
FSSE . . . . Foreign Service Sales Expense
FSSE . . . . Franciscan Sisters of St. Elizabeth (Roman Catholic religious order)
FSSJ . . . . Franciscan Sisters of St. Joseph (Roman Catholic religious order)
FSSP . . . . Federation des Salaries du Secteur Prive (South Vietnam)
FSSU . . . . Federated Superannuation Scheme for Universities (British)
FST . . . . Field Suitability Test
FST . . . . Finite Sampling Time
FST . . . . First National Stores, Inc. (NYSE symbol)
FST . . . . Fixed Service Tower
FST . . . . Foreign Service Tour (Military)
FST . . . . Forged Steel (Technical drawings)
FST . . . . Free Southern Theater
FST . . . . Frequency Shift Transmission
FST . . . . Full-Scale Tunnel (Aerospace)
FST . . . . Funkstelle (Radio station) (German military – World War II)
FST . . . . Fuzed Silica Tube
FSTC . . . . Farmington State Teachers College (Maine)
FSTC . . . . Fayetteville State Teachers College (North Carolina)
FSTC . . . . Foreign Science and Technology Center (Army)
FSTD . . . . Flight Simulation Test Data
FSTDY . . . . . . Final Semester Temporary Duty (Air Force)
FSTI . . . . Formed Steel Tube Institute
FSTR . . . . Fallschirmtruppen (Parachute Troops) (German military)
FSTV . . . . Full-Scale Test Vehicle (NASA)

FSU . . . . Ferry Service Unit
FSU . . . . Field Storage Unit (Military)
FSU . . . . Florida State University
FSU . . . . Foundation for Spiritual Understanding
FSUC . . . . Federal Statistics Users' Conference
FSUSA . . . . . . Finance School, United States Army
FSV . . . . Feline Fibrosarcoma Virus
FSV . . . . Final Stage Vehicle
FSV . . . . Final Storage Vehicle
FSVB . . . . Fort Smith & Van Buren R. R. (AAR code)
FSVM . . . . Frequency Selective Voltmeter
FSW . . . . Flexible Steel Wire
FSWMA . . . . . Fine and Specialty Wire Manufacturers Association
FSWR . . . . Flexible Steel Wire Rope
FSWT . . . . Free Surface Water Tunnel
FSWW . . . . . . First Society of Whale Watchers
FT . . . . Factory Test
FT . . . . Federal Triangle (Washington, DC)
FT . . . . Field Training (AFROTC)
FT . . . . Filing Time (Time a message is presented for transmission)
FT . . . . Fire Control Technician
FT . . . . Fire-Tube (Scotch-Type) Boiler
FT . . . . Firing Tables (Military)
FT . . . . Fixed Tone
FT . . . . Flame Tight
FT . . . . Flat Template
FT . . . . Flight Test (Report)
FT . . . . Fluorescent Target
FT . . . . Flush Threshold (Technical drawings)
FT . . . . Foam Tape
FT . . . . Fog Trumpet (Navigation charts)
FT . . . . Foot (or Feet)
FT . . . . Foreign Transaction
FT . . . . Formal Training (Military)
FT . . . . Fort
FT . . . . Fourier Transform
FT . . . . Free Throw (Basketball)
FT . . . . Freeport Minerals Company (NYSE symbol)
FT . . . . Frequency Tolerance
FT . . . . Full Terms
FT . . . . Fume-Tight (Technical drawings)
FT . . . . Functional Test
F-T . . . . Follow Through
F & T . . . . Fuel and Transportation
FTA . . . . Federation of Tax Administrators
FTA . . . . Fiches Typologiques Africaines
FTA . . . . Film Training Aid
FTA . . . . Flexographic Technical Association
FTA . . . . Fluorescent Treponemal Antibody (Test)
FTA . . . . Food Tray Association
FTA . . . . Forward Transfer Admittance
FTA . . . . Free the Army (Bowdlerized version) (Barracks graffiti; also, title of antimilitary play)
FTA . . . . Free Trade Association (European)
FTA . . . . Fuel Treatment Apparatus
FTA . . . . Fun, Travel, Adventure (Sarcastic alternate to FTA -- Free [bowdlerized] the Army)
FTA . . . . Future Teachers of America
FTA-ABS . . . . . Fluorescent Treponema Antibody - Absorption Test
FTAF . . . . Flying Training Air Force
FTAO . . . . Foreign Technology Activity Office(r)
FTAR . . . . Following Transmitted As Received
FTAS . . . . Federation of Turkish-American Societies (Later, Turkish-American Associations)
FTB . . . . Fails to Break
FTB . . . . Fleet Torpedo Bomber
FTB . . . . Flight (or Flying) Test Bed
FTB . . . . Full to Bursting (Reply to question, "Have you had enough to eat?")
FTBA . . . . Food Tray and Board Association
FTBF . . . . Frequency Tuned Bandpass Filter
FTC . . . . Fast Time Constant (RADAR)
FTC . . . . Federal Trade Commission (Independent government agency)
FTC . . . . Fixed Tantalum Capacitor
FTC . . . . Flight Test Center
FTC . . . . Flying Training Command (Air Force)
FTC . . . . Freon Tank Container
FTC . . . . Frequency Time Control
FT-C . . . . Foot-Candle (Illumination)
FTCA . . . . Federal Tort Claims Act
FTCC . . . . Fixed Temperature Compensating Capacitor
FTCC . . . . Flight Test Coordinating Committee (Air Force)

FTCD . . . . Fellow of Trinity College, Dublin
FTCL . . . . Fellow of Trinity College of Music, London
FTCP . . . . Flight Test Change Proposal
FTCR . . . . Functional Test Change Request
FTD . . . . Fails to Drain
FTD . . . . Femoral Total Density
FTD . . . . Field Training Detachment
FTD . . . . Flight Test Division
FTD . . . . Flight Test Drawing
FTD . . . . Foreign Technology Division (AFSC)
FTD . . . . Formal Technical Documents
FTD . . . . Freight Traffic Division
FTD . . . . Frequency Translation Distortion
FTDA . . . . . . Florists' Telegraph Delivery Association
FTDC . . . . . . Field Testing and Development Center
FTDIP . . . . . . Flight Test Division, Internal Project (Navy)
FTE . . . . Factory Test Equipment
FTE . . . . Flight Test Evaluation
FTE . . . . Foote Mineral Company (NYSE symbol)
FTE . . . . Full-Time Equivalent (Employees, students)
FTE . . . . Functional Test Equipment
FTEC . . . . . . Federal Trial Examiners Conference
FTECS . . . . . . Field Training Equipment Concentration Site (Army)
FTEM . . . . . . Factory Test Equipment Manufacturing
FTF . . . . Faellesraadet for Danske Tjenestemands-og Funktionaerorganisationer (Federation of Civil Servants' and Salaried Employees' Organizations) (Denmark)
FTF . . . . Functional Test Flight
FTFC . . . . . . Functional Test Flight Checklist
FTFI . . . . . . Florida Tropical Fish Industries
FTGDV . . . . . Footage Dives (Military)
FTI . . . . Facing Tile Institute
FTI . . . . Federal Tax Included
FTI . . . . Fellow of the Textile Institute (British)
FTI . . . . Film Thickness Indicator
FTI . . . . Fixed Target Information (Army)
FTI . . . . Foreign Trade Institute (Mexico)
FTI . . . . Foreningen Teknisk Information (Swedish Society on Technical Communication)
FTI . . . . Frequency Time Indicator (or Intensity) (RADAR)
FTID . . . . . . Flight Test Information Drawing
FTIMA . . . . . . Federal Tobacco Inspectors Mutual Association
FTL . . . . Fast Transit Link (Rapid-transit term)
FTL . . . . Federal Telecommunications Laboratory (Air Force)
FTL . . . . Flying Thread Loom
FTL . . . . Flying Tiger Line, Inc.
FTL . . . . Formal Technical Literature
FT-L . . . . Foot-Lambert
FTLB . . . . . . Foot-Pound
FTM . . . . Fan-Type Marker
FTM . . . . Film Thickness Monitor
FTM . . . . Flexible Theatre Missile
FTM . . . . Flight Test Missile (Air Force)
FTM . . . . Force/Torque Module (NASA)
FTMC . . . . . . Frequency and Time Measurement Counter
FTO . . . . Fleet Torpedo Officer (British)
FTO . . . . Flight Test Operations
FTO . . . . Fourier Transform Operator
FTP . . . . Federal Theater Project
FTP . . . . Fixed (or Full) Throttle Position (NASA)
FTP . . . . Fleet Training Publication
FTP . . . . Flight Test Program
FTP . . . . Fracture Toughness Parameter
FTP . . . . Functional Test Procedure
FTPF . . . . . . Francs-Tireurs et Partisans Francais (France)
FTPS . . . . . . Fellow of the Technical Publishing Society
FTR . . . . Fails to Reproduce
FTR . . . . Fan Thrust Reverser
FTR . . . . Fast Test Reactor
FTR . . . . Federal Telephone and Radio
FTR . . . . Film Tracing Reproduction
FTR . . . . Final Technical Report
FTR . . . . Flag Tower (Maps and charts)
FTR . . . . Flash Triangulation Reduction
FTR . . . . Flight Test Report
FTR . . . . Fruehauf Corporation (NYSE symbol)
FTR . . . . Full Time Regular (Civil Service employee category)
FTR . . . . Functional Test Report
FTRAC . . . . . Full-Tracked Vehicle
FTRF . . . . . . Freedom to Read Foundation

FTRM . . . . . . Flight Test Request Memorandum
FTRT . . . . Flight Test Release Ticket
FTS . . . . Facsimile Text Society
FTS . . . . Factory Test Set
FTS . . . . Factory Training School
FTS . . . . Faith Theological Seminary
FTS . . . . Federal Telecommunications System (of GSA)
FTS . . . . Field Training Services (Army)
FTS . . . . Flexible Test Station
FTS . . . . Flight Termination System
FTS . . . . Flight Test Sketch
FTS . . . . Flight Test Support
FTS . . . . Flying Training School
FTS . . . . Frequency Time Standard
FTS . . . . Funeral Telegraph Service
FTT . . . . Fever Therapy Technician (Navy)
FTT . . . . Flanged Tongue Terminal
FTT . . . . Free Territory of Trieste
FTT . . . . Fuel Transfer Tool
FTT . . . . Full Time Temporary (Civil Service employee category)
FTTD . . . . . . Full Time Training Duty (Army)
FT & TW . . . . Desk, Combination Flat Top and Typewriter
FTU . . . . Field Torpedo Unit
FTU . . . . First Training Unit
FTU . . . . Freeman Time Unit (Psychology)
FTU . . . . Frequency Transfer Unit
FTUB . . . . . . Free Trade Unions of Burma
FTUC . . . . . . Federal Trade Union Congress (European)
FTUP . . . . . . Free Trade Unions of the Philippines
FTV . . . . Flight Test Vehicle (Air Force)
FTW . . . . Federation of Telephone Workers
FTW . . . . Fizean Toothed Wheel
FTW . . . . Free Trade Wharf
FTWG . . . . . . Flight Test Working Group
FTWO . . . . . . Flight Test Work Order
FTWS . . . . . . Federal Train Wreck Statute
FTX . . . . Field Training Exercise
FTZ . . . . Federal Trade Zone
FTZB . . . . . . Foreign Trade Zone Board
FU . . . . Fire Unit (Military)
FU . . . . Follow-Up
FU . . . . Foul(ed) Up (To describe a confused, mixed-up situation, person, or action) (Bowdlerized version)
FU . . . . Frederick Ungar (Publisher)
FU . . . . Freeman (Time) Unit (Psychology)
FUA . . . . Farm Underwriters Association
FUA . . . . Fire Unit Analyzer (Military)
FUA . . . . Follow-Up Amplifier
FUA . . . . Frente Unita Angolana (Angolan United Front)
FUACE . . . . . Federation Universelle des Associations Chretiennes d'Etudiants (Universal Federation of Christian Students Associations)
FUB . . . . Facility Utilization Board
FUB . . . . Front de l'Unite Bangala (Bangala United Front)
FUBAR . . . . . Fouled Up Beyond All Recognition (Slang) (See FU)
FUBB . . . . . . Fouled Up Beyond Belief (Slang) (See FU)
FUD . . . . Fire Up Decoder
FUDE . . . . . . Federacion Universitaria Democratica Espanola (Spanish union of students)
FUDR . . . . . . Fluorodeoxyuridine
FUEN . . . . . . Federal Union of European Nationalities
FUFO . . . . . . Full Fuzing Option
FUH . . . . Fondazione Universale Hallesint (Italy)
FUIF . . . . . . Fire Unit Integration Facility (Military)
FUILA . . . . . Federazione Unitaria Italiana Lavoratori Abbigliamento (Italian Amalgamated Federation of Garment Workers)
FUL . . . . Front Uni Liberateur de la Guinee Portuguesa et des Isles du Cap Vert (United Liberation Front of Portuguese Guinea and Cape Verde)
FULICO . . . . . Fidelity Union Life Insurance Company
FULPIA . . . . . Federazione Unitaria Lavoratori Prodotti Industrie Alimentari e dello Zucchero e dell'Alcool (Amalgamated Federation of Food Processing, Sugar and Liquor Industries' Workers) (Italy)
FULS . . . . . . Federazione Unitaria Lavoratori dello Spettacolo (Amalgamated Federation of Entertainment Workers) (Italy)
FUMTU . . . . . Fouled Up More Than Usual (See FU)
FUN . . . . Florida United Numismatists
FUNA . . . . . . Front d'Union Nationale de l'Angola (National Union Front of Angola)
FUNC . . . . . . Force de l'Union National Cambodge (Cambodia)
FUNL . . . . . . Federation of Unions of Workers and Employees of North Lebanon
FUNOP . . . . . Full Normal Plot (Data processing)
FUNSA . . . . . Fabrica Uruguaya de Neumaticos, SA (A tire manufacturer)
FUNU . . . . . . Force d'Urgence des Nations Unies

FUNY . . . . Free University of New York
FUO . . . . Fever of Undetermined Origin (Medicine)
FUOP . . . . Fix Up On Printer (Have technician add or change an effect by means
       of optical printing) (Motion-picture production)
FUP . . . . Facility Utilization Plan
FUP . . . . Fusion Point
FUPOSAT . . . . Followup on Supply Action Taken
FUR . . . . Failure, Unsatisfactory or Removal
FUR . . . . Failure or Unsatisfactory Report
FUREPT . . . . . . (And) Further Report To (Army)
FURN . . . . Furnish (or Furniture)
FURPO . . . . . . Full Utilization of Rural Program Opportunities
FURS . . . . Failure or Unsatisfactory Report System
FURTS . . . . . . Furnished This Station (Army)
FUS . . . . Focused Ultrasonic Surgery
FUSA . . . . . . First United States Army
FUSAG . . . . . . First United States Army Group
FUSE . . . . . . Federation for Unified Science
FUSLA . . . . . . Friends of the United States of Latin America
FUT . . . . Fire Until Touchdown (Apollo) (NASA)
FUT . . . . Fleet Utility
FUTA . . . . . . Federal Unemployment Tax Act
FUW . . . . Federation of University Women
FV . . . . Flush Valve (Technical drawings)
FV . . . . Flux Valve
FV . . . . Folio Verso (On the back of the page)
FV . . . . Forward Visibility
FV . . . . Fruit and Vegetable Division (or ARS, Department of Agriculture)
FVA . . . . Flying Veterinarians Association
FVB . . . . First Virginia Bankshares (NYSE symbol)
FVC . . . . Fixed Vacuum Capacitor
FVC . . . . Forced Vital Capacity
FVD . . . . Fuel Vapor Detector
FVM . . . . Fluid Vacancy Model
FVMMA . . . . . Floor and Vacuum Machinery Manufacturers' Association
FVO . . . . Fluidic Valve Operator
FVP . . . . Feasibility Validation Program
FVP . . . . Fluid Velocity Potential
FVPA . . . . . . Flat Veneer Products Association
FVPB . . . . . . Flight Vehicle Power Branch
FVR . . . . Fiber Volume Ratio
FVR . . . . Functional Vestibular Reserve (Orientation)
FVR . . . . Fuse Voltage Rating
FVS . . . . Flight Vehicle Structure
FVSC . . . . . . Fort Valley State College (Georgia)
FVWU . . . . . . Free Visayan Workers' Union (Philippines)
FW . . . . Fairbanks Whitney Corporation (NYSE symbol) (Wall Street slang name:
       "Fuzzy Wuzzy") (Delisted; later, Colt Industries, Inc.)
FW . . . . Field Weakening
FW . . . . Field Worship (British Army)
FW . . . . Filament Wound
FW . . . . Fire Wall (Technical drawings)
FW . . . . Fixed Wing (Aircraft)
FW . . . . Focke-Wulf (A German fighter plane)
FW . . . . Fog Whistle (Navigation charts)
FW . . . . Foot Wide
FW . . . . Formula Weight
FW . . . . Fresh Water (Technical drawings)
FW . . . . Fresh Water (Vessel load line mark)
FW . . . . Full Wave
FWA . . . . Farmers and World Affairs
FWA . . . . Federal Works Agency (Abolished, 1949)
FWA . . . . Filler Wire Addition
FWA . . . . First Word Address
FWA . . . . Forward Wave Amplifier
FWA . . . . Full Wave Amplifier
FWA . . . . Future Weapons Agency (Army)
FWAA . . . . . . Football Writers Association of America
FWAC . . . . . . Full-Wave Alternating Current
FWAD . . . . . . Fort Wingate Army Depot
FWAS . . . . . . Failure Warning and Analysis System
FWAS . . . . . . Flight Warning and Analysis System
FWB . . . . First Wisconsin Bankshares (NYSE symbol)
FWB . . . . Fort Worth Belt Railway Company (AAR code)
FWB . . . . Four-Wheel Brake
FWB . . . . Free-Will Baptists
FWBA . . . . . . Full-Wave Balanced Amplifier
FWBC . . . . . . Fort Wayne Bible College (Indiana)
FWBR . . . . . . Full-Wave Bridge Rectifier
FWC . . . . Fair Weather Current

FWC . . . . Fleet Weather Central
FWC . . . . Foil Wound Coil
FWC . . . . Foster Wheeler Corporation (NYSE symbol)
FWC . . . . Fourdrinier Wire Council
FWCC . . . . . . Friends World Committee for Consultation (Quakers)
FWCL . . . . . . Field Wire Command Link (Army)
FWCNG . . . . . Florida West Coast Nuclear Group
FWD . . . . Fort Worth & Denver Railway Company (AAR code)
FWD . . . . Forward
FWD . . . . Four-Wheel Drive
FWD . . . . Fresh Water Damage
FWDA . . . . . . Federal Wholesale Druggists Association
FWDBL . . . . . . Forward Bomb Line
FWDC . . . . . . Full-Wave Direct Current
FW & DC . . . . Fort Worth and Denver City Railway Company
FWDCT . . . . . . Fresh Water Drain Collecting Tank
FWDP . . . . . . Foreign Weapon Development Program
FWE . . . . Finished with Engines
FWEA . . . . . . Finnish Workers' Educational Association
FWF . . . . Far West Financial Corp. (NYSE symbol)
FWFWA . . . . . . Fresh Water Fish Wholesalers Association
FWG . . . . Facility Working Group
FWG . . . . Factory Work Group
FWG . . . . Flexible Wave Guide
FWGIP . . . . . . Federation of Workers of Government of India Presses
FWHF . . . . . . Federation of World Health Foundations
FWHM . . . . . . Full Width at Half Maximum
FWHMA . . . . . Feed Water Heater Manufacturers Association
FWI . . . . Federation of West Indies
FWI . . . . French West Indies
FWL . . . . Fixed Word Length
FWL . . . . Foundation for World Literacy
FWL . . . . Fraternity of the Wooden Leg
FWLERD . . . . . . Far West Laboratory for Educational Research and Development
FWMAF . . . . . . Free World Military Assistance Forces (Vietnam)
FWMAO . . . . . . Free World Military Assistance Organization
FWNEOFAP . . . Funds Will Not Be Entrusted to Others for Any Purpose (Army)
FWO . . . . Fleet Wireless Officer (British)
FWOC . . . . . . Federation of Western Outdoor Clubs
FWOP . . . . . . Furloughed Without Pay
FWP . . . . Federal Writers' Project (Obsolete)
FWP . . . . Flight Watch Point
FWPCA . . . . . . Federal Water Pollution Control Administration (Department of the
       Interior) (Later, FWQA of Environmental Protection Agency)
FWQA . . . . . . Federal Water Quality Administration (Formerly, Federal Water
       Pollution Control Administration)
FWR . . . . Free Wheel Rectifier
FWR . . . . Full-Wave Rectifier
FWRC . . . . . . Federal Water Resources Council
FWRU . . . . . . Full-Wave Rectified Unfiltered
FWS . . . . Filament Wound Structure
FWS . . . . Filter Wedge Spectrometer
FWS . . . . Fleet Work Study (Navy)
F & WS . . . . . Fish and Wildlife Service (Department of the Interior)
FWSAB . . . . . . Federation of Women Shareholders in American Business
FWSG . . . . . . Fleet Work Study Group (Navy)
FWSSUSA . . . . Federation of Workers' Singing Societies of the United States of America
FWT . . . . Fair Wear and Tear
FWT . . . . Forward Wave Tube
FWTUC . . . . . . Free Workers' Trade Union Congress (Aden)
FWU . . . . Fort Wayne Union R. R. (AAR code)
FWVA . . . . . . Finnish War Veterans in America
FWWMR . . . . . Fire, Water, Weather, Mildew Resistant
FX . . . . Fighter Experimental
FX . . . . Foreign Exchange (Business and trade)
FXD . . . . Flash X-Ray Device
FXF . . . . Flash X-Ray Facility
FXP . . . . Fleet Exercise Publication (Navy)
FY . . . . Fiscal Year
FYA . . . . For Your Attention
FYC . . . . Fission Yield Curve
FYDO . . . . . . Five-Year Design Objectives
FYDP . . . . . . Fiscal Year Development Plan
FYDP . . . . . . Five-Year Defense Plan (or Program)
FYFS & FP . . . Five-Year Force Structure and Financial Program (DOD)
FYI . . . . For Your Information
FYIG . . . . . . For Your Information and Guidance
FYK . . . . First York Corporation (American Stock Exchange symbol)
FYMP . . . . . . Five-Year Materiel Program (Military)
FYP . . . . Five-Year Plan

FYPB . . . . Five-Year Planning Base (Army)
FYPP . . . . Five-Year Procurement Program (Army)
FYSA . . . . Foundation for Youth and Student Affairs
FYTDY . . . . . . Final Year Temporary Duty (Air Force)

FZA . . . . Fellow of the Zoological Academy
FZIA . . . . First Zen Institute of America
FZM . . . . Floating Zone Melting
FZS . . . . Fellow of the Zoological Society (British)

G

G . . . . Air or Army National Guard (Military aircraft identification prefix)
G . . . . Gage
G . . . . Game
G . . . . Games Played (Sports statistics)
G . . . . Garage
G . . . . Gauche (Left)
G . . . . Gauge
G . . . . Gauss
G . . . . Gear
G . . . . Gelaendegaengig (Having cross-country mobility) (German military –
  World War II)
G . . . . Gelding
G . . . . Gender
G . . . . General
G . . . . General Audiences (All Ages Admitted) (Movie rating)
G . . . . General Intelligence
G . . . . Generally Labeled (Compound, with radioisotope)
G . . . . Genitive (case) (Grammar)
G . . . . German
G . . . . Ghost
G . . . . Gibbs Function
G . . . . Giga (A prefix meaning multiplied by one billion)
G . . . . Gilbert (A unit of magnetomotive force)
G . . . . Gilt (Bibliography)
G . . . . Girder (Technical drawings)
G . . . . Glass
G . . . . Glider
G . . . . Gloom
G . . . . Goal (A position in lacrosse, soccer, hockey, etc.)
G . . . . Gold
G . . . . Good (Condition) (Antiquarian book trade and numismatics)
G . . . . Gourde (Monetary unit in Haiti)
G . . . . Government
G . . . . Grain
G . . . . Gram (Metric)
G . . . . Grand (Slang term for $1,000)
G . . . . Gravel (Maps and charts)
G . . . . Gravity (or the force or acceleration produced by it)
G . . . . Great
G . . . . Green (light or buoy) (Navigation charts)
g . . . . Greenwich Meridian (Lower branch)
G . . . . Greenwich Meridian (Upper branch)
G . . . . Greenwich Time
G . . . . Greyhound Corporation (NYSE symbol)
G . . . . Grid (Electronics)
G . . . . Groschen (Monetary unit in Austria)
G . . . . Gross
G . . . . Ground
G . . . . Ground Swell
G . . . . Group
G . . . . Gruppenfuehrer (Squad Leader) (German military)
G . . . . Guanine
G . . . . Guard (Position in football, basketball, etc.)
G . . . . Guardian
G . . . . Guide
G . . . . Guilder (Dutch monetary unit) (Modification of gulden)
G . . . . Guinea (Coin or sum of money) (British)
G . . . . Gulden (Monetary unit in the Netherlands)
G . . . . Gulf (Maps and charts)
G . . . . Gun
G . . . . Gusts (Meteorology)
G . . . . Gynoecium (Botany)
G . . . . Gyromagnetic Ratio

G . . . . Transport Plane (Navy symbol)
G . . . . Unit of Acceleration (Military)
G (Suit) . . . . . Antigravity Suit (Air Force clothing for supersonic flight)
G-1 . . . . Personnel Section of an Army or Marine Corps Division (or Marine
  brigade or aircraft wing) General Staff; the Officer in Charge of this
  Section
G-2 . . . . Military Intelligence Section of an Army or Marine Corps Division (or
  Marine brigade or aircraft wing) General Staff; the Officer in Charge
  of this Section
G-3 . . . . Operations and Training Section of an Army or Marine Corps Division
  (or Marine brigade or aircraft wing) General Staff; the Officer in
  Charge of this Section
G-4 . . . . Logistics Section of an Army or Marine Corps Division (or Marine
  brigade or aircraft wing) General Staff; the Officer in Charge of this
  Section
G-5 . . . . Civil Affairs Section of an Army Division or Brigade General Staff; the
  Officer in Charge of this Section
G-11 . . . . . . Hexachlorophene
4-G . . . . Selective Service Class (for Registrant Exempt from Service During Peace
  [Surviving Son or Brother])
GA . . . . Gage (or Gauge)
Ga . . . . Gallium (Chemical element)
GA . . . . Gamblers Anonymous
GA . . . . Games Ahead (Baseball)
GA . . . . Garrison Adjutant (British military)
GA . . . . Gas or Air
GA . . . . Gas Amplification
GA . . . . Gasoline Stowage and Fuel System Man (Navy)
GA . . . . Gastric Analysis
GA . . . . Gated Attenuation (Data processing)
GA . . . . Gauge Man (Navy)
GA . . . . Gear Assembly
GA . . . . General Accounting
GA . . . . General Agent (Business and trade, especially insurance)
GA . . . . General of the Army
GA . . . . General Assembly
GA . . . . General Assistance (A form of public charity)
GA . . . . General Atomic (Division of General Dynamics Corp.)
GA . . . . General Automation, Inc.
GA . . . . General Average (Insurance)
GA . . . . Geological Abstracts
GA . . . . Geometrical Acoustics
GA . . . . Georgia
GA. . . . . . . Georgia R. R. (AAR code)
GA . . . . Gibberellic Acid (Biochemistry)
GA . . . . Gland Anlage
GA . . . . Glen Alden Corporation (NYSE symbol)
GA . . . . Glide Angle (Aviation)
GA . . . . Glutamic Acid (Biochemistry)
GA . . . . Go Ahead (or resume sending) (Communications)
GA . . . . Goals Against (Hockey)
GA . . . . Government Agency
GA . . . . Graduate in Agriculture
GA . . . . Grant Aid
GA . . . . Ground-to-Air (Missile)
GA . . . . Ground Attacker Aircraft
GA . . . . Gypsum Association
GA . . . . L-Glutamic (acid) and L-Alanine (Copolymer)
G-A . . . . . . General Atomics (Division of General Dynamics Corporation)
G/A . . . . . . Ground-to-Air (Communications, weapons)
G & A . . . . . General and Administrative
GAA . . . . . . Gain Adjuster Adapter
GAA . . . . . . Gay Activists' Alliance (An organization)

GAA . . . . General Account of Advances
GAA . . . . General Agency Agreement (Navy)
GAA . . . . Grenfell Association of America
GAA . . . . Ground Area Attainable
GAA . . . . Groupement Atomique Alsacienne Atlantique (French)
GAAC . . . . . . Graphic Arts Advertisers Council
GAAE . . . . . . Graphic Arts Association Executives
GAAP . . . . . . Generally Accepted Accounting Principles
GAATV . . . . . Gemini Atlas/Agena Target Vehicle
GAB . . . . General Adjustment Bureau (Insurance)
GAB . . . . General Arrangements to Borrow
GABA . . . . . . Gamma-Aminobutyric Acid
GAC . . . . GAC Corp. (Formerly, General Acceptance Corporation) (NYSE symbol)
GAC . . . . Galvanized Aircraft
GAC . . . . General Advisory Committee (to the AEC)
GAC . . . . General Agency Check
GAC . . . . Gimbal Angle Change
GAC . . . . Goodyear Aerospace Corporation
GAC . . . . . . Grilled American Cheese (Sandwich) (Waitress's call to a short order cook)
GAC . . . . Grumman Aircraft Corporation
GAC . . . . Gustavus Adolphus College (Minnesota)
GACSU . . . . . Singapore Government Administrative and Clerical Services' Union
GACTI . . . . . . General Arbitration Council of the Textile Industry
GAD . . . . Gallium Arsenide Diode
GAD . . . . Glutamic Acid Decarboxylase (Enzyme)
GAD . . . . Government Actuary's Department
GAD . . . . Grants Administration Division (Environmental Protection Agency)
GADH . . . . . . Gastric Alcohol Dehydrogenase (Enzyme)
GADL . . . . . . Ground-to-Air Data Link
GADNA . . . . . Gduei Noar (Youth Battalions) (Israel)
GADO . . . . . . General Aviation District Office (FAA)
GADR . . . . . . Guided Air Defense Rocket
GADS . . . . . . Goose Air Defense Sector
GAE . . . . General Administrative Expense (A budget appropriation title)
GAE . . . . General American English
GAE . . . . Gibbs Absorption Equation
GAEC . . . . . . Goodyear Aircraft and Engineering Corporation
GAEC . . . . . . Greek Atomic Energy Commission
GAEC . . . . . . Grumman Aircraft Engineering Corporation
GAES . . . . . . Gas Appliance Engineers Society
GAF . . . . GAF Corp. (Formerly, General Aniline & Film Corporation) (NYSE symbol)
GAF . . . . German Air Force (German Luftwaffe)
GAF . . . . Government Affairs Foundation
GAF . . . . Growth of the American Family (A study)
GAFA . . . . . . German-American Football Association
GAFB . . . . . . George Air Force Base
GAFB . . . . . . Goodfellow Air Force Base (Texas)
GAFB . . . . . . Griffis Air Force Base
GAFD . . . . . . Guild of American Funeral Directors
GAFPG . . . . . General Aviation Facilities Planning Group
GAFS . . . . . . Gentile Air Force Station
GAFSC . . . . . German Air Force Southern Command
G/A/G . . . . . . Ground-to-Air-to-Ground
GAGDT . . . . . Ground-to-Air-to-Ground Data Terminal (Air Force)
GAH . . . . Games at Home (Baseball)
GAI . . . . Gate Alarm Indicator (RADAR)
GAI . . . . General Accounting Instructions
GAI . . . . Geophysical Associates International
GAI . . . . Gibbs Absorption Isotherm
GAI . . . . Governmental Affairs Institute
GAI . . . . Guaranteed Annual Income
GAIF . . . . . . Gimbal Angle Information Failure
GAINS . . . . . Gimballess Analytic Inertial Navigation System
GAIT . . . . . . Government and Industry Team
GAIU . . . . . . Graphic Arts International Union (Merger of International Brotherhood of Bookbinders and Lithographers and Photoengravers International Union)
GAJ . . . . Gaseous Axisymmetric Jet
GAJ . . . . Guild of Agricultural Journalists
GAK . . . . Garlock, Inc. (NYSE symbol)
GAL . . . . Gallium Arsenide LASER
GAL . . . . Gallon(s)
GAL . . . . Gas-Analysis Laboratory (NASA)
GAL . . . . Gimbal Angle Loss
GAL . . . . Guggenheim Aeronautical Laboratory
GAL . . . . Guinea Airways, Limited
GALCIT . . . . . Guggenheim Aeronautical Laboratory (at California Institute of Technology)
GALOVAL . . . Grappling and Lock-On Validation
GAM . . . . General Aeronautical Material
GAM . . . . General American Investors Company, Inc. (NYSE symbol)

GAM . . . . Graduate Aerospace Mechanical Engineering
GAM . . . . Ground-to-Air Missile
GAM . . . . Guaranteed Annual Minimum
GAM . . . . Guest Aerovias Mexico, SA
GAM . . . . Guided Aircraft Missile
GAMA . . . . . . Gas Appliance Manufacturers Association
GAMA . . . . . . Guitar and Accessory Manufacturers Association of America (Formerly, NAMMM)
GAMAS . . . . . Gulf Atomic Mobile Assay System
GAMC . . . . . . General Agents and Managers Conference of Nalu
GAMD . . . . . . Generale Aeronautique Marcel Dassault (Switzerland)
GAMIS . . . . . . Graphic Arts Marketing Information Service (Printing Industries of America)
GAMM . . . . . Gesellschaft fuer Angewadte Mathematik und Mechanik (German Association for Applied Mathematics and Mechanics)
GAMMA . . . . Guns and Magnetic Material Alarm (Weapon-detecting device to prevent skyjacking)
GAMP . . . . . . Global Atmospheric Measurements Program (National Science Foundation)
GAMS . . . . . . Girls Against More Skirt (Group opposing below-the-knee fashions introduced in 1970)
GANC . . . . . . Groupe d'Action Nationale Comerounaise (Cameroonian National Action Group)
GANO . . . . . Georgia Northern Railway Company (AAR code)
GAO . . . . . . General Accounting Office (of the US government)
GAO . . . . . . General Administrative Order
GAO . . . . . . General Agricultural Officer (Ministry of Agriculture, Fisheries, and Food) (British)
GAO . . . . General American Oil Company of Texas (NYSE symbol)
GAOW . . . . . General Accounting Office, Washington
GAP . . . . General Antenna Package (COMSAT)
GAP . . . . General Assembly Program
GAP . . . . Ghetto Arts Program
GAP . . . . Goodyear Associative Processor (Data processing)
GAP . . . . Government Aircraft Plant
GAP . . . . Grant Air Program (DOD)
GAP . . . . Great Atlantic & Pacific Tea Company, Inc. (NYSE symbol)
GAP . . . . Group for the Advancement of Psychiatry
GAP . . . . Group Attainment Program
GAP . . . . Guided Antitank Projectile
GAPA . . . . . . Greek-American Progressive Association
GAPA . . . . . . Ground-to-Air Pilotless Aircraft (Early US test missiles)
GAPAN . . . . . Guild of Air Pilots and Air Navigators
GAPE . . . . . . General Aviation Pilot Education (Safety project)
GAPE . . . . . . Ground Anchor Placement Equipment
GAPL . . . . . . Group Assembly Parts List
GAPT . . . . . . Graphical Automatically Programmed Tools
GAR . . . . Garrett Corporation (NYSE symbol) (Delisted)
GAR . . . . German Army
GAR . . . . Gimbal Angle Rate (or Readout)
GAR . . . . Grand Army of the Republic
GAR . . . . . . Growth Analysis and Review
GAR . . . . Guided Airborne (or Aircraft) Rocket
GARB . . . . . . Green, Amber, Red, Blue (Priority of the airways)
GARB . . . . . . Guided Anti-Radiation Bomb
GARC . . . . . . Graphic Arts Research Center (Rochester Institute of Technology)
G Arch . . . . . Graduate in Architecture
GARD . . . . . . Gamma Atomic Radiation Detector
GARD . . . . . . General American Research Division
GARD . . . . . . Graphic Analyzer of Resistance Defects
GARD . . . . . . Grumman-Alderson Research Dummy (Aircraft ejection seats)
GARDAE . . . . Gathers Alarms, Reports, Displays and Evaluates
GARF . . . . . . Graphic Arts Research Foundation
GARIOA . . . . Government and Relief in Occupied Areas (Post-World War II)
GARL . . . . . . Group Action Request Lists
GARMI . . . . . General Aviation Radio Magnetic Indicator
GARP . . . . . . Global Atmospheric Research Program (National Academy of Sciences)
GAS . . . . Gasoline
GAS . . . . General Adaptation Syndrome (Medicine)
GAS . . . . General Automotive Support
GAS . . . . Giant Air Shower
GAS . . . . Giant Attribute Survey
GAS . . . . Guild of All Souls (British)
GAS . . . . Northern Illinois Gas Co. (NYSE symbol)
GASBIINDO . . . Gabungan Serikat Buruh Islam Indonesia (Federation of Indonesian Islamic Trade Unions)
GASC . . . . Gas-Analysis Sample Container (Apollo) (NASA)
GASC . . . . Georgia, Ashburn, Sylvester & Camilla R. R. (AAR code)
GASDSAS . . . Gust Alleviation and Structural Dynamic Stability Augmentation
GASERBUN . . . Gabungan SB2 Non-Vakcentral (Federation of Non-Affiliated Trade Unions) (Indonesia)
GASH . . . . . . Guanidine Aluminum Sulfate Hexahydrate (Insecticide)

237

GASL . . . . General Activity Simulation Language
GASL . . . . General Applied Science Laboratories, Inc.
GASM . . . . . . Graphic Arts Spray Manufacturers
GASP . . . . Gas Annulus Sizing Program
GASP . . . . General Academic Simulation Program (Data processing)
GASP . . . . Gevic Arithmetic Simulation Program
GASP . . . . Grand Accelerated Space Platform
GASP . . . . Gravity-Assisted Space Probe (NASA)
GASP . . . . Greater (name of city) Alliance to Stop Pollution
GASP . . . . Group Against Smog and Pollution
GASS . . . . Great Analog Signal Saver
GASS . . . . Guidance Accuracy Study for SPRINT (Missile) (Army)
GASSER . . . . . Geographic Aerospace Search RADAR
GASSP . . . . . . Gas Source Seismic Section Profiler
GAST . . . . Geraeteausgabestelle (Equipment distributing point) (German military - World War II)
GAT . . . . Gateway Industries, Inc. (NYSE symbol)
GAT . . . . Gemini-Agena Target
GAT . . . . General Analysis Technique
GAT . . . . General Aviation Transponder
GAT . . . . Generalized Algebraic Translator (Data processing)
GAT . . . . Georgetown Automatic Translation (Data processing)
GAT . . . . Greenwich Apparent Time
GAT . . . . . . Ground-to-Air Transmitter
GAT . . . . Ground Attack Tactics (for air delivery of weapons against a ground target)
GATAE . . . . . . Graphic Arts Trade Association Executives
GATB . . . . General Aptitude Test Battery
GATBY . . . . . General Aptitude Test Battery
GATD . . . . . . Graphic Analysis of Three-Dimensional Data
GATE . . . . . . GARP Atlantic Tropical Experiment (National Academy of Sciences)
GATE . . . . . . GAT Extended (Data processing)
GATF . . . . Graphic Arts Technical Foundation
GATR . . . . Ground-to-Air Transmitting-Receiving (Station)
GATT . . . . General Agreement on Tariffs and Trade (Organization, and the concept it represents, concerned with adjustment of tariffs between 73 member nations)
GATT . . . . Ground-to-Air Transmitter Terminal
GATU . . . . . . Geophysical Automatic Tracker Unit
GATV . . . . . . Gemini-Agena Target Vehicle (NASA)
GATX . . . . General American Transportation Corporation
GA (UN) . . . . . General Assembly of the United Nations
GAUSS . . . . . . Gravity Association for Universal Scientific Study
GAW . . . . Gram Atomic Weight
GAW . . . . . . Guaranteed Annual Wage
GAW . . . . . . Guided Atomic Warhead
GAWAM . . . . Great American Wife and Mother (Slang)
GAWR . . . . . . Gross Axle Weight Rating (Auto safety)
GAWS . . . . . . Grandmothers of America in War Service (World War II)
GAWU . . . . . . General Agricultural Workers' Union (Kenya)
GAY . . . . Government Accumulation Yard
GAYIG . . . . . . Gallium Substituted Yttrium Iron Garnet
GAZS . . . . Gesamtverzeichnis Auslaendischer Zeitschriften und Serien (Cumulative List of Foreign Periodicals and Serials)
GB . . . . Galaxy Books (Oxford University Press)
GB . . . . Gall Bladder (or a patient with an affliction of this organ) (Medicine)
GB . . . . Games Behind
GB . . . . General Background
GB . . . . General Board (Military judicial or investigative body)
GB . . . . General Bronze Corporation
GB . . . . Glass Bowl
GB . . . . Glide Bomb (Air Force)
GB . . . . Gold Bond (Bond payable in gold coin)
GB . . . . Good-bye (Amateur radio)
GB . . . . Governing Body
GB . . . . Granby Mining Company, Ltd. (NYSE symbol)
GB . . . . Grand Bounce (Suspension or dismissal) (Slang)
GB . . . . Great Britain
GB . . . . Greenish Blue
GB . . . . Grid Bearing (Navigation)
GB . . . . Grounded Base
GB . . . . Guidebook
GB . . . . Gunboat (Naval)
G/B . . . . Government Boat
GBA . . . . Give Better Address (Communications)
GBA . . . . Grupo Buenos Aires
GBA . . . . Gustin-Bacon Manufacturing Company (NYSE Symbol) (Delisted)
GBBA . . . . . . Glass Bottle Blowers Association of the United States and Canada
GB/BHE . . . . . Gesamtdeutscher Block/Bund der Heimatvertriebenen und Entrechteten (All-German Bloc/Union of Expellees)
GBC . . . . Greenland Base Command

GBC . . . . . . Ground-Based Computer
GBCSCMC . . . General Board of Christian Social Concerns of the Methodist Church
GBD . . . . Grain Boundary Dislocation
GBDV . . . . . . Gate Breakdown Voltage
GBE . . . . Gilt Beveled Edges
GBE . . . . Knight Grand Cross, Order of the British Empire
GBF . . . . Great Books Foundation
GBF . . . . Ground-Based Field
GBG . . . . . . General Baking Company (NYSE symbol) (Delisted)
GBH. . . . . . . Gamma Benzene Hexachloride
GBI . . . . Gable Industries, Incorporated (Formerly, Central Foundry Co.) (NYSE symbol)
GBI . . . . Grace Bible Institute (Nebraska)
GB & I . . . . . Great Britain and Ireland
GBII . . . . Ground-Based Infrared Instrumentation
GBIIS . . . . . . Ground-Based Infrared Instrumentation System
GBiP . . . . . . German Books in Print
GBJ . . . . Glass Bell Jar
GBL . . . . Government Bill of Lading
GB/L . . . . . . Government Bill of Lading
GBM . . . . . . Gain Band Merit
GBM . . . . . . Glass-Bonded Mica
GBM . . . . . . Glomerular Basement Membrane
GBM . . . . . . Glycerine Ball Memory
GBMA . . . . . . Golf Ball Manufacturers Association
GBMA . . . . . . Great Britain Ministry of Aviation
GBO . . . . Goods in Bad Order
GBP . . . . Gain-Bandwidth Product
GBP . . . . Galactose-Binding Protein (Biochemistry)
GBP . . . . Gas Bearing Part
GBPA . . . . . . Gettysburg Battlefield Preservation Association
GBR . . . . Give Better Reference
GBR . . . . Grain Boundary Relaxation
GBR . . . . Ground-Based Radiometer
GBR . . . . Gun, Bomb and Rocket
GBS . . . . Gall Bladder Series (Radiography)
GBS . . . . General Bancshares Corporation (NYSE symbol)
GBS . . . . George Bernard Shaw
GBS . . . . Ground-Based Scanner
GBSCA . . . . . . Greater Blouse and Skirt Contractors Association (Later, Greater Blouse, Skirt and Undergarment Association)
GBSM . . . . . . Guild of Better Shoe Manufacturers
GBSR . . . . . . Graphite-Moderated Boiling and Superheating Reactor (AEC)
GBT . . . . Graded Base Transistor
GBT . . . . Ground-Based Telemetry
GBV . . . . Gate Breakdown Voltage
GBV . . . . Glass (or Globe) Ball Valve
GBW . . . . . . Green Bay & Western R. R. (AAR code)
GBW . . . . . . Guild of Book Workers
GB & W . . . . . Green Bay and Western Railroad Company
GC . . . . Gain Control
GC . . . . Gas Chromatograph (or Chromatography)
GC . . . . General Circular
GC . . . . General Counsel
GC . . . . General Cueing
GC . . . . Generic Code
GC . . . . Geneva Convention (Relative to protection of civilian persons in time of war) (Army)
GC . . . . Gentleman Cadet (British)
Gc. . . . . Gigacycle (Measurement)
GC. . . . . Glucocorticoid (Endocrinology)
GC . . . . Golf Club
GC . . . . Gonorrhea Case (Medical slang)
GC . . . . Government Contribution
GC . . . . Governors' Conference
GC . . . . Graham County R. R. (AAR code)
GC . . . . Grand Chancellor
GC . . . . Grand Chaplain
GC . . . . Grand Chapter
GC . . . . Grand Commander
GC . . . . Grand Cross
GC . . . . Great Circle
GC . . . . Greenland Cruiser
GC . . . . Grid Course (Navigation)
GC . . . . Grolier Club
GC . . . . Ground Control
GC . . . . Grounded Collector
GC . . . . Group Captain
GC . . . . Guanine, Cystine (Biochemistry)
GC . . . . Guidance Computer
GC . . . . Guidance Control

GC .... Gun Captain
GC .... Gun Control
G & C...... Guidance and Control
GCA .... Gain Control Amplifier
GCA .... Garden Club of America
GCA .... Gauge Control Analyzer
GCA .... GCA Corp. (NYSE symbol)
GCA .... General Claim Agent
GCA .... Geophysics Corporation of America
GCA .... Girls Clubs of America
GCA .... Glass Crafts of America
GCA .... Green Coffee Association (of New Orleans or of New York City)
GCA .... Greeting Card Association
GCA .... Greyhound Club of America
GCA .... Ground-Controlled Aircraft
GCA .... Ground-Controlled Approach (for lateral and vertical guidance of landing aircraft through use of ground RADAR and radio communications)
GCA .... Grounded Cathode Amplifier
GCA .... Guidance and Control Assembly
GC & A..... Guidance, Control and Airframe
GCAD ...... Granite City Army Depot
GCAL ...... Gram Calorie
GCB .... Generator Control Breaker
GCB........ Knight Grand Cross of the (Order of the) Bath (British)
GCBR ...... Gas-Cooled Breeder Reactor
GCBS ...... Ground Control Bombing System
GCC .... General Commission on Chaplains & Armed Forces Personnel
GCC .... Georgian Court College (New Jersey)
GCC .... Giannini Controls Corporation
GCC .... Gogebic Community College (Michigan)
GCC .... Good Counsel College (New York)
GCC .... Government Contract Committee (Government agency)
GCC .... Grand Canyon College (Arizona)
GCC .... Greenfield Community College (Massachusetts)
GCC .... Ground Control Center (Aviation)
GCC .... Group Change Control
GCC .... Grove City College (Pennsylvania)
GCC .... Guidance Checkout Computer
GCCA ...... Graphic Communications Computer Association (of Printing Industries of America)
GCCA ...... Greater Clothing Contractors Association
GCCW ...... United Gas, Coke and Chemical Workers of America
GCD .... Gain Control Driver
GCD .... General and Complete Disarmament
GCD .... Gold Coupling Dendrite
GCD .... Great Circle Distance
GCD .... Greatest Common Denominator
GCD .... Greatest Common Divisor
GCE .... General Certificate of Education (British)
GCE........ Ground Checkout Equipment (Aerospace)
GCE .... Ground Communications Equipment
GCE .... Ground Control Equipment
GCEP ...... Governing Council for Environmental Programmes
GCESq ..... Geodetic Communications and Electronics Squadron (Air Force)
GCF........ General Contract Finance Corporation (NYSE symbol) (Delisted)
GCF........ Greatest Common Factor
GCF........ Ground Communications Facility (NASA)
GCFAP ..... Guidance & Control Flight Analysis Program
GCFI ...... Gulf and Caribbean Fisheries Institute
GCFR ...... Gas-Cooled Fast Reactor (for commercial atomic power)
GCFT ...... Gonorrhea Complement Fixation Test
GCG .... Gravity-Controlled Gyro
GCG .... Ground Command Guidance
GCG .... Guidance Control Group (Military)
GCGS ...... Gravity-Controlled Gyro System
GCH .... Guidance Capsule Handling
GCH .... Knight Grand Cross of the Guelphic Order of Hanover
GCI .... Gannett Company Incorporated (NYSE symbol)
GCI .... Gray Cast Iron
GCI .... Ground Control Intercept (RADAR)
GCIA ...... Granite Cutters' International Association of America
GCIE ...... Knight Grand Commander of the Indian Empire (British)
GCIS ...... Ground Control Intercept Squadron
GCJB ...... Guidance Checkout (or Computer) Junction Box
GCK .... Grid-Controlled Klystron
GCL........ Ground Control Landing (Aviation)
GCL........ Guidance Control Laboratory (Aerospace)
GCL........ Guild of Catholic Lawyers
GCM .... General Circulation Model (Data processing)
GCM .... General Counsel's Memorandum (Internal Revenue Service)
GCM .... General Court-Martial

GCM .... Global Circulation Model (National Center for Atmospheric Research)
GCM .... Good Conduct Medal
GCM .... Greatest Common Measure
GCMA ...... Government Contract Management Association of America
GCMC ...... Good Conduct Medal Clasp
GCMG ...... Knight Grand Cross of St. Michael and St. George (British)
GCMI ...... Glass Container Manufacturers Institute
GCMO ...... General Court-Martial Order
GCMP ...... General Court-Martial Prisoner
GCMP....... Greater Cleveland Mathematics Program (Education)
GC-MS ..... Gas Chromatography - Mass Spectrometry
GCMSC ..... George C. Marshall Space Flight Center (Also known as MSFC)
GCN .... Gage Code Number
GCN .... Greenwich Civil Noon
GCNA ...... Guild of Carillonneurs in North America
GCNR ...... Gas Core Nuclear Rocket
GCO .... Genesco, Inc. (NYSE symbol)
GCO .... Georgetown College Observatory
GCO .... Ground Cutout
GCO .... Guidance Control Officer (Aerospace)
GCO .... Gun Control Officer (Navy)
GCP........ Generalized Computer Program
GCP........ Guidance Control Package
GCP .... Guild of Catholic Psychiatrists
GCR .... Gain Control Range
GCR .... Galactic Cosmic Ray
GCR .... Galvanocutaneous Reaction
GCR .... Gas-Cooled Reactor
GCR........ General Cigar Company, Inc. (NYSE symbol)
GCR........ Grand Central Rocket Co.
GCR .... Grignard's Chemical Reaction
GCR .... Ground-Controlled RADAR
GCRA ...... Giant Chinchilla Rabbit Association
GCRE ...... Gas-Cooled Reactor, Experimental (AEC)
GCRI ...... Georgetown Clinical Research Institute (FAA)
GCRI ...... Gillette Company Research Institute
GCRP ...... Galactic Cosmic Ray Particle
GCS .... Gate-Controlled Switch
GCS........ Graphic Communications Section
GCS........ Ground Communications System
GCS........ Guidance and Control Section
GCS........ Gyroless Control System
Gc/s ...... Gigacycles Per Second (IEEE)
GCSA ...... Galloway Cattle Society of America
GCSAA...... Golf Course Superintendents Association of America
Gc/sec .... Gigacycles Per Second (AIP)
GCSF....... Gulf, Colorado & Santa Fe Railway Company (AAR code)
GC & SF .... Gulf, Colorado and Sante Fe Railway Company
GCSI ...... Knight Grand Commander of the Order of the Star of India (British)
GCSM ...... Ground Composite Signal Mixer
GCSS....... Global Communications Satellite System
GCSS....... Ground-Controlled Space System
GCStJ ..... Knight Grand Cross, Order of St. John of Jerusalem (British)
GCSU ...... Government Clerical Services' Union (Ceylon)
GCSW ...... Graduate Certificate of Social Work
GCT........ General Classification Test (Military)
GCT........ Glass Cloth Tape
GCT........ Great Circle Track
GCT........ Greenwich Civil Time
GCT........ Greenwich Conservatory Time
GCT........ Ground Checkout and Test
GCTA....... Ground Commanded Television Assembly (Apollo) (NASA)
GCTS ...... Ground Communication Tracking Systems
GCU .... Ground Checkout Unit
GCU........ Ground Control Unit (Aerospace)
GCU .... Guidance Coupler Unit
GCUUSA .... Greek Catholic Union of the United States of America
GCV .... Gross Caloric Value
GCVO ...... Knight Grand Cross of the Royal Victorian Order (British)
GCW .... Garden City Western Railway Company (AAR code)
GCW .... Global Chart of the World (Air Force)
GCW .... Gross Combination Weight (for tractor and loaded trailer)
Gd .... Gadolinium (Chemical element)
GD .... Gate Driver
GD .... General Delivery
GD......... General Design
GD .... General Diagram
GD .... General Discharge
GD .... General Dispensary
GD .... General Duty
GD .... General Dynamics Corporation (NYSE symbol)

GD . . . . Geographic Distribution
GD . . . . God Damn
GD . . . . Good Delivery (Business and trade)
GD . . . . Grand Deacon (Masonry)
GD . . . . Grand Division
GD . . . . Grand Duchess
GD. . . . . Grand Duchy
GD . . . . Granddaughter
GD . . . . Grand Duke
GD . . . . Gravimetric Density
GD . . . . Grown Diffused
GD . . . . Gudermannian Amplitude
G-D . . . . General Dynamics Corporation
G & D . . . . . . Grosset & Dunlap (Publisher)
GDA . . . . Galvo-Drive Amplifier
GDA . . . . Global Data Area
GDA . . . . Gun-Defended Area
GD/A . . . . General Dynamics/Astronautics
GDAAA . . . . . Gift and Decorative Accessories Association of America
GDAP. . . . . . . GEOS (Geodetic Earth-Orbiting Satellite) Data Adjustment Program
GDAS. . . . . . . Ground Data Acquisition System
GDB . . . . General Duties Branch (RAF)
GDC . . . . Gardner-Denver Company (NYSE symbol)
GDC . . . . General Development Corporation
GDC . . . . General (Purpose) Digital Computer
GDC . . . . General Dynamics Corporation
GDC . . . . Geocentric Dust Cloud
GDC . . . . Geodetic (or Geomagnetic) Data Center (Environmental Science Services Administration)
GDC . . . . Geophysical Data Center
GDC . . . . Governmental Defence Council (British)
GDC . . . . Grand Director of Ceremonies (Masonry)
GDC . . . . Groupe des Democrates Camerounais (Cameroonian Democratic Group)
GDC . . . . Guidance Data Converter (Aerospace)
GDC . . . . Gun Direction Computer
GDCA . . . . . . Great Dane Club of America
GDCh. . . . . . . Gesellschaft Deutscher Chemiker
GDCI . . . . Gypsum Drywall Contractors International
GDDS. . . . . . . Gamma Dose Detector System
GDE . . . . Gibbs-Duhem Equation
GDE. . . . . Ground Data Equipment (Electronics)
GDF. . . . . Gas Dynamic Facility (Air Force)
GDF. . . . . Ground Decommutation Facility
GDF. . . . . Group Distributing Frames
GDG . . . . Gas Discharge Gauge
GDG . . . . Group Display Generator
GDGA . . . . . . Garment Dyers Guild of America
GDGIP . . . . . . Gas-Driven Gyro Inertial Platform (Aerospace)
GDH . . . . Growth and Differentiation Hormone (Endocrinology)
GDHS. . . . . . . Ground Data Handling System
GDHSWT. . . . . General Dynamics High-Speed Wind Tunnel
GDI . . . . God Damned Independent (College slang for student not affiliated with a fraternity or sorority)
GDI . . . . Ground Detector Indicator
GDIFS . . . . . . Gray and Ductile Iron Founders' Society (Later, Cast Metals Federation)
GDIS . . . . Gier-Dunkle Integrating Sphere
GDL. . . . . Gas Dynamics Laboratory
GDL. . . . . Gladstone-Dale Law
GDL. . . . . Glass Delay Line
GDLG . . . . . . Gadolinium Iron Garnet
GDM . . . . Geodetic Distance Measurement
GDM . . . . Grid Dip Modulator
GDMO . . . . . . General Duties Medical Officer
GDNCE . . . . . Guidance
GDO . . . . Garage Door Opener
GDO . . . . Grid-Dip Oscillator
GDO . . . . Gross Domestic Output (Economics)
GDOP . . . . . . Geometric Dilution of Precision
GDP. . . . . Gaede Diffusion Pump
GDP. . . . . Gaseous Discharge Principle
GDP. . . . . Grid Driving Power
GDP . . . . Gross Domestic Product (Economics)
GDP. . . . . Grounded into Double Plays (Baseball)
GDP. . . . . Guanosine Diphosphate (Biochemistry)
GDP . . . . Gun Director Pointer (Naval gunnery)
GDP(CL) . . . . . Gun Director Pointer (Cross Leveler) (Naval gunnery)
GDP(L) . . . . . Gun Director Pointer (Leveler) (Naval gunnery)
GDP(P) . . . . . Gun Director Pointer (Pointer) (Naval gunnery)
GDP(SS) . . . . . Gun Director Pointer (Sight Setter) (Naval gunnery)
GDP(T) . . . . . Gun Director Pointer (Trainer) (Naval gunnery)
GDR . . . . Geodetic Data Reduction

GDR . . . . German Democratic Republic (East Germany)
GDR . . . . Giant Dipole Resonance
GDR . . . . Graphic Depth Recorder
GDR. . . . . Guard Rail
GDRC. . . . . . . Gyro Drift Rate Compensation
GDS. . . . . Gas Dynamic System
GDS. . . . . Ground Display System
GDSA . . . . . . Goal-Directed Serial Alternation
GDSF . . . . . . Gesellschaft fuer Deutsch-Sowjetische Freundschaft
GDT. . . . . Glow Discharge Tube
GD/T. . . . . . . General Dynamics/Telecommunications
GDU . . . . Graphic Display Unit
GDV. . . . . General Development Corp. (NYSE symbol)
GDW . . . . Golden West Financial Corp. (NYSE symbol)
GE . . . . Federal Republic of Germany (NATO)
GE . . . . Gas Ejection (Opening) (Technical drawings)
GE . . . . Gastroenterology (Medicine)
GE. . . . . General Electric Company (NYSE symbol)
GE . . . . Geoscience Electronics
Ge. . . . . Germanium (Chemical element)
GE . . . . Gilt Edges (Bookbinding)
GE . . . . Gimbal Electronics
GE. . . . . Good Evening (Amateur radio)
GE. . . . . Great Exuma (Bahama Islands)
GE . . . . Ground Equipment
GE . . . . Grounded Emitter
GE . . . . Group Engineer
GE . . . . Guanidoethyl
GE. . . . . Gyro Error (Navigation)
GEA . . . . Gravure Engravers Association
GEA. . . . . Greater East Asia (Used by Japanese in such terms as War of Greater East Asia and Greater East Asia Co-Prosperity Sphere) (World War II)
GEAG. . . . . . . General Electric Airborne Guidance
GEANS. . . . . . Gimbaled Electrostatic-Gyro Aircraft Navigation System
GEAP . . . . . . General Electric Atomic Power
GEAPS . . . . . Grain Elevator and Processing Superintendents
GEAV. . . . . . . Guidance Error Analysis Vehicles (Air Force)
GEB. . . . . Gerber Products Company (NYSE symbol)
GEB . . . . Guiding Eyes for the Blind
GEBA . . . . . . Government Excess Baggage Authorization
GEBCO. . . . . . General Bathymetric Chart of the Oceans (International Hydrographic Bureau)
GEC. . . . . General Electric Company
GEC . . . . General Electrodynamics Company
GEC . . . . General Equipment Command (Army - Equipment and support of Engineers and Quartermaster)
GEC. . . . . Government Employees Council
GECECS . . . . . General Electric Chemical Engineering Calculation System
GECOM . . . . . General Compiler (Data processing)
GECOMIN . . . . Generale Congolaise des Minerais (Congo)
GECOS . . . . . General Comprehensive Operating Supervisor (or System)
GED. . . . . Gasoline Engine Driven
GED. . . . . General Educational Development (Test)
GED. . . . . Group on Electronic Devices
GED. . . . . Guanidoethyl Disulfide
GED. . . . . Gunn Effect Device
GEDP . . . . . . General Educational Development Program (Army)
GEDT . . . . . . General Educational Development Test
GEE. . . . . General Evaluation Equipment
GEE. . . . . Group for Environmental Education
GEEIA . . . . . . Ground Electronics Engineering Installation Agency (Air Force)
GEEK . . . . . . Geomagnetic Electrokinetograph (Equipment for exploring ocean depths)
Ge Engr . . . . . Geological Engineer
GEEP . . . . . . General Electric Electronic Processor
GEERS . . . . . Groupe d'Etudes Europeen des Recherches Spatiales
GEESE . . . . . General Electric's Electronic System Evaluator
GEF. . . . . Gauss Error Function
GEF. . . . . Gel Electrofocusing
GEF. . . . . Gradient Elution Fractionation
GEF. . . . . Ground Equipment Failure (Air Force)
GEFA . . . . . . Gulf-European Freight Association
GEFAP . . . . . Groupement Europeen des Associations Nationales de Fabricants de Pesticides (European Group of National Pesticide Manufacturers' Associations)
GEFFA . . . . . Gesellschaft fuer Forstliche Arbeitswissenschaft
GEFP . . . . . . Guild of Ethical Funeral Practice
GEG . . . . Gamma Eta Gamma (Fraternity)
GEGR . . . . . . General Grant National Memorial
GEGS. . . . . . . General Electric Guidance System (Aerospace)
GEI . . . . Gosudorstvenue Energeticheskoe Izdatel'stvo
GEICO . . . . . . Government Employees Insurance Company

GEK .... Geomagnetic Electrokinetograph (Equipment for exploring ocean depths)
GEL .... General Electric Laboratory
GELAC ..... Georgia Division, Lockheed Aircraft Corporation
GELAP ...... General Electric Computer Analysis Program
GELFAC ..... Gel Frontal Analysis Chromatography
GEM .... Gemini Fund Inc. (NYSE symbol)
GEM .... Giant Earth Mover (Machine)
GEM .... Government-Education-Medical
GEM .... Ground Effect Machine
GEM .... Guidance Evaluation Missile
GEM .... Gunn Effect Material
GEMA ..... Gesellschaft fuer Musikalische Auffuhrung
GE/MAC .... General Electric Measurement and Control
GEMAGS .... General Electric Magnetically Anchored Gravity System
GEMO ..... Ground Electronic Maintenance Officer (Navy)
GEMPPS ..... Groupe d'Etudes Mathematiques de Problemes Politiques et Strategiques (France)
GEMS ...... Generalized Evaluation Model Simulator (NASA)
GEMS ...... Global Environmental Monitoring System
GeMSAEC ... General Medical Sciences and Atomic Energy Commission
GEMSIP ..... Gemini Stability Improvement Program (NASA)
GEN .... General (Military)
GEN .... General Electric Network (Data processing)
GEN .... General Telephone & Electronics Corporation (NYSE symbol) (Wall Street slang name: "Jennie") (Later, GTE)
GEN .... Generator
GENA ..... Great Eastern Numismatic Association
GENC ..... General Electric Nose Cone (Aerospace)
GENDARME... Generalized Data Reduction, Manipulation, Evaluation
GENDEP .... General Depot (Military)
GENDET .... General Detail (Coast Guard)
GENDIS .... General Distribution (Pentagon security classification code)
GENDISP .... General Dispensary (Military)
GENDYN .... General Dynamics
GENENG .... Generalized Engine (Data processing)
GENESCO ... General Shoe Corporation (Acronym now official name of firm)
GENESYS ... Graduate Engineering Education System
GENL ...... General
GENLED .... General Ledger
GENMISH .... US Military Mission with the Iranian Gendarmerie
GENOT .... General Notice
GENPRL ..... General Precision Laboratory
GENSUP ..... General Support (Army)
GENSV ..... General Service (Military)
GENTEL ..... General Telephone & Electronics Corporation
GEO .... Central of Georgia Railway Company (NYSE symbol) (Delisted)
Geod E...... Geodetic Engineer
GEOG ..... Geography
GEOIS ..... Geographic Information System (Data processing)
GEOL ..... Geology
Geol E...... Geological Engineer
GEOLOC .... Geographical Location (Military)
GEOM ...... Geometry
GEON ...... Gyro Erected Optical Navigation
GEOREF ..... Geographic Reference System (Civil Defense)
GEOS ...... Geodetic Earth-Orbiting Satellite (NASA)
GEOSCAN ... Ground-Based Electronic Omnidirectional Satellite Communications Antenna
GEOSS ...... Geophysical Survey System (Naval Oceanographic Office)
GEP .... Goddard Experiment Package (NASA)
GEP .... Ground Effects Phenomenon
GEP .... Gulf Environmental Measurements Program
GEPAC ..... General Electric Programmable Automatic Comparator
GEPB ...... Grievance and Employment Policy Board (Army)
GEPC ...... German External Property Control Commission (Minden) (Allied German Occupation Forces)
GEPDS ..... General Electric Process Design System
GEPEXS ..... General Electric Parts Explosion System
GEPL ...... General Equipment and Packaging Laboratory (Army)
GER .... General Engineering Research
GER .... Goodyear Engineering Report
GER .... Great Eastern Railway (British)
GERA ...... Guard's Expense in Returning Absentee
GERE ...... Gewerkschaft Erdoel-Raffinerie Emsland (West Germany)
GEREP ..... Generalized Equipment Reliability Evaluation Procedure
GERM ...... Ground Effect Research Machine
GERMDF ..... German Ministry of Defense
GERO ...... George Rogers Clark National Historical Park
GERS ...... Groupe d'Etude et Recherches Sous-Marin
GERSIS ...... General Electric Range Safety Instrumentation System

GERT .... Graphical Evaluation and Review Technique
GERTS ...... General Electric Range Tracking System (Aerospace)
GERV ...... General Electric Reentry Vehicle (Aerospace)
GES .... General Educational Services (Corporation)
GES .... General Electric Semiconductor
GES .... Ground Electronic System
GES .... Ground Equipment System
GESAC ..... General Electric Self-Adaptive Control System
GESAMP .... Group of Experts on the Scientific Aspects of Marine Pollution (UN)
GESCO..... General Electric Supply Corporation
GESOC ..... General Electric Satellite Orbit Control
GEST ...... Gemini Slowscan Television
GESTAPO ... Geheime Staats Polizei (Secret State Police) (German)
GESyN .... Groupement d'Etude du Synchrotron National (France)
GET .... Getty Oil Company (NYSE symbol)
GET .... Ground-Elapsed Time (Aerospace)
GETA ...... General Equipment Test Activity (Army)
GETA ...... Government Employees Training Act
GETEPE..... Groupo Executivo de Trabalhos e Estudos de Projetos Espaciais (Brazil)
GETIS ...... Ground Environment Team of the International Staff (NATO)
GETLO ..... Obtain by Local Purchase (Military)
GETMA ..... Obtain by Local Manufacture (Military)
GETOL ..... Ground-Effect Take-Off and Landing
GETR ...... General Electric Test Reactor
GETS ...... Ground Equipment Test Set
GETT ...... Gettysburg National Military Park
GEU........ Grossesse Extra-Uterine (Medicine)
GeV .... Giga Electron Volt
GEV........ Ground Effect Vehicle
GEVIC ..... General Electric Variable Increment Computer
GEWA ...... George Washington Birthplace National Monument
GEWP...... George Washington Memorial Parkway (National Park Service designation)
GF .... Games Finished (Baseball)
GF .... Gap Filler (RADAR)
GF......... General Foods Corporation (NYSE symbol)
GF .... Generator Field
GF .... Generic Failure
GF .... Georgia & Florida R. R. (AAR code)
GF .... Girl Friend (Slang)
GF .... Glass Fiber
GF .... Globular-Fibrous (Biochemistry)
GF .... Glomerular Filtrate (Physiology)
GF .... Goals For (Hockey)
GF .... Gold Field
GF .... Goldflow
GF .... Ground Fog (Meteorology)
GF .... Growth Fraction (Endocrinology)
G & F...... Georgia & Florida Railroad
GFA .... General Freight Agent
GFA .... Gloucester Fisheries Association
GFA....... Good Fair Average (Insurance)
GFA .... Grain Futures Administration (Superseded by Commodity Exchange Administration, 1936)
GFA .... Gun Fire Area
GFAE ...... Government-Furnished Aerospace Equipment
GFAEL ..... Government-Furnished Aeronautical Equipment List
GFB........ Government Facilities Brochure
GFC........ Gas-Filled Counter
GFC........ Gel Filtration Chromatography
GFC .... George Fox College (Oregon)
GFC........ Gibraltar Financial Corporation of California (NYSE symbol)
GFC........ Grand Falls Central R. R. (AAR code)
GFCE ...... Government-Furnished Capital Equipment
GFCES ..... Glider Flight Control Electronics Subsystem
GFCM ..... General Fisheries Council for the Mediterranean
GFCS ...... Gaseous Flowmeter Calibration Stand
GFCS ...... Gun Fire Control System
GFCSMT ... Generalized Fire-Control System Maintenance Trainer (Spacecraft) (Navy)
GFD........ Gap-Filler Data (RADAR)
GFD........ Gallons per Square-Foot per Day
GFD........ Group Finance Department
GFDC...... Group Fire Distribution Center (Army)
GFDD...... Gun Fire Detection Device
GFDL ...... Geophysical Fluid Dynamics Laboratory (National Oceanic and Atmospheric Administration)
GFDNA ..... Grain and Feed Dealers National Association
GFE........ Gibbs Free Energy
GFE........ Government-Furnished Equipment
GFERR ..... Government-Furnished Equipment Requirements Request
GFF .... Granolithic Finish Floor (Technical drawings)
GFFAR ..... Guided Folding Fin Aircraft Rocket

GFG . . . . . . Governor's Foot Guard
GFH . . . . Gifford-Hill & Company Inc. (NYSE symbol)
GFHR . . . . . . Gas-Filled Hydrophobic Region
GFI . . . . . . Gap-Filler Input (RADAR)
GFI . . . . . . Government Free Issue
GFI . . . . Ground-Fault Interrupter (Electric shock preventive device)
GFIT . . . . . . Glass Fiber Insulation Tubing
GFL . . . . Ground Fire Locator
GFLS . . . . . . Ground Fire Locating System
GFLU . . . . . . General Federation of Labor Unions (Syria)
GFM . . . . . . Glass Fiber Material
GFM . . . . . . Government-Furnished Material (or Missile)
GFM . . . . . . Greyhound Food Management
GFMA . . . . . . Gold-Filled Manufacturers Association
GFME . . . . . . Government-Furnished Missile Equipment
GFMS . . . . . . Gaseous Flow Measuring System
GFMVT . . . . . General Foods Moisture Vapor Transmission
GFN . . . . . . General Finance Corporation of Delaware (NYSE symbol) (Delisted)
GFO . . . . Gap-Filler Output
GFO . . . . . . Gas-Fired Oven
GFO . . . . . . Gulf, Mobile & Ohio R. R. Company (NYSE symbol)
GFP . . . . Government Full Period
GFP . . . . Government-Furnished Parts
GFP . . . . Government-Furnished Property
GFPM . . . . . . Gas Fission Products Monitor
GFR . . . . Gap-Filler RADAR
GFR . . . . Gas-Filled Rectifier
GFR . . . . German Federal Republic (West Germany)
GFR . . . . Glass-Fiber Reinforced
GFR . . . . Glomerular Filtration Rate (Physiology)
GFR . . . . Government Facilities Request
GFRP . . . . . . Glass-Fiber-Reinforced Plastic
GF/RP . . . . . . Gap Filler/Reporting Post (RADAR)
GFRS . . . . . . Ground Forces Replacement Service
GFRT . . . . . . Gas-Filled Rectifying Tube
GFS . . . . Girls' Friendly Society of the USA
GFSS . . . . . . Gunfire Support Ship
GFST . . . . . . Ground Fuel Start Tank
GFT . . . . Glass Fabric Tape
GFTU . . . . . . General Federation of Trade Unions (Various countries)
GFU . . . . . . Glazed Facing Units (Technical drawings)
GFUT . . . . . . Ground Fuel Ullage Tank
GFV . . . . Guided Flight Vehicle
GFW . . . . . . Gesellschaft fuer Weltraumforschung (Society for Space Research) (Germany)
GFWC . . . . . . General Federation of Women's Clubs
GG . . . . Gamma Globulin (Medicine)
GG . . . . Gas Generator
GG . . . . Gewehrgranate (Rifle grenade) (German military - World War II)
Gg . . . . Gigagram
GG . . . . Government Girl
GG . . . . Governor General
GG . . . . Great Gross
GG . . . . Green Giant Co. (NYSE symbol)
GG . . . . Grenadier Guards (British military)
GG . . . . Groove Gauge
GG . . . . Ground Guidance (Aerospace)
G/G . . . . Ground-to-Ground (Communications, weapons, etc.)
GGA . . . . Grounded Grid Amplifier
GGA . . . . Gulf General Atomic (Commercial firm)
GGAR . . . . . . Gas-Guided Aircraft Rocket
GGC . . . . Golden Gate College (California)
GGC . . . . Ground Guidance Computer
GGD . . . . Great Granddaughter
GGE . . . . Generalized Glandular Enlargement (Medicine)
GGE . . . . Gradient Gel Electrophoresis
GGE . . . . Ground Guidance Equipment
GGIA . . . . . . Granite Grit Institute of America
GGL . . . . Gravity-Gradient Libration (Damper)
GGL . . . . Ground Glass
GGM . . . . . . Ground-to-Ground Missile
GGMA . . . . . . Glassine and Greaseproof Manufacturers Association
GGMA . . . . . . Government Gold Mining Areas
GGMWA . . . . Grace of God Movement, Women of Africa (Women's division of 3HO Foundation)
GGO . . . . Glavnaya Geofizicheskaya Observatory (Main Geophysical Observatory) (USSR)
GGPA . . . . . . Graduate Grade-Point Average (Higher education)
GGR . . . . Ground Gunnery Range
GGS . . . . Gravity Gradient Satellite
GGS . . . . Gravity Gradient Sensor

GGS . . . . . . Ground Guidance System (Aerospace)
GGSE . . . . . . Gravity Gradient Stabilization Experiment
GGT . . . . . . Gravitational Gradient Torque
GGTS . . . . . . Gravity Gradient Test Satellite (NASA)
GH . . . . General Hospital
GH . . . . General Host Corp. (NYSE symbol)
GH . . . . Good Housekeeping (A publication)
GH . . . . Grid Heading (Navigation)
GH . . . . Ground Handling
GH . . . . Growth Hormone (Endocrinology)
GH . . . . Guardhouse
GHA . . . . . . Grassland Husbandry Adviser (Ministry of Agriculture, Fisheries, and Food) (British)
GHA . . . . . . Greenwich Hour Angle
GHA . . . . . . Gyro Header Assembly
GHAA . . . . . . Group Health Association of America
GhAF . . . . . . Ghanaian Air Force
GHC . . . . . . Gating Half-Cycle (Data processing)
GHC . . . . . . Generalized Hyperbolic Class
GHC . . . . . . Grays Harbor College (Washington)
GHC . . . . Gulf Life Holding Company (NYSE symbol)
GHCS . . . . . . Good Housekeeping Check Sheet
GHE . . . . . . Gauss Hypergeometric Equation
GHE . . . . . . Gibbs-Helmholtz Equation
GHE . . . . . . Ground Handling Equipment
GHF . . . . . . Gauss Hypergeometric Function
GHG . . . . . . Governor's Horse Guard
GHH . . . . . . Galveston, Houston & Henderson R. R. (AAR code)
GHH . . . . . . Helme (George W.) Company (NYSE symbol) (Delisted)
GHL . . . . Guard House Lawyer (Military slang)
GHM . . . . . . Guaranteed Hourly Minimum
GHOST . . . . . Global Horizontal Sounding Technique (Meteorology)
GHP . . . . Gas High Pressure
GHQ . . . . . . General Headquarters (Military)
GHRF . . . . . . Growth Hormone Releasing Factor
GHS . . . . . . Ground Handling System (Aerospace)
GHS . . . . . . Grunberg Hydrofoil System
GHSG . . . . . . Guest Housing (Army)
GHT . . . . . . Golden Hour Tango
GHW . . . . . . Guaranteed Hourly Wage
GHX . . . . . . Ground Heat Exchanger
GHz . . . . Gigahertz
GI . . . . Galvanized Iron
GI . . . . Gastrointestinal (Medicine)
GI . . . . Geheimer Informant
GI . . . . General Index
GI . . . . General Issue
GI . . . . Gideons International
Gi . . . . Gilbert
GI . . . . Gimbel Brothers, Inc. (NYSE symbol)
GI . . . . Globin Insulin
GI . . . . Government of India
GI . . . . Government Issue (Army)
GI . . . . Green Island (Plant pathology)
GI . . . . Gross Investment
GI . . . . Gunner Instructor (British Navy)
GI . . . . Soldier (Wartime slang)
GI (Bill) . . . . . Veterans Benefits Act, Public Law 345, 1944
GI (Insurance) . . Popular Name for US Government Life Insurance (available to military personnel in World War II)
GIA . . . . . . Garuda Indonesian Airways, Ltd.
GIA . . . . Gemological Institute of America
GIA . . . . Goodwill Industries of America
GIA . . . . Gregorian Institute of America
GIA . . . . Groupement des Independants Africains (Independent Africans Group)
GIA . . . . Gummed Industries Association
GIAC . . . . . . General Industry Advisory Committee
GIAM . . . . . . Global Impacts of Applied Microbiology (International conferences)
GIB . . . . Gibson Greeting Cards, Inc. (NYSE symbol) (Delisted)
GIB . . . . Guy In the Back (Air Force slang)
GIBAIR . . . . . Gibraltar Airways, Ltd.
GIBI . . . . Gabungan Importir Buku Indonesia
GIBS . . . . . . Guy-In-The-Back-Seat (Copilot) (Air Force slang)
GIC . . . . General Improvement Contractors Association
GIC . . . . Groupement de l'Industrie Chimique (France)
GIC . . . . Guilde Internationale des Cooperatrices
GICG . . . . . . Glaze Icing (Aviation)
GICL . . . . . . Gila Cliff Dwellings National Monument
GICLDC . . . . . GI Civil Liberties Defense Committee
GICORP . . . . . Government Industry Cooperative Oyster Research Program
GID . . . . General Installation Dolly

GID	Giddings & Lewis Inc. (NYSE symbol)
GIDEP	Government-Industry Data Exchange Program
GIDP	Grounded into Double Plays (Baseball)
GIE	Ground Instrumentation Equipment
GIER	General Industrial Equipment Reserve
GIF	Gravito-Inertial Force
GIF	Gulf It to FORTRAN (Translator)
GIFCO	Gruppo Nazionale di Fisica Cosmica
GIFS	Gray Iron Founders Society
GIGI	Gamma Inspection of Grain Integrity
GIGO	Garbage In, Garbage Out (Data processing)
GIIP	Groupement International de l'Industrie Pharmaceutique des Pays de la CEE (International Pharmaceutical Industry Group for the EEC Countries)
GIIR	Government Idle Industrial Reserve
GIIV	Gated Image Intensifier Viewer
GIL	Gaseous Ion LASER
GIL	Gilbert Flexi-Van Corp. (NYSE symbol)
GIL	Green Indicating Lamp
GILMER	Guardian of Impressive Letters and Master of Excellent Replies
GIM	Gaining Inventory Managers
GIM	Generalized Information Management System
GIM	Glass Insulation Material
GIMRADA	Geodesy, Intelligence & Mapping Research & Development Agency (Army)
GIMS	Ground Identification of Missions in Space
GIMU	Gimballess Inertial Measuring Unit
GIN	Gimbaled Integral Nozzle
GINJIM	Great Inland Navigators, not Just Imbibing Mariners
GIO	Gas Identification Officer
GIO	Government Information Organization
GIP	Galvanized Improved Plow (Steel)
GIP	Gastric Inhibitory Peptide (Biochemistry)
GIP	Gaussian Image Point
GIP	Great Indian Peninsular R. R.
GIP	Great Irish Painter (of Jack B. Yeats, ca. 1905)
GIPS	Ground Information Processing System
GIPSE	Gravity Independent Photo-Synthetic Gas Exchanger
GIPSY	General Information Processing System
GIQ	Giant Imperial Quart (of beer)
GIRD	General Incentive for Research and Development (Canada)
GIRD	Good Industrial Relations Directors (Meetings sponsored by Master Printers of America)
GIRLS	Generalized Information Retrieval and Listing System
GIRLS	Global Interrogation Recording and Location System
GIRO	General Instructions for Routing and Reporting Officers
GIRS	Gimballess Inertial Reference System
GIRSS	General Information Retrieval System Simulation
GIRT	Groupe des Independants et Ruraux Tchadiens (Chadian Independent and Rural Group)
GIS	Gastrointestinal Series (Radiology)
GIS	General Installation Subcontractor
GIS	General Mills, Inc. (NYSE symbol)
GIS	Generalized Information System (IBM)
GIS	Geoscience Information Society
GIS	Graphic Input System
GIS	Greatness Is Simplicity (Also see SIG)
GIS	Guild for Infant Survival
GISAT	Ground Identification of Satellites
GISC	Government Information Services Committee (Special Libraries Association)
GISC	Grail International Student Center
GISMO	General Interpretative System for Matrix Operations (Data processing system used in engineering) (Navy)
GISPA	Guide to International Scientific Publications and Associations
GISS	Goddard Institute for Space Studies
GIT	Gastro-Intestinal Tract
GIT	General Information Test
GIT	Georgia Institute of Technology
GIT	Graph Isomorphism Tester
GIT	The Great Ideas Today (A publication)
GIT	Group Inclusive Tour (Travel)
GITT	Glucose Insulin Tolerance Test (Medicine)
GIU	General Intelligence Unit (US, London)
GIUK	Greenland, Iceland, United Kingdom
GIW	Glass-Insulated Wire
GIW	Gulf Intracoastal Waterway
GIWW	Gulf Intracoastal Waterway
GJ	Goldreich-Julian (PULSAR theory)
GJ	Grapefruit Juice (Restaurant slang)
GJ	Greenwich & Johnsonville Railway (AAR code)
GJC	Gainesville Junior College (Later, Cooke County Junior College) (Texas)
GJC	Grand Junction Canal
GJD	Grand Junior Deacon (Masonry)
GJ(O)	Grand Junction Office (AEC)
GJP	Galactic Jupiter Probe (NASA)
GJW	Grand Junior Warden (Masonry)
GK	General Cable Corporation (NYSE symbol)
GKA	Garter King of Arms
GKA	Grounded Kathode Amplifier
GKC	Gilbert Keith Chesterton (British journalist and author)
GKI	General Kinetics, Incorporated
GKO	Gosudarstvennyi Komitet Oborony (State Defense Committee) (USSR) (World War II)
GKSS	Gesellschaft fuer Kernenergieverwertung in Schiffbau und Schiffahrt (Atomic power) (Germany)
GL	Gage Length
GL	Gas LASER
GL	General Ledger
GL	Gothic Letter
GL	Grade Line
GL	Graduate in Law
GL	Grand Larceny
GL	Grand Lodge (Masonry)
GL	Grand Lot
GL	Great Lakes (Vessel load line mark)
GL	Great Lakes Dredge & Dock Co. (NYSE symbol)
GL	Grenade Launcher
GL	Grid Leak
GL	Ground Level
GL	Gun Lay(er)(ing)
GL	L-Glutamic (acid) and L-Lysine (Copolymer)
GLA	General Laboratory Associates
GLA	General Ledger Account
GLA	Gross Leasable Area
GLAC	Glacier National Park
GLAD	GLOTRAC (Global Tracking) Adjustment
GLANCE	Global Lightweight Airborne Navigation Computer Equipment
GLASLA	Great Lakes - St. Lawrence Association
GLB	Gas (or Grease) Lubricated Bearing
GLB	Glass in Barrels (Freight)
GLB	Glass Block
GLB	Globe-Union, Inc. (NYSE symbol)
GLBA	Glacier Bay National Monument
GLBC	Great Lakes Basin Commission
GLC	Gas-Liquid Chromatography (Analytical chemistry)
GLC	Gate Leakage Current
GLC	General Learning Corporation (of Time, Inc.)
GLC	Global LORAN Navigation Charts (Air Force)
GLC	Great Lakes Commission
GLC	Greater London Council
GLCA	Gallery of Living Catholic Authors
GLCA	Glen Canyon National Recreation Area
GLCA	Great Lakes Colleges Association
GLD	Gas Leak Detector
GLD	Gould, Inc. (NYSE symbol)
GLD	Gross Logical Design
GLDS	Gemini Launch Data System
GLDT	Gas LASER Discharge Tube
GLE	Grade Level Equivalent (Educational testing)
GLEAM	Graphic Layout and Engineering Aid Method
GLEEP	Graphite Low Energy Experimental Pile (Nuclear reactor) (British)
GLEP	Group for Lunar Exploration and Planning
GLF	Gaussian Lens Formula
GLF	General Telephone Company of Florida (NYSE symbol)
GLH	Glue Line Heating
GLHA	Great Lakes Harbor Association
GLHS	Great Lakes Historical Society
GLI	Gamma Linac Instrumentation
GLI	General Time Corporation (NYSE symbol) (Delisted)
GLIBAD	Glider Badge (Military decoration)
GLIC	General Ledger Identification Code
GLINT	Gospel Literature International (An organization); or Gospel Literature in National Tongues (The organization's work); formerly, Gospel Light International
GLIPAR	Guide Line Identification Program for Antimissile Research (ARPA)
GLIPAR	Guide Lines for Investigations, Planning and Research
GLIS	Gleaner Life Insurance Society
GLLO	Great Lakes Licensed Officers' Organization
GLM	Global Marine Inc. (NYSE symbol)
GLM	Government-Loaned Material
GLM	Graduated Length Method (of learning to ski) (Later, Accelerated Length Method)
GLM	Grand Livre du Mois (Best-selling book of the month) (France)

GLM . . . . Great Lakes Megalopolis (Proposed name for possible "super-city" formed by growth and mergers of other cities)
GLMA . . . . . . Great Lakes Mink Association
GLMI . . . . Great Lakes Maritime Institute
GLN . . . . Glidden Company (NYSE symbol) (Delisted)
GLN . . . . Glutamine (Amino acid)
GLNTC . . . . . . Great Lakes Naval Training Center
GLO . . . . General Land Office (Became part of Bureau of Land Management, 1946)
GLO . . . . Goddard Launch Operations (NASA)
GLO . . . . Ground Liaison Officer (Military)
GLO . . . . Gunnery Liaison Officer (Navy)
GLOBECOM . . Global Communications System (Air Force)
GLOC . . . . . . Ground Line of Communications
GLOCOM . . . . Global Communications System
GLOMB . . . . . Glide Bomb (Air Force)
GLOMEX . . . . Global Meteorological Experiment (Also known as GARP)
GLOP . . . . Gevic Logic Operation Program
GLOPAC . . . . . Gyroscopic Low-Power Attitude Control
GLORIA . . . . . Geological Long-Range Inclined ASDIC
GLOTRAC . . . . Global Tracking (RADAR)
GLOW . . . . . . Gross Lift-Off Weight
GLP . . . . Gelled Liquid Propellant
GLP . . . . General Fireproofing Co. (NYSE symbol)
GLP . . . . Government Lent Property
GLP . . . . Guide Line Paper (of Washington Standardization Officers) (Military)
GLPA . . . . . . Great Lakes Pilotage Administration (Department of Transportation)
GLQ . . . . Greater than Lot Quantities
GLR . . . . Glass LASER Rod
GLR . . . . Graphic Level Recorder
GLR . . . . Grolier, Inc. (NYSE symbol)
GLRC . . . . Gas-Liquid Radiochromatography (Chemical/biochemical analysis)
GLS . . . . General Lighting Service
GLS . . . . Graduate Library School
GLS . . . . Great Lakes Screw
GLS . . . . Green LASER System
GLS . . . . Gypsy Lore Society
GLSA . . . . General Ledger Subsidiary Account
GLSA . . . . Great Lakes Seaplane Association
GLSM . . . . . . Gold Life Saving Medal
GLT . . . . Gas LASER Tube
GLT . . . . Guide Light
GLU . . . . Gambia Labour Union
GLU . . . . Global Land Use (NASA)
GLU . . . . Glutamic Acid (Amino acid)
GLV . . . . Gemini Launch Vehicle (NASA)
GLV . . . . Globe Valve
GLV . . . . Gross Leukemia Virus
GLW . . . . Corning Glass Works (NYSE symbol) (Wall Street slang name: "Glow Worm")
GLWB . . . . . . Glazed Wallboard (Technical drawings)
GLY . . . . Glycine (Amino acid)
GLZ . . . . General Bronze Corporation (NYSE symbol) (Delisted)
GM . . . . Gainesville Midland R. R. (AAR code)
GM . . . . Geheimer Mitarbeiter
GM . . . . Geiger-Mueller (Counter)
GM . . . . General Maintenance (Army)
GM . . . . General Manager
GM . . . . General Medicine
GM . . . . General Merchandise
GM . . . . General Mortgage (Bonds)
GM . . . . General Motors Corporation (NYSE symbol)
GM . . . . Gentil Membre (Guest of Club Mediterranee, a vacation cooperative)
GM . . . . Geometric Mean
GM . . . . George Medal (British)
GM . . . . Gold Medal
GM . . . . Good Morning (Amateur radio)
GM . . . . Gradient Mixer (Chromatography)
GM . . . . Gram (Metric)
GM . . . . Grand Master (Masonry)
GM . . . . Greenwich Meridian
GM . . . . Grid Modulation
GM . . . . Ground Malfunction
GM . . . . Guard Mail
GM . . . . Guided Missile
GM . . . . Gunmetal
GM . . . . Gunner's Mate
G/M . . . . Guided Missile
GMA . . . . . . Gas Metal Arc
GMA . . . . General Mental Ability
GMA . . . . Glycol Methacrylate
GMA . . . . Government Modification Authorization

GMA . . . . . . Grocery Manufacturers of America
GMA . . . . Guided Missile Ammunition
GMAA . . . . . . Gold Mining Association of America
GMAC . . . . . . General Motors Acceptance Corporation
GMAD . . . . . . General Motors, Allison Division
GMAD . . . . . . General Motors Assembly Division
GMAIC . . . . . Guided Missile and Aerospace Intelligence Committee
GMAJCOM . . Gaining Major Command (Military)
GMAT . . . . . . Greenwich Mean Astronomical Time
GMAW . . . . . Gas Metal Arc Welding
GMB . . . . General Mortgage Bond
GMB . . . . Good Merchantable Brand
GMB . . . . Grand Master of the Bath (British)
GMB . . . . Guided Missile Brigade (Army)
GMBE . . . . . . Grand Master of the (Order of the) British Empire
GmbH . . . . . . Gesellschaft mit Beschraenkter Haftung (Company with limited liability)
GMBL . . . . . . Gimbal
GMC . . . . General Medical Council (British)
GMC . . . . General Military Course
GMC . . . . General Monte Carlo Code (Data processing)
GMC . . . . General Motors Corporation
GMC . . . . Georgia Military College
GMC . . . . Gordon Military College (Georgia)
GMC . . . . Ground Mobile Cenetheodolite
GMC . . . . Guided Missile Committee
GMC . . . . Guided Missile Control
GMC . . . . Gun Motor Carriage
GMCB . . . . . . Gunner's Mate, Construction Battalion (Navy rating)
GMCBG . . . . . Gunner's Mate, Construction Battalion, Armorer (Navy rating)
GMCBP . . . . . Gunner's Mate, Construction Battalion, Powderman (Navy rating)
GMCF . . . . . . Guided Missile Control Facility
GMCM . . . . . . Guided Missile Counter-Measures
GMCO . . . . . Guided Missile Control Officer
GMD . . . . General Medical Corp. (NYSE symbol)
GMD . . . . Geometric Mean Distance
GMD . . . . Geometrodynamics
GMD . . . . Ground Meteorological Detector
GMD . . . . Guided Missile Division
GMDEP . . . . . Guided Missile Data Exchange Program (Navy)
GMDRL . . . . . General Motors Defense Research Laboratory
GMDS . . . . . . German Military Documents Section (of AGO, Army) (World War II)
GME . . . . General Micro-Electronics
GME . . . . German Minimum Economy (Allied German Occupation Forces)
GME . . . . Gilt Marbled Edges (Paper)
GME . . . . Guided Missile Evaluator
GMF . . . . Glass Manufacturers Federation
GMF . . . . Guided Missile Facilities
GMFC . . . . . . Guided Missile Fire Control
GMFCS . . . . . Guided Missile Fire Control System
GMI . . . . General Motors Institute (Company-financed engineering school)
GMIA . . . . . . Gelatin Manufacturers Institute of America
GMIE . . . . . . Grand Master of the Order of the Indian Empire (British)
GMIP . . . . . . General Motors Improvement Project (Investigating team sponsored by consumer-advocate Ralph Nader)
GMJC . . . . . . Green Mountain Junior College (Vermont)
GMK . . . . Gyromagnetic Kompass
GML . . . . Galvanometer-Mirror Lightbeam
GML . . . . Guided Missile Laboratory
GML . . . . Guided Missile Launcher
GMLS . . . . . . Guided Missile Launching System
GMMA . . . . . Gloucester Master Mariners Association
GMMG . . . . . Grand Master of the Order of St. Michael and St. George
GMMTA . . . . . Groupement des Moyens Militaires de Transport Aerien (France)
GMO . . . . . . Gill-Morrell Oscillator
GMO . . . . . . Gulf, Mobile & Ohio R. R. (AAR code)
GM & O . . . . Gulf, Mobile & Ohio Railroad Company (Later, Illinois Central Gulf Railroad)
GMOO . . . . . Guided Missile Operations Officer
GMP . . . . Garrison Military Police (British)
GMP . . . . Good Manufacturing Practices (FDA)
GMP . . . . Grand Master of the Order of St. Patrick
GMP . . . . Grass Model Polygraph
GMP . . . . Guanine Monophosphate
GMPR . . . . . . General Maximum Price Regulation (World War II)
GMQ . . . . . . Good Marketable Quality
GMR . . . . . . General Mobilization Reserves
GMR . . . . Geometric Mean Radii
GMR . . . . Ground Mapping RADAR
GMR . . . . Ground Mobile RADAR
GMR . . . . Ground Movement RADAR
GMRMR . . . . . General Mobilization Reserve Materiel Requirement

GMRS........ General Mobilization Reserve Stock
GMRSO ..... General Mobilization Reserve Stockage Objective
GMRWG ..... Guided Missile Relay Working Group (Navy)
GMS .... Gas Measurement System
GMS .... Gelatin Matrix System
GMS .... Gemini Mission Simulator
GMS .... General Material Services
GMS .... General Medical Services
GMS .... General Military Science
GMS .... General Milk Sales
GMS .... Generation Management Station
GMS .... Gravitational Mass Sensor
GMS .... Gravity Measuring System
GMS .... Ground Maintenance Support
GMS........ Ground Mapping (or Marking) System
GMS .... Guidance Monitor Set (Aerospace)
GMS .... Guided Missile School
GMS .... Guided Missile System
GM & S ..... General Medicine and Surgery
GMSA .... German Minesweeping Administration (Allied German Occupation Forces)
GMSER ...... Guided Missile Service Report
GMSI .... Grand Master of the Order of the Star of India (British)
GMSO ...... German Mine Supplies Organization (Allied German Occupation Forces)
GMSR .... Guided Missile Service Record
GMSR .... Gunner's Mate, Ship Repair (Navy rating)
GMSRP...... Gunner's Mate, Ship Repair, Powderman (Navy rating)
GMST....... General Military Subjects Test
GMSU ...... General Maritime Stevedores' Union (Philippines)
GMSU ...... Guided Missile Service Unit (Air Force)
GMT .... Gas Missile Tube
GMT .... Geiger-Mueller Tube
GMT .... General American Transportation Corporation (NYSE symbol)
GMT .... General Military Training
GMT .... Geo-Marine Technology
GMT .... Greenwich Mean Time
GMT .... Guided Missile Target
GMTC ...... Glutamate Manufacturers Technical Committee
GMTI .... Ground Moving Target Indicator
GMTOA ..... Green Mountain Textile Overseers Association
GMTRB...... General Military Training Review Board
GMTS....... Guided Missile Test Set
GMU .... Guided Missile Unit
GMV .... Gram Molecular Volume
GMV .... Guaranteed Minimum Value
GMVL ...... Geldersche Maatschappij van Landbouw (Netherlands)
GMW .... Gram Molecular Weight
GMW .... Guevara-McInteer-Wageman
GMZFO ..... Gouvernement Militaire de la Zone Francaise d'Occupation (Military Government of the French Zone of Occupation) (of Germany)
GN .... Golden Number (Number used to fix the date of Easter)
GN .... Good Night (Amateur radio)
GN .... Grand National (Automobile racing)
GN .... Great Northern Railway Company (NYSE symbol) (Delisted)
GN .... Green (Maps and charts)
G:N........ Glucose:Nitrogen (Ratio)
G & N...... Guidance and Navigation (System) (Apollo) (NASA)
G in N ..... Graduate in Nursing
GNA .... Graysonia, Nashville & Ashdown R. R. (AAR code)
GNAT ...... General Numerical Analysis of Transport (Computer program)
GNB .... Gould National Batteries, Inc. (NYSE symbol) (Later, GLD)
GNC .... General Nursing Council
GNC .... Global Navigation and Planning Chart (Air Force)
GNC .... Goddard Network Control (NASA)
GN & C..... Guidance, Navigation, and Control
GNCCA ..... Grand National Curling Club of America
GNCS ...... Guidance, Navigation and Control System
GND .... Ground
GNE .... Gross National Effluent
GNE .... Guidance and Navigation Equipment
GNEC ...... General Nuclear Engineering Corporation
GNEM ...... Global Network for Environmental Monitoring
GNESIT...... Greater New England Society of Inhalation Therapists
GNF .... Gannett Newspaper Foundation
GNFMS ..... Gaseous Nitrogen Flow Measuring System
GNG .... Gaussian Noise Generator
GNH .... Grand National Hunt (British)
GNI........ Great Northern Iron Ore Properties (NYSE symbol)
GNI .... Gross National Income (Economics)
GNL .... Georgia Nuclear Laboratory (AEC)
GNMA ...... Government National Mortgage Association (Nickname: "Ginnie Mae")
GNMS ...... Gaseous Nitrogen Measuring System

GNN .... Ginn & Company (NYSE symbol) (Delisted)
GNN .... Great Northern Nekoosa Corp. (NYSE symbol)
GNO .... Gino's Inc. (NYSE symbol)
GNP .... Gas, Nonpersistent
GNP .... Gross National Product (Economics)
GNR .... Gaseous Nuclear Rocket
GNR .... Great Northern Railway (British)
GNR .... Gunner
GNRA ...... Gateway National Recreation Area (New York) (Department of the Interior)
GNRE....... Gross National Recreation Experience (Refers to cost of recreation in relation to gross national product)
GNRP....... General Neighborhood Renewal Plan
GNRY ...... Great Northern Railway
GNRY....... Gunnery
GNS .... Grain Neutral Spirits (Alcohol)
GNSH ...... Grey Nuns of the Sacred Heart (Roman Catholic religious order)
GNSR ...... Great North of Scotland Railway
GNTC ...... Girls' Naval Training Corps (British)
GNV .... Gesellschaft fuer Nukleare Verfahrenstechnik (Commercial firm)
GNW .... Genesee & Wyoming R. R. (AAR code)
GNY .... German Navy
GNYCFS..... Greater New York Council for Foreign Students
GO .... Gasoffizier (Gas Officer) (German military - World War II)
GO .... General Office(r)
GO .... General Order(s)
GO .... Generaloberst (Full general) (German military - World War II)
GO .... Gentil Organisateur (Employee of Club Mediterranee, a vacation cooperative)
GO .... Government Operations Committee (US Senate)
GO .... Graphitic Oxide
GO .... Guest Option (Hotel plan, Hilton hotels)
GO .... Gulf Oil Corporation (NYSE symbol)
GOA .... General Operating Agency
GOA .... Government-Owned Aircraft
GOA .... Group, Operations Analysis (Air Force)
GOAD ...... Group of Ancient Drama
GOALS...... General Operations and Logistics Simulation (Boeing)
GOAT ...... Gerber Oscillogram Amplitude Translator
GOAT ...... Goes Over All Terrain (Vehicle)
GOATS...... Group Operational Access Tester System (AT & T)
GOB........ General Officers Branch (Air Force)
GOB .... Glass Oceanographic Buoy
GOB .... Ground Order of Battle
GOBC ...... Ground Observer Corps (Canada)
GOBEP ..... Generalized One-Boson Exchange Potential
GOBSII ..... Gabungan Organisasi Buruh Serikat Islam Indonesia (Federation of Indonesian Moslem Trade and Labor Unions)
GOC .... Gas-Operated Core
GOC .... General Officer Commanding
GOC .... Grosseinkaufsgesellschaft Osterreichischer Consumvereine
GOC .... Ground Observer Corps
GOC .... Gulf Oil Company
GOC .... Gunnery Officer's Console (Army)
GOCAP ..... Graphic Output Circuit Analysis Program
GOCC ...... Geodetic Operations Control Center (NASA)
GOCO ...... Government-Owned, Contractor-Operated (Facility)
GO/CO ..... Government-Owned / Contractor-Operated (Facility)
GOCOM..... General Officer Command (US Army Reserve)
GOCR ...... Gated-Off Controlled Rectifier
GOD .... Government-Owned Depot
GOE .... Gas, Oxygen, Ether (Anesthesiology)
GOE .... Government-Owned Equipment
GOE .... Ground Operation Equipment
GOE/RPIE.... Ground Operational Equipment/Real Property Installed Equipment
GOES....... Geostationary Operational (or Orbit) Environmental Satellite (Environmental Science Services Administration)
GOF .... Good Old Friday (Slang)
GOF .... Government-Owned Facility
GOFAR ..... Global Ocean Floor Analysis and Research (Navy)
GOGO ...... Government-Owned, Government-Operated
GOH .... German Order of Harugari
GOI........ Government of Indonesia
GOI .... Government-Owned Installation
GOK .... God Only Knows (Facetious diagnosis for a puzzling medical case)
GOM .... God's Medicine; also, God's Own Medicine (Morphine) (Slang)
GOM .... Government-Owned Material
GOM ...... Grand Old Man (A venerated man, especially in a specific field)
GOMA ...... Good Outdoor Manners Association
GOMAC ..... Government Microcircuit Applications Conference
GOMAC ..... Groupement des Opticiens du Marche Commun (Common Market Opticians' Group)

GOMALCO . . . Gobel O'Malley Company (Entertainer George Gobel's firm; O'Malley is business manager)
GOO . . . . Get Oil Out (An organization in Santa Barbara, California)
GOOD EGGS . . Geriatric Order of Old Dolls Who Encourage the Generation Gap Singlemindedly (Tongue-in-cheek teachers' organization)
GOOS . . . . . . Gunnery Officers Ordnance School
GOP . . . . General Operational Plot
GOP . . . . General Outpost (Army)
GOP . . . . Government-Owned Property
GOP . . . . . . Grand Old Party (The Republican Party)
GOP . . . . . . Ground Observer Post
GOPL . . . . . . General Outpost Line
GOR . . . . . . General Ocean Research (Navy ship symbol)
GOR . . . . . . General Operating Room
GOR . . . . . . General Operational Requirements (Army)
GOR . . . . . . Gordon Jewelry Corp. (NYSE symbol)
GORF . . . . . Goddard's Optical Research Facility (Goddard Space Flight Center)
GORG . . . . . General Officers Review Group (Air Force)
GORID . . . . . Ground Optical Recorder for Intercept Determination
GORX . . . . . Graphite Oxidation from Reactor Excursion (Engineering computer code)
GOS . . . . . . General Operating Specification (Air Materiel Command)
GOS . . . . . . Geodetic Optical System
GOS . . . . . . Global Observing Systems (Weather)
GOSP . . . . . Golden Spike National Historic Site
GOSPLAN . . . From the Russian for Central Planning Commission
GOSS. . . . . . Ground Operational Support System (MSFC)
GOSSTRAKH . . Gosudarstvennoe Strakhovanie (State insurance) (USSR)
GOST . . . . . . Goddard Satellite Tracking
GOT . . . . . . Glutamic Oxaloacetic Transaminase (Biochemistry)
GOTS . . . . . Gravity-Oriented Test Satellite (NASA)
GOU . . . . . . General Outdoor Advertising Company, Inc. (NYSE symbol) (Delisted)
GOU . . . . . . Grupo de Oficiales Unidos (Group of United Officers) (Argentine)
GOV . . . . . . Generator Output Voltage
GOV . . . . . . Governor
GOVMAR . . . Governor, Marshall Islands
GOVT. . . . . . Government
GOX . . . . . . Gaseous Oxygen
GOYA . . . . . Greek Orthodox Youth of America
GP. . . . . Games Played (Hockey)
GP . . . . Gas, Persistent
GP. . . . . General Paresis (or Paralysis) (Medicine)
GP. . . . . General Pause (Music)
GP. . . . . General Practice (or Practitioner) (of medicine)
GP. . . . . General Provision
GP . . . . General Public (Merchandising slang)
GP . . . . General Purpose (Military)
GP . . . . Generalized Programming
GP . . . . Geographical Position
GP . . . . Geometric Progression
GP. . . . . Georgia-Pacific Corporation (NYSE symbol)
GP. . . . . Giant Pulse
GP. . . . . Gimbal Package
GP. . . . . Gimbal Platform
GP. . . . . Gimbal Point
GP. . . . . Glide Path
GP. . . . . Gloria Patri (Glory to the Father)
GP . . . . Glucose Phosphate
GP. . . . . Glycerophosphate
GP. . . . . Glycolyl Phthalate
GP. . . . . Government Property
GP. . . . . Graded Program
GP. . . . . Grand Passion
GP. . . . . Gratitude Patient (A nonpaying patient) (Medical slang)
GP. . . . . Great Primer
GP. . . . . Ground Pneumatic
GP. . . . . Group
GP . . . . Guinea Pig
GP . . . . Gun Pointer (Naval gunnery)
GP. . . . . Gyro Package
GP. . . . . Movie Rating for "Parental Guidance Suggested (All Ages Admitted)" (Later, PG)
GP (Gas). . . . . Persistent Chemical Agent Gas
GPA . . . . . . General Passenger Agent
GPA . . . . . . General Public Assistance (A form of public charity)
GPA. . . . . . . General Purchasing Agency (Allied German Occupation Forces)
GPA . . . . . . General-Purpose Amplifier
GPA . . . . . . Glycerine Producers Association
GPA . . . . . . Grade-Point Average (Education)
GPA . . . . . . Ground Plane Antenna
GPA . . . . . . Grounded Plate Amplifier
GPA . . . . . . Guidance Platform Assembly (Military)

GPAD . . . . . . Gallons Per Acre (per) Day (Irrigation)
GPAS . . . . . . General-Purpose Airborne Simulator
GPAT . . . . . . General-Purpose Automatic Test
GPATS . . . . . General-Purpose Automatic Test System (Air Force)
GPB . . . . General-Purpose Buffer
GPB . . . . Geon Process Butadiene
GPB . . . . . . Government Patents Board (Functions transferred to Secretary of Commerce, 1961)
GPBS . . . . . . Gas Pressure Bending System
GPC . . . . . . Gallons Per Capita
GPC . . . . . . Gauge Pressure Control
GPC . . . . . . Gel Permeation Chromatography
GPC . . . . . . General-Purpose Computer
GPC. . . . . . . Genuine Parts Company (NYSE symbol)
GPC . . . . . . Geocentric Pendulum Control
GPC . . . . . . Ghana Publishing Company
GPC . . . . . . Golay Pneumatic Cell
GPC . . . . . . Ground Power Contactor
GPC . . . . . . Gypsum-Plaster Ceiling (Technical drawings)
GPCA . . . . . Great Pyrenees Club of America
GPCD . . . . . Gallons Per Capita (per) Day
GPC-ERR. . . . General Passenger Committee-Eastern Railroads
GPCP . . . . . Great Plains Conservation Program
GPCR . . . . . Great Proletarian Cultural Revolution (Red China)
GPCT . . . . . George Peabody College for Teachers (Tennessee)
GPD. . . . . . . Gallons Per Day
GPDC . . . . . General-Purpose Digital Computer
GPDS . . . . . General Purpose Display System
GPE . . . . . . Gas Power Exchange
GPE . . . . . . General Precision Equipment Corporation (NYSE symbol) (Delisted)
GPE . . . . . . General-Purpose Equipment
Gp E . . . . . . Geophysical Engineer (An academic degree)
Gp Engr . . . . . Geophysical Engineer
GPER . . . . . General Plant Equipment Requirements
GPERF . . . . . Ground Passive Electronic Reconnaissance Facility
GPES . . . . . Ground Proximity Extraction System
GPF . . . . . . Gas Proof
GPF . . . . . . General-Purpose Forces
GPF . . . . . . Generalized Production Function (Industrial economics)
GPF . . . . . . Geuder, Paeschke & Frey Company
GPF . . . . . . Groove between Parallel Folds
GPFL . . . . . Group Flashing (Navigation signal lights)
GPG . . . . . . Gaertnerische Produktionsgenossenschaft
GPG . . . . . . General Planning Group
GPG . . . . . . Grains Per Gallon (Unit of measure for water hardness)
GPH. . . . . . . Gallons Per Hour
G Ph . . . . . . Graduate in Pharmacy
GPHA. . . . . . Great Plains Historical Association (Later, IGP)
GPI . . . . General Paralysis of the Insane is literal meaning, but is also medical slang for eccentricity
GPI . . . . General Precision, Incorporated
GPI . . . . General-Purpose Interface
GPI . . . . Gingival-Periodontal Index (Dentistry)
GPI . . . . Grain Products Irradiator (AEC)
GPI . . . . Ground Point of Intercept
GPI . . . . Ground Position Indicator (Dead-reckoning computer)
GPIN . . . . . . Groupement Professionnel de l'Industrie Nucleaire (Belgium) (Also known as NIC)
GPIP . . . . . . Glide Path Intercept Point
GPL . . . . . . General Precision Laboratory
GPL . . . . . . Geographic Position Locator (Navigation)
GPL . . . . . . Giant Pulse LASER
GPL . . . . . . Gimbal Pickoff Loop
GPLD . . . . . Government Property Lost or Destroyed (or Damaged)
GPLS . . . . . Giant Pulse LASER System
GPM . . . . . . Gallons Per Mile
GPM . . . . . . Gallons Per Minute
GPM . . . . . . General-Purpose Missile
GPM . . . . . . Geopotential Meter
GPM . . . . . . Grand Past Master (Masonry)
GPM . . . . . . Groups (of code transmitted) Per Minute (or Message) (Communications)
GPMA . . . . . Gasoline Pump Manufacturers Association
GPMMA . . . . Grain Processing Machinery Manufacturers Association
GPMS. . . . . . Gross Performance Measuring System (Air Force)
GPN . . . . . . General Performance Number
GPN . . . . . . Glass Plate Negative
GPNITL . . . . . Great Plains National Instructional Television Library
GPO . . . . . . General Post Office (British)
GPO . . . . . . General-Purpose Oscilloscope
GPO . . . . . . Giant Portland Cement Company (NYSE symbol)
GPO . . . . . . Government Printing Office

GPOA	Guild of Prescription Opticians of America
GPOCC	Group Occulting (Navigation signal lights)
GPP	General Plant Projects
GPP	Great Northern Paper Company (NYSE symbol) (Later, GNN)
GPP	Ground Power Panel
GPP	Gyro Pitch Position
GPR	General-Purpose Radiometer
GPR	General-Purpose Receiver
GPR	General-Purpose Relay
GPRA	Gouvernement Provisionnel de la Republique Algerienne (Provisional Government of the Algerian Republic)
GPRA	Government Public Relations Association
GPRR	General-Purpose Radio Receiver
GPRT	General-Purpose Radio Transmitter
GPS	Gallons Per Second
GPS	General Problem Solver (Data processing)
GPS	General-Purpose Simulation
GPS	Generality and Problem Solving
GPS	Germany Philatelic Society
GPS	Ground Processing System (Aviation)
GPS	Guinea Pig Serum
GPS	Gyroscope Parameter Shift
GPSDIC	General-Purpose Scientific Document Image Code (System) (National Bureau of Standards)
GPSDW	General Purpose Scientific Document Writer (National Bureau of Standards)
GPSS	General Process Simulation Studies (or System)
GPSS	General-Purpose Simulation System
GPSSM	General-Purpose Surface-to-Surface Missile (Army)
GPSU	Ground Power Supply Unit (Aerospace)
GPT	General Portland Cement Company (NYSE symbol)
GPT	Geometric and Positional Tolerance (Drafting symbol)
GPT	Glass Precision Tubing
GPT	Glass Probe Thermistor
GPT	Glutamic-Pyruvic Transaminase (Biochemistry)
GPT	Grid Pool Tank
GPT	Guidance Position Tracking (Aerospace)
GPTE	General Purpose Test Equipment
GpTh	Group Therapy
GPTI	General-Purpose Terminal Interchanges (Airline communication system) (Raytheon Co.)
GPU	General Public Utilities Corp. (NYSE symbol)
GPU	Generating Power Unit
GPU	Gosudarstvennoe Politicheskoe Upravlenie (Government Political Administration) (Soviet secret service organization, also known as OGPU)
GPU	Ground Power Unit
GPV	General Public Service Corporation (NYSE symbol) (Delisted)
GPV	Gereformeerd Politiek Verbond
GPV	Gyroscope Pickoff Voltage
GPVB	General-Purpose Video Buffer
GPVEH	General-Purpose Vehicle
GPW	Geneva Convention Relative to Treatment of Prisoners of War, 12 August 1949 (Army)
GPW	Georgia Power Co. (NYSE symbol)
GPW	Great Plains Wheat, Inc.
GPW	Gypsum-Plaster Wall (Technical drawings)
GPW 1929	Geneva Convention Relative to the Treatment of Prisoners of War, 27 July 1929 (Army)
GPX	Generalized Programming Extended
GPX	Greyhound Package Express
GPY	General Plywood Corporation (American Stock Exchange symbol)
GQ	General Quarters (General Alert) (Navy)
GQ	Gentlemen's Quarterly (A publication)
GQ	Grumman Corporation (NYSE symbol)
GQA	Get (or Give) Quick Answer
GQG	Grand Quartier-General (French GHQ)
GR	Gamma Ray
GR	Gas Ratio
GR	Geared Radial (Aircraft engine)
GR	General Radio
GR	General Reconnaissance (Marine Corps)
GR	General Research
GR	General Reserve
GR	Georgius Rex (King George of England)
GR	German Reports
GR	Germanium Rectifier
GR	Goodrich (B. F.) Company (NYSE symbol)
GR	Government Regulation
GR	Government Report
GR	Grab Rod
GR	Grand Recorder
GR	Grasse River R. R. Corporation (AAR code)
GR	Graves Registration (Military)
GR	Greece (NATO)
GR	Grid Resistor
GR	Grid Return
GR	Grooved Roofing (Lumber)
GR	Ground Range
GR	Group Report
GR	Gunnery Range
G-R	Goldbarg-Rutenberg (Enzyme unit)
GR's	Government Regulations
GRA	Gamma Ray Amplification
GRA	Governmental Research Association
GRA	Grace (W. R.) & Company (NYSE symbol)
GRA	Graduate Research Assistant
GRA	Grant Aid (Military)
GRA	Grass Roots Association
GRA	Guild for Religious Architecture
GRA	Gyro Reference Assembly
GRAAL	Graph Algorithm (Data processing)
GRACE	Graphic Arts Composing Equipment
GRACE	Group Routing and Charging Equipment (British)
GRACO	Gray Company, Inc.
GRAD	Gradient
GRAD	Graduate
GRAD	Graduate Resume Accumulation and Distribution (Data processing)
GRAE	Gouvernement de la Republique de l'Angola en Exile (Government of the Republic of Angola in Exile)
GRAF	Graphic Addition to FORTRAN (Data processing)
GRAID	Graphical Aid (Data processing)
GRAP	Greatest Response Amplitude Probability
GRAPD	Greatest Response Amplitude Probability Data
GRAPE	Gamma Ray Attenuation Porosity Evaluator
GRAPE	Graphical Analysis of Program Execution (Data processing)
GRAR	Government Report Authorization and Record
GRAR	Grinding Arbor
GRARR	Goddard Range and Range Rate (Tracking system) (NASA)
GRAS	Generally Recognized (or Regarded) As Safe (FDA term)
GRASER	Gamma Ray Amplification by Stimulated Emission of Radiation
GRASP	Generalized Retrieval and Storage Program
GRASP	Greater Rensselaer Alcoholic Service Project
GRASS	Ground-to-Air Scanner Surveillance
GRB	Geophysics Research Board
GRB	Government Reservation Bureau
GRB	Granatbuechse (Antitank grenade rifle) (German military - World War II)
GRBDS	Gyroscopes-Rate Bomb-Direction System
GRBM	Global Range Ballistic Missile (Air Force)
GRC	Gale Research Company
GRC	Gerontology Research Center (HEW)
GRC	Government of the Republic of China
GRC	Granite City Steel Company (NYSE symbol) (Delisted)
GRC	Guard Ring Capacitor
GRCA	Golden Retriever Club of America
GRCA	Grand Canyon National Park
GRCD	German Rhine Coordinating Directorate (Allied German Occupation Forces)
GrCr	Grande Croix
GRCSW	Graduate Research Center of the Southwest (Formerly, Southwest Center for Advanced Studies)
GRD	Geophysics Research Directorate (US)
GRD	Greatest Response Data
GRD	Ground Detector
GRD	Ground Resolved Distance (Satellite camera)
GRDF	Gypsum Roof Deck Foundation (Technical drawings)
GRE	Gamma Ray Experiment
GRE	Graduate Record Examination (Higher education)
GRE	Graduate Reliability Engineering
GRE	Ground Reconstruction Electronics (Used in photographing moon) (NASA)
GRE	Gulf Resources & Chemical Corp. (NYSE symbol)
GREB	Galactic Radiation Experiment Background Satellite (Navy transit satellite)
GRED	Generalized Random Extract Device (Data processing)
GREEN	Guild to Revive Exhausted Nurses
GREMAS	Genealogische Recherche mit Magnetband-Speicherung (Organic chemistry coding system)
GREMEX	Goddard Research Engineering Management Exercise (NASA)
GREPAT	Greenland Patrol (Navy)
GRETI	Groupe Romand pou l'Etude des Techniques d'Instruction (Switzerland)
GRF	Garbell Research Foundation
GRF	Gelatin, Resorcinol, and Formaldehyde
GRF	Golden Rule Foundation
GRF	Grassland Research Foundation

GRF . . . . Gravity Research Foundation
GRF . . . . Ground Repetition Frequency
GRFMA . . . . . Grand Rapids Furniture Market Association
GRFO . . . . Gun Range Finder Operator
GRFX . . . . Grinding Fixture
GRG . . . . Gastroenterology Research Group
GRH . . . . Greer Hydraulics, Inc. (American Stock Exchange symbol)
GRHQU . . . . . Gruppen-Hauptquartier (Group Headquarters) (German military – World War II)
GRI . . . . Gospel Recordings, Incorporated
GRI . . . . Government of the Ryukyu Islands
GRI . . . . Gravure Research Institute
GRI . . . . Guaranteed Retirement Income
GR-I . . . . Government Rubber-Isobutylene
GR et I . . . . . . Georgius Rex et Imperator (George, King and Emperor) (British)
GRID . . . . . . Graphic Remote Integrated Display
GRID . . . . Graphic Reproduction by Integrated Design
GRIN . . . . Graphical Input (Language) (Data processing)
GRIN . . . . Grapline Input (Data processing)
GRIN-2 . . . . . Graphical Interaction (Language) (Data processing)
GRINS . . . . . . General Retrieval Inquiry Negotiation Structure
GRIP . . . . Gemini Reentry Integration Program (Aerospace)
GRIPHOS . . . General Retrieval and Information Processor for Humanities Oriented Studies
GRIT . . . . Graduated Reduction in Tensions (Cold War term)
GRITS . . . . . . Goddard Range (and Range Rate) Instrumentation Tracking System (NASA)
GRJC . . . . Grand Rapids Junior College (Michigan)
GRL . . . . General Instrument Corporation (NYSE symbol)
GRL . . . . Grundrichtungslinie (Base line, a gunnery term) (German military – World War II)
GRM . . . . Global Range Missile
GRM . . . . Guarded Relay Multiplexer
GRM . . . . Guidance Rate Measurement
Gr N . . . . Graduate Nurse
GRN . . . . Gram-Negative (Bacteriology)
GRN . . . . Greenville & Northern R. R. (AAR code)
GRNC . . . . . . Group Number No Count (Military communication)
GRNR . . . . . . Grand River Railway Company (AAR code)
GRO . . . . General Routine Order(s)
GROCAP . . . . Gross Capability Estimator (Air Force)
GROOVE . . . . Generated Real-Time Output Operations on Voltage-Controlled Equipment (Data processing)
GROPAC . . . . Group Pacific
GROW . . . . . . Group Relations Ongoing Workshops
GRP . . . . Gamma Ray Projector
GRP . . . . Gaussian Random Process
GRP . . . . Gelatin Rigidized Panel
GRP . . . . Glass-Reinforced Plastic
GRP . . . . Gram-Positive (Bacteriology)
GRP . . . . Greatest Response Probability
GRP . . . . Ground Relay Panel (Aerospace)
GRP . . . . Grundrichtungspunkt (Base point, a gunnery term) (German military – World War II)
GRPJ . . . . Glass-Reinforced Plastic Joint
GRQU . . . . . . Gran Quivira National Monument
GRR . . . . Geneva Radio Regulations
GRR . . . . Georgetown R. R. (AAR code)
GRR . . . . Greek Research Reactor
GRREG . . . . . Graves Registration (Military)
GRRR . . . . . . Goddard Range and Range Rate
GRS . . . . Gamma Radiation Source
GRS . . . . Gamma Radiation Spectrometer
GRS . . . . Gamma Ray Spectrum
GRS . . . . General Radio Service (Canada)
GRS . . . . German Research Satellite (NASA)
GRS . . . . Government Rubber Styrene (A plastic substitute for rubber) (World War II)
GRS . . . . Grass (Maps and charts)
GRS . . . . Graves Registration Service (Military)
GRS . . . . Gravity Reference Signal (or System)
GRS . . . . Gyro Reference System (Aerospace)
GRSA . . . . . . Great Sand Dunes National Monument
GRSE . . . . . . Gamma Ray Spectrometric Equipment
GRSM . . . . . . Great Smoky Mountains National Park
GRSP . . . . . Glass-Reinforced Structural Plastic
GRT . . . . Gamma Ray Telescope
GRT . . . . Gamma Ray Tube
GRT . . . . Gross Registered Tons (Navigation)
GRT . . . . Ground Resistance Tester
GRTC . . . . . . Green River Test Complex
GRTE . . . . . . Grand Teton National Park
GRTM . . . . . . Geared Roller Test Machine

GRU . . . . Glavnoe Razvedivatelnoe Upravlenie (Chief Administration for Intelligence) (Division of the General Staff of the Soviet Army) (USSR)
GRUB . . . . . . Grocery Update and Billing
GrUff . . . . . . Grand Ufficiale (Grand Officer)
GRW . . . . General Railway Warrants (US Military Government, Germany)
GRW . . . . Greater Washington Investors, Inc. (NYSE symbol)
GRWS . . . . . . Gimbaled Reaction Wheel Scanner
GRWT . . . . . Gross Weight
GRX . . . . General Refractories Company (NYSE symbol)
GRY . . . . Gray Drug Stores, Inc. (NYSE symbol)
GS . . . . Galvanized Steel
GS . . . . Games Started (Baseball)
GS . . . . Gap Separation
GS . . . . Gastric Shield
GS . . . . General Schedule (Federal employee job classification GS-1 to GS-18)
GS . . . . General Secretary
GS . . . . General Semantics
GS . . . . General Sessions
GS . . . . General Service is literal translation, but used in sense of "excessively keen," or "overly acute" (British Army)
GS . . . . General Staff (Military)
GS . . . . General Superintendent
GS . . . . General Support (Army)
GS . . . . Geochemical Society
GS . . . . Geological Survey (Department of the Interior)
GS . . . . German Silver
GS . . . . Gerontological Society
GS . . . . Gillette Company (NYSE symbol)
GS . . . . Girl Scouts of the USA
GS . . . . Glide Slope (Aviation)
GS . . . . Gold Standards
GS . . . . Government Service
GS . . . . Grade System
GS . . . . Grammar School
GS . . . . Grand Secretary
GS . . . . Grand Steward (Masonry)
GS . . . . Grandson
GS . . . . Ground Speed (Aviation)
GS . . . . Ground Station (Aerospace)
gs . . . . Group Specific (Antigen)
GS . . . . Group Structured (Counseling Group)
GS . . . . Guardship
GS . . . . Guidance Station (or System) (Aerospace)
GS . . . . Gunnery School (Air Force)
GS . . . . Gunnery Sergeant
GS . . . . Gyrostabilizer
G/S . . . . General Support (Military)
G-S . . . . Gallard-Schlesinger (Chemical manufacturing corporation)
GSA . . . . Garden Seed Association
GSA . . . . General Services Administration
GSA . . . . Genetics Society of America
GSA . . . . Geological Society of America
GSA . . . . Germanistic Society of America
GSA . . . . Girl Scouts of America
GSA . . . . Glide Slope Antenna
GSA . . . . Gourd Society of America
GSA . . . . Gross Soluble Antigen
GSA . . . . Guild of Saint Alban
GSAP . . . . . . Gun Sight Aiming Point
GSB . . . . Gold Surface Barrier
GSB . . . . Grand Sword-Bearer (Masonry)
GSB . . . . Gypsum Sheathing Board (Technical drawings)
GSBI . . . . . . Gabungan Serikat Buruh Indonesia (Federation of Indonesian Trade Unions)
GSBR . . . . . Gravel-Surface Built-Up Roof (Technical drawings)
GSC . . . . General Staff Corps (Military)
GSC . . . . Geodetic Spacecraft
GSC . . . . Glenville State College (West Virginia)
GSC . . . . Group Study Course
GSC . . . . Guidance Shipping Container
GSC . . . . Guidance System Console (Aerospace)
GSCA . . . . . . Gordon Setter Club of America
GSCARNGARP . . General Staff Committees on Army National Guard and Army Reserve Policy
GSCC . . . . . . General Steel Casting Corporation
GSCO . . . . . . Guidance Sustainer Cut-Off (Aerospace)
GSCW . . . . . . General Society of Colonial Wars
GSCW . . . . . . Georgia State College for Women
GSD . . . . General Supply Depot
GSD . . . . General Support Division (Air Force)

GSD . . . . General Systems Division (of IBM)
GSD . . . . Grand Senior Deacon (Masonry)
GSDA . . . . . . Ground Speed Drift Angle
GSDB . . . . . . Geophysics & Space Data Bulletin (Air Force)
GSDC . . . . . . Get Set Day Care Program
GSDCA . . . . . German Shepherd Dog Club of America
GSDF . . . . . . Ground Self-Defense Force (Japan)
GSDFJ . . . . . . Ground Self-Defense Force Japan
GSDN . . . . . . Garden Supply Dealers National
GSDO . . . . . . General (Aviation) Safety District Office
GSDS . . . . . . Goldstone Duplicate Standard
GSE . . . . Ground Service Equipment (Air Force)
GSE . . . . Ground Support Equipment (Air Force)
GSECP . . . . . . Ground Support Engineering Change Proposal (Aerospace)
GSED . . . . . . Ground Support Equipment Division (Naval Air Engineering Center)
GSEE . . . . . . Geniki Synomospondia Ergaton Hellados (General Confederation of Greek Labor)
GSES . . . . . . Ground Support Equipment Section
GSETD . . . . . . General Systems Engineering and Technical Direction
GSF . . . . General Support Force (Air Force)
GSF . . . . Georgia Southern & Florida R. R. (AAR code)
GSF . . . . Grenade Safety Fuze
GSF . . . . Ground Support Facilities (Later, MGE) (Aerospace)
GSF . . . . Gulf Sea Frontier
GS & F . . . . . . Georgia Southern and Florida Railway Company
GSFC . . . . . . Goddard Space Flight Center (NASA)
GSFLT . . . . . . Graduate School Foreign Language Test
GSFSR . . . . . . Ground Safety and Flight Safety Requirements
GSFU . . . . . . Glazed Structural Facing Units (Technical drawings)
GSG . . . . Garment Salesmen's Guild of New York
GSG . . . . General Support Group (Army)
GSG . . . . Ground Systems Group
GSGS . . . . . . Geographical Section General Staff (British)
GSH . . . . Gas Space Heater
GSHR . . . . . . Gandhi Society for Human Rights
GSHR . . . . . . Grand Slam Home Runs (Baseball)
GSI . . . . General Safety Inspector (Aviation)
GSI . . . . General Service Infantry
GSI . . . . General Steel Industries, Inc. (NYSE symbol)
GSI . . . . Geophysical Service, Incorporated
GSI . . . . Government Source Inspection
GSI . . . . Ground-Speed Indicator
G & SI . . . . . . Gulf and Ship Island Railroad Company
GSISEA . . . . . Government Service Insurance System Employees' Association (Philippines)
GSK . . . . Gamble-Skogmo, Inc. (NYSE symbol)
GSK . . . . General Storekeeper (Navy)
GSK . . . . George S. Kaufman (American playwright, 1889-1961)
GSL . . . . Girls' Service League
GSL . . . . Great Somalia League
GSL . . . . Ground Systems Laboratory
GSM . . . . General Stores Material (Navy)
GSM . . . . Gold Star Mothers
GSM . . . . Ground Signal Mixer
GSM . . . . Guild of Saint Matthew
GSMD . . . . . . General Society of Mayflower Descendants
GSME . . . . . . Ground Support Maintenance Equipment
GSMFC . . . . . Gulf States Marine Fisheries Commission
GSNC . . . . . . General Steam Navigation Company (British)
GSO . . . . General Staff Officer
GSO . . . . Ground Safety Office(r) (Air Force)
GSO . . . . Ground-Speed Oscillator
GSO . . . . Ground Support Operations
GSO . . . . Gyro Storage Oven
GSOR . . . . . . General Staff Operational Requirements (Army)
GSP . . . . Genealogical Society of Pennsylvania
GSP . . . . General Semantic Problem
GSP . . . . General Strike for Peace
GSP . . . . Geodetic Satellite Program
GSP . . . . Girl Scouts of the Philippines
GSP . . . . Good-Service Pension (British Navy)
GSP . . . . Graphic Subroutine Package (Data processing)
GSPA . . . . . . Grain Sorghum Producers Association
GSPCA . . . . . German Shorthaired Pointer Club of America
GSPO . . . . . . Gemini Spacecraft Project Office (NASA)
GSPO . . . . . . Ground Systems Project Office
GSQ . . . . Generalized Sinusoidal Quantity
GSQC . . . . . . Ground Surveillance Qualification Course (Army)
GSR . . . . Galvanic Skin Response (Physiology)
GSR . . . . Galvanic Stimulation Rate
GSR . . . . General Service Recruit
GSR . . . . General Support Reinforcing (Army)

GSR . . . . Germanium Stack Rectifier
GSR . . . . Glide Slope Receiver
GSR . . . . Green Shoe Manufacturing Company (NYSE symbol)
GSR . . . . Grid Space Relay
GSR . . . . Ground Surveillance RADAR
GSR . . . . Group Selective Register
GSS . . . . General Service School (Army)
GSS . . . . General Supply Schedule
GSS . . . . Geo-Stationary Satellite
GSS . . . . Gilbert and Sullivan Society
GSS . . . . Global Satellite System
GSS . . . . Global Surveillance System (Air Force)
GSS . . . . Ground Support Systems (Aerospace)
GSSF . . . . . . General Supply Stock Fund (Air Force)
GSSF . . . . . . Ground Special Security Forces
GSSO . . . . . . General Stores Supply Office
GSSq . . . . . . Geodetic Survey Squadron (Air Force)
GSSR . . . . . . Ground Support System Review (Aerospace)
GSSS . . . . . . Ground Support System Specification (Aerospace)
GST . . . . Flying Boat (Russian aircraft symbol)
GST . . . . General Staff with Troops
GST . . . . Genstar, Ltd. (NYSE symbol)
GST . . . . Geographical Specialist Team (Army)
GST . . . . Gesellschaft fuer Sport und Technik
GST . . . . Greenwich Sidereal Time
GST . . . . Ground Sensor Terminal
GSTC . . . . . . Gorham State Teachers College (Maine)
GSTS . . . . . . German Student Travel Service
GSU . . . . General Service Unit (Marine Corps)
GSU . . . . General Support Unit (Army)
GSU . . . . Geographically Separated Units (Military)
GSU . . . . Glazed Structural Unit (Technical drawings)
GSUB . . . . . . Glazed Structural Unit Base (Technical drawings)
GSUC . . . . . . Ground Stub-Up Connection (Aerospace)
GSUSA . . . . . Gallipoli Society in the United States of America
GSUSA . . . . . General Staff, United States Army
GSV . . . . Gas Service Company (NYSE symbol)
GSV . . . . Globe Stop Valve (Technical drawings)
GSV . . . . Grumman Submersible Vehicle
GSV . . . . Guided Space Vehicle (Air Force)
GSW . . . . Great Southwest R. R., Inc. (AAR code)
GSW . . . . Great Western Sugar Company (NYSE symbol) (Delisted)
GSW . . . . Gunshot Wound (Medicine)
GS of W . . . . . Grand Superintendent of Works (Masonry)
GSW 1812 . . . General Society of the War of 1812
GSWA . . . . . . Gold Star Wives of America
GSWR . . . . . . Galvanized Steel Wire Rope
G & SWR . . . . Glasgow and South-Western Railway
GSWT . . . . . . General Staff with Troops
GSX . . . . General Signal Corporation (NYSE symbol)
GSY . . . . Gulf Science Year (1970)
GT . . . . Game Theory
GT . . . . Garbage Truck
GT . . . . Gas Tight
GT . . . . Gas Turbine
GT . . . . Gemini-Titan
GT . . . . General Technical Aptitude Area
GT . . . . Generation Time
GT . . . . German Translation
GT . . . . Gilt Top (Bibliography)
GT . . . . Good Templar
GT . . . . Goodyear Tire & Rubber Company (NYSE symbol)
GT . . . . Gran Turismo (Grand Touring) (Automotive term)
GT . . . . Grand Theft
GT . . . . Grand Tiler (Masonry)
GT . . . . Grand Treasurer (Masonry)
GT . . . . Grease Trap
GT . . . . Gross Tonnage
GT . . . . Ground Track
GT . . . . Ground Transmit
GT . . . . Group Transformation
GT . . . . Gutta (Drop of liquid)
G-T . . . . Gross Ton
GTA . . . . Gas Tungsten Arc
GTA . . . . Gear Train Analyzer
GTA . . . . Glass Tempering Association
GTA . . . . Glycerol Triacetate (Chemical)
GTA . . . . Graduate Teaching Assistant
GTA . . . . Graphic Training Aid
GTA . . . . Gravure Technical Association
GTA . . . . Ground Training Aid (Aerospace)

GTAC . . . . . . Ground-to-Air Cycle
GTAV. . . . . . . General Transport Administrative Vehicle
GTAW . . . . . . Gas Tungsten Arc Weld(ing)
GTC. . . . . . . Gain Time Control
GTC. . . . . . . Gas Turbine Compressor
GTC. . . . . . . General Transistor Corporation
GTC. . . . . . . Georgia Teachers College
GTC . . . . . . Good Till Canceled (as in a brokerage order)
GTC . . . . . . Good Till Countermanded
GTC. . . . . . . Government Training Centre (British)
GTC . . . . . . Guidance Transfer Container
GTC. . . . . . . Gulf Transport R. R. (AAR code)
GTCP . . . . . . Gas Turbine Compressor and Power Unit
GTD. . . . . . . Gear Test Data
GTD. . . . . . . Geometrical Theory of Diffraction
GTD. . . . . . . Ground Target Detection
GTD. . . . . . . Guaranteed (NYSE symbol)
GTDS . . . . . . Goddard Trajectory Determination System (NASA)
GTE . . . . Geipipari Tudomanyos Egyesulet
GTE . . . . Gilt Top Edge (Bibliography)
GT & E . . . . . General Telephone & Electronics Corporation
GTEA . . . . . . Group Test Equipment Assembly
GTF . . . . Generalized Transformation Function
GTF . . . . Glucose Tolerance Factor
GTF . . . . Government Test Facility
GTF . . . . Guidance Test Fixture
GTG . . . . Gas Turbine Generator
GTG . . . . Ground-to-Ground
GTGS. . . . . . Gas Turbine Generator Set
GTH. . . . . . . Gonadotrophic Hormone (Endocrinology)
GTI . . . . Grand Turk Island
GTIP . . . . . . Ground Tilt Isolation Platform
GTL . . . . Gas Transport LASER
GTL. . . . . . . Gas Turbine Laboratory (MIT)
GTM . . . . . . General Traffic Manager
GTM . . . . . . Good This Month
GTM . . . . . . Ground Test Missile
GTM . . . . . . Group Talk Microphone
GTMO . . . . . Guantanamo Bay, Cuba
GTMS. . . . . . Ground Target Marking System
GTN . . . . Glomerulo-Tubulo Nephritis (Medicine)
GTO . . . . Gate Turn Off (Data processing)
GTOL. . . . . . Ground Take-Off and Landing
GTOW . . . . . Gross Take-Off Weight (of an aircraft)
GTP . . . . Gas Turbine Power Unit
GTP . . . . General Test Plan
GTP . . . . Guanosine Triphosphate (Biochemistry)
GTPS . . . . . . Gas Turbine Power System
GTPSS . . . . . Good Test Plan Summary Sheets
GTR . . . . Gantry Test Rack (Aerospace)
GTR . . . . Government Transportation Request
GTR . . . . Ground Test Reactor (Air Force)
GTRR . . . . . . Georgia Institute of Technology Research Reactor
GTRY . . . . . . Grand Trunk Railway
GTS . . . . Gas Turbine Ship
GTS . . . . General Trouble Shooting
GTS . . . . Graphics Terminal Services (or System)
GTS . . . . Ground Telemetry Subsystem
GTS . . . . Ground Terminal System
GTS . . . . Guidance Test Set (Aerospace)
GTS . . . . Gyro Tilt Signal
GTSA . . . . . . German Telecommunications Statistics Agency
GTSS . . . . . . Gas Turbine Starting System
GTT . . . . Generated Target Tracking
GTT . . . . Glucose Tolerance Test (Medicine)
GTT . . . . Guttae (Drops of liquid)
GTTC . . . . . . Gulf Transportation Terminal Command
GTTF . . . . . . Gas Turbine Test Facility
GTTS . . . . . . Gyro Transfer Table System
GTU. . . . . . . Ground Test Unit
GTU. . . . . . . Gulf States Utilities Company (NYSE symbol)
GTUC. . . . . . Ghana Trades Union Congress
GTV. . . . . . . Gas Toggle Valve
GTV. . . . . . . Gate Valve
GTV. . . . . . . Ground Transport Vehicle
GTV. . . . . . . Growth Test Vehicle
GTV. . . . . . . Guidance Test Vehicle
GTV. . . . . . . Guided Test Vehicle
GTW . . . . . . Good This Week
GTW . . . . . . Grand Trunk Western R. R. (AAR code)
GTW . . . . . . Gross Take-Off Weight

GTX . . . . Gran Turismo Experimental
GTX . . . . Ground Transport Express (Airport baggage computer)
GTY. . . . . . . Grant (W. T.) Company (NYSE symbol)
GU . . . . Empresa Guatemalteca de Aviacion (Aviateca) (Guatemalan Airlines)
GU. . . . . Gasschutzunteroffizier (Gas Noncommissioned Officer) (German military - World War II)
GU . . . . Gastric Ulcer
GU . . . . Genitourinary (Medicine)
GU . . . . Georgetown University (Washington, DC)
GU . . . . Grafton & Upton R. R. (AAR code)
GU . . . . Guam
GU . . . . Guidance Unit (Military)
GUA . . . . Guidance Unit Assembly
GUA . . . . International Guards Union of America
GUARD. . . . . . Government Employees United Against Discrimination (An organization)
GUB. . . . . . . Government Union of Burma
GUBI . . . . . . Gemeinschaft Unabhangiger Beratender Ingenieurbueros (Association of German Consulting Engineers)
GUC . . . . Groupe d'Union Comerounaise (Group for Cameroonian Union)
GUCO . . . . . . Guilford Courthouse National Military Park
GUID . . . . . . Guidance
GUIDE . . . . . Guidance for Users of Integrated Data Processing Equipment
GUIDO . . . . . Guidance and Navigation Officer (NASA)
GUKR . . . . . . Glavnoe Upravlenie Kontrrazvedkoi (Chief Administration for Counter-intelligence) (of the Ministry of War) (USSR) (World War II)
GUL. . . . . . . Gulton Industries, Inc. (NYSE symbol)
GULFCOBASESERVUNIT . . Gulf Coast Base Service Unit
GULFCON . . . Gulf Control
GULFSEAFRON . . Gulf Sea Frontier
GULP. . . . . . General Utility Library Program
GUM . . . . . . Gosudarstvennyi Universal'nyi Magazin (Government Department Store) (Moscow)
GUNSGT . . . . Gunnery Sergeant
GUP. . . . . . . Gas Under Pressure
GUPAC . . . . . Gulf Permanent Assistance Committee (Persian Gulf)
GUPPY. . . . . Greater Underwater Propulsive Power (Type of submarine)
GURC . . . . . . Gulf University Research Corporation
GUSTO. . . . . Guidance Using Stable Tuning Oscillations
GUTS . . . . . . Georgians Unwilling to Surrender (Organization founded by former governor, Lester Maddox)
GUV . . . . Gerecht und Volkommen (Correct and Complete) (German)
GUX . . . . . . Grand Union Company (NYSE symbol)
GUY . . . . General Public Utilities Corporation (NYSE symbol)
GV . . . . Genital Vein
GV. . . . . Gentian Violet (A dye)
GV. . . . . Goerz-Visier (Bomb sight manufactured by Goerz Company) (German military - World War II)
GV . . . . Grande Vitesse (Fast train) (France)
GV . . . . Gravimetric Volume
GV . . . . Grid Variation (Navigation)
GV . . . . Ground Visibility
GVA . . . . General Visceral Afferent (Neurology)
GVA . . . . Gyroscope Vibration Absorber
GVB . . . . Guaranteed Voltage Breakdown
GVC . . . . Grand View College (Iowa)
GVC . . . . Graphics Vendor Control
GVC . . . . Guild Vector Colorimeter
GVE . . . . General Visceral Efferent (Neurology)
GVF . . . . Garnisonsverwendungsfaehig Feld (Fit for garrison duty in the field) (German military - World War II)
GVF. . . . . . . Grazhdanskii Vozdushnyi Flot (Civil Air Fleet) (USSR)
GVH. . . . . . . Garnisonsverwendungsfaehig Heimat (Fit for garrison duty in zone of interior) (German military - World War II)
GVH . . . . . . Graft Versus Host (Medicine)
GVHD . . . . . . Graft Versus Host Disease
GVHR. . . . . . Graft Versus Host Reaction(s) (Medicine)
GVI . . . . Gas Vent Institute
GVL . . . . Graniteville Company (NYSE symbol) (Wall Street slang name: "Grannie")
GVN . . . . Government of Vietnam
GVO . . . . Graeber-Verwaltungsoffizier (Graves Registration Officer) (German military - World War II)
GVP . . . . Geneeskundige Versorging Politte (Netherlands)
GVS. . . . . . . Government Vehicle Service (Postal Service)
GVS. . . . . . . Ground Vibration Survey
GVT. . . . . . . Gated Video Tracker
GVT. . . . . . . Gravity Vacuum Transit
GVT . . . . Gravity Vacuum Tube System (High-speed ground transportation)
GVWR . . . . . Gross Vehicle Weight Rating (Auto safety)
GW . . . . Air Force Guide for Writing
GW . . . . General Warning
GW . . . . General Will (Collectivist theory of government)

GW . . . . George Washington University (Washington, DC)
GW . . . . Gigawatt
GW . . . . Grenzwache (Frontier guard) (German military - World War II)
GW . . . . Gross Weight
GW . . . . Guerrilla Warfare
GW . . . . Guided Weapon (Air Force)
GW . . . . Gulf & Western Industries, Inc. (NYSE symbol)
G & W . . . . . . Gulf and Western Industries, Inc.
GWAA . . . . . . Garden Writers Association of America
GWAA . . . . . . Golf Writers Association of America
GWB . . . . Gypsum Wallboard (Technical drawings)
GWC . . . . George Williams College (Illinois)
GWC . . . . Global Weather Central
GWC . . . . Guard Well Capacitor
GWCA . . . . . . George Washington Carver National Monument
GWD . . . . (Gar) Wood Industries, Inc. (NYSE symbol) (Delisted)
GWD . . . . Grinding Wheel Dresser
GWETA . . . . . Greater Washington Educational Television Association
GWF . . . . Galveston Wharves R. R. (AAR code)
GWF . . . . Gating Wave Form
GWF . . . . Great Western Financial Corporation (NYSE symbol)
GWG . . . . Gaussian Wave Group
GWh . . . . Gigawatt-Hour
GWI . . . . Government-Wide Index (Later, USGRDR)
GWI . . . . Grinding Wheel Institute
GWI . . . . Ground Water Institute
G & WI . . . . . Gulf and Western Industries, Inc.
GWIBIT . . . . . Guild of Washington Incompetent Bureaucratic Idea Throatcutters
 (An organization rumored to have been active in World War II)
GWIGWO . . . . Good Will In, Good Will Out (Data processing)
GWJ . . . . Glue Weld Joint
GWJC . . . . . . Gardner Webb Junior College (North Carolina)
GWM . . . . Guaranteed Weekly Minimum
GWMC . . . . . . Galvanized Ware Manufacturers Council
GWOA . . . . . . Guerrilla Warfare Operational Area (Army)
GWP . . . . Government White Paper
GWP . . . . Gross World Product
GWR . . . . General War Reserves (Army)
GWR . . . . Great Western Railway (Prior to nationalization) (AAR code)
GWRI . . . . . . Ground Water Resources Institute

GWS . . . . GEEIA (Ground Electronics Engineering Installation Agency) Workload Schedule
GWS . . . . Geneva Convention for the Amelioration of the Condition of the Wounded and Sick in Armed Forces in the Field, 12 August 1949 (Army)
GWS 1929 . . . . Geneva Convention for the Amelioration of the Condition of the Wounded and Sick of Armies in the Field, 27 July 1929 (Army)
GWS-A & L . . Girl Watchers Society - Ankle & Leg Division
GWSF . . . . . . Georgia Warm Springs Foundation
GWS Sea . . . . Geneva Convention for the Amelioration of the Condition of the Wounded, Sick and Shipwrecked Members of the Armed Forces at Sea, 12 August 1949 (Army)
GWT . . . . Glazed Wall Tile (Technical drawings)
GWT . . . . Gross Weight
GWTA . . . . . . Gift Wrappings and Tyings Association
GWTB . . . . . . Glazed Wall Tile Base (Technical drawings)
GWTUF . . . . . Government Workers' Trade Union Federation (Ceylon)
GWTW . . . . . . "Gone with the Wind," a novel by Margaret Mitchell; also, a motion picture
GWU . . . . Gambia Workers' Union
GWU . . . . General Workers Union (Malta)
GWU . . . . George Washington University
GWU . . . . Great Western United Corp. (NYSE symbol)
GWU . . . . International Glove Workers' Union of America
GWW . . . . Guaranteed Weekly Wage
G/XMTR . . . . . Guidance Transmitter
GXP . . . . Georgia-Pacific Plywood Company (NYSE symbol) (Delisted)
GY . . . . General Tire & Rubber Company (NYSE symbol)
GY . . . . Gray (Buoy) (Maps and charts)
GY . . . . Greenish Yellow
GYK . . . . Giant Yellowknife Mines (American Stock Exchange symbol)
GYM . . . . General Yardmaster (Railroading)
GYN . . . . Gynecology
GYP . . . . Ghana Young Pioneers
GYP . . . . Gyro Yaw Position
GYRO . . . . . . Gyroscope
GYSGT . . . . . . Gunnery Sergeant
Gz . . . . Graetz number
GZ . . . . Ground Zero (Atomic detonation)
GZT . . . . Greenwich Zone Time
GZTS . . . . Guilford-Zimmerman Temperament Survey

H

H . . . . Altitude
H . . . . Amplitude of a Tide
H . . . . Atmospheric Head
H . . . . Hail
H . . . . Haler (Monetary unit in Czechoslovakia)
H . . . . Half
H . . . . Hall
H . . . . Hamiltonian Function
H . . . . Handily
H . . . . Harbor (Maps and charts)
H . . . . Hard(ness) (Of pencil leads)
H . . . . Hatch (Technical drawings)
H . . . . Hauch (Film)
H . . . . Haze (Weather reports)
H . . . . Headquarters
H . . . . Heat(er)
H . . . . Heavy
H . . . . Heavy Sea (Weather reports)
h . . . . Hecto (A prefix meaning multiplied by 100)
H . . . . Height
H . . . . Helicopter (Navy symbol) (Obsolete)
H . . . . Helicopter (When the second letter or only letter) (Designation for all US military aircraft)
H . . . . Helium
H . . . . Hence
H . . . . Henry (Unit of measurement) (Electricity)
H . . . . Heres (Heir)
H . . . . Heroin (Slang)
H . . . . Hic (Here)
H . . . . High
H . . . . Hits (Baseball)
H . . . . Holding Instructions Issued (Aviation)
H . . . . Holy
H . . . . Home
H . . . . Honor
H . . . . Horizontal
H . . . . Horn
H . . . . Horse
H . . . . Hospital Plane (When suffixed to Navy plane designation)
H . . . . Hostile (Military)
H . . . . Hot
H . . . . Hour(s)
H . . . . House
H . . . . Humidity
H . . . . Hundred
H . . . . Hupp Corporation (NYSE symbol) (Delisted)
H . . . . Hurricane Evacuation – General (Military aircraft identification prefix)
H . . . . Husband
H . . . . Hussars
H . . . . Hydrant
H . . . . Hydrodynamic Head
H . . . . Hydrogen (Chemical element)
H . . . . Hydrolysis
H . . . . Mustard Gas
H . . . . Nondirectional Radio Homing Beacon (Navigation charts)
H . . . . Search/Rescue (When the first letter of a pair) (Designation for all US military aircraft)
h . . . . Planck Constant (Symbol)
H . . . . Tide Correction
H (Bomb) . . . . . Hydrogen Bomb
H to H . . . . . . Heel to Heel
H^2 . . . . Deuterium
H^3 . . . . Tritium

1-H . . . . Selective Service Class (for Registrant Not Currently Subject to Processing for Induction)
4H . . . . Head, Heart, Hands, and Health (as in 4H organizations)
HA . . . . Half Add
HA . . . . Handelsabgabe
HA . . . . Hatch Act
HA . . . . Headquarters Administration Division (Coast Guard)
HA . . . . Heavy Artillery
HA . . . . Hectare
HA . . . . Hectocotylized Arm
HA . . . . Heeres-Atmer (Service oxygen breathing apparatus) (German military – World War II)
HA . . . . Hemadsorption (Medicine)
HA . . . . Hemagglutination
HA . . . . High Altitude
HA . . . . High-Angle
HA . . . . Hoc Anno (This Year)
HA . . . . Home Address
HA . . . . Horse Artillery
HA . . . . Horticultural Abstracts
HA . . . . Hospital Apprentice (Navy rating)
HA . . . . Hot Air
HA . . . . Hour Angle (Navigation)
HA . . . . Housing Allowance (Military)
HA . . . . Housing Assistance (HUD)
HA . . . . Human Adaptability
HA . . . . Hyaluronic Acid
H & A . . . . . . Health and Accident (Insurance)
HAA . . . . Haitian-American Association
HAA . . . . Hearing Aid Amplifier
HAA . . . . Heater Amplifier Assembly
HAA . . . . Heavy Antiaircraft
HAA . . . . Height Above Airport
HAA . . . . Helicopter Association of America
HAA . . . . Hepatitis Associated Antigen
HAA . . . . Honduran-American Association
HAA . . . . Hotel Accountants Association of New York City
HAA . . . . Housing Assistance Administration (HUD)
HAAC . . . . . . Hydraulic Actuator Assembly Container
HAAFE . . . . . Hawaiian Army and Air Force Exchange (Military)
HAATC . . . . . High Altitude Air Traffic Control
HAAW . . . . . Heavy Antitank/Assault Weapon (Army)
HAB . . . . Hazards Analysis Board (Air Force)
HAB . . . . Hearing Aid Battery
HAB . . . . High Altitude Bombing (Military)
HAB . . . . Horizontal Axis Bearing
HABGT . . . . . Hutt Adaptation of the Bender-Gestalt Test
HABP . . . . . . Hypersonic Arbitrary Body Program (NASA)
HABS . . . . . . Historic American Buildings Survey (Library of Congress)
HAC . . . . Haitian Air Corps
HAC . . . . Hawaii Aeronautics Commission
HAC . . . . Herbicide Assessment Commission
HAC . . . . High-Aluminous Concrete
HAC . . . . Hines Administrative Center (VA)
HAC . . . . Holland America Cruises (Formerly, Holland-America Line)
HAC . . . . Honourable Artillery Company (British)
HAC . . . . House Appropriations Committee (US Congress)
HAC . . . . Housing Assistance Council
HAC . . . . Hughes Aircraft Corporation
HAC . . . . Hydroballistic Advisory Committee
HACI . . . . . . Hughes Aircraft Company, International Division
HACOM . . . . . Headquarters Area Command
HAD . . . . Hawaii Air Defense

HAD.......	Heat-Actuated Device
HAD.......	High-Altitude Density (Sounding rocket)
HAD.......	High-Altitude Diagnostic (Unit) (Rocket launcher)
HAD.......	Horizontal Array Dipole
HAD.......	Hospital Administrator (or Administration)
HADA......	Hawaiian Defense Area
HADC......	Holloman Air Development Center
HADD......	Hawaiian Air Defense Division
HADES.....	Hypersonic Air Data Entry System
HADIZ.....	Hawaiian Air Defense Identification Zone
HADM.....	Heavy Atomic Demolition Munition (Military)
HADOPAD...	High-Altitude Delayed Opening Parachute Actuation Device
HADS.....	Hawaii Air Defense System
HAEE......	Harwell Atomic Energy Establishment
HAEH......	Horizontal Axis Electrical Hairspring
HAESZ.....	Husipari Allatorvosi Ellenorzo Szolgalat
HAF......	Headquarters Air Force
HAF	Hebrew Arts Foundation
HAF	Helms Athletic Foundation
HAF......	High Altitude Fuze (to activate weapons)
HAF......	Hypersonic Aerothermaldynamic Facility
HAFB.....	Holloman Air Force Base
HAFE.....	Harpers Ferry National Historical Park
HAFMED ...	Headquarters, Allied Forces Mediterranean
HAFO.....	Home Accounting and Finance Office
HAFTB.....	Holloman Air Force Test Base
HAG	Hold for Arrival of Goods
HAGR	Hamilton Grange National Memorial
HAHT.....	Hypersonic Arc-Heated Tunnel (Langley Research Center) (NASA)
HAI........	Handwriting Analysts, Incorporated
HAI........	Hemagglutination Inhibition
HAIC......	Hearing Aid Industry Conference
HAIC......	Hetero-Atom-In-Context
HAIRS.....	High-Altitude Test and Evaluation of Infrared Sources
HAKASH....	Hayl Kashish (Elderly Army) (Israel)
HAL........	Haftarbeitslager
HAL.......	Halliburton Company (NYSE symbol)
HAL.......	Hamburg-Amerika Linie (Hamburg-America Steamship Company)
HAL.......	Hawaiian Airlines, Limited
HAL.......	Heuristically-Programmed Algorithmic (Name of computer in film, "2001: A Space Odyssey")
HAL.......	Hindustan Aeronautics, Limited
HAL.......	Holland-America Line (Later, Holland-America Cruises)
HALCON	High-Altitude Long-Focus Convergent Mapping System
HALE......	Haleakala National Park
HALFSEE....	Headquarters, Allied Land Forces Southeastern Europe
HALO......	High Altitude, Low Opening (Parachute)
HALO......	Hughes Automated Lunar Observer (NASA)
HALPRO	Halverson Project (World War II plan to bomb Japan from China)
HaLV	Hamster Leukemia Virus
HAM	Hearing Aid Microphone
HAM	Heavy Atom Method
HAM	Heavy Automotive Maintenance
HAM	High-Speed Automatic Monitor
HAM	Hymns Ancient and Modern
HAMCO	HAWK (Homing All the Way Killer) Assembly and Missile Check-Out
HAMD	Helicopter Ambulance Medical Detachment
HAMP.....	Hampton National Historic Site
HAMP.....	High-Altitude Measurement Probe
HAMS......	Headquarters and Maintenance Squad
HAMS......	Hour Angle of the Mean Sun (Navigation)
HAMTC....	Hanford (Washington) Atomic Metal Trades Council
HAN	Hex Aluminum Nut
HANA	Halibut Association of North America
HANA.....	Helvetia Association of North America
HANDS.....	High-Altitude Nuclear Detection Studies (National Bureau of Standards)
HANE......	Hereditary Angioneurotic Edema (Medicine)
HANE......	High-Altitude Nuclear Explosion
HANG	Hawaiian Air National Guard
HAO	High Altitude Observatory (Boulder, Colorado) (National Bureau of Standards)
HAOC	Haynes-Apperson Owners Club
HAP.......	Heredopathia Atactica Polyneuritiformis
HAP.......	High-Altitude Platform
HAP.......	High-Altitude Probe
HAP.......	Honeycomb Aluminum Panel
HAP.......	Horizontal Axis Pivot
HAP.......	Hydroxylammonium Perchlorate
HAPDAR	Hard Point Demonstration Array RADAR
HAPDEC	Hard Point Decoys
HAPI	Holding As Previously Instructed (Aviation)
HAPO......	Hanford Atomic Products Operations (General Electric Company)
HAPPE	High-Altitude Particle Experiment (NASA)
HAR.......	Harbor
HAR.......	Harvey Aluminum, Inc. (NYSE symbol)
HAR.......	Honorary Air Reserve (Air Force)
HARA.....	High-Altitude RADAR Altimeter (NASA)
HARAS.....	Hughes Active RADAR Augmentation System
HARC.....	High-Altitude RADAR Controller
HARCFT....	Harbor Craft
HARCO....	Hyperbolic Area Coverage (Navigation)
HARDEX....	Harbor Defense Exercise (Navy)
HARDTS....	High-Accuracy RADAR Transmission System
HARE.....	High-Altitude Recombination-Energy Propulsion
HARE	Hydrazine Auxiliary Rocket Engine
HARIS......	High-Altitude Radiological Instrumentation System
HARK.....	Hardened Reentry Kill (Air Force)
HARLS.....	Horse Antiserum to Rabbit Lymphocytes
HARP	Halpern's AntiRADAR Point
HARP	High-Altitude Relay Point
HARP	High-Altitude Research Project (Military)
HARP	High-Altitude Rocket Probe (Army)
HARP	Honeywell Acoustic Research Project
HARPY	Hydrofoil Advanced Research Study Program
HARSAP	Harbor Survey Assistance Program (Naval Oceanographic Office)
HART	Hardened Amplifier for Radiation Transients
HART	Hypervelocity Aircraft Rocket, Tactical
HARTS......	Hardening Technology Studies Program
HARVAN....	Harriman and Vance (Code name for 1968 Paris peace talks on Vietnam, derived from the surnames of US negotiators W. Averell Harriman and Cyrus R. Vance)
HARYOU-ACT..	Harlem Youth Opportunities Unlimited - Associated Community Teams (A kind of Peace Corps for Harlem area of New York City)
HAS.......	Helical Antenna System
HAS.......	Helicopter Air Service
HAS.......	Helicopter Avionics System (Air Force)
HAS.......	High-Altitude Sampler
HAS.......	Holograph Assessment System
HAS.......	Hospital Administrative Services
HAS.......	Hover Augmentation System
HAS.......	Hydraulic Adjustable Speed
HASC......	Headquarters Air Service Command (Air Force)
HASC......	House Armed Services Committee
HASCO.....	Haitian-American Sugar Company
HASHS.....	Honeywell's Anti-Square Hat Society
HASL	Health and Safety Laboratory (of AEC)
HASP	High-Altitude Sampling Plane
HASP	High-Altitude Sounding Program (Navy)
HASP	High-Altitude Sounding Projectile
HASP	Houston Automatic Spooling Priority System (Data processing)
HASPID....	House Armed Services Permanent Investigations Subcommittee (US Congress)
HAST	High Altitude Supersonic Target
HASTI.....	High-Altitude Strike Indicator
HASVR.....	High-Altitude Space Velocity RADAR
HAT.......	Hat Corporation of America (NYSE symbol) (Later, HCA Industries, Inc.)
HAT.......	Hawaiian Archives for Tsunamis
HAT.......	Height Above Runway Touchdown Zone Elevation (Aviation)
HAT.......	High-Altitude Target
HAT.......	High-Altitude Testing (Sounding rocket)
HAT.......	High-Altitude Transmitter
HAT.......	Hypoxanthine, Aminopterin, and Thymidine (Biochemistry)
HATF.....	Hydraulic Actuator Test Fixture
HATO......	Handling Tool
HATRAC	Handover Transfer and Receiver Accept Change (SAGE)
HATS	Helicopter Attack System
HATS	High-Accuracy Targeting Subsystem
HATS	High-Altitude Terrain Contour Data Sensor
HATS	High-Altitude Test Stand
HATS	Hour Angle of the True Sun (Navigation)
HATS	Huntsville Association of Technical Societies (Alabama)
HATU.....	Heavy Air Training Unit
HATU	Heavy Attack Training Unit
HATV.....	High-Altitude Test Vehicle
HATWING ..	Heavy Attack Wing
HAU.......	Hebrew Actors Union
HAV.......	Heavily Armed Vessels
HAV.......	High-Accuracy Voltmeter
HAV.......	Hot Air Vulcanization
HAVEN.....	Help Addicts Voluntarily End Narcotics (An organization)
HAVO.....	Hawaii Volcanoes National Park
HAVOC	Histogram Average Ogive Calculator
HAW	Hawaii

HAW . . . . Heavy Antiarmor Weapon
HAW . . . . Heavy Assault Weapon
HAWIK . . . . . . Hamburg-Wechsler-Intelligenztest fuer Kinder (Intelligence
       test for children)
HAWK . . . . . . Have Alimony, Will Keep
HAWK . . . . . . Homing All the Way Killer (Small missile)
HAWSEAFRON . . Hawaiian Sea Frontier
HAX . . . . Helicopter Armored Experiment
HAY. . . . . Hayes Albion Corp. (NYSE symbol)
HAYSTAQ . . . . Have You Stored Answers to Questions? (Data processing)
HAZ . . . . Heat-Affected Zone
HAZEL . . . . . . Homogeneous Assembly Zero Energy (AERE)
HB . . . . Half Bound (Bibliography)
HB . . . . Half Breadth
HB . . . . Halfback (Football position)
HB . . . . Hampton & Branchville R. R. (AAR code)
HB . . . . Hard Black (Of pencil leads)
HB . . . . Hard-Boiled (Egg)
HB . . . . Heart Block (Medicine)
HB . . . . Heavy Barrel (In reference to a rifle)
HB . . . . Heavy Bombardment (or Bomber)
Hb . . . . Hemoglobin
HB . . . . High Band
HB . . . . High Boilers
HB . . . . His Beatitude or His Blessedness
HB . . . . Hit Batsman (Baseball)
HB . . . . Homing Beacon (Aviation)
HB . . . . Horizontal Bands (on buoys, beacons)
HB . . . . Horizontal Bomber
HB . . . . Hose Bib
HB . . . . House Bill (in state legislatures)
HB . . . . Housebreaking
HB . . . . Household Goods / Baggage
HB . . . . Human Being (Slang)
H/B . . . . Handbook
HbA . . . . Adult Hemoglobin (Physiology)
HBA . . . . . . Honest Ballot Association
HBAb . . . . . . Hepatitis B Antibody (Immunology)
HBAg . . . . . . Hepatitis B Antigen (Immunology)
HBAT . . . . . . Having Been Assigned to This Organization (or Headquarters)
HBAVS . . . . . . Human Betterment Association for Voluntary Sterilization
HBB . . . . . . Hoover Ball & Bearing Company (NYSE symbol)
HBC . . . . . . Homogeneous Boundary Condition
HBC . . . . Honeywell Business Computer
HBC . . . . Hydrogen Bubble Chamber
HBC . . . . Hudson's Bay Company
HBD . . . . Has Been Drinking (Medical notation)
HBD . . . . Hydroxybutyric Dehydrogenase
HBDC . . . . . . Home Base Development Committee (Navy)
HBDMA . . . . . Hat Block and Die Makers Association
HbF . . . . Fetal Hemoglobin (Physiology)
HBF . . . . Hauptbahnhof (Main Railroad Station) (Germany)
HBGM . . . . . . Hypersonic Boost-Glide Missile
HBI . . . . Hindustan Bible Institute
HBJ . . . . Harcourt, Brace, Jovanovich, Inc. (NYSE symbol)
HBL . . . . Heeresbetriebsstofflager (Army gasoline-supply depot) (German
     military - World War II)
HBL . . . . Heublein, Inc. (NYSE symbol)
HBM . . . . . . Heavy Ballistic Missile
HBM. . . . . . . His (or Her) Britannic Majesty
HBM . . . . Horizontal Boring Mill
HBMS . . . . . . His (or Her) Britannic Majesty's Service
HBN . . . . Hazard Beacon
HBP . . . . High Blood Pressure (Medicine)
HBP . . . . Hit By Pitcher (Baseball)
HBP . . . . Hydraulic Bench Press
HBPA . . . . . . Horsemen's Benevolent and Protective Association
HBR . . . . Has Been Reviewed
HBRACW . . . . Has Been Reviewed and Concurred With
HBS . . . . . . Half Bar Symbology
HBS . . . . Hanks Balanced Salt (Solution)
HBS . . . . Harbor Boat Service (Military)
HBS . . . . Harvard Business School
HBS . . . . Helicopter Blade Slap
HBS . . . . Hoboken Shore R. R. (AAR code)
HBS . . . . Hot Blade Stripper
HBSAA . . . . . Hack and Band Saw Manufacturers Association of America
HBSS . . . . . . Hanks Balanced Salt Solution (Cell incubation medium)
HBSS . . . . . . Hospital Bureau of Standards and Supplies
HBT . . . . Houston Belt & Terminal Railway Company (AAR code)
HB & T . . . . . Houston Belt & Terminal Railway Company

HBUA . . . . . . Hungarian Baptist Union of America
HBW . . . . . . Harcourt, Brace & World, Inc. (NYSE symbol) (Later, HBJ)
HBWR . . . . . . Halden Boiling Heavy Water Reactor
HC . . . . Habitual Criminal
HC . . . . Half Calf
HC . . . . Half Chest
HC . . . . Hand Control (Technical drawings)
HC . . . . Hannibal Connecting R. R. (AAR code)
HC . . . . Hard Copy
HC . . . . Headquarters Command (Military)
HC . . . . Heater Cord
HC . . . . Heating Cabinet
HC . . . . Heating Coil
HC . . . . Held (or Hold) Covered
HC . . . . Helene Curtis Industries, Inc. (NYSE symbol)
HC . . . . Helicopter Council
HC . . . . Helium Circulation (System)
HC . . . . Heralds' College (British)
HC . . . . Hexachloroethane (Organic chemistry)
HC . . . . High Capacity
HC . . . . High Carbon (Steel)
HC . . . . High Church
HC . . . . High Commissioner
HC . . . . High-Compression
HC . . . . High Conditioners (Psychology)
HC . . . . Hippocampal
HC . . . . Historical Commission
HC . . . . Hockey Club
HC . . . . Holy Communion
HC . . . . Holy Cross
HC . . . . Home Care
HC . . . . Honoris Causa (For the Sake of Honor)
HC . . . . Hors Concours (Not Competing)
HC. . . . . Hospital Corps(man) (Navy)
HC . . . . Hot and Cold
HC . . . . Hour Circle
HC . . . . House of Commons (British)
HC . . . . House of Correction
HC . . . . Hydraulic Cylinder
HC . . . . Hydrocarbon
HC . . . . Hydrocortisone (Endocrinology)
HC . . . . Hysteresis Comparator
HC. . . . . Screening Smoke (Mixture)
HCA . . . . . . Absent by Reason of Being Held by Civil Authorities (Military)
HCA . . . . Harness and Cable Assembly
HCA. . . . . . . HCA Industries, Inc. (Formerly, Hat Corporation of America) (NYSE
     symbol)
HCA . . . . . . Hobby Clubs of America
HCA . . . . . . Hotel Corporation of America (NYSE symbol) (Delisted)
HCA . . . . Human Component Analysis
HCA. . . . . . . Hunting-Clan Air Transport Ltd.
HCAA . . . . . Hebrew Christian Alliance of America
HCB . . . . . . Heaviside-Campbell Bridge (Electronics)
HCB . . . . Hoopes Conductivity Bridge (Electronics)
HCB . . . . House of Commons Bill (British)
HCBI . . . . . . Health Conference for Business and Industry
HCC . . . . . . Harlem Cultural Council
HCC . . . . Heliax Coaxial Cable
HCC . . . . Hollow Copper Conductor
HCC . . . . Hollywood Comedy Club
HCC . . . . Holyoke Community College (Massachusetts)
HCC . . . . Honeycomb Corrugated Construction
HCC . . . . Hunt (Philip A.) Chemical Corporation (NYSE symbol)
HCCA . . . . . Horseless Carriage Club of America
HCCG . . . . . . Discharge (from Military Service) under Honorable Conditions,
     Convenience of Government
HCCM . . . . . . Discharge (from Military Service) under Honorable Conditions,
     Convenience of Man
HCD. . . . . . . Heavy Chain Disease (Protein)
HCD. . . . . . . High Current Density
HCD. . . . . . . High Current Diode
HCD. . . . . . . Hoffman Core Driver
HCD. . . . . . . Horizontal Correlation Distance
HCDP . . . . . . Discharge (from Military Service) under Honorable Conditions,
     Dependency Existing Prior to Enlistment
HCE . . . . Human-Caused Error
HCEA . . . . . Holland Cheese Exporters Association
HCEBT . . . . . Houston Cotton Exchange and Board of Trade
HCEE . . . . . . Discharge (from Military Service) under Honorable Conditions, Expiration
     of Enlistment
HCF . . . . Heat Control Filter

HCF	Height Correction Factor
HCF	Highest Common Factor (Mathematics)
HCF	Hungarian Cultural Foundation
HCFD	Hydro-Chemical Form Die (Tool)
HCG	Hermanas Catequistas Guadalupanas (Roman Catholic women's religious order)
HCG	Horizontal Location of Center of Gravity
HCG	Human Chorionic Gonadotrophin (Endocrinology)
HCHC	High Carbon, High Chrome
HCHS	Handicapped Children's Home Service
HCI	Hierarchically Classified Index
HCI	High Current Inductor
HCI	Hughes Communications International (Hughes Aircraft Company)
HCIS	House Committee on Internal Security (Formerly, HUAC)
HCJ	High Court of Justice
HCJB	High Court Junior Beadle (Ancient Order of Foresters)
HCJC	Henderson County Junior College (Texas)
HCJC	Howard County Junior College (Texas)
HCJW	High Court Junior Woodward (Ancient Order of Foresters)
HCL	High Cost of Living (Slang)
HCL	Horizontal Center Line
HCl	Hydrogen Chloride
HCL	International Hod Carriers', Building and Common Laborers' Union of America (Later, Laborers' International Union of North America)
HCLA	Hungarian Catholic League of America
HCLE	Humanities Center for Liberal Education
HCM	Haitian Campaign Medal
HCM	Halifax Conservatory of Music
HCM	Harshaw Chemical Company (NYSE symbol) (Delisted)
HCM	His (or Her) Catholic Majesty
HCMA	Hotel Credit Managers Association
HCMS	Discharge (from Military Service) under Honorable Conditions, Medical Survey
HCMU	Discharge (from Military Service) under Honorable Conditions, under Age of Authorized Enlistment
HCMW	Discharge (from Military Service) under Honorable Conditions, Minor Enlisted Without Consent, under 18 at Time of Discharge
HCMW	United Hatters, Cap and Millinery Workers International Union
HCN	Hydrocyanic Acid (Inorganic chemistry)
HCN	Hydrogen Cyanide (Inorganic chemistry)
HCO	Hangar Control Officer (Navy)
HCO	Harvard College Observatory
HCO	Horizontal Control Operator (Military)
HCP	Hangar Control Position (Navy)
HCP	Hard Copy Printer
HCP	Hepatocatalase Peroxidase
HCP	Hexachlorophene (Germicide)
HCP	Hexagonal Close-Packed (Crystallography)
HCP	Horizontal Candle Power
HCP	Hydrazine Catalytic Plenum
HCP	Hypervelocity Countermeasures Program
HCPNY	Harbor Carriers of the Port of New York
HCPS	Horizontal Candle Power Seconds
HCQ	Hot Carrier Quad
HCR	Haut-Commissaire des Nations Unies pour les Refugies
HCR	High Chief Ranger (Ancient Order of Foresters)
HCR	High Cross Range
HCRW	Hot and Cold Running Water
HCS	Harvey Cushing Society
HCS	High Carbon Steel
HCS	High Court Secretary (Ancient Order of Foresters)
HCS	Home Civil Service (British)
HCS	Human Chorionic Somatomammotropin
HCSA	House Committee on Space and Astronautics (US Congress)
HCSB	High Court Senior Beadle (Ancient Order of Foresters)
HCSBC	Historical Commission, Southern Baptist Convention
HCSHT	High Carbon Steel, Heat-Treated
HCSLP	Hungarian Committee of Socialist Labor Party
HCSS	Home and Colonial School Society (British)
HCSW	High Court Senior Woodward (Ancient Order of Foresters)
HCT	Heater Center Top
HCT	Hematocrit (Medicine)
HCT	High Court Treasurer (Ancient Order of Foresters)
HCT	Hollow Cathode Tube
HCT	Hot Cathode Tube
HCT	Hull Collector Tank
HCT	Hydraulic Components Test
HCTS	House Call Tax Service
HCU	Helium Charging Unit
HCU	Homing Comparator Unit
HCU	Hydraulic Cycling Unit

HCUND	Hospitality Committee for United Nations Delegations
HCV	Hull Check Valve
HCV	Hydraulic Control Valve
HCVD	Hypertensive Cardiovascular Disease (Medicine)
HCZ	Hydrogen Convection Zone
HD	Hand Drawn
HD	Hansen's Disease (Leprosy) (Medicine)
HD	Harbor Defense (Military)
HD	Hard-Drawn (Metallurgy)
HD	Head
HD	Hearing Distance (Medicine)
HD	Heavy-Duty
HD	High Density
HD	Hilda Doolittle (Pen name of American poet, 1886-1961)
HD	Historical Development
HD	Historical Division (Air Force)
HD	Home Defence (British)
HD	Honorable Discharge
HD	Horizontal Drive
HD	Horse-Drawn
HD	Hourly Difference
HD	Hudson Bay Mining & Smelting Co., Ltd. (NYSE symbol)
HD	Humanitarian Deferment (Military)
HD	Hurricane Deck
H/D	Holddown
H & D	Hardened and Dispersed
HDA	Headquarters, Department of the Army
HDA	Heavy Duty Amplifier
HDA	High Duty Alloys, Ltd.
HDA	Horizontal Danger Angle (Navigation)
HDAC	Heavy Duty Air Cylinder
HDAP	Heavy Duty Automatic Press
HDAS	House Defense Appropriations Subcommittee (US Congress)
HDATZ	High Density Air Traffic Zone
HDB	Horizontal Dynamic Balancing
HDBA	Horizontal Dynamic Balancing Adjustment
HDBK	Handbook
HDC	Harbor Defense Command (Army)
HDC	Helicopter Direction Center
HDC	Holder in Due Course (Owner or holder of a negotiable instrument at some future time)
HDC	Holston Defense Corporation
HDC	Hough Development Corporation (Cleveland)
HDC	Housing Development Corporation (Washington, DC)
HDCG	Honorable Discharge, Convenience of Government (Military)
HDCM	Honorable Discharge, Convenience of Man (Military)
HDCR	Hard Chromium
HDCS	Human Diploid Cell Strains (Immunology)
HDD	Heavy Duty Detergent
HDD	Higher Dental Diploma (British)
HDD	Homopolar Disk Dynamo
HDD	Human Disorientation Device
HDDP	Honorable Discharge, Dependency Existing Prior to Enlistment (Military)
HDDR	High-Density Digital Recording
HDDS	High-Density Data System
HDDS	Honorable Discharge, Dependency Arising Since Enlistment (Military)
HDE	Homogeneous Differential Equation
HDED	Heavy Duty Enzyme Detergent
HDEE	Honorable Discharge, Expiration of Enlistment (Military)
HDEP	High-Density Electronic Packaging
HDF	Handle Door Fastener
HDF	Hartmann Dispersion Formula
HDF	High-Frequency Direction Finding
HDF	Horizontal Distributing Frame
HDG	Heading
HDG	Hot Dip Galvinization
HDI	Hawaiian Development Irradiator (AEC)
HDI	Horizontal Display Indicator
HDI	House Dress Institute
HDIF	Heavy-Duty Industrial Filter
HDIP	High Dose Immune Paralysis
HDIR	Heavy-Duty Industrial Relay
HDIV	Hughes Dynamic Imagery Viewer
HDL	Handelman Co. (NYSE symbol)
HDL	Harry Diamond Laboratory (Military) (Formerly, DOFL)
HDL	High-Density Lipoproteins (Medicine)
HDM	Hizbia Dighill e Mirifle (Somali Political Party)
HDM	Hudson & Manhattan R. R. (AAR code)
HDMA	Hardwood Dimension Manufacturers Association
HDMS	High-Density Memory System
HDMS	Hizb Dastur Mustaghil Somalia (Somali Independent Constitution Party)

HDMW . . . . . . Honorable Discharge, Minors Enlisted w/o Consent, Under 18 at Discharge
HDN . . . . Hemolytic Disease of Newborn
HDN . . . . Heyden Newport Chemical Corporation (NYSE symbol) (Delisted)
HDNPRSGR . . Headquarters Squadron Personnel Group
HDP . . . . Hexose Diphosphate
HDP . . . . High Detonation Pressure
HDP . . . . Horizontal Data Processing
HDPE . . . . . . High-Density Polyethylene (Plastics)
HDPS . . . . . . High-Density Power Supply
HDR . . . . Hand Rail
HDR . . . . High Definition RADAR
HDR . . . . Home Dockyard Regulations (Navy)
HDR . . . . Holddown and Release
HDRR . . . . . . Holloman Development Research Report (Air Force)
HDRSS. . . . . . High Data Rate Storage System
HDS . . . . Hospital Discharge Survey (Public Health Service)
HDS . . . . Hydrodesulfurization
HDS . . . . Hydrogen Detection System
HDSW. . . . . . Handwoerterbuch der Sozialwissenschaft (Dictionary of the Social Sciences)
HDT . . . . Heat Distortion Temperature
HDT . . . . Hi-Pot Dwell Time
HDTMA. . . . . Heavy-Duty Truck Manufacturers Association
HDV. . . . . . . Horse-Drawn Vehicle
HDW . . . . . . Hydrodynamic Welding
HDX . . . . Half Duplex
HDY . . . . Heavy Duty
HDZ . . . . Haubarkeitsdurchschnittszuwachs
HE . . . . Handling Equipment
HE . . . . Hardware Evaluator (NASA)
HE . . . . Hardware Executive
HE . . . . Hawaiian Electric Co., Inc. (NYSE symbol)
HE . . . . Hearing Examiner
HE . . . . Heat Engine
HE . . . . Heavy Equipment
HE . . . . Heavy Enamel
HE . . . . Height of Eye
He . . . . Helium (Chemical element)
HE . . . . Hematoxylin and Eosin (Biological stain)
HE . . . . High Efficiency
HE . . . . High Explosive
HE . . . . His Eminence
HE . . . . His Excellency
HE . . . . Hollis & Eastern R. R. (AAR code)
HE . . . . Horizontal Equivalent
HE . . . . Human Engineering
HE . . . . Human Enteric (Virology)
HE . . . . Hydraulics Engineer
HE . . . . Hydrogen Embrittlement
H & E . . . . . . Hemotoxylin and Eosin (Histology)
H & E . . . . . . Heredity and Environment
HEA . . . . High-Efficiency Antireflection (Coating)
HEA . . . . Higher Education Act
HEA . . . . Hot Electron Amplifier
HEAA . . . . . . High Explosive, Antiaircraft (Shell)
HEAD . . . . . . Health Emergency and Dispensary, Inc. (New Orleans clinic)
HEADCOM . . . Headquarters Command (Military)
HEAF . . . . . . Heavy End Aviation Fuel
HEAO. . . . . . High-Energy Astronomical Observatory (NASA)
HEAP . . . . . . Helicopter Extended Area Platform
HEAP . . . . . . High Explosive - Anti-Personnel (Rocket)
HEAP . . . . . . High Explosive Armor-Piercing (Projectile)
HEAR . . . . . . Hearing Education through Auditory Research (Foundation)
HEAR . . . . . . Hospital Emergency Area Radio (Illinois Hospital Association)
HEART . . . . . Household Employment Association for Reevaluation and Training (An organization)
HEAT . . . . . . High Enthalpy Arc Tunnel (NASA)
HEAT . . . . . . High Explosive Antitank (Projectile)
HEAT . . . . . . Human Erythrocyte Agglutination Test
HEB . . . . Hepar Embryonis Bovis (Embryonic bovine liver cells used in tissue culture studies of viruses) (Medicine)
HEB . . . . Hollow Electron Beam
HEBC . . . . . . Heavy Enamel Bonded Cotton (Insulation)
HEBDC . . . . . Heavy Enamel Bonded Double Cotton (Insulation)
HEBDP. . . . . . Heavy Enamel Bonded Double Paper (Insulation)
HEBDS . . . . . Heavy Enamel Bonded Double Silk (Insulation)
HEBP . . . . . . Heavy Enamel Bonded Paper (Insulation)
HEBS . . . . . . Heavy Enamel Bonded Silk (Insulation)
HEBS . . . . . . High Energy Battery System
HEC . . . . Hazeltine Electronics Corporation
HEC . . . . Heavy Enamel Single Cotton (Insulation)
HEC . . . . High Emission Cathode

HEC . . . . High-Energy Chemistry
HEC . . . . Hoffman Electronics Corporation (NYSE symbol)
HEC . . . . Hollerith Electronic Computer
HECC . . . . . . Hooker Electro-Chemical Company
HECMAR . . . . Human Engineering Criteria for Maintenance and Repair (General Electric, NASA)
HECP . . . . . . Harbor Entrance Control Post
HECRE. . . . . . High-Energy Cosmic Ray Experiment (Balloon flight) (NASA)
HECTOR . . . . Hot Enriched Carbon-Moderated Thermal Oscillator Reactor (British)
HECV . . . . . . Heavy Enamel Cotton Varnish (Insulation)
HECVES . . . . Harbor Entrance Control Vessel
HED . . . . Hall Effect Device
HED . . . . Haut-Einheits-Dosis (Unit Skin Dose)
HED . . . . Human Engineering Data
HED . . . . Hydraulically Extendable Dipperstick (for tractors)
HEDC . . . . . . Hasselblad Electric Data Camera
HEDC . . . . . . Heavy Enamel Double Cotton (Insulation)
HEDCOM . . . . Headquarters Command
HEDCV . . . . . Heavy Enamel Double Cotton Varnish (Insulation)
HEDRON . . . . Headquarters Squadron
HEDRONFAIRWING .. Headquarters Squadron Fleet Air Wing
HEDS . . . . . . Heavy Enamel Double Silk (Insulation)
HEDS . . . . . . High Explosive, Discarding Sabot
HEDSUPPACT . . Headquarters Support Activities
HEDSV . . . . . Heavy Enamel Double Silk Varnish (Insulation)
HEEB . . . . . . High-Energy Electrolyte Battery
HEED . . . . . . High-Energy Electron Diffraction
HEEDTA . . . . Hydroxyethylenediaminetetracetic Acid (Organic chemistry)
HEENT . . . . . Head, Ears, Eyes, Nose, Throat
HEEP . . . . . . Highway Engineering Exchange Program (IBM)
HEF . . . . Hearth Electric Furnace
HEF . . . . Heat-Curing Epoxy Film
HEF . . . . High Energy Forming
HEF . . . . High Energy Fuel (Air Force)
HEF . . . . Hospital Employees' Federation of Australia
HEF . . . . Human Ecology Fund
HEFA . . . . . . Higher Education Facilities Act
HEFG . . . . . . Hall Effect Function Generator
HEFU . . . . . . High-Energy Firing Unit (Army)
HEG . . . . Hall Effect Generator
HEG . . . . Heavy Enamel Single Glass (Insulation)
HEGIS . . . . . . Higher Education General Information Survey (US Office of Education)
HEGR . . . . . . High Energy Gamma Ray
HEH . . . . His (or Her) Exalted Highness (Term applied only to personages of British India)
HEHF . . . . . . Hanford Environmental Health Foundation (AEC)
HEHO. . . . . . Herbert Hoover National Historic Site
HEI . . . . Heat Exchange Institute
HEI . . . . High Explosive Incendiary
HEI . . . . Human Engineering Institute
HEI . . . . Humidity-Electronic Indicator
HEIAS. . . . . . Human Engineering Information and Analysis Service (Tufts University)
HEIB . . . . . . Home Economists in Business
HEIC . . . . . . Honourable East India Company (British)
HEICS. . . . . . Honourable East India Company's Service (British)
HEIT . . . . . . High Explosive Incendiary (Shell) Traced (i.e., fitted with tracer)
HEK . . . . Heavy Enamel Single Cellophane (Insulation)
HEL . . . . Hugoniot Elastic Limit
HEL . . . . Human Engineering Laboratory (Army)
HELASRON . . . Helicopter Antisubmarine Squadron
HELB . . . . . . High Energy LASER Beam
HELBAT. . . . . Human Engineering Laboratories Battalion Artillery Test (Army)
HELCAR . . . . Helicopter Collision Avoidance RADAR
HELEN . . . . . Hydrogenous Exponential Liquid Experiment
HELI. . . . . . . Helicopter
HELIPATH . . . Helicopter Position and Terrain Height
HELITEAM . . . . Helicopter Team
HELL . . . . . . Higher Education Learning Laboratory (of Youth Pride, Inc.)
HELO . . . . . . Helicopter
HELO . . . . . . High Energy Liquid Oxidizer
HELP . . . . . . Helicopter Electronic Landing Path (Army)
HELP . . . . . . Help Establish Lasting Peace
HELP. . . . . . . Heroin Emergency Life Project
HELP . . . . . . High Energy Lightweight Propellant
HELP . . . . . . Highway Emergency Locating Plan
HELP. . . . . . . Home Education Livelihood Program (New Mexico)
HELP. . . . . . . Housewives Elect Lower Prices (New York women's lobby group)
HELP . . . . . . Hughes Emergency Locator Pack
HELPR . . . . . Handbook of Electronic Parts Reliability
HELPS . . . . . . Helmet-Position Sensing System
HELREC . . . . . Health Record(s)

HELS . . . . . . High Energy LASER System
HEM . . . . . Hall Effect Multiplier
HEM . . . . . . Hemisphere Fund, Inc. (NYSE symbol)
HEM . . . . . Hybrid Electromagnetic (Wave)
HEMA . . . . . Hydroxyethyl Methacrylate
HEMAC . . . . . Hybrid Electromagnetic Antenna Coupler
HEMAR . . . . . Human Engineering Criteria for Maintenance and Repairs (Space station) (NASA)
HEMIS . . . . . Hemisphere
HeNe . . . . . Helium-Neon
HENRE . . . . . High Energy Neutron Reactions Experiment (AEC)
HEO . . . . . . Higher Executive Officer
HEO . . . . . . Higher Executive Order
HEOB . . . . . High Energy Organic Battery
HEOC . . . . . Higher Education Opportunities Committee
HEOEBS . . . . High Energy Organic Electrolyte Battery System
HEOS . . . . . Highly Eccentric (or Elliptical) Orbit Satellite
HEP . . . . . . Hall Effect Probe
HEP . . . . . . High Energy Particle
HEP . . . . . . High Energy Phosphate (Biochemistry)
HEP . . . . . . High Energy Physics
HEP . . . . . . High Explosive Plastic
HEP . . . . . . High-School Equivalency Program
HEP . . . . . . Higher Education Panel
HEP . . . . . . Hole-Electron Pair
HEP . . . . . . Human Engineering Plan
HEp . . . . . . Human Epithelial (Cells)
HEP . . . . . . Hydrazine Electrolysis Plenum
HEP . . . . . . Hydroelectric Plant
HEP . . . . . . Hydroelectric Power
HEP . . . . . . Hydrogen Embrittlement Proof
HEPA . . . . . High Efficiency Particulate Air
HEPC . . . . . Hydro-Electric Power Commission (Ontario, Canada)
HEPCAT . . . . Helicopter Pilot Control and Training
HEPDEX . . . . High Energy Proton Detection Experiment
HEPL . . . . . High Energy Physics Laboratory (Stanford University)
HEPP . . . . . Hoffman Evaluation Program and Procedure (Hoffman Electronics Corporation)
HEPP . . . . . Northwest Association of Horticulturists, Entomologists and Plant Pathologists
HEP-T . . . . . High Explosive Plastic Tracer (Military)
HER . . . . . . Harvard Educational Review
HER . . . . . . Helena Rubinstein, Inc. (NYSE symbol)
HER . . . . . . High Energy Ray
HER . . . . . . Horizontal Earth Rate
HER . . . . . . Human Error Rate
HER . . . . . . Hyper-Environmental RADAR
HERA . . . . . High Explosive Rocket Assisted
HERALDS . . . . Harbor Echo Ranging and Listening Devices
HERAP . . . . . Human Error Research and Analysis Program
HERDET . . . . Hereby Detached from Duty Assigned (Military)
HERF . . . . . High Energy Rate Forging (Metalworking)
HERF . . . . . High Energy Rate Forming
HERJ . . . . . High Explosive Ramjet (Rocketry)
HERMES . . . . Heavy Element and Radioactive Material Electromagnetic Separator (British)
HERO . . . . . Hazards of Electromagnetic Radiation to Ordnance
HERO . . . . . Historical Evaluation and Research Organization
HERO . . . . . Hot Experimental Reaction of O Power
HERS . . . . . Home Economics Reading Service (Recipe clipping service)
HERTS . . . . . Hertfordshire (British)
HES . . . . . . Hamlet Evaluation Survey (South Vietnam)
HES . . . . . . Head End Steering
HES . . . . . . Heavy Enamel Single Silk (Insulation)
HES . . . . . . Hess Oil & Chemical Corporation (NYSE symbol) (Delisted)
HES . . . . . . High Explosive Spotting
HES . . . . . . History of Education Society
HES . . . . . . Homeowners Emergency Services, Inc.
HES . . . . . . Hughes Earth Station
HESO . . . . . High Energy Solid Oxidizer
HESO . . . . . Hospital Educational Services Officer
HEST . . . . . HEAF (Heavy End Aviation Fuel) Emergency Service Tanks
HEST . . . . . High Explosives Simulation Technique
HESV . . . . . Heavy Enamel Single Silk Varnish (Insulation)
HET . . . . . . Heavy Equipment Transporter
HET . . . . . . High Explosive (Shell) Traced (i.e., fitted with tracer)
HET . . . . . . Hydroxyethyl Terephthalate (Chemistry)
HETF . . . . . Hill Engineering Test Facility (Air Force)
HETOC . . . . Hudson-Essex-Terraplane Owners Club
HETP . . . . . Height Equivalent to a Theoretical Plate
HETP . . . . . Hexaethyl Tetraphosphate (Organic chemistry)

HETS . . . . . . Height Equivalent to a Theoretical Stage
HETS . . . . . . High Energy Transfer Stage
HETS . . . . . . High Environment Test System (Air Force)
HETS . . . . . . Hyperenvironmental Test System (Air Force)
HEU . . . . Hydroelectric Unit
HEUS . . . . . . High Energy Upper Stage (NASA)
HEW . . . . Department of Health, Education, and Welfare
HEW . . . . Hanford Engineering Works
HEW . . . . Hewitt-Robins, Inc. (NYSE symbol) (Delisted)
HEWH . . . . . . High Explosive Warhead
HEXHD . . . . . Hexagonal Head
Hf . . . . Hafnium (Chemical element)
HF . . . . Hageman Factor (in blood plasma)
HF . . . . Half
HF . . . . Handwriting Foundation
HF . . . . Harassing Fire (Military)
HF . . . . Hard Firm (Of pencil leads)
HF . . . . Hartree-Fock (Orbitals) (Atomic structure)
HF . . . . Hazard Function
HF . . . . Haze Filter (Photography)
HF . . . . Heeresfahrzeug (Army vehicle) (German military - World War II)
HF . . . . Height Finding (RADAR)
HF . . . . High Frequency (Electronics)
HF . . . . Hold Fire (Military)
HF . . . . Home Fleet (British)
HF . . . . Home Forces (British Military)
HF . . . . House of Fabrics, Inc. (NYSE symbol)
HF . . . . Hull Filter
HF . . . . Human Factors
HF . . . . Hydrofluoric Acid (Inorganic chemistry)
HF . . . . Hydrogen Fluoride (Inorganic chemistry)
H/F . . . . Held For
HFA . . . . Hard Fibres Association
HFA . . . . Hardened Flexible Array
HFA . . . . Heavy Field Artillery
HFAA . . . . . . High-Frequency Airborne Antenna
HFAA . . . . . . Holstein-Friesian Association of America
HFAF . . . . . . Hawaii Foundation for American Freedoms
HFBA . . . . . . Hebrew Free Burial Association
HFBR . . . . . . High Flux Beam Reactor (AEC)
HFC . . . . Hard Filled Capsules (Pharmacy)
HFC . . . . High-Frequency Choke
HFC . . . . High-Frequency Correction
HFC . . . . High-Frequency Current
HFC . . . . Holy Family College (California, Pennsylvania, Wisconsin)
HFC . . . . Household Finance Corporation (NYSE symbol)
HFC . . . . Human Factors Checklists (Navy)
HFCAA . . . . . Hatters' Fur Cutters Association of America (Formerly, HFCAUS)
HFCAUS . . . . Hatters Fur Cutters Association of the United States (Later, HFCAA)
HFCC . . . . . . Henry Ford Community College (Michigan)
HFD . . . . Helium Fill to Distribution Unit (Aerospace)
HFD . . . . Horizon Flight Director (Aircraft)
HFD . . . . Human Factor Division (Air Research and Development Command) (Air Force)
HFDA . . . . . . Hospital Food Directors Association
HFDF . . . . . . High-Frequency Direction Finder
HF/DF . . . . . High-Frequency Direction Finding (Electronics)
HFE . . . . Heat-Flow Experiment
HFE . . . . Helmholtz Free Energy
HFE . . . . Human Factors in Electronics
HFE . . . . Human Factors Engineering
HFEF . . . . . . Hot Fuel Examination Facility (AEC)
HFET . . . . . . Heilmann-Feynman Electrostatic Theorem
HFF . . . . High-Frequency Furnace
HFF . . . . Hydraulic Fluid Filter
HFF . . . . Hypervelocity Flow Field
HFFF . . . . . . Hungarian Freedom Fighters Federation
HFFF . . . . . . Hypervelocity Free Flight Facility
HFG . . . . Harmonic Frequency Generator
HFG . . . . Human Factors Group
HFI . . . . High Fidelity Institute
HFI . . . . Hunt Foods and Industries, Inc. (NYSE symbol) (Delisted)
HFIAW . . . . . International Association of Heat and Frost Insulators and Asbestos Workers
HFIC . . . . . . Home Furnishings Industry Committee
HFIP . . . . . . Hexafluoroisopropanol (Chemistry)
HFIR . . . . . . High Flux Isotope Reactor (AEC)
HFJ . . . . High-Frequency Jammer
HFL . . . . Helium Fill Line
HFL . . . . Human Factors Laboratory (National Bureau of Standards)
HFM . . . . Hold for Money (Business and trade)
HFMF . . . . . Hone-Finish Monolithic Floor (Technical drawings)

HFMS . . . . Human Factors Measurement System
HFO . . . . Half Fare Order (Aviation)
HFO . . . . High-Frequency Oscillator
HF & OR . . . . Human Factors and Operations Research (Army)
HFORL . . . . . . Human Factors Operation Research Laboratory (Air Force)
HFP . . . . Helical Flight Path
HFP . . . . Helium Fuel-Tank Pressurization
HFP . . . . Hostile Fire Pay (Special pay for hazardous duty) (Military)
HFPCS . . . . . . Health Facilities Planning and Construction Service
HFPO . . . . Hexafluoropropylene Oxide
HFPS . . . . . . Hay Fever Prevention Society
HFPS . . . . Home Fallout Protection Survey (Formerly, EFPH) (Civil Defense)
HFR . . . . High Flux Reactor (Netherlands)
HFR . . . . High-Frequency Resistor
HFR . . . . Hold for Release
HFR . . . . Human Factors Research
HFRA . . . . . . Honorary Fellow of the Royal Academy
HFRE . . . . Hydraulic Fluid Replenishment Equipment
HFRT . . . . . . High-Frequency Radio Transmitter
HFS . . . . Heavy Flushing Spray
HFS . . . . Holy Family Seminary (Connecticut)
HFS . . . . Human Factors Society
HFS . . . . Hyperfine Structure
HFS . . . . Hypothetical Future Samples (Statistics)
HFSU . . . . Heat Flux Sensing Unit
HFSV . . . . . . High Flow Shutoff Valve
HFT . . . . High-Frequency Transceiver
HFTS . . . . Human Factors Trade Studies (Navy)
HFU . . . . Heeres-Funkstelle (Army radio station) (German military – World War II)
HFV . . . . Horizontal Flight Vector
HFWA . . . . . . High-Frequency Wave Analyzer
HFWF . . . . . . Hired Farm Working Force
HFX . . . . High-Frequency Transceiver
HG . . . . Hand Generator
HG . . . . Harmonic Generator
HG . . . . Hectogram(s)
HG . . . . Heliogram
HG . . . . High German (language, speech, etc.)
HG . . . . His (or Her) Grace
HG . . . . Holy Ghost
HG . . . . Home Guard (British)
HG. . . . . Homing Guidance
HG . . . . Horse Guards (British)
HG . . . . Hull Gage
Hg . . . . Hydrargyrum (Mercury) (Chemical element)
HG . . . . Hydrogen Generator
HG . . . . Hypobranchial Gland
H & G . . . . . Harden & Grind (Technical drawings)
HGA . . . . . . Heptagonal Games Association
HGA . . . . . . High Gain Antenna
HGA . . . . . . Hobby Guild of America
HGA . . . . . . Hop Growers of America
HGA . . . . . . Hotel Greeters of America
HGB. . . . . . . Hemoglobin
HGB . . . . . . Hot Gas Bonder
HGCB . . . . . Household Goods Carriers' Bureau
HGD . . . . . . Hourglass Device (Military decoration)
HGDH . . . . . His (or Her) Grand Ducal Highness
HGE . . . . . . Handling Ground Equipment
HGF. . . . . . . Human Growth Foundation
HGF. . . . . . . Hyperglycemic-Glycogenolytic Factor (Endocrinology)
HGG . . . . . . Hot Gas Generator
HGH. . . . . . . Hughes & Hatcher, Inc. (NYSE symbol)
HGH . . . . . . Human Growth Hormone (Endocrinology)
HGH . . . . . . Hyperglycemic-Glycogenolytic Factor (Later, Glucagon) (Endocrinology)
HGL . . . . . . Hausgemeinschaftsleitung
HGL . . . . . . High Gain Link
HGL . . . . . . High Go Low Test
HGMS . . . . . Helicopter Gravity-Measuring System (Naval Oceanographic Office)
HGN . . . . . . Hypogastric Nerve (Anatomy)
HGO . . . . . . Hepatic Glucose Output (Physiology)
HGPRT . . . . . Hypoxanthine-Guanine Phosphorilbosyltransferase
HGPS . . . . . . High Grade Plow Steel
HGR. . . . . . . Haubitzgranate (Howitzer shell) (German military – World War II)
HGR . . . . . . High Group Receiving
HGRF . . . . . . Hot Gas Radiating Facility
HGS . . . . . . Hyberbolic Grid System
HGSE . . . . . . Harvard Graduate School of Education
HGSE . . . . . . Hot Gas Soldering Equipment
HGSHS . . . . . Harvard Group Scale of Hypnotic Susceptibility
HGSW . . . . . . Horn Gap Switch

HGT . . . . . . High Group Transmitting
HGTVC . . . . . Hot Gas Thrust Vector Control
HGWA . . . . . Household Goods for Warders Association
HH . . . . Half Hard (Metallurgy)
HH . . . . Handhole
HH . . . . Hard of Hearing
HH . . . . Hashomer Hatzair
HH . . . . Heavy Hydrogen
HH . . . . High-Powered, Nondirectional Radio Homing Beacon (Navigation)
HH . . . . His (or Her) Highness
HH . . . . His Holiness
HH . . . . Houdaille Industries, Inc. (NYSE symbol)
HH . . . . Humbert Humbert (Character in Vladimir Nabokov's "Lolita")
HHA . . . . . . Hickory Handle Association
HHB . . . . . . Headquarters and Headquarters Battery
HHb . . . . . . Reduced Hemoglobin
HHBLG . . . . . Hobby Horse Brigade of the Legion of Guardsmen
HHC. . . . . . . Headquarters and Headquarters Company
HHC . . . . . . Hovercraft-Helicopter Carrier
HHCL . . . . . . H-Hour Coordinating Line (Army)
HHD . . . . . . Doctor of Honorary Humanities
HHD . . . . . . Doctor of Humanities
HHD . . . . . . Headquarters and Headquarters Detachment (Army)
HHE . . . . . . Helium to Heat Exchanger
HHE . . . . . . Herringer-Hulster Effect
HHE . . . . . . Household Economics Research Division (of ARS, Department of Agriculture)
HHE . . . . . . Household Effects
HHEFG . . . . . Hughes Hall Effect Function Generator
HHEG . . . . . . Hughes Hall Effect Generator
HHES . . . . . . Hex Head Electrical Squib
HHF . . . . . . Household Furniture (Insurance)
HHFA . . . . . . Housing and Home Finance Agency (Terminated, 1965; functions taken over by HUD)
HHFC . . . . . . H. H. Franklin Club
HHG . . . . . . Household Goods
HHGFAA . . . . Household Goods Forwarders Association of America
HHH. . . . . . . Hubert Horatio Humphrey
HHHH . . . . . Head, Heart, Hands, and Health (as in 4H organizations)
HHHMU . . . . Hydrazine Hand-Held Maneuvering Unit
HHI . . . . Harness Horsemen International
HHLR . . . . . . Horace Hardy Lestor Reactor
HHM . . . . . . Sisters of the Holy Humility of Mary (Roman Catholic religious order)
HHMS . . . . . . His Hellenic Majesty's Ship
HHMU . . . . . Hand-Held Maneuvering Unit (NASA)
HHN . . . . . . Hot Hydrogen Nozzle
HHP . . . . . . Hydraulic Hand Pump
HHS . . . . . . Helpers of the Holy Souls (Roman Catholic women's religious order)
HHS . . . . Hex Head Squib
HHT . . . . . . Headquarters and Headquarters Troop (Army)
HHV . . . . . . Help Hospitalized Veterans (An organization)
HHV . . . . . . High Heat Value
HHW . . . . . . Higher High Water
HHWI . . . . . . Higher High Water Interval
HI . . . . Harcost Industries
HI . . . . Harris-Intertype Corporation (NYSE symbol)
HI . . . . Hat Institute
HI . . . . Hawaii
Hi . . . . Hiburnium (Supposed chemical element, discovered 1922)
HI . . . . High
HI . . . . High Impact
HI . . . . High Intensity
HI . . . . Holton Inter-Urban R. R. (AAR code)
HI . . . . Hospital Insurance
HI . . . . Hostesses Internationales (French date service)
HI . . . . Hudson Institute
HI . . . . Humidity Index
HI . . . . Hydriodic Acid (Inorganic chemistry)
HI . . . . Hydrogen Iodide (Inorganic chemistry)
H and I . . . . Harassment and Interdiction
HIA . . . . . . Handkerchief Industry Association
HIA . . . . . . Health Industries Association
HIA . . . . . . Heart Infusion Agar
HIA . . . . . . Held (or Hold) in Abeyance (Military)
HIA . . . . . . Histadruth Ivrith of America
HIA . . . . . . Holiday Inns, Inc. (NYSE symbol)
HIA . . . . . . Horological Institute of America
HIA . . . . . . Hospital Industries' Association
HIAA . . . . . . Health Insurance Association of America
HIAA . . . . . . Hobby Industry Association of America
HIAC . . . . . . High Accuracy (RADAR)

HIAD	Handbook of Instructions for Aircraft Designers
HIADS	Hawaiian Integrated Air Defense System
HIAFSB	Handbook of Instructions for Air Force Subsystem Designers
HIAGSED	Handbook of Instructions for Aircraft Ground Support Equipment Designers
HIALS	High-Intensity Approach Lighting System (Airport runways)
HIAPSD	Handbook of Instructions for Aerospace Personnel Subsystem Designers
HIARA	Hail Insurance Adjustment and Research Association
HIAS	Hebrew Immigrant Aid Society
HIASD	Handbook of Instructions for Aerospace Systems Design
HIB	Herring Industries Board (British)
HIB	High Impedance Bridge
HIBAL	High Altitude Balloon
HIBEX	High Impulse Booster Experiments
HIC	Happy Irish Celebration
HIC	Health Insurance Council
HICAPCOM	High Capacity Communication system
HICAT	High-Altitude Clear Air Turbulence (Aviation)
HICLASS	Hierarchical Classification (Indexing)
HICO	Hastings Instrument Company
HICOG	High Commissioner for Germany
HICOM	High Command
HICOM	(Allied) High Commission(er), Germany
HICOMRY	High Commissioner of Ryukyu Islands
HICOMTERPACIS	High Commissioner Trust Territory, Pacific Islands
HID	Headache, Insomnia, Depression (Syndrome)
HIDA	Home Improvement Dealers Association of America
HIDAD	Helicopter Insecticide Dispersal Apparatus, Dry
HIDAF	Helicopter Insecticide Dispersal Apparatus, Fog
HIDAL	Helicopter Insecticide Dispersal Apparatus, Liquid
HIDAN	High Density Air Navigation
HIDE	High-Absorption Integrated Defense Electromagnetic Warfare System
HIE	Height Integration Equipment
HIE	Hibernation Information Exchange (Navy)
HIEAT	Highest Temperature Equaled for All Time (Meteorology)
HIEFM	Highest Temperature Equaled for the Month (Meteorology)
HIES	Hadassah Israel Education Services (Jerusalem)
HIESE	Highest Temperature Equaled So Early (Meteorology)
HIESL	Highest Temperature Equaled So Late (Meteorology)
HIF	Health Information Foundation
HIF	High Impedance Follower
HIF	Human Initiated Failure
H of IF	House of Ill Fame
HIFAR	High-Frequency Fixed Array RADAR
HIFC	Hog Intrinsic Factor Concentrate
HIFI	High-Intensity Food Irradiator
HI-FI	High-Fidelity (Usually, in reference to home sound-reproducing equipment)
HIFOR	High-Level Forecast (Meteorology)
HIG	Hermetically Sealed, Integrating Gyros
HIG	Honeywell Integrating Gyro
HIG	Hypervelocity Intercept Guidance
HIGED	Handbook of Instructions for Ground Equipment Designers
HIGH GASSER	High Geographic Aero-Space Search RADAR
HIGS	Hypervelocity Interceptor Guidance Simulation
HIGSS	Hypervelocity Intercept Guidance Simulator Study
HIH	His (Her) Imperial Highness
HIHAT	High Resolution Hemispherical Reflector Antenna Technique
HI-HICAT	High, High Altitude Clear Air Turbulence (Aviation)
HII	Health Insurance Institute
HII	High Input Impedance
HII	Host International, Incorporated (NYSE symbol)
HIJ	Sisters of the Holy Infant Jesus (Roman Catholic religious order)
HIJMS	His Imperial Japanese Majesty's Ship
HIL	High Intensity Light
HILAC	Heavy-Ion Linear Accelerator (AEC)
HIM	High-Intensity Microphone
HIM	His (Her) Imperial Majesty
HIMD	Handbook of Instructions for Missile Designers
HIMR	Handbook of Inspection Maintenance Requirements
HIMS	Heavy Interdiction Missile System
HIN	High-Intensity Noise
HING	High-Intensity Noise Generator
HIOMT	Hydroxyindole O-Methyltransferase (Biochemistry)
HIP	Hanford Isotopes Plant
HIP	Health Insurance Plan (of Greater New York)
HIP	High-Impact Pressure
HIP	Highly Ionized Plasma
HIP	Horizontal Injection Press
HIP	Hot Isostatic Pressure (Metals)
HIPA	Home Improvement Products Association
HIPAC	Hitachi Parametron Automatic Computer
HIPAR	High-Power Acquisition RADAR
HIPEG	High Performance External Gun
HIPERNAS	High Performance Navigation System
HIPIR	High Power Illuminator RADAR (Army)
HIPO	Hospital Indicator for Physicians' Orders
HIPR	High Internal Phase Ratio
HIPRI	High Priority
HIPS	Hyper-Intense Proximal Scanning
HIPSA	Hallicrafters Incremental Power Spectrum Analyzer
HIQ	Housing Intelligence Quotient
HIR	Handbook of Inspection Requirements (Navy)
HIR	Helicopter Instrument Rules
HIR	Walker (Hiram)-Gooderham & Worts, Ltd. (NYSE symbol)
HIRAC	High Random Access
HIRAN	High-Precision SHORAN (Short Range Navigation)
HIRD	High-Intensity Radiation Device
HIRDL	High-Intensity Radiation Development Laboratory
HIRES	Hypersonic In-Flight Refueling System
HIRF	High-Intensity Reciprocity Failure
HIRL	High-Intensity Runway Lights (Aviation)
HIRS	High-Impulse Retrorocket System
HIS	Health Interview Survey (National Institutes of Health)
HIS	Heavy Ion Source
HIS	Hic Iacet Sepulters (Here Lies Buried)
HIS	Histidine (Amino acid)
HIS	History (or Historical)
HIS	Hit Indicator System
HIS	Hospital Information System (Data processing)
HIS	Siegel (Henry I.) Co., Inc. (NYSE symbol)
HISE	High Interference Signalling Environment
HISS	High-Intensity Sound Simulator (or System)
HISSBI	Hispunan Serikat Buruh Indonesia (Federation of Indonesian Trade Unions)
HIST	High Input Shock Test
HIST	History
HISTEP	High-Speed Integrated Space Transportation Evaluation Program
HIT	Health Indication Test (Engine system)
HIT	Holtzman Inkblot Test (Psychology)
HIT	Hughes, Induced Turbulence
HIT	Hypersonic Interference Technique
HIT	Hypervelocity Impulse Tunnel
HITS	High-Speed Integrated Test System
HIUS	Hispanic Institute in the United States
HIVAC	High Value Asset Control
HIVOS	High Vacuum Orbital Simulator
HIXAT	Highest Temperature Exceeded for All Time (Meteorology)
HIXFM	Highest Temperature Exceeded for the Month (Meteorology)
HIXSE	Highest Temperature Exceeded So Early (Meteorology)
HIXSL	Highest Temperature Exceeded So Late (Meteorology)
HIY	Holiday Institute of Yonkers
HJ	Hic Jacet (Here Lies)
HJ	Honest John (A type of short range, unguided Army rocket)
HJ	Howard Johnson Company (NYSE symbol)
HJB	Hydrodynamic Journal Bearing
HJC	Hagerstown Junior College (Maryland)
HJC	Harcum Junior College (Pennsylvania)
HJC	Hibbing Junior College (Minnesota)
HJC	Highland Junior College (Kansas)
HJC	Hinds Junior College (Mississippi)
HJC	Holmes Junior College (Mississippi)
HJC	Holyoke Junior College (Massachusetts)
HJC	Hutchinson Junior College (Kansas)
HJD	Heterojunction Device
HJL	Honest John Launcher
HJP	Hand Jewel Pusher
HJP	Heat Jacketed Pump
HJPP	Heat Jacketed Proportioning Pump
HJR	Honest John Rocket
HJR	House Joint Resolution
HJ Res	House Joint Resolution
HJS	Hic Jacet Sepultus (Here Lies Buried)
HK	Heater Kit
HK	Hoeheres Kommando (Higher Command) (German military - World War II)
HK	House of Keys (Isle of Man)
HK	Human Kidney
HKA	Hong Kong Airways, Ltd.
HKF	Halbkettenfahrzeug (Half-track vehicle) (German military - World War II)
HKM	Harbison-Walker Refractories Company (NYSE symbol) (Delisted)
HKM	Hypervelocity Kill Mechanism (Air Force)
HKR	Hooker Chemical Corporation (NYSE symbol) (Delisted)
HKSU	Hong Kong Seamen's Union
HKT	Hollow Kathode Tube

HKT . . . . Hot Kathode Tube
HL . . . . Half-Life (of radioactive elements)
HL . . . . Hand Lantern
HL . . . . Head Linesman (Football)
HL . . . . Hecla Mining Co. (NYSE symbol)
HL . . . . Hectoliter
HL . . . . Height-Length
HL . . . . Helium Level
HL . . . . Herpetologists' League
HL . . . . High Level
HL . . . . Hinge Line (Technical drawings)
HL . . . . Histocompatibility Locus
HL . . . . Hoc Loco (In This Place)
HL . . . . Horizontal Line
HL . . . . Hot Line (Alert system)
HL . . . . House of Lords (British)
HL . . . . Hydrodynamics Laboratory (MIT)
HL . . . . Hygienic Laboratory (US)
HLA . . . . Hat Leather Association
HL-A . . . . Human Lymphocyte - Antigen (System for recognizing foreign tissue)
HLAS . . . . . . Handbook of Latin American Studies
HLAS . . . . . . Hot Line Alert System
HLB . . . . Harvard Library Bulletin
HLB . . . . Hydrophile-Lipophile Balance (Biochemistry)
HLBB . . . . . . Home Loan Bank Board
HLC . . . . House of Lords Cases (Law) (British)
HLCS . . . . . . Heat Limiter Control Switch
HLD . . . . Helium Leak Detector
HLE . . . . Hydrogen Line Emission
HLF . . . . Hallicrafters Company (NYSE symbol) (Delisted)
HLF . . . . Heart and Lung Foundation
HLF . . . . High Loss Ferrite
HLF . . . . Horizontal Line Frequency
HLFM . . . . . . High-Level Flux Monitor
HLG . . . . HAWK Logistics Group (Army)
HLG . . . . Homing Level Gage
HLH . . . . Heavy-Lift Helicopter
HLH . . . . Human Luteinizing Hormone
HLHS . . . . . . Heavy-Lift Helicopter System
HLI . . . . Highland Light Infantry (British)
HLI . . . . Holmium LASER Illuminator
HLL . . . . High-Level Language
HLL . . . . Hill Corporation (NYSE symbol) (Delisted)
HLM . . . . High Latitude Mode
HLM . . . . High-Level Mixer
HLN . . . . Holland Furnace Company (NYSE symbol) (Delisted)
HLN . . . . Hyperplastic Liver Nodules
HLNE . . . . . . Hillsboro & Northeastern Railway Company (AAR code)
HLO . . . . High Latitude Operation
HLO . . . . Holly Oil Company (NYSE symbol)
HLP . . . . Hypersonic Local Pressure
HLR . . . . Helicopter LASER Range-Finder
HLR . . . . Heller (Walter E.) International Corp. (NYSE symbol)
HLRM . . . . . . High Level Radio Modulator
HLS . . . . Heavy Lift System
HLS . . . . Heavy Logistics System
HLS . . . . Hoc Loco Situs (Laid in This Place)
HLS . . . . Holograph Letter Signed
HLSE . . . . . . High Level, Single Ended
HLT . . . . Hilton Hotels Corporation (NYSE symbol)
HLTL . . . . . . High-Level Transistor Logic
HLTTL . . . . . High-Level Transistor Translator Logic
HLV . . . . Herpes-Like Virus
HLW . . . . Higher Low Water
HLWI . . . . . . Higher Low Water Interval
HLY . . . . Holly Sugar Corporation (NYSE symbol)
HLZ . . . . Helicopter Landing Zone
HM . . . . Half Morocco
HM . . . . Hallmark
HM . . . . Handmade
HM . . . . Harbor Master
HM . . . . Harmonic Mean (Music)
HM . . . . Headmaster or Headmistress
HM . . . . Heavy Maintenance (Ordnance)
HM . . . . Heavy Mobile
HM . . . . Hectometer (100 meters)
HM . . . . His (or Her) Majesty
HM . . . . Hoc Mense (In This Month)
HM . . . . Hollow Metal (Technical drawings)
HM . . . . Home Mission
HM . . . . Homestake Mining Company (NYSE symbol)

HM . . . . Homogenization Medium
HM . . . . Hospital Corpsman (Navy rating)
HM. . . . . Hydrogen MASER
H/m . . . . Henry per Meter
HMA . . . . . . His (or Her) Majesty's Airship (British)
HMA . . . . . . Hoist Manufacturers Association
HMA . . . . . . Home Manufacturers Association
HMA . . . . . . Hot Melt Applicator
HMAC . . . . . . Health Manpower Advisory Council
HMAS. . . . . . His (or Her) Majesty's Australian Ship
HMB. . . . . . . Homatropine Methyl Bromide (Medicine)
HMB. . . . . . . Hops Marketing Board (British)
HMBA . . . . . . Hebrew Master Bakers Association
HMBS . . . . . . His Majesty's British Ship
HMC . . . . . . Heroin, Morphine and Cocaine (Mixture) (Slang)
HMC . . . . . . His (or Her) Majesty's Customs
HMC . . . . . . Historical Manuscripts Commission (British)
HMC. . . . . . . Howitzer Motor Carriage
HMC . . . . . . Hundred Million Club
HMC . . . . . . Hyoscine, Morphine, and Cactine (Tablets)
HMCS . . . . . . His (or Her) Majesty's Canadian Ship
HMCS . . . . . . His (or Her) Majesty's Civil Service
HMD . . . . . . Hammond Corp. (NYSE symbol)
HMD . . . . . . Helmet-Mounted Display
HMD . . . . . . Heterodyne Matrix Detector
HMD . . . . . . Hyaline Membrane Disease
HMD . . . . . . Hydraulic Mean Depth
HMDA . . . . . . Hydrostatic Motor Driven
HMDA . . . . . . Hexamethylenediamine (Organic chemistry)
HMDAA . . . . . Hydroxymethyl Diacetone Acrylamide
HMDBA . . . . . Hollow Metal Door and Buck Association
HMDF . . . . . . Hollow Metal Door and Frame (Technical drawings)
HMDS. . . . . . Hexamethyldisilazane (Organic chemistry)
HMDS. . . . . . Hexamethyldisiloxane (Organic chemistry)
HME. . . . . . . Hull, Mechanical, Electrical (Ship equipment) (Navy)
HM & E . . . . . Hull - Mechanical and Electrical (Ship equipment) (Navy)
HMEA . . . . . . Hatters Machinery and Equipment Association
HMED. . . . . . Heavy Military Electronics Department
HMEED. . . . . . Heavy Military Electronic Equipment Division (General Electric Company)
HMF. . . . . . . High Magnetic Field
HMF. . . . . . . His (or Her) Majesty's Forces
HMFF . . . . . . Hoc Monumentum Fieri Fecit (Caused This Monument to Be Made)
HMFI . . . . . . Her Majesty's Factory Inspectorate (Department of Employment) (British)
HMG . . . . . . Heavy Machine Gun
HMG . . . . . . His (or Her) Majesty's Government
HMG . . . . . . Human Menopausal Gonadotrophin (Endocrinology)
HMGB . . . . . . His (or Her) Majesty's Gun-Boat
HMGF . . . . . . High Modulus Glass Fiber
HMGI . . . . . . Hotel-Motel Greeters International
HMH . . . . . . His (or Her) Majesty's Household
HMI . . . . Hahn-Meitner-Institut fuer Kernforschung (West Germany)
HMI . . . . Handbook of Maintenance Instructions
HMI . . . . His (or Her) Majesty's Inspector
HMI . . . . Hoist Manufacturers Institute
HMI . . . . Horticultural Marketing Inspectorate (Ministry of Agriculture, Fisheries, and Food) (British)
HMI . . . . House Magazine Institute
HMIMF . . . . . His (or Her) Majesty's Indian Military Forces
HMIN . . . . . . His (or Her) Majesty's Indian Navy
HML. . . . . . . Hammermill Paper Company (NYSE symbol)
HML . . . . Hammond Metallurgical Laboratory (Yale)
HML. . . . . . . Heeresmunitionslager (Army ammunition depot) (German military - World War II)
HML . . . . His (or Her) Majesty's Lieutenant
HML . . . . Horace Mann League of the USA
HMM . . . . . . Heavy Meromyosin (Biochemistry)
HMMFC . . . . . House Merchant Marine and Fisheries Committee
HMN . . . . . . Heptamethylnonane (Fuel)
HMO . . . . . . Health Maintenance Organization (Proposed US health care plan)
HMO . . . . . . Heart Minute Output (Physiology)
HMO . . . . . . Hueckel Molecular Orbitals
HMP . . . . . . Handmade Paper
HMP. . . . . . . Harper's Magazine Press
HMP. . . . . . . Hexamethylphosphoramide (Chemical)
HMP. . . . . . . Hexose Monophosphate (Biochemistry)
HMP. . . . . . . High Melting Point
HMP. . . . . . . Hoc Monumentum Posuit (He Erected This Monument)
HMP. . . . . . . Humidity Monitoring Panel
HMP. . . . . . . Hydraulic Maintenance Panel
HMPA . . . . . . Hexamethyl Phosphoric Triamide
HMPMA . . . . . Historical Motion Picture Milestones Association

HMRA . . . . . . Hadassah Medical Relief Association
HMRP . . . . . . Hurricane Microseismic Research Problem (Aerology)
HMS . . . . Harmonic Multiplier Source
HMS . . . . Hierarchical Memory Storage (Data processing)
HMS . . . . Hind Mazdoor Sabha (India)
HMS . . . . His (or Her) Majesty's Service
HMS . . . . His (or Her) Majesty's Ship
HMS . . . . His (or Her) Majesty's Steamer
HMSA . . . . . . Hardware Manufacturers Statistical Association
HMSA . . . . . . Hawk Mountain Sanctuary Association
HMSO . . . . . . His (or Her) Majesty's Stationery Office
HMSO . . . . . . Honolulu Magnetic and Seismological Observatory
HMSS . . . . . . Hospital Management Systems Society
HMT . . . . Hexamethylenetetramine (Organic chemistry)
HMT . . . . His (or Her) Majesty's Trawler
HMT . . . . . . Hydrazine Monopropellant Thruster
HMTS . . . . . . Her Majesty's Telegraph Ship
HMTT . . . . . . Hexamethyl Trithiane
HMU . . . . Hydraulic Mock-Up
HMV . . . . His Master's Voice (Phonograph records)
HMW . . . . . . Hamilton Watch Company (NYSE symbol)
HMW . . . . . . High Molecular Weight
HMWC . . . . . . Health of Munition Workers Committee (British) (World War I)
HN . . . . Head Nurse
HN . . . . Hospitalman (Nonrated enlisted man) (Navy)
HN . . . . Host Nation
HN . . . . Human Nutrition Research Division (of ARS, Department of Agriculture)
HN . . . . Hutchinson & Northern Railway Company (AAR code)
HNA . . . . . . Hanna (M. A.) Company (NYSE symbol) (Delisted)
HNA . . . . . . Harrison Narcotic Act
HNA . . . . . . High Nickel Alloy
HNB . . . . . . Horn & Hardart Baking Company of New Jersey (American Stock Exchange symbol)
HNC . . . . . . Higher National Certificate (British)
HND . . . . . . Higher National Diploma (British)
HNE . . . . . . Harriman & Northeastern R. R. (AAR code)
HNG . . . . . . Houston Natural Gas Corp. (NYSE symbol)
HNGL . . . . . . Helium Neon Gas LASER
HNH . . . . . . Handy & Harman (NYSE symbol)
HNI . . . . . . Health News Institute (Defunct)
HNI . . . . . . Holmes and Narver, Incorporated
HNL . . . . . . Helium Neon LASER
HNL . . . . . . Hourly Noise Level
HNM . . . . . . Hanna Mining Co. (NYSE symbol)
HNM . . . . . . Hertzberg-New Method (Standard periodical binding)
HNM . . . . . . Hexanitromannite (Organic chemistry)
HNP . . . . . . Herniated Nucleus Pulposus (Medicine)
HNP . . . . . . High Needle Position (on dial)
HNPA . . . . . . Home Numbering Plan Area (AT & T)
HNPF . . . . . . Hallam Nuclear Power Facility (AEC)
HNS . . . . . . Hamilton Normal School
HNS . . . . . . Hanes Corp. (NYSE symbol)
HNS . . . . . . Hexanitrostilbene (High explosive)
HNS . . . . . . Holy Name Society
HNSF . . . . . . Hungarian National Sports Federation
HNZ . . . . . . Heinz (H. J.) Company (NYSE symbol)
HO . . . . Hale Observatories (Formerly, Mount Palomar and Mount Wilson Observatories)
HO . . . . Handelsorganisation
HO . . . . Head Office
HO . . . . High Oblique (Aerospace)
HO . . . . Holdover (Theater)
Ho . . . . Holmium (Chemical element)
HO . . . . Holy Day of Obligation
HO . . . . Home Office (British)
HO . . . . Hostilities Only (Applied to men who joined for duration of war only) (British Navy) (World War II)
HO . . . . House Officer
HO . . . . Hydrographic Office (Terminated 1963; later, NOO) (Navy)
HO . . . . Observation Helicopter
HOA . . . . . . Hands Off - Automatic
HOA . . . . . . Heavy Observation Aircraft
HOA . . . . . . Hechalutz Organization of America
HOA . . . . . . Home Owner Association
HOAP . . . . . . Housing Opportunity Assistance Program (Federal Home Loan Bank Board)
HOB . . . . . . Half-Octave Bandwidth
HOB . . . . . . Height (Depth) of Burst
HOB . . . . . . Hobart Manufacturing Co. (NYSE symbol)
HOB . . . . . . Homing on Offset Beacon
HOBE . . . . . . Horseshoe Bend National Military Park
HOBO . . . . . . Homing Optical Bomb

HOBOS . . . . . . Homing Bomb System (North American Rockwell Co.)
HOBS . . . . . . High Orbital Bombardment System
HOC . . . . . . Heavy Oil Cracking (Process) (Petroleum industry)
HOC . . . . . . Height Overlap Coverage (RADAR)
HOC . . . . . . High Output Current
HOC . . . . . . Hurricane Operations Center
HOCUS . . . . . . Hand or Computer Universal Simulation (Simulation modeling method)
HOD . . . . . . Heat of Detonation
HOD . . . . . . Hebrew Order of David
HODS . . . . . . Hydrographic Oceanographic Data Sheets
HOE . . . . . . Hydraulically Operated Equipment
HOF . . . . . . Hall of Fame
HOFR . . . . . . Home of Franklin D. Roosevelt and Vanderbilt Mansion National Historic Sites
HOFS . . . . . . Hydrogen-Oxygen Fuel System
HOG . . . . . . Homing Optical Guidance
HOGS . . . . . . Homing Optical Guidance System
HOH . . . . . . Hereford Otter Hounds
HOHI . . . . . . Handbook of Overhaul Instructions
HOI . . . . . . Handbook of Overhaul Instructions (Navy)
HOI . . . . . . Headquarters Office Instruction
HOI . . . . . . Headquarters Operating Instructions (Air Force)
HOJ . . . . . . Home on Jamming
HOJO . . . . . . Howard Johnson (Restaurant chain) (Slang)
HOKS . . . . . . Hind Oil Kamger Sabha (India)
HOL . . . . . . Higher Order Language (Data processing)
HOL . . . . . . Holiday
HOL . . . . . . House of Lords (British)
HOLC . . . . . . Home Owners' Loan Corporation (Terminated, 1942)
HOLUA . . . . . . Home Office Life Underwriters Association
HOM . . . . . . Hoskins Manufacturing Company (American Stock Exchange symbol)
HOME . . . . . . Homestead National Monument
HOMO . . . . . . Highest Occupied Molecular Orbitals
HOMOCO . . . . . . Homemakers and Mothers Cooperatives, Inc.
HOMP . . . . . . Halifax Ocean Meeting Point
HON . . . . . . Hold Off Normal
HON . . . . . . Honeywell, Inc. (NYSE symbol) (Formerly, M-H)
HON . . . . . . Honorable
HOO . . . . . . Hanford Operations Office (AEC)
HOP . . . . . . Helicopter Operations
HOP . . . . . . Helium Oxidizer-Tank Pressure
HOP . . . . . . High Oxygen Pressure
HOPE . . . . . . Health Opportunity for People Everywhere (Philanthropic project operating hospital ship)
HOPE . . . . . . Health Organization to Preserve the Environment
HOPE . . . . . . Help Obese People Everywhere (An organization)
HOPE . . . . . . Highly-Instrumented Orbiting Primate Experiment
HOPE . . . . . . Homes of Private Enterprise (An organization)
HOPE . . . . . . Housing Our People Economically
HOPE . . . . . . Hydrogen-Oxygen Primary Extraterrestrial (Fuel cell) (NASA)
HOPI . . . . . . Handbook of Operating Instructions (Navy)
HOPS . . . . . . Helmet-Mounted Optical Projection System
HOPS . . . . . . Heterodyne Optical Optimization Communication System with Stops (NASA)
HOR . . . . . . Heliocentric Orbit Rendezvous
HOR . . . . . . Home of Record
HORAD . . . . . . Horizontal RADAR Display
HORECA . . . . International Union of National Associations of Hotel, Restaurant and Cafe Keepers
HORSE . . . . . . Heavy Operational Repair Squadron Engineer (Air Force)
HOS . . . . . . Howard Stores Corporation (NYSE symbol) (Delisted)
HOS . . . . . . Hydrographic Office Scale (Obsolete)
HOSC . . . . . . Hardened Operational Site Concept
HOSC . . . . . . History of Science Cases
HOSI . . . . . . Handbook of Service Instructions
HOSP . . . . . . Hospital
HOSP . . . . . . Hot Springs National Park
HOSPRATS . . . Hospital Rations (Navy)
HOSS . . . . . . Halo Orbit Space Station (NASA)
HOSS . . . . . . Homing Optical System Study
HOSTWOY . . . Home of Selection and Completion of Travel Within One Year is Authorized (Military)
HOT . . . . . . Hand Over Transmitter
HOT . . . . . . Horizontal Output Transformer
HOT . . . . . . Horizontal Output Tube
HOT . . . . . . Human Old Tuberculin
HOTAC . . . . . . Helicopter Optical Tracking and Control
HOTBUN . . . . . . Have Not Yet Begun to Fight (Simulated war game)
HOTCE . . . . . . Hot Critical Experiments (AEC)
HOTLIPS . . . . . . Honorary Order of Trumpeters Living in Possible Sin
HOTRAN . . . . . . Hover and Transition (Simulator)
HOU . . . . . . Houston Lighting & Power Company (NYSE symbol)

HOVE . . . . . . Hovenweep National Monument
HOVI . . . . Handbook of Overhaul Instructions
HOVI . . . . Hopewell Village National Historic Site
HOVVAC . . . . Hovering Vehicle Versatile Automatic Control
HOW . . . . Happiness of Womanhood (Anti-feminist women's group)
HOWT . . . . . . Howard Terminal R. R. (AAR code)
HOW-TO . . . . Housing Operation with Training Opportunity (Office of Economic Opportunity)
HP . . . . Half Pay
HP . . . . Handling and Propulsion
HP . . . . Handmade Paper
HP . . . . Hard Point
HP . . . . Hauptpunkte (Crystallography)
HP . . . . Haut Parleur (Loudspeaker)
HP . . . . Helmerich & Payne, Inc. (NYSE symbol)
HP . . . . Hewlett-Packard Company
HP . . . . High Pass (Electronics)
HP . . . . High Performance
HP . . . . High Potency
HP . . . . High Power
HP . . . . High Pressure (Turbines)
HP . . . . High-Pressure Cylinder (Especially, a locomotive cylinder)
HP . . . . High Priest
HP . . . . High Priority
HP . . . . Highly Purified
HP . . . . Hire Purchase
HP . . . . Holding Pattern (Aviation)
HP . . . . Holiday Pay (Army)
HP . . . . Homeopathic Pharmacopoeia
HP . . . . Horizontal Parallax (Navigation)
HP . . . . Horizontal Polarization
HP . . . . Horse Power
HP . . . . Hot Pack or Pad (Physical therapy)
HP . . . . Hot Pilot (An egotistic flying cadet) (Air Force slang)
HP . . . . Hot-Pressed (Paper)
HP . . . . House Physician
HP . . . . Houses of Parliament (British)
HP . . . . Hydrostatic Pressure
HP . . . . Hypertension and Proteinuria
HP . . . . Hypertransfused Polycythemic
HP . . . . Hysterical Personality
H-P . . . . Handley-Page Ltd.
H-P . . . . High-Purity
H & P . . . . . . History and Physical (Examination) (Medicine)
HPA . . . . Head Post Assembly
HPA . . . . Head of a Procuring Activity (Army)
HPA . . . . High Power Amplifier
HPA . . . . High Pressure Air
HPA . . . . Hydraulic Pneumatic Area
HPAA . . . . . . High Pressure Air Accumulator
HPAAS . . . . . High Performance Aerial Attack System
HPAC . . . . . . Hydro-Press Accessory (Tool)
HPAG . . . . . . High Performance Air-to-Ground
HPAS . . . . . . High Performance Adhesive System
HPB . . . . Congregation of Handmaids of the Precious Blood (Roman Catholic religious order)
HPB . . . . Hand-Printed Books
HPB . . . . Helena Petrovna Blavatsky (Famous 19th-century occultist)
HPB . . . . Hinged Plotting Board
HPC . . . . Helicopter Performance Computer
HPC . . . . Hercules, Inc. (Formerly, Hercules Powder Company) (NYSE symbol)
HPC . . . . High Point College (North Carolina)
HPC . . . . Howard Payne College (Texas)
HPC . . . . Hydraulic Package Container
HPCA . . . . . . Hiroshima Peace Center Associates
HPCC . . . . . . High Performance Control Center (Aerospace)
HPCGS . . . . . (Frank-Massy) Household Purchasing Characteristics Generating System (Marketing)
HPCRB . . . . . Hydraulic Power Control Relay Box
HPD . . . . Hard Point Defense
HPD . . . . High Performance Drone
HPD . . . . High Power Density
HPD . . . . Hydraulic Pump Discharge
HPDI . . . . . . Hard Point Defense Interceptor
HPDLRL . . . . . High Power Diffraction Limited Raman LASER
HPDS . . . . . . Hard Point Defense System
HPER . . . . . . Health, Physical Education, and Recreation
HPF . . . . Harbor Patrol Fleet
HPF . . . . High Pass Filter
HPF . . . . High Power Field (Microscopy)
HPF . . . . Highest Possible Frequency (Electronics)

HPFC . . . . . . High Performance Fuel Cell
HPFM . . . . . . Hydro-Press Form (Tool)
HPG . . . . Hall (W. F.) Printing Company (NYSE symbol)
HPG . . . . High Power Generator
HPG . . . . Human Pituitary Gonadotrophin (Endocrinology)
HPG . . . . Hyper-Pure Germanium
HPGC . . . . . . Heading Per Gyro Compass (Navigation)
HPGC . . . . . . Hypopressure Gas Chromatography
HPH . . . . Hamischfeger Corp. (NYSE symbol)
HPH . . . . High Pressure Hose
HPH . . . . Horsepower-Hour
HPHD . . . . . . High Pressure High Density
HP-HR . . . . . . Horsepower-Hour
HPI . . . . Hardwood Plywood Institute
HPI . . . . Heavy Positive Ion
HPI . . . . Heifer Project, Incorporated
HPI . . . . Helme Products, Incorporated (NYSE symbol)
HPI . . . . High Performance Interceptor
HPI . . . . History of Present Illness
HPI . . . . Hydraulic Pressure Indicator
HPIP . . . . . . High Pressure Intensifier Pump
HPIR . . . . . . High Power Illuminator RADAR
HPIS . . . . . . High Performance Insulation System
HPJ . . . . High Power Jammer
HPJ . . . . High Pressure Jet
HPJC . . . . . . Highland Park Junior College (Later, Highland Park College) (Michigan)
HPK . . . . High Power Klystron
HPKA . . . . . . High Power Klystron Amplifier
HPL . . . . High Power LASER
HPL . . . . Human Placental Lactogen
HPLF . . . . . . High-Pressure Low-Flow
HPLJ . . . . . . High Pressure Liquid Jet
HPLR . . . . . . Hinge Pillar (Technical drawings)
HPM . . . . . . Head Positioning Mechanism
HPM . . . . . . Horizontal Panel Mount
HPM . . . . . . Human Potential Movement (Psychotherapy)
HPM . . . . . . Hydraulic Punching Machine
HPMA . . . . . Hardwood Plywood Manufacturers Association
HPMA . . . . . . High-Power Microwave Assembly
HPMA . . . . . . Hydroxypropyl Methacrylate
HPMV . . . . . . High Pressure Mercury Vapor
HPN . . . . Heavy Primary Nuclei
HPN . . . . High Pass Network
HPN . . . . Horsepower Nominal
HPO . . . . High Pressure Oxygen
HPO . . . . Highway Post Office (Bus or truck equipped with mail distribution facilities)
HPOT . . . . . . Helipotentiometer
HPOX . . . . . . High Pressure Oxygen
HPP . . . . Half Page Printer
HPP . . . . Harvard Project Physics
HPP . . . . Hydraulic Pneumatic Panel
HPPS . . . . . . Hughes Post Processor, Surveyor
HPPTS . . . . . . Hydraulic Package Pressure Test Set
HPR . . . . Halden Reaktor Prosjekt (Norway)
HPR . . . . Heart Profile Recorder
HPR . . . . High Polymer Rheology
HPR . . . . Hughes Photoelectric Reader
HPR . . . . Human Performance Reliability
HPRF . . . . . . Hypersonic Propulsion Research Facility
HPRR . . . . . . Health Physics Research Reactor (ORNL)
HPS . . . . Hardened Power System
HPS . . . . Health Physics Society
HPS . . . . Heat Protection System
HPS . . . . Hermetic Pivoting Seal
HPS . . . . High Pressure Steam (Technical drawings)
HPS . . . . High Protein Supplement
HPS . . . . Hull Pressure Switch
HPS . . . . Hybrid Propulsion System
HPS . . . . Hydraulic Power Section (Later, HPU: Hydraulic Pumping Unit)
HPS . . . . Hydraulic Power Supply
HPSA . . . . . . Hellenic Philatelic Society of America
HPSA . . . . . . Hydraulic Package Servovalve Actuator
HPSC . . . . . . Heading Per Standard Compass (Navigation)
HPSC . . . . . . Hydraulic Package Storage Container
HPSD . . . . . . High Power Switching Device
HPSTGC . . . . . Heading Per Steering Compass (Navigation)
HPT . . . . American Home Products Corporation (NYSE symbol) (Later, AHP)
HPT . . . . Hexamethylphosphorsauretrimide
HPT . . . . High Pot Tester
HPT . . . . High Pressure Test

HPT . . . . Horizontal Plot Table
HPT . . . . Hydrocylic Pressure Testing
HPTD . . . . . . High Point, Thomasville & Denton R. R. (AAR code)
HPTP . . . . . . Hydraulic Power Transfer Panel
HPTS . . . . . . High-Performance Third Stage (Rocket) (Army)
HPU . . . . Hydraulic Power Unit
HPU . . . . Hydraulic Pumping Unit
HPV . . . . Helium Pressure Vessel
HPV . . . . High-Passage Virus
HPV . . . . High Power Veractor
HPV . . . . High Pressure Valve
HPV-DE . . . . . High-Passage Virus (Grown in) Duck Embryo (Cells)
HPV-DK . . . . . High-Passage Virus (Grown in) Dog Kidney (Cells)
HQ . . . . Headquarters
HQ . . . . Highly Qualified
HQ . . . . Hoc Quaere (Look for This; See This)
HQBA . . . . . . Headquarters Base Area
HQC . . . . . . Handling Quality Criteria
HQC . . . . . . Headquarters Command (Air Force)
HQC . . . . . . High "Q" Circuit
HQC . . . . . . High "Q" Coil
HQC . . . . . . Hydraulic Quick Coupler
HQC . . . . . . Hydroxyquinoline Citrate
HQ-CAP . . . . . Headquarters, Civil Air Patrol
HQCOMDUSAF . . Headquarters Command, United States Air Force
HQCS . . . . . . Heraldic Quality Control System
HQDP . . . . . Headquarters, Department of the Pacific (Marine Corps)
HQES . . . . . . High-Quality Exitaxial Silicon
HQMC . . . . . . Headquarters, Marine Corps
HQS . . . . . . High-Quality Silicon
HQ & SERV. . . Headquarters and Service (Marine Corps)
HQSQ . . . . . . Headquarters Squadron
HQT . . . . . . Halogen Quenched Tube
HQTC . . . . . . High "Q" Tuned Circuit
HQ USAF . . . . Headquarters United States Air Force
HR . . . . Hair Space Between Letters (Proofreader's mark)
HR . . . . Handling Room
HR . . . . Heart Rate
HR . . . . Heat Resisting (Technical drawings)
HR . . . . Height Range (RADAR)
HR . . . . Helium Rebottled (System)
HR . . . . Helium, Refrigerated
HR . . . . Hemorrhagic Retinopathy
HR . . . . High Resistance
HR . . . . High Run
HR . . . . Highland Railway (British)
HR . . . . Home Rule
HR . . . . Home Run (Baseball)
HR . . . . Homoreactant (Medicine)
HR . . . . Hose Rack
HR . . . . Hospital Recruit
HR . . . . Hour
HR . . . . House of Representatives
HR . . . . Human Reliability
HR . . . . Humanitarian Reassignment (Military)
HR . . . . Humidity, Relative
HR . . . . International Harvester Company (NYSE symbol)
H & R . . . . . Harper & Row (Publisher)
H & R . . . . . Holding and Reconsignment (Military)
HRA . . . . . . Heat Rate Acceleration
HRA . . . . . . Heavy Replaceable (or Replacement) Assembly
HRA . . . . . . Hemispherical Reflective Antenna
HRA . . . . . . Highest Rank Aboard
HRA . . . . . . Honorary Royal Academician (British)
HRA . . . . . . Human Resources Administration (New York City)
HRA . . . . . . Hydraulic Rotary Actuator
HRAF . . . . . . Human Relations Area Files
HRAS . . . . . . High-Rate Activated Sludge (Waste treatment)
HRAT . . . . . . Hampton Roads Army Terminal
HRB . . . . H. & R. Block, Inc. (NYSE symbol)
HRB . . . . . . Highway Research Board
HRBC . . . . . . Horse Red Blood Cells
HRC . . . . . . Hardwood Research Council
HRC . . . . . . Helium Research Center
HRC . . . . . . Howard Research Corporation
HRC . . . . . . Human Resources Center
HRC . . . . . . Hybrid Receiver Circuit
HRD . . . . . . High Resolution Display
HRD . . . . . . Human Resources Development (An affiliate of International Correspondence Schools)
HRD . . . . . . Hydraulic Rate Damper

HRDL . . . . . . Hudson River Day Line R. R. (AAR code)
HRE . . . . Holy Roman Emperor (or Empire)
HRE . . . . Homogeneous Reactor Equipment
HRE . . . . Hubbard Real Estate Investments (NYSE symbol)
HRE . . . . Hydrazine Rocket Engine
HRE . . . . Hypersonic Research Engine (NASA)
HREBIU . . . . . Hotel and Restaurant Employees and Bartenders International Union
HREC . . . . . . Health Record
HRES . . . . . . High Resolution Electronic System
H Res . . . . . . House Resolution, United States House of Representatives
HRET . . . . . . Hospital Research and Educational Trust
HREU . . . . . . Hotel and Restaurant Employees and Bartenders International Union
HRF . . . . Height Ranger Finder
HRF . . . . Hussmann Refrigerator Company (NYSE symbol) (Delisted)
HRF . . . . Hypersonic Rarefied Flow
HRFA . . . . . . Hudson River Fisherman's Association
HRFA . . . . . . Hungarian Reformed Federation of America
HRH . . . . High Rate Heat
HRH . . . . His (or Her) Royal Highness
HRI . . . . Height-Range Indicator (Electronics)
HRI . . . . Horizon Reference Indicator (Aerospace)
HRI . . . . Horticultural Research Institute
HRIO . . . . . . Height-Range Indicator Operator
HRIP . . . . . . Hic Requiescat in Pace (Here Rests in Peace)
HRIP . . . . . . Highway Research in Progress
HRIR . . . . . . High-Resolution Infrared-Radiometer
HRIS . . . . . . High Repetition Illuminator System
HRIS . . . . . . Highway Research Information Service (of Highway Research Board)
HRJ . . . . High-Range Juno (Survey meter for radiation)
HRL . . . . Heat Rejection Loop
HRL . . . . High Refraction Layer
HRL . . . . High Repetition LASER
HRL . . . . Horizontal Reference Line (Technical drawings)
HRL . . . . Hughes Research Laboratories (Hughes Aircraft Co.)
HRL . . . . Human Resources Laboratory (Air Force)
HRLI . . . . . . High Repetition LASER Illuminator
HRLIS . . . . . . High Repetition LASER Illuminating System
HRLS . . . . . . High Repetition LASER System
HRO . . . . Homes Registration Office
HRO . . . . Housing Referral Office (Air Force)
HRP . . . . Heat-Resistant Phenolic
HRP . . . . Heat Resisting Plastic
HRP . . . . Holding and Reconsignment Point (Army)
HRP . . . . Human Reliability Program
H & RP . . . . . Holding and Reconsignment Point (Army)
HRPA . . . . . . Hebrew Religious Protection Association of Greater New York
HRPC . . . . . . High Range Pressure Control
HRPI . . . . . . High Resolution Pointable Imager
HRR . . . . Heat Rejection Radiator
HRR . . . . High Reliability Relay
HRR . . . . High Resolution RADAR
HRRC . . . . . . Human Resources Research Center
HRRI . . . . . . Human Resources Research Institute
HRRL . . . . . . Human Resources Research Laboratory (Air Force)
HRRO . . . . . . Human Resources Research Office
HRS . . . . Heading Reference System
HRS . . . . High Resolution System
HRS . . . . Home Reunion Society (British)
HRS . . . . Honorary Reserve Section
HRS . . . . Hospital Reading Society
HRS . . . . Hot Rolled Steel
HRS . . . . Hovering Rocket System
HRSD . . . . . . Hard Rock Silo Development
HRSS . . . . . . Hrvatska Republikanska Seljacka Stranka
HRT . . . . Hartwell R. R. (AAR code)
HRT . . . . Helmholtz Reciprocal Theorem
HRT . . . . High-Rate Telemetry (NASA)
HRT . . . . High Resolution Tracker
HRT . . . . Hiring, Retention, and Tenure (of college professors)
HRT . . . . Homogeneous Reactor Test
HRTS . . . . . . High Risk Test Site
HRV . . . . Heat Rate Variability
HRV . . . . Hydraulic Relief Valve
HRV . . . . Hypersonic Research Vehicle
HRW . . . . Holt, Rinehart & Winston, Inc. (NYSE symbol) (Delisted)
HRZ . . . . Hertz Corporation (NYSE symbol) (Delisted)
HS . . . . Half Strength
HS . . . . Half Subtractor
HS . . . . Handset
HS . . . . Hardstand
HS . . . . Harness or Saddlery

HS	Hartford & Slocomb R. R. (AAR code)
HS	Head Suppression
HS	Heat Shield (Aerospace)
HS	Heaviside (Ionosphere)
HS	Helicopter Squadron, Antisubmarine
HS	Hemstitched
HS	Heparitin Sulfate (Biochemistry)
HS	Herpes Simplex
HS	Hic Situs (Laid Here)
HS	High School
HS	High Speed
HS	Hinged Seat
HS	Historical Survey
HS	Hoc Sensu (In This Sense)
HS	Home Secretary (British)
HS	Honorary Secretary
HS	Horizon Scanner
HS	Horizon Sensor
HS	Horizontal Shear
HS	Horizontal Stripes (as on buoys, beacons)
HS	Hospital Ship
HS	Hot Spraying
HS	Hot Stuff (Slang)
HS	House Surgeon
HS	Hydraulic Supply
HS	Hydraulic System
HS	Hydrofoil Ship
HS	Hypersonic
H & S	Headquarters and Service (Battery) (Army)
HSA	Harvard Student Agencies (Inc.)
HSA	Herb Society of America
HSA	High Specific Activity (Radioisotope)
HSA	High Strength Adhesive
HSA	Hispanic Society of America
HSA	Holly Society of America
HSA	Hospital Savings Association
HSA	Human Serum Albumin
HSA	Hymn Society of America
HSAA	Health Sciences Advancement Award (National Institutes of Health)
HSAC	House Science and Astronautics Committee (US Congress)
HSAP	Honeycomb Sandwich Aluminum Panel
HSAS	Hard Stability Augmentation System
HSAS	Hypertrophic Subaortic Stenosis (Medicine)
HSA-UWC	Holy Spirit Association for the Unification of World Christianity
HSB	Heat Shield Boost
HSB	Hermetically Sealed Bushing
HSB	High-Speed Bus
HSBA	Horizontal Static Balancing Adjustment
HSBP	High-Speed Bench Press
HSBR	High-Speed Bombing RADAR
HSC	Hampden-Sydney College (Virginia)
HSC	Harsco Corporation (NYSE symbol)
HSC	Heat Sterilization Compound
HSC	High-Speed Carry
HSC	Higher School Certificate (British)
HSC	Home Products Safety Council
HSC	House Space Committee (US Congress)
HSC	Human Skin Collagen
HSC	Humboldt State College (California)
HSCA	Horizontal Sweep Circuit Analyzer
HSCC	Heavy Specialized Carriers Conference
HSCP	High-Speed Card Punch (Data processing)
HSCR	High-Speed Card Reader (Data processing)
HSCR	High Sub-Chief Ranger (Ancient Order of Foresters)
HSCT	Hughes Satellite Communications Terminal
HSD	Hardsite Defense (Army)
HSD	Hawker-Siddeley Dynamics
HSD	Height Sensing Device
HSD	Hit Scoring Device
HSD	Horizontal Situation Display
HSD	Hydropneumatic Suspension Device
HSDA	High-Speed Data Acquisition
HS-DARS	High-Speed - Data Acquisition and Reduction System
HSDL	High-Speed Data Link
HSDM	High-Speed Die Mounter
HSDP	Hardsite Data Processor (Army)
HSDT	High-Speed Distributor Transmitter
HSE	Hic Sepultus Est (Here Lies Buried)
HSEAD	Historical Society of Early American Decoration
HSEF	High School Evangelism Fellowship
HSERC	Historical Society of the Evangelical & Reformed Church

HSES	Hughes Satellite Earth Station
HSEUBC	Historical Society of the Evangelical United Brethren Church
HSF	Hartford Seminary Foundation
HSF	Hawaiian Sea Frontier
HSF	Hotel Sundry Fund (Air Force)
HSF	Hypothalamic Secretory Factor
HSFF	High-Speed Force Feed
HSFS	High-Speed Flight Station (NASA)
HSG	Holy Shroud Guild
HSG	Hydro-Shift Gun
HSGP	High School Geography Project
HSGT	High-Speed Ground Transportation
HSH	His (or Her) Serene Highness (Used for certain Continental European princes or princesses)
HSI	Handbook of Service Instructions
HSI	High Solar Intensity
HSI	High Strand Intensity
HSI	Horizontal Situation Indicator
HSJ	Honey-Combed Sandwich Joint
HSK	Heat Sink Kit
HSK	Honorary Surgeon of the King
HSKPG	Housekeeping
HSL	High-Speed Launch
HSL	High-Speed Logic
HSLA	High-Strength Low-Alloy (Steel)
HSLLC	High-Speed Liquid-Liquid Chromatography
HSL'S	Hlinkova Slovenska L'udova Strana
HSLWI	Helical Spring Lock Washer Institute
HSM	Hand and Shoe Monitor (Radiation detection)
HSM	Hard Structure Munition
HSM	Hardened Silo Missile
HSM	Hart, Schaffner & Marx (NYSE symbol)
HSM	Health Services and Mental Health Administration (See also HSMHA) (HEW)
HSM	His (or Her) Serene Majesty
HSMA	Hotel Sales Management Association
HSMHA	Health Services and Mental Health Administration (HEW) (Also see HSM)
HSMS	High-Speed Microwave Switch
HSMSR	Hardsite Missile Site RADAR (Army)
HSN	Hughes Sports Network (Formerly, SNI)
HSNP	Hawker-Siddeley Nuclear Power Company, Ltd. (British)
HSNY	Holland Society of New York
HSP	Half-Shade Plate
HSP	High-Speed Printer (Data processing)
HSP	High-Speed Pulse
HSP	Hospital Corporation of America (NYSE symbol)
HSP	Hot Stamping Press
HSP	Human Serum Prealbumin
HSPA	Hawaiian Sugar Planters' Association
HSPA	High-Speed Parallel Adder
HSPC	Heat Sterilizable Potting Compound
HSPT	High School Placement Test
HSPTP	High-Speed Paper Tape Punch (Data processing)
HSR	Hampshire Swine Registry
HSR	High School Percentile Rank
HSR	High-Speed Rail
HSR	High-Speed Reader (Data processing)
HSR	High-Speed Relay
HSRA	Harvard-Smithsonian Reference Atmosphere
HSRA	Hollow Shaft Rotary Actuator
HSRC	Highway Safety Research Center (University of Michigan)
HSRI	Highway Safety Research Institute (University of Michigan)
HSRO	High-Speed Repetitive Operation
HSRP	High-Speed Rotary Prism
HSRS	Hurricane Supersonic Research Site
HSS	Habitability Support System
HSS	Heeres-Sauerstoffschutzgeraet (Service oxygen breathing apparatus) (German military - World War II)
HSS	High-Speed Steel
HSS	High Spread Shears
HSS	History of Science Society
HSS	Honeycomb-Supported Screen
HSS	Hull Seal Section
HSS	Hybrid Simulation System
HSSA	Handbag Supply Salesmen's Association
HSSG	Heeres-Sauerstoffschutzgeraet (Service oxygen breathing apparatus) (German military - World War II)
HSSG	High-Speed Symbol Generator
HSSG	Holograph Stress Strain Gauge
HS & SS	Headquarters and Service Squadron
HSST	Heavy Section Steel Technology (AEC)

HST . . . . Harmonic and Spurious Totalizer
HST . . . . Harry S Truman
HST . . . . Hawaiian Standard Time
HST . . . . Heat Shrinkable Tubing
HST . . . . High-Speed Telemetry
HST . . . . Homogenate Survival Time
HST . . . . . . Hot Shot Tunnel
HST . . . . Hypersonic Transport (Aircraft)
HST . . . . Virus named for Hamazaki, Sato, Takahashi, and Tani, principal
            investigators (Medicine)
HSTC . . . . . . Henderson State Teachers College (Arkansas)
HSTP . . . . . . Heat Sterilization Test Program
HSTRA . . . . . High Strength Thermal Resistant Alloy
HSTS . . . . . . Horizontal Stabilizer Trim Setting
HSTT . . . . . . High-Speed Test Track
HSU . . . . . . Hardin-Simmons University (Texas)
HSU . . . . . . Hydraulic Supply Unit
HSUNA . . . . . Humanist Student Union of North America
HSUS . . . . . . Humane Society of the United States
HSV . . . . Head Suppression Valve
HSV . . . . Hull Solenoid Valve
HSV . . . . Hydraulic Selector Valve
HSW . . . . . . Helena Southwestern R. R. (AAR code)
HSY . . . . Hershey Foods Corp. (NYSE symbol)
HSZD . . . . . . Hermetically Sealed Zener Diode
HT . . . . Half-Time (Survey) (Shipping)
HT . . . . Halftone (Photoengraving)
HT . . . . Halt and Transfer
HT . . . . Hand Translation
HT . . . . Handling Time
HT . . . . Hawaiian Telephone Company (NYSE symbol) (Delisted)
HT . . . . Hawaiian Territory (Prior to statehood)
HT . . . . Hawaiian Theater (Military)
HT . . . . Hawaiian Time
HT . . . . Headed Type
HT . . . . Heat
HT . . . . Heat Treat
HT . . . . Heavy Tank
HT . . . . Height
HT . . . . Height of Target
HT . . . . Height Technician (Air Force)
HT . . . . Height Telling (RADAR)
HT . . . . Herd Test
HT . . . . High Temperature
HT . . . . High Tension
HT . . . . High Tide
HT . . . . Hoc Tempore (At This Time)
HT . . . . Hoc Titulo (In, or Under, This Title)
HT . . . . Hollow Tile (Technical drawings)
HT . . . . Homing Terrier
HT . . . . Horizontal Tabulation
HT . . . . Horsed Transport (Military)
HT . . . . Hospital Train
HT . . . . House Trailer
HT . . . . Hydrotherapy
HT . . . . Hydroxytryptamine
HT . . . . Hypertropia
HT . . . . Hypodermic Tablet
HTA . . . . . . Harness Tracks of America
HTA . . . . . . Heavier Than Air (Aircraft)
HTA . . . . . . High-Temperature Adhesive
HTA . . . . . . High Temperature Alloy
HTB . . . . . . Hair Tuning Bar
HTC . . . . . . Harris Teachers College (Missouri)
HTC . . . . . . Harris Transducer Corporation
HTC . . . . . . Hebrew Teachers College (Massachusetts)
HTC . . . . . . Hepatoma Tissue Culture
HTC . . . . . . High-Temperature Coil
HTC . . . . . . Highway Traffic Control
HTC . . . . . . Hughes Tool Company
HTC . . . . . . Huston Tillotson College (Texas)
HTC . . . . . . Hydraulic Temperature Control
HTC . . . . . . Hydraulic Test Chamber
HTC . . . . . . Hydrofoil Test Craft
HTCI . . . . . . High Tensile Cast Iron
HTD . . . . . . Hand Target Designator
HTD . . . . . . Horizontal Tactical Display
HTDS . . . . . . Hydrofoil Tactical Data System
HTDU . . . . . Horizontal Tactical Display Unit
HTE . . . . . . Hydraulic Test Equipment
HTF . . . . Heat Transfer Fluid

HTFC . . . . . . High-Temperature Fuel Cell
HTFMI . . . . . Heat Transfer and Fluid Mechanics Institute
HTFX . . . . . . Heat Treat Fixture
HTGR . . . . . . High-Temperature Gas-Cooled Reactor (AEC)
HTGR-CX . . . . High-Temperature Gas Reactor Critical Experiment
HTH . . . . Hexagon Tungsten Honeycomb
HTH . . . . High-Temperature Heater
HTH . . . . High-Test Hypochlorite
HTI . . . . Hand Tool Institute
HTI . . . . Horizontal Tactics Indicator
HTJ . . . . H-Plane Tee Junction
HTL . . . . Heat Transfer Laboratory (MIT)
HTL . . . . High-Temperature Lacquer
HTL . . . . High Threshold Logic
HTL . . . . High Turbulence Level
HTLT . . . . . . Hughes Transportable Link Terminal
HTLTR . . . . . . High-Temperature Lattice Test Reactor
HTM. . . . . . . Hard Tube Modulator (Electronics)
HTM . . . . Heat Transfer Meter
HTM . . . . High-Temperature Materials
HTM . . . . High-Temperature Metallography
HTMP . . . . . . High-Temperature Thermomechanical Processing (Alloy heat resistan
HTN . . . . Heterodyne
HTN . . . . Houghton Mifflin Co. (NYSE symbol)
HTO. . . . . . . Highway Transportation Officer (Army)
HTO. . . . . . . Horizontal Take-Off
HTO. . . . . . . Hospital Transfer Order
HTP . . . . Hardness Test Plan (Army)
HTP . . . . High Test Hydrogen-Peroxide
HTP . . . . Humidity Test Procedure
HTP . . . . Hydroxytryptophan
H-T-P . . . . . . A House, a Tree, a Person (Psychological drawing test)
HTPB . . . . . . Hydroxyl-Terminated Polybutadiene
HTR . . . . Halt and Transfer
HTR . . . . Harvard Theological Review (A publication)
HTR . . . . Heater
HTR . . . . High-Temperature Reactor (Atomic energy)
HTR . . . . High-Temperature Resistor
HTR . . . . Highway Traffic Regulation
HTR . . . . Hitachi Training Reactor (Japan)
HTR . . . . Homogeneous Thorium Reactor
HTRDA . . . . . High-Temperature Reactor Development Associates
HTRE . . . . . . Heat Transfer Reactor Experiment
HTRK . . . . . . Half-Track (A type of military vehicle)
HTS . . . . Hamden Testing Services, Inc.
HTS . . . . Harness Tracks Security (An organization)
HTS . . . . Hawaiian Tracking Station
HTS . . . . Heat Transfer Section
HTS . . . . Heat Transfer System
HTS . . . . Heat Transport Section (Apollo) (NASA)
HTS . . . . Heat-Treated Steel
HTS . . . . Height-Telling Surveillance
HTS . . . . High Tensile Steel
HTS . . . . High Tensile Strength
HTS . . . . Hybrid Test Set
HTS . . . . Hydraulic Test Set (or Station)
HTSC . . . . . . Highway Traffic Safety Center (Michigan State University)
HTSUP . . . . . Height Supervisor (RADAR)
HTT . . . . Heavy Tactical Transport
HTT . . . . High-Temperature Thermomechanical Treatment (Steel forging)
HTT . . . . Hook Tongue Terminal
HTTR . . . . . . Heat Treat
HTU . . . . Heat Transfer Unit
HTU . . . . Height of Transfer
HTV . . . . Herpes-Type Virus
HTV . . . . Homing Test Vehicle
HTV . . . . Hypersonic Test Vehicle (Air Force)
HTW . . . . High-Temperature Water
HTW . . . . High-Temperature Wire
HTW . . . . Hoosac Tunnel & Wilmington R. R. (AAR code)
HTX . . . . Health-tex, Inc. (NYSE symbol)
HTXRD . . . . . High-Temperature X-Ray Diffraction
HTY . . . . Henry Holt & Company (NYSE symbol) (Delisted)
HU . . . . Harvard University
HU . . . . Hydroxyurea
HU. . . . . Hyperemia Unit
HUAC . . . . . . House Un-American Activities Committee (Later, HCIS)
HUBA . . . . . . Hudson Bay R. R. (AAR code)
HUC . . . . . . Hebrew Union College (California, New York, Ohio)
HUCO . . . . . Hughes NADGE Consortium
HUCR . . . . . . Harvard University Character Recognizer (Data processing)

HUCR . . . . Highest Useful Compression Ratio (Aerospace)
HUD . . . . Department of Housing and Urban Development
HUD . . . . Heads-Up Display (Air Force)
HUFF-DUFF . . . High-Frequency Direction Finder
HUFSM . . . . . . Highway Users Federation for Safety and Mobility
HUG . . . . Head of Units Group (American Library Association)
HUGO . . . . . . Highly Unusual Geophysical Operation (A meteorological research vehicle)
HUK . . . . Hunter-Killer (Operations against submarines)
HUKFORLANT . . Hunter-Killer Forces, Atlantic (Navy)
HUKP . . . . Hostile, Unknown, Faker, and Pending (Used in SAGE to designate certain tracks and raids)
HUKS . . . . Hunter-Killer Submarine (Navy)
HUMID . . . . . . Hughes Unit Malfunction Isolation Detector
HUMINT . . . . . Human Intelligence
HUMRRO . . . . . Human Resources Research Office (CONARC)
HUMS . . . . Humanitarian Reasons
HUNTEST . . . . . Hunting and Testing (Apollo) (NASA)
HUP . . . . Helicopter Utility (Piasecki)
HUP . . . . Hospital Utilization Project (Western Pennsylvania)
HUREP . . . . . . Hurricane Report
HURRAH . . . . . Help Us Reach & Rehabilitate America's Handicapped (State-Federal rehabilitation program)
HUS . . . . Helicopter Utility Squadron
HUSAFICPA . . . Headquarters, United States Army Forces in Central Pacific Area
HUSTLE . . . . . Helium Underwater Speech Translating Equipment
HUTR . . . . Hubbell Trading Post National Historic Site
HUTRON . . . . Helicopter Utility Squadron
HV . . . . Hauptverwaltung
HV . . . . Heating and Ventilation
HV . . . . High Velocity
HV . . . . High Voltage
HV . . . . High Volume
HV . . . . Hypervelocity
H-V . . . . Height-Velocity
HVA . . . . Hauptverwaltung Aufklaerung (Main Administration for Intelligence) (East Germany)
HVA . . . . Heeresverwaltungsamt (Army Administration Office) (German military – World War II)
HVA . . . . Homovanillic Acid
HVAC . . . . . . Heating, Ventilating, and Air Conditioning (Building construction)
HVAP . . . . . . High Velocity, Armor-Piercing (Projectile)
HVAP . . . . . . Hypervelocity, Armor Piercing (Missiles)
HVAPDS . . . . . High Velocity, Armor-Piercing, Discarding Sabot (Projectile)
HVAP-T . . . . . Hypervelocity Armor Piercing - Tracer (Military)
HVAR . . . . . . High Velocity Aircraft Rocket
HVAT . . . . High Velocity Antitank (Projectile)
HVB . . . . Hauptverbandplatz (Clearing station) (German military – World War II)
HVB . . . . High Voltage Bias
HVC . . . . Hayden's Virbunum Compound (Medicine)
HVC . . . . High Voltage Connector
HV & C . . . . . Heating, Ventilating, and Cooling
HVD . . . . Height Velocity Diagram
HVD . . . . High Velocity Detonation
HVD . . . . Hypertensive Vascular Disease
HVDC . . . . . . High Voltage Direct Current
HVDF . . . . High and Very-High-Frequency Direction Finding
HVDP . . . . . . Heavy Drop (Military)
HVE . . . . High Vacuum Environment
HVE . . . . High Vacuum Evaporator
HVE . . . . High Voltage Engineering Corporation (NYSE symbol)
HVEC . . . . . . High Voltage Engineering Corporation
HVEM . . . . . . High-Voltage Transmission Electron Microscopy
HVES . . . . High Vacuum Evaporation System
HVF . . . . Harmonically Varying Field
HVG . . . . Haveg Industries, Inc. (NYSE symbol) (Delisted)
HVG . . . . High Voltage Gradient
HVH . . . . Herpesvirus Hominis
HVI . . . . Home Ventilating Institute
HVJ . . . . Hemagglutinating Virus of Japan (Medicine)
HVL . . . . Half-Value Layer
HVL . . . . Heeresverpflegungslager (Army ration depot) (German military – World War II)
HVL . . . . High Voltage Laboratory (MIT)
HVM . . . . High-Voltage Mode
HVM . . . . Hydraulic Valve Motor
HVM . . . . Sisters, Home Visitors of Mary (Roman Catholic religious order)
HVMVI . . . . . . High Voltage Mercury Vapor Isolator
HVO . . . . Hackfleisch Verordnung
HVP . . . . Half Value Period
HVP . . . . Heart Valve Prostheses

HVP . . . . High Vacuum Pump
HVP . . . . High Voltage Pump
HVPI . . . . Holland Vocational Preference Inventory
HVPR . . . . High-Voltage Phase Retard
HVPS . . . . High Voltage Power Supply
HVR . . . . Helicopter Visual Rules
HVR . . . . High-Vacuum Rectifier
HVR . . . . High Voltage Rectifier
HVR . . . . High Voltage Relay
HVR . . . . High Voltage Resistor
HVRA . . . . Heating and Ventilating Research Association (British)
HVRL . . . . High Voltage Research Laboratory (MIT)
HVS . . . . High Voltage Switch
HVS . . . . Hypersonic Vehicle Shield
HVSCR . . . . . . High-Voltage Selenium Cartridge Rectifier
HVSS . . . . Horizontal Volute Spring Suspension (Projectile)
HVST . . . . High Voltage Switching Transistor
HVT . . . . High Voltage Termination
HVT . . . . High Voltage Tester
HVT . . . . High Voltage Transformer
HVTP . . . . High Velocity, Target Practice (Projectile)
HVTPDS . . . . . High Velocity, Target Practice Discarding Sabot (Projectile)
HVTP-T . . . . . . Hypervelocity Target Practice - Tracer (Military)
HVV . . . . Hamburger Verkehrsverbund (Hamburg, West Germany, subway)
HVW . . . . High Voltage Waveform
HVW . . . . High Voltage Wire
HVWS . . . . . . Hebrew Veterans of the War with Spain
HVY . . . . Heavy
HW . . . . Half Wave
HW . . . . Hauptwachtmeister (First Sergeant) (German military – World War II)
HW . . . . Head Width
HW . . . . Head Wind (Navigation)
HW . . . . Headwaiter
HW . . . . Heavy Wall
HW . . . . Heavy Water
HW . . . . Herewith (Enclosures)
HW . . . . High Water
HW . . . . Hit Wicket
HW . . . . Hot Water
HW . . . . Howmet Corp. (NYSE symbol)
H/W . . . . Highway
HWA . . . . Hackensack Water Company (NYSE symbol)
HWA . . . . Hot Wire Anemometer
HWAA . . . . . . Heereswaffenamt (Army Ordnance Office) (German military – World War II)
HWB . . . . Handwoerterbuch
HWBR . . . . . . Half Wave Bridge Rectifier
HWC . . . . Hoerner Waldorf Corporation (NYSE symbol)
HWC . . . . Hot Water Circulating (Technical drawings)
HWCTR . . . . . Heavy-Water Components Test Reactor
HWCU . . . . . . Heated Window Control Unit
HWEP . . . . . . Hot Wire Emissive Probe
HWF & C . . . . High Water Full and Change
HWGCR . . . . . Heavy Water-Moderated Gas-Cooled Reactor
HWI . . . . Hardware Wholesalers, Incorporated
HWI . . . . Head Width Index
HWI . . . . Helical Washer Institute
HWI . . . . High Water Interval
HWL . . . . Hauptwiderstandslinie (Main line of resistance in a delaying action) (German military – World War II)
HWL . . . . High Water Line (Technical drawings)
HWL . . . . Hot Water Line
HWM . . . . High Water Mark (Maps and charts)
HWN . . . . Hazard Warning Network
HWNA . . . . . . Hosiery Wholesalers National Association
HWO . . . . Homosexual World Organization
HWOC . . . . . . Hotel Waldorf Astoria (American Stock Exchange symbol)
HWOCR . . . . . Heavy Water-Moderated Organic-Cooled Reactor (AEC)
HWOST . . . . . High Water Ordinary Spring Tides (Maps and charts)
HWP . . . . Half-Wave Plate
HWP . . . . Heavy Water Plant (AEC)
HWP . . . . Hewlett-Packard Company (NYSE symbol)
HWQ . . . . High Water Quadrature
HWR . . . . Half-Wave Rectifier
HWR . . . . Heavy Water Reactor (AEC)
HWR . . . . Hot Water Return
HWS . . . . Hot Water Soluble
HWT . . . . Hypersonic Wind Tunnel
HWTC . . . . . . Highway Traffic Control
HWY . . . . Highway
HX . . . . High Index (Aviation)
HXBT . . . . Helicopter Expendable Bathythermograph (NOO)

HXQ . . . . Hard X-Ray Quanta
HXR . . . . Hudson & Manhatton Corp. (American Stock Exchange symbol)
HY . . . . Hypobranchial (Gland)
HYACS . . . . . Hybrid Analog-Switching Attitude Control System for Space Vehicles
HYAS . . . . . . Hydro Gasification (Gas from coal fuel)
HYCOL . . . . . Hybrid Computer Link
HY-COM . . . . Highway Communications
HYCOTRAN. . . Hybrid Computer Translator
HYD. . . . . . . Hydraulic
HYD. . . . . . . Hydrometals, Inc. (NYSE symbol)
HYDAC . . . . . Hybrid Digital-Analog Computing (System) (Satellite)
HYDAPT . . . . Hybrid Digital-Analog Pulse Time
HYDRA. . . . . Hydrographic Digital Positioning and Depth Recording (System) (NOO)
HYDRO. . . . . Hydrographic Office (Later, NOO) (Navy)
HYDRSS . . . . High Data Rate Storage Subsystem (NASA)
HYFES . . . . . Hypersonic Flight Environmental Simulator
HYGAS. . . . . . Hydrogen Gasification

HYK. . . . . . . Huyck Corp. (NYSE symbol)
HYLA . . . . . . Hybrid Language Assembler
HYMA . . . . . . Hebrew Young Men's Association
HYP . . . . Harvard, Yale, and Princeton Universities
HYPERDOP. . . . Hyperbolic Doppler
HYPREM . . . . . Hyper-Response Electric Motor
HYSTAD . . . . . Hydrofoil Stabilization Device
HYSURCH . . . . Hydrographic Surveying and Charting (System) (NOO)
HYTAC. . . . . . Hydraulic Tachometer
HYTREC . . . . . Hydrospace Target Recognition, Evaluation and Control
HYTRESS . . . . . Hyway Test Recorder and Simulator System
HYVIA . . . . . . Hyper-Velocity Interceptor Armament
HZ. . . . . Hazeltine Corporation (NYSE symbol)
Hz . . . . Hertz (Cycles per second)
HZN . . . . Horizon Corp. (NYSE symbol)
HZYO. . . . . . . Hashomer Hatzair Zionist Youth Organization

I

I . . . . Angle of Incidence
I . . . . Fighter (Russian aircraft symbol)
I . . . . I-Beam (Structural metal shape)
I . . . . Id (That)
I . . . . Imperator or Imperatrix (Emperor; Empress)
I . . . . Imperial
I . . . . Incendiary (Bomb)
I . . . . Incisor (Dentistry)
I . . . . Incomplete
I . . . . Independent
I . . . . Indicated (or Indicative)
I . . . . Indicator
I . . . . Industrial
I . . . . Infantry
I . . . . Infield
I . . . . Inhibitory
I . . . . Initial
I . . . . Initial Approach (Aviation)
I . . . . Inner
I . . . . Input
I . . . . Inside
I . . . . Inspector
I . . . . Instantaneous
I . . . . Institute (or Institution)
I . . . . Instrument Correction
I . . . . Instrumental (or Instrumentation)
I . . . . Intelligence
I . . . . Interbank (Credit cards)
I . . . . Interceptor
I . . . . Interlocked Metallic Armor (Technical drawings)
I . . . . Intermediate (Vessel load line mark)
I . . . . International
I . . . . Interstate (Highway)
I . . . . Intestine
I . . . . Inverter
I . . . . Iodine (Chemical element)
I . . . . Ionic Strength
I . . . . Iraqi
I . . . . Iron
I . . . . Island (Maps and charts)
I . . . . Israeli
I . . . . One (Roman numeral)
I¹³¹ . . . . Radioactive Iodine
IA . . . . Immediately Available
IA . . . . Impedance Angle
IA . . . . Implementing Agency
IA . . . . In Absentia
IA . . . . Incorporated Accountant
IA . . . . Incremental Analysis (Statistics)
IA . . . . Indian Army
IA . . . . Indicated Altitude (Navigation)
IA . . . . Indirect Addressing
IA . . . . Infected Area
IA . . . . Infra-Audible (Sound)
IA . . . . Initial Appearance (RADAR)
IA . . . . Initial Authorization
IA . . . . Inspection Administration (Navy)
IA . . . . Instrument Abstracts
IA . . . . Intemperate to Alcohol (An alcoholic) (Slang)
IA . . . . Inter Alia (Among Other Things)
IA . . . . Interface Amplifier
IA . . . . International Alliance of Theatrical Stage Employees and Moving Picture Machine Operators of the United States and Canada (Also, IATSE)

IA . . . . International Angstrom
IA . . . . Interval Availability
IA . . . . Intra-Arterial (Physiology)
IA . . . . Intra-Articular (Orthopedics)
IA . . . . Iowa
IA . . . . Iraqi Airways
IA . . . . Isolation Amplifier
IA . . . . Issuing Agency
IAA . . . . Independent Airlines Association
IAA . . . . Indian Association of America
IAA . . . . Indoleacetic Acid (Organic chemistry)
IAA . . . . Instrumental Activation Analysis
IAA . . . . Insurance Accountants Association
IAA . . . . Interim Access Authorization
IAA . . . . Interment Association of America
IAA . . . . International Academy of Astronautics
IAA . . . . International Acetylene Association
IAA . . . . International Advertising Association
IAA . . . . International Aerospace Abstracts
IAA . . . . International Allergy Association
IAA . . . . International Apple Association
IAA . . . . International Association of Allergology
IAA . . . . International Aviation Affairs (FAA)
IAA . . . . Intimate Apparel Associates
IAA . . . . Iodoacetic Acid
IAAA . . . . . . Integrated Advance Avionics for Aircraft
IAAAA . . . . . Intercollegiate Association of Amateur Athletes of America
IAAB . . . . . . Inter-American Association of Broadcasters
IAABO . . . . . International Association of Approved Basketball Officials
IAAC . . . . . . International Association for Analog Computing
IAAC . . . . . . International Association of Art Critics
IAADF . . . . . Inter-American Association for Democracy and Freedom
IAADS . . . . . Integrated Anti-Airborne Defense System
IAAE . . . . . . International Association of Agricultural Economists
IAAF . . . . . . International Amateur Athletic Federation
IAAFA . . . . . Inter-American Air Force Academy (Operated by US Air Force to provide training for Latin American countries)
IAAHU . . . . . International Association of Accident and Health Underwriters
IAAI . . . . International Association of Arson Investigators
IAALD . . . . . . International Association of Agricultural Librarians and Documentalists
IAAM . . . . . . International Association of Auditorium Managers
IAAM . . . . . . International Association of Automotive Modelers
IAAO . . . . . . International Association of Assessing Officers
IAAP . . . . . . International Association of Amusement Parks
IAAP . . . . . . International Association for Analytical Psychology
IAAP . . . . . . International Association of Applied Psychology
IAARC . . . . . . International Administrative Aeronautical Radio Conference
IAASE . . . . . . Inter-American Association of Sanitary Engineering
IAATCD . . . . . If Authorized by Air Traffic Control, DME (Distance Measuring Equipment) May Be Used (Aviation)
IAATI . . . . . . International Association of Auto Theft Investigators
IAB . . . . Industrial Advisory Board (World War II)
IAB . . . . Industrial Arbitration Board (British)
IAB . . . . Interagency Board of Examiners (Civil Service Commission)
IAB . . . . International Abstracting Board (International Council of Scientific Unions)
IABA . . . . . . Inter-American Bar Association
IABA . . . . . . International Air Brokers Association
IABBS . . . . . . International Amateur Boat Building Society
IABC . . . . . . International Association of Business Communicators
IABF . . . . . . Inter-American Bar Foundation
IABG . . . . . . International Association of Botanic Gardens
IAB-ICSU . . . . Abstracting Board - International Council of Scientific Unions

IABLA . . . . . . Inter-American Bibliographical and Library Association
IABO . . . . . . International Association of Biological Oceanography (of International Union of Biological Sciences)
IABPAI . . . . . International Association of Blue Print and Allied Industries
IABPBD . . . . . International Alliance of Bill Posters, Billers and Distributors
IABS . . . . . . International Abstracts of Biological Sciences
IABSE . . . . . . International Association for Bridge and Structural Engineering
IABSOIW . . . . . International Association of Bridge, Structural and Ornamental Iron Workers
IAC . . . . Indian Airlines Corporation
IAC . . . . Industry Advisory Committee (World War II)
IAC . . . . Industry Advisory Council (Formerly, DIAC)
IAC . . . . Information Analysis Center (DOD)
IAC . . . . Instrument Array Cable
IAC . . . . . . Insurance Advertising Conference
IAC . . . . Integrating Assembly (or Associate) Contractor
IAC . . . . Integration, Assembly, and Checkout
IAC . . . . Intermediate Air Command (Air Force)
IAC . . . . International Advisory Committee (ANSI)
IAC . . . . . . International Air Convention
IAC . . . . International Algebraic Compiler
IAC . . . . International Analysis Code (Meteorology)
IAC . . . . International Astronautical Congress
IAC . . . . Interview-After-Combat
IACA . . . . . . Independent Air Carriers Association
IACA . . . . . . Inter-American College Association
IACA . . . . . . Inter-American Cultural Association
I-ACAC . . . . . Inter-American Commercial Arbitration Commission
IACB . . . . . . Indian Arts and Crafts Board (Department of the Interior)
IACB . . . . . . Inter-Agency Consultative Board
IACB . . . . . . International Association of Convention Bureaus
IACC . . . . . . Industrial Analysis and Control Council
IACC . . . . . . Integrating Assembly and Checkout Contractor
IACC . . . . . . Inter-Agency Cartographic Committee
IACC . . . . . . Inter-American Cultural Council
IACCP . . . . . . Inter-American Council of Commerce and Production
IACD . . . . . . International Association of Clothing Designers
IACE . . . . . . International Air Cadet Exchange
IACED . . . . . . Inter-African Advisory Committee on Epizootic Diseases
IACH . . . . . . Inter-Association Committee on Health
IACHR . . . . . Inter-American Commission on Human Rights (OAS)
IACI . . . . Inter-American Children's Institute (OAS)
IACI . . . . Irish American Cultural Institute
IACID . . . . . . Inter-American Center for Integral Development (OAS)
IACM . . . . . . International Association of Concert Managers
IACME . . . . . International Association of Crafts and Small and Medium-sized Enterprises
IACOMS . . . . . International Advisory Committee on Marine Sciences
IACP . . . . . . International Association of Chiefs of Police
IACP . . . . . . International Association for Child Psychiatry and Allied Professions
IACRL . . . . . . Italian-American Civil Rights League
IACS . . . . . . Inertial Attitude Control System (Aerospace)
IACS . . . . . . Integrated Armament Control System
IACS . . . . . . International Annealed Copper Standard
IACS . . . . . . International Arms-Control Symposium
IACW . . . . . . Inter-American Commission of Women (OAS)
IAD . . . . Immediate Action Directive
IAD . . . . Initiation Area Discriminator (RADAR)
IAD . . . . Inland Steel Company (NYSE symbol)
IAD . . . . . . Institute for American Democracy
IAD . . . . Integrated Airbase Defense
IAD . . . . Integrated Automatic Documentation (System)
IAD . . . . Internal Absorbed Dose
IAD . . . . . . International Astrophysical Decade
IADA . . . . . . Independent Aeronautical Dealers Association
IADA . . . . . . International Atomic-Development Authority (Proposed by Bernard M. Baruch, 1946, but never created)
IADB . . . . . . Inter-American Defense Board
IADB . . . . . . Inter-American Development Bank (Also, IDB)
IADC . . . . . . Inter-American Defense College (Washington)
IADC . . . . . . Inter-American Development Commission
IADF . . . . . . Inter-American Association for Democracy and Freedom
IADL . . . . . . International Association of Democratic Lawyers
IADPC . . . . . . Inter-Agency Data Processing Committee
IADR . . . . . . International Association for Dental Research
IADS . . . . . . International Agricultural Development Service (Department of Agriculture)
IADS . . . . . . International Association of Dental Students
IADS . . . . . . International Association of Department Stores
IADWS . . . . . Interim Air Defense Weapon System (Army)
IAE . . . . Infrared Auroral Emission
IAE . . . . Institute of Atomic Energy (Academy of Sciences, USSR)

IAE . . . . Institute of Automobile Engineers
IAE . . . . Integral of Absolute Error
IAEA . . . . . . Inter-American Education Association
IAEA . . . . . . International Atomic Energy Agency
IAEACPD . . . . Inter-American Emergency Advisory Committee for Political Defense
IAEC . . . . . . International Atomic Energy Committee
IAECOSOC . . . Inter-American Economic and Social Council (UN)
IAEI . . . . International Association of Electrical Inspectors
IAEL . . . . . . International Association of Electrical Leagues
IAES . . . . . . International Association of Electrotypers and Stereotypers
IAESC . . . . . . Inter-American Economic and Social Council
IAESC . . . . . . International Association of Evening Student Councils
IAESTE . . . . . International Association for the Exchange of Students for Technical Experience
IAF . . . . Indian Air Force
IAF . . . . Indium Arsenide Filter
IAF . . . . Indonesian Air Force
IAF . . . . Industrial Areas Foundation
IAF . . . . Initial Approach Fix (Aviation)
IAF . . . . Institute on American Freedoms
IAF . . . . Instrument Air Filter
IAF . . . . International Abolitionist Federation
IAF . . . . International Aeronautical Federation
IAF . . . . International Astronautical Federation
IAF . . . . Italian Air Force (Regia Aeronautica Italiana) (World War II)
IAFA . . . . . . Inter-American Foundation for the Arts
IAFAE . . . . . . Inter-American Federation for Adult Education
IAFC . . . . . . Instantaneous Automatic Frequency Control
IAFC . . . . . . Inter-American Freight Conference
IAFC . . . . . . Interim Airframe Change
IAFC . . . . . . International Association of Fire Chiefs
IAFD . . . . . . International Association on Food Distribution
IAFE . . . . . . International Association of Fairs and Expositions
IAFF . . . . . . International Air Freight Forwarder
IAFF . . . . . . International Association of Fire Fighters
IAFI . . . . . . Infantile Amaurotic Family Idiocy (Medicine)
IAFP . . . . . . International Alliance of Film Producers
IAFWNO . . . . . Inter-American Federation of Working Newspapermen's Organizations
IAG . . . . Interagency Advisory Group (Civil Service Commission)
IAG . . . . Inter-Association Group
IAG . . . . International Association of Geodesy
IAG . . . . International Association of Gerontology
IAGA . . . . . . International Association of Geomagnetism and Aeronomy
IAGAL . . . . . . Industry Advisory Group for Air Logistics
IAGC . . . . . . Instantaneous Automatic Gain Control (RADAR)
IAGC . . . . . . International Association for Geochemistry and Cosmochemistry
IAGFA . . . . . . International Association of Governmental Fair Agencies
IAGFCC . . . . . International Association of Game, Fish and Conservation Commissioners
IAGLO . . . . . . International Association of Governmental Labor Officials
IAGLP . . . . . . International Association of Great Lakes Ports
IAGM . . . . . . International Association of Garment Manufacturers (Absorbed by NOSA)
IAGMA . . . . . Illuminating and Allied Glassware Manufacturers Association
IAGS . . . . . . Inter-American Geodetic Survey
IAH . . . . International Association of Hydrogeologists (of International Union of Geological Sciences)
IAH . . . . International Association of Hydrology
IAHA . . . . . . Inter-American Hospital Association
IAHA . . . . . . Inter-American Hotel Association
IAHA . . . . . . International Arabian Horse Association
IAHFIAW . . . . International Association of Heat and Frost Insulators and Asbestos Workers
IAHP . . . . . . Institutes for the Achievement of Human Potential
IAHP . . . . . . International Association of Horticultural Producers
IAHR . . . . . . International Association for the History of Religions
IAHR . . . . . . International Association for Hydraulic Research
IAHU . . . . . . International Association of Health Underwriters
IAI . . . . Informational Acquisition and Interpretation
IAI . . . . International African Institute
IAI . . . . International Association for Identification
IAI . . . . Israel Aircraft Industries, Ltd.
IAI . . . . Istituto Affairi Internazionali (Institute for International Affairs) (Italy)
IAIAA . . . . . . International Association for Iranian Art and Archaeology
IAIABC . . . . . International Association of Industrial Accident Boards and Commissions
IAIAS . . . . . . Inter-American Institute of Agricultural Sciences (OAS)
IAIC . . . . . . International Association of Insurance Counsel
IAICM . . . . . . International Association of Ice Cream Manufacturers
IAIE . . . . Inter-American Institute of Ecology
IAIES . . . . . . Institute for Advanced Interdisciplinary Engineering Studies (Purdue University)
IAII . . . . Inter-American Indian Institute (OAS)
IAIP . . . . Inorganic Ablative Insulative Plastic

IAIP . . . . International Association of Independent Producers
IAIP . . . . International Association of Individual Psychology
IAIU . . . . Insurance Agents International Union
IAJAM . . . . . . Industrial Association of Juvenile Apparel Manufacturers
IAJC . . . . Inter-American Juridical Committee
IAJE . . . . Internacia Socio de Juristoj-Esperantistoj (International Association of Esperantist Lawyers)
IAJRC . . . . International Association of Jazz Record Collectors
IAK . . . . Internationales Auschwitz-Komitee (International Auschwitz Committee)
IAL . . . . International Algebraic Language (Replaced by ALGOL)
IAL . . . . International Algorithmic Language
IAL . . . . International Association of Laryngectomees
IAL . . . . International Association of Limnology
IAL . . . . International Association of Theoretical and Applied Limnology
IALA . . . . International African Law Association
IALA . . . . International Association of Lighthouse Authorities
IALA . . . . International Auxiliary Language Association
IALC . . . . Instrument Approach and Landing Chart (Aviation)
IALC . . . . International Association of Lions Clubs
IALC . . . . International Association of Lyceum Clubs
IALF . . . . Inter-American Literacy Foundation
IALL . . . . International Association of Law Libraries
IALP . . . . International Association of Logopedics and Phoniatrics
IALS . . . . International Association of Legal Science
IALSSA . . . . . . International Air Line Stewards and Stewardesses Association
IAM . . . . Incidental Amplitude Modulation
IAM . . . . Institute of Appliance Manufacturers
IAM . . . . Interactive Algebraic Manipulation (Data processing)
IAM . . . . International Association of Machinists (Later, International Association of Machinists and Aerospace Workers)
IAMAM . . . . . . International Association of Museums of Arms and Military History
IAMAP . . . . . . International Association of Meteorology and Atmospheric Physics
IAMAT . . . . . . International Association for Medical Assistance to Travelers
IAMAW . . . . . . International Association of Machinists and Aerospace Workers
IAMC . . . . Indian Army Medical Corps
IAMC . . . . . . Institute for Advancement of Medical Communication
IAMCA . . . . . International Association of Milk Control Agencies
IAMCR . . . . . International Association for Mass Communication Research
IAMFES . . . . . International Association of Milk, Food and Environmental Sanitarians
IAMFPA . . . . . International Association of Mouth and Foot Painting Artists
IAMFS . . . . . . International Association of Milk and Food Sanitarians
IAML . . . . International Association of Music Libraries
IAMLT . . . . . . International Association of Medical Laboratory Technologists
IAMM & D . . . Institute for Advanced Materials, Mechanics, and Design (Army Materiel Command)
IAMPTH . . . . . International Association of Master-Penmen and Teachers of Handwriting
IAMR . . . . . . Institute of Arctic Mineral Resources (University of Alaska)
IAMS . . . . Instantaneous Audience Measurement System
IAMS . . . . International Association of Microbiological Societies
IAMW . . . . . . Improved Antimateriel Warhead
IAMWH . . . . . Improved Antimateriel Warhead
IAN . . . . Instituto de Asuntos Nucleares (Colombia)
IANAP . . . . . . Interagency Noise Abatement Program
IANC . . . . International Airline Navigators Council
IANC . . . . Invest-in-America National Council, Inc.
IANEC . . . . . . Inter-American Nuclear Energy Commission (OAS)
IANF . . . . Inter-Allied Nuclear Force
IANU . . . . Italo-American National Union
IAO . . . . In and Out (of clouds) (Aviation)
IAO . . . . Information Activities Office(r) (Military)
IAO . . . . Intermittent Aortic Occlusion (Medicine)
IAO . . . . Internal Automation Operation
IAO . . . . International Academy of Orthodontics
IAOD . . . . . . In Addition to Other Duties (Military)
IAOL . . . . International Association of Orientalist Libraries
IAOR . . . . International Abstracts in Operations Research
IAP . . . . Incentive Awards Program (of the federal government, administered by CSC)
IAP . . . . Initial Aiming Point (Gunnery)
IAP . . . . Initial Approach (Aviation)
IAP . . . . Inlet Absolute Pressure
IAP . . . . Inorganic Ablative Plastic
IAP . . . . Instrument Approach Procedure (Aviation)
IAP . . . . International Academy of Pathology
IAP . . . . International Academy of Proctology
IAP . . . . International Airport
IAP . . . . International Association of Planetology
IAPA . . . . Inter-American Police Academy
IAPA . . . . Inter-American Press Association
IAPB . . . . Inter-Allied Personnel Board (World War II)
IAPB . . . . International Association for the Prevention of Blindness

IAPC . . . . Instituto de Aposentadoria e Pensoes dos Comerciarios (Brazil)
IAPC . . . . Inter-American Peace Committee (OAS)
IAPC . . . . International Association for Pollution Control
IAPES . . . . . . International Association of Personnel in Employment Security
IAPESGW . . . . International Association of Physical Education and Sports for Girls and Women
IAPF . . . . Inter-American Peacekeeping Force
IAPG . . . . Interagency Advanced Power Group
IAPH . . . . International Association of Ports and Harbors
IAPHC . . . . . . International Association of Printing House Craftsmen
IAPI . . . . Institute of American Poultry Industries
IAPIP . . . . International Association for the Protection of Industrial Property
IAPLLT . . . . . . Interamerican Program for Linguistics and Language Teaching
IAPMO . . . . . International Association of Plumbing and Mechanical Officials
IAPN . . . . International Association of Professional Numismatists
IAPO . . . . Industrial Accountable Property Officer (Air Force)
IAPO . . . . International Association of Physical Oceanography
IAPP . . . . International Association of Police Professors
IAPPW . . . . . . International Association of Pupil Personnel Workers
IAPS . . . . International Association of Pipe Smokers Clubs
IAPSC . . . . . . Inter-African Phytosanitary Commission
IAPSO . . . . . . International Association of Physical Sciences of the Oceans (of International Union of Geodesy and Geophysics)
IAPSP . . . . . . Inter-American Program for Social Progress (AID)
IAPT . . . . International Association for Plant Taxonomy
IAPTA . . . . . . International Allied Printing Trades Association
IAPW . . . . . . International Association of Personnel Women
IAQ . . . . International Association for Quality
IAR . . . . Inactive Air Reserve
IAR . . . . Individual Action Report
IAR . . . . Interagency Rate
IAR . . . . Interment is Authorized for the Remains of (Military)
IAR . . . . Intersection of Air Routes
IAR . . . . Inventory Adjustment Report (Military)
IAR . . . . Isobaric Analog Resonance (Nuclear structure)
IARA . . . . Inter-Allied Reparations Agency (Brussels)
IARA . . . . International Association of Rebekah Assemblies (IOOF)
IARB . . . . Inspection Analysis Review Board
IARC . . . . International Agency for Research on Cancer
IARCC . . . . . . Interagency Arctic Research Coordinating Committee (National Science Foundation)
IARE . . . . International Association of Railway Employees
IARF . . . . International Association for Religious Freedom
IARI . . . . Industrial Advertising Research Institute
IARIGAI . . . . . International Association of Research Institutes for the Graphic Arts Industry
IARIW . . . . . . International Association for Research into Income and Wealth
IARMI . . . . . . International Association of Rattan Manufacturers and Importers
IARO . . . . Indian Army Reserve of Officers
IARS . . . . International Anesthesia Research Society
IARSC . . . . . . International Association of Religious Science Churches
IARSEP . . . . . . Institute Africain de Recherches Sociales et Economiques pour l'Education Populaire (African Institute of Social and Economic Research for Popular Education)
IARU . . . . International Amateur Radio Union
IARW . . . . . . International Association of Refrigerated Warehouses (Formerly, NARW)
IAS . . . . Immediate Access Storage
IAS . . . . India-America Society
IAS . . . . Indian Astronautical Society
IAS . . . . Indicated Air Speed
IAS . . . . Institute for Advanced Studies (Army)
IAS . . . . Institute of Aeronautical Sciences
IAS . . . . Institute of Aerospace Sciences (Later, AIAA)
IAS . . . . Institute of American Strategy
IAS . . . . Institute of Andean Studies
IAS . . . . Institute for Atmospheric Sciences (Environmental Science Services Administration)
IAS . . . . Instrument Approach System
IAS . . . . Integrated Avionics System
IAS . . . . Interest Assessment Scales
IAS . . . . International Accountants Society
IAS . . . . International Association of Siderographers
IAS . . . . International Aviation Service (of FAA)
IAS . . . . Intrusion Alarm System
IAS . . . . Supreme Council of the Independent Associated Spiritualists
IASA . . . . Indo-American Sports Association
IASA . . . . Institute for Atomic Sciences in Agriculture
IASA . . . . Insurance Accounting and Statistical Association
IASA . . . . International Air Safety Association
IASA . . . . International Association of Sound Archives
IASAP . . . . . . Intercollegiate Association for Study of the Alcohol Problem

IASC	Inter-American Safety Council
IASC	International Association of Seed Crushers
IASD	Interatrial Septal Defect (Medicine)
IASDI	Inter-American Social Development Institute
IASH	International Association of Scientific Hydrology
IASH	Israeli Academy of Sciences and Humanities
IASI	Inter-American Statistical Institute (OAS)
IASLIC	Indian Association of Special Libraries and Information Centres
IASM	Independent Association of Stocking Manufacturers
IASOR	Ice and Snow on Runway (Aviation)
IASP	International Arts and Sciences Press
IASP	International Association for Social Progress
IASP	International Association for Suicide Prevention
IASPEI	International Association of Seismology and Physics of the Earth's Interior
IASRA	International Arthur Schnitzler Research Association
IASS	International Association for Shell Structures
IASSD	International Association of School Security Directors
IASSMD	International Association for the Scientific Study of Mental Deficiency
IASSW	International Association of Schools of Social Work
IASTA	Institute for Advanced Studies in the Theatre
IASY	International Active Sun Years
IAT	Indicated Air Temperature
IAT	Individual Acceptance Tests
IAT	Inside Air Temperature
IAT.	Institute for Advanced Technology
IAT	Institute of Animal Technology (London)
IAT	Institute for Applied Technology (National Bureau of Standards)
IAT	Interionic Attraction Theory
IAT	Italian Atomic Time
IATA	International Air Transport Association
IATA	International Amateur Theatre Association
IATA	Is Amended to Add
IATC	India America Trade Council
IATC	Inter-American Travel Congress
IATC	International Air Traffic Communications
IATC	International Association of Tool Craftsmen
IATC	International Association of Torch Clubs
IATCB	Interdepartmental Air Traffic Control Board
IATCR	International Air Traffic Communications Receiver Station
IATCS	International Air Traffic Communications Station
IATCT	International Air Traffic Communications Transmitter Station
IATD	Is Amended to Delete
IATE	International Association for Temperance Education
IATL	International Academy of Trial Lawyers
IATOD	In Addition To Other Duties (Military)
IATR.	Is Amended to Read
IATSC	International Aeronautical Telecommunications Switching Center
IATSE	International Alliance of Theatrical Stage Employees and Moving Picture Machine Operators of the United States and Canada (Also, IA)
IATTC	Inter-American Tropical Tuna Commission
IATUL	International Association of Technological University Libraries
IAU	International Association of Universities
IAU	International Astronomical Union
IAU	Italian Actors Union
IAUF	Interamerican Underwater Festival
IAUPL	International Association of University Professors and Lecturers
IAV	Indium Antimode Veractor
IAV	Inventory Adjustment Voucher
IAVA	Industrial Audio-Visual Association
IAVC	Instantaneous Automatic Volume Control (Electronics)
IAVCM	International Association of Visual Communications Management (Formerly, SRE)
IAVFH	International Association of Veterinary Food Hygienists
IAVG	International Association for Vocational Guidance
IAW	Improved Antimateriel Warhead
IAW.	In Accordance With
IAW	International Alliance of Women - Equal Rights, Equal Responsibilities
IAW	International Association of Wholesalers
IAW	Isotopic Atomic Weight
IAWA	Independent American Whiskey Association
IAWA	International Association of Wood Anatomists
IAWH	Improved Antimateriel Warhead
IAWMC	International Association of Workers for Maladjusted Children
IAWP	International Association of Women Police
IAWPR	International Association for Water Pollution Research
IAWR	Institute of Air Weapons Research (Air Force)
IAWS	Intercollegiate Association of Women Students
IAYM	International Association of Youth Magistrates
IAZ	Inner Artillery Zone
IB	Iberia-Lineas Aereas Espanolas (Air Lines of Spain)

IB	In Bond (Wines and spirits)
IB	Inbound
IB	Incendiary Bomb
IB	Inclusion Body (Cytology)
IB	Index of Body Build (Anatomy)
IB	Infantry Battalion (Army)
IB	Infectious Bronchitis (Veterinary medicine)
IB	Information Bulletin
IB	Inner Bottom (Technical drawings)
IB	Instruction Book
IB	Intelligence Branch
IB	International Broadcasting
IB	Interpreter's Bible
IB	Invoice Book
IBA	Igniter Booster Assembly (Aerospace)
IBA	Ignorant Bloody Aircrafthand (British Royal Air Force slang)
IBA	Independent Bankers Association
IBA	Independent Bar Association
IBA	Indolebutyric Acid
IBA	Inspection by Attribute
IBA	Institute for Bioenergetic Analysis
IBA	Institute of British Architects
IBA	International Bar Association
IBA	International Bridge Academy
IBA	International Briquetting Association
IBA	Investing Builders Association
IBA	Investment Bankers Association of America (Later, Securities Industry Association)
IBAA	Independent Bankers Association of America
IBAA	Italian Baptist Association of America
IBAHP	Inter-African Bureau for Animal Health and Protection
IBASF	Intervals Between Aircraft in Stream Type Formation
IBB	Intentional Bases on Balls (Baseball)
IBB.	International Brotherhood of Bookbinders (Later, Graphic Arts International Union)
IBBA	Inland Bird Banding Association
IBBA	International Brangus Breeders Association
IBBM	Iron Body Bronze-Mounted
IBBRIS	International Biodeterioration Bulletin Reference Index (A publication) (British)
IBBY	International Board on Books for Young People
IBC	Input Bias Current
IBC	Interboard Committee for Christian Work in Japan
IBC	International Biotoxicological Center
IBC	International Brightness Coefficient
IBC	International Business Corporation
IBC	Interstate Brands Corporation (NYSE symbol)
IBC	Inverted Bowl Centrifuge
IBCA	Department of Interior Board of Contract Appeals
IBCA	International Braille Chess Association
IBCC	Intra-Bureau Change Committee
IBCS	Integrated Battlefield Control System (Army)
IBD	Inhabited Building Distance (Army)
IBD	Institute of Business Designers
IBDA	Indirect Bomb-Damage Assessment
IBDM	Interim Bomber Defense Missile
IBDT	Insulation Breakdown Tester
IBE	International Bureau of Education
IBEC	International Bank for Economic Cooperation
IBEC	International Basic Economy Corporation
IBECO	Inboard Booster Engine Cutoff
IBED	Inter-African Bureau for Epizootic Diseases
IBEE	International Builders Exchange Executives
IBEG	International Book Export Group
IBEN	Incendiary Bomb with Explosive Nose
IBEW	International Brotherhood of Electrical Workers
IBF	Immature Brown-Fat (Cells)
IBF	International Badminton Federation
IBFD	International Bureau of Fiscal Documentation
IBFM	Institute of Broadcasting Financial Management
IBFMP	International Bureau of the Federations of Master Printers
IBFO	International Brotherhood of Firemen and Oilers
IBFS	International Benjamin Franklin Society
IBG	International Boxing Guild
IBH	Initial Beachhead (Military)
IBHD	Initial Beachhead (Military)
IBI	Insulation Board Institute
IBI	Intermittent Bladder Irrigation (Medicine)
IBI	International Broadcast Institute
IBI	Internationales Burgen Institut (International Castles Institute) (Also, ICI)
IBI	Interpersonal Behavior Inventory (VA)

IBI . . . . Invoice Book Inbound (Business and trade)
IBIA . . . . Institute of British Industrial Art
IBID . . . . International Bibliographical Description
IBIT . . . . ICBM Blast Interference Test
IBJ. . . . . Industrial Bank of Japan
IBJ . . . . Instrument Bearing Jewel
IBK . . . . Infectious Bovine Kerato-Conjunctivitis (Veterinary medicine)
IBKA . . . . . . Ikatan Buruh Kereta Api (Railroad Workers' Union) (Indonesia)
IBKB . . . . . . Ikatan Buruh Kendaaran Bermotor (Motor Transport Workers' Union) (Indonesia)
IBL. . . . . Interior Ballistics Laboratory (Aberdeen, Md.) (Army)
IBL. . . . . International Brotherhood of Longshoremen
IBLA . . . . . . Inter-American Bibliographical and Library Association
IBM . . . . Intercontinental Ballistic Missile
IBM . . . . International Brotherhood of Magicians
IBM . . . . International Business Machines Corporation (NYSE symbol)
IBMA . . . . . Independent Battery Manufacturers of America
IBMS . . . . . . Ion Beam Mass Spectrometer
IBN . . . . Identification Beacon
IBN . . . . Institute Belge de Normalisation (Brussels, Belgium)
IBNS . . . . . . International Bank Note Society
IBO . . . . International Broadcasting Organization
IBO . . . . Invoice Book Outbound (Business and trade)
IBOP . . . . . . International Balance of Payments Reporting System
IBOP . . . . . . International Brotherhood of Operative Potters
IBP. . . . . Initial Boiling Point
IBP. . . . . Inner (Edge of) Basal Piece
IBP . . . . Institute for Better Packaging
IBP. . . . . Insulated Binding Post
IBP. . . . . International Balance of Payments
IBP. . . . . International Biological Program (National Research Council)
IBP. . . . . Ion Beam Projector
IBP. . . . . Iowa Beef Processors, Inc. (NYSE symbol)
IBPM . . . . . . International Brotherhood of Paper Makers (Later, United Paper Workers International Union)
IBPMS. . . . . Indirect Blood Pressure Measuring System
IBPOEW . . . . . Improved Benevolent Protective Order of Elks of the World
IBR. . . . . Infra-Black Region
IBR. . . . . Institute for Basic Research (National Bureau of Standards)
IBR . . . . Institute of Boiler and Radiator Manufacturers
IBR. . . . . Integral Boiling Reactor
IBRD . . . . . . International Bank for Reconstruction and Development (Also known as World Bank)
IBRL. . . . . . . Initial Bomb Release Line
IBRM . . . . . . Institute of Boiler and Radiator Manufacturers
IBRO . . . . . . International Brain Research Organization
IBRV. . . . . . . Infectious Bovine Rhinotracheitis Virus
IBS. . . . . Impulse Balance System
IBS. . . . . Institute for Basic Standards (National Bureau of Standards)
IBS . . . . Intercollegiate Broadcasting System
IBS . . . . International Bach Society
IBS. . . . . International Benchrest Shooters
IBS . . . . International Bible Students
IBS. . . . . Ion Beam Scanning
IBS. . . . . Island Base Section
IBSA . . . . . . International Barber Schools Association
IBSHR . . . . . . Integral Boiling and Superheat Reactor
IBT. . . . . India-Burma Theater (World War II)
IBT. . . . . Instrumented Bend Test
IBT. . . . . Insulation Breakdown Tester
IBT. . . . . International Bridge & Terminal Company (AAR code)
IBT. . . . . International Brotherhood of Teamsters, Chauffeurs, Warehousemen and Helpers of America
IBT. . . . . Irrational Beliefs Test (Psychology)
IBTA . . . . . . International Baton Twirling Association of America and Abroad
IBTS . . . . . . International Beer Tasting Society
IBTTA . . . . . . International Bridge, Tunnel and Turnpike Association
IBTU. . . . . . . Instructors Basic Training Unit
IBU . . . . Ikatan Buruh Umum (General Workers' Union)
IBV . . . . Inspection by Variables
IBVE. . . . . . . Isobutyl Vinyl Ether
IBVM . . . . . . Institute of the Blessed Virgin Mary (Sisters of Loretto) (Roman Catholic religious order)
IBW . . . . Intelligence Bandwidth
IBW . . . . Ion Beam Weapon
IBWM . . . . . . International Bureau of Weights and Measures
IBY . . . . International Biological Year
IBY . . . . . . International Book Year (1972) (UNESCO)
IBZ . . . . Internationale Bibliographie der Zeitschriftenliteratur (International Index to Periodicals)
IC . . . . Ice Crystals

IC . . . . Iceland (NATO)
IC . . . . Iesus Christus (Jesus Christ)
IC . . . . Illinois Central R. R. (AAR code)
IC . . . . Immediate Constituent
IC . . . . In Charge Of
IC . . . . Index Catalogue
IC . . . . Index Correction (on a sextant)
IC . . . . Indicator and Control
IC . . . . Inertial Component
IC . . . . Infinite Capitalism (Book title)
IC . . . . Informal Communication
IC . . . . Information Center (Army)
IC . . . . Information Circular
IC . . . . Initial Conditions
IC . . . . Initial Course (Navigation)
IC . . . . Inlet Contact
IC . . . . Input Circuit
IC . . . . Input Current
IC . . . . Inspected and Condemned (Military)
IC . . . . Inspiration Consolidated Copper Company (NYSE symbol)
IC . . . . Inspiratory Capacity (Physiology)
IC . . . . Inspiratory Center (Physiology)
IC . . . . Institute of Charity (Rosminians)
IC . . . . Instruction Counter (Data processing)
IC . . . . Instrument Correction
IC . . . . Intake Closes (Valve position)
IC . . . . Integrated Circuit (Electronics)
IC . . . . Interceptor Command
IC . . . . Interchange Center
IC . . . . Intercommunications
IC . . . . Interfaith Compassionists
IC . . . . Interim Change
IC . . . . Interim Commission
IC . . . . Interim Committee
IC . . . . Interior Communication
IC . . . . Interior Communications Electrician (Navy rating)
IC . . . . Internal Combustion
IC . . . . Internal Connection (Electronics)
IC . . . . International Conference
IC . . . . International Control
IC . . . . Internment Camp
IC . . . . Internuclear Company
IC . . . . Interstitial Cells (Histology)
IC . . . . Intracerebral (Medicine)
IC . . . . Intracranial
IC . . . . Intracutaneous (Medicine)
IC . . . . Islamic Congress
IC . . . . Jesus (First and third letters of His name in Greek)
I/C . . . . In Charge Of
I/C . . . . Interchange
I & C . . . . . . Installation and Check (Military)
I & C . . . . . . Installation and Checkout (Spares)
I & C . . . . . . Installation and Construction (Military)
ICA . . . . Imperial Corporation of America (NYSE symbol)
ICA . . . . Individual Combat Actions (Army)
ICA . . . . Industrial Communications Association
ICA . . . . Ingenieros Civiles Asociados (Mexican construction company)
ICA . . . . Instituto de Ciencia Animal (Cuba)
ICA . . . . Integrated Circuit Array
ICA . . . . Integrated Conformal Array
ICA . . . . Intermuseum Conservation Association
ICA . . . . International Cartographic Association
ICA . . . . International Catholic Auxiliaries
ICA . . . . International Chefs' Association
ICA . . . . International Chiropractors Association
ICA . . . . International Claim Association
ICA . . . . International Coffee Agreement
ICA . . . . International Commission on Acoustics
ICA . . . . International Communication Association
ICA . . . . International Cooperation Administration (Later, Agency for International Development)
ICA . . . . International Co-operative Alliance
ICA . . . . International Council on Archives (UNESCO)
ICA . . . . Italian Charities of America
IC4A . . . . . . Intercollegiate Association of Amateur Athletes of America
ICAA . . . . . . Investment Counsel Association of America
ICAAAA . . . . . Intercollegiate Association of Amateur Athletes of America
ICAC . . . . . . International Committee for Accounting Co-operation
ICAC . . . . . . International Cotton Advisory Committee
ICAD . . . . . . Integrated Control and Display
ICAD . . . . . . International Committee for Automobile Documentation

ICAE . . . . . . International Commission of Agricultural Engineering
ICAE . . . . . . International Conference of Agricultural Economists
ICAF . . . . . . Industrial College of the Armed Forces
ICAF . . . . . . International Committee of Aeronautical Fatigue
ICAI. . . . . . . International Commission for Agricultural Industries
ICAITI . . . . . . Instituto Centroamericano de Investigacion y Technologia Industrial (Central American Research Institute for Industry)
ICALU . . . . . . International Confederation of Arab Labour Unions
ICAME . . . . . . International Center for the Advancement of Management Education (Stanford University)
ICAMR . . . . . . Interagency (or Interdepartmental) Committee for Applied Meteorological Research
ICAN . . . . . . International College of Applied Nutrition
ICAN . . . . . . International Commission for Aid Navigation
ICAO . . . . . . International Civil Aviation Organization
ICAP . . . . . . Inter-American Committee for the Alliance for Progress
ICAR . . . . . . Integrated Command Accounting and Reporting
ICARES . . . . . . Institut International Catholique de Recherches Socio-Ecclesiales (International Catholic Institute for Socio-Religious Research) (Later, FERES)
ICARUS. . . . . . Inter-Continental Aerospacecraft-Range Unlimited System
ICAS . . . . . . Institute of Combined Arms and Support (Fort Leavenworth, Kansas) (Army)
ICAS . . . . . . Interdepartmental Committee for Atmospheric Sciences (US)
ICAS . . . . . . Intermittent Commercial and Amateur Service (Radio)
ICAS . . . . . . International Council of the Aeronautical Sciences
ICAS . . . . . . International Council of Aerospace Sciences
ICASALS . . . . . International Center for Arid and Semi-Arid Land Studies (Texas Technological University)
ICATU. . . . . . International Confederation of Arab Trade Unions
ICB . . . . Inertia Compensated Balance
ICB . . . . Interior Control Board
ICB . . . . International Computer Bibliography (A publication of National Computing Center)
ICB . . . . International Container Bureau
ICBA . . . . . . International Community of Booksellers' Associations
ICBBA. . . . . . International Cornish Bantam Breeders' Association
ICBC . . . . . . Inclined Cleated Belt Conveyor
ICBC . . . . . . Interagency Committee on Back Contamination (Aerospace)
ICBD . . . . . . International Council of Ballroom Dancing
ICBLB . . . . . . International Committee for Breaking the Language Barrier
ICBM . . . . . . Intercontinental Ballistic Missile
ICBMS . . . . . . Intercontinental Ballistic Missile System
ICBO . . . . . . International Conference of Building Officials
ICBO . . . . . . Interracial Council for Business Opportunity
ICBP . . . . . . International Council for Bird Preservation
ICBPA . . . . . . Insurance Company and Bank Purchasing Agents Association
ICBS . . . . . . Incorporated Church Building Society (British)
ICBS. . . . . . . Interconnected Business System
ICBS . . . . . . International Cigar Band Society
ICBT. . . . . . . Intercontinental Ballistic Transport
ICBWR . . . . . . Improved Cycle Boiling Water Reactor
ICC . . . . Association Internationale de Chimie Cerealiere
ICC . . . . Ice Crystal Cloud
ICC . . . . Image Converter Camera
ICC . . . . Independence Community College (Kansas)
ICC . . . . Indian Claims Commission
ICC . . . . Indian Cultural Center
ICC . . . . Indiana Central College
ICC . . . . Industrial Communication Council
ICC . . . . Institute of Chinese Culture
ICC . . . . Integrated Chip Circuit
ICC . . . . International Chamber of Commerce
ICC . . . . International Children's Centre
ICC . . . . International College in Copenhagen (Denmark)
ICC . . . . International Computaprint Corporation
ICC . . . . International Computation Center (Rome, Italy) (Sponsored by UNESCO)
ICC . . . . International Conference on Communications
ICC . . . . International Congregational Council
ICC . . . . International Control Commission (Composed of representatives of Canada, India, and Poland, and charged with supervising the cease-fire in Laos established at Geneva Conference of 1962)
ICC . . . . International Controls Corporation
ICC . . . . International Cooperation Council
ICC . . . . International Cricket Conference
ICC . . . . Interstate Commerce Commission (Independent government agency)
ICC . . . . Inventory Control Center (of Field Army Support Command)
ICC . . . . Italian Culture Council
ICCA . . . . . . Infants' and Children's Coat Association
ICCA . . . . . . Initial Cash Clothing Allowance (Military)
ICCA . . . . . . Intercontinental Corrugated Case Association

ICCA . . . . . . International Consumer Credit Association
ICCAS . . . . . . International Center for Communication Arts and Sciences
ICCAT . . . . . . International Commission for the Conservation of Atlantic Tunas
ICCB . . . . . . Intermediate Configuration Control Board (Western Electric)
ICCB . . . . . . International Catholic Child Bureau
ICCC . . . . . . International Conference of Catholic Charities
ICCC . . . . . . International Conference of Coordination Chemistry
ICCC . . . . . . International Council of Christian Churches
ICCE . . . . . . International Congress on Combustion Engines
ICCE . . . . . . International Council of Commerce Employers
ICCF . . . . . . International Correspondence Chess Federation
ICCH . . . . . . International Catholic Confederation of Hospitals
ICCICA. . . . . . Interim Co-ordinating Committee for International Commodity Arrangements
ICCP . . . . . . Intelligence Civilian Career Program (Army)
ICCP . . . . . . International Conference on Cataloging Principles
ICCP . . . . . . International Council for Children's Play
ICCPC . . . . . . International Computation Center's Preparatory Committee
ICCTA . . . . . . International Consultative Council of Travel Agents
ICCUS . . . . . . International Claims Commission of the United States (Department of State) (Abolished, 1954)
ICCY . . . . . . International Cultural Centers for Youth
ICD . . . . Immune Complex Disease
ICD . . . . Industrial Cooperation Division
ICD . . . . Industry Cooperation Division (Navy)
ICD . . . . Institute for the Crippled and Disabled
ICD . . . . Interface Control Document (Apollo) (NASA)
ICD . . . . Interface Control Drawing
ICD . . . . International Circulation Distributors, Inc.
ICD . . . . International Classification of Diseases
ICD . . . . International College of Dentists
ICDA . . . . . . Infantry Combat Developments Agency (Army) (Pronounced Ick-da)
ICDA . . . . . . International Catholic Deaf Association
ICDA . . . . . . International Classification of Diseases Adapted
ICDA . . . . . . International Cooperative Development Association
ICDC . . . . . . Industrial and Commercial Development Corporation (Kenya)
ICDI . . . . . . Imperial Court, Daughters of Isis
ICDM . . . . . . Industrial Civil Defense Management
ICDMA. . . . . . Independent Carbon-Dioxide Manufacturers Association
ICDO . . . . . . International Civil Defence Organization
ICDP . . . . . . Intelligence Career Development Program
ICDP . . . . . . International Confederation for Disarmament and Peace
ICE . . . . Illness-Correctional Environments
ICE . . . . Increased Combat Effectiveness
ICE . . . . Initial Combat Employment (of new munitions)
ICE . . . . Input-Checking Equipment
ICE . . . . Institution of Civil Engineers (British)
ICE . . . . Integrated Circuits Engineering Corporation
ICE . . . . Integrated Cooling for Electronics
ICE . . . . Intelligence and Counterespionage (Fictitious organization in the Matt Helm series of books and movies)
ICE . . . . Internal Combustion Engine
ICE . . . . International Center for the Environment (Proposed)
ICE . . . . International Commercial Exchange
ICE . . . . International Cultural Exchange
ICEC. . . . . . . International Conference on Education in Chemistry
ICEC . . . . . . International Council for Exceptional Children
ICED . . . . . . Interprofessional Commission on Environmental Design
ICEDS. . . . . . Insurance Company Education Directors Society
ICEF . . . . . . International Council for Educational Films
ICEI . . . . . . Internal Combustion Engine Institute
ICEL. . . . . . . International Committee on English in the Liturgy
ICEM . . . . . . Incremental Cost Effectiveness Model
ICEM . . . . . . Intergovernmental Committee for European Migration
ICEM . . . . . . Inverted Coaxial Magnetron
ICEPAT . . . . . Iceland Patrol (Navy)
ICER . . . . . . Information Centre of the European Railways
ICER. . . . . . . Infrared Cell, Electronically Refrigerated
ICER . . . . . . Institute for Central European Research
ICES . . . . . . Integrated Civil Engineering System (Data processing)
ICES . . . . . . International Council for the Exploration of the Sea
ICES. . . . . . . International Cultural Exchange Service
ICESA. . . . . . Interstate Conference of Employment Security Agencies
ICESC . . . . . . Industry Crew Escape Systems Committee
ICET. . . . . . . Institute for the Certification of Engineering Technicians
ICETEX . . . . . Instituto Colombiano de Especializacion Tecnica en el Exterior (Colombia)
ICF . . . . Installation Confinement Facility (Army)
ICF . . . . Inter-Bureau Citation of Funds (Navy)
ICF . . . . Intercommunication Flip-Flop (Data processing)
ICF . . . . International Canoe Federation
ICF . . . . International Casting Federation

ICF . . . . Intracellular Fluid (Physiology)
ICF . . . . Intrinsic Coercive Force
ICF . . . . Iota-Cam Fiberscope
ICF . . . . Italian Catholic Federation Central Council
ICFA . . . . Independent College Funds of America
ICFATCMUTAI . . Is Cleared for Access to Classified Material Up to and Including
ICFC . . . . Industrial and Commercial Finance Corporation (British)
ICFC . . . . International Centre of Films for Children
ICFI . . . . Iota-Cam Fiberscope Instrument
ICFLPRMFS . . . Items are not Available Through Cannibalization, Fabrication, or Local Procurement or Replacement from Maintenance Float Stock
ICFPW. . . . . . . International Confederation of Former Prisoners of War
ICFS. . . . . Iota-Cam Fiberscope (Also, ICF)
ICFTU . . . . . . International Confederation of Free Trade Unions
ICFTUE . . . . . . International Center of Free Trade Unionists in Exile
ICG . . . . Indocyanine Green (Liver function test) (Medicine)
ICG . . . . Inflight Coverall Garment (Apollo) (NASA)
ICG . . . . Integrated Combat Group (Air Force)
ICG . . . . International Commission on Glass
ICG . . . . International Congress of Genetics
ICG . . . . Interviewer's Classification Guide
ICGICIP . . . . . Icing in Clouds and in Precipitation (Meteorology)
ICGIP. . . . . . . Icing in Precipitation (Meteorology)
ICGS . . . . International Catholic Girls' Society
ICH . . . . Incumbent Come Home (Political humor) (Pronounced "itch")
ICH . . . . Induction-Conduction Heating
ICH . . . . Infectious Canine Hepatitis (Veterinary medicine)
ICH . . . . Inhalation Cycle Histogram (Biometrics)
ICH . . . . Institute of Hispanic Culture
ICHC . . . . International Committee for Horticultural Congresses
ICHCA . . . . . . International Cargo Handling Coordination Association
ICHDA . . . . . . International Cooperative Housing Development Association
ICHDR . . . . . . Intersociety Commission for Heart Disease Resources
ICHE . . . . International Councils on Higher Education (Formerly, CHEAR)
ICHMH. . . . . . Interstate Clearing House on Mental Health
ICHPER. . . . . . International Council on Health, Physical Education and Recreation
ICHS . . . . International Committee of Historical Sciences
ICI. . . . . Imperial Chemical Industries
ICI. . . . . Information Concepts, Incorporated
ICI. . . . . Initial Capabilities Inspection (Military)
ICI. . . . . Inter-American Cooperative Institute
ICI. . . . . International Castles Institute
ICI. . . . . International Commission on Illumination
ICI . . . . Investment Casting Institute
ICI. . . . . Investment Company Institute
ICI. . . . . Italian Cultural Institute
ICIA . . . . International Credit Insurance Association
ICIA . . . . International Crop Improvement Association
ICIANZ. . . . . . Imperial Chemical Industries of Australia and New Zealand, Ltd.
ICIAP . . . . Interagency Committee on International Aviation Policy (State Department)
ICIASF . . . . . . International Congress on Instrumentation in Aerospace Simulation Facilities
ICIC. . . . . Interdisciplinary Committee on Institutes and Conferences
ICICLE . . . . . . Integrated Cryogenic Isotope Cooling Equipment
ICID . . . . International Commission on Irrigation and Drainage
ICIDCA . . . . . Instituto Cubano de Investigaciones de los Derivados de la Cana de Azucar
ICIE. . . . . International Council of Industrial Editors
ICIE. . . . . International Council of Industrial Engineers
ICIP . . . . International Conference on Information Processing (Paris, 1959)
ICIPE . . . . International Center for Insect Physiology and Ecology
ICIR . . . . In Commission, In Reserve (Navy vessel status)
ICIRA . . . . Instituto de Capacitacion e Investigacion en Reforma Agraria
ICIREPAT. . . . . International Committee on Information Retrieval Among Examining Patent Offices
ICIRO. . . . . . . Interim Commission of the International Refugee Organization
ICIS . . . . Interdepartmental Committee on Internal Security
ICIT . . . . Instituto Cubano de Investigacione Technologicas
ICITA . . . . . . International Cooperative Investigations of the Tropical Atlantic (Navy)
ICITO. . . . . . . Interim Commission for the International Trade Organization
ICJ . . . . International Commission of Jurists (of the United Nations)
ICJ . . . . International Court of Justice
ICJC . . . . Immaculate Conception Junior College (New Jersey)
ICJUB . . . . . . Intercontinental Jet Unmanned Bomber
ICJW . . . . International Council of Jewish Women
ICL . . . . Incoming Line
ICL . . . . Instructional Center Library
ICL . . . . Instrument Calibration Laboratory
ICL . . . . Integrated Configuration List
ICL . . . . International Christian Leadership

ICL . . . . International Computers, Limited (Great Britain)
ICL . . . . International Council for Christian Leadership
ICLA . . . . . . International Committee on Laboratory Animals
ICLA . . . . . . International Comparative Literature Association
ICLM . . . . . . Inter-California Line in Mexico R. R. (AAR code)
ICLM . . . . . . International Christian Leprosy Mission
ICM . . . . Improved Capability Minuteman (or Missile) (Air Force)
ICM . . . . Indian Campaign Medal
ICM . . . . Initiator Command Module
ICM . . . . Instantaneous Center of Motion
ICM . . . . Institute for Composite Materials
ICM . . . . Instrumentation and Communications Monitor
ICM . . . . Integrated Circuit Mask
ICM . . . . Intercostal Margin (Anatomy)
ICM . . . . Interim Catalog Module (MEDLARS)
ICM . . . . International Congress of Mathematicians
ICMA . . . . . . International Circulation Managers Association
ICMA . . . . . . International City Management (formerly, Managers') Association
ICMC . . . . . . International Catholic Migration Commission
ICME . . . . . . International Conference on Medical Electronics
ICMI . . . . . . International Commission on Mathematical Instruction
ICMICA . . . . . International Catholic Movement for Intellectual and Cultural Affairs
ICMLT. . . . . . International Congress of Medical Laboratory Technologists
ICMMP . . . . . International Committee of Military Medicine and Pharmacy
ICMP . . . . . . Interchannel Master Pulse
ICMPH . . . . . International Center of Medical and Psychological Hypnosis
ICMR . . . . . . Instrument Calibration and Maintenance Record
ICMS . . . . . . Integrated Circuit and Message Switch
ICMS . . . . . . International Commission on Mushroom Science
ICMST . . . . . International Conference on Machine Searching and Translation
ICMW . . . . . . Inherent Corrective Maintenance Workload
ICN . . . . In Christi Nomine (In the Name of Christ)
ICN . . . . Index of Community Noise
ICN . . . . Interim Change Notice
ICN . . . . International Chemical and Nuclear Corporation (NYSE symbol)
ICN . . . . International Council of Nurses
ICN . . . . Intromogenous Computer Network
ICNA . . . . . . Infants' and Children's Novelties Association
ICNAF . . . . . International Commission for the Northwest Atlantic Fisheries
ICNF . . . . . . Irredundant Conjunctive Normal Formula
ICNI . . . . . . Integrated Communication, Navigation, Identification (System)
ICNND. . . . . . Interdepartmental Committee on Nutrition for National Defense
ICNP . . . . . . International Commission on National Parks
ICNV . . . . . . International Committee on Nomenclature of Viruses
ICO . . . . Illinois College of Optometry
ICO . . . . Immediate Commanding Officer
ICO . . . . In Case Of
ICO . . . . Input Current Offset (Data processing)
ICO . . . . Integrator Cut-Off
ICO . . . . Interagency Committee on Oceanography
ICO . . . . International Coffee Organization
ICO . . . . International Commission for Optics
ICOA . . . . . . International Castor Oil Association
ICOBLA . . . . . International Committee for Breaking the Language Barrier
ICOC . . . . . . Instructions for Commodores of Convoys (Navy)
ICOCS . . . . . Interim Circuit Order Control System (Bell System)
ICOGRADA . . . International Council on Graphic Design Associations
ICOH . . . . . . International Congress on Occupational Health
ICOHH . . . . . International Concatenated Order of Hoo-Hoo
ICOHTEC. . . . . International Cooperation in History of Technology Committee
ICOLD . . . . . . International Commission on Large Dams of the World Power Conference
ICOM . . . . . . International Council of Museums
ICOMI . . . . . . Industria e Commercio de Mineros, SA
ICOMOS. . . . . International Council of Monuments and Sites
ICOMP. . . . . . Iceland Ocean Meeting Point (Navy)
ICON . . . . . . Integrated Control
ICONS . . . . . Information Center on Nuclear Standards (American Nuclear Society)
ICONS . . . . . Isotopes of Carbon, Oxygen, Nitrogen, and Sulfur (AEC project)
ICOPA . . . . . International Conference of Police Associations
ICOR . . . . . . Intergovernmental Conference on Oceanic Research
ICOS . . . . . . International Committee of Onomastic Sciences
ICOSS . . . . . Inertial-Command Off-Set System
ICOTS . . . . . Interagency Committee for Transportation Safety (Department of Transportation)
ICP . . . . Indian Communications Project
ICP . . . . Instructor Control Panel
ICP . . . . Instrumentation Calibration Procedure
ICP . . . . Integral Circuit Package
ICP . . . . International Council of Psychologists
ICP . . . . Inter-University Case Program

ICP	Inventory Control Point
ICP	Item Control Point
ICPA	International Commission for the Prevention of Alcoholism
ICPA	International Cooperative Petroleum Association
ICPAC	Instantaneous Compressor Performance Analysis Computer
ICPB	Inert Components Processing Building
ICPC	Interrange Communications Planning Committee
ICPE	Inventory Control Point Europe
ICPFF	Incentive Cost Plus Fixed Fee
ICPHS	International Council for Philosophy and Humanistic Studies
ICPI	Insurance Crime Prevention Institute
ICPI	Intersociety Committee on Pathology Information
ICPIGP	Internationale Chretienne Professionelle pour les Industries Graphiques et Papetieres (International Federation of Christian Trade Unions of Graphical and Paper Industries)
ICPO	International Criminal Police Organization
ICPOA	Intelligence Center, Pacific Ocean Areas
ICPP	Idaho Chemical Processing Plant (AEC)
ICPR	Industrial Cost and Performance Report
ICPR	Inter-University Consortium for Political Research
ICPRB	Interstate Commission on Potomac River Basin
ICPS	International Conference on the Properties of Steam
ICPTO	International China Painting Teachers Organization
ICPU	International Catholic Press Union
ICPUAE	International Conference on the Peaceful Uses of Atomic Energy
ICR	In-Commission Rate
ICR	Inductance-Capacitance-Resistance
ICR	Input and Compare Register
ICR	Instantaneous Center of Rotation
ICR	Institute for Cancer Research
ICR	Institute for Cooperative Research
ICR	Institute for Creative Research
ICR	Integral Cesium Reservoir
ICR	International Congress of Radiology
ICR	Interrupt Control Register
ICR	Intracranial Reinforcement
ICR	Ion Cyclotron Radiation (or Resonance)
ICR	Island Creek Coal Co. (NYSE symbol) (Delisted)
ICRA	Interagency Committee on Radiological Assistance
ICRC	International Committee of the Red Cross
ICRD	Index of Codes for Research Drugs (A publication)
ICRD	Interior Committee on Research and Development
ICRDA	Independent Cash Register Dealers Association
ICREPAT	International Cooperation in Information Retrieval Among Examining Patent Offices
ICRF	Imperial Cancer Research Fund (British)
ICRH	Institute for Computer Research in the Humanities (New York University)
ICRICE	International Centre of Research and Information on Collective Economy
ICRL	Individual Component Repair List (DOD)
ICRP	International Commission on Radiological Protection
ICRPG	Interagency Chemical Rocket Propulsion Group
IC & RR	Inventory Control and Requirements Review Board (CNO)
ICRS	Index Chemicus Registry System (A publication of Institute for Scientific Information)
ICRS	Institute of Contemporary Russian Studies (Fordham University)
ICRSC	International Council for Research in the Sociology of Co-operation
ICRU	International Commission on Radiological Units and Measurements
ICS	Impulse Conducting System (Physiology)
ICS	Income & Capital Shares, Inc. (NYSE symbol)
ICS	Indian Civil Service
ICS	Induction Communications System
ICS	Industrial Control System
ICS	Infrared Calibration System
ICS	Infrared Camera System
ICS	Infrared Communications System
ICS	Infrared Countermeasures System
ICS	Insert Card Section
ICS	Instrumentation and Control Subsystem
ICS	Integrated Combat Ship
ICS	Integrated Combat System
ICS	Integrated Command System
ICS	Interagency Communications System
ICS	Intercommunications System
ICS	Intercostal Space (Anatomy)
ICS	International Chamber of Shipping
ICS	International College of Surgeons
ICS	International Conrad Society
ICS	International Correspondence School
ICS	International Crocodilian Society
ICS	Interphone Control Station
ICSA	International Correspondence Society of Allergists
ICSAB	International Civil Service Advisory Board
ICSAC	International Confederation of Societies of Authors and Composers
ICSAL	Integrated Communications System, Alaska (Air Force, FAA)
ICSBC	Interstate Council of State Boards of Cosmetology
ICSC	Interim Communications Satellite Committee
ICSC	International Communications Satellite Consortium
ICSC	International Council of Shopping Centers
ICSDW	International Council of Social Democratic Women
ICSEM	International Commission for the Scientific Exploration of the Mediterranean
ICSH	International Committee for Standardization in Haematology
ICSH	Interstitial Cell-Stimulating Hormone
ICSHB	International Committee for Standardization in Human Biology
ICSID	International Centre for Settlement of Investment Disputes
ICSID	International Council of Societies of Industrial Design
ICSISP	International Center for Science Information Services in Phytovirology
ICSPE	International Council of Sport and Physical Education
ICSPFT	International Committee on the Standardization of Physical Fitness Tests
ICSS	International Commission on Signs and Symbols
ICSS	Inter-University Committee on the Superior Student
ICSSD	International Committee for Social Sciences Documentation
ICST	Integrated Combined System Test
ICSTO	International Civil Service Training Organization
ICSU	International Council of Scientific Unions
ICSU AB	International Council of Scientific Unions Abstracting Board
ICSW	Interdepartmental Committee on the Status of Women
ICSW	International Conference of Social Work
ICSW	International Council on Social Welfare
ICT	Image Converter Tube
ICT	Inflammation of Connective Tissue (Medicine)
ICT	Insect Carrier Toxicant
ICT	Institut fuer Chemie der Treibstoffe (West Germany)
ICT	Institute of Computer Technology
ICT	Insulated (or Insulating) Core Transformer
ICT	Insulin Coma Therapy
ICT	Integrated Circuit Tester
ICT	Integrated Computer Telemetry
ICT	International Computers and Tabulators, Ltd.
ICT	International Council of Tanners
ICT	International Critical Tables
ICTA	Institute of Certified Travel Agents
ICTA	International Center for the Typographic Arts
ICTA	International Confederation for Thermal Analysis
ICTASD	International Convention on Transistors and Associated Semiconductor Devices
ICTBA	Infants', Children's and Teens' Wear Buyers Association
ICTD	Inter-Channel Time Displacement
ICTE	Inertial Component Test Equipment
ICTMM	International Congresses on Tropical Medicine and Malaria
ICTOC	Independent Corps Tactical Operations Center
ICTP	Intensified Combat Training Program
ICTP	International Center for Theoretical Physics (Trieste)
ICTR	International Center of Theatre Research
ICTRM	Interagency Committee on the Transportation of Radioactive Materials
ICTS	International Catholic Truth Society
ICTU	Iraqi Confederation of Trade Unions
ICTU	Irish Congress of Trade Unions
ICU	Indicator Control Unit
ICU	Infrared Command Unit
ICU	Instruction Control Unit
ICU	Intensive-Care Unit (of a hospital)
ICU	Intermediate Care Unit
ICU	International Christian University (Tokyo)
ICUA	Institute for College and University Administrators
ICUA	Interdenominational Church Ushers Association
ICUE	International Committee on the University Emergency
ICUIS	Institute on the Church in Urban-Industrial Society
ICUMSA	International Commission for Uniform Methods of Sugar Analysis
ICUP	International Catholic Union of the Press
ICUS	Inside Continental United States (Military)
ICV	Internal Correction Voltage
ICV	Interphase Chromosome Volume
ICVA	International Council of Voluntary Agencies
ICW	In Connection With
ICW	India-China Wing (World War II)
ICW	Inter-American Commission of Women
ICW	International Chemical Workers Union
ICW	International Council of Women
ICW	Interrupted Continuous Waves (Electronics)
ICWA	Institute of Current World Affairs
ICWAR	Improved Continuous-Wave Acquisition RADAR (Army)

ICWG . . . . . . International Co-operative Women's Guild
ICWI . . . . International Car Wash Institute
ICWM . . . . . . Interdepartmental Committee on Weather Modification (Military)
ICWM . . . . . . International Committee on Weights and Measures
ICWP . . . . International Council of Women Psychologists
ICWP . . . . Interstate Conference on Water Problems
ICWR . . . . Interagency Committee on Water Resources
ICWSG . . . . . Infants' and Children's Wear Salesmen's Guild
ICWU . . . . . . International Chemical Workers Union
ICY . . . . International Cooperation Year (1965) (20th Anniversary of UN)
ICYE . . . . International Christian Youth Exchange
ICYF . . . . International Catholic Youth Federation (Later, WFCY)
ICYRA . . . . . Inter-Collegiate Yacht Racing Association (of North America)
ICZ . . . . Intertropical Convergence Zone
ICZ . . . . Isthmian Canal Zone
ICZN . . . . . . International Commission on Zoological Nomenclature
ID . . . . Idaho
ID . . . . Idea (Slang)
ID . . . . Ideal Toy Corp. (NYSE symbol)
ID . . . . Identification
ID . . . . Immediate Delivery
ID . . . . Immunodiffusion
ID . . . . Immunological Distance (in primate phylogeny)
ID . . . . Index of Dissimilarity
ID . . . . Indicating Device
ID . . . . Induced Draft
ID . . . . Industrial Development
ID . . . . Industrial Dynamics (Management analysis)
ID . . . . Infectious Disease (Medicine)
ID . . . . Infective Dose
ID . . . . Information Distributor
ID . . . . Inniskilling Dragoons (Military) (British)
ID . . . . Inside Diameter
ID . . . . Inside Dimensions
ID . . . . Institute of Distribution
ID . . . . Intellectual Digest
ID . . . . Intelligence Department (Army)
ID . . . . Intelligence Duties
ID . . . . Interdisciplinary
ID . . . . Interferometer and Doppler
ID . . . . Interior Department
ID . . . . Intermodulation Distortion
ID . . . . Intradermal
ID . . . . Item Description
ID(Card) . . . . . Identification Card
I & D . . . . Incision and Drainage (Medicine)
ID/50 . . . . Infective Dose, Median
IDA . . . . Idaho Power Company (NYSE symbol)
IDA . . . . Immediate Damage Assessment
IDA . . . . Immortalis Dei Auspicio (With the Help of God)
IDA . . . . Industrial Design Award
IDA . . . . Industrial Diamond Association of America
IDA . . . . Input Data Assembler
IDA . . . . Inspekteur der Artillerie (Inspector of Artillery) (German military – World War II)
IDA . . . . Institute of Defense Analyses
IDA . . . . Integro-Differential Analyzer
IDA . . . . Interactive Differential Analyzer
IDA . . . . Intercollegiate Dramatic Association
IDA . . . . International Defenders of Animals (An organization)
IDA . . . . International Development Association (An agency of the International Bank for Reconstruction and Development)
IDA . . . . International Dredging Association
IDA . . . . Ionospheric Dispersion Analysis (Air Force)
IDA . . . . Isotopic Dilution Analysis
IDAA . . . . . . International Doctors in Alcoholics Anonymous
IDAC . . . . . . Interconnecting Digital-Analog Converter
IDACON . . . . . Iterative Differential Analyzer Control
IDACS . . . . . . Integrated Detection and Classification Station
IDAD . . . . . . Internal Defense and Development (Army)
IDAP . . . . Industrial Design Assistance Program (National Design Council, Canada)
IDAP . . . . . . Internal Development and Assistance Program
IDAP . . . . . . Iterative Differential Analyzer Pinboard
IDAS . . . . . . Iterative Differential Analyzer Slave
IDAST . . . . . . Interpolated Data and Speech Transmission (Data processing)
IDB . . . . Illicit Diamond Buyer (or Buying)
IDB . . . . Inductance Decade Box
IDB . . . . Inter-American Development Bank (Also, IADB)
IDB . . . . Intercept During Boost
IDB . . . . Inter-Dynamic Balance

IDB . . . . Interpreter's Dictionary of the Bible
IDC . . . . Image Dissector Camera
IDC . . . . Imperial Defence College (British)
IDC . . . . Industrial Development Corporation
IDC . . . . Information Design Change
IDC . . . . Information and Direction Center
IDC . . . . Information Dynamics Corporation
IDC . . . . Infrared Detector Cryostat
IDC . . . . Input Display Console (Data processing)
IDC . . . . Interceptor Distance Computer
IDC . . . . Inter-Department Correspondence
IDC . . . . Interdepartmental Committee
IDC . . . . Interdepartmental Communication
IDC . . . . Interest During Construction
IDC . . . . International Development Conference
IDC . . . . International Development Corporation (Proposed corporation to combine Alliance for Progress and Agency for International Development)
IDC . . . . Intransit Data Card
IDC . . . . Iodine Dextrin Color
IDC . . . . Item Detail Card (Military)
IDCCC . . . . . Interim Data Communications Collection Center
IDCNA . . . . . Insulation Distributor Contractors National Association
IDCS . . . . . . Image Dissector Camera System
IDCS . . . . . . Initial Defense Communication Satellite (NASA)
IDCS . . . . . . Integrated Data Coding System
IDCSP . . . . . Initial (or Interim) Defense Communication Satellite Program (or Project)
IDD . . . . Industrial Development Division (Vietnam)
IDD . . . . Inter-Director Designation
IDD . . . . Interface Design Document
IDDD . . . . . . International Direct Distance Dialing (AT & T)
IDDRG . . . . . International Deep Drawing Research Group
IDDS . . . . . . Integrated (or Improved) Data Display System
IDE . . . . Infrared Decoy Evaluator
IDE . . . . Institute for Democratic Education (Absorbed by Anti-Defamation League of B'nai B'rith)
IDE . . . . Interim Data Element (Army)
IDEA . . . . . . Index for Design Engineering Applications (Data retrieval service) (Product engineering)
IDEA . . . . . . Inductive Data Exploration and Analysis (Data processing)
IDEA . . . . . . International Downtown Executives Association
IDEA . . . . . . Isolation of Dimensions and Elimination of Alternatives
I/D/E/A . . . . . Institute for Development of Educational Activities (of Charles F. Kettering Foundation)
IDEAS . . . . . . International Development – Economics Awareness System
IDEC . . . . . . Interior Design Educators Council
IDECS . . . . . Image Discrimination, Enhancement, Combination, and Sampling (Electronic optical system)
IDEEA . . . . . . Information and Data Exchange Experimental Activities
IDEN . . . . . . Instituto de Engerharia Nuclear (Brazil)
IDENT . . . . . . Identification
IDEP . . . . Industry Data Exchange Program
IDEP . . . . Inter-Agency Data Exchange Program
IDEP . . . . Inter-Department Data Exchange Program (Air Force)
IDEP . . . . Interservice Data Exchange Program (DOD)
IDEP . . . . Ion Density Electronics Package
IDES . . . . Integrated Defense System
IDF . . . . Integrated Data File
IDF . . . . Intermediate Distributing Frame
IDF . . . . International Dairy Federation
IDF . . . . International Democratic Fellowship
IDF . . . . International Diabetes Federation
IDFF . . . . Internationale Demokratische Frauenfoederation (Women's International Democratic Federation)
IDFOR . . . . . . Idle Waiting Convoy Forward (Vessel status) (Navy)
IDFR . . . . Identified Friendly (Military)
IDG . . . . Individual Drop Glider
IDG . . . . Inspector of Degaussing (Navy)
IDGIT . . . . . . Integrated Data Generation Implementation Technique
IDHEC . . . . . Institut des Hautes Etudes Cinematographiques (French institute for the study of the motion picture)
IDHF . . . . Integrated Data Handling System
IDHS . . . . . . Intelligence Data Handling System
IDI . . . . Improved Data Interchange
IDI . . . . Industrial Designers' Institute
IDI . . . . Industrial Development Institute (France)
IDI . . . . Institut de Droit International (Institute of International Law)
IDI . . . . International Development Institute (Proposed Agency for International Development program)
IDI . . . . Ion Dipole Interaction
IDIC . . . . Internal Dose Information Center (ORNL)
IDIIOM . . . . . . Information Displays, Incorporated, Input-Output Machine

IDIOT........ Instrumentation Digital On-Line Transcriber
IDIU........ Interdivisional Information Unit (Department of Justice intelligence unit)
IDL........ Ideal Basic Industries, Inc. (NYSE symbol)
IDL........ Index to Dental Literature
IDL........ Instrument Development Laboratories
IDL........ Interdisciplinary Materials Laboratory (Various universities)
IDL........ International Date Line
IDL........ Isotope Development, Limited
IDLC....... Integrated Digital Logic Circuit
IDLIS....... International Desert Locust Information Service
IDLOD...... Idle Waiting to Load (Shipping)
IDLR....... Instrumentation Development Laboratory Report
IDL & RS.... International Data Library and Reference Service
IDLT....... Identification Light
IDM........ Induced Dipole Moment
IDM........ Interdiction Mission (Air Force)
IDM........ Interpolating Delta Modulator
IDN........ In Dei Nomine (In God's Name)
IDNF....... Irredundant Disjunctive Normal Formula
IDO........ Idaho Operations Office (AEC)
IDO........ Identification Officer (Military)
IDO........ Industrial Development Organization (UN)
IDO........ Infrared Drying Oven
IDO........ Inspekteur der Ordnungspolizei (Inspector of Uniformed Police) (German military – World War II)
IDO........ International Disarmament Organization (Proposed)
IDO........ International District Office
IDOC....... International Documentation on the Contemporary Church (A publication)
IDOE....... International Decade of Ocean Exploration (1970's)
IDP........ Industrial Data Processing
IDP........ Initial Delay Position (Military)
IDP........ Inosine Diphosphate
IDP........ Instructor Display Panel
IDP........ Integrated Data Presentation
IDP........ Integrated Data Processing
IDP........ Interface Design Plan (Air Force)
IDP........ Intermodulation Distortion Percentage
IDP........ Internal Distribution Publication (Navy)
IDP........ Isotope Development Program (AEC)
IDPA....... Inland Daily Press Association
IDPC....... Integrated Data Processing Center
IDPM....... Initial Draft Presidential Memorandum
IDPS....... Integrated Data Processing System
IDPT....... Image Dissector Photomultiplier Tube
IDQ........ Industrial Development Quotient
IDQA....... Individual Documented Quality Assurance
IDR........ Incremental Digital Recorder
IDR........ Indian Defense Rules
IDR........ Infantry Drill Regulations
IDR........ Initial Design Review
IDR........ Inspection Discrepancy Report
IDR........ Instrumentation Development Request
IDR........ Interim Development Report
IDR........ Intermittent-Duty Rating
IDR........ Internal Development Report
IDR........ Invoice Discrepancy Report
IDRA....... International Desert Racing Association (Automobile racing)
IDRC....... Industrial Development Research Council
IDR & DS.... International Directory of Research & Development Scientists
IDREA...... Idle Other Reasons (Vessel status) (Navy)
IDS........ Identification Section
IDS........ Image Display System
IDS........ Indicator Drive Screw
IDS........ Inertial Data System
IDS........ Inertial Doppler System
IDS........ Infrared Detection System
IDS........ Instrument Development Section
IDS........ Integrated Data Store (or System)
IDS........ Integrated Display Situation
IDS........ International Development Services
IDS........ International Documents Service
IDS........ International Dostoevsky Society
IDS........ Investors Diversified Services, Inc. (Mutual funds)
IDS........ Ion Drift Semiconductor
IDSA....... Industrial Designers' Society of America
IDSB....... Independent Double Side Band
IDSC....... International Die Sinkers' Conference
IDSM....... Inertial Dampened Servomotor
IDSO....... International Diamond Security Organization
IDSOT...... Interim Daily System Operational Test (Navy)
IDSS....... Interlingua Division of Science Service

IDSTO...... Idle Used for Storage (Shipping)
IDT........ Image Dissector Tube
IDT........ Implantation Doping Technique
IDT........ Ion Doping Technique
IDT........ Isodensitracer
IDTOC...... Independent Division Tactical Operations Center (Army)
IDTS....... Improved Doppler Tracking System
IDTS....... Instrumentation Data Test Station
IDTS....... Instrumentation Data Transmission System
IDTSC...... Instrumentation Data Transmission System Controller
IDTW....... International Union of Doll and Toy Workers of the US and Canada (Later, International Union of Dolls, Toys, Playthings, Novelties and Allied Products of the US and Canada)
IDU........ Idoxuridine (A drug)
IDU........ Infrared Detection Unit
IDU........ Intermittent Drive Unit
IDU........ International Dendrology Union
IDV........ Integrating Digital Voltmeter
IDWA....... Intra-Divisional Work Authorization
IDZ........ Inner Defense Zone
IE........ Id Est (That Is)
IE........ Index of Enrichment
IE........ Index Error (Navigation)
IE........ (Order of the) Indian Empire
IE........ Indo-European
IE........ Industrial Electronics
IE........ Industrial Engineer(ing)
IE........ Information and Education (Army)
IE........ Infrared Emission
IE........ Initial Equipment (Navy aircraft)
IE........ Inside Edge
IE........ Installation Equipment (Army)
IE........ Internal Environment
I/E........ Ingress/Egress
IEA........ Immunoelectro Adsorption
IEA........ Import Entitlement Agreement (Special type of currency) (United Arab Republic)
IEA........ Indian-Eskimo Association of Canada
IEA........ Industrial Editors Association
IEA........ Instituto de Energia Atomica (Brazil)
IEA........ Instruments, Electronics, and Automation (Exhibit)
IEA........ Interment Exchange of America
IEA........ International Economic Association
IEA........ International Education Act
IEA........ International Education Association
IEA........ International Executives Association
IEA........ International Project for Evaluation of Educational Achievement
IEA........ Intravascular Erythrocyte Aggregation
IEAF....... Imperial Ethiopian Air Force
IEAHC...... Institute of Early American History and Culture
IEB........ Industrial Evaluation Board (BDSA)
IEB........ Infanterie-Ersatzbataillon (Infantry replacement training battalion) (German military – World War II)
IEB........ International Exhibitions Bureau
IEC........ Industrial Electrification Council
IEC........ Institut d'Etudes Congolaises (Congolese Institute of Studies)
IEC........ Integrated Electronic Central
IEC........ Integrated Equipment Component
IEC........ International Electric Corporation
IEC........ International Electrotechnical Commission
IEC........ Interstate Electronics Corporation
IEC........ Intra-Epithelial Carcinoma
IEC........ Inverse Electrode Current
IEC........ Ion-Exchange Chromotography
IEC........ Iso-Echo Contour
IEC........ Item Entry Control
I & EC...... Industrial and Engineering Chemistry (A publication of American Chemical Society)
IECEC...... Intersociety Energy Conversion Engineering Conference
IECEJ...... Institute of Electronic Communications Engineers of Japan
IECI....... Industrial Electronics and Control Instrumentation
IECO....... Inboard Engine Cutoff
IED........ Impact Energy Density
IED........ Independent Exploratory Development (Navy)
IED........ Initial Engine Development (Air Force)
IED........ Institute for Educational Development
IED........ Instrumental Engineering Division (Weather Bureau)
IED........ Ion Exchange Desalination
IEDES...... Institut d'Etude du Developpement Economique et Social (France)
IEE........ Induced Electrical Effect
IEE........ Induced Electron Emission

IEE......... Inner Enamel Epithelium (Dentistry)
IEE .... Institute of Environmental Engineers
IEE......... Institution of Electrical Engineers (British)
IEEE .... Institute of Electrical and Electronics Engineers
IEES........ International Education Exchange Service (State Department)
IEF......... International Eye Foundation
IEF......... Isoelectric Focusing
IEF......... Israel Education Fund
IEF......... Italian Expeditionary Force
IEFC....... International Emergency Food Council (Post-World War II)
IEG .... Information Exchange Group (National Institutes of Health)
IEHA .... International Economic History Association
IEI......... Indeterminate Engineering Items
IEI......... Industrial Education Institute
IEI......... Industrial Engineering Institute
IEI......... Institute for Educational Innovation (Became Education Development Center)
IEIS .... Integrated Engine Instrument System
IEL........ Information Exchange List (Military)
IEL........ Iowa Electric Light & Power Company (NYSE symbol)
IELS....... Isotope Exciter Light Source
IEM .... Institute of Experimental Meteorology (USSR)
IEM .... Ion Exchange Membrane
IEMC ...... Independent Electronic Music Center
IEMC ...... Industrial Equipment Manufacturers Council
IEN .... Industrial Equipment News (A publication)
IENGF ..... Istituto Electrotecnico Nazionale Gallileo Ferraris
IEO........ Incoherent Electronic Oscillator
IEO .... International Exchange Office
IEOCS ..... Interim Equipment Order Control System (Bell System)
IEOP........ Immunoelectroosmophoresis
IEP........ Indicateu Electronique de Pilotage (Electronic Pilotage Indicator) (Aviation)
IEP........ Information Exchange Program (or Project) (Military)
IEP........ Instrument for Evaluation of Photographs
IEP........ Integrated Engineering Program
IEP........ Intext Educational Publishers
IEP........ Inverted Energy Population
IEPA ...... International Economic Policy Association
IER .... Industrial Equipment Reserve
IER .... Infanterie-Ersatzregiment (Infantry replacement training regiment) (German military - World War II)
IER........ Inherent Equipment Reliability
IER .... Institute of Educational Research
IER........ Institute of Engineering Research (University of California)
IER........ Institute for Environmental Research (Environmental Science Services Administration)
IER........ Institute of Exploratory Research (Army)
IER........ Interim Engineering Report
IER........ Inventory Equipment Requirement
IERC....... International Electronic Research Corporation
IEREGEM .... Institut Equatorial de Recherches et d'Etudes Geologiques et Minieres
IERI ...... Illuminating Engineering Research Institute
IERS....... Inventory Equipment Requirement Specification
IES........ Id, Ego, Superego (Test) (Psychology)
IES........ Illuminating Engineering Society
IES........ Inductive Energy Storage
IES........ Industrial Engineering Services
IES........ Institute for Earth Sciences (Environmental Science Services Administration)
IES .... Institute of Environmental Sciences
IES .... Institute of European Studies
IES........ Internal Environment Simulator
IES .... International Exchange Service (For publications) (Smithsonian Institution)
IES........ Ion Energy Selector
IES........ Ion Engine Simulator
IES........ Ion Engine System
IES .... Irish Emigrant Society
IESA....... Instituto de Estudios Superiores de Administracion (Institute of Higher Studies of Administration) (Venezuela)
IESA....... Insurance Economics Society of America
IESC....... International Executive Service Corps
IESD....... Instrumentation and Electronic Systems Division (NASA)
IESM ...... Inductive Energy Storage Modulator
IESS....... International Encyclopedia of the Social Sciences
IESS....... Ion Engine System Section
IET........ Impact Excited Transmitter
IET........ Implanted Electrode Technique
IET........ Initial Engine Test
IET........ Institute of Educational Technology (British)
IET........ Interest Equalization Tax
IET........ Interval Embossed Tube

IETF .... Initial Engine Test Facility
IEU .... Input Expansion Unit
IEX .... Industria Electrica de Mexico, SA (NYSE symbol) (Delisted)
IEY .... International Education Year (UN designation)
IF .... Ice Fog
IF .... Immunofluorescence
IF .... Importance Factor (Statistics)
IF .... In Full
IF .... Industrial Fund
IF .... Information Feedback
IF .... Infrared
IF .... Infrared Filter
IF .... Initiation Factor (Protein biosynthesis)
IF .... Interferon (Biochemistry)
IF .... Intermediate Frequency (Electronics)
IF .... Intermittent Frequency
IF .... International Federation of American Homing Pigeon Fanciers
IF .... Interstitial Fluid
IF......... Intrinsic Factor (Biochemistry)
IF .... Ipse Fecit (He Did It Himself)
IF .... Ipso Facto (By the Fact Itself)
I-F........ Intermediate Frequency (Electronics)
IFA .... Incomplete Freund's Adjuvant
IFA .... Industrial Forestry Association
IFA .... Institute of Foresters of Australia
IFA .... Instituto de Fomento Algodonero (Bogota, Colombia)
IFA .... Institutt for Atomenergi (Norway)
IFA .... Integrated Feed Antenna
IFA .... Intercollegiate Fencing Association
IFA .... Intermediate Frequency Amplifier (or Attenuator)
IFA .... International Federation of Actors
IFA .... International Fertility Association
IFA .... International Festivals Association
IFA .... International Filariasis Association
IFA .... International Fiscal Association
IFA .... International Footprint Association
IFA .... International Franchise Association
IFA .... International Frisbee Association
IFA .... Istituto di Fisica dell'Atmosfera (Institute of Atmospheric Physics) (Italy)
IFAC ...... International Federation of Automatic Control
IFALPA ..... International Federation of Air Line Pilots Associations
IFAMP ..... If Approach Missed Proceed (Aviation)
IFAN ...... Institut Fondemental D'Afrique Noire
IFAN ...... Institut Francais d'Afrique Noire (French Institute of Black Africa)
IFAP....... International Federation of Agricultural Producers
IFARS ..... Individual Flight Activity Reporting System (Navy)
IFAS....... International Federation of Aquarium Societies
IFATCA..... International Federation of Air Traffic Controller Associations
IFATCC ..... International Federation of Associations of Textile Chemists and Colourists
IFB........ Invitation for Bid (Military)
IFBA ...... International Fire Buff Associates
IFBPW...... International Federation of Business and Professional Women
IFBSO....... International Federation of Boat Show Organisers
IFBWW ..... International Federation of Building and Wood Workers
IFC .... If Clause
IFC .... Improved Flotation Chamber
IFC .... Incremental Frequency Control
IFC .... Industrial Frequency Changer
IFC .... Infrared Fire Control
IFC .... Instantaneous Frequency Correlation
IFC .... Integrated Fire Control (RADAR)
IFC .... Intellectual Freedom Committee (American Library Association)
IFC .... Inter-Faith Compassionists
IFC .... International Finance Corporation (Affiliate of International Bank for Reconstruction and Development)
IFC .... International Fisheries Commission (US and Canada)
IFCA ...... International Federation of Catholic Alumnae
IFCATI ..... International Federation of Cotton and Allied Textile Industries
IFCC ...... International Federation of Camping and Caravanning
IFCC ...... International Federation of Children's Communities
IFCCA ..... International Federation of Community Centre Associations
IFCCTE ..... International Federation of Commercial, Clerical and Technical Employees
IFCJ....... International Federation of Catholic Journalists
IFCM ...... International Federation of Christian Metalworkers Unions
IFCMU ..... International Federation of Christian Miners' Unions
IFCN ...... Interfacility Communication Network
IFCO ...... Interreligious Foundation for Community Organization
IFCP....... International Federation of Catholic Pharmacists
IFCS....... Infrared Fire Control System

ACRONYMS AND INITIALISMS DICTIONARY

IFCS . . . . Integrated Flight Control System
IFCS . . . . International Federation of Computer Sciences
IFCTIO . . . . . . International Federation of Commercial Travelers Insurance Organizations
IFCTU . . . . . . International Federation of Christian Trade Unions (Often uses initialism CISC, based on name in French, to avoid confusion with ICFTU)
IFCTUBWW . . . International Federation of Christian Trade Unions of Building and Wood Workers
IFCUAW . . . . . International Federation of Christian Unions of Agricultural Workers
IFD . . . . Idealization to Frustration to Demoralization
IFD . . . . In Flagrante Delicto (Caught in the Act)
IFD . . . . In-Flight Deployment
IFD . . . . Infrared Detector
IFD . . . . Initial Fill Date (Army)
IFD . . . . Interfiber Distance
IFD . . . . Inter-Fighter Director
IFDA . . . . Institutional Food Distributors of America (Later, NAWGA)
IFDA . . . . International Foodservice Distributors Association
IFDS . . . . Integrated Flagship Data System (Navy)
IFE . . . . Image Feature Extraction
IFE . . . . Institute of Fire Engineers
IFE . . . . Internal Field Emission
IFEM . . . . Institute of Fireplace Equipment Manufacturers
IFEMA . . . . . . Industrial Finishing Equipment Manufacturers Association
IFEMS . . . . . . International Federation of Electron Microscope Societies
IFEP . . . . In-Flight Experiments Panel
IFES . . . . International Fellowship of Evangelical Students
IFF . . . . Identification, Friend or Foe (Military)
IFF . . . . Institute for the Future
IFF . . . . International Film Foundation
IFF . . . . International Flavors & Fragrances, Inc. (NYSE symbol)
IFF . . . . International Flying Farmers
IFF . . . . Ionized Flow Field
IFFA . . . . Institut fuer Forstliche Arbeitswissenschaft
IFFA . . . . International Federation of Film Archives
IFFCO . . . . . . Indian Farmers Fertiliser Cooperative, Ltd. (Gujarat, India)
IFFJ . . . . International Federation of Free Journalists of Central and Eastern Europe and Baltic and Balkan Countries
IFFJP . . . . International Federation of Fruit Juice Producers
IFFPA . . . . . . International Federation of Film Producers' Associations
IFFS . . . . International Federation of Film Societies
IFF/SIF . . . . . Identification, Friend or Foe/Selective Identification Feature
IFFTU . . . . . . International Federation of Free Teachers' Unions
IFGA . . . . International Federation of Grocers' Associations
IFGO . . . . International Federation of Gynecology and Obstetrics
IFH . . . . In-Flight Helium
IFI . . . . In-Flight Insertion
IFI . . . . International Fabricare Institute (Formerly, AIL and NID)
IFHE . . . . International Federation of Home Economics
IFHP . . . . International Federation for Housing and Planning
IFHTP . . . . . . International Federation for Housing and Town Planning
IFI . . . . Industrial Fasteners Institute
IFI . . . . Iterated Fission Expectation
IFIA . . . . International Federation of Ironmongers and Iron Merchants Associations
IFIAT . . . . . . International Federation of Independent Air Transport
IFIDA . . . . . . Independent Film Importers and Distributors of America
IFIF . . . . International Federation of Industrial Organizations and General Workers' Unions
IFIF . . . . International Federation for Internal Freedom (Later, Castalia Foundation)
IFIM . . . . International Flight Information Manual
IFINS . . . . . . If Instrument Conditions Encountered (Aviation)
IFIP . . . . International Federation for Information Processing
IFIPS . . . . . . International Federation of Information Processing Societies
IFIS . . . . Instrument Flight Instructors School (Navy)
IFIS . . . . Integrated Flight Instrument System
IFJ . . . . International Federation of Journalists
IFJU . . . . International Federation of Fruit Juice Producers
IFK . . . . Installations Fragenkommission (CEE) (Later, International Commission on Rules for the Approval of Electrical Equipment)
IFL . . . . Icelandic Federation of Labor
IFL . . . . International Friendship League
IFLA . . . . International Federation of Landscape Architects
IFLA . . . . International Federation of Library Associations
IFLC . . . . International Frequency List Committee
IFLOT . . . . . . Intermediate Focal Length Optical Tracker
IFM . . . . In-Flight Maintenance
IFM . . . . Instantaneous Frequency Measurement
IFM . . . . Instrument Flag Motor
IFM . . . . Integrating Fluctuation Meter
IFM . . . . International Falcon Movement
IFM . . . . International Fund for Monuments

IFMA . . . . . . Institutional Food Manufacturers Association
IFMA . . . . . . Interdenominational Foreign Mission Association of North America
IFMC . . . . . . International Folk Music Council
IFME . . . . . . International Federation for Medical Electronics
IFMIS . . . . . . Integrated Facilities Management Information System
IFMP . . . . . . International Federation for Medical Psychotherapy
IFMS . . . . . . In-Flight Management System
IFMSA . . . . . International Federation of Medical Student Associations
IFNE . . . . . . International Federation for Narcotic Education
IFO . . . . Identified Flying Object (Air Force)
IFO . . . . Improved Fiber Optics
IFO . . . . International Field Office (FAA)
IFOA . . . . . . Isotta Fraschini Owners' Association
IFOB . . . . . . Improved Fiber Optics Bundle
IFOCAP . . . . . Institut de Formation pour les Cadres Paysans
IFOFSAG . . . . International Fellowship of Former Scouts and Guides
IFOMA . . . . . Independent Fuel Oil Marketers of America
IFOP . . . . . . Institut Francais d'Opinion Publique (French Institute of Public Opinion)
IFOR . . . . . . International Fellowship of Reconciliation
IFORS . . . . . . International Federation of Operational Research Societies
IFOS . . . . . . International Federation of Ophthalmological Societies
IFOV . . . . . . Instantaneous Field of View
IFP . . . . Institut Francais du Petrole (French Institute of Petroleum)
IFP . . . . Institute of Physical Problems (USSR)
IFP . . . . International Fixed Public
IFPA . . . . . . Independent Fluorspar Producers Association
IFPA . . . . . . Industry Film Producers Association
IFPA . . . . . . International Federation of Photographic Art
IFPA . . . . . . Isoelectric Focusing in Polyacrylamide (Gel) (Biochemical analysis)
IFPAAW . . . . International Federation of Plantation, Agricultural and Allied Workers
IFPCS . . . . . . International Federation of Unions of Employees in Public and Civil Services
IFPCW . . . . . International Federation of Petroleum and Chemical Workers
IFPE . . . . . . Institute of Fiscal and Political Education
IFPEC . . . . . Independent Film Producers Export Corporation
IFPFP . . . . . Individual Flight Plans from This Point
IFPI . . . . . . International Federation of the Phonographic Industry
IFPM . . . . . . In-Flight Performance Monitor
IFPM . . . . . . International Federation of Physical Medicine
IFPRA . . . . . Interamerican Federation of Public Relations Associations
IFPW . . . . . . International Federation of Petroleum Workers
IFPWA . . . . . International Federation of Protestant Workers' Associations
IFR . . . . Image to Frame Ratio
IFR . . . . Increasing Failure Rate
IFR . . . . In-Flight Refueling
IFR . . . . Infrared Filter Radiometer
IFR . . . . Instrument Flight Recovery (NASA)
IFR . . . . Instrument Flight Rules (Aviation)
IFR . . . . Internal Function Register
IFRA . . . . . . International Foundation for Research in the Field of Advertising
IFRA . . . . . . International Fund-Raising Association
IFRB . . . . . . International Frequency Registration Board (of the ITU)
IFRC . . . . . . Instantaneous Frequency Correlation
IFRF . . . . . . International Flame Research Foundation
IFRI . . . . . . International Fund-Raising Institute
IFRIS . . . . . . Intelligence Finished Reports Information Subsystem (Data processing)
IFRO . . . . . . Internal Feed Rate Override
IFRU . . . . . . Interference Frequency Rejection Unit (Military)
IFS . . . . Identification, Friend or Foe, Switching Circuit
IFS . . . . In-Flight Safety
IFS . . . . Inshore Fire Support Ship (Navy symbol)
IFS . . . . Integrated Facilities System (Army)
IFS . . . . Integrated Flight System
IFS . . . . Intermediate Frequency Strip
IFS . . . . International Federation of Settlements and Neighbourhood Centres
IFS . . . . International Federation of Surveyors
IFS . . . . International Film Seminars
IFS . . . . Interrelated Flow Simulation
IFS . . . . Irish Free State
IFSAL . . . . . . Integral Frequency Scan Approach and Landing
IFSC . . . . . . Instituto de Formacao Social e Corporativa (Portugal)
IFSCC . . . . . . International Federation of Societies of Cosmetic Chemists
IFSDA . . . . . . International Federation of Stamp Dealers' Associations
IFSNC . . . . . . International Federation of Settlements and Neighbourhood Centres
IFSO . . . . . . International Federation of Sanitarians Organizations
IFSP . . . . . . International Federation of Societies of Philosophy
IFSPO . . . . . . International Federation of Senior Police Officers
IFSPS . . . . . . International Federation of Students in Political Sciences
IFSR . . . . . . International Flight Service Receiver Site
IFSS . . . . . . International Flight Service Station (FAA)
IFST . . . . . . International Federation of Shorthand and Typewriting

279

IFST . . . . International Flight Service Transmitter Site
IFSTA . . . . . . International Fire Service Training Association
IFSW . . . . **International Federation of Social Workers**
IFSWA . . . . . . International Figure Skating Writers Association
IFT . . . . In-Flight Text (Air Force)
IFT . . . . Input Frequency Tolerance (Data processing)
IFT . . . . **Institute of Food Technologists**
IFT . . . . Interfacial Test
IFT . . . . Intermediate Frequency Transformer
IFT . . . . International Federation of Translators
IFT . . . . International Frequency Tables
IFT . . . . Ion Focusing Technique
IFTA . . . . In-Flight Thrust Augmentation
IFTA . . . . . . **International Federation of Teachers' Associations**
IFTA . . . . . . International Free Trade Area
IF TACCAR . . . Intermediate Frequency Time Averaged Clutter Coherent Airborne RADAR
IFTAD . . . . . . Initial and Final Terminal Arrival Date (Army)
IFTC . . . . **International Film and Television Council**
IFTF . . . . Inter-Faith Task Force
IFTR . . . . International Federation for Theatre Research
IFTS . . . . In-Flight Test System
IFTU . . . . **International Federation of Trade Unions**
IFTU . . . . Iraq Federation of Trade Unions
IFTW . . . . . . International Federation of Tobacco Workers
IFTWA . . . . . International Federation of Textile Workers' Associations
IFU . . . . Intelligence Field Unit (Navy)
IFUN . . . . . . If Unable
IFUW . . . . . . International Federation of University Women
IFVLS . . . . . . If Flight Visibility Becomes Less Than
IFVR . . . . If Visibility Remains (Aviation)
IFWA . . . . . . International Federation for Works of Art
IFWEA . . . . . International Federation of Workers Educational Associations
IFWHA . . . . . International Federation of Women's Hockey Associations
IFWJ . . . . Indian Federation of Working Journalists
IFWL . . . . . . International Federation of Women Lawyers
IFY . . . . Independent Fission Yield
IFYC . . . . International Federation of Young Cooperators
IFYGL . . . . . International Field Year for the Great Lakes
IG . . . . Imperial Gallon
IG . . . . Indo-Germanic (Language, etc.)
IG . . . . Industriegewerkschaft (Industrial Trade Union) (West Germany)
IG . . . . Inertial Guidance
IG . . . . Inner Gimbal
IG . . . . Inner Guard (Masonry)
IG . . . . Inspector General (Air Force, Army, Marine Corps)
IG . . . . Institute of Geophysics (University of California)
IG . . . . Instructor Guide
IG . . . . Intendant-General
IG . . . . Interessen Gemeinschaft
IG . . . . Intestinal Groove
IG . . . . Irish Guards (Military unit)
IGA . . . . Independent Grocers Alliance Distributing Company
IGA . . . . Industry and General Applications
IGA . . . . Inhaled Gas Analyzer
IGA . . . . Inner Gimbal Axis
IGA . . . . International Geneva Association
IGA . . . . International Geographical Association (Esperantist)
IGA . . . . International Golf Association
IGA . . . . International Graduate Achievement
IGA . . . . Internationale Gartenbauausstellung
IGA . . . . Interstate Gambling Activities
IGA . . . . Ion Gun Assembly
IGAAS . . . . . Integrated Ground/Airborne Avionics System
IGACS . . . . . . Integrated Guidance and Control System
IGAEA . . . . . International Graphic Arts Education Association
IGAS . . . . International General Assembly of Spiritualists
IGAS . . . . International Graphic Arts Society
IGAS . . . . International Graphoanalysis Society
IGB . . . . Interference Guard Bands
IGB . . . . Internationales Gewerkschafts Buro (International Trades Union Office) (Germany)
IGC . . . . Indiana Gas Corporation (NYSE symbol)
IGC . . . . Institute for Graphic Communications
IGC . . . . Intellectually Gifted Children
IGC . . . . Intermagnetics General Corporation
IGC . . . . International Garden Club
IGC . . . . International Geophysical Committee (Also, CIG)
IGC . . . . **International Grassland Congress**
IGC . . . . Ion Gun Collector
IGC . . . . Isothermal Gas Chromatography
IGCA . . . . . . Italian Greyhound Club of America

IGCC . . . . . . Intergovernmental Copyright Committee
IGCG . . . . . Inertial Guidance and Calibration Group (Air Force)
IGCI . . . . . . Industrial Gas Cleaning Institute
IGCR . . . . . . Intergovernmental Committee on Refugees (Post-World War II)
IGD . . . . Inspector General's Department
IGE . . . . In-Ground Effect (Aviation)
IGE . . . . Instrumentation Ground Equipment
IGE . . . . International Geophysical Extension
IGE . . . . International Guiding Eyes
IGESUCO . . . . International Ground Environment Sub-Committee (NATO)
IGF . . . . Inspector-General of Fortifications (British)
IGF . . . . International Graphical Federation
IGF . . . . International Gymnastic Federation
IGFA . . . . . Inspector General, Foreign Assistance (Department of State)
IGFA . . . . . Interessen Gemeinschaft der Farbenindustrie Aktiengesellschaft (A dye trust) (Germany)
IGFA . . . . . . **International Game Fish Association**
IGFET . . . . . Insulated Gate Field Effect Transistor
IGFM . . . . . Internal Gamma Flux Monitor
IGFPIL . . . . . International Grotius Foundation for the Propagation of International Law
IGFVP . . . . . Interservice Group for Flight Vehicle Power (Military)
IGGI . . . . . . Inter-Governmental Group for Indonesia
IGI . . . . Inner Grid Injection
IGIA . . . . . . Interagency Group on International Aviation
IGIP . . . . . . Institute of Geophysics and Interplanetary Physics
IGIPAS . . . . . Interagency Group on International Programs in Atmospheric Science
IGK . . . . Infanteriegeschuetz – Kompanie (Infantry howitzer company) (German military – World War II)
IGL . . . . Ideal Gas Law
IGL . . . . Information Grouping Logic (Data processing)
IGL . . . . Infrared Gunfire Locator
IGL . . . . **International Minerals & Chemical Corporation (NYSE symbol)**
IGL . . . . Ionized Gas LASER
IGLOSS . . . . . Integrated Global Ocean Station System (Ocean information and forecasting service)
IGM . . . . International Grail Movement
IGM . . . . Internationale Gesellschaft fuer Moorforschung (International Society for Research on Moors)
IGM . . . . Iterative Guidance Mode (NASA)
IGMG . . . . . Internationale Gustav Mahler Gesellschaft (International Gustav Mahler Society)
IGN . . . . International-Great Northern R. R. (AAR code)
I-GN . . . . . . International-Great Northern Railroad Company
IGO . . . . Intergovernmental Organization (Generic term)
IGOA . . . . . . Independent Garage Owners of America
IGOR . . . . . . Instrument Ground Optical Recording
IGOR . . . . . . Intercept Ground Optical Recorder (NASA)
IGORTT . . . . . Intercept Ground Optical Recorder Tracking Telescope
IGOSS . . . . . Integrated Global Ocean Station System (Also see IGLOSS)
IGP . . . . Institute of the Great Plains (Formerly, GPHA)
IGP . . . . International Guild of Prestidigitators
IGP . . . . Investment Guaranty Program (AID)
IGR . . . . Infanteriegranate (Infantry howitzer shell) (German military – World War II)
IGRF . . . . . . International Geomagnetic Reference Field
IGS . . . . Imperial General Staff
IGS . . . . Improved Gray Scale
IGS . . . . Indicator Group Speed
IGP . . . . Inertial Guidance Package (or Platform)
IGS . . . . Inertial Guidance System (NASA)
IGS . . . . **Institute of General Semantics**
IGS . . . . International Geranium Society
IGSA . . . . . . International Golf Sponsors' Association
IGSP . . . . . . Institute for Gravitational Strain Pathology
IGT . . . . Inspector-General to the Forces for Training (British)
IGT . . . . **Institute of Gas Technology**
IGT . . . . Ionization Gauge Tube
IGU . . . . International Gas Union
IGU . . . . International Geographical Union
IGV . . . . Inlet Guide Vane
IGWF . . . . . International Garment Workers' Federation
IGWU . . . . . International Glove Workers' Union of America
IGY . . . . **International Geophysical Year**
IGY-WDC . . . . International Geophysical Year, World Data Center
IH . . . . In Home (Men's lacrosse position)
IH . . . . Incipient Heavies (Slang for rising young bureaucrats in the foreign policy field)
IH . . . . Infectious Hepatitis
IH . . . . Innateness Hypothesis (Linguistics)
IH . . . . **Inside Height**
IH . . . . **International Harvester Company**

IH . . . . International Holdings Corp. (NYSE symbol)
I/H . . . . Industria del Hierro (Part of a large Mexican industrial complex)
IHA . . . . Interim Housing Allowance (Military)
IHA . . . . International Hahnemannian Association
IHA . . . . International Hotel Association
IHA . . . . International House Association
IHAC . . . . . . Industrial Health Advisory Council (British)
IHAS . . . . . . Integrated Helicopter Avionics System (Navy)
IHATIS . . . . . International Hide and Allied Trades Improvement Society
IHB . . . . Indiana Harbor Belt R. R. (AAR code)
IHB . . . . International Hydrographic Bureau
IHC . . . . Immaculate Heart College (California)
IHC . . . . Indirectly Heated Cathode
IHC . . . . International Help for Children
IHC . . . . Ionic Heated Cathode
IHCA . . . . . . In Hands of Civil Authorities (Military)
IHCA . . . . . . International Hebrew Christian Alliance
IHD . . . . Indian Head, Inc. (NYSE symbol)
IHD . . . . International Hydrological Decade (UNESCO)
IHD . . . . Ischemic Heart Disease
IHE . . . . Institute of Home Economics (of ARS, Department of Agriculture)
IHE . . . . Intermediate Heat Exchanger
IHEA . . . . . . Industrial Heating Equipment Association
IHEU . . . . . . International Humanist and Ethical Union
IHF . . . . Industrial Hygiene Foundation of America
IHF . . . . Inhibit Halt Flip-Flop (Data processing)
IHF . . . . Institute of High Fidelity
IHF . . . . Integrated Hazard Function
IHF . . . . International Hockey Federation
IHF . . . . International Hospital Federation
IHF . . . . Inverse Hyperbolic Function
IHF . . . . Israel Histadrut Foundation
IHFAS . . . . . . Integrated High-Frequency Antenna System
IHFM . . . . . . Institute of High Fidelity Manufacturers
IHI . . . . Integrated Hit Indicator
IHI . . . . Ishikawajima-Harima Heavy Industries Co., Ltd. (Japan)
IHIA . . . . . . Include This Headquarters Information Addressee (Army)
IHIS . . . . . . Integrated Hit Indicator System
IHJ . . . . International Heroines of Jericho (Later, General Conference of Grand
          Courts Heroines of Jericho, Prince Hall Affiliation, USA)
IHK . . . . Industrie und Handelskammer
IHK . . . . Ionic Heated Kathode
IHL . . . . International Hockey League
IHL . . . . International Homeopathic League
IHM . . . . Daughters of the Immaculate Heart of Mary (Roman Catholic religious
          order)
IHM . . . . Sisters of the Immaculate Heart of Mary (California Institute of the Most
          Holy and Immaculate Heart of the BVM) (Roman Catholic religious
          order)
IHM . . . . Sisters, Servants of the Immaculate Heart of Mary (Roman Catholic
          religious order)
IHN . . . . In His Name
IHO . . . . Impeded Harmonic Operation
IHO . . . . International Hydrographic Organization
IHOU . . . . . . Institute of Home Office Underwriters
IHP . . . . Indicated Horsepower
IHP . . . . Inositol Hexaphosphate
IHP . . . . Institute for Human Progress
IHP . . . . International Hydrographic Program
IHPA . . . . . . Imported Hardwood Plywood Association
IHPH . . . . . . Indicated Horsepower Hour
IH/QAS . . . . . Indian Head (Maryland) - Quality Assurance Department
          (Naval ordnance station)
IHR . . . . Increased Hazard Rate
IHRA . . . . . . Increasing Hazard Rate Average
IHS . . . . Contraction of Greek word for Jesus; initials may also represent, or be
          taken to represent: In Hoc Signo, Vinces (In this sign, thou shalt con-
          quer); In Hoc Salus (In this cross is salvation); Iesus Hominum Salvator
          (Jesus, Saviour of Men)
IHS . . . . Indian Health Service
IHS . . . . Information Handling Services
IHS . . . . Infrared Horizon Sensor
IHS . . . . IPCO Hospital Supply Corp. (NYSE symbol)
IHS . . . . Isotope Heat Source
IHS . . . . Italian Historical Society of America
IHSA . . . . . . Iodinated Human Serum Albumin
IHSBR . . . . . . Improved High-Speed Bombing RADAR
IHSD . . . . . . Inertial Height Sensing Device
IHT . . . . Impact Hand Tool
IHT . . . . Institute of Heat Technology
IHTU . . . . . . Interservice Hovercraft Trials Unit

IHX . . . . Intermediate Heat Exchanger (Nuclear power)
II . . . . Ikebana International
II . . . . Image Intensifier
II . . . . Immigrant Inspector (Immigration and Naturalization Service)
II . . . . Ingot Iron
II . . . . Initial Issue
II . . . . Input Impedance
II . . . . Instituto Interamericano
II . . . . Intransit Inventory
II . . . . Inventory and Inspection Report
II . . . . Irish Institute
I/I . . . . Indorsement Irregular (Banking)
I/I . . . . Inventory and Inspection Report (Army)
IIA . . . . If Incorrect Advise
IIA . . . . Image Intensifier Assembly
IIA . . . . Incinerator Institute of America
IIA . . . . Information Industry Association
IIA . . . . Institute of Internal Affairs
IIA . . . . Institute of Internal Auditors
IIA . . . . Insurance Institute of America
IIA . . . . International Information Administration (Department of State)
          (Transferred to USIS, 1953)
IIA . . . . International Institute of Agriculture
IIA . . . . Invention Industry Association of America
I & IA . . . . . Interior and Insular Affairs
IIAA . . . . . . Institute of Inter-American Affairs (UN)
IIAC . . . . . . Infrared Information and Analysis Center (University of Michigan)
IIAE . . . . . . Instituto de Investigacion Aeronautica y Espacial (Argentina)
IIAF . . . . . . Imperial Iranian Air Force
IIAI . . . . . . International Institute of American Ideals
IIAILS . . . . . . Interim Integrated Aircraft Instrumentation & Letdown System
IIAS . . . . . . International Institute of Administrative Sciences
IIASA . . . . . . International Institute of Applied Systems Analysis
IIB . . . . Institut International de Bibliographie
IIB . . . . Institut International des Brevets
IIC . . . . Igniter Initiator Cartridge (or Container)
IIC . . . . Image Interpretation Cell
IIC . . . . Interceptor Identification Capability
IIC . . . . International Institute for Conservation of Historic and Artistic Works
IIC . . . . International Institute for the Conservation of Museum Objects
IIC . . . . Isotopes Information Center (ORNL)
IICA . . . . . . Instituto Interamericano de Ciencias Agricolas (Inter-American Institute
          of Agricultural Sciences)
IICBM . . . . . . Intermediate Intercontinental Ballistic Missile
IICC . . . . . . International Institute for Study and Research in the Field of Commercial
          Competition
IICE . . . . . . Institute for Internal Combustion Engines
IICMSD . . . . . International Institute for Comparative Music Studies and Documentation
IICP . . . . . . International Intersociety Committee on Pathology
IID . . . . Image Intensifier Device
IID . . . . Integrated Instrument Development
IID . . . . Intrinsic Infrared Detector
IID . . . . Ion Implantation Doping
IIDP . . . . . . Integrated Instrument Development Program
IIDT . . . . . . Ion Implantation Doping Technique
IIE . . . . Initial Ion Event
IIE . . . . Institut International de l'Epargne
IIE . . . . Institute of International Education
IIE . . . . Inter-American Institute of Ecology (Ecological Society of America)
IIE . . . . International Institute of Embryology (Later, ISDB)
IIEA . . . . . . International Institute for Environmental Affairs
IIEC . . . . . . Inter-Industry Emission Control (Program)
IIEL . . . . . . Institut International d'Etudes Ligures
IIEP . . . . . . International Institute for Educational Planning
IIF . . . . Institut International du Froid (International Institute of Refrigeration)
IIF . . . . Intense Irregular Field
IIFA . . . . . . International Institute of Films on Art
IIG . . . . Illuminated Internal Graticule
IIHA . . . . . . Intercollegiate Ice Hockey Association
IIHR . . . . . . Iowa Institute of Hydraulic Research
IIHS . . . . . . Insurance Institute for Highway Safety
IIHSC . . . . . . Inter-Industry Highway Safety Committee
III . . . . Information International, Incorporated
III . . . . Insurance Information Institute
III . . . . Inter-American Indian Institute
IIIC (LN) . . . . International Institute of Intellectual Cooperation of the League of
          Nations
IIIS . . . . . . Interim International Information Service (World War II)
IIL . . . . Induction Ion LASER
IIL . . . . Institute of Industrial Launderers

IILI . . . . Instituto Internacional de Literatura Iberoamericana (International Institute of Iberoamerican Literature)
IILR . . . . Institute of International Labor Research
IIMC . . . . International Institute of Municipal Clerks
IIMS . . . . Ion Implantation Manufacturing System
IIN . . . . Instituto Interamericano del Nino (Inter-American Children's Institute) (Uruguay)
IIN . . . . Item Identification Number
IINS . . . . Image Intensifier Night Sight
IINSE . . . . . . International Institute of Nuclear Science and Engineering
IIO . . . . Image Intensifier Orthicon
IIO . . . . Institute for International Order
IIOE . . . . International Indian Ocean Expedition (Navy)
IIP . . . . Index of Industrial Production
IIP . . . . Inorganic Insulative Plastic
IIP . . . . Instantaneous Impact Point
IIP . . . . Institut International de la Presse (International Press Institute)
IIP . . . . Interceptor Improvement Program
IIP . . . . International Ice Patrol
IIP . . . . International Institute of Philosophy
IIPC . . . . Image Intensifier Plumbicon Camera
IIPO . . . . Illinois Inventory of Parent Opinion
IIPR . . . . Installation Inspection Procedure Report
IIR . . . . Image Interpreter Response
IIR . . . . Integrated Instrumentation RADAR
IIR . . . . Intermediate Infrared
IIR . . . . International Institute of Refrigeration
IIRA . . . . International Industrial Relations Association
IIRB . . . . Institut International de Recherches Betteravieres (International Institute for Sugar Beet Research)
IIRG . . . . Institut International de Recherches Graphologiques
IIRR . . . . Institute of Industrial Race Relations
IIRR . . . . International Institute of Rural Reconstruction
IIS . . . . Industrial Information Service
IIS . . . . Infrared Imaging System
IIS . . . . Infrared Instrumentation System
IIS . . . . Inspection Instruction Sheet
IIS . . . . Inspections and Investigations Staff (Vietnam)
IIS . . . . Institut International de la Soudure (International Institute of Welding)
IIS . . . . Institut International de Statistique (International Statistical Institute)
IIS . . . . Institute for Intercultural Studies
IIS . . . . Institute of International Studies
IIS . . . . Integrated Insulation System
IIS . . . . Ion Implantation Study
IISA . . . . Institut International des Sciences Administratives (International Institute for Administrative Sciences)
IISD . . . . If Incorrect Service Direct (Aviation)
IISL . . . . International Institute of Space Law
IISO . . . . If Incorrect Service Originator (Aviation)
IISRP . . . . . . International Institute of Synthetic Rubber Producers
IIT . . . . Illinois Institute of Technology
IIT . . . . Image Intensifier Tube
IIT . . . . Inclinable Indexing Table
IIT . . . . Institut Interafricain du Travail
IIT . . . . Institut International du Theatre (International Theater Institute)
IITA . . . . International Institute of Tropical Agriculture (Ibadan, Nigeria)
IITRI . . . . Illinois Institute of Technology Research Institute
IITS . . . . Igniter Initiator Test Set
IIU . . . . Input Interface Unit (Data processing)
IIV . . . . Image Intensifier Viewer
IIVD . . . . Image Intensifier Viewing Device
IIW . . . . International Institute of Welding
IIYA . . . . Institute for International Youth Affairs
IJ . . . . Im Jahre (In the Year) (German)
IJA . . . . Institute of Jewish Affairs
IJA . . . . Institute of Judicial Administration
IJA . . . . International Jugglers Association
IJAB . . . . Internationaler Jugendaustausch und Besucherdienst der Bundesrepublik Deutschland (International Youth Exchange and Visitor Service of the Federal Republic of Germany)
IJAJ . . . . Intentional Jitter Antijam (Military)
IJBS . . . . Integrated Joint Broadband System (Army)
IJC . . . . International Joint Commission (US/Canada)
IJC . . . . Itasca Junior College (Minnesota)
IJC . . . . Itawamba Junior College (Mississippi)
IJCAI . . . . International Joint Conference on Artificial Intelligence
IJCS . . . . Integrated Joint Communication System (Army)
IJCS-PAC . . . Integrated Joint Communication System - Pacific (Military)
IJE . . . . Inverse Joule Effect
IJJU . . . . Intentional Jitter Jamming Unit (Military)
IJLB . . . . International Jewish Labor Bund

IJMA . . . . Infant and Juvenile Manufacturers Association
IJN . . . . Imperial Japanese Navy
IJRCS . . . . . . International Joint Rules Committee on Softball
IJS . . . . Institute of Jazz Studies
IJS . . . . Interrupt Jet Sensor
IJWU . . . . International Jewelry Workers Union
IK . . . . Indicator Kit
IK . . . . Infanteriekolonne (Infantry supply column) (German military - World War II)
IK . . . . Inner Keel
IK . . . . Interlake, Inc. (NYSE symbol)
I/K . . . . Inspector/Killer
IKA . . . . International Kitefliers Association
IKC . . . . International Kennel Club of Chicago
IKET . . . . Individual Knowledge Evaluation Test
IKF . . . . International Kart Federation
IKF . . . . International Kraft Federation
IKFC . . . . International Knife and Fork Clubs
IKH . . . . Ihre Kingliche Hoheit (His Royal Highness) (German)
IKI . . . . International Potash Institute
IKIP . . . . Institut Keguruan dan Ilmu Pendidikan (Name of many Indonesian schools)
IKL . . . . Isanmaallinen Kansanluke (National Patriotic Movement) (Finland)
IKN . . . . Inmont Corp. (Formerly, Interchemical Corp.) (NYSE symbol)
IKOR . . . . Immediate Knowledge of Results
IKS . . . . Integrated Key Set (Data processing)
IKUE . . . . Internacia Katolica Unuigo Esperantista (International Catholic Esperanto Union)
IL . . . . Bomber (Russian aircraft symbol)
IL . . . . Illinois
IL . . . . Illinois Central Industries, Inc. (NYSE symbol)
IL . . . . In Ladestreifen (Loaded in clips) (German military - World War II)
IL . . . . Including Loading
IL . . . . Incoming Letter
IL . . . . Index Lists (DOD)
IL . . . . Indicating Light
IL . . . . Inside Layer (Technical drawings)
IL . . . . Inside Left (Soccer position)
IL . . . . Inside Length (Technical drawings)
IL . . . . Instrumentation Laboratory
IL . . . . Interline
IL . . . . Intermediate Loop
IL . . . . International League (Baseball)
IL . . . . L'Internationale Liberale
I & L . . . . Installations and Logistics
ILA . . . . Instrument Landing Aid (or Approach)
ILA . . . . Instrument Low Approach (Aircraft landing method)
ILA . . . . Insulin-Like Activity
ILA . . . . International Language for Aviation
ILA . . . . International Laundry Association
ILA . . . . International Law Association
ILA . . . . International Leprosy Association
ILA . . . . International Longshoremen's Association
ILAADS . . . . . Interim Low Altitude Air Defense System
ILAAS . . . . . . Integrated Light Aircraft Attack (or Attack Avionics) System
ILAB . . . . Bureau of International Labor Affairs (Department of Labor)
ILAB . . . . International League of Antiquarian Booksellers
ILAF . . . . Identically Located Acceleration and Force (Aerospace)
ILAG . . . . Abbreviation of German Phrase Meaning "Prison camp for civilians"
ILAR . . . . Institute of Laboratory Animal Resources
ILAS . . . . Instrument Landing Approach System
ILAS . . . . Instrument Low-Approach System (Aircraft landing method)
ILAS . . . . Interrelated Logic Accumulating Scanner
ILBA . . . . International League for Bolivarian Action
ILBB . . . . Improved Life Blower Bearing
ILC . . . . Independent Labor Congress (Nigeria)
ILC . . . . Initial Launch Capability (Aerospace)
ILC . . . . Institute of Land Combat (Army)
ILC . . . . Integrated Logic Circuit
ILC . . . . International Labelling Centre
ILC . . . . International Labor Conference (A section of the International Labor Organization)
ILC . . . . International Latex Corporation
ILC . . . . International Law Commission (UN)
ILC . . . . International Legal Center (Formerly, SAILER)
ILCA . . . . International Lightning Class Association
ILCCS . . . . . . Integrated Launch Control and Checkout System
ILCEP . . . . . . Inter-Laboratory Committee on Editing and Publishing (Navy)
ILCF . . . . Inter-Laboratory Committee on Facilities (Navy)
ILCK . . . . Inductosyn Linearity Checkout Kit
ILCOP . . . . . . International Liaison Committee of Organizations for Peace
ILCS . . . . Induction Loop Communications System

ILC (UN) . . . . . International Law Commission of the United Nations
ILD . . . . Information Lead Distance
ILD . . . . International Labor Defense (An organization)
ILDA . . . . International Lutheran Deaf Association
ILE . . . . Isoleucine (Amino acid)
ILEA . . . . Inner London Education Authority (British)
ILEI . . . . International League of Esperantist Teachers
ILF . . . . Indian Local Forces (Military) (British)
ILF . . . . International Landworkers' Federation
ILFI . . . . International Labour Film Institute
ILFO . . . . International Logistics Field Office (Army)
ILG . . . . Instrument Landing Guidance
ILG . . . . Irish Linen Guild
ILGB . . . . International Laboratory of Genetics and Biophysics
ILGPNWU . . . . International Leather Goods, Plastic and Novelty Workers' Union
ILGWU . . . . . . International Ladies' Garment Workers' Union
ILH . . . . Jus Liberorum Habens (Possessing the Right of Children)
ILI . . . . Indiana Limestone Institute
ILI . . . . Injection LASER Illuminator
ILI . . . . Instant Lunar Ionosphere
ILI . . . . Institute of Life Insurance
ILI . . . . Inter-African Labour Institute
ILI . . . . Interamerican Labour Institute
ILIC . . . . In-Line Integrated Circuit
ILIC . . . . International Library Information Center
ILIR . . . . In-House Laboratory Independent Research Program (Army)
ILL . . . . Illinois
ILL . . . . Input Logic Level
ILL . . . . Institute of Lifetime Learning
ILL . . . . Interlibrary Loan
ILLIAC . . . . . . Illinois Automatic Computer
ILLLTV . . . . . . Integrated Low Light Level Television
ILLRI . . . . Industrial Lift and Loading Ramp Institute
ILLT . . . . Illinois Terminal Railroad Company
ILM . . . . Independent Landing Monitor (RADAR – TV landing guidance)
ILM . . . . Institute of Labour Management
ILMA . . . . Incandescent Lamp Manufacturers Association
ILMP . . . . Integrated Logistic Management Program
ILMT . . . . Intermediate-Level Maintenance Training
ILN . . . . Idle Line Network
ILN . . . . International Logistics Negotiations (Military export sales)
ILNY . . . . International League of New York
ILO . . . . In Lieu Of
ILO . . . . International Labor Office (A section of the International Labor Organization) (UN)
ILO . . . . International Labor Organization
ILOSS . . . . . . Integrated LASER Optical Sight Set
ILOST . . . . . . International Liaison Center of Schools of Cinema and Television
ILOUE . . . . . . In Lieu of Until Exhausted (Military)
ILP . . . . In-Line Printer
ILP . . . . Independent Labour Party (British)
ILP . . . . Index to Legal Periodicals (A journal)
ILP . . . . International Logistics Program
ILPA . . . . International Labor Press Association
ILPBC . . . . . . International League of Professional Baseball Clubs
ILPF . . . . Ideal Low Pass Filter
ILR . . . . In-Line Reciprocator
ILR . . . . Indicating Light Relay
ILR . . . . Infanterie-Lehrregiment (Infantry demonstration regiment) (German military – World War II)
ILR . . . . International Luggage Registry (Computer system for recovery of airline luggage)
ILRA . . . . Inbred Livestock Registry Association
ILRA . . . . International Log Rolling Association
ILRIS . . . . Intermediate Long-Range Interceptor System
ILRM . . . . International League for the Rights of Man
ILRV . . . . In-Line Relief Valve
ILRV . . . . Integral Launch and Reentry Vehicle
ILS . . . . Incorporated Law Society (British)
ILS . . . . Infrared Live Scanner
ILS . . . . Inspection Lot Size
ILS . . . . Instrument Landing System (Aviation)
ILS . . . . Integrated Logistic Support (DOD)
ILS . . . . Integrated Logistics System
ILS . . . . Interferometric LASER Source
ILS . . . . International Latitude Service
ILS . . . . International Learning Systems
ILS . . . . International Lunar Society
ILS . . . . International Salt Company (NYSE symbol) (Delisted)
ILS . . . . Interstate Land Sales (HUD)
ILSA . . . . Insured Locksmiths and Safemen of America

ILSAP . . . . . . Instrument Landing System Approach
ILSE . . . . Interagency Life Sciences Supporting Space Research and Technology Exchange
ILSMP . . . . . . Integrated Logistic Support Management Plan
ILSMT . . . . . . Integrated Logistic Support Management Team
ILSO . . . . Incremental Life Support Operations
ILSO . . . . Integrated Logistic Support Office (DOD)
ILSP . . . . Integrated Logistic Support Plan (or Program)
ILSPIP . . . . . . International Logistics Supply Performance Improvement Program
ILSS . . . . Integrated Life Support System (NASA)
ILSTAC . . . . . Instrument Landing System and TACAN
ILSW . . . . Interrupt Level Status Word
ILT . . . . In Lieu Thereof (Military)
ILTE . . . . Industria Libraria Tipografica Editrice
ILTF . . . . International Lawn Tennis Federation
ILTTA . . . . . . International Light Tackle Tournament Association
ILW . . . . International Low Water
ILWU . . . . International Longshoremen's and Warehousemen's Union
ILX . . . . Inland Molasses Company (American Stock Exchange symbol)
I-L YA . . . . . . Inter-Lake Yachting Association
ILZ . . . . Illinois Zinc Company (American Stock Exchange symbol)
ILZRO . . . . . . International Lead Zinc Research Organization
ILZSG . . . . . . International Lead and Zinc Study Group
IM . . . . Im Mittel (On an Average) (Germany)
IM . . . . Imperial Measure
IM . . . . Impulse Modulation
IM . . . . In Maintenance
IM . . . . Index Medicus (A publication)
IM . . . . Infectious Mononucleosis
IM . . . . Informal Memo
IM . . . . Inner Marker (Part of an instrument landing system) (Aviation)
IM . . . . Inspection Manual
IM . . . . Inspection Memorandum
IM . . . . Inspector of Machinery
IM . . . . Institute of Medicine (National Academy of Sciences)
IM . . . . Instructor's Manual
IM . . . . Instrument Man (Air Force)
IM . . . . Instrumentation and Measurement
IM . . . . Intelligence Memorandum
IM . . . . Intensity Modulation
IM . . . . Interceptor Missile
IM . . . . Interim Memorandum
IM . . . . Intermediate Modulation
IM . . . . Intermodulation
IM . . . . Internal Memorandum
IM . . . . International Mining Corporation (NYSE symbol)
IM . . . . Intramuscular (Medicine)
IM . . . . Inventory Manager (Military)
IM . . . . Isle of Man
I & M . . . . Inspection and Maintenance
I & M . . . . Installation and Maintenance
IMA . . . . Impedance Matching Attenuator
IMA . . . . Indian Military Academy
IMA . . . . Industrial Marketing Association
IMA . . . . Industrial Medical Association
IMA . . . . Institute for Mediterranean Affairs
IMA . . . . Interchurch Medical Assistance
IMA . . . . Intermediate Maintenance Activity
IMA . . . . International Management Association
IMA . . . . International Mineralogical Association
IMA . . . . Ion Microprobe Analyzer
IMA . . . . Irish Medical Association
IMA . . . . Islamic Mission of America
I & MA . . . . . . Inventory and Management Analysis
IMAA . . . . . . Industrial Medical Administrators' Association
IMACE . . . . . . Association des Industries Margarinieres des Pays de la CEE (Association of Margarine Industries of the EEC Countries)
IMAP . . . . . . Immediately After Passing (Aviation)
IMAS . . . . . . Industrial Management Assistance Survey (Air Force)
IMAT . . . . . . Integrated, Modification and Trial
IMAU . . . . . . International Movement for Atlantic Union
IMAW . . . . . . International Molders' and Allied Workers' Union of North America (AFL-CIO)
IM & AWU . . . International Molders' & Allied Workers' Union (AFL-CIO)
IMB . . . . Input Memory Buffer (Data processing)
IMB . . . . Institute of Microbiology
IMB . . . . Instrument Material Bulletin
IMB . . . . Intercontinental Medical Book Corp.
IMBA . . . . . . International Media Buyers Association
IMBE . . . . . . Institute for Minority Business Education
IMBEX . . . . . International Men's and Boys' Wear Exhibition

ACRONYMS AND INITIALISMS DICTIONARY

IMBLMS...... Integrated Medical and Behavioral Laboratory Measurement System
IMBT .... Iron Masters Board of Trade
IMC........ Image Motion Compensation
IMC .... Initial Marks (Held) Constant (Psychology)
IMC .... Instructional Materials Center
IMC .... Instrument (Flight) Meteorological Conditions (Aviation)
IMC .... Integrated Maintenance Chart (or Concept)
IMC .... Integrated Microwave Circuit
IMC .... Integrated Monolithic Circuit
IMC .... Intercollegiate Musical Council
IMC .... International Mailbag Club
IMC .... International Maritime Committee
IMC .... International Meteorological Committee
IMC .... International Micrographic Congress
IMC .... International Minerals and Chemical Corporation
IMC .... International Mining Corporation (NYSE symbol) (Later, IM)
IMC .... International Missionary Council
IMC .... International Multifoods Corporation (NYSE symbol)
IMC .... International Music Council
IMC .... Item Management Coding (Army)
IMC .... Item Master Card (Military)
IMCA ...... International Motor Contest Association
IMCAS ..... Interactive Man/Computer Augmentation System
IMCC...... Integrated Missile Control Center (NASA)
IMCD ...... Input Marginal Checking and Distribution
IMCE ...... International Meeting of Cataloging Experts
IMCO...... Improved Combustion
IMCO...... Intergovernmental Maritime Consultative Organization
IMCO...... International Metered Communications
IMCP ...... Item Management Coding Program
IMCS ...... International Movement of Catholic Students
IMD .... Indian Medical Department
IMD .... Information Media Department
IMD .... Institute for Muscle Disease
IMD .... Intercept Monitoring Display
IMD .... Intermittent Motion Driver
IMDA ...... International Mail Dealers Association
IMDC ...... Interceptor Missile Direction Center
IMDES ..... Item Management Data Element Standardization
IMDI ...... International Management and Development Institute
IMDO...... Installation and Materiel District Office (FAA)
IME .... Industria Machine Electroniche
IME .... Institute of Makers of Explosives
IME .... Institution of Mechanical Engineers (British)
IMEDE ..... Institut pour l'Etude des Methodes de Direction de l'Enterprise (A management development institute) (Lausanne, Switzerland)
IMEKO ..... International Measurement Confederation (Hungary)
IMEM ...... International Mass Education Movement
IMEO ...... Initial Mass in Earth Orbit (NASA)
IMEP ...... Indicated Mean Effective Pressure (Aerospace)
IMER ...... Institute for Marine Environmental Research (Great Britain)
IMF .... Impossible Mission Force (Fictitious group of undercover agents in TV series, "Mission: Impossible")
IMF .... Intense Magnetic Field
IMF .... Intermediate Maintenance Facility
IMF .... Internal Magnetic Focus
IMF .... International Marketing Federation
IMF .... International Metalworkers' Federation
IMF .... International Ministerial Federation
IMF .... International Monetary Fund
IMF .... International Motorcycle Federation
IMF .... Interplanetary Magnetic Field
IMF .... Interstate Motor Freight System (NYSE symbol) (Delisted)
IMF .... Israel Music Foundation
IMF .... Iuliu Maniu American Romanian Relief Foundation
IMF/IBRD .... International Monetary Fund and International Bank for Reconstruction and Development
IMFP ...... Interaction Mean Free Path (Astrophysics)
IMFSS...... Integrated Missile Flight Safety System
IMFWUNA.... International Molders and Foundry Workers Union of North America (Later, IM & AWU)
IMG....... Inferior Mesenteric Ganglia
IMG....... Informational Media Guaranty
IMGCN ..... Integrated Missile Ground Control Network
IMH....... Inlet Manhole (Technical drawings)
IMHEP ..... Ideal Man Helicopter Engineering Project
IMI .... Ignition Manufacturers Institute
IMI .... Imperial Metal Industries, Ltd. (British)
IMI .... Improved Manned Interceptor (Proposed plane) (Air Force)
IMI .... Infrared Measurement Instrument
IMI .... Integrally Molded Insulation

IMI .... International Maintenance Institute
IMI .... International Marketing Institute
IMI .... International Masonry Institute
IMI .... Istituto Mobiliare Italiano (Italy)
IMIB....... Inland Marine Insurance Bureau
IMIMI ..... Industrial Mineral Insulation Manufacturers Institute
IMIP....... Industrial Management Improvement Program
IMIR....... Interceptor Missile Interrogation RADAR
IMIS ...... Integrated Management Information System (Air Force)
IMITAC..... Image Input to Automatic Computers
IMJ .... Infrared Miniaturized Jammer
IMK .... Increased Maneuverability Kit
IMK .... Injection Molding Kit
IMK .... Instrument Marking Kit
IMKR ...... Inner Marker, Instrument Landing System (Aviation)
IML .... Inside Mold Line (Technical drawings)
IML .... Irradiated Materials Laboratory
IMLSS...... Integrated Maneuvering and Life Support System (NASA)
IMM....... Immune (or Immunization)
IMM ...... Institution of Mining and Metallurgy
IMM....... Integrated Maintenance Management
IMM....... Integrated Maintenance Manual
IMM....... Integrated Materiel Management
IMM....... International Monetary Market (Chicago Mercantile Exchange)
IMMA....... Ion Microprobe Mass Analyzer
IMME ...... Isobaric Multiplet Mass Equation
IMMED ..... Immediate
IMMIRS..... Integrated Maintenance Management Information Retrieval System (DOD)
IMMP ...... Integrated Maintenance Management Plan
IMMS ..... Indore Mill Mazdoor Sangh (Indore Textile Labour Association) (India)
IMMS ..... International Material Management Society
IMMT ...... Integrated Maintenance Management Team
IMN .... Indicated Mach Number
IMN .... Internal Mix Nozzle
IMNS ..... Imperial Military Nursing Service (British)
IMO....... Improper Order
IMO....... Inter-American Municipal Organization
IMO ...... International Meteorological Organization (Later, World Meteorological Organization)
IMP .... Imperial
IMP .... Implement
IMP .... Improved Maintenance Program (Air Force)
IMP .... Impulse Generator
IMP .... Independent Motion Picture Company
IMP .... Industrial Management Program
IMP .... Industrial Mobilization Planning
IMP .... Inflatable Micrometeoroid Paraglide
IMP .... Inosine Monophosphate
IMP .... Input Message Processor
IMP .... Instrumented Monkey Pod
IMP .... Integrated Maintenance Plan
IMP .... Integrated Memory Processor
IMP .... Integrated Monitoring Panel
IMP .... Integrating Motor Pneumotachograph
IMP .... Interface Management Plan (Air Force)
IMP .... Interface Message Processor (Data processing)
IMP .... International Match Point (Game of bridge)
IMP .... International Micro-Print Preservation, Inc.
IMP .... Interplanetary Magnetometer Probe
IMP .... Interplanetary Measurement Probe
IMP .... Interplanetary Monitoring Platform (Aerospace)
IMP .... Interplanetary Monitoring Probe (A spacecraft)
IMP .... Intra-Industry Management Program (Small Business Administration)
IMPA ...... International Motor Press Association
IMPACT ..... Implementation Planning and Control Technique (Data processing)
IMPACT ..... Improved Manpower Production and Controller Technique (Navy)
IMPACT ..... Integrated Managerial Programming Analysis Control Technique (Air Force)
IMPACT ..... Inventory Management Program and Control Technique (Data processing)
IMPATT...... Impact Avalanche and Transit Time
IMPBA ..... International Model Power Boat Association
IMPDAA ..... Independent Motion Picture Distributors Association of America
IMPI ...... International Microwave Power Institute
IMPL ...... Illustrated Maintenance Parts List
IMPPA ..... Independent Motion Picture Producers Association
IMPRESS ..... Interdisciplinary Machine Processing for Research and Education in Social Sciences (Data processing system) (Dartmouth College)
IMPRINT..... Imbricated Program for Information Transfer (Data processing)
IMPS ...... Inpatient Multidimensional Psychiatric Scale
IMPS ...... Integrated Master Programming and Scheduling
IMPS ...... Interface Message Processors (Data processing)

IMPS . . . . Interplanetary Measurement Probes
IMR . . . . Individual Medical Record
IMR . . . . Informal Memorandum Report
IMR . . . . Institute of Masonry Research
IMR . . . . Institute for Materials Research (National Bureau of Standards)
IMR . . . . International Medical Research
IMR . . . . Inventory Management Record (Military)
IMRA . . . . . . Infrared Monochromatic Radiation
IMRA . . . . . . International Mission Radio Association
IMRAN . . . . . . International Marine Radio Aids to Navigation
IMREP . . . . . . Immediately Report
IMRL . . . . . . Individual Material Readiness List (DOD)
IMRO . . . . . . Internal Macedonian Revolutionary Organization (World War II)
IMRO . . . . . . Interplant Material Requisition Order
IMS . . . . Image Motion Simulator
IMS . . . . In-Flight Management System
IMS . . . . Indian Medical Service
IMS . . . . Indirect Measuring System
IMS . . . . Industrial Management Society
IMS . . . . Industrial Mathematics Society
IMS . . . . Industrial Methylated Spirit
IMS . . . . Information Management System
IMS . . . . Infrared Measuring System
IMS . . . . Institute on Man and Science (Formerly, Council on World Tensions)
IMS . . . . Institute of Management Sciences
IMS . . . . Institute of Marine Science
IMS . . . . Institute of Mathematical Statistics
IMS . . . . Instrumented Measuring System
IMS . . . . Integrated Maintenance System
IMS . . . . Integrated Mapping System
IMS . . . . Interim Meteorological Satellite
IMS . . . . International Metallographic Society
IMS . . . . International Military Staff (NATO)
IMS . . . . International Musicological Society
IMS . . . . Interplanetary Mission Support
IMS . . . . Inventory Management and Simulator
IMS . . . . Irradiance Measuring System
IMSA . . . . . . International Motor Sports Association
IMSA . . . . . . International Municipal Signal Association
IMSC . . . . . . Industry Missile and Space Conference
IMSC & D . . . . Inventory Manager Stock Control and Distribution (Military)
IMSN . . . . . . Internal-Mix Spray Nozzle
IMSO . . . . . . Initial Materiel Support Office (Army)
IMSOC . . . . . . Interceptor Missile Squadron Operations Center (Air Force)
IMSR . . . . . . Interplanetary Mission Support Requirements
IMSS . . . . . . Inflight Medical Support System (Skylab) (NASA)
IMSSCE . . . . . . Interceptor Missile Squadron and Supervisory Control Equipment
IMSSS . . . . . . Interceptor Missile Squadron Supervisory Station
IMST . . . . . . Institute of Marine Sciences and Technology
IMT . . . . International Military Tribunal (Post-World War II)
IMTE . . . . . . International Military Tribunal for Europe
IMTFJ . . . . . . International Military Tribunal for Japan
IMTP . . . . . . Industrial Mobilization Training Program
IMTS . . . . . . Improved Mobile Telephone Service
IMU . . . . Inertial Measurement Unit
IMU . . . . International Mailers Union
IMU . . . . International Mathematical Union
IMUA . . . . . . Inland Marine Underwriters Association
IMUA . . . . . . Interservice Materiel Utilization Agency (Military)
IMVIC . . . . . . Indol Test, Methyl-Red Test, Voges-Proskauer Reaction, and
        Citrate Test (Medicine)
IMW . . . . International Map of the World
IN . . . . Idaho Nuclear (AEC)
IN . . . . Illinois Northern Railway (AAR code)
IN . . . . Inch
IN . . . . Indian Navy
IN . . . . Indiana
In . . . . Indium (Chemical element)
IN . . . . Infantry (Army)
IN . . . . Instructor Navigator
IN . . . . Instrument Note
IN . . . . Internal Note
IN . . . . Intranasal
I & N . . . . . . Immigration and Naturalization (Service)
INA . . . . INA Corp. (NYSE symbol)
INA . . . . Independent Newsletter Association
INA . . . . Industrija Nafta (State-owned company) (Yugoslavia)
INA . . . . Initial Approach (Aviation)
INA . . . . Inspector of Naval Aircraft
INA . . . . Institution of Naval Architects (British)
INA . . . . Insurance Company of North America

INA . . . . International Newsreel Association
INA . . . . International Normal Atmosphere
INA . . . . Iron Nickel Alloy
INA . . . . Isonicotinic Acid
INA . . . . Jena Nomina Anatomica (Anatomy)
INAA . . . . . . Instrumental Neutron Activation Analysis
INACDUTRA . . Inactive Duty Training (Air Force)
INACS . . . . . . Interstate Airways Communications Station
INACTFLTPAC . . Inactive Fleet, Pacific Fleet
INACTLANT . . . Inactive Fleet, Atlantic Fleet
INACTPAC . . . . Inactive Fleet, Pacific Fleet
INAD . . . . . . Inadequate
InAF . . . . Indian Air Force
INAH . . . . . . Instituto Nacional de Antropologia e Historia (Mexico)
INA/IC . . . . . . Inactive-In Commission, In Reserve (Vessel status)
INA/IS . . . . . . Inactive-In Service, In Reserve (Vessel status)
INA/OC . . . . . . Inactive-Out of Commission, In Reserve (Vessel status)
INA/OS . . . . . . Inactive-Out of Service, In Reserve (Vessel status)
INAP . . . . . . Integrated Neutron Activation Prediction (Code system)
INAS . . . . . . Industrial Naval Air Stations
INAS . . . . . . Inertial Navigation and Attack System
INB . . . . In Bono (In Good Order)
INB . . . . Industrial National Corp. (NYSE symbol)
INBEL . . . . . . Informations Belges (Belgian Information Agency)
INC . . . . Idaho Nuclear Corporation
INC . . . . Igniter Nozzle Closure
INC . . . . In Cloud (Aviation)
INC . . . . In Nomine Christi (In the Name of Christ)
INC . . . . Incorporated
INC . . . . Input Control System (Military)
INC . . . . International Numismatic Commission
INC . . . . Item Name Code (Military)
INCA . . . . . . Idaho Nuclear Code Automation (AEC)
INCA . . . . . . Information Council of the Americas
INCA . . . . . . Integrated Catalog Algorithm
INCA . . . . . . Integrated Communications Agency (Air Force)
INCA . . . . . . Integrated Navigation and Communications, Automatic
INCA . . . . . . International Newspaper and Colour Association
INCAIR . . . . . . Including Air
INCAP . . . . . . Institute of Nutrition of Central America and Panama
IncB . . . . Inclusion Body (Cytology)
INCB . . . . . . International Narcotics Control Board
INCBE . . . . . . Israel National Committee on the Biosphere and Environment
INCC . . . . . . International Newspaper Collectors' Club
INCD . . . . . . Incorporated
INCE . . . . . . Institute of Noise Control Engineering
INCFO . . . . . . Institute of Newspaper Controllers and Finance Officers
INCH . . . . . . Integrated Chopper
INCH . . . . . . International Center for High Quality Scrap (Scrap salvage)
INCIDI . . . . . . Institut International des Civilisations Differentes (International Institute
        of Differing Civilizations)
INCINC . . . . . . International Copyrights Information Center
INCL . . . . . . Inclosure
INCL . . . . . . Including
INCO . . . . . . Instrumentation and Communications Officer (NASA)
INCO . . . . . . International Nickel Company
INCODEL . . . . Interstate Commission on the Delaware River Basin
INCOMEX . . . . International Computer Exhibition
INCON . . . . . . Installation Console
INCORP . . . . . Incorporated
INCR . . . . . . Increase
INCR . . . . . . Increment
INCRA . . . . . . International Copper Research Association
INCWF . . . . . . Indian National Cement Workers' Federation
IND . . . . In Nomine Dei (In God's Name)
IND . . . . Indiana
IND . . . . Indianapolis (Indiana) (Airport symbol)
IND . . . . Induced Nuclear Disintegration
IND . . . . Industry
IND . . . . Intercept Director (Military)
IND . . . . Investigational New Drug (Application) (FDA)
INDAIR . . . . . . Identification of Aircraft
INDE . . . . . . Independence National Historical Park
Ind E . . . . . . Industrial Engineer
INDE . . . . . . Instituto Nacional de Electricidad (Guatemala)
INDEC . . . . . . Instituto de Desarrollo de la Comunidad
INDEC . . . . . . Interdepartmental Committee
INDELSEC . . . Industrial Electronic Security
INDEP . . . . . . Independent
INDIGO . . . . . Intelligence Division Gaming Operations
INDIV . . . . . . Individual

INDMAN . . . . Industrial Manager
INDMGR . . . . Industrial Manager
INDO . . . . . . Intermediate Neglect of Differential Overlap (X-ray diffraction)
INDOR . . . . . . Internuclear Double Resonance
INDUS . . . . . . Industry
INDUSMIN . . . Industrial Mineral Service (Midland, Ontario)
INE . . . . Incorrect Negative Expectancy (Psychometrics)
INE . . . . Inertial Navigation Element
INEAC . . . . . . Institut National pour l'Etude Agronomique du Congo (National Institute for the Study of Agronomy in the Congo)
INED . . . . Institut National d'Etudes Demographiques
INEWF . . . . . . Indian National Electricity Workers' Federation
INF . . . . Infantry
INF . . . . International Naturist Federation
INF . . . . Irredundant Normal Formula
INFANT . . . . . Iroquois Night Fighter and Night Tracker
INFANTS . . . . Interested Future Attorneys Negotiating for Tot Safety (Student legal action organization)
INFBAT . . . . . . Infantry Battalion (Army)
INFEREX . . . . . Inference Execution Language
INFO . . . . Information
INFO . . . . Information Network for Operations (Data processing)
INFO . . . . International Fortean Organization
INFOCEN . . . . Information Center
INFOES . . . . . . In-Flight Operational Evaluation of a Space System
INFOL . . . . . . Information Oriented Language (Computer program)
INFONAC . . . Instituto de Fomento Nacional (Industrial promotion agency) (Nicaragua)
INFOREQ . . . . Information Requested
INFORM . . . . . International Reference Organization in Forensic Medicine
INFORMAL . . . Information for Avionics Laboratory
INFRAL . . . . . . Information Retrieval Automatic Language (Data processing)
INFX . . . . Inspection Fixture
ING . . . . Inactive National Guard
ING . . . . Inertial Navigation Gyro
ING . . . . Ingenieur
ING . . . . Intense Neutron Generator
INGA . . . . Inspection Gage
INGAA . . . . . . Independent Natural Gas Association of America
Ing B . . . . Ingenium Baccalaureus (Bachelor of Engineering)
Ing D . . . . Ingenium Doctor (Doctor of Engineering)
Ing M . . . . Ingenium Magister (Master of Engineering)
INGO . . . . . . Industrial Non-Governmental Organization
InGP . . . . Indol Glycerophosphate (Biochemistry)
InGPS . . . . . . Indoleglycerolphosphate Synthetase (Biochemistry)
INH . . . . Improved Nike Hercules (Missile)
INH . . . . Isonicotinic Acid Hydrazide ("Wonder drug" for treatment of tuberculosis)
INI . . . . In Nomine Iesu (In the Name of Jesus)
INI . . . . Incipient Nonequilibrium Index
INI . . . . Interface Noise Inverter
INI . . . . International Nursing Index (A publication)
INI . . . . Intranuclear Inclusion
INIC . . . . Ideal Current Negative Immittance Converter
INIS . . . . International Nuclear Information System
INISWF . . . . . . Indian National Iron and Steel Workers' Federation
INIT . . . . Initial
INJ . . . . In Nomine Jesu (In the Name of Jesus)
INLAN . . . . . . Instant Language (Trademark) (Data processing)
INLE . . . . Instituto Nacional del Libro Espanol
INLO . . . . In Lieu Of
INLR . . . . Item No Longer Required
INM . . . . Inspector of Naval Machinery
INM . . . . Inspector of Naval Material
INM . . . . Interception Mission (Air Force)
INMM . . . . . . Institute of Nuclear Materials Management
INMWF . . . . . . Indian National Mine Workers' Federation
INO . . . . Issue Necessary Orders
INOAVNOT . . If Not Available Notify this Office at Once
INOC . . . . . . Iraqi National Oil Company (Government company)
INOP . . . . Inoperative
INP . . . . If Not Possible
INP . . . . In Pace (In Peace)
INP . . . . International News Photos
INP . . . . Interpace Corp. (Formerly, International Pipe & Ceramics Corp.) (NYSE symbol)
INPBM . . . . . . Information Not Provided By Manufacturer
INPC . . . . O-Isopropyl N-Phenylcarbamate (Herbicide) (Also, IPC)
INPFC . . . . . . International North Pacific Fisheries Commission
INPFC-US . . . . International North Pacific Fisheries Commission, United States Section
INPI . . . . Instituto Nacional de Promocion (National Institute of Industrial Promotion) (Peru)

INPI . . . . Instituto Nacional de Proteccion a la Infancia (Mexico)
INPIBOL . . . . . Instituto Promotor de Inversiones en Bolivia
INPRA . . . . . . International Public Relations Association
INPRODE . . . . Instituto Profesional para el Desarrollo (Professional Development Institute) (Colombia)
INPRONS . . . . Information Processing in the Central Nervous System
INPS . . . . Istituto Nazionale della Prevedenza Sociale (Italy)
INQ . . . . Inquiry
INQUA . . . . . . International Association for Quaternary Research
INR . . . . Insilco Corp. (Formerly, International Silver Company) (NYSE symbol)
INR . . . . Institut National de Radiodiffusion (Belgium)
INR . . . . Institute of Nuclear Research (Poland)
INRA . . . . Institut National de la Recherche Agronomique (France)
INRA . . . . Instituto Nacional de Reforma Agraria (Cuba)
INREP . . . . . . Installation Damage Report (Air Force)
INREPL . . . . . Incoming Replacement (Army)
INREQ . . . . . . Information Requested
INREQS . . . . . Information Requests (Army)
INRF . . . . International Nutrition Research Foundation
INRI . . . . Iesus Nazarenus Rex Iudaeorum (Jesus of Nazareth, King of the Jews)
INS . . . . Immigration and Naturalization Service (Department of Justice)
INS . . . . Inches
INS . . . . Inertial Navigation System
INS . . . . Inspection Division (Coast Guard)
INS . . . . Institute for Naval Studies
INS . . . . Institute for Nuclear Study (Japan)
INS . . . . Insurance
INS . . . . Integrated Navigation System
INS . . . . International Navigation System
INS . . . . International News Service (Merged with United Press to form UPI)
INS . . . . Interstation Noise Suppression
INS . . . . Ion-Neutralization Spectroscopy
INS . . . . Iron Nickel System
I-NS . . . . Inter-Nation Simulation (Simulation of international relations)
INSA . . . . Institute National de Science Applique (France)
INSACS . . . . . Interstate Airways Communication System
INSAFI . . . . . . Instituto Salvadoreno de Fomento Industrial (Industrial promotion agency) (El Salvador)
INSAIR . . . . . . Inspector of Naval Aircraft
INSATRAC . . . . Interception with Satellite Tracking
INSAV . . . . . . Interim Shipboard Availability (Navy)
INSCAIRS . . . . Instrumentation Calibration Incident Repair Service
INSCRUIT . . . . Inspector of Navy Recruiting and Naval Officer Procurement
INSDC . . . . . . Indian National Scientific Documentation Centre
INSDEN . . . . . Inspector of Dental Activities
INSDOC . . . . . Indian National Scientific Documentation Center (New Delhi)
INSEA . . . . . . International Society for Education through Art
INSEC . . . . . . Internal Security
INSEE . . . . . . Institut National de la Statistique et des Etudes Economiques (National Institute of Statistics and Economic Research) (France)
INSENG . . . . . Inspector Naval Engineering Material
INSERM . . . . . Institut National de la Sante et de la Recherche Medicale (France)
INSFOPAL . . . . Instituto Nacional de Fomento Municipal
INSGEN . . . . Inspector General (Navy)
INSGENPAC . . Inspector General, Pacific Fleet and Pacific Ocean Areas
INSH . . . . Inspection Shell
INSHOREPAT . . Inshore Patrol
INSILCO . . . . . International Silver Company (Acronym now used as firm's name)
INSINSTR . . . . Inspector-Instructor, Naval Reserve
INSITE . . . . . . Institutional Space Inventory Technique (Data processing)
INSITE . . . . . . Integrated Sensor Interpretation Techniques
INSMACH . . . . Inspector of Naval Machinery
INSMAT . . . . . Inspector of Naval Material
INSNAVMAT . . Inspector of Navigational Material
INSORA . . . . . Instituto de Organizacion Racional (Universidad de Chile)
INSORD . . . . Inspector of Ordnance
INSORDINC . . Inspector of Ordnance in Charge
INSP. . . . . Inspect(or)
INSPAT . . . . . . Inshore Patrol
INSPEC . . . . . . Information Service for Physics, Electrotechnology and Control (IEE)
INSPEL . . . . . . International Journal of Special Libraries (A publication)
INSPETRES . . . Inspector of Petroleum Reserves
INSP-INSTR . . . Inspector-Instruction (Marine Corps)
INSPIRE . . . . . . Institute for Public Interest Representation (Georgetown University)
INSRADMAT . . Inspector Radio Material
INSSCC . . . . . Interim National Space Surveillance Control Center
INST . . . . In Nomine Sanctae Trinitatis (In the Name of the Holy Trinity)
INST . . . . Instant
INST . . . . Institute (or Institution)
INST . . . . Instructor
INSTA . . . . . . Inter-Nordic Standardization

INSTAAR..... Institute of Arctic and Alpine Research (University of Colorado)
INSTAR...... Inertialess Scanning, Tracking and Ranging
INSTARS..... Information Storage and Retrieval System
INSTEP...... Indian Steel Training and Education Program (India)
INSTL....... Installation
INSTN....... Institut National des Sciences et Techniques Nucleaires (France)
INSURV ..... Board of Inspection and Survey (Navy)
INT .... Ad Interim Specification (Navy)
INT .... Infrared Nondestructive Testing
INT .... Intelligence and Law Enforcement Division (Coast Guard)
INT .... Interest
INT .... International
INT .... International Industries (NYSE symbol)
INT .... Intersection
INT .... Interstate R. R. (AAR code)
INT .... Iodonitro Tetrazolium Violet
INTA ...... Instituto Nacional de Tecnica Aeronautica (Spain)
INTA ...... Instituto Nacional de Tecnologia Agropecuaria (Argentina)
INTA ...... International New Thought Alliance
INTAAS ..... Integrated Aircraft Armament System
INTAC ...... Intercept Tracking and Control Group
INTAL ...... Instituto para la Integracion de America Latina
INTAMEL .... International Association of Metropolitan City Libraries
INTAPUC .... International Association of Public Cleansing
INTAVA ..... International Aviation Association
INTC .... Intelligence Corps
INTCO...... International Code of Signals
INTCP ...... Intercept(or)
INTECOM .... International Council for Technical Communication
INTELCEN ... Intelligence Center
INTELCENPAC.. Intelligence Center Pacific Ocean Areas
INTELSAT ... International Telecommunications Satellite Organization
INTERASMA... Association Internationale d'Asthmologie (International Association of Asthmology)
INTERATOM . Internationale Atomreactorbau (Germany)
INTERCOM ... Intercommunication System
INTERDICT ... Interference Detection and Interdiction Countermeasures Team (Electromagnetic compatibility programs)
INTERFILM ... International Inter-Church Film Centre
INTERHYBRID.. Association Intercontinentale du Mais Hybride
INTERMAG ... International Conference on Magnetics
INTERMILPOL .. International Military Police (NATO)
INTERMTRA ... Intermediate Training (Naval Air)
INTERPET .... International Petroleum Company
INTERPOL .... International Criminal Police Organization
INTERPRON .. Photo Interpretation Squadron
INTEXT...... International Textbook Company
INTIP .... Integrated Information Processing
INTIPS ...... Integrated Information Processing System
INTL .... International
INTMED ..... Intermediate
INTMED ..... Internal Medicine
INTMS ...... Internal Messenger Service (Hotels)
INTNS ...... In Transit
INTO....... Inhibited Nitrogen Tetroxide
INTO....... Intelligence Officer (Army)
INTOP ...... International Business Operations Game (Developed at University of Chicago)
INTOSAI ..... International Organization of Supreme Audit Institutions
INTPN ...... Interpretation
INTPR....... Interpret
INTR .... Intermittent
INTRAFAX ... Facsimile System (Western Union trade name)
INTRAN ..... Input Translator (Data processing)
INTRATA..... International Trading and Credit Company of Tanzania (Formerly, Tanganyika)
INTREDIS .... International Tree Disease Register System for Literature Retrieval in Forest Pathology (National Agricultural Library)
INTREPT ..... Intelligence Report
INTREX...... Information Transfer Experiments (MIT)
INTSUM ..... Intelligence Summary
INTUC ...... Indian National Trades Union Congress
INTV .... Instrumentation Television
INTVW...... Interview
INTWF ...... Indian National Textile Workers' Federation
INUS .... Inside the United States
INV .... In-Line Needle Valve
INV .... Inductive Null Voltage
INV .... Inventory
INV .... Invoice
INVES ...... Investigate (or Investigation)

INVOF ...... In the Vicinity Of
INVSTAR..... Investigate and Report
INWATS ..... Inward Wide Area Telephone Service (Bell System)
INX .... Inexco Oil Co. (American Stock Exchange symbol)
IO .... Image Orthicon
IO .... In Order
IO .... Incoming Orders
IO .... India Office
IO .... Indian Ocean
IO .... Industrial Operations
IO .... Information Officer
IO .... Initial Only
IO .... Injector Orifice
IO .... Input-Output (Electronics)
IO .... Institute for Oceanography (Environmental Science Services Administration)
IO .... Intake Opens (Valve position)
IO .... Intelligence Office(r)
IO .... Intercept Officer
IO .... Interpretive Operation
IO .... Intraocular
IO .... Inventory Objective
Io .... Ionium (Radioactive isotope of thorium)
IO .... Irish Office
IO .... Issuing Office
IO .... Iterative Operation
I-O .... Input-Output
I/O .... Input/Output (Data processing)
I/O .... Inspecting Order
I & O ...... Intake and Output
IOA .... Institute of Actuaries
IOA .... Institute of Outdoor Advertising
IOA .... International Olympic Academy
IOAT ...... International Organization Against Trachoma
IOB .... Input-Output Buffer (Data processing)
IOBB ...... Independent Order of B'nai B'rith
IOBC ...... Infantry Officer Basic Course
IOC .... Image Orthicon Camera
IOC .... Image Orthicon Control
IOC .... In Our Culture
IOC .... In-Out Converter
IOC .... Indirect Operating Costs
IOC .... Initial Operational Capability (Air Force)
IOC .... Initial Order Condition
IOC .... Input Offset Current
IOC .... Input/Output Controller (Data processing)
IOC .... Intergovernmental Oceanographic Commission (UNESCO)
IOC .... International Olympic Committee
IOC .... Interstate Oil Compact
IOC .... Iron Ore Company of Canada (Labrador)
IOC .... Iterative Orbit Calculator
IOC .... Permanent Intergovernmental Oceanographic Commission
IOCA ...... Independent Oil Compounders Association
IOC/B & CC .. Intergovernmental Oceanographic Commission – Bureau and Consultative Council
IOCC ...... Infantry Officer Career Course (Army)
IOCC ...... Input-Output Control Center (or Command) (Data processing)
IOCC ...... Interstate Oil Compact Commission
IOCD ...... Initial Operation Capability Date (Military)
IOCP ...... Indian Overseas Communication Project
IOCS ...... Input-Output Control System (Data processing)
IOCS ...... Instant Ocean Culture System
IOCU ...... Input/Output Control Unit (Data processing)
IOCU ...... International Office of Consumers' Unions
IOCV ...... International Organization of Citrus Virologists
IOD .... Imperial Order of the Dragon
IODC ...... Input Output Data Channel (Data processing)
IODC ...... Input Output Delay Counter (Data processing)
IOE .... Instrumentation Operations Engineer
IOE .... International Office of Epizootics
IOE .... International Organization of Employers
IOF .... Independent Order of Foresters
IOF .... International Oceanographic Foundation
IOFC ...... Indian Ocean Fishery Commission
IOFT ...... Institution on Farm Training
IOG .... Intercollegiate Opera Group
IOGA ...... Industry-Organized Government-Approved
IOGE ...... Integrated Operational Ground Equipment
IOGT ...... International Order of Good Templars
IOH .... Institute of Heraldry (DOD)
IOH .... Item(s) on Hand
IOI .... Interim Operating Instructions

IOIC	Integrated Operational Intelligence Center
IOIS	Integrated Operational Intelligence System
IOJ	International Organization of Journalists
IOJD	International Order of Job's Daughters
IOKDS	International Order of the King's Daughters and Sons
IOL	Initial Outfitting List (for advanced naval bases)
IOL	Instantaneous Overload
IOL	Intermediate Objective Lens
IOLM	International Organization for Legal Metrology
IOLV	Independent Order Ladies of Vikings
IOM	Indian Order of Merit
IOM	Inert Operational Missile
IOM	Innovator of the Month
IOM	Institute of Medicine (National Academy of Science)
IOM	Institute of Metals (British)
IOM	Inter-Office Memorandum
IOM	Isle of Man
I/OM	Input/Output Multiplexer (Data processing)
IOMA	Independent Oxygen Manufacturers Association
IOMP	International Organization for Medical Physics
IOMS	Interim Operation Meteorological System
IOMTR	International Office for Motor Trades and Repairs
ION	Institute of Navigation
ION	Isthmo-Optic Nucleus (or Nuclei) (In midbrain of chick)
IOO	Inspecting Ordnance Officer
IOOF	Independent Order of Odd Fellows
IOOSF	Integrated Orbital Operations Simulation Facility
IOOTS	International Organization of Old Testament Scholars
IOP	Input/Output Package (Data processing)
IOP	Input/Output Processor (Data processing)
IOP	Institute of Pyramidology
IOP	Intraocular Pressure
IOP	Iowa Power & Light Company (NYSE symbol)
I & OP	In and Out Processing
IOPAB	International Organization for Pure and Applied Biophysics
IOPB	International Organization of Plant Biosystematists
IOPC	Interagency Oil Policy Committee
IOPS	Input-Output Programming System (Data processing)
IOQ	Institute of Quarrying
IOR	Independent Order of Rechabites
IOR	Input-Output Register (SAGE)
IOR	International Offshore Rule (Yachting)
IOR	International Order of Runeberg
IORM	Improved Order of Red Men
IORS	Inflatable Occupant Restraint System
IOS	Image Optical Scanner
IOS	Image Orthicon System
IOS	Independent Order of Svithiod
IOS	Indian Ocean Ship
IOS	Indian Ocean Site
IOS	Input-Output Skip (Data processing)
IOS	Institute of Optimization and Systems Theory (Stockholm)
IOS	Integrated Operation System (Transportation)
IOS	International Organization for Standardization
IOS	Investors Overseas Services, Ltd. (Firm which sells mutual funds in foreign countries)
IOSA	International Oil Scouts Association
IOSL	Independent Order of St. Luke
IOSM	Independent Order of Sons of Malta
IOSS	Indian Ocean Station Support
IOSS	Integrated Ocean Surveillance System (Navy)
IOSTA	Institut d'Organisation Scientifique du Travail en Agriculture
IOT	Individual Operation Test
IOT	Induction Output Tube
IOT	Initial Orbit Time (Aerospace)
IOT	Input-Output Termination (Data processing)
IOT	Ipsilateral Optic Tectum
IOTA	Information Overload Testing Aid (or Apparatus)
IOTA	Institute of Theoretical Astronomy (University of Cambridge)
IOTA	Integrated Online Text Arrangement
IOTC	Infantry Officers Training Camp
IOTC	International Originating Toll Center (Bell System)
IOU	I Owe You (Business and trade slang)
IOU	Immediate Operation Use
IOV	Independent Order of Vikings
IOV	Input Offset Voltage
IOVC	In the Overcast (Aviation)
IOVST	International Organization for Vacuum Science and Technology
IOW	In Other Words
IOW	Inert Ordnance Warehouse
IOW	Isle of Wight

IP	Ice Point
IP	Identification Peculiarity
IP	Identification Point
IP	Identification of Position
IP	Identity Preserved (Wheat) (US Department of Agriculture)
IP	Impact Point
IP	Impact Prediction
IP	Impact Predictor (NASA)
IP	Implementation of Plan
IP	Improvement Program
IP	In Place (Dancing)
IP	Incentive Pay
IP	Incisoproximal
IP	Index of Performance
IP	India Paper
IP	Industrial Participation (Civil Defense)
IP	Industrial Planning
IP	Industrial Police
IP	Industrial Production
IP	Inertial Platform
IP	Initial Point (Military)
IP	Innings Pitched
IP	Input Power
IP	Institute of Petroleum (British)
IP	Institute of Physics (USSR)
IP	Instructor Pilot
IP	Intercept Point (Air Force)
IP	Interchangeable Solid and Screen Panels (Technical drawings)
IP	Intermediate Pressure
IP	International Paper Company (NYSE symbol)
IP	International Pharmacopoeia
IP	Interphalangeal (Anatomy)
IP	Interscience Publishers
IP	Intraperitoneal (Medicine)
IP	Iron Pipe
IP	Iso-electric Point
IP	Item Processing
I & P	Indexed and Paged
IPA	Including Particular Average (Insurance)
IPA	Independent Publishers' Association (Canada)
IPA	Industrial Perforators Association
IPA	Industrial Publicity Association
IPA	Institute of Public Administration
IPA	Institute of Public Affairs
IPA	Intermediate Power Amplifier (Electronics)
IPA	International Paddleball Association
IPA	International Phonetic Alphabet
IPA	International Phonetic Association
IPA	International Platform Association
IPA	International Police Academy (Formerly, Inter-American Police Academy)
IPA	International Police Association
IPA	International Psychoanalytical Association
IPA	International Publishers Association
IPA	Isopentenyladenosine (Biochemistry)
IPA	Isophthalic Acid
IPAA	Independent Petroleum Association of America
IPAA	Industrial Photographers Association of America
IPAA	International Prisoners' Aid Association
IPAC	Information-Processing and Control (Systems laboratory) (Northwestern University)
IPAD	Incoming Procurement Authorization Document (Air Force)
IPADAE	Integrated Passive Action Detection Acquisition Equipment
IPANY	Individual Psychology Association of New York
IPAS	Independants, et Paysans d'Action Sociale (Right-wing political party of independents and peasants) (France)
IPASE	Instituto de Providencia e Assistencia dos Servidores do Estado (Brazil)
IPAT	Institute for Personality and Ability Testing (Champaign, Illinois)
IPB	Illustrated Parts Breakdown
IPB	Inert Processing Building
IPB	Installation Property Book (Military)
IPB	International Peace Bureau
IPBM	Interplanetary Ballistic Missile (Air Force)
IPC	Illinois Power Company (NYSE symbol)
IPC	Image Products Company
IPC	Industrial Process Control (by computers)
IPC	Industrial Property Committee (US Military Government, Germany)
IPC	Industrial Publishing Company
IPC	Information Processing Center
IPC	Institut Politique Congolais (Congolese Political Institute)
IPC	Institute of Paper Chemistry
IPC	Institute of Pastoral Care

IPC . . . . Institute of Printed Circuits
IPC . . . . Instrumentation Package Container
IPC . . . . Integrated Procedures Control
IPC . . . . Inter-African Phytosanitary Commission
IPC . . . . Intermediate Processing Centers
IPC . . . . Intermittent Positive Control (Aviation)
IPC . . . . International Petroleum Company
IPC . . . . International Planning Corporation
IPC . . . . International Plasma Corporation
IPC . . . . International Poliomyelitis Congress
IPC . . . . International Poplar Commission
IPC . . . . International Publishing Corporation (England)
IPC . . . . Investors Planning Corporation
IPC . . . . Iraqi Petroleum Company
IPCC . . . . O-Isopropyl N-Phenylcarbamate (Herbicide) (Also, INPC)
IPCC . . . . Information Processing in Command and Control (Air Force)
IPCCIOS . . . . . Indo-Pacific Council of the International Committee of Scientific Management
IPCCS . . . . Information Processing in Command and Control Systems
IPCEA . . . . . . Insulated Power Cable Engineers Association
IPCO . . . . Idaho Power Company
IPCOG . . . . . . Informal Policy Committee for Germany
IPCOG . . . . . Interdepartmental Planning Committee on Germany (US)
IPCS . . . . Institution of Professional Civil Servants (British)
IPD . . . . Impact Prediction Data
IPD . . . . Improved Point Defense
IPD . . . . In Praesentia Dominorum (In the presence of the Lords of Session)
IPD . . . . Individual Package Delivery
IPD . . . . Insertion Phase Delay
IPD . . . . Institute for Professional Development
IPD . . . . Integrated Pin Diode
IPD . . . . Inventory of Psychosocial Development
IPD . . . . Isotope-Powered Device
IPD . . . . Issue Priority Designator
IPDA . . . . International Periodical Distributors Association
IPDA . . . . Intra-Pulse Demodulation Analysis
IPDL . . . . Isotopes Process Development Laboratory (AEC)
IPDP . . . . Intervals of Pulsations of Diminishing Period
IPDSMS . . . . . Improved Point Defense Surface Missile System
IPE . . . . Incentive PERT Events
IPE . . . . Industrial Plant (or Production) Equipment
IPE . . . . Information Processing Equipment
IPE . . . . Initial Portable Equipment
IPE . . . . Interpret Parity Error
IPE . . . . Inverse Photoelectric Effect
IPEA . . . . Independent Poster Exchanges of America
IPECS . . . . . . Integrated Power and Environmental Control System
IPEE . . . . Inclination of a Plane to the Plane of the Earth's Equator (Aerospace)
IPEE . . . . Instituto de Pesquisas e Estudos Economicos (Brazil)
IPEPLAN . . . . Instituto de Pesquisa e Planejamento (Brazil)
IPER . . . . Industrial Production Equipment Reserve
IPET . . . . Independent Professional Electronic Technicians
IPEU . . . . International Photo-Engravers Union of North America (Later, Lithographers and Photoengravers International Union)
IPEX . . . . International Printing Exhibition
IPF . . . . In-Process Factor
IPF . . . . Initial Protective Force
IPFA . . . . Insurance Premium Finance Association
IPFC . . . . Indo-Pacific Fisheries Council
IPG . . . . Induction Plasma Gun
IPG . . . . International Planning Group (Belgium, Germany, Netherlands)
IPG . . . . Interproject Group
IPG . . . . Interpublic Group of Companies, Inc. (NYSE symbol)
IPG . . . . Isotope Power Generator
IPGP . . . . Illegal Possession of Government Property
IPGS . . . . Intercollegiate Program of Graduate Studies
IPH . . . . International Association of Paper Historians
IPHC . . . . International Pacific Halibut Commission
IPI . . . . Identified Friendly Prior to Interception (Military)
IPI . . . . Immigration Patrol Inspector (Immigration and Naturalization Service)
IPI . . . . In Partibus Infidelium (In the countries, lands, or regions of unbelievers)
IPI . . . . Individually Planned (or Prescribed) Instruction (Education)
IPI . . . . Institute of Poultry Industries
IPI . . . . Interchemical Printing Inks
IPI . . . . International Pesticide Institute
IPI . . . . International Press Institute
IPI . . . . Intrapair Interval
IPI . . . . Inventory, Print, and Index (System)
IPI/MIS . . . . . . Individually Planned Instruction/Management and Information System
IPIP . . . . Information Processing Improvement Program
IPIR . . . . Immediate Photograph Intelligence Report (Military)

IPIR . . . . Initial Photographic Interpretation Report (Air Force)
IPIR . . . . Institute for Public Interest Representation (Georgetown University)
IPIS . . . . Instrument Pilot Instructor School (Air Force)
IPIx . . . . International Plant Index (A publication)
IPJP . . . . Interpost Junction Panel
IPK . . . . International Packers, Ltd. (NYSE symbol) (Delisted)
IPK . . . . International Prototype Kilogram
IPKO . . . . International Information on Peace-Keeping Operations
IPL . . . . Identified Parts List
IPL . . . . Indianapolis Power and Light Company (NYSE symbol)
IPL . . . . Information Processing Language (Data processing)
IPL . . . . Initial Program Load (Data processing)
IPL . . . . Interconnected Porosity Level
IPL . . . . Interim Parts List (Navy)
IPLV . . . . Intermediate Payload Launch Vehicle
IPM . . . . Illuminations Per Minute
IPM . . . . Immediate Past Master (Masonry)
IPM . . . . Impulses Per Minute
IPM . . . . Inches Per Minute
IPM . . . . Incidental Phase (or Pulse) Modulation
IPM . . . . Industrial Preparedness Measures
IPM . . . . Inner Peace Movement
IPM . . . . Interference Prediction Model
IPM . . . . International Prototype Meter
IPM . . . . Interpersonal Perception Method (Psychology)
IPM . . . . Interruptions Per Minute
IPMA . . . . In-Plant Printing Management Association
IPMA . . . . International Personnel Management Association
IPMANA . . . . . Interstate Postgraduate Medical Association of North America
IPMP . . . . Industrial Plant Modernization Program (Air Force)
IPMS . . . . Infinite Periodic Minimal Surface
IPMS . . . . Integrated Program Management System (Navy)
IPMS . . . . International Polar Motion Service
IPMS/USA . . . . International Plastic Modelers Society/US Branch
IPN . . . . Infectious Pancreatic Necrosis (Disease)
IPN . . . . Inspection Progress Notification
IPN . . . . Instrument Plan Number
IPO . . . . Installation Planning Order
IPO . . . . Installation Production Order
IPO . . . . Instantaneous Power Output
IPO . . . . Intellectual Property Owners (Patent lobby)
IPO . . . . International Parents' Organization
IPOR . . . . International Population Research Center (University of California)
IPP . . . . Imaging Photopolarimeter
IPP . . . . Impact Prediction Point (NASA)
IPP . . . . India Paper Proofs
IPP . . . . Infrared Pointer Package
IPP . . . . Inspired Partial Pressure
IPP . . . . Intrapleural Pressure (Biology)
IPP . . . . Inverse Polarity Protection
IPP . . . . Ionospheric Propagation Path
IPP . . . . Isothermal Pressure Profile
IPPA . . . . Inspection, Palpation, Percussion, Auscultation (Medicine)
IPPA . . . . Instant Potato Products Association
IPPA . . . . International Printing Pressmen and Assistants' Union of North America
IPPAU . . . . . . International Printing Pressmen & Assistants' Union of North America
IPPB . . . . Intermittent Positive Pressure Breathing
IPPDSEU . . . . International Plate Printers, Die Stampers & Engravers' Union of North America
IPPF . . . . International Penal and Penitentiary Foundation
IPPF . . . . International Planned Parenthood Federation
IPPI . . . . Instructional Procedures Preference Inventory
IPPMA . . . . . . In-Plant Powder Metallurgy Association
IPPR . . . . Intermittent Positive Pressure Respiration
IPPS . . . . International Plant Propagators' Society
IPPSA . . . . . . Israel-Palestine Philatelic Society of America
IPQ . . . . International Philosophical Quarterly (A publication)
IPQ . . . . Intimacy Potential Quotient
IPQC . . . . In-Process Quality Control
IPR . . . . Inches Per Revolution
IPR . . . . Individual Pay Record (Military)
IPR . . . . Informal Progress Report
IPR . . . . Institute of Pacific Relations
IPR . . . . Institute of Public Relations (British)
IPR . . . . Interim Progress Report
IPR . . . . Internal Progress Report
IPR . . . . Interpersonal Process Recall
IPR . . . . Istituto per le Pubbliche Relazioni (Italian public relations institute)
IPRA . . . . In-Place Repairable Assembly
IPRA . . . . International Paddle Racket Association
IPRA . . . . International Peace Research Association

IPRA........	International Public Relations Association
IPRB........	Inter-Allied Postwar Requirements Bureau (World War II)
IPRO.......	International Patent Research Office
IPS........	Impact Predictor System
IPS........	Inches Per Second
IPS........	Industrial Planning Specification
IPS........	Information Processing System
IPS........	Institute of Polar Studies (Ohio State University)
IPS........	Institute for Policy Studies
IPS........	Instructions Per Second (Data processing)
IPS........	Instructor Power Supply
IPS........	Instrumentation Power Supply (or System)
IPS........	Integrated Power System
IPS........	Interceptor Pilot Simulator (SSTM)
IPS........	International Confederation for Plastic Surgery
IPS........	International Phenomenological Society
IPS........	International Pipe Standard
IPS........	Interpretative Programming System
IPS........	Interruptions Per Second
IPS........	Introductory Physical Science (Project) (Education)
IPS........	Ion Plating Supply
IPS........	Iowa Public Service Co. (NYSE symbol)
IPS........	Iron Pipe Size
IPSA.......	Incremental Microwave Power Spectrum Analyzer (Air Force)
IPSA.......	Independent Postal System of America (Alternative to US Postal Service)
IPSA.......	International Political Science Association
IPSC.......	Information Processing Standards for Computers
IPSF.......	International Pharmaceutical Students' Federation
IPSFC......	International Pacific Salmon Fisheries Commission
IPSP.......	Inhibitory Postsynaptic Potential (Physiology)
IPSRA......	International Professional Ski Racers Association
IPSS.......	Institute of Planetary and Space Science
IPSSB......	Information Processing Systems Standards Board (American Standard Association) (Later, Board of Standards Review of ANSI)
IPSSG......	International Printers Supply Salesmen's Guild
IPST.......	Israel Program for Scientific Translations (an agency of the Government of Israel)
IPT........	Indexed, Paged, and Titled
IPT........	Induction Plasma Torch
IPT........	Industrial Power Tube
IPT........	Initial Production Test (Army)
IPT........	Internal Pipe Thread
IPTA.......	International Piano Teachers Association
IPTAR......	Institute for Psychoanalytic Training and Research
IPTH.......	Immunoreactive Parathyroid Hormone (Endocrinology)
IPTS.......	International Practical Temperature Scale (National Bureau of Standards)
IPTT.......	Internationale du Personnel des Postes, Telegraphes et Telephones (Postal, Telegraph and Telephone International)
IPU........	Interface and Priority Unit
IPU........	International Peasant Union
IPU........	Inter-Parliamentary Union
IPV........	Infectious Pustular Vulvovaginitis (Veterinary medicine)
IPV........	Inner Pilot Valve
IPV........	Intrinsic Payload Value
IPVS.......	Ion Pump Vacuum System
IPW........	Interrogation Prisoner of War
IPW........	Interstate Power Company (NYSE symbol)
IPY........	Inches Per Year
IPY........	International Polar Year
IPY........	Ion Pair Yield
IQ.........	I Quit (Smoking)
IQ.........	Idem Quod (The Same As)
IQ.........	Indefinite Quantity
IQ.........	Intelligence Quotient (Psychological and educational testing)
IQ.........	Internal Quality
IQ.........	International Quorum of Motion Picture Producers
IQ.........	Investment Quality Trends (A publication)
IQ.........	Iowa Quality (of pigs)
IQ.........	Questor Corp. (NYSE symbol)
IQA........	Inertial Quality Attitude
IQA........	Inspection Quality Assurance
IqAF.......	Iraqi Air Force
IQC........	Industrial Quality Control
IQC........	International Quality Centre
IQED.......	Id Quod Erat Demonstrandum (That Which Was to Be Proved)
IQI........	Image Quality Indicator
IQL........	Intermediate Query Language
IQN........	Inner Quantum Number
IQO........	Initial Quantity Order
IQR........	Interquartile Range
IQS........	International "Q" Signal

IQ & S......	Iron, Quinine, and Strychnine (Elixir)
IQSY.......	International Year of the Quiet Sun (1964-65)
IR.........	Ice on Runways (Aviation)
IR.........	Image Rejection
IR.........	Immunization Rate
IR.........	Independent Research
IR.........	Industrial Relations
IR.........	Informal Report
IR.........	Information Report
IR.........	Information Retrieval
IR.........	Infrared
IR.........	Infrared Equipment (Navy)
IR.........	Infrared Radiation
IR.........	Infrared Radiometer
IR.........	Ingersoll-Rand Company (NYSE symbol)
IR.........	Inland Revenue (British)
IR.........	Inside Radius (Technical drawings)
IR.........	Inside Right (Soccer position)
IR.........	Insoluble Residue
IR.........	Inspection Rejection
IR.........	Inspection Release
IR.........	Instantaneous Relay
IR.........	Instruction Register (Data processing)
IR.........	Instrument Reading
IR.........	Instrumentation Report
IR.........	Insulation Resistance
IR.........	Intelligence Ratio
IR.........	Intelligence Report
IR.........	Intelligence Review
IR.........	Interim Report
IR.........	Internal Reliability
IR.........	Internal Report
IR.........	Internal Resistance
IR.........	Internal Revenue
IR.........	Internal Review (Army)
IR.........	Interpretation Report
IR.........	Interrogation Report
IR.........	Interrogator-Responder
IR.........	Interval Rate (Army)
IR.........	Invention Report
IR.........	Investigation Record
Ir.........	Iridium (Chemical element)
I & R......	Initiative and Referendum
I & R......	Intelligence and Reconnaissance
IRA........	Independent Regulatory Agency (US Government)
IRA........	Indian Rights Association
IRA........	Integrated RADOME Antenna
IRA........	Intercollegiate Rowing Association
IRA........	Internal Revenue Act
IRA........	International Racquetball Association
IRA........	International Reading Association
IRA........	International Recreation Association
IRA........	International Rodeo Association
IRA........	International Roleo Association (Later, International Log Rolling Association)
IRA........	Iranian Airways Company
IRA........	Irish Republican Army
IRA........	Ithaca Railroad Association
IRAA.......	Independent Refiners Association of America
IRAA & A...	Increase and Replacement of Armor, Armament and Ammunition (Naval budget appropriation title)
IRAC.......	Industrial Relations Advisory Committee
IRAC.......	Infrared Advisory Center
IRAC.......	Intelligence Resources Advisory Committee (to supervise US intelligence budget)
IRAC.......	Interagency Records Administration Conference (Washington, DC)
IRAC.......	Interdepartment Radio Advisory Committee (Aviation)
IRAC.......	Interfraternity Research and Advisory Council
IRACQ......	Infrared Acquisition RADAR
IRACQ......	Instrumentation RADAR and Acquisition Panel
IRAD.......	Inbound Radial (Aviation)
IRAD.......	Independent Research & Development
IRADDS.....	Infrared Air Defense Detection System
IRAH.......	Infrared Active Homing
IRAH.......	Infrared Alternate Head
IRAM.......	Improved Reliability and Maintainability
IRAM.......	Institut de Recherche et Application des Methodes de Developpement
IRAN.......	Inspect(ion) and Repair as Necessary (Aviation)
IRAP.......	Industrial Research Assistance Program (Canada)
IRAP.......	Interagency Radiological Assistance Plan (AEC)
IRAR.......	Impulse Response Area Ratio

IRAS........ Infrared Attack System
IRAS........ Institute on Religion in an Age of Science
IRAS........ Integrated RADOME Antenna Structure
IRASA....... International Radio Air Safety Association
IRASER...... Infrared Amplification by Stimulated Emission of Radiation
IRASI....... Internal Review and System Improvement
IRAT........ Institut de Recherches d'Agronomie Tropicale et de Culture Vivrieres (Food and agricultural research foundation supported by France and several African states)
IRATE....... Intelligence Review and Assessment Task Element (Study of the effectiveness of the air war in Southeast Asia)
IRATE....... Interim Remote Area Terminal Equipment (Air Force)
IRB........ Impulse Resistance Bridge
IRB........ Inducto-Ratio Bridge
IRB .... Industrial Readjustment Branch
IRB .... Industrial Relations Board
IRB........ Inner Radiation Belt
IRB .... Irish Republican Brotherhood
IRBM ...... Intermediate-Range Ballistic Missile
IRC........ Industrial Reconstruction Corporation
IRC........ Industrial Relations Counselors, Inc.
IRC........ Information Recovery Capsule
IRC........ Information Resources Center (of Mental Health Materials Center)
IRC .... Infrared Countermeasures (Military electronics)
IRC........ Inland Revenue Commissioners (British)
IRC........ Inspection Record Card (Navy)
IRC........ Institutional Research Council
IRC .... Internal Revenue Code
IRC........ International Railways of Central America (NYSE symbol) (Delisted)
IRC........ International Rainwear Council
IRC........ International Red Cross
IRC........ International Relations Committee (American Library Association)
IRC........ International Reply Coupon
IRC........ International Rescue Committee
IRC........ International Research Council
IRC........ International Resistor Center
IRC........ International Rice Commission
IRC........ Ion Recombination Chamber
IRC........ Ionosphere Research Committee
IRC .... Irregular Route Carrier
IRC .... Item Responsibility Code
IRCA....... International Radio Club of America
IRCA ...... International Railway Congress Association
IRCAT...... Infrared Radiometer Clear Air Turbulence (Instrument)
IRCC ...... International Radio Consultative Committee
IRCCM ..... Infrared Counter-Countermeasures (Military electronics)
IRCD ...... Information Retrieval Center on the Disadvantaged (ERIC)
IRCDP...... International Research Career Development Program (Public Health Service)
IRCM ...... Infrared Counter-Countermeasures (Military electronics)
IRC & M .... Increase and Replacement of Construction and Machinery (Naval budget appropriation title)
IRCOPPS..... Interprofessional Research Commission on Pupil Personnel Services
IRCPPFI ..... Industrial Relations Council for the Plumbing and Pipe Fitting Industry
IRCS....... Infrared Communications System
IRCS....... Italian Red Cross Society
IRCT....... International Research on Communist Techniques
IRD .... Infrared Detector
IRD .... Isotopes and Radiation Division (American Nuclear Society)
IRD .... Itinerant Recruiting Detail
I/RD ...... Institutes and Research Divisions (National Institutes of Health)
IR & D ..... Independent Research and Development
IRDC ...... International Rubber Development Committee
IRDL ...... Information Retrieval and Display Language (Data processing)
IRDO ...... Infrared Drying Oven
IRDS....... Infrared Detecting Set
IRDU ...... Infrared Detection Unit
IRE .... Immediate Ready Element (Military)
IRE........ Infrared Engineering
IRE........ Institute of Radio Engineers (Later, IEEE)
IRE........ International Association of Railway Employees
IREC....... Increase and Replacement of Emergency Construction (Ships) (Naval budget appropriation title)
IREM ...... Institute of Real Estate Management
IREM ...... Integrated Regional Environmental Management Project
IREN ...... Instituto de Investigacion de Recursos Naturales
IREP ...... Interdisciplinary Research Equipment Program
IREX....... International Research and Exchanges Board
IRF........ Immediate Reaction Force (Military)
IRF........ Induced Radiation Flux
IRF........ Instant Ready Force (Military)

IRF........ International Rectifier Corporation (NYSE symbol)
IRF........ International Reform Federation
IRF........ International Road Federation
IRF........ International Rowing Federation
IRF........ Interrogation Repetition Frequency (RADAR beacon)
IRF........ Islands Research Foundation
IRFAA...... International Rescue and First Aid Association
IRFB....... International Radio Frequency Board
IRFED ...... Institut de Recherche et de Formation en vue du Developpement Harmonise (France)
IRFNA ..... Inhibited Red Fuming Nitric Acid
IRG .... Industrial Reprocessing Group
IRG .... Infrared Generator
IRG .... Initial Review Group (National Institutes of Health)
IRG .... Integrated Rate Gyro
IRG .... Interdepartmental Regional Group (Army)
IRG .... Internationale des Resistants a la Guerre
IRGAR ..... Infrared Gas Radiation
IRGL ...... Infrared Gunfire Locator
IRGRD ..... International Research Group on Refuse Disposal
IRH .... Infrared Heater
IRH .... Inspection Requirements Handbook (Navy)
IRH .... Institute for Research in Hypnosis
IRHF....... Integral Radiative Heat Flux
IRHO ...... Institut de Recherches pour les Huiles et Oleagineux
IRHR ...... Institute for Research in Human Relations
IRI .... Immunoreactive Insulin
IRI .... Industrial Research Institute
IRI .... Information Retrieval, Incorporated
IRI .... Infrared Imagery
IRI .... Infrared Instrumentation
IRI .... Institution of the Rubber Industry (British)
IRI .... Integrated Range Instrumentation
IRI .... Istituto per la Riconstruzione Industriale (Institute for Industrial Reconstruction) (Government holding company) (Italy)
IRIA .... Infrared Information and Analysis
IRIA .... Institut de Recherche d'Informatique et d'Automatique (France)
IRIC .... Infrared Image Converter
IRIC....... Inter-Regional Insurance Conference
IRICON ..... Infrared Vidicon Tube
IRIG .... Inertial Reference Integrating Gyro
IRIG .... Inter-Range Instrumentation Group
IRIS .... IBM Recruitment Information System
IRIS .... Increased Readiness Information System
IRIS .... Information Resources Information System (Library of Congress)
IRIS .... Infrared Image Scanner
IRIS .... Infrared Information Symposia (Navy)
IRIS .... Infrared Interferometer Spectrometer
IRIS .... Intelligence Reports Information Subsystem (Data processing)
IRIS-M ..... Infrared Interferometer Spectrometer - Michelson
IRK .... Infrared Kit
IRL........ Industrial Reactor Laboratories (New Jersey)
IRL........ Information Retrieval Language (Data processing)
IRL........ Infrared Lamp
IRL........ Infrared Lens
IRL........ Institute for Rational Living
IRL........ Interrogation and Locating
IRLA ...... International Religious Liberty Association
IRLAS ..... Infrared LASER
IRLCS ..... International Red Locust Control Service
IRLDA ..... Independent Retail Lumber Dealers Association
IRLS .... Interrogation, Recording, and Locating System (Naval Oceanographic Office)
IRM .... Illinois Railway Museum
IRM .... Improved Risk Mutuals
IRM .... Infrared Mapper
IRM .... Infrared Measurement
IRM .... Innate Release Mechanism (Endocrinology)
IRM .... Integrated Range Mission (Military)
IRM .... Interim Research Memo
IRM .... Isothermal Remanence
IRM .... Isothermal Remanent Magnetization
IRMA ...... Information Referral Manual
IRMA ...... Infrared Miss-Distance Approximator
IRMFSG ..... Inter-Range Missile Flight Safety Group
IRMJ ...... Infrared Miniaturized Jammer
IRMP ...... Infrared Measurement Program
IRMP ...... Interservice Radiation Measurement Program
IR/MRBM..... Intermediate-Range/Medium-Range Ballistic Missile
IRMS ...... Infrared Mapping System
IRN .... Internal Reference Number

ACRONYMS AND INITIALISMS DICTIONARY

IRN . . . . Ironton R. R. (AAR code)
IRNV . . . . Increase and Replacement of Naval Vessels (Naval budget appropriation title)
IRO . . . . Industrial Relations Office
IRO . . . . Inland Revenue Office(r) (British)
IRO . . . . Internal Revenue Office(r)
IRO . . . . International Refugee Organization
IRO . . . . International Relief Organization (Post-World War II)
IROAN . . . . . Inspect and Repair Only as Necessary (Military)
IROD . . . . Instantaneous Readout Detector (Satellite instrument)
IRODS . . . . . . Inertial Rate of Descent Sensor
IROPG . . . . . . Inter-Range Operations Planning Group (White Sands Missile Range)
IROR . . . . Inspection, Repair, Overhaul and Rebuild
IROS . . . . Increase Reliability of Operational System
IROT . . . . Infrared on Target
IRP . . . . Individualized Reading Program (Education)
IRP . . . . Industrial Readiness Planning
IRP . . . . Inertial Reference Package
IRP . . . . Information Resources Press (Washington, DC)
IRP . . . . Infrared Preamplifier
IRP . . . . Infrared Radiation Profile
IRP . . . . Infrared Responsive Phosphor
IRP . . . . Initial Receiving Point
IRPA . . . . International Radiation Protection Association
IRPD . . . . Industrial Relations and Personnel Development (Canadian publication)
IRPL . . . . Interservice Radio Propagation Laboratory
IRPM . . . . Infrared Physical Measurement
IRPP . . . . Industrial Readiness Planning Program
IRPP . . . . Infrared Pointer Package
IRQC . . . . Infrared Quantum Counter
IRR . . . . Immediate (or Individual) Ready Reserve (Army)
IRR . . . . Improved Rearming Rates (Military)
IRR . . . . Individual Retirement Record (Air Force)
IRR . . . . Industrial Retaining Ring Company
IRR . . . . Infrared Radiometer
IRR . . . . Infrared Receiver
IRR . . . . Institute for Reactor Research (Switzerland)
IRR . . . . Institute of Rubber Research
IRR . . . . Intelligence RADAR Reporting
IRR . . . . Internal Rate of Return (Finance)
IRR . . . . Israeli Research Reactor
IRRA . . . . Industrial Relations Research Association
IRRAD . . . . . . Infrared Range and Detection
IRRB . . . . International Rubber Research Board
IRRC . . . . International Relief and Rescue Committee (Post-World War II)
IRRD . . . . International Road Research Documentation System (OECD)
IRRI . . . . International Rice Research Institute (Philippines)
IRRM . . . . Information Requested in Above Referenced Message (Army)
IRRMP . . . . . . Infrared RADAR Measurement Program
IRRPOS . . . . . . Interdisciplinary Research Relevant to Problems of Our Society (Later, RANN) (National Science Foundation)
IRRT . . . . International Relations Round Table (American Library Association)
IRS . . . . Inactive Reserve Section (Military)
IRS . . . . Inboard Rotating Shield
IRS . . . . Independent Research Service
IRS . . . . Induction and Recruiting Station (Marine Corps)
IRS . . . . Ineligible Reserve Section
IRS . . . . Information Retrieval System
IRS . . . . Infrared Reconnaissance Set
IRS . . . . Infrared Reflective Spectra
IRS . . . . Infrared Spectroscopy
IRS . . . . Input Read Submodule
IRS . . . . Instrumentation RADAR Set
IRS . . . . Integrated Rate System
IRS . . . . Internal Revenue Service (Treasury Department)
IRS . . . . International Radio Silence
IRS . . . . International Rorschach Society
IRS . . . . Ionospheric Radio Signal
IRS . . . . Isotope Radiography System
IRSAC . . . . Institut pour le Recherche Scientifique en Afrique Centrale (Brussels)
IRSAC . . . . Institut de Recherches Scientifiques au Congo
IRSC . . . . Internal Revenue Service Centers
IRSCOT . . . . . . Infrared Structural Correlation Tables (A publication)
IRSE . . . . Instrument Systems Engineering
IRSFC . . . . . . International Rayon and Synthetic Fibers Committee
IRSG . . . . International Rubber Study Group
IRSGHL . . . . . . Infrared Systems and Guidance Heads Laboratory
IRSI . . . . International Remote Sensing Institute
IRSLL . . . . . . Image Recording System, Low Light
IRSM . . . . Infrared Systems Manufacturing
IRSO . . . . Infrared Solder Oven

IRSP . . . . Infrared Spectrometer
IRSS . . . . Inertial Reference Stabilization System
IRSS . . . . Infrared Search Set
IRSS . . . . Infrared Sensor System
IRSSO . . . . . . Infrared Search Set Operator
IRST . . . . Infrared Search and Track
IRSTS . . . . . . Infrared Search-Track System
IRT . . . . Individual Reliability Test
IRT . . . . Infinite-Resolution Trimmer
IRT . . . . Infrared Thermometer
IRT . . . . Infrared Tracker
IRT . . . . Infrared Tube
IRT . . . . Initialize Reset Tape
IRT . . . . Institute for Rapid Transit
IRT . . . . Interboro Rapid Transit (A New York City subway line)
IRT . . . . International Research and Technology, Inc.
IRT . . . . Interrogator-Responser-Transponder (Military)
IRTA . . . . Independent Retail Tobacconists Association of America
IRTC . . . . Infantry Replacement Training Center
IRTCM . . . . . . Integrated Real-Time Contamination Monitor (Module)
IRTD . . . . Infrared Target Detector
IRTF . . . . Intermediate Range Task Force
IRTRAN . . . . . Infrared Transmitting
IRTS . . . . International Radio and Television Society
IRTU . . . . International Railway Temperance Union
IRTWG . . . . . . Interrange Telemetry Working Group
IRU . . . . Industrial Rehabilitation Units (British)
IRU . . . . Inertial Reference Unit
IRU . . . . International Radium Unit
IRU . . . . International Relief Union
IRUS . . . . Infantry Rifle Unit Study (Army)
IRV . . . . Inspiratory Reserve Volume
IRW . . . . Infrared Window
IRW . . . . International Rocket Week
IRWC . . . . International Registry of World Citizens
IRY . . . . Intertype Corporation (NYSE symbol) (Later, HI)
IRZ . . . . Inner Radiation Zone
IS . . . . Independent Shoemen of America
IS . . . . Indexing in Source
IS . . . . Industrial Service (Equipment specifications)
IS . . . . Infantry School (Army)
IS . . . . Information Separator (Data processing)
IS . . . . Information Series
IS . . . . Information Service
IS . . . . Infrasonic
IS . . . . Initial Shortage
IS . . . . Initiation Supervisor
IS . . . . Input Simulator
IS . . . . Instrumentation Ships Project (Navy)
IS . . . . Insulating Sleeve
IS . . . . Integrally Stiffened
IS . . . . Integrated Satellite (Military spacecraft)
IS . . . . Integrating Support
IS . . . . Intercostal Space
IS . . . . Interior Surface
IS . . . . Intermediate School
IS . . . . Internal Shield (Electronics)
IS . . . . Interservice
IS . . . . Interstage Section
IS . . . . Interstate
IS . . . . Interval Signal
IS . . . . Intra-Spinal (Injection)
IS . . . . Invalided from Service (Medical) (Navy)
IS . . . . Inventory Schedule
IS . . . . Irish Society
IS . . . . Islands
I & S . . . . Inspection and Security
I & S . . . . (Board of) Inspection and Survey
I & S . . . . Interchangeability and Substitute
ISA . . . . Ignition Separation Assembly
ISA . . . . Independent Shoemen of America
ISA . . . . Inductee Special Assignment
ISA . . . . Innkeepers Society of America
ISA . . . . Instrument Society of America
ISA . . . . Insulating Siding Association
ISA . . . . Insurance Service Associates
ISA . . . . Intermediate Specific Activity (Radioisotope)
ISA . . . . International Schools Association
ISA . . . . International Security Affairs (DOD)
ISA . . . . International Security Agency
ISA . . . . International Shipmasters Association of the Great Lakes

ISA . . . . International Sign Association
ISA . . . . International Silk Association
ISA . . . . International Skeeter Association
ISA . . . . International Sociological Association
ISA . . . . International Standard Atmosphere
ISA . . . . International Standards Association
ISA . . . . International Studies Association
ISA . . . . Inter-Plant Shipping Authority
ISA . . . . Iranian Students Association
ISAA . . . . . . Insurance Service Association of America
ISABEL . . . . . . Iso Status Accumulating Binaries (Using) Extraordinary Logic
ISAC . . . . . . Industrial Safety Advisory Council (British)
ISAC . . . . . . Instrumentation System Assessment Center
ISAC . . . . . . International Security Affairs Committee
ISAC . . . . . . Interuniversity Southeast Asia Committee (of the Association for Asia Studies)
ISACC . . . . . . Initial Satellite Command and Control
ISAD . . . . . . Information Science and Automation Division (of ALA)
ISADPM . . . . . International Society for the Abolition of Data Processing Machines
ISAE . . . . Internacia Science Asocio Esperantista (International Esperantist Scientific Association)
ISAF . . . . Intermediate Super-Abrasion Furnace
IsAF . . . . Israeli Air Force
ISAGE . . . . . . International Symposium on Antarctic Glaciological Exploration
ISAGEX . . . . . International Satellite Geodesy Experiment
ISAGL . . . . . . International Shipmasters Association of the Great Lakes
ISAM . . . . . . Integrated Switching and Multiplexing (IBM)
ISAP . . . . Information Sort and Predict
ISAP . . . . International School Art Program
ISAP . . . . . . South American Petroleum Institute
ISAS . . . . Institute of Space and Aeronautical Science
ISAS . . . . Isotopic Source Assay System
ISASNP . . . . . International Symposium on Aerospace Nuclear Populsion
ISAUS . . . . . . Indonesian Students Association in the United States
ISAUS . . . . . . Iranian Students Association in the United States
ISAV . . . . Instituto de Sistemas Audio-Visuales (Institute of Audio-Visual Media) (Colombia)
ISAW . . . . . . International Society of Aviation Writers
ISB . . . . Independent Sideband
ISB . . . . International Society of Biometeorology
ISBC . . . . Interdepartmental Savings Bond Committee (Military)
ISBC . . . . International Society of Bible Collectors
ISBD . . . . International Standard Bibliographic Description (Library of Congress)
ISBE . . . . International Society for Business Education
ISBIC . . . . . . Interservice Balkan Intelligence Committee (World War II)
ISBN . . . . International Standard Book Number (Library of Congress)
ISC . . . . Idaho State College
ISC . . . . Imperial Service College (British)
ISC . . . . Index of Status Characteristics
ISC . . . . Indian Staff Corps
ISC . . . . Indoor Sports Club
ISC . . . . Industrial Security Committee
ISC . . . . Inertial Start Command
ISC . . . . Infrared Sightline Control
ISC . . . . Intelligence Subject Code
ISC . . . . Interamerican Society of Cardiology
ISC . . . . Interface Signal Chart
ISC . . . . International Sericultural Commission
ISC . . . . International Society of Cardiology
ISC . . . . International Softball Congress
ISC . . . . International Space Congress
ISC . . . . International Statistical Classification
ISC . . . . International Student Conference
ISC . . . . International Sugar Council
ISC . . . . International Supreme Council of World Masons
ISC . . . . Inter-Service Sports Council (Military)
ISC . . . . Interstage Section Container
ISC . . . . Interstate Commerce
ISC . . . . Interval Selection Circuit
ISC . . . . Iowa State College
ISC . . . . Irreversibly Sickled Cell
ISC . . . . Italian Space Commission
ISCA . . . . . . International Senior Citizens Association
ISCA . . . . . . Irish Setter Club of America
ISCAN . . . . . . Inertialess Steerable Communications Antenna
ISCAN . . . . . . International Sanitary Convention for Air Navigation
ISCAY . . . . . . International Solidarity Committee with Algerian Youth
ISCB . . . . Interallied Staff Communications Board (World War II)
ISCB . . . . . . International Society for Cell Biology
ISCBA . . . . . . Insulating Siding Core Board Association
ISCC . . . . Intersociety Color Council

ISCC . . . . . . Intersociety Cytology Council
ISCD . . . . . . International Society for Community Development
ISCE . . . . International Society of Christian Endeavor
ISCEH . . . . . . International Society for Clinical and Experimental Hypnosis
ISCET . . . . . . International Society of Certified Electronics Technicians
ISCLT . . . . . . International Society of Clinical Laboratory Technologists
ISCM . . . . . . International Society for Contemporary Music
ISCO . . . . . . Initial Systems Check-Out
ISCO . . . . . . Instrumentation Specialties Company
ISCOM . . . . . . Island Commander (Navy)
ISCOMADEIRA . . Island Commander Madeira
ISCOMAZORES . . Island Commander Azores
ISCOMBERMUDA . . Island Commander Bermuda
ISCOMFAROES . . Island Commander Faroes
ISCOMGREENLAND . . Island Commander Greenland
ISCOMICELAND . . Island Commander Iceland
ISCONA . . . . . Istituto per la Contability Nazionale
ISCOSS . . . . . . International Symposium on the Chemistry of the Organic Solid State
ISCP . . . . International Society of Clinical Pathology
ISCP . . . . Inventory Stock Cataloging Program
ISCP . . . . Iowa State College Press
ISCPET . . . . . Illinois State-Wide Curriculum Study Center in the Preparation of Secondary School English Teachers
ISCS . . . . Intermediate Science Curriculum Study
ISCT . . . . Ito System Color Television (Japan)
ISCYRA . . . . . . International Star Class Yacht Racing Association
ISD . . . . Induction System Deposit
ISD . . . . Industrial Systems Division
ISD . . . . Information Systems Division (NASA)
ISD . . . . Infrared Suppression Device
ISD . . . . Initial Search Depth
ISD . . . . Institute of Surplus Dealers
ISD . . . . Internal Security Division (Department of Justice)
ISD . . . . Interstate Stores, Inc. (NYSE symbol)
ISDB . . . . International Society of Developmental Biologists (Formerly, IIE)
ISDI . . . . International Social Development Institute
ISDN . . . . Institute for the Study of Developing Nations
ISDRA . . . . . . International Sled Dog Racing Association
ISDS . . . . Inadvertent Separation and Destruct System (Aerospace)
ISE . . . . Independent Ship Exercise (Navy)
ISE . . . . Individual Ship Exercises
ISE . . . . Instrumentation Suitability Evaluation
ISE . . . . Integral Squared Error
ISE . . . . Intercept System Environment (Army)
ISE . . . . International Society of Endocrinology
ISE . . . . Interpret Sign Error
ISEA . . . . Industrial Safety Equipment Association
ISEA . . . . Institut de Science Economique Appliquee (France)
ISEEP . . . . . . Infrared Sensitive Element Evaluation Program
ISEK . . . . International Society of Electromyographic Kinesiology
ISEO . . . . Institute of Shortening and Edible Oils
ISEP . . . . International Society for Educational Planners
ISER . . . . Instituto Superior de Educacao Rural
ISES . . . . International Society of Explosives Specialists
ISEU . . . . International Stereotypers-Electrotypers Union of North America
ISF . . . . Integrated Subject File
ISF . . . . International Science Foundation
ISF . . . . International Shipping Federation, Ltd.
ISF . . . . International Society for Fat Research
ISF . . . . International Softball Federation
ISF . . . . International Spiritualist Federation
ISF . . . . Interstitial Fluid (Physiology)
ISF . . . . Ionizer, Slab Fabrication
ISFA . . . . Intercoastal Steamship Freight Association
ISFA . . . . International Scientific Film Association
ISFADPM . . . . . International Society for the Abolition of Data Processing Machines
ISFNR . . . . . . International Society for Folk-Narrative Research
ISFR . . . . International Society for Fluoride Research
ISFSC . . . . . . International Society of Food Service Consultants
ISG . . . . Immune Serum Globulin
ISG . . . . Imperial Standard Gallon
ISG . . . . Interconnected Systems Group
ISG . . . . Internal Shutter Grid
ISG . . . . Interservice Group
ISGA . . . . . . International Stained Glass Association
ISGA . . . . . . International Study Group for Aerogrammes
ISGC . . . . . . International Society of Guatemala Collectors
ISGE . . . . . . International Society of Gastroenterology
ISGS . . . . . . Illinois State Geological Survey
ISGS . . . . . . International Society for General Semantics
ISH . . . . International Society of Hematology

ISHAM . . . . . . International Society for Human and Animal Mycology
ISHC . . . . International Siberian Husky Club
ISHI . . . . International Society for the History of Ideas
ISHM . . . . International Society for Hybrid Microelectronics
ISHR . . . . Intermediate Scale Homogeneous Reactor
ISHS . . . . International Society for Horticultural Science
ISI . . . . Indian Standards Institution
ISI . . . . Indian Statistical Institute
ISI . . . . Industrial Static Inverter
ISI . . . . Initial Support Increments (Army)
ISI . . . . Institute for Scientific Information
ISI . . . . Intercollegiate Society of Individualists
ISI . . . . Internally Specified Index
ISI . . . . International Safety Institute
ISI . . . . International Statistical Institute
ISI . . . . International Students, Incorporated
ISI . . . . Interstimulus Interval
ISI . . . . Intersymbol Interference
ISI . . . . Ion Source Injector
ISIA . . . . Ice Skating Institute of America
ISIA . . . . International Snowmobile Industry Association
ISIC . . . . Immediate Superior in Command (Military)
ISIC . . . . International Standard Industrial Classification
ISIC . . . . Intersymbol Interference Corrector
ISIM . . . . International Society of Internal Medicine
ISINC . . . . . . Immediate Superior in Command (Military)
ISIR . . . . In Service, In Reserve (Vessel status) (Navy)
ISIS . . . . Institute of Scrap Iron and Steel
ISIS . . . . Integral Spar Inspection System
ISIS . . . . Integrated Strike and Interceptor System
ISIS . . . . International Satellite for Ionospheric Studies (NASA-Canada)
ISIS . . . . International Science Information Services (Earth sciences data center in Dallas, Texas)
ISIS . . . . International Student Information Service
ISIS . . . . Interstate Settlement Information System (AT & T)
ISK . . . . Ion Source Kit
ISKON . . . . . International Society for Krishna Consciousness
ISL . . . . Information Search Language
ISL . . . . Institute of Space Law
ISL . . . . Internal Standard Line
ISL . . . . International Soccer League
ISL . . . . Item Study Listings
ISLF . . . . Improved Saturn Launch Facility
ISLFD . . . . . . Incorporated Society of London Fashion Designers
ISLIC . . . . . . Israel Society of Special Libraries and Information Centers
ISLLSL . . . . . International Society for Labor Law and Social Legislation
ISLRS . . . . . . Inactive Status List Reserve Section
ISLS . . . . Interrogation Side Lobe Suppression
ISLW . . . . . . Indian Spring Low Water
ISLWF . . . . . International Shoe and Leather Workers' Federation
ISM . . . . Iesus Salvator Mundi (Jesus, Savior of the World)
ISM . . . . Industrial, Scientific, and Medical
ISM . . . . Industrial Security Manual
ISM . . . . Infrared Systems Manufacturing
ISM . . . . Initial Segment Membrane
ISM . . . . Institute of Sanitation Management
ISMA . . . . . . International Shipmasters Association of the Great Lakes
ISMA . . . . . . International Superphosphate Manufacturers' Association
ISMA . . . . . . Inter-State Manufacturers Association
ISMDA . . . . . Independent Sewing Machine Dealers of America (Defunct)
ISME . . . . . . International Society for Musical Education
ISMET . . . . . . Inter-Service Metallurgical Research Council (British)
ISMG . . . . . . Interim Scientific and Management Group
ISMH . . . . . . International Society of Medical Hydrology
ISML . . . . . . Instituto Sperimentale dei Metalli Leggeri
ISMUN . . . . . International Student Movement for the United Nations
ISN . . . . Internment Serial Number
ISN . . . . Inter-Plant Shipping Notice
ISNP . . . . . . International Society of Naturopathic Physicians
ISNU . . . . . . Illinois State Normal University
ISNV . . . . . . Institute for the Study of Nonviolence
ISNY . . . . . . Insurance Society of New York
ISO . . . . Imperial Service Order (British)
ISO . . . . Individual System Operation
ISO . . . . Information Services Officer
ISO . . . . Information Systems Office (Library of Congress)
ISO . . . . Insurance Services Office
ISO . . . . International Science Organization
ISO . . . . International Standardization Organization
ISO . . . . Interplant Shipping Order
ISOD . . . . . . International Sports Organization for the Disabled

ISODATA . . . . . Iterative Self-Organizing Data Analysis Technique A (Data processing)
ISOMATA . . . . . Idyllwild School of Music and the Arts (California)
ISONIAZID . . . Isonicotinic Acid Hydrazide ("Wonder drug" for treatment of tuberculosis)
ISOPAR . . . . . . Improved Symbolic Optimizing Assembly Routine
ISOPEP . . . . . . Isometric Piping Efficiency Program
ISOSJ . . . . Institute of Social Order of the Society of Jesus
ISOTEC . . . . . . Isotope Thermoelectric Converter
ISP . . . . Independent Studies Project (Navy)
ISP . . . . Industrial Security Program (Air Force, Army)
ISP . . . . Information Systems Program (National Science Foundation)
ISP . . . . Infrared Spectrophotometer
ISP . . . . Instantaneous Sound Pressure
ISP . . . . Institute of Store Planners
ISP . . . . Integrated Support Plan
ISP . . . . Interamerican Society of Psychology
ISP . . . . Intergovernmental Science Programs
ISP . . . . Internationale des Services Publics (Public Services International)
ISP . . . . Inverse Sampling Procedure
ISP . . . . Isotope Separation Power
ISP . . . . Italian Society of Physics
ISP . . . . (From the Italian for) Serum-Precipitable Iodine (Medicine)
ISPA . . . . . . International Screen Publicity Association
ISPA . . . . International Sporting Press Association
ISPH . . . . . . Institut Superieur de Pedagogie du Hainaut (Belgium)
ISPL . . . . . . Incremental System Programming Language (Data processing)
ISPMB . . . . . . International Society for the Protection of Mustangs and Burros
ISPO . . . . . . Instrumentation Ships Project Office (Navy)
ISPP . . . . . . International Society for Portuguese Philately
ISPW . . . . . . International Society for the Psychology of Writing
ISQD . . . . . . Identification System for Questioned Documents (Book title)
ISR . . . . Impulse Sequencing Relay
ISR . . . . Industrial Security Regulations (DOD)
ISR . . . . . . Information Service Representative (Veterans Administration)
ISR . . . . Information Storage and Retrieval (Data processing) (Also, IS & R)
ISR . . . . Infrared Spectral Radiometer
ISR . . . . Institute of Semiconductor Research (USSR)
ISR . . . . Institute for Social Research
ISR . . . . Integral Superbeat Reactor
ISR . . . . Interim Scientific Report
ISR . . . . Internal Scientific Report
ISR . . . . . . International Society of Radiology
ISR . . . . International Synthetic Rubber Company (United Kingdom)
ISR . . . . Intersecting Storage Rings (Atom smasher)
IS & R . . . . . . Information Storage and Retrieval (Data processing) (Also, ISR)
ISRAC . . . . . . ITT Secure Ranging and Communications System
ISRAD . . . . . . Institute for Social Research and Development (University of New Mexico)
ISRB . . . . . . Inter-Service Research Bureau (British)
ISRD . . . . International Society for Rehabilitation of the Disabled
ISRO . . . . . . Isle Royale National Park
ISRS . . . . Information Search and Recording System (of UMREL)
ISRS . . . . . . Integrated Status Reporting System
ISRSM . . . . . . International Symposium on Rocket and Satellite Meteorology
ISRT . . . . . . Istituto Storico della Resistenza in Toscana (Italy)
ISRU . . . . . . International Scientific Radio Union (Also, URSI)
ISS . . . . Ignition Shielding System
ISS . . . . Image Sensor System
ISS . . . . Independent Sweep System
ISS . . . . Inductive Storage Switch
ISS . . . . Inertial Sub System (Navy)
ISS . . . . Infrared Sensor System
ISS . . . . Infrared Surveillance Set
ISS . . . . Institute of Salesian Studies
ISS . . . . Institute for Space Studies (NASA)
ISS . . . . Institute for Strategic Studies (Later, IISS)
ISS . . . . Instituto Superiore di Sanita (Italy)
ISS . . . . Instrument Servo System
ISS . . . . Instrumentation Support Service
ISS . . . . Integration Support Service
ISS . . . . Interco, Inc. (Formerly, International Shoe Company) (NYSE symbol)
ISS . . . . Interim Standard Set
ISS . . . . Intermediate Service School (Military)
ISS . . . . International Schools Service
ISS . . . . International Social Service (Later, TAISSA)
ISS . . . . International Students Society
ISS . . . . International Sunshine Society
ISS . . . . Interservice Supply Support (Military)
ISS . . . . Interstage Section Shell
ISS . . . . Involuntary Servitude and Slavery
ISS . . . . Ion-Scattering Spectrometry
ISSA . . . . International Social Security Association

ISSA . . . . Interservice Support Agreements (Military)
ISSAC . . . . . . Integrated Surface Search and Attack Coordinate
ISSB . . . . Inter-Service Security Board (British)
ISSC . . . . International Social Science Council
ISSC . . . . Interservice Sports Council
ISSC . . . . Interservice Supply Support Committee (or Coordinator) (Military)
ISSCB . . . . . . International Society for Sandwich Construction and Bonding
ISSCC . . . . . . International Solid State Circuits Conference
ISSCT . . . . . . International Society of Sugar Cane Technologists
ISSE . . . . International Sight and Sound Exposition
ISSEP . . . . . . Integrated System Safety Engineering Plan
ISSET . . . . . . International Symposium on Space Electronics
I & SSFR . . . . . Investigation and Security Service Field Representative (Veterans Administration)
ISSG . . . . Illustrated Shipboard Shopping Guide (Navy)
ISSI . . . . International Social Science Institute
ISSL . . . . Initial Spares Support List
ISSMFE . . . . . . International Society of Soil Mechanics and Foundation Engineering
ISSP . . . . Interservice Supply Support Program (Military)
ISSR . . . . Information Storage, Selection, and Retrieval (Data processing)
ISSRO . . . . . . Interservice Supply Support Records Office (Military)
ISSS . . . . Installation Service Supply Support
ISSS . . . . Institute for the Study of Sport and Society
ISSS . . . . International Society for Socialist Studies
ISSS . . . . International Society of Soil Science
ISSS . . . . International Society for the Study of Symbols
ISST . . . . International Society of Skilled Trades
ISST . . . . Involuntary Second SEA (Southeast Asia) Tour (Air Force)
ISSTA . . . . . . Israel Student Tourist Association
IST . . . . Indexing Slide Table
IST . . . . Information Science and Technology
IST . . . . Initial Support Team (Military)
IST . . . . Insulin Shock Therapy (Psychiatry)
ISTA . . . . International Seed Testing Association
ISTAR . . . . . . Image Storage Translation and Reproduction
ISTC . . . . Indiana State Teachers College
ISTC . . . . Interdepartmental Screw Thread Committee (Departments of Commerce and Defense)
ISTC . . . . International Shade Tree Conference
ISTC . . . . International Society for Training and Culture
ISTC . . . . International Student Travel Conference
ISTC . . . . Iowa State Teachers College
ISTD . . . . Imperial Society of Teachers of Dancing
ISTD . . . . Inter-Service Topographical Department (British)
ISTDA . . . . . . Institutional and Service Textile Distributors Association
ISTF . . . . International Society of Tropical Foresters
ISTIM . . . . . . Interchange of Scientific and Technical Information in Machine Language
ISTM . . . . International Society for Testing Materials
ISTMH . . . . . . Indefinite Substitute Temporary Mail Handler (US Postal Service employee classification)
ISTRACON . . . Interstation Supersonic Track Conferences
ISTSP . . . . . . Independent Schools Talent Search Program
ISU . . . . International Scientific Union
ISU . . . . International Seaman's Union
ISU . . . . International Skating Union
ISU . . . . International System of Units
ISU . . . . Iowa Southern Utilities (Southern Iowa Railway) (AAR code)
ISU . . . . Iowa State University
ISU . . . . Italian Service Unit (Italian prisoners of war who became volunteers in the Allied war effort)
ISU . . . . Southern Iowa R. R. (AAR code)
ISUDS . . . . . . Iterative Scheme Using a Direct Solution
ISUM . . . . Intelligence Summary
ISUSAIC . . . . . Intelligence School, United States Army Intelligence Center
ISUSE . . . . . . International Secretariat for the University Study of Education
ISV . . . . Input Signal Voltage
ISV . . . . International Scientific Vocabulary
ISV . . . . Interorbital Space Vehicle
ISVE . . . . Istituto di Studi per lo Sviluppo Economico (Institute for the Study of Economic Development) (Italy)
ISVR . . . . Institute of Sound and Vibration Research (Southampton University, England)
ISVS . . . . Integrated Secure Voice System
ISVS . . . . International Secretariat for Volunteer Service
ISW . . . . Intermediate Scale Warfare
ISWC . . . . International Society for the Welfare of Cripples
ISWG . . . . Imperial Standard Wire Gauge
ISWU . . . . Iron and Steel Workers' Union (India)
ISZ . . . . Iskustvennyi Sputnik Zemil (USSR)
IT . . . . Immediate Transportation

IT . . . . Immunity Test
IT . . . . Implosive Therapy (Type of behavior therapy)
IT . . . . Improved Tartar
IT . . . . In Transitu (In Transit)
IT . . . . Income Tax Unit Rulings (US Internal Revenue Service)
IT . . . . Index Translationum (UNESCO)
IT . . . . Indian Territory (in United States)
IT . . . . Information Theory
IT . . . . Inner Temple
IT . . . . Input Translator
IT . . . . Inspection Tag
IT . . . . Institute of Technology (Air Force)
IT . . . . Internal Thread
IT . . . . Internal Translator
IT . . . . International Tolerance
IT . . . . Interstate Theft
IT . . . . Interval Timer
IT . . . . Inventory Transfer
IT . . . . Isomeric Transition (Radioactivity)
IT . . . . Italy (NATO)
IT . . . . Item Transfer
I & T . . . . Installation and Test (Army)
ITA . . . . Independent Television Authority (British)
ITA . . . . Individual Task Authorization
ITA . . . . Industrial Truck Association
ITA . . . . Initial Teaching Alphabet (See i/t/a)
ITA . . . . Institut du Transport Aerien (Institute of Air Transport)
ITA . . . . Institute of Theoretical Astronomy (Leningrad, USSR)
ITA . . . . Intermediate Thrust Arc
ITA . . . . International Temperance Association
ITA . . . . International Touring Alliance
ITA . . . . International Twins Association
ITA . . . . Ionization Test Apparatus
i/t/a . . . . Initial Teaching Alphabet (A 44-symbol alphabet planned to simplify beginning reading by representing sounds more precisely)
ITAA . . . . International Transactional Analysis Association
ITAC . . . . Interagency Textile Administrative Committee
ITACS . . . . . . Integrated Tactical Air Control System
ITAE . . . . Integrated Time and Absolute Error
ITAL . . . . Instituut voor de Toepassing van Atoomenergie in de Landboury (Netherlands)
ITAL . . . . Inventory Trial Allowance List
ITAMVETS . . . . Italian American War Veterans of the United States
ITAR . . . . International Traffic in Arms Regulation (US)
ITAR . . . . Interstate Transportation in Aid of Racketeering
ITAS . . . . Indicated True Air Speed (Aviation)
ITAS . . . . Interamerican Travel Agents Society
ITB . . . . Industrial Training Board (British)
ITB . . . . Integral Terminal Block
ITB . . . . Integrated Test Block
ITB . . . . International Training Branch (US Office of Education)
ITB . . . . Ion Thruster Beam
ITB . . . . Island Tug and Barge R. R. (AAR code)
ITBL . . . . Incompressible Turbulent Boundary Layer
ITBS . . . . Iowa Test of Basic Skills
ITC . . . . Illinois Terminal R. R. (AAR code)
ITC . . . . Imperial Tobacco Company (of Great Britain and Ireland) Limited
ITC . . . . Inclusive Tour Charter
ITC . . . . Independent Television Corporation
ITC . . . . Indiana Technical College
ITC . . . . Industrial Training Council
ITC . . . . Infantry Training Center (Army)
ITC . . . . Inland Transport Committee (UN)
ITC . . . . Instructor Training Course
ITC . . . . Integrated Telemetry Complex
ITC . . . . Interchurch Transportation Council
ITC . . . . International Tin Council
ITC . . . . International Toastmistress Clubs
ITC . . . . International Traders Club
ITCA . . . . Intertropical Convergence (Trade winds)
ITCA . . . . Independent Television Companies Association (British)
ITCA . . . . International Typographic Composition Association
ITCA . . . . Irish Terrier Club of America
ITCAN . . . . . . Inspect, Test, and Correct as Necessary
ITCC . . . . International Technical Communications Conference (Society for Technical Communication)
ITCP . . . . Integrated Test and Checkout Procedures
ITCZ . . . . Inter-Tropical Convergence Zone
ITD . . . . Inception-to-Date
ITD . . . . Infrared Target Detector
ITD . . . . Integral Trap Door (Technical drawings)

ITD . . . . Interchannel Time Displacement
ITD . . . . Interface Timing Diagram
ITDA . . . . Integrated Tunnel Diode Amplifier
ITDE. . . . . Interchannel Time Displacement Error (Magnetic recording)
ITDU . . . . Infrared Tracking Display Unit
ITE. . . . . Input Test Equipment
ITE. . . . . Institute of Telecommunications Engineers
ITE. . . . . Institute of Traffic Engineers
ITE. . . . . I-T-E Imperial Corp. (NYSE symbol)
ITEC . . . . Infrared Techniques for Electronics Committee
ITED . . . . Iowa Tests of Educational Development
ITEWS . . . . . . Improved (or Interim) Tactical Electronic Warfare System
ITF . . . . Institut Textile de France
ITF . . . . Institute of Tropical Forestry (Department of Agriculture)
ITF . . . . Interactive Terminal Facility
ITF . . . . International Transport Workers' Federation
ITF . . . . Interstate Transportation of Fireworks
ITF . . . . Inverse Trigonometric Function
ITFCS . . . . . . Institute for Twenty-First Century Studies
ITFMSG . . . . . Interscience Technological Forecasting Methodology Study Group
ITFO . . . . International Trade Fairs Office (Commerce Department)
ITFS . . . . Instructional Television Fixed Service (Educational TV)
ITG . . . . Industrial Tachometer Generator
ITG . . . . Industry Technology Group (Air Force)
ITG . . . . Institute Technical Group
ITG . . . . Integrated Terminal Guidance
ITGA . . . . Isothermogravimetric Analysis
ITGD . . . . Interstate Transportation of Gambling Devices
ITGWF . . . . . . International Textile and Garment Workers' Federation
ITh . . . . Interthecal (Anesthesiology)
ITHL . . . . Internal Triangular Hinge Ligament (of scallops)
ITI . . . . International Technical Institute of Flight Engineers
ITI . . . . International Theatre Institute
ITI . . . . International Thrift Institute
ITIC . . . . International Tsunami Information Center
ITIC . . . . Inter-Tribal Indian Ceremonial Association
ITIN. . . . . Itinerary
ITIPI . . . . Interim Tactical Information Processing and Interpretation
ITIS . . . . Integrated Tank Insulation System
ITIS . . . . Internal Translation Information Subsystem (Data processing)
ITIU . . . . Inventory Temporarily in Use (Army)
ITK . . . . Itek Corp. (NYSE symbol)
ITL . . . . Incoming Transaction Listing
ITL . . . . Industrial Test Laboratory (Navy)
ITL . . . . Integrate-Transfer-Launch (Complex) (at Cape Kennedy) (Aerospace)
ITL . . . . Integration, Test, and Launch
ITL . . . . Intent to Launch
ITL . . . . Inverse Taper Lens
ITLC . . . . Instant Thin-Layer Chromatography
ITLT . . . . Interstate Transportation of Lottery Tickets
ITM . . . . Induction Tube Modulation
ITM . . . . Inspector of Torpedoes and Mines (Navy)
ITM . . . . Institute of Thread Machiners
ITM . . . . Interceptor Tactical Missile (Air Force)
ITM . . . . Interim Technical Memorandum
ITM . . . . Internal Technical Memorandum
ITMA . . . . . . Institute for Training in Municipal Administration
ITMG . . . . . . Integrated Thermal Micrometeoroid Garment (Spacesuit)
ITMIS . . . . . . Integrated Transportation Management Information System (Army)
ITMRC . . . . . . International Travel Market Research Council
ITN . . . . Independent Television News (British)
ITN . . . . Interim Technical Note
ITO . . . . Inspecting Torpedo Officer (Navy)
ITO . . . . Installation Transportation Office(r) (Air Force)
ITO . . . . Interim Technical Order
ITO . . . . International Trade Organization
ITO . . . . Invitational Travel Order (Army)
ITOFCN . . . . . Interim Technical Order Field Change Notice (Air Force)
ITOM . . . . . . Interstate Transportation of Obscene Matter
ITOP . . . . . . Integrated Test Operate Panel
ITOR . . . . . . Intercept Target Optical Reader
ITOS . . . . . . Improved TIROS Operational Satellite (ESSA)
ITOS . . . . . . Iterative Time Optimal System
ITP . . . . Idiopathic Thrombocytopenic Purpura (Medicine)
ITP. . . . . Inferior Thalamic Peduncle
ITP. . . . . Initial Trial Phase
ITP. . . . . Inosine Triphosphate
ITP. . . . . Inspection Test Procedure
ITP. . . . . Integrated Test Program
ITPA . . . . . . Illinois Test of Psycholinguistic Abilities
ITPA . . . . Independent Telephone Pioneer Association

ITPB . . . . Integrated Test Program Board
ITPFF . . . . . . Interstate Transportation of Prize Fight Films
ITPMG . . . . . . Interstate Transportation of Prison-Made Goods
ITPR . . . . Infrared Temperature Profile Radiometer
ITQ . . . . International Thesaurus of Quotations
ITR. . . . . In Transit Rendezvous
ITR. . . . . Infantry Training Replacement
ITR. . . . . Inlet Temperature Rise
ITR. . . . . Inspection Test Report
ITR. . . . . Instrumentation Tape Recorder
ITR. . . . . Intense Thermal Radiation
ITR . . . . Interim Technical Report
ITR . . . . Interim Test Report
ITR . . . . Internal Technical Report
ITR. . . . . Intra-Ocular Tension Recorder
IT/R . . . . Inventory Transfer Receipt
ITS . . . . Ignition Test Simulator
ITS. . . . . Improved Third Stage (of Minuteman rocket)
ITS. . . . . In-Tank Solidification
ITS. . . . . Independent Triggering System
ITS. . . . . Industrial Television Society
ITS. . . . . Infinite Time Span
ITS. . . . . Information Transmission System
ITS. . . . . Infrared Tracking System
ITS. . . . . Institute for Telecommunication Sciences (Department of Commerce)
ITS. . . . . Institute of Temporary Services
ITS. . . . . Integrated Trajectory System
ITS . . . . International Technogeographical Society
ITS . . . . International Trade Secretariat(s)
ITS. . . . . Intersectional Transportation Service
ITS. . . . . Ion Thrust System
ITSA . . . . Installation and Test Support Associate Contractor (Air Force)
ITSA. . . . . Institute for Telecommunications Science and Aeronomy (Environmental Science Services Administration)
ITSA . . . . Interstate Transportation of Stolen Aircraft
ITSB . . . . Interstate Transportation of Strikebreakers
ITSC . . . . International Telecommunications Satellite Consortium
ITSC . . . . Interstate Transportation of Stolen Cattle
ITSMV . . . . . . Interstate Transportation of Stolen Motor Vehicle
ITSO . . . . Instrument Technician Service Organization
ITSP . . . . Interstate Transportation of Stolen Property
ITT. . . . . Incoming Teletype
ITT. . . . . Indicator Time Test (Chemistry)
ITT . . . . Individual Technical Training (Military)
ITT . . . . Institute of Textile Technology
ITT . . . . Insulin Tolerance Test (Physiology)
ITT. . . . . International Telephone and Telegraph (NYSE symbol) (Wall Street slang name: "It Girl," the sobriquet for early movie star Clara Bow)
ITT. . . . . Inter-Theater Transfer (Army)
IT and T . . . . . International Telephone and Telegraph Company
ITTAC . . . . . . International Telegraph and Telephonic Advisory Committee
ITTC . . . . International Towing Tank Conference
ITTCOM . . . . . International Telephone & Telegraph World Communications, Inc.
ITTCS . . . . . . International Telephone and Telegraph Communications System
ITTE . . . . Institute of Transportation & Traffic Engineering (UCLA)
ITTE . . . . Interim Terminal Test Environment (FAA)
ITTF . . . . International Table Tennis Federation
ITTF . . . . International Telephone and Telegraph, Federal
ITTFL . . . . . . International Telephone & Telegraph Federal Laboratories
IT & TS . . . . . International Turtle and Tortoise Society
ITTT . . . . Institute of Transportation, Travel, and Tourism
ITTTA . . . . . . International Technical Tropical Timber Association
ITU . . . . Income Tax Unit
ITU . . . . International Telecommunication Union (A specialized agency of the United Nations)
ITU . . . . International Temperance Union
ITU . . . . International Typographical Union
ITUA . . . . Independent Trade Union Association (Turkey)
ITUC . . . . Irish Trade Union Congress
ITUR. . . . . Interstate Transportation of Unsafe Refrigerators
ITURM . . . . . . International Typographical Union Ruling Machine
ITV . . . . Industrial Television
ITV . . . . Instructional Television
ITVAC . . . . . . Industrial Transistor Value Automatic Computer
ITVB. . . . . International Television Broadcasting
ITVSDA . . . . . . Independent Television Service Dealers' Association
ITWF . . . . International Transport Workers' Federation
ITWG . . . . Interface Technical Working Group
ITWI . . . . Interstate Transmission of Wagering Information
ITWP . . . . . . Interstate Transportation of Wagering Paraphernalia
ITY . . . . International Tourist Year

ITZ . . . . Inter-Tropical Convergence Zone
IU . . . . Immunizing Unit (Medicine)
IU . . . . Indianapolis Union Railway Company (AAR code)
IU . . . . Instrument Unit (NASA)
IU . . . . Interference Unit (Military)
IU . . . . Interlingue Union
IU . . . . International Units (Vitamins)
IU . . . . International Utilities Corporation (NYSE symbol)
IU . . . . Interval of Uncertainty (Psychology)
IUA . . . . Inertial Unit Assembly
IUA . . . . International Union of Architects
IUAA . . . . International Union of Advertisers Associations
IUAA . . . . International Union of Alpine Associations
IUADM . . . . . . International Union of Associations of Doctor-Motorists
IUAES . . . . . . International Union of Anthropological and Ethnological Sciences
IUAI . . . . International Union of Aviation Insurers
IUAJ . . . . International Union of Agricultural Journalists
IUAO . . . . . . International Union for Applied Ornithology
IUAT . . . . International Union Against Tuberculosis
IUB . . . . International Union of Biochemistry
IUB . . . . International Universities Bureau
IUBS . . . . International Union of Biological Sciences
IUC . . . . International Underwater Contractors, Inc.
IUC . . . . International Union of Crystallography
IUC . . . . International University Contact for Management Education
IUC . . . . Inter-University Committee for Debate on Foreign Policy
IUC . . . . Interuniversity Council
IUCD . . . . Intrauterine Contraception (or Contraceptive) Device
IUCI . . . . Inter-University Committee on Israel (Later, America-Israel Cultural
             Foundation)
IUCME . . . . . . International University Contact for Management Education
IUCN . . . . International Union for Conservation of Nature and Natural Resources
IU Cr . . . . International Union of Crystallography
IUCRCB . . . . . Inter-University Committee for Research on Consumer Behavior
IUCSTP . . . . . . Inter-Union Commission on Solar-Terrestrial Physics
IUCTG . . . . . . Inter-University Committee on Travel Grants
IUCW . . . . International Union for Child Welfare
IUD . . . . Industrial Union Department (of AFL-CIO)
IUD . . . . Institute for Urban Development
IUD . . . . Intrauterine Device (A contraceptive)
IUDR . . . . Iododeoxyuridine (Drug for cancer)
IUDZG . . . . . . International Union of Directors of Zoological Gardens
IUE . . . . International Union of Electrical, Radio and Machine Workers
IUE . . . . International Union for Electroheat (Also, IUE-H)
IUEC . . . . International Union of Elevator Constructors
IUE-H . . . . . . International Union for Electroheat (Also, IUE)
IUEW . . . . International Union of Electrical Workers
IUF . . . . Interamerican Underwater Festival
IUF . . . . International Union of Food-Workers
IUFA . . . . International Union of Family Organizations
IUFDT . . . . . . International Union of Food, Drink and Tobacco Workers' Associations
IUFO . . . . International Union of Family Organizations
IUFRO . . . . . . International Union of Forest Research Organizations
IUGG . . . . International Union of Geodesy and Geophysics
IUGM . . . . International Union of Gospel Missions
IUGS . . . . International Union of Geological Sciences
IUH . . . . Instantaneous Unit Hydrograph
IUHPS . . . . . . International Union of the History and Philosophy of Science
IUHR . . . . International Union of Hotel, Restaurant and Bar Workers
IUJHUSC . . . . International Union of Journeymen Horseshoers of the United States and
             Canada
IUL . . . . Institute of Urban Life
IULA . . . . International Union of Local Authorities
IULC . . . . Independent United Labor Congress (Nigeria)
IULCS . . . . . . International Union of Leather Chemists Societies
IULCW . . . . . . International Union of Liberal Christian Women
IULEC . . . . . . Inter-University Labor Education Committee
IULIA . . . . International Union of Life Insurance Agents
IUMI . . . . International Union of Marine Insurance
IUMMSW . . . . International Union of Mine, Mill and Smelter Workers
IUMSWA . . . . . Industrial Union of Marine and Shipbuilding Workers of America
IUNS . . . . International Union of Nutritional Sciences
IUOE . . . . International Union of Operating Engineers
IUOTO . . . . . . International Union of Official Travel Organizations (Later, WTO)
IUP . . . . Installed User Program (Data processing)
IUP . . . . Irish University Press
IUP . . . . Israel Universities Press
IUPA . . . . International Union of Practitioners in Advertising
IUPAC . . . . . . International Union of Pure and Applied Chemistry
IUPAP . . . . . . International Union of Pure and Applied Physics
IUPM . . . . International Union for Protecting Public Morality

IUPPE . . . . . . Independent Union of Plant Protection Employees
IUPS . . . . International Union of Physiological Sciences
IUPW . . . . International Union of Petroleum Workers
IUR . . . . International Union of Railways
IUR . . . . Inter-User Reliability
IURC . . . . International Underwater Research Corporation
IURGRQR . . . . Item Urgently Required (Army)
IURN . . . . Institut Unifie de Recherches Nucleaires
IUS . . . . International Union of Speleology
IUS . . . . International Union of Students
IUSA . . . . International Underwater Spearfishing Association
IUSDT . . . . . . International Union of Social Democratic Teachers
IUSSI . . . . International Union for the Study of Social Insects
IUSTFI . . . . . . Institute on United States Taxation of Foreign Income
IUSY . . . . International Union of Socialist Youth
IUT . . . . Institut Universitaire de Technologie
IUTAM . . . . . . International Union of Theoretical and Applied Mechanics
IUUW . . . . International Union, United Welders
IUVDT . . . . . . International Union Against the Venereal Diseases and the Trepone-
             matoses
IUW . . . . Inshore Underwater Warfare
IUWDS . . . . . . International Ursigram and World Days Service
IV . . . . In Verbo (Under the Word)
IV . . . . Increased Value
IV . . . . Initial Velocity (Ballistics)
IV . . . . Input Voltage
IV . . . . Interventricular
IV . . . . Intervertebral
IV . . . . Intravenous (Medicine)
IV . . . . Inverted Vertical (Aircraft engine)
IV . . . . Invoice Value
IV . . . . Iodine Value
IVA Cr . . . . . . Independent Voters Association (Political organization in North Dakota,
             1918-1932)
IVA . . . . Ingenjoersveten Skapsakademien (Sweden)
IVA . . . . Inlet Vane Actuator
IVA . . . . Intravehicular Activity
IVA . . . . Inventory Valuation Adjustments
IVALA . . . . . . Integrated Visual Approach and Landing Aid (System) (RADAR)
IVAM . . . . Interorbital Vehicle Assembly Mode
IVAR . . . . Insertion Velocity Adjust Routine (NASA)
IVBA . . . . International Volleyball Association
IVC . . . . Imperial Valley College (California)
IVC . . . . Industrial View Camera
IVC . . . . Inferior Vena Cava (Anatomy)
IVC . . . . Integrated Vacuum Circuit
IVC . . . . Permanent Committee for the International Veterinary Congresses
IVCD . . . . Intraventricular Conduction Defect (Pathology)
IVCF . . . . Inter-Varsity Christian Fellowship of the United States of America
IVD . . . . Image Velocity Detector
IVD . . . . Information Viewing Device
IVDBA . . . . . . Imperial Valley Dune Buggy Association
IVDS . . . . Independent Variable Depth SONAR
IVE . . . . Image of Vocational Education
IVFRC . . . . . . In Visual Flight Rules Conditions
IVFZ . . . . International Veterinary Federation of Zootechnics
IVG . . . . Institutet fuer Verkstadsteknisk Forskning (Institute for Production
             Engineering Research) (Sweden)
IVI . . . . Incremental Velocity Indicator (NASA)
IVI . . . . Independent Voters of Illinois
IVI . . . . Initial Ventricular Impulse
IVI . . . . Internal Vibration Isolator
IVIC . . . . Instituto Venezolano de Investigaciones Cientificas
IVIS . . . . International Visitors Information Service
IVJC . . . . Intervertebral Joint Complex
IVMB . . . . Internationale Vereinigung der Musikbibliotheken (International
             Association of Music Libraries)
IVMS . . . . Instrumented Vibration Measuring System
IVO . . . . Input Voltage Offset
IVP . . . . Initial Vapor Pressure
IVP . . . . Inspected Variety Purity (Agriculture)
IVP . . . . Instituto Venezolano de la Petroquimica
IVP . . . . Intravenous Pyelogram (Radiology)
IVP . . . . Ion Vacuum Pump
IVS . . . . Independent Vertical System
IVS . . . . Infrared Viewing Set
IVS . . . . Input Voltage Supply
IVS . . . . International Voluntary Services
IVSD . . . . Interventricular Septal Defect (Pathology)
IVSI . . . . Instantaneous Vertical Speed Indicator (NASA)
IVSU . . . . International Veterinary Students Union

IVT . . . . Internationale Vereinigung der Textileinkaufsverbande (International Association of Textile Purchasing Societies)
IVT . . . . Intravenous Transfusion (Medicine)
IVU . . . . International Vegetarian Union
IVV . . . . Instantaneous Vertical Velocity
IVVI . . . . Instantaneous Vertical Velocity Indicator
IW . . . . Indirect Waste
IW . . . . Inside Width
IW . . . . Inspector of Works
IW . . . . International Wattier (Process) (A method of making transparencies for rotogravure plates)
IW . . . . Isle of Wight
IW . . . . Isotopic Weight
IWA . . . . Independent Watchmen's Association
IWA . . . . Institute of World Affairs
IWA . . . . Insurance Workers of America
IWA . . . . International Wheat Agreement
IWA . . . . International Women's Auxiliary to the Veterinary Profession
IWA . . . . International Woodworkers of America
IWBS . . . . Congregation of the Incarnate Word and Blessed Sacrament (Roman Catholic women's religious order)
IWBS . . . . . . Integral Weight and Balance System (Aviation)
IWC . . . . Incarnate Word College (Texas)
IWC . . . . Inland Waterways Corporation
IWC . . . . International Whaling Commission
IWC . . . . International Wheat Council
IWC . . . . Iowa Wesleyan College
IWCA . . . . . . International World Calendar Association
IWCA . . . . . . Irish Wolfhound Club of America
IWCCA . . . . . . Inland Waterways Common Carriers Association
IWCI . . . . Industrial Wire Cloth Institute
IWCS . . . . . . Integrated Weapons Control System
IWCS . . . . . . Integrated Wideband Communications System (Military)
IWCS . . . . . . Interceptor Weapon Control System
IWCS . . . . . . International Wood Collectors Society
IWCT . . . . . . International War Crimes Tribunal
IWD . . . . Iron or Wood (Freight)
IWDA . . . . . . Independent Wire Drawers Association
IWDS . . . . . . International World Day Service
IWE . . . . Institute of Water Engineers (British)
IWEWSULOTATDTO . . I Wish Everyone Would Stop Using Letters of the Alphabet to Designate Their Organizations (Originated by Bea von Boeselager in "Line o' Type," Chicago Tribune)
IWFA . . . . Intercollegiate Women's Fencing Association
IWFA . . . . . . Iowa-Illinois Gas & Electric Company (NYSE symbol)
IWG . . . . Iowa-Illinois Gas & Electric Company (NYSE symbol)
IWGC . . . . . . Imperial War Graves Commission (British)
IWGCSFIPERM . . Inter-Service Working Group for Cooperation & Standardization of Foto Interpretation Procedures, Equipment & Related Matters

IWI . . . . Irreversible Warmup Indicator (to detect whether frozen foods have risen above an acceptable temperature level) (Pronounced, "ee-wee")
IWISTK . . . . . . Issue While in Stock
IWIU . . . . . . Insurance Workers International Union
IWL . . . . International Walther League
IWL . . . . Italian Welfare League
IWLA . . . . . . Izaak Walton League of America
IWO . . . . International Vine and Wine Office
IWOC . . . . . . International Wizard of Oz Club
IWP . . . . Indicative World Plan
IWP . . . . Internal Working Paper
IWP . . . . International Working Party
IWR . . . . Isle of Wight Railway (British)
IWRC . . . . . . Independent Wire Rope Center (or Core)
IWRMA . . . . . Independent Wire Rope Manufacturers Association
IWS . . . . Industrial Water Supply
IWS . . . . Inland Waterway Service
IWS . . . . Institute of Wood Research (Michigan Technological University)
IWS . . . . International Wool Secretariat (Australia, New Zealand, South Africa)
IWSA . . . . . . International Water Supply Association
IWSA . . . . . . International Workers Sport Association
IWSB . . . . . . Insect Wire Screening Bureau
IWSCA . . . . . Irish Water Spaniel Club of America
IWSG . . . . . . International Wool Study Group
IWSM . . . . . . Integrated Weapon Support Management
IWSOE . . . . . International Weddell Sea Oceanographic Expedition
IWST . . . . . . Integrated Weapon System Training (Air Force)
IWT . . . . Inland Waterway Transport
IWTO . . . . . . International Wool Textile Organization
IWU . . . . Illegal Wearing of Uniform
IWU . . . . Illinois Wesleyan University
IWVA . . . . . . International War Veterans' Alliance
IWW . . . . Industrial Workers of the World ("Wobblies")
IWW . . . . Intracoastal Waterway
IWWA . . . . . . International Wild Waterfowl Association
IWWP . . . . . . International Who's Who in Poetry (A publication)
IX . . . . In Christo (In Christ)
IX . . . . Unclassified Miscellaneous (Navy ship symbol)
IXF . . . . Industrial X-Ray Film
IXR . . . . Integrated X-Ray Reflection
IY . . . . Imperial Yeomanry (British)
IY . . . . Ionized Yeast
IYC . . . . International Youth Congress
IYHF . . . . International Youth Hostel Federation
IYRU . . . . International Yacht Racing Union
IZ . . . . Interfacial Zone
IZS . . . . Insulin Zinc Suspension
IZY . . . . International Zoo Yearbook

J

J . . . . Irradiation Correction
J . . . . Jack (Technical drawings)
J . . . . January
J . . . . Join
J . . . . Joiner (Machinery)
J . . . . Joint
J . . . . Joist (Technical drawings)
J . . . . Joule
J . . . . Journal, Journalism
J . . . . Judean or Yahwistic (Used in biblical criticism to designate Yahwistic
          material)
J . . . . Judge
J . . . . July
J . . . . June
J . . . . Junior
J . . . . Jupiter
J . . . . Jus (Law)
J . . . . Justice (i.e., a judge; plural is JJ)
J . . . . Jute-Asphalted (Nonmetallic armor)
J . . . . Juvenile
J . . . . Mechanical Equivalent of Heat (Symbol)
J . . . . Radiant Intensity (Symbol)
J . . . . Standard Oil Company (NYSE symbol) (Wall Street slang name:
          "Jersey")
J-1 . . . . Personnel Section of a Joint Military Staff; the Officer in Charge of
          this Section
J-2 . . . . Intelligence Section of a Joint Military Staff; the Officer in Charge of
          this Section
J-3 . . . . Operations and Training Section of a Joint Military Staff; the Officer
          in Charge of this Section
J-4 . . . . Logistics Section of a Joint Military Staff; the Officer in Charge of
          this Section
JA . . . . Jack Adapter
JA . . . . Job Analysis
JA . . . . Jockey's Association
JA . . . . Joint Agent
JA . . . . Judge Advocate
JA . . . . Jump Address
JA . . . . Junior Achievement (A youth organization)
J/A . . . . Joint Account
JAA . . . . Judge Advocates Association
JAACS . . . . . John A. Andrew Clinical Society
JAAF . . . . . . Japanese Army Air Force
JAAF . . . . . . Joint Action Armed Forces
JAAF . . . . . . Joint Army and Air Force
JAAFAR . . . . Joint Army-Air Force Adjustment Regulations
JAAFCTB . . . . Joint Army-Air Force Commercial Traffic Bulletin
JAAFPC . . . . Joint Army-Air Force Procurement Circular
JAAFU . . . . . Joint Anglo-American Foul Up (Armed services slang) (World War II)
JAAOC . . . . . Joint Antiaircraft Artillery Operations Center (Military)
JAAP . . . . . . Joint Airborne Advance Party (Military)
JAARS . . . . . Jungle Aviation and Radio Service, Inc. (Mission plane service)
JAAS . . . . . . Jewish Academy of Arts and Sciences
JAB . . . . Joint Activity Briefing (Military)
JAB . . . . Joint Amphibious Board (Military)
JABOWA . . . . Janak-Botkin-Wallis (Data processing program regarding forest growth;
          named for three men involved in program)
JABS . . . . . . Journal of Applied Behavioral Science
JAC . . . . Jet Age Conference
JAC . . . . Jet Aircraft Coating
JAC . . . . Jeunesse Acricole Catholique (Catholic Farm Youth) (Congo--Brazzaville)
JAC . . . . Jeunesse Anarchiste Communiste (French student group)
JAC . . . . Joint Aircraft Committee (World War II)

JAC . . . . Joint Apprenticeship Council
JAC . . . . Joint Arms Control
JAC . . . . Journal of Applied Chemistry (Refers to either USSR or British
          publication)
JACC . . . . . . Joint Airborne Communication Center
JACC . . . . . . Joint Automatic Control Conference
JACC/CP . . . . Joint Airborne Communications Center/Command Post
JACCI . . . . . . Joint Allocation Committee Civil Intelligence (of US and Great Britain)
          (World War II)
JACE . . . . . . Joint Allied Communications Element
JACE . . . . . . Joint Alternate Command Element
JACFU . . . . . Joint American-Chinese Foul Up (World War II slang)
JACKPOT . . . . Joint Airborne Communication Center and Command Post
JACL . . . . . . Japanese-American Citizens League
JACM . . . . . . Journal of the Association for Computing Machinery
JACO . . . . . . Joint Actions Control Office
JACS . . . . . . Joint Action in Community Service
JACS . . . . . . Journal of the American Chemical Society
JACSPAC . . . . Joint Air Communications of the Pacific
JADB . . . . . . Joint Air Defense Board
JADE . . . . . . Japanese Air Defense Environment
JADE . . . . . . Junior Administrator Development Examination
JADF . . . . . . Japan Air Defense Force
JADF . . . . . . Joint Air Defense Force
JADITBHKNYC . . Just a Drop in the Basket Helps Keep New York Clean
          (Antilitter campaign)
JADOC . . . . . Joint Air Defense Operation Center
JAE . . . . Jaeger Machine Company (NYSE symbol)
JAEC . . . . . . Japan Atomic Energy Commission
JAEC . . . . . . Joint Atomic Energy Commission
JAEIP . . . . . . Japan Atomic Energy Insurance Pool
JAERI . . . . . . Japan Atomic Energy Research Institute
JAF . . . . Jordanian Air Force
JAF . . . . Journal of American Folklore
JAF . . . . Judge Advocate of the Fleet
JAFC . . . . . . Japan Atomic Fuel Corporation
JAFNA . . . . . Joint Air Force-NASA
JAFP . . . . . . Jewish Agency for Palestine
JAFPUB . . . . . Joint Army-Air Force Publication
JAG . . . . Judge Advocate General (Air Force, Army, Navy)
JAGAR . . . . . Judge Advocate General Area Representatives
JAGC . . . . . . Judge Advocate General's Corps
JAGD . . . . . . Judge Advocate General's Department (Air Force, Army)
JAGO . . . . . . Jugendarrestgeschaeftsordnung (Germany)
JAGOS . . . . . Joint Air-Ground Operations System (Military)
JAI . . . . Jami'at Al Islan
JAI . . . . Jewish Agency for Israel (Later, United Israel Appeal)
JAI . . . . Joint Staff Administrative Instruction (Military)
JAI . . . . Juvenile Amaurotic Idiocy (Medicine)
JAIEG . . . . . Joint Atomic Information Exchange Group (DOD)
JAIF . . . . . . Japan Atomic Industrial Forum
JAIM . . . . . . Job Analysis and Interest Measurement
JAJC . . . . . . Journalism Association of Junior Colleges
JAKIS . . . . . . Japanese Keyword Indexing Simulator
JAL . . . . Japan Air Lines
JAL . . . . Jet Approach and Landing Chart
JALC . . . . . . Jet Approach and Landing Chart
JALPG . . . . . Joint Automatic Language Processing Group
JAM . . . . Job Assignment Memo
JAMA . . . . . . Journal of the American Medical Association (A periodical)
JAMAC . . . . . Joint Aeronautical Materials Agency (Military)
JAMAG . . . . . Joint American Military Advisory Group
JAMMAT . . . . Joint Military Mission for Aid to Turkey

JAMPAC . . . . . Jamming Package (Air Force)
JAMPACK . . . . Jamming Package
JAMPO . . . . . Joint Allied Military Petroleum Office (NATO)
JAMTO. . . . . . Joint Airlines Military Traffic Office
JAMTRAC . . . . Jammers Tracked by Azimuth Crossings (RADAR)
JAN. . . . . Jantzen, Inc. (NYSE symbol)
JAN. . . . . January
JAN. . . . . Jet Aircraft Noise
JAN. . . . . Joint Army and Navy
JAN. . . . . Judgment Analysis (Psychology)
JANAF . . . . . . Joint Army-Navy-Air Force
JANAIR . . . . . Joint Army-Navy Aircraft Instrument Research
JANAP . . . . . . Joint Army-Navy-Air Force Publication
JANAST . . . . . Joint Army-Navy-Air Force Sea Transportation Message
JANCOM . . . . . Joint Army-Navy Communications
JANET . . . . . . Joint Army-Navy Experimental and Testing Board
JANFU . . . . . . Joint Army-Navy Foul Up (Military slang) (Bowdlerized version)
JANGO . . . . . Junior Army-Navy Guild Organization (Organization of teenage
         daughters of military officers, who helped out in war work) (World
         War II)
JANGRID . . . . Joint Army-Navy Grid
JANIC . . . . . . Joint Army-Navy Information Center
JANIS . . . . . . Joint Army-Navy Intelligence Studies
JANMAT. . . . . Joint Army-Navy Machine Tools Committee
JANMAT. . . . . Joint Army-Navy Material
JANMB. . . . . . Joint Army and Navy Munitions Board (Terminated, 1947)
JANNAF . . . . . Joint-Army-Navy-NASA-Air Force Interagency Propulsion Committee
JANOT . . . . . Joint Army-Navy Ocean Terminal
JANP . . . . Joint Army-Navy Publication
JANPPA . . . . . Joint Army-Navy Petroleum Purchase Agency
JANS . . . . Jet Aircraft Noise Survey
JANSRP . . . . . Jet Aircraft Noise Survey Research Program
JANTAB . . . . . Joint Army and Navy Technical Aeronautical Board
JANWSA . . . . . Joint Army-Navy War Shipping Administration
JAOC . . . . . . Joint Air Operations Center
JAP . . . . Jewish Agency for Palestine
JAP . . . . Joint Acceptance Plan
JAP . . . . Joint Apprenticeship Program (Department of Labor)
JAP . . . . Journal of Applied Physics
JAPA . . . . Jane Addams Peace Association
JAPA . . . . Japan Area
JAPCO . . . . . . Jamestown Paint and Varnish Company
JAPCO . . . . . . Japan Atomic Power Company
JAPIA . . . . . . Japan Auto Parts Industries Association
JAPO . . . . Joint Area Petroleum Office
JAPS . . . . Japanese American Philatelic Society
JAPSS . . . . . . Joint Automated Planning Support System (of JOPS) (Military)
JAQ . . . . Job Activities Questionnaire
JARE . . . . Japanese Antarctic Research Expedition
JARRP. . . . . . . Japan Association for Radiation Research on Polymers
JAS . . . . Jazz Arts Society
JAS . . . . Jewish Agricultural Society
JAS . . . . Job Analysis Schedule (Department of Labor)
JAS . . . . Journal of Aerospace Science
JASA . . . . Jewish Association for Services for the Aged (New York City)
JASA . . . . Joint Antisubmarine Action
JASA . . . . Journal Acoustical Society of America
JASAR . . . . . . Jittered and Swept Active RADAR
JASASA . . . . . Joint Air-Surface Antisubmarine Action
JASB . . . . Journal of the Anthropological Society of Bombay
JASB . . . . Journal of the Asiatic Society of Bengal
JASCO . . . . . . Joint Assault Signal Company (Small unit in Pacific amphibious warfare)
         (World War II)
JASDA . . . . . . Julie Automatic Sonic Data Analyzer (Navy)
JASDF . . . . . . Japanese Air Self-Defense Force
JASG . . . . Joint Advanced Study Group
JASIS . . . . Journal of the American Society for Information Science
JASS . . . . Joint Anti-Satellite Study
JASSC . . . . . . Japan-America Society of Southern California
JASTOP . . . . . Jet Assist Stop
JASU . . . . Jet Aircraft Starting Unit
JASW . . . . Japan-America Society of Washington
JAT . . . . Jam Angle Tracking
JAT . . . . Jugoslovenski Aerotransport (Yugoslav Air Transport)
JATCCCP. . . . . Joint Advanced Tactical Command, Control and Communications
         Program (Military)
JATMA . . . . . . Japan Automobile Tire Manufacturers Association
JATO . . . . Jet-Assisted Take Off (Aviation)
JATP . . . . Jazz at the Philharmonic
JATP . . . . Joint Air Transportation Plan
JATS . . . . Joint Air Transportation Service

JAVA . . . . Jamaica Association of Villas and Apartments
JAWPB . . . . . . Joint Atomic Weapons Publications Board
JAWPM . . . . . Joint Atomic Weapon Planning Manual
JAWPS . . . . . . Joint Atomic Weapons Publication System
JAWS . . . . Joint Arctic Weather Stations (Canada-US)
JAWYS . . . . . . Join Airways
JAX . . . . Jacksonville, Fla. (Airport symbol)
JAYCEES . . . . . (United States) Junior Chamber of Commerce
JB . . . . Jet Bomb
JB . . . . John Bull (The typical Englishman)
JB . . . . Joint Army-Navy Board
JB . . . . Joint Bond
JB . . . . Junction Box (Technical drawings)
JB . . . . Junior Beadle (Ancient Order of Foresters)
JB . . . . Juris Baccalaureus (Bachelor of Laws)
JB . . . . Stetson Hat (After John Batterson Stetson, 19th-century American hat
         manufacturer) (Slang)
J-B . . . . Jet Barrier
J & B . . . . Justerini & Brooks (Scotch)
JBA . . . . Jewel Bearing Assembly
JBA . . . . Junction Box Assembly
JBA . . . . Junior Bluejackets of America
J-BAR . . . . . . Jet Runway Barrier
JBC . . . . Jewish Book Council of America
JBC . . . . Johnson Bible College (Tennessee)
JBC . . . . Joint Blood Council
JBD . . . . Jet Blast Deflector
JBDAAFES . . . . Joint Board of Directors, Army-Air Force Exchange Service
JBES . . . . Jodrell Bank Experimental Station (British)
JBFSAW . . . . . Joint Board on Future Storage of Atomic Weapons
JBG . . . . Jewish Board of Guardians
JBHCPIUA . . . Journeymen Barbers, Hairdressers, Cosmetologists and Proprietors'
         International Union of America
JBIA . . . . Jewish Braille Institute of America
JBMA . . . . John Burroughs Memorial Association
JBMTO . . . . . . Joint Bus Military Traffic Office
JBP . . . . Jettison Booster Package (NASA)
JBS . . . . John Birch Society
JBS . . . . Joly Black Screen
JBT . . . . Jewelers Board of Trade
JBU . . . . John Brown University (Arkansas)
JBUSDC . . . . . Joint Brazil-United States Defense Commission
JBUSMC . . . . . Joint Brazil-United States Military Commission
JC . . . . Jack Cover
JC . . . . Jesus Christ (Jesus Christus)
JC . . . . Job Corps
JC . . . . Jockey Club
JC . . . . Joint Compound (Plumbing)
JC . . . . Joule Cycle
JC . . . . JOVIAL (Joule's Own Version of the International Algorithmic Language)
         Compiler (Data processing)
JC . . . . Julius Caesar
JC . . . . Junior College
JC . . . . Jurisconsult
JC . . . . Justice Clerk
JC . . . . Juvenile Court
JCA . . . . Jewelry Crafts Association
JCA . . . . Jewish Colonization Association
JCA . . . . Joint Church Aid (Biafra relief program in late 1960's)
JCA . . . . Joint Commission on Accreditation of Universities (Military)
JCA . . . . Joint Communication Activity
JCA . . . . Joint Communications Agency (Military)
JCA . . . . Joint Construction Agency
JCAC . . . . Joint Civil Affairs Committee
JCADIS. . . . . . Joint Continental Aerospace Defense Integration Staff (Military)
JCAE . . . . Joint Committee on Atomic Energy (of the US Congress)
JCAFU . . . . . . Joint Committee of the Autonomous Federations and Unions (Comite
         d'Entente des Federations et Syndicats Autonomes d'Algerie) (Algeria)
JCAH . . . . Joint Commission on Accreditation of Hospitals
J Can B. . . . . . Juris Canna Baccalaureus (Bachelor of Canon Law)
J Can D . . . . . Juris Canna Doctor (Doctor of Canon Law)
J Can M . . . . . Juris Canna Magister (Master of Canon Law)
JCAR . . . . Joint Commission on Applied Radioactivity
JCAS . . . . Joint Civil Affairs Committee
JCA-USA . . . . Joint Church Aid - United States of America (Also see JCA)
JCB . . . . Joint Communications Board
JCB . . . . Journal of Creative Behavior
JCB . . . . Juris Canna Baccalaureus (Bachelor of Canon Law)
JCB . . . . Juris Civilis Baccalaureus (Bachelor of Civil Law)
JCBA . . . . Jewish Conciliation Board of America
JCBC . . . . Joint Committee on Building Codes

JCBC . . . . Jute Carpet Backing Council
JCC . . . . Jamestown Community College (New York)
JCC . . . . Janney Cylinder Company
JCC . . . . Jarvis Christian College (Texas)
JCC . . . . Job Corps Camp
JCC . . . . Joint Communications Center
JCC . . . . Joint Computer Conference
JC of C . . . . . Junior Chamber of Commerce
JCCA . . . . . . Joint CONEX (Container Express) Control Agency
JCCDG . . . . . . Joint Command and Control Development Group (DOD)
JCCLE . . . . . . Joint Committee on Continuing Legal Education
JCCOMNET . . Joint Coordination Center Communications Network
JCCRG . . . . . . Joint Command and Control Requirements Group (Joint Chiefs
of Staff) (DOD)
JCCSC . . . . . . Joint Command and Control Standards Committee
JCD . . . . Juris Canonici Doctor (Doctor of Canon Law)
JCD . . . . Juris Civilis Doctor (Doctor of Civil Law)
JCDA . . . . . . Junior Catholic Daughters of America
JCDSG . . . . . . Joint Civil Defense Support Group
JCDSIPS . . . . . Joint Continental Defense Systems Integration Planning Staff (Air Force)
JCEB . . . . . . Joint Council on Educational Broadcasting
JCEC . . . . . . Joint Chapters - Educational Council
JCEC . . . . . . Joint Communications-Electronics Committee
JCEE . . . . . . Joint Council on Economic Education
JCEG . . . . . . Joint Communications-Electronics Group
JCENS . . . . . . Joint Communications Electronic Nomenclature System
JCEPC . . . . . . Joint United States/Canada Civil Emergency Planning Committee
JCET . . . . . . Joint Council on Educational Television
JCFR . . . . . . Junior College of Flat River (Missouri)
JCI . . . . Joint Communications Instruction
JCI . . . . Junior Chamber International
JCIHCA . . . . . Joint Council to Improve Health Care of the Aged
JCJC . . . . . . Jefferson City Junior College (Missouri) (Discontinued operation, 1958)
JCJC . . . . . . Jersey City Junior College (New Jersey)
JCJC . . . . . . Jones County Junior College (Mississippi)
JCK . . . . Joint Commission on Korea
JCL . . . . Job Control Language (Data processing)
JCL . . . . Johnny Come Lately (Slang)
JCL . . . . Junior Classical League
JCL . . . . Juris Canonici Licentiatus (Licentiate in Canon Law)
JCL . . . . Juris Civilis Licentiatus (Licentiate of Civil Law)
JCLC . . . . . . Joint Committee (of Congress) on the Library of Congress
JCLE . . . . . . Joint Committee on Library Education
JCLS . . . . . . Junior College Libraries Section (Association of College and Research
Libraries)
JCM . . . . Jeunesse Chretienne Malgache (Malagasy Christian Youth)
JCM . . . . Juris Civilis Magister (Master of Civil Law)
JCMIH . . . . . Joint Commission on Mental Illness and Health
JCN . . . . Job Change Notice (Form)
JCN . . . . Job Control Number
JCOC . . . . . . Joint Civilian Orientation Conference (DOD)
JCOT . . . . . . Joint Committee on College Teaching
JCP . . . . Japanese Communist Party
JCP . . . . Joint (Congressional) Committee on Printing
JCP . . . . JOVIAL (Joule's Own Version of the International Algorithmic Language)
Control Program (Data processing)
JCP . . . . Jungle Canopy Penetration
JCP . . . . Junior Collegiate Players (Later, Associate Collegiate Players)
JCP . . . . Penney (J. C.) Company (NYSE symbol)
JCPDS . . . . . . Joint Committee on Powder Diffraction Studies
JCPOA . . . . . Joint Council of Post Office Associations (South Africa)
JCPS . . . . . . Joint Center for Political Studies
JCR . . . . Jeunesse Communiste Revolutionnaire (French student group)
JCR . . . . Joint Council for Repatriation
JCR . . . . Junior Common Room (in British colleges and public schools)
JCRA . . . . . . Jewish Committee for Relief Abroad
JCRR . . . . . . Joint Commission on Rural Reconstruction
JCS . . . . Jewish Chautauqua Society
JCS . . . . Joint Chiefs of Staff (United States)
JCSAN . . . . . Joint Chiefs of Staff Alerting Network (Military)
JCSLHG . . . . . Joint Center for the Study of Law and Human Genetics
JCSM . . . . . . Joint Chiefs of Staff Memorandum (Military)
JCSO . . . . . . Joint Chiefs of Staff Organization
JCSS . . . . . . Jesus Christ Superstar (Rock opera)
JCSTC . . . . . . Joint Council for Scientific and Technical Communication (British)
JCT . . . . Jordan Cosmological Theory
JCT . . . . Junction
JCU . . . . John Carroll University (Ohio)
JCULS . . . . . . Joint Committee on the Union List of Serials
JCUS . . . . . . Joint Center for Urban Studies
JCV . . . . Joule-Clausius Velocity

JD . . . . J-Band Detector
JD . . . . Job Description (Department of Labor)
JD . . . . Joint Determination
JD . . . . Joint Dictionary (Dictionary of US Military Terms for Joint Usage)
JD . . . . Julian Date (or Day)
JD . . . . Junior Deacon
JD . . . . Junior Dean
JD . . . . Juris Doctor (Doctor of Jurisprudence)
JD . . . . Jurum Doctor (Doctor of Laws)
JD . . . . Justice Department
JD . . . . Juvenile Delinquency (or Delinquent)
JDA . . . . Japanese Defense Agency
JDA . . . . Jefferson Davis Association
JDA . . . . Joint Defense Appeal
JDA . . . . Juvenile Delinquency Act
JDC . . . . American Jewish Joint Distribution Committee
JDC . . . . Japan Documentation Center (Columbia University)
JDC . . . . Jet Deflection Control
JDC . . . . Jeunesse Democratique Camerounaise (Cameroonian Democratic Youth)
JDC . . . . Job Description Card
JDC . . . . Joint Distribution Committee (Short form of American Jewish Joint
Distribution Committee)
JDCS . . . . . . Joint Deputy Chiefs of Staff
JDENL . . . . . . Joined by Enlistment (Military)
JDEP . . . . . . Juvenile Delinquency Evaluation Project
JDFR . . . . . . Joined From (Military)
JDIND . . . . . . Joined by Induction (Military)
JDL . . . . Jewish Defense League
JDP . . . . Job Development Program
JDPC . . . . . . Joint Defense Production Committee (Later, Joint War Production
Committee) (World War II)
JDREENL . . . . . Joined by Reenlistment (Military)
JDS . . . . John Dewey Society
JE . . . . Jamin Effect (Electronics)
JE . . . . Jamming Equipment
JE . . . . Jerseyville & Eastern R. R. (AAR code)
JE . . . . Jet Engine
JE . . . . Jet Exhaust
JE . . . . Job Estimate
JE . . . . Joshi Effect (Electronics)
JE . . . . Joule Effect (Electronics)
JEA . . . . Jesuit Educational Association
JEA . . . . Joint Engineering Agency
JEA . . . . Joint Export Agent
JEA . . . . Joint Export Association (Department of Commerce)
JEA . . . . Journalism Education Association
JEAB . . . . . . Journal of the Experimental Analysis of Behavior
JEAL . . . . . . Junction Emitting Avalanche Light
JEB . . . . Joint Economy Board (Army-Navy)
JEB . . . . Joint Electronics Board
JEBG . . . . . . Japan Electronics Buyers' Guide
JEBM . . . . . . Jet Engine Base Maintenance
JEC . . . . Japanese Electrotechnical Committee
JEC . . . . Joint Economic Committee (of Congress)
JECA . . . . . . Jewel Cave National Monument
JECB . . . . . . Jet Engine Control Bearing
JECC . . . . . . Joint Economic Committee of Congress
JECI . . . . Jeunesse Etudiante Catholique Internationale (International Young
Catholic Students)
JECMB . . . . . Joint Executive Committee on Medicine and Biology
JEDEC . . . . . Joint Electron Device Engineering Councils
JEDS . . . . . . Japanese Expeditions to the Deep Sea
JEE . . . . Japan Electronics Engineering
JEE . . . . Journal of Engineering Education
JEEP . . . . . . General Purpose 1/4-ton Military Utility Vehicle
JEEP . . . . . . Joint Effort Evaluation Program (Military)
JEEP . . . . . . Joint Emergency Evacuation Plan (Military)
JEEP . . . . . . Joint Environmental Effects Program (Military)
JEEP . . . . . . Joint Establishment Experimental Pile (Atomic energy)
JEF . . . . Jacobi Elliptic Function
JEF . . . . Jefferson Lake Sulphur Company (NYSE symbol) (Delisted; see JFL)
JEF . . . . Jeunesses Europeennes Federalistes
JEFF . . . . . . Jefferson National Expansion Memorial National Historic Site
JEFM . . . . . . Jet Engine Field Maintenance
JEGP . . . . . . Journal of English and Germanic Philology
JEI . . . . Japan Electronics Industry
JEI . . . . Journal of Economic Issues
JEIA . . . . . . Japanese Electronic Industries Association
JEIA . . . . . . Joint Electronics Information Agency
JEIA . . . . . . Joint Export-Import Agency (Munich) (Allied German Occupation Forces)
JEIDA . . . . . . Japanese Electronic Industries Development Association

JEIPAC . . . . . Japanese Electronic Information Processing Automatic Computer
JEL . . . . Jeunesses Europeennes Liberales (Liberal European Youth)
JELC . . . . . . Joint Effort against Lefthanded Complications
JEM . . . . Jerusalem and the East Mission
JEM . . . . Jordon Electronic Manufacturing Company
JEMC . . . . . . Joint Engineering Management Conference
JEN . . . . . . Junta de Energia Nuclear (Spanish nuclear agency)
JENAKAT . . . . Jeunesse Nationale Katangaise (Katangan National Youth)
JENER . . . . . Joint Establishment for Nuclear Energy Research
JEOCN . . . . . Joint European Operations Communications Network
JEOL . . . . . . Japan Electron Optics Laboratory Company
JEOLCO . . . . Japan Electron Optics Laboratory Company
JEP . . . . Jet Engine Processor
JEPIA . . . . . . Japan Electronic Parts Industry Association
JEPUNA . . . . . Jeunesse du Puna
JES . . . . Japan Electronics Show
JES . . . . Jet Ejector System
JES . . . . John Ericsson Society
JESSI . . . . . . Junior Engineers' and Scientists' Summer Institute
JET . . . . Jam Exceeds Threshold
JET . . . . Job Element Text
JET . . . . Job Express Transportation
JET . . . . Jobs-Education-Training (Organization in Buffalo, New York)
JET . . . . Jobs Evaluation and Training
JET . . . . Joint Economic Team(s)
JET . . . . Joint Effort for Talent (Navy)
JET . . . . Jointly Endorsed Training (Union-management)
JETD . . . . . . Joint Electronics Type Designator
JETDS . . . . . Joint Electronics Type Designation System (Military)
JETEC . . . . . Joint Electron Tube Engineering Council
JETP . . . . Jet Propelled
JETP . . . . Journal of Experimental and Theoretical Physics
JETR . . . . . . Japan Engineering Test Reactor
JETRO . . . . . Japan External Trade Relations Organization
JETS . . . . . . Junior Engineering Technical Society
JEV . . . . Japanese Encephalitis Virus
JF . . . . Jack Field
JF . . . . Jet Flap
JF . . . . John Flanagan (Designer's mark, when appearing on US coins)
J & F . . . . . . Job & Function (Air Force)
JFACT . . . . . Joint Flight Acceptance Component Testing
J-FACT . . . . . Joint Flight Acceptance Composite Test (Gemini) (NASA)
JFAP . . . . . . Joint Frequency Allocation Panel
JFDA . . . . . . Jewish Funeral Directors of America
JFEA . . . . . . Japan Federation of Employers Association
JFEA . . . . . . Joint Foreign Exchange Agency (Berlin) (Post-World War II, Germany)
JFED . . . . . . Junction Field Effect Device
JFET . . . . . . Junction Field-Effect Transistor
JFH . . . . Jam Frequency Hopper
JFI . . . . Jet Flight Information
JFIAP . . . . . . Joint Foreign Intelligence Assistance Program
JFK . . . . John Fitzgerald Kennedy
JFKC . . . . . . John F. Kennedy Center for the Performing Arts
JFKSC . . . . . John F. Kennedy Spaceflight Center (Also known as KSC)
JFL . . . . Jefferson Lake Petrochemicals (American Stock Exchange symbol)
JFL . . . . Joint Frequency List
JFLA . . . . . . Jewish Free Loan Association
JFM . . . . Jet Flap Model
JFM . . . . Jeunesses Federalistes Mondiales
JFM . . . . Job Function Manual
JFM . . . . Jupiter Flyby Mission (Aerospace)
JFP . . . . Joint Frequency Panel
JFRC . . . . . . James Forrestal Research Center (Princeton University)
JFS . . . . Jet Fuel Starter
JFS . . . . Jewish Family Service
JFS . . . . Jewish Friends Society
JFSG . . . . . . Joint Feasibility Study Group (Air Force)
JFSNY . . . . . Jewish Folk Schools of New York
JFTCG . . . . . Joint Flight Test Control Group
JFTS . . . . . . Jet Fuel Thermal Stability
JFTU . . . . . . Jordan Federation of Trade Unions
JFV . . . . Jupiter Flyby Vehicle (Aerospace)
JG . . . . Jagdgeschwader (Fighter wing) (German military - World War II)
JG . . . . Jockeys' Guild
JG . . . . Junior Grade
JGA . . . . Juxtaglomerular Apparatus (Histology)
JGB . . . . Jewish Guild for the Blind
JGC . . . . Journal of General Chemistry
JGC . . . . Juxtaglomerular Cells
JGE . . . . Journal of General Education
JGH . . . . Jig Grinder Head

JGM . . . . Jig Grinding Machine
JGN . . . . Junction Gate Number
JGR . . . . Journal of Geophysical Research
JGS . . . . James Griffiths & Sons R. R. (AAR code)
JGSDF . . . . . Japanese Ground Self-Defense Forces
JGTC . . . . . . Junior Girls' Training Corps (British) (World War II)
JGW . . . . Junior Grand Warden (Masonry)
JGWTC . . . . . Jungle and Guerrilla Warfare Training Center (Army)
JH . . . . Juvenile Hormone (Endocrinology)
JHA . . . . John Howard Association
JHA . . . . Juvenile Hormone Analog
JHAS . . . . . . John Herron Art School (Indiana)
JHCNHS . . . . . John Henry Cardinal Newman Honorary Society
JHGSOWA . . . Joint Household Goods Shipping Office, Washington Area (Military)
JHHGSO . . . . Joint Household Goods Shipping Office (Military)
JHI . . . . John Hancock Investors, Inc. (NYSE symbol)
JHM . . . . Virus named for Dr. J. Howard Mueller (Medicine)
JHMO . . . . . . Junior Hospital Medical Officer
JHPS . . . . . . Judaica Historical Philatelic Society
JHS . . . . Journal of Hellenic Studies
JHSC . . . . . . Johnstown & Stony Creek R. R. (AAR code)
JHU . . . . Johns Hopkins University (Maryland)
JI . . . . Case (J. I.) Company (NYSE symbol) (Delisted)
JI . . . . Jazz International
JI . . . . Jersey Institute
JI . . . . Job Instruction
JIB . . . . Jewish Information Bureau
JIB . . . . Joint Intelligence Bureau (British)
JIBEI . . . . . . Joint Industry Board of the Electrical Industry
JIC . . . . Jewelry Industry Council
JIC . . . . Joint Industrial Council
JIC . . . . Joint Industry Conference
JIC . . . . Joint Intelligence Center
JIC . . . . Joint Intelligence Committee
JICA . . . . . . Joint Intelligence Center, Africa
JICA . . . . . . Joint Intelligence Collecting Agency
JICACBI . . . . . Joint Intelligence Collecting Agency, China, Burma, India (World War II)
JICAME . . . . . Joint Intelligence Collecting Agency, Middle East (World War II)
JICANA . . . . . Joint Intelligence Collecting Agency, North Africa (World War II)
JICARC . . . . . Joint Intelligence Collecting Agency, Reception Committee (Navy Department)
JICHS . . . . . . Joint Industrial Conference on Hydraulic Standards
JICPOA . . . . . Joint Intelligence Center, Pacific Ocean Areas
JICS . . . . . . Joint Intelligence Coordination Staff (Central Intelligence Agency)
JICST . . . . . . Japan Information Center of Science and Technology
JICUF . . . . . . Japan International Christian University Foundation
JIE . . . . Junior Institute of Engineers
JIEE . . . . Japanese Institute of Electrical Engineers
JIEP . . . . Joint Intelligence Estimate for Planning
JIFDATS . . . . . Joint In-Flight Data Transmission System (Army)
JIG . . . . Joint Intelligence Group (Military)
JIG . . . . Joule Impulse Generator (Electronics)
JIGS . . . . . . Joule Impulse Generator System (Electronics)
JIGTSC . . . . . Joint Industry-Government Tall Structures Committee
JIIST . . . . . . Japan Institute for International Studies and Training
JIL . . . . Jet Induced Lift
JILA . . . . . . Joint Institute for Laboratory Astrophysics (located at University of Colorado)
JIM . . . . Job Instruction Manual
JINR . . . . . . Joint Institute for Nuclear Research
JIOA . . . . . . Joint Intelligence Objectives Agency
JIP . . . . Joint Installation Plan
JIPMER . . . . . Jawahrlal Institute of Postgraduate Medical Education and Research (India)
JIR . . . . Jewish Institute of Religion
JIR . . . . Job Improvement Request
JIS . . . . Japanese Industrial Standard
JIS . . . . Jet Inlet System
JIS . . . . Jewish Information Society of America
JIS . . . . Job Information Service (Department of Labor)
JIS . . . . Joint Intelligence Staff
JISC . . . . . . Japanese Industrial Standards Committee
JISPB . . . . . . Joint Intelligence Studies Publishing Board
JIT . . . . Job Information Test (Military)
JIT . . . . Job Instruction Training
JIT . . . . Joint Interest Test (Navy)
JITC . . . . . . Jewelry Industry Tax Committee
JITF . . . . . . Joint Interface Test Force (Military)
JJ . . . . Judges
JJ . . . . Justices
JJC . . . . Jackson Junior College (Florida; Michigan)

JJC .... Jiffy Junction Connector
JJC .... Joliet Junior College (Illinois)
JJN .... Newberry (J. J.) Company (NYSE symbol)
JJS .... James Joyce Society
JJSS .... Jean-Jacques Servan-Schrieber (French publisher)
J-J S-S .... Jean-Jacques Servan-Schrieber (French publisher)
JJSWC ...... Jiffy Junction Single Wire Connector
JJWC ...... Jiffy Junction Wire Connector
J/K .... Joule per Kelvin
JKC .... Julian & Kokenge Company (NYSE symbol)
Jkg .... Joules per Kilogram
JKKB ...... Jeunesse du Kwilu-Kwango-Bateke (Kwilu-Kwango-Bateke Youth)
JKS .... Julius Kayser & Company (NYSE symbol)
JKT .... Job Knowledge Test (Military)
JL .... Javan LASER
JL .... Jones & Laughlin Steel Corporation (NYSE symbol)
JL .... Joule's Law (Electronics)
JL .... Jurin Law (Electronics)
JL .... Just Looking (A browser) (Retail slang)
J & L ...... Jones & Laughlin Steel Corp.
JLA .... Jet Lift Aircraft
JLA .... Jewish Librarians Association
JLB .... Jewish Labor Bund
JLC .... Jewish Labor Committee
JLC .... Joint Logistics Committee
JLC .... Junction Latching Circulator
JLC & E .... Jonesboro, Lake City and Eastern Railroad
JLE .... Jet Lift Engine
JLF .... Joint Landing Force
JLFB ...... Joint Landing Force Board
JLH .... Journal of Library History (A publication)
JLMIC ...... Japan Light Machinery Information Center
JLMSA ...... Jewish Liturgical Music Society of America
JLO .... Junction Light Output
JLP .... Jamaica Labour Party
JLPC ...... Joint Logistics Plans Committee
JLPG ...... Joint Logistics Plans Group (Military)
JLPPG ...... Joint Logistics and Personnel Policy Guidance (Military)
JLRB .... Joint Logistics Review Board (Military)
JLRSE ...... Joint Long-Range Strategic Estimates (Military)
JLRSS ...... Joint Long-Range Strategic Study (Military)
JLS .... Jet Lift System
JLT .... Junior Lord of the Treasury
JM .... Johns-Manville Corporation (NYSE symbol) (Wall Street slang name: "Jump")
JM .... Juris Magister (Master of Laws)
JMA .... Japan Meteorological Agency
JMA .... Japan Microphotography Association
JMA .... Japanese Military Administration
JMA .... Jewelry Manufacturers Association
JMA .... Jewish Music Alliance
JMA .... Junior Management Assistant
JMA .... Junior Military Aviator
JMAC ...... Joint Munitions Allocation Committee
JMAHEP .... Joint Military Aircraft Hurricane Evacuation Plan
JMB .... Jewelers Memorandum Bureau
JMB .... Joint Meteorological Board
JMC .... Jerden Manufacturing Corporation
JMC .... Joint Maritime Commission
JMC .... Joint Meteorological Committee
JMC .... Journal of Medicinal Chemistry
JMCAA ...... Jewish Ministers Cantors Association of America
JMCA ...... Judges, Marshals and Constables Association
JMCP ...... Jefferson Medical College of Philadelphia
JMD .... Joint Monitor Display
JMDC ...... Joint Manual Direction Center (Air Force)
JMEM ...... Joint Munitions Effectiveness Manual (Military)
JMF .... Jewish Music Forum
JMG .... Joint Meteorological Group (DOD)
JMI .... Jackson and Moreland, Incorporated
JMI .... John Muir Institute
JMJ .... Jesus, Maria, Joseph (Jesus, Mary, Joseph)
JMMF ...... James Monroe Memorial Foundation
JMN .... Jeweled-Orifice Misting Nozzle
JMNCL ...... Jeunesse du Mouvement National Congolaise - Lumumba (Youth of the Lumumba Wing of the Congolese National Movement)
JMPAB ...... Joint Materiel Priorities and Allocation Board (Military)
JMPTC ...... Joint Military Packaging Training Center
JMRO ...... Joint Medical Regulating Office
JMRO ...... Joint Military Regulating Office
JMRP ...... Joint Meteorological Radio Propagation Committee (British)

JMRT ...... Junior Members Round Table (American Library Association)
JMS .... James (Fred S.) & Co., Inc. (NYSE symbol)
JMS .... John Milton Society
JMSAC ...... Joint Meteorological Satellite Advisory Committee
JMSDF ...... Japanese Maritime Self-Defense Force
JMSPO ...... Joint Meteorological Satellite Program Office
JMT .... Job Methods Training
JMTB ...... Joint Military Transportation Board
JMTC ...... Joint Military Transportation Committee
JMTG ...... Joint Military Terminology Group
JMU .... Jamshedpur Mazdoor Union (India)
JMUSDC .... Joint Mexican-United States Defense Commission
JMVB ...... Joint Merchant Vessels Board (World War II)
JN .... Jet Navigation Charts (Air Force)
JN .... Johnson Noise (Thermal noise, that made by a resistor at a temperature above absolute zero)
J-N .... Jet Navigation
JNA .... Jena Nomina Anatomica (Anatomy)
JNACC ...... Joint Nuclear Accident Coordinating Center
JNCG ...... Japan Nuclear Codes Group
JND .... Just Noticeable Difference (Psychology)
JNE .... Ja Niin Edespain (And So On) (Finland)
JNF .... Jewish National Fund
JNHAC ...... Jewish National Home for Asthmatic Children
JNJ .... Johnson & Johnson (NYSE symbol)
JNL .... Japanese National Laboratory
JNPI .... Jetevator Null Position Indicator
JNR .... Japan National Railways
JNR .... Junior
JNRI .... Joint Nuclear Research Institute (USSR)
JNS .... Jet Noise Survey
JNSC ...... Joint Navigation Satellite Committee
JNU .... Universal Jet Navigation Charts (Air Force)
JNVOA .... Jewish Nazi Victims Organization of America
JNW .... Joint Committee on New Weapons and Equipment
JNWPU .... Joint Numerical Weather Prediction Unit
JO .... Job Order
JO .... Joint Organization
JO .... Journalist (Navy rating)
JO .... Junior Officers
JOA .... Joint Operating Agreement
JOAD ...... Junior Olympic Archery Development
JOB .... Just One Break (An organization devoted to securing employment for physically handicapped workers)
JOBS ...... Job Opportunities for Better Skills
JOBS ...... Job Opportunities in the Business Sector (Program)
JOC .... Jeunesse Ouvriere Chretienne Internationale (International Young Christian Workers)
JOC .... Jewish Occupational Council
JOC .... Joint Operations Center
JOC .... Joint Organizing Committee (Global Atmospheric Research Program)
JOC .... Journal of Organic Chemistry (Refers either to US or USSR publication)
JOD .... Joint Occupancy Data (Military)
JOEG ...... Joint Operations Evaluation Group
JOEG-V .... Joint Operations Evaluation Group, Vietnam (Air Force)
JOFL ...... Johnstown Flood National Memorial
JOG .... Joint Operating Group (SLA/ASIS)
JOG .... Joint Operations Graphic (Military)
JOG .... Joint Operations Group (DOD)
JOHNNIAC .. Johns (Von Neumann) Integrator and Automatic Computer
JOHPER .... Journal of Health, Physical Education, Recreation
JOIDES .... Joint Oceanographic Institutions for Deep Earth Sampling
JOIN .... Job Orientation in the Neighborhoods
JOKI .... John F. Kennedy National Historic Site
JOL .... Jonathan Logan, Inc. (NYSE symbol)
JOLA ...... Journal of Library Automation
JOM .... Jeunesse Ouvriere Marocaine (Moroccan Working Youth)
JOM .... Job Operation Manual
JOM .... Job-Oriented Manual
JOMA ...... Journal of Military Assistance
JOMN ...... Jeweled-Orifice Misting Nozzle
JOMU ...... John Muir National Historic Site
JON .... Jeweled-Orifice Nozzle
JOOD ...... Junior Officer of the Deck (Navy)
JOOMS .... Junior Observers of Meteorology (Trainees for government service to replace Weather Bureau men who had gone to war) (World War II)
JOOS ...... Job-Oriented Organizational Structure
JOOW ...... Junior Officer of the Watch
JOP .... Joint Operating Plan
JOP .... Joint Operation Procedure
JOPA ...... Junior Officers and Professional Association

JOPM....... Joint Occupancy Plan Memo
JOPM....... Joint Operation Procedure Memorandum
JOPR .... Joint Operation Procedure Report
JOPREP...... Joint Operational Report (Military)
JOPS .... Joint Operational Planning System (Military)
JOR .... Jet Operations Requirements
JOR .... Job Order Request
JOR ...... Joint Operations Requirements (Military)
JOR .... Jorgensen (Earle M.) Company (NYSE symbol)
JOS....... Jeunesse Ouvriere du Senegal (Senegalese Working Youth)
JOS .... Job Order Supplement
JOS .... Jostens, Inc. (NYSE symbol)
JOSA ...... Journal of the Optical Society of America
JOSCO ..... Joint Overseas Shipping Control Office
JOSPRO ..... Joint Ocean (or Overseas) Shipping Procedure
JOSS .... JOHNNIAC (Johns [Von Neumann] Integrator and Automatic Computer)
         Open Shop System (Data processing)
JOSS .... Joint Overseas Switching System (Military)
JOT .... Jam On Target
JOTR .... Joshua Tree National Monument
JOTS ...... Job-Oriented Training Standards
JOTU ...... Joint Organization of Trade Unions (Finland)
JOUAM ..... Junior Order United American Mechanics
JOVE .... Job Placement, On-the-Job Training, Vocational Counseling, Education
         (for ex-convicts) (Southern California)
JOVE....... Jupiter Orbiting Vehicle for Exploration
JOVIAL ..... Joule's Own Version of the International Algorithmic Language (Data
         processing)
JOWOG ..... Joint Working Group
JOY .... Job Opportunity for Youth (NASA employment program)
JOY........ Joy Manufacturing Company (NYSE symbol)
JP .... Fighter (Russian aircraft symbol)
JP .... Jack Panel
JP .... Jacobi Polynomial
JP .... Japan Paper
JP .... Jarrow Press, Inc.
JP .... Jefferson-Pilot Corp. (NYSE symbol)
JP .... Jet Penetration
JP .... Jet Petroleum
JP .... Jet Pilot
JP .... Jet Pipe
JP .... Jet Power
JP .... Jet Propellant (or Propelled; Propulsion)
JP .... Junction Panel (or Point) (Electronics)
JP .... Junge Pioniero
JP .... Junior Partner (i.e., a husband) (Slang)
JP .... Justice of the Peace
J & P ...... Joists and Planks (Technical drawings)
JPA .... Jack Panel Assembly
JPA .... Japan Procurement Agency
JPA .... Jesuit Philosophical Association of the United States and Canada
JPA .... Joint Passover Association of the City of New York
JPA .... Joint Planning Activity (DOD)
JPAP .... Jet Penetration Approach
JPB .... Joint Planning Board
JPB .... Joint Production Board (US and British)
JPB .... Joint Purchasing Board
JPBS....... Jettison Pushbutton Switch
JPC .... Jack Patch Cord
JPC .... Jeunesse Progressiste Casamancaise (Casamance Progressive Youth) (Senegal)
JPC .... Joint Planning Committee
JPCRD ...... Journal of Physical and Chemical Reference Data
JPD .... Jeunesse Progressiste Dahomeenne (Dahomey Progressive Youth)
JPDR .... Japan Power Demonstration Reactor
JPF .... Jewish Peace Fellowship
JPFT .... Jewish Philanthropic Fund of 1933
JPFT .... Joiner Pilaster Fumetight (Technical drawings)
JPG .... Jefferson Proving Ground (Military)
JPG .... Job Proficiency Guide
JPGC .... Joint Power Generation Conference
JPL .... Jet Propulsion Laboratory (NASA)
JPL .... Job Parts List
JPM .... Jet Piercing Machine
JPM .... Morgan (J.P.) & Co. (NYSE symbol)
JPMA ...... Juvenile Products Manufacturers Association
JPMR .... Joint Projected Manpower Requirements (Military)
JPN .... Japan Fund, Inc. (NYSE symbol)
JPNT .... Joiner Pilaster Nontight (Technical drawings)
JPO .... Joint Petroleum Office
JPO .... Joint Project Office(r)
JPOAA ...... Junior Panel Outdoor Advertising Association

JPP....... Jalkeen Puolenpaiuan (Afternoon) (Finland)
JPP .... Japan Paper Proofs
JPPL....... Joint Personnel Priority List
JPPRI ...... Jewish Policy Planning and Research Institute (Synagogue Council of
         America)
JPR .... Joint Procurement Regulations (of Army and Air Force)
JPRS ...... Joint Publications Research Service (Department of Commerce)
JPS .... Jeunesse Populaire Senegalaise (Senegalese People's Youth)
JPS .... Jewish Publication Society of America
JPS .... Joint Planning Staff (US and Great Britain) (World War II)
JPS .... Journal of Polymer Science
JPSA ...... Jewish Pharmaceutical Society of America
JPSA ...... Joint Program for the Study of Abortion
JPSA ...... Junior Philatelic Society of America
JPSC ...... Joint Production Survey Committee
JPT........ Jet Pipe Temperature
JPT .... Job Progress Ticket
JPTF....... Joint Parachute Test Facility (DOD)
JPTO .... Jet Propelled Take-Off
JPW .... Job Processing Word
JPWC ...... Joint Postwar Committee
JQ .... Job Questionnaire
JR .... Joint Resolution (Usually, of the US Senate and House of Representatives)
JR .... Jonkheer (Netherlands)
JR .... Junior
JRA .... Job Release Analysis
JRAS ...... Journal of the Royal Asiatic Society
JRATA ..... Joint Research and Test Activity
JRB .... Joint Radio Board
JRC .... Jet Reaction Control
JRC .... Joint Railroad Conference
JRC .... Joint Reconnaissance Center (Military)
JRC .... Junior Red Cross
JRCC ...... Joint Regional Continuing Committee (Later, RCEAC) (Civil Defense)
JRCC ...... Joint Rescue Coordination Center (Military)
JRCS ...... Jet Reaction Control System
JRDA ...... Jeunesse du Rassemblement Democratique Africain (Youth of the African
         Democratic Rally)
JRDACI...... Jeunesse du Rassemblement Democratique Africain de Cote d'Ivoire (Youth
         of the African Democratic Rally of the Ivory Coast)
JRDB ...... Joint Research and Development Board
JRDOD ..... Joint Research and Development Objectives Document (Military)
JRF .... Jewish Reconstructionist Foundation
JRF .... Judicial Research Foundation
JRI........ Jail Release Information
JRL .... Jet Research Laboratory
JRL .... Julie Research Laboratory
JRM .... Joule-Rowland Method (Electronics)
JRMTO ..... Joint Rail Military Traffic Office
JRPM ...... Joint Registered Publications Memorandum
JRR .... Japanese Research Reactor
JRS .... Japanese Rocket Society
JRS........ John R. Sinnock (Designer's mark, when appearing on US coins)
JRSO ...... Jewish Restitution Successor Organization
JRT .... Job Relations Training
JS .... Jack Screw
JS .... Jet Stabilization
JS .... Jet Stream
JS .... Jet Study
JS .... Jetevator Sensor
JS .... Jettison Signal
JS .... Job Specification (Department of Labor)
JS .... John R. Sinnock (Designer's mark, when appearing on US coins)
JS .... Joint Support (Military)
JS .... Junior Scholastic (A publication)
JS .... Just Scale
J/S .... Jamming to Signal
JSA .... Jammer System Analysis
JSA .... Japan Silk Association
JSA .... Jesuit Seismological Association
JSA .... Jewelers Security Alliance of the US
JSA .... Jewelers Shipping Association
JSA .... Jewish Society of Americanists
JSA .... Journeymen Stone Cutters Association of North America
JSA .... Junior Statesmen of America
JSAC ...... Jet Strategic Airlift Capability (of Military Air Command)
JSAG ...... Joint Service Advisory Group
JSAP ...... Joint Statement of Agreed Principles (US-USSR)
JSAS ...... Jammer System Analysis Simulator
JSAS ...... Journal Supplement Abstract Service (American Psychological Association)
JSB .... Bachelor of Judicial Science

JSB	Jaswant Singh and Bhattacharji (Staining method for blood cells, named for its discoverers) (Medicine)
JSB	Jewish Society for the Blind
JSB	Jewish Statistical Bureau
JSC	Jackson State College (Mississippi)
JSC	Johnson Service Company (NYSE symbol)
JSC	Joint Security Control
JSC	Joint Service Committee (Military)
JSC	Joint Setup Cost
JSC	Joint-Stock Company
JSC	Joint Strategic Committee
JSC	Joly Steam Calorimeter
JSC	Journal of Structural Chemistry
JSCA	Japanese Spaniel Club of America
JSCA	Journeymen Stone Cutters Association of North America
J Sc D	Doctor of Juridical Science
JSCM	Joint Service Commendation Medal (Military)
JSCO	Joint Staff Communications Office (Military)
JSCP	Joint Strategic Capabilities Plan (Military)
JSCR	Job Schedule Change Request
JSCS	Junior Slovak Catholic Sokol
JSD	Doctor of Juridical (or Judicial) Science (or Doctor of the Science of Law)
JSD	Jeunesse Social Democrate (Social Democratic Youth) (Malagasy)
JSD	Jewish Society for the Deaf
JSDA	Japanese Self-Defense Agency
JSE	Jam Strobe Extractor
JSEAC	Joint Societies Employment Advisory Committee
JSEP	Joint Services Electronics Program (Military)
JSESPO	Joint (Maritime Administration - Navy) Surface Effect Ship Program Office
JSF	Japan Scholarship Foundation
JSF	Junior Statesmen Foundation
JSFA	Journal of the Science of Food and Agriculture
JSGOMRAM . .	Joint Study Group on Military Resources Allocation Methodology
JSHS	Junior Science and Humanities Symposium
JSI	Job Satisfaction Inventory (Guidance)
JSI	Journal of Social Issues
JSIA	Joint Service Induction Area
JSIPS	Joint System Integration Planning Staff
JSK	Jeunesse du Sud-Kasai
JSL	Joint Support List (Military)
JSL	Journal of Symbol Logic (A publication)
JSM	Master of Judicial Science
JSMA	Joint Sealer Manufacturers Association
JSN	Job Sequence Number
JSO	Joint Service Office
JSOC	Joint Ship Operations Committee
JSOP	Joint Strategy Objective Plan (Military)
JSP	Japan Socialist Party
JSP	Joint Staff Planners (Joint Chiefs of Staff)
JSPC	Joint Strategic Plans Committee (Military)
JSPG	Joint Strategic Plans Group (Military)
JSPS	Japan Society for the Promotion of Science
JSR	Japan Science Review
JSRC	Joint Ship Repair Committee
JSS	Journal of the Siam Society
JSSC	Joint Strategic Survey Council (DOD)
JSTPS	Joint Strategic Target Planning Staff (DOD)
JSVA	Jewish Socialist Verband of America
JSWPB	Joint Special Weapons Publications Board
JSY	Jersey Airlines
JTA	Joint Table of Allowance
JTA	Joint Tenancy Agreement (Military)
JTA	Journal of Thermal Analysis
JTAC	Joint Technical Advisory Committee (Electronics)
JTASB	Joint Tactical Air Support Board
JTB	Joint Bar
JTB	Joint Transportation Board (Military)
JTC	Joint Telecommunications Committee (Military)
JTC	Joule-Thomson Coefficient (Electronics)
JTC	Joule-Thomson Cooler (Electronics)
JTC	Junior Training Corps (British)
JTCCG	Joint Technical Configuration Control Group (Military)
JTCG/ME	Joint Technical Coordinating Group for Munitions Effectiveness (Military)
JTD	Joint Table of Distribution (Military)
JTDS	Joint Track Data Storage
JTE	Jamming Tactics Evaluation
JTE	Joule-Thomson Effect (Electronics)
JTETF	Joint Test Evaluation Task Force (Air Force)
JTF	Japan Textile Federation
JTF	Joint Task Forces (Military)

JTG	Joint Task Groups (Military)
JTI	Jydsk Teknologisk Institut (Technological Institute of Jutland) (Denmark)
JTLAS	Jet Transport Landing Approach Simulator
JTML	Junior Town Meeting League
JTO	Jeunesse Travailleuse Oubanguienne (Ubangi Working Youth)
JTO	Joint Technical Operations
JTO	Junction Temperature, Operating
JTR	Joint Termination Regulation
JTR	Joint Travel Regulation
JTRE	Joint Tsunami Research Effort
JTS	Job Training Standard
JTS	Joint Task Force
JTSA	Jewish Theological Seminary of America (New York)
JTSTR	Jet Stream
JTU	Jet Training Unit
JTUAC	Joint Trade Union Advisory Committee
JTV	Jet Test Vehicle
JU	Jeunesse Universelle
JUD	Jeunesse d'Union Dahomeene (Dahomean Youth Union)
JUD	Juris Utriusque Doctor (Doctor of Both Laws; i.e., Canon and Civil Law)
JUDGE	Judged Utility Decision Generator
JUG	Joint Users Group (Data processing)
JUL	July
JUL	Juris Utriusque Licentiatus (Licentiate in Both Laws; i.e., Canon and Civil Law)
JUMO	Junkers-Motor (Junkers aircraft engine) (German military - World War II)
JUMPS	Joint Uniform Military Pay System
JUN	June
JUNC	Jeunesse d'Union Nationale Congolaise (Congolese National Union Youth)
Jur M	Master of Jurisprudence
Jur Sc D	Doctor of Judicial Science (or Doctor of Science of Jurisprudence)
JUSMAG	Joint United States Military Advisory Group
JUSMAGG . . .	Joint United States Military Aid Group, Greece
JUSMAP . . .	Joint United States Military Advisory and Planning Group
JUSMG	Joint United States Military Group
JUSMMAT	Joint United States Military Mission for Aid to Turkey
JUSNC	Journal of the United States National Committee
JUSPAO	Joint United States Public Affairs Office (Vietnam)
JUSSC	Joint United States Strategic Committee
JUT	Jet Utility Transport
JUT	Jeunesse de l'Unite Togolaise (Togolese Unity Youth)
JUWTF	Joint Unconventional Warfare Task Force
JUWTFA	Joint Unconventional Warfare Task Force, Atlantic
JV	Japanese Vellum
JV	Journal Voucher (Accounting)
JV	Junior Varsity
JVA	Jewish Vacation Association (Superseded by Association of Jewish Sponsored Camps)
JVA	Junior Victory Army (World War II)
JVB	Joint Vulnerability Board
JVC	Japanese Victor Corporation
JVC	Jewelers Vigilance Committee
JVD	Junction Variactor Doubler
JVE	Jean's Viscosity Equation
JVP	Japanese Vellum Proofs
JVS	Joint Vocational School
JW	Jacket Water
JW	John Wiley (& Sons) (Publisher)
JW	Junior Warden (Masonry)
JW	Junior Wolf (A young philanderer) (Slang)
JW	Junior Woodward (Ancient Order of Foresters)
JWB	National Jewish Welfare Board
JWC	Jim Walter Corporation (NYSE symbol)
JWC	Junction Wire Connector
JWG	Joint Working Groups (Military)
JWGA	Joint War Games Agency (JCS) (DOD)
JWL	Jewel Companies, Inc. (NYSE symbol)
J & WO	Jettison and Washing Overboard
JWPC	Joint War Plans Committee
JWPC	Joint War Production Committee
JWPS	Joint War Production Staff
JWR	Joint War Room
JWT	J. Walter Thompson Company (NYSE symbol)
JWT	Jewel Tea Company, Inc. (NYSE symbol) (Later, JWL)
JWTC	Jungle Warfare Training Center
JWU	International Jewelry Workers' Union
JWV	Jewish War Veterans of the USA
JWVA	National Ladies Auxiliary, Jewish War Veterans of the USA
JWYCC	Jamestown-Williamsburg-Yorktown Celebration Committee
JYA	Junior Year Abroad (Collegiate term)
JYP	Jersey Central Power & Light Co. (NYSE symbol)

K

K . . . . Capacity
K . . . . Care; Carus; Cara (Dear One)
K . . . . Carissimus (Dearest)
K . . . . Cathode Tube
K . . . . Cellophane
K . . . . Electron capture (Radioactivity)
K . . . . Ionization constant (Chemistry)
K . . . . Kalendas (Calends)
K . . . . Kalium (Potassium) (Chemical element)
K . . . . Karat (Variant of "carat," C, q.v.)
K . . . . Kathode (Cathode)
K . . . . Kayser
K . . . . Keel
K . . . . Keg
K . . . . Kellogg Company (NYSE symbol)
K . . . . Kelvin (The absolute scale of temperature in which zero equals -273.1 degrees Centigrade)
K . . . . Kentish
K . . . . Kerosene
K . . . . Kerr Constant (Electronics)
K . . . . Key
k . . . . Kilo (A prefix meaning multiplied by 1000)
k . . . . Kilogram
k . . . . Kilohm
K . . . . Kinesthetic
K . . . . King
K . . . . King (Chess)
K . . . . Kip (1000 lb)
K . . . . Kitchen
K . . . . Klystron
K . . . . Knight (Chess or cards)
K . . . . Knit
K . . . . Knots (Nautical speed unit)
K . . . . Kollsman (When followed by altimeter setting) (Also see KOL) (Aviation)
K . . . . Kopeck (Monetary unit in Russia)
K . . . . Koruna (Monetary unit in Czechoslovakia)
K . . . . Kraftfahrwesen (Motor transport) (German military - World War II)
K . . . . Kraftrad (Motorcycle) (German military)
K . . . . Krona (Monetary unit in Sweden)
K . . . . Krone (Monetary unit in Denmark, Norway)
K . . . . Kroon (Monetary unit in Estonia)
K . . . . Kurus (Monetary unit in Turkey)
K . . . . Modified for use as target aircraft (Suffix to Navy plane designation)
k . . . . Multiplication Factor (or Constant)
K . . . . Potassium (Chemical element)
K . . . . Smoke (Weather charts)
K . . . . Tanker (Designation for all US military aircraft)
K . . . . Thermal Conductivity (Symbol)
K (Day) . . . . . Day Set for Strike or Assault by a Carrier's Aircraft; Corresponds to D-Day (Navy)
K9 . . . . Canine (K9 Corps - Army Dogs) (World War II)
KA . . . . Cathode
KA . . . . Concrete Arch (Bridges)
KA . . . . King of Arms
KA . . . . Kuwait Airways
KAA . . . . Keep-Alive Anode
KAB . . . . Katholieke Arbeidersbewegung (Netherlands)
KAB . . . . Keep America Beautiful, Inc.
KAC . . . . Kaman Aircraft Corporation
KAC . . . . Kinetics and Catalysis
KACC . . . . . . Kaiser Aluminum & Chemical Corporation
KACC . . . . . . Korean-American Chamber of Commerce
KACF . . . . . . Korean-American Cultural Foundation

KACIA . . . . . . Korea-American Commerce and Industry Association
KaDeWe . . . . . Kaufhaus des Westens (Department Store of the West) (Germany)
KADU . . . . Kenya African Democratic Union (A political party)
KAF . . . . Kenya Air Force
KAFB . . . . . . Keesler Air Force Base
KAFB . . . . . . Kirtland Air Force Base
KAFH . . . . . . Ku-Band Antenna Feed Horn
KAG . . . . Kelvin Astatic Galvanometer
KAI . . . . Korean Affairs Institute
KAIG . . . . . . Kearfott Acceleration Integrating Gyroscope
KAIS . . . . Korea Advanced Institute of Science
KAK . . . . Kungliga Automobil Klubben
KAL . . . . Kalamazoo Stove & Furnace (NYSE symbol)
KALD . . . . . . Kalamein Door
KALDAS . . . . . Kidsgrove ALGOL (Algorithmic Language) Digital Analogue Simulation (Data processing) (British)
KAM . . . . Kenya African Movement
KAM . . . . Kinematic Analysis Method
KAM . . . . Knudsen Absolute Manometer
KAN . . . . Kansas Power & Light Company (NYSE symbol)
KAN. . . . . . . Kriegsausruestungsnachweisung (Table of basic allowances) (German military - World War II)
KANS. . . . . . . Kansas
KANU . . . . . . Kenya African National Union (A political party)
KAO . . . . Kappa Alpha Order
KAP . . . . Kinematical Analysis Program
KAPL . . . . . . Knolls Atomic Power Laboratory (AEC)
KAR . . . . King's African Rifles (Military) (British)
KAS . . . . Kroeber Anthropological Society
KAS . . . . Kulanka Afka Somalyed
KASC . . . . . . Knowledge Availability Systems Center
KAT . . . . Kappa Alpha Theta (Sorority)
KATM . . . . . . Katmai National Monument
KATUSA . . . . Korean Augmentation to the United States Army
KATY . . . . . . Missouri-Kansas-Texas Lines (Railroad)
KAW . . . . Kawneer Company (NYSE symbol)
KAYSEE . . . . . Kansas City, Missouri (Slang)
KB . . . . Kaufman & Broad, Inc. (NYSE symbol)
KB . . . . Keyboard
KB . . . . Keyboard Button (Data processing)
kb . . . . Kilobar
kb . . . . Kilobit(s)
KB . . . . King's Bench (of law courts) (British)
KB . . . . Kitchen and Bathroom
KB . . . . Kitchen Biddy (Female kitchen worker) (Restaurant slang)
KB . . . . Kite Balloon (Air Force)
KB . . . . Knee Brace (Technical drawings)
KB . . . . Knight Bachelor or Knight Companion of the Bath (British)
KB . . . . Kulturbund
KBA . . . . Killed by Air (Military)
KBA . . . . Knight of St. Benedict of Avis
KBART . . . . . Kings Bay Army Terminal
KBC . . . . K-Band Circulator
KBD . . . . King's Bench Division
KBE . . . . Key Company (NYSE symbol)
KBE . . . . Keyboard Encoder (Data processing)
KBE . . . . Keyboard Entry (Data processing)
KBE . . . . Knight Commander of the (Order of the) British Empire
KBI . . . . Kawecki Berylco Industries, Inc. (NYSE symbol)
KBI . . . . Keyboard Immortals (Recording label)
KBIM . . . . . . Kongres Buruh Islam Merdeka (Free Islamic Trade Union Congress) (Indonesia)
KBKA . . . . . . Kongres Buruh Karata Api (Congress of Railway Workers) (Indonesia)

KBKI . . . . Kesatuan Buruh Kerakjatan Indonesia (Indonesian Democratic Workers' Federation)
KBM . . . . Karissimo Bene Merenti (To the Most Dear and Well-Deserving)
KBO . . . . Kite and Balloon Officer (Navy)
KBP . . . . Kappa Beta Pi (Society)
KBP . . . . Kite Balloon Pilot
kbps . . . . Kilo Bits Per Second
KBR . . . . Keebler Co. (NYSE symbol)
KBR . . . . Komplementbindungsreaktion
KBr . . . . Potassium Bromide
kbs . . . . Kilobits per Second
KBS . . . . Knight of the Blessed Sacrament
KBSI . . . . Kongres Buruh Seluruh Indonesia (All Indonesia Congress of Workers)
KBWP . . . . . Kernkraftwerk Baden-Wuerttemberg Planungsgesellschaft
KC . . . . Kanawha Central Railway Company (AAR code)
KC . . . . Kansas City, Missouri (Slang)
KC . . . . Karman Constant
KC . . . . Kennel Club
KC . . . . Kerr Cell
kc . . . . Kilocalorie
kc . . . . Kilocycle (Radio)
KC . . . . King's Counsel (British)
KC . . . . Knight(s) of Columbus
KC . . . . Knight Commander
KC . . . . Koruna Ceskoslovensky (Czechoslovakian monetary unit)
K of C . . . . . Knight(s) of Columbus
KCA . . . . . . Kansas City Area Office (AEC)
KCA . . . . Keeshond Club of America
KCA . . . . Keesings Contemporary Archives (British world-news digest service)
kcal . . . . Kilocalorie
KCAS . . . . . Knots Calibrated Airspeed
KCB . . . . Keyboard Change Button (Data processing)
KCB . . . . Knight Commander (of the Order of the) Bath
KCC . . . . Kansas City Connecting R. R. (AAR code)
KCC . . . . Keyboard Common Contact (Data processing)
KCC . . . . Keokuk Community College (Iowa)
KCCC . . . . . . Kansas City Computer Center (Phillips Petroleum Company)
KCCH . . . . . Knight Commander of Court of Honor
KCF . . . . Key-Click Filter
KCG . . . . Kaiser Cement & Gypsum Corp. (NYSE symbol)
KCH . . . . King's College Hospital
KCH . . . . Knight Commander of the Guelphic Order of Hanover (British)
KCI . . . . Key Club International
KCIE . . . . Knight Commander of the Indian Empire (British)
KCL . . . . Kern County Land Company (NYSE symbol) (Wall Street slang name: "Casey") (Delisted)
KCL . . . . King's College, London
KCL . . . . Knudsen Cosine Law
KCLU . . . . . . Korean Council of Organization (South Korea)
KCMG . . . . . Knight Commander of St. Michael and St. George (British)
KCMO . . . . . Kansas City, Mexico & Orient Railway (AAR code)
KCN . . . . Kit Control Number (Navy)
KCNW . . . . . Kelly's Creek & Northwestern R. R. (AAR code)
KCP . . . . Keene's Cement Plaster (Technical drawings)
KCPC . . . . . . Keene's Cement Plaster Ceiling (Technical drawings)
KCPS . . . . . . Kansas City Public Service R.R. (AAR code)
KCPS . . . . . . Kilocycles Per Second
KCRF . . . . . . Korean Conflict Research Foundation
KCS . . . . Kansas City Southern Railway Company (AAR code)
kcs . . . . Kilocycles Per Second
KC/S . . . . . . Kilocycles Per Second
KCSI . . . . Knight Commander of the Star of India (British)
KCT . . . . Kansas City Terminal Railway Company (AAR code)
KCT . . . . Kelvin Circulation Theorem (Electronics)
KCVO . . . . . Knight Commander of the Royal Victorian Order (British)
KD . . . . Keep It Dark (Say Nothing About It) (Slang)
KD . . . . Kiln-Dried (Lumber)
KD . . . . Knock(ed) Down (i.e., disassembled)
KD . . . . Pilotless Aerial Target (Navy)
KDA . . . . Katholischer Deutscher Akademikerinnen (Bund) (Union of German Catholic University Women) (Germany)
KDB . . . . Kelvin Double Bridge (Electronics)
KDC . . . . Keyed Display Console
KDCL . . . . . . Knocked Down, in Carloads
KDCP . . . . . . Kidney Disease Control Program (Public Health Service)
KDD . . . . Kokusai Denshin Denwa (Telegraph and telephone corporation) (Japan)
KDE . . . . Kidde (Walter) & Co., Inc. (NYSE symbol)
KDF . . . . Kalamein Door and Frame
KDF . . . . Knob Door Fastener
KDF . . . . Knocked Down Flat

KDF . . . . Kraft durch Freude (Strength through Joy Movement) (Pre-World War II, Germany)
KDFC . . . . . . Korea Development Finance Corporation
KDG . . . . The King's Dragoon Guards (British)
KDH . . . . Korean Direct Hire
KDLCL . . . . . Knocked Down, in Less than Carloads
KDP . . . . Known Datum Point
KDP . . . . Potassium Dihydrogen Phosphate (Chemical)
KDPS . . . . . . Kurdish Democratic Party of Syria
KDR . . . . Kappa Delta Rho (Fraternity)
KDR . . . . Keyboard Data Recorder (Data processing)
KDS . . . . Kathode Dark Space
KDS . . . . Keel Depth Simulator
KDT . . . . Kammer der Technik
KDT . . . . Kings Department Stores, Inc. (NYSE symbol)
KE . . . . Keene Corp. (NYSE symbol)
KE . . . . Kendall's Compound E (Cortisone)
KE . . . . Kerr Effect (Electronics)
KE . . . . Keuffel and Esser Co.
KE . . . . Kinetic Energy
KEA . . . . Knitwear Employers Association
KEAS . . . . . . Knots Equivalent Air Speed
KEC . . . . Kelly's Creek R. R. (AAR code)
KEEP . . . . . . Kyosato Education Experiment Project (Self-help program for Japanese farmers established by Americans in 1948)
KEH . . . . King Edward's Horse Regiment (Military) (British)
KEI . . . . Kresge Eye Institute
KEK . . . . Kappa Eta Kappa (Fraternity)
KEL . . . . Keller Industries, Inc. (NYSE symbol)
KELP . . . . . . Kindergarten Evaluation for Learning Potential (McGraw-Hill)
KELU . . . . . . Kristana Esperantista Ligo Usona
KELU . . . . . . Kuching Employees and Labourers' Union (Sarawak)
KEMO . . . . . Kennesaw Mountain National Battlefield Park
KEN . . . . Kendall Company (NYSE symbol)
KEP . . . . Kellner Eye Piece
KEPOA . . . . . Keep This Office Advised
KEPZ . . . . . . Kaohsiung Export Processing Zone (Reexport manufacturing complex) (Taiwan)
KEREN-OR . . . Jerusalem Institutions for the Blind
KERUK-NASI . . Kerukunan Nasional (Compaign for National Harmony) (Indonesia)
KES . . . . Keystone Consolidated Industries, Inc. (NYSE symbol)
keV . . . . Kiloelectron Volt
KEWB . . . . . . Kinetic Experiment on Water Boiler (AEC)
KF . . . . Knudsen Flow (Electronics)
KF . . . . Kosciuszko Foundation
KF . . . . Kossuth Foundation
KFAED . . . . . Kuwait Fund for Arab Economic Development
KFC . . . . Katholieke Film-Centrale
KFC . . . . Kentucky Fried Chicken
KFE . . . . Kathode Flicker Effect
KFEA . . . . . . Korean Federation of Education Associations
KFH . . . . Ku-Band Feed Horn
KFK . . . . Gesellschaft fuer Kernforschung (West Germany)
KFK . . . . Kernforschungszentrum Karlsruhe (West Germany)
KFL . . . . Kenya Federation of Labour
KFL . . . . Key Facilities List (AEC)
KFM . . . . Klystron Frequency Multiplier
KFM . . . . Kroehler Manufacturing Company (NYSE symbol)
KFO . . . . Killing Federal Officer
KFOC . . . . . . Kaiser-Frazier Owners Clubs of America
KFRST . . . . . Killing Frost (Meteorology)
KFS . . . . Kalman Filtering System
KFSR . . . . . . Karakul Fur Sheep Registry
KFT . . . . Kalman Filter Theory
KFTU . . . . . . Korean Federation of Trade Unions (North Korea)
KFUK . . . . . . Kristelig Forening for Unge Kvinder (Young Women's Christian Associations) (Denmark)
KFUM . . . . . . Kristelig Forening for Unge Maend (Young Men's Christian Associations) (Denmark)
KG . . . . Kampfgeschwader (Bombardment wing) (German military - World War II)
KG . . . . Kampfgruppen
kG . . . . Kilogauss
kg . . . . Kilogram(s)
KG . . . . Knight of the (Order of the) Garter (British)
KG . . . . Known Gambler (Police slang)
KG . . . . Kommandit Gesellschaft
KG . . . . Konsumgenossenschaften
KG . . . . Kresge (S. S.) Company (NYSE symbol)
KGA . . . . Kitchen Guild of America
KGB . . . . Kewaunee, Green Bay & Western R. R. (AAR code)

ACRONYMS AND INITIALISMS DICTIONARY

KGB . . . . Komitet Gossudarstvennoi Bezopastnosti (Committee of State Security)
            (Russian Secret Police)
KGC . . . . Knight of the Golden Circle
KGC . . . . Knight Grand Commander
KGC . . . . Knight Grand Cross
kgcal . . . . . . Kilogram Calorie
kg/cum . . . . . Kilograms Per Cubic Meter
KGE. . . . . . . Kansas Gas & Electric Company (NYSE symbol)
KGE . . . . Klein-Gordon Equation
KGE. . . . . . . Knights of the Golden Eagle
kgf. . . . . Kilogram-Force
KGF. . . . . . . Kriegsgefangener (Prisoner of War) (Germany)
kg-f . . . . Kilogram-Foot
KGH . . . . . . Knight of the Guelphic Order of Hanover
KGK . . . . . . Kabushkiki Goshi Kaisha (Partnership) (Japan)
kg-m . . . . . . Kilogram-Meter
kgps . . . . Kilograms Per Second
KGR. . . . . . . Kanonengranate (Shell for a gun) (German military - World War II)
KGS. . . . . . . Kate Greenaway Society
KGS. . . . . . . Ketogenic Steroid (Endocrinology)
kg/s . . . . Kilograms Per Second
KGST . . . . . . Kolcsonos Gazdasag Segitseg Tanacs
KGV . . . . . . Knight of Gustavus Vasa
KH . . . . King's Hussars (Military) (British)
KH. . . . . Knight of the Guelphic Order of Hanover (British)
KHB. . . . . . . King's Hard Bargain (British military slang for undesirable sailor or
            soldier)
KHb . . . . Potassium Hemoglobinate
KHC. . . . . . . Karen Horney Psychoanalytic Clinic
KHC. . . . . . . King's Honorary Chaplain (British)
KHIF . . . . . . Keeping House of Ill Fame
KHL . . . . Kennedy-Heaviside Layer (Electronics)
KHM . . . . . . King's Harbour Master (British)
KHP . . . . Koppers Hydrate Process
KHPI . . . . . . Khimicheskii Poglotitel Izvestkovyi (Chemical absorbent) (USSR)
KHS . . . . Knight of the Holy Sepulchre
KHT . . . . Kathode Heating Time
kHz . . . . Kilohertz (Electronics)
KI . . . . Kiwanis International
KI . . . . Kovats (Retention) Index
KIA . . . . Killed in Action
KIAS . . . . . . Knots Indicated Airspeed
KIC . . . . Kelley Island Time & Transport (NYSE symbol)
KID . . . . Allied Kid Company (NYSE symbol)
KIF . . . . Kodak Industrial Film
KIFIS . . . . . . Kollsman Integrated Flight Instrumentation System
KIH . . . . Kaiser-I-Hind (Indian medal)
KIK . . . . Kozawa, Iwatsuru and Kawaguchi (Factor involving injection of
            cancerous gastric juices into rabbits, named for its discoverers)
            (Medicine)
KIL . . . . Krypton Ion LASER
KILLS . . . . . . Ka-Inertial Launch & Leave System
KIM . . . . Keyboard Input Matrix (Data processing)
KIMCODE . . . . Kimble Method for Controlled Devacuation
KIMO. . . . . . Kings Mountain National Military Park
KIND . . . . . . Kindness in Nature's Defense (Elementary school course)
KIP . . . . Key Intelligence Position
KIR . . . . Kirsch Co. (NYSE symbol)
KIRP. . . . . . . Kodak Infrared Phosphor
KIS . . . . Keyboard Input Simulation (Data processing)
KISC . . . . . . Knowledge Industry Systems Concept (Publishing and education)
            (Pronounced "Kiss")
KISMIF . . . . . Keep It Simple, Make It Fun
KISS . . . . Keep It Simple, Sir (Data processing)
KISS . . . . Keep It Simple, Stupid (Bridge bidding term)
KISS. . . . . . . Key Integrative Social Systems
KIST. . . . . . . Korean Institute for Science and Technology
KISZ . . . . . . Kommunista Ifjusagi Szovetseg (Communist Youth Organization) (Hungary)
KIT . . . . Kaufman Ion Thrustor
KIT . . . . Kentucky & Indiana Terminal R. R. (AAR code)
KIXF . . . . . . Kodak Industrial X-Ray Film
kJ . . . . Kilojoule
KJ . . . . Knee Jerk (Medicine)
KJC . . . . Keystone Junior College (Pennsylvania)
KJCPL . . . . . Koninklijke Java-China-Paketvaart Lijnen
KJF . . . . Kutta-Joukowski Force
KJS . . . . Kansas Journal of Sociology
KJS . . . . Kodak Job Sheet
KJV . . . . King James Version (or Authorized Version of the Bible, 1611)
KK . . . . Kabushiki Kaishi (Joint stock company) (Japan)
KK . . . . Kaiser Koenigliche

kK . . . . Kilokayser
KK . . . . Kleinkaliber (Small caliber) (German military)
KKA . . . . . . Knights of King Arthur
KKE . . . . . . Kommunistikon Komma Ellada (Communist Party of Greece)
KKG . . . . . . Kappa Kappa Gamma (Sorority)
KKHL . . . . . . Klung Kidney-Heart-Lung (Machine)
KKK . . . . . . Kissel Kar Klub
KKK . . . . . . Ku Klux Klan
KKP . . . . . . Kappa Kappa Psi (Society)
KKT . . . . . . King's Knight (Chess)
KL . . . . Kelvin Law (Electronics)
KL . . . . Kidney Lobe
kL . . . . Kilolambert
kl . . . . Kiloliter(s)
KL . . . . Klebs-Loeffler (Bacteriology)
KL . . . . Knights of Lithuania
KL . . . . Kuala Lumpur (Malaysia)
K of L . . . . . . Knights of Labor
K of L . . . . . . Knights of Lithuania
KLA . . . . Klystron Amplifier
KLB . . . . Knight of the Order of Leopold (Belgium)
KLG . . . . Knudsen Leaf Gauge
KLH . . . . Knight of the Legion of Honor (France)
KLI . . . . King's Light Infantry (Military) (British)
KLIC . . . . . . Keyletter-in-Context (Data processing)
KLM . . . . KLM Royal Dutch Airlines (NYSE symbol)
KLM. . . . . . . Koninklijke Luchtvaart Maatschappij (Royal Dutch Airlines)
KLO. . . . . . . Klystron Oscillator
KLS . . . . Key Lock Switch
KLS . . . . Krypton LASER System
KLT . . . . Kansas City Power and Light Company (NYSE symbol)
KLT . . . . Kiloton (Nuclear equivalent of 1000 tons of high explosive)
KLT . . . . Klystron Life Test
KLTO . . . . . . Knurling Tool
KLU . . . . Kaiser Aluminum & Chemical Corporation (NYSE symbol)
KM . . . . Kabataang Makabayan (Nationalist Youth) (Philippines)
kM. . . . . Kilo-Mega
km . . . . Kilometer(s)
KM . . . . Kinetic Momentum
KM . . . . King and Martyr (Church calendars)
KM . . . . Kitchen Mechanic (Restaurant slang)
KM . . . . Klystron Mount
KM . . . . Knight of Malta
KMA . . . . . . Kvindelige Missions Arbejdere
KMAG . . . . . United States Military Advisory Group to the Republic of Korea
KMB. . . . . . . Kimberly-Clark Corporation (NYSE symbol)
kMc. . . . . . . Kilo-Megacycles
kMcs . . . . . . Kilomegacycles per Second (Army)
KME. . . . . . . Kappa Mu Epsilon (Society)
KMEF . . . . . . Keratin, Myosin, Epidermin, Fibrin (Biochemistry)
KMER . . . . . . Kodak Metal Etch Resist
KMF . . . . Koussevitzky Music Foundation
KMG . . . . . . Kerr-McGee Oil Industries, Inc. (NYSE symbol)
kmh . . . . Kilometers Per Hour
km/h . . . . . . Kilometers Per Hour
KMJ . . . . Knight of Maximilian Joseph (Bavaria)
KML . . . . Kane Miller (NYSE symbol)
KMMA . . . . . Knitting Machine Manufacturers Association
KMP. . . . . . . Katipunang Manggagawang Pilipino (Confederation of Trade Unions of
            the Philippines)
KMP . . . . . . Koyala Mazdoor Panchayat (India)
KMPP . . . . . . Kisan Mazdoor Praja Party (India)
kmps. . . . . . . Kilometers Per Second
KMR. . . . . . . Kwajalein Missile Range (Army)
KMRA . . . . . . Knitwear Mill Representatives Association
KMRT . . . . . . Kansas & Missouri Railway & Terminal Company (AAR code)
KMS. . . . . . . Keysort Multiple Selector
km/s . . . . . . Kilometers Per Second
KMSMRR . . . . Kapisanan ng mga Manggagawa Sa MRR (Manila Railroad Workers' Union)
            (Philippines)
KMT. . . . . . . Kennametal Inc. (NYSE symbol)
KMT. . . . . . . Kuo Ming Tang (Nationalist Party of China)
KN . . . . Kennecott Copper Corporation (NYSE symbol)
kN . . . . Kilonewton
KN. . . . . Klamath Northern R. R. (AAR code)
Kn . . . . Knudsen number
KN(s) . . . . . . Knot(s)
KNA . . . . Kex National Association
KNA . . . . Killed; Not Enemy Action
KNA . . . . Korean National Airlines
KNA . . . . Korean National Association

KNB . . . . Kansas-Nebraska Natural Gas Co., Inc. (NYSE symbol)
KNC . . . . Kamerun National Congress
KNC . . . . Kingcome Navigation R. R. (AAR code)
KNDP. . . . . . . Kamerun National Democratic Party
KNF. . . . . . . Klein-Nishina Formula
KNI . . . . Knight Newspapers Incorporated (NYSE symbol)
KNK . . . . Kompates Natrium Kernkraftwerk
KNL . . . . Knight of the Netherlands Lion
KNM . . . . . . Kenya National Museum
KNR . . . . . . King's National Roll
KNS. . . . . . . Kinney Services, Inc. (NYSE symbol) (Later, WCI)
KNS. . . . . . . Knight of the Order of the Royal Northern Star
KNSW . . . . . . Knife Switch
KNT. . . . . . . Knight-Knott Hotels Corporation (NYSE symbol)
KNX . . . . Kinney Company, Inc. (NYSE symbol)
KNY . . . . Coca-Cola Bottling Company of New York, Inc. (NYSE symbol)
KO . . . . Coca-Cola Company (NYSE symbol)
KO . . . . Commanding Officer (Military slang)
KO . . . . Contracting Officer (Also, CO)
KO . . . . Keep Off (i.e., avoid assuming the risk on an application, pending further investigation) (Insurance)
KO . . . . King's Own (Military unit) (British)
KO . . . . Klystron Oscillator
KO . . . . Knockout (Boxing)
KO . . . . Knockout (Partly cut out or loosened area which can be easily removed, as in a junction box) (Technical drawings)
KO . . . . Opposite of OK (German slang)
KO's . . . . . . Knockout Drops (A drug producing unconsciousness) (Slang)
KOA . . . . . . Knocked-On-Atom
KOB . . . . . . Kobacher Stores, Inc. (NYSE symbol)
KOB. . . . . . . Kriegsoffizier-Bewerber (Applicant for wartime commission) (German military - World War II)
KOC . . . . . . Kuwait Oil Company
KOCO . . . . . . Korea Oil Corporation
kOe . . . . Kilo-Oersted
KOE. . . . . . . Koehring Co. (NYSE symbol)
KOF . . . . . . Knitted Outerwear Foundation
KOG . . . . . . Kansas, Oklahoma & Gulf Railway Company (AAR code)
KOG . . . . . . Kindly Old Gentleman (Slang)
KO & G . . . . . Kansas, Oklahoma & Gulf Railway Company
KOH . . . . . . Potassium Hydroxide
KOHANMARNAS. . Komando Pertahanan Maritim Nasional (Indonesia)
KOL . . . . . . Kollsman (Also see K) (Aviation)
KOLI . . . . . . King's Own Light Infantry (Military) (British)
KOMAB . . . . . Korean Medical Abstracts (A publication)
KOMSOMOL . . . Communist Youth League (From the Russian)
KOP. . . . . . . Kickoff Point (Diamond drilling)
KOP. . . . . . . Koppers Company, Inc. (NYSE symbol)
KOPS . . . . . . Keep Off Pounds Sensibly (Club)
KOR . . . . . . King's Own Royal (Military unit) (British)
KOR . . . . . . Kodak Ortho Resist
KOR. . . . . . . Koracorp Industries, Inc. (NYSE symbol)
KOR . . . . . . Seaplane (Russian symbol)
KORR . . . . . . The King's Own Royal Regiment (British)
KORSTIC . . . . Korea Scientific and Technological Information Center
KOSAB . . . . . Korean Scientific Abstracts (A publication)
KOSB. . . . . . . The King's Own Scottish Borderers (British)
KOSCOT. . . . . Cosmetics for the Community of Tomorrow (Acronym used as brand name)
KOTRA . . . . . Korea Trade Promotion Corporation
KOV . . . . . . Key Operated Valve
KOYLI . . . . . . The King's Own Yorkshire Light Infantry (British)
KP . . . . Keratitis Precipitates (Medicine)
KP . . . . Key Personnel
KP . . . . Key Pulsing
KP . . . . Key Punch
KP . . . . Kick Plate
KP . . . . Kidney Pore
KP . . . . Kids of Preachers
KP . . . . Kill Probability
kp . . . . Kilopulse
KP . . . . Kinetic Potential
KP . . . . King Post
KP . . . . King's Proctor
KP . . . . Kitchen Police (Kitchen helpers) (Military)
KP . . . . Klein Paradox
KP . . . . Knight of Pius IX
KP . . . . Knight of St. Patrick
KP . . . . Knights of Pythias
KP . . . . Knotty Pine
KP . . . . Kommunistische Partei (Communist Party) (German)
KP . . . . Kurie Plot

KPA . . . . Klystron Power Amplifier
KPA . . . . Korea Procurement Agency
KPA . . . . Kraft Paper Association
KPC . . . . Key Punch Cabinet
KPC . . . . Kinetic Process Control
KPC . . . . Klystron Phase Control
KPC . . . . Knights of Peter Claver
KPC . . . . Kodak Photofabrication Center
KPD . . . . Kommunistische Partei Deutschlands
KP & D . . . . . Kick Plate and Drip
KPDSU . . . . . . Kommunistische Partei der Sowjetunion
KPGMPTM . . . Kesatuan Persekutuan Guru Melayu, Persekutuan Tanah Melayu (Federation of Malay Teachers' Unions, Federation of Malaya)
kph . . . . Kilometers Per Hour
KPH . . . . Komunisticke Partija Hrvatske
kpi . . . . Kips Per Square Inch
KPJ . . . . Komunisticka Partija Jugoslavije
KPK . . . . Kappa Phi Kappa (Fraternity)
KPKK . . . . . . Kraisparteikontrollkommission
KPM . . . . Kathode Pulse Modulation
KPM . . . . King's Police Medal
KPM . . . . Kronig-Penny Model
KPNO . . . . . . Kitt Peak National Observatory
KPNOB . . . . . Kitt Peak National Observatory
KPO. . . . . . . Keypunch Operator
KPO. . . . . . . Kommunistische Partei Oesterreichs
KPOWU . . . . . Kenya Petroleum and Oil Workers' Union
KPP . . . . Keeper of the Privy Purse
KPP . . . . Komunistyczna Partia Polski (Communist Party of Poland)
kpps . . . . Kilopulses Per Second
KPR . . . . Kodak Photo Resist
KPS . . . . Klystron Power Supply
KPSI . . . . . . Thousands of Pounds Per Square Inch
KPSM . . . . . . Klystron Power Supply Modulator
KPSS . . . . . . Kommunisticheskaia Partiia Sovetskogo Soiuza
KPU . . . . Kenya People's Union
KPU . . . . Kommunisticheskaia Partiia Ukrainy
KPUZ . . . . . . Kommunisticheskaia Partiia Uzbekistana
KQ . . . . Kansas Quarterly
KQCP. . . . . . . King's and Queen's College of Physicians (Ireland)
KQF. . . . . . . Krupp Quick-Firing Gun
KR . . . . Contractor (Navy)
KR . . . . Keesom Relationship
KR . . . . Keying Relay
kR . . . . Kilorayleigh
kR . . . . Kiloroentgen(s)
KR . . . . Kinetic Reaction
KR . . . . The King's Regiment (British)
KR . . . . The King's Regulations for the Army and the Army Reserves (British)
KR . . . . King's Rook (Chess)
KR . . . . Kipp Relay
KR . . . . Knowledge of Results
KR . . . . Kroger Company (NYSE symbol)
KR . . . . Krona (Sweden)
KR . . . . Krone (Denmark, Norway)
KR . . . . Kronur (Iceland)
Kr . . . . Krypton (Chemical element)
KRA . . . . Kickback Racket Act
KRA . . . . Kraftco Corp. (NYSE symbol)
KRB . . . . Kansas River Basin
KRB . . . . Krebs-Ringer Bicarbonate (Buffer solution)
KRC . . . . Knight of the Red Cross
KRC . . . . Kodak Reflex Camera
KRD . . . . King's Remembrance's Department (British)
KRE . . . . Knight of the Red Eagle
KREEP . . . . . . Potassium (Chemical symbol: K), Rare-Earth Elements, and Phosphorus (Acronym used to describe crust material brought from the moon by astronauts)
KRF . . . . Kathode Ray Furnace
KRF . . . . Knowledge of Results Feedback
KRI . . . . King's Royal Irish (Military unit) (British)
KRL . . . . Kathode Ray Lamp
KRL . . . . Kirckhoff Radiation Law
KRM . . . . Klein-Rydberg Method
KRO . . . . Kathode Ray Oscilloscope
KRO . . . . Katholieke Radio-Omroep (Netherlands)
KRP . . . . Kodak Relief Plate
KRQ . . . . Kentucky Romance Quarterly
KRR . . . . Kansai Research Reactor (Japan)
KRR . . . . The King's Royal Rifles (British Army Regiment)
KRRC . . . . . . The King's Royal Rifle Corps (British)

KRS	Kinematograph Renter's Society
KRT	Cathode-Ray Tube
KRTO	Kathode Ray Tube Oscillograph
KRTS	Kathode Ray Tube Shield
KRTT	Kathode Ray Tube Tester
KRU	Krueger Brewing Company (NYSE symbol)
KS	Kansas
KS	Katoptric System
KS	Keep Type Standing (Printing)
KS	Ketosteroid
KS	Key Seated (Freight)
KS	Kidney Sac
KS	King's Scholar (British)
KS	Kipling Society
KS	Kraemer System
KS	Kurze Sicht (Short Sight) (Germany)
KSA	Kite-Supported Antenna
KSA	Knight of Saint Anne
KSA	Kwajalein Standard Atmosphere
KSAA	Keats-Shelley Association of America
KSB	Kradschuetzen-Bataillon (Motorcycle Battalion) (German military – World War II)
KSC	Kennedy Space Center (NASA)
KSC	Kentucky State College
KSC	Komunisticka Strana Ceskoslovenska
KSC	Korean Service Corps
KSC	Kress (S. H.) & Company (NYSE symbol) (Delisted)
ksf	Kips per Square Foot
KSF	Quaker State Oil Refining Corporation (NYSE symbol)
KSFUS	Korean Student Federation of the United States
KSG	Knight of St. Gregory
KSH	Knight of St. Hubert
KSI	Knight of the Order of the Star of India
KSJ	Knight of St. Januarius
KSK	Kappa Sigma Kappa (Fraternity)
KSKJ	American Slovenian Catholic Union of the USA
KSL	Keyboard Simulated Lateral Telling
KSL	Kinsel Drug Company (NYSE symbol)
KSLI	The King's Shropshire Light Infantry (British)
KSM	Katubsanan sa Mamumio (Philippine United Labor Congress)
KSM	Korean Service Medal
KSMMP	Kin Seeking Missing Military Personnel (Organization of parents with sons missing in action with purpose of supplementing US government search for missing personnel) (Post-World War II)
KSMU	Komunistycha Spilka Molodi Ukrainy
KSN	Kit Shortage Notice
KSP	Keyset Panel
KSP	Kodak Special Plate
KSP	KVP Sutherland Paper Company (NYSE symbol) (Delisted)
KSR	Keyboard Send and Receive
KSS	Kellogg Switchboard and Supply
KSS	Keying Switching Station
KSS	Knight of St. Sylvester
KSS	Korea Stamp Society
KSSBI	Konfederasi Serikat Serikat Buruh Islam (Confederation of Islamic Trade Unions of Indonesia)
KST	King-Seeley Thermos Company (NYSE symbol) (Delisted)
KSTC	Kansas State Teachers College
KStJ	Knight Commander, Order of St. John of Jerusalem (British)
KSTN	Kriegsstaerke-Nachweisung (Table of organization) (German military – World War II)
KSTR	Kema Suspension Test Reactor (Netherlands)
KSU	Kansas City Southern Industries, Inc. (NYSE symbol)
KSU	Kansas State University
KSU	Kent State University (Ohio)
KSU	Key Service Unit (Bell Laboratories)
KSV	Knight of St. Vladimir
KSW	Knight of St. Wladimir
KSY	King Seeley Corporation (NYSE symbol)
KT	Contract (Navy)
KT	Katy Industries, Inc. (Formerly, Missouri-Kansas-Texas R.R. Company, with Wall Street slang name of "Katy") (NYSE symbol)
KT	Kentucky & Tennessee Railway (AAR code)
kt	Kiloton (One thousand tons of TNT equivalent)
KT	Kinetic Theory
KT	Knight (Chess)
KT	Knight(s) Templar
KT	Knight of the Thistle (British)
KT	Potassium Titanate
KTA	Knitted Textile Association
KTA	Potassium Turbo-Alternator
KTB	Kriegstagebuch (War Diary) (German)
KTE	Kennedy-Thorndike Experiment
KTFR	Kodak Thin Film Resist
KTH	Kungliga Tekniska Hoegskolan (Royal Institute of Technology) (Stockholm)
KTIBF	Kibris Turk Ischi Birlikleri Federasyonu (Cyprus Turkish Trade Unions Federation)
KTL	Kai Ta Loipa (Et cetera)
KTL	Kuratorium fuer Technik in der Landwirtschaft
KTMS	Knapp Time Metaphor Scale
KTN	Potassium Tantalum Niobate
KTNF	Kodak Timing Negative Film
KTO	Kraus-Thomson Organization (Publishing)
KTR	Keyboard Typing Reperforator (Data processing)
KTS	Kelvin Temperature Scale
KTS	Key Telephone Systems
KTS	Kwajalein Test Site
KTTC	Keesler Technical Training Center
KTU	Key Telephone Unit
KTUC	Kenya Trades Union Congress
KTX	Keith Railway Equipment Company (AAR code)
KTZ	Khar'kovskii Traktornyi Zavod
KU	Kentucky Utilities Co. (NYSE symbol)
Ku	Kurchatovium (Chemical element)
KUB	Kidney, Ureter, Bladder (Medicine)
KUED	Kodak Unitized Engineering Data (Eastman Kodak)
KV	Kerr Vector (Electronics)
KV	Kidney Valve
kV	Kilovolt(s)
KV	Kinematic Viscosity
KV	Knights of Vartan
KV	Kongsberg Vaapenfabrikk (Norway)
KV	Kriegsverwendungsfaehig (Fit for active service) (German military – World War II)
kVA	Kilovolt-Ampere
kV-A	Kilovolt-Ampere
KVAB	Krankenversicherungsanstalt Berlin
kVAH	Kilovolt-Ampere Hour
kVAM	Kilovolt Ampere Meter
kvar	Kilovar
kVAr	Kilovolt-Ampere Reactive
kvarh	Kilovar-Hour
kVCP	Kilovolt Constant Potential
KVG	Keyed Video Generator
KVK	Kriegsverdienstkreuz (War Service Cross) (German military decoration – World War II)
kVM	Kilovolt Meter
KVP	Kasernierte Volkspolizei
kVP	Kilovolts Peak
KVP	Kodak Vacuum Probe
KVPD	Kasernierte Volkspolizei-Dienststelle
KVS	Kelvin-Varley Slide (Electronics)
KVW	Kansas City, Kaw Valley R. R., Inc. (AAR code)
KW	Kampfwagen (Tank) (German military – World War II)
KW	Katabatic Wind
KW	Kelsey-Hayes Company (NYSE symbol)
kW	Kilowatt(s)
KW	Korean War
KWAJ	Kwajalein Atoll (Army)
KWC	K-Band Wave-Guide Circulator
KWC	Kentucky Wesleyan College
kWe	Kilowatts of Electric Energy
KWE	Knight of the White Eagle
kWh	Kilowatt-Hour
kWhm	Kilowatt Hour Meter
kWhr	Kilowatt Hour
KWIC	Keyword in Context (A punched-card or computer-based indexing system)
KWIT	Keyword in Title
KWK	Kampfwagenkanone (Tank gun) (German military – World War II)
KWL	Kalt Wenig Loslich (Not Very Soluble Cold) (Germany)
KWLF	Kodak Wratten Light Filter
kWm	Kilowatt Meter
KWOC	Key Word Out of Context (Indexing)
KWOT	Key Word Out of Title (Indexing)
KWOT	Kilometer-Wave Orbiting Telescope (NASA)
kWr	Kilowatts Reactive
KWU	Kansas Wesleyan University
KWU	Kraftwerksunion (West Germany)
KWY	Key Way
KXC	Keleket X-Ray Corporation
KXF	Kodak X-Ray Film
KY	Kentucky

KYCH ...... Knights York Cross of Honour
KYD........ Kilo Yard
KYERI ...... Know Your Endorsers - Require Identification (Advice to businessmen and others who cash checks for the public)
KYR........ Kayser-Roth Corporation (NYSE symbol)

KYTOON .... Kite Balloon
KZ......... Konzentrationslager (Concentration Camp) (Initials also used in medicine to indicate a psychiatric syndrome found in surviving victims of the World War II camps)
KZO........ Koninklijke Zout-Organon, NV (Netherlands) (Later, AKZO)

L

L . . . . Azimuthal or Orbital Quantum Number Total
L . . . . Cellulose Acetate
L . . . . Cleared to Land (Aviation)
L . . . . Coefficient of Inductance
L . . . . Cold-weather aircraft with special equipment such as skis or extra
                    insulation (Designation for all US military aircraft)
L . . . . Difference of Latitude
L . . . . Drizzle (Weather reports)
L . . . . An El or elevated railway
L . . . . Equipped with Search Light (Suffix to plane designation) (Navy)
L . . . . Fifty (Roman numeral)
L . . . . Glider Aircraft (When first letter in Navy aircraft designation)
L . . . . Kinetic Potential (Symbol)
L . . . . Ladestreifen (Ammunition clip) (German military - World War II)
L . . . . Lady
L . . . . Lake (Maps and charts)
L . . . . Lambert (Unit of brightness)
L . . . . Lancers
L . . . . Land(ing)
L . . . . Landplane
L . . . . Large (Size designation for clothing, etc.)
L . . . . Lat (Monetary unit in Latvia)
L . . . . Late
L . . . . Latent Heat
L . . . . Latin
L . . . . Latitude
L . . . . Launch
L . . . . Law
L . . . . Lead Sheath
L . . . . Leaf (Bibliography)
L . . . . League
L . . . . Learner
L . . . . Leather
L . . . . Leave
L . . . . Left (Direction)
L . . . . Left (side of a stage) (A stage direction)
L . . . . Legal Division (Coast Guard)
L . . . . Legitimate
L . . . . Lempira (Monetary unit in Honduras)
L . . . . Length
L . . . . Lens
L . . . . Letter
L . . . . Leu (Monetary unit in Romania)
L . . . . Lev (Monetary unit in Bulgaria)
L . . . . Levo (Configuration in chemical structure)
l . . . . Levorotary (or Levorotatory) (Chemistry)
L . . . . Lewisite (Chemical warfare)
L . . . . Liaison (Airplane designation)
L . . . . Liber (Book)
L . . . . Liberal
L . . . . Libra (Pound)
L . . . . Licentiate
L . . . . Lift
L . . . . Ligament(um)
L . . . . Light
L . . . . Lightning
L . . . . Limen or Threshold (Psychology)
L . . . . Line
L . . . . Line Assembly
L . . . . Liner (Nautical)
L . . . . Link
L . . . . Linnaean
L . . . . Lip

L . . . . Liquid
L . . . . Lira(s) (Italian monetary unit)
L . . . . Listed (on a securities exchange)
L . . . . Listening Post (in symbol only)
L . . . . Lit
L . . . . Litas (Monetary unit in Lithuania)
l . . . . Liter (Metric measure of volume)
L . . . . Lithium Chloride
L . . . . Locator (Aviation)
L . . . . Loch
L . . . . Locus (Place)
L . . . . Lodge
L . . . . Logair (Air Force contract aircraft identification prefix)
L . . . . Logarithm, Logarithmic
L . . . . Long
L . . . . Long, Rolling Sea (Weather charts)
L . . . . Longacre (James B.) (Designer's mark, when appearing on US coins)
L . . . . Longitude
L . . . . Lord
L . . . . Lorentz Unit
L . . . . Lost (RADAR)
L . . . . Lost (Sports statistics)
L . . . . Low
L . . . . Lumen (Unit of light)
L . . . . Sinclair Oil Company (NYSE symbol) (Delisted)
L . . . . Single Acetate
L . . . . Timber (Lumber) (Vessel load line mark)
LA . . . . Fighter (Russian aircraft symbol)
LA . . . . Lag Amplifier
LA . . . . Land Agent (Ministry of Agriculture, Fisheries, and Food) (British)
LA . . . . Language Age (Score)
La . . . . Lanthanum (Chemical element)
LA . . . . Latin America
LA . . . . Launch Analyst (Aerospace)
LA . . . . Laureate in Arts
LA . . . . Lava (Maps and charts)
LA . . . . Law Agent
LA . . . . Lead Amplifier
LA . . . . Leading Aircraftsman
LA . . . . Left Angle
LA . . . . Left Ascension
LA . . . . Left Atrium (Anatomy)
LA . . . . Left Auricle (Anatomy)
LA . . . . Legislative Affairs
LA . . . . Legislative Assembly
LA . . . . Leschetizky Association
LA . . . . Letter of Activation (Military)
LA . . . . Library Association (British)
LA . . . . Licentiate in Arts
LA . . . . Lieutenant-at-Arms
LA . . . . Lighter than Air (Aircraft)
LA . . . . Lightning Arrester
LA . . . . Linear Assembly
LA . . . . Linguoaxial
LA . . . . Link Allotter
LA . . . . Link Analysis
LA . . . . Literate in Arts
LA . . . . Local Agent
LA . . . . Local Authority
LA . . . . Logarithmic Amplifier
LA . . . . Long-Acting (Pharmacy)
LA . . . . Longitudinal Acoustic
LA . . . . Los Alamos (New Mexico) Scientific Laboratory (AEC) (Also, LASL)

LA . . . . Los Angeles (California) (Slang)
LA . . . . Louisiana
LA . . . . Louisiana & Arkansas Railway Company (AAR code)
LA . . . . Low Altitude
LA . . . . Low Approach (Aviation)
LA . . . . Lower Arm
L/A . . . . Landing Account (Shipping)
L/A . . . . Letter of Authority
L/A . . . . Lloyd's Agent
L & A . . . . . . Light and Accommodation (Optometry)
L & A . . . . . . Louisiana & Arkansas Railway Company
LAA . . . . LASER Attenuator Assembly
LAA . . . . League of Advertising Agencies
LAA . . . . Library Association of Australia
LAA . . . . Life Insurance Advertisers Association
LAA . . . . Light Antiaircraft (Guns)
LAA . . . . Light Army Aircraft
LAA . . . . Lithuanian Alliance of America
LAA . . . . Los Alamos Area Office (AEC)
LAA . . . . Los Angeles Airways
LAA . . . . Low Altitude Attack
LAAD . . . . . Latin American Agribusiness Development Corporation
LAADS . . . . . Los Angeles Air Defense Sector (ADC)
LAADS . . . . . Low Altitude Air Defense (or Delivery) System
LAAF . . . . . . Libby Army Airfield
LAAFS . . . . . Los Angeles Air Force Station
LAAM . . . . . . l-Ali-alpha Acetylmethadol (Form of methadone)
LAAM . . . . . Light Anti-Air Missile
LAAPD . . . . . Los Angeles Air Procurement District
LAAR . . . . . . Liquid Air Accumulator Rocket
LAAS . . . . . . Laboratoire d' Automatique et de ses Applications Spatiales (France)
LAAS . . . . . . Los Angeles Air Service, Incorporated
LAAV . . . . . Light Airborne ASW (Antisubmarine Warfare) Vehicle
LAAW . . . . . Light Assault Anti-Tank Weapon
LAB . . . . Laboratory
LAB . . . . Laboratory for Applied Biophysics (MIT)
LAB . . . . Landsforeningen til Arbejdsløshedens Bekaempelse
LAB . . . . Lead Acid Battery
LAB . . . . Leave Authorization Balance (Air Force)
LAB . . . . Linear Alkylbenzene (Chemistry)
LAB . . . . Lloyd Aereo Boliviano (Bolivian airline)
LAB . . . . Los Angeles Branch (AEC)
LAB . . . . Low Altitude Bombing (Military)
LABA . . . . . . Laboratory Animal Breeders Association
LABE . . . . . . Lava Beds National Monument
LABEL . . . . . . Law Students Association for Buyers' Education in Labeling (Student legal action organization)
LABIL . . . . . Light Aircraft Binary Information Link
LABP . . . . . . Latin American Book Programs (Defunct)
LABP . . . . . . Lethal Aid for Bomber Penetration
LABPIE . . . . . Low Altitude Bombing Position Indicator Equipment
LABROC . . . . . Laboratory Rocket
LABS . . . . . . Low Altitude Bombing System (Air Force)
LAC . . . . LASER Amplifier Chain
LAC . . . . Launch Analyst's Console (Aerospace)
LAC . . . . Leading Aircraftman (Great Britain, Canada)
LAC . . . . Liberty Amendment Committee of the USA
LAC . . . . Limiting Admissible Concentration
LAC . . . . Linear Absorption Coefficient
LAC . . . . Lithuanian American Council
LAC . . . . Load Accumulator
LAC . . . . Local Agency Check
LAC . . . . Lockheed Aircraft Corporation
LAC . . . . Longitudinal Aerodynamic Characteristics
LAC . . . . Los Angeles College
LAC . . . . Lunar Aeronautical Chart (Air Force)
LAC . . . . Lunar Astronautical
LACA . . . . . . Life Agency Cashiers Association of the United States and Canada
LACA . . . . . . Low Altitude Control Area
LACAP . . . . . Latin American Cooperative Acquisitions Program (or Project)
LACAS . . . . . LASER Applications in Close Air Support (Air Force)
LACAS . . . . . Low-Altitude Close Air Support (Military)
LACATA . . . . . Laundry and Cleaners Allied Trades Association
LACBWR . . . . . LaCrosse Boiling Water Reactor (AEC)
LACC . . . . . . Los Angeles City College
LACE . . . . . . LASER Aerospace Communications Experiment
LACE . . . . . . Launch Angle Condition Evaluator
LACE . . . . . . Liquid Air Collection Engine
LACE . . . . . . Liquid Air Cycle Engine (Aerospace plane engine concept)
LACE . . . . . Local Automatic Circuit Exchange (Communications)
LACES . . . . . London Airport Cargo Electronic-Data-Processing Scheme

LACES . . . . . . Los Angeles Council for Engineering Societies
LACM . . . . . . Los Angeles County Museum
LACO . . . . . . Los Angeles College of Optometry
LACOM . . . . . Low-Altitude Contour Matching
LACONIQ . . . Laboratory Computer On-Line Inquiry
LACR . . . . . . Low Altitude Coverage RADAR
LACS . . . . . . Los Angeles Copyright Society
LACSA . . . . . Lineas Aereas Costarricenses, SA (Costa Rican airline)
LACSD . . . . . . Los Angeles County Sanitation District
LACT . . . . . . Lease Automatic Custody Transfer
LACUNY . . . . Library Association of the City University of New York
LACW . . . . . . Leading Aircraftswoman
LAD . . . . Lactic Acid Dehydrogenase
LAD . . . . Landing Assist Device (Aviation)
LAD . . . . Language Acquisition Device
LAD . . . . Large Area Display
LAD . . . . LASER Acoustic Delay
LAD . . . . LASER Air Defense
LAD . . . . Left Anterior Descending (Artery)
LAD . . . . Left Anterior Digestive (Gland)
LAD . . . . Library Administration Division (of ALA)
LAD . . . . Light Aid Detachment (British military)
LAD . . . . Light Air Detachment
LAD . . . . Location Aid Device
LAD . . . . Logical Analysis Device
LAD . . . . Lunar Atmosphere Detector
LADA . . . . . . Light Air Defense Artillery
LADAR . . . . . LASER Detection and Ranging
LADAR . . . . . LASER Doppler RADAR
LADD . . . . . . Low Altitude Drogue Delivery
LADE . . . . . . Lineas Aereas del Estada (Argentine Air Force airline)
LADH . . . . . . Liver Alcohol Dehydrogenase (Enzyme)
LADIZ . . . . . Leaving Air Defense Identification Zone
LADS . . . . . . LASER Air Defense System
LADS . . . . . . Limited Attack Defense System
LADS . . . . . . Low Altitude Detection System (Air Force)
LAE . . . . Lead Angle Error
LAE . . . . Left Arithmetic Element
LAEC . . . . . . Los Angeles Electronic Club
LAED . . . . . . Large Area Electronic Display
LAEDP . . . . . . Large Area Electronic Display Panel
LAEP . . . . . . Large Area Electronic Panel
LAF . . . . Limited Amplifier Filter
LAF . . . . Living Arts Foundation
LAFB . . . . . . Lincoln Air Force Base
LAFC . . . . . . Latin-American Forestry Commission
LAFO . . . . . . Los Angeles Foundation of Otology
LAFTA . . . . . Latin-American Free Trade Association
LAG . . . . L'Aiglon Apparel, Inc. (American Stock Exchange symbol)
LAGE . . . . . . Los Angeles Grain Exchange
LAGG . . . . . . Fighter (Russian aircraft symbol)
LAGS . . . . . . LASER-Activated Geodetic Satellite (AFCRL)
LAGS . . . . . . Linguistic Atlas of the Gulf States
LAH . . . . Licentiate of the Apothecaries' Hall (Dublin)
LAH . . . . Lithium Aluminum Hydride (Inorganic chemistry)
LAHIVE . . . . . Low Altitude/High Velocity Experiment
LAHS . . . . . . Low-Altitude, High-Speed
LAI . . . . Leaf Area Index
LAI . . . . Linee Aeree Italiane (Italian airline)
LAI . . . . Loaded Applicator Impedance
LAI . . . . Low Altitude Indicator
LAIC . . . . . . Lithuanian-American Information Center
LAINS . . . . . Low Altitude Inertial Navigation System (Air Force)
LAIR . . . . . . Letterman Army Institute of Research
LAIS . . . . . . Loan Accounting Information System (Agency for International Development)
LAJ . . . . Los Angeles Junction Railway Company (AAR code)
LAK . . . . Lightweight Antenna Kit
LAL . . . . Laboratoire de l' Accelerateur Lineaire (France)
LAL . . . . Langley Aeronautical Laboratory (Air Force)
LAL . . . . Loudspeaker Acoustical Labyrinth
LAL . . . . Lower Acceptance Level
LAL . . . . Lower Acceptance Limit
LALLL . . . . . Low Altitude Low Light Level
LALO . . . . . . Low Altitude Observation
LAM . . . . Laminate
LAM . . . . . . Latin-American Mission (Air Force)
LAM . . . . . . Load Accumulator With Magnitude
LAM . . . . . . London Academy of Music
LAM . . . . Loop Addition and Modification (Data processing)
LAM . . . . . . Master of Liberal Arts
LAMA . . . . . . Lead Air Materiel Area (Air Force)

LAMA....... Livestock Auction Markets Association
LAMA ...... Local Automatic Message Accounting (Telephone)
LAMAR ..... Linear Elastic Matrix Analysis Routine
LAMCO ..... Liberian American-Swedish Minerals Company
LAMCS...... Latin American Military Communications System
LAME ...... Lake Mead National Recreation Area
LAMP....... LASER and MASER Patents
LAMP....... Library Addition and Maintenance Program
LAMP....... Low Altitude Manned Penetrator
LAMP....... Lunar Analysis and Mapping Program
LAMPF ..... Los Alamos Meson Physics Faculty
LAMPP ..... Los Alamos Molten Plutonium Program (AEC)
LAMPRE ..... Los Alamos Molten Plutonium Reactor Experiment (AEC)
LAMPS ..... Light Airborne Multi-Purpose System (Navy)
LAMS ...... Land Acoustical Monitoring System (NASA)
LAMS ...... Load Alleviation and Mode Stabilization (Air Force)
LAMTS ..... Launcher Adapter Missile Test Set
LAN....... Linea Aerea Nacional de Chile (Chilean airline)
LAN....... Local Apparent Noon (Navigation)
LANA...... Lithuanian American National Alliance
LANABS .... Light-Attack Navigation and Bombing System
LANAC..... Laminar Air Navigation and Anticollision (Air Force)
LANCRA .... Landing Craft (Navy)
LANCRAB ... Landing Craft and Bases (Navy)
LANCRABEU .. Landing Craft and Bases, Europe (Navy)
LANCRABNAW .. Landing Craft and Bases, Northwest African Waters (World War II) (Navy)
LANDCENT ... Allied Land Forces Central Europe
LANDCRAB ... Landing Craft and Bases (Military)
LANDENMARK .. Allied Land Forces Denmark
LANDFOR .... Landing Force
LANDIS ..... Low Approach Navigation Director System (Aircraft landing aid) (Air Force)
LANDNORWAY .. Allied Land Forces Norway
LANDSOUTH .. Allied Land Forces Southern Europe
LANDSOUTHEAST .. Allied Land Forces Southeastern Europe
LANE ...... Linguistic Atlas of New England
LANFORASCU .. Landing Force Air Support Control Unit (Navy)
LANG ...... Language
LANICA ..... Lineas Aereas de Nicaragua, SA (Nicaraguan airline)
LANNET..... Large Artificial Nerve Net
LANS .... Load Alleviation and Stabilization
LANSA ..... Lineas Aereas Nacionales Consolidadas, SA
LANT....... Atlantic (Navy)
LANTCOM ... Atlantic Command (Military)
LANTFLT ... Atlantic Fleet
LANTRESFLT .. Atlantic Reserve Fleet
LAO....... Licensing Authorities Office
LAOAR...... Latin American Office of Aerospace Research (Air Force)
LAOD....... Los Angeles Ordnance District (Military)
LAOS....... Laymen's Overseas Service
LAP....... Large Area Panel
LAP....... Lattice Assessment Program (Civil Defense)
LAP....... Launch Analyst Panel (Aerospace)
LAP....... Left Atrial Pressure (Biology)
LAP....... Leucine Aminopeptidase (Biochemistry)
LAP....... List Assembly Programing (Data processing)
LAP....... Load, Assemble, Pack (Army)
LAP....... Location Audit Program (Navy)
LAP....... Loide Aereo Nacional, SA (Brazilian airline)
LAP....... Loudspeaker Acoustical Phase-Inverter
LAP....... Low Altitude Penetration
LAP....... Low Altitude Performance
LAP....... Lyophilized Anterior Pituitary (Endocrinology)
LAPA....... Leukocyte Alkaline Phosphatase Activity
LAPA....... Lightweight Aggregate Producers Association
LAPAM..... Low-Altitude Penetrating Attack Missile (Proposed)
LAPB ...... Laboratories' Applied Physiology Branch (Army)
LAPC ...... Los Angeles Pacific College
LAPD ...... Los Angeles Air Procurement District
LAPDOG..... Low-Altitude Pursuit Dive on Ground
LAPES....... Low Altitude Parachute Extraction System (Military)
LAPFO ...... Los Angeles Procurement Field Office
LAPL .... Lead Allowance Parts Lists
LAPRE ..... Los Alamos Power Reactor Experiment
LAPS ...... LASER Profile System
LAPSS...... LASER Airborne Photographic Scanning System (Navy)
LAR ...... Limit Address Register
LAR .... Liquid Air Rocket
LAR .... Local Acquisition RADAR
LAR .... Long-Range Aircraft Rocket

LAR .... Low Altitude Release
LAR .... Low-Angle Reentry (Aerospace)
LAR .... Low Aspect Ratio
LARA ...... Light Armed Reconnaissance Aircraft (Air Force)
LARA ...... Low-Altitude RADAR Altimeter (Air Force)
LARC ...... Langley Research Center (NASA)
LARC ...... Large Automatic Research Computer
LARC ...... Library Automation Research and Consulting
LARC ...... Libyan-American Reconstruction Commission
LARC ...... Lighter, Amphibious, Resupply Cargo (Vessel)
LARC ...... Lindheimer Astronomical Research Center (Northwestern University)
LARC ...... Livermore Atomic Research Computer
LARC ...... Loose Actors Revolving Company (for producing plays; members include actors George C. Scott and Rod Steiger)
LARCF ..... Lithuanian American Roman Catholic Federation
LARCT....... Last Radio Contact (Aviation)
LARDS...... Low Accuracy RADAR Data Transmission System
LARGOS..... LASER-Activated Reflecting Geodetic Optical Satellite
LARIAT ..... LASER RADAR Intelligence Acquisition Technology
LARS .... Laboratory for Agricultural Remote Sensing
LARS .... LASER Angular Rate Sensor
LARVA...... Low Altitude Research Vehicular Advancements
LAS .... Laboratories of Applied Sciences (University of Chicago)
LAS .... Laboratory of Atmospheric Sciences (National Science Foundation)
LAS .... Landing Approach Simulator
LAS .... Large Astronomical Satellite (ESRO)
LAS .... LASER Anti-Flash System
LAS .... Launch Area Supervisor
LAS .... Launch Auxiliary System
LAS .... Lebanese-American Society of Greater New York
LAS .... Light-Activated Switch
LAS .... Limited Assignment Status (Military)
LAS .... Linear Alkylate Sulfonate (Liquid detergent)
LAS .... Liturgical Arts Society
LAS .... Longitudinal Air Spring
LAS .... Low-Alloy Steel
LAS .... Lunar Attitude System
LAS .... Lutheran Academy for Scholarship
LASA ...... Large Aperture Seismic Array (Nuclear detection device)
LASA ...... Latin American Studies Association
LASAIL..... Land-Sea-Air Interaction Laboratory
LASAM..... LASER Semi-Active Missile
LASAS ..... Latin American Secretariat for Academic Services
LASCA ..... Large Area Solar Cell Array
LASCO ..... Latin American Science Cooperation Office
LASCODOCS .. Linguistic Analysis of Spanish Colonial Documents
LASCR ..... Light-Activated Silicon-Controlled Rectifier
LASD ...... Latin American Serial Documents
LASER....... Learning Achievement through Saturated Educational Resources
LASER ..... Light Amplification by Stimulated Emission of Radiation
LASH ...... LASER Antitank Semiactive Homing
LASH ...... Legislative Action on Smoking and Health
LASH ...... Lighter Aboard Ship (Barge-carrying ship)
LASIL .... Land and Sea Interaction Laboratory (Environmental Science Services Administration)
LASL .... Los Alamos (New Mexico) Scientific Laboratory
LASLA ..... Laboratoire d'Analyse Statistique des Langues Anciennes (Laboratory for the Statistical Analysis of Ancient Languages) (University of Liege, Belgium)
LASO .... Low Altitude Search Option (Search mode of the BOMARC guidance system)
LASP....... Laboratory for Atmospheric and Space Physics (University of Colorado)
LASP....... Low Altitude Space Platform
LASP....... Low Altitude Surveillance Platform
LASPAU ..... Latin American Scholarship Program of American Universities
LASR ...... Laboratories for Astrophysics and Space Research (University of Chicago)
LASRM ..... Low Altitude Short Range Missile
LASRM ..... Low Altitude Supersonic Research Missile (Air Force)
LASS ...... Light-Activated Silicon Switch
LASS ...... Lighter-than-Air Submarine Simulator
LASS ...... Line Amplifier and Super Sync Mixer
LASS ...... Lunar Applications of a Spent Stage (Aerospace)
LASSO ..... Landing and Approach System, Spiral-Oriented
LASSO ..... Light Aviation Special Support Operations
LASSO ..... Lunar Applications of a Spent Stage in Orbit (Aerospace)
LASTA ..... Light Attendant Station (Coast Guard)
LASV ...... Low-Altitude Supersonic Vehicle (Air Force)
LAT .... Language Aptitude Test (Military)
LAT .... Latitude
LAT .... Learning Ability Test (Military)
LAT .... Level Above Threshold

LAT	Linear Accelerator Tube
LAT	Linseed Association Terms (Shipping)
LAT	Local Apparent Time
LAT	Lockheed Air Terminal
LATAF	Logistics Activation Task Force (Air Force)
LATH	Laos and Thailand Military Assistance
LATS	Lightweight Antenna Terminal Seeker
LATS	Long-Acting Thyroid Stimulator
LATT	LASER Atmospheric Transmission Test
LAUD	League of Americans of Ukrainian Descent
LAUK	Library Association of the United Kingdom
LAUM	Linguistic Atlas of the Upper Midwest
LAUSC	Linguistic Atlas of the United States and Canada (1930)
LAV	Lifting Ascent Vehicle
LAV	Linea Aeropostal Venezolana (Venezuelan airline)
LAVERS	Lake Vessel Reporting System
LAVM	Low Altitude Vulnerability Model (Aerospace)
LAVO	Lassen Volcanic National Park
LAW	League of American Wheelmen
LAW	Left Attack Wing (Women's lacrosse position)
LAW	Left-Handers Against the World
LAW	Legal Aid Warranty (Fund providing legal services in case of arrest)
LAW	Light Antiarmor Weapon
LAW	Light Antitank Weapon (Military)
LAW	Light Area Weapon
LAW	Light Assault Weapon
LAW	Local Air Warning
LAWASIA	Law Association for Asia and the Western Pacific
LAWDS	LORAN-Aided Weapons Delivery System
LAWRS	Limited Aviation Weather Reporting Station
LAWS	Leadership and World Society (An organization)
LAWSO	Lockheed Antisubmarine Warfare Systems Organization
LAWV	Lorain & West Virginia Railway Company (AAR code)
LAX	Los Angeles (California) (International airport symbol)
LB	Bachelor of Law
LB	Bachelor of Letters
LB	Bachelor of Literature
LB	Graduate in Letters
LB	Laboratory Bulletin
LB	Landing Barge(s)
LB	Left on Base (Baseball)
LB	Leg Bye (Cricket)
LB	Letter Box
LB	Library Bulletin
LB	Library Bureau (of Sperry Rand Corporation)
LB	Lifeboat
LB	Light Bombardment (Air Force)
LB	Light Bomber (Air Force)
LB	Light Bracket
LB	Limited Base (Air Force)
LB	Line Buffer (Data processing)
LB	Linoleum Base (Technical drawings)
LB	Local Battery (Radio)
LB	Local Board
LB	Low Band
LB	Lower Bearing
LB	Photographic Laboratory Specialist(s) (Navy)
LB	Pound
L/B	Light Bomber
LBA	Linear-Bounded Automaton
LBA	Lutheran Benevolent Association
LBA	Luxembourg Brotherhood of America
LBAB	Lima Bean Advisory Board
LBAD	Lexington-Blue Grass Army Depot
LBAF	Line Width, Black-to-White-Ratio, Area, Fixation Point
LBAK	Lightweight Broadband Antenna Kit
LBB	Life Blower Bearing
LBB	Linear Ball Bushing
LBBP	Laboratory of Blood and Blood Products (Public Health Service)
LBBSB	Left Bundle Branch System Block (Cardiology)
LBC	Land Bank Commission
LBC	Light Barrier Control
LBC	Line Balance Converter
LBC	Logistical Base Command (Korea)
LBC	London Bankruptcy Court
LBC	Lummer-Brodhum Cube
LBCC	Long Beach City College (California)
LBCD	Left Border Cardiac Dullness (Cardiology)
LBCL	Louisville Behavior Check List (Psychology)
LBD	Left Border of Dullness (Cardiology)
LBD	Lifting Body Development

LBD	Little Black Dress (Women's fashions)
LBDQ	Leader Behavior Description Questionnaire (Psychology)
LBE	Landing Barge, Emergency Repair
LBEA	Lutheran Braille Evangelism Association
LBF	Lactobacillus bulgaricus Factor (Bacteriology)
LBF	Louis Braille Foundation for Blind Musicians
LBG	Left Buccal Ganglion
LBH	Length, Breadth, Height
LBH	Local Board of Health (British)
LBI	Leo Baeck Institute
LBI	Library Binding Institute
LBI	Licensed Beverage Industries
LBJ	Lady Bird Johnson (Mrs. Lyndon Baines Johnson)
LBJ	Long Binh Jail (Vietnam)
LBJ	Lyndon Baines Johnson
LBK	Landing Barge, Kitchen
LBL	Laminar Boundary Layer
LBLS	Laminar Boundary-Layer Separation
LBM	Load Buffer Memory (Data processing)
LB/M	Pounds Per Minute
LBNP	Lower Body Negative Pressure (Boots) (Space flight equipment)
LBO	Line Building Out
LBP	Length Between Perpendiculars (Technical drawings)
LBP	Leucine-Binding Protein (Biochemistry)
LBP	Light Beam Pickup
LBP	Low Back Pain
LBP	Low Blood Pressure
LBP	Personnel Landing Boat (Navy symbol)
LBR	Local Base Rescue (Air Force)
LBR	Lowville & Beaver River R. R. (AAR code)
LBRC	Loft Bomb Release Computer
LBRF	Lower Branchial Filament
LBS	Laminar Boundary-Layer Separation
LBS	Landing Barge, Support
LBS	Large Bulb Ship
LBS	LASER Beam Surgery
LBS	LASER Bombing System
LBS	Lecithin Bile State (Medicine)
LBS	Line Buffer System (Data processing)
LBSC	Long Beach State College (California)
LBSCR	London, Brighton, and South Coast Railway
LBT	Chemical Laboratory Technician (Navy)
LBT	Clinical Laboratory Technology (Navy)
LBT	L-Band Tetrode
LBT	L-Band Transmitter
LBT	Linear Beam Tube
LBT	Low Bandpass Transformer
LBU	Launcher Booster Unit
LBV	Landing Barge, Vehicle
LBW	Leg Before Wicket (Cricket)
LBWSYD	Long Beach Naval Shipyard
LBY	Liberty Fabrics of New York (American Stock Exchange symbol)
LC	Label Clause
LC	Lake Central Airlines
LC	Lancaster & Chester Railway Company (AAR code)
LC	Lance Corporal
LC	Landing Craft
LC	Last Card
LC	Late Commitment (Reason for missed intercept) (Military)
LC	Launch Complex
LC	Launch Conference (Aerospace)
LC	Launch Corridor (Aerospace)
LC	Launch Cost
LC	Launching Control (Military)
LC	Laureate of Arts
LC	Laureate of Letters
LC	Law Courts
LC	Lead Covered
LC	Least Count
LC	Left Center (Stage direction)
LC	Legitimate Child
LC	Lethal Concentration
LC	Letter Contract
LC	Letter of Credit
LC	Level Control
LC	Level Crossing
LC	Liaison-Cargo (Air Force)
LC	Liberal Conservative
LC	Liberty Corp. (NYSE symbol)
LC	Librarian of Congress
LC	Library of Congress

LC	Lightly Canceled
LC	Limited Coordinating
LC	Line-Carrying
LC	Line Collector
LC	Line of Communication
LC	Line Connection
LC	Line of Contact (Military)
LC	Link Circuit
LC	Liquid Capacity
LC	Liquid Chromatography
LC	Load Carrier
LC	Load Cell
LC	Locked Closed
LC	Loco Citato (At the Place Already Cited)
LC	Logic Corporation
LC	Lord Chamberlain (British)
LC	Lord Chancellor (British)
LC	Loud and Clear
LC	Low Carbon (content, as low carbon steel)
LC	Low Conditioners (Psychology)
LC	Lower Canada
LC	Lower Case (i.e., small letters) (Typesetting)
LC	Lower Cylinder
L/C	Inductance/Capacitance
L/C	Landing Craft
L/C	Launch Control (Aerospace)
L/C	Learning Curve
L/C	Letter Contract
L/C	Letter of Credit
L/C	Light Case
L/C	Single Acetate Single Cotton (Insulation)
L of C	Line of Communication (Military)
LCA	Lake Carriers' Association
LCA	Lake Central Airlines
LCA	Landing Craft, Assault
LCA	Launch Control Analyst
LCA	Launcher Control Area (Missile)
LCA	Leveling Control Amplifier
LCA	Library Club of America
LCA	Line Clearance Airdrome (Air Force)
LCA	Longitudinal Chromatic Aberration
LCA	Lussazione Congenita dell'Anca (Congenital Hip Dislocation) (Medicine)
LCA	Lutheran Collegiate Association
LCAF	Lutheran Church in America Foundation
LCAO	Linear Combination of Atomic Orbitals
LCATA	Laundry and Cleaners Allied Trades Association
LCAVAT	Landing Craft and Amphibious Vehicle Assignment Table
LCB	Launch Control Building (NASA)
LCB	Longitudinal Position of Center of Buoyancy
LCB	Lord Chief Baron (British)
LCBA	Loyal Christian Benefit Association (Formerly, Ladies' Catholic Benevolent Association)
LCBB	"Life Can Be Beautiful" (Old radio program; nicknamed "Elsie Beebee")
LCBWR	LaCrosse Boiling Water Reactor (AEC) (Also, LACBWR)
LCC	Amphibious Command Ship (Navy symbol)
LCC	Landing Control Center
LCC	Landing Craft, Control
LCC	Langley Complex Coordinator (NASA)
LCC	Launch Command and Control
LCC	Launch Control Center
LCC	Launch Control Console
LCC	Library of Congress Classification
LCC	Life Cycle Costs (DOD)
LCC	Local Communications Complex
LCC	Local Communications Console
LCC	Lockheed California Company
LCC	London Communications Committee (World War II)
LCC	London County Council(or)
LCCA	Load Current Contacting Aiding
LCCA	London Church Choir Association
LCCB	Local Configuration Control Board
LCCE	Lee County Central Electric R. R. (AAR code)
LCCR	Leadership Conference on Civil Rights
LCD	Launch Control Design
LCD	Least (or Lowest) Common Denominator
LCD	Lightweight Ceramic Dome
LCD	Liquid Crystal Digital (Battery-powered wristwatch)
LCD	Liquid Crystal Display
LCD	Lumped Constant Dispersion
LCDHWIU	Laundry, Cleaning and Dye House Workers International Union
LCDR	Lieutenant Commander

LCDR	London, Chatham, and Dover Railway
LCDTL	Load-Compensated Diode Transistor Logic (Data processing)
LCE	Landing Craft, Emergency Repair
LCE	Launch Complex Equipment
LCE	Launch Control Equipment
LCE	Launch Countdown Exercise
LCE	Load Circuit Efficiency
LCE	Lone Star Industries (Formerly, Lone Star Cement Corp.) (NYSE symbol)
LCEB	Launch Control Equipment Building
LCEOP	Landing Craft, Engine Overhaul Parties
LCF	Landing Craft, Flak
LCF	Launch Control Facility
LCF	Least Common Factor
LCF	Longitudinal Position of Center of Flotation
LC(FF)	Landing Craft, Flotilla Flagship
LC(FF)	Landing Craft, Infantry (Flotilla Flagship) (Navy symbol)
LCFLOLS	Laterally Compounded Fresnel Lens Optical Landing System
LCFLOTSPAC . .	Landing Craft, Flotilla, Pacific Fleet
LCG	Landing Craft, Gunboat (Navy)
LCG	Left Cerebral Ganglion
LCG	Liquid-Cooled Garment (Spacesuit)
LCG	Logistics Control Group (Air Materiel Command)
LCG	Longitudinal Position of Center of Gravity
LCG	Low-Cost Generator
LCGB	Letzeburger Chreschtliche Gewerkschaftsbond (Confederation of Christian Trade Unions of Luxembourg)
LCGF	Longitudinal Ciliated Groove of Filament
LCGIL	Libera Confederazione Generale Italiana dei Lavoratori (Free Italian General Confederation of Workers)
LCG(L)	Landing Craft, Gun (Large)
LCG(M)	Landing Craft, Gun (Medium)
LCGP	Landing Craft, Group
LCGS	Lead Computing Gun Sight
LCH	Launching Charging Header
L Ch	Licentiatus Chirurgiae (Licentiate in Surgery)
LCHP	Local Control Hydraulic Panel
LCHR	Launcher (Aerospace)
LCI	Labor Cost Index
LCI	Landing Craft, Infantry
LCI	Launcher Control Indicator (Military)
LCI	Livestock Conservation, Incorporated
LCI	Locus of Control Interview (Psychology)
LCI	Low Cost Inertial
LCIDIV	Landing Craft, Infantry, Division
LCIE	Laboratoire Central des Industries Electriques (France)
LCIFLOT	Landing Craft, Infantry, Flotilla
LCI(G)	Landing Craft, Infantry Gunboat
LCIGRP	Landing Craft, Infantry, Group
LCIL	Landing Craft Infantry, Large
LCILFLOT	Landing Craft Infantry, Large, Flotilla
LCI(M)	Landing Craft, Infantry (Mortar Ship)
LCI(R)	Landing Craft, Infantry (Rocket Ship)
LCJ	Lord Chief Justice (of England)
LCJC	Lower Columbia Junior College (Washington)
LCK	Landing Craft, Kitchen
LCK	Legion of Christ the King
LCL	Labor Congress of Liberia, Incorporated
LCL	Lambert Cosine Law
LCL	Leading Catholic Layman
LCL	Less-than-Carload Lots
LCL	Licentiate of Civil Law
LCL	Lifting Condensation Level (Air Force)
LCL	Light Center Length
LCL	Local
LCL	Lot-Car Load
LCL	Lower Control Limit (QCR)
LCLA	Lutheran Church Library Association
LCM	Lake Champlain & Moriah Rail Road Company (AAR code)
LCM	Land Combat Missile
LCM	Landing Craft, Mechanized
LCM	Large-Core Memory (Data processing)
LCM	Launch Crew Member
LCM	Lead Coated Metal (Technical drawings)
LCM	Least Common Multiple (Mathematics)
LCM	Left Costal Margin
LCM	Liquid Curing Medium
LCM	London City Mission
LCM	Lower of Cost or Market
LCM	Lowest Common Multiple
LCM	Lymphocytic Choriomeningitis (Pathology)
LCM6	Landing Craft, Mechanized, MKVI (Navy symbol)

LCM8 . . . . . . Landing Craft, Mechanized, MKVIII (Navy symbol)
LCMA . . . . . . Lutheran Campus Ministry Association
LCMA . . . . . . Lutheran Church Men of America
LCMS . . . . . . Launch Control and Monitoring System
LCMS . . . . . . Logistics Command Management System
LCMS . . . . . . Lutheran Church - Missouri Synod
LCMSO . . . . . Landing Craft Material Supply Officer
LCN . . . . La Cosa Nostra (Our Thing)
LCN . . . . Landing Craft, Navigation
LCN . . . . Load Classification Number
LCNC . . . . . . Local Cartage National Conference
LCNR . . . . . . Liquid Core Nuclear Rocket
LCNT . . . . . . Link Celestial Navigation Trainer
LCO . . . . Launching Control Office(r)
LCOC . . . . . . Launch Control Officer's Console
LCOC . . . . . . Lincoln Continental Owners Club
LCOCU . . . . . Landing Craft, Obstruction Clearance Unit
LCOP . . . . . . Launch Control Officer's Panel
LCOSS . . . . . . Lead Computing Optical Sighting System
LCP . . . . Landing Craft, Personnel
LCP . . . . Launch Control Panel
LCP . . . . Left Circular Polarization
LCP . . . . Legislative Council for Photogrammetry
LCP . . . . Licentiate of the College of Preceptors (British)
LCP . . . . Liquid Cyclone Process (for making high-protein edible cottonseed flour)
LCP . . . . Logistic Capability Plan (Military)
LCPA . . . . . . Lincoln Center for the Performing Arts
LCP-FY . . . . . Logistic Capability Plan - Fiscal Year (Navy)
LCPG . . . . . . Logic Clock Pulse Generator
LCP(L) . . . . . Landing Craft, Personnel (Large)
LCPL . . . . . . Landing Craft, Personnel (Navy symbol)
LCPL . . . . . . Landing Craft - Personnel/Logistics
LCP(M) . . . . . Landing Craft, Personnel (Medium)
LCP(N) . . . . . Landing Craft, Personnel (Nested)
LCP(P) . . . . . Landing Craft, Personnel (Plastic)
LCP(R) . . . . . Landing Craft, Personnel (Ramp)
LCPS . . . . . . Licentiate of the College of Physicians and Surgeons (British)
LCPS . . . . . . Lithuanian Catholic Press Society
LCP(SY) . . . . Landing Craft, Personnel (Survey)
LCQ . . . . Launch Crew Quarters
LCR . . . . Inductance Capacitance Resistance
LCR . . . . Landing Craft, Rubber
LCR . . . . Light Chopping Reticle
LCR . . . . Liquide Cephalo-Rachidien (Cerebrospinal Fluid) (French)
LCR . . . . Liquido Cefaloraquideo (Cerebrospinal Fluid) (Spanish)
LCR . . . . Logistic Change Report (Military)
LCR . . . . Lung Configuration Recorder
LCRA . . . . . . Lower Colorado River Authority
LCRE . . . . . . Lithium Cooled Reactor Experiment (AEC)
LCR(L) . . . . . Landing Craft, Rubber (Large)
LCRM . . . . . . Launch Control Room
LCR(R) . . . . . Landing Craft, Rubber (Rocket)
LCR(S) . . . . . Landing Craft, Rubber (Small)
LCRU . . . . . . Landing Craft, Recovery Unit
LCRU . . . . . . Lunar Communications Relay Unit (Apollo) (NASA)
LCRVR . . . . . Little Change in River Stage
LCS . . . . Land Combat System
LCS . . . . Landing Craft, Support
LCS . . . . LASER Communications System
LCS . . . . Lathe Control System
LCS . . . . Launch Control Sequence (or Simulator or Subsystem)
LCS . . . . Launch Control System
LCS . . . . Leveling Control System
LCS . . . . Liaison Call Sheet
LCS . . . . Lincoln Calibration Sphere
LCS . . . . Line Coding Storage
LCS . . . . Lithuanian Cultural Society
LCS . . . . Loudness Contour Selector
LCSA . . . . . . Lewis and Clark Society of America
LCSB . . . . . . Launch Control Support Building (Missiles)
LCSCU . . . . . Launch Coolant System Control Unit
LCSE . . . . . . LASER Communication Satellite Experiment (NASA)
LCSI . . . . Logistic Control Shipping Instruction
LCS(L) . . . . . Landing Craft, Support (Large)
LCS(M) . . . . . Landing Craft, Support (Medium)
LCSO . . . . . . Launch Complex Safety Officer
LCSO . . . . . . Local Communications Service Order
LCS(R) . . . . . Landing Craft, Support (Rocket)
LCSR . . . . . . Landing Craft, Swimmer Reconnaissance (Navy symbol)
LCSS . . . . . . Laboratorio Central del Servicio de Sismologia
LCSS . . . . . . Land Combat Support Systems

LCSS . . . . . . Launch Control and Sequencer System
LCS(S) . . . . . Landing Craft, Support (Small)
LCSSP . . . . . . Laboratory of Chemistry and Solid-State Physics (MIT)
LCSU . . . . . . Lao Civil Servants' Union
LCT . . . . Laboratoire Central de Telecommunications
LCT . . . . Landing Craft, Tank
LCT . . . . Laplace-Carson Transform(s) (Mathematics)
LCT . . . . Latest Closing Time
LCT . . . . Launch Control Trailer
LCT . . . . Life Component Tester
LCT . . . . Local Civil Time
LCT . . . . Long Calcined Ton (Bauxite, etc.)
LCTA . . . . . . London Corn Trade Association
LCT(A) . . . . . Landing Craft, Tank (Armored)
LCTD . . . . . . Located
LCTL . . . . . . Large Component Test Loop (AEC)
LCTMP . . . . . Little Change in Temperature (Meteorology)
LCTS . . . . . . LASER Coherence Techniques Section
LCTSU . . . . . Launch Control Transfer Switching Unit (Aerospace)
LCU . . . . Launch Control Unit
LCU . . . . Utility Landing Craft (Navy symbol)
LCV . . . . Landing Craft, Vehicle
LCV . . . . League of Conservation Voters
LCVM . . . . . . Log Conversion Voltmeter
LCVP . . . . . . Landing Craft, Vehicle and Personnel (Navy symbol)
LCW . . . . Lutheran Church Women
LCX . . . . Launch Complex
LD . . . . Decisions Lost (Boxing)
LD . . . . Doctor of Letters
LD . . . . Labor Department
LD . . . . Lady Day (In old books)
LD . . . . Lamp Driver
LD . . . . Lateral Drift
LD . . . . Laus Deo (Praise Be to God)
LD . . . . Left Defense
LD . . . . Lethal Dose (Pharmacology)
LD . . . . Level Detector
LD . . . . Level Discriminator
LD . . . . Lifeboat Deck
LD . . . . Light on Dark
LD . . . . Light-Dark (Cycles)
LD . . . . Light Difference (Difference between amounts of light perceptible to the two eyes) (Ophthalmology)
LD . . . . Limited Duty Officer (Navy)
LD . . . . Line of Departure (Military)
LD . . . . Line Driver
LD . . . . Line of Duty (Military)
LD . . . . Linear Decision
LD . . . . Linz and Donawetz (Furnace) (Metallurgy) (Named after two plant sites in Austria)
LD . . . . Liquid Drop
LD . . . . List of Drawings
LD . . . . Load
LD . . . . Local Delivery
LD . . . . Logic Driver
LD . . . . London Docks
LD . . . . Long Delay
LD . . . . Long Distance
LD . . . . Long Duration
LD . . . . Low Drag
LD . . . . Low Dutch (Philology)
LD . . . . Lower Deck
LD . . . . Lymphocyte Defined
L/D . . . . Length-Diameter
L/D . . . . Lift-Drag (Ratio)
L & D . . . . . . Loans and Discounts (Banking)
L & D . . . . . . Loss and Damage
LD50 . . . . Lethal Dose, Median (Lethal for 50% of inoculated group)
LDA . . . . Line Driving Amplifier
LDA . . . . Localizer Directional Aid (Aviation)
LDA . . . . Lord's Day Alliance of the United States
LDA . . . . Lowest Designated Assembly
LDA . . . . Lutheran Deaconess Association
LDAO . . . . . . Lauryldimethylamine Oxide (Detergent)
LDAPS . . . . . Long Duration Auxiliary Power System
LDB . . . . Light Distribution Box
LDB . . . . Load Determining Bolt
LDB . . . . Low Drag Bomb
LDBE . . . . . . London Diocesan Board of Education
LDBLC . . . . . Low Drag Boundary Layer Control (Military)
LDC . . . . Laboratory Data Control (Commercial firm)

LDC . . . . Latitude Data Computer
LDC . . . . Laundry and Dry Cleaning International Union
LDC . . . . Learning Disordered Children
LDC . . . . Less-Developed Countries
LDC . . . . Library Development Center (Columbia University)
LDC . . . . Light Direction Center (Military)
LDC . . . . Line Directional Coupler
LDC . . . . Local Defense Center
LDC . . . . Logistics Data Center (Army)
LDC . . . . Long Distance Communications
LDC . . . . Lower Dead Center
LDCO . . . . . . Laundry and Dry Cleaning Operations (Military)
LDD . . . . LASER Detector Diode
LDD . . . . . . Letter of Determination of Dependency
LDDS . . . . . . Low-Density Data System
LDE . . . . Lagrange Differential Equation
LDE . . . . Linear Differential Equations
LDE . . . . Long-Delayed Echo
LDF . . . . Local Defense Forces
LDF . . . . . . NAACP Legal Defense and Educational Fund
LD is FFD . . . . Line of Departure is Friendly Forward Disposition (Army)
LDG . . . . Landing
LDG . . . . Left Digestive Gland
LDG . . . . Linear Displacement Gauge
LDG . . . . Longs Drug Stores, Inc. (NYSE symbol)
LDGO . . . . . . Lamont-Doherty Geological Observatory (Formerly, LGO) (Columbia University)
L-DGO . . . . . . Lamont-Doherty Geological Observatory (Formerly, LGO) (Columbia University)
LDH . . . . Lactic Dehydrogenase (Medicine)
L d'H . . . . Legion d'Honneur (French decoration)
LDHM . . . . . . London Diocesan Home Mission (or Missionary)
LDI . . . . Landing Direction Indicator (Aviation)
LDI . . . . Life Detection Instrument
LDI . . . . Linear Displacement Indicator
LDI . . . . Load Indicator
LDIN . . . . . . Lead-In Lighting (or Lights) (Aviation)
L Div . . . . Licentiate in Divinity
LDK . . . . Lower Deck
LDL . . . . Language Description Language
LDL . . . . Learned Doctor of Laws
LDL . . . . Liquid Delay Line
LDL . . . . Low-Density Lipoprotein(s) (Biochemistry)
LDLE . . . . . . Light Duty Lathe Engine
LDM . . . . . . LASER Drilling Machine
LDM . . . . . . Last Day of the Month
LDM . . . . . . Licentiate of Dental Medicine
LDMI . . . . . . LASER Distance Measuring Instrument
LDMS . . . . . . LASER Distance Measuring System
LDMS . . . . . . Lunar Distance Measuring System
LDMX . . . . . . Local Digital Message Exchange
LDN . . . . Leeds & Northrop Co. (NYSE symbol)
LDNA . . . . . . Long Distance Navigation Aid
LDO . . . . Limited Duty Officer
LDO . . . . Linear Diophantine Object
LDP . . . . Laboratory Distribution Panel
LDP . . . . Langmuir Diffusion Pump (Electronics)
LDP . . . . Language Data Processing
LDP . . . . Leaflet Dispensing Pod
LDP . . . . Leasco Corp. (NYSE symbol)
LDP . . . . Liberal Democratic Party (Japan)
LDP . . . . Lorentz Doppler Profile (Electronics)
LDPD . . . . . . Liberal-Demokratische Partei Deutschlands (Liberal Democratic Party of Germany) (East Germany)
LDPE . . . . . . Low-Density Polyethylene (Plastic)
LDPN . . . . . . Low-Density Phenolic Nylon
LD is PPOS . . . Line of Departure is Present Positions (Army)
LDPS . . . . . . L-Band Digital Phase Shifter
LDR . . . . Leader
LDR . . . . Level Distribution Recorder
LDR . . . . Light Dependent Resistor
LDR . . . . Linear Dynamic Range
LDR . . . . Log Dose Response (Biochemical analysis)
LDR . . . . Lorentz Double Refraction
LDR . . . . Low Data Rate (RADAR)
LDRA . . . . . . Low Data Rate Auxiliary
LDRC . . . . . . Lumber Dealers Research Council
LDRI . . . . . . Low Data Rate Input (RADAR)
LDRS . . . . . . LASER Discrimination RADAR System
LDRSP . . . . . . Leadership
LDRY . . . . . . Laundry

LDS . . . . Langmuir Dark Space (Electronics)
LDS . . . . LASER Deep Space
LDS . . . . LASER Drilling System
LDS . . . . Latter-Day Saints
LDS . . . . Laus Deo Semper (Praise to God Always)
LDS . . . . Licentiate in Dental Surgery
LDS . . . . Linear Dynamic System
LDS . . . . Liquid, Diesel-Cycle, Supercharged
LDS . . . . Lunar Drill System
LDSA . . . . . . Logistics Doctrine and Systems Agency (Army)
LDSc . . . . . . Licentiate in Dental Science (British)
LDSI . . . . . . Licentiate in Dental Surgery (Ireland)
LDSJ . . . . . . Little Daughters of St. Joseph (Roman Catholic religious order)
LDSR . . . . . . League of Distilled Spirits Rectifiers (Defunct)
LDSRCS . . . . . Licentiate in Dental Surgery in the Royal College of Surgeons (British)
LDSS . . . . . . Lunar Deep Seismic Sounding (Aerospace)
LDT . . . . Lakefront Dock & R. R. Terminal (AAR code)
LDT . . . . LASER Discharge Tube
LDT . . . . Level Delay Time
LDT . . . . Library Development Team
LDT . . . . Linear Differential Transformer
LDT . . . . Local Daylight Saving Time
LDT . . . . London Dipole Theory
LDV . . . . Lactic Dehydrogenase Virus
LDV . . . . LASER Doppler Velocimeter
LDV . . . . Linear Differential Vector
LDV . . . . Local Defense Volunteers (Later called Home Guards) (British) (World War II)
LDVE . . . . . . Linear Differential Vector Equation
LDW . . . . Left Defense Wing (Women's lacrosse position)
LDX . . . . Long Distance Xerography (Communications facsimile system)
LE . . . . Labor Exchange
LE . . . . Launching Equipment
LE . . . . Law Enforcement
LE . . . . Lead Engineer
LE . . . . Leading Edge (Aerospace)
LE . . . . Left End
LE . . . . Left Extremity
LE . . . . Left Eye
LE . . . . Lifting Eye
LE . . . . Light Equipment
LE . . . . Low Efficiency
LE . . . . Low Explosive (Military)
LE . . . . Lunar Ephemeris
LE . . . . Lupus Erythematosus
LEA . . . . Law Enforcement Assistance Program
LEA . . . . Line Equalizing Amplifier
LEA . . . . Local Education Authority (British)
LEA . . . . Long Endurance Aircraft
LEA . . . . Loop Extension Amplifier
LEA . . . . Loss Executives Association
LEA . . . . Lutheran Education Association
LEAA . . . . . . Lace and Embroidery Association of America
LEAA . . . . . . Law Enforcement Assistance Act
LEAA . . . . . . Law Enforcement Assistance Administration (Justice Department)
LEA/BZ . . . . . Vessel Leased to Brazil
LEA/CH . . . . . Vessel Leased to China
LEAD . . . . . . Law Students Exposing Advertising Deception (Student legal action organization)
LEAD . . . . . . Letterkenny Army Depot
LEADER . . . . . Lehigh Automatic Device for Efficient Retrieval (Data processing)
LEA/EC . . . . . Vessel Leased to Ecuador
LEA/FR . . . . . Vessel Leased to France
LEA/GR . . . . . Vessel Leased to Greece
LEAM . . . . . . Lunar Ejecta and Micrometeorites (NASA)
LEA/MX . . . . . Vessel Leased to Mexico
LEA/NE . . . . . Vessel Leased to Netherlands
LEA/NO . . . . . Vessel Leased to Norway
LEAP . . . . . . Labor Education Advance Program
LEAP . . . . . . Language for Expressing Associative Procedures (Data processing)
LEAP . . . . . . Leadership and Education for Advancement of Phoenix (Arizona)
LEAP . . . . . . Leading Edge Airborne PANAR
LEAP . . . . . . Lift-off Elevation and Azimuth Programmer
LEAP . . . . . . Lockheed Electronics Assembly Program
LEAP . . . . . . Lower Eastside Action Project (New York City)
LEAP . . . . . . Lunar Escape Ambulance Pack
LEA/PA . . . . . Vessel Leased to Panama
LEA/PE . . . . . Vessel Leased to Peru
LEA/PG . . . . . Vessel Leased to Paraguay
LEAPS . . . . . . Local Exchange Area Planning Simulation (Bell Laboratories)
LEAR . . . . . . Logistics Evaluation and Review

LEA/RU ...... Vessel Leased to Russia
LEAS .... Local Education Agencies
LEAS .... Lower Echelon Automatic Switchboard
LEA/UK ..... Vessel Leased to United Kingdom
LEA/UR ..... Vessel Leased to Uruguay
LEAVERATS ... Leave Rations
LEB .... London Electricity Board
LEB .... Lower Equipment Bay (Apollo) (NASA)
LEC .... Lake Erie College (Ohio)
LEC .... Livestock Equipment Council
LEC .... Local Employment Committee (Department of Employment) (British)
LEC .... Local Engineering Change (DOD)
LEC .... Lockheed Electronic Company
LEC .... Lumped Element Circulator
LEC .... Lunar Equipment Conveyor (Aerospace)
LECA ...... Lehman Caves National Monument
LECE .... Ligue Europeenne de Cooperation Economique (European League for
               Economic Cooperation)
LECS ...... Launching Equipment Checkout Set
LED .... Large Electronic Display
LED .... Law Enforcement Division (National Park Service)
LED .... Library Education Division (of American Library Association)
LED .... Light-Emitting Diode
LED .... Low-Energy Diffraction
LEDC ...... League for Emotionally Disturbed Children
LEDC ...... Local Economic Development Corporation
LEDC ...... Logistics Executive Development Course (Army)
LEDP ...... Large Electronic Display Panel
LEDT ...... Limited Entry Decision Table
LEE .... Lake Erie & Eastern R. R. (AAR code)
LEED ...... LASER-Energized Explosive Device
LEED ...... Low-Energy Electron Diffraction
LEEP ...... Law Enforcement Education Program (Department of Justice)
LEEP ...... Library Education Experimental Project (Syracuse University)
LEF .... Lake Erie, Franklin & Clarion R. R. (AAR code)
LEF .... Life Extension Foundation
LEF .... Lincoln Educational Foundation
LEF .... Linear-Energy Spectrophotofluorometry
LEF .... Liquid Expanded Film
LEFC ...... L-Band Electronic Frequency Converter
LEFM ...... Linear-Elastic Fracture Mechanics
LEFW ...... Lake Erie & Fort Wayne R. R. (AAR code)
LEG .... Legal
LEG .... Logistical Expediting Group
LEG .... Logistics Evaluation Group
LEGAL ..... League for Equitable General Aviation Legislation
LEGM ...... Low-Energy Gamma Monitor
LEG (UN) .... Department of Legal Affairs of the United Nations
LEH .... Lehigh Valley Industries, Inc. (NYSE symbol)
LEI .... Life Expectancy Inventory
LEID .... Low-Energy Ion Detector
LEJ .... Longitudinal Expansion Joint (Technical drawings)
LEK .... LASER Experimental Package
LEKOTEK .... Leksaker, Bibliotek (Program providing meaningful toys for mentally
               disturbed children; operates on the same principle as a lending library)
               (Name formed from Swedish words for "playthings" and "library")
LEL .... Lens-End-Lamp
LEL .... Lower Explosive Limit (of fuel vapor)
LELTS ...... Lightweight Electronic Locating and Tracking System
LELU ...... Launch Enable Logic Unit
LEM .... Laboratory of Electro-Modeling (USSR)
LEM .... Lake Exploration Module (University of Wisconsin)
LEM .... LASER Energy Monitor
LEM .... Lehman Corporation (NYSE symbol)
LEM .... Logical End of Media
LEM .... Logistic Element Manager
LEM .... Lunar Excursion Module (Also, LM) (NASA)
LEMAC ..... Leading Edge Mean Aerodynamic Chord
LEMAR ..... Legalize Marijuana (Acronym is used for name of an organization)
LEMDE ..... Lunar Excursion Module Descent Engine
LEML & AIA.. Locomotive Engineers Mutual Life and Accident Insurance Association
LEMRAS ..... Law Enforcement Manpower Resources Allocation (IBM program product)
LEMSIP ..... Laboratory for Experimental Medicine and Surgery in Primates
LEN .... Lake Erie & Northern Railway Company (AAR code)
LEN .... Linear Electrical Network
LEND ...... Lockheed Engineers for National Deployment
LEO .... Librating Equidistant Observer
LEO .... Low Earth Orbiting (Satellite)
LEO .... Lyon's Electronic Office
LEP .... Laboratoire d'Electronique de Physique (France)
LEP .... Large Electronic Panel

LEP .... Least Energy Principle
LEP .... Library of Exact Philosophy
LEP .... Lowest Effective Power
LEPEDEA ..... Low Energy Proton Electron Differential Energy Analyzer (NASA)
LEPI .... Litton Educational Publishing, Incorporated
LEPMA ..... Lithographic Engravers and Plate Makers Association
LEPOR ...... Long-Range and Expanded Oceanic Research
LEPR ...... LASER Electron Paramagnetic Resonance
LEPS ...... Launch Escape Propulsion System
LEPS ...... London-Eyring-Polanyi-Sato (Potential surfaces - chemical reactions)
LEPT ...... Long-Endurance Patrolling Torpedo
LEPW ...... Longitudinal Electric Pressure Wave
LER .... Launcher Equipment Room (Missiles)
LER .... Lerner Stores Corporation (American Stock Exchange symbol)
LER .... London Electric Railway
LERK ...... LASER Experimental Research Kit
LES .... Launch Enabling System
LES .... Launch Escape System (Apollo) (NASA)
LES .... Licensing Executives Society
LES .... Lilliput Edison Screw
LES .... Lincoln Experimental Satellites (Lincoln Laboratory, MIT)
LES .... Local Engineering Specifications (DOD)
LES .... Local Excitatory State
LES .... Loop Error Signal
LES .... Low-Energy Sputter
LES .... Lunar Escape System (NASA)
LES .... Support Landing Boat (Navy symbol)
LESA ...... Lake Erie Steam Association
LESA ...... Lunar Exploration System for Apollo
LESA ...... Lunar Extended Stay, Apollo (NASA)
LESC ...... Lunar-Environment Sample Container (Apollo) (NASA)
LESL ...... Law Enforcement Standards Laboratory (Law Enforcement Assistance
               Administration)
LESS ...... Least Cost Estimating and Scheduling
LESS ...... Lunar Escape System Simulator (NASA)
LET .... Laboratory of Electromagnetic Theory
LET .... Launch Escape Tower
LET .... Leading Edge Tracker
LET .... Lincoln Experimental Terminal (NASA)
LET .... Linear Energy Transfer (Radiology)
LET .... Linearer Energiegtransfer
LET .... Live Environment Testing
LET .... Logical Equipment Table
LET .... Lunar Energy Transfer
Let D ...... Doctor of Letters
LE-TE ...... Leading Edge - Trailing Edge (Aerodynamics)
LETS ...... Law Enforcement Teletype (or Teletypewriter) Service
LETS ...... Leading Edge Tracker Seeker
LETS ...... Linear Energy Transfer System
LETS ...... Lunar Experiment Telemetry System
LEU .... Launch Enable Unit
LEU .... Leucine (Amino acid)
LEV .... Launch Escape Vehicle
LEV .... Leichtverwundet; Leichtverwundeter (Slightly wounded; minor casualty)
               (German military - World War II)
LEV .... Levitz Furniture Corp. (NYSE symbol)
LEV .... Lifting Entry Vehicle
LEV .... Logistics Entry Vehicle
LEV .... Lunar Excursion Vehicle
LEVA ...... Lunar Extravehicular Visor Assembly (Aerospace)
LEWP ...... Line Echo Wave Pattern
LEWU ...... Lanka Estate Workers' Union (Ceylon)
LEX .... Lambda Epsilon Chi (Acronym is taken from the Greek letters, but also
               represents Latin word for law, area of interest for the society's members)
LEX .... Land Exercise (Marine Corps)
LEY .... Liberal European Youth
LEZ .... Lunar Equatorial Zone (Army Map Service)
LF .... Fighter Aircraft Fitted with Engine Rated for Low-Altitude Performance
LF .... The Lancashire Fusiliers (British military)
LF .... Launch Facility
LF .... Ledger Folio
LF .... Left Field(er) (Baseball)
LF .... Left Foot
LF .... Left Forward (Football)
LF .... Left Front
LF .... Left Fullback (Soccer position)
LF .... Lettering Faded
LF .... Life Float
LF .... Lightface (Type)
LF .... Limit of Flocculation
LF .... Line Finder (Teletype)

LF . . . . Lineal Feet
LF . . . . Linear Filter
LF . . . . Linefeed
LF . . . . Linoleum Floor (Technical drawings)
LF . . . . Load Factor
LF . . . . Locally Funded
LF . . . . Lost on Foul (Boxing)
LF . . . . Low Frequency (Electronics)
LFA . . . . Leading (formerly, Large) Families of America
LFA . . . . Left Fronto-Anterior (Anatomy)
LFA . . . . Local Freight Agent
LFA . . . . Lutheran Fraternities of America
LFAR . . . . . . Last Frame Address Register
LFB . . . . Left Fullback (Football)
LFB . . . . Leverage Fund of Boston (NYSE symbol)
LFB . . . . Limited Frequency Band
LFB . . . . Low-Frequency Beacon
LFBR . . . . . . Liquid Fluidized Bed Reactor
LFBR-CX . . . . Liquid Fluidized Bed Reactor Critical Experiment
LFC . . . . L-Band Frequency Converter
LFC . . . . Lake Forest College (Illinois)
LFC . . . . Laminar Flow Control (Military)
LFC . . . . Level of Free Convection
LFC . . . . Logic Flow Chart
LFC . . . . Low-Frequency Correction
LFC . . . . Low-Frequency Current
LFC . . . . Lunar Farside Chart (Air Force)
LFD . . . . Latest Finish Date
LFD . . . . Least Fatal Dose
LFD . . . . Low-Frequency Decoy
LFD . . . . Low-Frequency Disturbance
LFD . . . . Lutheran Foundation for Religious Drama
LFDA . . . . . . Land and Facilities Development Administration (HUD)
LFE . . . . Brotherhood of Locomotive Firemen and Enginemen (AFL-CIO)
LFE . . . . LFE Corp. (Formerly, Laboratory for Electronics, Inc.) (NYSE symbol)
LFE . . . . Logarithmic Feedback Element (Data processing)
LFEB . . . . . . Launch Facility Equipment Building (Missiles)
LFEN . . . . . . Laboratorio de Fisica e Engenharia Nucleores (Portugal)
LFF . . . . Light Filter Factor
LFG . . . . Lead Free Glass
LFG . . . . Low-Frequency Generator
LFI . . . . Linear Function Interpolator
LFI . . . . Low-Frequency Inductor
LFILIE . . . . . Libera Federazione Italiana Lavoratori Industrie Estrattive (Free Italian Federation of Workers in Mining Industries)
LFINT . . . . . . Low-Frequency Intersection
LFJ . . . . Low-Frequency Jammer
LFL . . . . LASER Flash Lamp
LFL . . . . League for Liberty
LFL . . . . Linear Field Line
LFLPU . . . . . . Libyan Federation of Labor and Professional Unions
LFM . . . . Landing Force Manual (Navy)
LFM . . . . Launch First Motion
LFM . . . . Linear Feet Per Minute
LFM . . . . Low-Frequency Modulation
LFM . . . . Low-Powered Fan Marker
LFM . . . . Lower Figure of Merit
LFMA . . . . . . Laminated Foil Manufacturers' Association
LFMER . . . . . Lovelace Foundation for Medical Education and Research
LF/MF . . . . . . Low Frequency, Medium Frequency
LFML . . . . . . Little Flower Mission League
LFMS . . . . . . Laminated Ferrite Memory System
LFNGFT . . . . . Landing Force Naval Gunfire Team
LFNS . . . . . . Low Frequency Navigation System
LFO . . . . Low-Frequency Oscillator
LFP . . . . Late Flight Plan
LFP . . . . Left Fronto-Posterior (Anatomy)
LFP . . . . Livestock Feed Program
LFPL . . . . . . Lewis Flight Propulsion Laboratory (NASA)
LFPS . . . . . . Licentiate of the Faculty of Physicians and Surgeons (Glasgow)
LFQ . . . . Light Foot Quantizer
LFR . . . . Inshore Fire Support Ship (Navy symbol)
LFR . . . . Low Flux Reactor
LFR . . . . Low/Medium Frequency Radio Range
LFRA . . . . . . League of Federal Recreation Associations
LFRAP . . . . . . Long Feeder Route Analysis Program (Bell System)
LFRC . . . . . . Latex Foam Rubber Council
LFRD . . . . . . Lot Fraction Reliability Deviation (Quality control)
LFS . . . . Amphibious Fire Support Ship (Navy symbol)
LFS . . . . Landing Force Support Ship (Navy)
LFS . . . . Launch Facility Simulator

LFS . . . . Liquid Flow System
LFS . . . . Logic Fault Simulator
LFS . . . . Logistics/Ferry Station
LFS . . . . Loop Feedback Signal
LFSA . . . . . . Landesverband Freier Schweizer Arbeiter (Swiss Association of Autonomous Unions)
LFSC . . . . . . Louisville Fear Survey for Children (Psychology)
LFSMT/S . . . . . Liquid Fuel Systems Maintenance Technician/Specialist (Aerospace)
LFSS . . . . . . Landing Force Support Ship (Navy)
LFST . . . . . . Largest Feasible Steerable Telescope
LFSV . . . . . . Landing Force Support Vehicle
LFSW . . . . . . Landing Force Support Weapon
LFT . . . . Ladd-Franklin Theory
LFT . . . . LASER Flash Tube
LFT . . . . Late Finish Time
LFT . . . . Launch Facility Trainer
LFT . . . . Leap-Frog Test
LFT . . . . Linear Flash Tube
LFTU . . . . . . Landing Force Training Unit (Marine Corps)
LFU . . . . Lunar Flying Unit (NASA)
LFV . . . . Low-Frequency Vibration
LFV . . . . Lunar Flying Vehicle (NASA)
LFVO . . . . . . Library Foundation for Voluntary Organizations
LFZ . . . . Laminar Flow Zone
LG . . . . Laclede Gas Company (NYSE symbol)
LG . . . . Landing Gear (Aircraft)
LG . . . . Landing Ground (Navy)
LG . . . . Large Grain
LG . . . . Lateral Gastrocnemius
LG . . . . Left Guard (Football)
LG . . . . Leichtgeschuetz (Light gun for airborne operations) (German military – World War II)
LG . . . . Level Gage
LG . . . . Lewis Gun
LG . . . . Life Guards
LG . . . . Light Gun
LG . . . . Line Generator (Data processing)
LG . . . . Linguogingival
LG . . . . Liquid Gas
LG . . . . Loop Gain
LG . . . . Low German (Language, etc.)
LGA . . . . La Guardia Airport (New York) (Airport symbol)
LGA . . . . Light-Gun Amplifier
LGAF . . . . . . Light Ground Attack Fighter
LGAR . . . . . . Ladies of the Grand Army of the Republic
LGB . . . . Lateral Geniculate Body
LGB . . . . Local Government Board
LGC . . . . Lunar Gas Chromatograph
LGC . . . . Lunar Module Guidance Computer (NASA)
LGCA . . . . . . London Gregorian Choral Association
LGCP . . . . . . Lexical-Graphical Composer Printer (Photocomposition)
LGD . . . . Lambda Gamma Delta (Society)
LGD . . . . Leaderless Group Discussion
LGE . . . . Logic Gate Expander
LGE . . . . Lunar Geological Equipment (NASA)
LGG . . . . Light Gun-Pulse Generator
LGL . . . . Lynch Corporation (American Stock Exchange symbol)
LGM . . . . LASER Ground Mapper
LGM . . . . Little Green Men (British term for space signals)
LGM . . . . Lloyd's Gold Medal
LGMS . . . . . . LASER Ground Mapping System
LGN . . . . Lateral Geniculate Nucleus
LGN . . . . Line Gate Number (Data processing)
LGO . . . . Lamont Geological Observatory (Later, Lamont-Doherty) (Columbia University)
LGO . . . . Low Gravity Orbit
LGOC . . . . . . London General Omnibus Company
LGP . . . . Lummer-Gehreke Plate
LGPN . . . . . . International Leather Goods, Plastic and Novelty Workers' Union
LGR . . . . Low Greek
LGR . . . . Low Group Receiving Unit
LGS . . . . Landing Guidance System (Aerospace)
LGS . . . . Lega dei Giovani Somali (Somali Youth League)
LGS . . . . Lunar Geophysical Surface
LGS . . . . Lunar Gravity Simulator
LGT . . . . Liquid Gas Tank
LGT . . . . Low Group Transmitting Unit
LGTA . . . . . . Ligue Generale des Travaillois Angolais (General League of Angolan Workers in Exile)
LGTH . . . . . . Length
LGU . . . . Ladies Golf Union

LGV....... Lymphogranuloma Venereum (Medicine)
LGW....... Longines-Wittnauer Watch Company (NYSE symbol) (Delisted)
LGWF ..... Libyan General Workers' Federation
LH .... Labor Hour (In contract work)
LH .... Larval Heart
LH .... Lateral Hypothalamic (or Hypothalamus)
LH .... Left Halfback (Soccer and football position)
LH .... Left Hand
LH .... Legion of Honour
LH .... Light Horse (Cavalry)
LH .... Lighthouse (Maps and charts)
LH .... Liquid Hydrogen
LH .... Lower Half
LH .... Lower Hold (Shipping)
LH .... Lues Hereditaria (Medicine)
LH .... Luteinizing Hormone (Endocrinology)
LH2 .... Liquid Hydrogen
LHA .... Amphibious Assault Ship (Navy symbol)
LHA .... Ladies Hermitage Association
LHA .... Landing Helicopter Assault (Ship) (Navy)
LHA .... Lateral Hypothalamic Area
LHA .... Lay Helpers' Association (British)
LHA .... Livestock Husbandry Adviser (Ministry of Agriculture, Fisheries, and
    Food) (British)
LHA ...... Local Hour Angle
LHA ...... Local Housing Authority
LHA ...... Lord High Admiral (British)
LHA .... Lower Half Assembly
LHB .... Bachelor of Humane Letters (or Bachelor of Literature, or Bachelor of
    the More Humane Letters)
LHB .... Left Halfback (Football)
LHB .... Lost Heart Beat (An attractive girl) (Slang)
LHC .... Lined Hollow Charge
LHC .... Liquid Hydrogen Container
LHC .... Lord High Chancellor (British)
LHC .... Loretto Heights College (Colorado)
LHC .... Lutheran Historical Conference
LHCP ...... Left Hand Circularly Polarized
LHD .... Doctor of Humane Letters (or Doctor of Humanities; Doctor of Letters;
    Doctor of Letters of Humanity; Doctor of Polite Literature; Doctor of
    the More Humane Letters)
LHD .... Load, Haul, Dump (Mining)
LHDC ...... Lateral Homing Depth Charge
LHDR ...... Left-Hand Drive
LHDS ...... LASER Hole Drilling System
LHE .... Lagrange-Helmholtz Equation
LHE .... Liquid Helium
LHF .... Lamp Heat Flux
LHFS ...... Ligand Hyperfine Structure
LHH .... Left-Hand Head
LH & HS .... Lutheran Hospitals and Homes Society
LHI....... Ligue Homeopathique Internationale (International Homeopathic League)
LHJ .... Ladies' Home Journal (A publication)
LHM .... Master of Humane Letters (or Master of the More Humane Letters)
LHOB ...... Longworth House Office Building
LHP .... Launcher Handling Procedure
LHR .... Left-Hand Rule
LHR .... Lehigh & Hudson River Railway Company (AAR code)
LHR .... Low Hybrid Resonance
L & HR ..... Lehigh and Hudson River Railway Company
LHRAA ..... Lutheran Human Relations Association of America
LHRF....... Luteinizing Hormone Releasing Factor
LH-RH/FSH-RH .. Luteinizing Hormone - Releasing Hormone / Follicle-Stimulating
    Hormone - Releasing Hormone
LHS .... Left-Hand Side
LHS .... Lunar Horizon Sensor (Aerospace)
LHSV ...... Liquid Hourly Space Velocity
LHT .... Lighthouse Tender (Navy symbol)
LHT .... Lord High Treasurer (British)
LHT .... Lunar Hand Tool (NASA)
LHTH ...... Left-Hand Thread
LHV .... Liquid Hydrogen Vessel
LHW....... Lees-Hromas-Webb (Theory)
LHW....... Left Half Word
LHW....... Lower High Water
LHWI ...... Lower High Water Interval
L Hy ...... Registered Hypnotist
LI .... Leitender Ingenieur (Chief engineer) (German military - World War II)
LI .... Letter of Intent
LI .... Level Indicator
LI .... Liberal Internationale (World Liberal Union)

LI .... License Inquiry (Police)
LI .... Licentiate of Instruction (or Licentiate Instructor)
LI .... Light Infantry
LI .... Ligue Internationale de la Representation Commerciale
LI. .... Line Item (Army)
LI .... Linguoincisal
LI .... Lions International
Li .... Lithium (Chemical element)
LI .... Lithographer (Navy rating)
LI .... Long Island R. R. (AAR code)
LI .... Loop of Intestine
LI .... Lot Indices
LI .... Low Intensity
L/I .... Labindustries (Commercial firm)
L/I .... Letter of Intent
L & I ...... Launch and Impact
LIA .... International Union of Life Insurance Agents
LIA .... LASER Industry Association
LIA .... Lead Industries Association
LIA .... Leather Industries of America
LIA .... Limiting Interval Availability
LIAA ...... Life Insurance Association of America
LIAB....... Life Insurance Adjustment Bureau
LIAC ...... Liberian International American Corporation (New York)
LIAC ...... Local Industry Advisory Committee (Civil Defense)
LIAMA ..... Life Insurance Agency Management Association
LIB........ Liberal
LIB........ Library
LIBA ...... Long Island Biological Association
LIBBA ..... Long Island Beach Buggy Association
LIBCO ..... Liberty Investors Benefit Insurance Company
LIBMAS .... Library Master File (FORTRAN program)
LIBNAT..... Library Network Analysis Theory
LIBO ...... Lincoln Boyhood National Memorial
LIBR....... Librarian
LIB (UN).... Headquarters Library of the United Nations
LIC .... Lacquer Insulating Compound
LIC .... LASER Image Converter
LIC .... Life Insurers Conference
LIC .... Linear Integrated Circuit
LIC .... Low Inertia Clutch
LICA ...... Land Improvement Contractors of America
LICALM .... LORAN Inertial Command Air-Launched Missile
LICCD...... Ligue Internationale Contre la Concurrence Deloyale (International
    League against Unfair Competition)
LICET ...... Library of Industrial and Commercial Education and Training
LiCl .... Lithium Chloride
LICM ...... Left Intercostal Margin (Anatomy)
Lic Med .... Licentiate in Medicine
LICOF ..... Land Lines Communications Facilities (Aviation)
LICOR ..... Lightning Correlation
LICP....... Lead Inventory Control Point
LICROSS.... League of International Red Cross Societies
LID .... Laboratory of Infectious Diseases (NIAID) (Became Laboratory of Viral
    Diseases)
LID .... LASER Intrusion Detector
LID .... Leadless Inverted Device
LID .... League for Industrial Democracy
LID .... Low-Iodine Diet (Medicine)
LIDAR ..... Light Detection and Ranging
LIDF....... Line Intermediate Distributing Frame
LIDH....... Ligue Internationale des Droits de l'Homme
LIDIA...... Liaison Internationale des Industries de l'Alimentation (International
    Liaison for the Food Industries)
LIDO ...... Logistics Inventory Disposition Order
LIDS....... LASER Illumination Detection System
LIDS....... Lithium Ion Drift Semiconductor
LIE .... Limited Information Estimation
LIE .... Line Islands Experiment (National Science Foundation)
LIED....... LASER Initiating Explosive Device
LIEF....... Launch Information Exchange Facility (NASA)
LIEFC...... Long Island Early Fliers Club
LIEN....... Ligue Internationale pour l'Education Nouvelle (World Education
    Fellowship)
LIEP....... LORAN Integrated Engineering Program
LIEPS ...... LORAN Integrated Engineering Program, Shed Light
LIETS ...... Land Integrated Equipment for Tactical Systems
LIEUT...... Lieutenant
LIF........ LASER Interference Filter
LIF .... Left Iliac Fossa (Medicine)
LiF........ Lithium Fluoride

LIF......... Lone Indian Fellowship
LIFE....... Language Improvement to Facilitate Education of Hearing-Impaired Children (A project of NEA)
LIFE....... LASER-Induced Fluorescence Emission
LIFE....... League for International Food Education
LIFE....... Lear Integrated Flight Equipment
LIFEL...... Limited Functional English Literacy
LIFESTA..... Lifeboat Station (Coast Guard)
LIFMOP..... Linearly Frequency-Modulated Pulse
LIFO....... Last In, First Out (Inventories last purchased are first sold) (Accounting)
LIFPL...... Ligue Internationale de Femmes pour la Paix et la Liberte (Women's International League for Peace and Freedom)
LIFSUM...... Airlift Summary Report (Air Force)
LIFT....... Link Intellectual Functions Tester
LIFT....... Logically Integrated FORTRAN Translator (UNIVAC)
LIG........ Leichte Infanteriegeschuetz (Light infantry howitzer) (German military - World War II)
LIHDC...... Low Income Housing Development Corporation (North Carolina)
LIHG....... Ligue Internationale de Hockey sur Glace (International Ice Hockey Federation)
LiI........ Lithium Iodide
LIIG....... Logistics Item Identification Guide (Military)
LIK........ Leichte Infanteriekolonne (Light infantry supply column) (German military - World War II)
LIL........ Lead-In-Light-System (Airport runway lighting)
LIL........ Lily-Tulip Cup Corporation (NYSE symbol) (Delisted)
LIL........ Long Island Lighting Co. (NYSE symbol)
LIL........ Lunar International Laboratory
LILA....... Ligue Internationale de la Librairie Ancienne (International League of Antiquarian Booksellers)
LILCO...... Long Island Lighting Company
LILOC..... Light Lyne Optical Correlation
LIM........ Laboratory Institute of Merchandising
LIM........ Leningrad Institute of Metals (USSR)
LIM........ Limit
LIM........ Linear Induction Motor (Magnetic rapid-transit car)
LIM........ Losing Inventory Manager (Army)
LIMB....... Liquid Metal Breeder (Reactor)
LIMDAT..... Limiting Date
LIMDIS..... Limited Distribution (Military security classification)
LIMDU...... Limited Duty (Navy)
LIMEA...... Low Iron Content Monoethanolamine
LIMIRIS..... LASER-Induced Modulation of Infrared In Silicon
LML........ Limited-Information Maximum Likelihood (Econometrics)
LIMP....... Lunar-Anchored Interplanetary Monitoring Platform (Aerospace)
LIMRF...... Life Insurance Medical Research Fund
LIMS....... Limb-Motion Sensor (System)
LIN........ Line Item Number (Army)
LIN........ Liquid Nitrogen
LINAC...... Linear (Electron) Accelerator
LINC....... Laboratory Instrument Computer (Medical analyzer)
LINC....... Learning Institute of North Carolina
LINCOS..... Lingua Cosmica (Artificial language consisting of radio signals of varying lengths and frequencies)
LINCOTT..... Liaison, Interface, Coupling, Technology Transfer
LINCS...... Language Information Network and Clearinghouse System
LINFT...... Linear Foot
LINS....... Lightweight Inertial Navigation System
LINS....... LORAN Inertial System
LIO........ Lionel Corporation (NYSE symbol)
LIOC....... Lighted Independent of Computer
LIODD...... LASER In-Flight Obstacle Detection Device
LIOH....... Lithium Hydroxide
LIP........ Latent Information Parameter
LIP........ Life Insurance Policy
LIP........ Local Initiatives Program (Canada)
LIP........ Lunar Impact Probe
LIPS....... Litton Industries Privacy System
LIQ........ Liquid
LIR........ Laboratory for Insulation Research (MIT)
LIR........ Limiting Interval Reliability
LIR........ Line Integral Refractometer
LIR........ Longitude Independent Reset
LIR........ Lost Item Replacement
LIRR....... Long Island Rail Road
LIS........ LARC Instruction Simulator
LIS........ LASER Illuminator System
LIS........ LASER Interferometer System
LIS........ Loop Input Signal
LIS........ Lutheran Immigration Service
LISA....... LARC Instruction Assembly

LISA....... Library and Information Science Abstracts
LISA....... Library Systems Analysis
LISA....... Life Insurance Society of America
LISA ...... Linear Systems Analysis
LISN ...... Line Impedance Stabilization Network
LISP ...... List Processor (Data processing)
LISST...... Library and Information Scholarship Today (A publication)
LIST....... Library and Information Science Today (Publication)
LISTS...... Library Information System Time-Sharing
LIT........ Lawrence Institute of Technology (Michigan)
LIT........ Light Interface Technology (Signal transmission)
LIT........ Light Intratheater Transport (Air Force)
LIT........ Light Ion Trough
LIT........ Litton Industries, Inc. (NYSE symbol)
LIT........ Location/Identification Transmitter (NASA)
LIT........ Low Impedance Transmission
Lit B ...... Bachelor of Letters (or Literature)
Lit D ...... Doctor of Letters (or Literature)
LITE....... Legal Information Through Electronics (Air Force)
LITFUND.... Fund for the Relief of Russian Writers and Scientists in Exile
LIT-LIT..... Committee on World Literacy and Christian Literature
Lit M ...... Master of Literature
LITR....... Low Intensity Test Reactor (ORNL)
Litt B ..... Bachelor of Letters (or Literature)
Litt D ..... Doctor of Humane Letters (or Humanities); Doctor of Letters (or Literature)
Litt L ..... Licentiate in Letters
Litt M ..... Master of Letters
LITVC...... Liquid Injection Thrust Vector Control
LIU .... Long Island University
LIU .... Wood, Wire and Metal Lathers International Union
LIUNA ..... Laborers' International Union of North America (AFL-CIO)
LIV .... Legislative Indexing Vocabulary
LIV .... Lunar and Interplanetary Vehicle
LIVC ...... Low Input Voltage Converter
LIVCR ..... Low Input Voltage Conversion and Regulation
LIVR ...... Low Input Voltage Regulation
LIW .... Loss in Weight
LIWB ...... Livermore Water Boiler
LJ .... Laufen Jahre (Current Year) (Germany)
LJ .... Libby, McNeill & Libby (NYSE symbol)
LJ .... Library Journal (Professional periodical)
LJ .... Life Jacket
LJ .... Line Judge (Football)
LJ .... Little Joe (Spacecraft) (NASA)
LJ .... Little John (Rocket) (Military)
LJ .... Lord Justice
LJA .... Lord Justice of Appeal
LJC .... Lamar Junior College (Colorado)
LJC .... Laredo Junior College (Texas)
LJC .... Lasell Junior College (Massachusetts)
LJC .... Lees Junior College (Kentucky)
LJC .... Loretto Junior College (Kentucky)
LJD .... Doctor of Letters of Journalism
LJEWU ..... Lanka Jatika Estate Workers' Union (Ceylon National Estate Workers' Union)
LJJ .... Lords Justices
LJL .... Little John Launcher (Missile)
LJLV ...... Little Joe Launch Vehicle (Missile)
LJP .... Liquid Junction Potential
LJR .... Lead Joint Runner
LJR .... Little John Rocket
LJ/SLJ ..... Library Journal/School Library Journal (A publication)
LK .... Lockheed Aircraft Corporation (NYSE symbol)
LKA .... Amphibious Cargo Ship (Navy symbol)
LKAA ...... Ladies Kennel Association of America
LKAB ...... Luossavaara-Kiirunavaara Aktiebolag
LKB .... Link-Belt Company (NYSE symbol) (Delisted)
LKF .... Linear Kalman Filter
LKK .... Lake Shore Mines, Ltd. (American Stock Exchange symbol)
LKP .... Lietuvos Komunistu Partija
LK & PRR ... Lahaina-Kaanapali & Pacific Railroad (Hawaii)
LKQCP...... Licentiate of the King's and Queen's College of Physicians (Ireland)
LKRT ...... Loyal Knights of the Round Table
LKS .... Liver, Kidney, Spleen (Medicine)
LKS .... Logan-Keck-Stickney (Method)
LKS .... Lucky Stores, Inc. (NYSE symbol)
LKSMB ..... Leninski Komunistychny Saiuz Moladzi Belarusi
LL .... Land Locomotion Laboratory (Army)
LL .... Landline (Aviation)
LL .... Large Letter
LL .... Late Latin (Language)

LL	Lateral Lip
LL	Laymen's League
LL	Lease-Lend (Bill) (World War II)
LL	Leased Line (Private telephone or Teletype line)
LL	Leaves (Bibliography)
LL	Legislative Liaison
LL	Lending Library
LL	Library Literature (A serial index)
LL	Light Line (Military)
LL	Light Load
LL	Light Lock
LL	Limited Liability (Finance)
LL	Limiting Level
LL	Lincoln Laboratory (MIT)
LL	Lincoln Library of Essential Information
LL	Lines (as in a book)
LL	Liquor Law
LL	Live Load
LL	Loco Laudato (In the Place Cited)
LL	Loftleidir H. F. (Icelandic Airlines)
LL	Loose Leaf
LL	Lord Lieutenant
LL	Lorillard (P.) Company (NYSE symbol) (Delisted)
LL	Loudness Level
LL	Low Latin (Language)
LL	Low Level
LL	Lower Left
LL	Lower Leg
LL	Lower Lid (Ophthalmology)
LL	Lower Limb (Lower edge of sun, moon, etc.) (Navigation)
LL	Lower Limen (Psychology)
LL	Lower Limit
L/L	Library Labels (Antiquarian book trade)
L/L	Lower Limit
L & L	Lewd and Lascivious
L es L	Licencie es Lettres
LLA	Lady Licentiate of Arts (Scotland)
LLA	Lend-Lease Administration (Defunct)
LLA	Luther League of America
LLAMA	Low-Level Acceleration Measurement Apparatus
LLAT	Lawrence Lowery Apperception Test
LLB	Bachelor of Law(s)
LLB	Little League Baseball
LLBA	Language and Language Behavior Abstracts
LLBBMA	Loose Leaf and Blank Book Manufacturers Association
LLBCD	Left Lower Border of Cardiac Dullness (Cardiology)
LLC	Law Certificate
LLC	Liberty Loan Corporation (NYSE symbol)
LLC	Liquid Level Control
LLC	Liquid-Liquid Chromatography
LLC	Low Liquid Cutoff
LLC	Luneberg Lens Commutator
LLCO	Licentiate of the London College of Osteopathy
LLCS	Liquid Level Control Switch
LLD	Doctor of Law(s)
LLD	Lactobacillus lactis Dorner (Bacteriology)
LLD	LASER Light Detector
LLD	Launcher Load Dolly
LLDB	Luc-Luong Dac-Biet (Vietnamese Special Forces)
LLE	Left Lower Extremity (Medicine)
LLE	Liquid Liquid Extraction
LLE	Long Line Effect
LLEIS	Lower Level End Item Subdivision (Army)
LLF	Laubach Literacy Fund
LLFM	Land Line Frequency Modulation
LLFPB	Linear, Lumped, Finite, Passive, Bilateral
LLG	Luggage and Leather Goods Salesmen's Association of America
LLGMA	Luggage and Leather Goods Manufacturers of America
LLI	La Leche League International
LLI	Latitude and Longitude Indicator
LLI	Ligula Length Index
LLI	Liquid Level Indicator
LLI	Lord-Lieutenant of Ireland
LLIL	Long Lead Item List
LLJJ	Lords Justices
LLK	Louis Leakey - Korongo (Anthropological skull)
LLL	Land Locomotion Laboratory
LLL	Lawrence Livermore Laboratory (University of California)
LLL	Left Lower Lobe (of lung) (Medicine)
LLL	Licentiate in Laws
LLL	Long-Line Loiter (Aircraft)

LLL	Love's Labour's Lost (Shakespeare)
LLL	Low-Level Logic
LLL	Low Light Level
LLL	Lutheran Laymen's League
LLLO	Lend-Lease Liaison Office
LLLTV	Low Light-Level Television (Night vision device) (Air Force)
LLM	Load Line Method
LLM	Lunar Landing Module
LLM	Master of Law(s)
LLMA	Leavers Lace Manufacturers of America
LLM (CL)	Master of Laws in Comparative Law
LLM (Int L) . .	Master of Laws in International Law
LLN	League for Less Noise
LLP	Lambda Limiting Process
LLP	LASER Light Pump
LLP	Line Link Pulsing
LLP	Live Load Punch
LLP	Long Lead Part
LLP	Lunar Landing Program
LLP	Lyman Laboratory of Physics (Harvard)
LLPE	Labor's League for Political Education (AFL) (Later merged into Committee on Political Education [COPE] of AFL-CIO)
LLPI	Linen and Lace Paper Institute
LLPN	Lumped, Linear, Parametric Network
LLQ	Left Lower Quadrant (of abdomen) (Medicine)
LLR	Line of Least Resistance
LLR	Load Limiting Resistor
LLRC	Local Labor Relations Board (Japan)
LLRC	Luneberg Lens Rapid Commutator
LLRF	Lunar Landing Research Facility
LLRF	Lunar LASER Range Finder
LLRI	Low-Level-Run-In
LLRM	Low-Level Radio Modulator
LLRP	Long Lead Repair Part
LLRV	Lunar Landing Research Vehicle
LLS	LASER Light Source
LLS	LASER Line Scanner
LLS	Liquid Level Sensor
LLS	Lunar Landing Simulator
LLSS	Lunar Logistics System (OMSF)
LLSS	LASER Light Source Station
LLSS	Low Level Sounding System (for measuring weather conditions)
LLSV	Lunar Logistics System Vehicle (OMSF)
LLT	Long Island Lighting Company (NYSE symbol) (Later, LIL)
LLT	Long Lead Time
LLTI	Long Lead Time Items
LLTT	Landline Teletype
LLTTY	Landline Teletype (Military)
LLTV	Low Light-Level Television
LLTV	Lunar Landing Training Vehicle
LLU	Lending Library Unit
LLV	Lunar Landing Vehicle (NASA)
LLV	Lunar Logistics Vehicle (NASA)
LLVPG	Large Launch Vehicle Planning Group (NASA)
LLW	Lower Low Water
LLWI	Lower Low Water Interval
LLX	Louisiana Land and Exploration (NYSE symbol)
LLY	Eli Lilly and Co. (NYSE symbol)
LLYP	Long Leaf Yellow Pine (Lumber)
LM	Land Mine (Military)
LM	Launch Mount
LM	Legion of Merit
LM	Licentiate in Medicine
LM	Licentiate in Midwifery
LM	Liggett & Myers, Inc. (NYSE symbol)
LM	Light Metals
LM	Liquid Metals
LM	List of Material (DOD)
LM	Litchfield & Madison Railway Company (AAR code)
LM	Local Manufacture
LM	Locator, Middle (Aviation)
LM	Locus Monumenti (Place of the Monument)
LM	Long Metre (Music)
LM	Longitudinal Muscle (Anatomy)
LM	Lord Mayor
LM	Lower Motor (Neurology)
LM	Luftmine (Aerial mine) (German military - World War II)
LM	Lumen
LM	Lunar Module (Also, LEM) (NASA)
LM	Middle Latitude (Navigation)
L/M	Line Per Minute (Data processing)

L/M . . . . List of Materials
LMA . . . . Last Manufacturers Association
LMA . . . . League for Mutual Aid
LMA . . . . Lingerie Manufacturers Association
LMA . . . . Lunar Meteoroid Analyzer
LMA . . . . Lunar Module Adapter
LMAFS . . . . . . Lookout Mountain Air Force Station
LMAL . . . . . . Langley Memorial Aeronautical Laboratory
LM/ATM . . . . . Lunar Module Apollo Telescope Mount
LMB . . . . Linear Motion Bearing
LMBC . . . . . . Lady Margaret Boat Club (of St. John's College, Cambridge) (British)
LMC . . . . Large Magellanic Cloud
LMC . . . . LASER Mirror Coating
LMC . . . . Lime-Magnesium Carbonate
LMC . . . . Liquid Metal Cycle
LMC . . . . Logistics Management Center (Army)
LMC . . . . Lon Morris College (Texas)
LMC . . . . Louisville Municipal College (Kentucky)
LMC . . . . Low Middling Clause (Business and trade)
LMCN . . . . . . Launch Maintenance Conference Network (Aerospace)
LMCR . . . . . . Liquid Metal Cooled Reactor
LMD . . . . LASER Microwave Division (Army)
LMD . . . . Liquid Metal Detector
LMD . . . . Long Metre Double (Music)
LMD . . . . Louisiana Midland Railway Company (AAR code)
LMD . . . . Lunar Meteoroid Detector (NASA)
LMDA . . . . . . Lunar Meteoroid Detector-Analyzer (NASA)
LMDE . . . . . . Lunar Module Descent Engine (NASA)
LME . . . . Liquid Mercury Engine
LME . . . . London Metal Exchange
LMEC . . . . . . Liquid Metal Engineering Center (AEC)
LMED . . . . . . Light Military Electronics Department
LMEE . . . . . . Light Military Electronics Equipment
LMES . . . . . . Laboratory for Meteorology and Earth Sciences (NASA)
LMF . . . . Last Meal Furnished
LMF . . . . Low and Medium Frequency
LMFBR . . . . . Liquid Metal Fast Breeder Reactor (AEC)
LMFR . . . . . . Liquid Metal Fueled Reactor
LMFRE . . . . . Liquid Metal Fueled Reactor Experiment
lm/ft² . . . . . . Lumen Per Square Foot
LMG . . . . LASER Milling Gauge
LMG . . . . Light Machine Gun
LMG . . . . Liquid Methane Gas
LMH . . . . Lady Margaret Hall (Oxford University)
LMH . . . . Light Metal Hydride
LMH . . . . Lipid Mobilizing Hormone (Endocrinology)
LMI . . . . Lawn Mower Institute
LMI . . . . Liquid Mercury Isolator
LMI . . . . Loaded Motional Impedance
LMI . . . . Logistics Management Institute
LMIC . . . . . . Liberty Mutual Insurance Company
LMIC . . . . . . Liquid Metals Information Center (AEC)
LMIS . . . . . . Labor Market Information System (Department of Labor)
LML . . . . Leesona Moos Laboratory
LMLR . . . . . . Load Memory Lockout Register
LM/LRV . . . . . Lunar Module/Lunar Roving Vehicle
LMM . . . . Library Microfilm and Materials Company
LMM . . . . . . Lines per Millimeter
LMM . . . . . . Locator at Middle Marker (Aviation)
lm/m² . . . . . . Lumen Per Square Meter
LMMA . . . . . . Lutheran Medical Mission Association
LMMC . . . . . . Labor-Management Maritime Committee
LMMF . . . . . . Local Maintenance and Management of Facilities (Military)
LMN . . . . Lanthanum Magnesium Double Nitrate
LMN . . . . Load Matching Network
LMNA . . . . . . Label Manufacturers National Association
LMO . . . . LASER Master Oscillator
LMO . . . . Lens-Modulated Oscillator
LMO . . . . Linear Master Oscillator
LMOA . . . . . . Locomotive Maintenance Officers' Association
LMP . . . . Laminated Metal Part
LMP . . . . Last Menstrual Period (Medicine)
LMP . . . . Library Material Processed
LMP . . . . Light Metal Products
LMP . . . . Liquid Monopropellant
LMP . . . . Liquid Oxygen Maintenance Panel
LMP . . . . Literary Market Place (A publication)
LMP . . . . Longitudinal Muscles of Pinnule
LMP . . . . Low Melting Point
LMP . . . . Lunar Module Pilot (Apollo) (NASA)
LMPRT . . . . . Locally Most Powerful Rank Test (Statistics)

LMR . . . . Launch Monitor Room
LMR . . . . Light Modulation Recording
LMR . . . . Lowest Maximum Range
LMRA . . . . . . Labor-Management Relations Act
LMRDA . . . . . Labor-Management Reporting and Disclosure Act
LMRR . . . . . . Lunar Module Rendezvous RADAR (NASA)
LMRS . . . . . . Lockheed Maintenance Recording System
LMS . . . . Lamson & Sessions Co. (NYSE symbol)
LMS . . . . Land Mass Simulator
LMS . . . . LASER Mapping System
LMS . . . . LASER Mass Spectrometer
LMS . . . . LEM (Lunar Excursion Module) Mission Simulator
LMS . . . . Licentiate in Medicine and Surgery (British)
LMS . . . . Linear Measuring System
LMS . . . . Liquid Metal System
LMS . . . . Load Matching Switch
LMS . . . . London Missionary Society
LMS . . . . Lunar Measuring System
LMS . . . . Lutheran Mission Societies
LMSA . . . . . . Labor-Management Services Administration (Department of Labor)
LMSC . . . . . . Liquid Metals Safety Committee (AEC)
LMSC . . . . . . Lockheed Missiles Space Company
LMSD . . . . . . Lockheed Missile System Division (Lockheed Aircraft Corporation)
LMSG . . . . . . Low Magnetic Saturation Garnet
LMSI . . . . . . Association of Lithuanian Foresters in Exile
LMSS . . . . . . Lunar Mapping and Survey System
LMST . . . . . . Learning of Middle Size Task (Psychology)
LMT . . . . Launch Motor Test
LMT . . . . Length, Mass, Time (Physics)
LMT . . . . Limit
LMT . . . . Local Mean Time
LMT . . . . Log Mean Temperature
LMT . . . . Louisiana Midland Transport R. R. (AAR code)
LMTBR . . . . . Liquid Metal Thorium Breeder Reactor
LMTC . . . . . . Launcher Maintenance Trainer Course
LMTD . . . . . . Logarithmic Mean Temperature Difference
LMTDNS . . . . . Launch Environment, Mission, Type, Design Number and Series (Missiles)
LMU . . . . Lincoln Memorial University (Tennessee)
LMU . . . . Line Monitor Unit
LMVD . . . . . . Lower Mississippi Division (Army Engineers)
LMW . . . . LASER Micro-Welder
LMW . . . . Low Molecular Weight
lm/W . . . . . . Lumens Per Watt
LMWP . . . . . . Labor-Management Welfare-Pension (Reports) (Department of Labor)
LMZ . . . . Leningradskii Metallicheskii Zavod
LN . . . . Air Liban (Lebanese Air Lines)
LN . . . . Landwirtschaftliche Nutzflaeche
LN . . . . League of Nations
LN . . . . Liaison
LN . . . . Line
LN . . . . Lip Nerve
LN . . . . Liquid Nitrogen
LN . . . . Local National(s)
LN . . . . Logarithm (Natural)
LN . . . . Louisville & Nashville R.R. Company (NYSE symbol, delisted; AAR code)
LN . . . . Lymph Node
L & N . . . . . . Louisville and Nashville Railroad Company
L of N . . . . . . League of Nations
LNA . . . . Lithium Nitrate Ammoniate
LNA . . . . Lithographers National Association
LNA . . . . Low Noise Antenna
LNAC . . . . . . Limited National Agency Check
LNAC . . . . . . Louisville, New Albany & Corydon R. R. (AAR code)
LNAH . . . . . . League of Night Adoration in the Home
LNC . . . . Landscape Nursery Council
LNC . . . . Laymen's National Committee
LNC . . . . Lincoln National Corporation (NYSE symbol)
LNC . . . . Local Naval Commander
LNC . . . . Low Noise Cable
LNC . . . . Lymph Node Cell(s)
LNCH . . . . . . Launch (Aerospace)
LND . . . . Limiting Nose Dive (Aerospace)
LNDC . . . . . . Lesotho National Development Corporation
LNDIS . . . . . . Landing Intermediate Station (Aviation)
LNE . . . . Lehigh & New England R. R. (AAR code)
LNE . . . . Liquid Nitrogen Evaporator
L & NE . . . . . Lehigh and New England Railroad Company
LNER . . . . . . London and North-Eastern Railway
LNG . . . . Liquefied Natural Gas
LNLA . . . . . . Lithuanian National League of America

LNLI . . . . . . League for National Labor in Israel
LNMP . . . . . . Last Normal Menstrual Period
LNO . . . . Laona & Northern Railway (AAR code)
LNOC . . . . . . Libya National Oil Company
LNP . . . . Lehn & Fink Products Corporation (NYSE symbol) (Delisted)
LNP . . . . Liquid Nitrogen Processing
LNP . . . . Low Needle Position (on dial)
LNPIB . . . . . . Loch Ness Phenomena Investigation Bureau
LNR . . . . Leonard Refineries, Inc. (NYSE symbol) (Delisted)
LNR . . . . Low Noise Receiver
LNR . . . . Luftnachrichten-Regiment (Air forces signal regiment) (German military – World War II)
L & NRR . . . . Louisville & Nashville Railroad
LNS . . . . Laboratory for Nuclear Science (MIT)
LNS . . . . Land Navigation System
LNS . . . . LASER Night Sensor
LNS . . . . Liberation News Service
LNS . . . . Lioville-Neumann Series
LNS . . . . London Normal School
LNT . . . . Launch Network Test
LNTS . . . . . . Liquid Nitrogen Transfer System
LNTWA . . . . Low Noise Traveling Wave Amplifier
LNU . . . . League of Nations Union
LNV . . . . Lanvin-Parfums, Inc. (NYSE symbol) (Later, LCR)
LNW . . . . Louisiana & North West R. R. (AAR code)
LNWR . . . . . London and North-Western Railway
LNX . . . . Lenox, Inc. (NYSE symbol)
LNY . . . . Lane Bryant, Inc. (NYSE symbol)
LNYT . . . . . . League of New York Theatres
LO . . . . Landsorganisasjonen i Norge (Norwegian Federation of Trade Unions)
LO . . . . Landsorganisationen i Sverige (General Federation of Swedish Trade Unions)
LO . . . . Larval Operculum
LO . . . . Launch Operations (or Operator) (NASA)
LO . . . . Law Officer
LO . . . . Layout (Graphic arts)
LO . . . . Letter Orders
LO . . . . Liaison Office(r)
LO . . . . Licensed Officer (US Merchant Marine)
LO . . . . Lift Off (Aerospace)
LO . . . . Linguoocclusal
LO . . . . Local Oscillator (Electronics)
LO . . . . Locator, Outer (Aviation)
LO . . . . Lock-On
LO . . . . Locked Open (Technical drawings)
LO . . . . Locked Oscillator
LO . . . . Logical Operation
LO . . . . London Office
LO . . . . Longitudinal Optic
LO . . . . Low Oblique (Aerospace)
LO . . . . Lubricating Oil
LO . . . . Lubrication Order
LO . . . . Lunar Orbiter (Aerospace)
L/O . . . . Letter of Offer
L/O . . . . Lift-Off
LO₂ . . . . Liquid Oxygen
LOA . . . . . Leave of Absence
LOA . . . . Left Occiput Anterior (A fetal position) (Obstetrics)
LOA . . . . . . Length Over-All (Technical drawings)
LOA . . . . . . Light Observation Aircraft
LOAC . . . . . Low Accuracy
LOAN/A . . . . Vessels Loaned to Army (Navy)
LOAN/C . . . . Vessels Loaned to Coast Guard (Navy)
LOAN/M . . . . Vessels Loaned to Miscellaneous Activities (US Maritime Academy, etc.) (Navy)
LOAN/S . . . . Vessels Loaned to States (Navy)
LOAN/W . . . . Vessels Loaned to War Shipping Administration (Navy) (Terminated, 1946)
LOAP . . . . . . List of Applicable Publications (Air Force)
LOAS . . . . . . Liftoff Acquisition System
LOB . . . . Launch Operations Branch (NASA)
LOB . . . . Launch Operations Building (NASA)
LOB . . . . Left on Base (Baseball)
LOB . . . . Limited Operating Base
LOB . . . . Line of Balance
LOB . . . . List of Bidders
LOB . . . . Loyal Order of the Boar
LOBAR . . . . . Long Baseline RADAR
LOBSTER . . . Long-Term Ocean Bottom Settlement Test for Engineering Research (Navy project)
LOC . . . . Large Optical Cavity (LASER design)
LOC . . . . Launch Operations Center (NASA)
LOC . . . . Launch Operations Complex (AMR/PMR)

LOC . . . . Launch Operator's Console (Aerospace)
LOC . . . . Liaison Officer Coordinator (Air Force)
LOC . . . . Library of Congress
LOC . . . . Lincoln Owners Club
LOC . . . . Lines of Communication
LOC . . . . Location
LOC . . . . Logistic Operation Center (Military)
LOC . . . . Lord of Creation
LOCA . . . . . . Loss of Coolant Accident (AEC)
LOCATE . . . . . Library of Congress Automation Techniques Exchange
LOCATS . . . . . Lockheed Optical Communications and Tracking System
LOCC . . . . . . Launch Operations Control Center
LOCCOZO . . . Line of Communications Combat Zone (Military)
LOCI . . . . Ligue des Originaires de Cote d'Ivoire (League of Ivory Coast Natives)
LOCI . . . . . . Logarithmic Computing Instrument
LOCK . . . . . . Logistical Operational Control Key (Army)
LOCO . . . . . Long Core
LOCP . . . . . . Logistics Control Office, Pacific (Army)
LOCPURO . . . Local Purchase Order
LOCS . . . . . . Librascope Operations Control System
LOCTRACS . . . Lockheed Tracking and Control System
LOD . . . . Launch Operations Department
LOD . . . . Launch Operations Directorate (NASA)
LOD . . . . Line of Dance
LOD . . . . Line of Departure
LOD . . . . Line of Direction
LOD . . . . Line of Duty
LODC . . . . . . Local Defense District Craft
LODCS . . . . . Lunar Orbiter Data Conversion System
LODESTAR . . . Logically Organized Data, Entry, Storage, and Recording
LODI . . . . List of Deleted Items
LODOR . . . . . Loaded, Waiting Orders or Assignment (Navy)
LODP . . . . . . Lunar Orbiter Data Printer
LODUS . . . . . Low Data Rate UHF Satellite
LOE . . . . Louisiana Eastern R. R. (AAR code)
LOEAT . . . . . Lowest Temperature Exceeded for All Time (Meteorology)
LOEFM . . . . . Lowest Temperature Exceeded for the Month (Meteorology)
LOESE . . . . . Lowest Temperature Exceeded So Early (Meteorology)
LOF . . . . Lecherous Old Fool
LOF . . . . Libbey-Owens-Ford Glass Company (NYSE symbol)
LOF . . . . Line of Fire
LOF . . . . Line of Force
LOF . . . . Local Oscillator Filter
LOF . . . . Local Oscillator Frequency
LOF . . . . Lowest Observed Frequency
LOFAR . . . . . Low-Frequency Acquisition and Ranging
LOFAR . . . . . Low-Frequency Analysis and Recording
LOFT . . . . . . Loss of Flow Test Facility (AEC)
LOFT . . . . . . Loss of Fluid Test (Radioactivity)
LOFT . . . . . . Low-Frequency Telescope (NASA)
LOFTI . . . . . . Low-Frequency Trans-Ionospheric Satellite
LOG . . . . Legion of Guardsmen
LOG . . . . Logarithm
LOGACS . . . . Low-G Accelerometer Calibration System (Air Force)
LOGAIR . . . . . Logistics Airlift (Military)
LOGAIRNET . . Logistics Air Network (Air Force)
LOGALGOL . . Logical Algorithmic Language
LOGAN . . . . . Logical Language
LOGANDS . . . Logical Commands
LOGBALNET . . Logistics Ballistic Missile Network (Air Force)
LOGCOMD . . . Logistical Command
LOGEL . . . . . . Logic Generating Language (Data processing)
LOGEX . . . . . Logistical Exercise
LOGFOR . . . . . Logistics Force (Military)
LOGFTC . . . . . Logarithmic Fast Time Constant
LOGIC . . . . . . LASER Optical Guidance Integration Concept (Missile guidance)
LOGIC . . . . . . Level of Greatest Item Control (DOD)
LOGIPAC . . . . Logical Processor and Computer
LOGIT . . . . . . Logical Inference Tester (NASA)
LOGLAN . . . . Logical Language
LOGLAND . . . Logistics Support for Land Operations (DOD)
LOGLAND . . . Logistics Transport by Land (Military)
LOGMIS . . . . . Logistics Management Information System (Army)
LOGR . . . . . . Logistical Ratio
LOGRAM . . . . Logical Program
LOGSEA . . . . Logistics Transport by Sea (Military)
LOGSUP . . . . . Logistical Support (Army)
LOH . . . . Light Observation Helicopter (Air Force)
LOHAP . . . . . Light Observation Helicopter Avionics Package
LOI . . . . Letter of Instruction
LOI . . . . Letter of Interest

LOI . . . . Limit of Impurities
LOI . . . . Limiting Oxygen Index
LOI . . . . Line of Induction
LOI . . . . List of Items
LOI . . . . Lunar Orbit Insertion (Aerospace)
LOIUSA . . . . . Loyal Orange Institution of United States of America
LOL . . . . Length of Lead (Actual) (Technical drawings)
LOL . . . . Little Old Lady (Slang)
LOLA . . . . . . Light Observation Light-Armored Aircraft
LOLA . . . . . . Lunar Orbit and Landing Approach (Simulator)
LOLAS . . . . . Location of Launching Site (Army)
LOLEX . . . . . Low-Level Extraction (Military aviation)
LOLI . . . . . . Loyal Orange Ladies Institution
LOM . . . . . . LASER Optical Modulator
LOM . . . . . . Launch Operations Manager (NASA)
LOM . . . . . . Legion of Merit (Military award)
LOM . . . . . . Limitation of Movement
LOM . . . . . . List of Modifications
LOM . . . . . . Locator at Outer Marker (Aviation)
LOM . . . . . . Lomas & Nettleton Mortgage Investors (NYSE symbol)
LOM . . . . . . Low-Frequency Outer Marker
LOM . . . . . . Loyal Order of Moose
LOM . . . . . . Lunar Orbital Map (Air Force)
LOMA . . . . . Life Office Management Association
LOMS . . . . . . Library Organization and Management Section (Library Administration
       Division of ALA)
LON . . . . Line of Nodes
LON . . . . Londontown Manufacturing Co. (NYSE symbol)
LONG . . . . . . Longitude
LONGV . . . . . Longevity
LONO . . . . . . Low Noise
LOOM . . . . . . Loyal Order of Moose
LOOW . . . . . Lake Ontario Ordnance Works
LOP . . . . Launch Operation (or Operator's) Panel (NASA)
LOP . . . . Leave on Pass
LOP . . . . Left Occiput Posterior (A fetal position) (Obstetrics)
LOP . . . . Left Outside Position (Dancing)
LOP . . . . Letter of Proposal (Military)
LOP . . . . Life of Program
LOP . . . . Line of Position (Electronics)
LOP . . . . Local Operating Procedures
LOP . . . . Local Operational Plot
LOPAIR . . . . . Long Path Infrared
LOPAR . . . . . Long Baseline Position and Rates (Guidance and tracking system) (Air Force)
LOPAR . . . . . Low-Power Acquisition RADAR
LOPC . . . . . . Lunar-Orbit Plane Change (NASA)
LOPG . . . . . . Live Oak, Perry & Gulf R. R. (AAR code)
LOP-GAP . . . . Liquid Oxygen Petrol, Guided Aircraft Projectile
LOPP . . . . . . Lunar Orbiter Photographic Project
LOPS . . . . . . Length of Patient Stay
LOPS . . . . . . Lunar Orbiting Photographic System
LOPU . . . . . . Logistics Organization Planning Unit
LO-QG . . . . . Locked Oscillator-Quadrature Grid (Data processing)
LOR . . . . Large Optical Reflector
LOR . . . . Loral Corporation (NYSE symbol)
LOR . . . . Lunar Orbital Rendezvous (NASA)
LORAC . . . . . Long-Range Accuracy (RADAR)
LORAD . . . . . Long-Range Active Detection
LORADAC . . . . Long-Range Active Detection and Communications System
LORAE . . . . . Long-Range Attitude and Event (Instrumentation system)
LORA-HOJ . . . Long Range - Home on Jam
LORAN . . . . . . Long-Range Aid to Navigation
LORAN DM . . . Long-Range Aid to Navigation Double Master
LORAN DS . . . Long-Range Aid to Navigation Double Slave
LORAN M . . . Long-Range Aid to Navigation Master
LORAN S . . . . Long-Range Aid to Navigation Slave
LORAPH . . . . . Long-Range Passive Homing System
LORBI . . . . . . Locked-On RADAR Bearing Indicator
LOREC . . . . . Long-Range Earth Current Communications
LORL . . . . . . Large Orbital Research Laboratory (NASA)
LORMONSTA . . . LORAN Monitor Station
LORO . . . . . . Lobe on Receive Only
LOROP . . . . . Long-Range Oblique Photography
LORS . . . . . . Long-Range SONAR
LORS . . . . . . Lunar Optical Rendezvous System
LORS . . . . . . Lunar Orbiting Reconnaissance System
LORSAC . . . . . Long-Range Submarine Communications
LORSTA . . . . . LORAN Transmitting Station
LORSU . . . . . . Long-Range Special Unit (Military)
LORTAN . . . . . Long-Range and Tactical Navigation System
LORV . . . . . . Low Observable Reentry Vehicle

LOS . . . . Liaison Office Support
LOS . . . . Line of Sight (Military)
LOS . . . . Loss of Signal
LOS . . . . Lunar Orbiting Satellite
LOSM . . . . . . Launch Operations Simulation Model
LOS of NA . . . Ladies Oriental Shrine of North America
LOSREP . . . . . Loss Report (Aircrew/Aircraft)
LOSS . . . . . . Large Object Salvage System (Navy)
LOSS . . . . . . Lunar Orbit Space Station (NASA)
LOSSYS . . . . Landing Observer's Signal System
LOST . . . . . . Linear One-Step Transition (Mathematical model for social grouping)
LOST/A . . . . . Vessels Lost by Accident, Collision or Similar Methods (Navy)
LOST/E . . . . . Vessel Lost Through Enemy Action (Navy)
LOST/P . . . . . Vessels Lost Due to Weather, Perils of the Sea or Similar Reasons (Navy)
LOT . . . . Large Orbiting Telescope
LOT . . . . Lateral Olfactory Tract
LOT . . . . Left Occipitotransverse (Anatomy)
LOT . . . . Load on Top
LOT . . . . Lock on Track
LOT . . . . Lower Outer Tube
LOTADS . . . . . Long-Term Worldwide Air Defense Study (Army)
LOTAS . . . . . Large Optical Tracker - Aerospace
LOTON . . . . . Long Tons Discharged or Loaded
LOTS . . . . . . Launch Operations Television System
LOTS . . . . . . Logistics Over the Shore (Military)
LOTS . . . . . . LORAN Operational Training School
LOTW . . . . . . Loaded on Trailers or Wagons (Freight)
LOU . . . . Louisville Gas & Electric Company (Kentucky) (NYSE symbol)
LOV . . . . Limit of Visibility
LOX . . . . Liquid Oxygen
LO-X . . . . . . Low Thermal Expansion (Synthetic ceramic)
LOXSL . . . . . Lowest Temperature Exceeded So Late (Meteorology)
LOZ . . . . Liquid Ozone
LP . . . . Land Plane
LP . . . . Large Paper
LP . . . . Large Particle
LP . . . . Large Post
LP . . . . Last Paid (Military)
LP . . . . Latent Period (Physiology)
LP . . . . Lateral Pyloric (Neuron)
LP . . . . Launch Platform
LP . . . . Launching Platoon (Army)
LP . . . . Laureate of Philosophy
LP . . . . Left Traffic Pattern (Aviation)
LP . . . . Light Perception
LP . . . . Limited Production
LP . . . . Line Printer (Data processing)
LP . . . . Linear Polarization
LP . . . . Linear Programming
LP . . . . Linguistic Problems
LP . . . . Linguopulpal
LP . . . . Liquefied Petroleum (Gas)
LP . . . . Liquid Propellant
LP . . . . Liquid Propellant Missile
LP . . . . Litter Patient
LP . . . . Livens Projector (Military)
LP . . . . Local Procurement (Military)
LP . . . . Local Purchase
LP . . . . Long Persistence
LP . . . . Long Picot
LP . . . . Long Play(ing) (Phonograph record)
LP . . . . Long Primer
LP . . . . Lord Provost (British)
LP . . . . Loss of Pay (Court-martial sentence) (Marine Corps)
LP . . . . Low Pass (Electronics)
LP . . . . Low Point
LP . . . . Low Power (Microscopy)
LP . . . . Low Pressure
LP . . . . Low-Pressure Cylinder (Especially, a locomotive cylinder)
LP . . . . Lower Peninsula (Michigan)
LP . . . . Lumbar Puncture
L/P . . . . Landplane
LPA . . . . Amphibious Transport (Navy ship symbol)
LPA . . . . La Posada Airways (Texas)
LPA . . . . Labor Policy Association
LPA . . . . Leaky Pipe Antenna
LPA . . . . Light Pulser Array
LPA . . . . Linear Power Amplifier
LPA . . . . Liquid Propellant Analysis
LPA . . . . Lithium Perchlorate Ammoniate
LPA . . . . Little People of America (An organization)

LPA	Local Public Agency
LPA	Log Periodic Antenna
LPAA	Log Periodic Array Antenna
LPARM	Liquid Propellant Applied Research Motor
LPB	Loan Policy Board (of SBA)
LPB	Louisiana & Pine Bluff Railway Company (AAR code)
LPB	Low-Level Penetration Bomb
LPBBA	Log Periodic Broad Band Antenna
LPC	Laboratory Pulse Compression
LPC	Landmarks Preservation Commission (New York City)
LPC	Leader Preparation Course
LPC	Leather Personnel Carriers (i.e., boots) (Army slang)
LPC	Linear Power Controller
LPC	Low-Pressure Chamber Technician (Navy)
LPCL	Laboratory Pulse Compression Loop
LP-CW	Long Pulse - Continual Wave
LPD	Amphibious Transport Dock (Navy ship symbol)
LPD	Landing, Personnel, and Dock (Navy)
LPD	Landing Platform, Dock (Navy symbol)
LPD	Landing Point Designator (Apollo) (NASA)
LPD	LASER Polarization Detector
LPD	Launch Point Determination
LPD	Least Perceptible Difference (Psychology)
LPD	Local Procurement Direct (Military)
LPD	Log Periodic Dipole
LPD	Low Performance Drone
LPDA	Log Periodic Dipole Array
LPDC	London Parcels Delivery Company
LPE	Launch Preparation Equipment (Army)
LPE	Limited Paperback Editions
LPF	Leukocytosis-Promoting Factor
LPF	Life Probability Function
LPF	Liquid Pressure Filter
LPF	Logically Passive Function
LPF	Low Pass Filter
LPF	Low Power Field (Microscopy)
LPF	Lutheran Peace Fellowship
LPFO	London Procurement Field Office
LPG	Landwirtschaftliche Produktionsgenossenschaft
LPG	Launch Preparations Group (NASA)
LPG	Liquefied Petroleum Gas
LPG	Liquid Propane Gas
LPGA	Ladies Professional Golf Association
LPGA	Louisiana Pecan Growers' Association
LPGG	Liquid Propellant Gas Generator
LPH	Amphibious Assault Ship (Navy symbol)
LPH	Landing Platform, Helicopter (Navy symbol)
LPHB	Low-Pressure Heating Boiler
LPI	Latent Photographic Image
LPI	Lightning Protection Institute
LPI	Louisiana Polytechnical Institute
LPI	Low Pressure Index
LPIA	Liquid Propellant Information Agency (Johns Hopkins University)
LPIU	Lithographers and Photoengravers International Union (Later, Graphic Arts International Union)
LPL	LASER-Pumped-LASER
LPL	Lightproof Louver (Technical drawings)
LPL	Long Pulse LASER
LPL	Lunar Projects Laboratory
LPLG	Left Pleural Ganglion
LPLR	Lock Pillar
LPM	Lane Photograph Method
LPM	LASER Phase Macroscope
LPM	Light Pulser Matrix
LPM	Lines Per Minute (Data processing)
LPM	Liters Per Minute
LPM	Long Peculiar Metre (Music)
LPM	Lunar Payload Module (Aerospace)
LPM	Lunar Portable Magnetometer (Apollo) (NASA)
LPMA	Lead Pencil Manufacturers Association
LPN	Licensed Practical Nurse
LPN	Longview, Portland & Northern Railway Company (AAR code)
LPN	Low Pass Network
LPNA	Lithographers and Printers National Association
LPO	Local Purchase Order
LPO	London Philharmonic Orchestra
LPO	Lunar Parking Orbit (Apollo) (NASA)
LPOX	Low-Pressure Oxygen
LPP	Lanka Prajatantrawadi Party (Ceylon)
LPP	Large Paper Proofs
LPP	LASER-Produced Plasma

LPP	Leader Preparation Program
LPP	Long Periodic Perturbation
LPP	Lunar Precepts Positioner
LPPC	Load Point Photocell
LPPH	Leningrad Prison Psychiatric Hospital (Later, LSPH)
LPR	Amphibious Transport (Small) (Navy ship symbol)
LPR	Late Position Report (Report of a flight which is off flight plan)
LPR	Late Procurement Request (Air Force)
LPR	Leadership Potential Rating (Army)
LPR	Liquid Propellant Rocket (Air Force)
LPR	Long-Playing Rocket (Aerospace)
LPR	Looper Position Regulator
LPR	Lynchburg Pool Reactor
LPRC	Library Public Relations Council
LPRE	Liquid Propellant Rocket Engine
LPS	L-Band Phase Shifter
LPS	LASER Power Supply
LPS	Launch Phase Simulator (NASA)
LPS	Lightproof Shade (Technical drawings)
LPS.	Linear Programming System (Data processing)
LPS	Local Process Specification
LPS	London & Port Stanley Railway Company (AAR code)
LPS	Lord Privy Seal (British)
LPS	Lunar Penetrometer System
LPS	Lunar Pilotage System
LPSC	Luxembourg Philatelic Study Club
LPSD	Logically Passive Self-Dual
LPSNY	Lithuanian Philatelic Society of New York
LPSO	Laboratory Procurement Supply Office
LPSS.	Amphibious Transport Submarine (Navy symbol)
LPT	Language Proficiency Test (Military)
LPT	Lehigh Portland Cement Company (NYSE symbol)
LPT	Low-Pressure Test
LPT	Low-Pressure Transducer
LPTD	Long Play Talkdown
LPTF	Low Power Test Facility (AEC)
LPTR	Livermore Pool Type Reactor
LPTS	Louisiana Presbyterian Theological Seminary
LPTV	Large Payload Test Vehicle
LPTW	Lake Providence, Texarkana & Western R. R. (AAR code)
LPU	League of Prayer for Unity
LPU	Life Preserver Unit
LPUU	Linear Programming Under Uncertainty
LPV	Lightproof Vent (Technical drawings)
LPV	Log Periodic V (Antenna)
LPW	Linear Polarized Wave
LPW	Longitudinal Pressure Wave
LPW	Lumens Per Watt
LQ	Last Quarter (Moon phase)
LQ	Lege Quaeso (Please Read)
LQ	Lordosis Quotients
LQ	Lowest Quadrille
LQ	Lutheran Quarterly
LQA	Living Quarters Allowance (Air Force)
LR	Laboratory Reagent
LR	Laboratory Report
LR	Ladder Rung
LR	Landing RADAR
LR	Large Ring
LR	Latency Relaxation
LR	Laufen Rechnung (Current Account) (Germany)
Lr	Lawrencium (Chemical element)
LR	Leave Rations (Military)
LR	Lee Rubber & Tire Corporation (NYSE symbol) (Delisted)
LR	Left Rear
LR	Letter Report
LR	Level Recorder
LR	Liaison Report (or Request)
LR	Line Relay
LR	Liquid Rocket
LR	Living Room
LR	Lloyd's Register (of Shipping)
LR	Load Ratio
LR	Lock Rail
LR	Log Run (Lumber)
LR	Long Range
LR	Lower Right
L/R	Leave Rations (Military)
L/R	Left Right
L/R	Locus of Radius
L & R	Lake and Rail

L & R . . . . . . Larceny and Receiving
LR3 . . . . LASER Ranging Retroreflector (NASA)
LRA . . . . Labor Research Associates (An organization)
LRA . . . . Labor Research Association
LRA . . . . Light Replaceable Assemblies
LRA . . . . Lithuanian Regeneration Association
LRA . . . . Long-Range Aviation (Army)
LRAC . . . . . . Long-Run Average Costs
LRADP . . . . . Long-Range Active Duty Program (Army)
LRAF . . . . . . Long-Range Air Force
LRAM . . . . . . Licentiate of the Royal Academy of Music (British)
LRB . . . . Local Reference Beam (Holography)
LRB . . . . London Rifle Brigade (British)
LRB . . . . Loyalty Review Board (Civil Service Commission) (Abolished, 1953)
LRBA . . . . . . Laboratoire de Recherches Balistiques et Aerodynamiques
LRBF . . . . . . Longitudinal Ridge of Basal Fold
LRBM . . . . . . Long-Range Ballistic Missile
LRBR . . . . . . Long-Range Ballistic Rocket
LRBS . . . . . . LASER Ranging Bombing System
LRC . . . . Labrador Retriever Club
LRC . . . . Langley Research Center (NASA)
LRC . . . . Lead Resistance Compensator
LRC . . . . Lenoir Rhyne College (North Carolina)
LRC . . . . Level Recording Controller
LRC . . . . Lewis Research Center (NASA)
LRC . . . . Liberia Refining Company
LRC . . . . Line Rectifier Circuit
LRC . . . . Logistics Readiness Center (Air Force)
LRC . . . . London Rowing Club
LRC . . . . Longitudinal Redundancy Check
LRC . . . . Luneberg Rapid Commutator
LRC . . . . Lung Rate Counter
L or RC . . . . . Leather or Rubber Covered (Freight)
LRCA . . . . . . Lithuanian Roman Catholic Alliance of America
LRCE . . . . . . Little Rock Cotton Exchange
LRCO . . . . . . Limited Remote Communication Outlets (ATCS)
LRCP . . . . . . Licentiate in the Royal College of Physicians (British)
LRCPE . . . . . Licentiate of the Royal College of Physicians (Edinburgh)
LRCS. . . . . . . LASER RADAR Cross Section
LRCS . . . . . . League of Red Cross Societies
LRCS . . . . . . Licentiate of the Royal College of Surgeons (British)
LRCS . . . . . . Load Relief Control System
LRCSE . . . . . Licentiate of the Royal College of Surgeons (Edinburgh)
LRD . . . . Landing and Recovery Division (NASA)
LRD . . . . Long-Range Data (RADAR)
LRDC . . . . . . Learning Research and Development Center (University of Pittsburgh)
LRDE . . . . . . Long-Run Deal Effect (Marketing)
LRDL . . . . . . Longitudinal Ridge of Dorsal Lip
LRE . . . . Liquid Rocket Engine
LREDA . . . . . Liberal Religious Education Directors Association
LRF . . . . LASER Range-Finder
LRF . . . . Launch Rate Factor
LRF . . . . Liver Residue Factor
LRF . . . . Low Refraction Layer
LRF . . . . Luteinizing (Hormone) Releasing Factor
LRFG . . . . . . Low Range Force Gauge
LRFI . . . . League for Religious Freedom in Israel (Later, American Friends of Religious Freedom in Israel)
LRFPS . . . . . . Licentiate of the Royal Faculty of Physicians and Surgeons (British)
LRI . . . . Lawndale Railway & Industrial Company (AAR code)
LRI . . . . Learning Resources Institute
LRI . . . . Left-Right Indicator
LRI . . . . Library Resources, Incorporated (Subsidiary of Encyclopaedia Britannica)
LRI . . . . Long-Range Interceptor
LRI . . . . Long-Range RADAR Input
LRIBA . . . . . . Licentiate of the Royal Institute of British Architecture
LRIM . . . . . . Long-Range Input Monitor (RADAR)
LRIR . . . . Low-Resolution Infrared Radiometer
LRK . . . . LASER Research Kit
LRL . . . . Lawrence Radiation Laboratory (AEC)
LRL . . . . Leakage Resistance Limit
LRL . . . . Limited Raman LASER
LRL . . . . Livermore Research Laboratory (Later, Ernest Orlando Lawrence Livermore Laboratory) (AEC)
LRL . . . . Lunar Receiving Laboratory (NASA)
LRLEI . . . . . . League for Religious Labor in Eretz Israel
LRLG . . . . . . Long-Range Logistics Guidance (Air Force)
LRLL . . . . . . Longitudinal Ridge of Lateral Lip
LRL-L . . . . . . Lawrence Radiation Laboratory, Livermore (AEC)
LRM . . . . Latching Relay Matrix
LRM . . . . Limited Register Machine

LRM . . . . Logarithmic Ratio Module
LRM . . . . Long-Range Missile Launcher
LRM . . . . Lower Reject Limit Median
LRM . . . . Lunar Reconnaissance Mission
LRM . . . . Lunar Reconnaissance Module
LRNA . . . . . . Laws Relating to the Navy Annotated (Military law)
LRNOD . . . . . Long-Range Night Observation Device (Army)
LRO . . . . Long-Range Objectives (Navy)
LRO . . . . Long-Range Order
LRO . . . . Low-Resistance Ohmmeter
LROG . . . . . . Long-Range Objectives Group (Navy)
LRP . . . . LASER Retinal Photocoagulator
LRP . . . . Late Receptor Potential (Photoreceptor) (Physiology)
LRP . . . . Long-Range Patrol (Army)
LRP . . . . Long-Range Penetration
LRP . . . . Long-Range Plans
LRPE . . . . . . Long-Run Price Effect (Marketing)
LRPF . . . . . . Liberal Religious Peace Fellowship
LRPG . . . . . . Long-Range Penetration Group (Military) (World War II)
LRPG . . . . . . Long-Range Proving Ground
LRPGD . . . . . Long-Range Proving Ground Division (Air Force)
LRPGR . . . . . Long-Range Planning Ground Rules
LRP/GWU . . . . Logistics Research Project, George Washington University
LRPPD . . . . . Long-Range Planning Purpose Document
LR-QR . . . . . Letter Requirement - Quick Reaction (Army)
LRR . . . . Long-Range RADAR
LRR . . . . Long-Range Requirements (Navy)
LRR . . . . Lot Rejection Report
LRRC . . . . . . Labor Relations and Research Center (University of Massachusetts)
LRRP . . . . . . Long-Range Reconnaissance Patrol (Army)
LRRP . . . . . . Lowest Required Radiated Power
LRRR . . . . . . LASER Ranging Retroreflection (Apollo II experiment) (NASA)
LRRS . . . . . . Limited Remaining Radiation Service (Unit) (Military)
LRS . . . . Lake Reporting Service
LRS . . . . Lamb-Rutherford Shift
LRS . . . . Lanyard Release Switch
LRS . . . . LASER Ranging System
LRS . . . . LASER Raster Scanner
LRS . . . . Laurinburg & Southern R. R. (AAR code)
LRS . . . . League of Religious Settlements
LRS . . . . Legislative Reference Service (Later, Congressional Research Service) (Library of Congress)
LRS . . . . Light Radiation Sensor
LRS . . . . Lightweight RADAR Set
LRS . . . . Limited Resources Specialty
LRS . . . . Linguistics Research System
LRS . . . . Logistics Requirements System (Navy)
LRS . . . . Long-Range Search
LRS . . . . Long Right Shift
L/R/S . . . . . . Library Rubber Stamps (Antiquarian book trade)
LRSK . . . . . . Long-Range Station Keeping
LRSM . . . . . . Lab for Research on the Structure of Matter
LRSM . . . . . . Long-Range Seismic Measurement
LRSS . . . . . . Long-Range Survey System (Military)
LRSTPP . . . . . Long-Range Scientific Technical Planning Program
LRT . . . . LASER Range-Finder Theodolite
LRT . . . . Last Resort Target (Military)
LRT . . . . Loki Ranging Transponder
LRT . . . . Long Range Typhon (Navy)
LRT . . . . Long Ring Timer
LRTGT . . . . . Last Resort Target (Military)
LRTM . . . . . . Long-Range Training Mission (Military)
LRTS. . . . . . . LASER Range-Finder Theodolite System
LRTS. . . . . . . Library Resources & Technical Services (Journal)
LRU . . . . Least Recently Used (Replacement algorithm) (Data processing)
LRU . . . . Less than Release Unit (Army)
LRU . . . . Line Removable (or Replaceable) Unit
LRU . . . . Line Replaceable Unit
LRU . . . . Little Rock University (Arkansas)
LRV . . . . Lunar Rover (or Roving) Vehicle (NASA)
LRWE . . . . . . Long-Range Weapons Establishment (Australia)
LRY . . . . Liberal Religious Youth
LS . . . . Labor Service (Military)
LS . . . . Lactose Synthetase
LS . . . . Land Service
LS . . . . Landesschuetzeneinheit (Regional defense force) (German military - World War II)
LS . . . . Landing Ship (Navy)
LS . . . . Lange Sicht (Long Sight) (Germany)
LS . . . . LASER System

LS . . . . Lastensegler; Lastensegelflugzeug (Cargo transport glider) (German military – World War II)
LS . . . . Late Scramble (Reason for missed interception) (Military)
LS . . . . Lateral Septum
LS . . . . Launch Service
LS . . . . Launch Site
LS . . . . Lead Sheet (Military)
LS . . . . Leading Seaman
LS . . . . Left Side
LS . . . . Legal Scroll
LS . . . . Lepidopterists' Society
LS . . . . Letter Service
LS – . . . . Letter Signed (Manuscript descriptions)
LS . . . . Leukemia Society
LS . . . . Level Switch
LS . . . . Library Science
LS . . . . Licentiate in Science
LS . . . . Licentiate in Surgery
LS . . . . Life Support (Aerospace)
LS . . . . Lifesaving Service (Coast Guard)
LS . . . . Light Ship or Vessel
LS . . . . Light Source
LS . . . . Lighthouse Service (Coast Guard)
LS . . . . Limestone
LS . . . . Liminal (or Least) Sensation (Psychology)
LS . . . . Limit Switch (Electronics)
LS . . . . Line Stretcher
LS . . . . Linnaean Society
LS . . . . Liquid Scintillation (Chemical analysis)
LS . . . . Liquid Sensor
LS . . . . Listed Securities
LS . . . . Literature Search
LS . . . . Local Sunset
LS . . . . Locus Sepulchri (Place of the Sepulchre)
LS . . . . Locus Sigilli (Place of the Seal) (Legal)
LS . . . . Logistical Support (Army)
LS . . . . London Scottish (Army regiment)
LS . . . . Long Shot (A photograph or motion picture sequence taken from a distance)
LS . . . . Longitudinal Section
LS . . . . Loudspeaker
LS . . . . Low Speed
LS . . . . Lower Structure
LS . . . . Lump Sum
LS — . . . . Summer (Vessel load line mark)
L–S . . . . Leap-Second
L–S . . . . Lumbo-Sacral
L/S . . . . Launching System
L & S . . . . . Launch & Servicing (Aerospace)
LSA . . . . Labor Services Agency
LSA . . . . Labor Surplus Area
LSA . . . . Land Service Assistant (Ministry of Agriculture, Fisheries, and Food) (British)
LSA . . . . Land Settlement Association (British)
LSA . . . . Large Spherical Array
LSA . . . . Lateral Spherical Aberration
LSA . . . . Law and Society Association
LSA . . . . Layton School of Art (Wisconsin)
LSA . . . . Lead Spring Assembly
LSA . . . . Leaving Scene of an Accident (Traffic offense charge)
LSA . . . . Left Sacro-Anterior (Anatomy)
LSA . . . . Leukemia Society of America
LSA . . . . Level Shift Amplifier
LSA . . . . Library Science Abstracts
LSA . . . . Library Services Act (1956)
LSA . . . . Licentiate of the Society of Apothecaries (British)
LSA . . . . Limited Space-Charge Accumulation (Electronics)
LSA . . . . Linear Servo Actuator
LSA . . . . Linguistic Society of America
LSA . . . . Lithuanian Students Association
LSA . . . . Little Sisters of the Assumption (Roman Catholic religious order)
LSA . . . . Longitudinal Spherical Aberration
LSA . . . . Low Specific Activity (Radioisotope)
LSAA . . . . . . Linen Supply Association of America
LSAC . . . . . . London Small Arms Company (Military)
LSAL . . . . . . Left Salivary (Gland)
LSAM . . . . . . Lumped Shell Analysis Method
LSAO . . . . . . Line Station Assembly Order
LSAPT . . . . . . Lunar Sample Analysis Planning Team (NASA)
LSAT . . . . . . Law School Admission Test
LSAT . . . . Logistic Shelter Air Transportable

LSB . . . . Bachelor of Life Science
LSB . . . . Landing Ship, Bombardment
LSB . . . . Launch Service Building
LSB . . . . Launcher Support Building
LSB . . . . Least Significant Bit
LSB . . . . Left Sternal Border
LSB . . . . London School Board
LSB . . . . Lower Sideband
LSB . . . . Mine Sweeping Boat (Navy symbol)
LSBC . . . . . . LaSalle & Bureau County R. R. (AAR code)
LSBR . . . . Large Seed-Blanket Reactor (AEC)
LSC . . . . Large-Scale Computer
LSC . . . . LASER Spectral Control
LSC . . . . Latrobe Steel Co. (NYSE symbol)
L Sc . . . . Laureate of Science
LSC . . . . Left Stage Center (A stage direction)
LSC . . . . Lens Sign Convention
LSC . . . . Limit Signaling Comparator
LSC . . . . Lincoln Sesquicentennial Committee (Government agency)
LSC . . . . Linear-Shaped Charge
LSC . . . . Liquid Scintillation Counter (or Counting)
LSC . . . . Loco Supra Citato (In the Place Cited Above)
LSCA . . . . . . Library Services and Construction Act (1963)
L Sc D . . . . . Doctor of the Science of Law
LSCE . . . . . . Launch Sequence and Control Equipment
LSCP . . . . . . Logistic Support Control Point (Military)
LSCR . . . . . . Ligue des Societes de la Croix-Rouge
LSCRRC . . . . . Law Students Civil Rights Research Council
LSCT . . . . . . Lamar State College of Technology (Texas)
LSCT . . . . . . LASER Spectral Control Technique
LSD . . . . Doctor of Library Science
LSD . . . . Doctor of Life Science
LSD . . . . Landing Ship Dock (Aerospace)
LSD . . . . Landing Ship, Dock (Navy symbol)
LSD . . . . Large Screen Display
LSD . . . . Large Steel Desk (Position given to ex-astronauts)
LSD . . . . LASER Signal Device
LSD . . . . Latching Semiconductor Diode
LSD . . . . Latest Start Date
LSD . . . . Launch Systems Data
LSD . . . . Least Significant Difference
£SD . . . . Librae, Solidi, Denarii (Pounds, Shillings, Pence)
LSD . . . . Lightermen, Stevedores, and Dockers
LSD . . . . Logarithmic Series Distribution (Statistics)
LSD . . . . Logistics Systems Division (Air Force)
LSD . . . . Low-Speed Data
L–S D . . . . . . Lunar Surface Drill
LSD 25 . . . . . Lysergsaeure Diethyamid (Lysergic Acid Diethylamine Tartrate) (Hallucinogenic drug)
LSDS . . . . . . Large Screen Display System
LSDS . . . . . . Low-Speed Digital System
LSDSP . . . . . . Latvijas Socialdemokratiska Stradnieku Partija
LSE . . . . Landing Signal Enlisted (Military)
LSE . . . . Launch Sequencer Equipment
LSE . . . . Launch Support Equipment
LSE . . . . Life Support Experiment
LSE . . . . London School of Economics
LSE . . . . London Stock Exchange
LSE . . . . Lunar Support Equipment
LSE . . . . Lunar Surface Experiment
LSEP . . . . Lifetime Sports Education Project (of Lifetime Sports Foundation)
LSEP . . . . Lunar Surface Experiment Package (NASA)
LSEV . . . . . . Lunar Surface Exploration Vehicle
LSF . . . . Lande Splitting Factor
LSF . . . . Least Square Fit
LSF . . . . Lightweight Strike Fighter (NATO Air Forces)
LSF . . . . Literary Society Foundation
LSF . . . . Louisiana Sugar Exchange
LSFF . . . . . . Flotilla Flagship Landing Ship (Navy symbol)
LSG . . . . Logistics Support Group
LSG . . . . Lone Star Gas Company (NYSE symbol)
LSH . . . . Landing Ship, Headquarters
LSHCNC . . . . . Local and Short Haul Carriers National Conference
LSHI . . . . Large-Scale Hybrid Integration
LSH(L) . . . . . . Landing Ship, Headquarters (Large)
LSH(S) . . . . . . Landing Ship, Headquarters (Small)
LSHV . . . . . . Laminated Synthetic High Voltage
LSI . . . . Lake Superior & Ishpeming R. R. (AAR code)
LSI . . . . Large-Scale Integration (of circuits) (Electronics)
LSI . . . . Largest Single Item
LSI . . . . LASER Surface Interaction

LSI . . . . Lear-Siegler, Incorporated (NYSE symbol)
LSI . . . . Leukemia Society, Incorporated
LSI . . . . Lunar Science Institute (Houston)
LSI . . . . Lunar Surface Instrument
LS & I . . . . . . Lake Superior & Ishpeming Railroad Company
LSIA . . . . Lamp and Shade Institute of America
LSIG . . . . Landing Craft, Infantry (Gunboat) (Navy symbol)
LSIL . . . . Landing Ship, Infantry (Large)
LSIM . . . . Landing Craft, Infantry (Mortar) (Navy symbol)
LSIR . . . . Landing Craft, Infantry (Rocket) (Navy symbol)
LSIS . . . . LASER Shutterable Image Sensor
LSIS . . . . League of Shut-In Sodalists
LSIT . . . . Linear Strip Ion Thruster
LSK . . . . Liquid Sample Kit
LSK . . . . Liver, Spleen, Kidney (Medicine)
LSL . . . . Life Sciences Laboratory
LSL . . . . Logistics Systems Laboratory
LSL . . . . Low Sight Lobe
LSLP . . . . Lump-Sum Leave Payment (Air Force)
LSM . . . . Lakeside & Marblehead R. R. (AAR code)
LSM . . . . Landing Ship, Medium (Navy)
LSM . . . . LASER Slicing Machine
LSM . . . . Launcher Status Multiplexer
LSM . . . . Letter Sorting Machine (US Postal Service)
LSM . . . . Linear Sequential Machine
LSM . . . . Logistic Support Manager
LSM . . . . Lunar Surface Magnetometer (NASA)
LSM . . . . Lysergic Acid Morpholide
LSM . . . . Master of Life Science
LSM . . . . Medium Landing Ship (Navy symbol)
LS/MFT . . . . . . Lucky Strike Means Fine Tobacco (Advertising slogan)
LSMR . . . . Medium Landing Ship (Rocket)
LS and MS . . . . Less Sleep and More Speed (Hobo slang)
LSMSO . . . . . . Landing Ship, Material Supply Officer (Navy)
LSN . . . . Line Stabilization Network
LSN . . . . Linear Sequential Network
LSN . . . . Load Sharing Network
LSNY . . . . . . Linnaean Society of New York
LSO . . . . Landing Signal Officer
LSO . . . . Launch Safety Officer (NASA)
LSO . . . . Leesona Corporation (NYSE symbol)
LSO . . . . Line Stabilized Oscillator
LSO . . . . London Symphony Orchestra
LSO . . . . Louisiana Southern Railway Company (AAR code)
LSOC . . . . . . Logistical Support Operations Center
LSP . . . . Left Sacroposterior (A fetal position, the breech position) (Obstetrics)
LSP . . . . Lincoln Society of Philately
LSP . . . . Line Synchronizing Pulse
LSP . . . . Linear Selenium Photocell
LSP . . . . Logistics Support Plan
LSP . . . . Low-Speed Printer
LSP . . . . Lunar Spectral Photometrics
LSP . . . . Lunar Surface Probe
LSPAFRO . . . . Lump-Sum Payment to Air Force Reserve Officers
LSPC . . . . . . Linear Selenium Photocell
LSPC . . . . . . Louisiana Sweet Potato Commission
LSPET . . . . . . Lunar Sample Preliminary Examination Team (NASA)
LSPH . . . . . . Leningrad Special Psychiatric Hospital (Formerly, LPPH)
LSPPO . . . . . . Lead Screw Position Pickoff
LSPS . . . . . . Limited Serial Project Slip
LSQ . . . . Line Squall (Meteorology)
LSR . . . . Laboratory for Space Research (Netherlands)
LSR . . . . Large Ship Reactor
LSR . . . . Launch Signal Responder (Aerospace)
LSR . . . . Light Sensitive Relay
LSR . . . . Light Sensitive Resistor
LSR . . . . Light Stopping Reticle
LSR . . . . Liner Seal Ring
LSR . . . . Load Storage Register
LSR . . . . Local Sunrise
LSR . . . . Logistics Support Requirements
LSR . . . . Loose Snow on Runway (Aviation)
LSR . . . . Luftschutzraum (Air raid shelter) (German military - World War II)
LSR . . . . Lynchburg Source Reactor
LSRF . . . . . . LASER Submarine Range Finder
LSRI . . . . Large Screen RADAR Indicator
LSRV . . . . . . Lunar Surface Roving Vehicle
LSS . . . . Laboratory Support Service
LSS . . . . Launch Sequency Simulator
LSS . . . . Launch Status Summarizer
LSS . . . . Launch Support Section

LSS . . . . Life Saving Service
LSS . . . . Life Support System
LSS . . . . Lifesaving Station (Maps and charts)
LSS . . . . Light Spot Scanner
LSS . . . . Limited Storage Site
LSS . . . . Line Scanner System
LSS . . . . Linking Segment Subprogram
LSS . . . . Liquid Scintillation Spectrometer
LSS . . . . Logistic Support Squadron
LSS . . . . Longitudinal Static Stability
LSS . . . . Lunar Surveying System
LSSA . . . . . . Lithuanian Student Scout Association (Later, Lithuanian Scouts Association College Division)
LSSC . . . . . . Logistic Support System Characteristics
LSSD . . . . . . Lunar Surface Sampling Device
LSSF . . . . . . Limited Service Storage Facility
LSSL . . . . . . Support Landing Ship (Large) MK III
LSSM . . . . . . Local Scientific Survey Module
LSSM . . . . . . Lunar Scientific Survey Module (NASA)
LSSO . . . . . . Library Science Student Organization
LSSP . . . . . . Lanka Sama Samaja Party (Ceylon)
LSSP . . . . . . Lunar Surveying System Program
LST . . . . Landing Ship, Tank
LST . . . . Large Space Telescope
LST . . . . Late Start Time
LST . . . . Light-Sensitive Tube
LST . . . . Line Scan Tube
LST . . . . Liquid Oxygen Start Tank
LST . . . . Liquid Storage Tank
LST . . . . Local Sidereal Time
LST . . . . Local Standard Time
LST . . . . Lowenstein (M.) & Sons, Inc. (NYSE symbol)
LST . . . . Lunar Surface Transponder
LSTF . . . . . . Lead Sulfide Thin Film
LST-G . . . . . . Large Steam Turbine-Generator
LST(H) . . . . . . Landing Ship, Tank (Casualty evacuation)
LSTT . . . . . . Lake Superior Terminal & Transfer Railway Company (AAR code)
LSU . . . . Labor Service Unit
LSU . . . . Landing Ship, Utility (Navy symbol)
LSU . . . . Louisiana State University
LSUNO . . . . . Louisiana State University in New Orleans
LSV . . . . Landing Ship, Vehicle
LSV . . . . Lunar Shuttle Vehicle (Aerospace)
LSV . . . . Lunar Surface Vehicle
LSV . . . . Lunar Survey Viewfinder
LSVC . . . . . . Lunar Surface Vehicle Communications
LSW . . . . LASER Spot Welder
LSW . . . . Least Significant Word
LSW . . . . Lifshitz-Slyozov-Wagner (Theory)
LSW . . . . Limit Switch
LSWMA . . . . . Lutheran Society for Worship, Music and the Arts
LSWR . . . . . . London and South-Western Railway
LSX . . . . Landing Ship Experimental (Navy)
LT . . . . Lake Terminal R. R. (AAR code)
LT . . . . Laminated TEFLON
LT . . . . Landed Terms
LT . . . . Landing Team
LT . . . . Language Translation (Data processing)
LT . . . . Laplace Transform
LT . . . . Large Tug (Army)
LT . . . . Lateral Tooth
LT . . . . Lawn Tennis
LT . . . . Lead Time
LT . . . . Left Tackle (Football)
LT . . . . Legal Tender (Currency)
LT . . . . Less Than
LT . . . . Letter Telegram
LT . . . . Level Trigger
LT . . . . Licentiate in Theology
LT . . . . Lid Tank
LT . . . . Lieutenant
LT . . . . Light
LT . . . . Light Tank
LT . . . . Light Trap
LT . . . . Line Telegraphy
LT . . . . Link Trainer Instructor
LT . . . . Local Time
LT . . . . Locum Tenens (In the Place of; a substitute)
LT . . . . Logic Theorist
LT . . . . Logic Theory (Computers)
LT . . . . Long Ton (2240 pounds)

ACRONYMS AND INITIALISMS DICTIONARY

LT . . . . Low Temperature
LT . . . . Low Tension
LT . . . . Low Torque
LT . . . . Lower Torso
LT . . . . Lug Terminal
LT . . . . Lymphotoxin
LT . . . . National Lead Company (NYSE symbol) (Later, NL)
LT . . . . Turn Left After Takeoff (Aviation)
L/T . . . . Line Telecommunications
L/T . . . . Loop Test (Aerospace)
1LT . . . . First Lieutenant (Army)
2LT . . . . Second Lieutenant (Army)
LTA . . . . Large Transport Airplane
LTA . . . . Leave Travel Allowance
LTA . . . . Legionarios Del Trabajo in America
LTA . . . . Leisure Time Activity
LTA . . . . Leveling Torquer Amplifier
LTA . . . . Lighter than Air (Aircraft)
LTA . . . . Linen Trade Association
LTA . . . . LM (Lunar Module) Test Articles
LTA . . . . Long-Term Arrangements (Department of State)
LTA . . . . Low Temperature Ashing
Lt B . . . . Bachelor of Literature
LTB . . . . Limited Test Ban (Nuclear testing)
LTB . . . . Line Term Buffer (Data processing)
LTB . . . . London Transport Board
LTB . . . . Low Tension Battery
LTBO . . . . . . Linear Time Base Oscillator
LTBT . . . . . . Limited Test Ban Treaty (Signed in 1963; prohibits testing of nuclear devices in certain environments)
LTC . . . . Lafferty Transportation Company (AAR code)
LTC . . . . Lawn Tennis Club (British)
LTC . . . . Lead Telluride Crystal
LTC . . . . Leaseway Transportation Corporation (NYSE symbol)
LTC . . . . Lieutenant Colonel (Army)
LTC . . . . Linear Transmission Channel
LTC . . . . Load Tap Changing
LTC . . . . Longitudinal Time Constant
LTC . . . . Loop Test Conference (Aerospace)
LTC . . . . Low Temperature Coefficient
LTC . . . . Low Temperature Cooling
LTD . . . . LASER Target Designator
LTD . . . . Limited
LTD . . . . Long Tank Delta
LTD . . . . Long Term Disability (Military)
LTDA . . . . . . Localizer Type Directional Aid (Aviation)
LTDR . . . . . . LASER Target Designator Receiver
LTDS . . . . . . Launch Trajectory Data System
LTE . . . . Large Table Electroplotter (Data processing)
LTE . . . . Large Thrust per Element
LTE . . . . Launch to Eject
LTE . . . . Linear Threshold Element (Data processing)
LTE . . . . Local Thermodynamic Equilibrium
LTE . . . . Low Thrust Engine
LTEA . . . . . . Leaf Tobacco Exporters Association
LTF . . . . LASER Terrain Follower
LTF . . . . Layman Tithing Foundation
LTF . . . . Lead the Force
LTF . . . . Lipotropic Factor
LTF . . . . Liquid Thermal Flowmeter
LTF . . . . Local Training Flight
LT/FM . . . . . Long Term/Frequency Modulation
LTFRD . . . . . . Lot Tolerance Fraction Reliability Deviation (Quality control)
LTFS . . . . . . LASER Terrain Following System
LTG . . . . Lieutenant General (Army)
LTG . . . . Lighting
LTGCC . . . . . Lightning Cloud-to-Cloud (Meteorology)
LTGCCCG . . . . Lightning Cloud-to-Cloud, Cloud-to-Ground (Meteorology)
LTGCG . . . . . Lightning Cloud-to-Ground (Meteorology)
LTGCW . . . . . Lightning Cloud-to-Water (Meteorology)
LTGH . . . . . . Lightening Hole (Engineering)
LTGIC . . . . . . Lightning in Clouds (Meteorology)
LTGL . . . . . . Lee-Tse-Goldberg-Lowe (Theory)
L Th . . . . Licentiate in Theology
LTH . . . . Luteotrophic Hormone (Endocrinology)
LTHA . . . . . . Long-Term Heat Aging
LTI . . . . Light Transmission Index
LTI . . . . Lowell Technological Institute (Massachusetts)
LTIOV . . . . . . Latest Time Information of Value (Military)
LTIRF . . . . . . Lowell Technological Institute Research Foundation
LTJC . . . . Lyons Township Junior College (Illinois)

LTJG . . . . Lieutenant Junior Grade (Navy)
LTL . . . . Less than Truckload
LTL . . . . Line-to-Line
LTL . . . . Lot Truck Load
LTM . . . . Line Type Modulation (Radio)
LTM . . . . Long-Term Memory
LTMS . . . . . . Lunar Terrain Measuring System
LTN . . . . Linear Time-Varying Network
LTO . . . . Landing and Takeoff
LTO . . . . Lot Time Order
LTOF . . . . . . Low Temperature Optical Facility
LTON . . . . . . Long Ton
LTOT . . . . . . Latest Time Over Target
LTP . . . . Let's Tax Plutocrats (Humorous interpretation of LTP - Limit on Tax Preferences)
LTP . . . . Library Technology Program (Formerly, Project) (ALA)
LTP . . . . Limit on Tax Preferences
LTP. . . . . Line Throwing Projectile
LTP . . . . Lower Trip Point
LTPO . . . . . . Lot Tolerance Percent Defective
LTPP. . . . . . . Lipothiamide Pyrophosphate
LTR . . . . Lander Trajectory Reconstruction (Program) (NASA)
LTR . . . . LASER Tank Range-Finder
LTR . . . . Lattice Test Reactor
LTR . . . . Letter
LTR . . . . Library Technology Reports (A publication)
LTR. . . . . Liquid Test Rig (Apollo) (NASA)
LTR . . . . Lockheed Training Reactor
LTR . . . . Loew's Corp. (Formerly, Loew's Theatres, Inc.) (NYSE symbol)
LTRF . . . . LASER Tank Range-Finder
LTRI . . . . Lightning and Transients Research Institute
LTRS . . . . . . LASER Target Recognition System
LTS . . . . Landfall Technique School (Navy)
LTS . . . . Language Teaching System
LTS . . . . Language Translation System
LTS . . . . Launch Telemetry Stations
LTS . . . . Launch Tracking System
LTS . . . . Linearity Test Set
LTS . . . . Link Terminal Simulator
LTS . . . . Load Transfer Switch
LTS . . . . Long-Term Stability
LTSH . . . . . . League of Tarcisians of the Sacred Heart
LTSPC . . . . . . L'Union Territoriale des Syndicats Professionelles Caledoniens (Territorial Federation of New Caledonian Unions of Private Employees)
LTSTA . . . . . . Light Station (Coast Guard)
LTT . . . . Landline Teletypewriter
LTT . . . . Light Tactical Transport
LTT . . . . Lunar Test Table
LTTAT . . . . . . Long Tank Thrust-Augmented Thor
LTTC . . . . . . Lowry Technical Training Center
LTTD . . . . . . Letter-Type Technical Directive (Navy)
LTTR . . . . . . Long-Term Tape Recorder
LTV . . . . Launch Test Vehicles
LTV . . . . Long-Term Vibration
LTV . . . . Long Tube Vertical
LTV . . . . LTV Corp. (Formerly, Ling-Temco-Vought, Inc.) (NYSE symbol)
LTWA . . . . . . Lawn Tennis Writers' Association of America
LU . . . . Ligue Universelle (Esperantiste)
LU . . . . Load Unit
LU . . . . Logical Unit
Lu . . . . Lutetium (Chemical element)
LU . . . . Luxembourg (NATO)
LU . . . . Upper Limen (Psychology)
LUA . . . . Liverpool Underwriters Association
LUAP . . . . . . Land Use Adjustment Program
LUB . . . . Lubricate
LUBA . . . . . . Limited Underwater Breathing Apparatus
LUC . . . . Lukens Steel Company (NYSE symbol)
LUCALOX . . . . Translucent Aluminum Oxide (Ceramic)
LUCE . . . . . . L'Unione Cinematografica Educativa (Italy)
LUCID . . . . . . Language Used to Communicate Information System Design
LUCID . . . . . . Language for Utility Checkout and Instrumentation Development
LUCOM . . . . . Lunar Communication (System)
LUD . . . . Lift-Up Door (Technical drawings)
LUD . . . . Ludlow Corp. (NYSE symbol)
LUE . . . . Left Upper Extremity
LUE . . . . Linear Unbiased Estimator (Statistics)
LUF . . . . Lowest Usable (or Useful) Frequency (Radio)
LUG . . . . Light Utility Glider
LUH . . . . Lumen Hour
LUHF . . . . . . Lowest Usable (or Useful) High Frequency (Radio)

LUJB . . . . Left Umbilical Junction Box (Aerospace)
LUL . . . . Left Upper Lobe (of lung) (Medicine)
LULA . . . . Loyola University of Los Angeles
LULAC . . . . . . League of United Latin American Citizens
LULS . . . . Lunar Logistic System
LUMAS . . . . . . Lunar Mapping System
LUME . . . . Light Utilization More Efficient
LUMF . . . . Lockheed Underwater Missile Facility
LUMO . . . . Lowest Unoccupied Molecular Orbitals
LUN . . . . Ludington & Northern Railway (AAR code)
LUPC . . . . Lighted Under Program Control
LUPF . . . . Linear Utility Prediction Function (Mathematics)
LUQ . . . . Left Upper Quadrant (of abdomen) (Medicine)
LUR . . . . London Underground Railway
LUS . . . . Load, Update, Subset
LUSEX . . . . . . Lunar Surface Explorer Simulation Program
LUSI . . . . Lunar Surface Inspection
LUST . . . . Latrine Urinal Shower Toilet (A unit of mobility equipment) (Military)
LUT . . . . Launch Umbilical Tower
LUT . . . . Loge Unie des Theosophes
LUTC . . . . Life Underwriter Training Council
LUV . . . . Let Us Vote (Organization dedicated to lowering voting age to 18)
LUV . . . . Light Utility Vehicle (Japanese pickup truck)
LUVO . . . . Lunar Ultraviolet Observatory (NASA)
LV . . . . Landing Vehicle
LV . . . . Launch Vehicle
LV . . . . Leave
LV . . . . Legal Volt
LV . . . . Lehigh Valley R. R. (AAR code)
LV . . . . Licensed Victualer
LV . . . . Light Vessel
LV . . . . Limit Value
LV . . . . Linear Velocity
LV . . . . Low Voltage
LVA . . . . Launch Vehicle Availability (Aerospace)
LV (A) (2) . . . . Landing Vehicle, Tracked (Armored) (Mark II) ("Water Buffalo," Canopy Type)
LVAR . . . . Lithuanian Veterans Association Ramove
LVB . . . . Left Ventricular Bypass (Artificial heart booster)
LVB . . . . Low-Voltage Bias
LVC . . . . Lebanon Valley College (Pennsylvania)
LVC . . . . Log Voltmeter Converter
LVC . . . . Low-Voltage Capacitor
LVCD . . . . Least Voltage Coincidence Detector
LVD . . . . Louvered Door
LVD . . . . Low-Velocity Detonation (or Drop)
LVDA . . . . Launch Vehicle Data Adapter (NASA)
LVDC . . . . Launch Vehicle Digital Computer (NASA)
LVDC . . . . Low-Voltage Direct Current
LVDS . . . . Liquid, Vee, Diesel-Cycle, Supercharged
LVDT . . . . Linear Variable (or Voltage) Differential (or Displacement) Transformer
LVE . . . . Linear Vector Equation
LVEA . . . . Lehigh Valley Electronic Association
LVF . . . . Legion des Volontaires Francais Contre le Bolchevism
LVF . . . . Linear Vector Function
LVF . . . . Low-Voltage Fast (Electronics)
LVFC . . . . Launch Vehicle Flight Control
LVFCS . . . . . . Launch Vehicle Flight Control System
LVG . . . . Left Visceral Ganglion
LVG . . . . Lehr-und-Versuchgut
LVH . . . . Landing Vehicle, Hydrofoil
LVH . . . . Left Ventricular Hypertrophy (Medicine)
LVHX . . . . Landing Craft, Hydrofoil, Experimental (Navy symbol)
LVI . . . . Laus Verbo Incarnato (Praise to the Incarnate Word)
LVI . . . . Levi Strauss & Co. (NYSE symbol)
LVI . . . . Local Veterinary Inspector (British)
LVK . . . . Amphibious Support Vehicle (Navy symbol)
LVL . . . . Level
LVL . . . . Long Vertical Left
LVM . . . . Launch Vehicle Monitor
LVM . . . . Light Vehicle Mine (Military)
LVM . . . . Line Voltage Monitor
LVN . . . . Low-Voltage Neon
LVO . . . . Launch Vehicle Operation
LVO . . . . LVO Corp. (NYSE symbol)
LVOD . . . . Launch Vehicles Operations Division
LVOR . . . . Low-Powered, Very High Frequency Omnirange
LVP . . . . Left Ventricular Pump (Heart pump)
LVP . . . . Light Valve Projector
LVP . . . . Low-Voltage Plate
LVP . . . . Low-Voltage Protection (Electronics)

LVPG . . . . Launch Vehicle Planning Group (Aerospace)
LVPS . . . . Low-Voltage Power Supply
LVR . . . . Laboratory of Virology and Rickettsial Diseases
LVR . . . . Line Voltage Regulator
LVR . . . . Long Vertical Right
LVR . . . . Low-Voltage Release (Electronics)
LVRIS . . . . Low Volume Ramjet Inlet System
LVRJ . . . . Low Volume Ramjet
LVRR . . . . Lehigh Valley Railroad
LVS . . . . Low Velocity Scanning
LVST . . . . Longitudinal Velocity Sorting Tube
LVT . . . . Landing Vehicle, Tracked (Unarmored)
LVT . . . . Linear Variable Transformer
LVT . . . . Linear Velocity Transducer
LVT . . . . Low-Voltage Tubular
LVT (1) . . . . . . Landing Vehicle, Tracked (Unarmored) (Mark I) ("Alligator")
LVT (2) . . . . . . Landing Vehicle, Tracked (Unarmored) (Mark II) ("Water Buffalo")
LVT (3) . . . . . . Landing Vehicle, Tracked (Mark III)
LVT (4) . . . . . . Landing Vehicle, Tracked (Unarmored) (Mark IV)
LVT (A) . . . . . . Landing Vehicle, Tracked (Armored) (Turret Type)
LVT (A) (1) . . . Landing Vehicle, Tracked (Armored) (Mark I) ("Water Buffalo," Turret Type)
LVT (A) (4) . . . Landing Vehicle, Tracked (Armored) (Mark IV)
LVT (A) (5) . . . Landing Vehicle, Tracked (Armored) (Mark V)
LVTE . . . . Landing Vehicle, Tracked, Engineer (Model 1)
LVTH . . . . Landing Vehicle, Tracked, Howitzer (Model 6)
LVTP . . . . Landing Vehicle, Tracked, Personnel (Military)
LVTR . . . . Low VHF Transmitter-Receiver
LVTU . . . . Landing Vehicle, Tracked, Unarmored (Navy)
LVUSA . . . . . . Legion of Valor of the United States of America
LVVS . . . . Liquidatie Vermogens Verwalting Sarphatistraat (Amsterdam, Holland)
LVW . . . . Landing Vehicle, Wheeled
LVZ . . . . Low-Viscosity Zone
LW . . . . Lacerated Wound
LW . . . . Landsteiner-Wiener (Serum)
LW . . . . Launch Window (Aerospace)
LW . . . . Left Wing
LW . . . . Light Wall
LW . . . . Light Warning
LW . . . . Limited War
LW . . . . Long Wave (Radio)
LW . . . . Louisville & Wadley R. R. (AAR code)
LW . . . . Low Water (Maps and charts)
L-W . . . . Landsverk-Wollan (Radiation survey meter)
L & W . . . . . . Living and Well
LWA . . . . Light Weight Armor
LWA . . . . Lightly Wounded in Action
LWA . . . . Long Wire Antenna
LWASV . . . . . . Lightweight Aircraft-to-Surface Vessel (Military)
LWB . . . . Light Water Breeder (Reactor) (AEC)
LWB . . . . Long Wheelbase
LWBR . . . . Light Water Breeder Reactor (AEC)
LWC . . . . Lightweight Concrete (Technical drawings)
LWC . . . . Lindsey Wilson College (Kentucky)
LWC . . . . Liquid Water Content
LWCS . . . . Limited War Capabilities Study
LWD . . . . Larger Word (Data processing)
LWD . . . . Loomis-Woods Diagram
LWD . . . . Low Water Datum (Data)
LWF . . . . Lutheran World Federation
LWF & C . . . . . Low Water Full and Change
LWG . . . . Lightweight Gun
LWHS . . . . Lightweight Headset (Apollo) (NASA)
LWHVR . . . . . . Lightweight High Velocity Rifle
LWI . . . . Load Wear Index
LWI . . . . Low Water Interval
LWIC . . . . Lightweight Insulating Concrete (Technical drawings)
LWII . . . . Long Wavelength Infrared Illuminator
LWIR . . . . Long Wavelength Infrared
LWIRC . . . . . . Limited Warfare Intelligence Reduction Complex
LWIU . . . . Laundry, Dry Cleaning and Dye House Workers International Union
LWIU . . . . Leather Workers International Union of America
LWL . . . . Length at Waterline
LWL . . . . Limited War Laboratory (Army)
LWL . . . . Load Water Line
LWL . . . . Low Water Line
LWM . . . . Low Water Mark
LWMEL . . . . . . Leonard Wood Memorial for the Eradication of Leprosy
LWML . . . . Lutheran Women's Missionary League
LWNA . . . . Lumber (Timber), Winter, North Atlantic (Vessel load line mark)
LWO . . . . Limited War Office (Air Force)

LWOP. . . . . . . Leave Without Pay (Civil Service)
LWOS . . . . . . Low Water Ordinary Springs
LWOST . . . . . Low Water Ordinary Spring Tides
LWP . . . . Limited War Plan(s)
LWP . . . . Load Water Plane
LWQ . . . . Low Water Quadrature
LWR . . . . Light-Water Reactor (AEC)
LWR . . . . Limited War Capability
LWR . . . . Local Wage Rate
LWR . . . . Lower
LWR . . . . Lutheran World Relief, Inc.
LWRS . . . . . . Lightweight Weather RADAR Set
LWS . . . . Lightweight Sight
LWS . . . . Lightweight System
LWS . . . . Low Water Sensitivity (Brake fluid designation)
LWSF . . . . . . Lightweight Strike Fighter
LW(STA) . . . . . Light Warning (Station)
LWT . . . . Amphibious Warping Tug (Navy symbol)
LWT . . . . Lightweight Transponder
LWT . . . . Lightweight Type (Anchor gear)
LWU . . . . LASER Welder Unit
LWU. . . . . . . Leather Workers International Union of America
LWUI . . . . . . Longshoremen's and Warehousemen's Union International
LWV. . . . . . . Lackawanna & Wyoming Valley R. R. (AAR code)
LWV. . . . . . . Landwirtschaftsversorgungsamt (German Land Economic Supply Office) (Post-World War II)
LWV . . . . League of Women Voters of the United States
LWVUS . . . . . League of Women Voters of the United States
LWW . . . . . . Launch Window Width
LWW . . . . . . Lightweight Weapon
LWWS . . . . . Lightweight Weapons Sight

LX . . . . Los Angeles Airways, Inc.
LX . . . . Low Index (Aviation)
LX . . . . Lux
LXA . . . . Load Index from Address
LXD . . . . LASER Transceiver Device
LXD . . . . Load Index from Decrement
LXFT . . . . . . Linear Xenon Flash Tube
LXT . . . . Linear Xenon Tube
LY . . . . Last Year's Model (Merchandising slang)
LY . . . . Linear Yard
LY . . . . Lykes-Youngstown Corp. (NYSE symbol)
LYaPAS. . . . . . Logicheskii Yazyk dlia Predstavleniya Algoritmov Sinteza Releinykh Ustroistv (A Programming Language for Logic and Coding Algorithm) (Book title)
LYC . . . . Lynch Communication Systems (NYSE symbol)
LYK . . . . Lykes Brothers Steamship Company, Inc. (NYSE symbol) (Later, LY)
LYR . . . . . . Lancashire and Yorkshire Railway (British)
LYS . . . . Lysine (Amino acid)
LZ . . . . Landing Zone
LZ . . . . Lubrizol Corp. (NYSE symbol)
LZA. . . . . . . Labor Zionist Alliance
LZCO. . . . . . . Landing Zone Control Officer (Air Force)
LZD . . . . Launch Zone Display
LZDF . . . . . . Launch Zone Display Flag
LZF . . . . Launch Zone Flag
LZGF . . . . . . Lewis Zero Gravity Facility
LZO. . . . . . . Launch Zone Override
LZOA. . . . . . . Labor Zionist Organization of America-Poale Zion
LZOC . . . . . . Lincoln Zephyr Owner's Club
LZT . . . . Local Zone Time
LWO . . . . Limited Warning Operation

M

M	Absolute Magnitude (Astronomy)
M	Mach Number
M	MacNeil (Herman A.) (Designer's mark, when appearing on US coins)
M	Magistrate
M	Magnaflux
M	Magnetic
M	Magnetization
M	Maiden
M	Mail
M	Main (Hand)
M	Majesty
M	Make
M	Male
M	Mammato
M	Maneuvering Ship (In speed triangle of relative movement problems)
M	Manila (Rope)
M	Manipulus (Handful)
M	Mano (Hand)
M	Manual
M	March
M	MARCOR, Inc. (Formerly, Montgomery Ward & Company, Inc.) (Wall Street slang name: "Monkey") (NYSE symbol)
M	Mare
M	Maria (Mary)
M	Marine Corps (When used as prefix with plane designation)
M	Maritime (Air mass)
M	Mark (Coin)
M	Marker (Beacon)
M	Markka (Monetary unit in Finland)
M	Marquis
M	Married
M	Mars
M	Marshal
M	Martyr
M	Masculine
M	Mass
M	Master
M	Mate (of a ship)
M	Mater (Latin)
M	Matins (Early morning prayers)
M	Mature Audiences (Movie rating) (Replaced by GP)
M	May
M	Mean (Arithmetic average)
M	Mean Square
M	Measure(s) (Music)
M	Measured Ceiling (Aviation)
M	Mechanical
M	Medicine or Medical
M	Medieval
M	Medium (Size designation for clothing, etc.)
M	Medium (or 2-engine) Plane
M	Mega (A prefix meaning multiplied by one million)
m	Melts at
M	Member
M	Membrana (Membrane) (Anatomy)
M	Memorandum
M	Memoria (Memory)
M	Memory
m	Meridian (Lower branch)
M	Meridian (Upper branch)
M	Meridies (Noon)
M	Meridional Parts
M	Mesh

m	Meta (Chemistry)
M	Metacenter
M	Metal
M	Metalsmith (Navy)
M	Meter(s)
M	Methodist
M	Metropolitan
M	Mezzo (Half)
M	Middle
M	Midfield (Men's lacrosse position)
M	Miles
M	Military
M	Mill(s)
M	Mille (Thousand, in roman numerals)
m	Milli- (A prefix meaning divided by 1000)
M	Million
M	Mine
M	Minesweeper (Navy)
M	Minim(s)
M	Minor
M	Minute(s)
M	Misce (Mix)
M	Miscellaneous
M	Missile (Air Force)
M	Missile carrier aircraft (Designation for all US military aircraft)
M	Missing
M	Mist
M	Mix(ture)
M	Mobilization (as in M-Day) (Military)
M	Mode
M	Model (in military nomenclature)
M	Moderate Sea or Swell (Weather charts)
m	Modulus
M	Molar (Dentistry)
M	Mole
M	Molecular Weight (Also, MW)
M	Moment
M	Monday
M	Monoplane
M	Monsieur (Mister) (French)
M	Monsoon
M	Mont, Monte, etc. (Italy and Sicily only)
M	Month
M	Monthly
M	Monumentum (Monument)
M	Moon
M	Morgan (George T.) (Designer's mark, when appearing on US coins)
M	Morning
M	Morphine (Slang)
M	Mortar
M	Mortgage
M	Mortis (Of Death)
M	Mother
M	Motor
M	Mountain
M	Mountain Standard Time (Aviation)
M	Mouth
M	Mucoid
M	Mud
M	Musculus (Muscle) (Anatomy)
M	Mustard Gas
M	Muster
M	Myopia

M . . . . One Thousand (Roman numeral)
M (Day) . . . . . Mobilization Day (Military)
3M . . . . Maintenance and Material Management (Navy)
3M . . . . Minnesota Mining & Manufacturing Company (Also, MMM)
MA . . . . Machine Accountant
MA . . . . Magma Arizona R. R. (AAR code)
MA . . . . Magnesium Association
MA . . . . Magnetic Amplifier
MA . . . . Mahogany Association
MA . . . . Maids of Athens (An organization)
MA . . . . Manifest Anxiety
MA . . . . Manpower Administration (Department of Labor)
MA . . . . Manufacturing Assembly
MA . . . . Map Analysis
MA . . . . Maritime Administration (Department of Commerce)
MA . . . . Marshalling Area (Military)
MA . . . . Massachusetts
MA . . . . Master Alarm
MA . . . . Master of Arts
MA . . . . Masurium
MA . . . . May Department Stores Company (NYSE symbol)
MA . . . . Mechanical Advantage
MA . . . . Mechano-Acoustic
MA . . . . Mediterranean Area
MA . . . . Medium Artillery
MA . . . . Memory Address (Data processing)
MA . . . . Menorah Association
MA . . . . Menstrual Age
MA . . . . Mental Age (Psychology)
MA . . . . Mercury-Atlas (Spacecraft) (NASA)
MA . . . . Message Assembler
MA . . . . Meter Amplifier
MA . . . . Meter Angle
MA . . . . Metric Association
MA . . . . Micro-Alloy
MA . . . . Microphone and Amplifier (Television)
MA . . . . Middle Ages
MA . . . . Military Academy
MA . . . . Military Assistant (Air Force)
MA . . . . Military Attache (Diplomacy)
MA . . . . Military Aviator
MA . . . . Mill Annealed
mA . . . . Milliampere(s)
MA . . . . Ministry of Aviation (England)
MA . . . . Missed Approach (Aviation)
MA . . . . Mission Accomplished (Air Force)
MA . . . . Missionarius Apostolicus (Missionary Apostolic)
MA . . . . Mobilization Augmentee (Military)
MA . . . . Mountain Artillery
MA . . . . Munitionsanstalt (Ammunition depot) (German military – World
         War II)
MA . . . . My Account
M/A . . . . Mess Attendant
M/A . . . . Monetary Allowance
M & A . . . . . Management and Administration
M & A . . . . . Missouri and Arkansas Railway Company
MAA . . . . Macroaggregated Albumin (Medicine)
MAA . . . . Manufacturers Aircraft Association
MAA . . . . Marineartillerieabteilung (Naval coast artillery battalion)
         (German military – World War II)
MAA . . . . Master of Applied Arts
MAA. . . . . . . Master-at-Arms (Navy)
MAA . . . . Master of Arms (Head of a ship's police) (British)
MAA . . . . Master Army Aviator
MAA . . . . Mathematical Association of America
MAA . . . . Maximum Authorized Altitude (Aviation)
MAA . . . . Mediaeval Academy of America
MAA . . . . Medical Assistance for the Aged
MAA . . . . Mid America Airlines
MAA . . . . Modeling Association of America
MAA . . . . Motel Association of America
MAAA . . . . . . Memoirs American Anthropological Association (Journal)
MAAC . . . . . Mutual Assistance Advisory Committee
MAACL. . . . . . Multiple Affect Adjective Check List (of Educational and Industrial
         Testing Service)
MAACP . . . . . Mediterranean Area Airlift Command Post
MAAF. . . . . . Mediterranean Allied Air Force
MAAF. . . . . . Mediterranean Allied Army Air Forces
MAAG . . . . . . Military Allied Assistance Group
MAAG . . . . . Military Assistance Advisory Group (Merged with US Military Assistance
         Command)

MAALOX . . . . Magnesium-Aluminum Hydroxide (Commercial antacid)
MAAM . . . . . . Medium Antiaircraft Missile
MAAN . . . . . . Mutual Advertising Agency Network
MAANPI . . . . Mutual Aid Association of the New Polish Immigration
MA Arch . . . . Master of Arts in Architecture
MAAS . . . . . . Manpower Allocation and Accounting Subsystem (Air Force)
MAAT . . . . . . MAC (McDonnell Aircraft Corporation) Acquisition and Attack Trainer
MAATC. . . . . Mobile Antiaircraft Training Center
MAAU . . . . . . Mexican-American Affairs Unit (US Office of Education)
MAAW . . . . . Medium Antitank Assault Weapon
MAAWS . . . . . Middle Atlantic Association of Women Sailors
MAB. . . . . . . Magazine Advertising Bureau (of MPA)
MAB. . . . . . . Magnetic Amplifier Bridge
MAB. . . . . . . Malfunction Analysis Branch (NASA)
MAB . . . . . . Management Analysis Branch (Vietnam)
MAB . . . . . . Manganese Alkaline Battery
MAB . . . . . . Maracaibo Oil Exploration Corporation (NYSE symbol) (Delisted)
MAB. . . . . . . Marine Air Base
MAB. . . . . . . Materials Advisory Board (National Research Council)
MAB . . . . . . Medical Advisory Board
MAB . . . . . . Member, Advisory Board
MAB . . . . . . Metropolitan Asylums Board (British)
MAB . . . . . . Missile Assembly Building
MAB . . . . . . Mobile Assault Bridge
MAB. . . . . . . Munitions Assignment Board (Anglo-American) (World War II)
MABA . . . . . . M-Aminobenzyl Amine
MABA. . . . . . Meta-Aminobenzoic Acid
MABCGT . . . . Mutual Adjustment Bureau of Cloth and Garment Trades, Inc.
MABDG. . . . . Marine Aircraft Base Defense Group
MABDW . . . . . Marine Air Base Defense Wing
MABLE . . . . . Miniature Autonetics Base Line Equipment
MABO . . . . . . Marianas-Bonins Group
MABP. . . . . . Mean Arterial Blood Pressure (Physiology)
MABRON . . . . Marine Air Base Squadron
MABS . . . . . . Maltese-American Benevolent Society
MABS . . . . . . Marine Air Base Squadron (Marine Corps)
MABS . . . . . . Mixed Air Battle Simulation
MABU . . . . . . Maschinengewehr-Eisenbetonunterstand (Machine-gun-reinforced
         concrete pillbox) (German military – World War II)
MAC . . . . MacDonald (E.F.) Co. (NYSE symbol)
MAC . . . . Machine-Aided Cognition (Computer project) (DOD)
MAC . . . . Magnetic Attitude Control
MAC . . . . Maintenance Advisory Committee (NSIA)
MAC . . . . Maintenance Allocation Chart
MAC . . . . Maintenance Analysis Center (FAA)
MAC . . . . Major Air Command (Later, MAJCOM)
MAC . . . . Malignancy-Associated Changes (Cancer)
MAC . . . . Maneuver Area Command (Army)
MAC . . . . Marine Amphibious Corps
MAC . . . . Marker and Cell (Computing technique) (NASA)
MAC . . . . Mass Absorption Coefficient
M Ac . . . . Master of Accounting
MAC . . . . Materials Analysis Company
MAC . . . . Maximum Allowable Concentration
MAC . . . . McDonnell Aircraft Corporation (NYSE symbol) (Later, MD)
MAC . . . . McLeod Aerating Cardiac
MAC . . . . Mean Aerodynamic Chord (Aerospace)
MAC . . . . Mediterranean Air Command (Military)
MAC . . . . Metacarpal Ash per Centimeter
MAC . . . . Middle Atlantic Conference
MAC . . . . Military Airlift Command (Formerly, Military Air Transport Service)
MAC . . . . Mine Advisory Committee (NAS-NRC)
MAC . . . . Model Airplane Club
MAC . . . . Motion Analysis Camera
MAC . . . . Motor Ambulance Convoy
MAC . . . . Movimento Anti-Colonialista (Anti-Colonialist Movement)
MAC . . . . Multiaction Computer
MAC . . . . Multiple Access Computer
MAC . . . . Multiple Address Code
MAC (Air) . . . . Munitions Assignment Committee (Air) (Washington)
MACA . . . . . . Mammoth Cave National Park
MACA . . . . . . Military Airlift Clearance Authority
MACABRE . . . . Material Ablation with Chemically Active Boundary Layers in
         Reentry (NASA)
MACAF. . . . . . Mediterranean Allied Coastal Air Forces
MACAL. . . . . . Military Airlift Command Airlift Operations Report
MACAM . . . . . Military Airlift Command Automated Management
MACAP. . . . . . Major Appliance Consumer Action Panel
MACB. . . . . . Missile Assembly Control Building
MACC . . . . . . Malaysian-American Chamber of Commerce
M Acc . . . . . . Master of Accountancy (or Accounting)

MACC . . . . . . Modular Alter and Compose Console (Data Processing)
M Acc's . . . . . Master of Accounts
MACCS . . . . . Manufacturing Cost Collection System
MACCS . . . . . Manufacturing and Cost-Control System (Data processing)
MACE . . . . . . Machine-Aided Composition and Editing
MACE . . . . . . Massachusetts Advisory Council on Education
MACE . . . . . . Master of Air Conditioning Engineering
MACE . . . . . . Military Airlift Capability Estimator
MACE . . . . . . Missile and Control Equipment Division, North American Aviation
MAC Eng . . . . Master of Air Conditioning Engineering
MACG . . . . . . Marine Air Control Group
MACG . . . . . Marshalling Area Control Group (Military)
MACH . . . . . . Machine
MA Chem . . . . Master of Applied Chemistry
MACHGR . . . . Machine Group
MACIMS . . . . . Military Airlift Command Integrated Management System
MAC(K) . . . . . Military Armistice Commission (Korea)
MACMIS . . . . Maintenance and Construction Management Information System
⠀⠀⠀⠀⠀⠀⠀⠀⠀(Data processing)
MACNIMAATZ . . . MacArthur, Nimitz, and Spaatz (Nickname for tripartite
⠀⠀⠀⠀⠀⠀⠀⠀⠀command in the Pacific of General of the Army Douglas MacArthur,
⠀⠀⠀⠀⠀⠀⠀⠀⠀Fleet Admiral Chester W. Nimitz, and Strategic Air Commander
⠀⠀⠀⠀⠀⠀⠀⠀⠀General Carl A. Spaatz) (World War II)
MACO . . . . . Marshalling Area Control Officer (Military)
MACOI . . . . . . Military Assistance Command Office in Vietnam (US)
MA in Comm . . Master of Arts in Communications
MACON . . . . . Maintenance Console
MACOPS . . . . Military Airlift Command Operational Phone System
MACOS . . . . . Man - A Course of Study (Title of course and of training centers at
⠀⠀⠀⠀⠀⠀⠀⠀⠀various universities)
MACOV . . . . . Mechanized and Army Combat Operations Vietnam
MACP . . . . . . Mission Analysis Computer Program
MACR . . . . . . Member of the American College of Radiology
MACR . . . . . . Minneapolis, Anoka & Cuyuna Range R. R. (AAR code)
MACR . . . . . . Missing Air Crew Report
MACRI . . . . . Mercantile Atlantic Coastal Routing Instructions
MACS . . . . . . Marine Air Control Squadron
MACS . . . . . . McDonnell Automatic Checkout System
MACS . . . . . . Medium-Altitude Communications Satellite
MACS . . . . . . Military Aeronautical Communications Service
MACS . . . . . . Missile Air-Conditioning System
MACS . . . . . . Multiple Application Connector System
MACS . . . . . . Multiproject Automated Control System
MACSS . . . . . Medium-Altitude Communications Satellite System
MACTELNET . . MAC (Military Airlift Command) Teletype Network
MACTRAC . . . . Military Airlift Command Traffic Reporting and Control System
MACTU . . . . . Mines and Countermeasures Technical Unit (Navy)
MACU . . . . . . Michigan Association of Colleges and Universities
MACV . . . . . . Military Assistance Command, Vietnam
MACV . . . . . . Multipurpose Airmobile Combat-Support Vehicle
MACVFR . . . . Make Altitude Changes Visual Flight Rules (Aviation)
MACW . . . . . . Missionary Association of Catholic Women
MAD . . . . Machine Analysis Display
MAD . . . . . . Madison Fund, Inc. (NYSE symbol)
MAD . . . . . . Magnetic Airborne Detector (Navy)
MAD . . . . Magnetic Anomaly Detection (or Detector)
MAD . . . . Maintenance Alert Directive (Aviation)
MAD . . . . Maintenance, Assembly, and Disassembly
MAD . . . . Management Analysis Division (NASA)
MAD . . . . . . Manufacturing Assembly Drawing
MAD . . . . . . Marine Air (or Aviation) Detachment
MAD . . . . Michigan Algorithmic Decoder (IBM)
MAD . . . . Mileage Accumulation Dynamometer
MAD . . . . Military Airplane Division
MAD . . . . . . Mine Assembly Depot (Navy)
MAD . . . . Minimal Aural Dose
MAD . . . . . . Multi-Aperture Device (Data processing)
MAD . . . . Multiple Access Device
MAD . . . . Multiple Audio Distribution (Communications)
MAD . . . . Multiply and Add
MAD . . . . Mutual Assured Destruction
MADAEC . . . . Military Application Division of the Atomic Energy Commission
MADAM . . . . Moderately Advanced Data Management (Data processing)
MADAM . . . . Multipurpose Automatic Data Analysis Machine
MADAP . . . . . . Maastricht Automatic Data Processing and Display System (Air traffic
⠀⠀⠀⠀⠀⠀⠀⠀⠀control)
MADAR . . . . . Malfunction Analysis Detection and Recording (Data processing)
MADARS . . . . Maintenance Analysis, Detection and Reporting System
MADDAM . . . . Macromodule and Digital Differential Analyzer Machine
MADDIDA . . . Magnetic Drum Digital Differential Analyzer

MADE . . . . . . Magnetic Device Evaluator (Data processing)
MADE . . . . . . Micro Alloy Diffused Electrode
MADE . . . . . . Minimum Airborne Digital Equipment
MADE . . . . . . Multichannel Analog-to-Digital Data Encoder
MADEPSQ . . . . Marine Air Depot Squadron
MADGE . . . . Microwave Aircraft Digital Guidance Equipment (Helicopters)
MADI . . . . . . Master Data Index
MADIS . . . . . Millivolt Analog-Digital Instrumentation System
M Adm . . . . . . Master of Administration
MADM . . . . . . Medium Atomic Demolition Munition (Military)
M Adm E . . . . Master of Administrative Engineering
MADOC . . . . Medical Analysis of Days of Care (Report)
MADP . . . . Main Air Display Plot
MADRE . . . . . Magnetic Drum Receiving Equipment
MADRE . . . . . Martin Automatic Data-Reduction Equipment
MADREC . . . . Malfunction Detection and Recording (Checkout system for aircraft)
⠀⠀⠀⠀⠀⠀⠀⠀⠀(Air Force)
MADS . . . . . . Mars Atmosphere Density Sensor
MADS . . . . . . Missile Attitude Determination System (LASER device) (Air Force)
MADS . . . . . . Mobile Air Defense System
MADS . . . . . . Mobile Airborne Defense Station Concept (Air Force)
MADT . . . . . . Microalloy Diffused Base Transistor
MADW . . . . . . Military Air Defense Warning Net
M Ae . . . . Master of Aeronautics
MAE . . . . . . Master of Art Education
MAE . . . . . . Master of Arts in Education
MAE . . . . McDonnell Airborne Evaluator (McDonnell Douglas Corporation)
MAE . . . . Mean Absolute Error
MAE . . . . Medical Air Evacuation
MAE . . . . Monroe Auto Equipment Co. (NYSE symbol)
MAE . . . . Mutual Assistance, Executive (Military appropriation)
MAECON . . . . Mid-America Electronics Conference
MA Ed . . . . . . Master of Arts in Education
MAEE . . . . . . Marine Aircraft Experimental Establishment
M Ae E . . . . . Master of Aeronautical Engineering
M Ae Eng . . . . Master of Aeronautical Engineering
MAELU . . . . . . Mutual Atomic Energy Liability Underwriters
M Aero E . . . . Master of Aeronautical Engineering
M Aero Eng . . . Master of Aeronautical Engineering
MAERP . . . . . . Mutual Atomic Energy Reassurance Pool
MAERU . . . . . . Mobile Ammunition Evaluation and Reconditioning Unit
M Ae S . . . . . . Master of Aeronautical Science
M Ae Sc . . . . . Master of Aeronautical Science
MAET . . . . Microwave Amplifier Electron Tube
MAET . . . . . . Missile Accident Emergency Team
MAF . . . . MacAndrews & Forbes Company (NYSE symbol)
MAF . . . . Magnetic Anisotropy Field
MAF . . . . Maintenance Action Form
MAF . . . . Major Academic Field
MAF . . . . Manpower Authorization File
MAF . . . . Marine Air Facility
MAF . . . . Marine Amphibious Forces (Army)
MAF . . . . Maximum Amplitude Filter
MAF . . . . Michoud Assembly Facility (NASA)
MAF . . . . Minimum Audible Field
MAF . . . . Missionary Aviation Fellowship
MAF . . . . Mixed Amine Fuel
MAFA . . . . . . Manchester Academy of Fine Arts
MAFA . . . . . . Middle Atlantic Fisheries Association
MAFAP . . . . . Minimum Altitude over Facility on Final Approach Course (Aviation)
MAFB . . . . Mitchell Air Force Base
MAFCA . . . . . Model A Ford Club of America
MAFCO . . . . . . Magnetic Field Code
MAFD . . . . . . Minimum Acquisition Flux Density
MAFE . . . . . . Maintenance of Air/FMF (Fleet Marine Force) Expeditionary Equipment
MAFI . . . . Medic-Alert Foundation International
MAFIA . . . . . Marimba and Fife Inspectors Association (Women's tongue-in-cheek
⠀⠀⠀⠀⠀⠀⠀⠀⠀organization) (Defunct)
MAFIA . . . . . Morte Alla Francia Italia Anelo (Death to the French is Italy's
⠀⠀⠀⠀⠀⠀⠀⠀⠀Cry), or Movimento Anti Francesi Italiano Azione (Italian Action
⠀⠀⠀⠀⠀⠀⠀⠀⠀Movement Against the French)
MAFL . . . . Multi-Aperture Ferrite Logic
MAFOG . . . . Mediterranean Area Fighter Operations Grid
MAFOR . . . . . . Marine Forecast (Pronounced "Mayfor")
MAFR . . . . . . Merged Accountability and Fund Reporting (Air Force)
MAFS . . . . . . Memoirs American Folklore Society (Journal)
MAFS . . . . . . Mobilization Air Force Specialty
MAFSC . . . . . Mobilization Air Force Specialty Code
MAFSI . . . . . . Manufacturers' Agents for Food Service Industry
MAG . . . . Magazine
MAG . . . . Magnavox Company (NYSE symbol) (Wall Street slang name: "Maggie")

MAG . . . . Magnetic
MAG . . . . Magnitude
MAG . . . . . . Marine Aircraft (or Aviation) Group
MAG . . . . Marker-Adder Generator
MAG . . . . Marketing Aids Group
M Ag . . . . Master of Agriculture
MAG . . . . Military Advisory Group
MAGA . . . . . . Medium-Accuracy Gyro Assembly
MAGAMP . . . . Magnetic Amplifier
MAGCON. . . . Magnetized Concentration (Lunar)
MAGDARR. . . . Magnavox Doppler and Ranging RADAR
M Ag Ec . . . . . Master of Agricultural Economics
M Ag Ed . . . . . Master of Agricultural Education
MAGGE . . . . . Medium-Altitude Gravity Gradient Experiment
MAGI. . . . . . . Master Group Information System (AT & T)
MAGI. . . . . . . Mathematical Applications Group, Incorporated
MAGI . . . . . . Multiarray Gamma Irradiator
MAGIC . . . . . American Military Advisory Group in China (Post-World War II)
MAGIC . . . . . Machine for Automatic Graphics Interface to a Computer
MAGIC. . . . . . Madison Avenue General Ideas Committee (New York City)
MAGIC. . . . . . Matrix Analysis via Generative and Interpretive Computations (Data processing)
MAGIC . . . . . MIDAC Automatic General Integrated Computation (Data processing)
MAGIC . . . . . Modified Action Generated Input Control
MAGIC. . . . . . Motorola Automatically Generated Integrated Circuits
MAGIS . . . . . Megawatt Air-to-Ground Illumination System
MAGLEV. . . . . Magnetic Levitation (Magnetic high-speed train)
MAGLOC. . . . . Magnetic Logic Computer
MAGMOD . . . Magnetic Modulator
MAGNOX . . . Magnesium Oxide
MAGp . . . . . . Military Airlift Group (Air Force)
MAGPIE . . . . . Markov Game Planar Intercept-Evasion Package (Data processing)
M Agr . . . . . . Master of Agriculture
M Agr E . . . . . Master of Agricultural Engineering
M Agr Eng. . . . Master of Agricultural Engineering
M Agr S . . . . . Master of Agricultural Science
M Agr Sc . . . . . Master of Agricultural Science
MAGSI . . . . . . Minimum Altitude at Glide Slope Intersection Inbound (Aviation)
MAGTAF . . . . Marine Air Ground Task Force
MAGTRAC . . . Magnetic Amplifier, Transistorized, Automatic Target Tracker
MAH . . . . Mahoning Coal Railroad (NYSE symbol)
MAH. . . . . . . Maleic Anhydride
MAHA . . . . . . Metropolitan Association of Handwriting Analysts
MAHC . . . . . . Maximum Allowable Housing Cost (Army)
MAI . . . . Magister in Arte Ingeniaria (Master of Engineering Art)
MAI . . . . Mantle Arm Index
MAI . . . . Material Annex Item (Military)
MAI . . . . Member of the Anthropological Institute (British)
MAI . . . . Member, Appraisal Institute (Designation awarded to appraisers of real property)
MAI. . . . . Military Assistance Institute
MAI . . . . Multiple Address Instruction
MAID . . . . . . Maintenance Automatic Integration Director (Data processing)
MAID . . . . . . Manual Intervention and Display
MAID . . . . . . Merger Acquisition Improved Decision (Data processing)
MAID . . . . . . Monroe Automatic Internal Diagnosis (Data processing)
MAIDS . . . . . Machine-Aided Information and Dissemination Systems
MAIDS . . . . . Multipurpose Automatic Inspection and Diagnostic Systems (Army)
MAIN. . . . . . . Medical Automation Intelligence (System)
MAIN . . . . . . Military Authorization Identification Number
MAINT . . . . . . Maintenance
MAINTRAIN. . . Maintenance and Training (in Complex Equipment)
MAIR . . . . . . Molecular Airborne Intercept RADAR
MAIRAIRMED . . Maritime Air Forces, Mediterranean (NATO)
MAIRMAR . . . . Marine Air Depot, Miramar, California
MAIRU . . . . . . Mobile Aircraft Instrument Repair Unit
MAIS . . . . . . Mechanical Aids for the Individual Soldier (Army)
MAISA . . . . . . Middle Atlantic Intercollegiate Sailing Association
MAISA . . . . . . Multiple Analytical Isoelectrofocusing Scanning Apparatus
MAJ . . . . Major (Military)
MAJ. . . . . Model Air Jet
MAJAC . . . . . Maintenance Anti-Jam Console (Air Force)
MAJAC . . . . . Monitor, Antijam, and Control
MAJC. . . . . . . Mount Aloysius Junior College (Pennsylvania)
MAJCOM . . . Major Command (Military) (Formerly, Major Air Command)
MAJCON . . . . Major Air Command Controlled (units)
MAJ GEN . . . . Major General
MAK . . . . Macke Co. (NYSE symbol)
MAK . . . . Medical Accessories Kit (Apollo) (NASA)
MAK . . . . Methylated Albumin Kieselguhr (Chromatography)
MAK . . . . Monopulse Antenna Kit

MAKSUTSUB . . Make Suitable Substitution
MAL . . . . Magnetic Armature Loudspeaker
MAL . . . . Maintain at Least (followed by altitude) (Aviation)
MAL. . . . . Malariology Technician (Navy)
MAL. . . . . Malayan Airways, Limited
MAL . . . . Materiel Allowance List
MAL . . . . Miller Airlines (Michigan)
MALD . . . . . . Master of Arts in Law and Diplomacy
MALDEF . . . . . Mexican American Legal Defense and Educational Fund
MALE . . . . Multi-Aperture Logic Element
MALF . . . . . . Mobile Aerobee Launch Facility
MALI . . . . . . Material Annex Line Item
MALIMET . . . . Master List of Medical Indexing Terms
MALIPR. . . . . . Material Annex Line Item Progress Report
MALLAR . . . . . Manned Lunar Landing & Return
MALN . . . . . . Mouvement Africain de Liberation Nationale (African Movement for National Liberation)
MALOS. . . . . . Maintenance and Logistics Space (System)
MALS . . . . . . Master of Arts in Liberal Studies
MALS . . . . . . Medium-Intensity Approach Light System (Aviation)
MA in LS . . . . Master of Arts in Liberal Studies
MA in LS . . . . Master of Arts in Library Science
MALT . . . . . . Military Adviser's Language Text
MALT . . . . . . Military Assistance Language Training
MALTA . . . . . Middle Atlantic Lawn Tennis Association
MAM . . . . . . Management Analysis Memorandum (DOD)
MAM . . . . . . Medium Automotive Maintenance
MAM . . . . . . Military Air Movement Number
MAM . . . . . . Military Assistance Manual
MAM . . . . . . Milliampere Minutes
MAM . . . . . . Missile Alarm Monitor
MAMA . . . . . . Management Accounting Maintenance Advertising, Inc.
MAMA . . . . . . Middletown Air Materiel Area
MAMB . . . . . Military Advisory Mission, Brazil
MAMBO . . . . . Mediterranean Association of Marine Biology and Oceanography
MA Mech . . . . Master of Applied Mechanics
MAMI . . . . . . Machine-Aided Manufacturing Information (Data processing)
MAMI . . . . . . Multiple Association Management Institute
MAMIE. . . . . . Minimum Automatic Machine for Interpolation and Extrapolation
MAMMA . . . . Men Against the Maxi-Midi Atrocity (Klosters, Switzerland, group opposing below-the-knee fashions introduced in 1970)
MAMOS . . . . Marine Automatic Meteorological Observing Station (Automatic system)
MAMOS . . . . Missouri Associated Migrant Opportunities Services
MAMRON . . . Marine Aircraft Maintenance Squadron
MAMS . . . . . . Military Aircraft Marshalling System
MAMS . . . . . . Missile Assembly and Maintenance Shop (NASA)
MAMS . . . . . . Modern Army Maintenance System
MAN . . . . . . Maintenance Alert Network (RCA)
MAN . . . . Manager (or Managing)
MAN . . . . Manpower, Inc. (NYSE symbol)
MAN . . . . Maschinenfabrik Augsburg-Neurnberg (Germany)
MAN . . . . . . Meaningful Assistance in the Neighborhood (of Legal Aid Bureau of George Washington University Law School)
MAN . . . . . . Microwave Aerospace Navigation
MAN . . . . . . Military Aviation Notice (Air Force)
MAN . . . . . . Molecular Anatomy
MAN's . . . . . . Military Aviation Notices (Air Force)
MANA . . . . . Manassas National Battlefield Park
MANA . . . . . Manufacturers' Agents National Association
MANAM . . . . Manual Amendment
MANDEC . . . . Maneuvering Decoy
MANDFHAB. . . Male and Female Homosexual Association of Great Britain
MANDS . . . . . Maintenance and Supply
MANFOR . . . . Manpower Force Packaging (Military)
MANFORCE. . . Manpower for a Clean Environment (Water Pollution Control Federation)
MANI. . . . . . . Ministry of Agriculture for Northern Ireland (British)
MANIAC. . . . . Mathematical Analyzer, Numerical Integrator and Computer
MANIP. . . . . . Manual Input
MANIX . . . . . Machine Aids to Nike-X (Army)
MANMED . . . . Manual of Medical Department (Navy)
MANMEDDEPT . . Manual of the Medical Department (Navy)
MANOP . . . . . Manual of Operation(s)
MANOVA . . . Multivariate Analysis of Variance (Statistics)
MANS. . . . . . . Map Analysis System (Data processing)
MANSAT. . . . . Manned Satellite
MANTRAC . . . Manual Angle Tracking Capability
MANTRAP . . . Management Training Program (of Center for Research in Business and Economics, University of Houston)
MANU . . . . . . Mozambique African National Union
MANZCP . . . . Member of the Australian and New Zealand College of Psychiatrists
MAO . . . . Magnetic Amplifier Output

ACRONYMS AND INITIALISMS DICTIONARY

MAO ...... Mailing Address Only (Military)
MAO ...... Master of Art of Oratory
MAO ...... Master of Obstetric Art
MAO ...... Monoamine Oxidase
MAO ...... Muhammadan Anglo-Oriental
MAOI ...... Monoamine Oxidase Inhibitor
MAOS ...... Magnetic Amplifier Output Stage
MAOT ...... Military Assistance Observer Team
MAOT ...... Missile Auxiliary Output Tester
MAP....... Macro-Assembly Program
MAP....... Maghreb-Arabe Presse (Maghreb Arab Press Agency)
MAP ...... Management Assistance for Profits
MAP....... Manifold Absolute Pressure (Air Force)
MAP ...... Manifold Air Pressure
MAP....... Manpower Absorption Plan (Department of Labor)
MAP....... Mars Atmosphere Probe
MAP....... Master All-Purpose (Project) (New York City court program)
MAP ...... Mathematical Analysis without Programming (Data processing)
MAP ...... Maximum Average Price
MAP....... Maximum a Posteriori
MAP....... Measurement Analysis Program (National Bureau of Standards)
MAP....... Medical Aid Post
MAP ...... Medical Assistance Program (Christian Medical Society)
MAP ...... Message Acceptance Pulse (Aerospace communications)
MAP .... Military Aid (or Assistance) Program
MAP....... Military Assistance Program
MAP ...... Military Association of Podiatrists
MAP....... Minimum Audible Pressure
MAP....... Ministry of Aircraft Production (British)
MAP....... Missed Approach Point (Aviation)
MAP....... Missed Approach Procedure (Aviation)
MAP....... Missile Application Propulsion
MAP....... Model and Program (Data processing)
MAP....... Modular Acoustic Panel
MAP ...... Multiple Allocation Procedure (PERT)
MAP ...... Multiple Array Processor
MAP....... Multiple Avoidance Program
MAP ...... Muscle Action Potential
MAP ...... Musical Aptitude Profile
MAP....... Mutual African Press Agency
MAP....... Mutual Aid Program
MAPA ...... Mexican-American Political Association
MAPAC ..... Military Assistance Program Advisory Group
MAPAG ..... Military Assistance Program Advisory Group
MAPAR..... Materials and Processes Acceptance Requirement
MAPCC ..... Military Assistance Program Country Code
MAPCHE .... Mobile Automatic Programed Checkout Equipment
MAP/CIO ... Military Assistance Program / Common Item Order
MAPCO..... Mid-American Pipeline Company
MAPED ..... Machine-Aided Program for Preparation of Electrical Programs
MAPHILINDO.. Malaya-Philippines-Indonesia
MAPI ...... Machinery and Allied Products Institute
MAPID ..... Machine-Aided Program for Preparation of Instruction Data
MAPL....... Manufacturing Assembly Parts List
MAPLA ..... Military Assistance Program Logistics Agency (Merged with Defense Supply
            Agency)
MAPMIS .... Manpower and Personnel Management Information System (Navy)
MAPNY ..... Maritime Association of the Port of New York
MAPOM .... Military Assistance Program Owned Materiel
MAPONY ... Maritime Association of the Port of New York
MAPP ...... Manpower and Personnel Plan (Army)
MAPP ...... Masking Parameter Printout (Data processing)
MAPP ...... Mathematical Analysis of a Perception and Preference
MAPP ...... Methylacetylene Propodiene
MAPP ...... Mid-Continent Area Power Planners Committee (Electric power)
MAPRC..... Mediterranean Allied Photographic Reconnaissance Command
MAPRES..... Mini Air Passenger Reservation System
MAPROS..... Maintain Production Schedules
MAPS ...... Machine Automated Parts System
MAPS ...... Maintenance Analysis and Procedures System (Data processing)
MAPS ...... Major Assembly Performance System
MAPS ...... Make-a-Picture Story (Psychological testing)
MAPS ...... Management Analysis and Planning System
MAPS ...... Middle Atlantic Planetarium Society
MAPS ...... Miniature Air Pilot System
MAPS ...... Missile Application Propulsion Study
MAPS ...... Monetary and Payments System (Committee) (American Bankers
            Association)
MAPS ...... Multiple Address Processing System
MAPS ...... Multisatellite Attitude Program System
MAPS ...... Multivariate Analysis and Prediction of Schedules

MAPSAD ..... Military Assistance Property Sales and Disposal
MAPT....... Military Assistance Program Training
MAPU ...... Multiple Address Processing Unit (Military)
MAPUC ..... Member of the Association for Promoting the Unity of Christendom
            (British)
MAPUC..... Modified Area Production Urgency Committee (World War II)
MAQ .... Measures for Air Quality (Program) (National Bureau of Standards)
MAQ .... Monetary Allowance in Lieu of Quarters
MAR....... Magnetic Amplifier Relay
MAR .... Maintenance Action Report
MAR .... Major Assembly Release (Military)
MAR .... Management Analysis Report (DOD)
MAR....... Manistee & Repton R. R. (AAR code)
MAR....... March
MAR....... Maremont Corporation (NYSE symbol)
MAR ...... Maritime Central Airways
M Ar ...... Master of Architecture
MAR .... Master of Arts in Religion
MAR....... Memory Address Register
MAR ...... Microanalytical Reagent
MAR....... Mid-Atlantic Ridge (of sea floor)
MAR....... Minimal Angle Resolution
MAR....... Minimum Acceptable Reliability
MAR ...... Movimiento de Accion Revolucionaria (Clandestine guerrilla
            organization formed by Mexican students)
MAR....... Multifunction Array RADAR
MAR....... Mythology of All Races (Book)
MARAD..... Maritime Administration (Department of Commerce) (Also, MA)
MARAIRWING .. Marine Aircraft Wing
MARALLWEAFITRARON .. Marine All Weather Fighter Training Squadron
MARBA ..... Mid-America Regional Bargaining Association
MARBASSCOL .. Marine Corps Basic School
MARBKS .... Marine Barracks
MARBO ..... Mariana-Bonins Command
MARBRIG .... Marine Brigade
MARC ...... Machine-Readable Catalog (Library of Congress)
MARC ...... Manpower Authorization Request for Change (Air Force)
MARC....... Matador Automatic RADAR Command
MARC....... Material Accountability Recoverability Code
MARC....... Metropolitan Applied Research Center (Corporation)
MARC....... Missions Advanced Research and Communications Center
MARC ...... Model "A" Restorers Club
MARC....... Moore Automatic Remote Control
MARCAD..... Marine Corps Aviation Cadet(s)
MARCAMP.... Marine Corps Accrued Military Pay System
MARCAN .... Maneuvering Reentry Control and Ablation Studies
MARCE ...... Materiel Asset Redistribution Center Europe (Military)
M Arch ..... Master of Architecture
M of Arch.... Master of Architecture
M Arch in CP.. Master of Architecture in City Planning
M Arch Des ... Master of Architectural Design
M Arch E ... Master of Architectural Engineering
M Arch Eng... Master of Architectural Engineering
MARCIA ..... Mathematical Analysis of Requirements for Career Information Appraisal
MARCO ..... Machine Referenced and Coordinated Outline
MARCOR..... Marine Corps
MARCORDISBOF .. Marine Corps Disbursing Office
MARCORMAN .. Marine Corps Manual
MARCORPS ... Marine Corps
MARCORSUPDEP .. Marine Corps Supply Depot
MARDIV .... Marine Division
MARENTS .... Modified Advanced Research Environmental Test Satellite (Air Force)
MAREP ...... Marine Environmental Prediction (US government)
MAREQSQ ... Marine Air Regulating Squadron
MARES/FORSTAT .. Marine Corps Automated Readiness Evaluation System / Status
            of Forces
MARFAIR .... Marine Fleet Air
MARFAIRWEST .. Marine Fleet Air, West Coast
MARG ...... Market Analysis Report Generator (Data processing)
MARGARFOR .. Marine Garrison Force
MARGILSAREA .. Marshalls-Gilberts Area
MARI ...... Mercantile Atlantic Routing Instructions
MARI .... Motivator and Response Indicator
MARINE ..... Management Analysis Reporting Information on the Naval Environment
            System
MARINEX ... Marine Express
MARINTRARON .. Marine Instrument Training Squadron
MARISP...... Maritime Strike Plan
MARITCOM... Maritime Commission
MARKAR .... Mapping & Reconnaissance Ku-Band Airborne RADAR
MARL ...... Mobile Acoustics Research Laboratory

MARLIN . . . . . Middle Atlantic Regional Information Network
MARLIS . . . . . Multiaspect Relevance Linkage Information System
MARLSR . . . . . Manufacturers Association of Robes, Leisurewear, Shirts and Rainwear
MARM . . . . . Middle Atlantic Regional Meeting (of American Chemical Society)
Mar Mech E . . Marine Mechanical Engineer
MARNAF . . . . Marquardt Navair Fuel (A boron slurry propellant for spacecraft)
MARP . . . . Manpower Allocation/Requirements Plan (Navy)
MARP . . . . . . Months After Receipt of Problem (Navy)
MARPAC . . . . . Headquarters, Department of the Pacific (Marine Corps)
MARPDA . . . . Mid-America Periodical Distributors Association
MARRS . . . . . Mechanized Ammunition Recording and Reporting System
MARS . . . . . . Machine Automated Realty Service
MARS . . . . . . Machinery Retrieval System
MARS . . . . . . Magnetic Airborne Recording System
MARS . . . . . . Maintenance Activities and Resources Simulation (Data processing)
MARS . . . . . . Maintenance Analysis and Recording Systems
MARS . . . . . . Management Analysis Reporting System (Data processing)
MARS . . . . . . Manned Aerodynamic Reusable Spaceship
MARS . . . . . Manned Astronautical Research Station (Space laboratory)
MARS . . . . . Marine Account Reconciliation Service
MARS . . . . . . Martin Automatic Reporting System
MARS . . . . . . Master Attitude Reference System
MARS . . . . . . Material Action Reporting System
MARS . . . . . . Media Alert and Response System (Public relations project devised by Pharmaceutical Manufacturers Association)
MARS . . . . . . Memory-Address Register Storage
MARS . . . . . . Meteorological Automatic Reporting Station (Canada)
MARS . . . . . . Mid-Air Recovery System (Rescue by helicopter) (Military)
MARS . . . . . . Military Affiliated Radio System (Amateur-operated radio stations)
MARS . . . . . . Miniature Attitude Reference System
MARS . . . . . . Mobile Atlantic Range Ships (Tracking ships)
MARS . . . . . . Monitor and Replenisher System
MARS . . . . . . Multi-Aperture Reluctance Switch (Data storage unit)
MARS . . . . . Multiple Artillery Rocket System (Army)
MARSA . . . . . Military Accepts Responsibility for Separation of Aircraft
MARSAM . . . . Multiple Airborne Reconnaissance Sensors Assessment Model
M Ar Sc . . . . . Master of Arts and Sciences
MARSO . . . . . . Marine Corps Shipping Order
MARSTA . . . . . Marital Status (Army)
MART . . . . . . Maintenance Analysis Review Technique
MART . . . . . . Mobile Automatic Radiation Tester
MARTAC . . . . Marine Automatic Rapid Test and Control
MARTC . . . . . Marine Air Reserve Training Command
MARTEC . . . . Martin Thin-Film Electronic Circuit
MARTEL . . . . . Missile Anti-RADAR and Television (Anglo-French missile)
MARTI . . . . . . Maneuverable Reentry Technology Investigation
MARTINI . . . . Massive Analog Recording Technical Instrument for Nebulous Indications
MARTRA & REPLCOMS . . Marine Training and Replacement Commands
MARTS . . . . . . Master RADAR Tracking Station
MARU . . . . . . Middle America Research Unit
MARV . . . . . . Maneuvering Anti-RADAR Vehicle
MARVEL . . . . . Mississippi Aerophysics Research Vehicle with Extended Latitude
MAS . . . . Lithuanian Catholic Youth Association Ateitis
MAS . . . . Management Advisory Services
MAS . . . . Manned Aerial Surveillance
MAS . . . . Marine Acoustical Services
MAS . . . . Mars Approach Sensor
MAS . . . . Maschinen-Ausleih-Station
MAS . . . . Masco Corp. (NYSE symbol)
MAS . . . . Master of Accounting Science
MAS . . . . Master of Applied Science
MAS . . . . Member of the Arundel Society (British)
MAS . . . . Metal Anchor Slots (Technical drawings)
MAS . . . . Mercury Analyzer System (Perkin-Elmer Co. instrument designation)
MAS . . . . Metastable Atomic State
MAS . . . . Midcourse Active System
MAS . . . . Military Agency for Standardization (NATO)
MAS . . . . Military Alert System
MAS . . . . Military Assistance Sales
MaS . . . . Milliampere-Second
MAS . . . . Missile Alignment Set
MAS . . . . Missile Auxiliaries System
MAS . . . . Mission Analysis Section
MAS . . . . Moksleiviu Ateitininku Sajunga
MAS . . . . Monetary Allowance in Lieu of Subsistence
MAS . . . . Mount Alvernia Seminary (Massachusetts)
MAS . . . . Mount Angel Seminary (Oregon)
MASA . . . . . . Mail Advertising Service Association International
MASA . . . . . . Military Automotive Supply Agency
MASA . . . . . . Mines' African Staff Association
MASAF . . . . . . Mediterranean Allied Strategic Air Force

MASAI . . . . . . Mail Advertising Service Association International
MA/SB . . . . . . Motor Antisubmarine Boat
MASC . . . . . . Magazine Advertising Sales Club
MA Sc . . . . . . Master of Applied Science
MASC . . . . . . Middletown Air Service Command (Air Force)
MASC . . . . . . Military Automotive Supply Center
MASCA . . . . . . Museum Applied Science Center for Archeology (University of Pennsylvania)
MASCON . . . . Mass Concentration (of gravitational pull)
MASCOT . . . . . Manned Shuttle Comprehensive Optimization and Targeting (NASA)
MASCOT . . . . . Meteorological Auxiliary Sea Current Observation Transmitter
MASCOT . . . . . Military Air-Transportable Satellite Communications Terminal
MASCOT . . . . . Motorola Automatic Sequential Computer Operated Tester
MASCU . . . . . . Marine Air Support Control Unit
MASD . . . . . . Mobile Air & Space Defense (Air Force)
MASDC . . . . . Military Aircraft Storage and Disposition Center
MASE . . . . . . McDonnell Airborne Sidewinder Evaluator (McDonnell Douglas Corporation)
MASER . . . . . Microwave Amplification by Stimulated Emission of Radiation
MASF . . . . . . Military Assistance Service Funded
MASG . . . . . . Marine Air Support Group
MASG . . . . . . Missile Auxiliary Signal Generator
MASH . . . . . . Manned Antisubmarine Helicopter
MASH . . . . . . Medical Aid for Sick Hippies (Volunteer medical group)
MASH . . . . . . Mobile Army Surgical Hospital (Acronym also used as title of a satirical film, 1970)
MASH . . . . . . Multiple Accelerated Summary Hearing (Deportation of illegal aliens) (Immigration and Naturalization Service)
MASIS . . . . . . Management and Scientific Information System
MASK . . . . . . Maneuvering and Seakeeping
MASL . . . . . . MA (Military Assistance) Articles and Services List (DOD)
MASL . . . . . . Military Assistance Articles and Services List
MASM . . . . . . Motorized Antenna Switching Matrix
MASq . . . . . . Military Airlift Squadron (Air Force)
MASRU . . . . . Marine Air Support RADAR Unit (DOD)
MASS . . . . . . Marine Air Support Squadron
MASS . . . . . . Massachusetts
M As S . . . . . . Master of Association Science
MASS . . . . . . Mechanically Accelerated Sabot System (Generation of high-density molecular beams)
MASS . . . . . . Modern Army Supply System
M As Sc . . . . . Master of Association Science
MASSCAL . . . . Mass Casualties (Military)
MASSDAR . . . Modular Analysis, Speedup, Sampling, and Data Reduction
MASSq . . . Military Airlift Support Squadron (Air Force)
MASSTER . . . . . Mobile Army Sensor System, Test, Evaluation, and Review
MASSTER . . . . . Modern Army Selected Systems Test Evaluation and Review (Antitank helicopter)
MAST . . . . . . Magnetic Annular Shock Tube
MAST . . . . . . Marine Stable Element
MAST . . . . . . Midlevel Positions in Administrative, Staff and Technical Services (Civil Service Commission)
MAST . . . . . . Military Assistance to Safety and Traffic (Army program)
MAST . . . . . . Minimum Abbreviations of Serial Titles (A publication)
MAST . . . . . . Missile Automatic Supply Technique
MAST . . . . . . Mobile Assembly Sterilizer for Testing
MAST . . . . . . Model Assembly Sterilizer for Testing
MAST . . . . . . Multiple Applications Storage Tube
MASTARAV . . Master Army Aviator
Mast AR Av Bad . . Master Army Aviator Badge (Army)
Mast Div Bad . . Master Diver Badge (Army)
MASTER . . . . . Matching Available Student Time to Educational Resources (Data processing)
MASTER . . . . . Miniaturized Sink-Rate Telemetering RADAR
MASTER . . . . . Multiple Access Shared Time Executive Routine (Data processing)
MASTIF . . . . . . Multiple Axis Space Test Inertia Facility (Training device for astronauts)
MASUA . . . . . Mid-America State Universities Association
MASW . . . . . . Master of Arts in Social Work
MASWg . . . . . . Military Airlift Support Wing
MASWT . . . . . Mobile Antisubmarine Warfare Target
MAT . . . . Machine Available Time
MAT . . . . Manual Arts Therapist
MAT . . . . Master of Arts in Teaching
MAT . . . . Material
MAT . . . . Materiel
MAT . . . . Mathematical Automata Theory
MAT . . . . Mattel, Inc. (NYSE symbol)
MAT . . . . Mechanical Aptitude Test
MAT . . . . Metropolitan Achievement Test
MAT . . . . Microalloy Transistor
MAT . . . . Military Air Transport

MAT........ Military Aircraft Types
MAT........ Minimal Aversion Threshold (to noise)
MAT........ Missile Adapter Tester
MAT........ Missile Anti-Tank
MAT .... Moscow Art Theater
MAT........ Multiple Access Test
MA in T ..... Master of Arts in Teaching
MATA ...... Motorcycle and Allied Trades Association
MATA ...... Musical Arena Theatres Association (Later, Musical Theatres Association)
MATACQ .... Material Acquisition
MATAF ..... Mediterranean Allied Tactical Air Force
MATB....... Military Air Transport Board
MATB....... Missile Auxiliary Test Bench
MATC....... Missile Auxiliaries Test Console
MATCH ..... Manpower and Talent Clearinghouse
MATCH ..... Materials and Activities for Teachers and Children
MATCH...... Multi-Element Assured Tracking Chopper
MATCO ..... Military Air Traffic Coordinating Office(r) (Air Force)
MATCON .... Microwave Aerospace Terminal Control (Air Force)
MATCU ..... Marine Air Tactical (later, Traffic) Control Unit (Marine Corps)
MATD ...... Mine and Torpedo Detector (SONAR) (Navy)
MATE ...... Master of Arts in the Teaching of English
Mat E ...... Materials Engineer
MATE....... McDonnell Airborne Trainer and Evaluator (McDonnell Douglas Corporation)
MATE....... Missile/Aircraft Test Equipment
MATE....... Mission Analysis Technique for Experiments
MATE ...... Modular Automatic Test Equipment
MATE ...... Multipurpose Automatic Test Equipment
MA (T Ed).... Master of Arts in Teacher Education
MATH...... Mathematics
Math D...... Doctor of Mathematics
MATHN..... Mathematician
MATI ...... Moscow Aviation Technology Institute (USSR)
MATIC ..... Multiple Area Technical Information Center
MATICO .... Machine Applications to Technical Information Center Operations
MATMU .... Mobile Aircraft Torpedo Maintenance Unit
MATNO ..... Material (Requested) is Not Available
MATP ...... Military Assistance Training Program
MATP ...... Missile Auxiliary Test Position
MATRE ..... Material Requested
MATRIX ..... Management Trial Exercise (Career orientation simulation)
MATRS ..... Miniature Airborne Telemetry Receiving Station
MATS ...... Mediterranean Air Transport Service
MATS ...... Military Air Transport Service (Later, Military Air Command)
MATS...... Missile Auxiliaries Test Set
MATSC..... Middletown Air Technical Service Command (Air Force)
MATSO ..... Material Requested Being Supplied (Military)
MATT ...... Mobile Acoustic Torpedo Target
MATTS ..... Multiple Airborne Target Trajectory System
MATU...... Marine Air Traffic Unit
MATV...... Master Antenna Television
MATW ...... Metal Awning Type Window
MAU .... Maintenance Analysis Unit
MAU .... Maintenance Augmenting Unit
MAU .... Modern American Usage (A publication)
MAU .... Mount Allison University (New Brunswick, Canada)
MAUDE ..... Morse Automatic Decoder
M Au E ..... Master of Automobile Engineering
M Au Eng .... Master of Automobile Engineering
MAULT...... Manual or Automatic Ultrasonic Laboratory Test
MA in Urb Pl .. Master of Arts in Urban Planning
MAUSED ..... Midwest Association of University Student Employment Directors
MAUTEL .... Microminiaturized Autonetics Telemetry
MAV .... Macrosiphum avenae Virus
MAV .... Magyar Allamvasutak
MAV .... Manpower Authorization Voucher
MAVAR..... Mixer Amplification by Variable Reactance
MAVAR ..... Modulating Amplifier Using Variable Reactance
MAVES ..... Manned Mars and Venus Exploration Studies
MAVIN...... Machine-Assisted Vendor Information Network
MAVS...... Manned Aerial Vehicle for Surveillance
MAW .... Marine Air Wing (Marine Corps)
MAW .... Medium Antiarmor (or Antitank) Weapon
MAW .... Medium Assault Weapon
MAW ...... Military Airlift Wing (Air Force)
MAW .... Minor Assist Work
MAW .... Mothers for Adequate Welfare
MAWC ..... Marine Air West Coast
MAWCS .... Mobile Air Weapons Control System (ESD)
MA/WD...... Material Annex / Weapons Dictionary (Military)
MAWg ...... Military Airlift Wing (Air Force)

MAWP ...... Marine Air Wing Pacific
MAWS ...... Marine Air Warning Squadron
MAX .... Maximum
MAXMAR .... Maximum Mobile Army
MAXSECON.. Maximum Security Communications
MAY........ Mays, Inc. (NYSE symbol)
MAYO ...... Mexican-American Youth Organization
MAZH ...... Missile Azimuth Heading (Air Force)
MB........ Bachelor of Medicine
MB........ Bachelor of Music
MB........ Magnetic Bearing (Navigation)
MB........ Main Base (Air Force)
MB .... Main Battery (Guns)
MB .... Make-Break
MB........ March-Bender Factor (Physiology)
MB........ Marine Barracks
MB .... Marine Base
MB........ Mechanized Battalion (Army)
MB .... Medical Board
MB .... Medium Bomber
MB .... Megabar
MB .... Megabit
MB .... Melbourne Bitter (Brand of beer) (Initialism used by Australians as slang for "inebriated")
MB .... Melt Back
MB .... Memory Buffer
MB........ Meridian & Bigbee R. R. (AAR code)
MB .... Message Business
MB .... Methyl Bromide
MB .... Methylene Blue
MB .... Midbody
MB .... Militia Bureau
mb .... Millibars
MB........ Milton Bradley Co. (NYSE symbol)
MB........ Missile Bomber
MB .... Monthly Breakdown (Used in atmospheric studies)
MB........ Mooring Buoy
MB .... Motor Boat
MB .... Municipal Borough
MB .... Munitions Board
MB........ Music for the Blind
M-B .... Make-Break
M/B .... Medium Bomber
M & B ..... Matched and Beaded
MBA ...... Master of Business Administration
MBA ...... Material Balance Area (AEC)
MBA ...... Merion Bluegrass Association
MBA ...... Migratory Bird Act
MBA ...... Military Benefit Association
MBA ...... Minimum Burst Altitude
MBA ...... Monument Builders of America
MBA ...... Mortgage Bankers Association of America
MBAA...... Master Brewers Association of America
MBAA ...... Messinian Benevolent Association "Aristomenis"
MBAA ...... Mini Bike Association of America
MBAAS ..... Master of Business Administration in Actuarial Science
MBAD...... Medical Badge
MB Adm .... Master of Business Administration
MBAG ...... Modulated Bayard-Alpert Gauge
MBAM ..... Main Beam Avoidance Maneuver
MBAS...... Mutual Benefit and Aid Society
MBAWS .... Marine Base Air Warning System
MBB ...... Make-Before-Break
MBB ...... Messerschmitt-Boelkow-Blohm (West German aircraft company)
MBB ...... Miniature Brushless Blower
MBC ...... Main Beam Clutter
MBC .... Manhattan Bible College (Kansas)
MBC .... Mary Baldwin College (Virginia)
MBC ...... Master of Beauty Culture
MBC ...... Maximum Breathing Capacity
MBC....... Mediterranean Bombardment Code
MBC ...... Miniature Bayonet Cap
MBC....... Miniaturized Ballistic Computer
MBC....... Minnesota Bible College
MBC....... Modified Brequet Cruise (SST)
MBC....... Morris Brown College (Georgia)
MBCA...... Mercedes-Benz Club of America
MBCA ...... Munitions Board Cataloging Agency
MBCC...... Massachusetts Bay Community College
MBCC ...... Migratory Bird Conservation Commission (A federal government body)

MBCM . . . . . . Baccalaureus Medicinae, Chirurgiae Magister (Bachelor of Medicine, Master of Surgery)
MBCMC . . . . . Milk Bottle Crate Manufacturers Council
MBCS . . . . . . Medium Bandwidth Compression System
MBCS . . . . Meteor Burst Communication System
MBD . . . . Macro Block Design
MBD . . . . Minimal Brain Damage
MBDA . . . . . . Metal Building Dealers Association
MBDET . . . . . Mobile Boarding Detachment (Coast Guard)
MBDG . . . . . . Marine Base Defense Group
MBE . . . . . . Member of the (Order of the) British Empire
MBE . . . . Mennonite Board of Education
MBE . . . . Missile-Borne Equipment
MB Ed . . . . . . Master of Business Education
MBF . . . . Military Banking Facility
MBF . . . . Milk Bottlers Federation
MBF . . . . Molecular Beam Facility (NASA)
MBF . . . . Thousand Board Feet (Lumber)
MBFR . . . . . . Mutual Balanced Force Reductions (NATO)
MBGE . . . . . . Missile-Borne Guidance Equipment
MBGS . . . . . . Missile-Borne Guidance Set
MBH . . . . Manual Bomb Hoist
MBH . . . . Michalls Brothers (NYSE symbol)
MBH . . . . Mit Beschraenkter Haftung (Limited Liability) (Germany)
MBH . . . . Thousands of BTU per Hour
MBI . . . . May Be Issued
MBIA . . . . . . Malting Barley Improvement Association
M Bi Ch. . . . . . Master of Biological Chemistry
M Bi E . . . . . . Master of Biological Engineering
M Biorad . . . . . Master of Bioradiology
M Bi Phy . . . . . Master of Biological Physics
M Bi S . . . . . . Master of Biological Sciences
MBK . . . . Madchen-Bibel-Kreise (Bible Reading Circles) (Germany)
MBK . . . . Multiple Beam Klystron
MBL . . . . Marine Biological Laboratory
MBL . . . . Master Bidders List
MBL . . . . Miniature Button Light
MBL . . . . Mobile
MBM . . . . Master of Business Management
MBM . . . . Thousand Feet Board Measure
MBMA . . . . . . Metal Building Manufacturers Association
MBMU . . . . . . Middle Belt Mineworkers' Union (Nigeria)
MBMU . . . . . . Mobile Base Maintenance Unit
MBN . . . . Mixed Base Notation
MBNA . . . . . . Monument Builders of North America
MBNAD . . . . . Marine Barracks, Naval Ammunition Depot
MBNAS . . . . . Marine Barracks, Naval Air Station
MBNMD . . . . . Marine Barracks, Naval Mine Depot
MBNOB . . . . . Marine Barracks, Naval Operating Base
MBNS . . . . . . Marine Barracks, Naval Station
MBNYD . . . . . Marine Barracks, Navy Yard
MBO . . . . Management By Objective
MBO . . . . Meacham Bridge Oscillator
MBO . . . . Monostable Blocking Oscillator
MBO . . . . Moving Base Operator
MBOH . . . . . . Minimum Break-Off Height
MBOU . . . . . . Member British Ornithologists Union
MBP . . . . Manhattan Bowery Project
MBP . . . . Manpack Battery Pack
MBP . . . . Maximum Boiling Point
MBP . . . . Mean Blood Pressure (Physiology)
MBP . . . . Mechanical Booster Pump
MBP . . . . Mid-Boiling Point
MBPA . . . . . . Military Blood Program Agency
MBPAS . . . . . Monthly Bulk Petroleum Accounting Summary (Army)
MBPC . . . . . . Munitions Board Petroleum Committee
MBPDA . . . . . Metropolitan Bag and Paper Distributors Association
MBPS . . . . . . Mechanical Booster Pump System
MBPS . . . . . . Megabits Per Second
MBPS . . . . . . Million Bits Per Second
MBR . . . . Marker Beacon Receiver
MBR . . . . Material Balance Report (AEC)
MBR . . . . Mechanical Buffer Register (Data processing)
MBR . . . . Member
MBR . . . . Memory Buffer Register (Data processing)
MBR . . . . Motivation By Rotation
MBR . . . . Moving Belt Radiator
MBR . . . . Multibomb Rack
MBRA . . . . . . Marathon Boat Racers Association
MBRA . . . . . . Multi-Beam Radiometer Antenna
MBRE . . . . . . Memory Buffer Register, Even (Data processing)

MBRF . . . . . . Midbrain Reticular Formation
MBRO . . . . . . Memory Buffer Register, Odd (Data processing)
MBRUU . . . . . May Be Retained Until Unserviceable
MBRV . . . . . . Maneuverable Ballistic Reentry Vehicle
MBS . . . . Magnetron Beam Switching
MBS . . . . Main "Bang" Suppressor
MBS . . . . Master of Basic Science
MBS . . . . Motor Bus Society
MBS . . . . Multicore Bar Solder
MBS . . . . Multiple Business System
MBS . . . . Mutual Broadcasting System
MB/S . . . . . . Megabit Per Second
MBSA . . . . . . Methylated Bovine Serum Albumin
MBSA . . . . . . Modular Building Standards Association
MBSA . . . . . . Munitions Board Standards Agency
MBSB . . . . . . Marine Barracks, Submarine Base
MB Sc. . . . . . Master of Business Science
MBSI . . . . . . Musical Box Society International
MBSM . . . . . . Mexican Border Service Medal
MBST . . . . . . Multiple Beam Switching Tube
MBT . . . . Main Battle Tank (Army)
MBT . . . . Marianna & Blountstown R. R. (AAR code)
MBT . . . . Mechanical Bathymetric
MBT . . . . Mercaptobenzothiazole
MBT . . . . Mercury Bombardment Thrustor
MBT . . . . Metal Bond Tape
MBT . . . . Mobile Boarding Team
MBTA . . . . . . Massachusetts Bay Transportation Authority
MBTI . . . . . . Manpower Business Training Institute
MBTI . . . . . . Myers-Briggs Type Indicator (A personality test)
MBTS . . . . . . Meteorological Balloon Tracking System
MBTWK . . . . . Multiple Beam Traveling Wave Klystron
MBUCV . . . . . Museo de Biologia de la Universidad Central de Venezuela
M Bus Ed . . . . . Master of Business Education
MBV . . . . Mexican Border Veterans
MBV . . . . Minimum Breakdown Voltage
MBVP . . . . . . Mechanical Booster Vacuum Pump
MBVPS . . . . . Mechanical Booster Vacuum Pump System
MBW . . . . . . Metropolitan Board of Works (British)
MBW . . . . . . Movement for a Better World
MBW . . . . . . Munitions Assignment Board (Washington)
MBWO . . . . . . M-Type Backward Wave Oscillator
MBY & D . . . . Maintenance, Bureau of Yards and Docks (Budget category) (Navy) (Obsolete; see FEC)
MC . . . . Machine Console
MC . . . . Machinery Certificate (Shipping)
MC . . . . Magister Chirurgiae (Master of Surgery)
MC . . . . Magnetic Clutch
MC . . . . Magnetic Core
MC . . . . Magnetic Course (Navigation)
MC . . . . Main Cock
MC . . . . Maintenance Console
MC . . . . Major Component
MC . . . . Mantle Cavity
MC . . . . Mantle Collar
MC . . . . Marginal Check (Computer)
MC . . . . Marginal Cost
MC . . . . Marine Corps
MC . . . . Maritime Commission (of Department of Commerce) (Merged with Federal Maritime Commission)
MC . . . . Marked Capacity (Freight cars)
MC . . . . Marketing Center (Veterans Administration)
MC . . . . Master of Ceremonies
MC . . . . Master of Chemistry
MC . . . . Master of Classics
MC . . . . Master Commandant
MC . . . . Master Control
MC . . . . Materiel Command (Air Force)
MC . . . . Matsushita Electric Industrial (American Depository Receipts) (NYSE symbol)
MC . . . . Medical Center
MC . . . . Medical Corps (Navy)
MC . . . . Medico-Chirurgical
Mc. . . . . Megacycles
MC . . . . Melamine Council
MC . . . . Member of Congress
MC . . . . Member of Council
MC . . . . Memorial Commission (Federal body)
MC . . . . Memory Control (Unit) (Data processing)
MC . . . . Message Composer (Communications; data processing)
MC . . . . Metaling Clause (Marine insurance)

MC . . . . Meter-Candle
MC . . . . Metric Carat (200 milligrams)
MC . . . . Michigan Central R. R. (AAR code)
MC . . . . Michigan Chemical Corp.
MC . . . . Miles on Course
MC . . . . Military Committee (NATO)
MC . . . . Military Construction
MC . . . . Military Cross
mC . . . . Millicurie(s) (Also, mCi)
MC . . . . Millipore Corporation (Bedford, Massachusetts)
MC . . . . Missile Checkout
MC . . . . Missile Command (Army)
MC . . . . Missile Compartment
MC . . . . Missile Container
MC . . . . Missile Control
MC . . . . Mission Control (NASA)
MC . . . . Mitochondrial Complementation
MC . . . . Mode Counter
MC . . . . Modular Computer
MC . . . . Momentary Contact (Electronics)
MC . . . . Moneda Corriente (Current Money) (Spain)
MC . . . . Monkey Cells
MC . . . . Montecatini Mining & Chemical Company (NYSE symbol) (Delisted)
MC . . . . Motorcycle
MC . . . . Movement Control (of troops)
MC . . . . Mucous Cell
MC . . . . Multiple Choice
MC . . . . Multiple Contact
MC . . . . Multiple Copy
MC . . . . Munitions Command (Army)
M-C . . . . Medico-Chirurgical
M-C . . . . Mineralo-Corticoid (Endocrinology)
M/C . . . . Marginal Credit (Business and trade)
MC's . . . . . . Military Characteristics (Technical specification document for nuclear bombs and warheads)
M & C . . . . . . Morphine and Cocaine (Mixture)
MCA . . . . Malayan Chinese Association
MCA . . . . Manufacturing Chemists Association
MCA . . . . Marine Corps Association
MCA . . . . Maritime Control Area
MCA . . . . Master of Commercial Arts
MCA . . . . Master Community Antenna
MCA . . . . Mastiff Club of America
MCA . . . . Material Control Adjustment
MCA . . . . Material Coordinating Agency
MCA . . . . Maternity Center Association
MCA . . . . MCA Incorporated (NYSE symbol)
MCA . . . . Mechanical Contractors Association of America
MCA . . . . Medical Correctional Association
MCA . . . . Methylcholanthrene (Chemical)
MCA . . . . Metropolitan Club of America
MCA . . . . Metropolitan Cycle Association (New York)
MCA . . . . Microwave Control Assembly
MCA . . . . Midwest Commuter Airlines
MCA . . . . Mid-West Compensation Association
MCA . . . . Midwest Curling Association
MCA . . . . Military Chaplains Association of the USA
MCA . . . . Military Construction Appropriation (or Authorization)
MCA . . . . Military Construction, Army (Appropriation)
MCA . . . . Millinery Credit Association
MCA . . . . Minimum Crossing Altitude (Aviation)
MCA . . . . Model Cities Administration (HUD)
MCA . . . . Movers Conference of America
MCA . . . . Multiple Classification Analysis (Aviation)
MCA . . . . Music Critics Association
MCA . . . . Musicians Club of America
MCAA . . . . . . Mason Contractors Association of America
MCAA . . . . . . Mechanical Contractors Association of America
MCAA . . . . . . Military Civil Affairs Administration (The Netherlands) (World War II)
MCAAF . . . . . Marine Corps Auxiliary Air Facility
MCAAS . . . . . Marine Corps Auxiliary Air Station
MCAB . . . . . . Marine Corps Air Base
MCABM . . . . . Manner Common Among Business Men
MCAC . . . . . . Military Common Area Control
MCAD . . . . . . Marine Corps Air Depot
MCAD . . . . . . Massachusetts Commission Against Discrimination
MCAD . . . . . . Military Contracts Administration Department
MCAF . . . . . . Marine Corps Air Facility
MCAF . . . . . . Marine Corps Air Field
MCAF . . . . . . Mediterranean Coastal Air Force Headquarters
MCAF . . . . . . Military Construction, Air Force

MCAFB . . . . . McConnell Air Force Base
MCAIR . . . . . . McDonnell Aircraft Corporation (Later, McDonnell Douglas Corp.)
MCALF . . . . . . Marine Corps Auxiliary Landing Field
M Can L . . . . . Master of Canon Law
MCAP . . . . . . Military Construction Authorized Program
MCAP . . . . . . Minority Contractors Assistance Project
MCAPI . . . . . . Mid-Continent Association of the Pet Industry
MCAR . . . . . . Military Construction, Army Reserve
MCARNG . . . . Military Construction, Army National Guard
MCAS . . . . . . Marine Corps Air Station (Navy)
MCASTRO . . . McDonnell Astronautics Company
MCAT . . . . . . Medical College Admission Test
MCAT . . . . . . Midwest Council on Airborne Television
MCAUTO . . . . McDonnell Automation Company
MCB . . . . Marine Construction Battalion
MCB . . . . Marine Corps Base
MCB . . . . Matheson, Coleman and Bell (Commercial firm)
MCB . . . . Metal Corner Bead (Technical drawings)
MCB . . . . Millwork Cost Bureau
MCB . . . . Mobile Construction Battalion
MCB . . . . Motor Cargo Boat
MCBA . . . . . . Master Car Builders' Association
MCBETH . . . . Military Computer Basic Environment for Test Handling
MCBF . . . . . . Mean Cycles Between Failures
MCBM . . . . . . Marine Corps Brevet Medal
MCBW . . . . . . Amalgamated Meat Cutters and Butcher Workmen of North America
MCC . . . . Main Communications Center
MCC . . . . Maintenance of Close Contact
MCC . . . . Maintenance Control Center (Military)
MCC . . . . Manned Control Car (AEC)
MCC . . . . Manual Combat Center (Air Force)
MCC . . . . Manual Control Center (Air Force)
MCC . . . . Map Collectors' Circle
MCC . . . . Marine Corps Commandant
MCC . . . . Marylebone Cricket Club (Governing body for cricket)
MCC . . . . Master Control Console
MCC . . . . Mechanically Compensated Crystal
MCC . . . . Media Club of Canada (Formerly, Canadian Women's Press Club)
MCC . . . . Mennonite Central Committee
MCC . . . . Mercury Control Center
MCC . . . . Mesta Machine Company (NYSE symbol)
MCC . . . . Midcourse Correction
MCC . . . . Military Climb Corridor (Aviation)
MCC . . . . Military Coordinating Committee
MCC . . . . Miniature Center Cap
MCC . . . . Miscellaneous Common Carrier
MCC . . . . Missile Compensating Control
MCC . . . . Missile Control Center (Air Force)
MCC . . . . Mission Control Center (NASA)
MCC . . . . Modified Close Control (Air Force)
MCC . . . . Modulation with Constant Control
MCC . . . . Monitored Command Code (Marine Corps)
MCC . . . . Motor Carrier Cases (ICC)
MCC . . . . Motor Control Center
MCC . . . . Movement Control Center
MCC . . . . Multicomponent Circuits
MCC . . . . Multiple Computer Complex
MCC . . . . Munitions Carriers Conference
MCC . . . . Muskegon Community College (Michigan)
MCCC . . . . . . Missile Combat Crew Commander
MCCCA . . . . . Marine Corps Combat Correspondents Association
MCCD . . . . . . Marine Corps Clothing Depot
MCC-H . . . . . Mission Control Center - Houston (NASA)
MCCL . . . . . . Mason City & Clear Lake R. R. (AAR code)
MCCM . . . . . . Mexican Chamber of Commerce of US
MCCOR . . . . . Motion Compensation - Coherent On Receive
MCCR . . . . . . Master Change Compliance Record
MCCR . . . . . . Medical Committee for Civil Rights
MCCS . . . . . . Master Calendar Control System (New York City courts' speedup system)
MCCT . . . . . . Multistrip Cesium Contact Thrustor
MCCTU . . . . . Mongolian Central Council of Trade Unions
MCCU . . . . . . Multiple Communications Control Unit (Data processing)
MCCUSCUSRPG . . . . Military Coordinating Committee, United States Element, Canada-United States Regional Planning Group
MCD . . . . Doctor of Comparative Medicine
MCD . . . . Magna Carta Dames, National Society
MCD . . . . Magnetic Circular Dichroism
MCD . . . . Manual Control Device
MCD . . . . Marginal Checking and Distribution
MCD . . . . Marr, Cahalan, and Dunn
MCD . . . . Mast Cell Degranulating (or Destroying) Peptide (Biochemistry)

MCD . . . . Master Clerical Data (Management system)
MCD . . . . McDonald's Corp. (NYSE symbol)
MCD . . . . Mean Corpuscular Diameter
MCD . . . . Member of the College of Dentists (British)
MCD . . . . Metacarpal Cortical Density
MCD . . . . Metal-Covered Door (Technical drawings)
MCD . . . . Metals and Ceramics Division (Air Force)
MCD . . . . Mid-Central District (ATSC)
MCD . . . . Military Contracts Department
MCD . . . . Minimum Cost Design
MCDA . . . . . . Manpower and Career Development Agency
MCDARS . . . . . Mechanized Cost Distribution and Reporting System
MCDAS . . . . . . Metropolitan Cities Drug Association Secretaries
MCDP . . . . Micro-Programmed Data Processor
MCDP . . . . . . Missionary Catechists of Divine Providence (Roman Catholic women's
          religious order)
MCDT . . . . Mean Corrective Down Time
MCE . . . . Marginal Cost Efficiency (Marketing)
MCE . . . . Master of Christian Education
MCE . . . . Master of Civil Engineering
MCE . . . . Maximum Capability Envelope
MCE . . . . Memphis Cotton Exchange
MCE . . . . Military Characteristics Equipment
MCE . . . . Missile Compensating Equipment
MCE . . . . Mission Control Equipment
MCE . . . . Montgomery Cotton Exchange
MCEAC . . . . . . Marine Corps Emergency Actions Center
MCEB . . . . Marine Corps Equipment Board
MCEB . . . . Military Communications-Electronics Board
MCEC . . . . . . Marine Corps Education Center
MC Ed . . . . . . Master of Commercial Education
M Ce Eng . . . . Master of Cement Engineering
MC Eng . . . . . Master of Civil Engineering
M Cer E . . . . . Master of Ceramic Engineering
MCEU . . . . . . Mobile Civil Emergency Unit
MCF . . . . Magic Chef, Inc. (NYSE symbol)
MCF . . . . Master Control File
MCF . . . . Matched Crystal Filers
MCF . . . . Medium Corpuscular Fragility
MCF . . . . Migrant Children's Fund
MCF . . . . Mode Change Flag
MCF . . . . Monolithic Crystal Filter
MCF . . . . Multi-Channel Fixed
MCF . . . . Multiple Cost Factor
MCF . . . . Mutual Coherence Function
MCF . . . . Thousand Cubic Feet
MC'F . . . . . . Micro-Complement Fixation (Quantitative immunochemistry)
$\overline{M}$CF . . . . Million Cubic Feet ($\overline{M}$ with bar)
MCG . . . . Man Computer Graphics
MCG . . . . Medical College of Georgia
MCG . . . . Michigan Gas Utilities Co. (NYSE symbol)
MCG . . . . . . Microwave Command Guidance
MCG . . . . Mobile Command Guidance
MCG . . . . Mobile Communication Group (Air Force)
MCG . . . . Moving Coil Galvanometer
MC & G . . . . . Mapping, Charting, and Geodesy
MCGCM . . . . . Marine Corps Good Conduct Medal
MCGP . . . . . . Member of the College of General Practitioners (British)
MCGp . . . . . . Mobile Communications Group (Air Force)
MCGS . . . . . . Microwave Command Guidance System (RADC)
M Ch . . . . Magister Chirurgiae (Master of Surgery)
MCH . . . . Massachusetts Council for the Humanities
MCH . . . . Maternal and Child Health (Service)
MCH . . . . Mean Corpuscular Hemoglobin
MCH . . . . Methylcyclohexane (Organic chemistry)
MCHC . . . . . . Mean Corpuscular Hemoglobin Concentration
M Ch E . . . . . Master of Chemical Engineering
M Chem E . . . . Master of Chemical Engineering
MCHR . . . . . . Medical Committee for Human Rights
M Chr Ed . . . . Master of Christian Education
MCHS . . . . . . Maternal and Child Health Service
MCI . . . . Malleable Cast Iron
MCI . . . . Marine Corps Institute
MCI . . . . Materials Cost Index
MCI . . . . Meridian Control Integrator
MCI . . . . Mexican Coffee Institute
MCI . . . . Microwave Communications of America, Incorporated
MCI . . . . Milk Can Institute
mCi . . . . Millicurie (Also, mC)
MCI . . . . Mottled Cast Iron
MCIRA . . . . . . Micro-Electronic Replacement Assembly

MCIS . . . . . . Multiple Corridor Identification System (Air Force)
MCJ . . . . Master of Comparative Jurisprudence
MCJC . . . . . . Mason City Junior College (Iowa)
MCJR . . . . . . Multi-Channel Jezebel Relay (Military)
MCK . . . . Maintenance Check
MCK . . . . . . Master Cook (Navy)
MCK . . . . McKesson & Robbins, Inc. (NYSE symbol) (Delisted)
MCKA . . . . . . Metal Cutting Knife Association
MCL . . . . Marine Corps League
MCL . . . . Master of Civil Law
MCL . . . . Master of Comparative Law
MCL . . . . Master Configuration List
MCL . . . . Metal Crystal Lattice
MCL . . . . Mid-Canada Line (RADAR warning chain of fence across Canada;
          sometimes called the McGill Fence)
MCL . . . . Midclavicular Line
MCL . . . . Miniature Cartridge Light
MCL . . . . Minimal Computer Load
MCL . . . . Moore & McCormack Lines, Inc. (NYSE symbol)
MCL . . . . Moving Coil Loudspeaker
MCL . . . . Multi-Color LASER
MCL . . . . Mushroom Canners League
MCLA . . . . . . Marine Corps League Auxiliary
MCLD . . . . . . Multi-Color LASER Display
MCLFDC . . . . Marine Corps Landing Force Development Center
MCLO . . . . . . Medical Construction Liaison Office(r) (Air Force)
MCLR . . . . . . Minimum Critical Leaching Rate
MCLWG . . . . . Major Caliber Lightweight Gun
MCM . . . . Machines for Coordinated Multiprocessing
MCM . . . . Magnetic Card Memory
MCM . . . . Magnetic Core Memory (Data processing)
MCM . . . . Manned Circumlunar Mission
MCM . . . . Mannes College of Music (New York)
MCM . . . . Manual for Courts-Martial
MCM . . . . Marine Corps Manual
MCM . . . . Master of Church Music
MCM . . . . Medical Corps, Merchant Marine, General Service (USNR officer
          designation)
MCM . . . . Member of the College of Musicians (British)
MCM . . . . Micro Circuit Module
MCM . . . . Military Characteristics Motor Vehicles
MCM . . . . Mine Countermeasures
MCM . . . . Minneapolis College of Music
MCM . . . . Monolithic Circuit Mask
MCM . . . . Monte Carlo Method (Data processing)
MCM . . . . Moving Coil Microphone
MCM . . . . Multiple Connected Motor
MCM . . . . Thousand Circular Mils
MC-M . . . . . . Medical Corps, Merchant Marine (USNR officer designation)
MCMA . . . . . . Machine Chain Manufacturers Association
MCMA . . . . . . Metal Cookware Manufacturers Association
MCMC . . . . . . Marine Corps Memorial Commission
MCMC . . . . . . Medicine Cabinet Manufacturers Council
MCMG . . . . . Man-Carrying Motion Generator (Space-flight simulation)
MCMI . . . . . . Malleable Chain Manufacturers Institute
MCMR . . . . . . Medical Corps, Merchant Marine, General Service (USNR officer
          designation)
MCMS . . . . . . Medical Corps, Merchant Marine, Special Service (USNR officer
          designation)
MCN . . . . Maintenance Control Number
MCN . . . . Management Control Number (Army)
MCN . . . . Manual Control Number
MCN . . . . Manufacturing Change Notice
MCN . . . . Master Control Number
MC,N. . . . . . . Military Construction, Navy (An appropriation) (Also, MCON)
MCNRF . . . . . Military Construction, Naval Reserve Facilities
MCO . . . . Magnetron Cut-Off
MCO . . . . Main Civilian Occupation
MCO . . . . Marine Corps Officer
MCO . . . . Marine Corps Order
MCO . . . . Massachusetts College of Optometry
M Co . . . . . . Master of Cosmology
MCO . . . . Mill Culls Out (Lumber)
MCO . . . . Missile Checkout
MCO . . . . Missile Control Officer
MCO . . . . Mission Control Operation
MCO . . . . Movement Control Officer
MCO . . . . Multiple Channel Oscilloscope
MCOA . . . . . . Music Center Opera Association (Los Angeles)
MCOAG . . . . . Marine Corps Operations Analysis Group
MCOGA . . . . Mid-Continent Oil and Gas Association

MCOHM . . . . . Military Community Oral Health Managers (Army)
MCOLF . . . . . . Marine Corps Outlying Landing Field
M Com . . . . . . Master of Commerce
M Com Adm. . . Master of Commercial Administration
M Comp L . . . . Master of Comparative Law
M Com Sc . . . . Master of Commercial Science
MCON . . . . . . Military Construction, Navy (Also, MCN and MILCON)
MConsE . . . . . . Member of Association of Consulting Engineers (British)
MCOP . . . . . . Major Command Orientation Program (Air Force)
MCOP . . . . . . Multiple Conductor, Oil-Resistant, Portable
MCOPR . . . . . Major Command of Primary Responsibility (Air Force)
MCOR . . . . . . Methodist Committee for Overseas Relief
MCOS . . . . . . Mission Control Operations Section
MCOT . . . . . . Missile Checkout Trailer
MCOT . . . . . . Missile Control Officer, Trainer
MCOW . . . . . . Medical College of Wisconsin
MCP . . . . Maintenance Control Point
MCP . . . . Malawi Congress Party (Nyasaland)
MCP . . . . Male Chauvinist Pig (Feminist term)
MCP . . . . Management Control Plan
MCP . . . . Manual Control Panel
MCP . . . . Manufacturing Change Point
MCP . . . . Massachusetts College of Pharmacy
M Cp . . . . Master of Chiropody
MCP . . . . Master of City Planning
MCP . . . . Master Control Program (Data processing)
MCP . . . . Materiel Command Procedure
MCP . . . . Member of the College of Preceptors (British)
MCP . . . . Memory-Centered Processing (or Processor) (System)
MCP . . . . Military Construction Plan (or Program)
MCP . . . . Mode Control Panel
MCP . . . . Model Cities Program
MCP . . . . Multi-Component Plasma
MCP . . . . Multiple Chip Package
MCPA . . . . . . Member of the College of Pathologists Australasia
MCPA . . . . . . Memory Clock Pulse Amplifier
MCPA . . . . . . Midwest College Placement Association
MCPAC . . . . . Military Construction Programs Advisory Committee
MCPD . . . . . . Marine Corps Procurement District
MCPH . . . . . . Metacarpal-Phalangeal
MCPL . . . . . . Members of Congress for Peace through Law (An organization)
MCPL . . . . . . Multiple-Cue Probability Learning (Psychology)
MCPO . . . . . . Master Chief Petty Officer (Navy)
MCPON . . . . . Master Chief Petty Officer of the Navy
MCPP . . . . . . Mecoprop (Weed-control chemical)
Mcps . . . . Megacycles Per Second (Also see MHz)
MCPS . . . . . . Member of the College of Physicians and Surgeons (British)
MCQP . . . . . . Milk Carton Quality Performing Council
MCR . . . . Maintenance Control Report
MCR . . . . Manufacturing Change Request
MCR . . . . Marine Corps Reserve
MCR . . . . Master Change Record
MCR . . . . Master of Comparative Religion
MCR . . . . Master Control Routine
M Cr . . . . Master of Criminology
MCR . . . . McCord Corporation (NYSE symbol)
MCR . . . . Medical Corps, General Service (USNR officer designation)
MCR . . . . Mediterranean Communication Region (Air Force)
MCR . . . . Methodists for Church Renewal
MCR . . . . Micrographic Catalog Retrieval
MCR . . . . Military Compact Reactor (AEC)
MCR . . . . Mission Control Routine
MCR . . . . Multi-Channel Receiver
MCRA . . . . . . Member of the College of Radiologists Australasia
MCRC . . . . . . Marketing Communications Research Center
MCRD . . . . . . Marine Corps Recruit Depot
McREL . . . . . . Mid-Continent Regional Educational Laboratory
MCREP . . . . . Military Committee Representative (to the North Atlantic Council)
MCRL . . . . . . Mapping and Charting Research Laboratory (Ohio State University)
MCRL . . . . . . Master Component Repair List (DOD)
MCRL . . . . . . Master Cross Reference Listing
MCROA . . . . . Marine Corps Reserve Officers Association
MCRP . . . . . . Maritime Coal, Railway & Power Company, Limited (AAR code)
MCRR . . . . . . Marine Corps Reserve Ribbon
MCRS . . . . . . Micrographic Catalog Retrieval System
MCRT . . . . . . Multi-Channel Rotary Transformer (Electronics)
MCRV . . . . . . Manned Command/Reconnaissance Vehicle
MCS . . . . Madras Civil Service (British)
MCS . . . . Maintenance Control Section (DCE)
MCS . . . . Malayan Civil Service
MCS . . . . Marine Cooks and Stewards Union

MCS . . . . Marine Corps Schools
MCS . . . . Marine Corps Station
MCS . . . . Marine Corps Supply Activity
MCS . . . . Master Circuit System
MCS . . . . Master of Commercial Science
MCS . . . . Master Control Station (or System)
MCS . . . . Mathematical Code System
MCS . . . . Medical Corps, Special Service (USNR officer designation)
Mcs . . . . Megacycles per Second (Also see MHz)
MCS . . . . Meridian Control Signal
MCS . . . . Merritt-Chapman & Scott Corporation (NYSE symbol) (Delisted)
MCS . . . . Meter-Candle Second
MCS . . . . Microwave Carrier Supply
MCS . . . . Microwave Communication System
MCS . . . . Military Communications Stations
MCS . . . . Mine Countermeasure Support (Military)
MCS . . . . Mine Countermeasures Ship (Navy symbol)
MCS . . . . Missile Control System
MCS . . . . Model-Controlled System (NASA)
MCS . . . . Motor Circuit Switch
MCS . . . . Multichannel Scaling (Mode)
MCS . . . . Multidirectional Category System
MCS . . . . Multiple Computer System
MCS . . . . Multipurpose Communications and Signaling
MCSA . . . . . . Meritorious Civilian Service Award
MCSA . . . . . . Michigan Council for the Study of Abortion
MCSA . . . . . . Midwest Collegiate Sailing Association
MCSA . . . . . . Military Construction Supply Agency (Later, Defense Construction Supply Center)
MCSA . . . . . . Moscow, Camden & San Augustine R. R. (AAR code)
MCSC . . . . . . Marine Corps Supply Center
MC Sc . . . . . . Master of Commercial Science
MCSC . . . . . . Medical College of South Carolina
MC Se . . . . . . Master of Commercial Service
MCSH . . . . . . Manhattanville College of the Sacred Heart (New York)
MCSH . . . . . . Maryville College of the Sacred Heart (Missouri)
MCSL . . . . . . Management Control Systems List (DOD)
MCSP . . . . . . Multiple Conductor, Shielded, Pressure-Resistant (Cable)
MCSS . . . . . . Military Communications Satellite System
MCSS . . . . . . Missile Checkout System Selector
MCSTSC . . . . . Military Communications System Technical Standards Committee (Army)
MCT . . . . Magnetic Core Tape
MCT . . . . Magnetic Core Tester
MCT . . . . Master of Christian Training
MCT . . . . Maximum Continuous Thrust (Aviation)
MCT . . . . Maxwell Color Triangle
MCT . . . . Mechanical Comprehension Test
MCT . . . . Medium Chain Triglyceride
MCT . . . . Microwave Ceramic Triode
MCT . . . . Missile Compensating Tank
MCT . . . . Movable Core Transformer
MCT . . . . Movement Control Team (Air Force)
MCT . . . . Multiple Compressed Tablet (Pharmacy)
MCT . . . . Multistrip Cesium Thrustor
MCTA . . . . . . Metropolitan Commuter Transportation Authority (Greater New York City) (Later, Metropolitan Transportation Authority)
MCTC . . . . . . Maritime Cargo Transportation Conference (of MTRB)
MCTG . . . . . . Model Change Training Guide
MCTI . . . . Metal Cutting Tool Institute
MCTR . . . . . . Mackinac Transportation Company (AAR code)
MCTS . . . . . . Master Central Timing System (NASA)
MCTSA . . . . . Military Clothing and Textile Supply Agency (Army - Merged with Defense Supply Agency)
MCTT . . . . . . Metal-Ceramic Transmitting Tube
MCU . . . . Machine Control Unit
MCU . . . . Manual Control Unit
MCU . . . . Medium Close Up (A photograph or motion picture sequence taken from a relatively short distance)
MCU . . . . Message Construction Unit
MCU . . . . Miniature Command Unit
MCU . . . . Monitoring Control Unit
MCUG . . . . . . Military Computers Users Group
MCV . . . . Maritime Commission, Victory Ship
MCV . . . . Mean Corpuscular Volume
MCV . . . . Medical College of Virginia
MC-V(G) . . . . Medical Officers (Qualified for General Detail) (USNR designation)
MC-V(S) . . . . . Medical Officers (Qualified for Specialist Duties) (USNR designation)
MCW . . . . Mallinckrodt Chemical Works
MCW . . . . Medical Corps, Women's Reserve (USNR officer designation)
MCW . . . . Metal Casement Window (Technical drawings)
MCW . . . . Modulated Continuous Wave (Radio)

MCWR . . . . . . Marine Corps Women's Reserve
MCX . . . . Minimum-Cost Expediting
MCZ . . . . Museum of Comparative Zoology (Harvard University)
MCZE . . . . . . Minimum When Control Zone Effective (Aviation)
MCZNE . . . . . Minimum When Control Zone Not Effective (Aviation)
MD . . . . Doctor of Medicine
MD . . . . Machine Direction
MD . . . . Magnetic Drum
MD . . . . Main Droite or Mano Destra (Right Hand)
MD . . . . Main Duct
MD . . . . Management Directive
MD . . . . Managing Director
MD . . . . Manu Dextra (With the Right Hand) (Music)
MD . . . . Manual Data
MD . . . . Marine Detachment
MD . . . . Maryland
MD . . . . Maximum Design Meter
MD . . . . McDonnell-Douglas Corp. (NYSE symbol)
MD . . . . Mean Deviation
MD . . . . Measured Depth (Diamonds)
MD . . . . Measured Drilling (Diamonds)
MD . . . . Medical Department
MD . . . . Medical Discharge (from military service)
MD . . . . Medium Duty
Md . . . . Mendelevium (Chemical element) (Preferred form, but also see Mv)
MD . . . . Mentally Deficient
MD . . . . Mess Deck (Naval)
MD . . . . Message Data
MD . . . . Message-Dropping (Military)
MD . . . . Messages per Day
MD . . . . Metal Deactivator
MD . . . . Meteorology Department (Navy)
MD . . . . Methyldichloroarsine
MD . . . . Microalloy Diffused
MD . . . . Middle Dutch (Language, etc.)
MD . . . . Millwall Dock (British)
MD . . . . Mine Depot (Naval)
MD . . . . Mine Disposal
MD . . . . Minute Difference
MD . . . . Miscellaneous Document
MD . . . . Mitral Disease (Pathology)
MD . . . . Months after Date or Month's Date
MD . . . . Motor Drive
MD . . . . Movement Directive
MD . . . . Multidomain (Grains in rocks) (Geophysics)
MD . . . . Multinomial Distribution (Statistics)
MD . . . . Municipal Docks (AAR code)
MD . . . . Muscular Dystrophy (Medicine)
MD . . . . Musical Director
M-D . . . . Modulation-Demodulation
M/D . . . . . . Man Day
M/D . . . . Memorandum of Deposits (Business and trade)
M & D . . . . . Medicine and Duty
MDA . . . . . . Magic Dealers Association
MDA . . . . . . Magnetic Deflection Amplifier
MDA . . . . . . Maintainability Design Approach
MDA . . . . . . Maintenance Depot Assistance (Air Force)
MDA . . . . . . Maintenance Design Approach
MDA . . . . . . Mapco, Inc. (NYSE symbol)
MDA . . . . . . Marking Device Association
MDA . . . . . . Master Design Award
MDA . . . . . . Master of Dramatic Art
MDA . . . . . . Master Dyers Association
MDA . . . . . . Material Disposal Authority
MDA . . . . . . Mento-Dextra Anterior
MDA . . . . . . Meteroid Detector-Analyzer
MDA . . . . . . Minimum Descent Altitude (Aviation)
MDA . . . . . . Minimum Detectable Amount (of radiation)
MDA . . . . . . Mobile Depot Activities (Air Force)
MDA . . . . . . Mothers for Decency in Action (Group opposing sex education in schools)
MDA . . . . . . Motor Discriminative Acuity (Psychology)
MDA . . . . . . Multiple Docking Adapter (Apollo) (NASA)
MDA . . . . . . Mutual Defense Assistance
MDAA . . . . . . Muscular Dystrophy Associations of America
MDAA . . . . . . Mutual Defense Assistance Act
MDAC . . . . . . Mutual Defense Assistance, General Area of China
MDAC/E . . . . McDonnell Douglas Astronautics Company/East
MDAC/W . . . . McDonnell Douglas Astronautics Company/West
MDAGT . . . . . Mutual Defense Assistance, Greece and Turkey
MDAIKP . . . . . Mutual Defense Assistance, Iran, Republic of Korea, and Philippines
MDANAA . . . . Mutual Defense Assistance, North Atlantic Area

MDAP . . . . . . Mutual Defense Assistance Pact (or Program)
MDAR . . . . . . Minimum Daily Adult Requirement
MDAS . . . . . . Miniature Data Acquisition System
MDB . . . . Mitglied des Deutschen Bundestages (German Federal Parliament)
MDB . . . . Multiple Drive Block
MDC . . . . Main Display Console
MDC . . . . Maintenance Data Collection (Military)
MDC . . . . Manhattan Drug Company
MDC . . . . Manual Direction Center (Air Force)
MDC . . . . Maryland Cup Corp. (NYSE symbol)
MDC . . . . Master Direction Center (Air Force)
MDC . . . . Materials Dissemination Center (Institute for Development of Educational Activities)
MDC . . . . McDonnell Douglas Corporation
MDC . . . . Meteorological Data Collection
MDC . . . . Metropolitan District Commission
MDC . . . . Mild Detonating Cord
MDC . . . . Milwaukee-Downer College (Later, Lawrence University) (Wisconsin)
MDC . . . . Missile Development Center (Air Force)
MDC . . . . Missile Direction Center
MDC . . . . Mobile Distress Call
MDC . . . . Mongoloid Development Council
MDC . . . . Montreal Diocesan College
MDC . . . . Movement Designator Code
MDC . . . . Multi-Device Controller
MDC . . . . Multilayer Dielectric Coating
MDCA . . . . . . Manufacturing Design Change Analysis
MDCB . . . . . . Moisture Detector Control Box
MDCC . . . . . . Master Data Control Console
MDCK . . . . . . Madin-Darby Canine Kidney
MDCS . . . . . . Maintenance Data Collection System (or Subsystem) (Navy)
MDCS . . . . . . Master Digital Command System
MDCS . . . . . . Mutual Defense Control Staff (Department of State)
MDCT . . . . . . Multi-Dimensional Compensatory Task
MDC-W . . . . . McDonnell Douglas Corporation - West
MDD . . . . Doctor of Dental Medicine
MDD . . . . Median Droplet Diameter
MDD . . . . Milligrams per square Decimeter per Day
MDD . . . . Mouvement Democratique Dahomeen (Dahomean Democratic Movement)
MDDA . . . . . . Mechanicsburg Defense Depot Activity (AEC)
MDDC . . . . . . Manhattan District Declassified Code (AEC)
MDE . . . . McDermott (J. Ray) & Company, Inc. (NYSE symbol)
MDE . . . . Missile Display Equipment
MDE . . . . Modern Drug Encyclopedia
MDE . . . . Modular Design of Electronics
MDENDET . . . Mobile Dental Detachment (Coast Guard)
M Des . . . . . . Master of Design
MDF . . . . Main Distributing Frame
MDF . . . . Manual Direction Finder (Radio)
MDF . . . . Medium-Frequency Direction Finding
MDF . . . . Mild Detonating Fuse
MDF . . . . Multiband Direction Finder
MDFMR . . . . . M-Day Force Materiel Requirement
MDFNA . . . . . Maximum Density Fuming Nitric Acid
MDFR . . . . . . Make Descent From (Aviation)
MDG . . . . Medical Director General (British Navy)
MDG . . . . Metal Density Gage
MDGD . . . . . . Mercury Doped Germanium Detector
MDH . . . . Magnetic Drum Head
MDH . . . . Malate Dehydrogenase
MDH . . . . Maneuver Director Headquarters (Military)
MDHTSNAGEJTR. . . . Movement of Dependents and Household Goods to Temporary Station(s) Not Authorized at Government Expense, Except as Prescribed in Joint Travel Regulations (Army)
MDI . . . . Magnetic Direction Indicator
MDI . . . . Management Development Institute
MDI . . . . Manual Data Input (SAGE)
MDI . . . . Master Direction Indicator
MDI . . . . Methylene di-p-phenyl Diisocyanate (Chemistry)
MDI . . . . Micro-Dosimetric Instrumentation
MDI . . . . Missile Distance Indicator
MDI . . . . Mobilization Day Increment (Military)
MDI . . . . Mobilization Day Index
MDI . . . . Multiple Display Indicator
MDIA . . . . . . Mouvement pour la Defense des Interets de l'Angola (Movement for the Defense of Angolan Interests)
M Did . . . . . . Master of Didactics
M Di E . . . . . Master of Diesel Engineering
MDIE . . . . . . Mother-Daughter Ionosphere Experiment
M Di Eng . . . . Master of Diesel Engineering
MDIF . . . . . . Manual Data Input Function (Data processing)

M Dip . . . . . . Master of Diplomacy
MDIS . . . . Manual Data Input Section
MDIU . . . . Manual Data Input Unit (Data processing)
M Div . . . . . . Master of Divinity
MDK . . . . Mechanical Disconnect Kit
MDK . . . . Montana-Dakota Utilities Company (NYSE symbol)
MDL . . . . Magnetic Delay Line
MDL . . . . Magnetic Double Layer
MDL . . . . Management Data List
MDL . . . . Master Data Library (NASA)
MDL . . . . Master of Divine Literature
MDL . . . . Master Drawing List
MDL . . . . . . Mercury Delay Line
MDL . . . . . . Microwave Delay Line
MDL . . . . Microwave Development Laboratories
MDL . . . . Mine Defense Laboratory (Panama City, Florida) (Navy)
MDL . . . . Miniature Display Light
MDL . . . . Minimum Detectable Limit
MDL . . . . . . Modular Dummy Load
MDLC . . . . . . Materiel Development and Logistic Command (Army – replaced Ordnance, Engineer, Signal, Chemical and Quartermaster Overall Commands)
MDLF . . . . . . Mobile Drydock Launch Facility
MDLP . . . . . Mobile Dryer Loan Program
MDLS . . . . . . Marine Data Logger System
MDM . . . . . . Magnetic Disc Memory
MDM . . . . . . Magneto-Optical Display Memory
MDM . . . . . . Manpower Determination Model (Military)
MDM . . . . . Mobile Depot Maintenance (Air Force)
MDM . . . . . . Monolithic Diode Matrix
MDM . . . . . . Movement for a Democratic Military
MDM . . . . . . Movimiento Democratico de Mozambique (Democratic Movement of Mozambique)
MDMR . . . . . . M-Day Mobilization Requirement
MDMS . . . . . Miss Distance Measuring System
MDN . . . . . . Mark der Deutschen Notenbank (East German currency)
MDN . . . . . . Movimiento Democratico Nacionalista (Political party in Guatemala)
MDNA . . . . . . Machinery Dealers' National Association
MDNA . . . . . Maximum Density Nitric Acid
MDNA . . . . . Mobilehome Dealers National Association
MDO . . . . . . Mobile District Office
MDOT . . . . . . Modular Digital Output Timer
MDP . . . . . . Ferrocarril Mexicano del Pacifico (AAR code)
MDP . . . . . . Magyar Dolgozok Partja
MDP . . . . . . Malfunction Detection Package
MDP . . . . . . Malicious Destruction of Property
MDP . . . . . . Manpower Development Program (Department of Labor)
MDP . . . . . . Mean Datum Plane
MDP . . . . . . Mento-Dextra Posterior
MDP . . . . . . Meredith Corp. (NYSE symbol)
MDP . . . . . . Meteorological Datum Plane
MDP . . . . . . Movimiento Democratico Peruano (Peruvian Democratic Movement)
MDPG . . . . . . Magnetic Digital-Pulse Generator
MDR . . . . . . Magnet Drum Recorder
MDR . . . . . . Magnetic Dipole Radiation
MDR . . . . . . Maintenance Data Report (Army)
MDR . . . . . . Maintenance Demonstration Report
MDR . . . . . . Maintenance Design Requirement
MDR . . . . . . Manual Data Room
MDR . . . . . . Master Data Record
MDR . . . . . . Memory-Data Register
MDR . . . . . . Metropolitan District Railway (London)
MDR . . . . . . Minimum Daily Requirement (of a vitamin, etc.)
MDR . . . . . . Mission Data Reduction
MDR . . . . . . Motor Driven Relay
MDR . . . . . . Multichannel Data Recorder
MDRM . . . . . . Mouvement Democratique de Renovation Malgache (Democratic Movement Malagasy Restoration)
MDRS . . . . . . Mobilization Designation Reserve Section
MDRS . . . . . . Mylar Diaphragm Rupture System
MDRT . . . . . . Million Dollar Round Table (of the NALU)
MDS . . . . . . Magnetic Drum System
MDS . . . . . . Mail Distribution Schedule (Air Force)
MDS . . . . . . Mail Distribution Scheme (Army)
MDS . . . . . . Main Dressing Station
MDS . . . . . . Maintenance Data System
MDS . . . . . . Maintenance Documentation System (Bell System)
MDS . . . . . . Malfunction Detection System (Gemini) (NASA)
MDS . . . . . . Mass Digital Storage
MDS . . . . . . Master of Dental Surgery
MDS . . . . . . Master Drum Sender
MDS . . . . . . Mennonite Disaster Service

MDS . . . . . . Meteoroid Detection Satellite (NASA)
MDS . . . . Mine Detection Set
MDS . . . . Minimum Detectable (or Discernible) Signal (Radio)
MDS . . . . . . Mission Design and Series (Military)
MDS . . . . Mohawk Data Sciences Corp. (NYSE symbol)
MDS . . . . Molybdenum Disulfide
MDS . . . . . . Montant de Soutien (A trade negotiating plan of EEC) (French expression means amount of support)
MDSC . . . . . . Management Data Service Center
MD Sc . . . . . . Master of Dental Science
MDSE . . . . . . Merchandise
MDSOR . . . . . . Monthly Depot Space and Operating Report
MDSS . . . . . . Magnetic Drum Storage System
MDSS . . . . . . Mass Digital Storage System
MDSV . . . . . . Manned Deep Space Vehicle
MDT . . . . Mean Down Time
MDT . . . . . . Mento-Dextra Transversa
MDT . . . . Mercury Dynamic Test
MDT . . . . Moderate
MDT . . . . . . Mountain Daylight Time
MDT . . . . . . Mutual Defense Treaty
MDTA . . . . . . Manpower Development and Training Act (Department of Labor)
MDTA . . . . . . Modulation, Demodulation, Terminal and Associated (Equipment)
MDTS . . . . . . Mobile Doppler Tracking Station
MDTS . . . . . . Modular Data Transaction System
MDTU . . . . . . Mobile Dockside Transfer Unit
MDU . . . . Message Decoder Unit
MDU . . . . . . Mine Disposal Unit
MDU . . . . . . Mobile Development Unit (Thailand)
MDV . . . . . . Doctor of Veterinary Medicine
MDV . . . . . . Master of Veterinary Medicine
MDV . . . . . . Mission Development Company (NYSE symbol) (Delisted)
MDV . . . . . . Mouvement Democratique Voltaique (Upper Volta Democratic Movement)
MDW . . . . . . Chicago (Illinois) (Midway Airport) (Airport symbol)
MDW . . . . . . Mars Departure Window
MDW . . . . . . Military Defence Works (British)
MDW . . . . . . Military District of Washington (DC)
MDW . . . . . . Minnesota, Dakota & Western Railway Company (AAR code)
MDW . . . . . . Multipair Distribution Wire
MDY . . . . . . Magnetic Deflection Yoke
MDY . . . . . . Midland Oil (NYSE symbol)
ME . . . . Magnetoelastic
ME . . . . Main Entry (Library science)
ME . . . . Maine
ME . . . . Malt Extract (Microbiology)
ME . . . . Managing Editor
ME . . . . Marbled Edges
ME . . . . Marine Engineer
ME . . . . Master of Education
ME . . . . Master of Elements
ME . . . . Master of Engineering
ME . . . . Maximum Effort
ME . . . . Measuring Element
ME . . . . Mechanical Efficiency
ME . . . . Mechanical Engineer
ME . . . . Medical Examiner
ME . . . . Metabolizable Energy
ME . . . . Metal Evaporated
ME . . . . Metalsmith (Navy)
ME . . . . Methodist Episcopal
ME . . . . Methods Engineering
ME . . . . Methyl
ME . . . . Micro-Electronic
ME . . . . Micrometeoroid Explorer (Satellite)
ME . . . . Middle East(ern)
ME . . . . Middle English (Language, etc.)
ME . . . . Military Electronics
ME . . . . Military Engineer
ME . . . . Milligram Equivalent or Milliequivalent (Also, MEQ)
ME . . . . Mining Engineer
ME . . . . Missile Electrician
ME . . . . Mistress of English
ME . . . . Miter End (Technical drawings)
ME . . . . Mobility Equipment (Military)
ME . . . . Modulation Efficiency
ME . . . . Molecular Electronics
ME . . . . Morristown & Erie R. R. (AAR code)
ME . . . . Most Excellent (In titles)
ME . . . . Mouvement Europeen (European Movement)
ME . . . . Movie Editor
ME . . . . Muhammadan Era

ME . . . . Multi-Engine
ME . . . . Muzzle Energy
M:E . . . . Myeloid:Erythrocyte (Ratio)
MEA . . . . Maintenance Engineering Analysis
MEA . . . . Master of Engineering Administration
MEA . . . . Mead Corporation (NYSE symbol)
MEA . . . . Medical Exhibitors Association
MEA . . . . Mercapto Ethyl Amine
MEA . . . . Metropolitan Economic Area
MEA . . . . Middle East Airlines Company
MEA . . . . Minimum Enroute IFR Altitude
MEA . . . . Monoethanolamine
MEA . . . . Multimode Error Analysis
MEA . . . . Music Editors Association
MEAB . . . . . . Maintenance Engineering Analysis Board
MEAC . . . . . . Mid-Eastern Athletic Conference
MEAD . . . . . . Memphis Army Depot
MEADS . . . . . Maintenance Engineering Analysis Data System
MEAFSA . . . . Middle East/Southern Asia and Africa South of the Sahara (Military)
MEAL . . . . . . Master Equipment Allowance (or Authorization) List (Military)
MEAPL . . . . . Manufacturing and Engineering Assembly Parts List (File)
MEAPS . . . . . Method of Ensemble Average of Periodic Systems
MEAR . . . . . . Maintenance Engineering Analysis Record (or Report) (Navy)
MEARS . . . . . Maintenance Engineering Analysis Records
MEASURE . . . . Metrology Automated System for Uniform Recall and Reporting (Navy)
MEAT . . . . . . Manpower Employment Assistance Training (Act) (Pennsylvania)
Me B . . . . Bachelor of Metaphysics
MEB . . . . Marine Expeditionary Brigade (Military)
MEB . . . . Master Electronics Board
MEB . . . . Medical Board
MEB . . . . Mercury Electron Bombardment
MEB . . . . Midlands Electricity Board (British)
MEB . . . . Military Early Bird
MEBA . . . . . . Marine Engineers' Beneficial Association
MEBA . . . . . . National Marine Engineers' Beneficial Association
MEBBAS . . . . . Mission Essential Bare Base Augmentation Sets (Air Force)
MEBD . . . . . . Medical Examining Board
MEBD . . . . . . Milcherzeugerberatungsdienst
MEBS . . . . . . Multicore Extruded Bar Solder
MEC . . . . Maine Central Railroad Company
MEC . . . . Manufacturing Engineering Council
MEC . . . . Marginal Efficiency of Capital (Banking)
M Ec . . . . Master of Economics
MEC . . . . Master of Engineering Chemistry
MEC . . . . Methodist Episcopal Church
MEC . . . . Metrology Engineering Center (Navy)
MEC . . . . Microwave Electronics Corporation
MEC . . . . Military Essentiality Class (or Code)
MEC . . . . Minnesota Electronic Corporation
MEC . . . . Mobility Equipment Center
MEC . . . . Mobility Equipment Command (Army)
MEC . . . . Molecular Energy Corporation
MECA . . . . . . Maintainable Electronics Component Assembly
MECA . . . . . . Malfunctioned Equipment Corrective Action
MECA . . . . . . Mercury Evaporation (or Evaporating) and Condensation (or Condensing) Analysis (NASA)
MECA . . . . . . Multi-Element Component Array
MECAR . . . . . Metropolitan Engineers Council on Air Resources
MECAS . . . . . Middle East Center for Arab Studies
MECCA . . . . . Minnesota Environmental Control Citizens Association
MECE . . . . . . Master of Electro-Chemical Engineering
MECH . . . . . . Mechanic
MECH . . . . . . Methodist Episcopal Church
MECHBAT . . . . Mechanized Battalion (Army)
ME Ch E . . . . . Master of Electro-Chemical Engineering
MECHINF . . . . Mechanized Infantry (Army)
MECO . . . . . . Main Engine Cut-Off (Aerospace)
MECO . . . . . . Manual Equipment Check-Out
MECOM . . . . . Middle East Command (Military)
MECOM . . . . . Mobility Equipment Command (Army)
MECP . . . . . . Multi-Elliptical Cavity Pump
MECR . . . . . . Maintenance Engineering Change Request
MECU . . . . . . Member of the English Church Union
MED . . . . Manhattan Engineer District (Developed atomic bomb; dissolved, 1946)
M Ed . . . . Master of Education
MED . . . . Master of Elementary Didactics
MED . . . . Master of English Divinity
MED . . . . Median
MED . . . . Median Erythrocyte Diameter
MED . . . . Medical
MED . . . . Mediterranean

MED . . . . Mediterranean Engineer Division (Army Engineers)
MED . . . . Medium
MED . . . . Message Entry Device
MED . . . . Microelectronic Device
MED . . . . Minimal Effective Dose
MED . . . . Minimal Erythema Dose
MED . . . . Mobile Energy Depot
MEDA . . . . . . Multiplex Electronic Doppler Analyzer
MEDAC . . . . . Medical Accounting (and Billing Process)
MEDAC . . . . . Mouvement de l'Evolution Democratique de L'Afrique Centrale (Central African Democratic Evolution Movement)
MEDAL . . . . . Micromechanized Engineering Data for Automated Logistics
MEDCAP . . . . Medical Civic Action Program (Army)
MEDCAT . . . . Medical Civic Action Teams
MEDCAT . . . . Medium Altitude Critical Atmospheric Turbulence
MEDCENT . . . . Central Mediterranean
MEDCOM . . . . Mediterranean Communications (Military)
MEDCON . . . . Medical Contingency Report (Air Force)
MEDCOOP . . . Medical Continuity of Operations Plan (Army)
MEDCORPS . . . Medical Corps (Air Force)
MEDDA . . . . . Mechanized Defense Decision Anticipation (AFSC)
MED-DENT . . . . Medical Dental Division (Air Force)
MEDERCO . . . . Mouvement de l'Evolution et de Developpement Rural - Congo (Movement for the Evolution and Rural Development - Congo) (Leopoldville)
MEDEVAC . . . . Medical Evacuation Team (Army)
MEDEVAL . . . . Medical Evaluation (Military)
MEDEX . . . . . Médecin Extension (Doctors' aides, or medics) (Military)
MEDFLY . . . . Mediterranean Fruit Fly
MEDH . . . . . . Maintainability Engineering Design Handbook
MEDI . . . . . . Mossbauer Effect Data Index
MEDIA . . . . . Magnavox Electronic Data Image Apparatus
MEDIA . . . . . Manufacturers Educational Drug Information Association
MEDIA . . . . . Missile Era Data Integration Analysis
MEDIA . . . . . Move to End Deception in Advertising (Student legal action organization)
MEDICAID . . . Medical Aid (Federal program providing financial assistance for medical expenses of individual needy citizens)
MEDICARE . . . Medical Care (Federal program providing financial assistance for medical expenses of individual senior citizens)
MEDICO . . . . Medical International Cooperation
MEDICO . . . . Model Experiment in Drug Indexing by Computer
MEDICOS . . . . Mediterranean Instructions to Convoys (World War II)
MEDIHC . . . . Military Experience Directed into Health Careers (DOD/HEW project)
MEDIUM . . . . Missile Era Data Integration - Ultimate Method
MEDLARS . . . . Medical Literature Analysis and Retrieval System
M Ed LS . . . . . Master of Education in Library Science
MEDMER . . . . Medical Emergency Report (Air Force)
MEDMIS . . . . Medical Management Information System (Army)
MEDOFCOM . . Medical Officer-in-Command (Military)
MEDOL . . . . . Medically Oriented Language
MEDP . . . . . . Medium Port
MEDRED . . . . Medical Unit Readiness Report (Air Force)
MEDSAC . . . . Medical Service Activity (Army)
MEDSARS . . . . Maintenance Engineering Data Storage and Retrieval System
Med Sc D . . . . Doctor of Medical Science (or the Science of Medicine)
MEDSERVC . . . Medical Service Corps (Military)
MEDSPECC . . . Medical Specialist Corps (Military)
MEDSUPDEP . . . Medical Supply Depot
MEDT . . . . . . Military Equipment Delivery Team
MEDUSA . . . . Multiple Element Directional Universally Steerable Antenna
MEE . . . . Mass Energy Equivalent
MEE . . . . Master of Electrical Engineering
MEE . . . . Mechanical Evaluation Equipment
MEE . . . . Minimum Essential Equipment
MEECN . . . . . Minimum Essential Emergency Communications Network (Military)
MEEF . . . . . . Mobile Equipment Employment File (Air Force)
MEEL . . . . . . Mission Equipment Essentiality List
ME Eng . . . . . Master of Electrical Engineering
MEETAT . . . . . Maximum Improvement in Electronics Effectiveness Through Advanced Techniques
MEF . . . . Maintenance Efficiency Factor
MEF . . . . Marine Expeditionary Force (Military)
MEF . . . . Maximal Expiratory Flow
MEF . . . . Mesopotamian Expeditionary Force (British)
MEF . . . . Middle East Forces (British)
MEF . . . . Mouse Embryo Fibroblast(s)
MEF . . . . Multiple Effect Flash (Evaporator) (Seawater conversion system)
MEF . . . . Musicians Emergency Fund
MEFA . . . . . . Metal Etching and Fabricating Association
MEFPAK . . . . Manpower and Equipment Force Packaging (Military)
MEG . . . . Madly Enthusiastic Grape-eater
MEG . . . . Magnetoencephalogram

MEG . . . . Management Evaluation Group (State Department)
MEG . . . . Miniature Electrostatic Gyro
MEGA . . . . . . Military Evaluation of Geographic Areas
MeGV . . . . . . Million Volts
MeGW . . . . . . Megawatt (Also, MW)
MeGWH . . . . . Megawatt-Hour
MEI . . . . Maintenance Engineering Inspection
MEI . . . . Manual of Engineering Instructions
MEI . . . . MEI Corp. (Formerly, Minnesota Enterprises, Incorporated) (NYSE symbol)
MEI . . . . Metals Engineering Institute
MEI . . . . Middle East Institute
MEIC . . . . . . Member of the Engineering Institute of Canada
MEIF . . . . . . Mobile Equipment Information File (Air Force)
MEIS . . . . . . Military Entomology Information Service
MEIU . . . . . . Middle East Interpretation Unit (British)
MEIU . . . . . . Mobile Explosives Investigation Unit
MEJ . . . . Marman Expansion Joint
MEJ . . . . Maximum Economic Justification
MEK . . . . Methyl Ethyl Ketone (Solvent)
MEL . . . . Maneuvering Element (Military)
MEL . . . . Many-Element LASER
MEL . . . . Marine Engineering Laboratory (Navy)
M El . . . . Master of Elements
MEL . . . . Master of English Literature
MEL . . . . Master Equipment List
MEL . . . . Minimum Equipment List
MEL . . . . Mistress of English Literature
MEL . . . . Mobile Erector Launcher (Military)
MEL . . . . Music Education League
MELABS . . . . . Microwave Engineering Laboratories, Inc.
MELG . . . . . . Middle East Liaison Group (Military)
MELISS . . . . . Mitsubishi Electric Corporation Literature and Information Search Service
M Elo . . . . . . Master of Elocution
MELP . . . . . . Mid-European Law Project
MELS . . . . . . Missions Essential Sub-Systems Lists (Navy)
MELSA . . . . . Metropolitan Library Service Agency
MELVA . . . . . Military Electronic Light Valve
MEM . . . . Mars Excursion Module
Me M . . . . . . Master of Metaphysics
MEM . . . . Member
MEM . . . . Minimal Essential Medium
MEMA . . . . . Microelectronic Modular Assembly
MEMA . . . . . Motor and Equipment Manufacturers Association
MEMI . . . . . . Master Equipment Management Index (Air Force)
MEML . . . . . . Master Equipment Management List (Air Force)
MEML . . . . . . Molecular Engineering and Material Laboratory (MIT)
MEMO . . . . . Medical Equipment Management Office (Air Force)
MEMO . . . . . . Memorandum
MEMOCS . . . . Mitsubishi Electric Corporation Multiterm Out of Context System
MEMP . . . . . . Maximization of Expected Maximum Profit (Econometrics)
MEMQ . . . . . Married Enlisted Men's Quarters
MEMS . . . . . . Microbial Ecological Monitoring System (Apollo) (NASA)
MEMS . . . . . . Multi-Effect, Multi-Stage
MEMU . . . . . . Manned Extravehicular Manipulating Unit
M En . . . . . . Master of English
MEN . . . . Master Equipment Number
MEN . . . . Menasco Manufacturing (NYSE symbol)
MEN . . . . Multiple Event Network
MENA . . . . . . Middle East News Agency
MENC . . . . . . Music Educators National Conference
MEND . . . . . . Massive Economic Neighborhood Development (New York City)
MEND . . . . . . Medical Education for National Defense
MENEX . . . . . Maintenance Engineering Exchange
M Eng . . . . . . Master of Engineering
M Eng . . . . . . Master of English
M Eng . . . . . . Mechanical Engineer
M-ENG . . . . . . Multi-Engined
M Eng & PA . . . Master in Engineering and Public Administration
M Ent . . . . . . Master of Entomology
MEO . . . . Major Engine Overhaul
MEO . . . . Manned Earth Orbit
MEO . . . . Manned Extravehicular Operation
MEO . . . . Mass in Earth Orbit (NASA)
MEOM . . . . . Manned Earth Orbit Mission
MEOP . . . . . . Maximum Expected Operating Pressure
MEOS . . . . . . Microsomal Ethanol-Oxidizing System (Biochemistry)
MEOV . . . . . Maximum Expected Operating Value (FCC)
MEOWS . . . . . Multimode Electro-Optical Weapon System
MEP . . . . Magnetic Energy Product
MEP . . . . Mahajana Eksath Peramuna Party (Ceylon)
MEP . . . . Management Engineering Program (Air Force)

MEP . . . . Manuals of Engineering Practice (ASCE)
MEP . . . . Mars Entry Probe
MEP . . . . Master of Engineering Physics
MEP . . . . Mean Effective Pressure
MEP . . . . Medical Education Program (Air Force)
MEP . . . . Minority Entrepreneurship Program (Small Business Administration)
MEP . . . . Minuteman Education Program (Air Force)
MEP . . . . Mission Effects Projector (Lunar exploration)
MEP . . . . Mobile Electric Power
MEP . . . . Motor End Plate
MEP . . . . Multi-Elliptical Pump
MEPA . . . . . . Master in Engineering and Public Administration
ME Phy . . . . . Master of Engineering Physics
MEPP . . . . . . Miniature End Plate Potential
MEPP . . . . . . Mobile Electric Power Plant
MEPS . . . . . . Modular Electrical Power Station
mEq . . . . Milliequivalent
MEQ . . . . Mission Equities Corp. (NYSE symbol)
MEQA . . . . . . Mechanized Equipment Assignment (AT & T)
MER . . . . Manned Earth Reconnaissance (Naval Air Electronic Systems Command project)
MER . . . . Manpower Evaluation Report (Military)
MER . . . . Mass Energy Relationship
MER . . . . Maximum Efficient Rate (Oil)
MER . . . . Merchant
MER . . . . Merrill Lynch, Pierce, Fenner & Smith (NYSE symbol)
MER . . . . Metal Etch Resist
MER . . . . Metal Evaporated Resistor
MER . . . . Minimum Energy Requirements
MER . . . . Mitteleuropaisches Reisebuero (Middle European Travel Bureau)
MER . . . . Multi-Element RADAR
MER . . . . Multiple Ejection Rack
MERA . . . . . . Molecular Electronics RADAR Arrays
MERC . . . . . . Music Education Research Council
MERCAST . . . . Merchant Ship Broadcast
MERCO . . . . . Mercantile Communications (Shipping)
MERCO . . . . . Merchant Ship Control
MERCON . . . . Universal Transversal Mercator Converter (Computer program)
MERCOS . . . . . Merchant Codes (Shipping)
MERCY . . . . . Medical Emergency Relief Care for Youth
MERDC . . . . . Mobility Equipment Research and Development Center (Army)
MERDIFF . . . . . Meridian Difference
MERDL . . . . . Medical Equipment Research and Development Laboratory (Army)
MERGE . . . . . Mechanized Retrieval for Greater Efficiency (Data processing)
MERGV . . . . . Martian Exploratory Rocket Glide Vehicle
MERIT . . . . . . Michigan Educational Research Information Triad, Inc.
MERM . . . . . . Material Evaluation Rocket Motor
MERS . . . . . . Multi-Element Radiometer System
MERSIGS . . . . . Merchant Signals (Shipping)
MERT . . . . . . Maintenance Engineering Review Team (Navy)
MERT . . . . . . Milwaukee Electric Railway & Transport Company (AAR code)
MERTS . . . . . Micropound Extended Range Thrust Stand (NASA)
MES . . . . Maintenance Electrolyte Solution (Physiology)
MES . . . . Manned Exploration Site
MES . . . . Master of Engineering Sciences
MES . . . . Melville Shoe Corporation (NYSE symbol)
MES . . . . Miniature Edison Screw
MES . . . . Missile Electrical Simulator
MES . . . . MOL (Manned Orbiting Laboratory) Environmental Shelter
MES . . . . More Effective Schools (Program)
ME(S) . . . . . . Methodist Episcopal, South
MESA . . . . . . Manned Environmental Systems Assessment (A project of NASA)
MESA . . . . . . Mechanics Educational Society of America
MESA . . . . . . Middle East Studies Association of North America
MESA . . . . . . Miniature Electrostatic Accelerometer
MESA . . . . . . Modularized Equipment Storage (or Stowage) Area (or Assembly) (Apollo) (NASA)
MESA . . . . . . Multiple Engagement Simulation Analyzer (Military)
ME/SA . . . . . Middle East/South Asia
MESAN . . . . . Mouvement de l'Evolution Sociale de l'Afrique Noire (Black African Social Evolution Movement)
MESBIC . . . . . Minority Enterprise Small Business Investment Company
ME Sc . . . . . . Master of Engineering Science
MESC . . . . . . Middle East Supply Center
MESCPL . . . . . Mess Corporal (Marine Corps)
MESF . . . . . . Mobile Earth Station Facility
MeSH . . . . . . Medical Subject Headings (National Library of Medicine)
MESL . . . . . . Microwave Electronic Systems, Limited
MESSAGE . . . . Modular Electronic Solid-State Aerospace Ground Equipment
MESSSGT . . . . Mess Sergeant (Marine Corps)
MEST . . . . . . Missile Electrical System Test

MET	Magic Eye Tube
MET	Management Engineering Team (Air Force)
MET	Manufacturer's Excise Tax
MET	Mechanical Engineering Technician
MET	Meteorology
MET	Methionine (Amino acid)
MET	Metromedia, Inc. (NYSE symbol)
MET	Midexpiratory Time (Medicine)
MET	Minimum Energy Trajectory
MET	Minimum Exposure Time
MET	Missile Escort Team (Air Force)
MET	Mission Environment Tape
MET	Mobile (or Modularized) Equipment Transporter (NASA)
MET	Modular Equipment Transporter (NASA)
MET	Molecular Electronic Technique
MET	Multiemitter Transistor
META	Metropolitan Educational Television Association (Canada)
METB	Metal Base
METC	Modesto & Empire Traction Company (AAR code)
METC	Mouse Embryo Tissue Culture
METCO	Metropolitan Council for Educational Opportunity (Boston)
METD	Metal Door
Met E	Metallurgical Engineer
METE	Mezogazdasagi es Elelmiszeripari Tudomanyos Egyesulet
METF	Metal Flashing
METG	Metal Grill
METIMP	Meteorological Equipment Improvement Program
METJ	Metal Jalousie
METLO	Metrological Equipment and Technical Liaison Officer (Navy)
METM	Metal Mold
METO	Maximum Except Takeoff (Power) (Air Force)
METO	Meteorological Officer (Air Force)
METO	Middle East Treaty Organization
METOF	Meteorological Office
METON	Measured Tons Discharged or Loaded (Shipping)
METOP	Maximum Expected Takeoff Power
METP	Metal Partition
METR	Metal Roof
METR	Meteorology
METRI	Military Essentiality Through Readiness Indices
METRIC	Multi-Echelon Technique for Recoverable Item Control
METRL	Meteorology
METRL	Metrology Requirements List (DOD)
METRO	Materiel Essential to Reconstitution Operations (Air Force)
METRO	Meteorological Equipment Terminal and Representative Observation
METROC	Meteorological Rocket
METS	Metal Strip
METS	Modularized Equipment Transport System (NASA)
MET/SAT	Meteorological Satellite
METU	Middle East Technical University (Ankara, Turkey)
METU	Mobile Electronics Technical Unit
METW	Municipality of East Troy, Wisconsin R. R. (AAR code)
MEU	Marine Expeditionary Unit
MEU	Message Encoder Unit
MEV	Manned Entry Vehicle
MeV	Mega (or Million) Electron Volts
MEVE	Mesa Verde National Park
MEW	Marine Early Warning
MEW	Microwave Early Warning (Radio) (Air Force)
MEW	Ministry of Economic Warfare (British)
MEWA	Motor and Equipment Wholesalers Association
MEWS	Missile Early Warning Station
MEWS	Missile Electronic Warfare System (Army)
MEWT	Micro-Electronic Weld Tester
MEWTA	Missile Electronic Warfare Technical Area (White Sands Missile Range)
MEWU	Malayan Estates Workers' Union
M Ex	Master of Expression
MEX	Military Exchange
MEX	"Temporary Rank" (Army slang)
MEXE	Military Engineering Experimental Establishment (British)
MEXSVM	Mexican Service Medal
MEZ	Mittel Europaische Zeit (Central European Time) (German)
MF	Machine Finish (Paper)
MF	Magazines for Friendship
MF	Main Feed (Technical drawings)
MF	Maintenance Factor
MF	Male to Female (ratio)
MF	Mantle Floor
MF	Mark Forward (Papers) (British)
MF	Marshall Field & Company (NYSE symbol)

MF	Master of Forestry
MF	Mastic Floor (Technical drawings)
MF	Material Factor
MF	Medal of Freedom
MF	Medium Frequency (Radio electronics)
MF	Metal Film
MF	Mezzo Forte (Moderately loud) (Music)
MF	Mi Favor (My Favor) (Spain)
mF	Microfarad
MF	Microfiche (Sheet microfilm)
MF	Microfilm
MF	Middle Fork R. R. (AAR code)
MF	Mill Finish
mF	Millifarad
MF	Ministry (or Minister) of Food (British)
MF	Mother Fooler (Bowdlerized version)
MF	Motor Field
MF	Motor Freight
MF	Multifrequency
MF	Multiplying Factor (Microscopy)
MF	Muscle Fiber
M/F	Marked For
M & F	Male and Female (components, as of connecting devices)
MFA	Malicious False Alarm (Firefighting)
MFA	Malta Fencible Artillery (British)
MFA	Marconi-Franklin Antenna
MFA	Master of Fine Arts
MFA	Mercantile Fleet Auxiliary (British)
MFA	Military Flying Area
MFA	Military Functions Appropriation
MFA	Movement for Federation of the Americas
MFA	Multi-Function Antenna
MFAA	Masters of Foxhounds Association of America
MFA & A	Monuments, Fine Arts and Archives (SHAEF) (World War II)
MFAB-F	Mobile Floating Assault Bridge-Ferry (Military)
MFAIRWEST . . .	Marine Fleet Air, West Coast
MFAR	Michigan Foundation for Advanced Research
MFB	Medial Forebrain Bundle
MFB	Message from Base
MFB	Metropolitan Fire Brigade (British)
MFB	MFB Mutual Insurance Co. (from Manufacturers Mutual Fire Insurance Co., Firemen's Mutual Insurance Co., Blackstone Mutual Insurance Co.)
MFB	Motional Feedback
MFBF	Minimum Film Boiling Flux
MFBM	Thousand Feet Board Measure (Lumber)
MFC	Magnesium Flat Cell
MFC	Magnetic Film Counter
MFC	Magnetic-Tape Field Scan
MFC	Manual Frequency Control
MFC	Microfilm Frame Card
MFC	Microfunctional Circuit
MFC	Military Frequency Changer
MFC	Minimal Flight Forecasting Charts (Air Force)
MFC	Modern Foods Council
MFC	Mouvement Familial Chretien, or Movimiento Familiar Cristano (Christian Family Movement)
MFCA	Miniature Figure Collectors of America
MFCC	Missile Flight Caution Corridor
MFCL	Master Fund Control List (Air Force)
MFCS	Magnetic Field Calibration System
MFCS	Missile Fire Control System
MFCT	Major Fraction Thereof
MFCU	Multi-Function Card Unit
MFD	Magnetic Frequency Detector
MFD	Magneto-Fluid Dynamic
MFD	Manufactured
MFD	Microfarad
MFD	Minimum Fatal Dose
MFD	Munford, Inc. (NYSE symbol)
MFDP	Mississippi Freedom Democratic Party
MFE	Magnetic Field Energy
MFE	Master of Forest Engineering
MFE	Mouvement Federaliste Europeen (European Federalist Movement)
MFED	Manned Flight Engineering Division (NASA)
MFED	Maximum Flat Envelope Delay
MF Eng	Master of Forest Engineering
MFF	MacFadden Foundation
MFF	Magnetic Flip-Flop (Data processing)
MFF	Matching Familiar Figures (Psychology)
MFG	Manufacturing
MFG	McQuay-Norris Manufacturing Company (NYSE symbol) (Delisted)

MFG .... Molded Fiber Glass
MFGA ...... Master Furriers Guild of America
MFH .... Master of Fox Hounds
MFH .... Military Family Housing
MFH....... Mobile Field Hospital
MFHA....... Medal for Humane Action (Military - Berlin Airlift, 1948-9)
MFHC ...... Missile Flight Hazard Corridor
MFI .... Magnetic Field Indicator (or Intensity)
MFI .... Major Force Issues (Army)
MFIC ...... Military Flight Information Center
MFIC ...... Mutual Federation of Independent Cooperatives (Later, Northeast Dairy
            Cooperative Federation)
MFIT .... Manual Fault Isolation Test
MFK .... Mill Fixture Key
MFKP ...... Multifrequency Key Pulsing
MFL....... Magnetic Field Line
MFL....... Maintain Flight Level (Aviation)
MFL....... Master of Family Life
MFL....... Mauritius Federation of Labor
MFL....... Mindanao Federation of Labor (Philippines)
MFL....... Mobile Field Laboratory
MFL ...... Modern Foreign Language
MFLU ...... Miyako Federation of Labor Unions (Ryukyu Islands)
MFM ...... Magnetic Forming Machine
MFM ...... Magneto Fluid Mechanic
MFM ...... Maximally Flat Magnitude
MFM ...... Micrometer Frequency Meter
MFM ...... Miniature Fluxgate Magnetometer
MFM ...... Missile Farm Monitor (Army)
MFM ...... Morrissey, Fernie & Michel Railway (AAR code)
MFMA ...... Maple Flooring Manufacturers Association
MFMA ...... Metal Findings Manufacturers Association
MFMA ...... Midwest Feed Manufacturers Association
MFMA ...... Monolithic Ferrite Memory Array
MFMI ...... Men for Missions International
MFN ...... Most-Favored-Nation (Tariff)
MFO ...... Master Frequency Oscillator
MFO ...... Military Forwarding Officer
MFOA ...... Municipal Finance Officers Association of US and Canada
MFOB ...... Minimum Fuel on Board (Aviation)
MFOD ...... Manned Flight Operations Division
MFOI ...... Major Force Oriented Issue (Military)
MFOW ...... Pacific Coast Marine Firemen, Oilers, Watertenders and Wipers
            Association
MFP .... Maximum Freezing Point
MFP .... Middle (or Mean) Free Path
MFP .... Minimal Flight Path
MFP ...... Mixed Fission Products
MFP .... Molecular Free Path
MFP ...... Monofluorophosphate (Colgate toothpaste ingredient)
MF(P) ...... Microfiche (Positive)
MFPB ...... Mineral Fiber Products Bureau
MFPG ...... Mixed Fission Products Generator (AEC)
MFPS ...... Member of the Faculty of Physicians and Surgeons (Glasgow)
MFPS ...... Modular Force Planning System
MFR....... Malfunction Rate
MFR....... Manufacture(r)
MFR ...... Master Facility Register (AEC)
MFR....... Memorandum for Record (Military)
MFR....... Middle French (Language, etc.)
MFR....... Model Form and Record
MFR....... Mouvement Familial Rural (Rural Family Movement)
MFR .... Multifrequency Receiver
MFRP ...... Midwest Fuel Recovery Plant (AEC)
MFRS ...... Manufacturers
MFS .... Fleet Minesweeper (Steel-hulled) (Navy symbol)
MFS....... Magnetic Field Strength
MFS....... Magnetic-Tape Field Search
MFS....... Malleable Founders' Society (Later, Cast Metals Federation)
MFS....... Manned Flying System
MFS....... Master of Food Science
MFS....... Master of Foreign Service
MFS....... Master of Foreign Study
MFS....... Medal Field Service (Canada)
MFS....... Mercury Feed System
MFS....... Military Flight Service
MFS....... Missile Firing Station
MFS....... Missile Fuse Set Servo
MFS....... Modern Fiction Studies (A publication)
MFS....... Modular Flexible Scheduling (Education)
MFS....... Mountain Fuel Supply Company (NYSE symbol)

MFS .... Multifunction Sensor
MFS .... Multiple Frequency Synthesizer
MF & S .... Magazine Flooding and Sprinkling
MFSA ...... Metal Finishing Suppliers' Association
MFSA ...... Methodist Federation for Social Action
MFSFU ..... Matt-Finish Structural Facing Units (Technical drawings)
MFSK ...... Multiple Frequency Shift Keying
MFSO ...... Missile Flight Safety Officer
MFSOP ..... Missile Flight Safety Operations Plan
MFSR ...... Magnetic Film Strip Recorder
MFSS ...... Medical Field Service School
MFT .... Magnetic Flow Transmitter
MFT....... Major Fraction Thereof
MFT....... Master of Foreign Trade
MFT....... Mean Free Time
MFT....... Mechanized Flame Thrower
MFT....... Medical Field Service Technician (Navy)
MFT....... Meson Field Theory
MFT....... Metal Film Resistor
MFT....... Multiprogramming Fixed Task (Data processing)
MFT .... Muscle Function Test
MFTD ..... Mobile Field Training Detachment (Military)
MFTF ..... Missionary Flight Training Foundation
MFTRS ..... Magnetic Flight Test Recording System
MFTU ..... Macau Federation of Trade Unions
MFU ...... Magnetic Force Upset (Metals)
MFU....... Monofluorourea
MFUW....... Magnetic Force Upset Welding
MFV....... Magnetic Field Vector
MFV....... Mars Flyby Vehicle (Aerospace)
MFV....... Microfilm Viewer
MFVD....... Maximum Forward Voltage Drop
MFVP....... Mauler Feasibility Validation Program
MFWC ...... Marine Fleet Air, West Coast
MFX....... Mirror Fusion Experiment (AEC)
MFY....... Mobilization for Youth
MFY....... Music for Youth
MFZ....... Mezzo Forzando (Music)
MG .... Machine-Glazed
MG .... Machine Gun
Mg .... Magnesium (Chemical element)
MG .... Major General (Also, M/G)
MG .... Make Good
MG ...... Manchester Guardian (A newspaper)
MG ...... Marine Gunner
MG .... Maschinengewehr
MG .... Medial Gastrocnemius
MG .... Message Generator
MG ...... Middle Gimbal
MG .... Military Government or Governor
MG ...... Mill Glazed
mg .... Milligram(s)
MG....... Missile Guidance
MG ...... Mixed Grain
MG .... Modified Guaranteed (Securities trading)
MG .... Monogram Industries, Inc. (NYSE symbol)
MG ...... Morris Garage (British automobile manufacturer; initialism used as name
            of sports car it produces)
MG .... Motor Generator
MG .... Multi-Gage
MG ...... Myasthenia Gravis Foundation
M/G ...... Major General (Also, MG)
M/G....... Miles Per Gallon
M & G ..... Mapping and Geodesy (Army)
MGA ...... Medium Gain Antenna
MGA ...... Meteorological and Geostrophysical Abstracts (American
            Meteorological Society)
MGA ...... Military Government Association
MGA ...... Monongahela Railway (AAR code)
MGA ...... Mushroom Growers Cooperative Association
MGAA ..... Medium Gain Autotrack Antenna
MGAC ..... Monongahela Connecting R. R. (AAR code)
MGAP ..... Magnetic Attitude Prediction
MGAT ..... Make Good a Track Of (followed by degrees) (Aviation)
MGB ...... Ministerstvo Gosudarstvennoi Bezopasnosti (Russia)
MGB ...... Motor Gunboat (British)
MGC ...... Machine-Gun Company or Machine-Gun Corps
MGC ...... Major Gain Control
MGC ...... Major General Commandant
MGC ...... Manual Gain Control
MGC ...... Metallized Glass Coil

MGC	Midcourse Guidance and Control
MGC	Middle Georgia College
MGC	Missile Guidance Computer
MGC	Missile Guidance and Control
MGCA	Men's Garden Clubs of America
MGCA	Mushroom Growers Cooperative Association
MGCC	Missile Guidance and Control Computer
MGCD	Maximum Gapless Coverage Distance
MGCR	Maritime Gas-Cooled Reactor
MGCR-CX	Maritime Gas-Cooled Reactor Critical Experiment
MGD	Magnetogasdynamic
MGD	McGregor-Doniger, Inc. (NYSE symbol)
MGD	Mercury Germanium Detector
MGD	Miehle-Goss-Dexter (North American Rockwell Corp.)
MGD	Military Geographic Documentation
MGD	Million Gallons Per Day
MGE	Maintenance Ground Equipment (Formerly, GSF)
MGE	Milwaukee Grain Exchange
MGE	Minneapolis Grain Exchange
M Ge E	Master of Geological Engineering
M Ge Eng	Master of Geological Engineering
M Geol E	Master of Geological Engineering
MGES	Maintenance Ground Equipment Section
MGF	Myasthenia Gravis Foundation
MGG	Memory Gate Generator (Data processing)
MGG	Missile Guidance Group
MGG	Mouse Gamma-Globulin
MGGS	Major General, General Staff
MGH	Massachusetts General Hospital
MGI	Management Games Institute (Raytheon Co.)
MGI	Member of the Gas Institute (British)
MGI	Metal Grating Institute
MGI	MGIC Investment Corp. (NYSE symbol)
MGI	Mobile Gamma Irradiator (AEC)
MGID	Military Geographic Information and Documentation
MGK	Modern Greek (Language, etc.)
MGKU	Mumbai Girni Kamgar Union (Bombay Mill Workers' Union) (India)
MGL	Magnanimous Green Leprechaun
MGLA	Massachusetts General Laws Annotated (A publication)
MGM	Metro-Goldwyn-Mayer (Motion picture production corporation) (NYSE symbol)
mgm	Milligram
MGMA	Medical Group Management Association
MGMC	Multiple Gun Motor Carriage
MGMT	Make Good a Magnetic Track Of (followed by degrees) (Aviation)
MGO	Marketing Group Office
MGO	Master General of Ordnance (British)
MGO	Military Government Officer
MGP	Maintenance Ground Point
M-GPD	Million US Gallons Per Day (AEC, OSW)
MGR	Manager
MGR	McGraw-Edison Company (NYSE symbol)
MGR	Medieval Greek or Middle Greek
MGR	Metal Glaze Resistor
MGR	Monseigneur
MGR	Monsignor
MGRA	Major-General, Royal Artillery (British)
MGRS	Ferrocarriles Nacionales de Mexico (AAR code)
MGRS	Military Grid Reference System
MGS	Marine Geophysical Survey (NOO)
MGS	Metal Gravel Stop
MGS	Missile Guidance Section (or Set, or System)
MGS	Moment Gyro System
MGSA	Military General Supply Agency (Merged with Defense General Supply Center)
MGSA	Modern Greek Studies Association
MGSC	Missile Guidance Set Control
MGSE	Mechanical Ground Support Equipment
MGSE	Missile Ground Support Equipment
MGST	Military Geography Specialist Team
MGT	Management
MGT	Meteorological and Geoastrophysical Titles
MGU	Military Government Unit
MGU	Mobile & Gulf R. R. (AAR code)
MGUN	Marine Gunner
MGV	Miniature Gate Valve
MGW	Murphy (G.W.) Industries, Inc. (NYSE symbol)
MGYSGT	Master Gunnery Sergeant (Marine Corps)
MGZ	Maschinengewehr-Zieleinrichtung (Machine-gun sighting mechanism) (German military – World War II)

MGZF	Maschinengewehr-Zielfernrohr (Machine-gun telescopic sight) (German military – World War II)
MH	Magnetic Heading
MH	Maleic Hydrazide (Plant-growth retardant)
MH	Malt House
MH	Manhours
MH	Marital History
MH	Master of Horticulture
MH	Master Hosts
MH	Master of Humanics
MH	Master of Hygiene
MH	Medal of Honor (Often erroneously called Congressional Medal of Honor)
MH	Melanophore Hormone (Endocrinology)
MH	Menstrual History
MH	Mental Health
MH	Military History
mH	Millihenry
MH	Ministry of Health (British)
MH	Miscellaneous Hardware
MH	Most Honorable
MH	Murine Hepatitis
M-H	Minneapolis-Honeywell Regulator Company (Later, HON)
M/H	Man-Hours
M/H	Miles Per Hour (Also, MPH)
MHA	Marine Historical Association
MHA	Master of Hospital Administration
MHA	Mean Horizontal Acceleration
MHA	Medal for Humane Action
MHA	Mental Health Administration
MHA	Minehunter, Auxiliary (Navy symbol)
MHA	Minimum Holding Altitude (Aviation)
MHA	Modified Handling Authorized (Air Force)
MHA	Mormon History Association
MHB	Master Horizontal Bomber
MHB	Maximum Hospital Benefit(s)
MHb	Myohemoglobin
MHBA	Medical-Dental-Hospital Bureaus of America
MHC	Major Histocompatibility Complex (Genetics)
MHC	Manufacturers Hanover Corporation (NYSE symbol)
MHC	Mars Hill College (North Carolina)
MHC	Minehunter, Coastal (Navy symbol)
MHC	Moisture Holding Capacity
MHC	Morgan Horse Club
MHC	Morris Harvey College (West Virginia)
MHC	Mount Holyoke College (Massachusetts)
MHCC	Mobile Housing Carriers Conference
MHCC	Multipak Heliax Coaxial Cable
MHCOA	Motor, Hearse and Car Owners Association
MHCP	Mean Horizontal Candlepower
MHCS	Mental Hygiene Consultation Service
MHD	Magnetohydrodynamic (Generator) (Electric power)
MHD	Medical Holding Detachment
MHD	Metering Head Differential
MHD	Minimum Hamming Distance (Data processing)
MHD	Minimum Hemolytic Dose
MHD	Monocular Head-Up Display
M & HDA	Medical and Hospital Department, Army
MHDF	Medium and High Frequency Direction-Finding Station
MHDNA	Mobile Home Dealers National Association
MHE	Master of Home Economics
MHE	Materials Handling Equipment (Military)
MHE	Missile Handling Equipment
MHE	Muzzle Hatch Electrical
MHEC	Muzzle Hatch Electrical Control
MHEDA	Material Handling Equipment Distributors Association
MHE Ed	Master of Home Economics Education
MHF	Master History File
MHF	Medium High Frequency
MHF	Meridian House Foundation
MHF	Mixed High Frequencies
MHF	Mixed Hydrazine Fuel
MHFA	Multiple Conductor, Heat & Flame Resistant, Armor Cable
MHFB	Mental Health Film Board
MHFR	Military Height-Finder RADAR Equipment
MHG	Middle High German (Language, etc.)
MHG	Miniature Hydrogen Generator
MHHW	Mean Higher High Water
MHI	Malone & Hyde, Incorporated (NYSE symbol)
MHI	Marine Hydrophysical Institute
MHI	Material Handling Institute
M Hi E	Master of Highway Engineering

M Hi Eng . . . . . Master of Highway Engineering
MHJ . . . . Microwave Hybrid Junction
MHJC . . . . . . Mary Holmes Junior College (Mississippi)
MHK . . . . Member of the House of Keys (Isle of Man)
MHL . . . . Mast Hull Loop
MHL . . . . . . Master of Hebrew Literature
MHL . . . . . . Master of Humane Letters
MHL . . . . . . Metastable Helium Level
MHL . . . . . . Minimum Helium Loss (System)
MHLTA . . . . . Men's Hat Linings and Trimmings Association
MHLW . . . . . . Mean Higher Low Water (Navigation)
MHM . . . . . . Mill Hill Missionaries
MHM . . . . . . Minimum Hardware Modification (Aircraft landing)
MHM . . . . . . Mount Hope Mineral R. R. (AAR code)
MHM . . . . . . Muzzle Hatch Mechanical
MHMA . . . . . Mobile Home Manufacturers Association
MHMC . . . . . Mental Health Materials Center
mho . . . . Reciprocal Ohm
M Ho Ec . . . . . Master of Household Economy
M Hor . . . . . . Master of Horticulture
M Ho Sc . . . . Master of Household Science
MHP . . . . . . McGraw-Hill, Inc. (NYSE symbol)
MHP . . . . Mental Health Project
MH PE & R . . Master of Health, Physical Education, and Recreation
MHR . . . . Member of the House of Representatives
MHR . . . . . . Miniature Helium Refrigerator
MHR . . . . . . Missile Hazard Report
MHRA . . . . . . Modern Humanities Research Association
MHRI . . . . . . Mental Health Research Institute (University of Michigan)
MHS . . . . Magnetomotive Hammer System
MHS . . . . Marine Hospital Service (Public Health Service)
MHS . . . . Marriott Corp. (NYSE symbol)
MHS . . . . Mechanical Handling System
MHS . . . . Military Historical Society
MHS . . . . Ministry (or Minister) of Home Security (British)
MHS . . . . . . Missile Hazard Space
MHS . . . . Moravian Historical Society
MHS . . . . Sisters of the Most Holy Sacrament (Roman Catholic religious order)
M/H/S . . . . . . Miles Per Hour Per Second
MHSCP . . . . . Mean Hemispherical Candlepower
MHSH . . . . . . Mission Helpers of the Sacred Heart (Roman Catholic women's religious order)
MHSS . . . . . . Materials Handling Support System (Military)
MHT . . . . Manhattan Industries, Inc. (NYSE symbol)
MHT . . . . Manufacturers Hanover Trust Co.
MHT . . . . Mean High Tide
MHT . . . . Meyer Hydraulic Theory
MHT . . . . Museum of History and Technology (Smithsonian Institution)
MHTA . . . . . Molten High Temperature Alloy
MHTL . . . . . . Motorola High Threshold Logic
MHTV . . . . . . Manned Hypersonic Test Vehicle
M Hu . . . . . . Master of Humanities
MHUD . . . . . Monocular Head-Up Display
MHV . . . . Manned Hypersonic Vehicle
MHV . . . . Mean Horizontal Velocity
MHV . . . . Mouse Hepatitis Virus (Medicine)
MHV . . . . Murine Hepatitis Virus
MHVDF . . . . . Medium, High, and Very High Frequency Direction-Finding Station
MHVPS . . . . . Manual High Voltage Power Supply
MHW . . . . . . Mean High Water
MHW . . . . . . Multi-Hundred Watt
MHWI . . . . . . Mean High Water Lunitidal Interval
MHWN . . . . . Mean High Water Neap (Tides)
MHWS . . . . . Mean High Water Springs
M Hy . . . . . . Master of Hygiene
MHz . . . . Megahertz (Megacycles per Second)
MI . . . . Mach Indicated
MI . . . . Madras Infantry (British)
MI . . . . Malleable Iron
MI . . . . Management Intern
MI . . . . Manual Input (Electronics)
MI . . . . Manufacturing Inspector
MI . . . . Mare Island, California (Site of naval base)
MI . . . . Marshall Islands
MI . . . . Master Index
MI . . . . Match Institute
MI . . . . Material Inspection
MI . . . . Meat Inspection Division (of ARS, Department of Agriculture)
MI . . . . Medical Illustrator
MI . . . . Medical Inspection
MI . . . . Melanophore Index

MI . . . . Memorial Inscription
MI . . . . Metabolic Index
MI . . . . Michigan
MI . . . . Middle Initial
MI . . . . Mile
MI . . . . Military Intelligence (Army)
MI . . . . Military Internee
MI . . . . Miller Integrator
MI . . . . Ministry of Information (British) (Acronym used in World War I; MOI used in World War II)
MI . . . . Missed Interception (Military)
MI . . . . Missouri-Illinois R. R. (AAR code)
MI . . . . Mitral Insufficiency
MI . . . . Monitor Inspection
MI . . . . Mounted Infantry
MI . . . . Movements Identification (Military)
MI . . . . Mutual Inductance
MI . . . . Myocardial Infarction (Medicine)
M-I . . . . Missouri-Illinois Railroad Company
M & I . . . . . . Marshall & Ilsley Bank
M & I . . . . . . Movements and Identification (Military)
MIA . . . . Marble Institute of America
MIA . . . . Marine Industries Association
MIA . . . Master of Industrial Arts
MIA . . . . Master of International Affairs
MIA . . . . Metal Interface Amplifier
MIA . . . . Miami (Florida) (International airport, symbol)
MIA . . . . Mica Industry Association
MIA . . . . Millinery Institute of America
MIA . . . . Minimum Instrument Altitude (Aviation)
MIA . . . . Missing in Action (Military)
MIA . . . . "Mouse in Able" Program
MIAA . . . . . . Mutual Insurance Advisory Association
MIAC . . . . . . Material Identification Accounting Code
MIADS . . . . . Minot Air Defense Sector (ADC)
MIAEF . . . . . Missed Interception Due to Airborne Equipment Failure (Air Force)
MIAPD . . . . . Mid-Central Air Procurement District
M I Arch . . . . Master of Interior Architecture
M I Arch Eng . . Master of Interior Architectural Engineering
MIARS . . . . . . Maintenance Information Automated Retrieval System (DOD)
MIB . . . . Manual Input Buffer (Data processing)
MIB . . . . Motor Inspection Building
MIB . . . . Mutual Inductance Bridge
MIBARS . . . . . Military Intelligence Battalion (Aerial Reconnaissance and Surveillance) (Army)
MIBB . . . . . . Missouri & Illinois Bridge & Belt R. R. (AAR code)
MIBiol . . . . . . Member of the Institute of Biology (British)
MIBK . . . . . . Methyl Isobutyl Ketone
MIBritE . . . . . . Member Institute of British Engineers
MIC . . . . Congregatio Clericorum Regularium Marianorum sub titulo Immaculatae Conceptionis Beatae Mariae Virginis (Marian Fathers) (Roman Catholic religious order)
MIC . . . . Maintenance Information Center (Navy)
MIC . . . . Maintenance Information Chart (DOD)
MIC . . . . . . Malayan Indian Congress
MIC . . . . Management Information Center
MIC . . . . Materials Irradiation Chamber
MIC . . . . . . Meat Importers' Council
MIC . . . . Medical Inter-Fraternity Conference
MIC . . . . Memory Interface Connection (Data processing)
MIC . . . . Michigan Instructional Computer
MIC . . . . Microdot, Inc. (NYSE symbol)
MIC . . . . Micrometer (A "mike")
MIC . . . . Microwave Integrated Circuitry
MIC . . . . Microwave Interference Coordination
MIC . . . . Minimal (or Minimum) Inhibitory Concentration
MIC . . . . Missionary Sisters of the Immaculate Conception (Roman Catholic religious order)
MIC . . . . Mississippi Industrial College
MIC . . . . Monitoring, Identification, and Correlation
MIC . . . . Monolithic Integrated Circuit
MIC . . . . Music Industry Council
M-IC . . . . . . Military-Industrial Complex
MICA . . . . . . Macro Instruction Compiler Assembler (Data processing)
MICA . . . . . . Mobile Industrial Caterers' Association
MICB . . . . . . Meck Island Control Building (Army)
MICBM . . . . . Mobile Intercontinental Ballistic Missile
MICCO . . . . . Model Inner City Community Organization (Washington, DC)
MICCS . . . . . Minuteman Integrated Command and Control System (Missiles)
Mic D . . . . . . Doctor of Microbiology
MICE . . . . . . Material Transfer, Information Transfer, Control Transfer, Energy Transfer

MICE ...... Member of the Institution of Civil Engineers (British)
MICE ...... Microelectronic Integrated Checkout Equipment
MICE ...... Mutual Insurance Council of Editors
MICG ...... Management Information Coordinating Group (Navy)
MICH ...... Michigan
MIChemE..... Member of the Institution of Chemical Engineers (British)
MICL ...... Missile In-Commission Level
MICM ...... Monolithic Integrated Circuit Mask
MICO ...... Midland Continental R. R. (AAR code)
MICOFT ..... Mutual Insurance Committee on Federal Taxation
MICOM ..... Missile Command (Army)
MICOMS..... Maintenance Information Concerning (the repair and operation of) Missile Systems
MICPAK ..... Modular Integrated Circuit Package
MICR ...... Magnetic Ink Character Recognition (or Reader) (Data processing technique used for automatic sorting of bank checks and in other applications)
MICR ...... Management Improvement and Cost Reduction Project Reporting System
MICRAM ..... Microminiature Individual Components Reliable Assembled Modules
MICROACE ... Microminiature Automatic Checkout Equipment
MICS ...... Management Information Control System (Navy)
MICS ...... Multiplex Interior Communications
MICV ...... Mechanized Infantry Combat Vehicle (Army)
MID ...... Management Information Division (Vietnam)
MID ...... Manpower Information Division (Navy)
MID ...... Master of Industrial Design
MID ...... Mid-Continent Telephone Corp. (NYSE symbol)
MID ...... Middle
MID ...... Military Intelligence Detachment
MID ...... Military Intelligence Division (War Department) (World War II)
MID ...... Minimal Inhibiting Dose
MID ...... Minimum Infective Dose (Bacteriology)
MID ...... Missile Intelligence Directorate (Army)
MIDA ...... Major Items Data Agency (Military)
MIDA ...... Mid-American International Development Association (Nigeria)
MIDAC ...... Management Information for Decision-Making and Control (Data processing)
MIDAC ...... Michigan (University of) Digital Automatic Computer
MIDAR ..... Microwave Detection and Ranging
MIDARM ..... Microdynamic Angle and Rate Monitoring System
MIDAS ...... Micro-Imaged Data Addition System
MIDAS ...... Miniature Data Acquisition System
MIDAS ...... Missile Defense Alarm (or Alert) System (Air Force)
MIDAS ...... Missile Intercept Data Acquisition System
MIDAS ...... Modified Integration Digital Analog Simulator (Air Force)
MIDAS ...... Multiple Input Data Acquisition System (Bell System)
MIDEASTFOR.. Middle East Force (Navy)
MIDES ...... Missile Detection System
Mid G ...... Graduate Midwife
MIDIZ ...... Mid-Canada Identification Zone
MIDOP ..... Missile Doppler
MIDOT ..... Multiple Interferometer Determination of Trajectories
MIDPAC ..... US Army Forces, Middle Pacific (Name commonly used for AFMIDPAC)
MIDS ...... Management Information Display System
MIDS ...... Movement Information Distribution Station
MIDU ...... Malfunction Insertion and Display Unit (Aviation)
MIDW ...... Midwestern
MIE ...... Mass Inertia Excitation
MIE ...... Master of Industrial Engineering
MIE ...... Master of Irrigation Engineering
MIE ...... Meteor Ionizing Efficiency
MIE ...... Minimum Ignition Energy
MIEC ...... Pax Romana, Mouvement International des Etudiants Catholiques (International Movement of Catholic Students)
MIEE ...... Member of the Institution of Electrical Engineers (British)
MIEETAT ..... Major Improvements in Electronics Through Advanced Technology
MI Eng ...... Master of Industrial Engineering
MIEU ...... Miscellaneous Industries Employees' Union (Aden)
MIF ...... Master Index File
MIF ...... Migration Inhibition (or Inhibitory) Factor (Biochemistry)
MIF ...... Milk Industry Foundation
MIF ...... Miners' International Federation
MIF ...... Mobile Instrument Facility
MIF ...... Monopulse Interference Filter
MIFAS ...... Mechanized Integrated Financial Accounting System (Department of State)
MIFD ...... Material Information Flow Device (Military)
MIFE ...... Minimum Independent Failure Element
MIFERMA ..... Mines de Fer de Mauritanie (Iron Mining Company of Mauritania)
MIFI ...... Missile Flight Indicator
MIFireE...... Member of the Institution of Fire Engineers (British)
MIFL ...... Master International Frequency List

MIFR ...... Master International Frequency Register
MIFR ...... Multiband Infrared Filter Radiometer
MIFS ...... Material Information Flow System (Military)
MIFS ...... Multiplex Interferometric Fourier Spectroscopy
MIG ...... Magnetized Ionized Gas
MIG ...... Management Information Guide (Reference series)
MIG ...... Metal-Inert-Gas (Underwater welding)
MIG ...... Mikoyan and Gurevich (Acronym used as designation for a Russian aircraft and is formed from the names of the aircraft's designers)
MIG ...... Miniature Integrating Gyroscope
MIG ...... Multilevel Interconnect Generator
MIH ...... Miles in the Hour
MIH ...... Molecule-Induced Homolysis (Chemistry)
MIH ...... Molt Inhibitory Hormone
MIHS ...... Malian Institute of Human Sciences
MII ...... Military Intelligence Interpreter
MII ...... Military Intelligence Interrogation
MIIA ...... Medical Information and Intelligence Agency (DOD)
MIIA ...... Mine Inspectors' Institute of America
MIIC ...... Pax Romana, Mouvement International des Intellectuels Catholiques (International Mouvement of Catholic Intellectuals)
MIICS ...... Master Item Identification Control System
MIID ...... Media Institutes for Institute Directors
MIIS ...... Miscellaneous Inputs Information Subsystem (Data processing)
MIJ ...... Maatschappij (Joint stock company) (Netherlands)
MIJ ...... Metal Insulator Junction
MIJARC ..... Mouvement International de la Jeunesse Agricole et Rurale Catholique (International Movement of Catholic Agricultural and Rural Youth)
MIJO ...... Missile Joint Optimization
MIK ...... Methyl Isobutyl Ketone (Chemical)
MIK ...... More in the Kitchen (Family dinner-table expression)
MIKER ...... Microbalance Inverted Knudsen Effusion Recoil
MIL ...... Malfunction Investigation Laboratory
MIL ...... Miles Laboratories, Inc. (NYSE symbol)
MIL ...... Military
MIL ...... Mothers-In-Law Club International
MIL ...... Moving Inspection Lot
MILA ...... Merritt Island Launch Area (NASA)
MILADGOVT .. Military Advisory Government
MILADGRU ... Military Advisory Group
MILC ...... Midwest Inter-Library Center (Formerly, Center for Research Libraries)
MILCEST ..... Military Communications Electronic Systems Technology
MILCOMSAT.. Military Communications Satellite
MILCON ..... Military Construction (Also, MCN and MCON) (Navy)
MILDDU ..... Military-Industry Logistics Data Development Unit
MILDEPS ..... Military Departments
MILDIP ...... Military Industry Logistics Data Interchange Procedures
MILIRAD ..... Millimeter Wave RADAR Fuze
MILocoE ..... Member of Institution of Locomotive Engineers (British)
MILPERSINS .. Military Personnel Information System
MILPHAP .... Military Provincial Health Assistance Program
MILR ...... Master of Industrial and Labor Relations
MILS ...... Member of the Incorporated Law Society (British)
MILS ...... Missile Impact Location System
MILSAT ..... Military Satellite
MILSCAP ..... Military Standard Contract Administration Procedures (DOD)
MILSIMDS ..... Military Standard Item Management Data System
MILSPEC ..... Military Specification
MILSPOT..... Military Standard Purchase Operating Technique
MILSTAAD ..... Military Standard Activity Address Directory
MILSTAMP ..... Military Standard Transportation and Movement Procedures
MILSTAN .... Military Agency for Standardization
MILSTD ..... Military Standard
MILSTEP ..... Military Standard Evaluation Procedure
MILSTEP ..... Military Supply and Transportation Evaluation Procedures
MILSTICCS ..... Military Standard Item Characteristics Coding Structure
MILSTIICS ... Military Standard Item Identification Coding System
MILSTRAMP .. Military Standard Transportation and Movement Procedure
MILSTRAP .. Military Standard Transaction Reporting and Accounting Procedures
MILSTRIP .. Military Standard Requisitioning and Issue Procedure
MILTAG ..... Military Technical Assistance Group
MILW ...... Chicago, Milwaukee, St. Paul & Pacific R. R. (AAR code)
MIM ...... Magnetic Interaction Mechanism
MIM ...... Maintenance Instructions Manual (DOD)
MIM ...... Metal Insulator Material
MIM ...... Mica Insulator Material
MIM ...... Modern Interface Modules (Data processing)
MIM ...... Moving Iron Microphone
MIMA ...... Minute Man National Historical Park
MIMarE..... Member of the Institute of Marine Engineers (British)
MIME ...... Member of the Institute of Mining Engineers

MIME . . . . . . Member of the Institution of Mechanical Engineers (British)
MIME . . . . . . Ministry of Information Middle East (British) (World War II)
MIMechE. . . . . Member of the Institution of Mechanical Engineers (British)
MIMinE. . . . . Member of the Institution of Mining Engineers (British)
MIMJ . . . . . . Metal Insulator – Metal Junction
MIMM . . . . . . Member of the Institute of Mining and Metallurgy (British)
MIMMS . . . . . Marine Corps Integrated Maintenance Management System
MIMO . . . . . . Man In, Machine Out (Data processing)
MIMOSA . . . . Mission Modes and Systems Analysis
MIMR. . . . . . May Institute of Medical Research
MIMS . . . . . . Medical Information Management System
MIMS . . . . . . Modular Isodrive Memory Series
MIMSq . . . . . Missile Maintenance Squadron (Air Force)
MIMunE. . . . . Member of the Institute of Municipal Engineers
MIMUSA . . . . Matrix Iteration Method of Unfolding Spectra (Data processing)
MIN. . . . . . . Minimum
MIN. . . . . . . Minister
MIN. . . . . . . Minor
MIN. . . . . . . Minute
MINA . . . . . . Member of the Institution of Naval Architects (British)
MINABB . . . . Minimum Abbreviations (of MAST)
MINAC. . . . . Miniature Navigation Airborne Computer
MINBATFOR . Minecraft Battle Force, Pacific Fleet
MIND . . . . . . Magnetic Integrator Neuron Duplicator
MIND . . . . . . Meeting Individual Needs Daily (Program of District of Columbia
School Board)
MIND . . . . . . Methods of Intellectual Development (National Association of Manu-
facturers)
MINDIV . . . . Mine Division (Navy)
Min E . . . . . Mining (or Mineral) Engineer
MINE . . . . . . Minneapolis Eastern Railway (AAR code)
MINEAC . . . . Miniature Electronic Auto-Collimator
MINEC. . . . . Military Necessity
MINECTRMEASSTA . . Mine Counter-Measure Station
MINEVDET . . . Mine Warfare Evaluation Detachment
MING . . . . . . Magnetic Induction Nuclear Gyroscope
MING . . . . . . Middle Class, Intelligent, Nice Girls
MINIAPS . . . . Minimum Accessory Power Supply
MINICOM . . . Minimum Communications
MINICS . . . . . Minimal-Input Cataloging System (British)
MINISID . . . . Miniature Seismic Intrusion Detector (DOD)
MINI-SUBLAB. . Miniature Submarine Laboratory
MINITAS. . . . . Miniature True Airspeed Computer
MINITEX . . . . Minnesota Interlibrary Teletex Experiment
MINLANT . . . . Mine Warfare Forces, Atlantic (Navy)
MINN . . . . . . Minnesota
MINNEMAST. . Minnesota Mathematics and Science Teaching Project
MINPAC. . . . . Mine Warfare Forces, Pacific (Navy)
MINRA . . . . . Miniature International Racing Association
MINRON . . . . Mine Squadron
MINS . . . . . . Mare Island Naval Shipyard (Navy)
MINS . . . . . . Miniature Inertial Navigation System
MInstCE. . . . . Member of the Institution of Civil Engineers (Changed 1946 to MICE)
MInstE . . . . . Member of the Institution of Engineers (British)
MInstGasE. . . . Member of the Institution of Gas Engineers (British)
MInstNA. . . . . Member of the Institution of Naval Architects (British)
MInstPet . . . . Member of the Institute of Petroleum (British)
MInstPI. . . . . Member of the Institute of Patentees and Inventors (British)
MInstT. . . . . . Member of the Institute of Technology (British)
MINSY. . . . . . Mare Island Naval Shipyard
MINT . . . . . . Materiel Identification and New Item Control Technique (AFLC)
MINU. . . . . . Mobile Instrument Investigation Unit
MINUET . . . . Minimum Energy Trajectory Model (Army)
MIO . . . . . . Management Information Office(r) (Air Force)
MIO . . . . . . Map Information Office (US Geological Survey)
MIO . . . . . . Marine Inspection Office (Coast Guard)
MIO . . . . . . Minimal Identifiable Odor
MIO. . . . . . . Mobile Issuing Office (Navy)
MIO . . . . . . Movements Identification Officer (Air Force)
MIOUDO. . . . Museo del Instituto Oceanografico de la Universidad de Oriente
MIP . . . . Maintenance Improvement Program
MIP . . . . Maintenance Index Page
MIP . . . . Malleable Iron Pipe
MIP . . . . Management Improvement Program (Air Force)
MIP . . . . Management Incentive Program
MIP . . . . Manual Index Page (SNMMMS)
MIP . . . . Manual Input Processing (or Program)
MIP . . . . Manufacturers of Illumination Products
MIP . . . . Marine Insurance Policy
MIP . . . . Material Improvement Plan (or Program) (Aviation)
MIP . . . . Materiel Improvement Project (Military)

MIP . . . . Mean Indicated Pressure
MIP . . . . Methods Improvement Program (IBM)
MIP . . . . Microwave Interference Protection
MIP . . . . Military Improvement Program
MIP . . . . Minimum Impulse Pulse
MIP . . . . Missile Impact Predictor (Air Force)
MIP . . . . Mixed Integer Programming (Data processing)
MIP . . . . Model Implementation Plan
MIP . . . . Modulated Interframe Plan
MIP . . . . Monthly Investment Plan (NY Stock Exchange)
MIP . . . . Mortgage Insurance Premium
MIP . . . . Most Important Person
MIP . . . . Movimiento Independiente Peruano (Peruvian Independent Movement)
MIPC . . . . . . Manifold Ignition Primary Charge
MIPE . . . . . . Magnetic Induction Plasma Engine
MIPE . . . . . . Modular Information Processing Equipment
MIPI . . . . . . Madjelis Ilmu Pengetahuan Indonesia (Council for Sciences of Indonesia)
MIPIR . . . . . . Missile Precision Instrumentation RADAR
MIPL . . . . . . Master Indentured Parts List
MIPP . . . . . . Maintainability Index Prediction Procedure
MIPP . . . . . . Milk Indemnity Payment Program
MIPR . . . . . . Military Interdepartmental Procurement (or Purchase) Request
MIPR . . . . . . Monthly Interim Progress Report
MIProdE. . . . . Member of the Institution of Production Engineers (British)
MIPS . . . . . . Maintenance Index Pages
MIPS . . . . . . Military Information Processing System
MIPS . . . . . . Missile Impact Prediction Set
MIR . . . . Magnetic Ink Read
MIR . . . . Material Inspection Report
MIR . . . . Material Investigators Reactor (NASA)
MIR . . . . Maverick Interim Report
MIR . . . . Medical Incident Report
MIR . . . . Memory–Information Register
MIR . . . . Memory Input Register
MIR . . . . Method of Integral Relations
MIR . . . . Minneapolis Industrial Railway Company (AAR code)
MIR . . . . Mission Inherent Reliability
MIR . . . . Movimiento de Izquierda Revolucionario (Venezuelan political party)
MIR . . . . Multiband Infrared Radiometer
MIR . . . . Multiple Internal Reflection (Spectroscopy)
MIR . . . . Multiplex Intensity Rules
MIR . . . . Music Information Retrieval (Data processing)
MIRA . . . . . . Monthly Index of Russian Accessions (Library of Congress)
MIRA . . . . . . Movimiento de Independencia Revolucionaria en Armas (Puerto Rico
independence group)
MIRACLE. . . . . Mokum Industrial Research Automatic Calculator for Laboratory and
Engineering
MIRACODE . . . Microfilm Information Retrieval Access Code
MIRAGE . . . . Microelectronic Indicator for RADAR Ground Equipment
MIRAID. . . . . Maintenance Information Retrieval Aid
MIRAK . . . . . Minimum Rocket (from the German)
MIRAN . . . . . Miniature Infrared Analyzer (Spectrometer)
MIRAN . . . . . Missile Ranging
MIRB . . . . . . Mutual Insurance Rating Bureau
MIRD . . . . . . Medical Internal Radiation Dose (Committee) (Society of Nuclear
Medicine)
MIRD . . . . . . Minor Irregularities and Deficiencies
MIRE . . . . . . Member of the Institution of Radio Engineers (British)
MIRED. . . . . . Micro-Reciprocal Degrees
MIREQ . . . . . Minimum Requirements Specified
MIRF . . . . . . Multiple Instantaneous Response File
MIROS . . . . . Modulation Inducing Retrodirective Optical System (NASA)
MIRP . . . . . . Manipulated Information Rate Processor
MIRPS . . . . . Multiple Information Retrieval by Parallel Selection
MIRR . . . . . . Materiel Inspection and Receiving Report
MIRROS . . . . . Modulation Inducing Reactive Retrodirective Optical System (NASA)
MIRS . . . . . . Military Intelligence Research Section (Navy)
MIRSE. . . . . . Multipurpose Imaging Radiometer Spectrometer Equipment
MIRST. . . . . . Multiple Infrared Scattered Light Recorder
MIRTAK. . . . . Martin Infrared Tracker
MIRV . . . . . . Multiple Independent(ly) (Targeted) Reentry Vehicle (Military)
MIS . . . . Man in Space
MIS . . . . Management Information Service
MIS . . . . Management Information Specialist
MIS . . . . Management Information Systems
MIS . . . . Manifold Interest Schedule
MIS . . . . Marketing Information System
MIS . . . . Mary Immaculate Seminary (Pennsylvania)
MIS . . . . Master of International Service
MIS . . . . Material Inspection Service (Navy)
MIS . . . . Mechanical Impact System

MIS . . . . Mechanical Interruption Summary (FAA)
MIS . . . . Median Iris Society
MIS . . . . Metal Insulated Structure
MIS . . . . Metal-Insulator-Semiconductor
MIS . . . . Military Intelligence Services (Army)
MIS . . . . Military Interim Specification (Army)
MIS . . . . Mine Issuing Ship
MIS . . . . Mississippi River Corporation (NYSE symbol)
MISA . . . . . . Military Industrial Supply Agency
MISC . . . . . . Miscellaneous
MISCO . . . . . McCall Information Systems Company
MISER . . . . . Manned Interceptor SAGE Evaluation Routine
MISER . . . . . Media Insertion Schedule Evaluation Report (Advertising)
MISER . . . . . Microwave Space Electronics Relay
MISFET . . . . . Metal-Insulator-Semiconductor Field-Effect Transistor
MISHAP . . . . Missiles High-Speed Assembly Program
MISI . . . . . . Management Information System Directorate
MISIAS . . . . . Management Information Systems Inventory and Analysis System (Navy)
MISMA . . . . . Major Item Supply Management Agency
Mis Mus . . . . Mistress of Music
MISP . . . . . . Management Information System Plan
MISP . . . . . . Manned Interceptor Simulation Program
MISPC . . . . . Mechanized Infantry Squad Proficiency Course (Army)
MISR . . . . . . Major Item Status Report
MISR . . . . . . Minimum Industrial Sustaining Rate
MISRE . . . . . Microwave Space Relay (Electronics)
MISREP . . . . Mission Report (Air Force)
MISS . . . . . . Man-in-Space Simulator
MISS . . . . . . Man in Space Soonest
MISS . . . . . . Miniature SOFAR System
MISS . . . . . . Missile Intercept Simulation System
MISS . . . . Mississippi
MISS . . . . . . Mississippian Railway (AAR code)
MISS . . . . . . Mobile Instrumentation Support System
MISS . . . . . . Mobile Integrated Support System
MISS-D . . . . . Minuteman Integrated Schedules Status and Data Systems
MISSIL . . . . . Management Information System Symbolic Interpretive Language
MISST . . . . . . Missile-Supersonic Transport
MIST . . . . . . Medical Information Service via Telephone (Alabama)
MIST . . . . . . Minimum Structure Module
MIST . . . . . . Minor Isotopes Safeguards Techniques (AEC)
MIST . . . . . . Multi-Input Standard Tape
MISTIC . . . . . Michigan State Integral Computer
MISTR . . . . . Management of Items Subject to Repair (Air Force)
MISTRAM . . . . Missile Trajectory Measurement (Air Force)
MIStructE . . . . Member of the Institution of Structural Engineers (British)
MIT . . . . Massachusetts Institute of Technology
MIT . . . . Massachusetts Investors Trust
MIT . . . . Master Instruction Tape (Data processing)
MIT . . . . Mercury Integrated Test
MIT . . . . Military Intelligence Translator
MIT . . . . Milled in Transit (Commodities)
MIT . . . . Milwaukee Institute of Technology
MIT . . . . Minimum Individual Training
MIT . . . . Miracidal Immobilization Test (Parasitology)
MIT . . . . Mobile Information Team (Thailand)
MIT . . . . Mono-Iodotyrosine
MITB . . . . . . Missile Interface Test Bench
MITE . . . . . . Microelectronic Integrated Test Equipment
MITE . . . . . . Miniaturized Integrated Telephone Equipment
MITE . . . . . . Missile Integration Terminal Equipment
MITE . . . . . . Multiple Input Terminal Equipment
MITGS . . . . . Marine Institute of Technology and Graduate Studies (Baltimore)
MITI . . . . . . Ministry of International Trade and Industry (Japan)
MITM . . . . . . Military Industry Technical Manual
MITMA . . . . . Military Traffic Management Agency
MITMS . . . . . Military/Industry Technical Manual Specifications (NPPO)
MITO . . . . . . Minimum Interval Take Off
MITOC . . . . . Missile Instrumentation Technical Operations Communications
MITP . . . . . . Miniature Template (Tool)
MITR . . . . . . Massachusetts Institute of Technology Reactor
MITRE . . . . . Massachusetts Institute of Technology - RAND Corporation Engineering
MITS . . . . . . Man-in-the-Sea Program (Navy)
MITS . . . . . . Man in the Street (The average man) (Usually "Mr. Mits")
MITS . . . . . . Missile Ignition Test Simulator
MITS . . . . . . Missile Interface Test Set
MITTS . . . . . Mobile IGOR (Intercept Ground Optical Recorder) Tracking Telescope System (Air Force)
MIU . . . . . . Malfunction Insertion Unit
MIU . . . . . . Message Injection Unit
MIU . . . . . . Mobile Inspection Unit (Military)

MIU . . . . Motor Impeller Unit
MIUTC . . . . . Military Intelligence Unit Training Center
MIUW . . . . . . Mobile Inshore Undersea Warfare (Navy)
MIV . . . . Main Instrumentation Van (NASA)
MIV . . . . Moody's Investor Service (NYSE symbol)
MIV . . . . Moving Ion Voltmeter
MIWE . . . . . . Member of the Institution of Water Engineers (British)
MIX . . . . Magnetic Ionization Experiment
MJ . . . . Manufacturers' Junction Railway Company (AAR code)
MJ . . . . Marine Jet
MJ . . . . Master of Journalism
MJ . . . . Mastic Joint (Technical drawings)
MJ . . . . Military Judge
MJAO . . . . . Mediterranean Joint Air Orders
MJB . . . . Missile Junction Box
MJB . . . . Moore Jig Borer
MJC . . . . Marshalltown Junior College (Iowa)
MJC . . . . Marymount Junior College (Florida; Virginia)
MJC . . . . Mercy Junior College (Missouri)
MJC . . . . Miami-Jacobs College (Ohio)
MJC . . . . Midway Junior College (Kentucky)
MJC . . . . Military Junior College
MJC . . . . Moberly Junior College (Missouri)
MJC . . . . Modesto Junior College (California)
MJC . . . . Montgomery Junior College (Maryland)
MJC . . . . Morse Junior College (Connecticut)
MJC . . . . Morton Junior College (Illinois)
MJC . . . . Muscatine Junior College (Iowa)
MJD . . . . . . Doctor of Medical Jurisprudence
MJF . . . . Multiple Juxtapositional Fixedness (Tongue-in-cheek description of unusually strong bonding between metal ions and some ligands)
MJG . . . . . . Moore Jig Grinder
MJGA . . . . . Midwest Job Galvanizers Association
MJI . . . . Member of the Journalists Institute
MJM . . . . . . Man-Job Match (Military)
MJP . . . . . . Master of Jewish Pedagogy
MJPS . . . . . . Mouvement des Jeunesses Progressistes Soudanaises (Sudanese Progressive Youth Movement) (Mali)
MJQ . . . . . . Modern Jazz Quartet (Musical group)
MJR . . . . . . Maintenance Job Request
MJS . . . . . . Member of the Japan Society
MJSA . . . . . Manufacturing Jewelers Sales Association
MJSA . . . . . Manufacturing Jewelers and Silversmiths of America
MJSA . . . . . Mouvement des Jeunesses Socialistes Africaines (African Socialist Youth Movement)
MJ & SA . . . Manufacturing Jewelers & Silversmiths of America
MJT . . . . Materials Joining Tool
MJT . . . . Multi-Jet Transport
MJUPG . . . . . Movimiento da Juventude da Uniao Popular da Guine (Youth Movement of Guinean People's Union)
MJUPS . . . . . Mouvement des Jeunes de l'Union Progressiste Senegalaise (Youth Movement of the Senegalese Progressive Movement)
MJV . . . . Mojud Hosiery Company (NYSE symbol)
MJW . . . . . . Mays, (J. W.) Inc. (NYSE symbol) (Wall Street slang name: "Say Hey," derived from nickname of baseball star Willie Mays, "The Say Hey Kid")
MK . . . . Mackey Airlines, Inc.
MK . . . . Marschkolonne (March column) (German military - World War II)
mK . . . . Millikelvin
MK . . . . Mit Kappe (With Cap) (German military)
MK . . . . Mit Kern (With Core) (German military)
MK . . . . Monkey Kidney
MKA . . . . . . Machine Knife Association
MKA . . . . . . Marine-Kuestenartillerie (Naval coast artillery) (German military - World War II)
MKC . . . . . . Kansas City, Missouri (Airport symbol)
MKC . . . . . . Marion Laboratories, Inc. (NYSE symbol)
MKC . . . . . . McKeesport Connecting R. R. (AAR code)
MKE . . . . . . Makina ve Kimya Endustrisi Kurumu (Mechanical and Chemical Industrial Establishment) (Turkey)
MKE . . . . McKee (Arthur G.) & Company (NYSE symbol)
MKE . . . . Molecular Kinetic Energy
MKG . . . . . . Magnetocardiogram
MKG . . . . . . Meter-Kilogram
MKH . . . . . . Mackintosh-Hemphill Company (NYSE symbol)
MKO . . . . . . Modification Kit Order
MKO . . . . . . Muskogee Company (NYSE symbol)
MKOWU . . . . Madras Kerosene Oil Workers' Union (India)
MKQCP . . . . . Member of the King's and Queen's College of Physicians (Ireland)
MKR . . . . . . Marker Radio Beacon
MKS . . . . Meter-Kilogram-Second (Physics)

MKS........ Microwave Keying Switch
MKSA ...... Meter, Kilogram, Second, and Ampere (System)
MKSS....... Microwave Keying Switching Station
MKT........ Missouri-Kansas-Texas R. R. (AAR code)
MKTP....... Mark Template (Tool)
MKTT....... Missouri-Kansas-Texas of Texas R. R. (AAR code)
MKU .... Mock-Up
MKUD ...... From the Russian for: People's Commissar for Internal Affairs (USSR)
MKW .... Magneto-Kinetic Wave
MKW .... Marles-Kuhlmann-Wyandotte (French)
MKW .... Munitionskraftwagen (Ammunition Truck) (German military – World War II)
ML........ Licentiate in Medicine
ML .... Licentiate in Midwifery
ML .... Machine Language (Data processing)
ML .... Magnetogasdynamics Laboratory (MIT)
ML .... Major Lobe
ML........ Mantle Length
ML........ Mantle Lip
ML .... Martin Marietta Corporation (NYSE symbol)
ML .... Master of Law(s)
ML .... Master of Letters
ML .... Master of Literature
ML .... Maximum Likelihood (Statistics)
ML .... Mean Level
ML........ Medieval Latin (Language)
ML........ Mexican League (Baseball)
ML .... Microwave Laboratory (Stanford University)
ML .... Middle Latin (Language, etc.)
ML .... Military Liaison
ML........ Military Payroll Money List
mL .... Millilambert
ml .... Milliliter(s)
ML .... Minelayer
ML........ Missile Launcher
ML .... Missile Liner
ML .... Mission Life (Aerospace)
ML .... Mission Load
ML .... Mixed Lengths
ML .... Mold Line (Technical drawings)
ML........ Molder (Navy)
ML .... Monarchist League
ML .... Moneda Legal (Legal Tender) (Spain)
ML........ Money List
ML .... Motor Launch
ML .... Muzzle-Loading
ML........ Myelogenous Leukemia (Medicine)
M/L........ Minelayer (British)
MLA........ Magnetic Lens Assembly
MLA .... Maine Lobstermen's Association
MLA .... Maneuver Load Alleviation (Aviation)
MLA........ Manpack Loop Antenna
MLA .... Maritime Law Association of the US
MLA .... Master of Landscape Architecture
MLA .... Mechanical Lubricator Association
MLA .... Medical Library Association
MLA .... Member of the Legislative Assembly
MLA .... Metal Lath Association
MLA .... Microwave Linear Accelerator
MLA .... Mistress of Liberal Arts
MLA .... Modern Language Association of America
MLA .... Music Library Association
MLAA ...... Modern Language Association of America
M La L ..... Master of Latin Letters
MLANA ..... Melkite Laymen's Association of North America
MLAR....... Mill Arbor
ML Arch ..... Master of Landscape Architecture
MLAT ...... Modern Language Aptitude Test (Military)
MLB........ Maritime Labor Board (Terminated, 1942)
MLB .... Metallic Link Belt
MLB .... Motor Lifeboat
MLBPA ..... Major League Baseball Players Association
MLC........ Main Lobe Clutter
MLC........ Major Landing Craft
MLC .... Master of Labor Contract
MLC .... Meat and Livestock Commission (British)
MLC .... Member of the Legislative Council
MLC........ Mesh Level Control
MLC........ Microelectric Logic Circuit
MLC........ Military Landing Craft
MLC .... Military Liaison Committee

MLC .... Mixed Leukocyte Culture
MLC .... Motor Launch, Cabin
MLC........ Motor Load Control
MLC........ Multi-Layer Circuit
MLC........ Multi-Lens Camera
MLC........ Multiplanar Link Chain
MLCAEC .... Military Liaison Committee to the Atomic Energy Commission
MLCB ...... Missile Launch Control Blockhouse
MLCB ...... Multilayer Circuit Board
MLCC ...... Mined Land Conservation Conference
MLCG ...... Missile Launcher Control Group
MLCIM ..... Marquette League for Catholic Indian Missions
MLCP ...... Mobile Land Command Post
MLCR ...... Medical Laboratory Contract Reports (Army)
MLCU....... Mill Cutter (Tool)
MLD .... Master of Landscape Design
MLD .... Median Lethal Dose
MLD .... Metachromatic Leukodystrophy (Medicine)
MLD .... Midland Valley R. R. (AAR code)
MLD .... Minimum Lethal Dose (Biology)
MLD .... Minimum Line of Detection (Air Force)
ML Des ..... Master of Landscape Design
MLDS ...... Motor Launch, Double Shelter
MLDU ...... Marriage Law Defence Union (British)
MLE .... Maximum Likelihood Estimate (Statistics)
MLEC....... Mouvement pour la Liberation de l'Enclave de Cabinda (Movement for the Liberation of the Cabinda Enclave)
ML Eng ..... Master of Landscape Engineering
MLEP ...... Multipurpose Long Endurance Plane
MLEV ...... Manned Lifting Entry Vehicle
MLF........ Maintenance Level Function
MLF .... Medical Liberation Front
MLF .... Medial Longitudinal Fasciculus
MLF .... Multi-Lateral Force (NATO)
MLF .... Multilateral Missile Fleet (NATO)
MLFA ...... Maine Lobster Fishermen's Association
MLFX ...... Mill Fixture (Tool)
MLG .... Main Landing Gear
MLG .... Middle Low German (Language)
MLGCV...... Movement for the Liberation of Portuguese Guinea and the Cape Verde Islands
MLGP....... Movimento de Liberacao da Guine Portuguesa (Portuguese Guinea Liberation Movement)
MLHW ..... Mean Lower High Water (Navigation)
MLI .... Magnetic Level Indicator
MLI .... Marker Light Indicator
MLI .... Master of Literary Interpretation
MLI .... Minimum Line of Interception (Air Force)
MLI .... Mixed Lymphocyte Interaction
MLI .... Multilayer Insulation
M Lit ...... Master of Letters (or Literature)
MLL .... Manned Lunar Landing (NASA)
MLL........ Master of Latin Literature
MLL .... Maynard Listener Library
MLL........ McCall Corporation (NYSE symbol) (Delisted)
MLL........ Mistress of Liberal Learning
MLLE ...... Mademoiselle
MLLES ..... Mademoiselles
ML Libr ..... Master of Law Librarianship
MLLP ...... Manned Lunar Landing Program
MLLW ..... Mean Lower Low Water
MLM .... Master of Landscape Management
MLM .... Mixed Level Matrix
MLMA ...... Metal Ladder Manufacturers Association
MLMA ...... Metal Lath Manufacturers Association
MLMS ...... Member of the London Mathematical Society
MLN .... McLean Trucking Company (NYSE symbol)
MLN .... Mid-Lateral Nerve
MLN .... Modern Language Notes (A periodical)
MLN .... Mouvement de Liberation Nationale (National Liberation Movement) (Dahomey)
MLN .... Movimiento de Liberacion Nacional (Movement for National Liberation) (Guatemala, Mexico)
MLN .... Multiple Length Number
MLNS....... Ministry of Labour and National Service (British) (World War II)
MLO........ Manipulative Learning Operation (in laboratory work)
MLO .... Manned Lunar Orbiter (NASA)
MLO .... Mauna Loa Observatory (Hawaii) (National Weather Service)
MLO .... Medical Laboratory Observer
MLO .... Military Landing Officer
MLOR ...... Maintenance/Logistics Observer Report

MLP .... Machine Language Program
MLP .... Metal Lath and Plaster (Technical drawings)
MLP .... Minimum Latency Programming
MLP .... Mirror Landing Procedures
MLP .... Multi-Level Programmer
MLPC ...... Management-Labor Policy Committee
MLPC ...... Multi-Layer Printed Circuit
MLPF ...... Miniature Low Pass Filter
MLPFS ..... Merrill Lynch, Pierce, Fenner & Smith (Stockbrokers) (Wall Street slang name: "Thundering Herd")
MLPNPP .... Mobile Low-Power Nuclear Power Plant
MLQ .... Modern Language Quarterly (A publication)
MLR .... Main Line of Resistance
MLR .... Mechanized Line Records (Bell System)
MLR .... Memory Lockout Register
MLR .... Midland-Ross Corporation (NYSE symbol)
MLR .... Minimum Latency Routine
MLR .... Mixed Leukocyte Reactions
MLR .... Monthly Letter Report
MLR .... Multiply and Round
MLR .... Muzzle-Loading Rifle
MLRA ...... Marriage Law Reform Association (British)
MLRB ...... Mutual Loss Research Bureau
MLRG ...... Muzzle-Loading Rifled Gun
MLRP ...... Marine Corps Long-Range Plans
MLRP ...... Marine Life Research Program
MLRS ...... Manual Launch – RADAR Search
MLS .... Manistique & Lake Superior R. R. (AAR code)
MLS .... Manned Lunar Surface (NASA)
MLS .... Master of Librarianship
MLS .... Mechanical Limit Stop
MLS .... Mechanical Limit Switch
MLS .... Medium Long Shot (A photograph or motion picture sequence taken from a relatively great distance)
MLS .... Microwave Landing System
MLS .... Microwave Line Stretcher
MLS .... Miniature Linguistic Systems
MLS .... Missile-Launching System
MLS .... Multiple Listing Service (Real estate)
MLSB ...... Member of the London School Board
ML Sc ..... Master of Library Science
MLSF ...... Mobile Logistic Support Forces
MLSR ...... Molder, Ship Repair (Navy)
MLSRC ..... Molder, Ship Repair, Cupola Tender (Navy)
MLSRF ..... Molder, Ship Repair, Foundryman (Navy)
MLSRM ..... Molder, Ship Repair, Molder (Navy)
MLST ...... Milstead R. R. (AAR code)
MLT .... Mass Loaded Transducer
MLT .... Master of Law and Taxation
MLT .... Mean Length per Turn
MLT .... Mean Low Tide
MLT .... Median Lethal Time (Radiation)
MLT .... Micro-Layer Transistor
MLT .... Mobile Laboratory Table
MLT .... Muexins-Length Theory
MLTG ...... Missile Launch Tube Group
MLTP ...... Ministers Leadership Training Program
MLU .... Memory Loading Unit (of FADAC) (Military)
MLU .... Miscellaneous Live Unit (Military)
MLU .... Mobile Laundry Unit
MLU .... Mobile Living Unit (Mobile home)
MLU .... Moroccan Labor Union
MLV .... McDonnell Launch Vehicle
MLV .... Murine Leukemia Virus (Also, MuLV)
MLV(M). ... Murine Leukemia Virus (Moloney)
MLVPS ..... Manual Low Voltage Power Supply
MLV(R) .... Murine Leukemia Virus (Rauscher)
MLVS ...... Mill Vise
MLW .... Mean Low Water
MLWI ...... Mean Low Water Lunitidal Interval
MLWN ...... Mean Low Water Neap (Tides)
MLWS ...... Mean Low Water Springs
MLX .... McLouth Steel Corp. (NYSE symbol)
MLY .... Molybdenum Corporation of America (NYSE symbol)
MM .... Machinery
MM .... Machinist's Mate
MM .... Made Merchantable
MM .... Maelzel's Metronome (Music)
MM .... Main Memory
MM .... Maintenance Manual
MM .... Majesties

MM .... Man-Month
MM .... Manmade (Diamonds)
MM .... Marilyn Monroe (Deceased American motion picture star)
MM .... Marine Midland Corporation (NYSE symbol)
MM .... Maritime Mobile
MM .... Martyres (Martyrs)
MM .... Maryknoll Missioners (Catholic Foreign Mission Society) (Roman Catholic religious order)
MM .... Master Mason (Freemasonry)
MM .... Master Mechanic
MM .... Master Monitor
MM .... Master of Music
MM .... Masters
MM .... Materials Management (AEC)
MM .... Medal of Merit
MM .... Megameter
MM .... Mercantile Marine or Merchant Marine
MM .... Messageries Maritimes (Forwarding agents)
MM .... Messieurs (Plural of Mister) (French)
MM .... Methyl Methacrylate
MM .... Microfilm
MM .... Middle Marker (in an instrument landing system)
MM .... Military Medal
MM .... Military Medicine
mm .... Millimeter (Metric)
MM .... Millimole
MM .... Minelayer Fleet (Navy symbol)
MM .... Minister of Munitions (British) (World War II)
MM .... Minute Man (Missile)
MM .... Mis-Mated (Merchandising slang)
MM .... Missile Master (Fire direction and coordination system)
MM .... Mission Module
MM .... Mistress of Music
MM .... Morality in Media (An organization)
MM .... Motor Magnet
MM .... Motor Maintenance (Army)
MM .... Motor Maintenance Aptitude Area
MM .... Mouse Encephalomyocarditis (Virus) (Medicine)
MM .... Much Married (Slang)
MM .... Mucous Membrane
MM .... Mutatis Mutandis (With the Necessary Changes)
M/M .... Man-Month
M of M ..... Maintenance of Membership (Labor unions)
MMA .... Auxiliary Minelayer (Navy symbol)
MMA .... MacRobertson-Miller Airlines, Ltd.
MMA .... Marine Maritime Academy
MMA .... Massachusetts Maritime Academy
MMA .... Massachusetts Military Academy
MMA .... Master of Municipal Administration
MMA .... Master of Musical Arts
MMA .... Merrill's Marauders Association
MMA .... Methylmethacrylate
MMA .... Metropolitan Magazine Association
MMA .... Microminiature Mixer Amplifier
MMA .... Mirror Manufacturers Association
MMA .... Monorail Manufacturers Association
MMA .... Multiple Module Access
MMAA ...... Merchandise Mart Apparel Association
MMAC ...... Medical Materiel Advice Code (Military)
MM Adm .... Master of Municipal Administration
M Ma E .... Master of Marine Engineering
M Ma Eng ... Master of Marine Engineering
M-MARP .... Mobilization Manpower Allocations/Requirements Plan (Military)
MMAT ...... Mobile Mine Assembly Team
MMB .... Master Menu Board (Military)
MMB .... Mercedarian Missionaries of Berriz (Roman Catholic women's religious order)
MMB .... Milk Marketing Board for England and Wales
MMB .... Mixer Manufacturers Bureau
MMBP ...... Military Medical Benefits Property
MMC .... Man Marketing Council (New York City)
MMC .... Manufacturing Methods Committee
MMC .... Marlennan Corporation (NYSE symbol)
MMC .... Mary Morston's Companions
MMC .... Materiel Management Code (Military)
MMC .... Maximum Material Condition
MMC .... Maximum Metal Concept
MMC .... Merchant Marine Council (Coast Guard)
MMC .... Midcourse Measurement Correction
MMC .... Minelayer, Coastal (Navy symbol)
MMC .... Missile Maintenance Crew

MMC . . . . Missile Motion Computer
MMC . . . . Mortar Motor Carrier
MMC . . . . Mount Marty College (South Dakota)
MMC . . . . Mount Mary College (Wisconsin)
MMC . . . . Mount Mercy College (Iowa; Pennsylvania)
MMCBE . . . . . Machinist's Mate, Construction Battalion, Equipment Operator
MMCF . . . . . . Million Cubic Feet
MMCMP . . . . . Mobilization, Military and Civilian Manpower Program
MMCS . . . . . . Multiple-Mission Command System (Aerospace)
MMCT. . . . . . . Maritime Mobile Coastal Telegraphy
MMD . . . . Manual of the Medical Department (Navy)
MMD . . . . Mass Median Diameter
MMD . . . . Master Makeup and Display
MMD . . . . . . Materiel Management Division (Army)
MMD . . . . . . Maximum Mixing Depths (Meteorology)
MMD . . . . Mean Mass Density
MMD . . . . Mean Mass Diameter
MMD . . . . . . Merchant Marine Detail
MMD . . . . . . Microwave Mixer Diode
MMD . . . . Minelayer, Fast (Navy ship symbol)
MMD . . . . . . Money Market Directory
MMD . . . . . . Moving Map Display
MMDC . . . . . . Manual Master Direction Center
MMDL . . . . . . Micro-Miniature Delay Line
MME . . . . Machinist's Mate, Engineman (Navy rating)
MME . . . . Madame
MME . . . . Master of Mechanical Engineering
M Me . . . . Master of Metaphysics
MME . . . . Master of Mining Engineering
MME . . . . Master of Music Education
MME . . . . Material Military Establishment (Formerly, OSRD)
MME . . . . Maximum Maintenance Effort (Military)
MME . . . . McNeil Corporation (Formerly, McNeil Machine & Engineering Company) (NYSE symbol)
MME . . . . Minimum Mean Estimate
MMEC . . . . . . Machinery-Metals Export Club
M Mech E . . . Master of Mechanical Engineering
MM Ed . . . . . Master of Music Education
M Med Sc . . . Master of Medical Science
MMEF . . . . . . Maximal Midexpiratory Flow (Medicine)
MM Eng . . . . Master of Mechanical Engineering
MMEP . . . . . . Minuteman Education Program (Military)
MMES . . . . . . Master Material Erection Schedule
MMES . . . . . . Mesdames
M Met . . . . . . Master of Metallurgy
M Met E . . . Master of Metallurgical Engineering
MMF . . . . Fleet Minelayer (Navy symbol)
mmf . . . . Magnetomotive Force
MMF . . . . Meals for Millions Foundation
MMF . . . . Member of the Medical Faculty
MMF . . . . Microelectronics Manufacturing Facility (Philco-Ford Corporation)
MMF . . . . Micromation Microfilm
MMF . . . . Micro-Membrane Filter
MMF . . . . Mobile Magnetic Field
MMF . . . . Moravian Music Foundation
MMF . . . . National Association of Master Mechanics and Foremen of Naval Shore Establishments
MMFD . . . . . . Micromicrofarad
MMFPA . . . . . Man-Made Fiber Producers Association
MMFPB . . . . . Mill Mutual Fire Prevention Bureau
MMFPI . . . . . Man-Made Fiber Producers Institute
MMFV . . . . . . Manned Mars Flyby Vehicle (Aerospace)
MMG . . . . Machinist's Mate, Industrial Gas Generating Mechanic (Navy rating)
MMG . . . . Medium Machinegun
MMH . . . . Maintenance Man Hours
MMH . . . . . . Monomethylhydrazine (Chemical)
MMHC . . . . . Massachusetts Mental Health Center
MMHS . . . . . Mechanized Mechanical Handling System
MMI . . . . Man Machine Interface
MMI . . . . Mechanized Manufacturing Information
MMI. . . . . . . Micro-Magnetic Industries
MMI . . . . Montana Myotis Leukoencephalitis (Virus) (Medicine)
M Mic . . . . . . Master of Microbiology
MMICS . . . . . Maintenance Management Information and Control System
M Mi E . . . . . Master of Mining Engineering
MMIS . . . . . . Maintenance Management Information System (Military)
MMIS . . . . . . Municipal Management Information System (Civil Defense)
MMIT . . . . . . Man-Machine Interrogation Technique
MMJC . . . . . . Meridian Municipal Junior College (Mississippi)
MMK . . . . Material Mark
MMKR . . . . . . Middle Marker (in a instrument landing system)

MML . . . . Massmutual Mortgage and Realty Investors (NYSE symbol)
MML . . . . Master of Modern Languages
MML . . . . Motor Movement Latency
MMM . . . . . . Maintenance Man Minute
MMM . . . . . . Maintenance and Material Management (Navy)
MMM . . . . . . Manned Mars Mission (NASA)
MMM . . . . . . Mars Mission Module
MMM . . . . . . Medical Missionaries of Mary (Roman Catholic women's religious order)
MMM . . . . . . Minnesota Mining & Manufacturing Company (Also known as 3M Company) (NYSE symbol)
MMM . . . . . . Modern Music Masters Society
MMM . . . . . . Mouvement Mondial des Meres (World Movement of Mothers)
MMM . . . . . . Multi-Mission Module
MMMA . . . . . Meat Machinery Manufacturers Association
MMMEP . . . . . Military Manpower Management Evaluation Project
MMMI . . . . . . Meat Machinery Manufacturers Institute
MMMIS . . . . . Maintenance & Material Management Information System
MMMOS . . . . Mobile Micrometeorological Observation System
MMMPC . . . . Maintenance and Material Management Project Center (Navy)
MMMR . . . . . Medical Material Mission Reserve (Military)
MMN . . . . . . Metallurgic et Mechanique Nucleaires (Belgium)
MMNIC . . . . . Main Mediterranean Naval Intelligence Center (Navy)
MMO . . . . . . Main Meteorological Office
MMO . . . . Monarch Machine Tool Company (NYSE symbol)
MMO . . . . . . Music Minus One (Recording label)
MMOG . . . . . Merchant Marine Officers Guild
MMP . . . . International Organization of Masters, Mates and Pilots of America
MMP . . . . Machined Metal Part
MMP . . . . Maritime Mobile Phone
MMP . . . . Merchant Marine Personnel Division (Coast Guard)
MMP . . . . Military Mounted Police
MMP . . . . . . Multiplexed Message Processor
MMPC . . . . . . Maritime Mobile Phone Coastal
MMPC . . . . . . Mobilization Material Procurement Capability
MMPDC . . . . . Maritime Mobile Phone Distress and Calling
MMPI . . . . . . Minnesota Multiphasic Personality Inventory (Psychology)
MMPNC . . . . Medical Materiel Program for Nuclear Casualties
MMPR . . . . . . Missile Manufacturer's Planning Report
MMPVS . . . . . Modified Military Pay Voucher System
MMR . . . . Machinist's Mate, Refrigeration (Navy rating)
MMR . . . . Management Milestone Records (Navy)
MMR . . . . Miniature Micropower Resistor
MMR . . . . Mobilization Materiel Requirement
MMRA . . . . . . Mobilization Material Requirement Adjustment
MMRBM . . . . Mobile Mid-Range Ballistic Missile (Air Force)
MMRC . . . . . . Materials and Mechanics Research Center (Army)
MMRI . . . . . . Multi Media Reviews Index
MMRP . . . . . . Missile Master Replacement Program
MMS . . . . British vessel corresponding to US YMS
MMS . . . . Machinist's Mate, Shop Mechanic (Navy rating)
MMS . . . . Manpower Management System (Marine Corps)
MMS . . . . Mass Memory System
MMS . . . . Master of Mechanical Science
MMS . . . . Mazdoor Mahajan Sangh (Textile Labor Association) (India)
MMS . . . . Merchant Marine Safety
MMS . . . . Metabolic Monitoring System
MMS . . . . Missile Mix Study
MMS . . . . Missile Monitor System (Army)
MMS . . . . Mobile Monitoring Station
MMS . . . . Modulation Measuring System
MMS . . . . Moravian Missionary Society
MMS . . . . Motor Minesweeper
MMS . . . . Multiplex Modulation System
MMS . . . . Munitions Maintenance Squadron (Air Force)
MMSA . . . . . . Mercantile Marine Service Association (British)
MMSA . . . . . . Military Medical Supply Agency (Later, Defense Medical Supply Center)
MMSA . . . . . . Mining and Metallurgical Society of America
MM Sc . . . . . Master of Mechanical Science
MM Sc . . . . . Master of Medical Science
MMSC . . . . . . Multi-Mode SONAR Console
MMSCFD . . . . Million Standard Cubic Feet per Day
MMSCV . . . . . Manned Military System Capability Vehicle
MMSE . . . . . . Minimum-Mean Squared Error
MMSR. . . . . . . Machinist's Mate, Ship Repair (Navy rating)
MMSR . . . . . . Master Materiel Support Record
MMSRE . . . . . Machinist's Mate, Ship Repair, Engine Operator (Navy rating)
MMSRI . . . . . Machinist's Mate, Ship Repair, Instrument Maker (Navy rating)
MMSRO . . . . . Machinist's Mate, Ship Repair, Outside Machinist (Navy rating)
MMSRS . . . . . Machinist's Mate, Ship Repair, Inside Machinist (Navy rating)
MMSS. . . . . . . Manned Maneuverable Space System
MMSS. . . . . . . Manual Mode Space Simulator

MMST ...... Multi-Mode Storage Tube
MMSW ...... International Union of Mine, Mill and Smelter Workers
MMT .... Marine Minerals Technology (National Oceanic and Atmospheric
                  Administration)
MMT .... Maritime Mobile Telegraph
MMT .... Master of Medical Technology
MMT .... Merchant Marine Technical Division (Coast Guard)
MMT .... Missile Maintenance Technician
MMT .... Multi-Mode Tonotron
MMT .... Multiple-Mission Telemetry (Aerospace)
MMTC ..... Marine Minerals Technology Center (Bureau of Mines)
MMTC...... Maritime Mobile Telegraph Calling
MMTC ..... Materiel Management Training Center (Military)
MMTD ...... Multi-Mode Tonotron Display
MMTDC .... Maritime Mobile Telegraph Distress and Calling
MMTV...... Mouse Mammary Tumor Virus
MMU .... Midcourse Maneuvering Unit (Aerospace)
MMU .... Modular Maneuvering Unit (Aerospace)
MMU .... Municipal Mazdoor Union (India)
M Mus ..... Master of Music
M Mus Ed .. Master of Music Education
M Mus (Mus Ed).. Master of Music in Music Education
M Mus (Mus Lit) .. Master of Music in Music Literature
M Mus (PSM) .. Master of Music in Public School Music
M Mus (W Inst) . Master of Music in Wind Instruments
MMV .... Monostable Multi-Vibrator
MMW ...... Mean Maximum Weight
MMX .... Magma Copper Company (NYSE symbol) (Delisted)
MMX .... Mastergroup Multiplex (Bell Laboratories)
MMY .... Mental Measurements Yearbook (Psychology)
MN .... Macherey, Nagel (& Co.) (West Germany)
MN .... Magnetic North
Mn .... Manganese (Chemical element)
MN .... Mantle Nerve
MN .... Manx Airlines, Ltd.
MN .... Master of Nursing
MN .... Material Number
MN .... Materiel Needs (Army)
MN .... Maxim Nordenfelt Gun
MN .... Meganewton
MN .... Meningopneumonitis
MN .... Merchant Navy
MN .... Mineman (Navy rating)
MN .... Minnesota
M-N .... Macherey, Nagel (& Co.) (West Germany)
m-N........ Meter-Newton
M Na ...... Master of Navigation
MNA .... Master of Nursing Administration
MNA ...... Missing, Not Enemy Action
MNA .... Mouvement National Algerien (National Algerian Movement)
MNA ..... Multi-Network Area (Term used in TV ratings)
MNAO...... Mobile Naval Airfield Organization
MN Arch.... Master of Naval Architecture
MNAS ...... Member of the National Academy of Sciences
MNAU ..... Mobile Naval Airfield Unit
MNBA ...... Minimum Normal Burst Altitude
MNBLE .... Modified Nearly Best Linear Estimator (Statistics)
MNC .... Major NATO Commanders
MNC .... Masonite Corporation (NYSE symbol)
MNC .... Mouvement National Congolais (Congolese National Movement)
MNC .... Multinational Corporation
MNC-K ..... Mouvement National Congolais (Congolese National Movement) (Kalonji
                  Wing)
MNC-L...... Mouvement National Congolais - Lumumba (Congolese National Movement)
                  (Lumumba Wing)
MNCPPC .... Maryland -National Capital Park and Planning Commission
MND .... Martin Nuclear Division (AEC)
MND ..... Midsummer Night's Dream (Shakespeare)
MND .... Minimum Necrosing Dose
MND .... Minister of National Defence (Canada)
MNDA ..... Missionary Sisters of Notre Dame des Anges (Roman Catholic religious
                  order)
MNE .... Master of Naval Engineering
MNE .... Master of Nuclear Engineering
MNE .... Modern English
MNECP ..... Mobile National Emergency Command Post (Air Force)
MN Ed ..... Master of Nursing Education
MN Eng .... Master of Naval Engineering
MNF .... Millers' National Federation
MNF .... Morehead & North Fork R. R. (AAR code)
MNF .... Multilateral Nuclear Force

MNG .... Microwave Negative Grid
MNH ...... Museum of Natural History (Smithsonian Institution)
MNI .... Madras Native Infantry (British)
MNI .... Minimum Number of Individuals (Statistics)
MNJ .... Middletown & New Jersey Railway Company (AAR code)
MNJTS ..... Mouvement National des Jeunes Travailleurs du Senegal (National
                  Movement of Young Workers of Senegal)
MNL .... Marine Navigating Light
MNL .... Medical Nutrition Laboratory (Army)
MNL .... Minnesota National Laboratory
MNLS...... Marine Navigating Light System
MNM .... Military Necessity Modification
MNMANY ... Men's Neckwear Manufacturers Association of New York
MNMIA .... Men's Neckwear Manufacturers Institute of America
MNORM..... Missile Not Operationally Ready - Maintenance (Air Force)
MNORP .... Missile Not Operationally Ready - Parts (Air Force)
MNOT ...... Magyar Nok Orszagos (National Council of Hungarian Women)
MNP .... Morton-Norwich Products, Inc. (NYSE symbol)
MNPD ...... Missile and Nuclear Programming Data
MNPS ...... Movimiento Nazionale Pan-Somalo (Pan-Somali National Movement)
MNPWR ..... Manpower
MNR .... McMaster Nuclear Reactor (Canada)
MNR .... Mean Neap (Tide) Rise
MNR .... Movimiento Nacional Reformista (National Reformist Movement)
                  (Honduras)
MNR .... Movimiento Nacionalista Revolucionario (National Revolutionary
                  Movement) (Bolivia)
MNS .... Master of Nursing Science
MNS .... Master of Nutritional Science
MNS .... Member of the Numismatical Society (British)
MNS .... Meta-Nitride Semiconductor
MNS .... Ministry of National Service (British) (World War I)
MNS .... Minneapolis, Northfield & Southern Railway (AAR code)
MNS .... Molded Nylon Screw
MN Sc ..... Master of Nursing Science
MNT .... Minnesota & Ontario Paper Company (NYSE symbol) (Delisted)
MNT .... Modern Network Theory (Electrical engineering computer)
MNT .... Mononitrotoluene
MNU .... Manati Sugar Company (NYSE symbol)
MNV .... Marion Power Shovel Company (NYSE symbol)
MNWEB ..... Merseyside and North Wales Electricity Board
MO .... Machine Operation
MO .... Mail Order (Business and trade)
MO .... Maintenance and Operating (Factor)
MO .... Make Offer
MO .... Management Office
MO .... Manual Output
MO .... Manually Operated
MO .... Masonry Opening (Technical drawings)
MO .... Mass Observation
MO .... Master of Obstetrics
MO .... Master of Oratory
MO .... Master Oscillator (Radio)
MO .... Master of Osteopathy
MO .... Medical Officer
MO .... Medium Oocyte
MO .... Memory Operation
MO .... Mesio-Occlusal
MO .... Method of Operation
MO .... Micro-Opaque
MO .... Ministerstvo Oborony (Ministry of Defense) (USSR)
MO .... Missouri
MO .... Mobile Station (Air Force)
MO .... Modus Operandi (Police term for distinctive techniques used by criminals)
MO .... Mohawk Airlines, Inc. (Obsolete)
MO .... Molecular Orbital (Atomic physics)
Mo .... Molybdenum (Chemical element)
MO........ Money Order
MO .... Monitor Output
MO .... Month
MO .... Monthly Order (Navy)
MO .... Movement Orders
MO .... Mustered Out (of military service)
MO .... Philip Morris, Inc. (NYSE symbol)
M & O ..... Machinery and Optics
M & O ..... Maintenance and Operations
M & O ..... Management and Organization
M & O ..... Manpower and Organization (Military)
M & O ..... Mobile and Ohio Railroad Company
MOA ...... Management Operations Audit (Navy)
MOA ..... Marine Office of America (Insurance company)

MOA . . . . Matrix Output Amplifier
MOA . . . . Medium Observation Aircraft
MOA . . . . Military-Assistance-Program Order Amendment
MOA . . . . Ministry of Aviation (British)
MOA . . . . . Music Operators of America
MOAA . . . . . . Mail Order Association of America
MOAMA . . . . Mobile Air Materiel Area
MOARS. . . . . . Mobilization Assignment Reserve Section (Military)
MOAT . . . . . . Missile on Aircraft Test
MOB . . . . Main Operating Base
MOB . . . . Missile Order of Battle
MOB . . . . Mobil Oil Corp. (NYSE symbol)
MOB . . . . Mobilization (or Mobilize)
MOB . . . . Money-Order Business
MOBCON . . . . Mobilization Construction Plan
MOBDES . . . . Mobilization Designee
MOBED . . . . . Mobile Education Demonstration
MOBEX . . . . . Mobile Excursion
MOBEX . . . . . Mobile Exploration (NASA)
MOBEX . . . . . Mobility Test Exercise (Military)
MOBIDAC . . . Mobile Data Acquisition System
MOBIDIC . . . . Mobile Digital Computer (Army)
MOBIS . . . . . . Management-Oriented Budget Information System
MOBL . . . . . . Macro-Oriented Business Language
MOBL. . . . . . . Main Operating Base LASER
MOBOT . . . . . Mobile Remote-Controlled Robot
MOBRASOP . . . Mobilization Requirements in Support of the Army Strategic Objectives
          Plan
MOBS. . . . . . . Mobile Hospitals (Military slang)
MOBS . . . . . . Multiple-Orbit Bombardment System
MOBTB . . . . . Mobilization Troop Basis (Army)
MOBU . . . . . . Mobilization Base Units
MOC . . . . . . Magnetic Optic Converter
MOC . . . . Maintenance Operations Center (Military)
MOC . . . . Manual Operations Control
MOC . . . . Master Operational Controller
MOC . . . . Master Operations Center
MOC . . . . . . Master Operations Console
MOC . . . . . . Master Operations Control
MOC . . . . Master Ordnance Configuration File (Navy)
MOC . . . . Mathematical Operations Computer
MOC . . . . . . Military Order of the Carabao
MOC . . . . Missile Operation Center (Air Force)
MOC . . . . Mission Operation Computer
MOC . . . . Supreme Pup Tent, Military Order of the Cootie
MOCA . . . . . . Minimum Obstruction Clearance Altitude (Aviation)
MOCA . . . . . Montezuma Castle National Monument
MOCAS . . . . . Mechanization of Contract Administration Service
MOCI . . . . . . Mound City Group National Monument
MOCO . . . . . . Machinery Overhaul Company
MOCOM. . . . . Mobility Command (AMC)
MOCON. . . . . Mobile Repair Parts Container
MOCP . . . . . . Missile Out of Commission for Parts
MOCR . . . . . . Mission Operations Control Room
MOCR . . . . . . Moores Creek National Military Park
MOD . . . . . . Magnetic-Optical Display
MOD . . . . . . Mail-Order Department
MOD . . . . . . Manned Orbital Development (Station)
MOD . . . . . . Manpower & Organization Division (Air Force)
MOD . . . . Mapping of Disease
MOD . . . . March on Drugs (An organization)
MOD . . . . Medical Officer of the Day (Military)
MOD . . . . Mesial, Occlusal, and Distal (Describes location of openings in a
          carious tooth) (Dentistry)
MOD . . . . Microfilm-Output Device
MOD . . . . . . Microwave Oscillating Diode
MOD . . . . Ministry of Defence
MOD . . . . Miscellaneous Obligation Document
MOD . . . . Modification (or Modify)
MOD . . . . . . Money-Order Department
MODA . . . . . . Motion Detector and Alarm (Army)
MODAC . . . . . Mountain System Digital Automatic Computer
MODAP . . . . . Modified Apollo (NASA)
MODAP . . . . . Multiple Operational Data Acquisition Program (Data processing)
MODAPS. . . . . Modal Data Acquisition and Processing System
MODASM . . . . Modular Air-to-Surface Missile
MODB . . . . . . Military Occupational Data Bank
MODD . . . . . . Military Order of Devil Dogs
MODDF . . . . . Military Order, Devil Dog Fleas
MODE . . . . . . Management of Objectives with Dollars through Employees (Department
          of Agriculture)

MODE . . . . . . Mid-Ocean Dynamic Experiment
MODE . . . . . . Monitor Data Equipment
MODEM . . . . . Modulator-Demodulator (Data-processing term)
MODEST . . . . Missile Optical Destruction Technique
MODHATR. . . . Modified Hatrack (Cyclone forecasting) (Navy)
MODI . . . . . . Modified Distribution
MODICON . . Modular-Dispersed-Control
MODILS . . . . . Modular Instrument Landing System
MODM . . . . . Magneto-Optical Display Memory
MODM . . . . . Manned One-Day Mission (NASA)
MODOR . . . . . Molecularized Doppler RADAR
MODS . . . . . . Manned Orbital Development System (NASA/Air Force)
MODS . . . . . . Manned Orbiting Development Station (Air Force)
MODS . . . . . . Military Orbital Development System Station (Formerly, MTSS)
          (Air Force)
MODS. . . . . . . Missile Offense/Defense System
MODTEPS . . . . Modular Toxic Environment Protective Suit (NASA)
MOE . . . . Mars Orbit Ejection
MOE . . . . Master of Oral English
MOE . . . . Measure of Effectiveness
MOE . . . . Telemetering Mobile Station (ITU designation)
MOED . . . . . . Morristown-Edison National Park Service Group
MOEP. . . . . . . Meteorological and Oceanographic Equipment Program
MOF . . . . Maximum Observed Frequency (Radio)
MOF . . . . Metal Oxide Film
MOF . . . . Ministry of Food (British)
MOFAP. . . . . . Ministry of Fuel and Power (British)
MOFW . . . . . . Military Order of Foreign Wars of the United States
MOG . . . . . . Material Ordering Guide
MOG . . . . Metropolitan Opera Guild
MO & G . . . . . Master Obstetrics and Gynaecology (British)
MOGA . . . . . . Microwave and Optical Generation and Amplification
MOGA . . . . . . Montana Outfitters and Guides Association
MOGAS . . . . . Motor Gasoline
MOGR . . . . . . Moderate or Greater
MOH . . . . Hydrological and Meteorological Mobile Station (ITU designation)
MOH . . . . Master of Otter Hounds
MOH . . . . Medical Officer of Health (British)
MOH . . . . Ministry of Health (British)
MOH . . . . Mohasco Industries, Inc. (NYSE symbol)
MOH . . . . Mohawk Airlines, Inc. (Obsolete)
MOHAT . . . . . Modular Handling and Transport
MOHATS . . . . Mobile Overland Hauling and Transport System (Air Force)
MOHO. . . . . . . Mohorovicic Discontinuity
MOHOLE . . . . A deep hole exploratory project (MOHO derived from last name of
          Andrija Mohorovici, Yugoslav seismologist who proposed the project)
MOI . . . . Main d'Oeuvre Indigene (Indigenous Manpower) (Congo – Leopoldville)
MOI. . . . . Mars-Orbit(al) Insertion (Aerospace)
MOI . . . . Maximum Obtainable Irradiance
MOI . . . . Methods of Instruction
MOI . . . . Military Occupational Information
MOI. . . . . Military Operations and Intelligence
MOI. . . . . Ministry of Information (British) (World War II)
MOI . . . . Moment of Inertia
MOI . . . . Monaco Oceanographic Institute
MOI. . . . . Multiplicity of Infection
MOIC . . . . . . Medical Officer in Charge or Command
MOIG . . . . . . Master of Occupational Information and Guidance
MOIL. . . . . . . Motor Oil
MOK . . . . Mohawk Carpet Mills, Inc. (NYSE symbol)
MOL . . . . Machine-Oriented Language (Data processing)
MOL . . . . Manned Orbiting Laboratory (NASA)
MOL . . . . Master of Oriental Languages
MOL . . . . Metallo Organic LASER
MOL . . . . Morrell (John) & Company (NYSE symbol) (Delisted)
MOLA . . . . . . Midwest Open Land Association
MOLAB . . . . . Mobile Laboratory (NASA)
MOLB . . . . . . Majestic Circle, Military Order of Lady Bugs of USA
MOLDS . . . . . Management On-Line Data System
MOLECOM . . Molecularized Digital Computer
MOLETRONICS. Molecular Electronics
MOLINA. . . . . Mouvement pour la Liberation Nationale (Movement for National
          Liberation)
MOLL . . . . . . Metallo Organic Liquid LASER
MOLLUS . . . . Military Order of the Loyal Legion of the United States
MOLMI . . . . . Moskovskii Ordena Lenina Meditsinskii Institut
MOLOC . . . . . Ministry of Labour Occupational Classification (Later, CODOT)
          (British)
MOLS . . . . . . Magnetic-Operated Limit Switch
MOLS. . . . . . . Mirror Optional Landing System (Aviation)
MOLS. . . . . . . Mutually Orthogonal Latin Square(s)

MOLSINK ... Molecular Sink of Outer Space (Vacuum testing chamber for spacecraft systems)
MOM ...... Manned Orbiting Mission
MOM ..... Men Our Masters (Anti-feminist women's group)
MOM ...... Middle of the Month
MOM ...... Military Official Mail (Air Force)
MOM ...... Military Ordinary Mail
MOM ...... Modified Operational Missile
MOMA ...... Madagasikara Otronin'ny Malagasy (Madagascar Led by Malagasy) (Formerly MONIMA)
MOMA ...... Museum of Modern Art (New York)
MOMAR ..... Modern Mobile Army (Military)
MOMC ..... Mount McKinley National Park
MOMCOM ... Man-on-the-Move Communications
MOMM ...... Motor Machinist's Mate (Navy rating)
MOMMSR ..... Motor Machinist's Mate, Ship Repair (Navy rating)
MOMP ...... Michigan Ordnance Missile Plant (Army)
MOMP ...... Mid-Ocean Meeting Place
MOMS ...... Mothers of Men in Service (World War II)
MOMS ..... Mothers for Moral Stability (Group opposing sex education in schools)
MOMS ...... Multiple Orbit - Multiple Satellite
MOM/WOW... Men Our Masters / Women Our Wonders (Anti-feminist organization)
MON ...... Mixed Oxides of Nitrogen
MON .... Monday
MON ...... Monetary
MON ...... Monitor (Navy ship symbol)
MON ...... Monon R. R. (AAR code and NYSE symbol) (Delisted)
MON ...... Motor Octane Number
MONAB ..... Mobile Naval Air Base
MONAL ..... Mobile Nondestructive Assay Laboratory (AEC)
MONECA ..... Motor Network Calculator
MONIMA .... Mouvement National pour l'Independance Malgache (National Movement for the Independence of Madagascar) (Became MOMA)
MONOB .... Mobile Noise Barge
MONOK..... Monitor Resumed Normal Operation (Aviation communications)
MONOS ..... Monitor Out of Service (Aviation communications)
MONT ...... Montana
MONY ..... Mutual of New York (Insurance company)
MOO ...... Milkbottles Only Organization
MOO ...... Money-Order Office
MOO C of S .. Management Office, Office, Chief of Staff
MOON ..... Meeting Our Operational Needs
MOOSE ..... Man (or Manual) Orbital Operations Safety Equipment (Space life-raft) (NASA)
MOOSE ..... Man Out of Space Easiest
MOOSE ..... Move Out of Saigon Expeditiously (Army project, Vietnam)
MOOSSE..... Manned Orbital Oceanographic Survey System Experiment
MOP ...... Manned Orbital Platform
MOP ...... Manner of Performance (Officer rating)
MOP ...... Manual Operations Panel
MOP ...... Manuscript on Paper
MOP ...... Masers a Ondes Progressives (French)
MOP ...... Memorandum of Policy
MOP ...... Mission Operations Plan
MOP ...... Missouri Pacific R. R. Company (NYSE symbol)
MOP ...... Mobility Operating Procedure (Military)
MOP ...... Model Operational Plan
MOP ...... Modulation on the Pulse
MOP ...... Mother-of-Pearl
MOP ...... Mustering-Out Pay (Military)
MOPA ...... Master Oscillator Power Amplifier (Radio)
MOPA ...... Modus Operandi - Personal Appearance (FBI computer procedure)
MOPAC ..... Missouri Pacific Railroad Company
MOPAR ..... Master Oscillator - Power Amplifier RADAR
MOPB ...... Manually Operated Plotting Board
MOPE ...... Method of Personnel Evaluation
MOPE ...... Multiple Object Parameter Estimation
MOPF...... Mobile Optical Propagation Facility
MOPH ...... Military Order of the Purple Heart of the USA
MOPIC ..... Motion Picture (Army)
MOPP ...... Mission-Oriented Protection Posture (Army)
MOPR ...... Manner of Performing Rating
MOPS ...... Man-Operated Propulsion System
MOPS ...... Military Operation Phone System
MOPS ...... Missile Operations
M Opt ...... Master of Optometry
MOPTAR .... Multiple Object Precision Tracking and Ranging
MOQ ...... Married Officer Quarters
MOR ...... Magneto-Optical Rotation
MOR ...... Management Operating Ratios

MOR ...... Mars Orbital Rendezvous
M Or ...... Master of Oratory
MOR ...... Medical Officer Report (Navy)
MOR ...... Memory Output Register
MOR ...... Merchandising and Operating Results
MOR ...... Middle of the Road (Music)
MOR ...... Missile Operationally Ready (Air Force)
MOR ...... Modulus of Rupture
MORA ...... Mount Rainier National Park
MORAL ..... Massachusetts Organization for the Repeal of Abortion Laws
MORBREPT ... Morbidity Report
MORBTGREPT.. Morbidity Telegraphic Report
MORC ...... Medical Officers' Reserve Corps
MORC ...... Midget Ocean Racing Club (or Class)
MORD ...... Military Operations Research Department
MORDS ..... Manned Orbital Research and Development System
MORE ...... Money, Opportunity, Responsibility and Equality (Of organization "MORE for Women")
MOREL ..... Michigan-Ohio Regional Educational Laboratory
MOREPS .... Monitor Station Reports
MOREST .... Mobile Arresting Gear (Navy)
MORL ...... Manned Orbital (or Orbiting) Research Laboratory (NASA)
MORL ...... Medium Orbital Research Laboratory
Mor M ...... Master Mortician
MORP ...... Medical and Occupational Radiation Program (HEW)
MORR ...... Morristown National Historical Park
MORS ...... Military Operations Research Symposia
M Or Sc ..... Master of the Science of Oratory
MORSEAFRON.. Moroccan Sea Frontier (Navy) (World War II)
MORSL ..... Mobilization Reserve Stockage List (Army)
MORT ...... Master Operational Recording Tape (SAGE)
MORT...... Missile Operation (or Ordnance) Readiness Test(ing)
MORTREP .... Mortar Bombing Report
MORU ...... Mount Rushmore National Memorial
MOS ...... Major Operating System (Army)
MOS ...... Management Operating System
MOS ...... Manufacturing Operating System (IBM)
MOS ...... Marking of Overseas Shipments
MOS ...... Material Ordering Schedule
MOS ...... Mathematical Off-print Service (American Mathematical Society)
MOS ...... Mechanical Oblique Sketcher
MOS ...... Metal-Oxide Semiconductor
MOS ...... Metal-Oxide-Silicon (Integrated circuit) (Electronics)
MOS ...... Military Occupational Specialty Specification Serial Number
MOS ...... Ministry of State (British)
MOS ...... Ministry of Supply (British)
MOS ...... Missile on Stand
MOS ...... Mission Operations System (NASA)
MOS ...... Morton Air Services, Ltd.
MOSAIC .... Mobile System for Accurate ICBM Control
MOSAR...... Modulation Scan Array RADAR (or Receiver)
MOSAW ..... Medium Operating Speed Automatic Weapon (Military)
MOSC ...... Military Occupational Specialty Code
MOSC ...... Military Oil Subcommittee (of North African Economic Board) (World War II)
MOSEL ..... Molten-Salt Epithermal Reactor
MOSES ...... Movable Search System
MOSES ..... Multi-Occupant Sealed Environment Simulator
MOSFET ..... Metal-Oxide-Semiconductor Field-Effect Transistor
MOSP ...... Master Ordnance Systems Pattern File (Navy)
MOSRD...... Motor Machinist's Mate, Ship Repair, Diesel Engineering Mechanic (Navy rating)
MOSRG ..... Motor Machinist's Mate, Ship Repair, Gasoline Engine Mechanic (Navy rating)
MOSS ...... Manned Orbital Space Station
MOSS...... Manned Orbital Space System (NASA/Air Force)
MOSS...... Military Overseas Shelter Survey (Civil Defense)
MOSS...... Monitor Output Signal Strength
MOSS...... Mothers of Sons in Service (World War II)
MOSS ...... Mutually Owned Society for Songwriters
MOSSA...... Northern Rhodesia Mine Officials and Salaried Staff Association
MOSSRS ..... Management Order Ship Status Reporting System
MOST ...... Management Operation System Technique
MOST ...... Manned Orbital Solar Telescope
MOST ...... Metal Oxide Semiconductor Transistor
MOST...... Mobile Optical Surveillance Tracker
MOSTA...... Midwest Old Settlers and Threshers Association
MOSTAB..... Modular Stability (Derivative program)
MOT ...... Manned Orbital Telescope (NASA)
MOT ...... "The March of Time" (Radio and motion picture series)
MOT........ Marine Oil Transportation R. R. (AAR code)

MOT . . . . Maximum Operating Time
MOT . . . . Military Ocean Terminal
MOT . . . . Ministry of Transport (British)
MOT . . . . Month of Travel (Military)
MOT . . . . Motor Operating Time
MOT . . . . Motorola, Inc. (NYSE symbol)
MOTARDIV . . . Mobile Target Division (Navy)
MOTBA . . . . . Military Ocean Terminal, Bay Area
MOTBY . . . . . Military Ocean Terminal, Bayonne
MOTC . . . . . . Montreal Tramways (AAR code)
MOTEL . . . . . . Motor Hotel
MOTF . . . . Manganese Oxide Thin Film
MOTG . . . . . . Marine Operational Training Group
MOTKI . . . . . Military Ocean Terminal, King's Bay
MOTOGAS . . . Motor Gasoline (Military)
MOTOR . . . . . Mobile Oriented Triangulation of Reentry
MOTOREDE . . Movement to Restore Decency (Group opposing sex education in schools)
MOTPICT . . . . Motion Picture
MOTS . . . . . . Minitrack Optical Tracking System (or Station) (NASA)
MOTS . . . . . . Mobile Optical Tracking System
MOTS . . . . . . Module Test Set
MOTSU . . . . . Military Ocean Terminal, Sunny Point
MOTU . . . . . . Mobile Optical Tracking Unit
MOTU . . . . . . Mobile Technical Unit
MOU . . . . Memorandum of Understanding
MOU . . . . Mountain States Telephone & Telegraph Co. (NYSE symbol)
MOUSE . . . . . Minimum Orbital Unmanned Satellite of the Earth
MOV . . . . Manned Orbiting Vehicle (NASA)
MOV . . . . Manuscript on Vellum
MOV . . . . Mass of Vehicle
MOV . . . . Metal Oxide Varistor
MOV . . . . Moshassuck Valley R. R. (AAR code)
MOVDHHG . . . Movement of Dependents and Household Goods in Advance of Permanent Change of Station Orders Is Authorized (Army)
MOVLAS . . . . Manually Operated Visual Landing Aid System
MOVP . . . . . . Military-Owned Vehicle Plan
MOVPER . . . . Supreme Council, Mystic Order Veiled Prophets of Enchanted Realm
MOVREP . . . . Movement Reports System
MOVS . . . . . . Military-Owned Vehicle Service
MOW . . . . . . Ministry of Work (British)
MOW . . . . . . Montana Western Railway (AAR code)
MOWASP . . . . Mechanization of Warehousing and Shipment Processing
MOWS . . . . . Manned Orbital Weapon System (or Station)
MOWT . . . . . Ministry of War Transport (British)
MOWW . . . . . Military Order of the World Wars
MOXIE . . . . . Men Organized to X-press Indignant Exasperation (Seattle group opposing below-the-knee fashions introduced in 1970)
MOXY . . . . . Model X-Y (AEC computer code)
MP . . . . Machine-Pressed
MP . . . . Magnetic Particle
MP . . . . Mains Propres (Personal Delivery)
MP . . . . Maintenance Period
MP . . . . Maintenance Point
MP . . . . Manifold Pressure
MP . . . . Manual Proportional (Attitude control system of Mercury spacecraft)
MP . . . . Manual Pulser
MP . . . . Master of Painting
MP . . . . Mathematical Programming
MP . . . . McIntyre Porcupine Mines, Ltd. (NYSE symbol)
MP . . . . Mechanical Part
MP . . . . Mechanical Printer
MP . . . . Medium Pressure
MP . . . . Meeting Point (Military)
MP . . . . Melting Point
MP . . . . Member of Parliament (British)
MP . . . . Mesiopulpal
MP . . . . Methodist Protestant
MP . . . . Methylpurine
MP . . . . Metropolitan Police
MP . . . . Mezzo Piano (Moderately soft) (Music)
MP . . . . Michoud Plant (NASA)
MP . . . . Microprint
MP . . . . Mile-Post
MP . . . . Military Pay
MP . . . . Military Police (Army)
MP . . . . Military Prohibitionist (Slang)
MP . . . . Minister Plenipotentiary
MP . . . . Minuteman Platform
MP . . . . Miscellaneous Paper or Publication
MP . . . . Missile Platform
MP . . . . Missile Positioning

MP . . . . Missouri Pacific R. R. (AAR code)
MP . . . . Mistress of Philosophy
MP . . . . Mixed Population
MP . . . . Monitor Panel
MP . . . . Monumentum Posuit (Erected a Monument)
MP . . . . Motion Picture Production (Navy)
MP . . . . Motor Potential
MP . . . . Mounted Police
MP . . . . Multiplier Phototube
MP . . . . Multipole
MP . . . . Multiprocessing (Data processing)
MP . . . . Municipal Police
MP . . . . My Pal (Slang)
M/P . . . . Mail Payment (Banking)
M/P . . . . Memorandum of Partnership (Business and trade)
M & P . . . . . Material and Process
M(P) . . . . . . Microfilm (Positive)
MPA . . . . . . Magazine Publishers Association
MPA . . . . . . Man-Powered Aircraft
MPA . . . . . . Maryland & Pennsylvania R. R. (AAR code)
M Pa . . . . . . Master of Painting
MPA . . . . . . Master Printers of America (Division of Printing Industries of America)
MPA . . . . . . Master of Professional Accountancy
MPA . . . . . . Master of Professional Arts
MPA . . . . . . Master of Public Administration
MPA . . . . . . Master of Public Affairs
MPA . . . . . . Mechanical Packing Association
MPA . . . . . . Medical Procurement Agency
MPA . . . . . . Metal Powder Association
MPA . . . . . . Methylphosphonic Acid
MPA . . . . . . Microwave Power Amplifier
MPA . . . . . . Midwestern Psychological Association
MPA . . . . . . Military Pay Area
MPA . . . . . . Military Personnel Appropriation
MPA . . . . . . Military Personnel, Army
MPA . . . . . . Military Police Association
MPA . . . . . . Miniature Photocell Activator
MPA . . . . . . Mission Phase Analysis
MPA . . . . . . Mission Profile Analysis
MPA . . . . . . Missionary Pilots Association
MPA . . . . . . Mobile Press Association
MPA . . . . . . Modern Poetry Association
MPA . . . . . . Motion Picture Alliance
MPA . . . . . . Motion Picture Alliance for the Preservation of American Ideals
MPA . . . . . . Mouvement Populaire de Liberation de l'Angola
MPA . . . . . . Multi-Parameter Analyzer
MPA . . . . . . Multi-Precision Arithmetic
MPA . . . . . . Music Publishers' Association of the United States
MPAA . . . . . Motion Picture Association of America
MPAB . . . . . Military Petroleum Advisory Board
MPAC . . . . . Military Pay and Allowance Committee
MPACS . . . . . Management Planning and Control System (IBM)
MPAD . . . . . Manpower Personnel Assignment Document
MP Adm . . . . Master of Public Administration
MPAMA . . . . Milk Products Advertising-Merchandising Association
MPAR . . . . . Maintenance Program Analysis Report
MPAS . . . . . Mission Planning and Analysis Division (Aerospace)
MPATI . . . . . Midwest Program for Airborne Television Instruction
MPB . . . . . . Machine-Pressed Bales
MPB . . . . . . Magnetic Particle Brake
MPB . . . . . . Master of Physical Biology
MPB . . . . . . Material Performance Branch (Air Force)
MPB . . . . . . Matrix Program Board
MPB . . . . . . Miniature Precision Bearing, Inc.
MPB . . . . . . Missing Persons Bureau
MPB . . . . . . Montpelier & Barre R. R. (AAR code)
MPB . . . . . . Mouvement Progressiste de Burundi (Progressive Movement of Burundi)
MPB . . . . . . Multilayer Printed Board
MPBA . . . . . Machine Printers' Beneficial Association of the United States
MPBP . . . . . Metal Polishers, Buffers, Platers and Helpers International Union
MPBR . . . . . Multipunch Bar
MPBW . . . . . Ministry of Public Building and Works
MPC . . . . . . Machine Punch Card
MPC . . . . . . Magnetic Particle Clutch
MPC . . . . . . Manpower and Personnel Council (DOD)
MPC . . . . . . Manpower Priorities Committee
MPC . . . . . . Manufacturing Plan Change
MPC . . . . . . Marginal Propensity to Consume (Econometrics)
MPC . . . . . . Materiel Program Code (Air Force)
MPC . . . . . . Maximum Permissible Concentration (Radiation)
MPC . . . . . . Mechanical Positioning Control

MPC	Mechanized Production Control
MPC	Member of Parliament of Canada
MPC	Metromedia Producers Corporation
MPC	Military Payment Certificate
MPC	Military Personnel Center
MPC	Military Pioneer Corps (British)
MPC	Military Police Corps
MPC	Minimal Flight Planning Charts (Air Force)
MPC	Minor Planet Center
MPC	Monterey Peninsula College (California)
MPC	Montreal Presbyterian College
MPC	Movable Platform Configuration
MPC	Multi-Path Core
MPC	Multiple Process Chart
MPC	Multi-Processor Computer
MPC	Multi-Program Control
MPC	Multi-Purpose Center
MPC	Multiple-Purpose Communications
MPCA	Magnetic Powder Core Association
MPCA	Markham Prayer Card Apostolate
MPCA	Miniature Pinscher Club of America
MPCB	Minuteman Parts Control Board
MPCC	Multi-Processor Computer Complex
MPCD	Minimum Perceptible Color Difference
MPCE	Music Publishers Contact Employees
MPCH	Methodist Protestant Church
MPCI	Military Police Criminal Investigation
MPCID	Military Police Criminal Investigation Detachment
MPCL	Mooney Problem Check List (Education)
MPCO	Military Police Company
MPCRI	Mercantile Pacific Coastal Routing Instructions
MPCSW	Multipurpose Close Support Weapon (Military)
MPD	Magnetoplasmadynamic
M Pd	Master of Pedagogy
MPD	Materials Physics Division (Air Force)
MPD	Materials Proximity Detector
MPD	Maximum Packing Depth
MPD	Maximum Permissible Dose (Radiation)
MPD	Medusa Portland Cement Company (NYSE symbol)
MPD	Military Pay Division, Finance Center, US Army
MPD	Missile Purchase Description (Army)
MPD	Movimiento Popular Dominicano (Dominican Popular Movement)
MPD	m-Phenylenediamine (Chemical)
MPDA	M-Phenylenediamine
MPDC	Mechanical Properties Data Center (Air Force)
MPDD	Meteorological Penetration Detection Development
MPDFA	Master Photo Dealers' and Finishers' Association
MPDI	Marine Products Development Irradiator
MPDI	Multipunch Die
MPDP	Manpower Development Program
MPDS	Mechanical Provisioning Data System
MPDT	Mean Preventive Downtime
MPE	Master of Physical Education
MPE	Maximum Permissible Exposure (AEC)
MPE	Minimum Potential Energy (Fission)
MPE	Monthly Project Evaluation
MPE	Moving Paper Electrophoresis
MPE	Multiple Phase Ejector
MPEA	Machine Printers and Engravers Association of the United States
MPEA	Meat and Poultry Export Association
MPEA	Motion Picture Export Association
MPEA	Mouvement Populaire d'Evolution Africaine (African People's Evolution Movement)
MPEAA	Motion Picture Export Association of America
MPECC	Multi-Processor Experimental Computer Complex
M Pe E	Master of Petroleum Engineering
M Pe Eng	Master of Petroleum Engineering
MPEG	Military Police Escort Guard
MPEL	Maximum Permissible Exposure Levels (Medicine)
MPEP	Metalworking Processes & Equipment Program
MPER	Material-in-Process Engineering Request
MPERR	Master Personnel Record
MPES	Mass Properties Engineering Section
MPF	Machine Parts Fabrication
MPF	Medical Passport Foundation
MPF	Methodist Peace Fellowship
MPF	Metropolitan Police Force (Scotland Yard) (London)
MPF	Mexico Pilgrims Foundation
MPF	Mizrachi Palestine Fund
MPF	Multi-Purpose Food (Refers to a specific combination of ingredients used in a food relief program)

MPFC	Multi-Purpose Fire Control System
MPFE	Motion Picture Film Editors
MPG	Magazine Promotion Group
MPG	Matched Power Gain
MPG	Max-Planck-Gesellschaft (Research organization)
MPG	Microwave Pulse Generator
MPG	Miles Per Gallon
MPG	Military Products Group
M Ph	Master of Philosophy
MPH	Master of Physical Education and Health
MPH	Master of Public Health
MPH	Miles Per Hour
M Ph	Mistress of Philosophy
MPH	Murphy (G. C.) Company (NYSE symbol)
M Phar	Master of Pharmacy
M Phar C	Master of Pharmaceutical Chemistry
M Pharm	Master of Pharmacy
M Ph C	Master of Pharmaceutical Chemistry
MPHE	Master of Public Health Engineering
MPH Ed	Master of Public Health Education
MPH Eng	Master of Public Health Engineering
MPHN	Master of Public Health Nursing
M Pho	Master of Photography
MPHPS	Miles Per Hour Per Second
M Ph S	Master of Physical Science
M Ph Sc	Master of Physical Science
MPHTM	Master of Public Health and Tropical Medicine
M Phy	Master of Physics
MPI	Magnetic Particle Inspection
MPI	Man Portable Illuminator
MPI	Mandsley Personality Inventory
MPI	Max Planck Institute
MPI	Mean Point of Impact (Air Force)
MPI	Message Pattern Indicator
MPI	Metal Powder Industries Federation
MPI	Military Procurement Instruction
MPI	Molded Plastic Insulation
MPI	Molecular Parameter Index
MPI	Morris Pratt Institute Association
MPI	Movimiento pro Independencia de Puerto Rico
MPI	Multiphasic Personality Inventory
MPIC	Message Processing Interrupt Count
MPIC	Motion Picture Industry Controllers
MPIC	Motion Picture Industry Council
MPIF	Metal Powder Industries Federation
MPJ	Mouvement Panafricain de la Jeunesse (Pan-African Youth Movement)
MPK	Microphone Probe Kit
MPL	Maintenance Parts Lists
MPL	Man Position Locator
MPL	Marine Physical Laboratory
MPL	Mars Probe Lander (Aerospace)
MPL	Master Parts List
MPL	Master of Patent Law
MPL	Master of Polite Literature
MPL	Metals Processing Laboratory (MIT)
MPL	Metering Pumps, Limited
MPL	Minnesota Power & Light Company (NYSE symbol)
MPL	Mistress of Polite Literature
MPL	Motion Picture Laboratories (Commercial firm)
MPL	Mouvement Politique Lulua (Lulua Political Movement)
MPL	Multiple Payload Launcher
MPLA	Movimento Popular de Libertacao de Angola (Popular Movement for the Liberation of Angola)
MPLE	Multi-Purpose Long Endurance (Aircraft)
MPM	Magnetic Phase Modulator
MPM	Main Propulsion Motor
MPM	Maintenance Planning Manual
MPM	Major Program Memorandum (Military)
MPM	Meters Per Minute
MPM	Microwave Power Meter
MPM	Miles Per Minute
MPM	Monocycle Position Modulation
MPM	Moving Presentation Mode
MPM	Multipurpose Meal
MPMA	Montford Point Marine Association
MP,MC	Military Personnel, Marine Corps (An appropriation)
MPMIC	Mechanical Properties of Materials Information Center
MPMIS	Military Police Management Information System
MP & MTD	Motion Picture & Medical Television Department (of AMA)
MPMUL	Military Production Master Urgency List
MPMV	Mason-Pfizer Monkey Virus

ACRONYMS AND INITIALISMS DICTIONARY

M-PMV......Mason-Pfizer Monkey Virus
MPN.......Master Part Number System
MPN.......Military Pay, Navy (Funding)
MPN.......Military Personnel, Navy (An appropriation)
MPN.......Mobile Pulse RADAR Navigational Aid
MPN.......Most Probable Number
MPNA......Midwest Professional Needlework Association
MPNC......Mouvement pour le Progres National Congolais (Movement for National Congolese Progress)
MPO.......Macedonian Patriotic Organization of US and Canada
MPO.......Managers, Proprietors, and Officials
MPO.......Maximum Power Output
MPO.......Metropolitan Police Office (British) (Familiarly called "Scotland Yard" from its site at New Scotland Yard)
MPO.......Military Pay Order
MPO.......Military Permit Office(r)
MPO.......Military Personnel Office
MPO.......Military Post Office
MPO.......Motion Picture Operator
MPOA......Medial Preoptic Area (Anatomy)
MPOI......Master Program of Instruction (Army)
MPOIS......Military Police Operating Information System
M Pol Sc....Master of Political Science
MPOS......Mobile Post Office Society
MPP.......Maintainability Program Plan
MPP.......Martens Polarization Photometer
MPP.......Master Program Plan
MPP.......Materiel Performance Package (Military)
MPP.......Member of Provincial Parliament (British)
MPP.......Most Probable Position (Navigation)
MPP.......Motion Picture Pioneers
MPP.......Multiple Particle Plasma
MPPA......Metal Powder Producers Association
MPPA......Music Publishers' Protective Association
MPPH......Motion Picture Phonographic Unit
MPPHA......Multiparameter Pulse Height Analyzer
MPPL......Multipunch Plate
MPPL......Multi-Purpose Programming Language
MPPM......Mission Prediction and Performance Module (Aerospace)
MPPWCOM...Military Police Prisoner of War Command
MPR.......Master Power Regulator
MPR.......Material Purchase Requisition
MPR.......Materials & Process Requirement (Navy)
MPR.......Mercury Plunger Relay
MPR.......Military Pay Record
MPR.......Military Personnel Record
MPR.......Mine Production Report
MPR.......Monthly Progress Report
MPR.......Monthly Project Report
MPR.......Music Power Rating
MPRC......Military Personnel Records Center
MPRC......Motion Picture Research Council
MPRE......Medium Power Reactor Experiment
MPRF......Motion Picture Relief Fund
M Pr Gph....Master in Professional Geophysics
MPRI......Merchant Pacific Routing Instructions (Shipping)
MPRJ......Military Personnel Records Jacket (Army)
M Pr M......Master of Preventive Medicine
M Prof Acc....Master of Professional Accountancy
MPRS......Madjelis Permusjawaratan Rakjat Sementara
MPS.......Magnetic Pole Strength
MPS.......Maintenance Problem Summary
MPS.......Management Policy Statement
MPS.......Manual Phase Shifter
MPS.......Marbled Paper Sides
MPS.......Maritime Postmark Society
MPS.......Master of Personnel Services
M Ps.......Master of Psychology
MPS.......Material Processing System
MPS.......Materiel Planning Study
MPS.......Mathematical Programming System (Data processing)
MPS.......Mechanical Phase Shifter
MPS.......Member of the Pharmaceutical Society (British)
MPS.......Member of the Philological Society (British)
MPS.......Member of the Physical Society (British)
MPS.......Merrill-Palmer School
MPS.......Meters Per Second
MPS.......Microphone Power Supply
MPS.......Microwave Phase Shifter
MPS.......Miles Per Second
MPS.......Military Production Specifications

MPS.......Minister of Public Security (British)
MPS.......Mission Parcels Society (British)
MPS.......Mission Preparation Sheet
MPS.......Mission Profile Simulator (NASA)
MPS.......Molecular Photoelectron Spectroscopy
MPS.......Motion Picture Service (Department of Agriculture)
MPS.......Mouvement Populaire Senegalais (Senegal Popular Movement)
MPS.......Mucopolysaccharide
MPS.......Multiprogramming System (Data processing)
MPSA......Master of Public School Art
MPSA......Military Petroleum Supply Agency (Later, Defense Petroleum Supply Center)
MPSC......Material Planning Schedule and Control (Division of Inspection Offices, Navy)
MPSC......Military Personnel Security Committee
MPSC......Military Provost Staff Corps (British)
MPSE......Motion Picture Sound Editors
MPSM......Master of Public School Music
MPSN......Microwave Pulse Shaping Network
MPSP......Military Personnel Security Program
MPSS......Multi-Purpose Sampling System
M Ps Sc....Master of Physic Sciences
M Ps Th....Master of Psycho-Therapy
MPSX......Mathematical Programming System Extended (Data processing)
MPT.......Maneuver Planning Table (NASA)
MPT.......Mean Pulse Time
MPT.......Mechanical Power Transmission
MPT.......Mercury Procedures Trainer
MPT.......Micro-Programming Technique
MPT.......Missile Preflight Tester
MPT.......Missile Procedure Trainer
MPT.......Mouvement Populaire Tchadien (Chadian Popular Movement)
MPT.......Mouvement Populaire Togolais (Togolese Popular Movement)
MPT.......Multiple Pure Tone (Sound)
MPTA......Mechanical Power Transmission Association
MPTCMA....Motion Picture and Television Credit Managers Association
MPTE......Multi-Purpose Test Equipment
MPTEDA....Mechanical Power Transmission Equipment Distributors Association (Later, Power Transmission Distributors Association)
MPTO......Methods and Procedures Technical Orders
MPTR......Mobile Position Tracking RADAR
MPTS......Metal Parts
MPTS......Mobile Photographic Tracking Station
MP(TSWG)...Military Police Tripartite Standing Working Group
MPU.......Main Propulsion Unit
MPU.......Miniature Portable Unit
MPU.......Motor Pressurization Unit
M Pub Adm...Master of Public Administration
MPUL......Military Production Urgencies List
MPUS......Military Production Urgencies System
MPV.......Magnetic Polarization Vector
MPV.......Military Pay Voucher
MPV.......Missouri Public Service Company (NYSE symbol)
MPVA......Maintain a Position VFR (Visual Flight Rules) and Advise (Aviation)
MPVO......Mestnaia Protivovozdushnaia Oborona (Local Anti-Air Defense) (USSR)
MPVSCS....Military Pay Voucher Summary and Certification Sheet
MPW.......Minneapolis-Moline Company (NYSE symbol)
MPWB......Multilayer Printed Wiring Board
MPWG......Minute-Man Parts Working Group (Missiles)
MPX.......Multiplex
MPX.......Multiprogramming Executive (Operating system)
MPY.......Maatschappij (Company) (Netherlands)
MPZ.......Mid-Continent Petroleum (NYSE symbol)
MPZ.......Modified Protamine Zinc (Insulin)
MQ.......Mack Trucks, Inc. (NYSE symbol) (Delisted)
MQ.......Marketing Quota
MQ.......Merit Quotient
MQ.......Multiplier Quotient Register (Data processing)
MQA.......Manufacturing Quality Assurance
MQC.......Marquette Cement Manufacturing Company (NYSE symbol)
MQF.......Mobile Quarantine Facility (NASA)
MQIL......Miniature Quartz Incandescent Lamp
MQL.......Miniature Quartz Lamp
MQN.......Magnetic Quantum Number
MQO.......Marksmanship Qualification Order (Marine Corps)
MQP.......Military Qualification Program
MQP.......Motor Qualification Program
MQT.......Military Qualification Test
MQT.......Motor Qualification Test
MQU.......Multiplier Quotient Unit
MR.......Machine Records
MR.......Machine Rifle

MR . . . . Machinery Repairman (Military)
MR . . . . Macrophage Rich
MR . . . . Manpower Requirements
MR . . . . Manufacturer's Representative
MR. . . . . . . Manufacturing Requisition
MR . . . . Map Reading
MR . . . . Map Reference
MR . . . . Marginal Return (Army)
MR. . . . . . . Marginal Revenue
MR. . . . . . . Marketing Research Division (of AMS, Department of Agriculture)
MR . . . . The Massachusetts Review
MR. . . . . . . Master of the Rolls (British)
MR. . . . . . . Material Request (or Requisition)
MR . . . . Mate's Receipt
MR . . . . Mathematical Review (A publication)
MR. . . . . . . McCloud River R. R. (AAR code)
MR. . . . . . . Medium Range
MR. . . . . . . Medium Range Planes (Navy)
MR . . . . Memorandum for Record
MR. . . . . . . Memorandum Report
MR . . . . Memory Register
MR . . . . Mercury-Redstone (NASA)
MR . . . . Message Repeat
MR . . . . Metabolic Rate
MR. . . . . . . Methyl Red (A dye)
MR . . . . Metropolitan Railway (London)
MR . . . . Mi Remesa (My Remittance) (Business and trade) (Spain)
MR . . . . Microminiature Relay
MR. . . . . . . The Middlesex Regiment (British)
MR . . . . Midland Railway (British)
MR . . . . Military Readiness
MR. . . . . . . Military Regulation
MR. . . . . . . Military Requirement
MR. . . . . . . Mill Run (Unselected lot of a manufactured product)
mr . . . . Milliroentgen
MR . . . . Mine-Run
MR . . . . Mineral Rubber
MR. . . . . . . Minister-Residentiary (Diplomacy)
MR. . . . . . . Ministry of Reconstruction (British) (World War I)
MR. . . . . . . Miscellaneous Report
MR. . . . . . . Mission Reliability
MR. . . . . . . Missionarius Rector (Missionary Rector)
MR. . . . . . . Mister
MR. . . . . . . Mobilization Regulation (Army)
MR . . . . Modification Requirement
MR. . . . . . . Modulation Response
MR . . . . Molasses Residuum
MR . . . . Monitor Recorder
MR. . . . . . . Monthly Report
MR. . . . . . . Monthly Review
MR . . . . Morning Report
MR. . . . . . . Motivation Research
MR. . . . . . . Municipal Reform(er)
MR. . . . . . . Mutual Responsibility (Movement within Anglican Communion to make its mission more efficacious)
M/R. . . . . . . Memorandum Receipt (Military)
M/R. . . . . . . Missiles & Rockets Magazine
M/R. . . . . . . Morning Report (Army)
M & R . . . . . Maintenance and Repairs
MRA . . . . . . Machine Records Activity
MRA . . . . . . Masonic Relief Association of USA and Canada
MRA. . . . . . . Maximum Rendezvous Altitude
MRA. . . . . . . Medium-Powered Radio Range (Adcock)
MRA . . . . . . Menswear Retailers of America
MRA . . . . . . Midwest Resources Association (Defunct)
MRA. . . . . . . Minimum Reception Altitude (Aviation)
MRA . . . . . . Model Reporting Area (for Blindness Statistics) (HEW)
MRA . . . . . . Moral Re-Armament (An organization)
MRA . . . . . . Mountain Rescue Association
MRA. . . . . . . Multiple Recording Accelerometer
MRAC . . . . . . Member of the Royal Agricultural College (British)
MRAC . . . . . . Meter-Reading Access Circuit (Bell Laboratories)
MRAD . . . . . Mass Random Access Disk
MRADS . . . . . Mass Random Access Data Storage (Data processing)
M Ra E . . . . . Master of Radio Engineering
M Ra Eng . . . . Master of Radio Engineering
MRAF . . . . . Marshal of the Royal Air Force (British)
MRAL . . . . . . Materiel Readiness Authorization List
MRAM . . . . . Member of the Royal Academy of Music (British)
MRAPCON . . . Mobile RADAR Approach Control
MRAS . . . . . . Manpower Resources Accounting System (Air Force)

MRAS . . . . . Member of the Royal Asiatic Society (British)
MRASB . . . . . Member of the Royal Asiatic Society of Bengal
MRASE . . . . . Member of the Royal Agricultural Society of England
MRB . . . . . . Magnetic Recording Borescope
MRB . . . . . . Magnetic Recording Boresight
MRB . . . . . . Material Review Board
MRB . . . . . . Mileage Rationing Board (World War II)
MRB . . . . . . Modification Review Board
MRB . . . . . . Motor Rescue Boat
MRB . . . . . . Mutual Reinsurance Bureau
MRBC . . . . . . Missouri River Basin Commission
MRBC . . . . . . Molded Rubber Blended Cover
MR-BD . . . . . Mercury-Redstone Booster Development (Spacecraft) (NASA)
MRBM . . . . . Medium-Range Ballistic Missile
MRBM. . . . . . Mid-Range Ballistic Missile
MRBP . . . . . . Missouri River Basin Project
MRC. . . . . . . Magnetic Rectifier Control
MRC . . . . . . Magnetic Research Corporation
MRC . . . . . . Maintenance Requirement Card
MRC . . . . . . Major Retail Center
MRC . . . . . . Marine Research Committee
MRC . . . . . . Marine Resources Council
MRC . . . . . . Market Research Council
MRC . . . . . . Marlin-Rockwell Corporation (NYSE symbol) (Delisted)
MRC . . . . . . Master of Rehabilitation Counseling
MRC. . . . . . . Material Redistribution Center
MRC . . . . . . Maximum Reverse Current
MRC . . . . . . Measurement Research Center (University of Iowa)
MRC. . . . . . . Medical Research Council (Formerly, Committee) (British)
MRC. . . . . . . Medical Reserve Corps
MRC. . . . . . . Metals Reserve Company
MRC . . . . . . Meteorological Research Committee (British)
MRC. . . . . . . Micro Research Corporation
MRC. . . . . . . Mississippi River Commission (Army)
MRC . . . . . . Monsanto Research Corporation
MRC. . . . . . . Moon's RADAR Coordinates
MRC. . . . . . . Morning Readiness Check
MRC . . . . . . Movement Report Center
MRCA . . . . . Multirole Combat Aircraft
MRCAS . . . . . Monetary Ration Credit Allowance System (Military)
MRCC . . . . . . Mercury Recovery Control Center
MRCC. . . . . . Molded Rubber Coupling Cushion
MRCC . . . . . Movement Report Control Center
MRCOG . . . . . Member of the Royal College of Obstetricians and Gynaecologists (British)
MRCP . . . . . Member of the Royal College of Physicians (British)
MRCP . . . . . Mobile RADAR Control Post
MRCPA . . . . . Mobilization Reserve Components Program of the Army
MRCS . . . . . . Maintenance Requirement Cards
MRCS . . . . . Member of the Royal College of Surgeons (British)
MRCS . . . . . Missile Range Calibration Satellite
MRCVS . . . . . Member of the Royal College of Veterinary Surgeons (British)
MRD . . . . . . Mandatory Retirement Date (Army)
MRD . . . . . . Master Requirements Directory (Military)
MRD . . . . . . Materiel Redistribution Division
MRD. . . . . . . Medical Research Division
MRD. . . . . . . Metal Rolling Door (Technical drawings)
MRD. . . . . . . Military Reference Data
MRD. . . . . . . Military Requirements Determination
MRD. . . . . . . Minimum Reacting Dose
MRD . . . . . . Mississippi River Division (Army Engineers)
MRD. . . . . . . Monostable Relay Driver
MRD . . . . . . Motor Receiving Dolly
MR & D . . . . . Material Redistribution & Disposal
MRDA. . . . . . Media Research Directors Association
MR & DA . . . . Material Redistribution and Disposal Administration
MRDC. . . . . . Medical Research & Development Committee (Army)
MRDC . . . . . Military Research and Development Center (US-Thailand)
MRDC. . . . . . Module RADAR Display Console
M & RDET . . . Maintenance and Repair Detachment
MRDF . . . . . . Malleable Research and Development Foundation
MRDF . . . . . Maritime Radio Direction Finding
MRDL . . . . . Mean Reciprocal Detection Latency
MRDS . . . . . Molded Rubber Duct System
MRDTI . . . . . Metal Roof Deck Technical Institute
M Re . . . . . . Master of Religion
MRE . . . . . . Master of Religious Education
MRE . . . . . . Mean Radial Error
MRE . . . . . . Microbiological Research Establishment (British)
MRE. . . . . . . Mid-Range Estimate
MR Ed . . . . . Master of Religious Education
M Re E . . . . . Master of Refrigeration Engineering

M Re Eng .... Master of Refrigeration Engineering
MRES ...... Material Requirements Estimation System (Navy)
M Ret .... Master of Retailing
MRF .... Maintenance Replacement Factor
MRF .... Meteorological Rocket Facility
MRF .... Midbrain Reticular Formation
MRF .... Multipath Reduction Factor (Electronics)
MRF .... Music Research Foundation
MRF .... Myopia Research Foundation
MRFU ...... Multiple Rocket Firing Unit
MRG ...... Magnetic Radiation Generator
MRG .... Master of Religious Guidance
MRG .... Material Review Group
MRG .... Medium Range
MRG....... Minorities Research Group (for helping homosexuals) (British)
MRH ...... Magnetic Recording Head
MRH .... Master of Russian History
MRH .... Mechanical Recording Head
MRH .... Mobile Remote Handler
mr/hr ...... Milliroentgens Per Hour
MRHS ...... Midwest Railway Historical Society
MRHV ..... Maintain Runway Heading for Vector (Aviation)
MRI .... Machine Records Installation (Military)
MRI .... Malt Research Institute
MRI .... Mass Retailing Institute (Formerly, Mass Merchandising Research Institute)
MRI .... Mean Rise Interval
MRI .... Medical Research Institute (Navy)
MRI .... Medium-Range Interceptor
MRI .... Mental Research Institute
MRI ...... Microwave Research Institute (Polytechnic Institute of Brooklyn)
MRI .... Midwest Research Institute
MRI ...... MILSTRIP (Military Standard Requisitioning and Issue Procedure) Routing Identifier
MRI ...... Miscellaneous RADAR Input
MRI ...... Monopulse Resolution Improvement
MRIA ...... Magnetic Recording Industry Association
MRIA ...... Member of the Royal Irish Academy
MRICC ..... Missile & Rockets Inventory Control Center (Army)
MRIF ...... MSH (Melanophore-Stimulating Hormone) Release Inhibiting Factor
MRIR ...... Medium-Resolution Infrared Radiometer (NASA)
MRIS ...... Maritime Research Information Service (Department of Transportation)
MRIS ...... Market Research Information System (Bell System)
MRIS ...... Material Readiness Index System (Military)
MRIS ...... Medical Research Information System (Veterans Administration)
MRIS ...... Mobile Range Instrumentation System
MRJ .... Microwave Rotary Joint
MRJ .... Miniature Revolving Joint
MRK....... Merck & Company, Inc. (NYSE symbol)
MRL .... Maintenance Requirements List
MRL ...... Manufacturing Reference Line
MRL....... Manufacturing Research Laboratory
MRL....... Marketing Research Library
MRL ...... Master Repair List (DOD)
MRL ...... Master Report List
MRL ...... Materiel Requirements List
MRL .... Medical Record Librarian
MRL ...... Medical Research Laboratory (Navy and Air Force)
MRL....... Medium-Powered Radio Range (Loop radiators)
MRL ...... Minerals Research Laboratory
MRL ...... Missionary Research Library
MRL ...... Movimento Revolucionario Liberal (Colombian political party)
MRL ...... Multiple Rocket Launcher
MRL....... Multiple Ruby LASER
MRLPC ..... Mouvement de Regroupement et de Liberation du Peuple Congolais (Movement for the Regroupment and Liberation of the Congolese People) (Leopoldville)
MRM ...... Mail Readership Measurement
MRM ...... Management Responsibility Matrix
MRM ...... Medical Repair Technician (Navy)
MRM ...... Medium-Range Missile
MRM ...... Metabolic Rate Monitor (Trademark)
MRM ...... Michelson Rotating Mirror
MRM ...... Miles of Relative Movement (Navigation)
MRML ..... Medium-Range Missile Launcher
MRMO ..... Mobilization Reserve Materiel Objective
MRMPO ..... Mobilization Reserve Materiel Procurement Objective
MRMR ..... Mobilization Reserve Materiel Requirement
MRMS ...... Monetary Ration Management System (Military)
MRMU ..... Mobile Radiological Measuring Unit
MRMU ..... Mobile Remote Manipulating Unit (Air Force)
MRN .... Maritime Radio Navigation

MRN .... Medium-Round Nose (Diamond drilling)
MRN .... Meteorological Rocket Network (NASA)
MRN .... Minimum Rejection Number
mRNA ...... Messenger Ribonucleic Acid
m-RNA ...... Messenger Ribonucleic Acid
MRNL ...... Medical Research and Nutrition Laboratory (Army)
MRO ...... Maintenance, Repair, and Operation
MRO ...... Management Review Officer
MRO ...... Manufacturing Rework Order
MRO ...... Marathon Oil Company (NYSE symbol)
MRO ...... Materiel Release Order
MRO ...... Mechanized RADAR Observer
MRO ...... Medical Regulating Office(r) (Army)
MRO ...... Message Releasing Officer
MRO ...... Mid-Range Objectives
MRO ...... Motor Route Order Number
MRO ...... Movement Report Office
MROL ...... Minimum Resolvable Object Length
MRP ...... Malfunction Reporting Program (Navy)
MRP ...... Manned Reusable Payload
MRP ...... Markov Renewal Program
MRP ...... Master of Regional Planning
MRP ...... Maximum Resolving Power
MRP ...... Mid-Range Plan (1969-70) (Military)
MRP ...... Military Rated Power
MRP ...... Missouri Portland Cement Company (NYSE symbol)
MRP ...... Monthly Report of Progress
MRP ...... Mouvement Republicain Populaire (Popular Republican Movement) (France)
MRP ...... Movimiento Republicano Progresista (Progressive Republican Movement) (Venezuela)
MRP ...... Multiplex Recording Photography
MRPA ...... Modified Random Phase Approximation
MRPARABAD .. Master Parachutist Badge
MRPC ...... Mercury Rankine Power Conversion (AEC)
MRPC ...... Mouvement de Regroupement des Populations Congolaises (Movement for the Regroupment of the Congolese People)
MRPF ...... Maintenance of Real Property Facilities
MRPL ...... Material Requirements Planning List
MRQ ...... Marquardt Corporation (NYSE symbol) (Wall Street slang name: "Mr. Q.") (Delisted)
MRR .... Maintenance, Repairs and Replacements (Military)
MRR .... Material Rejection Report
MRR .... Material Reliability Report
MRR .... Material Review Record (or Reports)
MRR .... Mechanical Reliability Report(s) (FAA)
MRR .... Mechanical Research Report
MRR .... Medical Research Reactor
MRR .... Medium-Range RADAR
MRR ...... Metal Removal Rate
MRR ...... Microelectronic Radio Receiver
MRR .... Miniature Reed Relay
MRR ...... Molecular Rotational Resonance
MRR ...... Monthly Review Report
MRRC ...... Materiel Requirements Review Committee
MRRC ...... Mechanical Reliability Research Center
MRRS ...... Magnetic Reed Rotary Switch
MRS .... Magnetic Reed Switch
MRS .... Magnetic Resonance Spectrum
MRS .... Malfunction Reporting System (Boeing)
MRS .... Management and Reporting System
MRS .... Manned Reconnaissance Satellite (Air Force)
MRS .... Manufacturers Railway Company (AAR code)
MRS .... Master Repair Schedule (Air Force)
MRS .... Materiel Repair System (Air Force)
MRS ...... Medical Receiving Station
MRS .... Memo Routing Slip
MRS .... Military Railway Service (Army)
MRS .... Mistress
MRS .... Mobilization Requirement Study
MRS .... Mobilization Reserve Stocks
MRS ...... Monorail System
MRS .... Morse Shoe, Inc. (NYSE symbol)
MRS .... Motor Rotation Stand
MRS .... Movement Report Sheet
MRS ...... Multipurpose Research System
MRSD ...... Maximum Rated Standard Deviation
MRSH ...... Member of the Royal Society of Health (British)
MRSI ...... Mobilization Requirements, Secondary Items
MRSO ...... Mobilization Reserve Stockage Objective
MRSPWC ..... Member of the Royal Society of Painters in Water-Colours (British)
MRSV ...... Maneuverable Recoverable Space Vehicle

MRSV . . . . Military Railway Service Veterans
MRT . . . . Maintainability Review Team (Navy)
MRT . . . . Medium-Range Typhon (Missile)
MRT . . . . Meridianal Ray Trace
MRT . . . . Mildew-Resistant Thread
MRT . . . . Military Rated Thrust
MRT . . . . . . Mobile RADAR Target
MRT . . . . Modified Rhyme Test
MRTA . . . . . . Marketing Research Trade Association
MRTC . . . . . . Mackay Radio and Telegraph Company
MRTE . . . . . . Master of Radio and Television Engineering
MRT Eng . . . . Master of Radio and Television Engineering
MRTP . . . . . . Military Reliable Tube Program
MRTS . . . . . . Master RADAR Tracking Station
MRU . . . . Machine Records Unit
MRU. . . . . . . Material Recovery Unit
MRU . . . . Message Retransmission Unit
MRU . . . . Microwave Relay Unit
MRU. . . . . . . Minimal Reproductive Units (Bacteriology)
MRU. . . . . . . Mobile Radio Unit (Air Force)
MRU . . . . . . Much Regret, I Am Unable
M Ru E . . . . . . Master of Rural Engineering
M Ru Eng . . . . Master of Rural Engineering
MRV . . . . Maneuverable Reentry Vehicle (Air Force)
MRV . . . . Minute Respiratory Volume
MRV . . . . Mixed Respiratory Vaccine
MRV . . . . Mouvement de Regroupement Voltaique (Upper Volta Regroupment Movement)
MRV . . . . Multiple Reentry Vehicles
MRVC . . . . . . Member of the Royal Veterinary College (British)
MRVLP . . . . . Maneuvering Reentry Vehicle for Low-Level Penetration
MRVP . . . . . . Methyl-Red, Voges-Proskauer (Medium) (Bacteriology)
MRW . . . . Morale, Recreation and Welfare (Military)
MRW . . . . . . Motor Wheel Corporation (NYSE symbol) (Delisted)
MRWC . . . . . Multiple Reading and Writing with Computing
MRX. . . . . . . Memorex Corp. (NYSE symbol)
MRY. . . . . . . Mallory (P. R.) & Company, Inc. (NYSE symbol)
MS. . . . . . . Machine Screw
MS. . . . . . . Machine Steel
MS. . . . . Machinery Survey (Shipping)
MS. . . . . Magnetic South
MS . . . . Magnetic Storage
MS. . . . . Magnetostriction
MS. . . . . . . Mail Steamer
MS . . . . Main Switch
MS . . . . Maintenance and Service
MS. . . . . Major Subject (Military)
MS . . . . Manuscript
MS . . . . Manuscript Society
MS. . . . . Margin of Safety (Engineering)
MS . . . . Mass Spectrometry
MS . . . . Master of Science
MS . . . . Master Sergeant
MS . . . . Master of Surgery
MS. . . . . Master Switch
MS. . . . . Material Specifications
MS. . . . . Maximum Stress
MS. . . . . McCrory Corporation (NYSE symbol)
MS . . . . Mean Square
MS. . . . . Measuring Set
MS. . . . . Measuring System
MS . . . . Medical Supplies (Military)
MS. . . . . Medical Survey (Navy)
MS . . . . Medium Shot
MS. . . . . Medium Steel
MS. . . . . Memoriae Sacrum (Sacred to the Memory of)
MS . . . . Memory System
MS . . . . Merchant Shipping
MS . . . . Mercury-Scout (Spacecraft) (NASA)
MS . . . . Metallurgical Society (of AIME)
MS . . . . Meteoritical Society
MS . . . . Metric System
MS. . . . . Middle South Utilities, Inc.
MS . . . . Mild Steel
MS . . . . Military Science
MS . . . . Military Service Act (British)
MS . . . . Military Standard
MS . . . . Military Survivors
ms . . . . Millisecond (Also, msec)
mS . . . . Millisiemens
MS . . . . Minesweeper (or Minesweeping)

MS . . . . Ministry of Shipping (British)
MS . . . . Ministry of Supply (Also MOS) (British)
MS . . . . Mint State
MS . . . . Misrair, SAE (Egyptian Airlines)
MS. . . . . Miss or Mrs. (Pronounced "Miz")
MS. . . . . Missile System
MS . . . . Mission Sisters of the Holy Ghost (Roman Catholic religious order)
MS. . . . . Missionaries of La Salette (France)
MS . . . . Missionary Society (British)
MS . . . . Mississippi
MS . . . . Mitral Stenosis (Medicine)
MS. . . . . Modal Sensation (Psychology)
MS . . . . Modal Sensitivity
MS. . . . . Model Station
MS. . . . . Modulation Sensitivity
MS . . . . Molar Solution (Chemistry)
MS. . . . . Month's Sight (Banking and commerce)
MS. . . . . Morphine Sulfate (Organic chemistry)
MS . . . . Motor Ship
MS. . . . . Motor Supports
MS . . . . Multiple Sclerosis (Medicine)
MS . . . . Muscle Strength
MS . . . . Office of Management Services (FAA)
M/S. . . . . . . Magnetostruction
M/S. . . . . . . Meters Per Second
M/S. . . . . . . Minesweeping
M & S . . . . . . Bureau of Medicine & Surgery (Navy)
M & S . . . . . . Maintenance and Supply
MSA . . . . Magazine Shippers Association
MSA . . . . Main Store Allocator
MSA . . . . Malaysia-Singapore Airlines
MSA. . . . . . . Management System Analysis
MSA . . . . Mariological Society of America
MSA. . . . . . . Marker Signal Attenuation
MSA . . . . Masonic Service Association of the United States
MSA. . . . . . . Massachusetts School of Art
MSA . . . . Master of Science in Agriculture
MSA . . . . Master of Science and Arts
MSA . . . . Master of Scientific Agriculture
MSA. . . . . . . Mechanical Signature Analysis
MSA. . . . . . . Medical Services Account
MSA. . . . . . . Medical Services Administration (HEW)
MSA . . . . Member of the Society of Apothecaries (British)
MSA . . . . Member of the Society of Arts (British)
MSA. . . . . . . Mesa Petroleum Co. (NYSE symbol)
MSA . . . . Metaphysical Society of America
MSA. . . . . . . Methanesulfonic Acid
MSA. . . . . . . Military Subsistence Agency (Merged with Defense Supply Agency)
MSA . . . . Milton Society of America
MSA . . . . Mine Safety Appliance
MSA . . . . Mineralogical Society of America
MSA. . . . . . . Minesweeper, Auxiliary (Navy symbol)
MSA. . . . . . . Minimum Safe Altitude (Aviation)
MSA . . . . Minimum Section Altitudes (Aviation)
MSA . . . . Missionary Sisters of the Assumption (Roman Catholic religious order)
MSA. . . . . . . Mouvement Socialiste Africain (African Socialist Movement) (Congo-- Brazzaville)
MSA. . . . . . . Museum Store Association
MSA . . . . Mutual Security Act
MSA . . . . Mutual Security Agency (Functions transferred to Foreign Operations Administration, 1953)
MSA . . . . Mycological Society of America
MSAC. . . . . . Moore School of Automatic Computers (University of Pennsylvania)
MSAC. . . . . . Mount Saint Agnes College (Maryland)
MSAC. . . . . . Murray State Agricultural College (Oklahoma)
MSAE . . . . . . Master of Science in Aeronautical Engineering
MS in AE. . . . . Master of Science in Aeronautical Engineering
MS in Aero E . . Master of Science in Aeronautical Engineering
MS (Ag) . . . . . Master of Science in Agriculture
MS in Ag . . . . Master of Science in Agriculture
MS (Ag E) . . . . Master of Science in Agricultural Engineering
MS in Ag E . . . Master of Science in Agricultural Education
MS in Ag Ec . . Master of Science in Agricultural Economics
MS Agr . . . . . Master of Science in Agriculture
MS in Agr . . . . Master of Science in Agriculture
MS in Agr Ed. . Master of Science in Agricultural Education
MSAM . . . . . . Master of Science in Applied Mechanics
MSAM . . . . . . Mobile Surface-to-Air Missile
MSAMP. . . . . . Master Ship Acquisition Milestone Plan
M San . . . . . . Master of Sanitation
MS in AN . . . . Master of Science in Agricultural Engineering

M San Sc	Master of Sanitary Science
MSAO	Medical Services Accountable Officer
MSAR	Mine Safety Appliances Research
MS Arch	Master of Science in Architecture
M Sa Sc	Master of Sacred Sciences
MSAT	Minnesota Scholastic Aptitude Test
MSATA	Motorcycle, Scooter and Allied Trades Association
MS in Aud & Sp ..	Master of Science in Audiology and Speech
MSB	Boat Minesweeper (Navy symbol)
MSB	Magnetic Susceptibility Bridge
MSB	Main Support Base (Air Force)
MSB	Maritime Subsidy Board (Maritime Administration) (Department of Commerce)
Ms B	Master of Bacteriology
MSB	Mesabi Trust (Units of Beneficial Interest) (NYSE symbol)
MSB	Minesweeping Boat
MSB	Montadale Sheep Breeders Association
MSB	Most Significant BIT (Data processing)
MSB	Motor Surfboat
MSB	Multnomah School of the Bible (Oregon)
MSBA	Master of Science in Business Administration
MS in BA	Master of Science in Business Administration
MSBC	Master of Science in Building Construction
MS in Bl Sc ...	Master of Science in Biological Sciences
MSBR	Military Strength Balance Report
MSBR	Molten-Salt Breeder Reactor (AEC)
MS Bus	Master of Science in Business
MSC	Madras Staff Corps (British)
MSC	Magnetic Surface Current
MSC	Magnetically Settable Counter
MSC	Maine Sardine Council
MSC	Mankato State College (Minnesota)
MSC	Manned Spacecraft
MSC	Manned Spacecraft Center, Houston, Texas (NASA)
MSC	Maple Syrup Council
MSC	Maritime Service Committee
MSC	Maryland State College
M Sc	Master of Science
MSC	Material Source Code
MSC	Medical Service Corps (Navy)
MSC	Medical Specialist Corps (Military)
MSC	Mediterranean Sub-Commission (Silva Mediterranea) (FAO)
MSC	Memory Storage Control
MSC	Message Switching Center (Data processing)
MSC	Metal Shielded Cabinet
MSC	Midwestern Simulation Council
MSC	Mile of Standard Cable
MSC	Military Sealift Command (Navy)
MSC	Milliwatts per Square Centimeter
MSC	Minesweeper, Coastal (Navy symbol)
MSC	Mirror Sign Convention
MSC	Mirror Streak Camera
MSC	Missionarii Sacratissimi Cordis (Missionaries of the Most Sacred Heart) (Roman Catholic men's religious order)
MSC	Missionarii Sancti Caroli (Missionaries of St. Charles) (Roman Catholic men's religious order)
MSC	Mississippi Central R. R. (AAR code)
MSC	Mississippi Southern College
MSC	Mississippi State College
MSC	Montana State College
MSC	Moorhead State College (Minnesota)
MSC	Morehead State College (Kentucky)
MSC	Morgan State College (Maryland)
MSC	Motor Speed Control
MSC	Motor Starting Contractor
MSC	Moved, Seconded, and Carried
MSC	Multiple Scan Correlator
MSC	Multiple Spindle Chucker
MSC	Multipotential Stem Cells (Hematology)
MSC	Multi-Service Center
MSC	Murray State College (Kentucky)
M & SC	Missile and Space Council (Defunct)
MS in C	Master of Science in Commerce
MSCA	Microwave Switch Control Assembly
MSCA	Missile Site Construction Agency (Army)
MSCA	Mixed Spectrum Critical Assembly
M Sc in Agr Eng ..	Master Science in Agricultural Engineering
M Sc in Agr Ex ..	Master of Science in Agricultural Extension
MSCB	Missile Site Control Building
MS in C & BA..	Master of Science in Commercial and Business Administration
MSCC	Manned Space-Flight Control Center (Air Force)
M Sc CE	Master of Science in Chromo-Electronic Science
M Sc D	Doctor of Medical Science
M Sc D	Doctor of the Science of Medicine
MSCE	Master of Science in Civil Engineering
MS in CE	Master of Science in Civil Engineering
M Sc Ed	Master of Science Education
MS in Cer	Master of Science in Ceramics
MS (Cer E) ...	Master of Science in Ceramic Engineering
MS in Cer E ..	Master of Science in Ceramic Engineering
MS in Cer Tech ..	Master of Science in Ceramic Technology
MSCH	Mode Switch Chassis
MS in Ch	Master of Science in Chemistry
MS (Ch E) ...	Master of Science in Chemical Engineering
MS in Ch E....	Master of Science in Chemical Engineering
MS in Ch Eng ..	Master of Science in Chemical Engineering
M Sch Mus ...	Master of School Music
MSCI	Mediterranean Secret Convoy Instructions (World War II)
M Sci Mil	Master of Military Science
M Sc L	Master of the Science of Law
M Sc M	Master of the Science of Medicine
M Sc in ME ...	Master of Science in Mechanical Engineering
M Sc Med	Master of Medical Science
MSCNY	Marine Society of the City of New York
M Sc O	Master of the Science of Oratory
MSC(O)	Minesweeper, Coastal (Old) (Navy symbol)
MS in Con	Master of Science in Conservation
MS Cons	Master of Science in Conservation
M Sc (Ost)	Master of Science in Osteopathy
MSCP	Master of Science in Community Planning
MSCP	Mean Spherical Candlepower
MS in CRP	Master of Science in City and Regional Planning
MSCS	Merchant Ship Control Service
MSCS	Miner Sentence Completion Scale (Vocational measurement)
M Sc Tech	Master of Technical Science
MSC(UN)	Military Staff Committee of the United Nations
MSCW	Mississippi State College for Women
MSD	Doctor of Medical Science
Ms D	Doctor of Metaphysics
MSD	Magnetic Storage Drum
MSD	Major Seismic Disturbance
MSD	Master of Science in Dentistry
MSD	Master of Scientific Didactics
MSD	Master Standard Data
MSD	Material Support Department
MSD	McNaney Spectroelectric Device
MSD	Mean Solar Day
MSD	Mean Square Deviation
MSD	Mean Square Difference
MSD	Merck, Sharp and Dohme (Commercial firm)
MSD	Metal Sensor Detection
MSD	Metering Suction Differential
MSD	Method of Steepest Descent
MSD	Military Sales Department
MSD	Minesweeper, Drone (Navy ship symbol)
MSD	Minimum Safe Distance
MSD	Missile Systems Division (Lockheed)
MSD	Motor Storage Dolly
MSD	Moving Scene Display
MSD	Multifrequency Signal Detector
MSD	Multi-Sensor Display
MSDC	Manual Slave Direction Center (RADAR site)
MS Dent	Master of Science in Dentistry
MS in Derm ..	Master of Science in Dermatology
MS Des	Master of Science in Design
MS Di	Master of Scientific Didactics
MSDI	Mayonnaise and Salad Dressings Institute
MSDL	Magneto-Strictive Delay Line
MSDM	Medium Speed Dynabit Memory
MSDO	Management Systems Development Office
MSDP	Missile Site Data Processor
MSDPS	Missile Site Data Processing System
MSDPSS	Missile Site Data Processing Subsystem
MSDS	Magnetic Storage Drum System
MS in Dt	Master of Science in Dietetics
MSE	Magnetic Strain Energy
MSE	Massachusetts Studies in English (A publication)
MSE	Massey-Ferguson Limited (NYSE symbol)
MSE	Master of Sanitary Engineering
MSE	Master of Science in Education
MSE	Master of Science in Engineering
MSE	Materiel Status Evaluation (Army)

MSE . . . . Mean Square Error (Statistics)
MSE . . . . Member of the Society of Engineers (British)
MSE . . . . Midwest Stock Exchange
MSE . . . . Milwaukee School of Engineering
MSE . . . . Missile Support Equipment
MSE . . . . Mission Support Equipment
MSE . . . . Mississippi Export R. R. (AAR code)
MS in E . . . . . Master of Science in Education
MS in E . . . . . Master of Science in Engineering
M Se A . . . . . . Master of Secretarial Arts
MSEA . . . . Medical Society Executives Association
msec. . . . . Millisecond
MS Ed . . . . . . Master of Sanitary Education
MS Ed . . . . . . Master of Science in Education
MSEE . . . . . . Master of Science in Electrical Engineering
MSEE . . . . . . Mean Square Error Efficiency (Statistics)
MS in EE . . . . Master of Science in Electrical Engineering
MSE (Elec) . . . Master of Science in Engineering - Electrical
MSEI . . . . Mean Square Error Inefficiency (Statistics)
MSEL . . . . . . Master of Science and English Literature
MS Elect E . . . Master of Science in Electrical Engineering
MSEM . . . . . Master of Science in Engineering Mechanics
MSEM. . . . . . . Mission Status and Evaluation Module
MS in EM . . . . Master of Science in Engineering Mechanics
MS in EM . . . . Master of Science in Engineering of Mines
MS in E Mgt . . . Master of Science in Engineering Management
MS Eng . . . . . Master of Sanitary Engineering
MS Eng . . . . . Master of Science in Engineering
MS Ent . . . . . . Master of Science in Entomology
MSEP . . . . . . Maintenance Standardization Evaluation Program (Air Force)
MSEP . . . . . . Mercury Scientific Experiment Panel
MS in EP . . . . Master of Science in Engineering Physics
MSEPS . . . . . . Modular Space Electrical Power Station
MSER . . . . . . Management System Evaluation Review
MS in ES . . . . Master of Science in Engineering Science(s)
M Se Sc . . . . . Master of Secretarial Science
M Se St . . . . . Master of Secretarial Studies
MSEUE . . . . . Mouvement Socialiste pour les Etats Unis d'Europe
MSF . . . . Congregatio Missionariorum a Sancta Familia (Congregation of the
　　　　　　　　Missionaries of the Holy Family) (Roman Catholic men's religious order)
MSF . . . . Master of the Science of Forestry
MSF . . . . Minesweeper, Fleet (Navy symbol)
MSF . . . . Mobile Striking Force (Military)
MSF . . . . Mobility Support Forces (Military)
MSF . . . . Month-Second-Foot (or Feet) (Measurement)
MSF . . . . Moroccan Sea Frontier (Navy)
MSF . . . . Mott Scattering Formula
MSF . . . . Multiaxial Stress Field
MSF . . . . Multistage Flash (Desalination method)
MSF . . . . Muscle Shock Factor
MSFC . . . . . . Marshall Space Flight Center (Also known as GCMSC)
MSFC . . . . Mutual Society of the French Community
MSFH . . . . . . Manned Space Flight Headquarters
MSFM . . . . . . Master of Science in Forest Management
MSFN . . . . . . Manned Space Flight Network
MS For . . . . . Master of Science in Forestry
MS in For . . . . Master of Science in Forestry
MSFX . . . . . . Master Fixture
MSG . . . . Madison Square Garden Corporation (NYSE symbol)
MSG . . . . Manufacturers Standard Gage
MSG . . . . Mapper Sweep Generator
MSG . . . . Master Sergeant (Army)
MSG . . . . Message
MSG. . . . . Microwave Signal Generator
MSG . . . . Miscellaneous Simulation Generator
MSG . . . . Monosodium Glutamate
MSGA. . . . . . . Master Gage
MSGCEN . . . . Message Center
MS in GE . . . . Master of Science in General Engineering
MSGM . . . . . . Master of Science in Government Management
MSG Mgt . . . . Master of Science in Game Management
MSGO . . . . . . Mediterranean Secret General Orders
MSGP . . . . . . Mobile Support Group (Military)
MS in Gp Engr . Master of Science in Geophysical Engineering
MSGR. . . . . . . Messenger
MSGR. . . . . . . Mobile Support Group
MSGR. . . . . . . Monseigneur
MSGR. . . . . . . Monsignor
MS in GSM . . . Master of Science in General Science and Mathematics
MSGT. . . . . . . Master Sergeant
MSH. . . . . Manhattan Shirt Company (NYSE symbol) (Later, MHT)

MSH . . . . Master of Staghounds
MSH. . . . . Mauler Seeker Head
MSH. . . . . Medical Self-Help
MSH . . . . Melanocyte-Stimulating Hormone (Endocrinology)
MSH . . . . Melanophore-Stimulating Hormone (Endocrinology)
MSHA . . . . . . Master of Science in Hospital Administration
MSHAA . . . . . Morocco Spotted Horse Association of America
MSHB . . . . . . Minimum Safe Height of Burst (Military)
MSHE . . . . . . Master of Science in Home Economics
MS in HE. . . . . Master of Science in Home Economics
MSH Ec . . . . . Master of Science in Home Economics
MS in H Ec. . . . Master of Science in Home Economics
MS Hort . . . . . Master of Science in Horticulture
MSH & Ph Ed . . Master of Science in Health and Physical Education
MS in HR . . . . Master of Science in Human Relations
MS Hyg . . . . . Master of Science in Hygiene
MSI . . . . Inshore Minesweeper (Navy symbol)
MSI . . . . Maintenance Support Index
MSI . . . . Manned Satellite Inspector
MSI . . . . Marketing Science Institute
MSI . . . . Maximum Speed Indicator
MSI . . . . Maxwell Scientific International (Inc.)
MSI . . . . Mean Spleen Index
MSI . . . . Medium-Scale Integration (Circuit packaging)
MSI . . . . Military Static Inverter
MSI . . . . Minesweeper, Inshore (Navy symbol)
MSI . . . . Moderate Scale Integration (Electronics)
MSI . . . . Movimento Sociale Italiano
MSI . . . . Multiple Spark Igniter
MSI . . . . Multi-Sensor Imagery
MSID . . . . . . Mass Spectrometric Isotope Dilution
MS in ID . . . . Master of Science in Industrial Design
MSIE . . . . . . Master of Science in Industrial Engineering
MS in IE . . . . Master of Science in Industrial Engineering
MS in IM . . . . Master of Science in Industrial Management
MS Ind E . . . . Master of Science in Industrial Engineering
MS in Ind Ed . . Master of Science in Industrial Education
MSIR . . . . . . Master of Social and Industrial Relations
MSIS . . . . . . Manned Satellite Inspection System
MSIS . . . . . . Mask Shop Information System (Bell Laboratories)
MSISL . . . . . . Moore School Information Systems Laboratory
MSJ . . . . Machine Screw Jack
MSJ . . . . Master of Science in Journalism
MSJ . . . . Multiple Subsonic Jet
MSK . . . . Magyar Statisztikai Kozlemenyek (Hungary)
MSK . . . . Medvedev, Sponheuer, Karnick (Earthquake intensity scale)
MSK. . . . . Mission Support Kit
MSK . . . . Mobility Support Kit
MSL . . . . Magnetic Surfaces Laboratory
MSL . . . . Maintenance Supply Liaison (Air Force)
MSL. . . . . Management Selection, Limited
MSL. . . . . Master of Sacred Literature
MSL. . . . . Master Scheduling Letter
MSL. . . . . Master of Science in Language
MSL. . . . . Master of Science in Linguistics
MSL. . . . . Mean Sea Level
MSL . . . . Meteorological Satellite Laboratory
MSL . . . . Midsternal Line
MSL. . . . . Minesweeping Launch (Navy ship symbol)
MSL. . . . . Missile
MSL. . . . . MSL Industries, Inc. (Formerly, Minneapolis & St. Louis Railway Co.)
　　　　　　　　(NYSE symbol)
MSLA . . . . . . Mouse Specific Lymphocyte Antigens
MSLC . . . . . . Missile Sites Labor Commission (A federal government body)
MSLCOMD . . . Missile Command
MSLO . . . . . . Master Layout
MSLR . . . . . . Manchester, Sheffield, and Lincolnshire Railway (British)
MS (LS) . . . . . Master of Science in Library Science
MS in LS . . . . Master of Science in Library Science
MSM . . . . Manhattan School of Music
MSM . . . . Manufacturing Standards Manual
MSM . . . . Mars Surface Module
MSM . . . . Master of Medical Science
MSM . . . . Master of Sacred Music
MSM . . . . Master Scheduling Manager
MSM . . . . Master of Science in Music
MSM . . . . Master Slave Manipulator
MSM . . . . Meritorious Service Medal (Army)
MSM . . . . Millimeter and Submillimeter Conference
MSM . . . . Minesweeper, River (Navy ship symbol)
MSM . . . . Mission Simulation Model

MSM . . . . Missouri School of Mines
MSM . . . . Montana School of Mines
MSM . . . . Motorized Switching Matrix
MSM . . . . Mouvement Social Mohutu (Mohutu Social Movement)
MSM . . . . Mouvement Solidaire Muluba (Muluba Solidarity Movement)
MSM . . . . Thousand Feet Surface Measure (Lumber)
MSMA . . . . . . Major Symphony Managers Association
MSMA . . . . . . Medical-Surgical Manufacturers Association
MSMA . . . . . . Metropolitan Symphony Managers Association
MSMC . . . . . . Master Schedule and Milestone Chart
MSMDA . . . . . Mutual Sewing Machine Dealers Association
MSME . . . . . . Master of Science in Mechanical Engineering
MS in ME . . . . Master of Science in Mechanical Engineering
MS in Mech . . . Master of Science in Engineering Mechanics
MS Mech E . . . Master of Science in Mechanical Engineering
MS in Med . . . . Master of Science in Medicine
MS in Met . . . . Master of Science in Metallurgy
MS Met E . . . Master of Science in Metallurgical Engineering
MS in Met E . . . Master of Science in Metallurgical Engineering
MSMG . . . . . Missionary Sisters of the Mother of God (Roman Catholic religious order)
MS Mgt E . . . Master of Science in Management Engineering
MSMR . . . . . . Missouri School of Mines Reactor
MSMS . . . . . . Meteorological Systems Management Section
MSMS . . . . . . Mutual Security Military Sales
MSMTH . . . . . Metalsmith (Navy)
MS in Mus . . . Master of Science in Music
MS in Mus Ed . . Master of Science in Music Education
MSMV . . . . . . Monostable Multi-Vibrator
MSN . . . . Manned Space Network
MSN . . . . Master of Science in Nursing
MSN . . . . Military Serial Number
MSN . . . . Mission
MS in N . . . . . Master of Science in Nursing
MSNA . . . . . . Mission Accomplished (Military)
MS in NE . . . . Master of Science in Nursing Education
MS in N Ed . . . Master of Science in Nursing Education
MS in Nr Ed . . Master of Science in Nursing Education
MS in NT . . . . Master of Science in Nuclear Technology
MS in Nucl E . . Master of Science in Nuclear Engineering
MSO . . . . Maintenance Standard Order
MSO . . . . Maintenance Support Office (Navy)
MSO . . . . Management Science Office
MSO . . . . Mars Surface Operation
MSO . . . . Master of the Science of Oratory
M So . . . . Master of Sociology
MSO . . . . Material Sales Order
MSO . . . . Military Service Obligation
MSO . . . . Military Supply Officer
MSO . . . . Minesweeper, Ocean
MSO . . . . Missile Safety Officer
MSO . . . . Mobile Switching Office (Bell System)
MSO . . . . Ocean Minesweeper (Nonmagnetic)
MSOC . . . . . . Marine Systems Operational Compiler
MSOCC . . . . . Multisatellite Operations Control Center (NASA)
MSOD . . . . . . Military Service Obligation Date
MSOE . . . . . . Multiband Spectral Observation Equipment
MSOP . . . . . . Measurement System Operating Procedure
MS Orn Hort . . Master of Science in Ornamental Horticulture
M So Sc . . . . . Master of Social Science
M So Se . . . . . Master of Social Service
M So W . . . . . Master of Social Work
MSP . . . . Magnetic Scalar Potential
MSP . . . . Maintenance Support Plan (Army)
MSP . . . . Maritime Shore Patrol
MSP . . . . Master of Science in Pharmacy
M Sp . . . . Master of Speech
MSP . . . . Maximum Sound Pressure
MSP . . . . Minimum Sustaining Power
MSP . . . . Minneapolis (Minnesota) (Airport symbol)
MSP . . . . Miscellaneous Small Parts
MSP . . . . Modular System Programs
MSP . . . . Mutual Security Program
MSPA . . . . . . Maine Sardine Packers Association
MS in PA . . . . Master of Science in Public Administration
MSPB . . . . . . Medical Specialist Preference Blank
MSPC . . . . . . Medical Specialist Corps
MSPE . . . . . . Master of Science in Physical Education
MS in PE . . . . Master of Science in Petroleum Engineering
MS in PE . . . . Master of Science in Physical Education
MS in P Ed . . . Master of Science in Physical Education
MS in Pet E . . . Master of Science in Petroleum Engineering

MSPH . . . . . . Master of Science in Poultry Husbandry
MSPH . . . . . . Master of Science in Public Health
MS in PH . . . . Master of Science in Public Health
MS in Phar . . . Master of Science in Pharmacy
MSPHE . . . . . . Master of Science in Public Health Engineering
MSPH Ed . . . . . Master of Science in Public Health Education
MS in Phy . . . . Master of Science in Physics
MSPL . . . . . . Master Plate
MSPO . . . . . . Military Support Planning Officer (Civil Defense)
MSPR . . . . . . Master Spares Positioning Resolver (Data processing)
MSPR . . . . . . Model State Packaging Regulation (National Bureau of Standards)
MS in PRE . . . . Master of Science in Petroleum Refining Engineering
MSpS . . . . . . Missionaries of the Holy Ghost (Roman Catholic men's religious order)
MSPS . . . . . . Modular Space Power Station
MS in PSM . . . . Master of Science in Public School Music
MS in Py Sc . . . Master of Science in Poultry Science
MSR . . . . Magnetic Shift Register
MSR . . . . Magnetic Storage Ring
MSR . . . . Main Supply Road (or Route)
MSR . . . . Material Status Report (AEC)
MSR . . . . McDonnell Simulator Recorder (McDonnell Douglas Corporation)
MSR . . . . Mean Spring Rise
MSR . . . . Mechanized Storage and Retrieval (Data processing)
MSR . . . . Merchant Ship Reactor
MSR . . . . Metal Seal Ring
MSR . . . . Metalsmith, Ship Repair (Navy)
MSR . . . . Meteorological Sounding Rocket
MSR . . . . Mineral-Surface Roof (Technical drawings)
MSR . . . . Minesweeper, Patrol (Navy ship symbol)
MSR . . . . Missile Site RADAR (Army)
MSR . . . . Molten-Salt Reactor (AEC)
MSR . . . . Monthly Status Report (Navy)
MSR . . . . Multijunction Semiconductor Rectifier
MSR . . . . Multispeed Repeater
MS (R) . . . . . . Master of Science in Research
MSRA . . . . . . Middle States Regatta Association
MS in Rad . . . . Master of Science in Radiology
MSRB . . . . . . Margaret Sanger Research Bureau
MSRB . . . . . . Metalsmith, Ship Repair, Blacksmith (Navy)
MSRC . . . . . . Medical and Surgical Relief Committee
MSRC . . . . . . Metalsmith, Ship Repair, Coppersmith (Navy)
MSRE . . . . . . Molten-Salt Reactor Experiment (AEC)
MSRE . . . . . . Moon Signal Rejection Equipment
MS in Rec . . . . Master of Science in Recreation
MS in Ret . . . . Master of Science in Retailing
MSRF . . . . . . Metalsmith, Ship Repair, Forger-Anglesmith (Navy)
MSRG . . . . . . Modular Shift Register Generator
MSRL . . . . . . Mobile Secondary Reference Laboratory
MSRP . . . . . . Missile, Space and Range Pioneers, Inc.
MSRPP . . . . . . Multidimensional Scale for Rating Psychiatric Patients
MSRS . . . . . . Metalsmith, Ship Repair, Sheet Metal Worker (Navy)
MSRS . . . . . . Missile Strike Reporting System
MSS . . . . Maintenance Support Schedule (Air Force)
MSS . . . . Make Suitable Substitution
MSS . . . . Manufacturers Standardization Society (Valves and fittings)
MSS . . . . Manuscripts
MSS . . . . Maritime Support Service
MSS . . . . Mass Storage System
MSS . . . . Master of Sanitary Science
MSS . . . . Master of Social Service
MSS . . . . Master of Social Studies
MSS . . . . Master Surveillance Station (Air Force)
MSS . . . . Mastergroup Surveillance System (AT & T)
MSS . . . . Medical Service School (Air Force)
MSS . . . . Metal Spring Seal
MSS . . . . Meteorological Satellite Section
MSS . . . . Methylprednisolone Sodium Succinate (Steroid)
MSS . . . . Microwave Switching Station
MSS . . . . Military Supply Standards (DOD)
MSS . . . . Missile Stabilization System
MSS . . . . Missile Station Select
MSS . . . . Mission Corporation (NYSE symbol) (Delisted)
MSS . . . . Mission Support Site (Army)
MSS . . . . Mixed Spectrum Superheater
MSS . . . . Modular Space Station
MSS . . . . Moored Sonobuoy System (Navy)
MSS . . . . Multibeam Steering System
MSS . . . . Multi-Spectral Scanner (or Sensor)
MSS . . . . Special Minesweeper (Navy symbol)
MSSA . . . . . . Military Subsistence Supply Agency (Later, Defense Subsistence Supply Center)

MSSA . . . . . . Missionary Servants of St. Anthony (Roman Catholic women's religious order)
MS Sc . . . . . . Master of Sanitary Science
MS Sc . . . . . . Master of Social Science
MSSC . . . . . . Military Standard and Specification Committee
MSSCC . . . . . . Multicolor Spin-Scan Color Camera (NASA)
MSSCE . . . . . Mixed Spectrum Superheater Critical Experiment
MSSCS . . . . . . Manned Space Station Communications System
MSSE . . . . . . Master of Science in Sanitary Engineering
MSSE . . . . . . Missile System Support Equipment
MSS & H . . . . . Master of Science in Speech and Hearing
MSSJ . . . . . . Missionary Servants of St. Joseph (Roman Catholic women's religious order)
MSSJ . . . . . . Multiple Subsonic Jet
MSSP . . . . International Association of Marble, Slate and Stone Polishers, Rubbers and Sawyers, Tile and Marble Setters' Helpers and Marble Mosaic and Terrazzo Workers' Helpers
MS in Sp . . . Master of Science in Speech
MSSR . . . . . . Mars Soil (or Surface) Sample Return
MSSR . . . . . . Mixed Spectrum Superheat Reactor
MSSS . . . . . . Manned Static Space Simulator
MSSS . . . . . . Master of Science in Social Science
MS in SS . . . . Master of Science in Sanitary Science
MS in SS . . . . Master of Science in Social Service
MSST . . . . . . Master of Science in Science Teaching
MSST . . . . . . Meldesammelstelle (Message center) (German military – World War II)
MSSVFI . . . . . Manufacturers Standardization Society of the Valve and Fittings Industry
MSSW . . . . . . Master of Science in Social Work
MS in SW . . . . Master of Science in Social Work
MST . . . . Association of Maximum Service Telecasters
MST . . . . Machine Shock Test
MST . . . . Magnetostrictive Transducer
MST . . . . Mass Spectrometer Tube
MST . . . . Master of Sacred Theology
MST . . . . Master of Science in Teaching
M St . . . . . . Master of Statistics
MST . . . . . . Master of Teaching
MST . . . . Maximum Service Telecasters
MST . . . . Mean (or Median) Solar Time
MST . . . . Mean (or Median) Survival Time (Bacteriology)
MST . . . . Memotron Storage Tube
MST . . . . Mercantile Stores Company, Inc. (NYSE symbol)
MST . . . . Mercury System Test (NASA)
MST . . . . Microsecond Trip
MST . . . . Military Science Training
MST . . . . Missile System Test
MST . . . . Mobile Service Tower (Aerospace)
MST . . . . Mobile Strike Team
MST . . . . Monolithic Systems Technology
MST . . . . Mountain Standard Time
MST . . . . Multimode Storage Tube
MST . . . . Multi-System Test
MS (T) . . . . . . Master of Science in Teaching
MSTA . . . . . Manufacturers Surgical Trade Association
MSTC . . . . . . Maryland State Teachers College
MSTC . . . . . . Massachusetts State Teachers College
MSTD . . . . . . Master Steward (Marine Corps)
M St E . . . . . . Master of Structural Engineering
MS (T Ed) . . . . . Master of Science in Teacher Education
M St Eng . . . . Master of Structural Engineering
M-STEP . . . . . Multi-State Teacher Education Project
MSTG . . . . Material Safety Task Group (Air Force)
MS in T & I . . . Master of Science in Trade and Industrial Education
MSTL . . . . . . Minneapolis & St. Louis Railway Company (AAR code)
MSTP . . . . . . Master Template
MSTPHC . . . . Multistop Time-to-Pulse Height Converter (NASA)
MSTP & SSM . . Minneapolis, St. Paul & Sault Ste. Marie Railway Company
MSTR . . . . . . Massena Terminal R. R. (AAR code)
MS in Trans E . . Master of Science in Transportation Engineering
MSTS . . . . . . Military Sea Transportation Service (Navy)
MSTS . . . . . . Missile Static Test Site (Air Force)
MSTS . . . . . Multi-Subscriber Time-Shared (Computer system)
MSTSO . . . . . Military Sea Transportation Service Office
MSTV . . . . . . Manned Supersonic Test Vehicle
MSU . . . . Material Salvage Unit
MSU . . . . . . Medical Service Unit (Air Force)
MSU . . . . . . Memphis State University
MSU . . . . . . Message Switching Unit
MSU . . . . . . Michigan State University
MSU . . . . Middle South Utilities, Inc. (NYSE symbol)
MSU . . . . Mid-Stream Urine Specimen

MSU . . . . Montana State University
MSUC . . . . . . Middle South Utilities Company
M Sur . . . . . . Master of Surgery
MSUS . . . . . . Mouvement Socialiste d'Union Senegalaise (Senegalese Socialist Movement)
MSV . . . . . . Magnetically Supported Vehicle
MSV . . . . . . Martian Surface Vehicle
MSV . . . . . . Mean Square Velocity
MSV . . . . . . Miniature Solenoid Valve
MSV . . . . Mississippi & Skuna Valley R. R. (AAR code)
MSV . . . . . . Molecular Solution Volume
MSV . . . . . . Murine Sarcoma Virus (Medicine)
MSVC . . . . . . Mount St. Vincent College (New York)
MSVD . . . . . . Missile and Space Vehicle Department
MSV(M) . . . . . Murine Sarcoma Virus (Moloney)
MSW . . . . . . Master of Social Welfare
MSW . . . . . . Master of Social Work
MSWD . . . . . Multi-System Weapon Delivery (Air Force)
MSX . . . . . . Multinucleate Nature, Spherical Shape, Unknown History
MSX . . . . . . Seaboard Oil Company (Delaware) (NYSE symbol)
M Sy Th . . . . Master of Systematic Theology
MT . . . . Empty (Slang)
MT . . . . Machine Tool
MT . . . . Machine Translation (Data processing)
MT . . . . Magnetic Tape
MT . . . . Magnetic Tube
MT . . . . Mail Transfer
MT . . . . Maintenance Trailer
MT . . . . Mandated Territory
MT . . . . Mantle Tentacle
MT . . . . Manual Test
MT . . . . Masoretic Text (Hebrew tradition)
MT . . . . Master of Teaching
MT . . . . Master Timer
MT . . . . Maximum Torque
MT . . . . Mean Tide
MT . . . . Mean Time
MT . . . . Mechanical Time
MT . . . . Mechanical Translation (Data processing)
MT . . . . Mechanical Transport
MT . . . . Medical Technologist
MT . . . . Megaton
MT . . . . Methyltryptophan (Biochemistry)
MT . . . . Methyltyrosine (Biochemistry)
MT . . . . Metric Ton (1,000 kilograms)
MT . . . . Microptic Theodolite
MT . . . . Military Training
MT . . . . Military Transport
mT . . . . Millitesla
MT . . . . Ministry of Transport (British)
MT . . . . Missile Technician (Navy rating)
MT . . . . Missile Test
MT . . . . Mode Transducer
MT . . . . Montana
MT . . . . More Than
MT . . . . Mortgage Trust of America (NYSE symbol)
MT . . . . Motor Tanker
MT . . . . Motor Transport
MT . . . . Mountain
MT . . . . Mountain Time
MT . . . . Multiple Transfer
M/T . . . . Measurement Tons
MTA . . . . . . MAC (Military Airlift Command) Transportation Authorization
MTA . . . . . . Maintenance Task Analysis
MTA . . . . . . Major Training Area (Army)
MTA . . . . . . Mass Thermal Analysis
MTA . . . . . . Medical and Technical Assistant
MTA . . . . . . Metropolitan Transit Authority (Initialism also title of folk song about Boston's transit system)
MTA . . . . . . Metropolitan Transportation Authority (Greater New York City)
MTA . . . . . . Military Testing Association
MTA . . . . . . Minimum Terrain-Clearance Altitude
MTA . . . . . . Missile Tube Air
MTA . . . . . . Mobility Test Article (Lunar-surface rover) (NASA)
MTA . . . . . . Monopulse Tracking Antenna
MTA . . . . . . Musical Theatres Association
MTAC . . . . . Mathematical Tables and Other Aids to Computation
MTACCS . . . . Marine Tactical Command and Control System
MTAF . . . . . . Mediterranean Tactical Air Force Headquarters
MTAI . . . . . . Meal Tickets Authorized and Issued (Army)
MTAI . . . . . . Minnesota Teacher Attitude Inventory

MT(ASCP) .... Registered Medical Technologist (American Society of Clinical
Pathologists)
MTB .... Main Terminal Board
MTB .... Maintenance Time Budget
MTB........ Maintenance of True Bearing
MTB .... Malayan Tin Bureau
MTB .... Marine Test Boat
MTB........ Medium Tank Battalion
MTB........ Message to Base
MTB........ Michigan Seamless Tube Co. (NYSE symbol)
MTB........ Motor Torpedo Boat
MTB .... Multichannel Triple Bridge
MTB .... Seaplane Bomber (Russian symbol)
MTBA ...... Machine Tool Builders' Association
MTBD ...... Mean Time Between Discrepancies
MTBE ...... Mean Time Between Events
MTBF ...... Mean Time Between Failures
MTBFF ..... Mean Time Between First Failure
MTBFL ..... Mean Time Between Function Loss
MTBM ...... Mean Time Between Maintenance
MTBMA ..... Mean Time Between Maintenance Action
MTBR ...... Mean Time Between Removal (or Repair, or Replacement)
MTBRON..... Motor Torpedo Boat Squadron
MTBSF ..... Mean Time Between System Failure
MTBSTC .... Motor Torpedo Boat Squadrons Training Center (Melville, Rhode Island)
MTC .... Maintenance Task Cycle
MTC .... Master Tape Control
MTC .... Master of Textile Chemistry
MTC........ Material Testing Center
MTC........ Materiel Testing Command (Army) (Merged with Weapons and Mobility
Command)
MTC........ Maximum Track Capacity
MTC........ Mechanical Transport Corps
MTC........ Medical Test Cabinet
MTC........ Medical Training Center
MTC .... Memory Test Computer (SAGE)
MTC........ Meteorological Training Center
MTC .... Military Training Cadets (A boys' World War II organization)
MTC .... Missile Test Center
MTC .... Missile Transfer Car
MTC........ Missile Tube Control
MTC .... Mission and Traffic Control
MTC........ Mitsui Toatsu Chemicals, Inc. (Japan)
MTC .... Mobile Target Carrier
MTC ...... Monsanto Company (NYSE symbol)
MTC ...... Morse Telegraph Club
MTC ...... Motor Transport Corps
MTC........ Mouvement Traditionaliste Congolais (Congolese Traditionalist Movement)
MTC........ Multiple Tube Counts
MTC........ Mystic Terminal R. R. (AAR code)
MTCA...... Military Terminal Control Area
MTCA ...... Minimum Terrain Clearance Altitude (Aviation)
MTCA ..... Ministry of Transport and Civil Aviation
MTCA...... Multiple-Terminal Communication Adapter (Data processing)
MTCC ..... Master Timing and Control Circuit
MTCC....... Military Air Transport Service (later, Military Airlift Command) Transport
Control Center
MTCF ..... Mean Time to Catastrophic Failure
MTCF...... Missile Tube Comparator Fixture
MT Ch ..... Master of Textile Chemistry
MTCS ..... Meteor Trail Communications System
MTCU ..... Magnetic Tape Control Unit
MTD ...... Manufacturing Technology Division (Air Force)
MTD ...... Maritime Trades Department (AFL-CIO)
MTD........ Master Tape Data
MTD ...... Master of Textile Dyeing
MTD........ Master Time Display
MTD ...... Material Test Directorate (Army)
MTD ...... Mean Temperature Difference
MTD........ Metacarpal Total Density
MTD ...... Metal Trades Department (AFL-CIO)
MTD........ Mobile Target Division (Mine Force)
MTD ...... Multiple Target Detection
MTDA...... Modification Table of Distribution and Allowances (Army)
MT Des ..... Master of Textile Design
MTDL...... Multiple Tap Delay Line
MTDS...... Marine Corps Tactical Data System
MTDS...... Marine Toebreak Data System
MTE ...... Master of Textile Engineering
MTE .... Maximum Temperature Engine
MTE .... Maximum Tracking Error

MTE .... Microwave Test Equipment
MTE .... Multipurpose Test Equipment
MTE .... Multisystem Test Equipment (Military)
MT Eng ..... Master of Textile Engineering
MTF .... Machine Tool Forum
MTF .... Mean Time to Failure
MTF ...... Mechanical Time Fuze
MTF ...... Men's Tie Foundation
MTF .... Mississippi Test Facility (NASA)
MTF .... Modulation Transfer Function
MTFA ...... Modulation Transfer Function Analyzer
MTFA ...... Modulation Transfer Function Area
MTFCI ..... Model T Ford Club International
MTFD ...... Minimum Tracking Flux Density
MTFR ...... Minnesota Transfer Railway (AAR code)
MTG ...... Main Turbogenerator
MTG ...... Meeting
MTG ...... Mortage (NYSE symbol)
MTG ...... Motor-Torque Generator
MTG ...... Multiple-Trigger Generator
MTG....... Multipurpose Target Generator
MTGS...... Metal-to-Glass Seal
MTH ...... Magnetic Tape Handler
M Th ...... Master of Theology
MTH....... Mount Hood R. R. (AAR code)
MTI .... Main Tank Injection
MTI .... Manitoba Technical Institute (Canada)
MTI .... Material Thickness Indicator
MTI .... Mechanics Technology, Incorporated
MTI ...... Metal Treating Institute
MTI ...... Military Training Instructor
MTI .... Moving Target Indicator (RADAR)
MTIC ...... Ministerio do Trabalho, Industria e Comercio
MTIE ...... Micro-Thrust Ion Engine
MTIF ...... Master Tailored Interest File (Navy)
MTIK ...... Moving Target Indicator Kit
MTIS ...... Maintenance Task Information System
MTK....... Medium Tank
MTL ...... Master Tape Loading
MTL ...... Matched Transmission Line
MTL....... Mean Tide Level
MTLD ...... Mouvement pour le Triomphe des Libertes Democratiques (Movement for
the Triumph of Democratic Liberties) (Algeria)
MTLP ...... Master Tape Loading Program
MTLP ...... Metabolic Toxemia of Late Pregnancy (Medicine)
MTM .... Marathon Manufacturing Company (NYSE symbol)
MTM .... Methods-Time Measurement (Management)
MTM .... Methods Time Measurement Association for Standards and Research
MTM ...... Modular Torque Motor
MTMA ..... Military Traffic Management Agency (Later, Defense Traffic Management
Service)
MT/MF ..... Magnetic Tape to Microfilm
MTMR ...... Military Traffic Management Regulation
MTMS ..... Metal-To-Metal Seal
MTMTS..... Military Traffic Management and Terminal Service
MTNA ...... Music Teachers National Association
MTNS ..... Metal-Thick Oxide-Nitride-Silicon
MTO ...... Medical Transport Officer
MTO ...... Mediterranean Theater of Operations, United States Army (Shortened
form of MTOUSA) (World War II)
MTO ...... Mission, Task, Objective
MTO ...... Mississippi Test Operations (NASA)
MTOB ...... Manned Test Operations Board (NASA)
MTOE ..... Modification Table of Organization and Equipment (Army)
MTON...... Measurement Ton
MTOS...... Metal-Thick Oxide-Silicon
MTOUSA .... Mediterranean Theater of Operations, United States Army (Sometimes
shortened to MTO) (World War II)
MTP .... Miniature Trimmer Potentiometer
MTP .... Missile Tube Pressurization
MTP........ Mobilization Training Program (Military)
MTP........ Mobilization Troop Program
MTP........ Montana Power Company (NYSE symbol)
MTP........ Multiple-Task Performance
MTPP ...... Material Test Procedure Pamphlet
MTPS ...... Magnetic Tape Plotting System
MTR ...... Magnetic Tape Recorder
MTR ...... Materials Testing Reactor (AEC)
MTR ...... Materials Testing Report
MTR ...... Maximum Tracking Range
MTR ...... Mean Time to Repair

MTR	Mean Time to Restore (Air Force)
MTR	Meinicke Turbidity Reaction
MTR	Military Temperature Range
MTR	Missile-Track RADAR (Air Force)
MTR	Monopulse Tracking Receiver
MTR	Montour R. R. (AAR code)
MTR	Moving Target Reactor
MTR	Multiple Thermocouple Reference
MTR	Multiple Track RADAR
MTR	Multiple Tracking Range
MTR	Multitrack Range
MTRB	Maritime Transportation Research Board (National Research Council)
MTRE	Magnetic Tape Recorder End
MTRE	Missile Test and Readiness Equipment
MTRF	Mark Twain Research Foundation
MTRI	Missile Test Range Instrumentation
MTRP	Machine Tool Retrofit Program
MTRS	Magnetic Tape Recorder Start
MTS	Machine-Tractor Stations
MTS	Magnetic Tape System
MTS	Mardan Test Set
MTS	Marine Technology Society
MTS	Marketing Technical Services
MTS	Maschinen-Traktoren-Station (Machine-Tractor-Stations) (Germany)
MTS	Mashinno-Traktornye Stantsii (Machine-Tractor-Stations) (USSR)
MTS	Master Test Station
MTS	Medical Testing Systems (Commercial firm)
MTS	Members of the Technical Staff (A generic term)
MTS	Memory Test System
MTS	Message Traffic Study
MTS	Meteoroid Technology Satellite
MTS	Michigan Terminal System (Data processing)
MTS	Military Test Satellite
MTS	Missile Test Station
MTS	Missile Training Squadron
MTS	Missile Tube Supply
MTS	Mobile Telephone Service
MTS	Mobile Tracking Station (NASA)
MTS	Mobile Training Set
MTS	Monthly Treasury Statement (Government)
MTS	Motor-Operated Transfer Switch
MTSC	Magnetic Tape "Selectric" Composer (IBM)
MTSC	Middle Tennessee State College
MT/SC	Magnetic Tape "Selectric" Composer (IBM)
MTSD	Military Transmission Systems Department (NORAD)
MTSE	Magnetic Tape Splicing Equipment
MTSGT	Master Technical Sergeant (Marine Corps)
MTSGT(C) ...	Master Technical Sergeant (Commissary) (Marine Corps)
MTSPS	Multiple Transducer Seismic Profiling System
MTSQ	Mechanical Time, Superquick
MTSS	Magnetic Tape Storage System
MTSS	Military Test Space Station (Later, MODS)
MT/ST	Magnetic Tape "Selectric" Typewriter (IBM)
MTSU	Magnetic Tape Search Unit
MTSU	Malayan Technical Services' Union
MTT	Magnetic Tape Terminal
MTT	Master of Textile Technology
MTT	Mean Transit Time
MTT	Medium Tactical Transport (Army)
MTT	Metropolitan Edison Company (NYSE symbol)
MTT	Microwave Theory and Technique
MTT	Mobile Training Team
MTT	Multiple Target Tracker
MTTEA	Marine Towing and Transportation Employers Association
MTTF	Mean Time to Failure (Quality control)
MTTFF	Mean Time to First Failure (Quality control)
MTTR	Mean Time to Restore (or Repair)
MTTU	Modular Timing Terminal Unit
MTU	Magnetic Tape Unit
MTU	Methylthiouracil
MTU	Metric Units
MTU	Missile Training Unit (Air Force)
MTU	Mist Therapy Unit (Medicine)
MTU	Mobile Training Unit
MTU	Multiplexer and Terminal Unit
MTUC	Macau Trade Union Council
MTUC	Malayan Trades Union Congress
MTUC	Mauritius Trades' Union Congress
MTUF	Mauritius Trades' Union Federation
MTUOP	Mobile Training Units Out for Parts
MTV	Mammary Tumor Virus

MTV	Management Television (Air Force)
MTV	Marginal Terrain Vehicle
M TV	Master of Television
MTV	Mean Transformed Value
MTV	Missile Test Vehicle
MTV	Munition Test Vehicle
MTV	Mutatur Terminatio Versiculi (The Termination of the Little Verse Is Changed)
MTVAL	Master Tape Validation
MTVC	Manual Thrust Vector Control
MTW	Main Trawl Winch
MTW	Marinette, Tomahawk & Western R. R. (AAR code)
MTW	Mobile Training Wing (Air Force)
MTW	Mountain Waves (Aviation)
MTWF	Metal Thru-Wall Flashing (Technical drawings)
MTWS	Manual Track While Scan
MTX	Morrell Tank Line (AAR code)
MTY	Major Typhlosole
MU	Machine Unit
MU	Maintenance Unit (Military)
MU	Markup
MU	Mass Units
MU	Methylene Unit
MU	Methylumbelliferone (Biochemistry)
MU	Mobile Unit
MU	Motor Union
MU	Mouse Unit (With reference to radium emanations)
MU	Multiple Unit
MU	Munitions Command
MU	Musician (Navy rating)
M/U	Mockup
MUA	Maximum Usable Altitude (Aviation)
MUB	Mueller Brass Company (NYSE symbol) (Delisted)
MUBIS	Multiple Beam Interval Scanner
MUC	Meritorious Unit Citation (Army award)
MUC	Meritorious Unit Commendation (Air Force award)
MUC	Mount Union College (Ohio)
MUCC	Michigan United Conservation Clubs
MUCOM	Munitions Command (Army)
MUCUSA	Missionary Union of the Clergy in the United States of America
MUD	Memory Unit Drum (Data processing)
MUD	Middle, Up, Down (in game of bridge)
MUD	Movimento da Unidade Democratica
MUDPAC	Melbourne University Dual-Package Analog Computer (Australia)
MUE	Meritorious Unit Emblem
MUF	Material Unaccounted For (AEC)
MUF	Maximum Usable Frequency (Aviation)
MUG	Manning Unit Group (Air Force)
MUI	Maritime Union of India
MUJCSA	Mining Unions' Joint Committee of South Africa
MUJE	Mechanics' Unions' Joint Executives (South Africa)
MUL	Master Urgency List
MULDEM	Multiplexer/Demultiplexer (Bell Laboratories)
MULL	Modern Uses of Logic in Law
MULTICS ...	Multiplexed Information and Computing Service
MuLV	Murine Leukemia Virus (Also, MLV)
MUMMS	Marine Corps Unified Materiel Management System
MUMP	Marshall - University of Michigan Probe (Rocket flight)
MUMS	Multiple-Use MARC (Machine-Readable Catalog) System (Library of Congress)
MUN	Munitions
MUN	Munsingwear, Inc. (NYSE symbol)
MUNBG	Munitions Building (Washington, DC) (Obsolete)
MUNC	Munitions Command (Army)
MUNI	Municipal
MUNIREP. ...	Munitions Report (Worldwide report of location and status of air munitions) (Military)
MUO	Maximum Undistorted Output
MUO	Municipal University of Omaha
MUO	Mutual of Omaha (NYSE symbol)
MUO	Myocardiopathy of Unknown Origin
Muon	Mu-Meson (An elementary particle)
MUP	Master of Urban Planning
MUPL	Military Urgency Planning List
MUPL	Mock-Up Planning
MUPO	Maximum Undistorted Power Output
MUPS	Multiple Utility Peripheral System (Data processing)
MUR	Mock-Up Reactor (NASA)
MUR	Murphy Oil Corporation (NYSE symbol)
MURA	Midwestern Universities Research Association
MURF	Material Utilization Reference File (Military)

MURG ...... Machine Utilization Report Generator
MURL ...... Mockup Release
MURP ...... Manned Upperstage Reusable Payload
MUS .... Magnetic Unloading System
MUS........ Manned Underwater Station
MUSA....... Multiple Unit Steerable Antenna (Electronics)
Mus AD ..... Doctor of Musical Arts
MUSAP ..... Multi-Satellite Augmentation Program
Mus B ...... Bachelor of Music
Mus Bac ..... Bachelor of Music
Mus D ...... Doctor of Music
Mus Doc .... Doctor of Music
MUSE....... Medical Use of Simulation Electronics
MUSE....... Mobile Utilities Support Equipment
MUSE ...... Monitor of Ultraviolet Solar Energy
Mus Ed B ... Bachelor of Music Education
Mus Ed D ... Doctor of Music Education
Mus Ed M ... Master of Music Education
MUSICOMP .. Music Composition
MUSLO ..... Morocco United States Liaison Office
Mus M ..... Master of Music
MUSRP ..... McGill University Savanna Research Project
MUSS....... Missile Unit Support System
MUST ...... Manned Undersea Station
MUST ...... Manpower Utilization System and Techniques (Department of State)
MUST ...... Maximum Utilization of Skills and Training (Civil Service Commission)
MUST ...... Medical Unit Self-Contained Transportable (Field hospital) (Army)
MUST ...... Mobile Underwater Surveillance Teams
MUSTARD .... Multi-Unit Space Transport and Recovery Device
MUT........ Mercury Unit Test
MUTA ...... Multiple Unit Training Assembly (Army)
MUTACI ..... Mutuelle des Autochtones de la Cote d'Ivoire (Mutual Association of the Natives of the Ivory Coast)
MUTS ...... Manual Unit Test Set
MUTT ...... Military Utility Tactical Truck
MUV .... Mobile Underwater Vehicle
MUW....... Music Wire
MUWO ..... Muir Woods National Monument
MUWS ..... Manned Underwater Station
MUX .... Multiplexing Equipment
MUY .... Murray Corporation of America (NYSE symbol) (Delisted)
MV .... Manpower Voucher (Army)
MV .... Mantle Vessel
MV......... Mariner V (Spacecraft)
MV......... Market Value
MV .... Mean Value
MV .... Mean Variation
MV .... Measured Value
MV .... Medicus Veterinarius (Veterinary Physician)
MV .... Medium Voltage
MV .... Megavolt
Mv......... Mendelevium (A chemical element) (Also see Md)
MV .... Methyl Violet (A dye)
MV......... Midland Valley R. R. (AAR code)
MV .... Million Volts
mV......... Millivolt
MV......... Motor Vessel
MV .... Multi-Vibrator
MV .... Muzzle Velocity (Ballistics)
MV......... Mycoplasmatales Virus
MV......... Merchant Vessel
M and V .... Meat-and-Vegetable (A canned ration) (Military) (World War I)
M of V ..... The Merchant of Venice (by Shakespeare)
MVA .... Machinists Vise Association
MVA .... Mean Vertical Acceleration
MVA .... Megavolt-Ampere
MVA .... Mevalonic Acid
MVA .... Missouri Valley Authority
MVA .... Modern Volunteer Army
MVA .... Motor Vehicle Accident (Military)
MVAR....... Megavar
MVAR ..... Megavolt-Ampere Reactive
MVARH ..... Megavar-Hour
MVAS ...... Milwaukee Vocational & Adult School
MVAU ...... Maximum Volt-Ampere Utilization
MVB .... Mechanical Vacuum Booster
MVB .... Multivesicular Body
MVB .... Multi-Vibrator
MVBD....... Multiple V-Belt Drive
MVC .... Manual Volume Control
MVC .... Mississippi Vocational College

MVC .... Missouri Valley Conference (Sports)
MVD .... Doctor of Veterinary Medicine
MVD .... Map and Visual Display
MVD .... Ministerstvo Vnutrennykh Del (Ministry of Internal Affairs) (Political police and security organization) (USSR)
MVD .... Motor Vehicle Driver Selection Battery (Army)
MVDF ...... Medium and Very High Frequency Direction-Finding Station
MVE .... Multivariate Exponential Distribution (Statistics)
MVE........ Murray Valley Encephalitis
MV Ed ..... Master of Vocational Education
MVF .... Missile Verification Firing
MVFR ...... Maintain Visual Flight Rules (Aviation)
MVFV ...... Manned Venus Flyby Vehicle
MVG .... Most Valuable Girl
MVG .... Mycoplasmatales Virus (from) Goat
MVI........ Merchant Vessel Inspection Division (Coast Guard)
MVI........ Mercury Vapor Isolator
MVI .... Metal Ventilator Institute
MVI .... Motor Vehicle Inspection
MVII .... Minnesota Vocational Interest Inventory
MVJC ...... Mount Vernon Junior College (Washington, DC)
MVL........ Mercury Vapor Lamp
MVL........ Mycoplasmatales Virus (from) Acholeplasma laidlawii
MVLA ...... Mount Vernon Ladies' Association of the Union
MVM .... Master of Veterinary Medicine
MVM .... Medium-Voltage Mode
mvm .... Million Vehicle Miles
MVMA ...... Motor Vehicle Manufacturers Association (Formerly, AMA)
MVMC ...... Motor Vehicle Maintenance Conference
MVMF ...... Ministerstvo Voenno-Morskogo Flota (Ministry of the Navy) (1950-53; merged into the MO) (USSR)
MVMT ...... Movement
MVN .... Median Ventricular Nerve
MVO .... Member of the Royal Victorian Order (British)
MVP .... Magnetic Vector Potential
MVP........ Maintenance Verification Plan
MVP........ Mechanical Vacuum Pump
MVP .... Most Valuable Player (Athletics)
MVPCB ..... Motor Vehicle Pollution Control Board (California)
MVPS ...... Manually Variable Phase Shifter
MVPS ...... Mechanical Vacuum Pump System
MVRA ...... Metropolitan Visiting and Relief Association (British)
MVRI ...... Mixed Vaccine, Respiratory Infections
MVS .... Magnetic Voltage Stabilizer
MVS........ Mechanical Vibration System
MVS........ Mennonite Voluntary Service
MVS .... Minimum Visual Signal
MVS .... Ministerstvo Vooruzhennykh Sil (Ministry of the Armed Forces) (1946-50; superseded by VM and MVMF) (USSR)
MVS........ Missile Velocity Servo
MVS........ Modularized Vehicle Stimulation (Program)
MVS........ Multiple Vibration System
MVSB ...... Motor Vehicle Storage Building (Army)
MV Sc ..... Master of Veterinary Science
MVSMA ..... Mechanical Vibrating Screen Manufacturers Association
MVSN ...... Milizia Voluntaria per la Sicurezza Nazionale (Italy)
MVSP....... Maintain Visual Separation (Aviation)
MVSS ...... Motor Vehicle Safety Standard
MVSS ...... Motor Vehicle Storage Shed (Army)
MVT........ Mt. Vernon Terminal R. R. (AAR code)
MVT .... Multiprogramming with a Variable Number of Tasks (Data processing)
MVTR ...... Moisture Vapor Transmission Rate
MVU .... Minimum Variance Unbiased (Statistics)
MVUE ...... Minimum Variance Unbiased Estimate (Statistics)
MVULE ..... Minimum Variance Unbiased Linear Estimator (Statistics)
MVV .... Maximum Voluntary Ventilation
MVV........ Mean Vertical Velocity
MVW .... Missile Viewing Window
MVWDU ..... Missile Viewing Window Deicing Unit
MVX .... Milwaukee Vinegar Company
MW .... Manual Word
MW .... Medium Wall
MW .... Medium Wave(band)
MW .... Megawatt
MW ...... Microwave
MW ...... Middle Welsh
mW .... Milliwatt
MW .... Mixed Widths
MW .... Molecular Weight (Also, M)
MW .... Most Worshipful
MW .... Most Worthy

MW . . . . Multiple Wounds
MW . . . . Music Wire
M/W . . . . Man-Week
M of W . . . . . Maintenance of Way (Railroading)
MWA . . . . . . Married Women's Association (British group fighting for economic equality for wives)
MWA . . . . . . Midwest Aviation, Inc.
MWA . . . . Modern Woodmen of America
MWA . . . . Momentum-Wheel Assembly
MWA . . . . Munitions of War Act (British)
MWA . . . . Mystery Writers of America
MWAA . . . . . . Movers' and Warehousemen's Association of America
MWARA . . . . . Major World Air Route Area
MWB . . . . Marine (or Motor) Whaleboat
MWB . . . . Maxwell-Wien Bridge
MWB. . . . . Multilayer Wiring Board
MWBAS . . . . . Mail Will Be Addressed to Show
MWC . . . . Magnetoionic Wave Component
MWC . . . . Mary Washington College (University of Virginia)
MWC . . . . Miltonvale Wesleyan College (Kansas)
MWC . . . . . . Minister for (or Ministry of) War Communications (British) (World War II)
MWC . . . . Monod-Wyman-Changeux (Model) (Enzymology)
MWCE . . . . . . Millimeter Wave Communications Experiment
MWCR . . . . . . Mercury-Wetted Contact Relay
MWCS. . . . . . . Mobile Weapons Control System
MWD . . . . Megawatt Day
MWD . . . . Metering Water Dispenser (Apollo) (NASA)
MWD . . . . Metropolitan Water District
MWD . . . . Millimeter Wave Device
MWD . . . . Molecular Weight Distribution
MWDDEA . . . . Mutual Weapons Development Data Exchange Agreement (NATO)
MWD/MTU. . . . Megawatt Days per Metric Ton of Uranium
MWDP . . . . . . Mutual Weapons Development Program (NATO)
MWDT . . . . . . Mutual Weapons Development Team (Military)
MWD/T. . . . . . Megawatt-Days per Ton
MWe . . . . Megawatts of Electric Power
MWE . . . . Millimeter Wave Experiment
MWFM . . . . . . Microwave Window Failure Mechanism
MWG . . . . Meteorological Working Group
MWG . . . . Missile Working Group
MWG . . . . Music Wire Gauge
MWGM . . . . . . Most Worthy (or Worshipful) Grand Master (Masonry)
MWH . . . . Megawatt-Hour
MWH . . . . Model Wave Height
MWI. . . . . Mantle Width Index
MWI . . . . Master Weavers Institute
MWI. . . . . Measured Workload Index (Aviation)
MWI . . . . Message-Waiting Indicator
MWIA . . . . . . Medical Women's International Association
MWJC . . . . . . Marjorie Webster Junior College (Washington, DC)
MWK . . . . Mohawk Rubber Co. (NYSE symbol)
MWL . . . . Malawi Women's League
MWL . . . . Mean Water Level
mWL . . . . Milliwatt Logic
MWLDA . . . . . Maine Wholesale Lobster Dealers Association
MWM . . . . Maxwell-Wagner Mechanism
MWM . . . . Millimeter Wave Mixer
MWMCA . . . . . Michigan Women for Medical Control of Abortion
MWO . . . . Meteorological Watch Office
MWO . . . . Midwest Oil Corporation (NYSE symbol)
MWO . . . . Millimeter Wavelength Oscillator
MWO . . . . Modification Work Order
MWOA . . . . . . Mizrachi Women's Organization of America
MWP . . . . Maneuvering Work Platform (NASA)
MWP . . . . Maximum Working Pressure
MWP . . . . Membrane Waterproofing
MWP . . . . Millimeter Wave Propagation
MWP . . . . Most Worthy Patriarch

MWPS. . . . . . . Multimeter Wave Power Source
MWR . . . . Mean Width Ratio
MWR . . . . Method of Weighted Residual
MWR . . . . Muncie & Western R. R. (AAR code)
MWRT . . . . . . Mobile Wing Reconnaissance Technical (Squadron)
MWS . . . . Microwave Station
MWSC. . . . . . . Midwestern Simulation Council
MWSG . . . . . . Marine Wing Service Group (Marine Corps)
MWSR. . . . . . . Magnetic Wire Shift Register
MWST . . . . . . Mean Weighted Skin Temperature
MWT . . . . Master of Wood Technology
MWT . . . . Millimeter Wave Tube
MWT . . . . Ministry of War Transport (British)
Mwt . . . . Thermal Megawatt (or TMW)
MWTC . . . . . . Ministry of War Time Communications (British) (World War II)
MWUSA . . . . . Minute Women of the United States of America
MWV . . . . Maximum Working Voltage
MWV . . . . Mexican War Veteran
MWW . . . . Manual Wire Wrap
MWW . . . . Municipal Waste Water
MWWF . . . . . . Manual Wire Wrap Fixture
MWWII . . . . . . Mothers of World War II
MWZ . . . . Manischewitz Company (American Stock Exchange symbol)
MX . . . . Maxwell
MX . . . . Multiplex
MXD . . . . Multiple Transmitter Duplicator
MXQ . . . . Modular X-Ray Quantometer
MXR . . . . Manning, Maxwell & Moore, Inc. (NYSE symbol) (Delisted)
MXR . . . . Mask Index Register
MY . . . . Man-Years
MY . . . . Marley Co. (NYSE symbol)
MY . . . . Million Years
MY . . . . Motor Yacht
M/Y. . . . . Marshaling Yards (Military)
MYBP . . . . . . Million Years Before Present (Geology)
MYCI . . . . Mirrer Yeshiva Central Institute
MYDIS . . . . . . My Dispatch (Military)
MYDW . . . . . . Multiple Yield Defense Weapon
MYF . . . . Methodist Youth Fellowship
MYG . . . . Maytag Company (NYSE symbol)
MYG . . . . Myriagram
MYI . . . . Metallic Yarns Institute (Defunct)
MYIM. . . . . . . Mylar Insulation Material
MYL . . . . Myrialiter
MYLTR . . . . . . (Reference) My Letter (Military)
MYM . . . . Mony Mortgage Investors (NYSE symbol)
MYM . . . . Myriameter
MYMGM. . . . . . My Mailgram (Military)
MYMS . . . . . . Mothers of Young Mongoloids (An organization)
MYMSG . . . . . My Message (Military)
MYO . . . . Murray Ohio Manufacturing Co. (NYSE symbol)
MYOB . . . . . . Mind Your Own Business (Slang)
MYP. . . . . Multiyear Procurement (DOD)
MYR. . . . . Myers (L.E.) Co. (NYSE symbol)
MYRAA . . . . . Model Yacht Racing Association of America
MYRAD. . . . . . My Radio (Military)
MYS . . . . Man-Year-Space (Army)
MYSER . . . . . . (Reference) My Serial (Military)
MYTEL . . . . . . My Telegram (Military)
MYW . . . . Multiple Yield Weapon
MZ . . . . Macy (R. H.) & Company, Inc. (NYSE symbol)
MZ . . . . Metalurgichen Zavod
MZ . . . . Monozygotic
MZF. . . . . Manganese Zinc Ferrite
MZ Sc . . . . . . Master of Zoological Science
MZSH. . . . . . . Missionary Zelatrices of the Sacred Heart (Roman Catholic women's religious order)

N

N . . . . Avogadro Number (Number of molecules in one gram-molecular weight
        of a substance)
N . . . . Flying Boat (Russian aircraft symbol)
N . . . . Haploid Number (Genetics)
N . . . . International Nickel Company of Canada, Ltd. (NYSE symbol)
N . . . . Nail
N . . . . Name
n . . . . Nano (A prefix meaning divided by one billion)
N . . . . Nasal
N . . . . National (American) form of screw threads
N . . . . Natus (Born)
N . . . . Nautical
N . . . . Navigate, Navigating, or Navigation
N . . . . Navy
N . . . . Negro, Negroid
N . . . . Nephew
N . . . . Nervus (Nerve) (Anatomy)
N . . . . Nested (Freight)
N . . . . Net
N . . . . Neuter
N . . . . Neutral
n . . . . Neutron
N . . . . New (NYSE symbol)
N . . . . Newfoundland Standard Time (Aviation)
N . . . . Newspaper
N . . . . Newton (Unit of force)
N . . . . Night (Approach and landing charts) (Aviation)
N . . . . Night Fighter (When suffix to plane designation) (Navy)
N . . . . Nitrogen (Chemical element)
N . . . . Nocte (At Night)
N . . . . Nominally Labeled (Compound, with radioisotope)
N . . . . Nominative
N . . . . None
N . . . . Noon
N . . . . Normal
n . . . . Normal (Of molecular structure) (Chemistry)
N . . . . Normal Solution
N . . . . Norse (Philology)
N . . . . North, Northerly, Northern
N . . . . Note
N . . . . Noun
N . . . . November
N . . . . Nuclear Propelled, when follows vessel classification, as CAG(N) (Navy)
N . . . . Number
N . . . . Number of cases in sample studied (Statistics)
N . . . . Number of variables involved (Statistics)
N . . . . Numeric
N . . . . Nun (Buoy)
N . . . . Nylon
n . . . . Refractive index
N . . . . Tilt Correction
2N . . . . Diploid Number (Genetics)
NA . . . . Nachrichten-Aufklaerung (Signal intelligence) (German military -
        World War II)
NA . . . . Nachrichtenabteilung (Signal battalion) (German military - World War II)
nA . . . . Nanoampere
NA . . . . Narcotics Anonymous
NA . . . . National Academy or Academician
NA . . . . National Airlines, Inc.
NA . . . . National Archives (of the United States)
NA . . . . National Army
NA . . . . National Association
Na . . . . Natrium (Sodium) (Chemical element)

NA . . . . Nautical Almanac
NA . . . . Naval Academy
NA . . . . Naval Aircraft
NA . . . . Naval Architect(s)
NA . . . . Naval Attaché (Diplomacy)
NA . . . . Naval Auxiliary
NA . . . . Naval Aviator
NA . . . . Neurotics Anonymous
NA . . . . New Associations (A publication) (Later, NAP)
NA . . . . Nicotinic Acid (Biochemistry)
NA . . . . No Account (Banking)
NA . . . . Noradrenaline
NA . . . . North America(n)
NA . . . . Not Applicable
NA . . . . Not Appropriated
NA. . . . . Not Assigned
NA . . . . Not Authorized
NA . . . . Not Available
NA . . . . Nucleic Acid (Biochemistry)
NA . . . . Numerical Aperture (Microscopy)
NA . . . . Nurse's Aide
NA . . . . Nursing Auxiliary
NA . . . . Office of Noise Abatement (FAA)
N/A . . . . Next Assembly
N/A . . . . No Account (Business and trade, banking)
N/A. . . . . . . No Action
N/A . . . . Non-Acceptance (Business and trade)
N/A. . . . . . . Not Above
N/A. . . . . . . Not Affected
N/A . . . . Not Applicable
NA^{24}. . . . . . . Radioactive Sodium
NAA. . . . . . . Naphthaleneacetic Acid (Chemical)
NAA . . . . Naphthylacetic Acid
NAA . . . . National Academy of Arbitrators
NAA . . . . National Aeronautic Association
NAA . . . . National Alumni Association
NAA . . . . National Arborist Association
NAA . . . . National Archery Association of the United States
NAA . . . . National Association of Accountants
NAA . . . . National Auctioneers Association
NAA . . . . Naval Attaché for Air
NAA. . . . . . . Neutron Activation Analysis
NAA . . . . New Art Association
NAA . . . . North American Aviation
NAA . . . . Northern Attack Area
NAA . . . . Not Always Afloat (Shipping)
NAAAA. . . . . . National Alliance of Athletic Associations
NAAAA . . . . . . National Auto Auction Association
NAAAP . . . . . North American Association of Alcoholism Programs
NAAB. . . . . . . National Architectural Accrediting Board
NAAB . . . . . . National Association of Animal Breeders
NAAB . . . . . . National Association of Artificial Breeders
NAABC . . . . . National Association American Business Clubs
NAABCV. . . . . National Association American Balloon Corps Veterans
NAABI . . . . . . National Association of Alcoholic Beverage Importers
NAAC . . . . . . National Aeroballistics Advisory Committee
NAACC . . . . . National Association for American Composers and Conductors
NAACC . . . . . National Association of Angling and Casting Clubs
NAACP . . . . . National Association for the Advancement of Colored People
NAAD . . . . . . National Association of Aluminum Distributors
NAAD. . . . . . . Navajo Army Depot
NAADC . . . . . North American Air Defense Command
NAADS. . . . . . New Army Authorization Documents System

NAAE ...... National Association of Afro-American Educators
NAAE...... North American Academy of Ecumenists
NAAF...... Naval Auxiliary Air Facility
NAAF...... Northwest African Air Force
NAAFA...... National Association to Aid Fat Americans
NAAFI...... Navy, Army and Air Force Institutes (Responsible for clubs, canteens, and provision of some items for messing of British armed forces)
NAAFW ..... National Association of Air Forces Women
NAAG ...... National Association of Attorneys General
NAAG ...... NATO Army Armaments Group
NAAIS ...... National Aircraft Accident Investigation School (FAA)
NAAJS ...... National Academy for Adult Jewish Studies
NAAMA ..... National Agricultural Advertising and Marketing Association
NAAMIC ..... National Association of Automotive Mutual Insurance Companies
NAAMM ..... National Association of Architectural Metal Manufacturers
NAAN ...... National Advertising Agency Network
NAANACM ... National Association for the Advancement of Native American Composers and Musicians
NAAO ...... National Association of Amateur Oarsmen
NAAO ...... National Association of Assessing Officers
NAAO ...... Navy Area Audit Office (London)
NAAOP ..... National Association for the Advancement of Older People
NAAP...... National Association of Advertising Publishers
NAAPPB ..... National Association of Amusement Parks, Pools and Beaches
NAAS...... National Agricultural Advisory Service (British)
NAAS ...... National Association of Art Services
NAAS...... National Aviation Assistance
NAAS...... Naval Area Audit Service
NAAS ...... Naval Auxiliary Air Station
NAAS...... Navy Aircraft Accounting System
NAASR...... National Association for Armenian Studies and Research
NAATC ..... Naval Air Advanced Training Command
NAATS ..... National Association of Auto Trim Shops
NAATTFO .... National Association of Alcohol & Tobacco Tax Field Officers
NAAW ...... National Association of Accordion Wholesalers
NAAWFS .... Naval Air All Weather Flight Squadron
NAB........ Nabisco, Inc. (Formerly, National Biscuit Company) (NYSE symbol)
NAB .... National Aircraft Beacon
NAB .... National Alliance of Businessmen
NAB .... National Associated Businessmen
NAB....... National Association of Bioengineers
NAB .... National Association of Broadcasters
NAB....... Naval Advanced Base
NAB .... Naval Air Base
NAB....... Naval Amphibious Base
NAB....... Navigation-Avoidance System
NAB........ Navigational Aid to Bombing (Air Force)
NAB........ New American Bible
NAB........ Nickel Alkaline Battery
NAB........ Not Above
NAB........ Nuclear Air Burst
NAB .... Nuclear Assembly Building
NAB........ Nut and Bolt
NABA...... National Alliance of Black Americans
NABA...... Naval Amphibious Base Annex
NABA...... North American Ballet Association
NABA...... North American Benefit Association
NABAC ..... National Association for Bank Auditors and Comptrollers (Later, BAI)
NABC ...... National Association of Basketball Coaches of the United States
NABC ...... North American Blueberry Council
NABCA ..... National Alcoholic Beverage Control Association
NABCM ..... National Association of Baby Carriage Manufacturers
NABCM ..... National Association of Brattice Cloth Manufacturers
NABD...... Naval Advanced Base Depot
NABDC ..... National Association of Blueprint and Diazotype Coaters
NABDCC .... North American Band Directors Coordinating Committee
NABE....... National Association of Bar Executives (Formerly, NCBE)
NABE...... National Association of Book Editors
NABE...... National Association of Business Economists
NABE...... Nuclear Air Burst Effect
NABER ..... National Association of Business and Educational Radio
NABET ..... National Association Broadcast Employees and Technicians
NABF...... National Amateur Baseball Federation
NABI ...... National Association of Biblical Instructors (Later, American Academy of Religion)
NABIM ..... National Association of Band Instrument Manufacturers
NABISCO .... National Biscuit Company (Acronym now used as company name)
NABM ...... National Association of Bedding Manufacturers
NABM ...... National Association of Blouse Manufacturers
NABM ...... National Association of Boating Magazines
NABM ...... National Association of British Manufacturers

NABOM ..... National Association of Building Owners and Managers
NABP...... National Association of Boards of Pharmacy
NABPARS .... Navy Automatic Broadcasting, Processing and Routing System
NABR...... National Association of Baby Sitter Registries
NABR...... Natural Bridges National Monument
NABS ...... National Advertising Benevolent Society (British)
NABS ...... National Association of Barber Schools
NABS ...... National Association of Black Students
NABS ...... Nuclear-Armed Bombardment Satellite
NABSC ..... National Association of Building Service Contractors
NABSP ..... National Association of Blue Shield Plans
NABT ...... National Association of Biology Teachers
NABTE ..... National Association for Business Teacher Education
NABTTI ..... National Association of Business Teacher-Training Institutions
NABU...... Naval Advanced Base Unit
NABU ...... Non-Adjusting Ball-Up (A hopeless state of confusion) (Military slang)
NABUG ..... National Association of Broadcast Unions and Guilds
NABW ...... National Association of Bank-Women
NAC .... National Achievement Clubs
NAC .... National Advisory Committee (or Council)
NAC .... National Advisory Council on Education of Disadvantaged Children
NAC .... National Aero Club
NAC....... National Agency Check (of security clearance)
NAC .... National Arts Club
NAC .... National Association of Cemeteries
NAC .... National Association of Concessionaires
NAC .... National Association of Coroners
NAC .... National Association of Counties
NAC ...... National Aviation Club
NAC .... National Aviation Corporation
NAC .... National Can Corporation (NYSE symbol)
NAC .... Naval Academy
NAC ...... Naval Air Center (Military)
NAC .... Naval Aircraftman (British)
NAC .... Non-Airline Carrier (Aerospace)
NAC .... North Atlantic Council
NAC .... Northeast Air Command
NACA ...... National Acoustical Contractors Association
NACA ...... National Advisory Committee for Aeronautics (Functions transferred to NASA, 1958)
NACA ...... National Agricultural Chemicals Association
NACA ...... National Air Carrier Association
NACA ...... National Armored Car Association
NACA ...... National Association of Cost Accountants
NACA ...... National Association of County Administrators
NACA ...... North American College of Acupuncture
NACAA ..... National Association County Agricultural Agents
NACAC ..... National Association of Catholic Alumni Clubs
NACAC. .... National Association of College Admissions Counselors
NACAF...... Northwest African Coastal Air Force (World War II)
NACARM .... Northwest America Civil Air Routes Manual
NACATS ..... North American Clear Air Turbulence Tracking System (Aviation)
NACBA ..... National Association of Church Business Administrators
NACBS...... National Association and Council of Business Schools
NACC ...... Narcotic Addiction Control Commission (New York)
NACC ...... National Advisory Cancer Council
NACC ...... National Agency Check Center
NACC ...... National Alliance of Czech Catholics
NACC ...... National Association of Catholic Chaplains
NACC ...... National Association of Collegiate Commissioners (Later, Collegiate Commissioners Association)
NACC. ..... National Automatic Controls Conference
NACC ...... Norwegian American Chamber of Commerce
NACCA ..... National Association of Claimants' Counsel of America (Also known as NACCA Bar Association) (Later, American Trial Lawyers Association)
NACCA ..... National Association of Consumer Credit Administrators
NACCA ..... National Association of County 4-H Club Agents
NACCAM .... National Coordinating Committee for Aviation Meteorology
NACCC ..... National Association of Citizens' Crime Commissions
NACD ...... National Association for Community Development
NACD ...... National Association of Container Distributors
NACD ...... National Association of Soil and Water Conservation Districts
NACDA ..... National Association of Collegiate Directors of Athletics
NACDR...... National Association of College Deans and Registrars
NACDS ..... National Association of Chain Drug Stores
NACE...... National Association of Corrosion Engineers
NACE....... National Association of County Engineers
NACECE ..... National Advisory Council on Extension and Continuing Education
NACED...... National Advisory Council on the Employment of the Disabled (British)
NACEL...... Navy Air Crew Equipment Laboratory (Philadelphia, Pennsylvania)
NACEO ..... National Advisory Council on Economic Opportunity

NACFL . . . . . . National Advisory Committee on Farm Labor
NACGC . . . . . National Association of College Gymnastic Coaches
NACGC . . . . . National Association of Colored Girls Clubs
NACGG . . . . . North American Commercial Gladiolus Growers
NACGM . . . . . National Association of Chewing Gum Manufacturers
NACI . . . . . . National Agency Check and Written Inquiries
NACIFO . . . . . National Association of Church and Institutional Financing Organizations
NACIO . . . . . Naval Air Combat Information Office(r)
NACIS . . . . . . Naval Air Combat Information School
NACJ . . . . . . National Association of Costume Jewelers
NACK . . . . . . Nonacknowledge Character (Data processing)
NACL . . . . . . National Advisory Commission on Libraries
NACL . . . . . . Nippon Aviatronics Corporation, Limited
NACLEO . . . . . National Association of Coin Laundry Equipment Operators
NACLIS . . . . . National Commission on Libraries and Information Science
NACLS . . . . . National Association of Commission Lumber Salesmen
NACLSO . . . . . National Assembly of Chief Livestock Sanitary Officials
NACM . . . . . . National Association of Chain Manufacturers
NACM . . . . . . National Association of Credit Management
NACO . . . . . . National Association of Consumer Organizations
NACO . . . . . . National Association of Counties
NACO . . . . . . Navy Cool (Gunpowder)
NACO . . . . . . Night Alarm Cut-Off
NACOA . . . . . If Not Available Your Command, Obtain Accounting Data from Administrative Command (Army)
NACOL . . . . . National Advisory Commission on Libraries
NACOM . . . . . National Communications (System)
NACOM . . . . Northern Area Command
NACOR . . . . . National Advisory Committee on Radiation
NACOS . . . . . National Communications Schedule
NACP . . . . . . National Association of Creamery Proprietors (British)
NACPA . . . . . National Association of County and Prosecuting Attorneys
NACPDCG . . . National Association of Catholic Publishers and Dealers in Church Goods
NACPRO . . . . National Association of County Park and Recreation Officials
NACR . . . . . . National Advisory Committee on Radiation
NACRC . . . . . National Association of County Recorders and Clerks
NACRCD . . . . National Advisory Council on Rural Civil Defense
NACRMR . . . . National Advisory Committee on Rhesus Monkey Requirements
NACRO . . . . . National Association for the Care and Resettlement of Offenders (British)
NACS . . . . . . National Association of Carpet Specialists
NACS . . . . . . National Association of Christian Schools
NACS . . . . . . National Association of Civic Secretaries
NACS . . . . . . National Association of College Stores
NACS . . . . . . National Association of Convenience Stores
NACS . . . . . . National Association of Cosmetology Schools
NACS . . . . . . Northern Area Communications System
NACSA . . . . . National Advisory Committee on Safety in Agriculture
NACSA . . . . . National Association of Casualty and Surety Agents
NACSB . . . . . Naval Aviation Cadet Selection Board
NACSCORP . . . Paperback Book Distributing Firm (Owned by members of National Association of College Stores)
NACSCS . . . . . National Advisory Council on Supplementary Centers and Services
NACSDA . . . . National Association of Commissioners, Secretaries and Directors of Agriculture (Later, NASDA)
NACSE . . . . . National Association of Casualty and Surety Executives
NACSPMR . . . . National Association of Coordinators of State Programs for the Mentally Retarded
NACTA . . . . . National Association of Colleges and Teachers of Agriculture
NACTEFL . . . . National Advisory Council on the Teaching of English as a Foreign Language
NACTFO . . . . . National Association of County Treasurers and Finance Officers
NACTU . . . . . Night Attack Combat Training Unit (Navy)
NACU . . . . . . National Association of Colleges and Universities
NACUA . . . . . National Association of College and University Administrators
NACUA . . . . . National Association of College and University Attorneys
NACUBO . . . . National Association of College and University Business Officers
NACUCDRL . . . National Association of College & University Chaplains and Directors of Religious Life
NACUFS . . . . . National Association of College and University Food Services
NACUSS . . . . . National Association of College and University Summer Sessions
NACUTSO . . . . National Association of College and University Traffic and Security Officers
NACVE . . . . . National Advisory Council on Vocational Education
NACW . . . . . . National Association of College Women
NACWC . . . . . National Association of Colored Women's Clubs
NACWPI . . . . . National Association of College Wind and Percussion Instructors
NAD . . . . National Academy of Design
NAD . . . . National Association of the Deaf
NAD . . . . Naval Air Depot

NAD . . . . Naval Air Detail
NAD . . . . Naval Air Division (British)
NAD . . . . Naval Ammunition Depot
NAD . . . . Nicotinamide-Adenine Dinucleotide (Biochemistry) (Preferred form, but also see DPN)
NAD . . . . No Apparent Defect (Shipping)
NAD . . . . No Appreciable Disease (Medicine)
NAD . . . . North American Datum
NAD . . . . North Atlantic Division (Army Engineers)
NAD . . . . Not on Active Duty
NAD . . . . Nothing Abnormal Detected
NAD . . . . Nuclear Accident Dosimetry
NADA . . . . . . National Association of Dealers in Antiques
NADA . . . . . . National Automobile Dealers Association
NADAC . . . . . National Damage Assessment Center
NADAF . . . . . National Association of Decorative Architectural Finishes
NADAG . . . . . National Association of Diocesan Altar Guilds of the Protestant Episcopal Church
NADAR . . . . . North American Data Recorder Airborne
NADASO . . . . National Association of Drug and Allied Sales Organizations
NADB . . . . . . National Aerometric Data Bank (Environmental Protection Agency)
NADC . . . . . . National Anti-Dumping Committee
NADC . . . . . . Naval Air Development Center
NADC . . . . . . Naval Ammunition Depot, Concord
NADC-AC . . . . Naval Air Development Center - Aerospace Crew Equipment Department
NADC-AE . . . . Naval Air Development Center - Aero-Electronic Technology Department
NADC-AI . . . . Naval Air Development Center - Aeronautical Instruments Laboratory
NADC-AP . . . . Naval Air Development Center - Aeronautical Photographic Experimental Laboratory
NADC-AR . . . . Naval Air Development Center - Aviation Armament Laboratory
NADC-ASW . . . Naval Air Development Center - Antisubmarine Warfare Laboratory
NADC-AW . . . Naval Air Development Center - Air Warfare Research Department
NADC-ED . . . . Naval Air Development Center - Engineering Development Laboratory
NADC-EL . . . . Naval Air Development Center - Aeronautical Electronic and Electrical Laboratory
NADC-MA . . . Naval Air Development Center - Aviation Medical Acceleration Laboratory
NADC-MR . . . . Naval Air Development Center - Aerospace Medical Research Department
NADC-ST . . . . Naval Air Development Center - Aero Structures Department
NADC-SY . . . . Naval Air Development Center - Systems Project Department
NADC-WR . . . . Naval Air Development Center - Air Warfare Research Department
NADD . . . . . . National Association of Distributors & Dealers of Structural Clay Products
NADDM . . . . . National Association of Daytime Dress Manufacturers
NADEFCOL . . . NATO Defense College
NADEM . . . . . National Association of Dairy Equipment Manufacturers
NADET . . . . . National Association of Distributive Education Teachers
NADEVCEN . . . Naval Air Development Center
NADFPM . . . . National Association of Domestic and Farm Pump Manufacturers
NADGE . . . . . NATO Air Defense Ground Environment
NADGECO . . . NATO Air Defense Ground Environment Consortium
NADGEMO . . . NATO Air Defense Ground Environment Management Office
NADI . . . . National Association of Display Industries
NADI . . . . Naval Ammunition Depot, Indiana
NADL . . . . . . National Association of Dental Laboratories
NADL . . . . . . Navy Authorized Data List
NADLCC . . . . National Association of Defense Lawyers in Criminal Cases
NADM . . . . . . National Association of Discount Merchants
NADM . . . . . . National Association of Doll Manufacturers
NADM . . . . . . Naval Administration
NADMC . . . . . Naval Air Development & Material Center
NADMR . . . . . National Association of Drug Manufacturers Representatives
NADMW . . . . . National Association of Direct Mail Writers
NADO . . . . . . Navy Accounts Disbursing Office
NADOP . . . . . North American Defense Operational Plan (NORAD)
NADP . . . . . . Nicotinamide-Adenine Dinucleotide Phosphate (Biochemistry) (Preferred form, but also see TPN)
NADPH . . . . . Nicotinamide-Adenine Dinucleotide Phosphate (Reduced) (Biochemistry) (Preferred form, but also see TPNH)
NADREPS . . . . National Armaments Directors Representatives
NADS . . . . . . Naval Air Development Station
NADS . . . . . . North American Dostoevsky Society
NADSA . . . . . National Association of Dramatic and Speech Arts
NADSC . . . . . National Association of Direct Selling Companies
NADU . . . . . . Naval Aircraft Delivery Unit
NADUS . . . . . National Association of Doctors in the United States
NADUSM . . . . National Association of Deputy United States Marshals
NADWAGNS . . National Association of Deans of Women and Advisers to Girls in Negro Schools
NADWARN . . . Natural Disaster Warning
NAE . . . . National Academy of Education

NAE . . . . National Academy of Engineering
NAE . . . . National Aeronautical Establishment (Canada)
NAE . . . . National Association of Evangelicals
NAEA . . . . . . National Aerospace Education Association (Formerly, NAEC)
NAEA . . . . . . National Art Education Association
NAEA . . . . . . Newspaper Advertising Executives Association
NAEB . . . . . . National Association of Educational Broadcasters
NAEB . . . . . . National Association of Educational Buyers
NAEB . . . . . . North African Economic Board (World War II)
NAEBM . . . . . National Association of Engine and Boat Manufacturers
NAEC . . . . . . National Aerospace (formerly, Aviation) Education Council (Later, NAEA)
NAEC . . . . . . National Association of Electric Companies
NAEC . . . . . . National Association of Elevator Contractors
NAEC . . . . . . National Association of Engineering Companies
NAEC . . . . . Naval Air Engineering Center
NAECON . . . . National Aerospace Electronics Conference (IEEE)
NAED . . . . . . National Association of Electrical Distributors
NAEF . . . . . . Naval Air Engineering Facility
NAEFTA . . . . . National Association of Enrolled Federal Tax Accountants
NAEGA . . . . . North American Export Grain Association
NAEHE . . . . . National Association of Extension Home Economists
NAELSI . . . . . Naval Air Electronics Shipboard Installation
NAEM . . . . . . National Association of Exhibit Managers
NAEMB . . . . . . National Academy of Engineering Marine Board
NAEO . . . . National Association of Extradition Officials
NAEOM . . . . . National Association of Electronic Organ Manufacturers
NAEP . . . . . . National Assessment of Educational Progress (Sponsored by Carnegie Corporation)
NAEPS . . . . . . National Academy of Economics and Political Science
NAES . . . . . . National Association of Educational Secretaries
NAES . . . . . . National Association of Episcopal Schools
NAES . . . . Naval Air Experimental Station
NAESU . . . . . . Naval Air Engineering Service Unit (Philadelphia)
NAESU . . . . . Naval Aviation Electronic Service Unit
NAEYC . . . . . National Association for the Education of Young Children
NAF . . . . National Amputation Foundation
NAF . . . . National Arts Foundation
NAF . . . . Naval Air Facility
NAF . . . . Naval Aircraft Factory
NAF . . . . Naval Avionics Facility
NAF . . . . Nernst Approximation Formula
NAF . . . . Netherland-America Foundation
NAF . . . . Nonappropriated Fund(s)
NAF . . . . Northern Attack Force
NAF . . . . Numbered Air Force
NAFA . . . . . . National Association of Fleet Administrators
NAFA . . . . . . North American Falconers Association
NAFAD . . . . . National Association of Fashion and Accessory Designers
NAFAG . . . . . NATO Air Force Armaments Group
NAFB . . . . . . National Association of Farm Broadcasters
NAFB . . . . . . National Association of Franchised Businessmen
NAFB . . . . . . Norton Air Force Base
NAFBRAT . . . . National Association for Better Radio and Television
NAFC . . . . . . National Association of Food Chains
NAFC . . . . . . Naval Air Ferry Command (World War II)
NAFC . . . . . . Northern Attack Force Commander (Navy)
NAFCA . . . . . North American Family Campers Association
NAFCE . . . . . . National Association of Federal Career Employees
NAFCI . . . . . . National Association of Floor Covering Installers
NAFCO . . . . . National Floor Products Company, Inc.
NAFD . . . . . . National Association of Flour Distributors
NAFEC . . . . . . National Aviation Facilities Experimental Center (of FAA) (Atlantic City, NJ)
NAFED . . . . . National Association of Fire Distributors
NAFEM . . . . . . National Association of Food Equipment Manufacturers
NAFFP . . . . . . National Association of Frozen Food Packers (Later, AFFI)
NAFGDA . . . . National Auto and Flat Glass Dealers Association
NAFI . . . . National Association of Fire Investigators
NAFI . . . . National Association of Flight Instructors
NAFI . . . . Naval Air Fighting Instructions
NAFI . . . . . . Naval Avionics Facility, Indianapolis
NAFIC . . . . . . National Association of Fraternal Insurance Counsellors
NAFIS . . . . . . Navigational Aid Flight Inspection System
NAFLI . . . . . . Natural Flight Instrument System
NAFLU . . . . . . National Association of Free Labor Unions (Philippines)
NAFM . . . . . . National Association of Fan Manufacturers
NAFM . . . . . . National Association of Flag Manufacturers
NAFM . . . . . . National Association of Furniture Manufacturers
NAFMAB . . . . . National Armed Forces Museum Advisory Board (Smithsonian Institution)
NAFMB . . . . . . National Association of FM Broadcasters
NAFMG . . . . . National Association of Foreign Medical Graduates

NAFS . . . . . . Naval Air Fighter School
NAFS . . . . . . Newark Air Force Station
NAFSA . . . . . . National Association of Foreign Student Advisors
NAFSLAC . . . . National Association of Federations of Syrian & Lebanese American Clubs
NAFSONW . . . Nonappropriated Fund Statement of Operations and Net Worth
NAFT . . . . . . Natural Adjuvant Factor Toxoid (Medicine)
NAFT . . . . . . Network for Analysis of Fireball Trajectories
NAFTA . . . . . North Atlantic Free Trade Area
NAFTF . . . . . National Association of Finishers of Textile Fabrics
NAFTRAC . . . . National Foreign Trade Council
NAFV . . . . National Association of Federal Veterinarians
NAG . . . . National Action Group (Anti-busing organization)
NAG . . . . National Association of Gagwriters
NAG . . . . National Association of Gardeners
NAG . . . . Naval Advisory Group
NAG . . . . Naval Analysis Group
NAG . . . . Naval Applications Group
NAG . . . . Negro Actors Guild of America
NAGA . . . . . . National Amputee Golf Association
NAGA . . . . . . Negro Actors Guild of America
NAGARD . . . . NATO Advisory Group for Aeronautical Research and Development
NAGBSPA . . . North American Game Breeders and Shooting Preserve Association
NAGC . . . . . . National Association for Gifted Children
NAGC . . . . . . Naval Armed Guard Center
NAGC . . . . . . Navy Astronautics Group
NAGC . . . . . . North American Gladiolus Council
NAGCD . . . . . National Association of Glass Container Distributors
NAGCM . . . . . National Association of Golf Club Manufacturers
NAGCO . . . . . Naval Air Ground Center
NAGE . . . . . . National Association of Government Employees
NAGE . . . . . . National Association of Government Engineers
NAGE . . . . . . NATO Air Defense Group Environment
NAGI . . . . National Association of Government Inspectors
NAGM . . . . . . National Association of Glove Manufacturers
NAGM . . . . . . National Association of Glue Manufacturers
NAGPORT . . . . North American Export Grain Association
NAGS . . . . . . National Association of Government Secretaries
NAGS . . . . . . Naval Air Gunners School
NAGSCT . . . . National Association of Guidance Supervisors and Counselor Trainers
NAGT . . . . . . National Association of Geology Teachers
NAGTC . . . . . North American Gasoline Tax Conference
NAGVG . . . . North American Association Greenhouse Vegetable Growers
NAH . . . . Not at Home
NAHA . . . . . . National Association of Handwriting Analysts
NAHA . . . . . . National Association of Hotel Accountants (Later, NAHMA)
NAHA . . . . . . North American Highway Association
NAHA . . . . . . Norwegian-American Historical Association
NAHAL . . . . . Noar Halutzi Lohem (Pioneering Fighting Youth) (Israel)
NAHB . . . . . . National Association of Home Builders of the United States
NAHB . . . . . . National Association of Homes for Boys
NAHC . . . . . . National Association of Housing Cooperatives
NAHCSP . . . . . National Association of Hospital Central Service Personnel
NAHD . . . . . . National Association of Hillel Directors
NAHDDM . . . . National Association of House and Daytime Dress Manufacturers
NAHDSA . . . . National Association of Hebrew Day School Administrators
NAHES . . . . . National Association of Home Economics Supervisors
NAHHIC . . . . . National Association of House to House Installment Companies
NAHICUS . . . . Nuclear Attack Hazards in the Continental United States
NAHM . . . . . . National Association of Hosiery Manufacturers
NAHMA . . . . . National Association of Hotel and Motel Accountants (Formerly, NAHA)
NAHP . . . . . . National Association of Horseradish Packers
NAHPA . . . . . . National Association of Hospital Purchasing Agents
NAHRMP . . . . . National Association of Hotel and Restaurant Meat Purveyors
NAHRO . . . . . National Association of Housing and Redevelopment Officials
NAHS . . . . . . National Association of Horological Schools
NAHSA . . . . . National Association of Hearing and Speech Agencies
NAHW . . . . . . National Association of Hardwood Wholesalers
NAI . . . . National Agricultural Institute
NAI . . . . National Apple Institute
NAI . . . . New Acronyms and Initialisms (A publication)
NAI . . . . No Action Indicated
NAI . . . . No-Address Instruction
NAI . . . . No Airborne Intercept (Fighter aircraft lacking airborne intercept RADAR)
NAI . . . . Northrop Aeronautical Institute
NAI . . . . Northrop Aircraft, Incorporated
NaI . . . . Sodium Iodide
NAIA . . . . . . National Association of Industrial Artists
NAIA . . . . . . National Association of Insurance Agents
NAIA . . . . . . National Association of Intercollegiate Athletics
NAIA . . . . . . North American Indian Association

NAIB . . . . National Association of Independent Business
NAIB . . . . National Association of Insurance Brokers
NAIC . . . . . . National Association of Insurance Commissioners
NAIC . . . . . . National Association of Investment Clubs
NAIC . . . . National Astronomy and Ionospheric Center (Cornell University
        (National Science Foundation)
NAICC . . . . . . Nuclear Accident Incident Control Center
NAICO . . . . . . Nuclear Accident and Incident Control Officer (Army)
NAICOM/MIS . . Navy-Integrated Command Management Information System
NAICP . . . . . Nuclear Accident and Incident Control Plan
NAIEC . . . . . . National Association for Industry-Education Cooperation
NAIEHS . . . . . National Association of Importers and Exporters of Hides and Skins
NAIEM . . . . . . National Association of Insect Electrocutor Manufacturers
NAIF . . . . No AI-Equipped Fighters (Air Force)
NAIFR . . . . . . National Association of Independent Food Retailers
NAIG . . . . Nippon Atomic Industry Group (Japan)
NAII . . . . National Association of Ice Industries
NAII . . . . National Association of Independent Insurers
NAIIA . . . . . . National Association of Independent Insurance Adjusters
NAIIU . . . . . . Not Authorized If Issued Under
NAIJ . . . . National Association for Irish Justice
NAIL . . . . Neurotics Anonymous International Liaison
NAILM . . . . . . National Association of Institutional Laundry Managers
NAILS . . . . . . Naval Aviation Integrated Logistic Support Task Force
NAIOP . . . . . . Navigational Aid Inoperative for Parts
NAIP . . . . National Association of Industrial Parks
NAIP . . . . National Association of Industrial Plants
NAIR . . . . Narrow Absorption Infrared
NAIRE . . . . . . National Association of Internal Revenue Employees
NAIREC . . . . . . Nimbus Arctic Ice Reconnaissance (Canadian project)
NAIRO . . . . . . National Association of Intergroup Relations Officials
NAIRU . . . . . . Naval Air Intelligence Reserve Units
NAIS . . . . National Association of Independent Schools
NAIS . . . . Night Attack Interdiction System
NAIT . . . . Naval Air Intermediate Training
NAIT(C) . . . . . Naval Air Intermediate Training (Command)
NAITE . . . . . . National Association of Industrial Teacher Educators
NAIW . . . . National Association of Insurance Women
NAJ . . . . Napierville Junction Railway Company (AAR code)
NAJA . . . . . . North American Judges Association
NAJAFRA . . . . National Jazz Fraternity
NAJCW . . . . . National Association of Jewish Center Workers
NAJD . . . . National Association of Journalism Directors (Later, JEA)
NAK . . . . Negative Acknowledge
NAKOSTA . . . . Natural Convection in the Stationary Condition (Computer program)
NAL . . . . National Accelerator Laboratory (AEC)
NAL . . . . . . National Aeronautical Laboratory
NAL . . . . National Agricultural Library (Department of Agriculture)
NAL . . . . National Airlines, Inc. (NYSE symbol)
NAL . . . . . . National Assistance League
NAL . . . . National Association of Laymen
NAL . . . . National Astronomical League
NAL . . . . . . Naval Aeronautical Laboratory
NAL . . . . New American Library (Publisher)
NAL . . . . Numerical Analysis Laboratory
NALA . . . . National Agricultural Limestone Association (Later, National Limestone
        Institute)
NALAM . . . . . National Association of Livestock Auction Markets
NALC . . . . National Association of Letter Carriers of the United States of America
NALC . . . . National Association of Life Companies
NALC . . . . . . National Association of Litho Clubs
NALC . . . . . . Navy Ammunition Logistics Code
NALC . . . . Negro American Labor Council
NALCC . . . . . . National Automatic Laundry and Cleaning Council
NALCM . . . . . National Association of Lace Curtain Manufacturers
NALCO . . . . . Naval Air Logistics Control Office
NALCO . . . . . Newfoundland and Labrador Corporation
NALCOLANT . . Naval Air Logistic Control Office Atlantic
NALCOPACREP . . Naval Air Logistic Control Office Pacific Representative
NALDEF . . . . . Native American Legal Defense and Education Foundation
NALF . . . . . . Naval Auxiliary Landing Field
NALGM . . . . . National Association of Leather Glove Manufacturers
NALHI . . . . . . National Authority for the Ladies Handbag Industry
NALI . . . . National Agricultural Limestone Institute (Later, National Limestone
        Institute)
NALI . . . . North Atlantic Lobster Institute
NALLD . . . . . . National Association of Language Laboratory Directors
NALLO . . . . . . National Association of License Law Officials
NALMC . . . . . . National Association of Lighting Maintenance Contractors
NALO . . . . . . Naval Air Liaison Officer
NALOH . . . . . National Association Legions of Honor

NALS . . . . National Association of Legal Secretaries
NALS . . . . National Association of Lumber Salesmen
NALS . . . . North American Lily Society
NALT . . . . National Association of the Legitimate Theatre
NALU . . . . . . National Association of Life Underwriters
NALUS . . . . . . National Association of Leagues, Umpires and Scorers
NAM . . . . an-Nahdah al-Wataniyyah al-Mauritaniyyah (The Call of Nationalism of
        Mauritania)
NAM . . . . National Account Management (Bell System)
NAM . . . . . . National Air Museum (of the Smithsonian Institution)
NAM . . . . National Association of Manufacturers
NAM . . . . Naval Aircraft Modification
NAM . . . . Naval Aviation Museum (Pensacola, Fla.)
NAM . . . . Nederlandsche Aluminium Maatschappij NV
NAM . . . . Network Analysis Model
NAM . . . . Newspaper Association Managers
NAM . . . . North America
NAM . . . . North American Mortgage Investors (NYSE symbol)
NAMA . . . . . . National Automatic Merchandising Association
NAMA . . . . . . National Automotive Muffler Association
NAMA . . . . . . Naval Aeronautical Material Area
NAMA . . . . . . North American Mycological Association
NAMAC . . . . . National Amateur Missile Analysis Center
NAMAC . . . . National Association of Men's Apparel Clubs
NAMAE . . . . . Northern Air Materiel Area, Europe
NAMAP . . . . . Northern Air Materiel Area, Pacific
NAMARCO . . . National Marketing Corporation (Philippines)
NAMATCEN . . Naval Air Material Center
NAMB . . . . . National Association of Merchandise Brokers
NAMB . . . . . . Naval Amphibious Base
NAMBAC . . . . National Association Men's and Boys' Apparel Clubs
NAMBO . . . . . National Association of Motor Bus Owners
NAMC . . . . . . Naval Aerospace Medical Center
NAMC . . . . . . Naval Air Materiel Center
NAMC . . . . . . Naval Air Materiel Command
NAMC . . . . . . North Atlantic Military Committee
NAMCC . . . . . National Association of Mutual Casualty Companies
NAMD . . . . . . National Association of Marble Dealers
NAMD . . . . . . National Association of Marine Dealers
NAMD . . . . . . National Association of Market Developers
NAMD . . . . . . Naval Ammunition Depot
NAMDB . . . . . National Association of Medical-Dental Bureaus
NAMDI . . . . . . National Marine Data Inventory
NAME . . . . . . National Association of Management Educators
NAME . . . . . . National Association for Minority Education
NAMESU . . . . . National Association of Music Executives in State Universities
NAMF . . . . . . National Association of Metal Finishers
NAMFI . . . . . . NATO Missile Firing Installation
NAMG . . . . . . Narrow-Angle Mars Gate (NASA)
NAMG . . . . . . National Association of Mining Groups
NAMH . . . . . . National Association for Mental Health
NAMHH . . . . . National Association of Methodist Hospitals and Homes
NAMI . . . . . . Naval Aerospace Medical Institute
NAMIA . . . . . . National Association of Mutual Insurance Agents
NAMIC . . . . . . National Association of Mutual Insurance Companies
NAMILCOM . . North Atlantic Military Committee
NAMILPO . . . . NATO Military Posture
NAMIM . . . . . National Association of Musical Instrument Mechanics
NAMISTESTCEN . . Naval Air Missile Test Center
NAML . . . . . . National Applied Mathematics Laboratory (National Bureau of Standards)
NAMM . . . . . National Association of Margarine Manufacturers
NAMM . . . . . National Association of Mass Merchandisers
NAMM . . . . . . National Association of Mirror Manufacturers
NAMM . . . . . National Association of Music Merchants
NAMMD . . . . National Association of Marinas and Marine Dealers
NAMMIS . . . . . Navy Aviation Maintenance and Material Support System
NAMMM . . . . National Association of Musical Merchandise Manufacturers (Later,
        GAMA)
NAMMW . . . . . National Association of Musical Merchandise Wholesalers
NAMO . . . . . National Association of Marketing Officials
NAMO . . . . . National Association of Multifamily Owners
NAMO . . . . . . Naval Aircraft Maintenance Orders
NAMOA . . . . . National Association of Miscellaneous Ornamental and Architectural
        Products Contractors
NAMOS . . . . . National Art Museum of Sport
NAMP . . . . . National Association of Magazine Publishers
NAMP . . . . . National Association of Marble Producers
NAMP . . . . . National Association of Meat Purveyors
NAMP . . . . . Naval Aircraft Maintenance Program
NAMP . . . . . . Non-Accounting Majors Program
NAMPBG . . . . National Association of Manufacturers of Pressed and Blown Glassware

NAMPPF . . . . . Nautical Air Miles Per Pound of Fuel
NAMPW . . . . . National Association of Meat Processors and Wholesalers
NAMRAD. . . . . Non-Atomic Military Research and Development (Subcommittee)
NAMRC . . . . . North American Marten Rabbit Club
NAMRL . . . . . . Naval Aerospace Medical Research Laboratory
NAMRU . . . . . Navy Medical Research Unit (World War II)
NAMS . . . . . . National Associated Marine Suppliers
NAMS . . . . . . Nurses and Army Medical Specialists
NAMSA . . . . . NATO Maintenance and Supply Agency
NAMSA . . . . . North American Multi-Hull Sailing Association
NAMSB. . . . . . National Association of Men's Sportswear Buyers
NAMSB. . . . . . National Association of Mutual Savings Banks
NAMSO . . . . . NATO Maintenance and Supply Organization (Formerly, NATO
 Maintenance Supply Service Agency)
NAMT . . . . . . National Association for Music Therapy
NAMT . . . . . . Naval Air Maintenance Trainer
NAMT . . . . . . Naval Aircraft Mobile Trainer
NAMTA . . . . . National Art Materials Trade Association
NAMTC . . . . . Naval Air Missile Test Center
NAMTRAGRU. . Naval Aviation Maintenance Training Group
NAMU . . . . . . Naval Aircraft Material (Utility)
NAMU . . . . . . Naval Aircraft Modification Unit
NAMU . . . . . . Nigerian African Mine Workers' Union
NAMW . . . . . . National Association of Ministers' Wives
NAN . . . . Nisi Aliter Notetur (Unless Otherwise Noted)
NANA . . . . . . N-Acetylneuraminic Acid (Biochemistry)
NANA . . . . . . National Advertising Newspaper Association
NANA . . . . . . North American Newspaper Alliance
NANA . . . . . . Northwest Alaska Native Association
NANAC . . . . . National Aircraft Noise Abatement Council
NANBPWC . . . National Association of Negro Business and Professional Women's Clubs
NANC . . . . . . National Association of New Careerists
NANCF . . . . . North Atlantic Naval Coastal Frontier
NAND . . . . . . Naval Ammunition and Net Depot
NANE . . . . . . National Association for Nursery Education
NANEP . . . . . Navy Air Navigation Electronic Project
NANEWS . . . . Naval Aviation News
NANFAC . . . . Naval Air Navigation Facility Advisory Committee
NANM . . . . . . National Association of Negro Musicians
NANP . . . . . . National Association of Naturopathic Physicians
NANPE . . . . . National Association of Newspaper Purchasing Executives
NANS . . . . . . Naval Air Navigation School
NANTDDDC . . National Association of Negro Tailors, Designers, Dressmakers and
 Dry Cleaners
NANTS. . . . . . National Association of Naval Technical Supervisors
NANWEP. . . . . Navy Numerical Weather Prediction
NAO . . . . Narco Scientific Industries, Inc. (NYSE symbol)
NAO . . . . National Association of Optometrists
NAO . . . . Naval Aviation Observer
NAOA . . . . . . National Apartment Owners Association
NAOC . . . . . . Naval Aviation Officer Candidate
NAOEJ. . . . . . National Association of Oil Equipment Jobbers
NAOO . . . . . . National Association of Optometrists and Opticians
NAOP. . . . . . . National Association of Operative Plasterers
NAOS . . . . . . NASA Aircrew Oxygen System
NAOS . . . . . . North Atlantic Ocean Station
NAOT . . . . . . National Association of Organ Teachers
NAOT . . . . . . Naval Air Operational Training
NAOTC . . . . . Naval Air Operational Training Command
NAOTS . . . . . Naval Aviation Ordnance Test Station
NAP. . . . . Narragansett Pier R. R. (AAR code)
NAP. . . . . National Association of Parliamentarians
NAP . . . . National Association of Postmasters
NAP. . . . . National Association of Publishers
NAP. . . . . Naval Air Priorities
NAP. . . . . Naval Aviation Pilot
NAP. . . . . Neighborhood Action Program (New York City)
NAP. . . . . New Associations and Projects (A publication) (Formerly, NA)
NAP. . . . . Noise Abatement Procedure
NAP. . . . . Nomina Anatomica Parisiensia
NAP. . . . . Nonagency Purchase
NAP . . . . Not at Present
NAP. . . . . Nuclear-Active Particles (Astrophysics)
NAP. . . . . Nuclear Auxiliary Power
NAPA. . . . . . . National Academy of Public Administration
NAPA . . . . . . National Amateur Press Association
NAPA . . . . . National Asphalt Pavement Association
NAPA . . . . . . National Association of the Partners of the Alliance
NAPA . . . . . . National Association of Performing Artists
NAPA . . . . . . National Association of Polish Americans
NAPA. . . . . . . National Association of Purchasing Agents

NAPA. . . . . . National Automotive Parts Association
NAPA. . . . . . National Police Officers' Association
NAPA. . . . . . North American Pizza Association
NAPAC. . . . . National Program for Acquisitions and Cataloging (Library science)
NAPALM . . . . National ADP (Automatic Data Processing) Program for AMC (Army
 Materiel Command) Logistics Management
NAPAN . . . . . National Association for the Prevention of Addiction to Narcotics
NAPB . . . . . . National Association of Professional Bureaucrats
NAPBL . . . . . National Association of Professional Baseball Leagues
NAPC . . . . . . National Association of Plumbing Contractors
NAPC. . . . . . National Association of Precancel Collectors
NAPCA. . . . . National Air Pollution Control Administration (Later, APCO)
NAPCA. . . . . National Association of Pipe Coating Applicators
NAPCA. . . . . National Association of Professional Contracts Administrators
NAPCR . . . . . National Association for Puerto Rican Civil Rights
NAPCU. . . . . Northwest Association of Private Colleges and Universities
NAPE . . . . . . National Alliance of Postal Employees
NAPE . . . . . . National Association of Power Engineers
NAPE . . . . . . Nuclear Attack Preparedness Evaluation
NAPECW. . . . National Association for Physical Education of College Women
NAPEM. . . . . National Association of Public Exposition Managers
NAPEP . . . . . National Association of Planners, Estimators & Progressmen
NAPET . . . . . National Association of Photo Equipment Technicians
NAPF . . . . . . National Association of Plastic Fabricators
NAPF . . . . . . Naval Aviation Publication Facility
NAPFE . . . . . National Alliance of Postal and Federal Employees
NAPFM. . . . . National Association of Packaged Fuel Manufacturers
NAP(G) . . . . Naval Aviation Pilot (Glider)
NAPH. . . . . . National Association of the Physically Handicapped
NAPH. . . . . . National Association of Professors of Hebrew
NAPHCC. . . . National Association of Plumbing-Heating-Cooling Contractors
NAPI . . . . . . National Appaloosa Pony, Incorporated
NAPI . . . . . . National Association of the Pet Industry
NAPIA . . . . . National Association of Public Insurance Adjusters
NAPIM . . . . . National Association of Printing Ink Makers
NAPL. . . . . . National Association of Photo-Lithographers
NAPL. . . . . . National Association of Police Laboratories
NAPM . . . . . National Association of Pattern Manufacturers
NAPM . . . . . National Association of Photographic Manufacturers
NAPM . . . . . National Association of Punch Manufacturers
NAPMM . . . . National Association of Produce Market Managers
NAPNE. . . . . National Association for Practical Nurse Education
NAPNES . . . . National Association for Practical Nurse Education and Service
NAPNM . . . . National Association of Pipe Nipple Manufacturers
NAPO . . . . . Naval Air Priorities Office
NAPO . . . . . United National Association of Post Office Craftsmen
NAPOLI . . . . National Politics (Behavioral science game)
NAPOMHWMGL . . National Association of Post Office Mail Handlers, Watchmen,
 Messengers and Group Leaders
NAPP . . . . . National Association of Play Publishers
NAPP . . . . . National Association of Priest Pilots
NAPP. . . . . . Naval Aviation Preparatory Program
NAPP . . . . . Neighborhood Adult Participation Project
NAPPA. . . . . National Association of Physical Plant Administrators of Universities &
 Colleges
NAPPA . . . . . National Association of Pupil Personnel Administrators
NAPPC. . . . . National Association of Party Plan Companies
NAPPH . . . . . National Association of Private Psychiatric Hospitals
NAPPO. . . . . National Association of Plant Patent Owners
NAPR . . . . . National Association for Pastoral Renewal
NAPRE . . . . . National Association Practical Refrigerating Engineers
NAPRW. . . . . Northwest African Photographic Reconnaissance Wing
NAPS . . . . . National Association of Postal Supervisors
NAPS . . . . . Naval Academy Preparatory School
NAPS . . . . . Night Aerial Photographic System
NAPS . . . . . North American Precis Syndicate
NAPSAA . . . . National Association of Public School Adult Administrators (Later,
 NAPSAE)
NAPSAC. . . . Naval Atomic Planning, Support and Capabilities Report
NAPSAE . . . . National Association of Public School Adult Educators
NAPSG. . . . . National Association of Principals of Schools for Girls
NAPSIC . . . . North American Power Systems Interconnection Committee (US and
 Canada) (Electric power)
NAPT . . . . . National Association of Physical Therapists
NAPT . . . . . Naval Air Primary Training
NAPTC . . . . . Naval Air Propulsion Test Center
NAPTC . . . . . Naval Aviation Primary Training Command
NAPT(C) . . . . Naval Air Primary Training (Command)
NAPTC-AED. . Naval Air Propulsion Test Center - Aeronautical Engine Department
NAPTC-ATD. . Naval Air Propulsion Test Center - Aeronautical Turbine Department
NAPTCRO . . . . Naval Air Primary Training Command Regional Office

NAPU . . . . Nuclear Auxiliary Power Unit
NAPUS . . . . . . National Association of Postmasters of the United States
NAPUS . . . . . . Nuclear Auxiliary Power Unit System
NAQF . . . . North Atlantic Quality Figure
NAR . . . . Narrow
NAR . . . . National Association of Rocketry
NAR . . . . . Navy Ammunition Reclassification
NAR . . . . New American Review (A publication)
NAR . . . . . No Answer (Action) Required
NAR . . . . North American Rockwell Corporation
NAR . . . . Northern Alberta Railways Company (AAR code)
NAR . . . . Not According to Routine
NAR . . . . Notice of Ammunition Reclassification (Navy)
NAR . . . . Numerical Analysis Research
NARA . . . . Narcotic Addict Rehabilitation Act
NARAD . . . . . . Naval Research and Development
NARAL . . . . . . National Association for Repeal of Abortion Laws
NARANEXOS . . Name, Rate, Service Number, and Expiration of Obligated Service (Navy)
NARANO . . . . Name, Rate and Service Number
NARAS . . . . . . National Academy of Recording Arts and Sciences
NARATE . . . . . Navy Advanced RADAR Automatic Test Equipment
NARB . . . . National Advertising Review Board
NARB . . . . National Association of Referees in Bankruptcy
NARBA . . . . . . North American Regional Broadcasting Agreement (To minimize interference between AM stations)
NARBW . . . . . . National Association of Railway Business Women
NARC . . . . National Association for Retarded Children
NARC . . . . Nonautomatic Relay Center
NARC . . . . North American Rockwell Corporation
NARCE . . . . . National Association of Retired Civil Employees (Later, NARFE)
NARCF . . . . . . National Association of Retail Clothiers and Furnishers
NARCO . . . . . . Narcotics Commission (UN)
NARCO . . . . . National Aeronautical Corporation
NARCOM . . . Narration, Commentary (Motion pictures)
NARCOM . . . . North Atlantic Relay Communication Satellite
NARD . . . . National Association of Retail Druggists
NARD . . . . . National Association of Rudimental Drummers
NARDA . . . . . . National Appliance and Radio–TV Dealers Association
NARDIC . . . . . Navy Research and Development Information Center
NARDIS . . . . . Navy Automated Research and Development Information System
NARDIV . . . . . Naval Air Reserve Divisions
NAREB . . . . . . National Association of Real Estate Boards
NAREB . . . . . National Association of Real Estate Brokers
NAREC . . . . . . Naval Research Electronic Computer
NAREE . . . . . National Association of Real Estate Editors
NAREIF . . . . . . National Association of Real Estate Investment Funds
NARF . . . . Native American Rights Fund
NARF . . . . Naval Air Rework Facility
NARF . . . . . . Nuclear Aerospace Research Facility (Air Force)
NARFE . . . . . National Association of Retired Federal Employees (Formerly, NARCE)
NARGUS . . . . . National Association of Retail Grocers of the United States
NARHC . . . . . National Association of River and Harbor Contractors
NARI . . . . National Association of Residents and Interns
NARI . . . . Nuclear Aerospace Research Institute (Air Force)
NARIC . . . . . National Rice and Corn Board (Philippines)
NARICM . . . . . National Association of Retail Ice Cream Manufacturers
NARKOMVNUDEL . . Narodnyi Komissariat Vnutrennikh Del (People's Commissariat of Internal Affairs) (Soviet secret police organization) (Also known as NKVD)
NARL . . . . Naval Arctic Research Laboratory
NARM . . . . . . National Association of Record Merchandisers
NARM . . . . . . National Association of Relay Manufacturers
NARMFD . . . . National Association of Retail Meat and Food Dealers
NARMIC . . . . . National Action/Research on the Military Industrial Complex
NARMU . . . . . Naval Air Reserve Maintenance Units
NAROCTESTSTA . . Naval Air Rocket Test Station
NARP . . . . National Association of Railroad Passengers
NARRD . . . . . National Association of Record Retailer Dealers
NARS . . . . . . National Archives and Records Service (of GSA)
NARS . . . . Non-Affiliated Reserve Section
NARS . . . . North Atlantic Radio System
NARSA . . . . . . National Automotive Radiator Service Association
NARSC . . . . . National Association of Reinforcing Steel Contractors
NARST . . . . . National Association for Research in Science Teaching
NARSTC . . . . . Naval Air Rescue Training Command
NART . . . . National Association Recreational Therapists
NARTB . . . . . National Association of Radio & Television Broadcasters
NARTC . . . . . National Association of Railroad Trial Counsel
NARTC . . . . . . Naval Air Research Training Command
NARTEL . . . . North Atlantic Radiotelephone

NARTRANS . . . North American Rockwell Training and Services
NARTS . . . . . . Naval Aeronautics Test Station
NARTS . . . . . . Naval Air Rocket Test Station
NARTU . . . . . . Naval Air Reserve Training Unit
NARUC . . . . . . National Association of Railroad and Utilities Commissioners
NARVRE . . . . . National Association of Retired and Veteran Railroad Employees
NARW . . . . National Association of Refrigerated Warehouses (Later, IARW)
NAS . . . . Narrow Angle Sensor
NAS . . . . National Academy of Sciences
NAS . . . . National Advocates Society
NAS . . . . National Aerospace Standards
NAS . . . . National Aerospace System (FAA)
NAS . . . . National Aircraft Standards
NAS . . . . National Airspace or Aviation System (FAA)
NAS . . . . National Aquarium Society
NAS . . . . National Association of Sanitarians
NAS . . . . National Association of Stevedores
NAS . . . . National Association of Supervisors
NAS . . . . National Audubon Society
NAS . . . . National Service Industries, Inc. (NYSE symbol)
NAS . . . . Naval Air Station
NAS . . . . Nocturnal Adoration Society
NAS . . . . Nonlinear Antenna System
NAS . . . . Nursery Association Secretaries
NAS . . . . Nursing Auxiliary Service (British)
NASA . . . . National Acoustical Suppliers Association
NASA . . . . . . National Aeronautics and Space Administration
NASA . . . . National Animal Speech Agency (Humorous)
NASA . . . . National Appliance Service Association
NASA . . . . National Association of Schools of Art
NASA . . . . National Association of Securities Administrators
NASA . . . . National Association of Synagogue Administrators
NASA . . . . . National Automobile Salesmen's Association
NASA . . . . North American Securities Administrators
NASA . . . . North American Swiss Alliance
NASAB . . . . . . National Association of Shippers Advisory Boards
NASACT . . . . National Association of State Auditors, Comptrollers and Treasurers
NASAE . . . . . National Association of Supervisors of Agricultural Education
NASAF . . . . . . Northeast African Strategic Air Force
NASAKOM . . . Nasional, Agama, Kommunist (Indonesian President Sukarno's policy of unity among National, Religious, and Communist forces)
NASAO . . . . . National Association of State Aviation Officials
NASAP . . . . . . Network Analysis for Systems Applications Program (Computer program) (NASA)
NASARR . . . . . North American Search and Ranging RADAR (Navy)
NASASP . . . . National Association State Agencies for Surplus Property
NASA-TR . . . . NASA Tank Reactor
NASB . . . . Navigational Aid Support Base
NASBCO . . . . . National Association of School Bus Contract Operators
NASBE . . . . . National Association of State Boards of Education
NASBERM . . . Naval Air Station Bermuda
NASBIC . . . . . National Association of Small Business Investment Companies
NASBLA . . . . . National Association of State Boating Law Administrators
NASBO . . . . . National Association of State Budget Officers
NASBOE . . . . . National Association of Supervisors of Business and Office Education
NASBP . . . . . . National Association of Surety Bond Producers
NASC . . . . . National Aeronautics and Space Council
NASC . . . . National Aircraft Standards Committee
NASC . . . . . National Association of Specialized Carriers
NASC . . . . National Association of Student Councils
NASC . . . . . . NATO Supply Center
NASC . . . . Naval Air Systems Command
NASC . . . . . . Naval Aviation Safety Center
NASC . . . . . . North America Supply Council
NASCAR . . . . . National Association for Stock Car Auto Racing
NASCAS . . . . . National Academy of Science Committee on Atmospheric Science
NASCD . . . . . . National Association of Soil Conservation Districts
NASCDD . . . . . National Association of State Civil Defense Directors
NASCL . . . . . North American Student Cooperative League
NASCO . . . . . National Academy of Sciences Committee on Oceanography
NASCOM . . . . NASA Worldwide Communications Network
NASCOM . . . . Naval Air Systems Command
NASCOP . . . . . NASA Communications Operating Procedures
NASCRIST . . . . Naval Air Station Corpus Christi
NASCS . . . . . National Association of Shoe Chain Stores
NASD . . . . National Association of Schools of Design
NASD . . . . National Association of Securities Dealers
NASD . . . . . . Naval Air Supply Depot
NASD . . . . Naval Aviation Supply Depot
NASDA . . . . . National Association of Sign and Display Advertisers

NASDA ..... National Association of State Departments of Agriculture (Formerly, NACSDA)
NASDAD .... National Association of Seventh-Day Adventist Dentists
NASDAQ .... National Association of Securities Dealers Automated Quotations (Over-the-counter stock quotations)
NASDIEGO ... Naval Air Station San Diego
NASDM ..... National Association of Special Delivery Messengers
NASDSE ..... National Association of State Directors of Special Education
NASDSSE .... National Association of State Directors and Supervisors of Secondary Education
NASDT ...... Naval Aviators' Speech Discrimination Test
NASDTEC .... National Association of State Directors of Teacher Education and Certification
NASDVA ..... National Association of State Directors of Veterans Affairs
NASDVE ..... National Association of State Directors of Vocational Education
NASE .... National Academy of School Executives
NASE .... National Association of Steel Exporters
NASEAB ..... Naval Air Systems Effectiveness Advisory Board
NASEAN ..... National Association for State Enrolled Assistant Nurses
NASF .... National Association of State Foresters
NASFAA ..... National Association of Student Financial Aid Administrators (Formerly, NSFAC)
NASFCA ..... National Automatic Sprinkler and Fire Control Association
NASFM ...... National Association of Store Fixture Manufacturers
NASFT ...... National Association for the Specialty Food Trade
NASGTMO ... Naval Air Station Guantanamo
NASGW ..... National Association of Sporting Goods Wholesalers
NASHAW .... National Association for Statewide Health and Welfare
NASIS ...... NASA Aerospace Safety Information System
NASIS ...... National Association for State Information Systems
NASJAX ..... Naval Air Station Jacksonville
NASL .... Naval Applied Science Laboratory
NASL .... North American Soccer League
NASLAKE .... Naval Air Station Lakehurst
NASLS ...... National Association of Small Loan Supervisors
NASM .... National Air and Space Museum (of the Smithsonian Institution) (Formerly, National Air Museum)
NASM ...... National Association of Schools of Music
NASM ...... National Association of Service Managers
NASM ...... National Association of State Militia
NASM ...... Naval Aviation School of Medicine
NASMBCM ... National Association of Sanitary Milk Bottle Closure Manufacturers
NASMD ..... National Association of School Music Dealers
NASMD ..... National Association of Sewing Machine Dealers (Defunct)
NASMD ..... National Association of Sewing Machine Distributors (Defunct)
NASMD ..... National Association of Sheet Metal Distributors
NASMD ..... National Association of Sheet Music Dealers
NASMHPD ... National Association of State Mental Health Program Directors
NASMI ...... National Association of Secondary Material Industries
NASMO ..... NATO Starfighter Management Office
NASN ...... National Air Sampling Network (Public Health Service)
NAS–NRC .... National Academy of Sciences – National Research Council
NASO ...... Natchez & Southern Railway Company (AAR code)
NASO ...... National Astronomy (or Astronomical) Space Observatory (NASA)
NASO ...... Naval Aviation Supply Office
NASORLO .... National Association of State Outdoor Recreation Liaison Officers
NASP ...... National Airport Systems Plan (FAA)
NASP ...... National Association of School Psychologists
NASP ...... Negro, Anglo-Saxon Protestant
NASPA ..... National Association of Student Personnel Administrators
NASPENSA ... Naval Air Station Pensacola
NASPM ..... National Association of Slipper and Playshoe Manufacturers
NASPO ..... National Airspace System Program Office (FAA)
NASPO ..... National Association of State Purchasing Officials
NASPSM .... National Association of Shirt, Pajama and Sportswear Manufacturers
NASPSPA .... North American Society for the Psychology of Sport and Physical Activity
NASQUON ... Naval Air Station Quonset Point
NASR ...... National Annual Symposium on Reliability (IEEE)
NASR ...... National Association of Swine Records
NASRA ..... National Association of State Retirement Administrators
NASRC ..... National Association of State Racing Commissioners
NASRP ..... National Association of Special and Reserve Police
NASRR ..... North American Search and Range RADAR
NASS ...... National Aids Support System
NASS ...... National Association of Secretaries of State
NASS ...... National Association of Specialized Schools
NASS ...... National Association of Suggestion Systems
NASS ...... National Association of Summer Sessions
NASS ...... Naval Air Signal School
NASSA ..... National Aerospace Services Association

NASSB ..... National Association of Supervisors of State Banks
NASSC ..... National Alliance on Shaping Safer Cities
NASSDE .... National Association of State Supervisors of Distributive Education
NASSDSE .... National Association of State Supervisors and Directors of Secondary Education
NAS/SEC .... National Academy of Sciences' Site Evaluation Committee
NASSHE .... National Association of State Supervisors of Home Economics
NASSP ..... National Association of Secondary-School Principals
NASSSA ..... National Association of State Social Security Administrators
NASSTA ..... National Association of Secretaries of State Teachers Associations
NASSTIE .... National Association of State Supervisors of Trade and Industrial Education
NASTBD ..... National Association of State Text Book Directors
NASTRAN .... NASA Structural Analysis
NASU ...... National Association of State Universities (Defunct)
NASU ...... North American Singers Union
NASULGC ... National Association of State Universities and Land Grant Colleges
NASUP ..... National Association on Service to Unmarried Parents
NASW ..... National Association of Science Writers
NASW ..... National Association of Social Workers
NASWF ..... Naval Air Special Weapons Facility
NASWHP..... National Association of Sheltered Workshops and Homebound Programs
NASWSO .... National Association of Soft Water Service Operators
NAT .... Nationality
NAT .... Native
NAT .... Natural
NAT .... Naval Air Training
NAT .... No Action Taken
NAT .... North African Theater (World War II)
NAT .... North Atlantic Regional Area (Aviation)
NAT .... North Atlantic Treaty
NATA ...... National Association of Tax Accountants
NATA ...... National Association of Tax Administrators
NATA ...... National Association of Teachers' Agencies
NATA ...... National Association of Temple Administrators
NATA ...... National Association of Transportation Advertising
NATA ...... National Athletic Trainers Association
NATA ...... National Automobile Transporters Association
NATA ...... National Aviation Trades Association
NATA ...... National Aviation Training Association
NATA ...... North Atlantic Treaty Alliance
NATAF ..... Northwest African Tactical Air Force (World War II)
NATAPROBU .. National Association of Professional Bureaucrats
NATAS ..... National Academy of Television Arts and Sciences
NATAS ..... North American Thermal Analysis Society
NATAW ..... National Association of Textile and Apparel Wholesalers
NATB ...... National Automobile Theft Bureau
NATB ...... Naval Air Training Base
NATBASES.... Naval Air Training Bases
NATC ...... National Air Taxi Conference
NATC ...... National Association of Taurine Clubs
NATC ...... Naval Air Testing Center
NATC ...... Naval Air Training Center (or Command)
NATCAS ..... Navigation, Air Traffic Control and Collision Avoidance System
NATCC ..... National Air Transport Coordinating Committee
NATCO ..... National Automatic Tool Company
NATCO ..... Navy Air Traffic Coordinating Officer
NATCOM .... National Communications Center (FAA)
NATCOM .... National Communications Symposium (IEEE)
NATD ...... National Association of Tobacco Distributors
NATDEFSM ... National Defense Service Medal
NATE ...... National Association of Teachers of English
NATE ...... National Association of Temple Educators
NATEC ..... Naval Air Training and Experimental Command
NATECHTRACEN .. Naval Air Technical Training Center
NATECHTRAU .. Naval Air Technical Training Unit
NATECOM .... Naval Airship Training and Experimentation Command
NATEL ..... Nortronics Automatic Test Equipment Language
NATESA ..... National Alliance of Television and Electronic Service Associations
NATESTCEN .. Naval Air Test Center
NATEX ...... National Stock Exchange
NATF ...... Naval Air Test Facility
NATFB ..... National Archives Trust Fund Board
NATIP ...... Navy Technical Information Program
NATIV ...... North American Test Instrument Vehicle (Air Force test rocket)
NATL .... National
NATL ...... National Agricultural Transportation League
NATL ...... Naval Aeronautical Turbine Laboratory
NATMC ..... National Advanced Technology Management Conference
NATNAVMEDCEN .. National Naval Medical Center (Bethesda, Maryland)
NATO ...... Narrow-Angle Target of Opportunity (Photography) (NASA)

NATO ...... National Association of Taxicab Owners
NATO...... National Association of Theatre Owners
NATO...... National Association of Trailer Owners
NATO ...... National Association of Travel Organizations (Later, DATO)
NATO ...... North African Theater of Operations (World War II)
NATO ...... North Atlantic Treaty Organization
NATO-AGARD .. NATO-Advisory Group for Aeronautical Research and Development
NATOELLA ... NATO-European Long Lines Agency
NATO-LRSS... NATO-Long-Range Scientific Studies
NATOPS ..... Naval Aeronautical Tactical Operations
NATOPS ..... Naval Air Training and Operating Procedures Standardization
NATO-RDPP .. NATO-Multilateral Research and Development Production Program
NATO-SC .... NATO Science Committee
NATOUSA.... North African Theater of Operations United States Army (World War II)
NATPE ..... National Association of Television Program Executives
NATR ...... Natchez Trace Parkway (National Park Service designation)
NATR ...... No Additional Traffic Reported (Aviation)
NATRFD ..... National Association of Television-Radio Farm Directors
NATRI ...... Navy Training Requirements Information
NATS ...... National Association of Teachers of Singing
NATS ...... Naval Air Transport Service
NATS ...... Nordisk Avisteknisk Samarbetsnaemnd (Scandinavian Newspaper Technical
          Cooperation Council)
NATSA ..... National Associated Truck Stops and Associates
NATSC ..... National Association of Training School Chaplains
NATSC ..... National Association of Trap and Skeet Clubs
NATSECM .... National Security Medal
NATSF ..... Naval Air Technical Services (or Support) Facility
NATSFERRY .. Naval Air Transport Service, Ferry Command (World War II)
NATSJA ..... National Association of Training Schools and Juvenile Agencies
NATSLANT ... Naval Air Transport Service, Atlantic Wing
NATSO ..... National Association of Truck Stop Operators
NATSOPA .... National Society of Operative Printers and Assistants (British)
NATSPAC .... Naval Air Transport Service, Pacific Wing
NATSYN ..... Natural and Synthetic (Type of long-wearing rubber, which is actually
          wholly synthetic)
NATT ...... Naval Air Technical Training
NATTC ..... Naval Air Technical Training Center or Command
NATTS ..... National Association of Trade and Technical Schools
NATTS ..... Naval Air Turbine Test Station
NATTU ..... Naval Air Technical Training Unit
NATU ...... National Association of Trade Unions (Philippines)
NATU ...... Naval Aircraft Torpedo Unit
NATURBTESTSTA .. Naval Air Turbine Test Station
NATVAS ..... National Academy of Television Arts and Sciences
NATWA ..... National Auto and Truck Wreckers Association
NATWP ..... Naval Air Transport Wing, Pacific
NAU ...... Nautec Corporation (NYSE symbol) (Delisted)
NAUA ...... National Automobile Underwriters Association
NAUI ...... National Association of Underwater Instructors
NAUL ...... Netherland-America University League
NAULAS ..... North American Union Life Assurance Society
NAUM ...... National Association of Uniform Manufacturers
NAUT ...... Nautical
NAUWS ..... Naval Advanced Undersea Weapons School
NAV ...... National American Veterans
NAV ...... Navigate (Navigation; Navigational; Navigator)
NAV........ Navy
NAV ...... Net Asset Value
NAVA ...... National Audio-Visual Association
NAVA ...... Navajo National Monument
NAVA ...... North American Vexillological Association
NAVACT..... (Communication directed to) All Navy Activities
NAVAD ..... Naval Administrator at (place)
NAVADCOM.. Naval Administrative Command
NAVADUNIT.. Naval Administrative Unit
NAVAER .... Navy Aeronautics
NAVAERORECOV.. Naval Aerospace Recovery Facility
NAVAGLOBE.. Long Distance Navigation System, Global (Air Force)
NAVAID ..... Navigation Aid
NAVAIR ..... Naval Air Systems Command
NAVAIREWORKF.. Naval Air Rework Facility
NAVAIRFAC .. Naval Air Facility
NAVAIRLANT . Naval Air Force, Atlantic Fleet
NAVAIRPAC .. Naval Air Force, Pacific Fleet
NAVAIRRES... Naval Air Reserve
NAVAIRSYSCO .. Naval Air Systems Command
NAVAIRSYSCOM.. Naval Air Systems Command
NAVAIRTRACEN .. Naval Air Training Center
NAVALOT.... Allotment Division (Navy)
NAVAMDEP... Naval Ammunition Depot

NAVANTRACOM .. Naval Air Advanced Training Command
NAVAR ..... Navigation RADAR
NAVARA .... Navy Appellate Review Activity
Nav Arch .... Naval Architect (Academic degree)
NAVAREAAUDSVC .. Naval Area Audit Service
NAVARHO .... Navigation and Radio Homing (Aviation)
NAVARMDEP.. Superintendent or Officer in Charge Naval Armament and/or
          Ammunition Depot at (place)
NAVASCOPE.. Airborne RADARscope Used in NAVAR (Air Force)
NAVASCREEN.. Navigation RADAR Screen (Air Force)
NAVAUD .... Navy Auditor
NAVAUDSVC.. Director, Naval Audit Service
NAVAUTH.... Naval Authority
NAVBASE .... Naval Base
NAVBMC .... Navy Ballistic Missile Committee
NAVBOILAB .. Navy Boiler Laboratory
NAVC ...... Naval Aviation Cadet
NAVCAD .... Naval Aviation Cadet
NAVCENFRACO .. Navy Central Freight Control Office
NAVCENT ... Allied Naval Forces Central Europe
NAVCG ..... Coast Guard Publications
NAVCLODEP.. Naval Clothing Depot
NAVCM ..... Navigation Countermeasures and Deception
NAVCOM ... Naval Communications
NAVCOMM... Naval Communications (System)
NAVCOMMSTA .. Naval Communication Station
NAVCOMMU.. Naval Communication Unit
NAVCOMPT .. Office of the Comptroller of the Navy
Nav Const ... Naval Constructor (Academic degree)
NAVCONTRACEN .. Naval Construction Training Center
NAVCONVHOSP .. Naval Convalescent Hospital
NAVCOSSACT. Naval Command Systems Support Activity (Military)
NAVDAC .... Navigation Data Assimilation Computer
NAVDET .... Naval Detachment
NAVDIS ..... Naval District
NAVDISCBAR.. Naval Disciplinary Barracks
NAVDISP .... Naval Dispensary
NAVDIST .... Naval District
NAVDOC .... Navy Department Orientation Course
NAVDOCKS .. Bureau of Yards and Docks Publications (Navy) (Obsolete)
Nav E ...... Naval Engineer (Academic degree)
NAVELEX .... Naval Electronic Systems Command
NAVELEXSYSCOM .. Naval Electronics Systems Command
NAVENGRXSTA.. Naval Engineering Experiment Station
NAVEODFAC.. Naval Explosive Ordnance Disposal Facility
NAVEU...... US Naval Forces in European Waters
NAVEXAM ... Naval Examining Board
NAVEXOS.... Executive Office of the Secretary Publications (Navy)
NAVFAC .... Naval Facility
NAVFACENGCOM .. Naval Facilities Engineering Command
NAVFACENSYSCOM .. Naval Facilities Engineering Systems Command
NAVFE...... Naval Forces Far East
NAVFEC ..... Naval Facilities Engineering Command
NAVFLIGHTPREPSCOL .. Naval Flight Preparatory School
NAVFOR .... US Naval Forces
NAVFOREU ... US Naval Forces Europe (Later, NAVEU)
NAVFORGER.. US Naval Forces Germany
NAVFORJAP .. Naval Forces, Japan
NAVFORKOR.. Naval Forces, Korea
NAVFROF .... Navy Freight Office
NAVFUELDEP.. Naval Fuel Depot
NAVGEN .... Navy General Publications
NAVGUN .... Naval Gun Factory (Later, NWF)
NAVH ...... National Aid to Visually Handicapped (An organization)
NAVHOME ... US Naval Home (Philadelphia)
NAVHOSP.... US Naval Hospital
NAVHT ..... National Association of Vocational Homemaking Teachers
NAVIC ..... Navy Information Center
NAVICERT ... Navigation Certificate (Paper issued by British government to merchant
          vessel, certifying that cargo was noncontraband; that is, not
          consigned to Germany) (World War II)
NAVINSGEN.. Naval Inspector General
NAVINTEL ... Naval Intelligence
NAVION .... North American Aviation, Inc. (Also used to refer to light aircraft
          of World War II)
NAVJAG .... Judge Advocate General's Office Publications (Navy)
NAVJAP..... US Naval Forces, Japan
NAVLIS ..... Navy Logistics Information System
NAVLO ..... Naval Liaison Officer
NAVLOGSIP.. Navy Logistic Support Improvement Plan
NAVMAG .... US Naval Magazine

NAVMAR . . . . . Naval Forces, Marianas
NAVMAT. . . . . Naval Material Command
NAVMATINST. . Navy Material Instruction
NAVMATMOCON . . Navy Material Movement Control Plan
NAVMC . . . . . Marine Corps Publications
NAVMED. . . . . Naval Forces, Mediterranean (Formerly, NAVNAW)
NAVMED . . . . . Naval Medicine
NAVMEDIS . . . Navy Medical Information System
NAVMINCOMEASTA. . Navy Mine Countermeasures Station
NAVMINDEFLAB . . Navy Mine Defense Laboratory
NAVMINDEP. . Naval Mine Depot
NAVMIS . . . . . Naval Mission
NAVMUTAID . . Navy Mutual Aid
NAVNAW . . . . US Naval Forces, Northwest African Waters (Later, NAVMED)
NAVNETDEP . . Naval Net Depot
NAVNORSOLS . . Naval Forces, Northern Solomons (World War II)
NAVNORTH. . . Allied Naval Forces, Northern Europe
NAVNZ . . . . Naval Forces, New Zealand (World War II)
NAVOBSY. . . . Naval Observatory
NAVOCEANO . . Naval Oceanographic Office (Also known as NOO)
NAVOCS . . . . Naval Officer Candidate School
NAVOPFAC . . Naval Operation Facility
NAVORD . . . . Naval Ordnance Publications
NAVORD . . . . Naval Ordnance Systems Command
NAVORDSYSCO. . Naval Ordnance Systems Command
NAVORDSYSCOM . . Naval Ordnance Systems Command
NAVORDSYSSUPPO . . Naval Ordnance Systems Support Office
NAVPECO. . . . Naval Production Equipment Control Office
NAVPERS . . . . Bureau of Naval Personnel
NAVPERS . . . . Naval Personnel
NAVPERSRANDLAB. . Navy Personnel Research and Development Laboratory
NAVPHIL . . . . Naval Forces, Philippines
NAVPHOTOCEN . . Naval Photographic Center
NAVPORCO . . Naval Port Control Office
NAVPORCOF. . Naval Port Control Officer
NAVPOWFAC. . Naval Powder Factory
NAVPREFLIGHTSCOL . . Naval Preflight School
NAVPRIS . . . . Naval Prison
NAVPRO. . . . . Naval Plant Representative Office
NAVPROV. . . . Naval Proving Ground (Dahlgren, Virginia)
NAVPUBSCONBD . . Navy Department Publications Control Board
NAVPUR . . . . Navy Purchasing Office
NAVRADSTA . . Naval Radio Station
NAVRECONTECHSUPPCEN . . Naval Reconnaissance & Technical Support Center
NAVREGS . . . . Navy Regulations
NAVREL . . . . . Navy Relief Society
NAVRES . . . . . Naval Reserve
NAVRESLAB. . . Naval Research Laboratory
NAVRESMIDSCOL. . Naval Reserve Midshipmen's School
NAVRETRAINCOM . . Naval Retraining Command
NAVROUTE . . . Navy Routing Office
NAVRYUKYUS . . Naval Forces, Ryukyus (World War II)
NAVS. . . . . . National Anti-Vivisection Society
NAVS. . . . . . National Association of Variety Stores
NAVS. . . . . . Navigation System
NAVSANDA . . Bureau of Supplies and Accounts Publications (Formerly, NSA; now obsolete) (Navy)
NAVSAT . . . . . Navigational Satellite
NAVSEA . . . . Naval Avionics Support Equipment Appraisal
NAVSEC . . . . . Naval Ship Engineering Center
NAVSECGRU. . Naval Security Group
NAVSECGRUDET . . Naval Security Group Detachment
NAVSECPHILA. . Naval Ship Engineering Center, Philadelphia
NAVSECSTA . . US Naval Security Station
NAVSEG. . . . . Navigation Satellite Executive Steering Group
NAVSHIPLO . . US Navy Shipbuilding Office
NAVSHIPS. . . Bureau of Ships Publications (Navy) (Obsolete)
NAVSHIPSA . . US Navy Shipbuilding Scheduling Activity
NAVSHIPSYSCOM . . Naval Ship Systems Command
NAVSHIPYD . . Naval Shipyard
NAVSMO . . . . Navigation Satellite Management Office
NAVSO . . . . . Naval Supply Office
NAVSPASUR . . Naval Space Surveillance System
NAVSTA . . . . Naval Station
NAVSTAR . . . . Navy Study of Transport Aircraft Requirements
NAVSTRIP . . . . Navy Standard Requisitioning and Issuing Procedure
NAVSUPFORANT . . Naval Support Forces, Antarctica
NAVSUPRANDFA. . Naval Supply Research and Development Facility
NAVSUPSYSCOM . . Naval Supply Systems Command
NAVTA. . . . . . National Automatic Vendors' Trade Association
NAVTAC . . . . Tactical Navigation System

NAVTECHJAP . . Naval Technical Mission to Japan
NAVTECHTRACEN . . Naval Air Technical Training Center
NAVTECMISEU. . Naval Technical Mission in Europe
NAVTORPSTA . . Naval Torpedo Station
NAVTRADEVCEN . . Naval Training Device Center
NAVTRADISTCEN . . Naval Training and Distribution Center
NAVTRAFSAT. . Navigational/Traffic-Control Satellite
NAVTRANSAIR . . (For) Naval Transport Aircraft Class Travel, Priority is Hereby Certified
NAVTRANSCO. Naval Transportation Coordinating Office
NAVTRASCOL . . Naval Training School
NAVTRASTA . . Naval Training Station
NAVUWSES . . . Naval Underwater Systems Engineering Center
NAVWAG . . . . Naval Warfare Analysis Group
NAVWARCOL . . Naval War College
NAVWEPS . . . . Bureau of Naval Weapons (Obsolete)
NAVWESPAC . . US Naval Forces Western Pacific
NAVWPNQUALASSURO. . Naval Weapons Quality Assurance Office
NAVWPNSERVO. . Naval Weapons Services Office (Also known as WEPSO or NWSO)
NAW . . . . National Agricultural Workers Union
NAW . . . . National Association of Wholesalers
NAW . . . . Nationales Aufbauwerk
NAW . . . . Northwest African Waters
NAWA . . . . . . National Apple Week Association
NAWA . . . . . . National Association of Women Artists
NAWAC . . . . National Weather Analysis Center
NAWAF . . . . . Navy with Air Force
NAWAPA . . . . North American Water and Power Alliance
NAWAR . . . . . Navy with Army
NAWAS . . . . . National Warning System (Civil Defense)
NAWB . . . . . . National Association of Wine Bottlers
NAWC . . . . . . Naval War College
NAWCAS . . . . National Association of Women's and Children's Apparel Salesmen
NAWCC . . . . National Association of Watch and Clock Collectors
NAWCM. . . . . National Association of Wiping Cloth Manufacturers
NAWD . . . . . . Notice of Award
NAWDC . . . . National Association of Women Deans and Counselors
NAWF . . . . . . North American Wildlife Foundation
NAWFC . . . . . National Association of Wholesale Fur Cleaners
NAWG . . . . . National Association of Wheat Growers
NAWGA . . . . National-American Wholesale Grocers' Association
NAWIC . . . . . National Association of Women in Construction
NAWL . . . . . . National Association of Women Lawyers
NAWLA . . . . . National-American Wholesale Lumber Association
NAWM. . . . . . National Association of Wool Manufacturers (Later, American Textile Manufacturers Institute)
NAWMD . . . . National Association of Waste Material Dealers
NAWMP . . . . . National Association of Waste Material Producers
NAWPA. . . . . . North American Water and Power Alliance
NAWPB . . . . . National Association of Wholesale Pie Bakers
NAWPC . . . . . National Aircraft War Production Council (World War II)
NAWR . . . . . . National Assembly of Women Religious
NAWS . . . . . . National Aviation Weather System
NAWTPD . . . . Naval All Weather Testing Program Detachment
NAWTS . . . . . National Association of World Trade Secretaries
NAWU . . . . . . National Agricultural Workers Union
NAWWO . . . . National Association of Woolen and Worsted Overseers
NAXSTA . . . . Naval Air Experimental Station
NAYGTA . . . . North American Youth Glider Training Association
NAYRU. . . . . . North American Yacht Racing Union
NAZI . . . . . . Nationalsozialistische Deutsche Arbeiterpartei (National Socialist German Workers' Party, 1919-45)
NB. . . . . Narrow Band (Electronics)
NB. . . . . Naval Base
NB . . . . Nebraska
NB. . . . . New Brunswick (Canadian province)
NB. . . . . Nimbus (Meteorology)
Nb. . . . . Niobium (Chemical element) (See Cb)
NB . . . . No Ball
NB. . . . . No Bias (Relay) (Electronics)
NB . . . . No Bid(ders)
NB. . . . . Nonbattle (Army)
NB . . . . North Britain (i.e., Scotland)
NB. . . . . Northampton & Bath R. R. (AAR code)
NB. . . . . Northbound
NB. . . . . Not Bent (Freight)
NB . . . . Nota Bene (Note Well)
NBA. . . . . Narrow Band Allocation
NBA. . . . . Narrow Band Analyzer
NBA. . . . . Narrow Beam Adapter
NBA. . . . . National Band Association
NBA. . . . . National Bankers Association

NBA . . . . National Bankruptcy Act
NBA . . . . National Bar Association
NBA . . . . National Basketball Association (Professional basketball league)
NBA . . . . National Boat Association
NBA . . . . . National Book Awards
NBA . . . . . National Bowling Association
NBA . . . . National Boxing Association of America
NBA . . . . . . National Braille Association
NBA . . . . National Button Association
NBA . . . . . . Nickel Base Alloy
NBAA . . . . . . National Business Aircraft Association
NBAD . . . . . . Naval Bases Air Defense
NBADA . . . . . . National Barrel and Drum Association
NBAO . . . . New Brunswick Area Office (AEC)
NBAWADU . . . National Black Anti-War Anti-Draft Union
NBBA . . . . . . Northeastern Bird Banding Association
NBBB . . . . . . National Better Business Bureau
NBBDA . . . . . National Burlap Bag Dealers Association
NBBMA . . . . . . National Beauty and Barber Manufacturers Association
NBC . . . . . National Baseball Congress of America (Semiprofessional baseball)
NBC . . . . National Beagle Club
NBC . . . . . . National Beef Council
NBC . . . . National Board for Certification in Dental Technology
NBC . . . . . . National Book Committee
NBC . . . . . National Book Council (Great Britain)
NBC . . . . National Bowling Council
NBC . . . . National Braille Club
NBC . . . . National Broadcasting Company
NBC . . . . National Broiler Council
NBC . . . . . National Bus Company (British)
NBC . . . . Natural Background Clutter
NBC . . . . Navy Beach Commando
NBC . . . . Neumann Boundary Conditions
NBC . . . . Nostalgia Book Club
NBC . . . . . Nuclear, Biological, and Chemical (Warfare)
NBC . . . . Number Base Conversion
NBCA . . . . . . National Bituminous Concrete Association
NBCC . . . . . . National Baby Care Council
NBCC . . . . . . National Bidders Control Center
NBCC . . . . . . National Bituminous Coal Commission (Functions transferred to Department of the Interior, 1939)
NBCC . . . . . . National Budget and Consultation Committee
NBCC . . . . . . National Bureau for Co-operation in Child Care (British)
NBCL . . . . . . National Beauty Culturists' League
NBCSDA . . . . . National Broom Corn and Supply Dealers Association
NBCSI . . . . . . National Board of the Coat and Suit Industry (Defunct)
NBCU . . . . . . National Bureau of Casualty Underwriters
NBCW . . . . . . National Bird Cage Week
NBD . . . . Narrow Band Detector
NBD . . . . Negative Binomial Distribution (Statistics)
NBD . . . . Neutral Beam Divider
NBDA . . . . . National Barrel and Drum Association
NBDA . . . . . . National Bicycle Dealers Association
NBDL . . . . . . Narrowband Data Line
NBE . . . . Neutron Binding Energy
NBE . . . . Nominal Band Edge
NBE . . . . Nuclear Binding Energy
NBEA . . . . . . National Business Education Association
NBEDC . . . . . National Black Economic Development Conference
NBEOPS . . . . . National Board of Examiners for Osteopathic Physicians and Surgeons
NBER . . . . . . National Bureau of Economic Research
NBF . . . . Narrow Band Filter
NBF . . . . National Boating Federation
NBFA . . . . . . National Business Forms Associates
NBFAA . . . . . National Burglar and Fire Alarm Association
NBFFO . . . . . National Board of Fur Farm Organizations
NBFM . . . . . . Narrowband Frequency Modulation
NBFU . . . . . . National Board of Fire Underwriters
NBG . . . . National Bank of Greece
NBG . . . . No Blasted Good (Slang)
NBG . . . . No Bloody Good (British slang)
NBG . . . . Nuclear Beta Gage
NBGQA . . . . . National Building Granite Quarries Association
NBH . . . . National Bellas Hess (Inc.) (Commercial firm)
NBHA . . . . . . National Builders' Hardware Association
NBHCA . . . . . National Belgian Hare Club of America
NBI . . . . Nathaniel Branden Institute
NBI . . . . Norges Byggforskningsinstitutt (Norwegian Building Institute)
NBIT . . . . . . New Bedford Institute of Technology (Massachusetts)
NBK . . . . Nebelkerze (Smoke-candle) (German military - World War II)
NBL . . . . National Business League

NBL . . . . Naval Biological Laboratory (Oakland, California)
NBL . . . . New Brunswick Laboratory (AEC)
NBL . . . . Night Bombardment-Long Distance (Air Force)
NBL . . . . Not Bloody Likely (British slang)
NBLCC . . . . . National Black Lay Catholic Caucus
NBLE . . . . . . Nearly Best Linear Estimator (Statistics)
NBLP . . . . . . National Bureau for Lathing and Plastering
NBLU . . . . . . Naval Base Labour Union (Singapore)
NBMAIA . . . . . National Broom Manufacturers and Allied Industries Association
NBMB . . . . . National Bus Military Bureau
NBMC . . . . . . National Bar Mitzvah Club
NBMC . . . . . . National Businessmen's Council
NBMDA . . . . . National Building Material Distributors Association
NBME . . . . . . National Board of Medical Examiners
NBMG . . . . . Navigation Bombing and Missile Guidance System
NBMGS . . . . Navigation Bombing and Missile Guidance System
NBMR . . . . . NATO Basic Military Requirements
NBN . . . . Narrow Band Network
NBN . . . . Narrow Band Noise
NBNA . . . . . National Bank of North America (New York)
NBO . . . . Navy Bureau of Ordnance
NBOA . . . . . National Ballroom Operators Association
NBP . . . . Narodowy Bank Polski
NBP . . . . National Booster Program
NBP . . . . National Braille Press
NBP . . . . National Business Publications
NBP . . . . Neutral Bitter Principle (Pharmacy)
NBP . . . . Normal Boiling Point
NBPA . . . . . . National Building Products Association
NBPA . . . . . . Navy Board for Production Awards
NBPDW . . . . . National Brotherhood of Packinghouse and Dairy Workers
NBPE . . . . . . National Board of Podiatry Examiners
NBPE . . . . . . National Board of Polygraph Examiners
NBPI . . . . . . National Board for Prices and Incomes (Great Britain)
NBPRP . . . . . National Board for the Promotion of Rifle Practice (Army)
NBPW . . . . . National Brotherhood of Packinghouse Workers
NBR . . . . National Board of Review of Motion Pictures
NBR . . . . Non-Breathing
NBR . . . . North British Railway
NBR . . . . Null Balance Recorder
NBRF . . . . . . National Biochemical Research Foundation
NBRMP . . . . . National Board of Review of Motion Pictures
NBRSA . . . . . National Bench Rest Shooters Association
NBS . . . . Bureau of Ships Publications (Later, NAVSHIPS; now obsolete) (Navy)
NBS . . . . National Bookkeepers' Society
NBS . . . . National Broadcasting Service (of New Zealand)
NBS . . . . National Bureau of Standards (Department of Commerce)
NBS . . . . National Button Society
NBS . . . . Netherland Benevolent Society of New York
NBS . . . . Neutral Buoyancy Simulator
NBS . . . . New British Standard (Imperial wire gage)
NBS . . . . Night Bombardment-Short Distance (Air Force)
NBSA . . . . . . National Bakery Suppliers Association
NBSBL . . . . . National Bureau of Standards Boulder Laboratories
NBSC . . . . . . National Black Sisters' Conference
NBSDI . . . . . National Brands Soft Drinks Institute
NBSR . . . . . . National Bureau of Standards Reactor
NBSS . . . . . . Naval Beach Signal Section
NBT . . . . Narrow-Beam Transducer (National Ocean Survey)
NBT . . . . Navigator Bombardier Training (Air Force)
NBT . . . . Nederlandse Bond van Middelbare en Hogare Technici (Netherlands Union of Professional Engineers)
NBT . . . . Nimbus Beacon Transmitter
NBT . . . . Nitro Blue Tetrazolium
NBTA . . . . . . National Bus Traffic Association
NBTC . . . . . . New Brunswick Teachers College
NBTL . . . . . . Naval Boiler and Turbine Laboratory
NBTR . . . . . . Narrowband Tape Recorder
NBTS . . . . . . National Blood Transfusion Service
NBTS . . . . . . New Brunswick Theological Seminary
NBTS . . . . . . Northern Baptist Theological Seminary
NBW . . . . Noise Band Width
NBWA . . . . . National Beer Wholesalers' Association of America
NBY . . . . Nearest Besselian Year
NC . . . . Nashville, Chattanooga & St. Louis R. R. (AAR code)
NC . . . . National Cash Register Company (NYSE symbol; later, NCR)
NC . . . . National Coarse (Thread)
NC . . . . National Cooperatives (Association)
NC . . . . Naval Correspondence
NC . . . . Navigation Computer
NC . . . . Navigation Console

NC . . . . Navy Cross
NC . . . . Network Controller
NC . . . . New Caledonia
NC . . . . New Construction (Navy)
NC . . . . New Crop
NC . . . . Nickel-Clad
NC . . . . Nippon Club
NC . . . . Nitro Cellulose
NC . . . . No Change
NC . . . . No Charge
NC. . . . . No Circuits
NC . . . . No Connection (Technical drawings) (Radio)
NC . . . . No Contest (Sports)
NC . . . . No Cost
NC. . . . . Noise Criterion
NC . . . . Non-Callable (A type of bond)
NC . . . . Noncollectible
NC . . . . Nonlinear Capacitance
NC . . . . Normally Closed (Switch)
NC. . . . . North American Coal Corp. (NYSE symbol)
NC . . . . North Carolina
NC . . . . Northern Command
NC . . . . Northern Consolidated Airlines, Inc.
NC . . . . Nose Cone
NC . . . . Not Carried
NC . . . . Nuclear Capability
NC . . . . Nuclear Congress
NC . . . . Nucleus of Ciliated Cell
NC . . . . Nuestra Cuenta (Our Account) (Business and trade) (Spain)
NC . . . . "Nuff Ced" (Enough Said) (Slang)
NC. . . . . Numerical Control(s)
NC . . . . Nurse Corps (Military)
N/C. . . . . New Charter (Navigation)
N/C. . . . . No Change
N/C. . . . . Numerical Control
NCA . . . . National Camping Association
NCA . . . . National Canners Association
NCA . . . . National Capital Award
NCA . . . . National Cashmere Association
NCA . . . . National Cathedral Association
NCA . . . . National Ceramic Association
NCA . . . . National Charcoal Association
NCA . . . . National Cheerleaders Association
NCA . . . . National Chiropractic Association (Later, American Chiropractic Association)
NCA . . . . National Civic Association
NCA . . . . National Club Association
NCA . . . . National Coal Association
NCA . . . . National Coffee Association of United States of America
NCA. . . . . . . National Command Authorities
NCA . . . . National Commission on Accrediting
NCA . . . . National Composition Association
NCA . . . . National Confectioners Association of the United States
NCA . . . . National Constructors Association
NCA . . . . National Contesters Association
NCA . . . . National Costumers Association
NCA . . . . National Council on Alcoholism
NCA . . . . National Council on the Arts
NCA . . . . National Coursing Association
NCA . . . . National Cranberry Association
NCA . . . . National Creameries Association
NCA . . . . Naval Command Assistant
NCA . . . . Naval Communications Annex
NCA . . . . Navy Contract Administrator
NCA . . . . Neurocirculatory Asthenia (Medicine)
NCA . . . . Newfoundland Club of America
NCA . . . . Non-Contractual Authorization
NCA . . . . Non-Organic Ceramic Adhesive
NCA . . . . North Central Association of Colleges and Secondary Schools
NCA . . . . Northern Consolidated Airlines
NCA . . . . Northwest Computing Association
NCAA . . . . . . National Collegiate Athletic Association
NCAA . . . . . . Naval Civilian Administrators Association
NCAB. . . . . . . National Cancer Advisory Board
NCAB. . . . . . . National Collegiate Athletic Bureau
NCAB . . . . . . National Committee for Amateur Baseball
NCAB. . . . . . . National Cyclopedia of American Biography
NCAB. . . . . . . Navy Contract Adjustment Board
NCAC . . . . . . National Council of Acoustical Consultants
NCAC . . . . . . National Council Against Conscription
NCAC . . . . . . Northern Combat Area Command (Burma)

NCAD . . . . . . New Cumberland Army Depot
NCADH . . . . . National Committee Against Discrimination in Housing
NCAE. . . . . . . National Center for Audio Experimentation
NCAE . . . . . . National Conference on Aeronautical Electronics
NCAE . . . . . . National Conference on Airborne Electronics
NCAE . . . . . . National Council of Agricultural Employers
NCAEG . . . . . National Confederation of American Ethnic Groups
NCAEI . . . . . . National Conference on the Application of Electrical Insulation
NCAF. . . . . . . National Committee Against Fluoridation
NCAG . . . . . . National Council on the Arts and Government
NCAHUAC . . . National Committee to Abolish the House Un-American Activities Committee
NCAI . . . . National Congress of American Indians
NCAI . . . . National Council of American Importers
NCAIE . . . . . . National Council of the Arts in Education (Later, ACAE)
NCAIL . . . . . . National Council Against Illegal Liquor
NCALL . . . . . . National Council on Agricultural Life and Labor
NCAMI . . . . . . National Committee Against Mental Illness
NCAN . . . . . . National Coalition of American Nuns
NCAP. . . . . . . Neighborhood Community Action Program
NCAP. . . . . . . Night Combat Air Patrol
NCAP. . . . . . . Nucleotide Column Affinity for Purification (Biochemical analysis)
NCAPC . . . . . National Center for Air Pollution Control (of Public Health Service)
NCAPO . . . . . National Council of Adoptive Parents Organizations
NCAR . . . . . . National Center for Atmospheric Research (National Science Foundation)
NCAR. . . . . . . National Conference on the Administration of Research
NCARB. . . . . . National Council of Architectural Registration Boards
NCASI . . . . . . National Council of the Paper Industry for Air and Stream Improvement
NCAT. . . . . . . National Program for Clear Air Turbulence (Air Force)
NCATE . . . . . National Council for Accreditation of Teacher Education
NCAWA . . . . . National Coinamatic Auto Wash Association
NCAWE . . . . . National Council of Administrative Women in Education
NCAWRR. . . . . National Committee Against War, Racism and Repression
NCAYR . . . . . National Chaplains Association for Youth Rehabilitation
NCB. . . . . National Cargo Bureau
NCB . . . . National Classification Board (American Trucking Association)
NCB. . . . . National Coal Board (British)
NCB. . . . . National Collection of Industrial Bacteria (Great Britain)
NCB. . . . . National Conservation Bureau
NCB. . . . . Naval Communications Board
NCB. . . . . Naval Construction Battalion (or Brigade)
NCB . . . . Navy Comptroller Budget
NCB. . . . . New Crime Buffer
NCB. . . . . Nickel Cadmium Battery
NC & B. . . . . . Naval Courts & Boards
NCBA. . . . . . . National Catholic Bandmasters' Association
NCBA. . . . . . . National Chinchilla Breeders of America
NCBC. . . . . . . Naval Construction Battalion Centers
NCBE . . . . . . National Conference of Bar Examiners
NCBE . . . . . . National Conference of Bar Executives (Later, NABE)
NCBFAA . . . . . National Customs Brokers and Forwarders Association of America
NCBI . . . . National Cotton Batting Institute
NCBJS . . . . . . National Council of Beth Jacob Schools
NCBL . . . . . . Natural Convection Boiling Loops
NCBM . . . . . . National Council on Business Mail
NCBP. . . . . . . National Conference of Bar Presidents
NCBVA . . . . . National Concrete Burial Vault Association
NCBW . . . . . . National Cage Bird Week Association
NCC . . . . National Carbon Company
NCC . . . . National Castings Council
NCC . . . . National Climatic Center (National Oceanic and Atmospheric Administration)
NCC . . . . National Company of Crossbowmen
NCC . . . . National Computer Center (of Internal Revenue Service)
NCC . . . . National Computing Center (England)
NCC . . . . National Conference on Citizenship
NCC . . . . National Container Committee
NCC. . . . . National Coordinating Council on Drug Abuse Education and Information (Later, NCCDE)
NCC . . . . National Cotton Council of America
NCC . . . . National Council of Churches of Christ in the USA
NCC. . . . . National Crime Commission
NCC . . . . National Cryptologic Command (National Security Agency)
NCC . . . . National Cultural Center (Smithsonian Institution)
NCC . . . . Navigation Computer Control
NCC . . . . Navigation Control Console
NCC . . . . Navy Cost Center
NCC . . . . Newspaper Comics Council
NCC . . . . Nitrogen Charging Console
NCC . . . . NORAD Control Center

NCC . . . . Normal-Control Children (Psychology)

NCC . . . . North Central College (Illinois)

NCC . . . . Northwest Christian College (Oregon)

NCCA . . . . . . National Catholic Camping Association

NCCA . . . . . . National Cedar Chest Association

NCCA . . . . . . National Center for Child Advocacy

NCCA . . . . . . National Chemical Credit Association

NCCA . . . . . . National Clergy Conference on Alcoholism

NCCA . . . . . . National Coil Coaters Association

NCCA . . . . . . National Concrete Contractors Association

NCCA . . . . . . National Council for Critical Analysis

NCCAS . . . . . . National Center of Communication Arts and Sciences

NCCB . . . . National Citizens Committee for Broadcasting

NCCB . . . . National Conference of Catholic Bishops

NCCB . . . . . National Council to Combat Blindness

NCCBI . . . . . . National Coordinating Committee of the Beverage Industry

NCCC . . . . . National Catholic Cemetery Conference

NCCC . . . . . National Conference of Catholic Charities

NCCC . . . . . National Council of Corvette Clubs

NCCCCA . . . . National Collegiate Cross Country Coaches Association

NCCCD . . . . . National Center Confraternity of Christian Doctrine

NCCCR . . . . . National Citizens Committee for Community Relations

NCCCWA . . . . National Cotton Compress and Cotton Warehouse Association

NCCD . . . . . . National Center for Chronic Disease Control (Public Health Service)

NCCD . . . . . . National Council on Crime and Delinquency

NCCDAEI . . . . National Coordinating Council on Drug Abuse Education and Information

NCCDE . . . . . National Coordinating Council on Drug Education (Formerly, NCC)

NCCdL . . . . . . Nuova Camero Confederale del Lavoro (New Confederated Chamber of Labor) (Italy - Trieste)

NCCE . . . . . . National Center for Citizens in Education

NCCEM . . . . . National Council of Catholic Employers and Managers

NCCEWV . . . . National Coordinating Committee to End the War in Vietnam

NCCF . . . . . . National Commission on Consumer Finance

NCCF . . . . . . National Council on Community Foundations

NCCFL . . . . . National Catholic Conference on Family Life

NCCGDP . . . . . National Council of Chairmen of Graduate Departments of Psychology

NCCHI . . . . . . National Cap and Cloth Hat Institute

NCCI . . . . . . National Council on Compensation Insurance

NCCIJ . . . . . . National Catholic Conference for Interracial Justice

NCCJ . . . . . . National Conference of Christians and Jews

NCCL . . . . . . National Council of Coal Lessors

NCCLS . . . . . National Committee for Clinical Laboratory Standards

NCCM . . . . . National Council of Catholic Men

NCCMT . . . . National Committee for Careers in Medical Technology

NCCN . . . . . National Council of Catholic Nurses

NCCPA . . . . . National Cinder Concrete Products Association

NCCPA . . . . . National Council of College Publications Advisers

NCCPB . . . . . National Council of Commercial Plant Breeders

NCCR . . . . . . New Construction/Conversion Requirements System

NCCRE . . . . . National Consumers Committee for Research & Education

NCCS . . . . . . National Catholic Community Service

NCCS . . . . . . National Christ Child Society

NCCS . . . . . . National Command and Control System

NCCS . . . . . National Council for Community Services to International Visitors

NCCUSL . . . . . National Conference of Commissioners on Uniform State Laws

NCCV . . . . . . New Construction and Conversion

NCCW . . . . . National Council of Catholic Women

NCCWHO . . . . National Citizens Committee for the World Health Organization

NCCY . . . . . . National Committee for Children and Youth

NCCY . . . . . . National Council of Catholic Youth

NCCYSA . . . . . National Conference of Catholics in Youth Serving Agencies

NCD . . . . No Can Do (From pidgin English)

NCD . . . . North Central Division (Army Engineers)

NCD . . . . Not Considered Disqualifying

NCD . . . . Notice of Credit Due

NCDA . . . . . . National Center for Drug Analysis (St. Louis) (FDA)

NCDAC . . . . . National Civil Defense Advisory Council

NCDAI . . . . . . National Clearinghouse for Drug Abuse Information (Chevy Chase, Maryland)

NCDC . . . . . . National Catholic Development Conference

NCDC . . . . . . National Committee for the Day Care of Children

NCDC . . . . . . National Communicable Disease Center (Public Health Service)

NCDC . . . . . . Naval Contract Distribution Center

NCDCF . . . . . National Civil Defense Computer Facility

NCDD . . . . . . No Change in the Due Date

NCDH . . . . . National Committee Against Discrimination in Housing

NCDM . . . . . Numerical Control Drafting Machine

NCDO . . . . . . Navy Central Disbursing Office

NCDRC . . . . . . National Catholic Disaster Relief Committee

NCDS . . . . . . National Center for Dispute Settlement (American Arbitration Association)

NCDT & EBASE . . Naval Combat Demolition Training and Experimental Base (Maui, Hawaii)

NCDU . . . . . . Naval Combat Demolition Unit

NCE . . . . National College of Education (Illinois)

NCE . . . . National Committee on the Emeriti

NCE . . . . New Catholic Edition (Bible)

NCE . . . . New Catholic Encyclopedia

NCE . . . . Newark College of Engineering (New Jersey)

NCE . . . . No Change in Estimates

NCE . . . . Nuclear Capability Exercise (Army)

NCEA . . . . . . National Catholic Educational Association

NCEC . . . . . . National Committee for an Effective Congress

NCEDL . . . . . National Committee for Effective Design Legislation

NCEE . . . . . . National Catholic Educational Exhibitors

NCEEF . . . . . National Committee for Electrical Engineering Films

NCEFF . . . . . National Committee for Education in Family Finance

NCEHAI . . . . . National Committee on Ethics of the Hearing Aid Industry

NCEHELP . . . . National Conference of Executives of Higher Education Loan Plans

NCEL . . . . . . Naval Civil Engineering Laboratory (FEC)

NCEL . . . . . . Navy Contractor Experience List

NCEMC . . . . . National Committee on the Education of Migrant Children

NCEO . . . . . . National Center for Exploitation of the Oceans

NCEP . . . . . . National Center for Education in Politics

NCER . . . . . . National Conference on Electromagnetic Relays

NCERD . . . . . National Center for Educational Research and Development (HEW)

NCERT . . . . National Council of Educational Research and Training (India)

NCES . . . . . . National Center for Educational Statistics (US Office of Education)

NCET . . . . . . National Council for Educational Technology (British)

NCEW . . . . . National Conference of Editorial Writers

NCEY . . . . . . National Committee on Employment of Youth

NCF . . . . National Cancer Foundation

NCF . . . . National Civics Federation

NCF . . . . Nerve Cell Food

NCF . . . . Newton-Cotes Formula

NCFA . . . . . . National Cat Fanciers' Association

NCFA . . . . . . National Collection of Fine Arts (Smithsonian Institution)

NCFA . . . . . . National Consumer Finance Association

NCFA . . . . . . North Central Field Area

NCFAE . . . . . National Council of Forestry Association Executives

NCFC . . . . . . National Commercial Finance Conference

NCFC . . . . . . National Council of Farm Cooperatives

NCFDA . . . . . National Council on Federal Disaster Assistance

NCFL . . . . . . National Catholic Forensic League

NCFM . . . . . National Commission on Food Marketing

NCFNP . . . . . National Committee for a Freedom Now Party

NCFP . . . . . . National Conference for Fluid Power

NCFPC . . . . . National Center for Fish Protein Concentrate (Fish and Wildlife Service)

NCFR . . . . . . National Council on Family Relations

NCFRF . . . . . National Cystic Fibrosis Research Foundation

NCFS . . . . . . National College of Foot Surgeons

NCFS . . . . . . National Committee on Films for Safety

NCFSD . . . . . NORAD Cost Factors and System Data (Air Force)

NCG . . . . Coast Guard Publication (Later, NAVCG)

NCG . . . . National Council for the Gifted

NCG . . . . Network Control Group

NCG . . . . Nuclear Cratering Group (Army Corps of Engineers)

NCG . . . . Null Command Generator

NCGA . . . . . . National Committee on Governmental Accounting

NCGA . . . . . . National Corn Growers Association

NCGA . . . . . . National Cotton Ginners Association

NCGC . . . . . National Catholic Guidance Conference

NCGCC . . . . . National Convention of Gospel Choirs and Choruses

NCGE . . . . . National Council for Geographic Education

NCH . . . . National Chemsearch Corp. (NYSE symbol)

NCH . . . . National Clearing House (Public Health Service)

NCH . . . . National Committee on Housing

NCH . . . . National Council on the Humanities

NCHA . . . . . National Campers and Hikers Association

NCHA . . . . . National Capital Housing Authority

NCHA . . . . . National Cutting Horse Association

NCHE . . . . . National Committee on Household Employment

NCHM . . . . . National Center for Housing Management

NCHMT . . . . . National Capital Historical Museum of Transportation

NCHP . . . . . National Corporation for Housing Partnerships

NCHP . . . . . Nickel-Chromium Honeycomb Panel

NCHRP . . . . . National Cooperative Highway Research Program

NCHS . . . . . National Center for Health Statistics (of OSG)

NCHS . . . . . National Coalition of House Staffs (Interns and resident physicians)

NCHS . . . . . National Committee on Homemaker Service

NCHSR & D . . . National Center for Health Services Research and Development (HEW)

NCHWPPTA . . . National Conference of Health, Welfare and Pension Plans, Trustees and Administrators
NCI . . . . National Cancer Institute (of National Institutes of Health)
NCI . . . . National Cheese Institute
NCI . . . . Natural Casing Institute
NCI . . . . Naval Cost Inspector
NCI . . . . No-Cost Item
NCIC . . . . . . National Crime Information Center (FBI)
NCIC . . . . . . National Crop Insurance Council
NCICA . . . . . . National Counter Intelligence Corps Association
NCIESD . . . . . National Conference on International Economic and Social Development
NCIH . . . . National Conference on Industrial Hydraulics
NCIJC . . . . . . National Council of Independent Junior Colleges
NCIMA . . . . . . National Cellulose Insulation Manufacturers Association
NCIMC . . . . . National Council of Industrial Management Clubs
NCIMS . . . . . National Conference on Interstate Milk Shipments
NCIO . . . . National Council on Indian Opportunity
NCIP . . . . National Council for Industrial Peace
NCIR . . . . National Conference on Industrial Research
NCIS . . . . Navy Cost Information System
NCISC . . . . . . Naval Counterintelligence Support Center
NCIT . . . . National Committee for Insurance Taxation
NCITD . . . . . . National Committee on International Trade Documentation
NCJAVM . . . . . National Council on Jewish Audio-Visual Materials
NCJC . . . . . . National Conference of Judicial Councils
NCJCC . . . . . . National Council of Jewish Correctional Chaplains
NCJCJ . . . . . . National Council of Juvenile Court Judges
NCJCS . . . . . . National Conference of Jewish Communal Service
NCJD . . . . National Congress of the Jewish Deaf
NCJE . . . . National Council for Jewish Education
NCJO . . . . . . National Council of Junior Outdoorsmen
NCJSC . . . . . . National Criminal Justice Statistics Center
NCJW . . . . . . National Council of Jewish Women
NCL . . . . National Central Library (British)
NCL . . . . National Chemical Laboratory
NCL . . . . National Consumers League
NCL . . . . Navy Calibration Laboratory
NCLA . . . . . . National Council of Local Administrators of Vocational Education and Practical Arts
NCLC . . . . . . National Catholic Liturgical Conference
NCLC . . . . . . National Child Labor Committee
NCLC . . . . . . National Council of Labour Colleges
NCLC . . . . . National Council on Legal Clinics
NCLCH . . . . . National Civil Liberties Clearing House
NCLI . . . . National Committee for Labor Israel
NCLIS . . . . . . National Commission on Libraries and Information Sciences
NCLP . . . . National Conference on Law and Poverty
NCLP . . . . Numerically Controlled Line Plotter
NCLPGA . . . . . North Carolina Liquefied Petroleum Gas Association
NCLS . . . . National Committee for Liberation of Slovakia
NCL & SW . . . National Conference of Lawyers and Social Workers
NCLT . . . . Night Carrier Landing Trainer (Navy)
NCLTA . . . . . National Cigar Leaf Tobacco Association
NCM . . . . National Acme Company (NYSE symbol) (Delisted)
NCM . . . . . . Nicaraguan Campaign Medal
NCM . . . . Noise Cancelling Microphone
NCM . . . . Noncorrosive Metal
NCM . . . . Non-Crew Member
NCM . . . . Northern Conservatory of Music (Maine)
NCM . . . . Numerical Controlled Machine
NCMA . . . . . . National Ceramic Manufacturers Association
NCMA . . . . . . National Concrete Masonry Association
NCMA . . . . . . National Contract Management Association
NCMA . . . . . . National Council of Millinery Associations
NCMA . . . . . . Newspaper Credit Managers' Association
NCMC . . . . . . NORAD Cheyenne Mountain Complex
NCMDA . . . . . National Coin Machine Distributors Association
NCME . . . . . . National Council on Measurement in Education
NCMEA . . . . . National Catholic Music Educators Association
NCMF . . . . . . National Church Music Fellowship
NCMFST . . . . . National Committee for Motor Fleet Supervisor Training
NCMH . . . . . . National Committee on Maternal Health
NCMHI . . . . . National Clearinghouse for Mental Health Information (HEW)
NCMI . . . . National Council of Music Importers
NCMLB . . . . . National Council of Mailing List Brokers
NCMP . . . . . . National Commission on Materials Policy
NCMPA . . . . . National Corrugated Metal Pipe Association
NCMRED . . . . . National Council on Marine Resources and Engineering Development
NCMS . . . . . . National Classification Management Society
NCMS . . . . . . National Council of Marine Sciences
NCMT . . . . . . Numerically Controlled Machine Tool

NCMTA . . . . . National Council of Marine Trade Associations
NCMTE . . . . . National Council on Medical Technology Education
NCN . . . . New Caledonian Nickel Co.
NCN . . . . Northern & Central Gas Corp., Ltd. (NYSE symbol)
NCNA . . . . . . National Council on Noise Abatement
NCNA . . . . . North China News Agency
NCNASA . . . . . National Council of Naval Air Station Associations
NCNASEO . . . National Council of Naval Air Stations Employee Organizations
NCNC . . . . . . National Captive Nations Committee
NCNC . . . . . . National Council of Nigeria and the Cameroons
NCNC . . . . . . National Council of Nigerian Citizens
NCNGD . . . . . Not Crushed or Not Ground
N/CNO . . . . . Navy/Chief of Naval Operations
NCNPSA . . . . . National Conference of Non-Profit Shipping Associations
NCNW . . . . . . National Council of Negro Women
NCO . . . . National Credit Office
NCO . . . . Noncommissioned Officer (Military)
NCO . . . . North American Coal Corporation (NYSE symbol) (Delisted)
NCOA . . . . . . National Council on the Aging
NCOA . . . . . . Noncommissioned Officer Association
NCOBQ . . . . . Noncommissioned Officer Bachelor Quarters
NCOC . . . . . . National Council on Organized Crime
NCOIC . . . . . Noncommissioned Officer-in-Charge (Military)
NCOLP . . . . . Noncommissioned Officer Logistics Program (Army)
NCOMD . . . . . National Committee on the Observance of Mothers' Day
NCOMP . . . . . National Catholic Office for Motion Pictures
NCOOM . . . . Noncommissioned Officers' Open Mess
NCOPA . . . . . National Conference of Police Associations
NCORT . . . . . . National Catholic Office for Radio and Television
NCOSTA . . . . . National Council of Officers of State Teachers Associations
NCP . . . . Natco Corporation (NYSE symbol) (Delisted)
NCP . . . . National Collegiate Players
NCP . . . . National Commission on Productivity
NCP . . . . National Council on Philanthropy
NCP . . . . Naval Capabilities Plan
NCP . . . . Netherlands and Colonial Philately
NCP . . . . Nickel-Chromium Panel
NCP . . . . Nitrogen Charge Panel (Later, MRAC)
NCP . . . . Noctilucent Cloud Particles
NCPA . . . . . . National Committee for the Prevention of Alcoholism
NCPA . . . . . . National Cottonseed Products Association
NCPAD . . . . . National Council on Psychological Aspects of Disability
NCPC . . . . . . National Capital Planning Commission
NCPC . . . . . . National Coal Policy Conference
NCPC . . . . . . National Collegiate Poultry Club
NCPC . . . . . . Nose Cone Protective Covering
NCPD . . . . . . Navy Current Procurement Directive
NCPDM . . . . . National Council of Physical Distribution Management
NCPEA . . . . . . National College Physical Education Association
NCPEA . . . . . . National Conference of Professors of Educational Administration
NCPEAM . . . . . National College Physical Education Association for Men
NCPEG . . . . . Navy Contractor Performance Evaluation Group
NCPER . . . . . . National Conference on Public Employee Retirement Systems
NCPI . . . . National Clay Pipe Institute
NCPI . . . . Navy Civilian Personnel Instructions
NCPL . . . . National Collegiate Parachuting League
NCPLA . . . . . . National Council of Patent Law Associations
NCPM . . . . . . National Clay Pot Manufacturers
NCPPC . . . . . . National Capital Park and Planning Commission
NCPR . . . . . . National Congress of Petroleum Retailers
NCPRV . . . . . National Council of Puerto Rican Volunteers
NCPS . . . . National Commission on Product Safety
NCPT . . . . National Congress of Parents and Teachers
NCPTO . . . . . . National China Painting Teachers Organization
NCPTWA . . . . . National Clearinghouse for Periodical Title Word Abbreviations (ANSI)
NCPWB . . . . . National Certified Pipe Welding Bureau
NCPYA . . . . . National Conference of Public Youth Agencies
NCR . . . . National Capital Region (Military)
NCR . . . . National Cash Register Company (NYSE symbol)
NCR . . . . No Carbon Required
NCR . . . . Nuclear
NCRA . . . . . . National Corrections Recreation Association
NCRA . . . . . . National Council of Research Administrators
NCRAC . . . . . National Community Relations Advisory Council
NCRC . . . . . . National Catholic Resettlement Council
NCRC . . . . . . National Committee for a Representative Congress
NCRC . . . . . . Nickel-Cadmium Rechargeable Cell
NCRD . . . . . . National Council to Repeal the Draft
NCRD . . . . . . National Council for Research and Development (Later, NRDA) (Israel)
NCRE . . . . . . National Conference on Research in English
NCRE . . . . . . Naval Construction Research Establishment

NCRFCL . . . . . National Commission on Reform of Federal Criminal Laws
NCRH . . . . National Center for Radiological Health (Public Health Service)
NCRL . . . . National Chemical Research Laboratory (South Africa)
NCRLC . . . . . . National Catholic Rural Life Conference
NCRLS . . . . . . National Committee of Religious Leaders of Safety
NCRND . . . . . National Committee for Research in Neurological Disorders
NCRP . . . . National Committee for Responsible Patriotism
NCRP . . . . National Council (formerly, Committee) on Radiation Protection and Measurements
NCRPC . . . . . . National Capital Regional Planning Council
NCRPM . . . . . . National Committee on Radiation Protection and Measurements (Later, NCRP)
NCRR . . . . National Center for Resource Recovery
NCRS . . . . National Committee for Rural Schools
NCRSA . . . . . . National Commercial Refrigerator Sales Association
NCS . . . . National Cartoonists Society
NCS . . . . National Cemetery System
NCS . . . . National Chrysanthemum Society
NCS . . . . National Commemorative Society
NCS . . . . National Communications System (GSA)
NCS . . . . National Conference on Solicitations
NCS . . . . Naval Communications Station (or System)
NCS . . . . Net Control Station (Communications) (Amateur radio)
NCS . . . . Nonwater Cooling System
NCS . . . . Nuclear-Chicago Solubilizer
NCS . . . . Nucleolar Channel System
NCS . . . . Numerical Control Society
NCSA . . . . National Carl Schurz Association
NCSA . . . . National Council of Seamen's Agencies
NCSA . . . . National Crushed Stone Association
NCSA . . . . National Customs Service Association
NCSAA . . . . . National Confectionery Salesmen's Association of America
NCSAB . . . . . National Council of State Agencies for the Blind
NCSAC . . . . . National Catholic Social Action Conference
NCSAC . . . . . Nuclear Cross-Section Advisory Committee (AEC)
NCSAG . . . . . Nuclear Cross Section Advisory Group
NCSAW . . . . National Catholic Society for Animal Welfare
NCSBEE . . . . . National Council of State Boards of Engineering Examiners
NCSC . . . . National Communication System Circulars
NCSC . . . . . . National Council on Schoolhouse Construction
NCSC . . . . . . National Council of Senior Citizens
NCSCCY . . . . . National Council of State Committees for Children and Youth
NCSCEE . . . . . National Council of State Consultants in Elementary Education
NCSCR . . . . . North Carolina State College Reactor
NCSCT . . . . . National Center for School and College Television
NCSE . . . . National Commission on Safety Education
NCSE . . . . National Committee on Secondary Education (of NASSP)
NCSEA . . . . . National Community School Education Association
NCSEA . . . . . National Council of State Education Associations
NCSF . . . . National College Student Foundation
NCSGC . . . . . National Council of State Garden Clubs
NCSH . . . . . . National Clearinghouse for Smoking and Health (Public Health Service)
NCSH . . . . . . Newton College of the Sacred Heart (Massachusetts)
NCSI . . . . National Communication System Instructions
NCSI . . . . National Council for Stream Improvement
NCSJ . . . . National Conference on Soviet Jewry
NCSL . . . . National Civil Service League
NCSL . . . . National Conference of Standards Laboratories
NCSL . . . . Naval Code and Signal Laboratory
NCSLA . . . . . National Conference of State Liquor Administrators
NCSLL . . . . . National Conference of State Legislative Leaders
NCSLO . . . . . . Navy Control of Shipping Liaison Officer
NCSM . . . . . . National Communication System Memoranda
NCSN . . . . . National Council for School Nurses (AAHPER)
NCSO . . . . . . National Council of Salesmen's Organizations
NCSO . . . . . . Naval Control Service Office (World War II British Routing Service)
NCSO . . . . . . Naval Control of Shipping Officer
NCSORG . . . . Naval Control of Shipping Organization
NCSP . . . . National Conference on State Parks
NCSPA . . . . . . National Corrugated Steel Pipe Association
NCSPAS . . . . . National Conference of State Pharmaceutical Association Secretaries
NCSPS . . . . . National Committee for Support of the Public Schools
NCSRA . . . . . National Conference of State Retail Associations
NCSS . . . . . . National Center for Social Statistics (HEW)
NCSS . . . . . . National Conference of Shomrim Societies
NCSS . . . . . . National Cooperative Soil Survey
NCSS . . . . . . National Council for the Social Studies
NCSSA . . . . . Naval Command Systems Support Activity
NCSSC . . . . . Naval Command Systems Support Center
NCSSFL . . . . . National Council of State Supervisors of Foreign Languages

NCSSIA . . . . . National Council of State Self-Insurers Associations
NCSSSA . . . . . National Conference of State Social Security Administrators
NCSTAS . . . . . National Council of Scientific and Technical Art Societies
NC & ST L . . . Nashville, Chattanooga & St. Louis Railway
NCSTS . . . . . National Conference of State Transportation Specialists
NCSTSR . . . . . National Conference of Superintendents of Training Schools & Reformatories
NCSU . . . . North Carolina State University
NCSW . . . . . National Conference on Social Welfare
NCSWCL . . . . . National Commission on State Workmen's Compensation Laws (Presidential)
NCSWD . . . . . National Center for Solid Waste Disposal
NCSWDI . . . . . National Combination Storm Window and Door Institute
NCSY . . . . . . National Conference of Synagogue Youth
NCTA . . . . National Cable (formerly, Community) Television Association
NCTA . . . . . . National Capital Transportation Agency
NCTA . . . . . . National Cattle Theft Act
NCTC . . . . . . National Catholic Theatre Conference
NCTC . . . . . . National Collection of Type Cultures (Bacteriology)
NCTC . . . . . . Naval Construction Training Center
NCTCA . . . . . National Collegiate Track Coaches Association
NCTE . . . . . . National Council of Teachers of English
NCTE . . . . . . National Council for Torah Education
NCTEPS . . . . . National Commission on Teacher Education and Professional Standards
NCTGA . . . . . National Christmas Tree Growers Association
NCTJ . . . . . . National Council for the Training of Journalists (Great Britain)
NCTM . . . . . . National Council of Teachers of Mathematics
NCTO . . . . . . Naval Central Torpedo Office
NCTO . . . . . . Navy Clothing and Textile Supply Office
NCTR . . . . . . National Center for Toxicological Research (FDA)
NCTR . . . . . . National Council on Teacher Retirement
NCTS . . . . . . National Council of Technical Schools
NCTS . . . . . . Northeast Corridor Transportation System (Boston to Washington high-speed transportation)
NCTSI . . . . . National Council of Technical Service Industries
NCTW . . . . . National Conference of Tuberculosis Workers
NCU . . . . Nitrogen Control Unit
NCU . . . . Nozzle Control Unit
NCUA . . . . . . National Credit Union Administration
NCUC . . . . . . Nuclear Chemistry Users Committee
NCUI . . . . . . National Center for Urban and Industrial Health (Public Health Service)
NCUP . . . . . . Newark Community Union Project (New Jersey)
NCUP . . . . . . No Commission Until Paid
NCUPM . . . . . National Council of United Presbyterian Men
NCURA . . . . . National Council of University Research Administrators
NCUSA . . . . . Navy Club of the United States of America
NCUTLO . . . . National Committee on Uniform Traffic Laws and Ordinances
NCV . . . . No Commercial Value (Business and trade)
NCVA . . . . . . National Center for Voluntary Action
NCVP . . . . . . Noncapsid Viral Protein
NCW . . . . National Council of Women of the United States
NCW . . . . Not Complied With (Military)
NCWA . . . . . National Candy Wholesalers Association
NCWC . . . . . National Catholic Welfare Conference (Later, USCC)
NCWC . . . . . National Council of Women Chiropractors
NCWFC . . . . . National Council of Women of Free Czechoslovakia
NCWM . . . . . National Conference on Weights and Measures
NCWTF . . . . . Naval Commander Western Task Force
NCWU . . . . . National Catholic Women's Union
NCWX . . . . . No Change in Weather (Aviation)
NCY . . . . National Cylinder Gas Company (NYSE symbol)
NCYC . . . . . . National Council of Yacht Clubs
NCYF . . . . . . National Crusaders Youth Federation
NCYI . . . . . . National Council of Young Israel
NCYP . . . . . . National Conference of Yeshiva Principals
ND . . . . Doctor of Naturopathy
ND . . . . Narodowa Demokracja
ND . . . . National Dairy Products Corporation (NYSE symbol) (Delisted)
ND . . . . National Debt
ND . . . . Naval Dispensary
ND . . . . Naval District
ND . . . . Navy Department
Nd . . . . Neodymium (Chemical element)
ND . . . . New Directions (Books)
ND . . . . Next Day (NYSE symbol)
ND . . . . Next Day's Delivery
ND . . . . No Date (of publication)
ND . . . . No Decision (Sports)
ND . . . . No Detect
ND . . . . No Drawing (Engineering)
ND . . . . Non-Delay (Military)
ND . . . . North Dakota

ND . . . . Nostra Domina, Notre Dame (Our Lady)
ND . . . . Not Dated (Banking, bibliography)
ND . . . . Nothing Doing (Amateur radio slang)
ND . . . . Nuclear Device
ND . . . . University of Notre Dame (Indiana)
NDA . . . . . . National Defense Act
NDA . . . . . . National Dental Association
NDA . . . . . . National Diploma in Agriculture
NDA . . . . . . National Door Association (Defunct)
NDA . . . . . . Neutral Detector Assembly
NDA . . . . . . New Drug Application (FDA)
NDA . . . . . . Non-Dimensional Analysis
NDA . . . . . . Nonresonant Deflection Amplifier
NDA . . . . . . Nuclear Device Association
NDAAF . . . . . National District Attorneys Association Foundation
NDAB . . . . . . Numerical Data Advisory Board (NAS-NRC)
NDAC . . . . . . National Defense Advisory Commission (World War II)
NDAC . . . . . . North Dakota Agricultural College
NDAC . . . . . . Nuclear Defense Affairs Committee (NATO)
N DAK . . . . . . North Dakota
NDAP . . . . . . Nationalsozialistische Deutsche Arbeiter-Partei
NDAPTA . . . . . National Drivers Association for the Prevention of Traffic Accidents
NDAT . . . . . . Nondestructible Aiming Target
NDB . . . . Naval Disciplinary Barracks
NDB . . . . Navy Department Bulletin
NDB . . . . Net Debit Balance
NDB . . . . . . Nondirectional Beacon
NDB(ADF) . . . . Nondirectional Beacon (Automatic Direction Finder)
NDBC . . . . . . National Dried Bean Council
NDBCA . . . . . . Navy Department Board of Contract Appeals
NDBLO . . . . . Not to Descend Below (Aviation)
NDBP . . . . . . National Data Buoy Project (National Ocean Survey)
NDBS . . . . . . National Data-Buoy System
NDBS . . . . . . Naval Despatch Boat Service
NDBULCUMED . . Navy Department Bulletins, Cumulative Editions
NDC . . . . National Dairy Council
NDC . . . . National Defence Contribution (British)
NDC . . . . National Defence Corps (British)
NDC . . . . National Defense Council (Netherlands)
NDC . . . . National Democratic Club
NDC . . . . National Development Corporation (Philippines)
NDC . . . . Navigational Digital Computer
NDC . . . . New Democratic Coalition
NDC . . . . New Dramatists Committee
NDC . . . . Nippon Decimal Classification (Library science)
NDC . . . . No Date Club (Brooklyn girls - no dates for the duration) (World War II)
NDC . . . . NORAD Direction Center
NDC . . . . Notre Dame College (Missouri, New Hampshire, Ohio)
NDC . . . . Nuclear Design Calculations (Program)
NDCA . . . . . . Nuclear Development Corporation of America
NDCC . . . . . . National Defense Cadet Corps
NDCD . . . . . . National Drug Code Directory (FDA)
NDC-PS . . . . No Drawing Change Project Slip
NDD . . . . National Diploma in Dairying
NDDC . . . . . . NORAD Division Direction Center (Army)
NDDP . . . . . . NATO Defense Data Program
NDD & RF . . . . Naval Dry Dock and Repair Facility
NDE . . . . National Defense Education
NDE . . . . No Delay Expected
NDE . . . . Nondestructive Evaluation
NDE . . . . Nonlinear Differential Equations
NDEA . . . . . . National Defense Education Act
NDEA . . . . . . National Defense Emergency Authorization
NDEI . . . . . . National Defense Education Institute
NDER . . . . . . National Defense Executive Reserve
NDERR . . . . . National Defense Executive Reserve Roster (of the CSC)
NDF . . . . Nacelle Drag Efficiency (Factor) (Aerospace)
NDF . . . . Naval Dairy Farm
NDF . . . . Neutral Density Filter
NDFA . . . . . . National Dietary Foods Association
NDFEA . . . . . Northwest Dried Fruit Export Association
NDFYP . . . . . Navy Department Five Year Plan
NDG . . . . National Dance Guild
NDG . . . . No Date Given
NDGA . . . . . . Nordihydroguaiaretic Acid (Antioxidant; food additive)
NDGL . . . . . . Neodymium Doped Glass LASER
NDGO . . . . . . Navy Department General Order
NDGW . . . . . . Native Daughters of the Golden West
NDH . . . . Natural Disaster Hospitals (Public Health Service)
NDH . . . . Neue Deutsche Hefte (A publication)

NDHA . . . . . . National District Heating Association
NDHFP . . . . . New Developments Human Factors Program (Navy)
NDHQ . . . . . . National Defence Headquarters (Canadian)
NDHS . . . . . . Nimbus Data Handling System
NDI . . . . Nondestructive Inspection (Military)
NDIC . . . . . . Nuclear Data Information Center (ORNL)
NDIR . . . . . . Nondispersive Infrared (Analyzer)
NDL . . . . Norddeutscher Lloyd (German steamship company)
NDL . . . . Nuclear Defense Laboratory (Army)
NDLB . . . . . . National Dock Labour Board (British)
NDM . . . . Ferrocarriles Nacionales de Mexico (AAR code)
NDM . . . . Neutron Dose Monitor
NDMA . . . . . . National Door Manufacturers Association
NDMA . . . . . . National Dress Manufacturers Association
NDMB . . . . . . National Defense Mediation Board (World War II)
NDMSP . . . . . Navy Department Mobilization Security Plan
NDNT . . . . . . Not Dressed nor Tanned
NDO . . . . Navy Disbursing Office
NDOS . . . . . . National Defense Operations Section (FCC)
NDP . . . . National Democratic Party (Rhodesia and Nyasaland)
NDP . . . . National Diocesan Press
NDP . . . . National Disclosure Policy
NDP . . . . Navy Department Personnel
NDP . . . . New Democratic Party (Canadian)
NDP . . . . Nuclear Desalination Plant
NDPA . . . . . . National Decorated Packaging Association
NDPA . . . . . . National Democratic Party of Alabama
NDPBC . . . . . National Duck Pin Bowling Congress
NDPC . . . . . . National (Military Information) Disclosure Policy Committee (Air Force)
NDPD . . . . . . National-Demokratische Partei Deutschlands (National Democratic Party) (East Germany)
NDPIC . . . . . Navy Department Program Information Center
NDPRP . . . . . National Defense Project Rating Plan
NDQ . . . . North Dakota Quarterly
NDR . . . . National Dog Registry
NDR . . . . Network Data Reduction
NDR . . . . Nondestructive Read (Data processing)
NDR . . . . Norddeutsche Rundfunk (West German radio network)
NDR . . . . Normal Daily Requirement (Military)
NDRB . . . . . . New Developments Research Branch (Navy)
NDRC . . . . . . National Defense Research Committee (of Office of Scientific Research and Development) (World War II)
NDRE . . . . . . Norwegian Defense Research Establishment
NDRF . . . . . . National Defense Reserve Fleet (Maritime Administration, Department of Commerce)
NDRI . . . . . . Naval Dental Research Institute
NDRO . . . . . . Nondestructive Readout
NDRS . . . . . . National Driver Register Service (Department of Transportation)
NDRS . . . . . . Nuclear Definition and Reporting System
NDS . . . . Navigation Display System
NDS . . . . Navy Display System
NDS . . . . Nuclear Detection Satellite
NDSA . . . . . . National Disposal Services Association
NDSB . . . . . . Narcotic Drugs Supervisory Body (UN)
NDSF . . . . . . North Dakota School of Forestry
NDSM . . . . . . National Defense Service Medal
NDT . . . . Ferrocarril Nacional de Tehuantepec (AAR code)
NDT . . . . Nil Ductility Temperature
NDT . . . . Non-Destructive Test(ing) (QCR)
NDTA . . . . . . National Defense Transportation Association
NDTC . . . . . . National Drug Trade Conference
NDTC . . . . . . Naval Device Training Center (Orlando, Fla.)
NDTIB . . . . . Non-Destructive Test and Inspection Building
NDTMA . . . . . National Drain Tile Manufacturers Association
NDTP . . . . . . Nuclear Data Tape Program
NDUC . . . . . . Nimbus Data Utilization Center
NDUSTA . . . . . New Duty Station (Navy)
NDV . . . . Newcastle Disease Virus
NDV . . . . Nuclear Delivery Vehicle
NDW . . . . Naval District Washington
NDY . . . . Nonresonant Deflection Yoke
NE . . . . National Emergency
NE . . . . Naval Engineer
NE . . . . Negative Expectancy (Psychometrics)
Ne . . . . Neon (Chemical element)
NE . . . . New Edition
NE . . . . New England
NE . . . . Nickel Equivalent (Coinage)
NE . . . . Nonessential
NE . . . . Norepinephrine (Biochemistry)
NE . . . . Northeast, Northeastern, Northeasterly

NE. . . . . Northeast Airlines, Inc. (Obsolete)
NE. . . . . Not Explosive
NE . . . . Nuclear Engineer
N/E. . . . . . . Not Exceeding (Business and trade)
NEA . . . . National Editorial Association
NEA . . . . National Education Association
NEA . . . . National Electronic Associations
NEA . . . . National Employment Association
NEA . . . . National Endowment for the Arts
NEA. . . . . . . Nelson & Albemarle Railway (AAR code)
NEA. . . . . . . Network Equivalent Analysis
NEA. . . . . . . Newspaper Enterprise Association (A syndicate)
NEA. . . . . . . Northeast Airlines, Inc. (Obsolete)
NEA. . . . . . . Null Error Amplifier
NEAA . . . . . . Norwegian Elkhound Association of America
NEABFGP . . . . New England Advisory Board for Fish and Game Problems
NEAC. . . . . . New English Art Club
NEAC. . . . . . Northeast Air Command
NEACP. . . . . . National Emergency Airborne Command Post (DOD)
NEACSS . . . . . New England Association of Colleges and Secondary Schools
NEADS . . . . . Near East and African Development Service
NEAF . . . . . . North East Air Force
NEAFC . . . . . Northeast Atlantic Fisheries Commission
NEAGC . . . . . National Early American Glass Club
NEAPD . . . . . Northeastern Air Procurement District
NEAR . . . . . . National Emergency Alarm Repeater (Civil defense warning system for homes)
NEARA . . . . . New England Antiquities Research Association
NEARNAVDIST . . Commandant of the Nearest Naval District
NEAT . . . . . . National Cash Register Electronic Autocoding Technique (Data processing)
NEB . . . . Nebraska
NEB . . . . Neisner Brothers, Inc. (American Stock Exchange symbol)
NEB . . . . New English Bible
NEB . . . . Noise Equivalent Bandwidth
NEB . . . . North Equatorial Belt
NEBA . . . . . . NASA Employees Benefit Association
NEBHE . . . . . New England Board of Higher Education
NEBMA. . . . . . Neben-Munitionsanstalt (Branch ammunition depot)
NEBR . . . . . . Nebraska
NEBW. . . . . . Non-Vacuum Electron Beam Welding
NEC . . . . National Economic Council
NEC . . . . National Egg Council
NEC. . . . . . . National Electric(al) Code
NEC . . . . National Electronics Conference
NEC. . . . . . . National Emergency Council (Abolished, 1939)
NEC . . . . National Exchange Club
NEC. . . . . . . Navy Enlisted Classification
NEC . . . . Navy Enlisted Code
NEC . . . . Negro Ensemble Company (A theater group)
NEC. . . . . . . Netherlands Electrotechnical Committee
NEC . . . . New England Council
NEC . . . . Not Elsewhere Classified
NEC. . . . . . . Nucleus of Epidermal Cell
NECA . . . . . . National Electrical Contractors Association
NECA. . . . . . National Employment Counselors Association
NECA . . . . . . Near East College Association
NECAP . . . . . Nutmeg Electric Companies Atomic Project
NECC. . . . . . Northern Essex Community College (Massachusetts)
NECCO. . . . . New England Confectionary Company
NECCO. . . . . Northern Essex Community College (Massachusetts)
NECDC . . . . . New England Consumer Development Council
NECH. . . . . . National Employment Clearing House (American Chemical Society)
NECHE. . . . . Northeastern Colorado Hail Experiment
NECM . . . . . New England Conservatory of Music (Massachusetts)
NECNVA . . . . New England Committee for Nonviolent Action
NECO. . . . . . Nuclear Engineering Company, Inc.
NECOLIM. . . . Neocolonialist, Colonialist, and Imperialist
NECP . . . . . . New England College of Pharmacy
NECPA . . . . . National Emergency Command Post Afloat
NECS . . . . . . National Electrical Code Standards
NECTP . . . . . Northeast Corridor Transportation Project
NED. . . . . . . New England Division (Army Engineers)
NED. . . . . . . New English Dictionary (i.e., the Oxford English Dictionary)
NED. . . . . . . New Enterprise Division (of Monsanto Corp.)
NED . . . . . . Normal Equivalent Deviation
NED. . . . . . . North, East, and Down
NED. . . . . . . Nuclear Engineering Directorate (Army)
NEDA . . . . . . National Economic Development Association
NEDA . . . . . . National Electronic Distributors Association
NEDA . . . . . . National Emergency Defense Airlift

NEDC . . . . . . National Economic Development Council (Nickname: Neddie) (British)
NEDECO. . . . . Netherlands Engineering Consultants
NEDL . . . . . . New England Deposit Library
NEDN. . . . . . Navy's Worldwide Environmental Data Network
NEDO . . . . . National Economic Development Office
NEDU. . . . . . Navy Experimental Diving Unit
NEE . . . . National Electrical Effect
NEEB . . . . . . North Eastern Electricity Board (British)
NEEC . . . . . . National Export Expansion Council (Department of Commerce)
NEEC. . . . . . Nuclear Explosion Effects Center
NEED . . . . . . National Environmental Education Development (Program of National Park Service)
NEED . . . . . . Near East Emergency Donations
NEED. . . . . . Negro Education Emergency Drive
NEEDS . . . . . Neighborhood Evaluation and Decision System (HEW)
NEEDS . . . . . New England Educational Data Systems
NEEP . . . . . . Nuclear Electronics Effects Program
NEES . . . . . . Naval Engineering Experiment Station
NEES . . . . . . New England Electric System
NEF . . . . National Educators Fellowship
NEF . . . . National Extra Fine (Thread)
NEF. . . . . . . Naval Emergency Fund (A budget category)
NEF . . . . Near East Foundation
NEF . . . . New Education Fellowship
NEF . . . . Noise Equivalent Flux
NEF . . . . Noise Exposure Forecast (Aircraft)
NEF . . . . Nurses Educational Funds
NEFA . . . . . . Non-Esterified Fatty Acid (Biochemistry)
NEFA . . . . . . North-East Frontier Agency (India)
NEFARS . . . . . Nuclear Effects from Analysis of Residual Signatures
NEFC . . . . . . Near East Forestry Commission
NEFCO. . . . . New England Fish Company
NEFD . . . . . . Noise-Equivalent Flux Density
NEFE . . . . . . New England Fish Exchange
NEFO. . . . . . National Electronics Facilities Organization
NEFOS . . . . . New Emerging Forces
NEFSA . . . . . National Education Field Service Association
NEG . . . . Negative
NEG . . . . Negligible
NEGRO . . . . . National Economic and Growth Reconstruction Organization (Negro entrepreneurial organization)
NEGRO . . . . . New England Grass Roots Organization
NEGRS . . . . . Negative Report Submitted (Army)
NEH . . . . National Endowment for the Humanities
NEH. . . . . . . Nuclear Effects Handbook
NEHA . . . . . . National Executive Housekeepers Association
NEHC . . . . . . National Extension Homemakers Council
NEHGS . . . . . New England Historic Genealogical Society
NEI . . . . National Eye Institute
NEI . . . . Netherlands East Indies
NEI . . . . New Equipment Introduction (Army)
NEI . . . . Noise Equivalent Input
NEI . . . . Noise Equivalent Intensity
NEI . . . . Non Est Inventus (It Has Not Been Found or Discovered)
NEI . . . . Not Elsewhere Indicated
NEI . . . . Nouvelles Equipes Internationales (Later, European Christian Democratic Union)
NEIC . . . . . . National Earthquake Information Center
NEIL . . . . . . Neon Indicating Light
NEIPG . . . . . National Electronic Industries Procurement Group
NEISA . . . . . New England Intercollegiate Sailing Association
NEISS. . . . . . National Electronic Inquiry Surveillance System (FDA)
NEIT . . . . . . New Equipment Introductory Team (Army)
NEIULS . . . . . Northeast Iowa Union List of Serials
NEK. . . . . . . Naval Equerry to the King
NEK. . . . . . . Norsk Elecktrotecnisk Komite (Oslo, Norway)
NEKOA . . . . . New England Knitted Outerwear Association
NEKOLIM. . . . Neocolonialist-Colonialist-Imperialist (Indonesia)
NEL. . . . . . . National Emancipation League (Nigeria)
NEL . . . . National Engineering Laboratory (British)
NEL. . . . . . . National Epilepsy League
NEL. . . . . . . Naval Electronics Laboratory
NEL . . . . Naval Explosive Laboratory
NEL . . . . Nonspecific Excitability Level (Animal behavior)
NELA . . . . . . National Electric Light Association
NELA . . . . . . New England Library Association
NELAT . . . . . Navy Electronics Laboratory Assembly Tester
NELC . . . . . . Naval Electronics Laboratory Center
NELIA . . . . . Nuclear Energy Liability Insurance Association
NELIAC . . . . . Naval Electronics Laboratory International Algebraic Compiler
NELINET . . . . New England Library Information Network

ACRONYMS AND INITIALISMS DICTIONARY

NELM........ Naval Forces Eastern Atlantic and Mediterranean
NELM...... Navy Elements Atlantic and Mediterranean
NELS...... National Environmental Laboratories (Proposed)
NEM...... Newmont Mining Corporation (NYSE symbol)
NEM...... Non-Electronic Maintenance
NEM...... Not Elsewhere Mentioned
NEMA...... National Eclectic Medical Association
NEMA...... National Electrical Manufacturers Association
NEMAG..... Negative Effective Mass Amplifiers and Generators
NEMCC..... Non-Essential Motor Control Center
NEMCH..... New England Medical Center Hospitals
NEMDA..... Northeastern Minnesota Development Association
NEMEA..... New England Media Evaluators Association
NEMI...... National Elevator Manufacturing Industry
NEMIC...... New England Materials-Instruction Center
NEMO...... Naval Edreobenthic Manned Observatory
NEMO...... Naval Experimental Manned Observatory
NEMO...... Nuclear Exchange Model
NEMP....... Nuclear Electromagnetic Pulse
NEMPS..... National Environmental Monitoring and Prediction System
NEMRIP..... New England Marine Resources Information Program
NEMS....... Non-External-Moving Surface (Aircraft)
NEN...... New Eyes for the Needy
NEN...... Stichting Nederlands Normalisatie-Instituut
NENYIAC.... Northeast-New York Inter-Agency Committee
NEO...... Near Earth Orbit
NEO...... Noncombatant Evacuation Order (Army)
NEO...... Northeast Oklahoma R. R. (AAR code)
NEO...... Northeastern Operations Office (NASA)
NEOB....... New Executive Office Building (Washington, DC)
NEOCOMP... New Computational Formulas
NEOP...... New England Order of Protection
NEP...... Nearest Equivalent Product
NEP...... New Economic Policy (Program of USSR, 1921-28; also US wage/price freeze and controls of Nixon Administration, 1971)
NEP...... New Equipment Practice
NEP...... Noise Equivalent Power
NEP...... Non-Electronic Part
N/EP...... Name on End-Paper (Antiquarian book trade)
NEPA...... National Environmental Policy Act
NEPA...... Northeast Pacific Area
NEPA...... Nuclear Energy Powered Aircraft
NEPC...... New England Power Company
NEPCO...... New England Provision Company
NEPD....... Noise Equivalent Power Density
NEPE...... Nez Perce National Historical Park
NEPEA...... New England Project on Education of the Aging
NEPEX...... New England Power Exchange
NEPIA...... Nuclear Energy Property Insurance Association
NEPOOL..... New England Power Pool
NEPPCO..... Northeastern Poultry Producers Council
NEPR...... NATO Electronic Parts Recommendations
NEPR...... Nuclear Explosion Pulse Reaction
NEPRS..... New Equipment Personnel Requirements Summary (Army)
NEPU...... Northern Elements Progressive Union (Nigeria)
NER...... National Educational Radio
NER...... Never-Exceed Redline (Aerospace)
NER...... Noise Equivalent Radiance
NERA...... National Emergency Relief Administration
NERAC...... New England Research Application Center (University of Connecticut)
NERC...... National Electric Reliability Council
NERC...... National Electronics Research Council
NERC...... National Environmental Research Center (Environmental Protection Agency)
NERC...... Nuclear Energy Research Center (Belgium) (Also known as CEEN)
NERCP..... Naval European Research Contract Program
NEREM..... Northeast Electronics Research and Engineering Meeting
NERF...... National Eye Research Foundation
NERHL..... Northeastern Radiological Health Laboratory
NERMLS.... New England Regional Medical Library Service
NERO...... Near Earth Rescue Operation (NASA)
NERO...... Nuclear Effects Rocket Operations
NEROC..... Northeast Radio Observatory Corporation
NERRA..... New Equipment Resources Requirements Analysis (Army)
NERSICA.... National Established Repair, Service and Improvement Contractors Association
NERV...... Nuclear Emulsion Radiation of Recovery Vehicle (Aerospace)
NERV...... Nuclear Energy Research Vehicle
NERVA..... Nuclear Engine for Rocket Vehicle Application (or Approach) (NASA)
NES....... Naval Experimenting Station
NES....... New England Electric System (NYSE symbol)
NES........ Non-Erasable Storage

NES........ Not Elsewhere Specified
NESA...... National Electric Sign Association
NESA...... Near East and South Asia (State Department)
NESA...... New England School of Art
NESBIC.... Netherlands Student's Bureau for International Cooperation
NESC...... National Electric Safety Code
NESC...... National Environmental Satellite Center (Formerly, National Weather Satellite Center; later, National Environmental Satellite Service)
NESC...... Naval Electronic Systems Command
NESC...... Nuclear Engineering and Scientific Congress
NESCAC..... New England Small College Athletic Conference
NESCNSC.... Net Evaluation Subcommittee, National Security Council
NESCO..... National Engineering Science Company
NESCO..... Nigerian Electricity Supply Corporation African Workers' Union
NESDEC..... New England School Development Council
NESEP..... Navy Enlisted Scientific Education Program
NESLA..... New England Shoe and Leather Association
NESMRA.... New England Super-Modified Racing Association
NESS...... National Emergency Steel Specification (World War II)
NESS...... National Environmental Satellite Service
NEST...... National Emergency Survivable Tropo System
NEST...... Nonelectric Stimulus Transfer
NEST...... Nuclear Explosive Simulation Technique
NESTEF..... Naval Electronic Systems Test and Evaluation Facility
NESTS..... Non-Electric Stimulus Transfer System
NET....... National Educational Television
NET....... Net Equivalent Temperature
NET....... Network
NET....... New Equipment Training (Army)
NET....... Newton Emission Theory
NET....... Nippon Educational Television (Japan)
NET....... Noise Equivalent Temperature
NET....... Not Earlier Than
NET....... Nuclear Effects Test
NET....... Nuclear Emergency Teams (DASA)
NET....... Nuclear Engineer Trainees (AEC)
NET....... Number of Element Types
NETA...... Northwest Electronic Technical Association
NETAC..... Nuclear Energy Trade Associations' Conference
NETAPPS.... Net Ad-Produced Purchases (Advertising)
NETCO..... North Western Employes Transportation Corporation (Successor to Chicago & North Western Railway)
NETF...... Nuclear Energy Test Facility
NETF...... Nuclear Engineering Test Facility
NETL...... National Export Traffic League
NETMA..... Nobody Ever Tells Me Anything (Executive complaint)
NETOPS..... Nuclear Emergency Team Operations
NETP...... New Equipment Training Program (Army)
NETR...... No Essential Traffic Reported (Aviation)
NETR...... Nuclear Engineering Test Reactor (Air Force)
NETRC..... National Educational Television and Radio Center
NETS...... National Electronics Teachers' Service
NETS...... Navy Engineering Technical Services
NETS...... Network Techniques
NEU....... National Employees' Union (Ceylon)
NEUC...... National Engine Use Council
NEUM...... Non-European Unity Movement
NEUS...... Northeastern United States
NEUS...... Nuclear-Electric Unmanned Spacecraft
NEUT...... Neutral(izing)
NEV....... Nevada
NEW....... National Electronics Week
NEW....... Navy Early Warning
NEW....... Net Explosive Weight
NEWA..... National Electrical Wholesalers Association
NEWA..... Nuclear Energy Writers Association (Defunct)
NEWCC.... Northeastern Weed Control Conference
NEWISA.... New England Women's Intercollegiate Sailing Association
NEWLON.... New London, Connecticut
NEW MOONS.. NASA Evaluation with Models of Optimized Nuclear Spacecraft
NEWRADS.... Nuclear Explosion Warning and Radiological Data System
NEWS...... Naval Electronic Warfare Simulator
NEWS...... Neighborhood Environmental Workshops (Program of Full Circle Associates, group serving the urban poor)
NEWS...... New-Product Early Warning System
NEXCO.... National Association of Export Management Companies
NEXT...... Near-End Crosstalk Loss
NEXT...... New/Experimental Techniques
NEYO..... New York City National Park Service Group
NEZP..... Nezperce R. R. Company (AAR code)
nF......... Nanofarad

393

NF . . . . National Fine (Thread)
NF. . . . . National Formulary (A publication listing standard drugs)
NF. . . . . National Foundation
NF. . . . . Nationale Front
NF . . . . Near Face (Technical drawings)
NF . . . . Neighborhood Final Fade
NF. . . . . Nested or Flat (Freight)
NF . . . . Neue Folge (New Series) (Bibliography)
NF . . . . Neutral Fraction
NF. . . . . New Franc (French currency)
NF . . . . Newfoundland (with Labrador, a Canadian province)
NF. . . . . Niederfrequenz (Audio frequency) (German military - World War II)
NF. . . . . Night Fighter Aircraft
NF. . . . . No Fool
NF. . . . . No Form
NF. . . . . No Funds (Banking)
NF. . . . . Noise Factor
NF. . . . . Noise Figure
NF. . . . . Nonferrous
NF. . . . . Norfolk (Virginia) (Navy Yard)
NF. . . . . Nonfundable
NF. . . . . Nonwhite Female
NF. . . . . Normal Formula
NF . . . . Norman French
NF. . . . . Nose Fuse
NF . . . . Not Fordable (Maps and charts)
NF . . . . Nouveau Franc (New Franc) (French monetary unit, introduced in 1960)
NF . . . . Nutrition Foundation
NF . . . . The Royal Northumberland Fusiliers (British)
N/F . . . . Night Fighter Aircraft
N/F . . . . No Funds (Banking)
NFA . . . . National Faculty Association of Community and Junior Colleges
NFA . . . . National Firearms Act
NFA. . . . . . . National Food Administration
NFA . . . . National Foundry Association
NFA . . . . National Freedom Academy
NFA. . . . . . . Naval Fuel Annex
NFA . . . . . . New Farmers of America
NFA . . . . . . Night Fighter Association
NFA. . . . . . . Nitrogen Filling Assembly
NFA. . . . . . . No Further Action (Shipping)
NFA. . . . . . . Nondeterministic Finite Automaton
NFA . . . . . . Northwest Fisheries Association
NFAA . . . . . . National Federation of Advertising Agencies
NFAA. . . . . . National Field Archery Association
NFAC . . . . . . National Foundation for Asthmatic Children at Tucson
NFACJC . . . . National Faculty Association of Community and Junior Colleges
NFAH . . . . . National Foundation on Arts and Humanities
NFB . . . . National Federation of the Blind
NFB . . . . Naval Frontier Base
NFBA . . . . . National Food Brokers Association
NFBC. . . . . . National Film Board of Canada
NFBC . . . . . . Newfoundland Base Command (Military)
NFBF . . . . . . National Farm Bureau Federation
NFBPWC . . . . National Federation of Business and Professional Women's Clubs
NFC . . . . National Film Carriers
NFC . . . . National Food Conference Association
NFC. . . . . . . National Football Conference (of NFL)
NFC . . . . National Freight Corporation (British)
NFC. . . . . . . Navy Finance Center
NFC. . . . . . . Negative Factor Counting
NFC. . . . . . . Negative Feedback Circuit
NFC . . . . . . Not Favorably Considered
NFCA . . . . . . National Fraternal Congress of America
NFCA. . . . . . National Fuel Credit Association
NFCAA . . . . . National Fencing Coaches Association of America
NFCC . . . . . . National Farm-City Committee
NFCC . . . . . . National Foundation for Consumer Credit
NFCCS . . . . . National Federation of Catholic College Students
NFCDA . . . . . National Family Council on Drug Addiction
NFCGC . . . . . National Federation of Coffee Growers of Colombia
NFCPG. . . . . National Federation of Catholic Physicians' Guilds
NFCS . . . . . . Night Fire Control Sight
NFCTA . . . . . National Fibre Can and Tube Association
NFCU. . . . . . Navy Federal Credit Union
NFD. . . . . . . National Faculty Directory
NFD. . . . . . . Naval Fuel Depot
NFD. . . . . . . No Fixed Date
NFDA . . . . . . National Food Distributors Association
NFDA . . . . . . National Funeral Directors Association
NFDC. . . . . . National Father's Day Committee

NFDC . . . . . . National Flight Data Center (FAA)
NFDCAMD . . . National Food, Drug & Cosmetic Association of Manufacturers and
Distributors
NFDMA . . . . . National Funeral Directors and Morticians Association
NFE. . . . . . . Nose Fairing Exit
NFE . . . . Not Fully Equipped (of aircraft) (Air Force)
NFEA . . . . . . Newspaper Farm Editors' Association
NFEAC . . . . . National Foundation for Education in American Citizenship
NFEC. . . . . . Naval Facilities Engineering Command (Formerly, Bureau of Yards
and Docks)
NFEC . . . . . . Newspaper Food Editors Conference
NFEMC. . . . . National Federation of Export Management Companies
NFER . . . . . . National Foundation for Educational Research (British)
NFER . . . . . . National Foundation for Eye Research
NFF . . . . The National Football Foundation and Hall of Fame
NFF . . . . Naval Fuel Facility
NFF . . . . Numbered Fleet Flagship (Navy)
NFFA . . . . . . National Folk Festival Association
NFFA . . . . . . National Frozen Food Association
NFFC . . . . . . National Film Finance Corporation (British)
NFFDA . . . . . National Frozen Food Distributors Association
NFFDF . . . . . National Fraternal Flag Day Foundation
NFFE . . . . . . National Federation of Federal Employees
NFFF . . . . . . National Fantasy Fan Federation
NFFGB . . . . . National Federation of Flemish Giant Breeders
NFFGRB . . . . National Federation of Flemish Giant Rabbit Breeders
NFFI . . . . . . Not Fit for Issue (Navy)
NFFS . . . . . . National Foundation of Funeral Service
NFFS . . . . . . Non-Ferrous Founders Society
NFG . . . . National Fuel Gas Company (NYSE symbol)
NFGC . . . . . . National Federation of Grain Cooperatives
NFGCA . . . . . National Federation of Grandmother Clubs of America
NFGMIC. . . . . National Federation of Grange Mutual Insurance Companies
NFGND . . . . . National Foundation for Genetics and Neuromuscular Disease
NFGNE . . . . . National Fund for Graduate Nursing Education
NFH . . . . National Fish Hatchery
NFHA . . . . . . National Fox Hunters Association
NFHC . . . . . . National Foot Health Council
NFHEA . . . . . National Farm Home Editors Association
NFHPER . . . . . National Foundation for Health, Physical Education, and Recreation
NFHTP . . . . . National Federation of Hebrew Teachers and Principals
NFI . . . . Narrow Fabrics Institute
NFI . . . . National Fisheries Institute
NFI . . . . Noise Figure Indicator
NFIA . . . . . . National Feed Ingredients Association
NFIB . . . . . . National Federation of Independent Business
NFIC . . . . . . National Foundation for Ileitis and Colitis
NFIP . . . . . . National Foundation for Infantile Paralysis
NFIR . . . . . . National Federation of Indian Railwaymen
NFIS . . . . . . Naval Fighting Instruction School
NFISYD . . . . . National Federation of Independent Scrap Yard Dealers
NFIU . . . . . . National Federation of Independent Unions
NFJC . . . . . . National Foundation for Jewish Culture
NFJM. . . . . . National Foundation for Junior Museums
NFJMC . . . . . National Federation of Jewish Men's Clubs
NFK . . . . Norfolk & Western Railway (NYSE symbol)
NFL. . . . . . . National Federation of Laymen
NFL. . . . . . . National Football League
NFL. . . . . . . National Forensic League
NFL. . . . . No Fire Line (Military)
NFLD . . . . . . Newfoundland (Canadian province)
NFLF . . . . . . National Family Life Foundation
NFLF . . . . . . Nylon Full-Line Filter
NFLPA . . . . . National Football League Players Association
NFLPA . . . . . National Free Lance Photographers Association
NFLPN . . . . . National Federation of Licensed Practical Nurses
NFLSV . . . . . National Front for the Liberation of South Vietnam
NFLU . . . . . . National Federation of Labor Unions (Philippines)
NFM . . . . . . Narodni Front Makedonije
NFM . . . . . . Narrowband Frequency Modulation (Radio)
NFM . . . . . . Noise Figure Meter
NFM . . . . . . Non-Ferrous Metal
NFMA . . . . . . National Footwear Manufacturers Association
NFMA. . . . . . Northwest Farm Managers Association
NFMC . . . . . . National Federation of Music Clubs
NFMC . . . . . . National Film Music Council (Defunct)
NFMD . . . . . . National Foundation for Muscular Dystrophy
NFME . . . . . . National Fund for Medical Education
NFMLTA . . . . National Federation of Modern Language Teachers Associations
NFMM . . . . . . National Fellowship of Methodist Musicians
NFMN . . . . . . National Fallout Monitoring Network

NFMP....... Non-Ferrous Metal Powder
NFMR ...... National Foundation for Metabolic Research
NFMS ...... Navy Fleet Material Support
NFMS....... Nitrogen Flow Measuring System
NFMS ...... Noise Figure Meter System
NFMSAEG.... Naval Fleet Missile System Analysis and Evaluation Group
NFND ...... National Foundation for Neuromuscular Diseases
NFO .... National Family Opinion
NFO .... National Farmers Organization
NFO .... Naval Flight Officer
NFO .... Navy Finance Office
NFOBA ..... National Fats and Oils Brokers Association
NFP........ Non-Flare Proton
NFP........ Normal Failure Period
NFP........ Northern Frontier Province (Kenya)
NFPA ...... National Fire Protection Association
NFPA ...... National Flaxseed Processors Association
NFPA ...... National Flexible Packaging Association
NFPA....... National Fluid Power Association
NFPA....... National Forest Products Association
NFPA....... Natural Family Planning Association of Connecticut
NFPB ...... National Friends of Public Broadcasting
NFPC....... National Federation of Priests' Councils
NFPEDA .... National Farm and Power Equipment Dealers Association
NFPOC ..... National Federation of Post Office Clerks (Later, UFPC)
NFPS ...... Naval Flight Preparatory School
NFPS ...... Navy Field Purchase Systems
NFPS ...... Nuclear Flight Propulsion System
NFPTE ..... National Federation of Posts' and Telegraphs' Employees (India)
NFPW....... National Federation of Petroleum Workers (India)
NFPW ...... National Federation of Press Women
NFQ .... Night Frequency (Aviation)
NFR........ No Further Requirement
NFR........ Nuclear Fission Reactor
NFRA ...... National Forest Recreation Association
NFRC ...... National Finals Rodeo Commission
NFRM ..... National Foundation for Research in Medicine
NFRW ..... National Federation of Republican Women
NFS........ National Federation of Settlements
NFS........ National Food Survey (British)
NFS........ Neutron Flux Spectra
NFS........ Nitrogen Flow System
NFS........ Not on Flying Status
NFS........ Not For Sale
NFS........ Nuclear Fuel Services, Inc.
NFSA ...... National Fertilizer Solutions Association
NFSA ...... National Food Service Association
NFSA ...... Navy Field Safety Association
NFSAIS .... National Federation of Science Abstracting and Indexing Services
NFSC ..... National Federation of Stamp Clubs
NFSD ...... National Fraternal Society of the Deaf
NFSE ...... National Federation of Sales Executives
NFSF ...... National Freedom Shrine Foundation
NFSHSAA .... National Federation of State High School Athletic Associations
NFSM ..... National Fraternity of Student Musicians
NFSMA ..... National Fruit and Syrup Manufacturers Association
NFS & NC ... National Federation of Settlements and Neighborhood Centers
NFSO...... Navy Fuel Supply Office
NFSPS ..... National Federation of State Poetry Societies
NFSS ...... National Fallout Shelter Survey (Civil Defense)
NFSU ...... Non-Flying Support Unit
NFT........ No Filing Time (Aviation)
NFTA ...... National Freight Traffic Association
NFTB ...... National Federation of Temple Brotherhoods
NFTB ...... Naval Fleet Training Base
NFTB ...... Nuclear Flight Test Base
NFTC ...... National Foreign Trade Council
NFTC...... National Furniture Traffic Conference
NFTS ...... National Federation of Temple Sisterhoods
NFTS ...... Naval Flight Training School
NFTSA ..... US Navy Field Training Supervisors Association
NFTW...... National Federation of Telephone Workers
NFTY ...... National Federation of Temple Youth
NFU....... National Farmers' Union (British)
NFU....... Not For Us (Communications)
NFVOA ..... Northern Fishing Vessel Owners Association
NFWA ..... National Farm Workers Association
NFWA ..... National Furniture Warehousemen's Association
NFWE ..... National Federation of Woman's Exchanges
NFWI ...... National Federation of Women's Institutes (British)
NFZ .... Nuclear Free Zone

NG .... Narrow Gage
NG .... National Guard(man)
NG .... National Gypsum Company (NYSE symbol)
NG .... Navy General (MCD files)
NG .... Nephridial Gland
NG .... New Genus
NG .... New Guinea
NG .... Nitroglycerin
NG .... No Go (i.e., an unacceptable arrangement)
NG .... No Good (Similar to IC-- Inspected and Condemned)
NG .... Normal Graduate
NGA ...... National Gallery of Art
NGA ...... National Glider Association
NGA ...... National Graphical Association (British printers' union)
NGA ...... Needlework Guild of America
NGAA ..... National Gift and Art Association
NGAA ..... National Girls Athletic Association
NGAA ..... Natural Gasoline Association of America
NGARP ..... National Guard and Army Reserve Policy
NGAUS ..... National Guard Association of the United States
NGB ...... National Garden Bureau
NGB ...... National Guard Bureau (Army)
NGC ...... National General Corporation (NYSE symbol)
NGC ...... National Guild of Churchmen
NGC ...... National Guinea Club
NGC ...... Near Galactic Catalog
NGC ...... New General Catalogue (Astronomy)
NGC ...... Noise Generator Card
NGC ...... North Georgia College
NGC ...... Nozzle Gap Control (Aerospace)
NGCC ..... National Guard Computer Center
NGCC ..... North German Coal Control (Post-World War II)
NGCDO .... North German Coal Distribution Organization (Post-World War II)
NGCM..... Navy Good Conduct Medal
NGCMS..... National Guild of Community Music Schools
NGD ...... National Grassland Demonstration (British)
NGDA ..... National Glass Dealers Association
NGDC ..... National Geophysical Data Center
NGE ...... New York State Electric & Gas Corporation (NYSE symbol)
NGF....... National Genetics Foundation
NGF ...... National Golf Foundation
NGF ...... Naval Gun Factory (Later, NWF)
NGF....... Naval Gunfire
NGF....... Nerve Growth Factor (A protein) (Biochemistry)
NGFLO..... Naval Gunfire Liaison Officer
NGFLT..... Naval Gunfire Liaison Team
NGFO ..... Naval Gunfire Officer
NGFT ..... National Guard on Field Training Exercises
NGG ...... Negative Grid Generator
NGI....... National Garden Institute
NGJC ..... North Greenville Junior College (South Carolina)
NGL ...... Natural Gas Liquids
NGL ...... Neodymium Glass LASER
NGL ...... Neon Glow Lamp
NGL ...... No Gimbal Lock
NGLIOGT.... National Grand Lodge, International Order of Good Templars
NGLO ..... Naval Gunfire Liaison Officer
NGLR...... Neodymium Glass LASER Rod
NGM...... Neutron-Gamma Monte Carlo (Data processing)
NGMA..... National Gadget Manufacturers Association
NGMA..... National Gas Measurement Association
NGNF ..... National Guard not in Federal Service
NGO....... National Gas Outlet
NGO ...... Non-Governmental Organization (Generic term)
NGOC..... North German Oil Control (Post-World War II)
NGOCS .... National Guard Officer Candidate School
NGP ...... Nano Glass Pellet
NGPA ..... Natural Gas Processors Association
NGPSA .... Natural Gas Processors Suppliers Association
NGPT ..... National Guild of Piano Teachers
NGQ ...... Non-Government Quarters
NGR ...... National Guard Regulations
NGRC ..... National Government of the Republic of China
NGRS...... National Goals Research Staff
NGS....... National Genealogical Society
NGS....... National Geodetic Survey (National Oceanic and Atmospheric Administration)
NGS ...... National Geographic Society
NGS ...... National Geriatrics Society
NGS ...... National Gladiolus Society
NGS ...... National Goldfish Society

NGS	Naval Gunfire Support
NGS	Neutral Grain Spirits
NGS	Niagara Share Corporation (NYSE symbol)
NGS	Nucleonic Gauging System
NGSM	National Gold Star Mothers
NGSMA	Natural Gasoline Supply Men's Association
NGSP	National Geodetic Satellite Program (NASA)
NGT	Noise Generator Tube
NGTC	National Grain Trade Council
NGTE	National Gas Turbine Establishment (British)
NGUS	National Guard of the United States
NGVR	New Guinea Volunteer Reserve
NGX	Northgate Exploration, Ltd. (NYSE symbol)
NH	Naval Home
NH	Naval Hospital
NH	Never Hinged
NH	New Hampshire
NH	New York, New Haven & Hartford R. R. (AAR code)
NH	Nonhygroscopic
NHA	National Handbag Association
NHA	National Hay Association
NHA	National Health Association
NHA	National Hide Association
NHA	National Hockey Association (to 1917)
NHA	National Holiness Association
NHA	National Housing Act
NHA	National Housing Administration
NHA	National Housing Agency (Superseded by HHFA, 1947; then by HUD, 1965)
NHA	Nationwide Hotel Association
NHA	New Homemakers of America
NHA	Next Higher Assembly (Engineering)
NHA	Northwest Hardwood Association
NHAIAC	National Highway Accident and Injury Analysis Center
NHAM	National Hose Assemblies Manufacturers Association
NHAS	National Hearing Aid Society
NHASA	National Handbag & Accessories Salesmen's Association
NHAW	Northamerican Heating and Airconditioning Wholesalers Association
NHB	National Housing Bank (Brazil)
NHC	National Health Council
NHC	National Housing Center
NHC	National Housing Conference
NHC	National Housing Council (of the HHFA) (Abolished, 1965)
NHC	National Hurricane Center
NHCA	National Hairdressers and Cosmetologists Association
NHCC	National Hebrew Culture Council
NHD	Not Heard (Communications)
NHDAA	National Home Demonstration Agents' Association
NHDC	National Home Demonstration Council
NHDI	Notch Die (Tool)
NHE	Nitrogen Heat Exchange
NHE	Normal Hydrogen Electrode
NHEA	National Higher Education Association
NHEDLP	National Housing and Economic Development Law Project
NHEF	National Health Education Foundation
NHENMA	National Hand Embroidery and Novelty Manufacturers Association
NHESA	National Higher Education Staff Association
NHF	National Health Federation
NHF	National Hemophilia Foundation
NHF	National Humanities Faculty
NHF	Naval Historical Foundation
NHFL	National Home Fashions League
NHFRA	National Hay Fever Relief Association
NHG	New High German
NHH	Neither Help nor Hinder
NHHRA	National Hereford Hog Record Association
NHI	National Health Insurance (British)
NHI	National Heart Institute (Later, NHLI) (of NIH)
NHI	National Hobby Institute
NHIC	National Home Improvement Council
NHK	Nippon Hoso Kyokai (Japan Broadcasting Corporation)
NHKG	Nova Hut' Klementa Gottwalda
NHKYA	National Hand Knitting Yarn Association
NHL	National Hockey League
NHL	Negro Heritage Library
NHL	Newhall Land & Farming Co. (NYSE sybmol)
NHL	Normal Human Lymphocyte
NHLA	National Hardwood Lumber Association
NHLA	National Housewives' League of America
NHLI	National Heart and Lung Institute (Formerly, NHI) (National Institutes of Health)
NHLPA	National Hockey League Players' Association
NHM	No Hot Metal (Photocomposition)
NHM	Nozzle Hinge Moment
NHMA	National Handle Manufacturers Association
NHMA	National Housewares Manufacturers Association
NHMILCOM . .	NATO HAWK Military Committee
NHMO	NATO HAWK Management Organization
NHO	Navy Hydrographic Office (Later, NOO)
NHOS	Naval Hospital
NHP	National Hamiltonian Party
NHP	National Housing Partnership (HUD)
NHP	Nitrogen High Pressure
NHP	Nominal Horsepower
NHP	Nuclear Heart Pacer
NHPAA	National Horseshoe Pitchers Association of America
NHPC	National Historical Publications Commission
NHPDA	National Honey Packers and Dealers Association
NHPMA	Northern Hardwood and Pine Manufacturers Association
NHPO	NATO HAWK Production Organization
NHQ	New Hungarian Quarterly
NHR	National Hunt Rules (British)
NHR	Net Histocompatibility Ratio
NHRA	National Hot Rod Association
NHRE	National Hail Research Experiment
NHRP	National Hurricane Research Project
NHRR	New Haven Railroad
NHS	National Health Service (British)
NHS	National Health Survey
NHS	National Honor Society
NHS	National Huguenot Society
NHS	Normal Human Serum
NHSA	National Highway Safety Administration (Formerly, NHSB; later, NHTSA) Department of Transportation)
NHSA	National Home Service Association
NHSA	National Horse Show Association of America
NHSA	Negro Historical Society of America
NHSACA	National High School Athletic Coaches Association
NHSB	National Highway Safety Bureau (Later, NHSA, then NHTSA) (Department of Transportation)
NHSC	National Health Service Corps (HEW)
NHSC	National Home Study Council
NHSD	National Health Survey Division (of OSG)
NHSR	National Hospital Service Reserve
NHSRA	National High School Rodeo Association
NHSS	National Herb Study Society
NHT	Nernst Heat Theorem
NHTSA	National Highway Traffic Safety Administration (Formerly, NHSB and NHSA) (Department of Transportation)
NHUC	National Highway Users Conference
NHV	New Haven Clock & Watch (NYSE symbol)
NHWRA	National Health and Welfare Retirement Association
NHX	National Homes (NYSE symbol)
NI	Native Infantry
NI	Naval Instructor (British)
NI	Naval Intelligence
NI	Neurological Institute
Ni	Nickel (Chemical element)
NI	Noise Index
NI	Normal Impurity (Metals)
NI	Northern Indiana Public Service Company (NYSE symbol)
NI	Northern Ireland
NI	Not Interested
NI	Not Issued
NI	Nuclear Industries, Inc.
NIA	National Ice Association
NIA	National Iceboat Authority
NIA	National Income Accounts
NIA	National Insurance Association
NIA	National Intelligence Authority
NIA	Navy Industrial Association
NIA	Nickel Iron Alloy
NIAA	National Industrial Advertisers Association
NIAA	National Institute of Animal Agriculture
NIAAA	National Institute of Alcohol Abuse and Alcoholism
NIAB	National Institute of Agricultural Botany (British)
NIAC	National Industry Advisory Committee (FCC)
NIAC	National Information & Analysis Center
NIAC	Nuclear Insurance Association of Canada
NIADA	National Independent Automobile Dealers Association
NIADA	National Institute of American Doll Artists
NIAE	National Institute of Agricultural Engineering (British)

NIAE . . . . . . National Institute for Architectural Education
NIAG . . . . . . NATO Industrial Advisory Group
NIAID . . . . . National Institute of Allergy and Infectious Diseases (of National
        Institutes of Health)
NIAL . . . . . . National Institute of Arts and Letters
NIAM . . . . . . National Institute of Advertising Management
NIAMD . . . . . National Institute of Arthritis and Metabolic Diseases (of National
        Institutes of Health)
NIAP . . . . . . Non-Inverting Amplifier Pair
NIAR . . . . . . National Institute of Atmospheric Research
NIAR . . . . . . Neutron-Induced Autoradiography
NIASO . . . . . National Insurance Actuarial and Statistical Association
NIB . . . . National Industries for the Blind
NIB . . . . National Information Bureau
NIB . . . . National Institute for the Blind
NIB . . . . Negative Impedance Booster
NIB . . . . Negative Ion Beam
NIB . . . . Negative Ion Blemish
NIB . . . . Non-Interference Basis
NIBCA . . . . . National Intercollegiate Boxing Coaches Association
NIBCO . . . . . Northern Indiana Brass Company
NIBID . . . . . National Investment Bank for Industrial Development (Greece)
NIBJL . . . . . . National Information Bureau for Jewish Life
NIBL . . . . . . National Industrial Basketball League
NIBMAR . . . . . No Independence Before Majority African Rule (British policy
        in regard to Rhodesia)
NIC . . . . National Indications Center (DOD)
NIC . . . . National Industrial Council
NIC . . . . National Institute of Credit
NIC . . . . National Interagency Council
NIC . . . . National Interfraternity Conference
NIC . . . . National Interstate Council of State Boards of Cosmetology
NIC . . . . National Inventors Council (Department of Commerce)
NIC . . . . Negative Immittance Converter
NIC . . . . Negative Impedance Converter
NIC . . . . Negative Ion Chamber
NIC . . . . Network Information Center
NIC . . . . Newspaper Indexing Center (Flint, Michigan)
NIC . . . . Newsprint Information Committee
NIC . . . . Not in Contract (Technical drawings)
NIC . . . . Nuclear Industry Consortium (Belgium) (Also known as GPIN)
NICAD . . . . . Nickel Cadmium
NICAP . . . . . National Investigations Committee on Aerial Phenomena
NICATELSAT . . Nicaraguan Telecommunication by Satellite (Commercial firm)
NICB . . . . . . National Industrial Conference Board (Later, Conference Board)
NICCO . . . . . New Inner City Community Organization (Washington, DC)
NICD . . . . . . National Institute on Crime and Delinquency
NICDA . . . . . National Imported Car Dealers Association
NICE . . . . . . National Institute of Ceramic Engineers
NICE . . . . . . Normal Input-Output Control Executive (Data processing)
NICEM . . . . . National Information Center for Educational Media
NICHHD . . . . . National Institute of Child Health and Human Development
NICHROME . . . Nickel-Chromium (Alloy) (Trade name)
NICJ . . . . . . National Institute of Consumer Justice
NICMA . . . . . National Ice Cream Mix Association
NICMA . . . . . National Industrial Cafeteria Managers Association
NICO . . . . . . Navy Inventory Control Office
NICOA . . . . . National Independent Coal Operators Association
NICOP . . . . . Navy Industry Cooperation Plan
NICP . . . . . . National Inventory Control Point (Military)
NICP . . . . . . Nuclear Incident Control Plan
NICRA . . . . . National Ice Cream Retailers Association
NICRA . . . . . Northern Ireland Civil Rights Association
NICRISP . . . . . Navy Integrated Comprehensible Repairable Item Scheduling Program
NID . . . . National Institute of Drycleaning (Later, IFI)
NID . . . . New International Dictionary (Webster's)
NID . . . . US Naval Intelligence Division (Usually, ONI)
NIDA . . . . . . National Independent Dairies Association
NIDA . . . . . . National Industrial Distributors Association
NIDA . . . . . . National Institute on Drug Abuse
NIDA . . . . . . Northeastern Industrial Developers Association
NIDA . . . . . . Numerically Integrated Differential Analyzer (Data processing)
NIDCC . . . . . National Internal Defense Coordination Center
NIDH . . . . . . National Institute of Dental Health
NIDM . . . . . . National Institute for Disaster Mobilization
NIDOC . . . . . National Information and Documentation Center
NIDR . . . . . . National Institute of Dental Research (of National Institutes of Health)
NIDS . . . . . . National Institute of Diaper Services
NIDS . . . . . . Navigation Instrument Development Unit
NIE . . . . National Institute of Education (Formerly, Office of Education) (HEW)
NIE . . . . National Intelligence Estimate

NIE . . . . Negative Ion Erosion
NIE . . . . Neutron Ionization Effect
NIEHS . . . . . National Institute of Environmental Health Sciences
NIEM . . . . . . National Industrial Engineering Mission
NIER . . . . . . National Industrial Equipment Reserve (of DMS)
NIESR . . . . . National Institute of Economic and Social Research (British)
NIEU . . . . . . Negro Industrial and Economic Union
NIF . . . . National Interfraternity Foundation
NIF . . . . Navy Industrial Fund
NIF . . . . Nickel Iron Film
NIF . . . . Nuclear Information File
NIFA . . . . . . National Intercollegiate Flying Association
NIFAC . . . . . Night Forward Air Controller (Aircraft)
NIFB . . . . . . National Institute of Farm Brokers
NIFDA . . . . . National Institutional Food Distributor Associates
NIFTE . . . . . . Neon Indicator Flashing Test Equipment
NIG . . . . Naval Inspector General
NIG . . . . Nude Ionization Gauge
NIGA . . . . . . Neutron-Induced Gamma Activity
NIGMS . . . . . National Institute of General Medical Sciences
NIGP . . . . . . National Institute of Governmental Purchasing
NIH . . . . National Institutes of Health (of Public Health Service)
NIH . . . . Not Invented Here (Industrial term)
NII . . . . National Industries, Incorporated (NYSE symbol)
NIICP . . . . . . No Increase in Contract Price
NIIP . . . . National Institute of Industrial Psychology
NIIS . . . . Niagara Institute for International Studies (Canada)
NIJC . . . . North Idaho Junior College
NIJS . . . . Nuklearni Institut (Jozef Stefan Nuclear Institute) (Yugoslavia)
NILA . . . . . . National Industrial Leather Association
NILE . . . . . . National Institute of Labor Education
NILECJ . . . . . National Institute for Law Enforcement and Criminal Justice (Law
        Enforcement Assistance Administration)
NILFP . . . . . . National Institute of Locker and Freezer Provisioners
NILN . . . . . . Nylon Insert Lock Nut
NIM . . . . Naval Inspector of Machinery
NIM . . . . Night Intruder Mission (Air Force)
NIM . . . . Normal Integration Mode
NIM . . . . Nuclear Instrumentation Module
NIM . . . . Nylon Insulation Material
NIMA . . . . . . National Insulation Manufacturers Association
NIMAC . . . . . National Interscholastic Music Activities Commission
NIMC . . . . . . National Institute of Management Counsellors
NIMC . . . . . . National Institute of Municipal Clerks
NIMCGA . . . . Northern Indiana Muck Crop Growers Association
NIMH . . . . . . National Institute of Mental Health (of Health Services and Mental Health
        Administration)
NIMJ . . . . . . Near Infrared Miniaturized Jammer
NIMLO . . . . . National Institute of Municipal Law Officers
NIMMP . . . . . National Institute of Marine Medicine and Pharmacology (Proposed) (NIH)
NIMP . . . . . . National Intern Matching Program
NIMPA . . . . . National Independent Meat Packers Association
NIMPHE . . . . . Nuclear Isotope Monopropellant Hydrazine Engine
NIMR . . . . . . National Institute for Medical Research
NIMR . . . . . . Navy Industrial Management Reviews
NIMS . . . . . . Nationwide Improved Mail Service (Postal Service)
NIN . . . . National Information Network (ASTIA)
NINA . . . . . . No Irish Need Apply (Classified advertising)
NINDB . . . . . National Institute of Neurological Diseases and Blindness (of
        National Institutes of Health)
NINDS . . . . . National Institute of Neurological Diseases and Stroke
NIO . . . . National Institute of Oceanography (British)
NIO . . . . Naval Inspector Ordnance
NIO . . . . Navigational Information Office
NIO . . . . Navy Institute of Oceanography
NIOBE . . . . . Numerical Integration of the Boltzmann Transport Equation
NIOC . . . . . . National Iranian Oil Company
NIOP . . . . . . National Institute of Oilseed Products
NIOSH . . . . . National Institute of Occupational Safety and Health
NIP . . . . Navy Interceptor Program
NIP . . . . Nipple
NIP . . . . Normal Impact Point
NIP . . . . Notice of Intelligence Potential (Military)
NIPA . . . . . . Non-Interference Performance Assessment
NIPCC . . . . . National Industrial Pollution Control Council (Department of Commerce)
NIPD . . . . . . Not in the Public Domain
NIPH . . . . . . National Institute of Public Health
NIPHLE . . . . . National Institute of Packaging, Handling and Logistic Engineers
NIPO . . . . . . Negative Input, Positive Output
NIPP . . . . . . National Intelligence Projection for Planning
NIPP . . . . . . Non-Impact Printing Process

NIPR	National Industrial Plant Reserve
NIPS	National Information Processing System (Military)
NIPS	Nationwide Integrated Postal Service (Postal Service)
NIPS	Naval Intelligence Processing System
NIPS	Navy Information Policy Summaries
NIPS.	New Inventory Pricing Systems
NIPSSA	Naval Intelligence Processing Systems Support Activity
NIR	Near Infrared Region
NIR	Nerve Impulse Recorder
NIR	Next Inferior Rank
NIR	Non-Inductive Resistor
NIRA	National Industrial Recovery Act
NIRA	National Industrial Recreation Association
NIRA	National Intercollegiate Rodeo Association
NIRA	National Inter-Racial Association
NIRAS	National Institute of Research and Advanced Studies (Proposed)
NIRB	National Industrial Recovery Board (Terminated 1935)
NIRB	Nuclear Insurance Rating Bureau
NIRC	National Industrial Relations Court (British)
NIRC	National Institute of Rug Cleaning
NIRC	Negative Ion Recombination Chamber
NIRD	National Institute for Research in Dairying (British)
NIREB	National Institute of Real Estate Brokers
NIRI	National Investor Relations Institute
NIRNS	National Institute for Research in Nuclear Science (British)
NIRO	Nike-Iroquois (Rockets)
NIRPL	Navy Industrial Readiness Planning List
NIRPO	Naval Industrial Reserve Ordnance Plant
NIRS	National Institute for Radiological Science (Japan)
NI & RT	Numerical Index and Requirement Table
NIRTS	New Integrated Range Timing System
NIS	National Industrial Services Corp.
NIS	National Institute of Science
NIS	National Intelligence Survey
NIS	Naval Intelligence School
NIS	Naval Investigative Service
NIS	Navy Inspection Service
NIS	Negative Ion Source
NIS	Network Information System (AT & T)
NIS	Neutron Inelastic Scattering
NIS	Nickel Iron System
NIS	Night Illumination System
NIS	Nordiska Ingenjoerssamfundet (Scandinavian Society of Engineers)
NIS	Not in Stock
NISA	National Industrial Sand Association
NISA	Nonjudicial Service Association
NISA	National Industrial Stores Association
NISA	National Institute of Supply Associations
NISARC	National Information Storage and Retrieval Center
NISBS	National Institute of Social and Behavioral Science
NISC	National Industrial Space Committee
NISC	National Intramural Sports Council
NISE	Normalized Integral Squared Error
NISEC	National Institute for the Study of Educational Change
NISEE	National Information Service for Earthquake Engineering (National Science Foundation)
NISOA	National Intercollegiate Soccer Officials Association
NISP.	National Information System for Psychology
NISP.	Navy Integrated Space Program
NISRA	National Intercollegiate Squash Racquets Association
NISS	National Institute of Social Sciences
NIST.	National Institute of Science and Technology (Philippines)
NIT	National Institute of Technology
NIT	National Instructional Television Center
NIT	National Intelligence Test (Psychology)
NIT	National Invitation Tournament (Basketball)
NIT	Negative Income Tax
NITA	National Industrial Television Association
NITEDEVRON . .	Night Development Squadron
NITL	National Industrial Traffic League
NITMDA	National Indoor Track Meet Directors Association
NITP.	Nibbling Template
NITPA	National Institutional Teacher Placement Association
NITPICKERS . .	National Institute of Technical Processors, Information Consultants, Keyword Experts, and Retrieval Specialists (Fictitious organization)
NITROS	Nitrostarch
NIU	Naval Intelligence Unit
NIU	Northern Illinois University
NIUC	National Independent Union Council
NIV	Negative Ion Vacancy
NIVA	National Independent Vendors Association

NIVRA	Nederlands Instituut van Register-Accountants
NIW.	National Industrial Workers Union
NIW.	Naval Inshore Warfare Project
NIW.	Nonlethal Incapacitating Weapon
NIWARS	Netherlands Interdepartmental Working Group on the Application of Remote Sensing
NIWKC	National Institute of Wood Kitchen Cabinets
NIWS	National Institute on Workshop Standards
NIWU	National Industrial Workers Union
NIYC	National Indian Youth Council
NIZC	National Industrial Zoning Committee
NJ.	New Jersey
NJ.	Niagara Junction Railway (AAR code)
NJ.	Nylon Jacket
NJA	National Jail Association
NJA	National Jogging Association
NJA	Nozzle Jetevator Assembly
NJAC.	National Joint Advisory Council (on labor-management relations) (British)
NJBBF	National Judo Black Belt Federation of the USA
NJC	Natchez Junior College (Mississippi)
NJC	Navarro Junior College (Texas)
NJC.	Navy Job Classification Manual
NJC	Newton Junior College (Massachusetts)
NJC	Norfolk Junior College (Nebraska)
NJCAA	National Junior College Athletic Association
NJCC	National Joint Computer Committee (of ACM, AIEE, IRE) (Superseded by AFIPS)
NJCC	Northeastern Junior College of Colorado
NJCF	National Juvenile Court Foundation
NJCS	National Jewish Committee on Scouting
NJCSE	National Jewish Civil Service Employees
NJDP	National Job Development Program
NJF	Scandinavian Agricultural Research Workers' Association
NJG.	Nice Jewish Girl (Slang)
NJHA.	National Junior Horticultural Association
NJHS.	National Junior Honor Society
NJIC	National Joint Industrial Council (Pharmacy) (British)
NJII.	New Jersey, Indiana & Illinois R. R. (AAR code)
NJIS	National Jewish Information Service (for the Propagation of Judaism)
NJMC	National Jewish Music Council
NJMDC	NORAD Joint Manual Direction Center (Military)
NJNY.	New Jersey & New York R. R. (AAR code)
NJP	Network Job Processing
NJP	New Jersey Power & Light Company (NYSE symbol) (Delisted)
NJP	Nonjudicial Punishment (Military)
NJPMB	Navy Jet Propelled Missile Board
NJVGA	National Junior Vegetable Growers Association
NJWB	National Jewish Welfare Board
NJZ.	New Jersey Zinc Company (NYSE symbol)
NK	Neck
NK.	Next of Kin
NK	Nomenklatur Kommission (German) (Commission on Nomenclature) (Anatomy)
NK	Not Known
NKA	National Kindergarten Association
NKCA	National Kitchen Cabinet Association
NKDF.	National Kidney Disease Foundation
NKF.	National Kidney Foundation
NKF.	Nene Kampffugzeng
NKF	Nonlinear Kalmar Filter
NKF	Norges Kjott og Fleskesentral
NKFD.	Nationalkomitee Freies Deutschland
NKK	Nippon Kokan (Steel company) (Japan)
NKM	New Park Mining Company (NYSE symbol)
NKO	Narodnyi Komissariat Oborony (People's Commissariat of Defense) (Existed until 1946) (USSR)
NKOA	National Knitted Outerwear Association
NKP.	New York, Chicago & St. Louis R.R. Company (NYSE symbol) (Wall Street slang name: "Nickel Plate") (Delisted)
NKPA	National Kraut Packers Association
NKS.	Norsk Kjemisk Selskap (Norwegian Chemical Society)
NKT.	None Kept in Town
NKVD.	Narodnyi Komissariat Vnutrennikh Del (People's Commissariat of Internal Affairs) (Soviet secret police organization) (Also known as NARKOMVNUDEL)
NL	National League of Professional Baseball Clubs
NL	National Liberal (British politics)
NL	Naval Lighter
NL	Navy League
NL.	Nebenlager (Branch camp) (German military - World War II)

NL . . . . Netherlands (NATO) (Also when used as license plate designation)
NL . . . . New Latin
NL. . . . . New Line
NL. . . . . New London, Connecticut
NL. . . . . Night Letter
NL. . . . . NL Industries, Inc. (Formerly, National Lead Company) (NYSE symbol)
NL . . . . No Layers (Aviation)
NL. . . . . No License (Traffic offense charge)
NL. . . . . Non Licet (It Is Not Permitted)
NL. . . . . Non-Linear
NL . . . . Non Liquet (It Is Not Clear)
NL . . . . Non-Locking
NL . . . . Non Longe (Not Far)
NL . . . . North Latitude
NL . . . . Not Listed
NL. . . . . Not Located
NL . . . . Nuevo Leon (Mexican province)
NLA . . . . . . National Lime Association
NLA . . . . . . National Locksmiths Association
NLA . . . . . . Netherlands Laureate of Arts in America (An organization)
NLA . . . . . . Non-Linear Amplifier
NLA . . . . . . Nonuniform Linear Array
NLA . . . . . . Northwestern Lumbermen's Association
NLAA. . . . . . National Legal Aid Association
NLABS . . . . . Natick Laboratories (Army)
NLADA . . . . . National Legal Aid and Defender Association
NLAPW . . . . National League of American Pen Women
NLB. . . . . . . National Lighting Bureau
NLB . . . . Nuclear Light Bulb
NLBA . . . . . . National Lead Burning Association
NLBA . . . . . . National Licensed Beverage Association
NLBC. . . . . . National Livestock Brand Conference
NLBMDA . . . . National Lumber and Building Material Dealers Association
NLC. . . . . . . Nalco Chemical Co. (NYSE symbol)
NLC . . . . . . National League of Cities (Formerly, American Municipal Association)
NLC . . . . . . National Legislative Conference
NLC. . . . . . . National Legislative Council
NLC. . . . . . . National Liberal Club (British)
NLC. . . . . . . National Liberation Committee (South Africa)
NLC. . . . . . . National Location Code (Civil Defense)
NLC . . . . . . National Lutheran Council
NLC . . . . . . Negro Labor Committee
NLC . . . . . . New Location Code (Military)
NLC. . . . . . . New Orleans & Lower Coast R. R. (AAR code)
NLC . . . . . . Noctilucent Clouds
NLC. . . . . . . Noise-Level Cable
NLC . . . . . . Norden Laboratories Corporation
NLCP . . . . . . Navy Logistics Capabilities Plan
NLCS . . . . . . National Lutheran Commission (formerly, Committee) on Scouting
NLD. . . . . . . National Legion of Decency (Later, National Catholic Office for Motion Pictures)
NLD. . . . . . . Naval Lighter (Pontoon) Dock
NLD. . . . . . . Not in Line of Duty (as, of an injury) (Military)
NLDA . . . . . National Livestock Dealers Association
NLDA . . . . . National Luggage Dealers Association
NLDF . . . . . . Naval Local Defense Forces
NLE . . . . National Livestock Exchange
NLE . . . . Nonlinear Element
NLEA . . . . . . National Lumber Exporters Association
NLEC . . . . . . National Lutheran Educational Conference
NLEMA . . . . . National Lutheran Editors and Managers Association
NLF . . . . National Liberal Federation (British)
NLF . . . . National Liberation Front (Aden; Vietnam)
NLF . . . . Navigation Light Flasher
NLF . . . . Nearest Landing Field
NLFA . . . . . . National Lamb Feeders Association
NLFA . . . . . . National Livestock Feeders Association
NLFED . . . . . Naval Landing Force Equipment Depot
NLFT . . . . . . No-Load Frame Time
NLG . . . . . . National Lawyers Guild
NLG . . . . . . North Louisiana & Gulf R. R. (AAR code)
NLG . . . . . . Nose Landing Gear
NLG . . . . . . Null Line Gap
NLGI . . . . . . National Lubricating Grease Institute
NLI . . . . National Limestone Institute
NLI . . . . Neodymium LASER Illuminator
NLI . . . . Noise Limit Indicator
NLISA . . . . . National League of Insured Savings Associations
NLKF . . . . . . Nonlinear Kálmán Filter
NLL. . . . . . . National Lending Library for Science and Technology (England)

NLL . . . . . . National Liberal League (Later, National League for Separation of Church and State)
NLL. . . . . . . Negative Logic Level
NLL. . . . . . . New Life League
NLLST . . . . . National Lending Library for Science and Technology (British)
NLM . . . . . . National Language Mediator
NLM . . . . . . National Library of Medicine (of National Institutes of Health)
NLM . . . . . . Noise-Level Monitor (SONAR)
NLMA . . . . . National Lumber Manufacturers Association
NLMC . . . . . . National League of Masonic Clubs
NLMF . . . . . . National Labor-Management Foundation
NLMF. . . . . . Nucleus of Longitudinal Muscle Fiber
NLMFA. . . . . No-Load Mutual Fund Association
NLN . . . . . . National League for Nursing
NLNA . . . . . National Landscape Nurserymen's Association
NLO. . . . . . . Naval Liaison Officer
NLOGM. . . . . Navy Liaison Office for Guided Missiles
NLONTEVDET . . New London Test and Evaluation Detachment
NLP . . . . . . National League of Postmasters of the United States
NLP . . . . . . National Library of Peiping
NLP . . . . . . Neglected Language Program
NLPGA . . . . National LP-Gas Association
NLPTL . . . . . National Lutheran Parent-Teacher League
NLR. . . . . . . Noise Load Ratio
NLR. . . . . . . Nonlinear Resistive
NLR. . . . . . . North London Railway
NLRA . . . . . . National Labor Relations Act
NLRB . . . . . . National Labor Relations Board
NLRBU . . . . . National Labor Relations Board Union
NLRG. . . . . . Navy Long-Range Guidance
NLRSS . . . . . Navy Long-Range Strategic Study
NLS . . . . . . National Linen Service Corporation (NYSE symbol; later NAS)
NLS . . . . . . Navigating Light System
NLS . . . . . . Negative Lens Systems
NLS . . . . . . Neodymium LASER System
NLS . . . . . . No-Load Speed
NLS . . . . . . No-Load Start
NLS . . . . . . Nonlinear Smoothing
NLS . . . . . . Nonlinear Systems
NLS . . . . . . On-Line System (Data processing)
NLSA . . . . . . National Liquor Stores Association
NLSA . . . . . . National Locksmith Suppliers Association
NLSBA . . . . . National Lincoln Sheep Breeders' Association
NLSC . . . . . . Navy Lockheed Service Center
NLSC . . . . . . Northeastern Louisiana State College
NLSMA. . . . . National Longitudinal Study of Mathematical Abilities
NLSMB . . . . . National Live Stock and Meat Board
NLSP . . . . . . Neighborhood Legal Services Program
NLSPA . . . . . National Live Stock Producers Association
NLSS . . . . . . Navy Logistic Systems School
NLT . . . . Net Long Ton
NLT . . . . Night Letter (Telegraphic communications)
NLT . . . . Not Later Than
NLT . . . . . . Not Less Than
NLTA . . . . . . National League of Teachers' Associations
NLTC . . . . . . National Livestock Tax Committee
NLTE . . . . . . Non-Local Thermodynamic Equilibrium
NLTS . . . . . . Near Launch Tracking System
NLU . . . . . . National Labor Union (Philippines)
NLUS . . . . . . Navy League of the United States
NLV. . . . . . . National Vulcanized Fibre Company (NYSE symbol) (Delisted)
NLVP . . . . . . NASA Launch Vehicle Planning Project
NLW. . . . . . . National Library Week
NLW . . . . . . Nominal Line Width
nm . . . . Nanometer
NM . . . . National Match
NM . . . . Nautical Mile(s)
NM . . . . Naval Magazine
NM . . . . Netherlands Museum
NM . . . . Neuromuscular
NM . . . . New Mexico
NM . . . . New Moon (Moon phase)
NM . . . . Night Message
NM . . . . Nitrogen Mustards
NM . . . . No Mark
NM . . . . No Message
NM . . . . Nocte et Mane (Night and Morning)
NM . . . . Nonmetallic
NM . . . . Nonwhite Male
NM . . . . Not Measured
N/m. . . . . . . Newton per Meter

N/M . . . . Not Marked (Business and trade)
N & M . . . . . Night and Morning
N/m² . . . . . . Newton Per Square Meter
NMA . . . . . . National Management Association
NMA . . . . . . National Medical Association
NMA . . . . . . National Microfilm Association
NMA . . . . . . National Mustang Association
NMA . . . . . . Navy Mutual Aid Association
NMA . . . . . . Negligee Manufacturers Association
NMA . . . . . . Nonresonant Magnetic Amplifier
NMA . . . . . . Northwest Mining Association
NMAA . . . . . National Machine Accountants Association
NMAA . . . . . National Metal Awning Association
NMAA . . . . . Navy Mutual Aid Association
NMAB. . . . . . National Materials Advisory Board
NMAC . . . . . . National Medical Audiovisual Center (of the National Library of
              Medicine)
NMAC . . . . . Near Midair Collision
NMAF . . . . . National Medical Association Foundation
NMAG . . . . . Naval Magazine
NMAP . . . . . Navy Military Assistance Programs
NMAS. . . . . . NATO Military Authorities
NMATP. . . . . . Navy Military Assistance Training Program
NMB . . . . . . National Marine Board (British) (World War I)
NMB . . . . . . National Mediation Board
NMB . . . . . . National Motel Brokers (An organization)
NMB . . . . . . National Mutual Benefit
NMB . . . . . . Naval Minecraft Base
NMB . . . . . . Naval Model Basin
NMB . . . . . . No Military Branch
NMB . . . . . . Noise, Measurement Buoy
NMB . . . . . . Not Member of a Branch
NMBF. . . . . . National Manufacturers of Beverage Flavors
NMC . . . . . . Marine Corps Publications (Later, NAVMC)
NMC . . . . . . National Manpower Council
NMC . . . . . . National Meteorological Center (National Weather Service)
NMC . . . . . . National Music Camp (Interlochen, Michigan)
NMC . . . . . . National Music Council
NMC . . . . . . Naval Material Command (Also, NMCOM; formerly, NMSE)
NMC . . . . . . Naval Medical Center
NMC . . . . . . Naval Missile Center
NMC . . . . . . Navigation Map Computer
NMC . . . . . . Navy Mail Clerk
NMC . . . . . . Navy Memorandum Correction
NMC . . . . . . Northern Michigan College
NMC . . . . . . Northern Montana College
NMC . . . . . . Northwest Michigan College
NMC . . . . . . Nuclear Measurements Corporation
NMC . . . . . . Nuclear Metal Conference
N & MC . . . . . Navy and Marine Corps (Medal)
NMCA . . . . . . National Meat Canners Association
NMCA . . . . . . Navy Mothers' Clubs of America
NMCB . . . . . . National Metric Conversion Board (Proposed)
NMCB . . . . . . National Munitions Control Board (World War II)
NMCB. . . . . . National Museum of Canada Bulletin
NMCC . . . . . National Military Command Center (DOD)
NMCDA . . . . . National Model Cities Directors Association
NMCJS. . . . . . Naval Member, Canadian Joint Staff
NMCLK . . . . . Navy Mail Clerk
NMCM . . . . . . Navy and Marine Corps Medal
N & MCM . . . . Navy and Marine Corps Medal
NMCOM. . . . . Naval Material Command (Also, NMC; formerly, NMSE)
NMCS . . . . . . National Military Command System
NMCSA . . . . . Navy Material Command Support Activity
NMCSS . . . . . National Military Command System Standards
NMCSSC . . . . National Military Command System Support Center
NMD . . . . . . Naval Mine Depot
NMDA . . . . . National Medical and Dental Association
NMDA . . . . . National Metal Decorators Association
NMDA . . . . . . Nonresonant Magnetic Deflection Amplifier
NMDCEF. . . . . National Medico-Dental Conference for the Evaluation of Fluoridation
NMDL . . . . . . Navy Management Data List
NMDL . . . . . . Navy Mine Defense Laboratory (NFEC)
NMDR . . . . . Nuclear Magnetic Double Resonance
NMDS . . . . . . Naval Mine Disposal School
NMDU . . . . . Newspaper & Mail Deliverers Union of New York and Vicinity
NMDY . . . . . Nonresonant Magnetic Deflection Yoke
NME . . . . . . National Military Establishment (Designated Department of Defense, 1949)
NME. . . . . . . Noise-Measuring Equipment
NME . . . . . . Nonsupervisory Manufacturing Engineer
NMEBA . . . . . National Marine Engineers' Beneficial Association

NMEF. . . . . . Naval Mine Engineering Facility
NMES . . . . . . Naval Marine Engineering Station
NMEX . . . . . . New Mexico
NMF . . . . . . National Medical Fellowships
NMF . . . . . . Naval Missile Facility
NMF . . . . . . Nonuniform Magnetic Field
NMFC . . . . . National Motor Freight Classification
NMFEC . . . . . National Medical Foundation for Eye Care
NMFHG . . . . National Master Farm Homemakers Guild
NMFMA . . . . National Mutual Fund Managers Association
NMFPA . . . . . Naval Missile Facility, Point Arguello
NMFRL . . . . . Naval Medical Field Research Laboratory
NMFS. . . . . . National Marine Fisheries Service (National Oceanic and Atmospheric
              Administration) (Formerly, Bureau of Commercial Fisheries)
NMFTA . . . . . National Motor Freight Traffic Association
NMG . . . . . . Navy Military Government
NMG . . . . . . Numerical Master Geometry (System)
NMGA . . . . . National Military Guidance Association
NMH . . . . . . Nautical Miles per Hour
NMHU . . . . . New Mexico Highlands University
NMI . . . . . . National Macaroni Institute
NMI. . . . . . . Nautical Mile(s)
NMI. . . . . . . No Middle Initial
NMI. . . . . . . Nuclear Metals, Incorporated
NMIA . . . . . . N-Methyl Indoxyl Acetate
NMIC . . . . . . National Meat Industry Council
NMIC. . . . . . National Missile Industry Conference
NMIL . . . . . . New Materiel Introductory Letter (Army)
NMIMT. . . . . . New Mexico Institute of Mining and Technology
NMIS . . . . . . Naval Manpower Information System
NMIT . . . . . . New Materiel Introductory Team (Army)
NMJC . . . . . . Northeastern Mississippi Junior College
NMJC . . . . . . Northwest Mississippi Junior College
NMJL. . . . . . National Mah Jongg League
NMK . . . . . . Niagara Mohawk Power Corporation (NYSE symbol)
NML . . . . . . National Castings Company (NYSE symbol) (Delisted)
NML . . . . . . National Magnet Laboratory
NML . . . . . . National Municipal League
NML . . . . . . National Music League
NML . . . . . . Nautical Mile(s)
NML . . . . . . Northwestern Mutual Life Mortgage (NYSE symbol)
NMLRA . . . . . National Muzzle Loading Rifle Association
NMM . . . . . . Neutron Magnetic Moment
NMM . . . . . . Nuclear Materials Management (AEC)
NMMA . . . . . National Macaroni Manufacturers Association
NMMFO . . . . Navy Maintenance Management Field Office
NMMI . . . . . New Mexico Military Institute
NMMM. . . . . Navy Maintenance and Material Management System (Also known as
              NMMMS, MMM, and 3M)
NMMMS . . . . Navy Maintenance and Material Management System (Also known as
              MMM, NMMM, and 3M)
NMN . . . . . . Nicotinamide Mononucleotide
NMN . . . . . . No Middle Name
NMN . . . . . . Normetanephrine (Chemical)
NMND . . . . . Naval Magazine and Net Depot
NMNH . . . . . National Museum of Natural History (Washington, DC)
NMNRU . . . . . Naval Medical Neuropsychiatric Research Unit
NMO . . . . . . Navy Management Office
NMO . . . . . . Normal Mode Operation
NMONA . . . . National Mail Order Nurserymen's Association
NMOP . . . . . National Mission Operating Procedures
NMOSAW . . . . Naval and Military Order of the Spanish-American War
NMP. . . . . . . N-Methylpyrrolidone
NMP . . . . . . National Maintenance Point
NMP . . . . . . Naval Management Program
NMP . . . . . . Navigational Microfilm Projector
NMP . . . . . . Net Material Product (Economics)
NMP. . . . . . . Not Machine Pressed
NMPA . . . . . National Music Publishers Association
NMPATA . . . . National Music Printers and Allied Trades Association
NMPB . . . . . National Millinery Planning Board
NMPC . . . . . National Maintenance Publications Center (Army)
NMPC . . . . . Niagara Mohawk Power Company
NMPF. . . . . . National Milk Producers Federation
NMPF. . . . . . Normal Magnitude Probability Function
NMPG . . . . . New Mexico Proving Ground
NMPO . . . . . Navy Motion Picture Office
NMPP. . . . . . Nouvelles Messageries de la Presse Parisienne (Press distribution agency)
NMPS. . . . . . Nautical Miles Per Second
NMPX . . . . . Navy Motion Picture Exchange
NMR . . . . . . National Military Representatives with SHAPE (NATO)

NMR . . . . National Museum of Racing
NMR . . . . Nautical Mile Radius Of
NMR . . . . Normal Mode Rejection
NMR . . . . Nuclear Magnetic Relaxation
NMR . . . . Nuclear Magnetic Resonance (Spectrum)
NMRA . . . . . . National Marine Representatives Association
NMRA . . . . . . National Mine Rescue Association
NMRA . . . . . . National Model Railroad Association
NMRC . . . . . . Navy Material Redistribution Center
NMR & DA . . . . Navy Material Redistribution and Disposition Administration
NMR & DO . . . Naval Material Redistribution and Disposal Office(r)
NMRG . . . . . . Navy Mid-Range Guidance
NMRI . . . . Naval Medical Research Institute
NMRL . . . . . . Naval Medical Research Laboratory
NMRN . . . . . . National Meteorological Rocket Network
NMRO . . . . . . Navy Mid-Range Objectives
NMRP . . . . Nuclear Magnetic Resonance Program
NMRS . . . . . . National Mobile Radio System
NMRT . . . . Nimbus Meteorological Radiation Tape (NASA)
NMRTC . . . . . . Navy and Marine Corps Reserve Training Center
NMRU . . . . . . Naval Medical Research Unit
NMS . . . . Ancient Egyptian Arabic Order Nobles of the Mystic Shrine
NMS . . . . National Measurement System (National Bureau of Standards)
NMS . . . . Naval Medical School
NMS . . . . Naval Meteorological Service
NMS . . . . Navy Mid-Range Study
NMS . . . . Nitrogen Measuring System
NMS . . . . Normal Mouse Serum
NMS . . . . Nuclear Materials Safeguards (AEC)
NM & S . . . . . Bureau of Medicine and Surgery Publications (Navy)
NMSA . . . . . . National Metal Spinners Association
NMSB . . . . Navy Manpower Survey Board
NMSC . . . . . . National Maple Syrup Council
NMSC . . . . . . National Merit Scholarship Corporation
NMSC . . . . . . Northwest Missouri State College
NMSD . . . . Naval Medical Supply Depot
NMSE . . . . Naval Material Support Establishment (After 1966, NMCOM or NMC)
NMSHC . . . . . Bureau of Medicine and Surgery Hospital Corps Publication (Later, NAVMED) (Navy)
NMSM . . . . . . New Mexico School of Mines
NMSO . . . . . . NATO Maintenance and Support Operation
NMSO . . . . . . Nuclear Missile Safety Office(r)
NMSQT . . . . . National Merit Scholarship Qualifying Test
NMSS . . . . National Multiple Sclerosis Society
NMSS . . . . National Multipurpose Space Station
NMSSA . . . . . . NATO Maintenance Supply Service Agency (Later, NAMSO)
NMSSS . . . . . . NATO Maintenance Supply Service System
NMST . . . . . . New Materials System Test
NMSU . . . . . . New Mexico State University
NMT . . . . National Museum of Transport
NMT . . . . Not More Than
NMT . . . . Number of Module Types
NMTA . . . . . . National Manpower Training Association
NMTA . . . . . . National Metal Trades Association
NMTBA . . . . . National Machine Tool Builders' Association
NMTC . . . . . . Naval Mine Testing Center
NMTC . . . . . . Naval Missile Testing Center
NMTC . . . . . . Nucleon-Meson Transport Code
NMTF . . . . Naval Mine Test Facility
NMTO . . . . . . Navy Material Transportation Office
NMTS . . . . National Milk Testing Service
NMTS . . . . . . Noise Measurement Test Set
NMU . . . . National Maritime Union of America
NMU . . . . Northern Michigan University
NMUC . . . . . . National Medical Utilization Committee (HEW)
NMVP . . . . Navy Manpower Validation Program
NMVSAC . . . . National Motor Vehicle Safety Advisory Council
NMVTA . . . . . National Motor Vehicle Theft Act
NMWA . . . . . . National Mineral Wool Association
NMWC . . . . . . New Mexico Western College
NMWIA . . . . . National Mineral Wool Insulation Association
NMWS . . . . . . Naval Mine Warfare School
NMWTS . . . . . Naval Mine Warfare Test Station
NMWTS . . . . . Naval Mine Warfare Training School
NMWU . . . . . . National Mining Workers' Union of Malaya
NMY . . . . Nonresonant Magnetic Yoke
NN . . . . Names
NN . . . . National Neighbors (An organization)
NN . . . . Necessary Nuisance (i.e., a husband) (Slang)
NN . . . . Nevada Northern Railway Company (AAR code)
NN . . . . Noon

NN . . . . Normalnull (Mean sea level) (Germany)
NN . . . . Not Nested (Freight)
NN . . . . Notes (Finance)
NN . . . . Nouns
NN . . . . Nucleon-Nucleon
N/N . . . . Not To Be Noted (Business and trade)
NNA . . . . National Neckwear Association
NNA . . . . National Newman Apostolate
NNA . . . . National Notary Association
NNA . . . . National Notion Association
NNAA . . . . . . National Newman Alumni Association
NNAC . . . . . . National Noise Abatement Council
NNAFS . . . . . National Newman Association of Faculty and Staff
NNAV . . . . . . Bureau of Navigation Publications (Later, BPN; then, NAVPERS) (Navy)
N/NAVEXOS . . Navy/Executive Offices
NNB . . . . National Needlecraft Bureau
NNBL . . . . . . National Negro Business League
NNC . . . . National Nudist Council
NNC . . . . Navy Nurse Corps
NNC . . . . Northern Navigation Company, Limited (AAR code)
NNC . . . . Northwest Nazarene College (Idaho)
NNC . . . . Nudist National Committee
NNCA . . . . . . National Newman Chaplains Association
NNCAA . . . . . National Negro County Agents Association
NNCF . . . . . . National Newman Club Federation
NNCSDC . . . . National Neutron Cross Section Data Center
NND . . . . Naval Net Depot
NND . . . . New and Nonofficial Drugs (Pharmacy)
NND . . . . Newport News Shipbuilding & Dry Dock Company (NYSE symbol) (Delisted)
NNE . . . . Nonstandard Negro English
NNE . . . . North-Northeast
NNEA . . . . . . National Negro Evangelical Association
NNEB . . . . . . National Nursery Examination Board
NNEC . . . . . . National Nuclear Energy Commission (Brazil)
NNES . . . . . . National Nuclear Energy Series (of AEC-sponsored books)
NNF . . . . National Nephrosis Foundation
NNF . . . . National Newman Foundation
NNF . . . . Northern Nurses Federation
NNFF . . . . . . Not Nested or Folded Flat (Freight)
NNFP . . . . . . Nuclear Nitrogen Fixation Plant
NNG . . . . Northern Natural Gas Company (NYSE symbol)
NNGA . . . . . . Northern Nut Growers Association
NNI . . . . Noise and Number Index
NNI . . . . Office of Naval Intelligence Publications
NNM . . . . No Neutral Mode
NNMC . . . . . . National Naval Medical Center (Bethesda, Maryland)
NNMSG . . . . . Non-Nuclear Munitions Safety Group (Air Force)
NNN . . . . No No Nanette (Broadway musical)
NNO . . . . Nord-Nord-Ouest (North-North-West) (French)
NNP . . . . Needle Nosed Probe
NNP . . . . Negative Node Point
NNP . . . . Net National Product (Economics)
NNPA . . . . . . National Negro Press Association
NNPA . . . . . . National Newspaper Promotion Association
NNPA . . . . . . National Newspaper Publishers Association
NNR . . . . New and Non-official Remedies (Publication)
NNRA . . . . . . National Negro Republican Assembly
NNRC . . . . . . National Nuclear Research Centre (South Africa)
NNRDC . . . . . National Nuclear Rocket Development Center (Also known as NRDS)
NNRDF . . . . . National Nuclear Rocket Development Facility
NNRF . . . . . . National Neurological Research Foundation
NNS . . . . National Natality Survey
NNS . . . . Neural Network Simulator
NNSB & DDCO . . Newport News Shipbuilding and Dry Dock Company
NNSC . . . . . . Neutral Nations Supervisory Commission
NNSS . . . . . . Navy Navigational Satellite System
NNSY . . . . . . Norfolk Naval Shipyard
NNTP . . . . . . National Nuclear Test Plan (Later, NNTRP)
NNTRP . . . . . National Nuclear Test Readiness Program (Formerly, NNTP)
NNW . . . . North-Northwest
NNWH . . . . . . Non-Normal Working Hours
NNX . . . . Northern Central Railway Company (NYSE symbol)
NNYD . . . . . . Norfolk Navy Yard (Virginia)
NO . . . . Natural Order (Botany)
NO . . . . Naval Observatory
NO . . . . Naval Officer
NO . . . . Navigation Officer
NO . . . . New Orleans (Louisiana)
No . . . . Nobelium (Chemical element)
NO . . . . Nonofficial
NO . . . . Non-Original

NO . . . . Normally Open (Switch)
NO . . . . North Central Airlines, Inc.
NO . . . . Norway (NATO)
NO . . . . Not Operational
NO . . . . Not Out
NO . . . . Nuestra Orden (Our Order) (Business and trade) (Spain)
NO . . . . Number
N/O . . . . (In the) Name Of (Business and trade)
N/O . . . . No Orders (Business and trade)
N/O . . . . Not Otherwise
NOA . . . . . . National Oceanographic Association
NOA . . . . . . National Onion Association
NOA . . . . . . National Opera Association
NOA . . . . . . National Optical Association
NOA . . . . . . National Orchestral Association
NOA . . . . . . Nature of Action (Military)
NOA . . . . . . New Obligational Authority
NOA . . . . . . Not Otherwise Authorized
NOAA . . . . . National Oceanic and Atmospheric Administration (Pronounced "Noah")
NOAB . . . . . National Outdoor Advertising Bureau
NOAC . . . . . . No Action Necessary
NOACT . . . . . Naval Overseas Air Cargo Terminal
NOALA . . . . . Noise-Operated Automatic Level Adjustment
NOAP. . . . . . Navy Oil Analysis Program
NOART . . . . . New Orleans Army Terminal
NOB . . . . . . Naval Operating Base
NOB . . . . . . Northwest Bancorporation (NYSE symbol)
NOB . . . . . . Nuclear Order of Battle
NOB . . . . . . Number of Bursts
NOBC . . . . . National Office for Black Catholics
NOBC . . . . . National Organization of Bar Counsel
NOBC. . . . . . Naval Officer Billet Classifications (or Code)
NOBDUCHAR . . Naval Operating Base, Dutch Harbor, Aleutians
NOBFRAN. . . . Naval Operating Base, San Francisco, California
NOBNEWT . . . Naval Operating Base, Newport, Rhode Island
NOBS. . . . . . Naval Observatory
NOBSOLO . . Naval Operating Base, Coco Solo, Canal Zone
NOBSY . . . . . Naval Observatory
NOBTRIN . . . . Naval Operating Base, Trinidad
NOC . . . . . . Northrop Corporation (NYSE symbol)
NOC . . . . . . Notation of Content (Aerospace)
NOC . . . . . . Notice of Contents (Indexing)
NOC . . . . . . Nuttall Ornithological Club
NOCA . . . . . North Cascades National Park
NOCC . . . . . Navigation Operational Checkout Console
NOCHA . . . . . National Off-Campus Housing Association
NOCM . . . . . Nuclear Ordnance Commodity Manager
NOCO . . . . . Noise Correlation
NOCONIT. . . . No Continuing Interest
NOCT . . . . . Navy Overseas Cargo Terminals
NOD . . . . . . Naval Ordnance Department (British)
NOD . . . . . . Night Observation Device
NOD . . . . . . Noise Output Device
NODAC . . . . . Naval Ordnance Data Automation Center
NODC . . . . . National Oceanographic Data Center (NOAA)
NODC . . . . . Naval Operating Development Center
NODEL . . . . . Not to Delay
NODESTA . . . . Will Not Depart This Station (Army)
NODEX . . . . . New Over the Beach Discharge Exercise
NODI . . . . . Notice of Delayed Items
NODI. . . . . . Notice of Delinquent Item
NODIS . . . . . No Distribution (Military security classification)
NODL . . . . . National Office for Decent Literature
NODM . . . . . . Ferrocarril Nor-Oeste de Mexico (Mexico North Western R. R.) (AAR code)
NOE . . . . . . Not Otherwise Enumerated
NOE . . . . . . Notice of Exception
NOELS . . . . . New Office Education Learning Systems
NOEU . . . . . Naval Ordnance Experimental Unit
NOF . . . . . . National Optical Font (Typography)
NOF . . . . . . National Osteopathic Foundation
NOF . . . . . . Naval Operating Facility
NOF. . . . . . . Network Operations and Facilities
NOF. . . . . . . NOTAM (Notice to Airmen) Office
NOFA . . . . . National Office Furniture Association
NOFI . . . . . . National Oil Fuel Institute
NOFIN. . . . . . No Further Information
NOFMA . . . . . National Oak Flooring Manufacturers Association
NOFORN . . . . No Distribution to Foreign Countries (Pentagon security classification code)
NOFORN . . . . Not Releasable to Foreign Nationals
NOFT. . . . . . Naval Overseas Freight Terminal

NOFT . . . . . Notification of Foreign Travel
NOG . . . . . . Nuclear Ordnance Group (Air Force)
NOGA . . . . . National Osteopathic Guild Association
NOGAD . . . . . Noise-Operated Gain-Adjusting Device
NOGL . . . . . Naval Ordnance Gage Laboratory
NoHo . . . . . . North of Houston Street (Artists' colony) (New York City) (Also see SoHo)
NOHOL . . . . . Not Holding (a given course or altitude) (Aviation)
NOHP . . . . . Not Otherwise Herein Provided
NOHSN . . . . National Organization of Hospital Schools of Nursing
NOI. . . . . . . Non-Operational Intelligence
NOI. . . . . . . Not Otherwise Identified
NOI. . . . . . . Not Otherwise Indexed
NOIBN. . . . . Not Otherwise Indexed by Name (Tariffs)
NOIBN. . . . . Not Otherwise Indicated (or Identified) by Name (Military)
NOIC. . . . . . National Oceanographic Instrumentation Center (National Oceanic and Atmospheric Administration)
NOIC. . . . . . National Osteopathic Interfraternity Council
NOIC. . . . . . Naval Officer-in-Charge
NOIFN. . . . . No Information Available
NOIO . . . . . Naval Ordnance Inspecting Officer
NOISE . . . . . National Organization to Insure a Sound-Controlled Environment
NOISE . . . . . Noise Information Service
NOJC. . . . . . National Oil Jobbers Council
NOJC . . . . . New Orleans Jazz Club
NOJC . . . . . Northern Oklahoma Junior College
NOK . . . . . . Nationales Olympisches Komitee
NOK . . . . . . Next of Kin (Military)
NOK . . . . . . Nordostschweizerische Kraftwerke AG (Switzerland)
NOL . . . . . . National Old Lacers
NOL . . . . . . Naval Ordnance Laboratory (NFEC)
NOL . . . . . . Normal Operational Loss (AEC)
NOLC . . . . . Naval Ordnance Laboratory Corona
NOL-MDI . . . . Naval Ordnance Laboratory Miss Distance Indicator
NOLO . . . . . No Live Operator
NOLPE . . . . . National Organization of Legal Problems of Education
NOM . . . . . . Natomas Company (NYSE symbol)
NOM . . . . . . Newspapers on Microfilm
NOM . . . . . . Nomenclature
NOM . . . . . . Nominal
NOM . . . . . . Nominate
NOMA . . . . . National Office Management Association
NOMA . . . . . National Oil Marketers Association
NOMAD . . . . Navy Oceanographic Meteorological Automatic Device (Navy)
NOMDA . . . . National Office Machine Dealers Association
NOMEN . . . . . Nomenclature
NOMIS . . . . . Naval Ordnance Management Information System
NOMMA . . . . National Ornamental Metal Manufacturers Association
NOMOTC . . . . National Organization of Mothers of Twins Clubs
NOMSS. . . . . National Operational Meteorological Satellite System
NOMTF . . . . . Naval Ordnance Missile Test Facility
NON . . . . . . National Organization for Non-Parents
NONA . . . . . Notice of Nonavailability
NONADD . . . Nonadditivity (Statistics)
NONCOM . . . Noncommissioned Officer (Military)
NONCOMECM . . Noncommunications Electronics Countermeasures (Military)
NONCOMJAM . . Noncommunications Jamming (Military)
NONE . . . . . New Orleans & Northeastern R. R. (AAR code)
NONEG . . . . Negative Replies Neither Required nor Desired
N/ONI. . . . . Navy/Office of Naval Intelligence
N/ONR . . . . . Navy/Office of Naval Research
NONTSDSL . . . Not Included in Technical Service Demand Stockage Lists (Army)
NOO . . . . . . Naval Oceanographic Office (Formerly, NHO or HO)
NOO . . . . . . Notice of Obligation (Military)
NOOD . . . . . Nitric Oxide Optical Detector
NOOS . . . . . Nuclear Orbit-to-Orbit Shuttle (NASA)
NOP . . . . . . National Oceanographic Program
NOP . . . . . . National Opinion Poll
NOP . . . . . . Naval Officer Procurement
NOP . . . . . . Naval Ordnance Plant
NOP . . . . . . Navy Objectives Plan
NOP . . . . . . Noncoherent Optical Processor
NOP. . . . . . . Nopco Chemical Co. (Formerly, National Oil Products Co.) (NYSE symbol) (Delisted)
NOP . . . . . . Not Otherwise Provided
NOP . . . . . . Not Our Publication
NOP. . . . . . . Notice of Procurement (Navy)
NOPB. . . . . . New Orleans Public Belt R. R. (AAR code)
NOPCL. . . . . Naval Officer Personnel Circular Letter
NOPCO . . . . . National Oil Products Company (See NOP)
NOPE. . . . . . New Orleans Port of Embarkation

NOPI . . . . . . Naval Ordnance Plant Institute
NOPL . . . . . . Naval Ordnance Plant, Louisville
NOPOL . . . . . No Pollution
NOPS . . . . . . Nike Operator Proficiency Scale (Army)
NOPS . . . . . . Noncoherent Optical Processing System
NOPT . . . . . . No Procedure Turn Required (Aviation)
NOQUIS . . . . . Nucleonic Oil Quantity Indication System (Air Force)
NOR . . . . . . National Organization for Rehabilitation (Ireland)
nor . . . . Nitrogen ohne Radikal (Chemical prefix)
NOR . . . . Nitrogen Oxide Reduction (Research in automotive air pollution)
NOR . . . . North Central Airlines, Inc.
NOR . . . . Norwich Pharmacal Company (NYSE symbol) (Delisted)
NOR . . . . . . Not Operationally Ready
NOR . . . . . . Notice of Readiness (Shipping)
NORAC . . . . . No Radio Contact (Aviation)
NORAD . . . . . North American Air Defense (Integrated United States-Canada command)
NORADCOC . . NORAD Combat Operations Center
NORAP . . . . . Northwestern Alumni Players
NORBS . . . . . Northern Base Section (Corsica)
NORC . . . . . . National Oceanographic Records Center
NORC . . . . . . National Opinion Research Center (University of Chicago)
NORC . . . . . . Naval Ordnance Research Calculator (or Computer) (Naval Ordnance Proving Ground)
NORCALSEC . . Northern California Section, Western Sea Frontier
NORD . . . . . Bureau of Ordnance Publication (Later, NAVORD) (Navy)
NORD . . . . . Naval Ordnance
NORDEK . . . . Norway-Denmark (and Finland) (Trade bloc)
NORDITA . . . . Nordic Institute for Theoretic Atomic Physics
NORDO . . . . . No Radio
NOREC . . . . . No Record
NOREP . . . . . . No Reply Received
NORI . . . . . . National Office for the Rights of the Indigent
NORM . . . . . . Normal(ize)
NORM . . . . . . Normetal R. R. (AAR code)
NORM . . . . . . Not Operationally Ready Maintenance
NORML . . . . . National Organization for the Reform of Marijuana Laws
NORMSHOR . . Normal Tour of Shore Duty
NORO . . . . . . Not Operationally Ready - Other
NORPAC . . . . North Pacific Area; North Pacific Force
NORPAC . . . . . Northern Pacific Railroad
NORR . . . . . . No Reply Received
NORRA . . . . . National Off Road Racing Association
NORRS . . . . . Naval Operational Readiness Reporting Systems
NORS . . . . . . Not Operationally Ready - Supply
NORSAIR . . . . Not Operationally Ready Supply Aeronautical Items Report (Navy)
NORSAR . . . . . Norwegian Seismic Array
NORSG . . . . . Not Operationally Ready Supply Grounding
NORSN . . . . . Not Operationally Ready Supply Non-Grounding
NORSOLS . . . . Northern Solomons Area
NORTH . . . . . . Northern Operations of Rail Transportation and Highways (Alaska)
NORTHAG . . . . North European Army Group (NATO)
NORVA . . . . . Norfolk, Virginia (Navy)
NORVAGRP . . Norfolk, Virginia Group (Navy)
NORWESSEAFRON . . Northwestern Sea Frontier
NORWESSEC . . Northwestern Sector, Western Sea Frontier
NOS . . . . National Ocean Survey (Formerly, Coast and Geodetic Survey) (National Oceanic and Atmospheric Administration)
NOS . . . . National Operational Satellite
NOS . . . . Naval Ordnance Station
NOS . . . . Night Observation Sight (Air Force)
NOS . . . . Nimbus Operational System
NOS . . . . Non-Oriented Satellite
NOS . . . . Norges Offisielle Statistikk (Norway)
NOS . . . . Not Otherwise Specified
NOS . . . . Not Otherwise Stated
NOS . . . . Numbers
NOSA . . . . . . National Outerwear and Sportswear Association
NOSC . . . . . . Naval Ordnance Systems Command
NOSE . . . . . . National Odd Shoe Exchange
NOSE . . . . . . Neighbors Opposing Smelly Emissions (Student legal action organization)
NOSEC . . . . . . Information which does not affect national security
NOSI . . . . Now Simultaneous
NOSLA . . . . . . National Oil Scouts and Landmen's Association
NOSM . . . . . . Navy Occupation Service Medal
NOSMO . . . . . Norden Optics Setting, Mechanized Operation (Air Force bombsight)
NOSS . . . . . . National Orbiting Space Station
NOSS . . . . . . Nimbus Operational Satellite System (GSFC/USWB)
NOSSOLANT . . Naval Ordnance Systems Support Office, Atlantic
NOSSOPAC . . Naval Ordnance Systems Support Office, Pacific
NOST . . . . . . Knights of the Square Table
NOST . . . . . . Nuclear Operational Systems Test

NOSTA . . . . . National Ocean Science and Technology Agency
NOSUM . . . . . Notice to Airmen Summary
NOT . . . . New Orleans Terminal R. R. (AAR code)
NOTAD . . . . . Notice to Airmen Address
NOTAL . . . . . Not at All
NOTAL . . . . . Not to, nor Needed by, All
NOTAM . . . . . Notice to Airmen (Air Force)
NOTAS . . . . . Notice to Airmen Summary
NOTB . . . . . . National Ophthalmic Treatment Board
NOTC . . . . . . National Ordnance Traffic Committee
NOTC . . . . . . National Over the Counter Clearance Corporation
NOTIFY . . . . . Needed Occupational Television Instruction for Youth (Project)
NOTIP . . . . . Night Observation Television in a Pod
NOTIP . . . . . Northern Tier Integration Project
NOTM . . . . . New Orleans, Texas & Mexico Railway Company (AAR code)
NOTO . . . . . . Numbering Tool
NOTOF . . . . . Notice to Airmen Office
NOTP . . . . . . New Orleans Times Picayune (A newspaper)
NOTR . . . . . . National Order of Trench Rats
NOTS . . . . . . Naval Ordnance Test Station
NOTU . . . . . . Naval Operational Training Unit
NOTUN . . . . . Notice of Unreliability
NOU . . . . Naval Ordnance Unit
NOUS . . . . . . Naval Order of the United States
NOV . . . . November
NOVEL . . . . . Narrative Output Vocabulary Editing Language (Psychiatric test)
NOVS . . . . . . National Office of Vital Statistics
NOW . . . . National Organization for Women
NOW . . . . Neighbors of Woodcraft
NOWWN . . . . National Organization of World War Nurses
NOX . . . . Nitrogen-Oxygen
NOXZEMA . . . Knocks Eczema (Acronym, brand name for skin cream, said to be taken from this phrase)
NOY . . . . Not Out Yet
NOZ . . . . New Process Company (American Stock Exchange symbol)
NOZ . . . . Nozzle
NP . . . . National Pipe
NP . . . . National Publishing Company (Philadelphia)
NP . . . . Naval Prison
NP . . . . Near Point
NP . . . . Needle Position (on dial)
Np . . . . Neper
Np . . . . Neptunium (Chemical element)
NP . . . . Net Proceeds
NP . . . . Neuropsychiatric or Neuropsychiatry
NP . . . . New Paragraph
NP . . . . New Permutations
NP . . . . New Providence
NP . . . . Newport (Rhode Island)
NP . . . . Nickel Plated (Guns)
NP . . . . Nisi Prius (Unless Before) (Law)
NP . . . . No Paging
NP . . . . No Place of Publication (Bibliography)
NP . . . . No Protest (Banking)
NP . . . . Nonparticipating (Insurance or finance)
NP . . . . Nonpropelled
NP . . . . Normal Pressure
NP . . . . Northern Pacific Railway Company (NYSE symbol) (Wall Street slang name: "Nipper") (Delisted)
NP . . . . Notary Public
NP . . . . Noun Phrase (Grammar)
NP . . . . Nucleophasmic (Index) (Cytology)
NP . . . . Nucleoprotein (Biochemistry)
NP . . . . Nursing Procedure
N/P . . . . Notes Payable
NPA . . . . Committee for a National Peace Academy
NPA . . . . National Paddleball Association
NPA . . . . National Paperboard Association
NPA . . . . National Parking Association
NPA . . . . National Parks Association
NPA . . . . National Particleboard Association
NPA . . . . National Patrolmen's Association
NPA . . . . National Personnel Associates
NPA . . . . National Pet Association
NPA . . . . National Petroleum Association
NPA . . . . National Pharmaceutical Association
NPA . . . . National Pigeon Association
NPA . . . . National Pilots Association
NPA . . . . National Pituitary Agency
NPA . . . . National Planning Association
NPA . . . . National Preservers Association

NPA . . . . National Proctologic Association
NPA . . . . National Production Authority (Functions merged into BDSA, 1953)
NPA . . . . National Prohibition Act
NPA . . . . National Psychological Association
NPA . . . . Naval Procurement Account
NPA . . . . Navy Postal Affairs Section Publication
NPA . . . . New People's Army (Communist guerrilla force) (Philippines)
NPA . . . . Nigerian Ports Authority Clerical Workers' Union
NPA . . . . Normal Pressure Angle
NPA . . . . Numbering Plan Area (Bell System)
NPAB . . . . . . Navy Price Adjustment Board
NPAC . . . . . . National Peace Action Coalition
NPAC . . . . . . National Program for Acquisitions and Cataloging (Library of Congress)
NPAC . . . . . . Navy Procurement Assignment Committee
NPACI . . . . . . National Production Advisory Council on Industry (British)
NPACOE . . . . National Panhellenic Association of Central Office Executives
NPACT . . . . . . National Public Affairs Center for Television
NPANX . . . . . Naval Potomac Annex
NPAP . . . . . . National Psychological Association for Psychoanalysis
NPB . . . . National Plant Board
NPB . . . . Non-Primate Biosatellite
NPB . . . . Norfolk & Portsmouth Belt Line R. R. (AAR code)
NPBA . . . . . . National Palomino Breeders Association
NPBE . . . . . . National Political Button Exchange (An organization)
NPBEA . . . . . National Poultry, Butter & Egg Association
NPBI . . . . National Pretzel Bakers Institute
NPBMA . . . . . National Paper Box Manufacturers Association
NPBSA . . . . . National Paper Box Supplies Association
NPC . . . . NASA Procurement Circular
NPC . . . . National Panhellenic Conference
NPC . . . . National Patent Council
NPC . . . . National Peach Council
NPC . . . . National Peanut Council
NPC . . . . National People's Congress (Nigerian political party)
NPC . . . . National Personnel Consultants
NPC . . . . National Petrochemical Company (Iran)
NPC . . . . National Petroleum Council
NPC . . . . National Pharmaceutical Council
NPC . . . . National Potato Council
NPC . . . . National Press Club
NPC . . . . National Productivity Council (India)
NPC . . . . National Public Relations Council of Health and Welfare Services
NPC . . . . National Publicity Council for Health and Welfare Services
NPC . . . . NATO Parliamentarians' Conference
NPC . . . . NATO Pipeline Committee
NPC . . . . Naval Photographic Center
NPC . . . . Near Point of Convergence
NPC . . . . Needle Punch Card
NPC . . . . Neuropsychiatry Clerical Procedure (Navy)
NPC . . . . Neuropsychiatry Clerical Technician (Navy)
NPC . . . . Ninety Pound Charge
NPC . . . . Non-Printing Character
NPC . . . . Northern Peoples Congress
NPCA . . . . . . National Pest Control Association
NP & CA . . . . National Parks & Conservation Association
NPCF . . . . . . National Pollution Control Foundation
NPCI . . . . National Potato Chip Institute
NP-CLT . . . . . Neuropsychiatry Clerical Procedure Technician (Navy)
NPCP . . . . . . Nairobi Peoples' Convention Party
NPD . . . . NASA Policy Directive
NPD . . . . Navy Procurement Directives
NPD . . . . Neimann-Pick's Disease
NPD . . . . Nominal Percent Defective
NPD . . . . North Polar Distance
NPD . . . . Nuclear Power Demonstration (Reactor) (Canada)
NP or D . . . . No Place or Date
NPDA . . . . . . National Plywood Distributors Association
NPDAA . . . . . National Pharmaceutical Direct Advertising Association
NPDC . . . . . . National Patent Development Corporation
NPDC . . . . . . National Poetry Day Committee
NPDE . . . . . . Nonlinear Partial Differential Equation
NPDEA . . . . . National Professional Driver Education Association
NPDF . . . . . . Normal Probability Distribution Function
NPDI . . . . Non-Performance of Duty because Imprisoned (Navy)
NPE . . . . National Plastic Exposition
NPE . . . . Navy Preliminary Evaluation
NPE . . . . Nuclear Photographic Emulsion
NPEA . . . . . . National Printing Equipment Association
NPEC . . . . . . National Panhellenic Editors' Conference
NPED . . . . . . Nuclear Powered Energy Depot
NPEF . . . . . . New Product Evaluation Form

NPF . . . . National Paraplegia Foundation
NPF . . . . National Park Foundation (Formerly, National Park Trust Fund Board)
NPF . . . . National Parkinson Foundation
NPF . . . . National Piano Foundation
NPF . . . . Naval Parachute Facility
NPF . . . . Naval Powder Factory
NPF . . . . Naval Procurement Fund (Budget appropriation title)
NPF . . . . Network Pulse Forming
NPF . . . . Newtonian Potential Function
NPF . . . . Not Provided For
NPFC . . . . . . Naval Publications and Forms Center
NPFC . . . . . . North Pacific Fur Seal Commission
NPFF . . . . . . Normal Probability Frequency Function
NPFFG . . . . . National Plant, Flower and Fruit Guild
NPFFPA . . . . National Prepared Frozen Food Processors Association
NPFI . . . . National Plant Food Institute
NPF & PP . . . . Naval Prison Farms and Prison Personnel (Budget appropriation title)
NPFS . . . . . . Naval Pre-Flight School
NPFS . . . . . . No Prior or Current Federal Service
NPFSC . . . . . North Pacific Fur Seal Commission
NPG . . . . National Portrait Gallery (Smithsonian Institution)
NPG . . . . Naval Proving Ground
NPG . . . . Nuclear Planning Group (NATO)
NPG . . . . Nuclear Power Group
NPGLINAC . . . Naval Postgraduate School Linear Accelerator
NPGTC . . . . . National Prairie Grouse Technical Council
NPH . . . . Natural Period in Heave
NPH . . . . Neutral Protamine Hegedorn (Insulin)
NPH . . . . North American Philips Corp. (NYSE symbol)
NPHWA . . . . National Presbyterian Health and Welfare Association
NPI . . . . National Parkinson Institute
NPI . . . . Neuro-Psychiatric Institute
NPIC . . . . . . Naval Photographic Interpretation Center
NPIP . . . . . . National Poultry Improvement Plan
NPIRI . . . . . . National Printing Ink Research Institute
NPITI . . . . . . National Project for the Improvement of Televised Instruction (National Association of Educational Broadcasters)
NPJPA . . . . . National Prune Juice Packers Association
NPK . . . . National Presto Industries, Inc. (NYSE symbol)
NPK . . . . Nodal Point Keying
NPL . . . . National Physical Laboratory (India)
NPL . . . . National Physics Laboratory
NPL . . . . National Puzzlers' League
NPL . . . . Neon Pilot Light
NPL . . . . New Product Line
NPL . . . . New Programming Language (Data processing)
NPL . . . . Nonpartisan League (Political party in North Dakota opposed by the IVA)
NPL . . . . Nonpersonal Liability
NPLEI . . . . . . National Police Law Enforcement Institute
NPM . . . . Navy Programming Manual
NPM . . . . Neptune Meter Company (NYSE symbol)
NPM . . . . Northern Pacific Railway (AAR code)
NPMA . . . . . National Piano Manufacturers Association of America
NPMR . . . . . National Premium Manufacturers Representatives
NPN . . . . National Petroleum News (A periodical)
NPN . . . . Negative-Positive-Negative (Transistor)
NPN . . . . Nonprotein Nitrogen (Chemistry)
NPNA . . . . . No Protest Non-Acceptance (Banking)
NPO . . . . Naval Port Officer
NPO . . . . Navy Post Office
NPO . . . . Navy Program Objectives
NPO . . . . Navy Purchasing Office
NPO . . . . Negative - Positive - Zero
NPO . . . . New Philharmonic Orchestra (British)
NPO . . . . Nuclear Propulsion Office
NPOAA . . . . National Police Officers' Association of America
NPOLA . . . . . Navy Purchasing Office, Los Angeles
NPOPR . . . . . Not Paid on Prior Rolls
NP & OSR . . . . Naval Petroleum and Oil Shale Reserve
NPP . . . . National Policy Paper (Army)
NPP . . . . National Prohibition Party
NPP . . . . National Promotion Plan
NPP . . . . Naval Propellant Plant
NPP . . . . Negative Picture Phase
NPPA . . . . . . National Pickle Packers Association
NPPA . . . . . . National Press Photographers Association
NPPA . . . . . . National Probation and Parole Association
NPPC . . . . . . National Pork Producers Council
NPPC . . . . . . National Power Policy Committee (World War II)
NPPC . . . . . . Nuclear Power Plant Company, Ltd.
NPPE . . . . . . Nuclear Power Propulsion Evaluation

NPPF . . . . National Poultry Producers Federation
NPPO . . . . Navy Program and Planning Office
NPPO . . . . Navy Publications and Printing Office
NPPR . . . . Non-Productive Procurement Directive
NPPS . . . . Navy Planning and Programming System
NPPS . . . . Navy Publications and Printing Service
NPPSBO . . . . . Navy Publications and Printing Service Branch Office
NPPSO . . . . . . Navy Publications and Printing Services Office
NPPTA . . . . . . National Public Parks Tennis Association
NPR . . . . Narodowa Partia Robotnicza (National Workers Party) (Poland)
NPR . . . . National Public Radio
NPR . . . . Naval Petroleum Reserve
NPR . . . . Naval Plant Representative
NPR . . . . Navy Procurement Regulation
NPR . . . . New Production Reactor (Electronic)
NPR . . . . Noise Power Ratio
NPR . . . . Nuclear Paramagnetic Resonance
NPR . . . . Nuclear Power Reactor
NPR . . . . Nuclear Pulse Rocket (NASA)
NPRA . . . . . . National Petroleum Refiners Association
NPRA . . . . . . Naval Personnel Research Activity
NPRA . . . . . . Newspaper Personnel Relations Association
NRPB . . . . . . National Research Planning Board
NPRB . . . . . . Northern Pacific Railway (AAR code)
NPRC . . . . . . National Personnel Records Center (National Archives and Records Service)
NPRF . . . . . . Northrop Pulse Radiation Facility
NPRI . . . . . . National Psychiatric Reform Institute
NPRO . . . . . . Navy Plant Representative Office
NPRR . . . . . . National Public Relations Roundtable
NPS . . . . National Park Service (Department of the Interior)
NPS . . . . National Philatelic Society
NPS . . . . Naval Postgraduate School
NPS . . . . Night Photographic System
NPS . . . . No Prior Service
NPS . . . . Nominal Pipe Size
NPS . . . . Normal Pipe Size
NPS . . . . Normalized Plateau Slope
NPS . . . . Nuclear Power System
NPSA . . . . . . National Paint Salesmen's Association
NPSB . . . . . . News Print Service Bureau
NPSC . . . . . . Naval Personnel Separation Center
NPSD . . . . . . Naval Photographic Services Depot (Hollywood)
NPSE . . . . . . National Premium Sales Executives
NPSH . . . . . . Net Positive Suction Head (Pumps)
NPSL . . . . . . National Professional Soccer League
NPSPA . . . . . National Pecan Shellers and Processors Association
NPSR . . . . . . No Primary Staff Responsibility (Army)
NPSRA . . . . . National Professional Squash Racquets Association
NPSRA . . . . . Nuclear-Powered Ship Research Association (Japan)
NPT . . . . National Pipe Thread
NPT . . . . National Taper Pipe Thread
NPT . . . . Neuropsychiatry Technician (Navy)
NPT . . . . New Periodical Titles (of British Union Catalogue of Periodicals)
NPT . . . . Nonproliferation Treaty (to halt the spread of nuclear weapons)
NPT . . . . Nonpyramidal Tract
NPT . . . . Normal Pressure and Temperature
NPT . . . . Northern Pacific Terminal R. R. (AAR code)
NPTA . . . . . . National Paper Trade Association
NPTA . . . . . . National Passenger Traffic Association
NPTA . . . . . . National Piano Travelers Association
NPTA . . . . . . National Postal Transport Association
NPTC . . . . . . National Postal and Travelers Censorship (Army)
NPTCO . . . . . National Postal and Travelers Censorship Organization
NPTFB . . . . . . National Park Trust Fund Board (Later, National Park Foundation)
NPTL . . . . . . National Police Testing Laboratories
NPTRL . . . . . Naval Personnel and Training Research Laboratory (Formerly, Personnel Research Activity)
NPU . . . . National Postal Union
NPU . . . . Naval Parachute Unit
NPU . . . . Ne Plus Ultra (No Further; i.e., the pinnacle of attainment)
NPU . . . . Net Protein Utilization
NPU . . . . Nitrogen Press Unit
NPV . . . . No Par Value
NPVLA . . . . . National Paint, Varnish and Lacquer Association
NPX . . . . National Phoenix Industries, Inc. (American Stock Exchange symbol)
NQ . . . . Notes and Queries
NQA . . . . Net Quick Assets
NQAA . . . . . . Nuclear Quality Assurance Agency
NQB . . . . National Quotation Bureau (Stock market)
NQB . . . . No Qualified Bidders

NQD . . . . Notice of Quality Discrepancy
NQHR . . . . . . National Quarter Horse Registry
NQPC . . . . . . National Quartz Producers Council
NQR . . . . Nuclear Quadrupole Resonance (Frequencies)
NQRR . . . . . . Nuclear Quadrupole Resonance Response
NQT . . . . Nonlanguage Qualification Test
NR . . . . Nachrichtenregiment (Signal regiment) (German military – World War II)
NR . . . . National Recovery Act (or Administration)
NR . . . . National Review (A publication)
NR . . . . Natural Rubber
NR . . . . Naval Reserve
NR . . . . Navigational RADAR
NR . . . . Navy Regulations
NR . . . . Near
NR . . . . Negative Resistance
NR . . . . Net Register (Shipping)
NR . . . . New Republic (A publication)
NR . . . . No Release
NR . . . . No Risk (Business and trade)
NR . . . . Noise Ratio
NR . . . . Non Repetatur (Not to Be Repeated)
NR . . . . Nonrated
NR . . . . Nonreactive (Relay)
NR . . . . Nonreturnable (Beverage bottles)
NR . . . . North American Rockwell Corporation (NYSE symbol)
NR . . . . Northern Range (Navigation)
NR . . . . Not Required
NR . . . . Nuclear Reactor
NR . . . . Nuestra Remesa (Our Remittance) (Business and trade) (Spain)
NR . . . . Number
NR . . . . Number of Runs
NR . . . . Nystagmus Recorder
NR . . . . Submersible Research Vehicle (Nuclear Propulsion) (Navy ship symbol)
N/R . . . . No Record
N/R . . . . Not Required
N/R . . . . Not Responsible For
N/R . . . . Notes Receivable
N/R . . . . Notice of Readiness (Shipping)
NRA . . . . National Reclamation Association
NRA . . . . National Recovery Act
NRA . . . . National Recovery Administration (Voided by Supreme Court, 1935)
NRA . . . . National Recreation Association
NRA . . . . National Reform Association
NRA . . . . National Register of Archives (Historical Manuscripts Commission) (British)
NRA . . . . National Rehabilitation Association
NRA . . . . National Renderers Association
NRA . . . . National Restaurant Association
NRA . . . . National Rifle Association of America
NRA . . . . Naval Radio Activity
NRA . . . . Naval Reserve Association
NRA . . . . Network Resolution Area
NRA . . . . No Repair Action (Military)
NRA . . . . Nonregistered Accountable (Military)
NRA . . . . Nuclear Radiation Absorber
NRAA . . . . . . National Railway Appliances Association
NRAB . . . . . . National Railroad Adjustment Board
NRAB . . . . . . Naval Reserve Aviation Base
NRAC . . . . . . National Resources Analysis Center
NRAC . . . . . . Naval Research Advisory Committee
NRACCO . . . . Navy Regional Air Cargo Control Office
NRAD . . . . . . No Risk After Discharge (Shipping)
NRAF . . . . . . Naval Reserve Auxiliary Field
NRAO . . . . . . National Radio Astronomy Observatory
NRAO . . . . . . Navy Regional Accounts Office
NRAS . . . . . . Navy Readiness Analysis System
NRAS . . . . . . Nuclear Release Authentication System (Seventh Army)
NRATUC . . . . Northern Rhodesian African Trades Union Congress
NRAU . . . . . . Nyasaland Railways Asian Workers' Union
NRAWU . . . . . Nyasaland Railways African Workers' Union
NRB . . . . National Religious Broadcasters
NRB . . . . Natural Rubber Bureau
NRB . . . . Naval Reactors Board
NRB . . . . Naval Repair Base
NRB . . . . Navy Recruiting Bureau
NRB . . . . Navy Reservation Bureau
NRB . . . . New York Air Brake Company (NYSE symbol) (Delisted)
NRB . . . . Nuclear Reactors Branch (AEC)
NRBC . . . . . . National Rare Blood Club
NRBC . . . . . . Nucleated Red Blood Cell
NRC . . . . National Ramah Commission

NRC........ National Reading Council
NRC .... National Records Center
NRC .... National Referral Center (of Library of Congress)
NRC........ National Reprographic Centre (for Documentation) (British)
NRC .... National Republican Club
NRC .... National Research Corporation
NRC .... National Research Council
NRC........ National Resources Committee (Functions transferred to National Resources Planning Board)
NRC........ National Rocket Club
NRC .... Natural Resources Council of America
NRC .... Naval Records Club
NRC........ Naval Retraining Command
NRC........ Netherlands Red Cross
NRC........ Neutron Radiation Capture
NRC........ New Right Coalition
NRC .... Normal Retinal Correspondence
NRC .... Nuclear Research Council
NRCA....... National Resources Council of America
NRCA....... National Retail Credit Association
NRCA ...... National Roofing Contractors Association
NRCC....... National Registry in Clinical Chemistry
NRCC....... National Research Council of Canada
NRCC ..... NORAD Region Combat Center (Military)
NRCd ...... National Reprographic Centre for Documentation (British)
NRCI ...... National Red Cherry Institute
NRC-NAS .... National Research Council - National Academy of Sciences
NRCP ...... Nonreinforced Concrete Pipe (Technical drawings)
NRCPS ..... National Research Council on Peace Strategy
NRCS....... Normalized RADAR Cross-Section
NRD .... National Range Division (Air Force)
NRD........ Negative Resistance Diode
NRD........ No Record of Destination (Aviation)
NRD........ Nuclear Radiation Detector
NRD........ Office of Naval Research and Development
NRDA ...... National Research and Development Authority (Formerly, NCRD) (Israel)
NRDC....... National Research Development Corporation (British)
NRDC....... Natural Resources Defense Council
NRDC....... Navy Research and Development Committee
NRDFS ..... Naval Radio Direction Finder Service
NRDL ..... Naval Radiological Defense Laboratory
NRDS...... Nuclear Rocket Detection System (NASA)
NRDS...... Nuclear Rocket Development Station (AEC)
NRDU-V ..... Navy Research and Development Unit - Vietnam
NRE........ Negative Resistance Effect
NRE........ Nuclear Radiation Effect
NRE........ Nuclear Rocket Engine
NREC....... National Resources Evaluation Center (of OEP) (Nuclear effects)
NRECA ..... National Rural Electric Cooperative Association
NREFA ..... National Real Estate Fliers Association
NREP ...... Name Removed from End-Paper (Antiquarian book trade)
NRES ...... Naval Receiving Station
NRF........ National Rowing Foundation
NRF........ Naval Reactor Facility
NRF........ Naval Repair Facility
NRF .... No Reflight
NRF........ No Reinforcement (Psychology)
NRF........ Nouvelle Revue Francaise (French periodical; initials also used on books published by Gallimard)
NRFA...... National Retail Florists Association (Defunct)
NRFA...... National Retail Furniture Association
NRFC ...... Navy Regional Finance Center
NRFEA ..... National Retail Farm Equipment Association
NRFF ...... National Research Foundation for Fertility
NRFI ...... Not Ready for Issue
NRFO....... Navy Regional Finance Office
NRFSA ..... Navy Radio Frequency Spectrum Activity
NRG ...... Nautical Research Guild
NRG .... Naval Research Group
NRGA ...... National Rice Growers Association
NRH........ Non-Ready Hours
NRHA ..... National Retail Hardware Association
NRHC....... National Rural Housing Coalition
NR & HC .... National Rivers and Harbors Congress
NRHS ...... National Railway Historical Society
NRI .... National Radio Institute
NRI .... Norris Industries, Inc. (NYSE symbol)
NRIMS ..... National Research Institute for Mathematical Sciences (South Africa)
NRIP....... Number of Rejected Initial Pickups
NRIPMVLIC ... Non-Resident Inter-Province Motor Vehicle Liability Insurance Card (for travel in Canada)

NRK........ Normal Rat Kidney
NRL .... National Registry for Librarians
NRL .... National Research Laboratory
NRL .... Naval Research Laboratory (ONR)
NRL........ Norlin Corp. (NYSE symbol)
NRL........ Normal Rated Load
NRLCA ..... National Rural Letter Carriers' Association
NRLDA ..... National Retail Lumber Dealers Association
NRLP ...... National Railway Labor Panel (World War II)
NRLSI ...... National Reference Library of Science and Invention (British)
NRM ...... Natural Remanent Magnetism (or Magnetization)
NRM .... Naval Reserve Medal
NRM ...... Nonroutine Maintenance
NRM .... Northern Rocky Mountains
NRMA ..... National Retail Merchants Association
NRMC ..... National Records Management Council
NRMC ..... Naval Records Management Center
NRMC ..... Naval Reserve Manpower Center
NRMCA .... National Ready Mixed Concrete Association
NRMCEN .... Naval Records Management Center
NRMEC..... North American Rockwell Microelectronics Company
NRMM ..... National Register of Microform Masters (Library of Congress)
NRMS ..... National Registry of Medical Secretaries
NRMS...... Naval Reserve Midshipmen's School
NRMU ..... Northern Rhodesia European Mineworkers' Union
NRN ...... Natural Radioactive Nuclides
NRO ...... Naval Research Objectives
NRO ...... Negative Resistance Oscillator
NROE...... Naval Reactor Organic Experiment
NROO ..... Naval Reactors Operations Office
NROPS ..... New Riders of the Purple Sage (Rock music group)
NROS ..... Naval Reserve Officer School
NROTC .... Naval Reserve Officers' Training Corps
NROTCBA .... National Reserve Officers' Training Corps Band Association
NRP........ Non-Registered Publication
NRP ...... Nonstationary Random Process
NRP ...... Normal Rated Power
NRP .... Notice of Research Project
NRPA ..... National Recreation and Park Association
NRPB ..... National Resources Planning Board (Abolished, 1943)
NRPC....... National Railroad Passenger Corporation (Government rail transportation)
NRPF ...... National Railroad Pension Forum
NRPIO ..... Naval Registered Publications Issuing Office
NRPM...... Non-Registered Publications Memoranda
NRPSA ..... National Retail Pet Supply Association
NRR .... Naval Research Reactor
NRR .... Naval Research Requirement
NRR .... Net Reproductive Rate
NRR .... Net Retail Requirements
NRR .... Nuclear Rocket Reactor
NRRC ...... Naval Research Reserve Company
NRRE ...... Netherlands RADAR Research Establishment
NRRL ...... Northern Regional Research Laboratory
NRRS ...... Naval Radio Research Station
NRRS ...... No Remaining Radiation Service (Unit) (Military)
NRRTUC .... Northern Rhodesian Reformed Trades Union Congress
NRS........ National Reemployment Service
NRS .... Naval Radio Station
NRS .... Naval Receiving Station
NRS .... Naval Recruiting Station
NRS .... Naval Research Section (Library of Congress)
NRS .... Navy Relief Society
NRS .... Night Reconnaissance System
NRS .... Normal Rabbit Serum
NRS .... Nuclear Radiation Shield
NRSSG ..... Nuclear Reactor Systems Safety Group (Air Force)
NRT .... National Repertory Theatre Foundation
NRT .... Navy Reserve Training
NRT .... Neighbours of the Roundtable
NRT .... Net Registered Ton
NRT .... Nonradiating Target
NRT .... Nonreal Time
NRT .... Normal Rated Thrust
NRT .... Norton Company (NYSE symbol)
NRT .... Notion Round Table
NRTA ...... National Retired Teachers Association
NRTC ...... Naval Reserve Training Center
NRT & CMA .. National Retail Tea and Coffee Merchants Association
NRTS ...... National Reactor Testing Station
NRTS ...... Not Reparable This Station
NRTS ...... Nuclear Reactor Testing Station (AEC)

NRTSC . . . . . . Naval Reconnaissance and Technical Support Center
NRU . . . . National Reactor Universal
NRU . . . . Neuropsychiatric Research Unit (Navy)
NRUTUC . . . . Northern Rhodesia United Trades Union Congress
NRV . . . . Non-Revenue (Passengers or cargo) (Transportation)
NRWC . . . . . . National Right to Work Committee
NRW-KA . . . National Registry of Willys-Knight Automobile
NRX . . . . NERVA (Nuclear Engine for Rocket Vehicle Application) Reactor Experiment (AEC)
NRX . . . . Nuclear Reactor, Experimental
NRZ . . . . Nonreturn to Zero
NRZC . . . . . . Nonreturn to Zero Change
NRZL . . . . . . Nonreturn to Zero Level
NRZM . . . . . . Nonreturn to Zero Mark
ns . . . . Nanosecond (100 billionth of a second) (Also, nsec)
NS . . . . National Society
NS . . . . National Special (Thread)
NS . . . . National Steel Corporation (NYSE symbol)
NS . . . . Naval School
NS . . . . Naval Shipyard
NS . . . . Naval Station
NS . . . . Near Side (Technical drawings)
NS . . . . Nederlandsche Spoorwegen
NS . . . . Nervous System
NS . . . . Neurosurgery, Neurosurgeon
NS . . . . New School
NS . . . . New Series (Bibliography)
NS . . . . New Side
NS . . . . New Style
NS . . . . New System (Data processing)
NS . . . . Next System (Data processing)
NS . . . . Nickel Steel
NS . . . . Nimbostratus (Meteorology)
NS . . . . Nitrogen Supply
NS . . . . Nitrogen System
NS . . . . Non-Scheduled
NS . . . . Non-Specified
NS . . . . Norfolk Southern Railway Company (AAR code)
NS . . . . Normal Saline
NS . . . . Normal Serum
NS . . . . North-South
NS . . . . Nostro Signore (Our Lord)
NS . . . . Not Significant
NS . . . . Not Specified
NS . . . . Not Sufficient
NS . . . . Nôtre Seigneur (Our Lord)
NS . . . . Nova Scotia (A Canadian province)
NS . . . . Nuclear Science
NS . . . . Nuclear Ship
NS . . . . Nuclear Submarine
NS . . . . Nuclear Systems
NS . . . . Numismatic Society
NSA . . . . National Secretaries Association (International)
NSA . . . . National Security Act
NSA . . . . National Security Agency (DOD)
NSA . . . . National Service Acts (British)
NSA . . . . National Shellfisheries Association
NSA . . . . National Sheriffs' Association
NSA . . . . National Shipping Authority (Department of Commerce)
NSA . . . . National Showmen's Association
NSA . . . . National Shuffleboard Association
NSA . . . . National Silo Association
NSA . . . . National Ski Association of America (Later, United States Ski Association)
NSA . . . . National Slag Association
NSA . . . . National Slate Association
NSA . . . . National Society of Auctioneers
NSA . . . . National Standards Association
NSA . . . . Naval Stock Account
NSA . . . . Naval Supply Account
NSA . . . . Neurosurgical Society of America
NSA . . . . Noise Suppressor Assembly
NSA . . . . Nonenylsuccinic Acid (Organic chemistry)
NSA . . . . North-South Acceleration
NSA . . . . Norwegian Seamen's Association
NSA . . . . Nuclear Science Abstracts (AEC)
NSA . . . . Nuclear Systems Analysis
NSAA . . . . . . National Ski Areas Association
NSAA . . . . . . National Supply Association of America
NSAA . . . . . . Norwegian Singers Association of America
NSAC . . . . . . National Society of Accountants of Cooperatives

NSAC . . . . . . National Spiritualist Association of Churches
NSAC . . . . . . Nova Scotia Agricultural College
NSAD . . . . . . National Society of Art Directors
NSAF . . . . . . Naval Supply Account Fund
NSAFC . . . . . National Service Armed Forces Act (British)
NSALO . . . . . National Security Agency Liaison Officer
NSAM . . . . . . National Security Action Memorandum
NSAM . . . . . . Naval School of Aviation Medicine
NSANL . . . . . Non-Sectarian Anti-NAZI League
NSAS . . . . . . Non-Scheduled Air Services
NSA-US . . . . National Spiritual Assembly of the Baha'is of the United States
NSB . . . . National Science Board (of the National Science Foundation)
NSB . . . . Naval Standardization Board
NSB . . . . Naval Submarine Base
NSB . . . . New York Shipbuilding Corporation (NYSE symbol) (Delisted)
NSB . . . . Newsprint Service Bureau
NSB . . . . Nonspecific Binder
NSB . . . . Northern Soviet Boundary
NSBA . . . . . . National Safe Boating Association
NSBA . . . . . . National School Boards Association
NSBA . . . . . . National Shrimp Breaders Association
NSBA . . . . . . National Small Business Association
NSBA . . . . . . National Sugar Brokers Association
NSBB . . . . . . National Society for Business Budgeting
NSBC . . . . . . National Shoeboard Conference
NSBC . . . . . . National Student Book Club
NSBD . . . . . . Narrow Spectral Band Detection
NSBEO . . . . . National Sonic Boom Evaluation Office (Air Force)
NSBMA . . . . . National Small Business Men's Association
NSBRO . . . . . National Service Board for Religious Objectors
NSBT . . . . . . Not Series By Title
NSBWC . . . . . National Safe Boating Week Committee
NSC . . . . National Safety Council
NSC . . . . National Security Council
NSC . . . . National Society of Cwens
NSC . . . . National Space Club
NSC . . . . National Space Council
NSC . . . . National Starch & Chemical Corporation (NYSE symbol)
NSC . . . . National Synthetics Collection (Smithsonian Institution)
NSC . . . . Naval Supply Center
NSC . . . . Navigation and Sensor Computer
NSC . . . . Navy Service Center
NSC . . . . Neurosecretory Cells
NSC . . . . Newtex Steamship Company (AAR code)
NSC . . . . Nippon Steel Corporation (Japan)
NSC . . . . Non-Service Connected
NSC . . . . Northeastern State College (Oklahoma)
NSC . . . . Numerical Sequence Code
NSCA . . . . . . National Shrimp Canners Association
NSCA . . . . . . National Soccer Coaches Association of America
NSCA . . . . . . Northwest Salmon Canners Association
NSCA . . . . . . Nova Scotia College of Art
NSCAR . . . . . National Society of the Children of the American Revolution
NSCC . . . . . . National Siamese Cat Club
NSCC . . . . . . North Shore Community College (Massachusetts)
NSCCA . . . . . National Society for Crippled Children and Adults
NSCCA . . . . . National Sports Car Club of America
NSCDA . . . . . National Society of Colonial Dames of America
NSCDRF . . . . National Sickle Cell Disease Research Foundation
NSCF . . . . . . National Student Christian Federation (Later, UCM)
NSCF . . . . . . Naval Small Craft Facilities
NSCIC . . . . . . National Soybean Crop Improvement Council
NSCID . . . . . . National Security Council Intelligence Directive
NSC & MP . . . National Stock Control and Maintenance Point
NSCO . . . . . . National Scientific Committee on Oceanography
NSCP . . . . . . National Society for Corporate Planning
NSCP . . . . . . Naval Stores Conservation Program
NSCR . . . . . . Nuclear Science Center Reactor
NSCRC . . . . . National Stock Car Racing Commission
NSCS . . . . . . Navy Supply Corps School
NSCSC . . . . . National School Calendar Study Committee
NSCSCC . . . . National Standard for Common System Component Characteristics
NSCSWD . . . . No Small Craft or Storm Warnings are Being Displayed (Weather)
NSCT . . . . . . Niagara, St. Catherines & Toronto R. R. (AAR code)
NSCTE . . . . . National Society of College Teachers of Education
NSD . . . . National Silage Demonstration (British)
NSD . . . . National Standard Company (NYSE symbol)
NSD . . . . Naval Supply Depot
NSD . . . . Navy Support Date
NSD . . . . Network Status Display
NSD . . . . Noise Suppression Device

NSD . . . . Non-Self-Destroying
NSDA . . . . . . National Sprayer and Duster Association
NSDA . . . . . . National Surplus Dealers Association
NSDA . . . . Naval Supply Depot Annex
NSDAP . . . . . . Nationalsozialistische Deutsche Arbeiterpartei (National Socialist German Workers', or NAZI, Party, 1919-45)
NSDAR . . . . . . National Society, Daughters of the American Revolution
NSDB . . . . National Science Development Board
NSDBE . . . . . . National Society, Daughters of the British Empire
NSDBR . . . . . . National Society, Daughters of the Barons of Runnemede
NSDC . . . . National Square Dance Convention
NSDC . . . . . . NORAD Section Direction Center (Military)
NSDCM . . . . . NORAD Section Direction Center Manual (Military)
NSDFB . . . . . . Nationalsozialistischer Deutscher Frontkaempferbund (Germany)
NSDJA . . . . . . Northern Sash and Door Jobbers Association
NSDM . . . . . . National Security Decision Memorandum (Air Force)
NSDP . . . . National Serials Data Program (Proposed for Library of Congress)
NSDP . . . . National Society of Dental Prosthetists
NSDP . . . . Norfolk Sample Drug Program
NSDS . . . . Neutron Spectrometer Digital System
NSDUP . . . . . . National Society, Daughters of Utah Pioneers
NSE . . . . National Sales Executives
NSE . . . . National Stock Exchange
NSE . . . . Navigation Support Equipment
NSE . . . . Nuclear Science and Engineering
NSE . . . . Nuclear Support Equipment
NSE . . . . Nuclear Systems Engineering
nsec . . . . Nanosecond (100 billionth of a second) (Also, ns)
NSEC . . . . . . National Service Entertainments Council (British)
NSEC . . . . Naval Ship Engineering Center
NSEC . . . . . . Nuclear Science and Engineering Corporation (Pittsburgh)
NSEEC . . . . . . Naval Shore Electronics Engineering Center (Terminated, 1966)
NSEF . . . . Navy Security Engineering Facility
NSF . . . . . . National Sanitation Foundation
NSF . . . . . . National Science Foundation
NSF . . . . National Sharecroppers Fund
NSF . . . . Naval Stock Fund
NSF . . . . Naval Supersonic Facility
NSF . . . . Naval Supply Force
NSF . . . . Naval Support Force
NSF . . . . Negotiated Search Facility (Information retrieval)
NSF . . . . Nitrogen Supply Flask
NSF . . . . Nonstock Fund
NSF . . . . Not Sufficient Funds (Banking)
NSF . . . . Nuclear Safety Facility
NSFA . . . . National Science Foundation Act
NSFAC . . . . . . National Student Financial Aid Council (Later, NASFAA)
NSFC . . . . National Society of Film Critics
NSFD . . . . Notice of Structural or Functional Deficiency
NSFH . . . . North-South Fine, Hundreds
NSF-I . . . . National Science Fair - International
NSFO . . . . . . Navy Special Fuel Oil
NSFR . . . . National Society of Fund Raisers
NSFT . . . . North-South Fine, Tens
NSFTD . . . . . . Normal, Spontaneous, Full Term, Delivery (Medicine)
NSFU . . . . North-South Fine, Units
NSG . . . . Naval Security Group
NSG . . . . Not So Good
NSGA . . . . . . National Sand and Gravel Association
NSGA . . . . . . National Sporting Goods Association
NSGA . . . . . Naval Security Group Activity
NSGC . . . . . . National Self Government Committee
NSGC . . . . . . National Swine Growers Council
NSGT . . . . Non-Self-Governing Territories (UN)
NSGW . . . . . . Native Sons of the Golden West
NSH . . . . Nashua Corp. (NYSE symbol)
NSH . . . . Not So Hot (Slang)
NSHA . . . . . . National Steeplechase and Hunt Association
NSHO . . . . . . Naval Service Headquarters, Ottawa, Canada
NSI . . . . National Service (Life) Insurance
NSI . . . . National Shoe Institute
NSI . . . . Noise Source Instrumentation
NSI . . . . Nonsatellite Identification
NSI . . . . Non-Standard Item
NSI . . . . Norton Simon, Incorporated (NYSE symbol)
NSI . . . . Nuclear Safety Institute
NSI . . . . Nuclear Services International
NSIA . . . . . . National Security Industrial Association
NSIAC . . . . . . National Student Involvement Assistance Center (Boston University)
NSIC . . . . . . Noster Salvator Iesus Christus (Our Saviour Jesus Christ)
NSIC . . . . Nuclear Safety Information Center (AEC)

NSIC . . . . . . Nuclear Strike Information Center
NSID . . . . . . National Society of Interior Designers
NSIT . . . . Not Safe in Taxis
NSJ . . . . Nuestro Señor Jesucristo (Our Lord, Jesus Christ) (Spanish)
NSJC . . . . . . Noster Salvator Jesus Christus (Our Savior Jesus Christ)
NSJC . . . . . . Notre Seigneur Jesus Christ (Our Lord, Jesus Christ)
NSKK . . . . . . Nationalsozialistisches Kraftfahr-Korps (Germany)
NSL . . . . National Scientific Laboratory, Inc.
NSL . . . . National Semiconductors, Limited
NSL . . . . National Standards Laboratory (Australia)
NSL . . . . National Story League
NSL . . . . Naval Supersonic Laboratory
NSL . . . . Norwood & St. Lawrence R. R. (AAR code)
NSL . . . . Nuclear Safety Line
NSLB . . . . . . Nationalsozialistischer Lehrerbund (NAZI Germany)
NSLI . . . . . . National Service Life Insurance
NSLIN . . . . . Nonstandard Line Item Number (Army)
NSLSRA . . . . National Society of Live Stock Record Associations
NSM . . . . . . National Security Medal
NSM . . . . . . National Selected Morticians
NSM . . . . Naval School of Music
NSM . . . . Neurosecretory Material
NSM . . . . Noise Source Meter
NSM . . . . . . Northern Student Movement
NSMA . . . . . National Scale Men's Association
NSMA . . . . . National Shoe Manufacturers Association
NSMA . . . . . . National Soup Mix Association
NSMAPMAWOL . . Not So Much a Programme, More a Way of Life (British television program)
NSMC . . . . . . National Student Marketing Corporation
NSMC . . . . . . Naval Submarine Medical Center
NSME . . . . . Nonstandard Measuring Equipment (Aviation)
NSMFA . . . . . North Sea Mine Force Association
NSMG . . . . . . Naval School of Military Government
NSMG & A . . . Naval School of Military Government and Administration
NSMO . . . . . . NASTRAN Systems Management Office (NASA)
NSMP . . . . . . National Society of Mural Painters
NSMPA . . . . . National Screw Machine Products Association
NSMR . . . . . . National Society for Medical Research
NSMRSE . . . . . National Study of Mathematics Requirements for Scientists and Engineers
NSMS . . . . . . National Sheet Music Society
NSMSES . . . . Naval Ship Missile Systems Engineering Station
NSMT . . . . . National Society of Medical Technologists
NSMW . . . . . . Naval Schools Mine Warfare
NSN . . . . No Stock Number
NSNA . . . . . National Student Nurses' Association
NSNA . . . . . Newcomen Society in North America
NSNC . . . . . . Nova Scotia Normal College
NSNEW . . . . . National Society of New England Women
NSO . . . . . . Naval Staff Officer
NSO . . . . . . No Spares Ordered
NSO . . . . Nuclear Safety Office(r) (Air Force)
NSOA . . . . . . National School Orchestra Association
NSOB . . . . . . New Senate Office Building
NSOEA . . . . . National Stationery and Office Equipment Association
NSOGA . . . . National Seniors' Open Golf Association
NSP . . . . National Society of Professors
NSP . . . . National Space Program
NSP . . . . National Stolen Property
NSP . . . . Navy Standard Part
NSP . . . . Navy Support Plan
NSP . . . . New Species
NSP . . . . Nonstandard Holding Pattern (Aviation)
NSP . . . . Non-Standard Part
NSP . . . . Northern States Power Company (NYSE symbol)
NSP . . . . Nose Shipping Plug
NSP . . . . Not Separately Priced
NSP . . . . Nuclear Strike Plan (Army)
NSPA . . . . . National Scholastic Press Association
NSPA . . . . . . National Society of Public Accountants
NSPA . . . . . . National Soybean Processors Association
NSPA . . . . . . National Split Pea Association
NSPA . . . . . . National Standard Parts Association
NSPB . . . . . . National Society for the Prevention of Blindness
NSPC . . . . . . National Security Planning Commission
NSPC . . . . . . National Society of Painters in Casein
NSPCA . . . . . National Society for the Prevention of Cruelty to Animals
NSPCB . . . . . National Society for the Preservation of Covered Bridges
NSPCC . . . . . National Society for the Prevention of Cruelty to Children
NSPD . . . . . . Naval Shore Patrol Detachment
NSPE . . . . . . National Society of Professional Engineers

NSPF .... Not Specifically Provided for
NSPFEA ..... National Spray Painting and Finishing Equipment Association
NSPI .... National Society for Programmed Instruction
NSPI .... National Swimming Pool Institute
NSPIE .... National Society for the Promotion of Industrial Education
NSPO .... Navy Special Projects Office
NSPO .... Nuclear Systems Project Office (Air Research and Development Command) (Air Force)
NSPP .... Nuclear Safety Pilot Plant (ORNL)
NSPR .... National Society of Pershing Rifles
NSPRA ...... National School Public Relations Association
NSPRDS ..... New Systems Personnel Requirements Data System (Navy)
NSPRM ...... National Society of Professional Resident Managers
NSPS .... National Ski Patrol System
NSPWA ...... National Society Patriotic Women of America
NSQ .... Neuroticism Scale Questionnaire
NSQCRE ..... National Symposium on Quality Control and Reliability in Electronics (IEEE)
NSR .... National Scientific Register
NSR .... Neutron Source Reactor
NSR .... Night Sky Radiation
NSR .... No Staff Responsibility (Army)
NSR .... Normal Sinus Rhythm (Physiology)
NSRA .... National Shoe Retailers Association
NSRA .... National Shorthand Reporters Association
NSRB .... National Security Resources Board (Functions transferred to ODM, 1953)
NSRC .... National Stereophonic Radio Committee
NSRDC ...... National Standards Reference Data Center
NSRDC ...... Naval Ship Research and Development Center
NSRDF ...... Naval Supply Research and Development Facility
NSRDS ...... National Standard Reference Data System (National Bureau of Standards)
NSRMCA .... National Star Route Mail Carriers Association
NSRP .... National Search and Rescue Plan
NSRP .... National States Rights Party
NSRP .... Nontechnical Support Real Property
NSRQCE ..... National Symposium on Reliability and Quality Control in Electronics
NSRS .... Naval Supply Radio Station
NSRT .... Near-Surface Radiation Thermometer
NSS .... National Sculpture Society
NSS .... National Serigraph Society
NSS .... National Slovak Society of the USA
NSS .... National Snapdragon Society
NSS .... National Speleological Society
NSS .... National Stockpile Site
NSS .... National Study Service
NSS .... Naval Strategic Study
NSS .... Neutron Spectrometer System
NSS .... Newburgh & South Shore Railway Company (AAR code)
NSS .... Nitrogen Supply System
NSS .... Normal Saline Solution
NSSA .... National Sanitary Supply Association
NSSA .... National Science Supervisors Association
NSSA .... National Skeet Shooting Association
NSSA .... National Skirt and Sportswear Association
NSSA .... National Suffolk Sheep Association
NSSA .... National Sunday School Association
NSSA .... Navy Space Systems Activity
NSSA .... North-South Skirmish Association
NSSAB ...... National Selective Service Appeal Board (of SSS)
NSSB .... National Society of Scabbard and Blade
NSSC .... National Society for the Study of Communication
NSSC .... Naval Ship Systems Command
NSSC .... Naval Supply Systems Command
NSSC .... Neutral Sulfite Semichemical (Pulp)
NSSCC ...... National Space Surveillance Control Center
NSSDC ...... National Space Science Data Center (NASA)
NSSDP ...... National Society, Sons and Daughters of the Pilgrims
NSSE .... National Society for the Study of Education
NSSEA ...... National School Supply and Equipment Association
NSSET ...... National Symposium on Space Electronics and Telemetry (IEEE)
NSSF .... National Shooting Sports Foundation
NSSF .... National Social Science Foundation (Proposed in 1966)
NSSFC ...... National Severe Storm Forecast Center
NSSFC ...... National Society of Student Film Critics
NSSFNS ..... National Scholarship Service and Fund for Negro Students
NSSG .... National Ski Study Group
NSSIC ...... National Student Strike Information Center (Brandeis University)
NSSL .... National Service Star Legion
NSSL .... National Severe Storms Laboratory (NOAA)
NSSL .... National Society of State Legislators
NSSM .... National Security Study Memorandum

NSSMA ...... National Spanish-Speaking Management Association
NSSO .... National Society of Student Organists
NSSO .... National Solar Space Observatory (NASA)
NSSO .... Navy Ships' Store Office (PX)
NS & SO .... Nervous System and Sense Organs
NSSP .... National Severe Storms Project (National Weather Service)
NSSR .... New School for Social Research
NSSS .... National Space Surveillance System
NSSSE ...... National Study of Secondary School Evaluation
NSSTC ...... National Small Shipments Traffic Conference
NSSTE ...... National Society of Sales Training Executives
NST .... National Symposium on Telemetering
NST .... Navy Shipboard Terminal
NST .... New Serial Titles (A publication of Library of Congress)
NST .... Noise Source Tube
NST .... Nonslip Tread (Technical drawings)
NST .... Not Sooner Than
NS & T ..... Naval Science and Tactics
NSTA .... National Science Teachers Association
NSTA .... National Security Traders Association
NSTA .... National Shoe Traveler's Association
NSTA .... National Squash Tennis Association
NSTC .... National Security Training Commission (Expired, 1957)
NSTC .... National Shade Tree Conference
NSTC .... Nebraska State Teachers College
NSTC .... Nova Scotia Technical College
NSTF .... National Scholarship Trust Fund (An affiliate of the Graphic Arts Technical Foundation)
NSTIC ...... Naval Science Technical Information Center (British)
NSTL .... National Strategic Target Line (or List)
NSTS .... National Sea Training Schools (British)
NSU .... National Sugar Refining Company (NYSE symbol) (Delisted)
NSU .... Naval Scout Unit
NSU .... Neckarsulm (Location in Wuerttemberg, Germany, of NSU Werke, automobile manufacturer; initialism used as name of its cars)
NSU .... Nitrogen Supply Unit
NSU .... Non-Specific Urethritis
NSUA ...... Nigerian Students Union in the Americas
NSUPSC ..... Naval Supply Systems Command (Formerly, Bureau of Supplies and Accounts)
NSV .... Nationalsozialistische Volkswohlfahrt (Germany)
NSV .... Negative Supply Voltage
NSV .... Non-Spinning Vehicle
NSV .... Nuclear Service Vessel
NSVP .... National School Volunteer Program
NSW .... New South Wales
NSW .... Northwestern Steel & Wire Company (NYSE symbol)
NSWA ...... National Social Welfare Assembly
NSWA ...... National Stripper Well Association
NSWDAHAC .. National Society Women Descendants of the Ancient and Honorable Artillery Company
NSWMA ..... National Soft Wheat Millers Association
NSWPP ...... National Socialist White People's Party (Formerly, American NAZI Party)
NSY .... Naval Shipyard
NSYA ...... National School Yearbook Association
NSYD ...... Naval Shipyard
NSYF .... Natural Science for Youth Foundation
NT .... Narrower Term (Cross-reference) (Indexing)
NT .... National Trust for Historic Preservation
NT .... Naval Training
NT .... Net Tons (Shipping)
NT .... New Testament (of the Bible)
NT .... New Translation
NT .... No Trace (Counterintelligence)
NT .... No Transmission
NT .... Nontight
NT .... Normal Tour
NT .... Norris-Thermador Corporation (NYSE symbol) (Delisted)
NT .... Northern Territory (Australia)
NT .... Novum Testamentum (New Testament)
NT .... Numbering Transmitter
N/T .... No Terms (Shipping)
NTA .... Narcotics Treatment Agency (Washington, DC)
NTA .... National Aviation Corporation (NYSE symbol)
NTA .... National Tax Association
NTA .... National Technical Association
NTA .... National Trappers Association of America
NTA .... National Tuberculosis Association
NTA .... Naval Technical Assistants
NTA .... Navy Technician Authorization
NTA .... Near-Terminal Area (Airports)

NTA........ Neher Tetrode Amplifier
NTA........ Nitrilotriacetic Acid (Chemical)
NTA .... Northern Textile Association
NTA .... Nuclear Test Aircraft
NTAA ...... National Travelers Aid Association
NTB........ Nederlandse Toonkunstenaarsbond (Netherlands Musicians' Union)
NTB........ Nontariff Barrier (Kennedy Round)
NTBR....... Not To Be Resuscitated
NTC........ National Teachers Corps
NTC .... National Telemetering Conference (IEEE)
NTC .... National Theatre Conference
NTC .... National Thrift Committee
NTC .... National Translations Center
NTC .... National Transportation Center (Large city situated at a key junction
             of rail, air, and highway transportation) (Postal Service)
NTC........ National Travel Club
NTC........ Naval Training Center
NTC........ Negative Temperature Coefficient
NTC........ Normal Tour of Duty Completed
NTC .... Norwich Terrier Club
NTC........ Nucleon Transport Code
NTCA ...... National Telephone Cooperative Association
NTCAVAL .... Notice of Availability
NTCC....... Nimbus Technical Control Center
NTCD ...... Newark Transportation Control Depot
NTD........ Non-Tight Door
NTD .... Nuclear Test Directorate (Air Force)
NTDC ...... Naval Training Devices Center
NT & DC..... Naval Training and Distribution Center
NTDO ...... Navy Technical Data Office (of the Office of Naval Material)
NTDPMA .... National Tool, Die and Precision Machining Association
NTDRA ..... National Tire Dealers and Retreaders Association
NTDS ...... Navy Tactical (or Technical) Data System (Computer system)
NTE........ National Teacher Examination
NTE........ Navy Technical Evaluation
NTE........ Navy Teletypewriter Exchange (Later, NTX)
NTE........ Neutron Transient Effect
NTE........ Not to Exceed (Aviation)
NTEA ...... National Tax Equality Association
NTEF ...... National Tennis Educational Foundation
NTER ...... Normalized Transmission Energy Requirement
NTF........ National Turkey Federation
NTF........ Navy Technological Forecast
NTF........ Nuclear Test Facility
NTFC...... National Television Film Council
NTFY....... Notify
NTH........ Norges Tekniske Hogskole
NTHP...... National Trust for Historic Preservation
NTI .... Naval Travel Instructions
NTI .... No Travel Involved (Military)
NTI .... Noise Transmission Impairment (Telephone)
NTIAC ..... Nondestructive Testing Information Analysis Center
NTID ...... National Technical Institute for the Deaf
NTIOC...... No Travel Involved for Officer Concerned (Military)
NTIP ...... National Turkey Improvement Plan
NTIR ...... Nontechnical Intelligence Report
NTIS ...... National Technical Information Service (Formerly, CFSTI) (Department of
             Commerce)
NTL........ National City Lines, Inc. (NYSE symbol)
NTL........ National Temperance League
NTL .... National Training Laboratories
NTL........ Neon Test Light
NTL .... New Tokaido Line
NTL........ No Time Lost (Military)
NTL........ Nuclear Technology Laboratory (Stanford University)
NTLA...... National Truck Leasing Association
NTLDO..... Navy Terminal Leave Disbursing Office
NTLF ...... Northern Troops and Landing Force
NTLS ...... National Truck Leasing Service (of National Truck Leasing Association)
NTM ...... Net Ton Mile (Shipping)
NTM ...... New Tribes Mission
NTMA ...... National Tank Manufacturers Association
NTMA ...... National Terrazzo and Mosaic Association
NTME ...... Naval Technical Missions in Europe
NTMICP .... National Topographic Map Inventory Control Point
NTMJ...... Naval Technical Missions in Japan
NTMP...... Nike Target Measurements Program
NTNF...... Norges Teknisk-Naturvitenskapelige Forskningsrad (Royal Norwegian
             Council for Scientific and Industrial Research)
NTO ...... Name To
NTO....... National Tenants Organization

NTO .... Naval Transport Officer
NTO .... Nitrogen Tetroxide
NTO .... No Try On (Purchaser did not have a fitting) (Merchandising slang)
NTO .... Not Taken Out (Insurance)
NTOMC ..... National Tung Oil Marketing Cooperative
NTOP...... New Technologies Opportunities Program (US government)
NTORS..... Naval Torpedo Station
NTP........ No Title Page (Bibliography)
NTP........ Nonzero Temperature Plasma
NTP........ Normal Temperature and Pressure
NTP........ Nuclear Test Plant
NTP .... Number of Theoretical Plates
NTP........ Numerical Tape Punch
NTPA ...... National Trotting Pony Association
NTPC...... National Technical Processing Center
NTPC...... National Temperance and Prohibition Council
NTPG ...... National Textile Processors Guild
NTPI ...... Navy Technical Proficiency Inspection
NTPL ...... Nut Plate
NTQ .... Nebennieren, Thymus, Quotient (Test) (Medicine)
NTR .... National General Corporation (NYSE symbol; later, NGC)
NTR .... National Tape Repository
NTR .... Navigational Time Reference
NTR .... Nernst-Thompson Rule
NTR........ No Traffic Reported (Aviation)
NTR........ Noise Temperature Ratio
NTR .... Nothing To Report
NTR .... Nuclear Test Reactor (Also known as GETR)
NTRA ...... National Trailer Rental Association
NTRC ...... National Tourism Review Commission
NTRS ...... Nationwide Trailer Rental System
NTS .... Narodno-Trudovoi Soyuz (National-Labor Federation) (Anti-Soviet
             organization in Western Europe)
NTS .... National Thespian Society
NTS .... National Traffic System (Amateur radio)
NTS .... National Transportation Survey (Department of Transportation)
NTS .... National Tulip Society
NTS .... Natsional'no-Trudovoi Soiuz
NTS .... Naval Target Subdivision (G-2, SHAEF)
NTS .... Naval Torpedo Station
NTS........ Naval Training School (or Station)
NTS........ Naval Transportation Service
NTS........ Navigator Training Squadrons (Air Force)
NTS........ Nevada Test Site (AEC)
NTS........ Nontariff Size
NTS .... Nordiska Tidningsutgivarnas Samarbetsnaemnd (Joint Council of Nordic
             Newspaper Publishers)
NTS .... North American Sugar Industries, Inc. (NYSE symbol) (Delisted)
NTS........ Not to Scale (Drafting)
NTS........ Nuclear Test Stage
NTSA ...... National Tay-Sachs Association (Later, NTSAD)
NTSA ...... National Technical Services Association
NTSA ...... National Traffic Safety Agency
NTSAD ..... National Tay-Sachs and Allied Diseases Association (Formerly, NTSA)
NTSB ...... National Traffic Safety Bureau
NTSB ...... National Transportation Safety Board (Department of Transportation)
NTSC ...... National Television System Committee
NTSC....... North Texas State College
NTSCH...... Naval Training School
NTSEA ..... National Trade Show Exhibitors Association
NTSR ...... National Tunis Sheep Registry
NTSRP...... Non-Technical Services Real Property
NTT........ New England Telephone & Telegraph Company (NYSE symbol)
NTTA ...... National Tobacco Tax Association
NTTC ...... National Tank Truck Carriers
NTTC....... Naval Technical Training Center
NTTCIW ..... National Technical Task Committee on Industrial Wastes
NTTF ...... Network Test and Training Facility
NTTR ...... Naval Torpedo Testing Range
NTTR ...... Nontactical Telecommunications Requirement (Army)
NTTTTI ...... National Truck Tank and Trailer Tank Institute
NTU........ Naval Training Unit
NTU........ Number of Transfer Units
NTUC ...... National Trade Union Congress (Singapore)
NTUC ..... National Trade Union Council (Hungary)
NTUC ..... National Trade Union Council for Human Rights
NTUC ..... Nigerian Trade Union Congress
NTUC ..... Nyasaland Trade Union Congress
NTVS....... Navy Television System
NTW ...... Nose, Tail, Waist (Aviation)
NTWA ...... National Turf Writers Association

NTWS . . . . . . Narrow Track While Scan
NTWS . . . . . . Nontrack While Scan
NTX . . . . National Teletypewriter Exchange
NTX . . . . Naval Teletypewriter Exchange (Formerly, NTE)
NTX . . . . "Night Letter" (Navy communications class)
NTY . . . . National Tea Company (NYSE symbol)
NTZ . . . . North Temperate Zone
NU . . . . Name Unknown
NU . . . . National Union
NU . . . . Nebraska University
NU . . . . Northeast Utilities (NYSE symbol)
NU . . . . Number Unobtainable
NUAAW . . . . . National Union of Agricultural and Allied Workers (British)
NUBE . . . . . . National Union of Bank Employees (Malaya)
NUC . . . . National Union Catalog (of American libraries)
NUC . . . . Navy Unit Commendation
NUC . . . . New University Conference
NUC . . . . Nuclear
NUCA . . . . . . National Utility Contractors' Association
NUCAL . . . . . National Union Catalog Author List
NUCDEF . . . . . Nuclear Defense
NUCDETS . . . . Nuclear Detonation Detection Reporting System
Nuc E . . . . . . Nuclear Engineer (Academic degree)
NUCLEX . . . . . Nuclear Industries Exhibition
NUCMC . . . . . National Union Catalog of Manuscript Collections (Library of Congress)
NUCOM . . . . . Numerical Contouring Mechanism
NUCP . . . . . . National Union of Czechoslovak Protestants in America and Canada
NUCREP . . . . . Nuclear Damage Report
NUCS . . . . . . National Union of Christian Schools
NUCSE . . . . . National Union of Czechoslovak Students in Exile
NUCW . . . . . . National Union of Commercial Workers (Malaya)
NUCWAR . . . . Nuclear War
NUCWPN . . . . Nuclear Weapon(s)
NUD . . . . Nebraska University Disease or N. Underdahl Disease (A disease of
        swine named both for the place where it was originally identified and
        for the person who isolated the causative agent)
NUDET . . . . . Nuclear Detonation
NUDETS . . . . . Nuclear Detection System (NORAD/ESD)
NUDETS . . . . . Nuclear Detonation Reporting System (Air Force)
NUEA . . . . . . National University Extension Association
NUERA . . . . . Nuclear Extended Range Aircraft (Proposed) (Air Force)
NUES . . . . . . National Union of Ethiopian Students
NUET . . . . . . National Union of Elementary Teachers (British)
NUF . . . . National Urban Fellows
NUF . . . . Natural Uranium Fuel
NUFFIC . . . . . Netherlands Universities Foundation for International Co-operation
NUFP . . . . . . Not Used for Production
NUGMW . . . . . National Union of General and Municipal Workers (British)
NUH . . . . Norske Ungdomsherberger
NUI . . . . National University of Ireland
NUIA . . . . . . National United Italian Associations
NUJ . . . . National Union of Journalists
NUL . . . . National Urban League
NULACE . . . . . Nuclear Liquid Air Cycle Engine
NULO . . . . . . NASA Unmanned Launch Operations
NULOR . . . . . Neuron Location and Ranging
NUM . . . . National Union Electric Co. (NYSE symbol)
NUMAR . . . . . Nuclear Magnetic Resonance
NUMEC . . . . . Nuclear Materials and Equipment Company
NUMIS . . . . . Navy Uniform Management Information System
NUNA . . . . . . Not Used on Next Assembly
NUOS . . . . . . Naval Underwater Ordnance Station
NUP . . . . National Union of Protestants
NUPAAWP . . . . National Union of Plantation, Agricultural and Allied Workers of the
        Philippines
NUPAD . . . . . Nuclear-Powered Active Detection System
NUPLEX . . . . . Nuclear Complex
NUPTE . . . . . National Union of Port Trust Employees (India)
NUPW . . . . . . National Union of Plantation Workers (Uganda)
NUPW . . . . . . National Union of Plantation Workers in Malaya
NUR . . . . Natchez, Urania & Ruston Railway Company (AAR code)
NUR . . . . Net Unduplicated Research
NUR . . . . Non-Uniformity Ratio
NURDC . . . . . Naval Undersea Research and Development Center (Formerly, NUWC)
NUS . . . . National Union of Seamen (British)
NUS . . . . National Union of Students (British)
NUS . . . . National Utility Service, Inc.
NUS . . . . Nuclear Utility Services
NUSAS . . . . . National Union of South African Students
NUSC . . . . . . Naval Underwater Systems Center (Formerly, NUSL)
NUSI . . . . . . National Union of Seamen of India

NUSL . . . . . . Naval Underwater Sound Laboratory (Later, NUSC)
N/USL . . . . . . Navy Underwater Sound Laboratory (Later, NUSC)
NUSOS . . . . . Nuclear Underwater Sound Source
NUSRL . . . . . Navy Underwater Sound Reference Laboratory
NUSUM . . . . . Numerical Summary Report (Military)
NUT . . . . National Union of Teachers (British)
NUTEX . . . . . Nuclear Tactical Exercise
NUUSFE . . . . . National Union of United States Forces Employees (South Korea)
NUWC . . . . . Naval Undersea Warfare Center (Later, NURDC)
NUWRES . . . . Naval Underwater Weapons Research and Engineering Station (Newport,
        Rhode Island)
NUWS . . . . . . Naval Underwater Weapons Station
NUWSEC . . . . Naval Underwater Weapons Systems Engineering Center
NV . . . . Naamloze Vennootschap (Limited company) (Netherlands)
NV . . . . Near Vertical (Aerospace)
NV . . . . Nevada
NV . . . . New Version (of the Bible)
NV . . . . Nonvintage (Wine)
NV . . . . Nonvoting (Business and trade) (Finance)
NV . . . . Nord-Viscount Corp.
NV . . . . North American Aviation, Inc. (Wall Street slang name: "Navy")
        (NYSE symbol; later, NR)
NV . . . . Nozzle Vanes
NVA . . . . National Variety Artists
NVA . . . . National Vista Alliance
NVA . . . . Negative Vorticity Advection (Aviation)
NvA . . . . Normalized Volt-Ampere
NVA . . . . North Vietnamese Army
NVAL . . . . . . Not Available
NVAS . . . . . . North Vietnamese Army Suspect
NVATA . . . . . National Vocational Agricultural Teachers' Association
NVB . . . . National Volunteer Brigade (South African equivalent of the British Home
        Guard)
NVB . . . . Night Vision Binocular
NVC . . . . Nederlandse Vakcentrale (Netherlands Trade Union Central)
NVCC . . . . . . Northern Virginia Community College
NVCZ . . . . . . N-Vinyl Carbazole
NVDA . . . . . . National Vitamin Distributors Association
NVE . . . . Non-Visual Eyepiece
NVF . . . . National Vitamin Foundation
NVF . . . . NVF Company (Formerly, National Vulcanized Fibre Company) (NYSE
        symbol)
NVG . . . . Night Vision Goggles
NVGA . . . . . . National Vocational Guidance Association
NVGI . . . . . . National Voluntary Groups Institute
NVL . . . . Night Vision Laboratory
NVM . . . . Nativity of the Virgin Mary
NVM . . . . Nonvolatile Matter
NVMS . . . . . . Night Visibility Measuring Set
NVN . . . . North Vietnam
NVOCC . . . . . Non-Vessel Owning Common Carrier (Transportation)
NVP . . . . Nevada Power Company (NYSE symbol)
NVPA . . . . . . National Visual Presentation Association
NVPO . . . . . . Nuclear Vehicle Projects Office (NASA)
NVR . . . . No Voltage Release (Electronics)
NVRS . . . . . . Numerical Value Rating System (Navy)
NVS . . . . Neutron Velocity Selector
NVS . . . . Night Vision System
NVSD . . . . . . National Vital Statistics Division (of OSG)
NVTS . . . . . . National Vocational Training Service
NVV . . . . Nederlands Verbond van Vakverenigingen (Netherlands Federation of
        Trade Unions)
NW . . . . Chicago & North Western Railway Company (NYSE symbol) (Delisted)
NW . . . . Naked Weight
nW . . . . Nanowatt
NW . . . . Net Weight
NW . . . . Neville and Winther's Acid
NW . . . . No Wind (Air) Position (Navigation)
NW . . . . Norfolk & Western Railway Company (AAR code)
NW . . . . North Wales
NW . . . . Northwest, Northwesterly, Northwestern
NW . . . . Northwest Airlines, Inc.
NW . . . . Nuclear Weapon
N & W . . . . . Norfolk and Western Railway Company
NWA . . . . . . National Wine Association
NWA . . . . . . Naval Warfare Analysis
NWA . . . . . . Naval Weapons Annex
NWA . . . . . . Northwest Airlines, Inc. (NYSE symbol)
NWAA . . . . . National Wheelchair Athletic Association
NWAAF . . . . . Northwest African Air Forces
NWAB . . . . . Necks With Any Boy (Slang)

NWAC . . . . . . National Weather Analysis Center (Air Force - Navy)
NWAC . . . . . . National Wheelchair Athletic Committee
NWAG . . . . . Naval Warfare Analysis Group
NWAHACA . . . National Warm Air Heating and Air Conditioning Association
NWAI . . . . Nuclear Weapons Acceptance Inspection
NWAIB . . . . . . Nuclear Weapon Accident Investigation Board
NWB . . . . National Wiring Bureau
NWB . . . . New War Department Building
NWB . . . . Non-Weight-Bearing
NWBA . . . . . . National Wheelchair Basketball Association
NWBC . . . . . . National Wooden Box Council
NWC . . . . National War College (DOD)
NWC . . . . National Warning Center (Civil Defense)
NWC . . . . National Water Commission
NWC . . . . National Waterfowl Council
NWC . . . . National Waterways Conference
NWC . . . . National Writers Club
NWC . . . . Naval War College
NWC . . . . Naval Weapons Center
NWC . . . . New World Club
NWC . . . . Northwest Cape
NWC . . . . Northwest College (Washington)
NWC . . . . Nuclear War Capability
NWCA . . . . . . National Water Carriers Association
NWCA . . . . . . National Woodcarvers Association
NWCA . . . . . . Navy Wives Clubs of America
NWCA . . . . . . Northwest Cherry Briners Association
NWCAA . . . . . National War College Alumni Association
NWCC . . . . . . Northwest Christian College (Oregon)
NWCCL . . . . . Naval Weapons Center Corona Laboratories
NWCG . . . . . . Nuclear Weapons Coordinating Group
NWCIEP . . . . . Nation-Wide Committee on Import-Export Policy
NWCME . . . . . National Winter Convention on Military Electronics (IEEE)
NWCR . . . . . . Nuclear Weapons Correction Report (Army)
NWCRB . . . . . Navy War Contracts Relief Board
NWD . . . . New World Dictionary
NWDA . . . . . . National Wholesale Druggists Association
NWDGA . . . . . National Wholesale Dry Goods Association
NWDS . . . . . . Navigation/Weapon Delivery System
NWDS . . . . . . Noah Worcester Dermatological Society
NWDS . . . . . . Number of Words
NWDSEN . . . . . Number of Words Per Entry
NWEB . . . . . . Northwestern Electricity Board (British)
NWEF . . . . Naval Weapons Evaluation Facility
NWEO . . . . . . Nuclear Weapon Employment Officer
NWER . . . . . . Nuclear Weapon Effects Research
NWET . . . . . . Nuclear Weapon Effects Test
NWF . . . . National War Formulary
NWF . . . . National War Fund
NWF . . . . National Wildlife Federation
NWF . . . . National Woman's Forum
NWF . . . . Naval Weapons Factory (Formerly, NGF)
NWF . . . . Naval Working Fund (Navy, Coast Guard)
NWF . . . . New World Foundation
NWF . . . . Numerical Weather Facility
NWFA . . . . . . National Wholesale Furniture Association
NWFI . . . . Non-Woven Fabrics Institute
NWFMA . . . . . Northwest Farm Managers Association
NWG . . . . National Wire Gauge
NWGA . . . . . . National Wool Growers Association
NWGA . . . . . . Northwest Guides Association
NWH . . . . Normal Working Hours
NWHA . . . . . . National Wholesale Hardware Association
NWI . . . . Netherlands West Indies
NWIP . . . . Naval Warfare Information Publication
NWIRP . . . . . . Naval Weapons Industrial Reserve Plant
NWIYRA . . . . . North West Intercollegiate Yacht Racing Association
NWJA . . . . . . National Wholesale Jewelers Association
NWL . . . . National Water Lift Company
NWL . . . . National Women's League of the United Synagogue of America
NWL . . . . Naval Weapons Laboratory
NWLB . . . . . . National War Labor Board (World War II)
NWLDYA . . . . National Wholesale Lumber Distributing Yard Association
NWMA . . . . . . National Woodwork Manufacturers Association
NWMC . . . . . . National Wool Marketing Corporation
NWMC . . . . . . Northwest Michigan College
NWMP . . . . . . North-West Mounted Police (now the RCMP) (Canada)
NWMS . . . . . . Nazarene World Missionary Society
NWN . . . . Non-White Noise
NWNSA . . . . . National Women's Neckwear and Scarf Association

NW-NW . . . . . No Work - No Woo (Slogan adopted by women war workers in Albina shipyards in Portland, Oregon, who agreed not to date men who were absent from work) (World War II)
NWO . . . . Non-Woven Oriented
NWO . . . . Nuclear Weapons Officer
NWP . . . . National Woman's Party
NWP . . . . Naval Warfare Publications
NWP . . . . Naval Weapons Plant
NWP . . . . Naval Weapons Publications
NWP . . . . North-West Provinces
NWP . . . . Northwestern Pacific R. R. (AAR code)
NWP . . . . Numerical Weather Prediction
NWPC . . . . . . National Women's Political Caucus
NWPCA . . . . . National Wooden Pallet and Container Association (Formerly, NWPMA)
NWPF . . . . . . National Water Purification Foundation
NWPMA . . . . . National Wooden Pallet Manufacturers Association (Later, NWPCA)
NWR . . . . Next Word Request
NWR . . . . North Western Reporter (Legal)
NWR . . . . Nuclear Weapons Report (Army)
NWRA . . . . . . National Wheel and Rim Association
NWRC . . . . . . National Weather Records Center (National Weather Service)
NWRC . . . . . . Naval Warfare Research Center
NWRC . . . . . . Naval Weapons Research Center
NWREL . . . . . Northwest Regional Educational Laboratory
NWRF . . . . . . Naval Weather Research Facility
NWRO . . . . . . National Welfare Rights Organization
NWS . . . . National Weather Service (Formerly, US Weather Bureau) (National Oceanic and Atmospheric Administration)
NWS . . . . National Winter Sports
NWS . . . . Naval Weapons Station
NWS . . . . Nimbus Weather Satellite
NWSA . . . . . . National Welding Supply Association
NWSA . . . . . . National Winter Sports Association
NWSA . . . . . . Nuclear Weapons Supply Annex
NWSB . . . . . . National Wage Stabilization Board (Superseded NWLB, 1945; terminated, 1947)
NWSC . . . . . . National Water Safety Congress
NWSC . . . . . . National Weather Satellite Center (Later, National Environmental Satellite Service)
NWSC . . . . . . National Weather Service Center
NWSD . . . . . . Naval Weather Service Division
NWSF . . . . . . Northwest Sea Frontier
NWSF . . . . . . Nuclear Weapons Storage Facility (Army)
NWSG . . . . . Nuclear Weapon Systems Surety Group (Army)
NWSO . . . . . . Naval Weapons Services Office
NWSO . . . . . . Naval Weather Service Office
NWSS . . . . . . Nuclear Weapons Support Section (Army)
NWSSG . . . . . Nuclear Weapons System Safety Group
NWSY . . . . . . Naval Weapons Station, Yorktown (Virginia)
NWT . . . . Nonwatertight
NWT . . . . Northwest Industries Inc. (NYSE symbol)
NWT . . . . Northwest Territories, Canada
NWT . . . . Northwestern Terminal R. R. (AAR code)
NWT . . . . Nylon Wire Tie
NWTA . . . . . . National Wool Trade Association
NWTI . . . . National Wood Tank Institute
NWT/S . . . . . . Nuclear Weapons Technician/Specialist
NWU . . . . Nebraska Wesleyan University
NWU . . . . Nose Wheel Up
NWUS . . . . . . Northwestern United States
NWWA . . . . . National Water Well Association
NWWC . . . . . National White Wyandotte Club
NX . . . . Not Exceeding
NXDO . . . . . . Nike-X Development Office (Army)
NXMIS . . . . . . Nike-X Management Information System
NXPM . . . . . . Nike-X Project Manager (Army)
NXPO . . . . . . Nike-X Program (or Project) Office
NXPRG . . . . . Nike-X Program Review Group (Army)
NXR . . . . Non-Crossing Rule
NXSM . . . . . . Nike-X System Manager (Army)
NXSMO . . . . . Nike-X System Manager's Office
NXSO . . . . . . Nike-X Support Office
NY . . . . Navy Yard
NY . . . . New Year
NY . . . . New York (City or State)
NY . . . . New York (Naval Shipyard)
NY . . . . New York Airways, Inc.
NY . . . . No Year
NY . . . . Nuclear Yield
NYA . . . . National Youth Administration (Terminated, 1943)
NYA . . . . National Youth Alliance

NYA . . . . New York Airways, Inc.
NYA . . . . Not Yet Answered
NYAB . . . . . . New York Air Brake Company
NYABIC . . . . . New York Association for Brain Injured Children
NYAIC . . . . . . New York Association of Industrial Communicators
NYAL. . . . . . . National Yugoslav Army of Liberation (World War II)
NYALR . . . . . . New Yorkers for Abortion Law Repeal
NYAM . . . . . . New York Academy of Medicine
NYAM . . . . . . New York Academy of Music
NYAMP . . . . . New York Advertising Media Planners
NYANA . . . . . New York Association for New Americans
NYAP. . . . . . . New York Assembly Program (Data processing)
NYAS . . . . . . New York Academy of Sciences
NYBA . . . . . . National Young Buddhist Association
NYBG . . . . . . New York Botanical Garden
NYBOS. . . . . . Navy Yard, Boston, Massachusetts
NYBT . . . . . . New York Board of Trade
NYC. . . . . Neighborhood Youth Corps (Department of Labor)
NYC . . . . New York Central R. R. (AAR code)
NYC . . . . New York City
NYCBAN. . . . . New York Center Beacon Alphanumerics (FAA)
NYCC . . . . . . New York Candy Club
NYCCC . . . . . New York City Community College
NYCDC . . . . . New York Curtain and Drapery Club
NYCE. . . . . . . New York Cocoa Exchange
NYCE . . . . . . New York Cotton Exchange
NYCER. . . . . . New York Conference on Electronic Reliability
NYCFMA . . . . New York Credit and Financial Management Association
NYCHA . . . . . New York Clearing House Association
NYCHARL. . . . Navy Yard, Charleston, South Carolina
NYCME . . . . . New York Clothing Manufacturers Exchange
NYCN . . . . . . New York Connecting R. R. (AAR code)
NYCSA . . . . . New York Coat & Suit Association
NYCSA . . . . . New York College Stores Association
NYCSE. . . . . . New York Coffee and Sugar Exchange
NYCSG . . . . . New York Constitution Study Group
NYC & STL . . . New York, Chicago and St. Louis Railroad Company
NYCTCG . . . . New York Cold Type Composition Group
NYD . . . . Navy Yard
NYD . . . . New York Dock Railway (AAR code)
NYD . . . . Not Yet Dead (Humorous variant of Not Yet Diagnosed)
NYD . . . . Not Yet Diagnosed (Medicine)
NYDCC . . . . . New York Drama Critics Circle
NYEWW . . . . New York Exchange for Woman's Work
NYF. . . . . New York Foundation
NYFBT . . . . . . New York Film Board of Trade
NYFC . . . . . . New York Film Critics
NYFD . . . . . . New York Fashion Designers
NYFFFBA . . . . New York Foreign Freight Forwarders and Brokers Association
NYFWA . . . . . New York Financial Writers Association
NYGBS . . . . . New York Genealogical and Biographical Society
NYGC . . . . . . New York Governor's Conference
NYGJB. . . . . . New York Guild for Jewish Blind
NYH . . . . New York & Honduras Rosario Mining Co. (NYSE symbol)
NYHS . . . . . . New York Historical Society
NYHT. . . . . . . New York Herald Tribune (Defunct newspaper)
NYIDA . . . . . New York Importers and Distillers Association
NYIT . . . . New York Institute of Technology
NYJ . . . . National Young Judaea
NYK . . . . New York (City)
NYK . . . . Nippon Yusen Kaisha (Japanese steamship company)
NYKGRP . . . . New York Group (Navy)
NYLB. . . . . . . New York & Long Branch R. R. (AAR code)
NYLS . . . . . . New York Law School
NYLSMA. . . . . New York Lamp and Shade Manufacturers Association
NYMA . . . . . New York City Metropolitan Area

NYMA . . . . . . New York Mounters Association
NYMC . . . . . . New York Medical College
NYME . . . . . . New York Mercantile Exchange
NYMI. . . . . . . Navy Yard, Mare Island, California
NYNH & H . . . New York, New Haven and Hartford Railroad Company
NYNOR . . . . . Navy Yard, Norfolk, Virginia
NYNS. . . . . . . New York Naval Shipyards
NYNYK . . . . . Navy Yard, New York, New York
NYO . . . . New York Operations (AEC)
NYOSL . . . . . New York Ocean Science Laboratory
NYO & W. . . . New York, Ontario and Western Railway Company
NYP . . . . Not Yet Published
NYPA. . . . . . . New York Port Authority
NYPC . . . . . . New York Pigment Club
NYPD. . . . . . . New York Police Department (Initialism also used as title of TV series)
NYPE . . . . . . New York Port of Embarkation
NYPE . . . . . . New York Produce Exchange
NYPFO . . . . . New York Air Force Procurement Field Office
NYPH. . . . . . . Navy Yard, Pearl Harbor, Hawaii
NYPHIL . . . . . Navy Yard, Philadelphia, Pennsylvania
NYPL . . . . . . New York Public Library
NYPORT . . . . Navy Yard, Portsmouth, New Hampshire
NYPS . . . . . . National Yellow Pages Service
NYPS. . . . . . . Navy Yard, Puget Sound (Bremerton), Washington
NYQ . . . . New York Quarterly (A publication)
NYR. . . . . New York Review (of Books)
NYR. . . . . Not Yet Reported (Air Force)
NYR. . . . . Not Yet Returned (Military)
NYRB . . . . . . New York Review of Books (A publication)
NYRMA . . . . . New York Raincoat Manufacturers Association
NYS . . . . New York Shavians
NYS. . . . . New York Shipbuilding Company
NYSA . . . . . New York Shipping Association
NYSC. . . . . . . New York Shipbuilding Corporation
NYSCS . . . . . New York State Colonization Society
NYSDA . . . . . New York Security Dealers Association
NYSE . . . . . . New York Stock Exchange
NYSF . . . . . . National Youth Science Foundation
NYSIIS . . . . . New York State Identification and Intelligence System
NYSSA . . . . . New York Society of Security Analysts
NYSW. . . . . . New York, Susquehanna & Western R. R. (AAR code)
NYT. . . . . New York Testing Laboratories, Inc.
NYT . . . . The New York Times
NYTCL . . . . . New York Temperance Civic League
NYTS . . . . . . New York Theological Seminary
NYU . . . . New York University
NYWASH . . . . Navy Yard, Washington, DC (Obsolete)
NYZP. . . . . . . New York Zoological Park
NYZS. . . . . . . New York Zoological Society
NZ . . . . New Zealand
NZ . . . . New Zealand National Airways Corporation
N-Z. . . . . Nike-Zeus (Missiles)
NZA . . . . Niobium Zinc Alloy
NZB. . . . . New Zealand Black (Mice hybrids)
NZD. . . . . New Zealand Division
NZE. . . . . North Zenith East
NZEF. . . . . . . New Zealand Expeditionary Force
NZF. . . . . Near Zero Field
NZFL . . . . . . New Zealand Federation of Labor
NZG . . . . Near Zero Gravity
NZLO . . . . . . New Zealand Liaison Officer
NZNB . . . . . . New Zealand Naval Board (Wellington)
NZOI. . . . . . . New Zealand Oceanographic Institute
NZP. . . . . National Zoological Park (Smithsonian Institution)
NZSEAFRON . . New Zealand Sea Frontier
NZW . . . . New Zealand White (Mice hybrids)

O

O . . . . Cleared to the Outer Marker (Aviation)
O . . . . Hora (Hour)
O . . . . Horizontal Opposed (Aircraft engine)
O. . . . . New Orleans (Louisiana) (Mint mark, when appearing on US coins)
O. . . . . Oberst (Colonel) (German military - World War II)
O . . . . Obiit (Died)
O . . . . Object
O . . . . Oblast (Governmental subdivision in USSR corresponding to a province or state)
O . . . . Observation Aircraft (Designation for all US military aircraft)
O . . . . Occasional (Concerning occurrence of species)
O . . . . Occident or Occidental
O . . . . Ocean (Maps and charts)
O . . . . Octavo (Book from 20 to 25 centimeters in height)
O . . . . October
O . . . . Oculus (Eye)
O . . . . Off
O . . . . Offered (NYSE symbol)
O . . . . Office(r)
O . . . . Office of Operations (Coast Guard)
O . . . . Official
O . . . . Ohio
O . . . . Ohm (Electricity)
O . . . . Oil
O . . . . Old
O . . . . Only
O . . . . Open (Dancing position)
O . . . . Opening
O . . . . Operation
O . . . . Opium (Slang)
O . . . . Optimus (Best)
O . . . . Oral(ly) (Medicine)
O . . . . Orange (Maps and charts)
O . . . . Order
O . . . . Ordinary
O . . . . Ordinis (By the Order of)
O . . . . Ordnance
O. . . . . Ordonnanzoffizier (Special-missions staff officer) (German military - World War II)
O . . . . Organized Naval Reserve
O . . . . Oriental
O . . . . Original
o . . . . Ortho (Chemistry)
O . . . . Os (Bone)
O . . . . Osphradium
O . . . . Outfield (Baseball)
O . . . . Outlet
O . . . . Over
O . . . . Overcast (Nautical)
O . . . . Owner
O . . . . Oxygen (Chemical element)
O1 . . . . Organized Naval Reserve Seagoing
O2 . . . . Organized Naval Reserve Aviation
1-O . . . . Selective Service Class (for Conscientious Objector Available for Alternate Service Contributing to Maintenance of National Health, Safety, or Interest)
OA . . . . Oblate Sisters of the Assumption (Roman Catholic religious order)
OA . . . . Obligation Authority (Military)
OA . . . . Office of the Administrator
OA . . . . Office of Applications (NASA)
OA. . . . . Omniantenna
OA . . . . On or About (Military)
OA . . . . On Account (Business and trade)

OA . . . . On Account of
OA . . . . Open Account
OA . . . . Operating Authorization
OA . . . . Operations Analysis
OA . . . . Orbital Assembly
OA . . . . Order of the Alhambra
OA . . . . Order of the Arrow
OA . . . . Oro Americano (American Gold) (Business and trade) (Spain)
OA . . . . Osborne Association
OA . . . . Other Articles
OA. . . . . Output Amplitude
OA. . . . . Output Axis
OA . . . . Over-All (Technical drawings)
OA . . . . Overhead Approach (Aviation)
OA . . . . Overtime Authorization
O/A . . . . On or About (Military)
O/A . . . . On Account
O/A . . . . Our Account (Business and trade)
O/A . . . . Outer Anchorage (Navigation)
O & A (Date) . . Oath and Acceptance Date (Date from which a military officer's commissioned service runs)
O of A . . . . . Order of Amaranth
OAA . . . . o-Aminoacetanilide (Chemical)
OAA . . . . Office of Aviation Affairs (Army)
OAA . . . . Old-Age Assistance (HEW)
OAA. . . . . Organisation des Nations Unies pour l'Alimentation et l'Agriculture (Food and Agriculture Organization of the United Nations)
OAA . . . . Oxaloacetic (or Oxalacetic) Acid
OAAA . . . . . . Outdoor Advertising Association of America
OAARD. . . . . . Office of the Assistant Administrator for Research and Development (HEW)
OAASA . . . . . Office of the Administrative Assistant to the Secretary of the Army
OAASN . . . . . Office of the Administrative Assistant to the Secretary of the Navy
OAB. . . . . Old-Age Benefits
OAB . . . . Olive Advisory Board
OAB. . . . . Overseas Affairs Branch (Department of the Army)
OABETA . . . . . Office Appliance and Business Equipment Trades Association
OAC . . . . Oceanic Area Control (Aviation)
OAC . . . . Operating Agency Code
OAC . . . . Operations Analysis Center
OAC . . . . Operations Analysis Chief (Air Force)
OAC . . . . Optimal Automatic Control
OAC . . . . Ordnance Ammunition Command (Army) (Merged with Munitions Command)
OAC . . . . Overseas Automotive Club
OACC . . . . . . Oceanic Area Control Centre
OACD . . . . . . Office of Agricultural and Chemical Development (of TVA)
OACETT . . . . . Ontario Association of Certified Engineering Technicians and Technologists
OACI . . . . Organisation de l'Aviation Civile Internationale (International Civil Aviation Organization)
OACS. . . . . . . Office of Assistant Chief of Staff
OACSC-E . . . . Office of the Assistant Chief of Staff for Communications-Electronics
OACSFOR . . . Office of the Assistant Chief of Staff for Force Development (Army)
OACSI . . . . . . Office of the Assistant Chief of Staff for Intelligence (Army)
OACT. . . . . . . Ormone Adrenocorticotropina (Medicine)
OAD . . . . Office of Administration
OAD . . . . Officers' Accounts Division (Navy)
OAD . . . . Officers' Assignment Division, The Adjutant General's Office (Army)
OAD . . . . Opening of Anterior Digestive (Gland)
OAD . . . . Operational Active Data (Navy)
OAD . . . . Operational Availability Data (Military)
OAD . . . . Operations Analysis Division

OADMS ..... Office of Automated Data Management Services (General Services Administration)
OAE .... Old Antarctic Explorer
OAE .... Optical Alignment Equipment
OAES ...... Ohio Agricultural Experimental Station
OAF........ Occidentale Afrique Francaise (French West Africa)
OAF........ Officer Assignment Folder (Military)
OAF........ Oxygen Alternate Fill
OAFB ...... Offutt Air Force Base
OAFC....... Office of Air Force Chaplains
OAFIE ...... Office of Armed Forces Information and Education
OAG .... Oblique Anterior Gauche (Left Anterior Oblique Position) (Medicine)
OAG .... Office of the Adjutant General
OAG .... Official Airline Guide (Publication)
OAH .... Organization of American Historians
OAH .... Overhead Air Hoist
OAI........ Office of Aeronautical Intelligence
OAIAC..... Operational Area Industry Advisory Committee (Civil Defense)
OAIDE ...... Operational Assistance and Instructive Data Equipment
OAIP .... Organic Ablative Insulative Plastic
OAIS ...... Opinion, Attitude, and Interest Survey (Testing)
OAK .... Oakland (California) (Airport symbol)
OAL .... Optical Alignment Equipment
OAL .... Ordnance Aerophysics Laboratory
OAL .... Ozark Air Lines, Inc.
OALMA ..... Orthopedic Appliance and Limb Manufacturers Association
OAM .... Office of Aerospace Medicine (NASA)
OAM .... Office of Automation and Manpower (Labor Department) (Also see OMAT)
OAM .... Orthopedic Appliance Mechanic (Navy)
OAMA ...... Ogden Air Material Area
OAMCE ..... Organization Africaine et Malgache de Cooperation Economique (Afro-Malagasy Organization for Economic Cooperation) (Later, Common Afro-Malagasy Organization)
OAME...... Orbital Attitude and Maneuvering Electronics
OAMP ...... Optical Analog Matrix Processing
OAMPI..... Office Africain et Malgache de la Propriete Industrielle
OAMS...... Orbit Attitude and Maneuvering System (NASA)
OANDOS .... Ordnance and Ordnance Stores (Coast Guard)
OANDR ..... Operation and Regulation
OANFE..... Operational Aircraft Not Fully Equipped
OAO .... One and Only (A favorite girl or boy friend)
OAO .... Orbiting Astronomical Observatory (NASA)
OAOI....... On and Off Instruments (Aviation)
OAP........ Observation Amphibian Plane (Coast Guard)
OAP........ Office of Aerial Phenomena (Air Force)
OAP........ Office of Air Programs (Environmental Protection Agency)
OAP .... Office of Aircraft Production (World War II)
OAP........ Office of Antarctic Programs (National Science Foundation)
OAP........ Office of Atomic Programs (DOD)
OAP........ Offset Aiming Point
OAP .... Old Age Pension(s)
OAP........ Organic Ablative Plastic
OAP........ Outlet Absolute Pressure
OAPC....... Office of Alien Property Custodian (World War II)
OAPEC ..... Organization of Arab Petroleum Exporting Countries
OAPM ...... Optimal Amplitude and Phase Modulation
OAR........ Office of Aerospace Research (Air Force)
OAR........ Office of Analysis and Review (Army, Navy)
OAR........ Operations Analysis Report
OAR .... Optical Angle Readout
OAR ...... Optical Automatic Ranging
OAR........ ORDALT (Ordnance Alteration) Accomplishment Requirement
OAR .... Ordnance Accomplishment Requirement (Navy)
OAR........ Ordnance Allowance Report (Navy)
OAR........ Ordnance Alternation Requirements
OAR........ Organized Air Reserve
OAR ...... Overhaul and Repair
OAR ...... Overtime Authorization Request
OARAC..... Office of Air Research Automatic Computer
OARB...... Oakland Army Base
OARC ..... Office of Air Research Calculator
OARC....... Ordinary Administrative Radio Conference
OARP .... Office of Advanced Research Programs (NASA) (Now, Office of Advanced Research and Technology)
OARS ...... Ocean Area Reconnaissance Satellite (Antisubmarine warfare)
OART....... Oakland Army Terminal
OART ...... Office of Advanced Research and Technology (NASA)
OAS....... Occupational Aspiration Scale (Education)
OAS ...... Occupied Areas Section (Military government)
OAS ...... Office for Advance Studies
OAS........ Office of the Assistant Secretary (Defense) (Navy)

OAS....... Ohio Academy of Science
OAS........ Old-Age Security
OAS........ Olley Air Service, Ltd.
OAS ...... On Active Service
OAS ...... Organisation de l'Armee Secrete (Secret Army Organization) (Algeria and metropolitan France)
OAS........ Organization of American States (Also see OEA)
OAS ...... Organization of Arab Students in the USA & Canada
OAS ...... Output Amplitude Stability
OA & S ... Other Arms and Services (Military)
OASD ...... Office of the Assistant Secretary of Defense (Comptroller)
OASDHI ..... Old-Age, Survivors, Disability, and Health Insurance (Programs) (Social Security Administration)
OASDI ...... Old-Age and Survivors Disability Insurance Program (of the Social Security Act)
OASF ...... Orbiting Astronomical Support Facility
OASI ...... Old-Age and Survivors Insurance
OASIS ...... Ocean All-Source Information System
OASMS..... Ordnance Ammunition Surveillance and Maintenance School
OASN ...... Office of the Assistant Secretary of the Navy
OASN(FM) ... Office of the Assistant Secretary of the Navy for Financial Management
OASN(I & L) .. Office of the Assistant Secretary of the Navy for Installations and Logistics
OASN(P & RF) .. Office of the Assistant Secretary of the Navy for Personnel and Reserve Force
OASN(R & D) .. Office of the Assistant Secretary of the Navy for Research and Development
OASP ...... Organic Acid Soluble Phosphorus
OASPL ...... Overall Sound Pressure Level
OASR ...... Office of Aeronautical and Space Research (NASA) (Now, Office of Advanced Research and Technology)
OASV....... Orbital Assembly Support Vehicle
OASYS ..... Order Allocation System
OAT .... Office for Advanced Technology (Air Force)
OAT ...... Operating Acceptance Test
OAT ...... Operating Ambient Temperature
OAT ...... Optical Adaptive Technique
OAT....... Outside Air Temperature (Aviation)
OAT ...... Overall Test
OAT....... Quaker Oats Company (NYSE symbol)
OATC ..... Oceanic Air Traffic Center
OATC...... Overseas Air Traffic Control
OATS ..... Office of Air Transportation Security (FAA)
OATS ..... Optimum Aerial Target Sensor
OATS ..... Original Article Tear Sheets (A publication)
OATS ..... Overall Test Set
OAU ...... Organization of African Unity
OAV ...... Operational Aerospace Vehicle
OAWR...... Office of Atmospheric Water Resources (Bureau of Reclamation)
OAYR...... Outstanding Airman of the Year Ribbon
OB .... Obstetrician, Obstetrics (Medicine)
OB .... Ocean Bottom
OB........ Octave Band
OB......... The Old Bailey (London court)
OB......... Old Boy (Communications operators' colloquialism)
OB......... Ombudsman for Business (Department of Commerce)
OB .... On Board
OB......... Opening of Books
OB......... Operating Base (Navy)
OB .... Operating Budget
OB......... Operational Base (Navy)
OB .... Order of Battle
OB........ Ordered Back
OB......... Ordnance Battalion (Navy)
OB......... Ordnance Board (Navy)
OB......... Ortsbatterie (Local battery) (German military - World War II)
OB......... Outboard
OB .... Output Buffer (Air Force)
OB......... Outside Broadcasts
OB........ Outward Bound
OB......... Overboard
OBA ...... Octave Band Analyzer
OBA ...... Office of Business Administration (NASA) (Later, Office of Administration)
OBA ...... Oxygen Breathing Apparatus
OBADRS.... Octave Band Automatic Data Reduction System
OBAN...... Operating Budget Account Number (Air Force)
OBAWS..... On-Board Aircraft Weighing System
OBB .... Old Battleship (Navy)
OBB .... Operation Better Block
OBC....... On-Board Checkout (Aircraft)
OBC ...... Ouachita Baptist College (Arkansas)

OBC	Outboard Boating Club of America
OBC	Oxide-Coated Brush Cathode
OBCE	On-Board Check-Out Equipment
OBD	Omnibearing-Distance
OBD	Operational Base Development
OBE	Office of Business Economics (Department of Commerce)
OBE	Officer (of the Order) of the British Empire
OBE	Overcome (or Overtaken) by Events
OBEM	One-Boson Exchange Model
OBEP	One-Boson Exchange Potential
OBES	Orthonormal Basis of an Error Space (Statistics)
OBF	Octave Band Filter
OBF	Operational Base Facility
OBFS	Octave Band Filter Set
OBGS	Orbital Bombardment Guidance System
OB-GYN	Obstetrics-Gynecology (Medicine)
OBH	Oil Bath Heater
OBH	Old Berkeley Hunt
OBH	Old Berkshire Hounds
OBI	Obligated Involuntary Officer (Military)
OBI	Office of Basic Instrumentation (National Bureau of Standards)
OBI	Omnibearing Indicator (Radio)
OBIFCO	On-Board In-Flight Checkout
OBINXTO	Obiit in Christo (Died in Christ)
OBIS	Optimum Burn-In Screening
OBJ	Object
OBJ	Operation Buster-Jangle (Atomic weapons testing)
OBL	Operational Base Launch (Air Force)
OBL	Order Bill of Lading (Shipping)
OBLAUTH	Obligation Authority (Army)
OBLN	Obligation
OBM	Oriental Boat Mission
OBMA	Outboard Boat Manufacturers Association
OBMC	Officers' Basic Military Corps (Air Force)
OBN	Office of Biochemical Nomenclature (NAS-NRC)
OBNR	Oil Burner Route (Aviation)
OBNREN	Oil Burner Entry Point (Aviation)
OBNREX	Oil Burner Exit Point (Aviation)
OBO	Official Business Only
OBO	Order By Order
OBO	Ore-Bulk-Oil (Supertanker)
OBOE	Observed Bombing of Enemy
OBP	Oil Breather Pressure
OBP	On-Base Percentage (Baseball)
OBP	On Board Processor
OBP	Open Break Position (Dancing)
OBP	Outer (Edge of) Basal Piece
OBPI	Organisasi Buruh Perkebunan Indonesia (Estate Workers' Union of Indonesia)
OBR	Office of Budgets and Reports
OBR	Overseas Business Reports (Department of Commerce)
OBS	Observed (Observer; Observation)
OBS	Obsolete (or Obsolescent)
OBS	Ocean Bottom Station
OBS	Office of Boating Safety (Department of Transportation)
OBS	Official Bulletin Station (Amateur radio)
OBS	Omnibearing Selector (Radio)
OBS	Optical Beam Scanner
OBS	Optical Beam Steering
OBS	Orbital Bombardment System
OBSD	Optical Beam Steering Device
OBSI	Organisasi Buruh Seluruh Indonesia (Plantation Workers' Union of Indonesia)
OBSN	Observation
OBSP	Obiit sine Prole (Died without Issue)
OBSPL	Octave Band Sound Pressure Level
OBSRON	Observation Squadron
OBSS	Ocean Bottom Scanning SONAR
OBST	Obstacle
OBST	Obstruction
OBU	Oklahoma Baptist University
OBV	Obligated Volunteer Officer (Military)
OBV	Ocean Boarding Vessel
OBW	Observation Window
OC	Object Class (Military)
OC	Observer Corps (Became ROC, 1941) (British)
OC	Obstruction Chart
OC	Odor Control
OC	Of Course
OC	Office of Censorship
OC	Office Copy

OC	Officer Candidate (Army)
OC	Officer Commanding (Marine Corps)
OC	Officers' Cook
OC	Official Classification
OC	Oil Cooler
OC	Old Carthusian
OC	Old Catholic
OC	Old Crop
OC	On Cards
OC	On Center (Technical drawings)
OC	On Course (Navigation)
OC	Only Child
OC	Open Circuit
OC	Open Contract
OC	Open Cover
OC	Operating Characteristic
OC	Operation Crossroads (Atomic weapons testing)
OC	Operational Capability
OC	Operations Center (Military)
OC	Operations Control
OC	Opere Citato (In the Work Cited)
OC	Order Canceled
OC	Order Card
OC	Order of Cistercians (Roman Catholic religious order)
OC	Ordo Charitatis (Fathers of the Order of Charity) (Roman Catholic religious order)
OC	Original Cover
OC	Outing Club
OC	Outlet Contact
OC	Output Computer
OC	Overcharge (Merchandising slang)
OC	Overcurrent
OC	Overseas Commands (Air Force)
OC	Oxygen Consumed
O/C	Object Classification
O/C	Officer-in-Charge (Army)
O/C	Old Charter (Business and trade)
O/C	Open Charter (Business and trade)
O/C	Over-the-Counter (Also, OTC)
O/C	Overcharge
O & C	Onset and Course (of a disease) (Medicine)
O & C	Operation and Checkout
O in C	Officer-in-Charge
OCA	Oceanic Control Area (ICAO)
OCA	Office de Commercialisation Agricole (Senegal)
OCA	Office, Comptroller of the Army
OCA	Office of Computing Activities (National Science Foundation)
OCA	Office of Consumer Affairs (US Postal Service ombudsman)
OCA	Ontario College of Agriculture
OCA	Ontario College of Art
OCA	Operation Crossroads Africa
OCA	Operational Control Authority
OCA	Organization of the Cooperatives of America
OCA	Osteopathic Cranial Association
OCA	Oxychloride Cement Association
OCAA	Oklahoma City-Ada-Atoka Railway Company (AAR code)
OCAC	Oceanic Air Traffic Control
OCAC	Office, Chief of Air Corps
OCAFF	Office, Chief of Army Field Forces
OCAL	The Oxford Companion to American Literature
OCAM	Organisation Commune Africaine et Malagache (Common Afro-Malagasy Organization)
OCAMA	Oklahoma City Air Materiel Area
OCAR	Office of the Chief, Army Reserve
OCAS	Office of Carrier Accounts and Statistics (of CAB)
OCAS	Officer-in-Charge of Armament Supply
OCAS	Ordnance Configuration Accounting System (Navy)
OCAS	Organization of Central American States
OCAU	Office de Cooperation et d'Accueil Universitaire (France)
OCAW	Oil, Chemical and Atomic Workers International Union
OCB	Officer Career Brief (Résumé) (Military)
OCB	Oil Circuit Breaker
OCB	Operations Coordination Board (National Security Council)
OCB	Output Current Booster
OCB	Override Control Bits
OCC	Object Class Code
OCC	Occupation
OCC	Office of the Comptroller of the Currency (Department of the Treasury)
OCC	Officers' Chief Cook
OCC	Ohio College of Chiropody
OCC	Operations Control Center

OCC . . . . Operations Control Console
OCC . . . . Orange Coast College (California) (Now OCJC)
OCC . . . . Ordo Carmelitarum Calceatorum (Carmelites)
OCC . . . . Organic Carbon Cycle
O & CC . . . . . Order and Change Control
OCCA . . . . . . Office, Chief of Civil Affairs
OCCA . . . . . . Officer(s) in Charge of Civilian Affairs (in newly occupied countries) (Army) (World War II)
OCCA . . . . . . Oil and Colour Chemists' Association
OCCA . . . . . . Overseas Communications Cooperation Association
OCCB . . . . . . Operational Configuration Control Board
OCC-E . . . . . . Office of the Chief of Communications-Electronics (Army)
OCCGERMDL . . Army of Occupation of Germany Medal
OC of Ch . . . . Office, Chief of Chaplains (Army)
OCCI . . . . Olympia Circulation Company, Incorporated
OCCIS . . . . . . Operational Command and Control Intelligence System (Army)
OCCM . . . . . . Office of Commercial Communications Management
OCCMDL . . . . Army of Occupation Medal
OCCMED . . . . Occupational Medicine (Army)
OCCMLC . . . . Office, Chief, Chemical Corps (Army)
OCCMLO . . . . Office, Chief Chemical Officer (Army)
OCCO . . . . . . Office of the Chief Chemical Officer
OCCS . . . . Operational Command and Control System (Army)
OCCS . . . . Optical Contrast Contour Seeker
OCCULT . . . . . Ordered Computer Collation of Unprepared Literary Texts
OCCWC . . . . . Office of Chief of Counsel, War Crimes (Allied German Occupation Forces)
OCCWS . . . . . Office of the Chief of Chemical Warfare Service
OCD . . . . Office of Child Development (HEW)
OCD . . . . Office of Civilian Defense (Within Office of Emergency Management) (World War II)
OCD . . . . Office of Community Development (HUD)
OCD . . . . Operational Capability Date
OCD . . . . Ordnance Classification Defect (Navy)
OCD . . . . Ordo Carmelitarum Discalceatorum (Discalced, or barefoot, Carmelites) (Roman Catholic religious order)
OCD . . . . Oxford Classical Dictionary
OCDE . . . . Organisation de Cooperation et de Developpement Economiques (Organization for Economic Cooperation and Development)
OCDM . . . . . . Office of Civil and Defense Mobilization (Merged with Office of Emergency Planning)
OCDMS . . . . . On-Board Check-Out and Data Management System
OCDR . . . . . . Office of Collateral Development Responsibility
OCDRE . . . . . . Organic-Cooled Deuterium Reactor Experiment
OCE . . . . . . Office, Chief of Engineers (Army)
OCE . . . . Office de Commercialisation et d' Exportation (Morocco)
OCE . . . . Office of Cultural Exchange (Department of State)
OCE . . . . Officer Conducting the Exercise (Navy, Coast Guard)
OCE . . . . Officer Corps Engineers
OCE . . . . Ontario College of Education
OCE . . . . Oregon, California & Eastern Railway Company (AAR code)
OCE . . . . Oregon College of Education
OCE . . . . Oscillating Current Element
OCEA . . . . . . OMGUS (Office of Military Government, United States) Civilian Employees Association
OCEAN . . . . . . Oceanographic Coordination, Evaluation and Analysis Network
OCEANAV . . . Oceanographer of the Navy
OCF . . . . Office, Chief of Finance (Military)
OCF . . . . Open Channel Flow
OCF . . . . Owens-Corning Fiberglas Corporation (NYSE symbol)
OC of F . . . . . Office of the Chief of Finance (Army)
OCF & A . . . . Office, Chief of Finance and Accounting (Army)
OCFP . . . . . . Office of Commercial and Financial Policy (Department of Commerce)
OCG . . . . Oxygen Consumption Gauge
OCH . . . . Outpatient Clinic (Hospital) (Veterans Administration)
OCHAMPUS . . . Office for the Civilian Health and Medical Program of the Uniformed Services
OCI . . . . Office of Computer Information (National Bureau of Standards)
OCI . . . . Outpatient Clinic (Independent) (Veterans Administration)
OCIAA . . . . . . Office of Coordinator of Inter-American Affairs (World War II)
OCIC . . . . Office Catholique International du Cinema (International Catholic Film Office)
OCINFO . . . . . Office of the Chief of Information (Military)
OCJC . . . . Orange Coast Junior College (California)
OCL . . . . Obstruction Clearance Limit (Aviation)
OCL . . . . Old Light Cruiser (Navy symbol)
OCL . . . . Operational Control Level
OCL . . . . Ordnance Circular Letter
OCL . . . . Outgoing Correspondence Log
OCL . . . . Overhaul Cycle Limit

OCLALAV . . . . Organisation Commune de Lutte Antiacridienne et de Lutte Antiaviaire (Joint Anti-Locust and Anti-Avarian Organization) (Formerly, OCLAV)
OCLAV . . . . . . Organisation Commune de Lutte Antiaviaire (Joint Anti-Avarian Organization) (Later, OCLALAV)
OCLL . . . . Office, Chief of Legislative Liaison
OCLUS . . . . . . Outside Continental Limits of United States
OCM . . . . Ordnance Committee Meeting
OCM . . . . Ordo Constantini Magni (International Constantinian Order)
OCM . . . . Organisation Civile et Militaire
OCM . . . . Origin of Columellar Muscle
OCMH . . . . . . Office of the Chief of Military History
OCMI . . . . Officer in Charge, United States Coast Guard Marine Inspection Office
OCMM . . . . . . Office of Civilian Manpower Management (Navy)
OCMODL . . . . Operating Cost Model
OCMS . . . . . . Onboard and Checkout Monitoring System (Aerospace)
OCMS . . . . . . Ordnance Command Management System
OCMS . . . . . . Ordnance Committee Meeting Standards
OCMU . . . . . . Ocmulgee National Monument
OCN . . . . Operation Completion Notice
OCN . . . . Organization Change Notice
OC-N . . . . Office of the Comptroller, Navy
OCNGA . . . . . Officer in Charge of National Guard Affairs
OCNO . . . . . . Office, Chief of Naval Operations
OCNPR . . . . . . Operation and Conservation of Naval Petroleum Reserves (Budget appropriation title)
OCO . . . . Office, Chief of Ordnance (Army)
OCO . . . . Office of Civil Operations (Vietnam)
OCO . . . . Open-Close-Open (Technical drawings)
OCO . . . . Operational Capability Objectives (Army)
OCO . . . . Operational Checkout
OCO . . . . Ordnance Corps Order
OCOFF . . . . . . Office of the Chief of Finance
OCOFT . . . . . Office of the Chief of Transportation (Army)
OCOMS . . . . . Office of Community Services
OCON . . . . . . Orders for Correction of Non-Conformance (Navy)
OCONUS . . . . Outside Continental United States
OCOO . . . . . . Osteopathic College of Ophthalmology and Otorhinolaryngology
OCORD . . . . Office, Chief of Ordnance (Army)
OC of ORD . . . Office, Chief of Ordnance (Army)
OCOT . . . . . . Office, Chief of Transportation (Military)
OCP . . . . Ocean Culture Product
OCP . . . . Office Cherifien des Phosphates
OCP . . . . Office of Civilian Personnel
OCP . . . . Ontario College of Pharmacy
OCP . . . . Operating Control Procedure (Military)
OCP . . . . Operations Control Plan
OCP . . . . Out of Commission for Parts
OCP . . . . Overseas Communication Project
OCPR . . . . . . Office of Collateral Policy Responsibility
OCQ . . . . Oneida Ltd. (NYSE symbol)
OCQM . . . . . . Office of Chief Quartermaster (Military)
OCR . . . . Office of Civil Rights (HEW)
OCR . . . . Office of Civilian Requirements (Division of War Production Board) (World War II)
OCR . . . . Office of Coal Research (Department of the Interior)
OCR . . . . Office of Collateral Responsibility
OCR . . . . Office of Coordinating Responsibility (Air Force)
OCR . . . . Oil Circuit Recloser
OCR . . . . Optical Character Reader (or Recognition) (Data processing)
OCR . . . . Optimum Charge Regulator
OCR . . . . Order of Corporate Reunion (British)
OCR . . . . Ordo Reformatorum Cisterciensium (Cistercians, Trappists) (Roman Catholic men's religious order)
OCR . . . . Organization Change Request
OC & R . . . . . Operations, Commitments and Requirements (Military)
OCRD . . . . . . Office, Chief of Research & Development (Army)
OCRS . . . . . . Organisation Commune des Regions Sahariennes (Common Organization of the Saharan Regions)
OCRS . . . . . . Organized Crime and Racketeering Section (Department of Justice)
OCS . . . . Obstacle (or Obstruction) Clearance Surface (Aviation)
OCS . . . . Ocean Culture System
OCS . . . . Office of Civilian Supply (Division under the War Production Board) (World War II)
OCS . . . . Office of Commercial Services (Department of Commerce)
OCS . . . . Office of Communication Systems (Air Force)
OCS . . . . Office of Community Services (Bureau of Indian Affairs)
OCS . . . . Office for Consumer Services (HEW)
OCS . . . . Office of Contract Settlement (Functions transferred to GSA, 1949; now obsolete)
OCS . . . . Officer Candidate School (Military)
OCS . . . . Officers' Chief Steward (Navy)

OCS......... Old Church Slavonic
OCS .... On-Board Checkout System
OCS .... Open-Circuit-Stable
OCS .... Operations Control System
OCS......... Optical Character Scanner
OCS .... Organe de Controle des Stupefiants
OCS .... Oriented Cellular Structure
OCS .... Outpatient Clinic Substation (Veterans Administration)
OCS......... Overspeed Control System
OC/S .... Office, Chief of Staff (Army)
OCSA ...... Office of the Army Chief of Staff
OCSA ...... Outstanding Civilian Service Award
OC of SA ... Office, Chief of Staff, Army
OCSAB...... Office of Contract Settlement Appeal Board (Abolished, 1952)
OCSIGO..... Office of the Chief Signal Officer
OCSO ...... Office of the Chief Signal Officer
OCSO ...... Order of Cistercian Nuns of the Strict Observance (Roman Catholic religious order)
OCSO ...... Order of Cistercians of the Strict Observance (Trappists) (Roman Catholic men's religious order)
OC of SptS ... Office of the Chief of Support Services (Army)
OCSPWAR .... Office of the Chief of Special Warfare (Army)
OCSS .... Office of the Chief of Support Services
OCT........ Octagon
OCT........ Octane
OCT........ October
OCT........ Office, Chief of Transportation (Army)
OCT .... Office of Critical Tables (NAS-NRC)
OCT........ Officer Candidate Test (Military)
OCT .... Orbital Circularization Technique
OCT........ Ornithine Carbamoyltransferase
OCTAP...... Of Concern to Air Passengers (Group affiliated with PATCO)
OCTI .... Ordnance Corps Technical Instruction
OCTL....... Open Circuited Transmission Line
OCTLA...... Out of Control Area (Aviation)
OCT/RR ..... Off Course Target/Remote Reference Display
OCTV ...... Open-Circuit Television
OCU .... Oklahoma City University
OCU .... Operational Control Unit
OCV .... Oil Check Valve
OCV........ Old Aircraft Carrier (Navy symbol)
OCV .... Overriding Cam Valve
OCW .... Oklahoma College for Women
OD .... Doctor of Optometry
OD .... Observed Drift
OD......... Oculus Dexter (Right Eye) (Medicine)
OD .... Officer of the Day (or Deck) (Navy)
OD .... Oil Desurger
OD .... Old Dutch
OD .... Olive Drab (Color often used for military clothing and equipment)
OD .... On Demand (Business and trade)
OD .... On Duty
OD .... Operations Directive
OD .... Optical Density
OD .... Ordnance Data (Inspection and test data)
OD .... Ordnance Department or Division
OD .... Ordnance Document (Navy)
OD......... Ordnungsdienst (Military police service) (German military - World War II)
OD .... Organization Development
OD .... Origin and Destination
OD .... Original Design
OD .... Outside Diameter
OD .... Outside Dimension
OD......... Overdose (of narcotics)
OD .... Overdraft, Overdrawn (Banking)
OD......... Overdrive
O/D .... On Demand
O/D .... Order of Deportation
O/D........ Overdraft (Banking)
O & D ...... Origin and Destination (Airlines)
ODA ...... Office of Debt Analysis (Department of the Treasury)
ODA .... Omnidirectional Antenna
ODA .... Operational Data Analysis
ODA .... Oscillating Doublet Antenna
ODA .... Oxydianiline (Chemical)
ODAA ..... Office of Dependent Area Affairs (Department of State)
ODALE..... Office of Drug Abuse Law Enforcement (Department of Justice)
ODAS....... Ocean Data Acquisition Systems
ODB .... Odontoblast
ODB....... Office of Dependency Benefits
ODB........ Opiate-Directed Behavior

ODB ...... Output to Display Buffer (Data processing)
ODC ...... Orbital Data Collector
ODC ...... Organization Development Council
ODC ...... Original Design Cutoff
ODC ...... Other Direct Costs
ODCC ..... On-Board Digital Computer Control
ODCM ..... Office of the Director of Civilian Marksmanship
ODCR...... Officer Distribution Control Report (Navy)
ODCSO .... Office of Data Collection and Survey Operations (Bureau of Labor Statistics)
ODCSOPS .... Office of the Deputy Chief of Staff for Military Operations (Army)
ODCSPER .... Office of the Deputy Chief of Staff for Personnel (Army)
ODD .... Obstacle Detection Device
ODD .... Old Destroyer (Navy symbol)
ODD........ Operator Distance Dialing
ODDP...... Office, Director of Development Planning (Air Force)
ODDRE..... Office of Director of Defense Research and Engineering
ODDS ...... Oceanographic Digital Data System (Navy)
ODECA ..... Organisation de Estados Centroamericanos (Organization of Central American States)
ODESSA ..... Ocean Data Environmental Science Services Acquisition (Buoy)
ODESSA ..... Organisation der Ehemaligen Schutzstaffel Angehoerigen (Organization of Former Members of the Elite Guard) (Founded after World War II to smuggle war criminals out of Germany and provide them with false identities)
ODF .... Optimal Decision Function
ODF........ Orientation Distribution Function
ODFFU..... Organization for Defense of Four Freedoms for Ukraine
ODFI .... Open Die Forging Institute
ODG .... Operational Design Group
ODG .... Orbit Data Generator (NASA)
ODGSE..... Operational Development Ground Support Equipment
ODGSO .... Office of Domestic Gold and Silver Operations (Department of the Treasury)
ODH .... Operations Directive Handbook
ODHWS .... Office of Defense Health and Welfare Services (World War II)
ODI........ Office of Director of Intelligence (Military)
ODI .... Office Document Index
ODI .... Open Door International, for the Economic Emancipation of the Woman Worker
ODI .... Overseas Development Institute (British)
ODIS .... Origin Destination Information System (US Postal Service)
ODJB....... Original Dixieland Jazz Band
ODK .... Omicron Delta Kappa (Fraternity)
ODL .... Office of Defense Lending (Department of the Treasury)
ODL .... Ostwald Dilution Law
ODM ...... Office of Defense Manpower
ODM ...... Office of Defense Mobilization (Transferred to Office of Defense and Civilian Mobilization, 1958)
ODM ...... Operational Development Memorandum
ODM ...... Optical Display Memory
ODM ...... Orbital Determination Module
ODM ...... Order of Mercy (Mercedarians) (Roman Catholic religious order)
ODM ...... Overseas Development Ministry (British)
ODMA ..... Office of the Director of Military Assistance
ODMC ..... Office for Dependents' Medical Care (Army)
ODMO ..... Office of Defense Management and Organization (Military)
ODN ...... Own Doppler Nullifier
ODNR...... Oxford Dictionary of Nursery Rhymes
ODOM..... Odometer
ODOP...... Offset Doppler
ODP .... Office of Defense Planning (of FRS)
ODP........ Offshore Drilling Platform
ODP........ Operational Development Plan (or Program)
ODP........ Orbit Determination Program
ODP........ Organized Reservists in Drill Pay Status
ODPI .... Office of Director Public Information (Military)
ODPPP ...... Operating Division Project Product Policy
ODR........ Office of Defense Resources (Civil Defense)
ODR .... Omni-Directional Range
ODR........ On Display Racks (Freight)
OD & RD.... Overseas Discharge and Replacement Depot
ODRE...... Office of Defense Research and Engineering
ODRI ...... Office of United States Defense Representative, India
ODRN .... Orbiting Data Relay Network
ODRS ...... Orbiting Data Relay System
ODRSS ..... Orbiting Data Relay Satellite System
ODS .... Operating-Differential Subsidy (Authorized by Merchant Marine Act of 1936)
ODS........ Operational Data Summary
ODS .... Operational Display System

ODS	Optical Docking System
ODS	Ordnance Delivery Schedule (Navy)
ODSB	Ocean Data Station Buoy
ODSD	Oversea Duty Selection Date (Air Force)
ODT	Ocean Data Transmitter
ODT	Office of Defense Transportation (Within Office for Emergency Management) (World War II)
ODT	Optical Data Transmission
ODTC	Optic Display Test Chamber
ODTF	Operational Development Test Facility
ODTS	Operational Development Test Site
ODTS	Optical Data Transmission System
ODU	Old Dominion University (Virginia)
ODU	Output Display Unit
ODV	Eau-de-Vie (Taken from the French pronunciation and used to refer to brandy)
ODVAR	Orbit Determination and Vehicle Attitude Reference
ODWIN	Opening Doors Wider in Nursing (Project)
ODWSA	Office of the Directorate of Weapon Systems Analysis (Army)
ODZ	Outer Defense Zone
Oe	Oersted
OE	Office of Education (HEW)
OE	Old English (Language) (i.e., before 1150 or 1200)
OE	Old Etonian (British)
OE	Omissions Excepted
OE	Operations Engineering
OE	Oregon Electric Railway (AAR code)
OE	Original Equipment (Automobile industry)
OEA	Oblate Education Association
OEA	Office of Economic Adjustment
OEA	Office Education Association
OEA	Operator Error Analysis
OEA	Organisation des Etats Americains
OEA	Organizacion de los Estados Americanos (Organization of American States)
OEA	Organizational Expense Accounts
OEA	Outdoor Education Association
OEA	Overseas Education Association
OEB	Organic Electrolyte Battery
OEBS	Organic Electrolyte Battery System
OEC	Odd-Even Check
OEC	Office of Export Control (World War II)
OEC	Ohio Edison Company (NYSE symbol)
OEC	Orbital Electron Capture
OEC	Orbiting Experimental Capsule
OEC	Ordnance Equipment Chart
OECD	Organisation for Economic Co-operation and Development (Formerly, OEEC)
OECE	Organisation Europeenne de Cooperation Economique
OECO	Outboard Engine Cutoff
OECON	Offshore Engineering Conference
OECQ	Organisation Europeenne pour le Controle de la Qualite (European Organization for Quality Control)
OED	Office of Economic Development (Bureau of Indian Affairs)
OED	Operational Engineering Detachment
OED	Orbiting Energy Depot
OED	Oxford English Dictionary
OEDP	Overall Economic Development Program (Bureau of Indian Affairs)
OEE	Office of Educational Exchange (Department of State)
OEEC	Organization for European Economic Cooperation (Later, OECD)
OEEO	Office of Equal Educational Opportunities (US Office of Education)
OEF	Overseas Education Fund of the League of Women Voters
OEG	Operations Evaluation Group (Military)
OEG	Organization and Equipment Guide (Army)
OEGCA	Old English Game Club of America
OEGT	Observable Evidences of Good Teaching
OEI	Oficina de Educacion Iberoamericana (Ibero-American Bureau of Education)
OEI	Optoelectronic Isolator
OEI	Overall Efficiency Index
OEIU	Office Employes International Union
OEL	Ordnance Equipment List (Navy)
OEL	Organizational Equipment List
OEM	Office of Emergency Management (World War II)
OEM	Office Equipment Maintenance
OEM	Office of Executive Management
OEM	On Equipment Materiel (Army)
OEM	Original Equipment Manufacturer
OEMI	Office Equipment Manufacturers Institute
OEN	Oak Industries (Formerly, Oak Electro-Netics Corp.) (NYSE symbol)
OEN	Odd-Even Nuclei

OENR	Organization for European Nuclear Research
OEO	Office of Economic Opportunity
OEO	Oversea Employment Office(r) (Air Force)
OEOB	Old Executive Office Building (Washington, DC)
OEP	Occupational Education Project
OEP	Office of Economic Programs (of BDSA)
OEP	Office of Emergency Preparedness (Formerly, Office of Emergency Planning)
OEP	Operational Employment Plan (Military)
OEPF	Optometric Extension Program Foundation
OEPP	Organisation Europeenne et Mediterraneenne pour la Protection des Plantes (European and Mediterranean Plant Protection Organization)
OEPS	Office of Educational Programs and Services
OER	Odd-Even Rule
OER	Office of Economic Research (Department of Commerce)
OER	Officer Effectiveness Report (Air Force)
OER	Officer Efficiency Report (Army)
OER	Officers' Emergency Reserve (British)
OER	Operational Equipment Requirement
OER	Operations Engineering Report
OER	Original Equipment Request
OER	Osmotic Erythrocyte Resistance
OER	Overhead Expenditure Request
OER	Oxygen Enhancement Ratio
OERC	Optimum Earth Reentry Corridor (Aerospace)
OERL	Officer Education Research Laboratory (Air Force)
OERP	Overseas Expenditure Reduction Program (Military)
OERS	Organisation des Etats Riverains du Senegal
OES	Office of Economic Stabilization (World War II)
OES	Official Experimental Station (Amateur radio)
OES	Orbital-Escape System (NASA)
OES	Order of the Eastern Star
OES	Overseas Educational Service
OESCA	Old English Sheepdog Club of America
OESD	Ocean Engineering System Development
OESS	Office of Engineering Standards Services (National Bureau of Standards)
OET	Objective End Time
OET	Office of Emergency Transportation (FAA)
OET	Official English Title
OET & E	Operational Employment Testing and Evaluation
OEW	Office of Economic Warfare (World War II)
OEW	Open End Wrench
OEW	Operating Empty Weight
OEW	Ordinary Electromagnetic Wave
OEX	Office of Educational Exchange
OF	Oceanographic Facility
OF	Odd Fellows
OF	Old Face (Typography)
OF	Old French
OF	Operating Forces (Navy)
OF	Operational Fixed
OF	Ophthalmological Foundation
OF	Optical Frequency
OF	Optional Form
OF	Orbitofrontal
OF	Osteopathic Foundation
OF	Outfield(er) (Baseball)
OF	Outside Face (Technical drawings)
OF	Overflow
OF	Oxidizing Flame
O/F	Oxidant/Fuel (Ratio)
OFA	Office of Financial Analysis (Department of the Treasury)
OFA	Old Farmer's Almanac
OFA	Oronite Fuel Additive
OFACS	Overseas Foreign Aeronautical Communications Statistician
OFAR	Office of Foreign Agricultural Relations (Department of Agriculture)
OFARS	Overseas-Foreign Aeronautical Receiver Station
OFAS	Overseas Flight Assistance Service
OFATS	Overseas-Foreign Aeronautical Transmitter Station
OFB	Operational Facilities Branch (NASA)
OFC	Office
OFC	Office of Fishery Coordination (World War II)
OFC	Oil Free Compressor
OFC	Old Fired Copper (Initialism once used as brand name for bourbon)
OFC	Operational Flight Control
OFCC	Office of Federal Contract Compliance (Department of Labor)
OFCM	Office of the Federal Coordinator for Meteorological Services and Research
OFCS	Office of Foreign Commercial Services (Department of Commerce)
OFD	Ocean Floor Drilling
OFDAP	Office of the Field Directorate of Ammunition Plants

OFDI . . . . Office of Foreign Direct Investments (Department of Commerce)
OFE . . . . Office of Federal Elections (General Services Administration)
OFE . . . . Office Francais d'Edition
OFE . . . . Optical Flight Evaluation
OFEA . . . . Office of Foreign Economic Administration (Lend-Lease) (World War II)
OFEC . . . . Office of Foreign Economic Coordination (World War II)
OFERRA . . . . . Office of Foreign Economic Relief and Rehabilitation Administration
OFF . . . . Office(r)
OFF . . . . Officer's Family Fund
OFFEN . . . . . . Offensive (Ammunition)
OFFL . . . . Official
OFFNAVHIST . . Office of Naval History
OFG . . . . Optical Frequency Generator
OFGR . . . . Objective Force Gross Requirement (Army)
OFHA . . . . . . Oil Field Haulers Association
OFHC . . . . . . Oxygen-Free, High-Conductivity (Copper)
OFK . . . . Oberfeldkommandantur (Military government area headquarters) (German
     military - World War II)
OFL . . . . Open Fault Locater
OFL . . . . Oxidizer Fill Line
OFLAG . . . . . . From the German for "Permanent prison camp for captured officers"
OFLIC . . . . Office of Foreign Liquidation Commission
OFLT . . . . Office of Foreign Labor and Trade (Department of Labor)
OFLUSE . . . . . For Official Use Only (Army)
OFM . . . . Observation File Maintenance
OFM . . . . Office of Financial Management (Bureau of the Budget; later, OMB)
OFM . . . . Office of Flight Missions (NASA)
OFM . . . . Ordnance Field Manual (Military)
OFM . . . . Ordo Fratrum Minorum (Order of Friars Minor) (Observant Franciscans)
     (Roman Catholic religious order)
OFM . . . . Organization Field Maintenance
OFM . . . . Oxygen Fill to Missile
OFMC . . . . . . Operational Fixed Microwave Council
OFM Cap . . . . Order of Friars Minor Capuchin (Capuchins) (Roman Catholic religious
     order)
OFM Conv . . . Order of Friars Minor Conventual (Conventuals) (Roman Catholic
     religious order)
OFMS . . . . Office of Financial and Management Services (Department of Labor)
OFN . . . . Organization for Flora Neotropica
O & FN . . . . . Ordnance and Facilities - Navy
OFO . . . . Office of Flight Operations
OFO . . . . Orbiting Frog Otolith (NASA experimental spacecraft)
OFP . . . . Oil Filter Pack
OFP . . . . On-the-Fly Printer
OFP . . . . Operating Force Plan
OFP . . . . Original Flight Plan
OFP . . . . Oscilloscope Face Plane
OFPA . . . . . . Order of the Founders and Patriots of America
OFPM . . . . . . Office of Fiscal Plans and Management (Bureau of Indian Affairs)
OFPRA . . . . . Office Francais de Protection des Refugies et Apatrides (France)
OFR . . . . Office of the Federal Register
OFR . . . . Office for Recruitment (American Library Association)
OFR . . . . Oil-Filled Resistor
OFR . . . . Old French (Language, etc.)
OFR . . . . Ordering Function Register
OFR . . . . Over Frequency Relay
OFRR . . . . . . Office of Foreign Relief and Rehabilitation (Obsolete)
OFRRO . . . . . Office of Foreign Relief and Rehabilitation Operation (Obsolete)
OFS . . . . Oceanographic Facilities and Support (Office for) (National Science
     Foundation)
OFS . . . . Octave Filter Set
OFS . . . . Office of Field Service (OSRD) (World War II)
OFS . . . . Office of Field Services (Later, Bureau of Domestic Commerce)
     (Department of Commerce)
OFS . . . . Optical Fuzing System
OFS . . . . Orange Free State
OFSB . . . . . . Ordnance Field Service Bulletin (Military)
OFSC . . . . . . Ordnance Field Service Circular (Military)
OFSC . . . . . . Organization and Finance Sub-Committee
OFSD . . . . . . Operating Flight Strength Diagram
OFT . . . . Operational Flight Trainer
OFTD . . . . . . Oxygen Furnace Tilt Drive
OFTDA . . . . . Office of Flight Tracking and Data Acquisition (NASA)
OFTMS . . . . . Output Format Table Modification Submodule
OFU . . . . Floating Units Division (Coast Guard)
OF/WST . . . . Operational Flight/Weapons System Trainer
OG . . . . Office of Geography (Department of the Interior)
OG . . . . Officer of the Guard
OG . . . . Ogden Corp. (NYSE symbol)
OG . . . . Oh, Gee! (Slang)
OG . . . . Oil Gage

OG . . . . Old Girl (A wife) (Slang)
OG . . . . Olympic Games
OG . . . . On Ground (Aviation)
OG . . . . Operation Greenhouse (Atomic weapons testing)
OG . . . . Optic Ganglion
OG . . . . Or Gate (Data processing)
OG . . . . Original Gum
OG . . . . Outer Gimbal
OG . . . . Outside Guard
O/G . . . . Opto/Graphic, Inc.
OGA . . . . . . Ornamental Growers Association
OGA . . . . . . Outer Gimbal Axis
OGB . . . . . . Osterreichischer Gewerkschaftsbund (Austrian Trade Union Federation)
OGC . . . . . . Office of General Counsel
OGC . . . . . . Order of the Golden Chain
OGC-N . . . . Office of General Counsel, Navy
OGDA . . . . . Oyster Growers and Dealers Association
OGE . . . . . . Oklahoma Gas & Electric Company (NYSE symbol)
OGE . . . . . . Operating (or Operational) Ground Equipment
OGE . . . . . . Out-of-Ground Effect
OGE/RPIE . . . Operating Ground Equipment/Real Property Installed Equipment
OGES . . . . . Operational Ground Equipment Section
OGF. . . . . . . Organic Gardening and Farming (A publication)
OGFP . . . . . Obtaining Goods by False Pretense
OGG . . . . . . Organic Geochemistry Group
OGI . . . . . . Ocean General, Incorporated
OGI . . . . . . Oculogyral Illusion (NASA)
OGI . . . . . . Outer Grid Injection
OGL . . . . . . Obscure Glass
OGL . . . . . . Outgoing Line
OGLA . . . . . Office Grade Limitations Act
OGLE . . . . . Organization for Getting Legs Exposed (Group opposing below-the-
     knee fashions introduced in 1970)
OGM . . . . . . Office of Grants Management (Public Health Service)
OGM . . . . . . Office of Guided Missiles
OGM . . . . . . Optimum Gradient Method
OGMC . . . . . Ordnance Guided Missile Center
OGMS . . . . . Ordnance Guided Missile School
OGO . . . . . . Orbiting Geophysical Observatory (NASA)
OGPU . . . . . Otdelenie Gosudarstvenni Politcheskoi Upravi (Special Government
     Political Administration) (Former Soviet secret service organization, also
     known as GPU)
OGR . . . . . . Ordnance, Gunnery and Readiness Division (Coast Guard)
OGR . . . . . . ORNL (Oak Ridge National Laboratory) Graphite Reactor
OGR . . . . . . Outgoing Repeater
OGRC . . . . . Office of Grants and Research Contracts (NASA)
OGS . . . . . . Obsolete General Supplies (Military)
OGS . . . . . . Optical Guidance System
OGSE . . . . . Operational Ground Support Equipment
OGSEL . . . . . Operational Ground Support Equipment List
OGSS . . . . . Organizazione Generale degli Studenti Somali (Organization of Somali
     Students)
OGT . . . . . . Outgoing Trunk
OGU . . . . . . Occupational Guidance Unit (British)
OGU . . . . . . Outgoing Unit
OGV . . . . . . Outlet Guide Vane
OGW . . . . . . Overload Gross Weight
OH . . . . Office Hours
OH . . . . Ohio
OH . . . . Ohmic Heating
OH . . . . On Hand
OH . . . . Open Hearth
OH . . . . Out Home (Men's lacrosse position)
OH . . . . Overhaul
OH . . . . Overhead
O/H . . . . Over-the-Horizon Transmission
O/H . . . . Overhaul
OHA . . . . . . Oral History Association
OHA . . . . . . Oscillator Housing Assembly
OHA . . . . . . Outside Helix Angle
OHBMS . . . . On His (or Her) Britannic Majesty's Service
OHC . . . . . . Order of the Holy Cross (Episcopalian religious order)
OHC . . . . . . Ottumwa Heights College (Iowa)
OHC . . . . . . Overhead Camshaft (Automotive term)
OHD . . . . . . Ordinary Hydrodynamic
OHD . . . . . . Organic Heart Disease (Medicine)
OHD . . . . . . Over-the-Horizon Detector
OHDETS . . . . Over-Horizon Detection System
OHE . . . . . . Office of the Housing Expediter (Terminated, 1951)
OHF . . . . . . Omsk Hemorrhagic Fever
OHG . . . . . . Old High German (Language)

OHGS . . . . . . Omega Hyberbolic Grid System
OHH . . . . Owen Harrison Harding (of the James W. Ellison novel, "I'm Owen Harrison Harding")
OHI . . . . Occupational Health Institute
OHI . . . . Ocular Hypertension Indicator
OHI . . . . Oil-Heat Institute of America
OHI . . . . Ordnance Handling Instructions
OHIA . . . . . . Oil Heat Institute of America
OHIR . . . . . . Operating House of Ill Repute
OHM . . . . Ohmmeter
OHM-CM . . . . Ohm-Centimeter
OHMS . . . . . . On His (or Her) Majesty's Service
OHP . . . . Oxygen at High Pressure
OHPO . . Organization Health Program Officer
OHPS . . . . . . Oil Hydraulic Power Switch
OHR . . . . Ontario Hydro-Research
OHR . . . . Operational Hazard Report (Air Force)
OHR . . . . Over-the-Horizon RADAR
OHS . . . . Office of Highway Safety (of BPR)
OHS . . . . Oil Hydraulic Assembly
OHS . . . . Open Hearth Steel
OHS . . . . Organ Historical Society
OHSGT . . . . . Office of High Speed Ground Transportation (Department of Transportation)
OHTS . . . . . . Oil-Hardened Tool Steel
OHV . . . . Overhead Valve
OI . . . . Office of Information
OI . . . . Office Instruction
OI . . . . Oil Immersed
OI . . . . Oil-Insulated
OI . . . . On Instruments (Aviation)
OI . . . . Opening of Intestine
OI . . . . Operations Instruction
OI . . . . Optimist International
OI . . . . Output Impedance
OI . . . . Owens-Illinois Glass Company (NYSE symbol)
OIA . . . . Ocean Industries Association
OIA . . . . Office of International Administration (Department of State)
OIA . . . . Oil Import Administration (Department of the Interior)
OIA . . . . . . Oil Insurance Association
OIA . . . . . . Outboard Industry Associations
OIAA . . . . . . Office of Inter-American Affairs (Later, BIAA)
OIAA . . . . . . Office of International Aviation Affairs (FAA)
OIB . . . . Official Information Base
OIC . . . . Office of Industrial Cooperation (AEC)
OIC . . . . Office of International Conferences (Department of State)
OIC . . . . Office of International Cooperation (in CAA)
OIC . . . . Officer in Charge
OIC . . . . Ohio Improved Chesters (Initialism itself now used as name of breed of swine)
OIC . . . . . . Okinawa Interboard Committee
OIC . . . . . . Opportunities Industrialization Center (Washington, DC)
OIC . . . . Organisation Internationale Catholique
OIC . . . . Organisation Internationale du Commerce
OICC . . . . . . Officer in Charge of Construction (Navy)
OICO . . . . . . Office of Integration and Checkout
OICRF . . . . . Office International du Cadastre et Regime Foncier
OICW . . . . . . Opportunities Industrial Center West
OID . . . . Order Initiated Distribution
OIDA . . . . . . Ordnance Industrial Data Agency
OIDP . . . . . . Oversea Internal Defense Policy (Army)
OIDPS . . . . . . Oversea Intelligence Data Processing System
OIE . . . . Office International des Epizooties (International Office of Epizootics)
OIE . . . . Optical Incremental Encoder
OIE . . . . Optical Infrared Equipment
OIE . . . . Organisation Internationale des Employeurs
OIEC . . . . . . Office International de l'Enseignement Catholique (Catholic International Education Office)
OIESA . . . . . . Office of International Economic and Social Affairs (Department of State)
OIF . . . . Office for Intellectual Freedom (American Library Association)
OIF . . . . Office of International Finance (Department of the Treasury)
OIFC . . . . . . Oil-Insulated, Fan-Cooled
OIG . . . . Office of the Inspector General (Army)
OIG . . . . Organisation Intergouvernementale
OIGR . . . . . . Office of Industrial Growth and Research (of BDSA)
OIH . . . . Oceanic Institute of Hawaii
OIH . . . . Ovulation-Inducing Hormone (Endocrinology)
OIHP . . . . . . Office International d'Hygiene Publique (UN)
OII . . . . Office of International Investment (Department of Commerce)
OI & I . . . . . . Office of Invention and Innovation (National Bureau of Standards)
OIJ . . . . Organisation Internationale des Journalistes (International Organization of Journalists)

OIL . . . . Oil Insurance, Limited (Bermuda)
OIL . . . . Operation Inspection Log
OIL . . . . Orbital International Laboratory
OIL . . . . Ordnance Investigation Laboratory
OILA . . . . . . Office of International Labor Affairs (Labor Department)
OIM . . . . Office of Industrial Managers (Navy)
OIM . . . . Office of Industrial Mobilization (of BDSA)
OIM . . . . Organic Insulating Material
OIML . . . . . . Organisation Internationale de Metrologie Legale (International Organization of Legal Metrology)
OIMS . . . . . . Oscillator Instability Measurement System
OI-N . . . . . . Office of Information, Navy
OINA . . . . . Oyster Institute of North America
OINC . . . . . . Officer-in-Charge (Navy)
OINCABCCTC . . Officer-in-Charge, Advanced Base Combat Communication Training Center (Pearl Harbor) (Navy)
OING . . . . . . Organisation Internationale non Gouvernementale
OINT . . . . . . Omni-Intersection (Aviation)
OIO . . . . Office of International Operations (of IRS)
OIO . . . . Oklahomans for Indian Opportunity
OIP . . . . Operational Improvement Plan
OIP . . . . Optical Image Processor
OIP . . . . Organic Insulative Plastic
OIPAAR . . . . . Office of Industrial Personnel Access Authorization Review (Army)
OIPC . . . . . . Organisation Internationale de Police Criminelle (International Criminal Police Organization [Interpol])
OIPC . . . . . . Organisation Internationale de Protection Civile (International Civil Defense Organization)
OIR . . . . Office of Industrial Relations (Navy)
OIR . . . . Office of Institutional Research
OIR . . . . Office of International Research (of National Institutes of Health)
OIR . . . . Office of International Resources (Department of State)
OIR . . . . Oficina Interamericana de Radio (Inter-American Radio Office)
OIR . . . . Organisation Internationale de Radiodiffusion
OIRE . . . . . . Optical Infrared Equipment
OIR-N . . . . . . Office of Industrial Relations, Navy
OIRSA . . . . . . Organismo Internacional Regional de Sanidad Agropecuaria (Regional International Organization of Plant Protection and Animal Health Care)
OIRT . . . . . . Organisation Internationale de Radiodiffusion et Television (International Radio and Television Organization)
OIS . . . . Occupational Interest Survey (Aptitude test)
OIS . . . . Office of Industrial Survey (Navy)
OIS . . . . Office of Information Services
OIS . . . . Operational Instrumentation System
OISA . . . . . . Office of International Science Activities (National Science Foundation)
OISC . . . . . . Oil-Insulated, Self-Cooling
OISE . . . . . . Ontario Institute for Studies in Education
OISP . . . . . . Overseas Internal Security Program
OISR . . . . . . Office of Interstate Sales Registration (HUD)
OISS . . . . . . Organizacion Iberoamericana de Seguridad Social (Ibero-American Social Security Organization)
OIST . . . . . . Operator Integration Shakedown Test
OISTV . . . . . . Organisation Internationale pour la Science et la Technique du Vide
OIT . . . . Object Identification Test
OIT . . . . Oblique-Incidence Transmission
OIT . . . . Office of International Trade (Department of Commerce)
OIT . . . . Organisation Internationale du Travail (International Labour Organization)
OITA . . . . . . Office of International Tax Affairs (Department of the Treasury)
OITF . . . . . . Office of International Trade Fairs (Department of Commerce)
OITF . . . . . . Office of International Trade and Finance (Department of State)
OITT . . . . . . Outpulser, Identifier, Trunk Test
OIV . . . . Office International de la Vigneet du Vin (International Vine and Wine Office)
OIWC . . . . . . Oil-Insulated, Water-Cooled
OIWR . . . . . . Office of Indian Water Rights (Bureau of Indian Affairs)
OJ . . . . Ohne Jahr (Without Date of Publication) (Bibliography)
OJ . . . . Open-Joisted (Technical drawings)
OJ . . . . Opium Joint
OJ . . . . Orange Juice
OJ . . . . Orthomode Junction
OJ . . . . Outer Jacket
OJC . . . . Orlando Junior College (Florida)
OJC . . . . Otero Junior College (Colorado)
OJCS . . . . . . Office of the Joint Chiefs of Staff
OJD . . . . Order of Job's Daughters
OJDYD . . . . . Office of Juvenile Delinquency and Youth Development (HEW)
OJPR . . . . . . Office for Jewish Population Research
OJS . . . . Las Oblatas de Jesus Sacerdote (Oblates of Jesus the Priest) (Roman Catholic women's religious order)
OJSA . . . . . . Orthomode Junction and Switching Assembly
OJT . . . . On-the-Job Training

OK .... All Right (From Old Kinderhook or Oll Korrect)
OK .... Ohne Kosten (Without Cost) (Germany)
OK .... Oklahoma
OK .... Outer Keel
OKA .... Otherwise Known As
OKG .... Oskarshamnsverkets Kraft Grupp Aktiebolag (Sweden)
OKH .... Oberkommando des Heeres (Army High Command, German) (World War II)
OKIS ...... Organsko Kemijska Industrija Skopje (Yugoslavia)
OKL .... Oberkommando der Luftwaffe (Air Force High Command, German) (World War II)
OKLA ...... Oklahoma
OKM .... Oberkommando der Kriegsmarine (Navy High Command, German) (World War II)
OKN .... Okmulgee Northern Railway Company (AAR code)
OKN .... Opticokinetic Nystagmus (Eye condition)
OKT .... Oakite Products, Inc. (NYSE symbol)
OKT .... Oakland Terminal Railway (AAR code)
OKU .... Omicron Kappa Upsilon (Fraternity)
OKW .... Oberkommando der Wehrmacht (Armed Forces High Command, German) (World War II)
OL .... Occupational Level
OL .... Ocean Letter
OL .... Oculus Laevus (Left Eye) (Medical)
OL .... Oil Level
OL .... Old Latin
OL .... Open Loop
OL .... Operating License
OL .... Operating Location
OL .... Operating Log
OL .... Or Less
OL .... Ordinary Leave (Military)
OL .... Outgoing Letter
OL .... Outside Left (Soccer position)
OL .... Overflow Level
OL .... Overhead Line
OL .... Overlap
OL .... Overload (Electricity)
O/L .... Operations/Logistics
OLA .... Office of Legislative Affairs
OLA .... Osteopathic Libraries Association
OLAC ...... Off-Line Adaptive Computer
OLAFS ..... Orbiting and Launch Approach Flight Simulator
OLAS ...... Organization of Latin American Solidarity (Cuba)
OLB .... Oertliche Landwirtschaftsbetriebe
OLB .... Open Loop Bandwidth
OLBR ...... Omaha, Lincoln & Beatrice Railway Company (AAR code)
OLBW ...... Open-Loop Bandwidth
OLC .... Oakleaf Cluster
OLC .... Office of Legal Counsel (Department of Justice)
OLC .... On-Line Computer (System)
OLC .... Ontario Ladies College
OLC .... Outgoing Line Circuit
OLC .... Overseas Liaison Committee (of the American Council on Education)
OLCA ...... On-Line Circuit Analysis (System)
OLCC ...... Our Lady of Cincinnati College (Ohio)
OLCR ...... Sisters of Our Lady of Charity of Refuge (Roman Catholic religious order)
OLD .... Odd Lot Dealer
OLD .... Office of Legislative Development (Bureau of Indian Affairs)
OLD .... Old Town Corporation (American Stock Exchange symbol)
OLD .... Open-Loop Damping
OLD ECC .... Ordinary Linear Differential Equations with Constant Coefficients (Mathematics)
OLDR ...... On-Time Data Reduction
OLDS ...... On-Line Display System (Data processing)
OLE .... Office for Library Education (American Library Association)
OLEA ...... Office of Law Enforcement Assistance
OLEYIS ..... Otel, Lokanta ve Eglence Yerleri Iscileri Sendikasi (Istanbul Hotel, Restaurant and Amusement Places Workers' Union) (Turkey)
OLF .... Old Low Franconian
OLF .... Orbital Launch Facility
OLF .... Outlying Field
OLG .... Old Low German (Language)
OLG .... Open Loop Gain
OLHMIS ..... On-Line Hospital Management Information System
OLIS ...... Oxide Layer Isolation Structure
OLL .... Organic Liquid LASER
OLL .... Output Logic Level
OLLA ...... Office of Lend-Lease Administration (World War II)
OLLC ...... Our Lady of the Lake College (Texas)
OLM .... Office for Laboratory Management (DOD)

OLM .... Olin Mathieson Chemical Corporation (NYSE symbol; later, OLN)
OLM .... On-Line Monitor
OLM .... Sisters of Charity of Our Lady of Mercy (Roman Catholic religious order)
OLMR ...... Organic Liquid Moderated Reactor
OLN .... Olin Corporation (NYSE symbol) (Formerly, OLM)
OLO .... On-Line Operation
OLO .... Orbital Launch Operation
OLOS ...... Observer Line of Sight
OLP .... Observation Landplane (Coast Guard)
OLP .... Office of Labor Production (WPB) (World War II)
OLP .... Outside Left Position
OLP .... Sisters of Our Lady of Providence (Roman Catholic religious order)
OLPARS .... On-Line Pattern Analysis and Recognition System (Data processing)
OLPS ...... On-Line Programing System (Data processing)
OLR .... Office of Legislative Reference (Bureau of the Budget; later, OMB)
OLR .... Open Loop Response
OLR .... Organisation Pour la Liberation du Rwanda (Organization for the Liberation of Rwanda)
OLR .... Overload Relay
OLRS ...... Optical LASER Ranging System
OLRT ...... On-Line Real Time
OLS .... Operational Launch Station
OLS .... Operational Lines of Succession (Defense readiness)
OLS .... Optical Landing System
OLS .... Orbiting Lunar Station (NASA)
OLS .... Ordinary Least Squares (Statistics)
OLS .... Original Line of Sight
OLS .... Sisters of Our Lady of Sorrows (Roman Catholic religious order)
O & LS ..... Ocean and Lake Surveys (Navy) (Budget appropriation title)
OLSC ...... On-Line Scientific Computer (Data processing)
OLSCA ..... Orientation Linkage for a Solar Cell Array
OLSE ...... Ordinary Least-Squares Estimators (Statistics)
OLSP ...... Office of Life Science Programs (NASA) (No longer in existence)
OLSS ...... Overseas Limited Storage Site (Military)
OLT .... Oddity-Learning Task (Psychology)
OLT .... Official Latin Title
OLT .... Orange Light
OL & T .... Owners, Landlords, and Tenants
OLTEP ...... On-Line Test Executive Program (Data processing)
OLUC ...... Office of Land Use Coordination (Department of Agriculture) (Abolished, 1944)
OLV .... Orbital-Launch Vehicle
OLVG ...... Open-Loop Voltage Gain
OLVP ...... Office of Launch Vehicle Programs (NASA) (No longer in existence)
OLYM ...... Olympic National Park
OM .... Occupation Medal (as used with special reference to Germany or Japan)
OM .... Oceanography and Meteorology
OM .... Office Manager
OM .... Officer Messenger
OM .... Old Man (Communications operators' colloquialism)
OM .... Old Measurement
OM .... Opera Mundi (Book-packaging firm based in Paris)
OM .... Operations Maintenance
OM .... Opticalman (Navy rating)
OM .... Order of Merit
OM .... Ordnance Mission
OM .... Ordo (Fratrum) Minimorum (Minims of St. Francis of Paul) (Roman Catholic men's religious order)
OM .... Organic Matter
OM .... Our Message
OM .... Outboard Marine Corporation (NYSE symbol)
OM .... Outer Marker (Part of an instrument landing system) (Aviation)
O & M ..... Operation and Maintenance
O & M ..... Organization and Management
O & M ..... Organization and Methods
OMA .... Office of Military Assistance
OMA .... Oklahoma Military Academy
OMA .... Operation and Maintenance (Army)
OMA .... Operation Medicare Alert
OMA .... Optical Manufacturers Association
OMA .... Optical-Mechanical Assembly (Apollo) (NASA)
O & MA .... Operation & Maintenance Activities
OMAI ...... Organisation Mondiale Agudas Israel (Agudas Israel World Organization)
O-MAN ..... Overhead Manipulator (for handling loads in a nuclear environment) (AEC)
OMAR ...... Optical Mark Reader (Data processing)
OMARNG .... Operation and Maintenance, Army National Guard
OMAT ...... Office of Manpower, Automation, and Training (Department of Labor) (Also see OAM)
OMB .... Office of Management and Budget (Formerly, Bureau of the Budget)
OMB .... Ordnance Maintenance Bulletin
OMB .... Outboard Motorboat

OMB . . . . Outer Marker Beacon (Aviation)
OMBE . . . . . . Office of Minority Business Enterprise (Department of Commerce)
OMBI . . . . Observation-Measurement-Balancing and Installation (Production analysis)
OMC . . . . Office of Munitions Control (Department of State)
OMC . . . . Official Mail Center (Air Force)
OMC . . . . Open Market Committee (Federal Reserve System)
OMC . . . . Operations Monitoring Computer
OMC . . . . Ordnance Missile Command (Later, Missile Command)
OMC . . . . Ordo Minorum Cappucinorum (Capuchins) (Roman Catholic men's religious order)
OMC . . . . Ordo Minorum Conventualium (Conventual Franciscans) (Roman Catholic men's religious order)
OMC . . . . Organic Molecular Crystal
OMC . . . . Oscar Mayer & Company (NYSE symbol)
OMCC . . . . . . Olin Mathieson Chemical Corporation (Later, Olin Corp.)
OMCI . . . . Organisation Intergouvernementale Consultative de la Navigation Maritime (Intergovernmental Maritime Consultative Organization)
OMCR . . . . . . Organic-Moderated Cooled Reactor
OMD . . . . Ocean Movement Designator
OMDM . . . . . . Opto-Mechanical Display Module
OME . . . . Office of Management Engineer
OME . . . . Office of Manpower Economics (Department of Employment) (British)
OME . . . . Office of Minerals Exploration (Department of the Interior)
OMEC . . . . . . Optimized Microminiature Electronic Circuit
OMEGA . . . . . Off-Road Mobility Evaluation and Generalized Analysis (Army)
OMEGA . . . . . Operation Model Evaluation Group, Air Force
OMEP . . . . . . Organisation Mondiale pour l'Education Prescolaire (World Organization for Early Childhood Education)
OMETA . . . . . Ordnance Management Engineering Training Agency (Army)
OMF . . . . Operation and Maintenance of Facilities
OMF . . . . Optical Matched Filter
OMF . . . . Oscillatory Magnetic Field
OMF . . . . Overseas Missionary Fellowship
OMFBAA . . . . Operation and Maintenance of Facilities Budget Activity Account (Army)
OMFBR . . . . . Organic-Moderated Fluidized Bed Reactor
OMFCA . . . . . Operation and Maintenance of Facilities Cost Account (Army)
OMFP . . . . . . Obtaining Money by False Pretense
OMFSCA . . . . Operation and Maintenance of Facilities Summary Cost Account (Army)
OMFT . . . . . . Optical Matched Filter Technique
OMG . . . . Office Machines Group (Business Equipment Manufacturers Association)
OMG . . . . Office of Military Government
OMGB . . . . . . Office of Military Government for Bavaria (US Military Government, Germany)
OMGBS . . . . . Office of Military Government for Berlin Sector (US Military Government, Germany)
OMGE . . . . . . Organisation Mondiale de Gastro-Enterologie (World Organization of Gastroenterology)
OMGH . . . . . . Office of Military Government for Hesse (US Military Government, Germany)
OMGUS . . . . . Office of Military Government, United States
OMGWB . . . . Office of Military Government for Wuerttemberg-Baden (US Military Government, Germany)
OMI . . . . Oblati Mariae Immaculate (Oblate Fathers of Mary Immaculate) (Roman Catholic religious order)
OMI . . . . Office of Management Improvement (Department of Agriculture)
OMI . . . . Ohio Mechanics Institute
OMI . . . . Operation Move-In (New York City)
OMI . . . . Operational Maintenance Instruction
OMI . . . . Ordnance Modifications Instructions
OMI . . . . Organisation Meteorologique Internationale
OMICA . . . . . Organized Migrants in Community Action (Florida)
OMIOM . . . . . Original Meaning Is the Only Meaning (Writing term)
OMIS . . . . . . Omission
OMIS . . . . . . Operational Management Information System (Data processing)
OMJ . . . . Orthomode Junction (Electronics)
OMK . . . . Omark Industries, Inc. (NYSE symbol)
OMKR . . . . . . Outer Marker, Instrument Landing System (Aviation)
OML . . . . Orbiting Military Laboratory
OML . . . . Outside Mold Line (Technical drawings)
OMLP . . . . . . Ohio Midland Light & Power Company (AAR code)
OMM . . . . Office of Minerals Mobilization (Later, OMSF) (Department of the Interior)
OMM . . . . Officer Messenger Mail
OMM . . . . Organisation Meteorologique Mondiale (World Meteorological Organization)
OMM . . . . Organo-Metallic Material
OMMA . . . . . Outboard Motor Manufacturers Association
OMMC . . . . . Officer Messenger Mail Center
O & M,MC . . Operations and Maintenance, Marine Corps
OMMI . . . . . . Orszagos Mezogazdasagi Minosegvizsgalo Intezet

OMMIC . . . . . Ordnance Maintenance Management Information Center (Navy)
OMMMSA . . . Oil Mill Machinery Manufacturers and Supply Association
OMMS . . . . . . Office of Merchant Marine Safety (Coast Guard)
OMM(S)C . . . . Officer Messenger Mail (Sub) Center
O & MN . . . . Operation and Maintenance, Navy
OMNITENNA . . Omnirange Antenna
OMO . . . . Ordinary Money Order
OMP . . . . Oriental Music-Tape & Publishers
OMP . . . . Output Makeup
OMPA . . . . . . Octamethyl Pyrophosphoramide (Insecticide)
OMPER . . . . . Office of Manpower Policy, Evaluation and Research (Department of Labor)
OMPF . . . . . . Official Military Personnel File
OMPRA . . . . . One-Man Propulsion Research Apparatus (NASA)
OMPSA . . . . . Organisation Mondiale pour la Protection Sociale des Aveugles (World Council for the Welfare of the Blind)
OMPUS . . . . . Official Munitions Production United States
OMR . . . . Officer Master Record (Air Force)
OMR . . . . Optical Mark Reader (Motorola)
OMR . . . . Optical Meter Relay
OMR . . . . Organic Magnetic Resonance
OMR . . . . Organic Moderated Reactor (AEC)
OMR . . . . Our Material Returned
OMRCA . . . . . Organic-Moderated Reactor Critical Assembly
OMRE . . . . . . Organic-Moderated Reactor Experiment (AEC)
OMRF . . . . . . Oklahoma Medical Research Foundation
OMRI . . . . . . Oklahoma Medical Research Institute
OMRO . . . . . . Ordnance Materials Research Office (Army)
OMRR . . . . . . Ordnance Material Research Reactor
OMRV . . . . . . Operational Maneuvering Reentry Vehicle
OMRW . . . . . Optical MASER Radiation Weapon
OMS . . . . Oesterreichische Mineraloel und Stickstoffwerke AG (Formed by merger of OMV and OSW)
OMS . . . . Office of Management Services (Department of Agriculture)
OMS . . . . Office of Marketing Services (of BDSA)
OMS . . . . Operational Meteorological Satellite (NASA)
OMS . . . . Optical MASER System
OMS . . . . Orbital Maneuvering Subsystem
OMS . . . . Orbital Multifunction Satellite
OMS . . . . Ordnance Machine Shop
OMS . . . . Organic Mass Spectroscopy
OMS . . . . Organisation Mondiale de la Sante (World Health Organization)
OMS . . . . Organizational Maintenance Shop
OMS . . . . Oriental Missionary Society
OMS . . . . Outdoor Microphone System
OMS . . . . Output per Man Shift
OMS . . . . Output Multiplex Synchronizer
OMS . . . . Overseas Mission Society
OMSA . . . . . . Orders and Medals Society of America
OMSF . . . . . . Office of Manned Space Flight (NASA)
OMSF . . . . . . Office of Minerals and Solid Fuels (Formerly, OMM) (Department of the Interior)
OMSq . . . . . . Organizational Maintenance Squadron (Air Force)
OMSRADS . . . Optimum Mix of Short Range Air Defense Systems
OMT . . . . Organizational Maintenance Technician (Army)
OMT . . . . Orthotropic Multicell Tank
OMTR . . . . . . Officer Master Tape Record (Army)
OMTS . . . . . . Organizational Maintenance Test Station (Army)
OMU . . . . Operational Mock-Up
OMV . . . . Master of Obstetrics
OMV . . . . Oesterreichische Mineraloelverwaltung AG (Later, OMS)
OMVTO . . . . . Office Motor Vehicle Transportation Officer (Army)
OMVWI . . . . . Operating Motor Vehicle While Intoxicated
ON . . . . Octane Number
ON . . . . Off Normal
ON . . . . Old Norse (Language, speech, grammar)
ON . . . . Onorevole (Honorable)
ON . . . . Operation Notice
ON . . . . Orthopedic Nurse
O/N . . . . Order Notify (Bill of lading) (Shipping)
ONA . . . . Overseas National Airways, Inc.
ONA . . . . Overseas News Agency
ONAC . . . . . . Office of Noise Abatement and Control (Environmental Protection Agency)
ONAP . . . . . . Orbit Navigation Analysis Program
ONC . . . . Office of New Careers (HEW)
ONC . . . . Olivet Nazarene College (Illinois)
ONC . . . . Operational Navigation Charts (Air Force)
ONC . . . . Ordinary National Certificate (British)
ONC . . . . Orthopedic Nursing Certificate
ONCORE . . . . On Command Restartable
OND . . . . Ophthalmic Nursing Diploma

ACRONYMS AND INITIALISMS DICTIONARY

OND . . . . Ordinary National Diploma (British)
ONEO . . . . . . Office of Navajo Economic Opportunity
ONERA . . . . . Office National d'Etudes et de Recherches Aerospatiales (France)
ONF . . . . . . Old Norman French (Language, etc.)
ONF . . . . . . Old Northern French (Language, etc.)
ONG . . . . Oklahoma Natural Gas Company (NYSE symbol)
ONG . . . . Organisation non Gouvernementale
ONH . . . . Office of Naval History
ONI . . . . Office of Naval Intelligence
ONI. . . . . . . Operator Number Identification (Bell System)
ONIG. . . . . . . Opera Nazionale Invalidi di Guerra (Italy)
ONIO . . . . . . Office of Naval Inspectors of Ordnance
ONIT . . . . Organisation Nationale Independante des Travailleurs (National Independent Organization for Workers) (Belgium)
ONM . . . . . . Office of Naval Material (Later, NMCOM)
ONO. . . . . . . Office of Naval Operations
ON-OFF. . . . . Oscillatory, Non-Oscillatory Flip-Flop (Data processing)
ONOP . . . . . . Office of Naval Officer Procurement
ONP . . . . Operating Nursing Procedure
ONPOSR. . . . . Office of Naval Petroleum and Oil Shale Reserves
ONR . . . . . . Office of Naval Research
ONRAP . . . . . Oficina Nacional de Racionalizacion y Capacitacion de la Administracion Publica (Peru)
ONRL . . . . . . Office of Naval Research, London
ONRRR . . . . . Office of Naval Research Resident Representative
ONS . . . . Off-Normal Switch
ONSIDIV . . . . On-Sight Surveys Division
ONT . . . . . . Ontario (Canadian province)
ONT . . . . . . Ontario Northland Railway (AAR code)
ONT . . . . Our New Thread (Clark thread designation)
ONU . . . . Ohio Northern University
ONU . . . . . . Organisation des Nations Unies (United Nations Organization)
ONUC . . . . . . Organisation des Nations Unies au Congo
ONULP . . . . . Ontario New Universities Library Project
ONW . . . . Office of Naval Weapons
ONW . . . . On Watch
ONW . . . . Oregon & Northwestern R. R. (AAR code)
ONWS . . . . . Office of Naval Weather Service
OO . . . . Naval Oceanographic Office (Also known as NOO; formerly, HO or NHO)
OO . . . . Observation Officer (Military)
OO . . . . Oceanographic Office
OO . . . . Ohne Ort (Without Place of Publication) (Bibliography)
OO . . . . Once Over (To examine cursorily) (Slang)
OO . . . . Operation Order (Military)
OO . . . . Operations Office (AEC)
OO . . . . Or Order
OO . . . . Ordnance Office(r)
OO . . . . Osobyi Otdel (Counterintelligence surveillance unit in military formation until 1943) (USSR)
O/O . . . . . . Office of Origin
O/O . . . . Order Of (Business and trade)
O & O . . . . . Owned and Operated (Radio and TV stations)
O to O . . . . . Out to Out (Technical drawings)
OOA . . . . . . Object of Affections (Slang)
OOA . . . . . . Office of Ocean Affairs (Navy)
OOA . . . . Optimum Orbital Altitude
OOAA . . . . . Olive Oil Association of America
OOAMA . . . . . Ogden Air Materiel Area (AFLC)
OOB . . . . . . Off-Off Broadway (Theater)
OOB . . . . Out of Bed (Medicine)
OOBE. . . . . . Out-of-the-Body Experience (Parapsychology)
OOC . . . . . . Office of Censorship
OOC . . . . . . Operating (Vehicle) without Owner's Consent (Traffic offense charge)
OOC . . . . . . Organized Occupational Curricula
OOC . . . . Over-Ocean Communications
OOD . . . . . . Office Operations Department
OOD . . . . . . Officer of the Deck (Navy)
OOE . . . . . . Opening of Oesophagus
OOG . . . . . . Office of Oil and Gas (Department of the Interior)
OOG . . . . . . Oscillating Output Geneva
OOI. . . . . . . Oxygen/Ozone Indicator
OOJ . . . . . . Obstruction of Justice
OOL . . . . . . Office of Oceanography and Limnology (Smithsonian Institution)
OOL . . . . . Operator-Oriented Language (Data processing)
OOLR . . . . . Ophthalmology, Otology, Laryngology, Rhinology
OOM . . . . . . Officers' Open Mess
OOM . . . . . . Open Ocean Mining
OON . . . . . . Odd-Odd Nuclei
OOO . . . . . Order of Owls
OOP . . . . . . Oceanographic Observations of the Pacific

OOP . . . . . . Office of Organization Planning
OOP . . . . . . Optimum Optical Pump
OOP . . . . . . Out of Plane
OOPS. . . . . . Off-Line Operating Simulator
OOPS. . . . . . Office for Operations in Political Systems
OOQ . . . . . . Officer of the Quarters
OOR . . . . . . Office of Ordnance Research (Later, Army Research Office)
OOR . . . . . . Oxygen/Ozone Recorder
OOS . . . . . . Orbit-to-Orbit Shuttle (NASA)
O & OS . . . . . Ordnance and Ordnance Stores (Navy)
OOSS . . . . . . Overseas Operational Storage Site
OOT . . . . . . Oil Out Temperature
OOTC . . . . . Old Old Timers Club
OOTE. . . . . . Out-of-Town Executive
OOW . . . . . . Officer of the Watch (Navigation)
OP. . . . . Observation Plane
OP . . . . Observation Post
OP. . . . . . . Office Pass
OP. . . . . Office of Personnel
OP. . . . . Office of Pesticides (Public Health Service)
OP. . . . . . . Oil Pressure
OP. . . . . . . Oil Pump
OP. . . . . . . Old Price (Riots) (Occurred for 67 nights, beginning December 30, 1808, opening night of rebuilt Covent Garden Theatre, London, because of new and higher prices; protestors won)
OP. . . . . . . Open Policy
OP. . . . . . . Open Position (Dancing)
OP. . . . . . . Operation
OP. . . . . . . Operation Plans
OP. . . . . . . Operational Priority
OP. . . . . . . Operational Procedure
OP. . . . . . . Opposite Prompt (i.e., the left side) (A stage direction)
OP. . . . . . . Optical Probe
OP. . . . . . . Orbital Period
OP. . . . . . . Order of Preachers (Dominicans) (Roman Catholic men's religious order)
OP. . . . . . . Ordnance Pamphlets
OP. . . . . . . Ordnance Personnel
OP. . . . . . . Ordnance Publications (Navy)
OP. . . . . . . Ordo Praedicatorum (Order of Preachers) (Dominicans) (Roman Catholic religious order)
OP. . . . . . . Other People's (Borrowed money, cigarettes, etc.) (Slang)
OP. . . . . . . Out of Print (Publishing)
OP. . . . . . . Outer Panel
OP. . . . . . . Outpost
OP. . . . . . . Output
OP . . . . Outside Production
OP. . . . . . . Over Pressure
OP. . . . . . . Overprint
OP. . . . . . . Overproof (Distilling)
O-P . . . . . . Oppenheimer-Phillips (Process)
O/P . . . . . . Ownership Purpose Code (Military)
OPA. . . . . . . Office of the Pardon Attorney (Department of Justice)
OPA . . . . . . Office of Population Affairs (HEW)
OPA . . . . . . Office of Price Administration (World War II)
OPA. . . . . . . Office of Program Appraisal
OPA. . . . . . . Office of Public Affairs (Environmental Protection Agency)
OPA . . . . . . Officer Personnel Act
OPA. . . . . . . Optoelectronic Pulse Amplifier
OPACS . . . . . Office of Price Administration and Civilian Supply (Name changed to Office of Price Administration) (World War II)
OPADEC . . . . Optical Particle Decoy
OPAL. . . . . . . Optical Platform Alignment Linkage
OPAL . . . . . . Orientation Program in American Law (of AALS)
OPANAL . . . . Operations Analysis (Navy)
OPATTYGEN . . Opinion of the Attorney General
OPB . . . . . . Office of the Publication Board (Department of Commerce)
OPB . . . . Old Picked Bumpers (Choice cigarette butts) (Australian slang)
OPB . . . . . . Other People's Butts (Cigarette butts garnered from ash trays) (Slang)
OPBMA . . . . Ocean Pearl Button Manufacturers Association
OPBU . . . . . . Operating Budget
OPC . . . . Office of Price Control (World War II)
OPC . . . . Office of Private Cooperation (State Department)
OPC . . . . Oil Policy Committee (US Office of Emergency Preparedness)
OPC . . . . . . Operational Control (Aviation)
OPC . . . . . . Orange Pigment Cell
OPC . . . . Ordnance Procurement Center (Army)
OPC. . . . . . . Out-Patient Clinic (Medicine)
OPC . . . . . . Overseas Press Club of America
OPCIT . . . . . Opere Citato (In the Work Cited)
OPCM . . . . . Operative Plasterers' and Cement Masons International Association of the United States and Canada

OPCO . . . . . . Operating Plan Change Orders (Coast Guard publication)
OPCO . . . . . . Outside Production Consignment Order
OPCODE . . . . Operations Code (Army)
OP-COM . . . . Operations-Communications
OPCON . . . . . Operation and Control
OPCON . . . . . Optimizing Control (Military)
OPCS . . . . Office of Population Censuses and Surveys (Department of Employment) (British)
OPD . . . . o-Phenylenediamine (Chemical)
OPD . . . . Office of Program Development (NASA)
OPD . . . . Officer Personnel Directorate (Army)
OPD . . . . Opened (NYSE symbol)
OPD . . . . Opening of Posterior Digestive (Gland)
OPD . . . . Operations Division (War Department General Staff) (World War II)
OPD . . . . Optical Particle Detector (for evaluating film quality)
OPD . . . . Optical Proximity Detector
OPD . . . . Out-Patient Department
OPD . . . . Out-Patient Dispensary
OPDAR . . . . . . Optical Detection and Ranging
OPDD . . . . . . Operational Plan Data Document (Military)
OPDEVFOR . . . Operations Development Forces
OPDL . . . . . . Office of Production and Defense Lending (Treasury Department)
OPDR . . . . . . Office of Primary Development Responsibility
OPE . . . . One-Pion Exchange (Nuclear)
OPE . . . . Orbiting Primate Experiment
OPE . . . . Oregon, Pacific & Eastern Railway Company (AAR code)
OPE . . . . Outer Planets Explorer (NASA)
OPEC . . . . . . Organization of Petroleum Exporting Countries
OPEDA . . . . . Organization of Professional Employees of the Department of Agriculture
OPEDC . . . . . . Overseas Private Enterprise Development Corporation (Proposed successor to Agency for International Development)
OPEI . . . . Office of Public Education and Information (NASA)
OPEI . . . . Outdoor Power Equipment Institute
OPEIU . . . . . . Office & Professional Employees' International Union
OPEM . . . . . . One-Pion Exchange Model
OPEMA . . . . . Oilfield Production Equipment Manufacturers Association
OPENAH . . . . Operational Evaluation of Armed Helicopters
OPEP . . . . . . Orbital-Plane Experiment Package (NASA)
OPERA . . . . . . Ordnance Pulses Experimental Research Assembly (Nuclear reactor)
OPET . . . . Organization, Personnel Equipment and Training (Group)
OPEVAL . . . . . Operational Evaluation (Navy)
OPEX . . . . . . Operational and Executive (UN)
OPF . . . . Official Personnel Folder (Military)
OPF . . . . Open Pore Foam
OPF . . . . Optical Propagation Facility
OPFAC . . . . . . Operating Facilities (Coast Guard publication)
OPFAD . . . . . . Outer-Perimeter Fleet Air Defense
OPG . . . . Office of the Postmaster General (Obsolete)
OPG . . . . Original Proof Gallon
OPG . . . . Outside Production Group
OPGT . . . . . . Outer Planets Grand Tour (NASA)
OPH . . . . Old Parliamentary Hand (Political) (British)
OPH . . . . Operational Propellant Handling
Oph D . . . . . . Doctor of Ophthalmology
OPHIR . . . . . . Organic Power and Heat Industrial Reactor (AEC)
OPHS . . . . . . Operational Propellant Handling System
OPHTS . . . . . Operational Propellant Handling Test Site
OPI . . . . Off-Site Production Inspection
OPI . . . . Office of Primary Interest
OPI . . . . Office of Public Information
OPI . . . . Oil Pressure Indicator
OPI . . . . Omnibus Personality Inventory (Guidance in education)
OPI . . . . Orbital Position Indicator
OPI . . . . Ordnance Procedure Instrumentations
OPI . . . . Ordnance Procurement Instructions
OPI . . . . Organophosphate Insecticide
OPI . . . . Outside Procurement (or Purchase) Inspection
OP & I . . . . . Office of Patents and Inventions
OP & I . . . . . . Office of Publications and Information (Department of Commerce)
OPIC . . . . Overseas Private Investment Corporation (US)
OPIL . . . . Opalescent Indicating Light
OPIM . . . . . . Order Processing and Inventory Monitoring (Data processing)
OPINTEL. . . . . Operational Intelligence
OPIRG . . . . . . Oregon Public Interest Research Group (Student organization)
OPK . . . . Opelika Manufacturing Corporation (NYSE symbol)
OPK . . . . Optokinetic
OPL . . . . Ocean Pressure Laboratory
OPL . . . . Operational
OPL . . . . Out-of-Phase Loading
OPL . . . . Outpost Line
OPL . . . . Overpaid Last Account

OPLAN . . . . . . Operation Plan
OPLE . . . . . . Omega Position Location Equipment (NASA)
OPLR . . . . Outpost Line of Resistance
OPM . . . . Office of Procurement and Material
OPM . . . . Office of Production Management (Superseded by WPB, 1942)
OPM . . . . Operating Plane Months (Navy)
OPM . . . . Operations Per Minute
OPM . . . . Operator Programming Method
OPM . . . . Optical Power Meter
OPM . . . . Optically Projected Map
OPM . . . . Oscillating Pressure Method
OPM . . . . Other People's Money (Wall Street term)
OPMG . . . . . . Office of Provost Marshal General (Also, PMGO)
OPMSO . . . . . Outside Production Material Sales Order
OPN . . . . Office of the Chief of Naval Operations (Also, OPNAV)
OPN . . . . Open
OPN . . . . Opercular Nerve
OPN . . . . Other Procurement, Navy
OPNAV. . . . . . Office of the Chief of Naval Operations
OPNG . . . . . . Opening
OPO . . . . Office of Personnel Operations (Army)
OPO . . . . Oil Pressure Out
OPO . . . . Optical Parametric Oscillator (Tunable LASER device)
OPO . . . . Orbiting Planetary Observatory
OPORD . . . . . Operations Order (Military)
OPOS . . . . . . Outside Production Operation Sheet
OPP . . . . Octal Print Punch
OPP . . . . Open-Pore Polyurethan (Plastic)
OPP . . . . Opposite
OPP . . . . Out of Print at Present
OPP . . . . Oxygen Partial Pressure
OPPD . . . . . . Omaha Public Power District
OPPE . . . . . . Office of Programming, Planning, and Evaluation
OPPI . . . . Organic Preparations and Procedures International (A publication)
OPPR . . . . . . Operating Program
OPPS . . . . . . Oxygen Partial Pressure Sensor
OPR . . . . Office of Primary Responsibility (Air Force)
OPR . . . . Office of Private Resources (Department of State)
OPR . . . . Office of Public Relations
OPR . . . . Old Prussian
OPR . . . . Operate (Operating; Operation; Operator)
OPR . . . . Operational Project Requirements
OPR . . . . Optical Page Reader (Data processing)
OPR . . . . Outpatient Rate
OPR . . . . Overall Pressure Ratio
OPRA . . . . . . Ohio Penal Racing Association
OPRD . . . . . . Office of Production Research and Development
OPRED . . . . . Operations Reduction (Government term)
OPREP. . . . . . Operational Reporting System (Military)
OPRFLT. . . . . . Operator Fault
OPRM . . . . . . Office of Program Review and Resources Management
OPRNL . . . . . . Operational
OPRRB . . . . . . Officer Personnel Record Review Board (Air Force)
OPRRE . . . . . . Office of Public Roads and Rural Engineering (Later, Bureau of Public Roads)
OPS . . . . Oblique Photo Sketcher
OPS . . . . Office of Pipeline Safety (Department of Transportation)
OPS . . . . Office of Price Stabilization (Terminated 1953)
OPS . . . . Office of Products Safety (FDA)
OPS . . . . Official Phone Station (Amateur radio)
OPS . . . . Oil Pressure Switch
OPS . . . . On-Line Process Synthesis (Data processing)
OPS . . . . Operational Power Supply
OPS . . . . Optical Processing System
OPS . . . . Optical Propagation Study
OPS . . . . Orbiting Primate Spacecraft
OPS . . . . Overhead Positioning System (AEC)
OPS . . . . Oxidizer Particle Size
OPS . . . . Oxygen Purge System (or Subsystem) (NASA)
OPS . . . . . . Supreme Temple Order Pythian Sisters
OP(S)ARMYJAG . . Opinion(s) of the Army Judge Advocate General
OPSC . . . . . . Office of Planning Standards and Coordination (HUD)
OPSET. . . . . . Optimal Set (of Parameters) (Hydrology)
OPSF . . . . . . Orbital Propellant Storage Facility
OPSI . . . . . . Ordnance Publications for Supply Index (Military)
OPSIM . . . . . Operational Simulator (Coast Guard)
OPSTR . . . . . . Operating Strength (Army)
OPT . . . . Oil Pressure Transmitter
OPT . . . . Optical
OPT . . . . Optical Point Transfer
OPT . . . . Optimum

OPT . . . . Optional
OPT . . . . Other People's Tobacco (Slang)
OPTA . . . . Organ and Piano Teachers Association
OPTAN . . . . . . Operations Target Analysis (of strike missions in North Vietnam)
OPTAR . . . . . . Operating Target
OPTAR . . . . . . Optical Automatic Ranging
Opt D . . . . . . Doctor of Optometry
OPTEC . . . . . . Optical Properties Technical Evaluation Center
OPTEV . . . . . . Operational Test and Evaluation
OPTEVFOR . . . . Operational Test and Evaluation Force (Navy)
OPTIC . . . . . . Optical Procedural Task Instruction Compiler
OPTICON . . . . Optical Tactical Converter (Electronic reader for the blind)
OPTRA . . . . . . Air Operational Training
OPTUL . . . . . . Optical Pulse Transmitter Using Leaser
OPU . . . . Operations Priority Unit
OPU . . . . Overseas Plexiglas Unit
OPV . . . . Ohms Per Volt (British)
OPW . . . . Ohio Power (NYSE symbol)
OPW . . . . . . Operating Weight (Air Force)
OPW . . . . . . Optical Window
OQ . . . . Officers Quarters (Military)
OQC . . . . . . Operator Quality Control (RADAR)
OQI . . . . Oil Quantity Indicator
OQL . . . . . . Observed Quality Level
OQL . . . . . . Outgoing Quality Level
OQL . . . . . . Outgoing Quality Limit
OQMG . . . . . . Office, Quartermaster General (Army)
OQP . . . . . . Optimum Qualification Procedure
OQR . . . . . . Officer's Qualification Record (Military)
OQTD . . . . . . Operational Qualifications Test Deficiency (Air Force)
OR . . . . Officer Records (Military)
OR . . . . Official Receiver
OR . . . . Official Records
OR . . . . Oleoresin
OR . . . . Omnidirectional Radio Range
OR . . . . Operating Resources
OR . . . . Operating Room (Medicine)
OR . . . . Operational Readiness
OR . . . . Operational Reliability (Army)
OR . . . . Operational Report
OR . . . . Operational (or Operations) Requirement
OR . . . . Operational Research Quarterly
OR . . . . Operationally Ready
OR . . . . Operations Research (Data processing)
OR . . . . Operations Room
OR . . . . Operculum Ridge
OR . . . . Opponents' Runs (Baseball)
OR . . . . Ordered Recorded
OR . . . . Ordnance Report
OR . . . . Oregon
OR . . . . Orienting Response (Psychology)
OR . . . . Other Ranks (Ranks other than officers) (Military)
OR . . . . Out of Range
OR . . . . Outside Radius (Technical drawings)
OR . . . . Outside Right (Soccer position)
OR . . . . Overall Report
OR . . . . Overhaul and Repair
OR . . . . Overseas Replacement
OR . . . . Owasco River Railway (AAR code)
OR . . . . Owner's Risk (Shipping)
O-R . . . . Oxidation-Reduction
O/R . . . . Office of Record
O/R . . . . On Request
O & R . . . . . . Ocean and Rail (Shipping)
O & R . . . . . . Overhaul and Repair (Navy)
ORA . . . . Office of Research Analysis (Air Force)
ORA . . . . Operations Research Analyst (Army)
ORA . . . . Output Register Address
ORA . . . . Organization de Resistance de l'Armee (France)
ORAAP . . . . . . Outstanding Reserve Airman Appointment Program
ORACLE . . . . . Oak Ridge Automatic Computer and Logical Engine
ORACLE . . . . . Organic Rankine Cycle
ORAD . . . . . . Office of Rural Areas Development (Department of Agriculture)
ORAD . . . . . . Outbound Radial (Aviation)
ORAF . . . . . . Organisation Regionale Africaine de la CISL
ORAL . . . . . . Oral Access to Library
ORAMCO . . . . Oriental American Trade Development Corporation
ORAN . . . . . . Orbital Analysis
ORATE . . . . . Ordered Random Access Talking Equipment
ORAU . . . . . . Oak Ridge Associated Universities (AEC)
ORB . . . . Oceanic Ridge Basalts

ORB . . . . Omnidirectional Radio Beacon
ORB . . . . Operational Research Branch (Canada)
ORB . . . . Owner's Risk of Breaking
ORBA . . . . Orde Baru (New Order) (Indonesia)
ORBIS . . . . . . Orbiting Radio Beacon Ionospheric Satellite (NASA)
ORBIS . . . . . . Ordering and Billing System
ORBIT . . . . . Oak Ridge Binary Internal-Translator
ORBIT . . . . . On-Line, Real-Time, Branch Information (IBM)
ORBIT . . . . . . Oracle Binary Internal Translator (Algebraic programming system)
ORBS . . . . . . Orbital Rendezvous Base System
ORC . . . . Office of Reserve Components (Army)
ORC . . . . Officers' Reserve Corps
ORC . . . . Operational Readiness Check
ORC . . . . Operational Reports Control (Military)
ORC . . . . Opinion Research Center
ORC . . . . Opinion Research Corporation
ORC . . . . Orange River Colony (Became Orange Free State)
ORC . . . . Order of Railway Conductors
ORC . . . . Order of the Red Cross
ORC . . . . Organized Reserve Corps
ORC . . . . Over Run Clutch
ORC . . . . Owner's Risk of Chafing
ORC . . . . Oxidation Resistant Coating
ORCA . . . . . Oregon Caves National Monument
ORCA . . . . . Organisme Europeen de Coordination des Recherches sur le Fluor et la Prophylaxie de la Carie Dentaire (European Organization for Research on Fluorine and Dental Caries Prevention)
ORCB . . . . . . Order of Railway Conductors and Brakemen
ORCCA . . . . Open Road Camper Clubs of America
ORCEN . . . . . Overseas Records Center (Military)
ORCON . . . . Observation Report Conversion (Program)
ORCON . . . . Organic Control
ORCV . . . . . . Overriding Cam Valve
ORD . . . . Office of Research and Development (Formerly, Office of Manpower Research and Office of Special Manpower Programs) (Manpower Administration, Department of Labor)
ORD . . . . Office of Rubber Director (WPB) (World War II)
ORD . . . . Operational Ready Date
ORD . . . . Operations Requirement Document
ORD . . . . Optical Rotary Dispersion
ORD . . . . Ordnance
ORD . . . . Overseas Replacement Depot (Military)
ORD . . . . Owner's Risk of Damage
ORDALT . . . . . Ordnance Alterations
ORDC . . . . . . Army Ordnance Corps
ORDC . . . . . . Ordnance Research and Development Center (Aberdeen Proving Ground, Maryland) (Navy)
ORDCAN . . . . Orders Cancelled (Air Force)
ORDCONCAN . . Orders Considered Cancelled (Air Force)
ORDCOR . . . . . Orders Corrected (Air Force)
ORDCORPS . . . Ordnance Corps (Army)
ORDDIS . . . . . Ordinary Discharge (Military)
ORDENG . . . . Ordnance Engineering
ORDIP . . . . . . Ordnance Alteration Installation Plan (Navy)
ORDIR . . . . . . Omnirange Digital RADAR
ORDLIS . . . . . Ordnance Logistics Information System (Navy)
ORDM . . . . . . Ordnance Corps Manual
ORDMOD . . . . Orders Modified (Navy)
ORDP . . . . . . Ordnance Corps Pamphlet (Army)
ORDRAT . . . . Ordnance Dial Reader and Translator
ORDVAC . . . . Ordnance Variable Automatic Computer (AEC)
ORE . . . . Obtained Radiation Emittance
ORE . . . . Ocean Research Equipment, Inc.
ORE . . . . Oceanographic Research Equipment
ORE . . . . Office of Regional Economics (Department of Commerce)
ORE . . . . Operational Readiness (Navy)
ORE . . . . Operational Readiness Evaluation (Military)
ORE . . . . Oregon
ORE . . . . Organisation Regionale Europeenne de la CISL
ORE . . . . Overtraining Reversal Effect
OREAP . . . . . Organisation Regionale de l'Est pour l'Administration Publique
OREG . . . . . . Oregon
ORELA . . . . . Oak Ridge Electron Linear Accelerator
OREO . . . . . . Orbiting Radio Emission Observatory (Satellite)
ORF . . . . Owner's Risk of Fire
ORF . . . . Owner's Risk of Freezing
ORFC . . . . . . Orifice
ORG . . . . Operations Research Group (Navy)
ORG . . . . Organization(al)
ORGALIME . . . Organisme de Liaison des Industries Metalliques Europeennes (Liaison Group for the European Engineering Industries)

ORGDP...... Oak Ridge Gaseous Diffusion Plant (AEC)
ORGL...... Organizational
ORGN ..... Organization
ORGY ...... Organization for the Rational Guidance of Youth (Fictitious
         organization in film, "The Man from ORGY")
ORH .... Operational Requirements Handbook
ORI .... Office of Research and Inventions
ORI .... Office of Road Inquiry (Later, Bureau of Public Roads)
ORI .... Operational Readiness Inspection (or Instruction)
ORI .... Operations Research, Incorporated
ORI .... Oregon Research Institute
ORI ...... Outdoor Recreation Institute
ORIA .... Oriental Rug Importers Association
ORIC .... Oak Ridge Isochronous Cyclotron
ORIC .... Operational Readiness Inspection Committee (NASA)
ORIG .... Origin(al)
ORINS ...... Oak Ridge Institute of Nuclear Studies
ORIT ...... Operational Readiness Inspection Test
ORIT ...... Organizacion Regional Interamericana de Trabajadores (Inter-
         American Regional Organization of Workers of the ICFTU)
ORL....... Observed Range Limit
ORL ...... Orbiting Research Laboratory (NASA)
ORL....... Ordnance Research Laboratory (Pennsylvania State University)
ORL....... Overrun Lights (Aviation)
ORL....... Owner's Risk of Leakage
ORLA .... Optimum Repair Level Analysis (Air Force)
ORLA ..... Orde Lama (Old Order) (Indonesia)
ORLL ...... Operational Reports - Lessons Learned (Army)
ORM .... Off Road Mobility
ORMA ...... Office of Refugee and Migration Affairs (Department of State)
OR/MC...... Operational Requirements / Military Characteristics
ORMI .... Oak Ridge Military Institute
ORMOA ..... Office for Relations with Military and Occupation Authorities
ORMU ...... Orbital Remote Maneuvering Unit
ORN .... Orange
ORNL ...... Oak Ridge National Laboratory
ORO .... Oak Ridge Operations Office (AEC)
ORO .... Operations Research Office
ORP....... Objective Rallying Point (Military)
ORP....... Optical Rotary Power
ORP....... Orbital Rendezvous Procedure
ORP....... Organ Recovery Program
ORP....... Outside Right Position (Dancing)
ORP....... Oxidation Reduction Potential
ORP....... Oxygen Reduction Potential
ORPHIC .... Organized Projected Hypotheses for Innovations in Curriculum
         (Educational planning)
ORPI ...... Organ Pipe Cactus National Monument
ORPICS .... Orbital Rendezvous Positioning, Indexing and Coupling System
ORPL ...... Overseas Replacement
ORPS ...... Overseas Return Placement System (Military)
ORPSU ...... Organized Reserve Port Security Unit
ORQA ...... Office of Reliability and Quality Assurance
ORR....... Oak Ridge Reactor
ORR....... Optical Ratio Reflector
ORR....... Orbital Rendezvous RADAR
ORR....... Orthographic RADAR Restitutor
ORR....... Owner's Risk Rates (Shipping)
ORRRC ...... Outdoor Recreation Resources Review Commission (Department of the
         Interior)
ORS........ Obligated Reserve Section (Air Force)
ORS........ Oceanographic Research Ship
ORS........ Octahedral Research Satellite (NASA)
ORS........ Office of Radiation Standards (AEC)
ORS........ Office of Rent Stabilization (Functions transferred to Office of Defense
        Mobilization, 1953)
ORS........ Office of Research and Statistics (Social Security Administration)
ORS........ Official Relay Station (Amateur radio)
ORS........ Old Red Sandstone
ORS........ Operations Research Society (British)
ORS........ Oral Surgeon
ORS........ Organization Rating Scale
ORS........ Originating Register Sender
ORS........ Orthopaedic Research Society
ORS........ Oscillographic Recording System
ORS........ Outboard Rotating Shield
ORS........ Oval Ring Seal
ORS........ Over Range Station (Aviation)
ORS........ Owner's Risk of Shifting
ORSA ..... Operations Research Society of America
ORSA .... Order of Recollects of St. Augustine

OR/SA ..... Operations Research/Systems Analysis
ORSAC ...... Oak Ridge Systems Analysis Code
OR/SAEC .... Operations Research/Systems Analysis Executive Course (Army)
ORSANCO.... Ohio River Valley Water Sanitation Commission
ORSORT ..... Oak Ridge School of Reactor Technology (AEC)
ORS(S) ..... Operational Research Section (Singapore)
ORT .... Operating Room Technician (Navy)
ORT .... Operational Readiness Test
ORT .... Operational Readiness Training (Air Force)
ORT .... Optical Rotary Table
ORT .... Optimum Resolution Technique
ORT .... Orbital Rendezvous Technique
ORT .... Order of Railroad Telegraphers (Later, Transportation-Communication
        Employees Union)
ORT .... Organization for Rehabilitation through Training (Acronym is used in
        names of several Jewish social welfare organizations)
ORT .... Overland RADAR Technology
ORTC .... Organized Reserve Training Center
ORTF ...... Office de Radiodiffusion Television Francaise (State-owned radio and
        television network) (France)
ORTP .... Operational Readiness Training Program (Army)
ORTT .... Operational Readiness Training Test (Army)
ORTU .... Organized Reserve Training Unit
ORTUAG.... Organized Reserve Training Unit, Vessel Augmentation (Military)
ORTUAM .... Organized Reserve Training Unit, Administration of Mobilization
ORTUAV .... Organized Reserve Training Unit, Aviation Support (Military)
ORTUEL .... Organized Reserve Training Unit, Electronics (Coast Guard)
ORTUF ..... Organized Reserve Training Unit, Coastal Force
ORTUPS .... Organized Reserve Training Unit, Port Security (Coast Guard)
ORTUPS(O) ... Organized Reserve Training Unit, Port Security (Operational)
ORTUR ..... Organized Reserve Training Unit, Rescue Coordination Center (Military)
ORU .... Optical Reference Unit
ORU........ Oral Roberts University (Oklahoma)
ORU........ Orange and Rockland Utilities, Inc. (NYSE symbol)
ORU .... Organization for Rebirth of Ukraine
ORUFE ..... Operational Research Unit, Far East
ORUS ...... Official Register of the United States
ORV .... Ocean Range Vessel (Air Force)
ORVAT..... Organizational Vehicle Automatic Tester
ORW .... Owner's Risk of Becoming Wet
ORWP...... Optical Radiation Weapon Program
ORZ .... Omnirange Zone
ORZ .... Outer Radiation Zone
OS .... Observation-Scouting Plane (When first two letters in Navy designation)
OS......... Ocean Station (Maps and charts)
OS......... Oculus Sinister (Left Eye) (Medicine)
OS .... Odd Symmetric
OS......... Off Stage
OS .... Official Station
OS .... Oil Solenoid
OS......... Oil Switch
OS .... Old Saxon (Language)
OS......... Old School
OS .... Old Series
OS .... Old Side
OS .... Old Style (Calendar, previous to 1752)
OS......... On Sale
OS......... On Sample
OS......... On Schedule
OS......... On Side
OS .... On Station (Military)
OS .... On Switch
OS .... One Shot
OS......... One Side
OS......... Only Son
OS .... Operating System
OS......... Operation Sandstone (Atomic weapons testing)
OS......... Operation Snapper (Atomic weapons testing)
OS .... Operational Sheets
OS .... Operational Supplements (Air Force)
OS .... Operator's Set
OS ...... Optical Scanning (Data processing)
OS .... Order of Servites
OS......... Order Sheet
OS .... Ordinary Seaman
OS......... Ordnance School (Army)
OS......... Ordnance Specifications (Navy)
OS......... Original Series
OS .... Oro Sellado (Standard Gold) (Spain)
Os .... Osmium (Chemical element)
OS .... Output Secondary (Electronics)

OS . . . . Outside
OS . . . . Outside Sentinel
OS . . . . Outsize (Of clothes)
OS . . . . Over the State (Regarding distribution)
OS . . . . Oversea (Military)
OS . . . . Oversize
OS . . . . Overspecificity (Psychometrics)
O/S . . . . Out of Service
O/S . . . . Out of Stock (Business and trade)
O/S . . . . Outstanding
OSA . . . . Office of the Secretary of the Army
OSA . . . . Official Secrets Act (British)
OSA . . . . Omnibus Society of America
OSA . . . . Optical Society of America
OSA . . . . Ordo (Eremitarum) Sancti Augustini (Augustinians) (Roman Catholic religious order)
OSA . . . . Overseas Supply Agency
OSAC . . . . . . Open Space Action Committee
OSAF . . . . . . Office of the Secretary of the Air Force
OSAL . . . . . . Opening of Salivary (Gland)
OSALSAA . . . . Office, Special Assistant for Logistical Support of Army Aircraft
OSALSTC . . . . Office, Special Assistant for Logistical Support of Tactical Communications
OSB . . . . Officer Selection Board
OSB . . . . Operations Stations Book (Navy)
OSB . . . . Order of St. Benedict (Roman Catholic men's religious order)
OSB . . . . Order of Shepherds of Bethlehem
OSB . . . . Order of the Stars and Bars
OSB . . . . Ordnance Supply Bulletin
OSB . . . . Ordo Sancti Benedicti (Order of Saint Benedict) (Benedictines) (Roman Catholic religious order)
OSBA . . . . . . Outlet and Switch Box Association
OSBM . . . . . . Office of Space Biology and Medicine (Proposed for NASA)
OSBM . . . . . . Ordo Sancti Basil Magni (Order of St. Basil the Great) (Roman Catholic men's religious order)
OSBS . . . . . . Oblate Sisters of the Blessed Sacrement (Roman Catholic religious order)
OSC . . . . Oblate Spherical Coordinates
OSC . . . . . . Oblati Sancti Caroli (Oblate Fathers of St. Charles) (Roman Catholic religious order)
OSC . . . . Orbit Shift Coil
OSC . . . . Order to Show Cause
OSC . . . . Ordnance Systems Command (Also, NOSC) (Formerly, Bureau of Naval Weapons)
OSC . . . . Oregon State College
OSC . . . . Organizational Supply Code (Army)
OSC . . . . Oscillator
OSC . . . . Oscillograph
OSC . . . . Out, See Copy (Proofreader's note)
OSC . . . . Overseas Settlement Committee (British) (World War I)
OSC . . . . Own Ship's Course
OSC . . . . Royal Clan, Order of Scottish Clans
OS Cam . . . . . Order of St. Camillus (Camillians) (Roman Catholic religious order)
OSCAR . . . . . Observation Schedule and Records
OSCAR . . . . . Operating Sequence Control Array (NASA)
OSCAR . . . . . Operations, Scheduling, Control, and Reporting
OSCAR . . . . . Optimum Survival Containment and Recovery
OSCAR . . . . . Orbiting Satellite Carrying Amateur Radio (Aerospace)
OSCP . . . . . . Oscilloscope
OSCPS . . . . . Oxygen Supply and Cabin Pressurization Section (Apollo) (NASA)
OSD . . . . Office of the Secretary of Defense
OSD . . . . Office of Student Detachment (Navy)
OSD . . . . Operational Support Directive (Military)
OSD . . . . Operational System Diagram
OSD . . . . Optical Scanning Device
OSD . . . . Order of St. Dominic
OSD . . . . Ordnance Supply Depot
OSD . . . . Overseas Settlement Department (British) (World War I)
OS/D . . . . . . Over, Short, and Damaged (Report) (Shipping)
OSD-BMC . . . Ballistic Missile Committee (of the OSD)
OSD/ISA . . . . Office of the Secretary of Defense for International Security Affairs
OSDP . . . . . . On-Site Data Processor (NASA)
OS & DR . . . . Over, Short and Damaged Report (Shipping)
OSE . . . . Ocean Science & Engineering, Inc.
OSE . . . . Omniforce Spatial Environment
OSE . . . . Operation Status Equipment
OSE . . . . Operational Support Equipment
OSE . . . . Union Mondiale pour la Protection de la Sante des Populations Juives et Oeuvres de Secours aux Enfants
OSF . . . . Odd Side Flat
OSF . . . . Order of St. Francis (Franciscans) (Roman Catholic religious order)
OSF . . . . Overgrowth Stimulating Factor (Cancer cause)

OSFC . . . . . . Ordinis Sancti Francisci Capuccini (Franciscan Capuchins) (Roman Catholic men's religious order)
OSFCW . . . . . Office of Solid Fuels Coordinator for War (World War II)
OSFD . . . . . . Office of Space Flight Development (NASA) (No longer in existence)
OSFI . . . . . . Open Steel Flooring Institute
OSFM . . . . . . Office of Spacecraft and Flight Missions
OSFP . . . . . . Office of Space Flight Programs (NASA) (No longer in existence)
OSFS . . . . . . Oblati Sancti Francisci Salesii (Oblate Fathers of St. Francis of Sales) (Roman Catholic religious order)
OSG . . . . Office of the Secretary General (UN)
OSG . . . . Office of the Solicitor General (Department of Justice)
OSG . . . . Office of the Surgeon General (of Public Health Service; later, absorbed by office of Assistant Secretary for Health and Scientific Affairs)
OSG . . . . Osphradial Ganglion
OSH . . . . Ordo Sancti Hieronymi (Hieronymites)
OSH . . . . Own Ship's Heading
OSHA . . . . . . Occupational Safety and Health Act (1970)
OSHA . . . . . . Occupational Safety and Health Administration (Department of Labor)
OSHA . . . . . . Office of Special Housing Assistance (HUD)
OSHJ . . . . . . Oblate Sisters of the Sacred Heart of Jesus (Roman Catholic religious order)
OSHT . . . . . . Grand Lodge Order of the Sons of Hermann in Texas
OSI . . . . Ocean Search, Incorporated
OSI . . . . Ocean Systems, Incorporated
OSI . . . . Oceanographic Services, Incorporated
OSI . . . . Office of Scientific Information (National Science Foundation)
OSI . . . . Office of Special Investigation (Air Force)
OSI . . . . Office of Strategic Information
OSI . . . . Overhead Supply Inventory
OSI . . . . Oyster Shell Institute
OSIA . . . . . . Office, Services and Information Agency (Military)
OSIC . . . . . . Optimization of Subcarrier Information Capacity
OSIGA . . . . . . Ohio State Inventory of Guidance Awareness
OSIGO . . . . . . Office of Chief Signal Officer
OSIP . . . . Operational Suitability Improvement Program (for aircraft)
OSIS . . . . Office of Science Information Service (National Science Foundation)
OSJ . . . . Oblates of St. Joseph (Roman Catholic religious order)
OSJ . . . . Sovereign Order of Saint John of Jerusalem
OSK . . . . Osaka Syosen Karsha (Japanese steamship company)
OSL . . . . Open/Short Locator
OSL . . . . Orbiting Space Laboratory
OSL . . . . Order of Saint Luke the Physician
OSL . . . . Outstanding Leg
OSM . . . . On Station Mode
OSM . . . . Ordnance Safety Manual (Military)
OSM . . . . Ordo Servorum Mariae (Order of Servants of Mary) (Servites) (Roman Catholic religious order)
OSM . . . . Organizacion Submarina Mexicana, SA
OSM . . . . Oxygen Steel Making
OSMM . . . . . . Office of Safeguards and Materials Management (AEC)
OSN . . . . Ocean Science News
OSN . . . . Office of the Secretary of the Navy
OSN . . . . Osphradial Nerve
OSNC . . . . . . Orient Steam Navigation Company (British)
OSO . . . . Ocean Systems Operations
OSO . . . . Orbiting Solar Observatory (A satellite)
OSO . . . . Ordnance Supply Office
OSOC . . . . . . Off-Site Originated Change
OSODS . . . . . . Office of Strategic Offensive and Defensive Systems (Navy)
OSP . . . . Obiit sine Prole (Died without Issue)
OSP . . . . Oblate Sisters of Providence (Roman Catholic religious order)
OSP . . . . Ocean Survey Program (Navy)
OSP . . . . Office of Scientific Personnel (NAS-NRC)
OSP . . . . Office of Surplus Property (Superseded by War Assets Corporation) (World War II)
OSP . . . . Offshore Procurement
OSP . . . . Operational Survival Plan (Civil Defense)
OSP . . . . Operations Support Plan (Navy)
OSP . . . . Order of St. Paul the First Hermit (Pauline Fathers) (Roman Catholic religious order)
OSP . . . . Outfitting Stock Point
OSP . . . . Outside Procured Stores
OSPA . . . . . . Organisation Sanitaire Panamericaine
OSPE . . . . . . Organizational Spare Parts and Equipment
OSPRO . . . . . . Ocean Shipping Procedures
OSR . . . . Office of Scientific Research (AFSC)
OSR . . . . Office of Security Review (DOD)
OSR . . . . Operational Scanning Recognition
OSR . . . . Operational Status Release (Navy)
OSR . . . . Operational Support Requirement (Military)
OSR . . . . Optical Scanning Recognition

OSR . . . . Optical Solar Reflector
OSR . . . . Optical Sound Recorder
OSR . . . . Optimum Ship Routing
OSR . . . . Ordnance Status Report
OSR . . . . Output Shift Register
OSR . . . . Output Signal Range
OSR . . . . Oversea Returnee
OSR . . . . Oxide Stable Resin
OSRD . . . . . . Office of Scientific Research and Development (World War II)
OSRD . . . . . . Office of Standard Reference Data (National Bureau of Standards)
OSREPL . . . . . Oversea Replacement (Military)
OSRET . . . . . . Oversea Returnee (Military)
OSRMD . . . . . Office of Scientific Research, Mechanics Division
OSS . . . . Ocean Surveillance Satellite
OSS . . . . Oceanic Scanning Spectrophotometer
OSS . . . . Office of Space Sciences (NASA)
OSS . . . . Office of Space Systems (Air Force)
OSS . . . . Office of Statistical Standards (Bureau of the Budget; later, OMB)
OSS . . . . Office of Strategic Services (World War II)
OSS . . . . Office of Support Services (Army)
OSS . . . . Offshore Surveillance System
OSS . . . . Old Submarine (Navy symbol)
OSS . . . . Opening of the Style Sac
OSS . . . . Operational Storage Site (Military)
OSS . . . . Optical Sight System
OSS . . . . Optical Surveillance System
OSS . . . . Orbital Space Station
OSS . . . . Own Ship's Speed
OSSA . . . . . . Office of Space Science and Applications (NASA)
OSSC . . . . . . Oblati Sacratissimi Cordis (Oblate Fathers of the Sacred Heart) (Roman Catholic religious order)
OSSC . . . . . . Ordnance Storage and Shipment Chart (Army)
OSSF . . . . . . Overseas Services Storage Facility
OSSN . . . . . . Other Specialty Serial Numbers (Air Force)
OSSP . . . . . . Outer Solar System Probe
OSSR . . . . . . Office of Selective Service Records
OSSR . . . . . . Own Ship's Speed Repeater
OSSS . . . . . . Optical Space Surveillance Subsystem
OSSS . . . . . . Orbital Space Station Study
OSSS . . . . . . Orbital Space Station System (of NASA)
OSST . . . . . . Offshore Storage Tank
OSsT . . . . Ordo Sanctissimae Trinitatis Redemptionis Captivorum (Order of the Most Holy Trinity) (Trinitarians) (Roman Catholic religious order)
OST . . . . Object Sorting Test
OST . . . . Objective Start Time
OST . . . . Office of Science and Technology (Executive Office of the President)
OST . . . . Operational Suitability Test (Air Force)
OST . . . . Optical Sensing Trigger
OST . . . . Orbit Stay Time
OST . . . . Order Shipping Time
OST . . . . Ordinary Spring Tides
OST . . . . Ordnance Special Training
OST . . . . Over Stress Testing
OSTAC . . . . . Ocean Science and Technology Advisory Committee
OSTD . . . . . . Office of Supersonic Transport Development (Obsolete) (Department of Transportation)
OSTD . . . . . . Ordnance Standards
OSTF . . . . . . Operational Silo Test Facility
OSTF . . . . . . Operational Suitability Test Facility
OSTF . . . . . . Operational System Test Facility (Air Force)
OSTG . . . . . . Ocean Science and Technology Group (Navy)
OSTI . . . . . . Office of Scientific and Technical Information (NASA)
OSTI . . . . . . Organization for Social and Technical Innovation
OSTIV . . . . . . Organisation Scientifique et Technique Internationale du Vol a Voile (International Technical and Scientific Organization for Soaring Flight)
OStJ . . . . . . Officer of the Order of St. John of Jerusalem (British)
OSTS . . . . . . Office of State Technical Services (Department of Commerce)
OSTS . . . . . . Operational Suitability Test Site
OSTV . . . . . . Operational Support Television (Military)
OSU . . . . Ohio State University
OSU . . . . Order of St. Ursula
OSU . . . . Oregon State University
OSUR . . . . . . Ohio State University Reactor
OSURF . . . . . Ohio State University Research Foundation
OSURO . . . . . Ohio State University Radio Observatory
OSV . . . . Ocean Station Vessel
OSV . . . . Okulierschnellverschluss
OSV . . . . . . Orbital Support Vehicle
OSV . . . . Oriented Space Vehicle
OSV . . . . Output Serving Voltage
OSW . . . . Oblique Shock Wave

OSW . . . . Oesterreichische Stickstoffwerke AG (Later, OMS)
OSW . . . . Office of Saline Water (Department of the Interior)
OSW . . . . Office of Secretary of War
OSW . . . . Office of Solid Wastes (Public Health Service) (Later, SWO)
OSWA . . . . . . Off-Shift Work Authorization
OSWAC . . . . . . Ordnance Special Weapons Ammunition Command (Later, Weapons Command)
OSWC . . . . . . Ordnance Special Weapons Command (Army) (Merged with Missile Command)
OSWD . . . . . . Office of Special Weapons Development (Army)
OS & Y . . . . . Outside Screw and Yoke
OT . . . . Objective Test (Psychology)
OT . . . . Observer-Target
OT . . . . Occupational Therapy (or Therapist)
OT . . . . Occupational Therapy Technician (Navy)
OT . . . . Ocean (Oversea) Transportation (Military)
OT . . . . Office of Telecommunications (Executive Office of the President)
OT . . . . Office of Territories (Department of the Interior)
OT . . . . Oil-Tight
OT . . . . Old Term
OT . . . . Old Terminology
OT . . . . Old Testament (of the Bible)
OT . . . . Old Timer (Communications operators' colloquialism)
OT . . . . Old Top (Communications operators' colloquialism)
OT . . . . Old Tuberculin
OT . . . . Olfactory Threshold
OT . . . . On Time
OT . . . . On Truck
OT . . . . One-Time
OT . . . . Operating Temperature
OT . . . . Operating Time
OT . . . . Operational Test
OT . . . . Oregon Trunk Railway (AAR code)
OT . . . . Organization Table
OT . . . . Orotracheal
OT . . . . Other Than
OT . . . . Other Time
OT . . . . Otis Elevator Company (NYSE symbol)
OT . . . . Overlap Technician
OT . . . . Overtime (Business and trade)
O/T . . . . Old Terms (Business and trade)
O/T . . . . Overtime (Business and trade)
OTA . . . . Office of Tax Analysis (Department of the Treasury)
OTA . . . . Office of Technology Assessment (Proposed congressional traffic control organization)
OTA . . . . Oil Trades Association of New York
OTA . . . . Omnidirectional Transmitter Antenna
OTA . . . . Operation Town Affiliations
OTA . . . . Organisation Mondiale du Tourisme et de l'Automobile (World Touring and Automobile Organization)
OTAC . . . . . . Ordnance Tank-Automotive Command (Army) (Merged with Weapons and Mobility Command)
OTACS . . . . . . Old Timer Assay Commissioners Society
OTAD . . . . . . Office of Tributary Area Development (of TVA)
OTAD . . . . . . Oversea Terminal Arrival Date (Army)
OTADA . . . . . Office of Tracking and Data Acquisition
OTAG . . . . . . Office of the Adjutant General (Army)
OTAN . . . . . . Organisation du Traite de l'Atlantique Nord (French equivalent of NATO)
OTANY . . . . . Oil Trades Association of New York
OTASE . . . . . Organisation du Traite de Defense Collective pour l'Asie du Sud-Est (French equivalent of Southeast Asia Treaty Organization)
OTB . . . . Off-Track Betting
OTB . . . . Open to Buy
OTB . . . . Ordnance and Terminal Ballistics
OTBSSC . . . . . Over Thirty But Still Swinging Club
OTC . . . . Objective, Time, and Cost
OTC . . . . Office of Temporary Controls
OTC . . . . Officer in Tactical Command (Air Force)
OTC . . . . Officers' Training Camp (World War I)
OTC . . . . Officers' Training Corps
OTC . . . . Old Timers' Club
OTC . . . . Operational Training Capability (Air Force)
OTC . . . . Order of Three Crusades
OTC . . . . Ordnance Training Command (Army)
OTC . . . . Organization for Trade Cooperation (GATT)
OTC . . . . Over-the-Counter (Pharmacy)
OTC . . . . Over the Counter (Stock)
OTC . . . . Overseas Trade Corporation (British)
OTC . . . . Oxygen Transfer Compressor
OTCA . . . . . . Overseas Technical Cooperation Agency (Japan)
OTCC . . . . . . Organic Thermal Control Coating

OTCLANT . . . . Fleet Operational Training Command, Atlantic (usually, COTCLANT)
OTCM . . . . . . Ordnance Technical Committee Minutes (Military)
OTCPAC . . . . Fleet Operational Training Command, Pacific (usually, COTCPAC)
OTCR . . . . . . Office of Technical Cooperation and Research (Department of State)
OTD . . . . Official Table of Distances
OTD . . . . On the Deck
OTD . . . . Optical Tracking Device
OTD . . . . Organ Tolerance Dose
OTDA . . . . . . Office of Tracking and Data Acquisition (NASA)
OTE . . . . Optical Tracking Electronics
OTE . . . . Outer Tube Equipment
OT & E . . . . . Operational Test and Evaluation (Military)
OTEP . . . . . . Operational Test and Evaluation Plan (Military)
OTES . . . . . . Optical Technology Experiment System
OTF . . . . Optical Transfer Function
OTF . . . . Optimum Traffic Frequency (Radio)
OTF . . . . Other Than Flat (Freight)
OTFE . . . . . . Optical Terminal Flight Evaluation
OTFR . . . . . . Overall Transfer Function Response
OTH . . . . Other Than Hand (Freight)
OTH . . . . . . Over-the-Horizon (RADAR)
OTHR . . . . . . Over-the-Horizon RADAR
OTI . . . . Official Test Insecticide
OTI . . . . Optics Technology, Incorporated
OTI . . . . Ordnance Technical Instructions (Navy)
OTI . . . . Oregon Technical Institute
OTI . . . . Oxide Throat Insert
OTIA . . . . . . Office of Technical Information Agency (Army)
OTIA . . . . . . Ordnance Technical Intelligence Agency
OTIEP . . . . . . Office of Technical Information and Educational Programs (NASA) (No longer in existence)
OTIG . . . . . . Office, the Inspector General
OTIS . . . . Occupational Training Information System
OTIS . . . . Oklahoma Teletype Interlibrary System
OTIS . . . . Operational Test Instrumentation Ship (Navy)
OTIS . . . . Ordnance Telemetry Instrumentation Station (Army)
OTIS . . . . Other Than Iron or Steel (Freight)
OTJ . . . . On the Job
OTJAG . . . . . . Office, the Judge Advocate General
OTKDF . . . . . . Other Than Knocked Down Flat (Freight)
OTL . . . . Oil Tight Light
OTL . . . . Operating Temperature Limit
OTL . . . . Operating Time Log
OTL . . . . Oxidizer Topping Line
OTLP . . . . . . Zero Transmission Level Point
OTM . . . . . . Office of Telecommunications Management (FCC)
OTMA . . . . . . Oilfield Tank Manufacturers Association
OTN . . . . Octal Track Number
OTN . . . . Operational Teletype Network
OTN . . . . Over the Nose
OTNG . . . . . . Observer Training (Army)
OTO . . . . Oil Temperature Out
OTO . . . . Out-to-Out
OTOCTA . . . . Optimum Technical Operational Concept to Accomplish
OTP . . . . Office of Telecommunications Policy
OTP . . . . Office of Trade Promotion (Department of Commerce)
OTP . . . . Open Top (Freight)
OTP . . . . Other Than Portable (Freight)
OTP . . . . Oxidizer Tanking Panel
OTPI . . . . . . On Top Position Indicator
OTPMG . . . . . Office, the Provost Marshal General
OTQ . . . . On the Quarter
OTR . . . . Observed Temperature Rise
OTR . . . . Occupational Therapist, Registered
OTR . . . . Operating Temperature Range
OTR . . . . Operational Time Record
OTR . . . . Organic Test Reactor
OTRA . . . . . . Other Than Regular Army
OTRA . . . . . . Oversea Theater Requisitioning Authority (Military)
OTRAC . . . . . Oscillogram Trace Reader (Data processing)
OTRACO . . . . . Office des Transports du Congo (Office of Transportation in the Congo)
OTRAR . . . . . Other Than Regular Army
OTRT . . . . . . Operating Time Record Tag
OTS . . . . Off the Shelf
OTS . . . . Office of Technical Services (Later, CFSTI; then, NTIS) (National Bureau of Standards)
OTS . . . . Officers' Training School
OTS . . . . Operational Test Site
OTS . . . . Optical Technology Satellite
OTS . . . . Optical Tracking System
OTS . . . . Orbital Transport Systems

OTS . . . . Organization of Tropical Studies (National Science Foundation)
OTS . . . . Out of Service
OTS . . . . Ovonic Threshold Switch
O/TSC . . . . . . Other Than Special Consultants (Military)
OTSG . . . . . . Office of the Surgeon General
OTSR . . . . . . Once-Through Superheat Reactor (AEC)
OTSZH . . . . . . Other Than Steel or Zinc Heads (Freight)
OTT . . . . Office of Traffic and Transportation
OTT . . . . One-Time Tape
OTT . . . . Oral Trade Tests (Department of Labor)
OTT . . . . . . Outgoing Teletype
OTTER . . . . . Operational Training, Test and Evaluation RADAR
OTU . . . . Office of Technology Utilization (NASA)
OTU . . . . Office du Tourisme Universitaire (France)
OTU . . . . Operational Taxonomic Unit (Numerical taxonomy)
OTU . . . . Operational Training Unit
OTU . . . . Outlet Company (NYSE symbol)
OTUS . . . . . . Office of the Treasurer of the United States
OTV . . . . Orbital Transfer Vehicle
OTWR . . . . . . Orthogonal-Wound Refrasil
OU . . . . Oculi Unitas (Both Eyes Together)
OU . . . . Oklahoma University
OU . . . . Open University
OUA . . . . . . Order of United Americans
OUAM . . . . . Order of United American Mechanics
OUBC . . . . . . Oxford University Boat Club
OUCC . . . . . . Oxford University Cricket Club
OUCTA . . . . . Order of United Commercial Travelers of America
OUD . . . . Operational Use Data
OUDS . . . . . . Oxford University Dramatic Society
OUEL . . . . . . Oxford University Engineering Laboratory
OUF . . . . Oxygen Utilization Factor
OUK . . . . . . Operation Upshot-Knothole (Atomic weapons testing)
OUL . . . . . . Orbital Utility Light
OUM . . . . . . Oxford University Mission
OUN . . . . Organizatsiia Ukrains' kykh Natsionalistiv
OUNC . . . . . . Office for the United Nations' Conference (NASA) (Ad hoc office)
OUNPSA . . . . . Office of United Nations Political and Security Affairs (Department of State)
OUNS . . . . . . Office of Urban Neighborhood Services (HUD)
OUO . . . . Official Use Only
OUP . . . . Oxford University Press
OUPT . . . . . . Output
OURD . . . . . . Ogden Union Railway & Depot (AAR code)
OURI . . . . . . Oklahoma University Research Institute
OURS . . . . . . Orangutan Recovery Service
OUSA . . . . . . Office, Under Secretary of Army
OUSAF . . . . . Office, Under Secretary of Air Force
OUSARMA . . . Office of the United States Army Attaché
OUSCS . . . . . Office of Urban Studies and Clearinghouse Services (HUD)
OUSN . . . . . . Office, Under Secretary of Navy
OUSOFA . . . . Office of the Under Secretary of the Army
OUSW . . . . . . Office of the Under Secretary of War (Obsolete)
OUT . . . . Organization for Unemployed Teachers
OUT . . . . Outlet
OUTBD . . . . . Outboard
OUTC . . . . . . Ordnance Unit Training Center (Military)
OUTRAN . . . . Output Translator (IBM)
OUTUS . . . . . . Outside the United States
OV . . . . Oil of Vitriol
OV . . . . Orbiting Vehicle (Aerospace)
OV . . . . Output Voltage
OV . . . . Over
OV . . . . Over Voltage
OVA . . . . . . Office of Veterans' Affairs
OVAC . . . . . Overseas Visual Aids Centre (British)
OVAM . . . . . Orbital Vehicle Assembly Mode
OVB . . . . . . Onafhankelijk Verbond van Bedrijfsorganisaties (Independent Federation of Industrial Organizations) (Netherlands)
OVBD . . . . . . Overboard
OVC . . . . . . Ontario Veterinary College
OVC . . . . . . Oxidizer Vent Control
OVCS . . . . . . Operational Voice Communication Subsystem
OVCST . . . . . Overcast
OVE . . . . . . On Vehicle Equipment
OVERS . . . . . Orbital Vehicle Reentry Simulator (NASA)
OVF . . . . Oxygen Vent Fill
OVFL . . . . . . Overflow
OVHD . . . . . Oval Head
OVHD . . . . . . Overhead
OVHL . . . . . . Overhaul

OVL . . . . Optically Void Liquid
OVLD. . . . . . Overload
OVLP . . . . . . Over Voltage Load Protection
OVM . . . . On Vehicle Materiel (Military)
OVM . . . . Orbiting Velocity Meter
OVNI . . . . . Objectos Volantes No Identicados (Unidentified Flying Objects)
OVP. . . . . . . Oil-Vapor Pump
OVP . . . . . . Outside Vendor Personnel
OVP . . . . . . Over Voltage Protection
OVPD . . . . . Overpaid
OVR . . . . Office of Vocational Rehabilitation (HEW)
OVR . . . . . . Over Voltage Relay
OVRD . . . . . Override
OVRN . . . . . Overrun
OVRO . . . . . Owens Valley Radio Observatory
OVS . . . . Optical Viewing System
OVS . . . . Overhaul Specification
OVSP . . . . . Overspeed
OVSR . . . . . . Office of Vehicle Systems Research (Later, Safety System Laboratory)
              (National Bureau of Standards)
OVT . . . . . . Occupational-Vocational-Technical Training
OVT. . . . . . . Overnite Transportation Company (NYSE symbol)
OVU. . . . . . Overseas Securities Company (American Stock Exchange symbol)
OVUREP . . . . . Overseas Unit Replacement (System)
OVV . . . . . . Optically Violently Variable (QUASAR)
OVV . . . . . . Over Voltage
OVWD . . . . . Operating Vehicle While Drunk
OW . . . . Obere Winkelgruppe (Angles above 45º) (German military - World War II)
OW . . . . Ocellus Width
OW . . . . Ohne Wert (Without Value) (Germany)
OW . . . . Old Welsh
OW . . . . Old Woman (A wife) (Slang)
OW . . . . One Way (Fare)
OW . . . . Order Wire (Military)
OW . . . . Ordinary Warfare
OW . . . . Outer Wing
OW . . . . Overseas Writers (Association)
O/W . . . . . . Oil in Water
OWA . . . . . . Optical Wholesalers Association
OWAA . . . . . . Outdoor Writers Association of America
OWAEC . . . . . Organization for West African Economic Co-operation
OWC . . . . . . Officers' Wives Club (Military)
OWC . . . . . . Ordinary Wave Component
OWC . . . . . . Ordnance Weapons Command (Later, Weapons Command)
OWE . . . . . . Operating Weight Empty (of space shuttle) (NASA)
OWE . . . . . . Optimum Working Efficiency
OWF . . . . . . On Weight of Fiber
OWF . . . . . . Optimum Working Frequency (Communications)
OWG . . . . . . Oil, Water, Gas
OWGL . . . . . Obscure Wire Glass
OWHA . . . . . Oliver Wendell Holmes Association
OWI . . . . . . Ocellus Width Index

OWI . . . . Office of War Information (World War II)
OWI . . . . Operating While Intoxicated (Traffic offense charge)
OWIU . . . . . . Oil Workers International Union
OWL . . . . . . National Order of Women Legislators
OWL . . . . . . Older Women's Liberation (Feminist group)
OWL . . . . . . Other Woman, Limited (An organization)
OWLS . . . . . Office Workers Link Shift (After-hours production workers) (World War II)
OWLS. . . . . . Operation Work Load Scheduling
OWM . . . . . . Office of War Mobilization (Succeeded by OWMR, 1944)
OWM . . . . . . Office of Weights and Measures (National Bureau of Standards)
OWMR . . . . . Office of War Mobilization and Reconversion (Succeeded OWM, 1944;
              became part of Office of Temporary Controls, 1946)
OWP . . . . . . One-Way Polar (Telegraph)
OWP . . . . . . Outer Wing Panel
OWPP . . . . . Office of Welfare and Pension Plans (Department of Labor)
OWR . . . . . . Obligated War Reserves (Army)
OWR . . . . . . Omega West Reactor (AEC)
OWRR . . . . . Office of Water Resources Research (Department of the Interior)
OWS . . . . . . Ocean Weather Ship
OWS . . . . . . Operational Weather Support
OWS . . . . . . Orbital Weapon System
OWS . . . . . . Orbital Workshop (NASA)
OWS . . . . . . Ordnance Weapon Systems (Army)
OWSJ . . . . . Order of the White Shrine of Jerusalem
OWU . . . . . . Office of War Utilities (WPB)
OWU . . . . . . Ohio Wesleyan University
OX . . . . Oxide (or Oxidizer)
OXA . . . . . . Oxalic Acid
OXFAM . . . . . Oxford Committee for Famine Relief (British)
OXID . . . . . . Oxidizer
OXM . . . . . . Oxford Industries, Inc. (NYSE symbol)
OXO . . . . . . Orbiting X-Ray Observatory (NASA)
OXP. . . . . . . Oxford Paper Company (NYSE symbol) (Delisted)
OXY . . . . . . Occidental Petroleum Corp. (NYSE symbol)
OXY . . . . . . Oxygen
OY . . . . Orange Yellow
OYA . . . . . . Orthodox Youth of America
OYP. . . . . . . Opportunities for Youth Program (Canada)
OZ . . . . Ounce
OZ . . . . Ozone
OZA . . . . . . Ozark Air Lines, Inc.
OZAR . . . . . Ozark National Scenic Riverways (National Park Service designation)
OZARC. . . . . . Ozone ARCAS (All-Purpose Rocket for Collecting Atmospheric Soundings)
              (Navy)
OZD . . . . . . Observed Zenith Distance (Navigation)
OZ-FT . . . . . Ounce Foot
OZIN . . . . . . Ounce Inch
OZ-IN . . . . . Ounce Inch
OZ-INS . . . . . Ounce Inches
OZO . . . . . . Orbiting Zoological Observatory to Track Animals
OZT . . . . . . Ounces Troy

P

P . . . . Aircraft (Wind triangle problems)
P . . . . Departure
P . . . . Office of Personnel (Coast Guard)
P . . . . Pacer
P . . . . Pacific Standard Time (Aviation)
P . . . . Page
P . . . . Pamphlet
P . . . . Paper
p . . . . Para (Chemistry)
P . . . . Parallax
P . . . . Parental
P . . . . Park
P . . . . Part
P . . . . Participle
P . . . . Partim (In Part)
P . . . . Past
P . . . . Paste
P . . . . Pastor
P . . . . Patchy (Decelerometer readings) (Aviation)
P . . . . Pater (Father)
P . . . . Patrol (Designation for all US military aircraft)
P . . . . Pawn (Chess)
P . . . . Pax (Peace)
P . . . . Pebbles
P . . . . Pengo (Monetary unit in Hungary until 1946)
P . . . . Penny
P . . . . People
P . . . . Per
P . . . . Perch
P . . . . Pere (Father)
P . . . . Perforation
P . . . . Perianth
P . . . . Pericardium
P . . . . Perimeter
P . . . . Period
P . . . . Perishable
P . . . . Peseta (Spanish and Latin American monetary unit)
P . . . . Peso (Spanish and Latin American monetary unit)
P . . . . Pharmacopoeia
P . . . . Philadelphia (Pennsylvania) (Mint mark, when appearing on US coins)
P . . . . Phillips Petroleum Company (NYSE symbol)
P . . . . Phosphorus (Chemical element)
P . . . . Photographic Reconnaissance Capability (When suffix to Navy aircraft designation)
P . . . . Piano (Softly) (Music)
P . . . . Piaster (Monetary unit in Spain, Republic of Vietnam, and some Middle Eastern countries)
p . . . . Pico (A prefix meaning divided by one trillion)
P . . . . Pie
P . . . . Pilaster (Technical drawings)
P . . . . Pilot
P . . . . Pinnule
P . . . . Pint
P . . . . Pipe
P . . . . Pitch (Technical drawings)
P . . . . Pitch or Pitcher (Baseball)
P . . . . Pius (Dutiful)
P . . . . Planed
P . . . . Plate (Electron tube) (Technical drawings)
P . . . . Pleasant
P . . . . Plug
P . . . . Plus (More)
P . . . . Point

P . . . . Point (Lacrosse position)
P . . . . Poise
P . . . . Polar (Air mass)
P . . . . Polar distance
P . . . . Polarization
P . . . . Pole
P . . . . Pond
P . . . . Ponendum (To Be Placed)
P . . . . Pope
P . . . . Population
P . . . . Port
P . . . . Position
P . . . . Post
P . . . . Post (After)
P . . . . Postage
P . . . . Posten (Sentry) (German military)
P . . . . Posterior
P . . . . Power (Mechanics)
P . . . . Practical Intelligence
P . . . . Precipitation Ceiling (Aviation weather reports)
P . . . . Predicate
P . . . . Premolar (Dentistry)
P . . . . Presbyterian
P . . . . Present
P . . . . President
P . . . . Pressure (Mechanics)
P . . . . Pridie (The Day Before)
P . . . . Priest
P . . . . Priestly code used in biblical criticism
P . . . . Primary
P . . . . Primus (First)
P . . . . Princeps (Prince)
P . . . . Principal
P . . . . Pro (For)
P . . . . Probability (Statistics)
P . . . . Probability Ratio
P . . . . Proconsul
P . . . . Professional (Civil Service employees designation)
P . . . . Proficiency
P . . . . Profit
P . . . . Prompt (i.e., the right side) (A stage direction)
P . . . . Proportion in a Specific Class
P . . . . Proposed Departure (Aviation)
P . . . . Protestant
P . . . . Proton
P . . . . Prototroch
P . . . . Publication
P . . . . Punch
P . . . . Punkt (Point) (German military)
P . . . . Pupil
P . . . . Purl (Knitting)
P . . . . Purple
P . . . . Pursuit (Airplane designation)
P(Day) . . . . . . Production Day (Army)
3P . . . . Three-Pole, or Triple Pole (Switch)
4P . . . . Four-Pole (Switch)
P^{32} . . . . Radioactive Phosphorus
PA . . . . Pan-American Airways
PA . . . . Par Autorite (By Authority) (France)
PA . . . . Paralysis Agitans
PA . . . . Parametric Amplifier
PA . . . . Parapsychological Association
PA . . . . Parents Anonymous

PA . . . . Parents' Association
PA . . . . Participial Adjective
PA . . . . Particular Average
PA . . . . Passenger Agent
PA . . . . Patient (Medical slang)
PA . . . . Pattern Analysis (Test)
PA . . . . Pending Availability
PA . . . . Pennsylvania
PA . . . . Pennsylvania Railroad Company (NYSE symbol; later, PC)
PA . . . . Per Annum (By the Year)
PA . . . . Performance Analysis
PA . . . . Permanent Appointment
PA . . . . Pernicious Anemia
PA . . . . Personal Affairs
PA . . . . Personal Appearance
PA . . . . Personal Assistant (British)
PA . . . . Philippine Army
PA . . . . Philippine Association
PA . . . . Phonocardiogram Amplifier
PA . . . . Phosphoarginine
PA . . . . Photodiode Amplifier
PA . . . . Phthalic Anhydride (Chemical)
PA . . . . Physics Abstracts
PA . . . . Picatinny Arsenal (Army)
pA . . . . Picoampere
PA . . . . Pinellas Area Office (AEC)
PA . . . . Point of Aim (Military)
PA . . . . Polar Atlantic (American air mass)
PA . . . . Polymer Adhesive
PA . . . . Port Agency (Army)
PA . . . . Position Approximate (Navigation)
PA . . . . Post Adjutant
PA . . . . Post Amplifier
PA . . . . Posterior Aorta
PA . . . . Power Amplifier
PA . . . . Power Approach (Aerospace)
PA . . . . Pre-Amplifier
PA . . . . Prefect Apostolic
PA . . . . Press Agent
PA . . . . Press Association
PA . . . . Pressure Altitude (Aviation)
PA . . . . Price Analyst
PA . . . . Prince Albert Coat (Slang)
PA . . . . Principle of Adding (New math)
PA . . . . Priority Aggregate
PA . . . . Private Account
PA . . . . Procurement Authorization
PA . . . . Production Adjustment
PA . . . . Program Account
PA . . . . Program Address
PA . . . . Program Analysis (Data processing)
PA . . . . Program Authorization
PA . . . . Prolonged Action
PA . . . . Proprietary Association
PA . . . . Prosecuting Attorney
Pa . . . . Protactinium (Chemical element)
PA . . . . Proto-Actinium
PA . . . . Provisional Allowance
PA . . . . Psychoanalyst
PA . . . . Psychological Abstracts
PA . . . . Psychological Age
PA . . . . Public Act
PA . . . . Public Address (Amplification equipment) (Communications)
PA . . . . Public Administration
PA . . . . Public Affairs
PA . . . . Public Assistance
PA . . . . Publication Announcement
PA . . . . Pulse Amplifier
PA . . . . Puppeteers of America
PA . . . . Purchasing Agent
PA . . . . Put Away (Papers) (British)
P/A . . . . Pilotless Aircraft
P/A . . . . Power of Attorney
P/A . . . . Private Account (Banking)
P & A . . . . . . Percussion and Auscultation (Medicine)
P & A . . . . . Personnel and Administration (Army)
P & A . . . . . Pioneer and Ammunition
P & A . . . . . Price and Availability
P & A . . . . . Procurement and Assignment
P in A . . . . . . Parallax in Altitude (Navigation)
PAA . . . . Pan American World Airways, Inc. (Also see PAN-AM and PN)

PAA . . . . Pennsylvania & Atlantic R. R. (AAR code)
PAA . . . . Peruvian-American Association
PAA . . . . Planar Array Antenna
PAA . . . . Polish Association of America
PAA . . . . Population Association of America
PAA . . . . Post Award Action
PAA . . . . Potato Association of America
PAA . . . . Power Amplifier Assembly
PAA . . . . Print Advertising Association
PAA . . . . Professional Archers Association
PAA . . . . Proprietary Association of America
PAAA . . . . . . Premium Advertising Association of America
PAABS . . . . . Pan-American Association of Biochemical Societies
PAAC . . . . . . Pacific and Asian Affairs Council
PAAC . . . . . . Program Analysis Adaptable Control
PAAO . . . . . . Pan-American Association of Ophthalmology
PAAP . . . . . . Peaceful Alternatives to the Atlantic Pact
PAAP . . . . . . Provisional Algal Assay Procedure (Test measuring impact of chemicals on algal growth)
PAB . . . . Panair do Brasil, SA
PAB . . . . Para-Aminobenzoic
PAB . . . . Patrick Air Force Base
PAB . . . . Petroleum Administrative Board (Terminated, 1936)
PAB . . . . Police Administration Building
PAB . . . . Price Adjustment Board
PAB . . . . Priorities Allotment Board
PAB . . . . Pulsed Adsorption Bed (Process)
PABA . . . . . . Para-Aminobenzoic Acid
PABA . . . . . . Progessive Angus Breeders Association
PABD . . . . . . Precise Access Block Diagram
PABLA . . . . . . Problem Analysis by Logical Approach
PABV. . . . . . . Pyro-Actuated Ball Valve
PABX . . . . . . Private Automatic Branch Exchange (or dial PBX) (Communications)
PAC . . . . Pacific
PAC . . . . Pacific Air Command (Air Force)
PAC . . . . Pacific Airmotive Corporation
PAC . . . . Pacific Automotive Corporation
PAC . . . . Pacific Telephone & Telegraph Company (NYSE symbol)
PAC . . . . Packaged Assembly Circuit
PAC . . . . Packard Automobile Classics
PAC . . . . Pan-Africanist Congress (South Africa)
PAC . . . . Pan American College (Texas)
PAC . . . . Pan-American Congress
PAC . . . . Parametric Amplifier Converter
PAC . . . . Parker Aircraft Corporation
PAC . . . . Partido Autentico Constitucional (Authentic Constitutional Party) (El Salvador)
PAC . . . . Peace Action Center
PAC . . . . Performance Analysis and Control
PAC . . . . Personal Analog Computer
PAC . . . . Pharmaceutical Advertising Club
PAC . . . . Phenacetin (Acetophenetidin), Aspirin, Caffeine
PAC . . . . Plasma Arc Chamber
PAC . . . . Plowshare Advisory Committee (AEC)
PAC . . . . Pneumatic Analog Computer
PAC . . . . Policy Advisory Center
PAC . . . . Policy Advisory Committee (of Office of Economic Opportunity local program)
PAC . . . . Political Action Committee
PAC . . . . Primary Address Code
PAC . . . . Printing Accountants Club
PAC . . . . Production Acceleration Capacity
PAC . . . . Program Adjustment Committee
PAC . . . . Program Advisory Committee
PAC . . . . Program Allocation Checker
PAC . . . . Programmable Automatic Comparator
PAC . . . . Public Affairs Committee
PAC . . . . Pure and Applied Chemistry (IUPAC)
PAC . . . . Pursuant to Authority Contained in
PAC . . . . Put and Call (Stock market)
PACADV . . . . . Pacific Fleet Advance Headquarters (Guam)
PACAF . . . . . . Pacific Air Forces (Air Force)
PACAFBASECOM . . Pacific Air Forces Base Command
PACB . . . . . . Pan-American Coffee Bureau
PACC . . . . . . Products Administration & Contract Control
PACCALL . . . . Pacific Fleet Calls (Radio call signs)
PACCIOS . . . . Pan American Council of International Committee of Scientific Management
PACCOM . . . . Pacific Fleet Communications Instructions
PACCS . . . . . Pan American Cancer Cytology Society
PACCS . . . . . . Post Attack Command and Control System (Military)

PACCS/ADA .. Post Attack Command and Control System/Airborne Data Automation
PACCT ...... PERT (Program Evaluation and Review Technique) and Cost Correlation Technique
PACD .... Pacific Division (Military)
PACE .... Packaged Cram Executive (Data processing)
PACE .... Passive Attitude Control Experimental (Satellite)
PACE .... Performance and Cost Evaluation
PACE .... Phased Array Control Electronics
PACE .... Plan for Action by Citizens in Education
PACE .... Planned Action with Constant Evaluation (Data processing)
PACE .... Precision Analog Computing Equipment
PACE .... Preflight Acceptance (or Automatic) Checkout Equipment
PACE .... Prelaunch Automatic Checkout Equipment
PACE .... Procedural Approach to the Composition of Essays (In book title)
PACE .... Professional Activities for Continuing Education (AEC)
PACE .... Professional Association of Consulting Engineers
PACE .... Programmed Automatic Communications Equipment
PACE .... Projects to Advance Creativity in Education (HEW)
PACED ..... Program for Advanced Concepts in Electronic Design
PACE/LV .... Preflight Acceptance Checkout Equipment-Launch Vehicle
PACEMAKER .. Public Agency Career Employment Maker (OEO project)
PACENS ..... Patient Census
PACER ...... Portable Aircraft Condition Evaluator Recorder
PACER ...... Program of Active Cooling Effects and Requirements
PACER ...... Program-Assisted Console Evaluation and Review (Air Force)
PACER ...... Programmed Automatic Circuit Evaluator and Recorder
PACES ...... Political Action Committee for Engineers and Scientists
PACE-S/C .... Preflight Acceptance Checkout Equipment for Spacecraft
PACEX ...... Pacific Exchange (System) (Military)
PACFLT...... Pacific Fleet
PACGO ...... President's Advisory Committee on Government Organization
PACH .... Public Administration Clearing House (1931-1956)
PACHEDPEARL .. Pacific Headquarters, Pearl Harbor, Hawaii (Navy)
PACIFY...... Parents and Alumni Committee Involved for Youth (Brown University)
PACIR ...... Practical Approach to Chemical Information Retrieval
PACKAGE ... Planned Aids for Cross-Culture Knowledge, Action and Growth in Effectiveness
PACM....... Pulse Amplitude Code Modulation
PACOM ..... Pacific Area Command (Military)
PACOR ...... Passive Correlation and Ranging
PACORE ..... Parabolic Corner Reflector
PACORNALOG .. Pacific Coast Coordinator of Naval Logistics
PACREP...... Port Activities Report (Navy)
PACRESFLT ... Pacific Reserve Fleet
PACS .... Pacific Area Communications System
PACS .... Post Attack Communication System
PACT .... Pan American Commission of Tampa
PACT .... Pay Actual Computer Time
PACT .... Philco Automatic Circuit Tester
PACT .... Plan of Action for Challenging Times (Educational program for low-income students)
PACT .... Portable Aircraft Calibration Tracker (NASA)
PACT .... Production Analysis Control Technique (Navy)
PACT .... Program for Automatic Coding Techniques (Data processing)
PACT .... Programmed Automatic Circuit Tester
PACT .... Project for the Advancement of Coding Techniques
PACT .... Provide Addict Care Today (New York City)
PACTA ...... Packed Tape Assembly
PACUSA ..... Pacific Air Command, United States Army
PACV .... Patrol Air Cushion Vehicle (Also called Hovercraft) (Navy)
PACV .... Personnel Air Cushion Vehicle
PAD .... Palestine Arab Delegation
PAD .... Pedagogischer Austauschdienst (Pedagogical Exchange Service)
PAD .... Permissible Accumulated Dose
PAD .... Petroleum Administration for Defense (Abolished, 1954)
PAD .... Phenacetin, Aspirin, Desoxyephedrine
PAD .... Pilotless Aircraft Division (Navy)
PAD .... Pontoon Assembly Detachment
PAD .... Port of Aerial Debarkation (Air Force)
PAD .... Power Amplifier Device
PAD .... Precise Access Diagram
PAD .... Preferred Arrival Date
PAD .... Presence & Amplitude Detector
PAD .... Professional Administrative Development (Medicine)
PAD .... Program Action Directive
PAD .... Propellant-Actuated Devices
PAD .... Public Affairs Division (Military)
PAD .... Public Assistance Division (District of Columbia)
PAD .... Pulse Averaging Discriminator
PADA .... Payroll Automation for Department of Agriculture
PADA .... Prespin Automatic Dynamic Alignment

PADAL ..... Pattern for Analysis, Decision, Action, and Learning
PADAR ...... Passive Airborne Detection and Ranging
PADAR ...... Program Approval Disposal and Redistribution (Army)
PADAT ...... Psychological Abstracts Direct Access Terminal
PADESM ..... Parti des Desherites de Madagascar (Party of the Deprived of Madagascar)
PADI .... Parti pour l'Avancement de la Democratie en Ituri (Party for Democratic Advancement in Ituri)
PADI .... Professional Association of Diving Instructors
PADL .... Pilotless Aircraft Development Laboratory (Navy)
PADLOC..... Passive Detection and Location of Countermeasures (Air Force)
PADOC ..... Pay Adjustment Document
PADP .... Proposal for Advanced Development Program
PADRA ..... Pass to Air Defense RADAR
PADRE ..... Portable Automatic Data Recording Equipment
PADRES...... Padres Asociados para Derechos, Religiosos, Educativos y Sociales (Organization of Mexican-American priests)
PADS .... Passive-Active Data Simulation
PADS .... Personnel Automated Data System (TIMMS)
PADS .... Precision Aerial Deliver (or Display) System
PADS .... Publications of the American Dialect Society
PADT .... Post-Alloy Diffusion Transistor
PAE .... Partes Aequales (Equal parts)
PAE .... Peoria & Eastern Railway (AAR code)
PAE .... Phase Angle Error
PAE .... Physical Aptitude Examination
PAE .... Port of Aerial Embarkation (Air Force)
PAEC .... Philippines Atomic Energy Commission
PAEI .... Purchasing Agents of the Electronic Industry
PAET .... Planetary Atmosphere Experimental (or Experiments) Test (NASA)
PAF .... Pacific Air Forces
PAF .... Pan American Foundation
PAF .... Philippine Air Force
PAF .... Portuguese Air Force
PAF .... Production Assembly Facility
PA & F ...... Percussion, Auscultation, and Fremitus (Medicine)
PAFAM ...... Performance and Failure Assessment Monitor
PAFB .... Patrick Air Force Base (Florida)
PAFE .... Place Accepted for Enlistment
PAFLU ...... Philippine Association of Free Labor Unions
PAFMECSA ... Pan-African Freedom Movement of East, Central and South Africa
PAFS .... Primary Air Force Specialty
PAFSC ...... Primary Air Force Specialty Code
PAG........ Pacific Cement & Aggregates, Inc. (NYSE symbol) (Delisted)
PAG........ Pargas, Inc. (NYSE symbol)
PAG........ Precision Alignment Gyrocompass
PAG........ Professional Activities Group
PAG........ Progress Analysis Group (Navy)
PAG........ Project Advisory Group
PAG........ Protective Action Guide (Federal Radiation Council)
PAGE...... Philatelic Association of Government Employees
PAGE ..... Piston Arrestment Gas Entrapment System (SPRINT launch cell)
PAGE...... Polyacrylamide Gel Electrophoresis
PAGE...... Preliminary Automated Ground Environment
PAGEL ..... Priced Aerospace Ground Equipment List
PAGEOS ..... Passive Geodetic Earth-Orbiting Satellite (NASA)
PAGICEP..... Petroleum and Gas Industry Communications Emergency Plan (FCC)
PAGL....... Pulsed Argon Gas LASER
PAGS .... Polish-American Guardian Society
PAGTU...... Pan-American Ground Training Unit
PAH........ Para-Aminohippuric (Biochemistry)
PAH........ Parts Application Handbook
PAH........ Phase Adjusting Hub
PAH........ Polycyclic Aromatic Hydrocarbon
PAHA ...... Polish American Historical Association
PAHC...... Pan American Highway Congresses
PAHC...... Pontifical Association of the Holy Childhood
PAHEL ..... Pay Record(s) and Health Record(s)
PAHO...... Pan American Health Organization (OAS)
PAI .... Parti Africain de l'Independance (African Independence Party) (Senegal and Upper Volta)
PAI .... Photographic Administrators, Incorporated
PAI .... Pirchei Agudath Israel
PAI .... Plunger Actuated Indexer
PAI .... Poale Agudat Israel of America
PAI .... Precise Angle Indicator
PAI .... Processed Apples Institute
PAI .... Public Affairs Institute
PAIB .... Polish-American Information Bureau
PAID .... Personnel and Accounting Integrated Data (System) (Veterans Administration)

PAIGC . . . . . . Partido Africano da Independencia da Guine e Cabo Verde (African Party for Independence of Guinea and Cape Verde)
PAIGH . . . . . . Pan American Institute of Geography and History (OAS)
PAIL . . . . Post Attack Intercontinental Link
PAIMEG . . . . . Pan American Institute of Mining, Engineering and Geology (Defunct)
PAINT . . . . . . Post Attack Intelligence
PAINT . . . . . . Primera Asociacion Internacional de Noticieros y Television (First International Newsreel and TV Association)
PAIP . . . . Production Acceleration Insurance Program
PAIR . . . . Performance and Integration Retrofit
PAIRC . . . . . . Polish American Immigration and Relief Committee
PAIRS . . . . . . Product Assurance Information Retrieval System (Boeing)
PAIS . . . . Padre Island National Seashore (National Park Service designation)
PAIS . . . . Project Analysis Information System (Agency for International Development)
PAIS . . . . Psychological Abstracts Information Services
PAIS . . . . . . Public Affairs Information Service
PAIT . . . . Program for Advancement of Industrial Technology (Canada)
PAK . . . . Panzer Abwehr Kanone (Means, "Cannon Against Armor") (German anti-tank gun)
PAK . . . . Power Amplifier Klystron
PAKISTAN . . . Nation in Asia, the name of which is said to be coined from Punjab (P), Afghan border states (A), Kashmir (K), Sind (S), and Baluchistan (TAN). Name also means "land of the pure" in Hindustani.
PAL . . . . Pacific Air Lines
PAL . . . . Paired-Associates Learning (Task) (Psychology)
PAL . . . . Pathology Laboratory (Test)
PAL . . . . Performance Assessment Logic
PAL . . . . Peripheral Access Lattices
PAL . . . . Permissive Action Link
PAL . . . . Permissive Arming Line (or Link)
PAL . . . . Personnel Accounting Level (Air Force)
PAL . . . . Personnel Augmentation List (Military)
PAL . . . . Phase Alternating Line (German color television system)
PAL . . . . Philippine Air Lines
PAL . . . . Police Athletic League (New York)
PAL . . . . Posterior Axillary Line
PAL . . . . Power Assist Lathe
PAL . . . . Prescribed Action Link (DOD)
PAL . . . . Princeton Accelerator Laboratory
PAL . . . . Prisoner-at-Large
PAL . . . . Process Assembler Language
PAL . . . . Programmed Application Library (Data processing)
PAL . . . . Psycho-Acoustic Laboratory (Harvard University)
PAL . . . . Pulsed Argon LASER
PALC . . . . . . Point Arguello Launch Complex
PALCO . . . . . Pan American Liaison Committee of Women's Organizations
PALCRU . . . . Pay and Allowances Accrue From (Air Force)
PALEA . . . . . Philippine Air Lines Employees' Association
PALI . . . . Pacific and Asian Linguistics Institute (University of Hawaii)
PALI . . . . Prince Albert's Light Infantry (Military) (British)
PALIS . . . . . . Property and Liability Information System
PALMS . . . . . Provisioning Automated Logistics Material System
PALR . . . . . . Permissive Action Link Report (Army)
PALS . . . . . . Permissive Action Link Systems
PALSA . . . . . Philippine Air Lines Supervisors' Association
PAM . . . . Pamphlet
PAM . . . . Personal Accounting Management
PAM . . . . Personnel Actions Memorandum (Military)
PAM . . . . Phased Array Module
PAM . . . . Phoenix Airborne Missile
PAM . . . . Pittsburgh, Allegheny & McKees Rocks R. R. (AAR code)
PAM . . . . Planning, Activation, Modification (Army reorganization)
PAM . . . . Portable Alpha Monitor
PAM . . . . Priorities and Allocations Manual (Army)
PAM . . . . Pulse Amplitude Modulation (Radio)
PAMA . . . . . . Pan American Medical Association
PAMA . . . . . . Polish Alma Mater of America
PAMA . . . . . . Pulse-Address Multiple Access (Satellite communications)
PAMAC . . . . . Parts and Materials Accountability Control
PAMC . . . . . . Pakistan Army Medical Corps
PAMCS . . . . . Phoenix Airborne Missile Control System
PAMD . . . . . . Price and Management Data
PAMDS . . . . . Price and Management Data Section (of a stock list) (Navy)
PAM-FM . . . . Pulse Amplitude Modulation–Frequency Modulation
PAMI . . . . . . Personnel Accounting Machine Installation
PAMN . . . . . Procurement Aircraft and Missiles, Navy (An appropriation)
PAMO . . . . . . Port Air Materiel Office
PAMPA . . . . . Pacific Area Movement Priority Agency (Military)
PAMPER . . . . Practical Application of Mid-Points for Exponential Regression
PAMS . . . . . . Portable Acoustic Monitoring System

PAMTGG . . . . Pan Am Makes the Going Great (Title of ballet choreographed by George Balanchine, taken from Pan American World Airways' slogan) (Pronounced "pam-ti-guh-guh")
PAMUSA . . . . Post-Attack Mobilization of the United States Army
PAMWA . . . . Pan American Medical Women's Alliance
PAN . . . . Partido Accion Nacional (Mexican political party)
PAN . . . . Pennsylvania Association of Notaries
PAN . . . . Peroxyacetyl Nitrate (Chemical)
PAN . . . . Polyacrylonitrile (Plastic)
PAN . . . . Positional Alcohol Nystagmus (NASA)
PAN . . . . Propodial Anlage
PANAGRA . . . Pan American–Grace Airways, Inc.
PANAIR . . . . . Panama Air Lines
PANALU . . . . Parti National Lumumba (Lumumba National Party)
PAN-AM . . . . Pan-American World Airways, Inc. (Also see PN and PAA)
PANAMAC . . . Pan-American Airways Communications System
PANAMIN . . . . Presidential Arm for National Minorities (Philippines)
PANAR . . . . . Panoramic RADAR
PAND . . . . . . Passive Air Navigation Device
PANDEX . . . . Name of an all-inclusive index covering fields of science, technology and medicine; composed of Greek prefix Pan meaning all and -Dex from word index
PANDS . . . . . Pay and Supply (Coast Guard)
PANFI . . . . . . Precision Automatic Noise Figure Indicator
PANHONLIB . . Panama, Honduras, and Liberia (Acronym used to refer to merchant ships operating under "flags of convenience")
PANIC . . . . . Planned Attack on Nine Inner Cities (to build education parks)
PANLIBHONCO . . Panama-Liberia-Honduras-Costa Rica
PANS . . . . . . Positioning and Navigation System
PANS . . . . . . Procedures for Air Navigation Services (ICAO)
PANSEAFRON . . Panama Sea Frontier
PANY . . . . . . Port Authority of New York (Later, PANYNJ)
PANY . . . . . . Platinumsmiths Association of New York
PANYNJ . . . . Port Authority of New York and New Jersey (Formerly, Port Authority of New York)
PAO . . . . Primary Action Office(r) (Military)
PAO . . . . Prince Albert's Own (Military unit) (British)
PAO . . . . Property Action Order
PAO . . . . . . Public Affairs Officer (Embassies)
PAOA . . . . . . Pan American Odontological Association
PAP . . . . Parti d'Action Paysanne (Farmers Actions Party) (Upper Volta)
PAP . . . . Partido Accion Popular (Popular Action Party) (Ecuador, Peru)
PAP . . . . Patrol Amphibian Plane
PAP . . . . People's Action Party (Malaya)
PAP . . . . Personnel Allocation Plan (Navy)
PAP . . . . Pierced Aluminum Plank (Technical drawings)
PAP . . . . Pilotless Aircraft Program
PAP . . . . Polyethylene Aluminum Polyethylene
PAP . . . . Product Assurance Plan (Army)
PAP . . . . Production Allocation Program
PAP . . . . Projected Average Progress
PAP . . . . Proton Attenuation Procedure
PAP . . . . Pulmonary Artery Pressure
PAPA . . . . . . Philippine Alien Property Administration (Post-World War II)
PAPA . . . . . . Probabilistic Automatic Pattern Analyzer (Data processing)
PAPCNY . . . . Portuguese American Progressive Club of New York
PAPERMAN . . . Payroll and Accounting, Personnel Management, Manpower Utilization (Air Force)
PAPPA . . . . . Pulp and Paper Prepackaging Association
PAPS . . . . . . Permissive Arming and Protection System (AEC)
PAQ . . . . Position Analysis Questionnaire
PAQ . . . . Process Average Quality
PAQR . . . . . . Polyacene Quinone Radical
PAR . . . . Parametric Amplifier
PAR . . . . Partido Accion Renovadora (Political party in El Salvador)
PAR . . . . Payload Adapter Ring
PAR . . . . Peacetime Airborne Reconnaissance
PAR . . . . Peak-to-Average Ratio (Communications)
PAR . . . . Pennsylvania Advanced Reactor (AEC)
PAR . . . . People Against Racism (Civil rights organization)
PAR . . . . Performance Analysis & Review
PAR . . . . Perimeter Acquisition RADAR (Air Force)
PAR . . . . Phased Array RADAR
PAR . . . . Physiological Aging Rate
PAR . . . . Postanesthetic Recovery Room (Medicine)
PAR . . . . Precision Aircraft Reference
PAR . . . . Precision Approach RADAR (Aviation)
PAR . . . . Princeton Applied Research Corp.
PAR . . . . Problem Analysis Report
PAR . . . . Production, Augmentation and Reliability
PAR . . . . Production Automated Riveting

PAR	Profile of Average Reflectivity
PAR	Program Adjustment Request (Navy)
PAR	Program Appraisal and Review
PAR	Progressive Aircraft Rework
PAR	Project Audit Report
PAR	Public Administration Review (A publication)
PAR	Pulse Acquisition RADAR (Military)
PARA	Paragraph
PARA	Policy Analysis and Resource Allocation (State Department)
PARABAT	Parachute Battalion (Army)
PARADE	Passive-Active Ranging and Determination
PARADROP	An Airdrop by Parachute
PARAFRAG	Parachute Fragmentation Bomb (Air Force)
PARAMEDIC	A Medical Service Person Qualified to Participate in Parachute Activities (Air Force)
PARAMI	Parsons Active Ring-Around Miss Indicator
PARAN	Parents Assume Responsibility, Act Now (Group opposing sex education in schools)
PARARESCUE	Rescue by Individuals Parachuted to Distressed Person(s) (Air Force)
PARASEV	Paraglider Research Vehicle (NASA)
PARASYN	Parametric Synthesis (Data processing)
PARATROOPS	Parachute Infantry (Military)
PARB	Perimeter Acquisition RADAR Building (Army)
PARC	President's Appalachian Regional Commission
PARC	Progressive Aircraft Repair Cycle
PARCA	Pan American Railway Congress Association
PARCA	Projectile Autopropulse Radio-guid Contre Avion (France)
PARD	Periodic and Random Deviation
PARD	Pilot Airborne Recovery Device (A balloon-parachute)
PARD	Pilotless Aircraft Research Division (Langley Research Center) (Later, Applied Materials and Physics Division)
PARD	Precision Annotated Retrieval Display (System) (Data processing)
PARDON	Pastors' Anonymous Recovery-Directed Order for Newness (Rehabilitation program for troubled clergymen)
PARDOP	Passive Ranging Doppler
PARDP	Perimeter Acquisition RADAR Data Processor (Army)
PAREC	Pay Record(s)
PAREN	Parenthesis (or Parentheses)
PAREX	Programmed Accounts Receivable Extra Service (Data processing)
PARGS	Parks and Recreation Girls Service
PARI	Parent Attitude Research Instrument (A questionnaire)
PARIS	Pulse Analysis-Recording Information System
PARL	Prince Albert RADAR Laboratory
PARM	Partido Autentico de la Revolucion de Mexicana (Mexican political party)
PARM	Post-Attack Resource Management System
PARM	Program Analysis for Resource Management
PAROS	Passive Ranging on Submarines (Navy)
PARR	Pakistan Atomic Research Reactor
PARRS	Psychological Abstracts Reference Retrieval System (Syracuse University)
PARS	Passenger (or Programmed) Airlines Reservation System
PARS	Pilotless Aircraft Research Station (NASA)
PARSEC	Parallax Second (Unit of interstellar-space measure)
PARSECS	Program for Astronomical Research and Scientific Experiments Concerning Space
PARSQ	Pararescue
PARSYN	Parametric Synthesis (Data processing)
PART	Pan American Round Tables in the USA
PART	Parts Allocation Requirements Technique
PART	Practical Aid in Resources & Technology, Inc.
PARTAC	Precision Askania Range Target Acquisition
PARTEI	Purchasing Agents of the Radio, TV, and Electronics Industries
PARTICO	Parti d'Interets Congolais (Party for Congolese Interests)
PARTNER	Proof of Analog Results Through a Numerical Equivalent Routine (Data processing)
PARU	Photographic and Reproduction Unit
PARU	Postanesthetic Recovery Unit (Medicine)
PAS	Pan American Sulphur Company (NYSE symbol)
PAS	Para-Aminosalicylic (Acid) (Organic chemistry)
PAS	Parametric Amplifier System
PAS	Passed to the Adjacent Sector
PAS	Patients' Aid Society
PAS	Payload Analysis Section
PAS	Percussive Arts Society
PAS	Perigee-Apogee Stage (or System) (Aerospace)
PAS	Periodic-Acid Schiff (A stain)
PAS	Personnel Accounting Symbol (Air Force)
PAS	Personnel Accounting System (Marine Corps)
PAS	Personnel Administration Section (Library Administration Division of ALA)
PAS	Phase Address System
PAS	Phase Array System

PAS	Physicians for Automotive Safety (An organization)
PAS	Pierce Arrow Society
PAS	Pilots Advisory Service
PAS	Pilot's Attack Sight (British)
PAS	Pioneer Aerodynamic Systems, Inc.
PAS	Plasma Arc System
PAS	Pneumatic Air Saw
PAS	Polish Academy of Sciences
PAS	Polish Astronautical Society
PAS	Posterior Area of (Loose) Skin
PAS	Power Apparatus and Systems
PAS	Precise Acquisition System
PAS	Primary Alerting System
PAS	Processed Array Signal
PAS	Product Assurance Survey
PAS	Professional Activity Study (HEW)
PAS	Professor of Air Science (Air Force)
PAS	Public Address System
PAS	Public Administration Service
PAS	Pump Actuator Set
PAS	Pyrotechnics Arming Switch
PA/S	Periodic Acid/Schiff (A stain)
PASA	Pacific American Steamship Association
PASA	Para-Aminosalicylic Acid (Organic chemistry)
PASAR	Psychological Abstracts Search and Retrieval
PASB	Pan American Sanitary Bureau (Executive organ of PAHO)
PASC	Pan American Standards Committee (Also known as COPANT)
PASCAL	Philips Automatic Sequence Calculator
PASCO	Pan American Sulphur Company (Houston)
PASEP	Passed Separately (Military)
PASG	Pulse Amplifier Symbol Generator
PASG	Pulse Analyzer Signal Generator
PASO	Pan American Sanitary Organization
PA/SO	Port Anti-Submarine Officer (Navy)
PASS	Parts Analysis Summary Sheet
PASS	Penetration Aids/Strike System
PASS	Precision Autocollimating Solar Sensor
PASSA	Pacific American Steamship Association
PASSIM	President's Advisory Staff on Scientific Information Management
PASSION	Program for Algebraic Sequences Specifically of Input-Output Nature
PAST	Professor of Air Science and Tactics
PASU	Pan-African Socialist Union (Southern Rhodesia)
PASU	Patrol Aircraft Service Unit
PASUS	Pan American Society of the United States
PAT	Parametric Artificial Talker
PAT	Passive Acoustic Torpedo
PAT	Passive Acting Tracking
PAT	Pattern Analysis Test
PAT	Peninsula Air Transport Company (Michigan)
PAT	Peninsular Air Transport
PAT	People's Action Team (South Vietnam)
PAT	Personnel Authorization Table (Air Force)
PAT	Physics Achievement Test
PAT	Picture Arrangement Test
PAT	Plenum Air Tread (Army amphibian vehicle)
PAT	Point After Touchdown (Football)
PAT	Position Adjusting Type
PAT	Pre-Admission Testing
PAT	Prediction Analysis Techniques
PAT	Preliminary Acceptance Trials (Navy)
PAT	Pressure Assembled Thyristor
PAT	Process Analysis Team
PAT	Programmer Aptitude Tester
PAT	Property and Accounting Technician (Navy)
PAT	Psycho-Acoustic Testing
PAT	Pulsed Amplifier Tube
PATA	Pacific American Tankship Association
PATA	Pacific Area Travel Association
PATA	Plenum Air Tread Amphibian (Army)
PATBOMRON	Patrol Bombing Squadron
PATC	Paroxysmal Atrial Tachycardia (Medicine)
PAT-C	Position, Attitude, Trajectory-Control
PATCA	Panama Air Traffic Control Area
PATCENT	Patching Central (Army)
PATCO	Professional Air Traffic Controllers Organization
PATE	Programmed Automatic Telemetry Evaluator
PATE	Programmed Automatic Test Equipment
PATELL	Psychological Abstracts Tape Edition Lease or Licensing
PATFOR	Patrol Force
PATH	Pituitary Adrenotrophic Hormone
PATH	Port Authority Trans-Hudson (New York)

PATH . . . . Preserve American Patriotic Holidays Committee
PATH . . . . Prospectors and Treasure Hunters Guild
PATI . . . . Passive Airborne Time-Difference Intercept (Navy)
PATMI . . . . . . Powder Actuated Tool Manufacturers' Institute
PATRA . . . . . . Printing, Packaging and Allied Trades Research Association
PATRDL . . . . . Pan American Tung Research and Development League
PATRIC . . . . . . Pattern Recognition Interpretation and Correlation
PATRON . . . . Patrol Squadron
PATS . . . . Personnel Assistance Teams (Military)
PATS . . . . Personnel in an Awaiting Training Status (Air Force)
PATS . . . . Preacademic Training Student (Military)
PATS . . . . Precision Altimeter Techniques Study
PATSU . . . . . . Patrol Aircraft Service Unit
PATT . . . . Partial Automatic Translation Technique
PATT . . . . Project for the Analysis of Technology Transfer (NASA)
PATTERN . . . . . Planning Assistance Through Technical Evaluation of Relevance Numbers (RAND Corp.)
PATWAS . . . . . Pilots Automatic Telephone Weather Answering Service
PATWING . . . . Patrol Wing (Later, Fleet Air Wing)
PATWINGLANTFLT . . Patrol Wing Atlantic Fleet
PATWINGSCOFOR . . Patrol Wings Scouting Force
PAU . . . . Pan American Union (Central organ and permanent secretariat of the OAS)
PAU . . . . Pattern Articulation Unit (Data processing)
PAU . . . . Pilotless Aircraft Unit
PAU . . . . Precision Approach – UNICOM (Aviation)
PAU . . . . Present Address Unknown
PAUCA . . . . . Providence Association of Ukrainian Catholics in America
PAUDGET . . . . Photometer, Automated Universal Distribution Gonielectric Type
PAUSE . . . . . . People Against Unconstitutional Sex Education
PAV . . . . Pay Adjustment Voucher (Military)
PAV . . . . Personnel Allotment Voucher
PAV . . . . Phase Angle Voltmeter
PAV . . . . Position and Velocity
PAV . . . . Poste-Avion (Airmail)
PAV . . . . Pressure Altitude Variation
PAV . . . . Propellant Actuated Valve
PAVA . . . . . . Polish Army Veterans Association of America
PAVE . . . . . . Position and Velocity Extraction
PAVE . . . . . . Professional Audiovisual Education Study
PAVE . . . . . . Programmed Analysis for Value Engineers
PAVFC . . . . . . Princeton Azimuthally-Varying-Field Cyclotron
PAVLA . . . . . . Papal Volunteers for Latin America
PAVM . . . . . . Phase Angle Voltmeter
PAVN . . . . . . People's Army of Vietnam
PAVS . . . . . . Pulmonary Arterial Vasoconstrictor Substance
PAVT . . . . . . Position and Velocity Tracking
PAW . . . . Percussive Arc Welder
PAW . . . . Petroleum Administration for War (World War II)
PAW . . . . . . Powered All the Way
PA of W . . . . Pentecostal Assemblies of the World
PAWA . . . . . . Pan American Women's Association
PAWAF . . . . . . Polish American Workmen's Aid Fund
PAWOS . . . . . Portable Automatic Weather Observing Station
PAWS . . . . . . Parachute Altitude Wind Sensor
PAWS . . . . . . Polar Automatic Weather Station
PAWS . . . . . Programmed Automatic Welding System
PAX . . . . Passenger
PAX . . . . Private Automatic Exchange (Telephone)
PAXCON . . . . Passenger Airlift Contract (Military)
PAYE . . . . . . Pay As You Earn (Student loan program)
PAYE . . . . . . Pay As You Enter
PAYMARCORPS . . Paymaster, Marine Corps
PAYS . . . . . . Patriotic American Youth Society
PAZA . . . . . . Pan American Zebu Association
PB . . . . Parts Breakdown
PB . . . . Passbook (Banking)
PB . . . . Passed Ball
PB . . . . Patrol Boat
PB . . . . Patrol Bomber
PB . . . . Penta-Borane
PB . . . . Peripheral Buffer
PB . . . . Permanent Bunkers
PB . . . . Pharmacopoeia Britannica (British Pharmacopoeia)
PB . . . . Phenobarbital
PB . . . . Phonetically Balanced (With reference to word lists)
PB . . . . Picket Boat (Navy)
PB . . . . Piebald
PB . . . . Pilotless Bomber (Air Force)
PB . . . . Pitney-Bowes, Inc.
PB . . . . Plugboard

Pb . . . . Plumbum (Lead) (Chemical element)
PB . . . . Pocket Book
PB . . . . Power Boiler
PB . . . . Prayer Book
PB . . . . Presiding Bishop (Episcopal Church)
PB . . . . Pressure Breathing
PB . . . . Primary Buffer (Chemistry)
PB . . . . Privately Bonded
PB . . . . Program Board
PB . . . . Property Book (Army)
PB . . . . Publications Board (Later, CFSTI; then, NTIS)
PB . . . . Publications Bulletin
PB . . . . Purplish Blue
PB . . . . Push Button
PB . . . . United Board & Carton Corporation (NYSE symbol) (Delisted)
PBA . . . . Patrolmen's Benevolent Association
PBA . . . . Pencil Beam Antenna
PBA . . . . Permanent Budget Account
PBA . . . . Pill Box Antenna
PBA . . . . Plant Breeding Abstracts
PBA . . . . Polar Bear Association
PBA . . . . Polish Beneficial Association
PBA . . . . Poultry Breeders of America
PBA . . . . Professional Bookmen of America
PBA . . . . Professional Bowlers Association of America
PBA . . . . Public Buildings Administration (Functions transferred to GSA, 1949)
PBAA . . . . . . Polybutadiene Acrylic Acid
PBAC . . . . . . Program Budget Advisory Committee
PBAN . . . . . . Polybutadiene-Acrylic Acid Acrylonitrile
PBAPRS . . . . . Program/Budget Accounting and Progress Reporting System (Proposed) (Navy)
PBB . . . . Parallel by Bit
PBB . . . . Private Boxes and Bags
PBC . . . . Pacific Bible College (California)
PBC . . . . Parallel By Character
PBC . . . . Pedal Branch of Columellar (Muscle)
PBC . . . . . . Pen and Brush Club
PBC . . . . People's Bicentennial Commission
PBC . . . . Point of Basal Convergence
PBC . . . . Practice Bomb Container
PBC . . . . Public Buildings Commission (Functions transferred to PBA, 1939)
PBCA . . . . . . Pacific Bible College of Azusa (California)
PBCA . . . . . . Paperboard Butter Chip Association
PBCE . . . . . . Pine Bluff Cotton Exchange
PBCS . . . . . . Post Boost Control System (Missile technology)
PBD . . . . Peabody-Galion Corp. (NYSE symbol)
PBD . . . . Phenylbiphenyloxadiazole (Chemistry)
PBD . . . . Precise Block Diagram
PBD . . . . Program Budget Decision (DOD)
PBE . . . . Paschen-Bach Effect
PBE . . . . Proton Balance Equation
PBE . . . . Proton Binding Energy
PBEC . . . . . . Public Broadcasting Environment Center (Corporation for Public Broadcasting)
PBEIST . . . . . Planning Board European Inland Surface Transport (Army)
PBF . . . . Plastic Bottle Feeder
PBF . . . . Power Burst Facility (AEC)
PBF . . . . Pulsetile Blood Flow
PBG . . . . Program and Budget Guidance
PBHP . . . . . . Pounds Per Brake Horsepower
PB-HTGR . . . . Peach Bottom High-Temperature Gas-Cooled Reactor
PBI . . . . Paper Bag Institute
PBI . . . . Partial Background Investigation
PBI . . . . Paving Brick Institute
PBI . . . . Philadelphia Bible Institute
PBI . . . . Pitch Boundary Indicator
PBI . . . . Pitney-Bowes, Incorporated (NYSE symbol)
PBI . . . . Plumbing Brass Institute
PBI . . . . Polybenzimidazole (Plastics)
PBI . . . . Poor Bloody Infantry (British military slang)
PBI . . . . Process Branch Indicator
PBI . . . . Projected Books, Incorporated
PBI . . . . Protein-Bound Iodine (Medicine)
PBIC . . . . . . Polybutylisocyanate
PBIF . . . . . . Pacific Bible Institute of Fresno (California)
PBJC . . . . . . Palm Beach Junior College (Florida)
PBK . . . . Phi Beta Kappa
PBKA . . . . . . Persatuan Buruh Kereta Api (National Railway Workers' Union) (Indonesia)
PBKB . . . . . . Persatuan Buruh Kendaraan Bermotor (Motorized Vehicle Workers' Union) (Indonesia)
PBL . . . . Philadelphia Belt Line R. R. (AAR code)

PBL . . . . Public Broadcast Laboratory
PBM . . . . Patrol Search Plane (Navy designation for Mariner aircraft)
PBM . . . . Permanent Bench Mark
PBMA . . . . . . Peanut Butter Manufacturers Association
PBMR . . . . . . Pennsylvania Bureau of Municipal Research
PBNE . . . . . . Philadelphia, Bethlehem & New England R. R. (AAR code)
PBO . . . . Property Book Officer (Army)
PBO . . . . Push-Button Operation
PBOS . . . . . . Planning Board for Ocean Shipping (Army)
PBP . . . . Pellin-Broca Prism
PBP . . . . Power Bias Panel
PBP . . . . Private Brand Proneness (Marketing)
PBP . . . . Program Board Panel
PBP . . . . Push-Button Panel
PBPS . . . . . . Post Boost Propulsion System (Aerospace)
PBR . . . . Pabst Blue Ribbon (Beer) (Used by barmaids)
PBR . . . . Patapsco & Back Rivers R. R. (AAR code)
PBR . . . . Patrol Boat, River (Navy symbol)
PBR . . . . Pebble-Bed Reactor (AEC)
PBR . . . . Pencil Beam RADAR
PBR . . . . Pigment-Binder Ratio (Weight)
PBR . . . . Plum Brook Reactor (AEC)
PBR . . . . Power Breeder Reactor
PBR . . . . Precision Bombing Range
PBR . . . . Pressurized Ballistic Range (NASA)
PBRA . . . . . . Practical Bomb Rack Adapter
PBRE . . . . . . Pebble-Bed Reactor Experiment
PBRESD . . . . . Polar Branch, Research Environmental Science Division (Army)
PBRF . . . . . . Plum Brook Reactor Facility (Lewis Research Center)
PBRS . . . . . . Push-Button Rotary Switch
PBS . . . . Parimutuel Betting System
PBS . . . . Parts Breakdown Structure
PBS . . . . Peninsular Base Section
PBS . . . . Periscope Bombsight Stabilizer
PBS . . . . Phosphate-Buffered Saline
PBS . . . . Podiatry Bibliographical Society
PBS . . . . Potere Battericida del Sangue (Bactericidal Property of the Blood)
            (Medicine)
PBS . . . . Prefabricated Bituminous Surfacing
PBS . . . . Program Board Stowage
PBS . . . . Program Breakdown Structure
PBS . . . . Project Breakdown Structure
PBS . . . . Protestant Big Sisters
PBS . . . . Public Broadcasting Service
PBS . . . . Public Buildings Service (of GSA)
PBS . . . . Push-Button Switch
PBSCMA . . . . . Peanut Butter Sandwich and Cookie Manufacturers Association (Later,
            PBMA)
PBSE . . . . . . Philadelphia-Baltimore Stock Exchange
PBSM . . . . . . Plastic Bonded Starter Mix
PBSW . . . . . . Push-Button Switch
PBT . . . . Para-Bandit Target
PBT . . . . Parity Bit Test
PBT . . . . Piggyback Tape (Data processing)
PBT . . . . Piggyback Twistor (Data processing)
PBT . . . . Poly-Bay Tier
PBT . . . . Polybenzothiazole (Plastics)
PBTS . . . . . . Proton Beam Transport System
PBUP . . . . . . Perforated Back-Up Plate
PBV . . . . Pedal Blood Vessel
PBV . . . . Post Boost Vehicle (Aerospace)
PBVM . . . . . . Presentation of the Blessed Virgin Mary (Roman Catholic women's
            religious order)
PBW . . . . Percussive Butt Welder
PBW . . . . Power by Wire (Flight control)
PBW . . . . Proportional Bandwidth
PBW . . . . Pulse Burst Wave
PBWF . . . . . . Pulse Burst Wave Form
PBX . . . . Plastic Bonded Explosive
PBX . . . . Private Branch Telephone Exchange
PBY . . . . Patrol Bomber (Navy designation for Catalina aircraft)
PBZN . . . . . . Peroxybenzoyl Nitrate
PC . . . . Civilian Personnel Division (Coast Guard)
PC . . . . Pacific Coast R. R. (AAR code)
PC . . . . Package Control(ler)
PC . . . . Pad Coordinator
PC . . . . The Panama Canal
PC . . . . Paper or Cloth (Freight)
PC . . . . Paper Copy
PC . . . . Parent Cells
PC . . . . PARSEC (Parallax Second)

PC . . . . Participation Certificate
PC . . . . Past Commander
PC . . . . Patres Conscripti (The Roman Senate in early days of Rome)
PC . . . . Patrol Craft
PC . . . . Patrol Vessel, Submarine Chaser (Navy)
PC . . . . Pay Clerk
PC . . . . Peace Corps
PC . . . . Penetrating Cell
PC . . . . Penn-Central Co. (NYSE symbol)
PC . . . . Percent; Percentage
PC . . . . Perpetual Curate (or Curacy)
PC . . . . Personal Correction
PC . . . . Personnel Carrier (A vehicle)
PC . . . . Petty Cash
PC . . . . Pharmaceutical Corps (After company name)
PC . . . . Pharmacy Corps (Army)
PC . . . . Phase Coherent
PC . . . . Philippine Constabulary
PC . . . . Phosphocreatine (Creatine phosphate; see CP) (Biochemistry)
PC . . . . Photocell
PC . . . . Photoconductor
PC . . . . Pickup Cargo
pC . . . . Picocoulomb
pC . . . . Picocurie
PC . . . . Pilotage Charts (Air Force)
PC . . . . Pitch Channel
PC . . . . Pitch Circle (Technical drawings)
PC . . . . Pittsburgh Commerce Institute
PC . . . . Plane Commander
PC . . . . Plasma Chromatography
PC . . . . Plastic Core
PC . . . . Platelet Concentrate
PC . . . . Point of Curve (Technical drawings)
PC . . . . Polar Continental (American air mass)
PC . . . . Police-Constable (British)
PC . . . . Poni Curavit (Caused to Be Placed)
PC . . . . Poor Clares of Ireland (Roman Catholic women's religious order)
PC . . . . Port Call
PC . . . . Post Cibum (After Meals) (Medicine)
PC . . . . Post Commander (Military)
PC . . . . Post Consulatum (After the Consulate)
PC . . . . Postal Clerk (Navy rating)
PC . . . . Postcard
PC . . . . Pour Condoler (To Offer Sympathy)
PC . . . . Power Contactor
PC . . . . Power Control (System)
PC . . . . Pre-Carrier
PC . . . . Preparatory Commission
PC . . . . Preparatory Committee
PC . . . . Pressure Controller
PC . . . . Prices Current
PC . . . . Primary Center
PC . . . . Printed Circuit
PC . . . . Printer Control
PC . . . . Private Corporation (Often follows office listing of an associated
            group, such as a group of physicians practicing together)
PC . . . . Privileged Character (A favored student) (Teen slang)
PC . . . . Privy Council(lor) (British)
PC . . . . Procurement Command (Army)
PC . . . . Producers' Council
PC . . . . Program Counter
PC . . . . Project Coordinator
PC . . . . Projector Charge
PC . . . . Propulsive Coefficient
PC . . . . Prospectors Club
PC . . . . Prosthetics Center (Veterans Administration)
PC . . . . Provisional Costs
PC . . . . Public Contracts
PC . . . . Publications in Climatology
PC . . . . Pulsating Current
PC . . . . Pulse Compression
PC . . . . Pulse Controller
PC . . . . Punched Cards
PC . . . . Purchase Card
PC . . . . Purchasing and Contracting
PC . . . . Purified Concentrate
PC . . . . Submarine Chaser (173 feet) (Navy symbol)
P/C . . . . Printed Circuit
P & C . . . . . . Procurement and Contracting
P & C . . . . . . Purchasing and Contracting
P & C . . . . . . Puts and Calls (Securities trading)

PCA . . . . Pacific Communications Area (Air Force)
PCA . . . . Paperweight Collectors' Association
PCA . . . . Papillon Club of America
PCA . . . . Parachute Club of America
PCA . . . . Parliamentary Commissioner for Administration (British)
PCA . . . . Parti Communiste Algerien (Algerian Communist Party)
PCA . . . . Passive Cutaneous Anaphylaxis
PCA . . . . Peak Clipping Amplifier
PCA . . . . Pekingese Club of America
PCA . . . . Perchloric Acid
PCA . . . . Pericruciate Association (Cortex, of cat)
PCA . . . . Permanent Change of Assignment
PCA . . . . Permanent Court of Arbitration
PCA . . . . Personal Cash Allowance
PCA . . . . Photo Cell Assembly
PCA . . . . Photovoltaic Cell Array
PCA . . . . Plane Circular Aperture
PCA . . . . Plasma Covered Antenna
PCA . . . . Point of Closest Approach
PCA . . . . Polar Cap Absorption
PCA . . . . Polycrystalline Alumina
PCA . . . . Poodle Club of America
PCA . . . . Pool Critical Assembly (AEC)
PCA . . . . Popular Culture Association
PCA . . . . Porsche Club of America
PCA . . . . Portland Cement Association
PCA . . . . Positive Controlled Airspace
PCA . . . . Pre-Contractual Authorization
PCA . . . . President's Council on Aging
PCA . . . . Print Council of America
PCA . . . . Printing Corporation of America
PCA . . . . Private Communications Association
PCA . . . . Process Control Analyzer
PCA . . . . Producers Commission Association
PCA . . . . Production Credit Association
PCA . . . . Program Change Analysis (DOD)
PCA . . . . Progressive Citizens of America
PCA . . . . Pulp Chemicals Association
PCA . . . . Pyrotechnic Control Assembly (NASA)
PCA . . . . Pyrrolidonecarboxylic Acid (Organic chemistry)
P & CA . . . . . Paying and Collecting Area
PCAA . . . . . . Pancretan Association of America
PCAC . . . . . . Partially Conserved Axial-Vector Current
PCAC . . . . . . Private College Admissions Center
PCAM . . . . . . Punched-Card Accounting Machines
PCAU . . . . . . Philippine Civil Affairs Unit (Army unit which supplied emergency subsistence after end of Japanese dominance) (World War II)
PCB . . . . Partido Comunista de Bolivia (Communist Party of Bolivia)
PCB . . . . Petty Cash Book (Business and trade)
PCB . . . . Plenum Chamber Burning
PCB . . . . Polychlorinated Biphenyl (Organic chemistry)
PCB . . . . Printed Circuit Board
PCB . . . . Process Control Block
PCB . . . . Proprietor of copyright on a work by a Corporate Body
PCBA . . . . . . Printed Circuit Board Assembly
PCBDA . . . . . Put and Call Brokers and Dealers Association
PCBS . . . . . . Plastic Connector Backing Shell
PCBS . . . . . . Positive Control Bombardment System (Air Force)
PCBS . . . . . . Printed Circuit Board Socket
PCBS . . . . . . Pupil Classroom Behavior Scale
PCBTS . . . . . Portable Cesium Beam Time Standard
PCC . . . . Package Carrier Committee
PCC . . . . Paid Circulation Council
PCC . . . . Panama Canal Company
PCC . . . . Parent and Child Center (Project Head Start)
PCC . . . . Pasadena City College (California)
PCC . . . . Peak Cathode Current
PCC . . . . Personnel Control Center (Air Force)
PCC . . . . Phosphate Carrier Compound
PCC . . . . Poison Control Center
PCC . . . . Polarity Coincidence Correlator
PCC . . . . Population Crisis Committee
PCC . . . . Portable Cable Checker
PCC . . . . Portland Cement Concrete
PCC . . . . Positive Control Communication
PCC . . . . Postal Concentration Center
PCC . . . . Pre-Compressor Cooling
PCC . . . . President of the Canteen Committee (Military) (British)
PCC . . . . President's Conference Committee
PCC . . . . Printed Circuit Conference
PCC . . . . Private Carrier Conference (of ATA)

PCC . . . . Process Control Computer
PCC . . . . Production Compression Capability
PCC . . . . Provincial Congress Committee
PCC . . . . Pulse Counter Chain
PCC . . . . Pyro-Convective Cooling
PC(C) . . . . . . Submarine Chaser (Control) (173 feet) (Navy symbol)
PCCA . . . . . . Pewter Collectors Club of America
PCCA . . . . . . Playing Card Collectors' Association
PCCA . . . . . . Postcard Collector's Club of America (Defunct)
PCCA . . . . . . Power and Communication Contractors Association
PCCB . . . . . . Project Configuration Control Board (Army)
PCCEMRSP. . . . Permanent Commission for the Conservation and Exploitation of the Maritime Resources of the South Pacific
PCCG . . . . . . Protestant Cinema Critics Guild (Later, PCG)
PCCI . . . . . . Paper Cup and Container Institute
PCCI . . . . . . Pre-Contract Cost Letter (Military)
PCCI . . . . . . President's Committee on Consumer Interests
PCCL . . . . . . People's Community Civic League
PCCL . . . . . . Pre-Contract Cost Letter (Navy)
PCCNL . . . . . Pacific Coast Coordinator of Naval Logistics
PCCP . . . . . . Pacific Coast Canned Pear Service
PCCS . . . . . . Positive Control Communications System
PCCS . . . . . . Program Change Control System
PCD . . . . Panama Canal Department
PCD . . . . Power Control and Distribution
PCD . . . . Precision Course Direction (Aerospace)
PCD . . . . Procurement and Contracts Division (NASA)
PCD . . . . Program Change Decision (Military)
PCD . . . . Pulmonary Clearance Delay
PCDI . . . . . . Per Capita Disposable Income
PCDI . . . . . . Pierce Die
PCDS . . . . . . Power Conversion and Distribution System
PCE . . . . Escort Vessel (180 foot) (Navy symbol)
PCE . . . . Page Communications Engineers, Inc. (Canada)
PCE . . . . Patrol Craft Escort
PCE . . . . Peripheral Control Element
PCE . . . . Polyarthrite Chronique Evolutive (Chronic Evolutive Polyarthritis) (Medicine)
PCE . . . . Program Cost Estimate
PCE . . . . Punch Card Equipment
PCE . . . . Pyrometric Cone Equivalent (Refractory industry)
PCEA . . . . . . Pacific Coast Electrical Association
PCE(C) . . . . . Patrol Vessel, Escort (Control) (180 feet) (Navy symbol)
PCEEO . . . . . President's Committee on Equal Employment Opportunity
PCEH . . . . . . President's Committee on Employment of the Handicapped
PCEM . . . . . . Parliamentary Council of the European Movement
PCE(R) . . . . . Patrol Craft, Escort (Rescue) (180 feet) (Navy symbol)
P Cert Ed . . . . Professional Certificate in Education
PCETF. . . . . . Power Conversion Equipment Test Facility
PCF . . . . Pacific American Corporation (NYSE symbol) (Delisted)
PCF . . . . Pacificulture Foundation
PCF . . . . Parti Communiste Francaise (French Communist Party)
PCF . . . . Peace Centers Foundation
PCF . . . . Potential Conflict Forecasts (Army)
PCF . . . . Potentially Critical Failures
PCF . . . . Pounds per Cubic Foot
PCF . . . . Power Cathode Follower
PCF . . . . Power per Cubic Foot
PCF . . . . Prairie Chicken Foundation
PCF . . . . Probability of Consequence Factor
PCF . . . . Processed Citation File
PCF . . . . Prothrombin Conversion Factor
PCF . . . . Pulse Compression Filter
PCF . . . . Pulse-to-Cycle Fraction
PCFA . . . . . . Pin, Clip and Fastener Association
PCFE . . . . . . Polytrifluorochloroethylene
PCFO . . . . . . Position Classification Field Office
PCFP . . . . . . Predicted Comparative Failure Probability
PCG . . . . Pacific Gas & Electric Company (NYSE symbol)
PCG . . . . Phonocardiogram
PCG . . . . Plains Cotton Growers
PCG . . . . Planning & Control Guide
PCG . . . . Printed Circuit Generator
PCG . . . . Protestant Cinema Guild (Formerly, PCCG)
PCG . . . . Pulsed Coaxial Gun
PCGM . . . . . Pacific Coast Garment Manufacturers
PCGN . . . . . Permanent Committee of Geographical Names (Later, BGN)
PCH . . . . Paroxysmal Cold Hemoglobinuria
PCH . . . . Patrol Craft Hydrofoil
PCH . . . . Prepare Chassis
PCH . . . . Submarine Chaser (Hydrofoil) (Navy symbol)

PC & H . . . . . . Packing, Crating, and Handling
PCHAR . . . . . . Printing Character (Data processing)
PCHE . . . . Poor Clare Nuns of the Holy Eucharist (Roman Catholic religious order)
PCHL . . . . Pacific Coast Hockey League (Later, Western Hockey League)
PCHT . . . . Packaging, Crating, Handling and Transportation (Army)
PCI . . . . Panel Call Indicator
PCI . . . . Partito Comunista Italiano (Italian Communist Party)
PCI . . . . Pattern of Cockpit Indication
PCI . . . . Pattern Correspondence Index
PCI . . . . Peripheral Command Indicator
PCI . . . . Photographic Credit Institute
pCi . . . . Picocurie
PCI . . . . Pilot Club International
PCI . . . . Pneumatic Circuit Indicator
PCI . . . . Portable Cesium Irradiator (AEC)
PCI . . . . Portable Compass Indicator
PCI . . . . Potato Chip Institute, International
PCI . . . . Prestressed Concrete Institute
PCI . . . . Product Cost Index
PCIFC . . . . . . Permanent Commission of the International Fisheries Convention
PCIJ . . . . Permanent Court of International Justice
PCIM . . . . Parti du Congres de l'Independance de Madagascar (Party of the Congress for Malagasy Independence)
PCIRO . . . . . . Preparatory Commission for International Refugee Organization
PCIS . . . . Professional Career Information Service (Department of Labor)
PCIYRA . . . . . . Pacific Coast Intercollegiate Yacht Racing Association
PCJ . . . . Pontifical College of Josephinum (Ohio)
PCJC . . . . Panola County Junior College (Texas)
PCK . . . . Pilot Check
PCK . . . . Pittsburgh Coke & Chemical Company (NYSE symbol) (Delisted)
PCK . . . . Printed Circuit Keyboard
PCKB . . . . Printed Circuit Keyboard
PCKT . . . . Printed Circuit
PCL . . . . Pacific Coast League (Baseball)
PCL . . . . Polycaprolactone
PCL . . . . Positive Control Line
PCL . . . . Preliminary Change Letter (Navy)
PCL . . . . Printed Circuit Lamp
PCL . . . . Process Capability Laboratory
PCL . . . . Project Control Ledgers (Navy)
PCL . . . . Pulse Compression Loop
PCLA . . . . Power Control Linkage Assembly
PCLK . . . . Pay Clerk
PCLO . . . . Passenger Control Liaison Office(r) (Army)
PCM . . . . Parallel Cutter Mechanism
PCM . . . . Parti Communiste Marocain (Moroccan Communist Party)
PCM . . . . Passive Countermeasure
PCM . . . . Phase-Change Materials
PCM . . . . Philippine Campaign Medal
PCM . . . . Pitch Control Motor
PCM . . . . Polyimide Composite Material
PCM . . . . Precision Condenser Microphone
PCM . . . . President's Certificate of Merit (Military award)
PCM . . . . Pulse Code Modulation (Electronics)
PCM . . . . Pulse-Count Modulation
PCM . . . . Punch-Card Machine (Data processing)
PCMA . . . . . . Post Card Manufacturers Association
PCMA . . . . . . Professional Convention Management Association
PCMB . . . . . . para-Chloromercuribenzoate
PCMC . . . . . . Provided Chief of Mission Concurs
PCMD . . . . . . Pulse Code Modulation Digital
PCME . . . . . . Pulse Code Modulation Event
PCM-FM . . . . . Pulse Code Modulation – Frequency Modulation
PCMI . . . . . . Phochromic Microimage (Data processing)
PCMI . . . . . . Plastic Container Manufacturers Institute
PCMK . . . . . . Piece Mark
PCML . . . . . . President's Committee on Migratory Labor
PCM-PS . . . . . Pulse Code Modulation, Phase-Shift
PCMR . . . . . . President's Committee on Mental Retardation
PCMS . . . . . . Punched Card Machine System
PCMTEA . . . . . Pulse Code Modulation and Timing Electronics Assembly
PCN . . . . Partido de Conciliacion Nacional (Party of National Conciliation) (El Salvador)
PCN . . . . Partido Conservador Nicaraguense (Nicaraguan Conservative Party)
PCN . . . . Parts Change Notice
PCN . . . . Point Comfort & Northern Railway Company (AAR code)
PCN . . . . Position Control Number
PCN . . . . Procedure Change Notice
PCN . . . . Procurement Control Number
PCN . . . . Product Control Number
PCN . . . . Program Control Number

PCN . . . . Pulse Compression Network
PCNB . . . . . . Pentachloronitrobenzene
PCNB . . . . . . Permanent Control Narcotics Board
PCNS . . . . . . Polar Coordinates Navigation System
PCNY . . . . . Proofreaders Club of New York
PCO . . . . Pest Control Operator
PCO . . . . Philadelphia College of Osteopathy (Pennsylvania)
PCO . . . . Pittston Company (NYSE symbol)
PCO . . . . Placement Contracting Officer (Army)
PCO . . . . . . Plant Clearance Order
PCO . . . . Prince Consort's Own (Military unit) (British)
PCO . . . . Printing Control Officer (Air Force)
PCO . . . . Procurement Contracting Officer
PCO . . . . Procuring Contract Office(r) (Navy)
PCO . . . . Program Comparator
PCO . . . . Prospective Commanding Officer
PCO . . . . Purchase Change Order
PCO . . . . Purchasing Contracting Officer
PCOB(UN) . . . . Permanent Central Opium Board of the United Nations
PCOGA . . . . . Pacific Coast Oyster Growers Association
PC & OR . . . . . Procurement, Commitment and Obligation Record (Navy)
P-COSWA . . . . Pugwash Conferences on Science and World Affairs
PCOYO . . . . . President's Council on Youth Opportunity (Defunct)
PCP . . . . Peace Corps Physician
PCP . . . . Peripheral Control Program
PCP . . . . Phenyl-Cyclohexyl-Piperidine
PCP . . . . Pilot Control Panel
PCP . . . . Planar Combat Problem
PCP . . . . Polaroid Color Pack Camera
PCP . . . . . . Postgraduate Center for Psychotherapy
PCP . . . . Preassembled Cable in Pipe
PCP . . . . Primary Control Program (Data processing)
PCP . . . . Printed Circuit Patchboard
PCP . . . . Processor Control Program
PCP . . . . Production Change Point
PCP . . . . Program (or Project) Change Proposal (DOD)
PCP . . . . Progressive Constitutional Party (Malta)
PCP . . . . Pulse Comparator
PCPA . . . . . . Panel of Consultants for the Performing Arts (of CFC)
PCPA . . . . . . Para-Chlorophenylalanine (Organic chemistry)
PCPA . . . . . . Protestant Church-Owned Publishers Association
PCPF . . . . . . President's Council on Physical Fitness (Formerly, PCYF)
PCPG . . . . . . Primary Clock Pulse Generator
PCPI . . . . Parent Cooperative Preschools International
PCPJ . . . . . . Peoples Coalition for Peace and Justice
PCPM . . . . . . PERT Cost Performance Measurement
PCPS . . . . . . Philadelphia College of Pharmacy and Science (Pennsylvania)
PCPS . . . . . . Pulse-Coded Processing System
PCPT . . . . . . Physical Combat Proficiency Test (Army)
PCQ . . . . . . Production Control Quantometer
PCQ . . . . . . Productivity Criteria Quotient
PCR . . . . Partidul Comunist din Rominia
PCR . . . . Peninsular Chemresearch (Calgon Corporation)
PCR . . . . Power Conversion Room
PCR . . . . Prestressed Ceramic RADOME
PCR . . . . Primary Cosmic Radiation
PCR . . . . Procurement Center Representatives (Small Business Administration)
PCR . . . . Program Change Request (DOD)
PCR . . . . Program Control Register
PCR . . . . Project on Corporate Responsibility
PCR . . . . . . Publication Contract Requirements
PCR . . . . Pulse Compression RADAR
PCRA . . . . . . Poland China Record Association
PCRC . . . . . . Paraffined Carton Research Council
PCRI . . . . Papanicolaou Cancer Research Institute
PCRS . . . . . . Poor Clergy Relief Society (British)
PCRV . . . . . . Prestressed Concrete Reactor Vessel (AEC)
PCS . . . . Pacific Command Ship
PCS . . . . Particle Counting System
PCS . . . . Patrol Craft Sweeper
PCS . . . . Patrol Vessel, Submarine Chaser (Control) (136 feet) (Navy symbol)
PCS . . . . Periodical Control System (Libraries)
PCS . . . . Permanent Change of Station (Military)
PCS . . . . Phase Combining System (Trademark) (A solubilizer in scintillation counting)
PCS . . . . Phase Compensator System
PCS . . . . Photo Correlation System
PCS . . . . Physical Control System
PCS . . . . Pitch Control System
PCS . . . . Planning Control Sheet
PCS . . . . Plastic Connector Shell
PCS . . . . Plausible Conflict Situations (Army)

PCS	Pointing-Control System
PCS	Portable Communications System
PCS	Position Classification Standard (Civil Service)
PCS	Position, Course, and Speed
PCS	Post, Camp, or Station (Military)
PCS	Posterior Concave Side
PCS	Power Conductor System
PCS	Power Conversion System
PCS	Primary Calibration System
PCS	Primary Conditioning Solution
PCS	Principal Clerk of Session
PCS	Print Contrast Signal (Data processing)
PCS	Process Control System
PCS	Production Control Section
PCS	Program Counter Store
PCS	Project Control System (Data processing)
PCS	Property Control System
PCS	Pump Control Sensor
PCS	Punched Card System
PCSA	Power Crane and Shovel Association
PCSC	Control Submarine Chaser (136 feet) (Navy symbol)
PCSC	Power Conditioning, Switching, & Control
PCSE	Pacific Coast Stock Exchange
PCSE	President's Committee on Scientists and Engineers
PCSE	Printed Circuit Soldering Equipment
PCSH	Pierce Shell
PCSP	Programmed Communications Support Program (Air Force)
PCSW	President's Commission on the Status of Women
PCT	Paper Crepe Tape
PCT	Papercraft Corporation (NYSE symbol)
PCT	Parti Communiste Tunisien (Tunisian Communist Party)
PCT	Partido Conservador Tradicional (Traditionalist Conservative Party) (Nicaragua)
PCT	Patent Cooperation Treaty (Proposed international treaty, Sweden, 1967)
PCT	Percent
PCT	Performance Correlation Technique
PCT	Personality Completion Test (Psychology)
PCT	Pharmacy and Chemistry Technician (Navy)
PCT	Planning & Control Techniques
PCT	Porphyria Cutanea Tarda (Drug)
PCT	Portable Camera-Transmitter
PCT	Potential Current Transformer
PCT	Pressure Concentration Temperature
PCT	Proximal Convoluted Tubule (of a nephron)
PCT	Pulse Compression Tube
PCTFE	Polychlorotrifluoroethylene
PCTP	Pierce Template
PCTR	Physical Constant Test Reactor (AEC)
PCTS	Portable Cesium Time Standard
PCTS	President's Committee for Traffic Safety
PCTV	Private Channel Television
PCU	Partido Conservador Unido (Chilean Catholic political party)
PCU	Portuguese Continental Union of the United States of America
PCU	Pound Centigrade Unit
PCU	Power-Conditioning Unit
PCU	Power Control Unit
PCU	Pressure Control Unit
PCU	Print Control Unit
PCU	Process Control Unit
PCUS	Propeller Club of the United States
PCV	Packed Cell Volume
PCV	Peace Corps Volunteer
PCV	Petty Cash Voucher
PCV	Pneumatic Control Valve
PCV	Positive Crankcase Ventilation (For automotive antipollution systems)
PCW	Previously Complied With
PCW	Primary Cooling Water (Reactor)
PCW	Princess Charlotte of Wales (Military unit) (British)
PCW	Proprietor of copyright on a Composite Work
PCWF	Philippine Communications Workers' Federation
PCWU	Port Commissioners Workers' Union (India)
PCY	Pittsburgh, Chartiers & Youghiogheny Railway (AAR code)
PCYF	President's Council on Youth Fitness (Later, PCPF)
PD	Doctor of Pedagogy
PD	Doctor of Pharmacy
PD	Doctor of Philosophy
PD	Dublin Pharmacopoeia
PD	Interpupillary Distance
PD	Paid

Pd	Palladium (Chemical element)
PD	Paralyzing Dose
PD	Partido Democrata (Democratic Party) (Chile)
PD	Passive Detection (Electronics)
PD	Peak Detector
PD	People's Democracy (Irish political party)
PD	Pepper Dust (An adulterating element)
PD	Per Diem
PD	Phase Discriminator
PD	Phelps Dodge Corporation (NYSE symbol)
PD	Photodiode
PD	Physics Department
PD	Pitch Diameter
PD	Planning Directive
PD	Plate Dissipation
PD	Point Defense
PD	Point Detonating (Projectile)
PD	Polar Distance (Navigation)
PD	Police Department
PD	Port of Debarkation
PD	Port Director
PD	Port Dues
PD	Position Description
PD	Position Doubtful (On a chart) (Nautical)
PD	Positive Displacement
PD	Postage Due
PD	Postal District
PD	Postdated
PD	Posterior Digestive (Gland)
PD	Potential Difference (Electricity)
PD	Power Distribution
PD	Preliminary Design
PD	Presidential Determination
PD	Prime Driver
PD	Printer Driver
PD	Priority Directive
PD	Prism Diopter
PD	Probability of Detection
PD	Procurement Directive
PD	Procurement Division
PD	Production Department
PD	Program Decoder
PD	Program Directive
PD	Projected Display
PD	Promotion Director
PD	Property Damage
PD	Proximity Detector
PD	Public Domain
PD	Pulpodistal
PD	Pulse Driver
PD	Pulse Duration
PD	Pulsed Doppler
PD	Punch Driver
PD	Purchase Description
PD	Pyloric Dilator (Neuron)
P & D	Pickup and Delivery
P & D	Pioneer and Demolition Section
PDA	Parenteral Drug Association
PDA	Parti Democratico da Angola (Democratic Party of Angola)
PDA	Patent Ductus Arteriosus (Medicine)
PDA	Patient Data Automation
PDA	Payroll Deduction Authorization
PDA	Peak Distribution Analyzer
PDA	Permanent Duty Assignment (Air Force)
PDA	Phenylenediamine (Chemistry)
PDA	Point Director Array
PDA	Poise Distribution Amplifier
PDA	Population Drainage Area (Civil Defense)
PDA	Pour Dire Adieu (To Say Farewell) (On visiting cards)
PDA	Predelivery Acceptance Test (NASA)
PDA	Predicted Drift Angle (Navigation)
PDA	Principal Development Activity (Navy)
PDA	Probability Density Analyzer
PDA	Probability Distribution Analyzer
PDA	Produktions und Dienstleistungsabgabe
PDA	Professional Drivers Association
PDA	Property Disposal Account (or Agent) (Military)
PDA	Proposed Development Approach (Navy)
PDA	Public Display of Affection (Slang)
PDA	Pug Dog of America
PDA	Pulse Demodulation Analysis

ACRONYMS AND INITIALISMS DICTIONARY

PDA	Pump Drive Assembly
PDAB	Physical Disability Appeals Board (Military)
PDAS	A Popular Dictionary of Australian Slang
Pd B	Bachelor of Pedagogy
PDB	Para-Dichlorobenzene (Moth balls)
PDB	Pee Dee Belemnite
PDB	Positive Displacement Blower
PDB	Price Decontrol Board (Post-World War II)
PDC	Package Designers Council
PDC	Parke, Davis & Company (NYSE symbol) (Delisted)
PDC	Parti Democrate Chretien (Christian Democratic Party) (Burundi)
PDC	Partido Democrata Cristiano (Democratic Christian Party) (Bolivia, Chile, El Salvador)
PDC	Partido Democratico Cristao (Christian Democratic Party) (Brazil)
PDC	Per Diem, Travel and Transportation Allowance Committee for Departments of the Army, Navy, and Air Force
PDC	Personnel Distribution Command
PDC	Photo-Data Card (Trademark) (Data processing)
PDC	Plastic Dielectric Capacitor
PDC	Polystyrene Dielectric Capacitor
PDC	Power Distribution and Control
PDC	Practice Depth Charge
PDC	Preliminary Diagnostic Clinic
PDC	Prevention of Deterioration Center
PDC	Private Diagnostic Clinic
PDC	Probability of Detection and Conversion
PDC	Professional Development Center
PDCG	Proficiency Data Card
PDC	Prosthetic Distribution Center (Veterans Administration)
PDC	Publications Distribution Center (Military)
PDC	Publishers' Data Center, Inc.
PDC	Pulse Duration Commutator
PDC	Pyrotechnic Devices Checker
PDCA	Painting and Decorating Contractors of America
PDCA	Purebred Dairy Cattle Association
PDCG	Partido Democracia Cristiana Guatemalteca (Political party in Guatemala)
PDCI	Parti Democratique de la Cote d'Ivoire (Democratic Party of the Ivory Coast)
Pdck	Probability of Detection Conversion and Kill (for an interceptor system) (Military)
PDCO	Property Disposal Contracting Officer (Military)
PDCP	Private Development Corporation of the Philippines
PDCS	Parallel Digital Computing System
PDCS	Prototype Die Casting Service
Pd D	Doctor of Pedagogy
PDD	Past Due Date
PDD	Physical Damage Division (Navy)
PDD	Physical Defense Division (Army)
PDD	Precision Depth Digitizer (Oceanography)
PDD	Preferred Delivery Date
PDD	Premodulation Processor - Deep Space - Data
PDD	Priority Delivery Date
PDD	Probability Density Distribution
PDD	Program Design Data
PDD	Property Disposal Division
PDD	Public Documents Department (Government Printing Office)
PDD/CRASH	Problem Drinking Driver / Court Referred Action for Safer Highways (Seattle, Washington, safety action program)
PDD/RDD	Priority Delivery Date/Required Delivery Date
PDE	Paroxysmal Dyspnea on Exertion
PDE	Partial Differential Equation
PDE	Propellent Disposition Effects
PDE	Prospective Data Element (Army)
PDF	Parkinson's Disease Foundation
PDF	Particle Distribution Function
PDF	Passive Direction Finding
PDF	Point Detonating Fuze
PDF	Post Defense Force
PDF	Principal Direction of Fire (Military)
PDF	Probability Density Function (Statistics)
PDF	Probability Distribution Function
PDFD	Pulsed Doppler Frequency Diversity
PDG	Parachute Drop Glider
PDG	Parti Democratique de Guinee (Democratic Party of Guinea)
PDG	People's Drug Stores, Inc. (NYSE symbol)
PDG	Precision Drop Glider (Military)
PDG	Professional Dyers Guild
P-DGs	Presidents-Directeurs Generaux
PDGA	Pteroyldiglutamic Acid
PDGDL	Plasma Dynamics and Gaseous Discharge Laboratory (MIT)
PDGS	Precision Delivery Glides System
PDH	Packaged Disaster Hospital (Public Health Service)
PDH	Passive Defense Handbook (Navy)
PDH	Past Dental History
PDHV-RDA	Parti Democratique de la Haute Volta-Rassemblement Democratique Africain (Democratic Party of Upper Volta-African Democratic Rally)
PDI	Parti Democratique de l'Independance (Democratic Independence Party) (Morocco)
PDI	Pilot Direction Indicator (Electronic communications)
PDI	Plumbing and Drainage Institute
PDI	Powered Descent Initiation (Aerospace)
PDI	Program Design, Incorporated (Commercial firm)
PDIC	Periodic
PDJ	Plaine des Jarres (South Vietnam)
PDJ	Precision Drill Jig
PDJB	Precision Drill Jig Bushing
PDK	Phi Delta Kappa (Fraternity in field of education)
PDKI	Persatuan Pegawai Departemen Kesehatan Indonesia (Union of Health Department Employees) (Indonesia)
PDL	Parts Difference List
PDL	Poverty Datum Line
PDL	Precision Delay Line
PDL	Product Disaster Loans (Small Business Administration)
PDL	Programmed Digital Logic
Pd M	Master of Pedagogy
PDM	Parti Democratique Malgache (Malagasy Democratic Party)
PDM	Pendant Drop Method
PDM	Percent Deviation from the Median
PDM	Physiological Data Monitor
PDM	Power Density Meter
PDM	Print Down Module
PDM	Project Design Memo
PDM	Publications Distribution Manager (Military)
PDM	Pulse-Duration Modulation (Radio)
PDMA	Peninsula Drafting Management Association
PDMFM	Pulse Duration Modulation - Frequency Modulation
PDMP	Positive Displacement Mechanical (or Metering) Pump
PDMS	Physiological Data Monitoring System
PDMS	Polydimethylsiloxane
PDN	Partido Democratico Nacional (National Democratic Party) (Chile)
PDN	Production
PDN	Properly Driven Net
PDNC	Presidents' Day National Committee
PDO	Property Disposal Officer (Military)
PDO	Publications Distribution Officer
PDOC	Proceed Directly on Course (Aviation)
PDOL	Publishers Discount Option List
PDP	Pilot District Project (Office of Economic Opportunity)
PDP	Positive Displacement Pump
PDP	Process Development Pile (AEC)
PDP	Procurement Data Package
PDP	Professional Development Document
PDP	Program (or Project) Definition Phase (DOD)
PDP	Program Development Plan (NASA)
PDP	Programmed Data Processor
PDP	Project Development Plan
PDPC	Position Display Parallax Corrected
PDPGM	Past Deputy Provincial Grand Master (Masonry)
PDPS	Parts Data Processing System
PDPS	Program Definition Phase Studies (Navy)
PDPT	Parti Democratique des Populations Togolaises (Togolese Democratic People's Party)
PDQ	Photo Data Quantizer
PDQ	Pretty Damn Quick
PDQ	Programmed Data Quantizer
PDR	Periscope Depth Range (SONAR)
PDR	Periscope Detection RADAR
PDR	Philippine Defense Ribbon
PDR	Physicians' Desk Reference (A publication)
PDR	Power Directional Relay
PDR	Precision Depth Recorder
PDR	Pre-Detection Recording
PDR	Predetermined Demand Rate
PDR	Preliminary Data Report
PDR	Preliminary Design Review
PDR	Pressurized Deuterium Reactor (AEC)
PDR	Priority Data Reduction
PDR	Process Dynamics Recorder
PDR	Processed Data Recorder
PDR	Program Drum Recording
PDR	Pulse Doppler RADAR
PDRC	Pressure Difference Recording Controller

PDRL . . . . Permanent Disability Retired List
PDRP . . . . Power Demonstration Reactor Program (AEC)
PDS . . . . Paid-During-Service (Magazine subscriptions)
PDS . . . . Performer Design Sheet
PDS . . . . Permanent Duty Station (Air Force)
PDS . . . . Personnel Daily Summary (Army)
PDS . . . . Personnel Data Summary
PDS . . . . Personnel Data System
PDS . . . . Personnel Delivery System
PDS . . . . Pneumatic Distribution System
PDS . . . . Power Distribution System
PDS . . . . Priority Distribution System (Military)
PDS . . . . Prisoner Detention System
PDS . . . . Procurement Data Sheet
PDS . . . . Program Development Section
PDS . . . . Programmable Data Station (or System)
PDS . . . . Propellant Dispersion System
PDS . . . . Pulse Doppler Seeker
PDS . . . . Punch Driver Selectric
PD/S . . . . Problem Definition/Solution
PDS-A . . . . . . Personnel Data System for Airmen (Air Force)
PDS-A(I) . . . . . Personnel Data System – Airmen (Interim) (Air Force)
PDS-C . . . . . . Personnel Data System – Civilian
PDSD . . . . . . Point Detonating Self-Destroying (Projectile)
P & DSEC . . . . Pioneer and Demolition Section (Army)
PDSMS . . . . . . Point-Defense Surface Missile System
PDS-O . . . . . . Personnel Data System – Officers (Air Force)
PDSP . . . . Personnel Data System Planning (Air Force)
PDT . . . . Pacific Daylight Time
PDT . . . . Panoramic Design Technique
PDT . . . . Parallel Data Transmission
PDT . . . . Pendleton Tool Industries, Inc. (NYSE symbol) (Delisted)
PDT . . . . Posting Data Transfer (Air Force)
PDT . . . . Postive Displacement Turbine
PDT . . . . Pre-Delivery Test
PDT . . . . Predictor Display Technique
PDT . . . . Pulse Delay Time
PDU . . . . Parti Dahomeen de l'Unite (Dahomean Unity Party)
PDU . . . . Parti Democrate Unifie (Unified Democratic Party) (Name replaced by
    Section Voltaique de Rassemblement)
PDU . . . . Phase Demodulation Unit
PDV . . . . Premodulation Processor – Deep Space – Voice
PDW . . . . Priority Delayed Weather (Aviation)
PDX . . . . Place Decrement in Index
PDY . . . . Peabody Coal Company (NYSE symbol) (Delisted)
PDY . . . . Principal Duty (Military)
PE . . . . Pacific Electric Railway (AAR code)
PE . . . . Patrol Vessel, Eagle (Eagle boat) (Navy symbol)
PE . . . . Permanent Echo (RADAR)
PE . . . . Personnel, Enlisted or Enlisted Personnel Division (Coast Guard)
PE . . . . Personnel Equipment (Air Force)
PE . . . . Petroleum Engineer
PE . . . . Philadelphia Electric Company (NYSE symbol)
PE . . . . Photoelectric
PE . . . . Physical Education
PE . . . . Pigment Epithelium
PE . . . . Pinion End
PE . . . . Pistol Expert
PE . . . . Planning Estimate
PE . . . . Plasma Emission (Spectrophotometry)
PE . . . . Polyethylene
PE . . . . Port of Embarkation
PE . . . . Position Error
PE . . . . Post Engineer (Army)
PE . . . . Post Exchange (Marine Corps)
PE . . . . Potential Energy
PE . . . . Powdered Extract (Pharmacy)
PE . . . . Preliminary Evaluation
PE . . . . Presiding Elder
PE . . . . Prime Equipment
PE . . . . Printer's Error
PE . . . . Probable Error (Statistics)
PE . . . . Processing Element
PE . . . . Production Engineering
PE . . . . Professional Education
PE . . . . Professional Engineer
PE . . . . Program Element
PE . . . . Project Engineer
PE . . . . Protestant Episcopal
PE . . . . Pulley End
PE . . . . Pulse Encoding (Data processing)

PE . . . . Purchased Equipment
P-E . . . . Precipitation-Evaporation
P/E . . . . Price/Earnings Ratio (Relation between price of a company's stock and
    its annual net income)
P/E . . . . Professional and Executive (Employment register) (British)
P & E . . . . Privileges and Elections Subcommittee (US Senate)
P & E . . . . Procurement & Expedition
P & E . . . . Propellants and Explosives (Military)
P of E . . . . . . Portal of Entry (Bacteriology)
PEA . . . . Pattern Error Analysis
PEA . . . . Plastics Engineers Association
PEA . . . . Pitch Error Amplifier
PEA . . . . Potash Export Association
PEA . . . . Primary Expense Account
PEA . . . . Program Element Administrator (Navy)
PEA . . . . Progressive Education Association (Became defunct in 1955)
PEAC . . . . . . Photoelectric Auto Collimator
PEACE . . . . . People Emerging Against Corrupt Establishments (Underground military
    newspaper)
PEACE . . . . . Project Evaluation and Assistance, Civil Engineering (Air Force)
PEAP . . . . . . Principal Error Axis for Position
PEARL . . . . . Committee for Public Education and Religious Liberty
PEARL . . . . . Performance Evaluation of Amplifiers from a Remote Location
PEAS . . . . . . Presbyterian Educational Association of the South
PEAT . . . . . . Pricing Evaluation for Audit Technique (Finance)
PEAT . . . . . . Programme Elargi d'Assistance Technique (Expanded Program of Technical
    Assistance) (UN)
PEAV . . . . . . Principal Error Axis for Velocity
Pe B . . . . Bachelor of Pediatrics
PEB . . . . Physical Evaluation Board (Military)
PEB . . . . Positive Expulsion Bladder
PEBA . . . . . . Purified Extract of Brucella Abortus
PEBCO . . . . . Program Evaluation and Budget Committee (American Library Association)
PEBD . . . . . . Pay Entry Base Date
PEBH . . . . . . Physical Evaluation Board Hospital (Military)
PEBL . . . . . . Port Everglades Belt Line Railway (AAR code)
PEBLO . . . . . Physical Evaluation Board Liaison Officer (Air Force)
PEC . . . . Palestine Economic Commission
PEC . . . . Peak Electrode Current
PEC . . . . Pedal Excretory Cell
PEC . . . . Perkin-Elmer Corporation
PEC . . . . Photoelectric Cell
PEC . . . . Planetary Entry Capsule
PEC . . . . Plant Equipment Codes (DOD)
PEC . . . . Positive Engagement Clutch
PEC . . . . Potasse et Engrais Chimiques
PEC . . . . Previous Element Coding
PEC . . . . Production Equipment Code
PEC . . . . Production Executive Committee
PEC . . . . Program Element Code
PEC . . . . Program Environment Control
PEC . . . . Propulsion Environmental Chamber
PECA . . . . . . Petroleum Equipment Contractors Association
PECAN . . . . . Pulse Envelop Correlation Air Navigation
PECBI . . . . . . Professional Engineers Conference Board for Industry
PECE . . . . . . Proposed Engineering Change Estimate
PECI . . . . Preliminary Equipment Component Index (or Inventory)
PECM . . . . . . Passive Electronics Countermeasures
PECO . . . . . . Pecos National Monument
PECOS . . . . . Program Environment Checkout System
PECR . . . . . . Program Error Correction Report
PECS . . . . . . Portable Environmental Control System (NASA)
PED . . . . Personnel Equipment Data
PED . . . . Photoemission Diode
PED . . . . Positive Expulsion Device
PED . . . . Program Element Directive
PED . . . . Promotion Eligibility Date (Military)
PED . . . . Pure Edge Dislocation
PED . . . . Pyramid Element Designator
PEDA . . . . . . Pedal Artery
PEDA . . . . . . Personnel/Equipment Data Analysis
Ped B . . . . . . Bachelor of Pedagogy
PEDC . . . . . . Personal Effects Distribution Center
Ped D . . . . . . Doctor of Pedagogy
PEDIN . . . . . . Peapod Dinghy
PE Dir . . . . . . Physical Education Director
Ped M . . . . . . Master of Pedagogy
PEDRO . . . . . Pneumatic Energy Detector with Remote Optics
PEDS . . . . . . Packaging Engineering Data System
PEE . . . . Photo Emission Effect
PEE . . . . Photoelectron Emission

PEE . . . . Program Estimating Equation
PEEC . . . . Personnel Emergency Estimator Capability
PEEK . . . . People for the Enjoyment of Eyeballing Knees (Group opposing below-the-knee fashions introduced in 1970)
PEEK . . . . Periodically Elevated Electronic Kibitzer
PEEP . . . . Pilot's Electronic Eyelevel Presentation (British)
PEEP . . . . Porous Electrode Electrostatic Precipitation
PEER. . . . . Planned Experience for Effective Relating
PEERC . . . . . . Production Engineering Education and Research Center
PEF . . . . Palestine Endowment Funds
PEF . . . . Palestine Exploration Fund
PEF . . . . Physical Electronics Facility
PEF . . . . Plastics Education Foundation
PEF . . . . Polyethylene Foam
PEF . . . . Program Estimating Factor
PEFCO . . . . . . Private Export Finance Corporation
PEFO . . . . Petrified Forest National Park
PEFR . . . . Peak Expiratory Flow Rate
PEG . . . . Pneumatic Explosion Generator
PEG . . . . Polyethylene Glycol
PEG . . . . Polyurethane Elastomer Genthane
PEG . . . . Principle of the Equivalent Generator
PEG . . . . Public Service Electric & Gas Company (NYSE symbol)
PEGE . . . . Program for Evaluation of Ground Environment
PEH . . . . Planning Estimate Handbook
PEH . . . . Plus Each Hour (Aviation)
PEI. . . . . Polyethyleneimine
PEI . . . . Porcelain Enamel Institute
PEI. . . . . Prince Edward Island (A Canadian province)
PEI. . . . . Professional Engineers in Industry
PEIC. . . . . Periodic Error Integrating Controller
PEJ . . . . Premolded Expansion Joint (Technical drawings)
PEK . . . . Phi Epsilon Kappa (Fraternity)
PEL . . . . Panhandle Eastern Pipe Line Company (NYSE symbol)
PEL . . . . Precision Elastic Limit
PEL . . . . Priests Eucharistic League
PELC . . . . Professional Engineers' Legislative Committee
PELL . . . . Papers on English Language and Literature (A journal)
PEM . . . . Philco Electronic Module
PEM . . . . Photoelectromagnetic
PEM . . . . Product Effectiveness Manual
PEM . . . . Production Engineering Measures (Army)
PEM . . . . Program Element Monitor
PEM. . . . . Project Engineering Memorandum
PEMA . . . . Process Equipment Manufacturers Association
PEMA . . . . Procurement of Equipment and Missiles, Army
PEMA . . . . Production-Equipment-Missile Agency (Army)
PEMARS . . . . . Procurement of Equipment and Missiles, Army Management and Accounting Reporting System
PEMEX . . . . . . Petroleos Mexicanos (Mexican government petroleum operating company)
P & EML. . . . . Personnel and Equipment Modification List (Air Force)
PEMS . . . . Professional Education of the Media Specialist
PEN . . . . International PEN (Official name; PEN, never spelled out in use, is said, however, to stand for poets, playwrights, editors, essayists, novelists)
PEN . . . . Penetration
PEN . . . . Program Error Note
PENAID . . . . . Penetration Aid (Air Force)
PENB . . . . Poultry and Egg National Board
PENG. . . . . . . Photo-Electro-Nystagmography (Medicine)
PENN. . . . . . . Pennsylvania
PENNA. . . . . . Pennsylvania
PENNSTAC . . . Penn State University Automatic Digital Computer
PENNTAP . . . . Pennsylvania Technical Assistance Program
PENRAD . . . . . Penetration RADAR
PENSAM . . . . . Penetration Survivability Assessment Model
PENTAC . . . . . Penetration for Tactical Aircraft (Air Force)
PENTENG. . . . Pentagon English (Pseudotechnical language)
PENW . . . . . . Penetrating Wound
PEO . . . . Pankypria Ergatiki Omospondia (Pancyprian Federation of Labour) (The "Old Trade Unions") (Cyprus)
PEO . . . . Petroleum Corporation of America (NYSE symbol)
PEO . . . . Planners for Equal Opportunity
PEO . . . . Production Engineering Order
PEO . . . . Program Evaluation Office
PEO . . . . Prospective Engineer Officer
PEOC . . . . Publishing Employees Organizing Committee (AFL-CIO)
PEP . . . . Pauli Exclusion Principle
PEP . . . . Peak Energy Product
PEP . . . . Peak Envelope Power
PEP . . . . Peer Evaluation Program (College of American Pathologists)

PEP . . . . PepsiCo, Inc. (NYSE symbol)
PEP . . . . Performance Effectiveness (or Evaluation) Program (Navy)
PEP . . . . Phosphoenolpyruvate
PEP . . . . Photoelectric Potential
PEP . . . . Physical Education Program
PEP . . . . Physiological Evaluation of Primates
PEP . . . . Piping Efficiency Program
PEP . . . . Planar Epitaxial Passivated
PEP . . . . Platform Electronic Package
PEP . . . . Platform Evaluation Program
PEP . . . . Political and Economic Planning
PEP . . . . Polyethylene Powder
PEP. . . . . Practical Engineering Paperwork
PEP . . . . Pratt & Whitney Engine Program (Aviation)
PEP . . . . Pre-Amplifier Extension Plug
PEP . . . . Preventive Enforcement Patrol (New York City police)
PEP . . . . Primate Equilibrium Platform
PEP . . . . Princeton Experimental Package
PeP . . . . Principal of Pedagogy (Academic degree)
PEP . . . . Product Engineering and Production
PEP . . . . Program Evaluation Procedure (Air Force)
PEP . . . . Promoting Enduring Peace
PEP . . . . Public Employment Program
PEP . . . . Pulse Echo Pattern
PEPA . . . . Petroleum Electric Power Association
PEPA . . . . Pulse Echo Pattern Analyzer
PEPAG . . . . . . Physical Electronics and Physical Acoustics Group (MIT)
PEPC . . . . Polynomial Error Protection Code (Data processing)
PEPC . . . . Potomac Electric Power Company
PEPCO . . . . . . Potomac Electric Power Company
PEPG . . . . Piezo-Electric Power Generator
PEPL. . . . . Preliminary Engineering Parts List
PEPMC . . . . . . Printing Estimators and Production Men's Club
PEPP . . . . Planetary Entry Parachute Program (NASA)
PEPP . . . . Professional Engineers in Private Practice
PEPR . . . . Precision Encoding and Pattern Recognition Device (Data processing)
PEPS. . . . . Priced Exhibit Preliminary System
PEPS . . . . Program Element Plan Supplement
PEPSS . . . . . . Programmable Equipment for Personnel Subsystem Simulation
PEPSU. . . . . . . Patiala and East Punjab States Union
PEPSY. . . . . . . Precision Earth-Pointing System
PEQ . . . . Personal Experience Questionnaire (Psychology)
PEQUA . . . . . Production Equipment Agency
PER . . . . Partido Estadista Republicano (Political party) (Puerto Rico)
PER . . . . Performance Evaluation Routine
PER . . . . PERT Event Report
PER . . . . Phase Engineering Report
PER . . . . Physical Examination Rate (Military)
PER . . . . Post Engineer Request
PERA . . . . Planning and Engineering for Repair and Alteration (Navy)
PERA . . . . Production Engineering Research Association (British)
PERAM . . . . . Personnel Action Memorandum
PERBUM . . . . . Persatuan Buruh Minjak (Federation of Oil Workers) (Indonesia)
PERBUPRI. . . . . Persatuan Buruh Perkebunan Republik Indonesia (Plantation Workers' Union) (Indonesia)
PERBUTI . . . . . Persatuan Buruh Textiel Indonesia (Textile Workers' Union) (Indonesia)
PERC . . . . Peace on Earth Research Center
PERCOM . . . . . Peripheral Communications
PERCOS . . . . . Performance Coding System
PEREF . . . . . . Personal Effects
PEREF . . . . . . Propellant Engine Research Environmental Facility
PERFW . . . . . . Perforating Wound
PERG . . . . Production Emergency Redistribution Group
PERG . . . . Production Equipment Redistribution Group
PERGRA . . . . . Permission Granted (Military)
PERHUTANI . . . Perusahaan Kehutanan Negara
PERI . . . . Pea Ridge National Military Park
PERI . . . . Photoengravers Research Institute
PERI . . . . Production Equipment Redistribution Inventory (Army)
PERI . . . . Production Equipment Reserve Inventory (Navy)
PERINTREPT . . Periodic Intelligence Report
PERINTSUM . . . Periodic Intelligence Summary (Army)
PERK . . . . Payroll Earnings Record Keeping
PERKAPPEN . . . Persatuan Karyawan Perusahaan Perkebunan Negara (State Estate Enterprise Workers' Union) (Indonesia)
PERL. . . . . Public Employee Relations Library (of Public Personnel Association)
PERM . . . . Permanent
PERMACAP . . . Personnel Management and Accounting Card Processor
PERMAFROST . . Permanent Frost
PERMINVAR. . . Permeability Invariant
PERMR . . . . . . Permanent Residence

PERMU . . . . . . Permanent Magnet Users Association
PERNOGRA . . . Permission Not Granted (Military)
PERS . . . . Personnel
PERSCO . . . . . Personnel Support of Contingency Operations (Military)
PERSCON . . . . Personnel Control (Military)
PERSD . . . . Personnel Department (Marine Corps)
PERSDEP . . . . . Personnel Deployment Report (Military)
PERSEXP . . . . . Personal Expense Money
PERSINS . . . . . Personnel Information System (Army)
PERSOF . . . . . . Personnel Officer (Navy)
PERSPROC . . . . Personnel Processing
PERSSEPCENT . . Personnel Separation Center
PERSTAT . . . . . Personnel Status Report (Military)
PERS & TRACOMD . . Personnel and Training Command
PERSTRAN . . . . Personal Transportation (Navy)
PERT . . . . Program Evaluation and Review Technique (Data processing)
PERTCO . . . . . Program Evaluation Review Technique with Cost
PERTRAN . . . . . Perturbation Transport (NASA)
PERUSA . . . . . . Perspectives - United States of America (History course)
PES . . . . Parent Egg Seed
PES . . . . Parts Engineering Support
PES . . . . Patent Examining System
PES . . . . Philosophy of Education Society
PES . . . . Photoelectric Scanner
PES . . . . Photoelectron Spectroscopy
PES . . . . Photojet Edge Sensor
PES . . . . Preexcitation Syndrome (Cardiology)
PES . . . . Production Engineering Service
PES . . . . Production Engineering Specification
PES . . . . Professional Examining Service
PESA . . . . Petroleum Electric Supply Association
PESA . . . . Petroleum Equipment Suppliers Association
PESD . . . . Program Element Summary Data
PESD . . . . Program Execution Sub-Directive (Army)
PESDS . . . . . . Program Element Summary Data Sheet (DOD)
P & ESI . . . . . Physical and Engineering Sciences Division (Army Research Office)
PESIC . . . . Parti du Progres Economique et Social des Independants Congolais Luluabourg (Party for Economic and Social Progress of the Congolese Independents in Luluabourg)
PESO . . . . Participation Enriches Science, Music and Art Organizations (Orlando, Florida)
PESR . . . . Precision Echo Sounder Recorder
PEST . . . . Parameter Estimation by Sequential Testing (Computer)
PEST . . . . Pesticide Evaluation Summary Tabulation
PESTF . . . . . . Proton Event Start Forecast (Solar weather information)
PET . . . . Panel on Education and Training (COSATI)
PET . . . . Panel on Educational Terminology (US Office of Education)
PET . . . . Parent Effectiveness Training (in book title)
PET . . . . Particle Electrostatic Thruster
PET . . . . Pentaerythritol
PET . . . . Performance Evaluation Test
PET . . . . Periodic Environmental Test
PET . . . . Pet, Inc. (NYSE symbol)
PET . . . . Philippine Earth Terminal
PET . . . . Photoemission Tube
PET . . . . Phototropic Energy Transfer
PET . . . . Physical Equipment Table
PET . . . . Point of Equal Time (Aviation)
PET . . . . Polyethylene Terephthalate
PET . . . . Portable Electronic Telephone
PET . . . . Portable Executive Telephone
PET . . . . Position-Event-Time
PET . . . . Preliminary Examination Team (NASA)
PET . . . . Pressurization Events Trainer
PET . . . . Process Evaluation Tester
PET . . . . Production Environmental Tests
PET . . . . Production Evaluation Test
PETA . . . . Portable Electronic Traffic Analyzer (British)
PETE . . . . Petersburg National Battlefield
PETE . . . . Pneumatic End to End
PETE . . . . Product Engineering Tribute to Excellence
PETF . . . . Polyethylene Terephthalate
PETI . . . . Percent of Travel Involved
PETN . . . . Pentaerythritol Tetranitrate (Explosive)
PETP . . . . Polyethylene Teraphthalate
PETR . . . . Preliminary Flight Test Report
PETRES . . . . . Petroleum Reserves (Navy)
PETRODEG . . . Petroleum Degrading (Agent)
PETS . . . . Pacific Electronics Trade Show
PETS . . . . Prior to Expiration of Term of Service (Reenlistments) (Military)
PETS . . . . Programmed Extended Time Sharing

PETSEC . . . . . . Petroleum Section (Allied Force Headquarters)
PETT . . . . Phototropic Energy Transfer Technique
PETV . . . . Planar Epitaxial Tuning Varactor
PETV . . . . Process Evaluation Test Vehicle
PEUA . . . . Pelvic Exam Under Anesthesia (Medicine)
PEVI . . . . Perry's Victory and International Peace Memorial National Monument
PEW . . . . Passive Electronics Warfare
PEX . . . . Per Example
PEX RAD . . . . . Programmed Electronic X-Ray Automatic Diffractometer
PEY . . . . Photoelectric Yield
PF . . . . Parallel Fold
PF . . . . Patrol Vessel, Frigate (Navy symbol)
PF . . . . Pedal Furrow
PF . . . . Perchlorye-Fluoride
PF . . . . Performance Factor
PF . . . . Permeability Factor
PF . . . . Phenol-Formaldehyde (Organic chemistry)
PF . . . . Photogrammetric Facility (Army)
PF . . . . Physicians Forum
PF . . . . Pianoforte (Soft, then loud) (Music)
pF . . . . Picofarad
PF . . . . Pioneer & Fayette R. R. (AAR code)
PF . . . . Piu Forte (A little louder) (Music)
PF . . . . Pneumatic Float
PF . . . . Popular Force (ARVN)
PF . . . . Position Failure
PF . . . . Pour Feliciter (To Congratulate)
PF . . . . Power Factor (Radio)
PF . . . . Pre-Flight
PF . . . . Procurator Fiscal
PF . . . . Protection Factor (Civil Defense)
PF . . . . Proximity Fuze (Bomb, rocket, or shell)
PF . . . . Pulse Frequency
PF . . . . Pulverized Fuel
P & F . . . . . . Plant and Facilities
PFA . . . . Papermakers Felt Association
PFA . . . . Parti de la Federation Africaine (African Federation Party)
PFA . . . . Participating Field Activity (DOD)
PFA . . . . Pierre Fauchard Academy
PFA . . . . Pioneer Fraternal Association
PFA . . . . Pitch Followup Amplifier
PFA . . . . Polish Falcons of America
PFA . . . . Post Flight Analysis
PFA . . . . Proportional Fluid Amplifier
PFA . . . . Pure Fluid Amplification
PFAM . . . . . . Programmed Frequency Amplitude Modulation
PFB . . . . Photo Flash Battery
PFB . . . . Pneumatic Float Bridge
PFB . . . . Pre-Formed Beams (SONAR)
PFB . . . . Provisional Frequency Board (ITU)
PFBA . . . . . . Polyperfluorobutyl Acrylate
PFBRG . . . . . . Pneumatic Float Bridge
PFC . . . . Pacific Finance Corporation
PFC . . . . Passed Flying College (British)
PFC . . . . Plan Filing Cabinet
PFC . . . . Plaque-Forming Cells
PFC . . . . Positive Feedback Circuit
PFC . . . . Praying for Corporal (Private First Class desirous of promotion, or female in wartime desirous of a boy friend)
PFC . . . . Preflight Console
PFC . . . . Primary Flight Control
PFC . . . . Private, First Class (Army)
PFCA . . . . . . Plastic Food Container Association (Defunct)
PFCD . . . . . . Primary Flight Control Display
PFCO . . . . . . Position Field Classification Officer
PFD . . . . Present for Duty
PFD . . . . Primary Flight Display
PFD . . . . Pulse Frequency Diversity (Electronics)
PFDA . . . . . . Post Flight Data Analysis
PFDA . . . . . . Pulse Frequency Distortion Analyzer
PFE . . . . Pfizer, Inc. (NYSE symbol)
PFE . . . . Post Flight Evaluation
PFE . . . . Program for Executives
PFEFES . . . . . Pacific and Far East Federation of Engineering Societies
PFEL . . . . . . Pacific Far East Line
PFES . . . . . . Pure Fluid Encoder System
PFF . . . . Pathfinder Force (British RADAR designation which became overall synonym for RADAR) (Military)
PFF . . . . Permanent Family File (Navy)
PFFC . . . . . . Parallel-Flow Film Cooling
PFFX . . . . . . Profiling Fixture

PFG . . . . Pittsburgh Forgings Company (NYSE symbol)
PFG . . . . Primary Frequency Generator
PFGX . . . . Pacific Fruit Growers Express
PFI . . . . Pacific Forest Industries
PFI . . . . Pet Food Institute
PFI . . . . Photo Finishing Institute
PFI . . . . Physical Fitness Index
PFI . . . . Picture and Frame Institute
PFI . . . . Pie Filling Institute
PFI . . . . Pipe Fabrication Institute
PFI . . . . Potlatch Forest, Incorporated (NYSE symbol)
PFIA . . . . Police and Firemen's Insurance Association
PFIAB . . . . . . President's Foreign Intelligence Advisory Board
PFIM . . . . Pure Fluid Impact Modulator
PFK . . . . Penick & Ford, Ltd., Inc. (NYSE symbol) (Delisted)
PFK . . . . Perfluorokerosene
PFK . . . . Programmed Function Keyboard (Data processing)
PFL . . . . Propulsion Field Laboratory
PFLOLS . . . . . Portable Fresnel-Lens Optical-Landing System
PFLP . . . . Popular Front for the Liberation of Palestine
PFM . . . . Pitch Followup Motor
PFM . . . . Plan for Maintenance (Navy)
PFM . . . . Power Factor Meter
PFM . . . . Pressure Flow Meter
PFM . . . . Pulse Forming Machine
PFM . . . . Pulse-Frequency Modulation (RADAR)
P & FM . . . . . Programs and Financial Management (Navy)
PFMA . . . . . . Pipe Fittings Manufacturers Association
PFMA . . . . . . Plumbing Fixture Manufacturers Association
PFMR . . . . . . Pasadena Foundation for Medical Research (California)
PFN . . . . Passamaquoddy Ferry & Navigation Company (AAR code)
PFN . . . . Pulse Forming Network
PFNA . . . . . . Pentecostal Fellowship of North America
PFNS . . . . . . Position Firing and Navigation System (Army)
PFNS . . . . . . Position Fixing Navigation System
PFO . . . . Pitch Followup Operation
PFO . . . . Postal Finance Officer
PFO . . . . Procurement Field Office(s)
PFP . . . . Pensions for Professionals (Inc.)
PFP . . . . Postage Forward Parcels
PFP . . . . Publishers for Peace (An organization)
PFR . . . . Part Failure Rate
PFR . . . . Penn Fruit Company, Inc. (NYSE symbol)
PFR . . . . Pfarrer (Pastor)
PFR . . . . Photoflash Relay
PFR . . . . Polarized Frequency Relay
PFR . . . . Precision Fathometer Recorder (Raytheon Co.)
PFR . . . . Preliminary Flight Rating
PFR . . . . Programmed Film Reader (System)
PFR . . . . Prototype Fast Reactor (Atomic energy)
PFRA . . . . . . Prairie Farm Rehabilitation Act (Canada)
PFRT . . . . Pre-Flight Rating Test
PFRT . . . . Preliminary Flight Rating Test (Air Force)
PFS . . . . Parallel Filter System
PFS . . . . Personal and Family Survival (Civil Defense)
PFS . . . . Pitch Followup System
PFS . . . . Precision Frequency Source
PFS . . . . Preflight School (Military)
PFS . . . . Press Fit Socket
PFS . . . . Programmable Frequency Standard
PFS . . . . Propellant Feed System
PFS . . . . Pure Fluid System
PFSV . . . . . . Pilot-to-Forecaster Service
PFT . . . . Paper, Flat Tape
PFT . . . . Pittsburgh, Fort Wayne & Chicago Railway Co. (NYSE symbol)
PFT . . . . Portable Flame Thrower
PFT . . . . Preflight Team (Air Force)
PFT . . . . Program Flying Training (Air Force)
PFT . . . . Projective Field Theory
PFTC . . . . . . Pestalozzi Froebel Teachers College (Illinois)
PFTM . . . . . . Preliminary Flight Test Memo
PFU . . . . Plaque Forming Unit
PFUA . . . . . . Pitch Follow-Up Amplifier
PFUJ . . . . . . Pakistan Federal Union of Journalists
PFUM . . . . . . Pitch Follow-Up Motor
PFUO . . . . . . Pitch Follow-Up Operation
PFUS . . . . . . Pitch Follow-Up System
PFV . . . . Pestalozzi-Froebel-Verband (Pestalozzi-Froebel Association)
PFV . . . . Pour Faire (To Make a Call) (France)
PFW . . . . Progressive Free Wave
PFWOAD . . . . Place from Which Ordered to Active Duty (Military)

PG . . . . Page
PG . . . . Paralysie Generale (General Paralysis) (Medicine)
PG . . . . Paregoric (Slang)
PG . . . . Parental Guidance Suggested (Some Material May Not Be Suitable for Pre-Teenagers) (Movie rating) (Formerly, GP)
PG . . . . Paris Granite
PG . . . . Patrol Vessel, Gunboat
PG . . . . Pay Group
PG . . . . Paying Guest
PG . . . . Pedal Ganglion
PG . . . . Pedal Groove
PG . . . . Pelham Grenville Wodehouse (British humorist)
PG . . . . Permanent Grade
PG . . . . Pharmacopoeia Germanica
PG . . . . Polyethylene Glycol
PG . . . . Postgraduate (Refers to courses or students) (Slang)
PG . . . . Power Gain
PG . . . . Preacher General
PG . . . . Pregnant
PG . . . . Press Gallery (US Senate)
PG . . . . Prisonnier de Guerre (Prisoner of War, POW)
PG . . . . Procter & Gamble Company (NYSE symbol)
PG . . . . Produktionsgenossenschaft
PG . . . . Program Guidance
PG . . . . Proof Gallon (Wines and spirits)
PG . . . . Prostaglandin (Biochemistry)
PG . . . . Protein Granule
PG . . . . Proving Ground
PG . . . . Public Gaol
PG . . . . Pulse Generator
PG . . . . Pyrolytic Graphite
P & G . . . . . Procter and Gamble Company
PGA . . . . . . Pendulous Gyro Accelerometer
PGA . . . . . . Phosphoglyceric Acid
PGA . . . . . . Power Gain Antenna
PGA . . . . . . Pressure Garment Assembly
PGA . . . . . . Professional Golfers' Association of America
PGA . . . . . . Professional Group Audio
PGA . . . . . . Pteroylglutamic Acid (Folic acid)
PGAC . . . . . . Professional Group – Automatic Control
PGAH . . . . . . Pineapple Growers Association of Hawaii
PGAL . . . . . . Phosphoglyceraldehyde
PGANE . . . . . Professional Group on Aeronautical and Navigational Electronics
PGAP . . . . . Professional Group – Antennas and Propagation
PGAR . . . . . . Provisional Government of the Algerian Republic
Pg B . . . . . . Bachelor of Pedagogy
PGB . . . . . . Pyrographalloy Boron
PGBA . . . . . . Piece Goods Buyers Association
PGBTR . . . . . Professional Group – Broadcast and Television Receivers
PGBTS . . . . . Professional Group – Broadcast Transmission Systems
PGC . . . . Per Gyro Compass (Navigation)
PGC . . . . Persian Gulf Command (World War II)
PGC . . . . Primordial Germ Cell
PGC . . . . . . Programmed Gain Control
PGC . . . . . . Proving Ground Command (Air Force)
PGC . . . . . . Pulsed Gas Crymography
PGCh . . . . . Past Grand Chaplain (Masonry)
PGCOA . . . . . Pennsylvania Grade Crude Oil Association
PGCP . . . . . . Professional Group – Component Parts
PGCS . . . . . . Professional Group – Communications Systems
PGCT . . . . . Professional Group – Circuit Theory
PGD . . . . Past Grand Deacon (Masonry)
PGD . . . . Phosphaogluconate Dehydrogenase
PGD . . . . Pinion Gear Drive
PGD . . . . Pulse Generator Display
PGDC . . . . . . Provincial Grand Director of Ceremonies (Masonry)
PGDF . . . . . . Pilot Guide Dog Foundation
PGDS . . . . . . Pulse Generator Display System
PGE . . . . Pacific Great Eastern Railway Company (Later, British Columbia Railway) (AAR code)
PGE . . . . Population Growth Estimation
PGE . . . . Pore Gradient Electrophoresis
PGE . . . . Portland Grain Exchange
PGE . . . . Professional Group – Education
PGE . . . . Prostaglandin E (Biochemistry)
PG & E . . . . . Pacific Gas and Electric Company
PGEC . . . . . Professional Group on Electronic Computers (of IRE)
PGED . . . . . . Professional Group – Electronic Devices
PGEM . . . . . . Professional Group – Engineering Management
PGEWS . . . . . . Professional Group on Engineering Writing and Speech (Institute of Radio Engineers; now IEEE)

PGF . . . . Prostaglandin F (Biochemistry)
PGG . . . . Pneumatic Ground Group
PGH. . . . . . . Patrol Gunboat, Hydrofoil (Navy)
PGH. . . . . . . Produktionsgenossenschaft des Handwerks
PGHFE . . . . . Professional Group - Human Factors in Electronics
PGI . . . . Philippine Geothermal, Incorporated
PGI . . . . Professional Group - Instrumentation
PGIE . . . . . . Professional Group - Industrial Electronics
PGII. . . . . . . Pesatawan Guruh Islam Indonesia (Islamic Teachers' Union) (Indonesia)
PGIT . . . . . . Professional Group - Information Theory
PGKI . . . . . . Persatuan Guru Katholik Indonesia (Indonesian Catholic Teachers' Union)
PGL . . . . People's Gas Company (NYSE symbol)
PGL . . . . Portable Gas LASER
PGL . . . . Pulsed Gas LASER
PGM . . . . Past Grand Master (Masonry)
PGM . . . . Patrol Vessel, Motor Gunboat (Navy symbol)
PGM . . . . Planetary Gearhead Motor
PGME . . . . . . Professional Group - Medical Electronics
PGMTT . . . . . . Professional Group - Microwave Theory and Techniques
PGN . . . . Phi Gamma Nu (Fraternity)
PGN . . . . Portland General Electric Co. (NYSE symbol)
PGNCS. . . . . . Primary Guidance, Navigation and Control System
PGNS. . . . . . . Primary Guidance and Navigation System (Apollo) (NASA)
PGNS. . . . . . . Professional Group - Nuclear Science
PGO . . . . Ponto-Geniculate-Occipital (Cortex)
PGO . . . . Positive Grid Oscillator
PGP . . . . Pico Glass Pellet
PGP . . . . Precision Gas Products (Commercial firm)
PGPEP . . . . . . Professional Group - Product Engineering and Production
PGPS . . . . . . Packaged Gas Pressure System
PGPT . . . . . . Professional Group - Production Techniques
PGR . . . . Precision Graphic Recorder
PGR . . . . Psychogalvanic Reflex (or Response) (Psychology)
PGRF . . . . . . Pulse Group Repetition Frequency
PGRFI. . . . . . Professional Group - Radio Frequency Interference
PGRI . . . . . . Persatuan Guru Republik Indonesia (Union of Teachers of the Republic of Indonesia)
PGRQC. . . . . . Professional Group - Reliability and Quality Control
PGS . . . . Parallel Gap Soldering
PGS . . . . Passive Geodetic Satellite
PGS . . . . Passive Gravity Stabilization
PGS . . . . Pennsylvania German Society
PGS . . . . Pennsylvania Glass Sand Corporation (NYSE symbol) (Delisted)
PGS . . . . Plane Grating Spectrograph
PGS . . . . Portable Ground Station
PGS . . . . Power Generation System
PGS . . . . Predicted Ground Speed (Navigation)
PGS . . . . President of the Geological Society (British)
PGS . . . . Propellant Gaging System
PGS . . . . Provincial Grand Secretary (Masonry)
PGSB . . . . . . Provincial Grand Sword-Bearer (Masonry)
PGSC . . . . . . Persian Gulf Service Command
PGSC . . . . . . Portable Gas Supple Cart
PGSD . . . . . . Past Grand Senior Deacon (Masonry)
PGSE . . . . . . Peculiar Ground Support Equipment (DOD)
PGSU . . . . . . Propulsion Gas Supply Unit
PGT . . . . Per Gross Ton (Shipping)
PGT . . . . Photo Glow Tube
PGT . . . . Potato-Extract Glucose-Thiamine Hydrogen Chloride (Medium)
PGT . . . . Power Grid Tube
PGTI . . . . . . Persatuan Guruh Teknik Indonesia (Technical Teachers' Union of Indonesia)
PGTTT. . . . . . Precision Gear Train Tools and Test
PGUE . . . . . . Professional Group - Ultrasonic Engineering
PGV . . . . Pierce Governor Company (NYSE symbol)
PGVC . . . . . . Professional Group - Vehicular Communications
PGW . . . . . . Parallel Gap Welding
PGW . . . . Past Grand Warden (Masonry)
PGW . . . . United Plant Guard Workers of America
PGWG . . . . . . Parliamentary Group for World Government
PGWU . . . . . . Petroleum and General Workers' Union (Aden)
PH . . . . Parker-Hannifin Corp. (NYSE symbol)
PH . . . . Pearl Harbor, Hawaii
PH . . . . Performance History
PH . . . . Photographer's Mate (Navy rating)
PH . . . . Pinch-Hitter (Baseball)
PH . . . . Plane Handler (Navy)
PH . . . . Power House
PH . . . . Precipitation Hardening
PH . . . . Previous History (Medicine)
PH . . . . Public Health
PH . . . . Purple Heart (Decoration given to personnel wounded in military service)

1PH . . . . Single-Phase
2PH . . . . Two-Phase
3PH . . . . Three-Phase
PHA . . . . Palomino Horse Association
PHA . . . . Phytohemagglutinin (Biochemistry)
PHA . . . . Poultry Husbandry Adviser (Ministry of Agriculture, Fisheries, and Food) (British)
PHA . . . . . . Presbyterian Historical Society
PHA . . . . Professional Horsemen's Association
PHA . . . . Public Housing Administration (or HHFA; disbanded 1965)
PHA . . . . Pulse Height Analysis
PHAA . . . . . . Percheron Horse Association of America
PHAA . . . . . . Positive High Angle of Attack
PHAP . . . . . . Provincial Health Assistance Program (Vietnam)
Phar B . . . . . Bachelor of Pharmacy
Phar D . . . . . Doctor of Pharmacy
Phar M . . . . . Master of Pharmacy
PHAROS . . . . . Phased-Array RADAR Operational Simulation (Army)
PHAROS . . . . . Phased Array RADAR for Overland Surveillance
PHASR . . . . . . Personnel Hazards Associated with Space Radiation (Satellite)
Ph B . . . . . . Bachelor of Pharmacy
Ph B . . . . . . Bachelor of Philosophy
Ph B . . . . . . Bachelor of Physical Culture
PHB . . . . Port Huron & Detroit R. R. (AAR code)
PHB . . . . Public Health Service Building
PHBA . . . . . . Palomino Horse Breeders of America
Ph B in Arch. . . Bachelor of Philosophy in Architecture
Ph B in Com . . . Bachelor of Philosophy in Commerce
Ph BD . . . . . . Doctor of Bible Philosophy
Ph B in Ed . . Bachelor of Philosophy in Education
PHBRZ . . . . . . Phosphor Bronze
Ph C . . . . Pharmaceutical Chemist
Ph C . . . . Philosopher of Chiropractic
PHCAA . . . . . . Public Health Cancer Association of America
PHCIB. . . . . . . Plumbing-Heating-Cooling Information Bureau
PHCLIS. . . . . . Protected Home Circle Life Insurance Society
Ph D . . . . Doctor of Pharmacy
Ph D . . . . Doctor of Philosophy
PH D . . . . Piled Higher and Deeper (Humorous interpretation of the Ph D degree)
PH D . . . . Pre-Pearl Harbor Dad (A humorous wartime degree)
PHD . . . . Pulse Height Discrimination
PHE . . . . Phenylalanine (Amino acid)
PH Eng . . . . . Public Health Engineer (Academic degree)
PHERMEX. . . . . Pulsed High Energy Radiographic Machine Emitting X-Rays
Ph G . . . . . . Graduate in Pharmacy
PHG . . . . Prototype Hydrofoil Gunboat
PhI. . . . . International Pharmacopoeia
PHI . . . . Phosphohexose Isomerase
PHI . . . . Position and Homing Indicator
PHIBCORPAC . . Amphibious Corps Pacific Fleet
PHIBCORPS . . . Amphibious Corps
PHIBDET . . . . . Amphibious Detachment
PHIBDETIND . . Amphibious Detachment India
PHIBEU . . . . . . Amphibious Forces Europe
PHIBFOR . . . . Amphibious Force
PHIBGROUP . . Amphibious Group
PHIBLANT . . . . Amphibious Force, Atlantic Fleet
PHIBNAW . . . . Amphibious Forces Northwest African Waters
PHIBPAC . . . . Amphibious Force, Pacific Fleet
PHIBRON . . . . Amphibious Squadron
PHIBSEU . . . . Amphibious Forces Europe
PHIBSFORPAC . . Amphibious Forces Pacific Fleet
PHIBSLANT . . . Amphibious Forces Atlantic Fleet
PHIBSPAC . . . . Amphibious Forces Pacific Fleet
PHIBSTRAPAC. . Training Command Amphibious Forces, US Pacific Fleet
PHIBSUKAY . . . Amphibious Bases United Kingdom
PHIBTRA . . . . Training Command Amphibious Forces
PHIBTRABASE . . Amphibious Training Base
PHIBTRAINLANT . Training Command Amphibious Forces, Atlantic Fleet
PHIBTRAINPAC. . Training Command Amphibious Forces, US Pacific Fleet
PHIBTRALANT . . Training Command Amphibious Forces, US Atlantic Fleet
PHIBTRANS . . . Amphibious Transport
PHIBTRAPAC . . Training Command Amphibious Forces, US Pacific Fleet
PHIBTRBASE . . . Amphibious Training Base
PHIBWARTRACEN . . Amphibious Warfare Training Center
Phi D . . . . . . Doctor of Philanthropy
PHIL. . . . . . . Philippines
Phil C . . . . . . Philosophy in Chiropractic
PHILCAG . . . Philippine Civil Assistance Group
Phil LD . . . . . Doctor of Lithuanian Philology
PHILO3. . . . . . Philosophy (or Philosophical)

PHILPUC .... Philippine Presidential Unit Citation Badge
PHILSEAFRON .. Philippine Sea Frontier
PHILSOM..... Periodical Holdings in the Library of the School of Medicine
　　　　　　　(Washington University School of Medicine)
PHIN .... Position and Homing Inertial Navigator
PHJC .... Penn Hall Junior College (Pennsylvania)
PHJC .... Poor Handmaids of Jesus Christ (Ancilla Domini Sisters) (Roman Catholic
　　　　　　　religious order)
PHJC .... Port Huron Junior College (Michigan)
PHK .... Porter (H. K.) Company, Inc. (NYSE symbol) (Delisted)
Ph L .... Licentiate of Pharmacy
Ph L .... Licentiate in Philosophy
PHL .... Periodical Holdings List (Libraries)
PHL .... Philadelphia (Airport symbol)
PHL .... Philips Industries, Inc. (NYSE symbol)
PHL .... Public Health Law
PHLAG ..... Phillips Petroleum Load and Go (System)
PHLH .... Phillips Head (Screw)
PHLODOT .... Phase Lock Doppler Tracking
Ph M .... Master in Pharmacy
Ph M .... Master of Philosophy
PHM .... Patterson-Harker Method
PHM .... Pharmacist's Mate (Navy rating)
PHM........ Phase Meter
PHMA....... Plastic Houseware Manufacturers Association
Phm B ...... Bachelor of Pharmacy
PHMDP..... Pharmacist's Mate, Dental Prosthetic Technician (Navy rating)
Phm G ..... Graduate in Pharmacy
PHMWO ..... Prospect Hill Millimeter Wave Observatory (Waltham, Mass.) (Air Force)
PHNY ...... Pearl Harbor Navy Yard
PHO........ Phenolic Heavy Oil
PHO .... Port Health Officer
PHOAC..... Photographer's Mate, Combat Aircrewman (Navy rating)
PHODEC..... Photometric Determination of Equilibrium Constants (Data processing)
PHOM ...... Photographer's Mate (Navy rating)
PHOSI ...... Preliminary Handbook of Operations and Service Instructions
PHOTAC..... Photo Typesetting and Composing (AT & T)
PHOTINT..... Photographic Intelligence (Military)
PHOTRIPART .. Photo Triangulation Party (Military)
PHP .... Packing-House Products (Food industry)
PHP .... Peace and Happiness through Prosperity (Japanese periodical)
PHP .... Performance, Hermeticality and Price
PHP .... PHP Company (Formerly, Pacific Hawaiian Products Company)
PHP .... Planetary Horizon Platform
PHP .... Pounds per Horsepower
PHP .... Propeller Horsepower
PHP .... Pump Horsepower
PHPA ...... Pacific Herring Packers Association
PHPC ...... Post-Hostilities Planning Committee (Navy) (World War II)
PHR .... Parts per Hundred of Rubber
PHR .... Peak Height Ratio
PHR .... Process Heat Reactor (Program) (AEC)
PHRA ...... Poverty and Human Resources Abstracts
PHS .... Pallottine House of Studies
PHS .... Photographic Historical Society
PHS .... Posthypnotic Suggestion (Psychology)
PHS .... Prepared Hessian Surfacing (Air Force)
PHS .... Printing Historical Society
PHS .... Public Health Service (HEW)
PHSA ...... Pearl Harbor Survivors Association
PHS of A .... Postal History Society of the Americas
PHSI........ Plant Health and Seeds Inspectorate (Ministry of Agriculture, Fisheries,
　　　　　　　and Food) (British)
PHT .... Phototube
PHT .... Physical Therapy Technician (Navy)
PHT .... Pitch, Hit and Throw (Youth competition sponsored by professional
　　　　　　　baseball)
PHU .... Pressure, Hydraulic Unit
PHV .... Phase Velocity
PHWR ...... Pressurized Heavy Water Reactor
PHYS ...... Physical
PHYS ...... Physics
PHYSBE ..... Physiological Simulation Benchmark Experiment
PHYSEXAM ... Physical Examination
PHYSL ...... Physiological
PI .... International Protocol
PI .... Packaging Institute
PI .... Paducah & Illinois R. R. (AAR code)
PI .... Paper Insulated
PI .... Partido Independente (Independent Party) (Costa Rica)
PI .... Patrol Inspector (Immigration and Naturalization Service)

PI.......... Perceptual Isolation
PI .... Performance Index
PI .... Periodic Inspection (Military)
PI .... Perlite Institute, Inc.
PI .... Personal Identification
PI .... Personal Income
PI .... Pharmacopoeia Internationalis
PI .... Philippine Islands
PI .... Photointerpreter (or Photointerpretation)
PI .... Piedmont Airlines
PI .... Pig Iron
PI .... Pigeon Trainer (Navy)
PI .... Pilotless Intercepter (Air Force)
PI .... Point of Impact
PI .... Point Initiating
PI .... Point Insulating
PI .... Point of Interception (Navigation)
PI .... Point of Intersection
PI .... Poison Ivy (Campers' slang)
PI .... Polyimide (Polymer)
PI .... Poni Iussit (Ordered to Be Placed)
PI .... Popcorn Institute
PI .... Position Indicator
PI .... Power Injection
PI .... Power Input
PI .... Present Illness
PI .... Pressure Indicator
PI .... Primacord Interstage
PI .... Principal Investigator
PI .... Private Investigator
PI .... Production Interval
PI .... Program Interrupter
PI .... Programmed Information (Data processing)
PI .... Programmed Instruction
PI .... Proportional-Plus Integral (Digital control)
PI .... Protamine Insulin
PI .... Protocol Internationale
PI .... Psychiatric Institute
PI .... Public Information
P & I .... Properties and Installations
P & I .... Protection and Indemnity (Business and trade)
PIA .... Pakistan International Airlines
PIA .... Perfumery Importers Association
PIA .... Peripheral Interface Adaptors (Data processing)
PIA .... Plastics Institute of America
PIA .... Plug-In Amplifier
PIA .... Positive Ion Accelerator
PIA .... Pre-Installation Acceptance
PIA .... Printing Industries (formerly, Industry) of America
PIA .... Public Information Act
PIA .... Pumice Institute of America
PIACS ...... Pacific Integrated Automatic Communications Systems (Military)
PIADL ..... Plum Island Animal Disease Laboratory (of ARS, Department of
　　　　　　　Agriculture)
PIANC ..... Permanent International Association of Navigation Congresses
PIAP....... Psychologists Interested in the Advancement of Psychotherapy
PIAPACS ..... Psychophysiological Information Acquisition, Processing, and Control
　　　　　　　System
PIARC ..... Permanent International Association of Road Congresses
PIASA...... Polish Institute of Arts and Sciences in America
PIAT....... Projector Infantry, Anti-Tank (British shoulder-controlled weapon)
PIB......... Papuan Infantry Battalion
PIB......... Parachute Infantry Battalion (Army)
PIB......... Photo Intelligence Brief
PIB......... Plug-In Blank
PIB......... Polar Ionosphere Beacon
PIB......... Polytechnic Institute of Brooklyn
PIB......... Product Improvement Bulletin
PIB......... Publishers Information Bureau
PIB .... Pulse Interference Blanker (Radio)
PIBAC ..... Permanent International Bureau of Analytical Chemistry of Human and
　　　　　　　Animal Food
PIBAL ...... Pilot Balloon
PIBD ...... Point Initiating, Base Detonating (Projectile)
PIBOL ..... Pilot Back Up Control
PIBS .... Polar Ionospheric Beacon Satellite (NASA)
PIC .... Pesticides Information Center (National Agricultural Library)
PIC........ Petrochemical Investing Corporation
PIC .... Photo Interpretation Center
PIC .... Photographic Industry Council
PIC .... Pickens R. R. (AAR code)

PIC .... Plastic Insulated Conductor
PIC .... Polyethylene Insulated Conductor
PIC .... Positive Ion Chamber
PIC .... Power Information Center
PIC .... Premium Industry Club
PIC .... Presbyterian Interracial Council
PIC .... Procurement Information Center
PIC .... Procurement Information for Contracts (AFSC)
PIC .... Professional Interfraternity Conference
PIC .... Program Interrupt Control (Data processing)
PIC .... Pulsed Ionization Chamber
PIC .... Pursuant to Instructions Contained in (Military)
PICA .... Power Industry Computer Applications
PICA .... Printing Industry Computer Associates, Inc.
PICA .... Private Investment Company for Asia, SA
PICA .... Procedures for Inventory Control Afloat (Navy)
PICAO ...... Provisional International Civil Aviation Organization (Later, ICAO)
PICB .... Peabody Institute of the City of Baltimore (Maryland)
PICC .... Provisional International Computation Center
PICCO ...... Pennsylvania Industrial Chemical Corporation (Trademark)
PICE .... Programmable Integrated Control Equipment
PICGC ...... Permanent International Committee for Genetic Congresses
PICIC ...... Pakistan Industrial Credit Investment Corporation
PICM .... Permanent International Committee of Mothers
PICO .... Product Improvement Control Office
PICOE ...... Programmed Initiations, Commitments, Obligations and Expenditures (AFSC)
PICOMM ..... Potter Instrument Coordinated Measuring Machine
PICOP ...... Philippine Industries Corporation of the Philippines
PICS .... Perpetual Inventory Control System
PICS .... Personnel Information Communication System (Data processing)
PICS .... Photography in Community Self-Development (Program of Master Photo Dealers and Finishers Association)
PICS .... Plug-in Inventory Control System (Bell System)
PICS .... Production Information and Controls
PICT .... Perceived Instrumentality of the College Test
PICUTP ..... Permanent and International Committee of Underground Town Planning
PID .... Pelvic Inflammatory Disease (Medicine)
PID .... Photo Interpretation Department (Military)
PID .... Pilot-Induced Decillation
PID .... Political Intelligence Department (British)
PID .... Procurement Information Digest
PID .... Project Implementation Directive (Air Force)
PID .... Proportional-Plus Integral-Plus Derivative (Digital control)
PID .... Protruded Intervertebral Disc (Medicine) (British)
PID .... Public Information Division (Military)
PIDA .... Pet Industry Distributors Association
PIDC .... Philadelphia Industrial Development Corporation
PIDE .... Policia Internacional e de Defesa do Estado (Police for the Control of Foreigners and Defense of the State) (Portugal and Portuguese Africa)
PIDL .... Position Involves Intermittent Duty at Isolated Locations
PIE .... Pacific Intermountain Express (NYSE symbol) (Wall Street slang name: "Pizza") (Delisted)
PIE .... Plug-In Electronics
PIE .... Program Interrupt Entry (Data processing)
PIE .... Publications Indexed for Engineering (A publication)
PIE .... Pulse Interference Eliminator (RADAR)
PIEA .... Pencil Industry Export Association
PIEA .... Petroleum Industry Electrical Association
PIEA .... Pre-Arrangement Interment Exchange of America
PIECOST .... Probability of Incurring Estimated Cost (Military)
PIES .... Packaged Interchangeable Electronic System
PIF .... Pilot Information File
PIF .... Place in Inactive File
PIF .... Point Initiating Fuze
PIF .... Prolactin-Inhibiting Factor (Biochemistry)
PIFS .... Plume-Induced Flow Separation
PIG .... Pendulous Integrating Gyro
PIG .... Phillips Ionization Gage
PIG .... Photo-Island Grid
PIG .... Pride, Integrity, Guts (Police alternative for the appellation applied to policemen by radical groups)
PIG .... Pulse Inert Gas
PIGA .... Pendulous Integrating Gyro Accelerometers
PIGA .... Pulsed Integrated Gyroscopic Accelerometer
PIGMI ...... Position Indicating General Measuring Instrument
PIGS .... Portable Inertial Guidance System
PIHM .... Polish Institute of Hydrology and Meteorology
PII .... Printing Industry Institute (A graphic arts training school)
PII .... Procurement Instrument Identification
PII .... Pueblo International, Incorporated (NYSE symbol)
PIIF .... Proteinase Inhibitor Inducing Factor (Biochemistry)

PIIM .... Planned Interdependency Incentive Method
PIIN .... Procurement Instruction Identification Number (Army)
PIIN .... Procurement Instrument Identification Numbering (System) (Navy)
PIK .... Payment in Kind
PIK .... Pickwick International (NYSE symbol)
PIK .... Portable Injection Kit
PIL .... Parti de l'Independance et de la Liberte (Party for Independence and Liberty) (Congo – Leopoldville)
PIL .... Percentage Increase in Loss (Statistics)
PIL .... Plastic Impregnated Laminate
PIL .... Processing Information List (Data processing)
PILAC ...... Pulsed Ion Linear Accelerator
PILC .... Paper-Insulated, Lead-Covered Cable
PILO .... Public Information Liaison Officer (Military)
PILOT ...... Payment in Lieu of Taxes
PILOT ...... Piloted Low-Speed Test (Aerospace)
PILP .... Pseudo-Infinite, Logarithmically Periodic
PIM .... Penalties In Minutes (Hockey)
PIM .... Plated Interconnecting Matrix
PIM .... Point of Intended Movement (Military)
PIM .... Polyphase Induction Motor
PIM .... Precision Indicator of the Meridian
PIM .... Precision Instrument Mount
PIM .... Product Information Memoranda
PIM .... Program Integration Manual
PIM .... Provincial Institute of Mining
PIM .... Pulse Intensity Modulation
PIM .... Pulse Interval Modulation
PIMA .... Paper Industry Management Association
PIMCO ...... Poultry Industry Manufacturers Council
PIME .... Pontifical Institute for Mission Extension
PIMK .... Portable Injection Molding Kit
PIMNY ...... Printing Industries of Metropolitan New York
PIMO .... Presentation of Information for Maintenance and Operation (DOD)
PIN .... P-type Intrinsic-N-type
PIN .... Plastics Industry Notes (Later, CIN)
PIN .... Police Information Network (San Francisco Bay area, California)
PIN .... Position Indicator
PIN .... Positive-Intrinsic-Negative
PIN .... Public Service Company of Indiana, Inc. (NYSE symbol)
PINA .... Parallax in Altitude (Navigation)
PINN .... Pinnacles National Monument
PINO .... Positive Input – Negative Output (Data processing)
PINS .... Persons in Need of Supervision (Classification for delinquent children)
PINS .... Portable Inertial Navigation System
PINSAC ..... PINS (Portable Inertial Navigation System) Alignment Console
PINT .... Purdue Interpretive Program
PIO .... Pilot-Induced Oscillation
PIO .... Position Iterative Operation
PIO .... Public Information Office(r)
PIOSA ...... Pan Indian Ocean Science Association
PIP .... Partido Independencia de Puerto Rico (Political party) (Puerto Rico)
PIP .... Partners in Progress (Government) (Civil rights)
PIP .... Peripheral Interchange Program (Data processing)
PIP .... Persistent Internal Polarization
PIP .... Personal Identification Project (Data processing)
PIP .... Personal Innovation Program
PIP .... Plant-in-Place
PIP .... Power Input Panel
PIP .... Prearrival Inspection Procedure
PIP .... Preparedness and Industrial Planning
PIP .... Probabilistic Information Processing
PIP .... Product Improvement Plan
PIP .... Production Improvement Program (Navy)
PIP .... Program Integration Plan
PIP .... Progressive Inspection Plan (Navy)
PIP .... Proof in Print
PIP .... Proximal Interphalangeal (Joint)
PIP .... Pulse Input Proportional (Electro-optical system)
PIP .... Pulsed Integrating Pendulum
PIPA .... Pacific Industrial Property Association
PIPA .... Pulsed Integrating Pendulum Accelerometer
PIPE .... Pipestone National Monument
PIPER ...... Pulsed Intense Plasma for Exploratory Research
PIPR .... Plant-in-Place Records
PIPR .... Polytechnic Institute of Puerto Rico
PIPS .... Pulsed Integrating Pendulums
PIQ .... Property in Question
PIQA .... Proofing, Inspection and Quality Assurance (Military)
PIQSY ...... Probes for the International Quiet Solar Year (OSS)
PIR .... Parachute Infantry Regiment

PIR . . . . Partido de la Izquierda Revolucionaria (Revolutionary Party of the Left) (Bolivia)
PIR . . . . Personnel Information Report
PIR . . . . Petrolite Irradiation Reactor (AEC)
PIR . . . . Philippine Independence Ribbon
PIR . . . . Plug-In Relay
PIR . . . . Precision Instrumentation RADAR
PIR . . . . Process and Indoctrinate Recruits
PIR . . . . Product Information Release
PIR . . . . Production Inspection Record
PIRA . . . . . . Prison Industries Reorganization Administration (Terminated 1940)
PIRAD . . . . . . Proximity Information, Range and Disposition
PIRD . . . . Program Instrumentation Requirements Document (NASA)
PIREP . . . . . . Pilot's Report (Pertaining to meteorological conditions)
PIREPS . . . . . Pilot Reports
PIRF . . . . . . Petroleum Industry Research Foundation
PIRFC . . . . . Pilot Requests Forecast
PIRG . . . . . . Public Interest Research Group (Formed by consumer-advocate Ralph Nader)
PIRINC . . . . . Petroleum Industry Research Foundation, Incorporated
PIRO . . . . . . Pictured Rocks National Lakeshore (National Park Service designation)
PIRS . . . . . . Philosopher's Information Retrieval System (Bowling Green State University)
PIRS . . . . . . Project Information Retrieval System (HEW)
PIRT . . . . . . Precision Infrared Tracking
PIRT . . . . . . Precision Infrared Triangulation
PIS . . . . Passive Infrared System
PIS . . . . Positive Ion Source
PIS . . . . Postal Inspection Service
PIS . . . . Product Information Specialist
PIS . . . . Pulse Integration System
PISAB . . . . . . Pulsed Illumination Source
PISAB . . . . . . Pulse Interference Separation and Blanking (RADAR)
PISP . . . . . . Pipe Springs National Monument
PISW . . . . . . Process Interrupt Status Word
PIT . . . . Performance Improvement Tests
PIT . . . . Peripheral Input Tape (Data processing)
PIT . . . . Permanent Income Theory (Econometrics)
PIT . . . . Photographic Interpretation Technique
PIT . . . . Pittsburgh (Airport symbol)
PIT . . . . Print Illegal and Trace
PIT . . . . Processing of Indexing Terms
PIT . . . . Programmed Instruction Text
PIT . . . . Projected Inactive Time (Data processing)
PIT . . . . Provincial Institute of Textiles
PITA . . . . . . Pacific International Trapshooting Association
PITA . . . . . . Provincial Institute of Technology and Art
PITAC . . . . . . Pakistan Industrial Technical Assistance Centre
PITC . . . . Phenylisothiocyanate (Chemistry)
PITI . . . . Principal, Interest, Taxes, Insurance (on house payments)
PITR . . . . . . Plasma Iron Turnover Rate
PITS . . . . . . Passive Intercept Tracking System
PITS . . . . . . Propulsion Integration Test Stand
PIU . . . . Photographic Interpretation Unit (Marine Corps)
PIU . . . . Pilot Information Utilization
PIU . . . . Plug-In Unit
PIUMP . . . . . Plug-In Unit Mounting Panel
PIV . . . . Peak Inverse Voltage (RADAR)
PIV . . . . Plug-In Valve
PIV . . . . Positive Infinitely Variable
PIV . . . . Post Indicator Valve
PIVED . . . . . . Plasma-Injection Vacuum Energy Diverter
PIW . . . . Plastic Insulated Wire
PIWC . . . . . . Petroleum Industry War Council
PJ . . . . Panel Jack
PJ . . . . Plastic Jacket
PJ . . . . Police Justice
PJ . . . . Presiding Judge
PJ . . . . Probate Judge
PJ . . . . Procurement Justification (Navy)
PJ . . . . Pulsejet
PJ's . . . . Pajamas (Slang)
PJBD . . . . . . Permanent Joint Board on Defense
PJC . . . . Paducah Junior College (Kentucky)
PJC . . . . Paris Junior College (Texas)
PJC . . . . Pensacola Junior College (Florida)
PJC . . . . Perkinston Junior College (Mississippi)
PJC . . . . Portland Junior College (Oregon)
PJC . . . . Post Junior College (Connecticut)
PJC . . . . Poteau Junior College (Oklahoma)
PJC . . . . Pratt Junior College (Kansas)
PJES . . . . . . Photojet Edge Sensor
PJF . . . . Peripheral Jet (Flat-bottom)

PJM . . . . Pennsylvania-Jersey-Maryland (Electric power pool)
PJM . . . . . . Postjunctional Membrane
PJM . . . . Power Jets Memorandum
PJP . . . . Police Judiciaire des Parquets (Investigatory Police of the Public Prosecutor) (Belgium)
PJPC . . . . . . Plug/Jack Patch Cord
PJR . . . . Power Jets Report
PJS . . . . Peripheral Jet (Skegs)
PJS . . . . Piezojunction Sensor
PJS . . . . Plug and Jack Set
PJSS . . . . . . PACAF (Pacific Air Forces) Jungle Survival School
PJT . . . . Pulse Jitter Tester
PK . . . . Pole Cat (Slang)
PK . . . . Post Box (Turkish)
PK . . . . Prausnitz-Kuestner (Reaction) (Immunology)
PK . . . . Pridie Kalendas (The Day Before the Calends)
PK . . . . Principal Keeper (Slang for a warden)
PK . . . . Psychokinesis
PKA . . . . Pi Kappa Alpha (Fraternity)
PkAF . . . . . . Pakistani Air Force
PKB . . . . Packard-Bell Electronics Corporation (NYSE symbol) (Delisted)
PKB . . . . Photoelectric Keyboard
PKB . . . . Portable Keyboard
PKC . . . . Position Keeping Computer
PKD . . . . Pi Kappa Delta (Society)
PKDOM . . . . . Pack for Domestic Use
PKF . . . . Persatuan Karyawan Fadjarbhakti (Fadjar Bhakti State Trading Enterprise Workers' Union) (Indonesia)
PKF . . . . Primary Kidney Fold
PKG . . . . Package
PKG . . . . Packaging Corporation of America (NYSE symbol) (Delisted)
PKHO . . . . . . Protivo-Khimicheskaia Oborona (Antichemical defense) (USSR)
PKHOW . . . . . Pack Howitzer (Marine Corps)
PKI . . . . Partai Komunis Indonesia (Communist Party of Indonesia)
PKL . . . . Pi Kappa Lambda (Society)
PKN . . . . Perkin-Elmer Corporation (NYSE symbol)
PKO . . . . Perdant par Knockout (Losing by a Knockout) (France)
PKP . . . . Persatuan Karyawan Permorin (Permorin Company Workers' Union) (Indonesia)
PKP . . . . Pre-Knock Pulse
PKR . . . . Parker Pen Company (NYSE symbol)
PKS . . . . Phi Kappa Sigma (Fraternity)
PKSEA . . . . . . Pack for Overseas
PKT . . . . Phi Kappa Tau (Fraternity)
PKU . . . . Phenylketonuria (Congenital metabolism disorder) (Medicine)
PkV . . . . Peak Kilovolts
PKWN . . . . . . Polski Komitet Wyzwolenia Narodowego
PL . . . . Palm Leaf (Reaction) (Medicine)
PL . . . . Paperleg (A favored student) (Teen slang)
PL . . . . Parish Line R. R. (AAR code)
PL . . . . Partial Loss (Insurance)
PL . . . . Partido Liberal (Liberal Party) (Bolivia, Chile)
PL . . . . Parts List
PL . . . . Pathet Lao
PL . . . . Perceived Level (Noise)
PL . . . . Perception of Light
PL . . . . Petty Larceny
PL . . . . Phase Line
PL . . . . Pipeline
PL . . . . Place
PL . . . . Plain Language (As opposed to coded message) (Military)
PL . . . . Plastic Laboratory (Princeton University)
PL . . . . Plateau Length
PL . . . . Platz (Square)
PL . . . . Players League (Major league in baseball, 1890)
PL . . . . Ploshchad (Square)
PL . . . . Poet Laureate
PL . . . . Position Line (Navigation)
PL . . . . Post Laundry (Army)
PL . . . . Preliminary Leaf (Bibliography)
PL . . . . Price List
PL . . . . Private Line
PL . . . . Procedure Library
PL . . . . Production Language
PL . . . . Programming Language (Data processing)
PL . . . . Progressive Labor (A faction of Students for a Democratic Society)
PL . . . . Propagation Loss
PL . . . . Proportional Limit
PL . . . . Psychological Laboratory
PL . . . . Public Law (An act of Congress)
PL . . . . Public Liability (Business and trade)
PL . . . . Public Library

PL . . . . Pulpolingual
P/L . . . . Plain Language
P/L . . . . Profit and Loss (Accounting)
PLA . . . . Pedestrian League of America
PLA . . . . People's Liberation Army (Communist China)
PLA . . . . Philatelic Literature Association
PLA . . . . Playboy Enterprises, Inc. (NYSE symbol)
PLA . . . . Poly-L-arginine (Biochemistry)
PLA . . . . Port of London Authority
PLA . . . . Practice Low Approach (Aviation)
PLA . . . . Private Libraries Association
PLA . . . . Proton Linear Accelerator
PLA . . . . Public Library Association
PLA . . . . Pulpolinguoaxial
PLA . . . . Pulverized Limestone Association
PLAA . . . . Positive Low Angle of Attack
PLAAR . . . . . . Packaged Liquid Air-Augmented Rocket
PLACE . . . . . . Position Location and Aircraft Communication Equipment
PLACE . . . . . . Programming Language for Automatic Checkout Equipment
PLAD . . . . Parachute Low-Altitude Delivery (Air Force)
PLADS . . . . . . Parachute Low-Altitude Delivery System
PLADS . . . . . . Pulsed LASER Airborne Depth Sounding System (Naval Oceanographic Office)
PLAMAM . . . . . Plano de Melhoramento da Alimentacao e do Manejo do Gado Leiteiro
PLAN . . . . Positive Locator Aid to Navigation
PLAN . . . . Problem Language Analyzer (Data processing)
PLANAT . . . . . North Atlantic Treaty Regional Planning Group
PLANET . . . . . Planned Logistics Analysis and Evaluation Technique (Air Force)
PLANIT . . . . . . Programmed Language for Interaction Teaching (Data processing)
PLANN . . . . . . Plant Location Assistance Nationwide Network
PLANNET . . . . Planning Network
PLAO . . . . Parts List Assembly Order
PLASTEC . . . . . Plastics Technical Evaluation Center (DOD)
PLAT . . . . Pilot-LOS (Line of Sight) Landing Aid TV
PLAT . . . . Platt National Park
PLATO . . . . . . Programmed Logic for Automatic Teaching Operations
PLATR . . . . Pawling Lattice Test Rig (United Nuclear Company)
PLAV . . . . Polish Legion of American Veterans
PLB . . . . Personal Locator Beacon (Military)
PLB . . . . Poor Law Board
PLC . . . . Pacific Logging Congress
PLC . . . . Perry-Link Cubmarine (A submersible vehicle)
PLC . . . . Platform Control
PLC . . . . Platoon Leader's Class
PLC . . . . Pneumatic Lead Cutter
PLC . . . . Polycaprolactone (Polymer)
PLC . . . . Poor Law Commissioners (British)
PLC . . . . Power-Line Carrier
PLC . . . . Power Line Communications
PLC . . . . Presbyterian Lay Committee
PLC . . . . Prime Level Code
PLC . . . . Products List Circular (Patents)
PLCA . . . . Pipe Line Contractors Association
PLCY . . . . Policy
PLD . . . . Personnel Letdown Device
PLD . . . . Phase Lock Demodulator
PLD . . . . Posterior Latissimus Dorsi
PLD . . . . Principle of Limit Design
PLD . . . . Probable Line of Deployment (Army)
PLD . . . . Procurement Legal Division (Later, Office of General Counsel) (Navy)
PLD . . . . Product Line Development
PLDC . . . . Preliminary List of Design Changes
PLDMI . . . . . . Precise LASER Distance Measuring Instrument
PLE . . . . Phased Loading Entry (Data processing)
PLE . . . . Pittsburgh & Lake Erie R. R. (AAR code)
PLEA . . . . Pacific Lumber Exporters Association
PLEI . . . . Public Law Education Institute
PLENAPS . . . . Plans for the Employment of Naval and Air Forces of the Associated Powers in the Eastern Theater in the Event of War with Japan
PLENCH . . . . . Pliers & Wrench (combination)
P & LERR . . . . Pennsylvania and Lake Erie Railroad
PLF . . . . Parachute Landing Fall (Military)
PLF . . . . Patient Load Factor
PLF . . . . Phase Lock Frequency
PLF . . . . Philippine Labor Federation
PLF . . . . Positive Lock Fastener
PLF . . . . Power for Level Flight (Aeronautics)
PLF . . . . Private Line Telephone
PLF . . . . Proposition Letter Formula
PLG . . . . Pleural Ganglion
PLG . . . . Poor Law Guardian (British)

PLG . . . . Pulsed Light Generator
PLGL . . . . Plate Glass
PLGS . . . . Partita Liberale Giovani Somali (Somali Liberal Youth Party)
PLGT . . . . Prototype Lunar Geologist Tool
P-LGV . . . . . . Psittacosis-Lymphogranuloma Venereum
PLI . . . . Partido Liberal Independiente (Independent Liberal Party) (Nicaragua)
PLI . . . . Partito Liberale Italiano (Liberal Party of Italy)
PLI . . . . Pilot Location Indicator
PLI . . . . Power Level Indicator
PLI . . . . Practising Law Institute
PLI . . . . Pre-Load Indicating
PLIB . . . . Pacific Lumber Inspection Bureau
PLIN . . . . Power Line Impedance Network
PLIW . . . . Pre-Load Indicating Washer
PLK . . . . Phi Lambda Kappa (Fraternity)
PLK . . . . Plucky Little King (Used by Western diplomats in Amman in reference to King Hussein of Jordan)
PLK . . . . Poincare-Lighthill-Kuo (Method)
PLL . . . . Phase-Lock(ed) Loop (NASA)
PLL . . . . Poly-L-lysine (Biochemistry)
PLL . . . . Positive Logic Level
PLL . . . . Prescribed Load List
PLLR . . . . Phase Lock Loop Receiver
PLLRC . . . . . . Public Land Law Review Commission
PLM . . . . Packaged Liquid Missile
PLM . . . . Passive Lunar Marker
PLM . . . . Product Line Manager
PLM . . . . Production-Line Maintenance (Air Force)
PLM . . . . Pulse-Length Modulation
PLMA . . . . . . Producers Livestock Marketing Association
PLMD . . . . . . Payload Mating Dolly
PLMR . . . . . . Post Launch Memorandum Report
PLN . . . . Partido Liberacion Nacional (National Liberation Party) (Costa Rica)
PLN . . . . Partido Liberal Nacionalista (Nationalist Liberal Party) (Nicaragua)
PLN . . . . Planning Research Corp. (NYSE symbol)
PLO . . . . Pacific Launch Operations (NASA)
PLO . . . . Palestine Liberation Organization
PLO . . . . Phase-Locked Oscillator
PLO . . . . Philippine Labor Organization
PLO . . . . Plough, Inc. (NYSE symbol (Delisted)
PLO . . . . Program Line Organization
PLO . . . . Project Line Organization
PLO . . . . Public Land Order (Interior)
PLO . . . . Pulsed LASER Oscillator
PLO . . . . Pulsed Locked Oscillator
PLOB . . . . . . Place of Birth
PLOO . . . . . . Pacific Launch Operations Office (NASA)
PLOP . . . . . . Planetary Landing Observation Package
PLOP . . . . . . Pressure Line of Position (Air Force)
PLOS . . . . . . Primary Line of Sight (Sextants)
PLP . . . . Parliamentary Labour Party (British)
PLP . . . . Parti de la Liberte et du Progres (Freedom and Progress Party) (Belgium)
PLP . . . . Pattern Learning Parser
PLP . . . . Post Launch Phase
PLP . . . . Product Liability Prevention (Conference)
PLP . . . . Progressive Labour Party (Bermuda)
PLPB . . . . . . Petroleum Labor Policy Board (Abolished, 1936)
PL & PD . . . . . Public Liability and Property Damage (Insurance)
PLPG . . . . . . Publishers' Library Promotion Group
PLPS . . . . Packaged Liquid Propellant System
PLPS . . . . Propellant Loading & Pressurization System
PLR . . . . Philippine Liberation Ribbon
PLR . . . . Portable LASER Range-Finder
PLR . . . . Pressure Level Recorder
PLR . . . . Program Life Requirement
PLR . . . . Public Lending Right (Royalty for books borrowed from public libraries) (British)
PL & R . . . . . Postal Laws and Regulations (Later, Postal Manual)
PLRACTA . . . . Position Location, Reporting and Control of Tactical Aircraft (Military)
PLRS . . . . Phase Lock Receiving System
PLS . . . . Palomar-Leiden Survey
PLS . . . . Parsons Language Sample
PLS . . . . Periodic Log System
PLS . . . . Pitch Limit Switch
PLS . . . . Plasma Light Source
PLS . . . . Please
PLS . . . . Pneumatic Limit Switch
PLS . . . . Portable Laboratory Salinometer
PLS . . . . President of the Linnaean Society (British)
PLS . . . . Private Line Service

PLS . . . . Professional Legal Secretary (Designation awarded by National
Association of Legal Secretaries)
PLS . . . . Propellant Loading System
PLS . . . . Pulsed LASER System
PLS . . . . Pulsed Light Source
PLS . . . . Purnell Library Service (Commercial firm)
PLSD . . . . . . Promotion List Service Date (Air Force)
PLSS . . . . Portable Life Support System (NASA)
PLSS . . . . . . Prelaunch Status Simulator
PLT . . . . Pacific Lighting Corporation (NYSE symbol)
PLT . . . . Pilot
PLT . . . . Pipeline Time
PLT . . . . Planar Tube
PLT . . . . Post Loading Test
PLT . . . . Private Line Telephone
PLT . . . . Private Line Teletypewriter
PLT . . . . Procurement (or Production) Lead Time
PLT. . . . . Programmed Learning Textbook
PLT . . . . Pulsed Light Theodolite
PLU . . . . Platoon Leaders Unit (Marine Corps)
PLU . . . . Plural
PLU . . . . Pressure Lubrication Unit
PLUCON. . . . . Plutonium Decontamination Emergency Teams
PLUM . . . . . . Payload Launch Module
PLUM . . . . . . Philippine Labor Unity Movement (of Federation of Industrial and Agrarian
Workers)
PLUNA . . . . . . Primeras Lineas Uruguayas de Navegacion Aerea
PLUS . . . . PERT Lifecycle Unified System
PLUS . . . . . . Procedures for Long Supply Assets Utilization Screening (DOD)
PLUTHARCO. . . Plutonium, Uranium, Thorium Assembly Reactivity Code
PLUTO . . . . . . Pipe Line Under the Ocean (British project) (World War II)
PLV . . . . Postlanding Vent (Apollo) (NASA)
PLV . . . . Power Limiting Valve
PLW . . . . Pre-Load Washer
PLY . . . . US Plywood Corporation (NYSE symbol; later, UPC)
PLZT . . . . Pb-based Lanthanum-doped Zirconate Titanates
PM. . . . . Chesapeake & Ohio - Pere Marquette Dist. (AAR code)
PM. . . . . Pad Mechanic (Aerospace)
PM. . . . . Painting Machine
PM. . . . . Parlor Maid
PM . . . . Past Master (Masonry)
PM. . . . . Pattern Maker
PM . . . . Paymaster
PM. . . . . Peculiar Meter
PM. . . . . Per Month
PM. . . . . Pere Marquette Railway Company (AAR code)
PM. . . . . Periodic Maintenance
PM. . . . . Permanent-Magnet (Loudspeaker)
PM . . . . Phase Modulation (Radio)
PM. . . . . Photomultiplier
PM. . . . . Physical Medicine
PM. . . . . Piae Memoriae (Of Pious Memory)
pm . . . . Picometer
PM . . . . Plus Minus (More or less)
PM. . . . . Police Magistrate
PM. . . . . Policy Memorandum (Military)
PM. . . . . Pontifex Maximus
PM. . . . . Portable Medium-Power (Plant) (AEC)
PM. . . . . Post Meridiem (After noon)
PM. . . . . Post Mortem (After Death) (Examination)
PM . . . . Postmaster
PM. . . . . Pounds per Minute
PM. . . . . Powder Metallurgy
PM. . . . . Preincubation Mixture
PM. . . . . Premolar (Dentistry)
PM . . . . Presystolic Murmur
PM. . . . . Preventive Maintenance
PM. . . . . Preventive Medicine (Also, PVNTMED)
PM. . . . . Priest and Martyr (Church calendars)
PM. . . . . Prime Minister
PM . . . . Principle of Multiplying (New math)
PM. . . . . Prize Money
PM. . . . . Pro Mille (Per Thousand)
PM . . . . Procurement and Material
PM . . . . Production Manager
PM . . . . Production Mode
PM . . . . Profit Motivated (Housing)
PM. . . . . Program
PM . . . . Project Manager
Pm. . . . . Promethium (Chemical symbol)
PM. . . . . Propulsion Memorandum

PM . . . . Provost Marshal
PM . . . . Public Management (A publication)
PM . . . . Publicity Man (Slang)
PM. . . . . Pulpomesial
PM . . . . Pulse Modulation
PM . . . . Purchase Memo
PM. . . . . Purchase Money
PM. . . . . Sisters of the Presentation of Mary (Roman Catholic religious order)
PMA. . . . . . . Pacific Maritime Association
PMA . . . . Peat Moss Association
PMA . . . . . . Pencil Makers Association
PMA. . . . . . . Personnel Management Assistance
PMA. . . . . . . Pharmaceutical Manufacturers Association
PMA . . . . . . Philadelphia Musical Academy
PMA . . . . . . Philippine Mahogany Association
PMA . . . . . . Phonograph Manufacturers Association
PMA . . . . Plastic Mockup Assembly
PMA . . . . . . Pole Mounted Amplifier
PMA . . . . . . Pre-Amplifier Module Assembly
PMA . . . . . . Precision Measurements Association
PMA. . . . . . . Primary Mental Abilities (Test)
PMA . . . . . . Procurement and Management Assistance (Small Business Administration)
PMA. . . . . . . Procurement Methods Analyst
PMA . . . . . . Production and Marketing Administration (Department of Agriculture)
(Functions dispersed, 1953)
PMA . . . . . . Pyromellitic Acid
PMAA. . . . . . Paper Makers Advertising Association
PMAC. . . . . . Parallel Memory Address Counter (Data processing)
PMANY . . . . . Pattern Makers Association of New York
PMAT . . . . . . Primary Mental Abilities Test (Education)
PMB. . . . . . . Palm Beach Co. (NYSE symbol)
PMB . . . . Physical Metallurgy Branch
PMB . . . . Polymorphonuclear Basophilic (Leucocytes)
PMB . . . . . . Potato Marketing Board (British)
PMB . . . . Program Management Board
PMBR . . . . . . Practice Multiple Bomb Rack
PMC . . . . Pennsylvania Military College
PMC . . . . . . People's Mandate Committee
PMC . . . . Phenolic Molding Compound
PMC. . . . . . . Phenylmercuric Chloride
PMC. . . . . . . Plutonia-Molybdenum Cermet
PMC. . . . . . . Pollen Mother Cell
PMC . . . . . . Powdered Metal Cathode
PMC . . . . . . Predictive Multisensor Correlation
PMC . . . . . . Premium Merchandising Club of New York
PMC . . . . . . Pressurized Membrane Container
PMC. . . . . . . Princeton Microfilm Corporation
PMC. . . . . . . Procurement, Marine Corps (An appropriation)
PMC . . . . . . Procurement Method Coding (DOD)
PMC . . . . Program Marginal Checking
PMC. . . . . . . Propellant Monitor and Control
P-M-C . . . . . . Pollen-Mother-Cell
PMCC . . . . . . Postmark Collectors' Club
PMCD . . . . . . Post Mortem Core Dump
PMCG . . . . . . Pyrrolidyl Methyl Cyclopentylphenyl Glycolate (Chemical)
PMCS . . . . . . Pulse-Modulated Communications System
PMCT . . . . . . PAL (Permissive Action Link) Management Control Team (Army)
PMCV . . . . . . Programmed Multichannel Valve (Chromatography)
PMD. . . . . . . Payload Mating Dolly
PMD. . . . . . . Payload Module Decoder (NASA)
PMD. . . . . . . Post Mortem Dump (Data processing)
PMD . . . . . . Preventive Maintenance Division (Air Force)
PMD. . . . . . . Primary Myocardial Disease
PMD . . . . . . Program Monitoring and Diagnosis
PMD. . . . . . . Progressive Muscular Dystrophy
PMD. . . . . . . Psychiatric Military Duty
PMDA. . . . . . Photographic Manufacturers and Distributors Association
PMDA. . . . . . Pyromellitic Dianhydride
PMDG . . . . . Pentamethylene Diguanidine
PMDL . . . . . . Post M-Day Deployment List (Military)
PMDS . . . . . . Property Management and Disposal Service (General Services
Administration)
PME. . . . . . . Passive Microelectronic Element
PME. . . . . . . Peace Movement of Ethiopia
PME. . . . . . . Pedal Mode Ergometer
PME. . . . . . . Photomagnetoelectric
PME . . . . . . Polymorphonuclear Eosinophile
PME. . . . . . . Precision Measuring Equipment
PME. . . . . . . Professional Military Education
PMEA . . . . . . Powder Metallurgy Equipment Association
PMEL . . . . . . Precision Measuring Equipment Laboratory

ACRONYMS AND INITIALISMS DICTIONARY

PMEMA ..... Powder Metallurgy Equipment Manufacturers' Association
PMEV .... Panel Mounted Electronic Voltmeter
PMF .... Pakistan Mazdoor Federation
PMF .... Permanent Magnetic Field
PMF .... Personnel Master File (Army)
PMF .... Pilot Mortar Fire
PMF .... Professional Medical Film
PMF .... Progressive Massive Fibrosis
PMFS ...... Pulsed Magnetic Field System
PMFWCMA ... Paper Mill Fourdrinier Wire Cloth Manufacturers Association
PMG .... Paymaster General (Navy)
PMG .... Permanent Magnet Generator
PMG .... Phase Modulation Generator
PMG .... Physiological Measurement Group
PMG .... Postmaster General
PMG .... Prediction Marker Generator
PMG .... Propodial Mucus Gland
PMG .... Provost Marshal General (Army)
PMGDINYC .. Production Men's Guild of the Dress Industry of New York City
PMGO ...... Office of Provost Marshal General
PMGS ...... Provost Marshal General's School, United States Army
PMH .... Past Medical History
PMH .... Production per Man-Hour
PMH/M...... Productive Man-Hours per Month (Navy)
PMI .... Past (or Previous) Medical Illness
PMI .... Point of Maximal Impulse
PMI .... Point of Maximum Intensity
PMI .... Postmyocardial Infarction (Syndrome) (Medicine)
PMI .... Pressed Metal Institute
PMI .... Preventive Maintenance Inspection
PMI .... Primary Measurement Instrument
PMI .... Program Management Instruction
PMI .... Pseudo Matrix Isolation
PMI .... Purchased Materials Inspection
PMIC ...... Personnel Management Information Center
PMIJ ...... Pulse Modulated Infrared Jammer
PMIP ...... Pan Malayan Islamic Party
PMIS ...... Passive Microwave Imaging System (NASA)
PMIS ...... Personnel Management Information System (NASA)
PMIS ...... Printing Management Information Systems
PMJ .... Pulse Modulated Jammer
PMJC ...... Pine Manor Junior College (Massachusetts)
PMK .... Panel Marking Kit
PMK .... Portable Molding Kit
PMKY ...... Pittsburgh, McKeesport & Youghiogheny R. R. (AAR code)
PML .... Pakistan Muslim League (Political party)
PML .... Pattern Makers' League of North America
PML .... Preliminary Materials List (NASA)
PML .... Promotion Management List (Pronounced "Pemell") (Air Force)
PMLA ...... Publications of the Modern Language Association of America
PMLO ...... Principal Military Landing Offices (British)
PMLV ...... Permanent Magnet Latch Valve
PMM .... Military Morale Division (Coast Guard)
PMM .... Penobscot Marine Museum
PMM .... Polymethyl Methacrylate (Chemical)
PMM .... Professional Music Men, Inc.
PMM .... Profile Milling Machine
PMM .... Pulse Mode Multiplex
PMMA ...... Polymethyl Methacrylate
PMMC...... Permanent Magnetic Movable Coil
PMMI ...... Packaging Machinery Manufacturers Institute
PMMP...... Preventive Maintenance Management Program
PMMR...... Passive Multichannel Microwave Radiometer (NASA)
PMMS...... Phrenicon Metabolic Monitoring System
PMMS...... Plainsong and Mediaeval Music Society
PMN .... Phenyl Mercuric Nitrate
PMN .... Polymorphonuclear
PMN .... Program Management Network
PMO .... Perroni, Martin, O'Reilly (Commercial firm)
PMO .... Principal Medical Officer
PMO .... Product Manufacturing Organization
PMO .... Profit Making Organization
PMO .... Project Management Office (Army)
PMO....... Psychiatric Military Officer
PMOA...... Prospectors and Mine Owners Association
PMOG ..... Philippine Marine Officers' Guild
PMOS...... Primary Military Occupational Specialty
PMP .... Packed Main Parachute
PMP .... Parent Mass Peak
PMP .... Parents' Magazine Press

PMP .... Parti du Mouvement Populaire de la Cote Francaise des Somalis (Popular Movement Party of French Somaliland)
PMP .... Parts, Materials and Packaging
PMP .... Pontifical Mission for Palestine
PMP .... Powdered Metal Part
PMP .... Premodulation Processor
PMP .... Previous Menstrual Period
PMP .... Professor of Moral Philosophy
PMP .... Program Management Plan
PMP .... Program Monitor Panel
PMP .... Progressive Merger Procedure (Econometrics)
PMP .... Project Master Plans (Navy)
PMP .... Protective Mobilization Plan
PMP .... Pulsed Microwave Power
PMPA ...... Permanent Magnet Producers Association
PMPM...... Perpetual Motion Poetry Machine
PMPMA .... Powder Metallurgy Parts Manufacturers Association
PMR .... Pacific Missile Range (Later, WTR)
PMR .... Parabolic Microwave Reflector
PMR .... Partidul Muncitoresc Romin
PMR .... Parts Material Requirements File
PMR .... Proton Magnetic Resonance
PM & R .... Physical Medicine and Rehabilitation
PMRA ...... Projected Manpower Requirements Account (Navy)
PMRL ...... Pulp Manufacturers' Research League
PMRM...... Periodic Maintenance Requirements Manual (Navy)
PMRMO .... Protectable Mobilization Reserve Materiel Objective (Army)
PMRMR .... Protectable Mobilization Reserve Materiel Requirements
PMRS ...... Physical Medicine and Rehabilitation Service
PMRSG .... Pacific Missile Range Study Group
PMS .... Pantone Matching System (Printing)
PMS .... Permanent Magnet Speaker
PMS .... Personnel Management System (Air Force)
PMS .... Phoenix Missile System
PMS .... Planned Maintenance System (SNMMS)
PMS .... Plastic to Metal Seal
PMS .... Polaris Missile System
PMS .... Post-Menopausal Syndrome (Medicine)
PMS .... Predicted Manning System (Military)
PMS .... Pregnant Mare's Serum (Endocrinology)
PMS .... Pre-Midshipmen School
PMS .... President of the Meteorological Society (British)
PMS .... Professor of Military Science
PMS .... Program Management Support
PMS .... Program Management System (Data processing)
PMSA ...... Posterior Middle Suprasylvian Area
PMS/DOD ... Performance Measurement System / Department of Defense
PMSFN ..... Planetary Manned Space Flight Network
PMSG ...... Pregnant Mare's Serum Gonadotrophin (Endocrinology)
PMSGT ..... Paymaster Sergeant (Marine Corps)
PMSP ...... Preliminary Maintainability and Spare Parts
PMSPS ..... Project Management Staffing Practices Study (Navy)
PMSR ...... Patternmaker, Ship Repair (Navy)
PMSR ...... Physical, Mental, Social, Religious ("Fourfold Life" symbol of American Youth Foundation)
PMSS ...... Personnel Mobility Support System (Military)
PMS & T .... Professor of Military Science and Tactics
PMT .... Medical Photography Technician (Navy)
PMT .... P-Methoxytoluene
PMT .... Payment
PMT .... Permanent Magnet Tester
PMT .... Permanent-Magnet Twistor (Memory) (Bell Laboratories)
PMT .... Phase Modulated Transmission
PMT .... Photomultiplier Tube
PMT .... Portable Magnetic Tape
PMT .... Power Microwave Tube
PMT .... Premenstrual Tension (Medicine)
PMT .... Prepare Master Tape
PMT .... Production Monitoring Test
PMT .... Program Master Tape
PMT .... Pulse Modulator Tube
PMTD ...... Post Mortem Tape Dump
PMTHP ..... Project Mercury Technical History Program (NASA)
PMTO ...... Project Manager Test Offices (Military)
PMU .... Portable Memory Unit
PMVR ...... Prime Mover (Technical drawings)
PMW .... Private Microwave (System)
PMW .... Progressive Mine Workers of America
PMW .... Prompt Mobilization Designation Withdrawn
PMX .... Private Manual Exchange
PMYOB..... Please Mind Your Own Business

PN . . . . North Pole
PN . . . . Pacific Communications Net (Air Force)
PN . . . . Pacific Northern Airlines, Inc.
PN . . . . Pan American World Airways, Inc. (NYSE symbol)
PN . . . . Part Number
PN . . . . Perceived Noise
PN . . . . Percussion Note (Physiology)
PN . . . . Performance Number
PN . . . . Personnelman (Navy rating)
PN . . . . Piedmont & Northern Railway Company (AAR code)
PN . . . . Please Note
PN . . . . Positive-Negative
PN . . . . Practical Nurse
PN . . . . Prior Notice Required
PN . . . . Promissory Note (Business and trade)
PN . . . . Pseudo-Noise
PN . . . . Pseudo-Random Number (Data processing)
PN . . . . Psychiatry-Neurology
PN . . . . Psychoneurotic (Cases, patients, etc.)
P/N . . . . Part Number
PNA . . . . Pacific Northern Airlines, Inc.
PNA . . . . Paper Napkin Association
PNA . . . . Parti Nationale Africain (African National Party) (Chad)
PNA . . . . Pentose Nucleic Acid
PNA . . . . Pioneer Natural Gas Co. (NYSE symbol)
PNA . . . . Polish National Alliance of the United States of North America
PNA . . . . Polynuclear Aromatic
PNAS . . . . Proceedings of the National Academy of Sciences (A publication)
PNAvQ . . . . . Positive-Negative Ambivalent Quotient (Psychology)
PNB . . . . Pacific Northwest Bell (AT & T)
PNB . . . . Perceived Noise Decibel (Sonic boom)
PNBF . . . . Peak Nucleate Boiling Flux
PNBMS . . . . . Pacific Northwest Bird and Mammal Society
PNC . . . . Permanente Cement Company (NYSE symbol) (Delisted)
PNC . . . . Philatelic-Numismatic Combination
PNC . . . . Programmed Numerical Control
PNC . . . . Prohibition National Committee
PND . . . . Paroxysmal Nocturnal Dyspnea
PND . . . . Parti des Nationalistes du Dahomey (Dahomean Nationalists Party)
PND . . . . Partido Nacional Democratico (National Democratic Party) (Dominican Republic)
PND . . . . Passive Navigation Device
PND . . . . Postnasal Drip
PND . . . . Present Next Digit
PNdB . . . . Perceived Noise Decibels
PNDG . . . . . . Pending
PNDM . . . . . . Project Non-Design Memo
PNE . . . . Peaceful Nuclear Explosives (Division of AEC)
PNE . . . . Practical Nurse's Education
PNF . . . . Partito Nazionale Fascista (National Fascist Party) (Italy)
PNF . . . . Peierls-Nabarro Force
PNF . . . . Penn Traffic Company (NYSE symbol)
PNF . . . . Postnuclear Fraction (Biochemical tissue analysis)
PNFD . . . . . . Present Not For Duty (Military)
PNG . . . . Persona Non Grata
PNG . . . . Philippine Newspaperworkers' Guild
PNG . . . . Professional Numismatic Guild
PNGWA . . . . . Papua and New Guinea Workers' Association (Australian New Guinea)
PNH . . . . Paroxysmal Nocturnal Hemoglobinuria
PNH . . . . Partido Nacional Hondureno (Honduran National Party)
PNH . . . . Public Service Company of New Hampshire (NYSE symbol)
PNI . . . . Paratai Nasionalis Indonesia (Nationalist Party of Indonesia)
PNI . . . . Punjab Native Infantry (India)
PNII . . . . Prentiss Normal and Industrial Institute (Mississippi)
PNL . . . . Pacific Naval Laboratory (British)
PNL . . . . Pacific Northwest Laboratory (AEC)
PNL . . . . Perceived Noise Level
PNL . . . . Pulsed Neodymium LASER
PNLA . . . . . . Pacific Northwest Library Association
PNLA . . . . . . Pacific Northwest Loggers Association
PNM . . . . Pan-Somali Nationalist Movement
PNM . . . . Partido Nacionalista de Mexicano (Nationalist Party of Mexico)
PNM . . . . People's National Movement (Trinidad)
PNM . . . . Pulse Number Modulation
PNMO . . . . . . Provided No Military Objection Exists
PNNCF . . . . . Pacific Northern Naval Coastal Frontier
PNO . . . . Pennroad Company (NYSE symbol)
PNOK . . . . . . Primary Next of Kin (Army)
PNP . . . . Parti National du Progres (National Progress Parties) (Congo - Leopoldville)
PNP . . . . People's National Party (Jamaica)

PNP . . . . Positive-Negative-Positive (Transistor)
PNPF . . . . Piqua Nuclear Power Facility (AEC)
PNPR . . . . . . Positive-Negative Pressure Respiration
PNR . . . . Passenger Name Record (Airlines)
PNR . . . . Pittsburgh Naval Reactors Office (AEC)
PNR . . . . Point of No Return (Aviation)
PNR . . . . Preliminary Negotiation Reports
PNR . . . . Prior Notice Required
PNRBC . . . . . Pacific Northwest River Basins Commission
PNS . . . . Parasympathetic Nervous System
PNS . . . . Philadelphia & Norfolk Steamship (AAR code)
PNS . . . . Portsmouth (NH) Naval Shipyard
PNS . . . . Professor of Naval Science
PNSA . . . . . . Peanut and Nut Salters Association
PNS & T . . . . Professor of Naval Science and Tactics (Naval ROTC)
PNSY . . . . . . Portsmouth Naval Shipyard
PNTA . . . . . . Pacific Northwest Trade Association
PNTC . . . . . . Parti National Travailliste Camerounais (Cameroonese National Workers' Party)
PNTCENS . . . . Patient Census Report
PNU . . . . Pneumatic Scale Corporation, Ltd. (NYSE symbol)
PNUA . . . . . . Partito Nazionale Unito Africa (National Party of United Africans) (Somalia)
PNUA . . . . . . Polish National Union of America
PNV . . . . Parti National Voltaique (Voltaic National Party)
PNVAL . . . . . Previously Not Available (Army)
PNVD . . . . . . Passive Night Vision Devices (Army)
PNVTS . . . . . Pyrotechnics No-Voltage Test Set
PNW . . . . Prescott & Northwestern R. R. (AAR code)
PNWC . . . . . . Pacific Northwest Writers' Conference
PNWL . . . . . . Pacific Northwest Laboratory (AEC)
PNY . . . . Piedmont Natural Gas Co., Inc. (NYSE symbol)
PNY . . . . Portuguese Navy
PNYA . . . . . . Port of New York Authority
PO . . . . Officer Personnel Division (Coast Guard)
PO . . . . Parking Orbit
PO . . . . Passport Office (Department of State)
PO . . . . Patent Office
PO . . . . Peroral or Per Os (By Mouth) (Medicine)
PO . . . . Personnel Officer
PO . . . . Pesticides Office (Environmental Protection Agency)
PO . . . . Petty Officer (Navy)
PO . . . . Pilot Officer
PO . . . . Planetary Orbit
PO . . . . Planning Objectives
Po . . . . Polonium (Chemical element)
PO . . . . Por Orden (By Order) (Spain)
PO . . . . Port Officer
PO . . . . Portugal (NATO)
PO . . . . Post Office
PO . . . . Postal Order
PO . . . . Postoperative
PO . . . . Power-Operated
PO . . . . Power Oscillator (Electronics)
PO . . . . Power Output
PO . . . . Presbyteri Oratorii (Oratorians)
PO . . . . Previous Orders
PO . . . . Privately Owned
PO . . . . Probation Officer
PO . . . . Program Objective
PO . . . . Program Originator
PO . . . . Project Officer (Navy)
PO . . . . Project Order (DOD)
PO . . . . Proposals Outstanding
PO . . . . Propylene Oxide (Chemistry)
PO . . . . Province of Ontario (Canada)
PO . . . . Provisioning Order
PO . . . . Purchase Order
PO . . . . Put Outs (Baseball)
P/O . . . . Project Office
P & O . . . . . . Paints and Oil
P & O . . . . . . Peninsular and Oriental Steam Navigation Company (Steamship line)
P & O . . . . . . Pickled and Oiled
PO'd . . . . Put Out (i.e., angry) (Bowdlerized version)
PO1 . . . . Petty Officer First Class (Navy)
PO2 . . . . Petty Officer Second Class (Navy)
PO3 . . . . Petty Officer Third Class (Navy)
POA . . . . Pacific Ocean Area (World War II)
POA . . . . Panel of Americans
POA . . . . Preoptic Area (of a neuron)
POA . . . . Primary Optic Afferents

POA....... Primary Optic Atrophy
POA ...... Provisional Operating Authorization (for nuclear power plant)
POA ...... Public Order Act
POAA...... Property Owners Association of America
POAC...... Pony of the Americas Club
POAE...... Port of Aerial Embarkation (Air Force)
POAHEDPEARL.. Pacific Ocean Areas Headquarters Pearl Harbor
POAN ...... Procurement of Ordnance and Ammunition - Navy
POAR....... Problem-Objective-Approach-Response (System of planning patient care) (Medicine)
POAR....... Project Order Action Request (Navy)
POAS ..... Pankypria Omospondia Anexartiton Syntechnion (Pancyprian Federation of Independent Trade Unions) (Cyprus)
POASP ..... Plans and Operations Automated Storage Program (Military)
POATSC.... Pacific Overseas Air Technical Service Command
POAU...... Protestants and Other Americans United (for Separation of Church and State)
POB....... Peanut Oil and Beeswax (Penicillin base)
POB....... Place of Birth
POB....... Point of Beginning
POB....... Post Office Box
POB....... Power Outlet Box
POBATO ..... Propellant on Board at Take-Off
POC....... Parti d'Opposition Congolais (Congolese Opposition Party)
POC....... Particulate Organic Carbon
POC....... Pick Off, Circuit
POC....... Planning Objective Coordinator
POC....... Port of Call
POC....... Post Oral Ciliary (Gland)
POC....... Power Control
POC....... Precision Oscillator Crystal
POC ...... Prisoners of Conscience (File of persons imprisoned for political or religious beliefs kept by Amnesty International)
POC....... Privately Owned Conveyance
POC....... Proceed(ing) on Course (Aviation)
POC ...... Process Operator Console
POC ...... Production Operational Capability
POC....... Professional Officer Course (AFROTC)
POCA...... Psychiatric Outpatient Centers of America
POCIBO .... Polar Circling Balloon Observatory
POCL ..... Project Office Change Letter
POCM ..... Partido Obrero y Campesino de Mexico (Mexican political party)
POCN ..... Purchase Order Change Notice
POCR ...... Program Objectives Change Request (DOD)
POCS...... Patent Office Classification System
PO & CS ..... Post Office and Civil Service Committee (Obsolete) (US Senate)
POD ...... Pay on Delivery (Business and trade)
POD ...... Payable on Death
POD ...... Place of Discharge
POD....... Port of Debarkation (Military)
POD....... Port of Delivery (Shipping)
POD....... Port of Discharge (Navy)
POD....... Post Office Department (Later, United States Postal Service)
POD....... Post Office Directory
POD....... Preflight Operations Division
POD....... Pulse Omission Detector
Pod D ...... Doctor of Podiatry
PODM ..... Preliminary Orbit Determination Method (Computer) (NASA)
PODRS ..... Patent Office Data Retrieval System
PODS...... Post Operative Destruct System
PODUC ..... Provided (Following Named) Officers Have Not Departed Your Command (Amend Assignment Instructions As Indicated) (Army)
POE ...... Panel on the Environment (of President's Science Advisory Committee)
POE....... Plank-On-Edge
POE....... Port of Embarkation (Military)
POE....... Port of Entry
POE....... Print Out Effect
POED ..... Program Organization for Evaluation and Decision
POETS ..... Phooey on Everything, Tomorrow's Saturday (Bowdlerized version)
POF ...... Pyruvate Oxidation Factor (Biochemistry)
POGO ..... Polar Orbiting Geophysical Observatory
POGR...... Poplar Grove National Cemetery
POGS...... National Association of Post Office and General Services Maintenance Employees (AFL-CIO)
POGT ..... Power-Operated Gun Turret
POH....... Pull-Out Harness
POI ...... Parking Orbit Injection
POI ...... Parti Oubanguien de l'Independance (Ubangi Independence Party)
POI ...... Personal Orientation Inventory (Psychology)
POI ...... Program of Instruction
POINTER..... Particle Orientation Interferometer (ASD)

POINTMAIL .. Letter Appointment in Mail
POIP ...... Potential Offender Identification Program
POIR ...... Project Officers Interim Report (Air Force)
POISE ..... Panel on Inflight Scientific Experiments (NASA)
POISE ..... Photosynthetic Oxygenation Illuminated by Solar Energy
POL ...... Pacific Oceanography Laboratories
POL ...... Parents of Large Families
POL ...... Petroleum, Oil, and Lubrication (Military)
POL ...... Problem-Oriented Language (Data processing)
POL....... Procedure-Oriented Language
POL ...... Provisional Operating License (for nuclear power plant)
POLA...... Project on Linguistic Analysis
POLAD ..... Political Adviser (Military)
POLEX ..... Polar Experiment
POLIC ..... Petroleum Intersectional Command
POLIS ..... Petroleum Intersectional Service
POLIT...... Political
POLITBUREAU .. Political Bureau (of USSR)
POLO...... Pacific Command Operations Liaison Office
POLTL ..... Political
POLYOX.... Polyethylene Oxide
POM ...... Phenomenon of Man (Project)
POM ...... Potomac Electric Power Company (NYSE symbol)
POM ...... Preparation for Overseas Movement (Military)
POM ...... Program Operation Mode
POM ...... Project Office Memo
POMAR..... Position Operational, Meteorological Aircraft Report
POMAS..... Procurement Office for Military Automotive Supplies
POMCUS .... Prepositioning of Materiel Configured to Unit Sets (Army)
POMH ...... National Association of Post Office Mail Handlers, Watchmen, Messengers, and Group Leaders
POMM ..... Preliminary Operating and Maintenance Manual (Military)
POMS ..... Panel on Operational Meteorological Satellites
POMSEE .... Performance, Operating and Maintenance Standards for Electronic Equipment
POMSIP .... Post Office Management and Service Improvement Program (Obsolete)
POMV ..... National Federation Post Office Motor Vehicle Employees (Later, APWU)
PONA ..... Paraffins, Olefins, Naphthenes, Aromatics
PONCHO .... Patrons of Northwest Culture Organizations (Seattle, Washington)
PONSE ..... Personnel of the Naval Shore Establishment (Report)
PONTA ..... Popular New Titles from Abroad (Book acquisition program for libraries)
PONY ..... Protect Our Nation's Youth (Baseball league) (Name usually written Pony)
PONY ..... Purpose of Neighborhood Youth (Foundation)
PONYA ..... Port of New York Authority
POO .... Panel on Oceanography
POO .... Post Office Order
POO .... Priority Operational Objective (Military)
POOD ..... Permanent Officer of the Deck (Day) (Navy)
POOD ..... Provisioning Order Obligating Document
POOFF...... Preservation of Our Femininity and Finances (Women's group opposing below-the-knee fashions introduced in 1970)
POOFF ..... Professional Oglers of Female Figures (Men's group opposing below-the-knee fashions introduced in 1970)
POP .... Para-Chlorophenylalanine
POP .... Pay One Price
POP .... Perpendicular Ocean Platform (Oceanography)
POP .... Placing Older People (North Carolina)
POP .... Point of Purchase (Advertising)
POP .... Posterior Odds Processing (Weather forecasting) (National Science Foundation)
POP .... Power On/Off Protection
POP .... Programmed Operators and Primitives (Data processing)
POP .... Project Objective Plan
POP .... Prompt Ordering Plan
POP .... Pump Optimizing Program
POPA...... Patent Office Professional Association
POPA...... Property Owners' Protection Association
POPAI..... Point-of-Purchase Advertising Institute
POPE ...... Parents for Orthodoxy in Parochial Education (Group opposing sex education in schools)
POPGUN .... Policy and Procedure Governing the Use of Nicknames (Army)
POPI ...... Post Office Position Indicator (A form of long-range position indicator) (Great Britain)
POPO...... Push-On, Pull-Off (Data processing)
POPR ...... Prototype Organic Power Reactor
POPS ...... People Opposed to Pornography in Schools (Group opposing sex education in schools)
POPSI..... Precipitation and Off-Path Scattered Interference (Report) (FCC)
POQ ...... Provided Otherwise Qualified (Military)
POR....... Partido Obrero Revolucionario (Revolutionary Workers' Party) (Bolivia)
POR....... Pay on Return (Business and trade)

POR . . . . Payable on Receipt (Business and trade)
POR . . . . Pilot Opinion Rating
POR . . . . Poor & Company (NYSE symbol) (Delisted)
POR . . . . Portec, Inc. (NYSE symbol)
POR . . . . Preparation of Replacements for Oversea Movement (Military)
POR . . . . Press on Regardless (Automotive marathon)
POR . . . . Project Officers Report
POR . . . . Purchase Order Request
PORAC . . . . . Peace Officers Research Association of California
PORACC . . . . . Principles of Radiation and Contamination Control
PORDA . . . . . . Personnel Officers of Research and Development Agencies
PORDIR . . . . . . Port Director
PORE . . . . Point Reyes National Seashore (National Park Service designation)
POREA . . . . . . Post Office Regional Employees' Association (Believed defunct)
POREP . . . . . . Position Report (Air Force)
PORI . . . . Portal Operational Readiness Instrumentation
PORR . . . . . . Purchase Order Revision Request
PORT . . . . . . Photo-Optical Recorder Tracker
PORTAPAK . . . Portable, Self-Contained, Instrument Package
POS . . . . Pacific Orchid Society of Hawaii
POS . . . . Period of Service
POS . . . . Photo Optic System
POS . . . . Point of Sale (Credit card computer)
POS . . . . Positive
POS . . . . Program Order Sequence
POS . . . . Publications de l'Office de Statistique (Luxembourg)
POS . . . . . . Pupil Observation Survey (Education)
POSA . . . . . . Patriotic Order Sons of America
POSB . . . . . . Post Office Savings Bank
POSD . . . . . . Personnel on Station Date (Army)
POSD . . . . . . Program for Optical System Design
POSD . . . . . . Project Operation Support Division (NASA)
POSDCORB . . . Planning, Organizing, Staffing, Directing, Coordinating, Reporting, and Budgeting (Principles of management) (DOD)
POSE . . . . . . Parents Opposed to Sex Education (An organization)
POSE . . . . . . Photogrammetric Ocean Survey Equipment
POSE . . . . . . Power Operational Support Equipment
POSH . . . . . . Port Outward-bound, Starboard Homeward-bound
POSIP . . . . . . Portable Ship's Instrumentation Package
POSITRON . . . Positive Electron
POSM . . . . . . National Association of Post Office and General Services Maintenance Employees (Later, APWU)
POSM . . . . . . Patient Operated Selector Mechanism (Pronounced "possum")
POSN . . . . . . Position
POSR . . . . . . Pupil Observation Survey (Education)
POSS . . . . . . Palomar Observatory Sky Survey
POSS . . . . . . Passive Optical Satellite Surveillance
POSS . . . . . . Photo-Optical Surveillance Subsystem
POSS . . . . . . Possession
POSS . . . . . . Prototype Optical Surveillance System
POSSE . . . . . . Parents Opposed to Sex and Sensitivity Education (An organization)
POSSE . . . . . . Progressive On-Slaught to Stamp Out Stock Errors (Navy)
POSSUM . . . . . Polar Orbiting Satellite System - University of Michigan (Designed by engineering students)
POST . . . . . . Peace Officer Standards and Training
POST . . . . . . Polymer Science and Technology (A publication of American Chemical Society)
POSTER . . . . . . Post Strike Emergency Reporting
POST-J . . . . . . Polymer Science and Technology - Journals (Chemical abstracts)
POSTP . . . . . . Posterior Probability (Computations)
POST-P . . . . . . Polymer Science and Technology - Patents (Chemical abstracts)
POSTPRO . . . . Postprocessor (Computer) (Coast Guard)
POT . . . . Pennsylvania-Ontario Transportation Company (AAR code)
POT . . . . Pitch-Orthogonal Thrust
POT . . . . Portable Outside Toilet (A unit of mobility equipment) (Military)
POT . . . . Potential
POT . . . . Proposition of Today Committee (California organization)
POTANN . . . . Potomac Annex (Navy Department) (Obsolete)
POTC . . . . . . PERT (Program Evaluation and Review Technique) Orientation & Training Center
POTS . . . . . . Plain Old Telephone Service (Humorous term for Long Lines Department of AT & T)
POTUS . . . . . . President of the United States
POUF . . . . . . Projects of Optimum Urgency and Feasibility
POV . . . . Peak Operating Voltage
POV . . . . Personally (or Privately) Owned Vehicle
POV . . . . Pinch-Off Voltage
POV . . . . Pittsburgh & Ohio Valley Railway Company (AAR code)
POV . . . . Plane of Vibration
POV . . . . Pneumatically Operated Valve
POV . . . . Purchase, Outside Vendors

POVORTAD . . . Positive Vorticity Advection (Meteorology)
POW . . . . . . Perception of Ward (Scales) (Psychology)
POW . . . . . . Prisoner(s) of War (Also, PW)
POW . . . . . . Progressive Order of the West
POWER . . . . . Professionals Organized for Women's Equal Rights (Feminist group)
PP . . . . Pacific Petroleums, Ltd. (NYSE symbol)
PP . . . . Pages
PP . . . . Panel Point (Technical drawings)
PP . . . . Papa (Pope)
PP . . . . Parcel Post
PP . . . . Paris Publications (Inc.)
PP . . . . Parish Priest
PP . . . . Part Paid (Business and trade)
PP . . . . Parti du Peuple (People's Party) (Burundi)
PP . . . . Partial Pressure
PP . . . . Partial Program
PP . . . . Parts Per
PP . . . . Passive Participle
PP . . . . Past Participle
PP . . . . Past President
PP . . . . Pater Patriae (The Father of His Country)
PP . . . . Pay Period
PP . . . . Peak to Peak
PP . . . . Pellagra Preventive (Factor) (Also see PPF) (Biochemistry)
PP . . . . Per Procurationem (By Proxy)
PP . . . . Peripheral Processor (Data processing)
PP . . . . Permanent Party
PP . . . . Personal Property
PP . . . . Petticoat Peeping (From one girl to another, in reference to dress disarrangement)
PP . . . . Physical Profile
PP . . . . Physical Properties
PP . . . . Pianissimo (Very softly) (Music)
PP . . . . Pickpocket
PP . . . . Piers Plowman (Middle English poem)
PP . . . . Pilot Punch
PP . . . . Piu Piano (More softly) (Music)
PP . . . . Plan Profile
PP . . . . Planned Parenthood
PP . . . . Planning Purpose
PP . . . . Plaster of Paris
PP . . . . Polar Pacific (American air mass)
PP . . . . Polypropylene
PP . . . . Pontificum (Of the Popes)
PP . . . . Post Pagado (Postage Paid) (Spain)
PP . . . . Post Paid
PP . . . . Post Partum (Medicine)
PP . . . . Post Position (Racing)
PP . . . . Postage Paid
PP . . . . Postponed
PP . . . . Postprandial (After Meals)
PP . . . . Pounds Pressure
PP . . . . Pour Presenter (To Present)
PP . . . . Power Package
PP . . . . Power Plant
PP . . . . Praepter Propter (Approximately) (Pharmacy)
PP . . . . Prepaid
PP . . . . Preprocessor
PP . . . . Present Position (Military)
PP . . . . Pressure-Proof (Technical drawings)
PP . . . . Principal Point
PP . . . . Private Property (Military)
PP . . . . Privately Printed
PP . . . . Production Processes
PP . . . . Professional Paper
PP . . . . Program(ming) Plan
PP . . . . Progress Payments (Military procurement)
PP . . . . Proletarian Party
PP . . . . Public Property
PP . . . . Punctum Proximum (Near Point)
PP . . . . Purchased Parts
PP . . . . Push-Pull (Technical drawings)
P/P . . . . Partial Pay (Air Force)
P/P . . . . Point-to-Point (Air Force)
P & P . . . . . . Packing and Preservation
P & P . . . . . . Production and Procurement (Military)
PPA . . . . Paper Pail Association
PPA . . . . Paper Plate Association
PPA . . . . Parcel Post Association
PPA . . . . Per Power of Attorney (Business and trade)
PPA . . . . Periodical Publishers Association
PPA . . . . Phenylpyruvic Acid (Chemical)

PPA .... Piper Aircraft Corporation (NYSE symbol) (Delisted)
PPA .... Pitch Precession Amplifier
PPA .... Polymer Permeation Analyzer
PPA .... Polyphosphoric Acid
PPA .... Popcorn Processors Association
PPA .... Poultry Publishers Association
PPA .... Power Plant Automation
PPA .... Powerplant Performance Analysis
PPA .... Presidents' Professional Association
PPA .... Princeton-Pennsylvania Accelerator (AEC) (Closed, 1972)
PPA .... Produce Packaging Association
PPA .... Professional Panhellenic Association
PPA .... Professional Photographers of America
PPA .... Professional Programmers Association
PPA .... Professional Putters Association
PPA .... Program Problem Area
PPA .... Pseudo Passive Array
PPA .... Public Personnel Association (Later, IPMA)
PPA .... Publishers' Publicity Association
PPA .... Pulse Plasma Accelerator
PPA .... Pulsed Power Amplifier
PPA .... Purple Plum Association
PPAA ...... Patres Amplissimi (Cardinals)
PPAUS ...... Peat Producers Association of the United States
PPB .... Parts Per Billion
PPB .... Planning-Programming-Budgeting (System)
PPB .... Positive Pressure Breathing (Aerospace)
PPB .... Precision Pressure Balance
PPB .... Production Parts Breakdown
PPB .... Provisional Parts Breakdown
PPB .... Provisioning Parts Breakdown
PPB .... Push-Pull Bearing
PPBD ...... Port of Palm Beach District (AAR code)
PPBDT...... Persatuan Buruh Pengendara Betja Dokar dan Tjikar (Dogcart and Bullock-cart Drivers' Union) (Indonesia)
PPBES ...... Program Planning-Budgeting-Evaluation System Project
PPBF....... Pan-American Pharmaceutical and Biochemical Federation
PPBG ...... Preliminary Program and Budget Guidance
PPBI .... Dewan Pimpinan Pusat Persatuan Pengendara Betja Indonesia (Central Board of Indonesian Betja Drivers' Association)
PPBS....... Planning-Programming-Budgeting System
PPBS....... Positive Pressure Breathing System (Aerospace)
PPC .... Paperboard Packaging Council
PPC .... Partial Pay Card
PPC .... Patrol Plane Commander
PPC .... Per Pupil Cost
PPC .... Philatelic Press Club
PPC .... Phillips Petroleum Company
PPC .... Photographic Processing Cells
PPC .... Picture Postcard
PPC .... Plant Pest Control Division (of ARS, Department of Agriculture)
PPC .... Plug Patch Cord
PPC .... Pour Prendre Conge (To Take Leave)
PPC .... Power Pack Charger
PPC .... Priority Placement Certificate (Military)
PPC .... Progressive Patient Care
PP & C ..... Production Planning and Control
PP & C ..... Project Planning and Control
PPCA ...... Plasma Prothrombin Conversion Accelerator
PPCAA ..... Parole and Probation Compact Administrators Association
PPCAA ..... Plasma Prothrombin Conversion Accelerator (Physiology)
PPCF ...... Plasma Prothrombin Conversion Factor (Physiology)
PPCS ...... Precision Pointing Control System (Engineering)
PPD .... Parti Progressiste Dahomeen (Dahomey Progressive Party)
PPD .... Partido Popular Democratico (Political party) (Puerto Rico)
PPD .... Parts Provisioning Document
PPD .... Payload Position Data
PPD .... Personnel Planning Data
PPD .... Personnel Priority Designator (Military)
PPD .... Pitch Phase Detector
PPD .... Postpaid
PPD .... Prepaid
PPD .... Program Planning Document
PPD .... Project Planning Directive
PPD .... Purified Protein Derivative (Tuberculin)
PPD .... Purolator, Inc. (NYSE symbol)
PPDA ...... para-Phenylenediamine
PPDB ...... Personnel Planning Data Book (Navy)
PPDD ...... Plan Position Data Display
PPDF ...... Poisson Probability Distribution Function
PPDMG ..... Popular Priced Dress Manufacturers Group, Inc.

PPDP .... Preliminary Project Development Plan (NASA)
PPDP .... Pre-Program Definition Phase
PPDR ...... Pilot Performance Description Record
PPDR ...... Production Packing Depth Range
PPD-S ..... Purified Protein Derivative-Standard
PPDSE...... International Plate Printers', Die Stampers' and Engravers' Union of North America
PPE .... Independent Union of Plant Protection Employees in the Electrical and Machine Industry
PPE .... Premodulation Processing Equipment
PPE .... Pre-Production Evaluation
PPE .... Prototype Production Evaluation
PPE .... Purchasing Power Equivalent
PREP....... Preparatory
PREP....... Preposition
PPF .... Palestine Pioneer Foundation
PPF .... Parti Populaire Francais
PPF .... Peacetime Planning Factors
PPF .... Pellagra-Preventive Factor (Also see PP) (Biochemistry)
PPF .... Provision of Production Facilities (Military)
PPF .... United Association of Journeymen and Apprentices of the Plumbing and Pipe Fitting Industry of the United States and Canada
PPFA ...... Planned Parenthood Federation of America
PPFF ...... Poisson Probability Frequency Function
PPFO ...... Paris Procurement Field Office
PPG .... Pacific Proving Ground (AEC)
PPG .... Periodical Press Gallery (US Senate)
PPG .... Personnel Processing Group
PPG .... Piezoelectric Power Generation
PPG .... Planned Procurement Guide
PPG .... Plasma Power Generator
PPG .... Polypropylene Glycol
PPG .... Power-Play Goal (Hockey)
PPG .... PPG Industries (Formerly, Pittsburgh Plate Glass Company) (NYSE symbol)
PPG .... Primary Pattern Generator (Bell Laboratories)
PPGM ...... Propulsion & Power Generation
PPGM ...... Past Provincial Grand Master (Masonry)
PPGSW ..... Past Provincial Grand Senior Warden (Masonry)
PPH .... Parts Per Hundred
PPH .... Post-Partum Hemorrhage
PPH .... Pounds Per Hour
PPH .... Pulses Per Hour
PPHA ...... Peak Pulse Height Analysis
PPHM ...... Parts Per Hundred Million
PPI........ Packing, Postage, and Insurance
PPI .... Parcel Post, Insured
PPI........ Personnel Planning Information
PPI........ Peter Paul, Incorporated (NYSE symbol)
PPI........ Phoenix Precision Instrument Company
PPI........ Pickle Packers International
PPI........ Pictorial Position Indicator
PPI........ Plan-Position Indicator (RADAR)
PPI........ Plastics Pipe Institute
PPI........ Policy Proof of Interest
PPI........ Present Position Indicator
PPJ .... Pressure Plane Joint
PPK .... Paramp Pump Klystron
PPK .... Parti Progressiste Katangais
PPK .... Punt, Pass and Kick (Youth competition sponsored by professional football)
PPL .... Pacific Power and Light Company
PPL .... Palmer Physical Laboratory (Princeton University)
PPL .... Pennsylvania Power & Light Company (NYSE symbol)
PPL .... Per Pupil Limitation
PPL .... Pergamon Press, Limited
PPL .... Plasma Physics Laboratory (Also known as PPPL)
PPL .... Plasma Propulsion Laboratory
PPL .... Preferential Planning List
PPL .... Preferred Parts List
PPLO ...... Pleuropneumonia-like Organisms (Bacteriology)
PPLS ...... Preferred Parts List System
PPM....... Parts Per Million (Chemistry)
PPM....... Peak Power Meter
PPM....... Periodic Permanent Magnet
PPM .... Personnel Program Manager (Navy)
PPM....... Pfaudler Permutit, Inc. (NYSE symbol) (Delisted)
PPM....... Phenylpropanolamine (Hydrochloride) (Decongestant)
PPM .... Position and Pay Management (Army)
PPM .... Prairie Print Makers
PPM....... Project Profile Manual
PPM .... Pulse Period Modulation
PPM....... Pulse Position Modulation (Radio)

PPM . . . . Pulses Per Minute
PPMA . . . . Plastic Products Manufacturers Association
PPMA . . . . Precision Potentiometer Manufacturers Association
PPMA . . . . Pulp and Paper Machinery Association
PPMFC . . . . . . Preprints on Precision Measurement and Fundamental Constants
     (National Bureau of Standards)
PPMI . . . . Pilot Plant Meat Irradiator (AEC)
PPMI . . . . Printed Paper Mat Institute
PPN . . . . Parti Progressiste Nigerien (Nigerian Progressive Party)
PPN . . . . Peroxypropionyl Nitrate (Chemical)
PPN . . . . Procurement Program Number (Military)
PP & NA . . . . Private Plants and Naval Activities
PPO . . . . Pleuropneumonia Organisms (Bacteriology)
PPO . . . . Polyphenoloxidase
PPO . . . . Polyphenylene Oxide (A thermoplastic)
PPO . . . . Port Postal Office
PPO . . . . Prior Permission Only
PPO . . . . Projected Program Objective
PPO . . . . Publications and Printing Office (Military)
PPP . . . . Peak Pulse Power
PPP . . . . Perpex Peristaltic Pump
PPP . . . . Phase Program Planning (NASA)
PPP . . . . Planning Purpose Proposal
PPP . . . . Platelet-Poor Plasma
PPP . . . . Propria Pecunia Posuit (Erected at His Own Expense)
P & PP . . . . . Pull and Push Plate
PPPA . . . . Pulp and Paper Prepackaging Association
PPPC . . . . Petroleum Pool Pacific Coast
PPPC . . . . Pipe Plug Producers Council
PPPEA . . . . . . Pulp, Paper and Paperboard Export Association of the United States
PPPI . . . . Precision Plan Position Indicator
PPPI . . . . Projection Plan Position Indicator
PPPI . . . . Pulp, Paper & Paperboard Institute (USA), Inc.
PPPL . . . . Princeton Plasma Physics Laboratory (Also known as PPL)
PPPRF . . . . . . Pan Pacific Public Relations Federation
PPQ . . . . Planning Purpose Quote
PPR . . . . Palomino Pony Registry
PPR . . . . Permanent Pay Record
PPR . . . . Photo-Plastic-Recording
PPR . . . . Polska Partia Robotnicza (Polish Workers' Party)
PPR . . . . Present Participle
PPR . . . . Prior Permission Required
PPR . . . . Proprietary Procurement Request
PPR . . . . Purchase Parts Request
PPRA . . . . . . Past President of the Royal Academy (British)
PPRA . . . . . . Preliminary Personnel Requirements Analysis (Navy)
PPRC . . . . . . Polish Peace Research Committee
PPRIBA . . . . . Past President of the Royal Institute of British Architects
PPRIC . . . . . . Pulp and Paper Research Institute of Canada
PPS . . . . Paper Publications Society
PPS . . . . Parliamentary Private Secretary (British)
PPS . . . . Parti Progressiste Soudanais (Sudanese Progressive Party)
PPS . . . . Partial Pressure Sensor
PPS . . . . Partido Popular Socialista (Popular Socialist Party) (Mexico)
PPS . . . . Partito Populare Somalo (Somali People's Party)
PPS . . . . Patchboard Programming System
PPS . . . . Payload Power Switch
PPS . . . . Photovoltaic Power Supply
PPS . . . . Plasma Power Supply
PPS . . . . Polonus Philatelic Society
PPS . . . . Polska Partia Socjalistyczna (Polish Socialist Party)
PPS . . . . Post-Postscriptum (Further postscript)
PPS . . . . Precision Power Supply
PPS . . . . Pre-Positioned Stock
PPS . . . . Primary Power Standard
PPS . . . . Primary Pressure Standard
PPS . . . . Primary Propulsion System (Spacecraft)
PPS . . . . Program Planning System (DOD)
PPS . . . . Programmable Patch System
PPS . . . . Programmable Power Supply
PPS . . . . Provisioning Performance Schedule
PPS . . . . Pulses Per Second (RADAR)
PPSA . . . . . . Pan-Pacific Surgical Association
PPSAWA . . . . . Pan Pacific and Southeast Asia Women's Association of the USA
PPSB . . . . Prothrombin, Proconvertin, Stuart Factor, Antihemophilic B Factor
     (Blood coagulation factors) (Medicine)
PPSC . . . . Physical Profile Serial Code
PPSD . . . . Polska Partia Socjaino-Demokratycana (Polish Social-Democrat Party)
PPSEI . . . . Progres Politique, Social et Economique de l'Itasy (Political, Social
     and Economic Progress of the Itasy)
PPSG . . . . Piston and Pin Standardization Group

PPSIA . . . . . . "Personal Property Shipping Information" (Pamphlet) Is Applicable
     (Military)
PPSJ . . . . Pressure Plane Swivel Joint
PPSMEC . . . . . Procurement, Precedence of Supplies, Material and Equipment
     Committee (Joint Communications Board)
PPSN . . . . Purchased Part Shortage Notice
PPSR . . . . Periodic Personnel Strength Report (Army)
PPT . . . . Parti Progressiste Tchadien (Progressive Party of Chad)
PPT . . . . Period Pulse Train
PPT . . . . Periodic Programs Termination (Data processing)
PPT . . . . Pitch Precession Torquer
PPT . . . . Pre-Production Tests (Army)
PPT . . . . Product Positioning Time
PPT . . . . Punched Paper Tape
PPTB . . . . Pin-Pack Test Board
PPTL . . . . Pulp and Paper Traffic League
PPTR . . . . Punched Paper Tape Reader (Data processing)
PPTT . . . . Persatuan Pegawai Tambang Timah (Tin Mine Employees' Union) (Indonesia)
PPTY . . . . Property
PPU . . . . Parti Populaire des Ueles (Ueles Peoples Party)
PPU . . . . Peoria & Pekin Union Railway Company (AAR code)
PPU . . . . Peripheral Processing Unit (Data processing)
PPV . . . . Propulsive Propellant Venting
PPVS . . . . Propulsion Propellant Venting System
PPVT . . . . Peabody Picture Vocabulary Test
PPW . . . . Pacific Power & Light Co. (NYSE symbol)
PPW . . . . Plane-Polarized Wave
PPW . . . . Ponderosa Pine Woodwork
P & PW . . . . . Publicity and Psychological Warfare
PPWA . . . . Ponderosa Pine Woodwork Association
PPWF . . . . Pakistan Petroleum Workers' Federation
PP-WP . . . . . . Planned Parenthood–World Population
PPWR . . . . . . Prepositioned War Reserves
PQ . . . . Parti Quebecois (Quebec separatist political party)
PQ . . . . Permeability Quotient
PQ . . . . Personality Quotient
PQ . . . . Philadelphia Quartz Co.
PQ . . . . Planetary Quarantine (NASA)
PQ . . . . Plant Quarantine Division (of ARS, Department of Agriculture)
PQ . . . . Previous Question (Parliamentary law)
PQ . . . . Province of Quebec, Canada
P & Q . . . . . . Peace and Quiet
P's & Q's . . . . . Of expression "Mind your P's and Q's." Exact origin unclear, but
     theories include: admonishment of pub-owners that British drinkers be
     aware of number of "Pints and Quarts" being marked on their accounts;
     warning to apprentice typesetters that "p" and "q" forms be carefully
     restored to correct case, since each could so easily be mistaken for
     the other; cautioning of French dancing masters that pupils be aware
     of position of their "Pieds" (feet) and "Queues" (wigs) in executing the
     deep bow of a formal curtsey.
P and Q . . . . . Prime Quality (Slang)
PQA . . . . Plant Quality Assurance
PQA . . . . Project Quality Assurance
PQAI . . . . Procurement Quality Assurance Instruction
PQAP . . . . Planned Quality Assurance Program (Navy)
PQAP . . . . Procurement Quality Assurance Program
PQC . . . . Paul Quinn College (Texas)
PQC . . . . Precision Quartz Crystal
PQC . . . . Production Quality Control
PQE . . . . Project Quality Engineering
PQEP . . . . Product Quality Evaluation Plan (Military)
PQGS . . . . Propellant Quantity Gage (or Gaging) System (Apollo) (NASA)
PQM . . . . Post Quartermaster (Marine Corps)
PQMC . . . . . . Philadelphia Quartermaster Center (Merged with Defense Clothing and
     Textile Supply Center)
PQMD . . . . . . Propellant Quantity Measuring Device
PQN . . . . Principal Quantum Number
PQS . . . . Production Quotation Support
PQS . . . . Promotion Qualification Score (Military)
PQT . . . . Polyquinazolotriazole
PQT . . . . Professional Qualification Test (of the National Security Agency)
PQZ . . . . Premium Quality Zinc
PR . . . . Panel Receptacle
PR . . . . Parachute Rigger
PR . . . . Parallax and Refraction
PR . . . . Parliamentary Report
PR . . . . Partido Radical (Radical Party) (Chile)
PR . . . . Partido Republicano (Republican Party) (Brazil)
PR . . . . Partido Revolucionario (Revolutionary Party) (Guatemala)
PR . . . . Partisan Review (A publication)
PR . . . . Patrol Vessel, River Gunboat (Navy symbol)

PR . . . . Pattern Recognition
PR . . . . Payroll
PR . . . . Percentile Rank
PR . . . . Performance Report
PR . . . . Performance Requirement
PR . . . . Peripheral Resistance
PR . . . . Permanens Rector (Permanent Rector)
PR . . . . Permissive Reassignment (Air Force)
PR . . . . Photographic Reconnaissance Aircraft
PR . . . . Pershing Rifles (Honorary military organization)
PR . . . . Photoreconnaissance (Air Force)
PR . . . . Pilot Rating
PR . . . . Pinch-Runner (Baseball)
PR . . . . Pitch Ratio
PR . . . . Plant Report
PR . . . . Populus Romanus (The Roman People)
PR . . . . Position Report (Air Force)
PR . . . . Post Request
PR . . . . Poste Recommandee (Registered Post)
PR . . . . Posterior Ridge
PR . . . . Pour Remercier (To Express Thanks)
Pr . . . . Praseodymium (Chemical element)
PR . . . . Preferred (NYSE symbol)
PR . . . . Preliminary Report
PR . . . . Pre-Raphaelite
PR . . . . Press Release
PR . . . . Pressure Ratio
PR . . . . Princess Royal's (Military unit) (British)
PR . . . . Principal Register (Data processing)
PR . . . . Printing Request
PR . . . . Priority Regulation
PR . . . . Prize Ring (Boxing)
PR . . . . Pro Rata
PR . . . . Procurement Regulations
PR . . . . Procurement (or Purchase) Request
PR . . . . Progress Report
PR . . . . Progressive Resistance
PR . . . . Project Report
PR . . . . Proportional Representation (in legislatures, etc.)
PR . . . . Pseudo Random
PR . . . . Public Relations
PR . . . . Puerto Rico
PR . . . . Pulse Rate
PR . . . . Punctum Remotum (Far Point)
PR . . . . Purchase Requests
PR . . . . Purplish Red
PR . . . . River Gunboat (Navy symbol)
P & R . . . . . . Philadelphia & Reading Railway
PRA . . . . Parabolic Reflector Antenna
PRA . . . . Parti du Regroupement Africain (African Regroupment Party)
PRA . . . . Partido Revolucionario Autentico (Authentic Revolutionary Party) (Bolivia)
PRA . . . . Pay Readjustment Act (1942)
PRA . . . . Personnel Research Activity (Later, NPTRL)
PRA . . . . Popular Rotocraft Association
PRA . . . . President of the Royal Academy (British)
PRA . . . . Probation and Rehabilitation of Airmen (Air Force)
PRA . . . . Program Reader Assembly (Data processing)
PRA . . . . Projected Requisition Authority (Army)
PRA . . . . Proust Research Association
PRA . . . . Psoriasis Research Association
PRA . . . . Psychological Research Associates
PRA . . . . Public Resources Association
PRA . . . . Public Roads Administration
PRA . . . . Puerto Rico Area Office (AEC)
PRAC . . . . . . Public Relations Advisory Committee
PRACSATS . . . . Practical Satellites
PRADOR . . . . . PRF (Pulse Repetition Frequency) Ranging Doppler RADAR
PRAF . . . . . . Passenger-Reserved Air Freight
PRAM . . . . . . Program Requirements Analysis Method
PRANG . . . . . . Puerto Rico Air National Guard
PRAP . . . . . . Provisions of Following Reference Apply (Army)
PRARS . . . . . . Pitch, Roll, Azimuth Reference System
PRAS . . . . . . Pension and Retirement Annuity System
PRAT . . . . . . Production Reliability Acceptance Test
PRAW . . . . . . Personnel Research Activity, Washington, DC (Navy)
PRB . . . . Personnel Records Branch (Army)
PRB . . . . Personnel Research Branch (Army)
PRB . . . . Population Reference Bureau
PRB . . . . Pre-Raphaelite Brotherhood
PRB . . . . Procurement Review Board
PRBA(AG) . . . . Personnel Research Board of the Army, Adjutant General

PRBT . . . . Precision Remote Bathythermograph
PRC . . . . Part Requirement Card
PRC . . . . Pension Research Council
PRC . . . . People's Republic of China (Mainland China)
PRC . . . . Personnel Readiness Center (Air Force)
PRC . . . . Personnel Reporting Code (Army)
PRC . . . . Petroleum Reserves Corporation
PRC . . . . Physical Review Council (DOD)
PRC . . . . Planned Requirements, Conversion
PRC . . . . Planning Research Corporation
PRC . . . . Plastic Roller Conveyor
PRC . . . . Post Roman Conditam (After the Founding of Rome)
PRC . . . . Prattsburgh Railway Corporation (AAR code)
PRC . . . . Preoral Ciliary (Gland)
PRC . . . . Printer Control
PRC . . . . Production Readjustments Committee (WPB)
PRC . . . . Products Research & Chemical Corp. (NYSE symbol)
PRC . . . . Professional Relations Council (American Chemical Society)
PRC . . . . Program Review Committee
PRC . . . . Propulsion Research Corporation
PRC . . . . Pyrotechnic Rocket Container
PRCA . . . . . . Parks, Recreation and Cultural Affairs Administration (New York City)
PRCA . . . . . . Puerto Rico Communications Authority
PRCF . . . . . . Plutonium Recycle Critical Facility (AEC)
PRCHT . . . . . . Parachute
Prcht Bad . . . . Parachutist Badge (Army)
PRCM . . . . . . Passive Radiation Countermeasure
PRCO . . . . . . Pacific Requisition Control Office (Navy)
PRCP . . . . . . President of the Royal College of Physicians (British)
PRCS . . . . . . Personal Report of Confidence as a Speaker (Psychology)
PRCS . . . . . . Polish Red Cross Society
PRCS . . . . . . President of the Royal College of Surgeons (British)
PRCS . . . . . . Process
PRCS . . . . . . Purchase Requisition Change Supplement
PRCUA . . . . . . Polish Roman Catholic Union of America
PRD . . . . Part Reference Designator
PRD . . . . Parti Democratique Dahomeen (Dahomey Democratic Party)
PRD . . . . Partial Reaction of Degeneration
PRD . . . . Partido Revolucionario Dominicano (Dominican Revolutionary Party)
PRD . . . . Personnel Readiness Date (Army)
PRD . . . . Personnel Records Division (Army)
PRD . . . . Personnel Research Division (Navy)
PRD . . . . Personnel Resources Data
PRD . . . . Piezoelectric Resonating Device
PRD . . . . Polaroid Corporation (NYSE symbol)
PRD . . . . Postal Regulating Detachment (Military)
PRD . . . . Printer Driver
PRD . . . . Printer Dump
PRD . . . . Proficiency Rating Designator
PRD . . . . Program Requirement Document (Air Force)
PRD . . . . Projected Rotation Date
PRD . . . . Public Relations Division
PR & D . . . . . . Personal Rest and Delay (Air Force)
PRDC . . . . . . Polar Research and Development Center (Army)
PRDC . . . . . . Power Reactor Development Company
PRDL . . . . . . Personnel Research and Development Laboratory (Navy)
PRDN . . . . . . Partido de Reconciliacion Democratica Nacional (Party of National Democratic Reconciliation) (Guatemala)
PRDP . . . . . . Power Reactor Demonstration Program (AEC)
PRDV . . . . . . Peak Reading Digital Voltmeter
PRE . . . . Petroleum Refining Engineer
PRE . . . . Portable RADAR Equipment
PRE . . . . Premier Industrial Corp. (NYSE symbol)
PRE . . . . Progressive Resistive Exercise
PRE . . . . Pulse Radiation Effect
PREAG . . . . . . Photographic Reconnaissance Equipment Advisory Group (Military)
PRE-ARM . . . . . People's Rights Enforced Against Riots and Murder (Vigilante group in New Jersey)
PREC . . . . Propulsion Research Environmental Chamber
PREC . . . . Public Revenue Education Council
PRECIS . . . . . . Preserved Context Index System (British National Bibliography)
PRECO . . . . . . Preparatory Commission of the United Nations Organization
PRECOMMDET . . Pre-Commissioning Detail (Navy)
PRECOMMSCOL . . Pre-Commissioning School (Navy)
PRED . . . . Prediction
PREDICT . . . . . Prediction of Radiation Effects by Digital Computer Techniques
PREF . . . . Preference
PREF . . . . Propulsion Research Environmental Facility
PRELIM . . . . . . Preliminary
PRELORT . . . . . Precision Long-Range Tracking RADAR
PREM . . . . Premium

PREMA . . . . . . Pulp Refining Equipment Manufacturers Association
PREP . . . . Peace Research and Education Project
PREP . . . . Persons Responsive to Education Problems (An organization)
PREP . . . . Prepare
PREP . . . . . . Product Reliability Evaluation Program
PREP . . . . Programmed Educational Package
PREP . . . . Project Return Evaluation Program
PREP . . . . Putting Research into Educational Practice (Information service of ERIC)
PREPARE . . . . Project for Retraining of Employable Persons as Relates to EDP
PREPRO . . . . . Preprocessor (Computer) (Coast Guard)
PRES . . . . Presentation
PRES . . . . . . President
PRES . . . . President of the Royal Entomological Society (British)
PRES . . . . Preston R. R. (AAR code)
PRESET . . . . . . Preset Spin Echo Technique
PRESFR . . . . . . Pressure Falling Rapidly (Meteorology)
PRESIGN . . . . Procedure Sign
PRESPROC . . . . Presidential Proclamation
PRESRR . . . . . . Pressure Rising Rapidly (Meteorology)
PRESS . . . . . . Pacific Range Electromagnetic Signature Studies (or System) (Military)
PRESS . . . . . . Parti Republicain Social du Senegal (Social Republican Party of Senegal)
PRESSAR . . . . Presentation Equipment for Slow Scan RADAR
PRESTO . . . . . Program for Rapid Earth-to-Space Trajectory Optimization (NASA)
PRESTO . . . . . Program Reporting and Evaluation System for Total Operations (AFSC)
PREV . . . . Previous
PREWI . . . . . . Press Wireless (A radio service for the transmission of news)
PRF . . . . Petroleum Research Fund
PRF . . . . Plutonium Reclamation Facility (AEC)
PRF . . . . Plywood Research Foundation
PRF . . . . Primary Reference Fuel
PRF . . . . Psychiatric Research Foundation
PRF . . . . Psychosynthesis Research Foundation
PRF . . . . Public Relations Foundation
PRF . . . . Puerto Rican Forum
PRF . . . . Pulse Recurrence Frequency (Radio)
PRF . . . . Pulse Repetition Frequency (RADAR)
PRF . . . . Purdue Research Foundation
PRFI . . . . Portable Range-Finder/Illuminator
PRG . . . . Philadelphia & Reading Corporation (NYSE symbol) (Delisted)
PRG . . . . Plastic Radial Grating
PRG . . . . Provisional Revolutionary Government (Vietcong)
PRGM . . . . . . Program
PRGMR . . . . . Programmer
PRGS . . . . President of the Royal Geographical Society (British)
PRH . . . . . . Petrol Railhead
PRHA . . . . President of the Royal Hibernian Academy
PRI . . . . La Prevention Routiere Internationale (International Prevention of Road Accidents) (An organization)
PRI . . . . Paint Research Institute
PRI . . . . Paleontological Research Institution
PRI . . . . Partido Revolucionario Institucional (Mexican political party)
PRI . . . . Partito Repubblicano Italiano (Republican Party of Italy)
PRI . . . . Peace Research Institute
PRI . . . . Performance Registry International
PRI . . . . Phosphate Rock Institute
PRI . . . . Photo RADAR Intelligence
PRI . . . . Pineapple Research Institute of Hawaii
PRI . . . . Preliminary Rifle Instruction
PRI . . . . President of the Royal Institution (British)
PRI . . . . Priority
PRI . . . . Priority Requirement for Information
PRI . . . . Processing Research Institute (Carnegie Mellon University)
PRI . . . . Pulse Rate Indicator
PRICE . . . . . . Pricing Review to Intensify Competitive Environment (Data processing)
PRIDCO . . . . . Puerto Rico Industrial Development Company
PRIDE . . . . People for Rehabilitating and Integrating the Disabled through Education (New York City)
PRIDE . . . . . . Perfection Requires Individual Defect Elimination
PRIDE . . . . . . Personal Responsibility in Daily Effort (Military Airlift Command's acronym for the Zero Defects Program)
PRIDE . . . . . . Priority Receiving with Inter-Departmental Efficiency (Data processing)
PRIDE . . . . . . Production of Reliable Items Demands Excellence (Navy)
PRIDE . . . . . . Professional Results in Daily Effort (Strategic Air Command's acronym for the Zero Defects Program)
PRIDE . . . . . . Programmed Reliability in Design Engineering
PRI-FLY . . . . . Primary Flight Control (on an aircraft carrier) (Navy)
PRIM . . . . Primary
PRIMAR . . . . . Program to Improve Management of Army Resources
PRIME . . . . . . Planning through Retrieval of Information for Management Extrapolation
PRIME . . . . . . Precision Recovery Including Maneuvering Entry (Air Force)
PRIME . . . . . . Priority Improvement Effort (DOD)

PRIME . . . . . . Priority Management Efforts (Army)
PRIME . . . . . . Priority Management Evaluation (Navy)
PRIME . . . . . . Program Independence, Modularity, Economy
PRIME . . . . . . Programmed Instruction for Management Education (American Management Association)
PRIMER . . . . . . Patient Record Information for Education Requirements (Data processing)
PRIMTRA . . . . Air Primary Training
PRIN . . . . Performance Risk Index Number
PRIN . . . . Principal
PRINCE . . . . . Parts Reliability Information Center (of NASA)
PRINCE . . . . . Programmed Reinforced Instruction Necessary to Continuing Education
PRIND . . . . . . Present Indications Are
PRINMUS . . . . Principal Musician (Marine Corps)
PRINT . . . . . . Pre-Edited Interpretive System (Data processing)
PRINT . . . . . . Public Release of Information and Transcripts (Student legal action organization)
PRIO . . . . International Peace Research Institution, Oslo (Norway)
PRIOR . . . . . . Program for In-Orbital Rendezvous (Antisatellite system) (Air Force)
PRIP . . . . Parts Reliability Improvement Program
PRIS . . . . Prisoner
PRISCO . . . . . Price Stabilization Corporation
PRISE . . . . . . Pennsylvania's Regional Instruction System for Education (Network of colleges and universities)
PRISE . . . . . . Program for Integrated Shipboard Electronics
PRISIC . . . . . . Photographic Reconnaissance Interpretation Section (Squadron) Intelligence Center (JICPOA)
PRISM . . . . . . Program Reliability Information System for Management (Polaris)
PRISM . . . . . . Programmed Integrated System Maintenance
PRISM . . . . . . Progressive Refinement of Integrated Supply Management
PRJC . . . . Pearl River Junior College (Mississippi)
PRJC . . . . Puerto Rico Junior College
PRK . . . . Pridie Kalendas (The Day Before the Calends)
PRK . . . . Primary Rat Kidney (Cells)
PRL . . . . Parti Republicain de la Liberte (Republican Party for Liberty) (Upper Volta)
PRL . . . . Personnel Research Laboratory (DOD)
PRL . . . . Petroleum Refining Laboratory (Pennsylvania State University)
PRL . . . . Photoreactivating Light
PRL . . . . Pioneering Research Laboratory (Massachusetts) (Army)
PRL . . . . Plastics Research Laboratory (MIT)
PRL . . . . Precision Reduction Laboratory
PRL . . . . Progressive Republican League
PRL . . . . Project Research Laboratory
PRL . . . . Propulsion Research Laboratory
PRL . . . . Publications Requirements List
PRLTRL & M . . . Printer, Lithographer and Multilith Operator (Navy)
PRM . . . . Parti de Regroupement Mauritanien (Mauritanian Regroupment Party)
PRM . . . . Partial Response Method
PRM . . . . Partially Reflecting Mirror
PRM . . . . Personal Radiation Monitor (Military)
PRM . . . . Pilots Radio Manual
PRM . . . . Preliminary Requirements Model (NASA)
PRM . . . . Programming and Resources Management (NASA)
PRM . . . . Pulse Rate Modulation
PRMG . . . . . . Piston Ring Manufacturers Group
PRN . . . . Partido Republicano Nacional (National Republican Party) (Costa Rica)
PRN . . . . Pridie Nonas (The Day Before the Nones)
PRN . . . . Pro Re Nata (Whenever Necessary) (Medicine)
PRN . . . . Procurement Reallocation Notice
PRN . . . . Pseudo-Random Noise
PRN . . . . Pseudo-Random Number
PRN . . . . Puerto Rican Cement Company, Inc. (NYSE symbol)
PRN . . . . Pulse Ranging Navigation
pRNA . . . . . . Polysomal Ribonucleic Acid
PRNC . . . . . . Potomac River Naval Command (Washington, DC)
PRNC . . . . . . Puerto Rico Nuclear Center
PRO . . . . Parallel Rod Oscillator
PRO . . . . Particle Reduction Oven
PRO . . . . Parts Release Order
PRO . . . . Personnel Relations Officer (for Shore Stations) (Navy)
PRO . . . . Pitch Response Operator
PRO . . . . Planned Requirements, Outfitting (Navy)
PRO . . . . Proline (Amino acid)
PRO . . . . Public Record Office (British)
PRO . . . . Public Relations Office(r) (Usually military)
PROBCOST . . . Probabilistic Budgeting and Forward Costing
PROBE . . . . . . Performance Review of Base Supply Effectiveness (Air Force)
PROC . . . . . . Programming Computer
PROCD . . . . . . Procedure (or Proceed)
PROCO . . . . . Programed Combustion (Ford Motor Co.)
PROCOM . . . . Procurement Committee
PROCOMP . . . . Process Compiler

PROCOTIP.... Promotion Cooperative du Transport Individuel Publique (Public cars for private use to reduce traffic congestion) (Also known as TIP) (France)
PROCTOT .... Priority Routine Organizer for Computer Transfers and Operations and Transfers
PRODAC..... Programmed Digital Automatic Control (Data processing)
PRODC...... Production Command (Army)
PRODUTAS ... Proceed on Duty Assigned (Military)
PROF .... Peace Research Organization Fund
PROF .... Professor
PROF .... Pupil Registering and Operational Filing (Data processing)
PROFAC ..... Propulsive Fluid Accumulator
Prof Eng ..... Professional Engineer (Academic degree)
PROFILE .... Programmed Functional Indices for Laboratory Evaluation (RAND Corp.)
PROFIT ...... Program for Financed Insurance Techniques
PROFIT ...... Programmed Reviewing, Ordering and Forecasting Inventory Technique
PROFP ...... Proficiency Pay
PROGOFOP... Program of Operation (Data processing)
PROJ .... Project
PROJ .... Projectile
PROL .... Priority Requirement Objective List
PROLAN ..... Processed Language (Data processing)
PROLLAP..... Professional Library Literature Acquisition Program
PROLOG..... Program Logistics
PROLT ...... Procurement Lead Time
PROM...... Program, Resources, Objectives, Management (Air Force Systems Command technique)
PROM...... Promote (or Promotion)
PROMPT ..... Program to Record Official Mail Point-to-Point Times (Postal Service program)
PROMPT ..... Project Management and Production Team Technique (Data processing)
PROMPT ..... Project Reporting Organization & Management Planning Technique
PRONTO..... Program for Numeric Tool Operation (Data processing)
PROOF..... Precision Recording (Optical) of Fingerprints
PROP .... Planetary Rocket Ocean Platform
PROP .... Pre-Release Orientation Program (Reformatory program)
PROP .... Profit Rating of Projects
PROP .... Propaganda
PROP .... Propeller
PROP .... Property
PROP .... Proposed
PROP .... Proposition
PROP .... Proprietor
PRO-PAY.... Proficiency Pay (Military)
PROPR ...... Proprietor
PRORA ..... Programs for Research on Romance Authors
PROSAM.... Programmed Single-Axis Mount (Military camera)
PROSI....... Procedure Sign (Aviation)
PROSIG ..... Procedure Signal (Navy)
PROSIGN .... Procedure Sign (Army)
PROSIM ..... Production System Simulator (Data processing)
PROSINE .... Procedure Sign
PROTN ...... Procedure Turn (Aviation)
PROV....... Provinciale (Dutch)
PROV....... Provision
PROV....... Provisional
PROVCORPV.. Provisional Corps, Vietnam
PROVER ..... Procurement for Minimum Total Cost Through Value Engineering and Reliability
PROVER ..... Procurement, Value, Economy, Reliability
PROVOST .... Priority Research Objectives for Vietnam Operations Support
PROWORD.... Procedure Word
PRP........ Platelet-Rich Plasma
PRP........ Position Report Printout
PRP .... Postbuckled Rectangular Plate
PRP .... Production Requirements Plan
PRP .... Production Reserve Policy
PRP........ Pseudo-Random Pulse
PRP .... Public Relations Personnel (Navy)
PRP .... Pulse Repetition Period (RADAR)
PRPA ...... Professional Race Pilots Association
PRPP....... Phosphorylribose Pyrophosphate
PRPUC...... Philippine Republic Presidential Unit Citation (Military award)
PRPUCE..... Philippine Republic Presidential Unit Citation Emblem
PRR ...... Pawling Research Reactor (AEC)
PRR .... Pennsylvania R. R. (AAR code)
PRR .... Producer's Reliability Risk
PRR .... Proton Relaxation Rate
PRR .... Pulse Repetition Rate (RADAR)
PRRA ...... Puerto Rico Reconstruction Administration (Terminated, 1955)
PRRFC...... Planar Randomly Reinforced Fiber Composite
PRRI....... Puerto Rico Rum Institute

PRRM .... Philippine Rural Reconstruction Movement
PRRPA ...... Puerto Rico Rum Producers Association
PRS .... Pacific Rocket Society
PRS .... Parti de la Revolution Socialiste (Party of Socialist Revolution) (Benin – Senegal)
PRS .... Partido de la Revolucion Socialista (Party of the Socialist Revolution) (Cuba)
PRS .... Pattern Recognition Society
PRS......... Pattern Recognition System
PRS .... Pennsylvania-Reading Seashore Lines (AAR code)
PRS .... Performing Right Society
PRS .... Personal Recording System
PRS .... Personnel Readiness System (Air Force)
PRS .... Philatelic Research Society
PRS .... Photo Resist Spinner
PRS .... Photographic Reconnaissance System
PRS .... Physically Restricted Status (Military)
PRS .... Pneumatic Reading System
PRS .... Precision Ranging System
PRS .... Precision Rotary Stripper
PRS .... President of the Royal Society (British)
PRS .... Pressure Reducing Station
PRS .... Production Recording System
PRS .... Property Recovery Section
PRS .... Propodial Sinus
PRS .... Pseudo-Random Sequence
PRS .... Public Relations Section (Library Administration Division of ALA)
PRSA ...... President of the Royal Scottish Academy
PRSA ...... Public Relations Society of America
PRSEC ...... Payroll Section
PRSL ...... Pennsylvania-Reading Seashore Lines
PRSN ...... Provisional Relative Sunspot Number (NASA)
PRSS....... Pennsylvania-Reading Seashore Lines
PRSSA...... Public Relations Student Society of America
PRT .... Parr Terminal (AAR code)
PRT........ Pattern Recognition Technique
PRT .... Periodic Reevaluation Tests
PRT .... Personal Rapid Transit (Computer-guided transit system)
PRT .... Personnel Research Test
PRT .... Philadelphia Reading Test (Education)
PRT .... Platinum Resistance Thermometer
PRT .... Portable Radiation Thermometer
PRT .... Portable Radio Telephone
PRT .... Power Recovery Turbine
PRT........ Procurement Review Team
PRT .... Production Reliability Tests
PRT .... Program Reference Table
PRT .... Prova di Restituzione Termica (Italian) (Medicine)
PRT ......,.. Pulse-Repetition Time
PRT .... Pulsed RADAR Transmitter
PRTD .... Portland Traction Company (AAR code)
PRTG ...... Printing
PRTOT ...... Prototype Real-Time Optical Tracker (Data processing)
PRTR ...... Plutonium Recycle Test Reactor (AEC)
PRTRL...... Printer, Lithographer (Navy)
PRTRM...... Printer, Offset Process (Navy)
PRU .... Photographic Reconnaissance Unit (Aircraft) (Marine Corps)
PRU .... Provincial Reconnaissance Units (Military)
PRU .... Unit of peripheral resistance
PRUC ...... Partido Revolucionario de Union Civico (Revolutionary Party for Civic Union) (Costa Rica)
PRUD ...... Partido Revolucionario de Unificacion Democratica (Revolutionary Party of Democratic Unification) (El Salvador)
PRV .... Peak Reverse Voltage
PRV .... Pearl River Valley R. R. (AAR code)
PRV .... Pressure Reducing Valve
PRV .... Pressure Relief Valve
PRW .... Percent Rated Wattage
PRW .... Pressurized Water Reactor
PRWD ...... Priority Regular World Day
PRWI ...... Prince William Forest Park (National Park Service designation)
PRWRA ..... Puerto Rican Water Resources Authority
PRWV ...... Peak Reserve Working Voltage
PRX .... Pressure Regulation Exhaust
PRX .... Purex Corp., Ltd. (NYSE symbol)
PRY .... Pittsburgh Railways Corporation (NYSE symbol)
PS .... Packing Sheet
PS .... Painting System
PS .... Paleontological Society
PS .... Palm Society
PS .... Paradoxical Sleep

ACRONYMS AND INITIALISMS DICTIONARY

PS . . . . Parity Switch
PS . . . . Parlor Snake (Slang for "to escort visitors around post")
PS . . . . Partido Socialista (Socialist Party) (Chile)
PS . . . . Parts Shipper
PS . . . . Passenger Service
PS . . . . Passenger Steamer
PS . . . . Passing Scuttle
PS . . . . Patient's Serum (Medicine)
PS . . . . Payload Shroud
PS . . . . Paymaster Sergeant
PS . . . . Pedal Sinus
PS . . . . Penal Servitude
PS . . . . Per Ship
PS . . . . Perception Schedule
PS . . . . Permanent Secretary
PS . . . . Personnel Subsystem
PS . . . . Phase Shift
PS . . . . Philippine Scouts
PS . . . . Photochemical System
PS . . . . Photographic Service
PS . . . . Picket Ships (Navy)
PS . . . . Pistol Sharpshooter (Army)
PS . . . . Pittsburg & Shawmut R. R. (AAR code)
PS . . . . Planning and Scheduling
PS . . . . Plastic Surgery (Medicine)
PS . . . . Plotting System
PS . . . . Point of Switch
PS . . . . Point of Symmetry
PS . . . . Police Sergeant
PS . . . . Polystyrene
PS . . . . Polysulfone
PS . . . . Port Security
PS . . . . Post Scriptum (Written Afterwards; a postscript)
PS . . . . Postal Service (US)
PS . . . . Potentiometer Synchro
PS . . . . Power Supply
PS . . . . Preliminary Study
PS . . . . Pressure Switch
PS . . . . Prior Service
PS . . . . Private Secretary
PS . . . . Privy Seal (British)
PS . . . . Process Specification
PS . . . . Procurement Specification
PS . . . . Program Summary
PS . . . . Project Slip
PS . . . . Prompt Side (of a stage) (i.e., the right side) (A stage direction)
PS . . . . Proof Shot (Ammunition)
PS . . . . Proton Synchrotron (AEC)
PS . . . . Psychonomic Society
PS . . . . Pubblica Sicurezza
PS . . . . Public Sale
PS . . . . Public School
PS . . . . Public Stenographer
PS . . . . Puget Sound, Washington, and Puget Sound Naval Shipyard
PS . . . . Pull Switch
PS . . . . Pulmonary Stenosis
PS . . . . Pulse Shaper
PS . . . . Pulse Stretcher
PS . . . . Purity-Supreme (Supermarkets)
PS . . . . South Pole
PS . . . . Transport (Russian aircraft symbol)
P-S. . . . . Pressure-Sensitive
P/S. . . . . Point of Shipment
P/S . . . . Power Section
P & S . . . . . . Packers and Stockyards
P & S. . . . . . Paracentesis and Suction (Medicine)
P & S. . . . . . Pay and Supply (Coast Guard)
P & S. . . . . . Pittsburg & Shawmut Railroad Company
P & S . . . . . Port and Starboard
PSA . . . . Pacific Science Association
PSA . . . . Pacific Southwest Airlines (NYSE symbol)
PSA . . . . Parti Solidaire Africain (African Solidarity Party) (Congo - Leopoldville)
PSA . . . . Particle Size Analyzer
PSA . . . . Partido Socialista Argentino (Moderate socialist political party) (Argentina)
PSA . . . . Philippine Sugar Association
PSA . . . . Philosophy of Science Association
PSA . . . . Photographic Society of America
PSA . . . . Phycological Society of America
PSA . . . . Pisces Society of America
PSA . . . . Pitch Servo Assembly

PSA . . . . Play Schools Association
PSA . . . . Pleasant Sunday Afternoon(s)
PSA . . . . Poetry Society of America
PSA . . . . Polysilicic Acid
PSA . . . . Portable Sound Analyzer
PSA . . . . Post Shakedown Availability
PSA . . . . Poultry Science Association
PSA . . . . Power and Servo Assembly
PSA . . . . President of the Society of Antiquaries (British)
PSA . . . . Professional Skills Alliance
PSA . . . . Public Service Announcement (Radio/TV)
P & SA . . . . . Packers and Stockyards Administration (Department of Agriculture)
PSAA . . . . . . Pakistan Students' Association of America
PSAA . . . . . . Polish Singers Alliance of America
PSAC . . . . . . Passive Satellite Attitude Control
PSAC . . . . . . Personnel Service Company (Army)
PSAC . . . . . . President's Science Advisory Committee (Executive Office of the President)
PSAD . . . . . . Prediction, Simulation, Adaptation, Decision (Data processing)
PSAL . . . . . . Public Schools Athletic League
PSANDT . . . . Pay, Subsistence, and Transportation (Military)
PSAP. . . . . . . Plane Stress Analysis and Plot (Data processing)
PSAT . . . . . . Preliminary Scholastic Aptitude Test
PSAUSA . . . . . Polish Socialist Alliance of the United States of America
PSB . . . . Parti Socialiste Belge (Belgian Socialist Party)
PSBH . . . . . . Pad Safety in Blockhouse
PSBLS . . . . . Permanent Space Based Logistics System
PSC . . . . Pacific Science Center
PSC . . . . Pacific Science Council
PSC . . . . Pacific Studies Center
PSC . . . . Palmer Skin Conductance
PSC . . . . Parallel to Serial Converter
PSC . . . . Parti Social Chretien (Christian Social Party) (Belgium)
PSC . . . . Parti Socialiste Camerounais (Cameroonese Socialist Party)
PSC . . . . Partido Social Cristiano (Social Christian Party) (Bolivia)
PSC . . . . Passed Staff College (British)
PSC . . . . Paul Smith College (New York)
PSC . . . . Peacetime Subcontract
PSC . . . . Pembroke State College (North Carolina)
PSC . . . . Per Standard Compass (Navigation)
PSC . . . . Philadelphia Suburban Corporation (NYSE symbol)
PSC . . . . Philander Smith College (Arkansas)
PSC . . . . Pittsburgh Steel Company (NYSE symbol) (Delisted)
PSC . . . . Polaroid Stereoscopic Chroncyclegraph
PSC . . . . Porcelain on Steel Council
PSC . . . . Portland State College (Oregon)
PSC . . . . Postal Service Center
PSC . . . . Posterior Subcapsular Cataracts
PSC . . . . Potentiometer Strip Chart
PSC . . . . Potomac State College (of West Virginia University)
PSC . . . . Power Supply Calibrator
PSC . . . . Procurement Source Code
PSC . . . . Product Safety Commission (Proposed) (HEW)
PSCP. . . . . . . Program Status Chart
PSC . . . . Program Structure Code
PSC . . . . Public Service Careers Program (Department of Labor)
PSC . . . . Public Service Commission (Usually, of a specific state)
PSC . . . . Public Service Company
PSCLA . . . . . Petroleum Supply Committee for Latin America
PSCO . . . . . . Pacific Scientific Company
PSCO . . . . . . Pennsylvania State College of Optometry
PSCP . . . . . . Palestine Symphonic Choir Project
PSD . . . . Doctor of Political Science
Ps D . . . . Doctor of Psychology
Ps D . . . . Doctor of Psychology in Metaphysics
PSD . . . . Doctor of Public Service
PSD . . . . Parti Social Democrate de Madagascar et des Comores (Social Democratic Party of Madagascar and Comores)
PSD . . . . Partido Social Democratico (Social Democratic Party) (Brazil, El Salvador)
PSD . . . . Passing Scene Display
PSD . . . . Past Start Date
PSD . . . . Personnel Services Division (Army)
PSD . . . . Phase-Sensitive Demodulator
PSD . . . . Phase-Sensitive Detector
PSD . . . . Pitch Servo Drive
PSD . . . . Power Spectral (or Spectrum) Density
PSD . . . . Procurement Surveys Division (NASA)
PSD . . . . Promotion Service Date
PSD . . . . Propellant Slosh Dynamics
PSD . . . . Propellant Storage Depot (NASA)
PSD . . . . Protective Serum Dilution

PSD . . . . Pseudosingle Domain (Behavior of grains in rocks) (Geophysics)
PSD . . . . Puget Sound Power & Light Company (NYSE symbol)
PSD . . . . Pulse Shape Discriminator
PSD . . . . Pure Screw Dislocation
PSDC . . . . . . Protective Structures Development Center (Military)
PSDF . . . . Popular Self-Defense Force (Local armed units protecting Vietnamese hamlets)
PSDI. . . . . . . Partito Socialista Democratico Italiano (Italian Social Democratic Party)
PSDP . . . . . . Personnel Subsystem Development Plan
PSDS . . . . . . Passing Scene Display System
PSDS . . . . . . Permanently Separated from Duty Station (Military)
PSE . . . . Passive Seismic Experiment (NASA)
PSE . . . . Phase Shifter, Electronic
PSE . . . . Pitch Steering Error
PSE . . . . Point of Subjective Equality (Psychology)
PSE . . . . Pressurized Subcritical Experiment
PSE . . . . Product Support Engineering
PSE . . . . Psychological Stress Evaluator (Lie detector)
PSE . . . . Pulse Sense
PSEA . . . . . . Physical Security Equipment Agency
PSEA . . . . . . Pleaters, Stitchers and Embroiderers Association
PSEC . . . . . . Picosecond
PSE & G . . . . Public Service Electric & Gas Company
PSEMA . . . . . Parti Social d'Education des Masses Africaines (African Party for Social Education of the Masses) (Upper Volta)
PSEP . . . . Passive Seismic Experiments Package (NASA)
PSEQ . . . . . . Pupil Services Expectation Questionnaire
PSF . . . . Panama Sea Frontier
PSF . . . . Panhandle & Santa Fe Railway Company (AAR code)
PSF . . . . Parti Social Francais
PSF . . . . Payload Structure Fuel (Ratio)
PSF. . . . . . . Permanent Signal Finder
PSF . . . . Philippine Sea Frontier
PSF . . . . Point Spread Function
PSF . . . . Pounds per Square Foot
PSF . . . . Prime Subframe
P & SF . . . . . Panhandle and Santa Fe Railway Company
PSFL. . . . . . . Puget Sound Freight Lines (AAR code)
PSFQ . . . . . . Pupil Services Fulfillment Questionnaire
PSG . . . . Pechiney-Saint-Gobain (France)
PSG . . . . Platoon Sergeant (Army)
PSG . . . . Pulse Sweep Generator
PSGR . . . . . . Passenger
PSGW . . . . . . Past Senior Grand Warden (Masonry)
PSH . . . . Pre-Select Heading
PSH . . . . Program Support Handbook
PSH . . . . Proximity Sensing Head
PSH . . . . Publications Statistiques Hongroises (Hungary)
PSI . . . . Pacific Semiconductors, Incorporated
PSI. . . . . Partai Socialis Indonesia
PSI. . . . . Partito Socialista Italiano (Italian Socialist Party)
PSI. . . . . Phenomenological Systems, Incorporated
PSI . . . . Plan Speed Indicator
PSI . . . . Pounds per Square Inch
PSI. . . . . Praed Street Irregulars (An organization)
PSI. . . . . Problem Solving Information (Apparatus)
PSI. . . . . Protosynthex Index
PSI . . . . Public Services International
P & SI . . . . . Pay and Supply Instruction (Coast Guard)
PSIA . . . . . . Paper Stock Institute of America
PSIA. . . . . . . Pounds per Square Inch Absolute
PSIA . . . . . . Professional Ski Instructors of America
PSIC. . . . . . . Passenger Service Improvement Corporation
PSICP . . . . . . Program Support Inventory Control Point
PSID. . . . . . . Patrol Seismic Intrusion Detector (DOD)
PSID. . . . . . . Pounds per Square Inch Differential
PSIEP . . . . . . Project in Scientific Information Exchange in Psychology
PSIG . . . . . . Pounds per Square Inch Gage
PSIL. . . . . . . Preferred Speech Interference Level
PSJ. . . . . Parallel Swivel Joint
PSJ . . . . Plane Swivel Joint
PSJ . . . . Pressure Switch Joint
PSK . . . . . . Phase-Shift Key
PSK . . . . Power Supply Kit
PSK . . . . Protection Survey Kit
PSL . . . . Peabody Short Line R. R. (AAR code)
PSL . . . . Photographic Science Laboratory (Navy)
PSL . . . . Physical Sciences Laboratory
PSL . . . . Pressure Sensitive Label
PSL . . . . Primary Standards Laboratory
PSLA . . . . . . Polish Sea League of America

PSLLS . . . . . . Pulsed Solid-State LASER Light Source
PSM . . . . Paste Striping Machine
PSM . . . . Peak Selector Memory (Data processing)
PSM . . . . Pennsalt Corp. (Formerly, Pennsalt Chemicals Corp.) (NYSE symbol)
PSM . . . . Personnel Systems Management (Air Force)
PSM . . . . Phase Shifter Module
PSM . . . . Pia Societas Missionum (Fathers of the Pious Society of Missions, Pallottini) (Roman Catholic religious order)
PSM . . . . Power Strapping Machine
PSM . . . . Power System Module
PSM . . . . Program Sensitive Malfunction
PSM . . . . Propellant Storage Module
PS & M . . . . . Personnel Supervision and Management Division of ASTSECNAV's Office (Absorbed into SECP, 1944)
PSMA . . . . . . Power Saw Manufacturers Association
PSMA . . . . . . Progressive Spinal Muscular Atrophy (Medicine)
PSMD . . . . . . Photo Selective Metal Deposition
PSMFC . . . . . . Pacific States Marine Fisheries Commission
PSMI . . . . . . Precise Ship Motion Instrument
PSMMA . . . . . Plastic Soft Materials Manufacturers Association
PSMR . . . . . . Parts Specification Management for Reliability
PSMSL . . . . . . The Permanent Service for Mean Sea Level
PS & N . . . . . Pittsburg, Shawmut & Northern Railroad Company
PSNA . . . . . . Phytochemical Society of North America
PSNCF . . . . . . Pacific Southern Naval Coastal Frontier
PSNCO . . . . . Personnel Staff Noncommissioned Officer (Military)
P & SNP . . . . Pay and Subsistence of Naval Personnel (Budget appropriation title)
PSNS . . . . . . Physical Science for Nonscience Students
PSNS . . . . . . Puget Sound Naval Shipyard
PSNSY . . . . . Puget Sound Naval Shipyard
PSO . . . . Pad Safety Officer (Aerospace)
PSO . . . . Paint Spray Outfit
PSO . . . . Pauli Spin Operator
PSO . . . . Pilot Systems Operator
PSO . . . . Political Survey Officers (Navy)
PSO . . . . Primary Standardization Office
PSO . . . . Principal Scientific Officer
PSO . . . . Procurement Services Office
PSO . . . . Provisions Supply Office
PSO . . . . Publicity Security Officer (Navy)
PSP . . . . Package Size Proneness (Marketing)
PSP . . . . Pad Safety Plan
PSP . . . . Parti Soudanais Progressiste (Sudanese Progressive Party) (Mali)
PSP. . . . . Partido Social Progresista (Social Progressive Party) (Brazil)
PSP. . . . . Parts Screening Program
PSP . . . . Patrol Seaplane
PSP. . . . . Pauli Sound Pressure
PSP. . . . . Pauli Speech Power
PSP . . . . Performance Standards Program
PSP . . . . Personal Success Program
PSP . . . . Phenolsulfonephthalein (for kidney function test)
PSP . . . . Pierced Steel Planking (Military)
PSP . . . . Planned Standard Programming (Data processing)
PSP . . . . Platform Sensor Package
PSP . . . . Postsynaptic Potential
PSP . . . . Power System Planning
PSP . . . . Primary Supply Point (Military)
PSP . . . . Primary Support Point (Military)
PSP . . . . Product Support Program
PSP. . . . . Program Support Plan
PSPL . . . . . . Priced Spare Parts List
PSPMW . . . . . International Brotherhood of Pulp, Sulphite and Paper Mill Workers
PSPP . . . . . . Preliminary System Package Plan
PSPP . . . . . . Program System Package Plan
PSPP . . . . . . Proposed System Package Plan
PSPS . . . . . . Paddle Steamer Preservation Society
PSPS . . . . . . Program Support Plan Summary
PSPT. . . . . . . Planar Silicon Power Transistor
PSQ . . . . . . Personal Security Questionnaire
PSR . . . . Pacific Sociological Review (A publication)
PSR . . . . Packed Snow on Runway (Aviation)
PSR . . . . Pain Sensitivity Range (Biometrics)
PSR . . . . Panoramic Stereo Rectification
PSR . . . . Parachute Status Report (Army)
PSR . . . . Partiia Sotsialistov-Revoliutionerov
PSR . . . . Passenger Standing Route Order (Army)
PSR . . . . Perfectly Stirred Reactor
PSR . . . . Performance Summary Report
PSR . . . . Petaluma & Santa Rosa R. R. (AAR code)
PSR . . . . Phase Sequence Relay
PSR . . . . Physicians for Social Responsibility

PSR . . . . Plow-Steel Rope
PSR . . . . Processor State Register
PSR . . . . Progress Summary Report
PSR . . . . Project Summary Report
PSR . . . . Public Service Company of Colorado (NYSE symbol)
PSRAAALAA. . . President's Special Representative and Adviser on African, Asian, and Latin American Affairs (Department of State)
PSRD . . . . Personnel Shipment Ready Date (Army)
PSRD . . . . Professional Standard Review Organization (Proposed)
PSRF. . . . . . . Profit Sharing Research Foundation
PSRI . . . . Particulate Solid Research Institute
PSRI . . . . Position Subject Return of Incumbent
PSRMA . . . . . . Pacific Southwest Railway Museum Association
PSRS. . . . . . . Position Subject to Rotating Shifts
PSRT . . . . Passive Satellite Research Terminal
PSS . . . . Parti de Solidarite Senegalaise (Senegalese Solidarity Party)
PSS . . . . Partito Socialista Somalo (Somali Socialist Party)
PSS . . . . Passenger Service Systems (Airlines)
PSS . . . . Patent Searching System (Data processing)
PSS . . . . Pauli Spin Susceptibility
PSS . . . . Personal Signaling System
PSS . . . . Personnel Subsystem (Air Force)
PSS . . . . Personnel Support System (Army)
PSS . . . . Physiological Saline Solution (Physiology)
PSS . . . . Planetary Scan System
PSS . . . . Plant Science Seminar
PSS . . . . Plunger Snap Switch
PSS . . . . Polystyrene Sulfonate (Organic chemistry)
PSS . . . . Postal Savings System (Terminated, 1966)
PSS. . . . . Postscripts
PSS . . . . Power Supply Section
PSS . . . . Power System Synthesizer
PSS . . . . Precancel Stamp Society
PSS . . . . Presbyteri Sancti Sulpicii (Sulpicians) (Roman Catholic men's religious order)
PSS . . . . Propellant Supply Subsystem
PSS . . . . Pushbutton Selection Station
P/S/S . . . . Price/Stern/Sloan (Publishers)
PSSA . . . . . . Pitch Starting Synchro Assembly
PSSB. . . . . . . Passing Stopped School Bus (Traffic offense charge)
PSSC . . . . Physical Sciences Study Committee (India)
PSSC . . . . Pious Society of Missionaries of St. Charles (Later, CS) (Roman Catholic men's religious order)
PSSEP . . . . . . Preliminary System Safety Engineering Plan
PSSG . . . . Physical Science Study Group
PSSMA . . . . . . Paper Shipping Sack Manufacturers' Association
PSSO . . . . . . Pass Slip Stitch Over (Knitting)
PSSR. . . . . . . Parallel-Shaft Speed Reducer
PSSTA . . . . . . Port Security Station (Coast Guard)
PST . . . . Pacific Standard Time
PST. . . . . Paired Selected Ternary (Data processing)
PST . . . . Periodic Self-Test (Data processing)
PST . . . . Petrie Stores Corp. (NYSE symbol)
PST . . . . Piston Shock Tunnel
PST . . . . Polaris Star Tracker
PST . . . . Post-Stimulus Time
PST . . . . Pressure Sensitive Tape
PS & T . . . . . . Pay, Subsistence, and Transportation (Military)
PSTC . . . . . . Pressure Sensitive Tape Council
PSTE. . . . . . . Personnel Subsystem Test and Evaluation
PSTEP . . . . . . Pre-Service Teacher Education Program (National Science Foundation)
PSTF. . . . . . . Profit-Sharing Trust Fund
PSTGC . . . . . . Per Steering Compass (Navigation)
PSTL. . . . . . . Postal
PSTMA . . . . . . Paper Stationery and Tablet Manufacturers Association
PS & TN . . . . . Pay, Subsistence and Transportation, Navy
PSTO . . . . . . Principal Sea Transport Officer
PSTV . . . . . . Potato Spindle Tuber Virus
PSU . . . . Parti Socialiste Unifie (United Socialist Party) (France)
PSU . . . . Pennsylvania State University
PSU . . . . Photosynthetic Unit
PSU . . . . Plasma Spray Unit
PSU . . . . Primary Sampling Unit (Statistics)
PSU . . . . South Puerto Rico Sugar Company (NYSE symbol) (Delisted)
PSUB . . . . . . Piston Supported Upper Bearing
PSUR . . . . . . Pennsylvania State University Reactor
PSURAO . . . . . Pennsylvania State University Radio Astronomy Observatory
PSurg . . . . . . Plastic Surgery (Medicine)
PSV . . . . Pilotage Sans Visibilite
PSV . . . . Positive Start Voltage
PSV . . . . Probability State Variable

PSVM . . . . Phase Sensitive Voltmeter
PSVM . . . . Phase Shift Voltmeter
PSVOA . . . . . . Purse Seine Vessel Owners Association
PSVOMA . . . . Purse Seine Vessel Owners Marketing Association
PSW . . . . Plasma Spray Welder
PSW . . . . Potentiometer Slidewire
PSW . . . . Powerplant Specific Weight
PSW . . . . Program Status Word
PSW . . . . Psychiatric Social Worker
PSWG. . . . . . . Pressure Sine Wave Generator
PSWR . . . . . . Power Standing Wave Ratio
PSWTUF . . . . . Public Service Workers' Trade Union Federation (Ceylon)
PSY . . . . Pillsbury Company (NYSE symbol)
PSYCH . . . . . . Psychology
PSYCHL . . . . . . Psychological
PSYOP . . . . . . Psychological Operations (Military)
PSYWAR . . . . . Psychological Warfare
PSYWPN . . . . . Psychological Weapon (Military)
PSZ . . . . Pressure Sealing Zipper
PT . . . . Motor Torpedo Boat (Navy symbol)
PT . . . . Pacific Time
PT . . . . Pain Threshold
PT . . . . Paper Tape
PT . . . . Paper Trooper (One who salvaged paper for war effort) (World War II)
PT . . . . Part
PT . . . . Paschale Tempore (Easter Time)
PT . . . . Past Tense
PT . . . . Patrol Torpedo Boat (Navy)
PT . . . . Payment
PT . . . . Pencil Tube
PT . . . . Peninsula Terminal (AAR code)
PT . . . . Performance Test
PT . . . . Persistent Tease (Slang) (Bowdlerized version)
PT . . . . Personal Trade (In some retail establishments, customers are assigned to salesmen in rotation. A customer who is the "PT" or personal client of a salesman is not counted as part of the salesman's share of customers)
PT . . . . Petty Theft
PT . . . . Photographic Intelligenceman (Navy rating)
PT . . . . Physical Therapy
PT . . . . Physical Training
PT . . . . Pint
PT . . . . Plastic Tube
Pt . . . . Platinum (Chemical element)
PT . . . . Plenty Tough (Slang)
PT . . . . Plenty Trouble (Slang)
PT . . . . Pneumatic Tube (Technical drawings)
PT . . . . Point
PT . . . . Point of Tangency
PT . . . . Point of Turn (Navigation)
PT . . . . Port
PT . . . . Positional Tolerancing
PT . . . . Post Town
PT . . . . Postal Telegraph Company (Terminated)
PT . . . . Potential Transformer
PT . . . . Primary Target (Army)
PT . . . . Primary Trainer (Aircraft)
PT . . . . Private Terms
PT . . . . Pro Tempore (For the Time Being)
PT . . . . Procedure Turn (Aviation)
PT . . . . Production Techniques
PT . . . . Production Test
PT . . . . Profile Template
PT . . . . Programmer and Timer
PT . . . . Propellant Transfer
PT . . . . Propeller Torpedo (Boat)
PT . . . . Prothrombin Time (Medicine)
PT . . . . Provincetown-Boston Airline, Inc.
PT . . . . Pulse Timer
PT . . . . Pulse Train
PT . . . . Punched Tape
PT . . . . Pupil Teacher
PT . . . . Pyramidal Tract
P/T . . . . Personnel and Training (Navy)
P & T . . . . . . Permanent and Total (Disability)
P & T . . . . . . Posts and Timbers (Technical drawings)
PTA . . . . National Postal Transport Association
PTA . . . . Paper and Twine Association
PTA . . . . Parent-Teacher Association
PTA . . . . Passenger Transport Authorities (British)
PTA . . . . People Taking Action (An organization)

ACRONYMS AND INITIALISMS DICTIONARY

PTA . . . . Phenyltrimethylammonium
PTA . . . . Phosphotungstic Acid
PTA . . . . Photographers' Telegraph Association
PTA . . . . Phototransistor Amplifier
PTA . . . . Pitch Trim Adjustment
PTA . . . . Plasma Thromboplastin Antecedent (Factor X) (Physiology)
PTA . . . . Pope & Talbot Line (AAR code)
PTA . . . . Post-Traumatic Amnesia (Medicine)
PTA . . . . Primary Target Area
PTA . . . . Prior to Admission
PTA . . . . Program Time Analyzer
PTA . . . . Proposed Technical Approach
PTA . . . . Protestant Teachers Association
PTA . . . . Proton Target Area
PTAC . . . . . . Plant Transportation Advisory Committee
PTAD . . . . Productivity and Technical Assistance Division (Mutual Security Agency) (Abolished, 1953)
PTAH . . . . . . Phosphotungstic Acid-Hematoxylin (A stain)
PTB . . . . Partido Trabalhista Brasileiro (Brazilian Workers' Party)
PTB . . . . Physikalisch-Technische Bundesanstalt (West Germany)
PTB . . . . Pressure Test Barrel
PTBR . . . . . . Punched Tape Block Reader (Data processing)
PTC . . . . Pacific Tin Consolidated Corporation (NYSE symbol)
PTC . . . . Pacific Tuna Conference
PTC . . . . Parti Travailliste Congolais (Congolese Labor Party)
PTC . . . . Passive Thermal Control (NASA)
PTC . . . . Patrol Vessel, Motor Torpedo Boat, Submarine Chaser (Navy symbol)
PTC . . . . Peoria Terminal Company (AAR code)
PTC . . . . Personnel Transfer Capsule (Undersea technology)
PTC . . . . Personnel Transfer Chamber
PTC . . . . Personnel Transport Carrier
PTC . . . . Phenylthiocarbamide
PTC . . . . Pipe and Tobacco Council
PTC . . . . Pitch Trim Compensator
PTC . . . . Plan to Clear (Aviation)
PTC . . . . Plasma Thromboplastin Component (Physiology)
PTC . . . . Pneumatic Temperature Control
PTC . . . . Pneumatic Test Console
PTC . . . . Positive Target Control
PTC . . . . Positive Temperature Coefficient
PTC . . . . Positive Transmitter Control
PTC . . . . Postal Telegraph Cable
PTC . . . . Power Testing Code
PTC . . . . Power Transfer Coefficient
PTC . . . . Power Transmission Council
PTC . . . . Pressure Transducer Calibrator
PTC . . . . Programmable Test Console
PTC . . . . Programmer Training Center
PTC . . . . Pulse Time Code
PTCA . . . . . . Pressure Technology Corporation of America
PTCA . . . . . . Private Truck Council of America
PTCAD . . . . . Provisional Troop Carrier Airborne Division
PTCC . . . . . . Pacific Division Transport Control Center
PTCCS . . . . . Polaris Target Card Computing System
PTCLD . . . . . Part Called (NYSE symbol)
PTCR . . . . . . Pad Terminal Connection Room
PTCRM . . . . . Partial Thermochemical Remanent Magnetization
PTCS . . . . . . Pax Tibi Cum Sanctis (Peace to Thee with the Saints)
PTCS . . . . . . Pressure Transducer Calibration System
PTCV . . . . . . Pilot-Operated Temperature Control Valve
PTDA . . . . . . Power Transmission Distributors Association
PTDP . . . . . . Preliminary (or Proposed) Technical Development Plan
PTDQ . . . . . . Polymerized Trimethyl Dihydro Quinoline
PTDS . . . . . . Photo Target Detection System
PTDTL . . . . . Pumped Tunnel Diode Transistor Logic
PTE . . . . Parathyroid Extract (Medicine)
PTE . . . . Parmelee Transportation Company (NYSE symbol) (Delisted)
PTE . . . . Peculiar Test Equipment
PTE . . . . Private (British)
PTE . . . . Production Test Equipment
PT & E . . . . . Progress Tests and Examinations
PTEC . . . . . . Plastics Technical Evaluation Center (Army)
PTETS . . . . . Pioneer Television and Electronic Technicians Society
PTF . . . . Patrol Torpedo Boat, Fast (Navy symbol)
PTF . . . . Plasma Thromboplastin Factor (Physiology)
PTF . . . . Police Training Foundation
PTF . . . . Power Test Fail
PTF . . . . Program Temporary Fix (Data processing)
PTF . . . . Propellant Tank Flow
PTFE . . . . . . Polytetrafluoroethylene
PTFMO . . . . . Peacetime Force Materiel Objective

PTFMPO . . . . . Peacetime Force Materiel Procurement Objective
PTFMR . . . . . Peacetime Force Materiel Requirements
PTFMR-A . . . . Peacetime Force Materiel Requirements – Acquisition (Army)
PTFMR-R . . . . Peacetime Force Materiel Requirements – Retention (Army)
PTG . . . . Parent-Teacher Group
PTG . . . . Piano Technicians Guild
PTG . . . . Pressure Test (or Transfer) Gauge
PTG . . . . Professional Technical Group
PTG . . . . Prothoracic Glands (in insects)
PTG . . . . Pulse Target Generator
PTGANE . . . . . Professional Technical Group on Aerospace and Navigation Electronics
PTGAP . . . . . Professional Technical Group on Antennas and Propagation
PTGAS . . . . . Professional Technical Group on Aerospace
PTGC . . . . . . Programmed Temperature Gas Chromatography
PTGEC . . . . . Professional Technical Group on Electronic Computers (Affiliated with IEEE)
PTGEWS . . . . Professional Technical Group on Engineering Writing and Speech (of the IEEE)
PTGRFI . . . . . Professional Technical Group on Radio Frequency Interference
PTGS . . . . . . Portable Telemetry Ground Station
PTGT . . . . . . Primary Target
PTGWO . . . . . Philippine Transport and General Workers' Organization
PTH . . . . Pallet Torque Hook
PTH . . . . Parathyroid Hormone
PTH . . . . Phenylthiohydantoin (Chemistry)
PTH . . . . Plated Through Hole
P Th B . . . . . . Bachelor of Practical Theology
PTI . . . . Persistent Tolerant Infection
PTI . . . . Personnel Transaction Identifier (Air Force)
PTI . . . . Philadelphia Textile Institute
PTI . . . . Physical-Technical Institute (USSR)
PTI . . . . Pictorial Test of Intelligence (Education)
PTI . . . . Porous Tungsten Ionizer
PTI . . . . Power Tool Institute (Formerly, Electric Tool Institute)
PTIWU . . . . . Posts and Telegraphs Industrial Workers' Union (India)
PTJA . . . . . . Plan to Join Airways
PTK . . . . Polishing Tool Kit
PTK . . . . Potentiometer Tapping Kit
PTL . . . . Pocket Testament League
PTL . . . . Pressure, Torque, and Load
PTL . . . . Primary Target Line (Military)
PTLA . . . . . . Praise the Lord Anyway
PTLA . . . . . . Publishers' Trade List Annual
PTM . . . . Pattern Transformation Memory
PTM . . . . Pneumatic Telescope Mast
PTM . . . . Portland Terminal Company (AAR code)
PTM . . . . Program Timing and Maintenance
PTM . . . . Program Timing and Miscellaneous (Electronics)
PTM . . . . Proof Test Model (NASA)
PTM . . . . Pulse Time Modulation (Radio)
PTM . . . . Pulse Time Multiplex
PTMS . . . . . . Pattern Transformation Memory System
PTMT . . . . . . Polytetramethylene Terephthalate (Plastic)
PTN . . . . Partido Trabhista Nacional (National Workers' Party) (Brazil)
PTN . . . . Procedure Turn (Aviation)
PTO . . . . Pacific Theater of Operations (World War II)
PTO . . . . Petrolane, Inc. (NYSE symbol)
PTO . . . . Please Turn Over (the page)
PTO . . . . Port Transportation Officer
PTO . . . . Power Take-Off
PTO . . . . Propellant Transfer Operation
PTO . . . . Protivo-Tankovaia Oborona (Antitank Defense) (in USSR field forces)
PTOA . . . . . . Projective Tests of Attitudes
PTOS . . . . . . Peacetime Operating Stock (Military)
PTP . . . . Paper Tape Perforator
PTP . . . . Paper Tape Punch
PTP . . . . Parti Togolais du Progres (Party for Togolese Progress)
PTP . . . . Peak to Peak
PTP . . . . People-to-People
PTP . . . . Point-to-Point
PTP . . . . Porous Tungsten Plug
PTP . . . . Primary Target Point (NASA)
PTP . . . . Programmed Turn Phase
PTPD . . . . . . Part Paid (NYSE symbol)
PTPI . . . . . . Professional and Technical Programs, Incorporated
PTPS . . . . . . Package Test Power Supply
PTPU . . . . . . Program Tape Preparation Unit
PTR . . . . Paper Tape Reader
PTR . . . . Parts Tool Requirements File
PTR . . . . Patuxent River (Navy)
PTR . . . . Perforated Tape Reader
PTR . . . . Photoelectric Tape Reader

465

PTR . . . . Physikalisch-Technische Reichsanstalt
PTR . . . . Plug-Type Receptacle
PTR . . . . Pool Test Reactor
PTR . . . . Pool Training Reactor
PTR . . . . Portable Tape Recorder
PTR. . . . . . . Position Track RADAR
PTR . . . . Precision Transmitter Receiver
PTR . . . . **Preliminary Technical Report**
PTR . . . . Pressure-Tube Reactor (AEC)
PTR . . . . Pre-Transmit Receiving
PTR . . . . Processor Tape Read
PTR . . . . Proof Test Reactor (AEC)
PTR . . . . Punched Tape Reader
PTRC . . . . . . Personnel & Training Research Center (Air Force)
PTRD . . . . . . Part Redeemed (NYSE symbol)
PTRJ . . . . . . Powered Thermocouple Reference Junction
PTS . . . . Parameter Test Setup
PTS . . . . Photogrammetric Triangulation System
PTS . . . . Pneumatic Test Set
PTS . . . . Pod Tail Section
PTS . . . . Port Townsend R. R. (AAR code)
PTS . . . . Precision Timing System
PTS . . . . Programmable Terminal System (Aviation)
PTS . . . . Programmer Test Station
PTS . . . . Propellant Transfer System
PTSA . . . . . . Parent-Teacher-Student Association (Nickname: "Pizza")
PTSE . . . . . . Paper Tape Splicing Equipment
PTSR . . . . . . Pressure Tube Superheat Reactor (AEC)
PTSS . . . . . . Princeton Time Sharing Services (Inc.)
PTT . . . . Cleveland & Pittsburgh R. R. Company (NYSE symbol)
PTT . . . . Pacific Telephone and Telegraph Company
PTT . . . . Partial Thromboplastin Time
PTT . . . . **Physical Therapist Technician**
PTT . . . . Postes, Telegraphes, et Telephones (Post, Telegraph, and Telephone) (General Post Office) (France)
PTT . . . . Production Type Test
PTT . . . . Program Technical Training
PTT. . . . . . . Push to Talk
PTTC . . . . . . Pacific Transportation Terminal Command (Army)
PTTI . . . . Postal, Telegraph and Telephone International
PTTI . . . . Precise Time and Time Interval
PTTL . . . . . . Press-to-Test Light
PTU . . . . Phenylthiourea (Medicine)
PTUC . . . . . . **Philippine Trade Union Council**
PTV . . . . Parachute Test Vehicle
PTV . . . . Peak to Valley
PTV . . . . Penetration Test Vehicle (Aerospace)
PTV . . . . Propulsion Test Vehicles
PTV . . . . Public Television
PTV . . . . Punched Tape Verifier
PTVA . . . . . . Propulsion Test Vehicle Assembly (NASA)
PTVD . . . . . . Portable Toxic Vapor Detector
PTW . . . . . . Pressure-Type Window
PTWF . . . . . . Pakistan Transport Workers' Federation
PTWT . . . . . . Photo-Type Traveling Wave Tube
PTX . . . . Polythermalex
PU . . . . Paid Up
PU . . . . Parts Used (Medicine)
PU . . . . Pick-Up (Business and trade)
PU . . . . Plant Unit(s)
Pu . . . . Plutonium (Chemical element)
PU . . . . Polyurethane
PU . . . . Power Unit
PU . . . . Pregnancy Urine (Medicine)
PU . . . . Propellant Utilization (Air Force)
PU . . . . Pullman Inc. (NYSE symbol)
PUA . . . . Polish Union of America
PUAA . . . . . . Public Utilities Advertising Association
PUAD . . . . . . Pueblo Army Depot
PUAS . . . . . . Postal Union of the Americas and Spain
PUB . . . . Publication
PUBC . . . . . . Presbyterians United for Biblical Concern
PUBINFO . . . . Office of Public Information (Formerly, Office of Public Relations) (Navy)
PUBL . . . . . . Publication
PUBLINX. . . . . Public Links (Amateur golf)
PUBS . . . . . . Publication Series
PUC . . . . Pacific Union College (California)
PUC . . . . Parti de l'Unite Congolaise (Congolese Unity Party)
PUC . . . . Permanent Unit Code
PUC . . . . Port Utilization Committee

PUC . . . . Presidential Unit Citation
PUC . . . . Production Urgency Committee (WPB)
PUC . . . . Provided You Concur
PUC . . . . Public Utilities Commission
PUD . . . . Partido Union Democratica (Political party in Guatemala)
PUD . . . . Pick-Up and Delivery (Business and trade)
PUD . . . . Planned Unit Development (Housing)
PUD . . . . Public Utility District
PUE . . . . Propellant Utilization Exerciser
PUEG . . . . . . Polyurethane Elastomer Genthane
PUFA . . . . . . Polyunsaturated Fatty Acid(s) (Dietetics)
PUFFS . . . . . . Passive Underwater Fire Control Feasibility Study
PUFFT. . . . . . Purdue University Fast FORTRAN Translator (Data processing)
PUG. . . . . . . Partially Underground (Military)
PUG . . . . Propellant Utilization and Gaging
PUK . . . . Parti d'Unite Katangaise (Katanga Unity Party)
PUL . . . . Publicker Industries, Inc. (NYSE symbol)
PULL . . . . . . Power for Underwater Logistics and Living
PULSAR . . . . . Pulsating Star
PULSAR. . . . . Pulsed Uniform LASER-Stimulated Artificial Radiation (Proposed acronymic designation for pulsars, in the event they are found to be artificially caused by intelligent life from outer space)
PULSE. . . . . . Public Urban Locator Service
PUM . . . . President of the United Mineworkers
PUMF. . . . . . Peaceful Uses of Military Forces
PUMP . . . . . . Protesting Unfair Marketing Practices (Student legal action organization)
PUN. . . . . . . Partido Union Nacional (National Union Party) (Costa Rica)
PUN. . . . . . . Precision Underwater Navigation
PUNA. . . . . . Parti de l'Unite Nationale (National Unity Party) (Congo)
PUNC. . . . . . Practical, Unpretentious, Nomographic Computer
PUNC . . . . . . Probable Ultimate Net Cost
PUNC. . . . . . Program Unit Counter
PUNGA . . . . . Parti de l'Unite Nationale Gabonaise (Party for Gabonese National Unity)
PUO . . . . Pyrexia (fever) of Unknown Origin (Commonly called Trench Fever)
PUP . . . . People's United Party (British Honduras)
PUP . . . . Peripheral Unit Processor (Data processing)
PUP . . . . Public Utilities Panel (EECE)
PUPA . . . . . . Polish Union Printers Association (Chicago)
PUR . . . . Partido de Unificacion Revolucionaria (Party of Revolutionary Unification) (Guatemala)
PUR . . . . Patch Unit Radio (Bell System)
PUR . . . . Port Utilities (AAR code)
PUR . . . . Purchase
PUR . . . . Purdue University Reactor
PUR . . . . Purdue University Research
PURA . . . . . . PACOM (Pacific Area Command) Utilization and Redistribution Agency
PURGE . . . . . Pearson Universal Random Generator
PURM . . . . . . Project for Utilization and Redistribution of Materiel (Air Force)
PURP . . . . . . Purpose
PURS . . . . . . Partido de la Union Republicana Socialista (Socialist Republican Union Party) (Bolivia)
PURS . . . . . . Program Usage Replenishment System
PURV . . . . . . Powered Underwater Research Vehicle (Navy)
PUS . . . . Parliamentary Under-Secretary
PUS . . . . Personnel Utilization Sheet
PUS . . . . Pharmacopeia of the United States
PUS . . . . Propellant Utilization System
PUS . . . . Propulsion Utilization System
PUSAS . . . . . Proposed United States of America Standard
PUSE . . . . . . Propellant Utilization System Exerciser
PUSH . . . . . . People United to Save Humanity (An organization)
PUSJDS . . . . . Pious Union of St. Joseph for Dying Sinners
PUSMM. . . . . Parti d'Union Socialiste des Musulmans Mauritaniens (Party for Socialist Unity of Moslems of Mauritania)
PUSS . . . . . . Pilots Universal Sighting System
PUT . . . . Programmable Unijunction Transistor
PUTERA. . . . . Pusat Tenaga Ra'ayat
PUTT . . . . . . Propellant Utilization Time Trace (Data processing)
PUUSNA . . . . . Polish Union of the United States of North America
PV . . . . Par Value (Finance)
PV . . . . Paravane (Anti-moored-mine device) (Naval)
PV . . . . Patrol Vessel
PV . . . . Photovoltaic
PV . . . . Pigment Volume
PV . . . . Pilot Vessel
PV . . . . Pipe Ventilated
PV . . . . Planuebergang (Grade crossing) (German military – World War II)
PV . . . . Plasma Volume (Medicine)
PV . . . . Polyoma Virus
PV . . . . Position Value

PV . . . . Post Village
PV . . . . Present Value
PV . . . . Pressurization Valve
PV . . . . Priest Vicar
PV . . . . Primary Valve
PV . . . . Prime Vertical
PV . . . . Professional Volunteer
PV . . . . Public Voucher
P/V . . . . Peak-to-Valley
PVA . . . . Paralyzed Veterans of America
PVA . . . . Polyvinyl Alcohol (Organic chemistry)
PVA . . . . Positive Vorticity Advection (Meteorology)
PVAC . . . . . . Polyvinyl Acetate (Organic chemistry)
PVB . . . . Portametric Voltmeter Bridge
PVC . . . . Peripheral Vasoconstriction
PVC . . . . Pigment Volume Concentration
PVC . . . . Polyvinyl Chloride (Organic chemistry)
PVC . . . . . . Position and Velocity Computer
PVC . . . . Potential Volume Change
PVC . . . . Premature Ventricular Contraction (Medicine)
PVC . . . . Pressure Vacuum Chamber
PVC . . . . Pressure Volume Control
PVCI . . . . . . Peripheral Vision Command Indicator
PVCS . . . . . . Portable Voice Communications System
PVD . . . . Paravisual Director (British)
PVD . . . . Peripheral Vascular Disease
PVD . . . . Physical Vulnerability Division (Air Force)
PVD . . . . Plan(ned) View Display (RADAR)
PVD . . . . Portable Vapor Detector
PVDC . . . . . . Polyvinyl Dichloride (Organic chemistry)
PVDL . . . . . . Precision Variable Delay Line
PVE . . . . Prolonged Vacuum Exposure
P & VE . . . . . Propulsion and Vehicle Engineering (A Marshall Space Flight Center laboratory)
PVF . . . . Peak Visibility Factor
PVF . . . . Polyvinyl Fluoride (Organic chemistry)
PVH . . . . Phillips-Van Heusen Corporation (NYSE symbol)
PVJC . . . . . . Palo Verde Junior College (California)
PVK . . . . Packaged Ventilation Kit (Civil Defense)
PVL . . . . Pressure to Vertical Locks
PVM . . . . Pneumonia Virus of Mice
PVM . . . . Potentiometric Voltmeter
PVM . . . . Pressure Vessel Material
PVM . . . . Projection Video Monitor
PVME . . . . . . Polyvinyl Methyl Ether (Organic chemistry)
PVMI . . . . . . Parish Visitors of Mary Immaculate (Roman Catholic women's religious order)
PVNTMED . . . . Preventive Medicine (Also, PM)
PVO . . . . Pacific Vegetable Oil Corp.
PVO . . . . . . Protivo-Voxdushnaia Oborona (Antiaircraft defense) (USSR)
PVOR . . . . . . Precision VHF Omnirange
PVP . . . . Polyvinylpyrrolidone (A plasma extender)
PVPO . . . . . . Plant Variety Protection Office (Department of Agriculture)
PVQ . . . . Personal Value Questionnaire (Navy)
PVR . . . . Precision Voltage Reference
PVRO . . . . . . Plant Variety Rights Office (Ministry of Agriculture, Fisheries, and Food) (British)
PVS . . . . Pecos Valley Southern Railway Company (AAR code)
PVS . . . . Performance Verification System
PVS . . . . Plexus Visibility Score (Medicine)
PVS . . . . Principal Veterinary Surgeon (British)
PVS . . . . Propellant Venting System
PVT . . . . Pressure, Volume, Temperature
PVT . . . . Private
PVT . . . . Production Verification Tests
PVTAEA . . . . . Philippine Virginia Tobacco Administration Employees' Association
PVTR . . . . . . Portable Video Tape Recorder
PVU . . . . Praire View University (Texas)
PVU . . . . Pressure to Verticle Locks, Unlocked
PVV . . . . Pressure, Vent, and Vacuum
PW . . . . Packed Weight
PW . . . . Pericardium Wall
PW . . . . Philadelphia & Western R. R. (AAR code)
pW . . . . Picowatt (A trillionth of a watt)
PW . . . . Pittsburgh & West Virginia Railway (American Stock Exchange symbol)
PW . . . . Post War
PW . . . . Prince of Wales' (Military unit) (British)
PW . . . . Prisoner(s) of War (Also, POW)
PW . . . . Psychological Warfare
PW . . . . Public Works
PW . . . . Publishers' Weekly (Trade periodical)

PW . . . . Pulse Width (RADAR)
P & W . . . . . . Pratt & Whitney (Aircraft engine manufacturer)
PWA . . . . Pacific Western Airlines
PWA . . . . Pharmaceutical Wholesalers Association
PWA . . . . Public Works Administration (All functions transferred to office of Federal Works Agency, 1943)
PWA . . . . . . Publishers' Weekly Announcements (Now called Forthcoming Books)
PWAA . . . . . . Paint and Wallpaper Association of America
PWAA . . . . . . Polish Women's Alliance of America
PWAFRR . . . . . Present Worth of All Future Revenue Requirements
PWB . . . . Pilot Weather Briefing
PWB . . . . Printed Wiring Board
PWB . . . . Psychological Warfare Branch (Allied Forces) (World War II)
PWB . . . . Pulling Whaleboat
PWBA . . . . . . Plane-Wave Born Approximation
PWBA . . . . . . Professional Woman Bowlers Association
PWBC . . . . . . Peripheral White Blood Cells
PWC . . . . Pacific War Council (World War II)
PWC . . . . Prisoner of War Cage, Camp, Command, or Compound
PWC . . . . Public Works Center (Navy)
PWC . . . . Pulse-Width Coded
PWCC of A . . . Pembroke Welsh Corgi Club of America
PWCEN . . . . . . Public Works Center
PWD . . . . Procurement Work Directive (Army)
PWD . . . . Psychological Warfare Division (Military)
PWD . . . . Public Works Department (Navy)
PWD . . . . Pulse-Width Detector (or Discriminator) (RADAR)
PWDC . . . . . . Philippine War Damage Commission (Post-World War II)
PWDEPT . . . . . Public Works Department
PWDI . . . . Program with Developing Institutions
PWE . . . . Pauli-Weisskoph Equation
PWE . . . . Prisoner of War Enclosure
PWE . . . . Pulse-Width Encoder
PWF . . . . Photoelectric Work Function
PWF . . . . Pulse Wave Form
PWFN . . . . . . Projection Weld Flange Nut
PWG . . . . Panzerwagen (Tank) (German military - World War II)
PWG . . . . Photoelectric Web Guide
PWH . . . . Pellet Warhead
PWH . . . . Precision Welding-Head
PWH . . . . Proprietor of copyright on a Work made for Hire
PWH . . . . Prototype Wave Height
PWI . . . . Permanent Ware Institute
PWI . . . . Physiological Workload Index (Aviation)
PWI . . . . Pilot Warning Indicator (or Instrument) (Aviation)
PWI . . . . Proximity Warning Indicator (or Instrument)
PWIB . . . . . . Prisoner of War Information Bureau (Post-World War II)
PWIF . . . . . . Plantation Workers' International Federation
PWJC . . . . . . Paine, Webber, Jackson & Curtis (Stockbrokers)
PWL . . . . Piecewire-Linear
PWM . . . . Pokeweed Mitogen (Genetics)
PWM . . . . Printed Wiring Master
PWM . . . . Pulse-Width Modulation (RADAR)
PWM-FM . . . . . Pulse-Width Modulation - Frequency Modulation (RADAR)
PWMS . . . . . . Public Works Management System (Navy)
PWO . . . . Prince of Wales' Own (Military unit) (British)
PWO . . . . Production Work Order
PWO . . . . Public Works Officer (Navy)
PWOR . . . . . . Prince of Wales' Own Royal (Military unit) (British)
PWP . . . . Parents Without Partners (An organization)
PWP . . . . Past Worthy Patriarch
PWP . . . . Plasticized White Phosphorus
PWP . . . . Polish Workers' Party
PWP . . . . Postwar Planning (World War II)
PWPP . . . . . . Professionwide Pension Plan (American Chemical Society)
PWQM . . . . . . Protection Water Quality Management
PWR . . . . Pilot Wire Regulator
PWR . . . . Power Wirewound Resistor
PWR . . . . Pressurized Water Reactor (AEC)
PWR . . . . Prince of Wales' Royal (Military unit) (British)
PWR . . . . Program Work Requirement
PWR . . . . Publication Work Request
PWRCB . . . . . . President's War Relief Control Board (World War II)
PWRR . . . . . . Prepositioned War Reserve Requirements
PWRR-MF . . . . Prepositioned War Reserve Requirements for Medical Facilities (Army)
PWRS . . . . . . Prepositioned War Reserve Stock
PWRS-MF . . . . Prepositioned War Reserve Stocks for Medical Facilities (Army)
PWS . . . . Parallel Working System
PWS . . . . Petrified Wood Society
PWS . . . . Phoenix Weapons System
PWS . . . . Predicted Wave Signalling

PWS .... Private Wire Service
PWS........ Psychological Warfare Service (Allied Forces) (World War II)
PWT .... Progressive Wave Tube
PWT .... Propulsion Wind Tunnel (Air Force)
PWU .... Pressure-Work Up
PWV........ Pittsburgh & West Virginia Railway (AAR code)
PWV........ Prince of Wales' Volunteers (Military) (British)
PWV........ Pulse Wave Velocity
P & WV ..... Pittsburgh & West Virginia Railway
PWW .... Project West Wing
PWWC ...... Post War World Council
PWWR....... Power Wire-Wound Resistor
PX .... Pedro Ximenez (A blending sherry)
PX .... Physical Examination (Medicine)
PX .... Please Exchange (Merchandising slang)
PX .... Post Exchange (Military)
PX .... Private Exchange
PX .... Pyroxene (Also PYX)
PXA .... Pulsed Xenon Arc
PXD .... Place Index in Decrement
PXI .... Pulse Xenon Illuminator
PX In ...... Time of Arrival (Aviation)
PXL .... Pulsed Xenon Lamp
PXLS ...... Pulsed Xenon Light Source
PXLSS...... Pulsed Xenon Light Source System
PXM ...... Projection X-Ray Microscope
PX Me ..... Report My Arrival or Departure (Aviation slang)
PXN....... Paramount Pictures Corporation (NYSE symbol) (Delisted)
PXO....... Prospective Executive Officer
PX Out ..... Take-off Time (Aviation)
PXR .... Plus-X-Reversal
PXS .... Pulsed X-Ray System

PXS .... Pulsed Xenon System
PXU .... Portable X-Ray Unit
PXV .... Pedro Ximenez Viejo (A blending sherry)
PY .... Patrol Vessel, Yacht
PY .... Prior Year
PY .... Program Year
PY .... Pure Oil Company (NYSE symbol) (Delisted)
PY .... Yacht (Navy symbol)
PYA ...... Pioneer Youth of America
PYA .... Pioneer Youth Authority (Ghana)
PYA .... Pittsburgh, Youngstown & Ashtabula Railway (NYSE symbol)
PYA .... Plan, Year, and Age (Insurance designations)
Py B .... Bachelor of Pedagogy
PYC .... Patrol Vessel, Yacht, Coastal (Navy symbol)
PYC .... Pay Your Cash (Australian slang)
PYE .... Protect Your Environment (Groups)
PYR .... Pitch, Yaw, Roll
PYX .... Pyroxene (Also PX)
PZ .... Panzerbrechend (Armor-piercing) (German military – World War II)
PZ .... Paole Zion (Labor federation) (Later, Labor Zionist Alliance)
PZ .... Phase Zero
PZ .... Pickup Zone
PZ .... Pie Zeses (May You Live Piously)
PZD .... Phase Zero Defense
PZDV ...... Panzer-Division (Armored Division) (German military)
PZI .... Protamine Zinc Insulin
PZL .... Pennzoil Company (NYSE symbol)
PZL .... Progressive Zionist League-Hashomer Hatzair
PZP .... Phase Zero Program
PZPR ...... Polska Zjednoczona Partia Robotnicza (Polish United Workers' Party)
PZS .... President of the Zoological Society (British)
PZT .... Piezoelectric Zirconate Titanate

Q

Q . . . . Chicago, Burlington, and Quincy Railroad (Slang)
Q . . . . Coefficient of Association (Statistics)
Q . . . . Drone (Designation for all US military aircraft)
Q . . . . Dynamic Pressure (NASA)
Q . . . . Pen name for Sir Arthur Quiller-Couch (1863–1944; English man of letters)
Q . . . . Polaris Correction
Q . . . . The Proportion Not in a Specific Class
Q . . . . Quadrans (Farthing)
Q . . . . Quadrillion BTU's
Q . . . . Quaere (Inquire)
Q . . . . Quality Factor
Q . . . . Quantity
Q . . . . Quart
Q . . . . Quarter; Quarterly
Q . . . . Quartermaster
Q . . . . Quarto (From 25 to 30 centimeters) (Bibliography)
Q . . . . Quasi
Q . . . . Queen
Q . . . . Queen (Chess)
Q . . . . Queensland Fever (Disease first noted in farmers of Queensland, Australia)
Q . . . . Query
Q . . . . Question
Q . . . . Quetzal (Monetary unit in Guatemala)
Q . . . . Quick
Q . . . . Quiescit (He Rests)
Q . . . . Quintal (Unit of weight)
Q . . . . Quire (Measure of paper)
Q . . . . Receivership or Bankruptcy (Designation used with NYSE symbols)
Q . . . . Respiratory Quotient (Also, RQ) (Physiology)
Q . . . . Semi-Interquartile Range or Quartile Deviation (Statistics)
Q . . . . Squall (Meteorology)
Q . . . . Symbol expressing very large energy figures
QA . . . . Quality Assurance
QA . . . . Quarters Allowance
QA . . . . Quaternary Ammonium (Chemistry)
QA . . . . Quick-Acting
QA . . . . Quiescent Aerial
QAB . . . . Queen Anne's Bounty
QAC . . . . Quadripartite Agreements Committee (Military)
QAC . . . . Quality Assurance Code
QAD . . . . Quality Assurance Directive
QAD . . . . Quality Assurance Directorate (Materials) (British)
QAD . . . . Quality Assurance Division
QAD . . . . Quick Attach-Detach
QADC . . . . . . Queen's Aide-de-Camp (British)
QADK . . . . . . Quick Attach-Detach Kit
QADS . . . . . . Quality Assurance Data System
QAE . . . . Quality Assurance Engineering
QAET . . . . . . Quality Assurance Evaluation Test
QAF . . . . Quality Assurance Function
QAFO . . . . . . Quality Assurance Field Operations
QAI . . . . Quality Assurance Instruction
QAIP . . . . Quality Assurance Inspection Procedure
QAK . . . . Quick Attach Kit
QAL . . . . Quality Assurance Laboratory
QAL . . . . Quarterly Accession List
QAL . . . . Quartz Aircraft Lamp
QAL . . . . Quebec Airways, Limited
QALL . . . . . . Quartz Aircraft Landing Lamp
QALTR . . . . . . Quality Assurance Laboratory Test Request
QAM . . . . Quality Assurance Manual

QAMDO . . . . . Quadripartite Agreed Materiel Development Objective (Military)
QAMR . . . . . . Quadripartite Agreed Materiel Requirement (Military)
QANTAS . . . . Queensland and Northern Territories Air Service (Now QANTAS Airways) (Australian airline)
QAO . . . . Quality Assurance Office (Navy)
QAO . . . . Quality Assurance Operation
QAP . . . . Quality Assurance Procedures (or Program, or Provisions) (Navy)
QAP . . . . Quanah, Acme & Pacific Railway (AAR code)
QAP . . . . Quinine, Atabrine, Plasmoquine (Treatment for malaria)
QAPED . . . . . Quadripartite Agreed Plans of Engineering Design (Military)
QAPET . . . . . Quadripartite Agreed Plans of Engineering Tests (Military)
QAPL . . . . . . Queensland Airlines Party Limited
QAPST . . . . . Quadripartite Agreed Plans of Service Tests (Military)
QAR . . . . Quality Assurance Representative
QAR . . . . Quick Access Recording
QAS . . . . Quality Assurance Service (Medicine)
QAS . . . . Quick Action Shuttle
QASC . . . . . . Quadripartite Armaments Standardization Committee (Military)
QASP . . . . . . Quality Assurance Standard Practice
QAST . . . . . . Quality Assurance Service Test (Nuclear)
QAVC . . . . . . Quiet Automatic Volume Control
QB . . . . Qualified Bidders
QB . . . . Quarterback (Football position)
QB . . . . Queen's Bays (Military) (British)
QB . . . . Queen's Bench (in Law Courts) (British)
QB . . . . Queen's Bishop (Chess)
QB . . . . Quiet Birdmen (An organization)
QBA . . . . Quality Brands Associates of America
QBA . . . . Quebecair, Inc.
QBAC . . . . . . Quality Bakers of America Cooperative
QBACI . . . . . . Quality Bakers of America Cooperative, Incorporated
QBAN . . . . . . Qui Bixit Annos (Who Lived —— Years)
QBD . . . . Queen's Bench Division (Military) (British)
QBI . . . . Quite Bloody Impossible (British slang, applied particularly to flying conditions)
QC . . . . Qualification Course
QC . . . . Quality Control
QC . . . . Quantitative Command
QC . . . . Quantum Counter
QC . . . . Quartz Crystal
QC . . . . Quebec Central Railway Company (AAR code)
QC . . . . Queen's Counsel (Only in a Queen's reign) (British)
QC . . . . Quench Correction
QC . . . . Quick Connect
QCA . . . . Queen Charlotte Airlines, Ltd.
QCC . . . . Qualification Correlation Certification
QCC . . . . Quick Connect Coupling
QCCARS . . . . . Quality Control Collection Analysis and Reporting System
QCD . . . . Quality Control Data
QCDR . . . . . . Quality Control Deficiency Report
QCE . . . . Quality Control Engineers
QCF . . . . Quartz Crystal Filter
QCFO . . . . . . Quartz Crystal Frequency Oscillator
QCH . . . . Quick Connect Handle
QCI . . . . Quality Control Information
QCI . . . . Quota Club International
QCIM . . . . . . Quarterly Cumulative Index Medicus
QCK . . . . Quick Connect Kit
QCL . . . . Quality Control Level
QCM . . . . Quality Control Manager
QCM . . . . Quality Control Manual
QCM . . . . Quality Courts Motels
QCM . . . . Quartz Crystal Microbalance

QCM	Quartz Crystal Monitor
QCO	**Quality Control Organization**
QCO	Quartz Crystal Oscillator
QCOP	Quality Control Operating Procedure
QCP	Quality Control Procedure
QCPE	Quantum Chemistry Program Exchange (Indiana University)
QCR	**Quality Control/Reliability**
QCR	**Quality Control Report**
QCR	Quality Control Representative
QCR	Quality Control Review
QCR	Quality Control Room
QCR	Quick Change Response (System)
QCR	Quick Connect Relay
QCS	Quality Control System
QCS	Quality Cost System
QCSC	Quadripartite Chemical, Biological, Radiological Standardization Committee (Military)
QCT	Questionable Corrective Task
QCTR	Quality Control Test Report
QCU	**Quality Courts United**
QCU	Quartz Crystal Unit
QCU	Quick Change Unit
QCUS	Quartz Crystal Unit Set
QCVC	Quick Connect Valve Coupler
QCW	Quadrant Continuous Wave
QCWA	Quarter Century Wireless Association
QD	**Quaque Die (Everyday) (Pharmacy)**
QD	Quarterdeck
QD	Quasi Dicat (As If, or, as Though, One Should Say)
QD	Quasi Dictum (As If Said; as Though It Had Been Said)
QD	Quasi Dixisset (As If One Had Said)
QD	Quater Die (Four Times a Day) (Pharmacology)
QD	Quick Disconnect
Q & D	Quick and Dirty
QDA	Quantity Discount Agreement
QDC	Quick Dependable Communications
QDC	Quick Disconnect Cap
QDC	Quick Disconnect Connector
QDC	Quick Disconnect Coupling
QDCC	Quick Disconnect Circular Connector
QDD	Quantized Decision Detection
QDH	Quick Disconnect Handle
QDK	Quick Detach Kit
QDK	Quick Disconnect Kit
QDL	Quick Disconnect, Large
QDM	Quick Disconnect, Miniature
QDN	Quick Disconnect Nipple
QDP	Quick Disconnect Pivot
QDRI	**Qualitative Development Requirement Information**
QDS	Quick Disconnect Series
QDS	Quick Disconnect, Small
QDS	Quick Disconnect Swivel
QDTA	Quantitative Differential Thermal Analysis
QDV	Quick Disconnect Valve
QE	Journal of Quantum Electronics (A publication)
QE	Quadrant Elevation
QE	Quality Engineering
QE	Quality Evaluation
QE	Quod Est (Which Is)
QE 2	Queen Elizabeth 2 (Luxury liner)
QEA	QANTAS Empire Airways, Ltd.
QEAE	Quaternary Ethylaminoethyl (Chemistry)
QEAV	Quick Exhaust Air Valve
QEC	Quantum Electronics Council
QEC	**Quick Engine Change**
QECA	Quick Engine Change Assembly
QECK	Quick Engine Change Kit
QECS	Quick Engine Change Stand
QECU	**Quick Engine Change Unit**
QED	Quantum Electrodynamics
QED	Quick Erection Dome
QED	Quick Text Editor
QED	Quod Erat Demonstrandum (Which Was the Thing to Be Proved)
QEF	Quod Erat Faciendum (Which Was to Be Made, or Done)
QEI	Quod Erat Inveniendum (Which Was to Be Found Out)
QEL	Quality Evaluation Laboratory
QEL	Quiet Extended Life
QElecSC	Quadripartite Electronic Standardization Committee (Army)
QEM	Quadrant Electrometer
QEM	Qualified Export Manager (Designation given by American Society of International Executives)

QEngrSC	Quadripartite Engineer Standardization Committee (Army)
QEO	Quality Engineering Operations
QEOP	**Quartermaster Emergency Operation Plan**
QEP	Quality Evaluation Program (College of American Pathologists)
QEP	Quality Examination Program
QER	Qualitative Equipment Requirements (Army)
QES	Quadrant Eleventh-Gram Second
QESCP	Quality Engineering Significant Control Points
QEST	Quality Evaluation System Tests
QEV	Quick Exhaust Valve
QEW	Queen Elizabeth Way (Canada)
QF	Quality Factor
QF	**Quick-Firer (Gun)**
QF	Quick Freeze
QFC	Quantitative Flight Characteristics
QFCC	Quantitative Flight Characteristics Criteria
QFCI	Quartermaster Food and Container Institute (Army)
QFF	Quadrupole Flip-Flop (Data processing)
QFI	Qualified Flight Instructor
QFIRC	Quick Fix Interference Reduction Capability
QFL	Quasi-Fermi Level
QFM	Quantized Frequency Modulation
QFO	Quartz Frequency Oscillator
QFP	Quartz Fiber Product
QFP	Quick Fix Program
QFT	Quantized Field Theory
QG	Quadrature Grid
QG	**Quartermaster General (Military)**
QG	Queen Groupie
QGRB	Grayson Robinson Stores, Inc. (NYSE symbol) (Delisted)
QGV	Quantized Gate Video (RADAR)
QH	Quaque Hora (Every Hour) (Pharmacy)
QH	Quartz Helix
QH	Quorn Hounds
Q2H	Every Second Hour (Medicine)
Q3H	Every Third Hour (Medicine)
Q4H	Every Fourth Hour (Medicine)
QHC	Queen's Honorary Chaplain (British)
QHP	Queen's Honorary Physician (British)
QHS	Queen's Honorary Surgeon (British)
QI	Quality Index
QI	**Quarterly Index**
QI	Quasi-Inertial
QI	Quota International
QIC	Quality Information Center
QIC	Quality Inspection Criteria
QIC	Quartz-Iodine Crystal
QID	Quater in Die (Four Times a Day) (Pharmacology)
QIE-AF	Qualified International Executive – Air Forwarding (Designation given by American Society of International Executives)
QIE-EM	Qualified International Executive – Export Management (Designation given by American Society of International Executives)
QIE-TM	Qualified International Executive – Traffic Management (Designation given by American Society of International Executives)
QIL	Quartz Incandescent Lamp
QIL	Quartz Iodine Lamp
QIP	Quartz Insulation Part
QIP	Quiescat In Pace (May He or She Rest in Peace)
QIT	Quality Information and Test (System)
QK	Queen's Knight (Chess)
QKT	Queen's Knight (Chess)
QL	Quality of Living
QL	Quantum Libet (As Much as Is Desired) (In medical prescriptions)
QL	Queen's Lancers (Military) (British)
QLAP	Quick Look Analysis Program
QLI	Quality of Life Index
QLIT	Quick Look Intermediate Tape
QLL	Quartz Landing Lamp (Aviation)
QLM	Quasi-Linear Machine
QLP	Quality Low-Priced (Art series)
QLR	Quebec Law Reports
QLSM	Quasi-Linear Sequential Machine
QLT	Quantitative Leak Test
QLT	Quasi-Linear Theory
QLTY	Quality
QM	Quadrature Modulation
QM	**Quality Memorandum**
QM	Quality of Merit
QM	Quantum Mechanics
QM	Quaque Matin (Every Morning) (Pharmacy)
QM	**Quarterly Memorandum**

QM . . . . Quartermaster

QM . . . . Queen's Messenger(s) (British)

QM . . . . Quinacrine Mustard (Chromosome stain)

QM . . . . Quo Modo (In What Manner)

QMA . . . . . . Qualitative Materiel Approach (Army)

QMA . . . . . . Quartermasters Association

QMAAC . . . . Queen Mary's Army Auxiliary Corps (The WAAC) (British)

QMAO . . . . . Qualified for Mobilization Ashore Only (Navy)

QMC . . . . . . Quadripartite Materiel Committee (Military)

QMC . . . . . . Quartermaster Clerk (Marine Corps)

QMC . . . . . . Quartermaster Corps (Army)

QMCLK . . . . . Quartermaster Clerk (Coast Guard)

QMCR . . . . . Quartermaster Corps Regulations

QMC & SO . . . Quartermaster Cataloging and Standardization Office

QMCTC . . . . . Quartermaster Corps Technical Committee

QMDEP . . . . . Quartermaster Depot

QMDK . . . . . Quick Mechanical Disconnect Kit

QMDO . . . . . Qualitative Materiel Development Objective (Army)

QMDPC . . . . . Quartermaster Data Processing Center

QMEPCC . . . . Quartermaster Equipment and Parts Commodity Center

QMFCI . . . . . Quartermaster Food and Container Institute

QMFCIAF . . . . Quartermaster Food and Container Institute for the Armed Forces

QMG . . . . . . Quartermaster General (Army)

QMGMC . . . . Quartermaster General of the Marine Corps

QMI . . . . Qualification Maintainability Inspection

QMIA . . . . . . Quartermaster Intelligence Agency (Merged with Defense Intelligence Agency)

QMIMSO . . . . Quartermaster Industrial Mobilization Services Offices

QMO . . . . . . Qualitative Materiel Objective (Army)

QMobSC . . . . Quadripartite Mobility Standardization Committee (Army)

QMORC . . . . . Quartermaster Officers' Reserve Corps

QMPA . . . . . Quartermaster Purchasing Agency

QMPCUSA . . . . Quartermaster Petroleum Center, United States Army

QMQB . . . . . Quick-Make, Quick-Break

QMR . . . . . . Qualitative Materiel Requirement (Army)

QMRC . . . . . Quartermaster Reserve Corps

QMREC . . . . . Quartermaster Research & Engineering Command (Army)

QMREFEA . . . . Quartermaster Research & Engineering Field Evaluation Agency (Merged with Troop Evaluation Test)

QMRL . . . . . . Quartermaster Radiation Laboratory (Army)

QMRPA . . . . . Quartermaster Radiation Planning Agency

QMS . . . . . . Quartermaster School (Army)

QMS . . . . . . Quartermaster Sergeant

QMS . . . . . . Quartermaster Stores

QMSGT . . . . . Quartermaster Sergeant (Marine Corps)

QMSO . . . . . . Quartermaster Supply Officer (Army)

QMSW . . . . . Quartz Metal Sealed Window

QMTOE . . . . . Quartermaster Table of Organization and Equipment (Units) (Military)

QMW . . . . . . Quartz Metal Window

QN . . . . Quantum Number

QN . . . . Quaque Nocte (Every Night) (Pharmacy)

QNMC . . . . . Quadripartite Nonmateriel Committee (Military)

QNS . . . . . . Quantity Not Sufficient (Pharmacy)

QNTY . . . . . . Quantity

QO . . . . Quaker Oats (Trade name)

QO . . . . Qualified in Ordnance (Navy)

QO . . . . Quartermaster Operation

QO . . . . Queen's Own (Military unit) (British)

QOC . . . . . . Quality of Conformance

QOCH . . . . . The Queen's Own Cameron Highlanders (British)

QOD . . . . . . Quality of Design

QOD . . . . . . Quantitative Oceanographic Data

QOD . . . . . . Quick-Opening Device

QOMAC . . . . . Quarter Orbit Magnetic Attitude Control

QON . . . . . . Quarter Ocean Net

QOR . . . . . . Qualitative Operational Requirement (Military)

QOR . . . . . . Queen's Own Royal (Military unit) (British)

QORGS . . . . . Quasi Optimal (or Optimum) Rendezvous Guidance System

QP . . . . Qualification Proposal

QP . . . . Quantum Placet (As Much as Is Desired)

QP . . . . Quasi-Peak

QP . . . . Queen Post

QP . . . . Quick Processing (Chemicals)

QPAM . . . . . Quantized Pulsed Amplitude Modulation

QPC . . . . . . Qatar Petroleum Company

QPI . . . . Quadratic Performance Index

QPIS . . . . . . Quality Planning Instruction Sheet

QPL . . . . . . Qualified Products List (Navy)

QPM . . . . . . Quantized Pulse Modulation

QPP . . . . . . Quality Program Provision

QPP . . . . . . Quantized Pulse Position

QPPC . . . . . . Quarterly Production Progress Conference (Navy)

QPR . . . . . . Quarterly Progress Report

QPRI . . . . . . Qualitative Personnel Requirements Information

QPRS . . . . . . Quarterly Project Reliability Summary (Navy)

QPS . . . . . . Qualified Processing Source

QPS . . . . . . Quantitative Physical Science

QPS . . . . . . Quiescent Power Supply

QPSC . . . . . . Quiescent Power Supply Current

QPSK . . . . . . Quad-Phase Shift Key

QQ . . . . Questionable Questionnaires

QQC . . . . . . Quantitative Quality Characteristics

QQH . . . . . . Quaque Hora (Every Hour) (Pharmacy)

QQP . . . . . . Quick Query Program

QQPR . . . . . . Quantitative and Qualitative Personnel Requirements

QQPRI . . . . . Quantitative and Qualitative Personnel Requirements Information

QQSC . . . . . . Quadripartite Quartermaster Standardization Committee (Military)

QR . . . . Quality Review

QR . . . . Quantitative Restrictions (International trade)

QR . . . . Quantity Required

QR . . . . Queen's Royal (Military unit) (British)

QR . . . . Quick Reaction

QR . . . . Quotation Request

Q & R . . . . . . Quality and Reliability

QRA . . . . Quality and Reliability Assurance

QRA . . . . Quick Reaction Alert

Q & RA . . . . . Quality and Reliability Assurance

QRAC . . . . . . Quality and Reliability Assessment Council

QRBM . . . . . . Quasi-Random Band Model

QRC . . . . . . Quick Reaction Capability (Electronics)

QRC . . . . . . Quick Response Capability (Military)

QRCC . . . . . . Quadripartite Research Coordination Committee (Military)

QRCC . . . . . . Query Response Communications Console

QRCR . . . . . . Quality Reliability Consumption Reports

QRDC . . . . . . Quartermaster Research and Development Command (Army)

QRDEA . . . . . Quartermaster Research and Development Evaluation Agency (Army)

QREC . . . . . . Quartermaster Research and Engineering Command

QRF . . . . Quadrature Rejection Frequency

QRG . . . . . . Quadrupole Residual Gas

QRGA . . . . . . Quadrupole Residual Gas Analyzer

QRGAS . . . . . Quadrupole Residual Gas Analyzer System

QRI . . . . Qualitative Requirements Information (Army)

QRICC . . . . . Quick Reaction Inventory Control Center (Army)

QRP . . . . Quick Reaction Program

QRPAO . . . . . Qualified Radium Plaque Adaptometer Operator (Navy)

QRPS . . . . . . Quick Reaction Procurement System (Army)

QRR . . . . Quadrature Rejection Ratio

QRR . . . . Quadrupole Resonance Response

QRR . . . . Quarterly Research Review

QRRI . . . . . . Qualitative Research Requirements Information (Army)

QRRR . . . . . . Distress call for emergency use only by amateur radio stations in an emergency situation

QRS . . . . Queen's Row Spare

QRTP . . . . . . Quick Response Targeting Program (Lunar)

QRU . . . . Queen's Row Unit

QRUS . . . . . . Queen's Row Unit Spare

QRV . . . . Quick Release Valve

QRY . . . . Quality and Reliability Year

QS . . . . Quantum Satis or Sufficit (A Sufficient Quantity) (Prescription term)

QS . . . . Quarter Section

QS . . . . Quarter Sessions

QS . . . . Quartermaster Sergeant

QS . . . . Quota Source

QSAL . . . . . . Quadripartite Standardization Agreements List (Military)

QSC . . . . Quality, Service, Cleanliness (McDonald's hamburger stands motto)

QSD . . . . Quality Surveillance Division (Navy)

QSE . . . . Qualified Scientists and Engineers

QSF . . . . Quasi-Static Field

QSF . . . . Quasi-Stationary Front

QSG . . . . Quasi-Stellar Galaxy

QSI . . . . Quality Salary Increase

QSI . . . . Quarterly Survey of Intentions (Bureau of the Census) (Became Consumer Buying Expectations Survey)

QSIC . . . . . . Quality Standard Inspection Criteria

QS & L . . . . . Quarters, Subsistence, and Laundry (Military)

QSM . . . . Quarter Square Multiplier

QSM . . . . Quasi-Linear Sequential Machine

QSO . . . . Quasibiennial Stratospheric Oscillation

QSO . . . . Quasi-Stellar (or QUASAR) Object

QSOP . . . . . . Quadripartite Standing Operating Procedures (Military)

QSR . . . . Quarterly Status Report

QSR . . . . Quarterly Summary Report

ACRONYMS AND INITIALISMS DICTIONARY

QSS . . . . Quadrupole Screw Ship
QSS . . . . Quasi-Stellar Source
QSSA . . . . Quasi-Stationary State Approximation
QSSP . . . . Quasi-Solid State Panel
QSSR . . . . Quarterly Stock Status Report
QSTAG . . . . . . Quadripartite Standardization Agreement (Military)
QSY . . . . Quiet Sun Year
QT . . . . Qualification Test
QT . . . . Quantity
QT . . . . Quart
QT . . . . Queuing Theory
QT . . . . Quick Test (Psychology)
QT . . . . Quiet (or Sub Rosa, as, "On the QT")
QTA . . . . Quadrant Transformer Assembly
QTAM . . . . . . Queued Telecommunications Access Method (Data processing)
QTB . . . . Quarry-Tile Base (Technical drawings)
QTDG . . . . . . Quaker Theological Discussion Groups
QTF . . . . Quarry-Tile Floor (Technical drawings)
QTOL . . . . Quiet Takeoff and Landing (NASA)
QTP . . . . Qualification Test Program (or Procedure)
QTP . . . . Quantum Theory of Paramagnetism
QTPC . . . . Quadripartite Technical Procedures Committee (Military)
QTPR . . . . Quarterly Technical Progress Report
QTR . . . . Qualification Test Report
QTR . . . . Quarry-Tile Roof (Technical drawings)
QTR . . . . Quarter(ly)
QTR . . . . Quarterly Technical Report
QTS . . . . Qualification Test Specification
QTS . . . . Quartz Thermometer Sensor
QTYDESREQ . . Quantity Desired as Requested
QU . . . . Queen's University (Canada)
QUADRADAR . . Four-Way RADAR Surveillance

QUAL . . . . Qualification
QUANTRAS . . . Question Analysis Transformation and Search (Data processing)
QUARPEL . . . . Quartermaster Water-Repellent Clothing (Military)
QUART . . . . . . Quality Assurance and Reliability Team
QUASAR . . . . . Quasi-Stellar Radio Source (Astronomy)
QUASER . . . . . Quantum Amplification by Stimulated Emission of Radiation
QUB . . . . Queen's University, Belfast (Ireland)
QUE . . . . Quebec (Canadian province)
QUEST . . . . . . Quality Electrical Systems Test (Interpreter)
QUEST . . . . . . Quality Utilization Effectiveness Statistically Qualified
QUEST . . . . . . Quantitative Utility Estimates for Science and Technology (RAND Corp.)
QUESTER . . . . . Quick and Effective System to Enhance Retrieval (Data processing)
QUESTOL . . . . Quiet Experimental Short Takeoff and Landing (Program) (NASA)
QUI . . . . Queen's University, Ireland
QUI . . . . Quincy R. R. (AAR code)
QUP . . . . Quantity per Unit Pack
QUP . . . . Quonset Point (Navy)
QV . . . . Quantum Vis (As Much as You Wish) (Pharmacy)
QV . . . . Qui Vixit (Who Lived)
QV . . . . Quod Vide or Quod Videte (Which See)
Q4V . . . . Quicker for Victory (World War II)
QVR . . . . Queen Victoria's Rifles (British)
QVT . . . . Quality Verification Test
QW . . . . Quarter Wave
QWA . . . . Quarter-Wave Antenna
QWD . . . . Quarterly World Day
QWG . . . . Quadripartite Working Group (Military)
QWL . . . . Quick Weight Loss
QWMP . . . . . . Quadruped Walking Machine Program (Army)
QWP . . . . Quarter Wave Plate
QY . . . . Quantum Yield
QZ . . . . Quartz

R

R . . . . Acknowledgment of Receipt (Message handling)
r . . . . Angular Yaw Velocity
R . . . . Army (Military aircraft identification prefix)
R . . . . Electrical Resistance
R . . . . Product Moment Coefficient of Correlation (Statistics)
R . . . . Rabbi
R . . . . RADAR Contact (A diagonal line through R indicates RADAR service
        terminated. A cross through R indicates RADAR contact lost.)
        (Aviation)
R . . . . Radfahrabteilung (Bicycle battalion) (German military – World War II)
R . . . . Radial
R . . . . Radiancy
R . . . . Radical
R . . . . Radio
R . . . . Radius
r . . . . Radius of Gyration
R . . . . Railroad (or Railway)
R . . . . Rain (Weather reports)
R . . . . Range
R . . . . Rank
R . . . . Rankine (Temperature)
R . . . . Rare (When applied to species)
R . . . . Rate
R . . . . Ratio
R . . . . Rays
R . . . . Reaction
R . . . . Read
R . . . . Real
R . . . . Rear
R . . . . Reaumur (Thermometric scale)
R . . . . Received
R . . . . Received Solid (Amateur radio)
R . . . . Recipe
R . . . . Reconnaissance (Designation for all US military aircraft)
R . . . . Recto (Bibliography)
R . . . . Rector, Rectory
R . . . . Rectum
R . . . . Red (Light, buoy, beacon)
R . . . . Redetermination
R . . . . Referee (Football)
R . . . . Reflection (Angle of)
R . . . . Refraction
R . . . . Refrigerator
R . . . . Regiment
R . . . . Regina (Queen)
R . . . . Registered
R . . . . Regulating
R . . . . Reigned
R . . . . Reiz (Stimulus)
R . . . . Relative Humidity
R . . . . Reliability
R . . . . Reluctance
R . . . . Replaceability
R . . . . Reports
R . . . . Reprint
R . . . . Republic(an)
R . . . . Requiescat (He Rests)
R . . . . Research
R . . . . Reserve
R . . . . Reside, Residence, or Resident
R . . . . Resistance (Factor)
R . . . . Resistor
R . . . . Respiration

R . . . . Respond; Response
R . . . . Responsorium (Responsory)
R . . . . Restricted (Military document classification)
R . . . . Restricted (Persons under 18 [16 in some localities] not admitted
        unless accompanied by parent or adult guardian) (Movie rating)
R . . . . Retarder (Slow) (On clock-regulators)
R . . . . Retired, Retiree
R . . . . Returning
R . . . . Reverse
R . . . . Rex (King)
R . . . . Reynolds Number (Viscosity) (Also, RN)
R . . . . Rial (Monetary unit in Iran)
R . . . . Richtkreis (Aiming circle, a gunnery term) (German military – World
        War II)
R . . . . Rifle
R . . . . Right (side of a stage) (A stage direction)
R . . . . Ring (Technical drawings)
R . . . . Riser (Technical drawings)
R . . . . Rises
R . . . . River
R . . . . Road
R . . . . Rod (Measurement)
R . . . . Roentgen
R . . . . Roger (All right or OK) (Communications slang)
R . . . . Roma(n)
R . . . . Rood
R . . . . Rook (Chess)
R . . . . Rotary Wing (Aircraft designation)
R . . . . Rotor
R . . . . Rough (Appearance of bacterial colony)
R . . . . Rough Sea
R . . . . Route
R . . . . Royal
R . . . . Rubber
R . . . . Ruble (Monetary unit in Russia)
R . . . . Rule
R . . . . Runic
R . . . . Runs (scored) (Baseball or cricket)
R . . . . Rupee (Monetary unit in India)
R . . . . Transport (Naval aircraft designation)
R . . . . Uniroyal, Inc. (Formerly, US Rubber Company) (NYSE symbol)
°R . . . . Degree Rankine
R (Day) . . . . . . Redeployment Day (Military)
3R . . . . Readin', Ritin', and Rithmetic (Also, RRR)
6R . . . . Remedial Readin', Remedial Ritin', and Remedial Rithmetic (Humorous
        interpretation of the three R's) (Also, RRRRRR)
RA . . . . Coast RADAR Station (Maps and charts)
RA . . . . High-Powered Radio Range (Adcock)
RA . . . . Rabbinical Assembly
RA . . . . Radioactive
Ra . . . . Radium (Chemical element)
RA . . . . Radius of Action
RA . . . . Rain (Meteorology)
RA . . . . Raise(d)
RA . . . . Random Access
RA . . . . Raritan Arsenal
RA . . . . Rate Action
RA . . . . Rate of Application
RA . . . . Rayon
RA . . . . Read Amplifier
RA . . . . Rear Admiral (Also, RADM)
RA . . . . Rear Artillery
RA . . . . Receiver Attenuation

RA . . . . Rectal Artery
RA . . . . Redstone Arsenal (Army)
RA . . . . Reduction of Area
RA . . . . Refer to Acceptor
RA . . . . Registration Act
RA . . . . Regular Army
RA . . . . Reimbursement Authorization
RA . . . . Release Authorization
RA . . . . Reliability Analysis
RA . . . . Relocation Assistance (HUD)
RA . . . . Rental Agreement
RA . . . . Repair Assignment
RA . . . . Republic Aviation Corporation (NYSE symbol) (Delisted)
RA . . . . Resident Agent
RA . . . . Resident Auditor
RA . . . . Resistor Assembly
RA . . . . Retinal Anlage
RA . . . . Retrograde Amnesia
RA . . . . Reverendus Admodum (Very Reverend)
RA . . . . Rheumatoid Arthritis (Medicine)
RA . . . . Right Arch (Masonry)
RA . . . . Right Ascension (Astronomy)
RA . . . . Robbery Armed
RA . . . . Rosin Acid
RA . . . . Rotary Assembly
RA . . . . Rotogravure Association
RA . . . . Royal Academy (or Academician) (British)
RA . . . . Royal Artillery (British)
RA . . . . Rueckwaertiges Armeegebiet (Rear area of an army) (German military)
R-A . . . . Response Errors (Statistics)
R/A . . . . Radius of Action (Air Force)
R/A . . . . Refer to Accepter (as, a check or draft) (Banking)
R & A . . . . . . Rules and Administration Committee (US Senate)
RAA . . . . Rabbinical Alliance of America
RAA . . . . Renewal Assistance Administration (HUD)
RAA . . . . Respiratory Aid Apparatus
RAA . . . . Right Angle Adapter
RAA . . . . Right Ascension Angle
RAAA . . . . . . Red Angus Association of America
RAACEF . . . . . Rear Admiral Aircraft Carriers, Eastern Fleet (British)
RA(A)EF . . . . . Rear Admiral (Administration) Eastern Fleet (British)
RAAF . . . . . . Royal Australian Air Force
RAAG . . . . . . Regional Aviation Assistance Group (FAA)
RAAN . . . . . . Repair Activity Accounting Number (Navy)
RAB . . . . Radio Advertising Bureau
RAB . . . . Rotating Arm Basin
RABAL . . . . . Radiosonde Balloon Wind Data
RABAR . . . . . Radiosonde Balloon Release
RABAR . . . . . Raytheon Advanced Battery Acquisition RADAR
RABR . . . . . . Rainbow Bridge National Monument
RABR . . . . . . Right Angle Bulkhead Receptacle
RABS . . . . . . Remote Air Battle Station
RAC . . . . RADAR Address Counter
RAC . . . . RADAR Area Correlator
RAC . . . . RADAR Azimuth Converter
RAC . . . . Radio Adaptive Communications
RAC . . . . Ram Air Cushion (Aerospace)
RAC . . . . Rapid Action Change (DOD)
RAC . . . . Rational Activity Coefficient
RAC . . . . Reactor Accident Calculation
RAC . . . . Read Address Counter
RAC . . . . Rear Admiral Commanding (British)
RAC . . . . Recessed Annular Connector
RAC . . . . Rectified Alternating Current (Radio)
RAC . . . . Reliability Analysis Center (Air Force)
RAC . . . . Reparable Assets Control
RAC . . . . Republic Aviation Corporation
RAC . . . . Request Altitude Change (Aviation)
RAC . . . . Request for Authority to Contract (Military)
RAC . . . . Requisition Advice Care
RAC . . . . Research Advisory Committee
RAC . . . . Research Advisory Council
RAC . . . . Research Analysis Corporation
RAC . . . . Research Analysis Corps (Army)
RAC . . . . Royal Agricultural College (British)
RAC . . . . Royal Arch Chapter (Masonry)
RAC . . . . Royal Armoured Corps (British)
RAC . . . . Royal Automobile Club (Controlling body of motor racing in Britain)
RAC . . . . Rubber Allocation Committee
RAC . . . . Rules of the Air and Air Traffic Control (ICAO Air Navigation Commission)

RACC . . . . . . Radiation and Contamination Control
RACC . . . . . . Regional Agricultural Credit Corporation
RACC . . . . . . Reporting Activity Control Card (Army)
RACC . . . . . . Research Aviation Coordinating Committee
RACCA . . . . . Refrigeration and Air Conditioning Contractors Association-National
RACE . . . . . . Random Access Computer Equipment
RACE . . . . . . Rapid Automatic Checkout Equipment
RACE . . . . . . Request Altitude Changes En Route (Aviation)
RACE . . . . . . Research on Automatic Computation Electronics
RACE . . . . . . Restoration of Aircraft to Combat Effectivity
RACEP . . . . . Random Access and Correlation for Extended Performance
RACES . . . . . Radio Amateur Civil Emergency Service (Civil Defense)
RACFI . . . . . . Radio and Communication Facilities Inoperative
RACFOE . . . . . Research Analysis Corporation Field Office, Europe (Army)
RACIC . . . . . . Remote Area Conflict Information Center (Battelle Memorial Institute)
RACNE . . . . . Regional Advisory Committee on Nuclear Energy
RACOB(WA).. . Rear Admiral Commanding Combined Operational Bases (Western Approaches) (Britain)
RACOMS . . . . Rapid Combat Mapping System (Military)
RACON . . . . . RADAR Beacon
RACON . . . . . Radio Beacon
RACS . . . . . . Random Access Communications System
RACS . . . . . . Remote Access Computing System
RACS . . . . . . Remote Automatic Calibration System
RAD . . . . Radford Arsenal (Army)
RAD . . . . Radian
RAD . . . . Radiation Absorbed Dose (Unit of measurement of radiation energy)
RAD . . . . Radiator
RAD . . . . Radio
RAD . . . . Radius
RAD . . . . Rapid Access Disk
RAD . . . . Rapid Automatic Drill
RAD . . . . Ratio Analysis Diagram (Metallurgy)
RAD . . . . Reference Attitude Display
RAD . . . . Regional Accountable Depot (Military)
RAD . . . . Reichsarbeitsdienst
RAD . . . . Released from Active Duty (Navy)
RAD . . . . Reported for Active Duty (Navy)
RAD . . . . Required Availability Date (Military)
RAD . . . . Requirements Action Directive
RAD . . . . Research and Advanced Development
RAD . . . . Reservists on Active Duty (Navy)
RAD . . . . Return to Active Duty (Military)
RAD . . . . Right Anterior Digestive (Gland)
RAD . . . . Rite Aid Corp. (NYSE symbol)
RAD . . . . Roentgen Administered Dose
RAD . . . . Royal Albert Dock (British)
RAD . . . . Rural Areas Development
RADA . . . . . . Radioactive
RADA . . . . . . Random Access Discrete Address (Army division-level battlefield radio communications system)
RADA . . . . . . Royal Academy of Dramatic Art (British)
RADAC . . . . . Rapid Digital Automatic Computing
RADACS . . . . . Random Access Discrete Address Communications System
RADAL . . . . . Radio Detection and Location
RADAN . . . . . RADAR Doppler Automatic Navigator
RADAN . . . . . RADAR Navigation
RADAR . . . . . Radio Detection and Ranging
RADARC . . . . . Radially Distributed Annular Rocket Chamber
RADAS . . . . . Random Access Discrete Address System
RADAT . . . . . RADAR Data Transmission
RADAT . . . . . Radio Direction and Track
RADAT . . . . . Radiosonde Observation Data
RADATA . . . . . RADAR Automatic Data Transmission Assembly
RADATAC . . . . Radiation Data Acquisition Chart
RAD(BPF). . . . . Rear Admiral Commanding Destroyers (British Pacific Fleet)
RADC . . . . . . Rome Air Development Center (ESD)
RADC . . . . . . Royal Army Dental Corps (British)
RADCC . . . . . Rear Area Damage Control Center
RADCM . . . . . RADAR Countermeasures and Deception (Military)
RADCON . . . . RADAR Data Converter
RADDEF . . . . . Radiological Defense (Army)
RADEM . . . . . Random Access Delta Modulation
RADEP . . . . . RADAR Departure
RADER . . . . . Rassemblement Democratique du Ruanda (Democratic Rally of Rwanda)
RADEX . . . . . Radiation Exclusion Plot (Chart of actual or predicted fallout)
RADFAC . . . . . Radiating Facility
RADFO . . . . . Radiological Fallout
RADHAZ . . . . . Radiation Hazards
RADI . . . . Radiographic Inspection

RADIAC ..... Radioactivity Detection, Indication, and Computation (Radiological measuring instruments)
RADIC ...... Radio Interior Communications
RADIC ...... Redifon Analog-Digital Computer (British)
RADIC ...... Research and Development Information Center
RADINT ..... RADAR Intelligence
RADIQUAD ... Radio Quadrangle (Military)
RADIR ...... Random Access Document Indexing and Retrieval
RADIST ..... RADAR Distance Indicator
RADL .... Radial
RADL .... Radiological (or Radiology)
RADLAB ..... Radiation Laboratory
RADLCEN .... Radiological Center
RADLDEF..... Radiological Defense (Military)
RADLFO ..... Radiological Fallout (Army)
RADLMON ... Radiological Monitor(ing)
RADLO...... Radiological Defense Officer
RADLOP ..... Radiological Operations
RADLSAFE.... Radiological Safety (Military)
RADLSO ..... Radiological Survey Officer
RADLSV ..... Radiological Survey
RadLV....... Radiation Leukemia Virus
RADLWAR .... Radiological Warfare (Military)
RADM...... Rear Admiral (Also, RA)
RADMON .... Radiological Monitoring
RADN....... Radiation
RADNOS..... No Radio (Military)
RADNOTE.... Radio Note (Military)
RADOME .... RADAR Dome (NASA)
RADON ...... RADAR Beacon
RADOP...... RADAR-Doppler (Missile tracking system)
RADOP...... RADAR/Optical Weapons (Military)
RADOP...... Radio Operator (Navy)
RADOPR ..... Radio Operator
RADOSE ..... Radiation Dosimeter Satellite (NASA)
RADOT...... Real-Time Automatic Digital Optical Tracker (NASA)
RADPLANBD . Radio Planning Board (Navy)
RADPROPCAST . Radio Propagation Forecast
RADREL ..... Radio Relay
RADRON .... RADAR Squadron (Air Force)
RADS ...... Radius
RADS ...... Ryukyu Air Defense System
RADSTA ..... Radio Station
RADU....... RADAR Analysis and Detection Unit (National Weather Service)
RADVS ..... RADAR Altimeter Doppler Velocity Sensor
RADWAR..... Radiological Warfare
RAE .... Radio Astronomy Explorer (Satellite)
RAE .... Right Arithmetic Element
RAE .... Right Ascension Encoder
RAE .... Royal Aircraft Establishment (Great Britain)
RAEDOT ..... Range, Azimuth and Elevation Detection of Optical Targets
RAES....... Royal Aeronautical Society
RAET ...... Range, Azimuth, Elevation, and Time
RAF .... Regular Air Force
RAF .... Research Aviation Facility (National Center for Atmospheric Research)
RAF .... Reserved Air Freight
RAF .... Reynolds Analogy Factor
RAF .... Royal Air Force (British)
RAF .... Royal Aircraft Factory (British) (World War I)
RAFA ...... Royal Air Forces Association
RAFAR..... Radio Automated Facsimile and Reproduction
RAFAX ..... RADAR Facsimile Transmission
RAFB ...... Randolph Air Force Base
RAFB ...... Royal Air Force Base
RAFD ...... Rome Air Force Depot
RAFP ...... Ryukyuan Armed Forces Police
RAFS ...... Royal Air Force Station (British)
RAFSC ..... Royal Air Force Staff College (British)
RAFT ...... Rear Admiral Fleet Train (British Pacific Fleet)
RAFT ...... Recomp Algebraic Formula Translator (Data processing)
RAFT ...... Regional Accounting and Finance Test (Military)
RAFTC ..... Royal Air Forces Transport Command
RAFVR ..... Royal Air Force Volunteer Reserve (British)
RAG....... Replacement Air Group
RAG....... Requirements Advisory Group (Air Force)
RAG....... River Assault Group (Military)
RAGE...... Radio Amplification of Gamma Emissions (Antiguerrilla weapon)
RAGF ...... Remote Air-Ground Facility (Aviation)
RAH....... Receiving Array Hydrophone
RAH....... Robins (A.H.) Co., Inc. (NYSE symbol)
RAI .... Radiation Applications, Incorporated

RAI......... Radioactive Interference (NASA)
RAI .... Radiotelevisione Italiana (Italian government-controlled radio and television company)
RAI .... Random Access and Inquiry
RAI .... Range Azimuth Indicator
RAIC ...... Radiological Accident and Incident Control
RAIC ...... Redstone Arsenal Information Center (Army)
RAID ...... RADAR Identification and Direction System
RAID ...... Recallable Airborne Infrared Display
RAIL ...... Runway Alignment Indicator Light (or Lighting) (FAA)
RAILS...... Remote Area Instrument Landing Sensor
RAILS...... Remote Area Instrument Landing System (Army)
RAINPAL..... Recursive Aided Inertial Navigation for Precision Approach and Landing (NASA)
RAIR...... Rapid Advancement in Reading (Education)
RAIR ...... Recordak Automated Information Retrieval (System)
RAL .... Ralston Purina Company (NYSE symbol)
RAL .... Rapid Access Loop
RAL .... Rear Admiral Alexandria (British)
RAL .... Reenlistment Allowance (Military)
RAL .... Remote Area Landing
RAL .... Resort Airlines, Inc.
RAL .... Rubber-Air-Lead (Tile)
RALACS ..... RADAR Altimeter Altitude Control System
RALI....... Remarried Association of Long Island
RALT ...... Range Light
RALV...... Random Access Light Valve
RaLV...... Rat Leukemia Virus
RAM .... RADAR Absorbing Material
RAM....... Radio Attenuation Measurement (Spacecraft for testing communications)
RAM....... Ramada Inns, Inc. (NYSE symbol)
RAM....... Random Access Memory (Data processing)
RAM....... Random Angle Modulation
RAM....... Range-Altitude Monitor
RAM .... Rapid Area Maintenance (Air Force)
RAM .... Raytheon Airborne Microwave
RAM .... Reentry Antimissile
RAM....... Reentry Attenuation Measurement (NASA)
RAM....... Repeating Antipersonnel Mine
RAM .... Research Aviation Medicine (Navy program of research into aerospace medical techniques)
RAM....... Resident Aerospace Medicine (Physician in specialty training) (Military)
RAM....... Resources Analysis and Management
RAM .... Revolutionary Action Movement
RAM ...... Right Ascension of the Meridian (Navigation)
RAM ...... Royal Academy of Music (British)
RAM ...... Royal Arch Mason
RAMA ..... Rome Air Materiel Area (Air Force) (Deactivated)
RAMAC..... Random Access or Memory Accounting
RAMAC ..... Random Access Method of Accounting and Control (Data processing)
RAMARK ..... RADAR Marker (Military)
RaM-BaM ..... Rabbi Moses ben Maimon (Maimonides) (Jewish philosopher, 1135-1204)
RAMC ...... Royal Army Medical Corps (British)
RA/MCC..... Restricted Area/Military Climb Corridor (Aviation)
RAMD...... Random Accessory Memory Device
RAMD ...... Receiving Agency Materiel Division (Military)
RAMIS ...... Rapid Access Management Information System
RAMIS ...... Rapid Automatic Malfunction Isolation System
RAMIS ..... Receiving, Assembly Maintenance, Inspection, Storage (Military)
RAMMIT ..... Reliability and Maintainability Management Improvement Techniques (Army)
RAMMS...... Responsive Automated Materiel Management System (Army)
RAMNAC.... Radio Aids to Marine Navigation Committee (British)
RAMONT..... Radiological Monitoring
RAMP...... RADAR Mapping of Panama
RAMP...... RADAR Modification Program
RAMP ...... Radiation Airborne Measurement Program
RAMP...... Random Access Mechanization of Phosphorus
RAMP...... Raytheon Airborne Microwave Platform (Sky station)
RAMP...... Recovered Allied Military Personnel
RAMPART .... RADAR Advanced Measurements Program for Analysis of Reentry Techniques (ARPA - Raytheon)
RAMPS ..... Repatriated American Military Personnel (World War II)
RAMPS ..... Resources Allocation and Multi-Project Scheduling
RAMS ...... Reduced-Size Antenna Monopulse System
RAMS ...... Remote Area Mobility Study
RAMS ...... Remote Automatic Multipurpose Station
RAMS ...... Right Ascension Mean Sun (Navigation)
RAMSA ..... Radio Aeronautics Mexicana, SA
RAMSS ..... Royal Alfred Merchant Seamen's Society (British)
RAMTAC..... Reentry Analysis and Modeling of Target Characteristics

RAN . . . . Read Around Number
RAN . . . . Reconnaissance/Attack Navigator
RAN . . . . Regional Air Navigation (ICAO)
RAN . . . . Repair Activity Accounting Number (Navy)
RAN . . . . Reporting Accounting Number
RAN . . . . Request for Authority to Negotiate
RAN . . . . Royal Australian Navy
RANCID . . . . . Real and Not Corrected Input Data (Data processing)
RANCOM . . . . Random Communication Satellite
RAND . . . . . . Research Applied to National Needs (National Science Foundation)
RAND . . . . . . Research and Development (Origin of name of RAND Corporation, a non-profit national defense research organization)
RANDAM . . . . Random-Access Nondestructive Advanced Memory
RANDID . . . . . Rapid Alphanumeric Digital Indicating Device
RANDO . . . . . Radiotherapy Analog Dosimetry
RANN . . . . . . Research Applied to National Needs (Formerly, IRRPOS) (National Science Foundation)
RANSA . . . . . Rutas Aereas Nacionales, SA (Venezuelan cargo airline)
RANT . . . . . . Reentry Antenna Test
RAN(V)R . . . . Royal Australian Naval (Volunteer) Reserve
RANXPE . . . . Resident Army Nike-X Project Engineer
RAO . . . . Radio Astronomical Observatory
RAO . . . . Regional Agricultural Officer (Ministry of Agriculture, Fisheries, and Food) (British)
RAOB . . . . . . Radiosonde Observation
RAOB . . . . . . Royal Antediluvian Order of Buffaloes
RAOC . . . . . . Royal Army Ordnance Corps (British)
RAOMP . . . . . Report of Accrued Obligations, Military Pay
RAP . . . . RADAR Aim Point
RAP . . . . Radical Action for People
RAP . . . . Radiological Assistance Plan (AEC)
RAP . . . . Random Access Program (or Projector)
RAP . . . . Rapid
RAP . . . . Regimental Aid Post
RAP . . . . Regression Analysis Program (Military)
RAP . . . . Releasable Assets Program
RAP . . . . Reliable Acoustic Path
RAP . . . . Reliability Assessment Prediction
RAP . . . . Right Angle Plug
RAP . . . . Right Atrial Pressure (Biology)
RAP . . . . Rocket-Assisted Projectiles
RAP . . . . Rupees, Annas, Pies (Denominations of Indian money)
RAPC . . . . . . Radio Administration Plenipotentiary Conference
RAPC . . . . . . Right Angle Pressure Cartridge
RAPC . . . . . . Royal Army Pay Corps (British)
RAPCO . . . . . Regional Air Priorities Control Office (Army)
RAPCOE . . . . Random Access Programming and Checkout Equipment
RAPCON . . . . RADAR Approach Control
RAPD . . . . . . Response Amplitude Probability Data
RAPEC . . . . . Rocket-Assisted Personnel Ejection Catapult
RAPECA . . . . Rassemblement du Peuple Camerounais (Camerounese People's Rally)
RAPID . . . . . . Relative Address Programming Implementation Device (Data processing)
RAPID . . . . . . Remote Access Planning for Institutional Development (Data processing)
RAPID . . . . . . Remote Access Procedure for Interactive Design (General Motors)
RAPID . . . . . . Research in Automatic Photocomposition and Information Dissemination
RAPID . . . . . . Rocketdyne Automatic Processing of Integrated Data (Data processing)
RAPID . . . . . . Ryan Automatic Plot Indicator Device
RAPIDS . . . . . Random Access Personnel Information Dissemination System (Army)
RAPIDS . . . . . Rapid Automated Problem Identification System (DOD)
RAPM . . . . . . Reliability Assessment Prediction Model
RAPP . . . . . . Reconciliation and Purification Program (Air Force)
RAPP . . . . . . Registered Air Parcel Post
RAPP's . . . . . Radiologists, Anesthesiologists, Pathologists, and Physiatrists
RAPPI . . . . . . Random Access Plan-Position Indicator (Air Force)
RAPR . . . . . . Right Angle Panel Receptacle
RAPRA . . . . . Rubber and Plastics Research Association (British)
RAPS . . . . . . Risk Appraisal of Programs System
RAPT . . . . . . Reusable Aerospace Passenger Transport
RAPTAP . . . . . Random Access Parallel Tape
RAP-TAP . . . . Releasable Assets Program - Transferable Assets Program (Navy)
RAPTUS . . . . . Rapid Thorium-Uranium-Sodium (Nuclear reactor)
RAR . . . . Radio Acoustic Ranging
RAR . . . . Random Age Replacement
RAR . . . . Read Around Ratio
RAR . . . . Record and Report
RAR . . . . . . Reduced Aspect Ratio
RAR . . . . Regular Army Reserve
RAR . . . . Reliability Action Report (or Request)
RAR . . . . Remove Audible Ring
RAR . . . . Repair as Required
RAR . . . . Report Authorization Record (or Request)

RAR . . . . Royal Army Reserve (British)
RAR . . . . Royal Australian Regiment
RARAD . . . . . RADAR Advisory
RARC . . . . . . Revoked Appointment and Returned to Civilian Status (Navy)
RARDE . . . . . Royal Armament Research & Development Establishment (British)
RARE . . . . . . Ram Air Rocket Engine
RARE . . . . . . Rehabilitation of Addicts by Relatives and Employers
RAREP . . . . . RADAR Report
RARF . . . . . . RADOME, Antenna and Radio Frequency (Integration)
RARI . . . . . . Reporting and Routing Instructions
RARU . . . . . . Radio Range Station Reported Unreliable (Message abbreviation)
RAS . . . . Rabbonim Aid Society
RAS . . . . RADAR Advisory Service
RAS . . . . RADAR Assembly Spares
RAS . . . . RADOME Antenna Structure
RAS . . . . Radula Sinus
RAS . . . . Reaction Augmentation System
RAS . . . . Rear Area Security (Army)
RAS . . . . Rectified Air Speed (Navigation)
RAS . . . . Reflector Antenna System
RAS . . . . Report Audit Summary
RAS . . . . Requirements Allocation Sheet
RAS . . . . Reticular Activating System (Diffuse network of neurons in the brain)
RAS . . . . Rheumatoid Arthritis Serum (Factor) (Medicine)
RAS . . . . Royal Aeronautical Society (British)
RAS . . . . Royal Asiatic Society (British)
RAS . . . . Royal Astronomical Society (British)
RASA . . . . . . Railway and Airline Supervisors Association (AFL-CIO)
RASC . . . . . . Rear Area Security Controller
RASC . . . . . . Rome Air Service Command (Air Force)
RASC . . . . . . Royal Army Service Corps (British)
RASCAL . . . . Random Access Secure Communications Antijam Link
RASCC . . . . . Rear Area Security Control Center
RASC/DC . . . . Rear Area Security and Area Damage Control (Military)
RASD . . . . . . Reference and Adult Services Division (Formerly, RSD) (of American Library Association)
RASE . . . . . . Royal Agricultural Society of England
RASER . . . . . Radio Amplification by Stimulated Emission of Radiation
RASER . . . . . Range and Sensitivity Extending Resonator (Electronics)
RASES . . . . . Republic Aviation Society of Engineers and Scientists
RASIDS . . . . . Range Safety Impact Display System
RASO . . . . . . Rear Airfield Supply Organization
RASP . . . . . . Refined Aeronautical Support Program
RASP . . . . . . Retrieval and Sort Processor (Data processing)
RASPE . . . . . Resident Army SENSCOM (Sentinel Systems Command) Project Engineer
RASS . . . . . . RADAR Attitude Sensing System
RASS . . . . . . Rapid Area Supply Support (Military)
RAST . . . . . . Radioallergosorbent Technique (Allergy test)
RASTA . . . . . Radiation-Augmented Special Test Apparatus (LASER)
RASTA . . . . . Radio Station (Coast Guard)
RASTAC . . . . Random Access Storage and Control (Data processing)
RASTAD . . . . Random Access Storage and Display (Data processing)
RASTAS . . . . . Radiating Site Target Acquisition System
RAT . . . . Ram Air Temperature
RAT . . . . Ram Air Turbine
RAT . . . . Ratio
RAT . . . . Reichsangestellten-Tarifertrag (Germany)
RAT . . . . Reliability Assurance Test
RAT . . . . Remote Area Terminal
RAT . . . . Remote Associations Test (Psychology)
RAT . . . . Repeat Action Tablet (Pharmacology)
RAT . . . . Rocket-Assisted Torpedo (Antisubmarine warfare)
RATA . . . . . . Rankine Cycle Air Turboaccelerator
RATAC . . . . . RADAR Analog Target Acquisition Computer
RATAC . . . . . Raytheon Acoustic Telemetry and Control
RATAN . . . . . RADAR and Television Aid to Navigation
RATAV . . . . . RADAR Terrain Avoidance
RATC . . . . . . Rate-Aided Tracking Computer
RATCC . . . . . RADAR Air Traffic Control Center
RATCON . . . . RADAR Terminal Control
RATE . . . . . . Rate Analysis and Transportation Evaluation (Student legal action organization)
RATE . . . . . . Remote Automatic Telemetry Equipment (Data processing)
RATEL . . . . . Radiotelephone
RATELO . . . . Radiotelephone Operator
RATER . . . . . Response Analysis Tester (NASA)
RATG . . . . . . Radiotelegraph
RATO . . . . . . Rocket-Assisted Takeoff (Flying)
RATP . . . . . . Regie Autonome des Transports Parisiens
RATR . . . . . . Reliability Abstracts and Technical Reviews (NASA)
RATS . . . . . . Ram Air Turbine System

RATS . . . . Rapid Area Transportation Support (Air Force)
RATS . . . . Rate and Track Subsystem
RATS . . . . . . Reconnaissance and Tactical Security (Teams) (Military)
RATS . . . . Remote Alarm Transmission System
RATS . . . . . . Remote Area Tactical (Location and Landing) System
RATS . . . . . . Remote Area Terminal System
RATSC . . . . . . Rome Air Technical Service Command (Air Force)
RATSCAT . . . . RADAR Target Scatter Site (RADAR program)
RATSEC . . . . . Robert A. Taft Sanitary Engineering Center
RATT . . . . Radio Teletype(writer)
RAU . . . . Railway African Union
RAV . . . . Random Access Viewer
RAV . . . . Restricted Availability
RAVC . . . . . . Royal Army Veterinary Corps (British)
RAVE . . . . . . RADAR Acquisition Visual-Tracking Equipment
RAVE . . . . . . Random Access Video Editing (Computerized film editing)
RAVE . . . . . . Random Access Viewing Equipment
RAVEC . . . . . . RADAR Vector
RAVEN . . . . . Ranging and Velocity Navigation
RAVU . . . . Radiosonde Analysis and Verification Unit
RAW . . . . Rapid American Withdrawal (Antiwar march sponsored by Vietnam Veterans Against the War)
RAW . . . . Ready and Waiting (Slang)
RAW . . . . Right Attack Wing (Women's lacrosse position)
RAWARC . . . . RADAR and Warning Coordination (Teletypewriter circuit)
RAWB . . . . . . Railroad and Airline Wage Board (Terminated, 1953)
RAWIE . . . . . . Radio Weather Intercept Element
RAWIN . . . . . . RADAR Wind Sounding
RAWIND . . . . . Radio Wind (Coast Guard)
RAWINSONDE . . Radiosonde and RADAR Wind Sounding (Upper air observation)
RAWS . . . . . . RADAR Altimeter Warning Set
RAWU . . . . . . Railway African Mineworkers Trade Union (Southern Rhodesia)
RAWX . . . . . . Returned Account Weather (Aviation)
RAX . . . . Remote Access (Data processing)
RAY . . . . Raybestos-Manhattan, Inc. (NYSE symbol)
RAYCI . . . . . . Raytheon Controlled Inventory (Data processing)
RAY-COM . . . . Raytheon Communications Equipment (Citizens band radiotelephone)
RAYSISTOR . . . Raytheon Resistor (Electro-optical control device)
RAYSPAN . . . . Raytheon Spectrum Analyzer
RAY-TEL . . . . . Raytheon Telephone (Citizens band radio)
RAZ . . . . Rolled Alloyed Zinc
RAZEL . . . . . . Range, Azimuth and Elevation
RAZON . . . . . Range and Azimuth Only
RAZPE . . . . . . Resident ARGMA (Army Rocket and Guided Missile Agency) Zeus Project Engineer
RAZS . . . . . . Rolled Alloyed Zinc Sheet
RB . . . . RADAR Beacon
RB . . . . Rate Beacon
RB . . . . Read Back (Communications)
RB . . . . Read Backward
RB . . . . Read Buffer
RB . . . . Reading & Bates Offshore Drilling Co. (NYSE symbol)
RB . . . . Reconnaissance Bomber
RB . . . . Red Book (Drug topics)
RB . . . . Relative Bearing (Navigation)
RB . . . . Renegotiation Board
RB . . . . Repeated Back (Communications)
RB . . . . Report Bibliography
RB . . . . Rescue Boat
RB . . . . Research Bulletin
RB . . . . Restricted Bulletin
RB . . . . Retractable Boom
RB . . . . Return to Bias
RB . . . . Reverse Blocked
RB . . . . Rifle Brigade
RB . . . . Right Fullback (Football)
RB . . . . Rigid Boat
RB . . . . Rigid Body
RB . . . . Road Bend
RB . . . . Roast Beef (Restaurant slang)
RB . . . . Rocket Branch
RB . . . . Rubber Base (Technical drawings)
Rb . . . . Rubidium (Chemical element)
R/B . . . . Radio Beacon
R & B . . . . . . Rhythm and Blues (Music)
RBA . . . . RADAR Beacon Antenna
RBA . . . . Radio Beacon Array
RBA . . . . Ranger Battalions Association
RBA . . . . Reentry Body Assembly
RBA . . . . Rescue Breathing Apparatus
RBA . . . . Roadside Business Association

RBA . . . . Rotary Beam Antenna
RBA . . . . Rotor Blade Antenna
RBA . . . . Royal Society of British Artists
RBAF . . . . . . Royal Belgian Air Force
RBAUS . . . . . . Romanian Baptist Association of United States
RBA WWII . . . . Ranger Battalions Association World War II
RBBSB . . . . . . Right Bundle-Branch System Block (Physiology)
RBC . . . . Radio Beam Communications
RBC . . . . Red Blood Corpuscle or Cell (Medicine)
RBC . . . . Red Blood Count (Medicine)
RBC . . . . Remote Balance Control
RBC . . . . Roller Bearing Corporation
RBC . . . . Rotating Beam Ceilometer (Aviation)
RbCl . . . . Rubidium Chloride
RBCNO . . . . . Rotating Beam Ceilometer Inoperative (Aviation)
RBCS . . . . . . Radio Beam Communications Set
RBD . . . . Right Border of Dullness
RBD . . . . Rubbermaid, Inc. (NYSE symbol)
RBDE . . . . . . RADAR Bright Display Equipment (FAA)
RBDNRQ . . . . Received But Did Not Return Questionnaire
RBDP . . . . . . Rocket Booster Development Program (Aerospace)
RBDS . . . . . . RADAR Bomb Directing Systems
RBE . . . . Radiation Biological Effectiveness
RBE . . . . Radiation Biological Equivalent
RBE . . . . Relative Biological Effectiveness (of stated types of radiation)
RBE . . . . Replacement Battery Equipment
RBEC . . . . . . Roller Bearing Engineers Committee
RBF . . . . Renal Blood Flow (Physiology)
RBFC . . . . . . Retract Before Firing Contractor
RBG . . . . Right Buccal Ganglion
RBGS . . . . . . Radio Beacon Guidance System
RBH . . . . Regimental Beachhead (Army)
RBHA . . . . . . Rotor Blade Homing Antenna
RBI . . . . Reed Roller Bit Company (NYSE symbol) (Delisted)
RBI . . . . Root Beer Institute
RBI . . . . Runs Batted In (Baseball)
RBL . . . . Radiation Biology Laboratory (Smithsonian Institution)
RBM . . . . Range Betting Method
RBM . . . . Robbins Mills, Inc. (NYSE symbol)
RBMU . . . . . . Regions Beyond Missionary Union
RBN . . . . Radiobeacon (Maps and charts)
RBO . . . . Russian Brotherhood Organization of the United States of America
RBOF . . . . . . Receiving Basins for Off-Site Fuels (AEC)
RBOUSA . . . . . Russian Brotherhood Organization of the United States of America
RBP . . . . Ratio Balance Panel
RBP . . . . Retractable Bow Propeller
RBP . . . . Riboflavin-Binding Protein (Biochemistry)
RBP . . . . Rocket Branch Panel
RBPCA . . . . . . Rare Breeds Poultry Club of America
RBPD . . . . . . Religious Book Publishing Division (of Association of American Publishers)
RBR . . . . Renegotiation Board Regulation
RBR . . . . Ruberoid Company (NYSE symbol) (Delisted)
RBS . . . . RADAR Beacon Sequencer (or System)
RBS . . . . RADAR Beam Sharpening
RBS . . . . RADAR Bomb Scoring
RBS . . . . RADAR Bombsight
RBS . . . . Random Barrage System
RBS . . . . Rare Books Section (Association of College and Research Libraries)
RBS . . . . Recoverable Booster System
RBS . . . . Remote Battle System
RBS . . . . Research for Better Schools, Inc.
RBS . . . . Royal Society of British Sculptors
RBSC . . . . . . RADAR Bomb Scoring Central
RBSE . . . . . . RADAR Beam Sharpening Element
RBSRA . . . . . . Red Berkshire Swine Record Association
RBSS . . . . . . Recoverable Booster Support System
RBT . . . . Radial Beam Tube
RBT . . . . Resistance Bulb Thermometer
RBTE . . . . . . Replacement Battery Terminal Equipment
RBV . . . . Return Beam Vidicon (Satellite camera)
RBW . . . . Relative Biologische Wirkungsweise
RC . . . . Radio Code Aptitude Area
RC . . . . Radio Compass
RC . . . . Range Correction
RC . . . . Rassemblement Congolais (Congolese Rally) (Buakvu)
RC . . . . Rate of Change
RC . . . . Rate Command
RC . . . . Ray Control
RC . . . . Rayon and Cotton (Freight)
RC . . . . Reaction Control
RC . . . . Read and Compute

RC	Reader Code
RC	Ready Calendar
RC	Reception Center (Army)
RC	Recirculatory Air
RC	Reconstruction Committee (British) (World War I)
RC	Record Change
RC	Records Check
RC	Recruiting Center
RC	Red Cell or Corpuscle (Medicine)
RC	Red China
RC	Red Cross
RC	Reduced Cueing
RC	Reference Cavity
RC	Reformed Church
RC	Regional Center
RC	Register of Copyrights (US)
RC	Registered Criminologist
RC	Regulatory Council (FAA)
RC	Rehabilitation Center
RC	Reinforced Concrete (Technical drawings)
RC	Release Clause
RC	Relief Claim
RC	Remote Control
RC	Reply Coupon
RC	Requirements Contract
RC	Reserve Corps
RC	Resistance Capacitance (or Resistor-Capacitor)
RC	Resolver Control
RC	Respiratory Center (Medicine)
RC	Responsibility Center (Air Force)
RC	Reverse Course (Aviation)
RC	Reverse Current
RC	Revised Code
RC	Right Center (Theatrical)
RC	Roll Channel
RC	Roller Coating
RC	Roman Catholic
RC	Rosin Core
RC	Rosslyn Connecting R. R. (AAR code)
RC	Royal Crown (Soft drink brand)
R/C	Rate of Climb
R/C	Request for Checkage (Navy)
R/C	Rubber-Capped
R & C	Rail and Canal
RCA	Rabbinical Council of America
RCA	Radio Club of America
RCA	RCA Corporation (Formerly, Radio Corporation of America) (NYSE symbol)
RCA	Reach Cruising Altitude (Aviation)
RCA	Red Cross Act
RCA	Request for Corrective Action
RCA	Review and Concurrence Authority
RCA	Ricinus communis Agglutinin (Immunology)
RCA	Rocket Cruising Association
RCA	Rodeo Cowboys Association
RCA	Royal Cambrian Academy (British)
RCA	Royal Canadian Academy (or Academician)
RCA	Royal Canadian Artillery
RCAA	Rocket City Astronomical Association
RCAB	Review and Concurrence Advisory Board
RCAC	Royal Canadian Armoured Corps
RCADV	Reverse Course and Advise (Aviation)
RCAF	Royal Canadian Air Force
RCAF(WD)	Royal Canadian Air Force, Women's Division
RCAG	Remote Controlled (or Center) Air-Ground Facility
RCALT	Reach(ed) Cruising Altitude (Aviation)
RCAMC	Royal Canadian Army Medical Corps
RCAPC	Royal Canadian Army Pay Corps
RCASC	Royal Canadian Army Service Corps
RCAT	Radio Code Aptitude Test
RCAT	Radio Controlled Aerial Target
RCB	Radiation Control Board
RCB	Reflection Coefficient Bridge
RCB	Remote Control Bandwidth
RCB	Retailers Credit Bureau, Inc. (New York metropolitan area)
RCB	Rubber Control Board
RCBW	Radiological Chemical Biological Warfare
RCC	International Society of Reply Coupon Collectors
RCC	RADAR Control Clouds
RCC	Radio Common Channels
RCC	Radio Communications Center
RCC	Radiochemical Centre

RCC	Radiological Control Center (Army)
RCC	Rag Chewers' Club (Amateur radio)
RCC	Range Control Center
RCC	Ratio of Charges to Costs
RCC	RCA Corporation Communications
RCC	Read Channel Continue
RCC	Reader Common Contact
RCC	Real-Time Computer Complex
RCC	Recovery Control Center
RCC	Red Cross of Constantine
RCC	Remote Communications Central
RCC	Remote Communications Complex
RCC	Remote Communications Console
RCC	Rescue Control Center
RCC	Rescue Coordination Center (Coast Guard)
RCC	Rescue Crew Commander
RCC	Reset Control Circuit
RCC	Resources Conservation Company
RCC	Riverside City College (California)
RCC	Roman Catholic Church (British)
RCC	Rough Combustion Cutoff
RCC	Royal Crown Cola Company (NYSE symbol)
RCC	Russian Corps Combatants
R & CC	Riot and Civil Commotion
RCCC	Regular Common Carrier Conference
RCCC	Royal Curling Club of Canada
RCCE	Regional Congress of Construction Employers
RCCF	Reserve Components Contingency Force
RCCH	Roman Catholic Church
RCCP	Reinforced Concrete Culvert Pipe (Technical drawings)
RCCPLD	Resistance-Capacitance Coupled
RCCS	Rate Command Control System
RCCS	Royal Canadian Corps of Signals
RCCUS	Republican Citizens Committee of the United States
RCD	RADAR Cloud Detection Report (Aviation)
RCD	Reconnaissance Cockpit Display
RCD	Regent's Canal Dock (British)
RCD	Regional Cooperation for Development (Iran, Pakistan, Turkey)
RCD	Reinforcement Control Depot (Air Force)
RCD	Relative Cardiac Dullness (Medicine)
RCD	Research Centers Directory
RCD	Rock Coring Device
RCD	Rocket Cushioning Device
RCDA	Religion in Communist Dominated Areas (Magazine)
RCDC	RADAR Course-Directing Center
RCDC	Radiation Chemistry Data Center (University of Notre Dame)
RCDC	Royal Canadian Dental Corps
RCDCB	Regional Civil Defense Coordination Boards
RCDEP.	Rural Civil Defense Education Program
RCDMB	Regional Civil and Defense Mobilization Boards
RCDNA	RADAR Cloud Detection Report Not Available (Meteorology)
RCDNE	RADAR Cloud Detection Report No Echoes Observed (Meteorology)
RCDS	Rural Community Development Service (Department of Agriculture)
RCE	Radio Communications Equipment
RCE	Rapid Changing Environment
RCE	Rapid Circuit Etch
RCE	Reaction Control Engine
RCE	Reliability Control Engineering
RCE	Religious of Christian Education (Roman Catholic women's religious order)
RCE	Royal Canadian Engineers
RCEA	Recreational Coach and Equipment Association
RCEAC	Regional Civil Emergency Advisory Committee (Formerly, JRCC) (Civil Defense)
RCEEA	Radio Communications and Electronic Engineers Association
RCEME	Royal Canadian Electrical and Mechanical Engineers
RCF	Ratio Correction Factor
RCF	Recall Finder
RCF	Relative Centrifugal Force
RCF	Remain on Company Frequency (Aviation)
RCF	Repair Cost Factor (Navy)
RCF	Rotating Cylinder Flap
RCFR	Royal Canadian Fleet Reserve
RCFU	Rotary Carton Feed Unit
RCG	Radio Command Guidance
RCG	Radioactivity Concentrate Guide (Formerly MPC - Maximum Permissible Concentration) (AEC)
RCG	Receiving
RCG	Restricted Categorical Grammar
RCG	Reverberation Control of Gain
RCG	Right Cerebral Ganglion
RCHG	Reduced Charge

RCI	RADAR Coverage Indicator
RCI	Read Channel Initialize
RCI	Reichhold Chemicals, Incorporated (NYSE symbol)
RCI	Research Consultants, Incorporated
RCI	Resident Cost Inspector
RCI	Respiratory Control Index (Biochemistry)
RCI	Royal Colonial Institute (British)
RCIA	Retail Clerks International Association
RCIA	Retail Credit Institute of America
RCIC	Red Cross International Committee
RCIC	Royal Canadian Infantry Corps
RCIE	Regional Council for International Education (University of Pittsburgh)
RCIL	Reliability Critical Item List
RCIUA	Regional Council of the Independent Unions of Algeria (Union Regionale des Syndicats Independants d'Algerie)
RCJ	Reaction Control Jet
RCJ	Reinforced Composite Joint
RCJ	Royal Courts of Justice (British)
RCK	Radio Check (Aviation)
RCK	Ramp Check (Aviation)
RCL	Radiation Counter Laboratories, Inc.
RCL	Radio Command Linkage
RCL	Ramped Cargo Lighter
RCL	Royal Canadian Legion
RCL	Ruby Crystal LASER
RCL	Ruling Case Law
RCLM	Runway Centerline Marking (Aviation)
RCLO	Reports Control Liaison Officer (Army)
RCLS	Runway Centerline Lights System (Aviation)
RCM	Aviation Radio and RADAR Countermeasures Technician (Navy)
RCM	La Republique des Citoyens du Monde (Commonwealth of World Citizens)
RCM	RADAR Countermeasures
RCM	Radio (or RADAR) Countermeasures
RCM	Radio-Controlled Mine (Military)
RCM	Range Change Method (Aircraft)
RCM	Rassemblement Chretien de Madagascar (Christian Rally of Madagascar)
RCM	Receipt of Classified Material
RCM	Red Cell Mass
RCM	Regimental Court-Martial
RCM	Religious Conceptionist Missionaries (Roman Catholic women's religious order)
RCM	Right Costal Margin (Medicine)
RCM	Rotor Current Meter
RCM	Royal College of Music (British)
RCMASA	Russian Consolidated Mutual Aid Society of America
RCMD	Rice Council for Market Development
RCMIS	Reserve Components Management Information System (Army)
RCMP	Royal Canadian Mounted Police (Formerly, RNWMP)
RCN	Reactor Centrum Nederland (Atomic power) (Netherlands)
RCN	Receipt of Change Notice
RCN	Record Control Number
RCN	Report Change Notice
RCN	Royal Canadian Navy
RCNAS	Royal Canadian Naval Air Station
RCNC	Royal Canadian Naval College (1943-1948)
RCNC	Royal Corps of Naval Constructors
RCNLR	Reconnaissance Long Range (Army)
RCNR	Royal Canadian Naval Reserve
RCN(V)R	Royal Canadian Naval (Volunteer) Reserve
RCO	RADAR Control Officer
RCO	Radio Control Operator
RCO	Remote Communication Outlet (ATCS)
RCO	Remote Control Office
RCO	Remote Control Oscillator
RCO	Rendezvous Compatible Orbit
RCO	Reports Control Officer (Army)
RCO	Representative Calculating Operation
RCO	Research Contracting Officer
RCOA	Radio Club of America
RCOA	Record Club of America
RCOC	Royal Canadian Ordnance Corps
RCP	RADAR Conversion Program
RCP	Rectangular Coordinate Plotter
RCP	Regional Conservation Program
RCP	Reinforced Concrete Pipe (Technical drawings)
RCP	Relative Competitive Preference (Marketing)
RCP	Reliability Critical Problem
RCP	Remote Control Panel
RCP	Restartable Cryogenic Propellant
RCP	Richmond Corporation (NYSE symbol)

RCP	Right Circular Polarization
RCP	Rotation Combat Personnel
RCP	Royal College of Physicians (British)
RCPA	Reserve Components Program of the Army
RCPA	Rural Cooperative Power Association
RCP(b)	Russian Communist Party (Bolsheviks)
RCPC	Raymond Concrete Pile Company
RCPC	Royal Canadian Postal Corps (Formerly, CPC)
RCPE	Royal College of Physicians, Edinburgh
RCPT	Receipt
RCR	Reactor Control Room
RCR	Reader Control Relay
RCR	Reciprocating Cryogenic Refrigerator
RCR	Retail Credit Co. (NYSE symbol)
RCR	Runway Condition Reading (or Report) (Aviation)
RCRBSJ	Research Council on Riveted & Bolted Structural Joints
RCRC	Reinforced Concrete Research Council
RCRC	Revoked Commission, Returned to Civilian Status (Navy)
RCRD	Record
RCRF	Rei Cretariae Romanae Fautores (Society of Roman Ceramic Archeologists)
RCRHRCS	Research Center for Religion and Human Rights in Closed Societies
RCRL	Reliability Critical Ranking List
RCS	RADAR Calibration Sphere
RCS	RADAR Collimator System
RCS	RADAR Control Ship
RCS	RADAR Cross Section
RCS	Radio Command System
RCS	Radio Communications Set
RCS	Rate Command System
RCS	Reaction Control System (or Subsystem) (Apollo) (NASA)
RCS	Rearward Communications System
RCS	Reentry Control System (Aerospace)
RCS	Reliable Corrective Action Summary
RCS	Remote Control Set
RCS	Remote Control System
RCS	Reports Control Symbol (Military)
RCS	Representative Conflict Situations (Army)
RCS	Requirement Clearance Symbol (Military)
RCS	Revenue Cutter Service (Coast Guard)
RCS	Richardson Co. (NYSE symbol)
RCS	Royal College of Surgeons
RCSC	Radio Component Standardization Committee (British)
RCSHSB	Red Cedar Shingle and Handsplit Shake Bureau
RCSI	Receipt for (or of) Classified Security Information
RCSS	Random Communication Satellite System
RCT	RADAR Control Trailer
RCT	Radiobeacon Calibration Transmitter
RCT	Receipts (NYSE symbol)
RCT	Regimental Combat Team
RCT	Repeat Cycle Timer
RCT	Resolver Control Transformer
RCT	Rorschach Content Test (Psychology)
RCT	Royal Corps of Transport (British Army)
RCTB	Reserve Components Troop Basis (Army)
RCTC	Regeneratively Cooled Thrust Chamber
RCTDPOVALCAN	Request Concurrent Travel of Dependents by Privately Owned Vehicle (ALCAN Highway or via Route Required) (Army)
RCTL	Resistance Coupled Transistor Logic
RCTL	Resistor-Capacitor Transistor Logic
RCTP	Reserve Component Troop Program
RCTSR	Radio Code Test, Speed of Response
RCU	RADAR Calibration Unit
RCU	Relay Control Unit
RCU	Remote Control Unit
RCU	Requisition Control Unit
RCU	Research Coordination Unit
RCU	Rocket Countermeasure Unit
RCUA	Remote Checkout Umbilical Array
RCUEP	Research Center for Urban and Environmental Planning (Princeton University)
RCV	Receive
RCV	Relative Conductor Volume
RCV	Restartable Cryogenic Vehicle
RCVG	Replacement Carrier Fighter Group (V is Navy code for Fighter)
RCVR	Receiver
RCVS	Royal College of Veterinary Surgeons (British)
RCW	Register Containing Word
RCWS	Remote Control Water Sampler
RCWS	Russian Children's Welfare Society
RCY	Rotating Coil Yoke
RCZ	Radiation Control Zone

RD . . . . RADAR Data	RDD . . . . Research and Development Division
RD . . . . RADAR Display	RDE . . . . RADAR Display Equipment
RD . . . . RADARman (Navy rating)	RDE . . . . Receptor-Destroying Enzyme
RD . . . . Radiation Detection	RDE . . . . Research and Development Establishment (British)
RD . . . . Radiological Defense (Equipment)	RDE . . . . Rotating Disc Electrode
RD . . . . Random Drift	RD & E . . . . . Research, Development, and Engineering
RD . . . . Reaction of Degeneration	R & DELSEC . . Research and Development Electronic Security
RD . . . . Read	RDEP . . . . Recruit Depot (Navy)
RD . . . . Readiness Date	RDF . . . . Radio Direction Finder (or Finding)
RD . . . . Recognition Differential	RDF . . . . Radio Distribution Function
RD . . . . Regional Director	RDF . . . . Reflection Direction Finding
RD . . . . Reinforcement Designee (Air Force)	RDF . . . . Royal Dublin Fusiliers (British)
RD . . . . Relay Drawer	RDFL . . . . Reflection Direction Finding, Low Angle
RD . . . . Relay Driver	RDFSTA . . . . . Radio Direction Finder Station
RD . . . . Renal Disease	RDFU-V . . . . . Research and Development Field Unit - Vietnam
RD . . . . Replenishable Demand	RDG . . . . Reading Company (NYSE symbol and AAR code) (Delisted)
RD . . . . Required Date	RDG . . . . Resolver Differential Generator
RD . . . . Research and Development	RDG . . . . Right Digestive Gland
RD . . . . Reserve Decoration (British)	RDI . . . . Radio Doppler Inertial
RD . . . . Restricted Data	RDI . . . . Released Data Index
RD . . . . Retention and Disposal	RDI . . . . Royal Designer for Industry
RD . . . . Retinal Detachment	RDIS . . . . Replenishment Demand Inventory System
RD . . . . Revolutionary Development (South Vietnam)	RDK . . . . Research and Development Kit
RD . . . . Right Defense	RDL . . . . Radioactive Decay Law
RD . . . . Rix Dollar	RDL . . . . Radiological Defense Laboratory (Navy)
RD . . . . Road	RDL . . . . Random Dynamic Load
RD . . . . Roof Drain	RDL . . . . Reciprocal Detection Latency
RD . . . . Round	RDL . . . . Regional Development Laboratory (Philadelphia, Pennsylvania)
RD . . . . Royal Dragoons (British)	RDL . . . . Remote Display Link
RD . . . . Royal Dutch Petroleum Company (NYSE symbol)	RDL . . . . Replaceable Display Light
RD . . . . Running Days	RDL . . . . Rim of Dorsal Lip
RD . . . . Rural Dean	RDL . . . . Ritter Company, Inc. (NYSE symbol) (Delisted)
RD . . . . Rural Delivery	RDL . . . . Rocket Development Laboratory (Air Force)
RD . . . . Rural District	RDM . . . . RADARman (Navy)
R/D . . . . Refer to Drawer (Banking)	RDM. . . . . . . Radial Distribution Method
R & D . . . . . . Read and Destroy	RDM. . . . . . . Radiation Damage Monitor
R & D . . . . . . Requirements and Distribution	RDM. . . . . . . Recording Demand Meter
R & D . . . . . . Research and Demonstration (Labor training)	RDM. . . . . . . Relay Driver Module
R & D . . . . . . Research and Development	RDME . . . . Range and Distance Measuring Equipment
R of D . . . . . . Reporter of Debate (US Senate)	RDMI . . . . Roof Drainage Manufacturers Institute
RDA . . . . Rassemblement Democratique Africain (African Democratic Rally)	RDMU. . . . . . . Range-Drift Measuring Unit
RDA . . . . Recirculation Duct Assembly	RDN. . . . . . . Rejection Disposition Notice
RDA . . . . Recommended Dietary Allowance	RDO . . . . Radio Readout
RDA . . . . Recommended Duty Assignment	RDO. . . . . . . Radiological Defense Officer (Civil Defense)
RDA . . . . Reliability Design Approach	RDO. . . . . . . Redistribution Order (Military)
RDA . . . . Research and Development Abstracts	RDO. . . . . . . Research and Development Objectives (Military)
RDA . . . . Research and Development, Army	RDO. . . . . . . Research, Development, and Operation (Military appropriation)
RDA . . . . Rome Daily American (An English-language newspaper in Italy)	RDP . . . . RADAR Data Processing
RDAF . . . . . . Royal Danish Air Force	RDP . . . . RADAR Digital Probe
RDAFCI. . . . . . Research and Development Associates, Food and Container Institute	RDP . . . . Ration Distributing Point (Military)
RDAR . . . . . . Reliability Design Analysis Report	RDP . . . . Remote Data Processor
RDARA . . . . . Regional and Domestic Air Route Area	RDP . . . . Research Data Publication (Center)
RDAS . . . . . . Reflectivity Data Acquisition System	RDP . . . . Ribulose Diphosphate (Biochemistry)
RDAU . . . . . . Remote Data Acquisition Unit	RDPB . . . . . . RADAR Data Plotting Board
RDB . . . . RADAR Decoy Balloon (Air Force)	RDPC . . . . . . RADAR Data Processing Center
RDB . . . . Ramped Dump Barge	RDPE . . . . . . RADAR Data Processing Equipment
RDB . . . . Research and Development Board	RDPM . . . . Revised Draft Presidential Memorandum
RDB . . . . Resistance Decade Box	RDPM . . . . Rotary Drive Piston Motor
RDB . . . . Round Die Bushing	RDPS . . . . . . RADAR Data Processing System
RDB . . . . Rural Development Board (British)	RDPS. . . . . . . Remote Docking Procedures Simulator
RDC . . . . RADAR Design Corporation	RdQ . . . . Reading Quotient
RDC . . . . Radiation Density Constant	RDR . . . . RADAR
RDC . . . . Radioactivity Decay Constant	RDR . . . . Reliability Design Review
RDC . . . . Rail Diesel Car	RDR . . . . Reliability Diagnostic Report
RDC . . . . Rapid Development Capability	RDR . . . . Remote Digital Readout
RDC . . . . Rate Damping Control	RDR . . . . Research and Development Report
RDC . . . . Reflex Digital Control	RDR . . . . Research Division Report
RDC . . . . . . Regional Dissemination Center (NASA)	RDR . . . . Ryder System, Inc. (NYSE symbol)
RDC . . . . . . Remote Data Collection (Data processing)	RDRD . . . . . . Remote Digital Readout
RDC . . . . Remote Detonation Capability	RDRSMTR. . . . . RADAR Transmitter
RDC . . . . Research and Development Command (Military)	RDS . . . . RADAR Display Console
RDC . . . . Rotary Dispersion Colorimeter	RDS . . . . Range Destruct System
RDC . . . . Royal Defence Corps (British)	RDS . . . . Raytheon Data Systems
RDC . . . . Rubber Development Corporation	RDS . . . . Rendezvous Docking Simulator (Aerospace)
RDC . . . . Rural Development and Conservation (Department of Agriculture)	RDS . . . . Research Defence Society (British)
RDC . . . . Rural District Council	RDS . . . . Research and Development Service (Army-Ordnance)
RDCF . . . . . . Restricted Data Cover Folder	RDS . . . . Research and Development Survey
RDCO . . . . . . Reliability Data Control Office	RDS . . . . Resistive Divider Standard
RDD . . . . Rassemblement Democratique Dahomeen (Dahomean Democratic Rally)	RDS . . . . Respiratory Distress Syndrome (Hyaline membrane disease)
RDD . . . . Reactor Development Division (of AEC)	RDS . . . . Revco D.S., Inc. (NYSE symbol)
RDD . . . . Required Delivery Date	RDS . . . . Revolving Discussion Sequence

RD & S	Research, Development, and Studies (Marine Corps)
RDS/M	Rounds Per Minute (Gunnery)
RDT	Rapid Decompression Test
RDT	Remote Data Transmitter
RDT	Reserve Duty Training (Military)
RDT	Rotational Direction Transmission
RDT & E	Research, Development, Testing, and Evaluation Programs (Military)
RDT & EN	Research, Development, Test and Evaluation, Navy (Funding)
RDTR	Research Division Technical Report
RDTSR	Rapid Data Transmission System for Requisitioning (Navy)
RDU	RADAR Display Unit
RDU	Receipt and Despatch Unit (Aircraft)
RDW	Right Defense Wing (Women's lacrosse position)
RDWW	United Slate Tile and Composition Roofers, Damp and Waterproof Workers Association
RDX	Research Department Explosive
RDY	Ready
RDY	Royal Dockyard
Re	Earth or Geocentric Radius
RE	Radiating Elements
RE	Radiation Effects
RE	Radio Electrician
RE	Radio Exposure
RE	Radium Emanation
RE	Raduala Edge
RE	Rare Earth
RE	Rate of Exchange
RE	Reading-Ease (Score) (Advertising)
RE	Real Estate
RE	Red Edges
RE	Redman Industries, Inc. (NYSE symbol)
RE	Reference
RE	Reformed Episcopal (Church)
RE	Regarding
RE	Repayable to Either
RE	Research and Engineering
RE	Reticulo-Endothelium (Medicine)
Re	Rhenium (Chemical element)
RE	Rifle Expert
RE	Right End
RE	Right Excellent
RE	Right Eye
RE	Royal Engineers (Military) (British)
RE	Royal Exchange (British)
RE	Rural Electrification
REA	Railroad Evangelistic Association
REA	Railway Express Agency (Later, REA Express)
REA	Reader R. R. (AAR code)
REA	Reentry Angle
REA	Religious Education Association
REA	Renal Anastomosis
REA	Request for Engineering Authorization
REA	Research Engineering Authorization
REA	Responsible Engineering Activity
REA	Rice Export Association
REA	Rocket Engine Assembly
REA	Rubber Export Association
REA	Rural Electrification Administration (Department of Agriculture)
REAC	React(ion) (Reactive; Reactor)
REAC	Reeves Electronic Analog Computer
REACK	Receipt Acknowledged
REACT	Radio Emergency Associated Citizens Teams (Acronym alone is now used as official organization name)
REACT	Register Enforced Automated Control Technique (Cash register-computing system)
REACT	Rese Engineering Automatic Core Tester
REACT	Resource Allocation and Control Technique (Management)
REACTS	Reader Action Service (ZIP code computer)
REACTS	Regional Educators Annual Chemistry Teaching Symposium
READ	RADAR Echo Augmentation Device
READ	Real-Time Electronic Access and Display (System)
READ	Remedial Education for Adults
READ	Reserve on Extended Active Duty (Military)
READI	Rocket Engine Analyzer & Decision Instrumentation
READJP	Readjustment Pay
READR	Remain in Effect After Discharge and Reenlistment (Refers to orders) (Army)
READS	Reno Air Defense Sector (ADC)
REALCOM	Real-Time Communications (RCA)
REAP	Remote Entry Acquisition Package
REAP	Rural Environmental Assistance Program (Department of Agriculture)
REAPT	Reappoint(ment)

REASM	Reassemble
REASON	Responding to Elderlies' Abilities and Sicknesses Otherwise Neglected (Baltimore, Maryland)
REASTAN	Renton Electrical Analog for Solution of Thermal Analogous Networks
REAT	Radiological Emergency Assistance Team (AEC)
REB	RADAR Evaluation Branch (ADC)
REB	Reentry Body
REB	Research Earth Borer
REB	Rocket Engine Band
REB	Roentgen Equivalent Biological
REBA	Relativistic Electron Beam Accelerator
REBAR	Reinforcing Bar
REBAT	Restricted Bandwidth Techniques
REBE	Recovery Beacon Evaluation
REC	Radiant Energy Conversion
REC	Rain Erosion Coating
REC	Real Estate Council
REC	Receipt
REC	Receiver
REC	Recommendation
REC	Record(ing)
REC	Recreation
REC	Regroupement des Etudiants Camerounais (Regrouping of Cameroonese Students)
REC	Request for Engineering Change
REC	Reserve Equalization Committee (Military)
REC	Ripling Electrochemical
RECAP	Reliability Evaluation Continuous Analysis Program
RECAU	Receipt Acknowledged and Understood
RECD	Received
RECE	Representacion Cubana del Exilio
RECG	Radioelectrocardiograph
RECGA	Research and Engineering Council of Graphic Arts Industry
RECGP	Recovery Group (Air Force)
RECH	Reformed Episcopal Church
RECIP	Reciprocate (Reciprocating; Reciprocation)
RECIPE	Recomp Computer Interpretive Program Expediter
RECIRC	Recirculate
RECMD	Recommend(ation)
RECMECH	Recoil Mechanism
RECMF	Radio and Electronic Component Manufacturers' Federation
RECNO	This Office Has No Record Of (Army)
RECOG	Recognition (or Recognize)
RECOMP	Recommended Completion
RECOMP	Redstone Computer
RECON	Reliability and Configuration Accountability System
RECON	Remote Console (NASA computer)
RECON	Retrospective Conversion of Bibliographic Records (Library of Congress)
RECONCO . . .	Reconnaissance Company (Military)
RECONN	Reconnaissance
RECP	Reciprocal (or Reciprocating)
RECPT	Receptacle
RECPT	Reception
RECRT	Recruit
RECSQUAD . . .	Reconnaissance Squadron (Army)
RECSTA	Receiving Station
RECSYS	Recreation Systems Analysis (Data processing)
RECT	Rectangle
RECT	Rectify
RECY	Recovery
RED	Railroad Employees' Department (of AFL-CIO)
RED	Range Error Detector
RED	Reduce (or Reduction)
RED	Resume Entry Device
RED	Review, Evaluation, Disposition Board
REDAP	Reentrant Data Processing
REDAS	Reduced to Apprentice Seaman (Navy)
REDCAPE	Readiness Capability (Military)
REDCAT	Readiness Requirement (Military)
REDCON	Readiness Condition (Military)
RED HORSE . . .	Rapid Engineer Development, Heavy Operational Repair Squadron, Engineering (Air Force)
REDISTR	Redistribution
REDNT	Redundant
REDO	RADAR Engineering Design Objectives
REDOPS	Ready for Operations (Reporting system) (DOD)
REDOX	Reduction and Oxidation
REDOX	Reductant - Oxidant
REDREP	Redeployment Report (Military)
REDSG	Redesignate
REDSOD	Repetitive Explosive Device for Soil Displacement

REDW . . . . Redwood National Park
REDY . . . . Recirculating Dialyzate (Artficial kidney dialysis system)
REE . . . . Rare-Earth Elements
REE. . . . . Reliance Electric Company (NYSE symbol)
REEC . . . . . . Regional Export Expansion Council (Department of Commerce)
REECO . . . . . Reynolds Electrical and Engineering Company
REEFER . . . . . Refrigerator, Refrigerated or Cold Storage (Airplane, railway car, truck)
REEG . . . . . . Radioelectroencephalograph
REENL . . . . . . Reenlist (Military)
REENLA . . . . . Reenlistment Allowance (Military)
REENLB . . . . . Reenlistment Bonus (Military)
REEP. . . . . . . Range Estimating and Evaluation Procedure (Data processing)
REF . . . . Range Error Function (Aerospace)
REF. . . . . Refer
REF . . . . Release of Excess Funds
REFCD . . . . . . Research and Education Foundation for Chest Disease
REFD. . . . . . . Refund
REFL. . . . . . . Reference Line
REFL. . . . . . . Reflectance (or Reflector)
REFP. . . . . . . Reference Papers (Army)
REFR. . . . . . . Refractory
REFRACDUTRA. . Release from Active Duty for Training (Army)
REFRAD . . . . . Release from Active Duty (Military)
REFRANACDUTRA. . Release from Annual Active Duty for Training (Army)
REFRD. . . . . . Refrigerated
REFRG . . . . . . Refrigerate (Refrigeration; Refrigerator)
REFT. . . . . . . Release for Experimental Flight Test
REFTS . . . . . . Resonant Frequency Tracking System
REFURDIS . . . . Reference Your Dispatch (Military)
REFURLTR . . . . Reference Your Letter (Military)
REG . . . . Radioencephalogram
REG . . . . Range Extender with Gain (Bell System)
REG . . . . Region
REG . . . . Register
REG . . . . Registered (NYSE symbol)
REG . . . . Regular
REG . . . . Regulate (Regulation; Regulator)
REG . . . . Rheoencephalography (Medicine)
REGAF . . . . . . Regular Air Force
REGAL . . . . . . Range and Elevation Guidance for Approach and Landing (Aviation)
REGD . . . . . . Registered
REGEN . . . . . . Regeneration (or Regenerative)
REGLN . . . . . . Regulation
REGR . . . . . . Regulator
REHAB . . . . . . Rehabilitate
REHVA . . . . . . Representatives of European Heating and Ventilating Associations
REI. . . . . Request for Engineering Information
REI. . . . . Reusable External Insulation (of space shuttle) (NASA)
REIC . . . . . . Radiation Effects Information Center (Battelle Memorial Institute)
REIL . . . . Runway End Identification Lights (FAA)
REINF. . . . . . . Reinforce
REINFD. . . . . . Reinforced
REINFG . . . . . Reinforcing
REINFM . . . . . Reinforcement
REINS. . . . . . . RADAR-Equipped Inertial Naval System
REINS. . . . . . . Radio-Equipped Inertial Navigation System
REIS . . . . Readiness Information System (Army)
REIT . . . . Real Estate Investment Trust (Generic term)
REJASE . . . . . Re-Using Junk As Something Else (Conversion of junk into reusable items)
REL . . . . Radio Engineering Laboratories
REL . . . . Rate of Energy Loss
REL . . . . Regional Education Laboratory
REL . . . . Relay
REL . . . . Release
REL . . . . Relief
REL . . . . Rescue Equipment Locker
RELACS. . . . . . RADAR Emission Location Attack Control System
RELBY. . . . . . . When Relieved By (Air Force)
RELC . . . . Reliability Committee
RELCV . . . . . . Regional Educational Laboratory for the Carolinas and Virginia
RELE. . . . . . . Radio Electrician
RELL . . . . Reinforced Education Learning Laboratory (of Youth Pride, Inc.)
RELOC . . . . . . Relocate(d) (or Relocation)
RELPAS . . . . . Restricted Express Lists / Physiological Activity Section (National Science Foundation)
REL-R . . . . . . Reliability Report
REM . . . . Range Evaluation Missile
REM . . . . Rapid Eye Movement
REM . . . . Raumbildentfernungsmesser (Stereoscopic range-finder) (German military - World War II)
REM . . . . Registered Equipment Management (Air Force)

REM . . . . Remove (or Removable)
REM . . . . Roentgen Equivalent Manual (AEC)
REMA . . . . . . Refrigeration Equipment Manufacturers Association
REMAB . . . . . Radiation Equivalent Manikin Absorption
REMAD . . . . . Remote Magnetic Anomaly Detection
REMAS . . . . . Radiation Effects Machine Analysis System
REMC . . . . . . Resin-Encapsulated Mica Capacitor
REMCAL . . . . . Radiation Equivalent Manikin Calibration
REMCO. . . . . . Rear Echelon Maintenance Combined Operation (Military)
REMD . . . . . . Rapid Eye Movement (Sleep) Deprivation
REME . . . . . . Royal Electrical and Mechanical Engineers (British)
REMG . . . . . . Radioelectromyograph
REMILOC . . . . Required Inservice Manyears in Lieu of Controls (Military)
REMIT. . . . . . Research Effort Management Information Tabulation
REML . . . . . . Radiation Effects Mobile Laboratory
REMP . . . . . . Research Group for European Migration Problems
REM-RAND . . . Remington Rand (Later, a division of Sperry-Rand)
REMS . . . . . . Rapid Eye Movement State
REMS . . . . . . Registered Equipment Management System (Air Force)
REMSA . . . . . Railway Engineering Maintenance Suppliers Association
REMT . . . . . . Radiological Emergency Medical Teams
REMT . . . . . . Relief Electronic Maintenance Technician
RENE . . . . . . Rocket Engine/Nozzle Ejector
RENEC . . . . . Regroupement National des Etudiants Camerounais (National Regrouping of Cameroonese Students)
RENFE . . . . . Red Nacional de los Ferrocariles Espanoles (National Network of Spanish Railways)
RENMR . . . . . Reconnaissance Medium Range (Army)
RENOT . . . . . Regional Notice (FAA)
RENT . . . . . . Reentry Nose Tip (Air Force)
REO . . . . Ransom E. Olds Co. (Automobile)
REO . . . . Rare Earth Oxide
REO . . . . Real Estate Owned (Banking)
REO . . . . Regenerated Electrical Output
REOC . . . . . . Report When Established on Course (Aviation)
REORG . . . . . Reorganize(d)
REOS . . . . . . Reflective Electron Optical System
REP. . . . . RADAR Evaluation Pod (Spacecraft)
REP . . . . Radical Education Project
REP . . . . Range Probable Error (Formerly, Range Error Probable) (Air Force)
REP . . . . Recovery and Evacuation Program (Marine Corps)
REP. . . . . Reentry Physics Program
REP. . . . . Rendezvous Exercise Pod (NASA)
REP. . . . . Repair (Repaired; Repairing)
REP. . . . . Repeat (Repeater; Repetition)
REP. . . . . Report
REP . . . . Reporting Point (Aviation)
REP. . . . . Represent(ative)
REP. . . . . Republic
REP . . . . Republic Corporation (NYSE symbol)
REP . . . . Research Expenditure Proposal
REP . . . . Reserve Enlisted Program (Military)
REP . . . . Retrograde Pyelogram (Medicine)
REP. . . . . Rocket Engine Processor
REP . . . . Roentgen Equivalent Physical
R-EP . . . . Rational-Emotive Psychotherapy (Also known as R-ET and RT)
REPAS . . . . . . Research, Evaluation, and Planning Assistance Staff (AID)
REPC . . . . . . Research and Engineering Policy Council (DOD)
REPCAT. . . . . Report Corrective Action Taken
REPCOMDESPAC. . Representative of Commander Destroyers, Pacific Fleet
REPDN . . . . . . Reproduction
REPDU . . . . . . Report(ing) for Duty (Military)
REPEA. . . . . . Research and Engineers Professional Employees Association
REPFORMAINT . . Representative of Maintenance Force
REPIN . . . . . . Reply if Negative
REPIS . . . . . . Reserve Personnel Management Information System (Military)
REPISIC . . . . . Report Immediate Superior in Command (Navy)
REPL. . . . . . . Replace (Replaced; Replacement)
REPM . . . . . . Representatives of Electronic Products Manufacturers
REPO . . . . . . Reporting Officer (Navy)
REPPAC. . . . . Repetitively Pulsed Plasma Accelerator
REPR . . . . . . Real Estate Planning Report (Military)
REPSHIPS. . . . . Reports of Shipments
REPSNO . . . . . Report(ing) through Senior Naval Officer
REPT. . . . . . . Report
REQ . . . . Request
REQ . . . . Require(ment)
REQ . . . . Requisition
REQAFA . . . . . Request Advise as to Further Action (Army)
REQANS . . . . . Request Answer By (Date)
REQAURQN . . . Request Authority to Requisition

REQD . . . . Required
REQDI . . . . . . Request Disposition Instructions (Army)
REQFOLINFO. . Request Following Information Be Forwarded This Office (Army)
REQIBO . . . . . Request Item be Placed on Back Order
REQID . . . . . Request If Desired
REQINT . . . . . Request Interim Reply by (Date) (Military)
REQMAD . . . . Request Mailing Address
REQN . . . . . . Requisition
REQSI . . . . . . Request Shipping Instructions
REQSSD . . . . . Request Supply Status and Expected Delivery Date (Army)
REQSUPSTAFOL . . Request Supply Status of Following (Army)
REQT . . . . Requirement
REQTAT. . . . . . It Is Requested That (Army)
REQTRAC . . . . Request Tracer Be Initiated
REQUCHRD . . . Request Unit of Issue Be Changed to Read (Army)
RER . . . . RADAR Effects Reactor
RER . . . . Radiation Effects Reactor (Air Force)
RER . . . . Receiver Exciter Ranging (NASA)
RER . . . . Rerun
RER . . . . Reusable-Expendable-Reusable
RER . . . . Rough (Surfaced) Endoplasmi Reticulum
RER . . . . Rubberized Equipment Repair
RERC . . . . . . Real Estate Research Corporation
RERL . . . . Residual Equivalent Return Loss
RES . . . . Record Evaluation System
RES . . . . Reliable Stores Corporation (NYSE symbol)
RES . . . . Relief Electronics Specialist
RES . . . . Ren Embryonic Suis (Embryonic swine kidney cells used in tissue culture
          studies of viruses) (Medicine)
RES . . . . Reprint Expediting Service
RES . . . . Research
RES . . . . Reserve
RES . . . . Reservoir
RES . . . . Resistance (Resistant; Resistor)
RES. . . . . Reticulo-Endothelial System (Medicine)
RES . . . . Royal Entomological Society (British)
RES I . . . . . . Research EMP (Electromagnetic Pulse) Simulator I (Air Force)
RESA . . . . . . Scientific Research Society of America
RESC . . . . . . Regional Educational Service Center
RESC . . . . . . Rescind (Rescinded; Rescinding)
RESC . . . . . . Rescue
RESCAN . . . . Reflecting Satellite Communication Antenna
RESCAP . . . . Rescue Combat Air Patrol
RESCU . . . . . Radio Emergency Search Communications Unit
RESCU . . . . . Rocket-Ejection Seat Catapult Upward (Aviation)
RESCUE. . . . . Referring Emergency Service for Consumers' Ultimate Enjoyment (Service
          plan of Recreational Vehicle Dealers of America)
RESCUE. . . . . Remote Emergency Salvage and Clean Up Equipment
RESDAT. . . . . Restricted Data (Atomic Energy Act of 1954)
RESDIST . . . . Reserve District
RESEP . . . . . . Reentry System Environmental Protection
RESER . . . . . . Reentry Systems Evaluation RADAR (Aerospace)
RESFLD . . . . . Residual Field
RESG . . . . . . Research Engineering Standing Group (DOD)
RES/IC . . . . . Reserve - In Commission (Vessel status)
RESID . . . . . . Residual
RESIG . . . . . . Resignation
RES/IS . . . . . Reserve - In Service (Vessel status)
RESISTORS. . . . Radically Emphatic Students Interested in Science, Technology and
          Other Research Studies (Princeton-Trenton, New Jersey, high-school
          computer group)
RESLAB . . . . . Research Laboratory
RESMA . . . . . Railway Electric Supply Manufacturers Association
RESOC . . . . . Research Sonobuoy Configuration
RES/OC . . . . . Reserve - Out of Commission (Vessel status)
RESOJET . . . . Resonant Pulse Jet
RES/OS. . . . . Reserve - Out of Service (Vessel status)
RESP . . . . Regulated Electrical Supply Package
RESP. . . . . . . Response
RESP. . . . . . . Responsible
RESPO . . . . . Responsible Property Officer (Army)
RESS . . . . . . RADAR Echo Simulation Study (or Subsystem)
REST. . . . . . . RADAR Electronic Scan Technique
REST. . . . . . . Reentry Environment & Systems Technology
REST. . . . . . . Reentry System Test Program
REST. . . . . . . Reporting System for Training (Navy)
REST. . . . . . . Restrict(ed) (Restriction; Restrictor)
RESTA . . . . . . Reconnaissance, Surveillance and Target Acquisition
RESTAT . . . . . Reserve Components Status Reporting (Army)
RESTRACEN . . . Reserve Training Center
RESV . . . . . . Reserve Fleet (Navy)

RESVR . . . . . . Reservoir
RET. . . . . Rational-Emotive Therapy (Psychology)
RET . . . . Relay Extractor Tool
RET . . . . Retain(er)
RET . . . . Retard
RET. . . . . Retired
RET . . . . Return
R-ET . . . . . . Rational-Emotive Psychotherapy (Also known as R-EP and RT)
RETA . . . . . . Refrigerating Engineers and Technicians Association
RETA . . . . . . Retrieval of Enriched Textual Abstracts
RETAIN . . . . . Remote Technical Assistance and Information Network (Data processing)
RETC . . . . . . Rat Embryo Tissue Culture
RETD . . . . . . Retired
RETIMP . . . . . Raleigh-Edwards Tensile Impact Machine Pendulum
RETL . . . . . . Rocket Engine Test Laboratory (Air Force)
RETMA . . . . . Radio-Electronics-Television Manufacturers Association (Later, Electronic
          Industries Association)
RETORC . . . . . Research Torpedo Configuration
RETR. . . . . . . Retract(able)
RETRAN . . . . Refined Trajectory Analysis
RETRO . . . . . Regional Environmental Training and Research Organization (Retraining
          program for unemployed space-industry workers)
RETRO . . . . . Retro Rocket
RETRO . . . . . Retroactive
RETS . . . . . . Renaissance English Text Society
REURAD . . . . Refer to Your Message (Military)
REURTWX . . . . Reference Your Telegraph Wire Exchange
REUSE. . . . . . Revitalize Effective Utilization of Supply Excess (Navy)
REV . . . . Reentry Vehicle
REV . . . . Revenue
REV . . . . Reverend
REV . . . . Reverse
REV . . . . Review
REV . . . . Revise
REV . . . . Revlon, Inc. (NYSE symbol)
REV . . . . Revolution
REV . . . . Rotor Entry Vehicle (NASA)
REVCUR . . . . Reverse Current
REVEL . . . . . Reverberation Elimination
REVOCON . . . Remote Volume Control
REVOP . . . . . Random Evolutionary Operation
REVR . . . . . . Receiver
REVS . . . . . . Reconnaissance Electro-optical Viewing System
REVS . . . . . . Rotor-Entry Vehicle System (Aerospace)
REW . . . . . . Reward
REWRC . . . . . Report When Established Well to Right of Course (Aviation)
REWSON . . . . Reconnaissance, Electronic Warfare, Special Operations, and Naval
          Intelligence Processing Systems
REX . . . . Rare-Earth Exchanged (Faujasite, a zeolite)
REX . . . . Real Time Executive Routine (Data processing)
REX . . . . Reduced Exoatmospheric Cross-Section
REX . . . . Reentry Experiment
REX . . . . Reflector Erosion Experiment (NASA)
REX . . . . Rex Chainbelt, Inc. (NYSE symbol)
REX . . . . Rexall Drug & Chemical Company (NYSE symbol) (Delisted)
RF . . . . Radial Flow
RF . . . . Radio Frequency
RF . . . . Range-Finder (Gunnery)
RF . . . . Rapid-Fire
RF . . . . Read Forward
RF . . . . Reception Fair (Radio logs)
RF . . . . Reducing Flame
RF . . . . Re-Flight
RF . . . . Refunding
RF . . . . Regional Force (ARVN)
RF . . . . Register Finder
RF . . . . Relative Flow (Rate)
RF . . . . Release (or Releasing) Factor (Protein biosynthesis)
RF . . . . Reliability Factor
RF . . . . Replacement Factor
RF . . . . Replicate Form
RF . . . . Representative Fraction
RF . . . . Republique Francaise (French Republic)
RF . . . . Reserve Force
RF . . . . Resistance Factor
RF . . . . Response Factor
RF . . . . Reticular Formation (Sleep)
RF . . . . Reverse Free
RF . . . . Rheumatic Fever
RF . . . . Rheumatoid Factor (Medicine)
RF . . . . Right Field(er) (Baseball)

RF . . . . Right Foot
RF . . . . Right Forward
RF . . . . Right Front
RF . . . . Right Fullback (Soccer position)
RF . . . . Ring Frame
RF . . . . Ripple Factor
RF . . . . Rodeo Foundation
RF . . . . Rough Finish
RF . . . . Royal Fusiliers (British)
RF . . . . Running Forward
RFA . . . . Radio Frequency Amplifier
RFA . . . . Radio Frequency Attenuator
RFA . . . . Radio Frequency Authorizations (Air Force)
RFA . . . . Recommendation for Acceptance
RFA . . . . Relieved from Assigned (Military)
RFA . . . . Request for Alteration
RFA . . . . Request for Analysis
RFA . . . . Request Further Airways (Aviation)
RFA . . . . Reserve Forces Act
RFA . . . . Right Fronto-Anterior
RFA . . . . Rocky Flats Area Office (AEC)
RFA . . . . Roll Follow-Up Amplifier
RFA . . . . Royal Field Artillery (British)
RFA . . . . Royal Fleet Auxiliary (British)
RFAA . . . . . . Relieved from Attached and Assigned
RFAD . . . . . . Released from Active Duty not Result of Demobilization
RFAED . . . . . . Readiness Forecast Authorization Equipment Data (Air Force)
RFALROU . . . . . Request Followup Action on Listed Requisitions Indicated Still Outstanding in Unit (Army)
RFAS . . . . . . Radio Frequency Attitude Sensor
RFASIX . . . . . Reserve Forces Act of 1955, Six Months Trainee
RFAT . . . . Relieved from Attached (Army)
RFATHREE . . . . Reserve Forces Act of 1955, Three Months Trainee
RFB . . . . Recording for the Blind
RFB . . . . Reliability Functional Block
RFB . . . . Request for Bid
RFB . . . . Roter Frontkaempferbund
RFC . . . . Radio Facility Charts
RFC . . . . Radio Frequency Chart (or Choke)
RFC . . . . Radio Frequency Compatibility
RFC . . . . Radio Frequency Crystal
RFC . . . . Reconstruction Finance Corporation (Abolished, 1957)
RFC . . . . Royal Flying Corps (British)
RFC . . . . Rugby Football Club
RFCA . . . . . . Reconstruction Finance Corporation Act (Obsolete)
RFCMC . . . . . . Reconstruction Finance Corporation Mortgage Company
RFCO . . . . . . Radio (or Range) Facilities Control Officer
RFCO . . . . . . Radio Frequency Checkout
RFCP . . . . . . Radio Frequency Compatibility Program
RFCSEUSG . . . Retirement Federation of Civil Service Employees of the United States Government
RFD . . . . Radiation Flux Density
RFD . . . . Radio Frequency Demodulator
RFD . . . . Reactor Flight Demonstration
RFD . . . . Reentry Flight Demonstration
RFD . . . . Released for Delivery
RFD . . . . Reporting for Duty
RFD . . . . Residual Flux Density
RFD . . . . Rural Free Delivery (of mail)
RFDS . . . . . . Royal Flying Doctor Service (Australia)
RFDT . . . . . . Reliability Failure Diagnostic Team
RFE . . . . Radio Free Europe
RFED . . . . . . Research Facilities and Equipment Division (NASA)
RFF . . . . Radio Frequency Filter
RFF . . . . Radio Frequency Fuze
RFF . . . . Random Force Field
RFF . . . . Relative Failure Frequency
RFF . . . . Research Flight Facility (Air Force)
RFF . . . . Resources for the Future, Inc.
RFFD . . . . . . Radio Frequency Fault Detection
RFG . . . . Radio Frequency Generator
RFG . . . . Rapid-Fire Gun
RFG . . . . Rate and Free Gyro
RFG . . . . Receive Format Generator
RFG . . . . Roofing
RFHCO . . . . . Rocket Fuel Handler Clothing Outfit (Protective suit)
RFHT . . . . . . Radio Frequency Horn Technique
RFI . . . . Radio Frequency Indicator
RFI . . . . Radio Frequency Interference
RFI . . . . Ready for Issue
RFI . . . . Request for Information

RFI . . . . Request for Investigation
RFI . . . . Request for Issue
RFIM . . . . . . Radio Frequency Interference Meter
RFJ . . . . Radio Frequency Joint
RFK . . . . Robert Francis Kennedy
RFL . . . . Radio-Frequency Laboratories
RFL . . . . Radio Frequency Lens
RFL . . . . Reduced Focal Length
RFL . . . . Refuel(ing)
RFL . . . . Reset Flux Level
RFL . . . . Resorcinol-Formaldehyde-Latex
RFL . . . . Rough Field Landing
RFLD . . . . . . Radio Frequency Leakage Detector
RFM . . . . Radio Frequency Modulation
RFM . . . . Reactive Factor Meter
RFM . . . . Refueling Mission (Air Force)
RFM . . . . Roll Follow-Up Motor
RFM . . . . Roll Forming Machine
RFM . . . . Runway Friction Measurement
RFMA . . . . . . Reliability Figure of Merit Analysis
RFMS . . . . . . Remote File Management System
RFMT . . . . . . Runway Friction Measurement Test
RFN . . . . Registered Fever Nurse
RFNA . . . . . . Red Fuming Nitric Acid
RFO . . . . Radio Frequency Oscillator
RFO . . . . Regional Field Officer (Civil Defense)
RFO . . . . Request for Factory Order
RFO . . . . Roll Follow-Up Operation
RFOFM . . . . . Records for Our Fighting Men (Collected phonograph records during World War II)
RF & OOA . . . Railway Fuel & Operating Officers Association
RFP . . . . Radio Finger Printing (Identification of wireless radio operators by individual keying characteristics)
RFP . . . . Radio Frequency Plasma
RFP . . . . Republicans for Progress
RFP . . . . Request for Proposal
RFP . . . . Requests for Purchases
RFP . . . . Richmond, Fredericksburg & Potomac R. R. (AAR code)
RFP . . . . Right Frontoposterior
RFPB . . . . . . Reserve Forces Policy Board (DOD)
RFPP . . . . . . Radio Frequency Propagation Program
RF/PF . . . . . . Regional Forces-Popular Forces (Republic of Vietnam) (Army)
RFQ . . . . Request for Quotation
RFR . . . . Radio Frequency Receiver
RFR . . . . Radio Frequency Relay
RFR . . . . Reject Failure Rate
RFR . . . . Royal Fleet Reserve (British)
RFRJ . . . . . . Radio Frequency Rotary Joint
RFS . . . . Radio Frequency Seal
RFS . . . . Range Frequency Synthesizer
RFS . . . . Ready for Sea (Navy)
RFS . . . . Regardless of Future Size
RFS . . . . Response Feedback System (NASA)
RFS . . . . Roll Followup System
RFS . . . . Rossendorfer Forschungs-Reaktor
RFS . . . . Rover Flight Safety
RFSE . . . . . . Radio Frequency Shielded Enclosure
RFSP . . . . . . Radioactive Fallout Study Program (Canada)
RFSP . . . . . . Rigid Frame Selection Program
RFT . . . . Right Frontotransverse
RFT . . . . Rotary Feed-Through
RFTL . . . . . . Radio Frequency Transmission Line
RFTO . . . . . . Ready for Takeoff (Aviation)
RFTS . . . . . . Radio Frequency Test Set
RFU . . . . Ready-For-Use
RFU . . . . Reliability Field Unit
RFUA . . . . . . Roll Follow-Up Amplifier
RFUM . . . . . . Roll Follow-Up Motor
RFUO . . . . . . Roll Follow-Up Operation
RFUS . . . . . . Roll Follow-Up System
RFV . . . . RADAR Film Viewer
RFV . . . . Resonant Frequency Vibration
RFVM . . . . . . Radio Frequency Voltmeter
RFW . . . . Reserve Feed Water (Technical drawings)
RFW . . . . Reversible Full Wave
RFWAC . . . . . Reversible Full Wave Alternating Current
RFWAR . . . . . Request for Work and Resources
RFWDC . . . . . Reversible Full Wave Direct Current
RFZ . . . . Rinforzando (Indicates sudden emphasis on phrases or small groups of notes) (Music)
RG . . . . Radio Guidance

RG........ Range
RG........ Rate Grown
RG........ Rate Gyro
RG........ Reader's Guide
RG........ Reagent Grade
RG........ Real Gas
RG........ Reception Good (Radio logs)
RG........ Red-Green
RG........ Reduction Gear(box)
RG........ Reserve Grade (Military)
RG........ Reset Gate
RG........ Resolving Gel (Biochemistry)
RG........ Reticulated Grating
RG........ Reverse Gate
RG........ Rheingold Corp. (NYSE symbol)
RG........ Right Guard (Football)
RG........ Rolled Gold
RGA....... Rate Gyro Assembly
RGA....... Republican Governors Association
RGA....... Residual Gas Analyzer
RGA....... Ring Guild of America
RGA....... Royal Garrison Artillery (British)
RGAA...... Radiochemical Gamma Activation Analysis
RGB....... Red Green Blue
RGB....... River Gunboat
RGC....... Rio Grande College (Ohio)
RGD....... Regular Geophysical Day
RGDU...... Rassemblement General pour le Desarmement Universel
RGE....... Red under Gold Edges (Books)
RGE....... Reduced Gravity Environment
RGF....... Range Gated Filter
RGF....... Rarefied Gas Field (or Flow)
RGG....... Rotating Gravity Gradiometer
RGG....... Royal Grenadier Guards (British)
RGH....... Rough
RGI....... Rio Grande Industries, Inc. (NYSE symbol)
RGK....... Reserv Glavnogo Komandovaniia (Reserve of the High Command) (USSR)
RGL....... Rate Gyroscope Limit
RGM....... Recorder Group Monitor
RGM....... Remote Geophysical Monitor
RGM....... Reversible Gelatin Matrix
RGM....... Rounds per Gun per Minute
RGMS...... Reversible Gelatin Matrix System
RGN....... Region
RGN....... Registered General Nurse
RGO....... Royal Greenwich Observatory
RGP....... Rate Gyro Package
RGP....... Riegel Paper Corp. (NYSE symbol) (Delisted)
RG PH..... Registered Pharmacist
RGR....... Range Gated Receiver
RGR....... Rassemblement de Gauche Republicain (Assembly of the Republican Left) (French political party)
RGS....... RADAR Ground Stabilization
RGS....... Radio Guidance System
RGS....... Rate Gyro System
RGS....... Remote Ground Switching
RGS....... Rene Guyon Society
RGS....... River Gaging Station
RGS....... Rochester Gas & Electric Corporation (NYSE symbol)
RGS....... Royal Geographical Society (British)
RGSA...... Ruffed Grouse Society of America
RGSAT..... Radio Guidance Surveillance and Automatic Tracking
RGT....... Resonant Gate Transistor
RGTP...... Rough Template
RGUB...... Revolutionary Government of the Union of Burma
RGV....... Rio Grande Valley Gas Company (NYSE symbol)
RGW....... Rat fuer Gegenseitige Wirtschaftshilfe
RGZ....... Recommended Ground Zero
RH........ Radiation Homing
RH........ Random House, Inc. (NYSE symbol)
RH........ Rankine-Hugoniot
RH........ Relative Humidity
Rh........ Rhesus (Blood factor)
Rh........ Rhodium (Chemical element)
RH........ Right Halfback (Soccer position)
RH........ Right Hand
RH........ Rockwell Hardness
RH........ Round Head
RH........ Round House (Maps and charts)
RH........ Royal Highlanders (British)
RH........ Royal Highness

RH........ Rueckwaertiges Heeresgebiet (Rear area of a group of armies) (German military)
RHA....... Records Holding Area
RHA....... Religious Heritage of America, Inc.
RHA....... Royal Hibernian Academy
RHA....... Royal Horse Artillery (British)
RHA....... Rural Housing Alliance
RHAF...... Royal Hellenic Air Force
RHAW...... RADAR Homing and Warning System
RHAWS..... RADAR Homing and Warning System
RHB....... RADAR Homing Bomb (Air Force)
RHB....... Regional Hospital Board
RHB....... Right Halfback (Football)
RHB....... Round Hole Broach
RHC....... Resetting Half-Cycle
RHC....... Right Hand Console
RHC....... Rosary Hill College (New York)
RHC....... Rotational Hand Controller
RHC....... Rubber Hydrocarbon
RHCI...... Radiant Heating and Cooling Institute
RHCSA..... Regional Hospitals Consultants' and Specialists' Association
RHD....... Radioactive Health Data
RHD....... Random House Dictionary
RHD....... Relative Hepatic Dullness (Medicine)
RHD....... Rheumatic Heart Disease (Medicine)
RHE....... Record Handling Electronics
RHE....... Reliability Human Engineering
RHE....... Reversible Hydrogen Electrode
RHE....... Rheem Manufacturing Company (NYSE symbol) (Delisted)
RHEB...... Right-Hand Equipment Bay (Apollo) (NASA)
RHEO...... Rheostat
RHF....... Right Heart Failure (Medicine)
RHFS...... Receiving Hospital Field Station
RHFS...... Round Hill Field Station (MIT)
RHG....... Royal Horse Guards (British)
RHGSA..... Russian Historical and Genealogical Society in America
RHH....... Right Hand Head
RHH....... Robertson (H.H.) Co. (NYSE symbol)
RHI....... Range-Height Indicator (RADAR)
RHI....... Relative Humidity Indicator
RHIA...... Radiation-Hardened Interfacing Amplifier
RHIB...... Rain and Hail Insurance Bureau
RHINO..... Range Height Indicator Not Operating (Aviation)
RHIP...... Rank Has Its Privileges (Military slang)
RHIR...... Rank Has Its Responsibilities (Military slang)
RHL....... Radiological Health Laboratory
RHL....... Reverse Half-Line (Feed)
RHLG...... Radiometric Homing Level Gage
RHM....... Relative Humidity Meter
RHM....... Roentgen per Hour at one Meter
RHMS...... Royal Hibernian Military School (Dublin)
RHO....... Railhead Officer (Military)
RHO....... Reichshaushaltsordnung (Germany)
RHO....... Rhodesian Selection Trust Limited (NYSE symbol) (Later, RNO; then, RST)
RHOGI..... RADAR Homing Guidance Investigation
RHP....... Radiant Heat Pump
RHP....... Rated Horsepower
RHPS...... Radiation-Hardened Power Supply
RHQ....... Regimental Headquarters
RHR....... Reheater
RHR....... Rohr Industries (NYSE symbol)
RHS....... Right-Hand Side
RHS....... Royal Historical Society (British)
RHS....... Royal Horticultural Society (British)
RHS....... Royal Humane Society (British)
RHSI...... Rubber Heel and Sole Institute
RHSJ...... Religious Hospitallers of St. Joseph (Roman Catholic women's religious order)
RHT....... Reynolds Hydrodynamic Theory
RHW....... Reversible Half-Wave
RHW....... Right Half Word
RHWAC..... Reversible Half-Wave Alternating Current
RHWACDC... Reversible Half-Wave Alternating Current - Direct Current
RHWDC..... Reversible Half-Wave Direct Current
RHX....... Rexham Corp. (NYSE symbol)
RI........ Chicago, Rock Island & Pacific R. R. Company (NYSE symbol and AAR code)
RI........ RADAR Input
RI........ Radiation Intensity
RI........ Radio Inertial
RI........ Radio Influence

RI . . . . Radio Inspector
RI . . . . Radio Interference
RI . . . . Range Instrumentation
RI . . . . Receiving Inspection
RI . . . . Recovery, Incorporated
RI . . . . Recruit Instruction (Navy)
RI . . . . Reflective Insulation (Technical drawings)
RI . . . . Refractive Index
RI . . . . Refractories Institute
RI . . . . Reinsurance
RI . . . . Reliability Index
RI . . . . Relative Intensity
RI . . . . Relaxation Instruction (Psychology)
RI . . . . Report of Investigation
RI . . . . Republik Indonesia
RI . . . . Require Identification
RI . . . . Rescue, Incorporated
RI . . . . Respiratory Illness (Medicine)
RI. . . . . Retention Index
RI . . . . Retroactive Inhibition (Psychology)
RI . . . . Reverberation Index
RI . . . . Rhode Island
RI . . . . Ring Index (A reference book)
RI . . . . Rotary International
RI . . . . Routing Identifier
RI . . . . Royal Institution (British)
RI . . . . Royal Irish (Military unit) (British)
RI . . . . Rubber Insulation (Technical drawings)
R et I . . . . . . Regina et Imperatrix (Queen and Empress)
R et I . . . . . . Rex et Imperator (King and Emperor)
RIA . . . . Radioimmunoassay
RIA . . . . Religious Instruction Association
RIA . . . . Remote Intelligence Acquisition
RIA . . . . Research Institute of America
RIA . . . . Rock Island Arsenal (Illinois) (Army)
RIA . . . . Royal Irish Academy
RIAA . . . . . . Record Industry Association of America
RIAC . . . . . . Regional Industry Advisory Committee (Civil Defense)
RIAC . . . . . . Research Information Analysis Corporation
RIAEC . . . . . . Rhode Island Atomic Energy Commission
RIAF . . . . . . Royal Indian Air Force
RIAF. . . . . . . Royal Iraqi Air Force
RIAL . . . . . . Religion in American Life
RIAR . . . . . . Requirements Inventory Analysis Report
RIAS . . . . . . Research Institute for Advanced Studies (Martin Marietta Corporation)
RIAS. . . . . . . Rundfunk Im Amerikanischen Sektor Berlins (Radio in American Sector) (West Berlin, Germany)
RIB. . . . . Railway Information Bureau
RIB. . . . . Ribbed
RIB. . . . . Rural Industries Bureau
RIBA . . . . . . Royal Institute of British Architects
RIC. . . . . RADAR Indicating Console (FAA)
RIC . . . . RADAR Input Control
RIC . . . . RADAR Intercept Calculator
RIC . . . . RADAR Intercept Control
RIC . . . . Radio Industry Council (British)
RIC . . . . Rafter Input Converter
RIC . . . . Record Identification Code (Navy)
RIC . . . . Repairable Item Code
RIC . . . . Rodeo Information Commission
RIC. . . . . Royal Institute of Chemistry (British)
RIC . . . . Royal Irish Constabulary
RICASIP . . . . . Research Information Center and Advisory Service on Information Processing (National Bureau of Standards – National Science Foundation)
RICC . . . . . . Reportable Item Control Code (Army)
RICE . . . . . . Regional Information and Communication Exchange
RICE. . . . . . . Rhode Island College of Education
RICH . . . . . . Richmond National Battlefield Park
RICM . . . . . . Registre International des Citoyens du Monde
RICM . . . . . . Right Intercostal Margin (Anatomy)
RICMO . . . . . RADAR Input Countermeasures Officer (Air Force)
RICMT . . . . . RADAR Inputs Countermeasures Technician
RICS. . . . . . . Range Instrumentation Control System
RID. . . . . RADAR Input Drum
RID . . . . Radio Intelligence Division (of the Federal Communications Commission)
RID. . . . . Range Instruments Development
RID. . . . . Reset Inhibit Drive
RID. . . . . Reset Inhibit Drum
RID. . . . . Review Item Discrepancy
RIDA . . . . . . Reverse Isotope Dilution Assay (Chemical analysis)

RIDC . . . . . . Regional Industrial Development Corporation (Southwest Pennsylvania)
RIDD . . . . . . Range Instrumentation Development Division
RIDE . . . . . . Research Institute for Diagnostic Engineering
RIDEQ . . . . . Revista Iberoamericana de Educacion Quimica (A publication)
RIDF. . . . . . . Random Input Describing Function (Data processing)
RIDIT . . . . . . Relative to an Identified Distribution Transformation (Pharmacology)
RIDL . . . . . . Radiation Instrument Development Laboratory
RIDL . . . . . . Ridge Instrument Development Laboratory (Navy)
RIDT . . . . . . Retrieval of Information via Online Terminal (Data processing)
RIE . . . . Research in Education (Monthly publication of ERIC)
RIE. . . . . Retirement Income Endowment (Insurance)
RIE. . . . . Royal Institute of Engineers (British)
RIE. . . . . Royal Institute of Engineers (Netherlands)
RIEC . . . . . . Royal Indian Engineering College (British)
RIEDAC . . . . . Research in International Economics of Disarmament and Arms Control (A program of Columbia University School of International Affairs)
RIEI . . . . Republic Industrial Education Institute (Republic Steel Corp.)
RIEM . . . . . . Research Institute for Environmental Medicine (Army)
RIF. . . . . Radio Interference Filter
RIF. . . . . Reading Is Fundamental (Program) (Smithsonian Institution)
RIF. . . . . Reduction in Force (Military)
RIF. . . . . Reliability Improvement Factor
RIF. . . . . Right Iliac Fossa (Anatomy)
RIF . . . . Royal Irish Fusiliers
RIFC. . . . . . . Radio In-Flight Correction
RIFC. . . . . . . Rat Intrinsic Factor Concentrate
RIFI . . . . Radio Interference Field Intensity (Meter)
RIFI . . . . Radio-Interference-Free Instrument
RIFMA . . . . . Roentgen-Isotope-Fluorescent Method of Analysis
RIFS . . . . Radioisotope Field Support
RIFS . . . . Reductions in Forces
RIFT . . . . . . Reactor-in-Flight Test (NASA)
RIFT/S . . . . . Reaction in Flight Test/System
RIG . . . . Radio Inertial Guidance
RIG . . . . Radio Interference Guard
RIGS . . . . . . Radio Inertial Guidance System
RIGS . . . . . . Resonant Infrasonic Gauging System
RIGS . . . . . . Runway Identifiers with Glide Slope
RII . . . . RADAR Intelligence Information
RII . . . . Raymond International, Incorporated (NYSE symbol)
RIIA . . . . . . Royal Institute of International Affairs (British)
RIK . . . . Replacement in Kind
RIL. . . . . Radio Influence Level
RIL. . . . . Radio Interference Level
RIL. . . . . Red Indicator Light
RILAMAC . . . . Research in Laboratory Animal Medicine and Care
RILEM. . . . . . Reunion Internationale des Laboratoires d'Essais et de Recherches sur les Materiaux et les Constructions (International Union of Testing and Research Laboratories for Materials and Structures)
RILM . . . . . . Repertoire International de la Litterature Musicale (International Repertory of Music Literature)
RILOP. . . . . . Reclamation in Lieu of Procurement (Navy)
RILS . . . . Ranging Integration Location System
RIM . . . . RADAR Input Mapper
RIM . . . . Radial Inlet Manifold
RIM . . . . Radioisotope Medicine
RIM . . . . Receipt, Inspection, and Maintenance (Air Force)
RIM . . . . Receiving Inspection and Maintenance
RIM . . . . Resident Industrial Manager
RIM . . . . Royal Indian Marine
RIM . . . . Rubber Insulation Material
RIMAS . . . . . Russian Independent Mutual Aid Society
RIMB . . . . . . Roche Institute of Molecular Biology
RIMC . . . . . . Reportable Items of Major Combinations (Army)
RIME . . . . . . Radio Inertial Missile Equipment
RIME . . . . . . Research Institute for Management Executives (Washington, DC)
RIMMS . . . . . RVNAF (Republic of Vietnam Air Force) Improvement and Modernization Management System
RIMOB . . . . . Reserve Indication of Mobilization (Army)
RIMP. . . . . . . Remote Input Message Processor
RIMPTF . . . . . Recording Industries Music Performance Trust Funds
RIMR . . . . . . Rockefeller Institute for Medical Research
RIMS . . . . . . RADAR In-Flight Monitoring System
RIMS . . . . . . Radiant Intensity Measuring System
RIMS . . . . . . Radio Interference Measuring System
RIN . . . . Record Identification Number
RIN . . . . Regular Inertial Navigator
RIN . . . . Rotor Impulsive Noise (Helicopters)
RIN . . . . Royal Indian Navy
RINA . . . . . . Resident Inspector of Naval Aircraft
RINA . . . . . . Royal Institution of Naval Architects (British)

RINAL .... RADAR Inertial Altimeter
RIND .... Research Institute of National Defense (Sweden)
RINF .... Rinforzando (Indicates sudden emphasis on phrases or small groups of notes) (Music)
RINM .... Resident Inspector of Naval Material
RINS. ...... Research Institute for the Natural Sciences
RINS .... Rotorace Inertial Navigation System
RINSORD .... Resident Naval Inspector of Ordnance
RINSPOW .... Resident Naval Inspector of Powder
RINT .... Radiation Intelligence
RIO .... RADAR-Intercept Officer (Navy)
RIO .... Reporting In and Out (Military)
RIO .... Resident Inspector Office (Coast Guard)
RIO .... Resident Inspector of Ordnance
RIO .... Retail Issue Outlets
RIO .... Ride-It-Out
RIOMETER .... Relative Ionospheric Opacity Meter
RIOPR ...... Rhode Island Open Pool Reactor (AEC)
RIOS .... Rotating Image Optical Scanner
RIOT .... Real-Time Input-Output Transducer (Translator)
RIOT .... Resolution of Initial Operational Techniques
RIP. .... RADAR Identification Point
RIP. .... RADAR Improvement Program
RIP. .... Radioimmunoprecipitation (Biochemistry)
RIP. .... Recoverable Item Program (Marine Corps)
RIP. .... Reduction Implementation Panel (DOD)
RIP. .... Register Indicator Panel
RIP. .... Reliability Improvement Program
RIP. .... Requiescat in Pace (May He, or She, Rest in Peace)
RIP. .... Retirement Improvement Program (Air Force)
RIP. .... Rural Industrialization Program (Department of Agriculture)
RIPC. ...... Regroupement des Independants et Paysans Camerounais (Regrouping of Independents and Farmers of the Cameroons)
RIPFCOMTF ... Rapid Item Processor to Facilitate Complex Operations on Magnetic Tape Files (Data processing)
RIPOM ...... Report (command indicated) If Present, Otherwise by Message (Navy)
RIPP .... RADAR Intelligence Photo Producer
RIPS .... Radio-Isotope Power Supply
RIPS .... Radio Isotope Power System
RIPS .... Range Instrumentation Planning Study (AFSC)
RIPWC ...... Royal Institute of Painters in Water-Colours (British)
RIQAP ...... Reduced Inspection Quality Assurance Program
RIR .... Range Illumination RADAR
RIR .... Receiving Inspection Report
RIR .... Redgrave Information Resources Corp. (Publisher)
RIR .... Reduction in Requirement (Air Force)
RIRAA ...... Russian Immigrants' Representative Association in America
RIRB .... Railway Insurance Rating Bureau
RIRCA ...... Rhode Island Red Club of America
RIRJ .... Research Institute of Religious Jewry
RIRS .... Reliability Information Retrieval System
RIRTI ...... Recording Infrared Tracking Instrument
RIS .... RADIAC Instrument System
RIS .... Ramjet Inlet System
RIS .... Range Instrumentation Ship
RIS .... Range Instrumentation Station
RIS .... Record Input Subroutine
RIS. .... Reports Identification Symbol (Aviation)
RIS. .... Retarded Infants Service
RIS .... Rotating Image Scanner
RISA. ...... Radioiodinated Serum Albumin (Medicine)
RISA .... Railway and Industrial Spring Association
RISC .... Remote Information Systems Center
RISD. ...... Rhode Island School of Design
RISE. ...... Research in Supersonic Environment
RISE. ...... Reusable Inflatable Salvage Equipment
RISM .... Repertoire International des Sources Musicales
RISM .... Research Institute for the Study of Man (Army)
RISOP. ..... Red Integrated Strategic Offensive Plan (Army)
RISS. ...... Range Instrumentation and Support Systems
RISS .... Refractive Index Sounding System
RISSB ...... Research Institute on the Sino-Soviet Bloc
RIT. .... RADAR Inputs Test
RIT. .... Radio Information Test
RIT. .... Radio Network for Inter-American Telecommunications
RIT. .... Receiver Incremental Tuning
RIT .... Refining in Transit
RIT. .... Rochester Institute of Technology (New York)
RIT. .... Rocket Interferometer Tracking
RIT. .... Rotary Indexing Table
RITA. ...... Recoverable Interplanetary Transport Approach

RITA .... Resist Inside the Army (Peace-movement slang)
RITA. ...... Reusable Interplanetary Transport Approach Vehicle
RITA .... Rural Industrial Technical Assistance (Latin American building program)
RITE .... Rapid Information Technique for Evaluation
RIU .... Railroad Insurance Underwriters
RIV. .... Radio-Influence Voltage
RIV .... Regolamento Internazionale Veicoli (Italian generic term meaning "International Regulation of Vehicles") (Initialism also refers to International Railway Wagon Union)
RIV .... Rivet
RIY .... Renaissance of Italian Youth
RIZ .... Radio Industry Zagreb (Yugoslavia)
RJ .... RADAR/Jimsphere
RJ .... Ramjet
RJ .... Road Junction (Maps and charts)
RJ .... Rotary Joint
R & J .... Romeo and Juliet (by Shakespeare)
RJA .... Ramjet Addition
RJA .... Reform Jewish Appeal
RJA .... Retail Jewelers of America
RJA .... Rotary Joint Assembly
RJAF .... Royal Jordanian Air Force
RJB .... Ruby Jewel Bearing
RJBE. ...... Relative Jostle Biological Effectiveness
RJC .... Ranger Junior College (Texas)
RJC .... Rochester Junior College (Minnesota)
RJDA .... Rassemblement des Jeunesses Democratiques Africaines (Rally of African Democratic Youth)
RJE .... Ramjet Engine
RJE .... Rayleigh-Jeans Equation
RJE .... Remote Job Entry (Data processing)
RJM .... Religious of Jesus-Mary (Roman Catholic women's religious order)
RJM .... Royal Jersey Militia
RJP. .... Reaction Jet Pipe
RJP. .... Remote-Job Processing
RJR. .... Reynolds (R.J.) Industries, Inc. (NYSE symbol)
RJR .... Rotary Joint Reed
RJRA .... Rotary Joint Reed Assembly
RJS .... Reaction Jet Stabilization
RJT .... Rassemblement des Jeunes Togolais (Togolese Youth Rally)
RJTV .... Ramjet Test Vehicle
RK .... Rabbit Kidney
RK .... Rassemblement Katangais (Katanga Rally) (Elisabethville)
RK .... Rucker Co. (NYSE symbol)
RK .... Run of Kiln
RKII. ...... Runge-Kutta Second Order
RKFDV ...... Reichskommissar fuer die Festigung Deutschen Volkstums
RKG .... Radiocardiogram
RKG. ...... Rockingham R. R. (AAR code)
RKKA ...... Raboche-Krest'ianskaia Krasnaia Armiia (Workers' and Peasants' Red Army) (Redesignated Soviety Army) (USSR)
RKKY ...... Ruderman-Kittel-Kasuja-Yosida
RKM .... Runge-Kutta Method
RKN. ...... Runge-Kutta-Nystroem (Formula)
RKO .... Radio-Keith-Orpheum (Motion picture production and exhibition firm, also active in broadcasting)
RKO. ...... Range Keeper Operator (Navy)
RKO. ...... Reichskassenordnung (Germany)
RKR .... Rocker
RKS .... Rockwell-Standard Corporation (NYSE symbol) (Later, ROK)
RKT .... Rocket
RKTSTA ...... Rocket Station
RKV .... Rabbit Kidney Vacuolating Virus (Medicine)
RKV. ...... Rose Knot Victor (Gemini tracking ship)
RKVA ...... Reactive Kilovolt-Ampere
RKY .... Roentgen Kymography
RL .... High-Powered Radio Range (Loop radiators)
RL .... Radiation Laboratory
RL .... Radio Liberty
RL .... Radiolocation
RL .... Rail
RL .... Raman LASER
RL .... Random Lengths (Lumber)
RL .... Reading List
RL .... Reduced Level
RL .... Reiz Stimulus Limen (Psychology)
RL .... Relay Logic
RL .... Release Load
RL .... Research Laboratory
RL .... Resistance Inductance (Circuit)
RL .... Restaurant Liquor (License)

RL . . . . Retarded Learner (Education)
RL . . . . Retirement Loss
RL . . . . Return Loss
RL . . . . Rhumb Line
RL . . . . Richfield Oil Corporation (NYSE symbol) (Later, ARC)
RL . . . . Right Line
RL . . . . Rinderleistungbuch
RL . . . . River Lines, Inc. (AAR code)
RL . . . . Rocket Launcher (Air Force)
RL . . . . Roof Ladder
R/L . . . . Rocket Launcher
R & L . . . . . . Rail and Lake
RLA . . . . Redevelopment Land Agency (Washington, DC)
RLA . . . . Regional Land Agent (Ministry of Agriculture, Fisheries, and Food) (British)
RLA . . . . Research Laboratory for Archeology (British)
RLA . . . . Restricted Landing Area (Aviation)
RLADD . . . . . RADAR Low Angle Drogue Delivery
RLAF. . . . . . . Royal Laotian Air Force
RLAS . . . . . . Rocket Lunar Attitude System
RLB . . . . Reliable (or Reliability)
RLBCD . . . . . Right Lower Border of Cardiac Dullness (Medicine)
RLBM . . . . . . Rearward Launched Ballistic Missiles
RLC . . . . Radio Liberty Committee
RLC . . . . Remote Line Concentrator
RLC . . . . Run Length Coding
RLCA . . . . . . National Rural Letter Carriers' Association
RLCA . . . . . . Religion and Labor Council of America
RLCS . . . . . . Radio Launch Control System
RLD . . . . RADAR Laydown Delivery
RLD . . . . Retail Liquor Dealer
RLD . . . . Rolled
RLE . . . . Request Loading Entry (Data processing)
RLE. . . . . . . Research Laboratory for Electronics
RLEA . . . . . . Railway Labor Executives Association
RLETFL . . . . . Report Leaving Each Thousand-Foot Level (Aviation)
RLF . . . . Relief
RLF . . . . Religion and Labor Foundation
RLF. . . . . . . Retrolental Fibroplasia (Eye disease in premature babies)
RLF . . . . Royal Literary Fund (British)
RLG . . . . Railing
RLG . . . . Royal Laotian Government
RLH . . . . Run Like Hell (Slang)
RLHS . . . . . . Railway and Locomotive Historical Society
RLHTE . . . . . Research Laboratory of Heat Transfer in Electronics (MIT)
RLI . . . . Radiation Level Indicator
RLI . . . . Rostral Length Index
RLIEVDP . . . . Request Line Items Be Expedited for Vehicles (or Equipment) Deadlined for Parts (Army)
RLL . . . . Right Lower Lobe (Lungs)
RLL . . . . Rim of Lateral Lip
RLL . . . . Rocket Launcher Locator
RLM . . . . Rearward Launched Missile
RLM . . . . Regional Library of Medicine (Pan American Health Organization)
RLM . . . . Reynolds Metals Company (NYSE symbol)
RLM . . . . Royal London Militia
RLMA . . . . . . Roll Label Manufacturers Association
RLMM . . . . . . Research Laboratory for Mechanics of Materials
RLMS . . . . . . RADAR Land Mass Simulation
RLMS . . . . . . Reproduction of Library Materials Section (Resources and Technical Services Division of ALA)
RLO . . . . RADAR Lock-On
RLO . . . . Regional Liaison Office (Military)
RLO . . . . Repairs Liaison Officer (Landing craft and barges) (Navy)
RLO . . . . Returned Letter Office
RLOS . . . . . . Retention Level of Supply (Navy)
RLP. . . . . . . Ruby LASER Pulse
RLPH . . . . . . Reflected Light Photohead
RLPL. . . . . . . Railway Labor's Political League
RLQ . . . . Right Lower Quadrant (of abdomen) (Medicine)
RLR . . . . Right Larval Retractor
RL & R . . . . . Rail, Lake, and Rail
RLS. . . . . . . RADAR Line of Sight
RLS . . . . Raman LASER Source
RLS . . . . Rim Latch Set
RLS . . . . Rocket Launching System
RLS . . . . Roll Limit Switch
RLS . . . . Rotary Limit Switch
RLS . . . . Ruby LASER System
RLSP. . . . . . . Ruby LASER Single Pulse
RLT . . . . Regimental Landing Team (Military)

RLT . . . . Relating To
RLT . . . . Reliability Life Test
RLT. . . . . . . Re-Order Lead Time (Navy)
RLT . . . . Ring LASER Technique
RLT . . . . Rolling Liquid Transporter (Army)
RLT. . . . . . . Russian Literature Triquarterly (A publication)
RLTA . . . . . . Reenlistment Leave Travel Allowance (Military)
RLTA . . . . . . Rhodesian Lawn Tennis Association
RLTO . . . . . . Regional Lime Technical Officer (Ministry of Agriculture, Fisheries, and Food) (British)
RLTS . . . . . . Radio Linked Telemetry System
RLTV . . . . . . Relative
RLU . . . . Relay Logic Unit
RLV . . . . Rauscher (Murine) Leukemia Virus
RLV . . . . Relieve
RLV . . . . Reusable Launch Vehicle
RLV . . . . Roving Lunar Vehicle
RLWY . . . . . . Railway
RLY . . . . Relay
RM. . . . . RADAR Mapper
RM. . . . . Radiation Measurement
RM. . . . . Radio Monitor
RM . . . . Radioman (Navy)
RM. . . . . Range Marks
RM . . . . Raw Material
RM . . . . Reaction Mass
RM . . . . Readout Matrix
RM. . . . . Receiver, Mobile
RM . . . . Receiving Memo
RM . . . . Reichsmark (German currency) (Later, DM)
RM . . . . Relative Mobility (of ions) (Chemistry)
RM . . . . Remedial Maintenance
RM. . . . . Research Materials (National Bureau of Standards)
RM. . . . . Research Memorandum
RM. . . . . Resident Magistrate
RM. . . . . Residential Members (Designation for real estate appraisers)
RM. . . . . Respiratory Movement
RM. . . . . Return Material (Navy)
RM . . . . Riding Master (British)
RM . . . . Ring Micrometer
RM. . . . . Room
RM. . . . . Routine Maintenance
RM . . . . Royal Mail
RM . . . . Royal Marine(s) (British)
R/M. . . . . . . Radiation/Meteoroid
R/M . . . . Revolutions Per Minute
R & M . . . . . . Redistribution and Marketing
R & M . . . . . Reliability and Maintainability (Navy)
R & M . . . . . Reports & Memorandum
RMA . . . . . . Radio Manufacturers Association
RMA . . . . . . Rice Millers' Association
RMA . . . . . . Right Mento-Anterior
RMA . . . . . . Robert Morris Associates (National Association of Bank Loan Officers and Credit Men)
RMA . . . . . . Royal Marine Artillery (British)
RMA. . . . . . . Royal Military Academy (For cadets of Royal Engineers and Royal Artillery; frequently referred to as Woolwich) (British)
RMA . . . . . . Royal Military Asylum
RMA. . . . . . . Rubber Manufacturers Association
R-MAD . . . . . . Reactor Maintenance, Assembly, and Disassembly (AEC)
RMAF . . . . . . Royal Moroccan Air Force
RMAX. . . . . . . Range, Maximum
RMB . . . . . . Radio Marker Beacon
RMB . . . . Royal McBee Corporation (NYSE symbol) (Wall Street slang name: "Rhumba") (Delisted)
RMC . . . . . . Captain of Royal Marines (Military) (British)
RMC . . . . Radiation Material Corporation
RMC . . . . Randolph-Macon College (Virginia)
RMC . . . . Raytheon Manufacturing Company
RMC. . . . . . . Reliance Manufacturing Company (NYSE symbol) (Delisted)
RMC. . . . . . . Rendezvous Mercury Capsule (NASA)
RMC. . . . . . . Residential Manpower Center (Job Corps)
RMC . . . . Rocket Motor Case
RMC . . . . Rocky Mountain College (Montana)
RMC . . . . Rod Memory Computer
RMC . . . . Rotary Mirror Camera
RMC. . . . . . . Royal Military College (For army cadets; often referred to as Sandhurst) (British)
RMCB . . . . . . Registered Mail Central Bureau
RMCM . . . . . . Return Material Credit Memo
RMCMI . . . . . . Rocky Mountain Coal Mining Institute

RMCO . . . . . . Raymond Manufacturing Company
RMD . . . . Ready Money Down (Means immediate payment)
RMD . . . . Repair and Modification Directive
RMD . . . . Retromanubrial Dullness (Medicine)
RMDA . . . . . . Request for Manufacturing Development Authorization
RMDI . . . . . . Radio Magnetic Deviation Indicator
RME . . . . Raw Materials
RME . . . . Request Monitor Entry (Data processing)
RMEC . . . . . . Refractory Metals Electrofinishing Corporation
RMEL . . . . . . Rocky Mountain Educational Laboratory (Closed)
RMF . . . . Reactivity Measurement Facility (AEC)
RMF . . . . Reflectivity Measuring Facility
RMF . . . . Royal Munster Fusiliers (British)
RMG . . . . . . Radar Mapper Gapfiller
RMG . . . . Relative Motion Gage
RMI . . . . Radio Magnetic Indicator
RMI . . . . Radiological Monitoring for Instructors (Civil Defense)
RMI . . . . Reaction Motors, Incorporated
RMI . . . . Reich Ministry of Interior
RMI . . . . Reliability Maturity Index (Polaris)
RMI . . . . Reliability Monitoring Index
RMI . . . . Rocket Motor Igniter
RMI . . . . . . Roll Manufacturers Institute
RMIA . . . . . . Rattan Manufacturers and Importers Association
RMIC . . . . . . Research Materials Information Center (ORNL)
RMICBM . . . . . Road Mobile Intercontinental Ballistic Missile
RMIP . . . . . . Reentry Measurements Instrumentation Package
RMIS . . . . . . Resource Management Information System
RMJM . . . . . . Recluse Missionaries of Jesus and Mary (Roman Catholic women's religious order)
RMK . . . . Remark
RML . . . . . . Radar Mapper, Long Range
RML . . . . Radar Microlink
RML . . . . Radio Microwave Link
RML . . . . Rescue Motor Launch (Air/sea rescue) (Navy)
RML . . . . Review of Metal Literature (American Society for Metals abstracting journal)
RML . . . . Right Middle Lobe (Lungs)
RML . . . . Rocky Mountain Laboratory (National Institutes of Health)
RML . . . . Rotating Mirror Laser
RMLI . . . . . . Royal Marine Light Infantry (British)
RMLP . . . . . . Regional Medical Library Program
RMM . . . . . . Radar Map Matching
RMM . . . . . . Rifle Marksman
RMM . . . . . . Ripple Mark Meter
RMMEA . . . . . Rolling Mill Machinery and Equipment Association
RMN . . . . . . Registered Mental Nurse
RMN . . . . . . Reserve Material (Account) Navy
RMO . . . . . . Radar Master Oscillator
RMO . . . . . . Radio (or Radar) Material Office (Navy)
RMO . . . . . . Records Management Office(r) (Military)
RMO . . . . . . Recruitment and Manning Organization (WSA)
RMO . . . . . . Regimental Munitions Officer (Army)
RMO . . . . . . Regional Medical Officer
RMO . . . . . . Royal Marine Office (British)
RMOC . . . . . Recommended Maintenance Operation Chart (Army)
RMP . . . . . . Reentry Measurement Program
RMP . . . . . . Regional Medical Program
RMP . . . . . . Research Management Plan
RMP . . . . . . Research & Microfilm Publications
RMP . . . . . . Right Mentoposterior
RMP . . . . . . Royal Marine Police
RMPA . . . . . Rocky Mountain Psychological Association
RMPR . . . . . Revised Maximum Price Regulation (World War II)
RMR . . . . . . Reflector Moderated Reactor
RMR . . . . . . Regional Maintenance Representative
RMROCK . . . . Rocket Motors Records Office Center (Navy)
RMS . . . . . . Radar Maintenance Spares
RMS . . . . . . Radar Mapping Set (or System)
RMS . . . . . . Radio Marker Station
RMS . . . . . . Radiological Monitoring System
RMS . . . . . . Railway Mail Service
RMS . . . . . . Range Measuring System
RMS . . . . . . Range Modification System
RMS . . . . . . Rathkamp Matchcover Society
RMS . . . . . . Recruiting Main Station (Military)
RMS . . . . . . Reentry Measurement System
RMS . . . . . . Remote Maneuvering System
RMS . . . . . . Remote Manipulator System
RMS . . . . . Resources Management System (Army)
RMS . . . . . . (Square) Root of Mean Square

RMS . . . . . . Royal Mail Steamship (or Service) (British)
RMS . . . . . . Royal Microscopical Society (British)
RMSE . . . . . . Root Mean Square Error
RMSP . . . . . Refractory Metal Sheet Program (Navy)
RMSP . . . . . Royal Mail Steam Packet Company
RMT . . . . . . Radiometric Moon Tracer
RMT . . . . . . Registry of Medical Technologists
RMT . . . . . . Right Mentotransverse
RMTE . . . . . Remote
RMTR . . . . . Redesigned Missile Tracking Radar (Army)
RMTS . . . . . Research Member of the Technical Staff
RMU . . . . . Remote Maneuvering Unit (NASA)
RMV . . . . . . Reentry Measurement Vehicle
RMV . . . . . . Remove
RMV . . . . . . Respiratory Minute Volume (Physiology)
RMVBL . . . . . Removable
RMVD . . . . . Removed
RMVG . . . . . Removing
RMVL . . . . . Removal
RMWAA . . . . Roadmasters and Maintenance of Way Association of America
RMWC . . . . . Randolph-Macon Woman's College (Virginia)
RMWR . . . . . Religious, Morale, Welfare and Recreation (Military)
Rn . . . . Radon (Chemical element)
RN . . . . Radio Navigation
RN . . . . Reception Nil (Radio logs)
RN . . . . Reference Noise
RN . . . . Registered Nurse
RN . . . . Rejection Notice
RN . . . . Research Note
RN . . . . Reynolds Number (Viscosity) (Also, R)
RN . . . . Royal Navy (British)
RN . . . . . . Ruritan National
RNA . . . . . . Religious Newswriters Association
RNA . . . . . . Republic of New Africa (Black separatist group)
RNA . . . . . . Ribonucleic Acid (Biochemistry)
RNA . . . . . . Robbery Not Armed
RNA . . . . . . Rotatable Nozzle Assembly
RNA . . . . . . Rough, Noncapsulated, Avirulent (with reference to bacteria)
RNA . . . . . . Royal Neighbors of America
RNAA . . . . . Radiochemical Neutron Activation Analysis
RNAA . . . . . Russian Nobility Association in America
R/NAA . . . . . Rocketdyne - North American Aviation
RNAC . . . . . Royal Nepal Airlines Corporation
RNAF . . . . . Royal Naval Air Force (British)
RNAF . . . . . Royal Netherlands Air Force
RNAMY . . . . Royal Naval Aircraft Maintenance Yard (British)
RNAS . . . . . Royal Naval Air Service (Precursor of Fleet Air Arm) (British)
RNAS . . . . . Royal Naval Air Station
RNATE . . . . . Royal Naval Air Training Establishment (British)
R-NAV . . . . . Random Navigation
RNB . . . . . . Received, Not Billed
RNB . . . . . . Royal Naval Barracks
RNBC . . . . . Royal Naval Beach Commando (British)
RNC . . . . . . Radio Non-Contingent
RNC . . . . . . Republican National Committee
RNC . . . . . . Royal Naval College (For future officers; often spoken of as Dartmouth) (British)
RNC . . . . . . Rumanian National Committee
RNCC . . . . . Royal Naval College of Canada (1911-1922)
RNCF . . . . . Royal Netherlands Chemical Foundation
RN & CR . . . . Ryde, Newport, and Cowes Railway (British)
RNCVR . . . . . Royal Naval Canadian Volunteer Reserve (World War I)
RND . . . . . . Royal Naval Division
RNEIAF . . . . . Royal Netherlands East Indies Air Force
RNEIN . . . . . Royal Netherlands East Indies Navy
RNF . . . . . . Receiver Noise Figure
RNFP . . . . . Radar Not Functioning Properly
RNG . . . . . . Army National Guard
RNG . . . . . . Random Noise Generator
RNG . . . . . . Range
RNGHQ . . . . Royal Navy General Headquarters (British)
RNI . . . . . . Ranco Incorporated (NYSE symbol)
RNIB . . . . . Royal National Institute for the Blind (British)
RNID . . . . . Royal National Institute for the Deaf (British)
RNIO . . . . . Resident Naval Inspector of Ordnance
RNIR . . . . . Reduction to Next Inferior Rank
RNIT . . . . . Radio Noise Interference Test
RNLAF . . . . . Royal Netherlands Air Force
RNLBI . . . . . Royal National Life-Boat Institution (British)
RNLI . . . . . Royal National Life-Boat Institution (British)
RNLO . . . . . Royal Naval Liaison Officer (British)

RNM . . . . Radio-Navigation Mobile
RNM . . . . Rassemblement National Malagache (National Malagasy Rally)
RNMD . . . . . . Registered Nurse for Mental Defectives
RNN . . . . Royal Netherlands Navy
RNN . . . . Royal Norwegian Navy
RNNAS. . . . . . Royal Netherlands Naval Air Service
RNO. . . . . . . Roan Selection Trust, Ltd (NYSE symbol) (Formerly, RHO; later, RST)
RNOAF. . . . . . Royal Norwegian Air Force
RNOC. . . . . . . Royal Naval Officers Club
RNoN . . . . . . Royal Netherlands Navy
RNP . . . . Rassemblement National Populaire (France)
RNP . . . . Ribonucleoprotein
RNPS . . . . . . Royal Naval Patrol Service (British)
RNR . . . . Rayonier Inc. (NYSE symbol) (Delisted)
RNR . . . . Royal Naval Reserve (British)
RNS . . . . RADAR Netting Station
RNS . . . . . . Religious News Service
RNS . . . . Reusable Nuclear Shuttle (NASA)
RNS . . . . Royal Naval School (British)
RNSC . . . . Rocket/Nimbus Sounder Comparison (NASA)
RNSC . . . . . . Royal Naval Staff College (British)
RNTWPA . . . . Radio-Newsreel-Television Working Press Association
RNU . . . . RADAR Netting Unit
RNV. . . . . . . Radio Noise Voltage
RNV. . . . . . . Random Noise Voltmeter
RNV . . . . . . Replacement Naval Vessels
RNV. . . . . . . Resistive Null Voltage
RN(V)R . . . . . Royal Naval (Volunteer) Reserve (British)
RNVSR . . . . . Royal Naval Volunteer Supplementary Reserve (World War II) (British)
RNWMP . . . . . Royal North West Mounted Police (Later, RCMP)
RNZAF . . . . . . Royal New Zealand Air Force
RNZN . . . . . . Royal New Zealand Navy
RNZN(V)R . . . Royal New Zealand Naval (Volunteer) Reserve
RO . . . . RADAR Observer
RO. . . . . RADAR Operator
RO. . . . . Radiation Office (Environmental Protection Agency)
RO. . . . . Radio Operator
RO. . . . . Range Operation
RO. . . . . Receive Only
RO. . . . . Receiving Office(r)
RO. . . . . Reconnaissance Officer
RO. . . . . Records Office(r) (Air Force)
RO. . . . . Recruiting Officer (Military)
RO. . . . . Reddish Orange
RO . . . . Regimental Orders (Army)
RO. . . . . Regional Office (r)
RO. . . . . Reporting Officer (Army)
RO. . . . . Requisitioning Objective (Military)
RO. . . . . Research Officer (British)
RO . . . . Reserve Order
RO. . . . . Retrofit Order (Navy)
RO. . . . . Reverse Osmosis (Desalination)
RO. . . . . Rework Order
RO . . . . Rough Opening (Technical drawings)
RO. . . . . Route Order (Military)
RO. . . . . Routine Order(s)
RO . . . . Routing Office(r) (Navy)
RO. . . . . Royal Observatory (British)
RO. . . . . Royal Octavo
R & O . . . . . . Rail and Ocean
ROA . . . . . . Radio Operator's Aptitude Test (Military)
ROA. . . . . . . Reserve Officers Association of the United States
ROA. . . . . . . Return on Assets (Finance)
ROA . . . . . . Right Occiput Anterior (A normal position of fetus at delivery) (Obstetrics)
ROA . . . . . . Rules of the Air
ROAD . . . . . . Reorganization Objective, Army Division (Military)
ROADS . . . . . Real-Time Optical Alignment and Diagnostic System (Module)
ROAM . . . . . Return on Assets Managed (Finance)
ROAMA . . . . . Rome Air Materiel Area (Air Force) (Deactivated)
ROAR. . . . . . Royal Optimizing Assembly Routine (Data processing)
ROAT . . . . . . Radio Operator's Aptitude Test
ROB . . . . RADAR Order of Battle
ROB . . . . Relieve of Booty (Crime term)
ROB . . . . Remaining on Board
ROB . . . . Report on Board (Navy)
ROB . . . . Reserve on Board
ROB . . . . Reserveoffizier-Bewerber (Reserve officer applicant) (German military - World War II)
ROBEPS . . . . . RADAR Operating Below Prescribed Standards
ROBIN . . . . . . Rocket Balloon Instrument (Air Force)

ROBO . . . . Rocket Orbital Bomber
ROBOMB. . . . . Robot Bomb (Air Force)
ROC. . . . . . . Receiver Operating Characteristics (Pyschophysical measurement)
ROC. . . . . Reduce Operating Costs (Air Force project)
ROC . . . . Reliability Operating Characteristic
ROC. . . . . . . Remote Operator's Console
ROC . . . . Republican Organizing Committee (Political organization in opposition to the NPL of North Dakota)
ROC. . . . . . . Required Operational Capability
ROC . . . . Reserve Officer Candidate
ROC . . . . Reusable Orbital Carrier
ROC. . . . . . . Rockower Brothers, Inc. (NYSE symbol)
ROC. . . . . . . Royal Observer Corps (British civilian aircraft observers) (World War II)
ROC . . . . Royal Ordnance Corps (British)
R/OC . . . . . . Receive Only Center
RO in C . . . . . Resident Officer-in-Charge (Navy)
ROCALDIS . . . Routine Calls May Be Dispensed With
ROCAP . . . . . Regional Office, Central America and Panama (AID)
ROCAPPI . . . . . Research on Computer Applications for the Printing and Publishing Industries
ROCAT . . . . . . Rocket Catapult
ROCC. . . . . . . Regional Operations Control Center (AT & T)
ROCID . . . . . Reorganization of Combat Infantry Division (Army)
ROCKET . . . . Rand's Omnibus Calculator of the Kinetics of Earth Trajectories
ROCKOON . . . Rocket Balloon (Navy)
ROCMAS . . . . Russian Orthodox Catholic Mutual Aid Society of USA
ROCMM . . . . . Regional Office of Civilian Manpower Management
ROCP . . . . . . RADAR Out of Commission for Parts (ADC)
ROCR. . . . . . . Remote Optical Character Recognition (Data processing)
ROCWMAS . . . Russian Orthodox Catholic Women's Mutual Aid Society
ROD. . . . . . . Repair and Overhaul Directive
ROD . . . . Required Operational Data
ROD. . . . . . . Reverse-Osmosis Desalination
ROD. . . . . . . Rise-Off Disconnect
R-O-D . . . . . . Rise-Off-Disconnect
RODAC . . . . . Reorganization Objectives Army Division, Army and Corps
RODATA . . . . Registered Organization Data Bank
RODIAC . . . . Rotary Dual Input for Analog Computation
RODS . . . . Real-Time Operations, Dispatching, and Scheduling (System) (TRW, Inc.)
ROE . . . . Reflector Orbital Equipment
ROE . . . . Return on Equity (Finance)
ROE . . . . Round Off Error
ROE . . . . Royal Observatory, Edinburgh (Scotland)
Roent M . . . . . Master of Roentgenology
ROF . . . . . . Reformed Ogboni Fraternity (Nigeria)
ROF . . . . Reporting Organizational File (Military)
ROF . . . . Robertshaw Controls Company (NYSE symbol)
ROFL . . . . . . Russian Orthodox Fraternity Lubov
ROFOR . . . . . Route Forecast (Aviation)
ROFT . . . . . . RADAR OFF Target
ROG . . . . . . Receipt of Goods
ROG . . . . Residency Operations Group
ROG . . . . . . Rise Off Ground
R-O-G . . . . . . Rise-Off-Ground
ROGOPAG . . . Rossellini, Jr.; Godard, Pasolini, Gregoretti (Title of episodic motion picture formed from surnames of its directors)
ROH. . . . . . . Regular Overhaul
ROH. . . . . Revolucni Odborove Hnutf
ROH. . . . . . . Rohm & Haas Company (NYSE symbol)
ROI . . . . Radio, Optical, Inertial
ROI . . . . Reliability Organization Instruction
ROI . . . . Report of Investigation
ROI . . . . Return on Investment
ROI . . . . Rotating Optical Interferometer
ROI . . . . Royal Industries, Inc. (NYSE symbol)
ROIC . . . . . . Resident Officer-in-Charge
ROICC . . . . . Resident Officer in Charge of Construction
ROID . . . . . . Report of Item Discrepancy (Army)
ROJ . . . . Range on Jamming
ROK. . . . . . . Republic of (South) Korea
ROK. . . . . . . Rockwell Manufacturing Co. (NYSE symbol)
ROKA . . . . . . Republic of Korea Army
ROKAF . . . . . Republic of Korea Air Force
ROKPUC . . . . Republic of Korea Presidential Unit Citation Badge
ROKPUCE . . . . Republic of Korea Presidential Unit Citation
ROL. . . . . . . Rollins, Inc. (NYSE symbol)
ROLS . . . . . . Recoverable Orbital Launch System
ROM . . . . . . Range of Movement
ROM . . . . . . Read-Only Memory (Data processing)
ROM . . . . . . Return on Market Value (Finance)
ROM . . . . Rough Order Magnitude (Army)

ROM . . . . Run of Mine
ROMAC . . . . . Range Operations Monitoring and Control
ROMACC . . . . Range Operational Monitoring and Control Center
ROMBUS . . . . Reusable Orbital Module Booster & Utility Shuttle
ROMEMO . . . . Reference Our Memorandum
ROMO . . . . . . Rocky Mountain National Park
ROMON . . . . . Receiving-Only Monitor
ROMOTAR. . . . Range-Only Measurement of Trajectory and Recording
ROMP . . . . . . Report of Obligation Military Pay
RON . . . . Receiving Only
RON . . . . Remaining Overnight (Aviation)
RON . . . . Research Octane Number
RON . . . . Ronson Corporation (NYSE symbol)
RONAG . . . . . Reserve Officers Naval Architecture Group
RONB . . . . . . Research-Octane-Number-Barrels
RONCOM . . . . Ronald Como, Inc. (Perry Como's production firm; Ronald is his son)
RONLY . . . . . . Receiver Only (Radio)
RONS . . . . . . Reserve Officers of the Naval Service
ROO . . . . Railhead Ordnance Officer
ROO . . . . Range Operations Officer
ROOSCH . . . . . Royal Order of Sputnik Chasers
ROOST . . . . . Reusable One-Stage Orbital Space Truck
ROOT . . . . . . Relaxation Oscillator Optically Tuned
ROP . . . . Record of Performance or Record of Production
ROP . . . . Reorder Point (Navy)
ROP . . . . Right Occiput Posterior (A normal position of fetus before delivery) (Obstetrics)
ROP . . . . Right Outside Position (Dancing)
ROP . . . . Roper Corporation (NYSE symbol)
ROP . . . . Run of Paper (Advertising which is to appear on no specified page)
ROP . . . . Run of Press (i.e., on an unspecified page or plate in web press set-up) (Printing)
ROPA . . . . . . Reserve Officers Personnel Act
ROPB . . . . . . Reserve Officers Promotion Board (Air Force)
ROPP . . . . . . Receive-Only Page Printer
ROPRA . . . . . Reserve Officer Performance Recording Activity
ROPS . . . . . . Range Operation Performance Summary
ROPS . . . . . . Roll Over Protection System (for tractors)
ROR . . . . Range Only RADAR
ROR . . . . Rate of Read
ROR . . . . Released on Own Recognizance (Law)
ROR . . . . Rocket on Rotor
ROR . . . . Rockton & Rion Railway (AAR code)
ROR . . . . Rorer-Amchem, Inc. (NYSE symbol)
RORA . . . . . . Reserve Officer Recording Activity
RORC . . . . . . Royal Ocean Racing Club (British)
RORET . . . . . Authorized Rotational Retention (Navy)
RORIS . . . . . . Remote Operated Radiographic Inspection System
RO/RO . . . . . . Rollon/Rolloff
ROS . . . . RADAR Distribution Switch
ROS . . . . Read-Only Storage (Data processing)
ROS . . . . Red Owl Stores, Inc. (NYSE symbol) (Delisted)
ROS . . . . Reduced Operational Status
ROS . . . . Remote Optical System
ROS . . . . Representative Observation Site (Weather observing facility) (Air Force)
ROS . . . . Return from Overseas (Military)
ROS . . . . Rochester Subway Company (AAR code)
ROS . . . . Rotating Optical Scanner
ROS . . . . Royal Order of Scotland
ROS . . . . Run of Schedule (Commercial announcement to be broadcast throughout the program schedule)
ROSA . . . . . . Record One Stop Association
ROSC . . . . . . Reserve Officers Sanitary Corps
ROSE . . . . . . Remotely Operated Special Equipment (AEC)
ROSE . . . . . . Retrieval by On-Line Search (Data processing)
ROSE . . . . . . Rising Observational Sounding Equipment
ROSIE . . . . . . Reconnaissance by Orbiting Ship-Identification Equipment
ROSIE . . . . . . Rooters Organized to Stimulate Interest and Enthusiasm (Women baseball fans, Cincinnati)
ROSO . . . . . . Relay Operated Sampling Oscilloscope
ROT . . . . RADAR on Target
ROT . . . . Range on Target
ROT . . . . Rate of Turn
ROT . . . . Remedial Occupation Therapy
ROT . . . . Reusable Orbital Transport
ROT . . . . Right Occipitotransverse
ROT . . . . Rotary
ROT . . . . Rotate
ROT . . . . Rule of Thumb
ROTAB . . . . . Rotable Table
ROTAC . . . . . Rotary Oscillating Torque Actuators

ROTC . . . . . . Reserve Officers Training Corps (Separate units for Army, Navy, Air Force)
ROTCC . . . . . Receiver-Off-Hook Tone Connecting Circuit
ROTCM . . . . . Reserve Officers Training Corps Manual
ROTE . . . . . . Range Optical Tracking Equipment
ROTEL . . . . . Rotational Telemetry
ROTI . . . . Recording Optical Tracking Instrument (Missiles)
ROTI . . . . Reinforced Oxide Throat Insert
ROTL . . . . . . Remote Office Test Line (Bell Laboratories)
ROTR . . . . . . Receive-Only Tape Reperforator
ROTR-S/P . . . Receiving Only Typing Reperforator - Series to Parallel
ROTS . . . . . . Range on Target Signal
ROTT . . . . . . Rate of Turntable
ROTV . . . . . . Reusable Orbital Transport Vehicle
ROU . . . . Republica Oriental del Uruguay
ROV . . . . Refined Oil of Vitriol
ROV . . . . Remote Optical Viewing
ROVD . . . . . . Relay Operated Voltage Divider
ROVNITE . . . . Remaining Over Night
ROVS . . . . . . Remote Optical Viewing System
ROW . . . . Relocate Out of Washington (Navy)
ROW . . . . Rheinische Olefinwerke
ROW. . . . . . . Right(s)-of-Way (Also, RW)
ROW . . . . Risk of War
RP . . . . Radiation Pressure
RP . . . . Radiation Protection
RP . . . . Radioplane Company
RP . . . . Raid Plotter
RP . . . . Rally Point (Air Force)
RP . . . . Rate Package
RP . . . . Readiness Potential
RP . . . . Real Property
RP . . . . Receipt Pass
RP . . . . Reception Poor (Radio logs)
RP . . . . Receptor Potential
RP . . . . Recommended Practice
RP . . . . Reddish Purple
RP . . . . Reference Pulse
RP . . . . Refilling Point
RP . . . . Reformed Presbyterian
RP . . . . Regius Professor
RP . . . . Reinforced Plastic
RP . . . . Release Point (Ground traffic)
RP . . . . Remote Pickup
RP . . . . Replacement Pilot (Navy)
RP . . . . Reply Paid (Communications)
RP . . . . Reporting Post (RADAR)
RP . . . . Reprint
RP . . . . Republic of Panama
RP . . . . Res Publica
RP . . . . Research Paper
RP . . . . Reserve Personnel (Air Force)
RP . . . . Resistance Plate
RP . . . . Retained Personnel
RP . . . . Return of Post
RP . . . . Return Premium
RP . . . . Reverendus Pater (Reverend Father)
RP . . . . Revertive Pulsing
RP . . . . Revision Proposal
RP . . . . Right Traffic Pattern (Aviation)
RP . . . . Rocket Projectile
RP . . . . Rocket Propellant (Air Force)
RP . . . . Ron Pair!
RP . . . . Round Punch
RP . . . . Rules of Procedure
RP . . . . Rupee(s)
RP . . . . Rust Preventive
RPA . . . . RADAR Performance Analyzer
RPA . . . . Radium Plaque Adaptometer (Navy)
RPA . . . . Random Phase Approximation
RPA . . . . Regional Plan Association
RPA . . . . Renewal Projects Administration (HUD)
RPA . . . . Request Present Altitude (Aviation)
RPA . . . . Reserve Personnel, Army
RPA . . . . Resultant Physiological Acceleration
RPA . . . . Retarding Potential Analyzer (NASA)
RPA . . . . Rubber Peptizing Agent
RPA . . . . Rust Prevention Association
RPAE . . . . . . Retarding Potential Analyzer Experiment
RPAG . . . . . . Retired Professionals Action Group (Formed by consumer-advocate Ralph Nader)

RPAO .... Radium Plaque Adaptometer Operator (Navy)
RPASMC ..... Rubber & Plastic Adhesive & Sealant Manufacturers Council (Later, Adhesive and Sealant Council)
RPB .... RADAR Plotting Board
RPB .... Regional Preparedness Board (Military)
RPB .... Research to Prevent Blindness, Inc.
RPB .... Resources Protection Board
RPBG .... Revised Program and Budget Guidance
RPC .... RADAR Planning Chart
RPC .... RADAR Processing Center
RPC .... Records Processing Center (Veterans Administration)
RPC .... Recruiting Publicity Center (Military)
RPC .... Reefed Parachute Canopy
RPC .... Regional Planning Commission
RPC .... Registered Publication Clerk (Navy)
RPC .... Reliability Policy Committee
RPC .... Remote Position Control
RPC .... Remote Power Controller
RPC .... Reno-Pericardial Canal
RPC .... Reparable Processing Centers
RPC .... Reply Post Card
RPC .... Report(ing) to Commander (Military)
RPC .... Republican Policy Committee
RPC .... Reversed-Phase Chromatography
RPC .... Reversed Phase Column
RPC .... Russian People's Center
RPCC .... Reactor Physics Constants Center (Argonne National Laboratory)
RPCCA ...... Red Poll Cattle Club of America
RPCF. ...... Reiter Protein Complement Fixation (Medicine)
RPCH .... Reformed Presbyterian Church
RPCI .... Regroupement des Partis de la Cote d'Ivoire (Regroupment of the Parties of the Ivory Coast)
RPCK .... Reno-Pericardial Canal, Kidney
RP/CL ...... Reporting Post, Coastal Low (RADAR)
RP/CM ...... Reporting Post, Coastal Medium (RADAR)
RPCP. ...... Reno-Pericardial Canal, Pericardium
RPCRAAIO.... Receive and Process Complaints and Requests for Assistance, Advice, or Information Only (Army)
RPD .... RADAR Planning Device
RPD .... RADAR Prediction Device
RPD .... Rapid
RPD .... Rapid American Corp. (NYSE symbol)
RPD .... Reflex Plasma Discharge
RPD .... Relative Power Density
RPD .... Rerum Politicarum Doctor (Doctor of Political Science)
RPD .... Reserves Available to Support Private, Noninterbank Deposits (Federal Reserve System)
RPD .... Resistance Pressure Detector
RPD .... Ruchnoi Pulemet Degtyarev (Light Machine Gun) (USSR)
RPDES ...... Research Program Development and Evaluation Staff (Department of Agriculture)
RPDL .... Radioisotope Process Development Laboratory (ORNL)
RPDS .... Retired Personnel Data System (Air Force)
RPE .... Reformed Protestant Episcopal
RPE .... Related Payroll Expense
RPE .... Ron Pair Enterprises (Division of Wilson, Inc.)
RPEA .... Regional Planning and Evaluation Agency (California State Board of Education)
RPEP .... Register of Planned Emergency Producers
RPF. .... Radio Proximity Fuze
RPF. .... Radiometer Performance Factor
RPF .... Rassemblement du Peuple Francais (Rally of the French People)
RPF. .... Real Property Facilities (Army)
RPF. .... Relaxed Pelvic Floor (Medicine)
RPF .... Renal Plasma Flow (Physiology)
RPFC .... Recurrent Peak Forward Current
RPFOD ...... Reported for Duty
RPG .... Radiation Protection Guide (AEC)
RPG .... Radioisotopic Power Generator (Navy)
RPG........ Religious Publishers Group
RPG .... Report Program Generator
RPG .... Right Pedal Ganglion
RPG .... Rocket-Propelled Grenade
RPG .... Rotary Pulse Generator
RPGPM...... Rounds Per Gun Per Minute
RPH .... Registered Pharmacist
RPH .... Rideout Pyrohydrolysis
RP/H .... Repairs, Heavy
RPHST....... Research Participation for High School Teachers (National Science Foundation)
RPI........ RADAR Precipitation Integrator (National Weather Service)

RPI........ Railway Progress Institute
RPI........ Real Property Inventory
RPI........ Rensselaer Polytechnic Institute (New York)
RPI........ Richmond Professional Institute (Virginia)
RPI........ Ridder Publications, Incorporated (NYSE symbol)
RPI........ Rose Polytechnic Institute (Indiana)
RPIA ...... Rocket Propellant Information Agency
RPIE ...... Real Property Installed Equipment (Air Force)
RPIO ...... Registered Publication Issuing Office
RPJ .... Rotary Pressure Joint
RPL .... Radiation Physics Laboratory (National Bureau of Standards)
RPL .... Radio-Photo Luminescent (Dosimetry)
RPL .... Reactor Primary Loop
RPL .... Recommended Provisioning List
RPL .... Repair Parts List (Army)
RPL .... Rocket Propulsion Laboratory (Air Force)
RPL .... Running Program Language
RP/L ...... Repairs, Light
RPLV ...... Reentry Payload Launch Vehicle
RPM .... RADAR Performance Monitor
RPM .... Rate Per Minute
RPM .... Real Property Management
RPM .... Registered Publications Manual (Navy)
RPM .... Regulated Power Module
RPM .... Reliability Performance Measure (QCR)
RPM .... Resale Price Maintenance
RPM .... Revenue Passenger Mile
RPM .... Revolutions Per Minute (e.g., in reference to phonograph records)
RPM .... Rotation Per Minute
RPMA ...... Real Property Maintenance Activities (Army)
RPMC ...... Remote Performance Monitoring and Control
RPMD ..... Resources Planning and Mobilization Division (of OEP)
RPMI ...... Revolutions-Per-Minute Indicator
RPMI ...... Roswell Park Memorial Institute (Buffalo, New York)
RPMIO ..... Registered Publication Mobile Issuing Office(r)
RPMO...... Radio Projects Management Office
RPMP ...... Register of Plan Mobilization Producers
RP,N ...... Reserve Personnel, Navy (An appropriation)
RPO .... Railway Post Office
RPO .... Regional Pests Officer (Ministry of Agriculture, Fisheries, and Food) (British)
RPO .... Revolution Per Orbit
RPO .... Rotor Power Output
RPO .... Royal Philharmonic Orchestra (British)
RPOC ...... Report Proceeding on Course (Aviation)
RPOCN...... Request for Purchase Order Change Notice
RPP........ RADAR Power Programmer
RPP........ Rechargeable Power Pack
RPP........ Regional Priority Program (Army)
RPP........ Removable Patch Panel
RPP........ Rendezvous Point Position
RPP........ Repair Parts Provisioning
RPP .... Reply Paid Postcard
RPP........ Request Present Position (Aviation)
RPP........ Requisition Processing Point
RPP........ Roll-Pitch Pickoff
RPPA ...... Republican Postwar Policy Association (Encouraged Republican Party to drop its isolationist viewpoint and take a stand for an American share in international collaboration after the war) (World War II)
RPPE ...... Research, Program, Planning, and Evaluation
RPPI....... Remote Plan Position Indicator (Navy)
RPPL ...... Repair Parts Price List
RPPQ ...... Request for Price Quotation
RPR .... Radio Physics Research
RPR .... Rapid Plasma Reagin (Card test) (for venereal disease)
RPR........ Read Printer
RPR .... Rear Projection Readout
RPR .... Roll-Pitch Resolver
RPRA ...... Railroad Public Relations Association
RPRC ...... Religious Public Relations Council
RPRC ...... Retired and Pioneer Rural Carriers of US
RPRD ...... Research Policy and Review Division (of OEP)
RPROP ..... Receiving Proficiency Pay (Military)
RPRRB ..... Real Property Resource Review Board
RPRS...... Random-Pulse RADAR System
RPRS...... Roll-Pitch Resolver System
RPRT....... Report
RPS .... Range Pad Service
RPS .... Range Positioning System
RPS .... Rapid Photo Screening
RPS .... Registered Publications System

RPS	Regulated Power Supply
RPS	Renal Pressor Substance
RPS	Response-Produced Stimulation
RPS	Revolutions Per Second
RPS	Right Pedal Sinus
RPS	Rotary Precision Switch
RPS	Rotating Passing Scuttle
RPS	Rotational Position Sensing (Data processing)
RPSCTDY	Return to Proper Station Upon Completion of Temporary Duty
RPS-DL	Registered Publications Section - District Library (Navy)
R & P SEC . . .	Radio and Panel Section (Navy)
RPSM	Registered Publication Shipment Memorandum
RPSM	Resources Planning and Scheduling Method
RPSML	Repair Parts Support Material List
RPS-PL	Registered Publications Section - Personnel Library (Navy)
RPSTL	Repair Parts and Special Tools List (Army)
RPT	Registered Physical Therapist
RPT	Repeat
RPT	Report
RPT	Request Programs Termination (Data processing)
RPT	Resident Provisioning Team
RPT	Rocket-Powered Target
RPT	Rocket Propulsion Technician (Air Force)
RPT	Rotary Power Transformer
R & PT	Rifle and Pistol Team (Navy)
RPTN	Repetition
RPU	Radio Phone Unit (Navy)
RPU	Radio Propagation Unit (Army)
RPU	Railway Patrolmen's International Union
RPU	Rectifier Power Unit
RPU	Registered Publication Unit
RPU	Remote Pickup Unit
RPU	Retention Pending Use (Air Force)
RPV	Remote Positioning Valve
RPV	Rhopalosiphum padi Virus
RPVT	Relative Position Velocity Technique
RPWDA	Retail Paint and Wallpaper Distributors of America
RPY.	Roll, Pitch, and Yaw
RQ.	Recovery Quotient
RQ.	Respiratory Quotient (Also, Q) (Physiology)
R/Q	Request for Quotation
R & QA	Reliability & Quality Assurance
RQC	RADAR Quality Control
RQC.	Reliability and Quality Control
RQDCZ	Request Clearance to Depart Control Zone (Aviation)
RQDP	Request, Quandary and Deferment Plan
RQECZ	Request Clearance to Enter Control Zone (Aviation)
RQMD	Richmond Quartermaster Depot (Merged with Defense General Supply Center)
RQMS	Regimental Quartermaster-Sergeant (British)
RQMT.	Requirement
RQN	Radial Quantum Number
RQN	Requisition
RQP	Resistor Qualification Program
RQR	Require (Required; Requirement; Requiring)
RQS	Rate Quoting System
RQS.	Ready Qualified for Standby
RQT	Resistor Qualification Test
RQTAO.	Request Time and Altitude Over (Aviation)
RQTP	Resistor Qualification Test Program
RQY	Relative Quantum Yield
RR	Radiation Response
RR	Radio Range
RR	Radio Receptor Co., Inc.
RR	Radio Regulations
RR	Railroad
RR	Rapid Rectilinear
RR	Rarely Reversed (Decisions in law)
RR	Raritan River R. R. (AAR code)
RR	Readout and Relay
RR	Receiving Report
RR	Recovery Room
RR	Recruit Roll (Navy)
RR	Recurrence Rate
RR	Redundancy Reduction
RR	Registered Representative (Wall Street stock salesman)
RR	Removal-Replacement
RR	Rendezvous RADAR (NASA)
RR	Renegotiation Regulations
RR	Repetition Rate
RR	Research Report

RR	Respiratory Rate (Medicine)
RR	Responsible Receiver
RR	Retro-Rocket (Army)
RR	Rifle Range
RR	Right Rear
RR	Right Reverend
RR	Rights Reserved
RR	Roll Roofing
RR	Running Reverse
RR	Rural Route
RR	Rush Release
R/R	Remove and Replace
R & R	Rate and Rhythm (of pulse)
R & R	Refueling and Rearming (Air Force)
R & R	Reporting and Requisitioning (Air Force)
R & R	Rest and Recuperation (Military)
R & R	Rock and Roll (Music)
R & R	Rock and Rye
R & R	Routing and Record Sheet (Air Force)
RRA	Religious Research Association
RRA	Rubber Reclaimers Association
R & RA.	Retraining and Reemployment Administration (Terminated 1947)
RRAD	Red River Army Depot
RRAF	Ready Reserve of the Armed Forces
RRAF	Royal Rhodesian Air Force
RRB	RADAR Reflective Balloon
RRB	Railroad Retirement Board
RRC	Radiation Resistance Cable
RRC	Radio Receptor Company
RRC	Receiving Report Change
RRC	Recruit Reception Center
RRC	Reentry Rate Command (NASA)
RRC	Regular Route Carrier
RRC	Report Review Committee (National Academy of Sciences)
RRC	Requirements Review Committee (Navy)
RRC	Road Runners Club of America
RRC	Rocket Research Corporation
RRC	Royal Red Cross (British)
RRC	Rubber Reserve Committee (Navy)
RRC	Rubber Reserve Company
RR & C	Records, Reports and Control
RRCN	Receiving Report Change Notice
RRCS	Railroad Communication System
RRCS	Reentry RADAR Cross Section
RRD	Receive, Record, Display
RRD	Reliability Requirements Directive
RRD	Resonant Reed Decoder
RR & D.	Reparations, Removal, and Demolition (Section) (Industry Branch, US Military Government, Germany)
RRDA	Rendezvous Retrieval, Docking & Assembly (of space vehicle or orbital station)
RRDA	Repetitive Report Distribution Audit
RRDR	Raw RADAR Data Recorder
RRE	RADAR Research Establishment (British)
RRE	Railroad Enthusiasts
RRE	Range Rate Error
RRE	Royal RADAR Establishment (British)
RR & E	Round, Regular and Equal (with reference to pupils of eyes)
RRep.	Records Repository (Air Force)
RRev.	Records Review (Air Force)
RRF	Racing Research Fund
RRF.	Rapid Reaction Forces (Army)
RRF	Reading Reform Foundation
RRF	Refrigeration Research Foundation
RRF	Resonant Reed Filter
RRF.	Revised Recommended Findings
RRFO	Rhine River Field Organization (Post-World War II)
RRFS.	Range Rate Frequency Synthesizer
RRG	RADAR Range Gate
RRG	Roll Reference Gyro
RRI	Range Rate Indicator
RRI	Revised Ring Index (A reference book)
RRI	Rocket Research Institute
RRIC	Race Relations Information Center (Nashville) (Defunct)
RRIC	RADAR Repeater Indicator Console
RRIN	Readiness Risk Index Number
RRIPM.	Rapid Response Interference Prediction Model
RRIS	Remote RADAR Integration Station
RRK	Retaining Ring Kit
RRL	Radio Research Laboratories (Japan)
RRL	Rayleigh Radiation Law

RRL .... Regimental Reserve Line
RRL .... Registered Record Librarian (Medicine)
RRL .... Reserve Retired List (Military)
RRL .... Ruby Rod LASER
RRM .... Rayleigh-Ritz Method
RRM .... Runaway Rotating Machine
RRMF .... RADAR Reflectivity Measuring Facility
RRMRP ...... Ready Reserve Mobilization Reinforcement Pool (Army)
RRMRS ...... Ready Reserve Mobilization Reinforcement System
RRO .... Rechnungslegungsordnung fuer das Reich (Germany)
RRO .... Renegotiation Regional Office
RROA .... Railroadians of America
RROC .... Rolls-Royce Owners' Club
R & ROTC ... Reserve & Reserve Officers' Training Corps (Army)
RROU .... Remote Readout Unit
RRP .... Radio Relay Pod
RRP .... Regional Project Research Program
RRP .... Relay Rack Panel
RRP .... Rotterdam-Rhine Pipeline (Oil)
RRPA .... Ruhr Regional Planning Authority (Post-World War II)
RRPB .... Retraining and Reemployment Policy Board
RRPS .... Ready Reinforcement Personnel Section (Air Force)
RRR .... Raleigh Research Reactor
RRR .... Range and Range-Rate
RRR .... Readin', Ritin', and Rithmetic (Also, 3R)
RRR .... Residual Resistance Ratio (Metal purity)
RRR .... Resistor-Reactor Rectifier
RRR .... Rework Removal Rate
RRRE .... RADAR Range-Rate Error
RRRRRR ..... Remedial Readin', Remedial Ritin', and Remedial Rithmetic (Humorous
                  interpretation of the three R's) (Also, 6R)
RRS .... RADAR Ranging System
RRS .... Radiation Research Society
RRS .... Radio Receiver Set
RRS .... Radio Recording Spectrophotometer
RRS .... Radio Relay Station (or System)
RRS .... Radio Research Station (British)
RRS .... Range Rate System
RRS .... Reaction Research Society
RRS .... Reed Relay Scanner
RRS .... Rendezvous RADAR System
RRS .... Retired Reserve Section
RRS .... Retrograde Rocket System
RRSTRAF .... Ready Reserve Strategic Army Forces
RRT .... Relative Retention Time
RRT .... Rendezvous RADAR Transponder
RRT .... Request for Review of Tooling
RRT .... Requirements Review Team
RRU .... Radio Research Unit (Army)
RRU .... Remington-Rand UNIVAC
RRU .... Remote Readout Unit
RRV .... Rotor Reentry Vehicle
RRW .... Radiation Resistant Wire
RRWU .... Rhodesia Railway Workers' Union
RS .... Radio Duties - Special
RS .... Radio Simulator
RS .... Radio Station (Maps and charts)
RS .... Radular Sac
RS .... Range Selector
RS .... Rauwolfia Serpentina (A plant, the root extract of which is used
                  medicinally)
RS .... Reading of Standard
RS .... Ready Service
RS .... Receiver Station
RS .... Receiving Ship or Station
RS .... Reception Station
RS .... Reconnaissance Squadron (Military)
RS .... Reconnaissance-Strike (Military)
RS .... Reconnaissance Strip (Military)
RS .... Record Separator (Data processing)
RS .... Recording Secretary
RS .... Recruiting Service
RS .... Recruiting Station
RS .... Rectal Sinus
RS .... Rectus-Sinister (System) (Biochemistry)
RS .... Reentry System
RS .... Reformed Spelling
RS .... Regular Station (Military)
RS .... Regulating Station
RS .... Regulation Station (Air Force)
RS .... Reinforcing Stimulus

RS .... Reizstoff (Tear gas) (German military)
RS .... Reminder Shock
RS .... Remote Station
RS .... Report of Survey
RS .... Republic Steel Corporation (NYSE symbol)
RS .... Research Summary
RS .... Research Systems
RS .... Reset Steering
RS .... Respiratory Syncytial (Virus) (Medicine)
RS .... Response-Stimulus
RS .... Return to Saturation
RS .... Reverberation Strength
RS .... Revised Statutes
RS .... Right Side
RS .... Ringer's Solution (Physiology)
RS .... Road Space
RS .... Roberval & Saguenay Railway Company (AAR code)
RS .... Rochelle Salt
RS .... Route Selector
RS .... Royal Scots (Military)
RS .... Royal Society
RS .... Rubble Stone
R/S .... Range Safety
R/S .... Range Surveillance
R/S .... Report of Survey (Army)
R/S .... Revolutions per Second
R/S .... Routing Slip (Air Force)
R & S ...... Range and Safety
R & S ...... Reenlistment and Separation (Military)
R & S ...... Reports and Statistics Branch (US Military Government, Germany)
RSA .... American Railway Supervisors Association
RSA .... RADAR Service Area
RSA .... RADAR Signature Analysis (Air Force)
RSA .... Railway Supply Association
RSA .... Redstone Arsenal (Huntsville, Alabama)
RSA .... Regional Science Association
RSA .... Rehabilitation Services Administration (Social and Rehabilitation Service,
                  HEW)
RSA .... Relative Specific Activity
RSA .... Remote Station Alarm
RSA .... Remote Storage Activities
RSA .... Renaissance Society of America
RSA .... Rental Service Association
RSA .... Republic of South Africa
RSA .... Research Security Administrators
RSA .... Rhetoric Society of America
RSA .... Right Sacro-Anterior
RSA .... Rotary Servo Actuator
RSA .... Royal Scottish Academy (or Academician)
RSA .... Rubber Shippers Association
RSA .... Rural Sanitary Authority (British)
RSAAF ...... Royal South African Air Force
RSAC .... Radiological Safety Computer (Program)
RSAF .... Royal Swedish Air Force
RSALT ...... Running, Signal and Anchor Lights
RSARR ...... Republic of South Africa Research Reactor
RSB .... Range Safety Beacon
RSB .... Reconnaissance Strike Bomber
RSB .... Reduced Size Blueprint
RSB .... Regimental Stretcher-Bearer
RSB .... Reticulocyte Standard Buffer
RSBA .... Rail Steel Bar Association
RSBS .... RADAR Safety Beacon System
RSC .... RADAR Sea Clutter
RSC .... RADAR Set Control
RSC .... Range Safety Center
RSC .... Range Safety Command
RSC .... Range Scheduling Committee
RSC .... Rat Skin Collagen
RSC .... Reactor Steam Cycle
RSC .... Regular, Slotted, Corrugated (Container)
RSC .... Relative System Capability
RSC .... Replacement and School Command
RSC .... Rescue Sub-Centre (Aviation)
RSC .... Reserve Service Control (Navy)
RSC .... Re-Start Capability
RSC .... Revised Statutes of Canada
RSC .... Right Stage Center (A stage direction)
RSC .... Royal Shakespeare Company (British)
RSC .... Russell Sage College (New York)
RSCC .... Republican Senatorial Campaign Committee

RSCG . . . . . . Radio Set Control Group
RSCH . . . . . . Ready Spares Chassis
RSCH . . . . . . Research
RSCIE . . . . . . Remote Station Communication Interface Equipment
RSCR . . . . . . Reserve Special Commendation Ribbon
RSCS . . . . . . Range Safety Command System
RSCS . . . . . . Rate Stabilization and Control System
RSCSA . . . . . . Railway Signal and Communications Suppliers Association
RSD . . . . Radiance Spectral Distribution
RSD . . . . Reentry Systems Department
RSD . . . . Reference Services Division (of ALA) (Later, RASD)
RSD . . . . Rolling Steel Door (Technical drawings)
RSD . . . . Royal Society, Dublin
RSDLP . . . . . . Russian Social-Democratic Labor Party
RSDLP(b) . . . . Russian Social-Democratic Labor Party (Bolsheviks)
RSDP . . . . . . Remote Site Data Processor
RSDRP . . . . . . Rossiiskaia Sotsial-Demokraticheskaia Rabochaia Partiia
RSDS . . . . . . RADAR Systems Design Section
RSDS . . . . . . Range Safety Destruct System
RSDU . . . . . . RADAR Storm Detection Unit
RSDWP . . . . . Russian Social Democratic Workers Party
RSE . . . . Raid Size Estimate
RSE . . . . Request Select Entry (Data processing)
RSE . . . . Resistance Soldering Equipment
RSE . . . . Royal Society of Edinburgh
RSEC . . . . . . Regional Science Experience Center
RSER . . . . . . Remote Sensing of Earth Resources
RSER . . . . . . Rotary Stylus Electronics Recorder
RSES . . . . . . Refrigeration Service Engineers Society
RSEU . . . . . . Remote Scanner-Encoder Unit (Bell Laboratories)
RSF . . . . Research Systems Facility
RSF . . . . Residual Support Force (After main force redeployment) (Military)
RSF . . . . Roll Sheet Feeder
RSF . . . . Russian Student Fund
RSFA . . . . . . Roller Skating Foundation of America
RSFPP . . . . . . Retired Servicemen's Family Protection Plan
RSFSR . . . . . . Russian Soviet Federated Socialist Republic
RSG . . . . Rate Signal Generator
RSG . . . . Receiving Stolen Goods
RSG . . . . Reference Signal Generator
RSG . . . . Regional Seat of Government
RSG . . . . Reichssiedlungsgesetz
RSG . . . . Relay Switch Group
RSG . . . . Resident Study Group (Army)
RSG . . . . Royal Scots Greys (Military unit) (British)
RSGB . . . . . . Radio Society of Great Britain
RSGS . . . . . . Ranges and Space Ground Support
RSH . . . . RADAR Status History
RSHA . . . . . . Reichssicherheitshauptampt (Central Security Office of the Reich) (NAZI Germany)
RSHM . . . . . . Religious of the Sacred Heart of Mary (Roman Catholic women's religious order)
RSHS . . . . . . Railroad Station Historical Society
RSI . . . . RADAR Scope Interpretation
RSI . . . . Receipt, Storage, and Issue (Army)
RSI . . . . Reflected Signal Indication (Air Force)
RSI . . . . Regional Safety Inspector (Ministry of Agriculture, Fisheries, and Food) (British)
RSI . . . . Replacement Stream Input (Military)
RSI . . . . Research Studies Institute
RSI . . . . Reynolds Securities, Incorporated (NYSE symbol)
RSI . . . . Rotary Shaft Indicator
RS & I . . . . . . Receipt, Stowage and Issue
RS & I . . . . . Rules, Standards, and Instructions
RSIC . . . . . . Radiation Shielding Information Center (ORNL)
RSIC . . . . . . Redstone Scientific Information Center (Army)
RSIS . . . . . . Radical Science Information Service (News service attempting to interrelate radical politics and scientific issues)
RSITA . . . . . . Reglement du Service international des Telecommunications de l'Aeronautique
RSIUFL . . . . . . Release Suspension for Issue and Use of Following Lots
RSJ . . . . Rolled-Steel Joist
RSK . . . . Russeks, Inc. (American Stock Exchange symbol)
RSL . . . . Radio Standards Laboratory (National Bureau of Standards)
RSL . . . . Reconnaissance and Security Line
RSL . . . . Remote Sprint Launching
RSL . . . . Royal Society of Literature (British)
RSL . . . . Royal Society, London
RSLA . . . . . . Range Safety Launch Approval
RSM . . . . Radiation Survey Meter (NASA)
RSM . . . . Reconnaissance Strategic Missile

RSM . . . . Reed Switching Matrix
RSM . . . . Regimental Sergeant Major (Army)
RSM . . . . Rivet Setting Machine
RSM . . . . Royal Society of Musicians (British)
RSMA . . . . . . Railway Supply Manufacturers Association
RSMA . . . . . . Railway Systems and Management Association
RSN . . . . Radiation Surveillance Network (Public Health Service)
RSN . . . . Reason
RSN . . . . Research Surveillance Network
RSNA . . . . . . Radiological Society of North America
RSNO . . . . . . Referral Service Network Office
RSNP . . . . . . Registered Student Nurse Program
RSO . . . . Railway Sorting Office
RSO . . . . Railway Suboffice
RSO . . . . Range Safety Officer
RSO . . . . Range Support Operation
RSO . . . . Reconnaissance and Survey Officer
RSO . . . . Regimental Supply Officer (Army)
RSO . . . . Research Ship of Opportunity
RSOC . . . . . . Remote Sensing Oceanography (Navy)
RSOP . . . . . . Reconnaissance, Selection, and Occupation of Position (Military)
RSOR . . . . . . Range Safety Operations Requirement
RSP . . . . RADAR Signal Processor
RSP . . . . Radio Switch Panel
RSP . . . . Range Solar Panel
RSP . . . . Range Sorting Program
RSP . . . . Rapid Site Preparation
RSP . . . . Rate Sensing Package
RSP . . . . Receiving Stolen Property
RSP . . . . Reconnaissance and Security Positions
RSP . . . . Reinforced Structural Plastic
RSP . . . . Render Safe Procedure
RSP . . . . Responder Beacon
RSP . . . . Right Sacroposterior
RSP . . . . Roll Stabilization Platform
RSP . . . . Roscoe, Snyder & Pacific Railway Company (AAR code)
RSPA . . . . . . Railway Systems and Procedures Association
RSPCA . . . . . . Royal Society for the Prevention of Cruelty to Animals
RSPL . . . . . . Recommended Spare Parts List
RSPS . . . . . . Range Solar Panel Substrate
RSPWC . . . . . Royal Society of Painters in Water-Colours (British)
RSQ . . . . Rescue
RSR . . . . Range Safety Report
RSR . . . . Ready Service Ring
RSR . . . . Regular Sinus Rhythm (Physiology)
RSR . . . . Republica Socialista Romania (Socialist Republic of Romania)
RSR . . . . Request for Scientific Research
RSR . . . . Required Supply Rate
RSR . . . . Research Study Requests
RSR . . . . Revised Supplementary Regulation
RSR . . . . Rocket Stabilized Rod
RSR . . . . Rotary Seal Ring
RSR . . . . Route Surveillance RADAR
RSROA . . . . . . Roller Skating Rink Operators Association of America
RSRS . . . . . . Radio and Space Research Station (British)
RSS . . . . RADAR Signal Simulator
RSS . . . . Range Safety System
RSS . . . . Reactant Service System
RSS . . . . Reference Sound Source
RSS . . . . Regiae Societatis Sodalis (Fellow of the Royal Society)
RSS . . . . Rehabilitation Support Schedule
RSS . . . . Relative System Sensitivity
RSS . . . . Residual Sum of Squares (Statistics)
RSS . . . . Resource Survey Satellite
RSS . . . . Retention Spermatemia Syndrome (Medicine)
RSS . . . . Rifle Sharpshooter
RSS . . . . Rigid Space Structure
RSS . . . . Rockdale, Sandow & Southern R. R. (AAR code)
RSS . . . . Rotary Shaft Seal
RSS . . . . Root-Sum-Square
RSS . . . . Rural Sociological Society
RSSC . . . . . . Remote-Site Simulator Console (NASA)
RSSEL . . . . . . Recommended Special Support Equipment List
RSSK . . . . . . Rigid Seat Survival Kit
RSSN . . . . . . Research Space Surveillance Network
RSSP . . . . . . Range Single Shot Probability (Military)
R & S SQ . . . . Repair and Salvage Squadron (Military)
RST . . . . Radiometric Sun Tracer
RST . . . . Read Symbol Table
RST . . . . Readability, Strength, Tone
RST . . . . Recovery Sequence Tester

RST. . . . . Reentry System Technology (Aerospace)
RST . . . . Register and Self-Test
RST . . . . Reinforcing Steel (Technical drawings)
RST . . . . Research Study Team
RST . . . . Reset-Set Trigger
RST . . . . Resin Skived Tape
RST. . . . . Right Sacrotransverse
RST . . . . Roan Selection Trust, Ltd. (NYSE symbol)
RST . . . . Routine Sequence Table
RSTK . . . . . . Relay Servicing Tool Kit
RSU . . . . Recorder Switch Unit
RSU . . . . Relay Storage Unit
RSV . . . . Random Sine Vibration
RSV . . . . Respiratory Syncytial Virus
RSV . . . . Revised Standard Version (of the Bible, 1952)
RSV . . . . Rous Sarcoma Virus
RSV-Br . . . . . Rous Sarcoma Virus-Bryan (Strain)
RSVP . . . . . . Radiation Spectral Visual Photometer
RSVP . . . . . . Really Sexy Vamp Pants (Slacks for evening wear by women)
RSVP . . . . . . Research Selected Vote Profile (Election poll)
RSVP . . . . . . Research Society for Victorian Periodicals
RSVP . . . . . . Respondez, s'il Vous Plait (The Favor of an Answer is Requested)
RSVP. . . . . . . Restartable Solid Variable Pulse (Motor)
RSVR . . . . . . Reservoir
RSVR . . . . . . Resolver
RSV-S-R . . . . Rous Sarcoma Virus-Schmidt-Ruppin (Strain)
RSW. . . . . . . Repeating Slide Wire
RSW . . . . Retarded Surface Wave
RSW . . . . Royal Scottish Watercolor Society
RSWC . . . . . . Right Side Up with Care
RSYN . . . . . . Reactor Synthesis
RT . . . . Rachidian Tooth
RT . . . . Radio Technician
RT . . . . Radio Telegraphy
RT . . . . Radio Telephone or Telephony
RT . . . . Radular Teeth
RT . . . . Range Timing
RT . . . . Range Tracking
RT . . . . Ranger Tab (Army)
RT . . . . Rate
RT . . . . Ratio Transformer
RT . . . . Rational Therapy (Short form for rational-emotive psychotherapy)
          (Also known as R-ET and R-EP)
RT . . . . Reaction Time
RT . . . . Reading Test
RT . . . . Readout Technique
RT . . . . Real Time
RT . . . . Receive-Transmit (Radio)
RT . . . . Receiving Tube
RT . . . . Record Transfer
RT . . . . Recreational Therapy
RT . . . . Recueillis Temporaires (Temporarily Taken In) (of unadoptable children)
          (France)
RT . . . . Reduction Tables
RT . . . . Register Ton
RT . . . . Registered Technician (American Registry of X-ray Technicians)
RT . . . . Rejection Tag
RT . . . . Related Terms (Indexing)
RT . . . . Relaxation Training (Psychology)
RT . . . . Released Time
RT . . . . Remote Terminals (Data processing)
RT . . . . Reperforator-Transmitter
RT . . . . Research and Technology
RT . . . . Reserve Training
RT . . . . Reset Trigger
RT . . . . Resistor Tolerance
RT . . . . Resistor Transistor
RT . . . . Resting Tension (Biology)
RT . . . . Retention Time
RT . . . . Return Ticket
RT . . . . Right
RT . . . . Right Tackle (Football)
RT . . . . Right Turn After Takeoff (Aviation)
RT . . . . River Terminal Railway (AAR code)
RT . . . . Rocket Target
RT . . . . Room Temperature
RT . . . . Round Table
RT . . . . Round Trip
RT . . . . Router Template
RT . . . . Running Title
RT . . . . Runup and Taxi (Air Force)

R/T . . . . Radio Telephony
R/T . . . . Receiver-Transmitter
R/T. . . . . Record of Trial (Army)
R/T . . . . Reperforator/Transmitter
R/T . . . . Research and Technology
R/T . . . . Rho/Theta
R & T . . . . . . Research and Technology
RTA . . . . RADAR Terrain Analysis
RTA . . . . Radically Tapered Antenna
RTA . . . . Rail Travel Authorization (Military)
RTA . . . . Railway Tie Association
RTA . . . . Reactivity Test Assembly
RTA . . . . Reciprocal Trade Agreement
RTA . . . . Refrigeration Trade Association of America
RTA . . . . Reliability Test Assembly
RTA . . . . Rise Time Analyzer
RTA . . . . Royal Thai Army
RTA . . . . Rubber Trade Association of New York
RTAC . . . . . . Regional Technical Aid Center (Agency for International Development)
RTACF. . . . . . Real-Time Auxiliary Computing Facility (Apollo) (NASA)
RTAD . . . . . . Router Adapter
RTAF . . . . . . Royal Thai Air Force
RTAG . . . . . . Range Technical Advisory Group
RTAM . . . . . . Resident Terminal Access Method (Data processing)
RTB . . . . Radial Time Base
RTB . . . . Radiodiffusion-Television Belge (Belgian radio and television)
RTB . . . . Resistance Temperature Bulb
RTB . . . . Return to Base (Military)
RTB . . . . Rocket Test Base
RTBM . . . . . . Recoverable Test Bed Missile
RTC . . . . RADAR Tracking Center (or Control)
RTC . . . . Range Telemetry Central (Aerospace)
RTC . . . . Ratchet
RTC . . . . Reader Tape Contact
RTC . . . . Real-Time Command (Data processing)
RTC . . . . Replacement Training Center
RTC . . . . Reserve Training Corps
RTC . . . . Reverse Transfer Capacitance
RTC . . . . Rochester Telephone Corporation (NYSE symbol)
RTCA . . . . . . Radio Technical Commission for Aeronautics
RTCA . . . . . . Radio & Television Correspondents Association
RTCC . . . . . . Real-Time Computer Complex
RTCM . . . . . . Radio Technical Commission for Marine Services
RTCS . . . . . . Real Time Computer System
RTCTO . . . . . Record Time Compliance Technical Order
RTCU . . . . . . Real-Time Control Unit
RTCU . . . . . . Router Cutter (Tool)
RTD . . . . Range Time Decoder
RTD . . . . Read Tape Decimal
RTD . . . . Real-Time Display
RTD . . . . Reliability Technical Directive
RTD . . . . Research and Technology Division (Air Force)
RTD . . . . Resistance Temperature Detector
RTD . . . . Return to Duty (Military)
RTDA . . . . . . Radio and Television Dealers' Association
RTDA . . . . . . Retail Tobacco Dealers of America
RTDA . . . . . . Returned Absentees
RTDC . . . . . . Rocket Thrown Depth Charge
RTDD . . . . . . Real-Time Data Distribution
RTDD . . . . . . Remote Timing and Data Distribution
RTDG . . . . . . Radio and Television Directors Guild
RTDHS . . . . . Real-Time Data Handling System
RTDR . . . . . . Reliability Test Data Report
RTDS . . . . . . Real Time Data System
RTE . . . . RADOME (RADAR Dome) Test Equipment
RTE . . . . Receiver Test Equipment
RTE . . . . Regenerative Turboprop Engines
RTE . . . . Reliability Test Evaluation
RTE . . . . Request to Expedite
RTE. . . . . Return to Earth (NASA)
RTE . . . . Route
RTE . . . . RTE Corp. (NYSE symbol)
RTED. . . . . . . Return-to-Earth Digital (NASA)
RTEM . . . . . . RADAR Tracking Error Measurement
RTES. . . . . . . Radio and Television Executives' Society
RTF . . . . Radio Transmission Facility
RTF . . . . Radiodiffusion-Television Francaise (French radio and television)
RTF . . . . Radiotelephone
RTF . . . . Reconnaissance Task Force
RTF. . . . . Resistance Transfer Factor (of microorganisms to drugs)
RTF . . . . Rocket Test Facility

ACRONYMS AND INITIALISMS DICTIONARY

RTF . . . . Rubber-Tile Floor (Technical drawings)
RTFD . . . . Royal Thai Forest Department
RTFM . . . . Router Form
RTFR. . . . . . . Reliability Trouble and Failure Report
RTFV. . . . . . . RADAR Target Folder Viewer
RTG . . . . Radioactive Thermal Generator
RTG . . . . Radioisotope Thermoelectric Generator
RTG . . . . Radiotelegraph
RTG . . . . Rare Tube Gas
RTG . . . . Reglement Telegraphique (Telegraph Regulations)
RTG . . . . Requirements Tape Generator (NASA)
RTG . . . . Reusable Training Grenade
RTG . . . . Royal Thai Government
RTGD . . . . . . Room Temperature Gamma Detector
RTGp . . . . . . Reconnaissance Technical Group (Air Force)
RTGp . . . . . . Reconnaissance Training Group (Air Force)
RTGp . . . . . . Retraining Group (Air Force)
RTGU . . . . . . Router Guide
RTGV . . . . . . Real Time Generation of Video
RTH . . . . Relay Transformer Header
RTH . . . . RKO Theatres Corporation (NYSE symbol)
RtHon . . . . . . Right Honourable
RTI . . . . Request for Technical Information (Military)
RTI . . . . Research Triangle Institute
RTI . . . . Rise Time Indicator
RTI . . . . Round Table International
RTIC . . . . Rotor Temperature Indicator and Control (Instrumentation)
RTIP . . . . RADAR Target Identification Point
RTIR . . . . Reliability and Trend Indicator Reports
RTIRS . . . . . . Real Time Information Retrieval System
RTK . . . . Record Test Kit
RTL . . . . Radial Transmission Line
RTL . . . . Refrigerated Transmission Line
RTL . . . . Regimental Training Line (Army)
RTL . . . . Reinforced Tile Lintel (Technical drawings)
RTL . . . . Resistor-Transistor Logic
RTLF. . . . . . . Association of Railway Trainmen and Locomotive Firemen
RTLO . . . . . . Regional Training Liaison Officer (Ministry of Agriculture, Fisheries, and Food) (British)
RTM . . . . RADAR Target Materiel
RTM . . . . Railway Transfer of Minneapolis (AAR code)
RTM . . . . Rapid Tuning Magnetron
RTM . . . . Real-Time Metric
RTM . . . . Real-Time Monitor
RTM . . . . Receiver-Transmitter-Modulator
RTM . . . . Reconnaissance Tactical Missile
RTM . . . . Representative Town Meeting
RTM . . . . Research Technical Memorandum
RTM . . . . Revenue Ton-Miles
RTM . . . . Running Time Meter
RTMA . . . . . . Radio and Television Manufacturers Association
RTMS . . . . . . RADAR Target Measuring System
RTMS . . . . . . Rocket Thrust Measuring System
RTN . . . . Radial, Tangential, Normal
RTN . . . . Radio Telescope Network
RTN . . . . Raytheon Company (NYSE symbol)
RTN . . . . Registered Trade Name
RTN . . . . Report Test Number (NASA)
RTN . . . . Return
RTN . . . . Return to Neuter
RTNDA . . . . . Radio-Television News Directors Association
RTO . . . . Rail Transportation Officer(s) (Military)
RTO . . . . Railway Traffic Officer
RTO . . . . Real-Time Operation
RTO . . . . Reliability Test Outline
RTO . . . . Report Time Over (Aviation)
RTOL . . . . . . Reduced Takeoff and Landing (Aviation)
RTOP . . . . . . Research and Technology Objectives and Planning (NASA)
RTOT . . . . . . Range Track on Target (Air Force)
RTP. . . . . . . Real-Time Position
RTP. . . . . . . Reinforced Thermoplastics
RTP. . . . . . . Remote Transfer Point
RTP . . . . Request to Purchase
RTP. . . . . . . Request for Technical Proposal (Military)
RTP . . . . Requirement & Test Procedures
RTP . . . . Resistor Test Program
RTPA . . . . . . Rail Travel Promotion Agency
RTQC . . . . . . Real-Time Quality Control
RTR . . . . Real-Time Readout
RTR . . . . Reliability Test Requirements
RTR . . . . Returning to Ramp (Aviation)

RTRC . . . . Radio Telemetry and Remote Control
RTRC . . . . Radio and Television Research Council
RTRC . . . . Regional Technical Report Centers (Department of Commerce)
RTRCDS. . . . . Real-Time Reconnaissance Cockpit Display System
RTRO . . . . . . Real-Time Readout
RTS. . . . . RADAR Target Simulator
RTS . . . . RADAR Test Set
RTS . . . . RADAR Tracking Station (Military)
RTS . . . . RADAR Tracking System
RTS . . . . Radio Teletypewriter Set
RTS . . . . Range Time Signal
RTS . . . . Range Timing System
RTS . . . . Reactive Terminal Service (International Telephone and Telegraph computer)
RTS . . . . Real-Time Simulation
RTS . . . . Recorded Time Signal
RTS . . . . Regional Technical Support (Military)
RTS . . . . Relay Test System
RTS . . . . Religious Tract Society (British)
RTS. . . . . Remote Targeting System
RTS . . . . Remote Tracking Site (Military)
RTS . . . . Remote Tracking Station
RTS . . . . Repaired This Station
RTS . . . . Research and Technical Services (Military)
RTS . . . . Research Test Site
RTS . . . . Return to Search
RTS . . . . Return(ed) to Service (Aviation)
RTS . . . . Return to Stores
RTS . . . . Rotary Thumbwheel Switch
RTS . . . . Royal Toxophilite Society (British)
RTS . . . . Russ Togs, Inc. (NYSE symbol)
RT/S. . . . . . . Refrigeration Technician/Specialist
RTSA . . . . . . RADAR Target Signature Analysis
RTSD . . . . . . Resources and Technical Services Division (of ALA)
RTSM . . . . . . Return to Stock Memo
RTSq. . . . . . . Reconnaissance Technical Squadron (Air Force)
RTSS. . . . . . . Real Time Scientific System
RTST. . . . . . . Radio Technician Selection Test
RTT. . . . . Radiation Tracking Transducer
RTT . . . . Radioteletypewriter
RTT . . . . Rate of Turntable
RTT. . . . . Rectangular Tongue Terminal
RTT. . . . . Remote Tuning Technique
RTT . . . . Return Trip Time
RTT. . . . . Ring Tongue Terminal
RTT . . . . Rocket-Thrown Torpedo
RTT . . . . Role-Taking Task
RTTA . . . . . . Range Tone Transfer Assembly (Apollo) (NASA)
RTTAA . . . . . . Railway Telegraph and Telephone Appliance Association
RTTC . . . . . . Real-Time Computer Complex (NASA)
RTTD. . . . . . . Real-Time Telemetry Data
RTTDS. . . . . . Real-Time Telemetry Data System
RTTP. . . . . . . Router Template
RTTS. . . . . . . RADAR Telephone Transmission System
RTTV . . . . . . Real-Time Television
RTTV . . . . . . Research Target and Test Vehicle
RTTY . . . . . . Radio Teletype
RTU . . . . RADAR Timing Unit
RTU . . . . Railroad Telegraphers Union
RTU . . . . Reinforcement Training Unit (Army)
RTU . . . . Remote Terminal Unit
RTU . . . . Replacement Training Unit (Military)
RTU . . . . Reserve Training Unit
RTU . . . . Response Test Unit
RTUM . . . . . . Revolutionary Trade Union Movement (Czechoslovakia)
RTV . . . . Real Time Video
RTV . . . . Recovery Test Vehicle
RTV . . . . Reentry Test Vehicle (Air Force)
RTV . . . . Research Test Vehicle
RTV . . . . Returned to Vendor
RTV . . . . Rocket Test Vehicle
RTV . . . . Room Temperature Vulcanizing
RTVP. . . . . . . Real Time Video Processing
RTW . . . . Right to Work
RTW . . . . Right Worshipful
RTWS . . . . . . Raw Type Write Submodule
RTX . . . . Rapid Transit Experimental (Gas-turbine bus)
RTX . . . . Report Time Crossing (Aviation)
RTX . . . . Riegel Textile Corp. (NYSE symbol)
RTZ . . . . Return-to-Zero
RT-Z . . . . Rio Tinto-Zinc
RU . . . . Are You? (Communication)

RU . . . . Range User
RU . . . . Rat Unit
RU . . . . Reading of Unknown
RU . . . . Release Unit (Army)
RU . . . . Reproducing Unit
RU . . . . Reserve Unit (Equal to one US dollar) (International finance)
RU . . . . Roentgen Unit
RU . . . . Rugby Union (Controlling body of British rugby football)
Ru . . . . Ruthenium (Chemical element)
R & U . . . . . . Repairs and Upkeep (Military)
R & U . . . . . . Repairs and Utilities
RUA . . . . Retailer's Uniform Agency
RUAT . . . . . . Report Upon Arrival Thereat (Army)
RUB . . . . Rubber
RUBD . . . . . . Rubberized
RUBSG . . . . . . Recovery Unit and Base Support Group (Air Force)
RUC . . . . Reporting Unit Code (Data processing)
RUC . . . . Riverine Utility Craft (Vehicle for transporting through shallow water and snow)
RUC . . . . Royal Ulster Constabulary
RUCA . . . . . . Russell Cave National Monument
RUD . . . . Rudder
RUDAEE . . . . . Report of Unsatisfactory or Defective Airborne Electronic Equipment
RUDAOE . . . . Report of Unsatisfactory or Defective Aviation Ordnance Equipment (Navy)
RUDI . . . . Regional Urban Defense Intercept
RUDI . . . . Report of Unsatisfactory or Defective Instrumentation
RUDM . . . . . . Report of Unsatisfactory or Defective Material (Aircraft) (Navy)
RUDMIN . . . . . Report of Unsatisfactory or Defective Mine (Navy)
RUDMINDE . . . Report of Unsatisfactory or Defective Mine, Depth Charge, of Associated Equipment (Navy)
RUDTORPE . . . . Report of Unsatisfactory or Defective Torpedo Equipment (Navy)
RUE . . . . Right Upper Entrance (Theatrical)
RUE . . . . Right Upper Extremity (Medicine)
RUF . . . . Rigid Urethane Foam
RUFAS . . . . . . Remote Underwater Fisheries Assessment System
RUG . . . . Recomp Users Group (Data processing)
RUH . . . . Range Users Handbook
RUI . . . . Royal University of Ireland
RUIN . . . . Regional and Urban Information Network (Washington, DC)
RUL . . . . Right Upper Lobe (of lung) (Medicine)
RUM . . . . Railwaymen's Union of Malaya
RUM . . . . Remote-Control Underwater Manipulator (Oceanography)
RUM . . . . Remote Unit Monitor
RUN . . . . Reduction Unlimited
RUNCIBLE . . . . Revised Unified New Compiler with Its Basic Language Extended (Data processing)
RUNEL . . . . . . Runway-End Lighting
RUP . . . . Ruppert (Jacob) (NYSE symbol)
RUQ . . . . Rifle Unqualified (Military)
RUQ . . . . Right Upper Quadrant (of abdomen) (Medicine)
RUR . . . . Rossum's Universal Robots (Acronym is title of play by Karel Capek)
RUR . . . . Royal Ulster Rifles
RUSDIC . . . . . . Russian Dictionary
RUSH . . . . Remote Use of Shared Hardware (Data processing)
RUSNO . . . . . Resident United States Naval Officer
RUT . . . . Rutland Railway Corporation (AAR code)
RUTOP . . . . . . Rutowski Optimization (Computer program)
RUU . . . . Rijksuniversiteit Utrecht (Netherlands)
RUUR . . . . . . Regrade Unclassified Upon Receipt (Air Force)
RV . . . . Rahway Valley R. R. (AAR code)
RV . . . . Rated Voltage
RV . . . . Reading and Vocabulary Test (Also, RVT) (Military)
RV . . . . Rear View (Technical drawings)
RV . . . . Recreational Vehicles
RV . . . . Reentry Vehicle
RV . . . . Reference Voltage
RV . . . . Reinforcement Value (Psychology)
RV . . . . Released Value (Freight)
RV . . . . Relief Valve
RV . . . . Renal Vessel
RV . . . . Rendezvous
RV . . . . Rescue Vessel
RV . . . . Research Vehicle
RV . . . . Research Vessel
RV . . . . Residual Volume
RV . . . . Retroversion
RV . . . . Revised Version (of the Bible, 1881)
RV . . . . Rifle Volunteers
RV . . . . Right Ventricle (of heart)
RV . . . . Runway Visibility

R/V . . . . Rear View
R/V . . . . Reentry Vehicle (Nosecone) (Aerospace)
R/V . . . . Relief Valve
RVA . . . . Reactive Volt-Ampere Meter
RVA . . . . Regular Veterans Association of the United States
RVA . . . . Relative Volt-Ampere
RVA . . . . . . Reliability Variation Analysis
RVA . . . . Remote Voltage Adjustment
RVB . . . . RADAR Video Buffer
RVB . . . . Revere Copper & Brass, Inc. (NYSE symbol)
RVBR . . . . . . Riveting Bar (Tool)
RVC . . . . Random Vibration Control
RVC . . . . Relative Velocity Computer
RVC . . . . Rifle Volunteer Corps (Military) (British)
RVC . . . . Royal Veterinary College (British)
RVCM . . . . . Republic of Vietnam Campaign Medal (Military award)
RVD . . . . RADAR Video Digitizer
RVD . . . . Relative Vertebral Density
RVDA . . . . . . Recreational Vehicle Dealers of America
RVDP . . . . . . RADAR Video Data Processor
RVDT . . . . . . Rotary Variable Differential Transformer
RVE . . . . RADAR Video Extractor
RVE . . . . Representative Volume Element
RVF . . . . Rift Valley Fever
RVF . . . . Roosevelt Field, Inc. (NYSE symbol)
RVFN . . . . . . Report of Visit of Foreign Nationals
RVFX . . . . . . Rivet Fixture
RVG . . . . Reference-Voltage Generator
RVG . . . . Reichsversorgungsgesetz (Germany)
RVG . . . . Right Visceral Ganglion
RVG . . . . Rotating Vertical Gradiometer
RVGG . . . . . . Rotating Vertical Gravity Gradiometer
RVH . . . . Right Ventricular Hypertrophy (Medicine)
RVI . . . . Recreational Vehicle Institute
RVIMI . . . . . . Rubella Virus-Induced Mitotic Inhibitor
RVM . . . . Reactive Voltmeter
RVN . . . . Republic of Vietnam
RVNAF . . . . . Republic of Vietnam Air Force
RVNAF . . . . . Republic of Vietnam Armed Forces
RVO . . . . Regional Veterinary Officer (British)
RVO . . . . Reichsversicherungsordnung (German insurance laws)
RVO . . . . Relaxed Vaginal Outlet (Medicine)
RVO . . . . Runway Visibility Observer (Aviation)
RVP . . . . Reid Vapor Pressure
RVPA . . . . . . Rivet Pattern
RVR . . . . Riviana Foods Inc. (NYSE symbol)
RVR . . . . Runway Visual Range (Aviation)
RVS . . . . Radius Vector Subroutine
RVS . . . . Reentry Vehicle Simulator
RVS . . . . Reeves Brothers, Inc. (NYSE symbol)
RVS . . . . Remote Viewing System
RVSSC . . . . . Reverse Self Check
RVSVP . . . . . . Respondez Vite, s'il Vous Plait (Please Reply at Once)
RVSZ . . . . . . Riveting Squeezer (Tool)
RVT . . . Reading and Vocabulary Test (Also, RV) (Military)
RVTO . . . . . . Reentry Vehicle Test and Observables (Air Force)
RVTOL . . . . . Rolling Vertical Take-Off and Landing
RVU . . . . Relief Valve Unit
RVW . . . . . . Ralph Vaughan Williams (British composer, 1872-1958)
RVW . . . . . . River Raisin Paper Company (NYSE symbol)
RVX . . . . Reentry Vehicle, Experimental
RW . . . . Radiation Weapon
RW . . . . Radiological Warfare
RW . . . . Radiological Warhead
RW . . . . Rail-Water (Shipping)
RW . . . . Rain Showers (Meteorology)
RW . . . . Ramo Wooldridge
RW . . . . Random Walk
RW . . . . Random Widths (Lumber)
RW . . . . Raw Water (Technical drawings)
RW . . . . Rawinsonde
RW . . . . Read and Write
RW . . . . Recreation and Welfare (Navy)
RW . . . . Recruiting Warrant
RW . . . . Reel and Wheel (Freight)
RW . . . . Restaurant Wine (License)
RW . . . . Rewind
RW . . . . Right Wing
RW . . . . Right Worshipful
RW . . . . Right Worthy
RW . . . . Rotary Wing (Aircraft)

RW. . . . . Runway
R/W . . . . Ramo-Wooldridge-Thompson Corporation
R/W . . . . Read/Write
R/W . . . . Right-of-Way (Also, ROW)
RWA. . . . . . . Railway Wheel Association
RWA. . . . . . . Rectangular Wave-Guide Assembly
RWA. . . . . . . Rippled Wall Amplifier
RWA. . . . . . . Rotary Wing Aircraft
RWB . . . . Rear Wheel Brake
RWBH . . . . . . Records Will Be Handcarried (Army)
RWC. . . . . . . Rainwater Conductor
RWC . . . . Read, Write, and Compute
RWC. . . . . . . Read-Write-Continue
RWC. . . . . . . Roberts Wesleyan College (New York)
RWD. . . . . . . Regular Way Delivery
RWD. . . . . . . Regular World Day
RWDSU . . . . . Retail, Wholesale and Department Store Union
RWE. . . . . . . Rheinisch-Westfaelisches Electrizitaetswerk (AG) (West Germany)
RWF . . . . Royal Welch Fusiliers (British)
RWG . . . . . . Radio Writers' Guild
RWG . . . . . . Reliability Working Group
RWG . . . . . . Rigid Wave-Guide
RWG . . . . . . Roebling Wire Gage
RWGM . . . . . . Right Worshipful Grand Master (Masonry)
RWGS. . . . . . Right Worthy Grand Secretary (Masonry)
RWGT. . . . . . Right Worthy Grand Templar (Masonry)
RWGW . . . . . Right Worthy Grand Warden (Masonry)
RWH. . . . . . . RADAR Warning and Homing
RWI . . . . . . Radio Wire Integration (Military)
RWI . . . . Read-Write-Initialize
RWI . . . . Regular World Interval
RWI . . . . Remote Weight Indicator
RWJC . . . . . . Roger Williams Junior College (Rhode Island)
RWK. . . . . . . The Queen's Own Royal West Kent Regiment (British)
RWK. . . . . . . Rework
RWL . . . . Relative Water Level
RWLB . . . . . Regional War Labor Board
RWLR . . . . . . Relative Water-Level Recorder
RWM . . . . . . Resistance Welding Machine
RWM . . . . . . Roll Wrapping Machine
RWMA . . . . . Resistance Welder Manufacturers Association
RWNBH . . . . . Records Will Not Be Handcarried (Army)
RWO . . . . . . Reimbursable Work Order (Navy)
RWO. . . . . . . Riddare af Wasa Order (Knight of the Order of Vasa) (Sweden)
RWP . . . . Radio Wave Propagation
RWP. . . . . . . Radio Working Party
RWP . . . . Rifle and Weapons Platoon (Army)
RWPG . . . . . . Real World Problem Generation

RWR . . . . Rail-Water-Rail (Shipping)
RWR . . . . Relative Weight Response
RWRC . . . . . . Remain Well to Right of Course (Aviation)
RWS . . . . Range While Search
RWS . . . . Reaction Wheel Scanner
RWS . . . . Reaction Wheel Systems
RWS . . . . Royal West Surrey (Regiment) (British)
RWSGW . . . . . Right Worshipful Senior Grand Warden (Masonry)
RWT . . . . Read Write Tape
RWV . . . . Read-Write-Verify
RWVD . . . . . . Real World Visual Display
RWVR . . . . . . Real World Vehicular Rate
RWY . . . . Runway
RX . . . . Reconnaissance-Experimental Aircraft
RX . . . . Report Crossing (Aviation)
RX . . . . Resolver-Transmitter
RX . . . . "Rush" (on Teletype messages)
RXM. . . . . . . Richardson-Merrell, Inc. (NYSE symbol)
RXP . . . . Radix Point
RXS . . . . RADAR Cross Section
RY . . . . Railway
RY . . . . Roll Yoke
Ry . . . . Rydberg
RYA . . . . Railroad Yardmasters of America
RYALM . . . . . . Relay Alarm
RYC . . . . Rural Youth Corps (Maine)
RYC . . . . Ryan Aeronautical Company (NYSE symbol) (Delisted)
RYE . . . . Retirement Year Ending (Army)
RYGD . . . . . . Railway Grand Division
RYM . . . . Reference Your Message (Army)
RYM-I . . . . . . Revolutionary Youth Movement I (Also known as "Weatherman") (A faction of Students for a Democratic Society)
RYM-II . . . . . . Revolutionary Youth Movement II (A faction of Students for a Democratic Society)
RYNA . . . . . . Railroad Yardmasters of North America
RYS . . . . Royal Yacht Squadron (British)
RYSS . . . . . . Restore Your Subjunctive Society
RZ . . . . Regiment de Zouaves
RZ . . . . Return-to-Zero
RZ . . . . Rueckenfallschirm mit Zwangsausloesung (Static-line, backpack parachute) (German military - World War II)
RZA . . . . Religious Zionists of America
RZF . . . . Riemann Zeta Function
RZL . . . . Return-to-Zero Level
RZM . . . . Return-to-Zero Mark
RZMA . . . . . . Rolled Zinc Manufacturers Association
RZS . . . . Rolled Zinc Sheet

S

S . . . . Antisubmarine (Designation for all US military aircraft)
S . . . . Following a figure, indicates number of 100-share lots in a transaction; e.g., 4s indicates 400 shares (NYSE symbol)
S . . . . Magnetic Solar Daily Variation
S . . . . Sabbath
S . . . . Sacral
S . . . . Sacred
S . . . . Sacrifice (Baseball)
S . . . . Saeculum
S . . . . Saint
S . . . . San Francisco (California) (Mint mark, when appearing on US coins)
S . . . . Sand
S . . . . Satang (Monetary unit of Thailand)
S . . . . Saturday
S . . . . Saturn
S . . . . Saxon
S . . . . Schilling (Monetary unit in Austria)
S . . . . School
S . . . . Scouting (Naval aircraft designation)
S . . . . Scuttle
S . . . . Sea-air temperature difference correction
S . . . . Seaman, as S1 (Seaman 1st class) (Navy)
S . . . . Seaplane (Navy)
S . . . . Search
S . . . . Sears, Roebuck & Company (NYSE symbol)
S . . . . Second(ary)
s . . . . Secondary (Chemistry)
S . . . . Secret
S . . . . Secretary
S . . . . Section
S . . . . See
S . . . . Seelenlaenge (Barrel length) (German military – World War II)
S . . . . Seite (Page) (Germany)
S . . . . Sen (Japanese monetary unit)
S . . . . Senate
S . . . . Senate Bill (with number)
S . . . . Sensation (Psychology)
S . . . . Sent (Communications)
S . . . . Senza (Without)
S . . . . Separation
S . . . . September
S . . . . Sepulchrum (Sepulchre)
S . . . . Sepultus (Buried)
S . . . . Series
S . . . . Sesquiplane (Navy)
S . . . . Set
S . . . . Sharp
S . . . . Shell
S . . . . Shilling(s) (British monetary unit)
S . . . . Ship
S . . . . Side
S . . . . Siemens
S . . . . Sign(ed)
S . . . . Signa (Mark a prescription)
S . . . . Signature
S . . . . Signor
S . . . . Silicate
S . . . . Silver
S . . . . Silversmith
S . . . . Simplex
S . . . . Simultaneous transmission of range signals and voice
S . . . . Sine (Without)
S . . . . Single

S . . . . Singular
S . . . . Sinister (Left)
S . . . . Sink
S . . . . Sire
S . . . . Situs (Placed)
S . . . . Sixteenmo (Book from 15 to 17 1/2 centimeters in height) (Bibliography)
S . . . . Slip
S . . . . Slope (Technical drawings)
S . . . . Slow
S . . . . Small (Size designation for clothing, etc.)
S . . . . Smooth (Appearance of bacterial colony)
S . . . . Smooth Sea
S . . . . Snow
S . . . . Socialist
S . . . . Society
S . . . . Socius or Sodalis (Fellow)
S . . . . Soft
S . . . . Sol (Monetary unit in Peru)
S . . . . Solid
S . . . . Solo (Music)
S . . . . Solubility
S . . . . Son(s)
S . . . . Soprano (Music)
S . . . . Sou (Monetary unit in France)
S . . . . South; Southerly; or Southern
S . . . . Spar (Buoy)
S . . . . Special
S . . . . Special Air Mission (Military aircraft identification prefix)
S . . . . Species
S . . . . Specific Factor
S . . . . Specific Surface
S . . . . Specification
S . . . . Speed
S . . . . Sphere or Spherical
S . . . . Spool
S . . . . Staff
S . . . . Stand(s)
S . . . . Standard
S . . . . Station
S . . . . Statute
S . . . . Steamer
S . . . . Steel
S . . . . Stem
S . . . . Stere (Metric)
S . . . . Stimulus
S . . . . Stock
S . . . . Stopping Power
S . . . . Straight
S . . . . Straight-In (Aviation)
S . . . . Subito (Immediately; suddenly) (Music)
S . . . . Subject (Psychology)
S . . . . Subject of a proposition in logic
S . . . . Submarine
S . . . . Substantive
S . . . . Succeeded
S . . . . Sucre (Monetary unit in Ecuador)
S . . . . Sulfur (Chemical element)
S . . . . Summary
S . . . . Summer (Load line mark)
S . . . . Sun
S . . . . Sunday
S . . . . Superb
S . . . . Superior

S . . . . Supply (Department aboard a carrier) (Navy)
S . . . . Surfaced
S . . . . Surplus
S . . . . Survey
S . . . . Suus (His)
S . . . . Switch
S . . . . Symbol for Entropy
S . . . . Symmetrical (Chemistry)
S . . . . United States Senate (When appended to legislative designations)
/S/ . . . . Signed (Before signature on typed copy of a document, original of which was signed)
S-1 . . . . Personnel Section in Army Brigades or smaller units, and in Marine Corps units smaller than a brigade; the officer in charge of this section; also refers to adjutant (1st staff section, brigades and lower units)
S-2 . . . . Intelligence Section in Army brigades or smaller units, and in Marine Corps units smaller than a brigade; the officer in charge of this section
S3 . . . . Systems and Software Simulator
S-3 . . . . Operations and Training Section in Army Brigades or smaller units, and in Marine Corps units smaller than a brigade; the officer in charge of this section
S4 . . . . Stanford School Scheduling System
S-4 . . . . Logistics Section in Army Brigades or smaller units, and in Marine Corps units smaller than a brigade; the officer in charge of this section
S5 . . . . Civil Affairs Officer (Army)
S^{35} . . . . Radioactive Sulfur
2-S . . . . Selective Service Class (for Registrant Deferred Because of Activity in Study)
SA . . . . Franciscan Sisters of the Atonement, Third Order Regular of St. Francis (Graymoor Sisters) (Roman Catholic religious order)
SA . . . . Safeway Stores, Inc. (NYSE symbol)
SA . . . . Sail Area
SA . . . . Salt Acid
SA . . . . Salt Added
SA . . . . Salvation Army
Sa . . . . Samarium (Chemical element) (Obsolete form; see Sm)
SA . . . . Sandia Area Office (AEC)
SA . . . . Savannah & Atlanta Railway Company (AAR code)
SA . . . . Scaling Amplifier
SA . . . . Schizophrenics Anonymous
SA . . . . Scientific Assistant (Ministry of Agriculture, Fisheries, and Food) (British)
SA . . . . Seaman Apprentice
SA . . . . Second Attack (Men's lacrosse position)
SA . . . . Secretary of the Army
SA . . . . Secundum Artem (According to Art)
SA . . . . Seiners Association
SA . . . . Select Address
SA . . . . Semiannual
SA . . . . Semiautomatic
SA . . . . Sense Amplifier
SA . . . . Sensitized Activated
SA . . . . Servo Amplifier
SA . . . . Sex Appeal (Slang)
SA . . . . Shaft Alley (Technical drawings)
SA . . . . Shipping Authority
SA . . . . Shop Accessory (Drawing)
SA . . . . Signature Analysis
SA . . . . Sine Anno (Without date of publication)
SA . . . . Single-Action (Firearm)
SA . . . . Sinu-Atrial (Physiology)
SA . . . . Sinuauricular
SA . . . . Sister of Arts
SA . . . . Slugging Average (Baseball)
SA . . . . Small Arms (All firearms other than cannon)
SA . . . . Smithsonian Associates
SA . . . . Snap Action
SA . . . . Sociedad Anonima (Stock company) (Spanish)
SA . . . . Societas Adunationis (Franciscan Friars of the Atonement) (Roman Catholic religious order)
SA . . . . Societe Anonyme (Limited company) (French)
SA . . . . Society of Actuaries
SA . . . . Society of Antiquaries (British)
SA . . . . Society of Arts (British)
SA . . . . Sociological Analysis (A publication)
SA . . . . Soluble in Alkaline Solution
SA . . . . Soprano, Alto
SA . . . . South Africa
SA . . . . South African Airways
SA . . . . South America
SA . . . . South Australia
SA . . . . Southern Association (Baseball league)
SA . . . . Special Action (Military)

SA . . . . Special Agent
SA . . . . Special Artificer (Navy)
SA . . . . Special Assignment
SA . . . . Specific Activity
SA . . . . Spectrum Analyzer
SA . . . . Splitting Amplifier
SA . . . . Springfield Armory (Army)
SA . . . . Standard Addition
SA . . . . State's Attorney
SA . . . . Statocyst Anlage
SA . . . . Stone Arch (Bridges)
SA . . . . Store Address
SA . . . . Sturmabteilung (Storm troopers) (NAZI Germany)
SA . . . . Sub Anno (Under the Year)
SA . . . . Subsistence Allowance
SA . . . . Sugar Association
SA . . . . Sulfonamide(s)
SA . . . . Summing Amplifier
SA . . . . Supplemental Agreement
SA . . . . Surface Area
SA . . . . Sustained Action (With reference to drugs)
SA . . . . Systems Analysis
S/A . . . . Sociedad Anonima (Corporation) (Spain)
S/A . . . . Societa Anonima (Italy)
S/A . . . . Special Activities (Air Force)
S/A . . . . Subject to Approval
S & A . . . . . . Bureau of Supplies and Accounts (Navy) (Obsolete)
S & A . . . . . . Safe (or Safety) and Arm (or Arming) Device
SAA . . . . . . Sanders Associates, Inc. (NYSE symbol)
SAA . . . . . . Satellite Attitude Acquisition
SAA . . . . . . Senior Army Advisor
SAA . . . . . . Servo Actuated Assembly
SAA . . . . . . Shakespeare Association of America
SAA . . . . . . Signal Appliance Association
SAA . . . . . . Single Article Announcement (American Chemical Society publication)
SAA . . . . . . Slot Array Antenna
SAA . . . . . . Small-Arms Ammunition
SAA . . . . . . Society for Academic Achievement
SAA . . . . . . Society for American Archaeology
SAA . . . . . . Society of American Archivists
SAA . . . . . . Society of Animal Artists
SAA . . . . . . Society for Applied Anthropology
SAA . . . . . . Society for Asian Art
SAA . . . . . . Some American Artists (An organization)
SAA . . . . . . South African Airways
SAA . . . . . . Southern Ash Association
SAA . . . . . . Special Assignment Airlift (Air Force)
SAA . . . . . . Specialty Advertising Association
SAA . . . . . . Speech Association of America
SAA . . . . . . Staff Administrative Assistant (Army)
SAA . . . . . . Standards Association of Australia
SAA . . . . . . Summary Activity Account (Army)
SAA . . . . . . Supima Association of America
SAA . . . . . . Surety Association of America
SAAARNG . . . Senior Army Advisor, Army National Guard
SAAB . . . . . . Svenska Aeroplan AB (Swedish automobile manufacturer; acronym used as name of its cars)
SAAC . . . . . . Seismic Array Analysis Center (IBM)
SAAC . . . . . . Special Assistant for Arms Control (Military)
SAACI . . . . . . Salesmen's Association of the American Chemical Industry
SAAD . . . . . . Sacramento Army Depot
SAAD . . . . . . San Antonio Air Depot (Air Force)
SAAD . . . . . . Small-Arms Ammunition Depot
SAAD . . . . . . Sperry Air Arm Division
SAAEB . . . . . . South African Atomic Energy Board
SAAF . . . . . . Sino-American Amity Fund
SAAF . . . . . . South African Air Force
SAAM . . . . . . Special Assignment Airlift Movement (Army)
SAAMA . . . . . . San Antonio Air Material Area
SAAMI . . . . . . Sporting Arms and Ammunition Manufacturers Institute
SAAP . . . . . . Saturn/Apollo Applications Program (NASA)
SAAP . . . . . . South Atlantic Anomaly Probe (NASA-CNAE)
SAAR . . . . . . Saw Arbor
SAARDT . . . . . . Syndicat Autonome des Agents de la Radiodiffusior du Togo (Autonomous Union of Radiobroadcasting Workers of Togo)
SAARF . . . . . . Special Allied Airborne Reconnaissance Force (Teams parachuted into POW areas to take supplies to prisoners or to help them get out) (World War II)
SAAS . . . . . . Science Achievement Awards for Students
SAAS . . . . . . Society of African and Afro-American Students
SAASC . . . . . . San Antonio Air Service Command (Air Force)

SAAT . . . . Satellite Attitude Acquisition Technique
SAATSC . . . . . San Antonio Air Technical Service Command (Air Force)
SAAU . . . . . . Selfreliance Association of American Ukrainians
SAAU . . . . . . Swiss Association of Autonomous Unions
SAAUSAR . . . . Senior Army Advisor, United States Army Reserve
SAAVS . . . . . . Submarine Acceleration and Velocity System
SAB . . . . Scientific Advisory Board (Air Force)
SAB . . . . Signal Aviation Branch
SAB . . . . Societe Anonyme Belge d'Exploitation de la Navigation Aerienne
          (Sabena Belgian World Airlines)
SAB . . . . Society of American Bacteriologists
SAB . . . . Solid Assembly Building
SAB . . . . Soprano, Alto, Bass
SAB . . . . Structural Adhesive Bond
SAB . . . . Supporting Assistance Bureau (Agency for International Development)
SAB . . . . System Advisory Board
SABAR . . . . . . Satellites, Balloons and Rockets (Air Force program)
SABCO . . . . . . Society for the Area of Biological and Chemical Overlap
SABE . . . . . . Society for Automation in Business Education
SABENA . . . . . Societe Anonyme Belge d'Exploitation de la Navigation Aerienne
          (Sabena Belgian World Airlines)
SABER . . . . . . SECNAV (Secretary of the Navy) Advisory Board on Educational
          Requirements
SABH . . . . Simultaneous Automatic Broadcast Homer
SABIR . . . . . . Semi-Automatic Bibliographic Information Retrieval
SABMAR . . . . . Service-Craft and Boats Machine Accounting Report (Navy)
SABMIS . . . . . . Seaborne (or Ship-Launched) Anti-Ballistic Missile Intercept System (Navy)
SABO . . . . Sense Amplifier Blocking Oscillator
SABP . . . . Skeletal Axis of Basal Piece
SABR . . . . Society for American Baseball Research
SABRE . . . . . . SAGE (Semi-Automatic Ground Environment) Battery Routing Equipment
SABRE . . . . . . Sales and Business Reservations Done Electronically
SABRE . . . . . . Secure Airborne Bombing RADAR Equipment
SABRE . . . . . . Self-Aligning Boost and Reentry (Air Force)
SABRF . . . . . . Skeletal Axis of Branchial Filament
SABRI . . . . . . Serikat Buruh Rokok Indonesia (Cigarette Workers' Union) (Indonesia)
SABU . . . . Self-Adjusting Ball-Up (A state of confusion which may, or may not,
          clear up of itself) (Military slang)
SABW . . . . Society of American Business Writers
SAC . . . . Saint Ambrose College (Iowa)
SAC . . . . Saint Anselm's College (New Hampshire)
SAC . . . . Saint Augustine's College (North Carolina)
SAC . . . . San Antonio College (Texas)
SAC . . . . Santa Ana College (California)
SAC . . . . Science Advisory Committee (Air Force)
SAC . . . . Self-Adjusting Clutch
SAC . . . . Semiautomatic Coding
SAC . . . . Serving Area Concept (Bell System)
SAC . . . . Servo Adapter Coupler
SAC . . . . Shipbuilding Advisory Council (British)
SAC . . . . Single Acting Cylinder
SAC . . . . Social and Athletic Club
SAC . . . . Societe Africaine de Culture (Society of African Culture)
SAC . . . . Society of the Catholic Apostolate (Pallottines)
SAC . . . . Special Area Code (Bell System)
SAC . . . . Specific Acoustic Capacitance
SAC . . . . Sprayed Acoustical Ceiling (Technical drawings)
SAC . . . . Standard Aircraft Characteristics
SAC . . . . Store and Clear
SAC . . . . Strategic Air Command
SAC . . . . Supreme Allied Command(er) (Headquarters in London) (World War II)
SAC . . . . Sveriges Arbetares Centralorganisation (Central Organization of Swedish
          Workers)
SAC . . . . Synchro Azimuth Converter
SACA . . . . . . Special Assistant for Consumer Affairs (White House) (Obsolete)
SACA . . . . . . Steam Automobile Club of America
SACA . . . . . . Study Advisory Committee on Aeronautics (National Academy of
          Engineering)
SACACCS . . . . . Strategic Air Command Automated Command Control System
SACAY . . . . . . SECNAV (Secretary of the Navy) Advisory Commission on Youth
SACB . . . . Subversive Activities Control Board (Later, Federal Internal Security
          Board)
SACC . . . . Science Action Coordinating Committee
SACC . . . . Supplemental Air Carrier Conference
SACC . . . . . . Supporting Arms Coordination Center (Air Force)
SACCEI . . . . . Strategic Air Command Communications-Electronics Instruction
SACCOMNET . . Strategic Air Command Communications Network
SACCS . . . . . . Strategic Air Command Communications (or Control) System
SACE . . . . . . Semiautomatic Checkout Equipment (DOD)
SACE . . . . . . Shore-Based Acceptance Checkout Equipment
SACEM . . . . . . Society for the Advancement of Continuing Education for Ministry

SACEUR . . . . . Supreme Allied Commander Europe (NATO)
SACHC . . . . . . Soviet-American Committee on Health Cooperation
SACL . . . . South African Confederation of Labour
SACL . . . . Space and Component Log
SACLAMP . . . . Strategic Air Command Low-Altitude Missile Program (Air Force)
SACLANT . . . . Supreme Allied Commander, Atlantic (NATO)
SACLANTCEN . . Supreme Allied Commander, Atlantic, Anti-Submarine Warfare
          Research Center
SACLANTREPEUR . . Supreme Allied Commander, Atlantic, Representative in Europe
Sac Lit D . . . . Doctor of Sacred Literature
SACLO . . . . . Strategic Air Command Liaison Officer
SACMAP . . . . . Selective Automatic Computational Matching & Positioning System
SACMDR . . . . . Site Activation Commander (Army)
SACMED . . . . . Supreme Allied Commander, Mediterranean
SAC/MEP . . . . Strategic Air Command/Minuteman Education Program
SACO . . . . . . Select Address and Contract Operate
SACO . . . . Sino-American Cooperative Organization (Guerrilla and intelligence
          agency) (World War II)
SACO . . . . . . Sveriges Akademikers Centralorganisation (Swedish Confederation of
          Professional Association)
SACOA . . . . . . Southern Appalachian Coal Operators Association
SACOD . . . . . . South African Congress of Democrats
SACOM . . . . . SECNAV (Secretary of the Navy) Advisory Commission on Manpower
SACOM . . . . . Southern Area Command (Military)
SACOPS . . . . . Strategic Air Command Operational Planning System
SACPO . . . . . . South African Colored People's Organization
SACRA . . . . . . Student Alliance for Christian Renewal in America
SACS . . . . Satellite Attitude-Control Simulator (NASA)
SACS . . . . Southern Association of Colleges and Schools
SACS . . . . Synchronous Altitude Communications Satellite
SACSA . . . . . . Special Assistant for Counterinsurgency and Special Activities
SACSEA . . . . . Supreme Allied Command(er), Southeast Asia
SACSIR . . . . . South African Council for Scientific and Industrial Research
SAC/SSW . . . . Special Assistant to the Chief of Staff for Special Warfare (Army)
SACTO . . . . . . Sacramento Test Operations
SACTTYNET . . . Strategic Air Command Teletype Network
SACTU . . . . . . South African Congress of Trade Unions
SACTW . . . . . . South African Council of Transport Workers
SAD . . . . Safety, Arming and Destruct
SAD . . . . Safety and Arming Device
SAD . . . . Selected Area (Electron) Diffraction
SAD . . . . Semiconductor Anticoincidence Detector
SAD . . . . Sentence Appraiser and Diagrammer
SAD . . . . Site Activation Division
SAD . . . . Situation Attention Display
SAD . . . . Soviet Air Defense
SAD . . . . Soviet Air Demonstration
SAD . . . . Special Artificer, Special Synthetic Training Devices (Navy)
SAD . . . . Sugar, Acetone, Diacetic Acid (Test)
SAD . . . . Support Air Direction (Navy)
SAD . . . . Sympathetic Aerial Detonation (Air Force)
S & AD . . . . . Science and Applications Directorate (NASA)
SADAP . . . . . . Simplified Automatic Data Plotter
SADE . . . . Sociedad Argentina de Escritores
SADE . . . . Superheat Advanced Demonstration Experiment
SADF . . . . South African Defence Forces
SADIC . . . . . . Solid-State Analog-to-Digital Computer
SADIE . . . . . . Scanning Analog-to-Digital Input Equipment (National Bureau of
          Standards)
SADIE . . . . . . Semiautomatic Defense Intercept Environment (Air Force)
SADL . . . . Spares Application Data List
SADL . . . . Sterilization Advanced Development Laboratory
SADL . . . . Sterilization Assembly Development Laboratory (NASA)
SADM . . . . Special Atomic Demolition Munitions
SADMG . . . . . . Special Artificer, Special Devices, Machine Gun Trainer (Navy)
SADP . . . . Synthetic Array Data Processor
SADR . . . . Six Hundred Megacycle Air Defense RADAR
SADRAM . . . . . Search and Destroy RADAR Attack Modification
SADS . . . . Semi-Automatic Defense System
SADS . . . . Semiconductor Anticoincidence Detection System
SADS . . . . Simulated Air Defense System (RADAR)
SADS . . . . Swiss Air Defense System
SADSAC . . . . . Sampled Data Simulator and Computer
SADSAC . . . . . Seiler ALGOL Digitally Simulated Analog Computer
SADSACT . . . . . Self-Assigned Descriptors from Self and Cited Titles (Automatic indexing)
SADT . . . . Self-Accelerating Decomposition Temperature
SADT . . . . Surface Alloy Diffused-Base Transistor
SADTC . . . . . . SHAPE (Supreme Headquarters Allied Powers Europe) Air Defense Tech-
          nology Center (Netherlands)
SAE . . . . Self-Addressed Envelope
SAE . . . . Simple Arithmetic Expression

SAE .... Site Acceptance Evaluation (Army)
SAE .... Society for the Advancement of Education
SAE .... Society of Automotive Engineers
SAE .... Spiral Aftereffect (Aerospace)
SAE .... Stamped Addressed Envelope
SAE .... Standard Average European
SAE .... Steering Angle Error
SAE .... Supersonic Aircraft Engine
SAEA .... Southwest Atomic Energy Associates
SAEB .... Self-Adjusting Electric Brake
SAEC .... Sumitomo Atomic Energy Commission (Japan)
SAEDA ...... Subversion and Espionage Directed Against US Army and Deliberate Security Violations
SAEDE ...... Sensory Aids Evaluation and Development Center (MIT)
SAEH .... Society for Automation in English and the Humanities
SAEI .... Sumitomo Atomic Energy Industries, Ltd. (Japan)
SAEMR ...... Small Arms Expert Marksmanship Ribbon (Military decoration)
SAES .... Special Assistant for Environmental Services (Military)
SAEW .... Ship's Advanced Electronic Warfare
SAF .... Santa Fe International Corp. (NYSE symbol)
SAF .... Scandinavian American Fraternity
SAF .... Secretary of the Air Force
SAF .... Shielding Analysis Form (Civil Defense)
SAF .... Society of American Florists
SAF .... Society of American Foresters
SAF .... South Africa
SAF .... Southern Attack Force (Navy)
SAF .... Spacecraft Assembly Facility (NASA)
SAF .... Spanish Air Force
SAF .... Special Action Force (Army)
SAF .... Spin Armed Fuze
SAF .... Sterilization Assembly Facility
SAF .... Strategic Air Force
SAF .... Super Abrasion Furnace
SAF .... Svenska Arbetsgivareforeningen (An employers' confederation) (Sweden)
SAFA .... School Assistance in Federally Affected Areas
SAFA .... Society for Automation in the Fine Arts
SAFA .... Solar Array Failure Analysis
SAFA .... Soluble Antigen Fluorescent-Antibody
SAFAA ...... Secretary of the Air Force, Administrative Assistant
SAFARI ..... Semi-Automatic Failure Anticipation Recording Instrumentation
SAFARI ..... Spiro Agnew Fans and Rooters, Incorporated
SAFB .... Scott Air Force Base
SAFB .... Shaw Air Force Base
SAFCB ...... Secretary of the Air Force Correction Board
SAFCO ...... Standing Advisory Committee on Fisheries of the Caribbean Organization
SAFCPM .... Safeguard Communications Program Manager (Army)
SAFCPMO ... Safeguard Communications Program Management Office (Army)
SAFCTF ..... Safeguard Central Training Facility (Army)
SAFE .... Satellite Alert Force Employment
SAFE .... Society of Associated Financial Executives
SAFE .... South American and Far East
SAFE .... Survival (formerly, Space) and Flight Equipment Association
SAFE .... System, Area, Function, Equipment
SAFEA ...... Survival (formerly, Space) and Flight Equipment Association
SAFE TRIP .... Students Against Faulty Tires Ripping in Pieces (Student legal action organization)
SAFGC ...... Secretary of Air Force General Counsel
SAFI .... Semiautomatic Flight Inspection (FAA)
SAFI .... Senior Air Force Instructor
SAFI .... Sholem Aleichem Folk Institute
SAFIE ...... Secretary of Air Force, Special Assistant for Installations
SAFIL ...... Secretary of the Air Force (Installations and Logistics)
SAFIN ...... Secretary of Air Force, Special Assistant for Intelligence
SAFIS ...... Secretary of Air Force, Office of Information Services
SAFITP ..... Safeguard Integrated Training Plan (Army)
SAFLL ...... Secretary of the Air Force, Office of Legislative Liaison
SAFLOG ..... Safeguard Logistic Command (Army)
SAFMA ...... Assistant Secretary of Air Force (Materiel)
SAFMP ...... Assistant Secretary of Air Force (Manpower & Personnel)
SAFMSC .... Safeguard Materiel Support Command (Army)
SAFO .... Secretary of the Air Force Order
SAFO .... Senior Air Force Officer (present)
SAFOC ...... Semi-Automatic Flight Operations Center
SAFOC ..... Syndicat Autonome des Fonctionnaires d'Oubangi-Chari (Autonomous Union of the Workers of Ubangi-Shari)
SAFOH ...... Society of American Florists and Ornamental Horticulturists
SAFOI ...... Secretary of the Air Force, Office of Information
SAFPACC .... Safeguard Public Affairs Coordinating Committee (Army)
SAFPC ...... Secretary of Air Force Personnel Council
SAFPLAN .... Submarine Area Frequency Plan (Navy)

SAFR .... Senior Air Force Representative
SAFRD ...... Assistant Secretary of Air Force (Research and Development)
SAFS .... Secondary Air Force Specialty
SAFSCOM .... Safeguard System Command (Army)
SAFSEA .... Safeguard System Evaluation Agency (Army)
SAFSL ...... Secretary of Air Force Space Liaison
SAFSM ...... Safeguard System Manager
SAFSO ...... Safeguard System Office (Army)
SAFSR ...... Society for the Advancement of Food Service Research
SAFTAC ..... Semiautomatic Facility for Terminal Area Control
SAFTCP..... Safeguard Tactical Communications Plan (Army)
SAFTCS ..... Safeguard Tactical Communications System (Army)
SAFTRANS... Safeguard Transportation System (Army)
SAFTU ..... South African Federation of Trade Unions
SAFUS ...... Under Secretary of the Air Force
SAG........ St. Apollonia Guild
SAG........ Scientific Advisory Group
SAG........ Screen Actors Guild
SAG .... Seismic Air Gun
SAG .... Signal Actuated Gate
SAG .... Significant Air Gap
SAG........ Society of Arthritic Gardeners
SAG........ Sowjetische Aktiengesellschaften (Soviet corporations in East Germany)
SAG........ Sozialistische Arbeitsgemeinschaft
SAG .... Systems Analysis Group
SAGA....... Saint-Gaudens National Historic Site
SAGA....... Society of American Graphic Artists
SAGA....... Stage and Arena Guild of America
SAGA....... System for Automatic Generation and Analysis
SAGE....... Semi-Automatic Ground Environment (US defense system)
SAGE .... Special Assistant for Growing Enterprises (Division of National American Wholesale Grocers Association)
SAGEM...... Societe d' Applications Generals d'Electricite & de Mecanique (France)
SAGFC ..... Southeastern Association of Game and Fish Commissioners
SAGGE...... Synchronous Altitude Gravity Gradient Experiment
SAGI ...... Specialty Advertising Guild International
SAGP....... Society for Ancient Greek Philosophy
SAGS ...... Semiactive Gravity-Gradient System (NASA)
SAGU....... Saguaro National Monument
SAGW...... Surface to Air Guided Weapon (British)
SAH........ Semi-Active Homer (Missiles)
SAH........ Society of American Historians
SAH........ Society of Architectural Historians
SAHC ...... Self-Aligning Hydraulic Cylinder
SAHF ...... Semiautomatic Height Finder
SAHI ...... Sagamore Hill National Historic Site
SAHSA ..... Servicio Aereo de Honduras, SA
SAHYB ..... Simulation of Analog and Hybrid Computers
SAI .... Schizophrenics Anonymous International
SAI .... Senior Army Instructor
SAI .... Societa Anonima Italiana (An incorporated company) (Italian)
SAI .... Specific Acoustic Impedance
SAI .... Sudden Auroral Intensity
SAI .... Sugar Association, Incorporated
SAIAS....... Ship Aircraft Inertial Alignment System
SAIC ...... School of the Art Institute of Chicago
SAIC ...... Small Arms Interpost Competition (Military)
SAIC ...... South African Indian Congress
SAIC ...... Switch Action Interrupt Count
SAID....... Semi-Automatic Integrated Documentation
SAID ...... Speech Auto-Instructional Device
SAID ...... Supplementary Aviation Information Display
SAIE....... Special Acceptance Inspection Equipment
SAIFER ..... Safe Arm Initiation from Electromagnetic Radiation
SAIL ...... Sea-Air Interaction Laboratory (Oceanography)
SAIL ...... Ship's Armament Inventory List (Navy)
SAILER ..... Staffing of African Institutions for Legal Education and Research (An organization) (Later, International Legal Center)
SAILS ..... Seagoing Assembly-Integration-Launch System
SAILS ..... Simplified Aircraft Instrument Landing System
SAIM ...... South America Indian Mission
SAIM ...... Systems Analysis and Integration Model
SAIMR ..... South African Institute for Medical Research
SAIMS ..... Selected Acquisitions, Information and Management System
SAINT ..... Satellite Inspector and Satellite Interceptor (Air Force spacecraft program)
SAIORG ..... Supreme Assembly, International Order of Rainbow for Girls
SAIP....... Societe d'France Applications Industrielle de la Physique
SAIP ...... Submarine Antenna Improvement Program (Military)
SAIR....... Saugus Ironworks National Historic Site

SAIR . . . . Semiannual Inventory Report (Air Force)
SAIRR . . . . . . South African Institute of Racial Relations
SAIS . . . . School of Advanced International Studies
SAIS . . . . Societa Agricola Italo-Somala (Italo-Somali Agricultural Society)
SAISA . . . . . . South Atlantic Intercollegiate Sailing Association
SAISAC . . . . . Ship's Aircraft Inertial System Alignment Console
SAITR . . . . . . Special Artificer, Instruments, Typewriter and Office Equipment Repairman (Navy)
SAIWR . . . . . . Special Artificer, Instruments, Watch Repairman (Navy)
SAJ . . . . St. Joseph Light & Power Company (NYSE symbol)
SAJ . . . . Society for the Advancement of Judaism
SAJC . . . . Spring Arbor Junior College (Michigan)
SAJH . . . . San Juan Island National Historic Park
SAJI . . . . Saw Jig
SAK . . . . Suomen Ammattiyhdistysten Keskuslitto (Confederation of Finnish Trade Unions)
SAKI . . . . Solartron Automatic Keyboard Instructor
SAL . . . . Seaboard Air Line R. R. (AAR code)
SAL . . . . Scientific Airlock
SAL . . . . Sensorineural Acuity Level (Medicine)
SAL . . . . Ship Authorized Leave
SAL . . . . Short Approach Light (FAA)
SAL . . . . Solar Arc Lamp
SAL . . . . Solar Array Leaf
SAL . . . . Sons of the American Legion
SAL . . . . South Atlantic League (Nickname: Sally) (Baseball)
SAL . . . . Special Ammunition Load
SAL . . . . Standard Acceptance Limits
SAL . . . . Subject Authority List
SAL . . . . Supersonic Aerophysics Laboratory
SALA . . . . Scientific Assistant Land Agent (Ministry of Agriculture, Fisheries, and Food) (British)
SALA . . . . Servicios Aeronauticos Latina America
SALA . . . . Solar Arc Lamp Assembly
SALA . . . . Southwest Alliance for Latin America
SALALM . . . . . Seminars on the Acquisition of Latin American Library Materials
SALE . . . . Silicon Avalanche Light Emitter
SALE . . . . Simple Algebraic Language for Engineers
SALES . . . . . . Ship Aircraft Locating Equipment
SALM . . . . . . Society of Air Line Meteorologists
SALORS . . . . . Structural Analysis of Layered Orthotropic Ring-Stiffened Shells (Computer program) (NASA)
SALS . . . . Short Approach Light System (Aviation)
SALS . . . . Solid-State Acoustoelectric Light Scanner
SALSU . . . . . . Singapore Admiralty Local Staff Union
SaLSUA . . . . . Sierra Leone Students Union of the Americas
SALT . . . . Sisters All Learning Together (Feminist group)
SALT . . . . Strategic Arms Limitation Talks
SALT . . . . Symbolic Algebraic Language Translator
SALTE . . . . . . Semi-Automatic Line Test Equipment
SALTI . . . . . . Summary Accounting for Low-Dollar Turnover Items (Army)
SALUT . . . . . . Sea, Air, Land and Underwater Targets (Navy)
SALV . . . . Salvage
Salv Div Bad . . Salvage Diver Badge (Army)
SALVDV . . . . . Salvage Dives
SALWIS . . . . . . Shipboard Air-Launched Weapons Installation System
SAM . . . . S-Adenosylmethionine (Biochemistry)
SAM . . . . School of Aerospace Medicine (Formerly, School of Aviation Medicine) (Air Force)
SAM . . . . School Apperception Method
SAM . . . . Selective Automatic Monitoring
SAM . . . . Self-Propelled Anthropomorphic Manipulator (Moon machine)
SAM . . . . Semantic Analyzing Machine
SAM . . . . Service Attitude Measurement (Bell System)
SAM . . . . Signal (System) for Assessment and Modification (of behavior) (Patented)
SAM . . . . Simulated Assignment Model
SAM . . . . Simulation of Analogue Methods (Data processing) (British)
SAM . . . . Single Application Method (College admissions)
SAM . . . . Sociedade Africana de Mocambique (African Society of Mozambique)
SAM . . . . Societe des Americanistes
SAM . . . . Society for Advancement of Management
SAM . . . . Society of African Missions
SAM . . . . Society of American Magicians
SAM . . . . Society for Asian Music
SAM . . . . Sort and Merge
SAM . . . . Space Available Mail (Military)
SAM . . . . Special Air Mission
SAM . . . . Stage Assembly and Maintenance (Building)
SAM . . . . Stratospheric Aerosol Monitor (NASA)
SAM . . . . Substitute Alloy Material (AEC)
SAM . . . . Subsynoptic Advection Model

SAM . . . . Surface-Active Material
SAM . . . . Surface-to-Air Missile
SAM . . . . Synchronous Amplitude Modulation
SAM . . . . System Accuracy Model
SAM . . . . System Activity Monitor (Data processing)
SAM . . . . System Analysis Machine (Data processing)
SAM . . . . System for Assessment and Modification (of Behavior)
S/AM . . . . . . Surface-to-Air Missile
SAMA . . . . . . Sacramento Air Materiel Area
SAMA . . . . . . Salem Maritime National Historic Site
SAMA . . . . . . Scientific Apparatus Makers Association
SAMA . . . . . . Student American Medical Association
SAMAA . . . . . Special Assistant for Military Assistance Affairs
SAMAE . . . . . Southern Air Materiel Area, Europe
SAMAP . . . . . Southern Air Materiel Area, Pacific
SAMAR . . . . . Surface-to-Air Missile Availability Report
SAMB . . . . . . Secondary Aircraft Maintenance Base
SAM-B . . . . . . School of Aviation Medicine - Brooks
SAMBA . . . . . Special Agents Mutual Benefit Association (FBI)
SAMBA . . . . . Systems Approach to Managing BUSHIPS (Bureau of Ships; later, NESC or ESC) Acquisition (Navy)
SAMBO . . . . . Strategic Anti-Missile Barrage Objects
SAMCTT . . . . . School of Aerospace Medicine Color Threshold Test
SAMCU . . . . . Special Airborne Medical Care Unit
SAMD . . . . . . Surface-to-Air Missile Development
S/AM-D . . . . . Surface-to-Air Missile Development
SAMe . . . . . . S-Adenosylmethionine (Biochemistry)
SAME . . . . . . Society of American Military Engineers
SAME . . . . . . Students Against Misleading Enterprises (Student legal action organization)
SAMFU . . . . . Self-Adjusting Military Foul Up (Slang)
SAMI . . . . . . Single Action Maintenance Instruction
SAMI . . . . . . Socially Acceptable Monitoring Instruments (Medicine)
SAMID . . . . . Ship Anti-Missile Integrated Defense (Program) (Navy)
SAMIS . . . . . Structural Analysis and Matrix Interpretation System
SAMLA . . . . . Southern Atlantic Modern Language Association
SAMMA . . . . . Stores Account Material Management Afloat
SAMMI . . . . . Signature Analysis Methods for Mission Identification
SAMMS . . . . . Standard Automated Material Management System
SAMOS . . . . . Satellite-Missile Observation System
SAMP . . . . . . Stuntmen's Association of Motion Pictures
SAMPE . . . . . Society of Aerospace Material and Process Engineers
SAM & R . . . . Ship Activation, Maintenance and Repair
SAMS . . . . . . Sampling Analog Memory System
SAMS . . . . . . Satellite Automonitor System
SAMS . . . . . . Ship's Alteration Management System (Navy)
SAMS . . . . . . Southern Appalachian Migrants (Cincinnati slang)
SAMSAT . . . . . Surface-to-Air Missile Servicing, Assembly and Test
SAM/SAT . . . . South America/South Atlantic Regional Area (Aviation)
SAMSO . . . . . Space and Missile Systems Organization (Merger of Ballistic Systems Division and Space Systems Division) (Air Force)
SAMSOM . . . . Support Availability Multi-System Operational Model
SAMSON . . . . System Analysis of Manned Space Operations
SAMTEC . . . . . Space and Missile Test Center (Air Force)
SAN . . . . Sandersville R. R. (AAR code)
SAN . . . . Severe Acoustic Noise
SAN . . . . Ship Account Number (Navy)
SAN . . . . Srpska Akademija Nauka i Umetnosti (Belgrade, Yugoslavia)
SAN . . . . Styrene-Acrylonitrile
SANA . . . . . . Specialty Advertising National Association
SANA . . . . . . State, Army, Navy, Air
SANB . . . . . . South African National Bibliography
SANCAD . . . . . Scottish Association for National Certificates and Diplomas
San D . . . . . . Doctor of Sanitation
SAND . . . . . . Sampling Aerospace Nuclear Debris
SAND . . . . . . Sorting and Assembly of New Data
SANDA . . . . . Supplies and Accounts
SANDASO . . . . Bureau of Supplies and Accounts (later, NSUPSC) Shipment Order (Navy)
SANDOCC . . . . San Diego Oceanic Coordinating Committee
SANE . . . . . . National Committee for a Sane Nuclear Policy ("SANE" alone now used as organization name)
San E . . . . . . Sanitary Engineer (Academic degree)
SANE . . . . . . Severe Acoustic Noise Environment
SANF . . . . . . Sanford Recreation Area
SANKA . . . . . Sans Caffeine (Acronym used as brand name)
SANOVA . . . . Simultaneous Analysis of Variance
SANR . . . . . . Subject to Approval No Risk
SANS . . . . . . Simplified Account - Numbering System
SANS . . . . . . South African Naval Service
SANSAN . . . . . San Francisco, San Diego (Proposed name for possible "super-city" formed by growth and mergers of other cities)
SANTA . . . . . Souvenir and Novelty Trade Association

SANU . . . . Sudan African National Union (Political party)
SAO . . . . Secret Army Organization (English initialism for OAS, terrorist group in Algeria and metropolitan France)
SAO . . . . Select Address and Operate
SAO . . . . Smithsonian Astrophysical Observatory
SAO . . . . Special Activities Office (Air Force)
SAO . . . . Special Artificer, Optical (Navy)
SAO . . . . Special Astrophysics Observatory
SAO . . . . Staff Administrative Office (Military)
SAO . . . . Support Air Observation (Navy)
SAOC . . . . . . Space and Astronautics Orientation Course
SAODAP . . . . . Special Action Office of Drug Abuse Prevention (Proposed Federal drug agency)
SAOS . . . . . . Select Address (and Provide) Output Signal
SAOT . . . . . . Semiactive on Target
SAOTA . . . . . . Shrimp Association of the Americas
SAP . . . . Scorched Aluminum Powder
SAP . . . . Scouting Amphibian Plan (Coast Guard)
SAP . . . . Semi-Armor-Piercing (Projectile)
SAP . . . . Share Assembly Program (Data processing)
SAP . . . . Ship Acquisition Plan (Navy)
SAP . . . . Shipboard Antenna Pedestal
SAP . . . . Single-Axis Platform
SAP . . . . Sintered Aluminum Powder
SAP . . . . Skeletal Axis of Pinnule
SAP . . . . Society for Adolescent Psychiatry
SAP . . . . Society for American Philosophy
SAP . . . . Society of Applied Spectroscopy
SAP . . . . Sodium Acid Pyrophosphate (Food additive)
SAP . . . . Soon As Possible
SAP . . . . Sozialistische Arbeiterpartei
SAP . . . . Spot Authorization Plan (WPB) (Obsolete)
SAP . . . . Spy Against Pollution (An organization)
SAP . . . . Supervisory Airplane Pilot
SAP . . . . Symbolic Address Program
SAP . . . . Symbolic Assembly Program
SAP . . . . Systems Assurance Program (IBM)
SAPA . . . . South African Press Agency
SAPAI . . . . . . Salesmen's Association of Paper and Allied Industries
SAPC . . . . . . Shipowners Association of the Pacific Coast
SAPC . . . . . . Small Arms Post Competition
SAPC . . . . . . Suspended Acoustical-Plaster Ceiling (Technical drawings)
SAPE . . . . Society for Automation in Professional Education
SAPE . . . . Solenoid Array Pattern Evaluator
SAPFU . . . . . . Surpassing All Previous Foul Ups (Military slang)
SAPhA . . . . . . Student American Pharmaceutical Association
SAPI . . . . Salesmen's Association of the Paper Industry
SAPIR . . . . . . System of Automatic Processing and Indexing of Reports
SAPL . . . . Society for Animal Protective Legislation
SAPL . . . . Spartan-Approved Parts List
SAPO . . . . Subarea Petroleum Office
SAPP . . . . Skeletal Axis of Palp
SAPP . . . . Sodium Acid Pyrophosphate (Meat additive)
SAPP . . . . Soul Assurance Prayer Plan
SAPPMA . . . . . San Antonio Procurement and Production Materiel Area (Military)
SAPR . . . . Semi-Annual Progress Report
SAPS . . . . Servico de Alimentacao da Providencia Social (Brazil)
SAPS . . . . Surety Agents Promotional Society
SAPUC . . . . . . Sintered Aluminum Powder-Clad Uranium Carbide
SAPW . . . . . . United Stone and Allied Products Workers of America
SAQS . . . . Single Agency Qualification Standards (Aviation)
SAR . . . . National Society, Sons of the American Revolution
SAR . . . . Sales Authorization Request
SAR . . . . Sea-Air Rescue
SAR . . . . Search and Rescue
SAR . . . . Selected Acquisition Report (Air Force)
SAR . . . . Semi-Annual Report
SAR . . . . Semi-Automatic Rifle (Army)
SAR . . . . Single-Axis Reference
SAR . . . . Single-Bit Alternation Recording
SAR . . . . Society of Authors Representatives
SAR . . . . Sons of the American Revolution
SAR . . . . South African Republic
SAR . . . . Special Aeronautical Requirement (Navy)
SAR . . . . Specific Acoustic Resistance
SAR . . . . Stable Auroral Red (Arc) (Geophysics)
SAR . . . . Storage Address Register
SAR . . . . Submarine Advanced Reactor
SAR . . . . Successive Accelerated Replacement
SAR . . . . Support Air Request (Net) (Navy communications)
SAR . . . . Synthetic Antenna RADAR

SAR . . . . Synthetic Array RADAR
SAR . . . . System Analysis Report
SARA . . . . Saratoga National Historical Park
SARA . . . . Search and Rescue Aid
SARA . . . . Sequential Automatic Recorder and Annunciator
SARA . . . . Still Another Response Averager
SARAH . . . . . . Search and Rescue and Homing
SARAH . . . . . . Semi-Active RADAR Alternate Head
SARAH . . . . . . Semiautomatic Range Azimuth and Height (Subsystem)
SARARC . . . . . Subauroral Red Arc
SARB . . . . State Air Resources Board
SARBE . . . . . . Search and Rescue Beacon
SARBIM . . . . . Serikat Buruh Industri Bahan Makanan Rakjat (People's Food Processors' Union) (Indonesia)
SARBUBSI . . . . Serikat Buruh Betjak Seluruh Indonesia (Pedicab Workers' Union) (Indonesia)
SARBUFIS . . . . Serikat Buruh Film Senidrama Indonesia (Union of Film Artists of Indonesia)
SARBUKRI . . . . Serikat Buruh Kristen Indonesia (Union of Christian Workers of Indonesia)
SARBUKSI . . . . Serikat Buruh Kehutanan Seluruh Indonesia (Forestry Workers' Union of Indonesia)
SARBUMRI . . . . Serikat Buruh Metaal Republik Indonesia
SARBUPRI . . . . Serikat Buruh Perkebunan Republik Indonesia (Plantation Workers' Union of the Republic of Indonesia)
SARBUTRI . . . . Serikat Buruh Textil Republik Indonesia (Textile Workers' Union) (Indonesia)
SARC . . . . Secure Airborne RADAR Control
SARC . . . . Systems Analysis and Research Corporation
SARCALM . . . . Synthetic Array RADAR Command Air-Launched Missile
SARCAP . . . . . Search and Rescue – Civil Air Patrol
SARCC . . . . . . Search and Rescue Coordination Center (Air Force)
SARCCUS . . . . South African Regional Committee for Conservation and Utilization of Soil
SARD . . . . Simulated Aircraft RADAR Data
SARD . . . . Special Airlift Requirement Directive (Air Force)
SARD . . . . Special Airlift Requirement Document (Army)
SARDA . . . . . . State and Regional Defense Airlift Plan (FAA, Civil Defense)
SARDC . . . . . . Small-Arms Research and Development Center (Army)
SARDET . . . . . Search and Rescue Detachment (Navy)
SARDIP . . . . . . Stricken Aircraft Reclamation and Disposal Program (Navy)
SARDPO . . . . . San Antonio Research & Development Procurement Office (Military)
SAREP . . . . . . Speech and Reading Enrichment Program
SARGUN . . . . . Synthetic Aperture RADAR Gun
SARIPADI . . . . Serikat Pamong Desa Indonesia (Village Officials' Union)
SARLA . . . . . . South African Rock Lobster Association (Defunct)
SARLANT . . . . Search and Rescue, Atlantic (Coast Guard)
SARNI . . . . . . Serikat Nelajan Indonesia (Sailors' Union) (Indonesia)
SAROAD . . . . . Storage and Retrieval of Aerometric Data (Environmental Protection Agency)
SARP . . . . Schedule and Report Procedure (NASA)
SARP . . . . Signal Automatic RADAR Processing
SARP . . . . Standards and Recommended Practices
SARS . . . . Secretary of the Army Research and Study (Fellowship)
SARS . . . . Single-Axis Reference System
SARS . . . . Solar Array Reorientation System
SARS . . . . Synthetic Array RADAR System
SARSIM . . . . . Search and Rescue Simulation (Coast Guard)
SART . . . . St. Alban's Repertory Theater
SART . . . . Seattle Army Terminal
SARTEL . . . . . Search and Rescue, Telephone (Coast Guard)
SARUS . . . . . . Search and Rescue Using Satellites (Air Force)
SAS . . . . Satellite Attack Sensor
SAS . . . . Scandinavian Airlines System
SAS . . . . Sections Administratives Specialisees (French Army)
SAS . . . . Self-Adaptive System
SAS . . . . Signal Analysis System
SAS . . . . Small Astronomy Satellite
SAS . . . . Snake Approach Scale (Psychology)
SAS . . . . Snap Action Switch
SAS . . . . Society for Applied Spectroscopy
SAS . . . . Society of Australasian Specialists
SAS . . . . Sodium Alkane Sulfonate (A detergent)
SAS . . . . Sodium Aluminum Sulfate
SAS . . . . Solar Array Structure
SAS . . . . Solar Array System
SAS . . . . Solar Aspect Sensor
SAS . . . . Sound Amplification System
SAS . . . . Southern Appalachian Studies
SAS . . . . Space Activity Suit
SAS . . . . Spacecraft Antenna System
SAS . . . . Special Air Service (British)
SAS . . . . Special Ammunition Site
SAS . . . . Special Ammunition Stockage (Army)

SAS . . . . Stability Augmentation System (FAA)
SAS . . . . Sterile Aqueous Suspension
SAS . . . . Stimulo-Auto-Soroterapia (Medicine)
SAS . . . . Supersonic Attack Seaplane
SAS . . . . Suspended Aluminosilicate
SAS . . . . Suspended Array System (of submarine detection)
SAS . . . . System Analysis Study
SASAT . . . . . . Shipboard Anti-Submarine Attack Teacher (Navy)
SASC . . . . Semi-Automatic Stock Control
SASCOM . . . . . Southern Atlantic Satellite Communication
SASCOM . . . . . Special Ammunition Support Command (Army)
SASD . . . . Static Adjustable Speed Drive
SASDT . . . . . . Ships and Aircraft Supplemental Data Tables (Navy)
SASE . . . . Self-Addressed Stamped Envelope
SASI . . . . Society of Air Safety Investigators
SASI . . . . Southern Association of Science and Industry
SASI . . . . System on Automotive Safety Information
SASIDS . . . . . Stochastic Adaptive Sequential Information Dissemination System
SASJ . . . . Self-Aligning Swivel Joint
SASK . . . . Saskatchewan (Canadian province)
SASM . . . . Society for Automation in Science and Mathematics
SASM . . . . Special Assistant for Strategic Mobility (Air Force)
SASN . . . . Special Assistant to the Secretary of the Navy
SASO . . . . Senior Air Staff Officer (British)
SASP . . . . Special Ammunition Supply Point
SASP . . . . Stand Alone Support Program
SASP . . . . State Agency for Surplus Property
SASS . . . . Society for the Advancement of Scandinavian Study
SASS . . . . Society for Automation in the Social Sciences
SASS . . . . Special Aircraft Service Shop
SASSE . . . . . . Synchronous Altitude Spin-Stabilized Experiment
SASSIF . . . . . . Self-Adjusting System of Scientific Information Flow
SASSY . . . . . . Supported Activities Supply System (Marine Corps)
SAST . . . . Service Announcements in Science and Technology (NTIS)
SAST . . . . Society for the Advancement of Space Travel
SASTE . . . . . . Semi-Automatic Shop Test Equipment
SASV . . . . Snap Action Spool Valve
SAT . . . . Safe Arming Time
SAT . . . . Saturday
SAT . . . . Scholastic Aptitude Test
SAT . . . . School Ability Test (Psychology)
SAT . . . . School of Applied Tactics (AAFSAT)
SAT . . . . Scientific Advisory Team (Navy)
SAT . . . . Security Alert Team (Military)
SAT . . . . Semiautomatic Test Equipment (NASA)
SAT . . . . Sennacieca Asocio Tutmonde (Nationless Worldwide Association)
                  (Promotes use of Esperanto)
SAT . . . . Silicon Annular Transistor
SAT . . . . Sine Acido Thymonucleico (Without Thymonucleic Acid)
SAT . . . . Snap Action Thermostat
SAT . . . . Speaker Authentication Technique
SAT . . . . Special Assistance Team (Navy)
SAT . . . . Specific Aptitude Test
SAT . . . . Stanford Achievement Test (Education)
SAT . . . . Static Air Temperature
SAT . . . . Stepped Atomic Time (National Bureau of Standards)
SAT . . . . Subscriber Access Terminal
SATA . . . . . . Sociedade Acoriana de Transportes Aereos, Ltda.
SATA . . . . . . Something About the Author (Reference publication)
SATA . . . . . . Student Air Travel Association
SATA . . . . . . Subsonic Aerodynamic Testing Association
SATAF . . . . . . Site Alteration Task Force (Air Force)
SATAM . . . . . . Syndicat Autonome des Travailleurs de la Alimentation de Madagascar
                  (Autonomous Union of Food Workers of Madagascar)
SATAN . . . . . . Satellite Active Nullifier (Antisatellite weapon)
SATAN . . . . . . Satellite Automatic Tracking Antenna
SATAN . . . . . . Sensor for Airborne Terrain Analysis
SATANS . . . . . Static and Transient Analysis, Nonlinear, Shells (Computer program)
                  (Navy)
SATAR . . . . . . Satellite for Aerospace Research (NASA)
SATB . . . . . . Soprano, Alto, Tenor, Bass (Music)
SATB . . . . . . Specific Aptitude Test Battery
SATC . . . . . . Students Army Training Corps
SATC . . . . . . Suspended Acoustical-Tile Ceiling (Technical drawings)
SATCC . . . . . Southern Air Traffic Control Centre (British)
SATCHMO . . . . Satchel Mouth (Nickname of late trumpeter Louis Armstrong)
SATCO . . . . . . Signal Automatic Air Traffic Control System
SATCO . . . . . . Supervisory Air Traffic Control Organizations (FAA)
SATCOM . . . . . Committee on Scientific and Technical Communication
SATCOM . . . . . Satellite Communications Agency (Army)
SATCOM . . . . . Scientific and Technical Communication

SATCOMA . . . . Satellite Communications Agency (AEC/DCA)
SATD . . . . . . Seattle Army Terminal Detachment
SATDPI . . . . . . Salesmen's Association of the Textile Dyeing and Printing Industry
SATE . . . . . . Semi-Automatic Test Equipment
SATEC . . . . . . Semi-Automatic Technical Control
SATEC . . . . . . Societe d'Aide Technique et de Cooperation (An independent French
                  company)
SATELCO . . . . . Satellite Telecommunications Company (Japanese-American firm)
SATFOR . . . . . Special Air Task Force (Navy)
SATFY . . . . . . Satisfactory
SATGA . . . . . . Societe Aerienne de Transport Guyane Antilles (French Guiana Air
                  Transport)
SATH . . . . . . St. Thomas National Historic Site
SATIF . . . . . . Scientific and Technical Information Facility (NASA)
SATIN . . . . . . SAGE (Semi-Automatic Ground Environment) Air Traffic Integration
SATIRE . . . . . Semiautomatic Technical Information Retrieval
SATK . . . . . . Strike Attack
SATO . . . . . . South American Travel Organization
SATO . . . . . . Synthetic Aircraft Turbine Oil
SATP . . . . . . Small Arms Target Practice (Navy)
SATP . . . . . . Stabilization, Acquisition, Tracking and Pointing
SATPATT . . . . . Satellite Paper Tape Transfer
SATR . . . . . . So As To Reach (Aviation)
SATRAC . . . . . Satellite Automatic Terminal Rendezvous and Coupling
SATRAM . . . . . Systeme d'Atterrissage a Trajectoires Multiples (Aviation)
SATS . . . . . . Short Airfield for Tactical Support (Marine Corps)
SATS . . . . . . Small Airfield (for) Tactical Support (Air Force)
SATSA . . . . . . Signal Aviation Test and Support Activity
SATSLAM . . . . Satellite-Tracked Submarine-Launched Antimissile
SATT . . . . . . Semi-Automatic Transistor Tester
SATT . . . . . . Strowger Automatic Toll Ticketing
SATU . . . . . . Singapore Association of Trade Unions
SATU . . . . . . South African Typographical Union
SATUC . . . . . . South African Trade Union Council
SATW . . . . . . Society of American Travel Writers
SAU . . . . Search Attack Unit
SAU . . . . Spectrum Analysis Unit
SAU . . . . Surface Attack Unit
SAUCERS . . . . . Saucer and Unexplained Celestial Events Research Society
SAUFI . . . . . . Sindacato Autonomo Unificato Ferrovieri Italiani (Autonomous Union of
                  Italian Railroad Workers)
SAU & G . . . . San Antonio, Uvalde & Gulf Railroad Company
SAUS . . . . . . Soccer Association of the United States
SAV . . . . Savannah Electric & Power Co. (NYSE symbol)
SAV . . . . Service Availability (AT & T)
SAV . . . . Stock at Valuation
SAV . . . . Student Alternatives to Violence (An organization)
SAVBOND . . . War Savings Bonds (Allotment for purchase) (Navy)
SAVE . . . . . . Save All Valley Environment (Livermore, California)
SAVE . . . . . . Service Activities of Voluntary Engineers
SAVE . . . . . . Shortages and Valuable Excesses (Navy)
SAVE . . . . . . Society of American Value Engineers
SAVE . . . . . . Stop Addiction through Voluntary Effort
SAVE . . . . . . Student Action Voters for Ecology (An organization)
SAVE . . . . . . System for Automatic Value Exchange (Data processing)
SAVER . . . . . Stowable Aircrew Vehicle Escape Rotoseat
SAVES . . . . . States Audiovisual Education Study
SAVOR . . . . . Single-Actuated Voice Recorder
SAW . . . . . . Semiautomatic Weapons
SAW . . . . . . Small Arms Weapon
SAW . . . . . . South Albuquerque Works (AEC)
SAW . . . . . . Special Air Warfare
SAWAS . . . . . South African Women's Auxiliary Services
SAWBET . . . . . Supply Action Will Be Taken
SAWC . . . . . . Special Air Warfare Center
SAWE . . . . . . Society of Aeronautical Weight Engineers
SAWF . . . . . . Special Air Warfare Force(s)
SAWg . . . . . . Strategic Aerospace Wing (Air Force)
SAWMARCS . . . Standard Aircraft Weapon Monitor and Release Control System
SAWRS . . . . . Supplementary Airway Weather Reports
SAWRS . . . . . Supplementary Aviation Weather Reporting Station
SAWS . . . . . . Small Arms Weapons System
SAX . . . . Southwest Airmotive Co. (NYSE symbol)
SAXA . . . . . . Slotted Array X-Band Antenna
SAXL . . . . . . Short-Arc Xenon Lamp
SAY . . . . Sayre & Fisher Brick Company (NYSE symbol)
SAZO . . . . . . Seeker Azimuth Orientation (Air Force)
SB . . . . Bachelor of Science
SB . . . . Sales Book
SB . . . . Savings Bank
SB . . . . Scouting-Bombing Plane (When prefixed to Navy aircraft designation)

SB	Scrieve Board
SB	Secondary Battery (Navy)
SB	Secondary Buffer (Chemistry)
SB	Securing Bands
SB	Section Base (Military)
SB	Selection Board
SB	Selective Bibliography
SB	Senate Bill (in state legislatures)
SB	Senior Beadle (Ancient Order of Foresters)
SB	Separately Binned
SB	Service Bulletin
SB	Shipbuilding (Navy)
SB	Shipping Board
SB	Short Bill
SB	Signal Battalion (Army)
SB	Signal Boatswain
SB	Simultaneous Broadcast(ing)
SB	Single Braid
SB	Sitzungsberichte (Used in German journals)
SB	Slow Burning
SB	Small Bonds
SB	Small Business
SB	Smooth Bore (Ballistics)
SB	Solid Body (Technical drawings)
SB	South Buffalo Railway Company (AAR code)
SB	Southbound
SB	Special Bibliography
SB	Splash Block
SB	Stabilized Breakdown
SB	Standard Bead
SB	Standard Brands, Inc. (NYSE symbol)
SB	Standby Base (Air Force)
SB	Stanford-Binet (Intelligence test)
SB	Statement of Billing
SB	Steamboat
Sb	Stibium (Antimony) (Chemical element)
SB	Stolen Base(s) (Baseball)
SB	Stove Bolt
SB	Straight Binary
SB	Stretcher-Bearer
SB	Stuffing Box
SB	Sub-Bituminous
SB	Submarine Base (Navy)
SB	Submarine Fog Bell (Mechanical) (Maps and charts)
SB	Supply Bulletin
SB	Support Box
SB	Switchboard (Navy)
SB	Switchboard Operator (Navy)
S/B	Selection Board (Military)
S/B	Should Be
S & B	Sterilization and Bath
S³ Bᴾ	System Source Selection Board Procedure (Air Force)
SBA	Shaped Beam Antenna
SBA	Sick Bay Attendant (Navy)
SBA	Small Business Administration
SBA	Standard Beam Approach (British aircraft landing method)
SB of A	Smaller Business of America
SBAAM	Small Business Association of Apparel Manufacturers
SBAC	Society of British Aircraft Constructors
SBAC	Society of British Aerospace Companies
SBAE	Stabilized Bombing Approach Equipment (Navy)
SBAMA	San Bernardino Air Materiel Area
SBANE	Smaller Business Association of New England
SBAP	Society of Business Advisory Professions
SBASI	Single Budge Apollo Standard Initiator (Aerospace)
SBB	Self-Balancing Bridge
SBB	Serikat Buruh Batik (Batik Workers' Union) (Indonesia)
SBC	Saint Basil's College (Connecticut)
SBC	Saint Benedict College (Indiana)
SBC	Saint Bernard College (Alabama)
SBC	Simpson Bible College (California)
SBC	Small Bayonet Cap
SBC	Solid Bowl Centrifuge
SBC	SONAR Breakout Cable
SBC	Sonora-Baja California Railway (AAR code)
SBC	Southeastern Bible College (Florida)
SBC	Southern Baptist College (Arkansas)
SBC	Southern Baptist Convention
SBC	Space Borne Computer
SBC	Standard Boundary Condition
SBC	Start Breguet Cruise (SST)

SBC	Stokely-Van Camp, Inc. (NYSE symbol)
SBC	Sue Bennett College (Kentucky)
SBC	Summary Billing Card
SBC	Sweet Briar College (Virginia)
SBCA	Saint Bernard Club of America
SBCA	Soybean Council of America
SBCC	Separate Bias, Common Control
SBCED	Santa Barbara (California) Citizens for Environment Defense
SBCO	Shipbuilding Company
SBCORP	Shipbuilding Corporation
SBCP	Spanish Base Construction Program
SB & CR	Stock Balance and Consumption Report
SBCS	Statni Banka Ceskoslovenska
SBCU	Sensor-Based Control Unit (Data processing)
SBD	"Dauntless" single-engine scout-bomber (Navy symbol)
SBD	Seaboard Air Line R. R. Company (NYSE symbol) (Later, SCI)
SBD	Standard Bibliographic Description
SBDC	Shipbuilding and Drydock Company
SBDC	Small Business Development Center
SBDC	Small Business Development Corporation
SBDL	Solid Blank Delay Line
SBDP	Serikat Buruh Djawatan Perindustrian (Department of Industry Workers' Union) (Indonesia)
SBDPU	Serikat Buruh Djawantan Pekerdjaan Umun (Public Works' Union) (Indonesia)
SBDT	Surface Barrier Diffused Transistor
SBE	Pimpinan Pusat Serikat Buruh Es (Ice Workers' Union) (Indonesia)
SBE	Simple Boolean Expression (Mathematics)
SBE	Solar Beam Experiment(s)
SBE	Subacute Bacterial Endocarditis (Medicine)
SBED	Serial Bit Error Detector
SBER	Self-Balancing Electronics Recorder
SBER	Subbit Error Rate
SBES	S-Band Exciter System
SBETC	Small Business Export Trade Corporation
SBEU	Singapore Bank Employees' Union
SBF	Scientific Balloon Facility
SBF	Short Backfire (Antenna)
SBF	Southern Baptist Foundation
SBFC	Standby for Further Clearance (Aviation)
SBG	Strategic Bomber Group
SBGI	Serikat Buruh Gelas Indonesia (Glass Workers' Union) (Indonesia)
SBGP	Serikat Buruh Gula Proklamasi (Sugar Workers' Union) (Indonesia)
SBGP	Strategic Bomber Group (Military)
SBGSN	Serikat Buruh Garam dan Soda Negeri (Salt Workers' Association) (Indonesia)
SBH	Scottish Board of Health
SBHEU	Singapore Business Houses Employees' Union
SBHRT	Serikat Buruh Hotel, Rumah-Makan dan Toko (Hotel, Restaurant and Shops' Workers' Union) (Indonesia)
SBI	Serikat Buruh Industri (Industrial Workers' Union) (Indonesia)
SBI	Soviet Bureau of Information
SBI	Steel Boiler Institute
SBI	Sterchi Brothers Stores, Incorporated (NYSE symbol)
SBIC	Small Business Investment Company (Generic term)
SBICo	Small Business Investment Company (Generic term)
SBII	Serikat Buruh Islam Indonesia
SBIL	Serikat Buruh Islam Indonesia (Central Islamic Labor Union of Indonesia)
SBIM	Serikat Buruh Industri Metal (Metal Industries Workers' Union) (Indonesia)
SBIR	Serikat Buruh Industri Ringan (Small Industry Workers' Union) (Indonesia)
SBJ	Serikat Buruh Jodium (Iodine Factory Workers' Union) (Indonesia)
SBJC	Santa Barbara Junior College (California)
SBK	Serikat Buruh Kehutanan (Indonesian National Forestry Workers' Union)
SBK	Serikat Buruh Kependjaaran (Prisons Workers' Unions) (Indonesia)
SBK	South Brooklyn Railway Company (AAR code)
SBK	Storer Broadcasting Company (NYSE symbol)
SBKA	Serikat Buruh Kereta Api (Railway Labor Union) (Indonesia)
SBKB	Serikat Buruh Kendaraan Bermotor (Union of Motorized Transport Workers) (Indonesia)
SBKP	Serikat Buruh Kementerian Pertahanan (Defense Ministry Union) (Indonesia)
SBL	Sealed Beam Lamp
SBL	Serikat Buruh Logam (Metal Workers' Union) (Indonesia)
SBL	Society of Biblical Literature (Formerly, SBLE)
SBL	Staphylococcal Bacteriophage Lysate
SBL	Styrene-Butadiene Latice
SBLE	Society of Biblical Literature and Exegesis (Later, SBL)
SBLGI	Serikat Buruh Listrik dan Gas Indonesia (Union of Electrical and Gas Workers) (Indonesia)
SBLI	Savings Bank Life Insurance
SBLP	Simplified Bank Loan Participation Plan (Small Business Administration)

SBLSA........ Small Business and Labor Surplus Advisor
SBM........ St. Louis, Brownsville & Mexico Railway Company (AAR code)
SBMA ...... Steel Bar Mills Association
SBME .... Society of Business Magazine Editors
SBMI .... School Bus Manufacturers Institute
SBMPL ...... Simultaneous Binaural Mid-Plane Localization (Audiometry)
SBMSI....... Serikat Buruh Minjak Shell Indonesia (Union of Oil Workers for Shell Indonesia)
SBMW ...... Serikat Buruh Maclaine, Watson (Maclaine Watson Company Workers' Union) (Indonesia)
SBN........ Standard Book Numbering
SBNL....... Submarine Base, New London (Connecticut) (Navy)
SBNO....... Senior British Naval Officer
SBNOWA .... Senior British Naval Officer, Western Atlantic
SBO .... Specific Behavioral Objectives (Air Transport Association)
SBOA .... Specialty Bakery Owners of America
SBOLS ...... Shadow Box Optical Landing System
SBOM....... Soy Bean Oil Meal
SBOSI....... Serikat Buruh Obat Seluruh Indonesia (All Indonesian Medicinal Factory Workers' Union)
SBOST ...... Slavonic Benevolent Order of the State of Texas
SBP .... Serikat Buruh Pegadaian (Pawnshop Workers' Union) (Indonesia)
SBP .... Serikat Buruh Penerbangan (Airways' Unions) (Indonesia)
SBP .... Society of Biological Psychiatry
SBP .... Space Borne Programmer
SBP .... Special Block Purchase
SBP .... Standard Brands Paints Co. (NYSE symbol)
SBPD ...... Society of Business Publication Designers
SBPG ...... Serikat Buruh Perusahaan Gula (Sugar Workers' Union) (Indonesia)
SBPI....... Serikat Buruh Pelabuhan Indonesia (Dockworkers' Union) (Indonesia)
SBPI....... Serikat Buruh Pendjahit Indonesia (Tailors' Union) (Indonesia)
SBPKB...... Serikat Buruh Persuahaan Kaju dan Bangunan (Indonesian Building, Road and Irrigation Workers' Union)
SBPP ...... Serikat Buruh Pelebuhan dan Pelajaran (Dockworkers' Union) (Indonesia)
SBPPK ..... Serikat Buruh Pendidikan, Pengadjaran dan Kebudjaan (Department of Education Workers' Union) (Indonesia)
SBPT....... Serikat Buruh Perhubungan dan Transport (Communications and Transportation Workers' Union) (Indonesia)
SBPT....... Serikat Buruh Pertambangan Timah (Tin Mine Labor Union) (Indonesia)
SBPU ...... Serikat Buruh Pekerdjaan Umum (Public Workers' Ministry Union) (Indonesia)
SBQ .... Serikat Buruh Qantas (Qantas Labor Union) (Indonesia)
SBR .... Seat Bucket Read
SBR .... Society for Biological Rhythm
SBR .... Styrene-Butadiene Rubber
SBRC ...... Santa Barbara Research Center (Hughes Aircraft Company)
SBRI....... Serikat Buruh Rokok Indonesia (Cigarette Factory Workers' Union) (Indonesia)
SB-RK ..... Bomber (Russian aircraft symbol)
SBRP ...... Sonic Boom Research Program
SBRRI...... Serikat Buruh Radio Republik Indonesia (Indonesian Broadcasting Workers' Association)
SBS .... Serially Balanced Sequence (Statistics)
SBS .... Single-Business Service
SBS .... Sisters of the Blessed Sacrament (Roman Catholic religious order)
SBS .... Spaniel Breeders Society
SBS .... Spanish Benevolent Society "La Nacional"
SBS .... Special Block Sale
SBS .... Straight Binary Second
SBS .... Strategic Balkan Services (World War II)
SBS .... Strategic Bombing Survey
SBS .... Swiss Benevolent Society of New York
SBSC ...... Saint Bernardine of Siena College (New York)
SBSC ...... Saint Bernard's Seminary and College (New York)
SBSC ...... Separate Bias, Single Control
SBSI....... Serikat Buruh Seluruh Indonesia (All Indonesian Laborers' Union)
SBSK ...... Samodzielna Brygada Strzelcow Karpackich (Poland)
SBSKK ..... Serikat Buruh Sepatu Keradjinan Kulit Karet (Shoe Workers' Union) (Indonesia)
SBStJ ...... Serving Brother, Order of St. John of Jerusalem (British)
SBSUSA...... Sport Balloon Society of the United States
SBT .... Serikat Buruh Tambang (Mine Workers' Union) (Indonesia)
SBT .... Serikat Buruh Teknik (Technicians' Union) (Indonesia)
SBT .... Serikat Buruh Tekstil (Textile Workers' Union) (Indonesia)
SBT .... Small Boat
SBT .... Sodium Bitartrate
SBT .... Space-Based Tug (NASA)
SBT .... Surface Barrier Transistor
SBT .... System Burning Time
SBTP....... Serikat Buruh Teknik dan Pelabuhan (Technical and Harbour Workers' Union) (Indonesia)

SBTS ...... Shore-Based Tracking System
SBTT....... Serikat Buruh Tambang Timah (Tin Mine Laborers' Union) (Indonesia)
SBTU ...... Serikat Buruh Teknik Umum (Indonesia)
SBU .... Saint Bonaventure University (New York)
SBV .... Semi-Automatic Bleeder Valve
SBVC ...... San Bernardino Valley College (California)
SBW .... Seaboard and Western Airlines, Inc. (American Stock Exchange symbol) (Later, SWA)
SBW .... Spectral Bandwidth
SBW .... Steel Basement Window
SBWG ...... Strategic Bomb Wing (Military)
SBWU ...... Singapore Bus Workers' Union
SBX .... S-Band Transponder
SBX .... Student Book Exchange
SBY .... Selby Shoe Company (NYSE symbol)
SBY .... Standby
SBZ .... Sowjetische Besatzungszone (Soviet Occupation Zone) (East Germany)
SC .... Sacra Congregatio (Sacred Congregation)
SC .... Sad Case (An unpopular person) (Teen slang)
SC .... Sales Costs
SC .... Salesianorum Congregatio (Congregation of St. Francis of Sales) (Salesian Fathers) (Roman Catholic religious order)
SC .... Salmagundi Club
SC .... Salvage Charges
SC .... Same Case (Law)
SC .... Sandia Corporation
SC .... Sanitary Corps
Sc .... Scandium (Chemical element)
SC .... School Certificate
SC .... Schwann Cell (Biology)
SC .... Seamen's Center
SC .... Seat Cabs
SC .... Security Council of the United Nations
SC .... See Copy
SC .... Self-Closing
SC .... Self-Contained
SC .... Senatus Consulto (By the Decree of the Senate)
SC .... Separate Cover
SC .... Sequence Counter
SC .... Service Club (Military enlisted men's club)
SC .... Service Command (Marine Corps)
SC .... Shaped Charge (of explosive)
SC .... Sharp Cash
SC .... Shell Transport & Trading Company, Ltd. (NYSE symbol)
SC .... Shipping Container
SC .... Ship's Cook (Navy)
SC .... Short Circuit
SC .... Signal Conditioner
SC .... Signal Corps (Army)
SC .... Sine-Cosine
SC .... Single Case
SC .... Single Circuit (Electricity)
SC .... Single Column
SC .... Single Comb
SC .... Single Contact (Switch)
SC .... Single Counter
SC .... Single Crochet
SC .... Single Crystal
SC .... Sisters of Charity (Roman Catholic religious order)
SC .... Sized and Calendered (Paper)
SC .... Skin Conductance
SC .... Small Caps (Printing term)
SC .... Smooth Contour (Technical drawings)
SC .... So-Called
SC .... Socialist Commentary (A publication)
SC .... Societas Fratrum Sacris Cordis (Brothers of the Sacred Heart) (Roman Catholic religious order)
SC .... Soil Characteristics
SC .... Solar Cell
SC .... Solid-State Circuits
SC .... Source Code
SC .... South Carolina
SC .... Southern California
SC .... Southern Conference
SC .... Spacecraft
SC .... Special Circuit
SC .... Special Circular
SC .... Special Constable
SC .... Specific Cueing
SC .... Spermatocyte
SC .... Spread Correlation

SC . . . . Spreading Coefficient
SC . . . . Staff College (Military)
SC . . . . Staff Corps
SC . . . . Stage Center (A stage direction)
SC . . . . Steel Casting
SC . . . . Stored Command
SC . . . . Stratocumulus (Meteorology)
SC . . . . Strike Command (Military)
SC . . . . Su Cuenta (Your Account) (Business and trade) (Spain)
SC . . . . Subcutaneous (Injection) (Medicine)
SC . . . . Submarine Chaser (110 foot)
SC . . . . Sudden Commencement
SC . . . . Sugar Coated
SC . . . . Summary Court (Navy)
SC . . . . Sumter & Choctaw Railway (AAR code)
SC . . . . Supercalendered (Paper)
SC . . . . Superimposed Current
SC . . . . Supervisory Control
SC . . . . Supply Catalog (Military)
SC . . . . Supply Control (Military)
SC . . . . Supply Corps
SC . . . . Support Command (Army)
SC . . . . Supreme Court
SC . . . . Surface Combustion (Reducing gas process)
SC . . . . Swimming Club
SC . . . . Synchro-Cyclotron
SC . . . . Systems Command (Air Force)
S-C . . . . Secret and Confidential Files (Navy)
S/C . . . . Service Ceiling
S/C . . . . Short Circuit
S/C . . . . Spacecraft/Capsule
S/C . . . . Statement of Charges (Army)
S/C . . . . Subcontractor(s)
S & C . . . . . . Shipper and Carrier (Business and trade)
S & C . . . . . . Sized and Calendered (Paper)
S & C . . . . . . Strategic and Critical Raw Material
S en C . . . . . . Sociedad en Comandita (Limited partnership company) (Spain)
SCA . . . . Saluki Club of America
SCA . . . . Satellite Committee Agency (Army)
SCA . . . . Schipperke Club of America
SCA . . . . School and College Ability (Test)
SCA . . . . Science Clubs of America
SCA . . . . Screen Composers' Association
SCA . . . . Selectivity Clear Accumulator
SCA . . . . Senior Citizens of America
SCA . . . . Service Cinematographique des Armees (France)
SCA . . . . Service and Compliance Administration (US wage/price controls agency)
SCA . . . . Shipbuilders Council of America
SCA . . . . Shooters Club of America
SCA . . . . Ski Council of America
SCA . . . . Society for Creative Anachronism
SCA . . . . Soybean Council of America
SCA . . . . Speech Communication Association
SCA . . . . Spinach Carbonic Anhydrase (Enzyme)
SCA . . . . Sterba Curtain Antenna
SCA . . . . Stock Company Association
SCA . . . . Student Conservation Association
SCA . . . . Subsidiary Communications Authorization (Facilities used to transmit background music to subscribing customers)
SCA . . . . Summary Cost Account
SCA . . . . Switch Control Assembly
SCA . . . . Switzerland Cheese Association
SCA . . . . Synagogue Council of America
SC of A . . . . . Samoyed Club of America
SCAAP . . . . . Special Commonwealth African Assistance Plan
SCAD . . . . . . Schenectady Army Depot
SCAD . . . . . . Small Current Amplifying Device
SCAD . . . . . . State Commission Against Discrimination
SCAD . . . . . . Subsonic Cruise Armed Decoy (Air Force)
SCADA . . . . . Student Coalition Against Drug Abuse
SCADAR . . . . Scatter Detection and Ranging
SCADS . . . . . Scanning Celestial Attitude Determination System
SCADS . . . . . Sioux City Air Defense Sector (ADC)
SCAEF . . . . . Supreme Commander, Allied Expeditionary Force (World War II)
SCAG . . . . . . Saigon Civil Assistance Group
SCAJAP . . . . Shipping Control Administrator Japan
SCAL . . . . . . Silver City Airways, Limited
SCALE . . . . . Space Checkout and Launch Equipment
SCALO . . . . . Scanning Local Oscillator
SCALP . . . . . Students Concerned About Legal Prices (Student legal action organization)
SCAM . . . . . . Subsonic Cruise Armed Missile/Decoy

SCAMA . . . . . Skewed Circular Arc Method of Analysis
SCAMA . . . . . Switching Conference and Monitoring Arrangement (NASA)
SCAMP . . . . . Sectionalized Carrier and Multipurpose Vehicle (Military)
SCAMP . . . . . Signal Conditioning Amplifier
SCAMP . . . . . Single Channel Amplitude Monopulse Processing
SCAMP . . . . . Space-Controlled Army Measurements Probe
SCAMP . . . . . Standard Configuration and Modification Program
SCAN . . . . . . Selected Current Aerospace Notices (NASA)
SCAN . . . . . . Self-Correcting Automatic Navigator
SCAN . . . . . . Southern California Answering Network (Electronic link of many libraries, communities, etc.)
SCAN . . . . . . Stock Market Computer Answering Service
SCAN . . . . . . Switched Circuit Automatic Network (Army)
SCAND . . . . . Single Crystal Automatic Neutron Diffractometer
SCANDOC . . . Scandinavian Documentation Center (Washington, DC)
SCANS . . . . . Scheduling and Control by Automated Network System
SCANS . . . . . System Checkout Automatic Network Simulator
SCAO . . . . . . Senior Civil Affairs Officer
SCAP . . . . . . Silent Compact Auxiliary Power
SCAP . . . . . . Supreme Commander of the Allied Powers in Japan
SCAPE . . . . . Self-Contained Atmospheric Personnel (or Protective) Ensemble (Suit) (Aerospace)
SCAR . . . . . . Satellite Capture and Retrieval
SCAR . . . . . . Scandinavian Council for Applied Research
SCAR . . . . . . Scientific Committee on Antarctic Research
SCAR . . . . . . Signal Conditioner Assembly Request
SCAR . . . . . . Special Committee on Atlantic Research
SCAR . . . . . . Special International Committee on Antarctic Research
SCAR . . . . . . Strike Control and Reconnaissance (Aircraft)
SCAR . . . . . . Subcaliber Aircraft Rocket
SCAR . . . . . . Submarine Celestial Altitude Recorder (Navy)
SCAR . . . . . . Sun Caliber Aircraft Rocket
SCARDE . . . . Study Committee on Analysis of Research, Development, and Engineering
SCARE . . . . . Students Concerned About a Ravaged Environment (Organization in Cloquet, Minnesota)
SCARF . . . . . Santa Cruz Acoustic Range Facility
SCARF . . . . . Side-Looking Coherent All-Range Focused
SCARF . . . . . Survey of Change and Residential Finance (Census Bureau)
SCARP . . . . . Society for Comic Art Research and Preservation
SCARS . . . . . SACEUR (Supreme Allied Commander Europe) Command Alerting Reporting System
SCART . . . . . Sperry Continuity and Resistance Tester
SCARWAF . . . . Special Category Army Personnel with Air Force
SCAS . . . . . . Southwest Center for Advanced Studies
SCAT . . . . . . School and College Ability Test (of ETS)
SCAT . . . . . . Security Control of Air Traffic
SCAT . . . . . . Service Command Air Transportation
SCAT . . . . . . Share Compiler-Assembler, Translator
SCAT . . . . . . Sheep Cell Agglutination Test
SCAT . . . . . . Small Car Automatic Transit (System)
SCAT . . . . . . South Pacific Combat Air Transport (World War II)
SCAT . . . . . . Space Communications and Tracking
SCAT . . . . . . Special Advisory Committee on Telecommunications
SCAT . . . . . . Speed Command Attitude/Target (FAA)
SCAT . . . . . . Speed Control Approach/Takeoff
SCAT . . . . . . Sperry Canada Automatic Tester
SCAT . . . . . . Submarine Classification and Tracking
SCAT . . . . . . Supersonic Commercial Air Transport (NASA)
SCAT . . . . . . Surface-Controlled Avalanche Transistor
SCATA . . . . . Survival Sited Casualty Treatment Assemblage
SCATANA . . . . Security Control of Air Traffic and Air Navigation Aids (FAA)
SCATE . . . . . Space Chamber Analyzer - Thermal Environment (NASA)
SCATE . . . . . Stromberg-Carlson Automatic Test Equipment
SCATER . . . . . Security Control of Air Traffic and Electromagnetic Radiations (during an air defense emergency)
SCATS . . . . . Scheduling and Tracking System
SCATS . . . . . Self-Contained Automatic Test System
SCATS . . . . . Sequentially-Controlled Automatic Transmitter Start
SCATS . . . . . Simulation, Checkout and Training System
SCA(UN) . . . . . Department of Security Council Affairs of the United Nations
SCAW . . . . . . Supreme Camp of the American Woodmen
SCAWU . . . . . Singapore Clerical and Administrative Workers' Union
Sc B . . . . Bachelor of Science
SCB . . . . Shipowners Claims Bureau
SCB . . . . Ships Characteristics Board
SCB . . . . Ship's Cook, Butcher (Navy)
SCB . . . . Silicon Cell Bridge
SCB . . . . Silver Cadmium Battery
SCB . . . . Software Control Board (Apollo) (NASA)
SCB . . . . Strictly Confined to Bed (Medicine)
SCBA . . . . . . Self-Contained Breathing Apparatus

SCBA . . . . . . Supreme Circle Brotherhood of America
Sc BAM . . . . . Bachelor of Science in Applied Mathematics
Sc BC . . . . . . Bachelor of Science in Chemistry
SCBC . . . . . . Southern California Bible College
SCBD . . . . . . Scan Conversion and Bright Display
Sc BE . . . . . . Bachelor of Science in Engineering
SCBL . . . . . . Scotts Bluff and Agate Fossil Beds National Monuments
Sc BP . . . . . . Bachelor of Science in Physics
SCBR . . . . . . Steam-Cooled Breeder Reactor
SCBS . . . . . . Saint Charles Borromeo Seminary (Pennsylvania)
SCC . . . . Sacra Congregatio Concilii (Sacred Congregation of the Council)
SCC . . . . Sage Control Center
SCC . . . . Satellite Control Center
SCC . . . . Scandinavian Collectors Club
SCC . . . . Sequence Control Chart
SCC . . . . Short-Circuit Current
SCC . . . . Single-Cotton Covered (To identify single-strand cotton-covered magnet wire)
SCC . . . . Sisters of Christian Charity (Roman Catholic religious order)
SCC . . . . Small Centre Contact
SCC . . . . Societe Chimique des Charbonnages (France)
SCC . . . . Society of Cosmetic Chemists
SCC . . . . Sports Car Club of America
SCC . . . . Standard Commodity Classification
SCC . . . . Standard Community Classification
SCC . . . . Standardized Cost Categories
SCC . . . . State Corporation Commission
SCC . . . . Stock Control Center (Army)
SCC . . . . Storage Connecting Circuit (Teletype)
SCC . . . . Strategic Communications Command (Army)
SCC . . . . Stress Corrosion Cracking (Metals)
SCC . . . . Student of Codrington College (Barbados)
SCC . . . . Supervisor Control Console
SCC . . . . Supply Control Center
SC(C) . . . . . . Submarine Chaser (Control) (110 foot)
SCCA . . . . . . Southeastern Cottonseed Crushers Association
SCCA . . . . . . Sports Car Club of America
SCCB . . . . . . Safety Change Control Board
SCCE . . . . . . School and College Conference on English
SCCEA . . . . . Strategic Communications Command Equipment Applications Directorate (Army)
SCCF . . . . . . Satellite Communication Control Facility
SCCH . . . . . . Society of Cinema Collectors and Historians
SCCO . . . . . . Security Classification Control Officer
SCCRI . . . . . . Swedish Cement and Concrete Research Institute
SCCS . . . . . . Special Consultative Committee on Security (OAS)
SCCS . . . . . . Standard Commodity Classification System
SCCS . . . . . . STRICOM (Strike Command) Command and Control System (Army)
SCCTSD . . . . . Society of Catholic College Teachers of Sacred Doctrine
SCCUS . . . . . . Swedish Chamber of Commerce of the United States
SCCW . . . . . . Scarritt College for Christian Workers (Tennessee)
SCD . . . . Doctor of Commercial Science
Sc D . . . . Doctor of Science
SCD . . . . S-Band Cassegrain Diplexer
SCD . . . . Satellite Control Department
SCD . . . . Semi-Conductor Division
SCD . . . . Service Computation Date (Military)
SCD . . . . Servo Chart Drive
SCD . . . . Signal Cancelling Device
SCD . . . . Soil Conservation District (Agriculture)
SCD . . . . Specification Control Drawing
SCD . . . . Spreading Cortical Depression
SCD . . . . State Civil Defense
SCD . . . . Subcarrier Discriminator
SCD . . . . Subcontract Deviation
SCD . . . . Subject Captain's Discretion (Aviation)
SCD . . . . Supply, Commissary and Disbursing (Navy)
SCD . . . . Surrey Commercial Dock (British)
SC & D . . . . . Stock Control and Distribution
Sc D in Ed . . . . Doctor of Science in Education
Sc D Govt . . . . Doctor of Science in Government
Sc D in Hyg . . . Doctor of Science in Hygiene
SC Div Bad . . . Second Class Diver Badge (Army)
SCDL . . . . Ship Configuration Detail List (Navy)
SCDL . . . . Stabilized Carbon Dioxide LASER
Sc D (Med) . . . Doctor of Medical Sciences
SCDMR . . . . . . Steam-Cooled D_2O Moderated Reactor (AEC)
SCD, OC of SA. . Staff Communications Division, Office, Chief of Staff (Army)
SCDP . . . . Southern Cooperative Development Program (Sponsored by Southern Consumers Education Foundation)
SCDS . . . . Signal Circuits Design Section

SCDSB . . . . . . Suppressed-Carrier Double Sideband
SCE . . . . Saturated Calomel Electrode
SCE . . . . Scan Conversion Equipment (TV)
SCE . . . . Schedule Compliance-Evaluation (Polaris)
SCE . . . . Selection Control Element
SCE . . . . Separated Career Employee
SCE . . . . Signal Conditioning Equipment
SCE . . . . Single Cycle Execute
SCE . . . . Situationally Caused Error
SCE . . . . Small Current Element
SCE . . . . Society of Carbide Engineers
SCE . . . . Society for Creative Ethics
SCE . . . . Solder Circuit Etch
SCE . . . . Southern California Edison Company (NYSE symbol)
SCE . . . . Special Conditioning Equipment
SCE . . . . Standard Calomel Electrode
SCE . . . . Stored Controlled Energy
SCE . . . . Superintending Civil Engineer (British)
SCEA . . . . Signal Conditioning Electronics Assembly
SCEA . . . . Society of Communications Engineers and Analysts
SCEAR . . . . . . Scientific Committee on the Effects of Atomic Radiation
SCEC . . . . South Central Electric Companies
SCEC . . . . Spaceborne Computer Engineering Conference
Sc Ed D . . . . . Doctor of Science in Education
SCEE . . . . Student Committee for Economic Education
SCEERR . . . . . Sacra Congregatio Episcoporum et Regularium (Sacred Congregation of Bishops and Regulars)
SCEF . . . . Southern Conference Educational Fund
SCEH . . . . Society for Clinical and Experimental Hypnosis
SCEI . . . . Safe Car Educational Institute
SCEL . . . . Signal Corps Engineering Laboratories
SCEP . . . . Study of Critical Environmental Problems (MIT)
SCEPTRE . . . . . System for Circuit Evaluation and Prediction of Transient Radiation Effect
SCEPTRON. . . . Spectral Comparative Pattern Recognizer
SCERT. . . . . . . Systems and Computers Evaluation and Review Technique (Data processing)
SCEWA . . . . . Society for Citizen Education in World Affairs
SCF . . . . S-Band Composite Feed
SCF . . . . Satellite Control Facility (Sunnyvale, California) (NASA)
SCF . . . . Save the Children Federation
SCF . . . . Schematic Concept Formation
SCF . . . . Self-Consistent Field(s) (Quantum mechanics)
SCF . . . . Sequential Compatibility Firing
SCF . . . . Single Cost Factor
SCF . . . . Single Crystal Filament
SCF . . . . Spacecraft Checkout Facility
SCF . . . . Spinning Continuous Filament
SCF . . . . Spinning Crucible Furnace
SCF . . . . Standard Cubic Foot
SCF . . . . Support Carrier Force
SCFA . . . . Slovak Catholic Federation of America
SCFBR . . . . . . Steam-Cooled Fast Breeder Reactor (AEC)
SCFEL . . . . . . Standard COMSEC (Communications Security) Facility Equipment List
SCFM . . . . Standard Cubic Feet per Minute
SCFMA . . . . . . Summer and Casual Furniture Manufacturers Association
SCFS . . . . S-Band Composite Feed System
SCG . . . . Screen Cartoonists Guild
SCG. . . . . Security Classification Guide
SCG. . . . . Society of the Classic Guitar
SCG. . . . . South Carolina Electric & Gas Company (NYSE symbol)
SCG . . . . Space Charge Grid
SCG . . . . Stored Cold Gas
SCGA . . . . Sodium-Cooled Graphite Assembly (AEC)
SCGC . . . . Society of Carnival Glass Collectors
SCH . . . . School
SCH . . . . Sequencer Chassis
SCH . . . . Shelter Complex Headquarters (Civil Defense)
SCH . . . . Society for Colonial History
SCH . . . . Spencer Chemical Company (NYSE symbol) (Delisted)
SCH . . . . Square Cartridge Heater
SCH . . . . Supporting Checkout
SCHAVMED . . . School of Aviation Medicine (Later, School of Aerospace Medicine) (Navy)
SCHLA . . . . . . School for Latin America (Military)
SCHMOO . . . . Space Cargo Handler and Manipulator for Orbital Operations
Sch Mus B . . . Bachelor of School Music
SCHO . . . . Standard Controlled Heterodyne Oscillator
SchP . . . . Ordo Clericorum Regularium Pauperum Matris Dei Scholarum Piarum (Piarist Fathers) (Roman Catholic religious order)
SCHWR . . . . . . Steam-Cooled Heavy Water Reactor

SCI . . . . Sacra Congregatio Indicis (Sacred Congregation of the Index)
SCI . . . . San Clemente Island
SCI . . . . Science
SCI . . . . Science Citation Index
SCI . . . . Science Curriculum Improvement (Study) (Education)
SCI . . . . Seaboard Coast Line Industries (NYSE symbol)
SCI . . . . Seamen's Church Institute of New York
SCI . . . . Sequential Comparison Index (Measures effect of chemical pollution in lakes and streams)
SCI . . . . Service Civil International (International Voluntary Service)
SCI . . . . Ship Controlled Intercept (RADAR) (Navy)
SCI . . . . Shipping Container Institute
SCI . . . . Ship's Capability Impaired (Navy)
SCI . . . . Simulation Councils, Incorporated
SCI . . . . Slot Cell Inserter
SCI . . . . Society of Chemical Industry
SCI . . . . Sponge and Chamois Institute
SCI . . . . Stein Collectors International
SCI. . . . . . . Structured Clinical Interview
SCI . . . . Supervisory Cost Inspector (Navy)
SCIA . . . . . . Signal Corps Intelligence Agency (Army) (Obsolete)
SCIAS . . . . . Supreme Council of the Independent Associated Spiritualists
SCIB. . . . . . . Significant Counterintelligence Briefs
SCIBP . . . . . . Special Committee for the International Biological Program (National Research Council)
SCIC . . . . . . Semiconductor Integrated Circuit
Sci D . . . . . . Doctor Science
SCID . . . . Small Column Insulated Delays
SCIDE . . . . . . Servicio Cooperativo Interamericano de Educacion
SCI-FI . . . . . Science Fiction (Also, SF)
SCIM . . . . . . Speech Communications Index Meter
SCIMPEX. . . . . Syndicat des Commercants Importateurs et Exportateurs de l'Ouest African (Union of Commercial Importers and Exporters of West Africa)
SCIP. . . . . . . Scanning for Information Parameters
SCIP. . . . . . . Ship's Capability Impaired for Lack of Parts
SCIRA . . . . . . Snipe Class International Racing Association
SCIS. . . . . . . Science Curriculum Improvement Study
SCISRS . . . . . Sigma Center Information Storage and Retrieval System
SCIT . . . . Sub-Committee on Interzonal Trade (Allied German Occupation Forces)
SCITEC . . . . . . The Association of the Scientific, Engineering and Technological Community of Canada
SCJ . . . . Congregatio Sacerdotum a Corde Jesu (Congregation of the Priests of the Sacred Heart of Jesus) (Roman Catholic religious order)
SCJ . . . . Siberian Chemistry Journal
SCJC . . . . . . Saint Catharine Junior College (Kentucky)
SCL . . . . Save a Cat League
SCL . . . . Seaboard Coast Line Railroad
SCL . . . . Selectively Cross Linked
SCL . . . . Senior Citizens League
SCL . . . . Shaped Charge Liner
SCL . . . . Signal Corps Laboratory (Army) (Obsolete)
SCL . . . . Sisters of Charity (of Leavenworth) (Roman Catholic religious order)
SCL . . . . Site Concurrence Letter
SCL . . . . Southeastern Composers' League
SCL . . . . Space Charge Limited
SCL . . . . Standard Classification List
SCL . . . . Student of the Civil Law
SCL . . . . Symbolic Correction Loader
SCL . . . . Symmetric Clipper
SCLC . . . . . . Southern Christian Leadership Conference
SCLC . . . . . . Space-Charge-Limited Current
SCLK . . . . . . Ship's Clerk
SCLL . . . . . . Sandia Corporation, Livermore Laboratory
SCLO . . . . . . Statistical Clearance Liaison Officer (Army)
Sc M . . . . . . Master of Science
SCM . . . . Sanctae Memoriae (Of Holy Memory)
SCM. . . . . . . SCM Corporation (Formerly, Smith, Corona, Marchant) (NYSE symbol)
SCM. . . . . . . Selective Complement Accumulator
SCM . . . . . . Sender's Composition Message (Cable)
SCM . . . . . . Service Command Module (Aerospace)
SCM. . . . . . . Signal Conditioning Module
SCM. . . . . . . Single Crystal Meteorite
SCM. . . . . . . Small-Core Memory (Data processing)
SCM. . . . . . . Solar Cell Module
SCM . . . . . . Special Court-Martial (Army)
SCM. . . . . . . State-Certified Midwife
SCM. . . . . . . Strouds Creek & Muddlety R. R. (AAR code)
SCM. . . . . . . Student Christian Movement
SCM. . . . . . . Summary Court-Martial
S & CM . . . . . Strategic and Critical Materials (Military)
SCMA . . . . . . Southern Cypress Manufacturers Association

SCME . . . . . . American Federation of State, County and Municipal Employees
SCMF . . . . . . Single Contact Midge Flange
Sc M in Hyg. . . Master of Science in Hygiene
SCMM . . . . . Sisters of Charity of Our Lady, Mother of Mercy (Roman Catholic religious order)
SCMM . . . . . Society of Catholic Medical Missionaries, Incorporated (Medical Mission Sisters) (Roman Catholic religious order)
SCMO . . . . . Summary Court-Martial Order
SCMR. . . . . . Surface Composition Mapping Radiometer (NASA)
SCMS . . . . . . Signal Command Management System
SCN . . . . . . Satellite Control Network
SCN. . . . . . . Schematic Change Notice
SCN. . . . . . . Self-Checking Number
SCN. . . . . . . Sensitive Command Network
SCN. . . . . . . Shipbuilding and Conversion, Navy
SCN. . . . . . . Ships Construction, Navy (Funding)
SCN. . . . . . . Show Cause Notice
SCN. . . . . . . Single Crystal Needle
SCN. . . . . . . Sisters of Charity (of Nazareth) (Roman Catholic religious order)
SCN. . . . . . . Specific Control Number
SCN. . . . . . . Specification Change Notice
SCN. . . . . . . Summary and Charge Number
SCN. . . . . . . Supply Corps, Navy
SCN. . . . . . . Sylvania-Corning Nuclear Corporation
SCNA . . . . . . Sudden Cosmic-Noise Absorption
SCNAWAF . . . . Special Category Navy with Air Force
SCNR. . . . . . Scientific Committee of National Representatives (NATO)
SCNR. . . . . . Solid-Core Nuclear Rocket (NASA)
SCNR. . . . . . Supreme Council for National Reconstruction (South Korea)
SCNS . . . . . . Self-Contained Navigation System (NASA)
ScO . . . . Scientific Officer (Ministry of Agriculture, Fisheries, and Food) (Also, SO) (British)
SCO . . . . Scovill Manufacturing Company (NYSE symbol)
SCO . . . . Selective Conscientious Objection
SCO . . . . Society of Commissioned Officers
SCO . . . . Southern College of Optometry (Tennessee)
SCO . . . . Staff Communications Office
SCO. . . . . . . Statistical Control Office(r)
SCO . . . . Subcarrier Oscillator
SCO . . . . Subcontract Consignment Order
SCOA. . . . . . Societe Commerciale de l'Ouest Africain (West African Commercial Society)
SCOBA . . . . . Standing Conference of the Canonical Orthodox Bishops in the Americas
SCOBO. . . . . Satellite Collection Buoy Observations
SCOC. . . . . . Short Circuit Output Current
SCODA . . . . . Scan Coherent Doppler Attachment
SCOFA . . . . . Shipping Control Office, Forward Area (Navy)
SCOFOR . . . . Scouting Force (Navy)
SCOHR . . . . . Students Committee on Human Rights
SCOLAR . . . . Standard Costing of Laboratory Resources
SCOLAVNMED. . School of Aviation Medicine (Later, School of Aerospace Medicine)
SCOLMA. . . . Standing Conference on Library Materials on Africa (British)
SCOMA. . . . Shipping Control Office, Marianas (Navy)
SCOMO . . . . . Satellite Collection of Meteorological Observations
SCONS. . . . . Shipment Control System (Military)
SCOOP . . . . . Scientific Computation of Optimum Procurement (Air Force)
SCOOP . . . . . Support Plan to Continuity of Operations Plan
SCOP . . . . . . Ferrocarril del Sureste (AAR code)
SCOP . . . . . . Single Copy Order Plan (Bookselling)
SCOPE . . . . . . Scientific Committee on Problems of the Environment
SCOPE . . . . . . Senior Citizens' Opportunities for Personal Enrichment (Federal anti-poverty program)
SCOPE . . . . . . Sequential Customer Order Processing Electronically
SCOPE . . . . . Service Center of Private Enterprise
SCOPE . . . . . Simple Checkout-Oriented Program Language
SCOPE . . . . . Special Committee on Paperless Entries (California inter-bank group)
SCOPE . . . . . . Special Committee on Problems of the Environment (of International Council of Scientific Unions)
SCOPE . . . . . . Stromberg Central Operations Panel - Electric
SCOPE . . . . . Student Council on Pollution and Environment (Organization conceived in late 1969 by then Secretary of the Interior, Walter J. Hickel)
SCOPE . . . . . . Subsystem for the Control of Operations and Plan Evaluation
SCOPE . . . . . . Summer Community Organization and Political Education Program
SCOPE . . . . . . Supportive Council on Preventive Effort (Ohio)
SCOPE . . . . . . System to Coordinate the Operation of Peripheral Equipment
SCOPP . . . . . School-College Orientation Program of Pittsburgh
SCOPT . . . . . Subcommittee on (Computer) Programming Terminology (of ACM)
SCOR . . . . . . Scientific Committee on Ocean Research (International Council of Scientific Unions)
SCOR . . . . . . Self-Calibrating Omni-Range

SCOR ...... Special Committee on Oceanographic Research
SCORAN..... Scorer and Analyzer (Computerized educational testing)
SCORDES .... Sferics Correlation Detection System
SCORE ...... Satellite Computer-Operated Readiness Equipment (SSD)
SCORE ..... Selective Conversion and Retention (Navy)
SCORE ...... Service Corps of Retired Executives (Small Business Administration)
SCORE ...... Signal Communication by Orbiting Relay Equipment (Radio)
SCORE ...... Street Corner Offense Reduction Experiment
SCORE ...... Student Competitions on Relevant Engineering
SCORN...... Special Committee Opposing Resurgent Nazism
SCORON .... Scouting Squadron
SCOROR .... Secretary's Committee on Research on Reorganization (Navy)
SCORU ...... Statistical Control and Operations Records Unit (Air Force)
SCOT ...... Satellite Communication Terminal
SCOT....... Scotland (or Scottish)
SCOT....... Standby Compatible One-Tape (System)
SCOT....... Steel Car of Tomorrow
SCOT....... Supplementary Checkout Trailer
SCOT....... Support-Coated Open-Tubular (Column) (Chromatography)
SCOTCH..... Summer Cultural Opportunities for Teams and Children (National music program)
SCOTNATS ... Scottish Nationalists
SCOTRACEN .. Scouting Training Center (Navy)
SCOTT ...... Synchronous Continuous Orbital Three-Dimensional Tracking
SCOTT ...... Synthetic Medium Older Tuberculin Trichloracetic Acid Precipitated
SCOTT-R..... Super-Critical, Once-Thru Tube Reactor (Experiment) (General Electric Company)
SCOUT ..... Surface-Controlled Oxide Unipolar Transistor
SCOWR...... Special Committee on Water Research (International Council of Scientific Unions)
SCP .... Brotherhood of Sleeping Car Porters
SCP .... SAGE Computer Program
SCP .... Satellite Cloud Photograph
SCP .... Schematic Change Proposal
SCP .... Sector Command Post (Military)
SCP .... Security Classification Procedure
SCP .... Servo Controlled Positioner
SCP .... Short Circuit Protection
SCP .... Single-Cell Protein
SCP .... Social Credit Party (Canadian)
SCP .... Societe Culinaire Philanthropique
SCP .... Society of California Pioneers
SCP .... Solar Cell Panel
SCP .... Sonobuoy Control Panel
SCP .... Spherical Candlepower
SCP .... Supply Cataloging Program
SCP .... Survey Control Point
SCP .... Systems Change Proposal
SCPA ...... Solar Cell Panel Assembly
SCPA ...... Southern Coal Producers Association
SCPCU ...... Society of Chartered Property and Casualty Underwriters
SCPD, OC of SA .. Staff Civilian Personnel Division, Office, Chief of Staff (Army)
SCPF .... Sacra Congregatio de Propaganda Fide (Sacred Congregation for the Propagation of the Faith)
SCPI .... Scientists' Committee for Public Information
SCPI .... Structural Clay Products Institute
SCPO....... Second Class Post Office
SCPO ...... Senior Chief Petty Officer (Navy)
SCPP .... Surveyor Command Preparation Program (Aerospace)
SCPRF ...... Structural Clay Products Research Foundation
SCPS ...... Servo-Controlled Positioning System
SCPT ...... SAGE Computer Programming Training
SCPT ...... Security Control Point
SCPTR ...... Standing Committee on Personnel Training and Readiness (Navy)
SCQ....... Sisters of Charity of Quebec (Grey Nuns) (Roman Catholic religious order)
SCQC...... Scout Crew Qualification Course (Army)
SCR .... Scanning Control Register
SCR .... Selective Chopper Radiometer
SCR .... Semiconductor-Controlled Rectifier
SCR .... Senior Common Room (in British colleges and public schools)
SCR .... Sequence Checking Routine
SCR .... Series Control Relay
SCR .... Servo Chart Drive
SCR .... Shift Count Register
SCR .... Signal Corps Radio (Followed by model number) (Army)
SCR .... Silicon-Controlled Rectifier (Electronics)
SCR .... Sodium Cooled Reactor (AEC)
SCR .... Solar Cell Radiation
SCR .... Solar Cosmic Ray
SCR .... Soviet Cybernetics Review (A publication)

SCR .... Spanish Communication Region (Air Force)
SCR .... Speed Change Rate
SCR .... Static Card Reader
SCR .... Strip Chart Recorder
SCR .... Structural Ceramic Panel
SCR .... Sub-Chief Ranger (Ancient Order of Foresters)
SCR .... Summary Control Report (Planning and Production) (Navy)
SCR .... Supersonic Combustion Ramjet
SCR .... System Control Routine
SCRA ...... Stanford Center for RADAR Astronomy
SCRA ...... Supreme Council of the Royal Arcanum
SCRAM ..... Selective Combat Range Artillery Missile
SCRAM ..... Several Compilers Reworked and Modified
SCRAM ..... Space Capsule Regulator and Monitor
SCRAM ..... Spares Components Reidentification and Modification (Program) (DOD)
SCRAM ..... Supersonic Combustion Ramjet Missile
SCRAMJET.... Supersonic Combustion Ramjet
SCRAP ..... Selective Curtailment of Reports and Paperwork (Navy)
SCRAP ..... Series Computation of Reliability and Probability (Data processing)
SCRAP ..... Simple Complex Reaction-Time Apparatus
SCRAP ..... Society for Completely Removing All Parking Meters
SCRAP ..... Students Challenging Regulatory Agency Proceedings (Student legal action organization)
SCRB ...... Structured Case Review Blank
SCRBA ..... Student Committee for the Right to Bear Arms
SCREL...... South Central Regional Educational Laboratory Corporation
SCRG ...... Stationary Cosmic Ray Gas
SCRI .... Scientists' Committee for Radiation Information
SCRIPT ...... Scientific and Commercial Subroutine Interpreter and Program Translator
SCRIS ...... Southern California Regional Information Study (Bureau of Census)
SCRJ ...... Supersonic Combustion Ramjet
SCRL ...... Skill Components Research Laboratory (Air Force)
SCRS ...... Strip Chart Recorder System
SCRT ...... Sealed Cathode Ray Tube
SCS .... Safety Control Switch
SCS .... Saint Charles Seminary (New York)
SCS .... Scan Converter (or Counter) System
SCS .... Section Control Station (RADAR)
SCS .... Short-Circuit-Stable
SCS .... Signal Communications System (Air Force)
SCS .... Silicon-Controlled Switch
SCS .... Single Channel Simplex
SCS .... Slaving Control System
SCS .... Slovak Catholic Sokol
SCS .... Slow Code Scanner
SCS .... Society of Civil Servants (British)
SCS .... Society of Clinical Surgery
SCS .... Society for Conservative Studies
SCS .... Society of Construction Superintendents
SCS .... Soil Conservation Service (Department of Agriculture)
SCS .... SONAR Calibration Set
SCS .... SONAR Communications Set
SCS .... Speed Class Sequencing
SCS .... Stability and Control System
SCS .... Statistical Control System
SCS .... Stiffened Cylindrical Shell
SCS .... Superintendent of Car Service
SCS .... Surface Compression Strengthened
SCS .... Swedish Colonial Society
SCS .... Sweeping Current Supply
SC & S ..... Strapped, Corded, and Sealed (as, of a package or bale)
SCSA ...... Siamese Cat Society of America
SCSA ...... Soil Conservation Society of America
SCSA ...... Supreme Council for Sport in Africa
SCSBM ..... Society for Computer Science in Biology and Medicine
SCSC ...... Saint Cloud State College (Minnesota)
SCSC ...... Secondary Curriculum Study Center (of NASSP)
SCSC ...... South Carolina State College
Sc SD ..... Doctor of Social Sciences
SCSD ...... School Construction Systems Development (Project) (of Educational Facilities Laboratories)
SCSH ...... Structural Carbon Steel Hard
SCSJA ...... Sisters of Charity of St. Joan Antida (Roman Catholic religious order)
SCSL ...... Sandia Corporation, Sandia Laboratory (Army)
SCSL ...... Sisters of Charity (of St. Louis) (Roman Catholic religious order)
SCSLP...... Smithsonian Center for Short-Lived Phenomena
SCSM ...... Structural Carbon Steel Medium
SCSO ...... Space Communications Station Operation
SCSS ...... Self-Contained Starting System
SCSS ...... Structural Carbon Steel Soft
SCST ...... Scan Converter Storage Tube

SCST	Society of Commercial Seed Technologists
SCT	Scan Conversion Tube
SCT	Sentence Completion Technique (or Test)
SCT	Sequence Checking Tape
SCT	Sioux City Terminal Railway (AAR code)
SCT	Spectral Control Technique
SCT	Structural Clay Tile (Technical drawings)
SCT	Subroutine Call Table
SCT	Sugar-Coated Tablet
SCT	System Compatibility Tests
SCTA	Southern California Timing Association
SCTC	Small Craft Training Center
SCTC	Submarine Chaser Training Center
SCTE	Society of Cable Television Engineers
SCTH	Service Center for Teachers of History
SCTI	Sodium Components Test Installation
SCTI	Solid Carbide Tool Institute
SCTL	Short-Circuited Transmission Line
SCTOC	Satellite Communications Test Operations Center
SCTRACEN	Submarine Chaser Training Center
SCTY	Security
SCU	Scanner Control Unit
SCU	Scottish Church Union
SCU	Service Command Unit
SCU	Single Conditioning Unit
SCU	Special Care Unit
SCU	Statistical Control Unit (Military)
SCU	Storage Control Unit
SCU	Sulfur-Coated Urea
SCU	Surface Control Unit
SCU	Synchronous Controller Unit
SCU	System Control Unit
SCUAE	State Committee on the Utilization of Atomic Energy (USSR)
SCUBA	Self-Contained Underwater Breathing Apparatus
SCUD	Subsonic Cruise Unarmed Decoy
SCUDS	Simplification, Clarification, Unification, Decimalization, Standardization
SCUL	Simulation of the Columbia University Libraries (Data processing research)
SCUM	Society for Cutting Up Men
SCUMRA	Societe Central de l'Uranium et des Minerals et Metaux Radioactifs (France)
SC(UN)	Security Council of the United Nations
SCUP	Society for College and University Planning
SCUS	Supreme Court of the United States
SCUSA	Student Conference on United States Affairs
SCV	Smooth, Capsulated, Virulent (Bacteriology)
SCV	Sons of Confederate Veterans
SCV	Speed Control Valve
SCV	Strip Chart Viewer
SCV	Subclutter Visibility
SCV	System Component Verification
SCVTR	Scan Converting Video Tape Recorder
SCW	Screw & Bolt Corporation of America (NYSE symbol)
SCW	Silicone Carbide Whisker
SCW	Society of Colonial Wars
SCW	State College of Washington
SCW	Superintendent of Contract Work (Navy)
SCWC	Special Commission on Weather Modification
SCWCU	Supreme Council of the Western Catholic Union
SCWEP	Spinnable Cotton Waste Equalization Program
SCWR	Supercritical Water Reactor
SCX	Solar Coronal X-Ray
SCX	Starrett (L. S.) Company (NYSE symbol)
SCY	Scan Converter Yoke
SD	Doctor of Science
SD	Safety Destructor
SD	Same Day
SD	Sample Data
SD	Sample Delay
SD	Sash Door
SD	Saturation Deficit
SD	Scientific Design (Group)
SD	Sea Damaged (Grain trade)
SD	Second Defense (Men's lacrosse position)
SD	Secretary of Defense
SD	Seize Detector
SD	Selenium Diode
SD	Self-Destroying (Projectile)
SD	Semantic Differential
SD	Semidiameter
SD	Senior Deacon (Masonry)
SD	Serologically Defined (Immunology)
SD	Service Dress
SD	Servus Dei (Servant of God)
SD	Several Dates
SD	Shell Destroying (Device)
SD	Short Delay
SD	Short Delivery
SD	Short Duration
SD	Sicherheitsdienst (Police system) (NAZI Germany)
SD	Sight Draft (Business and trade)
SD	Sine Dato (Undated book)
SD	Sine Die (Without Day)
SD	Single Deck (Navigation)
SD	Single Determination
SD	Single Domain (Grains in rocks) (Geophysics)
SD	Situation Display
SD	Skin Dose
SD	Slow Down
SD	Soft Drawn
SD	Solid Drawn
SD	South Dakota
SD	Space Daily
SD	Special Delivery
SD	Special Duty
SD	Specially Denatured
SD	Specification for Design
SD	Spectacle Dispenser (Navy technician)
SD	Spectral Distribution
SD	Spin Device
SD	Stage Direction
SD	Stage Door (Theatrical slang)
SD	Standard Deviation
SD	Standard Oil Company of California (NYSE symbol)
SD	Stands Detached (Freight)
SD	State Department
SD	Stereo Directional
SD	Steward (Navy rating)
SD	Storm Detection (RADAR)
SD	Stowage Drawer
SD	Straight Duty
SD	Strength Differential (Steel)
SD	Streptodornase (Medicine)
SD	Stronnictwo Demokratyczne (Democratic Party) (Poland)
SD	Superintendent of Documents (US Government Printing Office)
SD	Supply Department (Navy)
SD	Supply Depot
SD	Surveillance Drone (Air Force)
SD	Survival Dose
SD	Sweep Driver
SD	System Demonstration
SD	Systolic Discharge (Physiology)
S/D	Salaried Direct (Ratio)
S/D	Seadrome
S/D	Shut Down
S/D	Sight Draft (Banking)
S & D	Search and Destroy (Army)
S & D	Single and Double (Reduction gears)
S & D	Song and Dance Act (Slang)
SDA	Sacro-Dextra Anterior
SDA	Sequential Degradation Analysis
SDA	Seventh-Day Adventist
SDA	Significant Digit Arithmetic
SDA	Simple Doublet Antenna
SDA	Sleeve Dipole Antenna
SDA	Slow Down Area
SDA	Soap and Detergent Association
SDA	Source Data Automation (Data processing)
SDA	Special Duty Assignment
SDA	Specific Dynamic Action (of foods) (Physiology)
SDA	Spectral Distribution Analyzer
SDA	Spontaneous Divergent Academic (Test) (Education)
SDA	Statistical Distribution Analyzer
SDA	Step Down Amplifier
SDA	Students for Democratic Action
SDA	Succinic Dehydrogenase Activity (Medicine)
SDA	Supporting Data Analysis
SDA	Symbolic Disk Address
SDA	Symbols-Digits-Alphabetics
SDA	Systems Dynamic Analyzer
SDAA	Salt Distributors Association of America
SDAA	Servicemen's Dependents Allowance Act

SDAA . . . . Skein Dyers Association of America
SDAC . . . . Seismology Data Analysis Center
SDAD . . . . Satellite Digital and Analog Display
SDADS . . . . . . Satellite Digital and Display System
SDAE . . . . San Diego & Arizona Eastern Railway Company (AAR code)
S DAK . . . . . . South Dakota
SDAP . . . . Systems Development Analysis Program
SDAS . . . . Source Data Automation System
SDAS . . . . Systems Data Analysis Section
SDAT . . . . Spacecraft Data Analysis Team (NASA)
SDAT . . . . Stanford Diagnostic Arithmetic Test
SDB . . . . Salesians of Don Bosco
SDB . . . . Skill Development Base (Army)
SDB . . . . Society for Developmental Biology
SDB . . . . Square Die Bushing
SDB . . . . Strength & Dynamics Branch (Air Force)
SDBF . . . . System Development Breadboard Facility
SDBHS . . . . . . Seventh Day Baptist Historical Society
SDBL . . . . Sight Draft Bill of Lading Attached (Business and trade)
SDC . . . . Scientific Data Center
SDC . . . . Seismological Data Center (Environmental Science Services
               Administration)
SDC . . . . Seize Detector Control
SDC . . . . Self-Defense Corps (Vietnam)
SDC . . . . Shaft-Driven Counter
SDC . . . . Shipment Detail Card
SDC . . . . Signal Data Converter
SDC . . . . Single Drift Correction
SDC . . . . Situation Display Converter
SDC . . . . Society of Daily Communicants
SDC . . . . Society of the Divine Compassion
SDC . . . . Solid Dielectric Cable
SDC . . . . Southern Defense Command (Army)
SDC . . . . Space Data Corporation
SDC . . . . Space Defense Corporation
SDC . . . . Space Development Corporation
SDC . . . . Space Disturbance Center (Boulder, Colorado)
SDC . . . . Special Devices Center
SDC . . . . Stabilization Data Computer
SDC . . . . State Defense Council
SDC . . . . Static Dielectric Constant
SDC . . . . Structural Design Criteria
SDC . . . . Studebaker Driver's Club
SDC . . . . Submersible Decompression Chamber (Underwater tank)
SDC . . . . Submersible Diving Capsule
SDC . . . . Support Design Change
SDC . . . . System Designator Code
SDC . . . . System Development Corporation
SDCE . . . . Society of Die Casting Engineers
SD Comm. . . . . Doctor of Science in Commerce
SDCP . . . . Supply Demand Control Points
SDCT . . . . Slosson Drawing Coordination Test
SDCW . . . . . . San Diego College for Women (California)
SDD . . . . Second Development Decade (UN)
SDD . . . . Signal Data Demodulator
SDD . . . . Slow Down Density
SDD . . . . Specially Designated Distributor (Liquor)
SDD . . . . Store Door Delivery
SDD . . . . Systems Definition Directive
SDDP . . . . Sight Draft Documents against Payment (Banking)
SDDU . . . . Simplex Data Distribution Unit
SDE . . . . Self-Disinfecting Elastomer
SDE . . . . Simple Designational Expression
SDE . . . . Society of Data Educators
SDE . . . . Standard Data Element (Army)
SDE & C. . . . . Standard Data Element and Codes (Air Force)
SDECE . . . . . . Service de Documentation Exterieure et Contre Espionage (Intelligence
               organization) (France)
SDEG . . . . Special Doctrine Equipment Group (Army)
SDF . . . . Louisville (Kentucky) Standiford Airport (Airport symbol)
SDF . . . . Self-Defense Force (Japan)
SDF . . . . Single Degree of Freedom
SDF . . . . Social Democratic Federation (Political coalition)
SDF . . . . Sonic Depth Finder
SDF . . . . Spectral Density Function
SDF . . . . Static Direction Finder
SDF . . . . Strategic Defensive Forces (Army)
SDF . . . . Sudan Defence Force (British)
SDF . . . . Swedish Defense Forces
SDFC . . . . Space Disturbance Forecast Center (Environmental Science Services
               Administration)

SDG . . . . Scan Display Generator
SDG . . . . Screen Directors' Guild of America, Inc.
SDG . . . . . . Simulated Data Generator
SDG . . . . Situation Display Generator
SDG . . . . Smith-Douglass Company, Inc. (NYSE symbol) (Delisted)
SDG . . . . Special Development Groups (Navy)
SDG . . . . Subminiature Displacement Gyroscope
SDG . . . . Sucrose Density Gradients
SDGA . . . . . . Single Degaussing Cable
SDGE . . . . . . Situation Display Generator Element
SDH . . . . Styling Data Handling
SDH . . . . Succinic Dehydrogenase
SDHD . . . . . . Society of Daughters of Holland Dames
SDHE . . . . . . Spacecraft Data Handling Equipment
SDHIRS . . . . . Sub-District Headquarters Induction and Recruiting Station (Navy)
SDI . . . . Saudi Arabian Airlines
SDI . . . . Selected Descriptive Item
SDI . . . . Selective Dissemination of Information (System) (Data processing)
SDI . . . . Source Data Information
SDI . . . . Standard Data Interface (Data processing)
SDI . . . . Standard Deviation Interval (Medicine)
SDI . . . . State Disability Insurance
SDI . . . . Steel Deck Institute
SDI . . . . Steel Door Institute
SDIG . . . . Screen Directors International Guild (Absorbed by Directors Guild of
               America)
SDIP . . . . Specifically Designated Intelligence Position
SDIP . . . . System Description and Implementation Plan (Navy)
SDIT . . . . Service de Documentation et d'Information Techniques de l'Aeronautique
SDI/UC . . . . . State Disability Insurance – Unemployment Compensation
SDIZ . . . . Submarine Defense Identification Zone
SDJC . . . . San Diego Junior College (California)
SDK . . . . Shelter Deck
SDK . . . . Sigma Delta Kappa (Fraternity)
SDKPIL . . . . . Socjaldemokracja Krolestwa Polskiego i Litwy
SDL . . . . National Council, Sons and Daughters of Liberty
SDL . . . . Shaft Driver, Left
SDL . . . . Slow-Down Length
SDL . . . . Sonic Delay Line
SDL . . . . Space Disturbances Laboratory (Environmental Science Services
               Administration)
SDL . . . . Strip Delay Line
SDL . . . . Supporting Document List
SDL . . . . Systematic Design Language
SDL . . . . Systems Development Laboratories
SDLO . . . . . . State, Defense Liaison Office
SDLP . . . . . . Social Democratic and Labor Party (Ireland)
SDM . . . . National Association of Special Delivery Messengers (AFL-CIO)
SDM . . . . Samsonov Density Meter (Gravimetrics)
SDM . . . . Selective Dissemination of Microfiche
SDM . . . . Slow-Down Model
SDM . . . . Soma Dendrite Membrane
SDM . . . . Sons and Daughters of Malta
SDM . . . . Statistical Delta Modulation
SDM . . . . Sub-Division Manager
SDME . . . . . . Synchronous Data Modern Equipment
SD (Met) . . . . Doctor of Science in Metallurgy
SDMF . . . . . . Space Disturbance Monitoring Facility (Environmental Science
               Services Administration)
S-DMICC . . . . State-Defense Military Information Control Committee
SDN . . . . Secret Document Number
SDN . . . . Separation Designation Number
SDN . . . . Societe des Nations (League of Nations)
SDNCO . . . . . Staff Duty Noncommissioned Officer
SDO . . . . San Diego Gas & Electric Company (NYSE symbol)
SDO . . . . Ship Development Objective (Navy)
SDO . . . . Special Duty Only (Military)
SDO . . . . Specialist Duty Only (Navy personnel designation)
SDO . . . . Staff Duty Officer
SDO . . . . Station Duty Officer (Navy)
SDO . . . . Synthetic Drying Oil
SDOC . . . . . . Specific Direct Operating Costs
SDOPR . . . . . Sound Operator (Navy)
SDP . . . . National Society, Sons and Daughters of the Pilgrims
SDP . . . . Sacro-Dextra Posterior
SDP . . . . Sea Duty Pay (Navy)
SDP . . . . Sentry Dog Patrol
SDP . . . . Ship Development Plan (Navy)
SDP . . . . Signal Data Processor
SDP . . . . Silicon Diode Pellet
SDP . . . . Single Department Purchasing (Agency)

SDP . . . . Sirotherm Demineralization Process
SDP . . . . Site Data Processors
SDP . . . . Slow-Down Power
SDP . . . . Small Distribution Phenomena
SDP . . . . Smoke Dispersion Pod
SDP . . . . Solar Desalination Plant
SDP . . . . Spectral Dependence Photocurrent
SDP . . . . Standard Pressed Steel Company (NYSE symbol)
SDP . . . . Storage and Distribution Point (Military)
SDP . . . . Surface Deformation Pattern
SDP . . . . Survey Data Processing
SDP . . . . System Design Proposal (Navy)
SDP . . . . Systems Development Plan
SDPA . . . . Small Defense Plants Administration (Terminated, 1953)
SDPL . . . . Safeguard Data Processing Laboratory (Army)
SDPL . . . . Servomechanisms and Data Processing Laboratory (MIT)
SDPO . . . . Space Defense Project Office (AMC)
SDPR . . . . Sons and Daughters of Pioneer Rivermen
SDR . . . . Scientific Data Recorder
SDR . . . . Search Decision Rule (Data processing)
SDR . . . . Self-Decoding Readout
SDR . . . . Shaft Driver, Right
SDR . . . . Simple Detection Response
SDR . . . . Small Development Requirement (Military)
SDR . . . . SNAP (Systems for Nuclear Auxiliary Power) Development Reactor
SDR . . . . Sodium Deuterium Reactor
SDR . . . . Solution Development Record
SDR . . . . SONAR Data Recorder
SDR . . . . Special Drawing Rights (of International Monetary Fund)
SDR . . . . Splash Detection RADAR
SDR . . . . Strip Domain Resonance
SDR . . . . Successive Discrimination Reversal
SDR . . . . System Development Requirement (Air Force)
SDR . . . . System Discrepancy Report
SDRP . . . . Simulated Data Reduction Program
SDS . . . . Sample Display Service (Department of Commerce)
SDS . . . . Scientific Data System (Later, XDS)
SDS . . . . Servo Drive System
SDS . . . . Ship Defense System
SDS . . . . Sign-Digit Subtractor
SDS . . . . Signal Distribution System
SDS . . . . Simonds Saw and Steel Company (NYSE symbol) (Delisted)
SDS . . . . Sisters of the Divine Saviour (Roman Catholic religious order)
SDS . . . . Smoke Destruction System
SDS . . . . Societas Divini Salvatoris (Society of the Divine Saviour) (Roman Catholic men's religious order)
SDS . . . . Sodium Dodecyl Sulfate
SDS . . . . Sons and Daughters of the Soddies
SDS . . . . Sozialistischer Deutscher Studentenbund (Student political organization) (Germany)
SDS . . . . Spectrometer Digital System
SDS . . . . Splash Detection System
SDS . . . . Students for a Democratic Society
SDS . . . . Sudden Death Syndrome (in children)
SDS . . . . System Design Specification
SDSBE . . . . . . San Diego Symposium for Biomedical Engineering
SDSC . . . . San Diego State College (California)
SDSH . . . . Society Devoted to the Sacred Heart (Roman Catholic women's religious order)
SDSS . . . . Satellite Data System Spacecraft (Air Force)
SDSS . . . . Self-Deploying Space Station
SDSVF . . . . . . State Dependent State Variable Feedback (Rocket engine) (NASA)
SDT . . . . Sacro-Dextra Transversa
SDT . . . . Scientific Distribution Technique
SDT . . . . Sea Depth Transducer
SDT . . . . Serial Data Transmission
SDT . . . . Shell Destroying Tracer (Ammunition)
SDT . . . . Simulated Data Tape
SDT . . . . Source Distribution Technique
SDT . . . . Step-Down Transformer
SDT . . . . Surveillance Data Transmission
SDTK . . . . Supported Drift Tube Klystron
SDTP . . . . Startover Data Transfer and Processing (Program)
SDU . . . . Shelter Decontamination Unit
SDU . . . . Signal Display Unit
SDU . . . . Spectrum Display Unit
SDU . . . . Subcarrier Delay Unit
SDUK . . . . Society for the Diffusion of Useful Knowledge
SDV . . . . Scudder Duo-Vest, Inc. (NYSE symbol)
SDV . . . . Slowed Down Video (RADAR)

SDV . . . . Society of Divine Vocations (Vocationist Fathers) (Roman Catholic religious order)
SDV . . . . Swimmer Delivery Vehicle
SDW . . . . Southdown, Inc. (NYSE symbol)
SDW . . . . Standing Detonation Wave
SDW . . . . Swept Delta Wing
SDX . . . . Sunray DX Oil Company (NYSE symbol) (Delisted)
SE . . . . Sanford & Eastern R. R. (AAR code)
SE . . . . Sanitary Engineer
SE . . . . School of Engineering
SE . . . . Second Entrance (Theatrical slang)
Se . . . . Selenium (Chemical element)
SE . . . . Servel, Inc. (NYSE symbol) (Delisted)
SE . . . . Single End
SE . . . . Single-Ended, Cylindrical Boiler (Navy)
SE . . . . Single Engine
SE . . . . Single Entry (Bookkeeping)
SE . . . . Soil Extract
SE . . . . Solid Extract (Pharmacy)
SE . . . . Southeast; Southeasterly; Southeastern
SE . . . . Special Equipment
SE . . . . Spherical Equivalent
SE . . . . Stamped Envelope (Designation in Lonely Hearts columns)
SE . . . . Standard Error
SE . . . . Starch Equivalent
SE . . . . Starter Electrode
SE . . . . Steam Emulsion
SE . . . . Stock Exchange
SE . . . . Subcritical Experiment (AEC)
SE . . . . Sulfoethyl
SE . . . . Support Equipment (Military)
SE . . . . Sustaining Engineering
SE . . . . System Effectiveness (Army)
SE . . . . Systems Engineer(ing) (Data processing)
S/E . . . . Standardization/Evaluation
S & E . . . . . . Salaries and Expenses
S & E . . . . . . Surveillance and Entry
SEA . . . . American Sailing Education Association
SEA . . . . Marine Manufacturers Safety Equipment Association
SEA . . . . Safety Engineering Analysis
SEA . . . . Seasonal Employees in Agriculture
SEA . . . . Seatrain Lines, Inc. (NYSE symbol)
SEA . . . . Service Educational Activities (Military)
SEA . . . . Sheep Erythrocyte Agglutination (Test)
SEA . . . . Ship/Equipment/Alterations (Navy)
SEA . . . . Ships Editorial Association (Navy)
SEA . . . . Societe d'Electronique et d'Automatique (Became part of Compagnie Internationale d'Informatique)
SEA . . . . Southeast Airlines, Inc.
SEA . . . . Southeast Asia
SEA . . . . Specific Energy Absorption
SEA . . . . State Economic Area
SEA . . . . State Education Agency
SEA . . . . Statistical Energy Analysis (or Approach) (Vibration analysis)
SEA . . . . Students for Ecological Action (An organization)
SEA . . . . Subterranean Exploration Agency
SEA . . . . Sudden Enhancement of Atmospherics (NASA)
SEA . . . . System Engineering Analysis
SEA . . . . System Error Analysis
SEABEE . . . . . Construction Battalion (CB) (Acronym is a phonetic reference to a member of this Naval unit)
SEAC . . . . Social and Economic Archive Centre (British)
SEAC . . . . Society for Economic, Social, Cultural Study and Expansion in Central Africa
SEAC . . . . Southeast Asia Command
SEAC . . . . Standards Electronic Automatic Computer (National Bureau of Standards)
SEACDT . . . . . Southeast Asia Collective Defense Treaty
SEACOM . . . . . Southeast Asia Commonwealth
SEACORE . . . . Southeast Asia Communications Research
SEAD . . . . Seneca Army Depot
SEAD . . . . Survivable Electronic Air Defense
SEADAC . . . . . Seakeeping Data Analysis Center (Navy)
SEADAG . . . . . Southeast Asia Development Advisory Group (Department of State)
SEADS . . . . . . Survivable and Effective Air Defense System
SEAFRON . . . . Sea Frontier
SEAIC . . . . . . Southeast Asia Information Center
SEAIG . . . . . . Southeast Asia Information Group
SEAL . . . . Sea, Air, and Land
SEAL . . . . Sea, Air, and Land Capability (Refers to Navy personnel trained in unconventional warfare)
SEAL . . . . Signal Evaluation Airborne Laboratory (FAA)

SEALF . . . . . . Semi-Empirical Absorption Loss Formula (Radio)
SEALOR . . . . . Southeast Asia Operational Requirement
SEALR . . . . . . Southeast Asia Logistic Requirement
SEALS . . . . . . Sea, Air, Land Teams
SEALS . . . . . . Stored Energy Actuated Lift System
SEAM . . . . . . Sidewinder Expanded Acquisition Mode
SEAM . . . . . . Society for the Emancipation of the American Male
SEAM . . . . . . Subset Extraction and Association Measurement
SEAMAP . . . . . Scientific Exploration and Mapping Program
SEAMEO . . . . . Southeast Asian Ministers of Education Organization
SEAMIC . . . . . Southeast Asia Management Information Center (Navy)
SEAMORE . . . . Southeast Asia Mohawk Revision Program (Army aviation)
SEAN . . . . . . Syndicat des Enseignants Africains du Niger (African Union of Teachers of Niger)
SEAOR . . . . . . Southeast Asia Operational Requirements
SEAPRO . . . . . Southeast Asia Programs Directorate
SEAR . . . . Safeguard Emergency Action Report (Army)
SEAR . . . . System Engineering Analysis Report
SEARAM . . . . . Semi-Active RADAR Missile
SEARCH . . . . . Scientific Exploration and Research (Seventh-Day Adventist foundation)
SEARCH . . . . . System for Electronic Analysis and Retrieval of Criminal Histories (Project succeeded by National Crime Information Center) (Department of Justice)
SEARCH . . . . . System Evaluation and Reliability Checker
SEARCH . . . . . System for Exploring Alternative Resource Commitments in Higher Education (Data processing)
SEAS . . . . Sea Environment Acquisition System
SEAS . . . . Sea School (Marine Corps)
SEAS . . . . Ship/Equipment/Alterations Summary (Navy)
SEASC . . . . . . Scientific Exploration of the Atlantic Shelf Committee
SEASIA . . . . . . Southeast Asia
SEASTAG . . . . Southeast Asia Treaty Organization Standardization Agreement
SEAT . . . . Sociedad Espanol de Automoviles de Turismo (Spanish automobile manufacturer; acronym used as name of its cars)
SEATAF . . . . . Southern European Atomic Task Force
SEATELCOM . . Southeast Asia Telecommunications System
SEATIC . . . . . . Southeast Asia Translation and Interrogation Center (Navy)
SEATO . . . . . . Southeast Asia Treaty Organization
SEB . . . . Secondary Education Board
SEB . . . . Society for Economic Botany
SEB . . . . Source Evaluation Board (NASA)
SEB . . . . Southern Electricity Board (British)
SEB . . . . Staphylococcal Enterotoxin B
SEB . . . . Strip Electron Beam
SEB . . . . System Error Bridge
SEBA . . . . Staphylococcal Enterotoxin B Antisera
SEBBETSI . . . . . Serikat Buruh Beras dan Tapioca Seluruh Indonesia (Rice and Tapioca Workers' Union) (Indonesia)
SEBC . . . . South-Eastern Bible College (Florida)
SEBDA . . . . . . Serikat Buruh Daehrah Autonoom (Civil Servants' Union) (Indonesia)
SEBIAC . . . . . . Southeast Basins Inter-Agency Committee
SEBIC . . . . Secondary Emission Bombardment-Induced Conductivity
SEBIC . . . . Sustained Electron Bombardment Induced Conductivity
SEBM . . . . Society for Experimental Biology and Medicine
SEBS . . . . Submarine Emergency Buoyancy System
SEBUMI . . . . . . Serikat Buruh Minjak, Stanvac (Oil Workers' Union, Stanvac) (Indonesia)
SEBV . . . . Solder End Ball Valve
SEC . . . . Sanitary Engineering Center
SEC . . . . Scientific and Engineering Computation
SEC . . . . Scientific Estimates Committee
SEC . . . . Secant
SEC . . . . Second
SEC . . . . Secondary Electron Conduction
SEC . . . . Secondary Emission and Conduction
SEC . . . . Secret
SEC . . . . Secretary
SEC . . . . Section
SEC . . . . Secundum (According To) (Latin)
SEC . . . . Securities and Exchange Commission
SEC . . . . Social Economic Council (Sociaal Economische Raad) (Netherlands)
SEC . . . . Societe Europeenne de Culture (European Society of Culture)
SEC . . . . Society for Educative Communication
SEC . . . . Society of Exchange Counselors
SEC . . . . Soft Elastic Capsule (Pharmacy)
SEC . . . . Solar Energy Collector
SEC . . . . Solar Energy Concentrator
SEC . . . . Solid Electrolyte Capacitor
SEC . . . . South-Eastern Command
SEC . . . . Southeastern Conference (College sports)
SEC . . . . Sulphur Export Corporation

SECA . . . . . . Self-Employment Contributions Act (under which self-employed persons contribute to OASDI coverage for themselves)
SECAC . . . . . . Sectional Aeronautical Chart
SECAL . . . . . . Selected Calling System (Military)
SECAM . . . . . . Sequence de Couleurs avec Memoire (Color Sequence with Memory) (French color television system)
SECAN . . . . . . Standing Group Communication Security and Evaluation Agency Washington
SECAP . . . . . . Systems Experiment Correlation and Analysis Program
SECDA . . . . . . Southeastern Community Development Association
SECDEF . . . . . Secretary of Defense
SECE . . . . Selfhelp of Emigres from Central Europe
SECFLT . . . . . . Second Fleet (Atlantic) (Navy)
SECH . . . . Secant, Hyperbolic
SECIT . . . . Syndicat des Employes Indigenes du Commerce du Togo (Union of Indigenous Employees of Commerce of Togo)
SECNAV . . . . . Secretary of the Navy
SECO . . . . Self-Regulating Error-Correct Coder-Decoder
SECO . . . . Sequential Coding and Decoding
SECO . . . . Sequential Control (Data processing; Teletype)
SECO . . . . Sustainer-Engine Cutoff
SECOFF . . . . . Section Office
SECON . . . . . . Secondary Electron Conduction (Television camera system)
SECOR . . . . . . Sequential Collation of Range (Army program)
SECP . . . . (Division of) Shore Establishment and Civilian Personnel (Navy)
SECRA . . . . . . Secondary RADAR (RADAR beacon)
SECS . . . . Solar Electric Communication Satellite
SECS . . . . Stem Elevated Camera System
SECTASKFLT . . Second Task Fleet
SECTBASE . . . . Section Base (Navy)
SEC(UN) . . . . . Secretariat of the United Nations
SECUS . . . . . . Supreme Emblem Club of the United States
SECWAR . . . . . Secretary of War
SECY . . . . Secretary
SED . . . . Sanitary Engineering Division (MIT)
SED . . . . Scottish Education Department
SED . . . . Sedco, Inc. (NYSE symbol)
SED . . . . Shore Establishments Division (Navy)
SED . . . . Skin Erythema Dose (Medicine)
SED . . . . Solar Energy Density
SED . . . . Sound Energy Density
SED . . . . Sozialistische Einheitspartei Deutschlands (Socialist Union Party of the German Democratic Republic)
SED . . . . Space Environment Division (of NASA)
SED . . . . Spectral Energy Distribution
SED . . . . State Executive Director
SED . . . . Stray Energy Detector
SED . . . . Systems Effectiveness Demonstration
SEDA . . . . State Emergency Defense Airlift
SEDCOR . . . . . Specialty Electronics Development Corporation
SEDD . . . . Systems Evaluation and Development Division (NASA)
SEDEIS . . . . . . Societe d'Etudes et de Documentation Economiques Industrielles et Sociales (France)
SEDES . . . . . . Societe d'Etudes pour le Developpement Economique et Social (France)
SEDFRE . . . . . Scholarship, Education and Defense Fund for Racial Equality
SEDL . . . . Southwest Educational Development Laboratory
SEDPC . . . . . . Scientific and Engineering Data Processing Center
SEDR . . . . Service Engineering Department Report
SEDS . . . . Society for Educational Data Systems
SEDS . . . . System Effectiveness Data System (Air Force)
SEE . . . . Secondary Electron Emission
SEE . . . . Society of Environmental Engineers (British)
SEE . . . . Survival, Evasion, and Escape (Military)
SEE . . . . Systems Effectiveness Evaluation
SEE . . . . Systems Efficiency Expert
SEEA . . . . Societe Europeenne d'Energie Atomique
SEE ACT . . . . . Shore Electronic Engineering Activity (Navy)
SEEB . . . . Southeastern Electricity Board (British)
SEED . . . . Skill Escalation Employment Development
SEED . . . . Special Elementary Education for the Disadvantaged
SEED . . . . Supply of Essential Engineering Data
SEEK . . . . Search for Education, Elevation and Knowledge (Program)
SEEK . . . . Survival Escape and Evasion Kit (Navy)
SEEK . . . . Systems Evaluation and Exchange of Knowledge (Data processing)
SEEN . . . . Syndicat d'Etudes de l'Energie Nucleaire (Belgium)
SEEO . . . . Shore Electronic Engineering Office (Navy)
SEER . . . . Submarine Explosive Echo Ranging
SEER . . . . Supervisory Electronic Engineer (Radio)
SEER . . . . System for Electronic Evaluation and Retrieval (Data processing)
SEER . . . . Systems Engineering, Evaluation and Research
SEES . . . . System Effectiveness Engineering Section
SEF . . . . Seaboard Finance Company (NYSE symbol) (Delisted)

SEF . . . . Self-Extinguishing Fiber (Monsanto Co. trademark)
SEF . . . . Shielding Effectiveness Factor
SEF . . . . Simple Environment Factor
SEF . . . . Solar Energy Flux
SEF . . . . Sound Energy Flux
SEF . . . . Southern Education Foundation
SEF . . . . Space Education Foundation
SEF . . . . Surface Effect Ship
SEFAR . . . . . Sonic End Fire for Azimuth & Range
SEFD . . . . . . Solar Energy Flux Density
SEFIC . . . . . . Seventh Fleet Intelligence Center (Navy)
SEFLO . . . . . . Sequence Flow (Tracing technique)
SEFOR . . . . . . Southwest Experimental Fast Oxide Reactor (for commercial atomic
                power)
SEFR . . . . Shielding Experiment Facility Reactor (AEC)
SEFSP . . . . . . Space Experiment and Flight Support Program
SEFT . . . . . . Single Engine Flight Training
SEG . . . . Screen Extras Guild
SEG . . . . Sliding Electron Gun
SEG . . . . Society of Economic Geologists
SEG . . . . Society of Exploration Geophysicists
SEG . . . . Standardization Evaluation Group
SEG . . . . Systems Engineering Group (Air Force)
SEG . . . . Systems Evaluation Group
SEGBA . . . . . Servicios Electricos del Gran Buenos Aires, SA (Electrical utility)
                (Argentina)
SEH . . . . Societe Europeenne d'Hematologie
SEH . . . . Solar Equivalent Hours
SEI . . . . Society of Engineering Illustrators
SEI . . . . Special Experience Identifier (Military)
SEI . . . . Statistical Engineering Institute
SEI . . . . Stockpile Entry Inspection (Navy)
SEI . . . . Stray Energy Indicator
SEI . . . . System/Equipment Inventory
SEIAC . . . . . . Science Education Information Analysis Center (ERIC)
SEIC . . . . Solar Energy Information Center
SEIC . . . . System Effectiveness Information Central
SEIOD . . . . . . Spogli Elettronici dell'Italiano delle Origini e del Duecento
                (A lexical, morphological, and syntactical inventory of Old
                Italian texts)
SEIP . . . . System Engineering Implementation Plan
SEIS . . . . Submarine Emergency Identification Signal
SEISA . . . . . . South Eastern Intercollegiate Sailing Association
SEIT . . . . Satellite Educational and Informational Television
SEIT . . . . Supervisory Electronic Installation Technician
SEJ . . . . Sliding Expansion Joint (Technical drawings)
SEK . . . . Synomospondia Ergaton Kyprou (Cyprus Workers' Confederation) ("Free
                Labour Syndicats")
SEKF . . . . . . Sister Elizabeth Kenny Foundation
SEL . . . . Scout Esperanto League
SEL . . . . Southeastern Educational Laboratory
SEL . . . . Standard Elektrik Lorenz (Germany)
SEL . . . . Stanford Electronic Laboratory (Stanford University)
SEL . . . . Systems Engineering Laboratory
SELC . . . . South Eastern Louisiana College
SELCAL . . . . . Selective Calling (Radio)
SELF . . . . National Citizens Committee to Save Education and Library Funds
SELF . . . . Societe des Ecrivains Luxembourgeois de Langue Francaise
SELL . . . . Suomi, Eesti, Latvija, Lietuva (Finland, Estonia, Latvia, Lithuania)
SELNI . . . . . . Societa Elettronucleare Italiana (Power reactor) (Italy)
SELS . . . . Severe Local Storm
SELSYN . . . . . Self-Synchronous (Trade name) (Motor)
SELT . . . . SAGE Evaluation Library Tape
SELT . . . . Sheet Explosive Loading Technique
SELT . . . . Syndicat des Enseignements Laics (Union of Public School Teachers)
                (Togo)
SEM . . . . Scanning Electron Microscope (or Microscopy)
SEM . . . . Semi-Enriched Minimal (Agar)
SEM . . . . Society for Ethnomusicology
SEM . . . . Standard Error of the Mean
SEM . . . . Stray Energy Monitor
SEM . . . . Subarray Electronics Module (Data processing)
SEM . . . . System Engineering Management
SEMA . . . . . . Societe d'Etudes de Mathematiques Appliquees (France)
SEMA . . . . . . Specialty Equipment Manufacturers Association
SEMCOG . . . . Southeast Michigan Council of Governments
SEMCOR . . . . . Semantic Correlation (Machine-aided indexing)
SEMD . . . . . . Stray Energy Monitor Device
SEMH . . . . . . Service Engineering Man-Hours
SEMI . . . . . . Self-Evacuating Multilayer Insulation (System)

SEMIS . . . . . . State Extension Management Information System (Department of
                Agriculture)
SEMLAM . . . . . Semiconductor LASER Amplifier
SEMLAT . . . . . Semiconductor LASER Array Techniques
SEMO . . . . . . Systems Engineering and Management Operations (Military)
SEMP . . . . . . Simplified Early Maturities Participation Plan (Small Business Administration)
SEMP . . . . . . System Engineering Management Plan
SEMRE . . . . . SPRINT Electromagnetic Radiation Evaluation
SEMS . . . . . . Severe Environment Memory Series (Data processing)
SEMS . . . . . . Stray Energy Monitor System
SEMS . . . . . . Support Engineering Manhours System
SEMS . . . . . . System Engineering Management Standard
SEMT . . . . . . Science, Engineering, Medicine, and Technology (Series)
SEMTA . . . . . Southeast Michigan Transportation Authority
SEMTR . . . . . SPRINT Early Missile Test RADAR (Army)
SEMTR . . . . . Supervisory Electronic Maintenance Technician (Relief)
SEN . . . . Senator
SEN . . . . Senior
SEN . . . . Steam Emulsion Number
SEN . . . . Syndicat des Enseignants du Niger (Union of Nigerian Teachers)
SENA . . . . . . Seaport Navigation Company (AAR code)
SENA . . . . . . Societe d'Energie Nucleaire Franco-Belge Ardennes (Belgian-French power
                consortium)
SENAC . . . . . Servico Nacional de Aprendizagem Comercial (Brazil)
SENAI . . . . . . Servico Nacional de Aprendizagem Industrial (Brazil)
SENAVAV . . . . Senior Naval Aviator (Navy)
SENL . . . . Standard Equipment Nomenclature List
SENLOG . . . . . Sentinel Logistics Command
SENN . . . . . . Societa Elettronucleare Nazionale (Italy)
SENPO . . . . . . Sentinel Project Office (Army)
SENSCOM . . . . Sentinel Systems Command (Army)
SENSEA . . . . . Sentinel System Evaluation Agency
SENTA . . . . . . Societe d'Etudes Nucleaires et de Techniques Advances (France)
SENTRAB . . . . Syndicat des Travailleurs des Entreprises, Privees, Travaux Publics et
                Batiments (Union of Workers of Private Enterprises, Public Works and
                Buildings) (Togo)
SEO . . . . Senior Engineer Officer (Navy)
SEO . . . . Senior Executive Officer (British)
SEO . . . . Senior Experimental Officer (Ministry of Agriculture, Fisheries, and Food)
                (Also, SExO and SXO) (British)
SEO . . . . Sin Errores y Omisiones (Errors and Omissions Excepted) (Business and
                trade) (Spain)
SEODSE . . . . . Special Explosive Ordnance Disposal Supplies and Equipment (Army)
SEOPSN . . . . . Select-Operate-Sense
SEP . . . . Saturday Evening Post
SEP . . . . Scientific and Engineering Personnel
SEP . . . . Selective Employment Payments (British)
SEP . . . . Separate
SEP . . . . September
SEP . . . . Serial Entry Printer
SEP . . . . Slug Ejector Punch
SEP . . . . Society of Engineering Psychologists
SEP . . . . Society of Experimental Psychologists
SEP . . . . Solar-Electric Propulsion
SEP . . . . Somatic Evoked Potential
SEP . . . . Southern Education Program
SEP . . . . Space Electronic Package
SEP . . . . Spherical Error Probability
SEP . . . . Standard Electronic Package
SEP . . . . Student Expense Program (Civil Defense)
SEPA . . . . . . Southeast Pacific Area
SEPA . . . . . . Southeastern Power Administration (Department of the Interior)
SEPA . . . . . . Southeastern Psychological Association
SEPACFOR . . . . Southeast Pacific Force (Navy)
SEPC . . . . . . Space Exploration Program Council (NASA)
SEPCEN . . . . . Separation Center (Navy)
SEPE . . . . Seattle Port of Embarkation
SEPE . . . . Societe d'Edition et de Publications en Exlusivite
SEPEMIAG . . . . Societe d'Etudes pour l'Equipement Miniere, Agricole et Industrial du
                Gabon (Gabon Society for Study of Mining, Agricultural and Industrial
                Equipment)
SEPGA . . . . . . Southeastern Pecan Growers Association
SEPL . . . . South European Pipeline (Oil)
SEPM . . . . . . Society of Economic Paleontologists and Mineralogists
SEPO . . . . . . Space Electric Power Office (AEC)
SEPORT . . . . . Supply and Equipment Report (Army)
SEPOS . . . . . . Selected Enlisted Personnel for Overseas Service
SEPR . . . . Societe d'Etude de la Propulsion Par Reaction
SEPROS . . . . . Separation Processing
SEPS . . . . Solar Electric-Propelled Spacecraft
SEPS . . . . System/Equipment Population Summary

SEPSA ...... Society of Educational Programmers and Systems Analysts
SEPST ...... Solar Electric Propulsion System Technology
SEPT........ September
SEPTA ...... Southeastern Pennsylvania Transportation Authority
SEPTEL ...... Separate Telegram
SEQU .... Sequoia and Kings Canyon National Parks
SEQUR ...... Safety Equipment Requirements
SER .... Sandia Engineering Reactor
SER .... Serial
SER .... Serine (Amino acid)
SER .... Service, Employment, Redevelopment (Operation for Mexican-Americans)
SER .... Sierra R.R. (AAR code)
SER .... Smooth (Surfaced) Endoplasmic Reticulum
SER .... SNAP (Systems for Nuclear Auxiliary Power) Experimental Reactor
SER .... South-Eastern Railway (British)
SER .... Sua Eccellenza Reveréndissima (His Eminence)
SER .... Surface Electrical Resistivity
SERA ...... Services, Education, Rehabilitation for Addiction (New York City)
SERA ...... Sierra R. R. (AAR code).
SERAC ...... Southeastern Regional Arts Council
SERAPE ...... Simulator Equipment Requirements for Accelerating Procedural Evolution
SERB ...... Study of the Enhanced Radiation Belt (NASA)
SERBAUD..... Serikat Buruh Angkutan Udara (Airways' Union) (Indonesia)
SERBIUM..... Serikat Buruh Industri dan Umum (Industrial and General Workers' Union) (Indonesia)
SERBU ...... Serikat Buruh Umum (General Workers' Union) (Indonesia)
SERBUHI ...... Serikat Buruh Harian Indonesia (Newspaper Employees' Union) (Indonesia)
SERBUMAMI... Serikat Buruh Makanan dan Minuman (Food Workers' Union) (Indonesia)
SERBUMIKSI.. Serikat Buruh Minjak Kelapa Seluruh (Coconut Oil Workers' Union) (Indonesia)
SERBUMIT .... Serikat Buruh Minjak dan Tambang (Oil and Minerals Workers' Union) (Indonesia)
SERBUMUSI ... Serikat Buruh Muslimin Indonesia (Moslem Workers' Union of Indonesia)
SERBUNI ..... Serikat Buruh Unilever Indonesia (Unilever Employees' Union) (Indonesia)
SERBUPI ..... Serikat Buruh Perkebunan Indo (Plantation Workers' Union of Indonesia)
SERBUPRI..... Serikat Buruh Pertambangan Indonesia (Mining Workers' Union) (Indonesia)
SERD .... Social, Educational Research & Development, Inc.
SERDES ..... Serializer, Deserializer
SERE....... Survival, Evasion, Resistance and Escape (Military)
SEREB .... Societe pour l'Etude et la Realisation d'Engins Balistiques (France)
SERF........ Sandia Engineering Reactor Facility
SERF........ Space Environmental Research Facility
SERFORSOPACSUBCOM .. Service Force South Pacific Subordinate Command
SERJ........ Supercharged Ejector Ramjet (Aircraft engine)
SERL........ Sanitary Engineering Research Laboratory (University of California)
SERL........ Services Electronics Research Laboratory (British)
SERLANT..... Service Forces, Atlantic (Navy)
SERM .... Society of Early Recorded Music
SERMCE ..... Amalgamated Association of Street, Electric Railway and Motor Coach Employees of America
SERME ...... Sign Error Root Modulus Error
SERON ...... Service Squadron (Navy)
SERPAC ..... Service Forces, Pacific (Navy)
SERRON .... Service Squadron (Navy)
SERS....... Southern Education Reporting Service
SERS .... State Employees Retirement System
SERS....... Support Equipment Requirements Sheet
SERT....... Solar Electric Rocket Test
SERT .... Space Electric Rocket Test
SERT .... Spinning Satellite for Electric Rocket Test
SERTH...... Satisfactory Evidence Received This Headquarters
SERTOMA .... Service to Mankind (Meaning of name of Sertoma International Organization)
SERV ...... Single-Stage Earth-Orbital Reusable Vehicle
SERVCOMFMFPAC .. Service Command, Fleet Marine Force, Pacific
SERVDIV .... Service Division (Navy)
SERVE....... Serve and Enrich Retirement by Volunteer Experience (Staten Island, NY, project)
SERVFOR .... Service Force (Navy)
SERVHEL..... Service Record(s) and Health Record(s)
SERVLANT.... Service Force, Atlantic Fleet
SERVLANTSUBORDCOMD.. Service Force, Atlantic Fleet, Subordinate Command
SERVNO .... Service Number (Navy)
SERVon .... Marine Corps Air Service Squadron
SERVON .... Service Squadron (Navy)
SERVPA..... Service Record(s) and Pay Record(s)
SERVPAC..... Service Force, Pacific Fleet
SERVPAHEL... Service Record(s), Pay Record(s) and Health Record(s)
SERVREC..... Service Record(s)
SERVSOWESPAC .. Service Force, Southwest Pacific Fleet
SES .... Satellite Earth Station

SES .... Seafarers Education Service (British)
SES .... Secondary Electron Scattering
SES .... Section d'Eclaireurs-Skieurs (of Chasseurs Alpins, French Army)
SES .... Sequential Environmental Stress
SES .... Shahmoon Industries, Inc. (American Stock Exchange symbol)
SES .... Small Edison Screw
SES .... Society of Engineering Science
SES .... Society of Eye Surgeons
SES .... Socioeconomic Status (or Strata)
SES .... Soil Erosion Service (Became Soil Conservation Service, 1935)
SES .... Solar Energy Society
SES .... Solar Environment Simulator
SES .... SONAR Echo Simulator
SES .... Space Environment Simulator (NASA)
SES .... Space Erectable Structure
SES .... Standards Engineers Society
SES .... State Experiment Stations Division (of ARS, Department of Agriculture)
SES .... Steam Engine Systems Corp.
SES .... Strategic Engineering Survey (Navy)
SES .... Study of Education at Stanford (Stanford University)
SES .... Supervisory Electronics Specialist
SES .... Surface Effect Ship
SES .... Sustaining Engineering Services
SESA ...... Signal Equipment Support Agency
SESA ...... Social and Economic Statistics Administration (Department of Commerce)
SESA ...... Society for Experimental Stress Analysis
SESA ...... Standard Electrica, SA (Brazilian affiliate of ITT)
SESAC ...... Society of European Stage Authors and Composers
SESAM ...... Systeme Electronique de Selection Automatique de Microfilms
SESAME ...... Search for Excellence in Science and Mathematics Education (Graduate program at University of California at Berkeley)
SESAME ..... Service, Sort and Merge (Data processing term)
SESC ...... South Eastern State College (Oklahoma)
SESC ...... Surface Environmental Sample Container (Apollo) (NASA)
SESCO ...... Secure Submarine Communications
SESDA ...... Serikat Sekerdja Departemen Agama (Brotherhood of Employees of Department of Religious Affairs) (Indonesia)
SESE........ Secure Echo-Sounding Equipment (SONAR) (Navy)
SESKOAD .... Sekolah Staf dan Komando Angkatan Darat
SESL........ Space Environment Simulation Laboratory (NASA)
SESOC ...... Surface Effects Ship for Ocean Commerce
SESP........ Society of Experimental Social Psychology
SESP........ Space Experiment Support Program
SESPA...... Scientists and Engineers for Social and Political Action
SESPENDO ... Serikat Buruh Pegawai Negeri dan Daeran Otonom (Civil Servants Workers' Union) (Indonesia)
SESR........ Selected Equipment Status Report (Navy)
SESR........ Societe Europeenne de Sociologie Rurale (European Society for Rural Sociology)
SESS........ Space Environmental Support System
SESS........ Summer Employment for Science Students
SET .... Scientists, Engineers, Technicians
SET .... Security Escort Team (Military)
SET .... Selective Electronic Training (Navy)
SET .... Selective Employment Tax (British)
SET. .... Senior Electronic Technician (National Weather Service)
SET .... Sensory Evaluation Test (Army)
SET .... Simplified Engineering Technique
SET .... Solar Energy Thermionic Program (NASA)
SET .... Space Electronics and Telemetry
SET .... Synchro Error Tester
SET .... Syndicat des Enseignants du Togo (Union of Togolese Teachers)
SE & T ...... Supplies, Equipment and Training (Civil Defense)
SETA ...... Simplified Electronic Tracking Apparatus (Air Force)
SETAC ...... Sector Tactical Air Navigation (System)
SETAF...... Southern European Task Force
SETAR ...... Serial Event Timer and Recorder
SETC .... Solid Electrolyte Tantalum Capacitor
SETD .... Sledborne Event Time Digitizer
SETD .... Space Environment Test Division (NASA)
SE/TD ...... Systems Engineering and Technical Direction
SETE ...... Secretariat for Electronic Test Equipment
SETE ...... Support and Electronic Test Equipment
SETF....... SNAP (Systems for Nuclear Auxiliary Power) Experimental Test Facility
SET-GO ..... Support and Encouragement for Talent - Gateway to Opportunity (Project)
SETINA..... Southeast Texas Information Network Association
SETIS ...... Societe Europeenne pour l'Etude et l'Integration des Systemes Spatiaux
SETP....... Society of Experimental Test Pilots
SETS .... Solar Electric Test Satellite
SETS ...... Solar Energy Thermionic Conversion System (NASA)
SETS ...... Special Electron Tube Section

SETT .... Submarine Escape Training Tank
SETU .... Societe d'Etudes et de Travaux pour l'Uranium (France)
SEU .... Saint Edward's University (Texas)
SEU .... Southeastern University (Washington, DC)
SEU .... Subjective Expected Utility (Concept) (Psychology of union-management relations)
SEUS .... Southeastern United States
SEV .... Schweizerischer Elektrotechnischer Verein (Swiss)
SEV .... Scout Evaluation Vehicle
SEV .... Ship Exercise Vehicle
SEV .... Special Equipment Vehicle
SEV .... Surface Effects Vehicle (Military)
SEVA .... Standup Extravehicular Activity (Aerospace)
SEVAC ...... Secure Voice Access Console (Army)
SEVAS ...... Secure Voice Access Systems (Army)
SEVFLT ..... Seventh Fleet (Pacific) (Navy)
SEVOCOM ... Secure Voice Communications
SEVP .... Severance Pay (Military)
SEW .... Silicon Epitaxial Wafer
SEW .... SONAR Early Warning
SEWT .... Simulator for Electronic Warfare Training
SEX .... Summer Experiment Group (Summer work for engineering undergraduates)
SExO .... Senior Experimental Officer (Ministry of Agriculture, Fisheries, and Food) (Also, SEO and SXO) (British)
SEY .... Secondary Electron Yield
SEYM .... Secondary Electron Yield Measurement
SEYMS ..... Secondary Electron Yield Measurement System
SEYS .... Secondary Electron Yield System
SF .... Atchison, Topeka & Sante Fe Railway Company (NYSE symbol) (Later, SFF)
SF .... Fleet Submarine (Navy symbol)
SF .... Sacrifice Fly (Baseball)
SF .... Safety Factor
SF .... San Francisco (California)
SF .... Scale Factor
SF .... Science Fiction (Also, SCI-FI)
SF .... Scouting Force (Navy)
SF .... Sea Flood
SF .... Security Forces (Japanese army)
SF .... Semifinished (Steel or other material)
SF .... Senior Fellow
SF .... Separation Factor (Chemical analysis)
SF .... Sexagesimo-quarto (Book up to 7 1/2 centimeters in height) (Bibliography)
SF .... Sforzando (Indicates sudden emphasis on single note or chord) (Music)
SF .... Sherwood Foresters (Military unit) (British)
SF .... Shift Forward
SF .... Shipfitter (Navy)
SF .... Signal-Frequency
SF .... Single Feeder
SF .... Sinking Fund (Finance)
SF .... Slow Fire (Military)
SF .... Soils and Fertilisers (An abstracts journal)
SF .... Sons of the Holy Family
SF .... Sound and Flash
SF .... Source and Fissionable (Material) (Obsolete; see SS) (AEC)
SF .... Special Facilities
SF .... Special Forces (Military)
SF .... Spinal Fluid (Medicine)
SF .... Spontaneous Fission (Radioactivity)
SF .... Spot Face
SF .... Square Foot
SF .... Standard Form (Military)
SF .... Standard Frequency
SF .... Stock Fund
SF .... Stowage Factor (Shipping)
SF .... Stress Formula
SF .... Structure Function
SF .... Su Favor (Your Favor) (Spain)
SF .... Sub Finem (Near the End)
SF .... Success Factor
SF .... Sulfation Factor (of blood serum)
SF .... Surface Foot
SF .... Swedenborg Foundation
SF .... Syndicat des Fonctionnaires (Lao Civil Servants' Union)
S/F .... Store-and-Forward
S & F ...... Sound and Flash (Battalion) (Military)
SFA .... Saks Fifth Avenue (Retail clothing store)
SFA .... Scandinavian Fraternity of America
SFA .... Short Field Aircraft
SFA .... Show Folks of America
SFA .... Simulated Flight-Automatic

SFA .... Single-Frequency Approach (Aviation)
SFA .... Slide Fastener Association
SFA .... Slow Flying Aircraft
SFA .... Solid Fuels Administration (Terminated 1954)
SFA .... Soroptimist Federation of the Americas
SFA .... Southeastern Fisheries Association
SFA .... Southern Freight Association
SFA .... Spatial Frequency Analyzer
SFA .... Special Foreign Activities (Military)
SFA .... Subcommittee on Frequency Allocations
SFA .... Sunfinder Assembly
SFA .... Symphony Foundation of America
S & FA ..... Shipping and Forwarding Agent
SFAAW ..... Stove, Furnace and Allied Appliance Workers' International Union of North America (AFL-CIO)
SFAC .... Societe des Forges et Ateliers du Creusot (France)
SFAD .... Society of Federal Artists and Designers
SFADS ...... San Francisco Air Defense Sector (ADC)
SFAL .... Samuel Feltman Ammunition Laboratory (Army)
SFAPS ...... Space Flight Acceleration Profile Simulator (NASA)
SFAR .... Sound Fixing and Ranging
SFAW .... Solid Fuel Administration for War (World War II) (Terminated 1947)
SFAW .... Stove, Furnace and Allied Appliance Workers
SFB .... Sender Freies Berlin
SFB .... Structural Feedback
SFBA ...... Steamship Freight Brokers Association
SFBARTD ... San Francisco Bay Area Rapid Transit District
SFBNS ...... San Francisco Bay Naval Shipyard
SFC .... S-Band Frequency Converter
SFC .... Saint Francis College (Indiana, Maine, New York, Pennsylvania, Wisconsin)
SFC .... School Facilities Council of Architecture, Education and Industry
SFC .... Sergeant First Class
SFC .... Sight Fire Control
SFC .... Sioux Falls College (South Dakota)
SFC .... Space Flight Center
SFC .... Special Flight Charts (Air Force)
SFC .... Specific Fuel Consumption
SFC .... Spinal Fluid Count (Medicine)
SFC .... Supercritical Fluid Chromatography
SFC .... Superior Fine Cognac
SFC .... Surface
SFC .... Switching Filter Connector
SFC .... Synchronized Framing Camera
SFCB .... Shipfitter, Construction Battalion (Navy)
SFCBB ..... Shipfitter, Construction Battalion, Blacksmith (Navy)
SFCBM ..... Shipfitter, Construction Battalion, Mechanical Draftsman (Navy)
SFCBP ..... Shipfitter, Construction Battalion, Pipe Fitter and Plumber (Navy)
SFCBR ...... Shipfitter, Construction Battalion, Rigger (Navy)
SFCBS ...... Shipfitter, Construction Battalion, Steelworker (Navy)
SFCBW ..... Shipfitter, Construction Battalion, Welder (Navy)
SFCC .... Sisters for a Christian Community
SFCP .... Shore Fire Control Party (Air Force)
SFCRS ...... State-Federal Crop Reporting Service
SFCS .... Saint Fidelis College and Seminary (Pennsylvania)
SFCS .... Surveyor Flight Control Section
SFCS .... Survivable Flight Control System (Air Force)
SFCSI ...... Special Foreign Currency Science Information (Program) (National Science Foundation)
SFCSIP ..... Special Foreign Currency Science Information Program (National Science Foundation)
SFCW ...... San Francisco College for Women (California)
SFCW ...... Sweep Frequency, Continuous Wave
SFD .... Solar Flux Density
SFD .... Stouffer Foods Corporation (NYSE symbol) (Delisted)
SFD .... Sudden Frequency Deviation
SFD .... Systems Flexowriter Double Case
SFDS .... Standby Fighter Director Ship (Navy)
SFDT .... Signal Format Development Team (France)
SFE .... Safeguard Industries (NYSE symbol)
SFE .... Societe Francaise des Electriciens (France)
SFE .... Society of Fire Engineers
SFE .... Stacking Fault Energy (Alloy)
SFE .... Surface-Free Energy
SFEA .... Survival and Flight Equipment Association
SFEC .... Standard Facility Equipment Card(s) (Electrical accounting machine)
SFEL .... Standard Facility Equipment List (Electronics)
SFEM .... Segner's Fortified Edd Meat (Growth medium for phage)
SFENA ..... Societe Francaise d'Equipements pour la Navigation Aerienne
SFERMA .... Societe Francaise d'Entretien et de Reparation de Materiel Aeronautique (France)
SFF .... Santa Fe Industries, Inc. (NYSE symbol)

SFF . . . . Sea Frontier Force (Navy)

SFF . . . . Site Field Force (Army)

SFF . . . . Solar Forecast Facility (Air Force)

SFF . . . . Spiritual Frontiers Fellowship

SFFV . . . . Spleen Focus Formation Virus

SFG . . . . Staircase Function Generator

SFGD . . . . Shell's Flue Gas Desulfurization

SFGE . . . . San Francisco Grain Exchange

SFH . . . . Standard Fading Hour (National Bureau of Standards)

SFH . . . . Super Flux Harness

SFHS . . . . Society for French Historical Studies

SFI . . . . Sindacato Ferrovieri Italiani (Union of Italian Railroad Workers)

SFI . . . . Small Flow Indicator

SFI . . . . Societe Financiere Internationale (International Finance Society)

SFI . . . . Sport Fishing Institute

SFI . . . . Step Function Input

SFI . . . . Surveyor Fund, Incorporated (NYSE symbol)

SFIC . . . . San Francisco Information Center (Army Air Warning Service)

SFID . . . . Section Francaise de l'Internationale Ouvriere (French Section of the Workers International)

SFIO . . . . Societe Francaise de l'Internationale Ouvriere (French Socialist Party)

SFIR . . . . Specific Force Integrating Receiver (Air Force)

SFIT . . . . Standard Family Interaction Test (Psychology)

SFJ . . . . Swept Frequency Jamming

SFL . . . . Sequence Flash Lights (FAA)

SFL . . . . Society of Federal Linguists

SFM . . . . Simulated Flight-Manual

SFM . . . . Simulated Flow Method

SFM . . . . Surface Feet per Minute

SFM . . . . Swept Frequency Modulation

SFMA . . . . . . Soda Fountain Manufacturers Association

SFMA . . . . . . Southern Furniture Manufacturers Association

SFMA . . . . . . Subscription Fulfillment Managers Association (Later, FMA)

SFMF . . . . . . Student Foreign Missions Fellowship

SFMI . . . . . . Soft Fibre Manufacturers' Institute

SFML . . . . Standard Facility Material List (Electrical accounting machine)

SFN . . . . Scott, Foresman & Co. (NYSE symbol)

SFN . . . . Ship and Facilities, Navy

SFNA . . . . Stabilized Fuming Nitric Acid

SFNCTU . . . . . Swiss Federation of National-Christian Trade Unions

SFNSY . . . . . . San Francisco Naval Shipyard

SFO . . . . San Francisco (California) (Airport symbol)

SFO . . . . San Francisco Oakland Helicopter Airlines, Inc.

SFO . . . . Service Fuel Oil

SFO . . . . Simulated Flame Out (Aviation)

SFO . . . . Space Flight Operations

SFO . . . . Spoleczny Fundusz Oszczednosciowy

SFO . . . . Subfornical Organ

SFO . . . . Submarine Fog Oscillator (Maps and charts)

S & FO . . . . . Supply and Fiscal Officer

SFOB . . . . Special Forces Operational Base

SFOBB . . . . . . San Francisco-Oakland Bay Bridge

SFOC . . . . Space Flight Operations Complex (NASA)

SFOD . . . . San Francisco Ordnance District

SFOD . . . . Space Flight Operations Director (NASA)

SFOD . . . . . . Special Forces Operational Detachment (Army)

SFOF . . . . Space Flight Operations Facility (NASA)

SFP . . . . Shungwayah Freedom Party (Kenya)

SFP . . . . Sintered Ferrous Part

SFP . . . . Solar Flare Proton

SFP . . . . Spartan-Furnished Property

SFP . . . . Straight Fixed Price

SFP . . . . Super Flat Pack

SFP . . . . Sustainer Firing Package

SFP-ANGS . . . Standardization Field Panel for Artillery and Naval Gunfire Support (Army)

SFPE . . . . San Francisco Port of Embarkation

SFPE . . . . Society of Fire Protection Engineers

SFPM . . . . Surface Feet Per Minute

SFPOE . . . . . . San Francisco Port of Embarkation (Military)

SFPOMMPAB . . Society for the Prevention of Married Men Posing as Bachelors

SFPP . . . . Spruce Falls Power & Paper Company (AAR code)

SFPPS . . . . . . Shore Facilities Planning and Programming System (Navy)

SFPRL . . . . . . Spartan-Furnished Property Request List

SFPTU . . . . . . Swiss Federation of Protestant Trade Unions

SFQ . . . . Southern Folklore Quarterly

SFR . . . . Safety of Flight Requirements

SFR . . . . Schaefer (F & M) Corp. (NYSE symbol)

SFR . . . . Selective File Retrieval

SFR . . . . Sequenced Flashing Lights

SFR . . . . SFC Financial Corporation (NYSE symbol) (Delisted)

SFR . . . . Solar Flare Radiation

SFR . . . . Space Frame RADOME

SFR . . . . Submarine Fleet Reactor

SFRA . . . . . . Science Fiction Research Association

S and FRAN . . San Francisco (California) (Navy)

SFRB . . . . Atchison, Topeka & Santa Fe – DF Loaders (AAR code)

SFRC . . . . . . Soya Food Research Council

SFRD . . . . . . Atchison, Topeka & Santa Fe – Refrigerator Cars (AAR code)

SFRD . . . . . . Secret Formerly Restricted

SFRJ . . . . Solid Fuel Ramjet

SFRS . . . . . . Swept Frequency Radiometer System

SFS . . . . S-Band Feed System

SFS . . . . Saint Francis Seminary (Wisconsin)

SFS . . . . Saybolt Furol Second (Oil Viscosity)

SFS . . . . Senior Flight Surgeon (Army)

SFS . . . . Simplified Firing System

SFS . . . . Society for Freedom in Science

SFS . . . . Sonic Frequency System

SFS . . . . Star Field Sensor

SFS . . . . . . Surfaced Four Sides

SF & S . . . . . . Supporting Facilities and Services

SFSA . . . . . . Steel Founders' Society of America (Later, Cast Metals Federation)

SFSAFBI . . . . Society of Former Special Agents of the Federal Bureau of Investigation

SFSC . . . . . . San Francisco State College (California)

SFSCT . . . . . . Smooth-Face Structural Clay Tile (Technical drawings)

SFSD . . . . Star Field Scanning Device

S & FSD . . . . . Sea and Foreign Service Duty (A Navy pay status)

S & FSD(A) . . . Sea and Foreign Service Duty (Aviation) (A Navy pay status)

S & FSD(S) . . . Sea and Foreign Service Duty (Submarine) (A Navy pay status)

SFSE . . . . . . San Francisco Stock Exchange

SFSR . . . . Shipfitter, Ship Repair (Navy)

SFSRC . . . . . . Shipfitter, Ship Repair, Chipper-Caulker (Navy)

SFSRD . . . . . . Shipfitter, Ship Repair, Diver (Navy)

SFSRF . . . . . . Shipfitter, Ship Repair, Steelworker-Anglesmith (Navy)

SFSRL . . . . . . Shipfitter, Ship Repair, Driller-Reamer (Navy)

SFSRP . . . . . . Shipfitter, Ship Repair, Pipe Fitter-Plumber (Navy)

SFSRR . . . . . . Shipfitter, Ship Repair, Riveter (Navy)

SFSRS . . . . . . Shipfitter, Ship Repair, Shipfitter (Navy)

SFSRW . . . . . . Shipfitter, Ship Repair, Welder (Navy)

SFST . . . . Scherenfernrohrstand (Emplacement of battery commander's telescope) (German military – World War II)

SFSU . . . . Singapore Federation of Services' Unions

SFT . . . . Simulated Flight Tests

SFT . . . . Specific Financial Transactions

SFT . . . . Spiral Fin Tubing

SFT . . . . Squeeze Film Test

SFT . . . . Stop for Tea (British)

SFT . . . . Superfast Train

SFTC . . . . Sherman Fairchild Technology Center

SFTE . . . . . . Society of Flight Test Engineers

SFTIP . . . . . . Special Flight Test Instrumentation Pool

SFTS . . . . . . San Francisco Theological Seminary

SFTS . . . . Synthetic Flight Training System

SFTU . . . . . . Swiss Federation of Trade Unions

SFTW . . . . . . Stamps for the Wounded

SFU . . . . Signals Flying Unit (British)

SFU . . . . Societe de Fluoration de l'Uranium (An international nuclear fuel company)

SFUGE . . . . . . Singapore Federation of Unions of Government Employees

SFV . . . . Semliki Forest Virus

SFV . . . . Sight Feed Valve

SFWA . . . . . . Science Fiction Writers of America

SFWC . . . . . . Search for Critical Weakness

SFWC . . . . . . Supreme Forest Woodmen Circle

SFWM . . . . . . Swiss Federation of Watch Manufacturers

SFXR . . . . Super Flash X-Ray

SFY . . . . Standard Facility Years (FAA)

SFZ . . . . Scott & Fetzer Co. (NYSE symbol)

SFZ . . . . Sforzando (Indicates sudden emphasis on single note or chord) (Music)

SG . . . . Sawtooth Generator

SG . . . . Scanning Gate

SG . . . . Schutzgemeinschaft Gegen Meinungsterror (Guard Society Against Opinion Terror) (Germany)

SG . . . . Scots Guards

SG . . . . Screen Grid (Electrode or vacuum tube)

SG . . . . Secretary-General (UN)

SG . . . . Senior Grade

SG . . . . Set Gate

SG . . . . . . Shell Gland

SG . . . . Signal Generator

SG . . . . Single Groove (Insulators)

SG	Smoke Generator
SG	Snow Grains (Meteorology)
SG	Solicitor General
SG	Soluble Gelatin (Pharmacy)
SG	South Georgia Railway Company (AAR code)
SG	Specific Gravity (Also, SPGR)
SG	Stacking Gel (Biochemistry)
SG	Standardization Group (Air Force)
SG	Standing Group
SG	Steel Girder (Bridges)
SG	Structural Glass
SG	Su Giro (Your Draft) (Banking) (Spain)
SG	Sunset Gun (Military ceremonial)
SG	Surgeon General (Army and Air Force)
SG	Swamp Glider
SG	Sweep Generator
SG	Symbol Generator
S-G	Secretary-General (UN)
1SG	First Sergeant (Army)
SGA	Scientific Glass Apparatus Co., Inc.
SGA	Slave Gyro Assembly
SGA	Society of Governmental Appraisers
SGA	Society of Graphic Art (British)
SGA	Southern Natural Gas Company (NYSE symbol)
SGA	Spectrometric Gas Analysis
SGA	Split Group Aperture
SGA	Standards of Grade Authorization
SGA	Switch Group Assembly
SGAA	Stained Glass Association of America
SGACC	Secretariat General de l'Aviation Civile et Commerciale (France)
SGA of M-A .	Sod Growers Association of Mid-America
SGAS	Space Geodesy Altimetry Study (Raytheon Co.)
SGB	Schweizerischer Gewerkschaftsbund (Swiss Federation of Trade Unions)
SGB	Strain Gage Bridge
SGBI	Santa Gertrudis Breeders International
SGBIP	Subject Guide to Books in Print (A publication)
SGC	Saint Gregory College (Oklahoma)
SGC	Screen Grid Current
SGC	Simulated Generation Control
SGC	South Georgia College
SGC	Space General Corporation
SGC	Spartan Guidance Computer (Army)
SGC	Spherical Gear Coupling
SGC	Stabilizer Gyro Circuit
SGC	Superior Geocentric Conjunction
SGCA	Secretariat General a l'Aviation Civile (French Civil Aviation Secretariat)
SGCF	SNAP (Systems for Nuclear Auxiliary Power) Generalized Critical Facility
SGCS	Silicon Gate-Controlled Switch
SGCS	Slave Gyro Control System
SGD	Signed
SGD	Sui Generis Degree
SGDE	System Ground Data Equipment (RADAR)
SGDG	San Guarantie du Gouvernement
SGDI	Swaging Die
SGE	Secondary Grid Emission
SGE	Severable Government Equipment
SGE	Sigma Gamma Epsilon (Society)
SGES	Society of Grain Elevator Superintendents
SGEU	Singapore General Employees' Union
SGG	Sustainer Gas Generator
SGH	Surgical Hospital
SGHWR	Steam Generating Heavy Water Reactor (British)
SGI	Society for Gynecologic Investigation
SGI	Specific Gravity Indicator
SGI	Spring Garden Institute
SGIA	Sun Glass Institute of America
SGINDEX	System Generation Cross-Reference Index (NASA)
SGIS	Student Government Information Service
SGJ	Supersonic Gas Jet
SGJA	Sporting Goods Jobbers Association
SGJP	Satellite Graphic Job Processor (Data processing)
SGL	Society of Gas Lighting
SGL	Supermarkets General Corp. (NYSE symbol)
SGLC	Strain Gage Load Cell
SGLI	Servicemen's Group Life Insurance
SGLI	Slave Gyro Leveling Integrator
SGLO	Standing Group Liaison Officer to the North Atlantic Council
SGLS	Space-to-Ground Link Subsystem (NASA)
SGM	Sangamo Company (NYSE symbol)
SGM	Screen Grid Modulation
SGM	Sergeant Major (Army)
SGM	Society for General Microbiology (British)
SGM	Spark Gap Modulation
SGMAA	Sporting Goods Manufacturers Agents Association
SGMD	Swaging Mandel
SGMS	Shipboard Gravity Measuring System
SGMT	Subgroup Modem Terminal
SGN	Scan Gate Number
SGN	Signal Companies, Inc. (NYSE symbol)
SGN	Standing Group, North Atlantic Treaty Organization
SGN	Surgeon General of the Navy
SGO	Squadron Gunnery Officer
SGO	Surgeon General's Office
SGOG	Suppressor Grid Orbitron Gauge
SGOT	Serum Glutamic Oxaloacetic Transaminase (Biochemistry)
SGP	Schering Plough Corp. (NYSE symbol)
SGP	Secondary Gun Pointer (Navy)
SGP	Society of General Physiologists
SGP	Society of Ghana Philatelists
SGP	South American Gold & Platinum Company (NYSE symbol) (Delisted)
SGP	Specialty Glass Products, Inc.
SGP	Stabilized Gyro Platform
SGP	Standard Guidance Package
SGP	Sudeten German Party
SGPT	Serum Glutamic-Pyruvic Transaminase (Biochemistry)
SGR	Seminal Groove
SGR	Sodium Graphite Reactor (AEC)
SGRA	Sporting Goods Representatives Association
SGREP	Standing Group Representative (NATO)
SGS	Secretary of the General Staff (Army)
SGS	Signode Corporation (NYSE symbol)
SGS	Swivelling Gunner's Station
SGS	Symbol Generation and Storage (Data processing)
SGSFU	Salt-Glazed Structural Facing Units (Technical drawings)
SGSP	Single Groove, Single Petticoat (Insulators)
SGSR	Society for General Systems Research
SGSUB	Self-Glazed Structural Unit Base (Technical drawings)
SGT	Satellite Ground Terminal
SGT	Sergeant (Military)
SGTA	Servo Gear Train Assembly
SGTM	Societe Generale des Transports Maritimes (France)
SGTM	Strain Gauge Thrust Meter
SGTR	Standard Government Travel Request
SGTR	Standardized Government Travel Regulations
SGTS	Satellite Ground Terminal System
SGTS	Swing Grip Thermal Stripper
SGU	Sidewinder Generator Unit
S-G(UN)	Secretary-General of the United Nations
SGUS	Slovak Gymnastic Union Sokol of the USA
SGW	Senior Grand Warden (Masonry)
SGX	Seeger Refrigerator Company (NYSE symbol)
SGZ	Surface Ground Zero
SH	Sacrifice Hit (Baseball)
SH	Schenley Industries, Inc. (NYSE symbol)
SH	Schoolhouse
SH	Scleroscope Hardness
SH	Semester Hour
SH	Sequence History
SH	Serum Hepatitis (Medicine)
SH	Ship's Head (Heading) (Navigation)
SH	Ship's Service-Man (Navy rating)
SH	Sick in Hospital
SH	Social History
SH	Soldiers' Home (Government agency)
SH	Somatotrophic (Growth) Hormone (Endocrinology)
SH	Specified Hours
SH	Station Hospital (Military)
SH	Steel Heads
SH	Steelton & Highspire R. R. (AAR code)
SH	Sulfhydryl (Chemistry)
SH	Super High Frequency
S & H	Sperry & Hutchinson (Trading stamp company)
S & H	Sundays and Holidays
SHA	Sample and Hold Amplifier
SHA	Shapell Industries, Inc. (NYSE symbol)
SHA	Sidereal Hour Angle
SHA	Society for Historical Archaeology
SHA	Society for Humane Abortion
SHA	Solid Homogeneous Assembly
SHA	Southern Historical Association
SHA	Support Harness Assembly

SHAA . . . . Society of Hearing Aid Audiologists
SHACO . . . . . Shorthand Coding
SHAD . . . . Sharpe Army Depot
SHADRAC . . . . Shelter Housed Automatic Digital Random Access (Data processing)
SHAEF . . . . . . Supreme Headquarters, Allied Expeditionary Force (Europe) (World War II)
SHAFR . . . . . . Society for Historians of American Foreign Relations
SHAL . . . . . . Subject Heading Authority List (Data processing)
SHALOM . . . . . Synchronous Halo Monitor (NASA)
SHAME . . . . . . Save, Help Animals Man Exploits (Connecticut organization)
SHANE . . . . . Steerable Hydrophone Array, Nonlinear Element
SHANICLE . . . . Short Range Navigation Vehicle (System) (Air Force)
SHAPE . . . . . . Supersonic High-Altitude Parachute Experiment (NASA)
SHAPE . . . . . . Supreme Headquarters Allied Powers Europe (NATO)
SHAPM . . . . . . Ship Acquisition Project Manager (Navy)
SHARE . . . . . . Share Happily and Reap Endlessly (Hollywood women's charity organization)
SHARE . . . . . . Society to Help Avoid Redundant Effort (in data processing)
SHARE . . . . . . Systems for Heat and Radiation Energy
SHARP . . . . . . School Health Additional Referral Program (Public Health Service)
SHARP . . . . . . Ships Analysis and Retrieval Project (Navy)
SHAS . . . . Shared Hospital Accounting System (Data processing)
SHAVE . . . . . Sugar Hotel Alpha Victor Echo (Apollo 10 astronauts' code for shaving operation)
SHAWCO . . . . Students' Health and Welfare Centers Organization
SHB . . . . Second Harmonic Band
SHBD . . . . . . Serum Hydroxybutyrate Dehydrogenase (Biochemistry)
SHBG . . . . . . Sex-Hormone-Binding Globulin
SHC . . . . Sacred Heart College (Alabama; Kansas)
SHC . . . . Seton Hill College (Pennsylvania)
SHC . . . . Siena Heights College (Michigan)
SHC . . . . Southern Humanities Conference
SHC . . . . Spring Hill College (Alabama)
SHC . . . . Superheat Control (Boilers)
SHC . . . . Superior Heliocentric Conjunction
SHC . . . . Surveillance Helicopter Company (Army)
SHCA . . . . . . Safety Helmet Council of America
SHCA . . . . . . Siberian Husky Club of America
SHCJ . . . . Society of the Holy Child Jesus (Roman Catholic women's religious order)
SHD . . . . Subsistence Homestead Division
SHDC . . . . . . Sacred Heart Dominican College (Texas)
SHE . . . . Self-Help Enterprises (An organization)
SHE . . . . Semi-Homogeneous Experiment
SHE . . . . Spares Handling Expense
SHE . . . . Special Handling Equipment
SHE . . . . Standard Hydrogen Electrode
SHE . . . . Subject Headings for Engineering
SHED . . . . . . Settlement Houses Employment Development (Large group of settlement houses)
SHEL . . . . . . Shore ELINT (Electromagnetic Intelligence) System (Navy)
SHELREP . . . . . Shelling Report
SHEMA . . . . . . Steam Heating Equipment Manufacturers Association
S-HEMP . . . . . System - Hydraulic, Electrical, Mechanical, Pneumatic
SHEN . . . . . . Shenandoah National Park
SHEP . . . . . . Solar High-Energy Particles
SHF . . . . Shared High Frequency
SHF . . . . Sisters of the Holy Faith (Roman Catholic religious order)
SHF . . . . Sisters of the Holy Family (Roman Catholic religious order)
SHF . . . . Structures Heating Facility
SHF . . . . Super-High Frequency (Radio wave)
SHFA . . . . . . Single-Conductor, Heat and Flame Resistant, Armor (Cable)
SHFS . . . . . . Superhyperfine Structure
SHG . . . . . . Second-Harmonic Generation (LASER)
SHG . . . . Sheller-Globe Corp. (NYSE symbol)
SHG . . . . Short-Handed Goal (Hockey)
SHGM . . . . . . Society for the History of the Germans in Maryland
SHH . . . . Sociedad Honoraria Hispanica
SHI . . . . Sheet Iron
S-HI . . . . System-Human Interaction
SHIEF . . . . . . Shared Information Elicitation Facility (Data processing)
SHIELD . . . . . . Sylvania High Intelligence Electronic Defense
SHIL . . . . Shiloh National Military Park
SHIP . . . . Self-Help Issue Point (Army)
SHIP . . . . Standard Hardware Interface Program
SHIPACS . . . . . Ship Acquisition Study (Navy)
SHIPALT . . . . . Ship Alteration
SHIPDA . . . . . . Shipping Data
SHIPDAFOL . . . Shipping Data Follows
SHIPDTO . . . . . Ship on Depot Transfer Order
SHIPGO . . . . . Shipping Order
SHIPIM . . . . . . Ship Immediately
SHIPREQ . . . . . Ship to Apply on Requisition

SHIPS . . . . . . Shipment Planning System (Military)
SHIR . . . . Ship History and Inventory Record (Navy)
SHIRAN . . . . . S-Band High-Accuracy Ranging and Navigation
SHJC . . . . Sacred Heart Junior College (North Carolina; Pennsylvania)
SHK . . . . Schick Electric, Inc. (NYSE symbol) (Delisted)
SHL . . . . Sheller Manufacturing Corporation (NYSE symbol) (Later, SHG)
SHL . . . . Student Homophile League
SHLMA . . . . . . Southern Hardwood Lumber Manufacturers Association
SHM . . . . Shamrock Oil & Gas Corporation (NYSE symbol) (Delisted)
SHM . . . . Ship Heading Marker (Navigation)
SHM . . . . Simple Harmonic Motion
SHMI . . . . Saddlery Hardware Manufacturers Institute
SHMO . . . . . . Senior Hospital Medical Officer
SHMO . . . . . . Shadow Mountain National Recreation Area
SHNS . . . . . . Society of Head and Neck Surgeons
SHO . . . . Senior House Officer
SHO . . . . Student Health Organizations
SHOCK . . . . . Students Hot on Conserving Kilowatts (Student legal action organization)
SHODOP . . . . . Short-Range Doppler
SHOPAIR . . . . . Short Path Infrared
SHORAN . . . . . Short-Range Navigation
SHORDU . . . . . Shore Duty (Navy)
SHORVEY . . . . Shore Duty Survey
SHOT . . . . . . Society for the History of Technology
SHP . . . . Seeker Head Position
SHP . . . . Shaft Horsepower (Nautical)
SHP . . . . Single Highest Peak (Aerospace)
SHP . . . . Southern Hardwood Producers
SHP . . . . Standard Hardware Program
SHP . . . . Standard Holding Pattern (Aviation)
SHP . . . . Standard Holding Procedure (Aviation)
SHPC . . . . . . Scenic Hudson Preservation Conference
SHPTARBY . . . . Ship to Arrive By
SHQ . . . . Station Headquarters
SHQ . . . . Supreme Headquarters
SHR . . . . Sheraton Corporation of America (NYSE symbol) (Delisted)
SHR . . . . Spontaneously Hypertensive Rats
SHR . . . . Step-Height Ratio (Crystallography)
SHRAM . . . . . Short-Range Air-to-Surface Missile
SHRF . . . . . . Ship Regular Freight
SHS . . . . Sacred Heart Seminary (Michigan)
SHS . . . . Ship's Heading Servo
SHSLB . . . . . . Street and Highway Safety Lighting Bureau
SHSN . . . . . . Sod House Society of Nebraska
SHSS . . . . . . Stanford Hypnotic Susceptibility Scale (Psychology)
SHSWD . . . . . Society for Hospital Social Work Directors
SHT . . . . Society for the History of Technology
SHT . . . . Space Hand Tool (NASA)
SHTG . . . . . . Shortage
SHTN . . . . . . Short Ton
SHTT . . . . . . Societe Hoteliere et Touristique de Tunisie
SHU . . . . Seton Hall University (New Jersey)
SHV . . . . Solenoid Hydraulic Valve
SHV . . . . Sub Hoc Voce or Sub Verbo (Under This Word)
SHW . . . . Sherwin-Williams Co. (NYSE symbol)
SI . . . . Saintpaulia International
SI . . . . Salinity Indicator
SI . . . . Sample Interval
SI . . . . Sandwich Islands
SI . . . . Saturday Inspection (Slang)
SI . . . . Screen-Grid Input
SI . . . . Selective Identification
SI . . . . Semi-Insulating
SI . . . . Seriously Ill (Army)
SI . . . . Serra International
SI . . . . Sertoma International
SI . . . . Service Instruction
SI . . . . Shift-In (Data processing)
SI . . . . Shipping Instructions
SI . . . . Ship's Installation (Navy)
SI . . . . Short Interest (Brokerage)
SI . . . . Signal Interface
SI . . . . Signal to Intermodulation Ratio
Si . . . . Silicon (Chemical element)
SI . . . . Smithsonian Institution
SI . . . . Society of Illustrators
SI . . . . Soluble Insulin
SI . . . . Source Impedance
SI . . . . Spark Ignition
SI . . . . Special Instruction
SI . . . . Special Intelligence (Army)

SI .... Spectrum Index
SI .... Spokane International R. R. (AAR code)
SI .... Sports Illustrated (A publication)
SI .... Spot Inspection (Military)
SI .... Staff Inspector
SI .... Staten Island
SI .... Station Identification
SI .... Straight-In Approach (Aviation)
SI .... Structure-of-Intellect (Model)
SI .... Sulphur Institute
SI .... System Integration
SI .... Systeme International d'Unites (International System of Units)
S-I .... Sensation-Intuition (Jungian psychology)
S/I .... Signal/Intermodulation
S/I .... Subject Issue
S & I .... Stocked and Issued
SIA .... Air Intelligence Service (Italian)
SIA .... Sanitary Institute of America
SIA .... Securities Industry Association (Formerly, ASEF and IBA)
SIA .... Self-Insurers Association
SIA .... Self-Interstitial Atom
SIA .... Ski Industries America
SIA .... Societe Internationale d'Acupuncture (International Society of Acupuncture)
SIA .... Societe Internationale Arthurienne (International Arthurian Society)
SIA .... Society of Insurance Accountants
SIA .... Soroptimist International Association
SIA .... Sprinkler Irrigation Association
SIA .... Standard Instrument Approach (RADAR) (Aviation)
SIA .... Strategic Industries Association
SIA .... Subminiature Integrated Antenna
SIABA...... Sindacato Italiano Artisti Belle Arti (Italian Union of Fine Arts)
SIAC ...... Secretariat International des Artistes Catholiques
SIAC ...... Securities Industry Automation Corporation (NYSE/ASE)
SIAC ...... State Industry Advisory Committee (Civil Defense)
SIAD ...... Sierra Army Depot
SIAE....... Societa Italiana degli Autori ed Editori (Italy)
SIAM ...... Signal Information and Monitoring Service (American radio monitoring service)
SIAM ...... Society for Industrial and Applied Mathematics
SIAN ...... Societe Industrielle et Agriculturelle du Niari (Industrial and Agricultural Society of Niari)
SIAP....... Sociedad Interamericana de Planeficacion (Inter-American Planning Society)
SIAP....... Straight-In Approach
SIAT....... Single Integrated Attack Team
SIB .... Satellite Integrated Buoy
SIB .... Satellite Ionospheric Beacons (Military)
SIB .... Sociedade Interplanetaria Brasileira (Brazil)
SIBC....... Societe Internationale de Biologie Clinique (World Association of Anatomic and Clinical Pathology Societies)
SIBGE...... Societe Industrielle Bull General Electric
SIBS ...... Salk Institute for Biological Sciences
SIBS ...... Stellar-Inertial Bombing System
SIC .... High School Student Information Center
SIC .... Science Information Council (National Science Foundation)
SIC....... Scientific Information Center
SIC .... Secretaria de Industria e Comercio (Brazil)
SIC .... Security Intelligence Corps
SIC....... Semiconductor Integrated Circuit
SIC .... Servicio de Inteligencia Colombiano (Colombia)
SIC .... Servico de Intercambio de Catalogacao
SIC .... Silicon Insulating Compound
SIC .... Skills Inventory Coordinator
SIC .... Societe Internationale de Cardiologie (International Society of Cardiology)
SIC .... Societe Internationale de Chirurgie
SIC .... Special Interest Committee
SIC .... Specific Inductive Capacity
SIC .... Standard Industrial Classification (Code)
SIC .... Standard Inspection Criteria
SIC .... Structural Influence Coefficient
SIC .... Survey Information Center
SICA ...... Society of Industrial and Cost Accountants of Canada
SICC ...... Safeguard Inventory Control Center (Army)
SICM ...... Scheduled Input Control Method
SICN ...... Societe Industrielle de Combustibles Nucleaires (France)
SICO ...... Systems Integration and Checkout
SICOT ..... Societe Internationale de Chirurgie Orthopedique et de Traumatologie (International Society of Orthopedic Surgery and Traumatology)
SICOVAM .... Societe Interprofessionnelle pour la Compensation des Valeurs Mobilieres
SICR....... Specific Intelligence Collection Requirements

SICR .... Supply Item Change Record
SICS ...... Secondary Infrared Calibration System
SID .... Doctor of Industrial Science
SID .... Security and Intelligence Service (Army)
SID........ Seismic Intrusion Detector (Army)
SID .... Servizio Informazione Difesa (Defense intelligence service) (Italy)
SID .... Silver Iodine Generator
SID .... Situation Display (RADAR)
SID .... Society for Information Display
SID .... Society for International Development
SID .... Society for Investigative Dermatology
SID .... Source Image Distortion
SID .... Spiritus In Deo (Spirit Rests in God)
SID .... Sports Information Director
SID .... Standard Instrument Departure (Aviation)
SID .... Strategic Intelligence Digests (Military)
SID .... Sudden Ionospheric Disturbance (NASA)
SID .... Synchronous Identification System
SIDA ...... Swedish International Development Agency
SIDASE..... Significant Data Selection
SIDC....... Supply Item Design Change (Navy)
SIDD....... Scientific Information and Documentation Division (Environmental Science Services Administration)
SIDE....... Suprathermal-Ion-Detector Experiment (Apollo) (NASA)
SIDEC...... Stanford International Development Education Center (Stanford University)
SIDF....... Sinusoidal Input Describing Function (Data processing)
SIDL....... System Identification Data List (Navy)
SIDOR ..... Siderurgica del Orinoco (Government steel company) (Venezuela)
SIDS....... Societe Internationale de Defense Sociale (International Society of Social Defense)
SIDS....... Societe Internationale de Droit Sociale
SIDS ...... Spares Integrated Data System
SIDS....... Stellar Inertial Doppler System
SIDS....... Sudden Infant Death Syndrome
SIE....... Science Information Exchange (Smithsonian Institution)
SIE....... Servizio Informazioni Esercito (Italy)
SIE....... Single Instruction Execute
SIE....... Society of Industrial Engineers
SIE .... Surface Ionization Engine
SIEB ...... Satellite Interrogated Environmental Buoy
SIEC....... Societe Internationale pour l'Enseignement Commercial (International Society for Business Education)
SIECOP..... Scientific Information and Education Council of Physicians
SIECUS ..... Sex Information and Education Council of the United States
SIEGE....... Simulated EMP (Electromagnetic Pulse) Ground Environment (Air Force)
SIEPM....... Societe Internationale pour l'Etude de la Philosophie Medievale (International Society for the Study of Medieval Philosophy)
SIEUSE ..... Secretariat International de l'Enseignement Universitaire des Sciences de l'Education
SIF....... Science Information Facility (FDA)
SIF........ Scott Industrial Foam
SIF........ Secure Identification Feature
SIF........ Selective Identification Feature (Military decoder modification)
SIF........ Sound Intermediate Frequency
SIFAD...... Separate Ion Formation and Drift
SIFCC....... Senate Interstate and Foreign Commerce Committee
SIF/IFF ..... Selective Identification Feature/Identification Friend or Foe (Military)
SIFT ...... Share Interval for FORTRAN Translator
SIFT ...... Simplified Input for Toss (Data processing)
SIFTOR ..... Sifting of Information for Technology of Reactors (MIT-AEC study)
SIG .... Senior Interdepartmental Group (Department of State)
SIG .... Ship Improvement Guide
SIG .... Signal
SIG .... Signature
SIG .... Signore
SIG .... Silicon Insulated Gate
SIG .... Simplicity Is Greatness (Also see GIS)
SIG .... Southern Indiana Gas & Electric Company (NYSE symbol)
SIG .... Special Interest Group
SIG .... Special Investigative Group (DOD)
SIG .... Starfield Image Generator
SIG .... Stellar Inertial Guidance Signal
SIG/AH ..... Special Interest Group/Arts and Humanities
SIG/ALP .... Special Interest Group/Automated Language Processing
SIGBAT..... Signal Battalion (Army)
SIG/BC..... Special Interest Group/Biomedical and Chemical Information Systems
SIG/BSS ..... Special Interest Group/Behavioral and Social Sciences
SIGC ...... Signal Corps (Army)
SIGCEN ..... Signal Center (Military)
SIGCOR ..... Signal Corps

SIG/CR . . . . . . Special Interest Group/Classification Research
SIGE . . . . **Societe Internationale de Gastro-Enterologie**
SIG/ES . . . . . . Special Interest Group/Education for Information Science
SIG/IA . . . . . . Special Interest Group/Information Analysis Centers
SIGINT . . . . . . Signal Intelligence (Military)
SIGIR . . . . Special Interest Group on Information Retrieval (of Association for Computing Machinery)
SIG/LA . . . . . . Special Interest Group/Library Automation and Networks
SIGMA . . . . . . **Sealed Insulating Glass Manufacturers Association**
SIGMA . . . . . Site Information Generation and Material Accountability Plan (Army)
SIGMA . . . . . . Society of Independent Gasoline Marketers of America
SIGMA . . . . . . Standardized Inertial Guidance Multiple Application
SIGMAP . . . . . Special Interest Group for Mathematical Programming
SIGMAS . . . . . Signal Measurement and Analysis System
SIGMET . . . . . Significant Meteorological Information (Aviation)
SIGN . . . . Strap-Down Inertial Guidance and Navigation
SIGO . . . . Signal Officer
SIGPLAN . . . . Special Interest Group on Programming Languages (Association for Computing Machinery)
SIG/RT . . . . . . Special Interest Group/Reprographic Technology
SIGS . . . . Simplified Inertial Guidance System
SIGSEC . . . . . . Signal Security (Military)
SIH . . . . Schweizerisches Institut fuer Hauswirtschaft
SIH . . . . Societe Internationale d'Hematologie (International Society of Hematology)
SIH . . . . **Society for Italic Handwriting**
SIH . . . . Sonesta International Hotels Corp. (NYSE symbol)
SIHS . . . . **Society for Italian Historical Studies**
SIHT . . . . Space Impact Hand Tool (NASA)
SII . . . . Smith International, Incorporated (NYSE symbol)
SII . . . . Standard Identification for Individuals (Social security) (American National Standards Institute)
SII . . . . Sugar Information, Incorporated
SII . . . . Supervisory Immigrant Inspector (Immigration and Naturalization Service)
SIIAEC . . . . . . Secretariat International des Ingenieurs, des Agronomes et des Cadres Economiques Catholiques (International Secretariat of Catholic Engineers, Agriculturalists and Economists)
SIIC . . . . Secretariat International des Groupements Professionnels des Industries Chimiques des Pays de la CEE
SIIR . . . . Spares Item Inventory Record
SIL . . . . Semiconductor Injector LASER
SIL . . . . Seriously Ill List
SIL . . . . Service Information Letter
SIL . . . . Societe Internationale de la Lepre (International Leprosy Association)
SIL . . . . Sound Intensity Level
SIL . . . . Speech Interference Level
SIL . . . . Summer Institute of Linguistics
SIL . . . . Surge Impedance Loading
SIL . . . . Systems Integration Laboratory
SILAF . . . . . . Sindacato Italiano Lavoratori Appalti Ferroviari (Italian Union of Railroad Contract Workers)
SILAP . . . . . . Sindacato Nazionale Dipendenti Ministero Dei Lavori Pubblici (National Union of Employees in the Ministry of Public Welfare) (Italy)
SILCA . . . . . . Sindacato Italiano Lavoratori Cappellai ed Affini (Italian Federation of Hat and Allied Workers)
SILI . . . . Sindacato Nazionale Lavoratori Italcable (National Union of Italian Cable Workers)
SILO . . . . Security Intelligence Liaison Office (Central Mediterranean Forces) (Navy)
SILP . . . . Sindacato Italiano Lavoratori del Petrolio (Oil Workers' Union) (Italy)
SILP . . . . Sindacato Italiano Lavoratori Postelegrafonici (Italian Union of Postal and Telegraph Workers)
SILS . . . . Shipboard Impact Locator System
SILS . . . . Silver Solder
SILSP . . . . . . Safeguard Integrated Logistics Support Plan (Army)
SILTE . . . . . . Sindacato Italiano Lavoratori Telecomunicazioni (Italian Union of Telecommunications' Workers)
SILTS . . . . . . Sindacato Italiano Lavoratori Telefoni di Stato (Italian Union of Government Telephone Workers)
SILULAP . . . . . Sindacato Italiano Lavoratori Uffici Locali ed Agenzie Postelegrafonici (Italian Union of Local Post and Telegraph Office Workers)
SIM . . . . School of Industrial Management (MIT)
SIM . . . . Scientific Instrument Module (NASA)
SIM . . . . Selected Item Management
SIM . . . . Sergeant Instructor of Musketry
SIM . . . . Servizio Informazioni Militare (Italian)
SIM . . . . Simmons Company (NYSE symbol)
SIM . . . . Societe Internationale de la Moselle (International Moselle Company)
SIM . . . . Societe Internationale de Musicologie (International Musicological Society)
SIM . . . . Society for Industrial Microbiology
SIM . . . . Steatite Insulation Material

SIM . . . . Stellar Image Monitor
SIM . . . . Student Interracial Ministry
SIM . . . . Subtotal Integration Mode
SIM . . . . Systems Integration Model
SIMA . . . . Salon International de la Machine Agricole
SIMA . . . . Scientific Instrument Manufacturers' Association (British)
SIMAJ . . . . . . Scientific Instrument Manufacturers' Association of Japan
SIMBAD . . . . . Simulation as a Basis for Social Agents' Decisions (Data processing)
SIMC . . . . Silicon Integrated Monolithic Circuit
SIMC . . . . Societe Internationale pour la Musique Contemporaine (International Society for Contemporary Music)
SIMCA . . . . . . Societa Industrielle de Mecanique et Carrosserie Automobile (French)
SIMCOM . . . . . Simulation and Computer (Data processing)
SIMCOM . . . . . Simulator Compiler (Computer)
SIMCON . . . . . Scientific Inventory Management and Control
SIMCON . . . . . Simplified Control
SIMCON . . . . . Simulation Controller
SIMDEP . . . . . . Simulation Development Program (DASA)
SIME . . . . Security Intelligence, Middle East (Navy)
SIMEA . . . . . . Societa Italiana Meridionale per l'Energia Atomica (Italy)
SIMFAC . . . . . Simulation Facility
SIMHA . . . . . . Societe Internationale de Mycologie Humaine et Animale (International Society for Human and Animal Mycology)
SIMICOR . . . . Simultaneous Multiple Image Correlation
SIMILE . . . . . . Simulator of Immediate Memory in Learning Experiments
SIMM . . . . Symbolic Integrated Maintenance Manual
SIMO . . . . Societe Industrielle des Minerais de l'Ouest
SIMOC . . . . . . Simulated Occupant (People Machine) (Office of Civil Defense)
SIMOP . . . . . . Simultaneous Operation
SIMP . . . . Shipboard Integrated Maintenance Program (Navy)
SIMPAC . . . . . Simulation Package (Data processing)
SIMPP . . . . . . **Society of Independent Motion Picture Producers**
SIMPU . . . . . . Simulation Punch
SIMR . . . . Schenley Instant Market Reports
SIMS . . . . Student International Meditation Society
SIMS . . . . Symbolic Integrated Maintenance System
SIMSA . . . . . . Savings Institutions Marketing Society of America
SIMSI . . . . . . Selective Inventory Management of Secondary Items (Navy)
SIMSOC . . . . . Simulated Society
SIMSUP . . . . . . Simulation Supervisor
SIN . . . . Scientific Information Notes (A publication)
SIN . . . . Security Information Network
SIN . . . . Sensitive Information Network
SIN . . . . Sine
SIN . . . . Spanish International Network (Television)
SIN . . . . Study Item Number (Army)
SIN . . . . Support Information Network
SINA . . . . Society for Indecency to Naked Animals (A hoax organization)
SINACMA . . . . Sindacato Nazionale Dipendenti Corte dei Conti e Magistrature Amministrure (National Union of General Accounting Office Employees) (Italy)
SINAD . . . . . . Signal Plus Noise and Distortion
SINADIMID . . . Sindacato Nazionale Dipendenti Ministero Difesa (National Union of Ministry of Defense Employees) (Italy)
SINAF . . . . . . Sindacato Nazionale Dipendenti Ministero Agricoltura e Foreste (National Union of Ministry of Agriculture and Forestry Employees) (Italy)
SINAMAI . . . . Sindacato Nazionale e Dipendenti Ministero Africa Italiana (National Union of Former Italian Employees of African Ministry) (Italy)
SINAMIL . . . . . Sindacato Nazionale Dipendenti Ministero del Lavoro e Previdenza Sociale (National Union of Ministry of Labor and Social Security Employees) (Italy)
SINAMN . . . . Sindacato Nazionale Dipendenti Marina Mercantile (National Union of Merchant Marine Workers) (Italy)
SINAP . . . . . . Satellite Input to Numerical Analysis and Prediction (National Weather Service)
SINAPI . . . . . . Sindacato Nazionale Ministero Pubblica Istruzione (National Union of Ministry of Public Instructors) (Italy)
SINASCEL . . . . Sindacato Nazionale Scuola Elementare (National Union of Elementary School Teachers) (Italy)
SINB . . . . Southern Interstate Nuclear Board
SINCOE . . . . . Sindacato Nazionale Dipendenti Ministeri Industria e Commercio Estero (National Union of Ministry of Industry and Foreign Commerce Employees) (Italy)
SIND . . . . Strobe Intersection Deghoster
SINDAF . . . . . Sindacato Nazionale Dipendenti Amministrazioni Finanziarie (National Union of Financial Administration Employees) (Italy)
SIN-ETH . . . . . Swiss Institute of Nuclear Research – Eidgenoessische Technische Hochschule
SINEWS . . . . . Ship Integrated Electronic Warfare System(s)
SING . . . . Singular
SINH . . . . Sine, Hyperbolic

SINS . . . . Ship Inertial Navigational System
SINS . . . . Sindacato Scuola non Statale (Italian Union of Private Schools'
             Employees)
SIO . . . . Scripps Institution of Oceanography
SIO . . . . Ship's Information Officer (Navy)
SIO . . . . Sindacato Italiano Ostetriche (Italian Union of Midwives)
SIO . . . . Special Inquiry Officer
SIO . . . . Staged in Orbit
SIOD . . . . . . Sindacato Italiano Odonototecnici Diplomati (Italian Union of
             Odontotechnicians)
SIOE . . . . Special Issue of Equipment
SIOH . . . . Supervision, Inspection and Overhead
SIOP . . . . Single Integrated Operations Plan (Military)
SIP . . . . Satellite Information Processor
SIP . . . . Selma (Alabama) Interreligious Project
SIP . . . . Senior Intensified Program (Education)
SIP . . . . Short Irregular Pulses
SIP . . . . Simulated Input Processor (Data processing)
SIP . . . . Sindacato Italiano Pescatori (National Union of Fishermen) (Italy)
SIP . . . . Sociedad Interamericana de Psicologia (Inter-American Society of
             Psychology)
SIP . . . . Standard Inspection Procedure
SIP . . . . Standard Interest Profile
SIP . . . . Step in Place
SIP . . . . Student Insurance Producers Association
SIP . . . . Submerged Injection Process (Steelmaking)
SIP . . . . Supersonic Infantry Projectile
SIPA . . . . Somali Institute of Public Administration
SIPC . . . . Securities Investor Protection Corporation (Proposed government
             insurance agency for brokerage accounts) (Pronounced "Sipic")
SIPD . . . . Supply Item Provisioning Document (Navy)
SIPE . . . . Scientific Information Program on Eutrophication (University of Wisconsin)
SIPE . . . . Societe Internationale de Psychopathologie de l'Expression (International
             Society of Art and Psychopathology)
SIPES . . . . Society of Independent Professional Earth Scientists
SIPG . . . . Societe Internationale de Pathologie Geographique (International Society
             of Geographical Pathology)
SIPI . . . . Scientists' Institute for Public Information
SIPI . . . . Southwestern Indian Polytechnic Institute (New Mexico)
SIPI . . . . Supervisory Immigration Patrol Inspector (Immigration and Naturalization
             Service)
SIPO . . . . Spacecraft Integration Project Office
SIPOP . . . . . . Satellite Information Processor Operational Program
SIPRA . . . . Societa Italiana Pubblicita Per Azioni (Italian radio and television
             advertising company)
SIPRE . . . . . . Snow, Ice and Permafrost Research Establishment
SIPRI . . . . Stockholm International Peace Research Institute (Now, International
             Institute for Peace and Conflict Research)
SIPROS . . . . . Simultaneous Processing Operation System (Data processing)
SIPS . . . . Spartan Improved Performance Study (Army)
SIPSDE . . . . . Society of Independent and Private School Data Educators
SIPU . . . . Selective Inactivation Photo-Dynamic Unit
SIR . . . . Selected Item Reporting
SIR . . . . Selective Information Retrieval
SIR . . . . Serious Incident Report (Military)
SIR . . . . Signal-to-Interference Ratio
SIR . . . . Simultaneous Impact Rate
SIR . . . . Snow and Ice on Runways (Aviation)
SIR . . . . Societa Italiana Resine
SIR . . . . Societe Rorschach Internationale (International Rorschach Society)
             (Originally, Societe Internationale du Test de Rorschach et Autres
             Methodes Projectives)
SIR . . . . Society for Individual Responsibility (Defunct)
SIR . . . . Society for Individual Rights
SIR . . . . Society of Industrial Realtors
SIR . . . . Sound Isolation Room
SIR . . . . Special Information Retrieval
SIR . . . . Special Investigative Requirement
SIR . . . . Specification Information Retrieval System (Data processing)
SIR . . . . Staten Island Rapid Transit Railway Company (AAR code)
SIR . . . . Statistical Information Retrieval
SIR . . . . Submarine Intermediate Reactor
SIR . . . . Supersonic Infantry Rocket
SIR . . . . . . Suppliers Information Request
SIRA . . . . Scientific Research Association (British)
SIRA . . . . Strategic Intelligence Research and Analysis
SIRA . . . . System for Instructional Response Analysis
SIRC . . . . Spares Integrated Reporting and Control (System)
SIR(CICR) . . . . . Service International de Recherches (du Comite International de la
             Croix-Rouge)
SIRE . . . . Society for the Investigation of Recurring Events

SIRI . . . . Societe Internationale pour la Readaptation des Invalides
SIRIN . . . . . . Single Readiness Information System (NORRS)
SIRL . . . . Support Item Requirement List
SIRS . . . . Satellite Infrared Spectrometer (NASA)
SIRSA . . . . . . Special Industrial Radio Service Association
SIRT . . . . Staten Island Rapid Transit Railway Company
SIS . . . . Naval Intelligence Service (Italian)
SIS . . . . SAGE Interceptor Simulator
SIS . . . . Satellite Infrared Spectrometer
SIS . . . . Satellite Interceptor System
SIS . . . . Science Information Services (Franklin Institute)
SIS . . . . Secondary Injection System
SIS . . . . Secret Intelligence Service (British)
SIS . . . . Semiconductor-Insulator-Semiconductor
SIS . . . . Serving the Indigent Sick
SIS . . . . Short Interval Scheduling (Quality control)
SIS . . . . Shut-In Society
SIS . . . . Society of International Secretaries
SIS . . . . Spark Ignition System
SIS . . . . Specification Information System
SIS . . . . Spuria Iris Society
SIS . . . . Stage Interface Substitute
SIS . . . . Station Identification Store (Bell Laboratories)
SIS . . . . Stator Interstage Seal
SIS . . . . STEP (Scientific and Technical Exploitation Program) Information Subsystem
SIS . . . . Sterile Injectable Suspension
SIS . . . . Strategic Intelligence School (Military)
SIS . . . . Student International Service (Foundation)
SIS . . . . Submarine Integrated SONAR
SIS . . . . System Integration Support
SISC . . . . Statewide Information Steering Committee (California)
SISL . . . . . . Sons of Italy Supreme Lodge
SISMS . . . . . Standard Integrated Support Management System (Joint Chiefs of Staff)
SISP . . . . Sudden Increase of Solar Particles
SISR . . . . Selected Items Status Report (Army)
SISS . . . . Semiconductor-Insulator-Semiconductor System
SISS . . . . Societe Industrielle des Silicones (France)
SISS . . . . . . Societe Internationale de la Science du Sol
SISS . . . . Submarine Improved SONAR System
SISS . . . . Submarine Integrated SONAR System
SISS . . . . Synchronous Identification System Study
SISS . . . . System Integration Support Service
SISTER . . . . . Special Institution for Scientific and Technological Education and Re-
             search (In proposal stage, 1964, in Great Britain)
SISTRAN . . . . System for Information Storage and Retrieval and Analysis
SISUSA . . . . . Scotch-Irish Society of the United States of America
SIT . . . . Separation-Initiated Timer
SIT . . . . Sequential Interval Timer
SIT . . . . Silicon Intensifier Tube (or Target)
SIT . . . . Simulation Input Tape
SIT . . . . Situation
SIT . . . . Slosson Intelligence Test
SIT . . . . Society of Instrument Technology (British)
SIT . . . . Space Impact Tool
SIT . . . . Spaceborne Infrared Tracker
SIT . . . . Spontaneous Ignition Temperature
SIT . . . . Statement of Inventory Transaction
SIT . . . . Stevens Institute of Technology
SIT . . . . Stopping or Storage in Transit
SIT . . . . Storage Inspection Test (Navy)
SIT . . . . Sugar Industry Technologists
SIT . . . . System Integration Test
SITA . . . . Societe Internationale des Telecommunications Aeronautiques
SITA . . . . . . Students' International Travel Association
SITC . . . . Standard Industrial Trade Classification (International Trade Centre)
SITCOM . . . . . Situation Comedy (Television)
SITE . . . . Search Information Tape Equipment
SITE . . . . Spacecraft Instrumentation Test Equipment
SITES . . . . . . Smithsonian Institution Travelling Exhibition Service
SITK . . . . . . Sitka National Monument
SITL . . . . Southwestern Industrial Traffic League
SITP . . . . System Integration Test Program
SITPB . . . . . . System Integrated Test Program Board
SITPRO . . . . . Simplication of International Trade Procedures (Committee) (British)
SITREP . . . . . Situation Report
SITS . . . . SAGE (Semi-Automatic Ground Environment) Intercept Target Simulation
SITS . . . . Societe Internationale de Transfusion Sanguine (International Society of
             Blood Transfusion)
SITS . . . . System Integration Test Service
SITU . . . . Society for the Investigation of the Unexplained
SITVC . . . . . . Secondary Injection Thrust Vector Control

SIU .... Seafarers' International Union of North America
SIU .... Societe Internationale d'Urologie (International Society of Urology)
SIU .... Southern Illinois University
SIU .... Subsystem Interface Unit
SIU-AGLI .... Seafarers' International Union of North America (AFL-CIO); Atlantic, Gulf, Lakes and Inland Waters District
SIUCB ...... Societa Italiana della Union Chimique Belge
SIUFL ...... Suspend Issue and Use of Following Lots
SIU-IUP ..... Seafarers' International Union of North America (AFL-CIO); Inland-boatmen's Union of the Pacific
SIU-IUPW .... Seafarers' International Union of North America (AFL-CIO); International Union of Petroleum Workers
SIUM .... Southern Illinois University Museum
SIU-MCS .... Seafarers' International Union of North America (AFL-CIO); Marine Cooks and Stewards' Union
SIU-MFOW ... Seafarers' International Union of North America (AFL-CIO); Pacific Coast Marine Firemen, Oilers, Watertenders and Wipers Association
SIUNA ...... Seafarers' International Union of North America
SIUSM ...... Suspend from Issue and Use as Suspect Material
SIU-SUP .... Seafarers' International Union of North America (AFL-CIO); Sailors' Union of the Pacific
SIU-TSAW .... Seafarers' International Union of North America (AFL-CIO); Transportation Services and Allied Workers
SIV .... Survey of Interpersonal Values (Psychology)
SIVD .... Spacecraft Information Viewing Device
SIW .... Self-Inflicted Wound (Military)
SIW .... Sisters of the Incarnate Word and the Blessed Sacrament (Roman Catholic religious order)
SIWL ...... Single Isolated Wheel Load (Aviation)
SIXFLT ..... Sixth Fleet (Atlantic) (Navy)
SIXPAC ..... System for Inertial Experiment Pointing and Attitude Control
SIZ .... Security Identification Zone
SJ .... San Juan (Puerto Rico)
SJ .... Service Junior
SJ .... Slip Joint (Technical drawings)
SJ .... Societas Jesu (Society of Jesus) (Jesuits) (Roman Catholic men's religious order)
SJ .... Statens Jaernvaegar (Sweden)
SJ .... Sub Judice (Under Consideration)
SJA .... Staff Judge Advocate (Air Force)
SJAA ...... Swedish Journalists Association of America
SJART ...... San Jacinto Army Terminal
SJB .... St. Joseph Belt Railway (AAR code)
SJB .... Society of Jewish Bibliophiles
SJBA ...... Sephardic Jewish Brotherhood of America
SJBC ...... Saint John the Baptist, Clewer
SJC .... Sacramento Junior College (California)
SJC .... Saint John's College (California, Kansas, Maryland)
SJC .... Saint Joseph College (Connecticut; Maryland)
SJC .... Saint Joseph's College (Indiana, Maine, New Jersey, Pennsylvania)
SJC .... Sayre Junior College (Oklahoma)
SJC .... Sisters of St. Joseph of Cluny (Roman Catholic religious order)
SJC .... Snead Junior College (Alabama)
SJC .... Society of Jews and Christians
SJC .... Standing Joint Committee
SJC .... Supreme Judicial Court
SJCC ...... Saint John College of Cleveland
SJCC ...... Spring Joint Computer Conference
SJCPS ..... Society of Jewish Composers, Publishers and Songwriters
SJCW ...... Saint Joseph's College for Women (New York)
SJD .... Doctor of Juridical Science (or Doctor of the Science of Jurisprudence or Doctor of the Science of Law)
SJE .... Swivelling Jet Engine
SJFC ...... Saint John Fisher College (New York)
SJG .... South Jersey Gas Company (NYSE symbol) (Later, SJI)
SJI .... South Jersey Industries, Inc. (NYSE symbol)
SJI .... Steel Joist Institute
SJJC ...... Sheldon Jackson Junior College (Alaska)
SJJRA ..... Standard Jack and Jennet Registry of America
SJK .... Steam-Jacketed Kettle
SJL .... St. Jude's League
SJLC ...... St. Johnsbury & Lamoille County R. R. (AAR code)
SJLC ...... Single Junction Latching Circulator
SJM .... Smucker (J.M.) Co. (NYSE symbol)
SJM .... Special Joint Meeting
SJO .... St. Joe Mineral Corporation (NYSE symbol)
SJO .... Service Junior-Oil-Resistant
SJP .... Special Job Procedure (Navy)
SJP .... Standard Jet Penetration (Aviation)
SJPS ...... Saint John's Provincial Seminary (Michigan)
SJRT ...... St. Johns River Terminal Company (AAR code)

SJS .... Saint John's Seminary (Massachusetts)
SJS .... Saint Joseph's Seminary (District of Columbia; Illinois)
SJS .... Society of Jewish Science
SJSC ...... San Jose State College (California)
SJSS ...... Saint Joseph's Seraphic Seminary (New York)
SJT .... St. Joseph Terminal R. R. (AAR code)
SJT .... Service Junior – Thermoplastic
SJT .... Subsonic (or Supersonic) Jet Transport
SJU .... Saint John's University (Minnesota; New York)
SJV .... Sharing Joint Venture
SJWVUSA .... Sons of Jewish War Veterans of the United States of America
SK .... Sanitaetskompanie (Medical company) (German military – World War II)
SK .... Service Kit
SK .... Sinclair-Koppers Company
SK .... Station Keeping
SK .... Storekeeper
SK .... Streptokinase (Enzyme)
SK .... Studebaker Corporation (NYSE symbol) (Wall Street slang name: "Studie") (Later, SKW)
SKA .... Statens Kriminaltekniska Anstalt
SKA .... Studienkommission for Atomenergie (Switzerland)
SKA .... Switchblade Knife Act
SKAMP ..... Station-Keeping and Mobile Platform (Robot sailboat)
SKBM ...... Serikat Kaum Buruh Minjak (Federation of Oil Unions of Indonesia)
SKC .... Skill Corporation (NYSE symbol)
SKC .... Sky Clear (Meteorology)
SKCB ...... Storekeeper, Construction Battalion, Stevedore (Navy)
SKCMA ..... Steel Kitchen Cabinet Manufacturers Association
SKD .... Selve-Kornbegel-Dornheim (Name of a German small arms ammunition factory) (World War II)
SKD .... Storekeeper, Disbursing (Navy)
SKED ...... Schedule
SKED ...... Sort Key Edit (Library of Congress)
SKF .... Svenska Kullagerfabriken AB (Swedish manufacturer, especially of ball bearings; active in many countries)
SKG .... Skaggs Companies, Inc. (NYSE symbol)
SKG .... Spencer Kellogg & Sons (NYSE symbol)
SKI .... Sloan-Kettering Institute
SKILA ..... Southern Korean Interim Legislative Assembly
SKILL ...... Satellite Kill
SKINS ..... Supplemental Knowledge Incentive Notes (Scrip offered to students for good performance) (Experimental learning program)
SKIP ...... Skinner Investigation Platform
SKK .... Sowjetische Kontrollkommission
SKL .... Skill Level
SKL .... Smith Kline & French Laboratories (NYSE symbol)
SKM .... Sine-Kosine Multiplier
SKO .... Society of Kastorians "Omonia"
SKO .... Standard Kollsman Industries, Inc. (NYSE symbol)
SKP .... Station Keeping Position
SKR .... South Korea Republic
SKR .... Station Keeping RADAR
SKS .... Savezna Komisija za Standardizacija (Federal Commission for Standardization) (Yugoslavia)
SKS .... Soren Kierkegaard Society
SKS .... Station Keeping Ship
SKSL ...... Skaneateles Short Line R. R. (AAR code)
SKT .... Specialty Knowledge Test (Military)
SKT .... Storekeeper, Technical
SKV .... Storekeeper, Aviation (Navy)
SKVV ...... Schweizerischer Katholischer Volksverein
SKW .... Sparks-Withington Company (NYSE symbol)
SKW .... Studebaker-Worthington Inc. (NYSE symbol) (Formerly, SK)
SKW .... Suddeutsche Kalkstickstoffwerke (AG)
SKY .... Skyline Corp. (NYSE symbol)
SKY .... Standard Oil Company (Kentucky) (NYSE symbol)
SKYCAV .... Sky Cavalry
SL .... Safety Level (Army)
SL .... Sales Letter
SL .... Salvage Loss
SL .... Sample Laboratory
SL .... San Luis Obispo (Mexican state; city and county in California)
SL .... Sand-Loaded (Technical drawings)
SL .... Satellite-Like (Virus)
SL .... Savings and Loan
SL .... Sea Level
SL .... Searchlight
SL .... Secundum Legem (According to Law)
SL .... Seditious Libeler
SL .... Sensation Level (Audiometry)

SL . . . . Sergeant-at-Law
SL . . . . Servomechanisms Laboratory (MIT)
SL . . . . Shift Left
SL . . . . Shipowner's Liability (Business and trade)
SL . . . . Sick Leave
SL . . . . Signal Level
SL . . . . Silicon Lacquer
SL . . . . Sine Loco (Without Indication of Place)
SL . . . . Single Line
SL . . . . Sisters of Loretto at the Foot of the Cross (Roman Catholic religious order)
SL . . . . Sockellafette (Pedestal mount) (German military – World War II)
SL . . . . Solicitor-at-Law
SL . . . . Sound Locator
SL . . . . Source Level
SL . . . . Squadron Leader (British Royal Air Force)
SL . . . . Stage Left (A stage direction)
SL . . . . Standard Length
SL . . . . Standard of Living
SL . . . . Standard Location (Civil Defense)
SL . . . . Stock Length (Construction or manufacturing materials)
SL . . . . Stock Level
SL . . . . Stock List
SL . . . . Stomodeal Lip
SL . . . . Storage Location
SL . . . . Straight Line (Statistics)
SL . . . . Streamline
SL . . . . Sub-Lieutenant (British Navy)
SL . . . . Submarine Qualification Lapsed (Navy)
SL . . . . Suo Loco (In Its Place)
SL . . . . Support Line (Military)
SL . . . . Sydney & Louisburg Railway Company (AAR code)
S-L . . . . Short-Long (as, of a signal light's flash cycle)
S-L . . . . Sound Locator (Military)
S/L . . . . Sea Level
S/L . . . . Searchlight
S/L . . . . Speedletter
S & L . . . . . . Savings and Loan (Association)
S & L . . . . . . Supply and Logistics
S & L . . . . . . System and Logistics
S-of-L . . . . Ship-of-the-Line
SLA . . . . Saturn LM (Lunar Module) Adapter (NASA)
SLA . . . . Scottish Library Association
SLA . . . . Showmen's League of America
SLA . . . . Single Line Approach
SLA . . . . Slovak League of America
SLA . . . . Spacecraft LM (Lunar Module) Adapter
SLA . . . . Special Libraries Association
SLA . . . . Square Loop Antenna
SLA . . . . Standard Life Association
SLA . . . . Standard Location Area (Civil Defense)
SLA . . . . State Liquor Authority
SLA . . . . Strip Line
SLA . . . . Supply Loading Airfield
SLAB . . . . . . Students for Labelling Alcoholic Beverages (Student legal action organization)
SLAC . . . . . . Special Committee on Latin American Coordination
SLAC . . . . . . Stanford Linear Accelerator Center (AEC)
SLAC . . . . . . Stowage Launch Adapter Container
SLAD . . . . . . Salon Litteraire, Artistique et Diplomatique
SLAD . . . . . . Shipboard Landing Assist Device
SLAD . . . . . . SONAR Locator, Altimeter, and Depthometer
SLAG . . . . . . Safe Launch Angle Gate
SLAG . . . . . . Side Looking Air-to-Ground (RADAR)
SLAIT . . . . . . Study Group on Legal Aspects of Intermodal Transportation
SLAL . . . . . . Stowage Launch Adapter, Lower
SLAM . . . . . . Seeking, Locating, Annihilating, Monitoring (Army project, Vietnam)
SLAM . . . . . . Space-Launched Air Missile
SLAM . . . . . . Stowage Launch Adapter, Middle
SLAM . . . . . . Strategic (or Supersonic) Low Altitude Missile
SLAN . . . . . . Sine Loco, Anno, vel Nomine (Without Place, Year, or Name)
SLANG . . . . . . Systems Language
SLANT . . . . . . Simulator Landing Attachment for Night Landing Training
SLAP . . . . . . Sandia-Livermore Aeroheating Program
SLAPS . . . . . . Subscriber Loop Analysis Program System (Bell System)
SLAR . . . . . . Side-Looking Aerial (or Airborne) RADAR
SLAR . . . . . . Side Looking Array RADAR
SLAR . . . . . . Slant Range
SLARF . . . . . . Slant Range Fuze
SLASH . . . . . . Seiler Laboratory ALGOL Simulated Hybrid (Data processing)
SLASH . . . . . . Small Light Antisubmarine Helicopter

SLAST . . . . . . Submarine-Launched Anti-Surface Ship Torpedo
SLAT . . . . . . Sindacato Lavoratori Amministrativi e Technichi (Union of Administration and Technical Workers) (Somalia)
SLAT . . . . . . Special Logistics Actions, Thailand
SLATE . . . . . Small, Lightweight Altitude-Transmission Equipment (FAA)
SLATE . . . . . . Stimulated Learning by Automated Typewriter Environment
SLAU . . . . . . Stowage Launch Adapter, Upper
SLAVCA . . . . Sindacato Nazionale Lavoratori Vetro e Ceramica (National Union of Glass and Ceramics' Workers) (Italy)
SLB . . . . Schlumberger, Limited (NYSE symbol)
SLB . . . . Self-Lubricating Bearing
SLB . . . . Side-Lobe Blanking (RADAR)
SLBM . . . . . . Sea-Launched Ballistic Missile (DOD)
SLBM . . . . . . Space-Launched Ballistic Missile
SLBM . . . . . . Submarine-Launched Ballistic Missile(s) (Navy)
SLBP . . . . Spring-Loaded Ball Plunger
SLC . . . . San Luis Central R. R. (AAR code)
SLC . . . . Sarah Lawrence College (New York)
SLC . . . . Searchlight Control (Military)
SLC . . . . Side-Lobe Cancellation (RADAR)
SLC . . . . Side-Lobe Clutter
SLC . . . . Simulated Linguistic Computer
SLC . . . . Southeastern Louisiana College
SLC . . . . Southland Corp. (NYSE symbol)
SLC . . . . Space Launch Complex
SLC . . . . Straight-Line Capacitance (or Capacity)
SLC . . . . Sublingual Cleft
SLC . . . . System Life Cycle
SL & C . . . . . Shipper's Load and Count (Bills of lading)
SLCL . . . . . . Sierra Leone Council of Labour
SLCM . . . . . . Sea-Launched Cruise Missile
SLCRM . . . . . . Ship Life Cycle Reference Matrix (Navy)
SLCU . . . . . . Standard Landing Craft Unit
SLD . . . . Serum Lactate Dehydrogenase (Biochemistry) (Also, SLDH)
SLD . . . . Specific Language Disability (Education)
SLD . . . . Square Law Detection
SLDH . . . . . . Serum Lactate Dehydrogenase (Biochemistry) (Also, SLD)
SLE . . . . Saint Louis Encephalitis (Medicine)
SLE . . . . Society of Logistics Engineers
SLE . . . . Student Letter Exchange
SLE-of-L . . . Studio Lighting Equipment
SLE . . . . Systemic Lupus Erythematosus (Rheumatic disease)
SLEDGE . . . . . Simulating Large Explosive Detonable Gas Experiment
SLEEP . . . . . . Swedish Low Energy Experimental Pile (Atomic energy)
SLEM . . . . . . Solution of Linearized Equations of Motion
SLEMA . . . . . . Schiffli Lace and Embroidery Manufacturers Association
SLEP . . . . Second Large ESRO Project
SLEW . . . . . . Static Load Error Washout
SLF . . . . Saturn Launch Facility
SLF . . . . Savings and Loan Foundation
SLF . . . . Scientific Laboratory Facility
SLF . . . . Scot Lad Foods Inc. (NYSE symbol)
SLF . . . . Skandinaviska Lackteknikers Forbund (Federation of Scandinavian Paint and Varnish Technicians)
SLF . . . . Society of the Little Flower
SLF . . . . Special Landing Forces (Marine Corps)
SLF . . . . Straight Line Frequency
SLF . . . . Suction Line Filter
SLFC . . . . . . Survivable Low Frequency Communication
SLFCS . . . . . . Survivable Low Frequency Communications System (Air Force)
SLFO,EAMTMTS . . . . St. Louis Field Office; Eastern Area, Military Traffic Management and Terminal Service (Army)
SLFP . . . . Sri Lanka Freedom Party (Ceylon)
SLGA . . . . . . Stained and Leaded Glass Association
SLGM . . . . . . Surface-Launched Guided Missile
SLGW . . . . . . Salt Lake, Garfield & Western Railway Company (AAR code)
SLI . . . . Seal and Label Institute
SLI . . . . Shelf Life Item (Military)
SLI . . . . Signal Line Isolator
SLI . . . . Slick Airways, Incorporated
SLI . . . . Slide Lobe Indicator
SLI . . . . Society for Louisiana Irises
SLI . . . . Sound Level Indicator
SLIA . . . . . . Spiritual Life Institute of America
SLIC . . . . . . Selective Letters in Combination
SLICE . . . . . . Southwestern Library Interstate Cooperative Endeavor
SLICE . . . . . . Students Litigating Against Injurious Can Edges (Student legal action organization)
SLIGO . . . . . . Sand Lake Irish Gatherings Organization
SLIM . . . . . . Saint Louis Institute of Music
SLIM . . . . . . Standards Laboratory Information Manual

SLIM . . . . Submarine-Launched Inertial Missile
SLIN . . . . Standard Line Item Number (Army)
SLIP . . . . Skills Level Improvement Program
SLIP . . . . Symmetric List Processor (FORTRAN extension)
SLIS . . . . Shared Laboratory Information System
SLIS . . . . Social Legislation Information Service
SLL . . . . Signal Long Lines
SLLS . . . . Snap Lock Limit Switch
SLLS . . . . Solidstate LASER Light Source
SLM . . . . School for Latin America (Air Force)
SLM . . . . Sea-Launched Missile
SLM . . . . Ship-Launched Missile
SLM . . . . Sound Level Meter
SLM . . . . Subscriber Loop Multiplex (Bell System)
SLMA . . . . Shoe Lace Manufacturers Association
SLMA . . . . Southeastern Lumber Manufacturers Association
SLMAB . . . . . . Single Line Missile Assembly Building
SLME . . . . Select Manual Entry Switch
SLMM . . . . Simultaneous Compass Locator at Middle Marker (Aviation)
SLMM . . . . Sub-Launched Mobile Mine
SLN . . . . Service Link Network (Bell Laboratories)
SLN . . . . Societe le Nickel
SLND . . . . Sine Loco Nec Data (Without Indication of Place or Date of Printing)
SLOB . . . . Satellite Low Orbit Bombardment
SLOE . . . . Special List of Equipment (Air Force)
SLOM . . . . Simultaneous Compass Locator at Outer Marker (Aviation)
SLOMAR . . . . . Space Logistics Maintenance and Repair
SLOR . . . . Successive Line Overrelaxation
SLOR . . . . Swept Local Oscillator Receiver
SLOS . . . . Secondary Line of Sight (Sextants)
SLOS . . . . Sierra Leone Organization Society
SLOS . . . . Sun Line of Sight
SLOWPOKE . . . Safe Low Power Critical Experiment (Nuclear reactor) (AEC)
SLP . . . . Scouting Landplane
SLP . . . . Sea-Level Pressure
SLP . . . . Silicon Light Pulser
SLP . . . . Sine Legitima Prole (Without Lawful Issue)
SLP . . . . Socialist Labor Party
SLP . . . . Soft Lander Probe (Aerospace)
SLP . . . . Spring Loaded Pulley
SLP . . . . Supersonic Local Pressure
SLPA . . . . Silicon Light Pulser Array
SLPC . . . . St. Louis Production Center
SLPC . . . . Supported Liquid Phase Catalyst
SLPL . . . . Sea Loading Pipe Line (Technical drawings)
SLPM . . . . Silicon Light Pulser Matrix
SLPP . . . . Serum Lipophosphoprotein
SLPP . . . . Sierra Leone People's Party
SLR . . . . Sales Letter Report
SLR . . . . Sealright-Oswego Falls Corporation (NYSE symbol) (Delisted)
SLR . . . . Side-Looking RADAR
SLR . . . . Single-Lens Reflex (Camera)
SLR . . . . Slush on Runway (Aviation)
SLR . . . . Sound Level Recorder
SLR . . . . South Lancashire Regiment (British)
SLR . . . . Spin Lattice Relaxation
SLR . . . . Static Line Regulation
SLR . . . . Storage Limits Register
SLRA . . . . Suede and Leather Refinishers of America
SLRAP . . . . Standard Low Frequency Range Approach
SLRC . . . . San Luis Rey College (California)
SLRD . . . . Searchlight RADAR
SLRI . . . . Shipboard Long-Range Input
SLRN . . . . Select Read Numerically
SLRV . . . . Surveyor Lunar Roving Vehicle (Aerospace)
SLS . . . . Saint Lawrence Seaway Development Corporation (Department of Transportation)
SLS . . . . Saint Lawrence Seminary (Wisconsin)
SLS . . . . Sea-Land Service (AAR code)
SLS . . . . Sea Level Static
SLS . . . . Side-Lobe Suppression
SLS . . . . Side-Looking SONAR
SLS . . . . Silicon Light Source
SLS . . . . Sindicato Lavoratori della Somalia (Workers Union of Somali)
SLS . . . . Spacecraft Landing Strut
SLSA . . . . Slotting Saw
SLSAC . . . . . . Saint Lawrence Seaway Authority of Canada
SLSDC . . . . . . Saint Lawrence Seaway Development Corporation (Independent government agency)
SLSF . . . . St. Louis-San Francisco Railway Company (AAR code)
SLSM . . . . Silver Life Saving Medal

SLST . . . . St. Louis, San Francisco & Texas Railway Company (AAR code)
SLST . . . . Slightly Staining
SLT . . . . Salant Corp. (NYSE symbol)
SLT . . . . Searchlight
SLT . . . . Self-Loading Tape
SLT . . . . Ship Letter Telegram
SLT . . . . Solid Logic Technology (IBM)
SLT . . . . Specific Launch Trajectory
SLT . . . . Stress Limit Tests
SLT . . . . Sveriges Litografiska Tryekerier
SL & T . . . . . . Shipper's Load and Tally (Bills of lading)
SLTF . . . . Silo-Launch Test Facility
SLTO . . . . Sea-Level Takeoff
SLT & SDL . . . . Searchlight and Sound Locator (Navy)
SLTUF . . . . Sri Lanka Trade Union Federation (Sri Lanka Vurthiya Samithi Sammelanaya) (Ceylon)
SLTX . . . . Sales Tax
SLU . . . . Saint Lawrence University (New York)
SLU . . . . Saint Louis University (Missouri)
SLU . . . . Southern Labor Union
SLURBS . . . . . . Sleazy Suburbs
SLURREX . . . . . Slurry Reactor Experiment
SLV . . . . Satellite Launching Vehicle (Air Force)
SLV . . . . Soft Landing Vehicle (NASA)
SLV . . . . Space Launch Vehicle
SLV . . . . Space-Like Vector
SLV . . . . Standard Launch Vehicle
SLW . . . . Spectral Line Width
SLW . . . . Store Logical Word
SLW . . . . Straight-Line Wavelength
SLYP . . . . Short Leaf Yellow Pine (Lumber)
SLZ . . . . Schiltz (Joseph) Brewing Co. (NYSE symbol)
SM . . . . Master of Science
SM . . . . Medal of Service of the Order of Canada
SM . . . . Sa Majeste (His Majesty)
SM . . . . St. Marys R. R. (AAR code)
SM . . . . Salvage Mechanic (Navy)
Sm . . . . Samarium (Chemical element) (See Sa)
SM . . . . Sanctae Memoriae (Of Holy Memory)
SM . . . . Schwarz/Mann (Supply company in biochemistry and chemistry)
SM . . . . Scientific Memorandum
SM . . . . Secretary's Memorandum (Military)
SM . . . . Semimonthly
SM . . . . Senior Magistrate
SM . . . . Sequence Monitor
SM . . . . Sergeant-Major
SM . . . . Service Module (NASA)
SM . . . . Sheet Metal
SM . . . . Shell Model
SM . . . . Shelter Management (Civil Defense)
SM . . . . Shipment Memorandum (Navy)
SM . . . . Short Metre (Music)
SM . . . . Signalman (Navy)
SM . . . . Silver Medalist
SM . . . . Single Manager (Defense)
SM . . . . Sinistra Mano (Left Hand)
SM . . . . Sisters of Mercy (Roman Catholic religious order)
SM . . . . Small Pica
SM . . . . Societas Mariæ (Marists)
SM . . . . Society of Mary (Marianists)
SM . . . . Society of Medalists
SM . . . . Soil Mechanics
SM . . . . Solar Magnetospheric
SM . . . . Soldier's Medal
SM . . . . Sons of Malta
SM . . . . Special Memorandum
SM . . . . Spiegel, Inc. (NYSE symbol) (Delisted)
SM . . . . Staff Memorandum
SM . . . . Stage Manager
SM . . . . Standard Matched
SM . . . . Standard Missile
SM . . . . State Militia (e.g., NJSM - New Jersey State Militia)
SM . . . . Stationary Medium-Power (Plant) (AEC)
SM . . . . Statistiske Meddelelser (Denmark)
SM . . . . Statute Mile
SM . . . . Stipendiary Magistrate
SM . . . . Strategic Missile
SM . . . . Streptomycin (An antibiotic)
SM . . . . Stria Medullaris
SM . . . . Structures Memorandum
SM . . . . Student Manual (Civil Defense)

SM........ Submarine, Mine Laying
SM........ Summary Memorandum
SM .... Supply Manual
SM........ Surface Measure
SM........ Surgeon Major
SM........ Sustained Medication (Pharmacology)
SM........ System Manager (Air Force)
SM........ System Mechanics
SM........ Systolic Murmur (Physiology)
S-M ...... Schuetzenmine (Antipersonnel mine) (German military – World War II)
S/M ...... Sensory-to-Motor (Ratio)
S/M....... Submarine (British)
S/M....... Submarine Pay
S & M ..... Sadism and Masochism
S & M ..... Service and Maintenance
S & M ..... Supply and Maintenance (Army)
S & M..... Surfaced and Matched (Lumber)
SMA ...... Safe Manufacturers' Association
SMA....... San Manuel Arizona R. R. (AAR code)
SMA ...... Scale Manufacturers Association
SMA ...... Screen Manufacturers Association
SMA ...... Senior Military Attaché
SMA....... Sequential Multiple Analyzer
SMA ...... Sergeant Major of the Army
SMA ...... Service Merchandisers of America
SMA....... Ship's Material Account
SMA ...... Skymark Airlines
SMA ...... Society of Manufacturer's Agents
SMA....... Society of Maritime Arbitrators
SMA....... Soviet Military Administration
SMA....... Squadron Maintenance Area
SMA....... Stabilized Member Assembly
SMA....... State Mutual of America (An insurance company)
SMA ...... Steatite Manufacturers Association
SMA ...... Stoker Manufacturers Association
SMA ...... Stucco Manufacturers Association
SMA....... Styrene and Maleic Anhydride (Copolymer)
SMA....... Subject Matter Area
SMA....... Suggested for Mature Audiences (Motion pictures)
SMA....... Superplastic Metal Alloy
S & MA .... Supply and Maintenance Agency (System) (Army)
SMAB ...... Solid Motor Assembly Building (for Missiles)
SMAC...... Scientific Machine Automation Corporation
SMAC...... Sequential Multiple Analyzer and Computer
SMAC...... Serial Memory Address Counter (Computer)
SMAC...... Special Mission Attack Computer
SMAC...... Submicron Aerosol Collector
SMACK..... Society of Males Who Appreciate Cute Knees (Group opposing below-the-knee fashions introduced in 1970)
SMACNA .... Sheet Metal & Air Conditioning Contractors' National Association
SMACRATRACEN .. Small Craft Training Center
SMACS ..... Serialized Missile Accounting and Control System
SMACS ..... Simulated Message Analysis and Conversion Subsystem
SMAD...... Sowjetische Militaeradministration
SMAL...... System Material Analysis List
SMALGOL.... Small Computer Algorithmic Language
SMAMA..... Sacramento Air Material Area
SMART ..... Salton's Magical Automatic Retriever of Texts (Data processing)
SMART ..... Satellite Maintenance and Repair Techniques (Air Force)
SMART ..... Sequential Mechanism for Automatic Recording and Testing
SMART ..... Space Maintenance and Repair Techniques
SMART ..... Supersonic Military Air Research Track
SMART ..... Supersonic Missile and Rocket Track
SMART ..... System Malfunction Analysis Reinforcement Trainer
SMART ..... Systems Management Analysis, Research, and Testing
SMARTS .... Status Memory and Real Time System (AT & T)
SMAS ...... Switched Maintenance Access System (Bell Laboratories)
SMASF ..... Servicemen's Mutual Aid and Savings Fund (South Vietnam)
SMASH..... Students Mobilizing on Auto Safety Hazards (Student legal action organization)
SMATS ..... Speed-Modulated Augmented Thrust System
SMAW ...... Second Marine Aircraft Wing
SMB .... Bachelor of Sacred Music
SMB .... Societas Missionaria Bethlehem
SMB .... Sunbeam Corporation (NYSE symbol)
SMBA ...... Slovenian Mutual Benefit Association
SMBJ ...... Style Manual for Biological Journals
SMC .... SAGE (Semi-Automatic Ground Environment) Maintenance Control (RADAR)
SMC....... Saint Martin's College (Washington)
SMC........ Saint Mary's College (Indiana, Kansas, Michigan, Minnesota)

SMC....... Saint Michael's College (Vermont)
SMC ...... Scientific Manpower Commission
SMC ...... Service Men's Center (World War II)
SMC....... Sheet Molding Compound(s)
SMC....... Silicon Monolithic Circuit
SMC....... Smith (A. O.) Corporation (NYSE symbol)
SMC....... Southern Missionary College (Tennessee)
SMC....... Squared Multiple Correlation (Psychology)
SMC....... Standard Molding Corporation
SMC....... Stepper Motor Control
SMC....... Student Mobilization Committee (to End the War in Vietnam)
SMC....... Supply & Maintenance Command (Army)
S-M-C .... Sperm (or Spore) Mother-Cell
SMCAF ..... Society of Medical Consultants to the Armed Forces
SMCC...... Saint Mary's College of California
SMCC...... Santa Monica City College (California)
SMCC...... Society of Memorial Cancer Center
SMCO...... SAGE (Semi-Automatic Ground Environment) Maintenance Control Office (ADC)
SMD........ Doctor of Sacred Music
SMD........ Scheduling Management Display
SMD........ Serum Malic Dehydrogenase (Biochemistry)
SMD........ Ship Manning Document (Navy)
SMD........ Short Metre Double (Music)
SMD........ Singular Multinomial Distribution (Statistics)
SMD........ Stop Motion Detector
SMD........ Structures and Mechanics Division (NASA)
SMD........ Submanubrial Dullness (Medicine)
SMD........ Submarine Mine Depot
SMD ...... Submersible Mining Device
SMD ...... Surplus Materials Division
SMD ...... System Management Directive
SMD........ Systems Manufacturing Division (IBM)
SMD........ Systems Monitor Display
SMDC...... Saint Mary's Dominican College (Louisiana)
SMDC...... Sodium Methyl Dithiocarbamate (Chemical)
SM Dendrol ... Master of Science in Dendrology
SMDF...... SAGE (Semi-Automatic Ground Environment) Main Distributing Frame
SMD, OC of SA .. Staff Management Division, Office, Chief of Staff (Army)
SME........ Sales and Marketing Executives-International
SME ...... Sheet Metal Enclosure
SME ...... Society of Manufacturing Engineers (Formerly, ASTME)
SME ...... Standard Medical Examination (Military)
SME........ Surface Measuring Equipment
SMEADO..... Selected Major Exploratory Advanced Development Objective
SME of AIME .. Society of Mining Engineers of American Institute of Mining, Metallurgical, and Petroleum Engineers
SMEC ...... Strategic Missile Evaluation Committee (Air Force)
SME-1....... Sales and Marketing Executives-International
SMEK ...... Summary Message Enable Keyboard
SMELLS...... Someone Must Eliminate Libby Lagoon Smells (Hartford, Wisconsin, organization)
SMEP ...... Society for Multivariate Experimental Psychology
SMERE ..... SPRINT Missile Electromagnetic Radiation Evaluation (Army)
SMERSH ..... Abbreviation of Russian phrase meaning "Death to the Spies," and name of a special division of USSR state security organizations charged with elimination of internal opposition to the regime (From 1942 into post-war years) (Best known outside of USSR for role of its agents in the popular James Bond series of espionage stories)
SME/SC ..... SPRINT Missile Engineering/Service Course (Army)
SMET ...... Spacecraft Maneuver Engine Transients (Apollo program) (NASA)
SMETC ...... Swiss Mouse Embryo Tissue Culture
SMF........ Sales Manpower Foundation
SMF........ Scientific Marriage Foundation
SMF........ Screw Machine Feeder
SMF........ Singer Company (NYSE symbol)
SMF........ Site Modification Facility
SMF........ Society for the Maintenance of the Faith (British)
SMF........ Solar Magnetic Field
SMF........ Spectral Multilayer Filter
SMF........ Stable Matrix Form
SMF........ Static Magnetic Field
SMFL........ Science, Mathematics, Foreign Languages
SMG ...... Seismocardiogram
SMG ...... Solids Moisture Gage
SMG ...... Submachine Gun
SMGD...... Supply Management Grouping Designator (Navy)
SM Geol .... Master of Science in Geology
SMGP ...... Strategic Missile Group (Air Force)
SMH........ Society for Maritime History (Formerly, American Maritime Institute)
SMHA....... Southern Mutual Help Association

SM in Hyg .... Master of Science in Hygiene
SMI .... Secondary Metal Institute
SMI .... Shelter Management Instructor (Civil Defense)
SMI .... Simulation of Machine Indexing
SMI .... Spring Manufacturers Institute
SMI .... Springs Mills, Incorporated (NYSE symbol)
SMI .... Statute Miles
SMI .... Success Motivation Institute
SMI .... Super Market Institute
SMI .... Systems Measurement Instrument (Data processing)
SMIA .... Steel Management in Action (Bethlehem Steel Company)
SMIC .... Study of Man's Impact on Climate
SMICBM ..... Semi-Mobile Intercontinental Ballistic Missile
SMILE .... Significant Milestone Integration Lateral Evaluation (Data processing)
SMIPP ...... Sheet Metal Industry Promotion Plan
SMIS .... Safeguard Management Information System (Army)
SMIS .... Society for Management Information Systems
SMIS .... Supply Management Information System
SMISOP ..... Safeguard Management Information System Operating Program (Army)
SMIT .... Simulated Midcourse Instruction Test (NASA)
SMIT .... Spin Motor Interruption Technique
SMITE ...... Simulation Model of Interceptor Terminal Effectiveness
SMIU .... Stove Mounters' International Union of North America (AFL-CIO)
SMJ .... Society of Medical Jurisprudence
SMJC .... Saint Mary's Junior College (Minnesota; Missouri; North Carolina)
SML .... Saluda Motor Lines (AAR code)
SML .... Search Mode Logic
SML .... Semantic-Meta-Language
SML .... Serials Master List
SML .... Simulator Load
SML .... States Marine Lines
SML .... Support Material List
SML .... Symbolic Machine Language
SMLE .... Short Magazine Lee-Enfield Rifle
SMLM .... Soviet Military Liaison Mission (Army)
SMLO ...... Senior Military Liaison Officer
SMLS .... Saint Mary of the Lake Seminary (Illinois)
SMM .... Master of Sacred Music
SMM .... Safeguards and Materials Management (AEC)
SMM .... Sancta Mater Maria (Holy Mother Mary)
SMM .... Societas Mariae Montfortana (Missionaries of the Company of Mary, or Montfort Fathers) (Roman Catholic religious order)
SMM .... Specially Meritorious Medal
SMM .... Stress Memo Manual
SMM .... Supervisory Middle Management
SMM .... System Maintenance Manual
SMM .... Systems Maintenance Management (Data processing)
S & MMIS .... Supply and Maintenance Management Information System (Army)
SMMP ...... Screw Machine Metal Part
SMMS .... Shipbuilding Material Management Systems (Navy)
SMMT ...... Society of Motor Manufacturers and Traders
SMNA ...... Safe Manufacturers' National Association
SMO .... Secondary Market Operation
SMO .... Senior Medical Officer (Military)
SMO .... Small Magnetospheric Observatory (Satellite)
SMO .... So Much Of
SMO .... Squadron Medical Officer
SMO .... Stabilized Master Oscillator
SMO .... Supplementary Meteorological Office
SMO .... Supply Management Office (Air Force)
SMOA ...... Single Manager Operating Agency
SMOG ...... Initials are said to stand for either Smelost', Mysl', Obraz, Glubina (Boldness, Thought, Image, Depth) or Samoye Molodoye Obyedinenie Geniev (Youngest Federation of Geniuses) (Clandestine group of writers in Moscow, USSR)
SMOG ...... Smoke and Fog
SMON ...... Subacute Myeolooptic Neuropathy
SMOP .... So Much of Paragraph
SMOS .... Secondary Military Occupational Specialty
SMOTE ...... Simulation of Turbofan Engine (Air Force)
SMOW ...... Standard Mean Ocean Water
SMP .... St. Martin's Press
SMP .... Scanning and Measuring Projector
SMP .... Sine Mascula Prole (Without Male Issue)
SMP .... Smudge Pot
SMP .... Social Marginal Productivity
SMP .... Sound Motion Picture Technician (Navy)
SMP .... Special Maintenance Project (FAA)
SMPAD ...... Society of Motion Picture Art Directors
SMPC .... Saint Mary of the Plains College (Kansas)
SMPC .... Societe des Mines et Produits Chimiques (France)

SMPE .... Society of Marine Port Engineers
SMPO ...... Sound Motion Picture Operator (Navy)
S-MPR ...... Semi-Monthly Progress Reports (Navy)
SMPTE ...... Society of Motion Picture and Television Engineers
SMR .... Scheduled Maintenance Replacement
SMR .... Seminarians for Ministerial Renewal (An organization)
SMR .... Shield Mock-Up Reactor
SMR .... Side-Looking Mapping RADAR
SMR .... Small Missile Range
SMR .... Society of Mary Reparatrix (Roman Catholic women's religious order)
SMR .... Solid Moderated Reactor
SMR .... Somnolent Metabolic Rate (Medicine)
SMR .... Special Money Requisition
SMR .... Standard Mortality Rate
SMR .... Status Monitoring Routine
SMR .... Stock Management Report
SMR .... Switching Mode Regulator
SM & R ..... System Malfunction Report
SM & R ..... Source, Maintenance, and Recoverability (Navy)
SMRAS ...... Safeguard Maintenance and Reporting Analysis System (Army)
SMRD ...... Spin Motor Rotation Detector
SMRE ...... Submerged Repeater Monitoring Equipment (RADAR)
SMRGC ..... Sun-Maid Raisin Growers of California
SMRL ...... Submarine Medical Research Laboratory
SMRLH ..... Soldier's Mail, Rush Like Hell (On correspondence)
SMRT ...... Scheduled Maintenance Replacement Time
SMRVS ..... Small Modular Recovery Vehicle System (AEC)
SMS .... Marine Service Squadron
SMS .... Saint Mary's Seminary (Connecticut; Missouri)
SMS .... Saint Meinrad Seminary (Indiana)
SMS .... Satellite Motion Simulator
SMS .... Scientific Mission Support
SMS .... Semiconductor-Metal-Semiconductor
SMS .... Sequence Milestone System
SMS .... Ship's Missile System
SMS .... Ships Motion Simulator
SMS .... Silico-Manganese Steel
SMS .... Small Magnetospheric Satellite (NASA)
SMS .... Spares Management System
SMS .... Special Mint Set (Numismatics)
SMS .... Spin Motor Supply
SMS .... Standard Modular Systems
SMS .... Standard Molecular System
SMS .... Stationary Meteorological Satellite (NASA)
SMS .... Stores Management Set
SMS .... Strategic Missile Squadron (Air Force)
SMS .... Subject Matter Specialist
SMS .... Surface Missile System
SMS .... Switching and Maintenance Set
SMS .... Synchronous Meteorological Satellite (NASA)
SMS .... Synoptic Meteorological Sounding
SMS .... Systems Maintenance Sector
SMS .... Systems Maintenance Service
SMSA ...... Standard Metropolitan Statistical Area (Bureau of Census)
SMSB ...... Strategic Missile Support Base
SMSC ...... Southeastern Missouri State College
SMSD ...... Ship Magnetic Submarine Detector
SMSE ...... Systems Maintenance Sector (Electronics)
SMSG ...... School Management Study Group
SMSG ...... School Mathematics Study Group
SMSGT ..... Senior Master Sergeant
SMSH ...... Sisters of Sainte Marthe (of St. Hyacinthe) (Roman Catholic religious order)
SMSO ...... Subcontract Material Sales Order
SMSRL ..... Sarah Mellon Scaife Radiation Laboratory (University of Pittsburgh)
SMT .... Ship's Mean Time (Navigation)
SMT .... Shop Mechanic's Test
SMT .... Small Missile Telecamera
SMT .... Sowjetisches Militaertribunal
SMT .... Square Mesh Tracking (Air Force)
SMTA ...... Sewing Machine Trade Association
SMTG ...... Solid-State and Molecular Theory Group (MIT)
SMTI ...... Southeastern Massachusetts Technological Institute
SMTN ...... Smoky Mountain R. R. (AAR code)
SMTS ...... Synchronous Meteorological Test Satellite
SMU .... Self-Maneuvering Unit (Air Force)
SMU .... Sociedadas Mexicanas Unedas
SMU .... Southeastern Massachusetts University
SMU .... Southern Methodist University
S Mus D ..... Doctor of Sacred Music
SMUSE ..... Socialist Movement for the United States of Europe

SMV........ Santa Maria Valley R. R. (AAR code)
SMV........ Satellite Mutual Visibility
SMV........ Slow Moving Vehicle (Emblem to prevent rear-end collisions)
SMW .... Second Main Watch
SMW .... Sheet Metal Workers' International Association
SMW .... Slotted Metal Window
SMW .... Society of Magazine Writers
SMW .... Strategic Missile Wing (Air Force)
SMWC ...... Saint Mary of the Woods College (Indiana)
SMWG ...... Strategic Missile Wing (Air Force)
SMWIA ..... Sheet Metal Workers' International Association
SMWP ...... Strategic Mobility Work Project (Army)
SMX........ Submultiplexer Unit
SMY........ Scientific Man-Year
SN......... Sacramento Northern Railway (AAR code)
SN......... Science News (A publication)
SN......... Scientific Note
SN......... Seaman (Navy rating)
SN......... Secretary of the Navy
SN......... Secundum Naturam (Naturally)
SN......... Serial Number
SN......... Service Number (Military)
SN......... Shipping Note
SN......... Side Note
SN......... Signal-to-Noise Ratio
SN......... Sine Nomine (Without Name)
SN .... Solid Neutral
SN......... Special Nuclear (Material) (AEC)
SN......... Standard Oil Company (Indiana) (NYSE symbol)
Sn .... Stannum (Tin) (Chemical element)
SN......... Stock Number
SN......... Strouhal Number (Sound)
SN......... Supernatant (Chemistry)
S/N .... Serial Number
S/N .... Shipping Note (Business and trade)
S/N .... Shipping Number
S/N .... Signal-to-Noise Ratio
S/N .... Stock Number
SNA....... Student Naval Aviator
SNAB...... Stock Number Action Bulletin
SNACS ..... Share News on Automatic Coding Systems (Data processing)
SNACS ..... Single Nuclear Attack Case Study (DOD)
SNACS ..... Stock Number Assignment Control System (Air Force)
SNADIGC.... Sindacato Nazionale Dipendenti Ministero Grazia e Giustizia (National Union of Ministry of Justice Employees) (Italy)
SNAF ...... Soviet Naval Air Force
SNAFU ..... Situation Normal, All Fouled Up (Military)
SNAIAS ..... Ships' Navigation and Aircraft Inertial Alignment System (Navy)
SNAME ..... Society of Naval Architects & Marine Engineers
SNAP...... Senior Naval Aviator Present
SNAP...... Short Notice Annual Practice (Military)
SNAP...... Simplified Numerical Automatic Programmer (Data processing)
SNAP...... Small Nuclear Auxiliary Power
SNAP...... Society of National Association Publications
SNAP...... Space Nuclear Auxiliary Power
SNAP...... Standard Navy Accounting Procedures
SNAP...... Sterile Nitrogen Atmosphere Processing
SNAP...... Structural Network Analysis Program
SNAP...... Student Naval Aviation Pilot
SNAP...... Subsystem for Nuclear Auxiliary Power
SNAP...... Symbolic Network Analysis Program (Data processing)
SNAP...... Systems for Nuclear Auxiliary Power
SNAP(G) .... Student Naval Aviation Pilot (Glider)
SNAPTRAN ... Systems for Nuclear Auxiliary Power Transient (AEC)
SNARE ..... Sandia Nuclear Assembly for Reactor Experiments
SNAV ...... Sindacato Nazionale Attrazionisti Viaggianti (National Union of Traveling Entertainers) (Italy)
SNB........ Soviet News Bureau
SNB........ Swiss National Bank
SNBL....... Sioux City & New Orleans Barge Line (AAR code)
SNC........ Saint Norbert College (Wisconsin)
SNC........ Standard Navigation Computer
SNCC....... Student National (formerly, Nonviolent) Coordinating Committee
SNCF....... Societe Nationale des Chemins de Fer Francais
SNCM ...... Second Nicaraguan Campaign Medal
SND........ San Diego Imperial Corporation (NYSE symbol) (Delisted)
SND........ Sap No Defect
SND........ Selected Natural Diamond
SND........ Self-Powered Neutron Detector
SND........ Semiconductor Neutron Dosimeter
SND........ Sisters of Notre Dame (Roman Catholic religious order)

SND....... Static No Delivery
SNDC...... Serbian National Defense Council
SNDL...... Sandale R. R. (AAR code)
SNDL ..... Standard Navy Distribution List
SND-MB ... Selected Natural Diamond – Metal Bond
SNDO ..... Standard Nomenclature of Diseases and Operations
SNDS ..... Stock Number Data Section
SNDT ...... Shreemati Nathibai Domodar Thackersey Women's University (India)
SNDV ..... Strategic Nuclear Delivery Vehicles (Army)
SNE .... Severe Noise Environment
SNE .... Sony Corp. (NYSE symbol)
SNEA ..... Student National Education Association
SNEC ...... Saxton Nuclear Engineering Corporation
SNECI ..... Sindicato Nacional dos Empregados do Comercio e da Industria da Provincia de Mocambique (National Union of Commercial and Industrial Workers of Mozambique)
SNECIPA ... Sindicato Nacional dos Empregados do Comercio e da Industria da Provincia de Angola (National Syndicate of Workers of Commerce and Industry of the Province of Angola)
SNECM..... Societe Nationale d'Etude et de Construction de Moteurs d'Aviation (France)
SNEG...... Syndicat National des Enseignants de Guinee (National Union of Guinean Teachers)
SNEL ...... Special Nuclear Effects Laboratory
SNELPIF ..... Sindacato Nazionale Esperti Laureati Propagandisti Industrie Farmaceutiche (National Union of University Graduated Experts for Propaganda in Pharmaceutical Industries) (Italy)
SNEPT ...... Space Nuclear Electric Propulsion Test
SNES ...... Syndicat National de l'Enseignement Secondaire (National Union of Secondary Schoolteachers) (France)
SNET ...... Syndicat National de l'Enseignement Technique (National Union of Technical Schoolteachers) (France)
SNF .... Serb National Federation
SNF .... Silicon Nitride Film
SNF .... Solids Not Fat
SNF .... Spot Noise Figure
SNF .... System Noise Figure
SNFO..... Student Naval Flight Officer
SNFS ...... Student Naval Flight Surgeon
SNG ...... Sans Notre Guarantee (Without Our Guarantee) (Business and trade) (France)
SNG ...... Southern New England Telephone Co. (NYSE symbol)
SNG ...... Stabilization Network Group
SNG....... Substitute for (or Synthetic) Natural Gas
SNH....... Sperry & Hutchinson Co. (NYSE symbol)
SNI .... San Nicolas Island
SNI .... Sequence Number Indicator
SNI .... Societa Nazionale Italiana
SNI .... Societe Nationale d'Investissment du Cameroun
SNI .... Sports Network, Incorporated (Later, HSN)
SNI .... Syndicat National des Instituteurs (National Union of Teachers) (France)
SNIAS ..... Societe National Industrielle Aerospatiale (France)
SNIE ...... Sindacato Nazionale Insegnanti Elementari (National Union of Elementary Teachers) (Italy)
SNIE ...... Special National Intelligence Estimates
SNIR ...... Signal-to-Noise plus Interference Ratio
SNIRD ..... Supposedly Noiseless Infrared Detector
SNJM...... Sisters of the Holy Names of Jesus and Mary (Roman Catholic religious order)
SNK....... Swank, Inc. (NYSE symbol)
SNL....... Somali National League
SNL....... Spore Newsletter (A publication)
SNL....... Standard Name Line
SNL....... Standard Nomenclature List (Military)
SNL....... State Narcotic Law
SNL....... Sun Chemical Corporation (NYSE symbol)
SNLR ...... Services No Longer Required
SNM ...... Satellite Navigation Map
SNM ...... Senior Naval Member
SNM ...... Signal-to-Noise Merit
SNM ...... Society of Nuclear Medicine
SNM ...... Special Nuclear Material(s) (AEC)
SNMMMIS.... Standard Navy Maintenance and Material Management Information System (Also known as 3M)
SNMMMS ... Standard Navy Maintenance and Material Management System
SNMT...... Society of Nuclear Medical Technologists
SNO ...... Senior Naval Officer
SNO ...... Senior Navigation Officer
SNOAD..... Senior Naval Officer Adriatic (British)
SNOBAL..... String-Oriented Symbolic Language (Data processing)

SNOBS . . . . . . Society of the Nourishment of Body and Soul (Gourmet club in North Carolina)
SNOK . . . . . . Secondary Next of Kin (Army)
SNOL . . . . . . Senior Naval Officer, Landings (British)
SNOMed. . . . . Systematized Nomenclature of Medicine
SNOOP. . . . . . Students Naturally Opposed to Outrageous Prying (Student legal action organization)
SNOP . . . . . . Senior Naval Officer Present
SNOP. . . . . . . Systematized Nomenclature of Pathology (NCI)
SNORE . . . . . . Self-Noise Reduction
SNORT . . . . . . Supersonic Naval Ordnance Research Track
SNOW . . . . . . Standard Normal Ocean Water
SNOW TIME . . . . SAC-NORAD (Strategic Air Command – North American Air Defense) Operational Weapons Test Involving Military Electronics
SNP . . . . Scottish National Party
SNP . . . . Soluble Nucleoprotein
SNP . . . . Space Nuclear Propulsion
SNP . . . . Suspected, Not Proved
SNP . . . . Synchro Null Pulse
SNPA . . . . . . Societe Nationale des Petroles d'Aquitaine (France)
SNPJ . . . . . . Slovene National Benefit Society
SNPL . . . . . . Syndicate National des Pilotes de Lignes (France)
SNPM . . . . . . Standard and Nuclear Propulsion Module
SNPO . . . . . . Space Nuclear Propulsion Office (AEC-NASA)
SNPOA . . . . Space Nuclear Propulsion Office, Albuquerque
SNPOC . . . . Space Nuclear Propulsion Office, Cleveland
SNPON . . . . Space Nuclear Propulsion Office, Nevada
SNPRI . . . . . . Selected Nonpriority List Item(s)
SNR . . . . Schenectady Naval Reactors Office (AEC)
SNR. . . . . . . Signal-to-Noise Ratio (Electronics)
SNRAFU . . . . . Situation Normal – Really All Fouled Up (Military slang)
SNRC . . . . . . Severn Naval River Command
SNS . . . . Society of Neurological Surgeons
SNS . . . . Sundstrand Corporation (NYSE symbol)
SNS . . . . Sympathetic Nervous System (Physiology)
SNSE . . . . . . Society of Nuclear Scientists and Engineers (Defunct)
SNSL . . . . . . Sons of Norway Supreme Lodge
SNSL . . . . . . Standard Navy Stock List
SNSM. . . . . . Sindacato Nazionale Scuola Media (National Union of Intermediate Schoolteachers) (Italy)
SNT . . . . Selective Nuclear Transfer
SNT . . . . Silicon Needle Transducer
SNT . . . . Sindacato Nazionale Tabacchine (National Union of Women Tobacco Workers) (Italy)
SNT . . . . Society for Nondestructive Testing (Later, ASNT)
SNTC . . . . . . Syndicat National des Transporteurs de Cameroun (National Union of Cameroonese Transportation Workers)
SNTC . . . . . . Syndicat National des Travailleurs Congolais (National Union of Congolese Workers) (Leopoldville)
SNTFC . . . . . . Senior Naval Task Force Commander
SNTS . . . . . . Sindacato Nazionale Telefonici di Stato (National Union of State Telephone Workers) (Italy)
SNTS . . . . . . Studiorum Novi Testamenti Societas (Society for the Study of the New Testament)
SNU. . . . . . . American Snuff Company (NYSE symbol) (Delisted)
SNU. . . . . . . Somali National Union
SNUB . . . . . . Show Nothing Unless Bad
SNUD . . . . . . Stock Number User Directory (Air Force)
SNUJ . . . . . . Singapore National Union of Journalists
SNV . . . . Systema Nervoso Vegetativo (Medicine)
SNW . . . . . . Strategic Nuclear Weapon
SNY. . . . . . . Southern New York Railway (AAR code)
SNY. . . . . . . Spanish Navy
SO. . . . . Schenectady Operation (AEC)
SO. . . . . Scientific Officer (Ministry of Agriculture, Fisheries, and Food) (Also, ScO) (British)
SO. . . . . Scouting-Observation Plane (When prefixed to Navy aircraft designation)
SO . . . . Secretary's Office (Navy)
SO. . . . . Seller's Option (Business and trade)
SO. . . . . Send Only
SO. . . . . Senior Officer (Military)
SO. . . . . Sex Offender
SO. . . . . Shift-Out (Data processing)
SO. . . . . Shipment (or Shipping) Order (Business and trade)
SO. . . . . Ship's Option
SO. . . . . Shop Order
SO. . . . . Signal Officer
SO . . . . Slope Occurrence
SO. . . . . Slow Operate (Relay)
SO. . . . . Small Oocyte
SO . . . . Southern Airways, Inc.

SO. . . . . Southern Company (NYSE symbol)
SO . . . . Special Orders
SO. . . . . Spring Opening
SO. . . . . Staff Officer
SO. . . . . Standing Order(s)
SO. . . . . Stationery Office (British)
SO . . . . Stockage Objectives
SO. . . . . Stop Order
SO . . . . Stopover (Slang)
SO . . . . Strategic Outline Chart (Air Force)
SO . . . . Strikeouts (Baseball)
SO. . . . . Suboffice
SO . . . . Superior Old
SO . . . . Supply Officer
SO. . . . . Surveillance Officer
SO. . . . . Switching Oscilloscope
SO. . . . . Switchover
S/O . . . . Send Only
SOA. . . . . . . SCOA Industries, Inc. (Formerly, Shoe Corporation of America) (NYSE symbol)
SOA. . . . . . . Self-Optimizing and Adaptive
SOA. . . . . . . Separate Operating Agency (Air Force)
SOA. . . . . . . Smithsonian Office of Anthropology
SOA. . . . . . . Special Open Allotment
SOA. . . . . . . Special Operating Agency
SOA. . . . . . . Speed of Advance (Military)
SOA. . . . . . . Speed of Approach
SOA. . . . . . . State of the Art
SOA. . . . . . . Student Orientation Assistant
SOAA . . . . . . Staff Officers Association of America
SoAF. . . . . . . Soviet Air Force
SOAF . . . . . . Sultan of Oman Air Force
SOAI . . . . . . Service des Organisations Aeronautiques Internationales (France)
SOAMUS. . . . . Study of One-Atmosphere Manned Underwater Structures
SOAP . . . . . . Self-Optimizing Automatic Pilot
SOAP . . . . . . Society of Airway Pioneers
SOAP . . . . . . Spectrometric (or Spectrographic) Oil Analysis Program
SOAP . . . . . . Students Opposed to Advertised Pollutants (Student legal action organization)
SOAP . . . . . . Supply Operations (or Overhaul) Assistance Program
SOAP . . . . . . Symbolic Optimum Assembly Programming
SOAPD . . . . . Southern Air Procurement District
SOAR . . . . . . Safe Operating Area
SOAR . . . . . . Save Our American Resources (Boy Scout project)
SOAR . . . . . . Simulation of Airlift Resources (Air Force)
SOAS . . . . . . School of Oriental and African Studies (University of London)
SOASC(I) . . . . Senior Officer Assault Ships and Craft (India) (British)
SOB . . . . Second Overtone Band
SOB . . . . Senate Office Building
SOB . . . . Shortness of Breath (Medicine)
SOB . . . . Son of a Bitch
SOB . . . . Souls on Board (Aviation slang)
SOB . . . . Superior Official Bureaucrat (Satirical bureaucracy term)
SOB's . . . . . . Silly Old Buggers (Wardroom officers over the "advanced" age of 39) (British naval slang)
SOB's . . . . . . Sons of Bosses International (An organization)
SOBIGM . . . . . Sign Off Brother, I've Got Mine (Remark used by seamen who avoided risky assignments during World War II) (Also used as hoax by National Maritime Union for name of organization issuing pamphlet about low state of merchant marine service)
SOBLIN . . . . . Self-Organizing Binary Logical Network (OTS)
SOBP . . . . . . Sentral Organisasi Buruh Pantjasila (Central Organization of Pantjasila Labor) (Indonesia)
SOBRI. . . . . . Sentral Organisasi Buruh Republik Indonesia (Central Labor Organization of the Republic of Indonesia)
SOBSI. . . . . . Serikat Organisasi Buruh Seluruh Indonesia (All Indonesia Central Labor Organization)
SOC. . . . . . . Saint Olaf College (Minnesota)
SOC. . . . . . . Satellite Operations Center (Cape Kennedy)
SOC. . . . . . . Satellite Orbit Control
SOC. . . . . . . Schedule of Organizational Change (Air Force)
SOC . . . . . . Sector Operations Center (Air Force)
SOC. . . . . . . Self-Organizing Control
SOC. . . . . . . Single Orbit Computation
SOC. . . . . . . Social
SOC . . . . . . Socialist
SOC . . . . . . Society
SOC . . . . . . Society of Cinematologists
SOC. . . . . . . Southern Oregon College
SOC. . . . . . . Space Operations Center
SOC. . . . . . . Special Operations Command (Military)

SOC........ Specific Optimal Control
SOC........ Squadron Operations Center (Air Force)
SOC........ Standard Oil Company
SoC........ State of Consciousness
SOC........ Superior Oil Company (Nevada) (NYSE symbol)
SOC........ Superposition of Configuration (Atomic physics)
SOC........ Supra-Oescophageal Commissure
SOCABU..... Societe du Caoutchouc Butyl (France)
SOCALSEC... Southern California Sector, Western Sea Frontier
SOCAR...... Statement of Condition and Recommendation (Military)
SOCB....... Shop Order Control Board
SOCC....... Salvage Operational Control Center (On submarine rescue ship during
               salvage operation)
SOCC....... Satellite Oceanic Control Center
SOCCER..... Smart's Own Concordance Constructor, Extremely Rapid (Data processing)
SOCHINAFOR.. South China Force (World War II)
SOCIM...... Society of Connoisseurs in Murder
SO Cist .... Sacer Ordo Cisterciensis (Cistercian Order of the Common
               Observance, or Cistercian Fathers) (Roman Catholic religious order)
SOCK....... Save Our Cute Knees (Detroit group opposing below-the-knee fashions
               introduced in 1970)
SOCM....... Stand-Off Cluster Munitions
SOCMA..... Synthetic Organic Chemical Manufacturers Association of the United
               States
SOCMC..... Special Order of the Commandant of the Marine Corps
SOCO...... Standard Oil Company of California
SOCOBANQUE... Societe Congolaise de Banque (Congo)
SOCOFIDE ... Societe Congolaise du Financement de Development (Congo)
SOCOM..... Solar Communications
SOCOM..... Solar Optical (or Orbital) Communications
SOCONY.... Standard Oil Company of New York (Socony Mobile is now official
               name of firm)
SOCRATES.... Storage and Retrieval of Carrier Rates (Military shipments)
SOCRATES ... System for Organizing Content to Review and Teach Educational
               Subjects (Data processing)
SOCRATES.... System for Organizing Current Reports to Aid Technology and Science
SOCRED ..... Social Credit Party (Canadian)
SOCS....... Spacecraft-Orientation-Control System
SOD........ Seller's Option to Double
SOD........ Small Object Detector
SOD........ Special Operations Detachment (Military)
SOD........ Special Order Discharge
SOD........ Staff Operations Division (NASA)
SOD........ Superintendent of Documents (US Government Printing Office)
SOD........ Sustained Operational Date
SOD........ Systems Operational Description (or Design)
SODA....... Source Oriented Data Acquisition
SODA....... Stamp Out Drug Addiction
SODAC...... Source Data Collection
SODAR...... Sound Detecting and Ranging
SODB....... Science Organization Development Board (National Academy of Sciences)
SODEPALM ... Societe pour le Developpement et l'Exploitation du Palmier a Huile
               (Ivory Coast)
SODEPAX .... Committee on Society, Development and Peace (of the Roman
               Catholic Church and the World Council of Churches)
SODERN ..... Societe d'Etudes et Realisations Nucleaires
SODRS...... Synchronous Orbit Data Relay Satellite
SODS....... Saturn Operational Display System
SODTICIOAP.. Special Ordnance Depot Tool Identification, Classification, Inventory,
               and Obsolescence Analysis Program (Popularly called "Soda Cap")
SOE........ Secret Operations Executive (British research unit corresponding to OSS)
               (World War II)
SOE........ Sequence of Events
SOE........ Silver Oxide Electrode
SOE........ Slater Orbital Exponents (Atomic physics)
SOE........ Status of Equipment (Army)
SOE........ Super Orbit Entry
SOEASTPAC... Southeast-Pacific Force (Later, Command) (Navy) (World War II)
SOEP....... Solar-Oriented Experimental Package (NASA)
SOF........ Sound on Film
SOF........ Special Operations Force (Military)
SOF........ Spillover Factor
SOF........ Spreading Ocean Floor
SOF........ Status of Forces Agreement (International treaty)
SOF........ Storage Oscilloscope Fragments
SOF........ Strategic Offensive Forces (Army)
SOFA....... Status of Forces Agreement (International treaty)
SOFA....... Student Overseas Flights for Americans
SOFAR...... Sound Fixing and Ranging (Navy underground sound system)
SOFC....... Saturn Operational Flight Control
SOFCS...... Self-Organizing Flight Control System

SOFIX ...... Software Fix (Data processing) (NASA)
SOFNET..... Solar Observing and Forecasting Network (Air Force)
SOFPAC ..... Special Operating Forces, Pacific
SOFT .... Status of Forces Treaty
SOFTA ...... Shippers Oil Field Traffic Association
SOFTY ...... Southern Federation of Temple Youth
SOG .... Seat of Government (Washington, DC)
SOG .... Special Operations Group (Navy)
SOG .... Supra-Oesophageal Ganglion
SOGAT...... Society of Graphical and Allied Trades (British)
SOGp....... Special Operations Group (Air Force)
SOGREAH .... Societe Grenobloise, d'Etudes et d'Applications Hydrauliques (France)
SOH........ Standard Oil Company (Ohio) (NYSE symbol)
SOH........ Start of Heading (Data processing)
SOHI .... Sponsors of Open Housing Investment (An organization)
SOHIO ...... Standard Oil Company (Ohio)
SoHo .... South of Houston Street (Artists' colony in New York City) (Also see
               NoHo)
SOHR ...... Solar Hydrogen Rocket Engine
SOI .... Scripps Oceanographic Institution
SOI .... Signal Operation Instructions
SOI .... Southern Indiana Railway (AAR code)
SOI .... Space Object Identification
SOI .... Specific Operating Instruction
SOI .... Stimulus Onset Interval
SOIC .... Supply Officer in Command
SOINC ...... Supply Officer-in-Charge (Navy)
SOIS .... Space Object Identification System
SOK........ Supply Authorized (Supply OK)
SOKSI ...... Sentral Organisasi Karyawan Sosialis Indonesia (Central Organization of
               Indonesian Socialist Workers)
SOL........ Safe Operating Limit
SOL........ Shipowner's Liability (Business and trade)
SOL........ Simulation Oriented Language (Data processing)
SOL........ Sola Basic Industries, Inc. (NYSE symbol)
SOL........ Soldier Out of Luck (Military slang)
SOL........ Substitute Optical Landing System
SOL........ Sure Out of Luck (Bowdlerized version)
SOL....... System Oriented Language
SOLAN ..... Solid Angles
SOLANT .... South Atlantic Force (Later, Command) (Navy) (World War II)
SOLANTFOR .. South Atlantic Force (Navy)
SOLAR ..... Society of Loose Actors Revolving (SOLAR Theater, Inc.)
SOLARIS .... Submerged Object Locating and Retrieving Identification System
SOLAS ..... Safety of Life at Sea (Convention) (International sea rules)
SOLE ...... Society of Logistics Engineers
SOLION .... Solution of Ions (Office of Naval Research)
SOLISTRON... Solid-State Klystron
SOLMAR..... Space Logistics Maintenance and Rescue
SOLO...... Selective Optical Lock-On (Sighting device)
SOLO...... System for Ordinary Life Operations
SOLOG ..... Standardization of Certain Aspects of Operations and Logistics
SOLOMON... Simultaneous Operation Linked Ordinal Modular Network
SOLRAD .... Solar Radiation (Monitoring satellite) (Navy)
SOM .... See Our Message
SOM .... Self-Organizing Machine
SOM .... Socony Mobil Oil Company, Inc. (NYSE symbol) (Delisted)
SOM .... SONARman (Navy)
SOM .... Start-of-Message
SOME ...... Secretary's Office, Management Engineer (Navy)
SOMH ...... SONARman, Harbor Defense (Navy)
SOMIEX ..... Societe Malienne d'Importation et d'Exportation (Malian Import Export
               Company)
SOMIREN .... Societa Minerali Radiaettini Energia Nucleare
SOMISA ..... Sociedad Mixta Siderurgia Argentina (Steel producer in Argentina)
SOMISS ..... Study of Management Information Systems Support (Army)
SOMP....... Start-of-Message Priority
SOMP....... Sydney Ocean Meeting Point (Navy)
SOMS...... Service Order Mechanized (or Mechanization) System (AT & T)
SOMS ..... Synchronous, Operational Meteorological Satellite
SON .... Society of Nematologists
SON .... Sonotone Corporation (NYSE symbol)
SON .... Support of Other Nations (Military support furnished certain nations
               and funded by the Air Force)
SONA ..... School of Naval Administration, Leland Stanford University
SONAC ..... SONAR Nacelle (Sonacelle)
SONAR .... Sound, Navigation and Ranging
SONCM .... SONAR Countermeasures and Deception
SOND ..... Secretary's Office, Navy Department
SONIC ..... System On-Line Network for Information Control (Data processing)
SONOAN... Sonic Noise Analyzer

SONRD ..... Secretary's Office, Office of Research and Development (Navy)
SONS....... Seek Out New Suppliers
SONS ...... Society of Non-Smokers
SONS....... Statistics of Naval Shipyards
SOO .... Schenectady Operations Office (AEC)
SOO .... Soo Line Railroad Company (NYSE symbol)
SOOM ...... Saigon Officers Open Mess (Vietnam)
SOON ...... Sequence for Opportunities and Negatives (RAND Corp.)
SOOP ...... Submarine Oceanographic Observation Program
SOP........ Safety Operating Plan
SOP .... Seat of the Pants
SOP .... Secretaria de Obras Publicas
SOP .... Semi-Open Position (Dancing)
SOP .... Senior Officer Present
SOP .... Simulated Output Program (Data processing)
SOP........ Sleeping-Out Pass (British armed forces)
SOP........ Standard Operating Procedure
SOP........ Surface Oil Pickup
SOP .... Symbolic Optimum Program
SOPA ...... Senior Officer Present Afloat
SOP(A) ..... Senior Officer Present (Ashore) (Navy)
SOPAC ..... South Pacific Area and Force (Later, South Pacific Command) (Navy) (World War II)
SOPAC ..... Southern Pacific Railroad Company
SOPACBACOM.. South Pacific Base Command (Navy)
SOPACCOMS.. South Pacific Communications (Navy)
SOPAT ..... South China Patrol (Navy) (World War II)
SOPE ...... Simulated Off-the-Pad Ejection (NASA)
SOPHE ..... Society of Public Health Educators
SOPLASCO ... Southern Plastics Company
SOPMC ..... Society of Paper Money Collectors
SOPO ...... Society of Oral Physiology and Occlusion
SOPR ...... Spanish Open Pool Reactor (Atomic energy)
SOPR ...... Special Officer Personnel Requirements (Military)
SOPS ...... Shot Noise Optical Optimization Communication System with Stops (NASA)
SOPS ...... Spacecraft Operations Planning Section
SOPUS ..... Senior Officer Present, US Navy
SOQ .... Sick Officer Quarters
SOR .... Sampling Oscilloscope Recorder
SOR .... Sensor Operation Room
SOR .... Society of Rheology
SOR .... Specific Operational Requirement (Military)
SOR .... Stable-Orbit Rendezvous (NASA)
SOR .... Standard Operating Report
SOR .... Standard Operating Rules
SOR .... Subcarrier Oscillator Rack
SOR .... Successive Overrelaxation
SOR .... Systems Operational Requirement
S-O-R ..... Stimulus-Organism-Response
SORA ...... Secretary's Office, Records Administration (Navy)
SORAFOM.... Societe de Radiodiffusion de la France d'Outre-Mer (Society for Radio Broadcasting of Overseas France)
SORAP ..... Standard Omni Range Approach
SORC...... Signal Officers' Reserve Corps
SORC ...... Sound Ranging Control
SORC...... Southern Ocean Racing Conference
SORCS ..... Shipboard Ordnance Requirement Computer System (Navy)
SORD ...... Society of Record Dealers of America
SORD ...... Southwestern Order Retrieval and Distribution (Southwest Bell Telephone Co.)
SORD ...... Submerged Object Recovery Device
SORETUR.... Societe Rouennaise d'Etudes Urbaines
SORG ...... Submarine Operations Research Group (Navy)
SORIN ..... Societa Ricerche Impianti Nucleari (Italy)
SORNE(I).... Senior Officer, Royal Naval Establishment (India) (British) (World War II)
SORNG ..... Sound Ranging
SORO ...... Special Operations Research Office
SORR ...... Submarine Operations Research Report (Navy)
SORS ...... Sacro Occipital Research Society
SORS ...... Spacecraft Oscillograph Recording System
SORT ...... Slosson Oral Reading Tests
SORT ...... Staff Organizations Round Table (American Library Association)
SORT ...... Structures for Orbiting Radio Telescope
SORTE ..... Summary of Radiation Tolerant Electronics
SORTI ..... Satellite Orbital Track and Intercept (ARPA)
SORTI ..... Star-Oriented Realtime Tracking Instrument
SORTIE ..... Supercircular Orbital Reentry Test Integrated Environment
SOS .... Congress of Scientists on Survival
SOS .... Same Old Slum (Sailor slang for food) (Bowdlerized version)
SOS .... Same Old Stew (Military slang) (Bowdlerized version)

SOS .... Same Only Softer (Band leader's signal) (Slang)
SOS .... Sanity on Sex (Group opposing sex education in schools)
SOS .... Save Our Schools
SOS .... Save Our Ship (or Souls) (Improper popular explanation of three wireless letters with meaning sent as code-signal for extreme distress)
SOS .... Science of Survival
SOS .... Scientists on Survival
SOS .... Self-Organizing System
SOS .... Send Out Succor
SOS .... Senior Opportunities and Services (OEO)
SOS .... Service of Supply
SOS .... Share Operating System (Data processing)
SOS .... Si Opus Sit (If Needed) (Medicine)
SOS .... Signed-Off Sick
SOS .... Silicon on Sapphire
SOS .... Sisters of Service (Roman Catholic religious order)
SOS .... Slum on a Shingle (Army breakfast dish) (Bowdlerized version)
SOS .... The Sniping, Observation and Scouting (Course) (British military) (World War I)
SOS .... SOS Consolidated Inc. (NYSE symbol)
SOS .... Space Ordnance Systems, Inc.
SOS .... SPRINT Operations Shelter (Army)
SOS .... Squadron Officers School (Air Force)
SOS .... Stabilized Optical Sight
SOS .... Stamp Out Sickness (Committee) (San Francisco, California)
SOS .... Stamp Out Stupidity (Student group opposing drug abuse)
SOS .... Student-Originated Studies (National Science Foundation)
SOS .... Suborbital Sequence (NASA)
SOS .... Support Our Soldiers (Network of antiwar-oriented coffee houses located near military bases)
SOS .... Suspend Other Service (Business and trade)
SOS .... Suspension of Service (Pilots' strike)
SOS .... Symbolic Operating System (Data processing)
SOS .... Symmetry, Orbitals, and Spectra (Atomic physics)
SOSAL ..... School of Systems and Logistics
SOSD ...... Spatial Operational Sequence Diagram
SOSED ..... Secretary's Office, Shore Establishments Division (Incorporated into SECP, 1944)
SOSM....... Ship Overhaul Schedule Milestone (Navy)
SOSR ...... Spin on Straight Rail
SOSS ...... Satellite Optical Surveillance Station
SOSS ...... Shipboard Oceanographic Survey System
SOSSI...... Scouts on Stamps Society International
SOSSPA .... Service of Supply, South Pacific Area (Navy) (World War II)
SOSTEL .... Solid State Electric Logic
SOSU ...... Scout Observation Service Unit (Navy)
SOSUS ..... Sound and Surveillance System
SOSUS ..... Sound System for Underwater Surveillance
SOSVS ..... Sound Surveillance System
SOT .... Sensation of Transcendence
SOT .... Son of Temperance (A heavy drinker) (Slang)
SOT .... South Omaha Terminal (AAR code)
SOT .... Start of Tape
SOT .... Systems Operating Test
SOTA ...... State of the Art
SOTB ...... Secretary's Office, Transportation Branch (Navy)
SOTE ...... Standard Optical Test Equipment
SOTFE ..... Special Operations Task Force, Europe
SOTIM ..... Sonic Observation of the Trajectory and Impact of Missiles
SOTS ...... Synchronous Orbiting Tracking Stations
SOTT ...... Second Order Transition Temperature
SOTUS ..... Sequentially Operated Teletypewriter Universal Selector
SOU .... Southern Airways, Inc.
SOU....... Southern Railway Company (AAR code)
SOU....... Statens Offentlige Utredningar (Sweden)
SOUP ...... Students Opposing Unfair Practices (in advertising) (Student legal action organization)
SOURS ..... Subcommittee on Use of Radioactivity Standards (National Research Council)
SOUSAFE .... Status of United States Air Force Equipment
SOUTHCOM .. Southern Command (Military)
SOV....... Shut-Off Valve
SOV....... Solenoid Operated Valve
SOW .... Start of Word
SOW .... Statement of Work
SOW .... Sunflower Ordnance Works
SOWESPAC ... Southwest Pacific Command (Navy)
SOWESSEAFRON .. Southwest Sea Frontier (Navy)
SOWETO..... Southwestern Townships (South Africa)
SOWg....... Special Operations Wing (Air Force)
SOX....... Solid Oxygen

SP . . . . Motor Patrol Boat (Navy symbol)
SP . . . . San Pedro (California)
SP . . . . Sanctissime Pater (Most Holy Father)
SP . . . . Satellite Processor (Data transmission)
SP . . . . Scholarly Publishing (A publication)
SP . . . . **Scientific Paper**
SP . . . . Section Patrol (Navy)
SP . . . . Security Police (Air Force)
SP . . . . Security Publication (Navy)
SP . . . . **Self-Propelled (Military)**
SP . . . . Selling Price
SP . . . . Seminar Press
SP . . . . Semipostal
SP . . . . Sequential Phase
SP . . . . Servants of the Paraclete
SP . . . . Service Panel
SP . . . . Set Point
SP . . . . Shear Plate (Technical drawings)
SP . . . . Shift Pulses
SP . . . . **Shore Party (Navy)**
SP . . . . Shore Patrol(man)
SP . . . . **Shore Police (Navy)**
SP . . . . Short Page
SP . . . . Short Period
SP . . . . Short Persistence
SP . . . . Short Pulse
SP . . . . Silver Plate
SP . . . . Simmonds Precision Products, Inc. (NYSE symbol)
SP . . . . Simple Printing
SP . . . . Sine Prole (Without Bodily Issue) (Law)
SP . . . . Single Particle
SP . . . . Single Phase
SP . . . . Single Pole (Switch)
SP . . . . Single Programmer
SP . . . . Single Purpose Gun
SP . . . . Sisters of Providence (Roman Catholic religious order)
SP . . . . Slugging Percentage (Baseball)
SP . . . . Small Packet
SP . . . . **Small Paper (Printing)**
SP . . . . Small Plaque
SP . . . . **Smokeless Powder**
SP . . . . Snow Pellets (Meteorology)
SP . . . . Socialist Party
SP . . . . Society of Protozoologists
SP . . . . Sociolinguistics Program
SP . . . . Soil Pipe
SP . . . . Solid Propellant Missile
SP . . . . Solid Propellants
SP . . . . Southern Pacific Company (AAR code)
SP . . . . Spare Part
SP . . . . Special
SP . . . . Special Paper
SP . . . . Special Projects
SP . . . . **Special Propellants**
SP . . . . **Special Publication**
SP . . . . Special Purpose
SP . . . . Spherical Polar
SP . . . . Splash Plate
SP . . . . Square Punch
SP . . . . Stable Platform
SP . . . . Standard Holding Pattern (Aviation)
SP . . . . Standard Pile
SP . . . . **Standard Practice**
SP . . . . Standpipe
SP . . . . Starting Point
SP . . . . **Starting Price**
SP . . . . Static Pressure
SP . . . . Station Pressure (Meteorology)
SP . . . . Stern Post
SP . . . . Stirrup Pump
SP . . . . **Stop Payment (Banking)**
SP . . . . **Strategic Planning Chart (Air Force)**
SP . . . . Stretcher Party
SP . . . . Subject-Predicate
SP . . . . Subliminal Perception
SP . . . . Submarine Patrol (Navy)
SP . . . . Sub-Professional (Civil Service employees designation)
SP . . . . Successive Planometric (A discrimination task)
SP . . . . Summary Plotter (RADAR)
SP . . . . Summating Potential (Hearing)
SP . . . . Summus Pontifex (Supreme Pontiff, Pope)

SP . . . . Sunlit Period
SP . . . . Supraprotest
SP . . . . Suspicious Person
SP . . . . Switch Panel
S-P . . . . Systems and Procedures
S/P . . . . Seaplane
S/P . . . . Spare Parts
S & P . . . . . . Stake and Platform (Technical drawings)
S & P . . . . . . Standard and Poor's Corporation
SP4 . . . . Specialist 4 (Army)
SP5 . . . . Specialist 5 (Army)
SP6 . . . . Specialist 6 (Army)
SP7 . . . . Specialist 7 (Army)
SPA . . . . S-Band Power Amplifier
SPA . . . . Sacrum Palatium Apostolicum (Sacred Apostolic Palace, Vatican, Quirinal)
SPA . . . . **Salt Producers Association**
SPA . . . . Scatter Propagation Antenna
SPA . . . . Self-Phasing Array
SPA . . . . Servo Power Assembly
SPA . . . . Servo Preamplifier
SPA . . . . Signal Processing Auxiliary
SPA . . . . Signal Processor Assembly (NASA)
SPA . . . . Silicon Pulser Array
SPA . . . . **Singapore People's Alliance**
SPA . . . . Societa per Azioni (Appears after the name of a company) (Italian)
SPA . . . . Society for Personnel Administration (Later, IPMA)
SPA . . . . **Society of Philatelic Americans**
SPA . . . . Society of Professional Assessors
SPA . . . . Society for Public Administration
SPA . . . . Sodium Polyacrylate
SPA . . . . Solar Power Array
SPA . . . . **Songwriters Protective Association**
SPA . . . . **South Pacific Area (World War II)**
SPA . . . . **Southern Pine Association**
SPA . . . . Southwestern Power Administration (Department of the Interior)
SPA . . . . Sparton Corporation (NYSE symbol)
SPA . . . . Special Public Assistance
SPA . . . . Special-Purpose Aircraft (Drone vehicle) (Military)
SPA . . . . **Specialist, Physical Training Instructor (Navy rating)**
SPA . . . . Spectrum Analyzer
SPA . . . . Splice Plug Assembly
SPA . . . . State Planning Agency (Department of Justice)
SPA . . . . Strategic Posture Analysis (Army)
SPA . . . . Subject to Particular Average (Insurance)
SPA . . . . Sudden Phase Anomaly (NASA)
SPA . . . . Systems and Procedures Association
SPAA . . . . . . Spacecraft Performance Analysis Area
SPAA . . . . . . Systems and Procedures Association of America
SPAAC . . . . . . Syndicat du Personnel Africain de l'Aeronautique Civile (African Union for Civil Aviation Employees)
SPAAMFAA . . . Society for the Preservation and Appreciation of Antique Motor Fire Apparatus in America
SPAB . . . . Supply, Priorities and Allocations Board (World War II)
SPAC . . . . Secretary's Pesticide Advisory Committee (HEW)
SPAC . . . . Spacecraft Performance Analysis and Command (NASA)
SPAC . . . . Spatial Computer
SPACCS . . . . . Space Command and Control System
SPACE . . . . . . Council of AFL-CIO Unions for Scientific, Professional and Cultural Employees
SPACE . . . . . . Sales Profitability and Contribution Evaluator (Data processing)
SPACE . . . . . . Self-Programming Automatic Checkout Equipment
SPACE . . . . . . Self-Programming Automatic Circuit Evaluator
SPACE . . . . . . Sidereal Polar Axis Celestial Equipment
SPACE . . . . . . Space Program American Citizens' Effort
SPACE . . . . . . Spacecraft Prelaunch Automatic Checkout Equipment
SPACE. . . . . . . Special Political Agricultural Community Education
SPACE . . . . . . Sperry Program for Advancing Careers through Education
SPACE . . . . . . Symbolic Programming Anyone Can Enjoy
SPACECOM . . . Space Communications
SPACETAC. . . . Space and Tactical System Corporation
SPACG . . . . . . Syndicat du Personnel de l'Aeronautique Civile du Gabon (Union of Civil Aviation Employees of Gabon)
SPACON. . . . . Space Control
SPAD . . . . Satellite Position Prediction and Display
SPAD . . . . Satellite Protection for Area Defense (ARPA)
SPAD . . . . Seaway Port Authority of Duluth
SPAD . . . . Societe pour Aviation et ses Derives (French) (World War I airplane)
SPAD . . . . Space Patrol Active Defense (Air Force)
SPAD . . . . Space Patrol Antimissile Defense
SPAD . . . . Space Principles, Applications and Doctrine (Air Force Systems Command)

SPAD . . . . Sprint Air-Directed Defense
SPADATS . . . . Space Detection and Tracking System (Air Force)
SPADATSC . . . . Space Detection and Tracking System Center (Air Force)
SPADATSS . . . . Space Detection and Tracking System Sensors (Air Force)
SPADE . . . . . . Signal Processing and Display Equipment
SPADE . . . . . . Spare Parts Analysis, Documentation and Evaluation
SPADE . . . . . . Sparta Acquisition Digital Equipment
SPADE . . . . . . Sperry Air Data Equipment
SPADE . . . . . . Strike Planning and Damage Estimator (Military)
SPADES . . . . . . Solar Perturbation and Atmospheric Density Measurement Satellite
SPADETS . . . . . Space Detection Network (Military)
SPADL . . . . . . Spare Parts Application Data List
SPADS . . . . . . SPRINT Air Directed Defense System (Army)
SPAEF . . . . Societe des Petroles d'Afrique Equatoriale Francaise (French Equatorial African Petroleum Company)
SPALT . . . . . . Special Projects Alterations (Navy)
SPAM . . . . . . Society for the Publication of American Music
SPAM . . . . . . Soil-Plant-Atmosphere (Computer simulation model)
SPAM . . . . . . Special Aeronautical Material
SPAMA . . . . . . Spanish Air Materiel Area
SPAMAG . . . . . Space Medicine Advisory Group
SPAMMER . . . . Space Hammer
SPAMS . . . . . . Ship Position and Altitude Measurement System
SPAN . . . . . . Society of Philatelists and Numismatists
SPAN . . . . . . Solar Particle (or Proton) Alert Network (NASA)
SPAN . . . . . . Space Communications Network
SPAN . . . . . . Space Navigation
SPAN . . . . . . Statistical Processing and Analysis (Data processing)
SPAN . . . . . . Storage Planning and Allocation (Data processing)
SPAN . . . . . . Stored Program Alphanumerics (FAA)
SPAN . . . . . . Successive, Proportionate, Additive Numeration (Decision making)
SPANAT . . . . . Systems Planning Approach-North Atlantic (FAA)
SPANDAR . . . . Space and Range RADAR (NASA)
SPANRAD . . . . Superimposed Panoramic RADAR Display
SPAR . . . . . . SAC (Strategic Air Command) Peacetime Airborne Reconnaissance
SPAR . . . . . . Seagoing Platform for Acoustic Research (NOL)
SPAR . . . . . . Semper Paratus (Always Ready) (Coast Guard motto)
SPAR . . . . . . Society of Photographer and Artist Representatives
SPAR . . . . . . Staff Procurement Activity Requirement (Military)
SPAR . . . . . . Super-Precision Approach RADAR
SPAR . . . . . . Symbolic Program Assembly Routine
SPAR . . . . . . Synchronous Position Altitude Recorder
SPARC . . . . . . Shore-Establishment Planning Analyses and Review Coordination (Navy)
SPARC . . . . . . Slab Penetration and Reflection Calculation
SPARC . . . . . . Space Program Analysis and Review Council (Air Force)
SPARC . . . . . . Space Research Capsule (or Conic) (NASA)
SPARC . . . . . . Standards Planning and Requirements Committee (ANSI)
SPARC . . . . . . Steam Plant Automation and Results Computer
SPARC . . . . . . Support Planning Analysis Reporting and Control (Navy)
SPARCS . . . . . . Solar Pointing Aerobee Rocket Control System
SPARK . . . . . . Saboteurs for a Philistine America Redeemed from Kultur (From book, "Bringing Down the House," by Richard P. Brickner)
SPARK . . . . . . School Prevention of Addiction through Rehabilitation and Knowledge (New York State program)
SPARK . . . . . . Seminars on Practical Applications of Research Knowledge (Advertising Research Foundation)
SPARM . . . . . . Solid-Propellant Augmented Rocket Motor (Navy)
SPARM . . . . . . Sparrow Anti-Radiation Missile
SPARPS . . . . . . Spares and Repair Parts Support (Navy)
SPARS . . . . . . Semper Paratus (US Coast Guard Women's Auxiliary; name taken from Coast Guard motto)
SPARS . . . . . . Site Production and Reduction System
SPARS . . . . . . Space Precision Attitude Reference System
SPARSA . . . . . Sferics, Pulse, Azimuth, Rate, and Spectrum Analyzer
SPARTA . . . . . Sequential Programmed Automatic Recording Transistor Analyzer
SPARTA . . . . . . Special Antimissile Research Tests in Australia
SPARTAN . . . . Special Proficiency at Rugged Training and Nation Building (Training program for Green Berets) (Army)
SPARTAN . . . . System for Personnel Automated Reports, Transactions, and Notices (Census Bureau, NASA)
SPAS . . . . . . Solar Proton Alpha Spectrometer
SPASCOMT . . . Space Assignment Committee
SPASM . . . . . . Space Propulsion Automated Synthesis Modeling (Program)
SPAST . . . . . . Special Assistant (Navy)
SPASUR . . . . . Space Surveillance System (Navy)
SPAT . . . . Silicon Precision Alloy Transistor
SPATE . . . . . . Sergeant Production Automatic Test Equipment
SPATE . . . . . . Student Personnel Association for Teacher Education
SPATS . . . . . . South Pacific Air Transportation Service (Navy)
SPAYZ . . . . . . Spatial Property Analyzer
SPB . . . . Seaplane Base

SPB . . . . Ship's Plotting Board
SPB . . . . Silver-Plated Bronze
SPB . . . . Solar Particle Beams
SPB . . . . Surplus Property Board
SPBA . . . . . . Specialty Paper and Board Affiliates
SPBC . . . . . . Saint Paul Bible College (Minnesota)
SPBC . . . . . . Society of Professional Business Consultants
SPBI . . . . . . Serikat Buruh Pertjetakan Indonesia (Printing Workers' Union) (Indonesia)
SPBOT . . . . . . Stationers and Publishers Board of Trade
SPBP . . . . . . Society for the Preservation of Birds of Prey
SPC . . . . . . Saint Paul College (Washington, DC; Missouri; Virginia)
SPC . . . . . . Saint Peter College (Maryland; New Jersey)
SPC . . . . . . Saint Procopin College (Illinois)
SPC . . . . . . Salicylamide, Phenacetin (Acetophenetidin) and Caffeine (Pharmacy)
SPC . . . . . . Seattle Pacific College (Washington)
SPC . . . . . . Set Point Controller
SPC . . . . . . Shuttle Pin Clutch
SPC . . . . . . Silver-Plated Copper
SPC . . . . . . Society for Philosophy of Creativity
SPC . . . . . . Society for the Prevention of Crime
SPC . . . . . . Solar Pointing Control
SPC . . . . . . Solid-Propellant Combustion
SPC . . . . . . Solid-Propellant Conference
SPC . . . . . . South Pacific Commission
SPC . . . . . . Space Projects Center (NASA)
SPC . . . . . . Special Common (Projectile)
SPC . . . . . . Special Fuel Consumption
SPC . . . . . . Special Program Code (Navy)
SPC . . . . . . Specialist, Classification Interviewer (Navy rating)
SPC . . . . . . Specific Propellant Consumption
SPC . . . . . . Standard Products Committee (Navy)
SPC . . . . . . Static Power Converter
SPC . . . . . . Sterilizable Potting Compound
SPC . . . . . . Stored Program Command (or Control) (Gemini) (NASA)
SPC . . . . . . Subcontract Plans Committee
SPC . . . . . . Suspended Plaster Ceiling (Technical drawings)
SPCA . . . . . . Serum Prothrombin Conversion Accelerator (Factor VII)
SPCA . . . . . . Society for the Prevention of Cruelty to Animals
SPCA . . . . . . Southern Pulpwood Conservation Association
SPCA . . . . . . Special-Purpose Cable Assembly
SPCC . . . . . . Ship's Parts Control Center
SPCC . . . . . . Society for the Prevention of Cruelty to Children
SPCC . . . . . . Strength Power and Communications Cable
SPCK . . . . . . Society for Promoting Christian Knowledge (Publisher) (British)
SPCM . . . . . . Spanish Campaign Medal
SPCM . . . . . . Special Court-Martial
SPCMO . . . . . . Special Court-Martial Order
SPCMWOMJ . . . Special Court-Martial Without a Military Judge
SPCO . . . . . . Southern Pacific Company
SPCR . . . . . . Spare Parts Change Request
SPCS . . . . . . Selective Paging Communications System
SPCS . . . . . . Static Power Conversion System
SPCTYS . . . . . . Society for Prevention of Cruelty to Young Singers
SPCW . . . . . . Specialist, Chemical Warfare (Navy rating)
SPD . . . . Doctor of Political Science
SPD . . . . Scientific Passenger Pod
SPD . . . . Seaplane Depot Ship
SPD . . . . Service Project Drawing
SPD . . . . Sigma Phi Delta
SPD . . . . Situation Projected Display
SPD . . . . Society of Publication Designers
SPD . . . . Southern Procurement Division (Navy)
SPD . . . . Sozialdemokratische Partei Deutschlands (Social Democratic Party of Germany) (West Germany)
SPD . . . . Speech Processing Device
SPD . . . . Static Pressure Distribution
SPD . . . . Steamer Pays Dues (Shipping)
SPD . . . . Stored Program Decommutation (or Decoder)
SPD . . . . Subjective Probability Distribution
SPD . . . . Synchronizer for Peripheral Devices
SPD . . . . Synchronous Phase Demodulator
SPD . . . . System Program Director (or Directive) (Air Force)
SPDC . . . . . . Spare Parts Distributing Center (Navy)
SPDF . . . . . . Special Projects Data Facility
SPDF . . . . . . Swedish Post Defense Forces
SPDG . . . . . . Spiral Point Drill Geometry
SPDLTR . . . . . Speedletter
SPDRAB . . . . . Society for the Prevention of Disparaging Remarks About Brooklyn
SPDT . . . . . . Single Pole, Double Throw (Switch)
SPE . . . . Shaft Position Encoder
SPE . . . . Society of Petroleum Engineers (of AIME)

SPE . . . . Society of Plastics Engineers
SPE . . . . Society for Pure English
SPE . . . . Special Purpose Equipment
SPE . . . . Spherical Probable Error
SPE . . . . Sprague Electric Co. (NYSE symbol)
SPE . . . . Stored Program Element
SPE . . . . Subport of Embarkation
SPE . . . . System Performance Evaluation
SPE . . . . Systems Performance Effectiveness
SPEA . . . . Sales Promotion Executives Association
SPEAC . . . . . . Selma Project Education Alternatives Center (Alabama)
SPE of AIME . . Society of Petroleum Engineers of American Institute of Mining,
   Metallurgical and Petroleum Engineers
SPEAR. . . . . . . Source Performance Evaluation and Reporting
SPEAR. . . . . . . Stanford Positron-Electron Asymmetric Ring
SPEARS . . . . . . Satellite Photo-Electric Analog Rectification System
SPEBSQSA . . . . Society for the Preservation and Encouragement of Barber Shop Quartet
   Singing in America
SPEC . . . . Scientific Pollution and Environmental Control Society
SPEC . . . . Society for Professional Engineering Checkers
SPEC . . . . Specification (or Specify)
SPEC . . . . Staff of the Production Executive Committee (of the WPB) (Obsolete)
SPEC . . . . Stored Program Educational Computer
SPECA . . . . . . Society for the Preservation and Enjoyment of Carriages in America
SPECAT. . . . . . Special Category
SPECDEVCEN . . Special Devices Center
SPECO . . . . . . Steel Products Engineering Company
SPECOMME . . . Specified Command Middle East
SPECON . . . . . Systems Performance Effectiveness Conference
SPECTRE . . . . . Special Executive for Counterintelligence, Terrorism, Revenge, and
   Extortion (Fictitious organization whose agents were characters in late
   Ian Fleming's "James Bond" mysteries)
SPECTROL . . . . Scheduling, Planning, Evaluation and Cost Control (Air Force)
Sp Ed . . . . . . Specialist in Education (Academic degree)
SPED . . . . Subsistence Preparation by Electronic Defusion (Army field kitchen)
SPED. . . . . Sulfur, Phosphorus, Emission Detector (Chromatograph accessory)
SPEDAC . . . . . Solid-State, Parallel, Expandable, Differential Analyzer Computer
SPEDCO . . . . . Southeastern Pennsylvania Development Corporation
SPEDE. . . . . . . System for Processing Educational Data Electronically
SPEDIAT . . . . . Special Diary Transcript (Military)
SPEDTAR . . . . . Stored Program Educational Transistorized Automatic Computer
SPEE . . . . Society for the Promotion of Engineering Education
SPEED. . . . . . . Scheduled Procurement of Essential Equipment Deliveries (US Postal
   Service)
SPEED. . . . . . . Self-Programmed Electronic Equation Delineator
SPEED. . . . . . . Signal Processing in Evacuated Electronic Devices
SPEED. . . . . . . Study & Performance Efficiency in Entry Design
SPEED. . . . . . . Systematic Plotting and Evaluation of Enumerated Data (Data processing)
   (National Bureau of Standards)
SPEED. . . . . . . Systemwide Project for Electronic Equipment at Depots (Military)
SPEM . . . . Sindacato Petrolieri e Methanieri (Union of Oil and Methane Gas
   Workers) (Italy)
SPEMS . . . . . . Space Environment Monitoring System
SPENAVO . . . . Special Naval Observer
SPEOPT. . . . . . Special Optical Tracking System (NASA)
SPEP . . . . Society for Phenomenology and Existential Philosophy
SPEPD . . . . . . Space Power and Electric Propulsion Division (Formerly Nuclear Systems
   and Space Power Division) (NASA)
SPEPS . . . . . . Specialist, Motion Picture Service - Booker (Navy rating)
SPERM . . . . . . Secret Paper Reconstitution Mechanism (Device to reclaim documents
   that have been inadvertently shredded)
SPERT . . . . . . Schedule Performance Evaluation and Review Technique
SPERT . . . . . . Simplified Program Evaluation and Review Technique (Trademark)
SPERT . . . . . . Special PERT
SPERT . . . . . . Special Power Excursion Reactor Test (US reactor facilities)
SPERW . . . . . . Specialist, Recreation and Welfare Assistant (Navy rating)
SPES . . . . Servico de Propaganda e Educacao Sanitaria (Brazil)
SPET . . . . Solid Propellant Electric Thruster (Aerospace)
SPET . . . . Super Power Electron Tube
SPF . . . . Society for the Propagation of the Faith
SPF. . . . . Specialist, Firefighter (Navy rating)
SPF . . . . Specific-Pathogen Free
SPF . . . . Spectrophotofluorometer
SPF . . . . Suburban Press Foundation
SPF . . . . Survival Probability Function
SPF. . . . . Synthetic Phenolic Foam
SPFA . . . . Societe des Professeurs Francais en Amerique
SPFA . . . . Steel Plate Fabricators Association
SPFC . . . . Society for the Parents of Fugitive Children (Fictional organization in
   film "Taking Off")
SPFL. . . . . Southern Philippines Federation of Labor

SPFM . . . . Society of Priests for a Free Ministry
SPFP. . . . . Single Pass Fit Program
SPFT. . . . . Single-Pedestal Flat-Top (Desk)
SPFW . . . . Single Phase Full Wave
SPG . . . . Saint Paul Guild
SPG . . . . Scan Pattern Generator
SPG . . . . Screen Producers Guild
SPG . . . . Seed Pea Group
SPG . . . . Simple Phrase Grammar
SPG . . . . Sinusoidal Pressure Generator
SPG . . . . Society for the Propagation of the Gospel (British)
SPG . . . . Source Power Gain
SPG . . . . Specialist, Gunnery (Navy rating)
SPG . . . . Suburban Propane Gas Corporation (NYSE symbol)
SPGA . . . . Southeastern Pecan Growers Association
SPGCPS . . . . . Senior Policy Group for Canadian Production Sharing
SPGJ . . . . Society for the Propagation of the Gospel among the Jews (British)
SPGM . . . . Specialist, Gunnery, Aviation Free Gunnery Instructor (Navy rating)
SPGN. . . . . Specialist, Gunnery, Anti-Aircraft Gunnery Instructor (Navy rating)
SPGR . . . . Specific Gravity (Also, SG)
SPGT . . . . Serum Pyruvic-Glutamic Transaminase (Biochemistry)
SPGT . . . . Springfield Terminal Railway Company (AAR code)
SPH . . . . Stable Platform Housing
SPH . . . . Statement of Personal History
SPHD . . . . Special Pay for Hostile Duty (Military)
SPHE . . . . Society of Packaging and Handling Engineers
SPHF . . . . Spin-Polarized Hartree-Fock (Atomic wave-function)
SP-HL. . . . . . . Sun Present - Horizon Lost
SPHS . . . . Swedish Pioneer Historical Society
SPHT . . . . Super Pressure - High Temperature
SP-HT. . . . . . . Specific Heat
SP/HT. . . . . . . Specific Heat
SPHW . . . . Single-Phase Half Wave
SPI. . . . . Secretariats Professionnels Internationaux
SPI. . . . . Senior Patrol Inspector (Immigration and Naturalization Service)
SPI. . . . . Serum Precipitable Iodine (Medicine)
SPI. . . . . Service Pedalogique Interafricain
SPI. . . . . Society of Photographic Illustrators
SPI. . . . . Society of the Plastics Industry
SPI . . . . Society of Professional Investigators
SPI . . . . Spanish Paprika Institute
SPI. . . . . Specialist, Punched Card Accounting Machine Operator (Navy rating)
SPI. . . . . Standard Practice Instructions
SPI . . . . Standard Protective Item
SPI . . . . Synthetic Phase Isolation (Telemetry)
SPIA . . . . Solid Propellant Information Agency (Air Force)
SPIB . . . . Shetland Pony Identification Bureau
SPIB . . . . Southern Pine Inspection Bureau
SPIC. . . . . Sisters of Providence and of the Immaculate Conception (Roman Catholic
   religious order)
SPIC . . . . Students for Promotion of Identity on Campus (New York group
   promoting ethnic pride among Latin American students)
SPICE . . . . . . Solar Particle Intensity Composition Experiment (NASA)
SPICE . . . . . . Special Programs Increasing Counseling Effectiveness (Pennsylvania
   State Department of Public Instruction)
SPID. . . . . Submersible Portable Inflatable Dwelling
SPIDER . . . . . . Systematic Planning for the Integration of Defense Engineering and
   Research (Program)
SPIE . . . . Secretariat Professionnel International de l'Enseignement
SPIE . . . . Simulated Problem Input Evaluation
SPIE . . . . Society of Photo-Optical Instrumentation Engineers
SPIN . . . . Searchable Physics Information Notices (Computer tapes)
SPIN . . . . Southern California Police Information Network
SPIN . . . . Space Inspection
SPINDEX . . . . Selective Permutation Indexing (Library of Congress)
SPINE . . . . . . Simulated Program for Investigation of Nuclear Effects
SPIR . . . . Student Project for International Responsibility
SPIRAL . . . . . . Sperry Inertial RADAR Altimeter
SPIRE . . . . . . Spatial Inertial Reference Equipment
SPIREP. . . . . . Spot Intelligence Report (Air Force)
SPIRES . . . . . . Standard Personnel Information Retrieval System (Military)
SPIRES . . . . . . Stanford Physics Information Retrieval System
SPIRO. . . . . . . Students Protesting Illegal Real Estate Operators (Student legal
   action organization)
SPIRT . . . . . . Stock Point Interrogation/Requirements Technique
SPISE . . . . . . Special Projects in Science Education
SPIT . . . . Selective Printing of Items From Tape (Data processing)
SPIW . . . . Special-Purpose Individual Weapon (A rifle which fires flechettes or
   darts) (Pronounced "Spew")
SPJC . . . . Saint Petersburg Junior College (Florida)
SPK . . . . Spare Parts Kit

ACRONYMS AND INITIALISMS DICTIONARY

SPK . . . . Standard Packaging Corporation (NYSE symbol) (Wall Street slang name: "Sputnik") (Delisted)
SPL . . . . Simple Phrase Language
SPL . . . . Sine Prole Legitima (Without Legitimate Issue)
SPL . . . . Single Propellant Loading
SPL . . . . Sloane Physics Laboratory (Yale)
SPL . . . . Sound Pressure Level
SPL . . . . Space Physics Laboratory (Aerospace corporation)
SPL . . . . Space Programing Language
SPL . . . . Spare Parts List
SPL . . . . Special-Purpose Language
SPL . . . . Speed Phase Lock
SPL . . . . Spermatophore Length
SPL . . . . Standard Pulse LASER
SPL . . . . Staphylococcal Bacteriophage Lysate (Bacteriology)
SPLC . . . . . Ship Program Life Cycle (Navy)
SPLC . . . . . Standard Point Location Code (American Trucking Association and Association of American Railroads)
SPLI . . . . . . Spermatophore Length Index
SPLIT . . . . . . Sundstrand Processing Languages Internally Translated
SPLM . . . . . Space Programing Language Machine
SPLT . . . . . . Specialist, Link Trainer Instructor (Navy rating)
SPM . . . . . . Sedimentary Phosphate Method
SPM . . . . . . Self-Propelled Mount
SPM . . . . . . Semi-Permeable Membrane
SPM . . . . . . Short Particular Metre (Music)
SPM . . . . . . Sine Prole Mascula (Without Male Issue)
SPM . . . . . . Smaller Profit Margin
SPM . . . . . . Societas Patrum Misericordiae (Fathers of Mercy) (Roman Catholic religious order)
SPM . . . . . . Solar Proton Monitor
SPM . . . . . . Sound Powered Microphone
SPM . . . . . . Specialist, Mail Clerk (Navy rating)
SPM . . . . . . Spectrophosphorimeter
SPM . . . . . . Split Phase Motor
SPM . . . . . . Standard Process Manual
SPM . . . . . . Static Presentation Mode
SPM . . . . . . Strokes Per Minute
SPM . . . . . . Sun Probe-Mars (NASA)
SPM . . . . . . Superparamagnetic (Fraction in rock) (Geophysics)
SPM . . . . . . Support Program Management
SPM . . . . . . Synthetic Plasma Membrane(s) (Biochemistry)
SPMA . . . . . Shoe Pattern Manufacturers Association
SPMA . . . . . Soda Pulp Manufacturers Association
SPMA . . . . . Sump Pump Manufacturers Association
SPMC . . . . . Society of Professional Management Consultants
SPMM . . . . . Society for the Promotion of Mohammedan Missions
SPMRL . . . . Sulphite Pulp Manufacturers' Research League
SPMS . . . . . Surveyor Payload Mechanism Section
SPMS . . . . . System Program Management Surveys (Air Force)
SPN . . . . . . Separation Program Number (Military)
SPN . . . . . . Sponsor Program Number (Military)
SPNEA . . . . Society for the Preservation of New England Antiquities
SPO . . . . . . Sacramento Peak Observatory
SPO . . . . . . Sausages, Potatoes and Onions (Meaning a cheap restaurant which specializes in these) (British slang)
SPO . . . . . . Sea Post Office
SPO . . . . . . Senate Post Office
SPO . . . . . . Shore Patrol Officer (Navy)
SPO . . . . . . Short Period Oscillation
SPO . . . . . . Signal Property Office
SPO . . . . . . Slaving Pick-Off
SPO . . . . . . Sozialdemokratische Partei Oesterreichs
SPO . . . . . . Sozialistische Partei Oesterreichs
SPO . . . . . . Special Projects Office (Navy)
SPO . . . . . . Specialist, Inspector of Naval Material (Navy rating)
SPO . . . . . . Surplus Property Office (Transferred to War Assets Administration, 1947)
SPO . . . . . . System Program Office (Air Force)
SPO . . . . . . System Project Office
SPOAV . . . . Specialist, Inspector of Aviation Material (Navy rating)
SPOC . . . . . Single Point Orbit Calculator
SPOC . . . . . Spacecraft Oceanography Project (Navy)
SPOCK . . . . Simulated Procedure for Obtaining Common Knowledge
SPODA . . . . Society for the Prevention of Drug Addiction
SPODAC . . . . SITS (SAGE Intercept Target Simulation) Probability of Detection and Conversion
SPODP . . . . Single-Precision Orbit Determination Program (NASA)
SPOEN . . . . Specialist, Engineering Inspector (Navy rating)
SPOMCUS . . . Selective Prepositioning of Materiel Configured to Unit Sets (Army)
SPON . . . . . Sponsor
SPON . . . . . Statistical Profile of Old Norse

SPOOFS . . . . Society for the Promotion of Otherwise Overlooked Football Scores
SPOOK . . . . Supervisor Program Over Other Kinds (Data processing)
SPOOR . . . . Specialist, Ordnance Inspector (Navy rating)
SPOPE . . . . Specialist, Petroleum Technician (Navy rating)
SPOPS . . . . Special Operations
SPORT . . . . St. Petersburg (Fla.) Olympic Regatta Training
SPORT . . . . Space Probe Optical Recording Telescope (Army)
SPORTFOR . . . Support Force
SPOT . . . . . Satellite Positioning and Tracking
SPOT . . . . . Smithsonian Precision Optical Tracking
SPOT . . . . . Symptom Pattern Observation Technique (Aviation)
SPOTY . . . . Single Parent of the Year
SPP . . . . . . New York Society for the Prevention of Pauperism
SPP . . . . . . Scott Paper Company (NYSE symbol)
SPP . . . . . . Secular Periodic Perturbation
SPP . . . . . . Society of Private Printers
SPP . . . . . . Spare Parts Provisioning
SPP . . . . . . Specialist, Photographic Specialist (Navy rating)
SPP . . . . . . Straight Path Penetration
SPP . . . . . . Supra Pubic Prostatectomy (Medicine)
SPP . . . . . . Swaziland Progressive Party
SPP . . . . . . System Package Plan (or Program)
SPPA . . . . . Screen Process Printing Association, International
SPPC . . . . . Spare Parts Provisioning Card
SPPLB . . . . . Specialist, Photographer, Laboratory (Navy rating)
SPPMP . . . . Specialist, Motion Picture Production (Navy rating)
SPPPG . . . . Specialist, Photogrammetry (Navy rating)
SPPR . . . . . Specialist, Public Relations (Coast Guard)
SPPS . . . . . Specialist, Port Security (Coast Guard)
SPPS . . . . . Stable Plasma Protein Solution (Medicine)
SPPSG . . . . Science and Public Policy Studies Group (Newsletter)
SPPVM . . . . Specialist, V-Mail (Navy rating)
SPQ . . . . . . Stanford Parent Questionnaire (Psychology)
SPQCR . . . . Specialist, Communications Specialist, Cryptographer (Navy rating)
SPQIN . . . . Specialist, Communications Specialist, Radio Intelligence (Navy rating)
SPQR . . . . . Senatus Populusque Romanus (The Senate and People of Rome)
SPQR . . . . . Small Profits, Quick Returns
SPQRP . . . . Specialist, Communications Specialist, Registered Publication Clerk (Navy rating)
SPQTE . . . . Specialist, Communications Specialist, Technician (Navy rating)
SPR . . . . . . Satellite Parametric Reduction
SPR . . . . . . Seal Pressure Ratio
SPR . . . . . . Sense Printer
SPR . . . . . . Sequential Probability Ratio
SPR . . . . . . Shock Position Ratio
SPR . . . . . . Silicon Power Rectifier
SPR . . . . . . Simplified Practice Recommendation
SPR . . . . . . Society for Pediatric Research
SPR . . . . . . Society for Psychical Research
SPR . . . . . . Solid Propellant Rocket
SPR . . . . . . Spartans Industries, Inc. (NYSE symbol) (Delisted)
SPR . . . . . . Special Program Requirement
SPR . . . . . . Special Project Report
SPR . . . . . . Special Purpose RADAR
SPR . . . . . . Specialist, Recruiter (Navy rating)
SPR . . . . . . Sudden Pressure Relay
SPR . . . . . . Supplementary Progress Report
SPR . . . . . . System Performance Rating
SPR's . . . . . Small Parcels and Rolls (Postal Service)
SPRC . . . . . Society of Public Relations Counsellors
SPRD . . . . . Science Policy Research Division (of Congressional Research Service, Library of Congress)
SPRE . . . . . Society of Park and Recreation Educators
SPRE . . . . . Solid-Propellant Rocket Engine
S & P RES DIS . . Severn and Potomac Reserve District (Marine Corps)
SPRF . . . . . Sandia Pulsed Reactor Facility
SPRI . . . . . Scott Polar Research Institute (Cambridge, England)
SPRI . . . . . Sperm Reservoir Length Index
SPRINT . . . . Selective Printing (Data processing term)
SPRINT . . . . Solid Propellant Rocket Intercept Missile (ARPA/AMC)
SPRINT . . . . Special Police Radio Inquiry Network (New York City)
SPRINTER . . . Specification of Profits with Interaction under Trial and Error Response
SPRJ . . . . . Self-Powered Reference Junction
SPRS . . . . . Single Passenger Reservation System (DOD)
SPRS . . . . . Special Purpose RADAR Set
SPRT . . . . . Sequential Probability Ratio Test (Statistics)
SPS . . . . . . Saint Patrick Seminary (California)
SPS . . . . . . St. Patrick's Missionary Society
SPS . . . . . . Samples Per Second
SPS . . . . . . Saturn Propulsion System
SPS . . . . . . Scientific Power Switching

SPS .... Secondary Propulsion System (NASA)
SPS .... Service Propulsion System (NASA)
SPS .... Servo Parameter Shift
SPS .... Set Point Station
Sp S .... Sharp Shooter (Army)
SPS .... Ship Planning System
SPS .... Simple Phrase System
SPS .... Sine Prole Superstite (Without Surviving Issue) (Law)
SPS .... Single Pole Switch
SPS .... Society of Pelvic Surgeons
SPS .... Society for Pentecostal Studies
SPS .... Solar Panel Substrate
SPS .... Solar Probe Spacecraft (Pioneer satellite)
SPS .... SONAR Phase Shifter
SPS .... Southwestern Public Service Company (NYSE symbol)
SPS .... Space Power System
SPS .... Special Services (Military)
SPS .... Specialist, Personnel Supervisor (Women's Reserve) (Navy rating)
SPS .... Specialist, Shore Patrol and Security (Navy rating)
SPS .... Spectrum Planning Subcommittee (FCC)
SPS .... Spokane, Portland & Seattle Railway System (AAR code)
SPS .... Standard Pipe Size
SPS .... Standard Pressed Steel Company
SPS .... Static Power System
SPS .... Static Pressure System
SPS .... Statistical Performance Standards (Navy)
SPS .... Stator Pivot Seal
SPS .... Steady Potential Shift
SPS .... Stereo Photographic System
SPS .... Stored Program Simulator
SPS .... Submarine Piping System
SPS .... Submerged Production System (Deepwater platform) (Humble Oil)
SPS .... Symbolic Programming System (Data processing)
SPSA .... Senate Press Secretaries Association
SPSA .... Special Projects School for Air
SPSC .... Space Power Systems Conference
SPSD .... Space Power Systems Division (NASA)
SP-SDF ..... Socialist Party - Social Democratic Federation (Later, Socialist Party, USA)
SPSDM ..... Society for the Philosophical Study of Dialectical Materialism
SPSE .... Society of Photographic Scientists & Engineers
SPSI .... Serikat Pelajaran Seluruh Indonesia (Sailors' Union) (Indonesia)
SPSI .... Society for the Promotion of Scientific Industry (British)
SPSO .... Senior Principal Scientific Officer (Ministry of Agriculture, Fisheries, and Food) (British)
SPSP .... St. Peter and St. Paul (The Papal seal)
SPSP .... Solid Propellant Surveillance Panel (Military)
SPSS .... Specialist, Personnel Supervisor, V-10 (Navy rating)
SPSS .... Statistical Package for the Social Sciences (A publication)
SPSSI ...... Society for the Psychological Study of Social Issues
SPST .... Single-Pole, Single-Throw (Switch)
SPSTNODM ... Single-Pole, Single-Throw, Normally Open, Double-Make (Electronics relay)
SPSTP ...... Solid Propellant Rocket Static Test Panel (Military)
SPT .... School of Physical Training
SPT .... Shipper Pays Taxes
SPT .... Silicon Planar Transistor
SPT .... Silicon-Powered Transistor
SPT .... Small Perturbation Theory
SPT .... Society of Photo-Technologists
SPT .... Society for Projective Techniques
SPT .... Sound-Powered Telephone
SPT .... Space Power Tool
SPT .... Spare Parts Transfer
SPT .... Specialist, Teacher (Navy rating)
SPT .... Support
SPTA .... Southern Pressure Treaters Association
SPTC .... Specified Period of Time Contract
SPTD .... Signal Processor Techniques Department
SPTF .... Signal Processing Test Facility
SPTF .... Sodium Pump Test Facility (AEC)
SPTL .... Support Line
SPTLT ...... Specialist, Link Trainer Instructor (Navy rating)
SPT & PA .... Society for Projective Techniques and Personality Assessment
SP(TR) ..... Specialist (Transportation) (Coast Guard)
SPTRJ ...... Self-Powered Thermocouple Reference Junction
SPTW .... Single-Pedestal Typewriter (Desk)
SPU .... Specialist, Utility (Women's Reserve) (Navy rating)
SPU .... Student Peace Union
SPU .... Subsurface Propulsion Unit
SPUD .... St. Paul Union Depot Company (AAR code)

SPUD .... Society for Prevention of Unwholesome Diet (National Potato Council)
SPUD .... Solar Power Unit Demonstrator
SPUD .... Stored Program Universal Demonstrator
SPUR .... Single Precision Unpacked Rounded
SPUR .... Space Power Unit Reactor (Air Force)
SPUR .... Support for Promoting the Utilization of Resources (Esso Education Foundation)
SPURT ...... Small Primate Unrestrained Test
SPURT ...... Spinning Unguided Rocket Trajectory
SPURV ...... Self-Propelled Underwater Research Vehicle
SPV .... Southeastern Public Service Company (NYSE symbol)
SPV .... Special Purpose Vehicles
SPV .... Specialist, Transport Airman (Navy rating)
SPVEA ...... Superintendencia do Plano de Valorizacao Economica da Amazonia (Brazil)
SPW .... Sealed Power Corp. (NYSE symbol)
SPW .... Specialist, Chaplain's Assistant (Navy rating)
SPWA .... Steel Products Warehouse Association
SPWAR ...... Special Warfare
SPWC .... Society for the Punishment of War Criminals
SPWG .... Space Parts Working Group
SPWLA ...... Society of Professional Well Log Analysts
SPWR .... Small Pressurized Water Reactor
SPWSM ..... Spanish War Service Medal
SPWWIII ..... Society for the Prevention of World War III
SPX .... Simplex Instrument (Telegraphy)
SPX .... Superheat Power Experiment
SPXAC ...... Specialist, Archivist (Navy rating)
SPXAR ...... Specialist, Artist (Navy rating)
SPXBL ...... Specialist, Ballistics (Navy rating)
SPXC .... Saint Pius X Seminary (New York)
SPXCC ...... Specialist, Cable Censor (Navy rating)
SPXCG ...... Specialist, Crystal Grinder (Navy rating)
SPXCT ...... Specialist, Cartographer (Navy rating)
SPXDI ...... Specialist, Discharge Interviewer (Navy rating)
SPXED ...... Specialist, Engineering Draftsman (Navy rating)
SPXFP ...... Specialist, Fingerprint Expert (Navy rating)
SPXGU ...... Specialist, Gage Specialist (Navy rating)
SPXID ...... Specialist, Intelligence Duties (Navy rating)
SPXIR ...... Specialist, Interpreter (Navy rating)
SPXJO ...... Specialist, Journalist (Navy rating)
SPXKP. ..... Specialist, Key Punch Operator and Supervisor (Navy rating)
SPXNC ...... Specialist, Naval Correspondent (Navy rating)
SPXOP ...... Specialist, Special Project (Navy rating)
SPXPC ...... Specialist, Position Classifier (Navy rating)
SPXPI ...... Specialist, Pigeon Trainer (Navy rating)
SPXPL. ..... Specialist, Plastic Expert (Navy rating)
SPXPR ...... Specialist, Public Information (Navy rating)
SPXQM. ..... Specialist, Operations - Plotting and Chart Work (Navy rating)
SPXRL ...... Specialist, Research Laboratory (Navy rating)
SPXRS. ..... Specialist, Armed Forces Radio Service and Special Naval Radio Units (Navy rating)
SPXSB ...... Specialist, Telephone Switchboard Operator and Supervisor
SPXST. ..... Specialist, Strategic Services (Navy rating)
SPXTD ...... Specialist, Topographic Draftsman (Navy rating)
SPXTS. ..... Specialist, Air Stations Operations Desk - Time Shack (Navy rating)
SPXVA ...... Specialist, Visual Training Aids (Navy rating)
SQ. .... Squadron
SQ. .... Square
SQ. .... Stereoquadraphonic (Record playing system) (CBS)
SQ. .... Superquick
SQA .... Squaring Amplifier
SQA .... Supplier (or Surveyor) Quality Assurance
SQAD ...... Surveyor Quality Assurance Directive
SQAP ...... Supplemental Quality Assurance Provision
SQAR ...... Supplier Quality Assurance Representative
SQAT ...... Ship's Qualification Assistance Team (Navy)
SQB .... Squibb Corp. (NYSE symbol)
SQC .... Self-Quenching Control
SQC. .... Station Quality Control (RADAR)
SQC. .... Statistical Quality Control
SQCP ...... Statistical Quality Control Procedure
SQD. .... Self-Quenching Detector
SQD. .... Square D Company (NYSE symbol)
SQDC ...... Special Quick Disconnect Coupling
SQI .... Special Qualifications Identifiers (Army)
SQID ...... Semiconducting Quantum Interference Device
SQL .... School Quota Letter
SQL .... Space Qualified LASER
SQM .... Square Meter
SQMS. ...... Staff Quartermaster Sergeant

SQN	School Quota Number
SQN	Spin Quantum Number
SQO	Squadron Officer
SQQ	San Quentin Quail (A minor female) (Slang)
SQR	Square Root (Data processing)
SQR	Supplier Quality Rating
SQ3R	Survey, Question, Read, Review, Recite (Psychology)
SQS	Statistische Quellenwerke der Schweiz (Switzerland)
SQS	Stochastic Queuing System
SQT	Ship Qualification Test (Navy)
SQT	Sterilization Qualification Tests
SQT	System Qualification Tests
SQTT	Ship Qualifications Trial Team (Navy)
SQUID	Superconducting Quantum Interference Detector (or Device) (Magnetometry)
SQUIRE.....	Submarine Quickened Response
SQUOD	Selected Quantile Output Device (Electronics)
SR	Air Search RADAR Receiver (Shipborne)
SR	General Society, Sons of the Revolution
SR	Sarcoplasmic Reticulum
SR	Saturable Reactor
SR	Saturday Review (A magazine)
SR	Scanning Radiometer
SR	Scientific Report
SR	Scientific Research
SR	Scottish Rifles (British military unit)
SR	Seaman Recruit
SR	Seaplane Reconnaissance Aircraft
SR	Search RADAR
SR	Search and Rescue
SR	Section Report
SR	Sedimentation Rate
SR	Selective Ringing
SR	Self-Rectifying
SR	Semantic Reaction
SR	Senate Resolution
SR	Send and Receive
SR	Senior
SR	Senior Registrar
SR	Senior Reviewer
SR	Senor
SR	Sensitivity Ratio
SR	Sensitization Response
SR	Separate Rations
SR	Service Record
SR	Service Report
SR	Severe, Right-moving (Thunderstorm)
SR	Sex Ratio
SR	Shift Register
SR	Shift Reverse
SR	Shift Right
SR	Ship Repair Ratings
SR	Shipment (or Shipping) Request
SR	Shipping Receipt (Business and trade)
SR	Short Range
SR	Short Rate
SR	Sigma Reaction
SR	Silicon Rectifier
SR	Silicon Rubber
SR	Simulation Report
SR	Single Reduction
SR	Sinus Rhythm (Medicine)
SR	Sister
SR	Slant Range
SR	Slow Release (Electronics)
SR	Small Ring
SR	Social Register
SR	Socialist Revolutionary (Russia)
SR	Society of Rheology
SR	Solar Radiation
SR	Solid Rocket
SR	Soluble, Repository (With reference to penicillin)
SR	Sons of the Revolution
SR	Sound Ranging
SR	Sound Report
SR	Southern Railway Company (NYSE symbol)
SR	Spares Requirement
SR	Special Regulations (Military)
SR	Special Report
SR	Specification Requirement
SR	Speed Regulator
SR	Split Ring (Technical drawings)

SR	Staff Report
SR	Stage Right (A stage direction)
SR	Standard Range Approach (Aviation)
SR	Standardization Report
SR	Star Route (A type of rural postal delivery route)
SR	State Register
SR	Stateroom
SR	Stationery Request
SR	Statstjanstemannens Riksforbund (National Association of Salaried Employees in Government Service) (Sweden)
SR	Status Report
sr	Steradian
SR	Stimulus-Response
SR	Storage Room
SR	Stove or Range
Sr	Strontium (Chemical element)
SR	Study Regulation
SR	Study Requirement (Air Force)
SR	Styrene Rubber
SR	Su Remesa (Your Remittance) (Business and trade) (Spain)
SR	Subject Ratio
SR	Subscriber Register
SR	Summary Report
SR	Sunrise (Meteorology)
SR	Supplemental Report
SR	Supplementary Regulation
SR	Supporting Research
SR	Surveillance RADAR (Air Force)
SR	Swissair (Swiss Air Transport Co., Ltd.)
S-R	Stimulus-Response
S/R	Shipper/Receiver (Difference)
S/R	Shipping Request
S/R	Slant Range
SRA	Science Research Associates
SRA	Screw Research Association
SRA	Senior Residential Appraiser (Designation given by Society of Real Estate Appraisers)
SRA	Servicemen's Readjustment Act
SRA	Ship Radio Authorization (Army)
SRA	Shop Replaceable Assembly (DOD)
SRA	Short Reflex Arc
SRA	Simultaneous Range Adcock Antenna (Military RADAR)
SRA	Society of Research Administrators
SRA	Society of Residential Appraisers
SRA	Sociological Research Association
SRA	Southern Rural Action, Inc.
SRA	Spanish Refugee Aid
SRA	Special Refractories Association
SRA	Special Rules Area
SRA	Specialized Repair Activity
SRA	Station Representatives Association
SRA	Stock Record Account
SRA	Subminiature Rotary Actuator
SRA	Sugar Rationing Administration (Department of Agriculture) (Ceased functions, 1948)
SRA	Sulforicinoleic Acid (Organic chemistry)
SRA	Svenska Radio Aktiebologet
SRA	System Requirements Analysis
SRAA	Schoolboy Rowing Association of America
SRAC	Short Run Average Costs
SRAE	Solar Radio Astronomy Experiment
SRAF	Standby Reserve of the Armed Forces
SRAM	Short-Range Air-Launched Missile
SRAM	Short-Range Attack Missile (Navy)
SRAM	Some Remarks on Abstract Machines (Data processing)
SRAN	Stock Record Account Number
SRANA	Shrine Recorders Association of North America
SRANC	Southern Rhodesia African National Congress
SRAP	Service Record and Allied Papers
SRAP	Standard Range Approach
SRARAV	Senior Army Aviator
Sr AR Av Bad ..	Senior Army Aviator Badge
SRATUC	Southern Rhodesian African Trade Union Congress
SRB	Seaplane Repair Base
SRB	Self-Retaining Bolt
SRB	Service Record Book (Military)
SRB	Solar Reflectory Beacon
SRB	Spherical Roller Bearing
SRB	Styrene Rubber Butadiene
SRB	System Review Board
SRBA	Students for the Right to Bear Arms

ACRONYMS AND INITIALISMS DICTIONARY

SRBC........ Sheep Red Blood Cells
SRBC .... Susquehanna River Basin Compact (Maryland, Pennsylvania, New York)
SRBM ...... Short-Range Ballistic Missile
SRC .... Sacra Rituum Congregatio (Sacred Congregation of Rites)
SRC .... Sample Rock Container (NASA)
SRC .... Saturable Reactor Coil
SRC .... Science Research Council (British)
SRC .... Securities Research Company
SRC .... Signal Reserve Corps
SRC .... Silicon Readout Cell
SRC .... Silicon Rectifier Column
SRC .... Sound Ranging Control (Military)
SRC .... Southern Regional Council
SRC .... Southwest Radio Church (An organization)
SRC .... Southwest Research Corporation
SRC .... Standard Requirements Code (Military)
SRC .... Stock Record Card (Military)
SRC .... Strasburg R. R. (AAR code)
SRC .... Swiss Red Cross
SRC .... Systems Research Configuration
S/RC .... Send/Receive Center
SRCC ...... Senior Control Center (Air Force)
SRCC ...... Simplex Remote Communications Central
SRCC ...... Strikes, Riots, and Civil Commotions
SRCD ...... Society for Research in Child Development
SR-CEF ..... Schmidt-Ruppin Chick Embryo Fibroblast(s)
SRCM ...... Savonius Rotor Current Meter
SRCP ...... Special Reserve Components Program
SRCR ...... Stability Regulated Controlled Rectifier
SRD .... Secret Restricted Data
SRD .... Selective Radiation Dectector
SRD .... Service Revealed Deficiency (or Difficulty)
SRD .... Shift Register Drive
SRD .... Single Radial Immunodiffusion (Analytical biochemistry)
SRD .... Society for the Relief of Distress (British)
SRD .... Standard Reference Data
SRD .... Standard Repair Design (Navy)
SRD .... Step Recovery Diode
SRDC ...... Standard Reference Data Center
SRDE ...... Signals Research and Development Establishment (British)
SRDE ...... Smallest Replaceable Defective Element
SRDL ...... Signals Research & Development Laboratory (Army) (British)
SRDS ...... Single Requirements Determination System
SRDS ...... Standard Rate and Data Service
SRDS ...... Systems Research and Development Service (FAA)
SRE .... Sancta Romana Ecclesia (Most Holy Roman Church)
SRE .... Sanctae Romanae Ecclesiae (of the Most Holy Roman Church)
SRE .... Series Relay (Electronics)
SRE .... Society of Relay Engineers (British)
SRE .... Society of Reproduction Engineers (Later, IAVCM)
SRE .... Sodium Reactor Experiment (AEC)
SRE .... Standard RADAR Environment
SRE .... Surveillance RADAR Element
SREA ...... Society of Real Estate Appraisers
SREB ...... Southern Regional Educational Board
SREC ...... Southern Rice Export Corporation
SREL........ Space Radiation Effects Laboratory (Langley, Virginia) (NASA)
S-REM....... Sleep with Rapid Eye Movement
SRES........ Southern Railway Employees' Sangh (India)
SRF .... Salmonellosis-Resistance Factor
SRF .... Sam Rayburn Foundation
SRF .... Selected Reserve Force (Units) (of Army National Guard) (Discontinued, 1969)
SRF .... Self-Realization Fellowship
SRF .... Self-Resonant Frequency
SRF .... Semi-Reinforced Furnace
SRF .... Slovak Relief Fund
SRF .... Solar Radiation Flux
SRF .... Stable Radio Frequency
SRF .... Submarine Range-Finder
SRF .... Submarine Repair Facility
SRF .... Supported Ring Frame
SRF .... System Recovery Factor
SRFCMP ..... Self-Rising Flour and Corn Meal Program
SRFD ...... Society for the Rehabilitation of the Facially Disfigured
SRFF ...... Set Reset Flip-Flop (Data processing)
SRFI ...... Self-Rising Flour Institute
SRFI........ Sugar Research Foundation, Incorporated
SRG .... Schering Corporation (NYSE symbol) (Delisted)
SRG .... Servomotor Rate Generator
SRG .... Short Range

SRG .... Sine Random Generator
SRG .... Statistical Research Group (Princeton University)
SRGA ...... Stable Reactor, General, Atomic
SRGR ...... Short Range Guided Rocket
SRGS ...... Survivable Radio Guidance System (Military)
SRH .... Supply Railhead
SRHE ...... Society for Religion in Higher Education
SRHL ...... Southwestern Radiological Health Laboratory (HEW)
SRI .... Sacrum Romanum Imperium (The Holy Roman Empire)
SRI .... Servo Repeater Indicator
SRI .... Silicon Rubber Insulation
SRI .... Society for Rational Individualism
SRI........ Sorry (Communications operator's procedural remark)
SRI .... Southern Research Institute
SRI........ Space Research Institute
SRI........ Spectrum Resolver Integrator
SRI........ Speech Rehabilitation Institute
SRI........ Spring Research Institute
SRI........ Stanford Research Institute
SRI .... Surface Roughness Indicator
SRIAER ..... Scientific Research Institute for Atomic Energy Reactors (USSR)
SRIB .... Strike Route Information Book (Strategic Air Command)
SRILTA ..... Stanford Research Institute Lead Time Analysis
SRIP .... Ship Readiness Improvement Program (Navy)
SRIP .... Specification Review and Improvement Program (Navy)
SRJ .... Self-Restraint Joint
SRJ .... Standard-Range Juno (Survey meter for radiation)
SRJ .... Static Round Jet
SRJC ...... Santa Rosa Junior College (California)
SRK .... Serrick Corporation (NYSE symbol)
SRL .... Savannah River Laboratory (AEC)
SRL .... Save-the-Redwoods League
SRL .... Searle (G.D.) & Co. (NYSE symbol)
SRL .... Seeler Research Laboratory (Air Force)
SRL .... Student Religious Liberals
SRL .... Study Reference List
SRL .... Systems Research Laboratory
SRLD ...... Small Rocket Lift Device
SRM .... Scrim-Reinforced Material (Nonwoven sheets)
SRM .... Shift Register Memory
SRM .... Short-Range Missile (Projected; not to be confused with SRAM)
SRM .... Single Register Machine
SRM .... Solid Rocket Motor
SRM .... Specific Repair Methods (Boeing)
SRM .... Speed of Relative Movement
SRM .... Spiritual Regeneration Movement (Foundation of America)
SRM .... Square Root Mode
SRM .... Standard Reference Material
SRM .... Standard Repair Manual
SRM .... Strategic Reconnaissance Missile
SRMA ...... Silk and Rayon Manufacturers Association
SRMC ...... Stearns-Roger Manufacturing Company
SRML ...... Short-Range Missile Launcher
SRN .... Serial Reference Number
SRN .... Simulation Reference Number
SRN .... Southern Air Transport, Inc.
SRN .... State Registered Nurse
SRN .... Stretch Receptor Neuron
sRNA ...... Soluble Ribonucleic Acid
SRNC ...... Severn River Naval Command
SRNR ...... Stock Request Number
SRNS ...... Surveyor Retro Nozzle Structure
SRO .... Savannah River Operation (AEC)
SRO .... Senior Research Officer (Ministry of Agriculture, Fisheries, and Food) (British)
SRO .... Single-Room Occupancy (New York housing term)
SRO .... Society of Radio Operators
SRO .... Solar Radio Observatory
SRO .... Standing Room Only (Theater)
SRO .... Standing Route Order (Army)
SRO .... Statutory Rules and Orders
SRO .... Superintendent of Range Operations (NASA)
SRO .... Systems Reproduction Order
SR & O ..... Statutory Rules and Orders
SROKA ...... Second Republic of Korea Army
SRP .... Safeguard Readiness Posture (Army)
SRP .... Savannah River Plant (AEC)
SRP .... Seat Reference Point
SRP .... Selective Reenlistment Program (Air Force)
SRP .... Self-Recording Penetrometer
SRP .... Sierra Pacific Power Co. (NYSE symbol)

SRP .... Solar Radiation Pressure
SRP .... Sonobuoy Referenced Position (Navy)
SRP .... Source Record Punch
SRP .... Sozialistische Reichs-Partei
SRP .... Spin Recovery Parachute
SRP .... Standard Relative Power
SRPARABAD ... Senior Parachutist Badge
SRPDAA ..... Silk and Rayon Printers and Dyers Association of America
SRPI .... Scrap Rubber and Plastics Institute
SRPI .... Silk and Rayon Print Institute
SRPJ .... Self-Restraining Pipe Joint
SRPN .... Special Requisition Priority Number
SRPO .... Science Resources Planning Office (National Science Foundation)
SRPP........ Skeletal Rod of Palp
Sr Prcht Bad .. Senior Parachutist Badge (Army)
SRPS .... Sensor-Referenced Positioning System
SRR .... Search and Range RADAR
SRR .... Security Rules and Regulations
SRR .... Short-Range RADAR
SRR .... Slow Rotation Room (NASA)
SRR .... Special Reimbursement Rate
SRR .... Spurious Response Rejection
SRR .... Steering Reversal Rate
SRR .... Strategic Ready Reserve (Military)
SRR .... Supplementary Reserve Regulations (British Army)
SRR .... Support Requirements Records (Navy)
SRR .... Survival, Recovery and Reconstitution (Military)
SRRB........ Search and Rescue Radio Beacon
SRRC .... Sperry Rand Research Center
SRRT........ Social Responsibilities of Libraries Round Table (American Library Association)
SRS .... Satellite Receiving Station
SRS .... Scientific Reference Service (HEW)
SRS .... Secondary RADAR System
SRS .... Selenium Rectifier Stack
SRS .... Shipboard RADAR System
SRS .... Sidelooking RADAR System
SRS .... Sight Restoration Society
SRS .... Simulated Raman Scattering
SRS .... Simulated Remote Station
SRS .... Slow Reacting Substance
SRS .... Social and Rehabilitation Service (HEW)
SRS .... Societatis Regiae Socius (Fellow of the Royal Society)
SRS .... Solar Radiation Simulator
SRS .... Sound Ranging Set
SRS .... Sounding Rocket System
SRS .... Spaceborne Reconnaissance System
SRS .... Speech Reinforcement System
SRS .... Squad Radio Set
SRS .... State Revenue Society
SRS .... Statistical Reporting Service (Department of Agriculture)
SRS .... Strike Reporting System
SRS .... Structural Research Series
SRS .... Student Response System
SRS .... Submarine Reactor Small
SRS .... Subscriber-Response Systems (Study of cable TV)
SRS .... Supply Response Section (Navy)
SRS .... Surveillance RADAR Station
SRS .... Survey Research Service
S/RS........ Staff Returns (Marine Corps)
SRSA .... Scientific Research Society of America
SRS-A....... Slow-Reacting Substance of Anaphylaxis (Immunology)
SRSC .... Sul Ross State College (Texas)
SRSCC ...... Simulated Remote Station Control Center
SRSK .... Short Range Station Keeping
SRSS........ Sociological Resources for Secondary Schools
SRSS........ Sociological Resources for Social Studies (Project of American Sociological Association)
SRSS .... Solar Radiation Simulator System
SRSTA ...... Society of Roller Skating Teachers of America
SRT .... S-Band Radio Transmitter
SRT .... Sagittal Ray Trace
SRT .... St. Regis Paper Company (NYSE symbol)
SRT .... Search RADAR Terminal
SRT .... Sedimentation Rate Test
SRT .... Self-Repair Technique
SRT .... Serials Round Table (of ALA)
SRT .... Silica RADOME Technique
SRT .... Slow-Run-Through Trials (Navy)
SRT .... Solar Radiation Test
SRT .... Solar Radio Telescope

SRT .... Speech Reception Thresholds (Audiometry)
SRT .... Supporting Research and Technology
SRT .... Synchro and Resolver Transmission
SRTC .... Search RADAR Terrain Clearance
SRTC .... Society of Ration Token Collectors
SRTF .... Short-Range Task Force
SRTN .... Solar Radio Telescope Network
SRTU .... Ship Repair Training Unit
SRTUC ...... Southern Rhodesian Trade Unions Congress
SRU .... Seaplane Reconnaissance Unit
SRU .... Seiberling Rubber Company (NYSE symbol) (Delisted)
SRU .... Ship Repair Unit
SRU .... Ship Replaceable Unit
SRU .... Societe de Raffinage d'Uranium (France)
SRU .... Submarine Repair Unit
SRU .... Suspension and Release Units
SRV .... Satellite Reentry Vehicle
SRV .... Short-Range Viewer
SRV .... Society of Russian Veterans
SRV .... Space Rescue Vehicle
SRV .... Step Recovery Varactor
SRV .... Submerged Research Vehicle
SRVC .... Sine-Random Vibration Control
SRW .... Sherwin-Williams Company of Canada (American Stock Exchange symbol)
SRWg .... Strategic Reconnaissance Wing (Air Force)
SRWS .... Simplified and Regularized Writing System
SRWU .... Sudan Railways Workers' (Trade) Union
SRY .... Stanray Corporation (NYSE symbol) (Wall Street slang name: "Sorry")
SRZ .... Special Rules Zone
SRZF .... Synchro Resolver Zeroing Fixture
SRZLO ...... Supreme Royal Zuanna, Ladies of the Orient
SS .... Passing Stop Sign (Traffic offense charge)
SS .... Sacred Scripture
SS .... Safety Supplements (Air Force)
SS .... Saints (as in "SS Peter and Paul")
SS .... Saline Soak
SS .... Same Size
SS .... Sancti (Saints)
SS .... Sand Springs Railway Company (AAR code)
SS .... Saturated Solution (Pharmacy)
SS .... Schutzstaffel (Elite Guard) (NAZI Germany)
SS .... Science Service
SS .... Screw Steamer
SS .... Sea State
SS .... Second Stage
SS .... Secret Service
SS .... Secretary for Scotland
SS .... Secretary of State
SS .... Selective Service
SS .... Selective Signaling
SS .... Semi-Steel
SS .... Senior Scholastic (A publication)
SS .... Sentence Suspended
SS .... Senza Sordini (Played without mutes) (Music)
SS .... Sequential Switch
SS .... Serials Section (Resources and Technical Services Division of ALA)
SS .... Series Separate
SS .... Set Screw (Technical drawings)
SS .... Set Steering
SS .... Sharpshooter (Marine Corps)
SS .... Shelf Stock
SS .... Shimmy Showing (From one girl to another, in reference to dress disarrangement)
SS .... Ship Service
SS .... Shipside
SS .... Shortstop
SS .... Side Seam
SS .... Silver Star (Military award)
SS .... Simple Spike
SS .... Simplified Spelling
SS .... Single Scan
SS .... Single-Seated
SS .... Single Shot
SS .... Single Sideband
SS .... Single Signal
SS .... Single Stranded
SS .... Single Strength (Citrus juices)
SS .... Slop Sink
SS .... Small Signal
SS .... Soap Suds
SS .... Social Science

SS .... Social Security
SS .... Social Service
SS .... Society of St. Sulpice (Sulpicians) (Roman Catholic men's religious order)
SS .... Sodium Saccharin
SS .... Solid State
SS .... Source and Special (Material) (AEC)
SS .... Source of Supply
SS .... Sparingly Soluble
SS .... Special Series
SS .... Special Service (Vessel load line mark)
SS .... Special Session
SS .... Special Staff
SS .... Special Study
SS .... Specification for Structure
SS .... Spin-Stabilized (Rockets)
SS .... Staff Specialist
SS .... Staff Surgeon
SS .... Stainless Steel
SS .... Standard Frequency Station
SS .... Standard Score (Psychology)
SS .... Standardized Solution (Pharmacy)
SS .... Starlight Scope
SS .... Statistical Standards
SS .... Steamship
SS .... Steel Sash
SS .... Steering System
SS .... Sterile Solution
SS .... Straight Shank (Screw)
SS .... Straight Sided
SS .... Straits Settlements (in Malaya)
SS .... Style Sac
SS .... Submarine (Navy symbol)
SS .... Submarine Qualification (Navy)
SS .... Submarine Studies (by SORG)
SS .... Successive Stereometric (A discrimination task)
SS .... Sum of Squares
SS .... Summary Sheet
SS .... Sunday School, or Sabbath School
SS .... Sunset (Meteorology)
SS .... Super Speed
SS .... Super Sport (in automobile model name)
SS .... Supersonic
SS .... Supervisors Section (American Association of School Librarians)
SS .... Support System (Air Force)
SS .... Supra Scriptum (Written Above)
SS .... Surveillance Station (RADAR)
SS .... Sworn Statement
SS .... Synchro Standard
SS .... System Sensitivity
SS .... Systems Specifications
S/S .... Spectrum Signature
S/S .... Statement of Service (Military)
S & S ...... Schleicher and Schuell (Filter-paper company)
S & S ...... Stars & Stripes (Military newspaper)
S & S ...... Supply and Service (Army)
S of S ...... Secretary of State
S1S .... Surfaced or Dressed One Side (Technical drawings)
S2S .... Surfaced or Dressed Two Sides (Technical drawings)
S4S .... Surfaced or Dressed Four Sides (Technical drawings)
SSA .... Associate in Secretarial Science
SSA .... Cargo Submarine (Navy Designation)
SSA .... Secretary of State for Air (British)
SSA .... Seismological Society of America
SSA .... Selective Service Act
SSA .... Senior Scientific Assistant (Ministry of Agriculture, Fisheries, and Food) (British)
SSA .... Series of Standard Additions
SSA .... Shaw Society of America
SSA .... Sheath of Skeletal Axis
SSA .... Ship's Stores Ashore (Navy)
SSA .... Signal Security Agency (Navy)
SSA .... Signal Supply Agency
SSA .... Simian Society of America
SSA .... Simpler Spelling Association
SSA .... Sisters of St. Ann of Providence (Roman Catholic religious order)
SSA .... Sisters of St. Anne (Roman Catholic religious order)
SSA .... Slaving Signal Amplifier
SSA .... Sleeve Stub Antenna
SSA .... Soaring Society of America
SSA .... Social Security Act
SSA .... Social Security Administration (of HEW)

SSA .... Society of Security Analysts
SSA .... Solid State Abstracts
SSA .... Source Selection Activity (or Authority) (Military)
SSA .... Sportswear Salesmen's Association
SSA .... Steuben Society of America
SSA .... Studio Suppliers Association
SSA .... Style Sac Artery
SSA .... Sumi-E Society of America
SSA .... Synchro Signal Amplifier
SS of A .... Secular Society of America (Defunct)
SSAA ...... Skate Sailing Association of America
SSAAT ...... Sun Sensor Attitude Angle Transducer
SSAC ...... Secondary School Admissions Center
SSAC ...... Source Selection Advisory Council
SSAC ...... Space Science Analysis and Command (Team) (NASA)
SSAC ...... Sponsors' Standards Advisory Committee (American National Standards Institute)
SSAC ...... Suspended Sprayed Acoustical Ceiling (Technical drawings)
SSACT ...... Social Security Act
SSAL ...... Simplified Short Approach Light (FAA)
SSALS ...... Simplified Short Approach Light System (Aviation)
SSAN ...... Social Security Account Number
SSAO ...... Solid State Audio Oscillator
SSAR ...... Spin-Stabilized Aircraft Rocket
SSAT ...... Secondary School Admission Test Board
SSAWV ..... Sons of Spanish American War Veterans
SSB .... Fleet Ballistic Submarine (Navy symbol)
SSB .... Security Screening Board (Army)
SSB .... Selective Service Board
SSB .... Single Sideband (Communications)
SSB .... Social Security Board (Abolished, 1946)
SSB .... Society for the Study of Blood
SSB .... Source Selection Board
SSB .... Space Science Board (National Research Council)
SSBC ...... Stock Status Balance Card
SSB/DPUT ... Serikat Sekerdja Biro/Dinas Pembangunan Usaha Tani (Agricultural Development Service Workers' Union) (Indonesia)
SSBF .... Single Side Band Filter
SSBFH ..... Star-Spangled Banner Flag House
SSBG ...... Single Side Band Generator
SSBKD ..... Serikat Sekerdja/Buruh Ketapradja Djakarta Raja (General Union of Government Officials of Greater Djakarta) (Indonesia)
SSBKTN .... Serikat Sekerdja Bank Koporasi, Tani dan Nelajan Disingkat (Cooperative, Farmers and Fishers Bank Employees' Union) (Indonesia)
SSBN .... Fleet Ballistic Missile Submarine (Nuclear powered) (Navy symbol)
SSBPI .... Serikat Sekerdja Bank Pembangunan Indonesia (Indonesian Development Bank Employees' Union)
SSBPT ...... Serikat Sekerdja Balai Penelitian Tekstil (Textile Research Institute Workers' Union) (Indonesia)
SSBR .... Smooth-Surface Built-Up Roof (Technical drawings)
SSBS .... Sol Sol Balistique Strategique
SSBSC ...... Single Side Band Suppressed Carrier
SSBSCOM .... Single Side Band Suppressed Carrier Optical Modulator
SSBUS ...... South Slavic Benevolent Union Sloga
SSC .... Cruiser Submarine (Navy symbol)
SSC .... Missionary Sisters of St. Columban (Roman Catholic religious order)
SSC .... Sacramento State College (California)
SSC .... Savannah State College (Georgia)
SSC .... Second Stage Conduit
SSC .... Senior Service College (Army)
SSC .... Sensor Signal Conditioner
SSC .... Serial Shift Counter (Data processing)
SSC .... Ship Structure Committee
SSC .... Ship Systems Command (Also, NSSC; formerly, Bureau of Ships) (Navy)
SSC .... Shipbuilding Stabilization Committee
SSC .... Silver Star Citation
SSC .... Sisters of St. Casimir (Roman Catholic religious order)
SSC .... Socialist Scholars Conference
SSC .... Society of Silver Collectors
SSC .... Solar Stabilization Computer
SSC .... Solicitor, Supreme Court
SSC .... Solid-State Circuit
SSC .... Southeastern Simulation Council
SSC .... Southeastern State College (Oklahoma)
SSC .... Southern State College (Arkansas; South Dakota)
SSC .... Spacesuit Communicator (Apollo) (NASA)
SSC .... Spin Synchronous Clock
SSC .... Squadron Supervisory Console (Air Force)
SSC .... Squib Simulator Console
SSC .... Standard Saline Citrate
SSC .... Standards Steering Committee (ANSI)

SSC	Stores Stock Catalog
SSC	Submarine Supply Center
SSC	Sunshine Mining Company (NYSE symbol)
SSC	Supply Status Code (Army)
SSC	Supply Support Center (Navy)
SSC	Supply System Command (Navy)
SSC	Systems Science and Cybernetics
SS & C	Supersized and Calendered (Paper)
S and SC	Sized and Supercalendered
SSCA	Standard Schnauzer Club of America
SSCC	Congregatio Sacrorum Cordium (Fathers of the Sacred Heart) (Roman Catholic religious order)
SSCC	Second-Stage Conduit Container
SSCC	Space Surveillance Control Center
SSCC	Spin-Scan Cloud Camera (NASA)
SSCCB	Safeguard System Configuration Control Board (Army)
SSCD	Society of Small Craft Designers
SSCD	Start Sample Command Delayed
SSCDS	Small Ship Combat Data System
SS/CF	Signal Strength, Center Frequency
SSCH	Sisters of Ste. Chretienne (Roman Catholic religious order)
SSCI	Steel Service Center Institute
SSCI	Steel Shipping Container Institute
SSCK	Sister Servants of Christ the King (Roman Catholic religious order)
SSCM	Sisters of Saints Cyril and Methodius (Roman Catholic religious order)
SSCNS	Ship's Self-Contained Navigation System
SSCP	School Science Curriculum Project
SSCQT	Selective Service College Qualifying Test
SSCR	Spectral Shift Control Reactor (AEC)
SSCr	Stainless Steel Crown (Dentistry)
SSCS	Shipboard Satellite Communications System
SSCS	Side-Stick Control System
SSCS	Single Side-Band Communications System
SSCS	Space Suit Communications System
SSCS	Submarine SONAR Calibration Set
SSCS	Synchronous Satellite Communications System
SS & CS	Ship's Stores and Commissary Stores
SSCT	Shipboard Communications Terminal
SSCT	Solid-State Celestial Tracker
SSCT	Solid-State Control Transformer
SSCU	Special Signal Conditioning Unit
SSD	Doctor of Sacred Scripture
SSD	Institute of the Sisters of St. Dorothy (Roman Catholic religious order)
SSD	Sanctissimus Dominus (Most Holy Lord) (The Pope)
SSD	Scrap Salvage Division (Navy)
SSD	Seize Signal Detector
SSD	Semiconductor Silicon Detector
SSD	Sequence Switch Driver
SSD	Single-Station DOVAP (Doppler, Velocity, and Position)
SSD	Solid-State Detector
SSD	Solid-State Dosimeter
SSD	Space Systems Division
SSD	Specialized Storage Depot
SSD	Specialized Support Department (Air Force)
SSD	Specialized Support Depot (Army)
SSD	Staatssicherheitsdienst
SSD	Stabilized Ship Detector (Navy)
SSD	Subsoil Drain (Technical drawings)
SSD	Surveillance Situation Display
SSD	Systems Support Division (Air Force)
SS & D	Synchronization Separator and Digitizer
SSDB	Shore Station Development Board
SSDC	Space Science Data Center (NASA)
SSDG	Society for the Study of Development and Growth
SSDHPER	Society of State Directors of Health, Physical Education and Recreation
SSDK	Savannah State Docks (AAR code)
SSDMIC	Secretariat State-Defense Military Information Control Committee
SSDN	Sanctissimus Dominus Noster (Our Most Holy Lord, Jesus Christ)
SSDP	Serikat Sekerdja Djawalan Padjak (Brotherhood of Tax Office Employees) (Indonesia)
SSDPA	Soft-Serv Dairy Products Association
SSDR	Satellite Situation Display Room
SSDR	Subsystem Development Requirement
SSDRS	Safeguard System Design Release Schedule (Army)
SSDT	Society of Soft Drink Technologists
SSE	Scuola de Sviluppo Economico (Italy)
SSE	Self-Sustained Emission
SSE	Single Side-Band Exciter
SSE	Sisters of St. Elizabeth (Roman Catholic religious order)
SSE	Society of St. Edmund
SSE	Society for the Study of Evolution

SSE	Solid-State Electronics
SSE	South-Southeast
SSE	Special Support Equipment
SSE	Support Systems Engineering (Boeing)
SSE	System Safety Engineering
SSE	System Status Evaluation (Army)
SSE	System Support Engineering
SSE	System Support Equipment
S1S1E	Surfaced or Dressed One Side and One Edge (Technical drawings)
SSEA	Sentinel System Evaluation Agency (DOD)
SSEAT	Surveyor Scientific Evaluation Advisory Team (NASA)
SSEB	Source Selection Evaluation Board
SSEC	Selective Sequence Electronic Calculator (Data processing)
SSEC	Social Science Education Consortium
SSEC	Solid-State Electronic Chronograph
SSEL	Solid-State Electronics Laboratory (Stanford University)
SSEM	Space System Effectiveness Model
SSEP	System Safety Engineering Plan
SSES	Single Strip Engine System
SSF	Saybolt Seconds Furol (Oil viscosity)
SSF	Service Storage Facility
SSF	Service Support Force (Military)
SSF	Ship's Service Force (Navy)
SSF	Single-Seated Fighter
SSF	Single Side Band Filter
SSF	Single Solar Flare
SSF	Single Stage Fan
SSF	Society for the Study of Fertility (England)
SSF	Special Security Facility
SSF	Special Service Force (Canadian and US troops under combined command) (World War II)
SSF	Stainless Steel Fiber
SSF	Standard Saybolt Furol (Oil viscosity)
SSF	Style Sac Flap
SSFL	Steady-State Fermi Level
SSFM	Single Sideband Frequency Modulation
SSFT	Self-Sealing Fuel Tank
SSFVT	Subsystems Functional Verification Test (NASA)
SSG	Guided Missile Submarine (Navy symbol)
SSG	Search Signal Generator
SSG	Single Side Band Generator
SSG	Southern Society of Genealogists
SSG	Special Studies Group (Joint Chiefs of Staff) (Military)
SSG	Staff Sergeant (Army)
SSG	Supply Spectrum Generator
SSG	Sweep Signal Generator
SSG	System Safety Group
SSGA	Society of St. Gregory of America
SSGA	Sterling Silversmiths Guild of America
SSGC	Short System Ground Check
SSGD	Smoke Screen Generative Device
SSGDFB	Second Sight-Guide Dog Foundation for the Blind
SSGJ	Supersonic Gas Jet
SSGN	Guided Missile Submarine (Nuclear powered) (Navy symbol)
SSGp	System Safety Group (Air Force)
SSGS	Solid State Gamma Switch
SSGS	Standard Space Guidance System
SSGT	Staff Sergeant
SSH	Second Stage Hydraulics
SSH	Sharon Steel Corporation (NYSE symbol) (Delisted)
SSH	Social Sciences and Humanities (Series)
SSH	South Shore Line (AAR code)
SSHA	Survey of Study Habits and Attitudes (Education)
SSHB	Stainless Steel Helium Bottle
SSHJM	Sisters of the Sacred Hearts of Jesus and Mary (Roman Catholic religious order)
SSHJP	Servants of the Sacred Heart of Jesus and of the Poor (Roman Catholic women's religious order)
SSHP	Single-Shot Probability
SSHR	Spartan Safety Hazard Report
SSHS	Stainless Steel Helium Sphere
SSHSA	Steamship Historical Society of America
SSI	Second Stage Ignition
SSI	Sector Scan Indicator
SSI	Service Social International
SSI	Shaft Speed Indicator
SSI	Shoulder Sleeve Insignia (Military)
SSI	Smart Set International (Program to discourage drug abuse)
SSI	Society of Scribes and Illuminators
SSI	Solid State Inverter
SSI	Spacecraft System Integration

SSI . . . . Standing Signal Instructions
SSI . . . . Stockpile Surveillance Inspection
SSI . . . . Sucro-Sac-Ologists Society International
SSIA . . . . Shoe Service Institute of America
SSIA . . . . Specification Serial of Individual Assigned
SSIC . . . . Southern States Industrial Council
SSIE . . . . Smithsonian Science Information Exchange, Inc.
SSIE . . . . Solid Surface Interaction Experiment
SSII . . . . Solid State Image Intensifier
SSIM . . . . Statistical, Sampling Inventory Method
SSIP . . . . Subsystem Integration Plan
SSIR . . . . Special Security Investigation Requirement
SSIS . . . . Spacecraft System Integration Support
SSISS . . . . Spacecraft System Integration Support Service
SSJ . . . . Savez Sindikata Jugoslavije (Yugoslavia Federation of Trade Unions)
SSJ . . . . Self-Aligning Swivel Joint
SSJ . . . . Side Support Jack
SSJ . . . . Single Subsonic Jet
SSJ . . . . Sisters of St. Joseph (Roman Catholic religious order)
SSJ . . . . Sisters of St. Joseph of the Third Order of St. Francis (Roman Catholic religious order)
SSJ . . . . Societas Sancti Joseph Sanctissimi Cordis (St. Joseph's Society of the Sacred Heart, or Josephites) (Roman Catholic men's religious order)
SSJC . . . . Southern Seminary and Junior College (Virginia)
SSJE . . . . Society of St. John the Evangelist
SSJSM . . . . Sisters of St. Joseph of St. Mark (Roman Catholic religious order)
SSK . . . . Anti-Submarine Submarine (Navy symbol)
SSKDN . . . . . . Serikat Sekerdja Kementerian Dalam Negeri (Union of Workers in the Department of Interior) (Indonesia)
SSKP . . . . . . Serikat Sekerdja Kementerian Pertaganan (Ministry of Defense Workers' Unions) (Indonesia)
SSKP . . . . . . Single-Shot Kill Probability
SSL . . . . Congregation of Sisters of St. Louis (Roman Catholic religious order)
SSL . . . . Licentiate of Sacred Scripture
SSL . . . . Safety Systems Laboratory (Formerly, Office of Vehicle Systems Research) (Department of Transportation)
SSL . . . . Solid-State Lamp
SSL . . . . Solid-State LASER
SSL . . . . Space Science Laboratory
SSL . . . . Space Simulation Laboratory
SSLC . . . . Ship System Life Cycle (Navy)
SSLC . . . . Society of Savings and Loan Controllers
SSLE . . . . Subacute Sclerosing Leukoencephalitis (A disease)
SSLO . . . . Solid-State Local Oscillator
SSLORAN . . . . Skywave Synchronized Long-Range Aid to Navigation
SSLS . . . . Solid-State LASER System
SSLS . . . . Standard Space Launch System (BSD)
SSLT . . . . Solid-State Logic Timer
SSLT . . . . Stock Status Lag Time
SSLV . . . . Southern San Luis Valley R. R. (AAR code)
SSLV . . . . Standard Space Launch Vehicle
SSM . . . . Second-Stage Motor
SSM . . . . Ship Simulation Model (Navy)
SSM . . . . Signal Strength Monitor
SSM . . . . Silver Star Medal
SSM . . . . Single Sideband Modulation
SSM . . . . Sisters of St. Mary of the Third Order of St. Francis (Roman Catholic religious order)
SSM . . . . Sisters of the Sorrowful Mother (Third Order of St. Francis) (Roman Catholic religious order)
SSM . . . . Society of the Sacred Mission
SSM . . . . Solar Simulation Module
SSM . . . . Spark Source Mass Spectrography
SSM . . . . Squadron Sergeant Major
SSM . . . . Staff Sergeant Major
SSM . . . . Standard Surfacing Mat (Fiberglass)
SSM . . . . Subsynaptic Membrane
SSM . . . . Surface-to-Surface Missile
SSM . . . . System Support Management/Manager
SSMA . . . . School Science and Mathematics Association
SSMA . . . . Solid-State Microwave Amplifier
SSMA . . . . Spread-Spectrum Multiple Access (Satellite communications)
SSMB . . . . Ship's Service Man, Barber (Navy)
SSMC . . . . Second-Stage Motor Container
SSMC . . . . Ship's Service Man, Cobbler (Navy)
SSMCNP . . . . . Safeguard System Management Communications Network Program (Army)
SSMCS . . . . . . Synchronous Satellite Military Communication System
SSMD . . . . Silicon Stud-Mounted Diode
SSME . . . . Space Shuttle Main Engine (NASA)
SSMI . . . . Sister Servants of Mary Immaculate of Mariowka (Roman Catholic religious order)

SSMI . . . . Sisters Servants of Mary Immaculate (Roman Catholic religious order)
SSMIMA . . . . . Scissor, Shear and Manicure Implement Manufacturers Association
SSMIS . . . . Support Services Management Information System (Army)
SSML . . . . Ship's Service Man, Laundryman (Navy)
SSMM . . . . Space Station Mathematical Model
SSMMA . . . . . . Staple and Stapling Machine Manufacturers Association (Defunct)
SSMN . . . . Sisters of St. Mary of Namur (Roman Catholic religious order)
SSMO . . . . Sisters of St. Mary of Oregon (Roman Catholic religious order)
SSMP . . . . Safeguard System Master Plan (Army)
SSMS . . . . Solid-State Mass Spectrometer
SSMS . . . . Sons of Sherman's March to the Sea (An organization)
SSMS . . . . Submarine Safety Monitoring System
SSMSN . . . . . . Surface-to-Surface Mission
SSMT . . . . Ship's Service Man, Tailor (Navy)
SSMTG . . . . . . Solid State and Molecular Theory Group (MIT)
SSMV . . . . Single Shot Multivibrator
SSN . . . . Space Surveillance Network
SSN . . . . Specification Serial Number
SSN . . . . Switched Service Network
SS(N) . . . . Submarine (Nuclear-Powered) (Navy symbol)
SSND . . . . School Sisters of Notre Dame (Roman Catholic religious order)
SSND . . . . Solid-State Neutral Dosimeter
SSNF . . . . Source Spot Noise Figure
SSNPP . . . . . . Small Size Nuclear Power Plant
SSNY . . . . Swiss Society of New York
SSO . . . . Senior Scientific Officer (Ministry of Agriculture, Fisheries, and Food) (British)
SSO . . . . Single Sweep Operation
SSO . . . . Space Station Office
SSO . . . . Spares Shipping Order
SSO . . . . Special Service Officer (Military)
SSO . . . . Statistical Service Office(r) (Military)
SSO . . . . Steady-State Oscillation
SSO . . . . Submarine Oiler (Navy symbol)
SSO . . . . Submarine Supply Office
SSO . . . . System Service Order (Bell System)
SSO . . . . System Staff Office
SSOC . . . . Southern Student Organizing Committee
SSOE . . . . Special Subject Operational Evaluation
SSOFS . . . . Smiling Sons of the Friendly Shillelaghs
SSOG . . . . Spur Stepover Gear
SSOM . . . . . . Solid-State Optical MASER
SSP . . . . Association of the Sons of Poland
SSP . . . . SACEUR (Supreme Allied Commander, Europe) Schedule Program (Army)
SSP . . . . Scientific Subroutine Package (Data processing)
SSP . . . . Scouting Seaplane
SSP . . . . Seismic Section Profiler
SSP . . . . Sentence Synthesizing Program
SSP . . . . Ship's Stores Profit (Navy)
SSP . . . . Single-Shot Probability
SSP . . . . Society of St. Paul for the Apostolate of Communications (Pauline Fathers) (Roman Catholic religious order)
SSP . . . . Solid State Photodiode
SSP . . . . Solid State Pneumatics
SSP . . . . Solid State Preamplifier
SSP . . . . SONAR Signal Processor
SSP . . . . Source Selection Plan
SSP . . . . Standard Shop Practice
SSP . . . . Standby Status Panel
SSP . . . . Steam Service Pressure
SSP . . . . Submarine Transport (Navy symbol)
SSP . . . . Subsolar Point (Aerospace)
SSP . . . . Sustained Superior Performance
SSP . . . . System Support Program
SSPB . . . . Socket Screw Products Bureau
SSPB . . . . Swedish State Power Board (Atomic energy)
SSPC . . . . Missionary Sisters of St. Peter Claver (Roman Catholic religious order)
SSPC . . . . Solid-State Power Controller (NASA)
SSPC . . . . Steel Structures Painting Council
SSPE . . . . Subacute Sclerosing Panencephalitis (A disease)
SSPFC . . . . Stainless Steel Plumbing Fixture Council
SSPHS . . . . . . Society for Spanish and Portuguese Historical Studies
SSPL . . . . Solid State Pneumatic Logic
SSPMO . . . . . . SONAR Systems Project Management Office
SSPN . . . . Satellite System for Precise Navigation (Air Force)
SSPN . . . . Ship's Stores and Profit, Navy
SSPN . . . . System for Precise Navigation (Later, DNSS)
SSPO . . . . Strategic Systems Project Office (Navy)
SSPP . . . . Schedule Status Pre-Processor
SSPP . . . . Serikat Sekerdja Pamong Pradja (Public Officials' Union) (Indonesia)
SSPP . . . . Society for the Study of Process Philosophies

SSPS........ Spacecraft Support Planning Section
SSPSM ...... Serikat Sekerdja Pabrik Sendjata dan Mesiu (Armaments' Union) (Indonesia)
SSPTT .... Serikat Sekerdja Pos, Telegrap dan Telepon (National Postal, Telegraph and Telephone Employees' Union) (Indonesia)
SSPWR ...... Small-Size Pressurized Water Reactor (AEC)
SSQ .... Simple Sinusoidal Quantity
SSQ .... Station Sick Quarters
SSR .... RADAR Picket Submarine (Navy symbol)
SSR .... Secondary Surveillance RADAR
SSR .... Security Survey Report (AEC)
SSR .... Selenium Stack Rectifier
SSR .... Separate Superheater Reactor (AEC)
SSR .... Slate-Shingle Roof (Technical drawings)
SSR .... Soviet Socialist Republic
SSR .... **Special Scientific Report**
SSR .... Spin Stabilized Rockets
SSR .... Spotted Swine Record
SSR .... Staff Support Room
SSR .... Static Squelch Range
SSR .... Stock Status Report
SSR .... Sum of the Squared Residuals (Econometrics)
SSR .... Summarized Spares Requirement
SSR .... Supply Support Request (Military)
SSR .... Surface Slip Resistance
SSRC ...... **Social Science Research Council**
SSRC ...... Solid State Research Center
SSRC ...... Swedish Space Research Committee
SSRF ...... Shell-Supported Ring Frame
SSRG ...... Simple Shift Register Generator
SSRL....... Systems Simulation Research Laboratory
SSRM ...... Second Stage Rocket Motor
SSRN ...... RADAR Picket Submarine (Nuclear powered) (Navy symbol)
SSRN ...... Service Shop Requirement Notice
S-SRNA ..... Specific Soluble Ribonucleic Acid
SSRS .... Society for Social Responsibility in Science
SSRSB ...... **Safety and Special Radio Services Bureau** (of FCC)
SSS .... **Selective Service System**
SSS......... Self-Service Store
SSS .... Senior Service School (Military)
SSS .... **Sentinel-Spartan System**
SSS .... **Shevchenko Scientific Society**
SSS .... Ship's Service Stores
SSS .... Signal Switching System
SSS .... Sisters of Social Service (Roman Catholic religious order)
SSS .... Site Security Supervisor
SSS......... Small Scientific Satellite (NASA)
SSS......... Small Solar Satellite (NASA)
SSS .... Small Structures Survey (Civil Defense)
SSS .... Societas Sanctissimi Sacramenti (Fathers of the Blessed Sacrament) (Roman Catholic religious order)
SSS .... Society for the Suppression of Speculative Stamps (Now defunct)
SSS .... Solid State Switching
SSS .... Solid-State System
SSS .... SONAR Signal Simulator
SSS .... Space Station Simulator
SSS .... Space Surveillance System (Navy)
SSS .... Spacecraft System Support
SSS .... **Specific Soluble Substance** (Polysaccharide hapten)
SSS .... Spin Stabilized Spacecraft
SSS .... Spinning Space Station
SSS .... Stabilized Sighting System
SSS .... Standard Supply System (Army)
SSS .... Stepping Switch Scanner
SSS .... **Sterile Saline Soak**
SSS .... **Strategic Support Squadron** (Air Force)
SSS .... Stratum Super Stratum (Layer Over Layer)
SSS .... Strong Soap Solution
SSS .... Subject Specialists Section (Association of College and Research Libraries)
SSS .... Subjective Stress Scale
SSS .... Supply Screening Section (Navy)
SSS .... Symbolic Shorthand System
SSSA .... **Soil Science Society of America**
SSSB .... System Source Selection Board
SSSBP....... **System Source Selection Board Procedure** (Air Force)
SSSC .... Self-Service Supply Centers
SSSC .... Single Side-Band Suppressed Carrier
SSSC .... Space Science Steering Committee
SSSC .... Special Spectrum Study Committee
SSSC .... **Stainless Steel Sink Council**
SSSD .... Second-Stage Separation Device

SSSD ...... Solid-State Solenoid Driver
SSSI .... Steel Scaffolding and Shoring Institute
SSSJ .... Single Subsonic Jet
SSSJ .... Student Struggle for Soviet Jewry
SSSL .... Society for the Study of Southern Literature
SSSLF ..... South Slavonian Socialist Labor Federation
SSSM ...... Site Space Surveillance Monitor
SSSM ...... Subset-Specified Sequential Machine (Air Force)
SSSO ...... **Specialized Surplus Sales Office**
SSSP....... Society for the Study of Social Problems
SSSP....... Space Shuttle Synthesis Program (National Academy of Sciences)
SSSP....... System Source Selection Procedure
SSSR ...... SAGE (Semi-Automatic Ground Environment) System Status Report (ADC)
SSSR ...... Society for the Scientific Study of Religion
SSSR ...... Syracuse Scales of Social Relations (Education)
SSSS ...... Shallow Spherical Sandwich Shell
SSSS ...... Society for the Scientific Study of Sex
SSStJ ...... Serving Sister, Order of St. John of Jerusalem (British)
SST .... Sea Surface Temperature
SST .... Shipboard (Weapon) Suitability Test (Navy)
SST .... Solid-State Processor
SST .... Spacecraft System Test
SST .... Split Second Timing
SST .... **Stainless Steel**
SST .... **Supersonic Transport** (Projected commercial aircraft)
SST .... Target and Training Submarine (Navy symbol)
SSTC ...... Secondary School Theatre Conference
SSTC ...... Solid-State Timer-Controller
SSTC ...... Spacecraft System Test Console (NASA)
SSTDC ..... **Society of Stage Directors and Choreographers**
SSTF ...... Saturn Static Test Facility
SSTI .... Serikat Sekerdja Topografi Indonesia (Indonesian Topography Employees' Union)
SSTIR ...... Sea Surface Temperature Imaging Radiometer
SSTM ...... SAGE (Semi-Automatic Ground Environment) System Training Mission (ADC)
SSTM ...... System Support Technical Manager (Navy)
SSTS ...... Signaling and Supervision Techniques Study
SST-T-T...... Sound, Sense, Today, Tomorrow, Thereafter (Teacher's Guide, published by Department of Transportation, for promoting supersonic travel)
SSTU ...... SAGE (Semi-Automatic Ground Environment) System Training Unit (ADC)
SSTU ...... Seamless Steel Tubing
SSTV ...... Submarine Shock Test Vehicle
SSU .... Saybolt Seconds Universal (Oil viscosity)
SSU .... **Self-Service Unit**
SSU .... Sensor Simulator Unit
SSU .... Spacecraft Support Unit
SSU .... Special Service Unit (Military)
SSU .... Squadron Service Unit (Aircraft)
SSU .... Standard Saybolt Universal (Oil viscosity)
SSU .... Statistical Service Unit (Military)
SSU .... Strategic Services Unit (Formerly, OSS)
SSU .... Sunday School Union
SSU .... Sverges Socialdemokratiska Ungdomsforbund
SSUSN ...... **Society of Sponsors of the United States Navy**
SSV .... Seraphic Society for Vocations
SSV .... Ship-to-Surface Vessel
SSV .... Society for Vascular Surgery
SSV .... Space Shuttle Vehicle (NASA)
SSV .... Spool Selector Valve
SSV .... Static Self-Verification
SSVC ...... **Selective Service**
SSV/GC & N .. Space Shuttle Vehicle/Guidance, Control, and Navigation
SSVS ...... Slow Scan Video Simulator
SSW .... Safety Switch
SSW .... St. Louis Southwestern Railway Lines (AAR code)
SSW .... Secretary of State for War (British)
SSW .... Siemens-Schuckert Werke (Germany)
SSW .... South-Southwest
SSW .... Staggered Spondaic Word
SSWF ...... Sudden Short-Wave Fade
SSWG....... System Safety Working Group
SSWM....... Superimposed Surface Wave Modes
SSWU ...... Singapore Sawmill Workers' Union
SSWWS ...... Seismic Sea-Wave Warning System
SSX .... South Coast Corporation (NYSE symbol)
SSZ .... **Society of Systematic Zoology**
SSZ .... Specified Strike Zone (Army)
ST .... Chicago, Milwaukee, St. Paul & Pacific Railroad (NYSE symbol) (Later, CHG)

ST . . . . Missionarii Servi Sanctissimae Trinitatis (Missionary Servants of the Most Holy Trinity) (Roman Catholic men's religious order)
ST . . . . Saint
ST . . . . Scalar Totalizer
ST . . . . Schmitt Trigger
ST . . . . Schuler Tuning
ST . . . . Screw Terminal
ST . . . . Seaman Torpedoman
ST . . . . Sedimentation Time
ST . . . . Self Test
ST . . . . Sensitivity Training
ST . . . . Senza Tempo (Without regard to time)
ST . . . . Sequence Timer
ST . . . . Service Test
ST . . . . Set Trigger
ST . . . . Shipping Ticket (Military)
ST . . . . Shock Tube
ST . . . . Shock Tunnel
ST . . . . Short Ton (2000 lbs.)
ST . . . . Shrink Template
ST . . . . Single Throw (Switch)
ST . . . . Single Tire
ST . . . . Skin Test
ST . . . . Slight Trace
ST . . . . Societe Theosophique (Theosophical Society)
ST . . . . SONAR Technician (Navy rating)
ST . . . . Sons of Temperance
ST . . . . Sounding Tube
ST . . . . Special Text
ST . . . . Special Tools
ST . . . . Special Translation
ST . . . . Standard Time
ST . . . . Standardized Test (Psychology)
ST . . . . Start Timing
ST . . . . Static Test
ST . . . . Static Thrust
ST . . . . Statistisk Tabelvaerk (Denmark)
ST . . . . Steam Trawler
ST . . . . Steam Tug
ST . . . . Steel Truss (Bridges)
ST . . . . Stock Transfer
ST . . . . Storage Tube
ST . . . . Stratus (Meteorology)
ST . . . . Street
ST . . . . Summer Time (Daylight saving time)
ST . . . . Superintendent of Transportation
ST . . . . Surface Tension
ST . . . . Survival Time
ST . . . . Swept Tone
ST . . . . Symmetrical Tokamak
ST . . . . System Test
S/T . . . . Search/Track
S/T . . . . Shipping Ticket (Army)
S/T . . . . Sonic Telegraphy
S & T . . . . . . Stenographer and Typist (Examination) (Civil Service Commission)
S & T . . . . . . Supply and Transport
S of T . . . . . . Sons of Temperance
STA . . . . Serum Thrombotic Accelerator
STA . . . . Shipboard Transmitting Antenna
STA . . . . Shorebased Transmitting Antenna
STA . . . . Short-Term Arrangements (Department of State)
STA . . . . Short-Terms Abroad
STA . . . . Single Target Attack
STA . . . . Slaving Torquer Amplifier
STA . . . . Society of Typographic Arts
STA . . . . Softening Temperature of Ash
STA . . . . Solution Treat and Age (Metals)
STA . . . . Southern Textile Association
STA . . . . Special Temporary Authorization (FCC)
STA . . . . Staff Training Assistant (Army)
STA . . . . Stagger Tuned Antenna
STA . . . . Staley (A. E.) Manufacturing Company (NYSE symbol)
STA . . . . Store Accumulator
STA . . . . Straight-In Approach (Aviation)
STA . . . . Supersonic Tunnel Association
STAAS . . . . . Surveillance and Target Acquisition Aircraft System
STAB . . . . . . Supersonic Transport Advisory Board
STAC . . . . . . Science and Technology Advisory Committee (NASA)
STAD . . . . Special Temporary Aviation Duty
STADAD . . . . . Satellite Tracking and Data Acquisition Department
STADAN . . . . . Satellite Tracking and Data Acquisition Network

STADIN . . . . . Standing Administrative Instruction for Army Attachés
STADINAIR . . Standing Administrative Instruction for Air Attachés
STAE . . . . . . Second Time Around Echo
STAF . . . . . . Scientific and Technical Application Forecasts
STAFF . . . . . . Stellar Acquisition Flight Feasibility
STAFT . . . . . . Steerable Antenna Focusing Technique
STAG . . . . . . Special Task Air Group
STAG . . . . . . Standards Technical Advisory Group
STAG . . . . . . Straight-Talking American Government (Comedian Pat Paulsen's political party)
STAG . . . . . . Strategy and Tactics Analysis Group (Army)
STAG . . . . . . Submarine-Rocket Technical Advisory Group
STAGD . . . . . . Syndicat des Travailleurs de l'Administration Generale du Dahomey (Dahomean Union of General Administration Workers)
STAGE . . . . . . Simulated Total Atomic Global Exchange (DOD)
STAI . . . . State-Trait Anxiety Inventory (Psychology)
STAIR . . . . . . Structural Analysis Interpretive Routine
STALAG . . . . Stammlager (Prisoner-of-war camp) (German)
STALAGLUFT . . Stammlagerluft (Prisoner-of-war camp for airmen) (German)
STALO . . . . . . Stabilized Local Oscillator (RADAR)
STALOG . . . . Study of Automation of the Logistic System (Military)
STALOS . . . . Stabilized Tunable Local Oscillator
STAM . . . . . . Submarine Tactical Advanced Missile
STAM . . . . . . Surface Target Acquisition Model
STAMIC . . . . Set Theory Analysis and Measure of Information Characteristics
STAMO . . . . . Stable Automatic Modulated Oscillator
STAMP . . . . . Satellite Telecommunications Analysis and Modeling Program
STAMP . . . . . Space Technology Analysis and Mission Planning
STAMP . . . . . Standard Air Munitions Package
STANAG . . . . Standardized Agreement (NATO)
STANAVITO . . Syndicat des Travailleurs de Transport et de la Navigation du Togo (Union of Transport and Navigation Workers of Togo)
STANINE . . . . Standard Nine Score (Military)
STANLANCRU . . Standard Landing Craft Unit (Military)
STANO . . . . . . Surveillance, Target Acquisition, and Night Observation (DOD)
STANOLIND . . Standard Oil Company of Indiana
STANORD . . . . Standardization Order (Navy)
STANVAC . . . . Standard Vacuum Oil Company
STANY . . . . . . Security Traders Association of New York
STAP . . . . . . Special Technical Assistance Program
STAPP . . . . . . Simulation Tape Print Program
STAPP . . . . . . Single-Thread All-Purpose Program
STAQ . . . . . . Security Traders Automated Quotation (System)
STAQC . . . . . . Statistical Quality Control System (Military)
STAR . . . . . . Safe Teenage Rocketry
STAR . . . . . . Satellite Telecommunications Automatic Routing
STAR . . . . . . Science Teaching Achievement Recognition
STAR . . . . . . Scientific and Technical Aerospace Reports (NASA)
STAR . . . . . . Score, Teach and Record (Teaching machine)
STAR . . . . . . Selective Training and Retention (Navy)
STAR . . . . . . Self-Testing and Repairing (Computer self-repair)
STAR . . . . . . Shield Test Air Facility Reactor
STAR . . . . . . Ship-Tended Acoustic Relay (Military)
STAR . . . . . . Simultaneous Temperature Alarm Readout
STAR . . . . . . Space Technology and Advanced Research
STAR . . . . . . Space Thermionic Auxiliary Reactor
STAR . . . . . . Special Treatment and Review (Navy)
STAR . . . . . . Special Tube Analyzing Recorder
STAR . . . . . . Specialized Training and Reassignment (Army)
STAR . . . . . . Spectral Technology and Applied Research
STAR . . . . . . Speed Through Aerial Resupply (Air Force)
STAR . . . . . . Standard Telecommunications Automatic Recognizer (Data processing)
STAR . . . . . . Standard Terminal Arrival Route (Aviation)
STAR . . . . . . Standard Test Authorization & Report System (Navy)
STAR . . . . . . Statistical Table Assembly and Retrieval System (Proposed for Social Security Administration)
STAR . . . . . . Statistical Treatment of RADAR Returns
STAR . . . . . . Steerable Array RADAR
STAR . . . . . . Stellar Attitude Reference
STAR . . . . . . Strike, Transfers, Acquisitions, or Removals (Navy)
STAR . . . . . . Submarine Test and Research (Navy)
STAR . . . . . . Swedish Tactical Attack RADAR
STAR . . . . . . System for Telephone Administrative Response (Data processing)
STAR . . . . . . System Training Application Requirements
STARAD . . . . Starfish Radiation (Satellite) (NASA)
STARAN . . . . Stellar Attitude Reference & Navigation
STARCOM . . . . Strategic Army Communications System (Military)
STARE . . . . . . Steerable Telemetry Antenna Receiving Equipment
STARFIRE . . . . System to Accumulate and Retrieve Financial Information with Random Extraction (Data processing)
STARLAB . . . . Space Technology Applications and Research Laboratory (NASA)

STARS . . . . Satellite Telemetry Automatic Reduction System (NASA)
STARS . . . . Seaborne Tracking and Ranging Station
STARS . . . . Shell Theory Automated for Rotational Structures (Grumman Aircraft Engineering Corp.)
STARS . . . . Stabilized Twin-Gyro Attitude Reference System
STARS . . . . Stationary Automotive Road Simulator
STARS . . . . Study of Tactical Airborne RADAR System
STARS . . . . . . Support Tracking Analysis Reporting Systems
STARS . . . . Synchronized Time, Automated Reporting System
STARS . . . . System Test and Astronaut Requirement Simulation
STAR(S) . . . . . . Specialized Training and Reassignment (Student) (Military)
START . . . . Selection to Activate Random Testing (Module) (NASA)
START . . . . Space Test and Reentry Technology
START . . . . Space Transport and Reentry Tests
START . . . . Spacecraft Technology and Advanced Reentry Tests (Air Force)
START . . . . Story-Telling Automatic Reading Tutor
START . . . . Summary Tape Assistance Research and Training (Bureau of the Census)
START . . . . . . System of Transportation Applying Rendezvous Technique
STAS . . . . Safe to Arm Signal
STASH . . . . . . Student Association for the Study of Hallucinogens
STAT . . . . SEABEE Technical Assistance Team
STAT . . . . Statim (Immediately) (Latin)
STAT. . . . . . . Statistic
STAT . . . . Statute
STATE . . . . Simplified Tactical Approach and Terminal Equipment
STATIC . . . . . . Student Taskforce Against Telecommunication Information Concealment (Student legal action organization)
STATLIB . . . . . Statistical Computing Library (Bell System)
STATRAFO . . . Standard Transfer Order
STATSBOBP . . . Scale of Teacher Attitudes Toward Selective Behavior of Boy Pupils (Satirical)
STB . . . . Bachelor of the Science of Theology
STB . . . . Sacræ Theologiæ Baccalaureus (Bachelor of Sacred Theology)
STB . . . . Soprano, Tenor, Bass
STB. . . . . Sun's True Bearing (Navigation)
STC . . . . Sacramento Test Center
STC . . . . Satellite Test Center (Air Force)
STC . . . . Satellite Tracking Center (Sunnyvale, California)
STC . . . . Satellite Tracking Committee (Military)
STC . . . . Scandinavian Travel Commission (Later, Scandinavian National Travel Offices)
STC . . . . Security Time Control
STC . . . . Sensitivity-Time Control (RADAR)
STC . . . . Serving Test Center (Bell System)
STC . . . . SHAPE (Supreme Headquarters Allied Powers Europe) Technical Center (NATO)
STC . . . . Short Time Constant
STC . . . . Short Title Catalog
STC . . . . Simulation Tape Conversion
STC . . . . Single-Trip Container
STC . . . . Society for Technical Communication (Formerly, Society of Technical Writers and Publishers)
STC . . . . Sound Transmission Class (Followed by number, indicates FHA rating of sound insulating quality of a partition construction)
STC . . . . South Texas College
STC . . . . Space Test Center (Air Force)
STC . . . . Specific Thermal Capacity
STC . . . . Spectral Transfer Coefficient
STC . . . . Standard Telephone and Cables
STC . . . . Standard Transmission Code (Data processing)
STC . . . . State Teachers College
STC . . . . Stepchild
STC . . . . Stereo Tape Club of America
STC . . . . Supplemental Type Certificate
STC . . . . Systems Test Complex (NASA)
STCA . . . . Scottish Terrier Club of America
STCA . . . . Silky Terrier Club of America
STCA . . . . Skye Terrier Club of America
STCA . . . . Staffordshire Terrier Club of America
STCC . . . . Springfield Technical Community College (Massachusetts)
STCC . . . . Standard Transportation Commodity Code
STCO . . . . Supervisor Training Conference Outline (Air Force)
STCS . . . . Surveyor Thermal Control Section
STCT . . . . Small Transportable Communications Terminal
STCW . . . . . . System Time Code Word
STD . . . . Doctor of the Science of Theology
STD . . . . Sacræ Theologiæ Doctor (Doctor of Sacred Theology)
STD . . . . Salinity/Temperature/Depth (or Density)
STD . . . . Servo Tape Display
STD . . . . Ship Training Detachment
STD . . . . Skin Test Dose

STD . . . . Sledborne Time Digitizer
STD . . . . Society for Theological Discussion
STD . . . . Standard
STD . . . . Standard Test Dose
STD . . . . Storage Tube Display
STD . . . . Strain-Gauge Transient Dosimetry
STD . . . . Stripline Tunnel Diode
STD . . . . Subscriber Trunk Dialing (Telephone communications)
STDA . . . . Steward's Assistant (Navy)
STDA . . . . Stripline Tunnel Diode Amplifier
STDB . . . . Steward's Branch (Marine Corps)
STDC . . . . Southern Travel Directors Council
STDN . . . . Set the Date Now (Organization supporting the end of US military involvement in Indochina)
STDN . . . . Standardization
STDP . . . . Special Training Devices Program
STDS . . . . Snake Torpedo Destruction System
STDS . . . . Standards (Timber measurement)
STE. . . . . Sainte
STE . . . . Society of Tractor Engineers
STE . . . . Special Test Equipment
STE . . . . Special-Type Ellipsometer
STE . . . . Specific Temperature Excursion
STE . . . . Star Tracker Electronics (Apollo) (NASA)
STE . . . . Stockton Terminal & Eastern R. R. (AAR code)
STEA . . . . Surveyor Test Equipment Assembly
STEA . . . . Systems Test Equipment Assembly
STEAG . . . . . . Steinkohlen-Elektrizitaet AG (West Germany)
STEAP. . . . . . . Simulated Trajectories Error Analysis Program (NASA)
STEAP. . . . . . . Space Trajectory Error Analysis Program (NASA)
STECR . . . . . . Ships Tactical Environmental Control Receiver
STEDI . . . . Space Thrust Evolution and Disposal Investigation (Air Force)
STEDMIS . . . . . Ships Technical Data Management Information System (Navy)
STEEG . . . . . . Scanned Topographic Electroencephalograph
STEEP . . . . Safety Training for the Execution of Emergency Procedures (NASA)
STEG . . . . Staatliche Gesellschaft zur Erfassung von Ruestungsgut (German Public Corporation for the Collection and Distribution of War Material)
STEG . . . . Supersonic Transport Evaluation Group
STEIN . . . . System Test Environment Input
STEL . . . . Society of Telegraphic Engineers (British)
STEL. . . . . Studenta Tutmonda Esperantista Liga (An organization)
STELO . . . . . . Studenta Tutmonda Esperantista Liga (World League of Esperanto-Speaking Students)
STEM . . . . Shaped Tube Electrolytic Machining (GE)
STEM . . . . Socio-Technological-Economic-Military (DOD)
STEM . . . . . . Special Technical and Economic Mission
STEM . . . . Stay Time Excursion Module
STEM . . . . Stay Time Extension Module (NASA)
STEM . . . . Stellar Tracker Evaluation Missile
STEM . . . . Storable Tubular Extendable Member
STEMFAB. . . . . Storable Tubular Extendable Member Fabrication
STEMS . . . . . . Small Terminal Evasive Missile System
STEMS . . . . . . Society to Encourage Miniskirts (New York group opposing below-the-knee fashions introduced in 1970)
STENCH . . . . . Society to Exterminate Neo-Communist Harbingers
STEP . . . . Safeguard Test and Evaluation Program (Army)
STEP. . . . . Safety Test Engineering Program (AEC)
STEP . . . . School to Employment Program
STEP. . . . . Scientific and Technical Exploitation Program
STEP. . . . . Sequential Tests of Educational Progress (of ETS; given in 10th and 12th grades)
STEP. . . . . Ship Type Electronics Plan (Navy)
STEP. . . . . Simple Transition to Electronic Processing
STEP. . . . . Solutions to Employment Problems (A program of National Association of Manufacturers)
STEP. . . . . Space Terminal Evaluation Program
STEP. . . . . Standard Tape Executive Package
STEP. . . . . Standard Test Equipment Procedure
STEP. . . . . Statistical Trajectory Estimation Program (NASA)
STEP. . . . . Student Education Program
STEP. . . . . Student Transfer Education Plan (Defunct) (of the National Urban League)
STEP. . . . . Supervisory Tape Executive Program (Data processing)
STEPS . . . . . . Solar Thermionic Electrical Power System
STER . . . . System Training Equipment Requirement
STET. . . . . Specialized Technique for Efficient Typesetting
STET. . . . . Steward, Technical (Marine Corps)
STEVE . . . . . . Space Tool for Extravehicular Emergencies
STF. . . . . Satellite Tracking Facility (Air Force)
STF . . . . Signal Tracking Filter
STF . . . . Space Track Facility
STF . . . . Spin Test Facility (NASA)

STF . . . . Staff
STF . . . . Stauffer Chemical Company (NYSE symbol)
STF . . . . Stratiform (Meteorology)
STF . . . . System Test Facility
STFB . . . . Staatliche Forstwirtschaftsbetriebe
STFF . . . . . . Safeguard Tactical Field Force (Army)
STFR . . . . Stratus Fractus (Meteorology)
STFSGT . . . . . Staff Sergeant (Marine Corps)
STG . . . . Satellite Terminal Guidance
STG . . . . Space Task Group (Later, Manned Spacecraft Center) (NASA)
STG . . . . Space Telescope Guidance
STG . . . . Steering Task Group
STGAA . . . . . Shade Tobacco Growers Agricultural Association
STGAR . . . . . . Staging Area (Military)
STGB . . . . Staging Base (Military)
STGP . . . . . . Subcontract Task Group Procurement
STGT . . . . . . Secondary Target
STH . . . . Somatotrophic (Growth) Hormone (Endocrinology)
STI . . . . Scientific and Technical Information (System) (Canada)
STI . . . . Screw Thread Insert
STI . . . . Serum Trypsin Inhibitor (Medicine)
STI . . . . Service Tools Institute
STI . . . . Single Tooth Indexer
STI . . . . Small Towns Institute
STI . . . . Soybean Trypsin Inhibition (Physiology)
STI . . . . Space Technology, Incorporated
STI . . . . Specifications Technology, Incorporated
STI . . . . Speech Transmission Index
STI . . . . State Technical Institute
STI . . . . Steel Tank Institute
S & TI . . . . Scientific and Technical Information
STIAP . . . . . . Standard Instrument Approach
STIC . . . . Scientific and Technical Intelligence Center (DOD)
STIC . . . . Space Technical Information Control
STICTION . . . . Static Friction
STID . . . . Scientific and Technical Information Dissemination (NASA)
STIDAS . . . . . Speech Transmission Index Device (Using) Artificial Signals
STIF . . . . Scientific and Technical Information Facility (NASA)
STIF . . . . Spectral Transmission Interference Filter
STIFC . . . . . . Space Track Interim Fire Control
STIM . . . . Sensitiviiy Training Impact Model
STIMS . . . . . Scientific and Technical Modular System
STINFO . . . . . Scientific and Technical Information (Project) (DOD)
STINGS . . . . . Stellar Inertial Guidance System (Air Force)
STIPIS . . . . . Scientific, Technical, Intelligence and Program Information System (HEW)
STIR . . . . Scientific and Technical Intelligence Register
STIR . . . . Shield Test and Irradiation Reactor (AEC)
STIR . . . . SNAP (Systems for Nuclear Auxiliary Power) Shield Test Irradiation Reactor
STIT . . . . Signal Technical Intelligence Team (Army)
STIT-CONUS . . Scientific and Technical Information Team, Continental United States (Army)
STIT-EUR . . . . Scientific and Technical Information Team, Europe (Army)
STIT-FE . . . . Scientific and Technical Information Team, Far East (Army)
STJ . . . . Series Tee Junction
STJ . . . . Society of St. Teresa of Jesus (Roman Catholic women's religious order)
STJU . . . . . . St. John's University (Minnesota; New York)
STK . . . . Single Tone Keying
STK . . . . Situation Track Display
STK . . . . Soiuz Trudovogo Krest'ianstva (Union of Working Peasantry) (Russia)
STK . . . . Sturmkanone (Self-propelled assault gun)
STKF . . . . . . Stock Fund
STKFA . . . . . Stock Fund Accounting
STKFS . . . . . Stock Fund Statement
STKG . . . . . . Sturzkampfgeschwader (Dive-bomber wing) (German military – World War II)
STL . . . . Sacrae Theologiae Lector (Reader in Sacred Theology)
STL . . . . Sacrae Theologiae Licentiatus (Licentiate of Sacred Theology)
STL . . . . Safe Tow Length
STL . . . . St. Louis (Missouri) (Airport symbol)
STL . . . . Seatrain Lines, Inc. (AAR code)
STL . . . . Sequential Table Lookup
STL . . . . Simulated Tape Load
STL . . . . Space Technology Laboratories (AEC)
STL . . . . Special Tool List
STL . . . . Standard International Corp. (NYSE symbol)
STL . . . . Stockage List
STL . . . . Studio-to-Transmitter Link
STL . . . . Support Table Load
STL . . . . Systems Techniques Laboratory (Stanford University)
STLA . . . . . . Strip Transmission Line Adapter (or Assembly)

STLB & M . . . . St. Louis, Brownsville and Mexico Railway Company
STLF . . . . Southern Troops and Landing Force
STLI . . . . Statue of Liberty National Monument
STLI . . . . Stockage List Item(s)
STLO . . . . . . Scientific Technical Liaison Office (AFSC)
STLR . . . . . . Semitrailer
STL-SF . . . . . St. Louis-San Francisco Railway Company
STL-SF & T . . . St. Louis, San Francisco and Texas Railway Company
STLSW of T . . . St. Louis Southwestern Railway Company of Texas
STLT . . . . Small Transportable Link Terminal
STLT . . . . Studio-Transmitter Link-Television
STLU . . . . St. Louis University (Missouri)
STM . . . . Master of Arts in Theology
STM . . . . Master of the Science of Theology
STM . . . . Sacrae Theologiae Magister (Master of Sacred Theology)
STM . . . . Scientific, Technical, and Medical
STM . . . . Service Technique Militaire (Switzerland)
STM . . . . Service Test Model
STM . . . . Shielded Tunable Magnetron
STM . . . . Short-Term Memory
STM . . . . Special Test Missile
STM . . . . Spin Tuned Magnetron
STM . . . . Steward's Mate (Navy rating)
STM . . . . Structural Test Model
STM . . . . Surface-to-Target-to-Missile
STM . . . . Synthetic Timing Mode
STM . . . . System Training Mission
STMA . . . . . . Stuffed Toy Manufacturers Association
STMD . . . . . . Syndicat des Travailleurs des Municipalites du Dahomey (Union of Municipal Workers of Dahomey)
STME . . . . . . Stellar Television Monitor Equipment
STML . . . . . . Sindicato de Trabajadores Mineros de Llallagua
STMT . . . . . . Statement
STMU . . . . . . Special Test and Maintenance Unit
STN . . . . SAC (Strategic Air Command) Telephone Net (Air Force)
STN . . . . Satellite Tracking Network
STN . . . . Solar Telescope Network
STN . . . . Station
STN . . . . Stevens (J. P.) & Company, Inc. (NYSE symbol)
STNA . . . . . . Sons of Temperance of North America
STO . . . . Sea Transport Officer
STO . . . . Slater-Type Orbital (Atomic structure)
STO . . . . Small-Time Operator (Slang)
STO . . . . Stone Container Corporation (NYSE symbol)
STO . . . . Storekeeper (Coast Guard)
STO . . . . System Test Objectives
STOC . . . . . . Standard Tactical Operating Condition
STOL . . . . . . Short Takeoff and Landing (Aviation)
STON . . . . . . Short Ton
STOP . . . . Single Integrated Operations Plan (Not strictly an acronym, but STOP is correct; it is a master list of Communist targets for attack in event of war, drawn up by Department of Defense)
STOP . . . . . . Stable Ocean Platform
STOP . . . . . . Stop This Outrageous Purge (Group opposed to extremist measures used by segregationists in Arkansas; opposed by CROSS)
STOP . . . . . . Strategic Orbit Point
STOP . . . . . . Supersonic Transport Optimization Program (NASA)
STOP-NSA . . . Students to Oppose Participation in the National Student Association
STOPS . . . . . Supreme Temple Order Pythian Sisters
STOR . . . . . . Storage
STOR . . . . . . Summary Tape Operations Rental (Bureau of the Census)
STORC . . . . . Self-ferrying Trans-Ocean Rotary-wing Crane (Helicopter)
STORE . . . . . Storage Technology for Operational Readiness
STORE . . . . . Students to Observe Retail Establishments (Student legal action organization)
STORET . . . . . Storage and Retrieval (Data processing)
STOS . . . . . . Space Test Operations Section
STOT . . . . . . Scheduled Time Over Target
STOT . . . . . . Stockpile-to-Target
STOW . . . . . Side Transfer Optimum Warehousing
STOW . . . . . . System for Take-Off Weight
STP . . . . Sacrosanctae (or Sacrae) Theologiae Professor (Professor of Sacred Theology)
STP . . . . SAGE (Semi-Automatic Ground Environment) System Training Program
STP . . . . Satellite Tracking Program (of the Smithsonian Institution's Astrophysical Observatory)
STP . . . . Scientifically Treated Petroleum (A motor fuel oil additive) (Initials reported, by extension of meaning, also to stand for a hallucinogenic drug, DOM)
STP . . . . Selective Tape Print
STP . . . . Sewage Treatment Plant

STP . . . . Simultaneous Test Procedure (Statistics)
STP . . . . Simultaneous Track Processor
STP. . . . . Sodium Triphosphate
STP . . . . Special Technical Publication
STP . . . . Standard Temperature and Pressure
STP . . . . Standard (Normal) Temperature and Pulse (Medicine)
STP . . . . Sterilization Test Program
STP . . . . Storage Tube Processor
STP . . . . System Test Plan
STP . . . . Systems Training Program (RADAR)
STPD . . . . Standard Temperature and Pressure, Dry
STPF. . . . . Shield Test Pool Facility
STPG . . . . Spare-Time Production for Gain (FAO)
STPM . . . . Syndicat Togolais du Personnel de la Meteorologie (Togolese Union of Meteorological Personnel)
STPP. . . . . Sodium Tripolyphosphate
STPP . . . . Student Teacher Performance Profile
STPR. . . . . Semiannual Technical Progress Report
STPS . . . . Stern Teacher Preference Schedule
STPX . . . . Systems Training Program Exercise
STR . . . . Scientific Technical Report
STR . . . . Search and Track RADAR
STR . . . . Service Trouble Report
STR . . . . Special Theory of Relativity
STR . . . . Special Trade Representative
STR . . . . Standard Tool Request
STR . . . . Strength
STR . . . . Subject Terminal Control Release (Aviation)
STR . . . . Submarine Test Reactor
STR . . . . Submarine Thermal Reactor (AEC)
STR . . . . Submersible Test Rack
STR . . . . Summary Technical Report
STR . . . . Super Transportable RADAR
STRAAD . . . . . Special Techniques for Repair and Analyses of Airborne Damage (Navy)
STRAC . . . . . . Strategic Army Command (Acronym has come to mean "ordered" or "neat")
STRACS. . . . . . Small Transportable Communication Stations
STRAD . . . . . . Strategic Aerospace Division (Air Force)
STRAD . . . . . . Switching, Transmitting, Receiving and Distribution
STRADAP. . . . . Storm RADAR Data Processor (ESD)
STRAF . . . . . . Strategic Army Force
STRAFPOA. . . . Strategic Air Force, Pacific Ocean Area
STRAGL . . . . . Straggler Line (Military)
STRAIRPOA . . . Strategic Air Force, Pacific Ocean Areas
STRANGE . . . . SAGE (Semi-Automatic Ground Environment) Tracking and Guidance Evaluation System
STRAP. . . . . . . Star Tracking Rocket Attitude Positioning (System) (NASA)
STRAP. . . . . . . Stretch Assembly Program (IBM)
STRAT. . . . . . . Strategic
STRATAD . . . . . Strategic Aerospace Division (Air Force)
STRATCOM . . . Worldwide Strategic Communications System (Air Force)
STRATO. . . . . . Stratosphere
STRATWARM . . Stratospheric Warming
STRAW . . . . . . Simultaneous Tape Read and Write
STRC . . . . Science and Technology Research Center
STRC . . . . Scientific, Technical and Research Commission
STRC . . . . Switch Tail Ring Counter
STRD . . . . Short Tour Return Date (Military)
STREP . . . . Space Trajectory Radiation Exposure Procedure
STRESS . . . . . . Stop the Robberies, Enjoy Safe Streets (Detroit police unit)
STRESS . . . . . . Structural Engineering Systems Solver (Data processing)
STRI . . . . Smithsonian Tropical Research Institute
STRI . . . . Stones River National Battlefield
STRICOM . . . . Strike Command (Military)
STRIKFLTLANT . . Striking Fleet Atlantic
STRIKFORSOUTH . . Striking and Support Forces Southern Europe (Navy)
STRIP . . . . Specification Technical Review and Improvement Program (Navy)
STRIP . . . . Standard Taped Routines for Image Processing (National Bureau of Standards)
STRIVE . . . . . Standard Techniques for Reporting Information on Value Engineering
STRJ. . . . . Self-Powered Thermocouple Reference Junction
STROBE. . . . . . Satellite Tracking of Balloons and Emergencies
STROBES . . . . . Shared-Time Repair of Big Electronic Systems (Data processing)
STRT. . . . . Stewartstown R. R. (AAR code)
STRUDL . . . . . Structural Design Language
STS . . . . Office of State Technical Services (Department of Commerce) (Also see OSTS)
STS . . . . S-Band Transmitter System
STS . . . . Saint Thomas Seminary (Colorado; Connecticut; Kentucky)
STS . . . . Satellite Tracking Station
STS . . . . School Television Service
STS . . . . Science Talent Search

STS . . . . Security Termination Statement (Military)
STS . . . . Self-Test Select
STS . . . . Serological Test for Syphilis (Medicine)
STS . . . . Servo Test System
STS . . . . Ship to Shore
STS . . . . Solar Tracking System
STS . . . . SONAR Test System
STS . . . . Space Transportation System
STS . . . . Special Test System (Air Force)
STS . . . . Special Training Standard (Air Force)
STS . . . . Special Treatment Steel
STS . . . . Specific Tensile Strength
STS . . . . Stabilized Telescope System
STS . . . . Standard Test for Syphilis (Medicine)
STS . . . . State Technical Services
STS . . . . Static Test Stand
STS . . . . Stockpile to Target Sequence
STS . . . . Structural Transition Section
STS . . . . Supersonic Target System
STS . . . . System Trouble Shooting
STSA . . . . State Technical Services Act
STSM . . . . Surface-to-Target-to-Surface-to-Missile
STSS . . . . Sensitive Thrust Stand System
STT . . . . Sensitization Test
STT . . . . Signal Tracing Tester
STT . . . . Single Target Track (Navy)
STT . . . . Spacecraft Terminal Thrust
STT . . . . Spade Tongue Terminal
STT . . . . Stenographer, Medical (Navy)
STTE. . . . . Special Tools and Test Equipment
STTF. . . . . SONAR Test Tower Facility
STTK . . . . Suomen Teknillisten Toimihenkilojarjestojen Keskusliitto (Federation of Finnish Technical Functionary Organizations)
STTOT . . . . . . Single Target Track on Target
STU . . . . Service Trials Unit
STU . . . . Servo Test Unit
STU . . . . Signal Transfer Unit
STU . . . . Skin Test Unit
STU . . . . Standard Prudential Corp. (NYSE symbol)
STU . . . . Student
STU . . . . Styrelsen foer Teknisk Utveckling (Swedish Board for Technical Development)
STU . . . . Submarine Test Unit
STU . . . . Submersible Test Unit (Navy)
STU . . . . System Timing Unit
STUC . . . . Sarawak Trade Union Congress
STUC . . . . Scottish Trades Union Congress
STUC . . . . Singapore Trade Union Congress
STUD . . . . Standard Tractor, Universal with Dozer (Army)
STUFF. . . . . . . System to Uncover Facts Fast
STUKA . . . . . . Sturzkampfflugzeug (German) (Dive bomber)
STV . . . . Separation Test Vehicle
STV . . . . Solar Thermo Vacuum
STV . . . . Solidaridad de Trabajadores Vascos (Solidarity of Basque Workers) (In exile) (Spain)
STV . . . . Standard Test Vehicle
STV . . . . Subscription Television
STV . . . . Surveillance Television
STVM . . . . Semi-Trailer Van Mount
STW . . . . Stanley Warner Corporation (NYSE symbol) (Delisted)
STWE . . . . Society of Technical Writers and Editors (Later, STWP; then, STC)
STWP . . . . Society of Technical Writers and Publishers (Formerly, STWE; later STC)
STX . . . . Start of Text (Data processing)
STX . . . . Stewart-Warner Corporation (NYSE symbol)
STY . . . . Sterling Drug, Inc. (NYSE symbol)
STZ . . . . Sterling Drugs, Inc. (NYSE symbol)
SU . . . . Savings Unit
SU . . . . Sensation Units
SU . . . . Service Unit (Military)
SU . . . . Set Up (Freight)
SU . . . . Siedlungsunternehmen
SU . . . . Siemens Unit
SU . . . . Sindicato Unico (Confederation of Labor) (Italy -- Trieste)
SU . . . . Single Uptake (Boilers)
SU . . . . Sonics and Ultrasonics
SU . . . . Soviet Union (The USSR)
SU . . . . Standard Upkeep
SU . . . . Strontium Units (Atomic energy)
SU . . . . Student Union
SU . . . . Syracuse University
SUA . . . . Satellite Unfurlable Antenna

SUA . . . . Silver Users Association
SUA . . . . State Universities Association
SUAB . . . . Svenska Utvecklingsaktiebolaget (Swedish Corporation for Development)
SUADPS . . . . . Shipboard Uniform Automatic Data Processing System (Navy)
SUAS . . . . System for Upper Atmosphere Sounding
SUAWACS . . . . Soviet Union Airborne Warning and Control System
SUB . . . . Submarine
SUB . . . . Substitute
SUB . . . . Suburban Gas (NYSE symbol) (Delisted)
SUB . . . . Supplemental Unemployment Benefit(s)
SUBAD . . . . . . Submarine Air Defense
SUBAD . . . . . . Submarine Force, Pacific Fleet Administration
SUBADMI . . . . Submarine Force, Pacific Fleet Administration, Mare Island
SUBASE . . . . . . Submarine Base
SUB-BELL . . . . Submarine Fog Bell (Mechanical)
SUBCOM . . . . . Subordinate Command, Service Force, Pacific Fleet
SUBCOMNELM . . Subordinate Command, (US) Naval Forces, Eastern Atlantic and
         Mediterranean
SUBDIV . . . . . . Submarine Division (Navy)
SUBDIZ . . . . . . Submarine Defense Identification Zone
SUBEASTLANT . . Submarine Force, Eastern Atlantic
SUBIC . . . . Submarine Integrated Control Systems
SUBJ . . . . Subject
SUBLANT . . . . . Submarine Force, Atlantic Fleet
SUBM . . . . Submission (or Submit)
SUBMEDCEN . . Submarine Medical Center (Navy)
SUBNO . . . . . Substitutes Not Desired
SUBOK . . . . . Substitution Acceptable
SUBOR . . . . . . Subordinate
SUBORCOM . . Subordinate Command
SUBORCOMDSERVLANT . . Subordinate Command, Service Force, Atlantic Fleet
SUBORCOMDSERVPAC . . Subordinate Command, Service Force, Pacific Fleet
SUB-OSC . . . . Submarine Oscillator
SUBPAC . . . . . Submarine Force, Pacific Fleet
SUBPACAD . . . Submarine Force, Pacific Fleet, Administrative Command
SUBPACSUBORDCOM . . Submarine Force, Pacific Fleet, Subordinate Command
SUBROC . . . . . Submarine Rocket
SUBRON . . . . . Submarine Squadron
SUBRPIO . . . . Sub-Registered Publications Issuing Office
SUBRU . . . . . . Submarine Repair Unit
SUBS . . . . Subscriptions
SUBSCOFOR . . Submarines Scouting Force (Pacific Fleet)
SUBSELS . . . . . Subsisting Elsewhere
SUBSIS . . . . . . Subsistence
SUBSLANT . . . . Submarines, Atlantic Fleet
SUBSPAC . . . . . Submarines, Pacific Fleet
SUBSSOWESPAC . . Submarines, Southwest Pacific Force
SUC . . . . Southern Union College (Alabama)
SUC . . . . SuCrest Corporation (NYSE symbol)
SUCEE . . . . . . Socialist Union of Central-Eastern Europe
SUCKER . . . . . Society for Understanding Cats, Kangaroos, Elks and Reptiles (Slang)
SUCL . . . . . . Set Up, in Carloads (Business and trade)
SUCR . . . . Sunset Crater National Monument
SUDAER . . . . . Stanford University, Department of Aeronautics and Astronautics
SUDAM . . . . . Sunk or Damaged (Navy)
SUDS . . . . Satellite Undetected Duds
SUDS . . . . Silhouetting Underwater Detecting System
SUDS . . . . State's Urban Development Something-or-other (Slang for Urban
         Development Corporation, New York)
SUDS . . . . Submarine Detecting System
SUDT . . . . Silicon Unilateral Diffused Transistor
SUE . . . . Seismic Underwater Explorer
SUE . . . . Strontium Unit Equivalent
SUE . . . . Sudden Expansion
SUEDE . . . . . . Surface Evaluation and Definition
SUEL . . . . Sperry Utah Engineering Laboratory
SUEM . . . . Syndicat Unique des Enseignants de Mauritanie (Unitary Union of
         Mauritanian Teachers)
SUF . . . . Sufficient
SUFFER . . . . . . System Utility Facility for Easy Recovery (NASA)
SUG . . . . Southern California Gas Company (American Stock Exchange symbol)
SUG . . . . Southern Union Gas Co. (NYSE symbol)
SUG . . . . Suggest
SUHL . . . . Sylvania Universal High-Level Logic
SUI . . . . State University of Iowa
SUIAP . . . . . . Simplified Unit Invoice Accounting Plan
SUID . . . . Sudden Unexpected Infant Death
SULCL . . . . . . Set Up in Less than Carloads
SULF . . . . Speedball Up-Range Launch Facility (Army)
SULINAC . . . . Super Linear Accelerator (Space flight simulator)
SUM . . . . Surface-to-Underwater Missile

SUMC . . . . Space Ultrareliable Modular Computer
SUMCM . . . . . Summary Court-Martial
SUMCMO . . . . Summary Court-Martial Order
SUMED . . . . . . Suez-Mediterranean (Pipeline)
SUMMA . . . . . Superconducting Magnetic Mirror Apparatus
SUMPAC . . . . . Southampton University Man-Powered Aircraft (British)
SUMS . . . . Sperry UNIVAC Material System
SUMSEL . . . . . Sumatera Selatan
SUMT . . . . Sequential Unconstrained Minimization Technique
SUN . . . . Sun Oil Company (NYSE symbol)
SUN . . . . Sunday
SUN . . . . Sunset Railway (AAR code)
SUN . . . . Switching Unit
SUN . . . . Symbols, Units and Nomenclature
SUNA . . . . . . Seafarers' International Union of North America
SUNA . . . . . . Switchmen's Union of North America
SUNFED . . . . . Special United Nations Fund for Economic Development
SUNOCO . . . . . Sun Oil Company
SUNY . . . . State University of New York
SUNYA . . . . . . State University of New York at Albany
SUNYAB . . . . . State University of New York at Buffalo
SUNY BCN . . . State University of New York Biomedical Communication Network
SUO . . . . Shell Oil Company (NYSE symbol)
SUP . . . . Sailors' Union of the Pacific
SUP . . . . Single Unit Parameter
SUP . . . . Statistical Utility Program
SUP . . . . Superior
SUP . . . . Supplement
SUP . . . . Supply
SUP . . . . System Utilization Procedure
SUPARCO . . . . Space & Upper Atmospheric Research Committee (Pakistan)
SUPCEN . . . . . Supply Center
SUPCOM . . . . Support Command (Army)
SUPCOM . . . . Supreme Command
SUPCON . . . . . Superintending Constructor
SUPCOSTINS . . Supervisory Cost Inspector
SUPDEP . . . . . . Supply Depot
SUPG . . . . System Utilization Procedural Guide
SUPIER . . . . . . Supply Pier (Navy)
SUPINSMAT . . . Supervising Inspector of Naval Material
SUPINTREP . . . Supplementary Intelligence Report
SUPIR . . . . Supplementary Photographic Interpretation Report (Military)
SUPO . . . . Supply Officer
SUPOHDU . . . . Supply from Stock on Hand or Due in
SUPP . . . . Sarawak United People's Party
SUPPT . . . . . . Supply Point (Military)
SUPRAD . . . . . Supplementary Radio
SUPSAL . . . . . . Supervisor of Salvage
SUPSD . . . . . . Supersede
SUPSGT . . . . . Supply Sergeant (Marine Corps)
SUPSHIP . . . . . Supervisor of Shipbuilding (Navy)
SUPT . . . . Superintendent
SUPTNAVOBSY . . Superintendent, Naval Observatory
SUPVR . . . . . . Supervisor
SURANO . . . . . Surface RADAR and Navigation Operation
SURBAT . . . . . . Simultaneous Unlimited Rigorous Block Analytical Triangulation (Apollo
         program) (NASA)
SURC . . . . Syracuse University Research Corporation
SURCAL . . . . . Surveillance Calibration Satellite
SURCAP . . . . . Surviving Capability Plan (Military)
SURE . . . . Symbolic Utilities Revenue Environment (IBM)
SURF . . . . Support of User Records and Files (Data processing)
SURFSIDE . . . . . Small Unified Reactor Facility Systems for Isotopes, Desalting, and
         Electricity (AEC)
SURG . . . . Surgeon (or Surgical)
SURGE . . . . . . Sorting, Updating, Report Generating, Etc. (Data processing)
SURGEN . . . . . Surgeon General
SURI . . . . Syracuse University Research Institute
SURIC . . . . Surface Integrated Control (Navy)
SURIC . . . . Surface Ship Integrated Control System (BUSHIPS; later, ESC or NESC)
SURPIC . . . . . . Surface Picture (AMVER) (Coast Guard)
SURSAN . . . . . Superintendencia de Urbanizacao e Saneamento (Brazil)
SURSAT . . . . . . Survey Satellite (NASA)
SURTEMS . . . . Surface Temperature Measuring System
SURV . . . . Standard Underwater Research Vehicle
SURV . . . . Survival
SURVAL . . . . . Simulator Universal Radio Variability Library
SURVL . . . . . . Surveillance
SURVM . . . . . . Surveillance and Maintenance (Army)
SUS . . . . Saybolt Universal Second (Oil viscosity)
SUS . . . . Signal Underwater Sound

SUS . . . . Silicon Unilateral Switch
SUS . . . . Society of University Surgeons
SUS . . . . Stop Unnecessary Spending
SUS . . . . Sunshine Biscuits, Inc. (NYSE symbol) (Delisted)
SUSD . . . . . State University of South Dakota
SUSFU . . . . . Situation Unchanged, Still Fouled Up
SUSGR . . . . . Southwestern Union for the Study of Great Religions
SUSMOP . . . . Senior United States Military Observer Palestine
SUSNO . . . . . Senior United States Naval Officer
SUSP . . . . Suspend (or Suspension)
SUSS . . . . . . Sound Underwater Signal Source
SUT . . . . Satellite Under Test
SUT . . . . Set Up Time
SUT . . . . Sub Unit Test
SUTEC . . . . . Seneca Underwater Test and Evaluation Center
SUTRASFCO . . . Sindicato Unificado de Trabajadores de la Standard Fruit Company
      (Honduras)
SUU . . . . Suspension Unit
SUV . . . . Sumpter Valley Railway (AAR code)
SUVAT . . . . . Support Unit Vehicle Automatic Tester
SUVCW . . . . . Sons of Union Veterans of the Civil War
SUWU . . . . . . Skilled and Unskilled Workers' Union - Somali Republic
SUY . . . . State University R. R. (AAR code)
SV . . . . Sacra Virgo (Holy Virgin)
SV . . . . Sailing Vessel
SV . . . . Sanctitas Vestra (Your Holiness)
SV . . . . Satellite Virus
SV . . . . Secondary Valve
SV . . . . Selecta Vision (RCA brand name for tape cartridges of TV programs)
SV . . . . Selective Volunteer (Navy)
SV . . . . Self-Verification
SV . . . . Set Value
SV . . . . Silicone Varnish
SV . . . . Simian Virus (Medicine)
SV . . . . Simulated Video
SV . . . . Single Vibrations (Half cycles)
SV . . . . Sinus Venosus (Anatomy)
SV . . . . Slide Valve
SV . . . . Sons of Veterans
SV . . . . Space Vehicle
SV . . . . Stroke Volume (Physiology)
SV . . . . Sub Verbo (Under the Word)
SV . . . . Sub Voce (Under that Word)
SV . . . . Surface Vessel
S/V . . . . Surface Vessel
S/V . . . . Survivability/Vulnerability (Applied to ability of weapon systems to
      survive attacks) (Military)
SVA . . . . SEABEE Veterans of America
SVA . . . . Sectionalized Vertical Antenna
SVA . . . . Solar Vane Actuators
SVA . . . . Statistical Vibration Analysis
SVA . . . . Sun Valley Airlines
SVAD . . . . . . Savannah Army Depot
SVC . . . . Saint Vincent College (Pennsylvania)
SVC . . . . . . Service
SVC . . . . Service Command (Army)
SVC . . . . Sine Vibration Control
SVC . . . . Single Variable Control
SVC . . . . Society of Vacuum Coaters
SVC . . . . Space Vehicle Code
SVC . . . . Superior Vena Cava (Anatomy)
SVCP . . . . . . Special Virus Cancer Program (National Cancer Institute)
Svc Strs . . . . . Service Stars (Army)
SVD . . . . Societas Verbi Divini (Society of the Divine Word) (Roman Catholic
      men's religious order)
SVD . . . . Space Vehicles Division (NASA)
SVD . . . . Surveyor Vehicle Department
SVE . . . . Seagrave Corporation (NYSE symbol)
SVE . . . . . . Swept Volume Efficiency (Air Force)
SVE . . . . System Valve Engineering
SVEAA . . . . . Schweizerischer Verband Evangelischer Arbeiter und Angestellter (Swiss
      Federation of Protestant Trade Unions)
SVEAD . . . . . State Variable Estimation and Accuracy Determination
SVF . . . . Standard Vented Furnace
SVI . . . . Sound Velocity Indicator
SVI . . . . Spiritus Vini Industrialis (Industrial Alcohol) (Latin)
SVIB . . . . Strong Vocational Interest Blank (Psychology)
SVIC . . . . . . Shock and Vibration Information Center (NASA)
SVIO . . . . . . Superintending Veterinary Investigation Officer (Ministry of Agriculture,
      Fisheries, and Food) (British)
SVJC . . . . Skagit Valley Junior College (Washington)

SVL . . . . Sapphire Vacuum Lens
SVLB . . . . . . Sapphire Vacuum Lens Blank
SVLF . . . . . . Shipboard Very Low Frequency (Navy)
SVLL . . . . . . Short Vertical Lower Left
SVLR . . . . . . Short Vertical Lower Right
SVLTE . . . . . Services Valve Life Test Establishment (British)
SVM . . . . . . Semitrailer Van Mount
SVM . . . . Service Volontaire Mennonite (Mennonite Voluntary Service)
SVM . . . . Servomation Corp. (NYSE symbol)
SVN . . . . Statistiek van Nederland (Netherlands)
SVP . . . . Security Vehicle Patrol (Air Force)
SVP . . . . Seminal Vesicle Protein(s) (Biochemistry)
SVP . . . . S'il Vous Plait (If You Please)
SVP . . . . Society of Vertebrate Paleontology
SVP . . . . Sound Velocity Profile
SVP . . . . Supplemental Vacation Plan
SVR . . . . Slant Visual Range
SVR . . . . Spiritus Vini Rectificatus (Rectified Spirit of Wine)
SVRD . . . . . . Silicon Voltage Reference Diode
SVS . . . . Sav-A-Stop, Inc. (NYSE symbol)
SVS . . . . Secure Voice System
SVS . . . . Service School (Military)
SVS . . . . Sound Velocity Structure
SVS . . . . Spectroradiometer Visible System
SVS . . . . Spinning Vehicle Simulator
SVS . . . . Stabilized Viewing System
SVSC . . . . . . Space Vehicle Sectoring Code
SVT . . . . Solar Vacuum Telescope
SVT . . . . Spiritus Vini Tenuis (Proof Spirit of Wine)
SVT . . . . Stray Voltage Tester
SVT . . . . Suomen Virallinen Tilasto (Finland)
SVTM . . . . . . Shielded Voltage Tunable Magnetron
SVTP . . . . . . Sound, Velocity, Temperature, Pressure
SVU . . . . Super Valu Stores, Inc. (NYSE symbol)
SVUL . . . . . . Short Vertical Upper Left
SVUR . . . . . . Short Vertical Upper Right
SVV . . . . Sit Venia Verbo (Forgive the Expression) (Latin)
SW . . . . Salt Water
SW . . . . Seawater
SW . . . . Secretary of War (Obsolete)
SW . . . . Security Watch
SW . . . . Semiweekly
SW . . . . Senior Warden (Masonry)
SW . . . . Senior Wolf (An accomplished philanderer) (Slang)
SW . . . . Senior Woodward (Ancient Order of Foresters)
SW . . . . Sent Wrong (i.e., misdirected)
SW . . . . Shelter Warden (British Home Defence) (World War II)
SW . . . . Shipper's Weights (Bills of lading)
SW . . . . Ship's Warrant (Marine Corps)
SW . . . . Short Wave (Electronics)
SW . . . . Shotgun Wedding (Forced marriage) (Slang)
SW . . . . Sidewinder
SW . . . . Simple Wear
SW . . . . Single Weight
SW . . . . Slow Wave (Electroencephalograph)
SW . . . . Snow Showers (Meteorology)
SW . . . . Social Work(er)
SW . . . . Socket Weld
SW . . . . South Wales
SW . . . . Southwest; Southwestern; or Southwesterly
SW . . . . Southwest Airways Company
SW . . . . Special Weapon
SW . . . . Specific Weight
SW . . . . Spot Weld (Technical drawings)
SW . . . . Steel Worker
SW . . . . Stock Width (Construction or manufacturing materials)
SW . . . . Stone & Webster, Inc. (NYSE symbol)
SW . . . . Store Ward
SW . . . . Switchband Wound (Relay)
SWA . . . . Seriously Wounded in Action (Military)
SWA . . . . South-West Africa
SWA . . . . Southern Wholesalers Association
SWA . . . . Southern Woodwork Association
SWA . . . . Southwest Airways Company
SWA . . . . Standing Wave Apparatus
SWA . . . . Straight Wire Antenna
SWA . . . . Sweets Company of America, Inc. (NYSE symbol) (Delisted)
SWAA . . . . . . Slovak Writers and Artists Association
SWAC . . . . . . Special Warhead Arming Control
SWAC . . . . . . Standards Western Automatic Computer (National Bureau of Standards)
SWACS . . . . . . Space Warning and Control System (NORAD)

SWAD . . . . Special Warfare Aviation Detachment (Army)
SWAG . . . . . . Standard Written Agreement (Military)
SWAK . . . . Sealed With a Kiss (Correspondence)
SWAK . . . . . . Spinners and Weavers Association of Korea
SWALK . . . . . . Sealed With a Loving Kiss (Correspondence)
SWAMI . . . . . . Stall Warning and Margin Indicator
SWAMI . . . . . . Standing Wave Area Monitor
SWAMI . . . . . . Stanford Worldwide Acquisition of Meteorological Information (Weather prediction system)
SWANU . . . . . South-West African National Union
SWAP . . . . Sampling Work Action Patrol
SWAP . . . . Senior Worker Action Program
SWAP . . . . Student Woodlawn Area Project (Chicago, Illinois)
SWAPO . . . . . South-West Africa People's Organization
SWAPS . . . . . Special Wire Assembly Planning System
SWARMS . . . . . Small Warhead and Reentry Multiple System
SWAT . . . . . . Sidewinder Angle Tracking (Missiles)
SWAT . . . . Special Warfare Armored Transporter (A vehicle)
SWAT . . . . Special Weapons and Tactics (Police)
SWAT . . . . Stop Withholding All Taxes
SWAT . . . . Stress Wave Analysis Technique
SWATM . . . . . Shallow Water Anti-Traffic Mine (Military)
SWB . . . . Short Wheel Base
SWC . . . . Saline Water Conversion
SWC . . . . . . Short Wave Converter
SWC . . . . . . Single Wire Connector
SWC . . . . Soil and Water Conservation Research Division (of ARS, Department of Agriculture)
SWC . . . . Solar Wind Compensator (or Composition) (Apollo 11) (NASA)
SWC . . . . Special Warfare Center (Army) (Later, J. F. Kennedy Center for Special Warfare)
SWC . . . . . . Special Weapons Command
SWC . . . . . . Submersible Work Chamber
SWC . . . . . . Superior White Crystal (Sugar)
SWC . . . . Supreme War Council (World War I)
SWC . . . . . . Surface Weapons Control
SWCA . . . . . Silver Wyandotte Club of America
SWCEL . . . . . Southwestern Cooperative Educational Laboratory
SWCENT . . . . . Switching Central
SWCLR . . . . . Southwest Council of La Raza (Mexican-American organization)
SWCP . . . . . . Saline Water Conversion Program (Department of the Interior)
SWCP . . . . . . Society of the War of 1812 in the Commonwealth of Pennsylvania
SWD . . . . . . Senior Weapon Director (Air Force)
SWD . . . . Side Water Depth
SWD . . . . Sliding Watertight Door
SWD . . . . Smaller Word
SWD . . . . Standing Wave Detector
SWD . . . . Synchronous Wave Device
SWDB . . . . . . Special Weapons Development Board
SWDL . . . . . . Safe Winter Driving League
SWE . . . . Scalar Wave Equation
SWE . . . . Shift Word, Extracting
SWE . . . . Society of Women Engineers
SWEAT . . . . . Student Work Experience and Training
SWEB . . . . . . South Wales Electricity Board (British)
SWEDL . . . . . Southwest Educational Development Laboratory
SWEE . . . . . . Southwest Electronic Exhibit
SWEEP . . . . . Structures with Error Expurgation Program
SWEFCO . . . . Special Weapons Ferry Control Office(r)
SWEL . . . . . . Special Weapons Equipment List
SWELSTRA . . . Special Weapons Equipment List Single Theater Requisitioning Agency
SWESS . . . . . Special Weapons Emergency Separation System
SWET . . . . . . Simulated Water Entry Test
SWETTU . . . . Special Weapons Experimental Tactical Test Unit
SWF . . . . Sea Water Feed
SWF . . . . Shortwave Fadeouts
SWF . . . . Special Weapons Facility (Navy)
SWF . . . . Southwest Forest Industries (NYSE symbol)
SWF . . . . Suedwestfunk
SWFC . . . . . . Surface Weapons Fire Control
SWFPA . . . . . Structural Wood Fiber Products Association
SWFTU . . . . . Sudan Workers Federation of Trade Unions
SWFX . . . . . . Spotweld Fixture
SWG . . . . . . Scientific Working Group (EXAMETNET)
SWG . . . . . . Shuttle Working Group
SWG . . . . . . Sine Wave Generator
SWG . . . . . . Slotted Wave-Guide
SWG . . . . . . Society of Woman Geographers
SWG . . . . . . Special Working Group
SWG . . . . . Square Wave Generator
SWG . . . . . . Staff Working Group

SWG . . . . Standard Wire Gauge
SWG . . . . Stubs Wire Gage
SWGR . . . . . . Switchgear
SWHG . . . . . . Social Welfare History Group
SWI . . . . Salt Water Igniter
SWI . . . . Sine Wave Inverter
SWI . . . . Special World Intervals
SWI . . . . Stall Warning Indicator
SWI . . . . Standing Wave Indicator
SWI . . . . Steel Window Institute
SWIFT . . . . . . Selected Words in Full Title (Data processing)
SWIFT . . . . . . Software Implemented Finder Translator (Data processing)
SWIG . . . . . . Southwestern Irrigated Cotton Growers Association
SWIMS . . . . . Serialized Weapons Information Management System (Navy)
SWIMS . . . . . Ship Weapon Installation Manuals
SWIP . . . . . . Secret Work in Process
SWIP. . . . . . . Soil-Wheel Interaction Performance
SWIP . . . . . . Standing Wave Impedance Probe (Geophysical instrument)
SWIP . . . . . . Super-Weight Improvement Program (Navy)
SWIRS . . . . . . Solid Waste Information Retrieval System (Bureau of Solid Wastes, HEW)
SWISSAIR . . . . Swiss Air Transport Co., Ltd.
SWJ . . . . Single Wire Junction
SWJ . . . . Socket Wrench Joint
SWL . . . . Safe Working Load (Shipping)
SWL . . . . Short Wave-Length Limit
SWL . . . . Shortwave Listener (Radio)
SWL . . . . Single Wheel Loading (Aviation)
SWL . . . . Still Water Level
SWL . . . . Sulfite Waste Liquor
SWL . . . . Surface Wave Line
SWL . . . . Swingline Inc. (NYSE symbol) (Delisted)
SWLA . . . . . . Southwest Library Association
SWK . . . . Stanley Works (NYSE symbol)
SWM . . . . Shipboard Wave Meter
SWM . . . . Special Warfare Mission
SWM . . . . Spot Weld Machine
SWM . . . . Surface Wave Mode
SWMA . . . . . . Southwestern Monuments Association
SWNCC . . . . . State, War, Navy Coordinating Committee
SWO . . . . Solid Waste Office (Environmental Protection Agency)
SWO . . . . Square Wave Oscillator
SWO . . . . Staff Weather Officer
SWO . . . . Stud Welding Outfit
SWOC . . . . . . Special Weapons Operation Center (Army)
SWOC . . . . . . Steel Workers Organizing Committee (Became United Steelworkers of America)
SWOD . . . . . . Special Weapons Ordnance Devices
SWOG . . . . . . Special Weapons Overflight Guide
SWOP . . . . . . Special Weapons Ordnance Pamphlet
SWOPSI . . . . . Stanford Workshop on Social and Political Issues (Stanford University)
SWORD . . . . . Separated, Widowed, or Divorced (New York City organization)
SWORD . . . . . Shallow Water Oceanographic Research Data (System) (Naval Ordnance Laboratory and Naval Oceanographic Office)
SWP . . . . Safe Working Pressure
SWP . . . . Sherwin-Williams Paints
SWP . . . . Socialist Workers Party
SWP . . . . Soil-Test Water Probe
SWP . . . . Special Weapons Project (Military)
SWP . . . . Special Working Party (Military)
SWP . . . . Submersible Water Pump
SWP . . . . Summer Work Program
SWP . . . . Surface Wave Phenomena
SWPA . . . . . . Southwest Pacific Area (World War II)
SWPA . . . . . . Southwestern Power Administration (Department of the Interior)
SWPA . . . . . . Southwestern Psychological Association
SWPA . . . . . . Surplus War Property Administration (Terminated 1944)
SWPB . . . . . . Surplus War Property Board (Terminated 1945)
SWPC . . . . . . Smaller War Plants Corporation (World War II)
SWPD . . . . . . Smaller War Plants Division
SWPF . . . . . . Southwest Pacific Force
SWPSA . . . . . . Southwestern Peanut Shellers Association
SWR . . . . Serum Wassermann Reaction (Medicine)
SWR . . . . Sine Wave Response
SWR . . . . Standing-Wave Ratio (Voltage) (Electronics)
SWR . . . . Steel Wire Rope
SWR . . . . Switch Rails
SWRA . . . . . . Selected Water Resources Abstracts (Service of WRSIC)
SWRB . . . . . . Standing Wave Ratio Bridge
SWRHL . . . . . Southwestern Radiological Health Laboratory (Las Vegas)
SWRI . . . . . . Southwestern Research Institute
SWRJ . . . . . . Split Wing Ramjet

SWRL . . . . Southwest Regional Laboratory for Educational Research and Development
SWRM . . . . . . Standing Wave Ratio Meter
SWROM . . . . . Standing-Wave Read-Only Memory (Data processing)
SWS . . . . Sargent-Welch Scientific Co. (NYSE symbol)
SWS . . . . Seam Welding System
SWS . . . . Service-Wide Supply
SWS . . . . Shift Word, Substituting
SWS . . . . Slow Wave Sleep
SWS . . . . Sociologists for Women in Society
SWS . . . . Solar-Wind Spectrometer
SWS . . . . Space Weapon Systems (Air Force)
SWS . . . . Special Weapon Systems (Military)
SWS . . . . Still Water Surface
SWS . . . . Switch Stand
SWSA . . . . . . Southern Wood Seasoning Association
SWSF . . . . . . Society for a World Service Federation
SWSG . . . . . . Security Window Screen and Guard
SWSM . . . . . . Special Weapons Supply Memorandum (Army)
SWST . . . . . . Society of Wood Science and Technology
SWT . . . . Short Wave Transmitter
SWT . . . . Spiral Wrap Tubing
SWT . . . . Supersonic Wind Tunnel
SWT . . . . Switch Ties
SWTA . . . . . . Special Weapons Training Allowance
SWTC . . . . . . Special Weapon Technical Command (Navy)
SWTI . . . . . . Special Weapons Technical Instructions (Army)
SWTL . . . . . . Surface-Wave Transmission Line
SWTTEU . . . . . Special Weapons Test and Tactical Evaluation Unit
SWU . . . . Slovenian Women's Union
SWUS . . . . . . Southwest United States
SWVA . . . . . . Scottish War Veterans of America
SWVB . . . . . . Social Work Vocational Bureau
SWWIAH . . . . . Society of World War I Aero Historians
SWWF . . . . . . Speed-Welding Wire Feeder
SWWU . . . . . . Singapore Wood Workers' Union
SWX . . . . Swift & Company (NYSE symbol)
SX . . . . Pia Societas Sancti Francisci Xaverii pro Exteris Missionibus (St. Francis Xavier Foreign Mission Society, or Xaverian Missionary Fathers) (Roman Catholic religious order)
SX . . . . Southern Pacific Company (NYSE symbol) (Wall Street slang name: "Sopac")
SX . . . . Stability Index (Aviation)
SXA . . . . Stored Index to Address
SXBT . . . . Shipboard Expendable Bathythermograph (System) (Naval Oceanographic Office)
SXC . . . . Saint Xavier College (Illinois)
SXL . . . . Short-Arc Xenon Lamp
SXO . . . . Senior Experimental Officer (Ministry of Agriculture, Fisheries, and Food) (Also, SEO and SExO) (British)
SXP . . . . Saxon Industries, Inc. (NYSE symbol)
SXR . . . . Soft X-Ray Region
SXS . . . . Sigma Xi Society
SXS . . . . Stellar X-Ray Spectra
SXT . . . . Stable X-Ray Transmitter
SY . . . . Shipyard
SY . . . . Sperry Rand Corporation (NYSE symbol)
SY . . . . Square Yard
SY . . . . Steam Yacht
SYB . . . . Sybron Corp. (NYSE symbol)
SYBEAUXARTS . . Syndicat des Beaux Arts Africains (Union of African Fine Arts)

SYCATE . . . . . Symptom-Cause-Test
SYCOM . . . . . Synchronous Communications (Satellite)
SYD . . . . Scotland Yard
SYD . . . . Sum of the Year's Digits (Statistics)
SYDIA . . . . . . System Developer Interface Activity (Data processing)
SYE . . . . Skelly Oil Company (NYSE symbol)
SYH . . . . See You Home (Teen slang)
SYL . . . . Somali Youth League
SYM . . . . Secondary Yield Measurement
SYMAN . . . . . Symbol Manipulation (Data processing)
SYMAP . . . . . Synagraphic Mapping System (Computer-made maps)
SYMEVETOPHARSA . . Syndicat des Medecins, Veterinaires, Pharmaciens, et Sages Femmes Africains du Mali (Union of African Doctors, Pharmacists, Midwives and Veterinarians of the Mali Federation)
SYMPAC . . . . . Symbolic Program for Automatic Control
SYMS . . . . . . Secondary Yield Measurement System
SYNCOM . . . . Synchronous Communication Satellite (GSFC)
SYNDETS . . . . Synthetic Detergents
SYNERCAU . . . Syndicat National d'Etudes et de Recherches pour les Cooperatives Agricoles et leur Unions
SYNMAS . . . . . Synchronous Missile Alarm System
SYNSPADE . . . Symposium on the Numerical Solution of Partial Differential Equations (Book title, Academic Press)
SYNTAC . . . . . Synthetic Tactics
SYNTEEDISETO . . Syndicat des Travailleurs de l'Energie Electrique et de Distribution d'Eau du Togo (Union of Electrical Energy and Water Distribution Workers of Togo)
SYNTIRT . . . . . Syndicat des Travailleurs des Industries Reunies du Togo (Union of Workers of United Industries of Togo)
SYNTOL . . . . . Syntagmatic Organization Language (Data processing)
SYP . . . . Simplicity Pattern Company, Inc. (NYSE symbol)
SYS . . . . System
SYS . . . . Systron-Donner Corp. (NYSE symbol)
SYSCOM . . . . . Systems Command (Navy)
SYSCON . . . . . Systems Control
SYSEC . . . . . . System Synthesizer and Evaluation Center
SYSGEN . . . . . Systems Generation (Data processing)
SYSP . . . . Sixth-Year Specialist Program (Library science)
SYSTO . . . . . . System Staff Office
SYSTRAN . . . . Systems Analysis Translator (Data processing)
SYT . . . . Sweet Young Thing (An attractive girl) (Slang)
SYU . . . . Sudanese Youth Union
SZ . . . . Splash Zone
SZ . . . . Symington Wayne Corporation (NYSE symbol) (Delisted)
SZB . . . . Silver Zinc Battery
SZC . . . . Silver-Zinc Cell
SZEC . . . . . . Silver-Zinc Electrochemical Cell
SZECC . . . . . . Silver-Zinc Electrochemical Cell
SZM . . . . Stereo Zoom Microscope
SZM . . . . Synthetic Zeolite Molecule
SZO . . . . Student Zionist Organization
SZOR . . . . . . Sintered Zinc Oxide Resistor
SZOT . . . . . . Szakszervezetek Orszagos Tanacsa (National Trade Union Council) (Hungary)
SZP . . . . Surf Zone Process
SZP . . . . Synchro Zeroing Procedure
SZR . . . . Sintered Zinc Resistor
SZSB . . . . . . Silver-Zinc Secondary (or Storage) Battery
SZVR . . . . . . Silicon Zener Voltage Regulator

T

T	Air Temperature Correction
T	American Telephone & Telegraph Company (NYSE symbol) (Wall Street slang name: "Telephone")
T	Cleared Through (for landing and takeoff) (Aviation)
T	Meridian Angle
T	Military Sea Transportation Service Ship, when precedes vessel classification (Navy)
T	Octodecimo (Book from 12 1/2 to 15 centimeters in height) (Bibliography)
T	T-Bar (Structural Metal Shape)
T	Table
T	Tablespoon (Measure)
T	Tabulated (or Charted) LORAN Reading
T	Tace (Be Silent)
T	Tackle (Football position)
T	Tactual
T	Take Off (Aviation)
T	Taken
T	Taper
T	Tare
T	Target
t	Teaspoon (Measure)
T	Technical or Technician
T	Tee (Piping Joint, etc.)
T	Teeth (Technical drawings)
T	Teich (Pond) (German military)
T	Telegrapher (Navy)
T	Telephone
T	Teletype
T	Temperature
T	Tempo
T	Temporal
T	Temporary
T	Tempore (In the Time Of)
T	Tenero (Tender)
T	Tenor
T	Tense
T	Tension
T	Tensor
T	Tentative Target
T	Tera (A prefix meaning multiplied by one trillion)
T	Terminal or Termination
T	Territorial or Territory
T	Tertiary
t	Tertiary (Chemistry)
T	Tesla (Unit of magnetic flux density, one weber per square meter)
T	Test Equipment
T	Test Reactor (AEC)
T	Testament
T	Than
T	Theft
T	Thickness
T	Thief
T	Thread
T	Thunderstorm
T	Thymine
T	Tide Rips
T	Tied
T	Tiler (Freemasonry)
T	Time
T	Title (Bibliography)
T	Toe
T	Tome
T	Tomus (Volume)
T	Ton(s)
T	Tonnage (Shipping)
T	Tooth
T	Top
T	Torque
T	Toward (Altitude difference)
T	Town
T	Township
T	Trace of Precipitation (Less than 0.005 inch of rain or 0.05 inch of snow)
T	Traffic Headquarters
T	Trainer (Designation for all US military aircraft)
T	Transcription
T	Transferred (Navy)
T	Transformer
T	Transit
T	Transition or Transitional
T	Transitive
T	Translation
T	Transmitting
T	Tread (Stair details) (Technical drawings)
T	Treated
T	Triangle
T	Trichlorethylene
T	Trillo (Music)
T	Trinitas (The Trinity)
T	Triode
T	Triple
T	Tritium (Radioisotope of hydrogen, H^3)
T	Tropical (Load line mark, or air mass)
T	Trotter
T	Troy (A system of weights for precious metals)
T	Truce
T	True (Direction)
T	Truss
T	Tuesday
T	Tug (Navy)
T	Tun (Unit of liquid capacity)
T	Turkish
T	Tutti (Sing or play together) (Music)
T	Typhlosole
3T	Triple Throw
TA	Table of Allowances
TA	TACAN (Tactical Air Navigation System) Approach
Ta	Tantalum (Chemical element)
TA	Tape Adapter
TA	Tape Advance
TA	Target Area
TA	Tariff Act
TA	Task Analysis
TA	Task Assignment
TA	Tax Agent
TA	Tax Amortization (Plan)
TA	Teaching Assistant (in a university)
TA	Technical Analysis
TA	Technical Assistance (or Assistant)
TA	Telegraphic Address
TA	Temperature, Axillary
TA	Tension Arterielle (Blood Pressure) (Medicine)
TA	Terephthalic Acid (Chemistry)
TA	Terrain-Avoidance (Helicopter)
TA	Territorial Army
TA	Test Accessory
TA	Testantibus Actis (As the Acts Show)

TA . . . . Third Attack (Men's lacrosse position, until 1933)
TA . . . . Time and Attendance
TA . . . . Total Aboard (Aviation)
TA . . . . Total Alkaloids (Medicine)
TA . . . . Toxin-Antitoxin (Medicine)
TA . . . . Trade Agreements Act (of US)
TA . . . . Trading As
TA . . . . Traffic Agent or Traffic Auditor
TA . . . . Transamerica Corporation (NYSE symbol)
TA . . . . Transit Authority
TA . . . . Transition Altitude
TA . . . . Transportation Authorization
TA . . . . Transverse Acoustic
TA . . . . Travel Allowance
TA . . . . Trip Authorization
TA . . . . Triplex Annealed
TA . . . . True Altitude (Height) (Navigation)
TA . . . . Tuberculin, Alkaline
TA . . . . Turbulence Amplifier
TA . . . . Type Availability
T/A . . . . Table of Allowances
T/A . . . . Trading As
T/A . . . . Transfer of Accountability
T/A . . . . Type Availability
T & A . . . . Time and Attendance
T & A . . . . Tonsillectomy and Adenoidectomy (Medicine)
TAA . . . . Technical Assistance Administration (UN)
TAA . . . . Television Appliance Association
TAA . . . . Trade Adjustment Assistance
TAA . . . . Trade Agreements Act (of US)
TAA . . . . Trans-Australia Airlines
TAA . . . . Transcript of Absentee's Account
TAA . . . . Transit-Advertising Association
TAA . . . . Transportation Association of America
TAA . . . . Turbine Alternator Assembly
TAA . . . . Turkish-American Associations
TAABS . . . . . . The Army Automated Budget System
TAAD . . . . Terrain Avoidance Accessory Device
TAADC . . . . . . Theater Army Air Defense Command
TAADS . . . . . . The Army Authorization Document System
TAAG . . . . Technical Analysis and Advisory Group (Navy)
TAALS . . . . . . Tactical Army Aircraft Landing Systems
TAALS . . . . . . The American Association of Language Specialists
TAAM . . . . . . Transportation Army Aviation Maintenance
TAAN . . . . . . Trans-America Advertising Agency Network
TAAP . . . . . . Three-Axis Antenna Positioner
TAAR . . . . . . Target Area Analysis-RADAR
TAARS . . . . . . The Army Ammunition Reporting System
TAB . . . . Tabulate (Tabulation; Tabulator)
TAB . . . . Tactical Air Base
TAB . . . . Tamper Attempt Board
TAB . . . . Target Acquisition Battalion
TAB . . . . Technical Abstract Bulletin (ASTIA)
TAB . . . . Technical Assistance Board (of the United Nations)
TAB . . . . Telecommunications Advisory Board
TAB . . . . Traffic Audit Bureau
TABBSS . . . . . Tactical Bare Base Support Study (Air Force)
TABL . . . . Tropical Atlantic Biological Laboratory
TABP. . . . . . . Tetraminobenzophenone
TABS . . . . Tabulator Stops
TABS . . . . Tactical Airborne Beacon System
TABS . . . . Technical and Business Service
TABS . . . . Theater Air Base Survivability
TABS . . . . Transatlantic Book Service (British)
TABSIM . . . . . Tabulating Equipment Simulator
TABSOL . . . . . Tabular Systems-Oriented Language
TABSTONE . . . Target and Background Signal-to-Noise Evaluation
TABU . . . . . . Typical Army Ball-Up (Slang for a military muddle)
TABV . . . . Theater Air Base Vulnerability
TAB VEE . . . . Theater Air Base Vulnerability (Air Force)
TABWAG . . . . Tank Battle War Game
TABWDS . . . . Tactical Air Base Weather Dissemination System (Air Force)
TABWE . . . . . Tactical Air Base Weather Element (Air Force)
TAC . . . . Tactical
TAC . . . . Tactical Air Command (Air Force)
TAC . . . . Tactical Assignment Console
TAC . . . . Team Activity Chart
TAC . . . . Technical Applications Center (Air Force)
TAC . . . . Technical Area Coordinator
TAC . . . . Technical Assistance Committee (of the Economic and Social Council
of the United Nations)

TAC . . . . Technology Application Center (University of New Mexico)
TAC . . . . Temperature Altitude Chamber
TAC . . . . The Architects Collaborative (Design firm)
TAC . . . . Total Alkaloids of Cinchona (Medicine)
TAC . . . . Tracking Accuracy Control
TAC . . . . Trade Agreements Committee (An interagency committee of the
executive branch of US government)
TAC . . . . TRANSAC (Transistorized Automatic Computer) Assembler Compiler
TAC . . . . Transformer Analog Computer
TAC . . . . Transistorized Automatic Control
TAC . . . . Translations Activities Committee (Special Libraries Association)
TAC . . . . Translator, Assembler, Compiler
TAC . . . . Transonic Aerodynamic Characteristics
TAC . . . . Transportation Account Code
TAC . . . . Triallylcyanurate
TAC . . . . Turboalternator Compressor
TACA . . . . . . Tactical Air Coordinator, Airborne
TACA . . . . . . Test of Adult College Aptitude
TACAC . . . . . Theater Army Civil Affairs Command
TACADS . . . . Tactical Automated Data Processing System
TACAN. . . . . Tactical Air Navigation (System)
TACAN-DME . Tactical Air Navigation Distance Measuring Equipment
TACAP. . . . . Tactical Air Command Aircraft Profiler Capability
TACAV . . . . . Linea Aerea TACA de Venezuela
TACC . . . . . . Tactical Air Command Central (Air Force)
TACC . . . . . . Tactical Air Control Center
TACCAR . . . . Time Average Clutter Coherent Airborne RADAR
TACCO. . . . . Tactical Coordinator
TACCOM . . . Tactical Communication
TACCTA . . . . Tactical Commander's Terrain Analysis (Military)
TACDACS . . . Target Acquisition and Data Collection System
TACDEN . . . . Tactical Data Entry Unit (Army)
TACDEW . . . Tactical Advanced Combat Direction and Electronic Warfare
TACFIRE . . . . Tactical Fire Control System (of ADSAF)
TACFO . . . . . TASAMS (The Army Supply and Maintenance System) Coordination Field
Office
TACG . . . . . . Tactical Air Control Group (Air Force)
TACH . . . . . . Tachometer
TACIT. . . . . . Time-Authenticated Cryptographic Identity Transmission (Military)
TACLO . . . . . Tactical Air Command Liaison Officer
TACLOG. . . . Tactical-Logistical (Army)
TACMAR . . . Tactical Multifunction Array RADAR (Air Force)
TACNAV . . . Tactical Navigation System
TACO. . . . . . Tactical Coordinator
TACOC . . . . . Tactical Air Control Operation Center
TACOM . . . . Tactical Communications
TACOM . . . . Tank Automotive Command (Army)
TACOMM . . . Tactical Communications (Military)
TACOSS . . . . Tactical Container Shelter System (North American Rockwell)
TACP . . . . . . Tactical Air Control Party (Air Force)
TAC/R . . . . . Tactical Reconnaissance
TACREACT. . . Tactical Reconnaissance Reaction Aircraft
TAC RISE . . . Tactical Reconnaissance Intelligence System Enhancement (Air Force)
TACRON . . . Tactical Air Control Squadron
TACRV . . . . . Tracked Air Cushion Research Vehicle (DOD)
TACS . . . . . . Tactical Air Control System (Air Force)
TACS . . . . . . Theater Area Communications Systems (Military)
TACS . . . . . . Thruster Altitude Control System (NASA)
TACSAT . . . . Tactical-Communications Satellite (DOD)
TACSATCOM . Tactical Satellite Communications
TACT . . . . . . Transistor and Component Tester
TACT . . . . . . Transonic Aircraft Technology (Program)
TACT . . . . . . Truth About Civil Turmoil
TACTIC. . . . . Technical Advisory Committee to Influence Congress (Federation of
American Scientists)
TACTL . . . . . Tactical
TACV . . . . . . Tracked Air Cushion Vehicle (High-speed ground transportation)
TAD . . . . Tactical Action Display (SAGE)
TAD . . . . Tactical Air Direction
TAD . . . . Tactical Atomic Demolition (Munitions)
TAD . . . . Target Acquisition Data
TAD . . . . Target Activation Date
TAD . . . . Target Area Designator (Air Force)
TAD . . . . Technical Acceptance Date
TAD . . . . Technical Analysis Division (National Bureau of Standards)
TAD . . . . Technical Approach Demonstration
TAD . . . . Technical Approval Demonstration
TAD . . . . Temporary Additional Duty
TAD . . . . Temporary Attached Duty
TAD . . . . Thrust-Augmented Delta (NASA)
TAD . . . . Top Assembly Drawing

TAD . . . . Training Aids Division (Navy)
TADAR . . . . . Tactical Area Defense Alerting RADAR
TADAS . . . . . . Tactical Air Defense Alerting System (Army)
TADC . . . . . . Tactical Air Direction Center
TADC . . . . . . Training and Distribution Center (Navy)
TADF . . . . . . Thomas A. Dooley Foundation
TADIC . . . . . . Telemetry Analog-Digital Information Converter
TADJET . . . . . Transport Air Drop and Jettison Test (Air Force, Army)
TADM . . . . . Tactical Atomic Demolition Munitions (Military)
TADO . . . . . . Tactical Airlift Duty Officer
TADOR . . . . . Table Data Organization and Reductions
TADP . . . . . . Tactical Air Direction Post (Military)
TADP . . . . . . Toronto Anti-Draft Programme
TAD/P . . . . . . Terminal Area Distribution Processing
TADR . . . . . . Test Answer Document Reader
TADS . . . . . . Tactical Automatic Digital Switch
TADS . . . . . . Target and Activity Display System (Military)
TADS . . . . . . Teletypewriter Automatic Dispatch System
TADS . . . . . . Tracking and Display System
TADS . . . . . . Type (Command) Automated Data System (Navy)
TADSS . . . . . Tactical Automatic Digital Switching System
TADYL . . . . . Tom Dooley Youth League
TAEA . . . . . . Tangipahoa & Eastern R. R. (AAR code)
TAEC . . . . . . Thailand Atomic Energy Commission for Peace
TAEC . . . . . . Turkish Atomic Energy Commission
TAERS . . . . . The Army Equipment Record System
TAF . . . . Tactical Air Force
TAF . . . . Terminal Aerodrome Forecast (Also, TAFOR)
TAF . . . . Third Air Force
TAF . . . . Toxoid-Antitoxin Floccules
TAF . . . . Tumor-Angiogenesis Factor (Protein-induced tumor)
TAFB . . . . . . Tyndall Air Force Base
TAFCSD . . . . Total Active Federal Commissioned Service to Date
TAFDS . . . . . Tactical Airfield Fuel Dispensing System
TAFFS . . . . . . The Army Functional Files System
TAFG . . . . . . Two-Axis Free Gyro
TAFHQ . . . . . Tactical Air Force Headquarters
TAFI . . . . Technical Association of the Fur Industry
TAFIES . . . . . Tactical Air Forces Intelligence Exploitation System
TAFMSD . . . . Total Active Federal Military Service to Date
TAFNORNOR . . Allied Tactical Air Force Northern Norway (NATO)
TAFO . . . . . . Theater Accounting and Finance Office (Military)
TAFOR . . . . . Terminal Aerodrome Forecast (Also, TAF)
TAFS . . . . . . Training Aid Feasibility Studies
TAFSEA . . . . . Technical Applications for Southeast Asia (Air Force)
TAFUBAR . . . . Things Are Fouled Up Beyond All Recognition
TAFX . . . . . . Tapping Fixture
TAG . . . . Target Attitude Group (Advertising)
TAG . . . . Technical Advisory Group
TAG . . . . Technical Art Group
TAG . . . . Technical Assessment Group (Navy)
TAG . . . . . . Telecomputer Applications Group
TAG . . . . Tennessee, Alabama & Georgia Railway Company (AAR code)
TAG . . . . Terminating and Grounding
TAG . . . . Test Automation Growth
TAG . . . . . . The Acronym Generator (An RCA computer program)
TAG . . . . The Adjutant General (Army)
TAG . . . . The Association for the Gifted
TAG . . . . Time Arrive Guarantee
TAG . . . . . . Training Aids Guide (Navy)
TAG . . . . Trans-Atlantic Geotraverse (Project)
TAG . . . . Transient Analysis Generator
TAG . . . . Transport Air Group (Joint Army, Navy, and Marine Corps)
TAGA . . . . . . Technical Association of the Graphic Arts
TAGA . . . . . . Travel Agents Guild of America
TAGBDUSA . . . The Adjutant General's Board, United States Army
TAGC . . . . . . Tripped Automatic Gain Control
TAGER . . . . . Texas Association for Graduate Education and Research
TAGEX . . . . . Travel at Government Expense (Aviation)
TAGIS . . . . . . Tracking and Ground Instrumentation System
TAGIU . . . . . Tracking and Ground Instrumentation Unit (NASA)
TAGO . . . . . . The Adjutant General's Office
TAGRDCUSA . . The Adjutant General's Research and Development Command, United
States Army
TAGS . . . . . . Tactical Aircraft Guidance System (Air Force)
TAGS . . . . . . Teledyne Airborne Geophysical Services
TAGSUSA . . . The Adjutant General's School, Army
TAH . . . . Total Abdominal Hysterectomy (Medicine)
TAHA . . . . . . Tapered Aperture Horn Antenna
TAHQ . . . . . . Theater Army Headquarters
TAI . . . . Transports Aeriens Intercontinentaux (Privately owned French airline)

TAIC . . . . Technical Air Intelligence Center (Navy)
TAIC . . . . Tokyo Atomic Industrial Consortium
TAICH . . . . . . Technical Assistance Information Clearing House
TAID . . . . Thrust-Augmented Improved Delta (Launch vehicle)
TAILS . . . . . . Tactical Automatic Landing System (Aviation)
TAIR . . . . Terminal Area Instrumentation RADAR
TAISSA . . . . . Travelers Aid - International Social Service of America
TAIU . . . . Technical Aircraft Instrument Unit (Navy)
TAJ . . . . Thermal Arc Jet
TAJAG . . . . . . The Assistant Judge Advocate General (Army)
TAJF . . . . Thermo-Acoustic Jet Facility (MSFC) (NASA)
TAKC . . . . Theological Associate, King's College (London)
TAL . . . . Talley Industries, Inc. (NYSE symbol)
TAL . . . . Target Acquisition Laboratory
TAL . . . . Technische Akademie der Luftwaffe (Germany)
TAL . . . . Training Aids Library (Navy)
TAL . . . . Transalpine (Pipeline) (Western Europe)
TAL . . . . Transocean Air Lines
TALA . . . . . . Textile Association of Los Angeles
TALAR . . . . . Tactical Landing Approach Radio (or RADAR) (Aviation)
TALBE . . . . . . Talk and Listen Beacon (Radio)
TALC . . . . . . Tactical Airlift Center
TALC . . . . . . Take-A-Look-See
TALF . . . . . . Take a Look Foundation
TALO . . . . . . Tactical Air Liaison Officer (Air Force)
TALO . . . . . . Time After Liftoff
TALOG . . . . . Theater Army Logistical Command
TALOP . . . . . Terminology, Administrative, Logistical and Operational Procedures
(Military)
TALS . . . . . . The Army Language School
TALS . . . . . . Transport Approach and Landing Simulator
TALT . . . . . . Tracking Altitude
TALUS . . . . . Transportation and Land Use Study (Michigan)
TAM . . . . . . Tactical Air Missile (Air Force)
TAM . . . . . . Tangent Approximating Manifold
TAM . . . . . . Target Activated Munition (Air-delivered land mines)
TAM . . . . . . Technical Area Manager
TAM . . . . . . Thermal Analytical Model (Apollo) (NASA)
TAM . . . . . . Throw Away Maintenance
TAM . . . . . . Toxoid-Antitoxin Mixture (Medicine)
TAMA . . . . . . Technical Assistance and Manufacturing Agreement
TAMAC . . . . . Three-Axis Manual Attitude Controller
TAMC . . . . . . Tripler Army Medical Center
TAMCO . . . . . Training Aid for MOBIDIC Console Operations
TAMe . . . . . . Tolylsulfonylarginine Methyl Ester (Test) (Medicine)
TAMIRAD . . . . Tactical Mid-Range Air Defense Program (Army)
TAMIS . . . . . . Telemetric Automated Microbial Identification System
TAMMS . . . . . The Army Maintenance Management System
TAMS . . . . . . Token and Medal Society
TAMS . . . . . . Total Active Military Service
TAN . . . . Tactical Air Navigational Aid
TAN . . . . Tandem
TAN . . . . Tandy Corporation (NYSE symbol)
TAN . . . . Tangent
TAN . . . . Technische Arbeitsnorm
TAN . . . . Test Area North (AEC)
TAN . . . . Title Analytic (Bibliography)
TAN . . . . Total Ammonia Nitrogen
TAN . . . . Trainable Adaptive Network
TAN . . . . Transonic Aerodynamic Nozzle
TAN . . . . Transportes Aereos Nacionales, SA (Tan Airlines)
TAN . . . . Twilight All Night
TANC . . . . . . Total Absorption Nuclear Cascade
TANESCO . . . . Tanzania Electric Supply Company
TANG . . . . . . Tangential
TANH . . . . . . Tangent, Hyperbolic
TANKBAT . . . . Tank Battalion (Army)
TANS . . . . . . Terminal Area Navigation System
TANS . . . . . . Territorial Army Nursing Service
TANSTAAFL . . . There Ain't No Such Thing As a Free Lunch (Young Americans for
Freedom slogan; also, book title)
TANU . . . . . . Tanganyika African National Union (Political party)
TANY . . . . . . Typographers Association of New York
TAO . . . . TACAN (Tactical Air Navigation System) Only
TAO . . . . Technical Assistance Operations (UN)
TAO . . . . Terrain Avoidance Override
TAOC . . . . . . Tactical Air Operations Center
TAOC . . . . . . The Army Operations Center
TAOR . . . . . . Tactical Area of Responsibility (Military)
TAOS . . . . . . Travel Allowance on Separation (Military)
TA/OSD . . . . . Task Analysis/Operational Sequence Diagram

TAP	Tactical Action Programs
TAP	Tappan Co. (NYSE symbol)
TAP	Target Assignment Panel
TAP	Teacher's Aide Program
TAP	Technical Area Plan (Navy)
TAP	Technical Assistance Program
TAP	Technological Adjustment Pay
TAP	Technology Application Program (NASA)
TAP	Telemetry Antenna Pedestal
TAP	Terrestrial Auxiliary Power
TAP	Thermal Analysis Program
TAP	Three-Axis Package
TAP	Total Action Against Poverty (A federal government program)
TAP	Transferrable Assets Program
TAP	Transportes Aereos Portugueses, SARL (Portuguese Air Transport)
TAPAC	Tape Automatic Positioning and Control
TAPAT	Tape Programmed Automatic Tester
TAPCO	Thompson Products, Inc.
TAPE	Tactical Air Power Evaluation (Air Force)
TAPE	Tape Automatic Preparation Equipment
TAPE	Target Profile Examination Technique (RADAR analysis concept) (Air Force)
TAPE	Technical Advisory Panel for Electronics (Air Force)
TAPE	Trust for Agricultural Political Education (Organization of dairymen)
TAPER	Temporary Appointment Pending Establishment of a Register
TAPER	The Army Plan for Equipment Records
TAPER	Turbulent Air Pilot Environment Research (NASA-FAA project)
TAPITS	Tactical Airborne Processing, Interpretation and Transmission System (Military)
TAPLINE	Trans-Arabian Pipeline
TAPO	Termination Accountable Property Officer
TAPPI	Technical Association of the Pulp and Paper Industry
TAPR	Toxic Altitude Propulsion Research
TAPRE	Tracking in an Active and Passive RADAR Environment
TAPS	Tactical Area Positioning System
TAPS	TERCOM (Terrain Contour Mapping) Aircraft Positioning Systems (Air Force)
TAPS	Terminal Area Positive Separation (FAA)
TAPS	Trajectory Accuracy Prediction System (Air Force)
TAPS.	Transactions of American Philosophical Society (A publication)
TAPS	Trans-Alaska Pipeline System
TAPSC	Trans-Atlantic Passenger Steamship Conference
TAPU	Tanganyika African Postal Union
TAQ	Transient Airman Quarters (Air Force)
TAR	Tactical Air Reconnaissance
TAR	Technical Action Request (Army)
TAR	Terminal Area Surveillance RADAR
TAR	Terrain-Avoidance RADAR
TAR	Test Analysis Report
TAR	Thrust-Augmented Rocket
TAR	Track Address Register
TAR	Training and Administration of the Reserve
TAR	Truck and Rail
TAR	Turnaround Ratio
TARABS	Tactical Air Reconnaissance & Aerial Battlefield Surveillance System
TARAN	Tactical Attack RADAR and Navigation
TARAN	Test and Repair (or Replace) as Necessary
TARC	Tactical Air Reconnaissance Center (Shaw Air Force Base)
TARC	Television Allocation Research Committee (or Council)
TARC	The Army Research Council
TARC	Theater Army Replacement Command
TARCAP	Target Combat Air Patrol (Navy)
TARE.	Telegraphic Automatic Relay (or Routing) Equipment
TARE.	Telemetry Automatic Reduction Equipment
TARE	Transistor Analysis Recording Equipment
TARFU.	Things Are Really Fouled Up (Military slang) (Bowdlerized version)
TARGET	Team to Advance Research for Gas Energy Transformation (Group of US gas and gas-electric companies)
TARGET	Thermal Advanced Reactor, Gas-Cooled, Exploiting Thorium
TARGET	Transportation Accident Research Graduate Education and Training
TARL	Training Aids Research Laboratory (Air Force)
TARMAC	Tar Macadam
TARMOCS	The Army Operations Center System
TARP	Tactical Airborne Recording Package
TARP.	Tarpaulin
TARP.	Test and Repair Processor (Data processing)
TARS	Tactical Air Reconnaissance School (Air Force)
TARS	Tactical Air Research and Survey Office (Air Force)
TARS	Technical Assistance Recruitment Service (UN)
TARS	Teen Age Republicans
TARS	Terrain Analog RADAR Simulator
TARS	Theater Army Replacement System

TARS	Three-Axis Reference System (Used in reference to Titan missile)
TARSCC	Three-Axis Reference System Checkout Console
TARSLL	Tender and Repair Ship Load List (Navy)
TART	Task Analysis Reduction Technique (Navy)
TARTC	Theater Army Replacement and Training Command
TARVAN	Truck and Rail Van
TAS	Tactical Advisory Service (Department of Commerce)
TAS	Tactical Area Switching
TAS	Tampa Southern R. R. (AAR code)
TAS	Target Acquisition System
TAS	Telephone Answering Service (or System)
TAS	Terminal Address Selector
TAS	The Army Staff
TAS	Three-Axis Stabilization
TAS	Towed Array SONAR
TAS	Tracking Antenna System
TAS	Training Aids Section (Navy)
TAS	Transverse Air Spring
TAS	True Air Speed
TASA	Task and Skill Analysis
TASA	The Aircraft Service Association
TASA	The Assistant Secretary of the Army
TASAMS	The Army Supply and Maintenance System
TASAP	The Army Scientific Advisory Panel
TASAS	Transformer Analogue Servo Analyzer cum Synthesizer
TASC	Tabular Sequence Control
TASC	Technology and Society Committee (Palo Alto, California)
TASC	Terminal Area Sequencing and Control
TASC	Test Anxiety Scale for Children (Psychology)
TASC	The Analytic Sciences Corporation
TASC	Total Absorption Shower Cascade
TASC	Total Avionic Support Capability
TASCOM	Theater Army Support Command
TASCON	Television Automatic Sequence Control
TASD	Tactical Action Situation Display
TASD	Terminal Railway, Alabama State Docks (AAR code)
TASE	Tactical Air Support Element (Military)
TASER.	Tele-Active Shock Electronic Repulsion (Nonlethal weapon)
TASES.	Tactical Airborne Signal Exploitation System
TASF	Tactical Air Strike Force (Air Force)
TASFUIRA	Things Are So Fouled Up It's Really Amazing (Military slang) (Bowdlerized version)
TASI	Time Assignment Speech Interpolation (Telephone cables) (Bell System)
TASKFLOT. . . .	Task Flotilla
TASL	Theater Authorized Stockage List (Military)
TASMOL	Tactical Aircraft Support Model
TASO	Television Allocations Study Organization
TASOS	Towed Array SONAR System
TASP.	Telemetry Analysis and Simulation Program (Spacecraft) (NASA)
TAS-PAC	Total Analysis System for Production, Accounting, and Control (Data processing)
TASR	Terminal Area Surveillance RADAR
TASR	Torque Arm Speed Reducer
TASS	Tactical Air Support Section
TASS.	Tactical Avionics System Simulator
TASS	Technical Assembly System
TASS	Telegraphnoye Agentstvo Sovyetskovo Soyuza (Telegraph Agency of the Soviet Union) (News agency)
TASS	Towed Array SONAR System
TASSA	The Army Signal Supply Agency
TASSO	Tactical Special Security Office (Army)
TASSO	Transatlantic Air Safety Service Organization
TASSq.	Tactical Air Support Squadron (Air Force)
TAST.	Tactical Assault Supply Transport
TASTA	The Administrative Support, Theater Army
TAT	Tactical Armament Turret
TAT	Target Aircraft Transmitter
TAT	Technical Acceptance Team
TAT	Technical Approval Team
TAT	Technical Assistance Team (Air Force)
TAT	Tetanus Antitoxin (Medicine)
TAT	Thematic Apperception Test (Psychology)
TAT	Thrust-Augmented Thor (NASA)
TAT.	To Accompany Troops
TAT	Torpedo Attack Teacher (Navy)
TAT	Toxin-Antitoxin (Medicine)
TAT	Trace Acceptance Tester
TAT	Training and Technology
TAT	Transatlantic Telephone (Cable)
TAT	True Air Temperature
TAT	Turn-Around Time (Navy)

TAT . . . . Two-Axis Tracking
TAT . . . . Tyrosine Aminotransferase (Enzyme)
TATAWS . . . . . Tank, Antitank and Assault Weapons System (Army)
TATB . . . . . Theater Air Transportation Board
TATC . . . . . . Terminal Air Traffic Control
TATCO . . . . . Tactical Automatic Telephone Central Office (Military)
TATCS . . . . . Terminal Air Traffic Control System
TATDL . . . . . . Tabulated Assembly Technical Data List
TATP . . . . . . Two-Axis Tracking Pedestal
TATSA . . . . . Transportation Aircraft Test and Support Activity (Military)
TATTE . . . . . . Tactical Test Equipment
TAUN . . . . . Technical Assistance of the United Nations
TAUS . . . . . . Tobacco Association of United States
TAV . . . . . . Technical (or Tender) Availability (Navy)
TAVE . . . . . . Thor-Agena Vibration Experiment (NASA)
TAVET . . . . . Temperature Acceleration Vibration Environmental Tester
TAVIP . . . . . . Tahun Vivere Pericoloso (The Year of Living Dangerously) (President
    Sukarno's national policy in 1964) (Indonesia)
TAW . . . . Tactical Assault Weapon
TAW . . . . . . Toledo, Angola & Western Railway Company (AAR code)
TAW . . . . . . Twice a Week (Advertising frequency)
TAWC . . . . . . Tactical Air Warfare Center (Air Force)
TAWCS . . . . . Tactical Air Weapons Control System
TAWS . . . . . . Tactical Warfare Center (Army)
TAWS . . . . . . Technical Analysis Work Sheet
TAWS . . . . . . Thomasville Aircraft Warning System
TAWU . . . . . . Transport and Allied Workers' Union (Rhodesia, Nyasaland, and Kenya)
TAX . . . . . . Training Assessment Exercise
TAY . . . . Third Avenue Transit Corporation (NYSE symbol) (Delisted)
TAZ . . . . . . Theater Administrative Zone (Military)
TB . . . . Tangential Bracket
TB . . . . Tank Battalion (Army)
TB . . . . Tariff Bureau
TB . . . . Technical Bulletin
TB . . . . Telegraph Bureau
TB . . . . Temporary Buoy (Maps and charts)
Tb . . . . Terbium (Chemical element)
TB . . . . Terminal Block
TB . . . . Terminal Board
TB . . . . Test Bulletin
TB . . . . Thermobarometer
TB . . . . Thymol Blue (An indicator)
TB . . . . Tile Base (Technical drawings)
TB . . . . Time Base
TB . . . . Times at Bat (Baseball)
TB . . . . Torpedo Boat (Navy symbol)
TB . . . . Torpedo Bomber (or Bombing)
TB . . . . Total Bases
TB . . . . Total Blank (Entertainment slang for poor show town)
TB . . . . Total Bouts (Boxing)
TB . . . . Tractor Biplane
TB . . . . Traffic Bureau
TB . . . . Tranquility Base (Moon landing site)
TB . . . . Trial Balance (Bookkeeping)
TB . . . . Trial Balloon
TB . . . . Troop Basis
TB . . . . True Bearing (Navigation)
TB . . . . Tubercle Bacillus (Bacteriology)
TB . . . . Tuberculosis
TB . . . . Twin Branch R. R. (AAR code)
T/B . . . . Title Block (Technical drawings)
T & B . . . . . . Top and Bottom (Technical drawings)
T & B . . . . . . Turn-and-Bank Indicators
TBA . . . . Tables of Basic Allowances (Previously, Basic Tables of Commissioning
    Allowances) (Navy)
TBA . . . . Television Bureau of Advertising
TBA . . . . Tertiary Butyl Acetate
TBA . . . . Thiobarbituric Acid
TBA . . . . Tires, Batteries & Accessories
TBA . . . . To Be Activated
TBA . . . . To Be Added
TBA . . . . To Be Announced
T/BA . . . . Table of Basic Allowances (Military)
TBAI . . . . Temporary Base Activation Instruction
TBAN . . . . . . To Be Announced (Army)
TBAWRBA . . . . Travel by Military Aircraft, Military and/or Naval Water Carrier,
    Commercial Rail and/or Bus Is Authorized (Army)
TBB . . . . Temporal Bone Banks (Otology)
TBB . . . . Tenor, Baritone, Bass
T & BB . . . . . . Top and Bottom Bolt (Technical drawings)
TBC . . . . Television Briefing Console

TBC . . . . Thyroxin Binding Globulin (Medicine)
TBC . . . . Torrey Botanical Club
TBC . . . . Toss Bomb Computer
TBC . . . . Trunk Block Connector
TBCA . . . . . . Test Boring Contractors Association
TBD . . . . Target Bearing Designator (Navy)
TBD . . . . Terminal Bomber Defense (Army)
TBD . . . . To Be Declassified
TBD . . . . To Be Defined
TBD . . . . To Be Determined
TBD . . . . To Be Disbanded
TBD . . . . To Be Done
TBD . . . . Troubleshooting Block Diagram
TBD . . . . Twin Boundary Diffusion
TBDS . . . . . . Test Base Dispatch Service
TBE . . . . European Federation of Tile and Brick Manufacturers
TBE . . . . Tetrabromoethane
TBE . . . . To Be Expended
TBE . . . . Total Body Ergometer
TBE . . . . Tuberculin Bacillen Emulsion (Medicine)
TBEA . . . . . . Truck Body and Equipment Association
TBEX . . . . . . Tube Expander
TBF . . . . Two-Body Force
TBFX . . . . . . Tube Fixture (Tool)
TBG . . . . Testosterone-Binding Globulin (Biochemistry)
TBG . . . . Thyroxine-Binding Globulin (Biochemistry)
TBGAA . . . . . Travel By Government Automobile Authorized
TBGP . . . . . . Tactical Bomb Group (Air Force)
TBH . . . . Test Bench Harness
TBI . . . . Target Bearing Indicator (Military)
TBI . . . . Test Bench Installation
TBI . . . . Threaded Blind Insert
TBI . . . . To Be Inactivated
TBJ . . . . Turbulent Bounded Jet
TBK . . . . TEFLON Bonding Kit
TBL . . . . Terminal Ballistics Laboratory (Army)
TBL . . . . Thin Base Laminate
TBL . . . . Through Bill of Lading
TBL . . . . Turbulent Boundary Layer
TBLC . . . . . . Term Birth, Living Child (Medicine)
TBM . . . . Tactical Ballistic Missile (Air Force)
TBM . . . . Temporary Bench Mark
TBMA . . . . . . Textile Bag Manufacturers Association
TBMAA . . . . . . Travel By Military Aircraft Authorized
TBMD . . . . . . Terminal Ballistic Missile Defense (Army)
TBMO . . . . . . Test Base Material Operation
TBMX . . . . . . Tactical Ballistic Missile Experiment
TBN . . . . Tobin Packing Co., Inc. (NYSE symbol)
TBO . . . . Thermal Bakeout
TBO . . . . Time Between Overhaul
TBO . . . . Transactions by Others
TBOA . . . . . . Tuna Boat Owners' Association
t-BOC . . . . . . tert-Butyloxycarbonyl (Organic chemistry)
TBOI . . . . . . Tentative Basis of Issue (Army)
TBP . . . . Timing Belt Pulley
TBP . . . . Trainable Bow Propeller
TBP . . . . Tributyl Phosphate (Chemical)
TBP . . . . True Boiling Point
TBP . . . . Twisted Bonded Pair
TBP . . . . Two-Body Problem
TBPA . . . . . . Thyroxine-Binding Pre-Albumin (Biochemistry)
TBPA . . . . . . Transatlantic Brides and Parents Association
TBR . . . . Torpedo Bomber Reconnaissance Aircraft (Navy)
TBRI . . . . Technical Book Review Index
TBS . . . . Tablespoon
TBS . . . . Tactical Bomb Squadron (Air Force)
TBS . . . . Talk-Between-Ships (which are tactically maneuvering; also, the VHF
    radio equipment used for this purpose)
TBS . . . . Tape and Buffer System (Data processing)
TBS . . . . Tokyo Broadcasting System
TBS . . . . Toronto Baptist Seminary
TBS . . . . Training and Battle Simulation (SAGE)
TBS . . . . Translator Bail Switch
TB & S . . . . . . Top, Bottom, and Sides (Lumber)
TBSG . . . . . . Test Base Support Group
TBSP . . . . Tablespoon
TBT . . . . Terminal Ballistic Track
TBT . . . . Thallium Beam Tube
TBTO . . . . . . Tributlytin Oxide (Organic chemistry)
TBU . . . . Time Base Unit
TBV . . . . Thermal Bypass Valve

TBV . . . . Tubercle Bacillus Vaccine
TBW . . . . Titanium Butt Weld
TBW . . . . To Be Withheld
TBW . . . . Total Bandwidth
TBWG . . . . . Tactical Bomb Wing (Air Force)
TBWO . . . . . . Tuned Backward Wave Oscillator
TBX . . . . Tactical Ballistic Missile Experimental
TC . . . . Tabulating Card
TC . . . . Tank Car(s)
TC . . . . Tank Corps
TC . . . . Tape Core
TC . . . . Tariff Circular
TC . . . . Tariff Commission (US)
TC . . . . Tax Court (US)
TC . . . . Tea Council of the United States of America
TC . . . . Teachers College (Columbia University)
TC . . . . Teardown Compliance
Tc . . . . Technetium (Chemical element)
TC . . . . Technical Characteristics
TC . . . . Technical Circular
TC . . . . Technical College
TC . . . . Technical Communication
TC . . . . Telex Corporation (NYSE symbol)
TC . . . . Temperature Capability
TC . . . . Temperature Coefficient
TC . . . . Temperature Control
TC . . . . Temporary Constable
TC . . . . Tennessee Central Railway Company (AAR code)
TC . . . . Tennis Club
TC . . . . Teracycle
TC . . . . Terra Cotta (Technical drawings)
TC . . . . Terrain Clearance (Military)
TC . . . . Test Conductor
TC . . . . Test Console
TC . . . . Test Controller
TC . . . . Tetracycline
TC . . . . Tetrahedral Cubic (Metallography)
TC . . . . Thermal Conductivity
TC . . . . Thermocouple
TC . . . . Thrust Chamber (Air Force, NASA)
TC . . . . Till Countermanded
TC . . . . Time Check
TC . . . . Time Closing
TC . . . . Time Compensation
TC . . . . Time to Computation
TC . . . . Timing Channel
TC . . . . Tinned Copper
TC . . . . Toll Center
TC . . . . Toll Completing
TC . . . . Top Center (Valve position)
TC . . . . Top Chord
TC . . . . Top of Column
TC . . . . Total Chances
TC . . . . Total Cost
TC . . . . Touring Club
TC . . . . Town Clerk (or Councillor)
TC . . . . Tracking Camera
TC . . . . Traffic Collision
TC . . . . Traffic Commissioner (or Consultant)
TC . . . . Training Center
TC . . . . Training Circular (Military)
TC . . . . Training Command
TC . . . . Transaction Code (Military)
TC . . . . Transceiver Code (Navy)
TC . . . . Transcobalamin (Biochemistry)
TC . . . . Transistorized Carrier
TC . . . . Transmission Controller
TC . . . . Transportation Corps
TCM . . . . Tre Corde (With three strings, or release the soft pedal) (Music)
TC . . . . Trial Counsel
TC . . . . Tricycle Club (British)
TC . . . . Trim Coil
TC . . . . Trip Coil
TC . . . . Troop Carrier (Air Force)
TC . . . . Tropical Continental (American air mass)
TC . . . . True Course
TC . . . . Trusteeship Council
TC . . . . Turret Captain (Navy)
TC . . . . Type Certificate
T/C . . . . Thermocouple
T/C . . . . Time Charter (Shipping)

TCA . . . . Tanners' Council of America
TCA . . . . Tattoo Club of America
TCA . . . . Teach Cable Assembly (Robot technology)
TCA . . . . Teaching Curriculum Association (A generic term; not the name of a specific organization)
TCA . . . . Technical Cooperation Administration (Transferred to Foreign Operations Administration, 1953)
TCA . . . . Telemetering Control Assembly
TCA . . . . Templehof Central Airport (West Berlin)
TCA . . . . Terminal Control Area
TCA . . . . Textile Converters Association
TCA . . . . Theater Commander's Approval (Military)
TCA . . . . Thermal Critical Assembly (Atomic energy)
TCA . . . . Thoroughbred Club of America
TCA . . . . Thrust Chamber Assembly (Missile technology)
TCA . . . . Tile Council of America
TCA . . . . Tissue Culture Association
TCA . . . . Tithe Commutation Act (British)
TCA . . . . Trace Contamination Analysis
TCA . . . . Track Crossing Angle
TCA . . . . Trailer Coach Association
TCA . . . . Trans-Canada Airlines
TCA . . . . Tricarboxylic Acid (Cycle) (Biochemistry)
TCA . . . . Trichloroacetate (Organic chemistry)
TCA . . . . Trichloroacetic Acid (Organic chemistry)
TCAA . . . . . . Tile Contractors' Association of America
TCAB . . . . . . Tetrachloroazobenzene (Organic chemistry)
TCAF . . . . . . TEFLON Coated Aluminum Foil
TCAI . . . . . . Texas College of Arts and Industry
TCAM . . . . . . Telecommunications Access Method (Data processing)
TCAP . . . . . . Tactical Channel Assignment Panel (Military radio)
TCAP . . . . . . Tricyanoaminopropene (Organic chemistry)
TCAP . . . . . . Trimethylcetylammonium Pentachlorphenate (Organic chemistry)
TCAT . . . . . . Tape-Controlled Automatic Testing
TCB . . . . Take Care of Business (Teen slang)
TCB . . . . Tantalum Carbon Bond
TCB . . . . Thermal Compression Bond
TCB . . . . Time Correlation Buffer
T-CBA . . . . . . Transfluxor, Constant Board Assembly
TCBE . . . . . . Thermo-Compression Bonding Equipment
TCBI . . . . Television Center for Business and Industry
TCBM . . . . . . Transcontinental Ballistic Missile (Air Force)
TCBV . . . . . . Temperature Coefficient of Breakdown Voltage
TCC . . . . Tactical Control Center (Military)
TCC . . . . Tactical Control Computer
TCC . . . . Teachers College of Connecticut
TCC . . . . Technical Control Center
TCC . . . . Telecommunications Coordinating Committee (State Department)
TCC . . . . Television Control Center
TCC . . . . Temperature Coefficient of Capacitance
TCC . . . . Temporary Council Committee (NATO)
TCC . . . . Test Conductor Console
TCC . . . . Test Coordinating Center (Army)
TCC . . . . Thermo-Control Coating
TCC . . . . Therofor Catalytic Cracking
TCC . . . . Thiokol Chemical Corporation
TCC . . . . Thromboplastic Cell Component (Medicine)
TCC . . . . Time Compression Coding
TCC . . . . Toroidal Combustion Chamber
TCC . . . . Tracking and Control Center
TCC . . . . Traffic Control Center
TCC . . . . Transcontinental Corps (Amateur radio)
TCC . . . . Transport Control Center (Air Force)
TCC . . . . Transportation Control Card
TCC . . . . Transportation Control Committee (Navy)
TCC . . . . Troop Carrier Command (World War II)
TCCFU . . . . . . Typical Coastal Command Foul Up (RAF slang) (World War II)
TCCH . . . . . . Tracer Control Chassis
TCCM . . . . . . Thermal Control Coating Material
TCCPSWG . . . . Tactical Command and Control Procedures Standardization Working Group (Army)
TCCS . . . . . . Trace Contaminant Control System
TCD . . . . Task Completion Date
TCD . . . . Technical Contracts Department
TCD . . . . Tentative Classification of Damage
TCD . . . . Tentative Classification of Defects
TCD . . . . Tentative Classification of Documents
TCD . . . . Test Control Drawings
TCD . . . . Thermochemical Deposition
TCD . . . . Three-Channel Decoder
TCD . . . . Thyratron Core Driver

TCD	Time-Correlation Data
TCD	Transistor Chopper Driver
TCD	Trinity College, Dublin
TCDD	Tetrachlorodibenzo-p-dioxin
TCE	Temperature Coefficient of Expansion
TCE	Total Composite Error
TCE	Transportation-Communications Employees Union (AFL-CIO)
TCEA	Training Center for Experimental Aerodynamics (NATO)
TCESOM	Trichlorethylene-Extracted-Soybean-Oil Meal
TCF	Technical Control Facility
TCF	Troop Carrier Forces
TCF	Tunable Control Frequency
TCF	Twentieth Century Fund
TCFB	Trans-Continental Freight Bureau
TCFM	Temperature-Control Flux Monitor (NASA)
TCFNO	The Common Fund for Nonprofit Organizations (Ford Foundation)
TCG	Territorial College of Guam
TCG	Theatre Communications Group
TCG	Time Code Generator
TCG	Time Controlled Gain
TCG	Tooling Coordination Group
TCG	Transponder Control Group
TCG	Tucson, Cornelia & Gila Bend R. R. (AAR code)
TCG	Tune-Controlled Gain
TCGp	Tactical Control Group (Air Force)
TCGU	TEXACO Continuous Grease Unit
TCH	Temporary Construction Hole (Technical drawings)
TCH	Thiocarbohydrazide (Organic chemistry)
TCH	Transfer in Channel
TCHEP	Technical Committee on High Energy Physics (of the Federal Council for Science and Technology)
TCHHW	Tropic Higher High Water
TCHHWI	Tropic Higher High Water Interval
TCHLW	Tropic Higher Low Water
TCI	Tall Clubs International
TCI	Technology Communications, Incorporated
TCI	Temperature Control Instrument
TCI	Terrain-Clearance Indicator
TCI	Travel Consultants, Incorporated
TCI	Trunk Cut-In
TCI	Twentieth Century Interpretations (Series of books)
TCID	Tissue Culture Infectious (or Infective) Dose
TCIR	Technical Command Informal Reports (Army)
TCJ	Thermocouple Junction
TCJ	Turbulent Confined Jet
TCK	Thermo-Chemical-Kinetic
TCK	Track(ing)
TCK	Two-Cavity Klystron
TCL	Takeoff Cruise Landing
TCL	Transcon Lines (NYSE symbol)
TCL	Transistor Contact Land
TCL	Transistor Coupled Logic
TCL	Transportable Calibration Laboratory
TCL	Trap Control Line
TCL	Trinity College, London
TCL	Troposcatter Communications Link
TCLHW	Tropic Lower High Water
TCLLW	Tropic Lower Low Water
TCLLWI	Tropic Lower Low Water Interval
TCLSC	Theater COMSEC (Communications Security) Logistic Support Center (Army)
TCM	Teaching Career Month
TCM	Telemetry Code Modulation
TCM	Telephone Channel Monitor
TCM	Terminal-to-Computer Multiplexer
TCM	Terrain Clearance Measurement
TCM	Tissue Culture Medium
TCM	Transfluxer Constants Matrix
TCM	Twin-Cartridge Machine
TCMA	Tabulating Card Manufacturers Association
TCMA	Textile Chemical Manufacturers Association
TCMD	Transportation Control and Movement Document
TCN	Technicon Corp. (NYSE symbol)
TCN	Tracing Change Notice
TCN	Transportation Control Number (Air Force)
TCNCO	Test Control Noncommissioned Officer
TCNE	Tetracyanoethylene
TCNQ	Tetracyanoquinodimethane (Organic chemistry)
TCNT	Transpiration-Cooled Nose Tip
TCO	Tactical Control Officer (Army)
TCO	Technical Contracting Office (Navy)
TCO	Termination Contracting Officers

TCO	Test Control Officer
TCO	Time and Charges, Operate
TCO	Tjaenstemaennens Centralorganisation (Central Organization of Salaried Employees) (Sweden)
TCO	Transportation Company (Army)
TCO	Transportation Control Office(r) (Air Force)
TCO	Trunk Cut-Off
TCP	Task Change Proposal
TCP	Teachers College Press
TCP	Technical Change Proposal
TCP	Technical Cost Proposal
TCP	Temporary Change Procedure
TCP	Time, Cost, and Performance
TCP	Time-Limited Correlation Processing
TCP	Traffic Control Post
TCP	Trichlorophenoxyacetic Acid (Herbicide)
TCP	Tricresyl Phosphate (Organic chemistry)
TCPC	Tab Card Punch Control
TCPI	Transportation Club of the Petroleum Industry
TCPO	Third-Class Post Office
TCPTF	Target Cost Plus Target Fee
TCQC	Tank Crew Qualification Course (Army)
TCR	Tab Card Reader
TCR	Tantalum-Controlled Rectifier
TCR	Technical Change Request
TCR	Telemetry Compression Routine
TCR	Temperature Coefficient of Resistance
TCR	Tentative Cancellation Request
TCR	Terrain Clearance RADAR
TCR	Time Code Reader
TCR	Tooling Change Request
TCR	Tracer
TCR	Traffic Control RADAR
TCR	Transfer Control Register
TCR	Transportation Corps Release
TCR	Two-Color Radiometer
TCRE	Temperature Compensated Reference Element
TCREC	Transportation Research Command (Army)
TCRJ	Thermocouple Reference Junction
TCRM	Thermochemical Remanent Magnetization
TCRPA	Trans-Continental Railroad Passenger Association
TCS	Tanking Control System
TCS	Target Control System
TCS	Target Cost System
TCS	Teacher Characteristics Schedule
TCS	Telecommunications Control System (Data processing)
TCS	Television Camera System
TCS	Temporary Change of Station
TCS	Ternary Compound Semiconductor
TCS	Thermal Control Surface (or System)
TCS	Tool Clearance Slip
TCS	Traffic Control Station
TCS	Transducer Calibration System
TCS	Transportable Communications System
TCS	Transportation and Communications Service (of GSA)
TCS	Transportation Communications System
TCS	Tube Cooling Supply
TCSD	Telemetry and Communications Systems Division (Apollo) (NASA)
TCSMC	Transportation Corps Supply Maintenance Command (Army)
TCSP	Tactical Communications Satellite Program
TCSP	Tandem Cross-Section Program (Bell System)
TCSq.	Troop Carrier Squadron (Air Force)
TCT	Texas City Terminal Railway Company (AAR code)
TCT	Tin Can Tourists of the World
TCT	Tool Change Time
TCT	Total Composite Tolerance
TCT	Traffic Control Transponder
TCT	True Centerline Tested
TCTC	Transportation Corps Technical Committee
TCTL	Tactical
TCTM	Aircraft Time Compliance Technical Manuals
TCTO	Technical Compliance Technical Order
TCTO	Time Compliance Technical Order
TCTU	Turkish Confederation of Trade Unions
TCU	Tape Control Unit
TCU	Temperature Control Unit
TCU	Test Control Unit
TCU	Texas Christian University
TCU	Thrust Control Unit
TCU	Topping Control Unit
TCU	Torpedo Control Unit

TCU	Towering Cumulus (Meteorology)
TCU	Transmission Control Unit
TCU	Transportation-Communication Employees Union
TCU	Transportation, Communications, and Utilities
TCUA	Time-Critical, Unspecified Area
TC(UN)	Trusteeship Council of the United Nations
TCUS	Tax Court of the United States
TCV	Temperature Coefficient of Voltage
TCV	Temperature Control Valve
TCV	Troop Carrying Vehicle
TCV	Twentieth Century Views (Series of books)
TCVC	Tape Control Via Console
TCW	Time Code Word
TCW	Tinned Copper Weld
TCWG	Telecommunication Working Group
TCWg	Troop Carrier Wing (Air Force)
TCWH(I)	Teamsters, Chauffeurs, Warehousemen and Helpers of America; International Brotherhood of (Indiana)
TCZD	Temperature-Compensated Zener Diode
TD	Table of Distribution (Military)
TD	Tactical Division (Air Force)
TD	Tank Destroyer (Military)
TD	Tape Degausser
TD	Task Description
TD	Task Directive
TD	Teachta Dala (Member of Parliament) (Ireland)
TD	Technical Data
TD	Technical Demonstration
TD	Technical Design
TD	Technical Direction (or Directive)
TD	Telegraph Department
TD	Telemetry Data
TD	Telephone Department
TD	Temporary Disability
TD	Temporary Duty
TD	Territorial Decoration
TD	Test Data
TD	Test Directive
TD	Test Director
TD	Testing and Development Division (Coast Guard)
TD	Third Defense (Men's lacrosse position, until 1933)
TD	Thor-Delta (Satellite)
TD	Thoria Dispersed (Nickel)
TD	Threshold Detection
TD	Thymus Dependent (Cells) (Biochemistry)
TD	Tile Drain (Technical drawings)
TD	Time Delay
TD	Time of Departure
TD	Time Difference
TD	Timed Disintegration (Pharmacy)
TD	Timing Device
TD	Tons per Day
TD	Tool Design
TD	Tool Disposition
TD	Topographic Draftsman (Navy)
TD	Torpedo Dive Bomber Aircraft
TD	Total Depth
TD	Touchdown (Football)
TD	Track Data
TD	Track Display
TD	Tractor-Drawn
TD	Tradesman (Navy rating)
TD	Traffic Director
TD	Training Detachment
TD	Training of Documentalists
TD	Trajectory Diagram (Army)
TD	Transform Domain
TD	Transmitter Distributor
TD	Transverse Direction
TD	Treasury Decision
TD	Treasury Department (in References to Rulings)
TD	Treasury Division
TD	Treatment Day
TD	True Depth (Diamond drilling)
TD	Trust Deed
TD	Tunnel Diode
TD	Turbine Direct Drive
TD	Turbine Drive(n)
TD	Typographic Draftsman (Navy)
T/D	Temperature Datum
T/D	Time Deposit (Banking)
T & D	Transmission and Distribution
TDA	American Train Dispatchers Association
TDA	Table of Distribution and Allowances
TDA	Table of Distribution-Augmentation (Military)
TDA	Telemetric Data Analyzer
TDA	Textile Distributors Association (Formerly, TFDA)
TDA	The Disposables Association
TDA	Thermodifferential Analysis
TDA	Time Delay Amplifier
TDA	Toluenediamine (Organic chemistry)
TDA	Tracking and Data Acquisition
TDA	Tuning Device Assembly
TDA	Tunnel Diode Amplifier
TDAC	Tropical Deterioration Administrative Committee (of NDRC) (World War II)
TDAMTB	Tables of Distribution and Allowances Mobilization Troop Basis (Army)
TDAS	Thermocouple Data Acquisition System
TDAS	Tracking and Data Acquisition System
TDAS	Tunnel Diode Amplifier System
TDB	Technical Directive Board
TDB	Top Drawing Breakdown
TDB	Turbine-Driven Blower
TDC	Tactical Data Converter
TDC	Tank Destroyer Center (Army)
TDC	Target Data Collection
TDC	Technical Development Center
TDC	Technical Document Center
TDC	Teflon Dielectric Capacitor
TDC	Temperature Density Computer
TDC	Termination Design Change
TDC	Test Director Console
TDC	Time Data Card
TDC	Time Delay Closing
TDC	Time Distribution Card
TDC	Time Domain Coding
TDC	Tooling Design Change
TDC	Top Dead Center
TDC	Track Data Central
TDC	Training Device Center
TDC	Transportation Development Center (Cambridge, Massachusetts) (Department of Transportation) (Formerly, NASA Electronic Research Center)
TDC	Tube Deflection Coil
T & DC	Training and Distribution Center (Navy)
TDCC	Tactical Data Communications Center
TDCC	Transportation Data Coordinating Committee (National Bureau of Standards)
TDCE	Technical Direction Contract Effort
TDCK	Technisch Documentatie Centrum voor der Krijgsmacht (Netherland Armed Services Technical Documentation and Information Center)
TDCM	Transistor Driver Core Memory
TDCN	Time Delay Compression Network
TDCO	Torpedo Data Computer Operator (Navy)
TDCS	Target Detection-Conversion Sensor
TDCSP	Tactical Defense Communications Satellite Program
TDCT	Time Domain Coding Technique
TDCT	Tunnel Diode Charge Transformer
TDCTL	Tunnel-Diode Charge-Transformer Logic
TDCU	Target Data Control Unit
TDCU	Tinned Copper
TDD	Target Detecting Device
TDD	Technical Data Digest (Air Force)
TDD	Technical Development Division
TDD	Telemetry Data Digitizer
TDD	Tuberculous Diseases Diploma (British)
TDDL	Time-Division Data Link (Radio)
TDDO	Time Delay Drop-Out (Relay)
TDE	Technical Data Engineer
TDE	Tetrachlorodiphenylethane (Organic chemistry)
TDE	Time Displacement Error
TDE	Time Duration Error
TDE	Toluene-Dioxane-Ethanol (Scintillation fluid)
TDE	Total Differential Equation
TDEC	Technical Development Evaluation Center
TDEC	Technical Division and Engineering Center (FAA)
TDEC	Telephone Line Digital Error Checking
TDEP	Tracking Data Editing Program (NASA)
TDF	Temporary Detention Facility
TDF	Thin Dielectric Film
TDF	Time Domain Filter
TDF	Two Degrees of Freedom
TDG	Technical Design Guide
TDG	Test Display Generator

TDG........	Thiodigalactoside (Organic chemistry)
TDG........	Time-Delay Generator
TDG........	Twist Drill Gauge
TD & G.....	Tall, Dark and Gruesome (Teen slang)
TDH........	Terre des Hommes (An international organization)
TDH........	Total Dynamic Head (Aerospace)
TDH........	Tracking Data Handling
TDHHG.....	For Travel of Dependents Authorized Transportation of Household Goods (Army)
TDHS.......	Tape Data Handling System
TDI........	TACAN (Tactical Air Navigation) Distance Indicator
TDI........	Target Data Inventory
TDI........	Tear-Down Inspection
TDI........	Test Data Interpolation
TDI........	Textile Dye Institute
TDI........	Toluene Diisocyanate (Organic chemistry)
T & DI.....	Tool and Die Institute
TDIL.......	Target Detection, Identification, and Location
TDIO.......	Timing and Data Input-Output
TDIO.......	Tuning Data Input-Output
TDIP.......	Total Disability Income Provisions (Military)
TDIS.......	Terminal Data Input System
TDIS.......	Time Distance (Military)
TDL........	Target Development Laboratory (Eglin AFB)
TDL........	Task-Directed Learning
TDL........	Technical Document List
TDL........	Threshold Damage Level
TDL........	Threshold Detection Level
TDL........	Tunnel Diode Logic
TDLR.......	Terminal Descent and Landing RADAR
TDM........	Tandem
TDM........	Telemetric Data Monitor
TDM........	Ternary Delta Modulation
TDM........	Test Data Memorandum
TDM........	Thermal Diffusion Method
TDM........	Thermodynamic Molding
TDM........	Time-Division Multiplex(er) (Radio)
TDM........	Torpedo Detection Modification (SONAR)
TDM........	Trouble Detection and Monitoring
TDM........	Tunnel Diode Mixer
TDMA.......	Time Division Multiple Access (Computer control system)
TDMD.......	Time Division Multiplex Device
TDMRA.....	Texas Delaine-Merino Record Association
TDMS.......	Telegraph Distortion Measuring System
TDMS.......	Time Division Multiplexing System
TDMS.......	Transmission Distortion Measuring Set
TDMTB.....	Tables of Distribution Mobilization Troop Basis (Army)
TDN........	Target Doppler Nullifier (RADAR)
TDN........	Total Digestible Nutrients
TDN........	Travel is Directed as Necessary in Military Service
TDO........	Technical Development Objective
TDO........	Technical Directives Ordnance
TDO........	Telegraph Delivery Order
TDO........	Time Delay Opening
TDO........	Training Development Officer (British)
TDOT.......	Thorndike Dimensions of Temperament (Personality test)
TDP........	Target Director Post (RADAR)
TDP........	Technical Data Package
TDP........	Technical Development Plan
TDP........	Teledata Processing
TDP........	Temperature Density Plotter
TDP........	Thermal Death-Point
TDP........	Thermistor Detector Package
TDP........	Total Development Plan
TDP........	Tracking Data Processor
TDP........	Traffic Data Processing
TDP........	Traffic Demand Predictor (Aviation)
TDPA.......	Textile Data Processing Association
TDPB.......	Tactical Display Plotting Board
TDPF.......	Tail Damping Power Factor (Aviation)
TDPFO.....	Temporary Duty Pending Further Orders (Military)
TDR........	Tail Damping Ratio (Aviation)
TDR........	Teardown Deficiency Report
TDR........	Technical Data Report
TDR........	Technical Data Requests
TDR........	Technical Development Requirement
TDR........	Technical Directive Records
TDR........	Technical Documentary Report
TDR........	Temperature Depth Recorder
TDR........	Test Data Recorder
TDR........	Test Data Report
TDR........	The Drama Review (A publication)
TDR........	Time Delay Relay
TDR........	Time Domain Reflectometry
TDR........	Transistorized Digital Readout
TDR........	Trap Designator Register
TD/R.......	Test Disable/Reset
TDRF.......	Target Doppler Reference Frequency
TDRL.......	Temporary Disability Retired List (Military)
TDRS.......	Tracking and Data Relay Satellite System (NASA)
TDRTC.....	Tank Destroyer Replacement Training Center
TDS........	Tactical Data System
TDS........	Tape Data Selector
TDS........	Target Designation System (Navy)
TDS........	Teleflora Delivery Service
TDS........	Telemetry Decommutation System
TDS........	Temperature, Depth, Salinity
TDS........	Temporary Duty Station (Air Force)
TDS........	Ter Die Sumendum (To Be Taken Three Times a Day) (Pharmacy)
TDS........	Thermal Degradation Sample (Apollo)
TDS........	Time Delay Switch
TDS........	Time, Distance, Speed
TDS........	Time-Division Switching
TDS........	Torpedo Destruction System
TDS........	Total Dissolved Solids
TDS........	Track Data Simulator
TDS........	Track Data Storage
TDS........	Tracking and Data System (NASA)
TDS........	(Annual) Training Duty Status (Navy Reserve)
TDS........	Trap Designator Set
TDS........	(US) Treasury Daily Statement
TDS........	Tunnel Destruct System
T & DS.....	Tracking and Data System (NASA)
TDSQB.....	Time-Delay Squib (Navy)
TDT........	Target Designation Transmitter
TDT........	Target Destination Transmitter
TDT........	Test Dwell Time
TDT........	Translation and Docking Trainer
TDT........	Transonic Dynamics Tunnel (Langley Research Center)
TDT........	Tunnel Diode Transducer
TDT/FC.....	Tank Destroyer Tactical and Firing Center
TDTG......	True Date-Time Group
TDTL.......	Tunnel-Diode Transistor Logic
TDU........	Target Detection Unit
TDU........	Tracking Display Unit
TDU........	Trigger Delay Unit
TDU........	Tropendienstunfaehig (Unfit for service in tropics) (German military – World War II)
TDV........	Touchdown Velocity (Aviation)
TDV........	Tumbleweed Diagnostic Vehicle
TDWU......	Transport and Dock Workers' Union (India)
TDX........	Timken-Detroit Axle (NYSE symbol) (Later, TKR)
TDY........	Teledyne, Inc. (NYSE symbol)
TDY........	Temporary Duty
TDZ........	Touchdown Zone (Aviation)
TDZL.......	Touchdown Zone Lights (Aviation)
TE.........	Table of Equipment
TE.........	Tageseinfluesse (Weather factors, a gunnery term) (German military – World War II)
TE.........	Tampa Electric Co. (NYSE symbol)
TE.........	Task Element
TE.........	Technical Engineer
TE.........	Technical Exchange
TE.........	Technician (Communications) (Navy rating)
TE.........	Technological Engineer (A publication)
Te.........	Tellurium (Chemical element)
TE.........	Tenants by the Entirety (Real estate)
TE.........	Terminal Equipment
TE.........	Test Equipment
TE.........	Thalassia Extract
TE.........	Thermal Efficiency
TE.........	Thromboembolic (Medicine)
TE.........	Topographical Engineer
TE.........	Tornisterempfaenger (Pack-type portable receiver) (German military – World War II)
TE.........	Trailing Edge
TE.........	Transequatorial (Scatter)
TE.........	Transport Empty
TE.........	Transport Erector (Air Force)
TE.........	Transverse Electric
TE.........	Trial (and) Error
TE.........	Tuning Eye

TE	Turbine Electric Drive
TE	Twin Engine
T/E	Table of Equipment (Army)
T/E	Tactical Emergency
T/E	Thermoelectric
T & E	Test and Evaluation (Navy)
T & E	Time and Events
T & E	Training and Education
T & E	Travel and Entertainment (Internal Revenue)
TEA	Task Equipment Analysis
TEA	Technical Engineers Association
TEA	Test and Evaluation Agency
TEA	Tetraethylammonium (Organic chemistry)
TEA	Texas Electronics Association
TEA	Textile Export Association of the US
TEA	Tiselius Electrophoresis Apparatus
TEA	Titanic Enthusiasts of America (An organization)
TEA	Trade Expansion Act
TEA	Triethylaluminum (Organic chemistry)
TEAB	Tetraethylammonium Bromide (Organic chemistry)
TEAC	Tetraethylammonium Chloride (Organic chemistry)
TEACC	Trade Expansion Act Advisory Committee
TEAD	Tooele Army Depot
TEAE	Triethylaminoethyl (Organic chemistry)
TEA-ER	Traffic Executives Association, Eastern Railroads
TEAL	Tactics, Equipment and Logistics Conference (between US, Great Britain, Australia, and Canada) (Developed "duck" designations for Mallard and Gander military communications systems)
TEAL	Tasman Empire Airways, Limited
TEAM	Teacher Education and Media (Project)
TEAM	Technique for Evaluation and Analysis of Maintainability
TEAM	Test & Evaluation of Air Mobility
TEAM	The Electronic Association of Missouri
TEAM	The European-Atlantic Movement
TEAM	The Evangelical Alliance Mission
TEAM	Top European Advertising Media
TEAMS	Test Evaluation and Monitoring System
TEAM-UP	Test Evaluation Analysis Management Uniformity Plan (Army)
TEAP	Trajectory Error Analysis Program (NASA)
TEAS	Threat Evaluation and Action Selection (Civilian defense program)
TEAS	Thrust Evaluation and Action Selection (Aerospace)
TEASE	Tracking Errors and Simulation Evaluation (RADAR)
TEB	Tax-Exempt Bond
TEB	Textile Economics Bureau
TEB	Tone Encoded Burst
TEB	Triethylborane (Organic chemistry)
TEBROC	Tehran Book Processing Centre
TEC	Tarif Exterieur Commun (Common External Tariff) (for EEC countries)
TEC	Temporary Engineering Change
TEC	Temporary Extended Compensation (Labor)
TEC	Test Equipment Committee
TEC	Thermal End Cover
TEC	Thermal Expansion Coefficient
TEC	Total Electron Content
TEC	Total Estimated Cost
TEC	Tower En Route Control (Aviation)
TEC	Training Evaluation and Control
TEC	Transearth Coast (Aerospace)
TEC	Tripartite Engineering Committee (Allied German Occupation Forces)
T & EC	Test and Evaluation Command (Army)
TECA	Technical Evaluation and Countermeasures Assignment
TECA	Tower En Route Control Area (Aviation)
TECE	Teleprinter Error Correction Equipment
TECH	Technical (or Technician)
TECH	Technology
TECHAD	Technical Adviser (Navy)
TECHEVAL	Technical Evaluation (Navy)
TECHN	Technical (or Technician)
TECHREP	Technical Representative (Military)
TECHSAT	Technology Satellite
TECHSVS	Technical Services (Army)
TECHTAF	Technical Training Air Force
TECHTRA	Air Technical Training (Navy)
TECM	Test Equipment Commodity Manager
TEC-NACS . . .	Teachers Educational Council - National Association Cosmetology Schools
TECO	Turbine Engine Checkout
TECOM	Test and Evaluation Command (Army)
TECSTAR	Technical Career Structure of the Army
TECU	Thermoelectric Environmental Control Unit
TED	Test Engineering Division (Navy)

TED	Test, Experiment and Development
TED	Thermoelectric Device
TED	Thomas Edmund Dewey (Republican candidate for President, 1948)
TED	Threshold Erythema Dose (Medicine)
TED	Threshold Extension Demodulator
TED	Toledo Edison Company (NYSE symbol)
TED	Trace Element Doping
TED	Training Equipment Development
TED	Transaction Effective Date (Air Force)
TED	Transfer Effective Date (Military)
TED	Turbine Engine Division (Air Force)
TEDA	Theatre Equipment Dealers Association
TEDAR	Telemetered Data Reduction
TEDE	Temperature-Enhanced Displacement Effect
TEDES	Telemetry Data Evaluation System
TEE	Tape Editing Equipment
TEE	Test Equipment Engineering
TEE	Torpedo Experimental Establishment (British)
TEE	Trans-Europe Express (Continental high-speed train)
TEEL	Temporary Expedient Equipment List (Army)
TEEM	Trans-Europ-Express-Marchandises (European express freight train service)
TEF	Tear Efficiency Factor (Textiles)
TEF	Temperance Education Foundation
TEFA	Total Esterified Fatty Acid
TEFC	Totally Enclosed - Fan Cooled
TEFL	Teaching English as a Foreign Language
TEFLON	Tetrafluoroethylene Resin (Du Pont)
TEG	Test Element Group
TEG	Thermoelectric Generator
TEG	Top Edge Gilt (Bibliography)
TEGG	Thermogrip Electric Glue Gun
TEGMA	Terminal Elevator Grain Merchants Association
TEI	Tax Executives Institute
TEI	Temporary Engineering Instruction (Navy)
TEI	Thorne Ecological Institute
TEI	Transearth Injection (Aerospace)
TEI	Transfer on Error Indication
TEI	Trucking Employers, Incorporated
TEIC	Tissue Equivalent Ionization Chamber
TEJ	Transverse Expansion Joint (Technical drawings)
TEJA	Tutmonda Esperantista Jurnalista Asocio (World Association of Esperantist Journalists)
TEJO	Tutmonda Esperantista Junulara Organizo (World Esperantist Youth Organization)
TEK	Tektronix, Inc. (NYSE symbol)
TEK	Test Equipment Kit
TEK	Truppenentgiftungskompanie (Personnel decontamination company) (German military - World War II)
TEKSIF	Turkiye Tekstil ve Orme Sanayii Iscileri Sendikalari Federasyonu (National Federation of Textile Unions) (Turkey)
TEL	TelAutograph Corporation (NYSE symbol) (Delisted)
TEL	Telephone
TEL	Telescope
TEL	Tetraethyllead (Organic chemistry)
TEL	Training Equipment List
TEL	Transporter-Erector-Launcher (Air Force)
TEL	Tucson Engineering Laboratory
TELATS	Tactical Electronic Locating and Targeting System
TELB	Telephone Booth
TELCO	Telephone Company
TELCON	Telephone Conversation
TELECOM	Telecommunications
TELECON	Telephone (or Teletype) Conference (or Conversation)
TELEDAC	Telemetric Data Converter
TELEFLORA . . .	Telegraph Florists Delivery Service
TELEPAK	Telemetering Package
TELERAN	Television, RADAR and Air Navigation
TELESAT	Telecommunications Satellite
TELETYPE	Teletypewriter
TELEX	Automatic Teletypewriter Exchange Service (of Western Union)
TELFAD	Telephone Executive Leader for a Day (New England Telephone Company program for high school students)
TELPAK	Telephone Package
TELSCAR	Transmit Electronically Location Shippers' Car Advice Reports
TELSCOM	Telemetry-Surveillance-Communications
TELSIM	Teletypewriter Simulation
TELSUN	Television Series for United Nations (A foundation formed to produce, and telecast on a commercial basis, dramatized descriptions of UN activities)
TELUS	Telemetric Universal Sensor
TEM	Target Evaluation Maintenance

TEM	Temiskaming & Northern Ontario Railway (AAR code)
TEM	Temple Industries, Inc. (NYSE symbol)
TEM	Transmission Electron Microscope (or Microscopy)
TEM	Transverse Electromagnetic (Wave) (Radio)
TEM	Triethylenemelamine (Organic chemistry)
TEM	Typical Egg Mass
TEMA	Tubular Exchange Manufacturers Association
TEMAC	Temporary Active Duty
TEMACINS. . . .	Temporary Active Duty Under Instruction (Navy)
TEMADD	Temporary Additional Duty (Navy)
TEMADDCON .	Temporary Additional Duty in Connection with (Specified activity) (Navy)
TEMADDINS . .	Temporary Additional Duty Under Instruction (Navy)
TEMARS	Transportation Environmental Measurement and Recording System
TEMDU	Temporary Duty (Navy)
TEMDUINS. . . .	Temporary Duty under Instruction (Navy)
TEMED	N,N,N',N'-Tetramethylethylenediamine
TEMFLY.	Temporary Duty Involving Flying (Navy)
TEMFLYINS . .	Temporary Duty Involving Flying Under Instruction (Navy)
TEMINS	Temporary Duty under Instruction (Navy)
TEMP	Temperature
TEMP	Tempered
TEMP	Template
TEMP	Texas Educational Microwave Project
TEMPO	Tactical (or Technical) Military Planning Operation
TEMPO	Temporary
TEMPO	Time and Effort Measurement through Periodic Observation
TEMPO	Total Evaluation of Management and Production Output
TEMS	Test Equipment Maintenance Set
TEMWAIT	Temporary Duty Awaiting (Specified event) (Navy)
TEN	Total Excretory (or Excreted) Nitrogen
TENES	Teaching English to the Non-English Speaking
TENG	Technical Engineers Association
TENN	Tennessee
TENN	Tennessee R. R. (AAR code)
TENOC	Ten-Year Oceanographic Program (Navy)
TENS	Tension
TENT	Tentative
TEO	Test Equipment Operator
TEO	Transmittal Engineering Order
TEOSS.	Tactical Emitter Operational Support System
TEOTA	The Eyes of the Army
TEP	Tau Epsilon Phi (Fraternity)
TEP	Territory Enterprises Proprietary
TEPA	Tetraethylenepentamine (Organic chemistry)
TEPA	Triethylenephosphoramide (Organic chemistry)
TEPI	Training Equipment Planning Information (Military)
TEPP	Tetraethylpyrophosphate (Biochemistry)
TEPPS	Technique for Establishing Personnel Performance Standards (Navy)
TEPS	National Commission on Teacher Education and Professional Standards
TER	Tau Epsilon Rho (Fraternity)
TER	Training Equipment Requirements Plan
TER	Triple Ejector Rack
TERB	Terrazzo Base
TERC	Technical Education Research Center (Oklahoma State University)
TERCOM.	Terrain Contour Matching (ASD)
TERD	Turbine Electric Reduction Drive
TEREC	Tactical Electronic Reconnaissance (Aircraft)
TERENVSVC. . .	Terrestrial Environmental Services (Army)
TERI	Torpedo Effective Range Indicator
TERLS	Thumba Equatorial Launching Station (Indian rocket station)
TERM	Terminal
TERM	Terminate (Terminated; Termination)
TERP.	Terminal Instrument Procedure (Aviation)
TERPACIS	Trust Territory of the Pacific Islands
TERPS	Terminal Planning System (Military)
TERR.	Territory
TERRA	Terricide-Escape by Rethinking, Research, Action (An organization)
TERRES	**Territorial Residents**
TERS.	Triple Ejector Rack (Navy)
TERT.	Tracking/Erosion Resistance Tester
TES	Telemetry Evaluation Station
TES	Terminal Encounter System
TES	Territorial Experiment Stations Division (of ARS, Department of Agriculture)
TES	Thermal Energy Storage
TES	Thin Elastic Shell
TES	Tidal Electric Station
TES	Tungsten Electron Snatcher
TESA	Television and Electronics Service Association
TESL	Teaching English as a Second Language
TESMA	Theatre Equipment and Supply Manufacturers Association
TESOL	Teachers of English to Speakers of Other Languages
TEST.	Teen-Age Employment Skills Training, Inc.
TEST	Thesaurus of Engineering and Scientific Terms
TEST.	Transamerica Electronic Scoring Technique (Credit risk evaluation)
TESTRAN.	Test Translator (Data processing)
TESTS	Technical-Engineering-Science Training for Secretaries
TET.	Teacher of Electrotherapy
TET	Test Equipment Team (or Tester)
TET	Test Equipment Tool
TET	Tetrachloride
TET	Texas Eastern Transmission Corporation (NYSE symbol)
TET	Thermionic Emission Technique
TET	Titanium Elevon Track
TET	Transistor Evaluation Test
TET	Troop Evaluation Tests (Army)
TETA	Test Equipment Technical Adviser
TETA	Travelers Emergency Transportation Association (Sought to pool transportation of salesmen traveling similar routes) (World War II)
TETA	Triethyltetramine
TETRA	Terminal Tracking Telescope
TETRAC	Tension Truss Antenna Concept
TEU	Telemetry Equipment Unit
TEU	Test of Economic Understanding
TEU	Transducer Excitation Unit
TEUC	Temporary Extended Unemployment Compensation (Labor)
TEUN	Trust for Education on the United Nations
TeV	Teraelectron Volts
TEV	Thermoelectric Voltage
TEV	Today's English Version (of the Bible)
TeV	Trillion Electron Volts
TEVROC	Tailored Exhaust Velocity Rocket
TEW	Tactical Early Warning
TEW	Transverse Electric Wave
TEWDS	Tactical Electronic Warfare Deception System
TEWGp	Tactical Electronic Warfare Group (Air Force)
TEWS	Tactical Effectiveness of Weapons Systems (Army)
TEWS	Tactical Electronic Warfare Support
TEX	Automatic Teleprinter Exchange Service (of Western Union)
TEX	Tactical Fighter, Experimental (Airplane)
TEX	Texas
TEX	Tumbling Explorer
TEXACO	Texas Company
TEXDEALAM .	Textile Dealers Association of America
TEX MEX	Texas Mexican Railway Company
TEXTIR	Text Indexing and Retrieval (Data processing)
TF	Tabulating Form
TF	Tactical Fighter
TF	Tactile Fremitus
TF	Tallulah Falls Railway Company (AAR code)
TF	Task Force
TF	Tax Foundation
TF	Teaching Fellow
TF	Technological Forecasting
TF	Temperature Factor
TF	Temporary Fix
TF	Terrain-Following (Helicopter)
TF	Territorial Force
TF	Test Flight (Air Force)
TF	Thin Film
TF	Tile Floor (Technical drawings)
TF	Till Forbidden (i.e., repeat until forbidden to do so) (Advertising)
TF	Time Frame
TF	To Fill
TF	To Follow
TF	Tolstoy Foundation
TF	Torpedo Fighter Aircraft (Navy)
TF	Total Forfeiture (of all pay and allowances) (Army)
TF	Tracking Filter
TF	Trainer Fighter
TF	Training Film (Military)
TF	Transfer Factor
TF	Transfer Function
TF	Transferase Factor (Protein biosynthesis)
TF	Transmitter Frequency
TF	Trichlorethylene Finishing
TF	Tropical Fresh Water (Vessel load line mark)
TF	Trust Fund
TF	Tuberculin Filtrate (Medicine)
TF	Twentieth Century-Fox Film Corporation (NYSE symbol)
T/F	Transfer of Function (Military)
TFA	Textile Fabrics Association

TFA	Tie Fabrics Association
TFA	Total Fatty Acids
TFA	Transfer Function Analyzer
TFA	Transistor Feedback Amplifier
TFA	Transverse Film Attenuator
TFA	Trifluoroacetic Acid
TFA	Tube Failure Alarm
TFA	Two-Way Finite Automata
TFA	US Trout Farmers Association
TFAA	Track and Field Athletes of America
TFAA	Trifluoroacetic Anhydride
TFB	Taft Broadcasting Company (NYSE symbol)
TFB	Thin-Film Barrier
TFC	Tank Fire Control
TFC	Tantalum Foil Capacitor
TFC	The Felician College (Illinois)
TFC	Thin-Film Capacitor
TFC	Thin-Film Cell
TFC	Thin-Film Circuit
TFC	Time of First Call (Navy)
TFC	Toccoa Falls College (Georgia)
TFC	Total Fixed Cost
TFC	Traffic Control
TFC	Transfer Function Computer
TFC	Transfer Function, Cumulative
TFC	Transistorized Frequency Converter
TFC	Trigonometric Function Computer
TFC	Trustees for Conservation
TFC	Turret Fire Control
TFCA	Thin-Film Cell Array
TFCC	Tank Fire Combat Computer
TFCP	Technical Facility Change Procedure
TFCS	Tank Fire Control System
TFCS	Torpedo Fire Control System
TFCSD	Total Federal Commissioned Service Date
TFD	Terrain Following Display
TFD	Thin-Film Distillation
TFD	Thrifty Drug Stores Co., Inc. (NYSE symbol)
TFD	Total Frequency Deviation
TFD	Tube Flood and Drain
TFDA	Textile Fabric Distributors Association (Later, TDA)
TFDM	Tactical Fighter Dispensing Munition
TFDRL	Trustees of the Franklin Delano Roosevelt Library
TFDS	Tactical Ferret Display System
TFDS	Tactical Flag Data System
TFE	Terminal Flight Evaluation
TFE	Terrain-Following Evaluator
TFE	Tetrafluoroethylene (Organic chemistry)
TFE	Thermionic Fuel Element
TFE	Trainer Flight Equipment
TFE	Turbo-Fan Engine
TFF	Terrain-Following Flight
TFF	Total Feedwater Flow
TFF	Transverse Flow Fan
TFF	Tuning Fork Filter
TFF	Turbine Flow Function
TFFE	Terrain-Following Flight Evaluator
TFG	Tentative Force Guidance
TFG	Textile Foremen's Guild
TFG	Transmit Format Generator
TFGP	Tactical Fighter Group (Air Force)
TFH	Thick-Film Hybrid
TFH	Transfer Function Hazard
TFI	Table Fashion Institute
TFI	Tax Foundation, Incorporated
TFI	Textile Foundation, Incorporated
TFI	Theatre for Ideas (An organization)
TFI	Time from Ignition (Apollo) (NASA)
TFIB	Thin-Film Interface Barrier
TFL	Taiwan Federation of Labor (Nationalist China)
TFL	Tanganyika Federation of Labor
TFL	Time to Failure Location
TFL	Transient Fault Locator
TFM	Terminal Forecast Manual
TFM	Thin-Film Microelectronics
TFM	Transmitter Frequency Multiplier
TFM	Trifluoromethylnitrophenol
TFM	Two-Fluid Manometer
TFMA	Technical Facility Modification Authorization
TFN	Total Fecal Nitrogen
TFNS	Territorial Force Nursing Service

TFO	Tonto Forest Observatory
TFO	Transactions for Others
TFO	Tuning Fork Oscillator
TFOL	Tape File Octal Load
TFP	Teachers Freedom Party
TFP	Trees for People (An organization)
TFPC	Thin-Film Photovoltaic Cell
TFPCA	Thin-Film Photovoltaic Cell Array
TFPL	Texas Forest Products Laboratory
TFR	Television Film Recorder
TFR	Terrain-Following RADAR
TFR	Thin-Film Resist
TFR	Total Final Reports (Air Force)
TFR	Transfer Function Response
TFR	Trouble and Failure Report
TFR	Tubular Flow Reactor
T/FR	Top of Frame
TFS	Tactical Fighter Squadron (Air Force)
TFS	Terrain-Following System
TFS	Tin-Free Steel
TFS	Transverse Feed System
TFSC	Turbine Flow Sensor
TFSC	(From the Latin for) Franciscan Tertiaries of the Holy Cross
TFT	Tabular Firing Tables (Military)
TFT	Thermal Fatigue Test
TFT	Thin-Film Field-Effect Transistor
TFT	Thin-Film Technique (or Technology)
TFT	Thin-Film Transducer
TFT	Thin-Film Transistor
TFT	Threshold Failure Temperatures
TFU	Telecommunications Flying Unit (British)
TFV	Twin Falls Victory (Tracking ship) (NASA)
TFW	Tactical Fighter Wing (Air Force)
TFW	Tethered Free-Floating Worker
TFW	Thermoplastic Fan Wheel
TFW	Tropical Fresh Water
TFW	Turbulent Far Wake
TFWC	Tactical Fighter Weapons Center
TFWG	Tactical Fighter Wing (Air Force)
TFX	Tactical Fighter, Experimental (Air Force)
TFX-N	Tactical Fighter Experimental - Navy
TFX-O	Tactical Fighter Experimental - Offensive
TFX-R	Tactical Fighter Experimental - Reconnaissance
TG	Tail Gear
TG	Tape Gauge
TG	Task Group
TG	Technology Gap
TG	Telegram
TG	Telegraph
TG	Temporary Gentleman (British slang term for officer for duration of the war) (World War I)
TG	Terminal Guidance
TG	Texas Gulf, Inc. (NYSE symbol) (Wall Street slang name: "Tough Guy")
TG	Timing Gate
TG	Tollgate (Maps and charts)
TG	Torpedo Group
TG	Tracking and Guidance
TG	Traffic Guidance (Aviation)
TG	Tropical Gulf (American air mass)
TG	Type Genus
T-G	Transformational-Generative (Linguistics)
T/G	Tracking and Guidance
T & G	Tongue and Groove (Lumber)
TGA	Thermogravimetric (or Thermogravimetry) Analysis
TGA	Toilet Goods Association (Later, CTFA)
TGATS	Theatre Guild-American Theatre Society
TGB	Tongued, Grooved, and Beaded
TGBL	Through Government Bill of Lading
TGC	Theater Ground Commander (Military)
TGC	Thermocouple Gauge Control
TGC	Throttle Governor Control
TGC	Tomato Genetics Cooperative
TGCA	Texas Gun Collectors Association
TGCA	Transportable Group Control Approach
TGCS	Transportable Ground Communications Station
TGE	Transmissible Gastro-Enteritis
TGE	Tryptone Glucose Extract (Milk agar)
TGE	Tuscon Gas & Electric Co. (NYSE symbol)
TGF	Treasury Guard Force
TGFA	Triglyceride Fatty Acid (Biochemistry)
TGFB	Triglycine Fluoberyllate

TGG . . . . Temporary Geographic Grid
TGI . . . . Target Intensifier
TGIC . . . . . . Tobacco Growers' Information Committee
TGIF . . . . . . Thank God It's Friday (Meaning work-week is nearly over)
TGIF-OTMWDUM . . Thank God It's Friday - Only Two More Work Days Until
           Monday (Pentagon saying)
TGL . . . . Thin Glass Laminate
TGL . . . . Toggle
TGL . . . . Touch and Go Landing (Aviation)
TGL . . . . Triangular Guide Line
TGLC . . . . . . Total Gate Leakage Current
TGLVQ . . . . . Terminal Guidance for Lunar Vehicles (Aerospace)
TGM . . . . . . Turbine Generator Management
TGO. . . . . . . Time to Go (Apollo) (NASA)
TGO . . . . . . Tuned Grid Oscillator
TGP . . . . . . Tone Generator Panel
TGPWU. . . . . Transport, General and Port Workers' Union (Aden)
TGRLSS . . . . . Two-Gas Regenerative Lift Support System
TGS . . . . Target Generating System
TGS . . . . Telemetry Ground Station
TGS . . . . Terminal Guidance Sensor (or System)
TGS . . . . Tide Gage System
TGS . . . . Transportable Ground Station
TGS . . . . Triglycine Sulfate
TGSE . . . . . . Tactical (or Test) Ground Support Equipment
TGSS . . . . . . Terminal Guidance Sensor System
TGT . . . . Target
TGT . . . . Tenneco, Inc. (Formerly, Tennessee Gas Transmission Co.) (NYSE symbol)
TGT . . . . Thermocouple Gauge Tube
TGT . . . . Thromboplastin Generation (Test)
TGT . . . . True Ground Track
TGTP . . . . . . Tuned Grid - Tuned Plate
TGV . . . . Two Gentlemen of Verona (by Shakespeare)
TGWU . . . . . Transport and General Workers' Union (British)
TGX . . . . . . Tube-Generated X-Ray
TH . . . . Tally Ho (Air Force)
TH . . . . Technische Hochschule
TH . . . . Territory of Hawaii (to 1959)
Th . . . . Thorium (Chemical element)
TH . . . . Thursday
TH . . . . Thyroid Hormone (Thyroxine) (Endocrinology)
TH . . . . Today's Health (A publication)
TH . . . . True Heading
TH . . . . Two Hands
T & H . . . . . . Test and Handling (Equipment)
THA . . . . . . Taft-Hartley Act
THAI . . . . . . Thai Airways Company, Ltd.
THAM . . . . . Tris-Hydroxy Methyl Aminomethane
THART . . . . . Theodore Army Terminal
THAT . . . . . . Twenty-four Hour Automatic Teller (Trademark for self-service banking
           display panel)
Th B . . . . Bachelor of Theology
THB . . . . . . Third Harmonic Band
THB . . . . . . Toronto, Hamilton & Buffalo Railway Company (AAR code) (Nickname:
           To Hell and Back)
Th C . . . . Candidate of Theology
THC . . . . . . Target Homing Correlator
THC . . . . . . Tetrahydrocannabinol (Active principle of marijuana)
THC . . . . . . Tube Humidity Control
THCC . . . . . . Tube Heating and Cooling Control
THCF . . . . . . Thompson-Huston Company of France
Th D . . . . Doctor of Theology
THD . . . . . . Thread
THD . . . . . . Total Harmonic Distortion
THD . . . . . . Total Harmonic Distribution (Music)
THD . . . . . . Tube Heat Dissipator
THDI . . . . . . Thread Die
THE . . . . . . Tape Handling Equipment
THECC . . . . . Truck and Heavy Equipment Claims Council
THEED . . . . . Tetrahydroxyethylethylenediamine (Organic chemistry)
THEN . . . . . . Those Hags Encourage Neuterism (Organization opposed to NOW
           [National Organization for Women])
Theom L . . . . . Theomonistic Licensee
THEOR . . . . . Theoretical
THERM . . . . . Thermometer
THERMA . . . . . Transfer of Heat Reduced Magnetically
THERMO . . . . . Thermal and Hydrodynamic Experiment Research Module in Orbit
THERMO . . . . . Thermostat
THERMODYN . . Thermodynamics
THERP . . . . . . Technique for Human Error Rate Prediction
THF . . . . . . Tetrahydrofolic (Acid)

THF . . . . Tetrahydrofuran
THFA . . . . . . Three-Conductor, Heat and Flame Resistant, Armor Cable
THFR . . . . . . Three-Conductor, Heat and Flame Resistant, Radio Cable
THGA . . . . . . Thread Gage
THHP . . . . . . Tetrahydrohomopteroic (Acid)
THI . . . . Temperature Humidity Index
THI . . . . Theodor Herzl Institute
THI . . . . Thiokol Chemical Corporation (NYSE symbol)
THI . . . . Time Handed In (Navy)
THI . . . . Travelers Health Institute
THIEF . . . . . . The Human Initiated Equipment Failures
THIR . . . . . . Temperature-Humidity Infrared Radiometer
THIS. . . . . . . The Hospitality and Information Service (For diplomatic residents and
           families in Washington, DC)
THK . . . . Thick
Th L . . . . Licentiate in Theology
THL . . . . Thermoluminescence (Also TL)
THL . . . . Tuned Hybrid Lattice
THLS . . . . . . Turret Head Limit Switch
THM. . . . . . . John R. Thompson Company (NYSE symbol) (Delisted)
Th M . . . . Master of Theology
THM. . . . . . . Traveling Heater Method
THM . . . . . . Trotting Horse Museum
THOMIS . . . . . Total Hospital and Medical Information System
THOR . . . . . . Tape-Handling Option Routines
THOR . . . . . . Transistorized High-Speed Operations Recorder
THORAD . . . . . Thor Agena D (Rocket)
THOU. . . . . . . Thousand
THP . . . . Tetrahydropapaveroline
THP . . . . Through Hole Probe
THP . . . . Thrust Horsepower (Jet engines)
THPFB . . . . . . Treated Hard-Pressed Fiberboard (Technical drawings)
THQ. . . . . . . Theater Headquarters (Military)
THQ. . . . . . . Troop Headquarters
THR . . . . Threonine (Amino acid)
THR . . . . Thrust
THRB . . . . . . Theodore Roosevelt Birthplace National Historic Site
THRM . . . . . . Thermal
THRO . . . . . . Theodore Roosevelt National Memorial Park
THROT . . . . . Throttle
THRU . . . . . . Through
THS . . . . Target Homing System
THS . . . . Textile History Society
THS . . . . Theatre Historical Society
THS . . . . Thermostat Switch
THS . . . . Three-Stage Least Squares (Econometrics)
THS . . . . Tourist Hospitality Service (British)
THS . . . . Tube Heating Supply
THSA . . . . . . Traveling Hat Salesmen's Association
THT . . . . Teacher of Hydrotherapy (British)
THT . . . . Tetrahydrothiophene
THT . . . . Total Homing Time
THTA . . . . . . Thread Tap
THTO . . . . . . Threading Tool
THTR . . . . . . Theater
THU . . . . Thursday
THUD . . . . . . Thorium, Uranium, Deuterium
THUDD . . . . . Thermal Uplink Data Display (Data processing)
THUMS . . . . . Texaco, Humble, Union, Mobil, and Shell (Petroleum companies)
THURS . . . . . Thursday
THW. . . . . . . Torsion Head Wattmeter
THY . . . . Turk Haval Yollari AO (Turkish Airlines, Inc.)
THz . . . . Terahertz
TI . . . . Tape Inverter
TI . . . . Target Identification
TI . . . . Target Indicator
TI . . . . Teardown Inspection
TI . . . . Technical Inspection
TI . . . . Technical Instruction
TI . . . . Technical Intelligence
TI . . . . Temperature Indicator
TI . . . . Terminal Island (San Pedro) (Navy base)
TI . . . . Termination Instruction
TI . . . . Test Instrumentation
TI . . . . Texas Instruments, Inc.
TI . . . . Thread Institute
TI. . . . . TI Corporation of California (NYSE symbol)
TI . . . . Time Index
Ti . . . . Titanium (Chemical element)
TI . . . . Tobacco Institute
TI . . . . Total Immersion (Language study)

TI	Track Identity
TI	Track Imitation
TI	Track Initiator
TI	Traffic Identification
TI	Training Instructor
TI	Transmission Identification
TI	Treasure Island (San Francisco Bay) (Navy base)
TI	Tricuspid Insufficiency (Medicine)
TI	Troop Information
TI	Tungsten Institute
T/I	Torque/Inertia
TIA	Tactical Identification and Acquisition (Navy)
TIA	Target Identification and Acquisition
TIA	Tax Institute of America
TIA	Trans-International Airlines
TIA	Transportation Intelligence Agency
TIA	Trends, Indicators and Analyses (on the Southeast Asia war) (Classified Air Force document)
TIA	Tricot Institute of America
TIA	Trouser Institute of America (Absorbed by NOSA)
TIAA	Teachers Insurance and Annuity Association
TIAA	Timber Importers Association of America
TIAC	Technical Information Advisory Committee (AEC)
TIAC	Texas Instruments Automatic Computer
TIARA	Target Illumination & Recovery Aid
TIAS	Target Identification and Acquisition System
TIAS	Treaties and Other International Acts Series (State Department)
TIB	Technical Information Bulletin
TIB	Technical Information Bureau (British)
TIB	This I Believe Test (Education)
TIBA	Triiodobenzoic Acid
TIBC	Total Iron-Binding Capacity
TIBTPG	Texas Instruments Bourdon Tube Pressure Gauge
TIC	Tape Identification Card
TIC	Tape Intersystem Connection (Data processing)
TIC	Target Intercept Computer
TIC	Technical Information Capability
TIC	Technical Information Center (AEC)
TIC	Technical Institute Council
TIC	Technical Instructors Course (Air Force)
TIC	Technical Intelligence Center (Navy)
TIC	Technicon Integrator/Calculator
TIC	Time Interval Counter
TIC	Transducer Information Center
TIC	Travelers Corporation (NYSE symbol)
TIC	Tuned Integrated Circuit
TICA	Technical Information Center Administration (Conference)
TICA	Timpanogos Cave National Monument
TICCIT	Time-Shared Interactive Computer-Controlled Information Television (System)
TICE	Time Integral Cost Effectiveness
TICLER	Technical Input Check List/Evaluation Report
TICP	Theater Inventory Control Point (Military)
TICT	Tactical Intelligence Collection Team (Military)
TICTAC	Time Compression Tactical Communications
TICUS	Tidal Current System
TICWAN	Trailerable Intracoastal Waterway Aids to Navigation (Boat)
TID	Tactical (or Target) Information Display
TID	Technical Information Division (of Library of Congress)
TID	Ter in Die (Three Times Daily) (Pharmacology)
TID	Traveling Ionospheric Disturbance
TID	Troop Information Division
TIDAR	Texas Instruments Digital Analog Readout
TIDAR	Time Delay Array RADAR
TIDDAC	Time in Deadband Digital Attitude Control
TIDE	Tactical International Data Exchange
TIDOS	Table and Item Documentation System
TIDY	Track Identity
TIE	Technical Information Exchange (National Bureau of Standards)
TIE	Technical Integration and Evaluation (Apollo) (NASA)
TIE	Temporary/Intermittent Employee
TIE	Texas Information Exchange
TIE	The Institute of Ecology
TI & E	Troop Information and Education
TIED	Troop Information and Education Division
TIES	Transmission and Information Exchange System
TIF	Technical Information File
TIF	Telephone Influence Factor
TIF	The International Foundation
TIF	Thin Iron Film
TIF	True Involute Form
TIF	Tumor-Inducing Factor (Medicine)
TIFO	Technical Inspection Field Office, Office of the Inspector General
TIFS	Total In-Flight Simulation (or Simulator) (Air Force)
TIG	Teletype Input Generator
TIG	The Inspector General (Army)
TIG	Time in Grade
TIG	Tungsten-Inert-Gas (Underwater welding)
TIGR	Transmission Integrated Rotor
TIGR	Turbine-Integrated Geared Rotor
TIGRIS	Televised Images of Gaseous Region in Interplanetary Space
TIH	Their Imperial Highnesses
TIH	Tie Line
TIH	Total Installed Horsepower
TIHP	Total Installed Horsepower
TII	Talos Integration Investigation
TII	Texas Instruments, Incorporated
TII	Thomas Industries, Incorporated (NYSE symbol)
TIIAL	The International Institute of Applied Linguistics
TIIC	Technical Industrial Intelligence Committee (US Military Government, Germany)
TIID	Technical Industrial Intelligence Division (Allied Board set up to send experts into Germany to ferret out Germany's war-developed scientific secrets) (Post-World War II)
TIIF	Tactical Image Interpretation Facility
TIK	Target Indicator Kit
TIK	Transcontinental Investing Corp. (NYSE symbol)
TIL	Technical Information and Library Service
TIL	Temperature Indicating Label
TILL	Total Initial Lamp Lumens
TILRA	Tribal Indian Land Rights Association
TILS	Tactical Instrument Landing System
TIM	Tangential Inlet Manifold
TIM	TEFLON Insulation Material
TIM	Temperature Indicator Monitor
TIM	Test Instrumented Missile (Army)
TIM	Thailand Independence Movement (Communist-directed activity outside Thailand) (Merged with TPF)
TIM	Time Interval Measurement
TIM	Time Interval Meter
TIM	Time Meter
TIM	Topic Indexing Matrix
TIM	Transistor Information Microfile
TIMA	Technical Illustrators Management Association
TIMATION	Time Location System (Navy)
TIMI	Technical Information Maintenance Instruction
TIMIG	Time in Grade (Military)
TIMINT	Time Interval (Military)
TIMM	Thermionic Integrated Micro Module
TIMMS	Total Integrated Manpower Management System (Navy)
TIMP	Texas Instructional Media Project (Education)
TIMS	The Institute of Management Sciences
TIN	Temperature Independent (Ferrite computer memory core)
TIN	Temporary Instruction Notice
TIN	Transaction Identification Number
TINOP	Transponder Inoperative (Aviation)
TINR	Target Identification Navigation RADAR
TINS	Thermal Imaging Night Sight
TINS	Trans-Inertial Navigation System
TINSY	Treasure Island Naval Shipyard
TIO	Target Indication Officer (Navy)
TIO	Technical Information Office
TIO	Television Information Office
TIO	Transistorized Image Orthicon
TIO	Troop Information Officer
TIOH	The Institute of Heraldry (Army)
TIP	Target Impact Point
TIP	Target Input Panel
TIP	Task Initiation and Prediction
TIP	Technical Information Panel (AEC)
TIP	Technical Information Pilot (Announcement bulletin formerly published by Navy Research Section, Library of Congress)
TIP	Technical Information Pool
TIP	Technical Information Program
TIP	Technical Information Project (MIT)
TIP	Techniques in Product Selection (National Association of Manufacturers)
TIP	Teletype Input Processing
TIP	Tilt Isolation Platform
TIP	To Insure Promptness
TIP	Toxicology Information Program (National Library of Medicine)
TIP	Track Initiation and Prediction (RADAR)
TIP	Tracking Impact Prediction (of satellites)

TIP.........	Translation Inhibitory Protein
TIP.........	Transponder Interrogator Processor
TIP.........	Transport Individuel Publique (French auto cooperative) (Also known as PROCOTIP)
TIP	Troop Information Program
TIP	Tumor Inhibitory Principle (A cancer-inhibiting substance)
TIP.........	Turn In a Pusher (Organization combating drug traffic)
TIPACS......	Texas Instruments Planning and Control System
TIPC.......	Texas Instruments Pressure Controller
TIPE........	Transponder, Interrogator, Pinger and Echo Sounder
TIPI	Tactical Information Processing and Interpretation (Military)
TIPIC	Turkish Investment Promotion and Information Center (Subdivision of the Union of Chambers of Commerce, Industry, and Commodity Exchanges of Turkey)
TIPL.......	Teach Information Processing Language
TIPR.......	Tactics Inspection Procedures Report
TIPRO......	Texas Independent Producers and Royalty Owners Association
TIPS.......	Teaching Information Processing System
TIPS.......	Technical Information Processing System
TIPS.......	Technical Information and Product Service
TIPS.......	Techniques in Product Selection (National Association of Manufacturers)
TIPS.......	Telemetry Impact Prediction System (Air Force)
TIPS.......	Terminal Interface Processors (Data processing) (DOD)
TIPS.......	Test Information Processing System (Air Force)
TIPS.......	Total Information Processing System (Veterans Administration)
TIPS.......	Total Integrated Pneumatic System
TIPS.......	Transistorized Inverter Power Supply
TIPSY......	Task Input Parameter Synthesizer
TIPTOP.....	Tape Input/Tape Output (Data processing)
TIP TOP	Tax Information Plan and Total Owed Purchase Accounting
TIQRC	Toxicology Information Query Response Center (National Library of Medicine)
TIR	Target Illuminating RADAR (Air Force)
TIR	Target Indication Room (Navy)
TIR	Technical Information Release
TIR........	Technical Intelligence Report
TIR	Time in Range
TIR	Total Indicated Runout
TIR	Total Indicator Reading
TIR	Total Internal Reflecting
TIR........	Transaction Item Report (Navy)
TIRB.......	Transportation Insurance Rating Bureau
TIRC	Tobacco Industry Research Committee (Later, Council for Tobacco Research, USA)
TIREC......	TIROS (Television Infrared Observation Satellite) Ice Reconnaissance
TIRH.......	Theoretical Indoor Relative Humidity
TIRIS	Traversing Infrared Inspection System (Aviation)
TIRKS	Trunks Integrated Records Keeping System (Bell Laboratories)
TIROS	Television Infrared Observation Satellite (NASA)
TIRP	Total Internal Reflection Prism
TIRR.......	Tactics Inspection Results Report
TIS	Target Information Sheet (Air Force)
TIS	Target Information System
TIS	Technical Information Section (Navy)
TIS	Technical Information Service (AEC)
TIS	Temperature Indicating Switch
TIS	Test Instrumentation System
TIS	The Infantry School (Army)
TIS	Theater Intelligence Section (Navy)
TIS	Thermal Insulation System
TIS........	Tishman Realty & Construction Company, Inc. (NYSE symbol)
TIS........	Total Information Service (of Saturday Review)
TIS........	Total Information System (Data processing)
TISA	Technical Information Support Activities (Army)
TISC	Tire Industry Safety Council
TISEO......	Target Identification System, Electro-Optical (Air Force)
TISP	Technical Information Support Personnel (Department of Labor)
TISTHR	Tool Inspection Small Tools Historical Record
TIT	Thermo-Isolation Technique
TIT........	Total Insertion Time
TIT........	Treponema Immobilization Test (Medicine)
TIT	Turbine Inlet Temperature
TITE.......	Tijuana & Tecate Railway Company (AAR code)
TITH.......	Triiodothyronine (Endocrinology)
TIU	Tape Identification Unit
TIU	Target Indication Unit (Navy)
TIV	Time in View
TIW	TEFLON-Insulated Wire
TJ	Talk Jockey (Radio)
TJ	Tomato Juice
TJ	Triceps Jerk
TJ	Turbojet
TJA	Trial Judge Advocate (Army)
TJADC	Theater Joint Air Defense Command (Military)
TJAG	The Judge Advocate General (Army)
TJAGC	The Judge Advocate General's Corps (Army)
TJAGSA	The Judge Advocate General's School, US Army
TJB	Tijuana Brass (Defunct musical group)
TJB	Trench Junction Box
TJC	Temple Junior College (Texas)
TJC	Thornton Junior College (Illinois)
TJC	Trajectory Chart
TJC	Tyler Junior College (Texas)
TJD	Trajectory Diagram
TJE	Turbojet Engine
TJF	Time-to-Jitter Flag
TJI........	Tex Johnston, Incorporated
TJM	Tower Jettison Motor
TJOC	Theater Joint Operations Center (Military)
TJP	Turbo-Jet Propulsion
TJPOI.......	Twisted Jute Packing and Oakum Institute
TK	Tank
TK	Truck
TK	Tuskegee R.R. (AAR code)
TKA	Toy Knights of America
TKD	Tokodynamometer
TKD	Top Kit Drawing
TKE	Tau Kappa Epsilon (Fraternity) (Pronounced, "Teke")
TKG........	Tanking
TKG........	Tokodynagraph
TKKTFSLB	"The Kandy-Kolored Tangerine-Flake Streamline Baby" (Title of book by Tom Wolfe)
TKO........	Technical Knock Out (Boxing)
TKO........	Technische Kontrollorganisation
TKP	Theta Kappa Phi (Fraternity)
TKP	Turkiye Komunist Partisi
TKR	Tanker
TKR	Timken Company (NYSE symbol) (Formerly, TDX)
TKTS.......	Thermodynamic Kelvin Temperature Scale
TKW	Thermal Kilowatts
TL	Talk-Listen
TL	Target Language
TL	Team Leader
TL	Technical Letter
TL	Technical Library
TL	Terminal Limen
TL	Test Laboratory
TL	Test Link
TL	Texas League (Baseball)
Tl	Thallium (Chemical element)
TL	Thermoluminescence (Also THL)
TL	Thrust Line
TL	Thymic Lymphoma (Medicine)
TL	Tie Line
TL	Time, Inc. (NYSE symbol)
TL	Time Lengths
TL	Time Limit
TL	Title List
TL	Total Length
TL	Total Load (Engineering)
TL	Total Loss
TL	Trade-Last
TL	Transaction Listing
TL	Transmission Line (or Level)
TL	Transmittal Letter
TL	Transport Loaded
TL	Triple Lindy (Dance step)
TL	Truckload
T/L	Tactical Landing
T/L	Time Loan (Banking)
T/L	Training Literature
T & L	Thrift and Loans (Industrial loan company)
TLA	Temporary Lodging Allowance (Military)
TLA	Textile Labor Association (India)
TLA	Theatre Library Association
TLA	Time Line Analysis
TLa	Transition Layer
TLA	Transmission Line Assembly (or Adapter)
TLB	Temporary Lighted Buoy (Maps and charts)
TLB	Time-Life Books
TLC	Talcott National Corp. (NYSE symbol)
TLC	Tangent Latitude Computer

TLC . . . . Tender Loving Care
TLC . . . . Texas Lutheran College
TLC . . . . Thin Layer Chromatography (Analytical chemistry)
TLC . . . . Time Line Controller
TLC . . . . Total Lung Capacity (Physiology)
TLC . . . . Translunar Coast (Aerospace)
TLCA . . . . Tangent Latitude Computer Amplifier
TLCPC . . . . . . Trunk Line-Central Passenger Committee
TLD . . . . Technical Logistics Data (Army)
TLD . . . . Thermoluminescent Device (or Dosimetry)
TLDC . . . . Taiwan Land Development Corporation
TLDI . . . . Technical Logistics Data and Information (Army)
TLDIC . . . . Technical Logistics Data and Information
TLE . . . . Temperature-Limited Emission
TLE . . . . Thin-Layer Electrophoresis (Analytical chemistry)
TLE . . . . Thin Leading Edge
TLE . . . . Total Lipid Extract (Biochemistry)
TLE . . . . Toward Liberal Education (In book title)
TLE . . . . Tower Lighting Equipment
TLF . . . . Terminal Launch Facility
TLG . . . . Tail Landing Gear
TLG . . . . Telegraph
TLG . . . . Thin-Layer Gel (Filtration) (Biochemical analysis)
TLI . . . . Time-Life International
TLI . . . . Translunar Injection (Aerospace)
TLL . . . . Television LASER Link
TLM . . . . Technical Liaison Memo
TLM . . . . Telemeter (or Telemetry)
TLMG . . . . Telemetering
TLMI . . . . Tag and Label Manufacturers Institute
TLN . . . . Talon, Inc. (NYSE symbol) (Wall Street slang name: "Zipper") (Delisted)
TLN . . . . Torque Limiting Nut
TLO . . . . Technical Liaison Office (Military)
TLO . . . . Total Loss Only
TLO . . . . Training Liaison Officer (Ministry of Agriculture, Fisheries, and Food) (British)
TLP . . . . Tabular List of Parts
TLP . . . . Tapered Link Pin
TLP . . . . Torpedo Landplane (Navy)
TLP . . . . Total Loss of Pay (Court-martial sentence) (Military)
TLP . . . . Transient Lunar Phenomena
TLP . . . . Trouble Location Problem
TLPR . . . . Terrestrial Low-Power Reactor (AEC)
TLR . . . . Tape Loop Recorder
TLR . . . . Toll Line Release
TLR . . . . Tool Liaison Request
TLR . . . . Trailer
TLR . . . . Triangulation-Listening-Ranging (SONAR)
TLRP . . . . Track Last Reference Position
TLS . . . . Tactical Landing System
TLS . . . . Target Location System
TLS . . . . Telemetry Listing Submodule
TLS . . . . Testing the Limits for Sex (Psychology)
TLS . . . . Time Limited Signal
TLS . . . . Time Line Sheet
TLS . . . . (The) Times Literary Supplement (London)
TLS . . . . Total Logic Solution
TLSD . . . . Torque Limiting Screw Driver
TLSG . . . . Turret Lathe Stop Gauge
TLSP . . . . Transponder Location by Surface Positioning (RADAR)
TLSS . . . . Technical Library Services Section
TLT . . . . Transportable Link Terminal (AMC)
TLTK . . . . Tool Truck
TLTP . . . . Too Long to Print (Strip marking) (Aviation)
TLTR . . . . Translator
TLTS . . . . Tracking Loop Test Set
TLU . . . . Table Look Up (Data processing)
TLU . . . . Threshold Logic Unit
TLU . . . . Time of Last Update
TLV . . . . Target Launch Vehicle (NASA)
TLV . . . . Threshold Limit Value
TLV . . . . Time Like Vector
TLv . . . . Transition Level
TLW . . . . Test Load Wire
TLX . . . . Trans-Lux Corporation (American Stock Exchange symbol)
TLZ . . . . Titanium-Lead-Zinc
TLZ . . . . Transfer on Less Than Zero
TM . . . . Tactical Missile (Air Force)
TM . . . . Tactical Monitor
TM . . . . Talking Machine
TM . . . . Tangent Mechanism

TM . . . . Technical Manual (Military)
TM . . . . Technical Materiel Corporation (NYSE symbol) (Delisted)
TM . . . . Technical Memorandum
TM . . . . Technical Minutes
TM . . . . Technical Monograph
TM . . . . Telemetry
TM . . . . Temperature, Mean
TM . . . . Temperature Meter
TM . . . . Test Manual
TM . . . . Texas Mexican Railway Company (AAR code)
TM . . . . The Maccabees
TM . . . . Their Majesties
TM . . . . Thematic Mapper
TM . . . . Thermal Mapper
Tm . . . . Thulium (Chemical element)
TM . . . . Time, Mission
TM . . . . Time Modulation
TM . . . . Time Monitor
TM . . . . Titanium Chloride
TM . . . . Tone Modulation
TM . . . . Tons per Minute
TM . . . . Top Management
TM . . . . Torpedoman's Mate
TM . . . . Tractor Monoplane
TM . . . . Trade Mission
TM . . . . Trademark
TM . . . . Traffic Manager
TM . . . . Training Manual (Military)
TM . . . . Training Missions (Air Force)
TM . . . . Trainmaster (Railroading)
TM . . . . Transcendental Meditation
TM . . . . Transport Mechanism (Physiology)
TM . . . . Transverse Magnetic
TM . . . . Trench Mortar
TM . . . . Tropical Medicine
TM . . . . True Mean
TM . . . . Twisting Moment
T/M . . . . Telemetering (or Telemetry)
T/M . . . . Torque Meter
T & M . . . . Time and Material Contract
T & M . . . . Time and Materials
TMA . . . . Terminal Control Area (Aviation)
TMA . . . . Terminal Maneuvering Area (Aviation)
TMA . . . . Tetramethylammonium
TMA . . . . Theatrical Mutual Association
TMA . . . . Thermomechanical Analysis (or Analyzer)
TMA . . . . Tile Manufacturers Association
TMA . . . . Time-Modulated Antenna
TMA . . . . Tobacco Merchants Association of United States
TMA . . . . Toiletry Merchandisers Association
TMA . . . . Total Materiel Assets (Military)
TMA . . . . Trimellitic Anhydride (Chemistry)
TMA . . . . Trimethylaluminum (Organic chemistry)
TMAB . . . . . . Temporary Missile Assembly Building
TMAG . . . . . . Travel More Advantageous to the Government
TMAO . . . . . . Trimethylamine Oxide (Organic chemistry)
TMAO . . . . . . Troop Movement Assignment Order
TMB . . . . David W. Taylor Model Basin
TMB . . . . Task Maintenance Burden
TMB . . . . Tide Measuring Buoy
TMB . . . . Trimethoxyboroxine (Organic chemistry)
TMBL . . . . . . Tacoma Municipal Belt Line (AAR code)
TMBR . . . . . . Timber
TMC . . . . Thatcher Glass Manufacturing Company, Inc. (NYSE symbol) (Delisted)
TMC . . . . Three-Mode Control
TMC . . . . Times Mirror Company (NYSE symbol)
TMC . . . . Titan Missile Contractor
TMC . . . . Transport Movement Control (Military)
TMC . . . . Transportation Materiel Command (AMC - Mobility)
TMC . . . . Triple Molecular Collision
TMC . . . . Tube Moisture Control
TM-C . . . . Thomas Micro-Catalogs
TMCA . . . . . . Titanium Metals Corporation of America
TMCC . . . . . . Time-Multiplexer Communications Channels
TMCL . . . . . . Target Map Coordinate Locator (Military)
TMCOMP . . . . Telemetry Computation
TMCR . . . . . . Technical Manual Contract Requirement
TMCS . . . . . . Trimethylchlorosilane (Chemistry)
TMD . . . . Tactical Mission Data (Military)
TMD . . . . Telemetered Data
TMD . . . . Theoretical Maximum Density

TMDAG	This Mode of Transportation has been Determined to be More Advantageous to the Government
TM & DE	Test, Measuring and Diagnostic Equipment (Army)
TMDI	Transponder Miss Distance Indicator
TMDL	Technical Manual Data List (DOD)
TMDS	Tetramethyldisilazane (Organic chemistry)
TMDT	Total Mean Down Time
TME	Thrust Monopropellant Engine
TME	Torpedoman's Mate, Electrical (Navy rating)
TME	Transmissible Mink Encephalopathy
TMEA	Typewriter Manufacturers Export Association
TME/FH	Total Maintenance Effort per Flight Hour (Navy)
TMF	Telemetry Module Facility
TMF	Test Mode Fail (Apollo) (NASA)
TMF	Time Marker Frequency
TMG	Tactical Missile Group (Air Force)
TMG	Tetramethyl Guanidine
TMG	Thermal Micrometeorite Garment (Aerospace)
TMG	Thiomethylgalactoside (Organic chemistry)
TMG	Time Mark Generator
TMG	Track Made Good (Aviation)
TMGE	Thermo-Magnetic-Galvanic Effect
TMGRS	Trace Material Generation Rate Simulator
TMGS	Terrestial Magnetic Guidance System (Aerospace)
TMH	Tons per Man-Hour
TMH	Trainable Mentally Handicapped
TMHA	The Military Housing Association
TMHL	Triplet Metastable Helium Level
TMI	Tool Manufacturing Instruction
TMI	Tracking Merit Interception
TMI	Trans-Mars Injection (Aerospace)
TMI	Travel Managers International
TMICP	Topographic Map Inventory Control Point (Army)
TMIMIS	Technical Manual Integrated Management Informations Systems (DOD)
TMIS	Technical Meetings Information Service
TMIS	Total Management Information System
TMJ	Temporo-Mandibular Joint
TMK	Tiravita Munnerrat Kalam
TMK	Transistor Mounting Kit
TML	Tetramethyllead (Organic chemistry)
TML	Thermo-Mechanical Loading
TML	Three Mile Limit
TML	Titanium Metallurgical Laboratory
TMLE	Transient-Mode Liquid Epitaxy
TMM	Test Message Monitor
TMMB	Truck Mixer Manufacturers Bureau
TMMD	Tactical Moving Mad Display
TMMT	Technical Manual Management Team (DOD)
TMN	Transmission
TMO	Total Materiel Objective
TMO	Traffic Management Office(r) (Air Force)
TMO	Transportation Movements Office(r)
TMP	Technical Manual Plan (DOD)
TMP	Test Methods and Procedures
TMP	Thermal Modeling Program
TMP	Thermomechanical Processing
TMP	Transistor Mounting Pad
TMP	Transportation Motor Pool (Military)
TMP	Trimethylolpropane (Chemistry)
TMPO	Total Materiel Procurement Objective
TMPROC	Telemetry Processing
TMPRY	Temporary
TMPS	Test and Maintenance Panel Subassembly
TMR	Technical Memorandum Report
TMR	Thermistor Micropower Resistor
TMR	Time Meter Reading
TMR	Timer
TMR	Total Materiel Requirement (Military)
TMR	Triple Modular Redundancy (Data processing)
TMRBM	Transportable Medium-Range Ballistic Missile
TMRP	Technology Mobilization and Reemployment Program (Department of Labor)
TMS	Tactical Missile Squadron (Air Force)
TMS	Target Marking System
TMS	Telemetry Modulation System
TMS	Temperature Management Station
TMS	Temperature Measurement Society
TMS	Test Monitor System
TMS	Thrust Measuring System
TMS	Tidewater Marine Service, Inc. (NYSE symbol)
TMS	Time and Motion Study
TMS	Tissu Musculaire Specifique (French) (Medicine)

TMS	Traffic Measurement System
TMS	Trimethylsilyl (Organic chemistry)
TMS	Turbine Management Station
TMS	Turbulence Measuring System
TMS	Type, Model, and Series
T/M/S	Type, Model, and Series
TMSD	Total Military Service Date
TMSDEA	Trimethylsilyldiethylamine (Organic chemistry)
TMSDMA	Trimethylsilyldimethylamine (Organic chemistry)
TMSIM	Trimethylsilylimidazole (Organic chemistry)
TMT	Transonic Model Tunnel
TMT	Transportation Motor Transport (Military)
TMTC	Thru-Mode (or Tri-Mode) Tape Converter
TMTD	Tetramethylthiuram Disulfide (Thiram) (Organic chemistry)
TMTR	Thermistor
TMU	Tactical Mobile Unit (Police)
TMU	Thermal-Mechanical Unit
TMU	Time Measurement Unit (Basic MTM unit)
TMUS	Toy Manufacturers of the United States
TMV	Tobacco Mosaic Virus (Biochemistry)
TMV	Torpedoman's Mate, Aviation (Navy rating)
TMV	True Mean Value
TMW	Tactical Missile Wing (Air Force)
TMW	Thermal Megawatt (or Mwt)
TMW	Transverse Magnetic Wave
TN	Tariff Number
TN	Technical Note
TN	Telephone Number
TN	Tennessee
TN	Tentacular Nerve
TN	Test Number
TN	Texas & Northern Railway Company (AAR code)
TN	Thermonuclear
TN	Track Number
TN	Train
TN	Transfer on Negative
TN	True North
TNA	Tetranitroaniline (Organic chemistry)
TNA	The National Archives
TNA	Time of Nearest Approach
TNA	Total Nucleic Acid
TNA	Trinitroaniline (Organic chemistry)
TNB	Technical News Bulletin (National Bureau of Standards)
TNB	The New Brood
TNB	Thomas & Betts Company (NYSE symbol)
TNB	Trinitrobenzene (Explosive)
TNC	Theater Naval Commander
TNC	Too Numerous to Count
TNC	Track Navigation Computer
TNC	Track No Conversion
TNC	Trans-National Communications, Inc.
TNC	Trevecca Nazarene College (Tennessee)
TNC	Trinitrocellulose (Organic chemistry)
TNC	Tripartite Naval Commission (Allied German Occupation Forces)
TNCC	Tripartite Nuclear Cross-Sections Committee (British, Canadian, and U.S.)
TNCD	Ten Nation Committee on Disarmament (Defunct, 1960)
TNCL	Tail Number Configuration List (Navy)
TND	Turned
TNDS	Tactical Navigational Display System
TNEC	Temporary National Economic Committee (Congressional committee which studied the American economic system) (World War II)
TNF	Thin Nickel Film
TNF	Timing Negative Film
TNF	Transfer on No Overflow
TNG	Training
TNGLIT	Training Literature
TNHQ	Theater Navy Headquarters
TNI	Thin Nickel Iron
TNI	Traffic Noise Index (Department of Transportation)
TNIF	Thin Nickel Iron Film
TNK	Tank
TNL	Terminal Net Loss
TNM	Tetranitromethane (Organic chemistry)
TNM	Texas-New Mexico Railway Company (AAR code)
TNM	Tumor Classification System Derived from Symbols: T for Primary Tumor; N for Regional Lymph Node Metastasis; M for Remote Metastasis (Medicine)
TNO	Texas & New Orleans R. R. (AAR code)
TNO	Toegepast Natuurwetenschappelijk Onderzoek (Dutch Institute for Applied Scientific Research)
TNOC	Threads No Couplings

TNP . . . . Trinitrophenol (Organic chemistry)
TNPG . . . . The Nuclear Power Group (British)
TNR . . . . Tone Not Relevant
TNR . . . . Trainer
TNR . . . . Transit Nuclear Radiation
TNRE . . . . Transit Nuclear Radiation Effect
TNS . . . . Tank Nitrogen Supply
TNS . . . . Thermal Night Site
TNS . . . . Toronto Normal School
TNS . . . . Tunable Noise Source
TNSA . . . . The National Spiritual Alliance of the United States of America
TNSDUNSPHI . . The National Society to Discourage Use of the Name Smith for Purposes of Hypothetical Illustration
TNT . . . . Transient Nuclear Test (AEC)
TNT . . . . Trim, Neat and Terrific (Slang)
TNT . . . . Trinitrotoluene (Explosive)
TNTDL . . . . . Tabulated Numerical Technical Data List
TNTV . . . . . . Tentative
TNV . . . . Total Net Value
TNW . . . . . Tactical Nuclear Weapon
TNX . . . . Thanks (Communications operator's procedural remark)
TNX . . . . Trinitroxylene (Organic chemistry)
TNYTI . . . . . . The New York Times Index
TNZ . . . . Transfer on Nonzero
TO . . . . Games Taken Out (Baseball)
TO . . . . Table of Organization
TO . . . . Take Off (Aviation)
TO . . . . Tandem Outlet
TO . . . . Technical Observer
TO . . . . Technical Order
TO . . . . Telegraph Office
TO . . . . Telephone Office
TO . . . . Test Operation
TO . . . . Theater of Operations
TO . . . . Time Opening
TO . . . . Time-Out
TO . . . . Tincture of Opium
TO . . . . Tool Order
TO . . . . Traditional Orthography (Writing system)
TO . . . . Traffic Officer
TO . . . . Transportation Officer
TO . . . . Transverse Optic
TO . . . . Travel Order
TO . . . . A Turn Over (A prospective customer who cannot be sold by one clerk and is turned over to another) (Merchandising slang)
TO . . . . Turnout
TO . . . . Turnover (Number) (With reference to enzyme activity)
T/O . . . . Table of Organization
T/O . . . . Target of Opportunity
T/O . . . . Test Operation
T & O . . . . . Taken and Offered (Sporting) (British)
TOA . . . . Table of Allowances
TOA . . . . Terms of Agreement (Army)
TOA . . . . Theatre Owners of America
TOA . . . . . . Time of Arrival
TOA . . . . . . Total Obligational Authority
TOAC . . . . . Tool Accessory
TOAD . . . . . . Tobyhanna Army Depot
TOAL . . . . . . Total Ordnance Alteration Application List (Navy)
TOB . . . . Take-Off Boost
TOB . . . . Telemetry Output Buffer (Data processing)
TOBI . . . . . . Test of Basic Information (Education)
TOBWE . . . . . Tactical Observing Weather Element (Air Force)
TOC . . . . . . Tactical Operations Center (Air Force)
TOC . . . . Tanker Operational Circular
TOC . . . . . . Task Order Contract
TOC . . . . . . Technical Order Compliance
TOC . . . . . . Television Operating Center
TOC . . . . . . Theater of Operations Command
TOC . . . . . . Timing Operation Center
TOC . . . . . . Total Organic Carbon
TOC . . . . . . Transfer of Control
TOCC . . . . . Transfer of Control Card
TOCCWE . . . . Tactical Operations Control Center Weather Element (Air Force)
TOCN . . . . . . Technical Order Change Notice (Air Force)
TOD . . . . . . Technical Objective Directive (or Document) (Air Force)
TOD . . . . Technical Operations Department
TOD . . . . Time of Day
TOD . . . . Time of Delivery
TOD . . . . Todd Shipyards Corp. (NYSE symbol)
TOD . . . . Turn Over Device

TODA . . . . . . Third-Octave Digital Analyzer
TODAS . . . . . Typewriter-Oriented Documentation-Aid System
TODT . . . . . . Tool Detail
TOE . . . . Tables of Organization and Equipment
TOE . . . . Term of Enlistment (Military)
TOE . . . . Texas, Oklahoma & Eastern R. R. (AAR code)
TOE . . . . Top of Edge
TOE . . . . Total Operating Expense
TOE . . . . Trainborne Operational Equipment
TO & E . . . . . Table of Organization and Equipment
TOEFL . . . . . Test of English as a Foreign Language
TOEMTB . . . . Table(s) of Organization and Equipment Mobilization Troop Basis (Army)
TOES . . . . . . Trade-Off Evaluation System
TOF . . . . Time of Filing
TOF . . . . Time of Flight
TOFC . . . . . . Trailer on Flatcar (Railroad)
TOFCN . . . . . Technical Order Field Change Notice (Air Force)
TOFM . . . . . . Tooling Form
TOG . . . . . . Take Off Gross (Weight) (Aviation)
TOG . . . . . . Target-Observer-Gun (Method) (Army)
TOGA . . . . . . Tooling Gage
TOGW . . . . . Take-Off Gross Weight
TOHP . . . . . . Take-Off Horsepower
TOI . . . . Technical Operations, Incorporated
TOI . . . . Term of Induction (Military)
TOJ . . . . Track on Jamming
TOJ . . . . Tropicana Products, Inc. (NYSE symbol)
TOKAMAK . . . Toroidal Chamber Machine (for thermonuclear fusion) (Acronym formed from the Russian)
TOL . . . . Test-Oriented Language
TOL . . . . Tolerance
TOLCAT . . . . Take-Off and Landing Critical Atmosphere Turbulence
TOLEYIS . . . . Turkiye Otel, Lokanta ve Eglence Yerleri Isci Sendikalari Federasyonu (National Federation of Hotel, Restaurant and Amusement Places Workers' Unions) (Turkey)
TOLIP . . . . . . Trajectory Optimization and Linearized Pitch (Computer program)
TOLO . . . . . . Tool and Operation Liaison Order
TOLO . . . . . . Tooling Layout
TOLT . . . . . . Towing Light
TOM . . . . . . The Old Man
TOM . . . . . . Translator Octal Mnemonic
TOM . . . . . . Typical Ocean Model (Oceanography)
TOMCAT . . . . Telemetry On-Line Monitoring Compression & Transmission
TOMCAT . . . . Theater of Operations Missile Continuous-Wave Anti-Tank Weapon
TOMSI . . . . . Transfer of Master Scheduled Item
TONAC . . . . . Technical Order Notification and Completion System
TONLAR . . . . Tone-Operated Net Loss Adjusted Receiving
TONT . . . . . . Tonto National Monument
TOO . . . . . . Time of Origin (Communications)
TOOL . . . . . . Test Oriented Operated Language (Data processing)
TOP . . . . Temple Opportunity Program (Temple University)
TOP . . . . Temporarily Out of Print
TOP . . . . Test Outline Plan (Army)
TOP . . . . The Option Process (HUD)
TOP . . . . Torque Oil Pressure (Air Force)
TOP . . . . Total Obscuring Power (Smoke cloud)
TOP . . . . Turn Out Perfection (US Air Force Southern Command's acronym for the Zero Defects Program)
TOPA . . . . . . Tooling Pattern
TOPIC . . . . . Time Ordered Programmer Integrated Circuit (NASA)
TOPICS . . . . . Total On-Line Program and Information Control System (Japan)
TOPICS . . . . . Traffic Operations Program for Increasing Capacity and Safety
TOPNS . . . . . Theater of Operations
TOPO . . . . . . Topography
TOPO . . . . . . Tri-n-Octyl Phosphine Oxide (Organic chemistry)
TOPOCOM . . . Topographic Command (Army)
TOPPER . . . . . Toy Press Publishers, Editors, and Reporters
TOPR . . . . . . Taiwan Open Pool Reactor (AEC)
TOPS . . . . . . Take Off Pounds Sensibly (Club)
TOPS . . . . . . Telemetry On-Line Processing System (Data processing)
TOPS . . . . . . Telephone Order Personalities and Smiles (Organization of chief telephone operators)
TOPS . . . . . . Teleregister Omni Processing and Switching (Data processing)
TOPS . . . . . . The Operational PERT System
TOPS . . . . . . Thermal Noise Optical Optimization Communication System (NASA)
TOPS . . . . . . Thermoelectric Outer Planet Spacecraft (NASA)
TOPS . . . . . . Total Operations Processing System (Data processing)
TOPSEC . . . . . Top Secret
TOPSI . . . . . . Topside Sounder, Ionosphere (NASA)
TOPSY . . . . . Test Operations Planning System
TOPSY . . . . . Thermally Operated Plasma System

TOR	Tactical Operations Room (Air Force)
TOR	Technical Operating Report
TOR	Tentative Operational Requirement
TOR	Terms of Reference (Army)
TOR	Third Order Regular of St. Francis
TOR	Time of Receipt (Army)
TOR	Time of Reception (Communications)
TOR	Torque (or Torquing)
TOR	Torrington Company (NYSE symbol) (Delisted)
TOR	Traffic on Request (Aviation)
TORC	Traffic Overload Reroute Control
TORPCM	Torpedo Countermeasures and Deception
TORPRON	Torpedo Squadron
TORQUE	Technology on Research Quantitative Utility Evaluation
TORR	Torricelli
TORS	Time Order Reporting System
TOS	Tactical Offense Subsystem
TOS	Tactical Operations System (ADSAF)
TOS	Tape Operating System (Data processing)
TOS	Term of Service
TOS	Thermally and Oxidatively Stable
TOS	TIROS (Television Infrared Observation Satellite) Operational Satellite (or System) (NASA)
TOS	Top of Steel (Flooring)
TOS	Turkiye Ogretmenler Sendikasi
TOS	Type of Shipment
TOSBAC	Toshiba Scientific and Business Automatic Computer
TOSCO	The Oil Shale Corporation of America
TOSE	Tooling Samples
TOSF	Tertiary of Third Order of St. Francis (Roman Catholic religious order)
TOSR	Thermally and Oxidatively Stable Resin
TOSS	Test Operation Support Segment
TOSS	TIROS (Television Infrared Observation Satellite) Operational Satellite System (NASA)
TOSS	Turbine-Operated Suspension System (NASA)
TOSSA	Transient or Steady-State Analysis (Data processing)
TOT	Time on Tape (Military)
TOT	Time on Target (Artillery support)
TOT	Time over Target (Air support)
TOT	Time on Track
TOT	Time of Transmission (Communications)
TOT	Total
TOT	Transportation Office will Furnish the Necessary Transportation (Military)
TOT	Turbine Outlet Temperature
TOT	Turn-On Time
T/OT	Table of Organization (Tentative)
TOTE	Test-Operator-Test-Exit (Unit) (Psychology)
TOTEM	Theater Operations and Tactical Evaluation Model
TOTFORF	Total Forfeiture (of all pay and allowances) (Army)
TOTM	Trioctyl Trimellitate (Chemistry)
TOTO	Tongue of the Ocean (Area of the Bahama Islands) (Navy)
TOTP	Tooling Template
TOTRAD	Tape Output Test Rack Autonetics Diode
TOU	Trace Operate Unit
TOUS	Test on Understanding Science
TOV	Time Out of View
TOV	Tooele Valley Railway Company (AAR code)
TOVALOP	Tanker Owner Voluntary Agreement on Liability for Oil Pollution
TOVC	Top of Overcast (Aviation)
TOVD	Transistor-Operated Voltage Divider
TOW	Take-Off Weight
TOW	Tube-Launched, Optically-Tracked, Wire-Guided (Weapon)
TOWA	Terrain and Obstacle Warning and Avoidance
TOXREP	Toxic Incident Report
TP	Tank Piercing (Ammunition) (Military)
TP	Target Practice (Military)
TP	Teaching Practice
TP	Technical Pamphlet
TP	Technical Paper
TP	Technical Problem
TP	Technical Proposal
TP	Technical Publication
TP	Technographic Publication
TP	Telemetry Processor
TP	Teleprinter
TP	Temperature Probe
TP	Tempore Paschale (At Easter Time)
TP	Tentative Pamphlet
TP	Term Pass
TP	Test Point
TP	Test Position
TP	Testosterone Propionate
TP	Texas & Pacific Railway Company (AAR code)
TP	Thermosphere Probe
TP	Tie Plate (Technical drawings)
TP	Tie Point
TP	Time Pulse
TP	Timing Point
TP	Tin Plate
TP	Title Page (Bibliography)
TP	Toilet Paper (Slang)
TP	Top Priority
TP	Total Parts
TP	Total Points
TP	Total Pressure
TP	Total Protein
TP	Totally Positive
TP	Training Period (Military)
TP	Transfer on Positive
TP	Transforming Principle (Bacteriology)
TP	Transport Pilot
TP	Transportation Priority
TP	Travaux Publics (France)
TP	Treaty Port
TP	Treponema pallidum (A spirochete) (Medicine)
TP	Trigonometrischer Punkt (Triangulation Point) (German military)
TP	Triple Plays (Baseball)
TP	Triple Pole
TP	Tropical Pacific (American air mass)
TP	True Position
TP	True Profile (Technical drawings)
TP	Tryptophan Pyrrolase (Biochemistry)
TP	Tuberculin Precipitation
TP	Turboprop
TP	Turbopump
T/P.	Test Panel
T and P.	Texas and Pacific Railway Company
TPA	Tape Pulse Amplifier
TPA	Technical Publications Announcement
TPA	Telemetry Power Amplifier
TPA	Telephone Pioneers of America
TPA	Test Plans and Analysis
TPA	Test Project Agreement
TPA	Theta Phi Alpha (Sorority)
TPA	Timber Producers Association of Michigan and Wisconsin
TPA	Track Production Area (Air Force)
TPA	Transfer of Pay Account (Military)
TPA	Trans-Pacific Airlines, Ltd.
TPA	Travel by Personal Auto (or Travel by Privately Owned Conveyance Authorized) (Military)
TPA	Trim Power Assembly
TPA	Tunable Parametric Amplifier
TPAA	Travelers Protective Association of America
TPAR	Tactical Penetration Aids Rocket
TPB	Tetraphenylbutane (Organic chemistry)
TPB	Tryptone Phosphate Broth
TPBA	Thyroxine-Binding Prealbumin (Biochemistry)
TPBVP	Two-Point Boundary Value Problem
TPC	Technical Prime Contractor
TPC	Telecommunications Planning Committee (Civil defense)
TPC	Telephone Pickup Coil
TPC	Test Point Controller
TPC	Thermally Protected Composite
TPC	Thromboplastic Plasma Component (Medicine)
TPC	Time Polarity Control
TPC	Trade Policy Committee (Advisory to President)
TPC	Training Plans Conference
TPC	Transistor Photo Control
TPC	Travel by Privately Owned Conveyance Permitted for Convenience (Military)
TPC	Turbo Pump Control
TPCF.	Treponema pallidum Complement Fixation (Test)
TPCP	Trainer Power Control Panel
TPCV	Turbine Power Control Valve
TPD	Tape Playback Discriminator
TPD	Test Point Data
TPD	Time Pulse Distributor
TPD	Tons Per Day
TPDS	Tape Playback Discriminator System
TPDT	Triple-Pole, Double-Throw
TPE	Tactical Performance Evaluation
TPE	Total Potential Energy

TPE	Turbo-Propeller Engine
TPEA	Television Program Export Association
TPESP	Technical Panel on the Earth Satellite Program
TPF	Tactical Patrol Force (Police)
TPF	Thai Patriotic Front (Communist-directed activity outside Thailand) (Merged with TIM)
TPF	Trainer Parts Fabrication
TPF	Triangle-Pac Forest Products (NYSE symbol)
TPF	Two-Phase Flow
TPFW	Thermoplastic Fan Wheel
TPFW	Three-Phase Full Wave
TPG	Timing Pulse Generator
TPG	Trypticase, Peptone, Glucose
TPH	Theosophical Publishing House
TPH	Tons Per Hour
TPHC	Time-to-Pulse Height Converter
TPHSG	Troop Housing (Army)
TPHW	Three-Phase Half Wave
TPI	Tape Phase Inverter
TPI	Target Position Indicator
TPI	Task Parameter Interpretation
TPI	Teatro Popolare Italiano (Italian theatrical troupe)
TPI	Technical Proficiency Inspection
TPI	Teeth Per Inch (of cog wheels)
TPI	Tennessee Polytechnic Institute
TPI	Terminal Phase Initiation
TPI	Thermal Protection Investigation
TPI	Threads Per Inch
TPI	Timing Pulse Idler
TPI	Tons Per Inch
TPI	Treponema pallidum Immobilizing (Test)
TPI	Trim Position Indicator
TPI	Truss Plate Institute
TPI	Turns Per Inch
TPIA	Treponema pallidum Immune Adherence (Test)
TPL	Tabular Parts List
TPL	Technical Publications Library
TPL	Terminal Per Inch
TPL	Test Parts List
TPL	Test Point Logic
TPL	Texas Pacific Land Trust (NYSE symbol)
TPL	Training Parts List
TPL	Transistorized Portable Laboratory
TPL	Trap Processing Line
TPL	Turns Per Layer
TPLD	Test Planning Liaison Drawing
TPLS	Terminal Position Location System
TPM	Tape Preventive Maintenance
TPM	Telemetry Processor Module
TPM	Title Page Mutilated
TPM	Transmission and Processing Model
TPM	Tri-Plate Module
TPMA	Timber Products Manufacturers Association
TPMG	The Provost Marshal General (Army)
TPMP	Texas Pacific-Missouri Pacific Terminal R.R. (AAR code)
TPN	Triphosphopyridine Nucleotide (Biochemistry) (See NADP)
TPNEG	Travel Will Be Performed at No Expense to the Government (Military)
TPNG	Topping
TPNH	Triphosphopyridine Nucleotide (Reduced) (Biochemistry) (See NADPH)
TPO	Technical Planning Office
TPO	Telecommunications Program Objective (Army)
TPO	Tentative Program Objectives (Navy)
TPO	Traveling Post Office
TPO	Tryptophan Pyrrolase (Biochemistry)
TPO	Tuned Plate Oscillator
TPOM	Tube Propagation d'Ondes Magnetron
TPOS	Track Position
TPP	Teletype Page Printer
TPP	Thermally Protected Plastic
TPP	Thiamine Pyrophosphate (Diphosphothiamine) (Biochemistry)
TPP	Total Package Procurement (Government contracting)
TPP	Transducer Power Programmer
TPP	Trans-Pluto Probe
TPP	Two-Phase Principle
TPPC	Total Package Procurement Concept
TPPC	Trans-Pacific Passenger Conference
TPPD	Technical Program Planning Division (Air Force)
TPPD	Technical Program Planning Document
TPQI	Teacher-Pupil Question Inventory
TPR	Tape Programmed Row (Data scanner)
TPR	Technical Progress Report
TPR	Teleprinter
TPR	Telescopic Photographic Recorder
TPR	Temperature Profile Recorder
TPR	Temperature, Pulse, Respiration (Medicine)
TPR	Test Performance Recorder
TPR	Total Peripheral Resistance
TPR	Trained Personnel Requirements (Air Force)
TPR	Transmitter Power Rating
TPRC	Thermophysical Properties Research Center (Purdue University)
TPRI	Teacher-Pupil Relationship Inventory
TPRV	Transient Peak Reverse Voltage
TPS	Tandem Propeller Submarine
TPS	Tank Pressure Sensing
TPS	Tape Plotting System
TPS	Tape Punch Subassembly
TPS	Task Parameter Synthesizer
TPS	Technical Publishing Society
TPS	Telemetry Processing Station (NASA)
TPS	Terminal Performance Specification
TPS	Terminals Per Station
TPS	Test Pilot School (Navy)
TPS	Test Plotting System
TPS	Test Point Selector
TPS	Test Preparation Sheet
TPS	Thermal Protection System
TPS	Thermoplastic Storage
TPS	Total Product Support
TPS	Trail Pilot Sensor
TPS	Tramp Power Supply
TPS	Translunar Propulsion Stage
TPS	Tube Pin Straightener
TPSF	Telephonie sans Fil (Wireless telephony)
TPSI	Torque Pressure in Pounds per Square Inch (Air Force)
TPSN	Transposition
TPSN	Troop Program Sequence Number
TPSP	Tape Punch Subassembly Panel
TPSS	Thermal Protection System Selection
TPST	Triple-Pole, Single-Throw
TPT	Tail Pipe Temperature
TPT	Target Practice (Ammunition) With Tracer
TPT	Tetraisopropyl Titanate (Organic chemistry)
TPT	Thor Power Tool Company (NYSE symbol) (Delisted)
TPT	Time Priority Table
TPT	Transonic Pressure Tunnel (NASA)
TPT	Trenton-Princeton Traction Company (AAR code)
TP-T	Target Practice (Ammunition) with Tracer
TPTD	Test Pilot Training Division
TPTG	Tuned Plate Tuned Grid (Electronic tube)
TPU	Tape Preparation Unit
TPU	Trunk Processing Unit (Bell System)
TPU	Turbopower Unit
TPUC	Telephone Pickup Coil
TPUS	Transportation and Public Utilities Service (Later, part of Transportation and Communication Service, GSA)
TPV	Thermophotovoltaic
TPV	Transverse Pallial Vein
TPW	Tenth-Power Width
TPW	Title Page Wanting
TPW	Toledo, Peoria & Western R. R. (AAR code)
TP & W	Toledo, Peoria & Western Railroad
TPWBH	Tax Paid Wine Bottling House
TPWIC	Theater Prisoner of War Information Center
TPWU	Tanganyika Plantation Workers Union
TPWU	Tea Plantation Workers' Union (Kenya)
TQ	Tale Quale (Of conditions on arrival) (Business and trade) (France)
TQ	Thought Quality (Psychology)
TQC	Time, Quality, Cost
TQC	Total Quality Control
TQD	Ter Quaterve in Die (Three or Four Times a Day) (Pharmacology)
TQE	Technical Quality Evaluation (Polaris)
TQM	Transport Quartermaster
TQMG	The Quartermaster General (Army)
TQP	Transistor Qualification Program
TQT	Transistor Qualification Test
TQTP	Transistor Qualification Test Program
TR	Tape Reader
TR	Tape Recorder
TR	Tape Register
TR	Target Recognition
TR	Tariff Reform
TR	Technical Regulation

ACRONYMS AND INITIALISMS DICTIONARY

TR . . . . Technical Report
TR . . . . Technical Representative
TR . . . . Temperature Range
TR . . . . Temperature Recorder
TR . . . . Temperature, Rectal (Medicine)
TR . . . . Tempore Regis (In the Time of the King)
TR . . . . Terminal Rendezvous
TR . . . . Test Report
TR . . . . Test Request
TR . . . . Test Routine
TR . . . . Test Run
TR . . . . Texas Gulf Producing Company (NYSE symbol) (Wall Street slang name: "Teddy Roosevelt") (Delisted)
TR . . . . Theodore (Teddy) Roosevelt
TR . . . . Therapeutic Radiology
TR . . . . Time to Retrofire (Aerospace)
TR . . . . Tone Relevant
TR . . . . Tons Registered (Shipping)
TR . . . . Toothed Ring (Technical drawings)
TR . . . . Tootsie Roll Industries, Inc. (NYSE symbol)
TR . . . . Torpedo Reconnaissance Aircraft (Navy)
TR . . . . Total Regulation
TR . . . . Total Revenue
TR . . . . Trace
TR . . . . Tracking RADAR
TR . . . . Trailer
TR . . . . Trainer
TR . . . . Training Regulations (Military)
TR . . . . Transatlantic Review (A publication)
TR . . . . Transfer Reset
TR . . . . Transformation Ratio
TR . . . . Transformer-Rectifier
TR . . . . Transmit(ter)-Receive(r)
TR . . . . Transportation (or Travel) Request (Military)
TR . . . . Trial Report
TR . . . . Trip Report
TR . . . . Tritium Ratio (Measure of tritium activity) (AEC)
TR . . . . Trouble Report
TR . . . . Tuberculin R (New tuberculin)
TR . . . . Tunnel Rectifier
T/R . . . . Transportation Request (Military)
T/R . . . . Trust Receipt (Banking)
T & R . . . . Testing & Regulating Department (Especially, in a wire communications maintenance division)
TRA . . . . Tackle Representatives Association
TRA . . . . Tandem Rotary Activator
TRA . . . . Textile Refinishers Association
TRA . . . . Theodore Roosevelt Association
TRA . . . . Thoroughbred Racing Associations of the United States
TRA . . . . Tire and Rim Association
TRA . . . . Trade Relations Association
TRA . . . . Trane Company (The) (NYSE symbol)
TRA . . . . Transracial Adoption
TRA . . . . Travel Research Association
TRA . . . . Triaxial Recording Accelerometer
TRA . . . . La Tuyere a Reverse Aval (Concorde)
TRAAC . . . . . . Transit Research and Attitude Control (Navy satellite)
TRAB . . . . Triaminobenzene (Chemical)
TRAC . . . . Tandem Razor and Cartridge (Gillette Co.)
TRAC . . . . Telescoping Rotor Aircraft System
TRAC . . . . Text Reckoning and Compiling (Data processing)
TRAC . . . . Thermally Regenerative Alloy Cell
TRAC . . . . Tractor
TRAC . . . . Transportation Account Code
TRACALS . . . . Tracking Controls and Landing Systems (Proposed)
TRACALS . . . . Traffic Control Approach and Landing System (Aviation electronics)
TRACDR . . . . . Tractor-Drawn
TRACE . . . . . . Tactical Readiness and Checkout Equipment
TRACE . . . . . . Tape-Controlled Recording Automatic Checkout Equipment (Component of automatic pilot) (Aviation)
TRACE . . . . . . Task Reporting and Current Evaluation
TRACE . . . . . Taxiway Routing and Coordination Equipment (Aviation)
TRACE . . . . . . Test Equipment for Rapid Automatic Checkout and Evaluation (Pan-American Airways)
TRACE . . . . . . Tracing and Routing of Aircraft Coordinating Equipment
TRACE . . . . . . Tracking and Communications, Extraterrestrial
TRACE . . . . . . Transistor Radio Automatic Circuit Evaluator
TRACE . . . . . . Transportable Automated Control Environment
TRACEN . . . . . Training Center
TRACES . . . . . Technology in Retrospect and Critical Events in Science (IITRI)
TRACOMDLANT . . Training Command, Atlantic Fleet (Navy)

TRACOMDPAC . . Training Command, Pacific Fleet (Navy)
TRACOMDSUBPAC . . Training Command, Submarines, Pacific Fleet (Navy)
TRACOMDWESTCOAST . . Training Command, West Coast (Navy)
TRACOMP . . . . Tracking Comparison
TRACON . . . . . Terminal RADAR Approach Control (FAA)
TRADAD . . . . . Trace to Destination and Advise
TRADCOM . . . . Transportation Corps Research and Development Command (Army)
TRADE . . . . . . Tracking RADAR Angle Deception Equipment
TRADER . . . . . Transient Radiation Effects Recorder
TRADET . . . . . . Training Detachment (Navy)
TRADEX . . . . . Target Resolution and Discrimination Experiment (ARPA)
TRADIC . . . . . Transistor-Digital Computer (Air Force)
TRADIS . . . . . Tape Repeating Automatic Data Integration System
TRAE . . . . Transport Airlift Estimator (Air Force)
TRAEX . . . . . . Training and Experience (Military)
TRAFCO . . . . . Television, Radio and Film Communications (of the Methodist Church)
TRAIN . . . . . . Telerail Automated Information Network (Association of American Railroads)
TRAINBASEFOR . . Training Base Force, Pacific Fleet (Navy)
TRAINLANT . . . Training Atlantic Fleet (Navy)
TRAINRON . . . Training Squadron (Later, SERRON) (Navy)
TRAIS . . . . . . Transportation Research Activity Information Service (Projected for Department of Transportation)
TRAJ . . . . Trajectory
TRALANT . . . . . Fleet Training Command, Atlantic (Navy)
TRAM . . . . Test, Reliability, and Maintainability
TRAM . . . . . . Tracking RADAR Automatic Monitoring
TRAMP . . . . . . Test Retrieval and Memory Print (Data processing)
TRAMPS . . . . . Temperature Regulator and Missile Power Supply
TRANC . . . . . . Transient Center (Marine Corps)
TRANET . . . . . Tracking (Transit) Network (Navy)
TRANS . . . . . . Telemetry Redundancy Analyzer System
TRANS . . . . . . Transfer
TRANS . . . . . . Transformer
TRANS . . . . . . Transmittance
TRANS . . . . . . Transport (Transportable; Transportation)
TRANSAC . . . . Transistorized Automatic Computer
TRANSCOM . . Transportable Communications
TRANSDIV . . . . Transport Division (Navy)
TRANSEC . . . . Transmission Security (Communications)
TRANSF . . . . . . Transformer
TRANSFAX . . . Facsimile Transmission
TRANSGRPPHIBFOR . . Transportation Group Amphibious Forces (Navy)
TRANSGRPSOPAC . . Transport Group, South Pacific Force (Navy)
TRANSL . . . . . Translation
TRANSLANT . . . Transports, Atlantic Fleet (Navy)
TRANSM . . . . . Transmission
TRANSP . . . . . . Transparency
TRANSPAC . . . Trans-Pacific
TRANSPHIBLANT . . Transports, Amphibious Force, Atlantic Fleet (Navy)
TRANSPHIBPAC . . Transports, Amphibious Force, Pacific Fleet (Navy)
TRANSRON . . . Transport Squadron (Navy)
TRANSV . . . . . Transverse
TRAP . . . . Tank, Racks, Adapters, Pylons (Military)
TRAP . . . . Tape Recorder Action Plan (Committee) (NASA/Air Force)
TRAP . . . . Terminal Radiation Airborne Program
TRAP . . . . Tracker Analysis Program
TRAPAC . . . . . Fleet Training Command, Pacific (Navy)
TRAPATT . . . . . Trapped Plasma Avalanche Triggered Transit (Bell Laboratories)
TRAPP . . . . . . Training and Retention as Permanent Party (Army)
TRAR . . . . Total Radiation Absolute Radiometer (NASA)
TRASH . . . . . . Tsunami Research Advisory System of Hawaii
TRASTA . . . . . . Training Station (Navy)
TRAU . . . . Tanganyika Railway African Union
TRAVEL . . . . . Transportable Vertical Erectable Launcher
TRAWL . . . . . . Tape Read and Write Library
TRB . . . . Tapered Roller Bearing
TRB . . . . Torpedo Recovery Boat
TRB . . . . Trapped Radiation Belt
TRBP . . . . Trainable Retractable Bow Propeller
TRC . . . . Tape Reader Calibrator
TRC . . . . Tape Reader Control
TRC . . . . Tape Record Coordinator (Data processing)
TRC . . . . Technical Research Center
TRC . . . . Technical Resources Center (Syracuse University)
TRC . . . . Temperature Recording Controller
TRC . . . . Test Readiness Certificate
TRC . . . . Thermodynamics Research Center (Texas A & M University)
TRC . . . . Tithe Rent-Charge
TRC . . . . Toroidal Propellant Container
TRC . . . . Tracking, RADAR-Input, and Correlation

TRC	Trade Relations Council of the United States
TRC	Transportation Research Command
TRC	Trona Railway Company (AAR code)
TRC	Type Requisition Code
TRCA	Tricycle Racing Club of America
TRCC	Theodore Roosevelt Centennial Commission (Government agency)
TRCCC	Tracking RADAR Central Control Console (BMEWS)
TRCE	Tactical Radio Communications Equipment
TRD	Test Requirements Document
TRD	Thread
TRD	Trapped Radiation Detector
TRD	Turbine Reduction Drive
TRDC	Transport Research and Development Command (Army)
TRDI	Trim Die
TR & DL	Tung Research and Development League
TRDM	Tactical Reconnaissance Data Marking
TRDTO	Tracking RADAR Data Takeoff
TRE	Telecommunications Research Establishment (British)
TRE	Tidal Regenerator Engine
TRE	Timing Read Error
TRE	Tool Research and Engineering Corp. (NYSE symbol)
TRE	Transient Radiation Effect
TRE	True Radiation Emittance
TREAS	Treasurer
TREAT	Transient Radiation Effects Automated Tabulation
TREAT	Transient Reactor Test Facility (AEC)
TREAT	Treatment
TREC	Tracking RADAR Electronic Component
TRECOM	Transportation Research Command (AMC - Mobility)
TRED	Transmitting and Receiving Equipment Development
TREE	Transient Radiation Effects on Electronics
TREES	Transient Radiation Effects on Electronic Systems (Air Force)
TREND	Tradeoffs for Lifting Reentry Vehicle Evaluation and Nominal Design
TRESI	Target Resolution Extraction of Statistical Invariances
TRF	Tank Range-Finder
TRF	Thermal Radiation at Microwave Frequencies
TRF	Thyrotropin-Releasing Factor (Biochemistry)
TRF	Transportation Research Foundation
TRF	Tuna Research Foundation
TRF	Tuned Radio Frequency
TRF	Turf Research Foundation
TRFCS	Temperature Rate Flight Control System
TRFS	Trace Fuselage Station
TRG	Technical Research Group, Inc.
TRG	Trailing
TRGP	Tactical Reconnaissance Group (Air Force)
TRGT	Target
TRH	Technical Reference Handbook
TRH	Their Royal Highnesses
TRH	Thyrotrophin-Releasing Hormone (Biochemistry)
TRI	Tactical Reconnaissance/Intelligence
TRI	Technical Report Instruction
TRI	Technical Research Institute (Japan)
TRI	Textile Research Institute
TRI	Tin Research Institute
TRI	Tire Retreading Institute
TRI	Torsion Reaction Integrating
TRI	Total Response Index (Psychology)
TRI	Transponder Receiver Isolation
TRI	Transportation Research Institute (Carnegie-Mellon University)
TRI	Triangle Industries, Inc. (NYSE symbol)
TRI	Tricycle
TRI	Triode
TR-I	Translations Register - Index
TRIA	Telemetry Range Instrumentation Aircraft
TRIAC	Triiodothyroacetic Acid (Endocrinology)
TRIAL	Technique to Retrieve Information from Abstracts of Literature (Data processing)
TRIBE	Teaching and Research in Bicultural Education (Indian organization in Maine)
TRIC	Trachoma Inclusion Conjunctivitis (Agent) (Medicine)
TRIC	Trichlorethyelene
TRICAP	Triple Capability (Army)
TRICC	Tariff Rules of the Interstate Commerce Commission
TRICE	Transistorized Realtime Incremental Computer
TRICHLOR	Trichlorethylene
TRID	Track Identity
TRIDOP	Tri-Doppler
TRIG	Trigger
TRIGA	Training Reactor, Isotopes General Atomic
TRIGA	Training, Research, Isotope, Production, General Atomic (AEC)

TRIGA	Traitement Industriel des Gadoues (French company)
TRIM	Targets, Receivers, Impacts, and Methods
TRIM	Technical Requirements Identification Matrix
TRIM	Test Rules for Inventory Management
TRIM	Thin Region Integral Method
TRIM	Trails, Roads, and Interdiction Missions (or Multisensor) (Navy)
TRIM	Training Records and Information Management System
TRIM	Training Relation and Instruction Mission (Military) (Vietnam, France, United States)
TRIM	Training Requirements and Information Management System (Navy)
TRIM	Transformation of Imagery (Data processing) (NASA)
TRIMS	Transportation Integrated Management System (Air Force)
TRIN	Trans-International Airlines, Incorporated
TRIP	The Road Information Program, Inc.
TRIP	Transformation-Induced Plasticity (Steel)
TRIPLTEE	True Temperature Tunnel (Acronym pronounced, "Triple T")
TRIPOD	Transit Injector Polaris Derived (Aerospace)
TRIPOLD	Transit Injected Polaris Derived
TRISECT	Total Reconnaissance Intelligence System Evaluation and Comparison Technique
TRIT	Triiodothyronine (Endocrinology)
TRIUN	Department of Trusteeship and Information from Non-Self-Governing Territories of the United Nations
TRJ	Thermocouple Reference Junction
TRK	Tank Rangefinder Kit
TRK	Tidewater-Raymond-Kiewit, Inc.
TRK	Track
TRK	Truck
TRK	Trunk
TRKDR	Truck-Drawn
TRKG	Tracking
TRKHD	Truck Head
TRL	Thermodynamics Research Laboratory
TRL	Tool Room Lathe
TRL	Transistor Resistor Logic
TRL	Transuranium Research Laboratory (AEC)
TRLB	Temporarily Replaced by Lighted Buoy Showing Same Characteristic (Maps and charts)
TRLFSW	Tactical Range Landing Force Support Weapon
TRLP	Transport Landplane (Navy)
TRM	Task Response Module (Office furniture)
TRM	Thermal Remanent Magnetization
TRM	Thermal Resistance Measurement
TRM	Thermoremanence
TRM	Thermoremanent Magnetism (or Magnetization)
TRM	Thickness Readout Module
TRM	Time Ratio Modulation
TRM	Time Release Mechanism (Martin-Baker seat system) (Aviation)
TRM	Totally Reflective Mirror
TRML	Terminal
TRML	Tropical Research Medical Laboratory (Army)
TRMT	Treatment
TRN	Transitron Electronic Corporation (NYSE symbol) (Delisted)
tRNA	Transfer Ribonucleic Acid
TRNBKL	Turnbuckle (Aerospace)
TRNCAP	Training Capability (Military)
T & RNP	Transportation and Recruiting Naval Personnel (Budget appropriation title)
TRNR	Trainer
TRNSP	Transport(ation)
TRO	Technical Reviewing Office
TRO	Transportation Officer
TRO	Truck Route Order (Army)
TROCA	Tangible Reinforcement Operant Conditioning Audiometry
TRODI	Touchdown Rate of Descent Indicator
TROMEX	Tropical Meteorological Experiment
TROO	Transponder On-Off
TROPEX	Tropical Experiment (Proposed by BOMEX)
TROPICS	Tour Operators Integrated Computer System (Airline ticket system)
TRP	Television Remote Pickup
TRP	Terminal Rendezvous Phase
TRP	Thunderstorm Research Project (Environmental Science Services Administration)
TRP	Time to Repair Part
TRP	Timing Release Pin
TRP	Traffic Regulation Point
TRP	Trainable Retractable Propellers
TRP	Troop
TRPB	Thoroughbred Racing Protective Bureau
TRPO	Track Reference Printout
TRPS	Temperature Regulating Power Supply
TRQ	Torque

TRQ . . . . Total Requirements
TRR . . . . Tactical Range Recorder
TRR . . . . Tactical Reaction Reconnaissance
TRR . . . . Target Ranging RADAR
TRR . . . . Teaching and Research Reactor
TRR . . . . Tethered RADAR Reflector
TRR . . . . Thailand Research Reactor (Atomic energy)
TRR . . . . Theoretical Research Report
TRRA . . . . . . Terminal R. R. Association of St. Louis (AAR code)
TRRB . . . . Test Readiness Review Board (NASA)
TRR of ST L . . . Terminal Railroad Association of St. Louis
TRS . . . . Tactical RADAR System
TRS . . . . Tactical Radio Set
TRS . . . . Tactical Reconnaissance Squadron (Air Force)
TRS . . . . Technical Research Ship
TRS . . . . Test Research Service
TRS . . . . Test Research Station
TRS . . . . Tetrahedral Research Satellite
TRS . . . . Third Readiness State
TRS . . . . Ticket Reservation Systems, Inc.
TRS . . . . Time Reference System
TRS . . . . Transportable Relay Station
TRS . . . . Tree-Ring Society
TRSA . . . . . . Terminal RADAR Service Area
TRSD . . . . . . Total Radiance Spectral Distribution
TRSD . . . . . . Total Rated Service Date (Air Force)
TRSF . . . . Torque-Regulated Speed Follower
TRSH . . . . . . Trim Shell
TRSL . . . . . . Toms River Signal Laboratory (Army)
TRSP . . . . Total Radiance Spectral Polarization
TRSP . . . . . . Transport Seaplane (Navy)
TRSq . . . . Tactical Reconnaissance Squadron (Air Force)
TRSR . . . . . . Taxi and Runway Surveillance RADAR
TRSSGM . . . . . Tactical Range Surface-to-Surface Guided Missile
TRSSM . . . . . Tactical Range Surface-to-Surface Missile
TRSV . . . . Tobacco Ring Spot Virus
TRT . . . . Tempo di Restituzione Termica (Thermal Restitution Test) (Italian) (Medicine)
TRT . . . . Tuned Receiver Tuner
TRU . . . . Transmit-Receive Unit
TRU . . . . Transportable Radio Unit (Military)
TRU . . . . Transuranium Processing Plant (AEC)
TRUB . . . . . . Temporarily Replaced by Unlighted Buoy (Maps and charts)
TRUD . . . . . . Time Remaining Until Dive (Air Force)
TRUMP . . . . . Target Radiation Measurement Program
TRUMP . . . . . Target Radiometric Ultraviolet Measuring Program
TRUMP . . . . . Total Revision and Upgrading of Marine Corps Programs
TRUST . . . . . Trieste United States Troops
TRUT . . . . . . Time Remaining Until Transition (Air Force)
TRV . . . . Tank Recovery Vehicle (Army)
TRV . . . . Thrust Reduction Valve
TRV . . . . Timing Relay Valve
TRV . . . . Tobacco Rattle Virus
TRVM . . . . . . Transistorized Voltmeter
TRW . . . . Tactical Reconnaissance Wing
TRW . . . . TRW, Inc. (Formerly, Thompson Ramo Wooldridge, Inc.) (NYSE symbol)
TRWG . . . . . Tactical Reconnaissance Wing (Air Force)
TRWOV . . . . . Transit without Visa
TRY . . . . Teens for Retarded Youth (Program in Fairfax County, Virginia)
TRY . . . . Trypothan (Amino acid)
TS . . . . Tank Steamer
TS . . . . Taper Shank (Screw)
TS . . . . Taper Sided
TS . . . . Target Strength
TS . . . . Teacher Survey
TS . . . . Teachers Section (Library Education Division of ALA)
TS . . . . Temperature Sensitive
TS . . . . Temperature Switch
TS . . . . Tensile Strength
TS . . . . Tentative Specification
TS . . . . Terminal (or Greater) Sensation
TS . . . . Terminal Service
TS . . . . Test Solution (of a chemical) (Medicine)
TS . . . . Test Summary
TS . . . . Texas Pacific Coal & Oil Company (NYSE symbol) (Delisted)
TS . . . . Theosophical Society
TS . . . . Thoreau Society
TS . . . . Threaded Stud
TS . . . . Thunderstorm (Meteorology)
TS . . . . Tidewater Southern Railway Company (AAR code)
TS . . . . Time Shack (NAS operations desk)

TS . . . . Time Sharing (Data processing)
TS . . . . Timing Selector
TS . . . . Tip Speed
TS . . . . Too Short (Symbol stamped in shoes which are not actually of the size marked)
TS . . . . Tool Sharpness
TS . . . . Tool Steel
TS . . . . Tool Storage
TS . . . . Top Secret
TS . . . . Torpedo Station
TS . . . . Tough Situation (Bowdlerized version)
TS . . . . Tower Station
TS . . . . Tracking System
TS . . . . Training Ship
TS . . . . Transfer Set
TS . . . . Transient State
TS . . . . Transit Storage
TS . . . . Transmission Set
TS . . . . Transmittal Sheet (Military)
TS . . . . Transmitter Station
TS . . . . Transport and Supply
TS . . . . Transverse Section (Medicine)
TS . . . . Triple Strength
TS . . . . Tub-Sized
TS . . . . Tubular (Tracheal) Sound
TS . . . . Tuning Stability
TS . . . . Two-Stage Least Squares (Statistics)
TS . . . . Type Specification
TS . . . . Typescript
T-S . . . . Temperature-Salinity
T/S . . . . Target Seeker
T/S . . . . Test Stand
T/S . . . . Third Stage
T/S . . . . Thyroid:Serum (Radioiodide ratio)
T/S . . . . Transtage (Upper stage for Titan III C rocket)
T/S . . . . Turn-in-Slip (Military)
TSA . . . . Tamworth Swine Association
TSA . . . . Target Signature Analysis
TSA . . . . Targhee Sheep Association
TSA . . . . Telegraph System Analyzer
TSA . . . . Textile Salesmen's Association
TSA . . . . Time Series Analysis
TSA . . . . Time-Shared Amplifier
TSA . . . . Tolkien Society of America
TSA . . . . Track Supply Association
TSA . . . . Training Situation Analysis (Navy)
TSA . . . . Transportation Service, Army
TSA . . . . Transportation Standardization Agency (DOD)
TSA . . . . Trypticase Soy Agar
TSA . . . . Tumor-Specific Antigens (Immunology)
TSA . . . . Two-Step Antenna
T & SA . . . . . Task and Skills Analysis
TS in A . . . . . Theosophical Society in America
TSAA . . . . . . Tobacco Salesmen's Association of America
TSAB . . . . . . Theatre-Screen Advertising Bureau (Defunct)
TSAC . . . . . . Target Signature Analysis Center
TSAC . . . . . . Testing Accessories
TSAC . . . . . . Title, Subtitle, and Caption
TSAD . . . . . . Test System Analysis Directorate (Army)
TSAF . . . . . . Typical System Acquisition Flow
TSAR . . . . . . Throttlable Solid Augmented Rocket
TSAR . . . . . . Timed Scanned Array RADAR
TSAR . . . . . . Transmission Security Analysis Report
TSAZ . . . . . . Target Seeker-Azimuth
TSB . . . . Technical Service Bulletin
TSB . . . . Thrust Section Blower
TSB . . . . Transportation Services Branch (Air Force)
TSB . . . . Trypticase Soy Broth
TSB . . . . Twin Sideband
TSC . . . . Tactical Support Center
TSC . . . . Tanker Service Committee
TSC . . . . Tarleton State College (Texas)
TSC . . . . Technical Subcommittee
TSC . . . . Teledyne Systems Corporation
TSC . . . . Television Scan Converter
TSC . . . . Test Set Computer
TSC . . . . Test Set Connection
TSC . . . . Texas Southmost College
TSC . . . . Thermal Stress Crack(ing) (Plastics)
TSC . . . . Thermal Surface Coating
TSC . . . . Thermally Stimulated Conductivity (or Currents)

TSC	Thiosemicarbazide (Organic chemistry)
TSC	Total System Control (Architecture)
TSC	Total System Cost (Aviation)
TSC	Tractor Supply Company (NYSE symbol) (Delisted)
TSC	Transportable Communication System
TSC	Transportation Systems Center (Department of Transportation)
TSCA	Textile Supplies and Credit Association
TSCA	Tool Sub-Contract Authorization
TSCA	Top Secret Control Agency
TSCC	Telemetry Standards Coordination Committee
TSCC	Top Secret Control Channels (Military)
TSCDP	Technical Service Career Development Program
TSCF	Top Secret Cover Folder
TSCLT	Transportable Satellite Communications Link Terminal
TSCN	Trainer Specification Change Notice
TSCO	Top Secret Control Officer
TSCP	Top Secret Control Proceeding (Navy)
TSCRA	Texas and Southwestern Cattle Raisers Association
TSCS	Top Secret Control Section (Navy)
TSCT	Transportable Satellite Communication Terminal
TSD	Tactical Situation Display
TSD	TARAN (Tactical Attack RADAR and Navigation) System Data
TSD	Target Skin Distance
TSD	Technical Services Division (National Library of Medicine)
TSD	Technical Support Directorate
TSD	Temperature-Salinity-Density-Depth (Relationships) (Oceanography)
TSD	Theater Shipping Document
TSD	Theory of Signal Detectability (or Detection)
TSD	Torque Screwdriver
TSD	Total Spectral Density
TSD	Track Situation Display
TSD	Traffic Situation (Status) Display
TSD	Triple-Sequence Diffusion
TSDA	Theory of Signal Detection Analysis
TSDF	Target System Data File
TSDI	Tactical Situation Display Indicator
TSDK	Torque Screwdriver Kit
TSDS	Two-Speed Destroyer Sweeper (Military)
TSDU	Target System Data Update
TSE	Tactical Support Element
TSE	Test Scoring (or Support) Equipment
TSE	Test Set Electrical
TSE	Test Support Equipment
TSE	Texas South-Eastern R. R. (AAR code)
TSE	Turbo-Shaft Engine
TSEC	Taft Sanitary Engineering Center
TSEC	Telecommunications Security (Army)
TSED	Training Simulators Engineering Department
TSEE	Test Support Equipment Evaluation
TSEG	Tactical Satellite Communications Executive Steering Group
TSEI	Truck Safety Equipment Institute
TSEM	Transmission Secondary Emission Multiplier
TSF	Tab Sequence Format
TSF	Tactical Strike Fighter
TSF	Telegraphie sans Fil (Wireless Telegraphy)
TSF	Telephone Service Fitting
TSF	Tower Shielding Facility (AEC)
TSF	Transverse Shear Force
TSFC	Thrust Specific Fuel Consumption
TSFR	Transfer
TSG	Technical Specialty Group (AIAA)
TSG	The Surgeon General (Army)
TSG	Time Signal Generator
TSG	Tracking (or Test) Signal Generator
TSGA	Three Conductor, Shipboard, General Use, Armor Cable
TSGS	Time Series Generation System
TSGT	Technical Sergeant
TSGT(C)	Technical Sergeant (Commissary) (Marine Corps)
TSH	Their Serene Highnesses
TSH	Thermodynamic Suppression Head
TSH	Thyroid-Stimulating (Thyrotrophic) Hormone (Endocrinology)
TSI	Target Signature Investigation
TSI	Technical Standardization Inspection
TSI	Time Sterile Indicator
TSI	Triple Sugar Iron (Agar)
TSI	Tri-South Mortgage Investors (NYSE symbol)
TSI	Turkish Standards Institution
TSIA	Trading Stamp Institute of America
TSIAJ	This Scherzo Is a Joke (Used by American composer Charles Edward Ives)
TSIL	Time Significant Item List
TSIMS	Telemetry Simulation Submodule

TSIT	Technical Service Intelligence Team
TSJC	Trinidad State Junior College (Colorado)
TSK	Time Shift Keying
TSK	Torque Screwdriver Kit
TSKT	Test Kit
TSL	Test Set Logic
TSL	Test Stand Level
TSL	Texas Short Line Railway (AAR code)
TSL	Thin Shock Layer
TSL	Trouble-Shooting Loop
TSLS	Two-Stage Least Squares (Statistics)
TSM	Tactical Survey Meter
TSM	Target Signature Measurement
TSM	Target-to-Surface-to-Missile Path
TSM	Time Scheduled Maintenance
TSM	Ton Statute Mile
TSMC	Technical Supply Management Code
TSMC	Transportation Supply Maintenance Command
TSMG	Thompson Submachine Gun
TSMO	TACSATCOM (Tactical Satellite Communications) Management Office
TSN	Time Since New (Navy)
TSO	Technical Service Organization (A generic term)
TSO	Technical Standard Order
TSO	Technical Support Organization (AEC)
TSO	Tesoro Petroleum Corp. (NYSE symbol)
TSO	Test Site Office
TSO	Test Support Office
TSO	Thrust Section Observer
TSO	Time-Sharing Option (Data processing)
TSO	Time Since Overhaul (of engine, or other equipment)
TSO	Town Suboffice
TSO	Transportation Supply Officer
TSOP	Tactical Standing Operating Procedure
TSOR	Tentative Specific Operational Requirement
TSOSC	Test Set Operational Signal Converter
TSP	Teaspoonful
TSP	Technical Specification
TSP	Technical Support Package (NASA)
TSP	Temperature-Sensitive Period
TSP	Temporary Standard Practice (or Procedure)
TSP	Test Support Program
TSP	Thyroid-Stimulating Hormone of the Prepituitary Gland (Endocrinology)
TSP	Time Sorting Program
TSP	Torpedo Seaplane (Navy)
TSP	Traffic Service Position (Telephone)
TSP	Transshipment Point
TSP	Trial Shot Point
TSP	Tri-Service Program (Military)
TSP	Trisodium Phosphate (Inorganic chemistry)
TSPAK	Time Series Package (Bell System)
TSPS	Traffic Service Position System
TSQ	Time and Super Quick
TSR	Tactical Strike and Reconnaissance
TSR	Technical Study Report
TSR	Technical Summary Report
TSR	Test Schedule Request
TSR	Thermally Stable Resin
TSR	Tile-Shingle Roof (Technical drawings)
TSR	Time Status Register
TSR	Torpedo-Spotter Reconnaissance (Military)
TSR	Towed SONAR Response
TSR	Tower Shielding Reactors (ORNL)
TSR	Transistor Saturable Reactor
TSR	Trans-Siberian Railway
TSR	Traveling Stock Reserve
TSRC	Tubular & Split Rivet Council
TSRE	Tropospheric Scatter Radio Equipment
TSRL	Total Support Requirements List
TSRP	Technical Support Real Property
TSS	Tactical Strike System
TSS	Tangential Signal Sensitivity
TSS	Tape Search System
TSS	Technical Specification Sheet
TSS	Telecommunication Switching System
TSS	Teletype Switching Subsystem
TSS	Test Set Simulator
TSS	Thrust Stand System
TSS	Time-Shared (or Sharing) System (Data processing)
TSS	Toroidal Space Station
TSS	Toroidal Support Submarine
TSS	Transistor Servo Simulator

TSS	Transparent Semiconductor Shutter
TSS	Tropospheric Scatter System
TSS	Twin-Screw Steamer (Nautical)
TSSA	Telemetry Subcarrier Spectrum Analyzer
TSSA	Test Scorer and Statistical Analyzer (Data processing)
TSSC	Target System Service Charge
TS & SCP	Task, Schedule and Status Control Plan
TSSCS	Tactical Synchronous Satellite Communication System
TSSE	Tactical Security Support Equipment (Military)
TSSM	Total Ship Simulation Model
TSSPS	Tsentralniya Suvet na Profesionalnite Suyuzi (Central Council of Trade Unions) (Bulgaria)
TST	Temperature Sensing Transducer
TST	Test
TST	Thermistor Sterilization Test
TST	Threshold Setting Tracer
TST	Time-Sharing Terminals, Inc.
TSTA	Transmission, Signaling and Test Access
TSTFLT	Test Set Fault
TSTO	Test Site Tool Order
TSTO	Testing Tool
TSTP	Test of Selected Topics in Physics
TSTP	Thermistor Sterilization Test Program
TSTP	Traffic Safety Training Program
TSTR	Transistor
TSTS	Tail Section Test Stand
TSTS	Thrust Structure Test Stand
TSTS	Tracking System Test Set
TSU	Technical Service Unit
TSU	Texas Southern University
TSU	This Side Up
TSU	Time Standard Unit
TSU	Transfer Switch Unit
TSU	Tulsa-Sapulpa Union Railway Company (AAR code)
TSUS	Tariff Schedule of the United States
TSV	Terminal Stage Vehicle
TSVP	Tournez s'il Vous Plait (Please Turn Over; PTO)
TSW	Test Switch
TSW	Transfer Switch
TSW	Transmitting Slide Wire
TSW	Tropical Summer Winter (Vessel load line mark)
TSX	Telephone Satellite, Experimental
TT	Tablet Triturate (Pharmacy)
TT	Target Towing Aircraft (Navy)
TT	Technical Test
TT	Technical Translation (Former NTIS publication)
TT	Teetotaler (Slang)
TT	Telegraphic Transfer (of funds)
TT	Teletype
TT	Teletypewriter
TT	Tetanus Toxoid (Medicine)
TT	Thermal-Tow
TT	Thrust Termination
TT	Toledo Terminal R. R. (AAR code)
TT	Torpedo Tube(s)
TT	Tourist Trophy (Motorcycle racing) (British)
TT	Tracking Telescope
TT	Transit Time (of blood through heart and lungs)
TT	Transonic Tunnel (NASA)
TT	Trans-Texas Airways
TT	Tree Tops
TT	Tricycle and Tail Skid (Aerospace)
TT	Trigesimo-Secundo (Book from 10 to 12 1/2 centimeters in height) (Bibliography)
TT	Trinity Term
TT	Troop Test
TT	Tuberculin Tested (Milk)
T/T	Timing and Telemetry
T/T	Torpedo Tube
T/T	Travel/Tourism
TT's	Tripoli Trots (Term used by entertainers in World War II)
TTA	Test Target Array
TTA	Theatre Television Authority
TTA	**Thrust Termination Assembly**
TTA	**Transit-Time Accelerometer**
TTA	**Trans-Texas Airways**
TTA	**Travel Time Authorized**
TTAB	**Trademark Trial and Appeal Board (of Patent Office)**
TTAF	Technical Training Air Force
TTAT	Torpedo Tube Acceptance Trials (Navy)
TTB	Test Two Bits

TTC	Tape to Card
TTC	Target Track Central
TTC	Technical Training Center (Air Force)
TTC	Technical Training Command (Army Air Forces) (World War II)
TTC	Teletypewriter Center (Military)
TTC	Temperature Test Chamber
TTC	Tetrazolium Chloride
TTC	Texas Technological College
TTC	Tight Tape Contact
TTC	Tin Telluride Crystal
TTC	Tobacco Tax Council
TTC	Tow Target Cable
TTC	Tracking, Telemetry, and Command
TTC	Transient Temperature Control
TTC	Treasure Trove Club
TTC	Triphenyltetrazolium Chloride (Organic chemistry)
TTC	Tropic Test Center (Army)
TTC	Tube Temperature Control
TTCC	The Technical Cooperation Committee (Army)
TTCE	Tooth-to-Tooth Composite Error
TTCI	Transient Temperature Control Instrument
TTCP	The Technical Cooperative Program (US, UK, Canada, Australia) (Research)
TTCP	Tripartite Technical Cooperation Program (Military)
TTCS	Truck Transportable Communications Station
TTD	Technical Training Detachment
TTD	Transponder Transmitter Detector
TTDR	Tracking Telemetry Data Receiver
TTE	Telephone Terminal Equipment
TTE	Temporary Test Equipment
TTE	Tentative Tables of Equipment
TTE	Trailer Test Equipment
TTEC	Teletypewriter Technician
T & TEC	Trinidad & Tobago Electricity Commission
TTEM	Tooling Test Equipment Team
TTF	Tactical Task Force
TTF	Tanker Task Force
TTF	Time to Failure
TTF	Tone Telegraph Filter
TTF	Training Task Force
TTF	Transistor Test Fixture
TTFN	Ta Ta For Now
TTG	Time to Go (Air Force)
TTG	Travel with Troops Going
TTGD	Time-to-Go Dial
TTH	Thyrotrophic Hormone (Endocrinology)
TTHA	Triethylenetetraminehexaacetic Acid (Organic chemistry)
TTI	Tactical Target Illustration
TTI	Texas Transportation Institute
TTI	The Teachers, Incorporated
TTI	Time to Intercept (Missiles)
TTI	Transportation Technology, Incorporated
TTI	Tuck Tummy In (Slang)
TTIA	Tube Temperature Indication and Alarm
TTITS	Thrust Termination Initiator Test Set
TTK	Two Tone Keying
TTL	Teletype Telling
TTL	Through the Lens (Trademark of Spiratone, Inc.)
TTL	To Take Leave
TTL	Transistor-Transistor Logic
TTLS	Team Training Launch Station
TTM	Tactical Telemetry
TTM	Two-Tone Modulation
T/TM	Test and Training Monitor
TTMA	Truck Trailer Manufacturers Association
TTMA	Tufted Textile Manufacturers Association
TTMCFC	Theater Type Mobilization Corps Force Capabilities
TTMCFO	Theater Type Mobilization Corps Force Objective
TTMP	Tactical Targets Materials Program
TTMP	Transit Time Magnetic Pumping
TTMS	Telephoto Transmission Measuring Set
TTO	Transmitter Turn-Off
TTO	Travel and Transportation Order
TTP	Tactical Targeting Program
TTP	Tape-to-Print
TTP	Thermistor Test Program
TTP	Thrombotic Thrombocytopenic Purpura
TTP	Total Taxable Pay
TTP	Transverse Thrust Propeller
TTP	Turn Toward Peace (An organization; later, WWWCUS)
TT & P	Training, Transient and Patient

TTPC	Titanium Toroidal Propellant Container
TTPE.......	Total Taxable Pay Earned
TTPH	Team Trainer, Pearl Harbor
TTR	Tape-Reading Tripping Relay
TTR	Target-Track RADAR (Air Force)
TTR	Thermal Test Reactor
TTR	Thermal Timing Relay
TTR	Thermal Transpiration Ratio
TTR	Time-Temperature Recorder
TTR	Tonopah Test Range
TTR	Transient Thermal Radiation
TTR	Travel with Troops Returning
TTRB	Timken Tapered Roller Bearing
TTRC	Transistorized Thyratron Ring Counter
TTS	Target Trajectory Sensor
TTS	Telegraphic Transfers (of Money) (Banking)
TTS	Telemetry Transmission System
TTS	Temporary Threshold Shift
TTS	Test and Training Satellite (NASA)
TTS	Thermal Transfer Standard
TTS	Tissue Type Specific (Antigen)
TTS	Transponder Test Set
TTS	Transportable Telemetry Set
TTSA	Transitional Training Squadron, Atlantic (Navy)
TTSFP.......	Training Transition School (Squadron), Pacific Fleet (Navy)
TTSP.......	Transition Training Squadron, Pacific (Navy)
TTT	Time-to-Target
TTT........	Time to Turn (Ship or aircraft)
TTT	Transamerican Trailer Transport
TTT	Trilateral Tracking Technique
TTT	True Temperature Tunnel
TTTT.......	Tartar-Talos-Terrier-Typhon
TTU	Timing Terminal Unit
TTV	Tow Test Vehicle (Aerospace)
TTVM.......	Thermal Transfer Voltmeter
TTW	Total Temperature and Weight
TTWL	Twin Tandem Wheel Loading (Aviation)
TTX	Tetrodotoxin (A poison) (Biochemistry)
TTY	Teletypewriter
TU	Societe Tunisienne de l'Air
TU	Tanking Unit
TU	Tape Unit
TU	Task Unit
TU	Taxicrinic Unit (Data processing)
TU	Technical Service Unit (Military)
TU	Thank You (Communications operator's procedural remark)
TU	Thermal Unit
TU	Timing Unit
TU	Torah Umesorah–National Society for Hebrew Day Schools
TU	Toxic Unit (Medicine)
TU	Trade Union
TU	Traffic Unit
TU	Training Unit (Army)
TU	Trans Union Corp. (NYSE symbol)
TU	Transfer Unconditionally
TU	Transfer Unit
TU	Transmission Unit
TU	Transuranium
TU	Tritium Unit (AEC)
TU	Trout, Unlimited (An organization)
TU	Tupolev (Russian aircraft symbol; initialism taken from name of aircraft's designer)
TU	Turbidity Unit
TU	Turkey (NATO)
TuAF.......	Turkish Air Force
TUAL	Tentative Unit Allowance List (Air Force)
TUAR	Turning Arbor
TUB	Temporary Unlighted Buoy (Maps and charts)
TUB	Tubing
TUBE	Terminating Unfair Broadcasting Excesses (Student legal action organization)
TUBE	Trans-Urban Bicentennial Exposition
TUC	Technology Utilization Center
TUC	Temporary Unemployment Compensation (Labor)
TUC........	Trade(s) Union Council
TUC	Trades Union Congress (Great Britain)
TUC	Transportation, Utilities, Communications
TUCA	Turning Cam (Tool)
TUCN.......	Trades Union Congress of Nigeria
TUCOPS......	The Universal Coterie of Pipe Smokers
TUCR	Troop Unit Change Request
TUCSA	Trade Union Council of South Africa

TUE	Tuesday
TUEL	Trade Union Educational League
TUES	Tuesday
TUF	Tactical Undercover Function (Chicago police operation)
TUF	Trade Union Federation (British)
TUFCDF	Thorium-Uranium Fuel Cycle Development Facility (AEC)
TUFEC	Thailand-UNESCO Fundamental Education Centre
TUFF-TUG....	Tape Update of Formatted Files-Format Table Tape Updater and Generator (Data processing)
TUFI........	This Umbrella Folds Itself (Trademark for type of umbrella)
TUFX	Turning Fixture
TUG	Towed Universal Glider
TUG........	TRANSAC (Transistorized Automatic Computer) Users Group
TUI	Trade Union International
TUIAFW	Trade Unions International of Agricultural and Forestry Workers
TUIFU	The Ultimate in Foul Ups (Military slang)
TUIR	Time Until In Range
TULC	Trade Union Leadership Council
TULE	Transistorized Universal Logic Elements
TUM........	Trades Union Movement
TUMA	Tumacacori National Monument
TUN........	Transfer Unconditionally
TUN........	Tuning
TUNG	Tungsten
TUOC	Tactical Unit Operations Center
TUP	Technology Utilization Program
TUPE	Tanganyika Union of Public Employees
TUPE	Tupelo National Battlefield
TUR	Traffic Usage Recorder
TUR	Transurethral Resection (of prostate gland)
TURB	Turbine
TURBOALT....	Turbo Alternator
TURBOGEN ...	Turbo Generator
TURCO......	Turn Around Control (Navy)
TURPS.......	Terrestrial Unattended Reactor Power System
TUS	Treasurer of the United States
TUS	Tugboat Underwriting Syndicate
TUSA	Third United States Army
TUSAB	The United States Army Band
TUSAC	The United States Army Chorus
TUSAFG	The United States Air Force Group, American Mission for Aid to Turkey
TUSC	Technology Use Studies Center (Southeastern State College)
TUSLOG.....	The United States Logistics Group (Military)
TUUL	Trade Union Unity League
TUW........	Tung-Sol Electric, Inc. (NYSE symbol) (Delisted)
TUWC.......	Tactical Utilization Working Committee (Navy)
TUWR	Turning Wrench (Tool)
TUZI	Tuzigoot National Monument
TV	Television
TV	Terminal Velocity (Navy)
TV	Test Vehicle (Air Force)
TV	Tetrazolium Violet
TV	Thermal Vacuum
TV	Tidal Volume (Amount of air which moves in and out of lungs under given conditions) (Medicine)
TV	Tidewater Oil Company (NYSE symbol) (Later, TMS)
TV	Time Variation of Gain
TV	Total Volume
TV	Transfer Voucher
TV	Transport Vehicle
TV	Trichomonas Vaginalis (A protozoan) (Medicine)
T/V	Target Vehicle
T/V	Test Vehicle
TVA	Tax on Value Added (European manufacturing tax)
TVA	Temporary Variation Authority (or Authorization)
TVA	Tennessee Valley Authority
TVA	Textile Veterans Association
TVA	Thrust Vector Alignment
TVAC	Time Varying Adaptive Correlation
TvB	Television Bureau of Advertising
TVBS	Television Broadcast Satellite (NASA)
TVC	Temperature Valve Control
TVC........	Thermal Voltage Converter
TVC........	Throttle Valve Control
TVC	Thrust Vector Control (Aerospace)
TVC........	Time Varying Coefficient
TVC........	Timed Vital Capacity
TVC........	Torsional Vibration Characteristics
TVC........	Total Annual Variable Cost
TVCAM	Television Camera and Control Equipment
TVCS	Tyler Vocational Card Sort (Guidance)

TVD . . . . Toxic Vapor Detector
TVD . . . . True Vertical Depth (Diamonds)
TVD . . . . Tuned Viscoelastic Damper
TVDC . . . . . . Test Volts, Direct Current
TVDC . . . . . . Tidewater Virginia Development Council
TVDP . . . . . . Terminal Vector Display Unit
TVDY . . . . . . Television Deflection Yoke
TVE . . . . Test Vehicle Engine
TVE . . . . Thermal Vacuum Environment
TVED . . . . . . Tuned Viscoelastic Damper
TVEL . . . . . . Track Velocity
TVERS . . . . . . Television Evaluation and Renewal Standards (Student legal action
                organization)
TVFT . . . . . . Television Flyback Transformer
TVG . . . . Tavares & Gulf R. R. (AAR code)
TVG . . . . Threshold Voltage Generator
TVG . . . . Time Variation of Gain
TVG . . . . Time Varied Gain
TVG . . . . Triggered Vacuum Gap
TVI . . . . Television Interference (Communications)
TVI . . . . Transient Voltage Indicator
TVIC . . . . . . Television Interference Committee
TVIG . . . . . . Television and Inertial Guidance
TVIS . . . . . . Turbine Vibration Indication System
TVIST . . . . . . Television Information Storage Tube
TVK . . . . Toimihenkilo - ja Virkamiesjarjestojen Keskusliitto (Confederation of
                Intellectual and Government Workers) (Finland)
TVL . . . . Tenth Value Layer
TVL . . . . Transverse Vertical Longitudinal
TVL . . . . TraveLodge International, Inc. (NYSE symbol)
TVLADVP . . . . Travel Advance Payment (TDY)
TVLALWADV . . Travel Allowance Advance (in PCS)
TVLALWS . . . . Travel Allowance on Separation
TVM . . . . Tachometer Voltmeter
TVM . . . . . . Television Monitor (Video only)
TVM . . . . Track-Via-Missile
TVM . . . . Trailer Van Mount
TVM . . . . Transistorized Voltmeter
TVOR . . . . . . Terminal VHF (Very High Frequency) Omnirange (Radio)
TVOR . . . . . . Terminal Visual Omni-Range
TVP . . . . True Vapor Pressure
TVPPA . . . . . Tennessee Valley Public Power Association
TVQ . . . . Top Visual Quality
TVR . . . . Temperature Variation of Resistance (Electricity)
TVS . . . . Tactical Vocoder System
TVS . . . . Telemetry Video Spectrum
TVS . . . . Television Viewing System
TVSD . . . . . . Time Varying Spectral Display
TVSG . . . . . . Television Signal Generator
TVSM . . . . . . Time Varying Sequential Measuring (Device)
TVSM . . . . . Time-Varying Signal Measurement
TVSO . . . . . . Television Space Observatory
TVSS . . . . . . Television Systems Section
TVT . . . . Thermo Vacuum Test
TVU . . . . Total Volume Urine (in 24 hours)
TVX . . . . Target Vehicle Experimental (Air Force)
TW . . . . Tail Wind
TW . . . . Taxiway
TW . . . . Technical Works (Air Force)
TW . . . . Tempered Water
TW . . . . Temporary Warrant
TW . . . . Thermoplastic Wire
TW . . . . Tile Wainscot (Technical drawings)
TW . . . . Time Word
TW . . . . Trans-World Airlines, Inc.
TW . . . . Traveling Wave
TW . . . . Twister
TW . . . . Typewriter
T/W . . . . Thrust-to-Weight
TW3 . . . . That Was The Week That Was (Television program of English origin)
                (Also, TWTWTW)
TWA . . . . . . Textile Waste Association
TWA . . . . Tooling Work Authorization
TWA . . . . . . Toy Wholesalers Association of America
TWA . . . . Trailing Wire Antenna (on aircraft)
TWA . . . . . . Trans-World Airlines, Inc. (NYSE symbol)
TWA . . . . . . Traveling-Wave Amplifier
TWA . . . . Traveling Wave Antenna
TWASPIT . . . . Therapeutic Work Aid Station for Physically Inactive Thinkers
TWAT . . . . . . Traveling Wave Amplifier Tube
TWB . . . . Traveling Wave Beam (LASER)

TWC . . . . Tennessee Wesleyan College
TWC . . . . Texas Wesleyan College
TWC . . . . Texas Western College
TWD . . . . Tactical Weapons Delivery
TWD . . . . Tail Wags Dog (Airspace effects)
TWE . . . . Textile Waste Exchange
TWEA . . . . . . Trading with the Enemy Act
TWEB . . . . . . Transcribed Weather Broadcast
TWEP . . . . . . Terminate with Extreme Prejudice (To kill) (Counterintelligence)
TWERL . . . . . Tropical Wind, Energy Conversion, and Reference Level
TWERLE . . . . Tropical Wind, Energy Conversion and Reference Level Experiment
                (National Science Foundation)
TWF . . . . Trans-World Financial Company (NYSE symbol)
TWG . . . . . . Technical Working Group (of the Conference on the Discontinuance of
                Nuclear Weapon Tests)
TWG . . . . . . Telemetry Working Group
TWGC . . . . . Treatment of War Gas Casualties
TWHBEAA . . . . Tennessee Walking Horse Breeders' & Exhibitors' Association of America
TWHO . . . . . . The White House Office
TWHTA . . . . . Tennessee Walking Horse Trainers' Association
TWI . . . . Threat Warning Information (Air Force)
TWI . . . . Training within Industry (British)
TWIMC . . . . . To Whom It May Concern
TWIS . . . . . . Technical Writing Improvement Society
TWIS . . . . . . Technically Workable Ideal System (Industrial engineering)
TWITW . . . . . "The Wind in the Willows," a book by Kenneth Grahame
TWIU . . . . . . Tobacco Workers International Union
TWK . . . . Tool Welders Kit
TWK . . . . Traveling Wave Klystron
TWK . . . . Typewriter Keyboard
TWL . . . . Leased Teletypewriter Service
TWL . . . . Top Water Level
TWL . . . . Tuberculosis Welfare League
TWL . . . . Twin Wheel Loading (Aviation)
TWM . . . . . . Tape Wrapping Machine
TWM . . . . . . Traveling Wave MASER
TWM . . . . . . Two-Way Mirror
TWMR . . . . . Tungsten Water-Moderated Nuclear Rocket
TWN . . . . Twin Industries Corporation (NYSE symbol) (Delisted)
TWOATAF . . . . Second Allied Tactical Air Force Central Europe
TWOM . . . . . . Traveling Wave Optical MASER
TW/OT . . . . . . Travel Without Troops
TWP . . . . Technological War Plan
TWP . . . . Total Wave Pressure
TWP . . . . Transwestern Pipeline Company (NYSE symbol) (Delisted)
TWP . . . . Traveling Wave Phototube
TWPA . . . . . . Traveling Wave Parametric Amplifier
TWPL . . . . . . Teletypewriter, Private Line
TWPS . . . . . . Travelling Wave Phase Sifter
TWR . . . . Thermo Warning Receiver
TWR . . . . Threat Warning RADAR
TWR . . . . Threat Warning Receiver
TWR . . . . Tool Wear Rate
TWR . . . . Tower
TWR . . . . . . Trans-World Radio
TWR . . . . Traveling Wave Resonator
TWS . . . . Tactical Warning System
TWS . . . . Tactical Weapon System
TWS . . . . Tactical Weather Station
TWS . . . . Tail Warning Set
TWS . . . . Tartar Weapons System
TWS . . . . Terrier Weapons System
TWS . . . . Thermal Wire Stripper
TWS . . . . Track-While-Scan (Communications)
TWS . . . . Twin Wheel Stripper
TWSO . . . . . . Tactical Weapon Systems Operation
TWSR . . . . . . Track-While-Scan RADAR
TWSRO . . . . . Track While Scan on Receive Only
TWSRS . . . . . Track-While-Scan RADAR Simulator
TWT . . . . Transonic Wind Tunnel
TWT . . . . Travel With Troops
TWT . . . . . . Traveling-Wave Tube (Radio)
TWT . . . . Two-Way-Traffic-in-Ideas Conference (of Labor Party) (British)
TWTA . . . . . . Traveling Wave Tube Amplifier
TWTWTW . . . . That Was The Week That Was (Television program of English origin)
                (Also, TW3)
TWU . . . . Tata Workers' Union (India)
TWU . . . . Texas Woman's University
TWU . . . . Transport Workers' Union (British)
TWU . . . . . . Transport Workers' Union of America
TWUA . . . . . . Textile Workers Union of America

TWX . . . . Teletypewriter Exchange Service (Western Union) (Term also used generically for teletypewriter message)
TWX . . . . Time Wire Transmission
TWY . . . . Taxiway
TWZO . . . . . . Trade Wind Zone Oceanography
TX . . . . Texaco Inc. (NYSE symbol)
TX . . . . Texas
TX . . . . Torque Transmitter
TX . . . . Transmitter (General term)
TXF . . . . Texfi Industries, Inc. (NYSE symbol)
TXG . . . . Texas Gas Transmission Corporation (NYSE symbol)
TXH . . . . Transfer on Index High
TXI . . . . Texas Industries, Inc. (NYSE symbol)
TXI . . . . Transfer with Index Incremented
TXL . . . . Transfer on Index Low
TXN . . . . Texas Instruments, Inc. (NYSE symbol)
TXO . . . . Texas Oil & Gas Corp. (NYSE symbol)
TXRX . . . . . . Transmitter-Receiver
TXT . . . . Textron Inc. (NYSE symbol)
TXU . . . . Texas Utilities Company (NYSE symbol)
TY . . . . Total Yield
TY . . . . Tri-Continental Corporation (NYSE symbol)
TYC . . . . Two-Year(-Old) Course (Horseracing)
TYCOM . . . . . Type Commander

TYDAC . . . . . . Typical Digital Automatic Computer
TYG . . . . Temple Youth Group (Local groups of National Federation of Temple Youth, sometimes called TYG-ers, pronounced "Tigers")
TYG . . . . Trypticase, Yeast-extract, Glucose (Growth medium for phage)
TYL . . . . TANU (Tanganyika African National Union) Youth League (Tanganyika)
TYL . . . . Tyler Corp. (NYSE symbol)
TYP . . . . Transitional Year Program (Brandeis University)
TYP . . . . Typical
TYP . . . . Typography
TYPER . . . . Typographical Error
TYR . . . . Tyrosine (Amino acid)
TYS . . . . Tensile Yield Strength
TYSD . . . . Total Years Service Date
TZ . . . . Tactical Zone
TZ . . . . Tidal Zone
TZ . . . . Time Zero
TZD . . . . True Zenith Distance (Navigation)
TZE . . . . Transfer on Zero
TZG . . . . Thermofit Zap Gun
TZJ . . . . Tubular Zippered Jacket
TZM . . . . Titanium-Zirconium-Molybdenum
TZP . . . . Time Zero Pulse
TZV . . . . Tetra Zolium Violet

U

U . . . . Intensity Unknown (Meteorology)
U . . . . Intrinsic Energy (Physics symbol)
U . . . . Umpire (Baseball)
U . . . . Uncirculated
U . . . . **Unclassified**
U . . . . Uncle
U . . . . Under
U . . . . Unified
U . . . . Uniform
U . . . . Uniformly Labeled (Compound, with radioisotope) (Also, UL)
U . . . . Union(ist)
U . . . . Unit(s)
U . . . . United
U . . . . United Corporation (NYSE symbol)
U . . . . Universal
U . . . . University
U . . . . Unknown
U . . . . Unlimited (Aviation)
U . . . . Unoccupied
U . . . . Unpleasant
U . . . . Unrestricted (Aviation)
U . . . . Unsymmetrical
U . . . . Unwatched (with reference to a light) (Maps and charts)
U . . . . Up(per)
U . . . . Uranium (Chemical element)
U . . . . Urschrift (Original, as of a document) (German military)
U . . . . Use
U . . . . Utah
U . . . . Utility (Designation for all US military aircraft)
U . . . . You (Communications)
UA . . . . Ultra-Audible
UA . . . . **Uniform Allowance**
UA . . . . Union Association (Major league in baseball, 1884)
UA . . . . **United Air Lines, Inc.**
UA . . . . United Aircraft Corporation (NYSE symbol)
UA . . . . University of Arizona
UA . . . . Upper Arm
U/A . . . . Underwriting Account (Business and trade)
U/A . . . . Unit of Account (European Monetary Agreement)
UAA . . . . **Undergarment Accessories Association**
UAA . . . . United Action for Animals
UAA . . . . **United African Appeal**
UAA . . . . University Aviation Association
UAA . . . . User Action Analyzer
UAAS . . . . . . Ukrainian Academy of Arts and Sciences in the US
UAB . . . . Unemployment Assistance Board
UAB . . . . Until Advised By
UAC . . . . Union Army of Commemoration
UAC . . . . United African Company
UAC . . . . **United Aircraft Corporation**
UAC . . . . United American Croats
UAC . . . . . . **Utility Airplane Council**
UAC . . . . . . Utility Assemble Compool
UACC . . . . . . Universal Autograph Collector's Club (International)
UACC . . . . . . Upper Area Control Centre
UACL . . . . . . United Aircraft of Canada, Limited
UACTE . . . . . Universal Automatic Control and Test Equipment
UADE . . . . . . Universidad Argentina de la Empresa
UADPS . . . . . Uniform Automated (or Automatic) Data Processing System
 (NYSE symbol)
UADPS/INAS . . Uniform Automated (or Automatic) Data Processing System/Industrial Naval
 Air Station
UADW . . . . . . **Universal Alliance of Diamond Workers**

UAE . . . . Union of Arab Emirates
UAF . . . . Ultimate Asbestos Fibril
UAF . . . . Unit Authorization File
UAFSC . . . . . . Utilization Air Force Specialty Code
UAFS/T . . . . . Universal Aircraft Flight Simulator/Trainer
UAG. . . . . . . Universidad Autonoma de Guadalajara
UAHC . . . . . . **Union of American Hebrew Congregations**
UAI . . . . Union Academique Internationale (International Union of Academies)
UAI . . . . Union des Associations Internationales (Union of International Associations)
UAI . . . . Union Astronomique Internationale (International Astronomical Union)
UAI . . . . Universal Azimuth Indicator
UAI . . . . Urban Affairs Institute
UAIDE . . . . . . **Users of Automatic Information Display Equipment**
UAIM . . . . . . United Andean Indian Mission
UAJG . . . . . . Union d'Action des Jeunes de Guinee (Guinean Union of Youth Action)
UAL . . . . UAL, Inc. (Formerly, United Air Lines) (NYSE symbol) (Wall Street
 slang name: "You All")
UAL . . . . **Ukrainian American League**
UAL . . . . Unit Authorization List
UAL . . . . Upper Acceptance Limit
UAL . . . . Urea-Ammonia Liquor
UAM . . . . . . Underwater-to-Air Missile (Air Force)
UAM . . . . . . Union Africaine et Malgache (African and Malagasy Union) (Later,
 Common Afro-Malagasy Organization)
UAM . . . . . . **United American Mechanics**
UAMC . . . . . . Utility Assemble Master Compool
UAMPT . . . . . Union Africaine et Malgache des Postes et Telecommunications
UAN . . . . Uric Acid Nitrogen
UANM . . . . . . **United African Nationalist Movement**
UANM . . . . . . **Universal African Nationalist Movement**
UAO . . . . Und Andere Orte (And Elsewhere) (German)
UAO . . . . Unexplained Aerial Object
UAP . . . . Unidentified Atmospheric Phenomena
UAP . . . . United Aircraft Products
UAP . . . . **United Australia Party**
UAP . . . . Urea-Ammonium Phosphate
UAP . . . . Utility Amphibian Plane (Navy)
UAPA . . . . . . **United Amateur Press Association**
UAR . . . . Underwater Acoustic Resistance
UAR . . . . Underwater Angle Receptacle
UAR . . . . Uniform Airman Record
UAR . . . . United Arab Republic (Later, FAR)
UAR . . . . Upper Air Route
UAR . . . . Upper Atmosphere Research
UARCO . . . . . UARCO, Inc. (Formerly, United Autographic Register Company)
UAREP . . . . . Universities Associated for Research and Education in Pathology
UARL . . . . . . United Aircraft Research Laboratories
UARS . . . . . . Unmanned Arctic Research Submersible
UAS . . . . Union of African States
UAS . . . . Unit Approval System (for approval of aircraft materials, parts, and
 appliances) (FAA)
UAS . . . . Unmanned Aerial Surveillance
UAS . . . . Upper Atmospheric Sounder
UASCS . . . . . United States Army Signal Center and School
UASS . . . . . . Unmanned Aerial Surveillance System
UAT . . . . Ultraviolet Acquisition Technique
UAT . . . . Union Aeromaritime de Transport (Privately owned French airline)
UAT . . . . Until Advised by the Tower (Aviation)
UATE . . . . . . Universal Automatic Test Equipment
UATI . . . . . . Union des Associations Techniques Internationales (Union of International
 Engineering Associations)
UATP . . . . . . Universal Air Travel Plan (Commercial airlines credit system)
UAUM . . . . . . Underwater-to-Air-to-Underwater Missile (Air Force)

UAUOC . . . . . United American Ukrainian Organizations Committee
UAW . . . . International Union, United Automobile, Aerospace and Agricultural Implement Workers of America
UAX . . . . United Automatic Exchange
UB . . . . Underwater Battery
UB . . . . United Brands Co. (NYSE symbol)
UB . . . . United Brethren in Christ
UBA . . . . Undenatured Bacterial Antigen
UBA . . . . Union of Burma Airways
UBA . . . . United Breweries of America
UBAEC . . . . . . Union of Burma Atomic Energy Centre
UBARI . . . . . . Union of Burma Applied Research Institute
UBBA . . . . United Boys' Brigades of America
UBBR . . . . University Bureaus of Business Research
UBC . . . . Universal Buffer Controller
UBC . . . . University of British Columbia
UBCHEA . . . . . United Board for Christian Higher Education in Asia
UBCJ . . . . United Brotherhood of Carpenters and Joiners
UBCL . . . . Union of Black Clergy and Laity of the Episcopal Church
UBCW . . . . United Brick and Clay Workers of America
UBD . . . . Utility Binary Dump (Data processing)
UBDMA . . . . . United Better Dress Manufacturers Association
UBEA . . . . United Business Education Association
UBF . . . . Universal Boss Fitting
UBF . . . . Universal Buddhist Fellowship
UBFC . . . . Underwater Battery Fire Control
UBFCS . . . . . . Underwater Battery Fire Control System (Navy)
UBHC . . . . Unburned Hydrocarbon
UBI . . . . Ultraviolet Blood Irradiation
UBI . . . . Universal Battlefield Identification
UBITRON . . . . Undulating Beam Interaction Electron Tube
UBM . . . . Ultrasonic Bonding Machine
UBO . . . . Uinta Basin Observatory
UBO . . . . US Tobacco Company (NYSE symbol)
U–BOAT–S . . . Unterseeboot (German submarine)
UBP . . . . Underwater Battery Plot (Antisubmarine warfare)
UBP . . . . United Bermuda Party
UBPVLS . . . . . Uniform Boiler and Pressure Vessel Laws Society
UBRF . . . . Upper Branchial Filament
UBS . . . . Uniform Bearing Stress
UBS . . . . United Bible Societies
UBS . . . . United Biscuit Company of America (NYSE symbol) (Delisted)
UBS . . . . Universal Builders Supply Company
UBSA . . . . United Business Schools Association
UBSO . . . . Uinta Basin Seismological Observatory
UBT . . . . Universal Boattail Thor (NASA)
UBT . . . . Universal Book Tester (Measures performance of binding)
UBTM . . . . United Bellows Tankage Module
UBV . . . . Ultraviolet–Blue–Visual (Photometric system)
UBX . . . . US Borax & Chemical Corporation (NYSE symbol) (Delisted)
UC . . . . Umbilical Cable (or Connector)
UC . . . . Una Corda (With one string or with the soft pedal) (Music)
UC . . . . Under Charge
UC . . . . Under Construction
UC . . . . Undercarriage
UC . . . . Unemployment Compensation
UC . . . . Union Camerounaise (Cameroonese Union)
UC . . . . Unit Cooler
UC . . . . University of California
UC . . . . Unoperated Control
UC . . . . Upper Canada
UC . . . . Upper Case (i.e., capital letters) (Typography)
UC . . . . Upper Cylinder
UC . . . . Urbis Conditae (From the Foundation of the City; that is, of Rome)
UC . . . . Utah International, Inc. (Formerly, Utah Construction & Mining Co.) (NYSE symbol)
UC . . . . Utility Cargo
U/C . . . . Unclassified
UCA . . . . Unitized Component Assembly
UCA . . . . Universal Calibration Adapter
UCACEP . . . . . United Council of Associations of Civil Employees of Pakistan
UCAR . . . . University Corporation for Atmospheric Research
UCAS . . . . Uniform Cost Accounting Standards
UCAS . . . . Union of Central African States
UCAVJ . . . . . . Union Continentale Africaine des Villes Jumelees (Continental African Union of Twin Cities)
UCB . . . . Union Chimique Belge (Belgium)
UCB . . . . Union Chimique–Chemische Bedrijven (Belgium)
UCBC . . . . Parti de l'Unite et da la Communaute Belgo-Congolaise
UCC . . . . Umbilical Checkout Cable
UCC . . . . Unadjusted Contractual Changes

UCC . . . . Uniform Commercial Code
UCC . . . . Uniform Credit Code
UCC . . . . Union Camp Corporation (NYSE symbol)
UCC . . . . United Cancer Council
UCC . . . . United Church of Christ
UCC . . . . United Electric Coal Companies (NYSE symbol) (Delisted)
UCC . . . . Universal Copyright Convention
UCC . . . . University of Corpus Christi (Texas)
UCC . . . . Utility Control Console
UCCA . . . . . United Ukrainian Congress Committee of America
UCCE . . . . . . Union des Capitales de la Communaute Europeenne (Union of Capitals of the European Community)
UCCE . . . . . . Universal Craftsmen Council of Engineers
UCCF . . . . . . United Campus Christian Fellowship
UCCRS . . . . . Underwater Coded Command Release System
UCCS . . . . . . Ultrasonic Chemical Cleaning System
UCCS . . . . . . Universal Camera Control System
UCD . . . . Unchanged Charge Distribution (Fission)
UCD . . . . University College, Dublin
UCD . . . . Usual Childhood Diseases (Medicine)
UCDEC . . . . . Union Chretienne Democrate d'Europe Centrale (Christian Democratic Union of Central Europe)
UCDP . . . . . . Uncorrelated Data Processor
UCDWN . . . . . Until Cleared Down (Aviation)
UCDWR . . . . . University of California Division of War Research
UCE . . . . Unit Checkout Equipment
UCE . . . . Unit Correction Entry
UCEA . . . . . . Union Chimique Elf-Aquitaine (France)
UCEA . . . . . . University Council for Educational Administration
UCEA . . . . . . Used Clothing Exporters Association of America
UCEC . . . . . . Utility Commission Engineers Conference
UCEMT . . . . . University Consortium in Educational Media and Technology
UCF . . . . Union Culturelle Francais
UCF . . . . Unit Control File (Air Force)
UCF . . . . United-Carr, Inc. (Formerly, United-Carr Fastener Corporation) (NYSE symbol) (Delisted)
UCF . . . . United Cat Federation
UCF . . . . United Cooperative Farmers, Inc.
UCFA . . . . . . Union pour la Communaute Franco-Africaine (Union for the Franco-African Community) (Niger)
UCFC . . . . . . United Community Funds and Councils of America
UCFE . . . . . . Unemployment Compensation, Federal Employees
UCG . . . . Unidirectional Categorical Grammar
UCHD . . . . . . Usual Childhood Diseases
UCI . . . . Union Cycliste Internationale (International Cyclists' Union) (World governing body for amateur bicycle racing)
UCI . . . . Unit Construction Index
UCI . . . . United Charity Institutions of Jerusalem
UCI . . . . Utility Card Input
UCIIM . . . . . . Unione Cattolica Italiana Insegnanti Medi
UCIS . . . . Uprange Computer Input System
UCISS . . . . . . Union Catholique Internationale de Service Social (Catholic International Union for Social Service)
UCJ . . . . Unsatisfied Claim and Judgment (State driver insurance)
UCJG . . . . . . Alliance Universelle des Unions Chretiennes de Jeunes Gens (World Alliance of Young Men's Christian Associations)
UCK . . . . Union Culturelle Katangaise (Katangan Cultural Union)
UCL . . . . Union Oil Company of California (NYSE symbol)
UCL . . . . Update Control List
UCL . . . . Upper Control Limit (QCR)
UCL . . . . Urea Clearance (Test) (Medicine)
UCLA . . . . . . University of California, Los Angeles
UCLG . . . . . . United Cement, Lime and Gypsum Workers International Union
UCLJ . . . . University of California, La Jolla
UCLM . . . . . . Unity of Czech Ladies and Men
UCLRL . . . . . . University of California Lawrence Radiation Laboratory
UCLT . . . . Until Cleared to Land by the Tower (Aviation)
UCM . . . . Can You Come and See Me?
UCM . . . . Union Commerce Corp. (NYSE symbol)
UCM . . . . Union des Croyants Malagaches (Malagasy Christian Union)
UCM . . . . University Christian Movement (Formerly, NSCF)
UCMJ . . . . . . Uniform Code of Military Justice
UCMP . . . . . . Union Catalog of Medical Periodicals
UCMS . . . . . . United Christian Missionary Society
UCMT . . . . . . Unglazed Ceramic Mosaic Tile (Technical drawings)
UCN . . . . Union Civica Nacional (National Civic Union) (Dominican Republic)
UCNC . . . . . . Union Carbide Nuclear Corporation
UCO . . . . Union Corp. (NYSE symbol)
UCO . . . . Universal Weather Landing Code
UCO . . . . Utility Compiler
UCOL . . . . . . Union des Colons du Katanga (Settlers' Union of Katanga)

UCON ...... Utility Control
UCOS....... Uprange Computer Output System
UCP........ Unified Command Plan
UCP........ United Country Party (Australia)
UCP........ Utilities Conservation Program (Navy)
UCP........ Utility Control Program
UCPA....... United Cerebral Palsy Associations
UCPF....... United Church Peace Fellowship
UCPN....... Union des Chefs et des Populations du Nord (Union of Chiefs and Peoples of the North) (Togo)
UCPTE ...... Union pour la Coordination de la Production et du Transport de l'Electricite (Union for Coordinating Production and Distribution of Electricity)
UCR........ Committee on Uniform Crime Records
UCR........ Unconditioned Response
UCR........ Uniform Crime Reports (Federal Bureau of Investigation)
UCR........ Unsatisfactory Condition Report
UCR........ Utah Coal Route (AAR code)
UCRC....... United Civil Rights Committee
UCRI .... Union Civica Radical Intransigente (Left-wing radical political party) (Argentina)
UCRL .... University of California Radiation Laboratory
UCRP .... Union Civica Radical del Pueblo (Moderate radical political party) (Argentina)
UCS .... Unconditioned Stimulus
UCS .... Underwater Cable System
UCS .... Underwater Communications System
UCS .... Uniform Chromaticity Scale (Illuminant)
UCS .... Union of Concerned Scientists
UCS .... United Community Services
UCS .... United Computing Systems
UCS .... Universal Cargo Sling
UCS .... Universal Character Set (Data processing)
UCS .... Universal Classification System
UCS .... Universal Connector Strip
UCS .... Universal-Cyclops Steel Corporation (NYSE symbol) (Later, CYL)
UCSB ...... University of California at Santa Barbara
UCSC ...... University of California at Santa Cruz
UCSD ...... Universal Communications Switching Device
UCSD ...... University of California, San Diego
UCSL ...... Union Congolaise des Syndicats Libres (Congolese Union of Free Syndicates) (Leopoldville)
UCSUS ..... Ukrainian Catholic Students of the United States
UCT .... United Commercial Travelers
UCT .... University of Cape Town (South Africa)
UCTA ...... Urine Collection/Transfer Assembly (Apollo) (NASA)
UCTC ...... Union Camerounaise des Travailleurs Croyants (Cameroonese Union of Believing Workers)
UCTS ...... United Church Training School
UCV .... Uncontrolled Variable
UCV....... United Confederate Veterans
UCW .... United Church Women
UCW ...... United Church Women of the National Council of Churches
UCWE....... Underwater Countermeasures & Weapons Establishment (British)
UCWR ...... Upon Completion Thereof Will Return to (Air Force)
UCX .... Unemployment Compensation, Ex-Servicemen
UCX....... University Computing Co. (NYSE symbol)
UCY .... United Caribbean Youth
UCYM ..... United Christian Youth Movement
UD........ Unavoidable Delay
UD .... Undesirable Discharge (Military)
UD........ Undetected Defect
UD........ University of Denver
UD........ Unlisted Drugs (A publication)
UD........ Upper Deck (Naval)
UD........ Urban District
UD........ Urethral Discharge (Medicine)
UD........ Uridine Diphosphate
UD........ Ut Dictum (As Directed)
UD........ Utility Dog (Degree of obedience training)
U-D .... University of Detroit
UDA....... Ulster Defense Association
UDA....... Ultrasonic Detergent Action
UDA ...... Union for Democratic Action
UDA....... Universal Detective Association
UDAA....... Unlawfully Driving Away Auto
UDB....... Updata Buffer (Data processing)
UDC....... Ultrasonic Doppler Cardioscope (Heartbeat monitor)
UDC....... Underdeveloped Countries
UDC ...... Uniao Democratica Caboverdeana (Cape Verde Democratic Union)
UDC ...... United Daughters of the Confederacy

UDC .... Universal Decimal Classification
UDC........ Up-Down Counter
UDC........ Upper Dead Center
UDC........ Urban Development Corporation (New York State agency)
UDC........ Urban District Council
UDC........ User Designation Codes (Navy)
UDC ...... Usual Diseases of Childhood
UDCA ...... Undesirable Discharge, Trial by Civil Authorities (Navy)
UDCA....... Union de Defense des Commercants et Artisans
UDCCS ..... Uniform Data Classification Code Structure (Navy)
UDD........ Union Democratique Dahomeene (Dahomey Democratic Union)
UDDC....... Urban Design and Development Corporation
UDDE....... Undesirable Discharge, Desertion without Trial (Navy)
UDDF....... Up and Down Drafts (Meteorology)
UDDIA ...... Union Democratique pour la Defense des Interets Africains (Democratic Union to Defend African Interests)
UDDL....... Ultrasonic Dispersive Delay Line
UDE........ Underwater Detection Establishment (British)
UDE........ Union Douaniere Equatoriale (Equatorial Customs Unions)
UDEAC...... Union Douaniere et Economique de L'Afrique Centrale (Central African Customs and Economic Union)
UDEAO...... Union Douaniere des Etats de l'Afrique et l'Ouest (Customs Union of West African States)
UDEC....... United Digital Electronic Computer
UDEFEC ..... Union Democratique des Femmes Camerounaises (Cameroonese Democratic Women's Union)
UDEL ...... Union des Editeurs de Litterature (France)
UDENAMO ... Uniao Democratica Nacional de Mocambique (Mozambican National Democratic Union)
UDETA ..... Unsymmetrical Diethyltriamine
UDETO...... Union Democratique Togolaise (Togolese Democratic Union)
UDF........ UHF (Ultra-High Frequency) Direction Finder
UDF........ Upside Down Flipper
UDFAA...... Upholstery and Decorative Fabrics Association of America
UDFE ...... Undesirable Discharge, Fraudulent Enlistment (Navy)
UDFMA ..... Upholstery & Drapery Fabric Manufacturers Association
UDFT ...... Union Democratique des Femmes Tunisiennes (Democratic Union of Tunisian Women)
UDG ...... United-Greenfield Corporation (NYSE symbol) (Delisted)
UDH........ Universal Die Holder
UDIT ...... Union pour la Defense des Interets du Tchad (Union for the Defense of Chadian Interests)
UDITS...... Universal Digital Test Set
UDJM....... Union Democratique de la Jeunesse Marocaine (Democratic Union of Moroccan Youth)
UDJV ...... Union Democratique de la Jeunesse Voltaique (Voltaic Democratic Youth Union)
UDK .... Upper Deck
UDL........ Ultrasonic Delay Line
UDL........ Uniform Data Link
UDL........ Unit Detail Listings (Air Force)
UDL........ Up Data Link
UDM ...... United Merchants & Manufacturers (NYSE symbol)
UDM ...... Universal Drafting Machine Corporation
UDM ...... Upright Drilling Machine
UDMH ...... Unsymmetrical Dimethylhydrazine
UDN ...... Underwater Doppler Navigation
UDN ...... Uniao Democratica Nacional (National Democratic Union) (Brazil)
UDOFT...... Universal Digital Operational Flight Trainer (Navy)
UDOP....... UHF (Ultra-High Frequency) Doppler System
UDP........ Unification du Droit Prive
UDP........ Uridine Diphosphate (Biochemistry)
UDPG....... Uridine Disphosphate Glucose (Biochemistry)
UDPGA...... Uridine Disphosphate Glucuronic Acid (Biochemistry)
UDPT....... Union Democratique des Populations Togolaises (Democratic Union of Togolese People)
UDR........ Ulster Defense Regiment
UDR........ Universal Digital Readout
UDR........ Usage Data Report
UDR ...... Utility Data Reduction
UDRC....... Utility Data Retrieval Control
UDRI ...... University of Dayton Research Institute (Ohio)
UDRO....... Utility Data Retrieval Output
UDRP ...... Uridine Diribose Phosphate (Biochemistry)
UDS........ Ultraviolet Detector System
UDS........ Union Democratique Senegalaise (Senegalese Democratic Union)
UDS........ Utilization and Disposal Service (of General Services Administration)
UDSG....... Union Democratique et Sociale Gabonaise (Gabonese Democratic and Social Union)
UDSM ..... Union des Democrates Sociaux de Madagascar (Union of Social Democrats of Madagascar)

UDSM	Union Departemental de Syndicats du Mungo (Departmental Union of the Trade Unions of Mungo) (Cameroon)
UDSR	Union Democratique et Socialiste de la Resistance (Democratic and Socialist Resistance Union)
UDSR	United Duroc Swine Registry
UDT	Underdeck Tonnage
UDT	Underwater Demolition Team (Navy)
UDT	Universal Data Transcriber (Navy)
UDT	Utility Dog Tracker (Degree of obedience training)
UDTI	Universal Digital Transducer Indicator
UDTPHIBSPAC	Underwater Demolition Teams, Amphibious Forces, Pacific Fleet (Navy)
UDU	Underwater Demolition Unit
UDUAL	Union de Universidades de America Latina
UDUF	Undesirable Discharge, Unfitness (Navy)
UDV	Union Democratique Voltaique (Voltaic Democratic Union)
UDW	Ultra-Deep Water
UDY	United Dye & Chemical Corporation (NYSE symbol)
UE	United Electrical, Radio and Machine Workers of America
UE	University Extension
UE	Until Exhausted
UE	Ultrasonic Engineering
UE	Unit Entry
UE	Unit Equipment (as authorized to an Air Force unit)
UEA	Ulex europeus Agglutinin (Immunology)
UEA	Union Europeenne de l'Ameublement (European Furniture Federation)
UEA	United Epilepsy Association
UEA	Universal Esperanto Association
UEAC	Union des Etats de l'Afrique Centrale
UEAC	Unit Equipment Aircraft
UEAC	United European American Club
UEB	Ultrasonic Epoxy Bonder
UEBC	Union Espanola Benefica de California
UEC	Union Electric Company
UEC	Union Europeenne de la Carrosserie (European Union of Coachbuilders)
UEC	Union Europeenne des Experts Comptables Economiques et Financiers (European Union of Public Accountants)
UEC	United Engineering Center
UEC	Unmanned Equipment Cabinet
UECA	Underground Engineering Contractors Association
UECB	Union Europeenne des Commerces du Betail
UECL	Union Europeenne des Constructeurs de Logements (European Union of Independent Building Contractors)
UED	United Electro Dynamics, Inc.
UEE	Unit Essential Equipment
UEEB	Union des Exploitations Electriques en Belgique
UEF	Uniform Electric Field
UEF	Union des Femmes Federalistes
UEF	Union Europeenne Feminine (European Union of Women)
UEF	United Engineering & Foundry Company (NYSE symbol) (Delisted)
UEFA	Union of European Football Associations
UEIC	United East India Company
UEL	Upper Explosive Limit
UEM	Union Electrica Madrilena (Spain)
UEM	Unite Electromagnetique (Electromagnetic Unit)
UEMS	Union Europeenne de Medecine Sociale (European Association of Social Medicine)
UENDC	Union Europeenne des Negociants Detaillants en Combustibles
UEO	Union de l'Europe Occidentale (Western European Union)
UEOA	Union des Etudiants Ouest Africains (Union of West African Students)
UEP	Underwater Electric Potential
UEP	Uniform External Pressure
UEP	Union Electric Company (NYSE symbol)
UEP	Union Europeenne de Paiements
UEP	Union Europeenne de Pedopsychiatres (European Union for Child Psychiatry)
UEPR	Unsatisfactory Equipment Performance Report (Military)
UER	Union Europeenne de Radiodiffusion (European Broadcasting Union)
UER	Unites d'Enseignement et de Recherche (Units of Teaching and Research) (University of Paris)
UER	Unsatisfactory Equipment Report
UERD	Underwater Explosives Research Division (Navy)
UERE	Ultrasonic Echo Ranging Equipment
UERL	Underwater Explosives Research Laboratory
UERMWA	United Electrical-Radio Machine Workers of America
UERS	Unusual Event Recording System (Jet transport)
UERT	Union Explosivos-Rio Tinto (Spain)
UESA	Ukrainian Engineers' Society of America
UESK	Unit Essential Spares Kit (Military)
UET	Unit Equipment Table (Military)
UET	United Engineering Trustees
UET	Universal Engineer Tractor (Later, BEST) (Army)
UETA	Universal Engineer Tractor, Armored (AMC - Mobility)
UETRT	Universal Engineer Tractor, Rubber-Tired (AMC - Mobility)
UEW	United Electrical Workers
UEX	Unexcelled Chemical Corporation (NYSE symbol)
UF	Ultra-Filtration
UF	Ultra-Fine
UF	Underground Feeder
UF	Unified Forces (Military)
UF	United Fruit Company (NYSE symbol) (Later, UB)
UF	United Fund
UF	University of Florida
UF	Upper Air Fallout (Civil Defense)
UF	Urea Formaldehyde
UF	Used For
U/F	Unit of Fire (Army)
UFA	Unesterified Fatty Acids
UFA	Uniform Firearms Act
UFA	Union des Femmes d'Algerie (Union of Algerian Women)
UFA	Universum-Film Aktien-Gesellschaft (German motion picture company)
UFA	Until Further Advised
UFA	Use Frequency Analysis
UFAC	Unlawful Flight to Avoid Custody
UFAED	Unit Forecast Authorization Equipment Data
UFAP	Unlawful Flight to Avoid Prosecution
UFAS	Unified Flight Analysis System (NASA)
UFAT	Unlawful Flight to Avoid Testimony
UFC	Unidirectional Filamentary Composite
UFC	Uniform Freight Classification
UFC	United Free Church (Scotland)
UFC	Universal Flight Computer
UFCA	United Film Carriers Association
UFCC	Uniform Freight Classification Committee
UFCE	Union Federaliste des Communautes Ethniques Europeennes (Federal Union of European Nationalities)
UFCG	Underwater Fire Control Group
UFCS	Underwater Fire Control System
UFCS	Universal Fire Control System
UFCT	United Federation of College Teachers (AFL-CIO)
UFD	Ultra-Fast Detection
UFD	Universal Firing Device (Military)
UFDC	United Federation of Doll Clubs
UFDC	Universal Flight Director Computer
UFE	Union des Groupements Professionnels de l'Industrie de la Feculerie de Pommes de Terre
UFEMAT	Union des Federations Nationales des Negociants en Materiaux de Construction de la CEE (Union of National Federation of Building Materials Merchants in the EEC)
UFEMTO	Union des Femmes du Togo (Togolese Women's Union)
UFER	Mouvement International pour l'Union Fraternelle entre les Races et les Peuples (International Movement for Fraternal Union among Races and Peoples)
UFESA	United Fire Equipment Service Association
UFF	Ufficiale (Official, Officer)
UFF	University Film Foundation
UFFVA	United Fresh Fruit and Vegetable Association
UFG	US Freight Company (NYSE symbol)
UFI	Union des Foires Internationales (Union of International Fairs)
UFI	Universal Fermi Interaction
UFIDA	Union Financer Internationale pour le Developpement de l'Afrique (International Financial Union for the Development of Africa)
UFJC	United Fund for Jewish Culture
UFL	United Financial Corporation of California (NYSE symbol)
UFLC	Union Internationale des Femmes Liberales Chretiennes (International Union of Liberal Christian Women)
UFM	University for Man (Manhattan, Kansas)
UFM	Upper Figure of Merit
UFMA	United Fur Manufacturers Association
UFMA	Upholstered Furniture Manufacturers Association
UFMA	Upholstery Fabric Manufacturers Association
UFN	Union Franco-Nigerienne (French-Niger Union)
UFN	Until Further Notice
UFN	U.S. Financial (NYSE symbol)
UFO	Unidentified Flying Object ("Flying saucers")
UFO	US & Foreign Securities Corporation (NYSE symbol)
UFOA	Union des Femmes d l'Ouest Africain (West African Women's Union)
UFOD	Union Francaise des Organismes de Documentation
UFOP	Ultra-Fast-Opening Parachute
UFOPIA	Unidentified Flying Objects Phenomena Investigations, Australia
UFP	United Federal Party (Northern Rhodesia)
UFPA	University Film Producers Association
UFPC	United Federation of Postal Clerks (Formerly, NFPOC)
UFR	Under Frequency Relay

UFRWO . . . . . . United Federation of Russian Workers' Organizations of USA and Canada
UFS . . . . Unnormalized Floating Subtract
UFSA . . . . . . Ukrainian Free Society of America
UFSJ . . . . . . Unitarian Fellowship for Social Justice
UFT . . . . Ultrasonic Frequency Transformer (or Translator)
UFT . . . . United Federation of Teachers (New York)
UFTR . . . . . . University of Florida Teaching Reactor
UFU . . . . Utility Flight Unit (Navy)
UFV . . . . Unsymmetrical Free Vibration
UFW . . . . United Furniture Workers of America
UFWOC . . . . . United Farm Workers Organizing Committee
UG . . . . Underground (Technical drawings)
UG . . . . United Gas, Inc. (NYSE symbol) (Formerly, UGC)
UG . . . . Universal Government
UGA . . . . Underwriters Grain Association
UGA . . . . Unity Gain Amplifier
UGB . . . . Union Giovantu Benadir (Benadir Youth Union) (Somalia)
UGB . . . . Unity Gain Bandwidth
UGBW . . . . . . Unity Gain Bandwidth
UGC . . . . Ultrasonic Grating Constant
UGC . . . . United Gas Corporation (NYSE symbol) (Later, UG)
UGC . . . . Unity Gain Crossover
UGC . . . . Universal Guided Column
UGC . . . . University Grants Commission (India)
UGC . . . . University Grants Committee (British)
UGCAA . . . . . Union Generale des Cooperatives Agricoles d'Approvisionnement
UGCW . . . . . . United Glass and Ceramic Workers of North America
UGDP . . . . . . University Group Diabetes Program (Study group involving 12 medical schools)
UGEAO . . . . . Union General e des Etudiants d'Afrique Occidentale (General Union of West African Students)
UGEC . . . . . . Union Generale des Etudiants Congolais (General Union of Congolese Students)
UGEED . . . . . Union Generale des Etudiants et Eleves Dahomeens
UGEG . . . . . . Union Generale des Etudiants Guineens (General Union of Guinean Students)
UGEM . . . . . . Union Generale des Etudiants du Maroc (General Union of Moroccan Students)
UGEMA . . . . . Union Generale des Etudiants Musulmans d'Algerie (General Union of Moslem Students of Algeria)
UGET . . . . . . Union Generale des Etudiants Tunisiens (General Union of Tunisian Students)
UGF . . . . Unidentified Growth Factor
UGF . . . . United Givers Fund
UGGI . . . . . . Union Geodesique et Geophysique Internationale (International Union of Geodesy and Geophysics)
UGI . . . . UGI Corp. (Formerly, United Gas Improvement Co.) (NYSE symbol)
UGI . . . . Union Geographique Internationale (International Geographical Union)
UGJA . . . . . . United Galician Jews of America
UGL . . . . Utility General
UGLIAC . . . . . United Gas Laboratories Internally Programmed Automatic Computer
UG/M . . . . . . Umdrehungen je Minute (Revolutions Per Minute) (Germany)
UGOC . . . . . . United Greek Orthodox Charities
UGPA . . . . . . Undergraduate Grade-Point Average (Higher education)
UGR . . . . Ultrasonic Grain Refinement
UGR . . . . Universal Graphic Recorder (Raytheon Co.)
UGRR . . . . . . Underground Railroad (A smuggling system) (Criminal slang)
UGS . . . . Union de la Gauche Socialiste
UGSA . . . . . . Union Generale des Syndicats Algeriens (General Federation of Algerian Trade Unions)
UGT . . . . Union General de Trabajadores de Espana (General Union of Spanish Workers) (In exile)
UGT . . . . Upgrade Training (Military)
UGTA . . . . . . Union Generale des Travailleurs Algeriens (General Union of Algerian Workers)
UGTAN . . . . . Union Generale des Travailleurs d'Afrique Noire (General Union of Workers of Black Africa)
UGTC . . . . . . Union Generale des Travailleurs du Cameroun (General Union of Workers of Cameroon)
UGTC . . . . . . Union Generale des Travailleurs Centrafricains (General Union of Central African Workers)
UGTCI . . . . . . Union Generale des Travailleurs de la Cote d'Ivoire (General Union of Workers of the Ivory Coast)
UGTD . . . . . . Union Generale des Travailleurs du Dahomey (General Union of Dahomey Workers)
UGTK . . . . . . Union Generale des Travailleurs du Kamerun (General Union of Workers of the Cameroon)
UGTM . . . . . . Union Generale des Travailleurs du Maroc (General Union of Workers of Morocco)
UGTM . . . . . . Union General des Travailleurs de Mauritanie (General Union of Workers of Mauritania)

UGTS . . . . . . Union Generale des Travailleurs du Senegal (General Union of Workers of Senegal)
UGTT . . . . . . Union Generale Tunisienne du Travail (General Federation of Tunisian Workers)
UGW . . . . United Garment Workers of America
UH . . . . Unit Heater (Technical drawings)
UH . . . . Upper Half
UH . . . . US Home Corp. (NYSE symbol)
UHA . . . . Ukrains'ka Halyts'ka Armiia
UHA . . . . Ultra-High Altitude
UHA . . . . Upper Half Assembly
UHAA . . . . . . United Horological Association of America
UHC . . . . Under Honorable Conditions
UHCMWIU . . . United Hatters, Cap and Millinery Workers International Union
UHCS . . . . . . Ultra-High Capacity Storage
UHF . . . . Ultra-High Frequency (Electricity of radio waves)
UHF . . . . United Health Foundations
UHF . . . . Unrestricted Hartree-Fock (Wave-Function)
UHFDF . . . . . Ultra-High-Frequency Direction Finder
UHFF . . . . . . Ultra-High Frequency Filter
UHFG . . . . . . Ultra-High Frequency Generator
UHFJ . . . . . . Ultra-High-Frequency Jammer
UHFO . . . . . . Ultra-High-Frequency Oscillator
UHFR . . . . . . Ultra-High-Frequency Receiver
UHG . . . . Urban History Group
UHJA . . . . . . United Hungarian Jews of America
UHMW . . . . . Ultra-High Molecular Weight
UHP . . . . Ultra-High Purity
UHP . . . . University of Hawaii Press
UHPFB . . . . . Untreated Hard Pressed Fiber Board
UHR . . . . Ultra-High Resistance
UHR . . . . Ultra-High Resolution
UHRA . . . . . . United Hunts Racing Association
UHS . . . . Ultra-High Speed
UHS . . . . Unitarian Historical Society
UHS . . . . United HIAS Service
UHS . . . . Universalist Historical Society
UHSA . . . . . . United Halsingian Society of America
UHT . . . . Ultrasonic Hardness Tester
UHT . . . . United Hebrew Trades of the State of New York
UHT . . . . Universal Horizontal Tail (Aviation)
UHTREX . . . . . Ultra-High Temperature Reactor Experiment (AEC)
UHTV . . . . . . Unmanned Hypersonic Test Vehicle
UHV . . . . Ultra-High Vacuum
UHVC . . . . . . Ultra-High Vacuum Chamber
UHVS . . . . . . Ultra-High Vacuum System
UI . . . . Underwear Institute
UI . . . . Unemployment Insurance
UI . . . . United Inches
UI . . . . Urban Institute
UI . . . . Ut Infra (As Below)
U/I . . . . Unidentified
U/I . . . . Unit of Issue (Army)
UIA . . . . Ukrainian Institute of America
UIA . . . . Unemployment Insurance Act (Canada)
UIA . . . . **Union of International Associations**
UIA . . . . **Union Internationale contre l'Alcoolisme**
UIA . . . . **Union Internationale des Architectes** (International Union of Architects)
UIA . . . . **Union Internationale des Avocats**
UIA . . . . Union Internationale des Syndicats des Industries Alimentaires
UIA . . . . United Israel Appeal
UIA . . . . Uranium Institute of America
UIAA . . . . Union Internationale des Associations d'Alpinisme (International Union of Alpine Associations)
UIAA . . . . Union Internationale des Association d'Annonceurs (International Union of Advertisers Associations)
UIAA . . . . Union Internationale des Assureurs Aeronautiques
UIACM . . . . . . Union Internationale des Automobile-Clubs Medicaux (International Union of Associations of Doctor-Motorists)
UIAL . . . . United Italian American League
UIALC . . . . . . United-Italian American Labor Council
UIAPME . . . . . Union Internationale de l'Artisanat et des Petites et Moyennes Entreprises (International Association of Crafts and Small and Medium-Sized Enterprises)
UIARVEP . . . . . Unione Italiana Agenti Rappresentati Viaggiatori e Piazzisti (Italian Union of Agents and Travelers)
UIAT . . . . Union Internationale des Syndicats des Industries de l'Alimentation et des Tabacs
UIB . . . . Union Internationale des Maitres Boulangers (International Union of Master Bakers)
UIB . . . . Unione Italiana Bancari (Italian Union of Bank Employees)

UIBC . . . . Unsaturated Iron-Binding Capacity

UIBPIP . . . . . . United International Bureau for the Protection of Intellectual Property

UIBWM . . . . . Trade Unions International of Workers of Building, Wood and Building Materials Industries

UIC . . . . Ultraviolet Image Converter

UIC . . . . Union of International Conventions

UIC . . . . Union Internationale des Chemins de Fer (International Union of Railways)

UIC . . . . Unit Identification Code (Army)

UIC . . . . United Industrial Corporation (NYSE symbol)

UICA . . . . Union of Independent Colleges of Art

UICANY . . . . . United Irish Counties Association of New York

UICC . . . . Union Internationale Contre le Cancer (International Union Against Cancer)

UICGF . . . . . . Union Internationale du Commerce en Gros de la Fleur

UICM . . . . Union Internationale Catholique des Classes Moyennes (International Catholic Union of the Middle Classes)

UICN . . . . Union Internationale pour la Conservation de la Nature et de Ses Ressources (International Union for Conservation of Nature and Natural Resources)

UICP . . . . Uniform Inventory Control Points System (Military)

UICPA . . . . . . Union Internationale de Chimie Pure et Appliquee (International Union of Pure and Applied Chemistry)

UICSM . . . . . . University of Illinois Committee on School Mathematics

UICT . . . . Union Internationale Contre la Tuberculose (International Union Against Tuberculosis)

UICWA . . . . . . United Infants' and Children's Wear Association

UID . . . . Unemployment Insurance Department

UIDA . . . . Union Internationale des Organisations de Detaillants de la Branche Alimentaire (International Federation of Grocers' Associations)

UIDAC . . . . . . Unione Italiana Dipendenti Aziende Commerciali ed Affini (Italian Union of Commercial and Allied Workers)

UIE . . . . UNESCO Institute for Education

UIE . . . . Union Internationale d'Electrothermie (International Union for Electroheat)

UIE . . . . Union Internationale des Etudiants (International Union of Students)

UIEC . . . . Union Internationale de l'Exploitation Cinematographique (International Union of Cinematograph Exhibitors)

UIEIS . . . . Union Internationale pour l'Etude des Insectes Sociaux

UIEO . . . . Union of International Engineering Organizations

UIEP . . . . Union Internationale des Entrepreneurs de Peinture

UIES . . . . Union Internationale pour l'Education Sanitaire

UIES . . . . Union Internationale d'Etudes Sociales (International Union for Social Studies)

UIF . . . . Ultraviolet Interference Filter

UIF . . . . Unfavorable Information File (Military)

UIF . . . . Universal Intermolecular Force

UIFI . . . . Union Internationale des Fabricants d'Impermeables

UIFL . . . . Union Internationale des Federations de Detaillants en Produits Laitiers

UIHE . . . . Union Internationale de l'Humanisme et de l'Ethique

UIHPS . . . . Union Internationale d'Histoire et de Philosophie des Sciences

UIIG . . . . Union Internationale de l'Industrie du Gaz (International Gas Union)

UIJDC . . . . Union Internationale de Jeunesse Democrate Chretienne (International Union of Young Christian Democrats)

UIJS . . . . Union Internationale de la Jeunesse Socialiste (International Union of Socialist Youth)

UIL . . . . Unione Italiana del Lavoro (Italian Union of Labor)

UIL . . . . United Illuminating Co. (NYSE symbol)

UILA . . . . Unione Italiana Lavoratori Assicurazioni (Italian Union of Insurance Workers)

UILAM . . . . . . Unione Italiana Lavoratori Albergo e Mensa (Italian Union of Hotel and Restaurant Workers)

UILC . . . . Unione Italiana Lavoratori Chimici (Italian Union of Chemical Workers)

UILE . . . . Union Internationale pour la Liberte d'Enseignement (International Union for the Liberty of Education)

UIL-GAS . . . . Unione Italiana Lavoratori Aziende Gas (Italian Union of Gas Workers)

UILIA . . . . Unione Italiana Lavoratori Industrie Alimentari (Italian Union of Food-Processing Workers)

UILIC . . . . Unione Italiana Lavoratori Imposte Consumo (Italian Union of Food Tax Levy Workers)

UILM . . . . Unione Italiana Lavoratori Metallurgici (Italian Metalworkers' Union)

UILPEM . . . . . Unione Italiana Lavoratori Petrolieri e Metanieri (Italian Union of Oil and Methane Gas Workers)

UILS . . . . Unione Italiana Lavoratori Saccariferi (Italian Union of Sugar Industry Workers)

UILT . . . . Unione Italiana Lavoratori delle Terra (National Union of Landworkers) (Italy)

UILT . . . . Unione Italiana Lavoratori Tessili (Italian Union of Textile Workers)

UILTRAS . . . . . Unione Italiana Trasporti ed Ausiliari del Traffico (Italian Union of Transport Workers and Auxiliary Services)

UILVECA . . . . . Unione Italiana Lavoratori Vetro, Ceramica ed Abrasivi (Italian Union of Glass, Ceramics and Abrasive Workers)

UIM . . . . Ufficio Informazioni Militare (Office of Military Information) (Italian)

UIM . . . . Union Internationale Motonautique (Union of International Motorboating)

UIM . . . . Unione Italiana Marittimi (Italian Union of Seamen)

UIMC . . . . Union Internationale des Services Medicaux des Chemins de Fer (International Union of Railway Medical Services)

UIMJ . . . . Union Internationale des Maisons de Jeunesse (Service de la FIJC)

UIMP . . . . Union Internationale pour la Protection de la Moralite Publique

UIN . . . . United States & International Securities (NYSE symbol)

UINF . . . . Union Internationale de la Navigation Fluviale (International Union of Inland Navigation)

UINL . . . . Union Internationale du Notariat Latin (International Union of Latin Notaries)

UIO . . . . Union Internationale des Orientalistes (International Union of Orientalists)

UIO . . . . Utility Iterative Operation

UIOF . . . . Union Internationale des Organismes Familiaux (International Union of Family Organizations)

UIOOT . . . . . . Union Internationale des Organismes Officiels de Tourisme (International Union of Official Travel Organizations)

UIP . . . . Union Internationale d'Associations de Proprietaires de Wagons de Particuliers (International Union of Private Railway Truck Owners' Associations)

UIP . . . . Union Internationale de Patinage (International Skating Union)

UIP . . . . Union Internationale de Physique Pure et Appliquee

UIP . . . . Union Internationale des Publicitaires

UIP . . . . Union Interparlementaire

UIP . . . . Unione Italiana Pescatori (Italian Union of Fishermen)

UIPC . . . . Union Internationale de la Presse Catholique

UIPCG . . . . . . Union Internationale de la Patisserie, Confiserie, Glacerie

UIPD . . . . Ulrich's International Periodicals Directory

UIPE . . . . Union Internationale de Protection de l'Enfance (International Union for Child Welfare)

UIPM . . . . Union Internationale de Pentathlon Moderne

UIPM . . . . Union Internationale de la Presse Medicale (International Union of the Medical Press)

UIPPI . . . . Union Internationale pour la Protection de la Propriete Industrielle

UIPVT . . . . Union Internationale Contre le Peril Venerien et la Treponematose (International Union Against the Venereal Diseases and the Treponematoses)

UIR . . . . University Industrial Research

UIR . . . . Upper Flight Information Region (Aviation)

UIRC . . . . Universal Interline Reservations Code

UIRD . . . . Union Internationale de la Resistance et de la Deportation (International Union of Resistance and Deportee Movements)

UIS . . . . Ulster-Irish Society

UIS . . . . Unemployment Insurance Service (Labor)

UIS . . . . Union Internationale de Secours (International Relief Union)

UIS . . . . Unit Identification System

UISA . . . . United Inventors and Scientists of America

UISAE . . . . Union Internationale des Sciences Anthropologiques et Ethnologiques (International Union of Anthropological and Ethnological Sciences)

UISB . . . . Union Internationale des Sciences Biologiques (International Union of Biological Sciences)

UISC . . . . Unreported Interstate Shipment of Cigarettes

UISE . . . . Union Internationale de Secours aux Enfants

UISM . . . . Union Internationale des Syndicats des Mineurs (Miners' Trade Unions International)

UISN . . . . Union Internationale des Sciences de la Nutrition (International Union of Nutritional Sciences)

UISP . . . . Union International des Societes de la Paix (International Union of Peace Societies)

UISPP . . . . Union Internationale des Sciences Prehistoriques et Protohistoriques (International Union of Prehistoric and Protohistoric Sciences)

UISSM . . . . . . Union Internationale des Syndicats des Industries Metallurgiques et Mecaniques

UISTAF . . . . . . Union Internationale des Syndicats des Travailleurs Agricoles et Forestiers et des Organisations des Paysans Travailleurs

UISTICPS . . . . Union Internationale des Syndicats des Travailleurs des Industries Chimiques, du Petrole et Similaires

UIT . . . . Union des Independants de Tananarive (Union of Independents of Tananarive)

UIT . . . . Union Internationale des Telecommunications (International Telecommunication Union)

UIT . . . . Unit Impulse Train

UITAM . . . . . . Union Internationale de Mecanique Theorique et Appliquee (International Union of Theoretical and Applied Mechanics)

UITBB . . . . Union Internationale des Syndicats des Travailleurs du Batiment, du Bois et des Materiaux de Construction (Trade Unions International of Workers of the Building, Wood and Building Materials Industries)

UITP . . . . Union Internationale des Transports Publics (International Union of Public Transport)

UIU . . . . Upholsterers' International Union of North America

UIU . . . . Upper Iowa University

UIUSD . . . . . . Union Internationale Universitaire Socialiste et Democratique (International Union of Social Democratic Teachers)
UIV . . . . Union Internationale des Villes et Pouvoirs Locaux (International Union of Local Authorities)
UIW . . . . United Iron Workers
UIWU . . . . . . United Israel World Union
UIWV . . . . . . United Indian War Veterans, USA
UJ . . . . Union Jack
UJA . . . . United Jewish Appeal
UJB . . . . Umbilical Junction Box
UJB . . . . United Jersey Banks (NYSE symbol)
UJC . . . . Union de la Jeunesse Congolaise (Congolese Youth Union)
UJC . . . . Union Junior College (New Jersey)
UJC . . . . Urbana Junior College (Ohio)
UJCD . . . . . . Union de la Jeunesse de la Cote d'Ivoire (Ivory Coast Youth Union)
UJD . . . . Utriusque Juris Doctor (Doctor of Either Law; i.e., Canon Law or Civil Law)
UJDG . . . . . . Union de la Jeunesse Democratique Gabonaise (Union of Democratic Youth of Gabon)
UJDK . . . . . . Union de la Jeunesse Democratique du Kongo (Union of Democratic Youth of the Congo)
UJEKO . . . . . Union de la Jeunesse Congolaise (Congolese Youth Union)
UJH . . . . International Union of Journeymen Horseshoers of the United States and Canada
UJNR . . . . . . United States – Japan Cooperative Program on Natural Resources
UJS . . . . Universal Jamming System
UJT . . . . Ultrasonic Journal Tester
UJT . . . . Unijunction Transistor
UK . . . . Unabkoemmlich (Indispensable, irreplaceable) (German military – World War II)
UK . . . . Union Carbide Corporation (NYSE symbol) (Wall Street slang name: "Ukulele")
UK . . . . Union Katangaise (Katanga Union)
UK . . . . United Kingdom of Great Britain and Ireland
UK . . . . University of Kansas
UK . . . . Urokinase (Enzyme)
UKA . . . . United Kingdom Alliance
UKAEA . . . . . United Kingdom Atomic Energy Authority
UKARC . . . . . United Kingdom Agricultural Research Council
UKB . . . . Universal Keyboard (Data processing)
UKC . . . . Ukrainian Gold Cross
UKC . . . . University of Kansas City (Later, University of Missouri at Kansas City)
UKCIS . . . . . United Kingdom Chemical Information Service
UKCR . . . . . United Kingdom Communication Region (Air Force)
UKIP . . . . . . United Kingdom Import Plan
UKML . . . . . United Knitwear Manufacturers League
UKMRC . . . . . United Kingdom Medical Research Council
UKNR . . . . . University of Kansas Nuclear Reactor
UKW . . . . . . Ultrakurzwelle (Ultrashort wave) (Germany)
UKWE . . . . . Ultrakurzwellenempfaenger (Very-high-frequency receiver) (Germany)
UL . . . . Ulitsa (Street)
UL . . . . Ultra-Linear
UL . . . . Underwriters' Laboratories (Inc.) (Also, ULI)
UL . . . . Uniformly Labeled (Compound, with radioisotope) (Also, U)
UL . . . . Unilever Limited (NYSE symbol)
UL . . . . Union List
UL . . . . Universal League
UL . . . . Unterlafette (Bottom carriage) (German military – World War II)
UL . . . . Up Left (The rear left portion of a stage) (A stage direction)
UL . . . . Up Link (Data processing)
UL . . . . Upper Leg
UL . . . . Upper Limb (Upper edge of sun, moon, etc.) (Navigation)
UL . . . . Upper Limit
ULAA . . . . . . United Latin Americans of America
ULAJE . . . . . Union Latino-Americaine des Jeunesses Evangeliques (Union of Latin American Evangelical Youth)
ULAPC . . . . . Union Latino-Americaine de la Presse Catholique
ULAST . . . . . . Union Latino Americana de Sociedades de Tisiologia (Latin American Union of Societies of Phthisiology)
ULC . . . . United Labor Congress (Nigeria)
ULC . . . . Universal Load Cell
ULC . . . . Upper Left Center (The rear left center portion of a stage) (A stage direction)
ULCA . . . . . . Ukrainian Life Cooperative Association
ULCER . . . . . Underwater Launch Control Energy Requirements
ULCER . . . . . Underwater Launch Current and Energy Recorder
ULCM . . . . . United Lutheran Church Men
ULD . . . . Ultrasonic Leak Detector
ULD . . . . Ultrasonic Light Diffraction
ULD . . . . Unit Logic Device
ULDEST . . . . . Ultimate Destination (Army)

ULDMI . . . . . . Ultra-Precise LASER Distance Measuring Instrument
ULE . . . . Ultra-Low Expansion (Trademark, Corning Glass Works)
ULEA . . . . . . University Labor Education Association
ULF . . . . Ultra-Low Frequency
ULFJ . . . . . . Ultra-Low Frequency Jammer
ULFO . . . . . . Ultra-Low Frequency Oscillator
ULG . . . . Upholstery Leather Group
ULI . . . . Underwriters' Laboratories, Incorporated (Also, UL)
ULI . . . . Union pour la Langue Internationale Ido (Union for the International Language Ido)
ULI . . . . Universal Logic Implementer
ULI . . . . Urban Land Institute
ULIA . . . . . . Unattached List, Indian Army
ULL . . . . Unitarian Laymen's League
ULLS . . . . . . Ultrasonic Liquid Level Sensor
ULLV . . . . . . Unmanned Lunar Logistics Vehicle (OMSF)
ULM . . . . Ultrasonic Light Modulator
ULM . . . . Undersea Long-Range Missile (Proposed)
ULM . . . . Underwater Launch Missile
ULMS . . . . . . Undersea (or Underwater) Long-Range Missile System (Navy)
ULO . . . . United Labour Organization (Burma)
ULO . . . . Unmanned Lunar Orbiter (NASA)
ULP . . . . Unfair Labor Practice
ULP . . . . Utility Landplane (Navy)
ULPA . . . . . . United Lightning Protection Association
ULPR . . . . . . Ultra-Low-Pressure Rocket
ULR . . . . Ultra-Linear Rectifier
ULRA . . . . . . United Lithuanian Relief Fund of America
ULRSA . . . . . Union and League of Romanian Societies of America
ULS . . . . Ultraviolet Light Stabilizer
ULS . . . . Union List of Serials
ULS . . . . United Lutheran Society
ULS . . . . University Libraries Section (Association of College and Research Libraries)
ULSP . . . . . . Unified Legal Services Program
ULT . . . . Ultralow Temperature
ULT . . . . Uniform Low-Frequency Technique
ULT . . . . Unione per la Lotta alla Tubercolosi (Union of Anti-Tuberculosis Association Workers) (Italy)
ULT . . . . United Lodge of Theosophists
ULTC . . . . . . Urban Library Trustees Council
ULTRACOM . . . Ultraviolet Communications
ULTRA-X . . . . . Universal Language for Typographic Reproduction Applications
ULZP . . . . . . United Labor Zionist Party
UM . . . . Unable to Maintain (Aviation)
UM . . . . Under-Mentioned (i.e., mentioned later in a document)
UM . . . . Underwater Mechanic
UM . . . . Unione Maniferro (Somalia)
UM . . . . University of Massachusetts
UM . . . . University of Miami (Florida)
UM . . . . Unscheduled Maintenance
UM . . . . Upper Motor (Neurons)
U/M . . . . Unit of Measure
U of M . . . . . . University of Michigan
UMA . . . . . . Ultrasonic Manufacturers Association
UMA . . . . . . Union de Mujeres Americanas (United Women of the Americas)
UMa . . . . Ursa Major (IAU)
UMAD . . . . . Umatilla Army Depot
UMANA . . . . . Ukrainian Medical Association of North America
UMAP . . . . . University of Michigan Assembly Program
UMASS . . . . . Unlimited Machine Access from Scattered Sites (Data processing)
UMB . . . . Union Mondiale de Billard (World Billiards Union)
UMBA . . . . . . United Mortgage Bankers of America
UMBR . . . . . . Unclad-Metal Breeder Reactor (AEC)
UMBR . . . . . . Universal Multiple Bomb Rack
UMC . . . . Uniform Motion Coupling
UMC . . . . Uniform Moving Charge
UMC . . . . Union du Moyen-Congo (Union of the Middle Congo)
UMC . . . . Unit Mail Clerk
UMC . . . . United Methodist Church
UMC . . . . United Motor Courts
UMC . . . . Universal Match Corporation
UMCA . . . . . . Uraba, Medellin and Central Airways, Inc.
UMD . . . . Ultrasonic Material Dispersion
UMD . . . . Unit Manning Document
UME . . . . Uniform Manufacturers Exchange
UME . . . . Unit Mobility Equipment
UME . . . . Urethane Mixing Equipment
UMEC . . . . . . Union Mondiale des Enseignants Catholiques (World Union of Catholic Teachers)
UMEJ . . . . . . Union Mondiale des Etudiants Juifs (World Union of Jewish Students)

UMF........ Ultra-Microfiche
UMF........ Uniform Magnetic Field
UMFC...... United Methodist Free Churches
UMHK...... Union Miniere du Haut Katanga (Mining Company of Upper Katanga)
UMHP....... Union Mondiale des Societes d'Histoire Pharmaceutique (World Organization of Societies of Pharmaceutical History)
UMI........ Udruzena Metalna Industrija (Belgrade, Yugoslavia)
UMI........ Unit Movement Identifier (Army)
UMi........ Ursa Minor (IAU)
UMIPS...... Uniform Material Issue Priority System (Navy)
UMIS....... Urban Management Information System
UMJL...... Union Mondiale pour un Judaisme Liberal
UMKC...... University of Missouri - Kansas City
UML....... Universal Mission Load (Military)
UMLER...... Universal Machine Language Equipment Register (Railroads)
UMM....... United Merchants & Manufacturers, Inc. (NYSE symbol)
UMMIPS..... Uniform Materiel Movement and Issue Priority System
UMML...... University of Miami Marine Laboratory (Florida)
UMMZ...... University of Michigan Museum of Zoology
UMNO...... United Malays National Organization
UMO....... United Molasses Company, Ltd. (American Stock Exchange symbol) (Delisted)
UMOC...... Ugly Man on Campus (Contest)
UMOFC..... Union Mondiale des Organisations Feminines Catholiques (World Union of Catholic Women's Organizations)
UMOL...... Unmanned Orbital Laboratory
UMOSBESL... Union Mondiale des Organisations Syndicales sur Base Economique et Sociale Liberale (World Union of Liberal Trade Union Organizations)
UMOSEA..... Union Mondiale des Organismes pour la Sauvegarde de l'Enfance et de l'Adolescence (World Union of Organizations for the Safeguard of Youth)
UMP........ Upper Mantle Project
UMP....... Upper Merion & Plymouth R. R. (AAR code)
UMPR....... Uniform Military Personnel Record
UMR....... Unit Mail Room (Air Force)
UMR....... Unsatisfactory Material Reports (Military)
UMR....... Upper Maximum Range
UMREL...... Upper Midwest Regional Educational Laboratory, Inc.
UMRR...... University of Missouri Research Reactor
UMS....... Unfederated Malay States
UMS....... United Missionary Society
UMS....... Universal Maintenance Standards
UMS....... Universal Military Service
UMS....... Unmanned Multifunction Satellite
UMSE....... Unmanned Surveillance Equipment
UMT....... Ultrasonic Material Testing
UMT....... UMC Industries (Formerly, Universal Match Corporation) (NYSE symbol)
UMT...... Union Marocaine du Travail (Moroccan Labor Union)
UMT....... Universal Microwave Trainer
UMT........ Universal Military Training (Participants known as Umtees) (US Army) (Post-World War II)
UMTA....... Urban Mass Transportation Act
UMTA....... Urban Mass Transportation Administration (Department of Transportation)
UMTD....... Using Mails to Defraud
UMTS...... Universal Military Training Service (or System)
UMTSA...... Universal Military Training and Service Act
UMU....... United Mineworker's Union
UMW....... Ultra-Microwaves
UMW...... United Mine Workers of America
UMWA...... International Union, United Mine Workers of America
UN........ Unilever NV (NYSE symbol)
UN........ United Nations
UN........ Uranium Nitride
UNA....... Ukrainian National Association
UNA....... Underwear-Negligee Associates
UNA....... United Artists Corporation (NYSE symbol) (Delisted)
UNAAA..... Ukrainian National Aid Association of America
UNAAF..... Unified Action Armed Forces (Military)
UNAC..... United Nations Appeal for Children
UNACOM.... Universal Army Communication System
UNADS...... UNIVAC Automated Documentation System (Data processing)
UNAEC...... United Nations Atomic Energy Commission (Superseded by Disarmament Commission, 1952)
UNAECC..... United Nations Atomic Energy Control Commission
UNAF....... Universities National Anti-War Fund
UNAKI...... Union des Colons Agricoles du Kivu (Union of Agricultural Settlers of Kivu) (Congo - Leopoldville)
UNAM...... Universidad Nacional Autonoma de Mexico
UNAMACE... Universal Automatic Map Compilation Equipment
UNAP...... Union Nationale Progressiste (National Progressive Union) (Burundi)
UNAPOC.... United National Association of Post Office Craftsmen

UNAR...... Unable Approve Altitude Requested (Aviation)
UNAR...... Union Nationale Ruandaise (Ruanda National Union)
UNARU..... Union Nationale Africaine du Ruanda-Urundi (African National Union of Ruanda-Urundi)
UNASABEC... Union Nationale des Syndicats Agricoles Forestiers, des Bois, de l'Elevage, et de la Peche du Cameroun (National Union of Farmers, Fishermen, Forest Guards and Timber Workers of Cameroon)
UNAT...... Union Nationale des Agriculteurs Tunisiens (National Union of Tunisian Farmers)
UNATRACAM.. Union des Associations Traditionelles du Cameroun (Union of Traditional Associations of Cameroon)
UNATRACO.. Union Nationale des Travailleurs du Congo (National Union of Workers of the Congo)
UNAUS..... United Nations Association of the United States
UNA-USA.... United Nations Association of the United States of America
UNB....... Universal Navigation Beacon
UNB....... University of New Brunswick (Canada)
UNC....... Unified Coarse Thread
UNC....... United Nations Command
UNC....... United Network Company (New TV broadcasting network)
UNC....... United Nuclear Corporation (NYSE symbol)
UNC....... Universal Navigation Computer
UNC....... University of North Carolina
UNC....... University of Northern Colorado (Formerly, Colorado State College)
UNCA...... United Nations Correspondents Associated
UNCACK.... United Nations Civil Assistance Command, Korea
UNCAST.... United Nations Conference on Applications of Science and Technology (1963)
UNCC...... Union Nationale des Cheminots du Cameroun (National Union of Railway Workers of Cameroon)
UNCCP..... United Nations Conciliation Commission for Palestine
UNCDF..... United Nations Capital Development Fund
UNCF...... United Negro College Fund
UNCIO..... United Nations Conference on International Organization (San Francisco, 1945)
UNCIP..... United Nations Commission for India and Pakistan
UNCITRAL... United Nations Commission on International Trade Law
UNCLE..... United Network Command for Law and Enforcement (Fictitious intelligence organization in various television series)
UNCMAC.... United Nations Command Military Armistice Commission
UNCOK..... United Nations Committee on Korea
UNCOL..... Universal Computer Oriented Language (Data processing)
UNCP...... United Nations Conference of Plenipotentiaries
UNCR...... United Nations Command (Rear)
UNCTAD.... United Nations Conference on Trade and Development
UNCURK.... United Nations Commission for the Unification and Rehabilitation of Korea
UND....... Urgency of Need Designator
UNDC...... United Nations Disarmament Commission (Also known as DC)
UNDEL..... Unione Nazionale Dipendenti Enti Locali (National Union of Local Government Employees) (Italy)
UNDERSECNAV.. Under Secretary of the Navy
UNDEX..... United Nations Index (A publication)
UNDI...... United Nations Document Index
UNDP...... United Nations Development Programme
UNE....... United Nations European Headquarters (Geneva, Switzerland)
UNE....... Universal Nonlinear Element
UNEASICO... Union des Etudiants et Anciens des Instituts Sociaux de Congo (Congolese Union of Students and Former Students of Social Institutes)
UNEC...... Union National des Etudiants Camerounais (National Union of Cameroonese Students)
UNEC...... United Nations Education Conference
UNECO..... Union Economique du Congo (Economic Union of the Congo) (Usumbura)
UNECOLAIT.. Union Europeenne du Commerce Laitier
UNEDA..... United Nations Economic Development Administration
UNEF...... Unified Extra Fine (Thread)
UNEF...... United Nations Emergency Force (to separate hostile forces of Israel and Egypt)
UNEM...... Union Nationale des Etudiants du Maroc (National Union of Moroccan Students)
UNESCO.... United Nations Educational, Scientific and Cultural Organization
UNESOB.... United Nations Economic and Social Office in Beirut
UNEXSO.... International Underwater Explorers Society
UNF....... Unified Fine (Thread)
UNF....... Union Freight R. R. (AAR code)
UNFB...... United Nations Film Board
UNFDAC.... United Nations Fund for Drug Abuse Control
UNFICYP.... United Nations Forces in Cyprus
UNFP....... Union Nationale des Forces Populaires (National Union of Popular Forces) (Political party) (Morocco)

UNFT . . . . Union Nationale des Femmes de Tunisie (National Union of Tunisian Workers)

UNFURNOTE . . Until Further Notice

UNG . . . . Union Gas Company of Canada (American Stock Exchange symbol)

UNGA . . . . . . United Nations General Assembly

UNH . . . . Uranyl Nitrate Hexahydrate

UNHCR . . . . . United Nations High Commissioner for Refugees

UNI . . . . Unionamerica, Incorporated (NYSE symbol)

UNI . . . . United States International Airways

UNI . . . . Unity Railways Company (AAR code)

UNIA . . . . . . Universal Negro Improvement Association (Organization led by Marcus Aurelius Garvey)

UNIADUSEC . . Union Internationale des Associations de Diplomes Universitaires en Sciences Economiques et Commerciales

UNIAPAC . . . . Union Internationale des Associations Patronales Catholiques

UNIATEC . . . . Union Internationale des Associations Techniques Cinematographiques (International Union of Technical Cinematograph Associations)

UNIC . . . . . . United International Club, Inc.

UNIC . . . . . . United Nations Information Centre

UNICA . . . . . Union Internationale du Cinema d'Amateurs (International Union of Amateur Cinema)

UNICCAP . . . . Universal Cable Circuit Analysis Program (Bell System)

UNICE . . . . . Union des Industries de la Communaute Europeenne (Union of Industries of the European Community)

UNICEF . . . . . United Nations Children's Fund (Acronym taken from former name United Nations International Children's Emergency Fund)

UNICHAL . . . . Union Internationale des Distributeurs de Chaleur (International Union of Heating Distributors)

UNICO . . . . . Union pour les Interets du Peuple Congolais (Union for the Interests of the Congolese People)

UNICOL . . . . Union des Colons de la Province Orientale (Union of Settlers in Orientale Province)

UNICOM . . . . Unified Communications (Radio station)

UNICOM . . . . Universal Components (Construction)

UNICOM . . . . Universal Integrated Communication System (Military)

UNIDAHO. . . . Union des Independants du Dahomey (Independents Union of Dahomey)

UNIDO. . . . . . United Nations Industrial Development Organization

UNIDROIT . . . . Institut International pour l'Unification du Droit Prive (International Institute for the Unification of Private Law)

UNIF . . . . Uniform

UNIFET . . . . . Unipolar Field-Effect Transistor

UNIFOR . . . . . Unified Forces (Military)

UNI-FREDI . . . Universal Flight Range & Endurance Data Indicator

UNIGABON . . Union Interprofessionnelle du Gabon (Inter-Trade Union of Gabon)

UNIMA. . . . . . Union Internationale de Grands Magasins (International Union of Department Stores)

UNIMOD. . . . . Unified Modular Plant (Atomic energy)

UNIO. . . . . . . United Nations Information Organization

UNIP . . . . United National Independence Party (Northern Rhodesia)

UNIPAC . . . . . Unit Packaging

UNIPEDE. . . . . Union Internationale de Producteurs et Distributeurs d'Energie Electrique (International Union of Producers and Distributors of Electrical Energy)

UNIPOCONGO . . Union des Populations Rurales du Congo (Union of Rural People of the Congo)

UNIPOL . . . . . Universal Procedure Oriented Language

UNIPRO . . . . . Unite et Progres du Burundi (Unity and Progress of Burundi)

UNIPRO . . . . . Universal Processor (Data processing)

UNIRAR . . . . . Universal Radio Relay

UNIS . . . . United Nations International School

UNISA . . . . . . University of South Africa

UNISCAMTA . . Union Territoriale des Syndicats de Cadres, Agents de Maitrise, Techniciens et Assimiles du Senegal (Territorial Union of Leaders, Supervising Personnel and Related Workers of Senegal)

UNISCO . . . . . Union des Interets Sociaux Congolais (Congolese Union of Social Interests)

UNISTAR. . . . . UNIVAC Storage and Retrieval System (Data processing)

UNIT . . . . Universal Numerical Interchange Terminal

UNITAR . . . . . United Nations Institute for Training and Research

UNITEC . . . . . University Information Technology Corporation

UNITEL . . . . . Universal Teleservice (Satellite information service)

UNITEL. . . . . . University Information Technology Corporation (MIT-Harvard)

UNIUM. . . . . . Union Nationale des Intellectuels et Universitaires Malgaches (National Union of Intellectuals and University People of Madagascar)

UNIV . . . . Universal

UNIV . . . . University

UNIVAC . . . . . Universal Automatic Computer

Univ D . . . . . Doctor of the University (Academic degree)

UNJBS . . . . . . United Nations Joint Board of Strategy

UNK . . . . Unknown

UNKRA . . . . . United Nations Korean Reconstruction Agency

UNLA. . . . . . . Unione Nazionale per la Lotta contra l'Analfabatismo (Union for the Struggle Against Illiteracy) (Italy)

UNLAM . . . . . Universitas Lambung Mangkurat

UNLIS . . . . . . United National Life Insurance Society

UNLL . . . . United Nations League of Lawyers

UNM . . . . Unified Miniature

UNM . . . . United Nations Medal

UNMAC . . . . . United Nations Mixed Armistice Commission

UNMC . . . . . . United Nations Mediterranean Commission

UNMEM . . . . . United Nations Middle East Mission

UNMOGIP . . . . United Nations Military Observer Group for India and Pakistan

UNMSC . . . . . United Nations Military Staff Committee

UNO . . . . Union Nacional Odriista (Peruvian political party)

UNO . . . . United Nations Organization

UNOC . . . . . . Union Nationale des Ouvriers Congolais (National Union of the Congolese Workers)

UNO-CARA-PEN . . Union Internationale pour la Cooperation Culturelle (International Union for Cultural Co-operation)

UNODIR . . . . Unless Otherwise Directed

UNOGIL . . . . . United Nations Observer Group in Lebanon

UNOINDC . . . . Unless Otherwise Indicated

UNOLS . . . . . . University National Oceanographic Laboratory System (National Science Foundation)

UNOPAR. . . . . Universal Operator Performance Analyzer and Recorder

UNP. . . . . Union Nacional Paraguaya (Political party in Paraguay)

UNP. . . . . Union Pacific Corp. (NYSE symbol)

UNP. . . . . United National Party (Ceylon)

UNPA . . . . . . United Nations Postal Administration

UNPAC. . . . . . Union Pacific Railroad

UNPC . . . . . . United Nations Palestine Commission

UNPIK . . . . . . United Nations Partisan Infantry Korea

UNPOC . . . . . United Nations Peace Observation Commission

UNPS . . . . Universal Power Supply

UNR. . . . . Ukrains'ka Natsional'na Rada

UNR. . . . . Unarco Industries, Inc. (NYSE symbol)

UNR. . . . . Union pour la Nouvelle Republique (Union for the New Republic) (French political party)

UNREF . . . . . . United Nations Refugee Fund

UNREP . . . . . Underway Replenishment (Navy)

UNRISD . . . . . United Nations Research Institute for Social Development

UNROD . . . . . United Nations Relief Operation in Dacca

UNRPR . . . . . . United Nations Relief for Palestine Refugees

UNRR. . . . . . . Unable Approve Route Requested (Aviation)

UNRRA . . . . . . United Nations Relief and Rehabilitation Administration ("United Nations" in this body's name derives from the wartime alliance of this name, not from any affiliation with the postwar international organization)

UNRS . . . . Union pour la Nouvelle Republique Senegalaise (Union of the New Senegalese Republic)

UNRWA . . . . . United Nations Relief and Works Agency

UNRWAPRNE. . United Nations Relief and Works Agency for Palestine Refugees in the Near East (Pronounced: "Un wrap me")

UNS. . . . . Unified Special (Thread)

UNS. . . . . Unishops, Inc. (NYSE symbol)

UNSAC . . . . . United Nations Scientific Advisory Committee

UNSC . . . . . . United Nations Security Council

UNSC . . . . . . United Nations Social Commission

UNSCC . . . . . United Nations Standards Co-ordinating Committee

UNSCCUR . . . . United Nations Scientific Conference on the Conservation and Utilization of Resources

UNSCEAR . . . . United Nations Scientific Committee on the Effects of Atomic Radiation

UNSCOB . . . . United Nations Special Committee on the Balkans (Greece)

UNSCOP. . . . . United Nations Special Committee on Palestine

UNSDRI. . . . . . United Nations Social Defense Research Institute (UN/Italy)

UNSF . . . . United Nations Special Fund

UNSFH . . . . . . United Nations Security Forces, Hollandia

UNSG . . . . United Nations Secretary General

UNSJIAH . . . . Universitas Sjiah Kuala

UNSM . . . . . . United Nations Service Medal

UNSS . . . . . . United Nations Sales Section (for UN documents)

UNSTD . . . . . . Union Nationale des Syndicats des Travailleurs du Dahomey (National Union of Syndicates of Dahomey)

UNSTHV . . . . Union Nationale des Syndicats des Travailleurs de la Haute Volta (National Federation of Workers' Union of the Upper Volta)

UNSU . . . . United Nations Study Unit (Philatelic organization)

UNSVM . . . . . United Nations Service Medal

UNT. . . . . Undergraduate Navigator Training

UNTA. . . . . . . Union Nationale des Travailleurs Angolais (National Union of Angolan Workers in Exile)

UNTA. . . . . . . United Nations Technical Assistance

UNTAA . . . . . United Nations Technical Assistance Administration

UNTAF . . . . . . United Nations Technical Assistance Fellowship

UNTC. . . . . . . Union Nationale des Travailleurs Congolais (National Union of Congolese Workers)

ACRONYMS AND INITIALISMS DICTIONARY

UNTCI ...... Union Nationale des Travailleurs de Cote d'Ivoire (National Union of Ivory Coast Workers)
UNTCOK..... United Nations Temporary Committee on Korea
UNTD....... University Naval Training Division (Canada)
UNTEA...... United Nations Temporary Executive Authority (Administers territory of West Irian during transfer from the Netherlands to Indonesia)
UNTM ...... Union Nationale des Travailleurs du Mali (National Union of Malian Workers)
UNTN ...... Union Nationale des Travailleurs Nigeriens (National Union of Nigerian Workers)
UNTS....... Union Nationale des Travailleurs du Senegal (National Union of Workers of Senegal)
UNTS....... United Nations Treaty Series (Project) (University of Washington)
UNTSO ..... United Nations Truce Supervision Organization (Works in Middle East between Israel and Arab nations)
UNTT ...... Union Nationale des Travailleurs du Togo (National Union of Togolese Workers)
UNTT ...... United Nations Trust Territory
UNUMO ..... Universal Underwater Mobile (Robot)
UNV .... Universal Insurance Company (American Stock Exchange symbol) (Delisted)
UNWCC ..... United Nations War Crimes Commission ("United Nations" in this body's name derives from the wartime alliance of this name, not from any affiliation with the postwar international organization)
UNWLA ..... Ukrainian National Women's League of America
UNYFA ..... Ukrainian National Youth Federation of America
UNYOM..... United Nations Yemen Observation Mission
UO .... Undelivered Orders (Army)
UO......... Union R. R. of Oregon (AAR code)
U & O ...... Use and Occupancy (Real estate)
UOA .... Used on Assembly
UOC .... Ultimate Operating Capability
UOC .... Unequilibrated Ordinary Chondrites
UOC .... Union de l'Ouest Cameroun (Union of West Cameroon)
UOC .... Unusual Occurrence Control
UOCO ..... Union Oil Company
UODDL...... User-Oriented Data Display Language (Data processing)
UOEF ...... Union de Obreros Estivadores de Filipinos (Union of Longshoremen of the Philippines)
UOGC ...... United Order of the Golden Cross
UOHC ...... Under Other than Honorable Conditions (Military)
UOIW...... United Optical and Instrument Workers of America
UOJCA ..... Union of Orthodox Jewish Congregations of America
UOL....... Underwater Object Locator
UOL........ Utility Octal Load
UOMCA ..... United Orthodox Ministers & Cantors Association of America & Canada
UOMS....... Union des Originaires de Mauritanie du Sud (Union of Natives of South Mauritania)
UOMS ...... Unmanned Orbital Multifunction Satellite
UOO .... Undelivered Orders Outstanding (Military)
UOP........ Universal Oil Products Company (NYSE symbol)
UOPA....... Uranium Ore Processing Association
UOR .... Uniform Officer Record
UOS .... Undelivered Order Schedule
UOS........ Underwater Ordnance Station (Navy)
UOS........ Unmanned Orbital Satellite
UOT........ Uncontrollable Overtime
UOT........ Upper Outer Tube
UOTS...... United Order True Sisters
UOV .... Union Ouvriere du Viet-Nam (Vietnam Labor Union) (South Vietnam)
UOV .... Units of Variance
UP .... Oregon Short Line R. R. (AAR code)
UP .... Oregon-Washington R. R. & Navigation (AAR code)
UP .... Umbilical Pin
UP .... Under-Proof (Of spirituous liquors) (Distilling)
UP .... Under Provisions of
UP .... Union Pacific R. R. Company (NYSE symbol and AAR code)
UP .... Unit Price
UP .... United Presbyterian
UP .... United Press (Merged with International News Service to form UPI)
UP .... United Provinces (India)
UP........ University Presses (General term applied to presses of various universities)
UP .... Unrotated Projectile (Rocket)
UP........ Upper Peninsula (Michigan)
U/P .... Unit Price
U & P...... Uttering and Publishing
UPA........ Ukrains'ka Povstans'ka Armiia
UPA........ Uncooled Parametric Amplifier
UPA........ Uniao dos Populacoes de Angola (Angolan People's Union)
UPA........ Union of Poles in America
UPA........ Union Postale Arabe (Arab Postal Union)
UPA........ Unitary Pole Approximation

UPA .... United Patternmakers Association
UPA .... University Photographers Association of America
UPADI ..... Union Panamericana de Asociaciones de Ingenieros (Pan American Federation of Engineering Societies)
UPAE ...... Union Postal de las Americas y Espana (Postal Union of the Americas and Spain)
UPAJ ...... Union Panafricaine des Journalistes
UPAP ...... Urban Planning Assistance Program
UPC........ Uganda People's Congress
UPC........ Underwater Pipe Cutter
UPC........ Union des Populations du Cameroun (Cameroon People's Union)
UPC........ Union Progressiste Congolaise (Congolese Progressive Union)
UPC........ Unit Processing Code
UPC........ United Power Company (British)
UPC........ United Presbyterian Church
UPC........ U.S. Plywood - Champion Papers, Inc. (NYSE symbol) (Delisted; later, CHA)
UPCHUK .... University Program for the Comprehensive Handling and Utilization of Knowledge (Humorous)
UPCO...... Union Progressiste Congolaise (Congolese Progressive Union)
UPCS ...... Universal Philatelic Cover Society
UPDA ...... United Plastics Distributors Association
UPDMA ..... United Popular Dress Manufacturers Association
UPE .... Unit Proficiency Exercise
UPE .... Unitary Pole Expansion
UPECO...... Union Progressiste Congolaise (Congolese Progressive Union)
UPEQUA .... Union Progressiste de l'Equateur (Progressive Union of Equateur Province) (Congo - Leopoldville)
UPEU ...... Uganda Public Employees' Union
UPF .... Unofficial Personnel Folder
UPFAW..... United Packinghouse Food and Allied Workers
UPFM...... Union Progressive des Femmes Marocaines (Progressive Union of Moroccan Women)
UPG........ Union Progressiste Guineenne (Guinean Progressive Union)
UPGRADE .... University of Pittsburgh Generalized Recording and Dissemination Experiment
UPGS...... Unione Progressista della Gioventu Somala (Progressive Union of Somali Youth)
UPGWA ..... United Plant Guard Workers of America
UPHPISEC .... Union for the Protection of the Human Person by International, Social and Economic Cooperation
UPI .... United Press International
UPIGO ...... Union Professionnelle Internationale des Gynecologues et Obstetriciens (International Union of Professional Gynecologists and Obstetricians)
UPIN ...... United Press International Newspictures
UPIR....... Uniform Photographic Interpretation Report (Military)
UPIU .... United Paperworkers International Union
UPJ .... Upjohn Company (NYSE symbol)
UPK .... United Park City Mines Company (NYSE symbol)
UPM....... Union du Peuple Malgache (Malagasy People's Union)
UPM....... Union Progressiste Mauritanienne (Mauritanian Progressive Union)
UPNCA ..... United Pants and Novelties Contractors Association
UPNE ...... University Press of New England
UPO....... Undistorted Power Output
UPO .... Unit Personnel Office(r)
UPP .... Ultra Precision Parachute
UPP .... United Papermakers and Paperworkers (Later, United Paperworkers International Union)
UPP .... United People's Party (Sierra Leone)
UPP .... Utility Print Punch
UPPC ...... Universal Pin Pack Connector
UPPF ...... United Presbyterian Peace Fellowship
UPPN ...... United People's Party of Nigeria
UPR .... Ultraviolet Proton Radiation
UPR .... Union des Populations Rurales (Union of Rural People) (Lomela-Kasai)
UPR .... University of Puerto Rico
UPR .... Uranium Production Reactor
UPREAL ..... Unit Property Record and Equipment Authorization List
UPREC ...... Upon Receipt
UPREL ...... Unit Property Record and Equipment List
UPRGp ..... Unit Personnel Records Group (Air Force)
UPROCO..... Union Progressiste du Congo (Progressive Union of the Congo) (Niangara)
UPRONA..... Unite et Progres National (Unity and National Progress) (Burundi)
UPRP ...... Union des Paysans Ruraux et Progressistes (Union of Rural and Progressive Farmers) (Congo - Kasai)
UPRR ...... Union Pacific Railroad
UPS .... Under Provisions of Section (Military)
UPS .... Underground Press Syndicate
UPS .... Uninterruptable Power Supply
UPS .... Union Progressiste Senegalaise (Senegalese Progressive Union)
UPS .... Unit Personnel Section (Military)

UPS . . . . United Parcel Service
UPS . . . . Universal Polar Stereographic Grid
UPSA . . . . . . Ukrainian Professional Society of America
UPSS . . . . United Postal Stationery Society
UPSTAGE . . . . Upper Stage Guidance Experiment
UPSTART . . . . . Universal Parachute Support Tactical and Research Target
UPSTEP . . . . . . Undergraduated Pre-Service Teacher Education Program (National Science Foundation)
UPT . . . . Undergraduate Pilot Training (Air Force)
UP & T . . . . . Unit Personnel and Tonnage Tables
UPTAJS. . . . . . United Parent-Teachers Association of Jewish Schools
UPTC . . . . Union Panafricaine des Travailleurs Croyants (Pan-African Union of Believing Workers)
UPTP . . . . Universal Package Test Panel
UPTT . . . . Unit Personnel and Tonnage Table (Military)
UPU . . . . Universal Postal Union (Post Office)
UPUC. . . . . . . Unauthorized Publication or Use of Communications
UPV . . . . Unfired Pressure Vessel
UPVC. . . . . . . Unplasticized Polyvinyl Chloride
UPW. . . . . United Port Workers' Union (Ceylon)
UPW. . . . . United Public Workers of America
UPWA . . . . . . Union of Polish Women in America
UPWA . . . . . . United Packinghouse Workers of America
UPY . . . . Union of People's Youth (Bulgaria)
UQ . . . . Upper Quadrile
UQGS . . . . . . Uniform Quality Grading System (Tires)
UQL. . . . . Unacceptable Quality Level
UQP . . . . Universities and the Quest for Peace (An organization)
UR . . . . Unconditioned Response
UR . . . . Unfinanced Requirement(s) (Army)
UR . . . . Uniform Regulations
UR . . . . Unit Record (Data processing)
UR . . . . University Relations
UR . . . . University Review (A publication)
UR . . . . Unsatisfactory Report
UR . . . . Up Right (The rear right portion of a stage) (A stage direction)
UR . . . . Uti Rogas (Be It as You Desire) (Used by Romans to express assent to a proposition)
URA . . . . United Republicans of America
URA . . . . Universities Research Association
URA . . . . University Research Associates
URA . . . . Urban Renewal Administration (of HHFA) (Terminated)
URAC. . . . . . . Union des Republiques de l'Afrique Centrale (Union of Central African Republics)
URAD . . . . . . Your Radio (message) (Military)
URAEP . . . . . University of Rochester Atomic Energy Project
URAI . . . . Universities Research Association, Incorporated
URB . . . . Union Regionale de Bamileke (Regional Union of Bamileke) (Cameroon)
URB . . . . Unridable Bicycle
URB . . . . Uris Buildings Corporation (NYSE symbol)
URBK . . . . . . Union Rheinische Braunkohlen Kraftstoff (West Germany)
URBM . . . . . . Ultimate Range Ballistic Missile (Air Force)
URC . . . . UARCO, Inc. (NYSE symbol)
URC . . . . Utilities Research Commission
URC . . . . Utility Radio Communication
URCO . . . . . . Union des Ressortissants du Congo pour la Defense et la Promotion du Congo (Union of Congolese for the Defense and Promotion of the Congo)
URD . . . . Underground Residential Distribution (Cable)
URD . . . . Union Republicana Democratica (Democratic Republican Union) (Puerto Rico, Venezuela)
URDIS. . . . . . . Your Dispatch (Military)
URDP . . . . . . Ukrains'ka Revoliutsiino-Demokratychna Partiia
URE . . . . United Refining Co. (NYSE symbol)
UREHE . . . . . . Union for Research and Experimentation in Higher Education
UREKA . . . . . . Unlimited Resources Ensure Keen Answers
U-REST . . . . . . Universal Range, Endurance, Speed, and Time
URF . . . . Union des Services Routiers des Chemins de Fer Europeens (Union of European Railways Road Services)
URF . . . . United Republican Fund
URFDA-NYC . . United Retail Fish Dealers Association of New York City
URG . . . . Underway Replenishment Group
URG. . . . . Universal Radio Group
URG. . . . . Urgent
URGR . . . . . . Underway Replenishment Group (Military)
URI . . . . United Research, Incorporated
URI . . . . University of Rhode Island
URI . . . . Unpublished Research Information (Conducted by National Science Foundation)
URI. . . . . Upper Respiratory Infection (Medicine)
URII . . . . Ukrainian Research and Information Institute
URIPS . . . . Undersea Radioisotope Power Supply

URIR. . . . . Unified Radioactive Isodromic Regulator
URISA. . . . . . . Urban and Regional Information Systems Association
URJA . . . . United Roumanian Jews of America
URLTR. . . . . . . (Reference) Your Letter (Military)
URM . . . . University Reform Movement (in Latin America)
URM . . . . Unlimited Register Machine
URMGM . . . . . Your Mailgram (Military)
URMSG. . . . . . Your Message
URO . . . . United Rink Operators
URO . . . . Ustredni Rada Odboru (Central Council of Trade Unions) (Czechoslovakia)
UROBA . . . . . United Russian Orthodox Brotherhood of America
UROC. . . . . . . United Railroad Operating Crafts
URP . . . . Undergraduate Research Participation (National Science Foundation project)
URP . . . . Upper-Stage Reusable Payload
URPE . . . . Union for Radical Political Economics
URPE . . . . Union des Resistants pour une Europe Unie (Union of Resistance Veterans for a United Europe)
URQ . . . . Unsatisfactory Report Questionnaire
URR . . . . Union R. R.-Pittsburgh (AAR code)
URR . . . . Unit Readiness Report (Army)
URS . . . . UNESCO Relations Staff
URS . . . . Uniform Reporting System
URS . . . . United Research Service
URS . . . . Universal Reference System
URS . . . . Universal Regulating System
URSER. . . . . . . (Reference) Your Serial (Military)
URSI. . . . . Union Radio Scientifique Internationale (International Union of Radio Science)
URSNSC . . . . . Union Regionale des Syndicats du Nyong-et-Sanaga
URSP . . . . Universal RADAR Signal Processor
URSS . . . . Union des Republiques Socialistes Sovietiques (French for Union of Socialist Soviet Republics; USSR)
URSW . . . . . . Union Regionale des Syndicats du Wouri (Regional Union of Wouri Unions)
URT . . . . Unit Recruit Training (Army)
URT . . . . Universal RADAR Tracker
URT . . . . Utility Radio Transmitter
URTEL. . . . . . . Your Telegram
URTNA . . . . . . Union des Radio-Televisions Nationales Africaines (Union of African National Radio and Television Stations)
URUCO . . . . . Union Rurale Congolaise - Buta-Province Orientale (Congolese Rural Union)
URV . . . . Undersea Research Vehicle
URW . . . . Ultrasonic Ring Welder
URW . . . . United Rubber, Cork, Linoleum and Plastic Workers of America
URWA. . . . . . . United Railroad Workers of America
URY . . . . Union Railway of Memphis (AAR code)
US . . . . Ubi Supra (In the Place Mentioned Above)
US . . . . Uncle Sam
US . . . . Unconditional Selection
US . . . . Unconditional Surrender
US . . . . Unconditioned Stimulus
US . . . . Under Secretary
US . . . . Uniform System
US . . . . United Service
US . . . . United States (of America)
US . . . . Universal Service (News agency)
US . . . . Unserviceable
US . . . . Up Stage (Away from audience) (A stage direction)
US . . . . US Supreme Court Reports
US. . . . . Ut Supra (As Above)
U/S . . . . Unhelpful, Helpless, Useless Persons (From abbreviation for "unserviceable")
USA . . . . Ultraviolet Spectral Analysis
USA . . . . Underwater Society of America
USA . . . . Union of South Africa
USA . . . . Union Syndicale de l'Agriculture (Union of Agricultural Workers) (Morocco)
USA . . . . United Scenic Artists
USA . . . . United Shareholders of America
USA . . . . United Shareowners of America
USA . . . . United Shoppers Association
USA . . . . United Soccer Association
USA . . . . United States of America
USA . . . . United States Army
USA . . . . United Steelworkers of America
USA . . . . United Students for America
USA . . . . United Synagogue of America
USA . . . . Urban Sanitary Authority (British)
US of A . . . . . Under Secretary of the Army
USAA . . . . United States Armor Association
USAAA . . . . . . United States Army Audit Agency

USAAAWR .... United States Army Audit Agency, Washington Region
USAAB ...... United States Army Aviation Board
USAABELCTBD .. United States Army Airborne and Electronics Board
USAABMDA ... United States Army Advanced Ballistic Missile Defense Agency
USAABMU .... United States Army Aircraft Base Maintenance Unit
USAAC ...... United States Army Administration Center
USAACDA .... United States Army Aviation Combat Developments Agency (CDC)
USAACS ..... United States Army Ambulance Service Association
USAADB ..... United States Army Air Defense Board
USAADCEN ... United States Army Air Defense Center
USAADCENFB .. United States Army Air Defense Center and Fort Bliss
USAADEA .... United States Army Air Defense Engineering Agency (AEC) (Formerly USASADEA)
USAADS ..... United States Army Air Defense School
USAADVCOM .. United States Army Advance Command
USAAESWBD .. United States Army Airborne, Electronics and Special Warfare Board
USAAF ...... United States Army Air Forces
USAAFIME.... United States Army Air Forces in the Middle East
USAAFINO ... United States Army Aviation Flight Information and Nav-Aids Office
USAAFIO .... United States Army Aviation Flight Information Office
USAAFO ..... United States Army Avionics Field Office (Formerly USASAFO)
USAAFUK .... United States Army Air Forces in the United Kingdom
USAAGDPSC .. United States Army Adjutant General Data Processing Service Center
USAAGNG ... United States Army Advisory Group (National Guard)
USAAGPC .... United States Army Adjutant General Publications Centers
USAAGS ..... United States Army Adjutant General's School
USAAMC .... United States Army Artillery and Missile Center
USAAML ..... United States Army Aviation Materiel Laboratories
USAAMR & DL .. United States Army Air Mobility Research & Development Laboratory (Also, AMR & DL)
USAAMS .... United States Army Artillery and Missile School
USAAPSA .... United States Army Ammunition Procurement and Supply Agency
USAARC ..... United States Antiaircraft Replacement Center
USAARENBD .. United States Army Armor and Engineer Board
USAARMA ... United States Assistant Army Attaché
USAARMBD ... United States Army Armor Board
USAARMC ... United States Army Armor Center
USAARMHRU .. United States Army Armor Human Research Unit
USAARMS .... United States Army Armor School
USAARTYBD.. United States Army Artillery Board
USAARU ..... United States Army Aeromedical Research Unit
USAASC ..... United States Army Air Service Command
USAASO ..... United States Army Aeronautical Services Office
USAASTA .... United States Army Aviation Systems Test Activity
USAATBD .... United States Army Arctic Test Board
USAATC ..... United States Army Arctic Test Center
USAATCO.... United States Army Air Traffic Coordinating Officer(s)
USAAVCOM .. United States Army Aviation Materiel Command
USAAVLABS .. United States Army Aviation Materiel Laboratories
USAAVNBD .. United States Army Aviation Board
USAAVNC.... United States Army Avionics Center (CONARC)
USAAVNHRU .. United States Army Aviation Human Research Unit
USAAVNS .... United States Army Aviation School (CONARC)
USAAVNTA .. United States Army Aviation Test Activity
USAAVNTBD .. United States Army Avionics Test Board
USAAVSCOM.. United States Army Aviation Systems Command
USAB .... United States Army, Berlin
USABAAR .... United States Army Board for Aviation Accident Research
USABESRL .... United States Army Behavioral Science Research Laboratory
USABF ...... United States Amateur Baseball Federation
USABIOLABS .. United States Army Biological Laboratories
USABRL...... United States Army Ballistic Research Laboratories
USABVAPAC.. United States Army Broadcasting and Visual Activities, Pacific
USAC .... Union des Syndicats Autonomes Camerounais (Federation of Cameroonese Autonomous Unions)
USAC .... United States Air Corps
USAC .... United States Alpine Club
USAC .... United States Army Corps
USAC .... United States Auto Club
USAC .... Utah State Agricultural College
USACA ..... United States Allied Commission Austria
USACA ..... United States Army Communications Agency
USACAC .... United States Army Continental Army Command (CONARC)
USACAF ..... United States Army Construction Agency, France
USACAK .... United States Army Construction Agency, Korea
USACARMSCDA .. United States Army Combined Arms Combat Developments Agency
USACAS ..... United States Army Civil Affairs School
USACBRWOC.. United States Army Chemical, Biological, and Radiological Weapons Orientation Course
USACBRWOCAAB .... United States Army Chemical, Biological and Radiological Weapons Orientation Course Academic Advisory Board

USACCIA .... United States Army Chemical Corps Intelligence Agency
USACCL .... United States Army Coating and Chemical Laboratory
USACCTC .... United States Army Chemical Corps Technical Committee
USACDA .... United States Arms Control and Disarmament Agency
USACDC .... United States Army Combat Developments Command
USACDCADA .. United States Army Combat Developments Command Air Defense Agency
USACDCARMA .. United States Army Combat Developments Command Armor Agency
USACDCARTYA .. United States Army Combat Developments Command Artillery Agency
USACDCAVNA ... United States Army Combat Developments Command Aviation Agency
USACDCCA ... United States Army Combat Developments Command Combined Arms Agency
USACDCCAA ... United States Army Combat Developments Command Civil Affairs Agency
USACDCCAG.. United States Army Combat Developments Command Combat Army Group
USACDCCBRA .. United States Army Combat Developments Command Chemical-Biological-Radiological Agency
USACDCCEA .. United States Army Combat Developments Command Communications-Electronics Agency
USACDCCHA .. United States Army Combat Developments Command Chaplain Agency
USACDCCSSG .. United States Army Combat Developments Command Combat Service Support Group
USACDCDPFO .. United States Army Combat Developments Command Data Processing Field Office
USACDCEA ... United States Army Combat Developments Command Engineer Agency
USACDCEC ... United States Army Combat Developments Command Experimentation Command
USACDCFAA ... United States Army Combat Developments Command Field Artillery Agency
USACDCFINA .. United States Army Combat Developments Command Finance Agency
USACDCIA ... United States Army Combat Developments Command Infantry Agency
USACDCIAS... United States Army Combat Developments Command Institute of Advanced Studies
USACDCICAS.. United States Army Combat Developments Command Institute of Combined Arms and Support
USACDCIDDFO .. United States Army Combat Developments Command Internal Defense and Development Field Office
USACDCILC... United States Army Combat Developments Command Institute of Land Combat
USACDCINS .. United States Army Combat Developments Command Institute of Nuclear Studies
USACDCINTA .. United States Army Combat Developments Command Intelligence Agency
USACDCISA... United States Army Combat Developments Command Institute of Systems Analysis
USACDCISS ... United States Army Combat Developments Command Institute of Special Studies
USACDCJAA .. United States Army Combat Developments Command Judge Advocate Agency
USACDCMA .. United States Army Combat Developments Command Maintenance Agency
USACDCMPA .. United States Army Combat Developments Command Military Police Agency
USACDCMSA .. United States Army Combat Developments Command Medical Service Agency
USACDCNG .. United States Army Combat Developments Command Nuclear Group
USACDCOA... United States Army Combat Developments Command Ordnance Agency
USACDCPASA .. United States Army Combat Developments Command Personnel and Administrative Services Agency
USACDCQA... United States Army Combat Developments Command Quartermaster Agency
USACDCSA ... United States Army Combat Developments Command Supply Agency
USACDCSWA .. United States Army Combat Developments Command Special Warfare Agency
USACDCSWCAG ... United States Army Combat Developments Command Special Warfare and Civil Affairs Group
USACDCTA ... United States Army Combat Developments Command Transportation Agency
USACDEC .... United States Army Combat Developments Experimentation Center
USACE ...... United States Army Corps of Engineers (Merged with General Equipment Command)
USACENCDCSA ... United States Army Corps of Engineers National Civil Defense Computer Support Agency
USACGSC ... United States Army Command and General Staff College
USACHB ..... United States Army Chaplain Board
USACHS ..... United States Army Chaplain School
USACIECA.... United States Army Advisory Commission on International Educational and Cultural Affairs
USACISO .... United States Army Counterinsurgency Support Office, Okinawa
USACIU ..... United States Army Command Information Unit
USACMLC.... United States Army Chemical Center
USACMLCB... United States Army Chemical Corps Board
USACMLCS ... United States Army Chemical Center and School
USACMLCSCH .. United States Army Chemical Corps School
USACMLRDL .. United States Army Chemical Research & Development Laboratories
USACMS ..... United States Army Command Management School

USACOMZEUR . . United States Army Communications Zone, Europe
USACPEB . . . . . United States Army Central Physical Evaluation Board
USACRAPAC . . United States Army Command Reconnaissance Activities, Pacific Command
USACRF . . . . . United States Army Counterintelligence Records Facility
USACRREL . . . . United States Army Cold Regions Research and Engineering Laboratory
USACS . . . . . . United States Army Courier Service
USACSA . . . . . United States Army Combat Surveillance Agency
USACSC . . . . . United States Army Computer Systems Command
USACSR . . . . . United States Air Corps Specialist Reserve
USACSS . . . . . United States Army Chief of Support Services
USACSS . . . . . United States Army Combat Surveillance School
USACSSEC . . . . United States Army Computer Systems Support and Evaluation Command
USACSTA . . . . United States Army Courier Station
USACTC . . . . . United States Army Clothing and Textile Center
USACTMC . . . . United States Army Clothing and Textile Materiel Center
USACWL . . . . United States Army Chemical Warfare Laboratory
USAD . . . . United States Army Dispensary
USADATCOM . . United States Army Data Support Command
USADC . . . . . . United States Army Data Support Command
USADCJ . . . . . United States Army Depot Command Japan
USADEG . . . . . United States Army Dependents' Education Group
USADJ . . . . . . United States Army Depot, Japan
USADOFL . . . . United States Army Diamond Ordnance Fuze Laboratory (Later, HDL)
USADPC . . . . . United States Army Data Processing Center
USADRB . . . . . United States Army Discharge Review Board
USADSC . . . . . United States Army Data Services and Administrative Systems Command
USAE . . . . United States Army Engineer
USAEAGSC . . . United States Army, Europe, Adjutant General Support Center
USAEARC . . . . United States Army Equipment Authorizations Review Center
USAEB . . . . . . United States Army Engineer Board
USAEC . . . . . . United States Army Electronics Command
USAEC . . . . . . United States Atomic Energy Commission
USAECA . . . . . United States Army Electronics Command Computation Agency
USAECBDE . . . . United States Army Engineer Center Brigade
USAECFB . . . . . United States Army Engineer Center and Fort Belvoir
USAECOM . . . . United States Army Electronics Command
USAECR . . . . . United States Army Engineer Center Regiment
USAEDH . . . . . United States Army Engineer Division, Huntsville
USAEDLMV . . . United States Army Engineer Division, Lower Mississippi Valley
USAEDM . . . . . United States Army Engineer Division, Mediterranean
USAEDMR . . . . United States Army Engineer Division, Missouri River
USAEDNA . . . . United States Army Engineer Division, North Atlantic
USAEDNC . . . . United States Army Engineer Division, North Central
USAEDNE . . . . United States Army Engineer Division, New England
USAEDNP . . . . United States Army Engineer Division, North Pacific
USAEDOR . . . . United States Army Engineer Division, Ohio River
USAEDPO . . . . United States Army Engineer Division, Pacific Ocean
USAEDSA . . . . United States Army Engineer Division, South Atlantic
USAEDSP . . . . . United States Army Engineer Division, South Pacific
USAEDSW . . . . United States Army Engineer Division, Southwestern
USAEEA . . . . . United States Army Enlistment Eligibility Activity
USAEEC . . . . . United States Army Enlisted Evaluation Center
USAEFMA . . . . United States Army Electronics Command Financial Management Agency
USAEGD . . . . . United States Army Engineer Gulf District
USAEHA . . . . . United States Army Environmental Hygiene Agency
USAEHL . . . . . United States Army Environmental Health Laboratory
USAEIS . . . . . . United States Army Electronic Intelligence and Security
USAEMA . . . . . United States Army Electronics Materiel Agency (Formerly, USASSA)
USAEMCA . . . . United States Army Engineer Mathematical Computation Agency
USAEMSA . . . . United States Army Electronics Materiel Support Agency (Formerly, USASMSA)
USAENGCOMEUR . . . . . United States Army Engineer Command, Europe
USAEPA . . . . . United States Army Electronics Command Patent Agency
USAEPG . . . . . United States Army Electronics Proving Ground
USAEPMARA . . . United States Army, Europe, Personnel Management and Replacement Activity
USAERA . . . . . United States Army Electronics Command Logistics Research Agency
USAERDA . . . . United States Army Electronic Research & Development Agency
USAERDAA . . . United States Army Electronics Research and Development Activity (Fort Huachuca, Arizona)
USAERDAW . . . United States Army Electronics Research and Development Activity, White Sands (New Mexico)
USAERDL . . . . . United States Army Electronics Research and Development Laboratory (Formerly, USASRDL)
USAERG . . . . . United States Army Engineer Reactor Group
USAES . . . . . . United States Army Engineer School
USAESC . . . . . United States Army Electronics Support Command
USAETL . . . . . . United States Army Engineer Topographic Laboratories
USAEU . . . . . . United States Army Exhibit Unit
USAEUR . . . . . United States Army Europe
USAEWES . . . . United States Army Engineer Waterways Experiment Station

USAF . . . . United States Air Force
USAF . . . . United States Army Forces
USAF . . . . United Student Aid Fund
US of AF . . . . . Under Secretary of the Air Force
USAFA . . . . . . United States Air Force Academy
USAFABD . . . . United States Army Field Artillery Board
USAFACFS . . . . United States Army Field Artillery Center and Fort Sill
USAFACS . . . . United States Air Force Air Crew School
USAFAGOS . . . United States Air Force's Air-Ground Operations School
USAFAPC . . . . United States Air Force Airframe Production Contract
USAFAPS . . . . United States Air Force Air Police School
USAFAS . . . . . United States Army Field Artillery School
USAFB . . . . . . United States Army Field Band
USAFBI . . . . . . United States Army Forces in the British Isles
USAFBMD . . . . United States Air Force Ballistic Missile Division
USAFBMS . . . . United States Air Force Basic Military School
USAFBS . . . . . . United States Air Force Bandsman School
USAFBS . . . . United States Air Force Bombardment School
USAF CMR . . . . United States Air Force Court of Military Review
USAFD . . . . . . United States Air Force Dictionary
USAFE . . . . . . United States Air Force in Europe
USAFECI . . . . United States Air Force Extension Course Institute
USAFEL . . . . . . United States Air Force Epidemiological Laboratory
USAFETAC . . . . United States Air Force Environmental Technical Applications Center
USAFETPS . . . . United States Air Force Experimental Test Pilot School
USAFEURPCR . . United States Air Force European Postal and Courier Region
USAFFE . . . . . . United States Army Forces, Far East (World War II)
USAFFGS . . . . United States Air Force Flexible Gunnery School
USAFFSR . . . . . United States Air Force Flight Safety Research
USAFHD . . . . . United States Air Force Historical Division
USAFI . . . . United States Air Forces Institute
USAFI . . . . United States Armed Forces Institute
USAFIA . . . . . . United States Army Forces in Australia
USAFIB . . . . . . United States Army Aviation Flight Information Bulletin
USAFICPA . . . . United States Army Forces in Central Pacific Area
USAFIK . . . . . . United States Army Forces in Korea
USAFIME . . . . . United States Armed Forces in Middle East
USAFINZ . . . . . United States Army Forces in New Zealand
USAFISPA . . . . United States Army Forces in the South Pacific Area
USAFIT . . . . . United States Air Force Institute of Technology
USAFLANT . . . United States Air Forces, Atlantic
USAFMEPCR . . . United States Air Force Mideast Postal and Courier Region
USAFMEPCS . . . United States Air Force Mideast Postal and Courier Service
USAFMTC . . . . United States Air Force Marksmanship Training Center
USAFNS . . . . United States Air Force Navigation School
USAFOCS . . . . United States Air Force Officer Candidate School
USAFOF . . . . . United States Army Flight Operations Facility
USAFPAC . . . . United States Air Forces, Pacific
USAFPACPCR . . United States Air Force Pacific Postal and Courier Region
USAFPACPCS . . United States Air Force Pacific Postal and Courier Service
USAFPEB . . . . . United States Air Force Physical Evaluation Board
USAFPS . . . . . United States Air Force Pilot School
USAFR . . . . . . United States Air Force Representative
USAFR . . . . . . United States Air Force Reserve
USAFRS . . . . . United States Air Force Recruiting Service
USAFS . . . . . . United States Army Finance School
USAFSA . . . . . United States Army Forces in South America
USAFSAM . . . . United States Air Force School of Aerospace Medicine
USAFSAWC . . . United States Air Force Special Air Warfare Center
USAFSC . . . . . United States Army Food Service Center
USAFSE . . . . . . United States Air Force Supervisory Examination
USAFSG . . . . . United States Army Field Support Group
USAFSO . . . . . United States Air Forces Southern Command
USAFSOC . . . . United States Air Force Special Operations Center
USAFSOF . . . . United States Air Force Special Operations Force
USAFSOS . . . . United States Air Force Special Operations School
USAFSRA . . . . . United States Air Force Special Reporting Agency
USAFSS . . . . . . United States Air Force Security Service
USAFSTC . . . . . United States Army Foreign Science and Technology Center
USAFSTRIKE . . . United States Air Forces Strike Command
USAFTALC . . . . United States Air Force Tactical Airlift Center
USAFTARC . . . . United States Air Force Tactical Air Reconnaissance Center
USAFTAWC . . . United States Air Force Tactical Air Warfare Center
USAFTFWC . . . United States Air Force Tactical Fighter Weapons Center
USAFTS . . . . . United States Air Force Technical School
USAF-USPCR . . United States Air Force – United States Postal Courier Region
USAFWPO . . . . United States Air Force Water Port Liaison Office(r)
USAG . . . . United States Army Garrison
USAG . . . . . . United States Army in Greece
USAGETA . . . . United States Army General Equipment Test Activity
USAGG . . . . . . United States Army Group, American Mission for Aid to Greece

USAGIMRADA .. United States Army Geodesy Intelligence and Mapping Research and Development Agency
USAGSC . . . . . United States Army General Supplies Commodity Center
USAH . . . . United States Army Hospital
USAHEL . . . . . United States Army Human Engineering Laboratories
USAHOME. . . . United States Army Homes (Prefabricated houses, shipped overseas)
USAHTN . . . . . United States Army Hometown News Center
USAIB . . . . United States Army Infantry Board
USAIC . . . . . . United States Army Infantry Center
USAIC . . . . . . United States Army Intelligence Corps
USAICA . . . . . United States Army Interagency Communications Agency
USAID . . . . . . United States Agency for International Development
USAIDR . . . . . United States Army Institute of Dental Research
USAIDSC . . . . . United States Army Information and Data Systems Command
USAIDSCOM . . United States Army Information and Data Systems Command
USAIIC . . . . . . United States Army Imagery Interpretation Center
USAILG . . . . . United States Army International Logistics Group
USAIMS . . . . . United States Army Institute for Military Systems
USAINFHRU . . . United States Army Infantry Human Research Unit
USAINTB . . . . United States Army Intelligence Board
USAINTC . . . . United States Army Intelligence Center
USAINTC . . . . United States Army Intelligence Command
USAINTELMDA . . United States Army Intelligence Materiel Developments Agency
USAINTS . . . . . United States Army Intelligence School
USAIPSG . . . . . United States Army Industrial and Personnel Security Group
USAIRA . . . . . United States Air Attaché
USAIRC . . . . . . United States Army Ionizing Radiation Center
USAIRMILCOMUN .. United States Air Force Representative, UN Military Staff Committee
USAIRR . . . . . . United States Army Investigative Records Repository
USAIS . . . . . . United States Army Infantry School
USAITFG . . . . . United States Army Intelligence Threats and Forecasts Group
USAJFKCENMA . . . United States Army John Fitzgerald Kennedy Center for Military Assistance
USAJFKCENSPWAR .. United States Army John F. Kennedy Center for Special Warfare (Airborne)
USAJSC . . . . . United States Army Joint Support Command
USALA . . . . . United States Amateur Lacrosse Association
USALAPA . . . . United States Army Los Angeles Procurement Agency
USALCJ . . . . . United States Army Logistical Center, Japan
USALDJ . . . . . United States Army Logistics Depot, Japan
USALDRHRU . . . United States Army Leadership Human Research Unit
USALDSRA . . . . United States Army Logistics Doctrine, Systems and Readiness Agency (New Cumberland Army Depot, Harrisburg, Pennsylvania)
USALMC . . . . United States Army Logistics Management Center
USALS . . . . . . United States Army Language School
USALWL . . . . . United States Army Limited War Laboratory
USAM . . . . Unified Space Applications Mission
USAM . . . . . . Union des Syndicats Autonomes de Madagascar (Federation of Malagasy Autonomous Unions)
USAM . . . . . . United States Army Mothers Organization, National
USAMAPLA . . . United States Army Military Assistance Program Logistics Agency
USAMB . . . . . . United States Army Maintenance Board
USAMBRL . . . . United States Army Medical Biomechanical Research Laboratory (Walter Reed Army Medical Center)
USAMC . . . . . United States Army Materiel Command
USAMC. . . . . . United States Army Medical Corps
USAMC. . . . . . United States Army Missile Command
USAMC. . . . . . United States Army Mobility Command
USAMC. . . . . . United States Army Munitions Command
USAMCALMSA . . . . United States Army Materiel Command Automated Logistics Management Systems Agency
USAMCC. . . . . United States Army Metrology and Calibration Center
USAMCFSA . . . United States Army Materiel Command Field Safety Agency
USAMCI & SA . . . United States Army Materiel Command Installations and Service Agency
USAMD . . . . . . United States Army Missile Detachment
USAMDA . . . . United States Army Medical Depot Activity, Ryukyu Islands
USAMECOM . . . United States Army Mobility Equipment Command
USAMEDS . . . . United States Army Medical Service
USAMEDSVS . . United States Army Medical Service Veterinary School
USAMEDTC . . . United States Army Medical Training Center
USAMERDC . . . United States Army Mobility Equipment Research and Development Center
USAMERDL . . . United States Army Medical Equipment Research and Development Laboratory
USAMETA . . . . United States Army Management Engineering Training Agency
USAMICOM. . . United States Army Missile Command
USAMIDA . . . . United States Army Major Item Data Agency
USAMMA . . . . United States Army Medical Material Agency
USAMMCS. . . . United States Army Missile and Munitions Center School

USAMMT . . . . . United States Army Military Mail Terminal
USAMOAMA . . United States Army Medical Optical and Maintenance Activity
USAMOCOM . . United States Army Mobility Command
USAMP . . . . . United States Army Mine Planter
USAMPS . . . . . United States Army Military Police School
USAMRDC . . . . United States Army Medical Research and Development Command
USAMRL . . . . . United States Army Medical Research Laboratory
USAMRN . . . . . United States Army Medical Research and Nutrition
USAMRNL . . . . United States Army Medical Research and Nutrition Laboratory
USAMRU . . . . . United States Army Medical Research Unit
USAMS . . . . . United States Army Management School
USAMSMADHS .. United States Army Medical Service Meat and Dairy Hygiene School
USAMSSA . . . . United States Army Management Systems Support Agency
USAM & TTC.. United States Army Mechanical & Technical Training Center (Also called MECHTECH)
USAMU . . . . . United States Army Medical Unit
USAMUCOM . . United States Army Munitions Command
USAMUFD . . . . United States Army Medical Unit, Fort Detrick (Maryland)
USAN . . . . . . United States Adopted Name (Drugs)
USANAFBA . . . United States Army, Navy and Air Force Bandsmen's Association
USANC . . . . . United States Army Nurse Corps
USANCG. . . . . United States Army Nuclear Cratering Group
USANDL. . . . . . United States Army Nuclear Defense Laboratory
USANWCG . . . United States Army Nuclear Weapon Coordination Group
USANWSG . . . United States Army Nuclear Weapon Systems Surety Group
USANWTC . . . United States Army Northern Warfare Training Center
USAOAC. . . . . United States Army Ordnance Ammunition Command (Merged with Munitions Command)
USAOCBRL . . . United States Army Ordnance Corps Ballistic Research Laboratory
USAOCCCL . . . United States Army Ordnance Corps Coating & Chemical Laboratory
USAOCDPS . . . United States Army Ordnance Corps Development & Proof Services
USAOC & S . . United States Army Ordnance Center and School
USAOD. . . . . . United States Army Ordnance District
USAOGMS . . . United States Army Ordnance Guided Missile School
USAOMC . . . . United States Army Ordnance Missile Command (Later, Missile Command)
USAORDCORPS .. United States Army Ordnance Corps
USAORP . . . . . United States Army Oversea Research Program
USAORRF . . . . United States Army Ordnance Rocket Research Facility
USAOSANO . . . United States Army Oversea Supply Agency, New Orleans
USAOSANY. . . United States Army Oversea Supply Agency, New York
USAOSASF . . . United States Army Oversea Supply Agency, San Francisco
USAOSREPLSTA. . . United States Army Oversea Replacement Station
USAOSWAC. . . United States Army Ordnance Special Weapons-Ammunition Command
USAOWC . . . . United States Army Ordnance Weapons Command (Merged with Missile Command)
USAPA . . . . . . United States Army Photographic Agency
USAPC . . . . . . United States Army Petroleum Center
USAPC . . . . . . United States Army Pictorial Center
USAPDA . . . . . United States Army Physical Disability Agency
USAPDC . . . . . United States Army Property Disposal Center (Merged with Defense Logistics Services Center)
USAPDCE. . . . . United States Army Petroleum Distribution Command, Europe
USAPEB. . . . . . United States Army Physical Evaluation Board
USAPERSCEN . . United States Army Personnel Center
USAPG . . . . . . United States Army Participation Group
USAPHC . . . . . United States Army Primary Helicopter Center
USAPHS . . . . . United States Army Primary Helicopter School
USAPIC . . . . . United States Army Photointerpretation Center
USAPO . . . . . . United States Antarctic Projects Office
USAPRC . . . . . United States Army Physical Review Council
USAPRDC . . . . United States Army Polar Research and Development Center
USAPRO . . . . . United States Army Personnel Research Office
USAPSG . . . . . United States Army Personnel Security Group
USAPT . . . . . . United States Army Parachute Team
USAPWA . . . . United Stone and Allied Products Workers of America
USAQMC . . . . United States Army Quartermaster Corps (Merged with Supply & Maintenance Command)
USAQMCENFL .. United States Army Quartermaster Center and Fort Lee
USAQMS . . . . United States Army Quartermaster School
USAQMTC . . . United States Army Quartermaster Training Command
USAR . . . . United States Army Reserve
USARACS . . . . United States Army Alaska Communications Center
USARADBD. . . . United States Army Air Defense Board
USARADCOM.. United States Army Air Defense Command
USARADSCH . . United States Army Air Defense School
USARAE . . . . . United States Army Reserve Affairs, Europe
USARAL . . . . . United States Army, Alaska
USARC . . . . . . United States Army Reserve Center
USARCARIB . . . United States Army, Caribbean
USARCEN . . . . United States Army Records Center
USARCPC . . . . United States Army Reserve Components Personnel Center

USARDA . . . . . United States Army Regional Dental Activity
USARDL . . . . . United States Army Research and Development Laboratories
USARDORAG . . United States Army Research and Development Operational Research
     Advisory Group
USAREC . . . . . United States Army Recruiting Command
USARECSTA . . . United States Army Reception Station
USAREPG . . . . United States Army Electronic Proving Ground
USARET-RSGSTA . . United States Army Returnee - Reassignment Station
USAREUR . . . . United States Army, Europe
USAREURAGLO . . . United States Army, Europe, Adjutant General Liaison Office
USAREURORDCOM . . United States Army European Ordnance Command
USARFANT . . . United States Army Forces, Antilles
USARFT . . . . . United States Army Forces, Taiwan
USARHAW . . . . United States Army, Hawaii
USARIEM . . . . . United States Army Research Institute of Environmental Medicine
USARIS . . . . . . United States Army Information School
USARJ . . . . . . United States Army, Japan
USARLANT . . . United States Army Forces, Atlantic
USARMA . . . . United States Army Attache'
USARMIS . . . . United States Army Mission
USARMLO . . . . United States Army Liaison Officer
USARMY . . . . . Uncle Sam Ain't Released Me Yet
USARO . . . . . . United States Army Research Office
USARP . . . . . . United States Antarctic Research Program (National Science Foundation)
USARPA . . . . . United States Army Radio Propagation Agency
USARPAC . . . . United States Army, Pacific
USARPACINTS . . . United States Army Pacific Intelligence School
USARSA . . . . . United States Amateur Roller Skating Association
USARSO . . . . . United States Army Forces Southern Command
USARSO-PR . . . United States Army Forces, Southern Command - Puerto Rico
USARSOUTHCOM . . United States Army Forces Southern Command
USARSTRIKE . . . United States Army Forces Strike Command
USARSUPTHAI . . . United States Army Support, Thailand
USARV . . . . . . United States Army Vietnam
USARYIS . . . . . United States Army, Ryukyu Islands
USAS . . . . United States Air Service
USASA . . . . . . United States Army Security Agency
USASADEA . . . United States Army Signal Air Defense Engineering Agency (Now
     USAADEA)
USASAE . . . . . United States Army Security Agency, Europe
USASAFO . . . . United States Army Signal Avionics Field Office (Now USAAFO)
USASATCOMA . . United States Army Satellite Communications Agency
USASATC & S . . . United States Army Security Agency Training Center and School
USASATSA . . . . United States Army Signal Aviation Test Support Activity
USASC . . . . . . United States Army Signal Corps (Merged with Communications and
     Electronics Command)
USASC . . . . . . United States Army Subsistence Center
USASCA . . . . . United States Army Satellite Communications Agency
USASCAF . . . . United States Army Service Center for the Armed Forces
USASCC . . . . . United States Army Strategic Communications Command
USASCHEUR . . . United States Army School, Europe
USASCII . . . . . United States of America Standard Code for Information Interchange
USASCR . . . . . United States Army Support Center, Richmond
USASCS . . . . . United States Army Signal Center and School
USASCSA . . . . United States Army Signal Communications Security Agency
USASCSOCR . . United States of America Standard Character Set for Optical Character
     Recognition
USASCV . . . . . United States Army Support Command, Vietnam
USASEA . . . . . United States Army Signal Engineering Agency
USASESA . . . . United States Army Signal Equipment Support Agency
USASESS . . . . United States Army Southeastern Signal School
USASETAF . . . . United States Army Southern European Task Force
USASEXC . . . . United States Armed Services Exploitation Center
USASFV . . . . . United States Army Special Forces, Vietnam
USASG(Aus) . . . United States Army Standardization Group (Australia)
USASG(CA) . . . United States Army Standardization Group (Canada)
USASG(UK) . . . United States Army Standardization Group (United Kingdom)
USASGV . . . . . United States Army Support Group, Vietnam
USASI . . . . United States of America Standards Institute (Formerly, ASA; now ANSI)
USASIGC . . . . . United States Army Signal Corps (Merged with Communications &
     Electronics Command)
USASIMSA . . . . United States Army Signal Materiel Support Agency (Now USAEMSA)
USASIS . . . . . . United States Army Strategic Intelligence School
USASMC . . . . . United States Army Supply and Maintenance Command (AMC) (Formerly,
     QMC)
USASMSA . . . . United States Army Signal Materiel Support Agency (Now USAEMSA)
USASOS . . . . . United States Army Services of Supply
USASPSAE . . . . United States Army Special Services Agency, Europe
USASPTC . . . . . United States Army Support Center
USASPTCM . . . United States Army Support Center, Memphis
USASPTCP . . . . United States Army Support Center, Philadelphia

USASPTCR . . . . United States Army Support Center, Richmond
USASRDL . . . . . United States Army Signal Research and Development Laboratory (Later,
     USAERDL)
USASRU . . . . . United States Army Surgical Research Unit
USASSA . . . . . United States Army Signal Supply Agency (Now USAEC)
USASSAFMPO . . United States Army Signal Supply Agency, Fort Monmouth Procurement
     Office
USASSAMRO . . . United States Army Signal Supply Agency, Midwestern Regional Office
USASSAUSAEPGPO . . United States Army Signal Supply Agency, United States Army
     Electronic Proving Ground Procurement Office
USASSAWPO . . United States Army Signal Supply Agency, Washington Procurement
     Office
USASSAWRO . . United States Army Signal Supply Agency, Western Regional Office
USASSD . . . . . United States Army Special Security Detachment
USASSG . . . . . United States Army Special Security Group
USASTAF . . . . . United States Army Southern European Task Force
USASTAF . . . . . United States Army Strategic Air Forces in the Pacific
USASTC . . . . . United States Army Signal Training Center (Fort Gordon, Georgia)
USAS/TC & FG . . . United States Army School/Training Center and Fort Gordon (Georgia)
USASTCFM . . . United States Army Signal Training Command and Fort Monmouth
USASTRATCOM . . United States Army Strategic Communications Command
USASTRATCOM-A . . . United States Army Strategic Communications Command, Alaska
USASTRATCOM-CONUS . . United States Army Strategic Communications Command -
     Continental United States
USASTRATCOM-EUR . . . United States Army Strategic Communications Command - Europe
USASTRATCOM-PAC . . United States Army Strategic Communications Command - Pacific
USASTRATCOM-SIGGP-T . . . United States Army Strategic Communications Command
     Signal Group, Thailand
USASTRATCOM-SO . . United States Army Strategic Communications Command - South
USASTRATCOM-V . . United States Army Strategic Communications Command - Vietnam
USASUPCOM-CRB . . United States Army Support Command - Cam Ranh Bay
USASUPCOM-QN . . United States Army Support Command - Qui Nhon
USASUPCOM-SGN . . United States Army Support Command - Saigon
USASWS . . . . . United States Army Special Warfare School
USAT . . . . United States Army Transport
USATAC . . . . . United States Army Training Center, Engineer (Fort Leonard Wood,
     Missouri)
USATACOM . . . United States Army Tank-Automotive Command
USATAFO . . . . United States Army Transportation Aviation Field Office
USATATSA . . . . United States Army Transportation Aircraft Test and Support Activity
USATA(WH) . . . United States Army Transportation Agency (White House)
USATC . . . . . . United States Army Topographic Command
USATC . . . . . . United States Army Training Center
USATCA . . . . . United States Army Terminal Command/Atlantic
USATCD . . . . . United States Army Training Center, Air Defense
USATCEUR . . . United States Army Terminal Command Europe
USATC FA . . . . United States Army Training Center, Field Artillery
USATCFE . . . . . United States Army Transportation Center and Fort Eustis
USATCFLW . . . United States Army Training Center and Fort Leonard Wood
USATCG . . . . . United States Army Terminal Command, Gulf
USATCP . . . . . United States Army Terminal Command/Pacific
USATCRTSA . . . United States Army Transportation Corps Road Test Support Activity
USATDGL . . . . United States Army Terminal Detachment, Great Lakes
USATEA . . . . . United States Army Transportation Engineering Agency
USATEC . . . . . United States Army Test and Evaluation Command (AMC)
USATECOM . . . United States Army Test and Evaluation Command
USATIA . . . . . . United States Army Transportation Intelligence Agency
USATMACE . . . United States Army Traffic Management Agency, Central Europe
USATMC . . . . . United States Army Transportation Materiel Command
USATOPOCOM . . . United States Army Topographic Command
USATRC . . . . . United States Army Transportation Research Command
USATRECOM . . United States Army Transportation Research and Engineering Command
USATREOG . . . United States Army Transportation Environmental Operations Group
USATRFSTA . . . United States Army Transfer Station
USATSC . . . . . United States Army Terrestrial Sciences Center
USATSCH . . . . United States Army Transportation School
USATT . . . . . . Union des Syndicats Autonomes des Travailleurs Tchadiens (Federation of
     Autonomous Workers Unions of Chad)
USATTAY . . . . United States Army Transportation Test Activity, Yuma (Arizona)
USATTB . . . . . United States Army Transportation Terminal, Brooklyn
USATTC . . . . . United States Army Transportation Training Command
USATTC . . . . . United States Army Tropic Test Center
USATTCA . . . . United States Army Transportation Terminal Command, Atlantic
USATTCARC . . . United States Army Transportation Terminal Command, Arctic
USATTCG . . . . United States Army Transportation Terminal Command, Gulf
USATTCP . . . . United States Army Transportation Terminal Command, Pacific
USATTU . . . . . United States Army Transportation Terminal Unit
USATUC . . . . . United States Army Terminal Unit, Canaveral
USAW . . . . . . Underwater Security Advance Warnings (Navy)
USAWC . . . . . United States Army War College
USAWC . . . . . United States Army Weapons Command (AMC)

USAWECOM .. United States Army Weapons Command
USAWES ..... United States Army Waterways Experiment Station
USAWF .... United States Amateur Wrestling Foundation
USB .... Unified S-Band
USB .... Upper Sideband
USBA .... Union Syndicale des Bases Americaines (Union of American Base Workers) (Morocco)
USBA .... United States Brewers Association
USBATU ..... United States - Brazil Aviation Training Unit
USBBS .... United States Bureau of Biological Survey (Terminated, 1940; later, Fish and Wildlife Service)
USBE .... Unified S-Band Equipment
USBE .... United States Book Exchange
USBEP .... United States Bureau of Engraving and Printing
USBER .... United States Mission, Berlin
USBF .... United States Baseball Federation
USBF .... United States Brewers Foundation
USBF .... United States Bureau of Fisheries (Terminated)
USBFDC ..... United States Bureau of Foreign and Domestic Commerce
USBG ...... United States Botanic Garden
USBGA ..... United States Blind Golfer's Association
USBGN ...... United States Bureau on Geographical Names (Terminated, 1947; later, Board on Geographical Names)
USBIA .... United States Bureau of Insular Affairs
USBL .... United States Bureau of Lighthouses
USBLS .... United States Bureau of Labor Statistics
USBM ...... United States Bureau of Mines
USBMG ...... United States Berlin Mission in Germany
USBN .... United States Bureau of Navigation
USBNP ...... United States Bureau of Navy Personnel (Terminated)
USBP .... United States Border Patrol (Treasury Department)
USBPA ..... United States Bicycle Polo Association
USBPR ...... United States Bureau of Public Roads
USBR .... United States Bureau of Reclamation (Department of the Interior)
USBRO ..... United States Base Requirements Overseas
USBS .... Unified S-Band System (Radio)
USBS .... United States Bureau of Standards
USBSA ...... United States Beet Sugar Association
USBTA ..... United States Board of Tax Appeals (Later, the Tax Court of the United States)
USBWA ..... United States Basketball Writers Association
USC .... Ultrasonic Storage Cell
USC .... Under Separate Cover
USC .... Union Sociale Camerounaise (Cameroonese Social Union)
USC .... Unitarian Service Committee (Post-World War II)
USC .... United States Citizen
USC .... United States Code (Law)
USC .... United States of Colombia
USC .... United States Congress
USC .... United States Customs
USC .... United Strasser Club
USC .... Universal Specimen Chamber
USC .... University of Santa Clara (California)
USC .... University of South Carolina
USC .... University of Southern California
USC .... Up Stage Center (Away from audience) (A stage direction)
USCA .... Uniformed Services Contingency Act
USCA .... United States Code Annotated (Based on official USC)
USCA .... United States Copper Association
USCA .... United States Courts of Appeals
USCAC ...... United States Continental Army Command
USCAL ...... University of Southern California, Aeronautical Laboratory
USCAM ...... United States Civil Aviation Mission
USCANS ..... Unified S-Band Communication and Navigation System (NASA)
USCAR ...... United States Civil Administration, Ryukyu Islands
USCC .... Union des Syndicats Croyants du Cameroun (Federation of Cameroonese Believers Unions)
USCC .... United States Cancellation Club
USCC .... United States Catholic Conference (Formerly, NCWC)
USCC .... United States Chamber of Commerce
USCC .... United States Circuit Court
USCC .... United States Commercial Company
USCC .... United States Cotton Commission
USCC .... United States Court of Claims
USCC .... United States Criminal Code
USCC .... United States Criminal Court
USCC .... United States Customs Court
USCC .... United Student Christian Council in United States
USCCA ...... United States Circuit Court of Appeals
USCCEC ..... United States Committee for Care of European Children (Post-World War II)

USCCHO ..... United States Conference of City Health Officers
USCCPA ..... United States Court of Customs and Patent Appeals
USCDC ..... United States Civil Defense Council
USCEC ...... University of Southern California, Engineering Center
USCF .... United States Chess Federation
USCF .... United States Churchill Foundation
USCG .... United States Coast Guard
USCG .... United States Consul General
USCGA ..... United States Coast Guard Academy
USCGAD..... United States Coast Guard Air Detachment
USC-GARP ... United States Committee for the Global Atmospheric Research Program
USCGAS ..... United States Coast Guard Air Station
USCGASB .... United States Coast Guard Aircraft and Supply Base
USCGAUX ... United States Coast Guard Auxiliary
USCGB ...... United States Coast Guard Base
USCGC ...... United States Coast Guard Cutter
USCGD...... United States Coast Guard Depot
USCGR ...... United States Coast Guard Reserve
USCGRC .... United States Coast Guard Receiving Center
USCGR(T) ... United States Coast Guard, Reserve (Temporary)
USCGR(W)... United States Coast Guard, Reserve (Women)
USCGS ..... United States Coast and Geodetic Survey (Later, National Ocean Survey)
USC & GS .... United States Coast and Geodetic Survey (Later, National Ocean Survey)
USCGSCF .... United States Coast Guard Shore Communication Facilities
USCGTS .... United States Coast Guard Training Station
USCHS ...... United States Capitol Historical Society
USCHS ...... United States Catholic Historical Society
USCIA ...... United States Customs Inspectors' Association Port of New York
USCICC ...... United States Council of the International Chamber of Commerce
USCIIC ...... United States Civilian Internee Information Center (Army)
USCIIC(Br) .... United States Civilian Internee Information Center (Branch) (Army)
USCINCEMEAFSA ... United States Commander in Chief Middle East, Africa South of the Sahara, and Southern Asia (Military)
USCINCEUR .. United States Commander-in-Chief Europe
USCINCSO ... United States Commander-in-Chief, Southern Command
USCJE .... United Synagogue Commission on Jewish Education
USCL .... United Society for Christian Literature (British)
USCM ...... United States Conference of Mayors
USCMA...... United States Court of Military Appeals
USCMA ..... United States Crutch Manufacturers Association
USCMI ...... United States Commission on Mathematical Instruction
USCOA ...... Uniformed Services Contingency Option Act
USCOB ...... United States Commander, Berlin
USCOLD ..... United States Committee on Large Dams (of the International Commission on Large Dams)
USCONARC... United States Continental Army Command
USCPSHHM ... United States Committee to Promote Studies of the History of the Habsburg Monarchy
USCR .... United States Committee for Refugees
USCRA ...... United States Citizens' Rights Association
USCS .... United States Conciliation Service (Functions transferred to Federal Mediation and Conciliation Service, 1947)
USCS .... Universal Ship Cancellation Society
USCSB....... United States Communications Security Board
USCSC ...... United States Civil Service Commission
USCSC ...... United States Collegiate Sports Council
USCSC ...... United States Cuban Sugar Council
USCSE ...... United States Civil Service Examination
USCSRA ..... United States Cane Sugar Refiners' Association
USCSSB...... United States Cap Screw Service Bureau
USCT .... Union des Syndicats Confederes du Togo (Federation of Confederated Unions of Togo)
USCT .... United States Colored Troops (Civil War)
USCTA ...... United States Combined Training Association
USCUN...... United States Committee for the United Nations (Later, UNAUS)
USCV .... Union Scientifique Continentale du Verre
USCWCC ..... United States Conference for the World Council of Churches
USD .... Ultrasonic Separation Detector
USD .... Unified School District
USD .... United States Dispensatory (Pharmacy)
USD .... University Science Development (National Science Foundation)
USDA .... United States Department of Agriculture
USDA .... United States Disarmament Administration (Transferred to US Arms Control and Disarmament Agency, 1961)
USDAO...... United States Defense Attache Office
USDB .... United States Disciplinary Barracks
USDC .... United States Department of Commerce
USDC ...... United States District Court
USDD .... United States Department of Defense
USDELIADB ... United States Delegation, Inter-American Defense Board

USDESEA..... United States Dependent Schools, European Area
USDHE & W .. United States Department of Health, Education, and Welfare
USDI .... United States Department of the Interior
USDJ .... United States Department of Justice
USDJ .... United States District Judge
USDL .... United States Department of Labor
USDLGI ...... United States Defense Liaison Group, Indonesia (Army)
USDO........ United States Disbursing Officer
USDOC ...... United States Department of Commerce
USDOCO .... United States Documents Officer
USDOCOLANDSOUTHEAST .. United States Document Office Allied Land Forces
　　　　　　　　　Southeastern Europe
USDOD ...... United States Department of Defense
USDOI ...... United States Department of the Interior
USDR .... United States Divorce Reform
USDSA ...... United States Deaf Skiers Association
USDSEA ...... United States Dependent Schools, European Area (Army)
USDT .... United States Department of the Treasury
USE .... Underground Service Entrance
USE .... Undersea Scientific Expedition
USE .... Unified S-Band Equipment
USE .... Unit Support Equipment
USE .... United States Embassy
USE .... United States Envelope Company
USE .... UNIVAC Scientific Exchange (Data processing)
USE .... Unmanned Surveillance Equipment
USEASA ...... United States Eastern Amateur Ski Association
USECC ...... United States Employees' Compensation Commission (Functions transferred
　　　　　　　　　to Federal Security Agency, 1946)
USEES........ United States Naval Engineering Experiment Station (Annapolis, Maryland)
USEFP........ United States Educational Foundation in Pakistan
USEI........ United States Society of Esperanto Instructors
USELMCENTO .. United States Element Central Treaty Organization
USEO........ United States Engineer Office
USEP .... United States Escapee Program
USERS........ Uniform Socio-Economic Reporting System (Financial reporting system
　　　　　　　　　for voluntary health and welfare organizations)
USES .... United States Employment Service (Department of Labor)
USESF .... United States Exchange Stabilization Fund
USESSA...... United States Environmental Science Services Administration
USET .... United States Equestrian Team
USEUCOM.... United States European Command
USF .... Uniaxial Stress Field
USF .... United States Fleet
USF .... University of San Francisco (California)
USFA .... United States Forces in Austria
USFA .... United States Fuel Administration (Terminated)
USFAA ...... United States Fronton Athletic Association
USFADTC .... United States Fleet Air Defense Training Center
USFARS ...... United States Federation of Amateur Roller Skaters
USFC .... United States Foil Company
USFCC ...... United States Fire Companies Conference
USFET ...... United States Forces, European Theater (American headquarters for
　　　　　　　　　occupation of Germany after SHAEF was dissolved) (World War II)
USFF .... United States Flag Foundation
USFGC ...... United States Feed Grains Council
USFHA ...... United States Field Hockey Association
USFI .... Unione Sindacale Ferrovieri Italiani (National Union of Italian Railway
　　　　　　　　　Workers)
USFIA .... United States Forces in Australia
USFIP........ United States Forces in the Philippines
USFIS .... United States Foundation for International Scouting
USFK .... United States Forces, Korea
USFMIA ...... United States Fishmeal Importers Association
USFORAZ .... United States Forces in Azores
USFR .... United States Fleet Reserve
USFS .... United States Foreign Service (Department of State)
USFS .... United States Forest Service
USFS .... United States Frequency Standard
USFSA ...... United States Figure Skating Association
USFSS........ United States Fleet SONAR School
USFTA ...... United States Floor Tennis Association
USFU .... Unglazed Structural Facing Units (Technical drawings)
USFWS ...... United States Fish and Wildlife Service (Department of the Interior)
USG........ Ultrasonic Space Grating
USG........ United States Gage
USG........ United States Government
USG........ United States Gypsum Company (NYSE symbol) (Wall Street slang name:
　　　　　　　　　"Gyp")
USG........ United States Standard Gage
USGA ...... Ulysses S. Grant Association

USGA ...... United States Golf Association
USGLI ...... United States Government Life Insurance
USGPO...... United States Government Printing Office
USGRDR .... United States Government Research and Development Reports (National
　　　　　　　　　Bureau of Standards)
USGRDR-I .... United States Government Research and Development Reports Index
USGRR ...... United States Government Research Reports (National Bureau of Standards
　　　　　　　　　publication)
USGS........ United States Geological Survey
USH .... United Shoe Machinery Corporation (NYSE symbol) (Delisted)
USH .... USLIFE Corp. (NYSE symbol)
USHA ...... United States Handball Association
USHA ...... United States Housing Authority (Functions transferred to Public Housing
　　　　　　　　　Commissioner, 1947)
USHB ...... Uniformed Services Health Benefits
USHC........ United States Housing Corporation (Terminated, 1952)
USHDA...... United States Highland Dancing Association
USHG........ United States Home Guard
USHGA ...... United States Hop Growers Association
USHL ...... United States Hygienic Laboratory
USHMAC...... United States Health Manpower Advisory Council
USHO........ United States Hydrographic Office (Later, Naval Oceanographic Office)
USHP........ United States Helium Plant (Amarillo, Texas)
USHWA...... United States Harness Writers' Association
USI .... Ultraviolet Spectroheliographic Instrument
USI .... United Sons of Israel
USI .... United States Industries, Incorporated (NYSE symbol)
USIA .... United States Information Agency
USIAC ...... United States Inter-American Council
USIB........ United States Intelligence Board (National Security Council)
USIC ...... United States Information Center (Department of State)
USICID ...... United States National Committee, International Commission on Irrigation
　　　　　　　　　and Drainage
USIITA ...... United States Indian International Travel Agency, Inc.
USILA...... United States Intercollegiate Lacrosse Association
USINOA...... United States Immigration and Naturalization Officers' Association
USIP........ University of Stockholm Institute of Physics
USIPC........ Uniformed Services Indentification and Privilege Card
USIS ...... United States Information Service (Name used abroad for USIA offices)
USISA........ United States International Sailing Association
USITA ...... United States Independent Telephone Association
USITT ...... United States Institute for Theatre Technology
USIU .... United States International University
US JAYCEE ... United States Junior Chamber of Commerce
USJCC ...... United States Junior Chamber of Commerce (JAYCEES)
USJPRS...... United States Joint Publication Research Service
US-JTC ...... United States – Japan Trade Council
USK........ Ultrasonic Kit
USK........ United States Forces, Korea
USKA........ United States Kart Association (Defunct)
USKBA ...... United Strictly Kosher Butchers Association
USKBTC ...... United States Kerry Blue Terrier Club
USL .... Underwater Sound Laboratory (Navy)
USL .... United States Leasing International, Inc. (NYSE symbol)
USL .... United States Legation
USL .... United States Lines Company (NYSE symbol) (Delisted)
USL .... Up Stage Left (Away from audience) (A stage direction)
USLANT ...... United States Atlantic Subarea
USLCA ...... United States Lacrosse Coaches' Association
USLCMBA .... United States Letter Carriers Mutual Benefit Association
USLD .... Ultrasonic Link Detector
USLD .... Union des Syndicats Libres du Dahomey (Federation of Free Unions of
　　　　　　　　　Dahomey)
USLO ...... United States Liaison Office(r)
USLO...... University Students for Law and Order
USLSA ...... United States Livestock Sanitary Association
USLSO ...... United States Logistics Support Office
USLTA ...... United States Lawn Tennis Association
USM ...... Underwater-to-Surface Missile (Air Force)
USM........ United States Mail
USM........ United States Marine(s)
USM ...... United States Mint
USM ...... United States Minutemen
USM........ USM Corp. (Formerly, United Shoe Machinery Corp.) (NYSE symbol)
USMA...... United States Maritime Administration
USMA...... United States Military Academy
USMA...... United States Military Attaché
USMA...... United States Monopoly Association (For legal reasons, only the initialism
　　　　　　　　　is used by the group; it is never officially spelled out)
USMAC...... United States Marine Air Corps
USMAC...... United States Military Assistance Command

ACRONYMS AND INITIALISMS DICTIONARY

USMACSV.... United States Military Assistance Command for South Vietnam
USMACTHAI .. United States Military Assistance Command Thailand
USMAC/V .... United States Military Assistance Command, Vietnam
USMAG ..... United States Military Advisory Group
USMAPS ..... United States Military Academy Prep School
USMAPU ..... United States Military Academy Preparatory Unit
USMATS ..... United States Military Air Transport Service (Later, Military Airlift Command)
USMB....... United States Marine Barracks
USMC....... United States Marine Corps
USMC....... United States Maritime Commission (Functions transferred to Department of Commerce, 1950)
USMCA ..... United States Men's Curling Association
USMCAS ..... United States Marine Corps Air Station
USMCR ..... United States Marine Corps Reserve
USMCR(AF) ... United States Marine Corps Reserve (Aviation Fleet)
USMCR(AO)... United States Marine Corps Reserve (Aviation, Organized)
USMCR(AV)... United States Marine Corps Reserve (Aviation, Volunteer)
USMCR(F) .... United States Marine Corps Reserve (Fleet)
USMCR(LS) ... United States Marine Corps Reserve (Limited Service)
USMCR(NAV).. Aviation Volunteer Marine Corps Reserve (Naval Aviators)
USMCR(NAVO) .. Graduate Aviation Cadets, Volunteer Marine Corps Reserve
USMCR(NAVT).. Volunteer Marine Corps Reserve, Aviation Specialist Transport Pilot
USMCR(O).... United States Marine Corps Reserve (Organized)
USMCR(V).... United States Marine Corps Reserve (Volunteer)
USMCR(VS)... United States Marine Corps Reserve (Volunteer Specialists)
USMCR(W).... United States Marine Corps Women's Reserve
USMCSS .... United States Marine Corps Selective Service Selectee
USMCSSV .... United States Marine Corps Selective Service Volunteer
USMC(W) .... United States Marine Corps, Women
USMCWR..... United States Marine Corps Women's Reserve
USMECBL .... United States Mission to the European Communities in Belgium and Luxembourg
USMEMILCOMUN .. United States Members, United Nations Military Staff Committee
USMEOUN.... United States Mission to the European Office of the United Nations
USMH....... United States Marine Hospital
USMHS...... United States Marine Hospital Service
USMIAEAA ... United States Mission to the International Atomic Energy Agency in Austria
USMICC ..... United States Military Information Control Committee
USMID ...... Ultra-Sensitive Microwave Infrared Detector
USMILATTACHE .. United States Military Attaché
USMILCOMUN.. United States Delegation, United Nations Military Staff Committee
USMILLIAS ... United States Military Liaison Office
USMILTAG ... United States Military Technical Advisory Group
USMLMCINCGSFG .. United States Military Liaison Mission to Commander-in-Chief, Group Soviet Forces, Germany
USMM ...... Union Socialiste des Musulmans Mauritaniens (Socialist Union of Mauritanian Moslems)
USMM ...... United States Merchant Marine
USMMA ..... United States Merchant Marine Academy
USMMCC .... United States Merchant Marine Cadet Corps
USMNATOEROF .. United States Mission to the North Atlantic Treaty Organization and European Regional Organizations in France
USMP....... United States Mallard Project (Army)
USMS ...... United States Maritime Service
USMSGS..... United States Maritime Service Graduate Station
USMSMI ..... United States Military Supply Mission to India
USMSOS..... United States Maritime Service Officers School
USMSSB ..... United States Machine Screw Service Bureau
USMSTS ..... United States Maritime Service Training School
USMSTS ..... United States Maritime Service Training Ship
USMSTS ..... United States Maritime Service Training Station
USMT....... United States Military Transport
USMTMSA.... United States Military Training Mission to Saudi Arabia
USN........ Union des Scolaires Nigeriens (Union of Nigerian Scholars)
USN........ United States Navy
USNA....... United States National Army
USNA ...... United States Naval Academy
USNA ...... United States Naval Aircraft
USNAAS..... United States Naval Auxiliary Air Station
USNAC...... United States Naval Administrative Command
USNAC...... United States Naval Air Corps
USNACC..... United States Naval Member of the Allied Control Commission (Germany)
USNAMTC.... United States Naval Air Missile Test Center
USNAS...... United States Naval Air Service
USNAS...... United States Naval Air Station
USNATC..... United States Naval Air Training Center
USNATRA .... United States Naval Training
USNAVSO.... United States Navy Forces Southern Command
USNAVSOUTHCOM .. United States Navy Southern Command

USNAVYMILCOMUN .. United States Naval Representative, United Nations Military Staff Committee
USNC....... United States National Commission for UNESCO (of the Department of State)
USNC....... United States National Committee (IEC)
USNCB...... United States Naval Construction Battalion (SEABEES) (BUDOCKS; later, FEC or NFEC)
USNCEREL.... United States Naval Civil Engineering Research and Evaluation Laboratory
USNCFID .... United States National Committee for Federation Internationale de Documentation
USNC/IBP ... United States National Committee for the International Biological Program
USNC-IGY ... United States National Committee for the International Geophysical Year
USNCPNM ... United States National Committee for the Preservation of Nubian Monuments
USNCTAM ... United States National Committee on Theoretical & Applied Mechanics
USNDD ..... United States Naval Drydocks
USNEDS ..... United States Navy Experimental Diving Station
USNEL ..... United States Naval Electronics Laboratory
USNFR ...... United States Naval Fleet Reserve
USNG ...... United States National Guard
USNH ...... United States Naval Hospital
USNI .... United States Naval Institute
USN-I ...... United States Regular Navy - Inductee
USN-I-CB ... United States Regular Navy - Inductee - Construction Battalion
USNIP ...... United States Naval Institute Proceedings (Publication)
USN(I)(SA) ... United States Navy (Inductee) (Special Assignment)
USNLO ..... United States Naval Liaison Officer
USNM ...... United States National Museum (Smithsonian Institution)
USNMF...... United States Naval Missile Facility
USNMR ..... United States National Military Representative
USNMSC..... United States Navy Medical Service Corps
USNO ...... United States Naval Observatory
USNOTS ..... United States Naval Ordnance Test Station
USNP....... United States Naval Prison
USNPG...... United States Naval Proving Ground
USNPS ..... United States Naval Postgraduate School
USNR....... United States Naval Reserve
USNR....... United States Navy Regulations
USNRB ..... United States Naval Repair Base
USNRDL ..... United States Naval Radiological Defense Laboratory
USN(Ret)..... United States Navy (Retired)
USNRF...... United States Naval Reserve Force
USNR(F) ..... United States Naval Reserve (Force)
USNRL ..... United States Naval Research Laboratory
USNRM..... United States Merchant Marine Reserve
USNRM1 ..... United States Merchant Marine Reserve Seagoing
USNRM2 ..... United States Merchant Marine Reserve Coastal Defense
USNRO...... United States Organized Naval Reserve
USNRO1 ..... United States Organized Naval Reserve Seagoing
USNRO2 ..... United States Organized Naval Reserve Aviation
USNRS ...... United States Navy Recruiting Station
USNR & SL ... United States Navy Radio and Sound Laboratory (San Diego, California)
USNRSV..... United States Naval Reserve, Selective Volunteer
USNRV ..... United States Naval Reserve, Volunteer
USNR(W).... United States Naval Reserve (Women's Reserve)
USNS ...... United States Naval Ship (Civilian manned)
USNSA ..... United States National Student Association
USNSMC..... United States Naval Submarine Medical Center
USN-SV ..... United States Regular Navy Selective Volunteer
USNTC...... United States Naval Training Center
USNTDC..... United States Naval Training Device Center
USNTI ...... United States Navy Travel Instructions
USNTS ...... United States Naval Training School
USNUSL ..... United States Navy Underwater Sound Laboratory (BUSHIPS; later, ESC or NESC)
USNWC ..... United States Naval War College
USNWR...... United States News & World Report (A publication)
USO........ Under Secretary of the Navy's Office
USO .... United Service Organizations
USO........ Unmanned Seismological Observatory
USOA ..... United States Olympic Association
USOA...... United States Overseas Airlines
USOC ...... United States Olympic Committee
USOE ...... United States Office of Education
USOFA...... Under Secretary of the Army
USOFAF ..... Under Secretary of the Air Force
USOID ..... United States Oversea Internal Defense (Army)
USOM ...... United States Operations Mission
USOMC ..... United States Ordnance Missile Command
USP .... Ultra-Sensitive Position
USP .... Underwater Sound Projection

USP . . . . Unique Selling Proposition (Advertising)
USP . . . . United States Patent
USP . . . . United States Penitentiary
USP . . . . United States Pharmacopeia (Following name of a substance, signifies substance meets standards set by USP)
USP . . . . United States Playing Card Company (NYSE symbol) (Delisted)
USP . . . . Universal Signal Processor
USP . . . . Utility Seaplane (Navy, Coast Guard)
USP . . . . Utility Summary Program
USPA . . . . . . United States Passport Agency (Department of State)
USPA . . . . . . United States Polo Association
USPA . . . . . . United States Potters' Association
USPC . . . . . . Union des Syndicats Professionels du Cameroun (Federation of Professional Trade Unions of Cameroon)
USPC . . . . . . United States Pharmacopoeial Convention
USPC . . . . . . United States Pony Clubs
USPC . . . . . . United States Purchasing Commission
USPD . . . . . . Unabhaengige Sozialdemokratische Partei Deutschlands
USPDO . . . . . United States Property and Disbursing Officer
USP & DO . . . . United States Property and Disbursing Officer
USPEC . . . . . United States Paper Exporters Council
USPEPA . . . . . United States Poultry and Egg Producers Association
USPFO . . . . . United States Property and Fiscal Officer
USPHS . . . . . . United States Public Health Service
USPHSR . . . . . United States Public Health Service Reserve
USPL . . . . . . Unpriced Spare Parts List
USPLTA . . . . . United States Professional Lawn Tennis Association
USPO . . . . . . United States Patent Office (Commerce Department)
USPO . . . . . . United States Post Office (Later, US Postal Service)
USPP . . . . . . University Science Policy Planning (Program) (National Science Foundation)
USPPA . . . . . United States Pulp Producers Association
USPS . . . . . . United States Postal Service (Formerly, POD)
USPS . . . . . . United States Power Squadrons
USPSF . . . . . . United States Pigeon Shooting Federation
USPTA . . . . . United States Paddle Tennis Association
USPTA . . . . . United States Pony Trotting Association
USPWIC . . . . . United States Prisoner of War Information Center (Army)
USPWIC(Br) . . . United States Prisoner of War Information Center (Branch) (Army)
USQBR . . . . . United States Quarterly Book Review
USR . . . . United States (Supreme Court) Reports
USR . . . . United States Reserves
USR . . . . United States Shoe Corporation (NYSE symbol)
USR . . . . Up Stage Right (Away from audience) (A stage direction)
USRA . . . . . . United States Railroad Administration (Functions transferred to Department of the Treasury, 1939)
USRA . . . . . . United States Revolver Association
USRA . . . . . . Universities Space Research Association
USRAD . . . . . United States Fleet Shore Radio Station
USRCSI . . . . . United States Red Cedar Shingle Industry
USRD . . . . . . Underwater Sound Reference Division (Navy)
USREDA . . . . . United States Rice Export Development Association
USREPMILCOMUN . . United States Representative, United Nations Military Staff Committee
USREPOF . . . . . United States Navy Reporting Office(r)
USRL . . . . . . Underwater Sound Reference Laboratory (Navy)
USRNMC . . . . . United States Representative to NATO Military Committee
USRO . . . . . . United States Mission to NATO and European Regional Organizations
USRO . . . . . . United States Navy Routing Office
USRPA . . . . . United States Racing Pigeon Association
USRRC . . . . . United States Road Racing Championship
USRS . . . . . . United States Reclamation Service
USRS . . . . . . United States Revised Statutes
USRS . . . . . . United States Rocket Society
USRS . . . . . . United States Rowing Society
USRSG . . . . . United States Representative, Standing Group (Military)
USS . . . . Ultraviolet Scanning Spectrometer
USS . . . . Underwater Sound Source
USS . . . . Unified S-Band System
USS . . . . Union Syndicale Suisse (Swiss Federation of Trade Unions)
USS . . . . United Scholarship Service
USS . . . . United Seamen's Service
USS . . . . United States Naval Vessel
USS . . . . United States Senate
USS . . . . United States Ship
USS . . . . United States Standard
USS . . . . United States Steamer
USS . . . . United States Steel Corporation (Also, USSC)
USS . . . . United Swedish Societies
US of S . . . . . Under Secretary of State
USSA . . . . . . Underground Security Storage Association

USSA . . . . . . Union Suisse des Syndicats Autonomes (Swiss Association of Autonomous Unions)
USSA . . . . . . United Saw Service Association
USSA . . . . . . United States Salvage Association
USSA . . . . . . United States Security Authority (for NATO affairs)
USSA . . . . . . United States Ski Association
USSA . . . . . . United Sugar Sampler's Association (Defunct)
USSAC . . . . . United States Security Authority for CENTO Affairs
USSAF . . . . . United States Strategic Air Force (Later, Strategic Air Command)
USSAFE . . . . . . United States Strategic Air Forces in Europe
US-SALEP . . . . United States - South Africa Leader Exchange Program
USSAS . . . . . United States Security Authority for SEATO Affairs
USSB . . . . . . United States Shipping Board (Terminated, 1933)
USSBA . . . . . . United States Seniors Bowling Association (Later, Seniors Division of the American Bowling Congress)
USSBD . . . . . . United States Savings Bonds Division (Treasury Department)
USSBIA . . . . . United States Stone and Bead Importers Association
USSBS . . . . . . United States Strategic Bombing Survey
USSC . . . . . . United States Servas Committee
USSC . . . . . . United States Steel Corporation (Also, USS)
USSC . . . . . . United States Strike Command (Military combined Tactical Air Command and Strategic Army Command Force)
USSC . . . . . . United States Supreme Court
USSDP . . . . . . Uniformed Services Savings Deposits Program
USSE . . . . . . Ultrasonic Soldering Equipment
USSEA . . . . . United States Scientific Export Association
USSECMILCOMUN . . The Secretary, United States Delegation United Nations Staff Committee
USSEF . . . . . . United States Ski Educational Foundation
USSF . . . . . . United States Steel Foundation
USSFA . . . . . United States Soccer Football Association
USSG . . . . . . United States Standard Gage
USSG . . . . . . United States Storekeeper-Gauger
USSGA . . . . . United States Seniors Golf Association
USSGREP . . . . United States Standing Group Representative (NATO)
USSH . . . . . . United States Soldiers' Home
USSI . . . . Ultrasonic Soldering Iron
USSIA . . . . . United States Shellac Importers Association
USSLL . . . . . United States Savings and Loan League
USSOUTHCOM . . United States Southern Command (Air Force)
USSPA . . . . . United States Student Press Association
USSPG . . . . . United States Senate Photographers Gallery
USSR . . . . . . Union of Soviet Socialist Republics
USSRA . . . . . United States Squash Racquets Association
USSS . . . . . . United States Secret Service
USSS . . . . . . United States Steamship
USSS . . . . . . Unmanned Sensing Satellite System
USSTAF . . . . . United States Strategic Air Forces
USSTAF . . . . . United States Strategic and Tactical Air Forces
USSTAFE . . . . . United States Strategic Tactical Air Force, Europe
USSTRICOM . . United States Strike Command
USSWA . . . . . United States Ski Writers Association
UST . . . . Ultrasonic Transducer (Crystal) (Used in measuring human cardiac output)
UST . . . . Undersea Technology
UST . . . . Union Senegalaise du Travail (Senegalese Labor Union)
UST . . . . Union Socialiste Tchadienne (Chadien Socialist Union)
UST . . . . University of Saint Thomas (Texas)
USTA . . . . . . Union des Syndicats des Travailleurs Algeriens (Federation of Unions of Algerian Workers)
USTA . . . . . . United States Trademark Association
USTA . . . . . . United States Trotting Association (Governing body of harness racing U.S.)
USTA . . . . . . United States Twirling Association
USTB . . . . . . United States Travel Bureau
USTC . . . . . . United States Tariff Commission
USTC . . . . . . United States Transportation Commission (Proposed commission to consolidate CAB, ICC, and FMC)
USTCA . . . . . United States Track Coaches Association
USTD . . . . . . Union des Syndicats des Travailleurs du Dahomey (Federation of Workers Unions of Dahomey)
USTDA . . . . . United States Truck Drivers Association
USTES . . . . . . United States Training and Employment Service (Department of Labor)
USTFA . . . . . United States Trout Farmers Association
USTFF . . . . . United States Track and Field Federation
USTG . . . . . . Union Syndicale des Travailleurs de Guinee (Guinean Federation of Workers)
USTHF . . . . . United States Team Handball Federation
USTIIC . . . . . United States Technical Industrial Intelligence Committee
USTRC . . . . . United States Transportation Research Command (Army)
USTS . . . . . . Union Syndicale des Travailleurs du Soudan (Federation of Sudanese Workers) (Mali)
USTS . . . . . . United States Time Standard (National Bureau of Standards)

ACRONYMS AND INITIALISMS DICTIONARY

USTS . . . . United States Travel Service (Department of Commerce)
USTSA . . . . . . United States Targhee Sheep Association
USTTA . . . . . . United States Table Tennis Association
USTU . . . . Ultrasonic Test Unit
USU . . . . United States Rubber Reclaiming Company (American Stock Exchange
    symbol)
USUB . . . . Unglazed Structural Unit Base (Technical drawings)
USUCA . . . . . United Steel Workers' Union of Central Africa (Rhodesia and Nyasaland)
US/UK . . . . . . United States/United Kingdom
USUSA . . . . . . United Societies of the United States of America
USV . . . . United States Volunteers (Civil War)
USV . . . . Unmanned Strike Vehicle
USVB . . . . United States Veterans Bureau
USVBA . . . . . . United States Volleyball Association
USVH . . . . United States Veterans Hospital
USVMS . . . . . Urine Sample Volume Measurement System
USVT . . . . Universal Stray Voltage Tester
USW . . . . Ultra-Short Wave
USW . . . . Und So Weiter (And So Forth) (German)
USW . . . . Under Secretary of War (Obsolete)
USW . . . . Undersea Warfare
USW . . . . United Steelworkers of America
USWA . . . . . . United Shoe Workers of America
USWACC . . . . United States Women's Army Corps Center
USWACS . . . . United States Women's Army Corps School
USWAP . . . . . United Steel Workers' Association of the Philippines
USWB . . . . . . United States Weather Bureau (Later, National Weather Service)
USWBC . . . . . United States War Ballot Commission (World War II)
USWCA . . . . . United States Women's Curling Association
USWGA . . . . United States Wholesale Grocers' Association
USWI . . . . United States West Indies
USWLA . . . . . United States Women's Lacrosse Association
USWSRA . . . . United States Women's Squash Racquets Association
USWSSB . . . . United States Wood Screw Service Bureau
USWV . . . . . . United Spanish War Veterans
USX . . . . Ultra-Soft X-Ray
USY . . . . United Synagogue Youth
USYC . . . . United States Youth Council
USZI . . . . United States Zone of the Interior
UT . . . . Conference Internationale pour l'Unite Technique des Chemins de Fer
UT . . . . Ultrasonic Test
UT . . . . Ultra-Thin
UT . . . . Umbilical Tower (Aerospace)
UT . . . . Underway Trials (Shipbuilding)
UT . . . . Union Terminal Railway Company (AAR code)
UT . . . . United Territory
UT . . . . United Utilities, Inc. (NYSE symbol)
UT . . . . Universal Time (NASA)
UT . . . . Universal Trainer
UT . . . . Upper Torso
UT . . . . Urinary Tract (Medicine)
UT . . . . User Test
UT . . . . Utah
UT . . . . Utilities Man
UT . . . . Utility Boat
UTA . . . . Ultrasonic Thermal Action
UTA . . . . Union de Tranports Aeriens (Privately owned international airline)
    (France)
UTA . . . . Unit Training Assembly (Military)
UTA . . . . United Typothetae of America
UTA . . . . Urban Transportation Administration (HUD)
UTAC . . . . Union Tunisienne de l'Artisanat et du Commerce (Tunisian Union of
    Artisans and Merchants)
UTAD . . . . Utah Army Depot
UTAH . . . . Utah Railway Company (AAR code)
UTC . . . . "Uncle Tom's Cabin" (Title of book by Harriet Beecher Stowe)
UTC . . . . Union des Travailleurs Congolais (Union of Congolese Workers)
    (Leopoldville)
UTC . . . . Unit Time Coding
UTC . . . . Unit Training Center (Military)
UTC . . . . United Technology Center (A division of United Aircraft Corporation)
UTC . . . . United Technology Corporation
UTC . . . . Universal Time Coordinated
UTC . . . . University Teachers Certificate
UTC . . . . Urban Training Center
UTCD . . . . Uniunea Tineretului Comunist Dimitrovist
UTCPTT . . . . . Union Internationale des Organismes Touristiques et Culturels des Postes
    et des Telecommunications (International Union of Tourist and Cultural
    Associations in the Postal and Telecommunications Services)
UTD . . . . UTD Corporation (Formerly, Union Twist Drill Company) (NYSE symbol)
    (Delisted)

UTE . . . . Union Technique de l'Electricite (France)
UTE . . . . Universal Test Equipment
UTELRAD . . . . Utilization of Enemy Electromagnetic Radiations
UTF . . . . Underwater Tank Facility
UTF . . . . Underwater Test Facility (GE)
UTI . . . . Urinary Tract Infection (Medicine)
UTIA . . . . University of Toronto, Institute of Aerophysics
UTIAS . . . . . . University of Toronto, Institute for Aerospace Studies
UTICI . . . . Union Techniques des Ingenieurs Conseils (France)
UTIL . . . . Utility (or Utilization)
UTIRS . . . . United Tiberias Institutions Relief Society
UTJ . . . . Uterotubal Junction
UTL . . . . Unit Transmission Loss
UTL . . . . Universal Transporter Loader
UTM . . . . Union des Travailleurs de Mauritanie (Union of Workers of Mauritania)
UTM . . . . Uniunea Tineretului Muncitor
UTM . . . . Universal Test Message
UTM . . . . Universal Testing Machine
UTM . . . . Universal Transverse Mercator (Grid)
UTMCI . . . . . . Union des Travailleurs de la Moyenne Cote d'Ivoire (Union of Middle
    Ivory Coast Workers)
UTML . . . . Utility Motor Launch
UTO . . . . United Telephone Organizations
UTOA . . . . United Truck Owners of America
UTOCO . . . . . Utah Oil Company
UTP . . . . Unified Test Plan
UTP . . . . Unit Territory Plan
UTP . . . . Unit Test Plan
UTP . . . . Universal Tape Processor
UTP . . . . Unlisted Trading Privileges
UTP . . . . Upper Trip Point
UTP . . . . Uridine Triphosphate (Biochemistry)
UTP . . . . User Test Program (Army)
UTP . . . . Utah Power & Light Company (NYSE symbol)
UTP . . . . Utility Tape Processor
UTR . . . . Underwater Tracking Range
UTR . . . . Union Transportation Company (AAR code)
UTR . . . . University Teaching Reactor
UTR . . . . University Training Reactor (AEC)
UTR . . . . Unprogrammed Transfer Register
UTR . . . . Up Time Ratio
UTR . . . . Urticarial Transfusion Reaction
UTROAA . . . . Units to Round Out the Active Army
UTRON . . . . . . Utility Squadron (Navy)
UTRONFWDAREA . . Utility Squadron, Forward Area (Navy)
UTRP . . . . Underwater Tactical Range, Pacific
UTRR . . . . University of Teheran Research Reactor
UTS . . . . Ultimate Tensile Strength (or Stress)
UTS . . . . Umbilical Test Set
UTS . . . . Unified Transfer System (Computer to translate Russian to English)
UTS . . . . Union Theological Seminary
UTS . . . . Union des Travailleurs du Senegal (Senegalese Workers Union)
UTS . . . . Unit Training Standard
UTS . . . . Unit Trouble Shooting
UTS . . . . Universal Test Station
UTS . . . . Universal Thrust Stand
UTS . . . . Universal Time Standards
UTSE . . . . Urine-Transfer System (Apollo) (NASA)
UTSE . . . . United Transport Service Employees
UTS-FO . . . . . Union Territoriale des Syndicats - Force Ouvrieres (Territorial Federation
    of Trade Unions Workers' Force) (French Somaliland)
UTSI . . . . University of Tennessee Space Institute
UTSV . . . . Union Theological Seminary in Virginia
UTT . . . . Utility Tactical Transport
UTTAS . . . . . . Utility Tactical Transport Aircraft System (Military)
UTTC . . . . Universal Tape-to-Tape Converter
UTTS . . . . Union Territoriale du Senegal des Travailleurs (Senegalese Workers Union)
UTU . . . . Ultrasonic Test Unit
UTU . . . . Underway Training Unit
UTU . . . . United Transportation Union
UTUC . . . . Uganda Trades' Union Congress
UTUC . . . . United Trades Union Congress (India)
UTV . . . . Underwater Television
UTV . . . . Universal Test Vehicle (Military)
UTWA . . . . . . United Textile Workers of America
UTWING . . . . . Utility Wing (Navy)
UTWINGSERVLANT . . Utility Wing, Service Force, Atlantic (Navy)
UTWINGSERVPAC . . Utility Wing, Service Force, Pacific (Navy)
UTX . . . . Union Tank Car Company (NYSE symbol) (Delisted)
UU . . . . Ultimate User
UU . . . . Union University (Tennessee)

602

UUA	Unitarian Universalist Association
UUA	UNIVAC Users Association
UUARC	United Ukrainian American Relief Committee
UUC	United University Club (British)
UUCA	United Underwear Contractors Association
UUE	Use Until Exhausted
UUEW	United Unions for Employees and Workers (Lebanon)
UUFSJ	Unitarian Universalist Fellowship for Social Justice
UUGS	Unitarian and Universalist Genealogical Society
UUIP	Uppsala University Institute of Physics (Sweden)
UUM	Underwater-to-Underwater Missile (Air Force)
UUMA	Unitarian Universalist Ministers Association
UUR	Under Usual Reserves
UUSC	Unitarian Universalist Service Committee
UUT	Unit Under Test
UUV	Unter Ublicher Vorbehalt (Errors and Omissions Excepted) (German)
UUWF	Unitarian Universalist Women's Federation
UV	Ultraviolet
UV	Ultravisible
UV	Under Voltage
UV	Underwater Vehicle
UV	UV Industries, Inc. (Formerly, United States Smelting, Refining and Mining Co.) (NYSE symbol)
UVAR	University of Virginia Reactor
UVASER	Ultraviolet Amplification by Stimulated Emission of Radiation
UVC	Ultra-High Vacuum Chamber
UVC	Ultraviolet Communications System
UVD	Ultrasonic Vapor Degresser
UVD	Ultraviolet Detector
UVD	Undervoltage Device
UVDC	Urban Vehicle Design Competition
UVF	Ulster Volunteer Force
UVIL	Ultraviolet Inspection Light
UVIL	Ultraviolet Ion LASER
UVL	Ultraviolet Lamp
UVL	Ultraviolet LASER
UVL	Ultraviolet Light
UVLS	Ultraviolet Light Stabilizer
UVM	Ultraviolet Meter
UVM	Universitas Viridis Montis (University of the Green Mountains; i.e., University of Vermont)
UVMC	United Voluntary Motor Corps
UVP	Ultra-High Vacuum Pump
UVPJU	Uganda Vernacular, Primary and Junior Secondary Teachers' Union
UVPS	Ultra-High Vacuum Pumping Station
UVR	Ultraviolet Radiation
UVR	Ultraviolet Receiver
UVR	Ultraviolet Rocket
UVR	Under Voltage Relay
UVR	University of Virginia Reactor
UVS	Ultraviolet Spectrometer
UVS	United Voluntary Services
UVSC	Ultraviolet Solar Constant
UVSP	Ultraviolet Spectral Photometer
UVT	Ultraviolet Transmission

UVT	Ultraviolet Tube
UVT	United States Vitamin & Pharmaceutical Corporation (NYSE symbol) (Delisted)
UVT	Universal Voltage Tester
UVV	Universal Leaf Tobacco Company, Inc. (NYSE symbol)
UW	Ultrasonic Wave
UW	Unconventional Warfare
UW	United Weldors International Union
UW	University of Washington (State)
UW	Untere Winkelgruppe (Angles up to 45°) (German military – World War II)
U/W	Underwriter
U/W	Used With
UWA	Ukrainian Workingmen's Association
UWA	United Weighers Association
UWA	United Women of the Americas
UWAL	Underwater Wide Angle Lens
UWAL	University of Washington Aeronautical Laboratory
UWARC	United Whiteruthenian (Byelorussian) American Relief Committee
UWATU	Underway Training Unit
UWBS	Uniform Work Breakdown Structure
UWC	United Whelan Corporation (NYSE symbol) (Delisted)
UWC	Universal Water Charts (Air Force)
UWC	Universal Winding Company
UWDD	Undersea Warfare Development Division (Navy)
UWF	United World Federalists
UWGB	University of Wisconsin at Green Bay
UWI	University of the West Indies (Jamaica)
UWL	Underwater Launch
UWM	Uniform Wave Motion
UWM	United World Mission
UWM	University of Wisconsin at Milwaukee
UWNE	Brotherhood of Utility Workers of New England
UWO	University of Western Ontario
UWOA	Unclassified Without Attachment
UWOA	Unconventional Warfare Operations Area (Army)
UWPC	United World Press Cooperative (Later, The Peoples Media Cooperative)
UWR	Under Weight Rejector
UWRR	University of Wyoming Research Reactor
UWS	Undersea Weapon System
UWS	Unmanned Weather Station
UWT	Underwater Telephone
UWT	Uniform Wave Train
UWTR	University of Washington Training Reactor
UWUA	Utility Workers Union of America
UWW	University Without Walls (at Antioch College)
UXB	Unexploded Bomb
UXO	Unexploded Ordnance
UXOI	Unexploded Ordnance Incident
UY	Universal Youth
UYLNA	Ukrainian Youth League of North America
UYT	Udylite Corporation (NYSE symbol) (Delisted)
UZ	Uhrzuender (Clockwork fuze) (German military – World War II)
UZRA	United Zionist Revisionists of America
UZW	Und Zwar (That Is) (German)

V

V . . . . Deflection of the Vertical
V . . . . Five (Roman numeral)
V . . . . Five dollars (Slang)
V . . . . Five-year sentence (Criminal slang)
V . . . . Fixed-wing aircraft (Navy designation)
V . . . . Heavier-than-air aircraft or personnel with duties related thereto (Navy designation)
V . . . . Potential Difference (Symbol)
V . . . . A safe (Criminal slang)
V . . . . Staff transport (When V is the first of two letters in a military aircraft designation)
V . . . . Unusual Visibility
V . . . . Vacuum Tube
V . . . . Vagabond
V . . . . Value
V . . . . Valve (Technical drawings)
V . . . . Van
V . . . . Vanadium (Chemical element)
V . . . . Vapor
V . . . . Variable
V . . . . Variation
V . . . . Vector (Mathematics)
V . . . . Vein
V . . . . Velocity
V . . . . Venerable
V . . . . Vent
V . . . . Ventilator
V . . . . Ventral
V . . . . Venue
V . . . . Verb
V . . . . Vermessung (Survey) (German military)
V . . . . Verse
V . . . . Versicle
V . . . . Version
V . . . . Verso (Bibliography)
V . . . . Versus (Against)
V . . . . Verte (Turn over)
V . . . . Vertex
V . . . . Vertical in line (Aircraft engine)
V . . . . Very
V . . . . Vicar, Vicarage
V . . . . Vice (in a position or title)
v . . . . Vicinal (Chemistry)
V . . . . Victoria
V . . . . Victory (As in "the V campaign" in Europe, during World War II)
V . . . . Vide or Videte (See)
V . . . . Village
V . . . . Violet
V . . . . Violin
V . . . . Virgin
V . . . . Viscosity
V . . . . Viscount
V . . . . Visibility
V . . . . Vision
V . . . . Visual
V . . . . Visual Acuity
V . . . . Vixisti (You Lived)
V . . . . Vixit (He Lived)
V . . . . Vocative
V . . . . Voice
V . . . . Volt (or Voltage)
V . . . . Volti (Turn)
V . . . . Voltmeter

V . . . . Volume (Bibliography)
V . . . . Volunteer (US Naval Reserve)
V . . . . Vowel
V . . . . VTOL (Vertical Take-Off and Landing) or STOL (Short Take-Off and Landing) When V is the second or only letter in a military aircraft designation)
V (Bomb) . . . . . Vergeltungswaffe Bomb (German "vengeance weapon")
V-1 . . . . Pilotless flying bomb employed by the Germans (World War II)
V-2 . . . . Rocket bomb employed by the Germans (World War II)
VA . . . . Attack Squadron (Symbol)
VA . . . . Value Analysis
VA . . . . Verb, Active
VA . . . . Verbal Adjective
VA . . . . Verpflegungsausgabestelle (Rations distributing point) (German military - World War II)
VA . . . . Vesicular-Arbuscular (Endomycorrhizae) (Botany)
VA . . . . Veterans Administration
VA . . . . Vicar Apostolic
VA . . . . Vice Admiral (Also, VADM)
VA . . . . Vickers Armstrong Gun
VA . . . . Victoria and Albert Order (British)
VA . . . . Video Amplifier
VA . . . . Vincent's Angina (Medicine)
VA . . . . Virginia
VA . . . . Virus-Antibody
VA . . . . Visual Acuity
VA . . . . Visual Aid
VA . . . . Visual Approach (Aviation)
VA . . . . Visual Training Aid Specialist (Navy)
VA . . . . Vixit Annos (He Lived [a given number of] Years)
VA . . . . Voice of America
VA . . . . Volt-Ampere
VA . . . . Voltaire Alternative
VA . . . . Vorausabteilung (Advance detachment) (German military - World War II)
V-A . . . . Vickers-Armstrong, Ltd.
V & A . . . . . . Victoria and Albert Museum (London, England)
V and A . . . . . Valuable and Attractive (A marking used by RAF on such supplies as watches and cameras)
V of A . . . . . . Volunteers of America
VAA . . . . Vietnamese American Association
VAAC . . . . . . Vanadyl Acetylacetonate
VAB . . . . Vehicle Assembly Building
VAB . . . . Vertical Assembly Building (NASA)
VAB . . . . Vertical Axis Bearing
VAB . . . . Voice Answer Back
VABA . . . . . . Value Added by Advertising
VABPF . . . . . Vice Admiral British Pacific Fleet
VAC . . . . Alternating Current Volts
VAC . . . . V Amphibious Corps
VAC . . . . Vacant (or Vacate)
VAC . . . . Variable Air Capacitor
VAC . . . . Vector Analog Computer
VAC . . . . Video Amplifier Chain
VAC . . . . Vidicon Alignment Coil
VAC . . . . Visual Aid Console
Vac . . . . Volts Alternating Current
VAC . . . . Volunteer Adviser Corps
VACTL . . . . . Vertical Assembly Component Test Laboratory
VAD . . . . Velocity-Azimuth Display
VAD . . . . Voltmeter Analog-to-Digital Converter
VAD . . . . Voluntary Aid Detachment
VADA . . . . . . Versatile Automatic Data Exchange

VADA....... VFR (Visual Flight Rules) Arrival Delay Advisory (Aviation)
VADE....... Vandenberg Automatic Data Evaluation (or Equipment)
VADM...... Vice Admiral (Also, VA)
VAF........ Vendor Approval Form
VAFB....... Vandenberg Air Force Base (California)
VAH........ Heavy Attack Squadron (Symbol)
VAH........ Vertical Array Hydrophone
VAH........ Veterans Administration Hospital
VAI........ Vassar Attitude Inventory (Education)
VAK........ Versuchs-Atomkraftwerk Kahl
VAKT....... Visual, Association, Kinesthetic, Tactile (With reference to reading)
VAL........ Light Attack Aircraft (Symbol)
VAL........ Valine (Amino acid)
VAL........ Variable Angle Launcher
VAL........ Vehicle Authorization List (Military)
VAL........ Vortex Arc LASER
VALB....... Veterans of the Abraham Lincoln Brigade
VALL....... Vortex Arc LASER Light
VALP....... Vortex Arc LASER Pump
VALUE...... Visible Achievement Liberates Unemployment (DOD project for
                disadvantaged youth) (Air Force)
VAM........ Value Aluminizing Machine
VAM........ Vogel's Approximation Method
VAM........ Voltammeter
VAMCO..... Village and Marketing Corporation (Jamaica)
VAMOS..... Verified Additional Military Occupational Specialty
VAMP...... Value Analysis of Management Practices
VAMP....... Variable (or Visual) Anamorphic Motion Picture (Training device to
                provide realistic environment during simulated flight training)
VAMP....... Vietnam Ammunition Program
VAMP....... Vincristine Amethopterin (National Cancer Institute)
VAMP....... Visual-Acoustic-Magnetic Program (NOO)
VAN........ Variable Area Nozzle
VAN........ Vorlaeufige Arbeitsnormen
VANWACE ... Vulnerability Analysis of Nuclear Weapons in Allied Command,
                Europe (Army)
VAOR....... VHF Aural Omnirange
VAP........ Velocity Analysis Program
VAP........ Vertical Axis Pivots
VAPI....... Visual Approach Path Indicator (Aviation)
VAPS....... Volume, Article or chapter, Paragraph, Sentence (Numbers) (Indexing)
VAQ........ Visiting Airmen's Quarters (Air Force)
VAR........ Reactive Volt-Ampere
VAR........ Vacuum Arc Remelting (Steel alloy)
VAR........ Variable (or Variation)
VAR........ Varian Associates (NYSE symbol)
VAR........ Vereinigte Arabische Republik
VAR........ Video-Audio (or Visual-Aural) Range (Radio)
VAR........ Visual Aural Range
VAR........ Volt-Ampere Reactive
VAR........ Voltage Adjusting Rheostat
VAR........ Volunteer Air Reserve
VARA....... Vereiniging van Arbeiders Radio Amateurs
VARC....... Virginia Associated Research Center
VARICAP..... Variable Capacitor
VARIG...... Empresa de Viacao Aerea Rio Grandense
VARISTOR.... Variable Resistor
VARO....... Veterans Administration Regional Office
VART....... Volunteer Air Reserve Training (Air Force)
VARTU...... Volunteer Air Reserve Training Unit (Air Force)
VAS........ Vanadium-Alloys Steel Company (NYSE symbol) (Delisted)
VAS........ Vibration Analysis System
VAS........ Visual Analysis System
VAS........ Visual Attack System
VASC....... Verbal Auditory Screen for Children
VASCAR..... Visual Average Speed Computer and Recorder (Speed trap)
VASI....... Visual Approach Slope Indicator (FAA)
VASIS...... Visual Approach Slope Indicator System
VASP....... Variable Automatic Synthesis Program (NASA)
VASP....... Viacao Aeres Sao Paulo, SA (Brazil airline)
VASRD...... Veterans Administration Schedule for Rating Disabilities
VASS....... Visual Analysis Subsystem (Military)
VASSS...... Van Allen Simplified Scoring System (Tennis)
VAST....... Versatile Automatic Specification Tester
VAST....... Versatile Avionics Ship (or Systems) Test(er)
VAT........ Value-Added Tax
VAT........ Ventricular Activation Time
VAT........ Vibration Acceptance Test
VAT........ Visual Acquisition Technique
VAT........ Visual Action Time
VAT........ Voltage Amplifier Tube

VATE....... Versatile Automatic Test Equipment (Computers)
VATLS...... Versatile Automatic Target Locating System
VATLS...... Visual Airborne Target Locator System
VATS....... Vehicle Automatic Test System
VATS....... Versatile Avionics Test Shop
VAU........ Vertical Acceleration Unit
VAVS....... Veterans Administration Voluntary Service
VAW....... Vertical Arc Welder
VAX........ Heavy Attack Aircraft, Experimental
VB......... Bombing Plane (Navy symbol)
VB......... Dive Bomber Squadron (Navy symbol)
VB......... Valve Box
VB......... Vertical Beam (of light)
VB .... Vertical Bomb (Air Force)
VB......... Vir Bonus (A Good Man)
VB......... Voelkischer Beobachter
VB......... Volunteer Battalion (Military)
VBA .... Vanilla Bean Association
VBA .... Vegetarian Brotherhood of America
VBD .... Volta Bureau for the Deaf
VBF........ Bomber-Fighter Squadron (Navy symbol)
VBF........ Bombing-Fighting Aircraft (Navy symbol)
VBF........ Vibratory Bowl Feeder
VBGQ...... Vacuum Brazed - Gas Quenched
VBI .... Venetian Blind Institute
VBI .... Verein Beratender Ingenieure
VBJ .... Vacuum Bell Jar
VBL .... Vinblastine
VBL .... Voyager Biological Laboratory (NASA)
VBN....... Verbal Noun
VBOS ..... Veronal Buffered Oxalated Saline
VBP .... Vacuum Backing Pump
VBP .... Vortex Breakdown Position
VBPF ..... Variable Band Pass Filter
VBR .... Virginia Blue Ridge Railway (AAR code)
VBT .... Bombing, Torpedo Plane (Navy symbol)
VBU .... Vibrating Bag Unloader
VBW....... Video Bandwidth
VBWR ..... Vallecitos Boiling Water Reactor (AEC)
VC......... Color Vision
VC .... Composite Aircraft Squadron (Navy symbol)
VC......... Vacuolated Cell
VC......... Valuable Cargo
VC......... Valuation Clause
VC......... Vehicular Communications
VC......... Vender Contact
VC......... Venereal Case (Medical slang)
VC......... Versatility Code
VC......... Vertical Circle
VC......... Veterinary Corps
VC......... Vicar Choral
VC .... Vice Chairman
VC .... Vice Chancellor
VC .... Vice Consul
VC......... Victoria Cross (British)
VC......... Video Correlator
VC......... Vietcong
VC......... Vietnamese Communists
VC......... Vigilance Committee
VC......... Vir Clarissimus (A Most Illustrious Man)
VC......... Virginia-Carolina Chemical Corporation (NYSE symbol) (Delisted)
VC......... Virginia Central Railway (AAR code)
VC......... Visual Capacity (Acuity)
VC......... Visual Cortex
VC .... Vital Capacity
VC......... Vitreous Carbon
VC .... Vitrified Clay (Technical drawings)
VC......... Voice Coil
VC......... Voltage Comparator
VC......... Volume of Compartment (Technical drawings)
VC......... Volunteer Corps
VC......... Vuelta de Correo (Return Mail) (Spain)
VC's....... Vocal Chords (Musical slang)
VCA........ VCA Corp. (Formerly, Vanadium Corporation of America) (NYSE symbol)
VCA .... Vitrified China Association
VC of A.... Vizsla Club of America
VCAD...... Vertical Contact Analog Display
VCAS...... Vice-Chief of the Air Staff (British)
VCB........ Construction Battalion (USNR classification)
VCB........ Vertical Location of the Center of Buoyancy
VCB........ Virginia Commonwealth Bank Shares, Inc. (NYSE symbol)

VCB . . . . Visual Control Board
VCC . . . . Variable Ceramic Capacitor
VCC . . . . Vasoconstrictor Center (Physiology)
VCC . . . . Vertical Centering Control
VCC . . . . Video Coaxial Connector
VCC . . . . . . Vietcong Captured
VCC . . . . Visual Communications Congress
VCC . . . . Voltage Coefficient of Capacitance
VCC . . . . Voltage-Controlled Capacitor
VCCA . . . . . . Vintage Chevrolet Club of America
VCCUS . . . . . Venezuelan Chamber of Commerce of the United States
VCD . . . . Vapor Compression Distillation
VCD . . . . Variable-Capacitance Diode
VCD . . . . Vernier Engine Cutoff (Air Force)
VCD . . . . Voltage Crossing Detector
VCE . . . . Vapor Compression Evaporation
VCF . . . . Vapor Chamber Fin
VCF . . . . Verified Circulation Figure (Periodical publishing)
VCG . . . . Vectorcardiogram (Medicine)
VCG . . . . Vehicle Control Group
VCG . . . . Vertical Location of the Center of Gravity
VCG . . . . Voltage-Controlled Generator
VCH . . . . Veterinary Convalescent Hospital
VCHP . . . . . . Variable Conductance Heat Pipe
VCI . . . . Variety Clubs International
VCI . . . . Vibration Control Index
VCI . . . . Vietcong Infrastructure
VCIGS . . . . . Vice-Chief of the Imperial General Staff (British)
VCIM . . . . . . Varnished Cambric Insulation Material
VCK . . . . Video Camera Kit
VCK . . . . Vietcong Killed
VCL . . . . Vertical Center Line
VCL . . . . Voice Communications Laboratory
VCLO . . . . . . Voltage-Controlled Local Oscillator
VCM . . . . Vertical Cutter Motion
VCM . . . . Vibrating Coil Magnetometer
VCM . . . . Vinyl Chloride Monomer
VCM . . . . Volatile Condensable Material
VCM . . . . Voltage-Controlled Multivibrator
VCMA . . . . . . Vacuum Cleaner Manufacturers Association
VCN . . . . Vendor Contract Notice
VCN . . . . Vibrio-cholerae Neuraminidase
VCNO . . . . . . Vice Chief of Naval Operations
VCNTY . . . . . Vicinity
VCO . . . . Variable Cycle Operation
VCO . . . . Vehicle Control Officer (Air Force)
VCO . . . . Vertical Control Operator (Military)
VCO . . . . Voltage-Controlled Oscillator
VCOT . . . . . . VFR (Visual Flight Rules) Conditions on Top (Aviation)
VCP . . . . Vehicle Collecting Point
VCP . . . . Velocity Control Programmer
VCP . . . . Verdan Checkout Panel
VCPA . . . . . . Virginia-Carolina Peanut Association
VCPA . . . . . . Virginia Crab Packers Association
VCR . . . . Vacuum Contact Relay
VCR . . . . Variable Compression Ratio
VCR . . . . Victor Comptometer Corporation (NYSE symbol)
VCR . . . . Voltage Coefficient of Resistance
VCS . . . . Cruiser-Scouting Aircraft Squadron (Navy symbol)
VCS . . . . Vacuum Control Switch
VCS . . . . Vapor Coating System
VCS . . . . Vapor Cooling System
VCS . . . . Variable Correlation Synchronization
VCS . . . . Vasoconstrictor Substance (Physiology)
VCS . . . . Vehicular Communications System
VCS . . . . Ventral Collecting Sinus
VCS . . . . Vice Chief of Staff
VCS . . . . Video Communications System
VCS . . . . Video Contrast Seeker
VCS . . . . Vietcong Suspects Detained
VCS . . . . Virginia & Carolina Southern R. R. (AAR code)
VCS . . . . Visual Call Sign (Communications)
VCS . . . . Voice Communications System
VCS . . . . Voltage Calibration Set
VC of S . . . . . Vice Chief of Staff (Army)
VCSA . . . . . . Vice Chief of Staff, Army
VC of SA . . . . Vice Chief of Staff, Army
VC/SAF . . . . . Vice Chief of Staff, Air Force
VCSFO . . . . . Veterans Canteen Service Field Office (Veterans Administration)
VCSL . . . . . . Voice Call Signs List
VCSP . . . . . . Voice Call Signs Plan

VCSR . . . . . . Voltage-Controlled Shift Register
VCT . . . . Vitrified Clay Tile (Technical drawings)
VCT . . . . Voltage Control Transfer
VCT . . . . Voltage Curve Tracer
VCTD . . . . . . Vendor Contract Technical Data
VCU . . . . Virginia Commonwealth University
VCU . . . . Voltage Control Unit
VCVS . . . . . . Voltage-Controlled Voltage Source
VCXO . . . . . . Voltage-Controlled Crystal Oscillator
VCY . . . . Ventura County Railway Company (AAR code)
VCZ . . . . Vinylcarbazole (Organic chemistry)
VD . . . . Double Vibrations (Cycles)
VD . . . . Vapor Density
VD . . . . Various Dates (Bibliography)
VD . . . . Venereal Disease
VD . . . . Ventilating Deadlight (Technical drawings)
VD . . . . Ventricular Dilator (Neuron)
VD . . . . Vertical Drive
VD . . . . Video Decoder
VD . . . . Visiting Dignitary
VD . . . . Voltage Detector
VD . . . . Volunteer Decoration
VDA . . . . Vertical Danger Angle (Navigation)
VDA . . . . Video Distribution Amplifier
VDA . . . . Visual Discriminatory Acuity
VDA . . . . Volksbund fuer das Deutschtum im Ausland (NAZI Germany)
VDB . . . . Victor D. Brenner (Designer's mark, when appearing on US coins)
VDC . . . . Vasodilator Center (Physiology)
VDC . . . . Voltage to Digital Converter
VDC . . . . Voltage Doubler Circuit
VDC . . . . Volts Direct Current
VDCP . . . . . . Video Data Collection Program
VDCT . . . . . . Direct-Current Test Volts
VDCU . . . . . . Videograph Display Control Unit
VDCW . . . . . . Direct-Current Working Volts
VDD . . . . Video Detector Diode
VDD . . . . Visual Display Data
VDD . . . . Voice Digital Display
VDDI . . . . . . Verband Deutscher Diplomingenieure (West Germany)
VDDP . . . . . . Video Digital Data Processing
VDE . . . . Vacuum Deposition Equipment
VDE . . . . Variable Display Equipment
VDE . . . . Verband Deutscher Elektrotechniker (West Germany)
VDEL . . . . . . Venereal Disease Experimental Laboratory
VDF . . . . Very-High-Frequency Direction Finding
VDF . . . . Vibration Damping Fastener
VDF . . . . Video Frequency
VDFG . . . . . . Variable Diode Function Generator
VDG . . . . Venereal Disease Gonorrhea
VDG . . . . Vertical and Direction Gyro
VDG . . . . Vertical Display Generator
VDH . . . . Valvular Disease of the Heart (Medicine)
VDI . . . . Vat Dye Institute
VDI . . . . Verein Deutscher Ingenieure (Society of German Engineers)
VDI . . . . Vertical Display Indicator
VDI . . . . Voluntary Data Inquiry
VDJ . . . . Verband der Deutschen Journalisten
VDK . . . . Verband Deutscher Konsumgenossenschaften
VDL . . . . Van Diemen's Land (Former name of Tasmania)
VDL . . . . Variable Delay Line
VDL . . . . Vasodepressor Lipid (Medicine)
VDL . . . . Voice Direct Line
VDM . . . . Variable Direction Microphone
VDM . . . . Vasodepressor Material
VDM . . . . Vector Drawn Map
VDM . . . . Vehicle Deadlined for Maintenance
VDM . . . . Verbi Die Minister (Minister, or Preacher, of the Word of God)
VDM . . . . Vibration Damping Mount
VDM . . . . Video Delta Modulation
VDMS . . . . . . Video Delta Modulation System
VDN . . . . Varudeklarationsnamnden (Labeling system) (Sweden)
VDP . . . . Vacuum Diffusion Pump
VDP . . . . Vehicle Deadlined for Parts
VDP . . . . Vertical Data Processing
VDP . . . . Vibration Diagnostic Program
VDP . . . . Volunteer Reservists in Drill Pay Status (Navy)
VDPG . . . . . . Verband Deutscher Physikalischer Gesselschaften (West Germany)
VDPI . . . . . . Vehicle Direction and Position Indicator
VDPS . . . . . . Voice Data Processor System
VDQ . . . . Visual Display of Quality
VDR . . . . Vendor Data Request

VDR . . . . Venous Diameter Ratio (Cancer detection)
VDRG . . . . . . Vendor Data Release Group
VDRL . . . . . . Venereal Disease Research Laboratory
VDRT . . . . . . Venereal Disease Reference Test (of Harris)
VDS . . . . Vapor Detection System
VDS . . . . Variable-Depth SONAR
VDS . . . . Vasodilator Substance
VDS . . . . Vehicle Design Section
VDS . . . . Velocita di Sedimentazione (Sedimentation Rate) (Medicine)
VDS . . . . Vendor Data Service
VDS . . . . Vendor Direct Shipment
VDS . . . . Venereal Disease Syphilis
VDS . . . . Video Display System
VDS . . . . Visual Docking Simulator
VDSS . . . . . . Variable Depth SONAR System
VDT . . . . Varactor Diode Test
VDT . . . . Variable Deflection Thruster (Helicopters)
VDT . . . . Variable Density Tunnel
VDT . . . . Variable Differential Transformer
VDV . . . . Vozdushno-Desantnye Voiska (Airborne Troops) (An autonomous command) (USSR)
VD-VF . . . . . . Vacuum Distillation - Vapor Filtration
VDW . . . . Venus Departure Window
VDW . . . . Very Deep Water
VE . . . . Value Effectiveness
VE . . . . Value Engineering
VE . . . . Velocity Error
VE . . . . Vesicular Exanthema (Medicine)
VE . . . . Victory in Europe (as in VE-Day)
VE . . . . Visalia Electric R. R. (AAR code)
VE . . . . Visual Efficiency
VEA . . . . Value Engineering Audit
VEA . . . . Vehicle Engineering Analysis
VEA . . . . Veliger Escape Aperture
VEA . . . . Vocational Education Act
VEAB . . . . . . Volkseigener Erfassungs und Aufkaufbetrieb
VEAMCOP . . . . Viking Error Analysis Monte Carlo Program (Data processing)
VEB . . . . Variable Elevation Beam (RADAR)
VEB . . . . Venus Entry Body
VEB . . . . Volkseigene Betrieb
VEBA . . . . . . Vereinigte Elektrizitaets und Bergwerks, AG (Holding company) (Germany)
VEBW . . . . . . Vacuum Electron Beam Welder
VEC . . . . Value Engineering Change
VEC . . . . Vibration Exciter Control
VECO . . . . . . Vernier-Engine Cutoff (NASA)
VECOS . . . . . Vehicle Checkout Set
VECP . . . . . . Value Engineering Change Proposals (Navy)
VECR . . . . . . Vendor Engineering Change Request (DOD)
VED . . . . Vacuum Energy Diverter
VED . . . . Viscoelastic Damper
VEDAR . . . . . Visible Energy Detection and Ranging
VEDR . . . . . . Value Engineering Design Review
VEE . . . . Venezuelan Equine Encephalomyelitis (Veterinary medicine)
VEECO . . . . . Vacuum Electronics Engineering Company
VEEG . . . . . . Vector Electroencephalograph
VEEP . . . . . . Vice President
VEER . . . . . . Variable Emergence Electronically Rotated
VEF . . . . Variable Electronic Filter
VEF . . . . Viscoelastic Fiber
VEFCA . . . . . Value Engineering Functional Cost Analysis
VEG . . . . Value Engineering Guideline
VEG . . . . Volkseigenes Gut
VEGL . . . . . . Value Engineering Guideline
VEH . . . . Vehicle
VEH . . . . Veterinary Evacuation Hospital
VEH . . . . Volkseigener Handel
VEI . . . . Value Engineered Indicator
VEIS . . . . . . Vocational Education Information System
VEL . . . . Velocity
VEL . . . . Virginia Electric & Power Company (NYSE symbol)
VEM . . . . Value Engineering Model
VEM . . . . Vasoexcitor Material (Physiology)
VEM . . . . Vendor Engineering Memorandum
VEN . . . . Vendo Company (NYSE symbol)
VENT . . . . . . Ventilation
VEO . . . . Value Engineering Organization
VEP . . . . Value Engineering Program
VEP . . . . Vertical Extrusion Press
VEP . . . . Visual Evoked Potential
VEP . . . . Voter Education Project (An organization)

VEPCO . . . . . . Virginia Electric and Power Company
VEPG . . . . Value Engineering Program Guideline
VEPIS . . . . . . Vocational Education Program Information System
VEPR . . . . Value Engineering Program Requirements
VER . . . . Verification (or Verify)
VER . . . . Vertical Earth Rate
VER . . . . Visual Evoked Response
VERA . . . . . . Vision Electric Recording Apparatus (BBC)
VERAS . . . . . Vehicle Experimental de Recherches Aerothermodynamique et Structurale (Glider) (France)
VERB . . . . . . Victor Electrowriter Remote Blackboard (Educational device of Victor Comptometer Corporation)
VERC . . . . . . Vehicle Effectiveness Remaining Converter
VERDAN . . . . . Versatile Differential Analyzer
VERLORT . . . . Very-Long-Range Tracking (NASA)
VERNAV . . . . . Vertical Navigation System
VERNITRAC . . . Vernier Tracking by Automatic Correlation
VERT . . . . Vertical
VERTIJET . . . . Vertical Take-Off and Landing Jet (Aircraft)
VERTOL . . . . . Vertical Take-off and Landing (Also, VTOL)
VES . . . . Vacuum Evaporator System
VES . . . . Variable Elasticity of Substitution (Industrial production)
VES . . . . Veterans Employment Service (of USES)
VESC . . . . . . Vehicle Equipment Safety Commission
VESCA(S) . . . . Vessels and Cargo
VESI . . . . Victor Educational Services Institute (Educational division of Victor Comptometer Corporation)
VESIAC . . . . . Vela Seismic Information Analysis Center (University of Michigan)
VESP . . . . . . Value Engineering Supplier Program
VESR . . . . . . Vallecitos Experimental Superheat Reactor
VEST . . . . . . Volunteer Engineers, Scientists and Technicians (An organization)
VET . . . . Value Engineering Training
VET . . . . Verbal Test
VET . . . . Versatile Engine Tester
VET . . . . Veteran
VET . . . . Veterinary
VET . . . . Vidicon Electron Tube
VETF . . . . . . Value Engineering Task Force
VETS . . . . . . Vertical Engine Test Stand
VetSci. . . . . . Veterinary Science
VEV . . . . Vlaams Economisch Verbond
VEV . . . . Voice-Excited Vocoder
VEVERP . . . . . Vietnam Era Veteran Recruitment Program
VEW . . . . Volkseigene Wirtschaft
VEWS . . . . . . Very Early Warning System
VEWU . . . . . . Viet-Nam Educational Workers' Union (North Vietnam)
VF . . . . Fighter Plane (Navy symbol)
VF . . . . Fighter Squadron (Navy symbol)
VF . . . . Vector Field
VF . . . . Velocity Failure
VF . . . . Ventricular Fibrillation (Medicine)
VF . . . . Vertical File
VF . . . . Very Fair
VF . . . . Very Fine (Condition) (Antiquarian book trade and numismatics)
VF . . . . Vicarius Foraneus (Vicar-Forane)
VF . . . . Video Frequency
VF . . . . View Factor
VF . . . . Vision Frequency
VF . . . . Visual Field
VF . . . . Visual Flight (Aviation)
VF . . . . Vocal Fremitus
VF . . . . Voice Frequency (Communications)
VF . . . . Vulcanized Fiber
VFA . . . . Variation Flow Analysis
VFA . . . . Video Free America
VFA . . . . Video Frequency Amplifier
VF AW . . . . . . Fighter Squadron - All Weather
VFAX . . . . . . Heavier-Than-Air Fighter/Attack/Experimental (Aircraft)
VFB . . . . Fighter Bombing Plane (Navy symbol)
VFC . . . . Variable Frequency Control
VFC . . . . Very Fine Cognac
VFC . . . . VF Corporation (NYSE symbol)
VFC . . . . Voice Frequency Cable
VFC . . . . Voice Frequency Carrier (Channel)
VFC . . . . Voltage to Frequency Converter
VFCS . . . . . . Vehicle Flight Control System
VFCT . . . . . . Voice Frequency Carrier Teletype
VFD . . . . Volunteer Fire Department
VFDM . . . . . . Vsemirnaia Federatsiia Demokraticheskoi Molodezhi (World Federation of Democratic Youth)
VFER . . . . . . Veterans Federal Employment Representative (Civil Service Commission)

VFF . . . . Valence Force Field
VFF . . . . Voice Frequency Filter
VFGH . . . . Valley Forge General Hospital
VFH . . . . Vacuum Film Handling
VFHT . . . . Vacuum Film Handling Technique
VFI . . . . Vinyl Fabrics Institute
VFI . . . . Vocational Foundation, Incorporated
VFL . . . . Variable Focal Length
VFL . . . . Variable Focal-Length Lens
VFLA . . . . Volume Folding and Limiting Amplifier
VFM . . . . Vacuum Forming Machine
VFM . . . . Vertical Flight Maneuver
VF(M) . . . . Fighter Plane (Two-engine) (Navy symbol)
VF(N) . . . . Night Fighter Squadrons (Navy symbol)
VFO . . . . Vandenberg Field Office (Air Force)
VFO . . . . Variable Frequency Oscillator
VFOI . . . . Verband Deutscher Feinmechanischer und Optischer Industrie (West Germany)
VFON . . . . . . Volunteer Flight Officers Network
VFP . . . . Fighter Squadron, Photo
VFP . . . . Vacuum Fore Pump
VFPR . . . . Via Flight Planned Route (Aviation)
VFR . . . . Verein fuer Raumschiffahrt (Society for Space Travel) (Germany)
VFR . . . . Visual Flight Rules (or Regulations) (Aviation)
VFRA . . . . Volume Footwear Retailers Association
VFRSA . . . . . . VFR (Visual Flight Rules) Restrictions Still Apply (Aviation)
VFS . . . . Vapor Feed System
VFS . . . . Ventilated Flight Suit
VFSS . . . . Voice Frequency Signaling System
VFT . . . . Vacuum Friction Test
VFT . . . . Voice Frequency Terminal
VFTG . . . . Voice Frequency Telegraph
VFV . . . . Venus Flyby Vehicle
VFVC . . . . Vacuum Freezing, Vapor Compression (Desalination)
VFW . . . . Vereinigte Flugtechnische Werke
VFW . . . . Verwaltungsamt fuer Wirtschaft (Executive Committee for Economics) (German)
VFW . . . . Veterans of Foreign Wars of the USA
VFW . . . . Veterans of Future Wars (Facetious organization formed by Princeton students in 1930's)
VFY . . . . Verify
VG . . . . Light Transport Plane (Single-engine) (Navy symbol)
VG . . . . Velocity Gravity
VG . . . . Ventricular Gallop
VG . . . . Verbi Gratia (For Example)
VG . . . . Vertical Grain
VG . . . . Vertical Gyro
VG . . . . Very Good (Condition) (Antiquarian book trade and numismatics)
VG . . . . Vibration Greatness
VG . . . . Vicarius Generalis (Vicar-General)
VG . . . . Voltage Gain
V-G . . . . Vertical Gust
VGA . . . . Variable Gain Amplifier
VGA . . . . Vertical Gyro Alignment
VGAA . . . . . . Vegetable Growers Association of America
VGC . . . . Variable Gas Capacitor
VGC . . . . Viscosity Gravity Constant
VGCL . . . . . . Vietnam General Confederation of Labor
VGE . . . . Visual Gross Error
VGF . . . . Escort-Fighting Squadron (Navy symbol)
VGFTU . . . . . . Viet-Nam General Federation of Trade Unions (North Vietnam)
VGH . . . . Velocity, Normal Gravity and Height
VGH . . . . Veterinary General Hospital
VGI . . . . Vertical Gyro Indicator
VGN . . . . Virginian Railway Company (AAR code)
VGO . . . . Vacuum Gas Oil
VGP . . . . Vertical Ground Point
VGPI . . . . Visual Glide Path Indicator
VGS . . . . Escort-Scouting Squadron (Navy symbol)
VGS . . . . Vehicle Generating System
VGSI . . . . Visual Glide Slope Indicator
VGV . . . . Vacuum Gate Valve
VGW . . . . Variable Geometry Wing
VH . . . . Ambulance Plane (Navy symbol)
VH . . . . Rescue Squadrons (Navy symbol)
VH . . . . Vacuum Housing
VH . . . . Vent Hole (Technical drawings)
VH . . . . Very Heavy
VH . . . . Very High
VH . . . . Veterans Hospital
VH . . . . Vir Honestus (A Worthy Man)

V/H . . . . Velocity/Height
V/H . . . . Vulnerability/Hardness (Refers to a weapon system's weaknesses and capabilities in withstanding adverse operating environments)
VHA . . . . Very High Altitude
VHB . . . . Very Heavy Bombardment (Air Force)
VHC . . . . Vertical Hold Control
VHC . . . . Very Highly Commended
VHF . . . . Vacuum Hydrogen Furnace
VHF . . . . Very High Frequency (Electronics)
VHF/DF . . . . . Very High Frequency Direction-Finding
VHFF . . . . . . Very High Frequency Filter
VHFG . . . . . . Very High Frequency Generator
VHFI . . . . Very High Frequency Indeed (Ultra-high frequency) (British)
VHFJ . . . . Very High Frequency Jammer
VHFO . . . . . . Very High Frequency Oscillator
VHFOR . . . . . . Very High Frequency Omnirange
VHFR . . . . . . Very High Frequency Receiver
VHFT . . . . . . Very High Frequency Termination
VHMCP . . . . . Voluntary Home Mortgage Credit Program (of HHFA) (Terminated)
VHN . . . . Vickers Hardness Number
VHO . . . . Very High Output
VHP . . . . Variable Horse Power
VHP . . . . Very High Performance
VHP . . . . Very High Pressure
VHR . . . . Video to Hardcopy Recorder
VHRR . . . . . . Very High Resolution Radiometer (NASA)
VHRTG . . . . . Veterans' Hospital Radio and Television Guild
VHS . . . . Versatile High Speed (Copier)
VHS . . . . Victorian House of Studies
VI . . . . Variable Interval
VI . . . . Verb Intransitive
VI . . . . Vermiculite Institute
VI . . . . Vertical Interval (Mapmaking)
VI . . . . Vide Infra (See Below)
VI . . . . Video Integrator
VI . . . . Vinegar Institute
VI . . . . Virgin Islands
VI . . . . Viscosity Index
VI . . . . Visual Inspection
VI . . . . Volume Indicator (Radio equipment)
VIA . . . . Viacom International, Inc. (NYSE symbol)
VIA . . . . Virus Inactivating Agent (Medicine)
VIAS . . . . Voice Interference Analysis Set
VIB . . . . Vertical Integration Building
VIBROT . . . . . Vibrational-Rotational (Spectra) (Data processing)
VIBS . . . . Vocabulatory, Information, Block Design, Similarities (Psychology)
VIC . . . . Variable Instruction Computer
VIC . . . . Varnish Insulating Compound
VIC . . . . Vasoinhibitory Center (Medicine)
VIC . . . . Very Important Contributors (Political)
VIC . . . . Very Important Customer
VIC . . . . Veterinary Investigation Centre (Ministry of Agriculture, Fisheries, and Food) (British)
VIC . . . . Virgin Islands Corporation (of the Department of the Interior, intended to promote VI economic development)
VIC . . . . Virginia Intermont College
VICA . . . . . . Vocational Industrial Clubs of America
VICI . . . . Velocity Indicating Coherent Integrator
VICI . . . . Video Console Indexing
VICK . . . . . . Vicksburg National Military Park
VICO . . . . . . Virginia International Company
VICOED . . . . . Visual Communications Education
VICOM . . . . . Visual Communications Management
VID . . . . Virtual Image Display
VID . . . . Volunteers for International Development
VIDA . . . . . . Ventricular Impulse Detector and Alarm
VIDAC . . . . . Visual Information Display and Control
VIDAR . . . . . Velocity Integration, Detection and Ranging
VIDAT . . . . . Visual Data Acquisition
VIDC . . . . . . Virgin Islands Department of Commerce
VIDIAC . . . . . Visual Information Display and Control
VIDS . . . . . . Virtual Image Display System
VIE . . . . Vigilance, Initiative, Excellence (Aerospace Defense Command's acronym for the Zero Defects Program)
VIEW . . . . . . Visible, Informative, Emotionally Appealing, Workable (Package evaluation in marketing)
VIFC . . . . . . VTOL (Vertical Takeoff and Landing) Integrated Flight Control
VIFCS . . . . . . VTOL (Vertical Takeoff and Landing) Integrated Flight Control System
VIFSC . . . . . . VTOL (Vertical Takeoff and Landing) Integrated Flight System Control
VIG . . . . Vaccinia Immune Globulin (Medicine)
VIG . . . . Video Image Generator

VIG . . . . Video Integrating Group
VIG . . . . Visual Integrating Group
VIGS . . . . Visual Glide Slope
VIH . . . . Velocity Impact Hardening
VII. . . . . Vacuum Impregnated Inductor
VII. . . . . Viscosity Index Improver
VIIS . . . . Virgin Islands National Park
VIKA . . . . **Viking Air Lines**
VIL . . . . **Vivisection Investigation League**
VILP. . . . . . . Vector Impedance Locus Plotter
VIM . . . . Vendor Initial Measurement
VIM . . . . Vertical Improved Mail (Postal Service term for conveyorized handling of US mail in large modern buildings)
VIM . . . . Vibration Isolation Module
VIM . . . . Vinyl Insulation Material
VIMHEX . . . . . Venezuela International Meteorological and Hydrological Experiment (Colorado State University project)
VIMS . . . . Virginia Institute of Marine Science
VIN . . . . Vehicle Identification Number
VIND . . . . Vicarious Interpolations Not Desired
VINITI . . . . . . Vsesoyuznyy Institut Nauchnoy i Tekhnicheskoy Informatsii (All-Union Institute of Scientific and Technical Information) (USSR)
VINS . . . . Velocity Inertia Navigation System
VIO . . . . Veterinary Investigation Officer (Ministry of Agriculture, Fisheries, and Food) (British)
VIO . . . . . . **Visual Intercept Officer (Navy)**
VIOC . . . . Variable Input-Output Code
VIP . . . . **Value Improving Products**
VIP . . . . Value in Performance
VIP . . . . Variable Inductance Pickup
VIP . . . . **Variable Information Processing (Navy)**
VIP . . . . Variable Input Phototypesetter
VIP. . . . . Vasoactive Intestinal Peptide (Biochemistry)
VIP . . . . Versatile Information Processor (Data processing)
VIP . . . . **Very Important Passenger**
VIP . . . . **Very Important Person**
VIP . . . . **Very Important Poor**
VIP . . . . Visit-Investigate-Purchase (Department of Commerce program)
VIP . . . . Visual Identification Point
VIP . . . . Visual Information Projection
VIP . . . . Visual Input (System) (AT & T)
VIP . . . . Visual Integrated Presentation (Aviation)
VIP. . . . . Volunteers in Parks (New York City)
VIP . . . . Vulcanized Interlinked Polyethylene (Union Carbide Corp.)
VIPI . . . . **Very Important Person Indeed**
VIPI . . . . Volunteers in Probation, Incorporated
VIPP. . . . . . . Variable Information Processing Package
VIPS. . . . . . . Veterans in Public Service Act
VIPS. . . . . . . Voice Interruption Priority System
VIR . . . . Vendor Information Request
VIR . . . . Vulcanized India Rubber
VIRNS . . . . . . Velocity Inertia RADAR Navigation System
VIS. . . . . American Viscose Corporation (NYSE symbol) (Delisted)
VIS . . . . Veterinary Investigation Service (Ministry of Agriculture, Fisheries, and Food) (British)
VIS . . . . Vibration Isolation System
VIS. . . . . Visibility
VIS. . . . . Visual
VIS . . . . Visual Information System
VIS . . . . **Visual Instrumentation Subsystem**
VISA . . . . Voluntary International Service Assignments (of the Society of Friends)
VISION . . . . . Volunteers for Incommunity Service of Our Neighbors (Harvey, Illinois)
VISR. . . . . . . Virginia Institute for Science Research
VISSR . . . . . . Visible and Infrared Spin Scan Radiometer (NASA)
VISTA. . . . . . Variable Interlace System for Television Applications
VISTA. . . . . . Verbal Information Storage and Text Analysis (in FORTRAN computer language)
VISTA. . . . . . Viewing Instantly Security Transactions Automatically (Wall Street)
VISTA. . . . . . Visual Information for Satellite Telemetry Analysis
VISTA. . . . . . **Volunteers in Service to America (Domestic "poverty corps," similar to Peace Corps)**
VIT . . . . Variable Impedance Tube
VIT . . . . Very Important Traveler
VIT . . . . Vibration Isolation Table
VITA . . . . Volunteers for International Technical Assistance
VITAL. . . . . . Variably Initialized Translator for Algorithmic Languages (Data processing)
VITAP. . . . . . **Viking Targeting Analysis Program (NASA)**
VIU . . . . Voice Intercommunications Unit
VIV . . . . Venus IV (USSR spacecraft)
VIV . . . . Vivace (Lively) (Music)
VIV . . . . Vivid-Inventive-Vital (Spring fashions)

VIV . . . . Vlaamse Ingenieurs-Vereiniging
VIVA . . . . Victory in Vietnam Association
VIVA . . . . Virgin Islands Visitors Association
VIVA . . . . Voices in Vital America (An organization)
VIZ . . . . Videlicet (Namely)
VJ . . . . Vom Jahre (Of the year)
V-J . . . . **Victory-Japan (14 August 1945)**
VJB . . . . Verdan Junction Box
VJC . . . . Vallejo Junior College (California)
VJC . . . . Vermont Junior College
VJC . . . . Virginia Junior College
VK . . . . Ventral Wall, Kidney
VK . . . . Vertical Keel
VKA . . . . Volatile Keying Assembly
VKF . . . . Von Kármán Facility
VKIFD . . . . . . Von Karman Institute for Fluid Dynamics (Also, VKI)
VL . . . . Varia Lectio (Variant Reading)
VL . . . . Vario-Losser (Electronics)
VL . . . . Velar Lobe
VL . . . . **Vertical Ladder (Technical drawings)**
VL . . . . Vice-Lieutenant (British)
VL . . . . View Loss
VL . . . . **Violation of Lawful (Order) (Military)**
VL . . . . **Vision, Left**
VL . . . . Visual Laydown
VL . . . . Vulgar Latin
V-L . . . . Van Langenhoven (Rifle)
V/L . . . . Vapor-to-Liquid
VLA . . . . Very Large Array
VLA . . . . **Very Low Altitude**
VLA . . . . Video Logarithmic Amplifier
VLA . . . . Visual Landing Aid
VLA . . . . Volume Limiting Amplifier
VLAC . . . . **Vertical Lift Aircraft Council**
VLADD . . . . . Visual Low Angle Drogue Delivery
VLAP . . . . . . Vietnam Laboratory Assistance Program (Naval Oceanographic Office)
VLB . . . . **Glider (Special) (Navy symbol)**
VLB . . . . Vacuum Lens Blank
VLB . . . . Versuchs- und Lehranstalt fuer Brauerie
VLB . . . . Very Long Baseline
VLB . . . . Verzeichnis Lieferbarer Buecher (List of Deliverable Books, i.e., books in print) (Germany)
VLB . . . . Visual LASER Beam
VLBI. . . . . Very Long Baseline Interferometer (or Interferometry)
VLCC . . . . Very Large Cargo (or Crude) Carrier (Oil tanker)
VLCG . . . . Ventral Longitudinal Ciliated Groove
VLCR . . . . Variable Length Cavity Resonance
VLD . . . . Vacuum Leak Detector
VLD . . . . Vendor List of Drawings
VLD . . . . Visual Laydown Delivery
VLDL . . . . Very Low Density Lipoprotein(s) (Biochemistry)
VLE . . . . Visible Light Emission
VLEASS. . . . . . Very Long Endurance Acoustic Submarine Simulator
VLF . . . . Vertical Launch Facility
VLF . . . . **Very Low Frequency (Electronics)**
VLFD . . . . Via Low Frequency Direct
VLFJ . . . . Very Low Frequency Jammer
VLFR . . . . Very Low Frequency Receiver
VLFS . . . . Variable Low Frequency Standard
VLI . . . . Video Load Impedance
VLM . . . . Variable Length Multiply
VLM . . . . Vortex Lattice Method
VLN . . . . **Training Glider (Navy symbol)**
VLP . . . . Vaporizing Liquid Plenum
VLP . . . . Vertical Landing Point
VLPP. . . . . . . Very Low Pressure Pyrolysis
VLR . . . . **Transport Glider (Navy symbol)**
VLR . . . . **Very Long Range**
VLR . . . . **Very Low Range**
VLR . . . . Violation of Law of Road (Traffic offense charge)
VLR . . . . Voluntary Loss Rate (of Air Force officers resigning before retirement)
VLRSN . . . . . . **Violation of Lawful Regulation Issued by the Secretary of the Navy**
VLS . . . . Vacuum Loading System
VLS . . . . Vapor-Liquid-Solid
VLS . . . . Very Low Speed
VLU . . . . Vacuum Lifting Unit
v-LVN . . . . . . Ventral Lateral Ventricular Nerve
VLW . . . . Village Level Workers (India)
VM . . . . **V-Mail Specialists (Navy)**
VM . . . . Vasomotor
VM . . . . Vector Message

VM .... Velocity Meter
VM .... **Velocity Modulation**
VM .... Vertical Magnet
VM .... Vestibular Membrane (Medicine)
VM .... Vir Magnificus (Great Man)
VM .... Virgin and Martyr (Church calendars)
VM .... Voennoe Ministerstvo (Ministry of War) (1950-53; merged into the MO)
           (USSR)
VM .... Voice Modulation
VM .... Volksmarine
VM .... Voltmeter
VM .... Voyager Mars (Aerospace)
V/m .... Volt Per Meter
VMA .... Valve Manufacturers Association
VMA .... Vanillylmandelic Acid
VMA .... Vehicle Maintenance Area
VMAP....... Video Map Equipment
VMAVA ..... Verdun-Meuse-Argonne Veterans Association
VMB........ Marine Medium and Heavy Patrol Bomber Squadron (Land-based and
           seaplane) (Navy symbol)
VMBF....... Marine Fighter Bomber Squadrons (Navy symbol)
VMC .... Variable Message Cycle
VMC .... Variable Mica Capacitor
VMC .... Vasomotor Center (Physiology)
VMC .... Veritable Master of Crewelwork
VMC .... Villa Madonna College (Kentucky)
VMC .... Villa Maria College (Pennsylvania)
VMC .... Virginia Medical College
VMC .... Visual Meteorological Conditions (Aviation)
VMC .... Vulcan Materials Company (NYSE symbol)
VMCCA ..... Veteran Motor Car Club of America
VMCR ...... Volunteer Marine Corps Reserve
VMD .... Doctor of Veterinary Medicine
VMD .... Marine Photographic Squadron (Navy symbol)
VMF........ Marine Fighter Squadron (Navy symbol)
VMF .... Vacuum Melting Furnace
VMFI ...... Voltage Monitor and Fault Indicating
VMF(N) .... Marine Night Fighter Squadron (Navy symbol)
VMG .... Video Mapping Group
VMG .... Video Mixer Group
VMH .... Ventromedial Hypothalamic (or Hypothalamus)
VMH .... Victoria Medal of Honour
VMI .... Vibration Measurement Integrator
VMI .... Virginia Military Institute
VMIC....... Vermont Maple Industry Council
V/mil ...... Volt Per Mil
VMJ........ Marine Utility Squadron (Navy symbol)
VMK .... Vita-Metall-Keramik (German dental material for crowns and bridgework)
VML........ Marine Glider Squadron (Navy symbol)
VML........ Ventral Mantle Lip
VMM .... Vacuum Melting Module
VMM .... Vehicle Model Movement
VMM .... Vertical Milling Machine
VMM .... Video Map Module
VMN .... Ventromedial Hypothalamic Nucleus
VMN .... Ventromedial Nucleus
VMO .... Marine Observation Squadron (Navy symbol)
VMO .... Velocity-Modulated Oscillator
VMO(AS) .... Marine Observation Squadron (Artillery Spotting) (Navy symbol)
VM & P .... Varnish Makers' and Painters' Naphtha
VMR........ Marine Transport Squadron (Navy symbol)
VMRB....... Vereinigte Metallwerke Ranshofen-Berndorf (AG)
VMS........ Valve Mounting System
VMS........ Velocity Measurement System
VMS........ Vibration Measuring System
VMS........ Video Modulation System
VMSB....... Marine Scout Bombing Squadron (Navy symbol)
VMT........ Validate Master Tape
VMT........ Variable Mu Tube (Electronics)
VMT........ Velocity-Modulated Tube
VMT........ Very Many Thanks
VMTB....... Marine Torpedo Bomber Squadron (Navy symbol)
VMWWI ..... Victory Medal World War I
VMWWII ..... Victory Medal World War II
VN .... Training Plane (Navy symbol)
VN .... Verb Neuter
VN .... Vietnam
VN .... Visiting Nurse
VNA .... Air Vietnam
VNA .... Visiting Nurse Association
VNAF ...... Vietnam Air Force

VNAF I & M.. Vietnam Air Force Improvement and Modernization Program
           (Air Force)
VNC .... Variable Neutralizing Capacitor
VNE .... Velocity Never to Exceed
VNG .... Ventral Surface, Nephridial Gland
VNIC....... Voltage Negative Immittance Converter
VNIIMP ..... Vsesoiuznyi Nauchno-Issledovatel'skii Institut Miasnoi Promyshlennosti
VNL........ Variable Neodymium LASER
VNL........ Via Net Loss
VNMC ...... Vietnam Marine Corps
VNN .... Vietnam Navy
VNO .... Value Not Obtained
VNO .... Vornado, Inc. (NYSE symbol)
VNR........ Van Nostrand Reinhold (Publishers)
VO .... Battleship Observation Squadron (Navy symbol)
VO .... **Observation Plane (Navy symbol)**
VO .... Verbal Orders
VO .... Verbindungsoffizier (Liaison officer) (German military –
           World War II)
VO .... Vernehmungsoffizier (Interrogation officer) (German military –
           World War II)
VO .... Verordnung
VO .... Verpflegungsoffizier (Mess officer) (German military – World
           War II)
VO .... Very Old
VO........ Veterinary Officer (British)
VO .... Violation of (Local) Ordinance
VO .... Visa Office (Department of State)
VO........ Volatile Oil
VOA .... Voice of America
VOA .... Volunteers of America
VO of A .... Vasa Order of America
VO-AG ..... Vocational Agriculture (Education)
VOB........ Vacuum Optical Bench
VOB........ Vereinigung
VOC .... Observation Spotter Squadron (Navy symbol)
VOC .... Variable Oil Capacitor
VOC .... Verbal Orders of the Commander
VOC .... Voice-Operated Coder
VOC .... Volunteer Officer Candidate (Army)
VOCA....... Voltmeter-Calibrator
VOCG ...... Verbal Order Commanding General
VOCM ...... Vehicle Out of Commission for Maintenance (Military)
VOCO ...... Verbal Order Commanding Officer
VOCODER.... Voice Coder
VOCOM ..... Voice Communications
VOCP ...... Vehicle Out of Commission for Parts (Military)
VOCS ...... Verbal Orders Chief of Staff
VOD .... Vacuum Oxygen Decarburization (Stainless-steel processing)
VOD .... Veno-Occlusive Disease (of the liver)
VOD .... Via Omni Direct
VOD .... **Vision, Right Eye**
VODACOM ... Voice Data Communications
VODAT...... Voice-Operated Device for Automatic Transmission
VODER...... Voice Coder
VODER...... Voice-Operated Demonstrator
VODP ...... **Verbal Orders by Direction of the President**
VOE........ Venus Orbit Ejection
VOE........ Visual Order Error
VOE........ Vocational Office Education (NASA employment program)
VOEC ...... **Vegetable Oil Export Corporation**
VOF........ Observation Fighter Squadron (Navy symbol)
VOF........ Vsesoiuznoe Obshchestvo Filatelistov (or Fizioterapistov)
VOG .... **Observation Plane Squadron (Navy symbol)**
VOG .... Vanguard Operations Group
VOG .... Vectoroculogram
VOGAA ..... Voice-Operated Gain-Adjusting Amplifier (NASA)
VOGAD ..... Voice-Operated Gain Adjusting Device
VOGOV .... **Verbal Orders of the Governor**
VOI .... Vehicle Ordnance Installation
VOI........ Video Output Impedance
VOICE ..... Vocabulary of Intelligence Concept Expressions
VOICE ..... Voice of Informed Community Expression
VOICE ..... Volunteer Oil Industry Communications Effort (Program) (Phillips Petro-
           leum Co.)
VOIS ...... Visual Observation Instrumentation Subsystem (Lunar space program)
VOKS....... Vsesoiuznoe Obshchestvo Kul'turnoi Sviazi s Zagranitsei (All-Union
           Society for Cultural Relations with Foreign Countries) (USSR)
           (Initialism also used as title of periodical)
VOL........ Volume
VOL........ Volunteer

VOLAR . . . . . . Volunteer Army (Project, absorbed by MVA, 1972)
VOLCAS . . . . . Voice-Operated Loss Control and Suppressor
VOLTAN . . . . . Voltage Amperage Normalizer
VOM . . . . Volt Ohm Meter
VOM . . . . Volt Ohm Milliameter
VOMI . . . . Volksdeutsche Mittelstelle (NAZI Germany)
VON . . . . Von's Grocery Company (NYSE symbol) (Delisted)
VOP . . . . Valued as in Original Policy (Insurance)
VOP . . . . Very Old Pale (Wines and spirits)
VOP . . . . Very Oldest Procurable
VOPNAV . . . . Vice Chief of Naval Operations
VOPO . . . . . . Volkspolizei (Also, VP)
VOPR . . . . . . Voice-Operated Relay
VOQ . . . . Visiting Officers' Quarters (Military)
VOR . . . . Very-High-Frequency Omnidirectional Radio Range
VOR . . . . Very-High-Frequency Omnirange
VOR . . . . Visual Omni-Range
VORDAC . . . . . VHF (Very High Frequency) Omnidirectional Range / Distance-
        Measuring for Air Coverage
VOR-DME . . . . Very-High-Frequency, Omnirange, Distance-Measuring Equipment
VOR/DMET . . . Very-High-Frequency Omnirange/Distance-Measuring Equipment
        Compatible with TACAN
VORTAC . . . . . Very-High-Frequency Omnirange TACAN (Tactical Air Navigation)
VOS . . . . Observation Scout Plane (Navy symbol)
VOS . . . . Visicoder Oscillograph System
VOS . . . . Vision, Left Eye
VOS . . . . Voice-Operated Switch
VOSA . . . . . . Verbal Orders of Secretary of the Army
VOSAF . . . . . . Verbal Orders Secretary of the Air Force
VOT . . . . Very Old Tawny (Wines and spirits)
VOT . . . . Voice Onset Time
VOTAG . . . . . Verbal Orders of the Adjutant General
VOTE . . . . . . Victory Only Through Education (Program of Constructive Action, Inc.)
VOU . . . . Voucher
VOV . . . . Video Output Voltage
VOX . . . . Voice-Operated Transmission
VP . . . . Patrol Plane (Navy symbol)
VP . . . . Patrol Squadron (Navy symbol)
VP . . . . Vacuum Pickup
VP . . . . Vacuum Pump
VP . . . . Valve Positioner
VP . . . . Vapor Pressure
VP . . . . Variable Pitch (as, an aircraft propeller)
VP . . . . Variable Property
VP . . . . Variant Pinocytic (Cells) (Medicine)
VP . . . . Various Paging, Various Places of Publication (Bibliography)
VP . . . . Various Places
VP . . . . Various Publications
VP . . . . Velocity Pressure
VP . . . . Venereal Pamphlet (Navy)
VP . . . . Venous Pressure
VP . . . . Vent Pipe (Technical drawings)
VP . . . . Verb Passive
VP . . . . Vertical Planning
VP . . . . Vertical Polarization
VP . . . . Vest Pocket
VP . . . . Vice President
VP . . . . Viral Protein
VP . . . . Visa Petition
VP . . . . Voges-Proskauer (Bacteriology)
VP . . . . Volkspolizei (Also, VOPO)
VP . . . . Vorposten (Outpost) (German military)
VP . . . . Voting Pool (Said of disposition of stocks)
VP . . . . Vulnerable Point
VPA . . . . Vibration Pickup Amplifier
VPA . . . . Videotape Production Association
VPA . . . . Vote Profile Analysis
VPB . . . . Medium and Heavy Patrol Bomber Squadron (Land based and seaplane)
        (Navy symbol)
VPB . . . . Patrol-Bombing Plane (Navy symbol)
VPB . . . . Vertical Plot Board (Navy)
VPB(HL) . . . . . Patrol Bomber, 4-engine, Landplane (Navy symbol)
VPB(HS) . . . . . Patrol Bomber, 4-engine, Seaplane (Navy symbol)
VPB(ML) . . . . Patrol Bomber, 2-engine, Landplane (Navy symbol)
VPB(MS) . . . . Patrol Bomber, 2-engine, Seaplane (Navy symbol)
VPC . . . . Vacuum Pump Chamber
VPC . . . . Vapor Phase Chromatography
VPC . . . . Variable Padder Capacitor
VPC . . . . Visual Punch Card
VPC . . . . Voltage to Pulse Converter
VPC . . . . Volume-Pulse-Charge

VPCA . . . . Video Prelaunch Command Amplifier
VPCDS . . . . . . Video Prelaunch Command Data System (Air Force)
VPCF . . . . Ventral Peristomial Collar Fold
VPD . . . . Vapor-Phase Deacidification (of books and documents)
VPD . . . . Variation Per Day (Navigation)
VPD . . . . Vehicle Performance Data
VPD . . . . Vehicles Per Day (Military)
VPDF . . . . Vacuum Pump Discharge Filter
VPE . . . . Video Processing Equipment
VPF . . . . Vacuum Pump Filter
VPF . . . . Variable Parts Feeder
VPF . . . . Variable Phase Filter
VPF . . . . Vibratory Pan Feeder
VPG . . . . Variable-Rate Pulse Generator
VPGS . . . . Vice-President of the Geological Society (British)
VPH . . . . Variation Per Hour (Navigation)
VPH . . . . Vehicles Per Hour (Military)
VPH . . . . Volkspolizeihelfer
VPI . . . . Vendor Parts Index
VPI . . . . Virginia Polytechnic Institute
VPK . . . . Vest Pocket Kodak
VPKA . . . . Volkspolizeikreisamt
VPL . . . . Variable Pulse LASER
VPL . . . . Ventral(is) Posterolateral(is)
VPL . . . . Volunteer Prison League
VPLCC . . . . . . Vehicle Propellant Loading Control Center
VPLS . . . . Vice-President of the Linnaean Society (British)
VPM . . . . Vacuum Pumping Module
VPM . . . . Variation Per Minute (Navigation)
VPM . . . . Vehicles Per Mile
VPM . . . . Versatile Packaging Machine
VPM . . . . Vertical Panel Mount
VPM . . . . Vertical Polarization Mode
VPM . . . . Vibrations Per Minute
VPM . . . . Voix du Peuple Murundi (Voice of the Murundi People)
Vpm . . . . Volts Per Meter (Also, V/m)
VPM . . . . Volts Per Mil
VPMA . . . . . . Vegetable Parchment Manufacturers Association
VPMOS . . . . . Verified Primary Military Occupational Specialty
VPN . . . . Vendor Part Number
VPNL . . . . Variable Pulse Neodymium LASER
VPO . . . . Vapor Pressure Osmometer
VPO . . . . Vienna Philharmonic Orchestra
VPOF . . . . Vacuum-Processed Oxide Free
VPP . . . . Vacuum Pickup Pencil
VPP . . . . Value Payable by Post
VPP . . . . Variable Pitch Propeller
VPP . . . . Vertical Pinpoint
VPP . . . . Vertical Pouch Packager
VPP . . . . Viral Porcine Pneumonia (Veterinary medicine)
VPR . . . . Valveless Pulse Rocket
VPR . . . . Virtual PPI (Plan-Position Indicator) Reflectoscope (RADAR)
VPRGS . . . . . . Vice-President of the Royal Geographical Society (British)
VPRI . . . . Vice-President of the Royal Institute (British)
VPR-NMP . . . . Virtual PPI (Plan-Position Indicator) Reflectoscope with
        Navigational Microfilm Projector (RADAR)
VPRS . . . . Vice-President of the Royal Society (British)
VPS . . . . Vacuum Pickup System
VPS . . . . Vacuum Pump System
VPS . . . . Variable Parameter System
VPS . . . . Vatican Philatelic Society
VPS . . . . Vibrations Per Second
VPS . . . . Vibrator Power Supply
VPSA . . . . Vice-President of the Society of Antiquaries (British)
VPSB . . . . Veterans Placement Service Board (Post-World War II)
VPT . . . . Patrol-Torpedo Plane (Navy symbol)
VPT . . . . Vibratron Pressure Transducer
VPT . . . . Video Pulse Termination
VPT . . . . Volume-Price Trend (Finance)
VPU . . . . Vacuum Penetration Unit
VPUA . . . . Vibration Pick-Up Amplifier
VPW . . . . Vertically Polarized Wave
VPZS . . . . Vice-President of the Zoological Society (British)
VQ . . . . Virtual Quantum
VQA . . . . Vendor Quality Assurance
VQC . . . . Variable Quartz Capacitor
VQC . . . . Vendor Quality Certification
VQD . . . . Vendor Quality Defect
VQZD . . . . . . Vendor Quality Zero Defects
VR . . . . Transport Plane (Multiengine) (Navy symbol)
VR . . . . Transport Squadron (Navy symbol)

VR . . . . Variable Ratio (Reinforcement)
VR . . . . Variant Reading
VR . . . . Veeder Industries, Inc. (NYSE symbol)
VR . . . . Vehicle Recovery
VR . . . . Vendor Rating
VR . . . . Ventilation Rate
VR . . . . Verb Reflexive
VR . . . . Verification Receiver
VR . . . . Vicar Rural
VR . . . . Victoria Regina (Queen Victoria)
VR . . . . Vision, Right Eye
VR . . . . Vocal Resonance
VR . . . . Voltage Regulator
VR . . . . Voltage Relay
VR . . . . Vulcanized Rubber
VRA . . . . Vertical Reference Attitude
VRA . . . . Vocational Rehabilitation Administration (Became Social and Rehabil-
itation Service) (HEW)
VRA . . . . Voltage Reference Amplifier
VRA . . . . Voltage Regulator Alarm
VRA . . . . Voting Rights Act
VRAD . . . . . . Vertically Referenced Attitude Display
VRAH . . . . . . Vertical Receiving Array Hydrophone
VRAM . . . . . . Variable Random Access Memory (Data processing)
VRB . . . . Variable Reenlistment Bonus (Military)
VRB . . . . Vehicle Retaining Board
VRB . . . . VHF Recovery Room
VRB . . . . Voice Rotating Beacon
VRC . . . . Variable Reluctance Cartridge
VRC . . . . Vehicle Research Corporation
VRC . . . . Vibrating Reed Capacitor
VRC . . . . Viscometer Recorder-Controller
VRC . . . . Visible Record Computer
VRCI . . . . . . Variable Resistive Components Institute
VRD . . . . Vacuum Tube Relay Driver
VRD . . . . Voltage Regulating Diode
VRD . . . . Volunteer Reserve Decoration (British)
VRE . . . . Vibrating Reed Electrometer
VRE . . . . Voltage Regulator-Exciter
V Rev . . . . . . Very Reverend
VRF . . . . Vascular Research Foundation
VRF . . . . Versatile Repair Facility
VRFI . . . . . . Voice Reporting Fault Indicator
VRFWS . . . . . . Vehicle Rapid Fire Weapon System (Army)
VRG . . . . Visual Reference Gate (Aviation)
VRH . . . . Var-Hour Meter
VRH . . . . Vertical Receiving Hydrophone
VR(HL) . . . . . . Transport, 4-engine, Landplane (Navy symbol)
VR(HS) . . . . . . Transport, 4-engine, Seaplane (Navy symbol)
VRI . . . . Vehicle Research Institute (Society of Automotive Engineers)
VRI . . . . Victoria Regina Imperatrix (Victoria, Queen and Empress)
VRI . . . . Viral Respiratory Infection (Medicine)
VR et I . . . . . . Victoria Regina et Imperatrix (Victoria, Queen and Empress)
VRIS . . . . Vietnam Refugee and Information Services
VRK . . . . Video Recorder Kit
VRL . . . . Vertical Reference Line (Technical drawings)
VRL . . . . Vibration Research Laboratory (Stanford University)
VRM . . . . Variable Reluctance Microphone
VRM . . . . Vendor Receiving Memo
VRM . . . . Viscous Remanant Magnetization
VRM . . . . Voltage Regulator Module
VR(ML) . . . . . . Transport, 2-engine, Landplane (Navy symbol)
VRMS . . . . . . Voltage Root Mean Square
VR(MS) . . . . . . Transport, 2-engine, Seaplane (Navy symbol)
VRP . . . . Vapor Reheat Process
VRP . . . . Variable Reluctance Pickup
VRPF . . . . . . Voltage-Regulated Plate Filament
VRPS . . . . . . Voltage-Regulated Power Supply
VRR . . . . Vibrating Reed Relay
VRR . . . . Visual Radio Range
VRS . . . . Vehicular RADIAC System
VRS . . . . Video Reception System
VRS . . . . Video Relay System
VRS . . . . Visual Reference System
VRS . . . . Volunteer Reserve Section
VRS . . . . Vortex Rate Sensor
VRSA . . . . . . Voice Reporting Signal Assembly
VRSS . . . . . . Voice Reporting Signal System
VRT . . . . Vacuum Rectifying Tube
VRT . . . . Van Raalte Company, Inc. (NYSE symbol) (Delisted)
VRT . . . . Variable Reluctance Transducer

VRT . . . . Visual Recognition Threshold
VRT . . . . Voltage Reference Tube
VRT . . . . Voltage Regulator Tube
VRU . . . . Voice Response Unit
VRU . . . . Voltage Readout Unit
VS . . . . Antisubmarine Squadron (Symbol)
VS . . . . Search Plane (Navy symbol)
VS . . . . Shore-Based Search Squadron (Navy symbol)
VS . . . . Single Vibrations (Half cycles)
VS . . . . Vacuum Switch
VS . . . . Vapor Seal (Technical drawings)
VS . . . . Vectoring Service
VS . . . . Vent Stack (Technical drawings)
VS . . . . Ventral Sac
VS . . . . Verse
VS . . . . Versus
VS . . . . Vertical Speed
VS . . . . Vertical Stereoscopic (Photograph)
VS . . . . Vertical Stripes (on buoys, etc.) (Maps and charts)
VS . . . . Very Superior
VS . . . . Vesicular Sound (in auscultation of chest) (Medicine)
VS . . . . Vesicular Stomatitis (Medicine)
VS . . . . Veterinary Surgeon
VS . . . . Vibration Seconds
VS . . . . Vide Supra (See Above)
VS . . . . Video Selection
VS . . . . Visceral Sinus
VS . . . . Visible Supply
VS . . . . Visual Signaling (Military)
VS . . . . Voltaire Society
VS . . . . Volti Subito (Turn over quickly) (Music)
VS . . . . Volumetric Solution
VS . . . . Voluntary Sterilization
V of S . . . . . . Veterans of Safety
V1S . . . . V-groove on One Side (Lumber)
V2S . . . . V-groove on Two Sides (Lumber)
VSA . . . . Vancouver School of Art
VSA . . . . Vereinigung Schweizerischer Angestelltenverbande (Federation of Swiss
Employees' Societies)
VSA . . . . Vibrating String Accelerometer
VSA . . . . Viscoelastic Stress Analysis
VSA . . . . Voltage-Sensitive Amplifier
VSB . . . . Scout-Bombing Plane (Navy symbol)
VSB . . . . Vent and Supply Bay
VSB . . . . Vestigial Sideband (Radio)
VSB-AM . . . . . Vestigial Side Band - Amplitude Modulation
VSBF . . . . . . Vestigial Sideband Filter
VSC . . . . Valdosta State College (Georgia)
VSC . . . . Variable Speed Chopper
VSC . . . . Vehicle Sectoring Code
VSC . . . . Vehicle System Control
VSC . . . . Vincentian Sisters of Charity (Roman Catholic religious order)
VSC . . . . Virginia State College
VSC . . . . Vocations for Social Change (Employment clearinghouse)
VSC . . . . Voltage-Saturated Capacitor
VSCCA . . . . . . Vintage Sports Car Club of America
VSCF . . . . . . Variable-Speed Constant Frequency
VSCNY . . . . . . Vedanta Society of the City of New York
VSD . . . . Valve Solenoid Driver
VSD . . . . Variable-Speed Drive
VSD . . . . Vendor's Shipping Document
VSD . . . . Ventricular Septal Defect (Medicine)
VSD . . . . Versatile Signal Device
VSD . . . . Vertical Situation Display
VSDR . . . . . . Vieteljahrsheft zur Statistik des Deutschen Reichs (Germany)
VSF . . . . Vestigial Sideband Filter
VSF . . . . Vitreous Silica Fabric
VSG . . . . Vernier Step Gage
VSG . . . . Versatile Symbol (or Signal) Generator
VSI . . . . Vendor Shipping Instruction
VSI . . . . Vertical Signal (or Situation) Indicator (Helicopters)
VSI . . . . Very Seriously Ill (Army)
VSI . . . . Video Sweep Integrator
VSI . . . . VSI Corp. (NYSE symbol)
VSIP . . . . Valence State Ionization Potentials (of atoms)
VSK . . . . Verband Schweizerischer Konsumvereine
VSL . . . . Valley & Siletz R. R. (AAR code)
VSL . . . . Valve Signal Light
VSLI . . . . Veterans Special Life Insurance (VA)
VSM . . . . Vehicle State Monitor
VSM . . . . Vestigial Sideband Modulation

VSM . . . . Vibrating Sample Magnetometer
VSM . . . . Vietnam Service Medal (Military)
VSMF . . . . . . Visual Search Microfilm File (Data processing)
VSMOS . . . . . Verified Secondary Military Occupational Specialty
VSMS . . . . . . Video Switching Matrix System
VSN . . . . Scout-Training Plane (Navy symbol)
VSN(M) . . . . Training Plane, 2-engine (Navy symbol)
VSO . . . . Scout Observation Plane (Navy symbol)
VSO . . . . Valdosta Southern R. R. (AAR code)
VSO . . . . Very Special Old
VSO . . . . Very Stable Oscillator
VSO . . . . Very Superior Old
VSO . . . . Voluntary Service Overseas (Military)
VSOP . . . . . . Very Superior Old Pale (Wines and spirits)
VSP . . . . Vehicle Scheduling Program (Data processing)
VSP . . . . Vertical Speed (Aviation)
VSP . . . . Video Signal Processor
VSQ . . . . Very Special Quality
VSR . . . . Very Short Range
VSR . . . . Vibration Sensitive Relay
VSR . . . . Voltage Sensing Relay
VSRBM . . . . . Very-Short-Range Ballistic Missile
VSS . . . . Variable Slit Set
VSS . . . . Variable SONAR System
VSS . . . . Variable Stability System (Aviation)
VSS . . . . Vehicle System Simulator
VSS . . . . Velocity Sensor System
VSS . . . . Vertical Sounding System
VSS . . . . Vertical Spike Soderberg (Pot) (Aluminum processing)
VSS . . . . Vertical Support Structure
VSS . . . . Video Storage System
VSS . . . . Video Supervisory Signal
VSS . . . . Visual Simulation System
VSS . . . . Voice Signaling System
VSS . . . . Voltage Sensing Switch
VSS . . . . Voyager Spacecraft Subsystem (NASA)
VST . . . . Variable Stability Trainer
VSTC . . . . . . Vermont State Teachers College
V/STOL . . . . . Vertical/Short Takeoff and Landing (Aircraft)
VSTP . . . . . . Visual Satellite Tracking Program
VSTR . . . . . . Volt Second Transfer Ratio
VSTSC . . . . . Vandenberg Scientific and Technical Societies
VSTT . . . . . . Variable Speed Tactical Trainer
VSV . . . . Vesicular Stomatitis Virus
VSW . . . . Variable Sweep Wing
VSW . . . . Very Short Wave
VSW . . . . Voltage Standing Wave
VSWR . . . . . . Voltage Standing-Wave Ratio (Electronics)
VT . . . . Torpedo Plane (Navy symbol)
VT . . . . Vacuum Tube (Electronics)
VT . . . . Variable Thrust
VT . . . . Variable Time (Fuse) (Also known as a "proximity fuse")
VT . . . . Variable Transformer
VT . . . . Vehicle Theft
VT . . . . Verb Transitive
VT . . . . Vermont
VT . . . . Vertical Tabulation (Data processing)
VT . . . . Vertical Tail
VT . . . . Vetus Testamentum (The Old Testament) (Bible)
VT . . . . Vibration Testing
VT . . . . Visual Telegraphy
VT . . . . Visual Toss
VT . . . . Voice Tube (Technical drawings)
V & T . . . . . . Volume and Tension (of pulse)
VTA . . . . Vacuum Tube Amplifier
VTA . . . . Variable Transfer Address
VTA . . . . Varnished Tube Association
VTA . . . . Vision Test Apparatus
VTB . . . . Torpedo-Bombing Plane (Navy symbol)
VTB . . . . Velocity Test Barrel
VTB . . . . Vlaamsche Toeristenbond
VTC . . . . Variable Trimmer Capacitor
VTC . . . . Vehicular Traffic Control
VTC . . . . Vidicon Television Camera
VTC . . . . Voting Trust Certificates (A type of stock certificate)
VTC . . . . Voting Trust Company
VTCC . . . . . . Variable Temperature Compensation Capacitor
VTCS . . . . . . Variable Thermal Control Surface
VTD . . . . Aircraft (Training) (Navy symbol)
VTDC . . . . . . Vacuum Tube Development Committee (Columbia University)
VTE . . . . Variable Thrust Engine

VTE . . . . Vertical Tube Effects (or Evaporation) (Desalination)
VTE . . . . Vibration Test Equipment
VTE . . . . Vicarious Trial and Error (Psychology)
VTES . . . . . . Variable Thrust Engine System
VTF . . . . Vacuum Test Furnace
VTF . . . . Vertical Test Facility (NASA)
VTF . . . . Vertical Test Fixture
VTF . . . . Vertical Tracking Force (of a phonograph cartridge)
VTF . . . . Voltage Transfer Function
VTFT . . . . . . Value Task Force Team
VTI . . . . Valparaiso Technical Institute (Indiana)
VTI . . . . Volume Thickness Index
VTIP . . . . . . Visual Target Identification Point
VTL . . . . Vacuum Tube Launcher
VTL . . . . Variable Threshold Logic
VTM . . . . Vacuum Tube Module
VTM . . . . Vehicles to the Mile (Military)
VTM . . . . Voltage Tunable Magnetron
VTMS . . . . . . Vinyltrimethysilane (Organic chemistry)
VT(N) . . . . . . Night Torpedo Bomber Squadron (Navy symbol)
VTNS . . . . . . Voltage Tunable Noise Source
VTO . . . . Vertical Takeoff
VTO . . . . Visual Training Officer (Navy)
VTO . . . . Vocational Training Officer (Navy)
VTO . . . . Voltage Tunable Oscillator
VTOHL . . . . . Vertical Take-Off and Horizontal Landing
VTOL . . . . . . Vertical Takeoff and Landing (Acronym used for a type of aircraft)
(Also, VERTOL)
VTP . . . . Vandenberg Test Program
VTP . . . . Vendor Test Procedure
VTP . . . . Visual Transmitter Power
VTPA . . . . . . Vertical Turbine Pump Association
VTPR . . . . . . Vertical Temperature Profile Radiometer
VTPS . . . . . . Vibration Test Plotting System
VTR . . . . Vehicle Tracking Receiver
VTR . . . . Vendor Trouble Report
VTR . . . . Vertical Test Range
VTR . . . . Videotape Recording (or Recorder)
VTRS . . . . . . Videotape Recording System
VTRS . . . . . . Videotape Response System
VTS . . . . Variable Time Step
VTS . . . . Vertical Thrust Stand
VTS . . . . Vibration Test System (or Specification)
VTS . . . . Vocational Training Service
VTS . . . . Vote Tally System
VTSC . . . . . . Virginia Theological Seminary and College
VTSPS . . . . . . Vsesoyuznyy Tsentral'nyy Sovet Professional'nykh Soyuzov (All Union
Central Council of Trade Unions) (USSR)
VTT . . . . Vacuum Thermal Testing
VTT . . . . Vacuum Tube Transmitter
VTU . . . . Volunteer Reserve Training Unit (Coast Guard)
VTU . . . . Volunteer Training Unit
VTU(MMS) . . . . Volunteer Training Unit (Merchant Marine Safety)
VTV . . . . Vacuum Tube Voltmeter
VTVM . . . . . . Vacuum-Tube Voltmeter (Radio)
VTW . . . . Variable Transmission Window
VTX . . . . Vacuum Tube Transmitter
VU . . . . Utility Squadron (Symbol)
VU . . . . Volume Unit
VUA . . . . Valorous Unit Award (Army)
VUB . . . . Variational Upper Bound
VUCS . . . . . . Ventilation Umbilical Connector System
VUF . . . . Vertical Upward Force
VUMS . . . . . . Vyzkumny Ustav pro Matematickych Stroju (Research Institute for
Mathematical Machines) (Czechoslovakia)
VUNC . . . . . . Voice of United Nations Command
VUP . . . . Vela Uniform Platform
VUS . . . . Versatile Upper Stage (NASA)
VUTS . . . . . . Verification Unit Test Set
VUU . . . . Virginia Union University
VUV . . . . Vacuum Ultraviolet
VV . . . . Vacuum Valve
VV . . . . Velocity-Volume
VV . . . . Vent Valve
VV . . . . Verses
VV . . . . Vice Versa
VV . . . . Voice Vocoder
VV . . . . Vulva and Vagina (Physiology)
VVAW . . . . . . Vietnam Veterans Against the War
VVB . . . . Vereinigung Volkseigener Betriebe
VVBAA . . . . . . Venetian and Vertical Blind Association of America

VVC........ Variable Vacuum Capacitor
VVC........ Vertical Velocity Console
VVC........ Voltage Variable Capacitor (Electronics)
VVCC...... Viri Clarissimi (Most Illustrious Men)
VVCD...... Voltage Variable Capacitance Diode
VVD........ Voltage Variable Diode
VVDS....... Video Verter Decision Storage
VVEAB ..... Vereinigung Volkseigener Erfassungs und Aufkaufbetriebe
VVG .... Vereinigung Volkseigener Gueter
VVHR....... Vibration Velocity per Hour
VVI .... Vocational Values Inventory (Guidance in education)
VVM .... Vector Voltmeter
VVM .... Velocity Vector Measurement
VVMS...... Velocity Vector Measurement System
VVN .... Vereinigung der Verfolgten des Naziregimes
VVO .... Very Very Old
VVPP ...... Variable Volume Piston Pump
VVR........ Variable Voltage Rectifier
VVRM ...... Vortex Valve Rocket Motor
VVS .... Very Very Superior
VVS .... Voenno-Vozdushnye Sily (Army Air Forces) (Part of the MO) (USSR)
VVSS ...... Vertical Volute Spring Suspension (Technical drawings)
VVS-VMF .... Voenno-Vozdushnye Sily – Voenno-Morskogo Flota (Naval Air Force) (USSR)
VVT .... Velocity Variation Tube
VVTC...... Vendor-Vendee Technical Committee
VVV........ Vereinigung Volkseigener Veriage
VW .... Early Warning Squadron (Symbol)
VW .... Very Worshipful

VW .... Vessel Wall
VW .... Volkswagen (German automobile)
VWA .... Vacuum Window Assembly
VWA .... Vendor Working Authority
VWA .... Verband der Weiblichen Angestellten (Association of Female Employees) (West Germany)
VWC .... Villa Walsh College (New Jersey)
VWCA ...... Volkswagen Club of America
VWDU ...... Viewing Window Deicing Unit
VWF........ Vehicle Work Flow
VWH .... Vale of White Horse (Hounds)
VWH .... Vertical Weld Head
VWHA ...... Vertical Weld Head Assembly
VWL........ Variable Word Length
VWOA ...... Veteran Wireless Operators Association
VWP........ Variable Width Pulse
VWPI ...... Vacuum Wood Preservers Institute
VWR........ Volkswirtschaftsrat
VWR........ VWR United Corp. (NYSE symbol)
VWW .... Veterans of World War I of USA
VX .... Experimental Squadron (Symbol)
VX .... Vivas, Care (May You Live, Dear One)
VX........ Vxor Carissima (Most Dear Wife)
VXO .... Variable Crystal Oscillator
VY........ Various Years (Bibliography)
VYB........ Vivian, Younger and Bond, Ltd.
VZ........ Virtual Zero
VZD....... Vendor Zero Defect

W

W . . . . Coast Guard Ship, when precedes vessel classification (Navy)
W . . . . Tungsten (Chemical element)
W . . . . Wall
W . . . . Wanting
W . . . . War
W . . . . Warden
W . . . . Warehouse
W . . . . Warhead (Nuclear)
W . . . . Warm
W . . . . Warrant (A document entitling holder to purchase a given issue of stock)
W . . . . Waste
W . . . . Watch Time
W . . . . Water
W . . . . Water Vapor Content
W . . . . Watt
W . . . . Wave Height Correction
W . . . . Weather
W . . . . Weather aircraft equipped with meteorological gear (Designation for all US military aircraft)
W . . . . Web
W . . . . Wednesday
W . . . . Week
W . . . . Weight
W . . . . Welsh (or Welch)
W . . . . Wesleyan
W. . . . . West, Westerly, Western
W. . . . . Westinghouse (As in "Group W")
W. . . . . Westvaco Corp. (NYSE symbol)
W . . . . Wet
W . . . . Whip
W . . . . White (Light, buoy, beacon)
W . . . . White (Maps and charts)
W . . . . Wicket
W. . . . . Wide, Width
W . . . . Widow
W . . . . Wife
W . . . . Wind (Wind triangle problems)
W . . . . Winter (Vessel load line mark)
W . . . . Wire
W . . . . With
W . . . . Without voice facilities on range or radiobeacon frequency
W. . . . . Wolfram (Tungsten) (Chemical element)
W . . . . Women's Reserve, Unlimited Service (USNR officer designation)
W . . . . Won (Sports statistics)
W . . . . Wood
W . . . . Word
W . . . . Work
W . . . . Wrong
W/. . . . . With (in conjunction with other abbreviations)
1-W . . . . Selective Service Class (for Conscientious Objector Performing Alternate Service Contributing to Maintenance of National Health, Safety, or Interest)
3Ws . . . . "The Who, What, or Where Game" (Television show; also, WWW)
4-W . . . . Selective Service Class (for Conscientious Objector Who Has Completed Alternate Service Contributing to National Health, Safety, or Interest)
WA . . . . Independent Watchmen's Association
WA . . . . Wabash R. R. Company (NYSE symbol)
WA . . . . Warm Air
WA . . . . Washington (State)
WA . . . . Watertown Arsenal (Massachusetts) (Army)
WA . . . . Wave Form Analyzer
WA . . . . Welfare Administration (Became Social and Rehabilitation Service) (HEW)
WA . . . . West Africa

WA . . . . Western Airlines, Inc.
WA . . . . Western Approaches (to Great Britain and Ireland)
WA . . . . Western Australia
WA . . . . Western Railway of Alabama (AAR code)
WA . . . . Will Adjust
WA . . . . Wire Association
WA . . . . With Average (Insurance)
WA . . . . Women's Reserve, Aviation Nonflying Duties (USNR officer designation)
WA . . . . Woolwich Armstrong Gun
WA . . . . Word Add
WA . . . . Word After (Message handling)
WA . . . . Work Authorization
WA . . . . Workers Anonymous (Mythical organization devoted to helping human beings overcome their desire to lead productive lives; created by columnist Arthur Hoppe in satirizing short work-week and early retirement schemes)
WA . . . . Workshop Assembly (Torpedo)
WA . . . . Writing Ability
W/A . . . . Warrant of Arrest
W of A . . . . . Western Railway of Alabama
WAA . . . . War Assets Administration (For disposal of US surplus war property) (Post-World War II) (Terminated after 1946)
WAA . . . . Warden's Association of America
WAA . . . . Wartime Aircraft Activity
WAA . . . . Welded Aluminum Alloy
WAA . . . . Western Amateur Astronomers
WAA . . . . World American Airlift
WAAAF . . . . . Women's Auxiliary Australian Air Force
WAABI . . . . . National Women's Association of Allied Beverage Industries
WAAC . . . . . . West African Airways Corporation
WAAC . . . . . . Women's Army Auxiliary Corps (Name later changed to WAC) (World War II)
WAAD . . . . . Westinghouse Air Arm Division
WAADS . . . . . . Washington Air Defense Sector (ADC)
WAAE. . . . . . . World Association for Adult Education
WAAF. . . . . . . Women's Auxiliary Air Force (Functioned under direct command of RAF) (World War II) (British)
WAAFB . . . . . Walker Air Force Base
WAAJ. . . . . . . Water-Augmented Air Jet
WAAMA . . . . . Woman's Auxiliary to the American Medical Association
WAAMAC . . . . Weight, Alignment and Mass Center Determination Equipment
WAAMMS . . . . Women's Auxiliary of the American Merchant Marine (World War II)
WAAPM . . . . . Wide Area Anti-Personnel Mine (Military)
WAAS . . . . . . Women's Auxiliary Army Service
WAAS . . . . . . World Academy of Art and Science (Israel)
WAASC. . . . . . Women's Auxiliary Army Service Corps (British)
WAB . . . . Wabash Railroad System (AAR code)
WAB. . . . . Waffenabwurfbehaelter (Parachute weapons container) (German military - World War II)
WAB. . . . . Wage Adjustment Board (World War II)
WAB . . . . Water-Activated Battery
WAB . . . . Western Actuarial Bureau
WAB . . . . When Authorized By
WAB . . . . Wine Advisory Board
WABCO . . . . . Westinghouse Air Brake Company
WABTOC . . . . When Authorized by the Oversea Commander (Military)
WAC . . . . Wake Analysis and Control
WAC . . . . War Assets Corporation (Post-World War II) (Succeeded by War Assests Administration)
WAC . . . . Weapon Assignment Console
WAC. . . . . Women's Army Corps (Formerly, WAAC)
WAC . . . . Worked All Continents (Contacted at least one station on all continents) (Amateur radio)

WAC .... World Aeronautical Charts (Air Force)
WAC .... World Affairs Center for the United States
WAC .... Wright Aeronautical Corporation
WAC .... Write Address Counter
WACA ...... Walnut Canyon National Monument
WACA ...... Western Agricultural Chemicals Association
WACA ...... Women's Apparel Chains Associations
WACB ...... Women's Army Classification Battery
WACM ...... Western Association of Circuit Manufacturers
WACO ...... Written Advice of Contracting Officer (Military)
WACRES ..... Women's Army Corps Reserve
WACRI ...... West African Cocoa Research Institution
WACS .... Workshop Attitude Control System
WACSM ..... Women's Army Corps Service Medal
WACU ...... West African Customs Union
WACVA ..... Women's Army Corps-Veterans Association
WAD .... Weapon Assignment Display (Air Force)
WAD .... Work Authorization and Delegation
WAD .... Wright Aeronautical Division
WADC ...... Western Air Defense Command
WADC ...... Wright Air Development Center (Air Force)
WADD ...... Wright Air Development Division
WADEX ..... Words and Authors Index (Computer-produced index)
WADF ...... Western Air Defense Force
WADS ...... Wide Angle Display System
WADS ...... Wide Area Data Service
WADVBS ..... World Association of Daily Vacation Bible Schools
WAE .... When (or While) Actually Employed (Government short jobs)
WAE .... Wills and Administration of Estates (Law)
WAE .... World Association of Estonians
WAED ...... Westinghouse Aerospace Electrical Division
WAEPA ..... War Agencies Employees Protective Association
WAEPA ..... Worldwide Assurance for Employees of Public Agencies
WAERSA ..... World Agricultural Economics and Rural Sociology Abstracts
              (A publication)
WAF .... Wafer
WAF .... With All Faults
WAF .... Women in the Air Force
WAF .... Word Address Format
WAFB ...... Warren Air Force Base
WAFB ...... Wright Air Force Base
WAFC ...... West African Fisheries Commission
WAFE ...... Wives of the Armed Forces, Emeritus
WAFF ...... West African Frontier Force
WAFFLE .... Wide-Angle Fixed-Field Locating Equipment
WAFS ...... Women's Auxiliary Ferrying Squadron (Part of Air Transport Command)
              (World War II)
WAFS ...... Women's Auxiliary Fire Service (British) (World War II)
WAG .... Walgreen Company (NYSE symbol)
WAG .... Warfare Analysis Group (Navy)
WAG .... Water-Alternating Gas
WAG .... Wellsville, Addison & Galeton R. R. Corporation (AAR code)
WAGGGS .... World Association of Girl Guides and Girl Scouts
WAGR ...... Windscale Advanced Gas-Cooled Reactor
WAGS ...... Weighted Agreement Scores
WAI .... Walk Around Inspection
WAIF ...... World Adoption International Fund
WAIS ...... Wechsler's Adult Intelligence Scale
WAJ .... Water-Augmented Jet
WAJ .... World Association of Judges
WAK .... Water Analyzer Kit
WAL .... Watertown Arsenal Laboratory (Army)
WAL .... We Are Lost (Army)
WAL .... Western Air Lines, Inc. (NYSE symbol)
WAL .... Western Allegheny R. R. (AAR code)
WAL .... Wide Angle Lens
W-AL .... Westinghouse-Astronuclear Laboratory
WALDO ..... Wichita Automatic Linear Data Output
WALOPT .... Weapons Allocation and Desired Ground-Zero Optimizer (Military)
WALP ...... Weapons Assignment Linear Program
WAM .... Walleye Measurements Program
WAM .... Words a Minute
WAMA ...... Weight After Mars Arrival (NASA)
WAMIS ..... Water Management Information System
WAML ...... Watertown Arsenal Medical Laboratory (Army)
WAML ..... Wright Aero Medical Laboratory (Air Force)
WAMOSCOPE .. Wave-Modulated Oscilloscope
WAMPUM .... Wage and Manpower Process Utilizing Machines (Bureau of Indian Affairs)
WAMS ...... Women's Automotive Maintenance Staff
WAMTMTS ... Western Area, Military Traffic Management and Terminal Service
WAN .... Wang Laboratories, Inc. (NYSE symbol)

WANAP ..... Washington National Airport
WANL ...... Westinghouse Astronuclear Laboratories
WAO .... Weapons Assignment Officer (Air Force)
WAO .... Women's American ORT
WAOS ...... Wide Angle Optical System
WAP .... Wide-Angle Panorama (Photography) (NASA)
WAP .... Women's Action Program (HEW)
WAP .... Work Assignment Procedure
WAPC ...... Women's Auxiliary Police Corps (British) (World War II)
WAPD ...... Western Air Procurement District
WAPD ...... Westinghouse Atomic Power Division (AEC)
WAPET ..... West Australian Petroleum (Ltd.)
WAPOR ..... World Association for Public Opinion Research
WAPS ...... Weighted Airman Promotion System (Air Force)
WAPS ...... Women of the American Press Service (Accredited American women war
              correspondents) (World War II)
WAPS ...... World Association of Pathology Societies
WAPT ...... Wild Animal Propagation Trust
WAR .... Warner Company (NYSE symbol)
WAR .... We Are Ridiculous (Antiwar slogan)
WAR .... Whiteruthenian American Relief
WAR .... Women Against Rape (Organization in Iowa City, Iowa)
WARC ...... World Administrative Radio Conference
WARCAD .... War Department - Civil Affairs Division
WARDS ..... Welfare of Animals Used for Research in Drugs and Therapy
WARES ..... Workload and Resources Evaluation System
WAREX ..... Warrant Issued for Extradite
WARFI ..... Wisconsin Alumni Research Foundation Institute
WARHD ..... Warhead
WARLA ..... Wide Aperture Radio Location Array
WARM ...... Weapons Assignment Research Model (Military)
WARP ...... Worldwide Ammunition Reporting Program
WARS ...... Wide Area Remote Sensors
WART ...... Wenceslaus Anxiety Representation Taxonomy (Satirical psychology term)
WAS .... Wadley Southern Railway Company (AAR code)
WAS .... Wide Angle Sensor
WAS .... Wideband Antenna System
WAS .... Women's Addiction Service (National Institute of Mental Health)
WAS .... Worked All States (Contacted at least one station in all states)
              (Amateur radio)
WASAG ..... Washington Action Group
WASC ...... Western Association of Schools and Colleges
WASC ...... White, Anglo-Saxon Catholic
WASCO ..... War Safety Council
WASGFC .... Western Association of State Game and Fish Commissioners
WASH ...... Washer
WASH ...... Washington
WASHO ..... Western Association of State Highway Officials
WASP ...... War Air Service Pattern (or Program) (Department of Commerce)
WASP ...... Weather-Atmospheric Sounding Projectile (Research rocket)
WASP ...... Weightless Analysis Sounding Probe (NASA)
WASP ...... Westinghouse Advanced Systems Planning Group
WASP ...... White, Anglo-Saxon Protestant
WASP ...... Williams Aerial Systems Platform (One-man flying platform)
WASP ...... Window Atmosphere Sounding Projectile (NASA)
WASP ...... Women's Airforce Service Pilots (World War II)
WASPA ..... White Anglo-Saxon Protestant Ambulatory (Extension of WASP; indicates
              the necessity of being able-bodied as an additional requirement for
              success)
WASPS ..... White Appalachian Southern Protestants (Chicago slang)
WASPS ..... Women's Auxiliary Service Platoon
WASSP ..... Wire Arc Seismic Section Profiler
WAT .... Weapons Assignment Technician
WAT .... Wideband Adapter Transformer
WAT .... Word Association Test (Psychology)
WATA ...... Wisconsin Automatic Test Apparatus
WATA ...... World Association of Travel Agencies
WATC ...... Washington Terminal Company (AAR code)
WATR ...... Waterville R. R. (AAR code)
WATS ...... Wide Area Telephone (or Telecommunications) Service (American
              Telephone and Telegraph Company contract billing system)
WATS ...... Women's Auxiliary Training Service
WATU ...... Western Approaches Tactical Unit (Navy)
WATW ...... Wood Awning Type Window
WAVES ..... Women Accepted for Volunteer Emergency Service (US Navy Women's
              Reserve) (World War II and later)
WAVES ..... Women Appointed Volunteer Emergency Services (British) (World War II)
WAW .... Waynesburg & Washington R. R. (AAR code)
WAWA ...... Woolens and Worsteds of America
WAWF ...... World Association of World Federalists
WAX .... Weapon Assignment and Target Extermination

WAY . . . . World Assembly of Youth
WB . . . . Wachovia Corp. (NYSE symbol)
WB . . . . Wage Board (Wage-earning federal workers' classification)
WB . . . . Wallboard
WB . . . . Warehouse Book
WB. . . . . Warner Brothers Pictures, Inc. (NYSE symbol) (Delisted)
WB . . . . Water Ballast
WB . . . . Water Board
WB . . . . Water Box
WB . . . . Waybill
WB. . . . . Weather Bomber (Air Force)
WB. . . . . Weather Bureau (Later, National Weather Service)
Wb. . . . . Weber
WB. . . . . Weekly Bulletin (Army)
WB. . . . . Westbound
WB . . . . Wet Bulb (Thermometer, of a psychrometer) (Meteorology)
WB. . . . . Whale Boat
WB . . . . Wheel Base
WB . . . . Wideband (Radio)
WB . . . . Will Be
WB . . . . Women's Bureau (Department of Labor)
WB. . . . . Wood Base (Technical drawings)
WB. . . . . Word Before (Message handling)
WB. . . . . Work Bench
WB. . . . . Work Book
WB . . . . World Bank
WB. . . . . World Brotherhood
WB . . . . Write Buffer
W/B . . . . Will Be
WBA . . . . . . Washington Bar Association
WBA . . . . . . Wideband Amplifier
WBA . . . . . . Woman's Benefit Association
WBA . . . . . . World Boxing Association
WBAN . . . . . Weather Bureau, Air Force, Navy (Manuals)
WBAS . . . . . Weather Bureau Airport Station
WBAT . . . . Wideband Adapter Transformer
WBAWS . . . . Weather, Briefing, Advisory and Warning Service
WBB. . . . . . . Webb (Del E.) Corp. (NYSE symbol)
WBBA . . . . . . Western Bird Banding Association
WBC . . . . . . Wayland Baptist College (Texas)
WBC. . . . . . . Weather Bureau Central Office (Washington, DC)
WBC. . . . . . . Western Bancorporation (NYSE symbol)
WBC. . . . . . . Westinghouse Broadcasting Company
WBC. . . . . . . White Blood Cell (or Corpuscle), or White Blood-Cell Count (Medicine)
WBC . . . . . . Wideband Coupler
WBC . . . . . . Wien Bridge Circuit
WBC. . . . . . . Wilkes-Barre Connecting R. R. (AAR code)
WBC. . . . . . . World Boxing Council
WBCA . . . . . Wyandotte Bantam Club of America
WBCCI . . . . . Wally Byam Caravan Club International (Organization of Airstream trailer owners)
WBCO . . . . . Wallace Barnes Company
WBCT . . . . . Wideband Current Transformer
WBD. . . . . . . Wideband Data
WBDJ . . . . . Weltbund der Demokratischen Jugend
WBDL . . . . . Wideband Data Link
WBF . . . . Wood Block Floor (Technical drawings)
WBFA . . . . . Workmen's Benefit Fund of the USA
WBFA . . . . . Western Bohemian Fraternal Association
WBFP . . . . . Wood-Burning Fireplace
WBGT. . . . . Wet Bulb Globe Temperature
WBH . . . . . . Welsh Board of Health
WBHO . . . . . Weather Bureau Hurricane Forecast Office
WBI . . . . Ward Behavior Inventory
WBI . . . . Will Be Issued
WBI . . . . . . Wooden Box Institute
WBL . . . . . . Welbilt Corporation (NYSE symbol)
WBL. . . . . . . Western Biological Laboratories
WBL. . . . . . . Wideband LASER
WBL. . . . . . . Wood Blocking
WBLC . . . . . Water-Borne Logistics Craft
WBM . . . . . . Woman's Board of Missions
WBMA . . . . . Wirebound Box Manufacturers Association
WBMC . . . . . Weight Before Mars Capture (NASA)
WBMCR . . . . Wideband Multi-Channel Receiver
WBMO . . . . . Weather Bureau (later, National Weather Service) Meteorological Observation Station
WBN . . . . . . Well Behaved Net
WBN . . . . . . West by North
WBNL . . . . . Wideband Noise Limiting
WBNS . . . . . Water Boiler Neutron Source (Reactor) (AEC)

WBNV . . . . . . Wideband Noise Voltage
WBO. . . . . . . Weather Bureau Office (Later, National Weather Service)
WBO. . . . . . . Wideband Oscilloscope
WBO . . . . . . Wideband Overlap
WBO . . . . . . Wien Bridge Oscillator
WBP . . . . . . Wartime Basic Plan
WBR . . . . . . Warner Brothers Company (NYSE symbol) (Delisted)
WBR . . . . . . Water Boiler Reactor
WBR . . . . . . Whole Body Radiation
WBR . . . . . . Wideband Receiver
WBRBN . . . . . Will Be Reported by NOTAM (Notice to Airmen)
WBRH . . . . . . Weather Bureau (Later, National Weather Service), Regional Headquarters
WBRO . . . . . Weather Bureau (Later, National Weather Service), Regional Office
WBS. . . . . . . West by South
WBS . . . . . . Without Benefit of Salvage
WBS . . . . . . Work Breakdown Structure
WB-S . . . . . . Wage Board, Supervisor (Civil Service classification)
WBSA . . . . . Weather Bureau (later, National Weather Service) Synoptic and Aviation Reporting Station
WBSCB . . . . . Work Breakdown Structure Control Board (Army)
WBSI . . . . . . Western Behavioral Sciences Institute (La Jolla, California)
WBSP . . . . . Western Beet Sugar Producers (Defunct)
WBT . . . . Wet Bulb Temperature
WBT . . . . . . Wideband Transmitter (or Transformer)
WBTC . . . . . Waterways Bulk Transportation Council
WBTE . . . . . Weapon Battery Terminal Equipment (Air Force)
WBTS . . . . . Waco, Beaumont, Trinity & Sabine Railway Company (AAR code)
WBTV . . . . . Weather Briefing Television
WBV. . . . . . . Wideband Voltage
WBVCO . . . . . Wideband Voltage Controlled Oscillator
WC . . . . Wage Change
WC . . . . War Cabinet
WC . . . . War College
WC . . . . War Communications
WC . . . . Water Closet (A toilet)
WC . . . . Weapon Carrier
WC . . . . Weapons Command (Army)
WC . . . . West Central (London postal district)
WC . . . . West Coast Airlines, Inc.
WC . . . . Western Command
WC . . . . Wheel Chair
WC . . . . Width Codes
WC . . . . Will Call
WC . . . . Without Charge
WC . . . . Women's Reserve, Communications Duties (USNR officer designation)
WC . . . . Wood Casing
WC . . . . Work Card
WC . . . . Work Center
WC . . . . Work Circle
WC . . . . Work Control
WC . . . . Working Capital
WC . . . . Working Circle (Technical drawings)
WC . . . . Workmen's Compensation
WC . . . . Write and Compute
W/C . . . . Watts Per Candle (Electricity)
W/C . . . . Wave Change
WCA . . . . . . Weimaraner Club of America
WCA . . . . . . West Coast Airlines, Inc.
WCA . . . . . . Western College Association
WCA . . . . . . Wideband Cassegrain Antenna
WCA . . . . . . Women's Christian Association
WCA . . . . . . Workmen's Compensation Act
WCA . . . . . . World Campus Afloat (Cruise ship educational program)
WCA . . . . . . Worst Case Analysis
WCAB . . . . . Working Committee of the Aeronautical Board
WCAFS . . . . . Wideband Cassegrain Antenna Feed System
WCAI . . . . . . Water Conditioning Association International
WCAP . . . . . Westinghouse Commercial Atomic Power
WCASS . . . . . World Conference of Ashkenazi and Sephardi Synagogues
WCBSU . . . . . West Coast Base Service Unit (Navy)
WCC . . . . . . War Claims Commission (Abolished, 1954)
WCC . . . . . . Water-Cooled Copper
WCC . . . . . . Westchester Community College (New York)
WCC . . . . . . Western Carolina College (North Carolina)
WCC . . . . . . Westminster Choir College (New Jersey)
WCC . . . . . . Widows Consultation Center
WCC . . . . . . Wilson Cloud Chamber
WCC . . . . . . Work Control Center
WCC . . . . . . World Council of Churches
WCCA . . . . . West Coast Crossarm Association
WCCA . . . . . . Whiteruthenian (Byelorussian) Congress Committee of America

WCCA ...... Whooping Crane Conservation Association
WCCA ...... Worst Case Circuit Analysis
WCCC ...... Wayne County Community College (Michigan)
WCCE ...... West Coast Commodity Exchange
WCCE ...... World Council of Christian Education
WCCESSA .... World Council of Christian Education and Sunday School Association
WCCMORS .... West Coast Classified Military Operations Research Symposium
WCD .... Weapons Classification Defects (Navy)
WCD .... Work Center Description
WCD .... Workshop for Cultural Democracy
WCDB ...... Wing Control During Boost
WCDC ...... West Coast (Naval Publications) Distribution Center
WCDFMA .... Water Cooler and Drinking Fountain Manufacturers Association
WCDO ...... War Consumable Distribution Objective
WCE .... Waste Calcining Facility (AEC)
WCE .... Weapon Control Equipment
WCEMA ..... West Coast Electronic Manufacturers' Association
WCEU ...... World's Christian Endeavor Union
WCF .... Waste Calcination Facility (AEC)
WCF .... Water Conditioning Foundation
WCF .... White Cathode Follower
WCF .... World Congress of Faiths
WCF .... World Congress of Flight
WCFA ...... Wholesale Commission Florists of America
WCFPR ..... Washington Center of Foreign Policy Research
WCG .... Water-Cooled Garment
WCG .... Worldwide Church of God
WCGZ ...... World Confederation of General Zionists
WCH .... West Coast Handling
WCHEN ..... Western Council on Higher Education for Nursing
WCHI ...... Women's Council for the Histadrut in Israel
WCI .... Warner Communications (NYSE symbol) (Formerly, KNS)
WCI .... White Cast Iron
WCJC ...... Webster City Junior College (Iowa)
WCJC ...... Wharton County Junior College (Texas)
WCJE ...... World Council on Jewish Education
WCL .... World Confederation of Labour
WCL .... Wright Center of Laboratories
WCLA ...... West Coast Lumbermen's Association
WCLD ...... Water Cooled
WCLIB ..... West Coast Lumber Inspection Bureau
WCM .... Welded Cordwood Module
WCM .... Wired-Core Matrix
WCM .... Wired-Core Memory
WCM .... Word Combine and Multiplexer
WCMA ...... West Coast Mineral Association
WCMIA ..... West Coast Metal Importers Association
WCMR ...... Western Contract Management Region (Air Force)
WCO .... Western Coordination Office (NASA) (Now, Western Operations Office)
WCOF ...... Women's Catholic Order of Foresters
WCOTP ..... World Confederation of Organizations of the Teaching Profession
          (Also known as CMOPE)
WCP .... War Control Planners (An organization)
WCP .... Weapon Control Panel (Aviation)
WCP .... Welder Control Panel
WCP .... White Combination Potentiometer
WCP .... Wing Chord Plane
WCP .... Work Control Plan
WCPA ...... World Constitution and Parliament Association
WCPAB ..... War Contracts Price Adjustment Board (All functions dispersed, 1951)
WCPC ...... Weatherford College of Parker County (Texas)
WCPT ...... World Confederation for Physical Therapy
WCR .... Water-Cooled Reactor
WCR .... Water-Cooled Rod
WCR .... Watercooler
WCR .... Western Communication Region (Air Force)
WCR .... Wire Contact Relay
WCR .... Word Control Register
WCRA ...... Weather Control Research Association
WCRC ...... Water Conditioning Research Council
WCRSI ..... Western Concrete Reinforcing Steel Institute
WCS .... Weapons Control System
WCS .... White Cross Stores, Inc. (NYSE symbol)
WCS .... Writable Control Storage (Data processing)
WCSA ...... West Coast of South America
WCSI ...... World Centre for Scientific Information
WCSPA ..... West Coast Shrimp Producers Association
WCSS ...... Weapons Control System Simulator
WCSS ...... West Coast Sound School
WCT .... World Championship Tennis, Inc.
WCT .... Worthy Chief Templar

WCTU ...... Women's Christian Temperance Union
WCTU ...... Women's Connubial Temperance Union (Satirical)
WCU .... Water Cooler Unit
WCU .... West Coast University (California)
WCU .... Western Catholic Union
WCV .... Water Check Valve
WCW .... Western College for Women (Ohio)
WCW .... Wood Casement Window (Technical drawings)
WCWB ...... World Council for the Welfare of the Blind
WC/WO ..... Working Committee on Weather Operations
WD .... Decisions Won (Boxing)
WD .... (Qualified for) Deck Watch (USNR officer classification)
WD .... War Damage
WD. .... War Department (Created, 1789; became Department of the Army, 1947)
WD. .... Ward Foods, Inc. (NYSE symbol)
WD. .... Water Desurger
WD .... Weapon Director (SAGE)
WD .... Weather Division (Air Force)
WD .... Web Depth
WD .... Well Deck
WD .... Wet Dressing
WD .... When Directed
WD .... When Discovered
WD .... When Distributed (NYSE symbol)
WD .... Whole Depth
WD .... Wind Direction
WD .... Window Detector
WD .... Window Dimension (Technical drawings)
WD .... Withdrawn
WD .... Wood
WD .... Wood Door (Technical drawings)
WD .... Word Display
WD .... Work(ing) Day
WD .... Works Department
W/D. ...... Withdrawn
WDA .... Weapons Defended Area
WDA .... Western District Area (Air Force)
WDA .... Wheel Drive Assembly
WDA .... Wildlife Disease Association
WDA .... Withdrawal of Availability (Military)
WDAF ...... Western Desert Air Force
WDAHAC .... National Society Women Descendants of the Ancient and Honorable
          Artillery Company
WDB. ...... Wide Deadband (NASA)
WDC .... War Damage Commission (British)
WDC .... War Damage Corporation (World War II)
WDC .... Washington Document Center
WDC .... Western Defense Command (Army)
WDC .... Westinghouse Defense Center
WDC .... Wideband Directional Coupler
WDC .... World Data Center (National Academy of Sciences)
WDC .... World Development Corporation
WDC-A ..... World Data Center A
WDC-B ..... World Data Center B
WDCS ...... Women's Division of Christian Service (of the Board of Missions, The
          Methodist Church)
WDCSA ..... War Department Chief of Staff, US Army (Obsolete)
WDD .... Western Development Division (ARDC)
WDE. ...... Weapon Direction Equipment (Navy)
WDE .... Weapons Direction Evaluation
WDF. ...... Weapon Defense Facility
WDF. ...... Wood Door and Frame (Technical drawings)
WD/FE ..... Water Dispenser/Fire Extinguisher (Apollo) (NASA)
WDGF ...... War Department Ground Forces (Obsolete)
WDGI ...... Wholesale Dry Goods Institute
WDGO ...... War Department General Order (Obsolete)
WDGS ...... War Department General Staff (Obsolete)
WDHCB ..... War Department Hardship Claims Board (Obsolete)
WDI .... War Department Intelligence (Obsolete)
WDI .... Warhead Detection Indicator
WDI .... Weapon Data Index (Navy)
WDI .... Web Depth Index
WDI .... Wind Direction Indicator (Aviation)
WDI .... Wood and Iron (Freight)
WDL. ...... Wave-Guide Directional Localizer
WDL .... Western Development Laboratories
WDL .... Wien Displacement Law
WDL .... Wireless Data Link
WDL .... Workers' Defense League
WDM .... S.S. White Dental Mfg. Company (NYSE symbol) (Delisted)
WDM .... Wavelength Division Multiplex

ACRONYMS AND INITIALISMS DICTIONARY

WDM . . . . Weight after Departure from Mars (NASA)
WDMA . . . . . . Wholesale Druggists Merchandising Association
WDMB . . . . . . War Department Manpower Board (Obsolete)
WDMF . . . . . . Weak Disordered Magnetic Field
WDMO . . . . . . Weight before Departure from Mars Orbit (NASA)
WDO . . . . Web Depth Order
WDP. . . . . Weapons Direction Program
WDP. . . . . Wenner Difference Potentiometer
WDP. . . . . Wood Panel
WDP. . . . . Work Distribution Policy
WDPC. . . . . . . Western Data Processing Center
WDPMG-ID . . War Department Provost Marshal General, Investigation Division (Obsolete)
WDR . . . . Write Drum
WDS . . . . Weapons Designation (or Delivery) Systems
WDS . . . . Weapons Direction System
WDS . . . . Wood Dye Stain
WDS . . . . Woods Corp. (NYSE symbol)
WDS . . . . Word Discrimination Score
WDSS . . . . . . War Department Special Staff (Obsolete)
WDT. . . . . Warmth Detection Threshold
WDTC . . . . . . Western Defense Tactical Command
WDU . . . . Window Deicing Unit
WDV . . . . War Department Vehicle (Obsolete)
WDW . . . . . . Wholesale Dealer in Wines
WDW . . . . . . Wood and Wire (Freight)
WDYT. . . . . . What Do You Think
WDYTYCIWSS . . Why Don't You Take Your Change In War Savings Stamps (Cashier's sign) (World War II)
WE. . . . . War Establishment
WE. . . . . Watch Error (Navigation)
WE. . . . . Western Electric
WE. . . . . With Equipment (Army)
WE. . . . . Withholding Exemptions (Army)
WE. . . . . Women's Reserve, Engineering Duties (USNR officer designation)
WE . . . . World Education, Inc.
W/E . . . . Week Ending
WEA . . . . Wall Effect Amplifier
WEA . . . . Workers' Educational Association
WEAL . . . . . . Women's Equity Action League
WEAPD . . . . . . Western Air Procurement District
WEARCON . . . Weather Observation and Forecasting Control System
WEB. . . . . Wagner Earth Bridge
WEB . . . . War Engineering Board
WEB . . . . Webbing
WEBROCK . . . . Weather Buoy Rocket
WEBS . . . . Weapons Effectiveness Buoy System
WEC . . . . Wagner Electric Corporation (NYSE symbol) (Delisted)
WEC . . . . Warhead Electrical Connector
WEC. . . . . Westinghouse Electric Corporation (Also, WECO, WESCO)
WEC . . . . Whole Earth Catalog (A publication)
WEC. . . . . World Energy Conference
WEC . . . . Worldwide Evangelization Crusade
WECB . . . . . . Weapons Evaluation and Control Bureau (USACDA)
WECEN. . . . . . Weather Center (Air Force)
WECO. . . . . . . Western Electric Company
WECO. . . . . . . Westinghouse Electric Corporation (Also, WEC, WESCO)
WECOM . . . . . Weapons Command (Army)
WED. . . . . Weapons Engineering Duty (Navy)
WED. . . . . Wednesday
WEDAC . . . . . Westinghouse Digital Airborne Computer
WEDGE . . . . . Waterless Electrical Data Generating Effortless
WEDGE. . . . . . Weapon Development Glide Entry
WEDS . . . . . . Weapons Effect Display System (AEC)
WEE. . . . . Western Equine Encephalitis (Veterinary medicine)
WEEF . . . . . . Western Electric Educational Fund
WEF . . . . War Emergency Formula
WEF . . . . With Effect From
WEF . . . . World Education Fellowship
WEF . . . . World Evangelical Fellowship
WEFAX . . . . . Weather Facsimile Experiment (Environmental Science Services Administration)
WEFT . . . . . . Wings, Engines, Fuselage, Tail (System for identifying aircraft)
WE-H . . . . . . Weapons Employment Handbook (DASA)
WEI . . . . World Education, Incorporated
WEIU . . . . . . Women's Educational and Industrial Union
WEL . . . . Weapons/Equipment List
WEM . . . . . . Welfare of Enlisted Men (Air Force)
WEM . . . . . . West Essex Militia (British)
WEMA . . . . . Western Electronic Manufacturers Association
WEMA . . . . . Woven Elastic Manufacturers Association

WEMD . . . . . . Western Electronics Maintenance Depot
WEN . . . . Wien Alaska Airlines
WENOA . . . . . Weekly Notice to Airmen (FAA)
WEO . . . . Warehouse Economy Outlet (A & P Co.)
WEO. . . . . Where Economy Originates (A&P marketing slogan)
WEP . . . . Water Electrolysis Plenum
WEP . . . . Water-Extended Polyester
WEP . . . . Wisconsin Experiments Package
WEPA . . . . . . Welded Electronic Packaging Association
WEPCOSE . . . . Weapon Control Systems Engineering (Navy)
WEPSO . . . . . Naval Weapons Services Office (Also known as NWSO and NAVWPNSERVO)
WEPTU . . . . . Weapons Reserve Training Units (Navy)
WER . . . . Water Electrolysis Rocket
WERS . . . . . . War Emergency Radio Service
WERTS . . . . . Writers' Ever-Ready Textual Service (Rent-A-Script) (Satirical)
WES . . . . Water Electrolysis System
WES . . . . Waterways Experiment Station (of Army Corps of Engineers)
WES. . . . . Weather Editing Section (FAA)
WESA . . . . . . White Sands National Monument
WESCAR . . . . Western Carolines (Navy)
WESCARSUBAREA . . Western Carolines Subarea (Navy)
WESCO . . . . . Walnut Export Sales Company
WESCO. . . . . . Westinghouse Corporation (Also, WEC, WECO)
WESCOBASESERVUNIT. . West Coast Base Service Unit (Navy)
WESCOM . . . . Weapons System Cost Model
WESCON. . . . . Western Electronics Show and Convention (IEEE)
WESCOSOUNDSCOL. . West Coast Sound School (Navy)
WESED . . . . . . Weapons System Evaluation Division (DOD)
WESEG . . . . . Weapons Systems Evaluation Group (DOD)
WESO. . . . . . . Weapons Engineering Service Office (DOD)
W/E & SP . . . . With Equipment and Spare Parts
WESPAC . . . . . Western Pacific (Area) (Navy)
WESRAC . . . . . Western Research Application Center (University of Southern California)
WESSEAFRON . . Western Sea Frontier (Navy)
WEST . . . . . . Western Educational Society for Telecommunications
WEST . . . . . . Western Energy Supply & Transmission Associates
WEST . . . . . . Western Transportation Company (AAR code)
WEST . . . . . . Women's Enlisted Screening Test (Air Force)
WESTAF . . . . . Western Transport Air Force
WESTAR . . . . Waterways Experiment Station Terrain Analyzer RADAR
WESTCOMMRGN . . Western Communications Region
WESTE . . . . . . Weapons Effectiveness and System Test Environment (Air Force)
WESTLANT. . . . Western Atlantic Area
WESTNAVELEX . . Naval Electronics Systems Command; Western Division; Mare Island; Vallejo, Calif.
WESTOMP . . . . Western Ocean Meeting Point
WESTPAC . . . . Western Pacific Railroad
WESTPACBACOM . . Western Pacific Base Command (Navy)
WESTT . . . . . Weapon System Tactical Tester
WESYP . . . . . Weapons System Plan (Navy)
WET . . . . Weapons Effectiveness Testing
WET . . . . Wet Environment Trainer (Navy)
WETAC . . . . . Westinghouse Electronic Tubeless Analog Computer
WETARFAC . . . Work Element Timer and Recorder for Automatic Computing
WETM . . . . . Weather Team (Air Force)
WEU. . . . . Western European Union (NATO)
WEW . . . . Western Electronic Week
WEW. . . . . . . White Stores, Inc. (NYSE symbol) (Delisted)
WEWAS. . . . . . Water Equipment Wholesalers and Suppliers (Formerly, WEWSA)
WEWSA. . . . . . Water Equipment Wholesalers and Suppliers Association (Later, WEWAS)
WEY. . . . . Weyenberg Shoe Manufacturing Company (NYSE symbol)
WEZU. . . . . . . Witterungseinfluesse und Zeitunterschied (Weather factors and time difference) (German military – World War II)
WF. . . . . Wallace Business Forms, Inc. (NYSE symbol)
WF. . . . . Wash Fountain
WF. . . . . Water Filter
WF. . . . . Water Finish
WF. . . . . Western Folklore (Journal)
WF . . . . White Fathers
WF. . . . . White Female
WF. . . . . Won on Foul (Boxing)
WF. . . . . Write Forward
WF. . . . . Wrong Font (Typesetting) (Proofreader's mark)
W & F . . . . . . Water and Feed
WFA . . . . War Food Administration (Determined military, civilian, and foreign requirements for human and animal food, and for food used industrially) (World War II) (Terminated 1945)
WFA . . . . Western Falconry Association
WFA. . . . . White Fish Authority (British)
WFA . . . . Wide-Frequency Antenna

619

WFA . . . . World Friendship Association
WFB . . . . World Fellowship of Buddhists
WFBI . . . . . . Wood Fiber Blanket Institute
WFBMA . . . . . Woven Fabric Belting Manufacturers Association
WFC . . . . Committee on the World Food Crisis
WFC . . . . Wake Forest College (North Carolina)
WFC . . . . Walleye Filter Changer
WFC. . . . . . . War Finance Committee
WFC . . . . Weld Flange Connection
WFC. . . . . . . Wells Fargo & Company (NYSE symbol)
WFC . . . . Western Forestry Center
WFC. . . . . . . Wolf First Class (A philanderer) (Slang)
WFCA . . . . . . Western Forestry and Conservation Association
WFCMV . . . . . Wheeled Fuel-Consuming Motor Vehicle
WFCY . . . . World Federation of Catholic Youth
WFCYWG . . . . World Federation of Catholic Young Women and Girls (Later, WFCY)
WFD. . . . . . . World Federation of the Deaf
WFDY . . . . World Federation of Democratic Youth
WFE . . . . With Food Element
WFEA . . . . . . World Federation of Educational Associations
WFEB . . . . Worcester Foundation for Experimental Biology
WFEO . . . . . . World Federation of Engineering Organizations
WFEX . . . . . . Western Fruit Express
WFF . . . . World Friendship Federation
WFG . . . . Wave Form Generator
WFH. . . . . . . World Federation of Hemophilia
WFHJ . . . . World Federation of Hungarian Jews
WFI . . . . Wheat Flour Institute
WFI . . . . Wheelabrator-Frye (NYSE symbol)
WFI . . . . Wood Flooring Institute of America
WFIA . . . . . . Western Forest Industries Association
WFL. . . . . . . Woman's Freedom League
WFL. . . . . . . Wredemann-Frang Law
WFM . . . . . . Water Flow Meter
WFM . . . . . . Wave Form Monitor
WFM . . . . . . Wave-Guide Frequency Meter
WFM . . . . . . Western Federation of Miners
WFMH . . . . . . World Federation for Mental Health
WFN . . . . . . Weapons and Facilities, Navy
WFN . . . . . . Well Formed Net
WFN . . . . . . World Federation of Neurology
WFNA . . . . . . White Fuming Nitric Acid
WFNS . . . . . . World Federation of Neurosurgical Societies
WFO . . . . . . Wide Field Optics
WFOF. . . . . . Wide Field Optical Filter
WFOT. . . . . . World Federation of Occupational Therapists
WFP . . . . Warm Front(al) Passage (Meteorology)
WFP . . . . Wearout Failure Period
WFP. . . . . . . World Food Program (UN)
WFP. . . . . . . Worldwide Fast for Peace
WFPA . . . . . . World Federation for the Protection of Animals (Also known as FMPA and WTB)
WFPS . . . . . . Wild Flower Preservation Society
WFPT . . . . . . World Federation for Physical Therapy
WFS . . . . Wood Furring Strips (Technical drawings)
WFS . . . . Work Function Surface
WFS . . . . World Future Society
WFSA . . . . . . Wash Frock Salesmen's Association
WFSA . . . . . . World Federation of Societies of Anesthesiologists
WFSEC . . . . . . World Fellowship of Slavic Evangelical Christians
WFSt . . . . Wehrmachtfuehrungsstab (Armed Forces Operations Staff, German) (World War II)
WFSW. . . . . . World Federation of Scientific Workers
WFTC . . . . . . Western Flying Training Command (AAFWFTC)
WFTD . . . . . . Women's Flying Training Detachment (World War II)
WFTU . . . . . . World Federation of Trade Unions
WFU. . . . . . . War Frauds Unit
WFUNA . . . . . World Federation of United Nations Associations
WFY-USA . . . . World Federalist Youth - United States of America
WG . . . . Wartime Guidance (Air Force)
WG . . . . Water Gage
WG . . . . Wave-Guide
WG . . . . Weight Guaranteed
WG . . . . Welsh Guards (British military)
WG . . . . West German(ic)
WG . . . . Window Guard
WG . . . . Wine Gallon
WG . . . . Wing
WG . . . . Wire Gauge
WG . . . . With Grain
WG . . . . Working Group

4WG. . . . . . . Weather Group (4th) (Washington, DC) (Air Force)
WGA . . . . . . Wave-Guide Assembly
WGA . . . . . . Western Growers Association
WGA . . . . . . Wheat Germ Agglutinin (Biochemistry)
WGAE . . . . . . Writers Guild of America, East
WGAF . . . . . . West Germany Air Force
WGAW . . . . . . Writers Guild of America, West
WGB . . . . Weltgewerkschaftsbund (World Federation of Trade Unions)
WGC . . . . West Georgia College
WGC . . . . Western Gear Corporation
WGC . . . . World Gospel Crusades
WGC . . . . Worthy Grand Chaplain (Masonry)
WGCL . . . . . . Window Glass Cutters League of America
WGDA . . . . . . Watermelon Growers and Distributors Association
WGDL . . . . . . Wave-Guide Delay Line
WGDS . . . . . . Warm Gas Distribution System
WGEEIA . . . . . Western Ground Electronics Engineering Installation Agency
WGER . . . . . . Working Group on Extraterrestrial Resources (NASA)
WGETS . . . . . . Wayne George Encoder Test Set
WGF . . . . Wave-Guide Filter
WGF . . . . Wound Glass Fiber
WGFAR . . . . . Wenner-Gren Foundation for Anthropological Research
WGG . . . . Worthy Grand Guardian (Masonry)
WGI . . . . Work Glove Institute
WGI . . . . World Geophysical Interval
WGII . . . . Working Group on Internal Instrumentation (NASA)
WGJ . . . . Worm Gear Jack
WGL . . . . Washington Gas Light Company (NYSE symbol)
WGL . . . . Wave-Guide Load
WGL . . . . Weapons Guidance Laboratory
WGL . . . . Wire Gloss
WGL . . . . Wissenschaftliche Gesellschaft fuer Luftschiffahrt
WGM . . . . . . Wave-Guide Meter
WGM . . . . . . Weighted Guidelines Method (Navy)
WGM . . . . . . World Gospel Mission
WGMA . . . . . . Washington Gallery of Modern Art
WGMA . . . . . . Wet Ground Mica Association
WGNL . . . . . . Wave-Guide Nitrogen Load
WGO . . . . Wehrmacht-Graeberoffizier (Armed forces graves registration officer) (German military - World War II)
WGO . . . . Winnebago Industries, Inc. (NYSE symbol)
WGp . . . . Weather Group (Air Force)
WGP . . . . Wire Grid Polarizer
WGPMS . . . . . Warehousing Gross Performance Measurement System
WGR . . . . War Guidance Requirements
WGR . . . . Water Graphite Reactor Experiment (AEC)
WGR . . . . Working Group Report
WGS . . . . Wave-Guide Glide Slope
WGS . . . . Web Guide System
WGS . . . . World Government Sponsors
WGSIM . . . . . . Working Group on Satellite Ionospheric Measurements (NASA)
WGSJ . . . . . . Worm Gear Screw Jack
WGTC . . . . . . Working Group on Tracking and Computation (NASA)
WG-T-C . . . . . Wave-Guide-to-Coaxial (Aerospace)
WGW . . . . . . Wave-Guide Window
WH . . . . Wall Hydrant
WH . . . . Warhead
WH . . . . Water Heater
WH . . . . Watt-Hour(s)
WH. . . . . Wehrmacht-Heer (Marking on Army vehicles) (German military - World War II)
WH . . . . Western Hemisphere
WH . . . . White House
WH . . . . White Motor Company (NYSE symbol)
WH . . . . Withholding
W/H . . . . Withholding
WHA . . . . Washington Headquarters Association
WHA . . . . Weld Head Assembly
WHA . . . . Western History Association
WHA . . . . World Hockey Association
WHAM . . . . . . Winning the Hearts and Minds (of the people) (Vietnam pacification program)
WHAM . . . . . . Work Handling and Maintenance (Navy)
WHAP. . . . . . When (or Where) Applicable
WHASA . . . . . White House Army Signal Agency
WHB. . . . . . . The Wandering Hand Brigade (Men who are likely to take liberties with women)
WHBL . . . . . . World Home Bible League
WHBMA . . . . . Wood Hat Block Manufacturers Association
WHCA . . . . . . White House Communications Agency
WHCA . . . . . . White House Correspondents Association

ACRONYMS AND INITIALISMS DICTIONARY

WHD . . . . Wage and Hour Division (Department of Labor)
WHD . . . . Warhead
WHD. . . . . Weatherhead Co. (NYSE symbol)
WHD . . . . Western Hemisphere Defense
WHDM . . . . . . Watt Hour Demand Meter
WHDS . . . . . . Warhead Section (Military)
WHE . . . . Water Hammer Eliminator
WHECON . . . . Wheel Control
WHF. . . . . World Heritage Fund (UNESCO)
WHHA . . . . . . White House Historical Association
WHI . . . . Weekly Hospital Indemnity
WHI . . . . Western Highway Institute
WHIA . . . . . . Woolen Hosiery Institute of America
WHIM. . . . . . . Women Happy in Minis (Boise, Idaho, group opposing below-the-knee fashions introduced in 1970)
WHIP . . . . Wideband High Intercept Probability
WHIS . . . . . . Whiskeytown-Shasta-Trinity National Recreation Area
WHIST. . . . . . Worldwide Household Goods Information System for Traffic Management (Army)
WHL. . . . . Western Hockey League
WHL. . . . . Wheel
WHL. . . . . World Heritage List (UNESCO)
WHM . . . . . . Watt-Hour Meter
WHMA . . . . . . Women's Home Mission Association
WHMAA . . . . . Wool Hat Manufacturers Association of America
WHMI . . . . . . Whitman Mission National Historic Site
WHNPA . . . . . White House News Photographers Association
WHO . . . . War on Hunger Office (Department of State)
WHO . . . . White House Office
WHO . . . . . . World Health Organization (The pronunciation "who" is not acceptable) (United Nations affiliate)
WHO . . . . World Housing Organization
WHOI. . . . . . . Woods Hole Oceanographic Institution
WHP. . . . . Water Horsepower
WHP. . . . . White House Police Force (Later, Executive Protection Service)
WHPC . . . . . . Wage Hour and Public Contracts Divisions (Department of Labor)
WHPCD. . . . . . Wage and Hour and Public Contracts Divisions (Department of Labor)
WHR . . . . Waste Heat Removal
WHR. . . . . Watt-Hour
WHR . . . . Western Hemisphere Reserve
WHR. . . . . Whirlpool Corporation (NYSE symbol)
W-HR . . . . . . Watt Hour
WHRA . . . . . . Western Historical Research Associates
WHRC . . . . . . Washington Home Rule Committee
WHRC . . . . . . World Health Research Center
WHS . . . . Water Hydraulic Section
WHSE . . . . . . Warehouse
WHSS . . . . . . White House Signal Support
WHT. . . . . White
WHU . . . . Well Head Unit
WHWTCA . . . . West Highland White Terrier Club of America
WHX . . . . Wheeling-Pittsburgh Steel Corporation (NYSE symbol)
WI . . . . Oak Harbor, Whidbey Island, Washington (Naval base)
WI . . . . Wallops Island (off coast of Virginia)
WI . . . . Water Injection
WI . . . . West India
WI . . . . West Indies or West Indian
WI . . . . When Issued (NYSE symbol)
WI . . . . Wine Institute
WI . . . . Wisconsin
WI . . . . Within
WI . . . . Women's Institute (British)
WI . . . . Women's Reserve, Intelligence Duties (USNR officer designation)
WI . . . . Word Intelligibility
WI . . . . Wrought Iron
W & I . . . . . . Weighing and Inspection
WIA . . . . Wounded in Action (Military)
WIAP . . . . Wartime Individual Augmentation Program (Military)
WIAP . . . . Westinghouse Industrial Atomic Power
WIAS . . . . Whiteruthenian Institute of Arts and Science
WIB . . . . Weather Information Branch (Air Force)
WIBC . . . . Woman's International Bowling Congress
WIBIS . . . . . . Will Be Issued
WIC . . . . Washington International Center
WIC. . . . . . . Wax Insulating Compound
WIC. . . . . . . Windsor Institute of Complementology
WICA . . . . . . While in Control Area (Aviation)
WICA . . . . . . Wind Cave National Park
WICHIE. . . . . . Western Interstate Commission for Higher Education
WICR . . . . . . Wilson's Creek Battlefield National Park
WICS . . . . . . Women in Community Service (An organization)

WICZ . . . . . . While in Control Zone (Aviation)
WID . . . . Wean United, Inc. (NYSE symbol)
WID . . . . West India Dock
WIDF . . . . . . Women's International Democratic Federation
WIE . . . . Wiebolt Stores, Inc. (NYSE symbol)
WIE . . . . With Immediate Effect
WIEU . . . . . . Weekly Intelligence Estimate Update (Vietnam)
WIF . . . . West India Fruit & Steamship Company, Inc. (AAR code)
WIF . . . . West Indies Federation
WIG. . . . . . . Wing in Ground
WIGO . . . . . . What Is Going On? (Humorous definition of science)
WIL . . . . Ward Indicator Light
WIL . . . . White Indicating Light
WIL . . . . Wilson & Company, Inc. (American Stock Exchange symbol)
WILCO . . . . . Will Comply (Used after "Roger") (Radio term)
WILL . . . . . . Workshop Institute for Living-Learning
WILPF . . . . . . Women's International League for Peace and Freedom
WIM . . . . Washington, Idaho & Montana Railway Company (AAR code)
WIMA . . . . . . Writing Instrument Manufacturers Association
WIMC . . . . . . Whom It May Concern
WIMS . . . . . . Wartime Instruction Manual for Merchant Ships (For deck officers of the United States Merchant Marine; popularly known as the "Convoy Bible") (World War II)
WIMS . . . . . . Wave-Guide Impedance Measuring Set
WIMSA . . . . . Webster Institute for Mathematics, Science and Arts (Webster College)
WIN. . . . . . . Water-Insoluble Nitrogen (Fertilizer)
WIN. . . . . . . Weapons Interception (Military electronics)
WIN. . . . . . . Western Information Network
WIN. . . . . . . Winn-Dixie Stores, Inc. (NYSE symbol)
WIN. . . . . . . Work Incentive Program (Department of Labor)
WIN. . . . . . . Workshop in Nonviolence
WINA . . . . . . Webb Institute of Naval Architecture
WINA . . . . . . Witton Network Analyzer
WINC . . . . . . Western Interstate Nuclear Compact
WIND. . . . . . . Weather Information Network and Display
WINDEE . . . . Wind Tunnel Data Encoding and Evaluation (System) (Boeing Co.)
WINDS . . . . . Weather Information Network & Display System
WINE . . . . . . Webb Institute of Naval Engineering
WINKS . . . . . Women in Numerous Kitchens (World War II)
WINS . . . . . . Weapons and Integrated Navigation System
WINS . . . . . . Women in National Service (Name given by Ladies' Home Journal to American housewives and their teen-age daughters, "the greatest reserve strength of America") (World War II)
WINS . . . . . . Women's Industrial and National Service Corps (British) (World War II)
WIO. . . . . . . Women's International ORT
WIP . . . . Weapons Installation Plan (Navy)
WIP . . . . Work in Progress
WIPIS . . . . . . Who Is Publishing in Science (An Institute for Scientific Information publication) (Trademark)
WIPO . . . . . . World Intellectual Property Organization (Formerly, BIRPI)
WIPS . . . . . . Women in Production Service (A voluntary, semimilitary organization of women employees, primarily at the E.I. duPont de Nemours and Company, at Richmond, Va.) (World War II)
WIR . . . . Weapons Inspection Report (Navy)
WIR . . . . Weekly Intelligence Review
WIR . . . . West India Regiment
WIRDS . . . . . Weather Information Remoting and Display System
WIRE . . . . . . Weapons Interference Reduction Effort (Navy)
WIRES . . . . . Women in Radio and Electrical Service (World War II)
WIRF. . . . . . . Women's International Religious Fellowship
WIS . . . . Washington Inventory Service
WIS . . . . Weather Information Service (Air Force)
WIS . . . . Wisconsin
WISA . . . . . . West Indian Students Association
WISA . . . . . . Wholesale Interservice Supply Agreement (Military)
WISARD . . . . Wideband System for Acquiring and Recording Data
WISC . . . . . . Wechsler Intelligence Scale for Children (Education)
WISC . . . . . . Wisconsin
WISE . . . . . . Wholesalers Institutional Service Extension (Division of National American Wholesale Grocers Association)
WISP. . . . . . . Widerange Imaging Spectrophotometer (Naval Oceanographic Office)
WISP . . . . . . Women Strike for Peace
WISS . . . . . . Weekly Induction Scheduling System (Navy)
WISSA . . . . . Wholesale Interservice Supply Support Agreements (Military)
WIT . . . . Washington Institute of Technology
WIT . . . . Wisconsin Institute of Technology
WIT . . . . Witco Chemical Company, Inc. (NYSE symbol)
WITCH . . . . . Women Incensed Over Traditional Coed Hoopla (Feminist group)
WITCH . . . . . Women's International Terrorist Conspiracy from Hell (Feminist group)
WITNESS . . . . Wire Installation Tester for Negating Errors by Sequencing and Standardization

621

WITS . . . . Women in Technical Service (World War II)
WIU . . . . Water Injection Unit
WIU . . . . Western Illinois University
WIWP . . . . . . World Institute for World Peace
WIX . . . . Wickes Corporation (NYSE symbol)
WIZO . . . . . . Women's International Zionist Organization
WJ . . . . Watkins-Johnson Company (NYSE symbol)
WJA . . . . . . Woolen Jobbers Association
WJBU . . . . . . William Jennings Bryan University (Tennessee)
WJC . . . . . . Washington and Jefferson College (Pennsylvania)
WJC . . . . . . Wenatchee Junior College (Washington)
WJC . . . . . . William Jewel College (Missouri)
WJC . . . . . . Wingate Junior College (North Carolina)
WJC . . . . . . Wood Junior College (Mississippi)
WJC . . . . . . Worcester Junior College (Massachusetts)
WJC . . . . World Jewish Congress
WJC . . . . . . Worthington Junior College (Minnesota)
WJCC . . . . . Western Joint Computer Conference
WJCC . . . . . Women's Joint Congressional Committee
WJD . . . . . . Welded Joint Design
WJLC . . . . . . Wye Junction Latching Circulator
WJLCER . . . . Women's Joint Legislative Committee for Equal Rights
WJP . . . . Water Jet Pump
WJT . . . . World Journal Tribune (Defunct New York City afternoon newspaper)
WK . . . . Week
WK . . . . Well-Known
WK . . . . . . Westinghouse Air Brake Company (NYSE symbol) (Delisted)
WKA . . . . . . Waffenkarren (Weapons cart) (German military - World War II)
WKACC . . . . Work Accomplishment Code (Navy)
WKB . . . . . . Wentzel-Kramer-Brillouin (Method)
WKF . . . . Well Known Factor
WKNL . . . . . Walter Kidde Nuclear Laboratories, Inc.
WKR . . . . . . Whittaker Corp. (NYSE symbol)
WKR . . . . . . Wrecker
WKS . . . . . . Workshop
WKSC . . . . . Western Kentucky State College
WKT . . . . . . Wayne-Gossard Corp. (Formerly, Wayne Knitting Mills) (NYSE symbol)
WKU . . . . . . Waukesha Motor Company (NYSE symbol) (Delisted)
WKY . . . . . . West Kentucky Coal Company (NYSE symbol) (Wall Street slang name: "Whiskey") (Delisted)
WL . . . . Wagons-Lits (Railroad sleeping or Pullman cars in Europe)
WL . . . . Waiting List
WL . . . . Walther League
WL . . . . Water Line
WL . . . . Wavelength (Electronics)
WL . . . . . . Wehrmacht-Luftwaffe (Marking of Air Force vehicles) (German military - World War II)
WL . . . . Western League (Baseball)
WL . . . . Wheel Locks
WL . . . . Wheeler Laboratories, Inc.
WL . . . . Wide-Band Limiter
WL . . . . Wind Load
WL . . . . Wiring List
WL . . . . Women's Reserve, Legal Specialist Duties (USNR officer designation)
WL . . . . Work Light
WLA . . . . . . Warner-Lambert Pharmaceutical Company (NYSE symbol)
WLA . . . . . . Wescosa Lumber Association
WLA . . . . . . Western Literature Association
WLA . . . . . . Wire Line Antenna
WLA . . . . . . Women's Land Army (British) (World War II)
WLA . . . . . . Women's Land Army (Part of the United States Crop Corps) (World War II)
WLB . . . . . . National War Labor Board (World War II)
WLB . . . . . . Wallboard
WLB . . . . . . Weapons Logbook (Military)
WLB . . . . . . Wilson Library Bulletin (A publication)
WLC . . . . . . Well Logging Cable
WLCAC . . . . Watts Labor Community Action Committee (Los Angeles, California)
WLCC . . . . . Walker-Lybarger Construction Company (Colorado)
WLCS . . . . . Workload and Cost Schedule (Military)
WLD . . . . . . West Longitude Date
WLE . . . . . . Wheeling & Lake Erie Railway Company (NYSE symbol and AAR code)
WLF . . . . . . Workload Factor
WLF . . . . . . World Law Fund
WLFX . . . . . Welding Fixture
WLG . . . . . . Washington Liaison Group
WLI . . . . . . Women's League for Israel
WLJ . . . . . . Wilson Jones Company (NYSE symbol)
WLM . . . . . . Western Lumber Manufacturers
WLM . . . . . . Wire Line Modems
WLN . . . . . . Wiswesser Line Notation (Chemical Structure)
WLO . . . . . . Waterloo R. R. (AAR code)

WLR . . . . Water Level Recorder
WLRD . . . . . . Warning Light Relay Driver
WLS . . . . Welch Scientific Company (NYSE symbol) (Delisted)
WLSC . . . . . . West Liberty State College (West Virginia)
WLT . . . . Wallace & Tiernan, Inc. (NYSE symbol) (Delisted)
WLT . . . . Weighing Less Than
WLT . . . . Wire Line Timing
WLTAS . . . . . Wingfoot Lighter-Than-Air Society
WLTE . . . . . . Warrant Loss to Enlisted Status (Revocation of appointment) (Navy)
WLU . . . . Washington and Lee University (Virginia)
WM . . . . (Qualified for) Engineering Watch (USNR officer classification)
WM . . . . Water Meter
WM . . . . Watermark
WM . . . . Watt Meter
WM . . . . Wave Meter
WM . . . . Wehrmacht-Marine (Marking on Navy vehicles) (German military - World War II)
WM . . . . Welding Memorandum
WM . . . . Western Maryland Railway Company (NYSE symbol and AAR code) (Wall Street slang name: "Wet Mary")
WM . . . . White Male
WM . . . . White Metal
WM . . . . Wire Mesh
WM . . . . Without Margin
WM . . . . Women Marines
WM . . . . Work Measurement (Army)
WM . . . . Worshipful Master (Masonry)
W & M . . . . . Washburn and Moen (Wire Gage)
WMA . . . . . . Washington Metropolitan Area
WMA . . . . . . Welding Machine Arc
WMA . . . . . . Wentworth Military Academy (Missouri)
WMA . . . . . . World Medical Association
WMATA . . . . Washington (DC) Metropolitan Area Transit Authority
WMB . . . . . . War Mobilization Board
WMB . . . . . . Williams Co. (NYSE symbol)
WMBA . . . . . . Wire Machinery Builders Association
WMBTOPCITBWTNTALI . . We May Be the Only Phone Company in Town, but We Try Not to Act Like It (Slogan)
WMC . . . . . . Wallace-Murray Corporation (NYSE symbol)
WMC . . . . . . War Manpower Commission (Within the Office of Emergency Management) (World War II)
WMC . . . . . . Weapons and Mobility Command (Army)
WMC . . . . . . Weapons Monitoring Center
WMC . . . . . . Weapons Monitoring Console
WMC . . . . . . Western Maryland College
WMC . . . . . . Wool Manufacturers Council
WMC . . . . . . World Methodist Council
WMC . . . . . . World Missions to Children
WMCE . . . . . . Western Montana College of Education
WMCL . . . . . . William Mitchell College of Law (Minnesota)
WMCP . . . . . . Woman's Medical College of Pennsylvania
WMD . . . . . . Wind Measuring Device
WMDA . . . . . Woodworking Machinery Distributors Association
WMDAA . . . . . Watch Material Distributors Association of America
WMEC . . . . . . Western Massachusetts Electric Company
WMECO . . . . . Western Massachusetts Electric Company
WMF . . . . . . Wire Mattress Federation
WMG . . . . . . Wire Measure Gauge
WMG . . . . . . Wire Metallizing Gun
WMHS . . . . . . Wall-Mounted Handling System (AEC)
WMHY . . . . . . World Mental Health Year (1960)
WMI . . . . . . War Materials, Incorporated
WMI . . . . . . Washington Music Institute
WMI . . . . . . Wave-Guide Moisture Indicator
WMI . . . . . . Wildlife Management Institute
WMI . . . . . . World Meteorological Intervals
WMK . . . . . . Weis Markets, Inc. (NYSE symbol)
WMM . . . . . . World Movement of Mothers
WMMA . . . . . Woodworking Machinery Manufacturers Association
WMO . . . . . . Wing Maintenance Officer
WMO . . . . . . World Meteorological Organization (UN)
WMP . . . . . . War and Mobilization Plan (Air Force documents)
WMP . . . . . . Weather Modification Program
WMP . . . . . . Wiener Mapping Procedure
WMP . . . . . . With Much Pleasure (Meaning, "We accept the invitation")
WMPCES(P) . . . War Manpower Commission Employment Stabilization (Plan) (Terminated, 1945)
WMPL . . . . . . World Mission Prayer League
WMR . . . . . . Water Moderated Reactor
WMR . . . . . . Wide-Band Multichannel Receiver
WMR . . . . . . World Medical Relief

WMS . . . . Warehouse Material Stores
WMS. . . . . . . Waste Management System
WMS . . . . Water Management Section (Apollo) (NASA)
WMS . . . . Weapons Monitoring System
WMS . . . . Weather Mapping System
WMS . . . . Wesleyan Missionary Society
WMS . . . . Wind Measuring System
WMS . . . . Women in the Medical Service (Army)
WMS . . . . Women's Medical Specialist
WMS . . . . Work Measurement System (Postal Service)
WMS . . . . World Magnetic Survey
WMSC . . . . . . Weather Message Switching System
WMSC . . . . . . Women's Medical Specialists Corps
WMSL . . . . . Wichita Mountains Seismological Laboratory (Military)
WMSO . . . . Wichita Mountains Seismological Observatory
WMT . . . . . . Wal-Mart Stores (NYSE symbol)
WMT. . . . . . . Weighing More Than
WMT . . . . . . West Meridian Time
WMU . . . . . . Western Michigan University
WMV . . . . . . War Munition Volunteers (British) (World War I)
WMWN . . . . . Weatherford, Mineral Wells & Northwestern Railway Company (AAR code)
WN . . . . Will Not
WN . . . . Winch
WN . . . . Work Notice
WN . . . . . . World Neighbors
WNA . . . . . . Washington National Airport (FAA)
WNA . . . . . . Winter, North Atlantic (Vessel load line mark)
WNAAUS . . . . Women's National Aeronautical Association of the United States
WNAF . . . . . Women's National Aquatic Forum
WNAP. . . . . . Washington National Airport
WNB . . . . . . Will Not Be
WNBA . . . . . Women's National Book Association
WNDC . . . . . Women's National Democratic Club
WNEC . . . . . Western New England College (Massachusetts)
WNF . . . . . . Winfield R. R. (AAR code)
WNFGA . . . . Woman's National Farm and Garden Association
WNFR. . . . . . Winifrede R. R. (AAR code)
WNG . . . . . . Warning
WNI . . . . . . Women's National Institute
WNL . . . . . . Wave-Guide Nitrogen Load
WNL . . . . . . Within Normal Limits
WNLA . . . . . Witwatersrand Native Labor Association (Nyasaland)
WNM . . . . . . Washington National Monument
WNM . . . . . . White Noise Making (Psychology)
WNO . . . . . . Wharton & Northern R. R. (AAR code)
WNP . . . . . . Will Not Proceed
WNP. . . . . . . Will Not Process
WNP . . . . . . Wire Nonpayment
WNPC . . . . . Women's National Press Club (Later, WPC)
WNR . . . . . . Western NORAD Region
WNRC . . . . . Washington National Records Center
WNRC . . . . . Women's National Republican Club
WNRE . . . . . Whiteshell Nuclear Research Establishment (Canada)
WNS. . . . . . . Windsor Industries, Inc. (NYSE symbol) (Delisted)
WNSA. . . . . . Woman's National Sabbath Alliance
WNSEA. . . . . Wood Naval Stores Export Association
WNTF . . . . . Western Naval Task Force (Navy)
WNU . . . . . . Western Newspaper Union
WNW. . . . . . West-Northwest
WNY . . . . . . Washington (DC) Naval Yard
WO . . . . Wait Order
WO . . . . Walkover
WO . . . . War Office (British)
WO . . . . War Orientation (Navy)
WO . . . . Warning Order
WO . . . . Warrant Officer
WO . . . . Western Operation
WO . . . . Wireless Operator
WO . . . . Wind Offset
WO . . . . Without
WO . . . . Women's Reserve, Ordnance Duties (USNR officer designation)
WO . . . . Work Order
WO . . . . Write Out
W/O . . . . Water-in-Oil
W/O. . . . . . . Without
WO1 . . . . Warrant Officer 1 (Army)
WOA . . . . . . Warrant Officers Association of the United States of America
WOA . . . . . . Weapons Orientation Advanced
WOA . . . . . . Work Order Authorization
WOA . . . . . . World Airways, Inc. (NYSE symbol)
WOB . . . . . . Washed Overboard (Shipping)

WOC . . . . (Government Official Serving) Without Compensation
WOCT . . . . . . WAC (Women's Army Corps) Officer Candidate Test
WOCU . . . . . . War on Community Ugliness (Program)
WOD . . . . . . Washington & Old Dominion R. R. (AAR code)
WOD . . . . . . Without Dependents (Military)
WOD . . . . . . Woodward Iron Company (NYSE symbol) (Delisted)
WODA . . . . . . World Dredging Association
WODD . . . . . World Oceanographic Data Display
WODDIN . . . . Worldwide On-Line Data and Document Intelligence System
WODECO . . . . Western Offshore Drilling and Exploration Company
WOE . . . . . . Watchdogs on Environment
WOE . . . . . . Withdrawal of Enthusiasm (Airline pilots objection to "Welcome aboard" talks)
WOE . . . . . . Without Equipment
W/OE & SP... Without Equipment and Spare Parts
WOFI . . . . . . Wood Office Furniture Institute
WOFP. . . . . . Wearout Failure Period
WOG . . . . . . Water-Oil-Gas
WOG . . . . . . With Other Goods (Business and trade)
WOGA . . . . . Western Oil and Gas Association
WOGS . . . . . We Old Girls Survive (A teachers' club in Michigan)
WOH . . . . . . War on Hunger (Program)
WOHC . . . . . Warrant Officer Hospital Corps
WOHH . . . . . Women's Organization of Hapoel Hamizrachi
WOIS . . . . . . Worn Out in Service (Military)
WOJG . . . . . Warrant Officer Junior Grade
WOL . . . . . . War-Office Letter (An order or an instruction) (British)
WOL . . . . . . Wedge Opening Load
WOL . . . . . . Wharf Owner's Liability (Insurance)
WOM . . . . . . Weapons Output Makeup
WOM . . . . . . Wide-Band Optical Modulation
WOM . . . . . . Wometco Enterprises, Inc. (NYSE symbol)
WOMAN . . . . World Organization of Mothers of All Nations
WOMPI . . . . International Association of the Women of the Motion Picture Industry
WONAAC . . . . Women's National Abortion Action Coalition
WOO . . . . . . Western Operations Office (Later, Western Support Office) (NASA)
WOO . . . . . . World Oceanic Organization (Proposed)
WOP. . . . . . . Wing Outer Panel (Aviation)
WOP . . . . . . Without Payment
WOP . . . . . . Without Personnel
WOP . . . . . . Without Preference (Rating)
WOP . . . . . . Without Priorities
W/O/P . . . . . . Without Penalty
WOPE . . . . . Without Personnel and Equipment
WOQ . . . . . . Wave Officers' Quarters
WOQT . . . . . Warrant Officer Qualification Test
WORC . . . . . Washington Operations Research Council
WORSAM . . . . Worldwide Organizational Structure for Army Medical Support Study
WORTAC.... Westinghouse Overall RADAR Tester and Calibrator
WOS . . . . . . Wilson Ornithological Society
WOSAC . . . . Worldwide Synchronization of Atomic Clocks
WOSB . . . . . Weather Observation Site Building
WOSD. . . . . . Weapons Operational Systems Development (NORAD)
WOSL. . . . . . Women's Overseas Service League
WOT . . . . . . Wide Open Throttle
WOTCU . . . . . Wave-Off and Transition Control Unit
WOTR . . . . . Wolf Trap Farm Park (National Park Service designation)
WOTT. . . . . . Wolves on the Track (A group of philanderers looking for girls) (Slang)
WOU . . . . . . Work Opportunities Unlimited
WOV . . . . . . Warren & Ouachita Valley Railway Company (AAR code)
WOW . . . . . . War on Waste (Navy)
WOW . . . . . Woman Ordnance Worker
WOW . . . . . Women Our Wonders (Anti-feminist men's group)
WOW . . . . . Woodmen of the World
WOW. . . . . . Word on the Way
WOW . . . . . . Worn-Out Wolf (An aging philanderer) (Slang)
WOWAR . . . . Work Order and Work Accomplishment Record
WOWN . . . . Without Winch
WOWS . . . . . Women Ordnance Workers (A national voluntary organization) (World War II)
WOY . . . . . . Woodley Petroleum Company (NYSE symbol)
WP. . . . . War Plans
WP . . . . Waste Pipe (Technical drawings)
WP. . . . . Wastepaper
WP. . . . . Water Packed
WP. . . . . Water Propeller
WP. . . . . Water Pump
WP. . . . . Waterproof(ing)
WP. . . . . Way-Point
WP. . . . . Weather Permitting
WP. . . . . Weatherproof

WP........	Weight Penalty
WP........	West Point
WP........	West Virginia Pulp & Paper Company (NYSE symbol) (Delisted)
WP........	Western Pacific R. R. (AAR code)
WP........	Wheel of Progress
WP........	White Phosphorus (Military)
WP........	Wild Pitch (Baseball)
WP........	Will Proceed to
WP........	Wire Payment
WP........	Without Prejudice
WP........	Word Punch
WP........	Working Paper
WP........	Working Party
WP........	Working Point
WP........	Working Pressure
WP........	Worthy Patriarch
WPA.......	Water Pump Assembly
WPA.......	Western Pine Association
WPA.......	Western Psychological Association
WPA.......	Wheelchair Pilots Association
WPA.......	With Particular Average
WPA.......	Women's Prison Association
WPA.......	Works Progress Administration (Created, 1935, to operate public works projects for unemployed persons; name changed to Work Projects Administration, 1939; later, absorbed by Federal Works Agency, which was terminated in 1942)
WPA.......	Workshop of the Players Art (New York City)
WPA.......	World Parliament Association
WPA.......	World Presbyterian Alliance
WPAFB......	Wright-Patterson Air Force Base
WPB.......	Wall Plate Box
WPB.......	War Production Board (World War II)
WPB.......	Wastepaper Basket
WPB......	World Peace Brigade
WPB.......	Write Printer Binary
WPBC......	Western Pacific Base Command (Marianas) (World War II)
WPBEF......	West Pakistan Bank Employees' Federation
WPC.......	Washington Press Club (Formerly, WNPC)
WPC.......	Water Pollution Control
WPC.......	Watts Per Candle
WPC.......	Wedge Power Clamp
WPC.......	Weldable Printed Circuit
WPC.......	William Penn College (Iowa)
WPC.......	Wired Program Computer
WPC.......	Wisconsin Electric Power Company (NYSE symbol)
WPC.......	World Peace Congress
WPC.......	World Planning Chart (Aviation)
WPC.......	World Power Conference
WPCA......	Water Pollution Control Administration (Department of the Interior)
WPCA......	Wool Pullers Council of America
WPCC......	Wilson Pharmaceutical & Chemical Corporation
WPCF......	Water Pollution Control Federation
WPCND.....	Women's Patriotic Conference on National Defense
WPD.......	Western Procurement Division (Marine Corps)
WPD.......	Write Printer Decimal
WPE.......	West Pittston-Exeter R. R. (AAR code)
WPEC......	Weapons Production Engineering Center (Navy)
WPF.......	World Peace Foundation
WPF.......	World Prohibition Federation
WPFA......	William Penn Fraternal Association
WPFC......	Commission for Fisheries Research in the West Pacific
WPFL......	West Pakistan Federation of Labor
WPFM......	Wiping Form
WPG......	Waterproofing
WPG.......	West Point Graduate
W & PH......	Wage and Purchase Hire
WPHI.......	Western Pennsylvania Horological Institute
WPI.......	Wall Paper Institute
WPI.......	Waxed Paper Institute
WPI.......	Western Pacific Industries (NYSE symbol)
WPI.......	Wholesale Price Index
WPI.......	Worcester Polytechnic Institute
WPI.......	World Patent Index
WPJ.......	Weakened Plane Joint
WPL.......	War Plan(s) (Navy)
WPL.......	Waste Pickle Liquor (Industrial waste)
WPL.......	Worst Path Loss
WPLJ......	White Port and Lemon Juice (Title of both song and drink)
WPLO......	Water Port Liaison Office(r) (Air Force)
WPM.......	War Plan, Mid-Range
WPM.......	West Point-Pepperell, Inc. (NYSE symbol)
WPM.......	Wire-Wound Porous Material
WPM.......	Wood Plastic Material
WPM.......	Words Per Minute
WPM.......	Work Package Management
WPM.......	World Presbyterian Missions
WPMA......	Waterproof Paper Manufacturers Association
WPMA......	Writing Paper Manufacturers Association
WPMC......	Waxed Paper Merchandising Council
WPN.......	Weapon
WPN.......	West Penn Traction Company (American Stock Exchange symbol)
WPNTS......	War Plan Naval Transportation Service
WPO.......	Water for Peace Office (Department of State)
WPO.......	Water Programs Office (Environmental Protection Agency)
WPO.......	World Ploughing Organization
WPOD......	Water Port of Debarkation
WPOE......	Water Port of Embarkation
WPP.......	Waterproof Paper Packing
WPP.......	Weapons Production Program
WPP.......	Web Printing Press
WPP.......	Weibull Probability Paper
WPP.......	World Pen Pals
WPPC......	Warning Point Photocell
WPPC......	West Penn Power Company
WPPDA.....	Welfare and Pension Plans Disclosure Act (Department of Labor)
WPPSS.....	Washington Public Power Supply System
WPPW......	Association of Western Pulp and Paper Workers
WPR.......	Working Party on Rationing (Allied German Occupation Forces)
WPRI......	Wartime Pacific Routing Instructions (Navy)
WPS.......	War Plan, Short-Range
WPS.......	Water Pressure Switch
WPS.......	Water Purification System
WPS.......	Watt Per Steradian
WPS.......	Wave Power Source
WPS.......	Weapons Program Section
WPS.......	White Power Structure
WPS.......	Wisconsin Public Service Corporation (NYSE symbol)
WPS.......	With Prior Service
WPS.......	Women in Public Service
WPS.......	Words Per Second
WPS.......	World Politics Simulation
WPSA......	Welsh Pony Society of America
WPSA......	World's Poultry Science Association
WPSC......	Shipping Control War Plan (Navy)
WPSL......	Western Primary Standard Laboratory
WPSNY.....	Women's Philatelic Society of New York
WPTA......	Wooden Pail and Tub Association
WPU.......	Write Punch
WPUC......	Waste-Paper Utilization Council (Defunct)
WPW.......	Wolff-Parkinson-White (Syndrome) (Medicine)
WPWM......	Wide Pulse Width Modulation
WPWOD.....	Will Proceed Without Delay
WPY.......	White Pass & Yukon Route (AAR code)
WPY.......	World Population Year (1974) (UN)
WQA.......	Weld Quality Assurance
WQF.......	Wider Quaker Fellowship
WQI.......	Water Quality Index
WQI.......	Water Quality Instrument
WQM.......	Water Quality Management
WQMD.....	Water Quantity Measuring Device
WQO.......	Water Quality Office (Environmental Protection Agency)
WR.......	Wagons-Restaurants (Railroad dining cars)
WR.......	War Reserve
WR.......	War Risk
WR.......	Wardroom (Navy)
WR.......	Warehouse Receipt (Often negotiable)
WR.......	Wartime Report
WR.......	Wartime Requirements (Air Force document)
WR.......	Washroom
WR.......	Wassermann Reaction (Medicine)
WR.......	Water-Rail (Transportation)
WR.......	Wave-Guide, Rectangular
WR.......	Weapons Requirement (DOD)
WR.......	Wet Runway (Aviation)
WR.......	Wildlife Restoration (Association)
WR.......	Will Ross, Inc. (NYSE symbol)
WR.......	Wire Rope
WR.......	Wissenschaftsrat (Science Council) (Germany)
WR.......	With Rights (Securities)
WR.......	Women's Reserve (Navy)
WR.......	Work Request
W/R.......	Warehouse Receipt

W & R . . . . . . Water and Rail
W & R . . . . . . Welfare and Recreation (Navy)
WRA . . . . War Relocation Authority (Within Office of Emergency Management)
   (To provide for the relocation of persons whose removal seemed
   necessary for national security, and for their maintenance and super-
   vision) (World War II)
WRA . . . . Weapons Replaceable (or Replacement) Assembly
WRA . . . . Western Range Association
WRA . . . . . . Whiteware Research Association
WRAC . . . . . . Willow Run Aeronautical Center (Michigan)
WRAC . . . . . . Women's Royal Army Corps (British)
WRACELD . . . . Wounds Received in Action (Incurred in) Combat with the Enemy or in
   Line of Duty (Army)
WRAF . . . . . . Women's Royal Air Force (British)
WRAIN . . . . . Walter Reed Army Institute of Nursing
WRAIR . . . . . Walter Reed Army Institute of Research
WRAM . . . . . . Wide-Range Recording and Monitoring (System) (Radiation)
WRAMA . . . . . Warner Robins Air Material Area
WRAMC . . . . . Walter Reed Army Medical Center (Military)
WRAP . . . . . . Weapons Readiness Analysis Program (Navy)
WRAP . . . . . . Women's Radical Action Project (Feminist group)
WRB . . . . War Refugee Board (Terminated 1945)
WRBC . . . . . . Weather Relay Broadcast Center
WRBR . . . . . . Wright Brothers National Memorial
WRC . . . . War Resources Council (Terminated)
WRC . . . . Warnaco, Inc. (NYSE symbol)
WRC . . . . Water Resources Council
WRC . . . . Water-Retention Coefficient
WRC . . . . Weapons Release Computer (or Controller)
WRC . . . . Weather Relay Center
WRC . . . . . . Welding Research Council
WRC . . . . . . Well to Right of Course (Aviation)
WRC . . . . . . Women's Relief Corps
WRCB . . . . . . War Relief Control Board (President's)
WRCGR . . . . . Women's Reserve of the Coast Guard Reserve
WRCLA . . . . . Western Red Cedar Lumber Association
WRCNS . . . . . Women's Royal Canadian Naval Service (World War II)
WRD . . . . Western Recruiting Division
WRD . . . . Worm Runner's Digest (A satirical publication)
WRDC . . . . . . Westinghouse Research and Development Center
WRE . . . . Weapon Research Establishment
WRECISS . . . . . Weapons Research Establishment Camera Interception Single Shot
WREDAC . . . . . Weapons Research Establishment Digital Automatic Computer
WRENS . . . . . . Women's Royal Naval Service (WRNS) (Acronym is a phonetic reference
   to members of this British service branch)
WRESAT . . . . . Weapons Research Establishment Satellite (Australia)
WREST . . . . . . Washington Regional Engineers, Scientists, and Technicians
WREU . . . . Western Railway Employees' Union (India)
WRF . . . . Weak Radial Field
WRF . . . . Weibull Reliability Function
WRF . . . . Wheat Ridge Foundation
WRF . . . . World Rehabilitation Fund
WRG . . . . Wells, Rich, Greene, Inc. (NYSE symbol)
WRGH . . . . . . Walter Reed General Hospital
WRH . . . . World Radio Handbook
WRI . . . . Wachovia Realty Investments (NYSE symbol)
WRI . . . . War Resisters' International
WRI . . . . War Risks Insurance (British)
WRI . . . . Weatherstrip Research Institute
WRI . . . . Wire Reinforcement Institute
WRI . . . . Wire Rope Institute
WRL . . . . War Resisters League
WRL . . . . Wien Radiation Law
WRL . . . . Wing Reference Line
WRM . . . . War Readiness Materiel
WRM . . . . . . Water Removal Mechanism
WRMA . . . . . . Welded Ring Manufacturers Association
WRMRATE . . . . War Readiness Materiel Rating (Air Force)
WRMSTAT . . . . War Readiness Materiel Status (Air Force)
WRN . . . . Warren (SD) Company (NYSE symbol) (Delisted)
WRNOA . . . . . Washington Reef Net Owners Association
WRNS . . . . Women's Royal Naval Service (A member is familiarly called a "Wren")
   (British) (World War II)
WRNT . . . . Warrenton Rail Road Company (AAR code)
WRNWCA . . . . Western Red and Northern White Cedar Association
WRO . . . . War Records Office
WRO . . . . War Risks Only
WRO . . . . . . Water Rights Office (Bureau of Indian Affairs)
WRO . . . . Western Regional Office
WRO . . . . Work Release Order
WRP . . . . Water Resource Planning

WRP . . . . Weapons Release Programmer
WRP . . . . Wiener Random Process
WRPA . . . . . . Water Resources Planning Act (1965)
WRPC . . . . . . Weather Records Processing Centers
WRPSM . . . . . War Reserve Publication Shipment Memorandum
WRR . . . . Warm Run Record
WRRA . . . . . . Water Resources Research Act (1964)
WRRC . . . . . . Willow Run Research Center (Air Force)
WRRR . . . . . . Walter Reed Research Reactor
WRRS . . . . . . Wire Relay Radio System
WRS . . . . Walter Reed Society
WRS . . . . Water Recirculation System
WRS . . . . Wave Radiometer System
WRS . . . . Weather RADAR Set (or System)
WRS . . . . Western Pacific R.R. Company (NYSE symbol) (Later, WPI)
WRS . . . . Wide-Range Sensor
WRSFA . . . . . . Western Reinforcing Steel Fabricators Association
WRSIC . . . . . . Water Resources Scientific Information Center (Department of the Interior)
WRSK . . . . . . War Readiness Spares Kit
WRSP . . . . . . World Register of Scientific Periodicals
WRSq . . . . . . Weather Reconnaissance Squadron (Air Force)
WRT . . . . Warrior River Terminal Company (AAR code)
WRT . . . . Wright Hargreaves Mines, Ltd. (NYSE symbol)
WRTA . . . . . . Western Railroad Traffic Association
WRTB . . . . . . Wire Rope Technical Board
WRU . . . . Wave Run-Up
WRU . . . . Western Reserve University (Later, Case-Western Reserve University)
WRU . . . . Who Are You? (Communication)
WRV . . . . Water Relief Valve
WR(W) . . . . . . War Reserve (Weapon)
WRWg . . . . . . Weather Reconnaissance Wing (Air Force)
WRWK . . . . . . Warwick Railway Company (AAR code)
WRX . . . . Western Refrigerator Line Company (AAR code)
WRY . . . . World Refugee Year
WS . . . . Wallops Station (NASA)
WS . . . . Ware Shoals R. R. (AAR code)
WS . . . . Warner & Swasey Co. (NYSE symbol)
WS . . . . Waste Stack (Technical drawings)
WS . . . . Water Soluble
WS . . . . Water Supply
WS . . . . Water Surface (Elevation)
WS . . . . Weak Signals (Radio)
WS . . . . Weapon System
WS . . . . Weapons Specifications
WS . . . . Weather Station
WS . . . . Weatherstripping
WS . . . . West Saxon
WS . . . . Wetted Surface
WS . . . . White Sisters (Missionary Sisters of Our Lady of Africa) (Roman Catholic
   religious order)
WS . . . . Wilderness Society
WS . . . . Wildlife Society
WS . . . . Wind Speed
WS . . . . Wirtschaft und Statistik (Germany)
WS . . . . Withholding Statement
WS . . . . Work Statement
WS . . . . Work Stoppage
WS . . . . Worksheet
WS . . . . Writer to the Signet (British)
W/S . . . . Watts per Steradian
W & S . . . . Whisky and Soda
WSA . . . . War Shipping Administration (Within Office of Emergency Management)
   (World War II)
WSA . . . . Wave-Guide Slot Array
WSA . . . . Weapons Systems Analysis (Army)
WSA . . . . Weed Society of America
WSA . . . . Western Slavonic Association
WSA . . . . Wholesale Stationers' Association
WSA . . . . Workplace Standards Administration (Department of Labor)
WSA . . . . Writers' Sodality of America
WSAA . . . . . . Wave-Guide Slot Array Antenna
WSAAA . . . . . Western States Advertising Agencies Association
WSAD . . . . . . Weapon System Analysis Division (Navy)
WSAO . . . . . . Weapon System Analysis Office (Navy)
WSAS . . . . . . Weapon System Acceptance Schedule
WSASSA . . . . . Wholesale School, Art & Stationery Supplies Association
WSAT . . . . . . Weapon Systems Accuracy (formerly, Acceptance) Trials (Navy)
WSATO . . . . . War Shipping Administration Training Organization (Terminated)
WSAWD . . . . . White Sands Air Weather Detachment
WSB . . . . Wage Stabilization Board (Terminated, 1953)
WSB . . . . Wheat-Soya Blend

WSB . . . . Will Send Boat
WSBP . . . . . . Western Society of Business Publications
WSC . . . . Water Systems Council
WSC . . . . Weapon System Contractor
WSC . . . . Weapon System Costing (Navy)
WSC. . . . . Wesco Financial Corporation (NYSE symbol)
WSC. . . . . Western Simulation Council
WSC . . . . White Sisters of Charity of St. Vincent de Paul (Roman Catholic
religious order)
WSC . . . . Wing Security Control (Air Force)
WSC. . . . . Winona State College (Minnesota)
WSC. . . . . Wisconsin State College
WSC . . . . Working Security Committee (Navy)
WSC . . . . World Spiritual Council
WSC. . . . . Wrap-Spring Clutch
WSC. . . . . Writing Services Center
WSCC. . . . . . . Weapon System Configuration Control
WSCC. . . . . . . Western State College of Colorado
WSCCM . . . . . Weapon System Configuration Control Manual (Navy)
WSCF. . . . . . . World's Student Christian Federation
WSCOC . . . . . Wills Sainte Claire Owners Club
WSCS . . . . . . Weapon System Communications System
WSCSR . . . . . Weapons System Contract Status Report (Navy)
WSD. . . . . Weapon System Director
WSD. . . . . Wind Speed Detector
WSDC. . . . . . . Weapon System Design Criteria
WSDD. . . . . . . Weapon Status Digital Display
WSDL. . . . . . . Weapons System Development Laboratory
WSDP . . . . . . Weapons System Development Plan
WSD/TD . . . . . Weapon System Demonstration Test Directive
WSE . . . . Weapon System Engineering (Navy)
WSE . . . . Weapons and Support Equipment (Navy)
WSE . . . . Western Society of Engineers
WSEC . . . . . . Washington State Electronics Council
WSEC . . . . . . Watt-Second
WSECL . . . . . . Weapon System Equipment Component List
WSED . . . . . . Weapons Systems Evaluation Division
WSEG. . . . . . . Weapon System Evaluation Group (DOD and Air Force)
WSEIAC . . . . . Weapon System Effectiveness Industry Advisory Committee
WSEL . . . . . . Weapons System Engineering Laboratory
WSEM . . . . . . Weapon System Evaluation Missile
WSEP . . . . . . Waste Solidification Engineering Prototype Plant (AEC)
WSEP . . . . . . Weapon System Evaluation Program (Air Force)
WSET . . . . . . Weapon System Evaluation Test (Navy)
WSF . . . . Weather Support Force (Military)
WSF . . . . Week Second Feet
WSF . . . . Western Sea Frontier (Navy)
WSF . . . . World Sephardi Federation
WSG . . . . Wesleyan Service Guild
WSG. . . . . Winter Study Group
WSG . . . . Wire Strain Gage
WSG . . . . Worthiest Soldier in the Group
WSGA. . . . . . . Water Soluble Gum Association
WSGE . . . . . . Western Society of Gear Engineers
WSHGA . . . . . Washington State Holly Growers Association
WSHLD . . . . . . Windshield
WSI . . . . War Service Indefinite
WSI . . . . Wind Speed Indicator
WSI . . . . World Synoptic Interval
WSIC . . . . . . Watchmakers of Switzerland Information Center
WSIM . . . . . . Water Separation Index, Modified
WSIR . . . . . . White Sands Integrated Range
WSJ . . . . Order of the White Shrine of Jerusalem
WSJ . . . . Wall Street Journal (A newspaper)
WSJ . . . . Worm Screw Jack
WSL . . . . Weather Seal
WSLO. . . . . . . Weapon System Logistics Officer
WSLR . . . . . . Weapon System Logistic Reviews (Navy)
WSM . . . . Weapon Support Manager
WSM . . . . Weapon System Manager
WSM . . . . Western Society of Malacologists
WSM . . . . Wigner-Seitz Method
WSMA. . . . . . . Window Shade Manufacturers Association
WSMAC . . . . . Weapon System Maintenance Action Center
WSMC . . . . . . Weapons System Management Codes (Navy)
WSMO . . . . . . Weapon System Materiel Officer (Air Force)
WSMPA . . . . . Western States Meat Packers Association
WSMR. . . . . . . White Sands Missile Range (Air Force)
WSN . . . . Western Society of Naturalists
WSNSCA . . . . Washable Suits, Novelties and Sportswear Contractors Association
WSO . . . . Washington Standardization Officers

WSO . . . . . . Western Support Office (Formerly, Western Operations Office) (NASA)
WSOC . . . . . . Weapon System Operational Concept
WSOEA . . . . Wholesale Stationery and Office Equipment Association
WSP . . . . Washington School of Psychiatry
WSP . . . . Water Supply Point
WSP . . . . Weapon Systems Pouch
WSP . . . . Weibull Shape Parameter
WSP . . . . West Penn Power Company (NYSE symbol)
WSP . . . . Wide-Band Signal Processor
WSP . . . . Working Steam Pressure
WSPACS . . . . Weapon Systems Planning (or Programming) and Control System
WSPD . . . . . . Weapons System Planning Data (Navy)
WSPG. . . . . . . Weapon System Phasing (or Purchasing) Group
WSPG. . . . . . . White Sands Proving Ground (Air Force) (Obsolete)
WSPGL . . . . . Weapon System Program Guide List
WSPO . . . . . . Weapon System Project Office (Air Force)
WSPOP . . . . . Weapon System Phase-Out Procedure
WSq . . . . Weather Squadron (Air Force)
WSR . . . . War Service Regulation
WSR . . . . Warren & Saline River R. R. (AAR code)
WSR . . . . Weak Signal Reception
WSR . . . . Weapon System Reliability
WSR . . . . Weapons Spares Report (Navy)
WSR . . . . Weapons Status Report (Navy)
WSR . . . . . . Weather Surveillance RADAR
WSR . . . . Weekly Summary Report
WSR . . . . Wire Shift Register
WSR . . . . Wood-Shingle Roof (Technical drawings)
WSR . . . . World Students Relief
W/sr . . . . Watt Per Steradian
WSRI . . . . . . World Safety Research Institute
WSRR . . . . . . West Shore Railroad
WSS . . . . War Savings Staff
WSS . . . . Warfare Systems School (Air Force)
WSS . . . . Washington Steel Corp. (NYSE symbol)
WSS . . . . Weapon System Specification
WSS . . . . Winston-Salem Southbound Railway (AAR code)
WSS . . . . . . World Ship Society
WSSA . . . . . . Weapon System Support Activities
WSSA . . . . . . Weed Science Society of America
WSSA . . . . . . White Sands Signal Agency (Military)
WSSA . . . . . . World Secret Service Association
WSSC . . . . . . Weapon System Support Center
WSSC . . . . . . Weapon System Support Code (Navy)
WSSCA . . . . . White Sands Signal Corps Agency
WSSCL . . . . . Weapon System Stock Control List
WSSI . . . . . . Women's Social Service for Israel
WSSL . . . . . . Weapon Support Stock List
WSSL . . . . . . Western Secondary Standards Laboratory
WSSM. . . . . . . Weapon System Support Manager
WSSS . . . . . . Weapon System Storage Site
WSSSP. . . . . . Western States Small School Project
WST . . . . Water Supply Tank
WST . . . . Weapon System Test
WST . . . . Weapon System Trainer (Navy)
WST . . . . Weightlessness Simulation Test
WST . . . . Write Symbol Table
WSTA . . . . . . Weapon System Task Analysis
WSTA . . . . . . White Slave Traffic Act
WSTC . . . . . . Washington State Teachers College
WSTC . . . . . . Weapon System Total Complex
WSTC . . . . . . Willimantic State Teachers College (Connecticut)
WSTC . . . . . . Winston-Salem Teachers College (North Carolina)
WSTF . . . . . . White Sands Test Facility (NASA)
WSTI . . . . . . Welded Steel Tube Institute
WSTL . . . . . . Weapon System Test Laboratory
WSTM. . . . . . . White Sands Transverse Mercator (Army)
WSTP . . . . . . Weapon System Test Program
WSTS . . . . . . Weapon System Training Set
WSU. . . . . Washington State University
WSU. . . . . Wayne State University (Michigan)
WSUOPR . . . . Washington State University, Open Pool Reactor
WSV. . . . . Water Solenoid Valve
WSW . . . . . . West-Southwest
WSW. . . . . White Consolidated Industries, Inc. (Formerly, White Sewing Machine
Corp.) (NYSE symbol)
WSW . . . . White Sidewall (Tires)
WSWA. . . . . . . Wine and Spirits Wholesalers of America
WSWL . . . . . . Warheads and Special Weapons Laboratory
WSWMA . . . . Water and Sewage Works Manufacturers Association
WSWMA . . . . . Western States Weights and Measures Association

WSX . . . . Western Air Lines, Inc. (NYSE symbol) (Later, WAL)
WSYP . . . . . . White Sulphur Springs & Yellowstone Park R. R. (AAR code)
WT . . . . War Tax
WT . . . . Warning Tag
WT . . . . Wartime
WT . . . . Watch Time
WT . . . . Water Tank
WT . . . . Water Tender (Navy)
WT . . . . Water Thermometer
WT . . . . Water-Tube Boiler (Naval)
WT . . . . Watertight
WT . . . . Weapon Test
WT . . . . Weapons Technician (Air Force)
WT . . . . Weapons Tight (Weapons will engage only objects identified as hostile)
WT . . . . Weight
WT . . . . Whiffle Tree (Structural test)
WT . . . . Wind Tunnel
WT . . . . Winterization Test
WT . . . . Wireless Telegraphy; Wireless Telephony; Wireless Telephone
WT . . . . With Tape
WT . . . . Word Type
W/T . . . . Water Tight
W/T . . . . Wireless Telegraphy
WTA . . . . . Washington Technological Association
W/TAX . . . . . Withholding Tax
WTB . . . . Welttierschutzbund (World Federation for the Protection of Animals) (Also known as WFPA and FMPA)
WTBTSP . . . . . Watch Tower Bible and Tract Society of Pennsylvania
WTC . . . . Westcoast Transmission Company, Ltd. (NYSE symbol)
WTC . . . . Wire Test Chamber
WTC . . . . Women's Talent Corps
WTC . . . . Women's Theater Council
WTC . . . . Workload Transaction Code (Navy)
WTC . . . . World Trade Center (New York City)
WTCA . . . . . Water Terminal Clearance Authority (Army)
WTCA . . . . . . Welsh Terrier Club of America
WTCA . . . . . World Trade Centers Association
WTCB . . . . . Water Tender Construction Battalion (Navy)
WTCM . . . . . Weld Timer Control Module
WTD . . . . War Trade Department (British) (World War I)
WTD . . . . Watertight Door
WTD . . . . Wind Tunnel Data
WTD . . . . World Trade Directory (Department of Commerce)
WTE . . . . World Tapes for Education
WTF . . . . Western Task Force (Navy)
WTF . . . . Will To Fire
WTFAA . . . . . Washington Task Force on African Affairs
WTFDA . . . . . Worldwide TV-FM DX Association ("DX" is radio term meaning distance)
WTG . . . . Wind Tape Generation
WTH . . . . Worthington Corporation (NYSE symbol) (Delisted)
WTJ . . . . Wedge Type Jack
WTL . . . . Wyle Test Laboratories
WTLC . . . . . . Western Trunk Line Committee
WTM . . . . Wind Tunnel Memorandum
WTM . . . . . Wind Tunnel Model
WTN . . . . Western Technical Net (Air Force)
WTN . . . . Wind Tunnel Note
WTO . . . . Warsaw Treaty Organization
WTO . . . . World Tourism Organization
WTOS . . . . . . Western Test Range Office of Safety (Air Force)
WTP . . . . Warrant to Pollute
WTP . . . . We, The People (An organization)
WTP . . . . Weapons Testing Program
WTP . . . . World Tape Pals (An organization)
WTPBC . . . . . . Wool Textiles Production Board of Control (British) (World War I)
WTR . . . . War Tax Resistance (An organization)
WTR . . . . Well to Right (Aviation)
WTR . . . . Western Test Range (Formerly, Pacific Missile Range)
WTR . . . . Westinghouse Test Reactor
WTR . . . . Work Transfer Request
WTR . . . . Wrightsville & Tennille R. R. (AAR code)
WTRC . . . . . . Weapon Test Reports Committee (AEC-DOD)
WTRZ . . . . . . Winterize
WTRZN . . . . . . Winterization
WTS . . . . War Training Service (of the Civil Aeronautics Administration) (Formerly Civilian Pilot Training) (World War II)
WTS . . . . Wind Tunnel Study
WTS . . . . Wing Tank Structure
WTS . . . . Women's Transport Service (British)
WTS . . . . Word Terminal Synchronous
WTSA . . . . . . Wood Turners and Shapers Association

WTSB . . . . Wood Turners Service Bureau
WTSC . . . . . . West Texas State College
WTTC . . . . . Western Technical Training Command (AAFWTTC)
WTV . . . . Water Tank Vessel (Navy)
WTWA . . . . . World Trade Writers Association
WTZ . . . . Wissenschaftlich-Technische Zentren
WU . . . . Wesleyan University
WU . . . . Western Union Corp. (NYSE symbol)
WU . . . . Work Unit
WU . . . . World Union
WUA . . . . Western Underwriters Association
WUA . . . . Work Unit Assignment (Navy)
WUAA . . . . . . Wartime Unit Aircraft Activity
WUC . . . . Work Unit Code
WUCM . . . . . Work Unit Code Manual
WUCT . . . . . . World Union of Catholic Teachers
WUCWO . . . . World Union of Catholic Women's Organizations
WUF . . . . World Union of Free Thinkers
WUFTU . . . . . World Union of Free Trade Unions
WUI . . . . Western Union International
WUIS . . . . . . Work Unit Information System (Defense Documentation Center)
WUJS . . . . . . World Union of Jewish Students
WULTUO . . . . World Union of Liberal Trade Union Organizations
WUM . . . . Women's Universal Movement
WUMP . . . . . . White, Urban, Middle Class, Protestant
WUMPS . . . . . Women Umpires (World War II)
WUMS . . . . . . Woman's Union Missionary Society of America
WUP . . . . Work Unit Plan (Navy)
WUPA . . . . . . Wupatki National Monument
WUPJ . . . . . . World Union for Progressive Judaism
WUR . . . . World University Roundtable
WUR . . . . Wurlitzer Co. (NYSE symbol)
WURB . . . . . . Western Utilization Research Branch
WUS . . . . World University Service
WUSL . . . . . . Women's United Service League (British)
WUT . . . . Warm Up Time
WUT . . . . Washburn University of Topeka (Kansas)
WUT . . . . Western Union Telegraph Co. (NYSE symbol)
WUTELCO . . . . Western Union Telegraph Company
WUTS . . . . . . Work Unit Time Standard
WUUN . . . . . . Women United for United Nations
WUX . . . . Western Union Exchange (Teleprinter)
WV . . . . Wall Vent (Technical drawings)
WV . . . . West Virginia
WV . . . . Wind Velocity (Speed and direction) (Navigation)
WV . . . . World Vision
W/V . . . . Weight/Volume (Concentration) (Chemistry)
W VA . . . . . . West Virginia
WVA . . . . World Veterinary Association
WVDC . . . . . . Working Voltage, Direct Current
WVE . . . . Water Vapor Electrolysis (Cell)
WVF . . . . World Veterans Federation
WVF . . . . World Veterans Fund
WVIT . . . . . . West Virginia Institute of Technology
WVL . . . . Warfare Vision Laboratory (Army)
WVMA . . . . . Women's Veterinary Medical Association
WVN . . . . West Virginia Northern R. R. (AAR code)
WVPA . . . . . . World Veterinary Poultry Association
WVS . . . . Water Vapor Sensor
WVS . . . . Women's Voluntary Services (Coordinated work of women for national service) (British) (World War II)
W-V(S) . . . . . . Women's Reserve, Emergency Duties (USNR commissioned officer designation)
WVSC . . . . . . West Virginia State College
W-V(S) (CEC) . . Women's Reserve, Civil Engineering Corps Duties (USNR commissioned officer designation)
W-V(S) (DC) . . Women's Reserve, Dental Corps Duties (USNR commissioned officer designation)
W-V(S) (H) . . . Women's Reserve, Hospital Corps Duties (USNR commissioned officer designation)
W-V(S) (MC) . . Women's Reserve, Medical Corps Duties (USNR commissioned officer designation)
W-V(S) (SC) . . . Women's Reserve, Supply Corps Duties (USNR commissioned officer designation)
WVT . . . . Water Vapor Transmission
WVT . . . . Watervliet Arsenal (Army)
WVTR . . . . . . Water Vapor Transmission Rate
WVU . . . . West Virginia University
WVWC . . . . . . West Virginia Wesleyan College
WW . . . . Walworth Company (NYSE symbol)
WW . . . . Warehouse Warrant

WW	Water–White
WW	Waterworks
WW	Weight Watchers, Inc.
WW	Wholesale Wine (License)
WW	Wilderness Watch, Inc. (An organization)
WW	Winchester & Western R. R. (AAR code)
WW	Wire Way (Technical drawings)
WW	Wire–Wound
WW	With Warrants (NYSE symbol)
WW	World War
WW	World–Wide
1WW	Weather Wing (1st) (California) (Air Force)
2WW	Weather Wing (2nd) (New York) (Air Force)
3WW	Weather Wing (3rd) (Nebraska) (Air Force)
4WW	Weather Wing (4th) (Colorado) (Air Force)
6WW	Weather Wing (6th) (Washington, DC) (Air Force)
7WW	Weather Wing (7th) (Illinois) (Air Force)
WWI	Whirlwind I
WWI	World War I
WWII	World War II
WWIII	World War III
WWA	Wallcovering Wholesalers Association
WWA	Western Writers of America
WWA	With the Will Annexed
WWA	Woolens and Worsteds of America (Association)
WWA	World Wide Airlines, Inc.
WWB	Writers War Board
WWBA.	Walt Whitman Birthplace Association
WWBA	Western Wooden Box Association
WWBPU	World Wide Baraca-Philathea Union
WWC	Walla Walla College (Washington)
WWC	Warren Wilson College (North Carolina)
WWC	Wavy Walled Cylinder
WWC	William Woods College (Missouri)
WWC	Woven Wire Cloth
WWCE	Western Washington College of Education
WWCP	Walking Wounded Collecting Post (Military)
WWCTU	World's Woman's Christian Temperance Union
WWD	Weather Working Days (Construction)
WWD	Women's Wear Daily (A publication)
WWF.	Waterside Workers' Federation of Australia
WWF.	Wire Wrap Fixture
WWF	World Wildlife Fund
WWFS	West Wales Field Society (British)
WWg	Weather Wing (Air Force)
WWIIHSLB	World War II Honorable Service Lapel Button
WWICS	Woodrow Wilson International Center for Scholars
WWIO	Worldwide Inventory Objective
WWIS	World Wide Information Services
WWLIS	Woodmen of the World Life Insurance Society
WWM	Weizsacker–Williams Method
WWM	Welded Wire Matrix
WWM	Wire Wrap Machine
WWMCCS	World–Wide Military Command and Control System (Defense)
WWML	Wood, Wire & Metal Lathers' International Union
WWMP	Western Wood Moulding Producers
WWN	With Winch
WWNSS	World–Wide Network of Standard Seismograph (Stations)

WWO	Wing Warrant Officer (British Royal Air Force)
WWP.	Washington Water Power Company (NYSE symbol)
WWP	Water Wall (Peripheral Jet)
WWP	Weather Wing Pamphlet (Air Force)
WWP.	Working Water Pressure
WWP.	World Weather Program (National Science Foundation)
WWPA	Western Wood Products Association
WWPA	Woven Wire Products Association
WWPMU	World-Wide Prayer and Missionary Union
WWR	Wire Wound Resistor
WWS	Water Wall (Side Skegs)
WWS	Women's Welfare Service
WWS	World Weather System
WWSA.	Walt Whitman Society of America
WWSD	Women's War Savings Division
WWSN	World-Wide Seismology Net (National Bureau of Standards)
WWSP	World Wide Surveillance Program (Military)
WWSSN	Worldwide Standardized Seismograph Network
WWTCA	World War Tank Corps Association
WWTS.	Waste Water Treatment System
WWV	Walla Walla Valley Railway Company (AAR code)
WWIVM	World War I Victory Medal
WWIIVM	World War II Victory Medal
WWVR	Wire Wound Variable Resistor
WWW	"The Who, What, or Where Game" (Television show; also, 3Ws)
WWW	Wolverine World-Wide, Inc. (NYSE symbol)
WWW	World Weather Watch
WWWI.	Widows of World War I
WWWCUS	World without War Council of the United States (Formerly, TTP)
WWWF	Worldwide Wrestling Federation
WWWTTUTWTU .	We Won't Write to Them Until They Write to Us (A servicemen's club)
WWWV	Women World War Veterans
WWY	Wrigley (William Jr.) (Delaware) (NYSE symbol)
WX	Weather
WX	Westinghouse Electric Corp. (NYSE symbol) (Wall Street slang name: "Wex")
WX	Wireless (Communications)
WxB	Wax Bite (Dentistry)
WXC.	Wilcox Oil Company (NYSE symbol) (Delisted)
WxP	Wax Pattern (Dentistry)
WXY	Waldorf System, Inc. (NYSE symbol) (Delisted)
WY.	Weyhaeuser Co. (NYSE symbol)
WY	Wyoming
WYAIO	Will You Accept, If Offered (the position of)
WYBL	Western Young Buddhist League
WYJCA	Wool Yarn Jobbers Credit Association
WYO	Wyandotte Industries (American Stock Exchange symbol)
WYO	Wyoming
WYR.	The West Yorkshire Regiment (British Army)
WYS.	Wyandotte Southern R. R. (AAR code)
WYT.	Wyandotte Terminal R. R. (AAR code)
Wz.	Warenzeichen (Trademark) (Germany)
WZ	Wissenschaftliche Zeitschrift (A publication)
WZO	Wein Zollordnung (Germany)
WZO	World Zionist Organization
WZOA	Women's Zionist Organization of America
WZT.	Wartegg-Zeichentest (Wartegg Test)

X

X . . . . Any point on a great circle
X . . . . By (As in 9 x 12)
X . . . . Christus
X . . . . Cross (As in X-roads)
X . . . . An Examination (Slang)
X . . . . Exchange
X . . . . Exclusive (Concession in a circus or carnival)
X . . . . Experimental (Military)
X . . . . Extra (As in x-hvy, or extra-heavy)
X . . . . Frost
X . . . . Intersect(ion)
X . . . . Mistake or Error
X . . . . Movie Rating for "Persons under 18 (16 in some localities) Not Admitted"
X . . . . No-wind distance between pressure pattern observations
X . . . . Parallactic angle
X . . . . Research (or Experimental) (Designation for all US military aircraft)
X . . . . Submersible Craft (Navy ship symbol)
X . . . . Ten (Roman numeral)
X . . . . A Toilet (Slang)
X . . . . US Steel Corporation (NYSE symbol) (Wall Street slang name: "Steel")
XA . . . . Crucible Steel Company of America (NYSE symbol) (Delisted)
XAAM . . . . . . Experimental Air-to-Air Missile (Air Force, NASA)
XAFH . . . . X-Band Antenna Feed Horn
XAL . . . . Xenon Arc Lamp
XAM . . . . Merchant Ship Converted to a Minesweeper (Navy symbol) (Obsolete)
XAP . . . . Merchant Transport (Ship symbol)
XAPC . . . . Merchant Coastal Transport, Small (Ship symbol)
XAS . . . . Experimental Air Specification Weapons (Navy)
XAS . . . . X-Band Antenna System
XASM . . . . Experimental Air-to-Surface Missile (Air Force, NASA)
XAT . . . . X-Ray Analysis Trial
XAV . . . . Auxiliary Seaplane Tender (Ship symbol)
XB . . . . Crossbar (Bell System)
XB . . . . Experimental Bomber
XB . . . . Exploding Bridgewire
XBR . . . . Experimental Breeder Reactor
XBT . . . . Expendable Bathythermograph (Naval Oceanographic Office)
XC . . . . Cross Country (Also, XCY)
XC . . . . Experimental Cargo Aircraft
XC . . . . Without the Right to Coupons (Finance)
XC . . . . X-Chromosome
X-C . . . . Ex-Coupon (Without the right to coupons, as of a bond) (Finance)
XCG . . . . Experimental Cargo Glider
XCL . . . . Armed Merchant Cruiser (Navy symbol)
XCONN . . . . . Cross Connection
XCS . . . . Cross-Country Skiing
XCT . . . . X-Band Communications Transponder
XCY . . . . Cross Country (Also, XC)
X-D . . . . Ex-Dividend (Without the right to dividend) (NYSE symbol)
X & D . . . . . . Experiment and Development (Flotilla) (Landing Craft)
XDE . . . . Xylene-Dioxane-Ethanol (Scintillation solvent)
XDH . . . . Xanthine Dehydrogenase
XDIS . . . . Ex-Distribution (NYSE symbol)
XDP . . . . X-Ray Density Probe
XDP . . . . X-Ray Diffraction Powder
XDPC . . . . X-Ray Diffraction Powder Camera
XDPS . . . . X-Band Diode Phase Shifter
XDS . . . . X-Ray Diffraction System
XDS . . . . Xerox Data Systems (Formerly, SDS)
XDT . . . . Xenon Discharge Tube
XE . . . . Experimental Engine (NASA)
Xe . . . . Xenon (Chemical element)

XECF . . . . Experimental Engine - Cold Flow Configuration (NERVA)
XEG . . . . X-Ray Emission Gauge
XEG . . . . Xerox Education Group
XES . . . . X-Ray Emission Spectra
XF . . . . Experimental Fighter
XF . . . . Extra Fine
XFA . . . . Cross Field Acceleration
XFA . . . . X-Ray Fluorescence Absorption
XFC . . . . X-Band Frequency Converter
XFD . . . . X-Ray Flow Detection
XFH . . . . X-Band Feed Horn
XFLT . . . . Expanded Flight Line Tester
XFM . . . . Expeditionary Force Message (Usually, EFM)
XFM . . . . X-Band Ferrite Modulator
XFQH . . . . Xenon-Filled Quartz Helix
XFT . . . . Xenon Flash Tube
XGAM . . . . Experimental Guided Air Missiles
XH . . . . Experimental Helicopter
XHM . . . . X-Ray Hazard Meter
XHR . . . . Extra High Reliability
XHV . . . . Extreme High Vacuum
X-I . . . . Ex-Interest (Without the right to interest) (Finance)
XIA . . . . X-Band Interferometer Antenna
XIC . . . . Transmission Interface Converter
XIM . . . . X-Ray Intensity Meter
XIN . . . . Ex (Without) Interest (Stock brokerage)
XIO . . . . Execute Input/Output
XIRS . . . . Xenon Infrared Searchlight
XIS . . . . Xenon Infrared Searchlight
XK . . . . X-Band Klystron
XL . . . . Excess Lactate
XL . . . . Extra Large
XLA . . . . X-Band Limiter Attenuator
XLC . . . . Xenon Lamp Collimator
XLDT . . . . Xenon LASER Discharge Tube
XLI . . . . Extra Low Interstitial
XLO . . . . Ex-Cell-O Corporation (NYSE symbol)
XLPS . . . . Xenon Lamp Power Supply
XLR . . . . Experimental Liquid Rocket (Air Force, NASA)
XLS . . . . Xenon Light Source
XLSS . . . . Xenon Light Source System
XLT . . . . Cross-Linked Polyethylene (Electronics)
XLT . . . . Xenon LASER Tube
XLWB . . . . Extra Long Wheel Base
XM . . . . Experimental Missile (Air Force, NASA)
XMIT . . . . Transmitter
XMS . . . . X-Band Microwave Source
XMS . . . . Xavier Mission Sisters (Catholic Mission Sisters of St. Francis Xavier) (Roman Catholic religious order)
XMT . . . . X-Band Microwave Transmitter
XMTR . . . . Transmitter
XN . . . . Ex-New (NYSE symbol)
XN . . . . Experimental (Navy)
XO . . . . Executive Officer (Military)
XO . . . . Experimental Officer (Ministry of Agriculture, Fisheries, and Food) (Also EO and ExO) (British)
XOB . . . . Xenon Optical Beacon
XOR . . . . Exclusive Or (Gates) (Data processing)
XOS . . . . Extra Outside (Clothing)
XP . . . . Express Paid
XP . . . . Xeroderma Pigmentosum
XPA . . . . X-Band Parametric Amplifier
XPA . . . . X-Band Passive Array

629

XPA . . . . X-Band Planar Array
XPA . . . . X-Band Power Amplifier
XPAA . . . . X-Band Planar Array Antenna
XPARS . . . . . . External Research Publication and Retrieval System (Department of State)
XPC . . . . Christus
XPD . . . . Cross-Polarization Discrimination
XPG . . . . Converted merchant ships, assigned to antisubmarine patrol or convoy escort (Navy symbol)
XPM . . . . Xerox Planning Model (A computerized representation of the Xerox Corporation's operations)
XPP . . . . Xi Psi Phi (Fraternity)
XPPA . . . . X-Band Pseudo-Passive Array
XPPA . . . . X-Band Pulsed Power Amplifier
XPR . . . . Ex (Without) Privileges (Stock brokerage)
XPS . . . . X-Band Phase Shifter
XPS . . . . X-Ray Photoelectron Spectroscopy
XPT . . . . Express Paid Telegraph
XPT . . . . X-Band Pulse Transmitter
XQ . . . . Cross-Question (Transcripts)
XQ . . . . Experimental Target Drone (Air Force, NASA)
XQH . . . . Xenon Quartz Helix
XR . . . . Without Rights (Stock brokerage)
XRB . . . . X-Band RADAR Beacon
XRCD . . . . . . X-Ray Crystal Density
XRD . . . . X-Ray Diffraction
X-REF . . . . . . Cross Reference
XRF . . . . X-Ray Fluorescence (Spectrometry)
XRII . . . . X-Ray Image Intensifier
XRL . . . . Extended Range Lance (Missile)
XRP . . . . X-Ray and Photofluorography Technician (Navy)
XRT . . . . Ex-Rights (NYSE symbol)
XRT . . . . X-Ray Technician (Navy)
XRX . . . . Xerox Corporation (NYSE symbol)
XS . . . . Christus
XS . . . . Cross-Section
XS . . . . Excess
XS . . . . Extra Strong
XSA . . . . X-Band Satellite Antenna
XSAL . . . . Xenon Short Arc Lamp

XSB . . . . Xavier Society for the Blind
XSECT . . . . . . Cross Section
XSF . . . . X-Ray Scattering Facility
XSL . . . . Experimental Space Laboratory
XSM . . . . Experimental Strategic Missile
XSM . . . . Experimental Surface Missile
X-SONAD . . . . Experimental Sonic Azimuth Detector
XSP . . . . Xi Sigma Pi (Fraternity)
XSPV . . . . Experimental Solid Propellant Vehicle
XSR . . . . X-Band Scatterometer RADAR
XSS . . . . Experimental Space Station (NASA)
XSTA . . . . X-Band Satellite Tracking Antenna
XSTD . . . . X-Band Stripline Tunnel Diode
XSTDA . . . . . . X-Band Stripline Tunnel Diode Amplifier
XT . . . . X-Ray Tube
XTA . . . . X-Band Tracking Antenna
XTAL . . . . Crystal
XTC . . . . Extendicare, Inc. (NYSE symbol)
XTLO . . . . Crystal Oscillator
XTO . . . . X-Band Triode Oscillator
XTR . . . . Xtra, Inc. (NYSE symbol)
XTWA . . . . X-Band Traveling Wave Amplifier
XTWM . . . . . . X-Band Traveling Wave MASER
XU . . . . Xavier University (Louisiana; Ohio)
XUV . . . . Extreme Ultraviolet
XVA . . . . X-Ray Vidicon Analysis
XVP . . . . Executive Vice President
XW . . . . Experimental Warhead
XW . . . . Without Warrants (NYSE symbol)
XWS . . . . Experimental Weapon System (or Specification)
XXS . . . . Extra Extra Strong
XXX . . . . International Urgency Signal
XYA . . . . X-Y Axis
XYAT . . . . X-Y Axis Table
XYL . . . . Ex-Young-Lady (i.e., a former sweetheart) (Slang)
XYL . . . . Former Young Lady (Wife) (Ham radio slang)
XYP . . . . X-Y Plotter
XYR . . . . X-Y Recorder
X Yr Dev . . . . Ten Year Device (US Army badge)

Y

ACRONYMS AND INITIALISMS DICTIONARY

Y......... Alleghany Corporation (NYSE symbol)
Y......... Doublecross (i.e., to betray) (Criminal slang)
Y......... Prototype (Designation for all US military aircraft)
Y......... Tanker (Army symbol)
Y......... Yard (Measure)
Y......... Year
Y......... Yellow (Buoy)
Y......... Yen (Japanese monetary unit)
Y......... Yeoman
Y......... Young Men's (or Women's) Christian Association (Short form of reference, especially to the group's building or specific facility, as "the Y swimming pool")
Y......... Younger or Youngest
Y......... Young's Modulus (of Elasticity) (Symbol)
Y......... Your
Y......... Yttrium (Chemical element) (Preferred form, but also see Yt)
Y......... Yukon Standard Time (Aviation)
YA........ Yaw Axis
YAA....... Yachtsmen's Association of America
YAAP...... Young Americans Against Pollution (Organization in Haverford, Pennsylvania)
YABA...... Yacht Architects and Brokers Association
YAC....... Young Adult Council of National Social Welfare Assembly
YADH...... Yeast Alcohol Dehydrogenase
YAEC...... Yankee Atomic Electric Company
YAF....... Young Americans for Freedom (An organization)
YAF....... Yugoslavian Air Force
YAG....... Miscellaneous Auxiliary (Navy ship symbol)
YAG....... Yttrium Aluminum Garnet
YAGL...... Yttrium Aluminum Garnet LASER
YAIC...... Young American Indian Council
YAK....... Yakovlev (Russian aircraft symbol; initialism taken from name of aircraft's designer)
YAL....... Yttrium Aluminum LASER
YAN....... Yancey R. R. (AAR code)
YANCON.... Yankee Conference (College sports)
YANGPAT.... Yangtze Patrol, Asiatic Fleet (Navy)
YANK...... Youth of America Needs to Know
YAP....... Yaw and Pitch
YAR....... York-Antwerp Rules
YARA...... Young Americans for Responsible Action
YAS....... Yaw Attitude Sensor
YASD...... Young Adult Services Division (of ALA)
YAT....... Yale & Towne Manufacturing Company (NYSE symbol) (Later, ETN)
YAVIS..... Young, Attractive, Verbal, Intelligent, and Successful
YAWF...... Youth Against War and Fascism
YB........ Yard Bird (Confined to camp) (Military slang)
YB........ Yearbook
YB........ Youngstown Sheet & Tube Company (NYSE symbol) (Wall Street slang name: "Yellow Belly") (Delisted)
Yb........ Ytterbium (Chemical element)
YBRA...... Yellowstone-Bighorn Research Association
YC........ Open Lighter (Navy symbol)
YC........ Y-Chromosome
YC........ Yacht Club
YC........ Yankee Conference (College sports)
YC........ Yard Craft (Navy symbol)
YC........ Yaw Channel
YC........ Yaw Coupling
YC........ Yeomanry Cavalry (Military) (British)
YCA....... Yachting Club of America
YCAP...... Youth Committee Against Poverty
YCC....... Youth Civic Center

YCC....... Youth Conservation Corps
YCCA...... National Youth Council on Civic Affairs
YCD....... Fueling Barge (Navy symbol)
YCD....... Youth Correction Division (Department of Justice)
YCF....... Car Float (Navy symbol)
YCF....... Yankee Critical Facility (Atomic energy)
YCF....... Young Calvinist Federation
YCI....... Young Communist International (Dissolved, 1943)
YCJCYAQFTJB.. Your Curiosity Just Cost You a Quarter for the Jukebox (Tavern sign)
YCK....... Open Cargo Lighter (Navy ship symbol)
YCL....... Young Communist League
YCLA...... Young Circle League of America
YCM....... Young Christian Movement
YCP....... Yaw Coupling Parameter
YCS....... Young Christian Students (College, high school, or international)
YCSM...... Young Christian Student Movement
YCTF...... Younger Chemists Task Force (American Chemical Society)
YCU....... Aircraft Transportation Lighter (Navy symbol)
YCV....... Aircraft Transportation Lighter (Navy symbol)
YCW....... Young Christian Workers (Later, Young Christian Movement)
YD........ Floating Derrick (Navy symbol)
YD........ Yard
Y & D..... Bureau of Yards and Docks (Obsolete) (Navy)
YDAA...... Yellow Dinitrophenylaspartic Acid
YDB....... Yield Diffusion Bonding
YDC....... Yaw Damper Computer
YDCA...... Young Democratic Clubs of America
YDDPA..... Youth Development and Delinquency Prevention Administration (HEW)
YDG....... Degaussing Vessel (Navy symbol)
YDI....... Youth Development, Incorporated
YDL....... Young Development Laboratories
YDSD...... Yards & Docks Supply Depot (Obsolete) (Navy)
YDT....... Diving Tender (Navy symbol)
YE........ Lighter, Ammunition (Navy symbol)
YE........ Yellow Edges
YE........ Yellow Enzyme
YEA....... Yaw Error Amplifier
YEB....... Yorkshire Electricity Board (British)
YEG....... Yeast Extract - Glucose (Medium)
YEH....... Reduced Yellow Enzyme
YELL...... Yellowstone National Park
YEPD...... Yeast Extract, Peptone, Dextrose (Medium)
YES....... Youth Education Services (Summer program)
YES....... Youth Employment Service (Department of Employment) (British)
YF........ Covered Lighter (Self-Propelled) (Navy symbol)
YF........ Provision Store Lighter (Navy symbol)
YF........ Range Tender (Navy Symbol)
YFB....... Ferryboat (Navy symbol)
YFB....... Launch (Navy symbol)
YFC....... Young Farmers' Club (British)
YFC....... Youth for Christ, International
YFD....... Yard Floating Dry Dock (Navy symbol)
YFN....... Covered Lighter (Non-Self-Propelled) (Navy symbol)
YFNB...... Large Covered Lighter (Navy symbol)
YFND...... Drydock Companion Craft (Navy symbol)
YFNX...... Lighter (Special Purpose) (Navy symbol)
YFP....... District Barge, Floating Power (Navy symbol)
YFP....... Floating Power Barge (Navy symbol)
YFR....... Refrigerated Covered Lighter (Self-Propelled) (Navy symbol)
YFRN...... Refrigerated Covered Lighter (Non-Self-Propelled) (Navy symbol)
YFRT...... Covered Lighter (Range Tender) (Navy symbol)
YFT....... Torpedo Transportation Lighter (Navy symbol)
YFTU...... Yugoslavia Federation of Trade Unions

YFU .... Harbor Utility Craft (Navy symbol)
YFU .... Yard Freight Unit
YFU .... Youth for Understanding
YF (XYL)..... Wife (Amateur radio slang)
YG........ Garbage Lighter (Self-Propelled) (Navy symbol)
YG .... Yellow(ish) Green
YG .... Yellow-Green Beacon (Aviation)
YG .... Young Spring & Wire Corporation (NYSE symbol) (Delisted)
YGL........ Yttrium Garnet LASER
YGN ...... Garbage Lighter (Non-Self-Propelled) (Navy symbol)
YGS........ Young Guard Society
YH........ Lighter, Ambulance (Navy symbol)
YH........ RADAR Beacon (Maps and charts)
YH........ Youth Hostel
YHA....... Youth Hostels Association
YHB....... House Boat (Navy symbol)
YHLC ...... Salvage Lift Craft, Heavy (Non-self-propelled) (Navy ship symbol)
YHT .... Heating Scow (Navy ship designation)
YHT .... Young-Helmholtz Theory
YIE .... Young Interference Experiment
YIG........ Yttrium Iron Garnet
YIGIB....... Your Improved Group Insurance Benefits
YIIJS ...... Young Israel Institute for Jewish Studies
YIL .... Yellow Indicator Lamp
YIP .... Willow Run Airport, Detroit, Michigan (Airport symbol)
YIVO ...... Yidisher Visnshaftlekher Institut (Yiddish Scientific Institute)
YJ........ RADAR Homing Beacon (Maps and charts)
YK........ RADAR Beacon (Maps and charts)
YKUF ...... Yiddisher Kultur Farband
YL........ Yellow (Maps and charts)
YL........ Young Lady (Amateur radio slang)
YLA........ Open Landing Lighter (Navy symbol)
YLC....... Young Life Campaign
YLI .... The Yorkshire Light Infantry (British Army)
YLI .... Young Ladies Institute
YLJ........ Yale Law Journal
YLLC ...... Salvage Lift Craft, Light (Self-propelled) (Navy ship symbol)
YLRL ...... Young Ladies Radio League
YM........ Dredge (Navy symbol)
YM .... Yeast Extract - Malt Extract (Medium)
YM .... Yellow Metal
YM .... Young Men's (Christian Association)
YM .... Your Message
YMA ...... Yarn Merchants Association
YMB....... Yeast Malt Broth
YMCA ..... Young Men's Christian Association
YMCU ..... Young Men's Christian Union
YMD ...... Your Message Date
YME....... Young's Modulus of Elasticity
YMF ...... Young Musicians Foundation
YMFS ...... Young Men's Friendly Society (British)
YMHA ..... Young Men's Hebrew Association
YMI....... Young Men's Institute
YMLC...... Salvage Lift Craft, Medium (Non-self-propelled) (Navy ship symbol)
YMP ...... Motor Mine Planter (Navy symbol)
YMS........ Auxiliary Motor Minesweeper (Navy symbol)
YMS....... Yield Measurement System
YMT....... Motor Tug (Navy symbol)
Y & MV ..... Yazoo and Mississippi Valley Railroad Company
YM - YWHA ..... Young Men's and Young Women's Hebrew Association
YN .... Net Tender (Navy symbol)
YN .... Yeoman (Navy rating)
YN .... Yes-No
YN .... Youngstown & Northern R. R. (AAR code)
YNG ...... Gate Vessel (Navy symbol)
YNHA ..... Yosemite Natural History Association
YNT....... Net Tender (Tug Class) (Navy symbol)
YO .... Fuel Oil Barge (Self-Propelled) (Navy symbol)
YO .... Yarn Over
YO .... Year-Old
Y/O....... Year-Old (Medicine)
YOAN ..... Youth of All Nations
YOB ...... Year of Birth
YOB....... Youth Opportunities Board
YOC....... Youth Opportunity Campaign (Civil Service Commission)
YOC ...... Youth Opportunity Centers
YOC ...... Youth Opportunity Corps
YOD ...... Year of Death
YOG ...... Gasoline Barge (Self-Propelled) (Navy symbol)
YOGN ..... Gasoline Barge (Non-Self-Propelled) (Navy symbol)
YOM ...... Year of Marriage

YON .... Fuel Oil Barge (Non-Self-Propelled) (Navy symbol)
YOS .... Oil Storage Barge (Navy symbol)
YOSE ...... Yosemite National Park
YOU ...... Youth Opportunities Unlimited (Project)
YOU ...... Youth Organizations United
YOUTHS .... Youth Order United Toward Highway Safety
YP........ Patrol Vessel (Navy symbol)
YP........ Yard Patrol
YP........ Yellow Pine
YP........ Yield Point (Ordinarily expressed in PSI)
YP........ Young People
YPA....... Yaw Precession Amplifier
YPD .... Floating Pile Driver (Navy symbol)
YPD .... Yaw Phase Detector
YPE....... Yoho Pitch Extractor
YPEC ...... Young Printing Executives Club of New York
YPF .... Yacimientos Petroliferos Fiscales (Argentina) (Oil agency)
YPFB ...... Yacimientos Petroliferos Fiscales Bolivianos (Bolivian oil company)
YPG .... Yuma Proving Ground (Arizona) (Army)
YPK .... Pontoon Stowage Barge (Navy symbol)
YPM....... Yale Peabody Museum
YPO....... Young Presidents' Organization
YPO....... Youth Programs Office (Bureau of Indian Affairs)
YPSCE ...... Young People's Society of Christian Endeavor
YPSL ...... Young Peoples Socialist League
YR .... Floating Workshop (Navy symbol)
YR........ Yaw Ring
YR........ Year
YR........ Young Republican
YRA....... Yacht Racing Association (British)
YRB .... Submarine Repair and Berthing Barge (Navy symbol)
YRBM ..... Submarine Repair, Berthing and Messing Barge (Navy symbol)
YRC....... Submarine Rescue Chamber (Navy symbol)
YRDH ...... Floating Dry Dock Workshop (Hull) (Navy symbol)
YRDM ..... Floating Dry Dock Workshop (Machinery) (Navy symbol)
YRL .... Covered Lighter (Repair) (Navy symbol)
YRNF ...... Young Republican National Federation
YRR....... Radiological Repair Barge (Navy symbol)
YRS .... Yugoslav Relief Society
YRST ...... Salvage Craft Tender (Non-self-propelled) (Navy ship symbol)
YS........ Stevedoring Barge (Navy symbol)
YS........ Yard Superintendent
YS........ Yellow Spot
YS........ Yield Strength (Ordinarily expressed in PSI)
YS........ Yoshida Sarcoma
YS........ Young Soldier(s)
YS........ Youngstown & Southern Railway Company (AAR code)
YSA....... Young Socialist Alliance
YSB .... Yacht Safety Bureau
YSB .... Yield Stress Bonding
YSD....... Seaplane Wrecking Derrick (Navy symbol)
YSD....... Youngstown Steel Door Company (NYSE symbol)
YSDB ...... Yield Stress Diffusion Bonding
YSE .... Yaw Steering Error
YSI .... Yellow Springs Instrument Company
YSL .... Yves Saint Laurent (French couturier)
YSM ...... Yangtze Service Medal
YSP .... Pontoon Salvage Vessel (Navy ship designation)
YSP .... Years Service for Severance Pay Purposes (Military)
YSR....... Sludge Removal Barge (Navy symbol)
YT .... Harbor Tug (Navy symbol)
Yt .... Yttrium (Chemical element) (Also see Y)
YT .... Yukon Territory, Canada
YTA....... Yiddish Theatrical Alliance
YTB .... Large Harbor Tug (Navy symbol)
YTCA ...... Yorkshire Terrier Club of America
YTEP .... Youth Training and Employment Project
YTHJ ...... Yeshivath Torath Hayim in Jerusalem
YTL .... Small Harbor Tug (Navy symbol)
YTM....... Medium Harbor Tug (Navy symbol)
YTS ...... Yuma Test Station
YTT .... Torpedo Testing Barge (Navy symbol)
YTX .... Planned District Craft (Navy symbol)
YU........ Yale University
YUBO....... Yucca House National Monument
YUK....... Youth Uncovering Krud (Antipollution organization in Schenectady, New York)
YUL .... Yale University Library
YV........ Drone Aircraft Catapult Control Craft (Navy symbol)
YVC....... Yellow Varnish Cambric
YVJC .... Yakima Valley Junior College (Washington)

YVP . . . . Youth Voter Participation (Massachusetts)
YVT . . . . Yakima Valley Transportation Company (AAR code)
YW . . . . Water Barge (Self-Propelled) (Navy symbol)
YW . . . . Young Women's (Christian Association)
YW . . . . Yreka Western R. R. (AAR code)
YWCA . . . . . . Young Women Committed to Action (Feminist group)
YWCA . . . . . . Young Women's Christian Association
YWCTU. . . . . . Young Women's Christian Temperance Union

YWF . . . . Young World Federalists
YWHA . . . . . . Young Women's Hebrew Association
YWHS . . . . Young Women's Help Society (British)
YWLL . . . . Young Workers Liberation League
YWN . . . . Water Barge (Non-Self-Propelled) (Navy symbol)
YWS . . . . Young Wales Society
YWT . . . . Yard-Walk-Throughs (Navy)
YWU . . . . Yiddish Writers Union

Z . . . . Administrative Aircraft (when a suffix to Navy plane designation)
Z . . . . Atomic Number (Symbol)
Z . . . . Azimuth Angle
Z . . . . Coriolis Correction
Z . . . . Greenwich Mean Time (Aviation)
Z . . . . Impedance (Symbol)
Z . . . . Lighter-than-air aircraft (Airship)
Z . . . . Vertical component of the earth's magnetic field
Z . . . . Woolworth (F. W.) Company (NYSE symbol) (Wall Street slang name: "Five & Dime")
Z . . . . Zenith
Z . . . . Zenith Distance (Astronomy)
Z . . . . Zero
Z . . . . Zinc (Chemical symbol is Zn)
Z . . . . Zloty (Monetary unit in Poland)
Z . . . . Zoll (Customs Duty) (Germany)
Z . . . . Zone
Z . . . . Zone Marker
Z . . . . Zone Meridian (Lower or upper branch)
Z . . . . Zuender (Fuze) (German military)
Z . . . . Zulu Time (Greenwich Mean Time)
ZA . . . . American Zinc, Lead & Smelting Company (NYSE symbol) (Delisted)
ZA . . . . Zero and Add
ZAAP . . . . . . Zero Antiaircraft Potential
ZAB . . . . Zinc-Air Battery
ZAED . . . . . . Zentralstelle fuer Atomkernenergie-Dokumentation beim Gmelin-Institut (Central Agency for Atomic Energy Documentation of the Gmelin Institute) (Germany)
ZAI . . . . Zero Address Instruction
ZAL . . . . Zale Corp. (NYSE symbol)
ZALIS . . . . . . Zinc and Lead International Service
ZAM . . . . . . Z-Axis Modulation
ZAMP . . . . . . Zeitschrift fuer Angewandte Mathematic und Physik (Switzerland)
ZANC . . . . . . Zambia National Congress - Southern Rhodesia
ZAP . . . . Zero and Add Packed
ZAP . . . . Zero Antiaircraft Potential (Missile)
ZAPB . . . . . . Zinc/Air Primary Battery
ZAPU . . . . . . Zimbabwe African People's Union (Southern Rhodesia)
ZAR . . . . Zeus Acquisition RADAR (Missile defense)
ZAS . . . . Zero Access Storage
ZAT . . . . Zantop Air Transport
ZAT . . . . Zinc Atmospheric Tracer
ZAV . . . . Zentralstelle fuer Arbeitsvermittlung (Germany)
ZB . . . . Crown Zellerbach Corporation (NYSE symbol)
ZB . . . . Zero Beat (Radio)
ZBE . . . . Zinc Battery Electrode
ZBL . . . . Zero-Based Linearity
ZBR . . . . Zero Beat Reception
ZBR . . . . Zero Bend Radius
ZBS . . . . Zivena Beneficial Society
ZBT . . . . Zeta Beta Tau (Fraternity)
ZC . . . . Zone Capacity
Z of C . . . . . Zones of Communications (Military)
ZCB . . . . Zinc-Coated Bolt
ZCC . . . . Zirconia-Coated Crucible
ZCD . . . . Zero Crossing Detector
ZCIC . . . . . . Zirconia-Coated Iridium Crucible
ZCMI . . . . . . Zion's Cooperative Mercantile Institution (Department store in Salt Lake City, Utah)
ZCN . . . . Zinc-Coated Nut
ZCR . . . . Zero-Temperature Coefficient Resistor
ZCS . . . . Zinc-Coated Screw
ZCW . . . . . . Zinc-Coated Washer

ZCZ . . . . Zavodi Crvena Zastava (Yugoslavia)
ZD . . . . Zener Diode
ZD . . . . Zenith Description
ZD . . . . Zenith Distance (Navigation)
ZD . . . . Zero Defects
ZD . . . . Zone Description
ZDA . . . . Zinc Development Association
ZDC . . . . Zens Defense Center
ZDC . . . . Zero Defects Council
ZDC . . . . Zinc Die Casting
ZDG . . . . . . Zinc-Doped Germanium
ZDMG . . . . . Zeitschrift der Deutschen Morgenlandischen Gesellschaft
ZDP . . . . Zero Defects Program (or Proposal)
ZDPA . . . . . . Zero Defects Program Audit
ZDPG . . . . . . Zero Defects Program Guideline
ZDPO . . . . . . Zero Defects Program Objective
ZDPR . . . . . . Zero Defects Program Responsibility
ZDR . . . . Zentraldeutsche Rundfunk
ZDR . . . . Zeus Discrimination RADAR (Missile defense)
ZDS . . . . Zinc Detection System
ZE . . . . Zenith Radio Corporation (NYSE symbol)
ZE . . . . Zero Effusion
ZE . . . . Zone Effect
ZEA . . . . Zero Energy Assembly
ZEBRA . . . . . Zero Energy Breeder Reactor Assembly (British)
ZEC . . . . Zero Energy Coefficient
ZEC . . . . Zinc-Electrochemical Cell
ZECC . . . . . . Zinc-Electrochemical Cell
ZEDRON . . . . Blimp Squadron (Later separated into BLIPRON and Blimp-HEDRON) (Navy)
ZEEP . . . . . . Zero Energy Experimental Pile (Nuclear reactor) (Canada)
ZEI . . . . Zero Environmental Impact
ZEL . . . . Zero-Length Launch (Air Force)
ZELL . . . . . . Zero Length Launching
ZEMTR . . . . . Zeus Early Missile Test RADAR (Army)
ZER . . . . Zero Energy Reflection
ZERC . . . . . . Zero Energy Reflection Coefficient
ZERT . . . . . . Zero Reaction Tool
ZES . . . . Zero Energy System
ZET . . . . Zero-Gravity Expulsion Technique
ZETA . . . . . . Zero-Energy Thermonuclear Assembly (AEC)
ZETR . . . . . . Zero-Energy Thermal Reactor (British)
ZEUS . . . . . . Zero-Energy Uranium System (British)
ZF . . . . Free Balloon (Navy symbol)
ZF . . . . Zero Frequency
Z/F . . . . Zone of Fire (Military)
ZFA . . . . Zeitschrift fuer Archaeologie (A publication)
ZFB . . . . Signals Fading Badly
ZFC . . . . Zirconia Fuel Cell
ZFE . . . . Zone of Flow Establishment
ZfG . . . . Zeitschrift fuer Geschichtswissenschaft (A publication)
ZFO . . . . Zone Francaise d'Occupation
ZFP . . . . Zyglo-Fluorescent Penetrant
ZFPT . . . . . . Zyglo-Fluorescent Penetrant Testing
ZFS . . . . Zero Field Splitting
ZG . . . . Zap Gun
ZG . . . . Zerstoerergeschwader (Twin-engine fighter wing) (German military - World War II)
ZG . . . . Zollgesetz (Germany)
ZG . . . . Zoological Gardens
ZGE . . . . Zero-Gravity Expulsion (or Effect or Environment)
ZGET . . . . . . Zero-Gravity Expulsion Technique
ZGG . . . . Zero-Gravity Generator

ZGH	Zonal Gravity Harmonic
ZGS	Zero Gradient Synchrotron (AEC)
ZGS	Zero-Gravity Simulator
ZH	Zinc Heads (Freight)
ZH	Zonal Harmonic
ZH	Zone Heater
ZHF	Zone Heat Flux
ZHR	Zirconium Hydride Reactor
ZI	Zero Input
ZI	Zonal Index
ZI	Zone of Interior (Military)
ZI	Zonta International
Z of I	Zone of Interior (Army)
ZIA	Zone of Interior Armies
ZIC	Zirconia-Iridium Crucible
ZIG	Zoster Immune Globulin
ZIP	Zinc Impurity Photodetector
ZIP	Zone Improvement Plan (Postal Service code)
ZIR	Zero Internal Resistance
ZISS	Zebulun Israel Seafaring Society
ZIX	Zinc Isopropyl Xanthate
ZJ	Zipper Jacket
ZK	Barrage Balloon (Navy symbol)
ZKB	Bomber (ZKB-26, etc.) (Russian aircraft symbol)
ZKD	Zagreb Kajkavian Dialect XXX (of Serbo-Croatian)
ZKD	Zentraler Kurierdienst
ZKN	Training Balloon (Navy symbol)
ZKO	Observation Balloon (Navy symbol)
ZKSK	Zentrale Kommission fuer Staatliche Kontrolle
ZL	Freezing Drizzle (Meteorology)
ZL	Zero Lift
ZL	Zloty
ZLC	Zero Lift Cord
ZLD	Zero Level Drift
ZLD	Zero Lift Drag
ZLD	Zodiacal Light Device
ZLDI	Zentralstelle fuer Luftfahrtdokumentation und Information (West Germany)
ZLG	Zero Line Gap
ZLL	Zero Length Launcher
ZLN	Zwiazek Ludowo Narodowy (National Democrats) (Poland)
ZLSM	Zeiss Light Section Microscope
Z-M	Zuckerman-Moloff (Sewage treatment method)
ZMAR	Zeus Multifunction Array RADAR
ZMC	Experimental Metal-Clad Airship (Navy)
ZMD	Zentralstelle fuer Maschinelle Dokumentation (West Germany)
ZMD	Zung Measurement of Depression (Scale)
ZMK	Zwiazek Mlodziezy Kommunistyczne
ZMMD	Zurich, Mainz, Munich, Darmstadt (A joint European university effort on ALGOL processors)
ZMP	Zwiazek Mlodziezy Polskiej
ZMRI	Zinc Metals Research Institute
ZMT	ZIP (Zone Improvement Plan) Mail Translator (Postal Service)
ZMWRP	Zwiazek Mlodziezy Wiejskiej Rzeczypospolitej Polskiej
ZN	Airship (Nonrigid) (Navy symbol)
Zn	Zinc (Chemical element)
ZNH	Airship, Air-Sea Rescue (Navy symbol)
ZNJ	Airship, Utility (Navy symbol)
ZNN	Nonrigid Training Airship (Navy symbol)
ZNO	Nonrigid Observation Airship (Navy symbol)
ZNP	Nonrigid Patrol Airship (Navy symbol)
ZNP	Zanzibar Nationalist Party
ZNR	Zinc Resistor
ZNS	Nonrigid Scouting Airship (Navy symbol)
ZnS	Zinc Sulfide
ZO	Zero Output
ZO	Zoological Origin
ZOA	Zionist Organization of America
ZOE	Zero-Energy
ZOE	Zinc Oxide-Eugenol (Dental cement)
ZOP	Zinc Oxide Pigment
ZOPI	Zero Order Polynomial Interpolator
ZOPP	Zero Order Polynomial Predictor
ZOR	Zinc Oxide Resistor
ZOS	Zapata Corporation (NYSE symbol)
ZPA	Zeus Program Analysis
ZPAR	Zeus Phased Array RADAR
ZPB	Zinc Primary Battery
ZPE	Zero Point Energy
ZPE	Zeta Phi Eta
ZPEN	Zeus Project Engineer Network

ZPFL	Zanzibar and Pemba Federation of Labour
ZPG	Airship Group (Navy symbol)
ZPG	Zero Population Growth (An organization)
ZPKK	Zentrale Parteikontrollkommission
ZPN	Impedance Pneumograph (Apollo) (NASA)
ZPO	Zeus Project Office
ZPPP	Zanzibar and Pemba People's Party
ZPPR	Zero Power Plutonium Reactor (AEC)
ZPR	Zero Power Reactor (AEC)
ZPRF	Zero Power Reactor Facility
ZPRON	Patrol (Lighter-Than-Air) Squadron (Navy symbol)
ZPRSN	Zurich Provisional Relative Sunspot Number (NASA)
ZPT	Zero Power Test
ZR	Freezing Rain (Meteorology)
ZR	Zentralrat
Zr	Zirconium (Chemical element)
ZR	Zone Refined
ZRC	Zenith Radio Corporation
ZRC	Zirconium Carbide
ZRK	Zentrale Revisionskommission
ZRN	Rigid Training Airship (Navy symbol)
ZrN	Zirconium Nitride
ZRN	Zurn Industries, Inc. (NYSE symbol)
ZRP	Rigid Patrol Airship (Navy symbol)
ZRP	Zero Radial Play
ZRS	Rigid Scouting Airship (Navy symbol)
ZRT	Zero Reaction Tool
ZS	Zero Shift
ZS	Zero and Subtract
ZS	Zero Suppress
ZS	Zoological Society (British)
ZSAT	Zinc Sulfide Atmospheric Tracer
ZSB	Zinc Storage Battery
ZSC	Zero Subcarrier Chromaticity
ZSC	Zinc Silicate Coat
ZSD	Zebra Stripe Display
ZSD	Zinc Sulfide Detector
ZSDS	Zinc Sulfide Detection System
ZSG	Zero Speed Generator
ZSGL	Zentrale Schulgruppenleitungen
ZSI	Zero Size Image
ZSL	Zjednoczone Stronnictwo Ludowe (United Peasants' Party) (Poland)
ZSN	Zoological Station of Naples
ZSPG	Zero-Speed Pulse Generator
ZSS	Zinc Sulfide System
ZST	Zinc Sulfide Tracer
ZST	Zone Standard Time
ZT	Zipper Tubing
ZT	Zone Time (Navy)
ZTA	Zeta Tau Alpha (Sorority)
ZTO	Zone Transportation Office(r) (Military)
ZTP	Zero Temperature Plasma
ZU	Zeitlich Untauglich (Temporarily unfit) (German military - World War II)
ZUP	Zone a Urbaniser de Priorite (Priority Urbanization Zone) (France)
ZUTRON	Airship Utility Squadron (Navy symbol)
ZUZZ	Zug- und Zerschneidezuender (Pull-and-cut igniter) (German military - World War II)
ZV	Zentralvorstand
ZV	Zu Verfugung (At Disposal) (Business and trade) (Germany)
ZVEI	Zentralverband der Electro-technischen Industrie (West Germany)
ZVR	Zener Voltage Regulator
ZVRD	Zener Voltage Regulator Diode
ZW	Zero Wear
ZWC	Zone Wind Computer
ZWL	Zero Wave Length
ZWO	Zuiver Wentenschappelijk Orderzock (Netherlands)
ZWP	Zone Wind Plotter
ZWV	Zero Wave Velocity
ZY	Zayre Corp. (NYSE symbol)
ZYP	Zefkrome Yarn Program (Dow Chemical Company)
ZZ	Zig-Zag
ZZ	Zingiber (Alternate name for myrrh) (Obsolete)
ZZ	Zu Zeit (At This Time) (Germany)
ZZ	Zugzuender (Pull igniter) (Germany military - World War II)
ZZA	Zamak Zinc Alloy
ZZC	Zero-Zero Condition
ZZD	Zig-Zag Diagram
ZZR	Zig-Zag Rectifier
ZZV	Zero-Zero Visibility